Main Street looking north on downtown Uniondale probably taken June 23, 1899. A June 28, 1899, "Banner" account identifies the scene as a display of McCormick machines sold that season in the Justus and Rogers Uniondale branch store. Photo from glass negative courtesy of Don Welch.

COMPILED BY THE
WELLS COUNTY HISTORICAL
SOCIETY

Turner Publishing Company
Publishers of America's History

Co-Produced by: Mark A. Thompson, Independent Publishing Consultant for Turner Publishing Company

Author: Wells County, Indiana Historical Society

Copyright © 1991 by Turner Publishing Company and Wells County Historical Society.

This book or any part thereof may not be reproduced without the written consent of the Author and Publisher

The materials were compiled and produced using available information; Turner Publishing Company regrets they cannot assume liability for errors or omissions.

Book Design: Elizabeth Dennis

Library of Congress Catalog Card No.: 91-067213

ISBN 978-1-68162-550-8

Limited Edition of 1,600 copies of which this book is number _____.

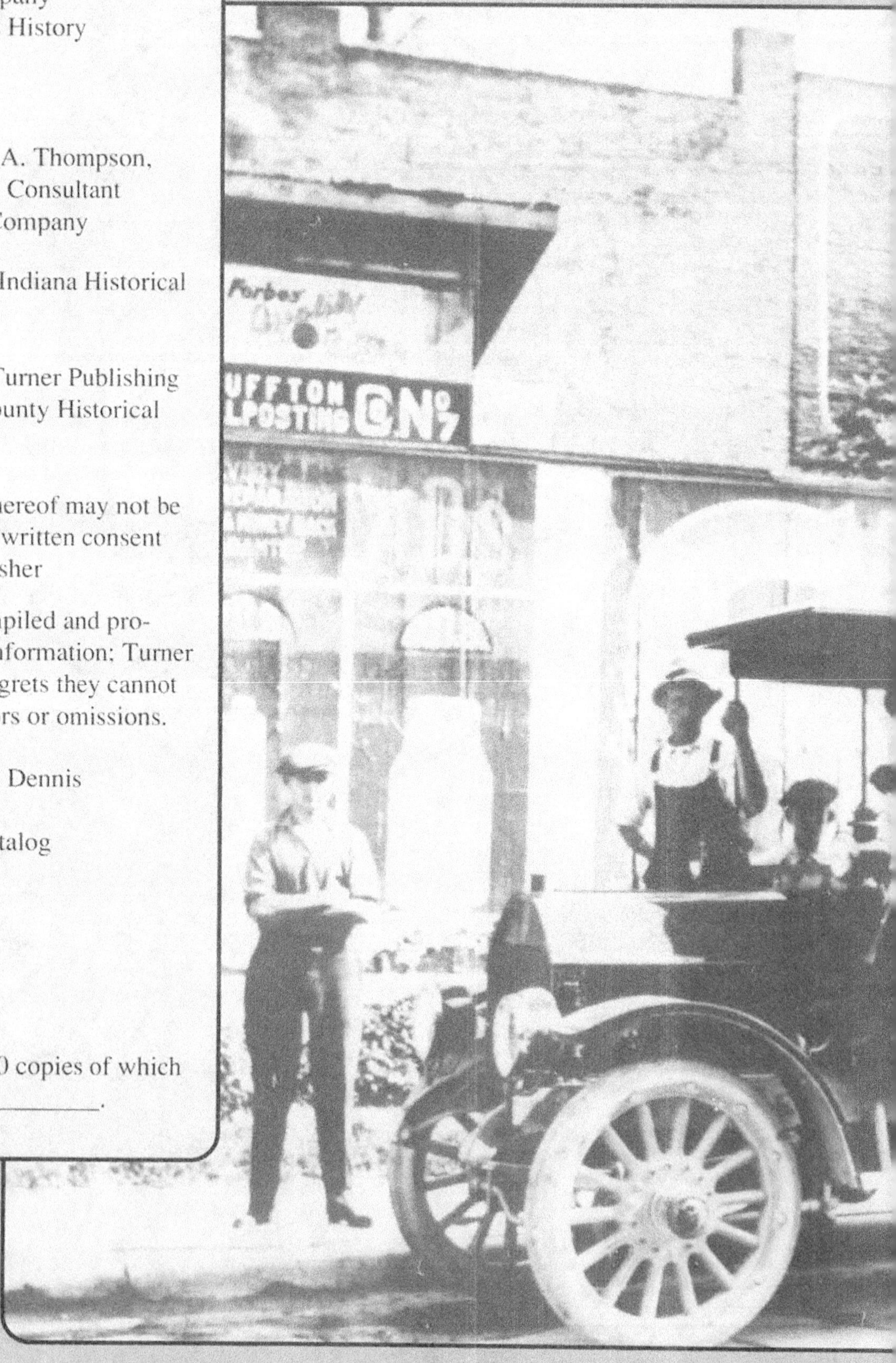

Bulger Trucking Company hauling boxes of Boss Mittens on West Washington Street near Main. Boss Mittens were produced in Bluffton in the top of the Curry Opera House on North Main.

The People's Dry Goods Store at the corner of South Johnson and West Market in Bluffton.

Table of Contents

Introduction 6
County Historical Society 8
County Historian 10
County History
    Town History 11
    Feature Stories 33
    Church History 57
    School History 105
    Club, Organization & Memorial History 135
    Business History 159
    Family History 237
Index 608

Introduction

Joyce (Day) Accavallo served as project chairiperson for the Wells County-Family History Book

"You could write a book about that!" — That's exactly what more than a thousand authors did. They wrote this book, telling the stories of their families, to be handed down to future generations.

This is the first volume published about Wells County people in seventy-three years. Prior to this, three books were published: the first, ***BIOGRAPHICAL and HISTORICAL RECORD of ADAMS and WELLS COUNTIES, INDIANA,*** was published in 1887 by The Lewis Publishing Co., Chicago. The second book to appear was ***BIOGRAPHICAL MEMOIRS of WELLS COUNTY, INDIANA***, in 1903 by B.F. Bowen, Logansport, Indiana. And in 1918, a two-volume ***STANDARD HISTORY of ADAMS and WELLS COUNTIES, INDIANA***, included a number of biographies and gave credit to O.E. Lesh of Bluffton as editorial advisor for the Wells County portion. The Lewis firm published this two-volume edition as well.

In the summer of 1990, the officers and directors of The Wells County Historical Society decided the publication of a family history book would help fulfill its mission in providing a printed record that updates the past seventy-three years. The ultimate goal would include every family that had ever lived here long enough to be included! The feature of the book would be to solicit all family histories, without any cost or obligation to the family. Five hundred words and one picture would be available to every family at no charge - additional words could be included for fifteen cents each, and an additional picture would cost five dollars. The book's printing and high quality binding would be paid from the pre-publication sale of the book for forty-five dollars and the sale of pages for businesses and organizations at two-hundred dollars per page for their history.

Churches and schools paid the actual publishing cost of one hundred dollars per page for their histories. Any excess revenue from the project would be put back in the book to include histories of past businesses, churches, and schools no longer in existence. Another important feature for the extra page is the inclusion of pictures reproduced here for the first time.

The Society's Board of Directors named a committee - Lyle Cotton, Alan Daugherty, Claudine Powell, Jim Foster and Paul Bender - to examine the financial feasibility of the project. They selected a book publisher, based on reputation and references, and more importantly, found the ideal person to serve as chairperson and editor-in-chief, Joyce (Day) Accavallo, with the support of her husband, Dennis, and young son, Charlie, agreed to accept the editorship, adding to her first-grade teaching duties at the Ossian School.

Joyce's qualifications were enhanced by the deep Wells County roots of her family. Her mother, Birdena, and her late father, Charles Day, have participated in the Society since its 1952 reorganization. Fondly known throughout the county as "Charlie," Mr. Day was respected for his ability as an educator and civic leader, and the authority on Liberty Township history. And Joyce's grandfather, William Henry Day, along with an uncle, Frank E. Day, were among the 1935 organizers of The Wells County Historical Society. Her intense interest and enthusiasm pulled the project together, keeping it on track and on schedule to a successful conclusion.

Each member of the original committee became a member of the Editorial Advisory Board, accepting a share of the work. Lyle Cotton handled the typing chores, assisted by Marilyn Minnich, Patty Mossburg, Susan Reed, Alan Daugherty, and Marge Haines. Alan Daugherty, with art and advertising talents, assumed the publicity role and provided advertising along with numerous news articles to encourage residents and former residents to submit their family stories. His wife, Regina, also helped research and write some of the histories of bygone organizations, etc. Craig Leonard, local professional historical and preservationist authority, gave Alan assistance with many of the pictures reproduced in the book.

Jim Foster, current President of the Society, readily volunteered his education background to oversee editing and proofreading. His able assistants were Barbara Elliott, Edwina Patton, Barbra Lesh, and Maro Bender. Editing was only concerned with readability by someone not familiar with the stories. The biographies in this volume are as submitted, and the Society does not assume any responsibility for error. It is recommended that any use of material presented be verified for further accuracy.

Mary Smith, the Society treasurer, assisted by her husband, John E., kept the necessary meticulous records of income, book sales records and serial numbers for the limited edition.

Paul L. Bender, immediate past-president of the Society, assisted by Charles Weterick, Herman Myers, and Claudine Powell, followed the business pages' histories; Marge Antrim solicited the schools' and Delores Polderman contacted organizations for their histories.

December 1, 1990, was the kick-off for submitting family histories. The end of February was set as a deadline; however, many learned too late about the book, in spite of heavy publicity, and the deadline was extended to April 30 to accommodate more submitters. Much work has to be done to still meet the promised book delivery by early December, 1991, as many books were ordered as Christmas gifts.

Early in the planning, a decision was made to make the volume more valuable by including an every-name index. This monumental task to be done after printer's proof pages were received, was accepted as a challenge by Susan Reed (and her computer), with index verification by Connie Sawyer and Mary Craig.

The *Wells County Family History* book has had township representatives helping gather the material and to make sales of the book, in every corner and crossroad in the county. These were: Jane Hamilton, Chester; Frances Clark, Liberty; Sharon McMillan, Jackson; Nancy Wagner, Nottingham; Claudine Powell and Susan Reed, Harrison/Bluffton; Vicki Seslar, Rockcreek; Frances Bayless, Lancaster; Melba Edwards, Union; and Mary Lou Woodard and Delores Polderman, Jefferson/Ossian. Melba Edwards also provided a photo-copying service (photographically) and Connie Brubaker assisted in photo-copying (Xerox).

Among the many providing valuable support services were Jim and Barbara Barbieri and their *News-Banner*, which day after day writes the history of Wells County; Eugene McCord, Joel Smekens, and others on the *News-Banner*, staff for stories and pictures; and Dave and Mary Jane Park, who have provided their Carnall

Insurance office as a downtown Bluffton location for our authors to drop off histories, place book orders, and finally to pick up the finished books and avoid mailing costs. These and untold others have graciously contributed time and talents without hesitation so that this book could become a reality.

It is with great pride that we dedicate this book, on behalf of those who participated in its production, and its more than a thousand authors, to our descendants in the years to come. We hope they will appreciate what their ancestors have done and will find enjoyment in the authors' presentations.

Paul L. Bender, Past-President for
The Wells County Historical Society
August 1, 1991

EDITOR AND EDITORIAL ADVISORY BOARD for the Wells County-Family History Book. Seated, (l. to r.) Claudine Powell, Joyce Day Accavallo, Editor-in-chief; James W. Foster. Standing: Alan Daugherty and Paul L. Bender. Lyle Cotton, the other member, was not available for the picture.

Township representatives who collected family histories, (l. tor.) - Francis Bayless, Jane Hamilton, Melba Edwards, Frances Clark, Claudine Powell and Sharon McMillan. Not pictured are Nancy Wagner, Susan Reed, Vicki Seslar, Delores Polderman and Mary Lou Woodard.

Gathered on the front steps of the Wells County Historical Museum are many of the Wells Countians who have worked on putting the family history book together. In the front row, (l. to r.): Jane Hamilton, Francis Clark, Barbara Elliott, Claudine Powell and Maro Bender. Second row: Frances Bayless, Mary Smith, John E. Smith, and Paul L. Bender. Third row: Alan Daugherty, Melba Edwards, Sharon McMillan, Marilyn Minnich and Barbra Lesh. Back row: Lyle Cotton, Patty Mossburg, Edwina Patton and Joyce Accavallo.

Wells County Historical Society

The Wells County Historical Museum at 420 West Market Street, Bluffton, was built in 1882 by Alvin Stewart. The style is French Second Empire. Listed in the National Register of Historic Places, 1979, it is carefully preserved and well-kept by members of the Wells County Historical Society.

The 100th anniversary of the organization of Wells County was February 2, 1937. Two years earlier a group of citizens was motivated by that Centennial to organize The Wells County Historical Society. They met in the small auditorium of the Community Building in Bluffton on February 13, 1935. It was well attended. Of the charter members, only Amos Gerber and Joe Seabold are active members today (1991).

The initial Society officers and directors were active in the community: President, Mrs. Fred J. Longden; 1st Vice President, Judge John F. Decker, 2nd Vice President, J. Edwin Reynolds; and Secretary; Mrs. J. Lawrence (Golda) Goodin. The Directors were Abram Simmons, W.A. Patton, William R. Barr, Dillon Myers, Charles C. Deam, Charles E. Sturgis, and Mrs. Ida Ashbaucher.

Their thinking and motivation is reflected in Article II of the original constitution: "Object - the general purpose of this Society shall be the promotion of historical study and investigation, generally, in the County of Wells; the discovery, collection, organization, preservation, and if practicable the publication of historical and archaeological facts pertaining to the County of Wells; the collection and preservation of books, pamphlets, papers, maps, genealogies, pictures, relics, manuscripts, letters, journals, field-books, and any and all other articles which will describe or illustrate the social, religious, political, industrial, or educational progress of the County of Wells; the dissemination of historical information to arouse interest in the past by publishing historical material in newspapers or otherwise; to see that our public archives are properly cared for; by holding meetings with addresses, lectures, papers, and discussions; and by marking historic buildings, sites, places, and trails." One is astounded by the all-encompassing breadth of vision these founding persons had. One is also greatly pleased by the manner in which many highly motivated persons since that time have sought to carry out the dictates of that mandate.

The first general membership meeting to adopt the constitution was held on June 4, 1935, with 27 present. Dues were $1.00 per year, with 78 members on the roll. Plans were initiated then for a Street Fair display in September to promote the Society and the coming Centennial Celebration in 1937.

1936 saw Dillon Myers as President, with continuing plans for the Centennial.

In 1937, with E.E. Sunier as President, Wm. R. Barr became general chairman of the Centennial Committee, and Dillon Myers chairman of the Planning Committee. The celebration was held as part of the Bluffton Free Street Fair in September. The court house plaza was used for Centennial activities and displays, and a Centennial parade was featured with each township taking part.

After the Centennial, interest waned and no further quorums could be gained to hold meetings.

The Society was dormant until November 1952 when an interested group met and initiated a reorganizational meeting held on December 1. Hermine Wiecking Colson was elected President; James McBride, 1st Vice President; Ora Lamm, 2nd Vice President; Edwina Patton, secretary-treasurer; and J.E. Reynolds, Margaret Powers, and Paul Bender as Directors.

The Society has continued to meet regularly and grow in membership since then. Its 1991 membership is 430, with members from across the country as well as Wells County.

Highlights of the past 39 years begin with the collection of Wells County material in a fourth-floor room of the Court House.

On November 17, 1961, the Wells County Historical Society entered into a 99-year lease agreement with the Wells County 4-H Association, for a .46 acre tract on the 4-H grounds. The Society moved a pioneer log cabin from the Paul Stout farm, southwest of Bluffton, to this tract.

Wells County Historical Society Presidents
1935 to 1991

President	Year(s)
Mrs. Fred Longden	1935
Dillon Myers	1936
Ed Sunier	1937
(Inactive period 1938 to 1951)	
Hermine Wiecking Colson	1952 through 1955
Leone Erick	1956
Warren McBride	1957 through 1959
Lloyd Ulmer	1960 through 1961
James Schultz	1962 through 1963
Jerry Fetters	1964
Paul Bender	1965 through 1968
Hersh Robbins	1969
Fred Hoeppner	1970 through 1971
Eugene McCord	1972
Harry Lindstrand	1973
Fred Tangeman	1974
Joyce Buckner	1975 through 1978
Herman Pence	1979
Fred Park	1980 through 1988
Paul Bender	1989 through 1990
James Foster	1991

In the 1960's it became apparent that to transact the business of this organization properly, it should be incorporated as a non-profit corporation and receive IRS approval for tax-exempt donations. Listed as incorporators were Paul L. Bender, Earl R. Deam, Mrs. Ethel Lamm, Mrs. Nora Biberstine, and Mary Shafer Kimmell.

In September, 1967, donations of local artifacts had made it necessary to seek larger and more easily accessible quarters for the museum. The museum was moved from the court house to the former home of Dr. and Mrs. Clarence H. Mead, located at 213 West Washington Street, Bluffton. It was May 11, 1969, however, before a formal dedication of the new facility was held. The museum was dedicated "to those who have preceded us, to whom we owe a great debt. We take great pride in the heritage left by their wisdom and foresight."

The Mead home at that time and now is owned by the Bluffton-Wells County Public Library although plans are currently underway to transfer ownership to the county, for the land to become public parking.

A dream of a permanent home for the Wells County Historical Museum became a reality with arrangements to purchase in 1974, from Ralph Jahn, the four-story Stewart-Studebaker home at 420 West Market Street. The purchase price was $25,000. Craig Leonard, historic preservation consultant, in his comprehensive *Architectural Atlas of Wells County*, lists the home as French Second Empire style, built in 1882, by the owner-builder-architect, Alvin Stewart. Stewart was the construction superintendent for the Lake Erie and Western Railroad, then being built through Wells County. In 1892, it became the home of John Studebaker, who had originally sold the land to Stewart. The front porch was added in 1920. The brick building to the east, once unattached, was built by Stewart as his office. The building is on the National Register of Historic Places.

Many members, some spending thousands of hours of volunteer work, have finished the interior in Victorian style, refurbished the exterior, and kept the surrounding lawn in excellent condition as a showplace that Wells County residents can be proud of. More than 10,000 catalogued items are housed and exhibited.

Besides the Museum, many other activities are or have been sponsored. Soon after its reorganization in 1952, a nearly complete file of old Wells County newpapers, belonging to the McBride family, was obtained and micro-filmed for deposit in the Bluffton-Wells County Public Library.

Officers of the Wells County Historical Society (1991). (l. to r.) Seated - Claudine Powell, 1st vice-president; James W. Foster, president; Mary Smith, treasurer. Standing - Marcia Hotopp, secretary; Paul L. Bender, immediate past-president.

Directors of the Wells County Historical Society (1991). (l. to r.) Barbara Elliott, Max Stinson, Alan Daugherty, Elmo Rieddle, Ramona Garton. Other 1991 directors, not in the photo, are: Lyle Cotton, Don Croy, Noah Yake, and Stan Gilbert.

Roger Swaim, publisher of the News-Banner, provided funding to complete the work and the News-Banner has continued to support this valuable project.

In the 1960's a complete census of all Wells County cemeteries was completed by many members working under the direction of Mrs. Clarence (Bea) Minniear. Bound copies were placed in the local library, Fort Wayne Library, Morman Library, the library in Washington, D.C., and the Museum library.

The Society was involved in the 1776-1976 *History of Wells County* edited by members Dorothy Rose and Joyce Buckner. This 232-page cloth-bound volume is a companion to the current *Wells County Family History*. A few copies of this book are still available for sale by the Society.

Another important publication was the previously mentioned *Architectural Atlas of Wells County*, by Craig Leonard. This spiral-bound limited edition is also available from the Society at this time. Three years of research went into this most thorough and complete site and structure survey of the entire county. Its 186 pages locate and picture many present and former buildings with descriptive information relative to date of construction and architect and builder, when known.

In 1976, as a part of the sesquicentennial celebration of the nation, the Society staged an Old American Craft Day. Held each October on the Museum grounds, its features displays and crafts of earlier pioneer days of Wells County. Other on-going annual events include the Annual Quilt Show, a Hobby and Collectors Show, and the annual Victorian Christmas Open House.

It is the goal of the Wells County Historical Society that the rich history and heritage of Wells County shall be preserved and continue to grow for the benefit of many future oncoming generations. This year's *Wells County Family History* book publication will be a significant contribution of the Society toward meeting that goal.

Wells County Historian

In 1981, the Indiana Historical Society and the Indiana Historical Bureau jointly requested the nomination of a local citizen to be named by them as "Wells County Historian." The criteria included: a person knowledgeable in local and state history; one who would be accessible to, and helpful to the public in all matters pertaining to local and state history; and one who would keep in touch with the state bureaus in matters of historical importance.

There was no question but that Fred F. Park should receive this nomination from the Wells County Historical Society's Board of Directors. The state bureau agreed and Park received the appointment as "Wells County Historian". He has held that position since then, fulfilling the state requirements, ever being the first source of county historical information for Wells County.

Fred "retired" in 1973, but only after serving more than forty years in education, twenty-nine of them as principal of Bluffton High School. He went on to lead in Wells County's Bicentennial efforts in 1976; serve as president of the Wells County Historical Society from 1980 through 1988; and put together a superb and unprecedented collection of Wells County History.

The numerous pictures Park has gathered have been made by him into many different slide presentations, which he has given to more than 100 community groups and vast numbers of citizens, enhancing the preservation of Wells County's heritage.

An outstanding contribution was the recording of his research in regular Historical Society newsletters, thus sharing his information with the membership.

Park received the well-earned "Community Service Award" for Wells County in 1965; and in 1982, he received the Bluffton Chamber of Commerce "Outstanding Citizen of the Year" award.

Fred F. Park has been an outstanding choice by the Indiana Historical Society and Bureau to be named as our first "Wells County Historian," an appointment he continues to merit today.

WELLS COUNTY TOWNS

A 1987 view of Domestic in southeastern Wells County.

Towns and Villages of Wells County

Banner City	1882	aa
Barbours Mills	1849	d
Batson Bridge		ff
Bee Creek	1846	v
Bluffton	1838	
Bly	1889	mm
Bracey		uu
Bull Skin		s
Chalfant's Corners	1870	mr
Choppeen	1848	c
Cora		
Coryville	1879	m
Craigville	1879	e
Cudahy	1896	ll
Curryville	1879	m
Derrick	1897	hh
Dillman	1880	j
Dodgerville		vv
Dogtown		j
Domestic	1884	o
Eagleville	1854	yy
Echo	1895	pp
Five Points		g
Fox	1859	ii
Greenfield	1828	dd
Greenville	1872	w
Greenwood	1828	dd
Jeff	1896	a
Keystone	1872	p
Kingsland	1883	i
Kingston	1841	ss
Kreps	1890	gg
Liberty Center	1878	h
Little Chicago		qq
Madduxville	1882	n
Markle	1850	n
McNatts	1890	u
Mechanicsburg		nn
Mt. Zion	1896	t
Murray	1839	z
Murray Road		mr
Netterfield	1870	dd
New Lancaster		z
Newville	1848	s
Nottingham	1848	y
Ossian	1850	v
Parkinson	1882	i
Petroleum	1894	l
Phenix	1889	f
Pleasant View		ww
Poneto	1880	w
Prospect		cc
Puckerville (Bluffton)	1835	
Pugney		zz
Reiffs Burgh	1853	ee
Reiffsburg	1853	ee
Ringville		o
Riverside	1912	x
Rockford	1849	d
Ruth	1890	jj
Slacum		
Sugar Grove		
Terrell		
Tocsin	1883	b
Tracy	1836	n
Travisville	1871	k
Union Station	1882	r
Uniondale	1882	r
Uniontown	1847	q
Vera Cruz	1870	s
Villa North		vv
Waikle	1869	aa
Walmerville		oo
Wellsburg	1855	vv
West Ossian	1870	kk
Winterville		rr
Worthington	1871	w
Worthington Crossing	1870	w
Zanesville	1854	c

Banner City

The younger generation of today probably have not heard of the name Banner City, or if they have they cannot tell where it was once located or perhaps even, care - but, why should they, living in today's busy and hectic world. Still, there are a few older people who remember the place and realize that at one time it was important to a few of our early pioneer families who settled in the region. My great grandfather, James Scott, went there to receive and send mail.

In the early part of 1860 a village sprang up along the Chicago and Atlantic Railroad just a mile west of the present day village of Uniondale. Banner City was on the dividing line between Union and Rockcreek Township. Mr. Roth, who owned the *Bluffton Banner* newspaper, named the little village in honor of his paper. There were about one hundred fifty inhabitants.

The first business house was established and started by Levi Waikel, who also operated a saw mill. He built the first town residence, and when the post office was established in 1882, he was the first postmaster. His father owned the first threshing machine brought to Union Township, and his brother William operated it for many years. During the year 1979 William Waikel handled over 42,000 bushels of grain.

In 1885 Andrew Brickley of Banner bought a saw mill from the Kelseys in Lafayette Township of Allen County. He moved it to Banner and there operated the Miller Brothers Handle and Bat Factory. For more information on Banner refer to the Biographical and Historical Record of Adams and Wells County of 1887, (Lewis Publishing Company) under the headings of William Waikel and Levi Waikel in Wells County

Bly

Bly at one time was a village located eight miles west of Bluffton on the Smoky Roe Pike (600 E). While no village exists there now, it is interesting to know that at the time of its founding in 1889, a post office was established. Tony Terrell was the first postmaster. At that time a short name was desired, so the name Bly, a three-letter word was selected. The name was obtained from the fact that Nellie Bly at that time had gained fame as the first woman to travel the world.

Boehmer

Boehmer "sprang up" on the Huntington-Wells County line. It didn't have a name at first, but a name was necessary as a railroad station was to be put there, so it had to have one. Joseph Boehmer, a bank cashier and Dr. Corey Evans, a surgeon and one-time mayor of Delphas, incorporated the Delphas, Bluffton, and Frankfort Railroad of Indiana on October 17, 1877. The Wells County Commissioners were persuaded to invest $30,000 in DB&F's capital stock. This was nearly enough money to build the approved fourteen miles of unballasted track between Bluffton and Warren.

Work began at Bluffton on this narrow guage road on July 8, 1878. By October 11, an excursion train was to run to Warren. It was made up of the engine, "Bluffton," and all the cars owned by the company, namely a coach, a box car and six flat cars. The patrons was treated at Warren to an ox roast, speeches, and band music. It was a gala occasion.

A year later, on October 8, 1879, Jacob C. Zent had the town site surveyed. The plat was not recorded until November 1, 1880. (Buckeye, a mile west, was surveyed on May 24, 1879, and recorded on October 1, 1879, by Samuel T. Jones and Loren B. Minn. It contained twelve lots.)

Dr. Evans supervised the first run from Warren through Delphas on December 16, 1879. He and Boehmer sold out to speculators in the East. By January 5, 1880, regular mail and express trains were running between Warren and Delphas.

Four lots on the north side of the railroad and ten on the south side are shown on the Boehmer plat. Front Street was the Huntington - Wells County Line and parallel to Front Street, and to the west was Back Street. These names were quite descriptive, of course, but not very imaginative!

The first store building was located north of the tracks and on the west side of Front Street. One half of the store carried a line of groceries and the other side calico and general merchandise. The store also served as the depot. A fifty-foot platform ran along the south side of the building and was used for loading and unloading. Just west of the platform was a pond. John Neff, a one-armed man, ran the business and operated the large warehouse south of the tracks. He lived in a house back of the store building.

Other operators of the store after John Neff were: Thomas Arnold, Don Gaiser, a Barr family, Tom Evans, Jim Jones and later John T. and Adeline Demning. One of their twins, Oliver Bryan, was killed in World War I and buried in Germany.

The railroad switch lay south of the tracks and ran west of Front Street. An offset in today's property fence shows its location.

Jim Jones made bridge rafters of oak and loaded them from this switch. Most of the bridges at this time were constructed of wood. His sawmill was about a mile north of the depot on the east side of the road.

Mail was delivered on horseback and was generally on time in the summer months. Possibly the first and only postmaster was William Mattlock (Matlock, Matlark), who died of a heart attack.

John Statlar operated his blacksmith shop on the east side of Front Street, just south of the railroad. He lived east of his shop along the south side of the tracks.

Boehmer also had a scale yard and elevator.

Some of the early families of the town were Amos Carroll, whose house was the last moved from Boehmer in 1927. John Weldon lived in a house that was weather boarded and plastered. Ed Gilbert's house was constructed of plank running up and down but was not plastered and was said to be the coldest in town. A Jackson family lived in a log house facing Back Street. There were three houses on Back Street. Other citizens of Boehmer were William Clannen, Charly and Alice Mossburg, Jimmy Irvin, and Dave Eubanks. At one time Boehmer had a population of fifty.

In February, 1886, John I. Clark endeavored to solicit $500.00 to build a church building. Interest was so favorable that in one day's time $700.00 was subscribed. There were four miles of muddy roads between Boehmer and Mt. Zion, where they attended church.

The Boehmer Methodist Protestant Class was organized by the Rev. E. Robinson on March 29, 1886, with eleven charter members. In 1887, the Rev. J.C. Macklin, pastor of the circuit, organized a board of trustees as follows: John J. Merriman, James Jones, George Sliger, A.L. Carroll, and William Melling.

Mr. Jacob Zent offered the church a lot for the building, but his wife refused to sign the deed. She did not want a church that close to her house. John I. Clark then offered a part of his orchard, but it too, was refused for the same reason, for it was just across the road.

On June 30, 1887, the board selected and secured a deed for the south part of the present party.

Timber was donated and Jim Jones sawed it in his mill. Ves Eiler built the church building and Martin Huggman assisted in finishing the interior and building and dressing the pews. The building was completed in the summer of 1888 at a cost of $1800.

One-room school houses dotted the country-side, spaced two miles apart, but Boehmer never had a school. When roads were really muddy the children would "coon the rail fences to school."

In 1886 the railroad, now known as the Clover Leaf, began laying heavy rails to change the road to standard guage. It was completed in one day on Sunday, June 26, 1887, and Monday morning was back on regular schedule.

The Marion, Bluffton, and Eastern Interurban was built in 1904, and crossed the Huntington - Wells County Line about half mile north of Boehmer. Its depot was known as Boehmer.

The railroad seemed to favor Buckeye, and business declined at Boehmer. Improved roads and increased production of the automobile took both people and business away from the community. Boehmer died. The last house was moved in 1927. The interurban quit running in 1932. The trains now run non-stop through there.

The Eiler family cemetery south of the church was preserved until about 1928. Now no trace of it can be found.

All that remains of the small pioneer village of Boehmer is the United Methodist Church and the parsonage, which was built in 1953.

CRAIGVILLE

For a small town in the center of a farming community, Craigville had about all that was needed in the late 1920s and through the 1930's. A trip to Bluffton, back then, was like going to Fort Wayne today. Going to Bluffton was considered a special trip to purchase something special, like a dress suit, new car, or to have family pictures taken at a real for sure photo studio, and to have a bigger selection of boy or girlfriends.

Craigville was a town of many businesses to support most local requirements of the local families, including: a cheese factory, tile mill, grain elevator, livestock yard, Railway Express office, Western Union office for sending money and messages to distant locations, cabinetmaker/carpenter, hardware (which provided many services such as gun repair, electrical machine shop, pressure water systems and general plumbing, etc.), garage/gasoline station (which provided sales/service for farm tractors and related equipment.) Also, there was service of all makes of automobiles - including one electric car, a U.S. Post Office, grocery store, meat market, live/dressed poultry, buying and selling of wild game pelts and cow hides, butchering of meat, shearing of sheep, theater featuring silent movies/medicine shows and vaudeville, barber shop, the home of Farmers State Bank (now known as "Farmers & Merchant Bank" in Bluffton), Craigville Telephone Company, blacksmith, harness and mower repair and personal shoe repair. In addition to the businesses, Craigville had two churches, a grade school and a high school (both in the same building which stands today).

Deihl's Lunchroom, Meat Market & Post Office in Craigville. (l. to r.) Harve Ginter, Esther Ginter (Peases), and Glennis McBarnes.

Life in Craigville was lots of fun for young and old alike. Each summer the merchants and town families would rope off one block of Main Street for games and fair booths. During the afternoon there would be a medicine show (by Gypsy Road Shows). After dark there would be outdoor movies. It was in the days when everyone helped each other with complete trust. If a car stopped along side any road, you stopped to give help. If a person was found walking

First store in Craigville in 1915.

Theatre in Craigville in 1920. At far left, Farmers State Bank.

View of Craigville looking north. Buggies are tied up in front of the Abbott-Reed Store which is the present location of the Craigville Telephone Company.

along a road, day or night, you stopped and offered a ride. Not everything was fun for the postmaster. In bad winter weather, and in the middle of the night, the railroad mail clerk would kick the mail bags out of the mail car with hope that the train was in or near Craigville. Many a morning, the postmaster would walk in the snow as far east as Curryville, before finding the mail. Another thing of interest was the burning of corn cobs under the automobile engines to heat the crankcase oil so the car could be started in severe winter weather. *Submitted by Robert and Max Deihl.*

CURRYVILLE

Curryville, located along the east boundary line of Wells county in Lancaster Township, was laid out by J.P. Drum and Peter Corey, on March 25, 1859. The village was laid out and named Coreyville in honor of Mr. Corey, but later the spelling of the name was changed to Curryville. It is possible that Mr. Corey (or Mr. Curry) was unable to write and he signed the official documents platting the land for the town with only his mark of an "X". The spelling may just have been an error on the part of the person filling out the legal forms. Although known as Curryville and being listed on most maps as Curryville, the official name was and will always be Coreyville.

The first church erected there was the United Brethren Church, built in 1877. The town had a railroad siding which was removed by the railroad and then once again installed to satisfy the desires of the local businessmen.

The Curryville Post Office was first established May 15, 1879, with Postmaster George W. Drum but was discontinued April 16 of the following year. Just a few days later on April 27, 1880, the post office was reestablished under Postmaster D.J. Cump and survived until June 29, 1907.

DILLMAN

The village of Dillman received its name from the Dillman families, one member of which was Sidney Dillman, who operated a blacksmith shop south of the crossroads. There were other Dillman families there also.

The first store building was erected by Robert Fornshell. He operated the store for several years. His store was located across from where the church is now. This store was first established 110 years ago. Soon after Fornshell went into business, Robert McFadden erected a building for a general store and post office. This was south of the crossroads on the west side.

The first school house was a small frame building built by Hugh Alexander, the trustee. It was built on the southwest corner of the intersection and later moved to the northeast corner, where it was later used as a store by Sherman Lemons.

In the year 1898 a two-room brick school building was erected which was razed to furnish material for the consolidated school at Jackson Center. At the time the first school house was built, the majority of the houses and stores were made from logs. There were several more houses in Dillman than now, several more north, south and west.

There have been several people who have owned and operated businesses in Dillman, namely: George Beard, A.T. Gilbert, George Lee, Luther Cruse, Woodard Pearson, Ed Lane, Christy Stark, Mrs. Long, Ben Good, Frank Malott, Clo Meadows, Ernest Graves, Thelma (Pat) Hicks, Larry Wright and Charles Greenfield.

There had been a store in the last store building almost continuously from 1904 until it burned in 1979. One year it was used as a school house. This was while the new consolidated building was being completed. There also was a restaurant in it at the time it burned.

There still is the church and also a beauty shop owned by Linda Walters.

The people who still live in Dillman are as follows: the John Walters family, the Chris Boots family, Mel Shideler, Rick Slusher, Ethel and Doris Blinn, Howard and Imo Howell, Frank and Claudine Slusher, the Jim Reynolds family, Dale and Inez Stambaugh, Jim and Wilma Crouch, the Gary Flaugher family and Chuck and Ardith Shideler.

EAGLEVILLE

Eagleville, north of Murray, was laid out by William J. Kirkpatrick on November 18, 1854. How the name of the town was obtained has not been learned. Although it did have a post office, little else is known. The town was a stop between Murray Road and Greenwood on the Bluffton to Fort Wayne (F.W., M&C.R.R.) railroad at least in the early 1870's.

JEFF

Jeff owed its existence almost entirely to the Standard Oil Company. The town was built up around the office and tool yard of the company. Most of the people living in Jeff were families engaged in the petroleum industry.

About twelve to fourteen families lived here when it had its largest population. The town received its name when a post office was placed here by the government.

The town was named for the owner of the general merchandise store, Jeff Jones. Jeff Jones later operated the Royal Crown Cola factory in Richmond. He sold the store to his father, John, who operated the store for many years. Other proprietors of the general merchandise store were: Charles Lucky, Sherman Hines, the Lloyd family and the Lewis family. All of the above mentioned merchants were located in a two-story frame building which has been remodeled for a garage.

A blacksmith shop across from the store on the south was operated by Edward Quisno for many years. Mr. Quisno was also our expert cabinet maker, a woodworker, tinkerer, and a teller of tall stores.

When the oil boom subsided Jeff suffered a decline in population. When Mr. Lewis was storekeeper, a disastrous fire destroyed most of the buildings on the southside of the road. A few years later a mysterious fire destroyed the blacksmith shop.

Doctor Underwood also ran a blacksmith shop north of Jeff on the banks of Prairie Creek. Most of the business district of Jeff was in the west part of the town, close to the present residence of the Krumdicks. Formerly a small store was operated by Virgil Booher and his wife, Pauline.

Former proprietors of the Booher Store were George Penrod, Nelson Runkle and Jess Meymer. Ray Penrod operated a garage and sold a variety of merchandise. Ray and wife Helen have both passed on; the house and garage are now vacant.

Still residing in Jeff is Maggie Williams. Living east in the corner is Lula Penrod, mother of Ken and Rond Penrod. The old log cabin once there was burned to the ground. Across from where the old cabin used to be, formerly owned by Robert and Kathern Slater, is now a new home owned by Brenda Buzzard and her son and daughter. On east down the road is a trailer home where Francis and Noreen Fuller live. The old Fuller home still stands; across from it is a new house built by Bill Copper, now owned by Dottie Gilbert and her four boys.

Now we go back south from the old cabin where Ed Merritt and family used to live; it is now owned by Myron and Barb Gearheart. Still farther south on part of the Gearheart ground live Howard (Red) and Helen Buckland in a trailer where used to stand a three-room house, formerly occupied by Ray and Helen Penrod. Across the road to the east, up on a hill, is a house where Don and Mary Kreisher live with their two girls. Down the road south from them on the same side of the road, a new house has been built by the Davis's, later sold to Paul and Margaret Fritz and two children. On up the road and back a lane live Jack and Barb Leas. Their children have all grown and moved away. Then on the corner, the home of the old Salem Church which still stands with a trailer beside it lives Glen Dawson. We must not forget that Art and Mildred Krumdick still live in Jeff, to the west of the old Penrod garage. That makes for about thirty people in all in 1991 who live at Jeff.

KEYSTONE

One recorded account relating to Keystone stated that it was located in about the center of Chester Township and was laid out by Luther Twibell, an early pioneer, on April 19, 1872. According to that account the name Keystone was chosen after an exciting contest was staged. How the name happened to be offered is best described in the following lines from history:

"Luther Twibell, the founder of Keystone, was a Virginian of Irish ancestry; was reared on plantation and late in his youth moved to Henry County, Indiana. In 1840, he accompanied his parents to Blackford County. He remained there with his parents until his marriage in his twentieth year on March 7, 1841. In the following October the young couple moved to Wells County and purchased 80 acres, a part of which was afterward platted as the site of Keystone. Young Mrs. Twibell was born in Pennsylvania of Dutch descent and it is supposed that the village was named as a tribute to her and the Keystone State of her nativity."

However, another consideration is taken from a newspaper account in February of 1870, which talked about the building of a mill by the West, Baldwin and Company firm, also known as the Keystone Lumber Company. It states that a portion of a Mr. Henry Barchman's farm adjoining the mill had already been laid out into lots with two new dwellings built and a third under way.

The Keystone post office was established January 20, 1871, with William E. Rust being the first postmaster.

Among the early settlers of Keystone were Eph Ruth, W.H. Templeton, James Bell, James Jackson, Henry Cottrill, Robert Travis, O.P. French, Mollie Ransopher, William Ellsworth, and Arthur Scott.

KINGSLAND

Kingsland was another town that came into existence when the Chicago and Erie Railroad was built. The town was first established about the year 1886 when a Presbyterian church was erected there. The early residents of Kingsland were: Daniel K. Hanna, Donaldson Wilson, David T. Wasson, and Evan L. Chalfant. In the early days Kingsland was a rival of other nearby trading communities. While history does not reveal any facts, old settlers say the name Kingsland was chosen from the fact that land in the vicinity was productive. In reference to the name Kingsland, it is supposed that there was a desire to indicate that the land was "fit for a king."

Al Forst furnished at one time the information that Kingsland was named after a civil engineer named Kingsland, who aided in surveying the Chicago and Erie Railroad.

The post office at this location was established as Parkinson on June 9, 1882, by Postmaster Ebenezer Parkinson, but the name was changed to Kingsland on April 21, 1884.

The most notable event in the history of Kingsland occurred on September 21, 1910, when two traction cars collided there killing thirty-four people and injuring many others.

LIBERTY CENTER

Liberty Center was so named for its geographical center of Liberty Township. History notes that Liberty Township was first settled in 1836 and 1837 by James Jackson and Henry Mossburg. G.H. King and Johnson King were the next to arrive.

View of Keystone looking north from the M W or A building. The Keystone School is partially in view at the top right.

McNatt in the Summer of 1915 (l. to r.) Billy Felton on porch, Felton by huckster wagon, Ellis Parker with brooms he made (grandfather of Delight Parker), salesman by Model T, Josie Holmes (wife of William) with baby (probably Charles), Doris Holmes and Dorcas Holmes sitting on running boards, Kitty Holmes (wife of Chas) sitting in Model T, Bill Holmes in Model T and Chas. Holmes in front of Model T, Fred Penrod in front of huckster wagon (father of Dorothy Gregg), Cal Slater is man with vest who had barbershop in corner of store, Harrison Coffield sitting on the porch (left), and Oliver Williams also on porch (right).

The township was organized and the first election held at the home of John Kings, the inspector, on the first Monday in April, 1842. There were only nine voters at this election. They were: James Jackson, Henry Mossburg, G.H. and Johnson King, Jacob First, John McFarren, David Goings, John Mounsey and John Hupp.

The first road opened through Liberty Township ran from Bluffton to Jackson Township, leaving the center of Liberty Township to the right (west). It was surveyed with a pocket compass about 1839 or 1840. It has long since been obliterated by farms. The next road was the present north and south road running through Liberty Center.

History further says that if any one man may claim the fatherhood of Liberty Center it is the late John W. Rinear. He came to Liberty Township in 1854. He helped clear the land at Liberty Center and part of his farm was the site for the town. In 1863, after returning from the war, he married Sarah C. First, a native of Liberty Township. On December 28, 1866, a daughter Hannah S. Rinear was born, the first native child of Liberty Center. She married John B. Funk of Liberty Center.

Actually Liberty Center was laid out November 12, 1878, by John Ernst and John Rinear.

In 1881 it had a post office, three general stores, a blacksmith and wagon shop, two sawmills, a tile factory, two physicians and a population of 125.

The Liberty Center Post Office was established by Joseph R. Walker, postmaster, on November 18, 1857 but discontinued on February 3, 1864. Postmaster Samuel J. Jackson reestablished it in May of 1875 and it was again discontinued on January 27, 1893.

MARKLE

Markle, according to history, was first platted in 1836 and was known as Tracy, being named for a man who owned land where the town was first laid out. The town did not grow very fast until 1850, when Dr. Joseph Scott erected the first permanent residence. It was at that time, although no authentic statement in history is available, that the name of the town was changed to Markle. The name Markle it was reported, was obtained from the name of a man named Markle, who also owned land which was used for a part of the town site.

Madduxville was a small town next to Markle on the east side and located in Wells County. Most if not all of the Tracy portion of Markle was in Hungtington County. Madduxville became a part of the town of Markle. The Tracy Post Office established in may of 1849 was renamed Markle in June of 1852 and George F. Miller served as the first postmaster.

MCNATT

McNatt is located one mile west of State Road 3 on Road 800. It derived its name from an early store owner by that name. In the beginning of the century it was a beehive of activity, enlarged by the oil boom of the area. This small town expanded to include a post office, a drug store, a blacksmith shop, two grocery stores, and a barber shop in the corner of the store, which had the usual cracker barrel, pot belly stove, and loafers' bench. The store at the corner has been discontinued; the other has been a market for years and enjoys a thriving business.

In the early years, two huckster wagons were in operation. Some of the early store owners were named Jones at both stores. Jones was a very familiar name in the area in the early years. The Len Jones who was a former owner of the present store is a grandfather of Cecil Schwob of Warren. Some of the other owners of this store were Bill and Charles Holmes, Cecil Jackson, father of James Jackson, the Bluffton building contractor.

In the spring of 1929 Ivan Williamson and his family came to McNatt as owners of the McNatt store. Ivan formerly had a filling station at his farm home one mile north of Blanche Chapel Church corner. Ivan had been victim of polio as a very young boy and had to use crutches. He had a very good business ability and made a success. In his later years his nephew Jack Monce worked with him. After Ivan's retirement Jack bought the store, built an addition to it, and made a supermarket out of it. In the meantime Ivan and Jack both built new homes. The town is a very neat and well-kept; all the homes not built new are remodeled.

Many years ago the store at the corner was closed and the building was removed. The site is now farm land. In the early days of the village a two story building housed the Odd Fellows Lodge and Rebeccas. Many family get-togethers were held on the bottom floor. Ora Lawrence, who lived next door in a log cabin, was a photographer. He took many pictures of area residents.

Roger Sills is now the owner of the McNatt store and also bought the Ivan Williamson home. *Submitted by Nova Coffield Schoeff*

View looking north on Main Street, Murray.

MT. ZION

An initial village at the northeast corner of Jackson Township was called Mt. Zion. It contained a church owned by the United Brethren which later held the Methodist Protestant membership. Documented as class-leader in one reference piece was Dr. Morrison, with steward being Thomas Arnold.

The town grew until it crossed the road going east into the northwest corner of Chester Township.

Mt. Zion established a post office on May 26, 1873, under Postmaster Isaac Neff, but it was discontinued in April of 1888. Three weeks later, Samuel D. Cloud serving as the new postmaster reestablished the post office and led its operation until the next discontinuance on February 15, 1905. Postmaster Charles Alvey Colbert reestablished Mt. Zion Post Office one last time on May 18, 1905 and it continued until April 30, 1917.

Wabash River bridge at Murray.

MURRAY

Murray was the site of the first white settlement in Wells County. There is no recorded information regarding the origin of the name Murray. The settlement was called Lancaster and often New Lancaster prior to receiving the name Murray,

Dr. Joseph Knox was the first white man to settle in Wells County or at any point between Fort Recovery, Ohio, and Huntington for that matter. His 1829 home was near the Murray location. His brothers, Vantress and Warner, soon joined him, but all of them left in 1832 over Black Haw War fear.

Allen and Isaac Norcross settled near this location in 1831. Both also left in 1832 due to the war, with only Allen returning afterward. Jacob Miller settled a short distance below Murray in 1832 and Henry Miller settled in the Dr. Knox clearing a little later. Both stayed there through the Black Haw War. Henry Miller's daughter was the first white child born in Wells County.

Bowen Hale opened a store on the Orman Pering farm near Murray, becoming the county's first merchant, and in 1832 the county's first mill was built at Murray by Jesse Gerhard. The first post office in Wells County was the Murray (Lancaster) Post Office (actually a mile from Murray) established on September 16, 1837, by Postmaster Bowen Hale. It was discontinued July 15, 1902. The first three or four months yielded him just twenty-five cents.

This settlement, first called Lancaster, later New Lancaster, actually began about 1833, but on October 17, 1839, the village of Murray was laid out by Jesse Gerhard. Subsequently W.H. Deam and Mr. Matthews made additions.

In the election to determine the county seat of Wells County, the village of Murray lost to the village of Bluffton by a single vote.

OSSIAN

According to history, the town of Ossian dates from the year 1869, when the Fort Wayne, Cincinnati and Louisville Railroad was built; but thirty years before that event,

Looking north on Jefferson Street in Ossian about 1910.

Ossian Lake Erie and Western Depot on the west side of the tracks between Mill and LeFever.

the country in the vicinity of Ossian was being settled and there was a small community on the site of the present town. A post office by the name of Bee Creek was established September 28, 1846, by Levi Young but the name was changed to Ossian on May 11, 1850.

After the railroad was built, some stores and buildings were erected near the railroad, but this settlement was called West Ossian (established October 8, 1870).

The Ossian community was first settled by Robert and William Craig, John Davis, John Snyder, James Ferguson, and Levi Young, who arrived there in 1837 and 1838. In 1838, Levi Young was the only resident upon the present site of Ossian. In 1845, he was joined by John Glass, who married into the Hatfield Family sometime during the following years. He was the first merchant of the little settlement. The opening of the Glass store in 1845 was the sign of coming growth. It was not convenient to go to Fort Wayne for supplies, so settlers began coming to the Glass store.

In those early days, the woods in that vicinity were full of wild game, pea vines were very high, and not a domestic animal could be found in the neighborhood. Other pioneers who arrived were Jonathan Eddy, Amos Schnoonover, and Mrs. Mary Wallace and their families. In 1846, the promise of a future town seemed so good that William Craig, John Ogden, and Squire LeFever laid out the town and advertised a sale of lots.

No official record tells how Ossian's name was selected, but old timers recall hearing it said that the town was named after a man named Ossian (pronounced Osh'an), a legendary character of Celtic literature. According to tradition, he was a bard, or poet, the son of Finn, and belonged to Ireland and to the third century A.D. Finn commanded the Fenians who were conquered in the Battle of Gabhra in 283. Stories about Ossian spread over Ireland and Scotland, and he was popularized again by the Irish literary revival. A great Ossianic revival was held in Scotland and word of this spread throughout the literary world. Apparently William Craig, at least, and possibly others of the early settlers at Ossian, were from Scotland and Ireland and they possibly suggested the name Ossian, as they had no doubt heard or read of him in the literature from their homeland.

In the 1880's Ossian swelled to 700 inhabitants. The Nimmons Stave Factory employed over 100. By 1900 the population had grown to 1000. Ossian bought their first piece of firefighting equipment in 1895 after several previously unsuccessful attempts to organize a hook and ladder company.

PETROLEUM

During 1893 John Bears cleared away an old rail fence to make way for the first store building in what was later to be known as Petroleum. The store was opened two weeks before Thanksgiving; John Kirkwood, a farmer living nearby, was the first customer. In March, 1894, Bears received his commission as postmaster.

On the fifth of June, 1894, Samuel Neher laid out the new town in lots.

In 1895, M.D. Williams and John Bears built the store building owned by the Petroleum Odd-Fellows (it is once again a store after the fireman used it as a meeting place). The next enterprises in order were a hoop mill owned by Ober and Mann, a saloon, and a livery barn.

From 1895 the oil-well companies started booming, and the new town grew from a few scattered buildings to a town of some size.

On January 23, 1896, the Odd-Fellows were instituted. In 1897 the United Brethren Church was constructed. In 1904 the C.B.C. Railroad Company put a line through Petroleum and stimulated business activities to a great extent. At that time came an elevator, lumber and coal yards, stock yards, a hardware store, a bank, a furniture store a millinery shop, an ice cream cream shop and others, until the town had five general stores and still was growing.

In 1915 the railroad was removed and from then on the town gradually declined to its present status.

Petroleum

Left - Charles Fisher, Petroleum mail carrier, in Petroleum ready to begin his route.
Middle - Charles Fisher delivering mail from Petroleum during the winter. Doctor Markley residence is in the background.
Bottom - View looking east on Market Street in Petroleum.

Petroleum had a hotel (the building where Donald Blair lives). The bank was the building next to where Merrill Myers has his business. Many changes have taken place over the years.

PONETO

In 1871 Simon Tappy laid out Worthington, named after the superintendent of the railroad. At that time there was only one building which was Mr. Tappy's residence. Through the efforts of Mr. Tappy and Dr. Doster, the two men were able to get a railroad station and located the land for a depot site. The name of the village was changed to Poneto when it was found that another Worthington Post Office existed. Dr. C.T. Melsheimer owned a saw mill at one time in Poneto.

Poneto had a street fair back in 1889. Poneto was a small town that had a lot of things going for it until the depression and World War Two.

I can remember when Poneto had two grocery stores, owners being Jesse Barrington and Joe Toman. There was a blacksmith shop and it was run by William Jones and Sons. The garage was run by Hott and Howard Smith. The Howard Smith family, including sons Robert and Allen and grandsons, still run the garage business in Poneto plus they added a trucking service.

There were two restaurants, Ulmer and Ray Foreman Lunch Room. There was a drug store, and it was run by George Nelson. There were two grain elevators, owned by Hosier Grain and H.C. Arnold and Son. There was a meat market, and ice house run by John Hardwidge. There was a tile mill run by J.W. Cook where they made 3" to 15" tile.

There were two banks, Farmer State Bank and Bank of Poneto. Two barber shops were run by Frank Stroup and by John Kunkel. Earlier, there was a barber shop operated by James Snyder. There was a shoe shop and repair shop that was operated by Fred Melick, who also repaired leather things.

The newspaper back in 1901 was the *Poneto Press* which was printed once a week and later printed twice a week.

Dr. Huffman was one that I can remember, but there were other doctors before him. There was a funeral home at one time. I can remember the train depot and the train stopped there. They had an interurban which went north and south. North bound time was 6:15 a.m. to 10:38 p.m. South bound 4:52 a.m. to 11:15 p.m. Mrs. Ida Ramsey was the local agent.

Tappy had a general machine shop, where they worked on all kinds of machinery. There were also two churches. One was of

Baptist denomination with preaching services every first and third Saturday evening, Sunday School every Sunday morning and 9:30 a.m. prayer meeting on Thursday evening at 7 p.m. The Methodist Church services were 9:30 a.m. and preaching monthly at 10:30 a.m. with prayer meeting on Wednesday evening at 7 p.m.

Standard Oil had a bulk plant in Poneto, with an oil agent that lived in Poneto. There were two gas stations, Shell and Standard Oil, and a hardware that was run by Hugh Rowe. They had a small courthouse. There was a creamer shop that was run by Rena Kizer.

The grade school in Poneto was just grades 1 through 8. The high school students went to Liberty Center, Chester Center, Jackson Center and Petroleum and Bluffton. The grade school closed the spring of 1944.

There were two cemeteries: one east of Poneto named Grove, and one north of Poneto in Liberty Township named McFarren.

The manager of the lumber yard was Mr. B. Holsinger.

Lee Kimmel was a constructor who built homes, and also built Chester Center and Jackson Center Schools.

Culver Manufacturing Company moved to Poneto about 1950 and made shoes for children in an old schoolhouse. They stayed a short time.

The library bookmobile came to Poneto. They had free shows in spring and summer. There isn't much there anymore; just Smith's garage, the two churches, one grain elevator and two beauty shops. *Marcella Sleppy McFarren*

ROCKFORD

This beautiful village, once holding over ninety inhabitants, is appropriately named, as it is situated at a ford where Rock Creek ripples poetically along over a fine rocky bed, and is in the southwest corner of Rock Creek Township. This is about seven miles west of Bluffton. The town was laid out in 1849. The Post Office, named Barber Mills, was established August 4, 1852, by Postmaster Emerson Barber (also a local mill owner). The post office was discontinued February 15, 1905. Rockford was laid out September 21, 1849, by Solomon Johnson and Matthew Davis. A general store was operated into more modern times under the ownership of Mark Swank. Later for a time a shop was continued by his daughter and son-in-law, Earl L. and Julie Beitenhouse. Stone was quarried out of Rockford for many years. One of two local churches still survives. The Friends Church Cemetery is located east of the creek and east of the edge of town.

PONETO

View looking south on Market Street in Poneto. Everything in view in the picture is now gone.

View looking east on Walnut in Poneto.

L. E. & W. Station in Poneto. Photo courtesy of Don Welch.

TOCSIN

Tocsin began in 1883 and is located primarily in Jefferson Township on US224, just two miles west of the Adams-Wells County line. Tocsin established a post office in July of 1882 under the leadership of Postmaster Samuel Kunkel.

The word Tocsin means alarm, and it is supposed that since Tocsin was the location of a large siding of the railroad and it was necessary for trains to sound an alarm at this point, the name Tocsin was devised.

UNIONDALE

Uniondale was a village of 100 inhabitants, in 1882, and was located three miles west of Kingsland, on the Chicago and Atlantic Railroad. George C. Ditzler surveyed and platted the village in 1882 as a station on the Chicago and Erie Railroad. He had sold his sawmill at Murray and as he had just taken a large contract from the old Chicago and Atlantic for supplying the railroad company with ties, bridge timbers and other building material, he leased two acres at the southwest corner of the Gardenour farm and there erected a new mill. He was soon employing fifty hands and a dozen teams, and before long it was the largest sawmill in Wells County, having a capacity of 15,000 feet. After its completion in May, 1882, Mr. Ditzler furnished all the building material required by the railroad for some distance on either side of Uniondale. It afterward became a general merchant mill. It furnished ties and timbers to several railroads and turned out 2,000,000 feet of lumber annually. Mr. Ditzler's residence was the first one completed at Uniondale, and his mill sawed the lumber for it, as well as for all the other buildings constructed in the village while he remained at the head of the business. His son Charles was the first child born in the town of Uniondale.

George C. Ditzler and Henry W. Lipkey are recorded as the founders of Uniondale. Henry W. Lipkey built and conducted the first store in Uniondale, and when a post office was established on January 21, 1886, he was appointed postmaster. He was also appointed agent for the railroad company. He probably had equal honors with Mr. Ditzler as "leading citizen." Mr. Lipkey opened his store soon after the village was platted and in November, 1883, formed a partnership with William Newhard. The latter afterward branched out into the grain business and built the first warehouse in town. Mr. Lipkey continued to develop as a merchant and a citizen and invested the proceeds of his large business in various lines.

Tocsin residential street. Photo courtesy of Don Welch.

In 1883 Union Station Plat was made of five and sixty-four one hundredths acres in the area east of Main Street and south about one and one-third blocks. It was recorded May 27, 1883. On November 5, 1883, William and Frederica Baber recorded the plat of the Baber Addition. It is on the west side of Main Street and south about one and one-third blocks. The Merchant's Addition Plat was recorded by Oscar Newhard, president of Uniondale Improvement Association and Margarette B. Strausbaugh in 1909. The Merchant's Addition is L-shaped. It extends north of Otto Street about one and one-third blocks and includes both sides of Lincoln Street up to the railroad. Nothing was ever recorded about the north side of the tracks until in the year 1973. Property lines there were very irregular.

Around 1900 the telephone was brought to Uniondale. Electricity came between 1911 and 1912. In 1915 the Gilbert Block was constructed, but it was destroyed by fire in the 1980s.

The State Bank of Uniondale closed during the depression of 1930. At that time Uniondale was a community of 300 people with 100 homes and a number of businesses. The Uniondale Exchange was opened at that time. This time was a place to cash checks; make deposits; pay electric, telephone and garbage bills, and apply for loans. The business men took turns, making a trip to Bluffton each day to take in the deposits and bring back cash for exchange. This was done at the two Bluffton banks.

There have been many businesses in Uniondale, such as a bakery, saw mill, lumber yard, cement block factory, hotel, theater, two restaurants, depot, tin shop, blacksmith shop, Western Union telegraph office, bank, two grain elevators, butcher shop, three groceries, mush factory, hardware store, three filling stations, three garages, tie barn, two barber shop three doctor's offices, harness shop, furniture store, mortuary, creamery, print shop, post office, telephone exchange office, electric, plumbing and heating shop, vault factory, two beauty shops, carpet weaving, race track and three churches, antique shop and body shop.

The former Lutheran church was made into the town hall, which is now used for various purposes. The former bank building is used as a meeting place for the town council and other meetings. A garage was built back of the town hall for the fire trucks.

There are two lodges - Knights of Pythias and Red Mens, with each having a Ladies' Auxiliary. Later there was the Lions Club. The Conservation Club was known as The Blue Goose.

There were three modes of transportation - the Interurban, known as the CB & C, the Erie Railroad, and the Jitney Bus. The CB &C (Cincinnati, Bluffton and Chicago) was completed from Huntington to Portland. It never got any further. It was sometimes called "the Corned Beef and Cabbage." The Erie Railroad, which was double tracked, ran from Chicago to Hoboken, New Jersey. The Jitney Bus ran from Huntington to Bluffton, stopping at Uniondale.

As of 1991, Uniondale has two churches, an elevator, garage, post office, beauty shop, machine shop, body shop, paint shop, two large trucking companies, large tire warehouse and vault warehouse.

In 1982 Uniondale celebrated the 100th Anniversary of the town. The streets were filled with booths of all kinds, such as eating, riding and souvenirs. The streets were also crowded with people from far and near, who came to help celebrate the historic event and meet old friends. There was a large parade with most county officials participating. Governor Orr of Indianapolis was one of the visitors. There was a combined church service on Sunday.

Uniondale is proud to be the home of our State Representative, Jeffery Espich; and for many years we had a State Senator - Von (Pat) Eichhorn. *Submitted by Ola Brickley*

UNIONTOWN

The village, originally laid out by Leonard Walker, was located in Union Township, Wells County; on December 6, 1847, it was registered at Bluffton, Indiana. The village consisted of a general store, blacksmith shop, sawmill, post office, and a one-room schoolhouse. In 1860, the first church building was erected. The businesses in this small village have all vanished from their foundations; even the streets are now all under cultivation. As for the church, the building is still being used to accommodate worshippers.

The village was located on the north side of a high bluff, skirted by the Eight Mile Creek on the south. The main street of the town was what is now Road 220 West. On the north, running east and west, was Washington Street. Center Street was the main street of the village, with Polk to the south and Jefferson was a north-south street. Jackson Street went east and west of Main. All the lots were sixty feet by one hundred and twenty feet. The outside corners of the village were marked by trees: On the northeast corner was a beech tree measuring ten inches in diameter; on the southeast corner was a mulberry measuring ten inches in diameter; on the southwest corner was a white oak measuring 28 inches in diameter; and on the northwest corner was another white oak measuring thirty inches in diameter. The village was measured off in chain and links: 100 links-four rods 66 feet-one chain.

Schoolhouse Number Two was built by Stephen Cartright, 1850/51, in the village

UNIONDALE

Top left - Uniondale soldiers of World War I. Top right - Main Street. Middle - Gilbert Block. Bottom left - Erie Railroad gas car in 1912. Bottom right - CB&C track in Uniondale besides Erie.

Vera Cruz

Top right - View looking southwest on Center Street at Mulberry. *Top left* - Post Office and store on Center and Wabash Streets. Photo courtesy of Don Croy. *Middle right* - Jerry Croy at the Corner Store located at Wabash and Center Streets about 1954. Photo courtesy of Don Croy. *Bottom left* - Bixler House Hotel stood at the corner of Center and Wabash Streets from the 1850s until 1885. *Bottom right* - Crayon drawing of two stores on South Mulberry Street. The building on the right was later moved to the east edge of Vera Cruz. Photo courtesy of Mr. and Mrs. Bill Garrett.

and was made of logs. The mill was located on the Eight Mile Creek in a bend shape so that water could be dammed up then and allowed to flow over to power a saw mill. There was an "ashery" which provided lye to make soap and hominy. A post office was just north of the church. Robert McBride donated land for the use of a cemetery and also an orchard. It is interesting to note that in the middle of section two one may find the remains of perhaps the first original burial ground used by the community. A few tombstones are still present, but the little site is completely covered with growth by nature and forgotten by mankind. This article written by Mary Osburn Yoquelet, whose parents, Willis and Mary Ethel Osborn were members of the Uniontown Church of Christ.

Vera Cruz

In the spring of 1841, three families, the Sauers, the Meyers, and the Moeschbergers, came to make their home six miles east of Bluffton. There were no roads, just a trail. In 1849 the settlers named the town Newville, because it was a new village. In 1870 it was incorporated and the name was changed to Vera Cruz, meaning "True Cross." The citizens met at the school house at 7:00 p.m. and the house was full. The people voted 49 to 1 in favor of incorporating. The boundaries were presented. The name was changed at that time to that of the post office, Vera Cruz. The motion carried by a large majority. After the meeting, several tunes were played by the Newville Brass Band.

The town had many industries that people of today would not know about. A woolen mill, a brickyard, a tannery, a harness shop, a hoop factory, a blacksmith shop, a well diggers, cheese factories, a buggy shop, taverns, jails, and two hotels. When the railroad came to Bluffton, the businesses started moving there also. In 1849 a Lutheran preacher named Kleinekaes organized a

Reform Lutheran Church and at that time a parsonage was built; it also served as a meeting house. As they began making preparation for the church, the material was unfortunately consumed by fire. In 1854 a frame church was built for the St. John Reformed people. Croy Machine Shop occupies that building now. In 1897 a brick church was built. It was destroyed by fire in 1980, but a new church was built in 1981.

The Evangelical Association at Vera Cruz was organized in 1853. Andrew Nicolai was in charge. They started with a membership of twenty. The house of worship, a frame building that will seat 250 people was dedicated in 1855. This frame building at 2715 SE Mulberry is used as Croy Machine Shop's warehouse. That was called the Albrecht Church.

The first Apostolic Church, just outside town, was erected in 1867. The members of the congregation came from many miles, hence they stayed for a day of worship.

When the Studabaker Bank in Bluffton closed during the depression, the town of Vera Cruz books showed a balance of $117.87. Noted under that in red it said, "Gone but not forgotten."

Another landmark is the brick Steinier store. Harry Lindstrand made a watercolor painting of it. In the early 1950s they showed movies on the store front. When they put in street lights they put a switch on the pole so the light could be turned off for the movies.

In 1905 a large hardware store owned by Ed Neuenschwander was built. In later years Cal Roush's Barber Shop occupied that corner. Many a new hair cut or a candy bar came through those doors. Rhonda's Clip & Curl now resides there.

A small building housed Godlip Rollie's saloon which later was Howard Croy's Upholstery Shop for many years. It still stands at the east end of the town. Howard is now ninety and still does a little work in his garage across the river.

In 1955 the Vera Cruz Opportunity School was started with an enrollment of 10. The town's original school building was used. Later new buildings were built.

The townspeople and the church co-sponsored an ice cream social in 1984. The Singing Sheriff and a local group entertained over 400 people. They were Charles and Kenny Walters, Lester Alexander and Roy Meyer.

As early as 1925 the children of Vera Cruz formed a group to go trick-or-treating on Halloween. Maybe their tricks would be upsetting your outhouse. The children still go around together in a group on a chosen night for their treats, but now the tricks are that you may be t-p'd or get your windows soaped.

As you enter Vera Cruz you travel over a new bridge built in 1985, but if you look to the side you'll see the old iron bridge built in 1887. It's part of the history of earlier days.

For more information about the history of Vera Cruz you can refer to the books: *Biographical History Record of Adams and Wells County 1887; History of Wells County 1776-1976; "From these Roots"* by Charles Joray. Also there is a poem by John Baumgartner called *"Mother's Lamp In the Window,"* which gives you a feel of the town in years gone by. *Submitted by Phyllis Croy*

ZANESVILLE

Zanesville, Indiana, was founded on March 4, 1849, by Leonard and James Walker. It is situated on the Allen-Wells County Line which divides the town in half east and west.

Zanesville probably got its name from Ebenezer Zane, who was authorized by Congress in 1796 to open a road through the Northwest Territory between Wheeling, Virginia, and Limestone (Maysville), Kentucky, to connect Pennsylvania and the east with the Kentucky settlements by a land route, usable the year round, and to supplement the Ohio River as an emigrant route. The first road in Ohio determined the important settlements of the following years; where it crossed the Muskingum, Zanesville

Zanesville's Main Street looking West in 1920.

(Ohio) developed; at the Hockhocking, Lancaster (Ohio); and at the Scioto, Chillicothe (Ohio).

By 1812 an east-west road ran from Chillicothe to Cincinnati and trails developed from Cincinnati to Greenville and Fort Wayne. Southern Indiana settlements were dependent upon this road and Zanesville's founder, Leonard Walker, came from such a settlement in Rush County, Indiana, to Zanesville. What would have been more fitting to name his town than Zanesville, as all or most of the people settling there would have some time or another depended on Ebenezer Zane's Road.

Through the years it has been a thriving community with several businesses and many community oriented groups. Presently the population is approximately 630 and we have around 231 homes. The Allen County section of town is served by emergency number 911, while the Wells County section is covered for emergencies by the Markle and Uniondale fire departments. Presently being built just three miles north of town is a new Southwest Allen County Fire Station that will be an asset to all of us.

We are fortunate to have three churches in town. The United Methodists are on the south edge of town, the United Brethren in Christ is near the middle of town, and the Church of God is located on the west edge of town. All three have an average attendance of 100 to 150. They all have active youth groups, children's club, choirs, and midweek prayer services. In addition the men and women of each church have active groups.

On Labor Day each year we celebrate Homespun Days. It consists of a flea market, food, fun, music and fellowship. There is also a parade through town that day.

The Zanesville Lions Club is quite active with about 25 members. They meet on the second and fourth Mondays usually at the clubhouse at the ball diamond.

The Zanesville Park is sponsored by the Lions and it is busy almost every night all summer. The Lions provide the concessions there.

A community group called ZANA (Zanesville Area Neighborhood) meets every third Monday at the Lions Clubhouse at 7:00 p.m. The organization began in February, 1986. It grew out of a February meeting of the town residents, who decided they did not want to pursue incorporation but would prefer a neighborhood association be formed. At that meeting 39 out of 40 voting preferred the association idea. Trav Holdman, who was the organizer of the town meetings, asked for a volunteer steering committee to take charge until an election could be held. The first board elected was Jim Vinson, Rita Zeddis, Dave Frick, Sandy Frick, Melba Edwards, Kenny Edwards, Trav Holdman, Sheldon Wright, and Don Roebuck.

In the years that followed we attended many meetings. Our main concern was the development of a sewer system for the town. Other betterments have taken a back seat, as this is such a pressing issue. We met with sewer and board of health officials, both state and local. We were three years arranging an entry into the Allen County Sewer District. We finally attained that goal in April, 1989. In April, 1990, we are still waiting on funding. ZANA takes in an area of six square miles, with the boundaries of Hamilton Road on the north, Prine and 200 west on the east, 1100N on the south, and Zubrick or 400W on the west. This is a total of 389 homes. The present board is Jim Vinson, president, John Schuhumacher, vice-president; Melba Edwards, secretary; Barb O'Connor, treasurer, Don Roebuck, Kenny Edwards, Dave Frick, Carolyn Kern, and Gigi Bell.

In 1990 ZANA with the sponsorship of the Lions, started a recycling program here.

The truck is manned every fourth Saturday of the month by various non-profit groups in the community and is located at the ballpark. We have had very good response to this.

Also in 1990 our nutrition site opened at the Lions Clubhouse. It has been very successful and serves our senior citizens very good lunches and provides a place for them to fellowship.

Zanesville has had its own post office since 1854. It is currently located on Allen County side of town. We have a grocery store, a gas station, a lawn service, a feed mill, a small engine repair, a Pizza carryout, a lawn mower sales, an appliance sales and repair, a pallet factory, a chimney sweep, a mowing service, a coal company, a greenhouse, a locker, a country store and auction, a landscaping service, a beauty shop, and a Surge dealer. These businesses are in or near town.

The children here attend Lafayette Central Elementary School and Ossian Elementary, according to which county they live in. The high school kids go to Norwell or Homestead, and the junior high students attended Norwell Middle or Woodside Middle School.

All of our churches are members of Tri-Township Emergency Relief. Union, Lafayette, and Pleasant Townships are involved, and the organization helps needy and deserving families each year with food, clothing, and utilities.

If you would like to know all about Zanesville's history you may want to go to your local library and read the Zanesville, Indiana, History 1849-1976. This is an account of Zanesville history and families compiled by Melba McBride Edwards and Rosemary Kumfer and typed for printing by Velma Harden. For the past several years Zanesville has had a newsy column in the *Bluffton Banner* and the *Huntington Tab*.

Second Wells County Courthouse built in 1844 and demolished in 1889.

Wells County Jail built in 1880.

Right - A 1991 view of the Bluffton Downtown streetscape in front of the courthouse. Yellow ribbons were tied to lamp posts, and on trees in honor of the soldiers involved in the Gulf War.

Left - Main and Market Streets in Bluffton in 1894.

Right - Downtown Bluffton at Market and Johnson Streets in 1991.

Left - Wasson Grocery and Craigville Post Office as it looked in 1958. Pete Wasson was Postmaster. Photo courtesy of Don and Madge (Wasson) Hetrick.

Right - Craigville depot first located at the railroad crossing at road 301 but later moved to a different Craigville location and used by the Craigville Telephone Company for storage. It survives at a location at Ryan and Edgerton Roads northeast of New Haven.

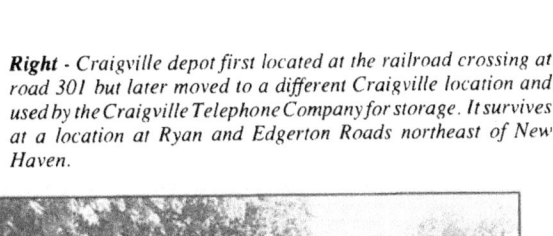

Left - In this 1987 view of Craigville in Lancaster Township, the post office is in view. It is now located in the old Bank building. Craigville still has an active business area.

Left - Curryville in a 1987 view, is located just west of the Wells and Adams County line in Lancaster Township.

Right - The round building at the right was the tile kiln at Echo, Jefferson Township. Echo photos courtesy of Velma Franke.

Left - Spading sod into a cart to make tile at the Echo Tile Mill.

Right - The saw mill and tile mill at Echo shared a common boiler.

Left - Remains of the Echo saw mill and tile mill after they burned down in 1923 or 1924.

Right - A 1987 view of Keystone.

Right - View looking north on Main Street, Liberty Center.

Left - Liberty Center State Bank built in 1907.

Right - View looking south on Main Street, Liberty Center.

Left - A 1987 view of McNatt in Jackson Township, which still retains its general store.

Right - A 1987 view of Mt. Zion located just south of IN 218.

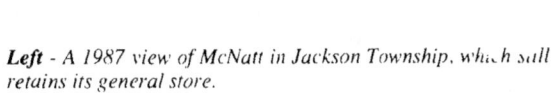

Left - The area of the earliest settlers and the first community in Wells County was Murray, which had its sesquicentennial in 1983. Murray came within one vote of becoming Wells County's county seat instead of Bluffton, which won a 3-2 decision for the designation back in 1838. This view is Murray in 1987. Photo courtesy of the Bluffton News-Banner.

Left - Main Street looking south in Ossian.

Right - Cochran Store and house in Phenix. Neighborhood center from 1919 until the early 1980s.

Left - Interior of the Cochran Store in Phenix as it looked in 1980.

Right - This is a 1987 view in Phenix of Nottingham Township. For many years the structure in the background was the store of the late Addie Cochran, who was a legend in her time as one of the veteran rural grocery-general store operators serving through an important era of Wells County history. Photo courtesy of the Bluffton News-Banner.

Left - In 1982, when Tocsin celebrated its 100th anniversary, the community had one business place in operation. The passing of the former railroad era and other genral economic developments changed the face of Tocsin. A half-century ago Tocsin had a number of stores, a lumberyard and other features. Today Tocsin has fine residents and churches in pleasant surroundings of a differant era and lifestyle. Photo courtesy of Bluffton News-Banner.

Right - Bluffton view looking south on Main at Washington in 1902.

Right - Uniondale Elevator powered by gasoline. Seventy-five cars of grain were shipped to Lima in 1894. The cars were 29-30 feet long with a capacity of 40,000 bushels.

Left - View looking east on Railroad Street in Uniondale in 1913. Photo courtesy of Mr. & Mrs. George Schwartz.

Right - View looking north on Main Street in Uniondale in 1910. Photo courtesy of Don Welch.

Left - Harness racing at the Uniondale track. Photo courtesy of Don Welch.

Right - View looking south on Main Street in Uniondale about 1910. Photo courtesy of Don Welch.

Left - The business district of Uniondale in 1987 looking north. This town celebrated its centennial in 1982.

A very early photo of Bluffton showing the south side of West Market Street.

The north side of West Market Street, Bluffton. The Studabaker Hardware is the present location of Murphy's Store.

Wells County Feature Stories

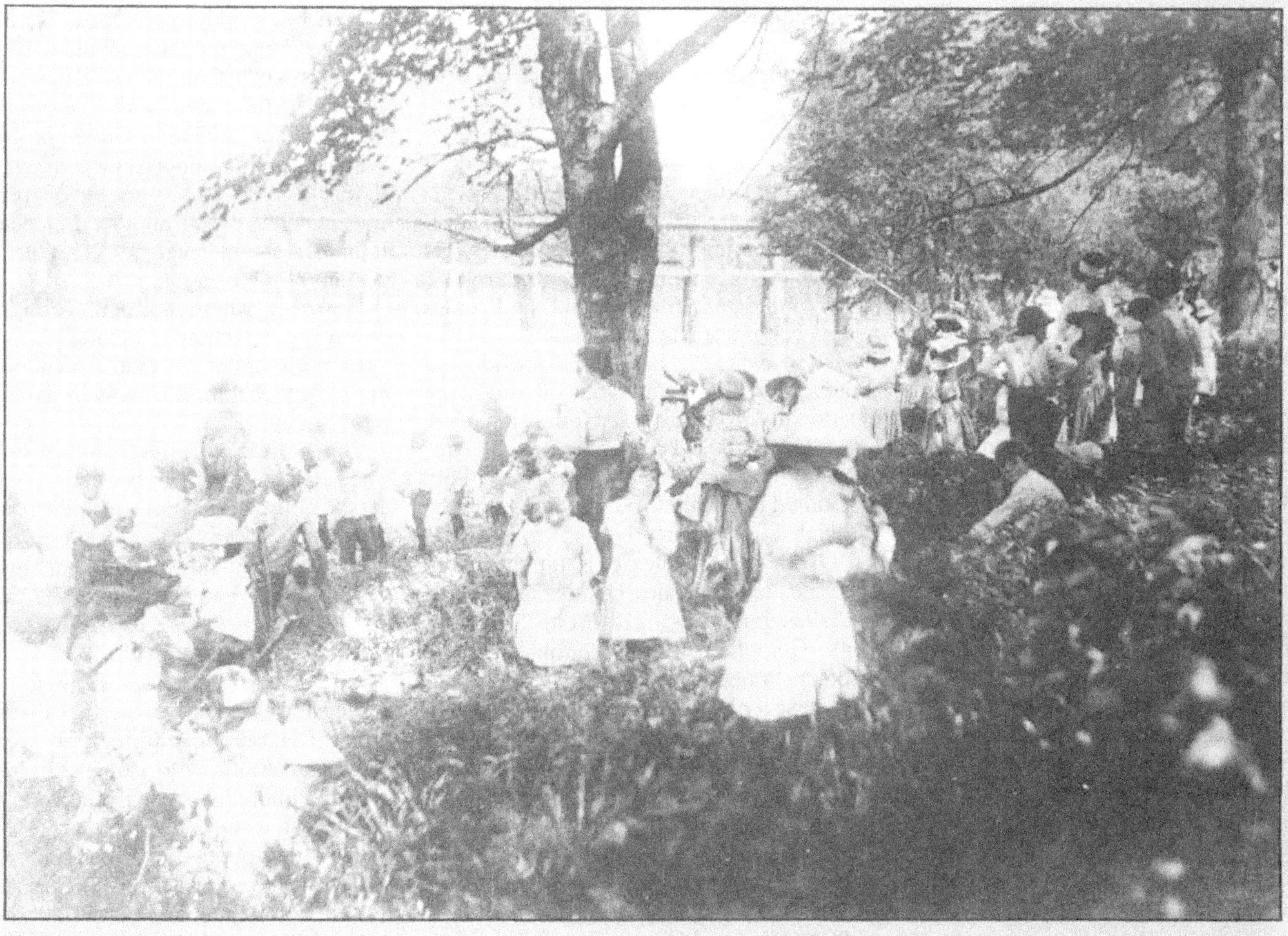

This group outing is located on the banks of the Wabash River in Bluffton once used during the Bluffton Street Fair as Fairland Park for the horse display and shows but currently named Kehoe Park, location of many outdoor presentations.

A Brief Political History of Wells County

If, in a discussion of politics, anyone should ask what have been the most influential features for Wells County, Indiana, over its 150-year history, the response might well be: the secret ballot and women.

These influences did not occur together and, in fact, came about 28 years apart.

Which became prominent first? The secret ballot.

Which did more to change the political complexion of the county? Women.

The secret ballot enables individual citizens to reflect their own minds without intimidation.

Women brought about closer scrutiny of candidates and brought about shifts in the political party holding power.

Wells County from its inception in 1837 became a political stronghold for the Democratic party in Indiana, along with other counties, including adjoining Adams County.

The secret ballot and women brought about a change in this climate, although it took a hundred ears to complete the process.

Politics in Wells County was dominated by men and the Democratic Party for more than four score years in the formative period of the county.

Today, the Republican Party has become the dominant power and women the deciding factor in many elections.

Use of the secret ballot for elections did not happen in Wells County until the city election in Bluffton in 1891.

In March, 1891, the Democratic Party decided that candidates for its slate for city offices would be determined under the new Indiana election law, which provided for use of what was described in news accounts of that day as the "popular Australian system of voting."

Republicans held to the party caucus for slating candidates.

Saturday, April 11, 1891, was fixed by the Democrats as the date for holding an election.

And, in 1892, the secret or Australian ballot was adopted countywide and records started being kept in county-level offices.

The Australian ballot originated in the mid-1800s, in Australia, made its way to England by 1872 and, in the United States of America, found its first use in 1888 in Louisville, Kentucky.

A dictionary definition of the Australian ballot: an official ballot printed at public expense on which the names of all nominated candidates and proposals appear and which is distributed only at the polling place and marked in secret.

Ballots were in use in Indiana by 1850 but they were not secret.

Each political party printed and supplied its own ballot on paper of a special color. As a voter approached a polling place, party workers offered him their ballot. If the voter wished to vote for candidates of different parties, he could cross out certain names and write in others.

But the colors of the ballot made it possible for everyone to see which party he was supporting.

Today, voting machines or computer punch cards are in use almost everywhere.

Voting machines were first used in the United States as early as 1892.

In the early 1970s, Wells County experimented with the bulky voting machine before adopting the computer election system of punch card ballots with the Bluffton City primary election in May 1975.

And, in 1976, the punch card ballot was used countywide and remains thus today.

But back to 1892.

In a national election that year, a man became the first and only resident of Bluffton to serve in the House of Representatives of the United States Congress. He was Augustus N. Martin, a lawyer, who was re-elected to subsequent two-year terms in 1894 and 1896 before losing out in an 1898 race.

In 1892, Wells County had 4,921 persons, all men, of course, cast ballots for one of four presidential candidates. In Wells County that election, the Democratic presidential candidate polled 2,725 votes, the Republican candidate 1,668, the Prohibition candidate 210 votes, and the Peoples Party candidate 318 votes.

Four years later, in the 1896 presidential election, Wells County voters found seven parties listed on their ballot. These included, in addition to the Democrats, Republicans, Prohibition and Peoples tickets, the Gold Standard Party, the National Party and the Socialist Labor Party.

Of the 6,038 votes cast for the seven presidential candidates, Democrats received 3,579, Republicans 2,212, Prohi 48, Peoples 149, Gold Standard 5, National 43, and Socialist Labor 2.

The seven presidential candidates in 1896 were the most Wells County voters were ever to find on their ballots until the year 1980 when eight appeared.

For those with short memories, the eight parties listed on the 1980 ballot were Democratic, Republican, American, Libertarian, Communist Party USA, Socialist Workers, Independent and Citizen.

The voter turnout in Wells County in 1980 was 10,677, about 84 percent of those eligible to vote. Even then, 232 voters did not vote for any of the eight presidential candidates.

History should note that in Wells County in 1980 Republicans polled 5,864 votes for that party's presidential candidate while the Democrat candidate receiving 3,760.

Of the remaining six parties, the Independent received 717 votes, Libertarian 85, American 8, Citizens 6, Socialist Workers 4 and Communist USA 1.

Through Wells County's 150 years of history, there have been other so-called minor parties and their candidates on ballots.

These minor parties have had names of Union Reform, Single Tax, Progressive, Farmer-Labor, Workers, Lafolette Progressive, Socialist, Farmers and Laborers, Socialist Democrat and Peoples.

The minor party peak occurred in 1912, a year in which former U.S. President Theodore Roosevelt ran under the banner of the Progressive Party against Democrat Woodrow Wilson, who was elected, and Republican William H. Taft. While Roosevelt placed third in the national presidential contest, he ran second in Wells County, polling 1,080 votes; Wilson received 2,758 and Taft 812. Wilson carried Indiana that year, followed in order by Roosevelt and Taft.

Only other minor party presidential candidates making indentation into voting patterns in Wells County were the election years of 1968, when, with five candidates for president, Alabama Governor George Wallace, running on an Independent Party slate, received 882 votes or 7.7 percent, and, in 1980, when another Independent, John Anderson, received 717 votes or 7 percent of the turnout.

However, where in all this voting is the power of the woman evident?

In 1920, under the 19th Amendment to the U.S. Constitution, women gained the right to vote.

The immediate effect of this suffrage was to give Wells County over 4,100 more person going to the polls, in addition to the 5,200 men already casting ballots.

Up to this time, the Democratic Party in Wells County had been outvoting the Republican Party about 3 to 2 in presidential election years.

Apparently there was little gratitude among the women for the fact that a national Democratic administration under President Woodrow Wilson had passed the suffrage amendment and pushed it to ratification by the states by 1920.

In Wells County in 1920, based upon an analysis of election figures recorded for that era, the Republican Party skimmed off over 2,400 of the 4,100 new women voters, while the Democratic Party gained only a little over 1,700.

The result was that the Democratic margin of victory that year in the presidential race in Wells County was pared to 223 votes.

By 1944, a time when the children of the women of 1920 would have reached voting age, Wells County "went Republican" for the first time in a presidential year, giving handsome, mustachioed Thomas Dewey its majority of votes over aging and ailing Franklin D. Roosevelt, who was making a successful bid for his fourth term as America's chief executive.

While the Democrats carried Wells County in 1920 by a vote of 4,653 to 4,430, the Republican Party took the nation by almost a 2 to 1 popular vote to elect as president Warren G. Harding over a long-since forgotten Democratic candidate by the name of James M. Cox.

By 1924, some of the newly franchised women must have become disenchanted because over 600 voters failed to go to the polls in Wells County that year. Of that number the Republican Party lost 500.

In the presidential race of 1928 in which Republican Herbert Hoover topped Democrat Al Smith, Wells County remained in the Democratic column by a bare 104 votes.

Election tallies of the period reveal that as many as 210 Democrats may have swung over to the Republican column and another 300 may have stayed away from the polls.

Again, in 1932, women may have been a factor as Wells County, along with the rest of America, wearied of the Great Depression and voted into the presidency Democratic Franklin D. Roosevelt (FDR).

A new voter surge was evident in 1932 as the total of 9,526 turning out at the polling places surpassed the previous record of 9,356 votes cast in 1920.

Voter interest and participation in Wells County continued high through the 1940 election with 10,257 voting in the presidential balloting. However, the next 20 years saw a slight decline in voter turnout and the 10,000 voter figure in Wells County was not attained again until the presidential election in 1960.

Republican Thomas Dewey carried Wells County by a 233 majority in 1944 over FDR but lost out nationally. Dewey was to lose out four years later, however, as President Harry S. Truman, a Missouri Democrat, carried Wells County by 438 votes and upset the national pollsters by winning re-election to the presidency.

But the lean years were coming for the Democrats in Wells County, especially in presidential voting years.

The Republican presidential candidate has won the majority of votes in Wells county in every presidential year since 1948 with the exception of 1964, when Texan Lyndon B. Johnson, elevated to the presidency with the assassination of President John F. Kennedy, won 60 percent of the Wells County vote over Arizona Senator Barry Goldwater.

That 60 percent victory margin in Wells County in 1964 established a record which was not to be surpassed until 1972 when Republican Richard M. Nixon, going for his second term as president, carried Wells county with 66 percent of the vote cast.

The record was short-lived, however, with the new mark of 70 percent of the Wells County vote cast going in 1984 to Republican candidate Ronald Reagan, who also was making a successful second term presidential bid.

The turnout in 1984 also set a new record for voter interest and participation.

A record 11,188 voters went to the polls.

The turnout was 80.4 percent of the 13,909 citizens registered and eligible to vote in 1984s presidential contest.

In the year 1944, in which Wells County gave presidential candidate Dewey a majority in a losing cause, the Republican Party candidates won seven of nine county-level offices.

The first woman ever elected to a Wells County office also occurred in 1944.

That woman was Mrs. Helen Harris, a Republican, who held the office of county recorder for four years, from 1944-48.

The recorder's office never has been won by a male since.

While the honor being the first woman elected to public office goes to Mrs. Harris, she was not the first to serve in a county-level capacity.

The first woman was Mrs. Lena Lantis, widow of Sheriff Orve Lantis.

Mrs. Lantis served 18 months as sheriff, only four months shy of a full two-year term, after her husband died in April 1936 as he started his second term as sheriff. Mrs. Lantis assumed the sheriff's post on May 1 as a result of her appointment to fill the vacancy by the Wells County Board of Commissioners.

Others to follow in county-level positions were Mrs. Lovie Fishbaugh, who was appointed as county auditor to complete the term of her husband, Clarence E. Fishbaugh, who died while holding the auditor's office; and Mrs. Iva Schwartz, who served the remainder of the term as county treasurer of her husband, David Schwartz, who died in 1951. She then was elected in her own right to the treasurer's office for two terms, serving from 1953-56.

Not only did Mrs. Harris break the mold in 1944 by being elected as a woman, but she also penetrated, as a Republican, public offices most often held by Democrats at the county level.

In 1944 also, Republicans poured into other offices in Wells County, capturing seven of nine posts, including sheriff, auditor, treasurer, coroner, surveyor and one county commissioner, as well as the recorder's position.

It was a great moment of victory for the Republican Party, which for decades had been one of the "minority" parties in Wells County.

Again, in the presidential voting year of 1944, Wells County voters gave Republican Thomas Dewey 5,648 votes to 3,804 for Democrat Franklin Roosevelt, who nonetheless was re-elected nationally to his fourth term in the White House.

Democrats in Wells County were to regain offices two years later, in 1946, with World War II over.

Many county-level offices were for two-year terms only in those times and, in 1946, the Democrats recaptured the offices of auditor and surveyor and, two years later, in 1948, the offices of recorder, sheriff, treasurer, coroner and commissioner.

Republicans were not idle in the ensuing year after the big losses in 1948, a year in which Democrat Harry S. Truman, in carrying Wells County, upset the national pollsters by winning re-election to the presidency of the United States over Republican Thomas Dewey.

In 1952, the Republicans won two of the three seats on the Wells County Board of Commissioners, establishing a "first ever" in history by holding the majority positions on that board. The triumph was sweet, although the party was to lose that hold two years later in 1954.

If the years had become lean through much of the 1960s for the Republican Party, it was coming to an end.

In 1968, the Republicans won two county commissioner offices to dominate the board again and the offices of recorder and surveyor. This was followed, in 1970, by capturing the offices of sheriff, treasurer and assessor.

Through much of the 1960s, Democrats gained offices because of little or no opposition from Republican candidates at election times. And most of these Democratic Party winners were returned to a second term in their respective offices.

In a recounting of Wells County political history, it would be remiss to forget a moment in 1982 in which a candidate running as an Independent won a county-level office.

Mrs. Joyce Harris, who had been elected in 1978 to the office of county clerk as a candidate on the Republican Party ticket, itself a first for that county office, declared herself an Independent four years later and was re-elected to the county clerk's post in 1982 despite opposition from her former party as well as the Democrats.

The Republican Party was not daunted, however. In the election of 1984, Republican victories took six of the seven county-level offices at stake and placed the party in control of not only the Board of Commissioners but also the County Council, a seven-member board, for the first time in Wells County history.

As a result of further Republican Party inroads in the election of 1986, Democrats were left with only four in county offices, the post of auditor and three positions on the County Council.

In 1990, Democrats made a net gain of one office, winning the sheriff's post for the first time in 20 years. *By Eugene McCord*

BLUFFTON BASEBALL

Bluffton's professional baseball team history included franchises in two minor leagues. A Bluffton team was a member of the Indiana State Baseball League during the summer of 1890 from May 1, to June 30. On June 30, 1890, the Bluffton Club was disbanded according to a Chronicle report after the Elkhart team disbanded. Bluffton was the newest team in the league and was asked to leave in order to "even up" the clubs. The Bluffton team and supporters were not happy about this decision to sacrifice their group.

In 1909 the city was a member of the Northern State Baseball League of Indiana and the city team took the pennant. The season ran from June 1, to September 19 with "Ducky" Eberts manager and captain of the team until June 28 when he left to play for a Hannibal, Missouri team. He was replaced by Herman Weber. Teams in the league were Bluffton Babes, Huntington Johnnies, Wabash Rockeries, Lafayette Wets, Marion Boosters and the Kokomo Wildcats.

In 1910, while with the same league, the Bluffton Babes again took the pennant. The opening dates for the Bluffton team was July 2 and the final game was played September 18, 1910. "Daddy" Orr was the manager of this team ending with 48 wins and 23 losses. Other teams and won-loss records in the league included Wabash, 45-27; Lafayette, 37-32; Marion Boosters, 30-39; Huntington Johnnies, 24-42; and the Logansport Whitecaps, 24-45.

May 24, 1911 was opening day for that year. While in the same league, the Bluffton team finished third out of six teams. This team was sometimes referred to as the Schocklies after the captain and manager Jack Schock. The season ran till July 29 when a lack of funds and fan support were blamed for the disbanding of the Bluffton Club. The Anderson team also disbanded. The Logansport team walked out after the June 20th game when they found out there was no money to pay their salaries. Also in the league were Lafayette Farmers (also called Wets, Marion Boosters, and Huntington Indians).

Between July 28 and July 31, 1911, efforts were made to revive the Northern State League of Indiana, but to no avail, and these efforts were abandoned by August 1, 1911. *(This article was compiled from local newspaper research notes of Barbra Lesh of the Wells County Public Library.)*

BLUFFTON POLAR EXPLORER

History books tell us Admiral Robert E. Peary was the first person to reach the North Pole, accomplishing the feat April 6, 1909, on his sixth attempt.

Nothing is said in these history books that a Bluffton doctor and surgeon might have been the first in 1907. Dr. Walter N. Fowler was a part if a five-man crew which formed the Walter Wellman Polar Expedition in 1906 for an attempt at "discovering" the North Pole by flying over it in a balloon.

Dr. Fowler was not aboard the Wellman Expedition balloon in its single assault on the polar region.

After the flight failed, Dr. Fowler returned to Bluffton in October, 1907, to reopen an office as a specialist on the eyes, ears and nose. The physician-surgeon had been gone from Bluffton six months.

The Wellman Expedition established its base camp at Spitsbergen on Svalbard Island, a Norwegian possession north of Norway and about 600 miles from the North Pole. The summer season had passed when the balloon airship "America" was taken from its shed on September 2 and made an ascent. Despite bad weather, Wellman found the airship performing well and made a decision that a start be made immediately for the North Pole. Aboard with Wellman were two other men identified only as Risenberg and Vandman. However, 30 miles from the Wellman base camp, the airship encountered a severe storm and was driven backward and landed on top of a glacier. The three men were rescued.

The flight had not been a planned one, but when the balloon's motor was found to be working in good order, Wellman cast off its anchor ropes attached to an accompanying steamer below and headed for the pole position some 600 miles away. It had been calculated earlier than a round trip of 1,200 miles could be made within a day's time of 12 hours. Encountering high winds and finding the airship being pushed backward, Wellman opened the balloon valves to permit the aircraft to descend quickly, landing on a glacier, where the balloon was secured.

Some 15 miles away, a rescue party directed by Dr. Fowler headed from the steamer and reached the glacier one and a half hours later. The three men who had occupied the airship were uninjured and all of the expedition's equipment was intact. Considerable difficulty was encountered in saving the airship, however, and the balloon had to be taken to pieces in order that it might be transported over the ice ridges and fissures to the ship at sea. This task was accomplished in two days, and on the evening of September 4, the expedition was back at Dane's Island, not far from the Wellman Camp.

Dr. Fowler, in addition to his medical knowledge, was an able mechanic and telegrapher and had entire charge of erecting and manipulating the suspension in the balloon's house. On numerous occasions, Wellman had written in his daily diary of the fine work of Dr. Fowler.

In one account, a letter sent to a Bluffton newspaper, Dr. Fowler related:

"Everyone is busy. We are working two shifts of men making gas for the big balloon and I tell you she is a hummer." "I made ascensions in large balloons in Paris but this is a whale compared to them. The work on the mechanical part of the airship is finished and inflation will be started...and then take about two weeks to suspend the car and load it and have everything in readiness." "I can imagine the thrill that will run through the patriotic American when the word comes that the great Wellman airship is off for the pole."

"It is absolutely impossible to get any idea of the size of this great ship which picks up and carries through the air at the rate of 15 miles an hour a load of more than 19,000 pounds and can keep it up for 1,200 miles."

"We can have the same motley assembly as a year ago (1906). English, French, German and Norwegian all spoken in our camp. Our laboring men are a fine lot of fellows and the two Frenchmen are a great improvement over last year."

Because one of the major concerns for the airship was the feared accumulation of snow or sleet on the more than half-an-acre area of the 250 foot long gas bag, hot air from the cooling mechanism of the two gasoline engines used to propel the airship was circulated within the bag. In addition, a device called an "equilabrator" eliminated the need for ballast and for venting gas. The device was designed to hold the altitude of the aircraft constant. Two parts, known as the "snake" and the "sausage," made up the device. The snake was a thick, rope-like structure covered with steel scales and designed to drag over the ice with the exposed points of the scales to cause a braking effect.

The sausage consisted of a 150-foot segmented tube containing 1,500 pounds of provisions. This unit was waterproof, capable of floating and covered with smooth steel scales.

These devices could be reeled in or out with winches as the need arose. To compensate for any accumulation of ice on the balloon, an appropriate length of the sausage could be reeled out to float along in the water or skim along over the ice.

Soon after the futile flight of the "America," Wellman closed up his expedition camp and the unit members disbanded for their respective homes. Dr. Fowler was met in New York City by his wife and the two made a visit to Washington before returning to Bluffton in mid-October.

In response to an inquiry, Dr. Fowler said he did not believe he would go again "even if there was an expedition" the following year (1908).

The North Pole expedition was not without its perils for the Bluffton doctor. He came near to losing his life by falling into a deep chasm in the ice while leading the rescue party from the ship to the downed Wellman balloon. Dr. Fowler told in an account that he was attempting to separate dogs which were fighting when the snow upon which he was standing slipped from under his feet and he was plunged into a chasm as far as the rope to which he was bound to his companions would let him go. The rope held and his companions succeeded in pulling him out of the chasm, where a fall would have meant certain death.

Wellman did not return to the Arctic region for another attempt, and it was not until 19 years later that a flight was made over the North Pole. Richard E. Byrd and Floyd Bennett of the United States accomplished the feat on May 9, 1926.

And history books so record it. *Submitted by Eugene McCord*

CHILDREN'S HOME

The building was constructed at a cost of $25,000 in 1929 by Clark Construction Co. Everett Brown, an architect, designed the plans of the building, which featured two wings for separation of the sexes.

It was designed to house about 30 children, but rarely did the population of the institution exceed 20 persons. Mrs. Vera Plan, who was juvenile officer and welfare director during the early years of the home, said that on the average from 15 to 20 children were in the home in the 1930s.

In 1929 this new children's home took the place of the former Wells County Orphanage which had been condemned by the state and refused a license to operate. It was constructed on the site of the former building situated three miles south and one-half mile east of Bluffton.

At the time of the new structure's erection, the institution was known as the Wells County Detention Home. The county commissioners, "against their will," according to a newspaper report, were pressured into changing the Wells County Orphanage to the Wells County Detention Home. A formality, but Circuit Court Judge Frank Gordon claimed that the change in name of the institution was necessary according to state law.

When the Welfare Department was created in 1936 and assumed control of aid to dependent children and operation of the two-story brick building, the institution became known as the Children's Home. As the Welfare Department began to place more and more children in private homes instead of the institution its population decreased to one child in January 1949.

That same month the county commissioners decided to abandon the home and recommended that it be used as a nursing and convalescent home. A home was found for the lone child on January 15 and it was announced that the Children's Home would close Feb., 1, 1949.

It became the Davis Nursing Home soon after it fell out of use as the children's home. Mr. and Mrs. Robert Davis operated the nursing home until 1954 when it became the South View Nursing Home under Mrs. Cora Anderson and her son Carl. They continued operating the nursing home there till the property was sold by the county on September 8, 1970. *(Taken from accounts in an article in the September 5, 1970 News-Banner.)*

CLINT PROUGH

Zanesville is and always has been a great sports oriented town. In basketball we had the great team of 1911. When baseball season came I thought I needed to get more information on Clint Prough so I could tell you more about him. Then lo and behold his daughter shows up at the U.B. Church. I had written a story a week before and I didn't know of the beautiful story that was going to enfold from that meeting. I feel this story is so important that I got permission to tell it to you first-hand.

I knew that Clint Prough was the son of Harrison and Jane Prough who lived two miles south of Zanesville on a farm. I knew that he was born in the late 80s and he went to Zanesville to school. I knew that he was married very young to a Dollie Walker, a daughter of Clark and Vine Walker, and they had a daughter, Arlene Carey of Huntington. I knew of his short baseball career with the Cincinnati Reds. I knew that he at some time divorced Dollie, and Arlene was raised in Zanesville by her grandparents. I

Thanksgiving 1907 - (l. to r.) Front row: Dalton Hanauer, Harrison Prough, Lyle Hanauer, Jane Cartwright Prough, Valentine Hanover. Second row: Mildred Davis Saal, John C. Davis, Nellie Prough Davis, Cora Prough, Frank Prough. Third row: Elizabeth Prough Hanauer, H. Clinton Prough, and Mary Prough Morrison.

didn't know" "the rest of the story." I needed more information and here was my chance. I went outside to talk to the Prough girls after church that morning.

Pharol told me she was Clint's daughter from a second marriage, and because of her family's feeling about divorce in those early days she had never met her half-sister in Huntington. I myself having three half-brothers, said to her "Gee, you better get to know her, you may not know what you are missing. Anyway you and your sister are not held responsible for what happened among family members a long time ago." I didn't know those words would have such an impact until I got a phone call from Pharol a few days later. She said, "Guess what? I jut met my sister today and she is a lovely person! I went home the day I was at Zanesville at church and I thought about what was said, and I called Arlene and said, "This is your half-sister, Pharol, would you like to get together?"

Of course the reply from another lovely lady, who I myself have since met, was "Yes!!" They both agreed they had a marvelous day together for the first time.

Pharol first found out she had a half-sister when she was 16 and her father took her to Knight's Store. It was there that Don Merchant innocently came over to her and said, "You sure look like your sister!"

Pharol and Arlene have many years to make up as they have lived the short distance, between Fort Wayne and Huntington, from each other for over half a century.

Pharol Pringle and Arlene Carey gave me some of Clint's story to relay to you. Clint married Dollie Walker at a young age and his dream was to play ball. Dollie's mother would not allow her daughter and small child to go traipsing over the country with a ballplayer husband and most mothers in that day and age would have agreed with her!

Pharol is not certain of the year her father played at different places. She knows he first started playing baseball in Zanesville. I'm sure he had many fans at the games here. Baseball was only a few years old and the National League was only born in 1876, just 11 years before Clint was born.

Clint's desire to play ball was so intense that he left his wife and small child in Zanesville and went on the road to play ball. He met Pharol's mother in Illinois and married her. During the years of 1911, 1912, 1913 he played at Birmingham, Alabama. It was in 1912 that he pitched one game for Cincinnati under manager Henry O'Day. He only played the one game, in which he pitched three innings, allowed seven hits, one base on balls and one strike out. He was six feet three, weighed 185 pounds and was very handsome. Because of his size, besides being nicknamed Bill he was called "Wee Willie." He played for the Coast League, being six years with Sacramento and five years with Oakland. He played games as far north as Seattle and as far south as Los Angeles. He then went with the Southern League, playing for Shreveport, Louisiana, in towns like Fort Worth, Dallas and El Paso. Clint was a pitcher for all these leagues.

About 1926, his arm went bad and he returned home to Indiana. Pharol remembers the trip home from Hamilton, Illinois, on Race Day in 1926 or 1927. She said the traffic to Indiana was bumper to bumper.

Clint played every and any game that was held around Zanesville at this time. He bought a farm because he didn't have any other trade to turn to, as baseball had been his life. He played a while for the bush league in Fort Wayne. He felt he was sort of a failure. My husband says that happens to a lot of famous sports people because their prime time is so short, and when that time is over they don't known what else to do! Clint died at the young age of 48. To us at Zanesville and to his children and grandchildren, he will never be considered a failure. Instead we will consider Clint Prough as our "Indiana Legend."

You'll find Clint in the Baseball Encyclopedia, but don't believe all you read there, as it says he was from Martle, Indiana (instead of Markle, Indiana, R.R. 1 near Zanesville). It says he was a right-handed pitcher, when he was left-handed, and it gives his birth date as November 25, 1888. In Pharol's mother's Bible, out of which her mother picked her name, it is recorded as November 28, 1887.

DEAM MEMORIES

Adam Deam, the father of the family, came to this (Wells) County in 1845, from Montgomery County, Ohio and established the first grain mill, which was located on the north bank of the Wabash River at Murray, on the site now known as the Harnish farm. He was father of nine children, all raised in this county.

Harrison Deam, the oldest son, and Robert Deam, the youngest son of Abram Deam, a son of the pioneer Adams Deam, recalled their happy childhood days at and around the old mill at Murray, and earlier in the day had the unusual experience of visiting their former home and finding a few of the old relics still in use. The party found the old hickory pegs in the barn, upon which they hung harness during their boyhood days. They also found the old grain bins in the same position and many other little things about the place brought back thoughts of the happy days. Upon entering the house the men recognized the stones now being used as steps as the stones formerly used in the mill.

Memories then drifted to the early political days in Bluffton, when J. P. Deam, the father of Herbert Deam, was elected a member of the town council and during whose administration the public improvements were brought up. Mr. Deam was emphatically in favor of sidewalks, and against considerable opposition he won his fight and a sidewalk was laid on the north side of Market Street from Main to Johnson. The people at the time prophesied that they had always walked in the road and could continue to do so and that the new improvement would bankrupt the community. The old plank road from Bluffton to Fort Wayne was again traveled, but the big topic of interest was the opening of the Lake Erie Railroad and the entrance into town of the first train. Mammoth crowds came from far and near to welcome the iron monster and on the cabin of the engine were, in gold letters, the word "Bluffton." *Information taken from a September 9, 1919, Evening Banner article.*

HOVERSTOCK CEMETERY

Hoverstock Cemetery is located in the northern part of Union Township on the south edge of the town of Zanesville. William Hoverstock and his wife Margaret donated the land on which the cemetery stands. There are many interesting scenes and objects in Wells County and in this cemetery you will find one of the most beautiful. This is the monument that was erected in the middle of the cemetery. It is the statue of William and Margaret and it is life size, said to be the exact image of the couple. The statue was made in Italy, carved from stone, at the cost of $1500 at that time. Some say the carving was made from a picture, others say the couple made a trip to Italy and posed for the carving. Below the statue is the inscription William Hoverstock 1815-1903 and Margaret Hoverstock 1820-1890. In the mound are buried the father and the mother of Mr. Hoverstock, along with him and his wife. William was the last to die of the group and the key to the vault was placed in the casket with his body, and after the burial, the padlock was closed. Some say the key was thrown into Eight Mile Creek! Later, the entrance to the mound was filled with dirt. The Zanesville School pupils remember walking to the cemetery with their teacher and being allowed to go in the vault the day of the funeral before the sealing. William's funeral was the most expensive on the Brindle Mortuary books. It cost $208 with a metallic casket! Today

Hoverstock Cemetery

Craig Lenwell with the George Bush stone.

New signs at Hoverstock.

Hoverstock statue.

the cemetery is lovely thanks to the loving care of caretaker Cal Burger. This past year he has seen that a wrought iron ornamental fence was placed around the statue area. The fence was handmade by Lynn Daffom a Union Township resident and native of the Zanesville area. Cal has also added new signs at the front of the cemetery. He was able to do this with the help of good friends Don Roebuck and Dick Thomas. William Hoverstock was also one of the great leaders of the church in Zanesville. He was well known for his generosity and humanitarianism.

Another interesting fact about the cemetery was discovered just this year by a young man of Zanesville, Union Township. Craig Lenwell, son of Kim and Glenda Lenwell was researching the names on the stones with his grandmother Peggy Thoma Roebuck. He came across a small single stone that reads simply GEORGE BUSH - FATHER - AGED 84 YEARS

Kingsland Wreck Victims

Mahl Paxon, after weeks of hard efforts, has succeeded in securing a photograph of every one of the forty-three passengers who were on the ill fated car, No. 233, which was completely wrecked at Kingsland on September 21, last (1910), and of whom forty-one were either killed outright or died within ten days from their injuries. These pictures he has mounted inside of a frame which is formed by the window frame taken from the wrecked car. The list of photographs includes those of the two passengers who escaped with their lives, Mr. W. Surgan and Fred Parkhurst. The only person ion the wreck whose pictures Mr. Paxson did not secure were those of the car crews and he may add these later. Mr. Paxson said Monday that he had arranged to display the pictures in their frame in the Peoples Store up until Saturday, and on Saturday and Sunday they will be in the window of J.E. McLain's Gallery. (This article is taken from the February 1, 1911, issue of the *Chronicle*.)

Lost Lakes

Situated near Jackson Center High School is a large peat bog, commonly referred to as Lost Lakes. Peat is formed by the decomposition of plants. Several million years ago the plants growing in the Lost Lakes began to decay. This process was repeated until peat had reached an average depth of sixty feet. If there had been great heat and pressure while this was happening the peat would have become coal.

In the United States peat is used mostly as a mulch and sometimes for cattle bedding. In Europe peat is dried, mixed with molasses and fed to cattle.

Before 1904 there was no road going through the Lakes. However, a road curved east around the lakes. In 1904 the Township graveled all the roads that were not already graveled. There was a Township vote on whether the road would be left as it was or whether it would be straightened to go

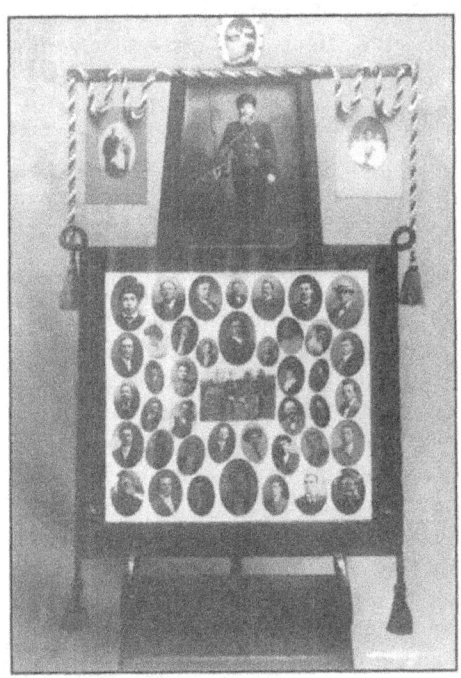
The caption on this assembled photo display created by Mahlon I. Paxson reads: "The frame above is the sash from a window of car No. 233 I.U.T. Co. wrecked Sep. 21, 1910, 1/2 mile north Kingsland, Ind. which 41 people were killed."

through the Lakes. The votes was to go straight through.

The road was put through on timbers while the Lakes were frozen over. When the spring thaw came the road sank. Every spring the road was filled and patched together until the year 1920.

One evening in 1920 the road was in condition at 11 o'clock, but the next morning there simply wasn't any road for about 100 feet. This chunk of road had broken loose from the rest of the fill and had slid to the west, leaving an abyss partially filled with water to the depth of 20 feet. The county filled the hole with clay and gravel.

A ditch was put through the Lakes in 1919-1920, which lowered the water level about four feet.

In 1932 the State took over the road to put through the highway. The contractors dipped peat for 60 feet until they hit blue clay. Then the excavation was filled with stone and black top was put on top of that. Even with this the road is sinking about three or four inches per year.

In later years, it hasn't settled as much as it did in early years. It has been resurfaced several times.

MOSSBURG CEMETERY

Rev. Henry and Jane Tharlkill Mossburg came to Wells County in 1836 and were one of the two families in Liberty Township. Rev. Henry officiated as minister in the Christian Church. They had nine children. Rev. Henry lost his health while serving in the War of 1812. When he knew the end was near, he selected a spot for his final resting place near their log cabin. He died on November 2, 1838, and was the first white man buried in Liberty Township. My grandfather Charles G. Mossburg, whose grandfather was James. T. Mossburg, son of Rev. Henry, related this story about the origin of the Mossburg Cemetery. When Rev. Henry died, his sons had to build fires around the grave for two days and two nights until the ground froze hard enough that the timber wolves couldn't dig up the grave. As they kept the fires built up at night they could see the red glowing eyes of the wolves watching them. Later on as a traveling band of gypsies passing thru the area were camped nearby, one of the women died and she was buried along with other Mossburg family members, thus becoming a cemetery. *Submitted by: James Richard Mossburg, great-great-great grandson of Rev. Henry Mossburg*

Magdalina Gottlieb Rolli who began the practice of placing the lamp in the window. Photo courtesy of Mrs. Bill Garrett.

Lamp which was used in the window from the mid 1920s as described in the poem by John H. Baumgartner. The lamp is now owned by Mrs. Rolli's granddaughter, Mrs. Bill Garrett of Bluffton.

MOTHER'S LAMP IN THE WINDOW

Many years ago, in this humble town
A family lived of common renown
Making their way the best they could-
Bread on the table, box filled with wood
Tater's in the bin, the barrel with its flour
Kraut in the jar-it smelled so sour!
Children coming home, what a happy sight!
Put the lamp in the window, it will soon be night.

This lamp was old, but as good as new
Many fond memories. I'm telling you,
Surround this lamp by the window there,
As mother was sitting in her rocking chair
Gazing up to her Maker as the saints of old
To the hills far away, so we are told.
Rocking her children to a sweet lullaby,
With the lamp in the window ne'er scarcely a cry.

From the angling road nearing this town
Stop on the bridge, to the right look down
Wabash and swimming hole where the old mill stood,
And what's left of the mill, is a few stumps of wood.
"What made this hole?" the young may ask.
The mill wheel was turning, the water rushed fast.
Her boys were swimming by the light of the moon.
The lamp's in the window in her living room.

Don't look for a castle as you drive further on,
Or a mansion with marble or pillars so strong;
But a neat old house real close to the street;
And if you go inside, it's quaint and neat.
The tables and chairs that set so well,
The cupboard and shelves from cinnamon smell.
And what I like best is the lovely sight
Of the lamp in the window burning so bright.

The church across the street with its belfry tower.
Hear the bell ring at the midnight hour.
Another year's past and a new begun;
The old was mingled with sadness and fun;
In health or sickness so their vows they made.
And so with new courage so unafraid
Much better she hopes the new will be.
She has the lamp in the window so all can see.

Why the lamp in the window, you might ask?
To keep it burning so long is quite a task
But love for her children has prompted this.
She has gone away, and her smile we miss.
As a light house standing by the stormy sea,
Only one remains, its lamplighter to be.
So hurry along is this sight you would see-
The lamp in the window by the maple tree.

So follow the road to the store of brick.
An old fashioned front with walls so thick
The steps are worn, though made of stone,
Inside it's different-how the years have flown!
The cracker barrel gone, the old coffee mill
Everyday grinding only on the Sabbath still.
She calls, "Supper's ready, children, stop your play."
The lamp's in the window at the close of day.

Next to the store was the blacksmith shop.
Only memories remain of this historic spot.
Mike with his hammer the anvil did ring,
Shrinking tires of steel was a wonderful thing;
Shoeing horses for farmers in the evening heat;
The bellows of the forge in rhythm would beat;
Sparks of the forge we could see in the dome,
The lamp's in the window it's time to go home.

The oil lamp gave way to the modern light
Standing on the shelf it's still all right.
The wood stove is gone there is another one there;
The house is real sturdy and in good repair;
The barn is empty with its clean swept floor,
No cows will come home when you open the door.
But one thing is there, I saw it last night-
The lamp in the window still burning so bright.

Let's reach out a hand to help each other-
This family did so to a suffering brother,
Don't think someone else the task might do,
For someone in want might be looking for you.
So let's love and help as the days go by,
Yes, we'll succeed if hard we try'
And if the Master will, there'll be in store
A lamp in our window on the other shore.

The Rollis house, which was about 120 years old when the poem was written, was located in the heart of the village of Vera Cruz. It was located where the St. John Church parking lot is now. The poem was written by John H. Baumgartner, May 1, 1964. The lamp tradition was continued even after her death by the family until the house was torn down.

View looking south on Mulberry at Center Street showing the Jacob Rolli house at left. House was demolished in 1968. The lamped window is the bottom left window on the right side of the building as seen here.

Palm Sunday Tornado of 1965

Mention tornadoes in Wells County and immediately to many minds comes the picture of the devastation wrought by the Palm Sunday twister of April 11, 1965, which left two dead, and 50 homes and farms demolished.

After leaving Wells County, the tornado smashed into southern Adams County, causing two deaths and extensive property losses there also, especially in the Berne area.

The tornado, or tornadoes as was later determined, entered Wells County on its southern boundary in Jackson Township about one-half mile east of Ind. 3 and moved diagonally from southwest to northeast across the lower portion of adjoining Chester Township and just north of the center of the easternmost township of Nottingham.

The path, described as 100 yards wide, cut a swath 18 miles long across Wells County's countryside, missing more populated areas.

In its wake, the twister, which struck about 8:30 p.m. left a woman and her 9-year-old daughter dead in their home at the north edge of the community of Keystone in Chester Township, leveled a church at Keystone as 12 members huddled under pews, and felled thousands of trees and hundreds of buildings.

At hospitals, 44 person, 14 of them from Adams County, were admitted for treatment of injuries. These included 41 at Caylor-Nickel Hospital in Bluffton, 11 at Blackford County Hospital in Hartford City, four at Wells Community Hospital in Bluffton and two at Huntington Memorial Hospital in Huntington.

There were others with minor injuries which were not attended by physicians or medical staff.

In Adams County, the tornado entered just west of Linn Grove, a community of about 275 persons, which was one of the hardest hit in the state.

All homes and business places in Linn Grove were damaged, most of them leveled to the ground.

Two died in Adams County.

Four miles northeast of Linn Grove, the town of Berne next felt the force of the tornado.

The blow hit the north and west edges of Berne, demolishing a furniture store and bowling alley along U.S. 27 with other property losses.

The extent of the property losses in Adams County included 25 businesses, primarily in Berne and Linn Grove, 134 dwellings damaged or total losses, 10 mobile homes, and over 100 autos.

The number of injured in Adams County was finally recorded at "100 plus."

Bluffton's National Guard unit was called out initially to patrol the devastated area in Wells and Adams Counties. Its guardsmen were partially relieved two days later by a National Guard unit from Portland.

Personnel from the American Red Cross moved into Bluffton to begin channeling aid to families and individuals urgently in need. These Red Cross people also spread out into the small towns to provide more direct help.

Wells County before the week was out was declared a disaster area, along with a dozen other counties of Indiana.

The Palm Sunday episode was not a single tornado over Indiana but rather a group of twisters, perhaps as many as 12, which struck across the state. The toll for Indiana from the mass onslaught was placed at 134 dead, more than 1,250 injured and property damage greater than $100 million.

President Lyndon B. Johnson made a rapid tour of tornado damaged areas in the vicinity of Elkhart, accompanied by Indiana Governor Roger Branigin, and pledged immediate emergency funds for what was termed "Indiana's worst disaster."

Bluffton was spared the blow of the tornado and became an oasis of mercy to storm victims.

The Bluffton Electric Power plant, along with its distribution lines, remained unscathed and was able to generate enough electricity to take care of most needs.

However, the Indiana and Michigan Electric Co. (I&M), which was supplying Bluffton with a purchased block of power, had 12 of its major electrical distribution lines, along with 54 steel towers, fall to the fury of the tornado. Numerous small communities and hundreds of farms were without power.

The loss of electricity to many of the farms placed a hardship on livestock since automatic feeders and water pumping systems would not function.

A creamery offered its transport vehicles to haul water to the communities of Berne and Linn Grove and other tank trucks carried water to farms from Bluffton.

The loss of the electrical distribution system of I&M resulted also in the shutdown of Franklin Electric Co. and Kitco Inc. in Bluffton and the Corning Glass Works Co. plant west of Bluffton.

While Bluffton electric patrons had power throughout the period, an estimated 85,000 customers of I&M were without electricity at least two days over portions of Indiana.

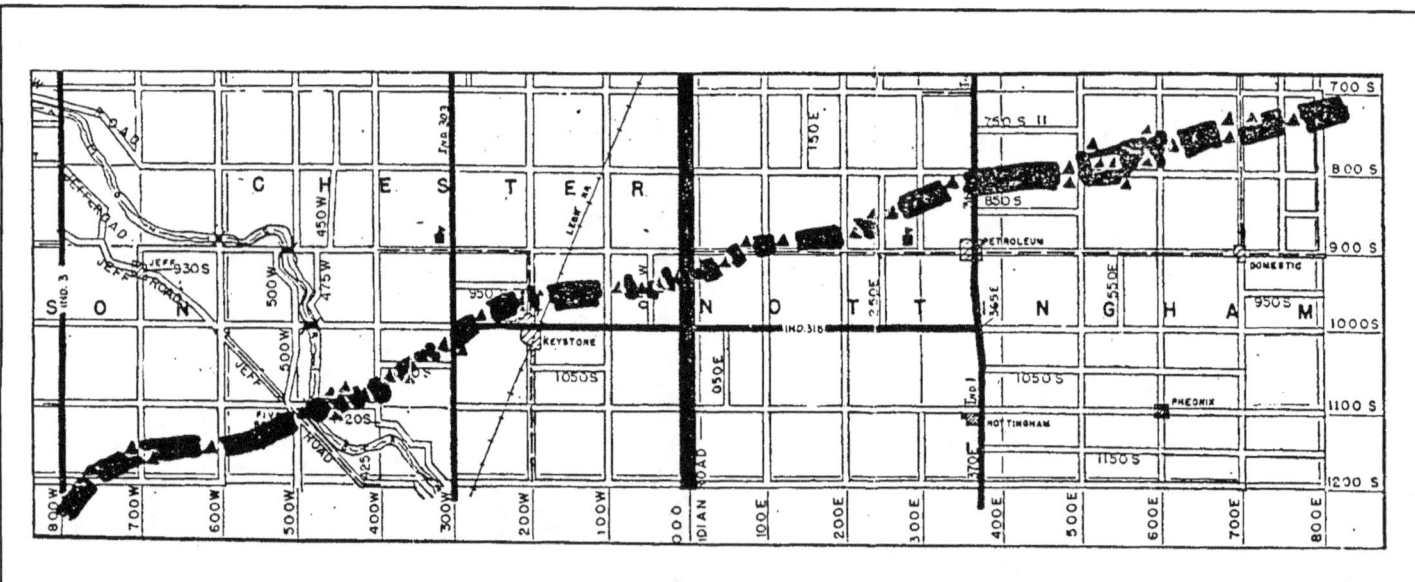

The 1965 Palm Sunday tornado entered Wells County across three townships and exited near County Roads 700S and 800E (upper right). Small triangles indicate homes and farms struck by the storm.

Pigeon Roost

Some years ago, Fred Park insisted that I write about an area in Lancaster Township, where many years ago huge numbers of pigeons roosted at night on knolls of land barely out of the water. This area probably also included a portion of Jefferson Township. The heart of the area must have been around the Pleasant Valley Church, more often called "Little Vine."

In Jefferson Township it probably included areas both north and east of Tocsin. The only basic information that I have was passed on to me from my father, John Carl Gallivan. He was born in 1884, and the time frame for all of this seems to have taken place before he was born. My grandfather died when my father was only seventeen. No doubt more of the information on the subject at hand came from Mr. David Pierce and Mr. Issac Clowser, who were neighbors.

In the height of this era, many young men would borrow their father's farm wagon and a lantern, and go out into these areas with clubs to harvest as many pigeons as they could. The pigeons could be sold for a good profit due to their large fat content.

There seems to be little doubt that these pigeons were the famous "passenger pigeons which are now extinct. There are history books that tell us that passenger pigeons were so numerous that at times they would blot out the sun. The only clear evidence that pigeons, in large numbers, were in this county are three open ditches. They are Pigeon Roost, Pigeon Roost #1, and Pigeon Roost #2. Some of the ditches that flow into them are the Raymond Gerber ditch and the Gallivan and Randall ditches. The main Pigeon Roost ditch forms the beginning of the Eight Mile, about one-half mile south of US 224. *Submitted by Victor E. Gallivan*

Pre-Historic Peoples of Wells County

It has been known since the French first explored the Middle West that there had been a race of people living there who were long since extinct. Mention was made by the explorers in their memoirs of the unique mound, earthworks, and fortifications made of earth, some huge and some small. Later, for want of a better name, these mystery people were called Mound-builders, and by the Indians "Allegwi."

Daniel Boone made mention of the fact that he had dug out pieces of pottery vessels and odd-shaped stone pipes merely by pushing the earth away with the toe of his moccasin.

Men especially trained in the work excavated hundreds of these mounds trying to find a clue as to who they were and where they came from. They discovered that the Indians of the historical period never did know the art of working stone into grooved axe-heads, tomahawks, and pestles. They merely found these objects where they had lain since the departure of the Mound-builders and put them to their own use. The Indians, however, did know the art of chipping arrow and spear heads from flint.

In Wells County evidences of these people have been discovered. Pieces of crude pottery have been found near the confluence of the Wabash River and the creek which enteres the Wabash just east of the White Bridge. Pottery has also been found farther east toward Vera Cruz. Examination of the pieces show that it is of a rude type decorated with lines and dots and made of clay, tempered with a powder manufactured by crushing mussel shells in mortar.

The land near where the pottery was discovered has been cultivated over so many times that is is now impossible to tell whether or not there had been mounds or earthworks there at one time. Flint arrow-heads have been found there in great numbers as well as grooved ax-heads of granite and other types of artifacts. All of these findings tend to prove the existence there, long ago, of mound-builders.

Skeletons have been found at different times in the county and a few years ago parts of a skeleton were dug from a sand or gravel pit near Liberty Center. In the Twin Hills just over the Wells-Jay county line were found several skeletons which were probably mound-builders. On the Huntington Road just out of Markle is a huge mound. The writer found a thigh bone which was undoubtedly moundbuilder and ancient. Relics which could have been made only by these mystery people were close by, which shows without a doubt that the skeletal material found in sand and gravel pits over the county was mound-builder.

At some future date when excavations have been made at different places known to be sites of the mounds of earthworks; when older people have been interviewed, who remember how the land in the county looked before it was cultivated; and when collections of relics known to have been found in the county have been examined, then something of interest can be told of the first citizens of the county. *Earl L. Romey*

Ouabache

The Ouabache (French spelling of the Indian name for Wabash) recreational and educational game preserve was established in 1933 as part of the CCC program. Its 1,089 acres were first known as the Wells County State Forest and Game Preserve.

In April, 1935, twenty men from Co. 586, Freetown, Indiana, under command of Lt. Louis Klaer, were transferred to the Wells County State Forest and Game Preserve to begin construction work on Camp Bluffton. They were housed in tents on an eroded pasture field, practically denuded of timber and grass, with a few scraggly oaks and hickory shoots, scattered here and there. The entire acreage showed the inevitable signs of abandonment; timber gone, top soil gone, gullies and erosion present.

July 1, 1935, Co. 1592 cadre was organized under the command of Lt. J. Ferris, Lt. Nyal Brooks, Lt. L. Klaer and Lt. Wayne

Pheasant brooder house and raccoon and animal display buildings at the Ouabache State Park.

At the Ouabache State Park, a small animal display building once housed several wild animals common to the area.

Houser, medical officer. A 21-acre lake (Kunkle Lake) was dug, several buildings built using local quarried stone, and quail and pheasant hatching and rearing areas built. Trees and shrubs were grown and planted. A 110 foot observation tower was constructed to watch for fires. A small zoo with bears, wildcats, foxes, skunks, coons, wolves, squirrels and other small animals was produced. Bison, elk and deer grazed in outside ranges near the tower. Picnic shelters were built along with tennis courts, a play field, and camping facilities. More recently, as Ouabache State Park, a swimming pool and shower and restroom facilities have been added.

RECALLING WELLS COUNTY FARMING

The farmer who owned no land moved often. March was the favored month for this. The oats must be sown if a crop was to be harvested.

Each season meant special work to be done. Spring was planting time—ground was tilled, prepared and seeds were planted just right. Gardens and truck patches were an important part of spring work. Don't forget spring cleaning—wiping down walls or repapering, washing windows and wood work, plus washing and airing winter blankets and bedding to be stored away for next year.

Summer came with plenty of lawn mowing, weeding gardens, gathering produce from the garden, preparing it for meals and canning as much as possible for winter use. Harvesting of oats and wheat was not easy work. Pop usually drove the horses pulling the binder which cut and tied the grain into sheaves. The oldest son served as "straw boss." Sis was good with driving the team of horses to the hay rope and feeding the animals. While dressed in men's overalls, long sleeved shirts, sun bonnets or straw hats tied on, gloves or heavy long stockings pulled on to protect hands and arms, the girls did their share of shocking the grain. It was usually very hot weather. The hard work was mixed with fun and joking as well as arguing and fussing. The younger kids carried jugs of cold water to the workers. Sometimes mom surprised the family "slaves" by putting weak lemonade or cold tea in the jug. If the jug wasn't emptied right away it was buried in the center of a shock of grain to keep it as cool as possible.

There was sweet corn to be prepared and dried. Apples were dried for dessert or pies to be enjoyed in the cold winter.

Fall came, school began, vegetables were harvested and hoarded for winter. The day the potatoes were harvested was usually cold and windy. Pop used a horse and single share plow to get the potatoes out of the ground. The kids picked up potatoes and put them in sacks ready to be hauled to the bins in the basement. Pumpkins were hauled to the basement ready for winter use for stewed pumpkin and yummy pumpkin pies.

Winter served as time for equipment repair.

Farming in the twenties and thirties was quite different than it is today. Farms had horses, cows, hogs, sheep, chickens, garden and truck patches, grape vines, and apple, cherry and pear trees. The foods on the table were grown on the farm and prepared in the home. The oldest daughter usually helped Mom with breakfast which might include freshly baked biscuits, fried sausage, steak, eggs, pancakes, plenty of good gravy, syrup, jellies, cooked cereals, plenty of rich milk for drinking and thick cream for Pop and Mom's "Old Reliable" coffee. All the things mentioned weren't served at each breakfast, but a lot of food was always ready because at least two hours of work was done before eating breakfast.

Dried corn was part of the diet. Sweet corn from the truck patch was picked, husked, cleaned and cut off the cob. It was spread on a cloth, placed so the sun would be on it most of the day. It was covered with a cloth to keep the flies off. Occasionally it was carefully stirred so it dried more evenly. Apples were peeled, cored, sliced and spread in the sun to dry, too. If the weather didn't cooperate and have sunny days, the drying was done partially and carefully in the oven of the kitchen range.

Green beans, tomatoes and some corn were canned. If money was available, peaches were bought and canned.

Butchering day was a busy one on a nice fall day. Some neighbors usually came to help. Much of the work was done outside. The fire was built under the huge iron kettle. Very hot water was needed to scald the hogs so hair could be scraped off easily. As the hog was cut into pieces, the extra fat was trimmed off and cut into smaller pieces. This fat was put in the large iron kettle to render the lard to be used for cooking and also made good cracklings to eat. Pork shoulders and hams were sugar cured. Sausage was ground and seasons while side meat was salted and packed away for future use.

Lean pork scraps were cooked to make a good broth. This was thickened with corn meal to make scrapple and set aside to cool. What a treat to have sliced scrapple fried for breakfast, served with hot syrup.

The butchered beef was chunked and cold packed for many good meals to come. Some of the steak was "fried down" and packed in stone jars and covered with lard for future use. One hind quarter was kept for slicing and frying during the winter. The good brown gravy from this was good on hot biscuits or corn bread. *Submitted by Eulala McLean*

UNION FARMERS ASSOCIATION

At the Union Center School house on Thursday, October 2, 1919, an address was given by H.,T. Walker, of Montpelier, to nearly a hundred farmers. After the address they organized their township by electing the following officers: Irel V. Pence, president; H.H. Neff, vice-president; Cliff Lipkey, secretary-treasurer.

Andy Elick, Mel Walters and Dell Wickliff were elected directors. Twenty-one joined the association at $5.00 each. They decided to make a drive within a few days and visit every farmer in the township.

LANCASTER TOWNSHIP FARMER'S ASSOCIATION

On Oct. 3, 1919, at Lancaster Chapel, commonly known as the Pugney Church, more than a hundred farmers and their wives listened very attentively to Mr. H.T. Walker, a most convincing and entertaining speaker from Montpelier. Music by the Craigville orchestra was very much appreciated. Miss Mary Thoma also delighted the audience with a selection on the flute, while Ruth Abbott and Esther Patterson sang two duets in a very pleasing manner.

After the address it was voted to organize Lancaster Township. Twenty-seven present joined the association at $5.00 each. These, with those who had previously joined, made a total of more than thirty, which was certainly a very creditable showing. Officers were elected as follows: N.J. Kleinknight, president; A.E. Hunt, vice president; Clem Wasson, secretary; Telfer Paxon, treasurer. Directors were Lantz Wasson, Jess Dailey, Dave Powell, Seth Snider and Ed Barger.

District leaders were from District 1—John Shady, Ray Wasson and D.T. Highley. District 2—Jess Dailey, Paul Scott and Barney Rupright. District 3 was Clem V. Wasson. District 4—Lewis Nordyke and David Powell. District 5—Isaiah Melching and Herman Schwartz. District 6—Charles Lash, Ott High and Lewis Mounsey. District 7—Denton Ratcliff, John Shafer, Shirley Hartman, Neal Crow and Bob Patterson. Distict 8—Ernest Nordyke and Oliver Durr. District 9—Charles King and Charles Lusk. District 10—Homer Fry and Ed Kolter. District 11—Curtis Shady, Ben Martin and Charles Patterson. District 12—Elmer Ratcliff, Sam Heckley and Dick Porter.

Besides these named as officers, the following joined the association: Chauncey Worthman, Sherman Paxson, Roy Allen, George Masterson and Frank Kershner. It was voted to make a canvass within a week so that canvassers could report at a meeting to be held the next Thursday evening, October 9, 1919, at the Bender School House. The success of this meeting was due in no small measure to the efforts of A.E. Hunt, temporary chairman, who had the meeting advertised thoroughly and the program carefully planned.

ROCKCREEK FOLKS

Mamie, Mamie, I've been thinking
Where would you and I be now
If the good old folks from Rockcreek
Had not come across the sea.
There's Gilberts, Brenards, Falks and Eichorns
Houtz and Lesh and Crum and Mast
Who would have cleared up woody Rockcreek
Built her roads and homes I'll ask.

There's Edris's in that bend at Rockford
The Bender's and Kershner's near Murray
Clines and Gordons, Sheets and Inskips
I'm glad to see you here today.

I know good folk you'll all remember
the good old times at Boiling Springs
The Haflicks, Millers, Lees and Ravers
at Picnics made those old wood ring.

Mamie, Mamie, I've been thinking
The Rockcreek folks it's plain to see
are just about the best folks living
The best that ever crossed the sea.

Recall the times at the Bender School house
There was the Masseys, Oldfathers, McAfee
Sellers, Duffs and Little Mamie
Always good as good could be.

— Author Unknown

The 1908 Bluffton Street Fair. The train brought folks from Fort Wayne and other towns around the area.

Top - *Abram Cline family in front of their new home built in 1898 at the southeast corner of Market and Williams Streets. Cline album photos courtesy Don Skinner.*

Below left - *Front parlor of the Cline house showing Victorian "home entertainment center", an upright piano.*

Below right - *Upstairs bathroom in Cline house.*

Above left - *Front stair hall in the Cline house.*

Above right - *View of the Cline kitchen including the stove and sinks. Note the third faucet for rain water used to rinse dishes.*

Bottom - *Cline basement laundry room including stove for heating irons and gas fired hot water tank. Also a drying rack for linens is in view.*

Top - View from the back parlor into dining room of Cline home.

Below left - View of Mr. Cline's upstairs study. Note the gas fired table lamp on the desk.

Below right - View of Mr. Cline's study showing the turret on the front of the house.

Above left - Cline dining room.

Above right - Mr. and Mrs. Cline's downstairs bedroom.

Bottom - Stood on present site of Bluffton Post Office until 1924 when it was moved to Oak and Townley Streets and demolished in 1977.

Top - *A 1908 post card of a bridge over Rockcreek. Location unknown.*

Below left - *Elias Tice and Chads Higgins, at the whip, hauling rock from the banks of the Wabash River for the foundation of the Court House. Photo courtesy of Pat Higgins.*

Below right - *Schwartz threshing ring. Photo courtesy of Mr. and Mrs. George Schwartz.*

Above left - *Crew works on the gravel road in front of the Prairie Church.*

Above right - *House of Frank Brickley being moved from Banner City to Uniondale. Photo courtesy of Mr. and Mrs. George Schwartz.*

Bottom - *Ray Bailey and Dave Schwartz moving the Frank Brickley home to Uniondale from Banner City. Photo courtesy of Mr. and Mrs. George Schwartz.*

Top - This oil well and pumping house was located on the Keane farm in Chester Township. Photo courtesy of Cheryl Powell.

Below left - View of oil well on the Chester Township Keane Farm. Photo included old derrick and storage tanks. Photo courtesy of Cheryl Powell.

Below right - Shows a typical pumping jack of a type used on Wells County oil wells. Photo courtesy of Indiana State Library.

Above left - Post card view of the Bluffton Community Building (City Hall) about 1940. Many local basketball games were held here till the local school built their gymnasium.

Above right - Chautauqua Grounds in Bluffton. View looking north on Indian Road One. Tent is pitched on the later site of the Airplane Service Station.

Bottom - Putting up tents for Street Fair Agricultural Exhibit on West Market Street about 1940.

Top - The old meets the new even in 1908 as a bull driven wagon is guided southward on the parade route on South Main Street over the interurban tracks and the brick pavement.

Below left - Booth at the 1908 Street Fair by Studabaker & Son Company.

Below right - The Studabaker Bank resting booth at the 1908 Street Fair. Location is directly in front of the bank (113 West Market).

Above left - The Davenport & Ehle 1908 Street Fair booth in front of their Rexall Drug Store on Market across the street from the front of the courthouse.

Above right - The north side of the 200 block of West Market during the 1908 Street Fair. The merchants worked together on this elaborate display. Band stage is set up in the street.

Bottom - The courthouse plaza during the 1908 Street Fair. View looking northwest.

Top - An event draws interest in front of the Agriculture Exhibit at the 1908 Bluffton Street Fair.

Below left - Free acts are a tradition of the Bluffton Street Fair. This act is underway over the 100 block of East Market Street. Just to the right of this scene was the Wells County Bank (now Farmer's and Merchants).

Below right - An act underway on a high stage built in the Market and Main intersection. Wells County Bank is on the right in this 1908 scene.

Above left - Labeled by the photographer, McLain, this 1908 Street Fair booth was by the Wood Light Lodge. The location is the Arnold Block across Main Street from the Courthouse. Deam Drug Store is below the Clayton dentist's office. A tailor by the name of Sands also had a shop on an upper level. The portion of the building to the right has been razed for parking.

Above right - Another local business display at the 1908 fair.

Bottom - Henry C. Arnold, dealer in grain had this display in the 1908 Street Fair at his store on 124 West Market.

Top - Jefferson Township parading down the 100 block of East Washington Street as part of the annual Street Fair march by all county students in the 1947 Fair.

Below left - Park School students in Street Fair parade.

Below right - Vera Cruz students in Street Fair parade.

Above left - Mounted horse patrol going through Street Fair parade in 1947, a traditional part of the fair.

Above right - Psi Iota Xi marches on West Market Street as part of an evening parade in the 1947 fair.

Bottom - American Legion Bank marches past the Bliss Hotel on South Main Street.

All photos this page - Views of Street Fair in the late 1940s.

Top - View of the White Bridge in February of 1980. When replaced, it was one of just a few iron structures spanning the Wabash River.

Below left - Taken from the top of the Courthouse tower looking north, this photo, taken by Jim Barbieri, News-Banner publisher and editor, shows Main Street blocked at Wabash in an early set-up stage of the Bluffton Street Fair. View is from about 1978.

Below right - A 1991 view of Veterans Park at Main and Arnold Streets. Memorial Day programs are now held there annually. Photo courtesy of Bluffton News-Banner.

Above left - The former Hoosier Grain property on Wabash was purchased by the city of Bluffton for $82,000 to accommodate the city's new recycling depot. Photo courtesy of Bluffton News-Banner.

Above right - The Kehoe Riverfront Park gazebo, which was dedicated in September of 1990. It was the third project of Bluffton revitalization after previously carrying out the Rivergreenway Trail and the Downtown Streetscape.

Bottom - One of the largest and most successful fund efforts of the Bluffton area's history raised about $160,000 to go with matching federal funds via the Bureau of Outdoor Recreation in the U.S. Dept. of Interior. This made possible the $320,000 Wells Community Swimming Pool next to the 4-H park. The fund drive one of several successful efforts led by Howard Rich, was channeled through the Wells County Foundation. Photo courtesy of Bluffton News-Banner.

Top - An event in a Street Fair in the late 1940s.

Below left - Another event in a Street Fair in the late 1940s.

Below right - The Carnell Building in flames December of 1982. The landmark stone front facade, a distictive construction feature when the building went up as the Studabaker Bank nearly 70 years earlier, was saved and the building reconstructed inside by developers Mick Cupp and Robert Troxel. Carnall Insurance and Carnell Abstract, both operated by David Park, moved to a new location on South Johnson Street. The vault inside the burned-out 113 West Market Street former bank building was intact and its contents okay. The Old-First National Bank had operated in this building until going to its new building in 1968. Photo courtesy of Bluffton News-Banner.

Above left - Interurban car stopping at Riverside south of Vera Cruz. Photo courtesy of Indian State Library.

Above right - A walnut table by Jacob Tribolet, who also made caskets for Herman Thoma. Jacob was Anna Tribolet Williamson's grandfather. He built the home at 418 West Market, Bluffton, which is currently occupied by the Don Strong family.

Bottom - Buffalo Bill Show comes to Bluffton in 1896 and paraded down Main Street. Photo courtesy of Indiana State Library.

Jenny and J. J. Wood at their cabin in Nottingham Township. Photo courtesy of Cheryl Powell.

Studabaker family reunion at the John Studabaker house where the Wells County Historical Museum is now.

Wells County Churches

Bluffton Universalist Church was originally built in 1878 on Bluffton's "Old Show Grounds" on the northeast corner of Williams and Cherry Streets. It was bought by the Disciples of Christ in 1898 and moved to the back of the lot to make room for a new auditorium.

Elhanan Presbyterian Church

The Elhanan Presbyterian Church, organized in 1843, was one of the earliest churches of the county and was located three miles east and 1/2 mile north of Ossian at the corner of Davis and Tocsin Roads. In 1845 a log church was built on ground donated by Robert Ewell for worship and burial. The Rev. John Nevins was the first pastor. Later an early member, James Ferguson, donated an acre of ground located across the road for the public cemetery, to be cared for by the trustees of the church. James Ferguson was trustee of Jefferson Township and one of the first road supervisors of the county. The land was a corner portion of the Ferguson farm. The Ferguson family that followed were faithful supporters of the church and served as elders and trustees.

In 1860, the Rev. M.M. Donaldson added the Elhanan parish to his ministry, in addition to the Murray and Pleasant Ridge (later the Ossian Presbyterian Church) churches.

In 1887, the church was a frame building (26 x 36) with a membership of approximately 40. The early elders were Alexander White, Charles Ferguson and James Ferguson. The Sunday school had 35 scholars, with Alexander White the Sunday School superintendent. At this time the Rev. Michael M. Lawson served, in addition to the Elhanan Church, the Presbyterian churches at Ossian and Kingsland.

In 1925, the church was dissolved; it merged with the Ossian Presbyterian Church in 1926. For the period of time that the Elhanan Church was pastored by the Ossian Presbyterian ministers, from the beginning of its organization in 1843, it was an independent and self-supporting church. *Submitted by Margie Ditmar*

Faith Evangelical United Brethren Church

The Faith Evangelical United Brethren Church is located at 402 West Mill Street, in Ossian, Indiana, a little town twelve miles south of the industrial city of Fort Wayne. The church was built in 1889, and the cost including the lot was $2,800.00. Until the building of the large Methodist Episcopal Church, it was the only brick house of worship in Ossian.

The trustees as elected at Zion Quarterly Conference, November 17, 1906, met in Ossian at the Rev. Millikin's and elected the following officers: John Beekner, president, George Smith, secretary, and John Caston, treasurer, for the purpose of buying property and building a parsonage. The parsonage was built in 1907.

The church denomination was known as "The Church of the United Brethren in Christ," being so named because of a meeting of Phillip William Otterbein and Martin Boehm, a reformed Mennonite preacher, in a revival meeting in the Isaac Long's barn. Mr. Otterbein, a German Reformed preacher, went up to Mr. Boehm, embraced him and said, "Wir sind Bruder," which means "we are brothers."

In 1892-93, the church was a mission. In 1893-94, we were on the Zanesville Circuit. In 1906, Ossian was changed to a Charge, including Ossian, Zion and Hebron. Zion was next to the Jackson School, southeast of Ossian (Echo). The Hebron Church was 1/4 mile south of the Caston School, northeast of Ossian. Zion left the Charge in the fall of 1925. Hebron merged with the Ossian Church on August 17, 1958. In 1971 to 1985, Prospect Church and Ossian were a Charge. Bethel was also with Ossian around 1918.

On November 16, 1946, the United Brethren and Evangelical Charge merged at Johnstown, Pennsylvania. We then became known as the "Evangelical United Brethren Church."

In 1968, we merged with the Methodist Church becoming a part of the newly formed United Methodist Church. We named ourselves the Faith United Methodist Church.

Many changes have taken place over the years. In 1931 under the leadership of the Rev. J.D. Smith, a basement was dug under the church. Most of the labor was donated by the men of the congregation. In 1940, under the leadership of the Rev. Walter House, new windows were installed at the cost of $1,0550.00. Florescent lights were installed. Walls and ceiling in the sanctuary were redecorated with celotex finishing; woodwork was varnished — all totaled $2286.55. On March 5th a dedication was held with a program and many visiting ministers present.

I recall that in 1925, under the leadership of the Rev. D.E. Hively, a revival meeting was held that lasted six weeks. The church was filled every night and some stood around the walls.

In 1944, under the leadership of the Rev. Ducker, we formed a missionary society. Mary Ault was elected president; Rosa Scherrer, vice-president; Hattie Shutt, treasurer; and Edna Freighner, secretary. That year we published a church paper called "The Tidings."

We had a male quartet composed of Charles Elzey, Ross Wickliffe, Ernest Middaugh and George Bushee. They, together with other talent of our church, put on programs at the rescue mission in Fort Wayne and other places throughout the vicinity.

The Joy Guild and The Dorcas Circle Ladies Aid was greatly appreciated by all the members.

In 1961, under the leadership of the Rev. Ferris Miller, the "Count On Me" class of the Sunday School adopted a Korean boy for $10.00 per month for 10 years. The idea

Faith Evangelical United Brethren Church Pastors

Year	Pastor	Year	Pastor
1889	W.Z. Roberts	1940-43	Rev. Walter House
1892-93	A mission	1944-45	Rev. Paul Ducker (he resigned)
1900-02	Rev. J.A. Kek		
1903	O.L. Richart	1946	Rev. Earl Bragg
1904	C.A. Spiller	1947-49	Rev. Harvey Fruth
1905-07	Rev. W.V. Milligan	1950-52	Rev. Ethel Hollingsworth
1908-09	Rev. S.A. Rhodes	1953-60	Rev. Lewis Strong
1910-13	Rev. J.W. Lower	1961-63	Rev. Ferris Miller
1914-15	Rev. W.E. Butler	1964-55	Rev. Jerry Fair
1916-17	Rev. Frank Grow	1967	Pastor William Oda
1918-20	Rev. Laura Belle Kline and Rev. Ethel Hollingworth	1968-69	Pastor Paul Burkett
		1970	Rev. David Bushong
1921	Rev. O.L. Richard	1971-6/77	Mrs. Wayne Everett Nigel (Wayne Everett died of cancer and is buried in Prospect Cemetery)
1922-24	Rev. Walter Roudebush		
1925-27	Rev. D.E. Hively		
1928	Rev. W.Z. Roberts		
1929-30	Rev. C.M. Eberly	6/77-1/80	Rev. John Stewart
1931-32	Rev. J.D. Smith	2/80-6/81	Rev. Glenda Wilcox
1933-35	Rev. Charles White	6/82-6/85	Rev. Paul Fredrick
1936-38	Rev. J.F. Bright	6/85-10/86	Rev. John Davis
1939	Rev. Charles Walker (died of cancer here)	10/86 -	Rev. David Harold

was conceived when Harvey Ault, the class teacher, refused Christmas gifts from the class, stating that the money should be used for something useful. Our church has supported two missionaries, the Sotherland family and the Bushongs, for several years.

Many gifts and memorials were given over the years. Some of them are the piano from the Ross family; the candleholder set from the Gilberts; offering plates by the Nigel Everett family; small ceiling lights by the John Simerman's; tape recorder by Ruth Heckley; organ light in memory of Yvonne Burton; piano lights in memory of Mr. and Mrs. Ross Wickliffe and Charlie Elzey; the large picture window by Fred Ault in memory of his wife, Agnes; the credenza by Ruth Elzey. Many memorials were made for the organ. The speaker system was given by Lucile Simerman in memory of her mother, Rose Smith. The flag was donated by Yvonne Burton. The cross was from the Joy Guild.

Progress was made over the years. The coal furnace with the central heat register in the middle of the sanctuary was replaced by a gas water system. Carpeting was installed. New ceiling lights and new pews were purchased, and insulation was put in the church.

In June, 1985, Prospect was taken off the Charge and a new leadership plan was in effect. With the departure of Pastor Paul Frederick to a church in McDaniels, Kentucky, Pastor John Davis assumed leadership of the Faith as well as the First U.M. Churches. The Faith parsonage, whose southeast corner in the living room was the scene of many weddings over the years, was rented to the Bethany Assembly of God minister.

Adverse conditions such as older members being laid to rest, young people getting married and moving away, others going away to college and many student pastors, have reduced our congregation of faithful people to a small closeknit family. Since the first church desired to be a station and since the Rev. Davis was transferred to a South Bend station by superintendent Riley Case and as our small congregation could not afford to pay a minister, on October 15th the vote was unanimous to merge with the First Church. *Submitted by Mary Ault*

KINGSLAND PRESBYTERIAN CHURCH

In 1886, under the direction of the Rev. Michael M. Lawson, minister of the Ossian Presbyterian Church, the Kingsland Presbyterian Church was organized. The church was located on the south side of highway 224 in Lancaster Township in the small village of Kingsland. Today a church is located on the spot where the old church stood. Early members in the church were L.F. Chalfant, who in 1925 was the oldest living member of the Ossian Presbyterian Church and the George, James, Levi, and Evan and Benjamin Fryback families.

The church was dissolved in 1904 and the members were received into the Ossian Presbyterian Church. *Submitted by Margie L. Ditmar*

MT. HOREB LUTHERAN CHURCH

Mt. Horeb Lutheran Church was situated on the banks of the historic Wabash River, 10 miles northwest of Bluffton in Rockcreek Township, near the covered bridge.

Rev. H. Wells, traveling missionary of the Synod of Northern Indiana, began a series of meetings in the Haiflich schoolhouse (a log structure about one mile northeast of the church) on June 9, 1859.

The following Sunday, 14 persons gave their names and requested to be organized into a Lutheran Church. On July 23, a meeting was held in Jacob Haflich's barn (now the Dick Greenawalt barn) at which time the organization was completed, with 19 charter members. William Wert, Samuel Haflich, Jacob Haflich, and Samuel Fate were elected as the first council.

Following the organization, they began to plan for the building of a house of worship. They decided to build on the banks of the river, between the residences of Jacob Haiflich, now the the Dick Greenawalt farm, and Samuel Haflich, later the Cover homestead, near the cemetery, a plot having been set aside for burial purposed as early as 1847.

Early in 1860 subscriptions were received for the building of the church. Samuel Haflich deeded a plot of ground to the church council for church and cemetery purposes. A contract was awarded to George Bailey and Isaac Taylor for the building of the house, which was to be "a good frame, finished in good style, 45 feet long, 30 feet wide, and 14 feet between floor and ceiling," at a price of $815.00. The building was completed and dedicated on September 30, 1860.

Rev. Wells served the congregation until the fall of 1864, when he resigned. About six months later a call was extended to Rev. A.J. Comer, three other congregations joining in the call and forming the Horb pastorate.

The original building served the congregation well until 1890, when it was remodeled and modernized to the extent of having a vestibule and steeple with a bell, a center aisle, Gothic windows with frosted glass, and a slate roof.

This building suffered two strokes of lightning. On March 17, 1934, there was a sort of internal explosion that blew out most of the window glass and scorched the tinsel decorations on the wallpaper. On June 4 of the same year it was struck again, setting the steeple afire. Considerable damage resulted, but the fire was finally controlled by the Markle Fire Department after the vestibule and steeple were destroyed. However, with the help of well wishers in the community, the building was repaired, but it lost some of its architectural symmetry.

During the early years of it existence, Mt. Horeb's membership was drawn from a rather wide territory, but with the building of other churches in the community and losses by death and removals, the member-

Mt. Horeb Lutheran Church

ship decreased to a point where it seemed it would have to disband.

Then largely through the efforts of Eulalia Lesh McElhaney, who has now been taken from the congregation, a renewed interest was kindled and younger persons with families were added to the membership. They were interested and were earnest in the work of the church.

During the summer of 1950 electric lights were installed and the church repapered. Owing to the liberal policy of the REMC and the cooperation of dealers, and the fact that there were persons in the congregation who were able and willing to give their time to the wiring and papering, it was not too expensive.

During the 94 years of Mt. Horeb's existence, the church was served by a number of pastors for varying lengths of time, but the record time was set by Rev. H.L. Walmsley, who began his career as a minister in 1931, at Mt. Horeb, and continued his ministry there until his death in 1965.

However, in spite of all efforts, with more deaths and families moving away, Mt. Horeb was forced to disband in the summer of 1954. After the Wabash Reservoir was put in it was recommended that the Horeb Cemetery be moved. So in the fall of 1970 it was moved from the original location along the Wabash to its present site on U.S. 224.

Mount Zion United Brethren in Christ Church

The following report is taken from records, conversations with individuals, and the first portion is taken from a report by Mrs. Vera Grove, written about 1959.

The first Mount Zion Church was built shortly after the Civil War, three-fourths of one mile south of Mount Zion, on ground donated by the father of Minta Williamson Bower. She remembers the church being made of hewn logs of good size. Residents of the community helped to erect the building.

The church was for all denominations; some of the ministers were the Reverands Sala, Ketterman and Kimmel. Mrs. Bowers remembers that the first service was conducted by the "Old Time Quakers," a group of women who were strangers to everyone.

Services were held Saturday night, Sunday morning and evening. The second church was built on the present site of the Benedict property and the old church was torn down. The new church was a neat frame building thirty by forty feet. It was called Bethel United Brethren Church and was dedicated in 1878 by Rev. S. Ervin. The membership was about thirty, the trustees were: D.L. Elliot, E. Morrison, Silas Poling, J.F. Barton, and James Coleman. The pastor was Rev. Biss.

This church was destroyed by fire of unknown original. D.P. Huffman said, "It was a serious blow to this little congregation, but they were men and women of determination; they at once set to build another house of worship." A tract of land twenty rods west of the old location was purchased from Louis Huffman, a Dunkard minister. A brick church was built, and it now stands as a monument to their faith. The church was dedicated in 1903 by Bishop Halleck Floyd. The minister was Rev. J.A. Rector and the trustees were Harvey Irick, Elijah Huffman, Silas Poling, Henry Fudge and Thomas Clampitt.

Mount Zion flourished as a community from 1898-1912, because of oil wells. During this period the church membership rose to 105, the largest in the history of the church. The highest Sunday School attendance was on January 18, 1910, when 133 attended. The boom resulted in a number of businesses, two blacksmith shops, hardware store, two saloons, three grocery stores, a restaurant, a mill and a drug store. The community was covered with rows of houses, of which a few remain.

Annual conferences were held at Mount Zion in 1887, 1907, 1913, 1926, 1934. Since 1941 annual conferences were held at the Rector Memorial United Brethren Campground, Muncie, Indiana.

The last Sunday at the Mount Zion Church was August, 1980. In attendance: Ethel Morrison Kincaid, Ruth Couch, Arizona Cloud Smith, Velma Grove Mann, Catherine White Wamsley, Hazel Confer, Opal Schemehorn Mounsey, Nancy Grove Baughman, another person from Mt. Zion and Rev. Luke Fetters.

In September, 1980 the land and church were sold for $2,000, to Sarah and Frank Frayer. The church land joins their farm, formerly the E.C. Pinney Farm. The Frayers sold the stained glass windows to someone in Fort Wayne. The church was torn down.

New Lancaster Church and The United Presbyterian Church of Murray

Much of the history of the Murray churches has been lost over the years. Many of the early Ossian Presbyterian Church records were lost when the Milo Gorrel farm burned in 1904. From past record we do know that on June 10, 1840, the first Presbyterian Church in the county was organized in the log home of Adam Hatfield, Jr. in Jefferson Township. It was named Bluffton Presbyterian Church, for location purposes, Bluffton being the closest larger settlement. The new church, with 22 charter members, later met in the log homes of Hiram Hatfield and John T. Glass in Jefferson Township.

In 1844, 19 members left and united with a new congregation being organized in Bluffton; the name of the original church was changed to Pleasant Ridge Church. It was in 1845 that plans were made to build a log church on the farm of Joseph Gorrell, southwest of what is now Ossian. Some of the members were opposed to the location of the new church and 13 members withdrew and formed the New Lancaster Church at New Lancaster (Murray).

In 1846, Joseph Gorrell and Adam Hatfield, Jr. secured the service of the Rev. Wilson M. Donaldson. The Donaldson family were early settlers in that part of Lancaster Township later known as Murray. It was at this time that, due to opposition to the location of the new church, 18 more members withdrew and formed the United Presbyterian Church of Murray.

In 1848, the Rev. Donaldson was installed as pastor of the Pleasant Ridge, Bluffton and New Lancaster churches; thus the total of five Presbyterian churches were in existence, with Elhanan in north Jefferson Township in existence in eight years from the beginning of the first church.

Records indicate that possibly the Adam Hatfield, Jr. and Hiram Hatfield families were among the families who left the original church to form the church at Murray. Hiram Hatfield was a ruling elder at the Murray Church, and it was not until 1867 that Hiram Hatfield moved his membership back to the Pleasant Ridge Church, located then in Ossian. Records show that Adam Hatfield, Jr.'s wife Martha died in 1840 and was buried in the old Henry Miller Cemetery, the first burial ground in the northern part of Wells County. Later her remains were moved to the Murray Cemetery.

It was in the year 1858 that the Rev. Donaldson gave up the Bluffton Church charge, as he wanted to bring in a new minister to the large area; he moved back to Murray where he resided until 1860, when he bought a farm west of the new settlement of Ossian. He then moved to Ossian and continued to serve the Pleasant Ridge and New Lancaster churches, and at this time added the parish of Elhanan Presbyterian Church to his charge. The Rev. Donaldson served the Pleasant Ridge, which in 1876 changed its name to the Ossian Presbyterian Church, and Elhanan Churches for 28 and 1/2 years.

We have no records of the later history of the Murray churches. The Murray Cemetery has many of the old graves and markers of the early settlers. *Submitted by Margie L. Ditmar*

SLACUM NEW LIGHT CHRISTIAN CHURCH

Two miles north of where Southern Wells School now stands was a red brick schoolhouse named Slacum. My great-uncle, the Rev. Bruce Mounsey, held a very successful revival meeting there and many souls were converted. They decided they needed a church, so a church was built just diagonally across from the school on land now owned by David Beavans. Bruce Mounsey was their first pastor. While this church was growing in numbers, my father, John H. Osborn, was the Sunday School Superintendent. When I was a boy, it was a must for me to go to Sunday School and church on a Sunday morning. Our family went there for several years.

Just north of the church was a good grocery and egg market run by John Bell and his son, Sherman. That store remained open for 75 years. The Bells had a round barn on their farm there.

Most of the people walked to church, but some came in buggies and a few in automobiles. Opal Bell was the piano player there for years. There was never any electricity in this church, just kerosene lamps hanging on the side wall for light. It was heated with potbelly stoves.

There was a church located just two miles south of Slacum called Chester Center, and my grandmother, Mary Ann Osborn, was in that church. When it was dedicated, she was eight years old. The Chester Center Church just lasted 40 years and was then sold at auction. Howard Smith bought it and tore it down. He moved the lumber to Reiffsburg and built a garage there just across the road east of the Reiffsburg Church.

This is some of the history of the Slacum Church reported by Paul Osborn, son of John H. Osborn, the superintendent there.

UNIONDALE WESLEYAN CHURCH

This church evolved out of a cottage prayer meeting that was held in various homes primarily in northern Wells County. In 1939 the suggestion came to hold services on Sunday mornings. Albert and Marjorie McCartney, who lived one mile west and five miles north of Uniondale, opened their home for these services. The Free Methodist Church out of Fort Wayne was first asked to come and hold services, which they did for awhile. The people were dissatisfied because this denomination did not allow a musical instrument to be used in the worship service. The Wesleyan Methodists were then asked to organize a church. They sent the Rev. Milo Bowsman and the Rev. Garl Beaver to preach and organize. The Rev. Floyd Titus became its first pastor, and as the church grew, it became too big for the home. Since many families were from the Uniondale area, the organization was moved to Uniondale. The congregation built their own church. Later a house was moved to the lot next to the church and remodeled for a parsonage.

Church attendance at times was between 100 and 150, with an average of about 50 members. One big event was the annual picnic, which was usually held at the State Forest. It was twenty years before there was a death in the church.

Some of the pastors were: The Rev. John Wilhoit, The Rev. Gordon Goodman, the Rev. Paul Shearhouse, the Rev. Clay, the Rev. Paul Titus, the Rev. H.S. Bollinger, the Rev. Woodrow Shields, the Rev. Vance Davison, the Rev. Eddie King, the Rev. Estel Eckert, and the Rev. James Mowat.

The church was disbanded by the Wesleyan Conference on Sept. 25, 1977, and all funds and assets were turned over to the district.

The church building was bought by Richard and Carol Shively of rural Uniondale and they established "The Oak Tree Antique Shop" in it. Now it is used for storage for another antique shop that they have in Bluffton. *Submitted by Forrest McCartney*

WALNUT LEVEL GERMAN BAPTIST CHURCH

The Walnut Level Church was located in Nottingham Township in Wells County. It was considered a sort of mother of churches in the eastern part of middle Indiana. Samuel Stump and George W. Studebaker did the first preaching. In 1866 the church was organized with 14 members. A structure was built in 1867 near Petroleum. The building was a frame building, 35 by 45 feet and could seat 500 people.

Jacob Warner, Amos Garrett, George Studebaker, and John Shigley were prominent members all during the life of Walnut Level Church. In 1876 Samuel Neher, minister from Allen County, Ohio, settled here and helped Elder Studebaker, so that the church grew considerably. There were 40 members in 1881. Lewis Huber, Samuel Fink, Joseph Engle, Daniel Shanks, and I.F. Yaney were men who worked very hard for this church.

Starting with a huge territory of several counties, its area was cut down by the organization of Pleasant Dale (1889), Hickory Grove (1882) and Blue Creek (1887), which was disbanded in 1905. The Walnut Level Church was disbanded in 1914, and the territory was divided between Pleasant Dale and Hickory Grove. The property was sold for $294.20. *Submitted by Barbara J. McKuras*

Murray United Presbyterian Church

First Reformed Church on the northeast corner of Washington and Oak Streets used until 1908.

Clockwise starting with top left - Africa Church and School located at the corner of county roads of 500S and 500W. The school (District #9) is still standing.

Murray Christian Church

Evangelical Church in Vera Cruz built on North Mulberry in 1855. The building is now a warehouse. The congregation merged with St. Johns. Photo courtesy Don Droy.

Early St. Johns Church built on the south side of Mulberry Street and is now the Croy Machine Shop. Photo courtesy Don Croy.

Original interior of the Craigville Evangelical United Brethern Chruch. Later became Craigville United Methodist Church till it closed and the congregation joined Lancaster Chapel.

Boehmer Church located on the Huntington-Wells County line on road 600W.

Saint Paul's Church Lutheran-Reform Built in 1880

St. Paul's Church

In the early years of the Lutheran Congregation in this community, the churches were in what was known as the Horeb Pastorate. In the beginning there were just the Horeb and St. Paul's Churches, and later on St. John, Mt. Zion, and St. Mark were organized.

During the ministry of Rev. I.C. Birk, sometime between 1918-1922, the St. John's congregation became too weak to support a pastor, so they joined with other churches in the community.

April 18, 1954, Mt. Zion decided to leave what is now known as the Uniondale Lutheran Parish and go in with the Hoagland Parish.

In 1954 the Horeb membership became too small to continue services so they decided to join other churches. St. Paul's was glad to welcome the majority of them into her membership.

In the fall of 1988 the Uniondale Lutheran Parish, which consisted of St. Paul's and St. Mark Lutheran Church, officially dissolved their long term association with each other making St. Paul's congregation the last of the five original churches that made up what was originally called the Horeb Pastorate.

St. Paul's Church was founded by Reformed and Lutheran families, who came here from Ohio and Pennsylvania. It was first organized on October 4, 1854, by the Reverend A. G. Dochandt.

Services were first held in a wooden schoolhouse which stood on what was known as the Crum farm at that time. The schoolhouse was west of the present church building, which is located at 1621 West 300 North in Rockcreek Township, and on the opposite side of the road, where the old cemetery now is.

That same schoolhouse was moved to its present location, directly across from the church on the Bayless Farm, which was the original Crum farm.

The St. Paul's Lutheran congregation was organized with eleven charter members on July 30, 1859, by Reverend Hugh Wells who was a traveling missionary of the Lutheran Synod. He became the pastor and served the Horeb and St. Paul's congregation until the fall of 1864, when he resigned. St. Paul's membership was 128 at that time.

During the ministry of Reverend Dechandt and Reverend Wells, a small brick church was erected and was dedicated on November 15, 1859. This first church had four plain glass windows, two on either side. It stood where the present church now stands. The site for the church and cemetery was given by Abraham Mast. The first person buried in the cemetery was Mikel Swartz in 1860. The bricks and lime was given by Henry Houtz. These bricks were made and fired on the Houtz farm which is now known as the Ed Houtz Farm. Mr. Houtz had the bricks made for the church and also for the Houtz house, in a field which is just east of the present Harold Lesh farm.

The two congregations worshipped in the old brick church until the year 1880, when it was torn down and a new and larger one was erected: the Lutherans and the Reforms uniting in the work.

The second church built is the present church building. It also had plain glass windows, four on either side and two on each side of the entrance hall. At the dedication service of the present church the Vera Cruz choir sang. The director of this choir was Gottieb Sauer. Ed Sauer, Ben Ashbaugher, Fred Ashbauger and Louise Sauer were members of this choir. After the dedication service was over the Abraham Mast family had the choir to their home for dinner. The Mast home was where the Howard Gilbert home was, west of the church and back the long lane.

In 1895 the plain glass windows were replaced with beautiful stained glass windows. In the earlier years of the church when these windows needed repairing they were taken to Ft. Wayne in a spring wagon, later on in a buggy and just a few weeks ago by automobile. The same time the windows were changed, the walls were frescoed. The pictures of Martin Luther and Zwingley were painted on the north wall, one on each side of the pulpit was another painting; a dove with the words above it "God is Love."

The present church also had a very high steeple when it was built, like most churches of that era. In 1913 that steeple was blown off and a much lower belfry was made which is the present one.

In the earlier years of the present church it was heated by a stove on either side of the center isle, which burned wood. The first lights were kerosene. Small swinging reflector lamps were fastened on the casing of each front window. Small low lamps sat on a round lamp shelf on the organ. A drop lamp from the ceiling on either side of the pulpit, and a large chandelier, which hung over the center isle. Many people can remember Oscar Bayless blowing each light through a curved tin tube.

The next heating system was a coal burning furnace and pressure gasoline lighting system. St. Paul's Church as had a few fires from both the pressure lighting system and the coal furnace, but nothing too serious.

The pressure gasoline system was replaced by electricity furnished from Delco Light Plant in the basement and later from the R.E.M.C. high line.

In 1911 the church was remodeled, a balcony was added. Sunday, April 2, 1911, was a re-dedication service. The Reverend S.E. Slater, D.D., the Lutheran pastor, and Reverend P.H. Weaver, B.D., the Reformed pastor, both taking part in the service.

When both the Reform and Lutheran congregations worshipped at St. Paul's, the Reforms would have church service following Sunday School and the Lutherans in the evening. Then the following Sunday the Lutherans had church service following Sunday School and the Reforms in the evening. There were two church services each and every Sunday.

In 1930, the Reformed congregation members left St. Paul's and united with other churches. An effort was made by the Lutheran congregation to buy the interest of the Reformed congregation. The money was raised, but was lost due to a bank failure.

St. Paul's has always had a very active Sunday School, which met every Sunday morning. During the earlier years of the church, the Sunday School was held jointly by the Reformed and the Lutheran congregation.

Classes were all on the main floor until 1911, when the balcony was added, then the Primary Department had their classes up there.

In 1947, a basement was put under the entire church building in memory of Gerald Lesh, Electrician Mate Second Class of the Naval Reserve, who lost his life serving his country in World War II. An oil furnace was also installed at the same time. Upon completion of the basement in 1947 the Primary Department moved from the balcony to the basement. In 1959 we had 40 children in our Primary Department being educated under very efficient teachers to become our future church.

In the summer of 1954, the front of the church was given a more worshipful look by the addition of an altar.

In the fall of 1958, the Altar cross, candelabra, vases, and offering plates were presented by Mrs. Florence Houtz and Mrs. Edna McAfee.

The old parsonage was torn down and salvaged by Perry Macon of Murray in the fall of 1965. The new parsonage was started that winter by Elmer Mossburg of Markle. Cost of the parsonage was $9,111.75, St. Paul's share. Open house for the parsonage was held on September of 1966. In 1988 St. Paul's sold their portion back to St. Mark's after dissolution of the Uniondale Lutheran Parish.

The new minister, Reverend Paul R. Hunteman, wife and family, came here in December 6, 1965, from Princeton, Indiana. St. Mark's and St. Paul's rented the Shively house on State Road 303 for them until the parsonage was completed.

In 1966 we began using bulletins for church and communion the first Sunday of every month, and also discontinued using grape juice and had grape wine for communion.

In 1968, with the new constitution of the church, two council members are elected for a term of three years. Councilmen whose term expired are Loren Decker and Boyd Sheets, who have served as church treasurer since 1946. Elected to serve as councilmen for 1968-1969-1970 were Robert D. Highlen and David McAfee, who received the office of church treasurer.

In 1972, Barbara Lesh was elected as a council member. She was the first lady to have been chosen. In 1973, the second lady was elected to the church council, Jeanne Gilbert. In 1977 she was the first lady to hold the office of president of the church council; then in 1979 she was the first lady to serve as superintendent of Sunday School.

Paneling was done in August from floor to level with bottom of windows. Ernest Lesh and Wayne Shadle were overseers of the work. The church was also painted inside. The work was done by Ardis Crum, Dana Cupp and Mark Harris. The ceilings were lowered and recessed ceiling lights were installed and the windows were painted on the outside.

I-beams were installed to support the bell. The work was done by Ray Bolinger and family. The bell has not been rung for at least 25 years from the year 1980.

During the past 132 years there have been 25 ministers serving St. Paul's. Of the 25 ministers only four of them are living:

Reverend E.A. Kreppert of Deland, Florida; Reverend Paul R. Hunteman of Uniondale, Indiana; Reverend Emil Bartos of Forrest, Illinois and Reverend Otto E. Dorsch of Zanesville, Indiana.

On the fifth of December, 1965, the Reverend Paul R. Huteman came to serve the Uniondale Lutheran Parish and was with us until his retirement the 31st of March, 1984. The Reverend Olney Eaton served as our vice-pastor until a new pastor was selected. Then on the 16th of July, 1984 the Reverend Emil Bartos came to be our new pastor until September of 1988. At that time the Reverend Otto E. Dorsch became our interim pastor and still remains so to this day.

St. Paul's congregation has always been interested in missionary work. The Adult Missionary Society was organized in April 1903, with 20 charter members who were: Mrs. Sadie Lesh, president; Ella Gilbert, vice-president; Winnie Hoffacker, recording secretary; Ada Decker, corresponding secretary; Mrs. M.R. Mohler, pastor's wife; Emma Bayless, Ella Stavor, Lydia Zoll, Ellen Eichhorn, Betty Lesh, Eliza Oldfather, Isabella McAfee, Minervia Staver, Lizzie Miller, Isabelle Decker, Lillie Decker, Rosa Lesh, Odessie Raber, Florence Houtz, and Susan Miller.

Ministers who have served the St. Paul's Church

Minister	Years	Minister	Years
Rev. Hugh Wells	1859-1864	Rev. D.F. Kain	1898-1901
Rev. A. Cromer	1865-1867	Rev. M.R. Mohlor	1902-1904
Rev. Fredrick Biddle	1868-1873	Rev. H.L. Greenwalt	1905-1908
Rev. William Waltman	1874-1876	Rev. S.E. Slater	1909-1913
Rev. T.G. Douglas	1877-1878	Rev. W.S. Oberholtzer	1913-1915
Rev. M.S. Morrison	1878-1879	Rev. H.C. Bixler	1915-1917
Rev. J.G. Jacoby	1879-1883	Rev. I.C. Birk	1918-1922
Rev. William Waltman	1883-1887	Rev. H.L. Greenwalt	1926-1930
Rev. T.A. Pattee	1888-1889	Rev. Harry L. Walmsley	1932-1965
Rev. A.J. Douglas	1889-1892	Rev. Paul R. Hunteman	1965-1984
Rev. J.H. Hoffman	1893-1894	Rev. Emil Bartos	1984-1988
Rev. Jabec Shaffer	1895-1896	Rev. Otto E. Dorsch	1988-present
Rev. Robert Atkin	1896-1898		

In the early years of the Society, the members served dinners at public farm sales; they not only helped the farmer, but also the Society's treasury.

On October 3, 1918, the Society bought a communion set. This communion set replaced the first one which was just the pitcher and a single cup of which everyone partook. Instead of wafers the bread was homemade, cut into thin strips and the minister would break it into individual pieces.

The Missionary Society celebrated their 25th Anniversary on May 6, 1928, at the St. Paul's Church with an open meeting. The 50th anniversary was held at the home of Reeta Gilbert at their regular meeting in 1953. Mrs. Lydia Zoll, the oldest charter and living member, was honored with a potted plant at this meeting. The 75th anniversary in 1978, was celebrated silently.

We had 28 members in 1959 and 20 live members and memoriam members have been made through our Society.

St. Paul's also had a young people's missionary society for several years. It was organized in 1906, with nine charter members who were: Ethel (Lamm) Bayless, Loye Bayless, Lela (Gilbert) Lesh, Irene (Farling) Lesh, Dwight Lesh, Ella (Orr) Lesh, Edna (Kleinknight) Lesh, Maud (Inskeep) Miller, and Myrl (McAfee) Miller.

The members donated food for the farm auction sales and helped work. In 1919, they joined with the adult group.

St. Paul's also had a society for the younger group, called the Mission Band. It was organized in 1903 with seven charter members who were Myrl Miller, Maud Miller, Ethel Bayless, Loye Bayless, Irene Lesh, Dwight Lesh and Lela Gilbert. This group later joined the Young People's Missionary Society.

In 1987 three Lutheran groups merged to form the "Evangelical Lutheran Church in America."

South Liberty Christian Church

In the year of 1875, John Mounsey was prompted by the Spirit of God that there should be religious services held in this community. Records show that John Mounsey rode horseback to George Hubbard's, who at that time lived five miles west of Warren, Indiana, to get his help to hold services, one per month, Saturday evening, Sunday morning, and Sunday evening in the No. 9 frame school house (Mounsey), where the No. 9 brick schoolhouse is standing now and was in the fall of 1875 in Liberty Township, Wells County, Indiana.

Roads were mostly mud in the "Good Old Days." Motorists who go speeding from place to place in high powered cars over smoothly paved highways would hardly be able to appreciate the lot of these Wells County pioneers who fought bumpy corduroy roads and a forest of trees and swampy land to establish a foundation for a church. In fact during certain rainy season of the year, mud rendered some roads very hard to get over. The people rode horseback, in wagons, and on sled to services.

The group organized February 4, 1877, while still in the schoolhouse. This was their creed, "We the undersigned committee throw ourselves together in church fellowship to watch over each other for good. Taking the Bible as the only rules of faith, and to practice, Christian our name, and Christian character our only test of fellowship." Some of the early family member names were Hubbard, Hupp, Jamison, Kimble, Gillem, Mounsey, Lewis, Hunnicutt, McClerry, Holsinger, Dolby, Wooster, Osborn, Jacobs, Grover, Eilar, Minnich, First, Landis, Foreman, Terhune, Musselman, Stinson, McKee, Brinneman, Brown, Shadle, Huffman, Godfrey, Gephart, Masterson, Garretson. Mendenhall and Murry appear on the records at the time of building and maintaining the first church.

On December 16, 1886, plans were made to build a church. They selected a northeast corner of section 32 of Liberty Township. They purchased one-fourth of an acre from David Dolby for $25.00 and the work was begun April 2, 1887, with Warren Thatcher's help. A building 34 x 44 was

First church turned and addition vestibule bell tower added - 1911.

Second church with vestibule and restrooms added - 1968.

New church 1978-1979

constructed and, on the fourth Sunday in January of 1888, the church was dedicated while Rev. Hubbert was pastor. At this time it was given the name of Dolby Chapel. It was also known as the Africa Church sometime in its earlier days. Later it was named The South Liberty Christian New-Lite Church after joining the Indiana Miami Reserve Christian New-Lite Conference, and still later the new-lite part was dropped.

If you were to have visited this church you would have found a pulpit like a big box and the choir in the northeast corner. Lights were of a chandelier type that pulled down and used oil. On March 9, 1907, another one-fourth of an acre was purchased from J. Perry Mounsey for $25.00 to be used for hitchracks. In 1910 a few automobiles began to take some of the space around the church and provide better transportation.

Then in 1911 the church building was turned around with the help of Billy Miller. They added Sunday School rooms, vestibule and a bell. Gas lights were added and later on electric lights. On October 28, 1911, it was dedicated while Rev. J.E. McCorkell was pastor. As the church grew various other improvements took place.

This church was destroyed by fire on September 25, 1952 while painters were cleaning paint from the sidewalk with an inflammable cleaning fluid.

Other family member names appear in the records at this time, being Payne, Richards, Boxell, Brown, Williamson, Harris, Colbert, Sills, Jackson, Crawford, Merriman, Knott, White, Garrison, Harrold, Gaiser, Noe, Leurance, Martin, Starr, Krinn, Bender, Zent, Penrod, Pond, Penny, Carroll, Markley, Micheal, Cossairt, Straw, Curry, Burkhart, Poling.

The people felt very deeply about the need to have a place to worship of their own, so once again they constructed a 36 x 50 church building, this time thinking ahead of the growing needs of the congregation. This building had a basement, electric heat and electric lights, and furniture from the old one was saved and used. It was dedicated July 5, 1953, while Rev. Elmer Engle was still pastor. Between 1961 and 1970 restrooms and vestibule were added to the front of the church. Also, classrooms were added in the basement. Still other family names appear on the records covering the period this church building was used such as Ruse, Betts, Oswalt, Fields, Jones, Westfall, Barr, Beavens, and Rains.

On September 1, 1977, this church was destroyed by fire after an electrical storm hit the breaker box shorting out an electric heater in the wall below it.

With some forethought, hard work and sacrifice another new church building, 36 x 60, one that would not burn so easily, was built and services began September 15, 1979. It was dedicated April 20, 1980 while Rev. Garry Wyatt was pastor. This church is still being used today with Sunday School and worship service on Sundays. There are midweek prayer meetings when weather permits.

The church as it is today gives us evidence of keeping alive the Spirit and tradition of the earlier church that was established by a people who believed in love and reverence for GOD. There are still descendants from the early pioneers attending services at this church.

Over the years various ministers were called from this church. Some were ones who lived in the community such as Bruce Mounsey, Roland Osborn, Carl Harris, Clayton Mounsey, Von Cossairt, Dewey Zent, Delmer Harrold, Wayne Dolby and Francis Huffman. The records show that we have had many more good spirit filled men from other places to lead us down through the years.

St. John United Church Of Christ

St. John United Church of Christ is located in Vera Cruz (formerly Newville) in Wells County. Many families from Adams County as well as Wells County attend this small but active church.

In the spring of 1841, three families came to make their homes in the dense forest six miles east of Bluffton. At that time there was just a trail to Bluffton. These were the families of Christian Sauer, John Moeschberger and Peter Meyer. They had come from Switzerland via Wayne County, Ohio. They were of the Reformed Church in Switzerland and were determined to abide by the counsel of the psalmist who had taught men, saying "Bless the Lord O my soul and forget not His benefits."

Other families came, too. Among them was a Lutheran family named Mueller. Mr. Mueller's efforts to secure a Lutheran minister brought Rev. Frederick Wynekin of the German Lutheran Church of Fort Wayne to preach a few times. In the '40s, Wynekin returned to Germany and upon his return to this country, he showed a decidedly strict Lutheran tendency. Soon after his return, he announced that strict adherence to the Lutheran faith would be the rule and that only Lutherans could receive the Holy Sacraments, as other believers were in error. Due to this position, his connection with the people was severed.

Other ministers served the community including Rev. Knabe from Adams County and then a Presbyterian minister who refused to conduct confirmation. This relationship was also quickly discontinued. During the last half of the year 1848, Dr. Jacob Bossard, pastor of the St. John Reformed Church of Fort Wayne, began to visit the Reformed people of Newville. He administered the Lord's Supper, performed baptisms, and visited people in their homes. Parents concerned about their young people sent them to Fort Wayne for instruction in the way of life. Dr. Bossard was a good preacher and a zealous worker.

In 1849, a Lutheran minister, Rev. Kleinekas, came and organized a Reformed and Lutheran Church. By now a considerable number of people had made their homes in this settlement, and there was a definite need for religious services. Therefore a parsonage was built (destroyed by fire circa 1987) where the minister lived on the first floor with the upper room used for services. This church was known as the Church of Peace. Unfortunately, a doctrinal controversy arose which resulted in terminating Rev. Kleinekas' ministry at the close of the first year.

This church was destroyed by fire in February 1980.

Other pastors served, one being Rev. Frederick Dechant, who came in 1855 after the church had been without a pastor for a few years. Some of the members of the Reformed and Lutheran Church had withdrawn and affiliated with the Evangelical Church. The balance affiliated with the Reformed segment.

In the year 1858, Mr. Rabel, a member of the church died. Because he felt richly blessed by God he showed his love by bequeathing $200.00 to the church. This would be the start of a fund for a new church building. After this great show of love another member, August Pauli, pledged $50.00 for a church bell. The balance needed for the church was raised by the congregation. Later that year the church was dedicated with Rev. H. Benz of Fort Wayne assisting in the ceremony. This building housed the worshipers for 53 years and is still being used as the Croy Machine Shop.

Immigration brought several French people into the community. They built a small church parsonage combination on the northern edge of Newville, known as the French protestant Church House. Its existence was of short duration and, after there was no hope of further pastoral care, their building became private property. On July 4th, 1863, Nicholas Klein, Gottleib Sauer and John Atz, acting for the German Reformed Church, traded their parsonage for the French Church Parsonage. This served as a parsonage until 1881.

In 1886 the first organ was purchased with Daniel Reinhart as organist for many years.

During this time Rev. John Stepler, now pastor of the church also served Reformed churches at Rockcreek and Union dale. In 1868 Stepler discontinued serving the

Uniondale and Rockcreek churches due to the large congregation in Newville and his illness.

Rev. Hullhorst came in 1869, recognized the spiritual desires of a group of people near Berne and shared the Word of God with them. In 1869 he organized the Cross Reformed Church (also known as the Church of the Cross). The next year this congregation was served along with the Newville charge. Then, in 1870, Rev. Hullhorst was instrumental in bringing the St. Luke congregation into a happy relationship with the church at Newville. The town's name was changed in 1870 to Vera Cruz, and these three congregations became known as the Vera Cruz Charge.

One pastor, Rev. Peter Vitz, who came in 1877, had the foresight to have the St. John German Reformed congregation buy the commanding corner in the town. This would be put to use in the year 1909 when the congregation decided to build a new church instead of remodeling the old one. The Rev. Oswald Vitz, son of Rev. Peter Vitz, was pastor at this time. The church was erected at the cost of $8500.00. The cornerstone laying was held June 20, 1909, and the dedication services were held November 14th the same year.

In 1934, the German Reformed Church joined the Evangelical Synod, and later in 1957, they joined the Congregational-Christian Churches. The church is now known as the St. John United Church of Christ.

The church was extensively remodeled in the year 1955 with new paneling, a new lectern, altar and pulpit.

On February 19, 1980, this church building was completely destroyed by fire of unknown origin. The only thing salvaged was the bell. This bell rings again from the new church. While the new church was being erected the congregation met in a building at the Vera Cruz Opportunity School. By November, the congregation was in the new church building although it was not completed. The present building is erected on the same lot as the old church and, because of insurance and donations from many friends and organizations, it was dedicated debt free January 11, 1981. The cost of this church was approximately $185,000.

The church though small, has been a light in several communities, as it has regularly attending members from Bluffton, Berne, Monroe, Geneva, Liberty Center, Craigville and areas around these towns.

At the present time there is no pastor. Our governing board consists of the following: Elders-Verlin Kauffman, Dan Frantz and Chester Smith: Deacons-Jack Wenger, Greg Kauffman and Ron Kipfer and Trustees-Ralph McAlhaney, Harold Steiglitz and Richard Kauffman.

Ministers who have served this congregation are as follows: Rev. Kleinekas, 1848; Rev. Chambour, 1850-55; Rev. Frederick Dechant, 1855-59; Rev. William Fenneman, D.D., 1859-63; Rev. Max Schultz, 1863; Rev. John Stepler, D.D., 1864-66; Rev. John Gehring, 1867-69; Rev. F. Hullhorst, 1869-72; rev. Abraham Bollinger, 1872-76; Rev. Peter Vitz, 1877-83; Rev. J. Otto Vitz, 1883-88; Rev. Henry Heusser, 1888-94; Rev. Christian Schoepfle, 1894-97; Rev. Oswald Vitz, 1897-1911; Rev. W.H. Schroer, D.C., 1911-18; Rev. Otto Scherry, 1918-30; Rev. Herbert Meckstroth, 1930-54; Rev. Louis Minsterman, 1955-62; Rev. Robert Oleson, 1963-66; Rev. John Dulin, 1967-74; Rev. Kent Ulery, 1975-79; Rev. John H.C. Niederhaus, 1980-84; Rev. Peter Smith 1985-91.

Present day church of St. John's Vera Cruz, which was dedicated in January of 1981.

Apostolic Christian Church

The roots of the Apostolic Christian Church can be traced directly to the emigration to America of several Swiss Mennonite families. This sect of people left their homeland in Europe to pursue greater freedom, both economically and spiritually, on this side of the Atlantic. In 1838, Christian Baumgartner and his family settled near Newville in Adams County. Under the guidance of his father, David Baumgartner, meetings were held in the various homes.

In 1852, two ministers named Ulrich Kipfer and Matthias Strahm joined the Baumgartner family. These two men kept and pondered the words of Samuel Frohlich which they heard in Switzerland and this started to grow, and they were not satisfied until they had this precious pearl in their hearts. So determined were these two men to find a sound religious faith, that in 1858 they set out on foot for Sardis, Ohio. Their objective was to visit with Isaac Gehring and Joseph Bella, ministers of the Apostolic Christian Church at Sardis, and to discuss the basic principals of the religious faith these two men espoused.

In a short time they were fully convinced they had truly found the "firm foundation" in Christ Jesus. Subsequently, they fully committed their lives to the Lord in repentance and embraced the new church. When these two men arrived back in the Newville community (a small town near the Adams-Wells County border, later named Vera Cruz), they enthusiastically told their relatives and friends of the new faith they acquired. It was with joy and conviction that they related the "new birth" experience and how God, in mercy, will grant peace of heart and mind to all who will surrender to the Lord and humbly follow His teachings. There was an immediate response to the gospel, resulting in the beginning of what is now known as the Bluffton Apostolic Christian Church.

In 1858, eighteen people were baptized in a pond near Newville. By 1867, the church community grew to the extent that a church building was required and was built near Newville. In 1897 the church membership had grown to 130, and new accommodations were needed. A new building was erected on the site seating 450 people. During these days the church was known as the Newville Apostolic Christian Congregation. In about 1900 when many families moved to Bluffton, and Newville faded as a settlement, the church became known as the Bluffton Apostolic Christian Church.

From 1935 to 1950 the church membership increased about fifty percent requiring additional space. Construction of the third (existing) church, which replaced the structure built in 1897, began in 1949. On August 6, 1950, the new church, which has a seating capacity of 1500 people, was dedicated. A Fellowship Hall was built in 1969 to accommodate various church function. In 1976 an addition to the church was constructed to provide additional Sunday School facilities.

In 1980, due to crowded conditions, the church decided to build a second church on the northeast edge of Bluffton. Bluffton North, which seats approximately 575 people, held its first services on Thanksgiving Day, 1982. With a concern for Christian care for the elderly of the community, the church felt a need to provide a retirement facility. Construction of "Christian Care Retirement Community" began in the fall of 1988 and it was opened to the public in December of 1989. Currently the facility consists of 64 nursing rooms, 17 residential apartments and 5 independent living duplex buildings.

The action of these first two sincere men of God precipitated a following that by 1991 has grown into two churches with approximately 1200 members and 550 Sunday School students from over 600 families. Thousands, over the years, have heard the glorious, pure and unadulterated gospel sounded from the pulpits by men chosen from the congregation. The doctrine of a born-again conversion, through repentance, remains strong in the church. Great emphasis is placed upon the price Christ paid in His sacrifice for sin and the ensuing responsibility of converted people to live their lives in harmony with the teachings of the Scripture.

Apostolic Christian Church Bluffton

Apostolic Christian Church Bluffton North

ASBURY CHAPEL UNITED METHODIST CHURCH

In the month of May in 1837, Robert Alexander, a local preacher, moved with his family to Jackson Township from Elkhart County, Ohio. He was a devout Christian, and when he heard of another local preacher, Brother John Ervin, who lived some distance away, he invited him to come and preach at the Alexander home.

Soon after that, a circuit riding missionary, Rev. George W. Bowers, made the Alexander home a regular preaching location. On Christmas Day in 1838 he organized a class of 11 members.

Later the congregation built a small frame church. This church was on a circuit with Montpelier. This congregation apparently disbanded about 1872.

With the coming of the oil boom of the 1890's the number of people in the area increased and Mr. J.C. Ziegler, an oil man from Montpelier, spearheaded the organization and building of the present Asbury Chapel.

In 1950, the building was enlarged and a basement was dug. In 1977, the interior of the sanctuary was completely redecorated and new furniture was installed. The United Methodist Women's group of the church has completely redone the kitchen and basement using proceeds from their annual bazaar.

At this time the attendance averages about 50 persons. The pastor is Rev. Joe O'Conner.

The church is located at the intersection of St. Rd. 3 and County Rd. 1100 S. in Jackson Township.

This article is based in a great part on a history of the church written in 1950 by Mrs. C.L. Smith who was a granddaughter of Robert Alexander.

BETHEL CHURCH

Bethel Church, just south of Bluffton on 300 South, has been known for a part of its near 150 year history as Bethel Methodist-Episcopal, but for the past several years it has been known simply as Bethel Church.

In the November 7th, 1890 edition of the Bluffton Chronicle it is stated that the organization of the church dates sometime between 1840 and 1842. In its earliest days it was on the circuit with the first M.E. Church of Bluffton, with the first minister probably Rev. Seth Smith.

The original church was a frame structure. In 1898 the congregation decided to build a new building at the same location. This building was designed by the famous Bluffton architect Cuno Kibele. It consisted of a Sunday School room and classrooms, connected with the auditorium by a sliding wood curtain. The red brick structure is of the Richardsonian Romanesque style of architecture. On March 1, 1984, Bethel Church had the honor of being officially added to the National Register of Historical Places. In 1986, an addition was begun to add restrooms, nursery facilities and a fellowship hall. The original structure was not altered except for an entrance at the rear of the building.

The original congregation of Bethel M.E. Church had its beginnings in Pennsylvania and the British Isles. It was a product of the "circuit rider" era of the 19th century. A gradual decline in membership began after World War II. Finally membership had declined to a few who desired to keep the small rural church alive.

In 1985 the trustees of Bethel Church turned over the duties to a new board and a new era began. Known simply as Bethel Church, it is now an independent church with no denominational ties. While the historic structure is a reminder of the past, it is most prepared to meet the future needs of the community.

The present minister, Patrick Harris was called to be full time pastor at Bethel in October, 1986. He is a graduate of Grace Theological Seminary in Winona Lake. His wife Katie and their three daughters, Christina, Stephanie and Jessica accepted the call to Bethel "not because it has a past, but, because it has a future."

Bethel Church demolished 1900-1904 (l. to r.) Marl Sawyer, James A. Storgeon, and George W. Caps.

Freddie and Harrold Poulson

Present Day Bethel Church shortly after construction, still showing old church.

Bethlehem Evangelical Lutheran Church and School

Bethlehem Evangelical Lutheran Church, a congregation of the Missouri Synod, is located at 6514 East and 750 North, Ossian, Indiana.

The first property was comprised of five acres of land, donated by Andrew Werling, Sr., located in Jefferson Township, Wells County, Indiana, which is about five and one-half miles southeast of Ossian.

In 1896, several members of St. Paul Lutheran Church, Preble, who lived in the community near Tocsin, expressed the desire to have a church and school in their own vicinity. The primitive roads, and the eight mile round trip by horse and buggy to church and school at Preble, prompted this desire.

On February 2, 1896, Bethlehem Evangelical Lutheran Church was constituted. Thirteen charter members signed that first constitution: Ernest Bauermeister Sr., Ernest Bauermeister Jr., Henry Bauermeister, Henry Berghorn, Martin Fackler, Karl Grewe, Ernest Meyer, Andrew Werling Sr., Andrew Werling Jr., Christian Werling, David Werling, George Werling, and John Werling. In February, 1897, Karl Stoppenhagen became the fourteenth member. At the outset, Bethlehem and St. Paul were served by the same pastor.

A wooden building, 40 feet long, 26 feet wide and 12 feet high, was erected by members at a cost of $850. This new church and school was dedicated to the glory of God on November 22, 1896.

In June of 1897, Bethlehem became officially independent of St. Paul, Preble, and was admitted as a member of the Lutheran Church - Missouri Synod in 1898.

July 25, 1897, construction of a parsonage, consisting of three rooms downstairs and two rooms upstairs, was begun. In August of 1897, a cellar was added and in April 1901, a summer kitchen was attached. The parsonage was further enlarged in the spring of 1910. This house still served as the teachers' building, standing north of the present school.

On October 3, 1897, the Reverend William Ludwig became the first pastor of Bethlehem, with an annual salary of $250.

The following is a chronology of official acts recorded: The first baptism was John David Paul Fackler, infant son of Martin and Louise Werling Fackler, baptized February 21, 1897. The second baptism was Otto David Karl Bauermeister, infant son of Ernest and Karoline Werling Bauermeister. Otto D.K. Bauermeister was a member of Bethlehem until his death on April 9, 1990.

The first recorded wedding was of Christian Grewe and Louise Bauermeister, April 29, 1897. An unrecorded wedding of Frederick Graft and Marie Bauermeister took place on November 25, 1896, in the original church-school.

The church records of St. Paul, Preble, record the death of an infant son of Henry and Friedericke Breier Bauermeister, December, 1896. As a consequence, on Christmas Day of 1896 a cemetery was established which still serves the congregation today. The first death on record for Bethlehem was that of Paul Fackler on March 14, 1897.

As the congregation quickly grew, the need for a larger church became evident. The cornerstone for a new church was laid on Sunday, June 15, 1913. This building was constructed using Suburban Bethlehem as the model at a cost of $12,000. The Building Committee consisted of Fred Graft, David Werling, Christian Franke, Karl Stoppenhage, Sr., and Ernest Bauermeister. The old frame church now served only as the school.

In 1939, electric lights were added to all buildings owned by the congregation. The next building program took place in January, 1948, when a new parsonage was planned. The lumber was milled by Andrew Werling, Jr., from timber donated by members. Dedication was held on April 24, 1949.

Music is an important part of Lutheran worship and, from its beginning, Bethlehem has incorporated organ music in its worship. The first pipe organ, donated by Andrew Werling, Sr., had bellows pumped by foot with every man 16 years or older taking his turn. The present pipe organ is an 18 rank, 15 stop Martin Ott pipe organ installed and dedicated in 1987.

The school was maintained by the congregation from the very beginning with the pastor serving as teacher. In 1935 it was resolved to secure a teacher for one year with an annual salary of $320. Henry F. Becker, a student, was then secured as the teacher of the school, thus becoming the first student-teacher at Bethlehem. Each year thereafter a supply teacher, or a student, served in the school until 1943.

Since that time, permanently called teachers have served in the school.

In the early history of the school, the students were responsible for the daily chores, such as sweeping the floors, carrying in the coal, firing of the cannonball (coal stove), and carrying in drinking water. Originally all classes were taught in German, then around World War I, English was added. German was discontinued about the time of World War II. School was in session regardless of the weather conditions. In 1936, with the temperature at -18 and deep snow, the school bus and students were stranded at the home of Otto Bauermeister overnight.

In the summer of 1946, improvements were begun on the school building, including the digging of a basement and the installation of a new furnace and stoker. Luther Dettmer and Company dug the basement with a total bill of $800.12. The new heating system was installed by Ashbacher's Tin Shop of Decatur, Indiana, for $905.

In 1955, a new brick school, with two large classrooms and a basement kitchen/cafeteria, replaced the old frame school. With numerous improvements over the years, this school building still serves the congregation today.

In 1978, Bethlehem students were involved in a car-bus accident sending 11 students to the hospital with injuries.

Presently serving the congregation as pastor is the Rev. William R. Brege, and as principal of the school is Mr. Jonathon P. Zinnel.

At total of 13 pastors and 41 teachers have served this congregation since its founding.

Bethlehem Lutheran Church had small beginnings but grew steadily over the years. The current membership is at 530 souls with 68 students enrolled in the school, 21 of them descendants of charter members.

Having recently celebrated the 90th Anniversary of the founding of our congregation, and the 10th Anniversary of the dedication of our new Sanctuary and Fellowship Hall, we continue to witness to our Savior Jesus Christ with humble appreciation of God's grace, and with joyous thanksgiving for the endless blessings, both physical and spiritual, which He gives to each of us. As our forefathers have in the past, so we continue to give all glory to God. We are reminded of the words of the Psalmist: "Not unto us, O Lord, not unto us, but unto Thy Name give glory, for Thy mercy and for Thy truth's sake." (Psalm 115:1). Our prayer is that many may come to know and believe the gospel which John 3:16 so beautifully proclaims: "For God so loved the world that He gave His only begotten Son, that whosoever believeth in Him should not perish but have everlasting life."

Bluffton First United Methodist Church

In the middle of November in 1838 there came riding, on horseback, into this village a young Methodist minister of 25 years of age. This young minister was the Rev. George W. Bowers. He was a member of what was known then as "The Portland Mission." He had been instructed by his bishop to carry the Methodist ministry to the people of Indiana.

After hearing this message from the Rev. Bowers, these Hoosier Pioneers banded themselves together and formed a religious society. This society was the beginning of the first Methodist congregation in Bluffton, Indiana.

The first three or four years the services of this society were held in the homes of members. As time went on, more members were added, and more room was needed. The new meeting place was in the courthouse on the corner of Main and Perry Streets. Services were held in the courthouse until 1847 when the first church was erected at the corner of Cherry and Johnson Streets where the First Baptist Church now stands. This was the home of the Methodists in Bluffton until October 13, 1872. The first Sunday School was organized in Bluffton in 1843. In the 1840s, the Methodists had again outgrown its facilities.

Plans for a new church building were submitted to the building committee. The committee suggested the lot on the northeast corner of West Washington and South Williams streets be purchased. A new church building made of brick was constructed. The new church building was dedicated on October 13, 1872, and the church was the church home until February, 1952.

In 1888, the First Methodist Church observed its fiftieth anniversary and was fortunate to have with the congregation, the Rev. George W. Bowers who delivered the first sermon in Bluffton and was the first minister to serve Bluffton. To make the occasion more impressive, a large oak tree was erected on the pulpit platform, a reminder of the first sermon he delivered standing under an oak tree in 1838.

The year 1938 brought the one hundredth anniversary year of this Methodist congregation. This eventful occasion, was celebrated on Sunday, November 17, 1938.

Bluffton United Methodist Church 1872-1952.

In the 1940s a building committee was appointed and instructed to accept pledges and funds for a new church. Anticipating the need for more land the trustees were authorized to purchase land east of the church. The last services were held in the old sanctuary on Sunday, February 10, 1952. Starting February 17, 1952, services were held in the City Building. Formal opening services were held May 3, 1953. The official dedication of the new church building was October 11, 1953.

In 1939, the major branches of Methodism consolidated and became the Methodist Church. In 1968, the Methodists consolidated with the Evangelical United Brethren Church and created what is now "The United Methodist Church."

Over the years in the United Methodist Church of Bluffton many have been called from its rank to work in various fields of Christian endeavor. Through them and from them the teachings and influences of our church have been felt, and are still being felt, far and wide in many areas of the world.

Since 1838, from this little group of worshipers of some 25 people, through trial and tribulation, successes and disappointments, we have now reached a membership of 671 and are still growing.

Bluffton United Methodist Church May 3, 1953 to the present.

THE BLUFFTON MULBERRY STREET WESLEYAN CHURCH

The Mulberry Street Wesleyan Church was first called the Bluffton Wesleyan Methodist Church. It was organized in 1886 by the Reverend R.V. Carter and the Reverend B.L. Couch. According to the earliest available record, Bluffton Wesleyan Methodist was a part of the Salamonia Circuit. The statistical report of 1888 shows the circuit consisting of four organized churches, but having only two buildings.

Although no record of charter members is available, it is thought that Mr. and Mrs. Will Sprowl, Tom Watson, Mrs. McFadden, and Mrs. Edington were among the first members.

Members worshipped in homes until 1889 when building plans were begun under the Rev. B.L. Couch. The church was completed in 1890 when the Rev. W.G. Moon was the pastor. It was a wooden structure containing one room and was located on the site of the present church. Tom Watson and Will Sprowl were the carpenters for the building, and they were assisted by members and friends of the church. An item from the *Bluffton Evening News* dated April 19, 1897, announced a service for the organization of a Sunday School.

The statistical records of 1913-1914 show a membership of 34 persons and one building valued at $1,000, with a total receipts for the year of $254.17 and an average Sunday School attendance of 50.

In 1920 a house was purchased and moved from the 100 block of West Washington Street to 917 South Mulberry Street and used as a parsonage. Then in 1956, while Earl and Rose Surface were serving as pastor, plans were started for building a new parsonage. The old parsonage was moved to a new location and sold. The new parsonage, which is the present one, was completed and dedicated on February 17, 1957 after G.C. Cockreil was installed as pastor.

The church has changed and endured even through adversities. One March 25, 1942, at about 3 o'clock in the morning, the church caught on fire. There was only a portion of the north wall standing and the floor was not burned, but everything else was completely destroyed.

The church had a building fund in the amount of $275.14. However, cash and pledges started coming in by mail and direct. Money was received on the first Sunday morning services of March 29, 1945. That service as held in the basement of the Park School. They raised approximately $3,200 with insurance in the amount of $2,000.

Plans for a new church were begun immediately. However, because of war-time restrictions, it was hard to obtain building materials. Some supplies were purchased before all the building materials were frozen on April 10, 1942.

The people worked on obtaining a permit to built and raising more money. They were refused a permit to build three different times. Finally, in July, 1942, a permit to replace the building was received with the cost not to exceed $5,000. With this restriction, the basement walls were poured and the excavating done by July 30, 1942.

Finally, on August 5th, a permit was granted without cost restrictions. Construction was started in earnest on September 1, 1942. By November 22, 1942, just eight months after the fire and less than three months after receipt of the unrestricted permit, the church was dedicated. On May 3, 1944, the *Bluffton New-Banner* carried an article telling of a note-burning service, signifying cancellation of all indebtedness against the building.

Another change took place on June 26, 1968, when the Pilgrim Holiness Church and the Wesleyan Methodist merged forming The Wesleyan Church. Thus, the name of the church changed to the Bluffton Wesleyan Church and then to the Mulberry Street Wesleyan Church. Also, there have been over 30 different pastors who have served the church faithfully over the past 100 years, as well as many faithful, committed, and wonderful members and lay people. May it please the Lord to continue to prosper His work in this place.

FORMER PASTORS
YEARS OF SERVICE

E. T. Span	1887-1888
E. L. Couch	1888-1890
W.G. Moon	1890-1892
(Supplied by Conference)	1892-1893
D.F. Gordon	1893-1894
G.W. Zike	1894-1896
C.A. Bilheimer	1900-1903
S.A. Mow	1903-1908
J.J. Coleman	1908-1910
H.T. Arnold	1910-1912
A.W. and Lydia Murphy	1912-1913
D.C. Dooley	1913-1915
Belle McClure	1915-1916
Henry Hanna	1916-1920
David Downing	1920-1921
A.B. Dayton	1921-1923
L.C. Tyndall	1923-1924
E.E. Spaugh	1924-1926
E.E. Hunte	1926-1934
Thomas Ballard	1934-1938
V.A. Vardaman	1938-1943
Glenn Appleman	1943-1946
E. Sterl Phinney	1946-1947
Russell Klinger	1947-1951
Roscoe Coleman	1951-1954
Earl and Rose Surface	1954-1956
G.C. Cockrell	1956-1961
Owen Heinzman	1961-1970
George Russell	1970-1973
Carl Roark	1973-1982
Garry D. Beecher	1982-

Boehmer United Methodist Church

Early one damp and dreary Sunday morning in February, 1886, John I. Clark and his twelve-year-old son Rufus walked the four miles to Mount Zion where they attended Children's Day exercises which were being held in connection with a revival meeting. In a short talk near the close of the service, Mr. Clark remarked that he wished for a church nearer his home. After the meeting, Mr. and Mrs. Thomas Arnold., owners of the store at Mount Zion, invited the Clarks to their home for dinner. During the afternoon, the possibilities of a church near Boehmer were discussed. Reverend Robinson (a circuit rider) promised to build a church if Mr. Clark could raise $500. So many were interested in the project that by Tuesday evening, a sum of $700 had been donated toward the building of the church.

The first Boehmer Methodist Protestant Class was organized by Reverend Robinson at the Roberts Schoolhouse, two miles west of Liberty Center on March 29, 1886, with eleven charter members. The class was placed in the Salamonie Circuit and elected officers and teachers and formed a Sabbath School, which met in the school until the new church was built. The first superintendent and his assistant were James Redding and Robert Campbell, and Aaron Moore was the first secretary of the class.

Reverend Robinson later resigned and Reverend John Neher was sent to finish the year. At the following annual church conference, Reverend J.C. Macklin was assigned as pastor of the Salamonie Circuit, which included Boehmer, Liberty Center, Blanche Chapel, Union Chapel, and West Liberty. Reverend Macklin organized a board of trustees with John Merrimen, James Jones, George Sliger, A.L. Carroll and William Melling serving. On June 30, 1887, the trustees selected and secured the deed for the south part of the present lot, purchased from Howard Thompson, and the erection of the new church was started.

The timber was donated and cut by the neighbors and was sawed by James Jones at his sawmill. Ves Eiler built the church and Martin Huffman assisted him in finishing the interior. They also made and dressed the pews. Due to a lack of funds, the work was halted in 1887 but resumed early in 1888 and the building was finished that summer at a total cost of $1800. The original church had one room and faced west.

By May 2, 1909, the Boehmer and Liberty Center churches had grown large enough to become a double station sharing the same pastor. By 1927, Boehmer realized the need for more room and the church was completely remodeled. A basement was dug and rooms added to the church, with rededication on December 4, 1927.

At the annual North Indiana Conference in May 1952, Boehmer and Liberty Center separated and became their own charge. Boehmer built a parsonage that year at a cost of just over $10,000. At the conference in 1953, Boehmer joined with Emmanuel near Rockford to form a circuit. They remained together until 1976 when Boehmer, for the first time, obtained its own minister, Barry Humble.

Early in 1985, it was decided to do remodeling work at the church. The sanctuary was plastered and painted, new windows and carpeting were installed, the woodwork was refinished, and a sixteen foot high steeple with a cross on top was placed on the belfry.

This helped prepare the congregation for the centennial celebration, held June 13 and 14, 1987. The centennial was two days of activities at the church with many former ministers and members attending. The cornerstone, sealed in 1927, was opened at that time.

Boehmer United Methodist Church is located three miles west and one-half mile south of Liberty Center on Wells-Huntington County Line. We are a country church with no center of population to draw from. The church is active in mission support, United Methodist Women's and United Methodist Youth Fellowship organizations, a Willing Workers Circle, and prayer chains for spiritual support.

Early Boehmer Church

Tradition has long played a strong role in the history of Boehmer, but we have never been afraid to look ahead and move forward when changing times and new ideas came along. Changes were talked and prayed about, and discussed thoroughly. All shoulders were put to the wheel; everyone worked together and another victory was won. We hope that God is pleased at the record made by Boehmer and pray that we will retain His favor in the future as we so richly have been rewarded by Him in the past hundred years.

Our name has always been Boehmer, and indeed we are "The Church by the Side of the Road"

Present Day Boehmer Church

Calvary Lutheran Church

Calvary Lutheran Church was "conceived" in December of 1954, when about a dozen people began holding worship services in the old Roxy Theater (109 E. Market). The American Lutheran Church officially recognized this "pregnancy" in May of 1955, when the young congregation was officially chartered by the ALC Mission Board. The church at this time moved Sunday services from the theatre to Psi Iota Xi Hall, at 115 1/2 S. Johnson Street.

After purchasing four acres of ground, on Highway One on the north edge of Bluffton, the congregation was officially "born" on November 24, 1957, when a new building was dedicated. On that morning Sunday School was held as usual in the Psi Ote Hall. At about 10:00 a.m. everyone journeyed to the new building, and assembled at the front door. Following the invocation and prayer and a responsive reading (Psalm 24:7-10), Harold Pett, representing the architect, handed the key to Clarence Bultemeir, the builder, who in turn presented the key to Joe Flowers, chairman of the building committee, who inserted the key in the door. The chairman of the congregation, the late Karl Horst, unlocked the door. The pastor, Daniel L. Steiner, opened the door and quoted Psalm 122:1; "I was glad when they said unto me; let us go into the house of the Lord." The people entered the church and the first of three dedicatory services on that day began.

The years have been good to Calvary Lutheran since that day. Of course there were days when it seemed as if the infant congregation would never survive. In retrospect those days of struggle have become good and pleasant years, because the fruits of these early labors are now evident. It was in 1975 that the education wing was completed and the building was not only beautiful but functional as well. Thus far the worship plant history of Calvary Lutheran.

The first year and one-half in the life of Calvary found the young church with two students pastors. The first was a young intern, Paul Stengel, who was sent by St. John's Lutheran Church of Fort Wayne to conduct services. He served about seven months. For the next year John Tangman, a young married seminarian, was the spiritual leader. It was in the fall of 1956 that the Rev. Daniel L. Steiner was installed as the church's first full time pastor, and he has served the congregation to the present time.

Calvary Lutheran has had a number of firsts. For a time the Bluffton Drive-In Theatre was used for early morning worship services. The church held the first church school for slow learners and has held special classes on Sunday. The church is also the first to broadcast live over the radio each Sunday.

There was no Lutheran Church in Bluffton during the first one hundred years of Wells County. Early in the history of Wells County there was a Mt. Horeb Lutheran Church just north and west of the old Cover Bridge, which burned a number of years ago. Early Lutherans worshiped at St. Mark's in Uniondale and St. Paul's in Rockcreek Township. Both of these congregations are members of the Evangelical Lutheran Church in America (ELCA). Calvary Lutheran Church, in Bluffton, was originally established as a congregation of the American Lutheran Church. Calvary Lutheran is now a congregation of the Evangelical Lutheran Church in America, a result of the merger of Lutheran Churches in January of 1988.

Present Chester Center Church

CHESTER CENTER CHRISTIAN CHURCH

The Chester Center Christian Church site was acquired on February 3, 1872, and the deed recorded on March 2, 1874. The site was purchased for $10.00 from Jesse and Catharine Thomas. The first structure was named the Christian Union Chapel Church with the Rev. Turner as the first pastor. The name of the church underwent at least two changes in succeeding years until it took on its present name.

A fire on January 25, 1896, destroyed all the early church records. A committee consisting of George Miller, Jess Miller, and T.M. Shields, brought the church history up-to-date. Many recall services being held in a log schoolhouse until a new building was constructed.

Trustees, in 1896, were Jesse Thomas, G.W. Miller, and Edward Ludlum. The church then had kerosene lamps on the walls and a round chandelier that pulled down from the ceiling with kerosene lamps arranged on it. Monthly dues of ten cents per member were collected for payment of the pastor's social security and retirement. The dues later increased to twenty-five cents.

In March, 1952, plans were made to remodel the one room church. Sunday School attendance had reached 238 and more room was needed. Fern Crosby submitted blueprints for the addition of a classroom and vestibule. Russ and Iona Harris purchased a half-acre of ground and sold it to the church for $1.00. Trustees at that time were Kenneth Nusbaumer, Russ Harris and Elis Braner; the pastor was Dewey Zent. In September 1962, Keith and Roger Lee finished construction of additional classrooms and the bathrooms.

Three members of the church congregation have become ministers: Vaughn Murray, Earl Murray, and Gene Betts. Dewey Zent pastored the church for sixteen years.

Former pastors include P.A. Drake, Bruce Mounsey, Mort Ross, O.A. Harris, George Johnson, John Robbins, Warren Wall, Hebert Ross, Jacob Frazier, Ed Oren, Joe White, Ernest Pursley, Ed Smith, Lester Howell, the Rev. Cross, Milton C. Wisley, Frances Huffman, Dewey Zent, Charles Swingley, Leonard Foster, Rufus Rumple, James Hall, Bill Jones, and Tony Robles. Gene Betts is the present pastor.

Drawing of the first church constructed in 1872.

Dillman Church

Abstract records show that on May 24, 1889, Charles W. and Florence Clampitt deeded one acre to the trustees of Dillman United Brethren Church for the price of $65.00. Shortly thereafter, Clampitts sold the farm to George W. and Mary M. Lee. Then, on Feb. 14, 1895, the trustees of the Dillman Church deeded .37 acres back to George and Mary Lee for $20.00. This property was part of the farm now owned by Ethel Blinn.

The building was started in the spring of 1889, the rough timber being furnished by Perry Kilander. The cutting and hauling to the mill were done by church people and friends. The sawed lumber was then hauled to the site where the church was to be built. The Dillman brothers, John, Ed, Jacob and Sidney built the new church building.

The new church was dedicated on Dec. 22, 1889, with Bishop Milton Wright officiating. The church was called Edwards Chapel, perhaps in honor of Bishop David Edwards who had served the United Brethren Church for many years.

The church house was remodeled in 1907 while the Rev. O.M. Wilson was pastor. A double floor was laid, rostrum changed, belfry put at the corner, and new seats purchased at a total cost of $1,400. The dedication service for these improvements was held on November 3, 1907.

In March, 1948, wind took off the south half of the roof, on a Friday, and on the following Sunday a torrential rain ruined the inside of the church. Sunday morning, men and women, wearing overshoes and wading water, drilled holes in the floor near the pulpit (east side) and let the water drain out. At the end of two weeks, during which "many were heartsick to think our place of worship was destroyed," two men, Frank Schweikhardt and Oscar Banter, made a tour of the community and found enough people interested, who responded with money to make the necessary repairs. Men and boys of the congregation did the work of taking up the floor and refinishing the furniture.

By the spring of 1951, attendance had grown until more classroom space was needed. Two classrooms were added. (These are now the pastor's study and the choir loft.) Some money had been donated for the need and again, the men of the church did the labor.

Shortly after the Rev. Ray Gant assumed charge of the work in 1955, the basement and the entrance on the south side of the church were added. The cost was over $5,000, but all labor was donated. There was no building fund, but when the basement and the new entrance were completed, which included an indoor restroom, all bills had been paid in full.

Dillman's first homecoming and Rally Day were held in 1960 using the basement facilities. Water was carried from a home across the road for these function. The church added a water well in the fall of 1961. The Rev. Dick Frederick was our pastor during these improvements.

Finally, a major project was completed in 1977, as a fellowship hall, kitchen, bathrooms, and nursery were added to the west side of the church. This project was a few years in the planning. The Rev. Archie Kent was instrumental in getting the building fund started. An auction was held at the parsonage one Saturday to begin the fund. Then a thermometer was posted showing the fund as it grew toward a goal of $10,000, the amount desired before the project was started. During the Rev. Mike Moore's pastorate, several floor plans were formulated, congregational meetings were held, and it was decided to break ground when the fund reached $8,000. Final plans were adopted with an estimated cost for the building of $25,000.

In the fall of 1976, ground was broken for the 44 x 60 structure, which included a new entrance and foyer on the south side of the church. With the exception of two phases of the construction, the labor was completed by the men, women, children, and friends of the church. The Lee brothers, Keith and Roger, ran the cement slab for the hall and Ralph Taylor plastered the ceilings. Building costs were maintained within the estimated $25,000 goal; however, it was decided to carpet the fellowship hall and furnish the kitchen. The project was completed in 1977 for a total cost of almost $35,000. The Rev. Victor Aviles was pastor when the project was completed.

Two parcels of land have been acquired, which allowed for church expansion. In 1975, Violet Banter donated the property to the north, now being used for a playground. The Theodore Allen property adjoined us on the south. In 1976 this property was purchased and the parking lot expanded. In 1990 Ethel Blinn donated approximately one acre to the Dillman Church.

The Dillman Church was a member of a circuit for many years. These were the Salamonie Circuit, the Van Buren Circuit, the Warren Circuit, the Mt. Zion-Dillman Circuit and Dillman-Fairview Circuit. Dillman-Fairview were yoked for a few years in the early 1970,s. Mt. Zion and Dillman owned the parsonage, which was located in Warren. When the Mt. Zion Church was disbanded, it was decided to sell that parsonage and purchase a parsonage closer to Dillman. The parsonage, located at 10358 W., 700 S, was purchased in the spring of 1967.

Thirty years ago, the Rev. Richard Frederick, in a college thesis wrote:

Dillman U.B. Church has had a fine, picturesque history. From present indications it looks also like it can expect a glorious future. As long as those people act on the faith that they have seen displayed in their forefathers, they will continue to have a true lighthouse for God in this rural community in Jackson Township, Wells County, Indiana.

Today, God's faith is still evident in the people of Dillman Church.

In order to accommodate our continuing growth, we are offering two morning services. Plans are also underway for building a new educational wing on to the church.

Pastor Greg Hockman is our senior pastor and Pastor David Hill is our assistant pastor.

We owe a tremendous debt to those who, in years gone by, have left for us such a rich heritage. May we who remain to carry on the work commit ourselves to following their example so that our next hundred years can be even more exciting than the first. Our best days are still ahead!

Epworth United Methodist Church

Two industrious women felt led by the spirit of the Lord to provide what had been neglected in Bluffton's westside neighborhood over the years. The two, Mrs. Julia Marcy and Sarah Gettle, came into neighborhood homes in 1898 to open Sunday School classes for the children.

In 1902, a one-room church was built on the corner of Wiley Ave. and Walmer St. The Sunday school members then became active in the Methodist Conference and set up a circuit with two established country churches, Prairie and Bethel Churches, and called themselves Epworth.

The members decided in 1914 to move their church building down the street to its present location at the corner of Cherry and Walmer Streets.

The women of the church had been meeting regularly over the years to sew. They carried their quilting frames from home to home and made comforts to sell to help pay the preacher's salary. The ladies also made and sold vegetable soup and other foods at a booth at the Bluffton Street Fair.

Between the years 1914 and 1928, the church was struggling to survive. With Mrs. March then in eternity and attendance down to 14 and less, some thought it was not worthwhile to continue. Others however, carried wood and coal from home and with their faith, kept the Church fires roaring through the 20s and the Great Depression.

By the 1937, there became a need for a larger building, funds were hard to come by, but Homer Gettle, son of Mrs. Sarah Gettle, and his wife, daughter of Mrs. Julia Marcy, loaned money interest-free for the building. The Reverend E.J. Maupin, who pastored at Epworth from 1916 to 1918, provided carpentry services for $20.00 a week.

The church addition was finished and dedicated Sept. 11, 1938. On April 19, 1953, Mrs. Homer Gettle turned the first spade of earth at a ground-breaking ceremony for the addition, which included a basement 40 by 50 feet, on the east side of the church to create the larger sanctuary and basement rooms that exist today. Mrs. Gettle also made a gift of $10,000 to purchase sanctuary furniture that still services the church.

In 1956 with Robert J. Johnson as pastor, the church started its first Bible School with an average attendance of 74 for those two weeks in June.

In 1959, Epworth became a station church and on June 1, the Reverend Keith David conducted the first morning worship service. Since then, Epworth has continued in service to its community. Pastors of various other churches in America got their first lessons at Epworth's Sunday School. Evangelist C. Wesley Dupin served Epworth until 1975 when he left to work with his evangelist father. During Pastor Dupin's service in April, 1974, Easter Sunday attendance saw the largest worship gathering in Epworth's sanctuary to that time: 298 attended morning worship.

Effective June 1, 1968, Epworth Methodist Church officially changed its name to Epworth United Methodist Church.

First Baptist Church of Bluffton

In 1991 the First Baptist Church will reach a climax of events in October of its sesquicentennial (150) year and in its present location at Cherry and Johnson Streets for ninety-five years.

"A few members of the Baptist denomination," according to historical accounts of the church, "met in Bluffton on the 14th day of October 1841 for the purpose of considering the propriety of organizing a new Baptist Church."

The five organizing Baptists were Fleming Johns, Elizabeth Johns, Rebecca Stahl, Henry B. Elston and Martha Grimes, all of whom had held membership earlier in Baptist churches in Ohio and Virginia.

Unsettled conditions for Baptists in regard to a church continued until 1855, when an agreement was reached with the Presbyterian denomination to use its meeting house for the sum of eight dollars per year, with the Presbyterians furnishing the wood for heat and lights. This arrangement continued for one year, until 1856, when the Baptists contracted for the use of the United Brethren Church on East Washington Street at Bennett St.

But Baptists had acquired, for fifty dollars, a lot on the northeast corner of Wabash and Williams Streets in 1850. However, unsettled conditions remained through the Civil War years and it was not until 1871 that a brick church building was erected on the site. The actual cash outlay for the structure was $1,800, since a large portion of the material and labor were donated. The sanctuary remained the Baptists' church home for twenty-five years.

By 1875, Baptists were having preaching every Sunday and had called a pastor for an annual salary of $600 and rent. The period was one of growth in membership, and the pastor's salary had been increased by 1884 to $1,000 a year.

With the erection of the Wabash Street Church, First Baptists became more settled and organized a Sunday School in 1871 and followed by forming a young people's group.

After a quarter of a century of use and with the increased development of the Sunday School and youth organization, Baptists discovered the building, according to church records, "too small and too much out of date." Sunday School officers wanted individual rooms for classes for the teaching of scripture.

Following what was described as "a good deal of private discussion," a group of about fifty church members met March 3, 1895, at a member's downtown store, with thirty-two of the men speaking in favor of a new site and a new church. Church records relate that all were "enthusiastic and willing to put their shoulders to the wheel and help turn it with their time and means."

A lot was acquired on the southwest corner of Cherry and Johnson Streets and a contract was awarded for erection of a church building, which still stands, for the sum of $11,500. The building cost did not include the furnishings and the organ. The sanctuary was dedicated by the Baptists in May, 1896, and a newspaper account of that date relates of the dedication services:

"The service began at 11 o'clock but an hour before that time the congregation gathered and filled the auditorium until, when the appointed time arrived and the curtain between it and the Sunday school room was raised, every inch of space on the ground floor and in the galleries was occupied and 1,900 people were within the walls."

Since the 1896 dedication, First Baptist Church has engaged in two remodeling programs, in 1915 and 1936; a major sanctuary rebuilding as a result of a June, 1946 fire; addition of an educational wing in 1970; and installation of a new organ in the fall of 1971.

The fire, on June 10, 1946, late on a Monday afternoon, caused an estimated $50,00 damage to the interior of the church, its sanctuary and its educational section. The Baptist congregation met in an auditorium of the City Building during the months of reconstruction before being able to return to occupancy of the Cherry Street building on Dec. 28, 1947.

An educational wing, an eleven-classroom, two-story addition, was completed and dedicated May 24, 1970, culminating a seven-year planning and financing effort. The construction contract cost was $106,578 and additional costs of equipment and furnishings boosted the total expenditure to nearly $120,000.

The following year, 1971, the congregation approved replacement of the church organ which had been installed in the sanctuary at the time of the building erection in 1896 and subsequently rebuilt following the 1946 fire.

Built and installed by the Lima Pipe Organ Company of Elida, Ohio, the new Beilharz organ, dedicated December 5, 1971, contains eighteen ranks for a total of 1,039 pipes and fourteen pistons. The organ has two manuals and pedal. The pipes for the three divisions are set into chests of aluminum construction.

Ministers who have served First Baptist Church of Bluffton over the nearly 150 years, and the year in which they began their ministry here, were:

Robert Tisdale, 1841; J.B. Allyn, 1848; Abel Johnson, 1852; S. Goodin, 1862; W.W. Robinson, 1864; C.A. Clark, 1872; W.W. Robinson, 1873 (second call); J.H. Rider, 1877; W.W. Tinker, 1885; D.R. McGregor, 1888; J.H. Green, 1891; W.W. Hicks, 1892; W.D. Chipp, 1898; C.S. Lester, 1899; W.C. Martin, 1904; E. Poulson, 1909; O.R. McKay, 1913; C.E. Odell, 1921; H.N. Spear, 1921; Morris H. Coers, 1935; H.T. Rafnel, 1941; J.U. Miller, 1946; W.E. Borne, 1949; Marvin E. Hall, 1955; Earl C. Gross, 1961; Edwin C. Gordon, 1965; Joe W. Elliott, 1969; Charles W. Darwin Jr., 1972; Donald E. Crellin, 1978

The Bell

A bell which has tolled over the Bluffton community for more than 115 years can be heard every Sunday morning ringing from the belfry of First Baptist Church at Cherry and Johnson Streets.

The bell came from the second courthouse erected in Bluffton as the governmental seat of Wells County. The courthouse, a two-story brick structure, was constructed in 1844-45 and was demolished in 1888 under an edict issued by a judge of Wells Circuit Court.

Weighing 722 pounds, the bell had its beginning in Bluffton in the nation's centennial year of 1876, when the Wells County Board of Commissioners purchased the device for the second courthouse.

After the second courthouse was condemned by the judge in 1888 and subsequently razed that same fall, the bell was acquired in 1889 by the First Baptist Church, which then was located in a brick building at the northeast corner of Wabash and Williams Streets.

Afterwards, the bell was moved to its present location with the completion and dedication in 1896 of the First Baptist Church sanctuary at the southwest corner of Cherry and Johnson Streets.

Every Sunday, that bell rings twice, once at the start of the church's worship services and again at the end.

The bell was bought by the county for the brick courthouse by County Commissioner Peter Studabaker on August 26, 1876. The price as $210.13.

First Church of God

In 1851 and 1852, David and James Keplinger, along with several other Church of God people from Ohio, came and organized a Church of God at Zanesville. There were 26 members in the first organization.

The Rev. David Keplinger, the first pastor for the Zanesville Church, traveled through Huntington, Whitley, LaGrange, DeKalb, Allen and Wells Counties - a 225 mile circuit - preaching fourteen to sixteen sermons each trip which lasted four weeks. Fredrick Kemp was appointed as the Rev. Keplinger's colleague, and the field of work was extended to Elkhart, Kosciusko, and Wabash Counties.

Ministers were appointed annually. In those early days, worship services were usually held in the schoolhouse. Following are a few names of the fine people who did so much in starting the congregation: Henry and Elizabeth Sink, Jacob and Rachel Soup, Jacob and Phoebe Haverstock, Grandmother Harmon and John Shoup.

In 1867, the congregation built its own house of worship. The building was completed and dedicated October 18, 1868, by the Rev. R.H. Bolton.

October 20, 1914, the Rev. C.I. Brown, president of Findlay College, dedicated a new bethel that we enjoy today. Active members who took a prominent part in the work of the church were: Daniel S. and Mary (Shoup) Keplinger, Conrad and Rebecca Knight, Jacob P. and Caroline Barnett, and their foster daughter Lavina (Kessler) Smuts.

The beautiful stained glass windows reveal the sacrifice those early leaders made for their edifice. Along with those just mentioned, the following names are found on the windows: Robert and Amanda Clark, James and Catherine Simonton, W.J. Beaty, Class 1, T. Clarence Clark, Philip and Mary Motz, and Henry and Elizabeth Sink.

In recent years, many improvements have been made on the church bethel. In 1947, a new concrete basement floor was put down, and later the walls were covered with knotty pine. In 1952, the stucco was removed and covered with redwood siding, painted white. In 1955-57 the ceiling was covered with tile, the walls paneled with mahogany wood, and new carpet laid.

In 1965, through the generosity of an anonymous donor, an organ was given to the church.

In 1967, construction of six classrooms, Pastor's study, baptistry, and extended nave were added to the west side of the building. A new furnace, furniture and carpet were installed. The next year, a parking lot was made on the west side.

The church celebrated its 100th year in the present building in 1968.

In 1989 the baptistry was removed and a portable baptistry was purchased.

The parsonage house, south of the church, was torn down in early 1991. The brick house just west of the church was purchased for the parsonage.

As a part of the General Conference, the church supports mission work in India, Bangladesh, and Haiti. In the last couple of years, the church has reestablished ties to the church in Czechoslovakia. Mission work has been extended to New Mexico, and Arizona.

In 1985, a purpose statement was written. It is as follows:

The Church with a Clear Purpose

Our purpose is to glorify God and give the praise and honor due him; to present Him message of salvation to all people, and provide opportunity for everyone to serve Him and find joy in Christian living through a caring church family.

The following is a list of pastors who served the church: David Keplinger, Fredrick Kemp, David Williams, A.B. Slyter, S.V. Sterner, the Rev. Anglemeire, Christian Sanda and E.B. Bell, Elias Bryan, E.B. Bell, J.B. Shock, W.W. Lovett, Joseph Bumpus, George Smith, Eddie Miller, I.W. Markley, N.W. Fuller, J.A. Wood, J.W. Boyd, J.E. McColley, R.D. Eden, the Rev. McClelland, E.M. Love, Miss Emma Isenberg, H.G. Herndeen, J.E. Primrose, J.G. Wise, G.A. Bartlebaugh, O.O. Tracy, C.E. Manes, B.T. Yeager, N.A. Gilliland, J.C. Manes, Victory Yeager, Sanford Ferguson, Harold Mishler, Earl Sleasman, Richard A. Wood, Joseph D. Lampton, John R. Beckler, R. Charles McKeown, Greg Peck and Ralph W. Thornton to the present.

Psalm 122:1 "I was glad when they said unto me, Let us go into the house of the Lord."

First Church of the Nazarene

According to the records, the Church of the Nazarene was organized on November 9, 1916. This followed a six-week revival meeting conducted by the Rev. and Mrs. U.E. Harding. The last week of the campaign was assisted by the nationally known "Uncle Bed" Robinson.

The Rev. Clyde E. Green was called as the first pastor. An agreement had already been entered into for the purpose of the church building at $2000, and on Sunday, December 10, 1916, the dedication was held, at which time over $1800 was raised. On January 6, 1917, the church building at the corner of Cherry and Williams Streets was purchased.

The new organization continued to grow in numbers and spiritually. By 1925, the church building had become too small. During the pastorate of M.M. Himler, the old frame church was torn down and a new brick structure was built. By 1937, the membership had grown to 150.

In 1945, the house next to the church on the east was purchased for a parsonage. During 1949-50, this property was remodeled.

In 1963, the property at 315 West Cherry Street was purchased and the home redecorated. It was dedicated as a Sunday School Annex unit on March 9, 1964.

In 1965, the church building at the corner of Williams and Cherry Streets underwent a major remodeling that doubled the church capacity to 250.

In the 1970's the church attendance reached around 200 persons. During the pastorate of the Rev. Walter Graeflin, the church started to see the need for new and expanded facilities to facilitate growth in the Bluffton Church of the Nazarene. In 1974, the property of 19.38 acres on Ellingham Pike was purchased. The home has been the parsonage for our pastors since that time.

In 1978, the point property of approximately 11 acres between Ellingham Pike and Hoosier Highway was purchased. It is the site of our present facility.

In 1985, during the pastorate of the Rev. Erwin Self, a large metal building was built near the parsonage on Nazarene Acres and served as a storage building for the church vans, tractor, and other equipment, and served as a gathering place for church functions.

In August of 1987, the Rev. Charles Fountain, Jr., accepted the pastorate of our church and moved to Bluffton with his wife Marsha and children Chip and Heather. They came from the North Carolina district.

In September of 1987, the ground was broken for the start of our present facility. It was completed in January of 1988. On January 17, 1988, the church had its final service in the Williams and Cherry Street facility. At the set time, the people of the church moved to the new facility on Ellingham Pike and Hoosier Highway for the conclusion of the morning worship service. It was a day of remembrance and a day of rejoicing in the Lord for the new facility and a new work for God.

On February 29, 1988, 388 people were present for the Dedication Service of the new facility. Dr. Bruce Taylor, former Northeast Indiana district superintendent, delivered the dedication message. Following this service, the church facilities were open to the public.

Since that time we have seen our church grown in number and spiritually. The 1990-91 Church Year saw an average church attendance of 197. Praise the Lord as we grow for Him in Bluffton, Indiana.

Pastors Who Have Served The Church

Pastor	Years	Pastor	Years
Rev. Clyde E. Green	1916-19	Rev. F.E. Cole	1935-36
Rev. E.E. Robinson	1919-19	Rev. C. Wesley Brough	1936-39
Rev. B.A. Fleming	1919-21	Rev. Evert Baker	1939-41
Rev. Floyd Henchell	1921-22	Rev. J.C. Duncan	1941-44
Rev. Clarence J. Quinn	1922-23	Rev. Harold E. Priddy	1944-46
Rev. Morris M. Himler	1923-26	Rev. E. Maury Ferguson	1946-50
Rev. J.W. & Mattie Wines	1926-26	Rev. Vance Davison	1950-58
Rev. G.H. Shaffer	1927-27	Rev. Walter G. Graeflin	1958-83
Rev. G.W. Henderson	1927-29	Rev. Erwin A. Self	1983-87
Rev. T.J. Wasson	1929-31	Rev. Charles A. Fountain, Jr.	1987
Rev. T.J. Beam	1931-35		

First Presbyterian Church of Bluffton

Wells County Presbyterianism had its beginnings in June, 1840, when services were held in a newly completed log barn in Jefferson Township. There were 22 charter members of the congregation, most of whom had come from Ohio. Now (1991) there are 350 active members.

After several years of traveling over poor roads to meet for services in members' homes, the congregation decided that a more easily accessible location was needed. Nineteen members of the original group formed the Bluffton Church, which was organized in August 24, 1844, under the leadership of the Rev. John Russ, who had been commissioned by the Presbytery of Miami for the task. The first group became known as the Pleasant Ridge congregation.

Services where held for 10 years in one of the other church buildings or in the old log court house which stood at the intersection of Main and Perry Streets. In 1853 the congregation obtained a site for building at the corner of Washington and Scott Streets; the structure, erected at a cost of $965, was dedicated on February 10, 1854.

This building was a barn-like frame structure 55 by 70 feet. Two woodburning stoves supplied the heat, and candles supplied lighting for worshippers who sat on hard, straight-backed pews. Elders rotated janitorial duties on a monthly basis until 1873.

When the traveling pastor arrived, services were a week-end occasion, beginning on Saturday and continuing through Sunday. Sunday School was held only during the summer, with classes meeting outdoors under shade trees. This building later became the old Sixby Opera House and still later the Sixby Mitten Factory.

In 1883 a brick building was built at the corner of Washington and Marion Streets at a cost of a little over $1200. In October, 1900, the building was rededicated after an extensive remodeling and addition, during which a pipe organ was installed.

Previous pastors have included: T. Raymond Allston, 1923-27; Walter M. Elliott, 1927-36; William Lichau, 1937-41; Arthur K. Koreteling, 1941-47; R. Dean Cope, 1947-53; Arthur W. Raabe, 1954-57; L. Henry Churchill, 1957-69; Philip M. Hazelton, 1969-85. The Rev. E. Wayne McLaughlin began his pastorate of the congregation in January of 1987.

During the pastorate of the Rev. Lichau, an extensive remodeling of the brick structure was completed. The Sunday School rooms were restructured, a balcony was removed from the sanctuary, and a complete redecoration was done. A glass-brick wall in the Sunday School area reflected the latest vogue in building materials.

The church has owned two parsonages. The first, on the corner of Wiley and Marion Streets, was judged to be too far from the church at Washington and Marion and was sold in 1912. A new manse was then purchased in the 300 block of West Cherry. It was sold in 1969, and the pastor for the first time purchased his own home.

At a congregational meeting on November 20, 1957, members voted to build a new church building on the Dustman Road on a seven-acre site donated by Mr. and Mrs. Orlen Sutton. Groundbreaking ceremonies were held March 20, 1960; the cornerstone was laid October 2, 1960, and the first worship services were held on Palm Sunday, March 26, 1961.

Once the major structure was completed, members of the congregation worked long hours laying tile, painting walls, painting exterior trim and landscaping the ground. On Sept. 30, 1962, the sanctuary and social hall portion of the building was dedicated.

In 1963, a second building phase was begun, with groundbreaking for the educational wing being held on March 21, 1965. Members not only painted and laid tile, they even unloaded bricks as they were trucked to the site. A ramp was built from the level of the narthex into the new wing to make the entire structure accessible to handicapped persons. The new structure was dedicated on May 15, 1966.

In 1977, with the addition of a youth wing, the original plans for the church structure were completed. The bell and cornerstone from the old church have been integrated into the landscaping of the Dustman Rd. site.

The Presbyterian Church as been a leader in community outreach. Programs at this time include: Boy Scout Troop 148, begun in 1964; Headstart, meeting at the church since 1967; Happy Hours, a luncheon/program for senior citizens, since November, 1973; Pre-school classes for three and four year-olds, since 1979; support of the Wells County Food Bank with 2¢ a meal collection, since 1990; and the sponsoring of a Yellow Ribbon Support Group for families with servicemen or women involved in Operation Desert Storm.

Members of the session in 1991 are Anne Pfeifer, Ted Smith, Rolland Coverdale, Deb Clark, Dean Engle, Tom Jackson, Dr. Rob Evans, Dewey Randall, and Tom Schwartz. Board of Deacons members include Iona Bergman, Pat Heign, Ruth Lowe, Dianne Schwarzkopf, Jolin Whicker, Jennifer Whicker, Lauretta Booror, Debbie Elkins, Tom Gibson, Mary Ann Landis, Stacie Randol, Steve Schwarzkopf, Bev Blessing, Karen Harrold, Elaine Beck, and Becky Steury. Trustees are Sally Kain, Ernie Beck, Pat Panos, Cindi Pastore, James D. Jackson, Sonia Shaw, Barbara Trubey, Dan Weldy, George Dunwiddie, Dorothy Hunt, Brian Schindler and Priscilla Jackson. Kim Durr is choir director, Steve Neuenschwander is organist, and Julie Coverdale is Christian Education Director.

Members of the church consider themselves "a middle-sized congregation—not too big and not too small. We believe in diversity and freedom of thought, yet we stand in a Christian tradition that holds to strong principles based on Biblical imperatives."

First United Church of Christ

The beginning of our church can be traced to those early country churches that were established by ministers or traveling missionaries.

On March 4, 1859 Reverend Freeland organized a German-Reformed Bible class in Bluffton for residents of German-Swiss ancestry. All of this helped lead to the establishment of our First Reformed Church in the period of 1882-1884.

The German Reformed Church of America was organized in the year of 1725 in Pennsylvania by a German school teacher, John Philip Boehm, who later was an ordained minister. At present, over 60 members can trace their lineage back to Rev. Boehm.

From 1882-1884 the First Reformed Church organized with three other county churches. With First Church showing good growth and a rising climb in membership, it decided to separate and become a charge of its own.

Organizations were formed, such as Ladies Aid Society, Womens Missionary Society, Sunday School, and Christian Endeavor in 1892.

With enthusiasm, dedication and a continued adherence to a slogan adopted earlier "We must stick together," the church continued to grow in witness for Christ as well as membership.

The First Church

A dream of a new church building took shape in 1905. Two years later on May 7, 1907, ground was broken on the new purchased lot on the corner of Marion and Cherry. The cornerstone was laid on July 21, 1907. The complete cost was $38,000.00.

The edifice, modified gothic in design, was built of red brick and Bedford stone and featured beautiful stained glass windows.

In 1934 there was a union of the Evangelical and Reformed Churches. In 1957 the Congregational Christian Church united with the Evangelical and Reformed Church forming the United Church of Christ.

In 1947 there was a need for expanded housing to meet the needs of the congregation. The interior remodeling was carefully planned to provide more classrooms, a pastor's study, a church office, a modern kitchen, a choir loft, and a remodeled chancel. The project also included a new bell, organ improvement, and an improved lighting system.

In 1964 an educational wing was added to the north of the church building. This unit included classrooms, the Painter Memorial Chapel, The Rider Lounge, and a foyer at the north street entrance.

A Heritage center has been developed incorporating one of the stained glass window panes from the first church building.

The First United Church of Christ is not all contained in bricks, windows, and songbooks, but it is also blessed with dedicated pastors who have inspired loyal Christian men and women to serve God, the Father, and his Son, Jesus Christ. These pastors along with dedicated lay persons and God's Spirit have made the First United Church of Christ what it is today.

Pastors from 1882 are C.F. Witthof; J.L. Bretz; A.L. Hassler; W.H. Xanders; S.U. Snyder; G.H. Souder; J.H. String; H.B. Diefenbach; B.E. Reemsnyder; W.A. Alspach; Matthew Worthman; Ralph Koch; Calvin M. Ley; associate pastors - Randy C. Rossman and Carole H. Green.

The Present Church

Keystone United Methodist Church

The history of our church begins with the history of Keystone. In 1868-1869 the Daughtery and Studebaker families, with monies subscribed, built a railroad from Ft. Wayne to Muncie. Along this railroad in 1871, the town of Keystone was platted. The Twibell Addition was on the east side of the road, and the Barchman Addition was on the west side.

Virtually paralleling the town's beginnings, was the religious interest which led to the official funding, in 1884, of what is today known as the Keystone United Methodist Church.

From comments of older citizens, it appears that at that time there had been in existence a log church on the east corner of the cross-roads, which had belonged to the United Brethren people.

In 1874, this log church was replaced by a one room brick schoolhouse. In those days they held singing schools, spelling bees, social functions, Sunday School and church, in the absence of churches, in the schoolhouses.

In March, 1884, a meeting was held in the schoolhouse resulting in the organization of the class with Robert Travis who became the first local preacher, with F.P. Risley and wife, W.K. Kershner and wife, Luther Twibell and wife, Anniah Irvin and wife, and David Hutchins and wife as charter members.

At the next quarterly meeting, held at the Eckrote Schoolhouse, on the Nottingham Circuit April 19, 1884, Keystone Church was admitted to the circuit with J.C. McLin as pastor with a salary of $200.

A subscription paper was circulated, and the amount of money raised was sufficient to go ahead with the building of the church.

The class met and elected F.P. Risley, Luther Twibell, W.K. Kershner, William Twibell, Samuel Irvin, W.H. Templeton, and D.A. Bryson, with instructions to go ahead with the building of a church.

William Twibell was given the task of overseeing the building if the church at $2.00 a day.

On June 2, 1884, Elias Thomas and Rhoda, his wife, who lived on the lot west of the church, deeded a lot for the sum of $50, in the Barchman Addition, for as long as it was used by the Methodist Church. Said deed is duly recorded in Book 11, page 421 of the records of Wells County.

Timbers for the building of the church were donated by Joseph Myers, Abraham Showalter, Ed Abshire, Jessie Thomas, Jacob Crosby, Albert Coddington, D.A. Bryson and Elias Thomas.

Hauling and labor donated was valued at $250. A church was erected at a cost of $1210.

The church was dedicated August 2, 1885 by Hugh Stackhouse, president of the Indiana Conference.

At the quarterly conference in August, 1885, the name of the circuit was changed from the Nottingham Circuit to the Keystone Circuit.

In 1886 the conference sent I.F. Ranspher as pastor. That same year the Rev. Udell of the United Brethren Communion came to the old schoolhouse and organized a United Brethren Church with 40 members.

By arrangement with the Trustees of our church, where services were held every other Sunday, the United Brethren Church was given the privilege of meeting in our church on the off Sunday.

The two Sunday Schools were combined as one, with Henry Cottrill as superintendent. The arrangement continued for approximately fifteen years.

In our church there was a succession of ministers for one and two years periods until 1900, when Ella Siebert was appointed pastor and served for three years. During her pastorate, the old parsonage, which later was the home of Mrs. Minnie Barner, was sold and a new parsonage was built, on the church lot, by Carl Poulson at a cost of $500.

During the next few years a constant growth continued.

In 1915-1916 the church decided on an extensive remodeling project. Due to the first World War some of the work was delayed until the war was over.

Movements were started towards consolidation in 1939. June 1, 1940 they voted and consolidated the M.E. and Methodist South. The new church was called "The Methodist Church."

The church has done extensive remodeling and redecorating many times and has been served by many pastors.

As wonderful as these material blessings were, and for which we are very thankful, they are not to be compared to the spiritual blessings that have been ours over the years. We look back with much joy to the brotherhood, good will and spiritual uplift we have enjoyed.

The Liberty Center Baptist Church

The first recorded entry of the Liberty Center Baptist Church was made at a service on June 16, 1855. The decision was made to invite delegates from Baptist churches in Bluffton, Montepelier, and West Union for the purpose of organizing a church. Tradition says that the early meetings were held in homes, in the log schoolhouse, or under an elm tree. The large tree remained standing in the school yard at Liberty Center, providing shade and rest for all, until about thirty years ago.

In October, 1855, Elder Abel Johnson was called to be the first pastor of the church and Charles Rinear was chosen as the first deacon. Both men served the church in various offices until their deaths.

A Sunday School was organized in 1865 and late in the year of 1866 plans for erecting a church building were discussed. In February 1867 the site was selected and agreed upon. The site, upon which a grocery store now stands, was donated by John Ernst. Much of the lumber and work was contributed by the members. The records says, "On the third Sabbath in January, 1869, the Liberty Center Baptist Church dedicated their new meetinghouse to the services of God."

By late 1879 the church building needed repairs because the floor had sunk. The congregation resolved to sell the structure and site and to secure a new location and build a new sanctuary. The building committee was first made up of the trustees, Joseph Garrett, John Spake, and John Ernst; later James Worster was added and Robert Crosdale was made treasurer of the building fund. Not such is known of the progress of the building except that the date on the building itself was 1883. This was the original brick structure, later remodeled, which was in use until November, 1951. The Rev. O.V. Fritz was pastor during this period.

Disaster came to the church on July 29, 1896, when the building was partially destroyed by a cyclone. At the next business meeting a motion was made to accept "the kind offer of the Methodist Church to use their building." The church as rebuilt and the dedication services were held February 14, 1897.

Over the years the membership of the church and the activity in the Sunday School increased. This brought to the congregation the realization that a larger building was needed.

A building fund was started in August, 1941, with Bertha Garrett being elected treasurer of the fund. Other members of the building committee were James Gordon, chairman, Mount Garrett, vice-chairman, Mrs. Dale Tinkel, secretary, Oline Rittenhouse, Lawrence Frantz, Homer Johnson, Mrs. Ora Heckman and Mrs. Joe Garrett.

The idea of a special Thanksgiving offering to be put into the building fund was proposed by Dale Tinkel. The idea was so well-received that an Easter offering was taken the following year. Since then two offerings have been received annually, at Easter and Thanksgiving, for this fund.

The groundbreaking ceremonies were held Easter Sunday in 1950 at which Fannie Garrett and Dolly Smith, two of the oldest members, turned the first shovelsful of dirt.

Construction was begun and the cornerstone laying ceremonies were conducted on October 1, 1950. The untiring efforts of the pastor, the Rev. W.C. Poulson, the sacrificial financial contributions, and the enormous amount of labor donated by members and friends, made it possible to dedicate the church with only a relatively small amount of indebtedness. The dedication services were held the week of November 18, 1951.

Over a period of 136 years, and under the leadership of 37 pastors, the church has shaped the lives of many people. Some have since moved to other communities and churches. Four men have gone out as ministers from the church: Omer Fisher, Bob Decker, Arnold Maggard and Ralph Galloway. Ralph was converted, licensed in 1959, and ordained in 1991 in the church. Also, several members have worked diligently at the state level for the church.

In contrast to the first services in the church which were held once a month, now there are three services a week. Along with the three services there are several active organizations: Choir, American Youth, American Baptist Women, and His Kids, a group of area children who meet after school at the church. For many years both the Ladies' Aid and Men's Brotherhood were very active in the church, but they no longer exist.

The Baptist, Methodist, and Boehmer Churches work harmoniously together in the annual Bible School. Also, the churches, along with the community, have an annual Pig Roast with proceeds going to the Liberty Center Community Park.

We thank God for the church and as we go into the next century, we pray her light will shine as bright as it did at her birth.

Murray Missionary Church

The Murray Christian Church was organized in a schoolhouse near the village of Murray, in Wells County, August 27, 1858. There were 40 charter members, including the: Galivans, Millers, Lees, Platters, Nashes, Markleys, and Harveys. The church was founded near where the first white settlers in Wells County were located by Rev. Samuel Minnich. The first church building was erected by this congregation one-half mile south of Murray, adjoining the public school building. It was a handsome frame building that was used until the year 1885 when the Presbyterian building was purchased. Although it has gone through some changes, it's the same building that's being used today. Mrs. Elizabeth (Miller) Harvey, the first white child born in the county, was a deaconess of this church for many years. From the time the church was founded in 1858 through 1927, the church had 25 pastors, including: Rev. Jennie Jones, the first woman pastor in the county and Rev. Jonathan J. Markley who pastored the church for 31 years.

Sunday, July 10, 1927, was a high day for the Old Murray Church. It was the day that their reconstructed church building was formally dedicated. The previous winter Rev. Samuel Frantz had been a very suc-

Fun and excitement were in the air this day in 1895 at the Murray Church where everyone was going on a picnic. Life and entertainment or recreation were simpler then - maybe better.

cessful revival meeting in which there were a number of conversions and additions to the church. Immediately the people began talking of church improvement. A committee was appointed, funds solicited, and work was begun in April. Two Sunday School rooms were added, the entrance was changed, the pulpit moved from the end to the side, a large choir platform was built, new carpet was purchased, and the building decorated anew both inside and out. The cost of the project was about $2000.

The Murray Church joined the Missionary Church Association 30 years ago, becoming "The Murray Missionary Church." The church now has a basement for fellowship meals and a second floor above it for additional Sunday School rooms. Many of the congregational families have called Murray "Home" for years.

Murray Missionary Church in 1990.

Old Salem United Methodist Church

From its beginning to the present day, the history of the Old Salem United Methodist Church has paralleled and has been an important part of the history of Wells County. Old Salem is located on County Road 700E, one-half mile south of St. Rd. 218 in Wells County. A short lane back of the church leads to the beautiful, serene church cemetery. Here many of the church members, from the early days of the church to the present, have been laid to rest.

The Old Salem Church, formerly known as the Gottschalk Settlement, came into existence when three religious families moved from Germany, finally settling in Wells County, Indiana. John and Jake Gottschalk and Michael Miller headed this group of pioneers. Services began in 1851, in the home of John Sauer, who owned the farm on which the church is presently located. Rev. Uphaus was the preacher assigned to the St. Mary's Circuit of the Evangelical Association which covered seven counties in Indiana and five counties in Ohio. After a time, services were moved to the home of Father Kreps, who lived one-half mile west of the present church. This was the cradle of the Old Salem Church, which was later called Salem Society. The church was renamed Old Salem to eliminate confusion due to another church not five miles away with the same name.

In 1852, services were held in the Lindsey Schoolhouse, one-half mile south of the present church. In 1855, Bishop John Sybert, dedicated a small log church built on the present site. In 1877, the log structure was torn down and our old sanctuary was built. During this horse and buggy era, the church had open wooden sheds with stalls around the south and west sides of the church. These enabled the members to put their horses in out of the bad weather while they worshipped. After undergoing numerous remodelings and changes, such as the sanctuary improvement of 1902, and the basement dedication of 1933, we came to a specific need of an educational unit in 1962. Plans for a remodeled sanctuary and the educational unit were drawn. Structural work began in August, 1964.

The women of Old Salem have been organized since the early days of the church. While their name has changed due to mergers, they continue to stress both foreign and home missions. For many years they served food at farm sales to earn money for their mission projects.

Our church opened its doors to the homeless churches of Linn Grove, Indiana, after the Palm Sunday 1965 tornado left a mass of debris behind. The pulpit was shared by Rev. Fred Orr of the United Church of Christ and Rev. Bob Bonewitz of the Old Salem and Linn Grove Calvary Evangelical United Brethren Churches. In 1966, May 1, we consecrated our remodeled sanctuary and educational unit.

Beginning in 1967, Old Salem had a reputation for putting on superb Gospel Sings. The church was always packed full and for good reason. Some of the top Gospel groups of radio and TV came to this country church to perform. Each summer since the early 1960s Old Salem has sponsored Vacation Bible School for children of the neighborhood. Recognizing the need of the handicapped, a chair lift was installed that could take a person to the basement or to the main floor and a wooden ramp was built outside.

Today our responsibility is great, but this is likewise our great opportunity, for by the way we meet the needs of church and community we can show our faith in God, our consecration to the cause of Christ. "Except the Lord build the church we labor in vain." The Old Salem Church has become a symbol of strength, comfort, and hope for many searching souls across the 140 years of its ministry. We are grateful for the labor of those who served before us. May we continue to lift up Christ and continue to be an effective witness worthy of the name Christian

Record of Ministers

Minister	Years	Minister	Years
Christian Glaus	1859-1861	John Rees	1909-1911
Mathias Hoelm	1861-1863	D.R. Heil	1911-1916
Christian Wessling	1863-1865	Byron G. Smith	1916-1919
Philip Parr	1864-1867	E.E. Haley	1919-1920
John Fuchs	1867-1869	F.D. Stemen	1920-1921
George Hertel	1869-1871	F.W. Launder	1921-1925
J.K. Troyer	1871-1873	F.J. Stedcke	1925-1930
Christian Glaus	1873-1875	J.M. Kistler	1930-1932
Enow R. Troyer	1875-1878	C.W. Schlemmer	1932-1933
Jacob Miller	1878-1880	F.D. Stemen	1933-1937
George Roederer	1880-1883	George Holston	1937-1947
C.C. Beyerer	1883-1886	Charles Young	1947-1948
John Hoffman	1886-1888	Clyde Walters	1948-1950
John Bruckert	1888-1890	Elmer Smith	1950-1951
J.H. Evens	1890-1893	Robert Cox	1951-1953
Michael Krueger	1893-1894	Cecil R. Smith	1953-1957
Nimrod J. Platz	1894-1897	Fuhrman Miller	1957-1961
Daniel D. Spangler	1897-1900	Bob Bonewitz	1961-1966
James H. Rilling	1900-1902	Vernon Denney	1966-1967
John F. Bockman	1902-1903	Homer Lynch	1967-1972
Leo J. Ehrhardt	1903-1904	Joe Bear	1972-1974
Edward Greiner	1904-1907	Gordon Neuenschwander	1974-1987
Jos. L. Buyer	1907-1909	Jerry Stout	1987-

The church in 1914.

The present church.

Ossian Presbyterian Church

June 10, 1840, the early church was established with the Rev. J.A. Ogden of Miami Presbytery, Greenville, Ohio, meeting with 11 families in the cabin of Adam Hatfield, Jr. on the south border of West Jefferson Township, with 22 charter members received by certificate from the Apple Creek Presbyterian Church of Ohio: Joseph Gorrell, Michael Harter, James Harris, Adam Hatfield, Jr., Daniel and Joseph Hatfield, John Riddle, David Truesdale, William Wallace, John and Wilson Gibson, and wives. Adam Hatfield Jr. had traveled the distance of 80 miles on foot to Miami Presbytery, Greenville, Ohio, with the petition requesting a Presbyterian Church be established in Wells County. The church was called Bluffton Presbyterian Church designating its location near the largest settlement of the region. Later the church met in the cabin of the Hiram Hatfield, and finally at the John T. Glass's, one mile west and three-quarters mile south of what is now Ossian.

Margaret Hatfield, teacher of the first township school, located on the Hatfield land, married John T. Glass in 1846, the second marriage in the township. John's older sister, Esther, was the wife of Joseph Gorrell. The Glass store in 1845 was the sign of the coming growth to the community.

In 1844, 19 members left uniting with the Presbyterian congregation being organized in Bluffton. At this time, the church was renamed the Pleasant Ridge Church. Plans were made to erect a log church on the Joseph Gorrell farm southwest of what is now Ossian (2059-800N). Due to opposition to the location of the church in 1845, 12 members withdrew forming the New Lancaster Presbyterian Church of New Lancaster (Murray).

In 1846, Joseph Gorrell and A. Hatfield secured the services of the Rev. Wilson M. Donaldson, a Murray pioneer family. This year, 18 more members withdrew and founded the United Presbyterian Church of Murray, leaving 17 members to move into the log church in 1847.

Joseph Gorrell, scholar, teacher, and accomplished vocalist, in 1887 was the oldest living resident in the county and of the Presbyterian faith 62 years; ordained elder 54 years. Elected 1847 Justice of the Peace, he served 29 years.

The Rev. Donaldson was installed as pastor of the Pleasant Ridge, Bluffton, and New Lancaster Churches in 1848. The Rev. Donaldson gave up the Bluffton charge in 1858, and after his wife Rachel Barnett died, he later married Elizabeth Egbert, and in 1860 bought a farm west of the new town of Ossian, building a home at what is now 102 Barnett. During this time he demitted the Murray Church, and took under his care the Elhanan Church northeast of Ossian, in addition to Pleasant Ridge. When the railroad and station was established on the Donaldson's farm in 1868, they platted the farm into town lots, establishing West Ossian, known as Donaldson's addition.

The Pleasant Ridge Church moved from the log church into a white frame building at Norwalt, between Young and LaFever Streets, in Ossian in 1866. The church accommodated 400 people, and had a Meneeley Bell and Mason & Hamlin organ. In 1876, the name changed to Ossian Presbyterian Church, and the Rev. Donaldson moved back to Pennsylvania to serve 10 years in the ministry after serving this area for 30 years. The Rev. Donaldson died in 1904; the body was returned to Ossian and services held in the church on Sunday following Sabbath School. He is buried in Oak Lawn Cemetery, Ossian.

The year 1900 brought plans for the present Ossian Church at 123 S. Jefferson. The building and furnishings were completely paid for at dedication in 1902, with church membership of 197.

A 100 year celebration was observed in 1940 with the Rev. Homer M. Keith presiding, the Rev. Wilson E. Donaldson, son of Wilson M. assisting.

In 1952 the unfinished portion of the basement was dug out making an additional room. Glass-Weisell Scholarship fund was established in 1959, offering low cost interest loans to college students. In 1961 under the leadership of the Rev. Milton Nolin, encouraged by a gift of stock from the Sherman Kattell family, the sanctuary was renovated and a Christian Education and Fellowship unit added. On March 25, 1962, the congregation worshipped in the new sanctuary, enjoying the Kattell lounge and added facilities. The basement was remodeled in 1964. The 125th Anniversary was celebrated in 1965. The Rev. Robert LaFollette, pastor, and Dr. Ralph Waldo Lloyd, previous minister, delivering the sermon.

The Glass Library was dedicated in 1979. One hundred forty years were celebrated in 1980 with the Rev. James Woodworth, pastor, and the Rev. Robert LaFollette, guest speaker. A drama of the founding of the early church was presented by several members. Recent additions to the church have been a bell choir and new manse.

June 10, 1990, the church celebrated 150 years of Pioneer Spirit with Pastor George Rogers and guest speaker the Rev. Robert Lafollette. The church membership is 266.

The Rev. Rogers, Chaplain (1st Lt.) Army Reserves, served at Fort Benning, Georgia for the duration of the Gulf War.

Ossian United Methodist Church

Carrying on the work of the founder of Methodism, John Wesley, the Ossian United Methodist Church has been an integral force in the Ossian Community since 1848. Methodism was first introduced as the St. Mary's Mission and has known several changes in its organization over the years. This mission territory extended from Ft. Wayne, south to the Wabash River, and took in a part of Adams, Huntington and Whitley counties. That same year, a society was begun at Prospect, four miles west of Ossian. In 1850 the Ossian Circuit was organized and Prospect became a part of it. Later a church was built at Prospect. Worship services were held in the frame school house which stood on the ground now occupied by the Elzey, Dickey, Haggard Funeral Home.

The church was built in 1853 on the present site. It was a 30' by 40' frame building, where the dining room and present annex now stand and faced south. Box, woodburning stoves furnished the heat and kerosene lamps proved the light.

By 1877, the membership had grown to 177 and the need for a larger edifice was evident. After a vote to begin construction in 1898, the present building was dedicated to the worship of God on February 18, 1900. Under the leadership of the Rev. J. Orr Powell, the Sunday School Annex was built in 1915 and the congregation was then the Methodist Episcopal Church.

In preparation for the Centennial Celebration when Rev. R. Edwin Green was pastor, very extensive projects were completed at a cost of 14,000 dollars. Interesting to note that in 1989, the cost of gas fired forced air furnaces for a new heating system was 15,000 dollars alone.

In 1960 when Rev. George Brunner was pastor, the educational unit was built on the south side and extending west. Carl Lee and Arden Gemmer worked together as the contractors.

In the 1970's a cathedral type accoustical tile ceiling, upholstered pews and revamping of the chancel were completed, and new wall to wall carpet was installed.

In the summer of 1985, with John W. Davis as pastor, the necessity for a new roof on the educational unit prompted the vote to build the roof higher, allowing more room for additional Sunday School class rooms. The entire building was roofed as well. The project became known as the "Upper Room" and is now completed and in use.

Four different parsonages have served as dwellings for the church's ministers. The present parsonage was built in the early 1970's in Rose Ann Heights under the donated service of the contractor, Richard Donaghy. The cost of construction was kept at a minimum by hours of volunteer services of both men and women of the church. Rev. Roy Laudermilk was its first occupant.

Changes in church government have taken place through the years, bringing about mergers in denominations and congregations. In 1939, the Methodist Episcopal, the Methodist Episcopal Church South, and the Methodist Protestant Church merged, becoming the Methodist Church.

The Evangelical Association organized by Jacob Albright and United Brethren Churches joined to form the Evangelical United Brethren Church in 1946.

In 1968 that church merged with the Methodist Church and is now known as the United Methodist Church.

Faith United Methodist was joined by the Hebron congregation of Northwest of Ossian in the early 1950's. In October, 1985, Faith and First Church merged to become the Ossian United Methodist Church. Ours is a connectional system, with itinerancy of its pastors, who are appointed by the North Indiana Conference to serve its 618 churches in the 37 northernmost counties of Indiana.

Organizations active within the church are the United Methodist Women, Methodist Youth Fellowship, Sunday School classes for all ages, a Wednesday morning Bible Study group, chancel choir, etc. We are aware of and share in the issues and concerns of the present age i.e., gun control, gambling, poverty, toxic landfill, AIDS, retirement homes for older adults, camps and camping of families, and all age groups, ethnic and racial groups.

In order to accommodate needs of the people, there are now two worship services every Sunday morning as the Rev. Dr. Robert Priest is the present pastor to the current membership of 337.

"Sons of the Congregation" who are serving in full time Christian service are the Rev. John Hunter, pastor of a Presbyterian Church in Florida, and Douglas L. Hadley, who will become a fully ordained elder at the 1991 session of Annual Conference at Purdue University in May.

A new Allen digital organ was installed the Spring of 1991. New carpeting in the annex was done in 1991.

The sacraments of baptism and holy communion are celebrated throughout the church year. Always conscious of the Lord's goodness to us, the "Welcome Mat" is out for anyone who desires to worship in this House of God.

Park United Brethren In Christ Church

Dedicated, friendly, concerned, caring, sharing, prayerful, fundamental, and Bible-believing are all words that can be used to describe Park United Brethren in Christ Church, located at the corner of East Ohio and Bennett Streets in Bluffton.

Since its beginning in 1938, Park United Brethren in Christ has endeavored to carry out its four major objectives of (1) providing opportunity for public worship, (2) bringing the lost into a personal relationship with Jesus Christ (3) helping each Christian grow in his faith, and (4) demonstrating God's love to the community.

Park Church started providing opportunity for public worship in 1939. The church originated at the Auglaize Annual Conference session of 1938 where a committee was established to explore the possibilities of establishing a United Brethren in Christ Church in the Bluffton area. The committee was chaired by the Reverend R.W. Rash who was at the time pastor of the Zanesville United Brethren in Christ Church.

After carefully surveying the Bluffton area, the committee felt the farming community of Bluffton would be ideal for a new church. Bases on their decision, a house at the church's present location was purchased. A Board of Trustees was appointed in June, 1938, and they immediately took on the not-so-small task of renovating and remodeling the house... preparing it for use as a house of worship. The Board of Trustees was comprised of George L. Springer, Vic Anderson, and the Reverend Rash.

The building project was finally completed and the church was officially organized... being named the Park United Brethren in Christ Church because of its location across the street from Washington Park. The church conducted its first prayer meeting on Friday, November 11, 1938, with 22 excited, eager, and thankful people in attendance.

Dedication ceremonies for the new church took place on December 4, 1938. At the time of the dedication there were six active members: Mr. and Mrs. George Springer, William Roberts, the Reverend and Mrs. Argo Suddeth, and Lamoine Springer (a junior member).

The George Springer family unselfishly gave of their time and energy to the new ministry. The late Lavina Springer served as the church's first class leader, George filled the capacity of Sunday School superintendent, and their son, Lamoine, was the Sunday School's first secretary. Many members of the George Springer family continue to serve at Park Church.

Park Church employed the Rev. Argo Suddeth as their first minister. Since the Rev. Suddeth, there have been several faithful ministers who have given strong leadership and guidance to the church. Pastors of the church have been: The Rev. Argo Suddeth, 1938-1939; The Rev. George Martin, 1939-1941; The Rev. S.A. Macklin, 1941-1945; The Rev. Kenneth Thornell, 1945 (three months); The Rev. R.G. Jewell, 1945-1951; The Rev. Sylvester Martin, 1951-1958; The Rev. Virgil Hull, 1958-1964 (February); The Rev. Dr. Lloyd Eby, 1964 (February-May); The Rev. Paul R. Fetters, 1964 (May)-1966; The Rev. John Goodwin, 1966-1968; The Rev. Tommy Williams, 1968-1969; The Rev. Paul E. Hirschy, 1969-1978; The Rev. James E. Sturgeon, 1978-1980; The Rev. Steven P. Howell, 1980-1987; The Rev. David Stephens, 1987-1988; The Rev. David Hedrick, 1989-.

It was during the Rev. George Martin's pastorate that plans were instigated for a building project. The church was experiencing growth in number and ministry, and more room was needed. Plans were to build a new and larger building at the rear of the property. The building project was completed, and the new building was dedicated in July of 1941.

Eleven years later plans again centered around another building program, this one bigger than any before. Ground was broken on June 8, 1952, for what has become the site of the present church. The new church building was to have a seating capacity of 216, and was to contain a choir area, a pastor's study, a full basement with Sunday School rooms and a junior chapel area. God's people once again joined together and a new church building was completed in the spring of 1953 and was dedicated on September 28 of the same year.

The former church building was converted into a temporary parsonage. In 1962 the temporary parsonage was connected to the church building... allowing additional space for an expanded worship area, a nursery, more classrooms, a fellowship hall and a kitchen. A house at 422 East Ohio was purchased and then sold in 1974 when the property at 1220 Ridgewood Drive was purchased to serve as the church parsonage.

The church has continued to change structurally to meet the needs of the congregation. A back section of the church was remodeled in 1985-86 to make room for a new nursery and to update the youth room.

A growing congregation made necessary in 1986-87 the remodeling of what was then called the "overflow area." Small classrooms were dismantled, walls torn down, new lighting and carpeting installed and many hours of labor resulted in a much-appreciated enlarged sanctuary.

Park United Brethren in Christ Church has seen several building phases since its beginning, has had numerous ministries go forth, and has seen hundreds of people walk through its doors, but its purpose has remained the same: to effectively communicate the Gospel of Christ by word and deed toward the end that all men and women shall be saved and become faithful disciples of Christ and responsible members of His Church.

The original Reiffsburg M. E. Church Building built in 1880.

REIFFSBURG UNITED METHODIST CHURCH

An obituary of Mrs. Barbara Shoemaker, who died at age 83 on August 14, 1921, indicated that she had settled with her parents on a farm at Reiffsburg in 1850, at a time when wolves could still be heard around the cabin. The paper reported the following about her Christian life:

She was baptized in the Christian faith in infancy. On February 21, 1856, she was converted and joined the Methodist Episcopal Church in a log church building that stood on the site now occupied by Myers Chapel. Sixty persons were converted in that meeting and they became the charter members of the Reiffsburg M.E. Church. She was the last surviving charter member of the Reiffsburg Church. For some years the class met in the school house and in private homes before the church at Reiffsburg was built. Thus she had 65-1/2 years of active Christian experience. She was the daughter of Samuel and Elizabeth Valentine. Samuel donated the land for the present Reiffsburg Church as well as two stained glass windows.

Our own Reiffsburg Church building has stood since 1880. A sanctuary was constructed and dedicated in August 1880. The physical appearance was different than it is today. The front of the church faced east with doors at the north and south ends and the men entered one and the women the other. Heat was supplied by two heating stoves approximately in the center of each side. The alter was located to the west, the choir in the northwest corner and the "Amen" section in the southwest corner. Hitching lots were to the south and west.

The first minister was the Rev. Henry C. Myers. In December, 1881, the church became part of a circuit which consisted of Bethel, Prairie, Poneto, and Reiffsburg. The present circuit includes only Poneto. A parsonage was later built at Reiffsburg where it remained until the present one was constructed in Poneto in 1917. In 1905 the church and sister churches of Poneto and Airline were remodeled.

Among the records and memories, we find many people who have contributed their time and talents to the church. Among these are Lorena "Rena" Dyson, who taught the young people for nearly 20 years. She had lots of class parties at her home and was always happy to see any of her former students when they came home to visit. Ben Leist is remembered as superintendent and for serving as song leader, and Paul Kizer for his many years of perfect attendance and service in several offices of the church. Charlotte Kizer has served as treasurer for approximately 30 years. Ernest and Verda King also donated many hours to the church. Goldie Haines was active for so many years in the church and women's organizations. We give thanks to Goldie's grandson, Steve, for the picture of the original church.

Every July there are a lot of old cranks around Reiffsburg—especially in the church parking lot! It is time for the annual Ice Cream Social. (The Ladies Aid minutes show the first "Social" was in August 1929, and the "Cream" was not homemade - maybe Fryback's?) The men have graduated over the years from 1 1/2 gallon freezers to 5 gallon ones, and they make from 65 to 70 gallons of ice cream for our friends, neighbors and people just passing through. The fellowship during this time is tremendous and is enjoyed by all. Of course the ladies of the church donate lots of pies and cakes to go with the ice cream.

The Reiffsburg Church has served the community for 135 years, during which time it has experienced growing pains such as finances, finding talented people to fill offices, sagging attendance and sorrows. But there have also been the mountaintop experiences of births, weddings, growth and seeing children and adults come to Christ. Combining all these happenings has brought the strength needed to attain this age. The church bell has rung for many occasions, both happy and sad ones, and has helped to ring in many a New Year.

The first women's group called the Ladies Aid was organized in 1917. Mrs. Lizzie Leist served as president for 17 years. In 1968 they became known as the United Methodist Women. Over the years the women of the church have helped with remodeling, spring cleaning, Vacation Bible School, and all other projects needing the extra boost. They even helped sand and varnish the pews during the last remodeling. Reading through the old meeting minutes, we see that they paid the janitor, part of the preacher's salary, and even paid for supplies for the Delco plant. They had lots of bake sales and ice cream socials and they pieced quilts and quilted quilts for people to make money. Very industrious ladies!

The members of the present church are hard-working and very special people (no names, because someone could accidentally be omitted) — you feel their love when you walk in the church. Our prayer is for many more years of service to the community.

The present Reiffsburg United Methodist Church.

SIX MILE CHURCH

On September 2, 1838, a small band of Christian followers met at the home of Tom and Rachael VanHorn (Hugh Studabaker farm S.E. of Bluffton) to form the Six Mile Church. Elder Hallet Barber, a circuit rider, was the organizer of the first church in Wells County. The first church building, a log structure, was built near the Six Mile Creek about one mile south of the present church on St. Rd. 116 east of Bluffton.

The minutes book of that first meeting include 74 signatures. Among them are William and Sarah Prillaman whose descendants (the Fay Hauk family) still attend Six Mile, and Solomon and Sarah Johnson whose descendants (the Marcia Johnson Hotopp family) are present members of Six Mile.

The church grew and in 1858 a wood frame building was constructed on what is now the west end of the Six Mile Cemetery. The entrance to the sanctuary was at the front, so late-comers would be encouraged to be on time. The building served a growing congregation until 1906, when a new cement block church and parsonage were built on the site of the present church.

Disaster struck when on February 12, 1914, this church was destroyed by fire. Only a single pew was saved. Undaunted, the congregation quickly built a crude wooden structure called a tabernacle in which to worship. The pews of this temporary building were of rough lumber. The floor was sawdust.

The present brick structure with its beautiful stained glass windows has housed the congregation since that time. It was dedicated on February 17, 1915, with its cost of $14,000 totally paid. The present ranch style parsonage was completed August, 1966, at the cost of $23,515.

Ministers serving extended pastorates were: James Atkinson (1843-1869), Guy T. Walters (1927-1937) and Max Andrew (1964-1975). Guy Walters, who served during the Depression years often received as salary, vegetables, meat and eggs from his parishioners. During those "hard times," he played a dedicated role in helping the church ladies at the Six Mile Street Fair Food Booth. Rev. Walters directed the youth in many plays which were given at neighboring churches and at the community building. Monies accumulated from these plays were used to defray expenses to Religious Youth Camp at Barbee Lake.

During the ministry of Max Andrew, Daily Vacation Bible School, which had begun in the 1920s, grew in spirit and numbers. Rev. Andrew was the first minister to live in the present parsonage.

Over the years there have existed many organizations including Christian Endeavor, Youth Groups, Ladies Aid, Missionary Society and Church Women United. The newly formed Missions Board is very active. Choir, Bible Studies and Discipleship and Membership classes have been integrally vital. The first Girl Scout troop in Wells County was organized at Six Mile by Grace Smith in about 1920. Sunday School began in 1876. Grade leveled materials were introduced in 1910 by Sarah (Sade) Markley, an elementary school teacher and principal at old Columbian School.

Beginning in the early 1900's came the spirit-filled traditions of Christmas. A huge live, candle-lit tree was the center of a loving, giving, and sharing Christmas service. Gifts from family members to each other, to the minister, Sunday School teachers, and officers of the church were distributed. For fire protection a bucket of water was placed near by. Included in the evening's celebration were recitations, songs, cantatas, and skits. Many times rescheduling of a little one's "piece" was caused by a necessary trip to the little building behind the church, as there existed no indoor plumbing. Climaxing the evening was the receiving of a brown bag containing an orange and hard candy purchased at a discount at Markley's Grocery (W. Market St., south side). After congregational singing of "Silent Night," candles were extinguished and worshippers, filled with the true Christmas spirit, bundled up to return to their homes.

In the early 1970's a new Christmas tradition started. The church women purchased a ten-foot tree and the kit for making Chrismon (religious) ornaments. The women spent many hours glueing tiny pearl beads and glitter to finish the many stars, crosses, Biblical creatures and symbols that adorn the tree. The Chrismon Service centers around the trimming of the tree with tiny white lights and the sparkling Chrismons. Hearts are drawn together in celebrating the advent of the Saviour's birth.

Six Mile continues to be friendly and dedicated to the teaching of Jesus as it attempts to follow the love and concern for others as exemplified by our Lord.

A more detailed historical account may be found in **150 Years of Six Mile Church History** available at the Wells County Museum and the public library.

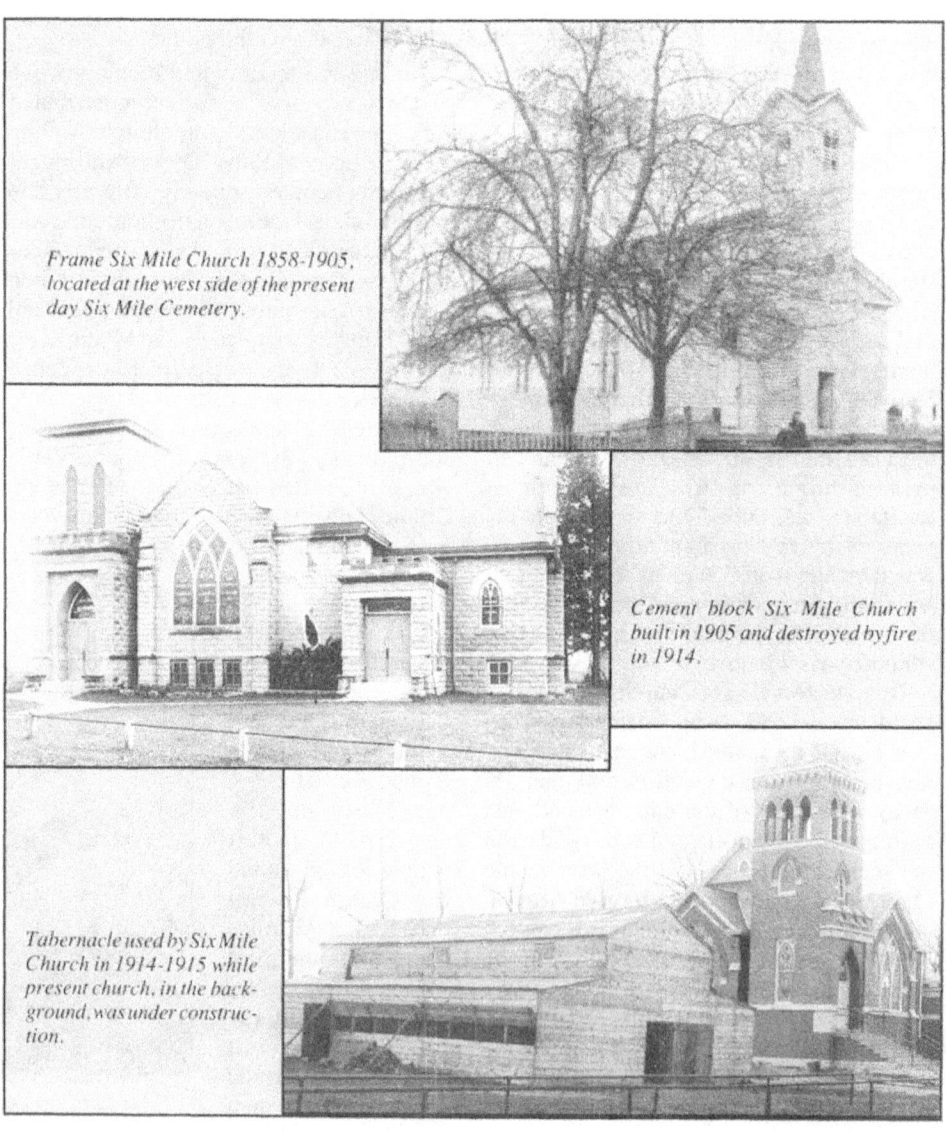

Frame Six Mile Church 1858-1905, located at the west side of the present day Six Mile Cemetery.

Cement block Six Mile Church built in 1905 and destroyed by fire in 1914.

Tabernacle used by Six Mile Church in 1914-1915 while present church, in the background, was under construction.

Former St. Joseph's Catholic Church. *Present St. Joseph's Catholic Church.*

St. Joseph's Catholic Church

According to the earliest history of Catholicism in Wells County, the Reverend Theodore Wilkin came on horseback to Bluffton in 1872. He celebrated mass in the home of Timothy Enright. Records show that two priests had visited Bluffton prior to 1872.

In 1875 the five original families joined to form a small mission congregation under the patronage of St. Joseph. They built a frame church building on West Cherry Street. The building was thirty by fifty feet and cost $1,300.00. This church was dedicated by Most Reverend Joseph Dwenger, second Bishop of Fort Wayne.

The parish grew slowly. Before the turn of the century several new Catholic families arrived in Wells County, including those of Ferdinand Effinger, William Fitzpatrick, John Moynihan, Tom Gallivan, Peter, Frank and Joe Barwiler, Charles Miller, the Arnolds and Fred Tangeman.

Other early families included those of Basil and John Kelley, Jacob Ehler, Adolph Leimgruber, Frank Tangeman and Alfonso Vachon, all of whom came after 1900.

In 1920 parishioners William Berling, Walter Shead, John Kelley, John Moynihan and John Belger requested of Bishop Alerding a resident pastor, and the Reverend Nicholas Keller was appointed. As Montpelier was a mission church, Father Keller served both parishes, having just one Sunday Mass in each.

Father Keller led the congregation in moving and enlarging the church building and building a rectory where the church had stood. A debt of $18,000.00 was incurred. Ferdinand Nusbaumer, grandson of Ferdinand Effinger, designed the buildings.

About the same time more families began to swell the numbers as well as the income and were a welcome addition to the parish. Among these were Floyd Sands, Robert Nash, Lee Wahman, Herman Geels and Walter Heller.

In the thirties the parish was proud of its John Kelley, who served as mayor of Bluffton, of its prominent merchants and professional people, including Cletus Geels, jeweler, Adolph Leimgruber and sons, Augustus Herman, Lawrence and sons-in-law, Ed Reidlinger and Joseph Strain, ice business, John Moynihan, gas company, John Belger, theater, Alfonso Vachon, monuments, Fred Tangeman, banker, Walter Heller, stone quarry, Lee Wahman, with the telephone company and Zander Malcolm, chiropractor.

The parish prayed and rejoiced with J. William Lester (now a Monsignor) not a parish son, but a grandson of Ferdinand Effinger, when he celebrated his first Mass in St. Joseph's church on August 26, 1945.

As the parish grew, having a problem accommodating the crowd even with three weekend Masses, the congregation was happy to have ten acres of ground at the north edge of Bluffton donated by E. J. Schaefer.

Mr. Schaefer and his partner, Wayne Kehoe, along with all the parish, donated generously to a building program in the late fifties. A handsome church and rectory were built, being dedicated on June 26, 1966, by the Most Reverend Leo A. Pursley, bishop of Fort Wayne-South Bend.

With each passing decade the parish became more keenly aware of the need for the religious education of its members and especially the children. The early seventies saw the parish capitalize on the dedicated effort of its pioneer volunteer religion teachers. Notable among these were Mrs. Floyd Sands, Mrs. Zander Malcolm, Mrs. Clemens Smekens and Mrs. Gletus Geels, augmented by the help of the pastor.

Now more dedicated people conducted Christian Doctrine classes for all grades including kindergarten and nursery age, classes held each Sunday between Masses. This includes preparing second graders for First Communion and eighth graders for the Sacrament of Confirmation.

The men of the parish remain generous both with time and funds for all parish functions. They have active chapters of the Knights of Columbus and St. Vincent de Paul Society.

Men and women participate as lectors, cantors and ministers of the Eucharist, while the young boys serve as acolytes.

Many men of the parish see each week their sons and grandsons serve the priest at Mass as they did in their youth.

Mrs. Clifton Baumgartner was church organist for more than forty years. Mrs. J. Raymond Cox is the present organist.

There are more than two hundred fifty families in the parish at this time.

An early parishioner, Ferdinand Effinger, originally plotted the Fairview Cemetery, reserving an area as a Catholic burying ground.

Dating back to the Civil War, young men and women of the parish have served in war and peace in some branch of the military.

Since the appointment of Father Keller, the following priests have served St. Joseph's: The Reverend Charles Girardot, The Reverend John Bapst, the Reverend Michael Kelner, the Reverend Aloysius Phillips, the Reverend John Roesler, the Reverend Robert Traub, Monsignor James Conroy and the present pastor, the Reverend Eugene Koers, who came in 1981.

St. Mark's Lutheran Church

In the spring of 1883, the Rev. J.C. Jacoby, D.D., pastor of the Horeb Pastorate, which consisted of the congregations of St. John's in Union Township, St. Paul's and Horab in Rockcreek and Mt. Zion at Five Mile, Pleasant Township in Allen County, began holding services in the Sugar Grove schoolhouse in Rockcreek Township, Wells County. His efforts resulted in the organization of St. Mark's on June 18, 1883, with twenty-three charter members.

A frame building was constructed and dedicated on October 7, 1883, in Uniondale, at the site of the present church building. Each of the five churches shared the same pastor, some meeting every Sunday and some every other Sunday. (See Horab Lutheran Church for more details). They also shared the expense of the parsonage which was located north of St. Mark's on the south west corner of the next street. In 1919, under the leadership of the Rev. I.C. Birk, a congregational meeting was held and committees were appointed to proceed with the necessary steps toward the erection of a new church. Bids were received shortly after, but due to high prices the construction plans were held in abeyance. In the meantime, the old church was moved north a block to a nearby lot purchased by the congregation and was used to house the church until the next building could be completed. Later, the town of Uniondale bought the building, and it is now known as the town hall.

Early in June, 1921, a contract was finally awarded to contractor U.G. Smuts at an approximated cost of $35,000. The service of groundbreaking was held on a Sunday afternoon in late June. Each church organization had a brief part in the service, which marked the culmination of a long unfulfilled ambition. The cornerstone for the new church was laid August 14, 1921. The sermon was preached by the Rev. A.B. Garman, D.D., missionary superintendent of the Michigan Synod. A "farewell service" in old St. Mark's was held Sunday morning, October 1, 1922, with the sermon being preached by the Rev. M.L. Stirewalt, D.D. The new St. Mark's, a brick building, was dedicated on Sunday, October 8, 1922. The dedicatory sermon was preached by the Rev. J.E. Whitteker, D.D., president of the Lutheran seminary at Maywood, IL. Dr. J.C. Jacoby, the venerable pastor who organized the church 39 years earlier, was present and delivered a sermon the evening of Dedication Day. Throughout the following week special services were held each evening, and Dedication Week was completed with a social gathering on Friday evening in the church basement. Yet today,

Old Uniondale Lutheran Parsonage

we are grateful to the Rev. I.C. Birk, who tirelessly worked on the drawing plans with the architect, A.A. Honeywell. This beautiful Gothic type church, with the lovely glass window, still today inspires those who come to worship here. The old parsonage was torn down in 1965 and the present modern one-story parsonage was built.

The faithful ministers of God who have served as pastors at St. Mark's are: Rev. J.C. Jacoby, 1879-1883; Rev. Wm. Waltman, 1883-1887; Rev. T.A. Pattee, 1888-1889; Rev. A.J. Douglass, 1889-1892; Rev. J.H. Hoffman, 1893-1894; Rev. Jabez Shaffer, 1895-1896; Rev. Robert Atkin, 1896-1898; Rev. D.F. Kain, 1898-1901; Rev. M.R. Mohler, 1902-1904; Rev. H.L. Greenawalt, 1905-1908; Rev. S.E. Slater, 1909-1913; Rev. W.S. Oberholtzer, 1913-1915; Rev. H.C. Bixler, 1915-1917; Rev. I.C. Birk, 1918-1922; Rev. E.A. Kreppert, 1922-1926; Rev. H.L. Greenawalt, 1926-1930; Rev. H.L. Walmsley, 1931-1965; Rev. P.R. Hunteman, 1965-1984 and Pastor Emeritus; Rev. Emil Bartos II, 1984-1988; and Rev. Wm. Peterson 1989-present. The Rev. A.J. Douglas won fame through his son, Lloyd Douglas, the author of *The Robe, The Big Fisherman, Magnificent Obsession* and others. In Lloyd Douglas's last book, *A Time To Remember,* he recalled his life in the Uniondale area and other small towns where his father preached. St. Mark's was the first pastorate for Rev. H.L. Walmsley, who served faithfully for 34 years until he died February, 1965, while in service to his flock.

On Sunday, October 8, 1972, St. Mark's celebrated its 50th Anniversary of the brick church and the 89th year of the congregation, with the affair attended during the day by more than 500 person. Dr. Gerald Miller was the guest church school speaker, relating his experience as a medical missionary in Africa. Church pastor Rev. Paul Hunteman's sermon was entitled *Mankind's Needs Are Met in Christ Jesus.* Afternoon speakers were Dr. Paul Krauss, a former pastor of Fort Wayne Trinity Lutheran Church and Dr. Herman Gilbert, a Rockcreek native and a former member of St. Paul's. A dinner was served at the town hall.

Uniondale United Methodist Church

The Uniondale Methodist Episcopal Church was organized in 1885 by Rev. Charles Murray who was appointed as pastor of the Markle Circuit. He served for two years, and then the congregation was transferred to the Ossian Circuit, with Rev. Henry Bridge as pastor. The early gathering of the Methodist Society was held in the Lutheran Church in Uniondale.

Charles Murray and Henry Bridge did not go to their churches in an automobile; Mr. Murray rode a white pony, and Mr. Bridge drove a horse and buggy and sometimes walked. There were no paved or gravel roads at that time.

The Rev. Mr. Bridge was the pastor who led the congregation in the 1886 construction of the little white Methodist Church, built on the lots now housing the Wilbert Vault plant; he remained as pastor in Uniondale for the next two years. Dedication services for the new house of worship were held in the John Haiflich woods, one-half mile east of Uniondale.

True to Methodist policy, the Uniondale charge was re-organized in 1892 to include: Uniondale, Rockford, Sparks Chapel, and Emmaus.

In 1900, a young man by the name of O.W. Singer became the pastor. He loved to play baseball with the boys. One Saturday afternoon they were playing ball in John Harsh's field, and one of the boys swore. Mr. Singer went to the young man and said, "If you cannot play ball without swearing, I will quit playing." The team could not afford to lose Singer, for he was a good ball player; thus there was no more swearing! He was very successful in his church work at Uniondale.

The buying of the first parsonage for this charge was promoted by Rev. R.S. Reed who was the pastor in 1902. At this time the Sparks Chapel Church was abandoned and removed from the charge.

Reverend Conde Hile served the charge from 1911 to 1914. A great revival moved among the membership and community resulting in growth and calls for a large house of worship. Roscoe Shaw became the pastor in 1915, and continued on to start a new church building the next year. By the time the new building was completed in 1917, Rev. Leroy Huddelson was pastor. At this time Uniondale and Rockford were the only churches on his charge.

To aid in the ministry to the people, a parsonage was built to the south of the church in 1922 while Rev. Wesley Pugh was the pastor.

Rev. Jep Jenson pastored between 1936-1939, and the people saw some big growth. Church records show that he baptized 99 person during his time at Uniondale. The grove of trees in back of the church, still enjoyed today, was planted while he was here.

The music program of the church was expanded in 1946 while Rev. Ed Rosier was pastor. The present piano, organ and Beckler Memorial chime system aided in the praise of God. The chimes continued to play each day at noon and six o'clock in the evening, sending out their beautiful music over the town of Uniondale.

In 1953 Uniondale became a one point charge, and the pastor then was Robert D. Wilburn, who stayed for five years.

Much needed Sunday School rooms were provided when a house north across the street was purchased in 1963. Property improvements included: the purchase of lots around the church and parsonage in 1965 for parking; the erection of a church office at the east end of the garage in 1973; the construction of a ramp entrance to the church basement in 1976; and the remodeling of the sanctuary to add an elevator-lift in 1988, making street parking, sanctuary and basement accessible to handicapped persons.

The church again became a two-point charge in 1984 with the addition of the Prospect United Methodist Church.

Two young men from the Uniondale Church went on to become ministers: Rev. Kenneth Fahl and Rev. Richard Harshman.

Under the leadership of Rev. Kent Biller, 1976-81 a nursery school was formed in 1979 to meet the needs of the young parents in the congregation. Also in February, 1980, he led the church to sponsor the first 'boat people' to be brought to Wells County from Vietnam. Many people in the community became involved in assisting Tran Man and his wife, Tran Nham Theim, both 20 years old, to become familiar with our language and customs. By November of that year the Tran family departed to join relatives in California. In February 1981, the church again stepped out to help Son Hong Lam, 49, and his sons, Minh, 14, and Hai, 13, also 'boat people' from Vietnam. This family was with us until August of 1981 when they went on to Oklahoma. Both boys are now college graduates.

We are thankful for those people who had a vision in 1885 that is still continuing today. We are grateful to the many pastors who gave a part of their lives that we might learn more about God.

We continue to believe "that where two or three are gathered in His name, there He is also," currently gathering for worship each Sunday Morning at nine o'clock with Rev. Joseph Haney as our pastor.

United Methodist Church of Poneto

The first organized church services were held in the Nottingham Township School House at the town of Worthington, later known as Poneto, 1870. The school was located at the corner of four townships: Nottingham, Chester, Harrison, and Liberty.

J.W. Paschall organized a class at Worthington, Feb. 25, 1878, with ten members becoming a part of the Bluffton Circuit. They continued meeting in the school house until the erection of the first building in 1880, at a total cost of $1200. The ground and the timber for this frame church building was donated by Simeon Tappy and his wife and was located a block west of the present church, which is located at 0035 East Walnut Street in Poneta, Indiana.

The first Sunday School was organized October 10, 1880, and the first report was made March 19, 1881, with Alexander Lee, superintendent.

On December 16, 1881, the Worthington Charge was changed to the Poneta Charge consisting of Bethel, Prairie, Reiffsburg and Poneta.

The first parsonage of this charge was purchased October 24, 1889, from P.M. Simons and wife. The trustees of the church were B.W. Shock, Z.T. Fetters and R.S. Hughes.

During the early history great interest was shown, and under the ministry of J.M. Haines, there were fifty conversions and fifty-seven joining church. Later E.J. Magor held a protracted meeting of 16 weeks and thirty-eight were converted. In the second year of David Wells (1901), there was an in-gathering of over one hundred souls.

Now the charge had progressed to a position where they purchased ground for a new church at Poneto from B.F. Starr and wife at the cost of $250. The present brick structure was erected in 1905, with many members donating time and money, $3657.17. The building was dedicated March 18, 1905, by S.F. Harter, pastor. The first Sunday School Superintendent of the new building was Charles Steube.

In the year of 1915, the church trustees deeded to the parsonage trustees a lot for the present parsonage. The first resident was J.R. Stelle and family.

Nineteen thirty-nine saw the merger of the M.E. South, M.E. North and Methodist Protestant Churches to become the Methodist Church. Then in 1968, the merger of the E.U.B. and Methodist Churches became the United Methodist Church.

Ministers Who Faithfully Served

1870	H.C. Gailbraith	1900-02	David Wells	1931-32	Dewitt Johnson	1951	F.T. Handley
1871	J.L. Ramsey	1903-94	Ralph Jones	1932	James McKnight	1952	Wilbur Thorne
1872-73	J.H. McMahon	1905-07	S.F. Harter	1933	James Bean	1953-56	Guy Johnson
1874	A. Douglas	1908-	J.H. McNary	1934-35	H.D. Neel	1957-58	Leon LaCoax
1875	J.H. Ramsey	1909-10	B.F. Hornaday	1936-37	Kenneth Smith	1959-61	Ernest Minegar
1876-77	J.W. Paschall	1911-12	Henry Lacy	1938-39	Paul Stephenson	1962-64	Stan Tobias
1878	T.W. Lincoln	1913-	D.A.J. Brown	1940-42	Clayton Steele	1965-66	Larry Schwartz
1879-80	H.C. Myers	1914-15	J.R. Stelle	1943-45	R.L. O'Dell	1967	Eugene Stolte
1881	J.N. Rhodes	1916-17	L.G. Carnes	1945	James Leist	1968-69	Lester Taylor
1882-83	Henry Bridges	1918	E.E. Wright	1945	Edward Burkhalte	1969	Greg Brendel
1884-85	J.B. Cook	1919	E.M. Foster	1946	Ferris Woodruff	1970-72	Richard Campton
1886-88	B.S. Hollopeter	1920-22	J.M. Stewart	1946	Tom Capin	1973-75	Tillman Nussbaum
1889-90	J.M. Haines	1923	J.K. Wyant	1947	John W. Omerod	1976-79	Eugne Rapson
1891	J.W. Walters	1924-25	J.H. French	1948	Homer Studabaker	1980-84	Neil Butcher
1892-93	R.H. Dempsey	1926-27	H.E. Forbes	1949	Bryce Fenig	1984-86	Richard Borgman
1894-95	J.L. Foster	1928-30	L.C. Wisner	1949-51	Max Morgan	1987-	Harold Wilson
1896-99	E.J Magor						

Superintendents

1983-84	Alexander Lee	1907-10	Alexander Lee	1932-39	Paul Oman	1970	Roger Lee
1885-89	Mrs. Henrietta Tappy	1911-15	Lewis Cobbum	1940-46	James Leist	1971-73	Robert Williams
1890-93	Alexander Lee	1916	H.C. Melick	1947-51	Mark Athan	1974-76	Galen Gray
1894-96	Charles Steube	1917-27	Fred Cobbum	1952-53	Robert Williams	1977	Dennis Rush
1897-99	Lewis Cobbum	1928	Edward Walker	1954-55	Carl Brinneman	1978-80	Robert Smith
1900-02	Charles Steube	1929	Fred Cobbum	1956-61	LaRoy Cobbum	1981-82	Dennis Reed
1903-04	George Gavin	1930	Dayton Musselman	1962-64	Robert Williams	1983-86	Derek Smith
1905-06	Charles Stuebe	1931	Edward Walker	1965-69	Don Athan	1987-	Steve Rush

ZANESVILLE UNITED BRETHREN IN CHRIST CHURCH

The Zanesville United Brethren Church is located in Northern Wells County in the town of Zanesville. The church was born in a little log cabin on 500W just one half mile south of 1100N in Union Township. This is the present farm of Marshall and Pearl Johnson. The cabin belonged to David Thomas (refer to his history in this book) who was a circuit riding preacher. He, along with the Henry Beabers and the Abraham Beabers, established later the College Corners Church just around the corner from the original.

Remember that this area was wilderness at that time. In fact the town of Zanesville had just been born on March 4, 1849, and the Thomases held their first meeting on April 8th one month later. From the log cabin in the wilderness the church moved to the College Corners schoolhouse. The year was still 1849 and soon after that a church building as erected next to the school. That church building is still standing across the road and is used as a barn on the Richard Caston residence. The congregation met here until 1855 when they moved to Zanesville. We are vague about where the meetings were held until 1857 when a frame church was built on the corner, where the Hartzlers live now, next to the old Shepler Garage building. This building is still standing (but in bad shape) on the Art Stock property on the south edge of town. The building was used until 1884 when a frame and brick building was erected on the south edge of town on old #303. This is the present site of the new Methodist Church building. In 1889 because of the convictions and sympathy with the old constitution of the United Brethren in Christ Church, William Hoverstock, Ballard Bowman, and others left the church and with the able leadership of Rev. C.L Culbertson, the new wood frame church was built, where it presently stands today on Broadway. The church was then referred to as the "radical middle church." The present building was erected about 1890 by Uncle Frank Sink.

It is said theat Mr. Haverstock dedicated ten acres of corn to the Lord which yielded 100 bushels per acre and netted the first $1000.00 for the Lord's House.

The church building has been remodeled several times. A floor furnace replaced the stoves in 1929. Two Sunday School rooms and a balcony were added on the northside of the building. In 1935-36, the floors were refinished, carpet replaced, and a new furnace installed. In 1938, the choir platform and altar, with two rooms on either side, were added. In 1954-55, at the cost of $13,000 a full basement, vestibule, basement entrance and larger furnace were added.

There is a long list of pastors from the time of the break away to the present. For more information on them you may refer to the History of the Zanesville United Brethren 1849-1889-1989 that can be found at the church library or the Archives at United Brethren headquarters in Huntington, Indiana.

In 1963 R.W. Rash became our paster. He was here until 1965. During that time the Baldwin organ was purchased and the fellowship hall was started. Rev. Donald Bender replaced Rev. Rash. While he was here, 1965-68, the red carpet was installed in the sanctuary. Rev. Hilas Custer came in 1968 and served until 1969. His replacement was Rev. Roger Hale who stayed until 1972. In 1972 Larry Taylor was placed in our midst to remain until 1986. Reverend Taylor holds the record of the number of consecutive years served here. Remaining here for 14 years he accepted a charge at the Good Shepherd Church in Huntington. During years the Taylors were here the parsonage was switched from the east side of the church to the west side, leaving the old study for the secretary. Also during this time Maxine Caley Brickley assumed the job of part time secretary. It was during these years that Zanesville Homespun Days were started by the church and they still continue today. It is celebrated every Labor Day and is a combination of food, fun and fellowship. When the Taylors moved to Huntington in 1986, Rev. George and Beverly Rhodifer moved in the parsonage to become our new pastor. Rev. Rhodifer is the present pastor of our church. During his years here a new sound system was installed, the Koinenia Ladies brought new carpet for the secretary's office and the pulpit area, the youth and the Koinenia also remodeled, painted, and wallpapered the basement, the nursery added some new cabinets and cribs, and Scott Taylor was hired as full time youth and music minister. Scott needed a place to live as he was newly married. The Orval Bugher house came up for sale right next door to the parsonage. It was purchased for $28,000 and Scott and Mary Ann and their new son Jordan live there now. Scott is a great asset to the church. He has engineered many fine cantatas and has a fine choir. The youth attendance has grown by leaps and bounds.

At the present time we are moving ahead in outreach and evangelism. We are very actively involved in Tri-Township Ministries (a combination of five area churches) and have developed a food bank ministry here in town for our area. Through this ministry we hope to lead people to Christ. We are also striving ahead to involve all the members of the church in a newly formed small group ministry. Our main concern is to reach the Zanesville Community with the message of eternal life, through Jesus Christ.

Zanesville United Methodist Church

The Zanesville First United Methodist Church originated as a United Brethren in Christ Church, with the first religious services being held April 8, 1849, in the home of Rev. David F. Thomas. In 1855, some members desiring a church closer to their homes moved services to the Zanesville schoolhouse. This officially organized the United Brethren in Christ Church of Zanesville, a part of the Auglaise Conference with circuit preacher Rev. William Greer. In 1857, a frame construction church was erected. In 1884 trustees purchased four lots at the south edge of Zanesville where a frame and brick church was built. With dimensions 45 x 60 feet and a cost of $3000, the new structure was dedicated in September 1884. An adjacent parsonage was also built at this time. In 1889, because of convictions and sympathy with the old constitution of the United Brethren in Christ Church, several members left the church to build another church two blocks west of the existing church. Those leaving the church opposed secrecy in the church and secret orders, such as the Masonic Order. They were known as the radical (Middle) church, and are still known today as the Zanesville United Brethren in Christ Church. Those remaining at the "Brick Church," the liberals, were part of the New Constitution Division of the Auglaise Conference. In 1891, two stoves were changed from the west end of the church, placing the entrance door in the center of the west side of the church and the pulpit toward the east. In 1903, the first furnace was installed for $600. In 1905 Adam Hamilton organized a class of young people called the "Willing Workers." The class originated from a successful revival under Rev. M.V. Millikin and became the first organized class of Sunday School. In 1918 under the ministry of D. Walter Zartman, a basement was dug under the sanctuary with additions of a new heating plant, elevated floor, new pews, gallery, stained glass windows, a private light system, and corner entrance. In the fall of 1922, some burning trash caused a fire from debris that blew into the bell tower. Due to the smoke, nobody could get close enough to set up a water brigade and it was feared that the entire building would be lost. Vern Botts, using his World War I gas mask, positioned himself in the tower and a bucket brigade was then successful. Evidence of this fire remained and foundation timbers were found visibly scarred during later demolition. In 1927, the United Brethren in Christ Church (liberal) became a separate station with Floyd L. Wilson being the first full-time pastor. During the ministry of Charles A. Thorn in 1935 the entire auditorium was redecorated and rededication services held. By 1944 the parsonage remodeling found inside water and plumbing a reality. On November 17, 1947, the Evangelical and the liberal United Brethren in Christ Church denominations merged and became known as the Evangelical United Brethren Church.

In 1968 the Evangelical United Brethren Church and Methodist Church united to become the United Methodist Church. The proper new church name became First United Methodist Church of Zanesville. Popular community names include Zanesville United Methodist, ZUM, or the "brick church." From 1968-1977 a yoked ministry was shared with Monson Chapel United Methodist Church. An educational unit addition was built and consecrated in 1986, with dedication and mortgage burning in 1979. Construction of a two-story addition to replace the 1884 sanctuary structure began in 1980. Stained glass windows and woodwork were restored and inserted in the new structure, which includes a church office, pastor study, classroom and restroom facilities, a walk-out lower level, and a new sanctuary with enlarged seating capacity. Consecration Service for the new structure was held September 27, 1981. The large stained glass window in the new structure remains in the same position as it was in the 1884 structure. This window location was the original front of the first sanctuary built at this site. Sixty pastors have served ZUM since its origination in 1849, the current pastor being Craig LaSuer.

Annually, ZUM offers Vacation Bible School in conjunction with other area churches. A church sponsored Nursery School opened on September 2, 1980. The ZUM Stik, a chocolate dipped fruit creation made its first appearance in 1981. Having made over 35,000 to date, the ZUM Stik trailer can be found making its rounds at community fairs and events. Christmas season finds members annually portraying a "Living Nativity Scene."

Fellowship through sports was created with a basketball team in 1971. A men's softball team was organized in 1978, with a women's team (Zumettes) following in 1986.

ZUM continues to give heavily to missions, having supported three work teams to Haiti since 1979. In 1986 ZUM began sponsoring a Z10-K, an annual walk/run to benefit missions. As a result of mission outreach, a community nutrition site for the elderly became a reality in Spring 1990.

With a current membership of 187, ZUM offers active prayer groups, Bible study groups, youth fellowship groups, Tape Ministry for shut-ins, men's and women's groups, prayer chains, Church Choir/Cantatas, Mens' and Women's Slow-pitch softball teams, Sunday School Class Fellowship/Friendship, Community Education/Inspiration Classes, and Summer Youth Church camps.

ZUM, a church with a place for everyone, was built to honor and glorify the Lord through worship, service, education, and fellowship.

Emmanuel Community Church

The Emmanuel Church began in 1850 with a group of neighbors meeting at the Redding Schoolhouse east of the corner 500 W and 300 N. in Rockcreek Township.

In 1857, one acre of ground located at 200 N. - 500 W., was purchased from the Schnolty family for $5.00. In the summer of 1867, a frame structure 32' x 56' was started and completed in 1868.

In 1892, the church was moved to 110 N. - 475 W., Rockford. The ground was purchased from Morgan and Mary Ware for $100. The church was rearranged and cement blocks were added to the outside. The church remained there until the structure was no longer safe.

The congregation leased for 100 years the disbanded Reformed Church for $1.00 and necessary repairs. By November of 1941, remodeling was completed; the church was dedicated and renamed Emmanuel Methodist Church.

Emmanuel was in the Marion Conference and shared a minister with Boehmer from 1953 to 1976.

On a cold, windy day, January 20, 1975, a fire in the church was discovered by Glen Wilburn. Despite the efforts of the Uniondale, Markle and Bluffton fire departments, the church suffered heavy damage.

The congregation then met at the Friend's Church building, formerly located at 100 N. in Rockford, until they could get Emmanuel restored.

The Rev. Joe Gibson was our minister from 1978 to 1981 and had faith in our ability to restore the Church. With several community benefits, prayer and hard work, the congregation returned in 1981.

Due to the small congregation, damage beyond insurance coverage, and financial obligations of the United Methodist Conference, the group decided to withdraw from the conference at this time and became a non-denominational church. They adopted the name Emmanuel Community Church.

Pastor Gerald L. Edris became our minister at that time. He had been a member of the church along with his parents and grandparents.

Our present minister is Pastor Bill Tennyson and family of Fort Wayne.

Our church address is 2115 N - 500 W., Bluffton, Indiana. *Submitted in loving memory of Ruth Reds*

McNatt United Methodist Church

In the beginning there was God, and our forefathers needed a meeting place to worship. The McNatt United Methodist Church, located at 9183 800 W. 90 S. was one of the early organizations of the Indiana Conference of the Methodist Protestant Church. Worship services were held in school houses since 1869.

In 1880, the first church building was completed, uniting the Pleasant Ridge (Ebersole School) and Hickory Grove classes of the Salomonie circuit, of which Antioch and Hamilton were members also. The McNatt site was half-way between Pleasant Ridge with thirty-five members and Hickory Grove with thirty members consolidated in 1878 under the name of McNatt Union Chapel Church.

The one-room frame building, forty-six by thirty-four feet, was dedicated April,

McNatt United Methodist Church

1880, and served the community until 1930. During the oil boom days, more people had moved into the community; therefore a larger building was needed.

In 1910, one and a half acres were purchased west of the church, and a five room house bought for one hundred dollars was moved in for a parsonage. Another room was added later and the house modernized.

The new church building was started back of the old church in the fall of 1931 during the pastorate of the Reverend George McKinley. Much labor and materials were donated. A bequest from John Beavans of $1500 started the building fund. The new church was dedicated February 7, 1932, free of debt. The cost was $7000. Restrooms and a kitchen were placed in the basement in 1948 to complete the modernization of the building.

Eleven years into our second hundred years, we have the assurance that God will be before us as we strive to do His will.

Emmanuel Community Church in 1991.

McNatt Union Chapel Church, which was the old McNatt Church from 1880 to 1932.

Petroleum United Methodist Church

Prairie Church

PETROLEUM CHURCH

In the fall of 1897, Rev. Allie Sipes, who was pastor of Phoenix and Nottingham churches, preached a sermon at the old Petroleum schoolhouse on the prospect of organizing a church at Petroleum. The next week Mrs. Sipes reported the matter to the United Brethern in Christ annual conference. Rev. Harry Meade was sent to the charge as pastor and immediately organized a class at the schoolhouse with the following trustees: L.K. Waldo, M.O. Williams, Carey Templin, Jacob Wolfe, and John Bears. George Kirkwood and John Bears were selected to canvass the community for funds and secured $1500.00 in pledges. William McDonald was selected as contractor, and the church was built at the cost of $1292.00. The seats were not put in until spring due to delay at the factory at Wabash. Dedication was held by Bishop Hott in May, 1898. John Bears served as trustee until 1937, and held the position of janitor for forty years. Note: The church was built on State Road 1 next to Harley Lewis, just to the north. The front steps still are there. This was known in conference as the Petroleum and Phoenix Circuit. Sometime in the early 1900's Gilead (the church located east of Balbec, IN) was added to the circuit. Gilead left the circuit in the 1950's.

The church was moved to the Hoppes lots (where it is today) and remodeled in the summer of 1939 at the approximate cost of $2500.00. On November 16, 1946, the church name was changed to Petroleum Evangelical United Brethren Church (EUB).

Sunday, July 28, 1963, a ground-breaking ceremony was held at the church at 9:30 a.m. for the new educational addition. The conference superintendent, Dr. M.W. Chambers, presided. The church pastor was Rev. Floyd Nevil and the contracting firm was Carl Easley and Son of Craigville. The cost of the addition was $16,000. In 1968, the church joined the Methodist conference, changing the name to Petroleum United Methodist Church.

When Petroleum and Phoenix split in 1978, the Petroleum Church bought the Phoenix share of the parsonage for $11,125.00.

On August 16, 1980, Henry Lynch became the first Missionary from our church.

In October, 1989, David Hughes became our pastor and still is.

PRAIRIE CHURCH

This church is located one and one-fourth miles west of State Road #1 on County Road 350 S. (Travisville Road).

Prairie Church was one of the earliest churches established in Wells County. Circuit riding Methodist ministers held church in schoolhouses and private homes as early as 1840; and in 1866, the existing sanctuary of the church was built on land donated by Jacob and Smithy Smith, and William S. and Rachel Nicely, and constructed with lumber furnished by the Hedges and Godspeed families.

Early members of the church were Lewis Buckles family, Joseph Sawyer family, William S. Nicely family, Robert M. Hedges family, John and Rachel Travis, Alexander and Susanna Lee, Ellen Smith, John and Rebecca Sawyer, Levi and Rebecca Neff, David Smith, Robert and Sophia Hedges, Jonas and Adeline Hedges, Harriet Goodspeed, O.E. Markley, Levi Merkey, Gestie Goodspeed, Della Rudy, Jessie Hare, Art Hedges family and Charles Merkey family.

Prairie (Methodist) Church was on a circuit with the Epworth Church in Bluffton until around 1948, and thereafter either Keystone, Blanche Chapel, Poneto, or Reiffsburg Methodist Churches, until being dropped from the Methodist Conference in 1967. At that time the Conference wanted the church to close, but since the land had been originally deeded to the Prairie Church Trustees, the congregation, under the leadership of Trustee Ralph Fyson, chose to keep the church open and the Conference relented and gave up any claim it had on the property. In 1974, Prairie joined the Indiana Yearly Meeting of Friends (Quaker), but in 1988 became nondenominational.

In 1959, with the money received from the sale of Prairie's share of the parsonage to the Epworth Church, and a private loan obtained with the help of Bluffton benefactor John W. Carnall, plans were started to remodel the church. Travisville contractor Vernon Melton removed the entrance hall and bell tower, and added a basement, classrooms and a restroom. In 1966, a Centennial Celebration was held and the mortgage was burned. In 1974, a trailer was set in to add more classroom space, pastor's study, and a fellowship room. In 1978, after extensive smoke damage from a furnace explosion, the sanctuary was remodeled.

Prairie's first minister was James Nash. Present minister is Kevin Keller and Church Trustees are Robert McFarren, Jeff Osborn, and Ethel Dedrick.

Prospect Methodist Church

The Prospect Methodist Church was the first church to be established in Union Township.

On October 30, 1848, a representative of the St. Mary's Mission located, at Fort Wayne, came to the home of Hezekiah Allen and organized a few people of the neighborhood into a Methodist class. The charter members were William Cotton, Hannah Cotton, John A. Lepper, Lousia Lepper, Absolem and Rhoda Housel, Thomas William and Phebe Quackenbush, Hannah Ady, Levi and Catherine Osborn, W.C. Webster, Hezekiah Allen and his wife. William Cotton was chosen class leader to take the minister's place when necessary. He was to lead prayer, keep records and give spiritual help when necessary.

On December 22, 1853, an acre of land was purchased from Levi Osborn for eight dollars and a log cabin was erected on the northeast corner. The Prospect Cemetery now covers the entire acre and every charter members is buried there.

A frame church was built across the road and dedicated on September 7, 1862. The belfry was added in 1890. This bell still hangs in the belfry of our church.

The present brick structure was dedicated on March 10, 1912. The trustees were Lewis Cotton, James Lipkey, William Lepper, Roswell Johns, Joseph Sonner, William Osborn, Frank Smith and William Platt.

The present trustees are Wendell Diehl, Tom Neuhauser, Genevieve Diehl, Anna Fullhart and Verdella DeWalt. The present minister is the Rev. Joe Haney.

Tocsin United Methodist

This church was first affiliated with a denomination that originally called themselves "German Methodists." Some of the earlier family names were Kleinknight and Heckley both of which area of German origin. Up until 1891 the church was called "Salem." They first met in a schoolhouse (Dailey) in Lancaster Township at 500 N and 500 E. The precise date of origin is unknown. In 1860 a tract of land was purchased from Sec. 11, Range 12 E. Township 27 N, now a portion of Munson family holdings. There is no record that a building was ever built. The congregation built on the east side of the road one-half mile south of US 224 on road 450 E. The land was purchased from a Mr. High and a Mr. James Dailey, both of whom were great-great uncles of mine. This building burned.

At that time the church was a member of the Auglaize Conference of the United Brethren in Christ, which was an Ohio Conference. After the fire some of the members attended the Liberty Class of the Methodist Episcopal Church which was later called Emmaus. The Emmaus Church was stuck by lightning in about 1927. Our congregation soon returned to the "Dailey Schoolhouse." Later still the church was located in the Tocsin School. This was a frame building which predates a brick building that currently houses a welding shop. In my lifetime Mr. Irvin Wasson and Margaret Garton (his sister) recalled attending church in the old Tocsin School.

In 1887 land was purchased on the north side of North Street in Tocsin. A frame church was built the same year. In 1915 the frame building was moved west and on the east side was built a large addition. A basement was placed under both buildings and brick veneer was placed around all of it. Mr. Garton told met that the rebuilding cost $12,000.00. Mr. Haldah Garton was a son of Margaret Garton. As a result of a dispute between the contractor and church officials, a lien was placed on the church. Saint Joseph Conference, to which the church joined in 1900, would not allow the church to be dedicated until the lien was removed in 1919. The undersigned was the youngest person in attendance at the dedication in August 1919, being only four months old.

For many years Tocsin Church was known for much musical talent. Children's Day and other events taxed the 400 seating capacity. Some people would come at 4:00 p.m. to get a seat. One of the greatest revivals was held in 1926. It must have lasted eight or nine weeks. The undersigned was seven years old and would have liked to have attended every night because of the good music.

In 1946 United Brethren in Christ and Evangelical Association merged into Evangelical United Brethren Church, both having taken the basis of their doctrines from the Methodist Church. In 1968 our denomination became affiliated with the United Methodist Church. Our present pastor is Steven W. Cunnington. *Submitted by Victor Gallivan.*

PROSPECT CHURCH. 169-20. 1862-1912

Bethlehem Lutheran Church in 1903.

Parade of "Tabernacle Boosters" on West Cherry Street, Bluffton at the time of the Billy Sunday Revival.

Wells County Schools

Bluffton class of 1926 taken at their twenty-fifth reunion. Photo courtesy Esther Carnall.

BEATTY SCHOOL

The first school in the Beatty School District of Jefferson Township was called Dody School and was located on the Lancaster-Jefferson Township line. It burned to the ground in approximately 1885. After the fire the new Beatty School was erected at the location one mile north of the township line within Jefferson Township, which was typical of most other schools of the era.

BENDER SCHOOL

District number seven in Rockcreek Township was commonly known as the Bender School, as the site was about one-half acre in size and had been a part of the Bender farm. On this small plot stood not only the school building but a coal shed. In addition, during some of the years, a small barn or stable existed in which horses were tied which had been driven to school by the students. This arrangement enabled those distant pupils to ride in a buggy or sleigh. What a luxury! This stable was also sometimes used as a gymnasium. The one-room school building was built in 1878 for a student population of from only 6 to 65.

BETHEL SCHOOL

Jefferson Township District #4 had for its first school a frame structure built prior to 1860. It was known as the Robb School. The second building was brick and was used only a few years when it was destroyed by fire in 1892. A third building, also of brick, was then built. These schools were built on land originally owned and donated by Amos Robb. The name, Bethel School, came from the Bethel Church erected nearby in 1873.

It has been recalled that one early teacher in this school did not rely on the hickory stick for punishment but would rather take disobedient students across her knee and pat their behinds vigorously. On one occasion the punishment backfired. When the teacher took the student across her knee to spank him, he bit her leg and did a real job of it. This same teacher, also in administering discipline, broke a slate over the head of a lad, leaving the frame hanging around his neck.

BLUFFTON BUSINESS COLLEGE

In 1905 the Bluffton Business College was graduating their first class of students. The college instructed classes on the second floor of the Grand Opera House (later to be renamed the Holiday Theatre) on the corner of Johnson and Washington Streets. It provided business training, review and post-graduate courses. Subjects included court reporting, bookkeeping, billing, stenography, foreign correspondence, typewriting, commercial law, office methods, banking, penmanship, spelling, correspondence and mathematics.

The school was in operation at least until 1911, as shown by different copies of their Bluffton Business College bulletins which have been saved. The bulletins were distributed to encourage others to take advantage of the courses offered at the college. Testimonials and other information were provided with many of the local students and their vocational progress being highlighted.

One student and graduate of the college, upon completing the bookkeeping course, secured a grade second to the highest in the state in the Government Civil Service Competitive Examinations. Another student, Curtis Fields, learned shorthand here while working at a local bank, and soon after secured a position as private secretary to President Hughes of DePauw University. Two years later he had the same position under John R. Mott, head of the Y.M.C.A.

Graduate Edwin Cravens became superintendent of the Red Cross Manufacturing Company. Graduate Miss Leona Cobbum was by 1911 in charge of the Indianapolis branch of the King Piano Company.

The college was endorsed by P.A. Allen, superintendent of Bluffton Public Schools. He had formerly been in charge of the Commercial Department of the Methodist College of Northern Indiana. R.S. Todd, president of the Studabaker Bank of Bluffton, was another prominent citizen who spoke highly of the school.

According to an August 19, 1869, advertisement in a local newspaper, an earlier attempt at a Bluffton Community College was made with an unknown success. The principal of the institution was P. Castle and classes were conducted over the Arnold and Company Drug Store, located in the McCleery and Melsheimer Building beginning September 1 of 1869. Classes included bookkeeping, penmanship, commercial law, and law of business. The best legal talent in Bluffton was engaged to lecture on Commercial Law according to the ad. There is no known relationship between the two schools.

BUNN SCHOOL

The Bunn School District #7 in Jefferson Township had a brick school building erected in 1882 on ground donated by Jacob Bunn. Two previous schools had existed. One was a one-room log school and the other one a single-room frame structure.

CALEY SCHOOL

Caley School was Union Township District #6 and was located on ground owned by Samuel Caley. It stood on a site one-quarter mile east of the proper place, which is located on old Indianapolis Road (State Road 3). A new fad in the early 1900s was to make the school homelike, so curtains were put up and laundered twice each year. Slate and slate pencils were common, and if a pupil forgot his slate rag, he used his sleeve to clean his slate.

Caley School, Union Township District #6 was built in 1888.

Bly School in 1919-1920 (l. to r.) Back row: Teacher-Harry Coleman, unknown, Jay McElhaney, Martha Prible, Leonard Krinn, Marion McElhaney, Ralph Kepinger, Bonewitz, Roy Jones. Second row: Mary Prible, Harold Prible, Nellie Noble, Edna Ware, Ona McElhaney, Silbert Harding, Edwin Prible, Beatrice Tarr, Alder Jones, Bergie Noble. Front row: Robert Bonewitz, Oscar Tarr, Claude Noble, Von Jones, Harry Krinn, Dean Hardin, Charles Day, and Wayne Pribble.

CASTON SCHOOL

The Caston School of that Jefferson Township District began as a large one-room frame building which was built on a farm owned by Abe Caston. In 1887 a one-room brick building was built and the frame structure was moved.

Conditions at this school were like those at about every other one-room school; common water bucket and cup, one or two large central heating stoves, and outside toilet facilities were at the back of the property. The back of the toilets were all open and when you made a call to them on a windy day, you had to hold on to your hat. And when it was zero outside, you had goose pimples.

In the school there was a large cupboard which was called the library. It held an interesting dictionary with a picture of a monkey on the front page. Everyone who came to school to visit got a chance to see the "monkey book."

CHESTER TOWNSHIP SCHOOL

The consolidated school building at Chester Center was the outgrowth of a need that had existed since the old building at Keystone was condemned for high school purposes in 1919. Actual construction work was not begun until the spring of 1922 by the contractors, Gordon and Reiff of Liberty Center, under the direction of architect Everty I. Brown of Bluffton.

Labor troubles hindered the work considerably during the first season, but by the time winter set in, the building had been enclosed and roofed. Work was resumed early in the spring of 1923, and the building was completed and occupied for school purposes on September 24, 1923. At the time, students from ten other Chester Township schools were consolidating into one school, which was called Chester Center. Those ten one-room schools were: McCallister, Slocum, Noe, Red, Chester, Gavin, Maddox, Shields, Five Points, and Keystone.

Chester Township School built in 1922 stood at the northeast corner of the present Southern Wells School site.

The Chester Center School was guided by trustee O.F. Tate during the years 1920 to 1928. His advisory board consisted of Win Noe, Otis Starr, William Twibell, and Lyman Zehner.

In the 1928 election John Osborn was elected trustee. Herschel Gilbert, Carl Huffman and James Ogle were elected to the advisory board.

Walter Krick was the first principal of the Chester Center Consolidated School. He was followed by Cary Mounsey, who relieved Krick before the 1924-25 school year. T.P. Charles replaced Mr. Mounsey before the 1928-29 year.

T.P. Charles was the school principal through the 1930-1931 school year. Then in the fall of 1931 Hugh Tate took over the reins of the school and was principal through the 1934 school year. H.T. Brunegraff was the principal during the 1934-35 year, and he was replaced by Hobart Black in the fall of 1935. Mr. Black remained as principal until the fall of 1937, and then Wayne Lee finished out as principal through the 30s.

John Osborn was elected trustee and served through 1932 with Carl Huffman, James Ogle, and Herschel Gilbert as his advisory board.

In the 1932 election Calvin Shadle was elected trustee. Cleophas Meyers, Francis Gilbert, and Curtis Arnold were elected to the advisory board. Mr. Arnold died during his term of office and was replaced by James Thomas.

In the 1936 election Everett Carnes was elected trustee of Chester Township. Those selected as advisory board members were Joe Pond, Harold Carter, and Omar Smith.

The Indians won their first tourney in 1936 when they won the Montpelier Blind Tournament.

Wayne Lee, who became principal in the fall of 1938, was the principal through the 1941 school year. Huber C. Settle became principal in the fall of 1941 and remained through the 1940s.

Keith Schowalter, a 1933 Chester graduate, was coaching the Indians during the 1939-40 season as the Indians beat Liberty Center 28-27 to win their first Sectional Crown.

Everett Carnes was re-elected to his second term as trustee in 1940 and served through 1944. Advisory board members serving with Mr. Carnes were Harold Carter, Joe Pond, and Jess Miller.

Then in the election of 1944, Edward Cochran was elected to head the Chester School Board. Also elected to the advisory board were Ed Carmichael, Leslie Hamilton and Charles Crosby.

In the 1948 election Edward Cochran was re-elected to head the school board. Charles Crosby, Herman Osborn and Win Noe were elected as advisory board members.

In the 1952 election Thurl Rogers was elected trustee to head the Chester School Board. Joe Pond, Olin Gilbert and Charles Crosby were elected to the advisory board.

Then in the 1956 election, Glen Jamision was elected trustee with Ward Showalter, Victory Mounsey, and Kenneth Kennedy elected to the advisory board.

Huber Settle, who became principal in

The original Columbian School Building, in the 1000 block of West Washington Street. A primary grade school used until 1961.

1941, was principal of the school until the fall of 1957. William Payne, former Indian coach, succeeded Mr. Settle as principal of the school, and continued through the 1965-66 school year.

Verlice Crosby was elected as trustee to head the school board in the 1960 election. Jim Ogle, Kenneth Kennedy and Ward Showalter were elected to the Chester Advisory Board.

In the November election for 1962, the four southern townships of Wells County voted to consolidate their schools. On January 1, 1963, Chester Center, Liberty Center, Jackson Center, and Petroleum became known as the Southern Wells Community Schools.

Early Nottingham Township Schools

There is no record to show there was any school taught in Nottingham Township until the public schools were established. The movement to establish the public schools was in 1849, and the first schools were commenced in the spring of 1850. The first election for school purposes was held in September, 1849, and some school officers elected, and in the same month an enumeration was taken showing the township was divided into districts pretty much as they are at the present time, and that there were then nine districts containing children of school age totaling 149.

At the election mentioned, Stanton Scott was elected trustee-treasurer and Jason B. Blackledge, trustee-clerk.

There were no funds at first with which to build schoolhouses and it was necessary for the patrons to volunteer and contribute their labor, which they did with few or no exceptions, going into the woods which surrounded the site on which the proposed building was to be erected, and cut the timber, hauled in the logs, and erected the "old log school house." All of the school districts did not have sufficient number of pupils to justify having school.

The first schools were all summer schools up to about 1856 or 1857 when the terms were changed to winter terms.

Some of the characteristics of these schools were: First, that they were surrounded by dense forests, through which the pupils of the incoming and rising generation beat their way, and made their own paths and roads, as they chose, or as best they could, as up to about this time no regular roads had been laid out and opened up. Besides the dense brush and undergrowth in many places, the principal difficulties they had to encounter was logs and swamps, and often they were glad of the logs to help them across the swamps. For though the forests were practically full of beasts, birds and vermin, the children were often quite as interesting to them as they were to the children, and each enjoyed the exchange of glances and community of interests, one about as much as the other. *(From the November 22, 1911, Chronicle newspaper account by Thomas E. Scott.)*

East Union Center School

Union Township Schools - Old Zion, Ormsby Central, College Corners

"The preservation of a free Government is the sole ground for encouraging the diffusion of knowledge and learning through the state. Not only was the system to be a public one, but it was meant to be a state-controlled, centrally administered organization," thus quoting from Article IX of the State Constitution of 1816.

Since the beginning of time, the purpose of education has been to learn about life and the meaning of that life, plus the method one should and can employ to live that life to the best of one's ability — a goal which millions of people throughout history have aspired to, but comparatively few have fully attained.

Union Township was organized in 1847 — a segment of the western part of a then two-part county, made up of Harrison Township and Rockcreek Township. Land sold for $2.50 per acre and the only neighbors of those early settlers were the Miami Indians, which fortunately were a friendly people to the white invaders. The early settlers in Union Township learned about the use herbs for medicines, the edible wild plants, fruits, etc., but the uppermost desire of those early parents was that their children could be taught those skills that could produce a new generation knowledgeable of the ways of life and able to gather the best things from that life.

Consequently, in 1848, the first Union Township School was erected of logs one mile south of Zanesville. "Old Zion School" or "Splinter" as it was named, had as its first teacher Abraham Beaber, who lived 3/4 mile south of the school.

Before the organization of Union Township, while Wells County was a two-township county, the children in Well County had the benefit of a circuit teacher, the first being Margaret Hatfield, who taught in the homes, spending one day and one night in each of the homes of that circuit.

Of the same type as the "Old Zion School" were the Ormsby School, Center School, and College Corners, all near Zanesville. These all were one-room log buildings; pupils sat on wooden benches and the teacher taught them from the only book the township possessed.

In 1851-52, John Kain started a school in the southern part of the township because he had a large family of boys and girls of school age and could not send them conveniently to any school then existing.

Teachers during the time of 1852 until in the 1920s took extra training at the Academy in Murray or at the Roanoke Seminary.

By 1906 there were ten schools in Union Township, four brick or block ones and six frame buildings. This did not include the town of Zanesville. The total number of pupils was 573. By that time in these little humble buildings, it is reported that they were well supplied with "modern seats, blackboards, and other aides to the pupils." By that date, there were pumps at all school sites to eliminate the lugging of water from neighboring homes. The common tin cup or long handled dipper was used by teacher and pupils alike. Each school was also provided with separate rest room facilities, situated apart from the main building for sanitary reasons!

School terms were from six to seven months per year. Wages of the average teacher during that period was $1.80 to $2.00 per day, and no discrimination was made between male or female as to qualifications, with the exception that the female who married had to quit teaching. All equipment the teacher desired as helpful in the education of the pupils was furnished by the teacher.

There were handicaps — lack of equipment, poor ventilation, inadequate heating from often smoking stoves, the unsanitary drinking and toilet facilities, and extra short recitation periods, yet there were happy times, such as spelling bees, ciphering contests, box socials, debating matches, programs of local talent — all were held in these little local schoolhouses at night.

If we were able to look back at those early times, we would catch glimpses of little children and those not so little, trudging across field, down dusty or muddy roadways, across snow that covered the fence rows, carrying their cold lunches packed in baskets or in individual little round tin pails; lard pails and molasses tins came in real handy for this. We might see them gathering in numbers as they neared the school, as more and more neighbor children joined. We could hear the chatter, laughter, singing, teasing, some quarrelling and all the tears that probably were shared by the "underdog" who could be the butt of cruel teasing. We would catch glimpses, of the short-stemmed field flowers clutched in little hands to present to an admired teacher, from whom the giver hoped to gain a pittance of recognition. As we look again, we would see some who drove their horses and buggies or rode into school.

In 1904, Union Township High School was built. W.H. Kain was trustee, E.J. Daughery, S.M. Caley, and Jonathan Seaman served on the advisory board. This was set to supply Union Township with its own high school, as previously those wanting a higher education needed to go to Bluffton, Ossian, or some boarding school.

The original school was built three miles south of Zanesville on land that was owned by John Lewis Warner. The date of the transaction was 1870. One of Mr. Warner's daughters, Anna Warner Bronner, and her husband, Jacob Bronner, sold 1.37 acres to the township in 1904 for $100. For some unknown reason the township, acting through trustee William Kain sold .50 acre back that same year for $50. (A daughter of the Bronner's, Guinevere Bronner Lesh, and her husband, Herschel Lesh, sold another acre for school use in the 1940's when David Schwartz was township trustee.)

What a giant step! A tie barn was erected for the convenience of having a place out of the weather to tie the horses which were used to carry the pupils and teachers.

Two graduates were produced in 1905; Eva Earl and Leon Newhouse. The year 1909 recorded no graduate, and in the year 1912, only one person, Iva Sink graduated. During early years, Union lost its high school commission and students were transferred to Ossian or Markle.

The tie barn sat on the south end of Union's acreage, Owen R. Bangs, beloved principal, held tight reign on more than the horses in that barn. I'm told lots of courting went on in there and nothing escaped his sharp eye.

Consolidation had its birth pangs during those early years as it was decided to centralize the total township school program. The little school houses relinquished their hold on the small groups and those pupils were integrated into the big, big central school, which was more properly called Union Center School.

Transportation was a problem, but as all problems have a way of finding solutions, the horse hack was brought into play. These were long, box-like carriages with bench-like seats along each side and uniquely enough, they had a heater! This heater was a little stove complete with the chimney protruding through the top. This was fired and lucky was they guy who sat near the stove! The motorized box-like hacks replaced those, but there were no heaters and sometimes those who rode the farthest nearly froze.

Progress speeds on as we catch glimpse after glimpse of new buses; in 1934, a new gym to replace the old barn; a new garage to house the buses, made from the bricks of the old one-room schools; changes in curriculum, methods; and as we run a boisterous course, the years spin by which can only be seen through the eyes of memory.

How often we recall the feverish search for knowledge and adventure in a multitude of words from the printed page.

When McNeely was principal, the students at times left their lunch buckets at home and ate soup, provided at school (1930's). Later, around 1940-41, Lucy Meyers was cook-janitor and the cafeteria began to take shape with the help of Mr. Frantz, who scrounged up some plates and utensils.

Union Center High School's largest graduating class was 26 in 1944; the smallest was in 1912, with one graduate. The total number graduating from Union Center High School was 825. Some high schools of today number that in one year, but for us quality has been a much more substantial consideration than quantity. Union Center High School has produced a wide spectrum of vocations — educators, doctors of medicine, doctors of chiropractics, nurses, many in various branches of service to our country, artists, musicians, business persons, architects, social workers, lawyers, merchants, horticulturists, Peace Corps workers, state representative, professional athletes, funeral directors, ministers of the Gospel, some of America's best farmers, a host of homemakers, mothers, fathers, grandfathers and grandmothers and a variety of other vocational persons.

An interesting point I read and have observed recently is the seemingly innovative idea that children n upper grades could well serve as teacher's helpers to the slow learning student in lower classes. Strange — this is the way it was done in the one-room school throughout those earlier years. Does history really repeat itself? In not all areas, of course, but some things that were good are still good today!

The high school program closed in 1962. High school and junior high students were transferred to Lancaster and Ossian, and the grade school remained at Union until the school's closing in May, 1968. At that time, the grade school children were divided between Rockcreek, Lancaster and Ossian.

A note of sadness comes creeping over me as I glance briefly in this hurried run through history. I saw Ole Union High with its stark empty windows peering out upon the world about. It was sorta' sad that it couldn't have a decent burial, as we would do for any other living vital being that had served its purpose. It was razed in 1981.

About 1964, a kindergarten was provided for Union Rockcreek students at Uniondale in Fuhrer's Garage. In 1968, it was closed and Rockcreek then had kindergarten. In the fall of 1968, Norwell was opened for all high school students of Northern Wells County.

The Union Center Alumni Association was established in 1926. It was a product of four of the graduates. Genevieve Walker Gaskill, Gladys Roe and her husband, Otis Schwartz, and Clifford Clark got together and decided to begin the meetings. They are still going on today. About 140 people met on the first Saturday of May, 1991, at the 4-H building in Bluffton to reminisce about old times. Six hundred fifty graduates, teachers and friends are on the mailing list yet.

Frog Pond School (l. to r.) Front row: Helen Leist, Velma Mowery, Lawrence Reaser, George Noble, Everett Reaser, Margaret Sellers, Ruby Moser, Justine Williams, Edith Onweller, Pearl Moser, Geraldine Williams. Back row: Earl Grove, Mearl Huffman, John Collins, Robert Melick, Glen Huffman, Howard Onweller, Audrey Pickering, Emma Reaser, Olive Onweller, Etta Lesh, Lucile Lambert (Henley), teacher. At that time A.R. Huyette was county superintendent of schools and Henry Johns was trustee of Nottingham Township.

Frog Pond School

Frog Pond School was in Nottingham Township, Wells County, Indiana. It stood on the north west corner of intersection 700 S. and 100 E. or one mile east and one mile south of Poneto. In the school year, 1918-1919, Frog Pond was typical of one-room country schools in Wells County.

The desks were graduated in sizes to accommodate all sizes of pupils, ranging from primer to eighth grade. The floors were wooden, and had been oiled. Each pupil provided his own transportation, mostly walking.

The teacher's desk was up front. Blackboards of slate covered the wall behind the teacher's desk. Many boxes of chalk were used during the year, in solving long compound interest problems, and in ciphering on Friday afternoons. Also spelling words were sometimes written on the board. In inclement weather, children played the game of "Jack" using the blackboard instead of their tablets. Pull-down maps were utilized in teaching geography.

A small corner cupboard held all the accessories provided by the school: a small world globe, several boxes of chalk, and erasers for the blackboard.

In the center of the room stood a large round coal-burning stove. Coal was stored in a nearby shed. At each side of the entrance hall, was a cloak room with shelves for lunch pails. High above the entrance hall was the belfry. One of the teacher's janitorial duties was ringing the bell to summon pupils from noon and recess recreation. A pump organ, played by either pupil or the teacher, provided music for singing and marching during morning exercises and holiday programs. A small bookcase, obtained from proceeds of a box-social, held books for outside reading. Water came from a pump outside. Matching the brick school house were two brick bathrooms, located at the back. *Submitted by Lucile Henley.*

Glass School

Glass School was in Jefferson Township District #5. James Glass gave the land for the first building, which was a log building. Later a frame building was built with a brick structure to follow even later. This pattern of log to frame to brick was typical of the local one-room school era.

Greenwood School

The Greenwood School in Jefferson Township north of Kingsland was built two and one-half miles south of Ossian and was a frame building. A brick structure was built in 1884 and probably got its name from the town of Greenwood, which was only one-quarter mile west of the school. The school house was the social center where box socials, spelling bees, and meetings of the Grange were held. The Grange often had debates on politics and also was the source of news of better farm practices, grain prices, etc.

Children were often punished for whispering by being required to sit on the front seats of the classroom. Often younger children learned things from listening to the teacher instruct classes for the older students. Classes were very short, so very little individual instruction could be given and often a teacher took a longer time on subjects he enjoyed and age groups he enjoyed while neglecting other subjects and groups he felt less desirable.

On Monday mornings, students came to school and often found evidence of a tramp having made his home there overnight or maybe a gang of gypsies or horse traders had camped under the big cottonwood tree, especially in later years after a well was dug on the property.

Haiflich School

The Haiflich School was a brick building built two miles north of the center of Rockcreek Township. School started at 9:00 and a teacher was often judged by the number of hours he was at the schoolhouse before 9:00. The "gym" consisted of the small school yard and sometimes a portion of a neighbor's field. The "floor" was Mother Earth and the "roof" often leaked. A variety of sports such as ball on board, tippy dup, dare base, blackman, pig tail, andy over, jumping, or fox and goose were participated in. Subjects taught were first, reading, writing, and arithmetic; then later added were U.S. History, geography, physiology, grammar and spelling. Dismissal was always 4:00 or later. Pupils were seated two to a desk and there were no school lunches.

Iron Bridge

Iron Bridge was located two miles west of the later Rockcreek Center location where a creek flows on the west side of the school yard. A bridge crossing Rock Creek, located on the highway which bounds the school yard on the north, gave the school its name. The first school was of logs and located south of where later buildings were located. The log structure was followed by a white frame or wooden building which was replaced by a brick structure in 1878.

No water wells were in the school yards in the early school days, so the township trustee usually furnished one water bucket and one tin cup for all to use. Water was carried from a neighbor's farm until 1904, when driven water wells were put in at all schools in the township. In 1878, trustee Haflich paid his teachers 65 cents a day.

No compulsary attendance law existed. There was no regular system of promotion and no near-at-hand high school, so most pupils' education ended with elementary or the first eight grades. The pupils decided what subjects they wanted to study and often decided when to pass to the next grade. No high school or college training was required for teaching, only the finishing of common school and passage of the state prepared examination. In those days many children, even beginners, walked a distance of two miles over mud and snow-covered roads to a school heated by only a wood-burning box stove.

Jackson Center School

Before 1937 Jackson Township took pride in its ten one-room school buildings that were served by faithful teachers. High school students were forced to enroll at Roll, Warren and Van Buren which were outside Wells County or in Chester Township here in Wells County.

Times were hard economically, and the entire country was still depressed from the 1929 episode. With the FDR administration came the "New Deal" innovations, and the country was beginning to cope with its high unemployment. One of FDR's ideas was the WPA (Works Progress Administration) which was a governmental agency responsible for many projects in Wells County - one being the construction of a high school that Jackson Township was scheduled to obtain. It was described in the history books as a fine, brick structure which would house grades 1-12 and could accommodate 400 students. This was the first time Jackson Township had one meeting place that united them, although there was already a strong church foundation established in the township.

In 1938, a hundred years after Jackson Township was set off as a separate unit of government (Sept. 4, 1837), a center of activity for the township finally existed with this beautiful structure. It was the last of eight consolidations in the county and served until another educational reorganization in the early 60s. In the spring of 1966, Jackson Township would no longer have a center because the consolidation of the four Southern Wells townships into a new complex housed in Chester Township opened in the fall of 1966. Many great memories were made for those students who attended or graduated from this institution and some centered around names such as: Lloyd Lieurance, Jim Love, Bill Hannah, Gladys Darrow, Beatrice Huffman, Harold Foust, Ray Bevington, Betty Cline, Jim Leas, Delight Parker, and many, many other great people.

Jackson School

The Jefferson Township School District #9 was called Jackson School. In 1886 a new brick school was built on the corner of the Graft farm. Before this the school had been a frame building located one-quarter mile east of the brick structure. This new building had two stoves and an entrance hall where the wood was stored which would be used in the stoves.

Materials used in school were slates, papers (if pupils had it), pencils, the blackboard, the Appleton Reader, and the McGuffy's Speller. There was a nice playground that had been improved with the planting of trees while John Ferguson was the school director. All of the play equipment, in early days, was homemade or brought from home. Sometimes the pupils made a playhouse and brought things from home to furnish it with.

Jackson Township School built in 1938 stood on the northwest corner of county roads 900w and 900s.

Jackson Center School during its construction. Photo courtesy of Marvin Day.

Lancaster Township School

In 1845, Lancaster Township was organized as a township unit under the law of 1816. An election was held and three trustees were elected on the 29th of August, 1845. The three trustees elected were William Hannah, Allen Clark and William Montgomery.

In 1847, the board met and laid the township off in school districts starting in the northeast corner of Range 12 with District No. 1 known in later years as the Daily School; District No. 2 was the Eagleville School; District No., 3 was the Donaldson School; No. 4 in the southwest part of the township; No. 5 was the Center School; No. 6 was the Bender School; No. 7 as the Wasson School; No. 8 as the Toll Gate; No. 9 as the Lamb School; and at a later date a district was made in Range 13 known as the Little School No. 10 and No. 11 was known as the Craigville School.

In 1856, the Indiana State Legislature passed a law providing that upon the petition of twenty householders in a township, there might be ordered an election, at which time three trustees should be chosen to manage the schools of the township.

The law of 1859 reduced the trustees to only one trustee to have charge of all the schools and the rest of the township business.

In 1856, it was decided that District No. 4 was too small and a new district was made which now is the Murray School. And the last district was made in the northeast part of the township known as the Swamp or Littlevine.

On May 7, 1853, there was a petition filed with the trustees of the township to hold an election for the purpose of levying a tax to build school houses in Lancaster Township. The election was held on the 6th of June, 1853, for the above said purpose and the final vote was 93 for a tax and 34 for no tax. A levy was made for 50¢ on the $100.00 valuation to raise money to build the school houses. On July 8, 1854, sealed bids were opened for the building of nine new frame school buildings.

Bids were accepted for the building of nine new buildings in districts No. 1, 2, 3, 4, 5, 6, 7, 8, 9, and 11. The average bid was $352. The bid was let to Jacob Myers, William Merriman and David Burgan. The trustees of the township at that time were Allen Clark, Nathaniel Greenfield and Alexander Delong.

In 1850, three more new school buildings were built by Enoch High in districts No. 3, 10 and 13 at a cost of $320.00 each. On June 6, 1868, the trustees opened bids for a new school building to be build in district No. 12. George Steele and Isaac Shady were the lowest bidders at $475.00.

The law of 1859 reduced the numbers of trustees from three to one. An election was held on April 4, 1859, and Nathaniel Greenfield was elected. He took office the following day, April 5, 1859.

In later years, the frame buildings were replaced by brick buildings. Several of these one room buildings were built by E.R. Davenport, trustee. In 1895, the two back rooms of Craigville School were built by Andy Reed, trustee. In 1899, the four-room building at Murray was built by Nelson Stafford, trustee. In 1903, the front part of the building at Craigville was built by Joel Fry, trustee. In 1910, the brick building known as the Little School was built by Dan Harsh, trustee. This building was used until 1928 when the students were sent to the Craigville School.

There came a time when these one-room schools were getting old and not very suitable for school purposes any more. A movement was started to consolidate these one-room buildings. Some of these were abandoned and the children were hauled to the Craigville and Murray schools.

In 1920, the trustee and advisory board started plans to build a high school and elementary school, and in December, 1921, the trustee and advisory board met and opened bids for a new school building to be built near the center of the township. Five acres of ground were bought from George Milholland for $1,250.00

Contracts were awarded to Hisey and Bebout for the general construction at $65,625.00. Bonds were issued for a period of fifteen years. Before the building was finished and equipment was bought, it was necessary to make a temporary loan to finish and equip the building. The total indebtedness at that time was about $113,000. This building was finished in the fall of 1922, and school started in it at that time. Students were all hauled by bus. Thirteen buses and 23 teachers were employed.

The first class to graduate from the high school was in the spring of 1923. The first principal was Gary E. Mounsey.

The building was built by the following township officers: A.E. Hunt, trustee; A.R. Huyette, Co. Supt.; Jess Dailey, Charles King, Raymond Wasson, and N.J. Kleinknight, advisory board.

To the trustee and the advisory board, after having the building built, came the obligation to meet bonds as they came due, and this was done by taxation. The boards met all of these payments as they came due through all their terms of office.

LIBERTY CENTER SCHOOL

The town of Liberty Center was founded about 1852. The first school was organized in 1896 with William C. Arnold as Town-

LANCASTER TOWNSHIP SCHOOLS

Murray School built in 1900 in Lancaster Township.

Craigville School, Lancaster District #11, housed both an elementary and high school and was built in 1903.

Lancaster Township School designed in 1922.

ship Trustee when the school was erected. The Advisory Board consisted of Oliver Markley, S.B. Vickery, and Lee Highlen. Jim Wooster was the first janitor and held this position for many years. Some of the first school teachers were Oscar Haegler, Sylvester Miller, Henry Snyder, Ruth Crosdale, Lily Morris Barcus, Jim Frantz and Orpha Ledbetter.

A.R. Huyette was county superintendent in 1909, Oscar Noe was principal and John Dean was township trustee.

To our knowledge four people are living that were among the first graduates - Mildred Boltin Sark, Sylvia Gephart Heath, Edith Baker McCloud and Ware Baker. The first graduate was Minnie Bundy McElhaney in 1898.

The schoolhouse that was erected in 1913, had as trustee John Dean and the board members were: C.R. Popejoy, L.A. Minniear and J.A. Johnson. The first year class had four graduates.

The children went to the Little Red School Houses and furnished their own transportation to the Liberty High School. After closing the district schools the children were transported into the Liberty Center School. The first school hack was pulled by horses with a small stove for heat with a stove pipe going out the side. The high school students drove horses and buggies and put the horses up for the day in several barns around over the town. The junior high school was organized in 1922.

Liberty Center was always noted for basketball. They first played outside, then in a barn near the school. Finally a gymnasium was built near the school. Several teams went to the sweet sixteen state tournament. The first team to go was in 1916 and again in 1923. After winning the sectional the team of 1964 made the "Believe It Or Not" record by playing nine overtimes in a game with Swayzee that Liberty Center finally lost.

The school was closed when Liberty, Chester, Jackson and Nottingham Townships consolidated and Southern Wells was built. The last class to graduate was in 1965. Many of the graduates went on to further their education into many professions around the world.

MILLIKEN SCHOOL

Milliken School got its name from Mr. Sam Milliken who owned the land it was built on. A brick structure replaced the earlier frame structure around 1880. This school was a part of the Jefferson Township system.

NEEDMORE SCHOOL

Needmore was the first Union Township School and was built in 1851-52 on a plot of land that was bought by Bunard Poirson from the government in 1836. The land had been sold to Jesse Folk in 1859. It was called Needmore because there were such a few pupils available that they needed more to keep it going.

This school was replaced with a new red brick building in 1884. Several of the scholars that went to the old and new school later married and settled in the community. Their children went to the school until 1923, when the school was abolished and all the pupils were taken by bus to the new Union Center High School.

OSSIAN SCHOOL

The Ossian High school was constructed on South Jefferson Street in 1925. This building was home to students in grades one through twelve. The school mascot was the Ossian Bear. The newspaper, known as the *"Bear Facts"*, first appeared in 1928. The school yearbook was called the Oracle and was first published in 1937. The school colors were red and white, and the school song was adapted from the Indiana University fight song. In 1953 a new gymnasium was added to the building.

In 1967, consolidation of Lancaster,

The 1964 Liberty Center basketball team holds record of nine overtimes in Regional tourney. (l. to r.) Kenny Huffman, Larry Garrett, Jerome Markley, Bruce Stanton, Dick Harris, Coach Richard Butt, John Collins, Jim Harris, Bill Day, Randy Raber, and Denny Archbold.

Liberty Center Commissioned High School built in 1913 replaced the first building from 1896. Both stood on the corner location of Main and Walnut. This building was demolished in 1973.

Rockcreek, Union, and Jefferson Townships created the North (Ossian) and South (Lancaster) High School campus while the new high school was being built on State Highway 224.

Norwell High School began in 1968, and the Ossian School became a junior high and elementary school. Kindergarten was added at that time. For three years prior to that time Kindergarten was held in the Presbyterian Church.

In 1978, the Norwell Middle School was built on to the west end of the high school and the Ossian building became an elementary school.

Ossian School continued to outgrow its capacity, so a new elementary school was attached to the existing gym on its west and south sides, and classes began in the new elementary building in the fall of 1989. In the summer of 1990, the three story brick school was torn down and hauled away. The very large cement stone plaque that rested at the very top of the roof line of the old school was preserved and placed in the south wall of the remodeled gym. The plaque reads, "Jefferson TWP. Schools 1926". The clock from the old study hall hangs on the wall of the new library.

PARK SCHOOL

A two-story brick school building was erected on the northwest corner of Ohio and Bennett Streets in 1882, serving children living east of Main Street in Bluffton. Named Washington Park School, it overlooked Bluffton's one-block square public park, Washington Park. This park, popular with both children and adults, included boat-swings, conventional swings and teeter-totters, horseshoes, a small wading and swimming pool, tennis courts, and covered pavillion for picnics and reunions.

The school building had two class rooms on the first floor for the first and second grades. Third and fourth grade rooms were on the second floor. Each room had 48 desks, the type on display at the Wells County Historical Museum. Each desk unit was fastened to the floor because the front of each desk was the seat for the pupil directly ahead. There was an opening in the upper right corner to hold an ink bottle, and a shelf below the desk top for books and tablets. Teachers' desks had a lift top for book and supply storage.

On the first day of school, students purchased their books from the local Progress Store on West Market Street, operated by J.E. (Ed) Reynolds - or if you were lucky, you might find someone who had a good used book to sell to you. Reynolds also sold paint, wallpaper, dishes and gift items.

There was one slate blackboard the length

Ossian High School was the first high school in the county outside of Bluffton. Originally built in 1879 it still stands at the northeast corner of Mill and Ogden Streets, but the building is greatly altered. Powers & Kibele designed the 1898 addition on the back.

Ossian Elementary in 1946.

of the front wall of each classroom, and a green burlap covered bulletin board on the back wall. Supplies were kept in tall cupboards. Each room had four ceiling-high windows to provide the maximum of natural lighting. The windows fitted loosely, letting winter snow drift in and pile up on the window sill. No doubt there were other small openings in the building. What excitement there was when an adventurous mouse was found hiding in the metal wastebasket!

Rest rooms were on the first floor. Coats, hats, and boots were left in a hallway between rooms where coat hooks were provided.

A belfry room was on the second floor where each school day the janitor pulled the rope to ring the bell for classes to begin.

Monthly fire drills were more exciting for those on the second floor. Each room here used an open, iron fire escape stairway on the west side of the building.

Reading, writing, and arithmetic were scheduled each day. For writing, the third grade used ink. Ink bottles and steel point pens were passed out from a wooden box, then collected at the end of the class exercise.

Recess led to a playground at the back of the building. Here were swings, teeter-totter and a merry-go-round.

Heating came from a separate building to the north where the janitor hand-fired a steam boiler. The janitor's duties included sweeping and oiling all the wood floors. Oiled sawdust was spread over the floors, then swept up with a push broom. A weekly chore was pushing a two-wheel hand cart to the Central School building for the few supplies available.

The location of Bluffton's three grade schools, Park, Central, and Columbian, was designed for students to have the shortest walking distance from their homes, four trips each day, since they walked home for lunch.

Finally, in May 1936, after 54 years, the building was torn down to make way for a newer, more efficient building. The country was still in the throes of the depression with money scarce. Public works, such as construction of school buildings, could receive help through the Works Projects Administration (WPA). The school board used WPA workers, and reportedly saved as much as 50% with a final cost of $38,000.

Construction of such a building using WPA relief labor was generally expected to take extra time. However, laying of brick began on August 1, 1936, and the building was finished ready for classes on February 2, 1937 - the 100th anniversary of the act authorizing the organization of Wells County. Howard Ullman, president of the school board, was given much credit for pushing the construction to completion in record time.

During the first semester of the 1936-37 school year with construction underway, Park students were bused each day to the Central School for morning classes (no study periods!), then home for lunch, with the afternoon free. In the afternoons, the first three grades of Central students used the classrooms after being at home during the morning. Both Park and Central teachers spent the whole day at school.

When the new Park School opened for the second semester in 1937, students found a bright new building with four classrooms on the main floor and a multi-use basement. There were entrances from Bennett Street on the east, and from Ohio Street on the west. The old wood corridor floor was now a beautiful brown tile. Returning to full day classes, the three grades (sometimes there were four grades, depending upon the number of students and school boundary lines which might be changed) found new tables and chairs replacing their old desks. The tables were made locally by the Patton-McCray firm which made furniture at their West Washington Street Factory. Each student's books and supplies were kept in individually assigned drawers. The cabinet of drawers, under the windows, was accessible only once in the morning and once for afternoon in order to avoid confusion. Children still went home for their lunch - this continued for the entire Park School era.

The basement contained the rest rooms, a room that would later be used for kindergarten, and a large meeting room with a small kitchen. This was the site of PTA and community meetings and other activities.

Classrooms continued to have wood floors, but now they were beautifully varnished and polished. Slate blackboards now covered both the front and back walls, while the wall opposite the windows contained coat closets with doors that when opened, recessed back into the closet.

Every year many extra-curricular activities were provided which were educational, interesting, enjoyable and fun.

May 26, 1972, was the last day for Park School, a fine neighborhood school; a victim of progress and consolidations and busing. Children would now be bussed to the new Eastside School and introduced to the school lunch program. The Park School building was remodeled to be used, as it is today, for the administrative offices of the Bluffton-Harrison Metropolitan School System. *(Material provided by Miss Georgiana Bender, who began her teaching career in 1931. She taught at Park School for 38 years, serving as principal for twenty years.)*

Washington Park School 1882 - 1936.

Park School 1937 - 1972.

Park School PTA

Mrs. Charles (Stella) Deam has been credited with organizing the first Parent Teachers Association (PTA) in Bluffton, and the first rummage sale.

A very early frame school house in Petroleum. It was erected about 1860 and its use was discontinued after the construction of the Petroleum Commissioned High School Building in 1899.

Petroleum School

Mrs. Deam was the first president of the new PTA at Park School. Miss Mary Weisell, principal at the school at that time, wrote about the organizing "that was a great occasion. We divided our (school) district, went out by twos and gave personal invitations wondering if anyone would come. We anxiously awaited the day. Mrs. Lew Dailey had a friend of hers to come over from Huntington to organize and get us set up.

"Our patrons came in on foot and on horseback until we were crowded in the cabin. Served coffee made on Mrs. Hixon's stove (she lived first house west) and homemade cookies. Got our cream from Mrs. Mary DeLong. Followed that manner of serving for several years."

When Miss Weisell advised the school's need for a Victrola (record player) and records, Mrs. Deam suggested a rummage sale, the first in Bluffton. Quoting again from Miss Weisell: "She advises we open shop. She, with her bicycle, brought in packages the size of bundles of baled hay; helped us mark and get our display ready. It was a success.

Mothers and teachers met after school for discussions relating to children and material items needed. These meetings were held in the fourth grade room on the second floor where there was a piano. At times, children gave short programs."

When the school moved from their 1882 building into the new 1937 building, the PTA continued to fund needed items for the children. These included books and bookcases for the school library, a stage and curtains, raincoats for school crossing guards, and a movie projector. Fund raising came from newspaper and scrap drives (during WWII). Another wartime project included the auctioning of rationed cans of food.

Many cans of food were sold and resold in the spirit of helping the school. The Park School PTA held their last meeting in May, 1972, when the school was closed. *(Material provided by Miss Georgiana Bender, Park School teacher and principal over a 38 year period. Miss Bender was given a lifetime membership in the local, state and national PTA in recognition of her devotion to children.)*

Petroleum School

The Petroleum School was in Nottingham Township, the fifth township to take its place among the nine Wells County units. It probably derived its name from Nottingham, England.

Nottingham Township was quite young when the school was built. The first settler, Joseph Blacklege, arrived on September 19, 1837. During the next year, when ten more families moved into the area, it could be said that the community actually began.

In 1843, before any schools were established, Mrs. Mary King taught school in a rude log cabin. Nottingham Township was the first township in Wells County to establish its school districts. In 1849, when Stanton Scott served as trustee, 149 children attended school in the nine log-school houses in the township. From 1870 to 1876, most of the log school houses were replaced by red brick structures, and the township was divided into twelve school districts.

In 1899 Petroleum School was built one mile west of the main crossroads under the direction of Samuel Gehrett, trustee. It housed grades on through twelve for all Nottingham Township students. A large barn was built on the lot for the teachers' and students' horses and buggies.

In 1910, an addition was added to the school on the north side under the leadership of trustee, Gus Baker. The rooms were for grades one and two, science, english, home economics and the coat halls were added. The cost of this addition was approximately $6,890. In 1924 under trustee James Carter's leadership, the remainder of the school, as it stood until torn down in 1974, was built.

The first basketball teams were known as the Petroleum Zippers. Later the teams became the Petroleum Panthers.

From 1903 to 1909 the high school was only three years, with 16 graduating. In 1910 the school started four years with only

Arthur Kirkwood graduating that year. From 1910 through 1966 Petroleum had 948 students graduating for a total of 964 graduating from Petroleum High School.

In 1966 Petroleum ceased admitting high school students. A new school, Southern Wells Junior and Senior High School, built in Chester Township, absorbed students from Petroleum, Chester Center, Liberty Center, and Jackson Township. A school housing grades one through six was built on the Southern Wells grounds. In 1974 the Petroleum School was torn down, with the Petroleum Lions Club using the grounds as a community park.

Poor Farm School

Harrison Township's District Number 7 was probably named the Poor Farm School because it was situated near the County Farm. It stood about thirty rods east of the County Farm crossroad and a few rods east of Six Mile Creek on the County Farm land. The brick school replaced an older frame house and was built in 1885 or 1886. The frame building stood directly west of the brick building. This was the school for the children from the Orphan's Home.

The school was only a few rods from the Six Mile Creek and most kids had skates. When the ice was good, they spent noons and recesses skating. One spring, when the ice was breaking up and large cakes were floating down the creek, someone thought of riding them. So at noon recess kids started up stream to ride a large cake down. Only two students had nerve enough to get on. When they were almost back to school, the ice lodged on some higher ground, the school bell rang and there was nothing to do but wade through ice water and spend the rest of the day sitting by the stove to dry out.

Poor Farm School of Harrison Township built near the County Farm and also serviced the children from the Orphan's Home.

care of stoves, sweeping, and keeping the blackboard and erasers clean. The subjects taught were spelling, reading, arithmetic, geography and penmanship. In front of the school house was a pump, in the winter the teacher would bring in a bucket of water. Each one had their own folding drinking cup. In the back of the school house was an outside toilet.

In the front door was a cloak room; with shelves on both sides, where metal dinner pails were kept. Under the shelves were hooks to hang coats. Inside the room was rows of seats, the teacher's desk faced all the pupils. Behind the teacher's desk was the blackboard the full width of the room and on each side of the room was a coal burning stove.

One school term was 89 days. Everyone walked to school no matter how bad the weather was.

At noon the older pupils would choose up sides and play baseball or a game called Duck on Davey. A large flat rock was used for the nest with a smaller rock called the duck.

Each player would have a rock and they would try to knock the duck off the nest.

It was not an easy task for the teacher to teach and keep records and be janitor also. The pay was very small according to the wages of today. Male teachers received $1.65 per day and female teachers $1.00 a day. Both parents often visited the school to check on the progress of every thing. At the close of the school year the parents had a big carry in dinner for everyone to enjoy.
Submitted by Aubry Clark Beavans

Roberts School - District #4

The Roberts School was located two miles west of Liberty Center in Liberty Township on the south west corner of the John Roberts farm. The little red brick school house had many memories for a great number of pupils. I have no way of knowing when the school house was built, perhaps before 1882. I have a record where the school started November 6, 1882, and ended March 17, 1883. The record shows that in 1882 there were 62 pupils that attended and the school was too small for that many pupils. Nothing but a Globe was found to instruct the students. The teacher taught eight classes in addition to taking

A 1901 design by architect Cuno Kibele, Rockcreek Township District #5 or Center School was nearly identical to a couple Harrison Township Schools (Hoover #8 and Poplar Grove #6). The only external difference is the fact that Poplar Grove had more vertical pieces in the belfry railing.

East Rockcreek School

East Rockcreek School

East Rockcreek Marker

Rockcreek Center School

Eight grades were taught by one teacher, who was nearly always a man. Sixty to seventy pupils were common. The school was located in the center of Rockcreek Township. The front hall had shelves on each side for dinner buckets and nails in the wall for coats. Everyone drank from the common waterbucket and toilets were in the back corner of the school yard.

Spelling, ciphering, and the query box were parts of the Friday night contests against other schools. When there was snow on the ground, horsedrawn bobsleds decked out with sleighbells carried kids to these contests. Box socials were often held to make money for some school ventures. The one-room school was torn down and replaced by the Rockcreek Township Consolidated and High School in 1922.

Rockcreek Township School

During the summer of 1922 there was much controversy concerning the development of a new consolidated school. This controversy ended with the closing of several small one-room school houses and the building of a new Rockcreek Township School which housed all twelve grades.

As the construction began many watched with great amazement. Children who once walked two or more miles to school would no longer walk to school. Instead they would ride "hacks" carrying fifteen to twenty children. Today they are called busses, which carry sixty to seventy children and make much longer routes. One freshman boy, Byrl Miller, drove a horse and buggy, picking up riders on his way to school.

A member of the faculty, Russell Stinson (who was honored by former Rockcreek students who put a brick in the new Hall of Fame Courtyard given in his memory), tripled his duties and abilities by being a fifth and sixth grade teacher, coach and "hack driver." Talk about versatility!

The school was not completed in time to start in September, the usual time; however, in October 1922, a grand opening and dedication was held with all twelve classes participating.

One of the first steps was the forming of an orchestra by Lewis Sawyer, principal and trombonist and Frank Young, a violinist and merchant. Mr. Young was the director. This orchestra was enjoyed by many children.

Mr. Sawyer, an alumni of Illinois University, suggested a contest to be held to compare words for a school song to be written to the tune of Illinois Loyalty. The contest was won by the late Cressie (McAfee) Falk, class of 1924, and is still used in the closing of our yearly Rockcreek Alumni meetings. The first school paper, printed in 1924, was called "The Limit"; later the name was changed to "The Spirit of Rockcreek." The school newspaper won many honors in school newspaper contests.

Because of his admiration for the old Brooklyn Dodgers, John Charles (Chick) Braden, class of 1927, suggested the name of Dodgers as the athletic team and school nickname. This nickname was selected from many entries by the student body.

Mr. Braden managed a semi-pro baseball team in 1950, and won a national championship in Japan.

Choosing the colors for the school was another issue settled by the student body. The chosen colors were blue and gold.

Sports were an interesting activity at Rockcreek, as they were with all small schools in Wells County. It was especially exciting when one of the smaller schools would beat one of the larger schools. The only time Rockcreek won the sectional tournament was in 1927.

A traveling trophy, "The Brick", was carried in a black bag from school to school. It was a great challenge to see which school could keep it the longest. The brick was for the first team and the "Milk Bottle" was for the second team.

Today it is the varsity and junior varsity teams. The Brick is in the Hall of Fame from Wells County. The Milk Bottle has never been located. We can't forget the girls' basketball team known as the "Bloomer Girls." Their traveling trophy was the "Rolling Pin," never located.

The first year to graduate students was 1923, with a total of three graduates. The last class was 1964, with a total of fifteen students. The grand total of graduates in the history of the school is 708 students. Our school continued as a K-6 grade school until 1979. At that time these students were sent to Lancaster and Ossian, a part of Northern Wells Community Schools. The school was torn down the summer of 1980. Again we were in a new consolidation with much controversy. The four upper townships of Wells County, Rockcreek, Union, Lancaster and Jefferson, consolidated for the new Norwell High School with the first graduating class of 1969.

The Alumni erected a marker at the site of the old school, 300 N. - 300 W. in Rockcreek Township. This concludes the history of our dearly beloved school, the Rockcreek Dodgers.

School Board Sells City Landmark - Former Baptist Church

The Bluffton school board has advertised the old Wabash Street schoolhouse. At a former effort the building failed to sell. It is now thought with the great scarcity of property in Bluffton, it may go, when again offered on October 4th.

This building has quite a reputation in Bluffton and is one of the old landmarks. When it was erected by the Baptist congregation it was the only brick church in the county and was much the finest in the county. The First Baptist organization of this city used the building for worship until they built the structure they now use on the corner of Cherry and Johnson Streets.

After being given up as a church the building was used as an apartment house, two families living in it. A front porch was added, and it served the purpose very well for that time. Afterward it was used by the Kindergarten Association, and for about two years it answered the purpose of a kindergarten. The Kindergarten Association turned the property over to the educational board of the city, and for two years it was used for the manual training department of the schools. Then it was rented to P.A. Allen and Will Lester for a business college, and many of the office men and women of today received a business education within its walls. Then the school board used it and two teachers were used for a short time.

Then it went to the athletic branch of the school and many a hot game of basketball has been played in the old structure. Here it was the basketball bug got into many breasts of the city, which had much to do with building the gymnasium on West Cherry Street. *(This article was published in the Evening Banner on August 11, 1919.)*

Scott School

The Nottingham Township District # 12 School has always been popularly known as the Scott School. The round log house at the Scott School was as indicated, built of timber in the manner referred to. The building was about 20 x 22 feet, cabled off, and roofed with clapboards held in place by weight poles. The chimney was made of sticks and mud, the floors of puncheons split from the timber, which, if it had been sawed and dressed would have made elegant finishing for the best of school house or residence of today.

The seats were made of linden, or bass wood saplings, eight to ten inches in diameter, split in halves and dressed with an ax and drawing knife with wooden pegs in each end for supports. The building was erected on a half acre of ground at the north west corner of section 32, in said township, bought of one Martha Marmon, of Logan County, Ohio, who was paid $1.25 for the plot, she making this price to "encourage the educational enterprises of the locality." It stood with the ends to the north and south, the door being in the south, and in the north end was a large open fire place which would take in about four foot wood. The back wall and jambs were built of clay, pounded in behind wooden supports, in moist condition, well saturated with salt to help form a glazing over the surface and give it durability.

About three feet from the floor, on each side, a couple of logs were cut and removed, almost the full length of the house, and in the spaces, two sashes to each opening were fitted for the glass, so they would slide past each other to let in air, and these were the windows. The cracks between the logs were chinked and plastered over with clay mortar.

For a writing desk for this house a black walnut slab or board about 3 1/2 or 4 inches thick, three feet wide and about twelve feet long, that had been used formerly by one of the patrons of the new school for a bench to dress leather on, as he had been a tanner by trade. This bench was laid on two trestle benches, one under each end. Can you realize what a superb writing desk this made as it was thus placed a little to one side of the center of the house, and that it was always a treat, a fair delight to be privileged to sit by it to study the lessons and write?

About 1862 the need of a new and better house was being felt and agitating the patrons of the Scott School, and owing to the fact that a house had been built a while before, one mile east of this one, there was a disposition to move the location farther west, and after considerable of wrangling, it was decided to build the new house on the southwest corner of the Scott Farm, one-fourth of a mile west in section 30, and in 1868 or '69, a new frame house was erected under the trusteeship of Thos. Aker.

About 1889 or 1890 the location was again changed back to the lot first secured of Mrs. Morman and a brick building erected under the supervision of trustee Wm. Higgins.

Four of Stanton Scott's children, two sons and two daughters, began and finished the common school here, and after further completing their equipment for the task, taught several terms, each, in the township, and one of them in Chester Township. They were Nathan M., Elizabeth, Elma Jane and Joshua.

Smoky Row School

The Harrison Township School District Number 6 was commonly known as Smoky Row. Legend has it that Smoky Row got its name from the continuous line of smoke in the air as the forests were cleared and burned on the new Range Line Road, or Smoky Row Pike as it is still sometimes called, which is now 600 E.

The first school was of logs and in the same vicinity as the next two structures. The second building was a frame structure on the Henry Steiner farm on the west side of the road. It was quite a distance back from the road and a short distance from the first crossroad south of 116 on 600E. The third building, which was also the last building to be used, was on the northwest corner of this same intersection and close to 600E. This final building was considered very up-to-date with its stone trim and imposing belfry. Pupils in this school came from families who were lately arrived from the "old countries" and so often acquired a language that was a mixture of the language spoken at home and the English spoken at school.

School consisted of two six or twelve-week terms, a winter and summer. Students could go to either or both. School was

Wells County Teachers' Institute meeting at the Sixbey Opera House (former Presbyterian Church) located southeast corner of Scott and Washington Streets, Bluffton.

never more than seven months long, even in later years. The teacher was boarded around with families and received from $5.00 to $10.00 per week in pay.

Health standards were never too high, and school was closed several times, once because too many parents refused to have children vaccinated for smallpox. The flu epidemic caused a closing, as did the first polio epidemic. Tonsilitis was a popular ailment. The most popular cures were a bag of assofoetida tied around the neck, a stink bug tied in a thimble, and an onion poultice of turpentine and lard. These are all served to keep people a good distance away, whether or not they cured the disease. For the juvenile delinquents of the day, the teacher kept a choice collection of assorted switches across two nails above the blackboard as a visible deterrent to mischief.

Union Township Center School

Union Township Center School was located in the center of Union Township and was built from brick during the year 1875 or 1876. The building would later become the Union Center High School.

Vera Cruz School

The school was first built in 1868 and had two classrooms, with the first four grades downstairs being taught by women and the four upper grades placed upstairs and taught by men. The school had a bell to call pupils to school each morning, afternoon, and at recess. A new building was built in 1896 and was made of brick. It also had two classrooms. This school building had a basement under the entire building and was heated with a furnace. Later the school was remodeled to include a dining room and a kitchen in the basement.

Wells County Teachers' Association

On Saturday, October 13, 1866, a convention of over 40 teachers assembled at the court house in Bluffton for the purpose of organizing a permanent Teacher's Association. The proceedings were harmonious. They assembled at 1:00 and organized by calling T.A.R. Eaton to the Chair, and appointing G.F. McFarren, secretary.

J.S. McCleery spoke "This convention has been called, at the solicitation of many teachers, for the purpose of forming a permanent Teacher's Association for Wells County, and also for the purpose of consulting together with reference to the time of holding our Teacher's Institute for the present year."

Others addressing the group were Mr. Cotton, Mr. Blue, Mr. Shinn, Mr. Eaton, and others. Shinn, Blue and Cotton were selected to draft a constitution and by-laws, to be submitted to the Association at its next regular meeting.

On motion, a committee of three from each township was appointed to solicit the future co-operation of the teachers not present at the Association. The following persons were appointed from the several townships, to wit:

Jackson: Charles Myers, John J. Good, and Robert McFadden; Chester: Jos. McDonald, Chambers Shadle, and Levi Bell; Liberty: Miss M. Mouncie, Miss T. Ewings, and Robert F. Gavin; Rockcreek: James A. Cotton, E.F. Cotton, and J.W. Walker; Union: Miss Mary Cotton, John H. Ormsby, and Geo. W. Scott; Nottingham: Miss Molly Watts, N.M. Scott, and Wm. Bloxom; Harrison: John B. King, Jonathan J. Markley, and F.M. McFadden; Bluffton: Miss Molly Burwell, Miss Lydia Bayha, Miss Laura Bugh; Lancaster: Daniel Hahns, Jas. Wasson, and E.H. Waugh; Jefferson: Michael C. Blue, Thomas W. Archbold, and Miss Mary Porter.

Pay ranged from $1.25 to $2 per day for teachers of Wells County the following year.

Zanesville School

The first school in Zanesville was a one-story frame building which stood directly south of Shepler's Garage, where Dan O'Brien's house now stands.

The only teacher I knew anything about was Mrs. John Carrol. I think she was the daughter of Dr. Weisel, who was a doctor here in Zanesville at that time. I would judge Mrs. Carrol was something like 30 years old in 1853. Here are the names of

The 1904 Keystone independent football team (note ball held by player in front), believed to be one of the earliest squads in Wells County. Notice the lack of protective equipment worn by the players. (l. to r.) Front row: Orval Lewis (standing), Fred Marsh, Bruce Barr, William Lambert, Levi Nutter (standing). Second row: Kenneth Kizer (standing), Burt Adams, Harley Murray, Earl French, Ed Adams(standing). Back row: Emery Merriman, Dr. DeWeese, and Ed Cochran.

some of her scholars: Albert Knight, Jay Michaels, William Bell, John Hesler, George Hesler, Jacob Lenington, Joe and Columbus Young.

Then about 1864 they built the two-story building. I went my first two terms in the lower room of this building. Then this building was condemned and torn down. About the year 1883, John Hesler and Hansy Enright were the last teachers to teach in the two-story building. Then they put a two-room building, one story. Later they divided the one room, making two rooms; which made three rooms in all.

While they were building the second brick building, they had school in a two-story building that stood about where the Alice Crum Beauty Shop now stands (site of Art Platt's Barber Shop in 1976). William M. Bel and Hansy Enright were the teachers; then school in the new building began in 1884. J.L. McBride was the principal of the Zanesville School in 1888. This building was used until about 1926, when it was discontinued and some of the children were taken to South Center (Union) and some to Lafayette Center, which has been continued up until the present time. *This information was given by Charles Clark, 86 years old, in 1962*

ZION SCHOOL

In 1848, Zion School was constructed and was the first school in Union Township. It was located one mile south of Zanesville. Zion School was built of round logs with a stick and mud chimney and a puncheon floor. It had a clapboard roof held in place by weight poles. Seats were made of basswood or linden trees which had been split into halves with pegs in each end for support. About thirty years later this school was overcrowded and new buildings were erected.

New Zion School (Splinter School) was located one-half mile south of the old Zion School on the west side of State Road 303. It was built as a result of the overcrowdedness of the Zion School. In the early 1900s the school was merged with Zanesville and a few students were sent to Union Center. For a few years the old school sat abandoned by the roadside. It was later sold to a family for a residence.

Top left - *Jackson Township District #3 known as the Dillman School. This two-room school had a counterpart built at the same time in Mt. Zion in 1898 but both have since vanished.*

Top right - *Reiffsburg School, Harrison township District #2, stood just north of Reiffsburg on state road one and built 1889.*

Middle - *Tocsin School (1886) located on US 224 in Tocsin still stands. This Jefferson Township District #10 school was later replaced by a larger school farther north of this location. Standing in front is Elizabeth (?) and Cora Stine. Photo courtesy of Madge Lobsiger.*

Bottom left - *Sugar Grove, Rockcreek Township District #1. Uniondale residents wanted this school built in their town but it stands a mile south of there and is today a private residence.*

Bottom right - *Classroom #2 in the Sugar Grove School, Rockcreek Township District #1.*

Top left - Keystone School of Chester Township built in 1896 and served till 1922.

Top right - Harrison Township District #8 school commonly known as the Hoover School. A common design in Wells County for early brick schools.

Middle - Vera Cruz School built in 1896 and was used for many years as the Opportunity School.

Bottom right - Harrison Township District #13 commonly known as Myers Chapel.

Bottom left - Poplar Grove School of Harrison Township. This second school built in 1903 in District #6 replaced an earlier brick structure which burned.

Top left - Batson Bridge School District #5 of Jackson Township built in 1897.

Top right - Tocsin School in Jefferson Township. This view was taken in 1908.

Middle - Nottingham Township School stood west of Petroleum from 1899 till 1967. This is a view of the original building.

Bottom left - First Liberty Center School built in 1896.

Bottom right - Nottingham School, District #11, built in 1898 stood on the north side of the town of Nottingham.

Top left - Poneto School. This 1898 building stood at the northwest corner of Meridian Road and Main Street until it burned in 1919.

Top right - Second Poneto School. This 1920 building cost $48,000.00

Middle - Bluffton High School at Oak and Central. The 1922 building was enlarged in 1965 and 1975.

Bottom right - Union Township School. This 1902 building stood until the late 1960's.

Bottom left - Central School as it looked when built in 1911. After it burned in 1938 it was greatly expanded and reopended in 1940 as the Bluffton High School.

Top left - Photo taken in 1907 of Bluffton Business College that was housed in old Baptist Church building on the northeast corner of Wabash and Williams.

Top right - Athletics has long been a part of local schools. This photo is of the Bluffton High School basketball team. (l. to r.) Front row: Bob Cummins, Donald Pursley, Joy Buckner, Hillard Walmer. Back row: Glynn Staker, Principal-Coach, A. G. Morris, Clyde Crawley, and Earl Moomaw.

Middle - The Faculty of the Adult Education Program in Wells County. (l. to r.) Carl Reeves; Mr. F. A. Cotton, County Supervisor; Marie Swisher; Floyd E. Grove; Clara Drew, representing Mrs. Risser; Elizabeth Cole; Harrison Prough; and Bertrand Handwork. Photo probably taken in the early 30's.

Bottom right - The Poplar Grove Learning Center (former elementary school) ended its service in 1991 with the full move to mainstreaming of all Wells and Adams Special Education students in the regular district schools for the fall. Photo courtesy Bluffton News-Banner.

Bottom left - Jackson Township School students marching in the street fair "School Parade" about 1950. The location is looking west on West Washington.

Bluffton-Harrison Schools

Our best records of the Bluffton-Harrison Schools' history began with Philemon A. Allen, who served as superintendent from 1881-1891 and again from 1907-1926; however, school in Bluffton actually had its beginnings before Superintendent Allen. During the early history of Bluffton, parents were the teachers. As the town grew, parents paid for a teacher and an unused building became a school house. One of the earliest examples was the use of the log court house as a school in 1844.

In 1848, in order to provide for free schools, the citizens of Indiana voted to support local taxes on personal and real property. This allowed for the construction of a few schools during the next two decades; however an organized building program did not begin until July 25, 1867, when bonds were issued to build a centrally-located, graded school. This two-story building was named Central. In September of 1881, Bluffton High School was organized in room 9 of the Central building. The three-year program graduated its first class of nine students in 1883. In 1885 the high school became a four-year program and was commissioned by the state in 1886. Bluffton High School received accreditation from the North Central Association of Colleges and High Schools in 1918, a distinction which continues to this day. On December 9, 1890, the new Bluffton High School was opened on the west side of the Central Building in the 500 block of West Washington Street.

William Wirt, an 1892 graduate of Bluffton High School, returned to Bluffton in 1899 to become superintendent of Bluffton Schools. In addition to Central and Bluffton High School, at the time of Mr. Wirt's return there was a Columbian School located in the west part of Bluffton and a Park School located in the east. During his tenure at Bluffton, Mr. Wirt initiated the year-round school, consisting of an 11 month school year divided into four equal sessions. Students were required to attend three of the four sessions. This innovative concept was utilized during the summers of 1905 and 1906. Mr. Wirt moved to Gary in 1907, and the program here was discontinued.

The Bluffton High School, which was later renamed P.A. Allen High School, was completed and the high school relocated to 428 Oak Street in September of 1923. The Central School, which had been rebuilt in 1910, continued to be used for high school classes. Shop classes were taught in the basement and music classes upstairs. Since P.A. Allen High School did not have a gym, physical education courses were taught in the Cherry Street gym, located on the southeast corner of Cherry and Morgan.

Central School was destroyed by fire on March 4, 1939. Sometime during late spring on early summer, Allen High School became an elementary school and the rebuilt Central School became the high school, which remained on Washington Street until 1954. With the completion of a New Jersey Street gymnasium, the P.A. Allen High School returned to the 428 South Oak Street location. On December 11, 1975, by action of the school board, P.A. Allen High School again became Bluffton High School.

Responding to the trend for consolidation across the state, a special election was held on July 11, 1961, resulting in the merger of the Bluffton City Schools and Harrison Township Schools to form the Bluffton-Harrison Metropolitan School District. The new Columbian School, located at 1225 West Washington Street, was dedicated at an open house the following December.

On March 4, 1973, East Side Elementary School held its open house. Later that year plans began to develop for construction at the secondary level. Four years later, on March 13, 1977, the Bluffton-Harrison Middle School and the P.A. Allen Auditorium addition at the high school were dedicated.

The current configuration of schools were effected in 1981 with the closing of Poplar Grove Elementary School. Although Poplar Grove continues to operate as a school building, it now houses special education students from both Adams and Wells Counties at the Poplar Grove Learning Center for the Adams-Wells Joint Services Cooperative.

Bluffton-Harrison Metropolitan School District Administration Building on 628 South Bennett Street.

Columbia School on 1225 West Washington Street.

Poplar Grove School Building - Adams-Wells Special Services Cooperative on 350 South State Road No. 1.

East Side Elementary School on 1100 East Spring Street.

Bluffton Middle School (Junior High) on 1500 Stogdill Road.

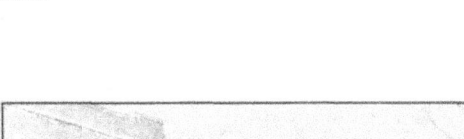

Bluffton High School on 428 South Oak Street.

Ossian Elementary in 1991.

Northern Wells Community Schools

In 1960, a Comprehensive Plan for Reorganization of School Corporations in Wells County was submitted to the state committee for the Reorganization of Schools. The plan was developed with the assistance of a committee whose members represented the different school corporations in Wells County. The plan recommended that three school corporations be created in Wells County. The name of the new school in the northern district was to be Northern Wells Community Schools and was to include all the schools in Union, Rockcreek, Jefferson and Lancaster Townships.

The plan created a five-member school board with one member representing each township and one at-large. The plan also designated the rights and powers of the school board and the disposition of all assets and liabilities of the former schools. At that time there existed schools in each of the four townships, each of which housed grades 1 through 12.

Since its creation in 1961, the Northern Wells Community Schools Corporation has grown from an enrollment in 1959-60 of 1857 students in grades 1 to 12 to enrollment of 2531 students in grades K to 12.

After creating the Northern Wells Community School Corporation, the school board moved forward to address the educational facility needs of the district. Norwell High School was completed in 1968 and was built in the center of the school district at the intersection of U.S. 224 and County Road 100 East. The new high school housed grades 9 to 12. Lancaster Central School and Ossian School were both reorganized to contain K-8, Rockcreek contained grades K-6 and Union School was closed.

Norwell Middle School was completed in 1979 and was built next to Norwell High School. The middle school housed grades 6 to 8 and added a swimming pool and additional outside athletic facilities to the existing high school complex. The middle school contained modern laboratory facilities and equipment for areas such as science, home economics, industrial arts, art, and physical education. Being located next to the high school enabled the corporation to adjust the

Lancaster Elemnetary in 1991.

Superintendents

J. McLean Benson,	1962-1970;
John McBride,	1970-1985;
Michael R. Sailsbery,	1985-

Member of the Board Of School Trustees

Walter Speheger	1962-1966
William Borror, Jr.	1962-1966
Rex Shutt	1962-1966
Clyde Barnes	1962-1969
Darrell Gilbert	1962-1966
Gilbert Bynum	1966-1971
Ervin Fox	1967-1970
Dean Roe	1967-1974
Marlowe Shepler	1967-1970
Robert Johnloz	1970-1981
Roger Allen	1971-1975
Allen Shatto	1971-1974
Jerald VanMeter	1972-1973
Edward J. Goetz	1974-1977
Phyllis Confer	1975-1982
Gerald Miller	1975-1982
Autie Lewis, Jr.	1976-1978
Thomas Woodward	1978-1985
Jack Ash	1979-1983
Kenneth Honegger	1981-1985
Mick Cupp	1983-1990
Bill Brubaker	1983-1987
Larry Reed	1983-1990
Vicki Hanselman	1985-1989
Mike Todd	1985-
Jim Beckstein	1987-1990
Sally Tinkel	1989-
Karen Dunn	1991-
Mike Krin	1991-
Arthur Windmiller	1991-

Norwell Middle School in 1991.

busing of secondary students to a central location. Lancaster Central and Ossian were both reorganize to house grades K to 5 and Rockcreek was closed.

In the summers of '79, '80, and '81, Ossian Elementary was renovated to create a more pleasant elementary atmosphere. Lancaster Central Elementary was renovated in 1986 to modernize the classrooms, remove asbestos and improve the educational atmosphere.

In 1989, a new building was completed to replace the old portion of Ossian Elementary School. The gymnasium was remodeled but the three-story portion was demolished upon completion of the school complex located southeast of the gymnasium. The new elementary school was developed on an expanded site to provide for a complete elementary education program. In the same year, a 50,000 square foot addition was attached to Norwell High School. The wing provided new facilities for science, vocational business education, and industrial technology education. The facility provided modern facilities to meet the new technological demands of high school education.

Norwell High School in 1991.

Southern Wells Community Schools

Southern Wells Jr.-Sr. High School was formed on January 1, 1963. The consolidation of Chester Center, Jackson Center, Liberty Center, and Petroleum took place due to a new policy of the Indiana Commission on General Education. The policy suggested that any school with an enrollment of less than 100 students that didn't offer two years of foreign language, could be forced to close.

After many meetings the school board decided to build Indiana's first circular Jr.-Sr. High School. Construction of the new school began in February of 1965. William Payne was chosen to be the principal of the new school; Lloyd Biberstine was the superintendent. Dedication of the new school occurred on November 27, 1966. On September 6 of the same year the first classes were held at the new consolidated Southern Wells Jr.-Sr. High School.

Southern Wells Elementary

In 1974, the Southern Wells Elementary School was constructed. Basically, this was the consolidation of the elementary townships schools. It was decided that bringing these schools together would be less expensive than updating each current building to make it reach state requirements.

The total coast of the elementary school was $1,516,445.00. This cost included things such as the general construction, mechanical work, electrical work, carpet, food service equipment, gym equipment, bleachers and casework.

Because the elementary is built in a pod-type manner, it is quite conducive to team teaching, and the utilization of staff members' strengths and skills. The building includes pods K-6 and facilities for special education. There are also special departments and teachers for art, music, speech and hearing, special education, and physical education.

Presently, there are approximately 38 staff members and 500 students in the elementary. Each member has an important job in getting the students ready for junior high and high school. The basic emphasis are on reading and mathematics. To help make learning fun, several clubs and special events are organized. For example, PRIME TIME FRIDAY NIGHT is a new occasion. Students come to the school Friday evening with a sack lunch and books to read. The three hour evening is divided into different periods where kids read, participate in special activities, and eat their supper. This event makes reading an enjoyable activity than can be shared with friends.

Staff in the elementary feel that excellence should be rewarded. That is why they invented THE RAIDER OF THE DAY award. Teachers nominate students for various tasks, such as doing good work on a paper or improving a skill. Then these names are put together in a drawing, and every day a student is drawn. That student gets the privilege of wearing a badge for that entire school day.

There are a lot of programs designed especially for sixth graders. Various clubs include Radio Club, Concession Club, Library Club, and Office Club. These jobs give students a chance to help out around the school by doing hands-on tasks. This provides experience and also self-esteem. Students are also given the chance to participate in choir and band.

Southern Wells Elementary School

Southern Wells Jr.-Sr. High School

Southern Wells Jr.-Sr. High School opened its doors in the 1966-67 school year to 575 students in grades 7 thru 12. These first students faced a difficult task in leaving behind their feelings of loyalty for their former schools in order to make the new school a success. In 25 years, all but the names and certain memories of the four township schools have been forgotten as the people united behind Southern Wells.

Since 1967 up until 1991, 1,950 students have received their high school diplomas from Southern Wells, giving the school an 87% graduation rate. This is very impressive for a small school like Southern Wells. The high school graduation rate shows how important education is to this community.

Not much has changed in the overall academic requirements for graduation at Southern Wells since it first opened. There has been a gradual increase in the number of credits needed for the high school diploma as Southern Wells became more competitive academically with the surrounding schools. In 1967, a student needed 32 credits covering the subject areas of English, mathematics, social studies, science and other elective courses. In 1979, a student had to earn 36 credits toward his or her diploma. Currently, in 1991, a student must earn 42 credits to graduate. Along with the regular high school diploma, Southern Wells adopted the Academic Honors Diploma in 1989. To earn this diploma a student most earn 47 credits covering a broad area of study, including difficult academic classes. Since the adoption of the Academic Honors Diploma, 11 of these special diplomas have been awarded.

A student at Southern Wells High School

Southern Wells High School

has the opportunity to study a wide range of subjects. Along with the basic requirements of English, social studies, mathematics, science, physical education and health, a student can choose courses that will prepare him or her for any occupation that he or she may desire. There are advanced biology, chemistry and physics for a student who wishes to become a scientist, doctor, or engineer. Since addition of a computer course in the fall of 1983, a student can learn to program and use computers in a society which is increasingly dependent on computers. A student may take business and accounting to prepare for a career in a management or a secretarial position. Psychology and sociology are two courses that will help a student better understand how to deal with people. If a student is interested in foreign cultures, he or she may take a foreign language. Also, Southern Wells offers vocational agribusiness, auto mechanics, industrial arts, health occupations, and home economics for vocational careers. There are other classes that may help mature special talent in the student. These classes involve art, choir, band, speech, and drama. All of these classes, plus a few other elective courses not earlier mentioned, combine to make Southern Wells a strong academic environment.

In addition to academics, a student may wish to join extracurricular activities. There are many clubs, organizations and societies that are available. Future Farmers of America (FFA) and Future Homemakers of American (FHA) are two of the most basic organizations that deal with traditional area of interest in this rural setting. A student who is interested in agriculture or other related agriculture fields could join FFA and get a head start on his career. A student who is interested in caring for the home and making it a better place for the family could join FHA and begin learning now.

A student who is interested in leadership roles may want to run for a class office or membership in Student Council. Sunshine Society is an organization for young women students who like to help others. For students interested in journalism or photography, there is the newspaper staff or the yearbook staff. Foreign language clubs allow students to lean more about foreign cultures than they would in a regular classroom environment. Students who achieve a 3.7 grade point average on a 4.0 weighted scale, and maintain a respectable attitude at and away from school, are eligible for membership in National Honor Society. ICE is a special organization for students who want to work while going to school. Campus Life is a club that brings students together to learn how to be better people. There are still more organizations that include band and choir, athletics and cheerleading.

To teach and advise students in their academic pursuits, and to sponsor their extracurricular activities, the Southern Wells faculty becomes directly involved in their students' lives. The faculty at Southern Wells cares as much for the students as they do about the students' grades. With a low teacher to student ratio, the teachers are able to devote more time to individual students in order to help them better understand the material. Sometimes, being a teacher means lending an ear to a student as much as teaching a class. Southern Wells teachers are dedicated to their students completely. Everyone at Southern Wells works together to ensure the best possible education for everyone.

Students who attend Southern Wells High School receive a well-rounded education. They can take the courses they need in order to obtain the career of their choice. While fulfilling their academic requirements, students enjoy the social scene in the various extracurricular activities. Most graduates of Southern Wells Jr.-Sr. High School can be proud of the education they received in this small town and rural setting.

SOUTHERN WELLS SPORTS

Sports came onto the scene at Southern Wells in 1967, the year the school opened. Basketball was the lone sport in the school's first year of existence. Mr. Tom Rethlake coached the first-ever Southern Wells boys' basketball team.

In 1968, sports really came into the spotlight. Four new sports teams were started for boys. The first Southern Wells baseball team took the field under the direction of Mr. Ross Myers. Mr. Warren Morton coached the track team while Mr. Gene Grogg led the cross country team. Under the guidance of Mr. Rethlake, the golfers hit the course for the first time.

With five sports already available for boys, there was only one sport missing. Then in 1972, the long awaited football program started. The first football team took the playing field under the watchful eye of Mr. Don Kistler.

After already having many sports for boys, the girls finally were able to participate on teams of their own. In 1976, all of the girls sports at Southern Wells were started. Mrs. Wendy Cavan was the coach of the first girls volleyball, basketball and track teams. Gymnastics was coached by Mrs. Myrna Levy.

Although Southern Wells hasn't been known to be a perennial power in sports, they have had their bright spots. The 1973 boys' basketball team won the school's first-ever ACAC tournament championship. Then in 1975 and 1976, the boys were ACAC conference champs. Also winning an ACAC Championship was the 1989 boys' cross country team. The most successful football team at Southern Wells was in 1979, when they were the County Co-Champs.

The only Sectional Championship ever recorded at Southern Wells happened in 1982. The 1982 boys' basketball team, under the direction of Mr. Jim Irwin, recorded the schools lone Sectional trophy. The team finished the season with remarkable 20-4 record.

There also are many sports that Jr. High students can participate in. Jr. High boys can participate in basketball, football, track and cross country. Meanwhile, girls can participate in basketball, track and volleyball.

Freshmen also have a variety of different sports. Boys and girls both can play Varsity sports if they make the team. Otherwise, boys can participate in basketball, football, baseball, track, golf and cross country, while girls have basketball, track and volleyball.

Overall, about half the students at Southern Wells participate in one sport or another.

Student authors of the Southern Wells School history (L to r.) Steve Biberstine, Alyssa Paxson, Staci Walters, and Monica Freel.

The 7th and 8th grades of Tocsin School in 1926-1927. The north room was for the elementary classes and the south room was for the high school class. The teacher at this time was Mr. Jesse Ferguson. (l. to r.) Front row: Lucy Garton Shaw, Isabel Byrd Gilbert, and Pauline Shoe. Seated middle row: Amaline Woodward, the teacher, Mr. Jesse Ferguson, and Dwight Gallivan. Back row: Robert Johnson, Naomi Johnson, Ruth Bright-Robertson, Erwin Franke, and Clayton Minniear. The grade school operated until the spring of 1941. Photo courtesy of Erwin Franke.

Shoemaker School in Harrison District #2. Location was near the fork of State Roads 216 (100S) and 316 at the Oubache State Park area.

Wells County Clubs/ Organizations and Memorial

Youth exhibits could be found in the early 1920's at crop shows sponsored by Farmer's Institutes. Pictured above are some Wells County youth showing off the corn which they grew. This was the beginning of 4-H in Wells County.

Bluffton Girl Scouts

The Girl Scout program began in Bluffton in 1937 under the sponsorship of Tri Kappa Sorority. It was during the presidency of Mrs. Truman (Julia) Caylor that the project began, and the sorority gave $100.00 to start the program. Roger Swaim, owner of the *Evening News-Banner*, encouraged the activity and supplied the sorority the names of 53 business men who might contribute money to get the program underway. A solicitation of the business men was made, and the project started in the spring of that year. The organization of the Girl Scout movement in Bluffton was through the co-operation of the Limberlost Girls Scout executives in Fort Wayne. Many visits were paid to Bluffton to enable the sorority to make the movement a huge success.

A visit to the schools enlisted enough little girls to form five lone troops. Meeting places for the Scouts were at the Bliss Hotel, Knights of Pythias Home and the Methodist Church. The scouts were taken to Lake Webster during the summers and were housed at the Bluffton Methodist cottage there - and also in the hotel, before the fishing season, June 15. A number of people were in charge of activities there: June Hiatt and Jim Murray, the swimming program, Marie Swisher Luce, crafts and Mary Williamson, nature study. A hike to North Webster from the lake cottage was a fun time, as was a ride on the paddle boat, the Dixie. At the lake cottage, each troop was seated at a separate table and girls were encouraged to say grace and participate in evening skits, which kept them busy and also encouraged their earning badges. Many times the sorority would send a school bus to take the Scouts roller skating in Huntington. The niceties of manners and etiquette were stressed and often the girls were taken into homes to be taught how to set a table.

In 1943, through the assistance of high school age students, a Girl Scout Camp - Camp A-Da-Hi, was established in the Harnish Orchards, north of town. There was only one permanent building, which housed the meals and was a center for craft projects. There were primitive facilities only and campfires were a highlight of the week. Tri Kappa husbands contributed labor for setting up the camp. One activity of this Girl Scout troop was a bike hike to Pleasant Lake for a week's outing. Francile Worthman (Mrs. Bob Anderson) was director of the camp assisted by Dot Webber (Mrs. Dick Wilkey). Some of the scouts at this camp were Beverly Buckner, Jo Fritz, Jane and Mary Lou Hamilton and Dottie Louden (Mrs. Joe Moore).

Some of the many workers were Mrs. Ralph (Martha) Santon, Mrs. Jess (Mary Hilma) Scott, Mrs. Gerald (Lois) Johnson, Mrs. E.R. (Grace) McNown, Mrs. Byrl (Dorothy) Masterson, Mrs. Roger (Celia) Swaim, Mrs. William (Dorothy) Gitlin, Mrs. Robert (Marilyn) Pickell, Mrs. George (Norma) Armstrong, Mrs. Rex (Jane) Bangs, Mrs. William (Barbara) Trubey, Mrs. William (Harriett) Thoma, Mrs. George (Martha) Bradley, Helen Lucas, Doris Athey, Mary Williamson, Mrs. Clifton (Ernestine) Baumgartner, Mrs. Mayme Tangeman, Mrs. Laura Thompson, Mrs. Homer (Dorothy) Markley, Mrs. Russell (Helen) Miller), Mrs. Jim (Barbara) Barbieri, Mrs. Herschel (Virginia) Robbins, Mrs. Robert (Martha) Green, Mrs. Morris (Vernice) Coers, Mrs. Roger (Gloria) Nelson, Mrs. Brooks (Joyce) Grandlienard, Mrs. Jack (Jean) Kober, Mrs. H.D. Brickley, Mrs. Lois Kunkel Noll, Mrs. Geo (Louise) Louden, Mrs. Gene (Jane) McCleery, Grace Iddings, Cathryn Monger, Erma Huyette, Mrs. Harold (Chella) Pettyjohn, Mrs. Justus (Mary) Webber, Mrs. Rem (Betty) Johnston, Jr., Mrs. Wm. (Levy) Fair, Mrs. Dianne (Brickley) Balaguras, and many, many, many more we have failed to list. Thanks to all who worked on the program - the Girls Scouts thank you! *Submitted by Catherine "Kate" Rix*

The First Girl Scout Troop in Wells County

The first Girl Scout Troop in Wells County was organized by Grace E. Smith about 1920. Grace was a young, enthusiastic teacher who had given up her job as a teacher in Liberty Center High School to come home and be head of the household after the death of her mother in February of 1919. She had had her college training at Defiance College in Ohio, where the emphasis was upon service to the community. Grace had a little sister twelve years younger than she, whom she loved dearly and for whom she wanted the best of education and the opportunity to have good times and wholesome fun. It so happened that that little sister had several good friends, most of them a part of the Six Mile Christian Church, located three miles south-east of Bluffton. Leaving her teaching job had created a vacant spot for Grace, for she was lively, fun-loving, and had a skill that was crying to be developed - that of working with young people. Finally, she did something about it. She went to her church pastor, the Rev. H.H. Short, and said, "Would you care if I organized a group of girls that would meet at the church and would be either a Campfire Girl or Girl Scout group?"

"Care?", the Rev. Short said, "Go ahead!" And "go ahead" she did. She investigated both the organizations she had in mind and found that the Girls Scouts, the newer organization, was better for the rural community of which these girls were a part. One deciding factor was that the Girl Scouts could start at age 10 years and Campfire girls, at that time needed to be 12 years of age. The wider age range fitted the group of girls better and the projects were better fitted to the interests of the girls.

So Girl Scouts became a reality at Six Mile. The name of this first group was the Oriole Troop and they used the orange and black of the oriole as their colors. The sponsor of the troop was the Six Mile (then Christian) Church. One thing was sure, there was very little money spent, for there just wasn't any available. Those were the pre-depression years when depression had already started in the rural community. Perhaps that was the best thing for the Scouts, for initiative was developed and money meant nothing.

The first girls to become the organization were: Frances Smith, the little sisters, daughter of A.J. and Minnie Walker Smith; Mildred Shoup and Edith Shoup, next door neighbors to the Smiths and daughters of Thomas N. and Rose Biberstine Shoup; Eva Chalfant and Lois Chalfant, daughters of Brent and Ida Captain Chalfant; Ada Steiner, daughter of Albert and Ethel Hauk Steiner; Musetta Short and Martha Ellen Short, daughters of the Rev. and Mrs. H.H. Short; Mildred Markley, daughter of Mr. and Mrs. Lee Markley; Edna Scherry, daughter of Mr. and Mrs John Scherry; Mildred Gifford, daughter of Mr. and Mrs. Thomas Gifford. Others who joined later were: Evelyn Captain, daughter of Lewis and Myrtle Arnold Captain; Catherine Cretor, who lived with the William Biberstine family; Mary Hauk, daughter of George and Fay Chalfant Hauk; Madeline Huffman, daughter of E.L. and Minnie Studabaker Huffman; Ina Kaeher; and Mabel Schwartz, daughter of Mr. and Mrs. David Schwartz.

In the beginning, the Girl Scouts attracted girls for a longer period and these girls were members well into their teen years. Thus, their activities were a little different from those the later Scouts did.

In the summer months nearly all the activities were out-of-doors. Hikes along the Six Mile Creek were common and camping became a favorite sport. The first was just over one night. It was along the Wabash, north west of Bluffton, a beautiful spot near the curve in State Road 116 which turns north to go toward Murray. The only tent the girls had was a large canvas stretched over a rope that was tied to two trees. In the night, it rained and the tent became practically a steambath. One girl thought she was ill because she was perspiring so much but, in the morning, found she was lying half way out of the tent. The girls were not entirely without protection, for Grace's father always accompanied the group on the camping trips. Not only was he protection, he also had a great interest in nature and was able to point out many interesting things to the girls.

After the first year the camps were longer - about a week and usually over a week-end. Those camps were held along the Salamonie River at a nice woods near Bellville Mill and just a short drive from Warren. The woods belong to a Mr. Powell who was very congenial and helped the girls find places to get necessary supplies and straw for the beds. He lived in an old house not far from the woods and often ambled back to see how we were getting along and to chat a while. He lived alone; the house would have been a dream to restore in this day.

Supplies were not much of a problem for the girls took with them ham, eggs, vegetables, butter and sometimes bread. Milk was available at a farm within walking distance. Water was no problem, for a clear stream of spring water flowed from the high bank of the river. At the spring it was cool enough to keep such things as butter and milk. The only problem was, the cooks had to scale the river bank on a tree and root stairway to get to the supplies. On one occasion the butter slipped from one scout's hands and sent rolling down the river bank. The girls took turns on the cooking job and used a stove made from a pice of sheet iron over some stones and an old piece of stove pipe to take care of the smoke. Other girls found wood and used just fallen pieces found in the woods. One rainy morning one girl was stationed with an umbrella over the stove to protect the eggs from too much rain.

It so happened that there was a one-room school house at the corner of Mr. Powell's woods and the outhouse there served as the Scout "rest room".

The tent which was home to the campers was borrowed and was just large enough for all the girls to lie down on their straw tics. A straw tick is a sack long enough for a bed and filled with straw, which was one of the by-products of the old threshing machine. Sometimes one needed to get up and shake the bed in order to remove the hard spots. One thunderstorm remains in the memory of all the troop. It was one of those summer storms with thunder, lightning, wind and lots of it. When the black clouds began rolling in, Grace said, "Shall we go to the school house or stay with the tent?" To a girl, they said, "Stay with the tent!" The girls held on to the poles and were down on their knees holding the tent to the ground. It looked for a while as though the tent, girls and all would go flying through the woods. But, after a while the storm was over. The most beautiful sunset broke through the clouds and the evening went on as usual.

The evenings were never to be forgotten with games and songs around the campfire, always ending with:

*Day is done,
Gone the sun
From the lake,
From the hills,
From the sky.
All is well; safely rest,
God is nigh.*

Although the week in camp was the highlight of the year, there were other activities. The troop formed a girls' choir that not only sang for church but sang for other functions as well. One time they sang for the Eel River Conference at Winona Lake. In that day that was a long way from home and the girls thought that was a big day.

Then there was the time they gave a minstrel show. Although some of it was done in black-face comedy, no one felt anything against black people. In fact, there was lots of emphasis on understanding all people. One project was to send a box of American dolls to children of Japan. Grace had a good friend, Lela Nordyke, who was a missionary in China and she often shared bits of letters and pictures with the girls.

The regular meetings of the troop were held in good parliamentary form, with the patrol leader conducting the meetings in keeping with strict rules. Each meeting had a business meeting and also a fun time. Sometimes there were pot-luck meals and queer things happened. There was the time everyone brought sandwiches, and who could forget the pie with no way to cut it? Someone suggested the axe (no one remembers why we had that) and so the Oriole troop became the first to cut a pie with the axe.

The Oriole Troop had an interest in smaller children and the sister of Ada Steiner was a sort of mascot for the group. There was also an animal that took part in some meetings. Shortie was a dachshund dog belonging to the Shoup family and it was practically impossible to go anywhere without Shortie, for he was truest of true friends to Edith. On one hike Shortie strayed long enough to find a skunk and was very unwelcome when he returned to his mistress. One year he went to camp and somehow found the ham we had brought; when he was discovered, he had an almost clean bone in his mouth. In spite of his inconvenience, the girls loved him and even made him a little uniform.

Those days were never to be forgotten by the girls of Oriole Troop. A big thank you is in their hearts to those who were so caring and willing to add to the happiness of a bunch of giggly girls.

May scouting last a long, long time!
Submitted by Frances Smith

LIBERTY CENTER GIRL SCOUTS

In the fall of 1964, the Liberty Center Girl Scouts were organized by Mrs. Paul (Nancy) Bonham and Mrs. Ivan (Katie) Beeks as members of the Limberlost Girl Scout Organization. They were assisted in organizing by Mrs. Dee Steffen, Mrs. Deeda Skiles, and Mrs. Beth Lampton. Approximately 60 girls joined in three full troops, Brownies, Juniors and Cadets. Some of the leaders who assisted over the years until 1973 were Mrs. Patti Penrod, Mrs. Shirley Sullivan, Mrs. Shirley Harshman, Mrs. Sue Clark, Mrs. Ross Myers, Mrs. Janet Schmidt, Mrs. Melba Cole, Mrs. Marilyn Meade, Mrs. Joan Elliott, Mrs. Ruth Stroud, and Mrs. B.J. Gray. Many others were also very important and helpful to the new troops.

The girls learned and practiced many camping skills, participated in Fine Arts and community projects, and learned caring and sharing for others. The Liberty Center Girl Scout Troops continued to flourish until 1973 when the Liberty Center School closed. Scouting continued on as the Southern Wells Girl Scouts.

SOUTH END BOYS' CLUB

In the fall of 1941 a group of 14 boys met in Washington Park and decided to start a boys club for the boys in the south end of Bluffton. It was to be ruled and governed by the boys and had its purpose to build better boys. Some of the things they stood for, as taken from their minutes, were (1) Discontinue smoking entirely. (2) Refusing of alcoholic beverages at all times. (3) Discontinue gambling entirely. (4) Be more attentive at church. (5) Be of more use to your family and community than you formerly were. (6) Show more interest towards this club.

That they enforced these rules is evident by the following notes. Claire Redding-excessive noise, found guilty and was suspended from the club over the week-end. Elmo Rieddle-profane language, found guilty and fined $.10 which he paid in full.

They sent the following letter to 157 men in Bluffton and received 50 cents from 85 of them for a one year membership.

"Past and Future of the South End Boys' Club

To associate you with the South End Boys' Club here are a few paragraphs telling action taken and planned by the boys' club.

The club was started so that boys might meet and spend their leisure hours away from home in a good warm place. It was to be more than just a meeting place—it has to be a place where eventually boys will become better boys.

They chose to set up a constitution and govern themselves. The first meeting was held in September 1941. The following were elected. Doc Miller, president, Chuck Ault, vice-president, Bill Stout, secretary, Russell Palmer, treasurer and Bill Sawyer, judge. A vacated house was obtained from Mr. J.A. McBride on 509 E. Townley Street for our club house. He gave us free rent and furnished us with a stove to heat the club.

Last Christmas the Rotary Club presented the South End Boys' Club with a fine radio. This gift was greatly appreciated, and if you should happen to belong to the Rotary Club, thanks again for your consideration.

For the future we plan an extensive recreation program consisting of softball and volleyball teams, enlargement of our club quarters, as our membership is growing. However, at present we haven't funds to carry out these plans.

This club is just like a stone at the top of a hill, once it gets started it will keep on rolling. Won't you give this club a shove by joining the South End Boys' Club? You won't be sorry, I am sure. Thanks again for everything."

Records show that 25 boys eventually belonged, but the life of the club was short because records show that just about every boy served in the Army, Navy, or Marines in World War II.

Bluffton Fire Department at the City Hall and Engine House on the northeast corner of Washington and Johnson Streeets now the location of the Wells County Republican Party.

The Minne Tonka Tribe No. 82 of the Red Men who had headquarters in Bluffton. This photo of the group in costume was taken at the 1908 Bluffton Street Fair as they participated in a parade. Location is Market Street in front of the Courthouse plaza looking west. Market Street was still brick at that time.

1949 Gamma Zeta members present organ keys to Ossian High School principal, Harry Andes and music teacher, Dorothy West. Presenting the keys are (l. to r.): Faye Hunter, Florence Yager, Principal Andes, Dorothy West, Vada Wilbaum.

Uniondale Knights of Pythias Lodge. Photo courtesy Mr. & Mrs. George Schwartz.

Bluffton Lions Club

On November 5, 1947, 150 Lions and their wives attended the Bluffton Lions charter night banquet at the Parlor City Country Club. Many attending in addition to the 23 charter members, were representing the sponsoring Fort Wayne Central Lions Club.

Local people, wishing the club success, were Mr. and Mrs. Fred Park representing Kiwanis, Mr. and Mrs. L.E. Templin from Rotary, and Mr. and Mrs. Homer Markley from the Chamber of Commerce. Glen O. Marsh, on behalf of the Country Club, gave the Lions a $25 gift.

Three of the 23 charter members are still active in our club today: William Fair, Paul Bender, and William Fryback. Other charter members were: Cloyd Farling, Jr., Wayne Bishop, James Murray, Lewis Captain, Luzerne Fishbaugh, Robert Mettler, Charles Baker, Hershel Baird, Max Coons, Charles Decker, Jr., Harold Fryhover, Joe Fudge, Ralph Higman, Wendell Larmore, Dennis Moser, Father A.N. Philips, Robert Spake, Walter Speheger, and Martin Tonner.

From that organizational banquet on, the Bluffton Lions Club has left its mark on the community with a host of projects, raising funds for the many worthwhile programs of Lionism. The Leader Dog program for the blind, the Lions Eye Bank, Cancer Control, Diabetes, and the Lions Club International Fund are all state and national programs supported by the club. In addition to these programs serving our area, other local projects include eye glasses and vision tests for the needy, hearing tests, and providing Leader Dogs for the blind.

Community betterment projects have been extensive. The first project in 1947 filled the need at the library for a special projector to aid bedfast patients in reading books. In 1950, a Lions newsstand was built on the courthouse plaza and run by the late Harold Nash, who was blind. In 1959, Lions mailed thousands of survey letters to Wells County senior citizens which resulted in the formation of today's Senior Citizen center.

Lions project funds helped establish Lion's Park on West Washington Street, and the park continues to receive the club's support annually. Each year, funds raised go back to the community to help make Bluffton a better place to live. For many years, a Cub Scout pack was sponsored, and currently a Boy Scout troop is supported for handicapped children at Poplar Grove School.

To raise money, we have sold sno-cones, cotton candy, brooms, light bulbs, oranges and grapefruit. Money raising events have included auctions and raffles and food and for many years the little red barn given away to the lucky ticket holder, was an annual street fair event. Once a Dale Carnegie course was sponsored to help our friends and neighbors develop more self confidence, improve memories, and improve the ability to deal with people (at least that's what the ad said.)

All of our fund raising ideas weren't resounding successes. Coloring books didn't sell too well, and a popping corn sale didn't go as expected. There was a little demand for an auto dimmer switch either. Culturally we sponsored "Rubinhoff and His Violin" for a well-attended concert at the community building. Evidently the Lion manning the spotlight didn't perform to Rubinoff's expectations. He kept screaming "keep the spot on ME." We don't know how disturbed he was, but when he walked off the stage he was never seen in Bluffton again. The Tommy Davis dance revues of the 50's and 60's with the local teacher and students were popular money makers for us. But Rookie Brown and the Satellites (basketball) was a financial bomb.

Around 1950 a donkey basketball game between the Lions and an all-star aggregation headed by Amos Gerber and Dwight Gallivan made money. With the Indiana popularity of basketball, we played against the Redheads, an all-girl team, held annual orange/grapefruit sales, and now, after 44 years, we've become the "Apple Dumplin' Gang" selling apple dumplings in the merchant's tent at the Bluffton Free Street Fair each year.

We're now committed to cleaning up litter along State Road 316, between Bluffton and the White Bridge, selling Lions Mints and Lions Candy, and trash bags. And for the most of those 44 years, our gum ball machines have been silently waiting for pennys all over town. This is all in the interest of our community while having a good time.

The good times are many, especially like the meeting night (always Tuesday evening at the Dutch Mill, except for the first year at the old Bliss Hotel), when Lion Dick Geist was scheduled to give a program about his World War II days as a diplomatic courier. Three or four of his fellow Lions, intending to play a joke on the rest of us, "spirited" him away with promise of dinner and refreshment in Fort Wayne, leaving us waiting at the Dutch Mill without a program. That was the infamous "Geist Heist" well documented in the news. A later kangaroo court severely punished the offenders. Justice will be done.

Our Lion Bill Trubey has honored our club by serving Lions International as a District Governor. Through his optometry profession he has led our club and others in providing help to distressed areas in Mexico and other Central American countries. Used eye glasses and fitting have been provided for their needy, along with donated ambulances, buses, trucks, medical supplies and other necessities.

It's been a great 44 years, with a terrific bunch of Lions. The names change as the years go by, but the enthusiasm, good fellowship and fun, and desire to be worthwhile servants to our community goes on and on and on.

1991 Members: (l. to r.) First Row- Jim Fritz, President, Paul Bender, Adrian Sprunger, Roy Johnson, Dan Weldy, Gene Edington, Deno Panos, Alan Daugherty, Tom Byanski, Terry Troxel, Bill Trubey. Second & Back Row- Bill Rhodes, Mike Myers, Tom Jackson, Larry Henkle, James Wyatt- Cabinet Secretary, Steve Skiles, Donald Sutton- Cabinet Treasurer, Gerald Kennerk- District Governor, Joe Moore, Bud Watters, Ann Platt, Tom Brenner, Ward Kowalke, Clyde Gray, Bill Fryback, Charles Weterick, Dick Wilkey, John Smith, Bob Deihl, Jeff Hewitt, Joe Smekens. Not present for picture- Reggie Bardo, Jack Barnes, Bob Bennett, Marty Braaksma, Ned Carnall, Maurice Dionne, Ned Emshwiller, Bill Fair, Steve Fischer, Jim Foster, Bob Greiner, Jody Holloway, Jerry Kizer, Tom Lockwood, Dick Mynatt, Ralph Nowak, Richard R. Reed, Dan Steiner.

PAST PRESIDENTS OF BLUFFTON LIONS

Year	Name	Year	Name	Year	Name
1947	Cloyd Farling, Jr.	1963	Ralph Nowak	1978	Dave Park
1948	Ralph Higman	1963	Ken Marks	1979	Robert Weidtholter
1949	Herschel Baird	1964	Earl (Bud) Watters	1980	Tom Jackson
1950	Charles Decker, Jr.	1965	Dan Steiner	1981	John Whicker
1951	Richard Swisher	1966	Ned Carnall	1982	Larry Henkle
1952	William Fryback	1967	Robert Bennett	1983	Milo Eiche
1953	Joe Moore	1968	Charles Kern	1984	Tom Byanski
1954	Paul Bender	1969	Adrian Sprunger	1985	Ward Kowalke
1955	Paul Neuhauser	1970	Doral Smith	1986	Randy Danielson
1956	James Murray	1971	Irv Harman	1987	Roy Johnson
1957	Dennis Moser	1972	Jack Collins	1988	Tom Lockwood
1958	Lewis Captain	1973	Bob Cooper	1989	Terry Troxel
1959	Carroll Schroeder	1974	Dick Mynatt	1990	Jim Fritz
1960	William Trubey	1975	James Colen	1991	Deno Panos
1961	Charles Boonstra	1976	Gail Allread		
1962	John Edris, Jr.	1977	Jeff Hewitt		

Wells County 4-H

Four-H in the United States first began in 1899, when Liberty Hyde Bailey of Cornell University started a junior naturalist program in New York State.

In 1900, W.B. Otwell, of the Illinois Farmers Institute, furnished seed corn to 500 boys who grew the corn for exhibits.

The idea of 4-H continued to spread as a county school superintendent, A.B. Graham, in Ohio, organized a boys and girls experiment club in 1902.

Indiana 4-H got its start from John Haines, Hamilton County School superintendent, with 93 boys in a junior corn club in 1904.

In 1914, the United States Congress passed the Smith-Lever Act which created the Cooperative Extension Service and allowed many counties to hire a county agent.

On August 1, 1914, Harry Gray began his work as county agent in Wells County. Later in 1914, the first state corn show was held with 60 entries. Mr. Gray continued to serve until July 31, 1918.

Mr. Gray, along with other county agents quickly learned that one way to persuade families to adopt new farming and homemaking practices was through introducing the innovative ideas to youth.

In Wells County, the Tocsin Farmers Institute began conducting youth exhibits with their annual crop show in the early 1920s. The Wells County 4-H program began to take shape with the arrival of county agent Earl C. Salisbury, who replaced Harry Gray. Mr. Salisbury served the county August 16, 1918 - August 15, 1923.

Four-H sewing clubs were organized in 1923 in Rockcreek and Lancaster Townships. The members worked under the guidance of their leaders Winifred Falk Thompson and Martha Salisbury.

Mrs. Ethel Edris became the first county 4-H Club leader when she helped to organize 4-H throughout the county. During the 1923 Street Fair, the first 4-H Club exhibit was held in the building at 115 South Johnson Street.

R.M. Roop arrived as county agent and worked in Wells County from October 1, 1923, to September 30, 1925. M.S. Smith, who served many years as county agent, arrived January 15, 1926, and remained until March 1, 1952.

The grounds around the Markle Dam served as the site of 4-H Camp in the late 1920s. Each camper was a member of an Indian tribe and participated in various tribe activities, classes, hikes, along with swimming in the Wabash River.

Four-H Club work continued to grow in the 1930s and 1940s due to the efforts of the 4-H leaders in each township. Many fine 4-H projects were exhibited at the Street Fair during this time.

The Wells County 4-H Association had its beginning on May 26, 1950, when a group of parents met with the 4-H leaders and decided to organize for the purpose of encouraging and supporting 4-H activities.

A set of by-laws, provided and recommended by Purdue University for such groups, was adopted and the association was later incorporated by the State of Indiana.

The immediate project of the association was to meet the need for a summer 4-H exhibit and judging which would then allow Wells County youth to participate in the State Fair. Thus in 1950, with tremendous increase in parent cooperation, a three day August fair was held at Fairland Park, along the Wabash River near the Dutch Mill Restaurant.

The fair was a success and strongly indicated the need for a permanent 4-H fair site and community center. The interest in such a site continued to grow and became so great that in October, 1950, the finance committee consisting of John Eichhorn, Harry Couch, W.R. Maddox and Vaughn Lipp was instructed to investigate the possibility of buying suitable land for this purpose.

On November 13, 1950, the 4-H Association voted unanimously to buy a tract of approximately 50 acres from Ware Baker for $29,970. This land was located on the south edge of Bluffton on State Road 1.

The site was chosen because of its convenient location in relation to the shopping and business area of Bluffton, availability of utilities, drainage, and general layout.

Numerous hours were spent by many volunteers in order to clear land and construct buildings at the 4-H park. Lumber cut from the trees was used to build the concession stand and the cattle barn.

The first fair at the new location was held August 14-16, 1951. Livestock was housed in tents, and home economics projects were displayed in a building adjacent to the park. A new concession building was operated by the Home Demonstration Clubs.

In 1953 a quonset style exhibit building was built. Several years later an upstairs was added in the front section along with concrete flooring in the back section. A heating system was also added which allowed the facility to be used throughout the year.

Wells County Rural Youth assisted with the construction of a concession stand used by their organization during the 4-H Fair. Later this building would be known as the 4-H Junior Leader Building.

A swine and sheep barn was built in 1959 and the addition of a show arena that same year connected the new barn to the cattle.

In 1962 another building was constructed to accommodate 4-H Fair exhibits and displays. The building was also utilized during the winter for boat and camper rental storage.

The caretakers house was built in 1963 and a new steel building was constructed in 1968 to replace the original concession stand. The Extension Homemakers Clubs operated the stand until the mid-1980s.

In 1969, the 4-H Association granted a ninety-nine year lease to the Bluffton Department of Parks and Recreation for the sum of one dollar to allow the construction of the Wells Community Pool. The three acre tract was located in the northwest corner of the 4-H Park.

The concrete bleachers were constructed in 1975 and have been used for a wide variety of events at the 4-H Park including the 1976 United States Bicentennial celebration and the 1989 Wells County Sesquicentennial celebration.

Through the years the 4-H Association had developed the park into an outstanding facility that is used not only by 4-H, but the entire community for many different events.

Today's 4-H Park has twelve building located on its nearly 40 acres and plans are in the development stages for a new multi-purpose building.

The major fund-raiser through the years for 4-H has been a pancake and sausage booth at the Bluffton Street Fair.

Dell Shaw and other volunteers on the 4-H Association decided upon the pancake and sausage menu since it could be served from early morning until evening at the Street Fair.

1989 marked the 40th year of the 4-H Pancake and Sausage Booth at the Street Fair.

The 4-H program in Wells county still remains the largest out-of school youth organization. Many new projects and activities have been added through the years that help to teach youth citizenship, leadership, responsibility and life skills.

1990 Wells County 4-H Fair Royalty. (l. to r.): Julie Baker-Princess, Jeremy Mounsey-Prince, Kevin Couch-King and Patty Girod-Queen.
Bottom Photo is the 1981 Wells County delegates to the State 4-H Junior Leader Conference. (l. to r.) Front row: Tami Decker, Shelley Price, and Jill Engle. Back row: Mike Witte, Mike Miller, Tim Stepp and David Lewandowski.

This is a listing if men and women who hav eserved as Extension Agents (either agriculture, home economics or youth) in Wells Coounty.

In the beginning these agents were know as "county agents" or "home ec agents".

In later years, assistant county agentswere employed to assist with the work load and to help with the youth programs. In the 1960's, youth agents evolved to work more closely with youth and volunteer leaders.

Harry Gray	1914-1918
Easrl C. Salisbury	1918-1923
R. M. Roop	1923-1925
Merrill S. Smith	1926-1952
Donald E. Frantz	1952-1958
Gertrude Glasgow	1953-1978
Hugh Reinhold	1958-1964
Eugene Eckrote	1963-1966
Paul Wharton	1964-1968
Hervey M. Kellogg	1965-1974
Merrill Jacks	1966-1969
Paul F. Houghes	1968-1972
Rex D. Jarrett	1970-1978
Marie Y. Kyle	1974-1974
David Lawrence	1974-1978
Phillip G. Stryker	1978-1980
Cynthnia K. Meeks	1979-1980
Roger A. Sherer	1979-
Paula Hook	1980-1989
Donald B. Kelso	1981-1987
G. John Caravetta	1988-1989
William Horan	1989-
Rebecca Haynes	1990

American Legion

Scarcely seven months after a thousand officers and enlisted men of the American Expeditionary Force, which had fought in Europe during World War I, had organized in Paris, France, on March 15-17, 1919, the American Legion, a post was formed in Bluffton, Indiana, and designated Grover Sheets Post 111.

Organization of the veterans of Wells County, who served during the World War I conflict, began in the fall of 1919 when a committee was formed, headed by Hoyt Hartman. The main topic of discussion at the time was whether to affiliate with the newly-formed American Legion, which had been formally recognized in a national meeting held May 8-10 in St. Louis, Missouri.

In Bluffton, on September 23, 1919, Dr. Fred Metts was made temporary president of the post organization. At a second meeting on September 30, the group voted to affiliate with the American Legion, and to name the post after the first Wells County serviceman killed in action in the war; hence the name Grover Sheets Post.

Dr. Metts was elected permanent chairman (commander); Earl "Tuck" Sawyer, secretary (adjutant), and James W. Stogdill, treasurer (finance officer).

Eligibility service dates for membership were established for any soldier, sailor, or Marine who served honorably between April 6, 1917 and November 11, 1918.

Adopted as the preamble to the Legion's constitution were the words: "For God and Country, we associate ourselves together for the following purposes: To uphold and defend the Constitution of the United States of America; to maintain law and order; to foster and perpetuate a 100 percent Americanism; to preserve the memories and incidents of our association in the Great War; to inculcate a sense of individual obligation to the community, state, and nation; to make right the master over might; to promote peace and good will on earth; to safeguard and transmit to posterity the principles of justice, freedom, and democracy; to consecrate and sanctify our comradeship by our devotion to mutual helpfulness".

Members of the post met twice monthly in the court room of the Wells County Courthouse in Bluffton from 1919 until 1922, when quarters were secured on the third floor of a building in the 100 block of West Market Street. A year later, the post headquarters were moved into the second floor of a building in the 200 block of West Market Street.

While the dream of a permanent headquarters or post always had been in the minds of those members of American Legion Post 111, it was not until 1943 that definite plans began to develop. It was five years that plans began to take form.

Thus, on July 23, 1949, a dedication program was staged, formally opening the permanent and present site at 111 West Washington Street. The total cost of erecting the building and equipping the facilities was $83,000.

The membership of American Legion Post 111 had reached a high of nearly 600 veterans by that date.

Already the Legion ranks were being supplemented by returning veterans of World War II of 1941 to 1946.

Within the next decade others were to join the American Legion, veterans of the Korean War period of 1950 to 1955; and another decade later, from a conflict in Vietnam that lasted over 10 years, came veterans of the Southeast Asia era which dated from 1961 to 1975. Other eligibility dates came as a result of confrontations in Beirut and in Grenada from August 24, 1982 to July 31, 1984, and in Panama from December 20, 1989 to January 31, 1990. In 1990-91, the United States participated in the United Nations Persian Gulf operations, Desert Shield and Desert Storm, would add more veterans.

Membership eligibility dates in the American Legion correspond to the times of those armed conflicts.

The American Legion Post membership today stands at a little more than 1,000. Its peak membership was a little over 1,300 a few years ago.

There are today only seven surviving Legion members of the World War I era of 1917-18.

For its own national organization, from the Bluffton post have come three Indiana state commanders. The first was Fred L. Wiecking in 1929-30. Others have been Robert M. Fritz in 1961-62 and James R. Zoll in 1971-72.

Commanders of Bluffton's Grover Sheets Post 111, American Legion, have been since its organization the following: 1919-Dr. Fred A. Metts; 1920-Hoyt Hartman; 1921-C.O. Rider; 1922-Earl Sawyer; 1923-Oris Huffman; 1924-Homer Marshall; 1925-Mearl High; 1926-Gerald Moon; 1927-Noah Miller; 1928-Ralph Davis; 1929-Noah Miller; 1930-Lee Wahman.

1931-Franklin Buckner; 1932-Jesse Dyson; 1933-F.D. Burchard; 1934-C.M. Lutz; 1935-Elmore Sturgis; 1936-Fleming French; 1937-Loren Poff; 1938-Omar Yarger; 1939-Clark Shumm; 1940-Raymond Haflich.

1941-Fred Huffman; 1942-Fred Groh; 1943-Harry K. Brown; 1944-William McBride; 1945-Harry B. Gavin; 1946-John W. Linn; 1947-Mervin S. Smith; 1948-Henry Troutman; 1949-Richard Huffman and Dale Decker; 1950-Donald Hammond.

1951-Ralph Higman; 1952-Joe H. Elzey; 1953-Robert M. Fritz; 1954-Richard S. Neff; 1955-Homer Baker; 1956-Arthur Scharlach and William H. Booher; 1957-James R. Zoll; 1958-Riley D. Kay; 1959-Linn E. Gregg; 1960-George Magley.

1961-Roy (Jake) Ehler; 1962-J.A. (Bill) Stipp; 1963-Harold Pett; 1964-Leon (Twig) Lindsey; 1965-Joe M. Jacobs; 1966-William G. Fritz; 1967-Paul R. Gagle; 1968-Jerry Leimgruber; 1969-Edwin H. Walter; 1970-Ralph (Barney) Pond.

1971-Robert Heckman; 1972-John H. Schwartz; 1973-Victor E. Gallivan; 1974-D.W. (Jim) Jeffries; 1975-Robert E. Mettler; 1976-Verlin Kauffman; 1977-Christopher R. Lewis; 1978-1979-James D. Dedrick; 1980-Sam E. Aeschliman.

1981-John P. Stroup; 1982-Harold L. Betz, Jr.; 1983-Thomas D. Stout; 1984-Richard Lockwood; 1985-James Berger; 1986-Craig Mann; 1987-Frank Lowe; 1988- John Herndon; 1989-Richard Lockwood; 1990-Paul Kautz.

Bluffton Rotary Club

In May of 1919, George L. Arnold and Will B. Gutelius arranged for a meeting of a few business and professional men to discuss the formation of a Bluffton Rotary Club. On June 6, 1919, a banquet was held at the Bliss Hotel officially beginning the Bluffton Rotary Club. The 25 charter members were joined by Rotarians from Fort Wayne, Muncie, Decatur, Huntington, and Marion to celebrate the formation of Bluffton's newest Service Club with its motto of "Service above Self." The Gaiety orchestra, and vocal solos by George Panos and Carl Shinkle, provided entertainment during the Charter meeting.

The charter members included:

J.R. Spivey, Will W. Weisell, Ralph S. Todd, Will B. Gutelius, Will R. Barr, W.A. Kunkel, Dr. Charles E. Caylor, Abram Simmons, George L. Arnold, Dr. Charles J. Blackman, C.A. Breece, George S. Morris, George L. Saunders, W.A. Patton, Lew W. Dailey, David Meyer, Fred J. Longden, Will H. Berling, John O. Cottingham, Alfred G. Saurer, Dr. Louis Severin, Earl R. McFarren, J. Edwin Reynolds, John W. Carnall and Homer R. Gettle.

W.A. Patton served as the club's first president. A long list of community leaders and business men have served the club as president over the past 72 years.

The Bluffton Rotary Club is a member of District 654 consisting of clubs in 60 cities located in the northern portion of Indiana. Bluffton Rotary has had three members serve as District Governor. The club's fourth president, W. R. Barr, was Governor of District 654, in 1926. Glen O'Laverty served in 1953, and Dr. Truman Caylor in 1965.

Over the years, the Bluffton Rotary Club has been active in a number of outstanding programs and projects, locally and internationally. To name a few, the Bluffton Rotary Club was instrumental in assisting and raising funds to build the Rotary wing for crippled children at the James Whitcomb Riley Hospital in Indianapolis; the Club has provided financial assistance for, among others, the Boy Scouts, scholarships for local youths, and educational meetings for students. More recently, the Club participated with other Rotary Clubs from around the world to raise 240 million dollars in order to eliminate polio throughout the world by the year 2000.

On October 16, 1990, the Bluffton Rotary Club dedicated the Ray Renollet Rotary Park as part of the River Greenway project. The Rotary Club is proud to provide this asset to the community as part of Bluffton's continued revitalization.

The Club's officers for 1991-92 includes Phil Swain as President, Ed Norris as President-elect, David Barth as vice-president, Don Skinner as secretary, William Cline as treasurer, and Dean Milligan as past President. Directors are Keith Huffman, John Stead, Dianne Witwer, Tess Dillman and Bruce Miller.

Bluffton Rotary Past Presidents

W.A. Patton	1919-20	Donald E. Frantz	1955-56
W.A. Kunkel, Sr.	1920-21	Corvin Briner	1956-57
George Saunders	1921-22	Truman Caylor	1957-58
William R. Barr	1922-23	Earl Dillon	1958-59
James R. Spivey	1923-24	Douglas N. Beaty	1959-60
Charles G. Dailey	1924-25	Don Harris	1960-61
Whorton Rogers	1925-26	Robert Cline	1961-62
W.A. Kunkel, Jr.	1925-26	James E. Smith	1962-63
Ralph S. Todd	1926-27	John R. Theime	1963-64
George Saunders	1926-27	Bruce Kephart	1964-65
Howard Ullman	1927-28	Howard Rich	1965-66
Louis Severin	1928-29	John L. Metz	1966-67
David Meyer	1929-30	Harry Walko	1967-68
Abraham Simmons	1930-31	Ronald Adams	1968-69
Frank Thompson	1931-32	Richard N. Matzen	1969-70
Paul J. Ritt	1932-33	John Seagrave	1970-71
J.L. Goodin	1933-34	Doyle Stern	1971-72
J.E. Reynolds	1934-35	Loren Lobsiger	1972-73
Max Markley	1935-36	Everett (Bill) Goshorn	1973-74
Walter Heller	1936-37	C. Lloyd Griffis	1974-75
Morris McCray	1937-38	Stanley Rigby	1975-76
John W. Carnall	1938-39	Richard Hartigan	1976-77
Ray Brown	1939-40	William F. Brockmann	1977-78
Delma Lockwood	1940-41	David L. Hanselman	1978-79
Fred Arend	1941-42	James D. Jackson	1979-80
W.A. Patton	1942-43	Don Skinner	1980-81
H. Brooks Smith	1943-44	Norm Kain	1981-82
Ray Renollet	1944-45	Timothy N. Mock	1982-83
Ward Huffman	1945-46	James C. Almdale	1983-84
Francis McFarren	1946-47	Gary D. Shaw	1984-85
Lawrence Williamson	1948-49	Harry L. White	1985-86
Deane Reynolds	1949-50	Jerry A. Reynolds	1986-87
Glen O'Laverty	1950-51	Gary L. Boone	1987-88
W.C. Ratliff	1951-52	Keith P. Huffman	1988-89
John T. Flaningam	1952-53	Bruce Miller	1989-90
William L. Cline	1953-54	Dean E. Milligan	1990-91
Gerald Heller	1954-55		

Creative Arts Council of Wells County

In the autumn of 1973, a group of individuals believed that there was a need for an organization to promote and sponsor cultural and educational activities of an artistic nature in Wells County. With funding through the Indiana Arts Commission, the Eli Lilly Endowment, and the financial contributions and efforts of one hundred and nineteen persons, the Creative Arts Council of Wells County was incorporated in 1974.

Since its inception, the Arts Council has become a viable part of the Bluffton-Wells County community. Funds and contribution annually from hundreds of individuals and businesses enables the Creative Arts Council to provide matching funds to all the county schools for special programs, as well as presenting concerts, lectures, exhibits, classes in art, crafts, ballroom dance and ballet, professional and community theater productions. The Arts Council sponsored a DAY IN THE PARK in 1980 and 1982, which featured local artists and their works, along with performances by the Cincinnati and Indianapolis symphonies. The Arts Council also sponsored PRETZEL FEST, arts and crafts festivals, in 1986, 1987 and 1988, which highlighted the present and historic Bluffton pretzel industry with crafts, cooking and literary contests, in addition to presenting artist and entertainment on the courthouse plaza.

Funding from the Indiana Arts Commission has provided Wells County with over $100,000 in grants since 1975. These funds have been used to promote arts in the community and encourage area artists.

The Creative Arts Council has occupied the former Dr. Clarence H. Mead home on West Washington Street since 1975, through a cooperative lease with the Bluffton-Wells County Public Library. This facility has provided a central location for the administration of the Arts Council, its gallery exhibits, classes, the annual Holiday Boutique, and meeting space for various community support groups such as Widow to Widow, the Writers and Hoosier Leather Guilds.

Former home & office of Dr. C.H. Mead on West Washington. Creative Arts Center 1975-1991

Right to left- Kelly Kober, representing Tri Kappa, presents gift of "Hannah's Place" water color painting by Harry Lindstrand to Marilynn Schwartz, Director for Creative Arts Council permanent collection 1984

Founders of the Creative Arts Council

Mr. & Mrs. Howard Almdale
Dr. & Mrs. L. Farrell Mock
Mr. & Mrs. Ware Baker
Mr. & Mrs. William Moser
Rev. & Mrs. F. Kaye Bass
Mr. & Mrs. Gene Moser
Dr. & Mrs. Louis Bradley
Dr. & Mrs. Jeno B. Mudrony
Beverly Buckner
Mrs. Patricia C. Niblick
Mr. & Mrs. Ned Carnall
Dr. & Mrs. Robert Nichols
Dr. & Mrs. Charles Caylor
Mr. & Mrs. Robert P. Nixon
Dr. & Mrs. Harold Caylor
Mr. & Mrs. Glen O'Laverty
Dr. & Mrs. Truman Caylor
Dr. & Mrs. Constantine Panos
Mrs. Lois S. Cline
Dr. & Mrs. David G. Pietz
Mr. & Mrs. Robert A. Cline
Dr. & Mrs. Neal C. Pitts
Dr. & Mrs. Jack T. Collins
Dr. & Mrs. B.K. Poindexter

Mr. & Mrs. John H. Edris, Jr.
Dr. & Mrs. Lawrence Purcell
Honor. Judge & Mrs. Eichhorn
Mr. & Mrs. Howard D. Rich
Dr. & Mrs. Jack L. Eisaman
Mr. & Mrs. R.N. Fitz Patrick
Mr. & Mrs. George Rittenhouse
Mayor & Mrs. William Fryback
Mr. & Mrs. E.J. Schaefer
Dr. & Mrs. Jess Scott
Mr. Victor E. Gallivan
Mr. & Mrs. Donald Rosie
Mr. & Mrs. William Garvey
Dr. & Mrs. Glenn Shaw
Mr. & Mrs. Kermit George
Mrs. Edith Shoemaker
Dr. & Mrs. William Gitlin
Mr. & Mrs. Robert Skiles
Dr. & Mrs. Russell E. Graf
Dr. & Mrs. Charles Smith
Mr. & Mrs. Kenneth Honegger
Mr. & Mrs. Clinton Sowards, Jr.
Mr. & Mrs. James S. Jackson
Dr. & Mrs. Dwight Stauffer

Dr. & Mrs. S. Bruce Kephart
Mr. & Mrs. August Streater
Mr. & Mrs. Kenneth Lampton
Dr. & Mrs. Don A. Strehler
Dr. & Mrs. Herbert Lohmuller
Dr. & Mrs. Pierre Talbert
Dr. & Mrs. Richard N. Matzen
Mr. & Mrs. Frederick Tangeman
Dr. & Mrs. Peter P. Mayock
Dr. & Mrs. James VanWinkle
Mr. & Mrs. Donald McArdle
Mr. & Mrs. John H. Waid
Dr. & Mrs. George W. Merkle
Dr. & Mrs. Alberto Waksman

Directors Of The Creative Arts Council

1976-79 Steven J. Neuenschwander
1979-80 Jayne Staley
1980-82 Mr. & Mrs. Walter Johnson
1983 Stepehen Smith
1983 Marilynn F. Schwartz

Crescent Chapter #48 Order Eastern Star

One hundred and ten years of Crescent Chapter Order of the Eastern Star began, dating from February 16, 1881. Twenty petitioners met at the residence of J.W. Tribolet for the purpose of making arrangements for the organization of a chapter of the Order of the Eastern Star. One a motion by Mary J. Todd, the name "Crescent" was adopted as the name of the chapter.

On March 22, 1881, a meeting for organization was held with the following present: J.J. Todd, Mary E. Mason, Lucy Karns, T.L. Wisner, Sarah Studabaker, Jacob Tribolet, Maggie McCleery, E.Y. Sturgis, Eliza A. Cook, W.S. Kapp, Mary Tribolet, Georgia A. Karns, Mary J. Todd, Mattie E. Gardiner, Addie B. Davenport, Delia W. Hale, Mattie North, Maggie Wisner, T.D. Wisner, Margaret A. Tribolet, Kate Kapp, J.W. Tribolet, Peter Studabaker, D.E. Bulger, Matilda Sturgis, H.L. Wisner, Samuel M. Karns, L.C. Davenport, W.D. Mason, G.T. Kocher, John North, J.P. Hale and Flo K. Kocher.

Crescent Chapter number 48 as duly constituted by T.L. Wisner, Special Duty Grand Patron of the State of Indiana on May 2, 1881. One of the by-laws stated: "meetings of the Chapter to be held on Monday after the full moon of each month; annual election of officers to be held on the stated communication preceding the festival of St. John the evangelist." Crescent Chapter was honored by a visit for the first time by a Worthy Grand Matron Nettie Ransford in 1883. Membership was 53 and dues 25 cents.

The town of Bluffton had no city water, no telephones, no Street Fair, but there were gas street lights in the business district. This was primarily a farm community until the oil boom in the southern townships. Population grew and so did the membership; therefore meetings were held in the Post Office. The rich heritage has endured 110 changing years because of the Christian teachings of the Order. A fifty year celebration was held in 1931, and a banquet followed the regular Chapter meeting. The electric signet was purchased in 1939. Star Point chairs and covers were added in 1944. During the Second World War, Crescent Chapter was a dependable source of volunteer labor for the Red Cross and the Selective Service Office. Crescent Chapter was instrumental in helping institute the Mississinewa, Portland and Muncie Chapters.

Crescent Chapter has sponsored numerous money making projects of which the proceeds were used by the Masonic Lodge for the purchase of the new kitchen equipment. The great event in this history was the move from the Masonic Hall (third floor) at 114-1/2 N. Main Street to the new Masonic Temple, 211 West Cherry. Dedication of the new temple was held October 21, 1967.

The pedestals and altar were constructed from solid walnut in 1967 by Bro. Edward Call. They were dedicated in 1969.

Crescent Chapter has been honored by the Grand Chapter of Indiana by having several Grand Chapter appointments: Mary E. Mason, Worthy Grand Matron, 1889; Jacob J. Todd, Worthy Grand Patron, 1884; Elmore J. Sturgis, Worthy Grand Patron 1946; Lyle J. Cotton, Worthy Grand Patron, 1977; Patricia Mossburg, Grand Warden, 1989, Gladys Cotton, District Deputy, 1971; and Patricia Mossburg, District Deputy,1981; Grand Representatives, Mildred Troutman, 1968, Gladys Cotton, 1978, and Nellie Fryback, 1990.

Crescent Chapter and the Masons sponsored Rainbow Assembly and a DeMolay Chapter for several years. New Star Point chairs were purchased during Nellie Fryback's Worthy Matron year in 1982-1983. A special project known as "The Homemade Apple Dumpling Booth" at the Bluffton Street Fair created fellowship and money to be used for local needs. Members have donated canned food to the Wells County Food Bank each Christmas. Crescent Chapter has been supportive of the Masonic Home in Franklin, IN. Two religious training students were supported by scholarships sponsored by Crescent Chapter. They were Rev. Tom French and Rev. Timothy Dilley.

Markle Chapter voted to join together with Crescent Chapter and consolidate in November, 1990. Emblems from the Markle Chapter were incorporated into Crescent's usage. With this consolidation our membership stands at 300 women and men, seeking to keep in mind the high ideals of life and citizenship as set forth in the principals of our Order.

We who have inherited Crescent Chapter wish to give a heartfelt "Thank You" to those faithful officers of loyal members who have left us with such a rich heritage.

Now we look forward with the hope we can carry on in that fine tradition and serve so that this Chapter will continue to be an asset to the Bluffton Community.

Elmore D. Sturgis- Worthy Grand Patron 1946

Gladys Cotton- District Deputy 1971, Grand Representative 1978

Lyle Cotton- Worthy Grand Patron 1977

Pat Mossburg-Grand Warder 1989, District Deputy 1981

Explorer Post 2150, BSA

Sponsored by the First United Methodist Church, Explorer Post 2150 was organized with eight high school young men on April 1, 1963. The leaders were Lyle J. Cotton and Ray Dunphy. The objectives of the Post were to give the young Explorers an opportunity to experience some strenuous outdoor activities, to be self-sufficient by learning their own way, to develop leadership skills, and to participate in activities which would make Bluffton a better place in which to live. All of this was to be accomplished in a wholesome atmosphere.

The Exploring program of the Boy Scouts of America is designed to develop those skills for students from high school through the age of 20.

1963 was a learning year. In 1964 the Post made their first canoeing trip on the Au Sable River in Michigan. Since then a canoeing trip into the Canadian Wilderness has been made each year except 1968. That year the Post took a three-week backpacking trip to the Philmont Scout Reservation in New Mexico. On July 4th the group celebrated our Nation's birthday at the 11,000 foot level.

Girls were admitted to the Post in 1975 and have been participating in all of the Post activities since then. Although the annual Wilderness trips are the main part of the program, the Post members have participated in many community projects; recycling, the All-City Cleanup, setting up the Red Cross Bloodmobile, and many others.

Now, twenty-eight years later, we have twenty-four Explorers. Ray Dunphy, post advisor, and Lyle J. Cotton, committee chairman, are still the active leaders.

Explorers portage to the next Canadian lake.

Sunset on a Canadian lake.

Explorers with trash from river road.

KIWANIANS

Community and youth service has been the watchword for 70 years of the Bluffton Kiwanis Club, which received its charter as a part of an international group of men on June 8, 1921.

The Kiwanis Club of Bluffton, seeking to build and keep a better community, measures its worth not alone on its accomplishments but also how its members have served together to contribute to the well-being of the community's citizenry.

Years before a 4-H organization came to this area, Bluffton Kiwanis was sending two young farm exhibitors to the International Livestock Exposition in Chicago each year.

Since the development of the nationwide 4-H Club organization, Kiwanis in Wells County has supported 4-H programs, projects, leadership conferences and the county's annual 4-H Fair. In the agricultural vein, Kiwanis has staged joint farm-city programs, dinners and other events over the years.

Kiwanis aid to youth projects has included the International Farm Youth Exchange, Junior Leadership Conferences, Boys State, Girls State, Junior Achievement, Police and Law Enforcement Career Schools, career days at universities, 4-H livestock exhibits and auctions and "homes" for short-term visits by students from a number of nations.

Contributions of Kiwanis have aided in building and equipping medical wings at Riley Children's Hospital in Indianapolis and help has gone to a medical clinic in India.

Funds have been provided locally so that those in hunger might have food and that both young and old might secure medical attention and better sight and hearing.

Kiwanis began its sponsorship in 1936 of Boy Scout Troop 140, which last June marked its 55th anniversary in the Bluffton community. The club in 1948 moved a frame structure as a scout hall to its present location on West Spring Street and each year since has borne the cost of the upkeep of the building and its heating. A Kiwanis committee maintains contact to assure leadership needs are met.

Leadership was given by Kiwanis to the Savings Bonds program of the 1940's and 1950's along with spearheading the use of "Victory Gardens" during the food-rationing days of World War II.

Because Kiwanians wanted Bluffton to remain the "Parlor City of Indiana," club members provided over a three-year period more than 3,000 tree seedlings free to residents and contributed in later years both funds and manpower toward the beautification of the banks of the Wabash River. Shrubbery on the plaza of the Wells County Courthouse was provided and installed by Kiwanians.

Kiwanis leadership also organized Little League baseball in the community, organized record hops, bought and installed playground equipment at the Wells County 4-H Park, gave funds and manpower to the continuing annual all-night party for Bluffton juniors and seniors to keep students off highways on year-end activities.

Over two decades Kiwanis has offered several thousands of dollars as interest-free loans to county students enrolled in colleges and universities. The loans have ranged from $300 to $1,000.

Every year for more than two decades, Kiwanians have acquired tickets and provided transportation to take over 500 third graders from all county schools to the Shrine Circus in Ft. Wayne.

A project for which Kiwanians have been proud is that of operating during the annual Bluffton Street Fair each fall an information booth where hundreds of lost items and scores of lost children have been reunited with their families. While scores of concessions, both local and foreign, seek sizeable profits from fair-goers, Kiwanians have been concerned solely with service toward others without renumeration.

Scores of 55-gallon barrels have been secured and repainted for placement in the city's parks and recreational area for use as trash receptacles. Kiwanians each spring in recent years also have walked the city's parks to clean them of trash and rubbish in readiness for summer activities.

Pianos have been donated by the club to both Southern Wells and Northern Wells High Schools and spotlight equipment to Bluffton High.

Kiwanis members support spiritual life of the community by making and distributing church directories, giving devotions in rest homes, and placing prayer tents at tables in restaurants.

For the veterans of America's wars confined to Veteran Administration Hospitals, Kiwanians have provided and continue to give programs twice yearly, primarily at the VA Hospital in Marion.

As early as 1939 Kiwanians here were pointing out the dangers of drug abuse and the effects of marijuana use. Materials still are being supplied to schools in the county.

For a three year period Kiwanis sponsored in the community "homes" for month-long visits of foreign students through the summer months to participate in normal American family life activities.

Because monies are necessary in most instances to maintain these programs, Kiwanis in Bluffton uses projects which give something in return in exchange for its fund-raising efforts.

Principal fund raising project of the Kiwanis Club for 33 years in the Kiwanis Travelogue of six programs.

From the Kiwanis Club, Dwight F. Gallivan served as Kiwanis Indiana District governor and as an international trustee.

Northern Wells Girl Scouts

Day Camp

The history of Girl Scouting in Northern Wells begins with four school systems and troops in each system. I have only been able to draw from two of the schools because of the closing of Rock Creek and Union Schools. To those who worked in Rock Creek and Union, I am sorry that I have little or no history to report.

According to those who were involved, Ossian Girl Scouting started in the late 30's to early 40's with Clover Drage as leader in 1940-41. Mrs. Norma Dalrymple Behning remembers having Mrs. Drage as her leader and Annetta Foshnight Hower as a troop member also.

In the early 50's Girl Scouting was revived with Vada Welbaum, Rosemary Smith, Bev Hunter and Jo Hadley as leaders. Other names mentioned were Ruth Hoover, Lillian Mahnensmith, and Mrs. Hilsmier. Violet Gibson was also involved in reorganizing with Keturah Wineland as another leader. The Psi Iota XI Sorority sponsored the troops.

Dr. Bev. Hunter told me of the hiking trips they took to the old covered bridge before it was burned, and how much fun they had by the river. The troops met at school, the United Methodist Church and sometimes at their homes. There was no day camp at that time so they took the girls to Oliver Lake camping.

Madiline Bailey became the leader in the 60's. No further history is available.

The early 70' is sketchy. I became involved in 1975 as day camp director.

The day camp in 1975 was held at the Ossian Conservation Club. We were all new at camping and fire building. That was one of the hottest summers we have had. We had a water tank brought in from the National Guard, because there was no water available.

The second year was a tad better but still very hot. We had about 100 girls turn out for camp. And of course we had a great time. We have had day camp every year except one since we have been at the Wells County Gun Club, State Park, and the Clarence Roth Farm. In 1989 we celebrated our 15th camp. Memories still linger of the highlights of day camps past. Once we built a full size wigwam with saplings carried from the woods, and covered it with old tentage. It was great.

We've hunted watermelon bandits, dressed dill pickles in their finest, made pond soup; it was delicious. We've hovered in the shelter singing very loud while severe storms raged overhead. Best of all were the camp fire sing-a-longs with Karen Gerbers and myself leading the singing. Lowell Tillman and Clarence Roth were our official sugar popcorn poppers.

The burnt marshmallows and sleepless nights will always be remembered by the leaders and girls.

Those from Lancaster area remember scouting starting in the late 40's and early 50's. The year book from 1950-51 shows about 30 fifth and sixth grade girls with Dorotha Sellers, Irene Wasson, Char Farling and Dorthy Shady as leaders or assistants.

Again in the year books from 1952-1966, there are pictures of the troops but no names. In 1966 there were 60 girls pictured from all levels of scouting.

I became a leader in 1974, for troop 95. There were six girls and we met at my home. We stayed together as a troop until the girls graduated from high school. Two of the girls, Angie Brubaker Landrum and Amy Ellerman Gillom were the first in Wells County and among the first ten in our council to receive their silver and gold awards, the highest awards given in Girl Scouting.

There were many changes during those years. The Girl Scout promise has changed three times. The Brownie promise is no longer used. The addition of five year olds as Daisy Scouts came in 1984. Amanda Brubaker was the first Daisy registered in Wells County. She is now a member of Troop 86 at Ossian School.

There are troops meeting in both Ossian and Lancaster Schools for each grade level, Kindergarten through fifth grade. At the middle school we have one troop.

Leaders have came and gone. The girls have changed their styles and ideas, but Scouting still continues to be lively and fun.

There have been many volunteers in the program in the last several years. There's not enough room to mention them all. I will try to list some of those I knew. Rose Frauhiger, Leslie Tillman, Maryann Rippenger, Barbara Keplinger, Dee Steffen, Janene Miller, Mary Hendricks, Jean Reef, Jean Glime, Ann Crismore, Sally Bracke, Janette Dickey, Judy Ellerman, Diane Schwartzkoph, Haslyn Harris, Mary Shaffer, Karen Gerbers, Emma Hobbs, Pamala Probst, Sandy Kerns, Kathy Price, Sheri Lynn Adam, Judy Adams, Kathy Privett, Kathy Green, Linda Wright, Pat Scott, Karen Platt, Bonnie Davis, Vera Ellenburg, Ruth Bingam, Lynn Babcock, Joan Bacon, Gina Urshel, Bonnie Fisher, Linda Dubach, Joan Payne, Lorane Lechleitner, Mary Robles, Diane Rush, and many more. A thank you doesn't seem like enough to say to those who had a roll in the lives of all girls that have been through the program.

One more very important person in our program is Ellen Hively, the field director for so many years. Her influence upon all the leaders and girls cannot be measured.

We have approximately 250 girls and 50 leaders in the program today. The present service team consists of Judy Kettring, Theresa Biberstine, Jan Schwartz, Roxianne Miser, Linda Forest, Cyndee Fiechter, Barbara Myers, Ruth Stuck, and Connie Brubaker.

Bluffton Optimist Club

Charter Optimist Honored - Shown above is Estel Rhodes (center) receiving special honors as one of the original Charter Optimist members at the clubs 20th Anniversary Celebration that was held May 12, 1984. Also pictured is Jerry Selking (left), Optimist Lieutenant Governor and Howard Luedtke (right), Governor of the Indiana Optimist District.

In early September of 1963, Bob Kyle visited his home town of Bluffton and convinced three men to take steps to form an Optimist Club. These men were Dick Holsinger, George Rittenhouse and Estel Rhodes.

Bob Kyle, who was living in Marion, was a member of the Marion Optimist Club, and realized the benefits that a club could bring to the youth, and the entire Bluffton community.

The three Bluffton men went to work, and a weekly meeting started after the Street Fair that year. By process of elimination, they found Tuesday morning breakfast to be the best meeting time, and the meetings were held at the Snug Restaurant, located at 126 W. Market Street.

They soon had 17 men pledged to the club. At that time, it took a membership of 25 to be admitted to Optimist International. The group struggled through the winter, never really meeting the required number. Several men, however, had jokingly promised to join once the group reached twenty-four members, thinking this would never happen!

In April of 1964, Dr. Wilhelm of the Fort Wayne Downtown Optimist Club, paid a visit to the Bluffton group and got the men fired-up. Within days the membership jumped to 30, and the club was officially recognized by Optimist International on May 5, 1964, becoming the 112th Optimist Club in Indiana.

Through the years the Bluffton Optimist Club has established many programs of lasting value. These include the Youth in Government Day for high school seniors, the Oratorical Contest, Bicycle Rodeo, Essay Contest, and the Respect for Law Day honoring law enforcement officers.

The sports programs which are sponsored by the club include a team sponsorship in the Little League Baseball program, the Parlor City Athletic Club Youth Basketball League, organization of the Tri-Star Basketball contest, and the popular Optimist Soccer League for grade school students of Wells County.

The major fund raisers for the club have included raffles and the sale of sausage sandwiches at the annual Bluffton Street Fair.

In 1987-88, Bluffton Optimist Member Ray Shaw served as Distinguished Governor of the Indiana North District of Optimist International. Other club members have served as lieutenant governor through the years.

In 1991, the Bluffton Optimist Club has nearly 50 men and women as members. The group meets each Tuesday morning at 6:45 a.m. at Traditions Restaurant, located at the south edge of Bluffton.

Past President Of the Bluffton Optimist Club

Richard Allen	1964-65
Richard Gerber	1965-66
Robert Steckbeck	1966-67
George Rittenhouse	1967-68
Tillman Gerber	1968-69
Raymond Lanternier	1969-70
Theodore Ellis	1970-71
Charles Sullivan	1971-72
Don Reeves	1972-73
Ray Shaw	1973-74
James Van Winkle	1974-75
Rex Jarret	1975-76
Gary Merritt	1976-77
Robert Maxwell	1977-78
Roger Schmidt	1978-79
Ronald Hanusin	1979-80
Dennis Zawodni	1980-81
Richard Shutt	1981-82
Larry Reed	1982-83
Roger Sherer	1983-84
Bill Hambrick	1984-85
Mike Graham	1985-86
Allyn Hines	1986-87
John Taylor	1987-88
Ray Paxson	1988-89
Larry Stromberg	1989-90
Tim Tobias	1990-91

Bay View Reading Club

In the fall of 1895, a group of Bluffton women recognized the need to form a second reading club to answer the demand for more intellectual growth opportunities for women of this area. Twelve local ladies, some who had visited at Bay View, MI, and learned of a study system developed there, formed the Bay View Reading Club.

Charter members were Georgiana (Mrs. P.A.) Allen, Lillian (Mrs. Frank) Asbaucher, Mary (Mrs. L.A.) Beeks, Josephine (Mrs. A.B.) Cline, Aldula (Mrs. James) Easton, Josephine (Mrs. Frank) Gordon, Anne (Mrs. Arthur) Huyette, Luella Kenagy (later Carnes), Mary (Mrs. Frank) Markley, Harriett ("Mrs. Dr.") McKinney, Emma (Mrs. Herman) Thoma, and Mae (Mrs. John) Winters.

Club meetings were held on alternate Tuesday afternoons from October to May, following a pattern still in existence 96 years later. The original programs followed the outlines set up in the Bay View magazine and two subjects were reported at each meeting, followed by a round-table discussion and a report on current events. The club motto of "More Light" was taken seriously, as the women expected to go home from their sessions more enlightened than when they arrived.

After World War I when subscription prices to the Bay View magazine rose to a prohibitive $1.00 (from 75 cents), which eventually caused the demise of the magazine, the local group selected programs of their own, planning them for a year in advance and printing their own program booklet. Miscellaneous topics were selected for study.

In the early 1900s this club joined the Federated Women's Clubs, joined with 22 other Wells County organizations in the heyday of women's clubs. Shortly after the depression, however, only Bay View and Foltz remained in the Federation of Women's Clubs, with these two clubs remaining federated until the mid sixties. Joined meetings of these two clubs are still held twice a year, with each club taking a turn at hostessing the other.

Today the Bay View Club, which is limited to a membership of 30 active members to allow the group to meet in homes, follows the historical pattern of bi-weekly meetings at which members take their semi-annual turn at presenting a review of a current non-fiction book or a topic of importance. In addition, a few culinary events brighten the intellectual scene, for the scholarly year begins with a fall luncheon and ends with the traditional May breakfast.

Officers for the 1990-91 year are Becky Salscheidier, president; Ethel Ley, vice president; Nedra Hiday, secretary-treasurer; and Geri Person, program chairman. Other members are: Lynne Apple, Barbara Barieri, Daisy Cox, Sue Dian, Mary Alice Eisaman, Bette Erxleben, Phyllis Hamilton, Marcella Hart, Pat Heig, Carolyn Huvendick, Carolyn McBride, Betty Johnston, Marge Lockwood, Dorothea Muir, Nancy Neuhauser, Betty O'Laverty, Irene Park (honorary), Marcella Phegley, Eunice Rosie, Vera Rudy, Carol Schamerloh, Mary Hilma Scott, Phyllis Shinn, Polly Stailey, Carol Stern, Rosemary Williams and Marty Wilson.

Bluffton Business and Professional Women

Bluffton Business and Professional Women were organized and chartered on August 21, 1956, becoming part of the state, national and international BPW.

OBJECTIVES: To elevate standards, promote interests, and extend opportunities to working women, as well as to help youth make career options.

COMMUNITY PROJECTS: Cancer and mental health; civic night with the WOMAN OF THE YEAR award; scholarship award; Young Careerist; and assisting YOUTH with CAREER OPTIONS.

Virginia Rowland served as State President and National Legislation Chairman; Ellen Mayne served as corresponding secretary; Janet Cooper, Estaleene Suman, Paula Hook, and presently Barbara Elliott have served as district directors.

Four charter members are still active: Bernice Anderson Ewing, Ellen Mayne, Mary Mitchell, and Rena Soper.

Present officers are: Gladys Cotton, president; Evelyn Priddy, vice-president; Betty Baker, secretary; and Ethel Clark, treasurer.

Bluffton Lodge #145, F&A.M.

Bluffton Lodge #145, Free and Accepted Masons, had its beginning early in the year 1853. Wells County had been organized as a county in 1837. Several Masons living in the area felt the need for a lodge in Wells County. Accordingly, a group of about twelve masons applied to the Grand Lodge of Free and Accepted Masons for a charter for a lodge in Bluffton. The application was received with favor by the Grand Lodge and on February 3, 1853, a dispensation for a lodge was granted.

After its founding in 1853, Bluffton Lodge #145, Freen and Accepted Masons leased quarters on an upper floor of the Bennett and Deam Building for nearly twenty years. This building was located at 116-118 North Main Street.

The officers for the first year of this lodge were Arthur M. Sanford, Worshipful Master; Oliver P. Gilham, Senior Warden; John Morgan, Junior Warden; Henry Courtney, Senior Deacon; David B. McClure, Junior Deacon; James A. Williams, Treasurer; James R. McCleery, Secretary; and William Freeman, Tyler.

In 1870, the lodge moved to a brick building, now the eastern part of the Murphy Store. In 1876, the Centennial Building, now housing the Penney Store, was built and the Masons moved into the third floor. The lodge, in 1890, moved to the third floor at 114 1/2 North Main Street. The lodge participated in the laying of cornerstones for some of the most prominent buildings in the community, mainly the new courthouse in 1889.

In 1956, a building program was initiated by the appointment of a building committee by Worshipful Master Linn Gregg, Sr.

The new Masonic Temple at 211 West Cherry Street is the result of years of planning. It was dedicated October 21, 1967. In addition to Bluffton Lodge #145, F&AM, the York Rite bodies, the Order of the Eastern Star, the Order of the Rainbow for Girls, and the Order of Demolay for Boys are associated. Their activities are conducted in the Temple.

Bluffton Community Women

The Bluffton Community Women is an organization formed for the common purpose of civic betterment. This purely local group holds strong to its friendly and relaxed atmosphere, proving that serving Bluffton and Wells County can be enjoyable.

The foundation of today's organization began in 1960 as Jaycee's Wives. In 1985, a landmark court decision allowed women to join the Jaycees, and the Jaycee Women organization was dissolved. In May of 1985, the Bluffton Community Women evolved.

The BCW is now involved in over 15 annual projects, benefiting citizens of all ages. Membership is open to any woman over 18 who enjoys serving her community.

The members of the Bluffton Community Women are proud to continue to serve our community, and be a part of the history of Wells County.

Church Women United Of Wells County

Church Women United is an ecumenical group of women organized to better serve the needy in the community, the nation, and the world. They meet together three times a year to learn of needs, act on them, and inspire the membership to learn from other units, state-wide.

On November 3, 1929, a group of women from the Methodist, Reformed, Baptist, and Presbyterian Churches of Bluffton met to organize a local branch of Federated Church Women.

For many years other denominations joined in the annual observance of World Day of Prayer, which was also held in other communities throughout the country.

On January 11, 1968, a meeting was held at the First United Methodist Church in Bluffton to discuss the proposal to broaden the interdenominational program to Church Women United. Mrs. Dwight Gallivan as in charge of the meeting, with fifteen churches represented.

A nominating committee, headed by Mrs. Paul Flowers, prepared a slate of officers who were installed on February 20, 1968 by the Rev. Robert Jackson of the First United Methodist Church. The officers selected for a two-year term were: President, Mrs. Dwight Gallivan, Vice-president, Mrs. Kenneth Eversole, Secretary, Mrs. Cletus Geels, and Treasurer, Mrs. John Higman.

Since then, women from more than 15 churches in Wells County meet to worship and celebrate World Day of Prayer, May Fellowship Day, and World Community Day. They also participate in the Fellowship of the Least Coin and projects for Church World Service such as the Blanket Sunday offering and making school, health, and sewing kits. A local project is an offering which provides vitamins for low-income mothers and children through the WIC program.

This active ecumenical group believes in the challenge. To whom much is given, much is required.

Past Presidents of Church Women United of Wells County (l. to r.) Seated: Mrs Dwight(Mary) Galaivan (68-70) 1st U.M.C., Mrs. Charles (Anna Lee) Ault (70-72) Old Salem U.M.C., Standing: Mrs. David (Clarabelle) Thompson (76-78) 1st U.M.C., Mrs. John (Carol) Meeks (82-84) Epworth U.M.C., Mrs. Susan Reed (84-86) 1st U.M.C., Mrs. Gale (Gail) Miller (86-88) 1st United Church of Christ, Mrs. Wayne (Jane) Hamilton (88-90) Poneto U.M.C., Mrs. John (Edna) Geist (90-92) 1st Presbyterian Church. Not present for picture: Mrs. Robert (Roma) McFarren (72-74) 1st Baptist, Mrs. Wendell (Bobbie) Oman (74-76) Epworth U.M.C. , Mrs. Lester (Mary) Sundling (78-80) 1st Presbyterian, and Mrs. George (Marlene) Schlagenhave (80-82) Six Mile United Church of Christ.

Foltz Literary Club

In 1890 May Foltz, Stella Mullen, and Henry Eichhorn graduated from Terre Haute Normal College. The two young ladies accepted employment with the Bluffton, Indiana schools. May Foltz, who was from Valley Mills, Indiana, was to be the science teacher and assistant principal of the high school.

May and Stella, upon their arrival in Bluffton, roomed together, as did Henry Eichorn and Charles Deam. Later May married Henry and Stella married Charles.

In 1891 May Foltz became the principal of the high school. That same year Mrs. Emma Dailey learned of a group of women in Marion who had formed a club to broaden their intellectual and spiritual horizons by a study of classical literature and such other subjects as were deemed conducive to such broadening. Mrs. Dailey immediately felt that such an organization among Bluffton women would be very desirable. She contacted some of her friends and explained the plan to them. It met with instant response.

A meeting was called and thirty-five invited women responded. The majority of them felt that it was too difficult an undertaking at that particular time, but a few of them formed an organization along the lines suggested. Mrs. Emma Dailey called Miss Foltz and asked her if she would lead the group. Despite her busy schedule, she consented. The nine ladies who became the charter members of the club were: Mrs. Amos (Addie Oppenheim) Cole, Mrs. Leander (Jessie Chaddock) Cook, Mrs. Joseph (Emma) Dailey, Mrs. Henry (May Foltz) Eichhorn, Mrs. James (Delia Wilson) Hale, Mrs. William (Anna) Marsh, Mrs. W.B. (Mary Wright) Nimmons, Mrs. Cyrene (Jenny Bassett) Warner, and Mrs. Lent (Dorothea Kellerman) Williamson.

In 1894 the group took the name of the May Foltz Circle, in honor of their leader, and a constitution and by-laws were adopted. This name was later changed to the Foltz Reading Circle, and in 1926, the organization took its present name, Foltz Literary Club.

After the first few years of the existence of the club, the services of a leader or teacher were dispensed with. Officers were elected yearly and study programs were planned.

On many occasions the club has brought outstanding lecturers to Bluffton as speakers.

The Foltz Literary Club is the oldest organization of its kind in Wells County with a constitution and by-laws. Through the years the club has maintained the original format of educational and cultural endeavors.

The 1991 active members are: Bonnie Ramsey, president; Jean Pfister, first vice-president; Amy Greiner, second vice-president; Marcia Schmeckebier, secretary; Betty Cline, treasurer; Jeanne Almdale, Lynn Babcock, Anita Dold, Barbara Elliott, Teresa Evans, Mary Gallivan, Eileen Garvey, Betty Griffis, Nancy Hewitt, Diane Humphrey, Betty Kephart, Martha Lindsay, Genevieve Lohmuller, Patricia McLaughlin, Edwina Patton, Jacquelyn Pietz, Beverly Rich, Marilynn Schwartz, Phyllis Smith, Mary Sundling, Justine Tangeman, Judy Tomlin, Betty Van Winkle, and Nancy Wagner.

The honorary members are Ernestine Baumgartner, Eunice Markley, Harriett Thoma, and Ruth Willey. The associate members are: Cheryl Flack, Elizabeth Leonard, Nina Jane Meyer, Elizabeth Patton and Sue Skinner.

Paradise Rebekah Lodge #83

Rebekah Lodges were organized as auxiliaries to Odd-Fellow Lodges, based on the degree work formulated by Schylur Colfax of South Bend, Indiana, in 1851. The Rebekah degree is based on the women of the Bible whose lives and sacrifices are beloved stories in that sacred record.

Rebekahs are pledged to comfort the sick, the bereaved, and the need. Therefore, the local lodge takes part in the national project of the Educational Foundation, the Eye Research project and the Pilgrimage to the Tomb of the Unknown Soldier in Arlington Cemetery. The state projects of the Arthritis Foundation, the fraternal home at Greensburg, and the Youth Pilgrimage to the United Nations are supported. The local concerns supported by the lodge are the Food Bank, the Utility Bank and Senioride.

The Charter for Paradise Rebekah Lodge #83 was issued by the Grand Lodge IOOF of Indiana, in 1872.

The original hand written Constitution and By-laws were not dated. This document was signed by G.F. Markley, John Bruno, and W.L. Fetters. Paradise Rebekah Lodge #83 has grown as a result of consolidation with other lodges: Mount Olive of Petroleum, in 1973; Harmony of Poneto in 1974; Shoupene of Zanesville in 1976; Augustus of Liberty Center, in 1982; and Olive of Decatur in 1991.

Members of the lodge who have served as elective state officers include the following:

Treva Sharp Miller (Petroleum) was president of the Rebekah Assembly of Indiana in 1957.

Jesse Haines (Petroleum) was Grand Patriarch of the Grand Encampment in 1962.

Velma Cavitt (Zanesville) was president othe Association of LAPM of Indiana in 1965.

Florence Clark (Liberty Center) was president of the Association of LAPM of Indiana in 1970.

Evelyn Plasterer (Decatur) was president of the Association of LAPM of Indiana in 1977.

Mabel White (Bluffton) was secon vice-president of the association of LAPM of Indiana in 1991.

Members of the lodge who have served as elective officers of District #31 include:

Bluffton: Carrie Kirkwood, Viola McCurdy, Harriet McAfee, Kate Stegekemper, Dorothy Smith, Edna Brown, Betty Edington, Ilah Hart, and Dorthea Ostrander.

Petroleum: Hattie Dickenson, Anna Dukes, Treva Sharp Miller, Lela Settle, and Mabel White.

Poneto: Enola Jones, Rena Mowery and Louella Ifer.

Zanesville: Zetta Lopshire, Vergie Woods, Velma Cavitt, Edna Smith, Neola Johnson, Martha Belle Dowty, Evelyn Johnson, Talitha Stickler and Mildred Edwards.

Liberty Center: Jennie Stroud, Florence Clark, Edith Humerickhouse, and Shirley Harshman.

Decatur: Helen Lister Call, Melvina Read, Evelyn Plasterer, and Mary Alice Kitson.

Psi Iota X Sorority Alpha Eta Chapter - Bluffton

The primary purpose of Psi Iota X, a national philanthropic sorority, is to do good and to bring pleasure to those less fortunate about us.

The first Psi Ote chapter was founded in Muncie, Indiana, on September 19, 1897. Today, in 1991, we have chapters in five states.

The Bluffton chapter, Alpha Eta, was organized on October 29, 1923. Charter members were: Alta Jane Carson, Edna Farling, Florence Fishbaugh, Dolly Hamilton, Zoe Malcolm, Dorothy Rippe, Mary Stine Shaffer, Mary Siford, Madge Spray, Elizabeth Stogdill, Mary Templin, and Irene Kelly Wiley.

In 1933 the Psi Otes purchased seven acres of land south of Bluffton from the Federal Land Bank for $1,00. It soon became known as "the Psi Ote Pool." For almost four decades children and adults learned to swim there, had picnics, fished, enjoyed the beach dances, and created many great memories.

Alpha Eta has had many projects during the years: bake sales, street fair booths, plant sales, bus trips, golf tournaments, sales of knives and cheeseballs, and our annual Christmas House Walk.

While Psi Iota X has become best known for its effort in the field of speech and hearing, it has continued its support of the Food Bank, Bi-County Services, Wells County Public, Creative Arts Council, Senior Ride, Wells County Literary Council, Junior Achievement and Riley Hospital.

We are often reminded of the challenges our founders faced and overcame to make our sorority the outstanding organization it is today as we try to help others.

Former "Psi Ote Castle"- Many Bluffton and Wells County residents recall when the Psi Ote Pool bathhouse and concession stand complex looked like this.

1923 Photo, Back row: Harriet Lambert, Virginia Costello, Mary Brown, Elizabeth Stogdill, Edna Skiles, Dolly Hamilton, Pauline Farr, Dorothy Rippe. Front row: Mary Shaeffer, Ila Kassler, Mary Thomas, Zoe Malcolm, Ella Caylor, Martha Thomas, Irene Huyette, Alda Jane Woodward.

Psi Iota Xi Gamma Zeta Chapter

Charter members of Gamma Zeta Chapter of Psi Iota XI Sorority- March 17, 1945. (l. to r.) Back row: Alberta Swaim, Ruth Wilburn, Rosemary Smith, Lois Johnson, Leona Mahnensmith, Joan McClain, Rosella Shull White, Lela Cossairt. Front row: Patty Blanton, Elizabeth Wert, Vada Welbaum, Marcelle Morrissey

Psi Iota Xi, a national philanthropic and cultural organization, was founded in Muncie, Indiana, on September 19, 1897. It has grown to more than 150 chapters nationwide.

A small group of women in Ossian, Indiana, decided they wanted to become part of this unique organization. On March 17, 1945, a charter was bestowed upon this group and Gamma Zeta Chapter of Psi Iota Xi became an important part of Ossian and Wells County.

The ritual was conducted by Grand President Ruth Hancock in the Psi Ote Hall in Bluffton. More than 100 members from chapters in Fort Wayne, Markle, and Bluffton attended. Alpha Nu Chapter of Markle was our sponsoring chapter.

The purpose of Psi Iota Xi is to give its time, money, and love to help people overcome difficulties. We are especially active in the field of speech and hearing. In fact, Psi Iota Xi has received national recognition for donating over a million dollars to speech and hearing and other philanthropic projects.

Locally, Gamma Zeta members have made major contributions to our community. In December of 1949, our sorority presented an organ to the Ossian School; in 1986 we established a fund for a child suffering from cerebral palsy and have since purchased a motorize wheelchair and computer for his use. We have recently instituted a fund for another child in our community who suffers from various physical problems.

Past and present members have dedicated their time and effort to several ongoing projects over the years. They include our adoption of a mental health patient and financial contributions to various cultural activities. We have also given money to Riley Hospital. Our sponsorships include Scout troops, Girls State representatives, and student volunteers at the Ossian Health Care Center.

Gamma Zeta's efforts have helped to make Ossian and Wells County a better place to live. We believe our future will be as rewarding as our past as we continue to focus our efforts on helping others.

Tri Kappa Beta Phi

Kappa, Kappa, Kappa was founded February 22, 1901, when seven friends from May Wright Sewell's Classical School for Girls in Indianapolis decided to form a club. They elected officers, adopted a constitution, and formally installed a sorority. The women decided to start sororities in their hometowns. The first local Tri Kappa sororities were in Bloomington and New Harmony.

The Bluffton Chapter of Tri Kappa, Beta Phi, was founded May 6, 1920. Lucille Blackman and Lois Kunkel were instrumental in the founding of Beta Phi. During the chapter's early years, money was raised through bake sales, tag day, a bingo booth at the Street Fair, card parties, and dances. In the 1920s, the Beta Phi chapter organized and supported the first kindergarten in Wells County. The kindergarten, which was held at Central School, averaged sixty pupils. In the 1930s, Beta Phi sponsored the first Girl Scout programs in Bluffton. The chapter provided equipment, meeting places, and leaders for the troops. Sponsorship continued until the Bluffton Girl Scouts joined the Limberlost Council in the 1960s. In 1931, the Alpha Associate Chapter was installed. Another associate chapter, Beta, was installed in 1961. The associate chapters were formed so that members of Beta Phi who have been actively involved for ten years or more could still be involved in Tri Kappa, but not as an active member.

For the past twenty years, Beta Phi has raised money by selling T-shirts and sweatshirts at the Street Fair, geraniums, pecans and chocolate-covered peanut butter Easter Eggs. The Red Stocking Follies, with community participation and support, has raised thousands of dollars for various charitable projects.

Tri Kappa promotes charity, culture and scholarship by helping families at Thanksgiving and Christmas, by sponsoring the high school art show, and by awarding numerous scholarships to college students. Tri Kappa has also supported many community projects, such as Senioride, the Wells Community Pool, the Dream Arboretum, and ARC.

The following verse is a fitting statement of Tri Kappa's purpose:

We shall pass through this world but once.
Any good, therefore, that we can do or any kindness that we
can show to any human being let us do it now.
Let us not defer or neglect it
For we shall not pass this way again.

4-H members Jerry Penrod, left, and Marion Flemming, right, with their Grand Champion Rabbits

4-H Club in 1934 was the "Just Us Jr. Leasder Club" from Rockcreek Township. Members (L-R) are: Mary Bailey Eichhorn, Mabeline Harnish Vickery, Helen Hasler Foust, Lucile Farling, Avis Fate Wright, Lillian Gemmell Engle, Magdalene Oldfather Hogg and Agnes Graham Miller.

IN MEMORY OF JAMES W. MURRAY

James W. Murray Birth 8/25/17-Died 1/16/87

Jim Murray was a positive influence in Bluffton. As an educator (teacher, principal, coach), he affected the lives of thousands of youngsters

He loved all sports, as a coach, referee, life guard, participant. He coached fifth and sixth grade and junior high basketball, and Junior Legion baseball. He lettered in swimming at Ball State, played kickball, baeball, basketball with the students, and played tennis, especially in retirement. After learning to sail in Venezuela, he started the Lake Tippecanoe Sailing Club.

Jim was a responsible citizen. As Navy lieutenant, J.G. in World War II, he was in the Aleutian Islands and an armed guard on merchant ships going to Murmansk, Russia. In Bluffton, he was a city councilman, board member of Clinic Hospital, member and president of Lion's Club. In Englewood, FL he helped get bike patsh for the people's safety.

Jim loved music. He sang in church choirs, played the organ, enjoyed concerts and listening to good music ("Stardust", his favorite).

He was a devout Christian and was active in First United Church of Christ.

Jim loved his family, and with his own hands built a house for them and one for his mother, plus a cottage at the lake.

He loved to travel and visited all 50 states, Canada, Mexico, Puerto Rico, Guatemala, Panama, Venezuela, Peru and nine European countries.

Jim died of cancer on Jan. 16, 1987.

The world is a better place for his having lived. We'll always remember Jim Murray.

WELLS COUNTY BUSINESSES

This old NCR cash register was purchased by Weisell Clothing Company in 1913 and used in the store location which later became Masterson's Men's Store on east Market. The cash register originally costing $1500.00 is still in working order and a part of the collection of the Wells County Historical Society.

"UNCLE BEN'S" BLUFFTON BUSINESS MEMORIES

B.F. Plessinger, "Uncle Ben", arrived in Bluffton from Ohio with his family on November 7, 1842, and the family moved into a small, one-room blacksmith shop on Morgan Street.

In the early forties, Bluffton was merely a little group of homes in the midst of a vast wilderness. The town proper was confined to a cluster of business houses about a block square with the houses scattered here and there on the higher places. The whole region which is now occupied by the southwestern residence and business section of town was one large swamp and forest. Everything south of South Street and west of Williams was wilderness. A large creek, starting in the swamp where the Lake Erie and Western railroad now is, ran east through the territory between what is now South Street and Central Avenue. South of this creek was a dense forest; so dense that when, as a small boy, he and his playmates used to go nutting, they had to leave one of their number on the north bank to yell out now and then so his companions could find their way back to the creek.

Uncle Ben's father had a shoe shop when they first moved to Bluffton but he soon sold this to Henry Walmer and started into the harness business. He sold this and started a grist mill where the Roy Stafford Mill is now located. The old mill was run by water power, power being obtained from an old mill race which has long since been abandoned. A saw mill was situated just above the grist mill where Starr's quarry is now located.

About 1853 Uncle Ben's father fitted him out with a team of mules and a wagon and for five years he hauled produce between Bluffton and Fort Wayne on the new plank road. In those days hogs and cattle were driven to Fort Wayne, the nearest shipping point. Up to five hundred hogs at a time were common.

In 1858, Uncle Ben took up plastering, brick and stone work. He first worked on the Walmer Shoe Shop and the Christman Bakery on East Market just east of where the picture show now is. *Taken from a February 7, 1919, Evening Banner article of the memories of B.F. Plessinger*

A.W. COTTON DESK AND WOOD SPECIALTY COMPANY

During the first year of the depression, 1930, Ancil W. Cotton organized the A.W. Cotton Desk and Wood Specialty Company to produce wood office desks and furniture specialities in the former Hartle Laundry building at 412 South Morgan Street in Bluffton.

The rent for this wood frame building was $5.00 per month. In 1933, the rent was increased to $6.00! His first employee was Chester Lucas who had been a supervisor on the Works Progress Administration (WPA) site, east of Bluffton, that would become the Ouabache State Park.

The first large office desk was purchased by Cotton's friend and high school classmate, Dr. William A. Gitlin. Dr. Gitlin had completed his medical residency and opened his office practice on East Market Street. This same desk was given to the Wells County Historical Museum in 1990 by Dr. Gitlin upon his retirement from active practice.

In 1934, Dr. Wendell Bucher, a brother-in-law of Frank Buckner (*Out-of-Bounds by Buck* in the *Bluffton Banner* and later *Bluffton News-Banner,* and Mayor of Bluffton 1935-1943), chief surgeon at Children's Hospital, Akron, Ohio, contacted Cotton to build physician's treatment room furniture for him. His idea was that wood furniture would be less intimidating to children than the then popular white painted metal and glass cabinets for instruments and examination tables. This order resulted in a new business direction.

In 1937, travel trailers had reached the market. One of these, empty, was purchased and outfitted with a complete set of physician's office and treatment room furniture to show the potential doctor customers in their own community. This new concept in furniture sold well throughout the Midwest, dictating construction in 1939 of a new manufacturing facility qt 1100 South Morgan Street in Bluffton.

At the end of World War II, television had arrived on the market and contracts were obtained from Capehart-Farnsworth,

The A.W. Cotton Desk and Wood Specialty Co., in 1930. (l. to r.) Dan Gilbert, Ancil Cotton and Chester Lucas.

Construction just completed in 1939 at 1100 South Morgan for the A.W. Cotton Company.

Magnavox, and Zenith to build their wood cabinets. At that time the factory was producing 124 cabinets per day with 80 employees. One of the products was an entertainment center that housed a television, radio and record player, as well as room for books and records.

After a 35 year history, Cotton sold the business and retired. The present building occupant (1991) is General Manufacturing, Inc. owned by Paul Reiff. *By Paul L. Bender*

ABBOTT-REED STORE

After eighteen years continuously in business at one place in Craigville, Alfred A. Abbott this week closed a transaction with his partner, Winniet Reed, by which he sold his one-half interest in the general store which they owned at that place. Mr. Reed became the sole owner of the stock of goods and will continue to operate the store. Mr. Abbott still owns the buildings which are used by the store. It appears that both of the partners were willing to sell, in order to escape from the confinement of the store, and after the annual invoice was completed Mr. Reed made an offer of either give or take so much, and Mr. Abbott accepted the offer and told Mr. Reed that he would sell. Although he had really been desirous himself of selling in order to get less confining work Mr. Reed is well pleased with his business place and enjoys a good patronage and the store makes a nice return on the investment. He became a partner of Mr. Abbott four years ago, at which time he came from Ohio City. Mr. Reed has been in the store so long that he probably will feel almost lost at being out of the business. *Taken from the Bluffton Chronicle, January 18, 1911.*

BANK OF UNIONDALE

The Bank of Uniondale opened for business on December 5, 1908, with the following officers: President H.W. Lipkey; Vice President P.E. Gilbert; Cashier J.A. Brickley.

In June, 1917, it was reorganized as a state bank, having been established as a private concern. At that time it assumed the name of the State Bank of Uniondale, and its capital stock was increased from $10,000 to $25,000, surplus and undivided profits of $2,000, average deposits $200,000. The bank was closed due to the depression in 1930.

Long time employees besides Mr. Brickley were Vaughn Scott, Loye Bayless, Naomi (Miller) Boulware, and Zelah (Brickley) Brown.

BAYHA TAILORING

Mr. George Bayha desires all his old friends and patrons to know that he has opened a tailoring establishment in the room above Erler's grocery, opposite Curry's Opera House, on Main Street, and desires them all to call and see him before having clothing made elsewhere. *Taken from the Bluffton Banner, November 17, 1876*

Bank of Uniondale whose teller's wall is on display at the Wells County Historical Museum.

Bliss Hotel

The Bliss House opened for business in April of 1884 as the largest and most plush of a number of hotels in Bluffton. It originally cost $10,000. The original two-story structure later was engulfed by further construction on all four sides—plus the addition of a third floor. The original sat several feet further from Main Street than the final structure. By 1900 the structure was virtually complete, the main changes which came after the turn of the century being the addition of large plate glass windows across the front.

James Humphrey was the first proprietor and continued in this capacity for a number of years. Jeffrey Bliss, founder of Bliss House, died Dec. 16, 1898. Bliss came to Bluffton in 1851 at age 26, and arrived to serve as clerk for his brother-in-law, John Studabaker, in the latter's grain business. He had been retired from active business when the Bliss building was constructed. Following his death, his widow, Lucinda, remained owner of the hotel until 1904, when she sold the building for $30,000 to a newly formed corporation.

The Bliss Hotel Company was founded by several influential businessmen, including the Blisses' son-in-law, "Colonel" Louis C. Davenport, William A. Kunkel, Sr., Abram Simmons and others. Mr. and Mrs. Cletus Geels, who sold the business and premises to the Ohio Oil Co. (who razed the building to build a gas station) bought control of the corporation in 1946 from a group of stockholders which included the late V.M. Simmons and William A. Kunkel Jr., sons of the original incorporators. *(Taken from News-Banner article at the time the hotel was to be razed.)*

Bluffton Farnsworth TV and Radio Corp.

A World War II factory which employed 350 to 400 person at its peak, operated in Bluffton for four years and four months, starting in August 1943. When it closed in January 1948, the work force had dropped to 140.

The Farnsworth Television and Radio Corp., was located in Bluffton to expand the WWII wartime production of Army communication equiptment. Farnsworth also had plants in Fort Wayne and Marion. A two story brick building in the 800 block of West Washington Street, known as the Patton-McCray building, had housed a furniture manufacturing firm from 1923 to 1942, owned and operated by W.A. Patton and Morris McCray, both of Bluffton. This

Bliss Hotel

(Center) - The Bliss Hotel after the turn of the century. (Upper left) - Staircase in the lobby area. (Upper right) - Dining room with the entrance to this area just left of the grand staircase. (Bottom left) - The lounge area. (Bottom right) - Registration and shop area interior. This area was in front right or southwest corner of the hotel

2600 square foot building was quickly converted and equipped so that 10 days after the plant site was accepted by Farnsworth, the first shipment of transmitters was made!

The north end of the building housed the Berling and Motz poultry processing plant, and a center section housed a clay pottery facility. Farnsworth occupied the south section.

Equipment made here was the BC 604 FM radio transmitter, used with the BC 603 receiver and the BC 605 intercom, for communications between army tanks and the military command. Production was 50 transmitters a day, a production schedule reached after being in operation only seven weeks. With the end of the war, production was terminated and the plant closed.

Shortly after the war ended and production of civilian goods was resumed, Farnsworth reopened the plant. It was revamped and highly mechanized to manufacture consumer radios. Three assembly lines were installed and table, portable, and automobile radios were made at the rate of 1500 per day. When the table radio market became saturated, Farnsworth closed the assembly plant and converted it to a warehouse. Nearly 300 employees were without a job.

Herman Zeps, later owner-manager of Bluffton FM radio station WCRD, came here from the General Motors plant at Kokomo, filling the position of quality control manager. Plant manager was William Henry Rupley; Morris McCray, personnel manager; Carl Shatto, superintendent; Bill Starr, industrial engineer; Roger Huffman, material control; and Ted Snyder, maintenance.

The warehouse operation came to an end in 1950. For a short period Franklin Electric (another wartime government contractor) used the building as a warehouse. After this, Duchess Pretzel founded their pretzel bakery (the first to make twisted pretzels west of Pennsylvania) in this building. They later sold to Bachmann Jacks who continued the pretzel bakery until January 3, 1959, when a $500,000 fire destroyed the building and its equipment. The pretzel company built a new ultra-modern plant on State Road 116 West, which was later sold to the Keebler Company. (*Material provided by Herman Zeps and Eugene McCord. McCord is editor-emeritus of the News-Banner.*)

Farnsworth Television and Radio Corporation located at Indiana and Washington in Bluffton.

Farnsworth employees in front of plant on West Washington in the summer of 1943.

THE BLUFFTON PHARMACY

The Bluffton Pharmacy at 312 South Main Street, Bluffton, Indiana was located in the former home of William and Rachel Morris. The business opened in 1969 with the comforts of a waiting room, a fireplace, living room furniture, a children's play area, and free coffee.

It was owned and operated for twenty years by George Rittenhouse and family: wife, Nina, sons, Kent, Greg, Brock and daughter Linda.

One of the first in Northeast Indiana to computerize and to use a fee system of pricing; deliveries were made to nursing homes and people at home. It closed in 1989, one of the last of the independent pharmacies in Indiana. Many people tell us they miss us, the pharmacy, and our services.

We want to thank the people of the area who allowed us to share their lives.

BLUFFTON TELEPHONE COMPANY

Starting from a humble little stock company, with an original 55 subscribers, under the name of the Bluffton Telephone Company, the growth of the company has been steady.

The company was organized in 1894 by local men as stockholders and directors as follows: W.H. Ernst, president; Hugh Dougherty, vice president; L.C. Davenport, treasurer; James W. Sale, secretary, and A.P. Oppenheim, manager. The original franchise was granted by LaVergne B. Stevens, at that time mayor of the city.

The company was reorganized February 10, 1896, under the name of the United

Telephone Company, after acquiring the Bluffton exchange, the Portland and the Hartford City exchanges.

In 1901 the company was merged with the Indiana Telephone Company with exchanges at Marion, Upland, Hartford City and Montpelier. Later the Huntington plant of the Huntington and Phoenix Telephone Company was acquired.

After the merger with the larger companies, James W. Sale was elected general manager, and C.H. Plessinger succeeded him as secretary.

Mr. Sale remained general manager of the company until he was succeeded by W.A. Patton, now general manager of the W.B. Brown Company.

Besides the local men named, in 1898 several other men were stockholders including S. Bender and D.A. Walmer of this city.

W.A. Patton was general manager of the company until August of 1914, when he was succeeded by C.A. Breece. Mr. Breece came here from Indianapolis, where he had been with the Central Union Company since 1901, as an engineer.

From its humble beginning the local company has grown until at the present time in the five exchanges of Marion, Huntington, Montpelier, Hartford City, and Bluffton, it has 1980 miles of toll wire and 21,451 miles of exchange wire, a total of 23,431 miles, almost enough to stretch around the earth.

B.B. Earley, local manager of the company, came to Bluffton January 1, 1918, from Shelbyville, where he had been manager of the Central Union Company there for five years. Mr. Early was active in local circles at Shelbyville and since coming to Bluffton has taken an active part in all civic affairs and has won a host of friends.

According to the announcement of Mr. Breece this morning, the present rates of the company of $3.00 per year for business phones, will remain in effect until December 1. This was the rate set by Postmaster General Burleson. The increase rates as applied for by the company are now before the public service commission and no decision has been rendered. *(This sketch was taken from an October 31, 1919, Evening Banner article. New equipment was being introduced into the two story phone company building owned by E.C. Vaughn and W.A. Patton. Then current phone service totaled 1327 telephones.)*

BLUFFTON THEATERS AND OPERA HOUSES

The Terrell Grand Opera House (later the Grand Theater) was of interest to local architectural consultant and preservationist Craig Leonard because it was the work of Cuno Kibele, one of the local architect/builders he was researching as a thesis in architectural preservation.

Kibble went to Muncie in 1904, shortly after the Grand was opened. The real credit for the design, however, probably should go to George Garnsey, a Chicago Theater designer brought into the project by Charles DeLacour, the Grand's promoter, who was also from Chicago. When the Grand was being razed, it was Garnsey's name alone which appeared on the cornerstone.

The Grand lost much of its original appearance after a fire in 1929 on the top floor, which was then removed. The auditorium was remodeled in time for the town centennial in 1936, at which time the balcony was perhaps removed. A balcony was mentioned in the accounts at the time it opened in 1904 and is shown on the 1912 Sanborn fire insurance maps of Bluffton, which are at the Historical Society Museum.

According to a November 19, 1902, article in the *Bluffton Chronicle,* oil-rich Nottingham township farmer, John W. Terrell, had Cuno Kibele prepare plans for an opera house to be financed by Terrell. July 1 of the next year it was reported that Terrell and Charles DeLacour of Chicago were ready to proceed if money and commitment from the Elks for an upstairs lodge were assured. A week later George Garnsey was preparing new plans.

Another week passed. Terrell ambushed his son-in-law outside the Terrell home, shot him in the leg, then followed him to a Bluffton doctor's office, where he shot him again, this time fatally. In August Terrell competed with the town of Petroleum for a site of a CB&C depot. Petroleum was fearful that Terrell's town, started around a depot, would replace Petroleum.

September 16, 1903, H.W. Wiley, a Chicago opera house builder, arrived to begin work on a building to include two 19 x 30 shops on the front, the Elks Lodge on the second and third floors, as well as the theater.

Kibele would serve as the construction superintendent on the project. On October 21, Terrell was taken by the sheriff from the Wells County Jail to the building site across the street to allow Terrell to lay the cornerstone of the opera house.

Construction continued with Terrell's financial investments throughout his trial. He was found guilty of murder in December of 1903. Terrell divested himself of his estate, including participation in the opera house before it opened in April, 1904, with a performance of a morality play, "Our New Minister." The Bluffton High School commencement was held there in June.

Bluffton New-Banner accounts in February and March of 1981 give additional history of the Terrell Opera House and Grand movie theater of later years (1930-75.) The articles were published as the demolition of the structure created a parking lot.

The Curry Opera House at 119 North Main was a three-story Italianate building built about 1875 with three business rooms in its first floor, offices across the facade on the two upper floors, and an auditorium with a later-added balcony on the upper floors behind the offices. The theater access was via a wide stair from the street.

James Whitcomb Riley was at Curry's on December 9, 1885, but the opera house

The Grand Opera House later to become the Holiday Theater. Built by Terrell, it was located on the southeast corner of Washington and Johnson which was east, across the street, from the jail (now the Public Library) and also south, across the street, from the fire station (now Wells County Republican Headquarters). The building was razed for parking.

BLUFFTON WHOLESALE GROCERY COMPANY

was short-lived. On December 10, 1891, a newspaper article relating the Wells County Farmer's Institute's inability to get the use of the new circuit court room, thus forcing them to the Curry Opera House, which was described "a place little better than an old barn." The upper floors of the building were heavily damaged by fire in 1977.

Sixbey Opera House stood in the one hundred block of East Washington. The old Presbyterian Church was sold to Charles C. Sixbey in February, 1884, and he turned it into a skating rink. In January, 1886, he moved his grocery to the rink building. About 1890 the Sixbey Opera House began operating in the same building and was still operating when the Grand was under construction.

Little is known about other theaters. The Mystic Theater, 115 S. Main, was in existence in 1912. A Bluffton clothier, Byrl Masterson, noted his first job as a projectionist at the Mystic. The Gaiety Theater was advertising movies in February of 1927. The Wells (later called the Roxy) Theater was located at 109 East Market in the late thirties and forties. *Research by Craig Leonard*

BLUFFTON WHOLESALE GROCERY COMPANY

After more than 30 years in a successful retail grocery business in Bluffton, John H. Painter developed an equally successful wholesale grocery business serving a 90-mile radius in twenty-four counties in Northern Indiana and Northwest Ohio.

In 1914, before the first World War, J.H. leased ground from the Nickel Plate Railroad on West Cherry Street where he built his first 40 x 60 room for storing and selling groceries wholesale. Finding that he could get boxcars of sugar and other staples, during war years, he began selling to other merchants and drop-shipping to others on the railroad lines was the foundation of this new business. In 1914 his son Paul joined the business, entering the military service in 1918, and returning to the business in 1921. In 1929 J.H. sold his retail grocery store located in the Thoma building in 118 S. Main Street to Max Himmelstein, a fresh fruit and vegetable merchant from Ft. Wayne. He then concentrated on expanding the wholesale business where his warehouse space was at a premium. He added on to the warehouse until he had a space of 50,000 square feet.

The business was incorporated in 1929 as the Bluffton Wholesale Grocery Company and business grew from $500,000 annually to over 5 million in 1949. It grew from one solid-tire International delivery truck, to a four truck fleet in 1935, and to 19 units in 1959. The company maintained and serviced all of their delivery equipment under the supervision of Dwight Maddux.

The company became a charter member of the United Buyers Corporation, (UBC)

Chicago, in 1935, which provided the buying and merchandising power of 50 cooperating wholesalers. Two of the major brands promoted were Deerwood, the top quality label, and Foodcraft.

A sales meeting was held every Friday night in the office. Rem Johnston, printer, was responsible for an up-dated price list for over 5000 items they sold for the Grocery Company, for each salesman. There were 14 salesmen personally soliciting accounts weekly from retail merchants in Bluffton and surrounding area for delivery the same week. Thirteen hundred and eighty merchants were served. The annual payroll of $305,000 supported a work force of 58. In 1946, an Institutional Department was set up in Fort Wayne on North Clinton St. A survey showed Fort Wayne to be more centrally located in the area being serviced, so, in 1953, the business moved to Fort Wayne with 168,000 square feet of area, a small package department, cash and carry department, and 2500 square ft. of refrigeration space. All facilities were organized and expanded for better service; special parking areas were assigned; and the staff was increased to eighty employees. In 1957, the business was consolidated with Bursley Company to form the original Food Marketing Corporation.

After his return from the service in 1921, Paul Painter joined his father in the business becoming salesman, buyer, and manager. Other Bluffton people associated with the business were Tom Hefty, who joined the company in 1935 as sales manager; Justus Webber and Vern Wasson, salesmen and buyers; Luzern Fishbaugh as warehouse superintendent; Mary Thompson Landis as office manager. Others who worked in the office included: Mary Starr, Florabelle Smith, Louise Barringer, Jeanne Bynum, and Mildred Huffman. Other long-time faithful employees included Harmon Brubaker, Marion and Ralph McFarren, Kay Conner, Laurence Conner, Jonathon Wyatt, Earl Perry, Kenneth Perry, Charles Reber, Forest and Harold Stinson, Don Reber, Olan Brickley, Russell Hay, and Arthur Harris.

Cupp's Store

Ray Cupp started in the store business on the north side of the tracks in Uniondale after purchasing the general store from Bill Meeks. After the Gilbert block was completed, Mr. Cupp went into business in the corner store. He was there until about 1940. His store reflected a more recent time than Jim Waid's, which started when there was no electricity or cars. Although from 1915 on most people had cars, a hitching rack remained outside the front door for those who still drove horses.

The store was opened by Mr. Cupp at 5:00 in the morning so he could catch the Fort Wayne traffic . . . People who worked at places like G. E. would stop to buy tobacco, gasoline, or cold meat for their lunches. He closed up at 10:00 or 11:00 in the evenings. On Saturday, he usually stayed open until midnight.

When a customer came in carrying his baskets of eggs, butter, etc., he saw a long room with different counters for each department along the two sides of the room. There were counters for groceries, meat, dry goods, hardware and drugs. Behind the counters were shelves that reached clear to the ceiling. A lifter was used to get something down from those shelves.

A great big old coal stove sat in the middle of the room. Its doors would be opened now and then for someone to spit in

---

Meet Us At The Institute	Cupp's Annual Institute Specials		Meet Us At The Institute
AS USUAL BROOMS 29c each Thursday, Feb. 23rd, Only!	YOU WILL RECALL THAT WE ALWAYS PUT ON A NICE LINE OF SPECIALS DURING THE WEEK OF THE JOINT UNION - ROCK CREEK FARMERS INSTITUTE, AND THIS YEAR WILL BE BIGGER AND BETTER THAN EVER! WE WILL HAVE SOMETHING NEW AND DIFFERENT FROM FORMER YEARS. DON'T MISS THIS YEAR.		ASK US ABOUT THE **100 lb. sack PURE CANE GRANULATED SUGAR** YOU MUST BE HERE!
P & G SOAP, 10 Bars for ....39c CLASSIC SOAP, 10 Bars for 33c	**Marbles --- Free To Every Boy & Girl --- Marbles** THURSDAY EVENING AFTER THE PROGRAM		**OYSTER SHELL CAR COMING** — Leave Your Order — 98c PER 100-LB. BAG
5-LBS SUGAR, limit, for ....29c PERFECT PEACHES, In Full Syrup, can ....21c GOOD BULK RICE, Pound ....7c PRUNES, Good Ones, pound ....15c BULK RAISINS, Pound ....11c MARUFAT BEANS, Pound ....9c CANNED CORN ....10c POST TOASTIES ....11c VAN CAMP PORK & BEANS ....9c GINGER SNAPS, 2 Lbs. for ....25c FIG BARS, 2 Lbs. for ....25c MATCHES— 6 Boxes for ....19c 5c ROLLS WAX PAPER, 2 for ....5c APPLE BUTTER, Quart Can ....22c MUSTARD, Quart Can ....22c 25c MAPLE SYRUP ....19c LILY WHITE FLOUR, Pastry ....89c PERFECT FLOUR, Bread $1.09	**CANDY** MIXED CANDY, 2 Pounds for ....25c ALL 5c CANDY BARS, 3 For ....10c CHOCOLATE DROPS, Per Pound ....15c SALTED PEANUTS, Per Pound ....15c SEE OUR DISPLAY OF 5c BARS IN SOUTH WINDOW **EXTRA SPECIAL** AN EXTRA GOOD BULK COFFEE, at Per Pound ....24c GALVANIZED PAILS ....19c GALVANIZED FOOT TUBS ....39c 4-QUART TIN PAILS ....11c BLUE GRANITE WASH PAN ....19c MEN'S 15c WORK SOX, Per Pair ....11c OIL CLOTH, Per Yard ....33c RED AND BLUE HANDKERCHIEFS ....7c 1 LOT BOY'S TICK MITTENS, Pair ....5c PERCALES, LIGHT AND DARK, Per Yard ....15c ENGLISH PRINTS, Per Yard ....20c SHIRTINGS, Per Yard ....14c GIVE US YOUR ORDER FOR **4 and 5 ft. Poultry Fence** FOR SPRING	**FOR SPRING** —We Will Have a Full Line of All Kinds of— HOUSE and BARN PAINT, INSIDE PAINT, LACQUER, TURPENTINE, LINSEED OIL, ETC. **PERFECTION OIL STOVES** DON'T MISS SEEING OUR DISPLAY! **RUGS—CERTAINTEED** YOU WILL HAVE TO SEE THE NEW PATTERNS TO APPRECIATE THEM! EACH—$8.75 ANOTHER NEW HIT IN RUGS WILL BE SHOWN AT THIS TIME, TOO **SINGLE ITEM SALE** ONE ONLY OF EACH OF THESE ITEMS WILL BE SOLD AT THIS PRICE! 1 Bicycle Tire ....Regular $2.00; 1 only at $1.49 1 Wheel Barrow ....Regular $5.00; 1 only at $3.98 5 Gal. Can Motor Oil ..Regular $4.00; 1 only at $2.69 1 Open Washer ....Regular $6.00; 1 only at $4.98 1 Closed Washer ....Regular $16.00; 1 only at $12.98 1 Cast Top Wilson Heater Reg. $12.; 1 only at $8.98 1 3-Burner Perfection Oil Stove ....Regular $22.50; 1 only at $18.50 1 12 Gauge Shot Gun Regular $8.50; 1 only at $6.39 1 Disc Wheel Dan Patch Wagon, ...Regular $5.00; 1 only at $3.98 **SPARTAN RADIOS** and **RADIO ACCESSORIES**		— See Our — **STONE CHICKEN FOUNTAINS** — For Water or Milk — 39c EACH — One Assortment of — **BASKETS** 19c EACH — We Have — **ALADDIN AND COLEMAN LAMP SUPPLIES** WE WILL HAVE A FULL LINE OF EVERYTHING FOR THE YOUNG CHICKENS THIS SPRING **EGG-A-DAY POULTRY MASH** 5c Per Pound **BLOCK SALT** 39c EACH 100-LB. BAG SALT ....98c 50-LB. BAG SALT 54c

a mouthful of tobacco juice. Chairs and benches were placed around for people to sit and visit with each other.

The eggs and butter were traded, and an order was given to a clerk who wrote it down and then went to fill it. The purchased articles were then placed in the farmer's baskets. This was before the time of paper bags.

The farmers brought in eggs, cream, butter and chickens — by the sack or crate. Some of the eggs were resold to the townspeople. The store made a profit of two cents a dozen on them. People also brought in beef hides, which the store bought at two cents a pound.

When the farmer brought his cream in, it was tested for the amount of butterfat, and he was paid accordingly. The cream was then placed in ten-gallon metal cans and sold to Schlosser Brothers of Fort Wayne. For years, Clifford Fryback drove the Schlosser truck that came to pick up the cream.

Some items were delivered to the store. Schaefer Hardware of Decatur made deliveries. There was also a meat truck and a bread truck.

In the store part, there were horse collars, radios, stove pipes, binder twine, block salt, and double-thumbed gloves.

At one time, the elevator and the store bought a truckload of salt together. This was done about twice a year. Families used much salt. It was placed in the animal's feed.

The double-thumbed gloves were used by the farmers who had to shuck their corn by hand. When one part of the glove was worn out, it could be turned around and worn the other way. The store purchased these by the gross.

Flour and sugar were bought in one hundred pound lots and resacked by hand. Crackers were bought in barrels. A little heat box with a light in it was used to "freshen" them up. The store also carried yard goods and threads of all kinds. There were chambers, lard cans, and all sorts of butchering tools, as the farmers did their own butchering at that time.

Candy treats were carried for the schools. Mr. Cupp made up sample bags and showed them to the teachers and bus drivers who ordered them as Christmas treats for their children. Churches also gave sacks of candy and oranges at Christmas time. Hundreds were made up by the store.

Everything was sacked. On Friday, the clerks sacked soup beans, sugar (five pounds for 19 cents), brown sugar (always sold in two pound bags), and flour. Flour was sold in twenty-five pound bags. There was a special flour room. It was screened so the mice couldn't get in. Cornmeal was kept there too.

Instead of super-saver stamps, there were Saturday night drawings. Customer's names were put in a lard can each week. On Saturday night a name was drawn for one prize. The winner had to be there in order to receive his prize. Nice items like end tables and little rocking chairs were given away.

On Saturday night several round flat cheeses called daisies might be sold. The sales might have helped by Mr. Cupp's mode of promotion. He often cut a slice of cheese into small pieces and passed around the samples. This whetted the appetite for everyone to buy a pound of cheese.

Often cheese, crackers, and bologna were bought and taken home for the family to eat that night as a treat.

Paper tape came in about 1929-30. This made wrapping sacks much easier. Prior to this, bags had to be tied up with string.

In the back of the store was a tank filled with coal oil for lamps. There was also a vinegar barrel. People brought in their own containers and filled them.

The store didn't start selling milk until about 1918. Previously the townspeople bought their milk from people around town who had cows, or from Henry Schwartz, who had a dairy route from his farm.

Eventually an ice cream cabinet appeared. Fryback's ice cream was sold. Four flavors were carried.

There was a large walk-in cooler in the back of the store. The meat was kept in this and wasn't displayed because there was no refrigerated show case. Mutschler's of Decatur supplied most of the meat. Mr. Cupp kept cattle on a farm and butchered a lot of those to sell in the store. He would order those killed and skinned. He did the cutting up.

The store kept chocolate, marshmallow and honey cookies. The latter came in a barrel. They were the size of a saucer and sold for ten cents a dozen.

Pop was being sold in 1927-1928.

The safe was blown just once. There might have been one or two break-ins a year, but no one was ever caught.

Reportedly, Bob Cupp counted eggs in the back room when he was a young fellow. When his friends walked through the alley and they got to cutting up, he would throw eggs at them through the back door. *By Mary Harris*

David Meyer Company

In the year 1898, David Meyer and J.J. Klopfenstine operated what was known as the Meyer and Klopfenstine Harness and Buggy Shop, located north of the courthouse. Two years later David Meyer had completed a two-story building and the firm moved into these new quarters where they continued as partners until May 25, 1919, at which time Mr. Meyer bought Mr. Klopfenstine's share of the business and the firm name was changed to The David Meyer Co., later to be changed to just David Meyer Company.

In 1903 the first first ventured into the automobile business when they purchased one of the very first Auburn cars to be manufactured. "Dave" would wind it up in front of the store and start out full of hope and confidence but before he got back he would usually have to call upon some goodhearted farmer to pull him into town. After several such trips he swore never to buy another automobile and this he stuck to until the year 1909, at which time he received an invitation to join a party on a test tour of the first four-cylinder car built by the Auburn Company. After taking the tour of 30 days over all kind of roads through Illinois, Wisconsin and up to Duluth, Minnesota, everything "went lovely," traveling about 3,000 miles with only one puncture. After this demonstration, Dave decided to take the agency for the Auburn car, as the buggy business at that time began to fall off. In this manner the firm ventured once again into the automobile business, and now the large cases once used for displaying harness were filled with all the popular automobile accessories and parts. In 1927, however, the firm dropped the Auburn Agency and began selling dependable Oakland and Pontiac cars.

Economy Store

Another change in the business district of Bluffton came to the surface Thursday morning when it was learned that Levenson and Son, operating the Economy Store on West Market Street, had obtained a lease on the adjoining room from the owners, Kunkel and Vaughn.

It is the intention of the Economy to expand but the proprietors have no positive statement to make at the present time. The room east of the Economy has been occupied by a restaurant for several years and upon the expiration of the present lease, the plans are to cut an arch through the east wall of the Economy and in this manner connect the two rooms.

It is understood that the restaurant lease will not expire before next March, but if arrangements can be perfected and a location obtained the restaurant will be moved at an earlier date.

The Economy Store was opened by Ezra Levenson in 1894 and the store has enjoyed a lively patronage from the date of opening. Ben, a son of Mr. Levenson, entered the business after graduating from school and has successfully managed the enterprise since 1913, although the senior Levenson has never retired from active management. The Economy has been operated for nearly a quarter of a century and has taken its place among the permanent and reliable business firms of Bluffton and Wells County.

The restaurant (Premer's Restaurant) is a present operated by Hi Premer, who has enjoyed an excellent business.

Several years ago, the room was occupied by Gus and Fred Plessinger, who operated a bakery and cafe but this firm suffered the loss of the location through a disastrous fire. When the room was remodeled, it was occupied by Nelle Krill as a millinery store. The room remained vacant some time after Miss Krill moved her millinery parlor to West Washington Street and at the time of the Kingsland wreck, the room was used as a temporary morgue, the victims of the disaster being carried to this location. Some time later another restaurant was opened by Ervin Throp, who later sold to Emanuel Nusbaum, whom it will be remembered, committed suicide in the rooms now occupied by the Hotel Annex. The Nusbaum estate sold the cafe to Spafford Church, who in turn disposed of his interest to Lowman and Premer who conducted the restaurant as a partnership for two years. Hi Premer then purchased Mr. Loman's interest and has successfully operated the eating house for nearly three years. *(This article was taken from the September 4, 1919 Evening Banner)*

Estey Piano Corporation

The history of Bluffton, Wells County, Indiana, would not be complete without some mention of what many consider to be the total musical instrument, the piano. Bluffton was once the piano capital of America. More pianos were built in and shipped from Bluffton than any other single point in the United States.

In the early 1900's the King Piano Co. was established in Bluffton and was followed by the H.C. Bay Co. During the late 20's and early 30's, when piano production was at its peak, the Bay Company utilized close to 1500 employees.

Superintendent of the Bay Company was. B.K. Settergren, who, upon the demise of the Bay Piano Company, established the Settergren Piano Co., which flourished briefly.

In the mid 30's Settergren attained the manufacturing rights and licenses to the Estey Piano, as established by Colonel Jacob Estey in 1869, and transferred these rights from New York to Bluffton.

B.K. Settergren Company manufactured baby grand pianos at this location at Bond and Lancaster in Bluffton. The building began as the Studabaker Scale Co. about 1870, was Brown Furniture 1906-23, and Settergren later became Estey Piano.

With the exception of the World War II years (1941-1945), Estey continued to produce and ship quality pianos through dealerships throughout the United States and in several foreign countries.

In 1969 (having changed ownership and now experiencing financial difficulties), in its 100th anniversary year, Estey started a process of moving the plant, which ultimately concluded in 1970.

For many years a local craftsman, Don B. Spake, was superintendent of the Estey Piano Corporation. It was through his expertise, design, and production skills that Estey achieved a high degree of success as one of Bluffton's outstanding products.

Forst Grocery Store

Frank Forst came to Bluffton sometime in the early 1880's. He worked first as a baker, then went into partnership with Robinson Hatfield, in the Star bakery. This partnership dissolved in a very few years, and he then started a partnership with his brother Emory. They started Forst Grocery Store, sometime during the first years of the 1890s.

The first place they had the business was in a small building at the west end of Miller Street on Oak. Later they bought out the C.M. Miller Grocery and moved to a small room west of the Morris 5¢ and 10¢ store.

Next they moved all the stock to a store east of the Studabaker bank that had been occupied by the Central Grocery. In the meantime, the youngest brother, Albert, entered into partnership with them. Earl, Emory's son, and Dana Omen, son of Emma Bayha Omen, worked as stock clerks and delivery boys there for several years.

The business was dissolved in 1912 when Emory went on the road as a traveling salesman for a wholesale grocery business.

Fryback Ice Cream Company

John Fryback went to work for Schlosser Bros. Creamery about 1919. Schlosser Bros. had three large plants, one in Fort Wayne, Plymouth and Frankfort, Indiana, respectively. They were, at the time, the largest butter producer in Indiana. Farms at that time were small and most farmers had a few cows and a few chickens and a few hogs, etc. People on the farm didn't need much cash because they raised everything that they needed. After the first World War things began to change. Roads were better and people began to get automobiles. They had to have money to pay property taxes so they began to sell some of their excess produce. Some farmers that were close to town sold milk each day house to house. There was a lot of raw milk sold at that time. Those farmers that lived further from town had fed their excess whole milk to hogs. Since there was no electricity on the farm to keep their milk sweet, they needed a market for sour cream to increase their income. The hogs did just as well on skim milk with a supplement of ground corn or wheat.

Schlosser Bros could buy this sour cram and make excellent butter after it was pasteurized and churned. They hired men like John Fryback that had a farm background as fieldman. It was their job to call on farmers and sell them a DeLaval separator to separate the whole milk into cream and skim milk. Then the fieldman would hire a man and furnish him a truck to buy this cream. They would usually go once a week and leave an empty five or ten gallon can and pick up the full cans. The cream would be taken to the cream station in Bluffton or Zanesville or other towns where it would be weighed and a sample was taken and tested for percent butterfat. A check would be drawn for the farmer that sold the cream and taken to him on his next pickup day. This business wasn't real competitive when it started but later Cloverleaf, Sherman White, and others got into the business, and in addition, several companies were buying whole milk. If you sold whole milk, you didn't have to wash that darn separator with its many discs.

Schlosser Bros saw this change coming and had started to get into the ice cream business. They had their company-owned cream stations, and by this time, 1927 or 1928, most country stores bought cream also. This gave them several outlets to sell ice cream. In addition, Cliff Fryback had a pony and wagon and sold Schlosser ice cream on a route through Bluffton at about this same time.

Things were going pretty well for them until the depression hit in 1929. The banks closed, and their assets were frozen. They couldn't pay their bills so they filed for bankruptcy.

They gave their fieldmen a chance to continue on their own. John Fryback had the Bluffton cream station on West Market Street (where Old First National Bank parking lot is located) where he had been selling Schlossers Ice Cream. He also had some customers where he had been selling butter and ice cream wholesale. He had a little stock in Schlosser Bros. which he sold. He bought a five gallon batch freezer and started to make his own ice cream.

Fryback's Ice Cream was born in the depression of 1929. John Fryback's son, Clifford, drove an ice cream route and made the ice cream on Sunday. There wasn't much packaged ice cream at that time but some of the first factory packed ice cream made in the United States was made here. Most of it was put into five gallon metal cans and the dealers sold hand dipped ice cream. Most people didn't have home freezers. If they wanted ice cream at this time, they had to walk or drive to the nearest ice cream store. Cones were three dips for a nickel.

After a few years, John hired Scotty Mills to make ice cream. He had purchased a ten gallon-batch freezer which used ammonia for a refrigerant and produced ice cream much faster. As the business grew, he moved further east on Market Street. Earl Fryback, John's brother, had taken Mr.

Bill, Clifford and John C. Fryback pictured in the store on Market Street about 1950.

Mills place as ice cream maker. (Cliff Fryback took a factory job during the second World War and wasn't very active in the business after that).

In 1946, Bill Fryback joined his father, Cliff, and Uncle in the business. We built a new plant and retail store on South Scott Extended (Garden Store now.) We moved the Market Street store to the corner of Washington and Johnson (Republican Headquarters now). Grant Habegger took over the wholesale routes, and we started making our own ice cream which we had purchased from Pet Milk for many years.

John Fryback died in June of 1963. Business was good for many years but Marsh Foodliners started selling ice cream as a loss leader for 99¢ a gallon and 69¢ or 79¢ on sale. That was the beginning of the end of the small ice cream companies as well as the end of many small grocery stores in the surrounding communities.

I got a chance to sell the wholesale business to Hawthorn Mellody about 1968. In 1971 I sold the retail business and ran successfully for mayor of Bluffton. That was the final chapter of Fryback's Ice Cream Co. *Submitted by Bill Fryback*

GLOVE AND MITTEN FACTORIES

Gloves were manufactured by the Boss Mitten Factory and by the Great Northern Glove Company. The Boss Factory, managed by A.J. Farr, was a branch with headquarters at Kewanee, Ill. Archie Cook managed the Great Northern. Between 75 and 100 girls and women were employed by the two companies.

GRIMES FOUNDRY

The George W. Grimes Company operated a foundry. H.L. Norris was the manager. This concern manufactured oil well supplies and gray castings. Large quantities of oil well supplies were shipped by this company to the great southwestern fields in Texas and Oklahoma.

HARRIS AND WETERICK DRUG STORE

On May 1, 1891, Charles Deam purchased his drug store at 103 South Main Street in Bluffton from Eli Foreman. Deam was the sole owner of the store until the turn of the century when James R. Spivey became a part owner and the store became known as Deam and Spivey. Samuel Weldy bought an interest in the firm in 1921 but sold his interest a few years later.

Don V. Harris, who had been employed as a pharmacist with Deam and Spivey since 1927, purchased an interest in the store on January 1, 1937, following the death of Spivey. Mrs. Spivey retained an interest in the firm which was then called Deam, Spivey, and Harris. Mr. Deam had been inactive in the store for a number of years, so with the death of Spivey, a pharmacist was added to the staff. Eventually Mrs. Spivey sold her interest in the store to Deam and Harris, and the name was changed to Deam and Harris Drug Store. This took place in 1941. Charles Weterick purchased an interest in the store in 1949.

In 1947, the Farmers and Merchants Bank purchased the room at 103 South Main

Harris and Weterick Drug Store in 1954 prior to the use of both rooms.

Don Harris and Charlie Weterick the last day of business in November 1972.

Street from A. Walter Hamilton so the drug store was forced to move. The 105 and 107 rooms next door were purchased from George Arnold. At this time only the 107 location was used by the firm. This move forced Dr. Jess Scott to relocate his office to South Johnson Street. Geels Jewelry which occupied the 105 room remained for a time.

In 1953, Mr. Deam sold his interest in the store to Don Harris and Charles Weterick and the firm changed its name to Harris and Weterick Drug Store. In 1964, the drug store was remodeled with a new front and modern fixtures installed.

Both rooms were now used by the drug store. The business continued in the location until November, 1972, when the rooms were sold to the Farmers and Merchants Bank for further bank expansion. The fixtures and merchandise were sold to the Hook Drug Company. Harris retired and Weterick became an employee of the Hook Drug Store on South Main Street. This ended 81 years of continuous operation of a drug store in the 100 block of South Main Street which was known as the Arnold Block.

A subsidiary of the drug store was the Bluffton Chemical Company which packaged and distributed Deam's Substitute for Smoke, a product for curing and smoking meat. This product was distributed in the Midwest for many years. With the passing of time and the advent of rural electrification and refrigeration, sales had declined, but it was still sold in limited quantities at the time the store closed. The store closing also terminated the Meat Smoke business.

HOOK'S GARAGE

Ralph Hook opened Hook's Garage in 1932 on the first block of West Walnut Street in Bluffton. It was located across the alley from the back door of J.C. Penny Co. When the building was purchased to be torn down for the American Legion hall, he moved the garage to a small building on the property of the Old Tile Mill off South Bond St. This belonged to Elmer Baumgartner. In 1958 Ralph bought the Walter Scholl house and garage at the corner of Silver and Bond. Mr. Scholl had the Oliver Tractor Dealership in a larger building just north of the garage building. The business remained in this building until the death of Ralph, when his son-in-law, Charles Ault, took over the business and moved it out on St. Rd. 116 North across from Erie Stone Company. Chuck continued the business until 1987 when health problems of his father caused him to close the shop. Ralph did all sorts of mechanical work, but was known for his machine work. He specialized in grinding valves, fitting pins, grinding heads, boring cylinders, and pinning cracked blocks at a time when other garages did not have the equipment or know-how. Ralph designed the letterhead for his business himself.

HOOSIER CONDENSED MILK COMPANY - BLUFFTON

Hoosier Condensed Milk Company was originally called Riverside Condensery. It was located on the north quadrant of the junction of State Roads 116 and 316 near Vera Cruz. State Road 316 is still called Church Road in that area. The land was purchased in 1908 from August and Rose Klein. This information was found in the abstract belonging to Howard Croy, 3338 S.W. Church Road. His present home is built on the former Riverside Condensery site. Francis Walters (age 89) lives diago-

Hoosier Condensed Milk Co. in Bluffton.

Central Dairy, Inc. in Ft. Wayne Indiana.

nally across the road, the only building still there at the crossroad, from the time of the condensery.

An interesting note - the writer was told that during the 1913 flood some milk had to be brought in by boat.

Riverside was incorporated October 6, 1909, with 2000 shares of common stock and 1000 shares of preferred stock at $100.00 par value per share. In January 1926 this was increased to 8000 shares (changes are recorded in Corporation Record Book I in the Recorder's Office).

A traction line, the Bluffton, Geneva, Celina and Eastern, served shipping needs for awhile. When it was discontinued, it necessitated a move to Bluffton and a name change to Hoosier Condensed Milk Co.

The new site of Hoosier was just west of the Lake Erie and Western Railroad (part of New York, Chicago, & St. Louis and part of the Nickle Plate Chain) on the north side of West Wiley Avenue. The H.C. Bay Piano Factory was on the south side, the present site of Sterling Casting.

A petition for a name change to Hoosier Condensed Milk Co. was filed September 2, 1919, and authorized February 2, 1920 (Page 63 of Wells Circuit Court Records).

Through additional purchases at various times, the following subsidiaries are recognized. Pioneer Ice Cream Co., on Lafayette Street, Central Dairy, on Brooklyn Avenue - both of Fort Wayne, Indiana, Rose Hill Dairy of Bluffton, and Central Dairy Products of Fort Wayne. Manufactured products offered for sale included: (1) 40% to 50% cream, (2) powdered milk, both skim and whole, (3) Mil-Ko-Lac, (4) ice cream mix, (5) condensed and sweetened condensed milk, (6) cottage cheese.

The cream was first shipped in refrigerated freight cars - 200 ten gallon cans. The cans were covered with ice during the summer to maintain quality. By the 1930's customers were wanting door to door delivery - so refrigerated semis were used. Six truck loads of cream weekly were shipped to Breyer Ice Cream and several loads to New York. Through World War II additional problems developed. The semis were allowed to carry just one extra tire. When a blowout occurred another tire would go out in a very short time. It took three way calling, often at night, to stop a truck returning empties to meet the semi carrying cream, to transfer the cream to the other semi. In the meantime, authorization for tires had to be arranged. A semi load carried 204 ten gallon cans.

Powdered and condensed milk was sent principally to bakeries and candy manufacturers until World War II. Then the powdered milk was also sent to South America and Europe.

Mil-Ko-Lac was sold mainly for chicken and animal feed. Ice cream mix was sold to ice cream manufacturers and, for several years, to Dairy Queen in Indiana before Hoosier was sold.

At first, Riverside and Hoosier did not open on Sundays. As milk amounts increased, it became impossible for some farmers to keep the extra day's milk cold enough. It was also difficult for Hoosier to hold that much extra milk. During the flush supply in the spring, the total pick up each day would reach 100 tons. Pennsylvania also had strict requirements to meet inspection.

Employees often became a part of the family type situation with second generation hired. When a special formula for orphan animals was ordered, spouses came in for a couple of days to man the packing line.

Hoosier Condensed Milk Co. and the four subsidiaries were sold in November, 1958 to Wayne Cooperative Milk Producers, Inc. of Fort Wayne, Mr. Amos Neuhauser, officer and manager continued to work for a couple years - celebrating 50 years in the dairy business. *By Lucille Neuhauser Venis*

JOHN A. MORRIS COMPANY

John A. Morris was born in Rush County, Indiana in 1856. he grew up in Lebanon, Indiana. In November, 1874, he, married Mary E. Powell, and they had four children, Flo (Mrs. Harry McFarren), Elizabeth (Mrs. C.B. Larrimer), William D., and George S. John A. was employed in Lebanon as a clerk in local stores. He distinguished himself by his commercial knowledge and ability even at an early age. He gradually acquired the capital and influence which enabled him to start a commercial career of his own.

John A. started in the wholesale business, traveling regularly all over the state of Indiana. His lines included glassware, dinnerware, and pottery. He enlarged the number of lines he sold until finally he had twelve or fourteen trunks of samples. He traveled by steam train, interurban, and electric car. He got to the point where he had to have a helper, who was his son William.

He decided to open an office and sample room in Bluffton. This was a second story on North Main Street. Rather than have to travel to see his customers, he decided to pay the expenses of his customers on buying trips to Bluffton. This made a nice trip for the customers at no expense to themselves.

The customers picked what they wanted and an order was written. This was done by hand and sent to the factory for attention. The merchandise was shipped directly to the customer, with the invoice coming to the Bluffton office. At this point the John A. Morris Company added on their commission and sent the invoices to their customers for payment. The invoices were also written by hand.

John A. Morris was the president of the company. Later it was operated by Compton O. Rider as President and General Manager; Ray Renollet, Vice President, Harry A. McFarren, Secretary and Treasurer; Harold Pettyjohn, Assistant Secretary and Treasurer; and C.F. Ault, Assistant General Manager.

When the Morris 5/10¢ to $1.00 Stores were sold to the G.C. Murphy Company, the Murphy Company also purchased the John A. Morris Company. Later this was sold to Ray Renollet and associates and was finally sold to D.L. Haffner. The company was closed in 1980. *Submitted by Ola I. Brickley*

Keystone Lumber Company

Messrs. West, Baldwin & Co., better known as the "Keystone Lumber Company," have erected a fine mill, 40 by 60 feet and three stories high, twelve miles south of Bluffton, at the point where the railroad crosses Scuffle Creek, near the residence of Mr. Henry Barchman. The mill is now in operation, turning out large quantities of splendid ash, walnut and poplar lumber. The members of this company command a large capital, and are making business brisk in their locality. They are bringing on and will soon have in running order a planer and handle machine. Most of their lumber will be shipped to Boston, though they have already contracts in Cincinnati amounting to $60,000.

A portion of Mr. Barchman's farm adjoining the mill has been laid out in lots, two new dwellings are up and a third under way, and we should not be surprised to see a flourishing village there within a very few years. The location is beautiful. So much for enterprise and capital. *From an article in the February 3, 1870, Bluffton Banner.*

L.L. Bender & Company

L.L. Bender was 30 years old when he started his own business. Born in a log cabin on the "Smoky Row Pike" two miles west of Bluffton, he gained his first experience on his father's dairy farm. Following this he was employed by his father at hardware stores in Yoder and Linden, Indiana. Returning to Bluffton, he purchased the variety and hardware store of Frank Young at 224 West Market, the same location where he was retired by his death at the age of 97.

Most of Young's stock was closed out and emphasis placed on bicycles and motorcycles. Thor and Indian were two popular makes. To promote sales, Everett and Bill Helms, employees, raced Bender's motorcycles in area races. The Helms brothers, with brothers Carl and Harry later opened their own business, Wells Electric Company.

A *Chicago Tribune* story in 1917 about Charles F. Kettering's new invention, Delco-Light, to provide electricity for farm homes, took Bender to Dayton, Ohio. As a result the Street Fair booth in front of the L.L. Bender store that and succeeding years prominently displayed this new farm lighting system and the many labor-saving appliances it could provide.

The store pioneered in other products new to the market. Electrical supplies, the first motor powered washing machines, Frigidaire (another Kettering development) electric refrigeration, vacuum cleaners, automatic oil-burners for furnaces, etc.

In 1929 the appliance business was sold to Dwight Fritz (Fritz Electric). Bender then represented the Delco-Light Company in Indiana, Ohio, and Michigan from Bluffton. The 1930 depression plus rapid expansion of rural power lines dictated a change where Bender repurchased hundreds of the Delco plants he had sold, rebuilt them and shipped them in truckloads to the Pennsylvania mountain area still too remote for power lines. At this time a battery factory was set up in a section of the then vacant Grimes Foundry on West Washington Street. Named the Power-Lite Battery Company, Bender made lead-acid glass jar cells for the Delco systems as well as automotive batteries.

The Gates Rubber Company invention of the V belt to replace round and flat leather belts made Bender a distributor of their products in Northeastern Indiana. Other wholesale electrical, plumbing and industrial supplies were added as the depression eased.

Always interested in the farm and farm animals, as a sideline, from the 1940's to the 1960's, Bender made annual trips to Texas, purchasing carloads of registered Hereford calves. Many of these were sold for 4H projects in northern Indiana. Other ventures were in Mexican burros and miniature horses.

As time and age crept up, Bender's activities slowed down. However, he continued to be active daily in the business until 1981. Jack Barnes purchased the store inventory which he closed out in order to open the Toggery in the Bender Building. *Submitted by Paul L. Bender*

L.L. Bender, age 92, and store front in 1976.

Display in front of L. L. Bender store at 1917 Free Street Fair.

Bender store in 1917. Dealer for W. B. Brown Co., Bluffton chandelier maker. Note their wood and stained glass fixtures hanging from ceiling, and on center table. (l. to r.) L. L. Bender, Elizabeth Bender, Bill Helms, and Fred Wilson.

173

Leader Company

Linked with the history of Wells County, the history of The Leader Company is truly a romance. Dating back to the time of land grants in Wells County, the ground upon which the big store now stands was first granted to Abraham Studabaker and was one of that Indiana pioneer's first properties in Wells County.

Abraham Studabaker then sold the ground back to the county, the old abstract of title reads, and it was later purchased by John and Peter Studabaker. That portion of the land now occupied by the clothing department of The Leader Company was sold by John Studabaker to George Arnold, father of H.C. Arnold. The lot now occupied by the shoe department was sold to Nathan Schlissinger, the widow, a sister of A. M. Rothchild, of the Rothchild and Co., Chicago, holding the land until it was finally purchased by Sam Bender and E.S. Walmer.

The Leader Company was founded by Sam Bender, who is now probably the oldest, and the pioneer merchant of Wells County.

Mr. Bender first came to Bluffton in 1871, October, and helped to make the Miller corn planter. He occupied the room upstairs over what is now the Bluffton Hardware Company. At that time the lower floor was occupied by a dry goods store run by Anthony Sunier.

According to Mr. Bender's own story he worked for $39.00 per month and boarded himself. He worked ten hours daily and says he saved $40.00 a month by working at night for seven and one-half cents per hour. Mr. Bender says he could have saved a little more, but there was a lodge on the third floor that asked him to lay off one night a week because of the noise he made.

In the spring of 1872 Mr. Bender went to Rockcreek Township and worked as a carpenter and ran a thrashing machine and clover huller. In those days this work was all done by horsepower. John C. Raver was his partner in the thrashing machine business.

In March, 1875, Mr. Bender was married and lived on a farm in Rockcreek Township until he was forced to leave on account of his health. So in 1879 he moved to Bluffton and worked for H.C. Arnold for two years. H.C. Arnold then ran a store in the rooms on Market and Main which is now occupied by the Leader Clothing, shoes and notions department.

In 1881, Mr. Bender formed a partnership with Jacob H. Houtz and opened a store in an old room just north of the Al Gutelius Drug Store. They sold dry goods, notions, groceries and shoes.

In 1884 they sold their stock to H.C. Arnold and bought a sawmill at Curryville. The same year Houtz and Bender bought 991 acres of timber land in Scioto County, Ohio, and in June of the next year they moved to Ohio and put in a new sawmill. In October, 1885, Mr. Bender bought out Mr. Houtz and the latter came to Bluffton.

For two years the two men lived in a sawmill shanty built by Amos Christ, William Randall and Mr. Bender in three days. In the spring of 1887 Mr. Bender graded land for a stock of goods and formed a partnership again with Mr. Houtz, the firm name being Bender and Houtz. He had sold all he had in Ohio but a team of horses and a long wagon, and in 1887 he drove back to Wells County in the covered wagon in one week, a distance of 200 miles.

Bender and Houtz then opened their stock of goods in the room now occupied by the dry goods department of The Leader Company. In about three months Mr. Houtz retired and the firm became S. Bender. This was the nucleus of the now great Leader Company.

In 1888 Philo Rogers bought a half interest and the firm name became Bender and Rogers. This firm continued for three years and in September, 1891, Mr. Rogers retired and the business was then changed the to The Leader.

In 1892, the store enlarged and took in the room now occupied by the shoe department and continued in those quarters and under Mr. Benders's active management for ten years. In the fall of 1902 a half interest was sold to E.S. Walmer and the firm name was known as Bender and Walmer until in February, 1903, W.R. Barr was taken into the firm and the corner room now occupied by the clothing department was taken over. In the fall of 1907 Mr. Walmer retired and Bender and Barr continued to run the store.

The next year, in 1908, the firm was incorporated as The Leader Company with a capital stock of $100,000 with the following stockholders: S. Bender, W.R. Barr, H.H. Bender, M.F. Burroughs, Frank Elmore, Inez Cravens, Charles L. Meriman, Fred H. Barr, and Nellie Neiderhouser. Since that time all stockholders have sold their interests, the last being M.F. Burroughs. The stockholders are now S. Bender, H.H. Bender and W.R. Barr.

Mr. Barr came to Bluffton from Fort Wayne in 1880, with his parents, at the age of 6 years. He started to school here the year Mr. Allen became superintendent of the schools. He secured his first job with G.F. McFarren during the summer and got $5 for his summer's work. He went through the public schools and went to Rochester, New York, with a party of civil engineers. He then came back to Bluffton and worked at the McFarren Clothing Company until he formed a partnership with Will Smith in 1898 and bought out the John W. Tribolet Clothing Store which occupied the corner room of the present Leader Store. They ran a clothing store there for five years, or until Barr bought out Mr. Smith and merged with Bender and Walmer.

For a few months in 1882 G.F. McFarren occupied the corner room with his clothing store, while the present building of McFarren Clothing Company was in course of construction.

A peculiar fact about the corner room of the Leader Company is, that it has always been a clothing store. George Arnold, father of H.C. Arnold, first occupied it with a clothing and general store and he sold it to John W. Tribolet and Bro. Then J.W. Tribolet ran the store until 1898. The Tribolets ran a clothing store there for thirty years, the firm name being originally Humphrey and Tribolet, J.L. Humphrey being the senior partner.

Shortly after the incorporation of The Leader Company a second corporation was formed known as The Leader Realty Company, for the purpose of handling the real estate of the company. The company now owns 46 feet of their frontage on Market Street, from the corner to the Davenport and Ehle Drug Store, the length of the block on Main, or back to Perry Street including the property occupied by the Overland Sales Company and Studabaker Grain and Seed Company, back along Perry Street to the Alley, forming an L.

The Leader Company now is one of the largest department stores in the county and is one of the most prosperous financially in the state.

The owners now have plans underway for a complete remodeling of their present building. Before the war started a complete set of plans had been compiled and building operations would have been underway before this time, had not the war interfered with the plans. The next few years may see an up-to-date fireproof building standing upon the site where Abraham Studabaker got his first land grant from the government and did his first trading with the American Indians. *This article is from the February 1, 1919, Evening Banner.*

Licking Men's Wear

Our family. William, Ruth, Linda, Betty Sue, Jacqueline, and Tom moved to Bluffton, Indiana in December 1955. We had lived in Hartford City, Indiana for about ten years prior to that date. William (Bill), after returning from the service in World War II, returned to his old job with Morris 5 & 10 Stores but after ten years with them he was offered a partnership with a friend to go into men's clothing business in Bluffton, Indiana. After five years we bought out the partner's shares, establishing Licking Men's Wear located at 113 S. Main Street. We remained there for twenty seven years. Due to Bill's health we closed out the business in 1983 and retired. The building has since been torn down and has become a parking lot for Farmers and Merchants Bank.

Our family of three daughters and one son grew up here in Bluffton. They all graduated from Bluffton High School and all graduated from college. Linda (Licking) Gerhold is a graduate of Indiana University School of Dental Hygiene. She, her husband, Gary and family live in Indianapolis, Indiana. They have two sons, one daughter: Michael, 20 years old, junior at Purdue University; Jennifer 17 years, high school junior; and Steven, 16 years old, sophomore in high school.

Betty Sue is also a graduate of Indiana University School of Dental Hygiene. She lives in Decatur, Indiana, but still commutes to work in Bluffton, in the office of Dr. Kerry Schamerloh. She has a son, Douglas Frantz, a freshman at Ball State University, and a daughter, Sara Lynn Frantz, who is graduating from Adams Central High School in May, 1991.

Our number three daughter, Jacqueline (Jacque) Goodwin is a graduate of Ball State University with a degree in marketing. She and her family, a daughter Erica, nine years old and a son Brad, eight years old, live in Raleigh, North Carolina. Jacque is working as office manager and sales of a Cellular Phone Company. She is also a consultant with Beauty Control Cosmetics of Dallas, Texas.

Last, but not least, is son Thomas, also a graduate of Indiana University in the School of Business. He, his wife, Brenda, and daughter Nicole, nine years, son, Will, four years, live in Winchester, Kentucky. Tom is in sales with RMSA (Retail Merchandise Service Automation) better known as inventory control system for retailers.

Bill and Ruth met at Kelly Field, Texas, during WWII and were married there February 17, 1945. Ruth was originally from Marion, North Carolina and Bill grew up in Greensburg, Indiana. They have belonged to the First United Methodist Church for thirty-five years. Bill has been a member of the Bluffton Kiwanis Club for over thirty-five years. He is past president of Bluffton Chamber of Commerce, past President of Kiwanis Club, past President Bluffton Retail Merchants, and belongs to American Legion and Bluffton Masonic Lodge.

We are now retired after working together for twenty-seven years. We enjoy our home, family, friends, some travel, reading, sewing, crafts and television.

The 1929 Packard Roadster, belonging to the Linn sisters (standing behind), parked in front of their shop at 112 South Johnson. Note the large spot-light mounted on the running board.

LINN BEAUTY SHOPPE

Genevieve and Justine Linn graduated from beauty school in 1926. Their first beauty shop was located in the basement of the Bliss Hotel on South Main Street. When the building at 112 South Johnson Street became available, they moved into it and did a thriving business for nearly twenty years.

Genevieve (Peg) and Justine worked from early morning until late at night marcelling, permanent waving, bobbing and hair dyeing, but those long hours were rewarding.

When the girls took their newly purchased 1929 Hudson roadster home to show their father O.T. Linn, his only remark, was "Oh, you girls, how foolish! You save your money." In only a few short weeks after the incident, the crash of 1929 occurred.

Genevieve retired in 1942 and moved to Fort Wayne, with her husband, Harold (Bill) Windmiller.

Justine, along with her husband, David Sprunger, had two daughters. She managed the shop for a year after Genevieve retired, and then sold the shop to Evelyn McCroy.

In 1945, the shop was purchased by John and Ruth Micklitsch who continue a beauty business at this same location as of this writing in 1991. *Submitted by Mary Lou Sprunger Phillips*

Licking Men's Wear as it appeared in 1957.

LONGFIELD IRIS FARM

Kathryn S. Wright of the American Iris Society asked Mrs. Paul Cook (Emma) and Mary Williamson to write the history of the Longfield Iris Farm, the relationship of E.B. Williamson and Paul H. Cook, and their relationship to the Longfield Iris Farm.

(Articles on Mr. Cook's iris breeding has been published in the A.I.S. Bulletins.)

Both men were hybridizers of iris (dwarf, median, tall bearded and species). Both introduced many iris, E.B. Williamson along with Mary, over 100 varieties, Paul Cook and Emma about 70 iris and six hemerocallis.

Edward Bruce Williamson (July 10, 1877-February 25, 1933) of Bluffton, Indiana, started breeding iris in 1909. Although he grew a number of species, his earliest work was with the Oncocyclus, particularly I. susiana and Regella I. korolkowl. From their offspring, E.B. Williamson named four: John W. Tribolet, Maude Tribolet, Margaret Tribolet, and Cherokee Maid. The Indiana winters were much too rugged for these species. After a particularly severe winter when many species were killed, E.B. Williamson dug up the remaining rhizomes and shipped them to B.Y. Morrison of Takoma Park, D.C., where the winters are milder. Cherokee Main and Maude Tribolet are listed in the 1929 Check List.

Following the removal of the apogons, E.B. Williamson began growing and breeding the pogoniris and some species. He produced Dorothea K. Williamson (named for his mother) from a cross (I. fulva XI, foliosa) in 1918. From the tall bearded, his first introduction was Lent A. Williamson (named for his father) (Amas X ...) in 1918, too.

At this time Paul Cook met E.B. Williamson through the mutual acquaintance of Paul's future wife Emma Carnes. Paul was breeding sweet peas and a few iris at this time. From that meeting the Cooks and Williamson became close friends, even forming a business venture, the Longfield Iris Farm. Both were enthusiastic iris breeders but their methods were different. E.B. Williamson's scientific work was with the Okonata (dragonflies), his hobby was the breeding of iris. E.B.W. was known as a "selective breeder." Iris breeding at that time was in its infancy. E.B.W.'s method was to try to develop a good landscape iris: large, well formed blossoms, interesting colors, a ship-like stem that withstood wind and rain, and a vigorous growing plant with numerous flowers on a stem which lengthened the season. Bruce would choose a seed parent with the above qualities and gather pollen from other flowers with good characteristics. These crosses would be made in exact numbers to produce every possibility. While E.B.W. was busy at the bank or collecting "bugs", his two daughters, Mary and Jane, would collect the pollen in the morning in little pill boxes and spend the afternoon applying the pollen to the seed parents, under the direction of their father. This method produced thousands of seedlings a year. One especially fruitful season produced 70,000 seedlings. Iris friends would travel to Bluffton each flowering season to help sort out the best of the crop. Mary and Jane also were included in this exciting venture, learning a great deal about iris from the adults.

Paul Cook's method was purely scientific. In the winters Paul studied the genetics of iris breeding, laid his plans for the next season's crosses, and figured mathematically the results of the crosses. When his seedlings flowered, he would compare, mathematically, the flowering results with those he had made two years previously on paper. The results again the paper count were amazingly accurate. A scientist from Cornell University told me, "Paul is one of the best geneticists in the country."

Paul Howard Cook (January 27, 1891-November 7, 1963) was born in Poneto, Wells County, Indiana. Paul became interested in plant breeding about 1910 after reading books by L.H. Bailey. He first bred small fruits, sweet peas, then iris, daffodils, tree peonies, gladiolas, and true lilies. He

LONGFIELD IRIS FARM

Williamson's Iris beds on West Market in Bluffton. View shows the buildings which face Morgan Street between Market and Wabash.

E. Bruce Williamson about 1910.

Mary Williamson about 1960.

was a charter member of the American Iris Society, and a member of that society's scientific committee.

Paul was a mail carrier so that he could have his afternoons free to breed iris. Emma Cook (Paul's wife) assisted Paul in all phases of his work, hybridizing, planting, sorting, as well as entertaining guests and creating meals at a moment's notice.

The first Longfield Iris Farm catalogue was very small, listing only Lent A. Williamson, Dorothea K. Williamson and Mary Williamson (a small amoena.) That was in 1922. The first full size catalogue was issued in 1925. The last catalogue was in 1958.

Mr. Williamson, along with other early iris breeders, produced new iris almost instantly because of his method of breeding and the earliness of the venture. On the other hand, Paul Cook, patiently and methodically, working on his "blue line", his "black line", his "red line", and his "pink line", did not introduce an iris until 1937, 17 years after his iris work started. His first tall bearded iris, named E.B. Williamson, won the Roman Gold Medal in 1938. From the iris E.B. Williamson, to his last introduction, the iris he introduced were winners.

Longfield Iris Farm introduced Mr. Cook's new varieties until it went out of business in 1958. Cook then introduced his own. After Mr. Cook left the business in 1929, Mary and Jane Williamson issued catalogues through 1935. Their father had become Research Associate at the Museum of Zoology, University of Michigan in 1928. In 1936 Jane married and left the firm. Mary Williamson was then manager until the firm closed its door. Anna Tribolet Williamson (Mrs. E.B. and mother of Mary and Jane) assisted Mary in the iris business. Although her name was never mentioned in the catalogue, she was a hard working member.

Longfield also introduced iris and hemerocallis for Mr. E.B. Lapham of Elkhart, Indiana; Mr. Don G. Waters of Elmore, Ohio; Mr. Walter Welch, Middlebury, Indiana; Mr. Clarence Jonas, Fort Wayne, Indiana; Mr. Robert H. McCormick, Columbus, Ohio; Dr. Franklin Cook, Evanston, Illinois; Mr. Stanley Clarke, Mrs. George D. Robinson, Battle Creek, Michigan; Mrs. Glen Kildow, Alexandria, Indiana; Mr. Franklin B. Meade, Fort Wayne, Indiana; and Mr. Wilmer Flory, Logansport, Indiana.

Awards to Paul H. Cook for his iris introduction: 2 Hybridizer awards, AIS 1945, Foster Memorial Plaque 1957, 3 Dykes Medals, Salbe Night in 1955; Whole Cloth 1962; Allegiance 1964, posthumously.

Two Roman Gold Medals, E.B. Williamson 1938; Whole Cloth 1961. Many other awards, Awards of Merit and Honorable Mentions were bestowed on his iris.

Iris awards to E.B. Williamson: Charter member of the American Iris Society; 1926-1932 Vice President of the American Iris Society; two Silver Medals awarded by A.I.S. (Highest award before Dykes Medal) for Geo. J. Tribolet 1926 and Cinnabar 1930.

Iris awards to Mary Williamson: 1940 Dykes Medal for Wabash. Wabash was introduced after Mr. Williamson's death. Mary Williamson, following the suggestion of Mrs. Ethel Anson Peckham, gathered pollen from the older Williamson amoenas such as Cantaile and using Dorothy Dietz as the seed parent, made the cross that eventually produced Wabash. Many Awards of Merit and Honorable Mentions to both E.B. and Mary Williamson.

Scientific achievements of E.B. Williamson: Curator of Insects at Carnegie Institute, Pittsburg, Pennsylvania; Curator at Vanderbilt University, at Nashville, Tennessee; 1905 elected to the Sigma XI, National honorary scientific society; 1912 Collaborator, Bureau of Entomology, U.S. Dept. of Agriculture; 1915 Charter member and Fellow elected to Entomology Society of America.

Made collecting trips to North, South and Central America and the West Indies. He wrote and published over 128 scientific papers, collected and named 14 new genera and 92 new species, and had the largest collection of dragonflies outside of the British Museum.

Markley Grocery

Markley Grocery, a name synonymous with the early grocery stores of Bluffton, was first opened on Main Street by George Markley and his son, Jesse. A nephew, Ralph Markley, started working for them at the age of 13, when they moved to West Market Street. Ralph and his brother, Homer, purchased a one-half interest in 1926, naming the store Markley Brothers. Later, purchasing the other one-half interest, the store continued at the same location until the death of Homer in 1967.

It was always operated as a friendly old-fashion hometown store. Country customers gathered around the stove, using it as a meeting place, as they brought homemade butter and eggs to trade on groceries. Eggs were candled in the back room, where potatoes were sacked by the peck and peanuts were roasted to sell in the big glass jar, where many a hand dipped in for a taste. Cheese came in a round wheel and was cut to size. Quarters and halves of beef and pork were cut to order of the customer. Sugar and salt came in barrels and were sold by the pound. Tobacco in plugs, candy and cookies from their cases were sold in bulk amounts. Vegetables were displayed in the front window and then taken to the cool basement each evening. Bananas hung from their stalks to be cut as wanted. Phone orders and delivery were a service. Throughout the years many wonderful clerks served the store. The store policy being the customer comes first, and the customer is always right.

McDowell Hard Wood Company

The McDowell Hard Wood Company, owned by Frank McDowell, bought hard wood timber. They prepared the timber for commercial uses.

McDowell Lumber Company

Mr. Frank T. McDowell purchased the lumber company from Mr. William Ditzler in 1919. The mill was destroyed by fire and rebuilt in 1921. At that time there were approximately eight other sawmills and hoop mills in Bluffton.

In the late years of the 18th century and throughout the 19th century, the sawmill was typically one of the most important industries in every small Midwestern town. It was the second oldest industry in Bluffton.

Wells County had very few gravel roads, and most of the logs were hauled into town by bob-sled, which gave work to many farmers during the winter period. Several of the mills used oxen to drag the logs to the mill from the log yard. All of the mills were located on the two railroads in Bluffton. People owning land were very fortunate to have a place to dispose of their timber. It gave them money to clear their land for farming.

Mr. McDowell was engaged in hoop manufacturing at Decatur from 1916 to 1920. Prior to this he operated the Bluffton News Stand, which he sold to K.B. Skiles in 1916.

My parents, Mr. and Mrs. Frank Matson, for five years operated the West Side Restaurant between the railroads on West Washington Street. After I arrived (fourth daughter) they decided to sell the restaurant and Dad would go to Decatur and work for Mr. McDowell at the hoop mill. In 1920 my father returned to Bluffton to be superintendent of the McDowell Lumber Company, where he was employed until the age of 75.

The sawmill served farmers of the community in a 25 mile radius, and also pro-

Frank McDowell

George Yates and Frank Matson on July 18, 1950.

duced lumber for the railroads, U.S. Navy and furniture manufacturing companies.

The white and burr oak were produced for the U.S. Navy as well as other ship builders to make and maintain the many ships built. Red oak, walnut, hard and soft maple, beech and sycamore were consumed locally for the building of homes and barns, etc. Elm was used for the manufacture of hoops and staves; basswood for barrel heads and ash and hickory for handles.

Mr. McDowell was a "go-getter" and over the years owned sawmills in the following towns: Decatur, Hartford City, Montpelier, Fort Wayne, Van Buren, Parker City and Redkey as well as Bluffton.

The Bluffton mill was closed on November 6, 1959, and was the oldest and longest operated sawmill in the community. The scarcity of good quality timber in the area prompted the closing of the mill.

Mr. McDowell passed away September 30, 1963. *Submitted by Mrs. John E. (Mary) Smith Bookkeeper 1937-1959*

MERCER LUMBER COMPANY

On February 7, 1899, Harry R. Swisher started invoicing the stock of the E.H. "Daddy" Montgomery Saw Mill and Lumber Yard located on West Wabash Street. Years later one thing that stuck in his memory most was that it had been the coldest February that he could remember.

Prior to coming to Bluffton, Mr. Swisher was connected with the Winters, Mercer and Brannum Lumber Company at Elwood, with headquarters in Chicago, and it was Mr. Fielding L. Mercer, who, along with Mr. Swisher, intended buying the Montgomery Yard and Mill, which they did after the invoice was completed.

After the deal was completed and the firm name established as the F.L. Mercer Lumber Co., everything went along fine and the business grew a little each year. During 1907 they sold to the New York Central R.R. alone, one million feet of hardwood to be used as car stock and ties. The regular run of business would average around 100 cars of hardwood shipped each year. In 1910 Mr. Mercer passed on and his share of the business was taken over by his heirs.

The company kept one or two men on the road buying timber all the time up until the year 1916, at which time hardwood became so scarce and hard to buy that they discontinued the saw mill.

On January 1, 1924, the Swisher family became sole owners of the Mercer Lumber Co., at which time they held a meeting and elected a board of directors as follows: Harry W. Swisher, president and treasurer; Fred Swisher, secretary; and directors being Mrs. Harry R. Swisher, George Swisher and Marie Swisher. Eventually the name was changed to Swisher Lumber Company.

MORRIS COMPANY

On Saturday, November 14, 1903, George S. Morris opened a small 5 and 10¢ store in Bluffton, Indiana. Mr. Morris was a young clothing clerk who wanted to get into business for himself. He had no money laid by, but did have his home, so he placed a mortgage on it for $750.00, and by working hard and long into the night, and by using his keen business judgement, he was determined to make a go of it and he did. By buying for cash with order and selling for cash, he soon paid off the mortgage.

He soon found that his judgement was good in that Fair Play to all was the best way. He conducted his business on a strictly cash basis, because it was fair to all. He bought the best merchandise and sold it at the lowest possible cash price, which was fair to the customer and the store.

He added clerks and other helpers to the store force as they were needed, and trained them to earn good wages and never expected anything of them that he would not do himself and the result proved his good judgement. This is a policy the Morris 5/10¢ to $1.00 Stores always maintained.

The store prospered and at that time had to move to a much larger room and better location. It had more floor space than any other store in Bluffton. He found a location in another city and took his best-trained young man and placed him as manager in that store. He continued this practice until they were operating stores in Ohio, Michigan, Illinois, and Indiana.

The Morris 5/10¢ to $1.00 Stores, Inc. was the largest 5¢ to $1.00 chain operating solely in the Middle West. All the officers and managers began work where Mr. Morris started - at the bottom - and grew with the company. Officers and managers of the company were selected from the ranks of the store managers.

This Company was incorporated in 1915 with eleven stores all in Indiana and the stock being sold to the employees only. The directors were George S. Morris, President; John A. Morris, Vice President; Harry A. McFarren, Secretary-Treasurer; Fred D. Bell, and Festus Rhoten. Many changes came to this organization. By 1956 the officials were Ray P. Brown, President and Merchandise Manager; Fred Arend, Vice President and General Manager; Harry A. McFarren, Secretary-Treasurer; Compton O. Rider, Merchandise Buyer; Ray Renollet, Merchandise Buyer; and Harold Pettyjohn, Assistant Secretary-Treasurer.

This company also owned the stock of the John A. Morris Company of Bluffton, Indiana, a manufacturers agent of 5/10¢ to $1.00 merchandise. Selling in nearly every state in the Midwest, this company as operated by Compton O. Rider, President and General Manager; Ray Renollet, Vice President; Harry A. McFarren, Secretary-Treasurer; Harold Pettyjohn, Assistant Secretary-Treasurer; and Fred Ault, Assistant General Manager.

During all these years of progress the company met its every obligation in each of the cities in which it operated a store, taking the attitude of a home owned store. It took part in contributing to worthy causes, such as Chamber of Commerce, Red Cross, etc., and also advertising in local newspapers. The managers, many of them, owned their homes and were active members in the cities' civic organizations.

Ossian Grain Company

The company was proud of its progress and the development of the organization which they built, and many of the many friends they had in the four states in which they operated. The company continued in this type of operation until 1956. They were operating 71 stores.

The business was sold to the G.C. Murphy Company in 1951. It was later sold to the Ames Department Stores.

NIMMONS AND COMPANY

William B. Nimmons learned the coopers' trade at age 14, being born in 1836. In 1870 he moved to Bluffton and engaged in the manufacture of staves and heading for oil barrels. He was the controlling member of the firm of Nimmons and Company.

In the years preceding and following the date of Mr. Nimmons' removal to this city the Standard Oil Company, even then one of the leading corporations of the country, used yearly an immense supply of oaken casks and barrels for the transportation of kerosene and kerosene products. It was before the day of the tank car and the pipe line as they are known today and the demand was much greater than at present. Mr. Nimmon' knowledge of this phase of the business, gained during his employment as barrel inspector at Cleveland, enabled him to grasp the possibilities in the manufacture of barrels for this use.

Suitable oak timber was plentiful and cheap in Wells County then and accordingly this vicinity was chosen as the scene of Mr. Nimmon' operations. A factory was established on a spot to the west of the present site of the Studabaker Elevator and it soon became one of the city's leading manufacturing institutions. There was no difficulty in disposing of the product at a profitable figure from the very first and the venture prospered from its inception.

Timber was hauled in from all parts of the county. Mr. Nimmons owned his own teams for that purpose and most citizens of Bluffton whose residence goes back to thirty years or longer have distinct recollections of the long wagon trains making their way to and from the factory almost daily.

The factory was discontinued here in 1892 when the oak timber began to fail and was moved to Malden, Missouri, and later to Pine Bluff, Arkansas, where it is still operated under the management of Mr. Rainey, Mr. Nimmons' foster son. The product of the factory is the same as it was when the plant was in operation here—oaken barrels for the use of the Standard Oil Company.

Mr. Nimmon' entire fortune was accumulated through the judicious purchase of timber and its manufacture into staves and headings. At one time he was widely interested in Wells County farm land through his timber investments but with the removal of his factory his interests in that direction have been removed.

A brother, Ebenezer Nimmons, was for a time a resident of Ossian. He operated a stave and heading factory there for a number of years, succeeding L.M. Cary in the ownership of the industry, which has been discontinued for a number of years. *(This sketch was taken from the death account of William B. Nimmons in the June 22, 1910, Bluffton Chronicle. Nimmons built and lived in the house on the southeast corner of Market and Oak.)*

NORTH-FRAZIER COMPANY

The North-Frazier Tile Company was managed and owned by L.N. Frazier. Drainage tiles of every description were manufactured.

OSSIAN GRAIN COMPANY

It was 1942 when Ken Rutledge moved from Ft. Wayne to Ossian with his wife, Evelyn, and daughter Janice. They shared with his mother-in-law, Ida Yaney, the big house next to the Levy Grain Company on West Mill Street at the Nickle Plate Railroad.

Ida and Ken both worked at the General Electric in Fort Wayne on the night shift. Ken started hauling coal for Ben Levy during the day. In 1948 he went into partnership with Ben Levy, Levy Grain Company and continued to learn the grain business.

Ken Rutledge

After Ben Levy's stroke and death. Ken became full owner and incorporated the business in May, 1951, as the Ossian Grain Company. The business served farmers of Wells County as a feed mill for livestock, coal for fuel, seed for crops, and a place to sell grain at harvest time. Grain was shipped by rail to ships in Toledo, Ohio, and Detroit, Michigan; and by truck to Decatur, Indiana. It is also remembered by local fisherman that the corn cob pile out back was the best place to dig for fishworms.

Ken sold the business on September 6, 1969, and moved his wife Evelyn to Largo, Florida. They lived there for ten years until Ken's unexpected death January 29, 1980.

His daughter, Janice Williams, still lives in Ossian and is a teacher at the Ossian Elementary School. She has two daughters, Michelle and Julie.

Painter Grocery Store

In the early part of the century into the 20's, the farmers came into town on Saturday nights to bring butter and eggs. It was necessary for clerks to candle eggs, weigh butter, and wrap it for special Saturday night delivery. After shopping in town, the farm families returned to trade the value of their produce for groceries. Bluffton was a Saturday Night town. Streets and stores were full of people shopping and visiting - it was the big event of the week.

John H. Painter's Grocery Store in 1899 was at 118 South Main Street in the Thoma building. The room was a long, rather narrow room with apples and melons displayed out in front, and inside there were cookies in bulk containers to the right, with dishes and cookware displayed from there to the back of the store. Along the left side there were counters and shelves with tobacco, candy, containers of oysters and fish, dill pickles in open barrels, and bananas suspended in a big bunch to be broken off and sold by the dozen. Sugar came in barrels, crackers in cases, and cheese in large rounds ready to cut and weigh up as sold. Canned goods were displayed on the shelves. In the center of the store between counters, the charge account book was located. When customers came in to pay, J.H. rewarded them with a bag of candy from the counter next to the record book.

As grocery business grew, more space was needed, and a balcony was built across the back of the room, with a center stairway under the 14 ft. ceilings, for displaying Haviland china, glassware, and Volrath cookware - all of finest quality. It was customary then to choose as holiday or anniversary gifts, a set of one matching

Painter Grocery - note the "Queensware" Dept. on the right side of the store: bowl and pitcher sets, Gone With The Wind lamps, Haviland dinnerware, etc.

plate, cup, and saucer from this merchandise, as well as complete sets.

Being before the self-serve era, many clerks were needed to serve the customers. One of the Friday afternoon jobs, in preparation for the busy Saturday, was to weigh up packages of 25¢ worth of granulated and brown sugar. Clerks needed to get up orders, deliver to the homes, measure, weigh, and package all purchases, along with restocking the shelves. Extra Saturday help included Mary and Dorothy Painter and extra street boys to carry things in and out for the farm trade. Virgie Gray Brubaker was a faithful, long time clerk in the store. J.H. had the reputation of being a hard task master, but tops in training and rewarding help. He and Charlie Deam, a long time friend, often agreed that they had the same discipline and work ethics in the training of help.

Bookkeeping had to include the knowledge of bartering and charge accounts, as well as how to handle cash sales. Most orders were taken over the telephone and daily deliveries were made to the homes. E. Bruce Williamson, President of Wells County Bank, was a close friend of J.H.'s, and they mutually respected each other's financial expertise. The change to self-serve and cash method of merchandising groceries created many changes for shoppers as well as merchants.

In 1927 many units of elaborate electric refrigeration were installed in the grocery store by L.L. Bender. This was the first of its kind and offered refrigeration for dairy products and produce.

J.H. was a very progressive merchandiser. He was a man with no formal schooling past third grade, but he had a world of practical experience to guide his decisions for improvements, and he was willing to invest in them. To him, no place could equal Bluffton as the ideal spot to live and work. When he was ninety years old, he expressed regret that he wasn't young enough to get into the new supermarket plan of merchandising. He was 93 when he died and was still stimulated and alert with visits from family and former employees. "Nothing Ventured - Nothing Gained" was one of his slogans along with "The Customer is Always Right." He was also heard to say, "Waste not - want not" and "A penny saved is a penny earned." This is the way he lived and the way he conducted his business.

Patton-McCray Company

The Patton-McCray Company was organized in 1923 by William A. Patton and Morris W. McCray, both of whom had been employed by the W.B. Brown Company. Mr. Patton and Mr. McCray purchased a brick building on West Washington Street, which had been the site of a clay pot factory, and started their furniture factory there. At first the factory made only beds. Later they expanded their line to include dressers and kneehole vanities. Still later they began turning out feet for living room furniture, and foot stools. In 1929, they purchased a building west of the factory, which had been occupied in former days by the Commercial Hotel, conveniently close to the Cloverleaf Railroad Station.

Buying another building was taking a chance in 1929, for the Studabaker Bank and the Wells County Bank had both failed; but they realized that they needed the space. The company weathered the Depression. One year they grossed only $35,000, but they managed to stay in business.

One interesting story concerns the bank holiday in 1932. All the banks in the United States were closed, and people lived on the cash they happened to have on hand and whatever credit they had. The day before the bank closed, someone passed the word to Morris McCray. Will Patton decided this was a good time to collect a bill someone in Muncie owed the company; so he rode the interurban to Muncie and came back with the cash. He hid the twelve hundred dollars in the house overnight; and the next day the Patton-McCray Company met its payroll in cash!

Some years later, when the Caylor-Nickel Clinic opened its hospital in 1940, the Patton-McCray Company supplied the wooden head and foot boards for the forty-six beds.

It was World War II which brought an end to the Patton-McCray Company. Materials were becoming hard to get; and some employees were leaving to work in war plants. So in 1942 the company went out of business. The building was rented to the Farnsworth Company and in 1954 was sold to the Duchess Pretzel Corporation. *Submitted by Edwina Patton*

People's Store

"Not the oldest, not the biggest, but the best." This is the motto of the People's Store, one of Bluffton's best established department houses, established in its present location eighteen years ago tomorrow (Sunday).

The People's Store was founded March 9, 1901, by Morton Olds, John Bishop and Bert Patterson. These gentlemen conducted the business, establishing a wide trade, for seven years.

On March 5, 1905, E.W. Walmer purchased the interests of Olds and Patterson and the business was conducted by Mr. Bishop and Mr. Walmer, the firm name being E.S. Walmer and Company, the store name, however, not being changed.

On July, 1910, Wm. C. (Carl) McBride was taken into the firm. He retained his interest for six years and sold out to Mr. Walmer August 10, 1916. On October 4, of the same year Mr. Walmer bought Mr. Bishop's interest and since that time has conducted the store himself.

Hilliard W. Walmer, son, and Mrs. Walmer have owned interest in the firm for several years, but their shares were always figured in with that of Mr. Walmer.

The late Chauncey E. Dragoo, who came here from Montpelier, Indiana, to take charge of the shoe department, was taken into the firm February 1, 1918. He died on February 19 of the same year, and February 28, M.M. Frisbie, present manager of the shoe department, took over Mr. Dragoo's interest.

Mr. Walmer is one of the leading business men of Bluffton. He was born in Bluffton on the present site of the opera house. He attended the Bluffton schools and was graduated from the Bluffton High School under Professor Allen in 1886.

His first job was with his brother, D.A. Walmer, in Montpelier. He graduated in June and on August first went to Montpelier and worked for the firm of H.C. Arnold and Co., for four years. At the end of that time he purchased an interest in the livery barn of W.M. McDermott and was in that business six months to a day. He sold out his interest May 10, 1891, and came back to Bluffton.

He went to work for his brother, Will Walmer, on the old Walmer farm, the homestead being the brick residence now owned by J.E. Reynolds.

On August 1, 1891, he started to work in the shoe department for Sam Bender and was there about two years during the time George Becker was manager of the Leader Store. After Mr. Becker went into business for himself, Mr. Walmer practically had the management of the store and on February 1, 1904, he bought a half interest in the business. The firm name was known as Bender and Walmer.

One year later the firm took in W.R. Barr and these three men conducted the business for four and one-half years. At the end of this time Mr. Walmer sold his interest to Bender and Barr for $20,000 and the building, now the middle room of the Leader Store, for $6000. This building was then known as the Schellisinger building.

Mr. Walmer purchased two-thirds interest in the People's Store without an inventory, on March 5, 1908. During his regime at the head of the business, he added the shoe department and greatly increased the business of the firm.

M.M. Frisbie, although practically a newcomer in Bluffton, has won hosts of friends during his residence here and is already one of the boosters of the city. He is in active charge of the shoe and ready-to-wear departments. *(This article is from the March 8, 1919, Evening Banner.)*

Petroleum Hardware

The Petroleum Hardware was a bustling center of business and social activity for over 60 years; however, my recollection of its long history spans only the last decade. I remember tiptoeing over creak wooden floorboards that blackened my bare feet in the summertime. I would crawl into the huge glass display case pretending it was my secret castle as I'd eavesdrop on the old cronies swapping stories around the potbelly stoves. I could hear the ding of the cash register as its money drawer popped open in the distance, and the smells of the store would envelop me, safe in my imaginary world. Sooner or later, a frowning pair of bespectacled eyes would peer through the glass to let me know I shouldn't be hiding in there. My dirty faced smile could generally turn the most serious reprimand into a piece of juicy fruit gum for, you see, a little girl wasn't liable to get in much trouble when the eyes behind those bifocals belonged to her great grandfather.

The Petroleum Hardware was established near the turn of the century and shortly thereafter my great grandfather, Ray Barnes, bought into the business with Calvin Risser and Amos Snyder. In 1933, his son and my grandad, Claude Barnes, joined the business.

Although my childhood memories reflect only a brief and final portion of a long-time business, my mother, Betty Mann, assured me her memories are much the same. Grandad even said his son, Charles, used to play in the same glass display I did. Here are some of my childhood recollections: the wooden stool Grandad Ray would typically be perched on throughout the day, the area of broken glass that littered a far corner, "Don't go near the broken glass with bare feet!" echoes in my mind as well as the screeching sound of window panes being cut to size, the pulley elevator to the second floor, the old crown top gasoline pumps and the rattle of nails being scooped out of wooden kegs.

A child remembers sights and sounds, but it's the smells of the hardware that are most vivid in my memory: lead pipe, the oily floorboards, jars of seed coated with fertilizer, and especially the oil soap

Petroleum Hardware

Claude Barnes (left) and his father Ray Barnes (right) in the early 1920's.

Claude Barnes and Kim Mann Durr inside Petroleum Hardware in 1966.

Grandad would use to clean his dirty hands after repairing someone's plumbing or wiring. My greatest joy was to accompany Grandad on one of his jobs in the country. Off we'd go in his Ford pick-up truck. I loved to watch him work, his powerful hands and the precision with which he worked his tools. The shrill whine of the power drill was the only thing that frightened me, but Grandad would kindly warn me to plug my ears when he'd turn it on. Mom said I followed in her footsteps as she had accompanied him the same way a generation earlier watching him install people's electricity and plumbing.

In a recent telephone conversation with Grandad Claude, I asked him some of the things he remembered most about the hardware. Here's some of what he had to say, "When I was in high school I had a battery shop upstairs. We built the first crystal set radio from a kit. Dad had the first gas pump in Petroleum, but that was at the grocery. Gas sold for less than 19 cents a gallon. Kerosene was ten cents a gallon. We sold a lot of horse collars for around $3 to $4 a piece, and plenty of wire fence. Farmers had all kinds of stock then, chickens, hogs, cows. Ten to twenty acres was a good size field back then. Nails would sell for 5 cents a pound and seed around 5 cents a scoop. The fellas would come and sit around the stove every night, Sam Warner, Les King, Frank Hanes, Dick and Lou Burgess. Sometimes we'd even pop popcorn on the stove."

The Petroleum Hardware was a typical small town mainstay of days gone by. After serving the rural community for over half a century, it closed its door in November, 1966. Great Grandad Ray was 85 years old and had never retired. *Submitted by Kim Durr*

Piano Capital of the World
King, Bay, Settergren, Estey

Never again in the history of the world will one city produce the quantity of pianos that once were manufactured in Bluffton. This Wells County town was indeed known as the world's Capital of Piano Manufacturing.

A.J. King Piano Company was the first of several piano manufacturers to be established in the city of Bluffton (1908). King already had a factory in Michigan but built facilities for the production of player and grand pianos at a West Wiley location between the railroad and Bond (now Sterling Casting). The famous King Upright Grand piano was a popular item in many homes in the beginning years of the 20th century. The Wells County Historical Museum owns one of these fine pianos.

Mr. B.K. Settergren came to Bluffton in 1914 to serve as the factory manager in the A.J. King Company plant. He continued in that position when H.C. Bay Piano Company purchased and took over plant operations in 1917.

Settergren's desire to vacation in his native country forced his resignation in 1922. However, on May 1, 1923, he established the B.K. Settergren Piano Company at the Brown Furniture Factory location on Lancaster Street. In 1929 Settergren chose to fight a volatile economy by purchasing the H.C. Bay Company which had gone into receivership in 1928. He also made a $10,000 purchase for the piano portion of a financially troubled New York firm, Estey Piano and Organ Company. Although the Estey name was part of the purchase, it was not used until 1935 when Settergren decided to drop his own name in favor of Estey Piano Corporation.

Piano manufacturing resumed in 1945 at the Lancaster plant after a brief World War II switch to tables and chairs. The business continued to flourish under the direction of Settergren's widow after his 1949 death. In 1964 she regained the business by default, having sold it two years earlier, but sold again to Ionox Investments who continued piano operations until the factory was closed permanently in 1970. The Wells County piano manufacturing business had survived for sixty-two years and provided a quality living for many of its citizens.

Some of the manufacturing equipment from Bluffton's Estey Factory was purchased by the Walter Piano Company of Elkart which at this time is one of only two piano manufacturers left in Indiana. The other is Kimball International in West Baden.

Besides Bay, Estey, and Settergren, other Bluffton piano labels have been Alexander, Alexander Bros., Bellman, Chase & Baker, Drachman, Lancaster, Malcolm Love, Meldorf, Metropolitan, N.W. Nelson, Purcell, Schumann, Soward, Vollmer, Vough and Wegman.

H.C. Bay Company, the largest piano factory in the world as it looked about 1925. The plant was originally built in 1908 as the King Piano Factory and stood at Wiley Avenue at the railroad.

Upright grand piano built by the King Piano Company in Bluffton. This item is currently a part of the collection of the Wells County Historical Museum.

Pinney Store In Mount Zion

Ernest and Lucy Stout Pinney moved from Darke County, Ohio, to Mt. Zion, India, in 1921. They had purchased a store building in Jackson Township. This store building had adjoining living quarters with it.

A country store had all the necessary items needed to keep a household and a farm running back through the 1920s and 1930s. In the dry goods area were bolts of material, thread and buttons. Some heavy work shoes were also available. The store soon became the gathering place for the local community, and many a yarn was spun on cold snowy nights. The men would sit on benches around the big pot-bellied stove discussing politics and the news of the day. The women would sit in a circle on high-backed wooden chairs exchanging the latest recipes and the happenings of the neighborhood.

Fourth of July was a special time in the town of Mt. Zion when sack races were won or lost and greased pigs were caught by a lucky guy.

Christmas time at the store meant that the children got a little sack of candy and of course an orange or apple and many times Santa Claus came to visit. The Pinney's had four girls. The oldest, Vera, married Guy Grove and he retired from Estey Piano Co. Beatrice married Nelson Huffman and she retired from teaching school from Jackson School. Nellie married Clifford Fryback and she retired from Franklin Electric. Mary Ellis, who had married Pete Ellis, retired from Norwell School. Earnest and Lucy Pinney had operated this country store for almost 40 years when they retired in 1960.
Submitted by Nellie Fryback

R.C. Meyer Store

My parents were Reuben C. Meyer and Mable C. Walter Meyer. My father ran a grocery store at Riverside for 21 years. It was a general store six miles east of Bluffton, on what now is called St. Rd. 116. The store was our business place as well as our home - we lived above the store.

R.C. (as he was called by all) decided on building a huckster. The first one was gray with sides that opened up and were propped by a large pole. The groceries were on racks, and underneath the truck was a place for eggs and chickens. Then in 1932 he designed a new huckster, but this one was going to be a grocery store on wheels. It was orange on the outside with his name on the sides; cusomers walked into it from the back. The groceries were on shelves on the sides and the racks were built so that the products would not fall from the shelves in case of a quick brake or stop.

In the back was a place on each side of the huckster to keep chickens he bought from the farmers; also on the sides were places for eggs to be kept. Also in the front of the huckster was an ice box, a small one, but efficient enough to keep cheese and meat inside. Also he had a gas heater in the huckster for the wintertime. He had six routes, one for each day of the week. The store was closed on Sundays and Christmas. He thought that if you couldn't make it in six days you certainly could not do it in seven. He also lived by the Golden Rule.

He got ice from the pits in Vera Cruz and stored this in the old condensery, which had a room with thick walls to keep the milk cool. The ice was stored in this room and sold in the summertime to those who had ice boxes. He and my mom ran a cider mill from the last of August well into October. They opened on Thursday only from 6:00 A.M. until 9:00 P.M. He used an old Buick engine to run the presses and hired men in the neighborhood to work that day of the week. He bought the condensery and it became our garage for the huckster, a place for the chickens and the eggs he had purchased and was also a garage for the car and pick-up truck. He used every bit of space for one thing or another. He also raised calves in that place. Nothing was to go to waste.

He and my Uncle Walt ran a broiler palnt in the old hotel in Vera Cruz. They sold the broilers to hotels and restaurants until the depression stopped them. The men butchered and cleaned the chickens in the back part of the plant. The front part had the incubators; the next room was for the chickens that had just hatched; the following room was for the larger chickens, until they were the right size for sale. There were the regular drawn and the New York drawn. It was like an assembly line from the front of the building to the back.

I was born and raised in a grocery store, and it was my home, my play house, and also my school. Yes, I learned quite a bit by listening to the customers that came in to buy or just visit. R.C. bought the 5 and 10 in Berne and sold things to customers as they were loading the truck to transport what was left to our store in Riverside.

Mom had a large garden out back of the store, and also raised chickens for our own use. We also had our own eggs, for you see, we did not live out of the store. To coin a phrase of my daddy, "We can't eat up the profits."

He was a progressive man, and this is what he learned from his parents. I was his only child and daughter, and he taught me many things: business, and of course the Golden Rule was there every day - not just on Sundays. He did a lot of work in the St. John's Reformed Church in Vera Cruz, and did lots of things for other people; those people know who they are. The church had a couple of ice cream socials beside the store.

I didn't know any other kind of life - so that life was normal for me. He was my father, my teacher, and the best friend I ever had. He was kind, but he also could be very strict.

He bought the Morisey House for taxes and it was moved in beside the store in 1932 - he connected that house to the store, via a back window, also put in a bathroom and made cabinets for the kitchen with sink, etc. This was my first real home. We always left and entered by the front door of the store. It was depression time, but it was a great life.
Submitted by Mrs. Ed (Justine) Rodenbeck

Red Cross Company

Pumps, windmills, hand cider presses and similar articles were manufactured by the Red Cross Manufacturing Company. It employed 100 men. The head of the concern was J.A. Ullman, who was assisted by his son, Howard Ullman, Sr.

Retail Merchant's and Manufacturer's Association

Increasing merchandising and manufacturing in the Bluffton and Wells County area was promoted as far back as 1906 when the organization called the Retail Merchant's and Manufacturer's Association accomplished their first apparent major success. The group secured a contract with W.B. Brown in early May of that same year whereby he agreed to move from Huntington to Bluffton with his factory under certain conditions. The terms provided for free rent for a five-year period, with an option to buy whatever buildings the association provided him at that time. He would also receive a $1,000 bonus to help cover moving costs for his machinery, as well as lost profits during the moving time.

His factory employed fifteen skilled workmen who moved with their families from Huntington. Mr. Brown assured Bluffton citizens that additional work force would be added soon due to the increased work space promised him from the association.

Shortly thereafter the association purchased the truck scale factory on North Union Street, including machinery, for $4,000 from the Toledo owners. The Brown

Company would later move to Bluffton and manufacture hardwood interiors, furniture and lighting fixtures.

The association was congratulated for their success but encouraged to continue their efforts, as "one factory isn't enough."

The factory committee continued immediately trying to raise additional money for the factory fund. They had $16,000 raised toward a goal of $30,000. A two percent subsidy for a factory fund was considered for the city or entire township.

SAWMILLS

Following is a letter written November 11, 1959 by Frank McDowell who closed the McDowell Lumber Company at Bluffton.

By request from the Historical Society, I am pleased to give you my version of the sawmill activities in the neighborhood of Bluffton for the past 60 years. There has been millions of feet of timber used in the operation of the various sawmills during that period.

"In the late years of the 18th century and the early years of the 19th the sawmill was the only industry in activity with few exceptions. There were several sawmills in operation at that time and extending several years in the 19th century."

White and burr oak was the most desired species for many mills, the clear lumber being sold to U.S. Navy as well as other ship builders to make and maintain the many ships built.

Red oak, walnut, hard and soft maple, also beech and sycamore were consumed locally for the building of homes and barns as well as many other uses. Elm was used for the manufacture of hoops and staves. Basswood was used for barrel heads; ash and hickory for handles.

Wells County had very few gravel roads and most of the logs were hauled into town by bob-sled which gave work to many farmers during the winter period. Several of the mills used oxen to drag the logs up to the mill from the log yards. All the mills were located on the two railroads in our city of Bluffton.

People owning land in the late 18th and early 19th century were very fortunate having a place to dispose of their timber giving them the money to clear their land for farming purposes.

I will give you the locations of the various mills that I recall were operating when I was quite a bit younger. North and McDowell Sawmill was located in the Northwest corner of the crossing of the Clover and Lake Erie Railroad.

Buck Handle Factory was located Southeast of the Clover Leaf and Lake Erie Railroad crossing which moved later to North and McDowell location.

Montgomery Sawmill, South along Lake Erie Railroad where Swisher Lumber Company is now located. Moving on south along the railroads, there was a band mill located where Bluffton Grocery Company was built.

Just on the south side of South Street was a Stave and Heading Plant operated by F.P. Adams. Also a small Hickory Handle Factory along Indiana Street, and another sawmill operated by Smith and Bell along Lake Erie tract north of Wiley Avenue.

Meyers and Fetters operated a Hoop Factory on North Marion Street on the banks of the Wabash River. This mill was destroyed by fire.

Speaking of other mills in operation from time to time, Charles Eaton operated a mill along the Clover Leaf Railroad just south of South Street, and Ober and Mann operated a Hoop Mill on South where the Hoosier Condensed Milk Company is now located which was sold to Lee and Charles Fetters after their mill was destroyed by fire on North Marion Street.

James Eaton owned the land and operated the mill on North Baldwin Street. He later leased the land and sold the mill to William Ditzler. This mill, including the real estate from Mr. Eaton, was sold to Frank McDowell in 1919 which he has operated ever since. This mill was destroyed by fire and rebuilt in 1921."

McDowell recalls the time where there were six and possibly eight mills operating in the early 1900s. The McDowell Mill, which was closed November 6, 1959, had been the longest and oldest operated sawmill in the community. The scarcity of good quality timber in this area prompted the closing of same.

THE STUDABAKER BANK

In 1838, John Studabaker came to Wells County traveling overland, when the county and the entire surrounding country was dense forest and swamp. He opened a little store in a log cabin on a plot of ground where the court house now stands. In a crude way, even back in those pioneer days, Mr. Studabaker did a little banking business storing furs, which in those days were accepted as legal tender in exchange for supplies of goods and clothing. All goods were hauled overland from Cincinnati, taking fifteen days, and the customers were mostly the red skinned Americans.

In 1844 Mr. Studabaker put up a two-story frame building a little south of his log cabin and was named agent for the American Fur Company. In 1852 he erected a brick building and four years later started the Exchange Bank in a building about where the offices of the Studabaker Grain and Seed Company now are.

In 1863 the Exchange Bank was merged into the First National Bank with a capital stock of $50,000. The directors were George Arnold, Sr., Jeffrey Bliss, Amos Townsend, and James VanEmon. Mr. Studabaker was elected president, H.C. Arnold, cashier, and Hugh Dougherty, assistant cashier.

During the trying days of the war of the rebellion Mr. Studebaker safely piloted the affairs of the institution, and in 1868 the bank was reorganized into a private bank, namely the Exchange Bank of John Studabaker & Co., composed of Mr. Studabaker, Hugh Dougherty and Peter Studabaker. The institution was known by this name until 1903 and the Exchange

Buck Handle Factory was located where Almco Steel is now located on North Oak Street Extended.

Studabaker Bank

The Studabaker Bank building was built at 113 West Market.

View of the interior taken from behind the counter facing the front of the bank building.

View of interior prior to 1913.

A recreation of a former photo scene of the bank following the rebuilding in 1914.

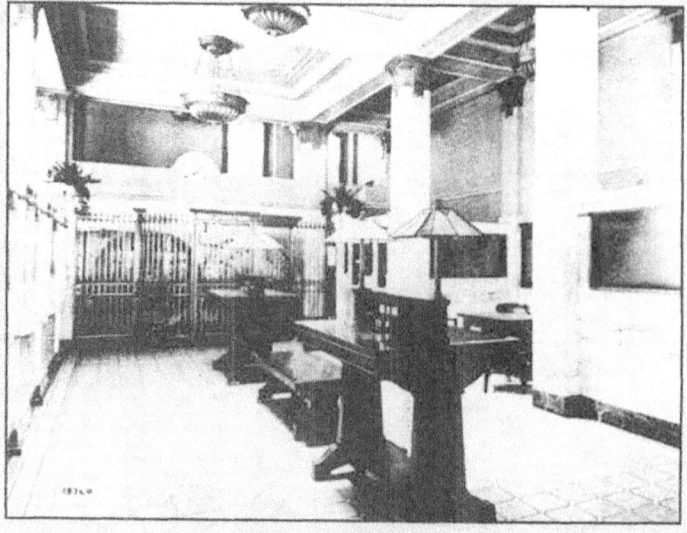
Interior of the rebuilt bank looking to the north.

Bank of John Studabaker was instrumental in bringing about many of the early successes in the business world of Wells County.

In the year 1903 the bank was again reorganized, this time as a state bank, Mr. Studabaker retiring, Mr. Dougherty remaining as president and both retaining their interest in the concern. The name was changed to The Studebaker Bank and the capital stock was increased to $200,000.

For many years the bank occupied the room now housing the ladies ready-to-wear department of the Leader Company, and was finally moved into a two-story brick building on the site of the present edifice. During the erection of the new building the bank was housed in the room now occupied by the Overland Automobile Company.

The present magnificent home of the bank (113 W. Market) was erected in 1913-1914. The vault alone is worth a visit, the large door weighing twelve tons. The bank occupies the entire first floor. The second floor is occupied by offices, five rooms of which have been furnished rent and heat free to the local Red Cross, since the beginning of the war.

Hugh Dougherty, now of the Fletcher Savings & Trust Company, of Indianapolis, was president of the bank from 1899 until 1904, when H.C. Arnold was elected president. He remained president until June, 1909, when he retired from the presidency and R.S.Todd was elected to that position.

Todd was a Bluffton product, having been a graduate of the Bluffton High School and of DePauw University, of which institution he has for the past eight years been a trustee. He entered the bank as errand boy when but fourteen years of age, and by his faithful wok and ability gradually rose to bookkeeper, assistant cashier, cashier and finally to the presidency. In addition to president and director of the bank, Mr. Todd has diversified real estate holdings and was an officer and director in various other local and outside corporations.

Mr. Todd's friends were fond of telling of his first job in Bluffton as "devil" in the old Chronicle office, which in those days was located in the back end of the second floor of the building occupied today by Linn & Saurer. Mr. Todd worked there two weeks for fifty cents and in drawing a bucket of water from a cistern where the Weisell Store now stands, lost the bucket in the well and was afraid to go back and collect his four bits. He still insisted that though he may owe D.H. Swaim for a rusty bucket, Mr. Swaim still owes him a half dollar.

John S. Gilliland has been with the bank for the past 28 years starting as bookkeeper and being promoted to assistant and cashier and then to vice presidency. The cashier, W.W. Rogers, started with the bank in 1905 as bookkeeper and is known by every farmer in the county, having been in active charge of all the farm sales which have dealt with the bank. The other personnel of the bank is as follows: assistant cashiers, C.B. Ratliff, A.H. Kirkwood, J.W. Stogdill; Misses Louise Barwiler, Thelma Lesh, Ruth Meyers; Chester Thorpe, J.F. Knoble and Wilbert Reynolds. *(This article come from the February 14, 1919 Evening Banner.)*

THE THOMA TRADITION

In 1849, Henry Thoma, a lad of 17, left his home in Ebersdorf, Germany, crossing the Atlantic in a sailing ship. He apprenticed to a cabinet maker in Findlay, Ohio - when finished in 1853, he looked for a location for his own shop. Arriving in Bluffton in October, 1853, he formed a partnership with Jacob Tribolet.

It was a furniture and undertaking business, established then on the exact location, at 116 South Main Street, until its closing in 1984.

Thoma and Tribolet dissolved their partnership, sometime in the 19th century period. Thoma's son, Herman, joined him at an early age and the firm became Thoma & Son. As the business grew, Henry and Herman purchased the Painter Grocery and Williamson Hardware locations, just to the south of their store.

Henry died in 1911. In 1922, Herman's son, William, joined him. To accommodate the funeral portion of the business, and to provide a facility for holding funerals instead of in the home, the store was remodeled and a chapel added. Morris McCray and Carl Shelley led in the operation of the

William H. Thoma

furniture store for many years, assisting William Thoma with the funeral home business as well. Later, Harry James, followed by John Maynard, managed the furniture section. Maynard, with his exceptional interior decorating ability and a pleasing personality, undertook the purchase of the furniture store by contract.

At the same time, in 1964, Howard Rich and William Thoma (Howard had joined Thoma earlier in the funeral business) moved the funeral home, now a separate business, to a newly-constructed modern facility at 308 West Washington Street. This became the Thoma-Rich Funeral Home, as it is today, continuing the Thoma tradition. The Thoma name continues as the oldest continuous business in Wells County.

The Thoma Furniture Store was closed in 1984 by Maynard. The building now houses several other businesses.

TONNER BODY WORKS

In 1920 Sylven Tonner purchased a small repair shop on W. Walnut St. in Bluffton. He retained employee Ralph Guiler. Here they made batteries and started repairing trucks and cars and "stretched" truck bodies by welding pieces of steel into the frames. His slogan: "If We Can't Make It Run, It Must Be a Snail."

In 1927 he moved to the Painter Building on E. Walnut, behind the Community Building. That same year John Painter, owner of Bluffton Grocery Company, asked Sylven to build a van for his business. Sylven also had a maintenance contract to repair and maintain all Bluffton Grocery Company trucks and equipment.

In 1929 Sylven owned the first power drill in Wells County. It weighed 25 pounds. At this location, Mr. Tonner first started building flat beds for hauling milk. In 1932, the first covered bed for milk hauling was built for the Hoosier Condensery, and The Tonner Body Works was born. From then on standard milk truck bodies of various sizes composed the major portion of their production. All the original bodies were hand-made. They also made semi-trailers for the condensery to haul canned milk to Philadelphia. They were some of the first long-distance refrigerated vans.

As business expanded, they designed and built tractor cabs and wood and steel van bodies. In 1939 they built Wells County's first library trailer. They built freight truck bodies, huckster wagons, passenger bus bodies, refrigerated bodies, egg bodies. He built Bluffton's first enclosed tanker fire truck body on which all ladders and equipment were enclosed.

Milk truck body built by Tonner Body Works.

Mr. Tonner would tackle any order, such as a body for a miniature circus (with crank-out sides); an elevator for Central Dairy for moving powdered milk to an upper level; an auger and elevator to load gravel into trucks; freight elevators for Bluffton Grocery Co.; a freight elevator for the Caylor-Nickel Clinic. (Mr. Tonner was approved to repair and service elevators in the state of Indiana.) He changed truck wheelbases, constructed sleeper truck cabs, made a stationary power plant with reversible gear box, and so on.

In 1946 he built his own 60' x 200' building on South State Road 1. Elmer Baumgartner, the contractor, poured the cement floor and put up the cement block walls. Sylven invented and built the rotary trowel used to trowel the floor.

Sylven and son Martin, along with Loren Lobsiger and Jake Felber, made the steel roof support rafters. Sylven bought four bomb carts from Army surplus to haul the roof supports to the building site. His employees put up these rafters and roof. There were no roof supports posts inside the building to inhibit movement.

Unfortunately, after only four years in his new building, Sylven Tonner was killed on June 3, 1950, in a plane crash near Cleveland in a privately owned plane that he was piloting. Ivan Moser and Dale Dunaway were killed also.

Sylvan's widow, Esther Tonner, continued the business for seven years. In 1957, Esther Tonner sold the inventory and equipment and rented the building to Mix-Mill, thereby bringing to an end the Tonner Body Works.

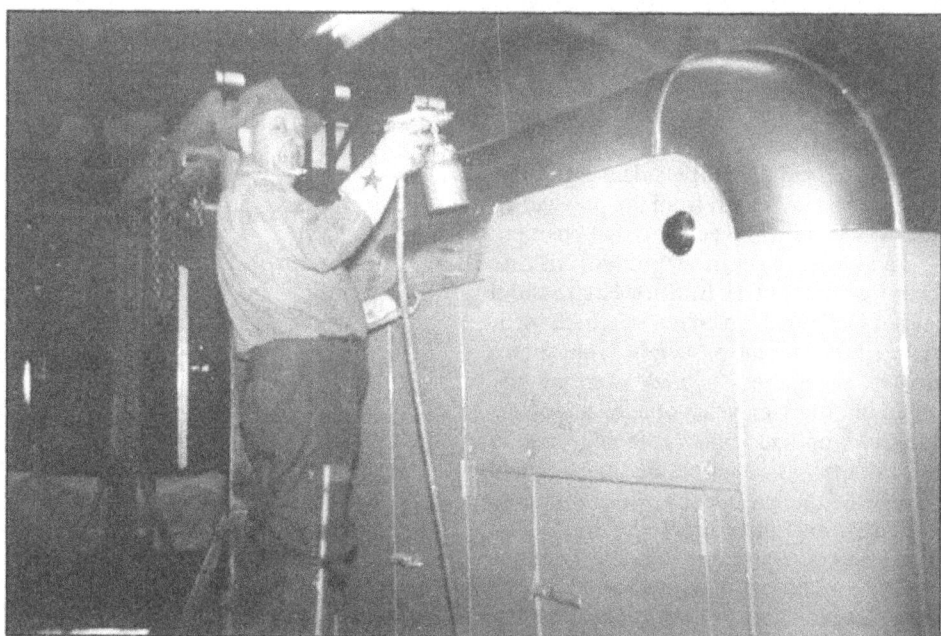

Sylven Tonner painting one of his milk truck bodies in 1947.

WALMER & ENGELER

Henry C. Arnold first established the firm known as Walmer & Engeler, in the room now occupied by the clothing department of The Leader Company, back in 1867. This firm was known as Arnold, Bliss & Company. It was composed of H.C. Arnold, James T. Arnold and Jeffrey Bliss. In 1869 George Arnold, Sr. was admitted to the firm.

In 1875 George Arnold and Jeffrey Bliss retired leaving the two partners. The two continued the business nine years when H.C. Arnold took charge of both Bluffton and the Montpelier store acquired in 1871.

In 1887 the Bluffton store was reorganized with two junior partners, F.F. Engeler and Jacob J. Baumgardner. Two years later, Godfrey Ashbaucher bought out the interest of Baumgardner. After time a Mr. Arnold retired from active service in the store, still retaining his interest. In 1909 Arnold sold his interest to D.A. Walmer, taking Walmer's interest in the Montpelier store. Walmer, Engeler & Co. then in 1902 purchased the interest of Ashbaucher, leaving the two present partners, F.F. Engeler and D.A. Walmer.

Walmer started his business career under the tutelage of M.M. Justus, who owned a butcher shop at that time, 1875. He then secured a position with George A. McFarren in a grocery store, leaving there in 1876 to work for his father, Henry S. Walmer, who ran a shoe shop in the building at present occupied by the Brickley Meat Market on East Market Street. Walmer worked there for two years, then working for John Dougherty in the lumber business, being woods boss of a gang of men cutting timber in the virgin forest near Montpelier. In September, 1880, he started work for the H.C. Arnold Company here, and took charge as a junior partner of the Montpelier store in 1884.

The firm in 1878, bought their present building which was built by George Gardner and the Ogden heirs, moving from the corner of Main and Market Streets. In 1903 occurred the disastrous fire, which gutted the building, causing a loss of $18,000 to the building and contents. The building was then remodeled and an extension of sixty feet built on, extending the building to the alley.

F.F. Engeler, junior partner, started work for H.C. Arnold when he was about fifteen years of age and worked so faithfully that he was taken in as partner in 1887. He has been with the store ever since and has had a large share in building the business and stock up to its present standard.

When Walmer and Engeler obtained control of the business they at once commenced to departmentize the store and employ later and more up-to-date methods in conducting a large department store. In this work they had the able assistance of George P. Becker.

Connected with the store for a number of years, and manager of the shoe department, was Alfred Saurer, now member of the furniture company of Linn & Saurer. At present Dana Woodward is manager and buyer of the shoe department, having been with the firm for the past two years. In charge of the carpet department is Mr. Ollum who has been with the firm some time and is also advertising manager and window trimmer. The firm occupies basement, first, second and third floors of their present building.

Walmer & Engeler Realty Company is an incorporated firm which controls the real estate of the Walmer & Engeler Company partnership. *(This article taken from the February 8, 1919, Evening Banner.)*

WEST SIDE RESTAURANT

My parents, Mr. and Mrs. Frank Matson, owned the West Side Restaurant for five

West Side Restaurant

years, before selling it in 1919. It was located in the 800 block of West Washington Street.

During this period the west part of Bluffton had many bustling enterprises, such as grocery stores, a meat market, a drug store, a barber shop, a pool room, and also a hotel.

A newspaper clipping of the time states that since the arrival of the piano factory, Mr. Matson had built up an excellent business and was enjoying very good patronage.

My older sister told me that, in that era, you could resell the bread or rolls left by the patrons. They said those "ornery" fellows from the piano factory would pepper the food so it couldn't be served again.

My expected arrival in June (the fourth daughter) was the reason for the closing of the restaurant. The cook, my mother, then became a full-time homemaker, and Dad went to work at the hoop mill in Decatur for Frank McDowell. *Submitted by Mary Matson Smith*

WHISTLE STOP ICE CREAM PARLOR

The Whistle Stop Ice Cream Parlor, located at 605 North Main Street in Bluffton, Indiana, just over the railroad track to the right, was built in 1976 by Bonnie and Norman Wall. The building behind the Whistle Stop known as the Yesteryear was also built by the Walls. The Whistle Stop Ice Cream Parlor and the Yesteryear Antique Shop were in the planning stages for more than three years before they were built. During that period the Walls collected the lumber and brick for the buildings and stored them. The Yesteryear was built from the dismantled remains of three old barns that once stood in Jay County. The brick Whistle Stop was built from the brick sorted and hand-cleaned during construction. They carefully cleaned and preserved a cornerstone date 1893. The walk between the two buildings was made from brick manufactured by the Star Brick Company which went out of business in the early 1900s. Norm dug the brick from an old lawn west of Bluffton, cleaned it and laid the new walk himself.

The chandeliers and wall clock in the Whistle Stop came from the old Keenan Hotel in Fort Wayne, and he also used marble from the hotel to make the tops for the ice cream tables. The street lights, outside, was salvaged from a Berne scrap pile.

The Whistle Stop Ice Cream Parlor and Yesteryear buildings, etc. were sold in May 1981 to Joe and Nellie Sleppy. Their daughter, Sandra Sleppy managed the ice cream parlor, and the Yesteryear building was remodeled for banquets and various parties for the community. The Sleppy's operated these businesses until 1984, when the Whistle Stop became the present Whistle Stop Video Shop and the Yesteryear became the Rustic Cove Restaurant. *Submitted by Nellie Sleppy*

WILLIAM STEFFEN

William Steffen was an enthusiast of farming and farm machinery from his youth. Born on a farm and farming with horses, he was happy when his father bought their first tractor, a Mogual, in 1916. William helped with a threshing ring and a steam-powered ditching machine. He went into partnership with his father in farming.

Later his places of employment were Covault Paint Shop, the piano factory, Jones and Ash Hardware, Ware Baker Implements and Dan Steffen Hardware. In 1931 he sold the first sixteen-foot John Deere combine in Indiana.

In 1937 he bought 28 acres at 3731 N. State Road Number One and started a repair shop in a hog house. In 1941 he took on the Minneapolis Moline Agency. He soon out-grew that place.

In 1944 he bought 200 feet in a cornfield from Wes Miller north of Bluffton on State Road One. He was the next after the Airplane Station and the Dutch Mill to build north of the bridge. Business was very good, and in 1951 he put up a Quonset building for storage.

In 1960, his son, Russel, became part owner. In 1970, he took on the Ford Agency and later the Oliver, Cockshutt and White. Business was very good and he enjoyed serving the community.

The business was sold in 1987 and the tract of land in 1989.

William Steffen was born in French township in 1901 to Peter and Elizabeth Schwartz Steffen. He married Mary Kaehr in 1923. They were the parents of three children, Mrs. (Warren) Marjorie Schladenhauffen of Angola, Russel Steffen of Bluffton, and Mrs. (Glen) Leota Reinhard of Ossian. William Steffen died in March, 1988.

WILLIAMSON HARDWARE COMPANY

Frank G. Thompson, manual training teacher and physical director in the Bluffton High School, became a partner in the business of the Williamson Hardware Company. Mr. Thompson purchased a part of the stock of the heirs of the late George T. and Lent Williamson.

The Williamson Hardware Company is one of the oldest established businesses in Bluffton, having been established in 1874. The business was purchased by the Williamson brothers from Jeoffrey Bliss, who had operated the business for a number of years before in the corner room now occupied by the Leader Company. The firm has occupied its present building about 37 years.

When plans now contemplated are complete, the Williamson Hardware Company will be one of the most up-to-date in this section of the state and will have probably the finest business rooms in the city.

The firm will occupy the two rooms east of the present room. The new business room will be completely remodeled and will be 40 feet wide and extend clear through to Walnut Street, as well as Market Street.

The entrance will be in the center of the room with two eight foot show windows on each side. On the west side of the room shelving will be constructed, reaching to the ceiling. On the east side the shelving will extend half-way up, and above that will be prism glass the entire length of the room, making it the best lighted room in the city. Prism glass will also be above the windows and transoms at the front of the building.

New and modern showcases will be installed down the center of the room as well as on each side.

Drinking fountain and ladies' rest room will be a feature of the new quarters. The ladies' rest room will be fitted up for the convenience of those from the rural districts who spend the day in the city.

The new room will have a concrete basement its entire length, making three full stories 40 feet wide and extending full half a block long. An electric elevator will be installed, situated so that all hardware can be unloaded from the drays onto the elevator, and then placed in its position in stock on any one of the three floors. A modern garage will be maintained in the rear of the ground floor for the company's machines. In its entirety the new building will contain 20,000 feet of floor space.

W.D. Clark and Ferdinand Mosiman have been with the Williamson Company for more than forty years. They were conversant with the stock when the business was purchased from Jeoffrey Bliss.

Col. W.L. Kiger, who for many years has been manager of the business, has been with the firm for the past 37 years. Mr. Kiger entered the business as a clerk and by his business ability worked into the managership. During the entire time Mr. Kiger has been with the firm, he has paid every bill by the company. Mr. Kiger has never been away from his desk more than one week at a time during his regime.

Frank Thompson is a popular and well-known young man and is the son-in-law of D.H. Swaim, publisher of the Evening News. During the time Mr. Thompson has made Bluffton his home, he has won a host of warm friends, both among the business men of the city and among the school children with whom he has been associated.

Mr. Thompson will resign his position in the high school and give his entire attention to the hardware business. (*This article was from the Tuesday, June 17, 1919, Evening Banner.*)

William Steffen's place of business in approximately 1952.

Right - Southeast corner of the Market and Johnson Street intersection.

Wickliffe Store in Zanesville taken about 1925. This building was built in 1890.

Keystone Store building is still standing on the east side of Main (200W).

View of the Bluffton Manufacturing Company about 1902. They produced farm implements and washing machines.

Left - This office set was built by the A.W. Cotton Company of Bluffton and sold to and only used by Dr. William A. Gitlin. It was built about 1936 at a cost of $225 and is currently a part of the collection in the Wells County Historical Museum.

"Bob" Wolf assisting "Ed" Moser at the Craigville Garage with the assembly of farm machinery.

The Deam Drug Store owned by Charles Deam was located in the Arnold Block across Main Street form the Courthouse. Although greatly altered, this portion of the block remains as a part of the Farmer and Merchant's Bank.

The Great Northern Glove Company building built in 1912 on East Washington behind the present Post office location. Later it was used by Franklin Electric.

Right - Number 2 block tower one-half mile east of Uniondale in 1893 with an Erie Railroad hand car. Charles Porter station master is on stairway platform. Section hands (l. to r.) are Melvin Wolf, William Holden (foreman), Chas. Gaskill, John Burnsides, and seated is one unknown and on the right, Emmet Strausbaugh.

Uniondale Depot in 1909. Charles Porter was the agent. Photo courtesy Mr. & Mrs. George Schwartz.

Clover Leaf Depot was built in 1902 and was Bluffton's last remaining depot when it was demolished in 1991.

Construction of the Erie Lackawanna track elevation near Uniondale.

Left - South Main Street looking North from Washington Street in 1951. Photo courtesy of Hersh Robbins.

Birdseye view of Uniondale looking east from the Erie water tower. Photo courtesy of Mr. & Mrs. Schwartz.

Early view of the Wasson grocery and Gas Station in Craigville prior to the addition of the Post Office.

Office of Dr. Frank Garrett on Main Street in Liberty Center as it looked about 1980.

Right - *John Waid General Store in Uniondale.*

Hall & Garton General Store in Tocsin located on the east side of Main. This is no longer standing. The bank and hardware were later built in 1890.

Bluffton Boot and Shoe Mfg. Co. located on the southwest corner of Indiana and Washington Streets. The building was built by the Bluffton Commercial Club in 1892 as inducement for a shoe company to locate here. The enterprise only survived for about two years. Later occupants included Patton-McCray Company, Farnsworth Radio, and Bachmann Pretzel.

The Hetrick-Wolf Grocery once located in Craigville on Market Street just west of Main (IN 301). Standing in front is Mrs. Robert (Tracy) Wolf who helped in the store. The south side of Craigville School can be seen, one block away, to the north.

Franklin Electric Co., Inc.

E. J. (Ed) Schaefer

T. W. (Wayne) Kehoe

World War II was still raging, both in Europe and in the Pacific, in November, 1944, when Franklin Electric Company was founded in Bluffton, Indiana, by E.J. (Ed) Schaefer and T.W. (Wayne) Kehoe. These two men, after successful careers in industry as electrical engineers, were convinced that they could develop a successful business by mass-producing small electric motors custom-designed for the specific needs of individual customers.

The choice of Bluffton as a location for this new company was largely a result of war-time circumstances. All employment was controlled by the War Manpower Commission, which told Ed and Wayne that there was no extra manpower in Indiana, and they could not start a company. However, after much argument and persuasion, and learning that the Farnsworth Company in Bluffton was completing a government contract and discharging employees, the commission relented and authorized starting the new company in Bluffton.

Both Ed and Wayne would probably be described today as workaholics, especially in the early days of the company when all their energies were needed to get the fledgling company off the ground. Their lifelong devotion was to the company, second perhaps only to their families. Both credit the early success of the company in part to the support and encouragement of their wives, Hildegarde and Ruth, respectively.

Ed Schaefer was born in Baltimore, Maryland, and was always interested in technical and engineering matters. He graduated from Baltimore Polytechnic Institute, one of the most academically demanding high schools in the nation, and from Johns Hopkins University with an electrical engineering degree. He worked for the General Electric Company, first in Schenectady, New York, then in Fort Wayne, Indiana, where he was head of electrical design for fractional horsepower motors, until he left to form Franklin Electric with Wayne. Ed has some 80 U.S. patents to his credit, most relating to electrical or mechanical aspects of electric motors. He has been active in church and civic projects, including the Caylor-Nickel Medical Research Foundation, and later personal interests of music, flower gardening and an occasional vacation at the ocean at Baltimore. While his first interest was technical, he is well read and informed on national and international matters.

Unlike Ed, Wayne Kehoe was a native Hoosier, born in the small community of Staunton. He graduated from Glen High School in Shelbyville, where he played baseball and basketball. He then attended and graduated from Rose Polytechnical Institute (now Rose-Hulman) at Terre Haute. After college he also worked for General Electric, first in Schenectady, then in Cleveland, Ohio. He left G.E. to become Chief Engineer for the Fort Wayne City Utilities. It was from this position that he joined Ed to found Franklin Electric. Wayne was active in technical societies, civic and church activities. He was head of the Bluffton Chamber of Commerce for a time, working for local business and industrial expansion in Wells County. His chief interests or hobbies were golf and Bridge.

Ed and Wayne were both friendly and congenial and willing to talk to anyone in the plant on ideas, complaints or suggestions. Probably nothing shows the character and abilities of these two men better than the respect and esteem with which they were and are held by co-workers at Franklin Electric, and the people of Bluffton and Wells County.

Finding a location for the new company in Bluffton was not easy for Ed and Wayne during the war when there was no new building, and all existing industrial buildings were being utilized for the war effort. They finally were able to rent the second floor of an old shoe factory in the 100 block of East Washington Street, then occupied by the Culver Manufacturing Company, a glove manufacturer.

Deciding on a company name, they had visions of national growth and decided against using their own names. The name picked was, of course, Franklin Electric Company, after Benjamin Franklin, who could be considered our nation's first electrical engineer.

When the company started in November, 1944, there was little civilian market for electric motors and the only significant customer was the Armed Forces. Franklin's first product was a lightweight generator for the U.S. Army Signal Corps. It was part of a 22 pound, backpack, gasoline- engine-driven generator set for powering radios of paratroopers and other assault troops. Employment at 1944 year-end was a grand total of five, the two founders and three other men. Production during 1945 consisted entirely of Army Signal Corp. generators. When the war ended in August, orders ceased. While everyone was, of course, glad the conflict was over, conversion to a peacetime economy and new products was not easy for a struggling new company.

Production of motors had been anticipated, but many months were needed before designs were completed, tooling and equipment obtained, and orders received. From a peak employment of nearly 100, employment dropped to about a dozen. These were tough times for Franklin and its employees. Orders were few and money scarce. Many vendors had misgivings about the young company and would sell for cash only. Some of the old time employees remember working only three days a week, and on occasion, being asked to delay cashing their paychecks until payment was received from a customer. A desk might consist of a sheet of plywood on two saw horses, with orange crates for bookcases. Early employees laugh now and think of these as "the good old days" but it was no laughing matter at the time, instead, deadly serious. A few employees thought the company would fail and left, but the great majority of employees had faith and not only stayed, but worked long, long hours along with Wayne and Ed. "The Canteen" in those days consisted of one lift-top pop cooler, operated on the honor system. While officially discouraged, some did go to Graden's service station behind Franklin for rolls, doughnuts, and candy during break.

In 1946, the principal pieces of equipment consisted of two lamination punch presses, one for stator and one for rotor, plus lathes for shafts and end bells. The presses were hand fed and the stators were hand wound. For varnish treatment, racks of stators were lowered by hoist into the varnish tank, drained, then put in a small batch oven to cure. Once the hoist support broke, dropping hoist, rack, and all into the tank, splashing varnish over a wide area and igniting it. The fire department was able to extinguish the fire with little building damage. The stator baking oven appeared undamaged, but when reloaded, it blew up. Mr. Culver, the building owner, was understandably upset over these events. When a similar fire occurred less than a week later, Mr. Culver delivered an ultimatum - either get out or buy the building. Ed and Wayne somehow managed to scrape together enough money to purchase the building in 1947. It didn't take long to fill the entire building. The second floor saw immediate use as the stator department, varnish tank-oven, and tool room. The first floor was primarily devoted to rotor and assembly departments. Shaft and end bell departments were located in the basement, with the punch press in the back room.

A little later, when the first 150 - ton automatic lamination press was ordered, it arrived by flat-bed trailer during, of all times, Street Fair. After maneuvering his long tractor/trailer through streets jammed with parked cars and back down narrow alleys, the truck driver vowed he would never return to Bluffton.

Application for the motors varied, but the largest use was for pumps, fans and blowers. In Franklin's entire history, the largest single use for their motors has been for pumping water from wells. Some other applications for these early motors included oil burners, garage doors, milk coolers and other farm equipment, tool and workshop motors, X-ray machines and even a tiny motor for electric erasers. Most pump motors at that time had fairly large enough opening with no screens, and it was not uncommon for a motor to be returned with a small animal or insect in it. They had crawled in for warmth and then died or were killed when the motor started. The repair department saved some of these mice, snakes, scorpions, toads, lizards, and large insects, and preserved them by dipping them in the varnish tank and baking. These amateur taxidermists had a collection of these "critters" mounted on a large board hanging over the repair department. The first plant expansion was a metal building added to the southeast part of the Washington Street building. Promptly dubbed "the sheep shed," it was cold in winter, hot in summer, and noisy when it rained.

A suggestion award system was instituted early in Franklin's history. Ed and Wayne recognized the talents and ideas of their co-workers and felt they should share in the economic benefits of suggestions that resulted in cost savings and improved quality. The first award was for $5.00 for suggesting a side opening in the test booth for diverting motors needing adjustment.

In 1948, the company paper, <u>Frankly Speaking,</u> covering company and employee news, was established. By this time, well over a hundred motors a day were being produced.

By 1950, the Washington Street plant was "bursting at the seams." Several departments were also located in the old Farnsworth Building on Washington Street; the offices were scattered between the Washington Street plant and two different areas of the New Bliss Hotel, across the street. These makeshift arrangements did not provide nearly enough room and were very inefficient, so it was decided something had to be done for more space. The company was successful enough by now that several neighboring communities were making overtures to Franklin Electric to move their city. However, Ed and Wayne wanted to stay in Bluffton and made a proposal to the Bluffton Chamber of Commerce for a new $200,000 building to be financed by $110,000 in loans to the company and the remaining $90,000 through a mortgage. The Chamber of Commerce realized the value of Franklin to the community and agreed to the proposal. A Chamber committee worked out the details and within four months the required funds had been pledged by local businessmen and citizens and a mortgage arranged. The loan was repaid as promised prior to the due date.

Ground was broken in early 1951 for the new plant, on East Spring Street, on 15 acres at Bluffton's south edge. The building was one story, measuring 200 x 248 feet including manufacturing and office areas. It was completed the following year for $217,000 with equipment raising the total to over $300,000. The original structure comprised 49,000 square feet and occupied what is now the northeast corner of the present building. Many additions have been made since and the Spring Street plant now covers over 400,000 square feet, over eight times the size of the original. For those agriculturally oriented, this is over 9 acres under roof.

Everyone was elated when the move could be made to the new building. However, business had grown so rapidly between the planning of the building and its completion that there was not room for all operations, and several departments remained in the Washington Street plant.

By the end of 1953, production had reached 1000 motors per day and the payroll included about 500 names. The Franklin Electric Credit Union has always been controlled by the employee shareholders, through the elected officers and committees.

The most significant product in Franklin's history was introduced in 1950 the submersible deep well pump motor for domestic water systems. Franklin had made motors for shallow well and jet pump water systems for some time, but the submersible water systems, with both pump and motor under water in the 4" diameter well, offered many advantages quietness, freedom from freezing, less space required, easy installation, and much greater pumping capacity and pressure. This water - lubricated submersible motor, designed especially for home water systems, has been Franklin's most successful product. This led also to the development of larger submersible motors, for 6" and 8" and larger wells for irrigation, commercial and industrial use, plus other uses such as mine de-watering. Other variations of these motors with hermetically sealed windings included submersible gasoline pumps, large sealless motors for commercial air conditioning, the oil field submersible motors, and the Sea-Mersible motor with its many applications for very deep submergence in the world's oceans.

Another new product, introduced in 1951, was the "Submatic" submersible sump pump motor. Franklin had made motors for upright column type sump pump for some time, but the Submatic opened new market possibilities. Advantages are that the pump and motor can be located out of sight below floor level and will continue pumping even when submerged. In addition to its basic use for domestic sump pumps, modifications have been utilized for hydrotherapy, sewage, and contractor pumps.

A pension plan was announced in November, 1953, for all Franklin employees. It was a non-contributory plan, with the company paying the entire cost of a special pension fund which could be used for no other purpose. Total pension benefits paid to retirees company - wide to date are approaching two million dollars.

The mid-fifties saw Franklin employment reach 600, and submersible motor production hit 700 per week. An addition was made to the back of the Spring Street plant in 1955, nearly doubling its size. New products included the 6" submersible motor, which eventually would extend through 60 horsepower, and the submersible gasoline pump motor, used to pump gasoline at service stations, where both the pump and motor are in the underground tanks. Some new motor applications included hospital beds, coolant pumps, new fans and blowers, a radial-arm saw motor and a large motor for Belle City Engineering, for an automated cattle feed grinder.

In April 1955, the employee bonus plan, originated in 1947, reached one million dollars. To commemorate this accomplishment and the company's tenth anniversary, $10.00 of each employee's bonus payment was paid in silver dollars.

About this time, cramped for space again, Franklin purchased the old Bluffton grocery building in west Bluffton for storage. It was used for about 12 years, until the property was donated to the Bluffton High School, who razed the building to use it as a parking lot. To provide even more room, two large air-supported buildings (dubbed balloon buildings) were temporarily erected west of the Spring Street plant.

In 1957, Wayne Kehoe left active management of Franklin to purchase and manage Belle City Engineering, which moved to Bluffton and became Mix-Mill, manufacturing automatic feed grinders and other farm equipment. Wayne remained on the Franklin Board of Directors, where his knowledge and experience continued to serve the company.

Bob Nixon had joined Franklin in 1952, and for thirty some years, as Vice President of Finance, guided the company through the intricacies of the financial world and made sure "the books" were kept correctly.

In 1959, a building program added to both the west and south sides of the plant, as well as doubling office area. Employment was about 850 and record customer sales of $12 million were attained that year. That was also the year Franklin became a publicly-held company with shares traded over-the-counter.

An interesting application was explored for keeping ports and channels open year-round, in ice-bound regions of the world, by pumping large amounts of water against the ice. The unit was called an "Aqua Therm" and consisted basically of a special propeller on a Franklin submersible motor, with mounting equipment and controls. A crew, including Bill Garvey of Franklin Electric, spent several weeks in the Antarctic testing it. Despite successful tests, the vast use envisioned by some, such as keeping the St. Lawrence seaway open year-round, never materialized. However, smaller units for keeping piers and docks ice-free, and variations used for aeration in fish hatcheries, sewage disposal plants, and manure pits did provide considerable submersible motor business in ensuing years.

Still other modifications of the submersible motor were tested and developed for use in large hermetically sealed air conditioning equipment. This led to the 6" and 10" sealed air conditioning motors, and considerable business, in later years, from Trane, York, Carrier, and other manufacturers of large commercial air conditioners.

The Sixties also was the beginning of the expansion to plants outside of Bluffton that was to make Franklin the national and international company that it is. The first satellite plant was built in Siloam Springs, Arkansas, a town roughly the size of Bluffton in northwest Arkansas, at the western edge of the Ozark Mountains.

With this project barely under roof in 1962, an agreement was reached to set up the first venture outside the United States. This was a 50% Franklin-owned operation in Dandenog, Victoria, Australia.

In the following year, 1963, Franklin Electric of Canada, Ltd. was established in Strathroy, Ontario, a town about 100 miles northeast of Detroit.

Within a year, still another new Franklin plant would open, a wholly-owned subsidiary named Franklin Electric Europa GmbH in Wittlich, West Germany.

In 1961, C.J. Balentine joined the company as vice president of engineering. An electrical engineering graduate of Princeton University, "Bal" came to Franklin from General Electric with 21 years of engineering and executive experience. Bal would later become president, and then chairman of the board before retiring in 1983.

In 1965, August L. (Augie) Streater joined Franklin as vice-president of engineering. An electrical engineering graduate of the University of Washington, he came to Franklin after 17 years experience in engineering and management at General Electric. He also served as chairman of the board before retiring some 20 years later.

1966 saw the one millionth submersible motor made at the Siloam Springs plant. Franklin at that time had made over four times as many submersible motors as any other manufacturer and each year made more than all other manufacturers combined.

In 1966 an election was held to see if production and maintenance workers wished to be represented by the IUE, AFL-CIO. The vote was 352-312 for the union, and the IUE was certified by the NLRB and the company. The union signed the first three - year contract in December.

Also in 1966, the Franklin Electric College Scholarship Program was announced. The program awarded each year a substantial scholarship to a high school graduating child of a Franklin employee. In 1974, it was increased to two scholarships awarded each year (for a period of four years each). Two scholarships have been awarded each year since.

Oil Dynamics, Inc. a company owned jointly by Franklin Electric and Goulds Pumps was formed in Tulsa, Oklahoma. Complete pumping systems, including motors, pumps and controls were, made for both primary and secondary recovery of oil.

Introduced in 1968 was a line of "Sea Mersible" motors for undersea operation. These were used for drive systems in deep submergence exploration and rescue submarines, and also for other undersea vehicles, off-shore oil wells, undersea hand tools, submarine winches, core drills, and commercial fishing equipment.

Joining Franklin in 1967 as vice president of manufacturing was Quentin D. Ponder. He came from several managerial posts at General Electric, and had bachelor, master, and doctor degrees from several universities. He became president of Franklin in 1981.

The early 1970's were generally good years for Franklin. In 1970, Franklin Electric was ranked in the top 1000 manufacturing companies in the country by Fortune Magazine, an unusual achievement and honor for a company only 25 years old.

1972 was a good year for Franklin with sales of $64 million, exceeding any previous year. Operations were greatly increased, both by expansion of the Bluffton and Siloam Springs plant, and acquisition of new ones.

International operations were also expanded when two new foreign subsidiaries were established, one in Johannesburg, South Africa, and the other in Brazil, South America.

In 1975, Franklin leased the Red Cross Mfg. building in southwest Bluffton for all scale and weighing operations in Bluffton until a new plant was purchased in Whiteville, North Carolina, and all scale and weighing divisions were consolidated there.

In 1976, several employees organized the Quarter Century Club of employees and retirees with 25 or more years of service.

Over the years, relations between the various Franklin plants and the labor unions involved were generally good and contracts usually reached harmoniously. However, in Bluffton in 1972, management and Local 802, IUE, AFL-CIO did not come to an agreement, and the union voted for a strike which began on December 10. It was an emotional period as the strike stretched into 1973. Affected were not only Franklin employees and their families, but the entire Bluffton community and beyond. Negotiations continued, and at last in April, a new contract was signed and the long strike ended.

In 1980, the 10 millionth fractional horsepower motor was assembled in Bluffton. A large new plant was purchased in Wilburton, Oklahoma, primarily for 6" submersible motor operations. Another international operation started in 1982, a 49% Franklin-owned plant in Monterey, Mexico.

In 1981, Conrad Balentine was named chairman of the board and Quentin Ponder, president. Bal retired two years later but remained on the board of directors.

When Franklin celebrated its 40th anniversary in 1984 and the Quarter Century Club produced a history book, over 20 millions motors had been produced.

Also in 1984, the Washington Street plant was razed and the land donated to the Caylor Nickel Medical Center.

In 1985, Quentin Ponder left the company and William Lawson joined Franklin from Skyline Corporation in Elkhart, Indiana, as president, and the following year as chairman of the board and chief executive officer. Bill has an engineering degree from Purdue University and a masters degree from Harvard School of Business.

The last half of the 1980's were years of many and significant changes for Franklin. Markets were different and economic conditions in many aspects of business nationwide were uncertain. Some of Franklin's lines were not profitable. After much study and consideration by Bill Lawson, other management, and the board of directors, it was decided to sell the packaging, weighing and scale division, and also the Jacksonville, Arkansas, plant which produced small motors. This was accomplished over a two year period and allowed Franklin to concentrate its skills and expertise on its original products, fractional horsepower and submersible motors. Employment dropped from a peak of about 3500 in all plants in 1980 to approximately 2000 in the late eighties. However, sales were considerably higher, despite this reduction in employees. This was accomplished by much effort, reorganization, and restructuring, resulting in a leaner, more efficient company.

Last year, 1990, was a good year with record earnings on sales of nearly $180 million. The number of plants, through sales and consolidation, has been reduced to ten, in Indiana, Bluffton and Jonesboro, and in Arkansas and Oklahoma in the United States plus internationally in Canada, Mexico, Germany, South Africa and Australia. Nearly a third of sales are from outside the United States.

Despite some health problems which limit his active participation, Ed Schaefer retains a keen interest in the company that has literally been his life. He has won numerous industry and community awards over the years but has remained a down-to-earth, friendly individual. Probably no one has had a greater impact on Bluffton and Wells County than this remarkable man.

In the 1990 Franklin Electric Annual Report, Bill Lawson outlines Franklin's position and outlook today -

Looking forward with confidence and optimism to a bright future.

Bluffton-Wells County Public Library

Although the people of Bluffton and Wells County established a library fund derived from ten percent of the proceeds of the sale of lots in Bluffton in 1827, it wasn't until 1902 that a formal library was formed. In the 1840's, a larger desk was ordered by the clerk to house the collection. P.A. Allen, in his first administration, 1881-91, founded a library which was comprised of 3,000 books which was located in the high school and was called the "Free City Library." When the city consented to accept the library from the school system in 1902 and to maintain a Free Public Library by resolution of council in 1903, Andrew Carnegie agreed to contribute $13,000 toward the total coast of the $18,909 required to build the Carnegie building at 223 West Washington in Bluffton. Miss Bertha Craven was hired as the librarian at a salary of $240 per year. Long time trustees serving more than ten years during this period were: Samuel Hitchcock, 1902-1912; May Eichhorn, 1902-1932; Jennie Simmons, 1902-1932; James Hale, 1903-1914; Catherine Alexander, 19107-1917; W.L. Kiger, 1908-1938; P.A. Allen, 1908-1942; Judge Charles E. Sturgis, 1914-1938; Emma Walbert, 1917-1937; and J. Frank Meyer, 1925-1938. In 1912, the Library Board granted permission to all students of Bluffton High School to use the library, and Harrison Township levied a tax to support the library. In 1914, Lancaster and Liberty Townships became part of the taxing district.

During the depression years, the library was forced to discontinue Sunday afternoon hours which had been in existence since the Carnegie was opened, and staff members were given vacations without pay. In the 1930s, Civil Works Project workers repaired the floors and walls in the basement and inventoried the collection, and the Works Project Administration provided a mending and cleaning woman. Miss Ida Ashbaucher was the librarian during the period 1919-1938. Other librarians serving for shorter periods of time were Mary Rothermal, 1909-1911; Isobel Dubois, 1911-1912; Nannie Jayne, 1912-1919; Marguerita McDonald, 1938-1940; and Elsa Strassweg, 1940-1944.

In 1920, the Board discussed a county library and finally, on March 4, 1937, all township petitions had been filed with the county commissioners. In November of the same year, a two cents levy was approved. In 1939, the Board met to discuss the best way to meet the needs of the county. Later that year, a twenty-foot semi-trailer, holding about 2,000 books and featuring three skylights and ventilators on the roof, was purchased. Trustees serving for terms longer than ten years in the decades from 1930-1950 were: Eunice Markley, 1932-1958; Charles Park, 1938-1949; William Thoma, 1938-1967; Marie Girod, 1938-1964; Charles Hogg, 1938-1949; Margaret Powers, 1941-1962; Beth Fryback, 1941-1958;

The Bluffton-Wells County Public Library built in 1903.

The Bluffton-Wells County Public Library nearing completion in June of 1991.

Lyle R. Willey, 1942-1962; Bertha Garrett, 1947-1966; and Ralph Baker, 1949-1965. Clara Sturgis served as librarian from 1944 to 1966 when she retired at the age of 70.

In the early 1950's, the record library was started through a donation by the Kiwanis Club and a listening room was established in the basement. Also in the 50's, the library began participating in the Indiana Film Circuit and the purchase of 16mm films. The newspaper microfilm collection was also initiated during this time period. In the early 1960's, the Library Board authorized the construction program which consisted of a two-floor addition to the rear of the Carnegie building. Mr. Compton Rider donated his valuable international doll collection, and the Foster Memorial Fund was established from the estate of Catherine Foster.

In 1965, the former residence of Dr. C.H. Mead was purchased from the Wells County Historical Society and was occupied by the newly formed Creative Arts Council. In 1970, the book trailer was replaced by a self-contained bookmobile featuring air-conditioning and the capacity for 3500 books. In 1978, the present Bookmobile, a modified recreational vehicle, was purchased. During the mid-1970's, art prints were added to the collection, an Indiana collection was separated for genealogical and local and Indiana historical research, large print books, musical cassettes, and an oral history program were initiated. Librarians during this period were Elizabeth Mason, 1966-1975, and Charles Joray, 1975-1982. In 1979, the Ossian Branch Library was opened in a store front owned by Charles Hissem on South Jefferson Street. The Branch has been successful and recently was moved to 207 North Jefferson, the former Hunter home, purchased by the Library Board for a new branch building in 1989. Board members serving ten years or more were: Cleme Reynolds, 1951-1961; Judge Joseph Eichorn, 1952-1962; David S. Thompson, 1954-1967; Barbara Barbieri, 1961-1976; Carolyn Edris, 1966-1978; Mary Alice Eisaman, 1968-1986; Elizabeth O'Laverty, 1972-1983; Anna Fullhart, 1973-1988; Catherine Rix, 1972-1982; and Charles Day, 1976-1988 and 1989-1990.

In 1986, it became apparent that books had usurped all the space for people in the library with only a few seats left for study and reading. In addition, the difficult steps meant the building was not accessible to the handicapped. A long-range plan was undertaken with exhaustive community, study and school surveys being taken. On September 6, 1988, the board voted to build a new library to replace the 83-year old Carnegie structure and the 25-year old addition. The original plan called for a building of 29,000 square feet at a cost of slightly more than three million dollars. This project did not receive approval of the Indiana Board of Tax Commissioners. In 1989, after receiving a cost estimate comparing renovation and a new structure, the board, consisting of Beryl J. Gray, president, Caroline Newell, Charles Day, Sue Dian, Dorothy Gitlin, Katherine Heaston, and Kent Sprunger, voted to build a 22,400 square feet library with the option of a meeting room increasing the size to approximately 22,900 square feet at a cost of $2.6 million to be funded with a General Obligation Bond. The site chosen was that of the former Wells County jail on property given the library by the Wells County Commissioners. This attractive, functional building, which is handicapped accessible, is located at 200 West Washington Street, just across the street from the original Carnegie building. Current board members are, Board President, Beryl J. Gray (1982-); Vice-President, Duane Miller (1990-); Secretary, Caroline Newell (1983-); Treasurer, James Foster (1990-); and members, Dorothy Gitlin (1988-); Ted Smith (1990-) and Alfred Norris (1990-). The present Library Director is Barbara J. Elliott. Marilyn R. Hite served as Director from 1982-1989.

City of Bluffton

Everett E. Faulkner
Mayor 1988 to Present

The common need and goals of individuals results in the gathering and joining together of people for their common good. This sharing of common purpose for mutual benefit accomplished the larger scope of tasks not possible by single individuals by themselves. This, we find, took place during the early pioneer days in the opening up of the wilderness.

Pioneers, and later settlers, chose advantageous sites and formed communities. The sites were very important as to their location, for resources, and the means to supply the community's livelihood. Some of the early communities blossomed at first, only to die out later, when essentials to sustain and cause community growth ran out or disappeared.

It becomes very evident and apparent that a community that survives is not so just because of happenstance. Bluffton is one such community that has much more than survived over the years, it has prospered. Frontier dangers, flood, droughts, fires, depressions and wars have tried the community's resolve and strengthen the peoples moral metal. Providence, working His hand in the community, is evident by the Bluffton Community's numerous churches, and the faith that is exercised there and in the everyday life of the community.

The remoteness of the early Bluffton community can be pointed out by the story of George Webster, a Marion builder, and his efforts to find Bluffton in 1841, when bids were being solicited for the construction of Wells County's second court house.

The story tells first of his failing to find anyone in Marion who had ever heard of Bluffton. He later heard that Bluffton was on the Wabash River, so he went to Peru, since Peru was also on the Wabash River. But here, too, no one had known or heard of Bluffton; so he journeyed up the Wabash River to Huntington where he did find people who knew of Bluffton and directed him on up the river. When he finally rode into Bluffton, along the Wabash River, after three days travel, he found a community of orderly homes and buildings along dirt streets.

The story not only describes Bluffton's remoteness, but also at that time "there were not any roads or communications except horseback". In spite of this isolation, the community's self-sufficiency in meeting its needs for growth and expansion continued to be met locally until later years.

The agricultural base of the Bluffton Community furnished the first products for commerce in the community's exchange outside the area. Grain and livestock were basic along with the lumber cut from the great forests.

Later in the 19th century, oil and natural gas finds would boom the area's economy. The community's small shops, mills and stores would supply the people with flour, shoes, hardware, harness, buggies, wagons, furniture and the like, all made in the community.

Outside commerce was benefited by the completion of the Fort Wayne plank road in 1851. It is hard today to imagine the absence of roads as it was then. The completion of this plank road and others to follow were important to the change starting to take place in the Bluffton community's growth. A community wide effort led by John Studabaker and Hugh Dougherty, at their great financial risk, financed the building of the south branch of the Lake Erie and Western Railroad from Ft. Wayne, that finally completed its construction into Bluffton in 1869. The first train to arrive in Bluffton was met by an enthusiastic crowd. An old cannon had been taken to the West Washington Street crossing and salutes were fired to greet the train. An extra heavy powder charge caused the cannon to explode, but fortunately no one was hurt.

Later, the electric interurban railway made a wide appearance through the state and in the Bluffton community, only to shortly be forced out by the rapid growing number of automobiles.

The people of the Bluffton community expressed a great pride in their city, which was evident by their progressiveness.

The Indiana State Legislature in 1851 granted a special charter incorporating the Town of Bluffton, with David Angel as Bluffton's first mayor. The incorporation encouraged business and commercial growth through an organized city government, which supported necessary municipal improvements.

The early needed improvements were gravel streets, surface drainage and a fire department. Dedicated residents formed the "Vigilant Hook and Ladder Company No. 1", a volunteer fire department on November 19, 1879, when their rules and bylaws were approved by the Bluffton Council. This growth and progress resulted in Bluffton being incorporated as a city by the State Legislature in 1883, with a city charter and E.C. Vaughn serving as mayor.

Growing communities, such as Bluffton, realized the need for sanitation and a safe drinking supply. To this end efforts were successful in 1886 to build the Bluffton Water Works, composed of a well, pumping station, 10,000 feet of water main, and 33 fire hydrants. This was followed in 1896 with the start of large construction and

Elected Officials 1988-92

Mayor	Everett E. Faulkner
Clerk-Treasurer	Christie A. Pretzel
City Council	James Phillabaum, Pres.
	Richard Haynes
	K. Thomas Terhune
	Robert Bate
	Mark Baller
Board of Works	Everett E. Faulkner
	James Philabaum
	Mark Baller
City Attorney	David Feeback
City Judge	Lyle J. Cotton

Department Heads

Chief of Police	Robert Frantz
Fire Chief	Gary Markley
Water Supt.	Edward C. Davis
Electric Supt.	Edward C. Davis
Street Commissioner	Robert L. Hite
Sewage Supt.	Robert Mohler
Park and Recreation	Eugene Edington
Animal Warden	Ronnie Weaver
Utility Office Mgr.	R.D. "Skip" Esmond

upgrading of the city sanitary and storm sewers, to be completed before the general street paving project work in 1898. In 1889, the year the present court house construction was started, electric street lighting went into operation. The city's beautiful tree-lined paved streets with fine buildings, electric lights and public water supply, were among the reasons Bluffton became known as the "Parlor City". This community progress over the years has continued even though times and conditions have changed. The basic community principle of individuals with common needs and goals working together still is necessary for community progress!

Most recently, Bluffton has received three distinguished honors over the last three years: 1989 All-American City Finalist; 1990 Outstanding Indiana Community of the Year; and the 1991 Governor's Recycling Award. Bluffton is a community which sees what needs to be done and does it!

Mayors Of Bluffton

David Angel	1851	James Plessinger	1898-1902
Samuel Decker	1852	John Mock	1902-1906
J.H. Buckles	1853	A.W. Hamilton	1906-1910
C.W. Beadsley	1854	Frank Smith	1910-1914
S.R. Karns	1855	John Mock	1914-1918
C.S. Burgan	1856	P.F. Hunt	1918-July 1921
J.E. Brown	1857	John Kelly	1921-1922
J.R. McCleery	1858	Frank Thompson	1922-1926
I.A. Godard	1859	Theo Harsh	1926-1930
W.R. Ferguson	1859	John W. Kelly	1930-May 1934
Robert Russell	1860	Gabriel T. Markley	May 1934-1935
Newton Burwell	1861-1865	Franklin Buckner	1935-1943
John McFadden	1865-1866	John H. Waid	1943-1948
C.G. Quick	1866-1868	John A. Johnston	1948-June 1951
Nelson Kellog	1868-1873	Silas Neff	June 1951-1952
Levi Mock	1873-1877	H.H. Robbins	1952-1956
Wm. Blackston	1877-1879	Robert Venis	1956-1960
David Smith	1879-1881	Charles Decker	1960-1968
E.C. Vaughn	1881-1883	Carl P. Goodwin	1968-1972
H.L. Martin	1883-1884	William Fryback	1972-1980
James Hale	1884-1889	John Flaningam	1980-March 1985
Martin Walbert	1889-1894	William Fryback	March 1985-1988
L.B. Stevens	1894-1897	Everett E. Faulkner	1988-present
James P. Hale	1897-1898		

Original Community Building, built in 1926 - now the City Building with Mayor, Clerk-Treasurer, and Utilities offices.

Police & Fire Building, built in 1971.

Bluffton Utilities city power plant on East Cherry Street.

Street Dept. (left) and Water Dept. (right) buildings at 612 East Spring Street.

Markle Medical Center

In the fall of 1963, the community of Markle, Indiana, needed a physician to replace Dr. Halden Woods, who had died in an auto accident about six months earlier. Markle was small and some in the community felt that there wouldn't be enough work for two doctors in Markle. The community had a fund-raiser and collected over $4,000 to help toward purchasing Dr. Wood's office and the furniture store beside it, in order to have space for a medical office in downtown Markle on Morse Street.

Dr. Gerald Miller was the first doctor to answer the call. He and his wife Mary moved to Markle in February, 1964, and opened the office in March. Dr. LeRoy Kinzer and wife Dawn moved to Markle the 1st of July of that year and joined the practice. Dr. Miller and Dr. Kinzer had been in residency together at the Lutheran Hospital, so they decided to practice together in Markle.

It wasn't long until the two doctors decided they needed a surgeon. Dr. Victor Binkley joined the practice in 1970. He came with good surgical skills and the practice expanded as Dr. Binkley also did surgery for other doctors at the Wells Community Hospital. At this time, the doctors stopped going to the Lutheran Hospital in Fort Wayne and the Huntington Hospital, because they were too busy delivering babies, giving anesthetics, and doing surgeries.

It was at this time that the Wells Community Hospital in Bluffton, Indiana, became their primary hospital.

In July, 1973, Dr. David Brown and his wife Sue joined the practice. He was from Pennsylvania and had to learn about "Hoosier Hysteria." Also in 1973, a second office was opened in Bluffton, Indiana. That same year also, Steve Binkley, a personal and family counselor, and his wife Char, came on staff. People in the community know him best as the Christian counselor who has helped them through stressful times in their lives.

The house in Bluffton soon became too small for the ever-increasing patient load and the number of doctors joining the staff, so in 1974, space was rented from the Wells Community Hospital, first floor, to see patients. Dr. Joe Greene and wife Cathy served with Markle Medical Center from 1975 to 1989 as a family physician.

The office space in the Markle office seemed to be getting smaller and the patient load larger, so a new office was constructed at 201 E. South St. in Markle in 1975.

In July, 1978, Dr. David Meek and wife Peg joined the practice. He has worked as a family physician but also has filled the niche of giving anesthesia for surgery.

In 1980, after finishing his residency in OB/GYN in Corpus Christi, Texas, Dr. Marcelo Gavilanez and wife Joan joined the practice. He has delivered many of the babies born in Wells County.

Markle Medical Center found itself too crowded at the Bluffton Office and negotiated with the Wells Community Hospital to take over the whole second floor of the hospital office building in 1986. This added better patient service and assisted with the new trend toward outpatient surgery and testing.

The Medical Corporation has furnished complete medical care to the Warren Memorial Methodist Home since 1971. Therefore, on July 2, 1986, the next office opening was a satellite in Warren, Indiana. More medical help was necessary with the expansion and Dr. Deb Miller was added to the medical staff.

There was an ever-increasing load of patients and another physician was needed. In 1990, Dr. John Wilson and his wife Gwen came on board. Keeping three offices staffed with doctors at all times keeps

Dr. Victor Binkley

Dr. David Brown

Dr. Marcelo Gavilanez

Dr. LeRoy Kinzer

Dr. David Meek

Dr. Deborah Miller

Dr. Gerald Miller

Dr. John F. Wilson

the doctors very busy. The three offices cover parts of two counties, with other patients coming from a wider market area. The end of the first 25 years of practice (1964-1989) showed over 16,000 active patients.

The success of Markle Medical Center lies with the personnel employed, the doctors, psychologist, office coordinators, nurses, receptionists, bookkeepers, insurance clerks, etc. This is a "people organization" (52 employees). The doctors only recently put into writing their mission statement, but it has been the guiding principle for Markle Medical Center since its inception in 1964. The mission statement is this:

Markle Medical Center exists to allow competent, properly trained Christian - oriented physicians an opportunity to provide compassionate and comprehensive medical care, and to carry out these activities with qualified personnel in a comfortable and congenial atmosphere, and to use sound business principles.

The following are practicing physicians with Markle Medical Center in 1991: Victor W. Binkley, M.D., general surgeon; David C. Brown, D.O., family practice; Marcelo Gavilanez, M.D., OB-GYN; LeRoy D. Kinzer, M.D., family practice; David A. Meek, M.D. family practice; Deborah L. Miller, M.D., family practice; Gerald L. Miller, M.D. family practice; John F. Wilson, M.D. family practice; Stephen N. Binkley, M.S., counselor.

National Oil & Gas, Inc.

Aerial view of National Oil & Gas offices built in 1958, surrounding present Airplane Station. Picture taken before two canopies covering gas pump islands were added in 1989.

National Oil & Gas, Inc. was incorporated in 1940 and has operated from the same location since 1931, when its founder, William Moser, started in the oil jobber business known as Moser Oil Company. Originally, they sold White Rose products from the National Refining Company in Findlay, Ohio.

Their trademark will be remembered by the older people as the young lad in black and white checkered britches holding the blackboard where the messages changed weekly. For instance, one might say: "Safety first, don't run others down." Or in the wintertime, referring to the temperature, one might say: "So what if it's O degrees, that's nothing." The original bulk plant and Airplane Service Station were built low, much nearer the riverbank level as we know it today. Later, when the Wabash River bridge was built in 1937, and Highway #1 and #124 were raised to their present dry levels, the service station, too, was raised to a higher elevation. The original airplane service station was Mr. Moser's idea. It was complete with a wing extending both ways over the body of the service station, with an actual propeller out front and the tail in the rear which housed the restrooms. In later years, the south wing was enclosed to house two service bays and the north wing still existed where the station operator, Eli Gerber, would park his Studebaker automobile in the shade. The service station was rebuilt from scratch in 1958 and vastly renovated in 1989 as a convenience store. Another feature of the airplane service station corner is the tree with a bear and squirrel perched on the limbs. Mr. Moser had this built from concrete by a gentleman from Pennville, Indiana. This one of a kind creation still exists long after the artist had moved on to California and has since passed away. Mr. Moser, himself, passed away in October, 1990.

Mr. Moser was truly an innovator. In the early 1930's, he had the first transport truck in the area built to his specifications. Transports in the 1904's hauled approximately 3,000 gallons, whereas today they haul 8,200-8,500 gallons. Early tank wagons delivering product in the rural areas held 500 gallons where today's tank wagons have 2,000-2,500 gallons. Early deliveries were made with five gallon buckets of gasoline hand-carried to the farmer's tank where it was then poured through a metal funnel. Needless to say, this required many trips back and forth from the tank wagon to the farmer's 55 gallon storage drum to complete the sale. Larger farmers may have had two 55 gallon drums and later in the 1940-50 period, 300 gallon overhead tanks came into existence. Today, 550 or 1,000 gallon skid tanks with electric metered pumps are more commonplace. Some farmers with large acreages even have 8,000 to 10,000 gallon underground storage tanks.

National Oil & Gas took over the Phillips

66 brand distribution and soon became Phillips' largest jobber in the State of Indiana as they embarked on a major building program, constructing new service stations in Fort Wayne, Decatur, Portland, Hartford City, Churubusco, Dunkirk, Berne, Wabash, Peru, Montpelier, Redkey, Markle, Geneva and Bluffton.

In more recent years, they have ventured into the convenience store field and now are expanding into new areas such as Angola, Huntington, North Manchester, Ossian, Auburn, Upland, Rome City, Monroeville, Lagro, Larwill, Pleasant Lake, South Whitley, Garrett, Petroleum, Syracuse, Urbana, LaFontaine, Huntertown, Stroh, Monroe, Columbia City and in the Ohio cities of Van Wert, Cecil and Wren.

Early officers in the corporation were William W. Wile, Jr. and Graydon G. Gibson, who along with Mr. Moser, guided the early expansion from the 1940's through the mid-sixties. Since that time, the present president, William Gene Moser, son of the founder; Edward Alberding, vice-president; Jay Kipfer, secretary-controller; and Tillman Gerber, treasurer, have supervised the corporate activities.

With the acquisition of Decatur Oil Company in 1979 and Shumaker Oil Company of Huntington in the early 80's, the company now represents Marathon Oil, Unocal and BP as well as Phillips 66. Petroleum products are delivered to farmers, heating oil customers, schools, commercial, industrial and municipal accounts over a 16 county area of Indiana and Ohio through tank wagon drivers operating out of 15 bulk plants scattered throughout this area.

The Airplane Service Station, built in 1931, was a landmark through the 1930's and 1940's. Located on the present site of National Oil's offices and the current Airplane Station at 407 North Main Street.

Moser Oil Company bulk plant on North Main Street in the early 1930's.

The company has been an active supporter in the Wells County community. They have been proud to be involved in Bluffton's Revitalization program, construction of the local swimming pool, sponsoring youth baseball teams, contributing to Dollars for Scholars in the Bluffton, Norwell and Southern Wells schools, United Way and Wells County and South Adams Fine Arts.

A sales promotion parade in Bluffton and area towns served by the Moser Oil Co., when they became distributors for the National Refining Co., selling Enarco products and White Rose gasoline in northeastern Indiana. Standing (l. to r.): Joel Malleer, Ralph Dailey, unknown, Ora Frauhiger, Levi (Speed) Maller, Oren Bowman, unknown, Perl Wittern, Earl Frauhiger with Wm. Frauhiger Sr. behind, Bruce McAfee, Eli Gerber, Airplane Station Manager, Bill Young, Kenny Moore, standing by gas pump. William Moser, owner of Moser Oil Co., two National Refining salesmen and Ben Becker. Musicians standing on truck: Paul Fisher, Orville Grim. Seated: Lloyd Gilliom, Ralph Baker, Chalmer Snyder, Bill Grim. Picture taken November 19, 1933.

News - Banner

In 1992 the News-Banner will celebrate its 100th anniversary.

Tracing from the time that the Evening News was established in September of 1892, a daily newspaper has been published in Bluffton every single day except for Sundays and a designated set of legal holidays over the 99-year span without missing an issue.

The Banner was begun as a separate daily newspaper in 1899. It was 30 years later that the News and Banner merged to form the News-Banner.

Within about six months of the 1892 launching by Harry Tribolet and Frank Dailey, the Evening News was purchased by David H. Swaim and his brother, W.T.T. Swaim for $100.

For more than 93 years, until June of 1986, the David Swaim family—he was followed by his son, Roger Swaim, and also Roger's wife, Celia Swiam—remained at the helm of the newspaper company.

In June 1986, James C. Barbieri, who joined the News-Banner 41 years ago in 1950 and has served in leadership posts most of that span, including years as general manager and editor, headed new purchasers in acquiring the News-Banner. Barbieri, then 57, became president and publisher while continuing as editor and general manager.

Joining in the purchase and leadership was George B. Witwer, then 27, who had marketing experience with Proctor and Gamble and newspaper experience at Ligonier in his father's company. Witwer became vice president and marketing director.

Before the Swaim family leadership, and prior to the News, the Banner, and the News-Banner, the early history of newspapers in Wells County was a story of publication which came and went in relatively short spans.

The westward movement in the nation was accompanied by vigorous expression from freedom-loving people who came with printing means of the day not long after the carving of each frontier.

In Wells County, "The Republican Bugle" appeared in 1847.

Others included "The People Press" from 1855-60, "The Regulator" in 1858, "The Blade" in 1859-60, "The Badger" in 1861, "The Shoe Fly" in 1872, "Little Lively" in 1872, "The Gem" in 1873-1875, "The Greenback Times" in 1878, and probably some more.

The Bluffton Chronicle was a weekly in which David Swaim participated. It was started in 1878 and continued for 40 years until 1918.

"The People's Press," back in 1855 had become "The Union" during the Civil War period and later the name was changed to "The Standard" in 1866, before becoming "The Chronicle" in 1868.

Were it not for a brief period more than century ago of the Chronicle's suspension amid financial difficulties in 1873, the News-Banner probably could claim to be celebrating its 136th direct-line anniversary this year, tracing back to the "People's Press" start.

George Arnold became Chronicle owner in 1878, and then W.T.T. Swaim and Asbury Duglay acquired it in 1888. Shortly afterwards David Swaim became a part owner. With Duglay's death in 1891, the two Swaims had the entire ownership. W.T.T. Swaim died in 1895. David Swaim, who shared in buying the fledgling Evening News in early 1893, was to go forth in an illustrious newspaper career that was heavily involved in the progress of Wells County.

The Banner name had appeared here as early as 1850 with newspapers under the name of "The Weekly Banner" being published sporadically.

Incidentally, that "Republican Bugle," traced back to 1847, actually was a Democratic paper in politics. Remember, the Republican party was not to be founded nationally until 1856. Thomas Smith, a Mexican War veteran, was the editor of the Bugle back in 1847. It had large type, with printing by a wooden press.

The Weekly Banner in 1850 was launched by Samuel Upton and Lewis Grove. Several publishers of Banner-named newspapers were noted through the years. In 1884 E.Y. Sturgis, a part-owner since the prior years, became sole owner. He and Arnold of the Chronicle argued the two sides of the city debate over launching the waterworks in 1886, as was noted in the waterworks centennial event in 1986.

In 1891 the Weekly Banner was sold to John Ormsby and P.A. Allen, who was to become distinguished as an educator here.

George Saunders was to emerge, however, as the leader of the Banner as a daily newspaper. The Banner became a daily in 1899, and in January of 1902, Saunders purchased it from Allen.

Saunders and David Swaim were competitors and leading citizens for years to come. Saunders served from 1922-26 as a state senator and then from 1926 to his death in 1931 as a state representative. He was a Democrat and operated the Banner as a Democratic newspaper. Swaim was a Republican but operated the News as an independent newspaper.

Roger G. Swaim, son of David Swaim, graduated from Bluffton High School in

The old building of the News-Banner showing the old press.

1915 but already had begun his newspaper career through going from a carrier-boy role as a lad, to helping out part-time during his later school years, and then to his full-time career.

In 1929, the Swaim-led News and the Saunders-led Banner merged to form the News-Banner. There were other stockholders, and such continued to be the case over the years, but the Swaim interest emerged as the majority one.

In the later years of his father's life, Roger G. Swaim became the leader in operation of the News-Banner, and he became the publisher, as well as president and editor and general manager, after the 1939 death of David H. Swaim.

Managing or city editor, the late Orin O. Craven who had 60 years service in the News and News Banner, and Eugene McCord, who retired in 1986 with 40 years of service but has resumed service on a part-time basis, were major, long-term contributors to News-Banner history. Joel Smekens, who was a carrier as a boy and joined the newspaper as a Linotype operator in 1963, became a state-claimed sports editor before moving on to his present position as managing editor.

Also with long involvement in the News-Banner progress and still active in 1991 are Marlene Holloway, business manager, who joined the newspaper in 1952 and Connie Edington, advertising manager, who started with the News-Banner in 1953.

Barbieri, the current publisher, led in preparations for and carrying out construction in 1975 of the News-Banner's modern newspaper building at 125 North Johnson Street. it replaced the former Workman Building location at 220 West Market Street—the Banner location after 1910 and then the News-Banner's home following the merger.

In 1975, with the new building, the News-Banner converted from "hot metal" to photo composition and offset printing. In 1980s, the progress was to continue into Apple computers and laserprinters for composition and MacIntoshes for composition and business purposes.

A "total market" publication, "The Echo" was added in 1986 to maximize market services. In 1988 the Ossian Journal was purchased from Edwin Peck along with the Sunriser-News. The Ossian Journal continues to be published as a weekly newspaper and the Sunriser-News as a shopper publication.

Barbieri won a series of awards, chiefly in investigative reporting in the 1980's, but also in news, news series, and editorial writing. Smekens won awards in sports and feature fields.

The News-Banner is most pleased to have a key daily role in the life and progress of Wells County—the vital newspaper role here for nearly a century, and one foreseen for the century to come.

The News-Banner's modern newspaper plant at 125 North Johnson Street, since 1975.

Pretzels, Inc. / Bachman Foods / Duchess Pretzels

Whether by accident or design, Bluffton is now the pretzel capital of Indiana. In 1954, as the story goes, two men from Baltimore, Maryland, set out for the midwest in search of the perfect spot for the first twisted pretzels west of Pennsylvania. A midwest location was desired for distribution purposes in order to be centrally located between several large cities. Traveling from Decatur to Huntington, car trouble ensued. Checking the map and discovering Bluffton only a few miles south of U.S. 224, the two soon found themselves in Lawrence Goodin's garage on West Market Street. In conversation with the civic-minded mechanic, the two men explained their mission and were soon led to Paul Bender, then president of the Chamber of Commerce. He directed the two entrepreneurs to the then vacant Farnsworth building once known as the Patton McCray building which was located on West Washington Street just west of where Cline Lumber currently stands. The mix of building, town and co-operative people must have impressed the two men because they chose to settle there and establish the Duchess Pretzel Corporation. One of those men was president of the company, Frank Elzey, and the other, vice president and sales manager, was my grandfather, Lorin L. Mann, Sr.

Granddaddy began operations with his son, William, and dad's dear like-a-brother friend, William Huggins. Both boys were only 18 and fresh out of high school. About a year later, Lorin Jr. (Jake) joined operations after serving in the Navy. The Duchess Pretzel 200 foot long production line from dough twister to final oven became an attraction for area residents. Many toured the plant to view the manufacture of pretzels with the product untouched by human hands in the process.

In 1962, Duchess merged with Bachman Foods of Reading, Pennsylvania. Dad remained while Bill Huggins subsequently parted the company to pursue other business ventures. Suddenly, and from an undetermined cause, fire swept the old 45,000 square foot building at 5:00 a.m. on January 2, 1969, levelling it in 60 minutes. Soon after, the parent company decided to rebuilt in the Bluffton area. On April 1, 1969, ground was broken for the new plant in the building currently housing the Keebler snack foods bakery on the north edge of town. On September 5, 1970, the new facility constructed by James Jackson Company and in full operation hosted an open house for Wells County. Visitors touring the three million dollar, 75,000 square-foot plant were impressed by the new facility lauded as the most automated and sanitary bakery in the country at the time. Bachman operated in its new location until the parent company decided to close its Bluffton plant in the fall of 1978.

At that point, my dad, who had been plant manager for several years, faced major career decisions. At 42 years of age with three children still at home, did he move to Bachman's Reading location, secure in a managerial position, or knowing the void left by Bachman's exit from the midwest, did he endeavor to capitalize on the many customers left without service? In the fall of 1978, with the instrumental return of William Huggins, the two formed a partnership in Pretzels Incorporated. The decision had been made. One 50 foot oven was assembled in a 12,000 - square - foot warehouse in Jasun Park at the south edge of town. With a handful of employees including Lu Ann Garton and Barb Gray, who are both still active in the company, and a totally manual packing process, the business commenced. The first pretzels ran off the line in the spring of 1979. Absent was the familiar click of the automated pretzel twisters made obsolete by the much more efficient and trouble-free extruding machines. Virtually all "twist" pretzels are now dye-cut with only a handful of manufacturers still featuring the mechanical dinosaurs.

The original Pretzels, Inc. building was outgrown by 1980. Ground was broken for a new 28,000 square foot structure just across the drive in Jasun Park where it is still located. Several building additions have been made to that structure through the past 10 years to accommodate production of a full array of pretzels: thins, sticks, rods and minis, as well as a complete line of cheese snacks. Primarily a private label company, Pretzels introduced its own brand names, "Will Yums" and "Harvest Road" in the mid-eighties. These successful product lines have led to nationwide distribution and into Canada. The bulk of the plant's production, however, remains with a 500-600 mile radius similar to that of the Duchess Company's original market area in the late fifties.

The current operation hosts a 66,456 - square - foot facility housing 3-104' ovens, its original 50' oven, with another full - size oven on order to meet with current production demands. There are 105 employees operating the highly automated, state-of-the-art bakery which houses the only automated rod packing machine in the world. The high-precision, computerized machinery is truly a tribute to technology. Pretzels, Inc. continues to grow as my family's third generation actively participates in the deep rooted business. In 1988, my brother, William Mann II (Chip), and Bill Huggin's son, Steve, joined the company after college graduation.

Today, Pretzels, Inc. thrives. Its fateful history is significant in Bluffton having become the Pretzel capitol of the midwest. All because, once upon a time, two men had car trouble. *Submitted by Kim Durr*

Bill Mann (left) and Bill Huggins (right) around 1954.

Bill Huggins (left) and Bill Mann (right) in the spring of 1991.

Thoma/Rich Funeral Home

The original "THOMA-TRIBOLET" building located at 116 S. Main Street, immediately South of the Court House. This building was built in the mid 1850's and used as a cabinet shop and furniture retail store. This is the building where the coffins were made and the undertaking business established. About the turn of the century the original Thoma building was moved from the 116 S. Main Street location immediately north into the alley, now known as Walnut Street. The building sat there and business continued to operate all the time the new brick building was being constructed at the 116 S. Main Street location. When the new building was completed the old frame building was moved from the alley to the corner of Scott and Cherry Streets, then the home of Herman Thoma, where it was used as a storage building for the Thoma operation.

The Thoma/Rich Funeral Home has its roots in Wells County dating back to the early 1850's when Henry Thoma left his farm home in Ebersdorf, Germany, at the age of 17 and sailed for America. He landed at Ellis Island in New York on June 7, 1849, and was processed through as an immigrant to the United States. He moved on to Findlay, Ohio, where he learned the cabinet maker's trade, serving as an apprentice for three years. At the same time he attended school at the Presbyterian Academy in Findlay. In October of 1853 he moved to Bluffton, Indiana.

As was the custom in Europe, furniture making and undertaking were a combination business. If you could make a cabinet, you could also make a coffin. In January of 1854, Henry Thoma and Jacob Tribolet embarked in the joint venture of furniture and undertaking business, under the firm name of Tribolet & Company. When there was a death in the community, the family would come to Mr. Thoma. Many times a notched hickory stick indicated the height and width of the person who died, and he would make the coffin in his cabinet shop. It was also the service of the undertaker to deliver the coffin to the home, place the body in the coffin, and then assist the family in making the funeral arrangements. The funeral conveyances were exceedingly primitive, many times using a spring wagon instead of a hearse. In 1855, Mr. Thoma made with his own hands the first horse drawn hearse used in Wells County. The Thoma/Rich Funeral Home still has this hearse, along with other horse drawn vehicles used by the Thomas.

Sometime in 1861, Jacob Tribolet left Bluffton to join the Civil War and the business partnership dissolved. Henry Thoma continued the business under his own name.

There came a son, Herman W. Thoma, and then a grandson, William H. Thoma. They grew up into the business through the same dateless processes of life. Henry Thoma died in 1913. His son, Herman Thoma, born in 1872, succeeded his father in the business and was among the first of the Indiana undertakers to pass requirements of the state license law in 1898. He died in 1946.

William Thoma was born in 1901. A graduate of DePauw University in 1922, he was licensed the same year after study at the Worsham School of Embalming, Chicago. He then became an active partner in the firm. He died in 1974.

Howard Rich had his training at the Indiana College of Mortuary Science and became a member of the firm in 1956. In 1961 Mr. Rich became a partner, and the firm name was changed to Thoma/Rich Funeral Home.

From 1853 until 1964 the establishment was located at 116 S. Main Street in Bluffton, Indiana. The building was a combination of three store fronts, housing the furniture business with the funeral operation tucked in the middle.

By the 1960's, it became evident that funeral customs were changing. The shift away from the traditional church funerals was declining. Larger, more convenient facilities were required to serve the public needs at the time of death. William Thoma and Howard Rich built an all new 80 by 100 feet traditional, colonial style building at 308 West Washington Street. The home was built to provide expanded facilities for funeral direction and greater comfort and convenience for those who call upon its services.

William Thoma died in 1974. Howard Rich purchased the remaining stock of the business from the Thoma family and has continued to operate the firm under the Thoma/Rich name.

Left: The Thoma's built the new brick building around the turn of the century at their 116 S. Main Street location. They later acquired the other two stores fronts to the south of them and incorporated the three buildings into the Thoma Furniture and Funeral Home operation. The funeral home was located in the center building. The funeral home was moved from this location in September of 1974.

Right: In 1974 the Thoma/Rich Funeral Home moved into their newly constructed colonial building at 308 W. Washington Street. This was the first all modern building built and designed for funeral service in North Eastern Indiana. The home was built to provide expanded facilities of comfort and convenience for those who call upon its services.

Wells Community Hospital

Wells County did not have a hospital until 1918. Surgery was performed in the home or doctor's office. Critically ill patients who could stand the trip, were transported to Fort Wayne on the interurban, or by car, for hospitalization and treatment.

Wells County citizens, recognizing the need, petitioned the County Commissioners as provided by Indiana statute, to appoint a hospital board. On March 5, 1917, Carl Bonham, J.A. McBride, Levi Huffman, and Albert Knight, together with the County Treasurer, H.W. Lipkey, organized as the Wells County Hospital Board. Together with Dr. I.N. Hatfield representing the doctors of the county, they quickly purchased the Goodyear-Springfield land at the south end of Main Street for $3,000.00. After visiting several new hospitals, Dr. Edward Allport of Cleveland was selected to design the building. Steel shortages and inflation from World War I dictated plan changes, with the building constructed with building tile instead of steel, and hardwood floors replacing terrazo. The general contract was awarded to J. Sam Ozee, Jr. of Matoon, Illinois for $28,194.00 on June 14, 1917. The cornerstone was laid on September 3, 1917, with participation by the local Masonic Lodge, and the building was completed and ready for the first patients the following June.

1917 - 1950

The first floor of the two-story building consisted of: janitor's room, supply room, laundry, kitchen, dining room, furnace and coal storage, emergency room, X-ray, seven-patient ward, and two isolation rooms. The second floor housed the general operating and emergency operating rooms, maternity beds and nursery. There was no elevator. A wide stone outside staircase led to the reception room on the main, or second floor.

The hospital had all modern features of the time: laundry chute, incinerator, sanitary wash basins, up-to-date patient call system, and steam heat. The bed capacity was 16, but before long was stretched to 25.

Wells County doctors who were responsible for the hospital's founding were: H.D. Brickley, Asa Brown, L.H. Cook, L.W. Dailey, R.M. Dickason, George E. Fulton, J.C. Fulton, O.G. Hamilton, I.N. Hatfield, B.E. Huffman, C.S. Mead, Fred A. Metts,

1950 - 1970

1970 - Present

George Morris, J.W. McKiney, J.L. Redding, Louis Severin, S.A. Shoemaker, L. Spaulding, and Erskin Summers. Charles Caylor moved his practice from Pennville to Bluffton that year (1917), and became associated with Wells County Hospital.

Three registered nurses from Chicago staffed the hospital, including Ina Agar, later Mrs. H.D. Brickley, serving as the first Superintendent. Others joining the nursing staff included: Mary Houser, Lulu (Summers) Hamilton, Vesta (Neff) Eversole, Esther (Laymond) Huffman, Deane (Ellingham) Baxter, Inez (Slough) Speheger, Cleo (Chalfant) Lewis, and Orpha Covault.

The first baby born in the new hospital, was Robert Egley, son of Chris and Helen (French) Egley of Petroleum, June 27, 1918.

Overcrowding brought about a $340,000 addition in April 1948, that was completed in 1950. This addition, to the back of the 1917 building, eliminated the long exterior flight of stairs to the front entrance. The hospital now had capacity for 75 patients.

In 1966, the hospital trustees saw the need for a long-range building program for the hospital. The first phase was a new wing in 1968; the second phase, 1977, a new building section across the front, with an attached physician's office building; and finally, an updating and remodeling of the section completed in 1950. During the phased construction, the original 1917 building was removed completely. In June 1969, the name was changed to Wells Community Hospital.

During recent years, with constant improvement of facilities and services, the hospital has been able to provide state-of-the-art technology and programs for its patients. Particularly important has been the last generation of CT scanning, mammography, ultrasound, automated laboratory equipment, and other diagnostic mediums, as well as Home Health Care Services, and educational programs. A highly-trained medical, nursing, and ancillary staff provide outstanding care, in all area.

The hospital opened their first Birthing Room in 1984. The popular areas have been expanded to include two more Labor/Delivery/Recovery/Postpartum (LDRP0 room in 198, where the mother labors, delivers and then completes her hospital stay in the same room.

Opened in 1991, the Wells Women's Health Center is the newest service, designed to enhance the quality of women's health throughout her life span.

Costs have been held down, while the hospital has been able to operate, since 1960, without county tax funds for operating.

The 1990 report showed gross revenue to be $6,698,469 and expenses of $6,632,677, leaving $65,792.00 after covering all cost and depreciation. In 1990, there were 1,555 inpatients and 3,477 emergency patients.

In 1973, the hospital inaugurated an Emergency Ambulance Service for Wells County. There were 244 runs that first years. In 1990, there were 1,190 runs. Today's regulations have practically eliminated the original volunteer EMT, who has served so well, requiring far more full-time emergency medical technicians.

There are eighteen active medical staff members, as well as many specialists on the courtesy staff, who regularly visit the hospital for patient services and consultations.

A 74 YEAR TRADITION OF FAMILY CARE

Old-First National Bank

Sixty years ago the business, resources, and personnel of a pair of two-year-old Wells County banks were merged to establish the Old-First National Bank.

The Old-First was formed in 1931 by the uniting of the Old National Bank and the First National Bank, two Bluffton institutions founded in March 1929.

Within the new bank, which has since grown to be the largest financial institution in Wells County, were combined the history and traditions of Bluffton banking activities from as early as the mid-19th century.

There were personnel from the old Studabaker Bank, founded by John Studabaker, a Wells County pioneer engaged in financial work as early as 1856. There were others who had worked at the old Wells County Bank and the Citizens Bank, and even some who had had connections with the numerous small banks which were in operation in the towns and villages of the county early in the present century.

Grew With Area

With them came the spirt of the small community bank, a spirit which was to mold the new bank as an integral part of the Bluffton and Wells County Community.

As the area grew, so did the Old-First. Its total resources, the prime indicator of a bank's health, swelled steadily and its other business grew proportionately.

In 1953 its headquarters in the 100 block of West Market Street underwent a major remodeling, unwittingly prophesying the day when the building would no longer be adequate to house the growing business and expanded services of the Old-First.

Acting with necessary foresight before that day arrived, the officers and directors of the bank moved to construct the beautiful new bank building at 304 West Market Street, which was unveiled in February of 1968 completing another significant chapter in the history of the Old-First.

Two Predecessors

That history began in 1929.

On March 9 of that year the Old National Bank was incorporated with Henry C. Paul as president, Frank H. Cutshall as vice president, F. William Hitzeman as cashier, James W. Stogdill as assistant cashier and F.J. Tangeman as trust officer and assistant cashier.

Serving on the board of directors were Paul, Cutshall, Hitzeman, Henry J. Bowerfind and Edward M. Wilson.

Main Office in Bluffton.

Twenty days later, on March 29, Charles M. Niezer and a group of businessmen organized the First National Bank. Niezer himself was president. The officers included Harry C. Fair as vice president, Harry C. Moore as executive vice president and cashier and R.N. Fitzpatrick and Howard E. Thomas as assistant cashiers.

On the board of directors were Niezer, Fair, Moore, F.F. Engeler, Ralph Morrow, David Meyer, W.A. Patton, Fred Potthoff, O.E. Shafer, William Spain and H.M. Ullman.

Representative from each of the two banks were to figure prominently in the history of the Old-First.

On September 17, 1931, the new bank was formed. From the Old National Bank came Paul and Cutshall, as chairman of the board and president, respectively. Also joining the Old-First from the Old National Bank were Stogdill as vice president, Tangeman as trust officer and assistant cashier, and Bowerfind, Wilson, and Hitzman as members of the board.

From the First National Bank, Fitzpatrick came as cashier, and Howard Thomas, who eventually became a vice president.

Long Term President

In 1938, after Cutshall retired, Stogdill was elected president of the bank. Stogdill's tenure as president of the bank spans thirty years of the institution's history, and it was under him that the bank realized its greatest growth.

His banking career began in 1915, when he joined the Studabaker Bank, after high school graduation. After the United States entered World War I, Stogdill enlisted in the Army and was commissioned a lieutenant. He was an artillery instructor at Army camps in South Carolina and Kentucky.

After the war he returned to the Studabaker Bank and worked there until it ceased operation in 1927. That same year the Citizens Bank was organized by area businessmen. Stogdill served there as assistant cashier until the operation was bought by the Wells County Bank. In 1929, the Old National Bank was organized and he started there as assistant cashier, working in that position until the consolidation of the two financial institutions in September 1931.

He became Old-First president in 1938, and the bank grew and prospered under his direction.

Ossian Office

SOME FROM 1ST NATIONAL

Fitzpatrick came to the bank as a cashier in the 1931 merger.

His banking career began April 1, 1922, when he accepted a position as bookkeeper in the Wells County Bank. When the First National was established in 1929, he was on the list of officers as an assistant cashier. Later he became cashier.

In 1938, when Stogdill became Old-First president, after Cutshall had retired, Fitzpatrick moved up to fill the vacated vice presidency, while continuing to hold the cashier's post.

In 1963, he retired from his cashier's role, but remained as vice president.

BUILDING'S HISTORY

The building which the Old First National Bank vacated in 1968 has a historic past with roots that extend back to the earliest Wells County banking and financial endeavors.

Begun in 1913 and completed in 1914, the building was the headquarters of the old Studabaker Bank. But, at the time it was completed, it was nearly 50 years younger than the bank itself.

John Studabaker was one of Bluffton's earliest and hardiest pioneer settlers. A man of energy and vision he worked in many ways to improve his chosen homeland in frontier Indiana.

He was one of the county's earliest railroad promoters and eventually headed the firm which made the first rail connection between Bluffton and Fort Wayne.

He owned and operated a general store at Main and Market Streets. Histories of early Wells County reveal that in 1856 he "commenced lending money and selling New York exchange in connection with his produce trade".

In 1863, together with George Arnold, Jeffrey Bliss, Amos Townsend, and James Van Emon, he organized the First National Bank of Bluffton, with a capital of $50,000.

NEW BANK FORMED

In 1868 the bank closed business. On New Year's Day, 1869, Studabaker, his brother Peter and their nephew, Hugh Dougherty, a Civil War hero, formed the Exchange Bank. Still later, the institution was renamed as the Studabaker Bank.

From the Studabaker General Store, the bank moved westward into a narrow, three story brick building in the 100 block on West Market Street. It operated in that building until 1913 when John Studabaker purchased an adjacent store building.

He then announced plans to tear down both buildings and construct a handsome new bank edifice. During the construction period, operations of the Studabaker Bank were carried on in a store building in the 100 block of North Main Street.

When the Studabaker Bank closed in 1927, the building became headquarters for, in short order, the Citizens Bank, the Wells County Bank, and the Old National Bank. In 1931, with the merger of the Old National and the First National, it became the home of the Old-First National Bank.

Veteran bank employees can recall many colorful scenes in connection with the long history of the bank and its buildings but they vow that none were quite so "quaint" as in some other Hoosier banks where "seed" corn and other agricultural supplies were stacked and sold along the wall.

WARY OF HOLD-UPS

With the John Dillinger era, in the 1920's and 1930's, bank workers developed an ingrained wariness.

The Old-First actually weathered one near hold-up. The incident came on Jan. 5, 1935, when Stogdill and police received a tip that a gang of robbers were preparing an elaborate plan for an early morning hold-up of the institution.

The bandits planned to capture bank janitor Harrison Kapp as he opened the doors early in the morning. They would then force him to let them inside. Then they planned to accost each of the employees as they arrived.

Stogdill notified police. State and city officers, armed with machine guns and wearing bulletproof vests, spent the night inside the bank. Other officers were in patrol cars and at other strategic points in the downtown area.

Stogdill notified Kapp to leave early for work. The janitor reached the building, went inside and turned on the lights without being apprehended by the would-be robbers.

Meanwhile, officers spotted a suspicious-looking car, which repeatedly drove past the front and rear of the building. Later the occupants of the car were seen to enter the old Ray Hotel, across Main St., from the Post Office.

BUSINESS AS USUAL

Bank employees arrived for work at the normal time and were told to "act normal" despite the presence of the hidden police officers and the possibility of a robbery. Fitzpatrick recalled wryly the difficulty of "acting normal" under such circumstances.

At 10 a.m. that morning police closed in on the gang in the old upstairs hotel room. They arrested six men and one woman, after capturing two of the men who fled on foot.

One of the men was released, as he had no part in the robbery plan. The others were brought to trial two days later and sentenced to prison terms on the same day.

Robbery attempts not withstanding, the Old-First grew and prospered through the years.

BOARD MEMBERS

1978	Lester Bauermeister	1929	F. Wm. Hitzeman
1929	Henry Bowerfind	1984	Garry Jones
1937	Dr. Harry D. Brickley	1983	Donald McArdle
1968	Dr. Charles H. Caylor	1934	Thomas McKiernan
1971	William L. Cline	1984	Robert J. Meyer
1929	Frank H. Cutshall	1985	Dean E. Milligan
1943	John H. Edris	1967	Herman W. Myers
1978	John H. Edris, Jr.	1929	Henry C. Paul
1983	Jeffrey Espich	1960	Edward J. Schaefer
1937	Frank F. Engeler	1960	Paul E. Shaffer
1938	Raymond N. Fitzpatrick	1938	James W. Stogdill
1961	Dr. Max M. Gitlin	1958	Ralph Tyndall
1946	James O. Gordon	1929	Edward Wilson
1967	C. Lloyd Griffis	1985	Ronald C. Wimmer
1943	Hoyt H. Hartman		

THE HISTORY CONTINUES

A key figure in the long history of the Old-First National Bank has been James W. Stogdill, who in 1990 celebrated 75 years in banking. Stogdill began his banking career on June 14, 1915.

Stogdill was president of Old-First until 1968, when he was succeeded by C. Lloyd Griffis, who had joined Old-First in January of 1963 as an executive vice president.

Griffis held the top post until Dec. 11, 1985, when he entered retirement. He was followed in the presidential seat by Dean E. Milligan, who had joined the firm in December, 1984 as an executive vice president.

Ongoing progress at the bank over the years included the opening of north and south branches of Bluffton in September of 1975. Further expansion came in June of 1988 when the Ossian branch bank was opened, with William H. Howard named as the Ossian branch manager.

Old-First also was the leader in Wells County in offering Automatic Teller Banking, with the first ATM machines placed in 1986.

On April 11, 1985, Old-First formed a one - bank holding company, Old-First National Corporation. In May of 1986, Old-First National Corp. announced its agreement to affiliate with Fort Wayne National Corporation. The merger took effect on March 1, 1987.

James W. Stogdill being presented with the Sagamore of the Wabash award in June of 1990. (l. to r.) Dean E. Milligan, President of OFNB 1986 to present, James W. Stogdill, President of OFNB 1938 to 1968, and Lloyd Griffis, President of OFNB 1968 to 1986.

ALMCO STEEL PRODUCTS CORPORATION

*Howard Almdale
President and CEO of
Almco Steel Products Corporation*

Almco Steel Products was founded and incorporated on August 26, 1946, by Hoard Almdale. The decision was made to locate in Bluffton after looking at many towns in the Midwest area. Construction of a small concrete block building was started in February, 1947. Some light presses and other necessary machinery were purchased and operations began in September, 1947.

As time went on, increasing competition in the small stamping field pushed the corporation into somewhat heavier stamping. We moved from approximately 100 ton equipment to 300-500 ton equipment.

Land was low on the north side of the plant and tremendous amounts of fill clay were added, to the extent that the News Banner described the pile of fill as the Bluffton mountain. However, the mountain disappeared as the site was leveled and the building extended. Press equipment with longer beds, great capacity (up to 1600 tons) and greater speed was continuously added, always with an eye to remaining competitive in our industry. Statistical process control and equipment to measure accurately to less than one thousandth of an inch became a byword throughout our operations.

For the most part, automotive and truck stampings were produced, but gradual diversification was successfully undertaken. Today we not only supply parts for the new automotive and truck industry, but also in aircraft, agriculture, electric motors, government/military contract work, as well as replacements parts for fraction of an ounce; the largest products (truck bumpers) weigh about 100 pounds.

Employment today, under a very competent staff that includes Jim Almdale, son of the founder, is about 100 people from not only Wells but contiguous counties. Almco has a sales network that penetrates Indiana, Ohio, Michigan, Illinois, and Iowa. With increasing customer diversification and attention and responsiveness to customer's needs, a continuing bent toward heavy and large stampings, increased capabilities in welding, assembly, robotics and parts finishing, and a strong quality control program, Almco is confident of future growth.

*James C. Almdale
Vice President of Almco Steel Products Corporation
and son of Howard Almdale*

Bluffton Chamber of Commerce

The Bluffton Chamber of Commerce has been active in one form or another since the early 1900s. The Chamber is a business association formed to advance the general welfare and prosperity of the Bluffton area, so that its citizens and all areas of its business community have ample opportunity to prosper.

The first organized group evolving from the business association concept was the Bluffton Commercial Club, an organization more social in nature than business related. After the Club's formation in 1901, its members worked toward bringing the Indiana Truck Scale Company to Bluffton. The group soon merged with the Bluffton Elks Club, which had acquired the meeting rooms located on the second floor of a building located in the two hundred block of West Market Street.

Not long after the informal dissolution of the Commercial Club, the Merchants and Manufacturing Association as established in yet another attempt to assist the further development of commerce in the area. Part of the progress this organization achieved included the establishment of the A.J. King Piano Company.

During 1914, local community leaders formed the first Bluffton Chamber of Commerce. In addition to manufacturing development, the newly formed association became more actively involved in assisting retail merchants in promotional events and advertising.

As the community grew, so did the efforts of the Chamber. In the 1950's, the members were instrumental in attracting the Corning Glass Company which became Bluffton's largest employer. This achievement encouraged the Chamber to further address the area of industrial development. Members of the Chamber and other industrial leaders were responsible for forming the first Bluffton Industrial Development Corporation, a for-profit corporation established to attract industry into a newly acquired industrial site.

Through the 60's and 70's, the Chamber continued to focus much of its effort and industrial development; through by 1980 and 1990 standards, this effort was more passive in nature. In addition, because of the popularity of Bluffton's downtown, the Chamber continuously battled what is, even in the 1990's, a seemingly never ending problem available parking. Also, through the years, the Chamber maintained a social environment that enabled business and community leaders to exchange ideas, and develop understanding and trust—crucial elements for public and private development.

In the late 80's and early 90's, the increasingly global and competitive economy brought significant changes to the ideals which had firmly entrenched the Chamber's course. The early 1980s brought about unforeseen changes that crippled the United States' and Indiana's economy. A recession, that to many seemed a depression, brought about plant closures and cutbacks. Corning Glass moved its Bluffton facility to another city, taking away hundreds of jobs. The nation's unemployment rose to over 10 percent.

Community leaders from both the public and private sectors realized that Bluffton could no longer depend on chance or fortunate circumstance - driven development. Bluffton began an aggressive approach to development that included a new organization called the Bluffton Revitalization Committee, Inc. This new committee focused a great deal of its attention to the downtown area through promotions, historic rehabilitation, and retail business recruitment. Revitalization maintained this focus from 1985 through 1988 until other Revitalization - born projects began to take on momentum.

Through the tremendous efforts of both Revitalization and the Chamber, a record $1.5 million was raised from private sources in the community. These fundraising efforts won Bluffton the honor of being an All-American City Finalist for 1989. Those dollars went into Revitalization planned projects known today as the Rivergreenway Trail, Kehoe Riverfront Park, and the downtown streetscape project.

On a parallel course of time, Bluffton Revitalization and the Bluffton Chamber of Commerce were negotiating a merger of sorts to develop an "umbrella" organization that would address all the development and business assistance needs of the community. It had become clear that precious financial resources were being stretched too thin.

In 1989, the Chamber and Revitalization formed an organization called Bluffton Horizons. Today, policy for community and economic development are established by two separate boards of directors, but administered from one central office located in the 200 block of south Main Street in downtown Bluffton. That office is run by a chief executive officer and one administrative assistant.

In 1990, Bluffton and the Bluffton Chamber of Commerce were awarded the first Outstanding Indiana Community of the Year award from the Indiana Chamber of Commerce. Bluffton won this distinguished award because of its tremendous efforts through public/private partnership to resolve an economic and community crisis.

In 1990 and 1991 the Bluffton Chamber and Revitalization, through the vehicle of Bluffton Horizons, experiences growing support and began focusing their attention on forming a solid organizational foundation for community growth.

CRAIGVILLE TELEPHONE COMPANY, INC.

Craigville's first telephone service was provided by the German Telephone Company, organized by John H. Barger in 1905. This early exchange served 60 customers with magneto telephones.

Due to World War I, the name of the company was changed in 1919 to the Craigville Telephone Company, Inc. Mr. Barger remained a director until his death in 1958.

Floyd Herman, son-in-law of Mr. Barger, became a director of the company and its secretary in 1930. He served as manager of the company until 1985, giving 55 years of full time service. Mr. Ehrman continued to serve the company by being on the board of directors until 1988.

In 1952 Howard F. Reinhard, son-in-law of Mr. Ehrman, became president of the company; he served as telephone lineman and repairman until 1977 when he became inside plant manager. Since Mr. Ehrman''s retirement, Mr. Reinhard serves as president and general manager.

Sometime during 1905-1919, the central office and the operators moved to the second floor of the house existing at 2409 N Main Street in Craigville. At one time, the barn on this property contained a sign reading the German Telephone Company. The central office remained at this location until 1961 when a new building was constructed at the company's present location, the former Abott and Reed Store, to house the office and the equipment. In 1963, the company cut over from the magneto system to dial service with direct distance dialing and extended area service with the Bluffton exchange. The company started to bury underground cable in 1965, and now about 85% of the cable is buried. This saves many headaches for the linemen, they no longer have to worry as much about ice, wind, or lightning storms, semi trucks or large farm equipment damaging the cable.

In 1978, they became the first company in Indiana to change a Stromberg-Carlson digital central office. At present, a new updated switch has been installed with completion taking place March 1, 1991. This update is allowing the company to go equal access, which means the customer has the privilege to choose the long distance carrier of their choice. It also allows us to go local automated message accounting (LAMA). This means the company will be doing their own recording of calls instead of having Indiana Bell, AT&T or GET doing it for us. In the near future, we are hoping to put all customers on private lines. At present 70% of our customers are private lines with the remaining customers on two party lines (at one time there were at least 10 parties to each line).

A new office area was added to the existing structure in 1984.

In the early 1960's the company asked the late Harry S. Lindstrand, a prominent Wells County artist, to design the company logo, which we use today.

As of February, 1991, the Craigville Telephone Company serves over 765 accounts with over 1350 telephones in Adams and Wells Counties.

In the 87 years of the company's existence, there have been at least 53 people involved with its operation. Many of those were operators or part time help used during emergencies such as snow, wind and/or ice storms.

Present employees of the Craigville Telephone Company are Howard Reinhard, president/manager; Lee Vongunten, asst. manager; Carl (Reinhard) Vongunten, secretary; Arvilla (Reinhard) Rodenbeck, asst. secretary; Keith Ehrman, Stephen Rodenbeck and Ronald Meyer, linemen.

The following is a list of full, part time and emergency help that could be recalled:

Operators: Gracie Bell, Theo Byerly, Lillian Diehl, Opal Drum, Inez (Frauhiger) Bauman, Christine Dubach, Enid Gahman, Marie Gerber, Lorraine High, Clara Isch, Goldier Kehrn, Elle Landis, Marjorie Myers, Doris Rauner, Ilene Reinhard, Mary Ann Reinhard, Agnes Schaefer, Marie Tschannen, and Tracy Wolfe.

Linemen: Roy Diehl, Amos Dubach, Robert Gahman, Ralph Freels, Earl Frauhiger, John Green, Walter Conrad, Mr. Lesh, Mr. Cooper, Floyd Ehrman, Noah Yake, Lamoin Barger, Donald W. Barger, Wayne Barger, Howard Reinhard, Carlton Reinhard, Arland Reinhard, Brian Netherland, Steve Shady, Don Double, Mike Leeth, Jeff Gerber, Keith Ehrman, Lee Vongunten, Stephen Rodenbeck, and Ronald Meyer.

Office Employees: John Barger, Walter Reed, Floyd Ehrman, Lola Ehrman, Howard Reinhard, Ilene Reinhard, Ada Gerber, Carlton Reinhard, Arland Reinhard, Arvilla (Reinhard) Rodenbeck, Carla (Reinhard) Vongunten, and Lee Vongunten.

We know names may have been omitted, but memories only go back so far. Old records were not kept.

The Craigville Telephone Company is in its fourth generation of family operation.

Dr. Byron Poindexter

Dr. Byron K. Poindexter owns the beautiful historic office building at 328 West Market where his dental office is located. Dr. Poindexter graduated from Indiana University School of Dentistry in June, 1958, with a Dr. of Dental Surgery degree. He and his wife, Patricia, moved to Bluffton where he opened his first dental office located in the Gal-Ham Building in August of 1958. He then moved his office to its current location on West Market in May, 1966.

Mrs. Poindexter is the former Patricia Hunley. The Poindexters are the parents of four children. There are two daughters, Devon Kay (Mrs. Donald Willey) and Gay Rachelle, and there are two sons, Byron Clay and Blake Theodore. They have one grandchild, Carson Landis Willey.

Dr. Poindexter is a member of First United Methodist Church, Elks, Masonic Lodge, Wells County Historical Society, Wells County Crime Stoppers, Mizpah Shrine, Scottish Rite, Indiana Dental Society, Isaac Knapp Dental Society, American Dental Society and Delta Sigma Delta Dental Fraternity. He is a past president of Wells County Crippled Children. He and his wife Patricia served two terms on the Bluffton High School All Night Party Committee. They also served on the Parents Advisory Board of Hillsdale College.

Dr. Byron Poindexter

DR. BYRON K. POINDEXTER
Dentistry

Farmers and Merchants Bank

Farmers and Merchants Bank of Bluffton began operations on January 2, 1917, in a two-story brick building in Craigville, Indiana.

Gideon Gerber, a farmer who had been born and raised on a farm east of Bluffton, was successfully managing a business known as the Craigville Elevator when a group of citizens asked him to organize and open a bank. The first meeting to form this bank was held on July 10, 1916. The bank opened its door to business in January of 1917.

During the late 1920's, when the number of Wells County banks had risen to 12, Gideon Gerber served as president of the Wells County Bankers Association.

In the years that ensued, Gideon Carter felt the burden of managing the elevator and the bank, while also renting out farms he owned. As the Great Depression set in, he was faced with the decision of choosing between farming and banking. Gideon's son, Amos, convinced him to sell the farms. Another decision was made to move the bank to Bluffton, where it would be more centrally located and could better serve the community.

With the help of Compton O. Rider, Fred J. Tangeman and others, a charter was obtained and the bank opened on January 3, 1933, at its present Main and Market Street location in Bluffton, Indiana. Now a bank with total assets of $102,903, the name was changed to Farmers and Merchants Bank for the new opening.

The bank's management team consisted of Gideon Carter, who headed the bank, Fred Tangeman and young Amos Gerber.

Times were not the best for starting a new venture or for moving a bank from Craigville to Bluffton. The impact of the Great Depression resulted in numerous bank foreclosures and mergers. During the early months of the new Bluffton bank's life, a national moratorium closed all banks temporarily. However, the Farmers and Merchants Bank of Bluffton and the Ossian State Bank were the first in the great Fort Wayne area allowed to reopen after the presidentially-declared moratorium.

In the difficult times of the 1930's, most banks merely hoped to survive. So when Farmers and Merchants Bank climbed above a half-million dollars in assets in 1936, the year of the Wells County Centennial, there was reason for mounting confidence.

On the occasion of the bank's 25th anniversary in 1958, bank remodeling programs were carried out doubling the bank's work

interior and providing a complete face change. In 1973, more renovation occurred when the bank moved into an area previously occupied by the Harris and Weterick Drug Store. A third phase of updating and remodeling the facility was instituted in mid-1900 with major interior changes creating a fresh business-like atmosphere.

In July 1983, Farmers and Merchants Bank proudly opened its first branch inside Scott's Food Stores, south of Bluffton in the Harrison Plaza.

In late 1985 the bank took action to become a part of Lincoln Financial Corporation of Fort Wayne. This decision has proven to be good for the bank and its customers.

In the 74-year history of Farmers and Merchants Bank, impressively there have been only three presidents: Gideon Gerber, who served through 1961; Amos Gerber, who ended an illustrious career after 60 years in banking, served from 1961 to 1987; and current president and chief executive officer, Gerald L. Babb, who was appointed to the position in 1987.

Farmers and Merchants Bank has long been a faithful civic partner in many projects in the community and Wells County over the years, and it will continue to be a leader in the years ahead.

Heyerly's

Heyerly's Market in Bluffton

Heyerly's Bakery in Ossian

Heyerly's Market in Bluffton, and Heyerly's Bakery in Ossian are among Wells County's longest running family businesses.

Ray and Herman Heyerly first established the Heyerly name in business in 1929 when they began running two bread routes. For two years they traveled the rural roads of Adams, Allen, and Wells Counties selling cold meat and bread. They purchased their bread from Vic Eichenberger's bakery in Berne during these early years.

In 1931, Gardener's Bakery in Ossian came up for sale. Ray and Herman's father, Albert Heyerly, purchased the business, and Heyerly's Bakery was established. Now, while baking their own products, they continued their bread routes. In 1936, they added a third route when their brother, Luster Heyerly, began a route of his own.

Through the years, customers expressed their desire to be able to purchase more than just meat and bread from the Heyerly brothers. So, in the late 1930s, the Heyerlys expanded their bread routes to include a full line of grocery items. In addition during these years, the bakery began adding more specialty items such as danish, cakes, rolls and pies to their product line. Now customers were offered produce, canned goods, dairy products, and a large selection of bakery products, in addition to cold meat and bread.

They were on the road with three huckster wagons until 1959 when they bought the Bluffton grocery store and a slaughter house from Otto Ratliff. In their new grocery store, the Heyerly brothers featured their own fresh baked goods, and meat which they butchered themselves. They also smoked their own meat products in the smoke house located at the grocery store. They continued selling beef and pork that they had butchered, until 1970, when they closed down the slaughter house.

In 1964, the bakery expanded its production and moved into the Sharp's Hardware building in Ossian where it is still located today. Since that time, the bakery has continued to add new items to its long list of products. In addition to being featured at Heyerly's Bakery and Heyerly's Market, the baked goods from the bakery are also available today at various location in Decatur and Berne.

During the growing years, the boys divided the responsibilities of these businesses between them. Ray took the responsibility for managing the bakery, and he has always been the head baker. Herman and Luster managed the grocery store where Herman specialized in meats while Luster coordinated all of the groceries and the produce department. Many of the boys' brothers and sisters also played an important role in making these businesses successful. In addition, Ray and Luster's children took an active part in the businesses, and they continue to do so today.

Ray's children, Ron, Stan, Lynn and Galen Heyerly, and Denise (Heyerly) Steffen are all active in the day to day operations of the bakery. They are involved in every aspect of the bakery from mixing and baking to decorating and delivering the products.

Luster's children, Herb Heyerly and Sue (Heyerly) Lantz are actively involved in running the grocery store where they continue the tradition of selling only top quality meats and, of course, baked goods from the bakery.

The businesses are now seeing a third generation of workers from the Heyerly family as Ray and Luster's grandchildren have begun getting involved in working at both businesses.

Through the years, the Heyerly family and their businesses have made a significant mark on the history of Wells County. Possibly the most notable of their contributions to the history books has been the 25 consecutive years in which Heyerly's Market and Bakery purchased the 4-H Grand Champion Steer. From 1962 to 1986 the Heyerly brothers were successful every year in their bid for the grand champion steer, and they continue to be active bidders every year at the 4-H auctions.

When the grocery store was purchased in 1959, there were some 25 local grocery establishments in Bluffton. Heyerly's is the only one among those that is still in business today. More than 60 years of hard work and friendly service have firmly established both of the Heyerly businesses in the pages of Wells County history.

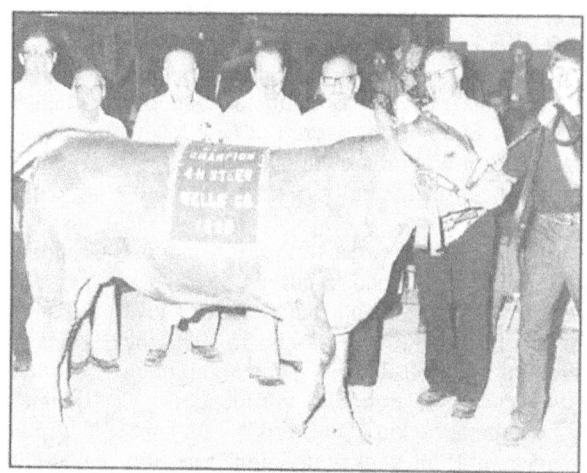
Grand Champion Steer

James E. Van Winkle O.D.

Dr. James E. Van Winkle on the corner of Johnson and Washington Streets.

The Bluffton, Wells County, Indiana, area has had optometric services through this practice for over 70 years. The visual needs of the community evolved from the testing and fitting of spectacles by jewelers to the visual assessment, care, and referral by university level optometric graduates, professionally licensed practitioners.

The current optometric practice of Dr. James E. Van Winkle, O.D. began with the practice of Dr. Homer R. Gettle in the 1920,s. Dr. Jess T. Scott, O.D., graduate of Northern Illinois College of Optometry in Chicago, joined him in late 1953, in an office area located in at 107 South Main Street. Dr. Scott purchased the practice in 1943 and acquired the location on the northwest corner of Washington and Johnson Streets in December, 1947. The site was remodeled and became his professional office on March 10, 1948.

Dr. James E. Van Winkle of Goshen, Indiana, joined the practice in mid-June, 1967, following his masters of optometry from Indiana University School of Optometry. His practice was interrupted by two years of military service during 1969-1971. He served as a captain in the U.S. Air Force, providing optometric care at Valdosta, GA during the Vietnam conflict.

Following his tour of military duty, Dr. Van Winkle entered into partnership with Dr. Scott. He and his wife, Betty (Inebnit), joined in the community life of Wells County and raised their children Andrew (Aug. 20, 1969) and Jennifer L. (April 14, 1972), at 1203 Echo Lane.

Upon Dr. Scott's retirement in 1987 after 52 years of practice, Dr. Van Winkle assumed the practice.

Optometric care has expanded over the years from simple techniques of evaluation of levels of near and farsightedness, to very precise appraisals of the internal as well as the external health of the eye. Spectacles are no longer the only eyewear available. The developments of the 1960,s made contact lens wearing more realistic; further manufacturing capabilities have expanded even this field today.

Continuous education requirements and manufacturer's products have broadened the type of care which can be offered in an optometric office. In this era there is greater public interest in health care and preventative health measures. Optometrist work very closely with allied health services to meet the specific need for optimum eye health care of their patients.

In early summer of 1991, Dr. Van Winkle will be moving into his new office facility at 105 Harvest Road. This will enable him to continue to expand his services to Bluffton and the surrounding communities.

New Offices for Dr. James E. Van Winkle under construction on 105 Harvest Road in the spring of 1991.

Kitco, Inc.

Kitco Eng. & Mfg. Company Inc. at its beginning in 1955. The 200 E. Spring Street location was once the Houser Eng. & Mfg. Company location.

The company started as Kitco Eng. & Mfg. Co., Inc. in 1955, founded by three former U.S. Rubber Co. employees: William Kelley, Carl Ihrcke, and Ray Tobin, from whose names was derived the name Kitco. Leonard C. Lindblom started with the company in 1956. This small company started with new ideas in design and production for close tolerance, flash-free rubber parts.

In 1956, the Dole Valve Co. of Chicago, Illinois, acquired the company, and it was a wholly-owned subsidiary. In 1962, the companies were acquired by Eaton Mfg., headquartered in Cleveland, Ohio.

In the interim, Mr. Kelley and Mr. Tobin left the company and Mr. Ihrcke had died. Leonard C. Lindblom became plant manager.

In 1968, Kitco Eng. & Mfg. Co., Inc. was made a division of Eaton, Yale & Towne, Inc. and the name was changed to Precision Molded Products Division. In 1970, Eaton Yale & Towne, Inc. became Eaton Corporation.

In 1976, Eaton Corporation determined rubber manufacturing did not fit their long-range plans. When it was learned that Eaton wanted to divest itself of Precision Molded Products Division, Leonard C. Lindblom successfully completed negotiations to purchase the division from Eaton. The divestiture transaction was official as of December 31, 1976. After an accumulated 22 years of experience, expansion and an outstanding reputation, it was only fitting to return to how it all started Kitco, an independent company. The same personnel, equipment, and facilities to manufacture precision molded rubber parts were retained.

Kitco has played a vital role in Wells County's history by providing the livelihood for many of the families in the area. Some of our employees have been employed at Kitco in excess of 30 years.

Kitco is a manufacturer of precision molded rubber parts to customer design and specifications, and we supply to the automotive appliance, business machines, home entertainment, food and beverage, and vending industries.

Today's corporate offices and modern manufacturing facility clearly show Kitco's extensive growth and expansion in 36 years.

Simpson Industries

Simpson Industries dates back to 1912 when R.J. Simpson first began repairing bicycles and motor cars in Litchfield, Michigan. For the next twenty years, he became involved in various business endeavors, including the selling of automobiles. In 1934, the Simpson-Ely Company became a subsidiary of Litchfield Manufacturing Company and began manufacturing oil pump covers for Ford V-8 engines. The orders soon multiplied and the Simpson Company became incorporated. The Company successfully diversified from that point.

Today, Simpson Industries produces machined parts and assemblies for original equipment manufacturers of automobiles, trucks, diesel engines, and farm equipment in the United States and Canada. The Company has manufacturing facilities in Michigan, Indiana, Ohio, North Carolina and Canada. Our Bluffton operation was added to the team in December of 1978 at 131 W. Harvest Road, Bluffton, Indiana.

In 1978 we started out with 32,000 square feet and 12 employees. In 1984 we added an additional 16,000 square feet, bringing us to our present 48,000 square feet. We presently have 65 employees. The operations manager is Gary Boone, who came to Bluffton from Litchfield, Michigan, where the company's corporate office is located.

Gary Boone, Operations Manager

Our customer base includes Ford, General Motors, Saturn, Borg Warner, Cummins, Chrysler and American Motors. Our employees are proud to have earned Ford's Q-1 and General Motors Targets for Excellence Awards.

Our future is bright for continuous growth in the community, along with a more diversified customer base.

STATE BANK OF MARKLE

According to old records, the first bank was organized in Markle, Indiana, in 1903. The bank operated under the name Farmers and Trade Bank until about 1920, when it was reorganized under the name of Markle State Bank and continued under that name until the bank was closed during the National Bank Holiday in the early 1930's. This organization was liquidated at that time, paying all depositors in full.

During that period, from the bank's closing until 1947, the Town of Markle was without a bank and was serviced by an exchange operated by the Markle Businessmen's Association which had purchased the bank building and equipment from the closed bank. The exchange was a convenient service but it could not meet the needs of the Markle community and as a result, signs of a lack of progress were noticed in the community.

A group of public-spirited businessmen in Markle associated themselves to organize a new bank. A charter for a new bank, known as the State Bank of Markle, was granted by the State Department of Financial Institutions and the Secretary of State on September 9, 1947. The new corporation was authorized for $35,000 capital, consisting of the 350 shares of common stock at $100.00 per share per value. Forty-six stockholders comprised the original organization. The original directors were Irvin I. Wolfcale, Vaughn L. Crow, Paul McGuffey, Floyd Thomas, Carl J. Freds, Albert E. Luther, and Howard T. Anderson. Officers were Irvin Wolfcale, President; Vaughn Crow, Vice President; and Howard Anderson, Secretary and Cashier.

The bank operated in the original bank building, which it purchased from the Markle Business Men's Association, until 1961 when a new building was built on the site where the bank is currently located. In 1976 construction was begun which doubled the size of the bank.

State Bank of Markle purchased the Randol Insurance Agency in 1985 and formed the Markle Insurance Services to provide additional services for customers.

In the 1980's it became apparent that if the bank were to continue as an independent bank, it would be necessary to expand its base of operations. Thus, in June of 1987 an office was opened in Bluffton to service the Wells County area.

Current members of the Board of Directors are Gerald L. Miller, M.D., Chairman, Donald L. Hoopingarner, James H. Davis, Jr., Douglas F. LeMaster, Jr., Bevan D. Best, Elmo Murrell, Richard L. Randol, and Rudy Frauhiger. Officers are Donald Hoopingarner, President and Trust Officer, George Keplinger, Vice President, Joh A. Smith, Vice President, Mark Wolf, Asst. Vice President, Marcella Hardin, Cashier and Asst. Trust Officer, Coleen Allred, Asst. Cashier, Sara Imel, Asst. Cashier and Branch Manager, and Billy J. Randol, Asst. Vice President of Markle Insurance Services.

State Bank of Markle in Markle

State Bank of Markle at 1705 Baker Place in Bluffton.

STEFFEN OIL COMPANY, INC.

Steve's Petroleum Service on July 1, 1964.

A family farm east of Craigville, Indiana, owned by his parents, Tobias and Martha Baumgartner Steffen, was the birthplace of Elmer Steffen on May 4, 1920. Born on his father's 31st birthday was unique in itself. Preceding many good times and some unfavorable events during their Christian walk of life, this couple usually were in a joyful frame of mind.

In those days there were many house and barn fires, either started by lanterns, lamps, or by wood burning stoves. Such was the case of a house fire in the spring after Elmer's first school year. The 80-acre farm was lost because of failure to make interest payment on the principal. Subsequently, Martha acquired encephalitis (sleeping sickness). A cash crop was important, so sugar beets were grown by many farmers as was practiced here. One particular year there were 10 acres of pickles, six acres of potatoes, and four acres of kidney beans, on the 80 acre farm. Needless to say, there was enough work for parents, six children and some outside labor force. It took more than a wagon load of oats to buy shoes and supplies for the school aged children

By the spring of 1934, the family had moved to another farm. This was considered the winding-down of the great depression. Here there was a "farm sale," disposing of all farm equipment and two horses. Riding a school bus, which went to Craigville, was a new experience. Further schooling at Lancaster was terminated after the ninth grade. Elmer had worked during the summer, paid by the month (12 to 18 dollars) on neighboring farms. It was during the winter of 1936-37 that the family moved to Villa North, Bluffton. He worked at a local glove factory before washing cars at service stations.

It was in Sunday School that he met Dee Freidinger from Bay City, Michigan. The draft came up after Pearl Harbor, and at the age of 21, Elmer went to the U.S. Army. After serving three years and 10 months in the ETO, Dee and Elmber began housekeeping in Bay City, Michigan, where home was to Dee and their first born son, Derrell. Dee's father, being a home builder, had ready-made employment for Elmer in October, 1945.

After two years, his father Tobias, passed away, after driving a tank wagon for the Wells County Co-op, a supplying company of petroleum products. Having been appointed executor of the will and while in the process of managing the estate, Elmer was hired to replace his dad. This was in September of 1947.

In the ensuing years the family increased to four. When they became of age, marriage was considered. Derrell married Sue Ramseyer, and teaches school; Marcia, a nurse, married Larry Belsley; Donn, after serving in the U.S. Naval Air Corps, now is an electrical engineer and married Karen Gramm; Allen, now a business partner, married Arlene Shifferly.

The entire family, working very little elsewhere, was instrumental in propagating the business, which was now known as Steffen Oil Company. Employment with the co-op was terminated July 1, 1964. Having established a close-knit relationship of friends in the business community, they were encouraged to continue to be served with petroleum products as had been established. Bulk plant facilities were purchased at 705 West Market St., Bluffton, on July 1, 1965, the beginning of Steve's Petroleum Service, and a formal contract was signed with Sun Oil Company. Initial deliveries were made on July 11, 1964, which was Allen's 11th birthday. Filling a combine in the field for Floyd Gerber was the first delivery on a Saturday afternoon, rendering service as a tank wagon owner-operator. Subsequently 55,000 gallons of underground gasoline storage was put in place during the next few months, at this same location.

The first full time employee, Chad Cochran, was hired to help serve the community in 1968, adding another delivery truck with much success.

In 1978 Steve's Petroleum Service had grown successfully and a new corporation was formed, Steffen Oil Co., Inc.

Several oil companies made offers to supply us product, but Sun Oil has prevailed at this writing. Allen joined the work force soon after high school, as his college days were brief. He has since assumed ownership with Chad, in 1980.

(l. to r.) Sue & Darrell Steffen, Arlene & Allen Steffen, Elmer & Dee Steffen, Marcia & Larry Belsley, and Karen & Donn Steffen.

THE DUTCH MILL

The Dutch Mill, "On the Banks of the Wabash," is a Bluffton Institution!

It all began with Glen Moser's dream of owning a restaurant. A dream that became a reality in July 1948, when he bought the Dutch Mill, not long after he returned from duty in the Armed Forces.

He knew the restaurant business from experience prior to the war, and the years he spent as a cook in the Navy added to his expertise.

In 40 years, Glen has turned the Dutch Mill from a one-room restaurant with three booths, 12 counter stools and a table into a 12-room establishment with a seating capacity of 500.

Over the years, that one room has grown to its present size as more dining rooms were added to accommodate the growing number of customers.

Completing the complex are a complete carry-out service and the Cupboard, where self-service is available.

Despite the fast food mania, the Dutch Mill began as a family business and remains that way today.

Adding to the family flavor of the business is the fact that all of Glen's children, Rose, Laura Bertsch, Julie, Emily, David and Daniel, have worked there at one time or are now employed there. His wife, Dina Fae, also worked there in earlier years.

The current owner of the Dutch Mill, Kenneth Steffen, started at the restaurant in 1950 at the age of 13 and has been associated with the business ever since.

The Dutch Mill Restaurant in 1948 with a seating capacity of 25 in one dining room.

The family theme continued with the Steffen family, with Ken's wife, Roberta and their children, Jeffrey, Angela McClain, Tobias and Elaine Olson, being employed at the Dutch Mill at various times.

Home-made pies have always been a specialty at the Dutch Mill, along with home-made muffins and rolls, served with the wide variety of food on the menu.

Seeking to provide the public with the best in food and service, the restaurant has continued the custom of grinding its own hamburger and cutting its own steaks. Baked fish, charbroiled chicken and stir fry foods and well as weight control meals are available for the health conscious customers.

Active in community affairs, Glen and Dina Fae Moser donated land to the recent Bluffton Revitalization project of Kehoe Park on the banks of the Wabash.

Through the years the Dutch Mill has been generous in helping anyone who was hungry and assisted many young people through high school and college by hiring them at the restaurant.

That same service and quality food are provided today as the Dutch Mill continues its role of a "Bluffton Institution."

The Dutch Mill Restaurant in 1991 with a seating capacity of 500 in twelve dining rooms.

The Fabri-Form Company

The Fabri-Form Company, founded by the late J.W. (Jack) Knight in 1943, in Byesville, Ohio, is a manufacturer of custom plastic products and a pioneer in the field of thick sheet thermoforming. The new company started with ten employees in a rented storeroom, and the chief market was the aircraft industry. Within one year, the business expanded to 35 employees.

In 1953, the company purchased property in Pekin, Indiana, and built a new plant to produce the first plastic refrigerator door liners. Today this plant is still a custom thermoforming operation and its principal products are now tote trays for various schools throughout the country.

At Byesville, The Fabri-Form Co was busy producing visors for military aircraft helmets and space suits. On February 20, 1962, Lt. Col. John. H. Glenn, Jr. first orbited the earth with a Fabri-form visor on his helmet.

A.J. Dragonette became CEO in 1970 while Shirley Knight remained as chairman of the board, a position she still holds today. It was during his tenure that Fabri-Form entered the field of returnable material handling system.

In 1981, John W. Knight, son of the founder, became CEO.

During the decade of the 80's, the Fabri-Form Company expanded its production of returnable handling systems. They added a production facility in the Detroit, Michigan, area in 1984. The plant was to supply the automotive industry with returnable packaging.

In 1990, the Bluffton, Indiana, area provided an ideal location for the establishment of a team concept facility. The strong support of the people and the local government officials make Bluffton a town with a future.

Fabri-Form of Bluffton is a major step for the Fabri-Form Company. Serving as a model for the industry, it will be the standard by which thermoforming companies will be measured in the 90's.

The company closed the Michigan operating in 1991, combining it with the new facility in Bluffton, Indiana.

The year 1990 was a year of prosperity for the Fabri-Form Company. During this year, Fabri-Form acquired Marks Transfer and Storage Co. to improve our shipping capabilities to customers and our other facilities. A new extruder line was added to the Byesville plant.

From our beginning as a manufacturer of aircraft canopies, to the development of the helmet visor on the first space suit, to our current focus on returnable material handling systems, our products have covered a wide range of industries. Our emphasis has always been on quality and engineering, which is a reputation we still enjoy after 48 years in business.

Cline Lumber Company, Inc.

1888 was the year that Albert B. and Mary Josephine Cline moved to Bluffton to begin the nucleus of the lumber business. After various ventures with other people, A.B. by 1920, became the sole owner of several lumber yard outlets, located at Van Buren, Warren, Liberty Center, Uniondale, Ossian, Geneva, Portland, Ridgeville, Pennville, Montpelier, Poneto and Bluffton. Also at this time, A.B. and his brother Charlie joined together with yards at Kendallville, Waterloo, Wolcottville, Avilla, and Butler.

Joining his father in the family business in 1920, Lloyd M. Cline and wife, Lois Shirley, became active stockholders and by the end of the 1920's Lloyd was the CEO of all operations. By this time, Poneto and Pennville were closed.

In 1948, William L. Cline graduated from DePauw University, then joined his father in the management of the lumber companies. A.B. Cline died in 1954, and Lloyd Cline died in 1961. From this point on, William L. Cline has been chief operating officer to the present time. Several noteworthy dates over the past 40 years: 1949 saw the Bluffton yard burn to the ground - only to be rebuilt. In 1975, the Portland Yard burned badly, but was restored. Also in the past 20 years, due to changing economic conditions in the country, Van Buren, Liberty Center, Uniondale, Geneva, Ridgeville and Montpelier have been closed. The active outlets at this writing are Ossian, Warren, Portland and Bluffton.

In 1974, the daughter of Martha Cline Colson (granddaughter of Lloyd M. Cline) and her husband, Don K. Skinner, moved to Bluffton to join in the management of the lumber outlets. The Skinners are representing the fourth generation in the retail lumber business.

Special mention should be made of deceased personnel who served in this business throughout the early years: Chauncey K. Reid, Charlie McCarty, George Louden and J. Ray Cox.

Cosmetology

Elizabeth McAfee

Elizabeth McAfee and Gladys (McAfee) Cotton, together have provided 100 years of professional hair care in the field of Cosmetology in the Wells County and surrounding area. They are the daughters of John McAfee, Jr. and Hazel (McCleery) McAfee.

Elizabeth, present owner of Market Place Beauty Salon, graduated from Betty Jean College of Cosmetology in Fort Wayne in 1937, after graduating from Rockcreek High School in 1935.

She first worked in the shops of Gelana Lesh, Goldie Sawyer, and the Linn sisters.

Elizabeth's first solely owned salon, established in 1941, was the Grand Beauty Shop, which was situated in the old Opera House building known as the Grand Theatre. The Grand Beauty Salon changed its name to the Holiday Beauty Salon when the theatre changed its name to The Holiday.

Elizabeth has continued to operate her salon in Bluffton, and for 55 years has provided professional cosmetology service to her customers. She continues to attend clinics and studies in the profession to learn and keep up with styles and fashion, as they do change with time. Elizabeth has practiced her profession by working each day in three inch high-heeled shoes.

Gladys (McAfee) Cotton

Gladys, known as "Glady" to most everyone, graduated from Rockcreek High School in 1946. She immediately enrolled in studies at Wayne University of Cosmetology in Fort Wayne, and upon graduation began working for her sister at the Grand Beauty Salon in Bluffton.

She married in 1947 and purchased a beauty salon in Uniondale when she and her husband settled near there. In 1948, this salon was sold and she returned to work in her sister's salon in Bluffton until 1957.

Gladys' Glamour Shop was opened at 327 E. Central in December of 1957. This shop, being in their home, permitted Gladys to work and yet be at home during her children's "growing up" years.

1991 will find her celebrating 45 years of serving others through the profession of cosmetology. It has been and continues to be a very rewarding, worthy profession. Continuing education through classes about new products, techniques and styles keep Gladys abreast of new style and fashion.

Elizabeth McAfee

Gladys (McAfee) Cotton

Gerber Furniture

Alvin and Ed Gerber started an upholstery business at the corner of Arnold and Mulberry Streets, and in 1947 decided to expand by building a larger store on State Road #1 north. They purchased one acre of land from Marion Meeks and started construction on the 14,400 square foot building. Contractors were Elmer and Cliff Baumgartner. This was the second business north of the railroad tracks. R S &M Studio was the first. In 1948, the store opened for business. The basement included a cabinet shop operated by Ervin Schwartz, an upholstery shop and finishing room. The first upholsterers were Jim Moser and Bob Brickley, with Viola Gerber, Ed's wife, doing the sewing. Later upholsterers were George Bixler, Ralph Stager, Charles Stanley and Monie Schwartz.

Harry Longenberger joined Alvin in carpet installation and continued for many years. Other installers included Howard Schwartz, Russell Gerber and Leon Gerber.

Drapery making was added with Viola Gerber, Katie Isch and Minnie Aschliman doing the sewing. Victor Gerber started employment in 1950, and continues today selling and installing drapery and blinds.

Involved in sales with the Gerbers were Vernon Gerber and later Robert Yergler. Roger Longenberger was hired in 1954, got involved in sales, and later did the buying.

A warehouse was added and a large awning was put on the entire front of the building, where for many years customers parked to shop.

When Ed Gerber decided to move to Florida, Alvin Gerber continued in the store until 1970. Harry and Roger Longenberger, long-time employees, purchased the business. The store name remained the same, and the same quality furniture has been kept. The cabinet shop and upholstery business were discontinued and these areas were turned into show rooms.

Devona Longenberger took over the bookkeeping duties along with Leah Johnson, who worked until 1987. Marilyn Longenberger started in 1972 in sales and helping with the Interior Design facet, where she remains.

In 1990 Alvin Gerber completely retired and the building was sold to the Longenbergers. The architecture has remained pretty much the same. With the five-laning of Road #1 in 1990, there was no longer room in the front to park, so a parking lot has been added to the south side of the building. The tradition of quality furniture has not changed in the 43 years in Bluffton.

James S. Jackson Co., Inc.

In 1947, the James S. Jackson Construction Company was founded by James S. and Mary Alice Jackson in a farm house on the south side of Bluffton. With a loan of $500.0, miscellaneous carpenter tools, a wheelbarrow and a second hand pick-up truck, Jackson Construction was on its way. Small repair jobs and some remodeling work kept the company busy until late fall when a tornado ripped through Wells County. Jim Jackson, with his small crew, literally worked his way through Wells County, putting together estimates and making repairs.

Later that year, Jim was recommended by a former employer for the construction of a new service station in Huntington, Indiana. This was the first commercial job for the company and a big boost.

The Jackson family grew along with the company. Sons Jim, Tom and Mick, and daughters Sally and Cindy all had a part in some aspect of the construction company.

Today, James S. Jackson Co., Inc. is run by James S., chairman, sons James D., president and Thomas K., executive vice president. The company specializes in industrial and commercial construction projects throughout Indiana and many other states. Instead of the family farm home, the headquarters are in a new office and warehouse located in Jason Park on Bluffton's south side. The construction company has continued to grow and prosper well into its second generation, as we hope it will into the third and beyond.

Ossian State Bank

Our history begins with the Farmers State Bank here in Ossian which was chartered November 1, 1912 and opened for business November 2, 1912. Shortly after beginning business, the Farmer State Bank purchased the Bank of Ossian, which had been in operation since 1904.

During the middle 1920's there were 12 banks serving Wells County, but, during the depression years of 1929 to 1933 their number diminished until the Farmers State Bank in Ossian was one of the three remaining banks in the county.

In accordance with the then existing law, banking corporations were required to be rechartered each 20 years, and on October 19, 1932, a new charter was issued to Ossian State Bank as successor of the Farmers State Bank. Following the bank holiday declared by the President in March 1933, and the revising of banking laws, this bank became a member of the Federal Deposit Insurance Corporation, with deposits insured up to $5,000.00. This law has been amended to give a maximum of $100,000.00 of insurance to our depositors, the cost of this insurance being borne by the bank.

The Farmers State Bank opened for business with Dr. E.W. Dyar as president; Leonard M. Springer, vice president; and John D. Hanna, cashier. The resources on opening were $15,650.41. At the close of 1990, total assets held were $54,327,000.00.

In 1948 the bank building was remodeled and in 1977 the present bank building was erected. Ossian State Bank remains the only independent bank in the county. Present directors are: Autie Lewis, Jr.; Joan Johnson; Robert B. Legge; Vernon R. Dowty; Edward Martz; W.J. Sorg, Jr.; and Peter L. Confer.

Smith's Garage and Trucking

Smith's Garage and Trucking of Poneto, Indiana, as it is known today, became a successful business started by Howard E. Smith in 1926.

The business in the Innskeep building, one block west of Meridian Road on Walnut Street in Poneto, was purchased from the bank. The previous owners were Amstutz and Nusbaum of Berne, Indiana. As well as operating the garage, Howard drove a school bus for eight years for Chester Center School. He also hauled mail from Fort Wayne to Muncie. He owned three straight trucks with which he hauled sugar beets into Decatur, Indiana, and hauled bagged sugar out of Decatur. Those who worked during the first years were Harold Hott, Dowell Singer, Eldie Burnau, Jerry McKee and Dayton Musselman, all of whom drove trucks for the business.

Property was purchased during the 1930's one block west, to prepare for moving into the old bank building across from the Innskeep building. After moving into the building, an addition was added for the servicing of automobiles, trucks, tractors, etc. Employees at this time were sons, Bob Smith and Allen Smith, and Doug Ginger, Eldie Burnau, Levi Reaser and Lawrence Reaser. One semi - truck was owned for which Howard, with the help of his wife Mary, made the bed of the trailer.

In 1961 the business moved to the building one block west of this site which was formerly a grocery store, post office, etc. In more recent years, the business has expanded and is now operates a full service garage and hardware department. In addition, they own and operate six semi trucks hauling grain, fertilizer, chemicals, etc. The business has grown into a family practice with sons, Bob and Allen, three grandsons, Derek Smith, Len Smith and Steve Rush. Other employees have been Bob Harris, Ken Flowers, Dennis Bulger, Vernon Stone and Bob Clifton.

Howard, age 86, still goes to the business each day. He and his wife, the former Mary Roof, reside in Poneto where they have lived and raised their three sons, Jack, Allen and one daughter Caroline Rush. *Submitted by Mr. and Mrs. Bob (Mary) Smith*

Sunier and Lockwood, Inc.

Sunier & Lockwood, Inc., 105 North Main Street, P.O. Box 497, Bluffton, is an insurance agency that has existed under that name, and in the same location, since 1926. It was at that time when Cecil C. Lockwood and E.E. Sunier purchased the business of Hitchcock and Fetters, located at 101 1/2 North Main Street, on the second floor of the McFarren Building, (now the Eley TV and Appliance Building). Samuel E. Hitchcock was the father-in-law of Ed Sunier. Hitchcock and Fetters had acquired the agency from a Mr. W.W. Greek who operated the agency in the late 1880's. The agency has been insuring Wells County people continuously for over 100 years.

The agency offers a full line of insurance, property and casualty, including auto, life, and health, with a staff of seven full-time agents: Cecil Lockwood, Jr., Phillip K. Lockwood, Thomas R. Lockwood, CPCU, Trudy Murray, Dolores E. Borton, Paula Jaskie, and Carol Souder.

Sunier & Lockwood, Inc., hopes to extend to the community its careful, competent service for at least one more century. The agency was established in Bluffton in 1878.

Trubey/Hullinger/Gutwein

Dr. Garold L. Johnson began his optometric practice in Fort Wayne after graduating from Northern Illinois College of Optometry in 1922. In the summer of 1932, he moved with his wife and daughter to Bluffton and established an office above the Deam and Spivey Drug Store (now Farmers and Merchants Bank building) across from the court house. The rent for the two room office was $8.00 per month, and coal was carried up the stairs in a scuttle. Neighboring offices were occupied at various times by lawyers George Mock, Joseph Eichhorn and George Davis.

In June 1953, Dr. Johnson's son-in-law, C.Wm. Trubey, graduated from Ohio State University School of Optometry and joined Dr. Johnson in his practice. Prior to college, Dr. Trubey assisted several years on the family farm near Colon, Michigan.

Drs. Johnson and Trubey, with realtor William Hall, erected a new office building at 206 N. Main in 1968, and the practice was moved to the new location.

In 1977, Dr. Sandra J. Jones of Ossian, a graduate of Indiana School of Optometry, expanded the practice to three. The title "Dr. Jones" was short-lived since one month after graduation she married Les Hullinger of Fort Wayne and became Dr. Hullinger.

Dr. Johnson passed away in January, 1978, after practicing 45 years in Bluffton. He was a life member of the American and Indian Optometric Associations.

After completing her O.D. degree at Indiana University School of Optometry in 1988, and serving a residency at West Point Military Academy, Dr. Dawn E. Gutwein, a native of Lafayette, Indiana, joined the practice in June, 1989.

Today the practice includes the three doctors; Michele Pastore, optometric technician; and optometric assistants and office personnel, Melba Cole, Kim Reinhard, Vicki Fiechter, Rosey Chidester, and Lisa Mann.

Woods Locker Service

The locker plant in Zanesville was purchased in October, 1956, by Myron Wayne and Mary Elizabeth Young Woods. They had devoted many hours serving the folks of Wells and other surrounding counties, slaughtering beef and hogs.

In January, 1984, Myron and Mary sold the locker to their son Douglas Dayton and his wife Debrah Kay Sheets Woods. Since their take over, it still has the same loving family tradition.

Doug and Debbie have added a meat market and deli since their purchase of their locker and making the business increase every year.

In 1990, the locker had added a smokehouse to the facility. This enables them to make their own smoked hams, bacon, sausage, cold meats, etc. the list goes on, and they're still making new items.

The deli specializes in its homemade salads, party trays and other special touches.

In the years to come Woods Locker will continue to serve the public in the same friendly way.

Delivery wagon on Main Street. "Transfer" companies hauled freight from the railroad depot to its local destination. This wagon belonged to Deam Livery on West Market Street, Bluffton.

Wells County Family History

The Sampson Thomas home in Union Township (900N and 1/2 mile west from the Markle-Zanesville road). (l. to r.): Lewis Thomas, Allie Thomas, Suzanne Caley, Kohr Thomas, and Monroe Thomas. Photo courtesy of Jane Anne Thomas, granddaughter of Lewis.

ABBOTT/MCDANIEL FAMILIES

Andrew V. Abbott was born in Kosciusko County, Indiana, July 17, 1843 (died January 7, 1921). Catherine (McDaniel) Abbott was born March 17, 1853 (died October 15, 1925) in Nottingham Township, Wells County. They were married October 5, 1872, in Wells County. They had eight children, Amanda Omelia (born September 12, 1873, died May 24, 1929), Charles Alexander born (July 3, 1877, died August 19, 1961), Osper Harvey (born May 22, 1880), George Washington (born February 10, 1883, died August 1955), Eva Luesynda (born January 28, 1887, died October 26, 1909), Willie Arthur (born March 18, 1890), Lola May (born March 16, 1893) and Nellie Florence (born February 24, 1896, died July 6, 1962).

Nellie Florence married Leo Joy McKuras April 27, 1916, in Jay County. Nellie and Leo had four children, Genieve, Wanda, Murray and Harley. Nellie and Leo moved to Reiffsburg in Wells County in 1928.

Andrew V. Abbott and Catherine (McDaniel) Abbott

Andrew was living with a Lesh family in 1850 and he really did not know very much of his family except he had a sister Amanda. He enlisted at Warsaw to fight in the Civil War from July, 1862, until July, 1865. He was wounded in the chest September 20, 1863, at the Battle of Chickamauga, Georgia, and in May of 1864 was in a hospital in New Albany, Indiana. In January and February, 1965, he was guarding prisoners of war in Elymira, New York. He was discharged from there July 12, 1865. He came to Wells County in 1870. In 1898 he applied for a pension because the wound he received in the war "kept him from working at any but the most easy" and then only for a short time.

Andrew and Catherine lived in Jay County and later moved to Kansas and worked in the oil fields for a few years and then returned to Jay County.

Catherine was the daughter of Alexander (born December 29, 1816, died August 27, 1899) and Mary (Evans) McDaniel. Both of them were born in Bedford, Pennsylvania and Mary died shortly after the birth of Catherine. Alexander married Frances Dawley September 11, 1853. Alexander and Frances had several more children.

Alexander is the son of Amos and Catherine McDaniel who arrived in Wells County in the 1840's and farmed in Nottingham Township. They both were born in Pennsylvania.

Refer to McKuras, Johnson and Shigley histories.

DENNIS AND JOYCE (DAY) ACCAVALLO

Dennis James Accavallo was born November 19, 1949, and grew up in Ridgefield Park, New Jersey. His parents are Anthony Francis Accavallo, Jr. (born January 1, 1916) and Rose Marie Samele Accavallo (born March 28, 1913). On June 26, 1938, Anthony (Tony) and Rose Accavallo were married. Rose Accavallo's parents were Juestina Dellernia Samele Pellechio (1893-1985) and Vincenzio Samele (1890-1928). Rose has a half-brother, Sal Pellechio (1930), from her mother's second marriage. In 1915, when Rose was two years old her parents left Cerignola, Foggia, Italy, and came to the United States. Rose still has two aunts, an uncle, and many cousins who live in Italy. Tony and Rose visited these relatives in Italy in 1983 and 1988. Tony's parents were Anthony Francis Accavallo (1883-1961) and Anotonett Taddata (1883-1969). Anthony was born in Pietrapartoe, Pontenza, Italy, and immigrated in 1906. Anotonett was from Castelmezzarno, Pontinza, Italy, and came in 1907 to Ellis Island. Tony's siblings are Nick (1907), Mary (1909), Carmela (1911), Kenny (1918) and Frances (1923). Tony was a driver and supervisor for REA until his retirement and Rose was a dress operator in New York City. Four children were born from this marriage: Roseann (1940), Vincent (1941), Anthony (1945), and Dennis (1949). This family still lives in New Jersey except for Vincent who resides in Lagrange, Ohio, and Dennis in Bluffton, Indiana.

July 1924, three generations who have lived at 209 W. Wabash St. on front porch. (L to R) Charles Day, Fido, John Buckner, Floretta (Buckner) Day and her husband William Henry Day

Dennis graduated from Ridgefield Park High School, Ridgefield Park, New Jersey, in 1967. He was active in sports and still holds the school track record for the broad jump. In 1972 Dennis graduated with a B.A. in psychology and secondary education from Yankton College in South Dakota. He never pursued a teaching career but instead became an air traffic controller in the F.A.A. Dennis began in 1974 at the Muncie Airport and in 1978 transferred to Baer Field in Fort Wayne. Since 1985 he has been employed by General Electric Supply Company in marketing. Dennis and Joyce (Day) Accavallo were married August 11, 1984

August 11, 1984 - Wedding day of Dennis and Joyce Accavallo. Back (L-R) Birdena and Charles Day, Tony and Rose Accavallo. Front (L-R) Joyce and Dennis Accavallo

Joyce Deanne Day was born September 29, 1952, in Bluffton, Indiana. Her parents are Charles Edward Day (May 14, 1913 - April 12, 1990) and Birdena Nadine (Voigt) Day (January 24, 1919). They were married May 20, 1944. Three children were born to Charles and Birdena: William Edwin (1946), Kent Owen (1949), and Joyce Deanne (1952). Joyce graduated from Southern Wells High School in 1970 and then received her B.S. in elementary education from Taylor University in 1974. In August, 1974, Joyce began teaching at Rockcreek Elementary in second grade. In 1979, Rockcreek was closed and later torn down and Joyce was transferred to Ossian Elementary. After ten years of teaching first grade in this building it was closed, and the new Ossian Elementary was constructed. Joyce continues to teach first grade and will begin her eighteenth year of teaching in the fall of 1991. Joyce came from a long line of educators as her parents, maternal grandmother, three aunts, an uncle, and many cousins have entered this field. As a small child, Joyce remembers always wanting to be a teacher of small children and never considered any other field.

July 1990, Charlie Accavallo on porch at Wabash Street home.

Charles Anthony Accavallo was born September 2, 1985, to Dennis and Joyce. He was named after both of his grandfathers. Each grandparent won a special place in Charles' (Charlie) heart. Because of distance, his Grandpa and Grandma Accavallo rely on telephone calls, letters, and vacations to get to know him. Grandma Day loves to read stories and play games with all her grandchildren. The Accavallos live at 209 West Wabash Street which is close to downtown Bluffton. After Charlie was born Grandpa Day would stop by and ask Charlie if he would like to go downtown. Because of the frequent walks, cookies and juice at the Snug, and visits to Murphys for a "little" candy, at an early age Grandpa Day was called "Downtown" by Charlie. This Wabash Street home was where Charles Day moved with his parents at the age of ten. Joyce enjoyed visiting her grandma at this home until her grandmother had to go to a nursing home. Six generations have now lived in this house. They are John J. Prible, John Buckner, Floretta (Buckner) Day, Charles Day, Joyce (Day) Accavallo, and Charles Accavallo. After much restoring with her parents help, Joyce moved into this house in 1980. Dennis and Joyce's wedding took place in this home with their families in attendance in 1984. The old pump organ, that had belonged to Joyce's grandmother and had been given to Joyce, was played at the wedding. Wells County holds many wonderful memories both past and present and the Accavallos feel it is a great place to live.

For more information see the Charles Day Family in this book.

AKER GRANDLIENARD

Randolph L. O'Donnell (born in 1865) and Sarah M. Walker (born in 1871) were married in the late 1880's and resided for several years in Nottingham, Indiana. They were the parents of four children, Charles D., W. Ray, Ada B., and Edwin Clyde. Ray O'Donnell was well-known in Bluffton, having operated the Cloverleaf Creamery there for several years.

William Aker married Martha Johnson in the late 1800's and they, too, resided in Nottingham for quite some time. They were the parents of six children, one of whom was V.H. Aker. V.H. Aker and Ada O'Donnell were married in 1909. They lived in Michigan for a short time and then moved to Oklahoma. V.H. became Superintendent of Sinclair Gasoline plants in Oklahoma and Texas. During those years two sons, Harry E. and Glenn L., and one daughter, Blanche R., were born to the Akers.

Vott and Ada (O'Donnell) Aker

V.H. and Ada Aker always had wished to return to Wells County to live. While still in Oklahoma, they purchased "Aker's Acres," a 100-acre farm in Nottingham Township, and returned with Harry Glenn and Blanche to live there for several years.

Harry married Ruby Miller of Huntington, and shortly thereafter they moved to Kansas, where Harry died in 1962. Glenn married Avis Kunkel and lived in Bluffton for several years before moving with his family to the Marshall County area in Northern Indiana. Later, they purchased a home and now reside near Etna Green in Kosciusko County.

Blanche married Max D. Grandlienard, a son of William and Ica French Grandlienard of Adams County after Max returned from serving as a sergeant in the European Theatre during World War II. Although Max was born and raised in Adams County, the Grandlienard family came to Wells County from Moutier, Switzerland in the middle-1800's.

Max and Blanche live on their farm in Harrison Township and are the parents of one daughter, Vicki. They farm approximately 600 acres of land in Wells County and are members of the Old Salem United Methodist Church. For many years Max has been teaching an adult Sunday School class and serving as chairman of the administrative board. Blanche is the administrative board secretary. Max and Blanche also served in the Harrison Township trustee's office from 1963 through 1970 and at one time or another have been active members of the Wells County Democratic Party, Harrison Township Farm Bureau, the Jefferson Club, C.R.O.P., and 5-County "JOBS, Inc."

After having lived in Southern California for several years, daughter Vicki returned to Wells County in 1989 with her husband, LeRoy W. Cramer. LeRoy farms with father-in-law Max, and Vickie is a computer programmer analyst. Vickie and LeRoy have three sons: David and Willie, who live in California, and DeWayne, who resides in Alabama. Vickie and LeRoy live at "Aker's Acres," which is now owned by Max and Blanche.

ADDINGTON FAMILY

The Addington family has been traced to my seventh generation, William Addington born in London, England, 1750. He came to America at the age of twenty and located in Culpepper County, Virginia. He married Margaret Cromwell in 1774.

That same year, the Revolutionary War broke out and he enlisted and served under General George Washington. He was present at the surrender of Lord Cornwallis in Yorktown, 1781.

Front - Alvis Patton, Dennis, Sarah. Back - Homer, Carson, Perry, Nancy, Mary Elizabeth, Belle

Sixth generation, Charles Cromwell Addington Sr., was born in Russel County, Virginia, 1777. He married Anna Doaty, 1802. They had seven boys and five girls. His second wife was Sarah Butcher, married 1840. They had three boys, one girl. He was 92 when he married his third wife Susannah Moore, 1869.

He was honored by a centennial birthday dinner with over one thousand in attendance, 533 were descendents. He rode to the church in his wagon, alighted without help; after preaching, he walked 1/4 mile to the festive event. He died at the age of 104.

His second child, Joseph Addington, and Nancy Esterling Addington were the great grandparents of Maybelle Addington Carter of the Carter family fame. They are great-great-grandparents of Mrs. Johnny (June Carter) Cash.

John and Laura Hunnicutt

Fifth generation, Charles Cromwell Addington, Jr., born 1807, died 1893, married Jane Lawson, 1830. They had four boys, three girls.

Fourth generations Henry Ellington Addington, born 1833, died 1903, married Elizabeth Gulley, 1856. They had six sons, four daughters.

Third generation Alvis Patton Addington, born 1857, died 1950, married Sarah Ellen Derting, 1879. She was born 1861, died 1943.

Their children and spouses were: William Perry, Carson, (Marjorie Frazier), Nancy, (Emmanuel Brinneman), Mary Elizabeth (William Patton Meade), Homer, (Evelyn Ratlif), Belle, (Jerome Kiser), Dennis (Lola Johnson).

Nancy's daughters: Mrs. Iva (Audrey) Moser, deceased, has four boys and one girl. Mrs. Ollie (Violet) Blumenhorst, deceased, has one daughter.

Homer's daughters, Mrs. James (Esther) Lockwood has one girl and one boy.

Carson located in Chicago with Belle and Dennis locating in Michigan. The others reside in Wells County.

Alvis "Patton" Addington came to Indiana in 1887 and bought a farm south of Bluffton. He was a farmer and road contractor and constructed several roads in Wells Count and surrounding counties.

The house was moved by horses and remodeled with several rooms being added. Many family dinners were enjoyed at the Addington home with several friends and relatives in attendance.

John, (Drusilla), Carl, (Lona), Charlie and Edith Daugherty, Mrs. Dowell (Louella) Ifer are all Addington descendants that reside in Wells County.

Henry and Emily Meade were good neighbors and introduced his brother, William Patton to Mary Elizabeth, with them later marrying.

Grandpa was active and in good health for his age. He was ill only three days prior to his death at age 93, September 28, 1950.

Mary Elizabeth, born February 10, 1888, died October 10, 1965, married William Patton Meade, 1904. He was born in 1879, died in 1945. Their children are: Vera (Shadle), infant, Velma (Huffman), Arnet, Mary (Hunnicutt), Alvis, Dorothy (Meyers).

I married Carl Hunnicutt on January 12, 1929. Our children are: Louella (Sproat), Kenneth, Louise (Campbell), Carlene (Griffin), Larry, Thomas and James Hunnicutt. *Submitted by Mary Meade Hunnicutt*

GARY LEE AFFOLDER

Gary Lee Affolder, the second son of Virgil Leroy and Mary Ellen (Beck) Affolder, was born on May 26, 1949. When Gary was two years old, the family moved to farm (where his folks still reside) on county road 450 east just 1 1/2 miles east and 3/4 mile north of the highway 1 and 224 crossroad. Gary and his brother Steve grew up there, where close neighbors, just to the south on the same mile, were his maternal grandparents, the Shannon Becks. The boys helped grandpa and dad with farming and attended Ossian High School. Gary graduated in 1967 and went on to become a tool and die maker, beginning his career at Hower Tool.

Gary met his future wife, Kathleen (Kathy) Jo Hirschy, born December 4, 1953, in Decatur, Indiana, to Melvin Martin and Mary Ellen (Confer) Hirschy, in February of 1972, prior to the marriage of Steve and Kathy's sister Judy. Gary and Kathy were the honor attendants in that wedding. Kathy graduated from Adams Central High School and was employed at GE in Decatur. On December 1, 1972, Gary and Kathy were married at the Cross United Church of Christ in Berne, Indiana, by the Rev. Robert Hegnauer. A son, Corey Lee, was born to them at the Lutheran Hospital in Fort Wayne, Indiana, on April 7, 1974. They purchased 3 1/2 wooded acres from Grandpa Beck's farm in 1976 and built a home there. On June 16, 1977, a daughter, Jill Ellen, completed their family.

Gary continues in his chosen profession. Kathy is active in church and community, teaching Sunday School, working in the women's group, coaching minor league, and assisting in social activities at the Ossian Health Care. Corey will graduate from Norwell High School in May of 1992. He has chosen the tool and die field as his career, and as a junior in high school, attended the Regional Vocational School in the afternoons of his school days. As an eighth grader at Norwell, Jill is active in sports, enjoys reading and music, and plans to go to college.

They attend the Decatur Church of God.

VIRGIL LEROY AFFOLDER

Virgil Leroy Affolder, born on August 6, 1920, son of Charles and Mary Ellen Hendricks Affolder, married Mary Ellen Beck, born December 23, 1919, daughter of Shannon Larimer and Nellie Lorinda Stogdill Beck, on November 15, 1941. Following their marriage, they lived with Mary Ellen's parents. Steven Lynn, their first son, was born on February 11, 1944. When Steve was 13 months old, Virgil was drafted into the Navy to serve in World War II. He was in the Navy from March of 1945 to April of 1946. Following his tour of military duty, he returned home and in November of 1946 he moved his family to Winchester, Indiana, where he, his father, and Uncle Elmer Affolder operated a wholesale Massey Harris implement dealership. Their second son, Gary Lee, was born in Winchester on May 26, 1949. Following the sale of the dealership in 1950, Virgil continued to work for the new owners. They moved back to Wells County on March 26, 1951, to a farm they purchased one and one-half miles east and three-fourths mile north of the highway 1 and 224 crossroad, just a few farms north of Mary Ellen's folk's farm. Initially they raised cattle and hogs along with field crops, but gradually they eliminated animal production and continued to raise only field crops.

Virgil and Mary Ellen Affolder

On March 4, 1972, Steve married widowed Judith Ellen Hirschy Beer (January 1, 1947); she was the mother of four children: Michelle Minnette (March 17, 1966), Penny Jo (April 21, 1967), Daniel Edward (January 24, 1969), and Samuel Melvin (August 27, 1971). On April 11, 1975, they became the parents of a son, Kriss Shannon. They live in French Township, Adams County.

On December 1, 1972 (after meeting and standing as maid of honor and best man at Steve and Judy's wedding), Gary married Kathleen Jo Hirschy, Judy's sister, daughter of Melvin and Mary Ellen Confer Hirschy (born December 5, 1953.) They have two children, Corey Lee (born April 7, 1974), and Jill Ellen (born on June 16, 1977.) Gary and Kathy purchased a farm in 1990 a half mile south of his folks' farm, which was bought by his great-grandfather Josiah Larimer Beck in 1881 and then by his grandfather Shannon Larimer Beck.

Virgil is semi-retired but continues to farm only his own farm, having farmed various area farms through the past 40 year

CLYDE W. ALBERSON

Joshua Alberson, my great-great-grandfather, moved from North Carolina to Wayne County, Indiana, where he married Catherine Deeter in 1826. Land was later purchased in Randolph County near Deerfield, where they reared their family. In 1840 they moved to Adams County near Domestic. A virgin forest, requiring much hard work, was cleared to make room for buildings and productive farm ground. As time passed a need for a burial ground was recognized and in 1863 he gave a portion of his land for the Alberson Cemetery, which is located one mile east of Domestic.

Charles, son of Joshua, married Mary Brown in 1846 and settled at Phenix in southern Wells County. A log cabin was erected in 1850, and he acquired several acres of land which remained in the family for generations. Eleven children were born to this marriage and some of their descendents still live in Wells County.

Philip, son of Charles, bought land near his father and built a large frame house. Oil having been discovered in this area during the 1800's, Philip had several high producing oil wells on his land. As the "oil boom" progressed, Philip and his wife Sarah opened their home as a boarding house and kept men who worked in the oil fields. Later Philip sold this farm to his son, William, and purchased a neighboring farm, where he built a house and barn, this being the farm which Clyde Alberson owns and where he lives.

The first store in Phenix was built by Philip Alberson and Dennis Reeves, later known as Cochran's Grocery.

William, "Little Willie," son of Philip, married Flossie Carter March 31, 1912. He enlarged his farming operation to include a steam engine and threshing machine, which threshed grain for many farmers in the area. The children born to this marriage were Milo, Clyde, Raleigh, Kenneth, and Lillie, who married Roy Harris and lives near Keystone, Indiana.

Clyde, son of William, was born in 1916 in Wells County and started to school at Mole Hill in Nottingham Township. This was a one-room schoolhouse with a "pot belly" stove for heat, and outside toilets. Later he was transferred to Petroleum High School when the one-room school houses were closed. Upon graduating in 1936, he moved to Muncie, Indiana, to seek employment. In 1937 he married Berneice Baker. They had one daughter, Joan, who gave them two grandchildren. Rinda Kay and James; their son Robert died in infancy. After a few years they moved back to Phenix, where Berneice died in 1968. In 1970 he married Norma Lou Kline, daughter of John Frederick Kline and Hazel Gertrude Brumbaugh Kline of Huntington County, Indiana. She had one son, Steven, of Bluffton, Indiana, who gave them a granddaughter, Melissa.

Schooled in industrial tooling, Clyde followed this occupation until retirement. He is a member of the Masonic Lodge, Tri State Gas Engine and Tractor Assn., Board of Trustees of the Alberson Cemetery, and he and his wife are active in The Order of the Eastern Star.

ALBERSON HARRIS

Roy and Lillie Alberson Harris, who married on May 18, 1940, have lived in Wells County their entire lives, except for the time that Roy spent in the Air Force during World War II. They were engaged in farming until their retirement, and are still living on their farm in Nottingham Township. Lillie belongs to the DAR and is a family genealogist. They have one daughter, Ann Wheeler, secretary to the Medical Director of Charter Beacon Hospital in Fort Wayne, and two grandchildren, Jarrod Hahn and Katherine Wheeler.

The Harris family were Quakers, who came from England and settled in North Carolina about 1750, later moving to Randolph County, Indiana. Roy's grandfather, Ivy Harris, came to Wells County after his discharge from the Civil War. He married Jane Carroll and lived in the Keystone area until his death in 1912. Their children were Guy, Bertha and Vivian.

Guy Harris (1883-1977) married Retta McGeath (1882-1960). With horses and wagon he earned $1.25 a day building gravel roads in southern Wells County. He was a farmer and Ohio Oil Company employee. Their children were Helen, Kathleen and Roy.

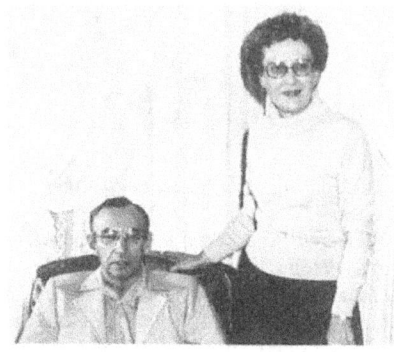

*Roy and Lillie (Alberson) Harris.
Taken 1980 40th wedding anniversary.*

Retta's parents were Pierce McGeath and Matilda Jane Starr. He was the son of James McGeath and Elizabeth Foreman who came from Henry County, Indiana, to Chester Township, Wells County, on February 18, 1839. The McGeath family were of Scotch-Irish descent, coming to America before the Revolutionary War, with many of them serving in that war. Some settled in Loudoun County, Virginia, and others moved on west to Indiana.

The Starr family were Quakers from Ireland and were early settlers in Pennsylvania; they later went to West Virginia and then on to Ohio. Retta's grandfather, Benjamin Starr, came from Hocking County, Ohio, to Chester Township, Wells County, on May 13, 1839. He married Matilda Jane Popejoy. The McGeaths and Starrs were farmers.

Lillie's great-great grandfather, Joshua Alberson, was a native of North Carolina. Her great-grandparents, Charles Alberson and Mary Brown Alberson, came to Wells County in 1850 and erected a log house near Phenix in Nottingham Township, where her grandfather, Phillip Alberson, was born in 1854. Phillip married Sarah Davis ar built a large frame house near the log house where Lillie's father, William, was born in 1890.

William married Flossie Carter, daughter of John Carter and Martha Sawyer Carter. Their children were Milo, Clyde, Raleigh, Lillie and Kenneth. Flossie died in 1944 and William was killed in an accident in 1965. The Alberson's were farmers; they had several oil wells on their land during the oil boom in southern Wells County.

John Carter, born in Ohio, served in the Civil War in both the infantry and cavalry. At one point in the war he was held prisoner and later released in an exchange of prisoners. Upon his discharge he came to Wells County.

The parents of Martha Sawyer Carter were James Sawyer and Ruth Haines. James Sawyer came from Ireland in 1840. He was a doctor and one of the early school teachers of Wells County.

ALEXANDER

In the spring of 1885, when the west was wild and unsettled, homesteaders were moving farther east in the United States to take up government claims. Among those were Lester Alexander's mother, Dessie, born in 1884 in Missouri. Lester's mother and his grandparents traveled in a covered wagon to Colby, Kansas. Lester's grandfather built a sod house and traveled 40 miles with a team and wagon to purchase lumber for the door and windows for the sod house. The covered wagon top was set on the ground and that is where the family lived until the sod house was built.

There were no neighbors closer than a mile but the first thing everyone thought was to build a schoolhouse, also made of sod. It was also used as a Sunday school and church, to which a minister would make his rounds about every month or two, preaching Sunday morning and night, coming by horseback most of the time. Neighbors would also gather at the schoolhouse for literary meetings and debates and spelling matches. Lester's mother, Dessie, recalls her school lunch every day was bread, spread with sugar. She never saw fruit until one day, being a good speller, she traded her headmark for a delicious apple from a schoolmate, who had apples sent to them by a relative from Missouri.

Lester and Edna Alexander

As a young lady, Lester's mother met Joe Alexander, born in Illinois, and they were married in 1902. Lester was the youngest of four children. When he was two years old the family moved to Allen County, Indiana, where farmland could be purchased at a much cheaper price per acre. In the mid-1930's Lester and his parents moved to Wells County, Indiana, where he met his wife, the former Edna Reusser, whose father was born in Switzerland and her mother in Indiana.

Lester served as Wells County Commissioner from 1970 to 1978.

Their son, Richard, a Purdue graduate and in the insurance business, lives near Muncie with his wife, Carolyn. Dick's children are Beth McCormick and Ben and Dan Alexander and two grandchildren, Courtney McCormick and Katie Alexander.

Their daughter, Rowena, a teacher, is married to Dr. James Mount and they, with their children, Carrie and Carter, live in Bedford, Indiana.

ALEXANDER CRUM

Gerald Alexander and Alice Crum were married June 12, 1960, at St. Mark's Lutheran Church, Uniondale, Indiana. He was the only son of the four children of Carl and Clellah Tribolet Alexander of Huntington County. Gerald, born October 11, 1916, on a farm south of Bippus, Indiana, attended schools in Huntington County, and graduated from Chester School in North Manchester. He came to Wells County in 1945, when the family bought a farm north of Uniondale. He farmed and worked for Legge Elevator 17 years.

Alice was the only daughter of the four children of Hubert (Buck) Crum and Clara Sink of Union Township, Wells County. She was born September 12, 1919, in Uniondale; started school at Sugar Grove, Rockcreek Township, and graduated from Union Center School. She was a beautician, factory worker, and, with Gerald, a farmer. (During WWII she, and others, rode the Victory Bus to G.E. in Fort Wayne.)

Gerald and Alice have no children. They live at the north edge of Uniondale, in the house they built in 1960.

Alice and Gerald Alexander

Both are active in St. Mark's Lutheran Church, belonging to the Men's and Women's organizations. Gerald was a member of the Lions Club when it was active in Uniondale.

Gerald's parents were married January 14, 1914, in Huntington. They were of English and German descent. His father had been a carpenter, railroader, and farmer. Both died at Wells County Hospital; Carl in April, 1957, Clellah on Easter Sunday, 1983. Gerald has three sisters: Lenchen, born March 15, 1919, married Jacob Houser; had five children; and lived in Wabash County. She died in 1979. Mary Ellen, born September 9, 1920, married John Urban Bender from Siberia, Indiana. She was in the U.S. Navy and also a U.S. Navy wife. They had six children, five surviving. They live in Bluffton six months and Sun City, Arizona, six months. Doris, born April 16, 1926, married Hilden Swihart; had five children; and lives in Berne, Indiana.

Both of Alice's parents were born in Union Township, Wells County. They were married June 17, 1916, in the Uniondale Telephone Office, where she worked. Hubert Crum had been a deputy sheriff, custodian, with his wife, at Union Center School, and retired from the County Highway Department. In 1969, he was killed at the south edge of Uniondale. Clara died in 1978 in her home in Bluffton. Hubert's grandparents, Samuel and Mary Braham Crum, and his father, John Henry Crum, of German descent, came from Dauphin County, Pennsylvania, to Wells County when John was 14. Hubert's mother, Emma Preskey, from Bluffton, was John's second wife. Clara's parents were Emmett and Corinthia Ann Gorman Sink. Corinthia's father, William Gorman, from Ireland, became a naturalized citizen, May 9, 1870, in Wells County. Alice's brothers: John Henry Crum, born March 17, 1916, married Beatrice Harris; had three children; and lives in Warsaw, Indiana. Merl, born June 12, 1921, married Esther McFarren; had two children and lived in Marion, Indiana. Merl died in 1985. Dean, born October 16, 1932, married Joan Huffman; had two children; retired from G.E. in Fort Wayne, and moved to Cherokee Village, Arkansas.

THE ALEXANDER/FRIAR FARM

This is the history of one farm and its family with a heritage rooted firmly in Jackson Township, Wells County. What appears to some as a mere patch of ground, has served others as home and livelihood with sorrows and joys.

1840 settlers to this area included nine children of John and Rhoda Alexander. Their son, James, purchased a 120-acre farm in Jackson Township, Section 5, southwest corner. James was killed in Texas during the Civil War. His brother, Hugh, purchased the farm in an estate settlement.

Hugh Alexander became known for his unique brick and tile making. The Alexander tile was flat on the bottom like a loaf of bread and fired in a beehive shaped kiln. Some of this brick was used to rebuilt the exterior walls of the still-standing original homestead after an 1870's fire.

Hugh, a school teacher and Jackson Township trustee, and his wife Charity had four children. Virgile became a druggist in Roll, Indiana. Almedia, a school teacher, married Morgan McClure, a Wells County rural mail carrier. Antoinettte, a music teacher, married Charley Friar, a worker in the oil fields. Frank helped his father with farming and the brick and tile company.

One of the biggest changes for all of Jackson Township was orchestrated in 1890 through the oil fields. Due to the high paying oil jobs, the Alexander Brick and Tile Company found it difficult to keep employees. Consequently, they quit production.

Charley Friar used his skill as a tool dresser in the Jackson Township oil wells. His wife, Antoinette, served as a payroll officer for the Ohio Oil Company.

In 1910, with the oil boom fizzling, Charley Friar realized many farmers had a surplus of poultry and eggs. The only buyers were the local grocery stores. He began to buy poultry and eggs which he shipped to a Fort Wayne Packing Company. By 1912, he was shipping a new product called "sweet cream" to the Cloverleaf Creamery in Marion.

During the 1930's a gradual transition from selling "sweet cream" to selling "whole milk" took place. This product was sent away daily in ten-gallon cans by milk trucks to different companies. There was very little profit for anyone. By the 1940's the average farmer made a living plus ten percent profit. Life on the Alexander farm was no exception as family members coped with the ups and downs all community farmers faced.

The Hugh Alexander farm was purchased in 1950 by grandson Victor Friar, son of Charley and Antoinette Friar, and his wife Reathel (Gentis). Victor continued with the family milking and farming business.

Victor and Reathel Friar, who celebrated their

63rd wedding anniversary on March 4, 1991, are the longest married couple in Jackson Township. They raised six children on their farm. Joaquin, a music and art teacher, married Rev. Roy Crawford. Ruth, an elementary teacher, married Dr. C.R. Woodbury. Robert, Ph.D., a professor at Ferris State College, married Fran Urban. Marrianna, a science teacher, married Fred Stricker. Donald, employed by Budd Manufacturing Company, married Beverly Youngblood. Geneva, an elementary teacher, married Michael Gilmer.

The Hugh Alexander/Victor Friar original brick house homestead. Built in 1863. Located Jackson Township, Section S, Southwest corner

Fifteen grandchildren and twelve great-grandchildren know that if the twelve-inch wall of the Alexander brick house could talk, it would be a message of perseverance and love.

HEZEKIAH ALLEN

Cyrus Allen relates to one of the early pioneers of Wells County, Indiana. Hezekiah Allen, born October 6, 1807, Montgomery County, New York State, was 11 years of age when his family settled in Trumbull County, Ohio. Hezekiah married Sarah Rinear, November 10, 1836, and the young couple settled first in Ohio and, 1847, made the move to Indiana, making a log cabin built by a brother to Hezekiah, Matthew Allen, their first home in Jefferson Township, Wells County, Indiana. The lands were all cleared and entered by Mr. Allen on the Indian Reserve. The patents for 36 acres were signed by President Zachary Taylor. The couple's children all married except Jonathan. Mary J. became the wife of Jacob Clark; Ransom married Elizabeth Todd; Isaac became the husband of Nancy Wilson and Emma married Perkins Scott. Mr. Allen's second marriage was to Elizabeth Hashman, and two children were born: Ida and Jasper N. The third marriage was to Mary A. Jennings Reed, and they had one child, Emma, now the wife of Pearl Scott - another early pioneer family of Wells County.

Cyrus Allen in his car - the latest model at the time.

Isaac and wife, Nancy, had two children, Sarah and Cyrus. Sarah never married and Cyrus continued to live on the homeplace until his later years in life. Cyrus Allen married Alice Glass, daughter of John and Emma McCorkle Glass, another early pioneer family of Jefferson Township, Wells County. The couple never had children. The Allen families are buried both in the Prospect and Ossian cemeteries. The early Glass, Scott and McCorkle families are all related to one another by marriage, and the lineage to these early pioneer families still exists today as for example - my mother, Mary A. Osburn Yoquelet relates to all three of these families; which makes myself, Eugene E. Yoquelet, a great-great-grandson to James Scott. The Allens are distantly related through marriage, as are the Glass family and McCorkles. The Allen homeplace is still in existence today and the fine home and buildings may be enjoyed by all who travel on the present Norwell blacktop road north of the school or a short distance west and south of Ossian.

ALLYN-EVANS

At the turn of the century, William and Mary Ann (Kindel) Allyn, lived near Poneto in Chester Township. Married in 1875, they had seven children: Myrtle Bessie (my great-grandmother), Frank, Golden, Rozelle (Guy), Florence, John, and Hazel. William was a farm implement dealer. At the same time, George and Lovina Evans lived south of Poneto in Harrison Township. They were married in 1874 and had six children: Samuel, Theodore, William Charles (my great-grandfather), Alfred, Nellie, and Earnest.

In 1900, William Evans worked as a farm hand on a nearby farm. He met Myrtle Allyn and they were married in 1901. My grandmother, Lucy Evans Hardy, remembers that their house sat at the beginning of a lane lined with sweet-smelling locust trees on the Allyn family property. The Allyns lived in the main farmhouse at the end of the lane. Since the railroad tracks ran alongside the property, she and her sister, were warned to hide from the "tramps" who followed the tracks passing by their house.

Around 1905, William Evans became a realtor and moved his family, which by then consisted of his wife, Myrtle, and two daughters, Lucy and Lillie, to Hartford city. About a year later, they moved to Indianapolis where they remained for almost ten years. During this time, the Evans family lived across the street from the Kenneth Hardy family and Lucy met Olin Ranchell Hardy, who would become her husband in 1925.

L to R — Back: Steven Hardy, Brenda Hardy, Jim Hardy, Murvin Murphy. Middle: Nick Hardy, Lucy Evans Hardy, Diana Busche, Shirley (Hardy) Murphy. Front: Samantha Hardy, Daniel Busche, Matthew Busche

Meanwhile, George and Lovina moved their family to Marion, where George opened a grocery on the "Soldier's Home corner". There, in Marion, they spent the rest of their lives.

Around 1916, the William Evans family, which now included Howard, who was born in 1913, moved to Kansas City for a few months and back to Marion, Indiana. After a short time, the Evanses returned to Indianapolis. William and Myrtle were eventually divorced and William finally returned to Marion, where he died in 1937. Myrtle married Harry Bucksot in later years and died in Indianapolis in 1961.

As fate would have it, my grandmother, Lucy, was re-introduced to Olin Hardy on a blind date after her family returned to Indianapolis. They were married on September 5, 1925, and had been married 58 wonderful years when Olin passed away in 1983. They had two children, Shirley Ann, born in 1929, and Olin Ranchell, Jr. (Jim), born in 1931.

My mother, Shirley, married Edward Ermal Craig on December 12, 1958. I was born on October 5, 1959, and lived in Indianapolis until my marriage to Mark William Busche, of Fort Wayne, on May 26, 1979.

Purely by chance, we purchased our home in Zanesville, on the Wells County side, in 1984. Our sons, Daniel Mark Hardy Busche and Matthew Jerome Busche, were born in Bluffton in 1985 and 1990. What a nice coincidence that I would find myself in Wells County, not too far from where my grandmother was born! *Submitted by Diana L. Busche*

DELORES ANDERSON

When I was a child, I played in a one-room log cabin built in the center of a large apple orchard, on land bought by my grandparents in 1896. They lived in the cabin until the brick house I grew up in was built. This was the era of the crank (and often cranky) telephone, sharing a party line with seven neighbors. Our phone number was two shorts and a long and friends who knew only digital numbers were amazed and sometimes not amused when the switchboard operator in Tocsin joined our conversations! We children were "verboten" to listen to neighbor's calls and especially any calls to the church parsonage.

Our needs were nearly supplied by the farm and a trip outside the county was an excursion. An ice cream cone was a luxury. In addition to the apples and cider, Mom had a five-acre "vegetable and berry truckpatch" and a separate flower garden. She raised chickens and, by hand, milked up to 35 cows twice a day. Dad did the farming and raised the livestock. My parents, however, shared the farming and parenting responsibilities. Mom would work in the fields when needed, and Dad would cook supper, hear our catechism, and see that we did our homework. The summer kitchen was a building separate from the house and a hub of year-round activity. Summer meals were prepared there to keep the house cool, rain water (collected in a cistern) was heated in a large copper boiler to do laundry and for bathing, and meat from the butchering activities was fried down and canned there. Hundreds of jars of vegetables, fruits, and preserves were processed each season, and apple cider was cooked down to apple butter. There was an oversized wooden bathtub with a copper lining - for pleasure from the hot summer or for Mom's tough scrubbing. Well water was powered by a windmill and lighting was provided by candles, oil lamps, or lanterns.

I went to Bethlehem Lutheran School when it was a one-room school with one teacher for eight grades. I graduated from Ossian High School and obtained a B.S. degree in business from Indiana University in Bloomington.

George Anderson and I were married in 1957 and we had a daughter, Kim Roberta. George was diagnosed terminally ill in 1958 and we moved back to the farm to live with my mother. He died in 1959. I now live in a house built on the "Back Forty."

Our daughter, Kim, married her high school sweetheart, Bruce Werling. They have two daughters, Nicole Renae and Allison Kate, and expect a third child in June, 1991. Kim is an R.N. and Bruce is employed by Lincoln Manufacturing in Fort Wayne. They bought a piece of the farm that is known as "Shortsplatz," where they built their home.

Central Soya Co., Inc., Fort Wayne, hired me in 1959. Today my job with this multi-national agribusiness firm entails global communications that take less time to connect than it did to ring three longs to call a neighbor. I can telephone or fax operations abroad - reaching Europe early in our business day and the Far East 12 hours later. I marvel at the changes in my lifetime - from living on a self-sufficient farm and isolated from the rest of the world, to being dependent on global business activities, economics, and world events for my livelihood. My family, neighbors, and friends, and this little piece of land in Wells County, are a sanctuary from the demands of these changing times!

JAMES VICTOR ANDERSON FAMILY

Records in the Anderson family Bible state the family moved from Butler County, Pennsylvania, to Warren Village, Trumbull County, Ohio, and then to Paulding County, Ohio. In the spring of 1936, James Victor (Vick) Anderson and his wife Georgianna Mae (Henrey) purchased their first homestead, on State Road 1 north of Bluffton, known as the South Wind Farm. One year later they sold this farm and purchased one east of Craigville. Vick was one of the founders of the Bluffton Park United Brethren Church. There were seven children born to the union:

Beulah married Raymond Weisman and returned to Scott, Ohio. They had two children, Gale and Sharon.

Donna (deceased) married George Yocum and returned to Celina, Ohio. They had three sons, Dean, Forrest, and Gene.

Naomi married Dale Osborn and they now live in Fort Wayne. They had three daughters, Joan, Janet, and Pauline.

Chloe (deceased) married James Kizer, and they adopted two daughters. Linda now resides in Florida. Sharon married Chris Allen and they reside in Bluffton with their daughter, Leah.

James F. "Andy" Anderson married Betty Thomas, and they reside in Bluffton. They are the parents of four children: James "Ron" married Jean Werling and they have two children — Cary and Cristin. They reside in Bluffton. Jerry married Judy Murray and they have three children: Holli, Jamie, and Ben. They reside in Fort Wayne. Janice married Steven Yager, and they have three children: Matt, Brian, and Julie. They also reside in Fort Wayne. Kevin married Marsha Dentel and they are the parents of two sons, Chad and Adam. They reside in Bluffton.

Lauretta married Dee Borror (deceased) and they had three children: Judy married Terry Werling; and they had two children, Ryan and Kelli. They reside in Ossian. Dennis married Pamela Sawyer and they had one daughter, Lisa. Lisa married Gunnar Heller and they have one son, Drew. Dennis' second marriage was to Linda Robbins, and they have two children, Eric and Erin. They reside in Wells County. Michael married Lynette Linton and they have two son, Justun and Jarrett. They reside in Fort Wayne.

Alice Arlene married Jack Wilson, and they live in Petroleum. They have two children: Bruce married Carol Jacobs and they have two children, Mark and Kimberly. Becky married Gary Stroud and they have three children: Craig, Natalie, and Blake. They reside in West Virginia.

RUTH ANDERSON FAMILY

Robert Riley Stanton and Iva Mariah Fish Stanton built a home in southern Wells County in the late 1800's. To them were born five children. Iva died at the birth of Fred Ivason. Fred's twin, who was stillborn, was placed in its mother's arms for burial. Fred, who never married, was raised by Robert Riley's brother, Zebulon Stanton, and his wife, Cora, who had two children of their own, Edith and Dallas Stanton. Robert Stanton, a carpenter, kept the other four children, Blanch Ruth, Lena Esther, Thurman Jennings, and Robert Howard, at home. Fred was a barber in Bluffton for several years.

Blanch Stanton and her husband, Elmer McDaniel, left Indian for Minnesota with five sons and two daughters.

Esther Stanton married Forrest Mosure and lived in Bluffton with their three children, Betty, Forrest Jr., and Mary Ann. After a period of illness, Esther moved to California to be with her daughter, Mary Ann Mendenhall, until her death.

Thurman Stanton, a barber in Wabash, was a landowner in Southern Wells County and there he spent his final years. He never married. He is buried in Woodlawn Cemetery.

Robert Howard Stanton married an Adams County girl, Rose Moyer, and moved to Detroit, Michigan, to work for Grinnel Brothers, a music company. Before he went to Detroit, he had gained experiences at the H.C Bay Piano Factory in Bluffton. To them was born one daughter, Ruth Joanne, who was married in Detroit to Robert Anderson, of Arkansas. They lived in Detroit, but upon the death of Thurman Stanton, purchased his homestead in Wells County. Robert Howard spent many years as a mechanical engineer in Detroit.

Benjamin Moyer, one of 12 children, including three sets of twins, and who referred to John and Emmarelis Cowans as uncle and aunt, was born in Wells County in the middle 1860's near Tocsin to George Moyer, who came to Wells County in the 1840's from Pennsylvania, and his wife, whose name has not been recalled.

Benjamin Moyer's wife, Dorcas, was a first cousin to three Wells County residents, Mrs. Charles (Jenny) Mock, Mrs. Bill (Ella) Blocker, and Mrs. Abe (Elsie) Bierie, who were descendants of an Adams County family, Charles Twigg and Eleanor Purcell Twigg.

Robert Howard Stanton and wife, Rose Moyer Stanton, returned to Southern Wells County from Detroit and lived with Thurman Stanton until their deaths — Rose in 1970 and Robert in 1983, and were buried in Woodlawn Cemetery, at the edge of Warren.

TOM ANTRIM FAMILY

Our family has roots in the Pennsylvania Dutch country of Reading and Pottstown, near Philadelphia, and the Chesapeake Bay Area of Maryland. The Teas side of the family dates back to 1822, with Issac Cirwithen fathering Sarah Emily, born in 1855. Sarah married George Hallowell Teas. Sarah and George had five sons. One son was Edward, born on October 7, 1876, in Milford, Delaware. He graduated from the Delaware Academy, and law school at Columbia University. He then married Margaret Pasquith from Oriole, Maryland, and they settled on Deal Island in the Chesapeake Bay.

Of their four children, Emily Maria was my mother, born on August 21, 1906. After graduating from high school, Emily traveled to Philadelphia to live with an aunt, in 1929. In spite of the depression, she found work, and married Clifford David Hudson, a recent graduate of the University of Pennsylvania, in chemical engineering. They married in 1933, and I was born in 1935.

My first memories include a house in the suburbs of Philadelphia with woods, paths with a winding creek, and safe spaces to play. This is not quite what we find there now.

Tom and Marge Antrim

In 1953, I married Thomas Antrim, whose mother, Rhea, and dad, Edgar, were from Pottstown, Pennsylvania. Rhea's mother was part of an acrobatic act (the base) with her stepdad as the "flyer" on a vaudeville circuit. Edgar was a general contractor, and built gas stations in the New Jersey area.

Tom and I have three sons, and shortly after the youngest, Andrew, was born, Tom had an offer to work at Franklin Electric in Bluffton. Since "safe places to play" were now hard to find, we thought Indiana sounded wonderful. Tom was a graduate of Drexel University in mechanical engineering.

In 1966, we moved to Wells County; "how unbelievable it was when he could drive to work in just minutes." Our sons, Steve, Bruce, and Andrew, attended Lancaster Elementary and Norwell High school. Steve went on to Purdue University, graduated, and now lives in Tennessee. Bruce attended Indiana University earning a BA, MBA and a law degree in 1991. Andrew attended Hanover College and Mercer University, earning first a BA and then his law degree.

At the present time, Bruce and his family live in Illinois, where his wife, Jan, is an elementary school principal. They have two children, Lucas, ten, and Joy, who is six. Andrew lives in Wells County, and is practicing law with Edris, Brown, Johnson and Feeback.

With the encouragement of my husband and sons I also graduated from Huntington College, St. Francis College, and Purdue University. For the past 15 years I have taught school in Wells County, first at Southern Wells, and for 14 years I have taught at Northern Wells.

Tom and I have been members of the First Presbyterian Church of Bluffton, serving as ordained elders.

I belong to the Indiana Association for Gifted Children, the National Associaton for Gifted Children, and Norwell Classroom Teachers, serving as their president for one term, treasurer, vice president, and negotiating team member for ten years. I am also a member of ISTA, NEA and a retired member of Delta Kappa Gamma and Kappa Kappa Kappa. *Submitted by Mrs. Tom (Marge) Antrim*

ARCHBOLD

Emmett and Mary Etta (Valentine) Archbold bought a home one and a half miles west of Ossian in the area that was known for years as Tile Town. This was in the late 1800's. There they raised a family of four boys and two girls. Emmett was a painter and wallpaper hanger by trade all his life. Their family consisted of Forrest, Marvin, John, George, Rosa, and Hattie. They are all deceased with the exception of Hattie.

Forrest and Georgie had no children. Marvin and Iva (Woods) had five children: Nellie, Glen, Mary (Dafforn), Paul and Ned. George and Geneva (Heckley) had no children. Russell and Rose (Archbold) Scherrer had three boys: Orville, Forrest, and Verlin. Fred and Hattie (Archbold) Shutt had two children: Mary (Shutt) Bragg and Robert.

John and Edna (Woods) Archbold had one son Harold and two daughters, Luella and Joan. Harold married Wilma Carnes. They had three children: Dean, Lyle, and Marilyn Lindquist. Luella married Wallace Updike and they had one son, Alan. Joan married Forace Hale Brewer and they have three daughters: Kay Reusser, Lyn Brewer, and Camille Havens.

John Archbold was a farmer, painter, and decorator. They lived one and a half miles west of Ossian for over 60 years. Harold was a painter, decorator, and farmer. Luella was a deputy auditor of Huntington County over 23 years. She is now retired. Joan Brewer was a lab and x-ray technician at the former Wells County Hospital and now is a retired Northern Wells teacher. She taught for 23 years.

PATRICK ARCHBOLD FAMILY

Patrick Archbold, son of Thomas and Mary (Kent) Archbold, was born 1782 in Westmoreland County, Pennsylvania, a sibling of: Rebecca (1781) who after 1850 married Joseph Johnson; Martha (1798-1873), who married Hazel Andrews; William who died young; Sarah Ann (179?-?), who married Perry Andrews; Sabertha (179?-1839) who married Jeremiah Andrews; and Thomas (1800-1871), who married Melinda "Linney Berry" Andrews. The father, Thomas, was a veteran of the Revolution and served five different periods from Chester and Fayette Counties, Pennsylvania. On March 18, 1806, Patrick married Francina "Fanny" McClain, also born 1783 in Westmoreland County, and it was about that time that they and his father Thomas and the rest of the family all removed to Harrison County, Ohio. Sometime later they moved on to Dohannon Township, Tuscarawas County, Ohio, where most of Patrick's siblings found their spouses.

Fanny's parents have not been traced, but a possibility may be a Joseph McClain who also removed to Tuscarawas County, Ohio, around the time of the Archbolds. The clue come from Joseph's will, which at the time of his death about 1828 mentions his "daughter Fanny." The children of Patrick and Fanny numbered ten and included: Joseph (1807-1870), who married Elyla Van Horn; John A. (Absolam ?) (1809-1885), who married Elizabeth Gibson, daughter of George W. and Rebecca (Reed) Gibson of Chester County, Pennsylvania. Thomas (1811-1893), who married Phebe Valentine; William, who died young; Lettice who married Amaziah Van Horn; Francina, who married Thomas Hoy; Rebecca (1827), who married Robert Green; Sarah (1824), who married Thomas Mullen; Mary, who married George Gibson; and Ann (1820-1884), who married William Gibson.

Patrick Archbold
1782 PA -1856 IN

After the death of Patrick's mother, Thomas remarried a Mary Liggett, likely a widow, in about 1826; she, too, had expired prior to 1835 when Thomas, at age 83, with several of his children and spouses, all removed to Adams County, Indiana. They were followed by several of Patrick and Fanny's children to the same area. Patrick was a respected farmer and justice of the peace in Tuscarawas County, Ohio, for several years, but finally, with most of his family gone, he and Fanny too packed a wagon for the long trail west to settle in Wells County, Indiana in 1847. There they lived the remainder of their lives in the renewed bliss of being surrounded by siblings, children, and grandchildren.

Patrick had served in the War of 1812 as a private under Captain William Stokes in the First Regiment, Second Battalion, of the Ohio Militia, and the traditional story is that when the call to arms came he was working in a field. He directly left his team and wagon on the spot, went to the cabin to collect his rifle and provisions, and proceeded without delay. In religion Patrick was a Presbyterian. This, however, was not traditional, for his grandfather, Patrick the first, born 1725, was a devout Catholic from Ireland. But for some reason or another Thomas his son refused to rear his children in the church, which lost him a measure of favor in his father's eyes. John, the other son of the first Patrick, did remain with his family in the Catholic Church, but Thomas must have been forgiven for he did receive his oldest son's measure in his father's will.

Even though Patrick lived less than ten years in Wells County prior to his death on January 3, 1856, he had become well-known and well-respected among the local citizens and his neighbors and other friends he'd made in Indiana, as well as all of his admiring descendants. Fanny continued to live a widow's life without him for another ten years. Her life ended on September 18, 1866, when she rejoined him in the glory of paradise.

AREND

Fred and Erma Arend came to Bluffton in 1936. Mr. Arend was born in Ohio, but he spent most of his earlier years in Elwood, Indiana.

Fred Arend became associated with the Morris Five and Dime Store in Elwood, Indiana. Later, after moving to Bluffton, Indiana, he was connected with the G.C. Murphy Co.

During Fred Arend's years in Bluffton, he was a member of the Rotary Club, and a member of the First United Methodist Church.

The Arends had four children: Linda, Ruth Ellen, James, and Kenneth.

Linda Arend Stebing and her husband, Don Stebing, have one daughter Gina, and all live in Fort Wayne.

Ruth Ellen Arend Roberts and her husband, Joe Roberts, live in Noblesville and they have four children: Karla, Mark, Brenda, and Julie.

James Arend married Norma Ring and they live in Indianapolis with their daughter, Lori.

Kenneth Arend lives in Fort Wayne and he has one daughter, Jami.

Emma Arend died in 1964. Fred Arend married Nadine Hammond in 1966. He died in May 1971.

ELLEN ARMSTRONG

Ellen Mae (Osborn) Armstrong, oldest of eight children, was born in 1932 to John and Leita Osborn. She was born at 9584E 900N, one mile east of Prospect Methodist Church and went to Ossian Elementary School, then Union Center School, where she graduated in 1950. With so many children in the family, Leita knew all the tricks. Ellen still remembers having the measles, because she was scolded for hiding in the bottom of the cupboard and reading comic books with a flashlight (bad for the eyes). Ellen helped with hand laundry, hanging it from the clothes line, strung between the trees. She spent time with friends, Isabel Borton and Betty Crist, at their house. At school, she sang in a girls' sextet, performed in school plays, and worked the lunch room. She did babysitting, shampooed hair, and did other odd jobs for the neighbors. In summers, she worked in Bluffton at the Dutch Mill, where she met her husband, Charles Ray Armstrong, born in 1928 in Fort Wayne to Opal Mae and Houston Tillman Armstrong. Ellen and Chuck lived in Fort Wane, Uniondale, and then Bluffton, while Chuck held various jobs with Central Dairy, Montgomery Ward's, the Bluffton Police Department, and McMahon Paper of Fort Wayne. Mark, Phil, and Ross were born in Bluffton. They moved to Indianapolis and raised their children in Lawrence, a northeast suburb.

Armstrongs — 1963
Back row: Phillip, Mark, Ross
Front row: Kent and Susan

Chuck was a salesman and manager for Aero Drapery (nineteen years) and is current owner of an upholstery company. Ellen did jobs in the community: doing laundries, ironing, and maintenance for a laundromat, though her first priority was always her children: Mark Steven (1951), Philip Doyle (1954), Ross Howard (1955), Kent Douglas (1958), and Susan Elizabeth (1959). Ellen and Chuck centered their lives on their children's activities, and have been active members of the Lawrence Church of the Nazarene since 1959. Ellen has taught Sunday School, helped with the nursery, and been in the choir for years. Chuck drove the church bus and worked with Boy Scouts. In addition to those organizations and Little League Baseball, the boys did paper routes, worked at the State Fairgrounds Coliseum and the Indianapolis 500 Speedway. They won various trips from the Indianapolis newspaper companies to Washington, D.C., Florida and other locations, a reward for their good salesmanship. This big family had the busiest (and loudest) house on the block. The kids (neighbors included) climbed the apple tree in the backyard, enjoyed fishing, and rode seven miles to the park in Castleton (86th Street) for swimming whenever they could.

1987
Charles and Ellen Armstrong

Instead of vacations, the family returned to Bluffton every holiday to visit with both sets of grandparents. They were in Bluffton the day of the Palm Sunday tornadoes (1960's). Ross was at Great-grandma Smith's house, and just before phones went dead, she called to say he was scared, and someone would have to come get him. Lights were out everywhere as they headed for Indianapolis. (Chuck had to work the next day.) Roads were blocked, and they drove many miles out of their way. No other cars were around. The usual two hour trip took five hours, until midnight. After the boys graduated from Lawrence Central High School, they worked at Aero Drapery as salesmen and installers. Mark was in the U.S. Army and served in the Vietnam War. He married Teresa Marlene (Wood) in 1972, daughter of Dewey J. and Clara Wood. After graduating from Indiana University, Indianapolis, B.S. Business Management, and from Kansas City Nazarene Theological Seminary in 1989, he is the pastor of the Nazarene Church in Perry, Florida. Their daughters were born in Indianapolis: Elizabeth Ann (1972) and Laura Elaine (1977). Elizabeth joined the U.S. Army, studying music at Norfolk, Virginia, as a clarinetist. She was disappointed this Christmas (1990), because at enlistment, they promised she would go home for the holidays, but the Persian Gulf War with Iraq started that fall, and nobody was allowed to leave the military bases. While in high school, Philip tried a job picking sweet corn, and found out he was not a farmer. The employer dropped him back at the house the first day and announced, "This is not a country boy." After graduation, he managed pizza parlors in Ohio, North Carolina, South Carolina, and Florida, then settled in Indianapolis. He married a high school classmate, Janet Faye (Sweeney), in 1976, daughter of Earl-Arn and Nellie Sweeney. They have two children: Christina Lynn (1979) and Douglas Howard (1986). He currently manages a carpet fashions store in Indianapolis. Ross is an installer for Aero Drapery. He married Karen Denise (Watkins) in 1978, and has one daughter, Katrina Denise (1980). Kent, a plant manager for Aero Drapery at Westfield, married Linda (Carney) in 1987, daughter of Lowell Adrian and Lucille (Lawson) Carney. While in high school, Kent tried corn detassling one summer, but decided he is not a farmer either. Susan was born a month before the move from Salem Street to Cotton Street in Lawrence. As a teenager, she did babysitting and told of many amusing but difficult experiences. One mother who had fixed the evening meal told her to serve the children, and put the pork chops back into the oven immediately. Susan forgot. While the kids were eating, the father breezed through the kitchen and yelled at the St. Bernard dog: "Well, go ahead. You might as well take them all." He moved the pan from the stove, where the dog was balancing himself, to the floor, and the dog finished up the leftovers. Susan played the clarinet in the marching band, sang with the Jubileers, and participated in a special humanities program, concentrating three subjects into a two hour study period. She died suddenly in a car accident in 1976 with her boyfriend, his brother and sister. The sister was the only survivor. Ellen and Chuck currently reside at 3709 Breen Drive, Indianapolis, near Lawrence. (Refer to Levi Osborn for previous ancestry.)

GEORGE ARNOLD FAMILY

George Arnold was descended from English settlers who immigrated to North Carolina in the early 1700's. After a series of migrations further west, most of that branch of the Arnold family was located near Greensville, Ohio, at the time of George Arnold's birth in 1818. As a young man, George taught school at various places near Greenville. In 1840 he married Ann Maria Welty (born 1813) of Gettysburg, Pennsylvania. They resided in Greenville for about two years, and then after a five-year period of farming under the severest pioneer conditions in Whitley County, Indiana, he and his family moved to Columbia City, Indiana. There George entered into partnership with Henry Swihart in a general store; he later bought out his partner and expanded the business successfully. The Arnolds left Columbia City in 1856 and relocated in Bluffton, Indiana, where George became a partner with John Studabaker in a dry goods concern. After a year, he bought out Mr. Studabaker's interest and became the sole proprietor of the business, which he continued to operate until 1878. He then sold the store and purchased the *Bluffton Chronicle,* a Republican weekly newspaper, which he and his younger son, Charles A. Arnold, published until 1888. In that year George Arnold commissioned the Fort Wayne architectural firm of Wing and Mahurin to design a commercial block located on South Main Street opposite the site of the present courthouse. The "Arnold Block" was widely copied later in other downtown buildings and in the design of the courthouse itself. Ann Maria Arnold died in 1889. George Arnold died in 1904.

Henry Clay Arnold (1843-1933), first son of George and Ann Maria Arnold, began working as a bookkeeper in John Studabaker's produce and banking business in 1856 at the age of thirteen. He later was employed by his father's firm in the same capacity. He served for a brief time in 1863 in the pay department of the U.S. Army and then returned to Bluffton to take the position of cashier in the First National Bank. In 1866 he organized the firm of Arnold, Bliss & Company, which operated stores in Bluffton and Montpelier, Indiana. He took an active part in various other businesses in and around Bluffton. In 1895, H.C. Arnold built "Wildwood," a 24-room mansion in the Queen Anne style on his portion of the Arnold family tract, which was located in the 600, 700, and 800 blocks of Main and Johnson Streets. The house was a local landmark until it was destroyed by fire in 1940.

Henry C. Arnold married Eliza Bulger (1842-1935) in 1867; their children were Lelia, (1868-1953), Affie (1871-?), Mary (1873-1959) George L. (1876-1972), and Henrietta (1879-?).

Sarah L. Arnold, third child of George and Maria Arnold, was born in 1844 and was married to her cousin, John B. Welty, of Gettysburg, Pennsylvania, in 1868. They had three children, all of whom died in infancy. Sarah was educated in the common schools of Bluffton and at the Fort Wayne College and the Methodist College at Delaware, Ohio. John Welty died in 1924; Sarah Arnold Welty died in 1932 in a tragic fire at her house, which was located at the south edge of the Arnold family tract on Main Street.

Charles A. Arnold, youngest child of George and Ann Maria Arnold, was born in 1852 and was married to Kate Wahl in 1877. He was educated in the common schools of Bluffton and at the Fort Wayne College. As a young man he taught in the Bluffton graded schools for a time and later clerked in the family dry goods store. In 1878 he and his father purchased the *Bluffton Chronicle,* which he published until 1888. He was later in the timber business at Monroe and Poneto, Indiana. In 1888 he was nominated by the Republican Party to be state senator, but was narrowly defeated in a heavily Democratic district. Kate Wahl Arnold died in 1901; Charles married Catherine Wisner (1860-1940) in 1905. Charles A. Arnold died in 1932.

The children of Charles and Kate W. Arnold were: Albert, Anna, Sherman, Margaret, Sarah and Donald. Sarah (Sally) Arnold (1890-1961) married Herman S. Wiecking in 1909 (see entry for Wiecking Family).

The George Arnold family plot is located in Fairview Cemetery near Bluffton.

ARNOLD/GILBERT

Dale Arnold and Ruth Eloise Gilbert were married on November 2, 1941. One year later he served in the Air Transport Command in World War II and was involved in the final stages of the war in Japan. He was in the service for three years. He worked in the carpenter trade for one year, then started to farm in Liberty Township. In 1954 we purchased a farm in Rockcreek Township and have lived there for thirty years.

Our family started with Linda in 1950, then Dick in 1953, Tom in 1955, and Rhonda in 1960. They all attended Rockcreek High School until it was vacated.

Linda is now living with her husband, Robert Pederson, in Copper Canyon, Texas, near Dallas. Their son, Eric, was born in Howell, Michigan, on April 24, 1985.

Dick and his wife, Lorri (Stoffer), and their three children live on the family farm, one half mile north of 300 N on 303. Their children are Dustin, born on March 11, 1981; Joel on March 14, 1985; and Lindsay on June 29, 1988.

Tom and Sue (Russell) have two children and live in Tocsin. Nathaniel was born on September 3, 1980, and Tera Sue was born on September 17, 1982.

Rhonda and her husband, Randy Hoopingarner, live in Fort Worth, Texas, having moved there in 1981. Amanda was born on May 14, 1982, and Brittany was born on February 12, 1990.

Dale's parents were Luster and Gertrude (Gertie Reece) Arnold; they were married in 1916. Their six children were as follows: Wanda Eileen, who died at birth; Dale, born October 13, 1918; Robert, born June 22, 1922; Marjorie, born December 3, 1923; Harold, born August 22, 1932; and Max, born April 24, 1937.

Luster was a son of Adam and Julia (Lanning) Arnold, a grandson of Moses and Mary Ann (Bartlemay) Arnold, and a great-grandson of Jacob and Chloe (Maddox) Arnold.

Gertrude (Luster's wife) was a daughter of John and Mary (Kimmer) Reece. Her brothers and sisters were Lottie, Anna, Charles, Vada, James, Arther, Molly and William. Their ancestors originated from North Carolina.

My father was John B. Gilbert, son of Martin and Elizabeth (Harvey) Gilbert. Other members of the family were George, Myrl, Maude, Paul and Martha.

Martin Gilbert was a son of Martin and Lydia (Houtz) Gilbert, who came to Wells County in 1829.

My mother was the oldest daughter of William and Myrtle (Bush) Dowty. They were married in 1898. Other members in the family were Lona (Jack), Ilow (Buckles) and Adam, who married Virginia Nevitt.

The other members of my family were: Darrell, Lowell, Lois, Joyce, David, Carol, and Janet.

In 1981 we retired from farming and moved to Uniondale.

ATHAN FAMILY

John Wilson Athan, born July 9, 1935, in Rockbridge County, Virginia met and married Evangeline Barton, born November 28, 1839, in Delaware County, Indiana. They were married April 2, 1857, and started housekeeping in a little house in Liberty Township (2992 address 200S. 1706 W.). Both were of Irish descent. They had three sons and eight daughters. Mary Jane born March 2, 1859; Nancy born January 6, 1861; Thomas, born November 2, 1862; Martha, born August 20, 1865; William born April 19, 1868; Malinda born August 24, 1870, Rosel Benjamin, born May 6, 1873; twins born and died August 27, 1875; Francis Jane, born November 7, 1876, and Elsie, born October 7, 1879. They moved to Bluffton in 1859. John Wilson died, March 27, 1880, and is buried in the Rockford Cemetery. Evangeline got work at the Bliss Hotel and raised her family, the youngest one (Elsie) being one-year old at her father's death. Evangeline died July 26, 1913.

One of their sons, Rosel Benjamin, better known as Ross, grew up in Bluffton and as a boy played with Herman Thoma. Herman's mother was Ross's Sunday School teacher. When Ross became of working age, he went north of Markle and hired to John Edgar as a farm worker.

Atkinson Edgar born September 22, 1809, came to America from England and married Mary Ann Mounsey born January 28, 1810. They had four children: Mary, born December 30, 1831; Sarah born December 10, 1833; John born March 28, 1836; and Jane born May 15, 1838.

One of their sons, John Edgar, married Zelda Ann Poling (born April 18, 1845) of Holland descent on March 27, 1871. Zelda Ann had 12 brothers and sisters. They set up housekeeping two miles north of Markle and had six children: John Edgar (born February 1872), Nora (born July 23, 1873), Almeda (born July 6, 1875), Atkinson (born December 2, 1877), Minnie (born April 4, 1879), and Ruth (born October 5, 1881).

Their daughter, Nora, married Ross Athan December 15, 1894. They lived near Markle as Nora's father passed away, and her mother moved to Huntington. Ross and Nora moved to the homeplace two miles north of Markle. Ross farmed all of his life. They had one son Mark, born on the home place near Markle, June 13, 1908. Nora died November 1919 and was buried in the Markle Cemetery. She was later moved by William Thoma, to the Grove Cemetery near Poneto.

In 1922, Ross married Neva Lowry (Perry) and they moved west of Poneto on 218. Ross died April 17, 1951, is buried in the Grove Cemetery beside Nora. Neva died in 1962 and was buried at Keystone Cemetery beside her former husband, Levi Lowry. Mark attended school at both Chester Center and Liberty Center and was graduated from Liberty Center. He met and married Eunice Hedges December 24, 1933. Eunice is the daughter of Arthur Clay and Effa Belle (Smith) Hedges. (refer to Hedges history in this book.) They set up housekeeping west of Five-Points in Chester Township, Wells County. The first hogs they sold for $2.65 cwt. Gross income for 1934 was $850.00 on 160 acres. In 1937 they moved to 100E-4926S and continued to reside there in 1991. A welder by trade, Mark started farming because of the Depression and still does. Eunice retired from Bluffton Harrison School System in May, 1977, and continues to work at Wells Community Hospital in 1991. Mark and Eunice have three children: Donald Rosel, born October 24, 1934; Rex Arthur, born January 31, 1936; and Mary Ann, born June 5, 1945. Donald married Linda Lou Rigby (from Jay County), September 15, 1963, and built their home at 4488S-200E (Ellingham Pike). They have three sons: Thomas Arthur, born April 21, 1967; Michael Andrew, born March 16, 1973; and Stephen Allen, born January 7, 1976. Thomas married Katrina Marie Brown who was from Bluffton in 1987. They have one son, Kedric Thomas, born April 10, 1988.

Rex married Karen Santon, from Bluffton, November 23, 1960. He graduated from Butler University and taught school for 12 years. He is now employed at Lincoln Life Insurance. Karen is a nurse. They live at Walnut Creek, California. They have two children: Julie Reneé, born December 14, 1961; and John, born July 15, 1964. Julie married Rich Newcomb August 31, 1991.

Mary Ann married Ronald Smith from Sweetser, Indiana. They both graduated from Ball State University and teach in the Pontiac, Michigan School System. They live in Waterford, Michigan. They had two sons: Jason Bradley, born May 10, 1969; and Cary born, born December 3, 1967. Cary passed away of cancer February 2, 1985 in his senior year of high school.

Refer to Hedges Family History in this book.

AULT - HOOK

Charles William (Chuck) Ault is the son of Charles Fredrick (Fred) born December 27, 1902, and Agnes Evelyn Myers Ault, born March, 1906. Fred was the son of Charles E. and Christina Elzey Ault and was born in Fort Wayne. Charles died when Fred was a small boy and "Teen" then married William Parker. Agnes was the daughter of William and Elva Kumfer Myers, who lived northeast of Ossian. After the death of Agnes in 1941, Fred married Ethelbelle Myers, a sister of Agnes. Chuck is an only child. Fred worked for the J.A. Morris Co., a jobber for five and ten cent stores. Anna Lee is the oldest child of Ralph Allen Hook, born September 17, 1903, and Caroll Schlagenhauf Hook, born January 12, 1907. Ralph was the son of Paul Dennis and Minnie Stover Hook. They were farmers near Eaton, Indiana. Caroll is the daughter of Henry and Eva Gottchalk Schlagenhauf. They were farmers in Wells County.

Back row: Rex Arthur Athan, Karen (Santon) Athan, Ronald Smith, Mary Ann (Athan) Smith, Linda Lou (Rigby) Athan, Donald Rosel Athan. Middle row: Jason Bradley Smith, Mark Athan, Eunice Gladys (Hedges) Athan, John Athan. Front row: Michael Andrew Athan, Katrina Marie (Brown) Athan, Thomas Arthur Athan, Julie Reneé (Athan) Newcomb, Stephen Allen Athan

*Chuck and Anna Lee Ault
October 1985*

Chuck, born June 16, 1927, and Anna Lee, born February 22, 1927, graduated from Bluffton High in 1945, were married in 1947, and have lived their entire married life in Harrison Township, Wells County (N.N. NE. 35-27-12). Chuck served in the army in Japan at the close of World War II. For several years he drove a truck picking up milk at farms in ten gallon milk cans. He later became a mechanic and took over Hook's Garage at the death of his father-in-law. Anna Lee is a housewife and in 1973 started driving a school bus for Bluffton-Harrison Schools. She is active in church and community as a volunteer. Chuck and Anna Lee have five sons. Stephen born October 27, 1948, married Jo Ann (Jody) Moore of Bluffton. During the Vietnam conflict, Steve spent one year in Vietnam operating a bulldozer. They have two sons, Andrew Charles, born June 3, 1977, and Adam Joseph, born April 26, 1985. In 1991, Steve works for PHD Co. at Fort Wayne. His hobby is restoring antique cars. Jody teaches at the Norwell Middle School. They live in Harrison Township, Wells County. Stanley K., born December 12, 1951, married Tami Lowrey of Antioch, California. Stan went to Rose-Hulman Institute of Technology and the University of Illinois, where he earned his doctorate in physics. He works at Livermore National Laboratory doing research. She is a registered nurse working for Glaxo Drug Company. they live at Antioch, California. Scott Alan, born February 2, 1953, married Robin Maury of Celina, Ohio. They have two daughters; Samantha Marie, born November 29, 1980, and Shawna Leigh, born November 29, 1983, and a son, Scott Aaron, born January 23, 1991. Scott went to Purdue and graduated from the professional pilot program. He is a corporate pilot flying out of Dayton, Ohio. Robin is a housewife and part-time model. They live at Englewood, Ohio. Stacey Charles, born November 3, 1956, married Brenda Lea Gentis. They have three children: Jonathan Charles, born June 19, 1985, Olivia Margaret, born April 22, 1987, and Anastasia Catherine, born May 3, 1989. Stacey received his BS degree in forestry from Michigan Technological University and his master's degree in wildlife from Texas Technology. He works for Dow-Corning at Midland, Michigan as a wildlife biologist. Brenda is a housewife. Stuart Henry born February 10, 1965, married Lora Renee Mechling. They have two daughters, Shannon Morae born June 4, 1983, and Sydney Nicole, born November 5, 1986. Stuart works for Mix Mill in Bluffton and also builds custom cabinets at his home. Lora is a medical laboratory technician at Caylor-Nickel Medical Center. They live in Harrison Township, Wells County.

BABCOCK FAMILY

James D. Babcock, my grandfather, was born April 24, 1848, Carroll County, Indiana, a son of Peleg III and Malinda McCart Babcock. He told me that when the first train was to arrive in Delphi, Indiana, his father allowed him to ride a horse into Delphi to see the train arrive; when it came the horse became frightened and ran home, and Grandfather had to walk home.

The family later moved to Jasper County, Indiana, and it was there that grandfather's parents died. His mother is buried in the Crocket Cemetery, southeast of Rensselaer, Indiana. His father died in 1859 in Illinois and is buried in Union County, Illinois.

James, following his parent's demise, was sent to live with an uncle near St. Joe, Missouri. This was during the Civil War. He told me that when he was plowing with a team of horses, Confederate soldiers confiscated the horses and left him with his plow in the ground with no horses.

As a young man he returned to Jasper County, Indiana, and on December 7, 1870, he and Viola Jane Cox were married in Rensselaer in Jasper County, Indiana, and their career as farmers began. Nine children were born, namely: Elmer, Mary Lamson, George, my father, Homer, Anna Gertrude Scott, Elizabeth Yeoman, Thomas, Ruby Graham and Frank.

In 1904 James sold his land in Jasper County and then purchased 220 acres in Sections 27 and 28 in Rock Creek Township, Wells County.

On February 12, 1910, George, my father, and Lorena Wilburn were married in the Methodist Parsonage in Uniondale, Indiana. They established their first home in Jordan Township, Jasper County, Indiana. On January 29, 1911, I was born at that location.

In 1911 James sold the land in Rock Creek Township and purchased land just north of Petroleum in Nottingham Township, Wells County. When I was about 30 days of age, my parents moved to the Nottingham Township farm which my father operated. He was a prudent man, an excellent farmer and cattle man. He died in Chicago, Illinois, on June 11, 1917, following surgery.

James died on December 15, 1927, in Bluffton; he is buried in Weston Cemetery at Rensselaer, Indiana.

My first days at school were at the Petroleum School, and then after my father's property was disposed of at a public auction, my mother and I moved to Rockford. There I attended the one-room school until the new Rock Creek Township School was built. I graduated from that school in 1929.

In September, 1930, my mother and I moved to Huntington County, first in Salamonie Township and then later to Rock Creek Township. On May 5, 1934, Margaret Allen and I were married at the Methodist Parsonage in Mount Etna. On Oct. 5, 1936, our first child, Emmalee, was born in the Wells County Hospital in Bluffton. James L., our second child, was also born at the Wells County Hospital, on April 7, 1939.

In 1941 we purchased land in Salamonie Township and we lived there until we moved to Bluffton in 1979. On January 26, 1948, George was born in the Huntington County Hospital in Huntington. In the election of November, 1950, I was elected trustee of Salamonie Township and served two terms and continued to operate the farm.

Emmalee graduated from the Salamonie Township School in 1954; she then attended and graduated from Parkview Hospital School of Nursing. In 1956 she and Norman Wade were married. They had three children: Scott is a graduate of Indiana University School of Business and is at the General Electric in Fort Wayne; Susan is a graduate of The Evansville University School of Physical Therapy, she is a physical therapist at a hospital in Durham, NC; Sarah is a student at DePauw University in Greencastle, Indiana.

James L. graduated from the Salamonie Township School in 1957 and the following year entered Indiana University. On June 9, 1963, he and Lynn Maish were married in the Presbyterian Church in Warsaw, Indiana. Lynn had graduated from the high school in Warsaw and from DePauw University School of Nursing. After graduating from the School of Medicine, James did a rotating internship at Parkland Memorial Hospital in Dallas, Texas, then one year at Camp El Toro in California and one year in DaNang, Vietnam. After discharge he returned to Indiana University to do his residency in orthopedic surgery; he is now an orthopedic surgeon at the Caylor-Nickel Clinic in Bluffton.

They have three children: Becky is a senior at Miami University in Oxford, Ohio. She has been accepted in the Indiana University School of Medicine; Julia is a junior at Depauw University; Michael is a senior at Norwell High School.

George graduated from the last class from Salamonie Township High School (1966) and was valedictorian of his class. He then enrolled at Indiana University, was elected into the Phi Beta Kappa National Scholastic Fraternity, and graduated from the School of Medicine in the class of 1973. On June 15, 1969, he and Janice Banter were married in the United Methodist Memorial Home Chapel in Warren. Janice had graduated from the Purdue University School of Nursing.

George did his internship and residency at the University of Kentucky, at Lexington. While they were in Lexington, Timothy was born on December 19, 1973, and Lisa was born on April 1, 1977. Timothy is a junior at Bluffton High School, and Lisa is in the eighth grade at Bluffton Middle School. George is a general surgeon at the Caylor-Nickel Clinic in Bluffton.

Early in 1985 Margaret experienced a reoccurance of multiple myeloma, and later she developed acute leukemia. She died on June 6, 1986, and is buried in the Elm Grove Cemetery in Bluffton.

On August 15, 1987 Mary Elizabeth Steiner and I were married in Calvary United Methodist Church in Linn Grove, Indiana. Mary Elizabeth graduated from Hartford Township High school and Ball State University, having earned both her Bachelor's and Master's degrees in Elementary Education. She first taught in the one-room eight-grades Yager School in French Township in Adams County. Later she taught at Petroleum, Portland, and Bluffton. She retired in 1982, having taught school for forty-three years. *(Harold G. Babcock)*

JOHN ELGIN BAILEY FAMILY

John Elgin Bailey (January 28, 1892 - April 1972) married Lydia Myrl Gilbert (August 3, 1894 - April 28, 1948) on January 2, 1913. They had two daughters, Anna Elizabeth Bailey and Mary Jane Bailey.

Anna Elizabeth (September 19, 1913) married Ivan Ralph Decker (November 21, 1912 - July 24, 1989) on June 25, 1938. They had eight children: Jayne Rosalyn, Joyce Elaine, Mary Elizabeth, Edward David, Myrl Jean, Ivan Ralph Jr., Carol June, and Philip Martin Decker.

Jayne Rosalyn, born June 23, 1939, married

Dale Lee Sullivan, born March 6, 1941, on March 15, 1963. They have three daughters: Diann Jayne (born September 11, 1963) who married Thomas Lee Metz (born December 9, 1963) on August 6, 1980; Julie Ann born August 25, 1968; and Jennifer Lee born August 21, 1973.

Joyce Elaine Decker was born June 18, 1941.

Mary Elizabeth Decker, born January 14, 1943, married James Henry Borne, born July 5, 1941, on November 10, 1962. They were divorced on August 19, 1986. They had three children: Nancy Elaine (December 6, 1963) who married Stephen Clifford Wise (January 16, 1961) on February 20, 1988; Elizabeth Ann (March 3, 1967) married Homayoun Honarmandian (December 3, 1961) on September 1, 1990; Richard James Borne was born January 16, 1968.

Edward David Decker (February 23, 1944) married Christine Suzanne Chaney (December 25, 1945) on Mary 25, 1963. They have four children: Cheri Rene Decker (January 2, 1964) who married Garrett Warren Hamilton (August 11, 1958) on July 26, 1986, and they have two children Erin Nichole (February 23, 1988), and Lucas Allen (November 22, 1989); Tami Suzanne Decker born December 31, 1964; Clinton Edward (December 18, 1966) married Jacqueline Michelle Meyer (May 13, 1968) on August 4, 1990; Dustin David Decker born May 20, 1971.

Myrl Jean Decker was born February 8, 1947.

Ivan Ralph Decker, Jr. (June 21, 1950) married Barbara Delores Fuentes (February 4, 1954) on March 1, 1985. They have three children: Catherine Joanna Decker born January 8, 1976, adopted December 5, 1986; Christopher Joseph Decker born May 21, 1979, adopted December 5, 1986; and Michael William Decker born March 24, 1986.

Carol June Decker was born March 15, 1952.

Philip Martin Decker was born January 6, 1958.

The other daughter of John Elgin and Lydia Myrl Bailey was Mary Jane Bailey (October 13, 1915), who married Robert Eldon Eichhorn (November 14, 1914) on November 30, 1937. They had two children: Jimmie Lee Eichhorn and Marilyn Joan Eichhorn.

Jimmie Lee Eichhorn (June 19, 1938) married Connie Mae Booth (June 14, 1939) on June 27, 1959. They have three children: Kent Allen born June 3, 1960; Cindy Sue (June 9, 1962) who married Leslie Jay Smith (April 20, 1963) on April 11, 1987. They have one son Jay Michael Smith born September 27, 1990; and Adam Lee Eichhorn who was born December 27, 1972.

Marilyn Joan Eichhorn (August 4, 1943) married Richard Allen Morris (November 17, 1941) on June 1, 1963. They have two children: Kevin Richard Morris (November 29, 1941) who married Deborah Eileen Meek (January 20, 1966) on December 20, 1986. They have one son Austin Mitchell Morris born April 4, 1990. Kami Jo Morris was born May 18, 1970.

BAKER

John Baker, Sr., and Susan (Hower) Baker were natives of Pennsylvania. When they were children, they moved with their parents into Ohio, where they grew up and were married. John Baker, Sr., was a cooper by trade and worked at that business until the end of his life in 1853. John Baker, Sr., and wife, Susan, came to Wells County about the year 1850. John Baker, Sr., and Susan had eight children: Sarah, Lydia, Mary A., Elizabeth, John Jr., Jacob, Martin and an infant who died at birth.

John Baker, Jr., attended the public schools of Jackson Township in Wells County, Indiana, until he was 18 years of age. He then enlisted in the army, becoming a member of Company E 75th Regiment Indiana Volunteers, December 6, 1863, and remained in the service of his country until the close of the war, being discharged, therefore, in August 1865. He was with Sherman in the great battle from Atlanta to the sea. After his return, he began to work at the carpenter's trade. He married Mollie (Hudson) Baker on October 31, 1874, in Wells County, Indiana. Her parents were Benjamin Hudson and Katie Ann (Mullen) Hudson. At one time, John Baker, Jr., owned two hundred and sixty-nine acres in Jackson Township which also supported 14 oil wells. He was engaged as a stock farmer and general farming. John Jr., and wife (Mollie) were members of the Christian Church. Mr. Baker was a member of the Masonic Lodge #246 in Warren, Indiana. Mr. Baker was a registered Democrat.

The Claire McMillan home that was built in 1896

In 1896, he built the house that Sharon and Claire McMillan live in now. He constructed the barn in 1901. The farm has been in the Baker family, or heirs, for over a hundred years. From the marriage of John Jr. and Mollie, three children were born: James W., born May 23, 1876, married Anna Good. They had three girls, Maxine, Helen, and Inez. Oscar E. was born November 29, 1883, and was married to Meda Click. No children were born to this union.

Benjamin Franklin (Frank) was born September 23, 1879, and married Mary Hannah Hayward. Frank was an oil pumper and a farmer. Mr. Baker built all new buildings on the farm where he lived. The gravel for the cement block house was from the river bottom which he owed. Four children were born to the marriage: Ethel, Hazel, Mildred, and Howard E.

Howard E. graduated from International Business College and went to Oklahoma to work in the oil fields. Upon returning to Indiana, he married Vernis A. (Custard) on July 21, 1934. Vernis was the daughter of A. Bert Custard and Nettie (Coffield) Custard.

Two daughters were born of this union. Lennyce E. (Baker) Powers was born on April 3, 1946. Lennyce is married to Laurence (Larry) Powers and resides at Greenwood, Indiana. She is a school teacher at the Perry Meridian High School. They have one daughter, Emily. Sharon K. (Baker) McMillan was born on March 10, 1943. Sharon is married to Claire T. McMillan. Sharon is rural mail carrier out of Warren Post Office. They have two daughters: Clarice, graduated from Ball State University in May, 1990; Kristi is a student at Ball State University.

Mr. Baker was trustee for Jackson Township, Wells County. He was the first school board member from Jackson Township in the consolidation of Southern Wells School Corp. Mr. Baker is a member of Masonic Lodge #246 in Warren, Indiana. He is also a member of Congregational Christian Church (now United Church of Christ) in Warren. Vernis is a member of the McNatt Methodist Church.

BAKER-PAXSON

Mahlon Irey Paxson was born November 11, 1842, in Jay county near Pennville. He entered the Civil War in 1862, at the age of twenty. He was a blacksmith during the war and served under General Sherman during his famous "march to the sea." Malon was discharged on April 19, 1864, and wrote in his diary; "I got shot with a bullet through the rim of my hat, which missed my head by one-half inch."

He married Rebecca Walker, a Quaker from Pennsylvania, in 1878 and came to the Petroleum area in 1886. In 1888 they built a house and barn (now the Dale Kirkwood farm) for a cost of $2,500. Mahlon and Rebecca had three sons; Telfer, Orville (Joe) and Sherman.

In 1912 Mahlon had a museum on East Wabash Street, containing mounted animals; Indian artifacts, such as arrowheads and axes; over three thousand guns from the 1700's (even one from Daniel Boone); and canes he hand-carved out of roots, grapevines and tree limbs. Mahlon died February 15, 1920, and is buried in the Pennville Cemetery. In February, 1921, the contents of the museum were sold to the State of Indiana Museum at Indianapolis.

*Rodney D. - Doris E. Paxson
June 16, 1990*

Telfer Paxson married Elva Eichhorn in 1920, and together they farmed and raised registered Jersey cattle in Lancaster Township, Wells County, until Telfer's death in 1937. They had three children: Wilda Bell, Rodney and Lois Dougherty.

Rodney Dallas Paxson was born on February 5, 1915. In 1934, he graduated from Lancaster High School and bought his first car, a 1922 Ford Coupe, for $21.00. Rodney began working at the Erie Stone Company operating a crane for twenty-five cents an hour.

Ira Glenn Baker was born March 19, 1894 to J.E. Baker and Sally Ware. He served in the last mounted cavalry (World War I) stationed at Fort Sheridan, Illinois, and on his returned to Wells County, married Edna Gerber in 1919. Their only daughter, Doris Elaine Baker, was born in 1920.

Ira served as trustee of Harrison Township during the Depression years of 1929 and 1930, and managed the License Branch in the early 1940's in the basement of the old Bliss Hotel. Ira and Edna farmed 214 acres in Harrison Township, Wells County, until Ira's death in 1981. His brothers, Ware and Hugh, and sisters, Edith McCloud and

Crystal Cotten are still living in the Bluffton area. Another sister, Grace Buckner Knapp, died in 1991.

In 1940, when Rodney and Doris were married, Doris was secretary for Northern Indiana Public Service Company, in Bluffton. In September, 1941, Rodney went to the Panama Canal Zone with the Panama Construction Corporation and operated a twelve yard shovel on the third set of locks.

For the following ten years, Rodney was in the road paving business, and in 1957 went into the transportation industry, hauling propane for the Blue Flame Gas Corporation. Paxon Leasing Corporation was formed in 1963, to haul liquid fertilizer, and both corporations were sold to California Liquid Gas Company on January 1, 1974.

In 1947, Rodney and Doris built a home one and one-half mile east of Bluffton on State Road #124, the area in which they still reside. They had four daughters and one son: Carolyn Raffa, Janis Case, Connie Pifer, Christie Mann and Kent Paxson.

Baker-Paxson history covers 105 years involvement in the Wells County Community. Doris Baker Paxson has lived on the same section of land for 71 years.

ROBERT L. BAKER FAMILY

Robert L. Baker was born in 1934 in Wells County, the third child of Boyde and Josephine Baker. He has two sisters, Betty Jane Stinson and Barbara Ann Garrett, both Wells County resident. He married Carol Ann Brookmyer, oldest child of Floyd and Norma (Korte) Brookmyer in 1958. They had five children: Timothy Martin, Michael Alan, Scott David, Steven Douglas, and Cindy Ann (Dafforn).

Timothy Martin Baker married Patricia Joan Douglass and two children were born of this marriage: Ryan Patrick in 1986 and Allison Mae in 1989. Michael Alan Baker married Sarah Louise Parkison and one child has been born of this marriage, Alexandria Louise in 1990. Scott David Baker married Amanda Renee Patterson and one child has been born of this union in 1988, Staci Danielle. Steven Douglas married Mischelle Deering in 1987. Steven has a stepson, Nathan James Ness, born in 1982. Cindy Ann Baker married Timothy James Dafforn in 1989.

Robert (Bob) is presently a foreman with Fox Contractors Corp. In the past he has been the proprietor of a construction company (1965 to 1974), and a full time farmer from 1975 to 1990. Carol had a ceramic shop and gives lessons one day a week; she works part-time at Northwestern Mutual Life Insurance Company in Berne. Bob and Carol both enjoy their family and grandchildren. They established their home in Wells County, buying the farm where they live from the Ralph Murrays in 1968. All of the original structures are gone and new buildings have been added to during their residence there.

JASON BANTER FAMILY

Jason Banter and Violet Ritchey were married in 1930 in Bluffton. He was a son of John W. and Lillie Herring Banter. He was born on February 7, 1906 and died in 1985. We were both born in Jackson Township. I was born December 29, 1910. We were away from Jackson Township for a few years, but upon the death of his mother we came back to the farm that he was born on. We have always been farmers. Jason also worked for the Wells County Highway in 1950 and 1960.

Jason and Violet Banter

We had nine children. Gene lives in New Castle, and Jack served in the army in Germany in 1954. He married Ruth Hunt and lives on a farm near North Manchester. They have two children, Maria and Mike. He is also a crane operator. Ellen graduated from St. Joseph Hospital School of Nursing as an R.N. She married Gary King. They live in Fort Wayne and have two daughters, Ann, and Sue, who is married to Todd Williams. Ileen, also a graduate from St. Joseph Hospital with an R.N., married William Maxwell and they have two children, William and Lisa. Linda is an R.N. graduate from St. Joseph Hospital. She married Wendell King and lives east of Bluffton and has two children, Lora and Chris, and a granddaughter, Ashton. Joyce, a doctor's assistant, married Don Thornett and lives in Fairfax, Virginia, with their three children, Julie, Eric and Amy. Rex, a veteran of the Vietnam War, married Mickie Gregerson, a St. Joseph R.N., is a farmer, and lives on the farm where I was born. They have four children, Sara, Sam, Dan, and Katie. Joan, also an R.N. from St. Joseph Hospital, is married to George Springer and lives east of Bluffton with their three children, George, Ben, and Susan. Wanda Mason is a respiratory technician and lives north of Bluffton with her daughter, Angie.

I still live on the farm which has been in the Banter name since 1849. I'm a member of the Dillman United Brethren Church, the Missionary Fellowship and Ladies Aid of the Church, and the Jackson Township Home Economics Club. *Submitted by Violet Banter*

JOHN W. BANTER

John W. Banter, son of Joseph and Elmira Jeffries Banter, was born one mile south and one-half mile west of Dillman in Jackson Township, Wells County, on April 18, 1863, the fourth child in a family of nine children.

He was born in a log cabin on the farm where he spent his entire life, at what is now 11404 W - 1000S. At the age of nine years, he burst the joint-water sac in his right knee jumping off a chicken-coop, leaving him with a stiff knee. There being two other John Banters in Jackson Township, he was always known as Crippled Johnny.

His parents had migrated here from Bavaria, Germany, and were so "Dutch," and slurred their words so much it was difficult to understand their name. Records show the name of Painter leaving Germany was changed to Bender around 1810, according to Wayland's History of the Shenandoah. From 1838 to 1860 records show that most Bender's had changed their name to Banter. They also show that they had their Negro slaves with them. And when they got to the Ohio River the slaves were told if they got them across the river the slaves could go free.

L to R: Frank Banter holding horse, Cora Banter next to him, Harley Banter, Roy Banter, (white shirt), Dad, Mother (Elsie on her lap) Mae and Walter. Picture taken about 1900 in house Zada (Banter) McMillan was born

His father's land grant, made on September 25, 1839, was patented in the name of John Banter. His father could neither read nor write English so probably never knew how his name was written on his deeds, U.S. Census reports or other papers.

He married Lillie Ann Herring, (whose birthday was September 12, 1866,) on October 20, 1883. She was born in Darke County, Ohio. To this union twelve children were born. Frank, Harley, Walter, Roy, Cora Belle, Mae, Elsie, Jesse, Oscar, Jay and Jason (twins) all of whom are deceased and Zada who lives in Monroe Township, Grant County.

Frank's son, Howard, Jason's son Rex, and Oscar's daughter's Ardith Shideler and Claramae Banter are residents of Jackson Township. Most of Harley's family are in Blackford County; one daughter lives in Indianapolis. Walter's family live in Grant County, along with most of Jay's family. Roy's two girls are in Oklahoma and Texas. Mae's son, Dale, is deceased, but his family is in Florida. The two of Jay's children living out of Grant County are in Anderson, Indiana, and Florida. Jason's family is mostly in Indiana, but one daughter lives in Fairfax, Virginia.

His daughter, Zada taught school in Jackson Township in the one-room school for three years, teaching at the then known schools of Jeff, Banter and Eversole under the supervision of Township Trustee, Clell Gilbert. She then married J. Paul McMillan and moved to Grant County, where she now lives.

Zada had one son, John, in Grant County and Claude B. and Claire T. McMillan who live in Wells County, and are employed at Franklin Electric in Bluffton.

HALLET BARBER

When Hallet Barber arrived in Wells County in the mid-1830's he found little more than wilderness and a few scattered farms in the early stages of clearing. His home was in Darke County, Ohio, but he traveled often three months at a time through much of Ohio and Indiana, preaching, baptizing and planting churches. In September, 1838, he established the first church in Wells County, Six Mile Christian Church in Harrison Township, followed by the Liberty Union Church and two years later by the Scuffle Creek Church in Chester Township. He further organized groups of churches into conferences, the first being the Bluffton Conference.

Hallet was born in central New York in 1798, married fifteen year old Sarah Vining in Delaware County, Ohio, in 1818, and entered the ministry in 1829. By that time he had eight children: Lovina (born 1820), Celestia (1821), Harrison (1823), Elizabeth (1825), Emerson (1827), and Ira Albern (1828). In 1833 they were living in central Ohio and had added Nina (1830) and Urania (1831) to the family. Then on to Darke County and the births of Chauncey (1834), Delphina (1836), and Nancy Jane (1839), before their final move in 1841 to Indiana, where Rosalinda (1842) and finally Orin (1846) were born.

After settling his family at the present site of Rockford, Hallet built one of the county's first grist and sawmills on Rock Creek, thus giving the name of Barber's Mills to the community's post office. Hallet continued his pastoral travels until in 1849 he contracted cholera while nursing an abandoned victim and died. So widely beloved was he, that a contemporary biographer of his noted the news of his death produced "a shock such as is seldom felt, even at the death of a good minister." He was the first person buried in Rockford Cemetery.

All of Hallet's children except Harrison, Nina, and Rosalinda are mentioned in his will of 1848. Lovina married Richard Tyler, and their son Myron followed his grandfather's footsteps in the ministry in Rhode Island. Hallet's sons Chauncey and Emerson also became clergymen, the latter quite prominent in Missouri, where his wife, the former Calista Pingry, died and he married Bethany Beardslee. In 1849 Albern wed Sarah Ann, daughter of Wells County pioneer Solomon Johnson, and the previous year his sister Urania became the wife of Solomon's son, Jonas Johnson. Urania remained in the area, as did Elizabeth, who became Mrs. Louis Witham, and Delphina, Mrs. George W. Davis. Elizabeth's daughter Esther also gave her hand to Jonas Johnson after her aunt Urania died in 1861. Less is known about Celestia, who married Samuel Baker, and Nancy Jane, who married Francis Pfeifer. Orin reportedly enlisted in the Union Army at the age of nineteen and was struck down by disease near the end of the Civil War. His mother Sarah was mercifully spared the grief, however, for she passed away in 1861. She joined Hallet in Rockford Cemetery, where they rest under a monument inscribed: "Though dead he yet speaketh."

BARBIERI-PASTORE

Jim (James Charles) Barbieri (born in Park Ridge, Illinois) arrived in Bluffton in June, 1950, after graduating from DePauw University, Greencastle, to join the Bluffton New-Banner. He had been employed in sports-news-feature writing on the Chicago American for a time during the college period. He married DePauw graduate Barbara Carolyn Forsell (born in Rockford, Illinois) on April 28, 1951, in Greencastle, Indiana. While Jim served overseas in the U.S. Army, Barbara taught school in Illinois. Over decades Jim has been a reporter, editor, advertising, circulation manager, and general manager of the New-Banner; and managed the project for the modern newspaper building completed in 1975. He won several major reporting-writing awards. He received Wells County's Distinguished Service Award and was made a Sagamore of the Wabash by Governor Bowen. He went to the White House for presidential sessions by invitations of Presidents Ford, Carter, and Reagan, including also a session with President Bush. Barbara taught first grade at Central School, 1953-54; became a member of Tri Kappa, 1954, and president, 1961; appointed trustee of the Bluffton-Wells County Public Library, 1961, as an addition to the Carnegie Library was built, and served as president of the board twice; past member of the Bluffton Park and Recreation Board (while the Community Pool was built); past member of the Wells County Creative Arts Council, served as president; charter member of the Friends of the Library, 1989.

The Barbieri/Pastore Family in February 1991. Lori and Chuck Barbieri with children, Ashley and Brent; Barbara and Jim Barbieri with Jim holding Stephen Pastore; Cindi and Steve Pastore; and Jenni Pastore

Jim and Barbara's children are Charles Edward Barbieri born November 9, 1954, and Cynthia Jean Barbieri born January 7, 1957, both graduates of Bluffton High School. The family are members of the First Presbyterian Church. In June of 1986, Jim became co-owner of the News Banner Publications, as well as President, Publisher and Editor. Barbara is Arts/Entertainment Editor, and Photographer, for the News-Banner. Charles, a graduate of DePauw and IU-Indianapolis law school, is a Michigan attorney and share-holder in Foster, Swift, Collins, and Smith law firm. He is married to Lorie Seitz (Monroe, Michigan). They have children, Ashley Ann, January 8, 1987; Brent Edward, November 14, 1990. Cynthia, is a graduate of Ball State University, and has an M.A. from IU-Fort Wayne. She is a special education teacher with Adams-Wells County Special Services Corporative. She is married to Stephen Pastore, construction foreman for James. S. Jackson Co. (He arrived in Bluffton when his father, Nick Pastore, served as project manager for the building of the Corning Plant.) They have two children, Jennifer Kristen, January 27, 1983; Stephen Nicholas, April 30, 1985.

BARCUS

The Barcus Family has been in Wells County, Indiana since the late 1850's. William Barcus and his wife Helen and their son James Ross moved from the Stuebenville, Ohio, area late 1850's. They settled on an 80-acre farm section twelve in Liberty Township.

William died when James Ross was seventeen years old. James stayed on the farm with his mother and worked and cleared the land. He married Ellen Crosdale. They had one son, William E., and one daughter, Lula, who married Fred Miller.

William E. married Lilie L. Morris. They had one son, Herman Morris Barcus. William and Lilie moved on the Barcus farm with their son Herman after James R. and wife moved to Liberty Center about 1926. James' wife died December 23, 1938. James R. died in August, 1943.

Herman M. married Edith Williamson January 21, 1939. William E. and Lilie moved to Liberty Center. Herman and Edith moved on the Barcus farm. Edith was the daughter of Joseph D. Williamson and Ethel Mae (Kline).

Three children were born to Herman and Edith: Janice Elaine, Jack Leon and James Allen.

William E. and Lilie, parents of Herman, died August, 1946, and January, 1949.

Janice E. married O. Floyd Soper June 5, 1960. Janice graduated from Parkview School of Nursing Fort Wayne and Floyd graduated from Ball State Teachers College. Janice is a nurse at Caylor-Nickel Hospital in Bluffton. Floyd teaches at Bluffton High School.

Janice and Floyd have two daughters: Sharon Kay born July 20, 1961; and Susan Lynn, born March 21, 1966.

Sharon Kay married Terry A. Cressman from New Dundee, Ontario, Canada, November 5, 1983. They have one son, Scott Joseph, born May 21, 1987, and one daughter, Sarah Elizabeth, born August 31, 1989. The Cressmans lived in Kitchner, Ontario, until the fall of 1990, when they moved to Sturgis, Michigan.

Susan Lynn married David Batdorff from Charlevoux, Michigan, April 7, 1988. They have one daughter, Rachal Elaine, born September 6, 1990. The Batdorff family lives near Albany, Indiana.

Jack L. Barcus married Karen Sue Shane from Bluffton, January 8, 1966. They have one daughter, Tammera Sue, born September 7, 1967, and one son, David Leon, born February 2, 1970.

Tammera Sue married Tim Garwood from Fort Wayne, September 28, 1985. They have one daughter, Melissa Sue, born August 6, 1989. The Garwoods live in Ossian, Indiana.

David L. Barcus is engaged in farming with his father, Jack, in Liberty Township. James A. Barcus is also engaged in farming after attending college, spending six years in the U.S. Navy, and driving a semi a few years.

Herman, Edith, and James A. still live on the Barcus Farm which Herman's great-grandfather settled on well over 100 years ago.

Three generations of the Barcus Family graduated from Liberty Center High School: Lilie L. Barcus, her son Herman and wife Edith, and their three children, Janice, Jack and Jim.

BARGER

John H. Barger, born March 10, 1872, and Elizabeth L. Peoples, born 1875, were married March 5, 1896. Four boys and three girls were born to this union: Orval, Floyd, Doyle, Glen, Alta, Lola, and Aleta. Glen, the third from the youngest, was born August 31, 1901. John H. had the house built in 1902 on his eighty acres in Lancaster Township. Glen remembers watering the newly planted trees in the front yard with the help of a goat and wagon.

Front: John H. Barger, Orval, Floyd, Dole, and Alto Back: Glen, Lola, Elizabeth, Aleta

February 18, 1925, Glen married Queenie H. Fiechter, born Jan. 18, 1903. Lena Rinehart, born

1863 and died 1942. Three children were born to Glen and Queenie: John Richard, born June 14, 1927, William Keith, born Jan. 9, 1930, and Carol Natalie born May 19, 1933. Glen continued farming, and also raised turkeys that were sold at Barr St. Market in Fort Wayne. He served on the advisory board for Lancaster Township when the east building addition was added to the Lancaster School. Glen died Oct. 25, 1981. He lived his entire life on this farm.

John R. married Barbara Louise Douglass, born June 2, 1931. They have three children: Debra Louise, born May 29, 1953, who married John Huskins, and they have three children, Natalie, Jordan, and Lauren; Kathryn Ann, born Dec. 10, 1954, married Barry Kolter, and they have three children, Travis, Jared and Kristen; and John Max, born Feb. 23, 1964. John R. has a farm in Adams County and farms the Lancaster Township farm.

Front: Carol Barger Stern, Queenie Barger, Barbara Douglass Barger, Doyle Stern and John R. Barger

William K. "Bill" married Cora V. Lucas born Sept. 8, 1934, and they have three children: Keith Allen, born October 2, 1954, married Karla Yost and they have one child, Elliot Samuel; Cynthia Sue, born march 7, 1959; Barry Neal, born Nov. 22, 1962, married Marilyn Blythe. Bill operated a landscaping nursery, then went into home construction. Bill died April 7, 1981.

Carol N. married Doyle Robert Stern, born June 12, 1932, and they have two boys: Timothy Robert, born Jan. 22, 1955, married Elizabeth Ellen Broyles; Mark Nathan, born Feb. 5, 1957, married Mary Suzanne McGaughy. They have a daughter, Ashley Nicole.

BARNES

Richard J. (Jack) Barnes and Mary Adahleen White were married in Ossian in January, 1942. Jack's parents were John and Anna Merley Barnes from Fulton County, Indiana. Adahleen's parents were Clyde and Dora Hoopengardner White who had always lived in Jefferson Township. Jack and Adahleen lived in LaPorte, Indiana, both before and after their marriage. Jack was a furniture salesman and Adahleen was a registered nurse, graduating from St. Joseph's School of Nursing in Fort Wayne in 1937. Their time there was interrupted by World War II. Jack's military service was in Georgia and the Pentagon. They also lived in several other areas of Indiana, Illinois, and Ohio, before moving to Jefferson Township in 1955, where they have lived ever since. After leaving the furniture business, Jack worked for General Electric and then as coordinator of the Alcohol and Drug Treatment Program at Parkview Hospital in Fort Wayne. Adahleen worked at Lutheran Hospital in Fort Wayne until 1985. They are noe both retired. They have three children, Elizabeth, Karen and Richard C.

Elizabeth (Betty) Barnes was born in LaPorte in October, 1942. She graduated from Ossian High School in 1960, and the University of Colorado in 1966, and St. Francis College in 1969. She is now teaching at the Columbian School in Bluffton. She married DeWayne Oakes in 1962. They have three children: Richard, Mary Anne and John.

Richard E. (Ted) Oakes was born in Denver, Colorado, in October, 1964, and graduated from Norwell High School in 1983. He married Jodi Foreman in 1988 and is a tool and die maker at K-K Tool and Design Inc. in Markle. Jodi is the daughter of Don and Marie Foreman of Bluffton and is an habilitation specialist for Bi-County Services in Bluffton.

Mary Anne Oakes was born in Bluffton in November, 1966. She married Scott Sherry in 1987 and is a student at Indiana University Extension in Fort Wayne. Both she and Scott, who is from Chicago, served in the Navy. Scott is a certified welder for Teco, Inc. They have two children: Erin, born September, 1988, and Kyle, born July, 1990.

John Oakes was born in Bluffton in November 1968. He graduated from Norwell in 1987, and is a tool and die maker for Melching's Machine Shop east of Ossian.

Jack and Adahleen Barnes' second daughter is Karen. She was born in LaPorte in January, 1947. She graduated from Ossian High School in 1965, Indiana University in 1973, and received an R.N. degree from Purdue University in 1982. She is currently working as an Intake Coordinator for Professional Care Management, Inc. in Allen county. She married Richard Gorrell in 1972 and they live in Leo, Indiana.

Richard C. Barnes was born in Joliet, Illinois in June, 1951. He graduated from Norwell in 1969. He and Linda Wood were married in 1971 and have three children: Derek, born February, 1972; Ian, born June, 1977, and Myah, born April, 1979. After their divorce, Richard married Judith Baker Bonar in 1989. They now live in Fort Wayne and he is a sales representative.

BARNES, SMITH, WINEGART

Katharine June, daughter of John and Fern Crabbs Nussdorfer, was born June 23, 1919 in Roanoke, Indiana. Her marriage was April 19, 1941, to Maurice J., son of David and Sofronia Dubbs Barnes. Their only child was Ellen Jeanne, born September 12, 1944. Maurice was killed November 6, 1944, in Germany in World War II.

Katharine Barnes was married September 25, 1948 to Max W., son of Raymond and Lois Whitacre Smith. His son was Durand L., born January 14, 1946, to Max and Alice Cross Smith. Alice passed away April 1, 1947. Max and Katharine moved to Wells County in February 1952. Their home was two miles south of Zanesville on old State Road 303, turn east, the first house on the north side. Durand lives on the farm at the present time. Max and Katharine had a son, W. Brooks, born March 18, 1953. Max passed away January 28, 1968. Brooks passed away September 30, 1972.

Ellen Jeanne Barnes was married September 19, 1964, to Gary W. son of Gail and Donnabelle Bolinger Bowersock. Their home is one mile south of Zanesville on 300W. on the southeast corner. Their children are Scott W., born, August 17, 1966, and Pamela J., born Oct. 16, 1968.

Durand Smith was married September 12, 1970, to Lavonne, daughter of Edward and Joy Seward. Their children are Jeannette S., born September 13, 1973, Darren P., born December 6, 1975, and Natalie D., born August 13, 1980.

Katharine Smith was married November 26, 1970, to Elwood I. son of Illie and Blanche Johnson Winegart. Her home at this writing is 11760 N. Marzane Road near Zanesville.

THE ERNST BAUERMEISTER FAMILY

The Ernst Bauermeister family history in Wells County began in 1892 when our great-grandparents, Ernest and Sophie Bauermeister, arrived from Minden, Westfalen, West Germany. Our grandparents, Henry and Fredricke Breier Bauermeister, also settled in Jefferson Township that same year. They had nine children: Frieda, Martha, Minna, Emma, Ernst, Agnes, Paul, Arthur and Mildred. Their first home was about one-fourth mile north of Bethlehem Lutheran Church. Later they purchased the farm on the corner of 1000N and 750E where they farmed for many years. Grandfather was born on September 2, 1866, and died in August of 1947. Our grandmother was born on May 4, 1870 and passed away on December 28, 1960. Ernst Bauermeister, our father, was born on January 4, 1902. He married Edna Gallmeyer, a resident of Adams County on November 29, 1924. They bought a farm five miles east of Ossian on road 750 E where they farmed until Dad passed away in 1966. Their family consisted of five children: LaVon, Lester, Norbert, Arline, and Glenn.

Mother was born on November 13, 1902, and died on October 16, 1983.

Lavon married Robert Scherer and they had five children: Keith, Bruce, Kevin, Robyn, and Barry. LaVon and Bob live near Hoagland, Indiana.

Picture is of Ernst and Edna Bauermeister in 1924

Lester, a well-known farmer in Jefferson Township, lives on his farm on road 1000N east of Ossian. He married Elva (Joey) Reinking and they had three children: Jeffrey, Dawn, and Heidi. Jeff is married to Lori McClain and they have three children, Whitney, Carlee and Briar. Dawn is married to Steve Crosby.

Norbert, also a well-known farmer who farmed in partnership with his brother Lester, now lives on the farm on 1000N and 750E. He is married to Alice Kukelhan and they have four children: Amy, Tina, Tony and Terry. Arline, now living in Oswego, Illinois, is married to John Koomjohn. Their children are Dirk, Lisa and Derek.

Glenn lives on the farm on 750E in Jefferson Township and is employed by the Indiana Department of Transportation. He is married to Pauline Hoffmann and has four children: Rod,

Ronda, Scott, and Brian. Ronda is married to David Flesch and has two children: Joshua and Lindsay.

BAUERMEISTER-LIMBACH

Ernest Konrad Dietrich Bauermeister and Sophia Wilhelmine Luise Limbach were married in 1862 in Windheim, Germany. They were the parents of eight children: Ernest Jr., Karl (Charles), William, Henry, Fred, Sophia, Marie, and Anna.

Ernest Bauermeister Family
Anna, Marie, William, Henry, Karl (Charles), Fred, Sophia, Sophia, Ernest Sr., Ernest Jr.

The first of the family to immigrate from Germany was Ernest Jr., who immigrated from Loh, Kreis-Minden, Providence of West Fahlen, Germany. He made his voyage to the port of New York, New York, on the vessel "Reihn" on or about October 3, 1880. The rest of the family members followed, with all of the family settling in Wells County except Karl, William, and Fred, who settled in the Fort Wayne area.

Ernest Jr. married Karoline Werling. Karl (Charles) married Charlotte Artman. William married Lizetta Oeting. Henry married Fredericke Breier. Fred married Anna Muller. Sophia married David Werling. Marie married Fred Graft. Anna married William Graft; after his death she married William Roembke.

NORWIN RICHARD BAUERMEISTER

Norwin R. Bauermeister is the son of Otto and Luella Bauermeister, born August 12, 1938, and twin brother of Norman Bauermeister.

He attended Bethlehem Lutheran Grade School and was a graduate of Ossian High School. In 1956 he joined the Army Reserves and completed his reserve duty. Since 1966, he has been self-employed with his brother Norman as a builder-contractor and also is engaged in farming.

He was married in 1966 to Martha (Thiele), daughter of Edward and Frieda Thiele (Sr.), and has two children. Brian Keith also attended Bethlehem Lutheran Grade School and was a Norwell High School graduate. He received a degree in Electronics Engineering from ITT Technical Institute of Fort Wayne. He is married, and with his wife, Lori, resides in Fort Wayne.

Marla is also a graduate of Norwell High School and completed her grade school education at Bethlehem Lutheran School. She is currently a freshman at Indiana University with a major in sports, marketing and management.

BAUERMEISTER-SWANK

Norman Robert (Butch) Bauermeister was born August 12, 1938, and is a twin son of Otto David Karl Bauermeister (March 17, 1897 - April 9, 1990) and Luella Glenora Young Bieberich Bauermeister (November 22, 1903).

Butch was baptized and confirmed at Bethlehem Lutheran Church, Ossian, Indiana. He attended Bethlehem Lutheran Grade School and graduated from Ossian High School in 1956. He was active in 4-H, raising rabbits and playing basketball while in high school. After graduation he joined the army reserves and was a member of the 890 Transportation Unit for six years. Butch worked for Donald Shive, Inc. as a carpenter until 1966, when he and his twin brother formed their own company, Bauermeister Builders.

On June 2, 1962 at Bethlehem Lutheran Church, Ossian, he married Joyce Ann Swank, daughter of Robert Christopher Swank (May 11, 1919) and Alma Priscilla Smith (September 1, 1923) of Allen County.

Joyce was baptized at Fairview Church of God, Yoder, Indiana, attended elementary school at Smith School and Pleasant Center School in Allen County. Joyce played with the band and graduated from Ossian High School in 1961. She was also a 10-year 4-H member. She attended Warner Beauty College and worked at General Electric and Magnavox in Fort Wayne.

Norman Bauermeister Family
Jodi, Alan Stephens, Zachary S., Brenda S. Joyce, Norman Bauermeister.

Butch and Joyce have two daughters who were both baptized and confirmed at Bethlehem Lutheran Church, Ossian.

Brenda Lee (January 4, 1964) attended Bethlehem Grade School and graduated from Norwell High School in 1982. She attended Purdue University, where she graduated with a Bachelors of Science degree in nursing in 1986. Brenda then moved to Indianapolis, where she was employed at the I.U. Medical Center, in the Transplant Unit. On October 22, 1988, she married Alan Lee Stephens (March 10, 1962), son of Cleo and Evona Montfort Stephens. Brenda and Alan now live in Elmhurst, Illinois, where Alan is in a surgical residence at Rush Presbyterian Hospital in Chicago. Brenda is a nurse for the Community Nursing Service of Loyola Hospital of Chicago. Brenda and Alan have one son, Zachary Robert (December 17, 1990).

Jodi Lynn (November 3, 1967) attended Bethlehem Lutheran Grade School and graduated from Norwell High School in 1986. Jodi then went to work for Scotts Foods in Bluffton, and later at J.C. Penny's in Southtown. In 1988 she worked at the Fort Wayne Country Club while attending I.U.P.U. campus in Fort Wayne. In 1989 Jodi transferred to Purdue campus in West Lafayette where she is currently a student. She works at the student union food service and registrar's office while working on her bachelor's degree in retail management.

Both Brenda and Jodi were 10-year 4-H members in Jefferson Township, receiving many honors in clothing and woodworking.

In 1978 Butch and his twin (Norwin) purchased the farm that was bought by their great-grandfather, Ernest Bauermeister Sr. in 1892.

Butch and Joyce built their home on a section of the farm that was platted in lots as part of the Kunkle addition of Tocsin, and was later purchased by Ernest Bauermeister, Sr., in 1898.

Butch is an active member of Bethlehem Lutheran Church. He enjoys using his woodworking skill building furniture. Joyce is a homemaker and a volunteer at Bethlehem Lutheran School as a secretary and helps in the church office.

BAUERMEISTER-YOUNG

Otto Bauermeister was the son of German immigrant, Ernest Bauermeister Jr. Otto's father came to the United States in 1881 and worked in Fort Wayne a short time before he moved to Adams County. There he worked for Bill Hilgeman for seven years and attended St. Paul's Lutheran Church at Preble, where he married his wife, Karoline Werling, on November 15, 1888. They had five children, Adolph, August, Otto, Hulda, and an infant daughter who was stillborn and buried at Bethlehem Lutheran Cemetery.

Several years after the immigration of Ernest Bauermeister Jr., Otto's grandfather, Ernest Bauermeister Sr., immigrated to the United States. On December 10, 1892, he purchased 40 acres of land from T.W. Archbold (corner of 800N and 650E). Ernest Sr. and another son, Henry, lived together and farmed the land. Henry purchased a farm on 1000N and the farm was sold to Otto's father. Otto's father farmed the land but did not live on the land for any length of time. The original barn was destroyed by fire (believed to have been set by a neighbor). The family, fearing that the house could also be destroyed, sold it to a Mr. Archbold, who moved it west three quarters of a mile on 800N. It was moved across the fields, using horses to pull the structure as it rolled upon huge logs. The move took two weeks of hard labor. This house still stands and is owned by Albert Meyer.

Otto and Luella Bauermeister 60th Anniversary November, 1989.

Otto purchased the farm in 1919, when he and a carpenter friend, George Henry travelled to Chicago and purchased from the Sears-Roebuck Catalog factory a new house and barn. Everything was pre-cut and marked and was delivered on the Erie Railroad in Tocsin. Hay wagons hauled the materials to the site (two miles north of Tocsin). barn cost a total of $1000 and the house $2,400 including all the windows and doors. These same buildings are still in use today.

In September of 1919 Otto married Alma Rutz. Otto and Alma had four children: Kurt, 1920-1920; Mildred, August 29, 1921 - May 10, 1989; Leona, 1924-1925; Halden, 1926-1927. After

Alma's death in January of 1929, Otto married Luella Young Bieberich on November 9, 1929. Luella's first husband, Edwin Bieberich, had died of a heart attack, leaving behind his wife and young daughter, Eileen (November 8, 1927). Luella is the daughter of Charles and Sophia Furhmann Young and had four siblings, Adelia, Alma, Fredrick, and Ludwig, who died as a young child. Otto and Luella together had three sons: Delbert (August 28, 1931); Norma (Butch) and Norwin, twins, born August 12, 1938.

Otto and Luella farmed and for several years and sold eggs that were shipped to New York by railroad. In 1978 the family farm was purchased by the next generation and is now owned and operated by Norman and Norwin Bauermeister.

Otto always enjoyed his kitty and visiting with friends and neighbors. Otto passed away on April 9, 1990. Luella lives in the home that she and Otto shared for 61 years. Luella is an active member of the Bethlehem Ladies Aid and makes beautiful quilts and hand work. Her family has many samples of her beautiful work to enjoy. There are five children, eleven grandchildren, and seven great-grandchildren.

FRANK BAYHA FAMILY

Frank Bayha, son of George, married Effie Stuver in 1891, moved to 914 W., Wabash were six children were born: Agnes, Charles, Mary, Paul, Ruth and Ralph.

Factory-made cigars replaced Frank's job as cigar maker, though he worked in his spare time for Herman Wiecking. He worked at the Brown chandelier factory until it closed, then at the Bay Piano Factory until his death in 1926.

In the spring of 1926, he moved to his father's house where his wife remained until 1955 when she moved to her daughter Mary's home.

Frank, a happy man, did not take life too seriously; a child at heart. There were always fireworks on the Fourth or a small sack of candy when the grocery bill was paid, no matter how short the money. He owned neither car nor carriage, but always had time for a chat or walk with family or friend.

Effie, a hard worker, popular with neighbors and friends, was always ready to help an ill neighbor or sit with a bereaved family. Her friends' visits continued when she became house bound.

The Frank Bayhas - 1906
Effie holding Ruth, Mary, Agnes holding Ralph, Charles, Frank

Agnes married young, then divorced. She became a Harvey girl in Clovis, New Mexico for two years. She then worked for Bluffton mitten factory, married and moved to Fort Wayne, where she remained until her death in 1952.

Charles left home early, moved to Pennsylvania where he married and had four children: John, Sarah, Franklin and Martha. He died in 1952.

Mary was born in 1900, educated in Bluffton Schools, a member of the Reformed Church, and a talented outgoing child. She ran errands, visited a wide circle of friends, young and old, and had enough freedom to pursue a variety of interests. She was a camp-fire girl under the instruction of Mrs. Charles Deam. Her hand sewn campfire dress is still a family heirloom.

After graduation she entered Terre Haut summer session, then taught at a one-room school that winter. She walked five miles morning and night in some of the worst weather Bluffton had for years. The next two years she taught third grade at Columbian, then married Floyd Thomas, a farmer in Union Township, Huntington County in 1921. They had five children: Floyd, Jr., Jane Anne, Dean, Bobbie and Phil. Mary had a beautiful voice, was a good homemaker and a caring farm wife and mother. She died in 1990.

Ralph was a baker. He stayed at the home his grandfather had built and died there in 1970. For a time he was a salesman for Laymens Wholesale Company, but was again working at a bakery when he died.

Ruth worked at Fort Wayne, but came to live at her sister Mary's home in 1942. Bobbie had encephalitis, which left him in a coma that lasted for twenty seven years before he died. Mary needed help as the family kept Bobbie at home for all those years. Ruth was a shy, caring person, selfless in service, a hard steady worker. She was a dear member of a close loving family and greatly missed at her death in 1972.

JOHANN GEORGE BAYHA FAMILY

Johann George Bayha's wife, Agnes, and six children arrived by covered wagon at Bluffton in 1852. He bought three lots from the Studebaker addition on Feb. 7, 1854 for $40.00. He paid $.25 a week on the mortgage. He sold the lots to the west, cut his timber and built his house in 1853. It still stands on the corner of Miller and Morgan.

George, Jr. was born in Wurtenberg, Germany in 1807. He came to America in 1832, arrived in New York, and went directly to Wheeling where he had relatives. He applied as soon as possible for naturalization papers, determined to become a good citizen. He married Agnes Hoblitizel, also from Wurtenberg, in 1832, at Pittsburgh, where their first child was born.

They returned to Wheeling, then began a slow journey across Ohio. George was tailoring from one small town to another. When they arrived in Bluffton, they knew they wanted to settle and raise their family. Four more children were born in Bluffton.

George, first tailor in Bluffton, started his own shop above where the Leader store stood on the N.W. corner of Wabash and Main. George was a quiet unassuming man, broad minded, well educated, intent on educating both boys and girls in his family. He wrote and spoke German and English, but allowed only English to be spoken in their home. He kept a journal of his travels which gave great insight into the family.

George was a draftsman and carpenter besides being a tailor. A hand carved high chair he made for his children and some tools he made are still family possessions.

Agnes was a quiet, shy woman, kept to herself, but was a good homemaker who taught her children manners.

The children were Lou, father of five, a Civil War veteran who fought all four days in the Gettysburg battles; Elizabeth died young; Lydia, an educator; Mary, wife of John Tribolet, mother of five; John moved to Kansas; Emma, wife of Jacob Omen, mother of three; Ellen, wife of Dan Tremaine; Eliza Jane (Lude) first tailoress in Bluffton; Frank, cigar maker and father of Mary Bayha Thomas.

May 1901 view of the home of Eliza Jane Bayha. Eliza on walk of brick. Nora Mapes inside fence.

Lou was a paper boy in Bluffton, then after the Civil War settled in Monongahela, Pennsylvania, a successful business man and photographer.

Lydia, a tailoress, chose instead to become an educator in Bluffton schools then California, and last in Kansas. She paid for music lessons for Mary Thomas and always encouraged her academically. Lydia was a stern, austere woman, but kind.

Lyde, small energetic, vivacious, well read, well traveled was a favorite of Mother's. She never married. She was employed as a tailoress by W.D. Mason until her death in 1926. My mother, Mary Thomas, ran errands for her from age five upwards and learned many skills from her. She was an amateur photographer, worked with and learned from friend and neighbor Ben Ashbaucher. Her home was always open to those in need and she was surrounded by friends and relatives all her life. *(Jane Anne Thomas)*

GERALD BAYLESS FAMILY

Gerald Dean Bayless (1906-) was the first child of Charles Homer Bayless (1886-1968) and Laura Ethel Hoffacker Bayless (1887-1949). He was born in Rockcreek Township, Wells County, Indiana, and graduated from Rockcreek High School.

Gerald married Iva Caroline Schwartz (1907-1967), also of Rockcreek Township, and they lived on the adjoining farm east of his parents' home on 300N. He engaged in farming with his father, Homer, and his brother, Max. Soybeans, first grown as a hay crop, became one of their cash crops. Soybean cooperative test plots with Purdue University were started in 1940 and continued until 1980.

When Gerald attended the Farmers Conference agronomy meetings held at Purdue, he became interested in producing hybrid seed corn. The first acre of hybrid seed was planted on Bayless land in 1934; six acres were planted in 1935. Gerald was one of the pioneers in the corn belt states for single cross corn and in 1940 planted his first acre of seed for commercial single cross sales. This was the beginning of the Bayless & Sons seed corn business, later known as Hybrids, Inc.

Gerald and Iva had three children: Peggy (1929-), Keith (1932-1985), and Charles Larry (1941-). As they grew old enough, they learned to walk on the stilts used for corn detasseling (their first ones were junior-sized, custom-made by 'Grandad Homer') and joined the detasseling crews. Larry frequently walked on stilts at the Bluffton Street Fair and 4-H Fair parades. All three graduated from Rockcreek High School. Keith, who completed a Purdue University short course, and Larry, a 1963 graduate of Purdue, joined the family seed business.

Peggy married Philip Costello (1929-), of Bluffton. Their sons Patrick and Kevin were born in Dayton, Ohio, graduated from high school in Appelton, Wisconsin, and from the University of Wisconsin-Madison. Their youngest son, Michael, was born in Escanaba, Michigan, graduated from Nowell High School and Purdue University. Patrick, a CPA, married Bonnie School, of Appleton. They and their children, Megan, Brent, and Kathryn, live in Appleton. Kevin, a para-legal, lives in California. Michael, an engineer, lives in Michigan. Peggy presently lives in the home place on 300N.

In 1954, Gerald and Iva moved to a newly constructed home just east of their original home, where Gerald still lives. Keith and his wife, Elizabeth Ann (Liz) Stahl (1935-), of Lancaster Township, moved into the older home. In 1970, they moved to a house south of Ossian on Highway 1. At about the same time, Keith started his own enterprise of growing seed corn for wholesale. Their children, Ann, Gay and Steve, are graduates of Norwell High School. Ann, a sales representative in California, has two sons, Caleb and Casey. Gay, a graduate of IPFW, is an interior designer. She lives in California and has a son, Seth. Steve, who continues the enterprise started by his father, married Jean Nowakowski, of Bluffton. They and their children, Brittany, Braden and Lauren, live in Union Township on 900N.

Larry married Carolyn Gearheart Hays (1943-), of Chester Township. Their home is across the road from Gerald. Their children, George Hays and Amanda (Amy) Bayless, graduated from Norwell High School. George married Tammy Hall, of Ossian. They and their sons, George, Benjamin and Andrew, live in Fort Wayne. Amy is majoring in elementary education at Butler University, Indianapolis. Larry's daughter, Lori Jo Bayless, is deceased, age four. His son, Lyle Bayless, lives in Texas.

Refer to the Homer Bayless family.

HOMER BAYLESS FAMILY

The Homer Bayless family can be traced back, on the paternal side, to James O. Bayless (1820-1890) and Harriett Bacon (1828-1872). They had a son, James Oscar Bayless (1858-1931) who came to Wells County, Indiana, from Miami County, Indiana, and married Emma Blanche Oldfather (1862-1938) of Wells County. Her lineage can be dated back to the Reverend John Philip Boehm, who is credited with the founding of the Reformed Church of America. He was first a school teacher, then later ordained as a minister in the church.

The Reverend Boehm was married to Anna M. Scherer. Their daughter, Anna Maria Boehm, married Hans Adam Mosser (1684-1770) who came to this country from the Palatinate in Germany in 1728 on the ship *James Goodwill*. They had a son Nicholas, (1738-1824) who married Catherine Ley, a daughter of Christopher Ley, who came to this country in 1732 on the ship *Loyal Judith*.

Nicholas and Catherine Mosser had a daugter, Anna Maria Mosser (1763-1835) who married John Nicholas Albert (1765-1831). Their son, David Albert, married Elizabeth Houtz (1806-1883). Their daughter, Lydia Albert (1831-1870) married Michael Oldfather (1826-1906) of Montgomery County, Ohio and they came to Wells County in 1853. Their fifth child was Emma Blanche Oldfather (1862-1938), who married James Oscar Bayless (1858-1931). The first child of Oscar and Emma Bayless was Charles Homer Bayless (1886-1968), which brings us to the subject of this article.

James Oscar Bayless, Emma Oldfather Bayless children: Homer, Ethel, Loye

Other children of Oscar and Emma Bayless were Ethel (1892-1971) and Loye Marie (1898-1985). Ethel married Ora Lamm, a prominent farmer in Rockcreek Township. Their children were Leota, Vadis, Opal Marie and Rex Lamm. Loye can be remembered as working for many years at the Uniondale Exchange Bank.

In 1886, Oscar and Emma purchased a 120-acre farm in Rockcreek Township, located across from St. Paul Lutheran Church on 300N. Much of the acreage was in timberland, which had to be cleared and burned. We understand one end of the lower floor of the bank barn was among the first in the county to be cemented and used for hog feeding. In about 1912, soybeans were planted on the farm and used for hay.

Homer Bayless (1886-1968) married Laura Ethel Hoffacker (1887-1949) a daughter of Henry and Etta Gilbert Hoffacker of Wells County. Homer had received teacher training in Angola and taught in some of the one-room schools in Rockcreek Township (Bender, Haiflich, Raber schools) before he took over farming of the home place when Oscar and Emma and their daughter, Loye, moved to Uniondale in 1915.

The children of Homer and Ethel Bayless were Gerald Dean (1906) Marjorie, deceased at age 30, Kenneth "Kay" Oscar (1909) and Max Henry (1911-1984).

Gerald married Iva C. Schwartz (1907-1967) of Wells County. Their children were Peggy (1929), Keith (1932-1985) and Charles Larry (1941).

Kay married Mary Smekens (1912) of Wells County. Their children were Betty (1930) and Sue (1936).

Max married Frances Mannix (1915) of Blackford County, Indiana. Their children were Ancil (1945) and John (1946).

KENNETH BAYLESS FAMILY

Kenneth (Kay) Oscar Bayless (1909-) was born in Rockcreek Township, the third child of Charles Homer Bayless (1886-1968) and Laura Ethel Hoffacker Bayless (1887-1949). A 1928 Rockcreek High School graduate, Kay worked at Dudlo Manufacturing in Fort Wayne, Indiana, until 1931 when he became an oil and gas distributor for Wells County Farm Bureau. His customers were small farmers with small equipment and sales ranged from five gallons kerosene to fifty gallon gasoline drums. Later on, as farms grew, storage tanks were larger. He had the first metered pump on his truck in the area. His tank carried a slogan which read, "It's Been O'Kay Since 31", until he sold his business in 1971.

Kay married Mary Smekens (1912-) in 1929, a daughter of Hubert (1881-1958) and Henrietta Smekens (1883-1959), natives of Belgium. Mary attended Bluffton High school and was employed by The Dutch Mill in Bluffton for twenty-thee years. She was an active member and Past Matron of Eastern Star, and an active volunteer for many groups.

Mary's father, Hubert, was from Brussels, and her mother, Henrietta, from Antwerp. They were married in Belgium and had two children, Henry V. Smekens (1904-50) and Victoria Smekens (1906-1989). These children remained in Belgium when their parents sailed to America in 1910 to settle in Huntington, Indiana. Hubert was a blacksmith and

Back (L to R) Will Chamberlain, Phillip Nelson, Brad Nelson, Andrew Nelson, Jana Day, Pandy Day, Scott Day, Betty Day, Marvin Day, Steve Day, Dave Seligman, Susan Day. Front (L to R) Jenny Chamberlain, Sue Nelson, Kenneth Bayless, Jill Day, Mary Bayless, Sarah Seligman, Daniel Day Seligman, Sally Day

was particularly fond of Belgian horses. While in Huntington, they had three more children: Mary (1912-), Julliette (Jolly Kelly) (1913-1985) and Clemen (Bud) Smekens (1915-). They lived in Huntington, Petroleum and Liberty Center before moving to Bluffton in 1923. Hubert's last blacksmith shop was in Rockford in the 1930's.

Kenneth and Mary Bayless

Kay and Mary's eldest daughter, Betty (1930-), married Marvin L. Day (1929-), son of Frank Day of Sebring, Florida, and Carrie Gordon Day (1900-1989). Their five children are Susan, Sally, Sarah, Scott and Steven.

Daughter Sue (1936-) married Philip E. Nelson, son of Brainard and Alta Nelson of Morristown, Indiana. Philip heads the Food Science Institute of Purdue University, Lafayette, Indiana. Sue also works at Purdue in Education. Their daughter, Jenny, a nurse, married William Chamberlain from Petoskey, Michigan. Son Andrew attends Purdue University, and youngest son, Bradley, is at West Lafayette High School, active in music and sports.

In his leisure time, Kay enjoys bowling and horseshoes. He and his brother, Max, were charter members of the local Horseshoe Club. Since retirement, Kay and Mary spent winter times in Arizona and Florida where Kay has won several horseshoe trophies. In 1985, he won first place in his class in the World Horseshoe Tournament in Lafayette, Indiana.

The Baylesses are members of the First United Church of Christ in Bluffton, and Kay has membership in three Masonic groups.

MAX BAYLESS FAMILY

Max Henry Bayless (1911-1984) was the youngest child of Charles Homer Bayless (1886-1986) and Laura Ethel Hoffacker Bayless (1887-1949). He was born in Rockcreek Township, Wells County, Indiana, and graduated from Rockcreek High School in 1930. He was a farmer except for the time he served in the infantry during World War II.

Max helped his father, Homer, and his brother, Gerald, farm what had been his grandparents', Oscar and Emma Bayless, farm until his marriage to Frances Mannix (1915). She was the only child of James and Nellie Cole Mannix from Blackford County, Indiana. She, too, was from the farm. In fact, she lived on only one farm before her marriage and continues to live on the 160 acres she and Max purchased in 1946 when they were married. It is located just inside Lancaster Township from Rockcreek Township on 200N.

Starting out on his own farm, Max raised both livestock and grain. He later sold the livestock and raised only grain. At one time, Max also produced, processed and sold popcorn, often being called the "Popcorn Man."

For a pastime, Max thoroughly enjoyed pitching horseshoes and earned several trophies. He belonged to a local club that engaged in horseshoe pitching in competition with clubs organized in surrounding counties. After retirement, he continued the sport while spending time in Arizona or Florida in winter months.

Max and Frances Bayless

Frances attended Ball State University and St. Francis College, training to be a teacher. The 1930's was not the easiest time to pursue a college degree. She taught ten years in Blackford County before her marriage, and afterwards fifteen years at Lancaster Elementary, Wells County. Since retirement, she has been involved in several volunteer services.

Max and Frances were members of the First United Church of Christ in Bluffton and participated in many of its activities.

Their oldest son, Ancil Louis Bayless (1945) married Marcella Berg, daughter of Nellie and Joseph Berg of Berrien Springs, Michigan. Ancil graduated from Lancaster High School and was in the service during the Vietnam conflict. Afterwards he attended Andrews University in Berrien Springs, Michigan. From Central YMCA College in Chicago, he received a degree in Respiratory Therapy, then an LPN degree from Sauk Valley Community College in Illinois. He and his family live in Keene, Texas, and he and Marcella work in Fort Worth, Texas. They have a son, Kristofor, seventeen, and a daughter Kristina, nine.

Their youngest son, John Allen Bayless (1946), married Diana Sue Burton, daughter of Roger and Lillian Burton of Huntington, Indiana. He too graduated from Lancaster High School. John attended Purdue University before serving in the Vietnam conflict (February 1966 - August 1968). Upon his discharge, he continued his studies, graduating from Huntington College and later earning a master's degree from Ball State University. He and his wife, Sue, live and work in Houston, Texas. (Refer to entry for Homer Bayless Family)

DOUGLAS NEIL BEATY, SR. AND EDITH GRACE (TODDIE) VAN HOOSE BEATY FAMILY HISTORY

Douglas Neil Beaty, son of Cletus Vane Beaty and Froan Paxon, raised by Floyd and Madge Huetison of Harrison Township, was born January 24, 1919, in Lomax, Indiana. Married Edith Grace (Toddie) Van Hoose May 7, 1941, in Hammond, Indiana. Died in Bluffton, Indiana February 15, 1987, and is buried at the Ossian Cemetery.

Edith Grace (Toddie) Van Hoose, daughter of

Neil, Billy, Toddie, Kevin and D.N. Jr. (Buck); picture taken January 1987.

Mack Van Hoose and May Morris, was born May 29, 1922, in East Chicago, Indiana.

Children born to this union:

Douglas Neil Beaty, Jr. (Buck) was born December 17, 1942, in East Chicago, Indiana. Married Janice Elaine Uptgraft, daughter of Weisell and Mary Uptgraft, December 22, 1963, in Petroleum, Indiana. They have two children: Dawn Rene Beaty born January 18, 1965, in Marion, Indiana. Billy May Beaty Kreigh was born July 29, 1948, in Bluffton, Indiana. Married Rex Alan Kreigh, son of J. Roger and Lucile Mackey Kreigh, January 7, 1967, in Bluffton, Indiana. They have two daughters: Regan Ann Kreigh born July 12, 1967, in Bellefonte, Pennsylvania; Erin Neille Kreigh born February 20, 1974, in Bluffton, Indiana. Kevin Mack Beaty was born April 16, 1952, in Bluffton, Indiana. Married Sara Lee Kaehr, daughter of Phil and Gloria Kaehr, August 8, 1973, in Bluffton, Indiana. They have two children: Jessica Lee Beaty born Jan. 16, 1978, in Bluffton, Indiana; Jared Neil Beaty born May 5, 1982, in Bluffton, Indiana.

JOSIAH LARIMER BECK

Josiah Larimer Beck, born on November 12, 1853, in Crawford County, Ohio, the son of Daniel and Nancy Larimer Beck, married Lydia Jane Kleinknight, born on August 14, 1855, also in Crawford County, Ohio, the daughter of Jacob and Elizabeth Miller Kleinknight. They moved to Wells County, Indiana, in 1881, to a farm one and one-half miles east and one-half mile north of the highways 1 and 224 crossroad. They had four children. Charles Sumner was born December 3, 1878; Maude was born in 1884; Laura was born in 1893; and Shannon Larimer was born on December 13, 1898.

Josiah and Larimer Beck and Lydia Jane Beck

255

Charles married Grace Inlow, who died at the age of 32. They had four children: Velma, Charles, Edith, and Carolyn, and lived in Peru, Indiana.

Maude, who died at the age of 26, married Walter Johnson. They had two children, Larimer and Elizabeth, and lived in Decatur. After Maude's death, Walter and the children moved to Findlay, Ohio.

Laura married Charles Shimer and they had three children, Alice, Lawrence, and Theo, and lived in Bluffton.

Shannon eloped with Nellie Lorinda Stogdill, born in Wells County on June 7, 1894. Following their Hillsdale, Michigan, marriage, they moved in and lived with Shannon's parents on the farm. After Grandpa Josiah's sudden death in April of 1925, Grandma Lydia continued to live with Shannon and Nellie. Lydia became an arthritic invalid, living the remainder of her days in a wheelchair and dying on August 20, 1938. Shannon and Nellie had one daughter, Mary Ellen, on December 23, 1919, who married Virgil Affolder on November 15, 1941.

Shannon and Nellie Beck

They had two sons, Steven Lynn born on February 11, 1944, and Gary Lee, born on May 26, 1949. Nellie suffered a cerebral hemorrhage and three weeks later she died on March 26, 1964.

Shannon continued to live on the farm. He would often eat at A local restaurant in Ossian where a renewed friendship with widowed Emma Grieder blossomed into romance. They were married on October 9, 1965. After many happy years together, Shannon's health began to seriously fail and he moved to the Ossian Health Care on December 27, 1989. Emma passed away on June 16, 1990, and Shannon died on December 24, 1990, having spent his entire life, except for the last year, living where he had been born.

MATTHEIS (MATTHIAS) BECK

Mattheis Beck was born in Wurtemberg, Germany, October 8, 1796. He was a farmer and his father was a furrier. He had a sister, Mary, who married Martin Heckley. Rosina Hoelle, daughter of Martin and Agnesia Stroblerin Hoelle, was born June 6, 1797. Her father was a miller. Mattheis and Rosina were married on February 3, 1819. They emigrated from Wurtemberg, circuit Sulz, Leidringen and landed in Baltimore on October 10, 1833.

Eight children were born to this union. Martin was born October 13, 1819, married Susan Price, and died April 5, 1895. Rosina was born March 30, 1821, married Conrad Glock and died April 29, 1889. Agnesia was born May 11, 1822, and died June 29, 1841. Magdelena was born January 20, 1826, and died September 30, 1826. Another Magdelena was born February 17, 1830, married Samuel Kreigh, and died November 16, 1881. Anna Marie was born June 27, 1834, married Henry Fuhrman and died August 24, 1908. Anna was born February 28, 1836, and died February 2, 1843. John Michael was born May 17, 1839, first married Mary Miller and then Melissa Bennett. He died August 9, 1907.

Mattheis was not compelled to serve in the German Army because one leg was several inches shorter than the other and he walked with a cane. He was an aristocratic looking man of some means.

The Beck family settled on a small farm outside West Newton, in Westmoreland County, Pennsylvania. This is where their last three children were born. They then went by steamboat down the Ohio and the Wabash Rivers to Fort Wayne, arriving in 1841. While living there, Agnesia, their daughter died. Her death was recorded at St. Paul's Evangelical Lutheran Church where the Beck's attended services.

While living in Fort Wayne, Mattheis purchased 240 acres of heavily timbered land in Jefferson Township, Wells County; and proceeded to clear it. On Monday he would take his gun and tools and walk out to his farm, work all week, then walk back on Saturday, a distance of 16 miles. He built a four-room log house. This home was considered a little less than a mansion. The family moved to the farm in 1841.

Their daughter Anna died at the age of seven and was buried in the front yard of the homestead. In later years she was moved to the Poe Cemetery to lie next to her parents. John Michael remained on the farm with his parents and took care of them until their deaths. Mattheis Beck died March 10, 1869 and Rosina died September 9, 1872.

Martin and Susan, who were married on September 9, 1852, continued to farm in Wells County. Their children were Samuel, Mary, John, Martin, Anna, Emma, and Llewellyn. Mary married Andrew McMillan White and John married Cora Snyder. They were the only descendants to have families. All the children are buried in either Poe or Elhanan Cemetery along with their parents. Mary died of typhoid fever stemming from a contaminated well. Her two eldest sons, Charles and Andrew, nearly died from this same disease.

At this point, the families began to leave Wells County and are now located in various places far and near.

THE BECK-SHIMER FAMILY

The Beck-Shimer family in Wells County dates back to the late 1800's. My great-grandparents Josiah and Lydia Beck and their two children, Charles and Maude, moved from Galion, Ohio. At that time they purchased a farm west of Tocsin in Jefferson Township. At the Tocsin homestead, my grandmother Laura was born in 1989, and in 1898 the youngest child, Shannon, was born.

Josiah was a farmer. Along with all the children, Laura helped on the farm and lived there until her marriage to Charles Nelson Robinson Shimer, known as Charlie, in 1909.

Charlie was the son of Obediah and Susanne Shimer. They had thirteen children: Effie, Margaret, Asa, Elmira, Verdie, Almedia, Clara, Florence, Edith, Sadie, Emma, Charles and Walter.

Obediah and his family lived northwest of Craigville. He made a living by farming and butchering. After Charlie and Laura were married, they moved down the road from Obediah. Charlie continued to help his father with the farming and butchering.

Charlie and Laura had three children: Alice in May, 1912, Lawrence in April, 1914, and Theo Marie in January, 1916. A few years after their marriage, Charles moved his family to the town of Tocsin and went to work at Preble.

In the 1920's Charlie moved his family to Bluffton where he worked at the Bay Piano Factory. He continued to work at the piano factory until right before the Depression, at which time he took a job repairing interurban tracks. In the mid-1930's, Charlie started to work as a carpenter and later went into business for himself building and remodeling homes.

Children of Laura and Charles Shimer, Alice, Lawrence, Theo, Marie

Alice Shimer graduated from Bluffton High School in 1931. She went to work at the Wells County Hospital in the kitchen as second cook in charge. In 1943, Alice went to work at Automatic Canteen Company of America in Fort Wayne. Alice then went to work in 1945 as the bookkeeper at the Hoosier Grain and Supply until 1977, when she retired. In 1963, Alice purchased a home on N. Marion Street and continues to live there. She enjoys watching the birds and squirrels that visit her yard.

Lawrence Shimer married Ruth Kershner from the Lancaster School area in 1935. They have two children: Roseanne and Ned. In 1977, Lawrence retired from NIPSCO after 25 years of service. Lawrence and Ruth continue to live in Fort Wayne. They have seven grandchildren and six great-grandchildren.

Theo Marie married Raymond "Buss" Musser in 1942. They had three children: Monty, Michael "Mick," and Rebecca "Becky".

I remember every December my parents and Aunt Alice would spend a weekend afternoon at the Hoosier Grain and Supply making evergreen grave blankets for the graves of my grandparents, who both died in 1953. While the grown-ups were busy working, I sat at my Aunt Alice's desk and played at her adding machine.

Alice Shimer and myself are the only members of the Beck-Shimer family who continue to live in Wells County, though all the rest of the family comes back home to visit with the family and friends.

GREG AND SHEILA BECKMAN

April 17, 1982, was the wedding day of Gregory B. Beckman and Sheila R. Johnson. The event took place at the Six Mile Church.

Greg was born in 1958 in Huntington County to Ronald and Charlene Beckman. After graduating

Greg and Sheila Beckman with Brian

from Huntington North High School in 1976, Greg earned his BA degree in business administration at Manchester College.

Shelia was born at the Wells Community Hospital in 1959. Her parents are Leon and Anna Johnson (see Leon Johnson history). She graduated valedictorian of her 1977 Bluffton High School class. In 1980 she graduated from IU of Fort Wayne as a dental hygienist.

Son, Brian Matthew was born December 26, 1986. Brian enjoys going to the library and attending pre-school. Rochelle Alaine was born May 9, 1991. She is busy growing.

Greg, and Sheila, Brian and Rochelle live in Fulton County.

GARY AND MARTHA BEECHER

Neither of us, Garry Beecher and Martha Tharp Beecher, are Wells County natives. We moved here in June, 1982. Something of ourselves and our background follows.

Martha is a native of Arkansas. She and her family moved to central Indiana in June, 1953. She graduated from Clinton Central High School, Michigantown, Indiana, in May 1963. She attended Frankfort Wesleyan College from 1964 to 1967 completing two and one-half years of college.

Garry was born in Decatur, Illinois, and lived in the same house all his growing-up years. He graduated from Dwight D. Eisenhower High School in June, 1966. He had pursued vocational electrical engineering. However, feeling called to ministry, he attended and graduated from Frankfort Wesleyan College in June, 1971, with an A.B. degree in Religion. In 1982 he completed his Master's degree in Ministries from Indiana Wesleyan University along with a 400 hour Unit in Chaplaincy Practicum from Fort Wayne Parkview Hospital.

Garry and Martha met at Frankfort Wesleyan College and married June 29, 1968, at Martha's home church, Kirklin Wesleyan Church. Three months later Garry became part-time minister in Martha's home church, where he served until June, 1972. They moved then to serve as full time minister to the Edgerton Wesleyan Church, Edgerton, Indiana, for eleven years. In June, 1982, they moved to Bluffton Mulberry Wesleyan Church as ministers, where they presently serve.

To this union were born two sons and one daughter: Greg Allen Beecher, born January 28, 1970, Frankfort, Indiana; Grant College Beecher, October 28, 1973, Paulding, Ohio; Melody Renee Beecher, August 19, 1975, Paulding, Ohio. Greg is currently in his third year of college at Indiana Wesleyan University pursuing a major in communications. Grant is a junior, and Melody a freshman at Bluffton High School.

Martha did child care in their home for eleven years until going back into public employment in the Wells County Department of Public Welfare October 31, 1988, as a clerk-typist.

Garry and Martha Beecher, Greg, Grant, and Melody

Garry's parents are Howard Beecher, Jr. and Beulah Callaway Beecher, and they still live in the same home Garry was reared in and which is located in Decatur, Illinois. His father is a welder retired from Caterpillar and his mother is a life-long homemaker. Garry has one brother who is a minister in Corydon, Indiana. Both his grandfathers were ministers. His family tree carries records back to lineage with the renowned Reverend Lyman Beecher, Reverend Henry Ward Beecher and Harriet Beecher Stowe.

Martha is child number eight of ten children. The youngest is the only one deceased. He was a Military Police killed during the Vietnam War. Both her parents are living in Kirklin, Indiana. Her father, James W. Tharp, Sr. is retired from self-employment. Her mother is a life-long homemaker. Her living siblings are residents of Indiana (six), Montana (one), and Missouri (two).

We enjoy living in Bluffton, Indiana. It has deep sense of community commitment and strong morals, to which we give strong allegiance. Thank you for making this community a welcoming place to live.

BENDER

The Wells County history of this particular line of the Bender name began in 1850 when John Bender and his wife Barbara (Mast) moved from their native Lebanon Colunty, Pennsylvania. John's father had the same name and was also born there. The couple first moved to Bluffton (only six months), then to farming locations in Rockcreek Township. The first farm was near Rockford. The second farm located near St. Paul's Church became known as the Bender Farm. John and Barbara retired to South Street in Bluffton just two years before his death but Barbara remained there about twenty-five years prior to her death.

Barbara was the mother of eleven children and at her death in 1902 five were still living. John Henry was the oldest of these five and lived on the Bender Farm. The remaining children, Mrs. William Susan Miller, W.P. (Will), Sam, and Jonathan also lived in Wells County.

As a boy John Henry helped his father clear the land known as the Bender Farm which, was purchased in 1852. He was educated in the local school of that neighborhood which became known as the Pennsylvania settlement of Rockcreek Township. Upon returning home after three years in the Civil War, John Henry engaged in the threshing business while cutting wood and husking corn during the winter.

John Henry married Eliza Raver in 1870. They resided on her parents Wells County farm. In 1881, John and Eliza purchased the Bender Farm and moved there. This couple's children included: Mrs. William (Cora Elen) Hefflefinger, John Daniel, William Henry, Della Jane, Louis Nelson, Charles Wilson, an unnamed infant, Mrs. Oliver (Ada Azora) Eichorn, Mrs. Jim (Barbara Nettie) Wilson, and Mrs. Claude (Maude Edna) Brickley.

John Henry's eldest son, John Daniel, was the fourth successive generation to be named John. John Daniel did not survive childhood. The next child, William Henry, was the first to carry on the Bender name from this linage. A later son, Louis, did again cary on the name John to his son.

Elva Gardenour, in 1897, became the bride of William Henry. Their first child named Velma L. was killed in Uniondale on July 22, 1899, at the age of one and one-half years. She was killed when she wandered into the path of a train. The engineer, seeing the child but unable to stop the train, had climbed to the front of the locomotive in an unsuccessful attempt to knock the young child off the tracks. Later children of the family included: Mrs. Albert (Juanita Irene) Spice, Fredrick Adonis who never married, Malcolm Dean who married Grace Eldeva Wamsley David, and Merline Keith, also known as Buzzy, who married Alice Elene Martin.

Both Malcolm and Buzzy have continued the Bender name through male children.

BENDER-BRADBURN

Paul L. Bender (1918) and Maro L. Bradburn (1920) celebrated their golden wedding anniversary this year (1991). They were married in West Lafayette, Indiana on April 6, 1941.

Maro is the daughter of Clifford R. Bradburn (1895-1973) and Gladys Terhune (1899-1969). Born at Barbers Mill (now Rockford) Indiana, she graduated Valedictorian of the 1938 class at P.A. Allen High School. After graduation, Maro was secretary at the Morris Company, Bluffton, until her marriage. Later she retired as secretary at National Oil and Gas, Inc., Bluffton.

Formerly active in Psi Iota Xi Sorority (Pres. 1958-59) and Bay View Literary Club, she has assisted in community projects. She is a member of First United Methodist Church, serving as a church trustee, administrative council member, and currently membership secretary.

Paul and Maro Bender

Paul is the son of Lawrence L. Bender (1883-1981) and Elizabeth A. Reiff (1884-1951). Born in Bluffton, he graduated from P.A. Allen High School in 1935 and Purdue University in 1939. He was an engineer and assistant production manager with Goodman Mfg. Co., Chicago, a heavy machinery manufacturer, until 1947, when they returned to

Bluffton to associate as partner in L.L. Bender & Co. In 1953 he entered the health care field with Wells County Hospital (later Wells Community Hospital). Serving as its Administrator, he retired in 1987.

Community service includes City Plan Commission (Secr. 1951-55); Mental Health Assn.; United Fund; Anthony Wayne Council Boys Scouts (Executive Board 1962-), (Silver Beaver Award 1966); Elm Grove Cemetery Assn., (Trustee 1951-); Allen-Wells Chapter Red Cross Board, Regional Blood Services (Vice-chairman 1986-), (Clara Barton Award 1987); Wells County Historical Society (Pres. 1966-70, 1989-91); Bluffton Lions Club (Pres. 1954); Elks Lodge. Professional organizations include American Institute of Electrical & Electronic Engineers, American Academy of Medical Administrators, Indiana Hospital Assn; former director Midwest Health Net. Biography included in *Indiana Lives* and several editions of *Who's Who,* Midwest.

In 1971, Bender received the Wells County Community Service Awards, and in 1987 was named a Sagamore of the Wabash.

He is a member of the First United Methodist Church, serving as trustee 1956-58 and Chairman of the Administrative Board 1982-84

Maro and Paul Bender have two children, Paul Lee, Jr. (1946), and Linda Maro (1947). Lee is an engineering graduate of Purdue, where he is a member of the administrative staff at the West Lafayette campus. His first marriage was to Cheryl Erwin and they have a daughter Elizabeth Maro Bender (1978). A second marriage (1985) is to Connie (VanEmon) Prichard who had two children, Jeremy and Jennifer Prichard. Daughter Linda is married (1973) to Carl M. Heuer. They live in Fort Wayne. Linda attended Ball State and Purdue and is a laboratory technician and the Red Cross Blood Services; Carl, a Purdue graduate, is a registered pharmacist with Walgreens in Fort Wayne.

BENDER-CHRISTMAN

V.O. (Vergie) Bender, born November 6, 1885, died May 5, 1975, was born to Jonathan and Amanda Staver Bender of Rockcreek Township. V.O. married Nov. 24, 1906, Jennie Christman, born July 27, 1886, died May 19, 1955, daughter of George and Mary Alice (Masterson) Christman. V.O. farmed and built their home on the George Christman Farm four miles west of Bluffton in Liberty Township. Four children were born to V.O. and Jennie: Verl, who married Marie Leffel Werner, Whitley County, deceased; Vera, who married Elroy Watson, living near Poneto and had one child, Patricia (Dyson); Marjorie, who married Willis Souder, had one son, Bill, and resided in DeKalb County; Maryalis, who married (Paul Stout). They are life long residents of Harrison Township.

Other children of Jonathan and Amanda Bender: Bessie, who married Frank Haflick; Advanti; Lawrence L. who married Lizzie Reiff; and Valley, who married Rea Renwick. Valley lived at LaGrange Merry Manor after living her married life at White Pigeon, Michigan and died in 1991; Lilah, who married Galen Gray; Winnifred, who married John Graham, Cario, in Richmond. All except Valley and Cario remained Wells County residents.

Jonathan, born in 1854, died in 1915, was the son of John, born in 1807 in Berks County, Pennsylvania, died in 1879 in Wells County, Indiana, and Barbara (Mast), born in 1815 in Berks County, Pennsylvania, died in 1902, in Wells County. Burial at St. Paul's, Rockcreek Township. Other related families: Yoder, Staehle or Stehly.

Amanda Staver's family came to Wells County from Montgomery County, Ohio. Jonathan married Sarah Rhoads. After her death he married Minerva Hoops. Amanda was one of eight known children: Lydia who married Isaih Langle; Mary, who married Jacob Wolfgang; Sarah, who married Jim Lesh; Eliza Jane, who married Allen Oldfather; Susannah E., who married Lemuel Miller; Samatha E., who married Phillip Eichhorn; John H., who married Barbara Miller. David, a nephew, was raised by Jonathan. Other related families: Swatzell, Dupes, Merkling, Sheets, Martin, Evans, Worrilaw, Perkes, Calvery, Harrison, Stainhouse.

V.O. (Vergie) & Jennie (Christman) Bender, Vera (Watson), Verl, Mary Alice (Stout) and Marjorie (Souder) about 1925.

Peter Christman, born in 1794 in Germany, died in 1876, in Huntington County, and Elizabeth (Wirth) Christman came to America in the 1840's and settled in Huntington County. Son Frederick, born in 1828 in Germany, died in 1897 in Wells County, married Catherine (Grossman) in Wabash County, came to Bluffton about 1856. He operated a bakery with son Frank, in the Christman Block across from the Community Building. A son, John, died young. Frederick bought a 120-acre farm (Christman Farm) for son, George. George (1862-1942) and Mary Alice (Masterson) (1863-1933), daughter of William Henry and Maria Perrin (Rockwell) Masterson were the parents of five daughters: Maude (1884-1958), Jennie (V.O. Bender) (1886-1955), Hazel (1888-1966), Morna (1891-1896), Chloe (1893-1946). Other related families: Miller, Studebaker, Whitehead, Weisskopft, Aschauer, Raw, Bick.

More family history refer to Wells County Library Genealogy.

FAMILY TREE - Roots-Branches-Twigs by Patricia (Watson) Dyson.

GEORGIANA BENDER

Georgiana Bender (1908) is the daughter of Lawrence L. Bender (1883-1981) and Elizabeth A. Reiff (1884-1951). She was enrolled at the Columbian School for one semester each of the first and second grades. After the third and fourth grades at Columbian, she went to Central School, where she graduated from the eighth grade, as was the custom at that time. She graduated from the Bluffton High School in 1925.

Miss Bender enrolled at Madam Blakers, Indianapolis, a private school for girls who wished to become teachers. Graduation here in 1927 gave her a teaching license. At that time there was a teacher surplus, and one year was spent as a substitute teacher. The following year she was hired to teach third grade of 36 students at the Columbian School at a salary of $90 per month. Here were grades one through four, with Sarah Markley, principal.

Georgiana Bender

In 1931 she transferred to the Park School, teaching third grade. Again, the Park School had four grades, with Lillian Roush as principal. During summer vacations, Miss Bender attended Butler University, receiving a bachelor of science degree in education in 1946. She continued her post-graduate studies at Indiana University, receiving a master's degree, and a lifetime elementary, elementary supervisor, and principal's license in 1956. She served as principal while teaching fourth grade at Park until her retirement in 1972.

The two-story Park School building, built in 1882, was razed in 1936 and the present building built at that time, at a cost of $38,000. The building now houses the superintendent and administrative offices of the Bluffton-Harrison School System.

Miss Bender was honored by the Park P.T.A., who presented her with a lifetime membership in 1965. She has been an active member of the Tri Kappa Sorority and the Delta Kappa Gamma Society International.

BENDER-REIFF

Lawrence L. Bender, son of Jonathan Bender (1854-1915) and Amanda Staver (1859-1942) was born November 21, 1883, in Harrison Township, Wells County. He married Elizabeth Alice Reiff, daughter of George L. Reiff (1856-1940) and Rose Bay (1864-1935), who was born June 9, 1884, in Liberty Township, Wells County, on November 22, 1903.

Lawrence and Elizabeth Bender

Their two children are Georgiana Bender, born February 22, 1908, and Paul L. Bender, born March 5, 1918. Paul married Maro L. Bradburn April 6, 1941.

Lawrence Bender operated a business under his name, L.L. Bender, from 1913 until his death in 1981. His wife, Elizabeth, died on January 1, 1951.

BENNETT

There was a small house in Chester Township across the road from the Salamonie River that was called "The River Edge Stock Farm" in which Larry Arment Bennett and Ruth Mable Thomas took up housekeeping. Seven girls and two boys were born to this union: Thelma Irene, Garnet Viola, Florence Leone, Verla Mae who died at birth, Marjorie Rose, Evelyn Ilene who was just few days old when she passed away, and Crystal Avis, and two sons, John Edward and Charles William. My father was born October 27, 1887, and passed away on September 22, 1966, at the age of 78.

Grandfather John A. Bennett was born November 4, 1856, in Chester Township in Wells County and passed away in 1926. He married Francis Rose Miller who was born August 6, 1864, and passed away in 1944. They were married October 28, 1883, in Wells County.

L to R: Crystal Bailey, Charles Bennett, John Bennett, Florence Penrod, Garnet Conner - 1989

My mother was a Thomas, and was born May 23, 1893, and passed away May 17, 1952. Her mother was Marjorie Thomas Crosby, died July 4, 1961, and was born in 1872.

My father Larry Arment Bennett was a farmer who drove a stock truck and dealt in livestock, etc.

I (Florence Penrod) spent my first school years in a one-room school called Noe School in Chester Township in Wells County. There were no buses, so we rode to school in a Model T Ford with side curtains and Lyman Zehner was the driver. My other years, I attended the Chester Center School and the Chester Center Christian Church beside it and graduated in 1936. At first we rode in a horse hack pulled by horses and then a school hack. I retired after almost 18 years at CTS plant in Berne, Indiana.

I married George W. Penrod, a farmer, and we have two sons, George Allan, a factory worker at Dana, and Paul Edward, a factory worker at Franklin Electric, and a daughter, Rebecca Ruth, a factory worker in Fort Wayne. We have six grandchildren: Ruth Elaine Boice, Ronda Lee Mathews, Mark Allan and Jon Michael, Jeremy and Kyle Penrod; and three great-granddaughters: Saran Christine, Carrie Elizabeth Penrod, and Kayle Nicole Boice.

I am an active member of the Chester Center Christian Church of Wells County. I have been privileged to hold different offices in the church. I enjoy crafts, reading and several hobbies. *(Florence L. Penrod)*

SYLVAN AND ALICE BERTSCH

Sylvan and Alice Bertsch are celebrating forty years of being downtown merchants in Bluffton as Bertsch Jewelry Store. For twenty years the store was located at 119 South Johnson Street. When Kenneth Green retired in 1971 we purchased Green's Jewelry Store and moved to our present location at the northwest corner of Market and Johnson Streets. This building has been a jewelry store since it was built in 1892. It began as E.E. Mosiman and Son, then became George Mosiman Jewelry, Mosiman and Green Jewelers, Green's Jewelry Store and Bertsch Jewelry. In the present building and ninety-nine years there have been only four proprietors. Built during the same period as the courthouse it has always been retained in the original style.

Sylvan Bertsch was born in Adams County. His father was a farmer at the time, but soon sold his farm and took his young family to Elgin, Illinois, where he was in charge of the crystal fitting for Elgin National Watch Company. Sylvan entered the jewelry business by going to Elgin Watch College. Then during World War II, he served in the U.S. Navy. He returned to Elgin Watch College and on becoming a watchmaker he worked for the Elgin Watch Company. In 1947 he returned to Bluffton to work for Mosiman and Green Jewelers. In 1944 he met and married a local girl (myself), Alice A. Arnold.

My family goes back to 1837, when Jacob Miller moved to Wells County as one of the earliest settlers. Also, Rev. Elijah Sutton, who preached the first sermon in Wells County was a great grandfather, as was George F. Burgan another early settler, Charles M. Miller, my grandfather, was the County Auditor when the courthouse was built and his name is on the cornerstone. My father, Cleo B. Arnold and my mother, Edith Miller Arnold each served several terms as City Clerk-Treasurer's of Bluffton, my father from 1936 to 1946, and my mother from 1946 to 1956.

Grandpa Miller built a home at 403 W. South Street in 1891 where they raised three children and two orphans. We moved into the house when we were young and my grandparents were elderly; so my two sisters and I were raised there also. Marjorie Carol Arnold and Edith Charlene Arnold were my sisters. They both graduated from high school here and after leaving for a while to attended college, they lived here for several years before moving away with their families.

We raised four children in Bluffton. Three daughters are married and living on the east coast in New Jersey and Connecticut. Our son and his wife live in Fort Wayne where he is an optometrist.

Four generations of our family have been members of the First United Methodist Church here. The churches, schools and library have always been important to this family. We are proud to see a new library being built for the future generations of this community. *(Alice Bertsch)*

BENEDICT AND ROSANNA RITTER BIBERSTEIN

Benedict Biberstein was born on December 18, 1795, in Bozingen near Biel, Switzerland. He married and had two children while living in Bozingen; however, both his wife and children died. Then Benedict married Rosanna Ritter in Wyttenbach, Switzerland, on June 1, 1826. While living in Switzerland, Benedict and Rosanna had five children: Jacob, Julia, Alexander, Ferdinand, and Rosanna.

In 1833 Benedict left his wife and small children in Switzerland and sailed for America to locate suitable land for purchase. He came to Wayne County, Ohio, which had become the home of a great many Swiss immigrants. He bought a piece of land in Paint Township, south of Mount Eaton. Benedict then returned to his native land and brought back his wife and four children. One child, Alexander had died four years earlier.

The Benedict Biberstein Family after his death. Back row: (left to right) Maria Louise (Mrs. Jacob Flora), Ferdinand, Emanuel and Phillip. Middle row: Rosanna (Mrs. Benedict Biberstein), Julia (Mrs. Jacob Wetter), Maria Susannah (Mrs. John Graber), and William. Front row: Lena (Mrs. Michael Henneford) and Rosanna (Mrs. Frederick Engeler)

Soon after Benedict's family settled on the land he had purchased in Wayne County, tragedy struck. Benedict and Rosanna's two youngest children, Ferdinand and Rosanna, died on the same day - September 10, 1834. This misfortune was lessened somewhat for Benedict and Rosanna when Rosanna gave birth to their sixth child, John Ferdinand (who was known as Ferd) on December 28, 1834.

Ten more children were born to Benedict and Rosanna while they were living in Wayne County. Their names are Alexander Martin, twins Rosanna Lena and Frederick, David, Maria Susannah, Maria Louise, Emanuel, William, Lena and Philip. One of the twins, Frederick, died when he was three days old and David died at the age of twenty-one in 1862 while serving his country during the Civil War. Alexander died at the age of twenty-three and Philip died a few weeks before his twenty-fifth birthday. The other children lived to a good age.

Benedict was a member of the German Reformed Church, in which faith he died. He was known as an active and energetic man of sterling honesty and had acquired a splendid reputation because of his many fine qualities.

Benedict is buried in Wayne County, Ohio. His surviving children all came to the Vera Cruz community in Wells County at different times.

Finally his widow, Rosanna, came to Vera Cruz with her youngest children who were still living at home. The 1870 census reveals that sixty-four year old Rosanna, who listed her occupation as "keeping house," was living with eighteen year old Lena and sixteen year old Philip.

Rosanna Ritter Biberstein died five years after this census was taken. She was buried in Vera Cruz Cemetery.

BIBERSTINE-HUNNICUTT

Roy and Ethel Leona (Hunnicutt) Biberstine were married June 19, 1920, at Six Mile Christian Parsonage (corner of 116 and Stogdill Road) by the Rev. W.D. Samuel. They moved into the Harman home on Dustman Road. They raised four children: Jogene, Betty Eileen, Doris Marie and V. Ted. They lived at 909 S. Main with Ethel's folks for a time; in 1929 they moved from 1125 S. Main to a home one mile south on State Road 1. Gravel from the property was sold to help pay for the big brick house and 40 acres of land.

Roy Biberstine and Ethel Leona Hunnicutt Biberstine

Roy, son of Frank and Nettie (Durr), with his brother Ralph, was raised on a farm on East Dustman Road, which was, over the years, also home to Ralph and his wife Elizabeth (Drewett), Don, Betty, Linda and Tom Sturgis, Ted and Phyllis Biberstine and family, Kenny, Marie (Murry), and Becky Gilliom, and Tim and Jean Biberstine. The property was sold in the 1970's to the Troxels.

Ethel, daughter of Ullysess and Delilah (Freel) lived on a farm west and north of Poneto with three sisters, Mary, Delcie, and Nellie and six brothers: Freddie (died age 9), Frank, Edson, Earl, Frank and Hugh. Her father moved houses. In 1915 the family moved to 909 S. Main.

Roy graduated from P.A. Allen High School in 1911. He joined the army February 8, 1918, and served overseas as a corporal in Co. F 49th Infantry. He was a registered professional engineer, a Wells County deputy, and later county surveyor (1923-1933); engineer for State Conservations Department (1940-1941), and Division Engineer in Fort Wayne District of State Highway Department (1941-1943). He was commissioned as Bluffton postmaster on December 21, 1942, by Franklin D. Roosevelt and assumed these duties February 1, 1943. He was a partner with Walter W. Heller in Bluffton Ready Mix and a partner with Lester Baker, St. Joe, Indiana, in Baker Road Co. Roy was a gentleman farmer; his wife, children, Bob Groh, and Kenny Gilliom tended the animals and farmed the land. Roy was especially proud of his herd of Registered Brown Swiss. He also enjoyed politics and was a member of Indiana Society of Professional Engineers, Kiwanis, Masons, Scottish Rite and Mizpah Shrine. He died August 27, 1966.

Roy Biberstine Farm

Ethel was a homemaker who tended to her home and to family and friends alike. She love to play the piano and was especially talented. If she heard a song, she could play it. She enjoyed her Home Forum Home Ec. Club and Delta Theta Tau Sorority and Eastern Star. Their friends, and their children's friends, still have fond memories of times spent in Roy and Ethel's home, barn, and land around the pits. After Ethel's death on January 4, 1986, her home and 40 acres were sold to Wendell B. King. Forty acres south of Beacon Road were sold to Richard A. Lockwood.

Jogene married Romanell (Reid), lives in La Porte, and has three children and five grandchildren. Betty (Sturgis) married Gene Kain (died 1986). She lives in Bluffton and has four children, two stepsons, and fourteen grandchildren. Doris married Forrest M. Woodward; they live in Kalamazoo, Michigan, and have four daughters and nine grandchildren. Ted married Phyllis (Jensen); they live in Bluffton and have five children and nine grandchildren.

LLOYD BIBERSTINE

The history of the Biberstine family starts in Bozingen which is now a part of Biel, Switzerland. Biberstine in Swiss comes from Biber meaning beaver and Stein meaning stone. Biberstine towns are in Switzerland, Austria and Germany.

Benedict Jr., born December 18, 1795, near Biel, married Rosanna Ritter, June 1, 1826. In 1834 they landed in New York before migrating to Mt. Eaton, Ohio and later to Vera Cruz, Indiana.

Emanuel, their son, married Albertine Bovine on April 20, 1869. Nine children Laura, Frank, Fred, Albert, Charles, Ida, Rose, William, and Chester were born.

William, born January 4, 1889, married Nora Pace, daughter of William and Mary Jane Stine Pace, on May 2, 1908. Two children, Lloyd, April 29, 1918, and Joan, October 12, 1925, were born.

William, a farmer in Harrison Township, died on May 9, 1960. Nora, born August 19, 1891, in Nottingham Township died January 1, 1980.

Lloyd, a 1939 Ball State graduate, began teaching at Rockcreek High School. May 2, 1940, he married Marcile Platt, born June 16, 1918. Two years later, April 7, 1942, twins, Richard Wayne and Barbara Kay, were born. On October 8, 1943, Judith Ann was born.

A move back to Wells County, purchase of a farm, and teaching at Liberty Center came next. October 16, 1946, Becky Jo was born.

Lloyd's teaching expanded to a principalship and superintendency of Southern Wells, while Marcile was busy taking care of their family.

Another child, William Lloyd, was born on April 2, 1954. The children's time was spent in school activities, helping farm, 4-H, Little League, and church activities. The entire family was active in the Six Mile Church.

May of 1960 became graduation time from Ball State for the twins, with teaching degrees. Richard has taught a sixth grade in the Bluffton-Harrison system since then. On June 12, 1965, he married Judith Morris, born February 17, 1942, a Huntington College graduate. Their family consists of Lisa, born January 19, 1971, Steven Wayne, born September 18, 1972, and Amy, born May 16, 1976.

Barbara Kay married Lynn Burroughs, born February 27, 1942, on March 21, 1964. They spent three years with the Air Force in Germany before returning home for the birth of Douglas Lynn on January 3, 1969. Tanya Michele was born on May 20, 1971.

Judith Ann, who has taught since 1964, was married June 14, 1964 to Michael Haley. Jeffrey Lynn was born on April 11, 1969. A second marriage on July 11, 1976 was to Roger Summers, born February 14, 1948. Megan Marie was born on October 8, 1977, and Joshua Craig on May 5, 1979.

Becky Jo taught at the Ossian School before marrying Robert Gibson, born June 4, 1944, on December 22, 1968. Children were Todd Alan, born August 20, 1971, Brian Wayne, born August 6, 1974, and Tricia Renee, born September 11, 1976.

William Lloyd married Renee Rachelle Frauhiger, born November 30, 1955, on September 28, 1974. Michelle Renee was born November 22, 1975.

JOHN BIDDLE FAMILY

John Biddle, a farmer, was born Nov. 1, 1799 in Pennsylvania. He married Susannah Bevington,

Biberstine Family
Seated: Richard Biberstine, Barbara Burroughs, Judy Summers, Lloyd Biberstine, Marcile Biberstine, Becky Gibson, William Biberstine. Middle row: Judy Biberstine Lynn Burroughs, Tanya Burroughs, Joshua Summers, Megan Summers, Tricia Gibson. Back row: Lisa Biberstine, Amy Biberstine, Steve Biberstine, Douglas Burroughs, Roger Summers, Jeff Haley, Rodd Gibson, Brian Gibson, Robert Gibson, Michelle Biberstine, Renee Biberstine

September 9, 1831 in Wayne County, Ohio. She was born June 3, 1809 in Pennsylvania. They came to Wells County sometime between 1853 and 1858., They owned NE 1/4 Sec 7 Township 28 Range 13, 160 acres.

He died June 7, 1862, and she died October 3, 1892. They are buried in Old Uniontown Cemetery near Zanesville. The cemetery was fenced to keep out the farmer's animals, but has had no other upkeep for years. It is in sad shape. To view the graves, one must climb a barbed wire fence and use cutters to clear the growth.

According to census records, John and Susannah had at least eight children. See Jacob Johnson entry for Elizabeth, the oldest child.

Alexander, born c1835 in Ohio, married first, Sarah Confer, second Sarah Gardner, January 20, 1868, third, Rebecca Nelson, February 25, 1869. Children: John, born c1859; Nelson born May 13, 1869, died November 7, 1951, married Alice Gibson; and another son and daughter.

Henry, born c1837, Ohio, died c1902, married Mary Peck, March 3, 1863. Rachel, born c1841, married Mathias Clark, June 13, 1858. Angeline, born c1844, Ohio, married John Todd, March 11, 1862. Mary born c1854, died October 10, 1863 and is buried in Old Uniontown Cemetery. Jacob, born c1849.

John, born October 1853, Ohio, died April 6, 1909, married Sarah Nelson, born 1855, died 1913. Children: Victor, born 1889 and James, born 1893, and according to census, at least four others.

John Biddle's great-grandfather, Andreas Bittle, came to American on the ship *Phoenix*, November 2, 1752. Andreas' son, Andrew, married Christina Cover, daughter of Daniel and Maria Kober. The Kober and Bittle families were charter members of the Reformed Church near Westminster, Maryland.

Andrew was a wagonmaster, carrying supplies during the Revolutionary War. Andrew and Christina lived in Frederick County, Maryland until about 1796, when he and his family moved to Woodford Township, Bedford-Huntington County border, Pennsylvania. After his death in 1812, his son Jacob (born c1770, died c1851, married Rachel Todd), and joined his brother-in-law Samuel Todd in Beaver County, Pennsylvania.

Rachel Todd's ancestors include the Todds, Warfields, and Pierpoints of Anne Arundel County, Maryland. The Todds came from England in 1651 and were the original patentees of land on which Annapolis was surveyed.

Jacob and Rachel migrated to Wayne County, Ohio by 1828. Here they joined other grandchildren of the Kober/Cover family.

John Biddle and Susannah Bevington were in Saltcreek Township, Wayne County, Ohio during the 1850 census. He is listed on the census as a minister. One source states that John's father had three sons who were ministers of the United Brethren Church.

John died within nine years after he came to Indiana. No record has been found concerning John serving as a minister in Indiana, but John and Susannah's Christian influence has extended to present day generations. Oh, how sweet the reunion will be one day!

BLACK

In 1856, Sarah and Demonthese Black homesteaded a home just one half mile east of Uniondale, Indiana. They had a son, George, who married Laura Lipkey and they built a home in Uniondale, which is still there across from the depot.

In 1817, William Herbert was born; Carrie was born next and she married Mr. McCague; they had two boys and one girl who all moved to Fort Wayne. Another daughter, Minnie, married Mr. Sonners, and they had three children and lived in rural Fort Wayne. Another daughter was born named Laura who lived in Fort Wayne but never married.

William Herbert married Rose Ellen Nicholson; they built a home in Uniondale and lived there all their lives. They had six children; Inez died at birth; Kenneth died at eight years old; Charles died at two years old; Cecile married Ed Gemmer from Columbia City and had one child, Maurine. Maurine married Jack Vetter from Fort Wayne and they moved to Houston, Texas. They have three children, Lynn Ann, Larry, and Sandra, who all live in Texas. Cecile's second marriage was to Charles Oglesby of Urbanna, Indiana, where they lived. Evah married Earl Green from Convoy, Ohio, and they had one child, Bonnie. Bonnie married David Caston of Decatur, Indiana, and they have two children, Marnie and Chris, and live in Decatur. Evah later married Abe Young of Bluffton.

Herbert W. Black married Martha Travis from Bluffton in 1928 and lived in Uniondale. He had a barber shop for many years, then he was head orderly at Caylor-Nickel Clinic. He died in 1969; Martha then married Lorin Mann Sr. in 1971. He was from Reading, Pennsylvania, and he died in 1982.

Herbert and Martha had three children: Carol Deane, who married Stanley Hoffacker of Liberty Center. They have four children: Candace L. who lives in Uniondale, Stacy Lee who lives in Indianapolis, Steven who lives in Indianapolis, Scott who married Sarah Noble of Carmel, Indiana, and lives in rural Leesburg, Indiana.

Adrienne married Doyt Davies and lives in Fort Wayne. They have one daughter Robin, living in Fort Wayne.

Michael Travis married Ruth Grave of Hilliard, Ohio, and they have three children: Angela, Tonya and Wendy. Michael married Daphne Johnslow and they live at North Webster, Indiana.

In 1903, William H. Black became the rural letter carrier of Uniondale in which position he served until 1933. He first delivered mail by horseback, then by horse and buggy, then by motorcycle, and finally the car. In appreciation, the patrons gave him meat and fresh produce.

Before he retired he was elected President of the Rural Letters Carrier Association of Indiana, which was a real honor. After retirement he had his own printing shop. Down through the years he was faithful to the Lutheran Church. The town had their own band and he played the trombone for a concert once a week.

His entire life he was a Republican, serving as precinct committeeman. After his death in 1948, his son Herbert was elected to that job until he died in 1969. His daughter, Carol Hoffacker, served in that capacity and is also chairman of the Republican Party in Wells County.

The Black name has deep roots over several generations in the town of Uniondale, Indiana.

LELA BLAIR-HOLLOWAY

In the Traditions Restaurant at Bluffton, Indiana, hangs a picture of the 1914 girls' basketball team of Petroleum High School. Mother, Carrie Eva Blocker Blair, is one of them. She graduated from Petroleum High School, then earned her teacher's license from Muncie Normal. She married John Oscar Blair. They lived at a farm east of what is now Franklin Electric, on the south edge of Bluffton. In 1915, Lela Marie Blair/Holloway was born here. Her father, John Blair, farmed and did "teaming," hauling stone and gravel with horses to help build county roads. After farming a few years, they moved to Petroleum and her father worked at H.C. Bay Piano Factory. Came the Great Depression, the factory closed and John Blair became custodian of Petroleum Consolidated School for almost twenty years. They belonged to Petroleum United Brethren Church. Mother, Carrie, was a Sunday School teacher and played the piano. She also sang in the Wells County Chorus and did volunteer work.

Lela's paternal grandparents were George M. (1861-1923) and Hannah E. (1862-1947) Holloway Blair, of Quaker lineage. They lived on their farm southeast of Petroleum, near the Coon Grade School. The family attended this school and a church north of Coon School. Lela's father, John had a sister, Estelle (Egly), and two brothers, Walter and Raymond. Lela's mother-in-law, Jennie Kirkwood Holloway, had been one of Lela's father's teachers at Coon School.

John O. Blair was united in marriage to Carrie E. Blocker on February 13, 1915 in Bluffton, Indiana.

Lela's maternal grandparents were George W. (1866-1942) and Dequestney (Cassie) (1871-1948) Williams Blocker. George W. was of Swiss descent. It is said that Grandmother Cassie had Indian heritage, though of Quaker descent. They had met at a singing school, a popular gathering place of young folk. They lived on the Blocker homestead, north of Domestic, which dated back to 1874. As they raised their six boys and two girls, they were devout Christians with a family altar, where each morning there was Bible reading and prayers. Acquaintances called them the "A, B, C's", as there were Alvin, Belvin, Carrie, then, Erma, Harold, Ervin, Sterling and Russell.

Lela's sister, Mary Louise, who attended Ball State Teachers College with Lela, became a teacher at Petroleum, and Lela in Lancaster Township in Wells County. Mary married George Muskoff, a pharmacist, and became a druggist's wife with three children in Navarre, Ohio.

Lela's brother, John Jr., a Petroleum High School basketball star, married Wanda Murray. He, a World War II veteran, attended Ball State, remained in Muncie, where he went into business. They raised three children.

Lela's brother, Carl, a Korean War veteran, graduated from Petroleum High School, married Lucille Ivins and remained in Nottingham Township, where they raised five children. Carl is employed at Franklin Electric.

Lela married John H. Holloway, (of

Episcopalian lineage), second son of Lee and Jennie Kirkwood Holloway, also a graduate of Petroleum High School who played on the basketball team. She went to Ft. Wayne as a bride in 1939. They raised four children. John retired from General Electric after thirty-four years. They had been married almost forty-seven years when John died in 1986. Lela spends her days doing volunteer work for South Wayne United Methodist Church, Rescue Mission, Allen County Cancer Society, singing with Southmoor Singers, playing the piano and enjoying thirteen grandchildren and a great-grandfather.

BLOXSOME-HEATH

We can date the Bloxsome family back the 1750 when our great-great-great-great-grandparents, Richard Bloxsome of Dundee, Scotland, and Anna, a native of Virginia, settled in Louisa County, Virginia. On a visit to the county seat there, we found many records stored in an old shoe box pertaining to the deeds and other legal matters these two were involved with while there. We were pleased to have some of these papers copied for our references. They were the parents of William, who settled in Belmont County and later in Clark County, Ohio. He was the father of James Bloxsome.

James and his wife, Ann (Robinson), were the parents of six children, one of them being my great-grandfather, James. This James was a Civil War veteran. He enlisted in Co. L, 34 Ind. Vol. Infantry. He saw much action in the South. Upon returning home after the war, on April 17, 1869, he married his sweetheart, Christena Tinsley. Before their marriage, Christena had taught school.

Front row: Natasha Heath, Kyle Heath, Roderick Heath. Back row: Bryan Heath, Kim Heath, Barbara Heath

They were the parents of five children, one being my grandfather, Arthur William, who was born February 23, 1871. He attended Marion Normal College in 1893, earning a teacher's certificate. He taught for a short while in Sugar Creek School in Nottingham Township, Wells County. Later he enrolled at the Medical College of Indiana, University of Indianapolis, graduating on March 29, 1897. He then began the practice of medicine, having an office in Montpelier, Indiana. Later he moved his office to Pennville, Indiana, remaining there until his death.

My grandfather married my grandmother, Irene (Romine), July 2, 1923. She was the daughter of William and Margaret Singer Romine. William, a timber buyer, was the son of Cornelius, who was the son of Noah and Eliza Jane Brown Romine of Virginia. Margaret was a daughter of William and Rhoda Connett Singer, who maintained a grocery store in Chester Township, at Poneto, Indiana. My grandmother, Irene, attended Muncie Normal College in Muncie, Indiana.

To my grandparents were born two daughters, Naomi and Grace. Grace, my aunt, married and lives in Fort Wayne and has two children, Diane and Michael.

Our mother, Naomi, born August 19, 1924, graduated from Chester Center High School in 1942. She received her nursing diploma from Ball Memorial Hospital School of Nursing, June 8, 1945. She and Roderick Nusbaumer of Keystone, Indiana, were married June 8, 1946, after he returned from World War II. He had served in the Navy Air Corps.

To my parents were born two children, Barbara and Kay. My brother graduated from Southern Wells High School and continued his education at Purdue University.

Barbara graduated with the first class at Southern Wells School. She attended Ball State Teacher's College at Muncie, Indiana. For a few years she worked in the office of the 3M paper plant. She and Hubert Heath were united in marriage and became the parents of three sons. (1) Bryan Heath, born December 26, 1968, who is married to Kim, and has a two-year-old daughter, Natasha. They reside in Hartford City, Indiana. (2) Roderick Heath, born February 12, 1976; and (3) Kyle Heath, born February 13, 1981, are currently students at Southern Wells School. The family presently resides in Chester Township.

PAUL BONHAM FAMILY

Paul and Nancy Bonham have lived in Wells County since 1955. Their farm is located in Liberty Township, Wells County, and has been in the Thompson-Bonham family for 128 years. The farm was deeded to Paul's great-grandfather, John Howard Thompson, in 1863 and then deeded to his grandmother, Mrs. (Asa) Emma Thompson Bonham, in 1902.

Paul's great-grandparents, Carey W. and Sarah E. Bonham, and his great-great-grandparents, Burdain and Nancy Bonham, are buried in the Sparks Cemetery in Wells County.

Paul Irvin Bonham was born in Huntington, Indiana, on October 21, 1928, to Elijah R. and Hattie Schilling Bonham of Warren, Indiana. He graduated from Warren High School and Purdue University with a Bachelor of Science Degree in Agriculture. He served in the Army in the Korean War as a first lieutenant with the 9th Field Artillery Battalion, 3rd Division. He was awarded the Bronze Star for Meritorious Service. Paul's twin brother, Richard Bonham, lives in Warren, Indiana. His sister, Carolyn Grigsby, lives in Neenah, Wisconsin.

Paul I. Bonham Family
Lauren, Julie, Nancy, Paul, Bill, Vivian

Nancy Joan Howard Bonham was born in Hammond, Indiana, on December 2, 1932, to Vane R. and Vivian Ellis Howard. She graduated from Hammond High School, and later from Indiana University with a bachelor of science degree, and a master of science degree in education. After teaching in Casper, Wyoming, and Hammond, Indiana, she and Paul were married on February 20, 1955. Nancy's brother, Vane E. Howard, lives in Houston, Texas. Her sister, Judith Gaye Vivian McCarty, resides in San Diego, California.

Paul and Nancy are the parents of four children: (1) Vivian Lynne was born January 25, 1956. She graduated from Southern Wells High School and Indiana University. She was married to John Alvin Blakeslee, September 1, 1979. They have four children: Julie Elise, born September 6, 1981; Abbey Lynne, born November 28, 1984; Seth Bonham, born December 5, 1986, and Lucas Paul, born March 10, 1989; (2) Julie Anne was born March 25, 1958. She died at the age of eight years old on May 6, 1966 from leukemia. Julie is buried in the Thompson Home Cemetery in Huntington County; (3) Lauren Gayle was born August 19, 1960. She graduated from Southern Wells High School, and from Indiana University in 1982. Laurie was married to Randall Lee Lockdall on July 26, 1986. They have a son, Matthew Bonham, born May 2, 1988 and Andrew Payne born April 18, 1991; (4) William (Bill) Bonham, was born October 3, 1962, and also graduated from Southern Wells High School. Bill attended Purdue University. He lives on a farm that was owned by his grandfather and his great-grandfather in Huntington County.

The Bonhams have always been interested in pubic affairs and have served in many capacities in the community. Paul was a member of the Wells County Area Plan Commission and the Board of Zoning Appeals from 1967 to 1987. In 1987 he was appointed Trustee of Liberty Township, and in 1990 was elected the Auditor of Wells County. Nancy was active in Girl Scouts for many years. She was named "Wells County Homemaker of the Year" in 1982. Presently she is a fourth grade teacher at the Lancaster Elementary School in the Norwell School District. Paul and Nancy are members of the Church of Christ of Warren, Indiana.

BOOKS FAMILY

The Books family has been represented in Wells County for six generations, beginning with Thommas Books in the first half of the nineteenth century to his present-day great-great-great grandson, Jeremy LaVaughn Books.

Four of the other great-great-great grandchildren of Thommas Books remain in Wells County—brothers Jason Beck and Bryan Beck, and Vicki Barrick-Markley, all of rural Ossian, and Debra Barrick of Bluffton. There are two other great-great-great granddaughters—Diana (Barrick) Zagrocki of Crown Point and Shari Barrick of Royal Oak, Michigan.

Thommas Books moved to Wells County from the Celina, Ohio, area sometime in the late 1830's. Among the family's prized possessions is a pocket-sized catechism book, printed in German and copywritten 1839, with a notation on the inside cover: "Thommas Books . . . his book, 1842."

Books is an uncommon name in the United States. Of Dutch derivation, it is locational in origin. First spelled "Boeke," it meant "dweller at, or near, a birch tree."

After migrating to America, many of our ancestors settled in Pennsylvania—where more than one-fifth of the 402 Books families in the United States today reside. The Books name is now found in 35 states, with Wisconsin, Indiana, Minnesota and Ohio—in addition to Pennsylvania—having the largest concentrations.

Thommas Books and his wife, whose name is not known, had three sons: George Washington Books, Andrew Jackson Books, and Horton Hamilton Books, from whom the current Wells County family traces its lineage.

The early Wells County Bookses lived in the southeaster party of the county, as evidenced by an elementary spelling book still in the family's possession. In one margin is written: "Horton Hamilton Books . . . this book bought in Buenna Visty (Beuna Vista, now Linn Grove) December 12, 1867." The book may have been a present, as it was purchased just five days prior to his 13th birthday.

Horton and Mary Elizabeth (Holloway) Books had nine children: Laura L. (born August 24, 1874); Leara E. (August 26, 1875); George Andrew (January 8, 1877); Lesty Ann (October 29, 1878); Leota Ethel (July 15, 1880); Loreta E. (June 3, 1883); Perry Alexander (January 13, 1886); Cory Jane (October 16, 1887), and James Grover (July 15, 1894).

Mary Books was the daughter of John Holloway and Louisa Holloway. She had one brother and four sisters: Milton F., Lydia S. (married name Ellsworth); Hannah E. (Blair); Jessica A. (Harris); and Christina (Rose).

Horton Books, who was born on December 17, 1850, died on September 8, 1904, and along with his wife is buried in the Alberson Cemetery just east of Domestic in Adams County. Mary Books was born October 3, 1852, and died at age 65 on January 4, 1918.

The next-to-last son of Horton and Mary, Perry Alexander, married Neva Grove on January 1, 1910. Neva, born in 1892, was one of ten children of Oliver and Margaret (Blair) Grove—eight of them girls.

Perry and Neva had two children—Edna (born July 19, 1910) and Virgil LaVaughn (September 12, 1912). Edna Books married Mearl Dukes of the Petroleum area on October 30, 1929; she died of kidney disease on January 24, 1989, in Largo, Florida. Virgil Books married Marjorie Edith Kreigh (a daughter of Glenn Kreigh and Viola Smith) on August 30, 1936. Marjorie Books, born July 16, 1918, died on July 3, 1971, from diabetes complications.

Perry Books owned a farm southeast of Petroleum, later purchasing 40 more acres close by. Like many others during the Great Depression, he lost the original farm and later sold the other 40 acres. He and Neva then rented a house and land on County Road 200N one mile east of Indiana.

Front: Virgil Books. Back: L to R: Elaine Beck, Gary Books, Joyce Moss

After Virgil and Marjorie married, they moved with Perry and Neva to a rented home and arm near 450E and 100N, east of Bluffton. Two years later, Virgil and Marjorie rented a house and farm ground from Charles Sturgis northeast of Bluffton. Following Neva Books's death in 1943, Perry moved in with Virgil and Marjorie at the Sturgis rental property.

By this time, Perry had recovered financially from the Depression, and he and Virgil purchased a 160-acre farm along Highway 1 north at its intersection with 500N.

In 1944, after Perry Book's death, Virgil sold the farm's livestock and machinery, letting the land go to a tenant. He went to work at the Dana Corp. in Fort Wayne as a machinist, retiring in April, 1977, after more than 30 years of service.

Virgil and Marjorie had four children, the great-great grandchildren of Thommas Books: Joyce Ann (born November 28, 1939); Marcia Lynne (May 5, 1942); Gary Wayne (March 1, 1946); and Elaine Kay (June 6, 1950). Marcia died of anemia on May 22, 1953, at age 11.

After Marcia's death, the large farm house and 80 acres of land five miles north of Bluffton were sold and a new ranch-style house was built on the remaining 80 acres.

Joyce Books married Merlin Barrick, the son of Olive and Millie. They had four children: Debra Barrick (born August 11, 1957); Diana Zagrocki (February 3, 1960); Vicki Barrick-Markley (September 7, 1961); and Shari Barrick (November 27, 1962). Joyce later married Jerry Moss, son of Walter and Marjorie of Arcola, and she and her husband live in Ossian.

On August 26, 1972, Gary Brooks married the former Lana Jane Johnloz, daughter of Robert and Olive Elizabeth. Son Jeremy LaVaughn was born December 27, 1973. They reside in Bluffton.

Elaine Books, on April 24, 1971 married Richard Beck, son of Ancel and Ruth. They have two sons—Jason Ryan (born November 3, 1973) and Bryan Michael (January 5, 1977).

Of the 160 acres purchased by Perry and Virgil Books in 1943, just a small parcel remains with the family today. Dick and Elaine Beck and their two sons reside in the ranch home built by Virgil and Marjorie Books in the 1950's; Virgil Books currently occupies an adjoining mobile home. Vicki Barrick-Markley and her husband, Kent, built a new home in the late 1980's just to the south of 500N along Highway 1.

All of the remaining acreage of the second 80-acre tract was sold to Paul Mills in the 1980's.

GARY BOONE FAMILY

Our family moved to Bluffton, Indiana in 1982, from Osseo, Michigan. Simpson Industries had opened a new plant in Jason Park, Bluffton, in 1978. Gary later was transferred here from Simpson's Litchfield, Michigan plant.

Gary was born October 1, 1942, to Harold and June Boone and grew up on a farm near Pittsford, Michigan. He graduated from Pittsford High School in 1961. He received a BA in Business Administration from Hillsdale College in 1972.

Ann (Packer) Boone was born March 9, 1945, to Charles and Phyllis Packer and grew up on a farm, near Jonesville, Michigan. She graduated from Jonesville High School in 1963. She attended Michigan State University from 1963-65, and later graduated with a BA in Psychology from IUPU, Fort Wayne, Indiana.

Gary and Ann were married at the United Methodist Church in Hillsdale, Michigan, in 1965. Children are Scott Aaron, born November 23, 1969, in Stuttgart, Germany, while Gary was stationed with the United States Army at Goeppingne, Germany. Scott graduated from Norwell High School in 1988 and received an AB degree in Horticulture/Landscaping from Vincennes University in 1990.

Stacie Lynn was born December 12, 1971, at Hilldale, Michigan. She graduated from Norwell High School in 1990 and is a sophomore at Indiana University at Bloomington.

Gary is presently operations manager at Simpson Industries. Ann is church secretary at Bluffton First United Methodist Church.

BORNE FAMILY

Jacob Borne was born in 1844 in Kenton, Berne, Switzerland, son of Christ and Catherine Wagner Borne and Ellen Jane Magley, born 1864 in Magley, Indiana, daughter of Conrad and Rosana (Betzberger) Magley, of Magley, Indiana, were married in 1878 and lived at 418 South Jersey Street until her death in 1928. Jacob Borne died in 1889.

Ellen Jane Borne became a practical nurse following her husband's death. She specialized in maternity and delivered over 50 babies including her own grandchild. No care of the sick was too hard for her willing hands and she was beloved by everyone who knew her. She helped at the Knights of Pythias Home during the flu epidemic in 1917-18.

Mrs. Harry Dwight (Ina Agar) Brickley was the first superintendent at the Wells County Hospital, opened in 1918, and she took Mrs. Ellen Jane Borne with her as a nurse. She was a life member of the First United Methodist Church in Bluffton.

Jacob and Ellen Jane Borne had two children, Louise Katherine Borne born 1879 and Charles Conrad Borne born 1881.

Louise Katherine Borne married Bert Hesher in 1900. He died in 1919. Two children were born one of which was born in 1904, died in 1924.

Josephine Hesher born 1906, and married Noble Shields in 1924. A daughter Katherine Jane was born in 1926. She now lives with her mother in Bradenton, Florida. Her second marriage was to Roy Sprowl, and a son, Wayne Sprowl, was born 1934. He lives in Birmingham, Alabama. Her third marriage was to Otto Weilemann who died in 1966.

L to R Back: Charles Borne, Bert Hesher. Middle: Grace Borne, Grandma Ellen Jane Borne, Elizabeth Borne (on lap), Louise Hesher. Front: Louise Borne, Frederick Hesher, Josephine Hesher

Charles Conrad Borne married Grace Andrew, daughter of James W. and Sarah E. Andrew of Warren in 1905. They had three daughters, Louise, born 1906, died 1967. Elizabeth, born 1908, still living and Patricia Jean, born 1924, died 1983.

Charles Conrad Borne was a life-long resident

of 515 South Jersey Street, Bluffton, until his death at 65 years in 1948. Charles worked many years for L.L. Bender Delco and was city electrician for Bluffton for 19 years from 1929 until his death in 1948. He was a member of the Volunteer Fire Department for 45 years until his death, from 1903 until 1948. He also drove the first "Cherry Picker" truck for the Electric Department in Bluffton. Charles Borne did not know the meaning of the word "FEAR".

Grace Andrew Borne was born in 1884 and died in 1968 at eighty-four years of age. Grace Borne was a homemaker all her married life.

Their daughter, Louise Borne, married Wendell W. Archbold of Ossian in 1934. A daughter, Lou Ann Archbold, was born in 1938. She is now a principal of Sequoia Junior High School in Fontana, California. Louise died in 1967 and Wendell in 1989.

Elizabeth Borne married Stanley Hansen in 1935. Three babies died at birth, Patricia Marie in 1937, David Borne Hansen, 1938 and Barbara Louise, 1942. In August 1943, they adopted James Myron Hansen for their son. Born February 27, 1942, James lives in Australia. December 27, 1943, a daughter, Elaine Jean Hansen was born. Elaine married Ray C. Gardiner in 1967. They have a daughter, Lisa Renee, born 1971, who is a student at the University of Southern Mississippi, Hattiesburg, Mississippi. They live at 110 Hemlock Drive, D'Iverbille, Mississippi 39532.

Elizabeth Borne Hanson married Albert Anthony Tschannen in 1971. They reside at 324 W. Washington St. Bluffton. From 1954 until 1966, Elizabeth Hansen owned and operated the City News stand on East Market Street, Bluffton.

Patricia Jean Borne, born 1924, was married to Kenneth D. Platt in 1943. Patricia was secretary at the First U.M. Church for thirty years. She died in 1983 and Kenneth died in 1972. Their children were John Stephen, David Borne Platt, 1948; killed in Vietnam 1969, Mark Andrew, born 1951, Marcia Ellen, born 1953, and Teresa Louise, born 1956. All are married.

Submitted by Josephine Hesher Weilemann of Bradenton, Florida, and her first cousin Elizabeth Borne Tschannen of Bluffton, the only two living members of the immediate Borne Family.

BORROR FAMILY

Allen Borror moved in 1890 to Indiana from the village of Borror's Corners, Ohio, a settlement south of Columbus, Ohio. Allen, his wife, Jenny, and son, Jobe, came to Bryant, Indiana, by horse and wagon where he purchased a farm. They had two more sons, Edward and Ross. Then the family moved to Petroleum (Wells County) around 1895 and opened a slaughter house.

Allen's son, Jobe, married Carrie Runyon in 1909. They moved to Linn Grove (known then as Buena Vista). Jobe worked at the Meshberger Brothers Stone Company. Daughter Lenna was born in 1910. A year later Jobe, Carrie, and Lenna moved back to Wells County, east of Petroleum, where Jobe began farming. Subsequent children born were a son, Richard Earl, in 1915 and a daughter, Evelyn Jane, in 1917. Then in 1921, twin boys, Glenn and Wrenn, were born. A second set of twin boys, Dee and Lee, were born in 1928. Lee, however, died at the age of three months. Jobe's wife, Carrie, died in 1954 at the age of 64, and Jobe died in 1975 at the age of 85. Both are buried in the Linn Grove Cemetery with infant son Lee.

Carrie (49 years) and Jobe (51 years) Borror taken at LaCross, Wisconsin 1938.

Daughter Lenna married Paul Bryant in 1929. Three children were born: Robert, Paul Jr. and Elizabeth Ann. Lenna passed away in 1984.

Son Richard Earl died in 1941 at the age of 26.

Daughter Evelyn Jane married Rollie Bullock in 1946. One son, Tony, was born.

Son Wrenn lives in Marion, Indiana, and has a son, Danny, and a daughter, Jill.

Son Glenn (who lived much of his life in Nottingham Township) lives west of Bluffton in Liberty Township. He has three sons: Earl Richard (married Karla Hoover, and they have two children, Sean and Manda) who lives in Liberty Township. Glenn Jr., who lives in Maccka City, Florida. Randy is married to Kim Bordonaro and lives in Fort Wayne.

Son Dee married Lauretta Anderson on August 13, 1948. They resided on a 40 acre farm on Dustman Road north of Bluffton. One daughter, Judy, and two sons, Dennis and Mike, are members of this family. Daughter Judy married Terry Werling June 7, 1969. They have a son, Ryan and daughter, Kelli. Son Dennis married Linda Robbins on October 7, 1972. Dennis has two daughters, Lisa and Erin, and a son, Eric. Lisa married Gunnar Heller on May 19, 1990, and they have a son, Drew. Son Mike married Lynette Litten on January 17, 1982, and they have two sons, Justin and Jarrett. Dee Borror passed away on September 19, 1988.

CEDRIC R. BOTTS FAMILY

Cedric R. Botts, second son of Vernon F. Botts and Mary Malinda Martin Botts, was born one and three-quarter miles west of Zanesville (Wells County) on "Knights Chicken Farm". According to father's diary entry "Monday October 6, 1942, Baby was born at 3:00 a.m., weight eight and three-fourths pounds. Dr. J.L. McBride came at 2:30, went after Sade Diff, got back 2:45, took Sade home p.m."

Younger brother, Douglas, born in same house in 1926. Older brother, Darrell, wasn't born in Wells County, but all three Botts lived in Wells, and graduated from Union Center High School. Darrell and Douglas were U.S. Army Paratroopers in World War II.

Vern died in 1929; and Mary and Donald McBride were wed in 1930. From this marriage five more children: Roger (deceased), Maurice, Melba (Mrs. K. Edwards), Mary Lou (Mrs. Kenneth Burkhart), and David McBride.

Cedric married Jean Richardson, second daughter of MacBride Richardson and Goldie Earhart Richardson, on December 25, 1943. They had five children: son Michael V., born in 1947, has a son Jason and daughter, Raven. Neenah S., born 1950, has two daughters, Amy and Shelley Baker. Nilah J. born in 1952, died in 1961 at the age of nine.

Chris L., born in 1955, has a son Justin and daughter Aaron Bates. Patrick C. born in 1964, has a son Benjamin and daughter Erica.

Back row: Chris, Neenah. Front row: Patrick, Cedric, Jean, Mike

Michael Botts graduated from Huntington North, and earned a B.S. degree in computer science at Purdue University. Michael was in the Vietnam war from 1965 to 1968. Neenah graduated from Huntington North, and is an L.P.N. Chris graduated from Huntington North, and graduated from Purdue University with a PhD in Educational Psychology and Science. Patrick graduated from Huntington North (Salutatorian), freshman at Purdue, and graduated from Ball State with a B.S. degree in Business Administration.

Cedric Botts served in the U.S. Navy in World War II from 1943 to 1946, G.I. boot camp, Mach. School at University of Minnesota, Packard Motor School, two years repairing P.T. motors in New Guinea in the South Pacific. After the war he worked at International Harvester, G.E., and fired steam engines on the Pennsylvania Railroad for one year. Then he went back to school for a degree in engraving, jewelry mfg., and diamond setting at New Castle, Pennsylvania; a master's degree in hand engraving at Washington D.C.; and a degree in watchmaking at Bradley University, Peoria. He owned a jewelry store in Markle (present address) for 17 years. He is a member of Markle Masonic Lodge, Scottish Rite, Fort Wayne, Veterans of Foreign Wars, Markle American Legion, Roanoke and Markle Volunteer Fire Dept. 1955-1991, holding offices of Chief and Assistant Chief. Also 17 years at G.E. and four years at C.T.S., Fort Wayne, he retired in 1987.

DARRELL BOTTS

Darrell B. Botts was born on January 16, 1923, in the Bott's house in Zanesville. He was the son of Vernon Botts and Mary Melinda Martin. The house he was born in belonged to Dr. E.H. Botts (died-1916), who raised Vern because he was his nephew. Here is Dr. Botts story:

"Dr. E.H. Botts, of Zanesville, is the son of David and Ellenor (Fordyce) Botts, both now deceased. He was born in Clinton County, Ohio, May 20, 1858, and was reared amid the scenes of rural life. He attended the graded schools at Genntown, Ohio, and came to Huntington County, Indiana, in 1881, securing employment on a farm in order to have the benefit of outdoor life. Two years later, in August, 1883, he was united in marriage with Miss Ida Young, a daughter of John Young, of Huntington County, Indiana, who was born in that county in March, 1864. When a boy he had a liking for the medical profession, which was shown even in his play. Being poor, and with nothing but his strong will and indomitable courage to carry him through the world, he rented a farm with the intention of making enough money to enable him to take a course in medicine. For two years he borrowed books, and after working all day in the fields would read until far into the night thus acquiring a rudimentary knowledge of his profession. He further pursued his studies for six years under the preceptorship of Dr. Ira E. Lyons, of Huntington, and later with Dr. E.S. Fisher, of Markle, Indiana. In the fall of 1889, he entered the Fort Wayne Medical College, in which he took a three year course, graduating in March, 1893. Immediately thereafter, Dr. Botts located at Zanesville, where he began his profession encumbered with a heavy debt. His practice soon became lucrative and exceeded his anticipations. Besides owning an eighty-acre farm in Huntington County, he enjoyed a large and lucrative practice. The Doctor has not had children of his own, but has taken into his family his brother's son, Vernon, who he is educating. Owing to his profession, he has held aloof from political work, but has kept himself informed on the issues of the day, being a supporter of Democratic principles. He conscientiously performs his professional duties, taking pride in keeping abreast with the times."

In 1929, when Darrell was six years old, his father died; and in November 1930, his mother married Don McBride. He attended Lafayette Central for first grade, and then he moved with his mother and stepfather to a farm south of Zanesville. From then on, he attended and graduated from East Union Center in 1941. In November 1941, he married Jane Ann Barnes, and soon after went to World War II. He served as a paratrooper, as did his brother Douglas, in Japan. While assigned there, the two met and their picture was shown in the Fort Wayne newspaper. At the same time, brother Cedric was stationed in New Guinea, with the U.S. Navy.

After World War II, Darrell enrolled at Purdue University where he graduated on February 10, 1946. He took a job coaching at Battleground, Indiana, and later at East Union Center. He has since managed several wire drawing plants over the country.

He was vice-president of Fort Wayne Metals, and manager of National Standard's plants in Corbin, Kentucky; Los Angeles, California; and Niles, Michigan. It was from the Niles plant that he retired. He enjoyed the opportunity of teaching at his alma mater, and then the involvement with research, development, and other people that he experienced through the years in industry. He never misses an alumni celebration for East Union Center, as he looks forward to it each year. At Union, he was involved in sports, and was a star at basketball and boxing.

Darrell and Jane lost two infants at birth; and then after Sandra was born, a son Darrell Steven was born on August 24, 1953. Susan was born on December 6, 1957. Sandra married Jeff Wise and they had three children. She is now married to Dale Vincent and their family lives in Clio, Michigan. She has three grandchildren. "Steve" as the family calls him is not married and works for the city of Fort Wayne, where he resides. Susan married Paul Flowers, who has two children, and they live in Mishawaka, Indiana. Darrel and Jane now live in South Bend, Indiana.

DOUGLAS BOTTS FAMILY

Douglas S. Botts was born just west of Zanesville on the Wells-Allen County line on April 29, 1926. He was the son of Vernon and Mary Martin Botts. The father, Vernon, died when he was three years old and the following year his mother married Don McBride. In 1933, he moved with his parents to Union Township, just a little south of Zanesville. He attended East Union Center but dropped out before graduation during his senior year. He was in the class of 1944.

Doug married Doris Bunsold, also of Union Township, in January 1947. They had three girls, Rita, Sheila, and Cynthia. Rita, born on December 21, 1947, is married to Clayton Linn Zeddis and they have two boys, Rodney (1968) and Bradford (1970). The Zeddises, former residents of Union Township, now live in a new house in Windfall Estates on Feighner Road.

Doug and Doris Botts
Rita, Sheila, Cindy

Rita works at K-Mart Distribution Center, and Linn at Zollners of Fort Wayne. Neither of their sons is married.

All the family has been involved in many community projects in the Zanesville area. Lions Club, ZANA, Little League, and other sporting activities take up lots of their free time. They are also members of the Zanesville Church of God, and play baseball for the teams there. Rod works for Auto Collision of Fort Wayne, and Brad is attending IUPU in Fort Wayne and works for Doug Edwards Mowing Service.

Cindy Watson, Sheila Wyss, Rita Zeddis

Sheila, born on January 24, 1952, has three girls: Michele Fisher (1969) and Chastity Fisher (1976), whose father is Steve Fisher; and Angel Wyss (1983) whose father is Les Wyss. Sheila is single and lives near Poe, Indiana. Michele is married to Scott Fornwalt and she has a little girl. They live in Ossian.

Cindy born on February 2, 1953, has two children: Buffy Cook (1970) and Matthew Cook (1971) whose father is Bruce Cook. Cindy is now married to Dan Watson and they have a small son, Ian. Cindy manages a McDonalds in Iverness, Florida. Buffy is married and has two children. Buffy and Mat also live in Florida.

After nine years of marriage, Doris died at the young age of 29 leaving three small children and her husband. All the family helped to take care of the children. In late 1958, Douglas married Evelyn La Claire and they moved to Lafayette Township. There Mark (1959) and Kelly (1961) were born. They live in the eastern states.

Linn and Rita Zeddis, Brad, Rod

Doug died in November, 1982, while a resident of Huntington. Most of his lifetime, he was an operator of large equipment and a truck driver. He was in World War II as a paratrooper in Japan. In his younger days he was very handsome and very talented. About 1953, he built his own home on State Road #1 in Ossian. He loved to draw, and had a heart of gold, but died a victim of alcohol. For more of his story refer to Don McBride, Cedric Botts, and Darrell Botts writings in this book.

BOWER FAMILY

The Bowers are of German descent. Joel Bower was born in Pennsylvania in 1824, a son of Simon and Hannah Bower. He moved to Fairfield County, Ohio, when he was a young man. It was there that he married Susannah (Susan) Shoemaker, a daughter of Henry and Sarah Shoemaker. Susan was born in Ohio in 1826.

Joel brought his family to Wells County, Indiana in 1853 and purchased eighty acres of woodland and a mile and half southwest of Reiffsburg. Their first house was a twenty by twenty-four feet, one-and-a-half story structure. Joel, a shoemaker by trade, not finding ample work to support his growing family, cleared the land and took to farming. He eventually purchased a total of five hundred and twenty acres.

Joel and Susannah had eleven children: Henry, Simon, E.J., Rebecca, twins Israel and Hannah, Willison, Jacob, Noah, Mahlon and Frank. Susannah died on March 2, 1889, and is buried in the Stahl Cemetery. Joel married Cynthia Arnold. They had two children: Joel D. and Cynthia. Joel died January 15, 1896, and is buried in the Garnand Cemetery.

C. Rosalee Stahl Bower, age 55, taken Aug. 9, 1990 on her birthday.

Joel's son, Mahlon, born 1865, married Eura Anna Rush, a daughter of Ishumal (Ishucal) Rush and Lydia Stanford, both natives of Virginia. Eura was born on September 23, 1868, in Wells County, Indiana. Mahlon and Eura had eight children: Ella Mae, Irvin R., Viola, Dewhite, Paul, twins Clara and Kari, Kari died in infancy and Gerald. Mahlon died February 10, 1907. Eura married Nelson May on July 20, 1919. She died January 4, 1944.

Paul was born on February 1, 1900. He married Florence B. Cline on June 19, 1930, in Fort Wayne, Indiana. Florence was born November 15, 1913, in Washington, the daughter of Fredrick Cline (born in New York) and Zepha Pace. Paul and Florence had seven children: Mahlon, Marvin, George E. (Ramona F. Carr), Lavelle (Rollie Sharp, Wendell Nierman), Paul L. (Gloria Kay Abner), Judy (James haven), Linda (James R. Ogle). Paul died on November 30, 1962 and is buried in the Stahl Cemetery. Florence resides in Poneto, Indiana.

Marvin C. was born June 28, 1933. He married C. Rosalee Stahl on November 21, 1955, in Huntington, Indiana. Rosalee was born August 9, 1935, to Lester V. and Cathryn E. Dolby Stahl, who reside in Huntington. Five children were born to Marvin and Rosalee: Gary A., Michael L., Diana K., Sondra S. and Kent P. Marvin presently lives in Poneto, Indiana.

Gary married Sheryl Hockenberry and they have two children, Angela R. (twelve) and Dennis A. (ten). Mike married Robin Franze Bleeky and has two stepsons. Chad A. (eleven) and Scott A. Bleeky (seven). Diana's first marriage to Randall Brown produced two children: Christie R. (eight) and Travis R. (seven). Her second marriage was to Bryce A. Brickely. They have a daughter Jessica L. (2). Sondra S. and Kent P., at this time are unmarried and reside in Bluffton, Indiana.

Our beloved mother C. Rosalee Stahl Bower passed away after a long courageous battle with cancer on Sunday, January 13, 1991. She was laid to rest in the Lancaster Cemetery in Huntington County, Indiana. Heavens most precious Rose will remain in our hearts and memories through eternity.

BOWER FAMILY

The Bower family lived on a farm south of Bluffton, adjacent to the Bracy Pumping Station. The huge tanks were a constant concern because of a feared oil leak and fire or tanks explosion.

Ephraim L. Bower was married to Catherine Hoover Masterson. The Masterson children were Frank, Mary and Jennie. Young Frank was killed in a motorcycle-side car accident. Mary married Bert Wasson and her children were Elizabeth and John. Jennie married Forrest Cummins and her children were Robert and Edna. Jennie later married Ralph Morrow - a daughter, Mary Jane.

The Ephraim Bower children were Zeffa, twins Carrie and Charles, and Mabel. Ephraim was a farmer and Kate taught school. Zeffa passed away at an early age. Carrie was employed at the Studabaker Bank. Charles was married to Bessie Miller, no children to this union. Charles was a born naturalist and he and Charles Deam, Bluffton naturalist, went on many field trips to see and study plants and shrubs. Mabel Naomi was married to C. Edwin Craven and their children were Herbert Edwin and Catherine Elizabeth.

BOWMAN

In 1859 or 1860, Adam Bowman, Jr., born September 3, 1825, died September 26, 1916, moved with his wife, Charlotte Schick, to Wells County, Indiana. They left Starke County, Ohio, around 1856 and moved in the interim to Elkart County, Indiana. To this union were born eleven children. Adam Bowman Sr. is reputed to be from Germany, and his wife, Elizabeth Spiecer, was from England. At the time of Adam Jr.'s death, there were nine children who survived him: Charles, Samuel, Adam Bruff, Henry, and Frank who at that time resided in Elkart County; also surviving him was Ed of Poneto, John of Hartford City, Mrs. Phillip Householder, Bluffton, and Mrs. Ida Cherry of Warren, Ohio. A son, William, had died September 21, 1910, in the Kingsland train wreck. One sister, Mrs. Margaret Stauffer of Starke County, Ohio, survived Adam Jr. Two brothers, Richard and Samuel, were already deceased.

One son of the above, Ed, married Jesse Roy of Elkart, Indiana. To that union were born five children, four of whom survived. One son, Roy, died in infancy. At this time, February 16, 1991, two children of this union survive. Robert, born February 17, 1903, and a younger sister Doris Zoll. Two others, Kenneth and Howard, are now deceased.

To the union of Robert Bowman and Chrystal Tricer (born June 3, 1905) were born two sons, Byrl (born April 4, 1940) and Roy (born April 15, 1944). Both sons attended the local public schools and have since obtained master's degrees

Roy resides in Indianapolis with his wife Jodie, and son Blake. Byrl currently resides in Kalamazoo, Michigan, having done so since receiving an undergraduate degree at Western Michigan University. To the union of Byrl and Mary have been born two daughters, Jennifer and Joanna, and one son, Bret.

BOWMAN

Dious Bowman, our father was born in Huntington County, Indiana, June 19, 1884. He was the son of Ellis and Lydia (Bond) Bowman. He married Netta Belle Ernst at Warren, January 19, 1905.

Our mother was born April 13, 1887. Her parents were George and Eliza Jane (Boll) Ernst. Grandpa Ernst was born in Ashtabula County, Ohio. His father, John Ernst, was born in Ohio in 1821 and died in the service in 1863. He was a member of Co. C.H. 42nd Regt., Ohio Volunteer Infantry, and was buried in the National Cemetery at St. Louis, Missouri.

Barber Shop in Jim Porter's Poolroom on North Main. First barber, George Harris, second barber D.E. Bowman, third barber, George Brice. Jim Porter at far right side.

George and Eliza Ernst lived in Peterson, Adams County, Indiana. Our parents, Dious and Netta Bowman, were residents of Wells County and were the parents of six children: Enid McDaniel, Edith Arnold, Ethel Dedrick, Eileen Miller, Harold, and Donald Bowman.

Our father's trade was barbering. Early in their marriage, he operated a barber shop in Tocsin. Later, he worked in several shops in Bluffton, including the Jim Porter Poolroom on North Main Street. In the early 30's, he owned a shop in Fort Wayne, at the site of the present Fort Wayne Newspapers Building located on West Main Street.

Our father died March 4, 1945, and mother continued to live at their 1225 W. Cherry residence until her death on March 11, 1967.

CATHERINE LUCILE (SMITH) BOWMAN

The log cabin where my mother was born in 1880 was located in a woods a mile south of Liberty Center, Indiana, and is now long-gone. She was Girthie Rinear, born to George F. and Ellen (McKee) Rinear. My father was Daniel B. Smith, son of Daniel H. and Catherine (Taylor) Smith. My grandfather, Daniel H. Smith, fought in the Civil War for the Army of the Potomac. He was wounded at Petersburg. My parents lived in Liberty Center from 1896 to 1908. Dad was a painter and paper hanger. They had three children: Kenneth, born in 1898, who died at six weeks of age; Catherine Lucile (me), born in 1902; and Esther Sophia, born in 1906. In 1908 my parents bought a general store in Mt. Zion, Indiana. At that time Mt. Zion was an oil boom town. The store also housed the men who worked in the oil fields. There were twelve beds, two men to a bed. Mother cooked their breakfast and supper each day, as well as packing a lunch box for each man to take with him to work for his noon meal. In another section of the building was the livery stable. We lived there until 1917. Then Dad took a job as a lineman for the Liberty Center Telephone Co. and we moved back to Liberty Center. I graduated from Liberty Center School a few years later. I married Oren Bowman in 1924 and we went to live with his mother, Rachael (Funk) Bowman on her farm. Oren's father, William E. Bowman, was killed in the 1910 Kingsland interurban wreck. Oren farmed and during thirty-two years of that time he also drove a school bus for the Liberty Center School. Oren and I had two sons, George Oren and Daniel Booker Bowman. George married and had two sons and one daughter. He was killed in 1958 in a motorcycle accident just south of Bluffton, Indiana. Daniel had three sons. He is now retired from a career in law enforcement and lives in Ohio.

HAROLD BOWMAN FAMILY

In the year 1857, two brothers, Richard S. Bowman and Adam Bowman, Jr., came to Wells County, Indiana, from Pigeon Run, Stark County, Ohio.

Richard settled on 160 acres of land in Lancaster Township located two miles east of Bluffton on what is now state road 124. Of recent years the farm has been known as the Byrd place. Our great-grandfather, Richard, and his wife, Mary Shaffer Bowman, cleared and farmed the 160 acres where they settled. Our great grandfather fought with the Union forces in the Civil and was wounded and decorated.

To them three children were born: John, Byron, and Jennie. John married and acquired land in central Lancaster Township, where he reared a large family; many of his descendants are still residents of the area. Jennie remained on the home place and, with her husband, Jack Byrd, reared seven children. Some of their descendants still live in the county. Byron, our grandfather, married Margaret Ulmer in 1889. To them one son and two daughters were born. They were Luster, our father, and Zora and Vera.

Harold and Irene Bowman, December 1975

Our father, Luster Bowman, and our mother, Anna Johnston, were married in 1905. Our mother was a daughter of Robert and Agnes Gordon Johnston. They were the parents of four children: Harold, Kenneth, James, and Cathryne. Harold is the only one living. Our father, Luster Bowman, was elected sheriff of Wells County and served two (two-year) terms in the early 1930's. He was the first Republican to be elected to that office in Wells County's 100 years. Our grandfather, Robert Johnston, was a Democratic sheriff at the turn of the century and his son, "Joke" Johnston, was a Democratic Sheriff in the mid teens.

In the mid-1920's, Roscoe and Edna Brown Murray moved to Bluffton, soon after buying the former Gettle Jewelry Store. The Murrays came from Muncie, where members of their family also had a jewelry business. Roscoe and Edna Murray had three children: Harold, Irene, and Ernest. Their daughter Irene and Harold Bowman met and were married a couple of years later. Harold and Irene recently observed their 63rd wedding anniversary.

Harold and Irene had two children. Their daughter, Pat (Patricia) is married to Richard D. Wolfcale. Pat is a retired nurse and her husband, Dick, is a retired Marine Corp. veteran, having served in both the Korean and Vietnam wars. They have four children. Their son, Richard, was married to the former Maria Leon. Richard was a former Air Force pilot and an investment consultant with Merill-Lynch. They had two children. Richard died unexpectedly in August, 1991.

Harold and Irene are still quite active in their church, First United Methodist, where they have been lifetime members. They are still active associates in the operation of The Bowling Center in Bluffton.

JAMES BOWMAN FAMILY

In the Bowman family tree, I, James L. Bowman, can trace back to my great-great-great-grandparents, Gideon and Alice (Sautbine) Bowman.

Gideon (1822-1896) and Alice had six children, one being my great-great-grandpa, William A. William (1860-1922). He married Abbagail (Studabaker) (1861-1950) who is one of eight children from Abram Studabaker and Louisa (Dewitt). William and Abbagail had nine children, one being my great-grandpa, Charles A. (1890-1983) "Pop" Bowman. Charles married Velma O. (Lenhart) (1893-1980). Velma's parents were E. Burt Lenhart (1871-1938) and Martha (Johnson) (1873-1947). E. Burt's parents were John H. Lenhart and Tillie (Stevens). Martha's parents were Rieklef B. Johnson and Louisa (Baker).

In about 1925, Charles Bowman and Orval Lenhart opened a general store in Rockford. Charles bought out the store a few years later. Orval moved to Wren, Ohio, and opened his own store. The store in Rockford closed in the 1940's due to World War II. After the store closed Charles worked with Jessie Dunn as a carpenter. Velma helped at the general store before it closed, and during the war she worked at the Farnsworth Factory. Velma also wrote the Rockford News for the News Banner. Charles and Velma had my great-uncles, Kenneth E. and Gail R., and my great-aunt, Madeline D. (Bowman) Mosure, and my grandpa James W.

Standing left to right: William C. and Jeromy E. Seated left to right: James W., Charles A. James L.

My grandpa worked in his father's general store and served in the U.S. Air Force three years during World War II. After the war, he worked with Jessie Dunn as a carpenter. While working on the Gallman Building, he met his future wife, Carolyn Joan Murray (1928-1989). James and Carolyn got married and now Grandpa has retired from working thirty-six years at Franklin Electric. My grandma, Carolyn, worked at the Morris 5 and 10, the Caylor Nickel Clinic, and the ASCS Office.

My grandma, Carolyn, had one brother, Gene E. Murray. Their parents were Harold E. Murray (1906-1978) and Vera L. (White) (1909 -1980). Harold's parents were Rosco E. Murray and Edna V. (Brown). Vera's parents were Albert "Pete" White (1887-1949), who owned a barber shop in Bluffton, and Arista L. (Stahl) (1889-1938). Roscoe's parents were James E. Murray and Eva E. (Stevens). Arista's parents were Thomas P. Stahl (1850-1922) and Zipporah E. (Hupp) (1850-1943). Albert's parents were Henry J. White and Isabelle (Bentz).

James and Carolyn (Murray) Bowman had three children, Keith Murray, William Charles, and Jeffrey Lee. Keith attended Purdue University and graduated from Fort Wayne Regional Vocational Center as a journeyman machinist. Keith and Nancy L. (Wilson) have two children, Kasandrea Michelle and Karolyn May Bowman. My father William, graduated from Lincoln Tech, and is married to Mary A. (McDaniel), the daughter of Lewis N. McDaniel (1902-1965) and Mildred (Wolfe) (1911-1989). William and Mary have two children, me, James Lewis, and my brother Jeromy Edward Bowman. Jeffrey attended Ivy Tech and is married to Sharon (Feemster).

JOHN A. BOWMAN FAMILY

Richard Bowman was born June 14, 1821, in Pennsylvania to Adam and Elizabeth Spicer Bowman. His family moved to Ohio when he was six years old.

In Starke County, Ohio, on June 22, 1848, Richard married Mary Shaefer, born December 23, 1822, of John W. and Eva Wagner Shaefer. Two sons were born while the family lived in Ohio: John Adam on April 19, 1850, and Byron Washington on December 16, 1852. They brought their family to Wells County in 1857 and settled in Lancaster Township. Viletta Jane was born February 22, 1862. In March 1887, they moved to Bluffton and lived at 1019 West Wabash Street. Richard died April 24, 1900. Mary died November 19, 1900, and they are buried in Fairview Cemetery.

John completed his education at the Bluffton High School and engaged in the mercantile trade in Bluffton. He was married December 28, 1876, to Elizabeth Emeline Williams, daughter of James S. Williams. Four children were born to this union: Harry Oliver, born October 8, 1877; Lewis Claude born November 29, 1878; Bonnie Albert, born

John Bowman Family about 1916
Back (L-R) Herman "Buck", Howard "Windy", Lavern "Jap", Mary Harris, Virgil "Jack", Dorothy Havens, Eva Hunt. Front (L-R) Robert, Nellie Potter, John, Eliza Jane, George

December 27, 1880; and Jesse Winfield, born June 22, 1882. Elizabeth died December 18, 1885

In 1886, John sold his goods to Albert Shepherd and purchased the good of Samuel Kunkle of Tocsin and became a resident of that new village. He was appointed postmaster of Tocsin on January 31, 1886.

On March 17, 1887, John married Eliza Jane Archbold, who was born near Tocsin, to William John and Lovina Yarger Archbold, both natives of Ohio. They had fourteen children: Eva Myrtle, born August 7, 1889, was married to Theodore Oman Hunt; Zola May was born November 25, 1890; Nellie Florence, born July 14, 1892, was married to Alva Potter; Ralph Wilmer was born March 13, 1894; Robert Wilson, born October 23, 1895, married Beatrice Eichhorn; George Dewey, born March 7, 1898, married Esther Anna Dailey; Herman J., born September 22, 1899, married Mattie (not known); Howard McKinley, born January 22, 1902, married (unknown); Elmer Laverne, born November 2, 1903, married Isabelle Peterson, Dorothy Elizabeth, born February 10, 1906, married Elbert E. Havens; Virgil Ray, born June 7, 1908, married Wilma Noll. All of the above children are deceased. Mary Lavina, born October 14, 1910, married Gerald Harris and lives in Bluffton. Three children were born to this union: Carolyn who married Ted Wemhoff and lives in Decatur with her husband and three sons, William, Gregory, and Michael; Sharon who married Robert Mayer and lives in Ossian with her husband and three children, Deborah, Jerry, and Sheri; Ronald who married Carol Webker and lives in Zanesville with their two daughters, Lee Ann and Ginger and Carol's son, Brian McGreavy.

BRADBURN-TERHUNE

Clifford R. Bradburn was born June 2, 1894, in Tipton County, Indiana. He was the son of William Bradburn (1857-1944) and Phoebe (Pheba?) H. Stevens (1866-1954) who were married March 14, 1866, in Tipton County. Phoebe was the daughter of Solomon Stevens (1840-1910) and Martha ? (1844-1927). Most of Clifford's lifetime was spent as a rural mail carrier out of the Bluffton post office.

On October 17, 1914 he married Gladys Terhune, daughter of Albert Terhune (1851-1934) and Susan Jones (1858-1919). Gladys was born August 28, 1899, near Mount Zion in Wells County. Gladys passed away on January 6, 1969, and Clifford died on April 11, 1973.

Clifford and Gladys Bradburn

Their five daughters are Irene, born 1915; Ruth, born 1916; Ruby, born 1918; Maro, born 1920; and Jane, born 1930. Irene is married to William "Pete" Watkins and presently residing in Berne, Indiana. They have one son, Richard E. Watkins. Ruth is married to Lester McIntire and now resides in Hartford City. They have two children, Lois McIntire Woolard and Dwight McIntire. Ruby married Joe Fudge and they live northeast of Fort Wayne. They have a daughter, Suzanne Fudge Sieveking. Maro married Paul L. Bender and they live in Bluffton. They have two children, Paul L. Bender, Jr. and Linda Bender Heuer. Jane lives in Jacksonville, Texas, and has two sons, James Low, M.D., and Brad Low, and a daughter, Kathy Low Stamper.

BRADEN, ROBERTS, SWANK

My grandparents, John and Frances Harris Braden (1849-1938) moved to Wells County from Ridgeville, Randolph County. My grandfather was a Civil War veteran; having attained rank of corporal, he served with Company E; 75th Indiana Infantry. John and Frances were the parents of ten children. My father, Franklin C. (Cad) Braden (1875-1928) was one of the six boys.

My father remembered his first home as a log cabin east of Rockford, Rockcreek Township. The family later moved into Rockford, and because of the size of the family, some of the children were raised in other homes. My father lived in the home of John and Mary Jane Roberts. Here he learned about farming. Most of the family were members of the Rockford Friends (Quaker) Church.

My great-grandfather, Robert D. Roberts, was born in Kentucky in 1811. In 1837 he moved to Wells County and entered 120 acres of government land in Rockcreek Township, section 32. My grandfather, also Robert D., was the son of Robert and his second wife, Abigal Redding Sparks. In 1878 Robert married Julia Ann Wyatt, daughter of John and Lucinda Tam Wyatt of Huntington County. My mother, Stella, was then born on December 7, 1881. The family continued to live on the land which was acquired in 1837.

The young people of the community attended the Rockford School, which was situated a short distance southwest of the village. School was usually in session seven months of the year, with large attendance, grades one through eight, and only one teacher. My parents received their education there.

Stella Roberts and Cad Braden were married in 1900. They built a new home on the land which they bought next to the Roberts farm. They were parents of three children, Ralph D., Edna M., and Ardis A.

My brother Ralph, now 86 years of age, graduated from Liberty Center High School in 1922. He married Alice Heckler from Monroeville, Indiana, his wife now for 63 years. They have two children, Neil Braden and Marva Thorn, both of Fort Wayne. Ralph retired from General Electric after 43 years of service. He was an instructor at the Winchester Gun Club in Fort Wayne. Trap shooting was his hobby, and at age 67 he became the oldest man ever to win the state event.

My sister Edna (1911-1978) was a graduate of Rockcreek in the class of 1928. She married Donald Dickie (1904-1966). They lived on a farm in Rockcreek Township. Edna was a wonderful homemaker; her hobbies were needlework and baking. They were parents of one daughter, Janice, who is married to Ronald Stork. They live in Elkhart County and both are teachers.

I attended the Rockford School until fifth grade, when the new Rockcreek School opened in the fall of 1922. I enjoyed riding in the Model T school bus and attending such a large school. Our teachers were the best - D.N. Decker, Russell Stinson, and Frank Day, to name a few. Graduating in 1930, I went on to Manchester College, received a degree in Elementary Education, and taught school for more than thirty years in Randolph and Wells Counties.

In 1939, I married Mark Swank (1909-1976), son of Charles and Carrie Summers Swank of Clear Creek Township, Huntington County, Mark was a graduate of Clearcreek High School. Mark was working in Piqua, Ohio, when we were married. We lived there a short time, then bought a little house in Rockford and moved back home. In 1944, Mark bought the Rockford General Store which he opened for a number of years. Later he worked in Bluffton at Schwartz Plumbing, from which he retired.

Our daughter, Julia, was born in 1945. She was a Rockcreek graduate. At Manchester College she received a B.S. and M.A. degrees and taught school in the Cincinnati, Ohio, area and in Wells County. While in Cincinnati, she met and married Earl Beitenhaus. They lived in Cincinnati for several years and then moved to Rockford.

I have three granddaughters: Heather, the oldest, is a graduate of Norwell High School and Purdue University, and received an M.A. degree from the University of Wisconsin. She is now married and lives in Indianapolis. Granddaughters Sara and Amy are high school students here in Wells County. (*Ardis Braden Swank*)

BREEDLOVE-LINTON

Oather Breedlove was born April 6, 1895, in Illinois. His ancestors went across Indiana, some north and some west into Illinois, where his father settled. Myrtle Lorene Philippi was born in Illinois, January 26, 1903. Her grandfather, Peter Philippi (January 26, 1835-October 24, 1903) came from Germany, meeting her grandmother, Mary C. Fischer (July 6, 1845-April 23, 1927) on the boat coming to America. They had four sons and five daughters. Oather and Myrtle were married November 27, 1920. They had three sons: Arthur, Emil, and Ivan Eugene, and three daughters: Deleen, Betty and Judy. The family moved to Nottingham Township, Wells County, in 1941 to the Petroleum area.

My mother was Lena M. Peel. Her father was Joseph Marion Peel, born November 23, 1861, in Franklin County, Ohio. His parents moved to Wabash Township, Adams County, Indiana, in 1867. They moved by covered wagons, the only means of transportation in those days. He helped his father clear 160 acres, where he grew to manhood along with his two brothers and seven sisters. Her mother, Carrie Mae Cook was born September 29, 1869, in Adams County, Indiana. Carrie was the first daughter of Jacob Cook and Frances Abnet. They had eight children.

Linda Platt, Theresa Breedlove, Emil and Ellen, Karen Murphy, Coralee Miller

Joseph farmed all his life on the same farm east of Berne and raised Belgian horses. One was registered Roscoe Peel #16444. After he sold it, Roscoe became Senior and Grand Champion of the New York Fair, New York. Joseph and Carrie were married July 30, 1887. They had fifteen children; my mother Lena was the twelfth one. She married John A. Linton, May 3, 1927. His family came from Ohio.

They had two daughters, Genevieve and Ellen Linton. Her second marriage was to Fred Johns, who lived in Nottingham Township, west of Petroleum, on November 17, 1939. He had two sons, Keith and Kent. They had one son, Ronald Henry Johns.

Emil I. Breedlove and Ellen Linton were married in Petroleum Church, June 26, 1949. They had four daughters. Linda married Jon Platt in 1969. They had one son, Stephen. Theresa was married to Alvin Waber in 1972, no children. A second marriage to Daniel Varner in 1978, no children. Karen married James Murphy on July 18, 1981, no children. He had two sons and one daughter. Coralee married Fred Miller Jr., November 17, 1979. They have one daughter, Tabitha, and one son, Brian.

We now live in Reiffsburg in the house my step-grandfather, Henry Johns, built in the 1950's on the west side of State Road 1, using the old filling station as part of the house. (*Emil and Ellen Linton Breedlove*)

BREWER

Forace Mahlon and Jennie Evelyn (March) Brewer moved from a farm near Garrett, Indiana to a 127-acre farm three miles southwest of Bluffton on the Hoosier Highway with eight children in 1929. On this farm six more children were born, all delivered at home except the last one.

The family raised watermelons, cantaloupes, and vegetables for sale at the home roadside market. Several swarms of bees produced honey, and hogs, cows, and chickens were raised to eat and sell. Some of the chickens were sold to nearby restaurants. The family canned over 1,000 jars of fruit, vegetables and meat each year.

The roadside market was moved into Bluffton and set up in a tent on the northwest corner of Main and Market Streets. A few months later, it was moved into a building at 116 N. Main Street where it existed for 15 years as a retail and wholesale business of fresh fruits and vegetables. Produce was brought in by truck and train from Michigan, Georgia, and South Carolina. The store motto was "Where you get a square deal." Many people gathered in the store by the pot-bellied stove on Saturday evening after doing their shopping. The store was sold in 1945.

Forace and Jennie Brewer Family, Christmas 1987. Standing left to right: Virginia, Lorene, Hertha, Jennie, Hale, Ines, Jean, Max, Ray Seated: Venita, Jennie, Luana

The family turned to tomatoes for income; hired help harvested them for the canning factory. After Mr. Brewer's death in January 1949, the farm became more diversified and raised grain and livestock. In 1965, Mix Mill bought the farm intending to build a factory on part of the land. The rest of the land was to be an experimental farm, but the plans did not materialize. The farm had since been resold. Jennie moved to Fort Wayne after the farm was sold to Mix Mill; she died in 1988.

Forace was active in community affairs and ran for County Treasurer in 1943. He was the Vice President of the District Duroc Association and showed hogs at local and state fairs. The family attended Prairie and Six Mile Churches. The children attended Poplar Grove Elementary School and Bluffton High School.

The surviving children are: N. Venita Messinger, Indianapolis, retired teacher; Lorene F. Oswalt (Dale), Bluffton, retired registered nurse; Hertha M. Kruckelberg (Kenneth), Moro, Illinios, housewife; Ines M. Gillespie (Robert), Wabash, retired lab and x-ray technician; Jennie V. Kralicek (John), Bryan, Ohio, retired lab and x-ray technician; E. Jean Holmes (Charles), Fort Wayne, registered nurse at Fort Wayne Allergy Consultants; Luana Stanley, Fort Wayne, systems manager at Allen County Public Library; F. Hale (Joan), Bluffton, retired farmer and Amtrak conductor; M. Max (Phyllis), Kendallville, Noble County High School principal and media specialist; W. Ray (Rosalda), Muncie teacher at Delta Middle School.

The deceased children are Ruth, Wanda, Dorothy, and Virginia.

FORACE BREWER FAMILY

Forace Hale Brewer and Evelyn Joan Archbold were married August 16, 1958, at Mulberry Street Wesleyan Church. Forace, of Bluffton, was the son of F.M. and Jennie Brewer. Joan, of Ossian, was the daughter of John E. and Edna Archbold. Forace was a farmer and Joan was the X-ray and laboratory technician at the Wells County (now Community) Hospital after graduating from Marion College, Marion, Indiana. They had three daughters.

In 1967, they both changed careers. Joan began teaching first grade at Rockcreek and Forace accepted a job on the Pennsylvania Railroad. During the following years, she taught third grade at Rockcreek, second and third grades at Lancaster and obtained a master's degree from St. Francis College. Forace worked for Conrail and later as a conductor for Amtrack passenger trains.

Their daughters are all graduates of Bluffton High School.

Kayleen Janele attended Taylor University and graduated from Purdue. She is married to John Reusser and they have three children: Amanda Kay, Christopher John and Lindsay Nicole. She writes articles for several magazines and works at a government job. They live in Port St. Lucie, Florida.

Lynette Elaine attended Kentucky Christian College and graduated from Indiana University. She is co-owner and manager of Ambassador Travel in Fort Wayne.

Camille Elise attended Indiana Wesleyan University and graduated from Ivy Tech. She works at North American Van Lines and is married to Ron Havens. They live in Fort Wayne and have hosted four exchange students.

Forace and Joan retired in 1991 and 1990, respectively. They live on their farm at 1652E - 350S, Bluffton.

BRICKLEY

Harry Dwight Brickley, M.D., was the son of Thomas Jefferson Brickley and Minnie Mosure Brickley. He was born in Bluffton, September 20, 1886. Living later on West Wabash Street, he was five when the first electric street lights were installed. The family moved to a farm in Rockcreek Township, where his sister Marie and brother Raymond were born. Jean Kober well chronicles this family and their ancestors under the entry GIROD-KOBER.

Doctor Brickley attended Valparaiso University, then returned to teach at Sugar Grove School in Uniondale and at Liberty Center. Returning to college, he subsequently was graduated as an M.D. from the Chicago College of Medicine and Surgery in 1913. After five years of practice in Chicago, he enlisted as a first lieutenant in the Army Medical Corps in World War I serving at Camp Mills (New York) Base Hospital. While stationed there, on September 9, 1918, he married Ina Agar, the ceremony taking place in New York City. His bride's parents, William Hoyle Agar, a civil engineer, and Jessie McGuire Agar from Manchester, England, had moved to Perth, Australia, where Ina was born. Moving then to Pullman, Illinois, Ina later became a registered nurse and was the first superintendent of the Wells County Hospital, during World War 1.

Dr. H.D. Brickley 1950's
Mrs. Ina M. Brickley

Dr. and Mrs. Brickley returned to Bluffton in 1920 and established an office in the 100 block of West Washington next to Sharp's Photo Studio. Following erection in 1925 of a medical building, which was located at Main and Cherry Streets, Dr. Brickley was joined by two other well known physicians, Drs. Clarence S. Mead and Orville G. Hamilton, and dentists, Drs. Paul Ritt and Alfred Keller. Over the years, many younger doctors began their careers practicing with Drs. Brickley, Mead and Hamilton. The last of them who succeeded to the practice and now is recently retired is the well-loved Dr. Constantine Panos.

Dwight, or H.D. to his friends, was a member of the Baptist Church, having been baptized in the Wabash River. He was a long time member of the Bluffton School Board, a director of the Old-First National Bank, and both a charter member and past president of the Kiwanis Club. He had been a member of the Masonic Lodge while in New York in World War I. Ina started the first Girl Scout troop in Bluffton, was advisor of Rainbow Girls, and was active in other civic functions. Dr. Brickley's chief avocation, however, was farming, an interest which has been continued by his family as the R.H. & D. Farms.

Dr. and Mrs. Brickley's first son, Thomas Raymond, died at age five. Their second son, Richard, is a retired general surgeon, is married to Suzanne Slusser, and is living in Indianapolis. His oldest child is Dinah Marie, who resides in Chicago. Other children are Sarah Jane, Richard Agar II, Laura Jean, and Andrew John, all of Indianapolis. Their third son, Harry Dwight, Jr. is also a retired general surgeon living in Indianapolis but traveling to Bluffton frequently on farm business. Their daughter, Jean Diann, with her husband, Nicholas J. Balaguras, owns Aristotle's Book Store in Bloomington. Their children are Jean Muir Whitlock, whose husband Todd is a dentist in Bloomington, John Dwight of Chicago, and Jeffrey Thomas.

Dr. Brickley died November 16, 1960, and Mrs. Brickley died December 20, 1990. They rest in Fairview Cemetery.

BRICKLEY FAMILY

Joshua A. Brickley, who was a member of an old and prominent family of Wells County, was a resident here since the early 1850's. Mr. Brickley was born in Rockcreek Township of Wells County, a son of Alfred and Barbara (Haiflich) Brickley. His great-great grandfather was Peter Brickley, who was born about 1720 in Germany. He died around 1800.

Brickley Country Home - Old Homestead

His great grandfather was Andrew Brickley, who was born in Pennsylvania in the late 1700's. He died in 1835. He married Susanne Flick and they migrated to Ohio in 1814. They were the parents of six children, one of whom was George Brickley, who married Bulinda Wolfcale. George and Bulinda are the grandparents of Joshua. They had ten children, one of them being Alfred, who was the father of Joshua.

Alfred was born in Ohio, as was his wife, Barbara, but grew up in Wells County. Alfred cleared away the forest and was prosperous farmer. Alfred died in 1907 and Barbara in 1916. Alfred served his country in the Civil War, enlisting in Company H, first Indiana Regiment. He was a member of the Lew Daily Post of Bluffton. To Alfred and Barbara were born twelve children, all of whom are deceased. They were: Lewis, husband of Alice Nash; Andrew, husband of Mary Lang; Joshua, husband of Mary Cecile Lesh; George, husband of Alice Crum; Bulinda, wife of John Ditzler; Adaline, wife of John Gardenour; Cora, wife of Frank Gardenour; William, Laura, Milo, Arnetta, and Sarah.

Joshua taught school from 1890 to 1908. He then became cashier at the Bank of Uniondale, which later became the State Bank of Uniondale. He and J.B. Miller owned and operated the grain elevator. His wife was Mary Cecile Lesh, daughter of James and Sarah (Staver) Lesh. Her brothers and sisters, all deceased, were Orlo Ervin, William Horton, Ada, Ellen, Grace, Edna, and Minnie.

To Joshua and Mary Cecile were born three children: Darrel K. and Brooks F., both deceased, and Ola I. of Uniondale.

Darrel married Luverne Blose of Springfield, Ohio, who now lives in Fort Wayne. Darrel and Luverne had two children: John, of Bay Village, Ohio, who is married to Joan Steinkraus; and Patricia, of Warren, Pennsylvania, married to David Metcalf. John and Joan have two children: Alan Chandler and Brynn Crystal. Patricia and David have two children: Kimberly Sue and Brian Alan. Brooks married Phyllis Dougal, deceased, of VanWert, Ohio.

Former barn on Jacob Brickley Homestead

Phyllis and Brooks had two boys: James A. and Stephen M. James lives in Rumson, New Jersey, and is married to Marjorie Colegrove. Their two children are Janice, wife of Robert Klein of Omaha, Nebraska and Douglas of Waco, Texas.

Stephen is single and lives in Atlanta, Georgia.

Ola is single and lives in the homeplace in Uniondale. She worked for forty six years at the John A. Morris Company of Bluffton.

RICHARD E. BRICKLEY

Richard was born on February 23, 1938. He is the son of Herbert (1900-1969) and Gladys (1907-1970) (Rohrabaugh) Brickley. Richard's great-great-great-grandfather came from Germany around 1720. Some of his ancestors went to Pennsylvania and some to Indiana (settled around Uniondale). Chester and Zora (Weikle) Brickley were Richard's grandparents. They lived northwest of Uniondale. They were farmers.

Richard married Judy Kahn of Kingsland [daughter of Bill (born 1909) and Vadis [Green] Kahn (1912-1987)] on June 27, 1959.

Richard came from a large family of seventeen children whose names are: Bryce, Dean, Bill, Alice Jacobs, Joan Knight, Elizabeth Heron, Lester, Freida Key, Chester, Dixie Osborn, Beatrice Huffman, Janet Marshall, Clarence, Jerry, George (January 26, 1946-July 23, 1966), and Dorthy Lewis.

Richard Brickley Family
Back row: Rick, Tom, Dick, Mick. Front row: Debbie, Judy and Richard Brickley

Judy also came from a large family of ten children whose names are: Paul, Bill, Tom, Jack, Connie Adams, Linda Lugenbill, Becky Koch, Sally Rehm (May 11, 1941-April 24, 1989), and Dixie Smith (December 31, 1937-August 25, 1989).

Richard and Judy attend Sonlight Church south of Bluffton on State Road #1.

Richard works as a laborer out of Local 213. He has worked at Franklin, Corning, GM in Marion, and Sterling Casting. Richard has helped many farmers in Wells County. He bowls in Bluffton, has played softball on the Corning and Old Timers Leagues, and currently plays for the Sonlight church team. He has watched his four sons play baseball, football, soccer, basketball, and softball.

Richard and Judy have four sons. Rick E. Brickley was born on October 8, 1959. He graduated from Bluffton High School in 1979. Rick is married to Debra Dawson, daughter of Gene and Irene Dawson of Travisville. Rick and Debbie attend Six Mile Church where Debbie is a Sunday School teacher. Debbie is a special education teacher at Bluffton High School. Rick works at Fasson in Fort Wayne. Rick enjoys bowling and playing softball. Rick and Debbie live in Poneto.

Richard and Judy's second son, Mick L. Brickley, was born on July 12, 1961. He graduated in 1979 from Bluffton High School. He attends Sonlight Church.

Richard D. Brickley was born on August 8, 1963. He graduated from Bluffton High School in 1983, and attended IU in Fort Wayne. Richard works at R.E.M.C. in Wabash. He married Tracy Engledow, daughter of Jack and Judy Engledow of Wabash. Richard and Tracy have two daughters: Andrea K. and Alyssa L. They also have a daughter, Amber Herron. Richard enjoys bowling, and he bowled his first 300 game this last fall. He also plays softball.

Thomas W. Brickley was born on January 2, 1971. He graduated from Norwell in 1989. Tom enjoys playing baseball, basketball, football and soccer. He plays softball for Sonlight Church and Ace Hardware. Tom joined the Air National Guard in April of 1989 for six years. His basic training was in Lackland, Texas, from July 24 to September of 1989, and he attended technical school from September to December, 1989, at Sheppard AFB. Tom is now working for Nipsco in Fort Wayne.

ROBERT W. BRICKLEY FAMILY

The Robert W. Brickley family moved to Rockcreek Township, Wells County, in April, 1964, from Huntington County. The home and ground were taken to make a part of the Huntington Reservoir for flood control.

Robert Brickley married Rosalyn A. (Stahl) Brickley. There were four children born to this union. The children are Louise Kay, Scott A., Kevin L., and Brian L.

Louise Kay married James E. Inskeep, and they have two children, Andrew Robert and Emily Roseanne.

Scott A. married Sandra L. (Sink) Brickley, and they have three children, Nicole Lynn, Jason Paul, and Jared Clinton.

Kevin L. married Donna M. (Temple) Brickley, and they have one child, Rachel Marie.

WILLIAM HERBERT BRICKLEY (HERB.)

Herb Brickley's great-great grandfather, Peter Brickley, came from Germany. Peter was born around 1720. He came to the U.S. and died around 1800. He had a large family. One member of this family was Andrew Brickley. Andrew married Susanna Flick, and they had eleven children. One of these children was David Brickley who was born December 21, 1804, in Pennsylvania and died February 9, 1887, in Indiana. David was married to Mary Wolfcale on November 15, 1828. Some of their children were Mary, Jonathan, and Andrew. Andrew Brickley, a Civil War Veteran, was born on November 15, 1837, and died on September 27, 1909. He was married to Sarah Wet. They had five children: William, born on May 11, 1869; Bertia, born on June 17, 1872, Effie, born on May 20, 1885, Clarence, born on February 20, 1889, and Chester, who was born on February 29, 1876, and died on January 27, 1948. Chester was married to Zora May Weikel November 29, 1899. They lived in Uniondale where he worked as a farmer. Chester and Zora had three children: William Herbert Brickley, Sarah (Brickley) Hatfield, and Edna (Brickley) Sanderson.

William Herbert Brickley was born on September 7, 1900, and died on November 13, 1969. He was married to Gladys Rohrabaugh on November 7, 1925. Gladys was born on January 14, 1907, and died on November 18, 1970. She was the daughter of Curtis Elmer Rohrabaugh and Estalla Fetterhoff. Herb worked as a farmer in Wells, Allen, and Adams counties. He also worked at the Hoosier Condensery and the Wells County Highway as a road grader. Herb liked his mules, Ginnie and Kate. They were show mules, and they got many first place ribbons when he showed them at fairs. Herb played horseshoe and fast-pitch softball in Uniondale and Markle. Most of all he loved to play cards, go to go-cart races, and attend Rockcreek basketball games.

Herb and Gladys had seventeen children, seventy-six grandchildren, ninety-eight great grandchildren, and one great-great grandchild. Of the seventeen children were: Bryce, born May 6, 1926. He went to the service from 1944 to 1946. Dean, born November 22, 1928, he married Gelene McDonald on July 24, 1948; William, born May 6, 1930, married Lois Brown on March 24, 1951 and went to the service from 1951 to 1953. Alice, born September 12, 1931, married Ralph Jacobs on September 9, 1951. Elizabeth, born September 27, 1932, married William Haron. Joan, born September 24, 1933, married Phyneal Knight on April 21, 1956. Lester, born January 22, 1935, married Maxine Lowe, on March 25, 1977. Frieda, born August 21, 1936, married Roland Key on June 18, 1958. Richard, born February 3, 1938, married Judy Kahn on June 27, 1959. Chester, born April 9, 1939, married Jeanne Maurer on April 1, 1967. Dixie born March 5, 1940, married Hank Osborn on July 2, 1960. Beatrice, born June 7, 1941, married John Huffman on February 2, 1963. Janet Marshall, born June 13, 1942.

Clarence, born August 15, 1943, married Debbie Nicholas on March 9, 1985. Jerry, born October 6, 1944, married Pat Lang on October 1, 1965. Jerry was in the service from October 1965 to October 1967. George, born January 26, 1946, died on July 23, 1966. Dorothy Lewis was born March 14, 1947.

BRINKMAN FAMILY

Our parents were Edward and Irma (Matson) Brinkman. They both lived most of their eighty plus years in Bluffton, Indiana.

Edward, or Ed as he was known in Bluffton, was the son of Henry and Ellen Brinkman of Fort Wayne. He was born July 25, 1883, and died in Bluffton September 17, 1967. His mother and father both came to this country from Germany. He lived in Fort Wayne until he was fifteen and then went to St. Louis, Missouri, until he came back to Bluffton in 1904. He worked in foundries and learned to be a molder and worked at this trade most of his life. His last six working years were spent at General Electric Company in Fort Wayne, from where he retired.

On August 23, 1905, he married Irma Matson. She was born in Montpelier, Indiana, on May 25, 1885, and died in Bluffton June 9, 1967. When she was three weeks old, her parents moved to Bluffton and she spent the rest of her life there. Her parents were Denial and Margaret Matson. Her mother was born in Ireland and her father was from Ohio of Scottish ancestors.

Our parents were true Hoosiers. They were never happy to be away from Bluffton for very long. They lived on West Central Avenue and their children were born and raised there. There were five daughters and three sons. Carl and Norman died as newborns, and Barbara died of pneumonia at fourteen months.

Dad, Mom and Jr. on leave from Navy

Their oldest daughter, Ruth, lived in Bluffton and was married to Howard Bowman. They are both deceased. They had two sons, Jerry and John, and three daughters, Mary, Nancy, and Rebecca.

Edna was married to Jack Cotton from Bluffton. They moved to Michigan and later to Arizona, where they both died. They had five sons, Max, Carlton, Jack Jr., Larry, and Robert and one daughter, Patricia.

Helen was married to Carl Brand from Bluffton and lived near Petroleum until he retired, and then moved to Angola. They had three sons, James, Donald, and Robert, and one daughter, Rosemary. Robert is deceased.

Mildred was married to John G. Summers and has lived in Three Rivers and Kalamazoo, Michigan, for 56 years. They have three sons, David, Thomas and Michael, and one daughter, Karen.

Edward Jr., married Evelyn Mills, from Tocsin and they also lived in Three Rivers and now in Kalamazoo. They have one son, Rodney, ad one daughter, Sandra.

All five children attended school in Bluffton and some of their teachers also taught their mother.

Although I am sure Mother and Dad would have been pleased to have their children stay in Wells County, they have scattered to many places: California, Arizona, Colorado, Texas, Oregon, New York, Florida, and Michigan.

Their home is still standing on Central Avenue and through the years has been kept up very nicely and still seems like home to Helen, Edward Jr., and myself.

There are numerous great and great, great grandchildren and they too are scattered throughout the country.

I remember one time when we took Mother and Dad to Phoenix, and then all the way home, they could hardly wait to get back to God's Country— Bluffton! *Submitted by Mildred Brinkman Summers, Edward Brinkman Jr., Helen Brinkman Brand*

BRINEMAN-MINNIEAR

Family of Clarence H. and Ingabee (Bee) Brineman Minniear

Clarence Hampton Minniear, the third child of Albert and Viola Perlina (Clark) Minniear, was born on December 21, 1901, in Liberty Township, Wells County Indiana. He was married on February 27, 1926 to Ingabee (Bee) Brineman, (November 6, 1905) in Liberty Center, Indiana. She was the daughter of Jefferson Daniel and Vernosha Belle (Croasdale) Brineman. They lived at Gary, Indiana, for thirty years and then returned to their farm located at Markle in 1953 on their retirement. Clarence H. Minniear died on November 23, 1984; burial was in Horeb Cemetery, Uniondale, Indiana.

Phyllis Dene Minniear, the first child of

Dean, Bill, Dorothy, Richard, Chester, Brice, Joan, Clarence, Beatrice, Warren, Elizabeth, Jerry, George.
Front row: Freida, Janet, Gladys, Herb, Dixie, Alice

271

Clarence Hampton and Ingabee (Bee) Brineman Minniear, was born on August 18, 1927, at Gary, Indiana. She is a Spanish-English teacher in the Porter County School System, having earned her AB degree from Valparaiso University and an MA from Indiana University. She was married on July 5, 1952, to Russell Floyd Franzman, who was born on November 8, 1927, at Cannelton, Indiana; the son of Oscar and Nellie (Robinson) Franzman. Russell served in the armed forces in Korea from 1946 to 1947. He is owner of a printing company at Hebron, Indiana.

Russell Hampton (Rusty) Franzman, the only child of Phyllis Dene (Minniear) and Russell F. Franzman, was born on February 1, 1957, at Porter County, Indiana. He attended Ferris State University at Big Rapids, Michigan, and was married on November 4, 1978, to Susanne Marie Lewandowski. She was born on September 30, 1954, at Gary, Indiana. She is the daughter of John J. and Catherine Jean (Smurdon) Lewandowski. The children of Russell and Susanne are: Chad Michael Franzman, born on August 7, 1978, at Hebron, Indiana; and Kathryn Dene Franzman, born on December 9, 1983, at Hebron, Indiana.

Doris Marie Minniear, second child of Clarence Hampton and Ingabee (Brineman) Minniear was born on July 2, 1930, at Gary, Indiana. She was a secretary to the dean of the American University Graduate School in Washington, D.C. and is currently serving as consultant in the student loan department of Ferris State University in Michigan. Her marriage to Charles R. Bayor occurred on October 10, 1947. He is the son of Charles and Martha (Mitckess) Bodinger, and later was adopted by his mother and step-father Hosea Bayor. He was born on September 18, 1926. He is a graduate of Valparaiso University and served in World War II.

Gregory Adam Bayor, the fifteenth generation and only child of Charles R. and Doris (Minniear) Bayor was born on July 14, 1948, at Gary, Indiana. He was one of the Eagle Boy Scouts selected to usher at the inauguration ceremonies of President Lyndon B. Johnson, on January 20, 1965, in Washington, D.C. He earned his degree from the University of Baltimore and is currently employed as Superintendent of Parks and Recreation at Rockville, Maryland. He was married on January 3, 1976, to Virginia Anne Gambrill. She was born on January 1, 1952, at Baltimore, Maryland, daughter of Paul M. and Sarah Ann (Anderson) Gambrill.

Doris Marie Minniear's second marriage was on August 10, 1963, to Aaron Lewis Andrews. He was born on November 15, 1920, in Birmingham, Ohio. He was the son of Lee and Merle (Couldtrip) Andrews and was the senior dean and founder of the Health and Allied Science Schools at Ferris State University in Michigan. He served in the Navy during World War II and the Korean War and was retired in the rank of commander. Aaron L. Andrews died on March 15, 1990, at Big Rapids, Michigan.

Suzannah Marie Andrews, the only child of Aaron Lewis and Doris Marie (Minniear) Andrews, was born on December 23, 1965, in Washington, D.C. A 1986 graduate of Ferris State University in Michigan, she is currently employed as a court and convention reporter. She was married on June 12, 1988, to Ian Bruce Barrie. He was born on July 20, 1963, at Highland Park, Michigan. He is the son of Bruce Leon and Barbara June (Rice) Barrie. A graduate of Collins Graphic School, he majored in advertising design and computer graphics.

VERNON BRINNEMAN FAMILY

These are the years from 1834 and into 1991 of the Vernon Edward Brinneman family.

Jefferson Brinneman was born April 2, 1834, to Daniel and Rebecca (Shaufer) Brinneman. He had a sister, Medora.

Mathias and Mary (Kesner) Glass were parents of John, Jacob, George, Daniel, Solomon, Susan Ann, Mary Ann, and Katherine. The sons all served in the Civil War.

Mathias and Mary Glass were buried in the "old" cemetery in northwest Bluffton, Indiana.

Jefferson Brinneman and Susan Ann Glass were married March 3, 1861. Children born to this union were Iliph Elmore, Solomon Wilmore, Mary Etta, Ida Ellen, Rachel Rebecca, Elza Allen, and three sets of twins. They were Mathias Emanuel and Jefferson Daniel; Margaret Katherine and Edward Marcellus; and Augustus Newton and Oscar Homer.

Jefferson died in 1881, leaving Susan a widow at age 39 with twelve children. She also raised two grandchildren, Clara Brinneman and Grant Frantz. Susan died in 1918. Susan and Jefferson were buried in the "old" Bluffton Cemetery.

Vernon and Mildred Brinneman

Augustus Newton Brinneman and Sarah Brown Romine were married June 2, 1916. Their son, Vernon Edward, was born April 20, 1918. Sarah Catherine had four children by an earlier marriage to Charles Romine. They are Clarence, Arthur, Minnie and Lloyd.

Vernon Edward Brinneman and Mildred Luella Killingbeck were married June 22, 1940, by the Rev. Morris Coers, in Bluffton, Indiana.

Mildred is a daughter of William and Dovie (Bellville) Killingbeck.

Children born to Vernon and Mildred were James Edward, December 13, 1942; Lorin Richard, December 26, 1947; and Kathryn Sue, February 27, 1957.

James joined the United States Marines upon graduation from high school in 1960. He fell in love with a California girl, Donna May Sharp, daughter of Donovan and Laurel Sharp. They were married April 26, 1963, by the Chaplain of his unit. They have three children: Laura Jean, March 17, 1964; Lawrence Ross, August 15, 1965; and Thomas Edward, February 19, 1971.

Laura Jean became the wife of Robert Gillespie, who also has seen duty in the military. They have no children as of this date.

Lawrence Ross and Rochelle Hinote were wed November 16, 1988. They became the parents of Ashley Nicole, February 20, 1990, and Shawn Ross, February 7, 1991.

Thomas Edward joined the National Forestry Service shortly after high school graduation in 1989.

Lorin Richard Brinneman and Frances Elizabeth Parr became husband and wife August 28, 1976. Children born to this union are Amber Dawn, August 24, 1977; Jessica Diane, June 1, 1981; and Shawna Lea, January 5, 1986.

Lorin has served in the United States. He and his brother, James, have both seen overseas duty.

Kathryn Sue Brinneman and Kent Duane Wolf married in 1974. Children born to this union are Jeremy Daniel, November 20, 1974; Jason Edward, January 8, 1977; and Michelle Reneé, October 20, 1983.

The union of Kathryn and Kent Wolf was dissolved in 1984.

Kathryn (Brinneman) Wolf and Jerry Wayne Powers, son of Bennie and Buelah Powers, were happily wed July 20, 1989. Jerrad and Jacob are Jerry's sons by an earlier marriage.

BRODT-BECKLER

From about 1570 A.D. to the time of emigration to America in 1832, over 400 years covers the span of my grandmother Brodt's family. Members of this family lived in Wurttemburg, Germany, before emigration.

The surname of the first and second generations of this Brodt family was Brottsehelm instead of Brodt. In the German language, the second syllable of this name is translated "a joker". This perhaps was the reason why Hans Brodt of the second generation dropped the Schelm syllable, retaining the simplified name of Brodt which occurred in 1650.

*Porch Balcony - Frank Beckler and John Beckler
Front - William and Elizabeth Beckler, Benjamin and Christena, Louis and Anna Beckler*

Hans Brodt of the third generation married Anna Weisser, the daughter of Jacob Weisser, the mayor of Grossaspach. A quote from the church record - "he was of good conduct benefactor of the poor, as well as ministry." To the church he presented the Ulmer Bible in 1729, which was printed in Germany. He died in May 31, 1729, under the ministry of the church.

Johann Brodt of the sixth generation was mayor of Klein, Wurttemburg. The site of this village is on the Neckar River surrounded by red wine vineyards.

The Brodt homestead is located in the village of Klein Ingersheim. John Fetzer who passed away in 1991 visited this home and took photographs in 1952.

Jakob Brodt of the seventh generation and his wife and family settled in Sugar Creek region, near New Philadelphia, Ohio. One of their children, Gottlieb, was my great-grandfather. He was born October 27, 1803, in Germany, died in Wells County, Indiana, September 7, 1871. He is buried in the Horeb Cemetery near Uniondale. He married Margaretta Seaman in Ohio in 1835.

They had eight children, Mary, Lana, Christena,

Catherine, Elizabeth, Rachel, Gottlieb, and John.

Mary Brodt married John Fetzer in Wells County, October 27, 1867. Their children were Barbara and John.

Lana Brodt married John Zimmerman, who owned the ice pond east of Bluffton.

Brodt homestead located in the village of Klein Ingersheim

Christena Brodt was born in Hocking County, Ohio, December 20, 1842, and died in Wells County in 1914. She married Benjamin Beckler. They were my grandparents. They had six children, William, Frank, John, who was my father, Louis, Elizabeth and Anna.

Catherine Elizabeth married John Harsh. They had three children, Edward, Mary, and Cora. John A. Fetzer was left as an orphan at the age of twelve. He lived with the Harsh family until he was seventeen.

Rachel married William Baber.

Gottlieb Brodt was born in 1850, died in 1882 - married Sara Jane Meeks.

John Brodt was married to Emma Sechler.

My parents, John W. Becker married to Grace Pearson of Blackford County. She was a daughter of William Harvey Pearson and Elizabeth Nelson Pearson.

My brother is John W. Beckler. His wife is Constance (Hill) of Decatur. They have four children, Gary of Xenia, Ohio, Kathy, who is married to Wayne Ley of Huntington. Gary's children are Aaron, Andrew, and Allissa. Cheryl Zoll, husband Marshall, who are residents of Greencastle, Indiana. Cheryl Marshall's children are Stephanie, Mitch, and Rachel. Timothy John Beckler of Bluffton, wife Tammy (Phipps). Tim's daughters are Alison and Laura.

The writer, Pauline Beckler Zoll was married to Sebert Zoll on July 20, 1968, he passed away March 1, 1979.

BROMAN

Ralph and Barbara Broman came to Wells County in 1953 for his employment as math and science teacher in the P.A. Allen High School. After completing his A.B. degree in 1950, Ralph served in the army during the Korean War. An instructor in chemical-bacteriological-radiological warfare, Ralph was assigned to the Presidio of San Francisco. He and Barb lived in California until his discharge in 1952, when they returned to Indiana. Ralph taught one year in Rush County. In 1954 Ralph contracted polio. He completed his M.A. degree from I.U. in 1960. Retiring in 1989, Ralph was a thirty-seven year career teacher.

Both of Ralph's parents were career teachers, starting at the ages of eighteen and seventeen in one-room schoolhouses. After their two children entered school, Rosa taught and studied for her B.S. degree, finishing at the age of 56. Roy taught and completed his A.B. degree, earning Phi Beta Kappa membership at I.U. His M.A. degree was earned at I.U. early in his forty year career at Mishawaka High School.

Ralph's parents were second generation immigrants from Sweden. Between 1870 and 1890 both grandfathers left Sweden with brothers and sisters to come to America, and both grandmothers came over with their parents. Eric Bowman and Anna Malmsten lived in Chicago, but they and John Nelson and Emelia Rapp settled near Chesterton in Porter County. Later, they lived in western Marshall County and eastern Stark County, where Ralph's parents grew up.

Barbara is descended from pioneers who arrived in America in the 1700's and wended their ways west to Indiana. The Millers were Holland Dutch who started from New Jersey and headed across Pennsylvania and Ohio. In 1835, Benjamin Miller and Jane Calvert from Virginia settled in Randolph County, Indiana. Also settling in Randolph County were her great-great-grandparents, Taylor and Mariah Thorn, who had started out from North Carolina in 1832. Newlyweds eighteen and fifteen years old, they walked most of the way.

Barbara's great-grandparents, Josiah and Isabel Jewett, married in Decatur County and moved to Carroll County in 1850. Their daughter married Samuel Hunt in Carroll County and in 1918 moved to Randolph County. In Randolph County Barbara's parents met and married; they, Everett and Nellie Hunt, began farming but in 1929 moved to Anderson.

Ralph and Barbara met while students at Ball State. Their first child, David Alan, born in Anderson in 1952, and wife Joyce Cylkowski from Detroit have two sons, Corey and Joseph, and live in Kokomo. Nancy Christina, born in 1954 in Bluffton, is married to Jeffrey Winkle from Cincinnati. They, with daughter Amberly, live in North Carolina. Robert Eric, born in 1955, and wife Karen Echols from Dallas live with sons Eric and Benjamin in Wisconsin. Nelson Arthur, born in 1957, lives in Bluffton with wife Linda (Herman) from Wells County and daughters, Angela and Allison. Carl Edwards, born in 1962, resides in Seattle. All five children attended college, four have degrees, and several are continuing their formal education.

LAWRENCE BROTHERS

The Lawrence (Larry) Brothers family moved to Zanesville, Indiana, seventeen years ago. Lora grew up in Ohio on an eighty-acre farm located in Van Wert County. She is one of eight children born to Frederick and Mildred Germann. She has five brothers and two sisters. Lora's father (now deceased) was a lifelong farmer in Ohio, and the farm has been in the Germann family for over two hundred years. Lora's mother, Mildred, is a resident of Convoy Care in Convoy, Ohio. Lora works at Lincoln National Life Insurance Co. in Fort Wayne, Indiana.

Lawrence Brothers, Lora, Lance, and Lorena

Lawrence is the only child of John and Erma Brothers (now deceased) of Huntertown, Indiana. Lawrence and his parents lived on a farm owned by his grandparents, Edward and Marie Bobay. John Brothers retired after working for 30 years at General Electric in Fort Wayne, Indiana. Brothers has been a tool grinder for over twenty years and is currently employed at Peace-Windamatic in Huntertown, Indiana.

The Brothers have two children. Their son, Lance, is a graduate of Norwell High School, Ossian, Indiana, and is a sophomore at Indiana University in Bloomington. Their daughter, Lorena, is a senior at Norwell High School and plans on entering college in the fall. The Brothers attend the Zanesville Church of God in Zanesville, Indiana.

BROWN

The Brown Family came from Rush County to Grant County, Indiana, in the late 1800's. Mahlon

Standing: Nelson, David, Joyce, Robert, Karen, Allison, Linda, Carl, Nancy. Sitting: Jim Sharp, Earl Sharp, Veral Broman Sharp, Jeff, Angel, Barbara, Ralph. Floor: Corey and Ben, Joseph, Amberly and Eric Christmas 1990

Deboyd Brown was born to Clara Love and Charles A. Brown on December 8, 1896, in Grant County, Indiana. He died on March 29, 1970 in Bluffton, Indiana and is buried at the Lancaster Cemetery in Huntington County, Indiana. He married Mildred Gertrude Beal February 15, 1919, at the Church of Christ in Warren, Indiana. Mildred was born in Huntington County, September 4, 1901, the daughter of Cora Alice Rittenhouse and Chester Hayes Beal. Mildred died March 28, 1979, and is buried at the Lancaster Cemetery in Huntington County. The children born to Mahlon and Mildred are, Maxine Lavon Moser of Wren, Ohio. Robert Leon Brown of Marion, Indiana. Helen Berniece Schnitz of Decatur, Indiana. Bertha Jean Malson of Fort Wayne, Indiana. Marvin Lewis Brown of Valparaiso, Indiana. Harold Dean Brown, deceased. Doris Joan Alexander of Franklin, Indiana. Carl Edwin Brown of St. Petersburg, Florida. Larry Wayne Brown of Greenfield, Indiana. Linda Kay Higgins of Plano, Texas, and Judith Diane Hoopingarner of Florissant, Missouri.

On July 17, 1918, Mahlon was notified that as a result of his physical examination, he was found by the local board for division #2, Grant County, Indiana to be qualified for military service. He went into town for daily training but the war ended before he was called into service. Later, three of his sons would serve the country. One in the Army, one in the Air Force and one in the Navy.

Mahlon and Mildred, with their five children, moved to Wells County from Huntington County, Indiana, in 1929. They first lived on a farm near Liberty Center. They lived there only a short time and then moved to Bluffton in 1930. During the next fourteen years, the family lived in several rental houses including one in Vera Cruz. In 1944, they purchased a home on the southeast corner of Main and Arnold Streets and that was the family home until 1966 when they moved to a smaller home at 316 South Wayne Street where they lived until they died. It was during the Great Depression when the family moved to Bluffton. Mahlon worked for a dairy and did carpentry work. Mahlon continued to do carpentry work the rest of his life. He joined the carpenter's union in 1941.

In 1930, the family's 17-month old son, Harold, died of spinal meningitis. Everyone was having trouble making ends meet at this time but people helped whenever they could. The Jahn Funeral Home provided their services in return for Mahlon doing some painting and carpentry work and driving the ambulance when needed.

The family were members of the Church of Christ in Bluffton, which was located on the southeast corner of Cherry and Johnson Streets. At about 1930, the congregation was too small to financially keep the doors open and the First Baptist Church across the street asked the few remaining families to join them. The family became faithful members of the First Baptist Church.

BROWN

Our Brown family can be dated from early English history including their settlement in Virginia in 1650. Our great-grandfather, John Sloan Brown, later settled in Clinton County, Ohio, where our grandpap, Daniel Routh Brown, was born. He married Sarah Emily Haynie. They had three children, Clarence, George Wilbert (1873), and Alice Erminnie (Carnes), before they were influenced by a relative to come to Wells County, "Which was building up fast!"

Grandpap taught school near Wilmington, Ohio, before moving to Wells County in 1879. They had a home northwest of Liberty Center, and later bought land one mile north of Mount Zion. He cleared the land and built a house and barn that became their "home place." He was a noted mathematician and carpenter who built many barns in that community. Three more children were born in Wells County—Mary Jane (Hensel and McHenry), Corina (Dawson), and Robert.

Our dad, George Wilbert (Bert), was a tool dresser in the oil fields when he was young. Because he didn't like horses, he was one of the first in Wells County to buy a "machine," as autos were then called. In 1900 he bought a one-cylinder 1899 Oldsmobile in Indianapolis and drove it home. A Mr. Haines from Kokomo, who was a car manufacturer, rode as far as Kokomo with him. On this trip three buggies were upset because the horses were frightened by the car. He felt like taking the car back. Soon he made it into a two-cylinder car.

(L-R) Bertha, Dortha, Mae, Dad, Mother, Mary, Edith, and Violet

About 1901 or 1902, the Warren Fair Association influenced dad and a Mr. Foust from Warren to run a race on the fairground's one-half mile track. They advertised it widely and a large crowd attended. Both cars developed engine trouble and neither finished the race. The Indianapolis Speedway has determined this was the first auto race in Indiana with paid admission.

Dad married Mamie Irena Ruble, daughter of James and Berthena Tharp Ruble, in 1905. He continued working in the oil fields until 1913 when he became manager of the Liberty Center Telephone Company. He held this position until his death in 1946.

In 1917, he took a leave of absence to work in the oil fields near Peru, Kansas. That same year he had to return to Liberty Center because of the draft for World War I. He didn't have to serve. We had gone to Kansas on the train but for his return he decided to drive his 1910 Ford. Later that year all eight of us made the trip back home to Liberty Center. It took one week — we had to stay in Missouri an extra day because of the gasless Sunday during the war. The next time you see a 1910 Ford in a parade, consider two adults and six girls making the eventful trip.

The six daughters are: Violet, who married George Jones and had three children: Jane, Wilbert, and Joan. Mae (deceased) married Edward H. Sprat. They had two children, Patricia and Edward, Jr. Edith married William R. Ward. They had two children, Rebecca and Ruth Mary. Mary married Dale Tinkel, two children, Bert Thomas and Sarah Sue. Dortha married Kenneth Small; four children: Timothy, Kathryn, Judith and Karen. Bertha married Omer Fisher, three children, Stephen, Millicent (Ann), and Cynthia.

BROWN

Return with me now to those early times of yesteryear, from out of the past comes the sound of, "Wild West in Wells County." The "Buffalo Bill Tent Show" had come to Bluffton and young Anna Brown, of dating age, attended the entertainment with her sister. It was here that Anna met William Travis and my heritage began.

Soloman and Jacob Brown grew up as brothers in Brownsville, Pennsylvania. Soloman came to Indiana, married Hanna Haiflich, in Wells County, and the union brought eleven children, seven reaching adulthood. Daughter Anna grew up with brothers, Amos, Lewis, William, Charles, and Jess, and sister, Sarah. Times were hard and everyone worked to help with daily life. Anna could remember, as a young child, she needed to stand on a box to manage her task of making the bread. Two of the boys married, two remained bachelors, the girls married, and Jess died in an accidental fire.

On December 20, 1899, at Poneto, Anna Brown married William Travis. William Travis' parents were Jeanette Grove and Thomas Travis. Times continued to be hard, but they managed to raise their children in love and security. Through an eight year period of illness of Bill, Anna kept the family going by raising their own food, and doing services for others to supplement their meager income. They lost a baby son their first year of marriage. A second son survived until age seven. Their third son, Ralph, became a musician and settled near Columbia City, before illness took his life at age thirty-five. They also had two daughters who have happy memories of growing up in Bluffton. Martha married Herbert Black, and lived in Uniondale, raising three children, Carol, Adrienne and Michael. Daughter DeVota married Lawrence Ross, of Ossian, in 1927. With young daughter, Marilyn, they lived in Indianapolis while Lawrence completed Pharmacy College. Returning to Bluffton, he worked at the Caylor-Nickel Clinic the remaining years of his life. A son, William, lived to be twenty-one, dying in a gun accident.

Marilyn married Craig Kleinknight in 1951, and moved to Indianapolis. Their Heavenly Bundles included daughters Kimberly and Krista, and a son, Mark Alden. Kim married David Brown and moved to New Jersey, now with daughter Hilary, age four. In 1989, DeVota Ross graduated from this life in May, and in November of that year, Kim and David were blessed as a son, Jacob Brown, came into this life - thus, bringing to full circle the Brown ancestry.

DARRELL E. BROWN FAMILY

Darrel E. Brown was born August 17, 1948, in Wells County. Darrell is the oldest of six children born to Edwin and Emojean Brown, all in Wells County.

Darrell graduated from Montepelier High School in 1966 and Purdue University in 1970. He married Connie Sue Williams in 1968. Darrell and Connie have two children: Michelle René Brown, born September 13, 1971, and Craig Matthew Brown, born March 16, 1974. Michelle graduated from Blackford High School in 1990 and is a student at Hanover College at this writing.

Darrel worked for the Soil Conversation Service from 1970 until 1978, when the family moved back to the family farm. He began farming the home farm and continues to this time. He is also working for the Soil Conservation Service again.

Darrell's wife, Connie, is the daughter of the

late Ivan A. Williams, Sr. and Mary Fuller Williams of rural Blackford County. Ivan, one of thirteen children, was born on April 18, 1919, to William and Annabelle Shivers Williams, who moved to Indiana from Lebanon, Missouri. Mary Fuller Williams, one of seven children, was born on September 23, 1928, to James Harley Fuller and Goldie Pearl Hizer Fuller. The Fullers were born in Blackford County, Indiana. Mary's maternal grandparents were Aaron M. Hizer and Sarah Elizabeth James Fuller.

Darrell and Connie's home is on the Blackford - Jay County line on a farm listed as a "Hoosier Homestead." Darrell's great-great-grandfather acquired the farm in 1851. According to earlier histories, Tom Haverfield's father, Nathan, was born near Wheeling, West Virginia, in 1797. Earlier Haverfields came to America from Ireland.

EDWIN V. BROWN FAMILY

Edwin Brown was born to William and Pearl Bell Marker Brown September 8, 1921, in Nottingham Township, Wells County. His great-grandfather was Phillip Brown, and Jacob Brown was his grandfather. Edwin's brothers are: Harold (deceased) Earl, Howard (deceased), Clyde and Joy.

Edwin married Emojean Inskeep at Liberty Center in 1943. Emojean's parents were Charles B. and Mary Elizabeth (Molly) Reece Inskeep. Her grandparents, William and Margaret (Dye) Inskeep came to Indiana from Ohio in 1853. John Alexander and Mary Emiline (Kimmer) Reece came to Indiana from North Carolina, moving to Plum Tree in 1894.

Top row L to R: Marcia, Darrell, Cynthia Bottom row L to R: Gloria, Marvin, Saundra

Edwin graduated from Montpelier in 1939, and from Purdue in 1943. He served in World War II, as a medical laboratory technician in the army in New Guinea for three years. Edwin taught school ten years in Wells County.

In 1936 William and Pearl took over the Haverfield-Marker farm, located on the Blackford-Jay County line. This farm is listed as a "Hoosier Homestead", acquired by Thomas Haverfield in 1851. This is the retirement home of Edwin and Emojean Brown. Edwin's grandparents were Daniel Monroe Marker and Mary Augustus (Haverfield) Marker.

Emojean was born in Rockcreek Township in 1923. Her sisters were: Dorotha (Mrs. Seved) Rochon (deceased 1979), Mary Esther (Mrs. Arthur) Line; Virginia (Mrs. Joe) Lieurance, Charlene (Mrs. Warren) Young, a brother, William (married Doris Vickrey). All six of the children graduated from Rockcreek High School.

Edwin and Emojean have six living children: Darrell E. 1948, married Connie Williams; their children are Michelle R., and Craig M. Marvin G. 1951, first marriage was to Angela Moore. Their children are: Eric A. and Jason P. Marvin's second marriage was (Spore) Bosstick. Mary's sons: Ronald, John, Shane and Joe Bosstick. Gloria J., 1953, married Bruce Osborn. Their children are: Jennifer B., Joshua K., Julie Ann. Marcia E., 1957, (married Thomas Davey). Their children are Beniah, Lydia, Amos, Anna, Naomi, John, Magdalen. Cynthia E., 1958 (married James Young). Their children are: Christina, Beth Ann, Phillip. Saundra Brown, 1959, her children are Amber D. and Jarred.

Edwin and Emojean Brown

Edwin spent twenty-five years as an employee of Soil Conservation Service (USDA), working in Jay, Blackford and Vigo Counties.

An additional 160 acres was purchased in 1962 and 1969. This land is farmed by Darrell and Craig Brown.

The children's interests while living on the farm in Blackford and Vigo counties were : 4-H, band, church youth groups, and campus life. Edwin, Darrell and Marvin farmed and raised cattle, hogs and sheep. Emojean is an Amway distributor.

Edwin and Emojean attend Blackford Baptist Temple Church near Hartford City.

Emojean is descended from a Revolutionary Soldier, Abraham Inskeep, who resided at Hampshire County, Virginia (now West Virginia). Emojean is a member of DAR, Francois Godfroy Chapter.

More information on Edwin Brown Family is on record in the Bluffton library.

JOY L. BROWN

Joy L. Brown was born on the Brown farm in Nottingham Township on the Wells-Blackford County Line on January 23, 1913. His parents were William and Pearl Marker Brown. There were six boys in their family, Harold, Earl, Howard, Clyde, Joy and Edwin.

Joy graduated from Petroleum High School in 1931. He continued to farm with his father until 1936; then his parents moved into Blackford County, four miles east of Montpelier on State Road 18.

On April 11, 1936, Joy was united in marriage to Pauline Arnold, who was born September 13, 1916. They continued to farm on the Brown farm where Joy was born. Pauline was the daughter of Theodore and Matilda Masterson Arnold. They lived in Nottingham and ran the country store.

Joy and Pauline had one son, Kent, who was born February 4, 1951. Kent married Dora Harper and they have two sons, Jayson, twenty-one and Wesley, ten years old. They have one grandson, Derrick. Kent graduated from Southern Wells High School in 1969. Kent then attended the Indianapolis Barber School and upon graduation, worked for seventeen years in the Boise Barber Shop in Montpelier, Indiana.

Frances Stepp Hart Brown and Joy L. Brown

Joy was elected to the board of Well County Commissioners in 1957. His term started January 1, 1958, as the terms at that time were for three years each. He served three years terms followed by three four years terms for a total of twenty-one years.

Joy and Pauline were married forty-nine years when Pauline passed away on May 4, 1985.

On January 16, 1988, Frances Stepp Hart and Joy were united in marriage. Frances was born in Wells County, Nottingham Township, on September 24, 1916, to C. Bert and Carrie Karns Stepp, the seventh of twelve children. (Ten of the twelve children are still living.) Frances graduated from Petroleum High School in 1935.

In April 1937, Frances was united in marriage to Delmar Hart, son of John W. and Flora Martin Hart of Blackford County. They had four children: Joyce Hart Lee of Montpelier, Indiana, Jerry W. Hart of Tustin, California, Judy Hart Herring of Keystone, Indiana, and Jeffrey Hart of Logansport, Indiana.

Delmar retired from the Montpelier Post Office in June 1973 after thirty-five years. He was a rural carrier when he retired. They lived in the Montpelier area thirty-seven years. In December, 1973, Delmar passed away. Frances continued living in Montpelier until January 1988, when she sold her home in Montpelier and married Joy Brown of Wells County and moved in his house, where they are currently living at 9533E 1200S, Montpelier, Indiana.

BROWN-MCCREERY

A little over three miles west of Poneto, Indiana, on State Road 218 in Chester Township, is where Arthur Shriver Brown was born on June 14, 1884. The middle child of Frank T. Brown and Martha Rose (Shriver) Brown, he was a premature baby weighing around three pounds. His mother kept him warm in a box on the oven door. As he grew, his mother rode a horse side saddle carrying him on a pillow.

Arthur Brown's parents came to Indiana from Guernsey County, Ohio, around 1876. His father and uncles came earlier to clear the land. The little house they lived in still stands behind the large two story brick home built in 1917.

He was called "Brownie" by his friends and neighbors. He went to Popejoy one-room school in Liberty Township. He graduated from Liberty Center High School. When he was twelve years old, his mother died of typhoid fever. He was taught to farm at an early age and always enjoyed it. He was active in the Republican party, the Elks Lodge, and all bodies of the Masonic Order. In 1913, he purchased an Overland, one of the first automobiles in Wells County. On September 1, 1920, he married Margaret

E. Higgins, daughter of George and Nellie (Thomas) Higgins of Six Mile. Grandfather, Frank T. Brown, was killed by a bull shortly after Dad and Mother's marriage.

Helen Brown McCreery, Robert H. McCreery

On May 9, 1923, I was born on a cold and icy day at the Wells County Hospital. Mother had to crawl up the steps, as the weather was extremely bad for that time of the year. I am an only child. Dad taught me, by the age of five, to help on the farm milking cows and tending animals. I have many fond memories of working with him. Dad died in 1975 at the age of ninety-one. Mother and dad were charter members of the Wells County Historical Society.

Mother was a member of the Neighborhood Home Demonstration Club of Chester Township, the State Board of Crippled Children, the Wells County Health Council, and helped to organize the Adams-Wells Association of Retarded Citizens. Mother died in 1988 at the age of 97.

I went to Chester Center School, graduating in 1941. I graduated from Ball State, earning a degree in elementary education. In 1947, while teaching in Indianapolis, I married Robert H. McCreery. He is a graduate of Purdue University in Metallurgical Engineering (1948). After our marriage, we lived and worked in Evansville, where Ann was born in August of 1954. In 1955, we moved to Muncie, where Sarah was born.

In June of 1960, we moved to Portland, Indiana, where I taught elementary school in Jay County. I am an elder in the First Presbyterian Church, an Associate member of Tri-Kappa, a volunteer at the Jay County Hospital, and an active member in the Republican Party. In 1986, we received a Hoosier Homestead Award, as the farm had been in the family for over one hundred years.

My husband, Robert H. McCreery, was Jay County's first successful heart transplant on Valentine's Day, 1990. He retired as senior vice president of Metallurgy in 1990 from Teledyne Portland Forge.

Ann McCreery Oswalt teaches Special Education at Mississinewa High School, Gas City, Indiana. She has one daughter, Courtney Anne Oswalt, eight years old, and lives in Blackford County. Sarah McCreery Wappes teaches business education at Warsaw High School, Warsaw, Indiana. *(Helen Brown McCreery)*

BRUBAKER-DALRYMPLE FAMILY

Billy Lee Brubaker was born in Huntington County, September 10, 1941, to Ralph D. and Mary A. Watson Brubaker. He was the youngest of seven children. Bill, as he prefers to be called, was raised in Huntington County and graduated from Warren High School in 1959. In 1960 he married Connie J. Dalrymple, a transplant from Wells County. She is the daughter of Velin J. and Mary Josephine Worster Dalrymple. Connie was born May 29, 1941, in Ossian, where she lived until June of 1953. She completed school and graduated from Warren High School in 1959.

Bill and Connie lived in the Warren area until 1962 when they moved to Tocsin, renting the home belonging to Mary Blue. In the spring of 1964, they moved to their present home near Uniondale.

Bill worked for the Wilbert Vault Works for four years. He went to work in Huntington at Yoeman Engineering in 1965, where he has been employed as a mold maker for 26 years. At the present he is shop supervisor at the Yoeman Riverfork Shop, Huntington.

Bill and Connie purchased the small restaurant in Uniondale (The Pleasant Inn) in 1972, but only kept it open for business for a short time.

Connie graduated from Warner Beauty College in 1959. She worked part time as a beautician for about ten years. She began driving school bus for Northern Wells Community School as a substitute in 1977, then driving full time in 1978. After six years she entered the education field as a teaching assistant where she is presently employed.

The Brubakers have been active in Boy Scouts, Cub Scouts, and Girl Scouts for several years. They are also members of the Markle United Methodist Church, Markle Masonic Lodge, and Emerald Chapter Order of Eastern Star.

Bill served on the Northern Wells Community School Board of Trustees from 1983 to 1987. In July of 1987, he was appointed to the Ossian School Building Corporation where he is serving as president.

Bill and Connie have five children: Lionel Kent, Matthew Lee, Angela Kay, Pamala Lynn, and Amanda Caroline. Lionel married DeLora Okuly on June 19, 1982. They have two children, Mary Elizabeth and Benajamin Joseph. They reside in Bluffton. Matthew married Rhonda Mahlie in April, 1982 and divorced in August, 1985. One son was born into the union, Matthew Lee II. Matthew and Matthew II live near Uniondale. Angela married Branley L. Landrum of Huntington County. They live in Bippus, Indiana. Pamala has one child Lacey Jo and they live in Berne, Indiana. Amanda is attending Ossian Elementary, presently in grade five.

The family is proud to have their home within the old Miami Indian Reservation. It is important to them as Bill's Great-Aunt Josephine C. Goodbow Watson was a full-blooded Miami Indian, a descendant of Little Turtle.

BRUMBAUGH AND SHIDLER

David Henry Brumbaugh was born on November 20, 1861 (son of Isaac and Rebecca (Waltz) Brumbaugh). He was married August 22, 1886, to Lavina Shidler, born February 18, 1865 (daughter of Aaron and Nancy (Strickler) Shidler).

They started housekeeping in Lancaster Township of Huntington County. David moved his family to Union Township of Wells County in 1903. His father, Isaac, was a contractor. He built the original main buildings of Huntington College, Horace Mann School, Loon Creek Church of the Brethren, and many fine brick homes, including his own. David was a farmer and carpenter. He built the buildings and the home on his farm, located north of Markle, Indiana.

Two children were born. Edward Merl was born on January 13, 1888, and he died on December 4, 1976. Edna Pearl was born on December 29, 1890, and she died on February 5, 1974.

Edna Pearl married Harry Cline, son of Jesse and Ann (Beatty) Cline in 1912. Two sons were born, Russell Ray on August 18, 1913, and Edward Fay on July 11, 1915.

Edward married Pearl Rarick (born July 16, 1891 and died October 2, 1972), daughter of John Henry and Lizzie (Shively) Rarick, in 1908. Edward was a farmer in Union Township and lived a mile north of Markle on the old Fox farm which he purchased in 1908. He served on the Advisory Board of Union Township many years, and as director of Huntington Mutual Insurance for 26 years. He was active in the Markle Church of the Brethren where he served as trustee. He played a trombone in the Erie and Markle bands. Pearl was a homemaker talented in crocheting, needlepoint, and embroidery. They lived their 64 years of married life in the same home.

Edward and Pearl were the parents of six children. Mark Ray was born September 14, 1908, and died in 1990. Paul Martin was born July 30, 1910. Doris Arlene was born October 14, 1912. Ruth Maxine was born February 16, 1918. John David was born October 8, 1922, and died in March of 1989. James W. was born August 23, 1924.

Mark Cline married Zedda M. Applegate (born July 6, 1915 and died April 14, 1990). She was the daughter of Otto Ward and Edna Blanch (Kistler) Applegate from Grass Creek, Indiana. Mark graduated from Manchester College. He started teaching at age eighteen at Union Center, Wells County. He taught at several Indiana schools, and was principal at Rockcreek in Wells County. The last 28 years of his career was spent in the math department of Clay High School, in South Bend. He retired in 1975 and resided in South Bend until his death. Mark and Zedda had two children, David M. was born December 21, 1940, and Mark Kay was born January 1, 1944.

Paul Martin Cline was named after Martin G. Brumbaugh, once Governor of Pennsylvania. Paul worked at the Markle Lumber Company before serving four years with the U.S. Army Quartermaster Corps, with one year in the Philippines. He married Marie Sweet (born February 16, 1920 and died December 25, 1963) in May, 1943. They were the parents of two children. Jayde S. born March 14, 1944. Duane was born September 26, 1959. After returning from service, Paul worked for Ditzler Lumber Company, and ten years later he operated his own sawmill.

From 1964 to retirement in 1975, he worked in maintenance at Baer Field, Fort Wayne. He married Madalyn Lavonne Gephart (born February 12, 1926) on August 26, 1966. They live in Markle and are active in the Markle Church of the Brethren. During his lifetime membership, he has served as treasurer, deacon, class teacher, trustee, and song leader. His grandfather and great-grandfather, Isaac, had served as song leaders in their churches likewise.

Doris Cline married Ward Ripley on June 5, 1935. They had three children. Carolyn Ruth was born September 12, 1936. Ronald Mark was born April 23, 1938. Robert Edward was born July 22, 1940. Doris married Herbert Rutenberg (born April 15, 1906, son of Christian Conrad and Ida (Johnkey) Rutenberg from Huntington County) on December 2, 1951. Doris worked at Model Engineering in Huntington, and then Royal Lace at Baer Field, Fort

Edward and Pearl Brumbaugh 1941
Back L to R: Doris, John, Mark, Ruth; Front L to R: Pearl, Paul, James, Edward

Ruth Cline married Jay H. Smith (born December 17, 1916, son of Arthur and Effie May (Hite) Smith) on December 25, 1940. Ruth and Jay are farmers living on farms in Union Township, in Huntington County, and Rockcreek, and Union Townships in Wells County. Jay drove a school bus for 15 years, while farming, and worked at G&H Fertilizer. After retiring from farming, Ruth worked ten years at the Dutch Mill in Bluffton as cook. Both have been active members of the Markle Church of Christ. They have driven the Alcan Highway to Alaska three times to visit their daughter, Cheryl, and family. They presently live in the homestead of Edward and Pearl, north of Markle. They have three children. Ardith Jay was born November 11, 1941. Sonja Sue was born January 14, 1943. Cheryl Ann was born September 23, 1949.

John David Cline married Emojean Jacobs (born June 1, 1928) daughter of Robert John and Emma (Detrick) Jacobs of Susquehanna, Pennsylvania) on April 1, 1951. John was a farmer in Union Township, and a member of the Markle Church of the Brethren. He is World War II, U.S. Army veteran and a member of American Legion Post 111 in Bluffton. He was on the Board of Directors of the Huntington Mutual Insurance Company. Emojean was an R.N., taking her nurses training at the Lutheran Hospital in Fort Wayne. She worked 11 years as a staff member at Wells Community Hospital and five years as a private nurse in Huntington. They lived in the homestead of David and Lavine. Emojean still lives there. They are the parents of two daughters. Melinda was born June 8, 1953. Jo Ann as born June 24, 1956.

James Cline married Roberta Sinks (native of Centralia, Illinois) in 1956. James graduated from Manchester College, and then Bethany Biblical Seminary, and is ministering in the Church of the Brethren. He served as a pastor in and near Seattle, Washington. He did social work for the city, working with first time offenders and drug addicts. James is musically inclined, playing the piano, organ, and other instruments. He plays the pipe organ at the Episcopal Church in Seattle. He and Roberta sing in the church choirs.

Roberta took nurses training in Chicago and worked as a surgical R.N. They are retired and reside in Seattle. Much of their time is spent in church and volunteer work. They have two children. James, was born March 25, 1958. Vickie Marie was born September 6, 1960.

ROSS AND BETTY BRYANT FAMILY

Ross Wayne Bryant was born on April 11, 1936, at 5776E 105ON, Ossian, Indiana. Ross was the second child of Vernon and Geneva (Greek) Bryant. He graduated from Ossian High School in 1954.

After graduation from high school, Ross worked at International Harvester and took college classes at the Purdue University Extension in Fort Wayne. After graduation from Purdue with an associates degree in industrial technology, he became employed at Peter Eckrich and Sons, Fort Wayne, in January, 1959.

Betty Lou Stevenson was born on January 16, 1939, in White County near Monticello, Indiana. Betty's parents are Walter and Mildred (Van Meter) Stevenson. She graduated from Buffalo High School in May, 1957. In September, 1957, Betty moved to Fort Wayne to attended International Business College. After graduation, she became employed at Peter Eckrich and Sons, where she met Ross.

Ross and Betty were married April 23, 1960, in Fort Wayne. They began married life living in Ossian in an apartment at 307 South Jefferson Street.

Ross and Betty continued working at Peter Eckrich and Sons until 1961. In October, 1961, Ross was activated with the Indiana Air National Guard during the Berlin Crisis for one year. He was stationed at Baer Field, Fort Wayne.

On January 10, 1962, their first daughter, Brenda Lee, was born. In 1962 after the Berlin Crisis, Ross returned to Peter Eckrich and Sons as a quality assurance inspector. In 1963 they moved to a home at 420 West Roe Street, Ossian. On November 11, 1963, their second daughter, Bonnie Lynne, was born. Brenda and Bonnie attended the Ossian Elementary School and graduated from Norwell High School.

Ross, Betty, Brenda, and Bonnie were members of the Faith United Methodist Church, Ossian.

Seated: Ross Bryant, Betty (Stevenson) Bryant Back: Brenda (Bryant) Blazier and Bonnie (Bryant) Reinhard

Brenda and Bonnie were very active in school activities and both were ten-year 4-H members. Ross and Betty made 4-H a family interest and all of them enjoyed many opportunities in the Wells County 4-H program. Betty served as a 4-H leader in Jefferson Township from 1975-1984. She also served on the 4-H Association and is chairman of the Indiana 4-H Foundation Committee. Ross and Betty each served on the 4-H Council. Brenda and Bonnie won many county, state, and national 4-H awards.

Bonnie graduated from Purdue University in 1987 and married Mark Alan Rinehart of Indianapolis on August 12, 1989.

In 1974 the family moved to 11887N 450E, Ossian, where Ross and Betty still live.

Betty became employed at Allen Dairy Products in 1984. In June, 1987, Ross began working for Johnson Controls, Ossian, because Eckrich had closed their Fort Wayne plant in 1986. Ross continues to enjoy farming and farms 160 acres in addition to his employment at Johnson Controls.

In September, 1991, their first grandchild will be born to Brenda and Joseph Blazier.

BRYANT

The Bryant family originated in England when Thomas Powell and Henrietta Howells were married in 1808. They immigrated to America from Leominster, England, in 1817.

Joseph, the sixth child of Thomas and Henrietta, and his wife, Margaret, settled in Indiana. Mary, the second child of Joseph and Margaret, married Boyd Ladd in 1837. Their oldest daughter, Olive, married William Bryant in 1881. They lived for twenty years on a farm near Swayzee, Indiana. They had four daughters and four sons. Their oldest son was Ozro Bryant.

Ozro married Laura Effie Echelbarger in 1901. They had three daughters: Myrl, Frances, Gaynelle, and one son, Vernon. Vernon was born on June 20, 1911.

In 1912 William and Ozro moved their families to Wells County east of Ossian when Vernon was one year old. They moved by train. This move included their household furnishings, livestock, machinery, etc. The reason for their move was to purchase land. Land in Wells County was a lot cheaper than land around Swayzee. Four months after their move, William was stricken with pneumonia and died in February, 1913.

Ozro and his wife purchased an 80-acre farm for $150 an acre on the Wells and Allen County Line, east of Ossian. Ozro, or "O.L." as he was called by his friends, was an outstanding farmer. He farmed 200 acres with horses. In 1921 he purchased a 10-20 International Titan tractor.

O.L. Bryant won the Indiana "Corn King" title in 1928 with his 127.45 bushel per acre yield from his farm. The following year his son, Vernon, won the 1929 top corn grower award. They continued to receive many awards for their outstanding corn production.

Front: Deanna (Bryant) Patton, Geneva (Greck) Bryant, Vernon Bryant, Guilia (Bryant) Maxwell Back: Ross Bryant, Lee Bryant

O.L. Brant and Son Farms were called the "Leveldale Farms." O.L. and Vernon were the first farmers in this part of the state to raise soybeans. In 1935, they raised their first hybrid seed corn, which was among the first in Indiana. Vernon was O.L.'s "right hand man" in all their farm projects. Together they farmed 407 acres, raised and sold certified hybrid seed corn, soybeans, and wheat. Hybrid seed corn sold for $7.00 per bushel.

Vernon married Geneva Geraldine Greek on June 21, 1931. Geneva was a daughter of Floyd and Flossie Greek of Allen County.

Vernon and Geneva moved to a 120-acre farm, which they purchased in 1936, at 5776E 1050N, east of Ossian, where they live today. Their children are Lee, Ross, Guilia, and Deanna.

Lee married Phyllis Schnepp in 1955. They have one son, Duane, who married Cynthia Rodriguez. They have two children: Erin and David.

Ross married Betty Stevenson in 1960. They have two daughters: Brenda (married Joseph Blazier) and Bonnie (married Mark Rinehart).

Guilia married Hugh Maxwell in 1957. They have three children: Douglas (married Charlotte Burman), Sherri (married Rod Tudor), and Barry.

Deanna married Robert Patten in 1959. They have two sons: Troy (married Wendy Shirley) and Tracy.

BUCKNER

The Buckner family originated in England. A descendant came to America and settled in Virginia as early as 1667. William Nicholas Buckner from Campbell County, Kentucky, moved to a farm in Wells County, Indiana, in 1855. This would be on the southwest corner of the intersection of 200S and 500W. My father, Franklin B. Buckner, was born in Bluffton on February 20, 1900. He was the son of Dr. George W. Buckner, a veterinarian, and Emma Adams Buckner. Franklin married Grace E. Baker, who lived in Liberty Township. They had three children: Barbara, Edward Adams, and Beverly. Edward, now deceased, married Gloria Eichhorn of Uniondale, and fathered three children, Bruce (of Las Vegas, Nevada); Sally (of Bluffton); and Bradley (of Kodiak, Tennessee). My father died in 1954 at the age of 54 of hypertension. He served Bluffton as mayor from 1935 through 1942 and was active in Democratic politics for many years. He had the distinction of being the first mayor to serve two consecutive four-year terms. During his terms the electric service was extended into the rural areas, and a program of sewer improvements was started. He also served a quarter of century as a news reporter and city editor for Bluffton newspapers. He was Sunday school superintendent for the Baptist Church, a past president of the Kiwanis Club, past commander of the American Legion Post 111 and a member of the Bluffton Masonic Lodge.

Franklin B. Buckner
Grace Buckner Knapp

Mother was elected City Clerk Treasurer of the city of Bluffton in 1956. She married Harry J. Knapp in 1960 and moved to Decatur, Indiana. She was past president of Psi Iota Xi sorority and was active in community affairs. She is presently living in Swiss Village in Berne, Indiana.

I graduated from P.A. Allen High School and attended both Indiana and Purdue Universities. I served in the WAVES (Navy) in World War II from 1943 to 1946. In 1947 I married Sherman T. Kumpf of Bluffton. He was with J.C. Penney Company for 40 years and retired as manager of the Cortland, New York, Penney store in 1980. I worked for 20 years as secretary at the State University of New York in Cortland. We have two sons, Scott and Michael, who were both born in Bluffton and who are both mechanical engineers trained at Union College. They both live in the Cortland area.

My sister, Beverly, also graduated from P.A. Allen High School. In addition, she graduated from Purdue University and has an M.S. degree from Michigan State in East Lansing, Michigan. She is a registered medical technologist and has done graduate work in management at Central Michigan University. Beverly retired from the Caylor-Nickel Medical Center in Bluffton in January 1991 as a special projects director. Her previous positions were as laboratory manager, personnel director, and director of research and development over a career of 35 years. (*Barbara Buckner Kumpf*)

DR. JOY BUCKNER FAMILY

Francis Marion Buckner, born October 9, 1867, was the eighth child of William Nicholas Buckner and Amelia Margaret Yelton Buckner. Having purchased land in Indiana, the William Nicholas Buckner family moved in 1855 from Campbell County, Kentucky, to Wells County, Indiana. The land is located eight miles west and one mile south of Bluffton. This presently is the SW corner of 200S and 500W. William was a farmer and a broommaker.

Francis Marion married Stella Doster April 6, 1891. They had three children. The first was Doster born April 7, 1892, died February 2, 1959. The second was a daughter, Dale, born September 21, 1892, died June 23, 1961. The third child was my father, Joy, born January 26, 1898, died February 6, 1975. Both families immigrated from England. The Buckners were farmers and horsemen. The Dosters were farmers.

Joy married Winifred Morse Terry August 7, 1926. Joy was a graduate of Bluffton High School and Indiana University Medical School. He was a practicing physician and surgeon at the Wells County Hospital. He served three terms as county coroner. He raised, trained and raced Standardbred horses, training on the family racetrack near Poneto. My mother, Winifred, was born August 30, 1901, died November 6, 1986. She graduated from the University of Iowa and was a reporter for the *Indianapolis Star* at the time of her marriage. Her family had located in Indianapolis having moved the offices of *The Horseman and Fair World*, a weekly newspaper devoted to the Standardbred horse, of which her father was owner, editor and publisher. Winifred was a member of the National Society, Daughters of the American Revolution. She was Organizing Regent of Captain William Wells Chapter of Wells County, Indiana.

Joy and Winifred had three daughters. Kathryn Annabelle born August 13, 1928, Joyce Terry born March 9, 1932, Caroline Elizabeth born June 7, 1937. They are all members of Daughters of American Revolution.

Kathryn (Kitty) graduated from Bluffton High School and Indiana University. She married Robert William Bonham, Jr, an attorney (September 3, 1950). They had one son, Robert William III, born July 19, 1955. Robert, Jr., died December 23, 1986. Kitty is currently mayor of Hartford City, Indiana. She has raised Standardbred horses.

Joyce (Jimmy) graduated from Bluffton High School and Indiana University. She was a merchandise buyer for Wolf and Dessauer Department Store in Fort Wayne before returning to Indiana University to become a teacher. She taught in Indianapolis and Bluffton before moving to Warren, Indiana and starting the *Warren Weekly*. She also trained Standardbred harness horses. She married David Thompson February 12, 1985. She is a past president of the Wells County Historical Society and, with Dorothy Rose, wrote the *Wells County History, 1876-1976*. Kitty and Joyce established the *Hoosier Horse Review*, a tabloid devoted to Standardbred horses.

Caroline married Stephen Foster Newell October 3, 1959. They have three boys. Christopher Stephen was born August 25, 1964, Scott Foster was born November 11, 1967, and Jonathan Andrew was born February 19, 1974.

BUCKNER (PACE-POFF)

The Buckner ancestors date back to 1631 in Oxford, England, where John Buckner was born. The family came to America in 1667, landing in Virginia; later they moved to Kentucky. Grandfather Charles Nicholas Buckner, born 1854, and Grandmother Sarah Josephine, born the same year, married in Peach Grove, Kentucky, and moved to Wells County, eventually to Liberty Center.

Our mother, Daisy Beulah, was born on a farm, September 1891. She was a telephone operator for the Liberty Center officer. It was located inside a local residence. She married Herman Harry Pace from Poneto on February 12, 1916. They settled on a farm near Liberty Center. Dad joined with two other performers and together they put on well received minstrel shows around the county during the Depression era.

A son was born, Robert Edwin, in 1918, living three days. On April 14, 1923, another son was born, James Dwight, named for their doctor and good friend, Dr. Dwight Brickley. A daughter, Bonnie Jean, was born November 8, 1925. Dwight and Bonnie attended Liberty Center High School. In the winter of 1936 a snow storm came up suddenly, and, after trying to reach home, they had to go back to Liberty Center and stay in different homes for two days.

Bonnie Jean Pace Poff, Dwight Pace

After graduating from school Dwight became a farmer with his father. He continues to live in the

house in which he was born. Flying and walking are his hobbies. In August, 1946, he married Hallie Marie Girod. After receiving her degree in nursing from Lutheran Hospital, she worked at Wells Community Hospital.

They had three sons. James Girod, a medical doctor, married Lucy Wagner. They have two children, Gina Marie and Jesse Girod. They live in Pensacola, Florida. Thomas Dwight, an optometrist, married Gilda Walz. They live in Phoenix, Arizona. Robert Harry, a school teacher at Southern Wells, married Kimberly Moyer. They have two children, Brian Robert and Stephanie Ann. They live near Liberty Center.

In August, 1946, Bonnie met Joseph Lauren Poff from Bluffton, a World War II veteran, who had been awarded the Bronze Star. They were married on November 1, 1947. Joe took advantage of the G.I. Bill and two years later received his degree from International Business College. He began work for the Wells County Co-op in 1950, managing the operation until 1966, when he had to retire because of ill health. Three children were born: Deborah Jane in September, 1948; David Lauren in December, 1949; and in September, 1961, Mark Andrew. They lived in Bluffton. The children graduated from Bluffton High School. Following in her father's footsteps, Deborah also graduated from International Business College and works at Farmers & Merchants Bank. She married Gregory Kauffman, who works in construction. They adopted two children, Bethany Jane and Bradley Joseph. Later a son was born, Brandon Gregory. David married Elanda Adams; he works with heavy equipment and Elanda manages the M.R.I. facility at Caylor-Nickle Medical Center. They have two children, Bret Lane and Brandi Jeau. Mark attended college in Fort Wayne. During high school he began work at the local radio station and has continued to work in radio communications as a disc jockey. Joe died in 1968. Bonnie has worked at the Bluffton Utilities office for the past twenty-five years.

GEORGE EMERY BUEL FAMILY

George, Edward, and another brother came from Maryland to settle in Indiana, in Wells and Huntington counties. At that time, their last name was spelled "Bull" and the date was in the 1880's. Edward settled in Huntington County about a mile south of Markle, on old S.R. 3. George settled in Wells County, and later purchased a 40-acre farm, located at 1584 N 400 W in Rockcreek Township, and added another forty acres, making a total of eighty acres, which is still intact at the "Homeplace" of the Buel family. It was inherited in 1979 by the three Buel children, at the time of the death of their father, Howard Buel.

The name change was made during the years of 1910 to 1912 from "Bull" to "Buel", and is confirmed through the signatures of Howard and Charles when they were practicing writing their names in their school books at that time. These books were found in the attic by the children upon the death of their step-mother, Faye Irene Buel, just this spring after her death in January, 1991. Some of these books are over 80 and 90 years old and still in reasonable condition.

George Emery Bull married Emma Luella Walters in the early 1890's, and they had five children, the first being Howard Lemuel Bull (at the time of his birth), Leota Irene Bull, Charles Emery Bull, Mary Elizabeth Bull, and George Brooks Bull (now Buel). George Buel is living in Rockford, Ohio, and is the only one of the five still living.

Births and deaths of the family are as follows, using the name of "Buel" as it appears on the tombstone in the Emmanuel Cemetery located a 2115 N 500 W, Rockcreek Township, Wells County, Bluffton, Indiana.

George Emery Buel, born July 10, 1864, died December 31, 1928, and his wife Emma Luella (Walters) Buel, born October 15, 1874, died April 16, 1922 and their five children.

Howard Lemuel Buel, born September 13, 1896, died May 26, 1979, Leota Irene (Buel) Cotton, born December 12, 1897, died September 5, 1985, Charles Emery Buel, born February 21, 1899, died January 1, 1968, Mary Elizabeth (Buel) Beerbower, born June 2, 1902, died December 31, 1976, and George Brooks Buel, born June 7, 1910, and living in Rockford, Ohio.

Howard Lemuel Buel was in the service of World War I, and was stationed at Wright-Patterson Air Force Base at Dayton, Ohio. He met and married Della Mae Hime during that time, and they lived on the Air Force Base where their first child was born. His name was Marvin and he lived only three days, dying of S.I.D.S, what we now call Sudden Infant Death Syndrome. Howard and Della moved back to the farm, after he was discharged from the service, to help his father with the farming which of course was done with horses.

Births and deaths of the Howard Buel family are as follows: Howard Lemuel Buel, born September 13, 1896, died May 26, 1979 and his wife Della Mae (Hime) Buel, born May 8, 1901, died July 6, 1935 and their five children:

Marvin, born and died in October, 1924 and buried in Dayton, Ohio, Eva Mae (Buel) Green, born October 5, 1926, died February 24, 1946, Arlene Rose (Buel) Gordon, born July 7, 1929, living in Rockcreek Township, Phoebe Ann (Buel) Boze, born March 15, 1932, living near Berne, Indiana, Roger Lee Buel, born October 17, 1933, living in San Jose, California.

Descendants of George Emery Buel include: five children, sixteen grandchildren, forty great-grandchildren and over thirty-four great-great-grandchildren.

BULGERS

Our grandfather, Thomas Martin Bulger, was born near Murray, June 25, 1848, the son of Joseph S. and Sarah E. Guthrie Bulger. They moved to Rockcreek Township when he was a small child. In 1863, his father died, after which they moved to Bluffton, where his mother died in 1873. His marriage to Ameret Isophene Davis took place in Wells County, January 19, 1881. Grandmother was born January 23, 1850, to William P. and Lucinda Richey Davis, who were among the earliest settlers of the county. William P. Davis was born in Green County, Tennessee, moving to Wells County in 1836. There were no roads, only heavy forests and rough prairies. Most of the early settlers had to cut their own roads. The first wedding in the county was that of Rebecca Davis and Robert Simison, sister of William P. Davis and our grandmother's aunt.

Thomas M. Bugler started the Bugler Trucking Co. as a dray line about 1880. From a single wagon truck he enlarged the business and motorized it. It was one of the city's business firms for over 75 years. He also served two terms as city councilman. They had two sons, Milton Claire and William Daily Bulger (Dail).

Our father Dail was born June 3, 1887, and was a partner in the company most of his life. On September 17, 1910, he married Ethel Jarrett at the home of her sister, Mrs. Charles (Addie) Mendenhall in Liberty Township. Ethel was the daughter of William B. and Jane Fuller Jarrett. The Jarretts were among the first settlers of Chester Township in the 1830's, and Jane Fuller was the daughter of Mary Godfrey Fuller of the Miami Indian Godfreys. William Jarrett was the son of Bentley and Emmaline Jarrett.

Bulger Trucking Company
Milton Claire Bulger - Driving, William Dailey Bulger - Standing on side of truck

Dail and Ethel Bulger were the parents of six children. He operated the trucking company until 1924, when he bought a farm in Liberty Township. Thomas and William graduated from Liberty Center. In 1930, we moved back to Bluffton where he again operated the Bulger Trucking Co. until about 1945, after which Thomas and sons continued in the business for several years. Our grandmother (Mrs. Thomas Bulger) lived with us for 18 years, I can't remember a time when she wasn't there when we were growing up. A former school teacher, she helped us with our homework and had many stories to tell about the "old days."

Brother Tom died in 1981, leaving Thomas Jr., who now resides on South Main Street and Theodore D. (Ted) of Knox, Indiana. Robert D. died in 1955, leaving two children, Sandra K. (Mrs. Ed Hiatt) and Dennis D. of rural Bluffton. Roger Claire retired from White Sands Missile Range after 22 years of service and now lives in El Paso, Texas.

Still living in the Bluffton area are:

William B. (Bill) Bulger who resides with his wife, the former Thelma List, at 932 North Main Street. They have one daughter, Judy (Mrs. Gary Wood), of Fort Wayne.

Jane Bulger (Mrs. Floyd) Schoeff of East Dustman Road. She has one daughter, Vickie Patterson Rehbein, and one son Douglas Bert Patterson, both of Bluffton.

And Mary Bulger Uptgraft (Mrs. Weisell) who recently moved to East Spring Street after living most of her life near Petroleum, where her husband was engaged in farming. They have three daughters, Janice (Mrs. Douglas) Beaty of Anderson, Sheila (Mrs. William) Fenton of Terre Haute, and Laura (Mrs. Nick) Chaney of rural Uniondale; and one son, James Weisell (Jim) Uptgraft of rural Keystone.

RICHARD L. BUMGARNER FAMILY

Richard L. Bumgarner was born on November 25, 1929, to Joe Bumgarner, (1907-1959) and Marie Dunn (1909-1984). He married Marylou Johnson (1933) on August 12, 1951. Their children are: (1)

Steven Lee Bumgarner, (May 13, 1953) who married (1973) Jill Borror (March, 1955), daughter of Lucille Steffen Borror (1926) and Wrenn Borror, (1921).

Their children are: Carrie Joe Bumgarner (April 1, 1975) and Kelli Marie Bumgarner (August 12, 1977). (2) Michael Joe Bumgarner (February 21, 1956) who married (1974) Sharlene Helms, daughter of Paul Helms (1920) and Virginia Helms (1929); she was born in September, 1956. (3) Keith Richard Bumgarner (November 28, 1960). He has a son, Jordon Keith Bumgarner, who was born on December 26, 1982, in Kent, Washington.

BUNN-CHRISTMAN

I am Berneice (Bunn) Christman, my parents were Don and Iva (Faus) Bunn; my paternal grandparents were Henry and Althea (Ade) Bunn, all Bluffton natives. My maternal grandparents were John and Cora (Foutz) Faus of rural Rockcreek Township.

My sisters and I are alumni of Bluffton High School. I graduated in 1930 and Evelyn graduated in 1935. Two of our brothers, and our triplet sisters did not survive infancy.

I was six years old in 1918, the year World War I armistice was signed. I remember Dr. Asa Brown stopping at our home long past midnight to visit two of my relatives who were ill. He would sit down, lay his head to the back of the chair and ask to be awakened in two hours. His rounds were endless, as people were dying by the thousands that year from the tragic flu epidemic.

In those days autos were few and there were no radios or TV's. I remember trudging with may parents through ten blocks of deep, soft snow to downtown Bluffton on Saturday shopping evening. My baby sister would be in a cradle-type sled made by my father, who was a cabinet-maker. Our last stop in shopping was at the Ashbaucher Music Store on Washington Street for records for our Edison Victrola.

When Dr. Charles Caylor, founder of the Caylor-Nickel Clinic, first opened an office in Bluffton, he became our family physician. We loved him over the years as we did his sons, Dr. Harold and Dr. Truman. My father's last heart attack was attended by Dr. Allen Nickel. Our family watched the birth and extraordinary development to national prominence of the Caylor-Nickel Clinic.

Before the depression, my father was employed by the H.C. Bay and B.K. Settergren Piano factories. During the depression he oversaw the masonry construction at the Wells County State Forest and Game Preserve (now Ouabache State Recreation Area). Virgil Simmons and Kay Kunkel held Indiana State Conservation posts in Indianapolis during the Roosevelt New Deal years. My father later became foreman of the maintenance crew at Baer Field. Many a snowy night he and his crew kept the runways clear when these storms blew in. My father's last employment was in security at the Estey Piano Factory.

My sister, Evelyn (Bunn) Babcock, died several years ago. My sister, Dayra (Bunn) Wagner, is widowed and lives in Muncie. I too am widowed and am a resident of Anderson. Dayra's daughter, Jan (Mrs. Dan Baker), lives in Bluffton.

Evelyn and I both were employed at the Bluffton Auto License Bureau under the management of Frank Smith.

My father's first cousin, Mrs. Tom (Nellie) McNeal still lives and is active at 102. *(Berneice Bunn Christman)*

KENNETH W. BURKHART FAMILY

Kenneth W. and Mary Lou (McBride) Burkhart were married on December 24, 1961, in the Clear Creek Church in Huntington County. Kenneth was the son of Willard E. and Vera Caroline (Walker) Burkhart of Clear Creek Township in Huntington County. Kenneth was serving with the U.S. Army in Fort Lewis, Washington, so the first year of their marriage they lived in Olympia, Washington. Mary Lou was employed in the payroll department of the Washington State Highway Department.

They returned to Zanesville in 1962, when they bought the Zanesville house from the estate of Mary Lou's grandmother, Almissa McBride. Kenneth worked at the International Harvester, and Mary Lou worked in the payroll department at Lincoln National Life Insurance Company.

Mary Lou and Kenneth Burkhart

Kenny and Mary Lou's first daughter, Beth Ann, was born on June 11, 1863, and their second daughter, Kimberly Kay, was born on August 17, 1965. Mary Lou decided to stay home with her children, so she started a day care center. They lived in Zanesville for ten years, and in 1973 they sold the Zanesville house to Kenneth W. and Melba L. Edwards. Melba is Mary Lou's sister. They then bought a home one-half mile south of Zanesville on 303. The home was located across the road from Mary Lou's homeplace.

Kenneth continued to work at the International Harvester and Mary Lou started up a day care center again in this house. During a total of about fifteen years in the day care business, Mary Lou had taken care of a total of 150 children; some of them were second generation children.

Beth Ann and Kimberly both graduated from Norwell High School. Beth Ann went on to Ball State College and graduated in 1985. She is presently employed at Maumee Industries in Fort Wayne. Kimberly went to International Business College, where she graduated in 1984. Kimberly is presently employed at Scott's Bakery in Fort Wayne.

Kenneth and Mary Lou moved to their farm on the Hosler Road in Huntington County in 1981, where Kenneth engaged in farming, cattle raising, and driving truck for Stoneco. Mary Lou is employed at the Legge Elevator Company, Inc., in Uniondale, as a bookkeeper.

BURLEIGH-BENNETT

My sister Doris (Dodie) and I "grew up in the newspaper business."

I was born August 8, 1926 and Doris on December 12, 1927, at Wells County Hospital to Roger and Celia Swaim. We were delivered by Dr. H.D. Brickley, as was my daughter, Kathy, twenty-six years later.

During our childhood we were in and out of the newspaper office on West Market Street almost every day, forming many friendships with the fine News-Banner people, I remember brass spittoons that were really used, green celluloid visors worn by some of the men, my grandfather's sleeve garters, cleaning out and filling the past pots and bulletins taped on the front windows . . . one bulletin announcing the death of John Dillinger.

(L to R) Janet Swaim Burleigh, Doris Swaim Bennett About 1930

There was also time to enjoy grandmother's and Aunt Helen's grape juice, and going with her on sewing visits with the Story sisters. Grandfather usually had us "in tow" at ball games, movies and at the "Snug," a local restaurant. He and our dad took us hunting for Mayapples and mushrooms, family motor trips, both long and short, were taken, a favorite being to Huntington's "Nick's Kitchen." Summers were spent at softball games and at the Psi Iote Pool. I remember our dad finishing his ice cream at Fryback's just in time to come home for lunch. I remember mother's cooking club, the seven "Sisters of the Skillet" whose recipes are still savored today by their children.

Doris and I took piano lessons for many years, mother being our first teacher. We sang in the Girls' Glee Club and I began voice lessons with David Baxter. This was the beginning of many years of being accompanied by my mother and singing in the church choir with my dad. Olive Grimsley Ratliff was director of the Glee Club and choir and was a positive influence. Our parents took us to many concerts, exposing us to the talents of many great musicians of the day.

Both Doris and I graduated from Bluffton High School in 1944 and 1945 respectively and became members of Tri Kappa. We attended DePauw together and met our husbands there. During those years we worked summers and many holidays at the News-Banner, selling ads, taking market reports by phone, reading proof, and getting local news items from passers-by and local merchants. Following our father's death we served as directors of the News-Banner from 1976 to 1986.

After graduating from DePauw in 1948, I taught public school music in Salem, Indiana, and in 1949 married James F. Burleigh, born July 3, 1924, of Springfield, Ohio. Jim was a World War II veteran, having serving in the army in Normandy and Germany. He was a prisoner-of-war and was held in the same camp as William Shelley of Bluffton (although they were unknown to each other at t' time). We first lived in Schenectady, New York, and Cleveland while Jim worked for G.E. and then moved to Bluffton where he became business manager of the paper. We then lived in Columbus, Indiana, Kent, Ohio, and finally Denver, Colorado, where we have lived for twenty-seven years. Jim was in sales with Polaroid Corp. and Sheaffer-

Eaton before his retirement, and I taught pre-school for eleven years before retiring.

Our children are Timothy Swaim Burleigh, born 1951, Kathryn Burleigh Denny (Mrs. Gordon), born 1953, and Andrew James Burleigh, born 1955. We have six grandchildren.

Following her graduation from DePauw, Doris (Dodie) taught kindergarten in Indianapolis and in 1951 married Jack D. Bennett of Rockford, Illinois. Jack was in sales before his retirement from Cosco. Their home for many years has been in Chagrin Falls, Ohio, where Dodie taught second-grade for eighteen years. She died January 2, 1989. Their children are: Peter Swaim Bennett, born 1953, and Sally (Mrs. Andrew Westman), born 1956. Sally has two children.

Roger and Celia's five grandchildren spent a great deal of time in Bluffton, enjoying their grandmother's cooking and the countless trips to the Dutch Mill. They were often put to work at the News-Banner stuffing papers, and those years formed some of their best memories: the Linotype machine, the rhythm of the press, the automatic binding machine, the teletype in the front window, Harry Schwartz riding his bicycle backward down the alley, Kaye Ivins setting their names in type and measuring their height against the door frame. Like us, they too came to feel a kinship with the News-Banner people. *(Janet Swaim Burleigh)*

BURNS

May of 1945 saw joyous celebrations for the ending war. Another momentous occasion for us was the birth of the first member of our Burns family in Wells County. Merlin John Burns was born May 12, 1945, the fourth and youngest son of Edmund and Susie (Mussetter) Burns. Ed was born in Illinois and Susie in South Dakota. His three older brothers — Virgil, Ed, and Ronald — had all been born in either Minnesota or South Dakota.

The horseshoe bend north of Poneto was Merlin's first home, but his parents then bought a farm one mile west of Poneto, where they lived until 1983. He attended Chester Center School, graduating in 1963. After Merlin attended International Business College, Uncle Sam felt his talents would be better utilized in a military setting. He spent the next two years as an NCO-company clerk with the 598th Transportation Company, 7th U.S. Army Europe, stationed in Kassel and Mannheim, Germany for 20 months. Their unit also assisted in the pullout of all U.S. troops from France in 1966.

Declining the Army's offer to attend OCS, Merlin returned to civilian life and eventually began employment at the Farmers and Merchants Bank in Bluffton. He spent 13 years with F&M (1968-1981), then accepted an offer to join the Bank of Montpelier as cashier. Eventually becoming vice-president of what became the Pacesetter Bank of Montpelier, Merlin served the Southern Wells-Montpelier banking community from 1981 until 1990 when health problems necessitated a disability retirement.

In July, 1970, Merlin was introduced by mutual friends to Terry Whaley, then residing in Muncie and employed by Ball State. Two months later they became engaged and they were married July 3, 1971, a year and a day after meeting, in St. Augustine Catholic Church, Rensselaer.

Terry is the oldest of the three daughters of Lawrence and Patricia (Wilbanks) Whaley of Newton County, Indiana. She graduated from Mt. Ayr School (now North Newton) and Ball State. She completed her Master's of Library Science degree from Indiana University in 1989 and has been employed as Reference and Adult Services Librarian at the Bluffton-Wells County Public Library since 1987.

Merlin and Terry have lived in Nottingham Township, southwest of Reiffsburg, since 1975. Their three sons have all been born in Wells County. Morgan Louis was born December 26, 1975; Conor Patrick on March 30, 1981; and Logan Timothy on December 21, 1983. All attend Southern Wells Schools.

The Burns Family
Logan, Terry, Morgan, Merlin, Conor

Merlin and the boys are members of St. Joseph's Catholic Church in Bluffton. Terry belongs to the Reiffsburg United Methodist Church, where she's assistant pianist and organist. Merlin is an avid golfer, and the boys are quickly learning. The family has always had Arabian horses to enjoy and a chocolate Labrador puppy has now joined the clan. Baseball occupies many summer hours and lots of sports are enjoyed, especially if they involve the University of Notre Dame. Terry enjoys reading and genealogy but has little time for either.

Spending time together as a family, enjoying visits with family and friends, and praising the Lord for blessings beyond measure keeps this family busy and happy.

EDWARD AND BETTY BUSHEE FAMILY

Edward and Betty were both born in Wells County.

Edward is a true native of Wells County, being born in Jefferson Township in 1930.

His family history says his great-grandparents, Jacob and Olive (Cave) Bushee, were married in 1847 in Hocking County, Ohio, and came to Union Township, Wells County, in 1850. Jacob cleared land on the Indian Reserve and settled his wife and family in a rude log cabin near a group of Hocking County, Ohio, men whom he assisted in rolling logs and erecting buildings. He was a chosen leader by the men. It was well-known that Jacob was never second in his work. He helped in building nearly all the early cabins. The history says perhaps no man did more for the pioneers, his heart always having a kindly feeling for the sick and distressed. He was even credited with saving the life of a neighbor Charles Earle. Jacob was an active politician in the early days of northern Wells County. He died January 11, 1901.

The Jacob Bushees had eight children, one of which was James, Edward's grandfather born June 22, 1859. He married Sarah Jane Flum (born August 8, 1862) on December 31, 1889. They had one daughter and five sons. Edward's father Harley (their first son) was born March 26, 1893. He married Dosha Letha Webster on February 14, 1922. They had one daughter and four sons, Edward being the youngest. Many of the family members were carpenters and farmers by trade.

Edward started first grade at Ossian and moved the same year to East Union where he graduated as valedictorian in 1948. He served two years in the Army at Camp Chaffee, Arkansas, Fort Sill, Oklahoma and in Salzburg, Austria.

Edward and Betty Bushee

Betty (DeBaillie) Bushee was born at Banner City near Uniondale in 1933 to Alberic and Martha (Colpaert) DeBaillie. Her parents were both born in Belgium. They came to America in the early 1900's and worked as farmers and farm laborers. She moved to Allen County; attended Lafayette Central School until tenth grade, moved to Noble County, and graduated from Rome City High School in 1951. She worked at General Electric in Fort Wayne and in the office at S.S. Kresge until she joined Edward in the Army. She came home when Edward went to Austria and worked at Western Auto in the office until their first son was born.

Edward and Betty met at a basketball game between Lafayette Central and East Union and were married March 1, 1952. They have two sons, Gregory of rural Uniondale, Jeffrey of Zanesville, and four grandchildren, Mandy, Andrew, Travis, and Meggan. They have been farmers in Union Township since Edward returned from the Army.

CALEY

The Caley descendants migrated to Wells County from areas in Virginia and Ohio. Samuel B. Caley was my great-great grandfather (his name and account of his life can be found in the Zanesville History Book). He was a mail carrier in that area in 1850 - his son, George Francis, also helped with mail carrying. This George Caley was my grandfather's father. George was born in 1835 and married Mary McBride, born in 1835. Their first son, Samuel M., my grandfather, was born in 1866. My grandfather was born and raised in Wells County and was a farmer all of his life, living 1 1/2 miles north of Markle, Indiana. Grandfather married Effie Brickly in 1877. They had three children, one died at infancy. Their oldest, George Clifford, my father, born in 1889, and a daughter, Vella. My grandfather, Sam, loved horses. When one of his favorite horses died, he had a horsehide coat made. It was very easy to identify Grandpap in the winter time. One of his last wishes was to be able to see the Kentucky Derby. He drove to Lexington, Kentucky, by himself in a little coupe when he was in his seventies. Shortly after, he had a massive stroke, and was bedfast for seven years. He died in 1946. He also loved to fish and sometimes would go to Webster Lake, Indiana, Miller's Landing, and I got to go along and cook. Grandmother Effie died before I was born. Grandfather Sam was on the advisory board of the first Union Center High School.

My father, George Clifford, married Cressie I. Haflich in 1911, shortly after graduation from Union School and Valparaiso College. He worked in the First National Bank in Warren for several years and then they had a Chevrolet Car Agency in Markle. My mother was one of the first ladies in the area to drive a horseless carriage, so she and my father would go to Detroit and drive their cars home for resale. Also my mother was a good pianist, having graduated from Muncie Conservatory before she was married. She played piano many times in a Markle movie house for the silent movies.

Dedication of the Allen-Wells County REMC Building Ossian, Indian, 1949 L to R: Hugh Abbott - Chrm, Public Service Comm. of Indiana, Lindsay Huffer-MFG. of Co-op, G.C. Caley - Pres. REMC, Gov Henry Schricker, Mayor Fort Wayne - Henry Branning Jr., Police Chief Eisenhut of Fort Wayne

They moved out to a farm, next house north of Grandfather's, around 1915 to help with the farming, as it had become too much for Grandfather. Also my Grandmother, Effie, was ill. My mother took care of her until her death in 1924. George Clifford and Cressie had four children: Jaunice, born 1916, William (Bill) Samuel, born 1922, Barbara, born 1926, and Donald, born 1931. My father continued farming all the years of child rearing. He started the Allen-Wells County R.E.M.C. and I recall many meetings at our home in 1935 through 1936 before they got their building at Ossian. He was president of this group for over 19 years. What a blessing to have electricity in the rural areas. All of the Caley children graduated from E. Union Center High School. Jaunice married Jack McClintic in 1934; William S. Caley, after the Navy R.O.T.C., graduated from Indiana University and married Marjorie Cockriel in 1948; Barbara graduated as an R.N. from the Lutheran Hospital and married Hubert Girvin in 1947; Don graduated from the Indiana University and went on into the Regular Air Force and married Jane in 1953.

Having lived through the depression era, I recall the togetherness of our farming neighbors. The steam threshing machine was run by a Mr. Line who went around to all the farmers, threshing wheat. At the end of the season, we would have an ice cream social at different farm homes each summer and have made ice cream and cake. The Brumbaughs, Pences, Thomases, Davises, Elicks, Spaids were all nearby farmers. Our social activities also included band concert nights in the summer at Markle. They pulled the band wagon out onto a blocked off street, and we heard great music weekly. Saturday nights were drawing nights, put on in Markle by the merchants; prizes were sugar and other staples, or sometimes cash. You also did your weekly grocery shopping and socializing. In the years before World War II, the town would show free movies outside — an early version of the drive-in movies.

My parents, Cliff and Cressie, always had a wonderful attitude and outlook on life - they always tried to encourage us on any new steps or adventure we attempted. They met with a very tragic car accident along with my Aunt Zoa and Uncle Curt Haflich in September, 1959. Coming home from the Bluffton Street Fair, at the intersection of State Road #116 and #303, an underage driver ran a stop sign, killing all of them plus a passenger in his car. Six years later, at this same intersection, a drunken driver ran the stop sign killing my brother, Bill and his four children instantly. There is so much I wish I could tell you about Bill and his wonderful family, but am limited on space. The children were devoted 4-H members and were on their way to the 4-H Fair. A Caley Memorial was set up that will go on forever through the Wells County 4-H Association. Each year an outstanding boy and girl is awarded a $50.00 savings bond in their memories.

I, Barbara, will add some facts on my life in this book under the Girvin History. My brother, Don, made a career in the Air Force after graduation from Indiana University and marrying. He spent his life all over this world piloting various planes fro the Air Force. He is now retired and lives with his wife, Elsa, north of San Francisco, California. He has two sons, and two grandchildren, who live nearby in California.

This ends my Caley line here in Wells County, Indiana. *Submitted by Barbara Caley Girvin*

WILLIAM CALEY FAMILY

Many have heard of the Caley 4-H Memorial Award and know that it is a great honor to have it bestowed upon them.

When David Isch and Clarice McMillan were named winners of the 1985 Caley 4-H Memorial Award, they knew it was a great honor.

They and other classmates had heard for several years about the award and why it was given. Of course, they did not know the people honored in memory, just as they were being honored for their 4-H and other qualities.

The Caley accident happened on Tuesday evening July 27, 1965.

Those who can hark back to twenty-six years ago. Many recall the numbness of a Wells County community as word spread of the crash at Ind. 116 and Ind. 303 (now County Road 300W) while the Caleys were enroute to the 4-H fair.

Killed were William Caley, forty-three; three sons: Kirby, fourteen; Kent, twelve; and Kevin, eight; and one daughter, Kris, eleven.

William and Marjorie Caley, Kirby, Kent, Kevin, and Kris

It happened at 7:45 p.m. when the Huntington Route 5 driver of another car went through the stop sign. The Caleys were eastbound on preferential Ind. 116. The other driver was southbound on 303.

The Caley auto flipped after the impact and landed on its top. The other driver, who escaped with only minor injuries, was prosecuted later, but it was too late.

William Caley was with the Canadian division of Bowmar Corp. He was a graduate of Indiana University. He and the family members were strong supporters of 4-H. They were going back to the fair after having been there earlier in the day. Kriss had won top honors in junior beef showmanship.

The recollections make it seem more real and yet unreal.

Especially because a good number remembered then and now that William Caley's parents and his aunt and uncle had been killed in a similar crash at that very same location in September of 1959 — while coming home from the Bluffton Street Fair.

It is fitting when an epic event is utilized in the positive form of the Caley Award — thereby extending in one symbolic way those lives that ended all too soon.

Certainly it is appropriate that young people of the caliber of Clarice and David should be recognized and encouraged through this award.

William's wife the former Marjorie Cockriel survived the crash and is now living in Florida.

EDWARD J. CALL

Edward Joseph Call was born May 8, 1913, in Lancaster Township, Wells County, Indiana, the fifth child of seven children of Joseph W. Call and Alverta Belle (Vaughn) Call. He lived and worked on his parents' farm until his graduation from high school in 1931. He then worked for farmers in the area until his marriage on December 23, 1934, to Mary Belle Wilson, daughter of Chancy Wilson and Pearl (Ruby) Wilson, after which he and his wife purchased a home at 815 S. Johnson Street Bluffton, Indiana, where they still reside.

Edward J. (Pete) and Mary Belle Call on golden wedding anniversary December 23, 1984

Pete, as he has always been known, worked at the Swisher Lumber Company several years, then went to the Home Lumber Company at Huntington, as assistant manager. While he was there the draft was begun and he was soon to be drafted. Work at the lumber company was slacking off and it was becoming necessary for the lumber company to lay off some of its workers. An older man working there was scheduled to be laid off, but because Pete knew he was soon to be drafted he requested that they keep the older man and Pete would quit. It was not yet his time to go into service, so he went to Baer Field and worked on the fire department until he was called. When his number was about to come up he enlisted in the Navy Seabees and went into the service in June, 1943. He served in New Guinea and the Philippines for two and a half years until the end of the war. He was discharged in October, 1945.

After coming home he was appointed the first Veteran's Service officer for Wells County. He had served in this office about a year when he became the Standard Oil agent for Standard Oil Company. In 1948 he went to work at the Bluffton Post Office, where he worked until his retirement on April 23, 1978.

During his life in Bluffton he has belonged to the First United Methodist Church and the American Legion, and was a member of the Bluffton Kiwanis Club for several years, and served one year as its president. While a member of the Kiwanis Club he was involved in the formation of the Little League of Wells County. He was a member of the Bluffton Fire Department for seventeen years and served as its fire chief for two or three years. He served on the Park Board for a time and has been interested in various civic projects.

He is active in the church and is a member of the board of directors of the Wells County Council on Aging. He was selected as the Council on Aging's "Older Hoosier for 1990" and went on to become the "Older Hoosier for Area III Council on Aging", which includes nine counties.

Although retired he is very active, playing golf, fishing, working in his one-acre garden and doing odd jobs for various people.

CAMPBELL

Our family came to Wells County well before the turn of the century. William Henry Campbell, who served in the Union Army during the Civil War, was of Scottish descent. He married a Welsh girl named Alice McCann. They raised their family in Boone County, Indiana. William had two boys, Jim and Carey, from a previous marriage. William and Alice had four children: Cory, Burt, Jess and Willie Henry.

Willie Henry Campbell (1869-1952) married an Irish lass, Ida Luelva McDonald (1871-1948). Willie was a farmer by trade, locating first in Mud Creek, Indiana. Next he operated a grocery store in the town of Pickard (nicknamed "Tailholt"), then a blacksmith shop in Deming and finally moved to a farm in Boone County. Before the family left southern Indiana, five children were born: Virgil (1893-1956), Cleo (died at 18 months), Doyle H. (1900-1990), Charles (1902-1976), and Margaret (1906-).

In 1902 Willie and his family moved to a farm near Murray, Indiana. Ten years later they moved to Bluffton, where he worked for the Interurban Electric Railroad. After being laid off because of age, he moved to another farm northeast of Bluffton.

His son, Doyle H., worked first for one of the piano factories, then a major industry in Bluffton. In 1923 he joined the U.S. Postal Service, where he worked until retiring in 1960. He was a Boy Scout leader in Bluffton as early as 1930. Doyle would also meet and eventually marry Helen J. Kershner (1902-1972).

Her grandfather, William Henry Kershner, and his wife Emma immigrated from Germany, settling first in Pennsylvania. They eventually came to Indiana, living on a farm near Murray. They had two sons, Henry and Frank, and three daughters, Bessie Brandyberry (later Mowery), Delia Capp, and Mamie Lobsiger.

Their son Henry M. (1867-1939) married Martha Simeral (1874-1932). Henry was owner and proprietor of the Kershner Grocery Store in Bluffton until he died. They had three children: Ray, Fern Karns and Helen Campbell.

Helen Kerschner and Doyle H. Campbell married in 1923. They had two children, Bill K. born 1929 and Peggy Jo, born 1931. Both grew up in Bluffton, Peggy marrying Lloyd Spichiger from Linn Grove and Bill marrying Nancy M. Mossburg, who lived in Liberty Center, Indiana, until she was fourteen.

Although both Bill and Nancy were born in Wells County, they did not meet until college, Indiana University in Fort Wayne. They were married February 3, 1951. The day before the wedding was the coldest February 2 ever recorded in Fort Wayne, Indiana - 17°. They took up residence in Bluffton, where Bill worked for Franklin Electric Company, Inc. until retiring in 1988. Nancy has worked at Caylor-Nickel since 1974. Five children were born of this union, which accounts for Nancy and Bill's active participation in scouting and school activities.

Nancy was Girl Scout leader at East Side School and a Cadet leader of the Methodist Church group. She was active in PTA at Park School, East Side, Poplar Grove and was on the PTA Council of Bluffton. Bill and Nancy were the first co-presidents of the Central Junior High PTA.

Bill joined scouting at the age of twelve. He advanced to the rank of Eagle Scout. He later served as Scoutmaster of Troop 141, Cubmaster of 3143 and Assistant Scout Master of Troop 142. As committee chairman of Post 2150 he accompanied the post on a trip to Philmont Scout Ranch in New Mexico and a canoe trip to Canada. He served as chairman for the three-county Limberlost District in 1971-1972.

Their five children are married and have nine children of their own. The children, spouses and grandchildren are as follows:

Son, James Allen (1952) married Carolyn Burns of Fort Wayne. One child, Kiersten E. (1990); son, David Kay (1954) married Vernie S. King of Bluffton. Children Liane R., (1981) and Brian K. (1985); daughter, Judy Ann (1956) married Anthony Thomas of Fort Wayne; children Merrie E. (1983) and Jacob C. (1985); son, Richard Lee (1960) married Susan A. Cotton of Bluffton. Children Andrew J. (1986), Stacy M. (1989) and Matthew R. (1990); daughter, Dian Kay (1963) married Randall G. Steffen of Bluffton. One child, Janelle M. (1988).

CAMPBELL FAMILY

William Henry Campbell (Scottish), married Alice McCann (Welsh). William and Alice lived in Boone County, Indiana. They had four children: Cory, Burt, Jess, and Willie.

Willie Henry Campbell (September 5, 1869 - September, 1952), married Ida Leulva McDonald (October 23, 1871 - winter 1948) (Irish). They came to Wells County from Boone County in the early 1900's. Their five children were: 1) Virgil (October 18, 1893 - October 4, 1956); 2) Cleo (died at eighteen months); 3) Doyle (February 25, 1900 - October 28, 1990); 4) Charles (June 30, 1902 - March 20, 1976); 5) Margaret (July 21, 1906 - currently living in California).

Virgil Campbell married Mary Schell. They had three children: 1) Doris Valeria Campbell, (October 12, 1916-). Valeria married Henry Lockwood and they had one son, Donald. She later married John Merkey who died in January 1990. 2) Ruth Elizabeth Campbell (January 30, 1917-). Ruth married Vaughn Ochsenrider, and married Kenneth Julian. Both husbands are deceased. 3) Dale Leveral Campbell (March 20, 1919 - June 20, 1986).

Dale married Kathryn Anna Mazelin (August 7, 1921-), from Berne, Indiana, on August 12, 1939. Dale drove a truck for many years. The last twenty-six years, he drove for Renner's Express based in Bluffton. They later moved their office and Dale moved to Lansing, Michigan. He retired from Renner's Express in 1976, and moved back to Bluffton. Dale and Kathryn have seven children. 1) Richard Lee Campbell (January 21, 1940-). Richard married Marjorie Reece of Sacramento, California, in 1961. They had two children. Richard later married Judi Itchner in August, 1966, and they have three daughters. 2) Jackie Ray Campbell (July 16, 1941), currently lives in Decatur, Indiana. 3) William Dean Campbell (January 7, 1943-) married Sandra Nicholson and they have four children. William lives in Enns, Austria. 4) Patricia Ann Campbell (April 25, 1944-), married Donnie K. Faus December 30, 1961 and had three sons. Patricia later married Walter Miller and they reside in Fort Wayne, Indiana. 5) Claudia Diane Campbell (April 12, 1945-) is single and lives in Bluffton. 6) Sandra Kay Campbell (November 30, 1947-), married Ronald Lee Oswalt from Poneto and they have three children. They live in Bluffton.

Richard Lee Campbell had the following children: 1) Randy JoAnn Campbell (February 14, 1962-) is married to Robert Leon and have two daughters, Jennifer JoAnn Leon, and Tara Michelle Leon. They live in Sacramento, California. 2) Brett Alan Campbell (May 19, 1963-) is married and lives in California. 3) Rory Michelle Campbell (June 21, 1969-). 4) Nicole Roseanne Campbell (October 30, 1971-). 5) Cristina Louise Campbell (April 26, 1977-). The three younger girls live with Richard and Judi in San Antonio, Texas. William Dean Campbell had the following children: 1) Debra Lynn Campbell (October 5, 1962-). 2) Douglas Lynn Campbell (September 8, 1963-) married Luetta Coffield and have two daughters, Ashley Linn Campbell (March 10, 1986-), and Derek Evan Campbell (February 14, 1989-). 3) Jon Michael Campbell (June 12, 1966-). 4) Jeffery Deane Campbell (October 7, 1969-) married Lori Kinsey and have one child, Sara Jade Campbell (September 26, 1990-). The four Campbell children all reside in Bluffton. Patricia Ann Campbell Miller had the following children: 1) Kent Adrian Faus (October 13, 1963-) married Ann Cline of Denver, Colorado. Presently serving in the Air Force and stationed in Germany. 2) Kelly Dale Faus (September 26, 1966-) married Carrie Smith of Indianapolis and they are living in Indianapolis. 3) Kris Samuel Faus (August 27, 1969-) lives in Fort Wayne, Indiana.

Sandra Kay Campbell Oswalt had the following children: 1) William "Todd" Oswalt (September 26, 1966-) living in Boston, Massachusetts. 2)

Ronald "Keith" Oswalt (July 9, 1970-) living in Bluffton. 3) Jill Ann Oswalt (October 26, 1976-) living in Bluffton. The seventh child of Dale and Kathryn Campbell was Marna Sue Campbell (January 12, 1949 - January 12, 1949.)

CAMPELL-LOCKWOOD-KUNKEL

William Henry Campbell (Scottish) married Alice McCann (Welsh) and lived in Boone County, Indiana. William was in the Civil War on the Union side. They had four children, Cory, Burt, Jess, and Willie.

Willie Henry Campbell (1869-1952) married Ida Leulva McDonald (Irish 1871-1948). They had five children: Cleo, Virgil, Doyle, Charles and Margaret. Willie started as a farmer located at Mud Creek, then moved to a farm near Levanon in Boone County and later moved on a farm in Wells County. He also worked for the Interurban Electric Railroad.

Virgil Campbell (1893-1956) married Mary Schell of Bryant, Indiana. They had three children, Valeria, Ruth and Dale. Virgil was farmer and later worked for Tokheim in Fort Wayne.

Valeria Campbell (1915) married Henry Lockwood. They had one son, Donald. Valeria later married John Merkey, who worked for Pennsylvania Railroad. He was a World War I veteran, sixty-eight years in American Legion Post III. They lived in Harrison Township for thirty-five years. on a farm and later moved to Barbee Lake. Valeria lives in Bluffton, Indiana.

Donald Lockwood (1932) married Betty Lou Fear of Petroleum, Indiana. They had two children, Donald and Debra. Donald graduated from Bluffton High School and was a sergeant in the Air Force during the Korean Conflict. He worked for General Electric in Fort Wayne for twenty-six years. They live in Harrison Township.

Donald (1954) married Debra Lynn Wasson. They have two children, Lindsay and Kyle. Donald graduated from Bluffton High School. He worked at General Electric and is now employed at General Motors in Fort Wayne. They live near Ossian, Indiana.

Debra (1956) married Stanley Alan Kunkel. They have two children, Brent and Chelsea. Debra graduated from Bluffton High School and is employed at Lincoln National Life Insurance Company in Ft. Wayne. They lived near Bluffton, Indiana.

CAMPBELL-MCFARREN

In a mid-sized house Walter Campbell and Mildred McFarren started a family in Liberty Township. They had two daughters and three sons through their marriage. Their names are Donna, Linda, Robert, Dennis, and Ronald.

Walter Campbell was born on March 23, 1923, to Walter and Louetta Campbell, Sr. Mildred McFarren was born on October 18, 1926 to Earnest and Della McFarren. They were married on January 19, 1946.

Our grandfather worked at Grissom Air Force Base in Bunker Hill making runways before the war. Then on January 18, 1943, he went into the military service right at the beginning of World War II. During the war he fought in the Battle of the Bulge then on December 5, 1945, he was discharged from the military service and began working at Ratliff Grocery Store in Bluffton. Our grandmother didn't work at a paying job before the war. She worked at Franklin Electric during the war and was laid off after the war ended. After the war, she occasionally worked at a tomato factory. She told us she really never had to work until she had kids to raise.

All of the kids went to the Liberty Center School for awhile but they soon moved into the consolidated Southern Wells High School. Donna, the oldest, graduated from school and married Carl Thompson on June 13, 1965. They had four children and they were Terry, Tim, Todd, and Curt. Donna and Carl were divorced and she married Harry Helms.

Linda graduated from high school and married Kenneth Gephart on July 28, 1968. Linda and Ken had three children and they were Tammy, Cliff, and Ryan.

Robert graduated from school and married Connie Uhrick in April of 1972. They had two children and they were Phillip and Carol.

Dennis graduated from school and married Dianne Krick on February 26, 1972. Dennis and Dianne had three children and they were Tracie, Sherry, and Denisa. After having their children, Dennis and Dianne went into mission work.

Ronald, the youngest, graduated from school and married Carol Skinner on May 26, 1972. They had three children named Heidi, Anthony, and Jeremy. Ron is now the deputy sheriff of Wells County.

Our grandmother and grandfather are the proud parents of five wonderful children. They also have fifteen grandchildren and one-great grandchild.

CAPS

George William Caps was born July 13, 1825, in Aumebauch-Newstat near Darmstat, Germany. His father, Christopher, was a native of Germany and a farmer. His mother, Anna Catherine Wurtenberger, ancestors being Huguenots, fled from France during wars and religious persecutions. There were six children but the two boys, George W. and Christopher W., came to American to escape so much military service. Christopher came to American earlier, while George came in May of 1854. Christopher operated a blacksmith shop in Newville, as it was known then (now Vera Cruz), after 1880.

George W. married Mary Elizabeth Marks at Vera Cruz. She had come to America in 1855. Christopher W. died of typhoid fever in 1859 and had no children.

Picture shows the three drawers you don't see unless you know where they are.

George W. and Mary E. lived at the Vera Cruz location where all the children were born. Then they moved to a farm owned by Mary E.'s brother along the Maumee River near Fort Wayne, Indiana. In 1878, George W. bought the 80-acre farm, southeast of Bluffton, for $2,800. They left the Maumee River farm early in the morning and walked, with a team of horses, what livestock they had, the rest of their possessions in the wagon, and got to the Bluffton farm at midnight. Their children were: Edward, Tillie, William, John, Rinehold, Lydia, Dora, George L., and Amos.

The Caps brothers, Edward, Rinehold, William and John, manufactured and installed printing presses in Kansas City until 1902. At that time they formed the Caps Brothers Manufacturing Company and produced the "Caps Car" until 1905, when the reorganized with more capital, into the Kansas City Motor Car Company. This company was in business until 1909 when the Ford mass production made individual manufacturing obsolete and unable to compete. Less than 20 of the Caps Cars were produced while the Kansas City Motor Car Company produced some 300 cars, buses, and trucks.

John continued work as shop foreman for the Moriarty Cadillac Company until 1916, when he moved to a farm in Leavenworth County, Kansas.

Tillie later in life moved to Lawrence, Kansas. Lydia lived in Fort Wayne, Indiana. Dora lived in Bluffton, Indiana. Amos died at six months. After the father, George W., died, George L. bought shares that belonged to the brothers and sisters and kept the farm southeast of Bluffton. That farm belonged to the Caps 109 years, from 1878 to 1987.

George W. came to American on a steamer, six weeks on the ocean. He played the violin for the entertainment on the boat, and also barbered.

Mary E. came to American on a sail boat, three months on the ocean, with very crowded and uncomfortable conditions.

The chest, at the Wells County Historical Museum, is the one Mary E. brought her belongings in from Germany, on a sail boat in 1855.

CHARLES CAPTAIN FAMILY

The Charles Frederick (Charlie) Captain family represents the third and fourth generations of this family in the United States. The founders of the Captain's were Solomon (1806) and Margaret (1809) Captain. Solomon was born in a valley in Switzerland in the small village of Roche shortly after the French armies swept through Switzerland during the French Revolution (1798).

The political changes, under French control, caused much confusion and dissatisfaction. By 1830 many Swiss had begun to demand political reforms. There was much unrest. Solomon, his wife, Margaret (born in France), and their small baby left Roche for the New World where they could live in a free democratic country. They came by boat across the ocean and then by a horse drawn wagon into the Old Northwest.

(L to R) Diana, Charles F., Bradley Lee, Timothy Linn, Charles (Chad) Captain

John E. Captain, Charlie's grandfather, and the youngest of six children, was born in Adams

County (1849). He married Mary Ann Sovine, also born in Adams County (1853). She was a daughter of Sophia (Garbar) Sovine and Frederick Sovine, both natives of Switzerland. Charlie's father, Charles Henry (1880) was the fourth of eleven children. He came to Wells County with his parents in 1900 where farm land was purchased four miles southeast of Bluffton. He started farming his own land known as "The Ideal Stock Farm" and this farm is still in the Captain family. He married Ruth Gregg in 1936, and Charles F. (1937) was their only child.

Ruth Gregg's grandparents, John Gregg (1829) and Fannie Wallace (1841) came to the United States from Ireland in 1850. They were married in 1858. Richard Gregg, one of their thirteen children, married Lavina Linn. Lavina was the third of seven children of Levi Linn (1831) and Caroline Meyers (1838). (See Linn Entry). Ruth was the second child and only daughter of three children.

Charles grew up on the farm and was very active in agricultural activities, particularly the raising and showing of registered Aberdeen Black Angus cattle. He had many Grand Champion animals. Upon graduation from high school he attended Purdue University.

Charles married Diana Maddux (See Maddux Entry) in April of 1960 Diana graduated with a master's degree in education from Ball State Teacher's College and has taught in the Bluffton Schools ever since. Charles and his sons still own and manage the Captain farms. In addition to farm management, Charles has been a supervisor at Kitco Inc. since 1965. They live southeast of Bluffton on a farm with their three sons, Charles Nathan (Chad), Bradley Lee, and Timothy Linn. The boys, like their father, have been active in 4-H, particularly in the beef project. The boys encouraged their father to switch to Chianina cattle. They are white and about the size of a horse so they were quite a contrast to the small Black Angus. The boys have won many honors with their cattle in state and national shows.

Chad graduated from Bluffton High School (1982) and Purdue University (1987). He works for Manville Inc. in Buffton, Indiana.

Brad graduated from Bluffton in 1988 and is a junior at Indiana University majoring in international business. Future planes include a degree in law.

Tim is a sophomore at Bluffton High School. He is active in running sports and show choir. He plans to attend Indiana University and obtain an elementary education degree.

CARNES-WALKER

Everett Wayne Carnes (1885) was married to Mable Chloe Walker (1898). Everett was the son of William Henry Carnes and Etta Noe. Etta was the daughter of David and Harriett Noe.

Chloe was the daughter of William Alvin Walker and Bertha Alice Farlow, born July 24, 1880, who were married on April 17, 1897. William was the son of William Walker and Mary Miller. Bertha was the daughter of William Riley Farlow and Mary McCrum.

Everett was one of six children: Eldon, Clyde, Ralph, Mildred, Alma and Everett.

Chloe was the oldest of eight children. The others were Blanch, Irene, who married Donald Thomas, Jerome, Claire, Howard, Wayne, and Fern, who married Charles Crosby.

Everett and Chloe have six children. Yvonne, born February 23, 1918, married Bernie Lofton on October 11, 1939. They have five children: Joy, Jack, June, Janet, Jamie and thirteen grandchildren. They live in Moline, Illinois. Monnah, born August 23, 1919, was married on October 17, 1943, to Earl Raber, born September 22, 1943. Monnah lives in Bluffton. They have three children, Donald Kent, who is married to Glenna Osborn, Bruce Lee, who is married to Mary Lou Kaehr, and has four children, and Connie Sue, who is married to Mike Bohme. Berthetta, born August 22, 1921, was married to Ked Chaney, (February 29, 1920), on July 9, 1949. They live in Fort Wayne. They have two boys, Jim and Tim. Mary Magdaline, born October 2, 1923, was married on July 7, 1944, to Howard Myers, born July 30, 1920. They live in Bluffton. They have two daughters, Linda and Debby and they have eight grandchildren. Jack Walker, born February 14, 1926, was married on November 10, 1945, to Mick, born March 1, 1926. They live at Columbia City. They have one son, Joe, who is married to Charlene Chaney and they have two sons, Chad and Travis. Carolyn Sue, born February 10, 1935, was married on December 13, 1985 to Jerry Lee Vaughn, born July 5, 1933. They live in Bluffton. They have three children, Theresa Joan (Terry), who is married to Ked Biberstine. They have two children, Ashley Vaughn and Zachary Ked. Sandra Lee is married to Kurt Reiners and has one son, Andrew Christopher. Scott Alan is single.

CARROLL

I will write off some few words, as regards Wells County early 20th century facts, as I recall them from boyhood to manhood. I was born in Buckeye in the first decade of this century. My parents Elbridge and Flora (Flo) Sliger Carroll, removed to Wells County about 1910. When we reached school age, we attended the Travisville District #9 one-room school which was built in 1881. The teachers, as I remember, were Ruth Markley, Charley Mendeth, Eva Kunkle, Chloe Grove and Victor Gavin. There was a huge coal stove in the school room that had to be stocked during cold weather. The teachers were allowed a little money to pay a student, with muscle, to keep the coal buckets full. The teacher's pay was less than twenty-five dollars per week. I know this because my mother, after her children had out grown the grade school, taught at Travisville during World War I. The male teachers, who were gone at that time, were being drafted or enlisted in the armed services. Mother taught one year at Travisville, also one year each, at Roberts and Reiffsburg. Mother drove a 1916 Ford which she had to crank as there weren't many cars with starters at that time or at least they were not in her price range. The teacher's salary was no secret as it was published annually in the local newspapers. I wonder if this is still done in Wells County? I thought it was a very good idea to know where the tax money went.

Most of the farm houses, in the first two decades of my life, were built without bathrooms, running water or electricity. The house my parents owned, about four miles from Bluffton, located on the Hoosier Highway, was a good example of the period. We used coal, oil, and gasoline lamps. Bath tubs were really standard galvanized laundry tubs. There was a good drilled water well within a few feet of our back door. Mother had both coal and wood stove and a tall burner oil stove for cooking. It seems people were able to do without many of the things that are necessary in today's layout. There was no radio in our home until my brother Arthur and I ordered parts from Sears Roebuck and put one together, that was about 1920. I think perhaps people today might be better off to go back to more reading and handwork.

My generation has grown up in a very interesting era. Looking back over the events and inventions that have come to be commonplace have placed us in an unique place in United States History. I wouldn't have missed it for anything. I also think back of how transportation has changed. I recall having watched funeral processions go by and there would be a nicely harnessed team of horses hitched at the front, followed by carriages, a few buggies, a few of what now have become antique autos being driven in low gear. My brother Arthur and I would, when the Indianapolis 500 mile race was going to be run, select a comfortable spot on the grass, between the house and the road, to watch the automobiles fly by - at perhaps forty mph or less. We would try to identify the make of autos and notice the states on the license plates. At that time, there were perhaps seventy makers or manufactures left. Samples of what we listed and would read were Hayne, Fearless, Overland, Regal, Paige, Marmon, Stutz, Buick, Studebaker, Reo, Oakland, Pierce-Arrow, Ford, Saxon, Maxwell, Cole, Davis, Packard, Franklin, Hupmobile, Cadillac to name a few.

Grandfather Sliger used to let me ride with him to the Liberty Center Blacksmith Shop. He would hitch up old Moll and Doll, his work team of horses, to his wagon, load up a few plow shares and other pieces that needed attention. It was less than five miles to the shop, but it seemed further. Grandfather did not believe in pushing his horses too much. He always fed and watered them quite well. I know about the watering since it was my job to pump the water and fill the one half hollow log he had converted to a trough. I forget the blacksmith's name, but Granddad told me that he had served a stretch of time in a penitentiary for killing a man. I wasn't too keen about loafing in that shop after that story. Granddad assured me that the man was safe and he would guarantee my safety. It was a self defense case. It seems some man, for whatever reason I was not told or I don't remember, came at him with an iron bar. The blacksmith had no choice but to throw a hammer, he was working with, at his assailant and the man died. The hammer had cracked his skull. The smithy did a good job on the shares. We left town and were back home at sundown. *(Clyde A. Carroll)*

CARTWRIGHT-CASTON

Susan Frances Cartwright was born September 10, 1860, to James S. Cartwright and Sarah Shafer at their farm home on State Road 1 at the south edge of Ossian. She was a Christian and a fine example for others.

Her paternal lineage led to John Cartwright, a religious and political refugee from England, who lived in the Province of Zeeland, Netherlands.

Matthew, his first child, was born in 1634 in Middleborough, and emigrated to St. Mary's County, Maryland. He was naturalized in 1671, married Sarah, and died in 1688.

Peter Cartwright, 1687-1751, their fourth son, of Norwood and Lapworth, married Judith Slye. She was the daughter of Robert Slye II and Priscilla Goldsmith, the granddaughter of Capt. Robert Slye and Susannah Gerard, eldest daughter of doctor and lawyer Thomas Gerard and Susannah Snow, daughter of John Snowe and Edyreth (Judith).

First Maryland legislatures met in the homes of Capt. Slye's Bushwood and Gerard's St. Clements.

Gerard moved to his land near the Washingtons and Lees, where two widowed daughters married, in turn, Colonel John Washington.

Cartwrights by generation: John; Matthew; Peter; Robert (c. 1725-1799) of Berkeley County, Virginia, married Margaret and had two children.

Their son, Nimrod John, born 1763, married Margaret, and had two sons, John and James I. He sold his land, moved to Mercer County, Pennsylvania, in 1810, then to Trumbull and Mahoning Counties, Ohio.

Both sons married daughters of John McCorkle and Isabelle Montgomery, who emigrated from Ulster in 1799, and settled in the Western Reserve in 1803.

1902 Family of Josephus Caston and Susan Cartwright Caston of Ossian, Indiana, Jefferson Township. Back row: (L-R) Ada, Charles, Bertha, Ned; Front: (L-R) Josephine, Susan Cartwright Caston, Russell, Josephus Caston

Susan Cartwright (eighth generation) married Josephus Caston, born April 17, 1877, son of John Caston and Elizabeth McDaniel. John was in the boot and leather business in Manchester, Ohio, and was able to purchase a section in Jefferson Township in 1832.

Josephus, "Seph" (1851-1923) was a teacher, farmer, and lumberman. He attended Methodist College and Valparaiso University. He farmed his land across from his father's and his children attended Caston School.

After the passing of Susan's father, James S., mother Sarah Cartwright moved to Ossian for convenience.

Josephus and Susan purchased the Cartwright farm and moved with their family. Their children were: Charles Caston (1880-1958), educator. He attended Valparaiso, Stanford University and others. His hobby was earning another degree in divinity and law. He married Edna Stanfield. Ada Caston (1882-1910) studied millinery design in Chicago. She was a proofreader at the *Chicago Tribune*. Her millinery shop was in Ossian. She married Ora Faust. Ned Leslie Caston (1889-1944), employed by Grand Trunk Railroad, married Clara Wurts. Their son, Leslie was a doctor. Bertha Caston (1884-1959). Typhoid dashed her hopes for a career as a young woman. Josephine Frances Caston (1895-1923) studied music at the European School in Fort Wayne, and was invited to teach. She preferred the Ossian area. Russell E. Caston (1898-1980) managed a lumber firm in Oklahoma City. He purchased the Sash and Door section and built custom homes. His family purchased the balance. He married Roxy Lyle.

CASH

Charles Alonzo Cash, known to all as Lonnie, was born in Jay County in 1867 and died in 1944. He married Amy Leona Gray, who passed away in 1957. They lived in and near Pennville most of their life with the exception of several years in Bluffton.

They were the parents of three children: Hilda, the oldest, was born in 1893 and died in 1952. She married Charles Miles, who was a prominent farmer in Blackford County. They raised a family of five children, three of whom are still living.

L to R Carl Cash, Hilda Miles, Ethel Cart, Lonnie Cash, Leona Cash

The other daughter, Ethel, was born in 1897 and passed away in 1981. She was married to Christian Cart of Balbec in Jay County. They had two children, Delores Grissell of Bluffton, and a son, Herley, who died in an automobile accident in 1960.

A son, Carl, was born in Jay County in 1906 and passed away May, 1989, in Bluffton. Carl farmed for a number of years and later worked for the Bluffton schools and Wells County Public Library. In earlier years, he was employed at H.C. Bay Piano Company in Bluffton, where everyone knew him as Casey. In 1927 he married Marguerite Matson, daughter of Frank and Jessie Carlson Matson. They enjoyed nearly sixty-two years of married life. They had two daughters: Dixie Carleen was born in 1932. She graduated from Rockcreek High School and married Billy Joe Randol of Markle in 1955. They had three children: Douglas, who married Duree Ward and resides at Zanesville, Julie, who is married to Ken Bannister and resides in Huntington, and Brian, married to Stacie Heign and resides in Markle. Dixie passed away in 1986 of leukemia.

Janet Ann, born in 1939, also graduated from Rockcreek High School, and married Roy D. Schoeff of Wells County in 1964. They have four children, all graduates of Southern Wells High School: Cara, a nurse at Lutheran Hospital in Fort Wayne; twins, Shelley and Sheryl, both married, Shelley to Todd Preston and residing in New Haven, and Sheryl to Carl Lusher and they live in Auburn. The son, Brad, is attending ITT in Fort Wayne.

The Carl Cashes have eight great-grandchildren, Holly and Carly Randol, Billy Murphy, Courtney, Zachary, Gabriel and Morgan Randol, and Colin Lusher.

ABRAHAM CASTON

Abraham was born in 1825 the son of Henry Caston and Nancy Crem. He married Clarissa Sisson and had five children: Nancy, John, Lewis, Mary A. and Elizabeth Jane. After Clarissa died, he married Chloe Freeland and they had six children: Amilia, Catherine, William, Ollie Samuel and Cassy.

He served in the Civil War and farmed for a living. He died of pneumonia February 29, 1888. His funeral was held in the Ossian Baptist Church, and he is buried in Oaklawn Cemetery in Ossian. Clarrisa died at the age of 27 and was buried in the Poe Cemetery. Chloe died from acute kidney trouble on March 5, 1913, and was buried next to Abraham in Oaklawn Cemetery in Ossian.

HENRY CASTON

Little is known of Henry Caston's life. He came to Akron, Ohio from Germany in the early

1911 Reunion at James S. Cartwright Homestead Home of Josephus Caston and Susan Frances Cartwright. Back row: 1. Elvin Hoover holding Dale 2. Bertha Caston Hoover 3. Josephine Caston 4. Fred Beatty 5. ___ Beatty 6. Will Johnston of L.A. 7. Charles Caston 8. Sanford Walker 9. Bessie Taylor Walker 10. Earl Deam and child 11. ___ Deam 12. Nellie Beatty Deam 13. Edna Beatty; Middle: Grace Dunwiddie @ child 2. Victory Beatty 3. Mrs. Victory Beatty 4. Andrew Cartwright 5. Lucy Cartwright Sterret 6. Genevieve Walker 7. Susan Cartwright Caston 8. Russell Caston 9. Josephus Caston 10. Alice Cartwright Taylor 11. Warren Taylor 12. Emma Cartwright Beatty 13. James K. Beatty; Lower: 1 ___ Dunwiddie 2. Corrine Hoover 3. daughter of Vic Beatty 4. Helen Hoover 5. daughter of Victor Beatty children 6. Virginia Walker 7. Moine Walker 8. Donald Dunwiddie 9. ___ Dunwiddie

1800's, then later came to the Wells County area and married Nancy Crem. They had seven children: Abraham, John, Henry, Nancy, Martha, Betsy, and Catherine. Nancy Crem Caston is buried in Poe Cemetery. Henry is believed to be buried in the Old Ossian Cemetery.

CAYLOR

David Samuel Caylor, who was born on March 5, 1825, in Ohio was the first member of the Caylor family known to have lived in Wells County. David had completed his medical education at Rush Medical College in Chicago, and practiced at Keystone, Indiana, until his practice was stopped by a stroke in 1897. He died in 1903.

Charles Eli, son of David Samuel and Alice Shockley Caylor was born April 17, 1870. Charles decided that he wanted to be a doctor in spite of the fact that his father was unable to pay for his education. However, Charles found that he could finance his own medical training by teaching grade school six months a year in Somerset, Wabash County, and attending the Kentucky School of Medicine the other six months. He finished medical school in 1892.

In 1893, Dr. Charles married Bessie Ferree and settled in the booming community of Nottingham, which had several hundred people, active gas and oil development, and no physician. At first he used a bicycle to make house calls, but with the help of his mother-in-law he was able to buy a horse and a two-wheeled cart. Dr. Charles' practice grew rapidly and on August 19, 1894, their older son, Harold D. Caylor, was born. In 1897, when the "inexhaustible" gas and oil were being exhausted, Dr. Caylor moved his family to Pennville, in Jay County, and January 10, 1900, the second son, Truman E., was born.

Charles E. Caylor

Much impressed by the group practice of the Mayo Clinic, Dr. Charles resolved to attempt something like this in Pennville, and in 1908 the Provident Hospital was chartered by the State.

Failure of the CB&C railroad caused Dr. Charles to move to Bluffton in 1918. The new Wells County Hospital had one surgery, no laboratory, no x-ray, and no elevator, so surgical patients had to be carried down to surgery on a litter.

In 1918 Harold graduated from Rush Medical School in Chicago, and almost immediately came down with active tuberculosis. In remission, Harold married Ella L. Cary in 1919, only to relapse again until 1921. Their daughter, Rebecca (married to Dr. Donald Meier), was born in 1924, and Patricia (married to Dr. William E. Symon, and after his death in 1967 to James Niblick), was born in 1925. Dr. Harold accepted appointment to the staff of the Mayo Clinic until 1929.

Truman married Julia Gettle in 1922 and graduated from Rush Medical School in 1923. Dr. Truman and Julia had three children.

Carolyn (married to Herman Wadlington) was born in 1923, Charles H. (married to Phyllis Strasberg) was born in 1925, and Constance (married to Joseph Carney) was born in 1929.

In the fall of 1929, at the beginning of the Great Depression, the three Drs. Caylor were ready to launch their experiment in group medicine from which the clinic and the clinic hospital grew. Their timing was bad, but their concept was good, and the Caylor-Nickel Medical Center has grown with the changes in medical practice and knowledge.

After completing his medical education, Dr. Charles H. Caylor, only son of Dr. Truman, joined the group in 1957 and at present is chairman of the Caylor-Nickel Medical Center Board.

Dr. Charles E. was killed in an accident in 1944, and Bessie Ferree Caylor died in 1957. In 1969, Ella Cary Caylor died. In 1972, Dr. Harold was married to Henrietta Noe Lee, who survives him. Dr. Harold died in 1986.

Julia Gettle Caylor died in 1960. Dr. Truman married Eva Graham in 1961, and after her death in 1979, married Suzanne Black in 1980. Dr. Truman died in 1988 and is survived by Suzanne B. Caylor.

Wife of Dr. Charles H. Caylor, Phyllis Strasberg Caylor, died in 1987.

TRUMAN E. CAYLOR, M.D.

Truman E. Caylor, M.D., a fifth-generation American, was descended from John Koehler, a German immigrant who indentured himself for three years in order to pay for his passage to Virginia in 1763. As with many who came through immigration, his name was spelled phonetically, and Koehler became Caylor.

In time, John Caylor moved west to the Miami Valley of Ohio. His son, Elias, born May 22, 1805, near Dayton, was said to have been the first white child born west of the Miami River.

In 1827, Elias, his wife Sarah, and their children moved to Henry County, Indiana, where in 1844 he was elected a minister in the Dunkard Church. He was ordained in 1857. His son, David Samuel Caylor, followed his father into the ministry, but later was graduated from Rush Medical College in Chicago, and went on to practice medicine in Independence, Greentown, and finally in Petroleum in Wells County. David and his third wife, Alice Shockley, had one son, Charles E.

Truman was born in Pennville, Indiana, on January 10, 1900, to Dr. Charles E. and Bessie Ferree Caylor. He had one brother, Harold D., who was five and a half years older. Dr. Charles E. practiced medicine in Nottingham during the oil boom days, then in Pennville where the boys grew up. Both liked school and did well in it.

Truman's hobbies were competitive sports and outdoor activities like camping and hunting. Once, as a young boy, he and a friend went camping along the Salamonie, using the river water like pioneers did. As they explored upriver the second day out, they discovered a dead horse in the water not far from their camp. They couldn't get home fast enough! In spite of that discovery, however, Truman continued to enjoy camping and hunting throughout most of his life.

Ever the entrepreneur, Truman began his working life at a very early age. Quick in mind and movement and able to run fast, his first job was dropping the go-devil into an oil well to set off the dynamite. Later on in grade school, he delivered groceries after school for a local store. By the time he got into high school, electricity was coming to Pennville, so Truman, at the age of 14, became an electrician. He ran his own business of wiring houses in his spare time. Within a year he had saved enough money to buy a Henderson one-cylinder motorcycle, his pride and joy. He later travelled to and from Bloomington on his cycle when he was a student at Indiana University.

Truman E. Caylor, M.D., 1900-1988

The first clinic building in Bluffton was built in 1917 on the corner of Main and Cherry. Truman wired the entire building by hand, using a bit and brace.

While at Indiana University, Truman became a member of Delta Upsilon fraternity and, because of his business experience, was appointed House Steward his second year there. He cleared $500 that year, which amount was used to purchase the land that the present D.U. house sits on.

Truman was graduated from the University of Wisconsin, then from Rush Medical College where he was a member of Phi Rho Sigma. He interned at Evanston General Hospital, then returned to Bluffton where he practiced medicine from 1924 to 1980, specializing in urology.

In 1922 Truman was married to Julia Gettle and they had three children: Carolyn Alice, Charles Homer, and Constance Joyce.

After Julia Caylor's death in 1960, Truman was married to Eva Abbott Graham of Miami Beach, Florida, in 1961. She died in 1979. In 1980 he was married to Suzanne Black of Indianapolis, whose father, Dr. C.S. Black of Warren, had been president of the Indiana State Medical Association the same year that Julia Gettle Caylor was president of the Indiana State Medical Association Auxiliary.

In their medical life, Dr. Charles E., Dr. Harold, and Dr. Truman were the ultimate physicians and surgeons. Their greatest joy was to serve their patients and to provide a clinic in the vanguard of medicine. Dr. Charles E. died in 1945. When Drs. Harold and Truman were retired in 1980, the Caylor-Nickel Clinic had 55 physicians, 700 employees, its own 201-bed hospital, and a research institute.

Truman died in his own hospital on July 31, 1988, as he had lived, loving God, people, nature, and the practice of medicine.

CAYOT-HUEBNER

Roy Cayot, son of Lewis Cayot and Beatrice Middleton, married Martha Huebner, daughter of William Huebner and Hanna Zilkie. They moved from Allen County to the Kingsland area in 1930. In 1936 they moved to the Zanesville area.

Roy (June 10, 1902-1957) and Martha (March 20, 1901-1984) had twelve children. Eleven of their children graduated from East Union; the youngest, Dale, graduated from Lancaster.

Harold married Edith Nix. They had six

children: Thomas, Dennis, Cheryl, Janell, Patricia, and Marcia. Eugene (Gene) married Glenna Smuts. They had five children: Ellen, Karen, Leslie, Bradley, and Carol. Cathleen (twin) married Donald Lloyd. They had eight children: Donna, Dianna, David, Donald, Dana, Dean, Danny (deceased) and Darlene. Ileen (twin) married Dean Kern. They had four children: Judy, Connie, Barbara, and Lisa. Marcella (twin) married Ora Shaw. They had ten children: Vickie, Peggy, Susan, Sandy, Russell (deceased), Kelly, Tammi (deceased) Robin, Shad, and Shane. Mildred (twin) married Edward Springer. They had four children: Hal, Arlin, Lee, and Scott. Manford married Marion Peters. They had four children: Tony, Ronald, Carl, and Craig. Robert married Janice Fairfield. Robert's children are James R. Edward and Marita. Richard married Joyce Michaels. They had six children: Kathy, Linda, Michael, Steven, Yvonne, and Clark. Carolyn married Rod Goebel. They had three children: Debra, Delain, and Danette. Marilyn married Robert Kaltenmark. They had three children: Sheri, Douglas, and Eric. Dale married Jane Mattox. They had two children: Adam and Brian.

CAYOT-SMUTS

Eugene Cayot (February 22, 1925 - October 24, 1985), the son of Roy Cayot and Martha (Heubner) Cayot (see Cayot), married Glenna Smuts, daughter of Ruthford Smuts (see Smuts) and Bertha (Volmar) Smuts, on May 1, 1948.

Eugene (Gene) ranked third in his graduating class at East Union Center High School. After graduation, he joined the U.S. Marine Corps, serving in the 4th Marine Division. He was awarded the Purple Heart after being wounded in action during the invasion of Iwo Jima in World War II. After the war, Gene attended steamfitters and plumbers training on the G.I. Bill. He worked for Geiger Radio and Appliances (see Geiger), and farmed.

Gene and Glenna bought a farm on 1100N in Union township, and moved to Wells County, August 1, 1951. In 1961, they put aside about thirty acres for wildlife habitat and planted many trees. They built a house on the farm in 1971.

In 1968, Gene and Glenna bought Geiger's business and changed the name to Cayot Heating and Appliances. Gene and Glenna and their two sons, Leslie and Bradley, ran the business. In 1977, Gene and Glenna bought the Odd Fellows building where their business is located.

Gene and Glenna are the parents of five children. Ellen is a dental hygienist, earning her degree at Indiana University. She is married to Danny Decker and has one son, Jess. She lives on a farm in Wells County.

Karen graduated from Ball State University with an M.A. degree. She is teaching in Noble County and lives in Zanesville.

Leslie is a licensed plumbing contractor. He lives in the farm house his parents bought in 1951.

Bradley is a licensed plumbing contractor. He is married to Debra (Hersher) Cayot. He has two daughters, Rachel and Paige. Brad's family lives in Lafayette Township, Allen County, in the house his grandfather, Ruthford Smuts, built (see Smuts). This is where Glenna grew up and attended Lafayette Central School. Carol earned an A.S. degree in commercial art in Indiana University. She is married to James Love III, and lived at Big Turkey Lake, Hudson, Indiana.

After Gene's death in 1985, Glenna, Bradley and Leslie incorporated the business and continue to operate Cayot Heating & Plumbing Corp. in Zanesville.

CHALFANT

My father, Brent Chalfant, was born November 14, 1887, to Abner and Emma Schock Chalfant in Harrison Township. Abner's father was Reason Chalfant, son of Chads Chalfant.

Brent married Ida May Captain. To this union were born Eva, Lois and Wendell. My parents were farmers but also owned and operated a sand and gravel pit for many years.

My first two years of school were in the Shoemaker one-room school. Transportation was a school hack drawn by two horses. A kerosene heater kept us warm in the winter. When my sister, Lois, was ready for school, my parents paid tuition for us to go to school in Bluffton. After Poplar Grove School was built, Lois graduated from eighth grade there. Brother Wendell went there all eight grades. We all graduated from Bluffton High School.

After eighth grade, school was over for many students. So I would have transportation to high school, my father traded a cow and some cash with another farmer for a pony and buggy. I drove the pony into a livery stable near downtown, then walked a few block to the high school on West Washington Street. My senior year, 1924, we had a school bus to ride.

I married Hugh "Jack" Reynolds of Linn Grove. He was an employee of Meshberger Brothers Stone Corporation. The company purchased a stone quarry near Willshire, Ohio, in 1933, where he was plant superintendent and we moved to Willshire, where I am still living. We had two children. Our son, Leon, is living in Brunswick, Ohio, and our daughter, Kathleen King, lives in Willshire, Ohio.

My sister, Lois, married Ivan Hammond of Poe, Indiana. She was a cake decorator for many years at Eavey's, when that was the first supermarket in the region, and also at Heyerly's and at Scott's in Columbia City. They had three daughters, Carolyn of Huntington, Janet of Bluffton, and Marianne of Leigh High Acres, Florida. Following the death of her husband, she married Ed Bauer, who is now deceased. Lois is now living in Huntington.

Brother Wendell married Marjorie Sawyer. After living several years in Bluffton, they moved to Wolcottville, Indiana. They had four children, Julie, Daniel and Robert, all of Fort Wayne, and James (deceased). Wendell and Marjorie are both deceased.

Highlights that I remember: Heche's huckster wagon from Vera Cruz would come to our place once a week. Mother traded eggs for groceries. The threshing machine coming in tooting a whistle, delighting the children. In the winter, when our church was having revival meetings, Father hitched the horses to a bobsled, which had straw to sit on and blankets to keep warm. We picked up neighbors along the road to church. Then, our church was not only an important part of our lives spiritually, but an miportant part of our social lives.

Lois and I were part of Baltimore Oriole Girl Scout Troop of the Six Mile Church, organized by Grace Smith in 1920, first in Wells County and thought to be first in Indiana. (*Eva M. Reynolds*)

CHALFANT

The Chalfant name is one of the earlier family names in Wells County, with many descendants still tracing their lineage back to them. Their history in the old country traces them to the Huguenot family de Chalfonte in Buckingham near London, England, in the southern part in Burnham Hundred. The name appears there as early as 1288 A.D. with several towns bearing the name. (Chalfton Common, Chalfont Grove, Chalfont St. Giles, Chalfton Park, and more.)

The Chalfant's emigrated to the U.S. in 1684 and settled in the Brandywine River area of Chester County, Pennsylvania. Here again we find the name mentioned at Chalfant Station.

The first Chalfant in Wells County was Chads Chalfant (born February 19, 1802, in Brownsville, Pennsylvania, and died February 10, 1883, in Wells County. Like his forefathers he was respected for his farming and carpentry skills. Methodists, Chad's grandfather had donated land for the Methodist Episcopal Church in Brownsville, Pennsylvania. He is buried under the pulpit of that church, which still exists along the river near Church Street.

Chads Chalfant married Nancy Ferguson in Perry County, Ohio. He moved to Indiana in 1837, and farmed in the southwest quarter of Section 25 of Harrison Township. He lived and died on this farm at age 82. He and his wife are buried at Bethel Cemetery. Their children are Elizabeth (1824), Lydia (1826), Mercy (1827), Robert (1829), Mary J. (1833), Reason (1835), Joseph (1837) and Sarah (1841). Before he died, Chads made each child a rocker and wrote their name on the bottom. I know of at least three of these still in existence today.

Upon his death, Chads Chalfant left part of his farm to his sons Reason and Robert. Robert was the father of four children, including his son Frank, who remained on the farm, marrying Mary Potts and became the step-father to Ralph Potts. Reason, living in the homeplace, had four children including: Clara (Alice) Chalfant Gentis who stayed on the farm until selling to Herman Pence in 1946.

Mercy Chalfant married John Poultney Sturgeon April 16, 1848. Their children were Clarinda (1849), Henry (1856), Sedora (1858), James (1861), and twins Mary and Nancy (1865). Mercy and John are buried at Bethel Cemetery.

James Sturgeon married Viola Linn in 1889. They were the parents of two sons Charles "Ray" (1890) and Hugh Linn (1891).

Hugh Linn Sturgeon married Mima Kleinknight in 1917; she died in 1946. Hugh died in 1974. They, too, are buried at Bethel Cemetery. They were the parents of three children, Ruth (1918), Robert (1921) and Alfred Wayne (1926).

Ruth married Ralph Potts Jr., step-son of Frank Chalfant on June 27, 1942. They eventually resided on the portion of the farm and original house of Robert Chalfant. They had one daughter, Susan (1951), who married Leon Gaiser in 1977. They are the parents of two children, Hilary Linn (1986) and Caleb (1988). After the death of Ralph Potts in 1987, the Pences sold the original Chalfant homestead house along with a few acres, to the Gaisers. It is a house rich in family history for them. The rocker Chads made for his daughter, Mercy, now rocks his great-great-great-great-grandchild on land he cleared and farmed.

CHADDS CHALFANT FAMILY

I am Viva Chalfant Schott. I've always lived in Harrison Township. My father was Harry Chalfant. The Chalfants are descendents of Chadds Chalfant who came to Pennsylvania in 1687. He was a wheelwright; built the first Methodist Church in

Brownsville in 1776. He instituted the Masonic Lodge there. He was buried under the pulpit of the church he built.

He had one daughter and six sons. Son Robert had ten children, one being Chadds Chalfant, who moved to Indiana in 1889. Chadd was married to Nancy Fergeson. They had eight children: Elizabeth A. (Sylvester Reynolds); Lydia, (Mrs. James Higgins); Mercy (John Sturgeon); Robert (died 1905); Mary J. (___Campbell); Reason, (Mary C. Valentine); Joseph F. (_____) Sarah, (Joe Cobbum). Chadds Chalfant died on November 10, 1842.

My great-grandfather was Reason Chalfant. He had four children: Abner, Robert, William and Alice. Abner married Emma Schock at Reifsburg Methodist Church. Emma and Abner had three children, Mellie Pearl (never married), Brent (married Ida Captain), Harry (married Blanche Helen Page, daughter of Robert Wiley Page).

Viva Chalfant Schott

Harry and Blanche were my parents. We lived southeast of Bluffton. Most of Chadds' children lived close to the Bethel Church where the older Chalfants are buried.

I am the oldest of three children. We lived on the farm now owned by the Dale Schenkels. We attended the Six Mile Church until 1929, when we moved to Bluffton. We all worked hard when I was growing up.

My brothers were Senior P. Chalfant (married H. Mary Mendenhall) and J.C. Chalfant (married Patricia Bickers and has one daughter Aimie Lee; he lives in Van Nuys, California.)

Abner's brother Robert had three children: Faye (Hauk) now at Swiss Village; Cleo Lewis, deceased; and Howard, also deceased. He served in World War I.

Abner's sister Alice was married to Charles Gentis. They had one daughter Mabel (McAfee). She had one daughter, Anna Louise McAfee Colen, now Mrs. Thurl Kaufman.

My uncle Brent and Aunt Ida had three children: Eva May Chalfant Reynolds, Lois D. Chalfant Hammond and Wendell C. Chalfant. Wendell has one daughter and three sons. They lived or live around Wolcotville and Fort Wayne. As there are no sons but Wendell's they will have to carry on the Chalfant name.

I married Terrell W. Schott on October 24, 1932. His parents lived near Petroleum. We had one son, John Terry Schott, who had one daughter and three sons and also adopted one daughter Amanda Lee Brown. My son died of cancer in 1989. My granddaughter, Margaret Faye McAfee, has three boys, Chad Yates, Bradley Yates and Andrew McAfee.

Zachary A. has no children, Victor has two daughters, Jessica and Alysa. John Douglas has one son, John Paul Julian.

My brothers: Senior P. Chalfant was in Africa in the second World War. He was called to service after graduation from Palmer Chiropractic College. He served in the Medical Corps. J.C. served in the Air Force and was with the group that dropped the first atomic bomb on Japan.

Our son enlisted in the Air Force. He was married and his daughter was born at Bergstron Air Force Hospital in Austin, Texas. Victory, Terry's second son, enlisted in the Marine Corps. He is now in the national guard at Bluffton.

CHALFANT-PRILLAMAN

The Chalfants came from Chalfant, England, in 1687 with William Penn's second expedition. Chadds Chalfant came to Wells County in 1837, and planted his family on the southwest quarter of section 25, Harrison Township. At the site of the home of Leon and Susan Gaiser. His son Reason (born 1835) gave Poneto, in which he had real estate interests, a bank. Reason's son, Robert D. (1869-1943) married Mary L. Prillaman in 1890. Besides a Shrapshire Sheep fancier, he was a skilled architect and carpenter, and built the house and barn, the present home of Charles and Diane Captain at 40873-200S.

Robert and Mary (Prillaman) Chalfant December 1940

Mary was the daughter of Lewis (1825) and Maria (Masterson), both charter members of Six Mile Church, who came to Wells County in 1838. Lewis owned approximately 800 acres which is a portion of the Ouabach State park. The Prillaman home is now the home of Mr. and Mrs. Robert Greiner, State Road 316 near the park. When Clarence and Geneva Croy lived there, Clarence created a huge cross, made from walnut beams from the original barn. This was placed in the sanctuary of the Six Mile Church. In order to attend Six Mile, Lewis and his family traveled by foot, horseback, buggy, or bobsled to ford the Wabash River. Besides farming, he taught school for $12.00 a month. Lewis Prillaman held many Harrison Township offices and in 1868 was the first Republican ever chosen as a commissioner.

The Prillaman reunion was for many years held at the home of Fred and Cora (Prillaman) McBride, now the Ritten-house. Since Mary (Prillaman) Chalfant was the only daughter of Lewis and Maria who married a farmer, her home was frequently the scene of good old fashioned food, such as, smoked ham, fried chicken, sweet corn, strawberry jam, and apple pie.

Robert and Mary Chalfant had three children: Fay Hauk, Cleo Lewis and Howard Chalfant.

JAMES O. CHANEY

James Otho Chaney is a full-blooded Zanesvillite, both sets of grandparents having been around Zanesville in early years. Otho Chaney, his grandfather (for whom he is named), lived on a farm, had a butcher shop, and the Zanesville Post Office at one time. For the family genealogy refer to John W. Walker and George Weaver.

James graduated from Lafayette School in 1940. There he was voted the "Most popular, Most talkative, and Best gum chewer." He had the distinction of being the lightest man on the basketball team. You guessed it, his leading sport was basketball; Hires Root Beer, his favorite drink; and "girl" his favorite subject. His future, a missionary to China. Well, Jim never got to China, but he probably has dug enough dirt that if he would have gone straight down, he would have been there now.

Jim married Gladys Louise Williams, daughter of Mr. and Mrs. Ernest Williams, of Springfield, Illinois.

Chaney Trenching was first established 26 years ago by James O. Chaney. While at the Illinois State Fair in August of 1950, Mr. Chaney first saw the backhoe. He returned to Akron, Indiana, where he purchased a "Hop To" backhoe with intentions of repairing tile ditches for farmers in the surrounding area.

Having the only backhoe available, he covered many miles driving the tractor down the road to and from jobs. While becoming more established, several farmers extended a helping hand in the business when they weren't busy with crops.

The Chaneys have three sons and two daughters. As the Chaney sons grew older they became engaged in work with their father and thus developed "Chaney & Sons Excavating."

Kendric lives in Markle. Nick has a house over by Norwell, and Ron lives near Zanesville. Susie is married to Ed Decker and lives near Eaton, Indiana. Charlene is married to Joe Carnes and resides at rural Markle. The Chaneys have sixteen grandchildren and six great-grandchildren who dearly love the family get togethers with grandma and grandpa.

With the growth of the business over the years, he purchased more equipment. In late 1989, the Chaney's large pole barn burned to the ground, and a lot of their equipment was destroyed. This didn't stop the Chaneys from going right on with the business. For about two years now, Jim and Louise have been retired but they still do lots of the running for the boys.

Jim and Louise, who live just a few miles west of Zanesville, are faithful members of the Zanesville United Brethren Church. In years past they have supported and done lots of work at the church's camp in Ohio. They also were one of the first to volunteer their time to the food bank. Jim and his boys have taken the time to work at getting a building leveled, and room for a trailer at the church for storage and office room.

For more information on their family refer to the *Zanesville History Book 1976*.

CHUPP FAMILY

Our family heritage in Wells County began when Gideon Chupp and Elizabeth Fredricks married and set up residence at the corner of North County Line Road and 100E. The family lived there for many years, and a son, Clark, later resided on the home place. The home was an old log cabin, which was later replaced with a cement block structure. Aside from Clark, the family moved elsewhere to Ohio, Illinois, Oklahoma, and Kansas.

Grandfather Gideon was born February 28,

1825, and died June 11, 1899. He was married once prior to Elizabeth and had a son, Jake. Grandmother Elizabeth was born June 6, 1829, and died July 21, 1915. She was married before and had four children: George, John and Fred Herman. The fourth child died at birth.

Gideon and Elizabeth had six children: Mary Platt, Laura Reed, Ellen Allen, and Clark Chupp. Two passed away at birth. All now are deceased.

Clark married Edith Florence Skinner and five children were born to them. They were: Forest Chupp, Mildred Coverdale Bair, Marguerite Odier, Roy Chupp, and Wanda Wheeler Hughes. Roy died at the age of five weeks.

We started to school at the Bethel School and later attended the Ossian School. We walked, then drove horse and buggy, and then finally rode the bus after that mode of transportation was available in the area.

Forrest passed away in 1970 with the others living in the Fort Wayne, Indiana or Celina, Ohio, area. Most of the Chupp descendants have not lived recently in Wells County except that Nancy Chupp Gass, Forrest's daughter, lived in Wells County for a period of time and her son Herbert, still lives there. Dinah Coverdale Hart, a granddaughter of Mildred Coverdale Bair, currently lives on the North County Line Road near Zanesville.

There are many interesting and humorous incidents that occurred over the years, but there is not enough space to permit the telling of these stories and yet be fair to all of the family members.

JAMES W. AND VEDA M. (PACE) CLAGHORN FAMILY

James William Claghorn and Veda Maxine Pace were married in Bluffton, Indiana, December 27, 1939. James W. was born on November 30, 1918, in Crittenden County, Kentucky, the first son of Walter E. and Berta E. (Duvall) Claghorn. Veda M. was the oldest daughter of Herman and Hazel Bell (Schwartz) Pace. James graduated from Bluffton High School in 1938 after moving to a farm south of Bluffton from Detroit, Michigan, in 1935. Veda graduated from Bluffton High School in 1939. James served in the Sixth Marine Division during World War II, where he was an amphibious "Duck" driver in the battle of Okinawa in the Pacific. Following the war, he was in the trucking business as an owner-operator and later as a driver for a National Oil & Gas gasoline tanker truck. In 1965, James went to work for Corning Glass Works as a security guard, where he worked until his retirement in 1982.

James and Veda live at 1880 South Hoosier Highway. They are the parents of five sons: James Lee of Hartford City, Indiana, who married Elizabeth Ann Kennedy and whose children are: Elise Annette, James Kennedy, and Amy Lee; William David of Keystone, Indiana, who is married to the former Rosemary Cupp and whose children are: Jeanette Lynne, Jeffery Lee (deceased), Jerry Lyle, Tawnya Sue (Cupp); Larry Wayne of Bluffton, Indiana, who is married to the former Linda Sue Bouse and whose children are: Cynthia Sue, Corinna Lynn, and Christopher Wayne; Ronald Eugene of Berne, Indiana, who is married to the former Grace Wulliman and whose children are: Angela Joe, Daniel Deron, and Bret W.; Leslie Allen of Bluffton, Indiana, who is married to the former Diane Kay Falk. Children are Mark Allen (deceased) and Elizabeth Ann.

ROBERT G. AND GERALDINE L. CLAGHORN FAMILY

Robert and Gerry were married June 11, 1950, at Epworth Methodist Church in Bluffton, Indiana. Robert was born October 22, 1930, in Detroit, Michigan, the third son of Walter E. and Berta E. (Duvall) Claghorn. Gerry was born October 6, 1932, in Wolcottville, Indiana, the second daughter of Clyde and Naomi Faye (Kemper) Mounsey. Gerry's paternal grandparents were Samuel T. and Minnie (Ustick) Mounsey, who lived in Chester Township of Wells County. Her maternal grandparents were George and Anna (Nash) Kemper of Bluffton.

Left to Right-Back row: Kent, Bob, Father Bob, Keith, Tim; Left to Right-Back row: Mother Gerry, Connie, Deb, Pam

Robert attended grades one through eight at Poplar Grove School and grades nine through twelve at P.A. Allen High School in Bluffton, graduating in 1948. Gerry graduated from Bluffton High School in 1950. After getting married in June, 1950, they were engaged in farming, while Robert also worked as a mechanic. Gerry worked for many years as a secretary for Ellenberger Realtors and is presently with Century 21 Troxel Realty. In 1964, Robert went to work at the newly constructed Corning Glass Works color television plant west of Bluffton, where he was a millwright and later an electrician. He worked there until 1986, when he went to work at the General Motors Truck Assembly Plant at Roanoke, Indiana. Robert and Gerry purchased the family farm from Robert's parents in 1958. They live at 5043S 500E, Bluffton, Indiana, and are the parents of four sons and three daughters, all of whom graduated from Bluffton High School.

Pamela Sue married Michael L. Spichiger of Linn Grove, Indiana. They are the parents of Jennifer Jo, Gary Michael, and Brandi Janelle Spichiger. They live in Louisville, Kentucky, where Mike is an insurance agent. Constance Elaine is married to James Reusser. Children are: Heather Rebecca, Heath Dean, and Holli Elaine Terhune. They live in Bluffton and Jim is engaged in farming. Keith Alan is married to Carla Inskeep. They both attended Ball State University. Children are Nicholas Keith, Benjamin Robert, and MacKenzie Jo. They live in Indianapolis, where Carla is an RN at Community Hospital and Keith is a real estate agent. Robert William married Toni Fate. Their son is Christopher Robert. Robert W. lives in Bluffton and has a floor covering installation business. Debra Kay graduated from Ball State University as an elementary school teacher. She married Larry Quade of Logansport, Indiana, who also graduated from Ball State with a degree in finance. They have one son, Robert Ryan. They live in Jasper, Indiana, where Larry is a purchasing agent for Kimbal Electronics Corporation. Kent Roger married Dianne Jersild. Dianne graduated from Ball State with a degree in business. Children are, Kristine Nicole and Matthew Kent. They live in Indianapolis, where Kent has a floor covering installation business. Timothy Lee married Teresa Taylor. Children are: Britton Lee, Jordon Glenn, and Andrea Fay. Tim is an upholsterer at Berne Furniture in Berne, Indiana. He also is swimming coach for the Bluffton-Harrison Middle School and assistant coach for the Bluffton High School varsity swim team.

WALTER E. JR. AND LELA K. (MINGER) CLAGHORN FAMILY

Walter E. Claghorn Jr. was born in Detroit, Michigan September 4, 1924, the second son of Walter E. Sr. and Berta E. (Duvall) Claghorn. He moved to a farm south of Bluffton with his parents from Detroit in 1935. He attended grade school at Poplar Grove and high school at P.A. Allen High in Bluffton. Walter had a lifetime love of motorcycles and airplanes, always having a motorcycle, also learning to fly and owning his own airplane. He served in the U.S. Navy during World War II as a

The Robert Claghorn Family

gun captain on the ISS *Yakima* in the Atlantic Theater. After getting out of the Navy, Walter went into the long distance hauling business with his own semi rig. On November 17, 1946, he was married to Lela Kathryn Minger. Lela is the daughter of Jay and Edith (Mallonee) Minger of Bluffton. Lela graduated from Bluffton High School and following high school worked at Caylor-Nickel Hospital as a lab technician. For a period of time, they owned and operated The Pine Village Truck Stop on Highway 37 at Elwood, Indiana. They later moved to a home south of Bluffton and Walter continued in the trucking business. They are the parents of five boys and one daughter: John Jay, who married Sandra Maupin; Alan Kent of Franklin, Indiana, who is married to the former Karey Duke, and whose children are Erin Nicole and Emily Lynn; Ted Michael, who lives south of Bluffton and is married to the former JoAnn Campbell and who has a daughter, Anna Louise; Gale Brian of Indianapolis, Indiana, who is married to the former Janice Heron and whose children are Dustin Jay and Stephanie Jo; Bradley Wayen of Bellbrook, Ohio, who is married to the former Vicki Clark and whose children are Bradley Wayne Jr. and Wesley Walter; Jean Ann of Anchorage, Alaska, who is married to Bob Lyles and whose children are Wendy Lee (Holsinger) and Chad Daniel Lyles. Walter died October 24, 1981. Lela continues to live at their home south of Bluffton and is employed at K-Mart in Bluffton.

WALTER AND BERTHA (DUVALL) CLAGHORN

Walter E. Claghorn was born June 9, 1896, at Marion, Kentucky. He graduated from Marion High School. Berta E. Duvall was born March 11, 1898, at Marion, Kentucky. They both attended East Central State Teachers College at Tishomingo, Oklahoma. After graduating and getting teacher's licenses, they taught school near Ada, Oklahoma, for a period of time. They then returned to Crittenden County, Kentucky, where they bought a small farm and Walter taught school at Stanley, Kentucky. They later moved to Detroit, Michigan, where Walter went into the construction business.

Berta and Walter Claghorn

As they traveled from their home in Detroit back to visit their relatives in Kentucky, they very often traveled through or near Bluffton, Indiana, and were always impressed with the excellent farm land they passed in this area and often remarked that they would like to settle near Bluffton. As if Lady Luck was with them, in 1928, Berta spied an advertisement in the Detroit News that said a minister from Bluffton, Indiana, would like to trade a 122 acre farm in Wells County, Indiana, six miles south of Bluffton, for a home in Detroit because he had accepted a pastorship there. After making a trip to look the farm over, they made the trade. They continued to live in Detroit until December of 1935, when they moved permanently to the farm south of Bluffton, where they lived until they sold the farm to their son Robert and his wife Gerry in 1958. Walter retired from farming and carpenter work at this time. They lived in a house that Walter had built just north of the home farm until 1985, when, because of Berta having had a stroke, they lived with Robert and Gerry. Since January, 1990, they had lived at Meadowvale Care Center in Bluffton. They are the parents of three sons: James W. Claghorn of 1880 South Hoosier Highway; Walter E. Claghorn Jr. who died in 1981; and Robert G. Claghorn of 5043S 500E Bluffton, Indiana. Walter and Berta have eighteen grandchildren, thirty-six great-grandchildren and two great-great grandchildren. They have been married seventy-three years on January 19, 1991.

CLYDE CLANIN FAMILY

In 1915, Dora A. Pence of Swayzee, Indiana, bought the 80-acre Harnish Fruit Farm three miles southeast of Bluffton, just west of the Hoosier Highway and east of the Frank Markley farms. Mr. Pence asked his hired hand, Clyde Clanin, to work the farm he had just bought. On March 1, 1915, Clyde, Florence and Maxine Clanin moved to the Harnish farm in Wells County. They moved everything they owned, including chickens and cow by horse-drawn wagon.

Clyde Clanin was born in 1887 southwest of Sweetser, Indiana. He was of Scotch-Irish and English descent. He was the oldest of eight children. His mother died when he was fourteen years of age, and it was necessary for him to quit school while in the eighth grade and stay at home to help his father care for the other seven children, who ranged from eight months to twelve years of age. His farming career in Wells County was stock farming along with grain farming. He loved horses and showed his Belgian horses at the Bluffton Free Street Fair along with other choice animals he owned. He drove a school bus in Harrison Township for eight years.

Florence Lugar Clanin was born in 1890 in Grant County near Jalapa, Indiana, close to the Mississinewa River. Florence was of German and Pennsylvania Dutch descent. She spent her childhood near an old Indian campground. She and her sister rode their horse to sing at the Indian Campground Church. At different times in her life she lived with her maternal grandmother, Martha Harter Renbarger, in and Indian log cabin. She was well-known for her Pennsylvania Dutch cooking by her relatives and the hay hands and threshing ring. Bountiful dinners or country-cured ham and fried chicken were served in the Clanin home along with homemade ice cream.

Maxine Clanin was born in 1911 near Jalapa, Indiana. Maxine started her school at the Travisville one-room schoolhouse, which consisted of eight grades and one teacher. She was transported to school in a red, horse-drawn school bus. In those days, schools never "let out" because of inclement weather. They had to use a huge box on runners as a sled drawn by horses to get to school sometimes. School hours in those days were from 8:30 a.m. until 4:00 p.m., and the country-school term ended the last of April

While living in Wells County, the Clanins encountered some hardships — the small pox epidemic, the 1918 flue epidemic and the Great Depression, the closing of the banks in Bluffton, and the suicide of their friend, who was a bank president.

Farm mortgage foreclosures were numerous in those days and the Union Central Life Insurance Company foreclosed the mortgage on the Clanin farm. One evening President Franklin D. Roosevelt broadcast on the radio and said, "If there is anyone within the sound of my voice who has farm mortgage foreclosure, please go to your nearest information, and I will see that you get a three-year mortgage moratorium." The Clanins went to Bluffton at ten o'clock that same evening and sent the telegram, and the mortgage was stopped, permitting the Clanins to remain on the farm for another three years.

Due to the Depression and low farm prices — three cents a pound for hogs and ten cents a dozen for eggs — they could not afford the farm near Bluffton. They bought a cheaper farm in Rockcreek Township near the Wabash River in Huntington County. Again they hitched their beautiful horses to their wagon and moved.

It was President Roosevelt who gave the Clanins another chance. Needless to say, the Clanins are staunch Democrats and always will be.

CLARK

The Clark family history has been traced to Sargent and Eunice (Irwin) Clark of Guilford County, North Carolina, in 1813. John I. Clark was the oldest son of Sargent and established a home on eighty acres of government ground in Huntington County. There he married Nancy Helms in 1846. Later they purchased a 69 acre farm in Liberty Township, Wells County. It was John I. who influenced the first minister to come into the community to hold a revival at Roberts School. From this revival came forth the Boehmer Church. John I. and his wife became the first church members. Four children were born to this union: Viola Minniear, Huntington County; Rufus, Liberty Township; Garnet Smith, Muncie; and Lester (1884) who lived his entire life in Liberty Township.

Lester and Myrtle Clark

Lester, my father, graduated from Liberty Center High School in 1903. Dad married Myrtle Shadle, daughter of Jame Newton and Caroline Penrod in 1930. My parents lived with my grandparents for six years, as grandfather needed care because of a stroke. They later purchased an 80-acre farm two miles west and a quarter mile north of Liberty Center. There was a small house on the farm; a new house was built a little later. My father was a well-known farmer and seed buyer for O.M. Scott & Sons in Ohio. Dad was very interested in the Mossburg Cemetery and always had a project going where he could improve the cemetery. Many times when we went for a drive, we ended up at the cemetery. Dad always wanted me to drive so he could look at growing crops in the neighborhood. He died in 1961. Mother was born in 1882 in

Chester Township. She was a homemaker, very active in the Boehmer Church, a Sunday school teacher, and did missions work. Mother was well-known for her bread baking and won many prizes. She died in 1962.

Ethel Clark at retirement party in 1983 from Franklin Electric

To this union seven children were born: Ruth E. Valentine, Fort Wayne; Helen V. Kirkwood, Bluffton; Aubry I. Beavans Keystone; Homer S. (wife Frances Speheger), died 1981; Harry E. (wife Frances Mendenhall), died 1970; Martha (infant), died 1918 at age ten months; Ethel L. Clark, Bluffton.

After I graduated from Liberty Center high School in 1938, I continued to live with my parents to help them during their illness. During the war I worked at Farnsworth in Bluffton for two years. Later I went to Franklin Electric, where I retired with 38 years of service. There I was active in the Quarter Century Club, having been an officer for ten years. I am now a member of Park United Brethren Church and am donating my time as secretary. I'm a member of the Business and Professional Women's Club, currently serving as treasurer. In 1984 I joined the Wells Community Hospital Auxiliary. I enjoy calling the Life-Line subscribers for a monthly check. We have over forty subscribers; sometimes I go to homes to install the units. The Life-Line helps the subscribers to stay at home and feel secure.

The John I. Clark farm was inherited by Lester, then passed to Harry, and a great-grandson, Barry Clark, now resides in the home. *(Ethel Clark)*

CLARK

Walter B. Clark was born in Frederick, Maryland c.1787. His wife Margaret DeGroff Clark was born in Gettysburg, Pennsylvania. It was said that her father was from Poland, and a brother, Abraham, was an inn proprietor near Baltimore. They were married in Pennsylvania and settled in Greencastle in 1811. They had six children: Amelia (born c. 1800), John B. (born 1810), Abraham (born c.1818), Jeremiah (born c.1820, died 1900), Catherine, and Washington. Walter served with Capt. Andrew Robison's Company in 1814 during the War of 1812. In 1833, they went to Wayne County, Ohio near Doyleston; in 1841 to Medina County, Ohio and to Wells County, Indiana after Margaret died in 1852. Walter was a farmer, a mechanic, and a manufacturer of saddle-trees. A descendant still has one of the cash books he kept in his business.

Jeremiah married Catherine Porter in January 1846 in Ohio. They had eight children: Virgil (1846-1928); James Porter (c.1851- married Dora Sutton); Walter (1852-1912, married Rose Niriter); Lantz Alanson (c.1855 married Amelia Caston); Mary Agnes (Mace) (1859-1927, married Charles R. White; Martha (married Elmer Allen); Alice (c.1865-1887); Laura (1868-1935, married Lafayette Gorrell). Virgil was born in Ohio, Laura in Johnson County, Missouri, and the rest in Wells County.

The descendants of Mary Clark and Charles White are listed under the biography of Charles White.

Jeremiah's brother Abraham married Catherine Rasor in 1841 in Medina County, Ohio. They had four children, all but the last born in Ohio. Margaret (c. 1843-1885, married John Hume Ferguson); George (c.1845-1864); James M. (c.1848-1926, married Eliza Bauman/Baughman); Mary J. (c.1858-1882, married Lewis Caston.) Among present day descendants of Abraham are the families of Harold Mahensmith, Hazel Woodward, Bernice Osborn, Viola Fitch and Camilla Henry, all grandchildren of John and Margaret Clark Ferguson.

BARRY CLARK FAMILY

I grew up in Liberty Township west of Liberty Center near the Huntington County line, the son of Harry and Frances (Mendenhall) Clark, grandson of Lester and Myrtle Clark and William and Lena (Jacob) Mendenhall. I was born in 1944, and enjoyed being a farm boy and am still active in farming. I went to Liberty Center High School, and attended Purdue University. After graduation from high school I married the former Nancy Cheryl Grove, daughter of Bob and Mary Grove of Bluffton. Much to my own surprise I graduated from Purdue with a B.S. degree in agriculture.

Shortly after graduation from Purdue my wife, daughter and I moved into the John I. Clark homestead. This house was built in the early 1880's and down the years served many purposes, such as a home for families, temporary church, and grain storage. This home is where my grandfather grew up, I grew up, and our children are growing up and have grown up.

Down through time my grandfather, father, and I have raised assorted agricultural livestock and products. Seed production was started by Lester Clark in 1937 and is still in production today.

Since high school (early 1960's) many changes have occurred and agriculture is no exception. Fences no longer exist, and big machine technology is apparent. Fertilizer, seed, and pesticide technology have changed the landscape of the predominant blout and pewamo soils.

Nancy and I have five children: Diana (Clark) Neuenschwander, born in 1968, to graduate from Purdue 1991 in industrial systems analysis.

Susan (Clark) Carrol, born in 1970, a Southern Wells graduate. Now she is a knowledgeable dental assistant.

Kathryn Clark, born 1974, a junior at Southern Wells possibly contemplating law school.

Aaron Clark, born 1976, a freshman at Southern Wells, active in band, undecided, but whatever he decides will be achieved.

Brett Clark, born 1978, a fifth grader at Southern Wells, likes basketball and neat clothes. Brett at this point dreaming of agriculture.

Nancy Clark (mother of above children) is a junior at Indiana-Purdue Fort Wayne, working toward double majors in psychology, and nursing. She is bound to be able to fulfill her dream of helping people.

Life is full of challenges, opportunities, disappointment, success and failure. Proper perception of all situations is vital. Every person is responsible for his own actions and feelings. The answer is in the power of God. With him we are never alone. In God we do trust after all.

Thank you for taking the time to read this short article.

May God bless you all. *(Barry E. Clark)*

CLARK-BEAVANS

Aubry I. Clark, the daughter of Lester E. (Myrtle Shadle) Clark, was born in Liberty Township, Wells County, in 1909. Aubry attended a little one-room brick school house called "Roberts School." The teacher taught eight classes. Inside was a shelf for dinner pails, underneath a place to hang coats. The school was heated by two pot-belly coal stoves; one on each side of the room. In front of the school was a pump. Each morning a bucket of drinking water was brought in. Each pupil had his or her own drinking cup. Behind the school was an outside toilet.

At noon, the boys played baseball or a game called "Duck on Davey" — each player trying to knock the Duck off the nest with a rock.

We lived one-fourth mile north of the school. Sometimes we would wait for the teacher, Charley Frantz, to bank the fires so we could walk home with him. He lived beyond our house.

Lester and Aubrey Beavans and family

I went to the Roberts School for five grades. After that school year, I rode in a horse-drawn bus to Liberty Center High School. Seats were lengthwise of the bus on each side. Father purchased a gentle driving mare and a Storm King Buggy for us to drive to school. My brothers, Homer and Harry, went along. Later, Ethel was enrolled in school. Mother had many white Leghorn hens and often we would take a big market basket of large white eggs to the store on our way to school and pickup a few groceries to stock our kitchen.

I graduated from Liberty Center High School in 1927. I worked at Fort Wayne Knitting Mills, Dudlow and General Electric.

Lester A. Beavans from Warren, Indiana, worked at Caswell Reunion at Huntington, and Ball Brothers at Muncie. During World War II, he was a machinist at Wiley and Lett at Marion, assembling airplane parts. In 1974, we moved from Warren to a 160-acre farm which we now own. Besides farming, he drove the school bus sixteen years for Chester Center School.

Lester and Aubrey were married June 3, 1931 To this union six children were born:

1933—Huber was born. Married to Bernadine (Scott) Beavans of Fort Wayne. He served in the Navy two years. Two children: Michael and Debra. Deceased 1974.

1935 - daughter, Mrs. Thomas (Norma) Berry of Marion. Three children: Steven, Patty and Pamela.

1938 - Dee Moine (Jane Marsh) Beavans of

DeBary, Florida. Served in the Army two years. Three children: Donna, Brenda, and Chris.

1940 - Morris (Alice Sicks) Beavans. DeBary, Florida One daughter, Lisa.

1943 - daughter, Mrs. Harold (Nancy) Sills of Marion, Indiana. Two children: Camela and Brian.

1944 - David (Irma Blevins) Beavans of Poneto, Indiana. Two children: Eric and Ryan.

Lester departed this life in November, 1980, at the Lutheran Hospital. He is buried in the Woodlawn Cemetery, Warren, Indiana.

His wife, Aubry, still lives on their country farm in Chester Township. She is an active member, pianist, clerk, and board member of the South Liberty Christian Church. *(Aubry Beavans)*

RUFUS B. CLARK

Rufus B. Clark was born January 9, 1874 in Liberty Township, Wells County. He was the son of John Irwin and Nancy Ann (Helm) Clark and grandson of Sargent and Eunice (Irwin) Clark. He lived his entire life in Liberty Township. He had one brother, Lester E. Clark and two sisters, Viola Minniear and Garnet Smith. December 4, 1898, he married Zora Burman, of Salamonie Township, Huntington County. He cleared some land from a Hickory grove two and a half miles west of Liberty Center. Here he built a house, barn and other farm buildings, which became known as the "Hickory Grove Farm." They lived here until Mr. Clark retired from farming. They then moved to Liberty Center, a few years before both of their deaths, which occurred in 1943.

To this union five children were born: Faye, who married Frank Schmidt, Howard R., who married Florence Anguish, Mary, who married Ralph Boltin, Edith, who married Clare Prible, and Harmon, who married Estalene Davis.

Mr. Clark was a member of the Boehmer Methodist Protestant Church and the Liberty Center IOOF Lodge. He held many offices in both. He was a stock holder and director of both the Liberty Center Bank and the Liberty Center Telephone Company. Mr. Clark was also a good carpenter. Many of the barns that he helped build in the community can still be seen.

He loved raising livestock. Some were purebred: Rose Comb Brown Leghorn chickens, Scotch Collie dogs, Hereford cattle, O.I.c. and Chester White hogs. He never liked to feed his hogs unless he had time to stand and watch them eat. Often in February, he would have an auction in his barn, selling these pedigreed hogs. Catalogues had been printed describing each animal. Buyers and bidders came from far and near. Many came on the Marion and Bluffton Interurban Line that stopped in front of the house. Many of the hogs that were sold would be crated and shipped on the freight car of the interurban. In the summers, he would take animals to show at fairs and often won awards.

Many summers, homecomings were held in the hickory grove surrounding the farm-house. Logs, topped with wide, thick planks, were arranged in the entertainment area to provide seating, and a stage or platform was built from materials borrowed from the nearby Boehmer Church. Crowds of people would arrive in horse drawn buggies and early model cars. A basket dinner was held at noon on tables made by pushing together the planks used for seats. Area churches were invited to attend the morning worship service. A speaker was engaged for the afternoon programs, along with local talent of readings and special music.

Mr. Clark was a kind, gentle and thoughtful man. He loved to visit with people. He was always interested and active in the civic affairs of the community. He was always ready and willing to help if there was sickness or a death or any need in the area.

CLINE

Albert Bradbury Cline was born November 1, 1863, son of William Washington and Harriet Chaffee Cline of Hartford City. He attended Asbury College in Greencastle, before it was renamed DePauw University. His pioneer spirit drove him to expand his interests to Wells County.

A.B. married Mary Josephine Phillips in 1888. Her parents were the Reverend and Mrs. Ner H. Phillips. "Joe" was educated at DePauw and was an early member of Kappa Kappa Gamma. They had two sons: Ner William, July 30, 1896, and Lloyd Maxwell, July 4, 1898. Ner died in 1916 from a motorcycle accident. His untimely death prompted the family to establish a memorial at a Christian school in China. Both Ner and Lloyd were members of Beta Theta Pi at DePauw.

Lloyd and Lois Shirey Cline, a native of Loogootee, were married on May 13, 1920. She attended DePauw as a member of Kappa Kappa Gamma and he served in world War I as second lieutenant in the U.S. Army. Lloyd followed A.B. as trustee of DePauw for twenty years and was building committee chairman for three major projects: Student Union, library and a men's dorm. Locally he served on the building committee throughout the time the Methodist Church built a new sanctuary and parsonage in the mid 1950's. Lloyd was a member of Scottish Rite, Shrine, Elks Lodge, American Legion and Kiwanis. Lois was a member of Tri Kappa, the Library Board and Foltz Literary Club.

They had two children: Martha, March 30, 1921, and William Lloyd, April 4, 1925. Martha graduated from DePauw in 1943 where she served as president of Kappa Kappa Gamma. She married U. Gordon Colson May 13, 1943. William Attended Purdue, served in the U.S. Navy during World War II, then graduated from DePauw in 1948.

Martha and Gordon lived in Paris, Illinois, where she was art buyer for Colson Calendar Manufacturing Company. Also she served on a youth center board, Eastern Illinois Mental Health Association, private kindergarten, literary club and owned and managed a travel agency and gift shop. After she retired, Bluffton became the family residence. Two daughters were born: Anne Colson Meo, October 31, 1945, and Sue Colson Skinner, September 25, 1948, both in Bluffton. Anne has two children, Kristen, October 2, 1975, and Nicholas Rae, February 22, 1978. They all live in Libertyville, Illinois. Sue and Don Skinner have two children: Gordon Scott, August 23, 1971 and Sarah Elizabeth, June 19, 1977. They all live in Bluffton.

William married Ellen Fry on June 20, 1952. Their daughter, Sandy Cline, married Stanley Heyerly in 1966. They have three daughters: Stacy, September 16, 1968; Laura, July 6, 1970, and Jennifer, June 8, 1972. All reside in Wells County. William is president of Cline Lumber Company, served as president of Indiana Lumber and Builders Supply Association in 1981, a director of Old First National Bank, a director of Indiana Lumbermens Insurance Company of Indianapolis, a member of the Rotary Club, Elks Lodge and American Legion.

ROBERT A. CLINE FAMILY

The migration of the Robert A. and Betty L. Cline family actually began with Mrs. Olive Grimsley, along with daugher Betty, coming to Bluffton in 1932. Mrs. Grimsley was hired as music supervisor for the Bluffton Public Schools, a position she held until 1950, when she married a fellow teacher, Mr. William C. Ratliff. Olive Grimsley Ratliff was well-known for successfully promoting music in the schools and the community. Also, she was Minister of Music at Bluffton First United Methodist Church for many years. Mr. Ratliff (W.C.) taught chemistry and biology at P.A. Allen High School, and influenced many students to go into the field of science. He was a successful farmer, too, and later helped to establish the Caylor Nickel Research Laboratory.

Betty Lou Grimsley was born in Moores Hill, Indiana. After coming to Bluffton with her mother in 1932, graduated from P.A. Allen High School in 1939. Then she attended Indiana University, graduating with a Bachelor of Public School Music degree. Betty taught choral music in Washington, Indiana, then Columbus, Ohio, (where she was living with husband, Bob) and finally, the greater number of years here in Wells County (Liberty Center, Jackson, and Southern Wells Jr.-Sr. High School). Currently Betty is a certified Director of Music at Bluffton First United Methodist Church, a position she has held since 1969. Betty, like her mother, has influenced many students to keep alive their interest in music, and has been active in church and community programs involving the fine arts.

Robert (Bob) Cline was born in Garrettsville, Ohio, son of Anthony M. and Bessie Wadsworth Cline. he graduated from Bedford, Ohio, High School in 1932, and then attended Hiram College for one year. He moved to Columbus, Ohio, where he worked for the State Bureau of Unemployment Compensation. As a member of the national guard, he was called into service in Ohio's 37th Infantry Division during World War II, and also served in the Korea War. He has served ten years on active duty and forty-six years to the present, in National Guard and Army Reserve organizations. He holds the retired rank of lieutenant colonel. It is interesting to note that Bob met Betty on a train, just prior to overseas duty in the South Pacific. During the three years he was away, they corresponded often, and upon his return were married in 1945 at the Bluffton First United Methodist Church.

After the Korean War, Bob and Betty settled in Bluffton where Bob worked for 21 years as accountant at Franklin Electric. After retirement, Robert was Wells County Veterans service officer for three years. Bob's interests and contributions to this community have been many: treasurer of the Wells County Republican Party (being made a Sagamore of the Wabash in 1988, Masonry, First United Methodist Church, great interest in genealogy, and other community endeavors.

Born to Betty and Bob Cline are three children, here listed with their families:

Carol Cline Higgins, husband Tom L. Higgins, children Amy and Joy (Bluffton, Indiana).

Davis Robert Cline, wife Judy Ellenberger Cline, children, Joseph and Bethany (Dephaven, Minnesota).

Wiliam Wadsworth Cline, wife Jane Steinhauer Cline, step-daughter April (Bluffton, Indiana).

JAMES ETHAN CLOUD

James Ethan Cloud was born September 15, 1918, in Van Buren, Indiana to Ethan James and

Lucy Francis Cloud. Mother was born to Isaac and Elizabeth James.

Grandmother James was a Duckwall. Mother and grandmother were both born one mile north of Dillman. Grandmother lived to 96 years of age at this location.

Father was born to John and Marguereta (Welch) Cloud. They settled in the northeast corner of Grant County.

The Clouds came from the countries of Ireland and England and were previously named MacCloud. They landed in Boston in 1800, moved to Pennsylvania. There they married into the Dutch community, then moved to Ohio and on to Indiana.

I was the youngest child of four girls and four boys. Dad died when I was two months old. Mother maintained a home for Josie, Dollie and myself. Mother died when I was twenty years old.

I moved to Warren and married Lois Thompson in 1937. We had two children, Rex and Agatha.

James E. Cloud and Helen L. Cloud

In 1942 I owned and operated two dump trucks. I went to Tennessee, and helped build the Milan Arsenal Plant where I hauled the first load of gravel into Camp Campbell when they started building it. I was drafted into the Army in 1943. In January of 1943 I was sent to Galveston, Texas, for three months training. I then spent 31 months in the Pacific. I was at Baker Island, the Hawaiian Islands, the Philippines and also Okinawa. After my discharge, I came home to Huntington, Indiana.

In 1945 Lois and I were divorced. I married Martha Creiger in 1947. We had two children, Debra and Melody.

I worked for Northern Indiana Public Service Company. In 1953 I moved to Poneto and started farming, then moved west of Bluffton on the Rockford Pike, then east of Murray and two Jackson Township. I always had a truck. I worked for National Oil and Gas, also Mosier Oliver and Hoosier Grain. I hauled John Deere equipment out of Iowa and Nebraska to the east coast. I also hauled International and Chrysler parts from Springfield, Ohio, Fort Wayne, Indiana and Detroit, Michigan to Mexico.

We sold out of farming in 1971 and moved west of Bluffton. We also had a home in Laredo, Texas. Martha died in 1980.

I married Helen Norton Benavides of Laredo, Texas, and Pennsylvania. We moved to Bluffton in 1982, I sold my truck and retired.

I served as: vice-president of the Circle W. Saddle Club; one term on the Jackson Township Advisory Board; one term as vice-president of the Liberty Center Lions Club; vice-president for one term, and one term as treasurer of the Full Gospel Businessman's Fellowship International.

I presently belong to the Liberty Center Lions Club, the Bluffton American Legion and Full Gospel Businessmans Fellowship International. I accepted Christ and was born again in 1981. God has been good to me and watched over me all of my life.

THE COCHRANS

William J. Cochran, born May 10, 1720, Ireland, married in 1748 to Hannah Michael, born 1713 in Londenderry, Ireland. He died 1813 in Monongah, West Virginia. Their great-grandson, Ezra H. Cochran, born January 20, 1852, in West Virginia, came by covered wagon to Henry County, Indiana, in 1880.

A year later his wife, Elizabeth Mae Fleming Cochran, came by train with the two older children, Estella and Edgar D. Cochran. In 1887, the Cochrans came by covered wagon to a forty-acre farm one mile east and one-and-a-half miles north of Keystone, Chester Township, Wells County. They raised five children.

Estella married Chris Flaugh, Montpelier, in 1902. They lost a son. Son Francis Joseph, married Roxie Locke. Both are deceased but have two sons, Joe Jr., and Danny, living in Benton Harbor, Michigan. There are several grandchildren.

Edgar D. graduated from Keystone High School, then served three years in Spanish American War. He spent two years in the Philippine Islands. On his return he became rural mail carrier out of Keystone, where he served for 30 years. He and Catherine B. Black were married September 4, 1905, and resided in Keystone until Edgar's death in 1951 and Katie's in 1965. Catharine (Katie) was born in Buckland, Ohio, and her family moved to Keystone in 1903. Before moving to Ohio, her family came to Pennsylvania. All but Katie moved on to Kansas and Oklahoma with the oil fields in the early 1900's. Edgar was trustee of Chester Township from 1953 until 1960.

Mary Cochran Burnett and Emma Cochran Russell lived in Chicago for many years. Emma has one son, Gene, living in Boonesville, Missouri. He and Mary Ann have a son, Ricky, living in Evansville, Indiana. Esta Cochran Speece taught the first and second grades at Chester Center for several years.

Edgar and Katie's first son, Melvin Russell, passed away at 16 months. Mary Elizabeth was born April 1, 1908. She married Vernon Cobbum, Bluffton, May 12, 1926. They had three sons. Don Alan, the second son, passed away at three months. In 1938 the Cobbums moved to Noble County, Indiana, where they have lived for fifty years. Their son, Brooks, married Ellen Moser and lives at Longwood, Florida. Their daughter, Karen, passed away leaving two daughters, Dawn Schuman, Indiana University and Kim Schuman, Longwood, Florida. Brooks and Ellen's son, Curtis, also lives in Longwood. Their son, Norman and wife, Margie, live in England. They have three children; Graham, Faith, and Alison.

Edgar D. an Katie Cochran

The second daughter, Eula B. who was born July 9, 1912, married Urshell Ellison December 30,1961. Urshell died February 29, 1988. Eula resides at Bridgman Estates, Bridgman, Michigan. Naomi Belle was born September 15, 1915, and died nine days later.

Edgar B. was born April 24, 1917. He attended Ball State and Indiana University, and taught in Southern Indiana and Merrillville, Indiana, for several years. He now resides in Crown Point, Indiana. He married Mary Jean Tyler February 22, 1941. She died in July, 1963. They had two children, Pamela Kay, born March 16, 1943, and Kent Alan, born September 20, 1952. Pam married Phil Baker in 1962 and they have two daughters, Dana and Dawn. The Bakers live in Morganton, North Carolina. Kent married Jayne Symmes in 1977 and lives in Crown Point, Indiana.

Ernest H. was born June 6, 1922. He resides in Crossville, Tennessee. He retired from Ryder Trucking Company. He married Vera Mae Minnich December, 1940. Vera Mae died April 15, 1984.

Sharon Diane was born March 31, 1942, and Gloria Sue on March 26, 1944. Sharon married Jack Clark August 14, 1960. Their daughter, Kelli, is married to Jim Warren and lives in Wameka, Wisconsin. Traci married Dan Hale, and lives in Pikeville, Tennessee. Mike and Jennifer have two children, Josh and Stephanie. They live in Crossville, Tennessee, as do Matt, Michelle and Nicholas.

Sue lives at Holmes Beach, Florida. She lost a son, Scott Smeckens, July 15, 1990. She was married to Len Olund May 13, 1988.

COCHRAN-ROSE

We can trace our great-great-great-grandfather, John Rose, to Virginia in 1760. His son, Anthony (1792) married Mary Woodring in 1820. Their son, John Rose (1830) married Rachel Teegarden (1832). One of their five children was my grandmother, Lucy J. (Rose) Cochran. I enjoyed staying on her farm in Nottingham Township, Wells County, and listening to great stories about her maternal side, the Teegardens, and her paternal side, the Roses. Her brothers and sisters were Nelson, Alice (Rose) Risser, Ellen (Rose) Haines, and William Rose. I remember them all from the beloved Rose reunions.

My grandmother Lucy married Benton C. Cochran and they raised a family on the farm. Grandmother sold eggs and butter when we went "to town" in Bluffton on Saturday nights.

Bee and Roger Stauffer and sons Jay, Jan, and Jerry-1948

Grandmother Lucy's mother was Rachel Teegarden, whose ancestors have been traced back eleven generations to Christian Teegarden (1650-1702). He married Maria Tilman (1648-1714). Rachel was the daughter of Daniel Teegarden (1793-1873), granddaughter of Aaron T. (1754-1823) and great-granddaughter of Abraham (1689-1753), who was the son of Christian. The Teegardens were land owners and made swords in Solingen, Germany. I especially treasure an antique set of inlaid knives made in Solingen and my grandmother Rachel's black cloak.

Abraham was baptized on May 19, 1689, in the Reformed Church at Solingen, Germany. On September 1, 1736, he and his family arrived in Philadelphia on the ship "Harle." He died in 1753 near Hargerstown, Washington County, Maryland.

Bee Cochran came to Wells County when she was in seventh grade and lived in Nottingham Township until her graduation from Petroleum High School in 1933. She graduated from Ball State Teachers College, white cap and gown, in 1935, and taught at Chester Center School. In 1938, Bee married Roger J. Stauffer, an educator. They moved to Ohio, where Bee remained at home raising her family until 1962. Then she earned a B.S. degree from Ohio Northern University, followed by a master's degree in Education from Wright State University in 1972.

Bee (Cochran) Stauffer is an active member of Delta Kappa Gamma International Honorary Society, University Women's Club, Alpha Delta Omega Sorority, Mercer County Chapter of Ohio Genealogical Society, Mercer County Retired Teachers, Ohio Retired Teachers and National Retired Teachers' Associations. She is on the board for Mercer County Family Crisis of Ohio and does volunteer work for Scholarships in Education. Bee has participated in "Faith by Phone" for the United Methodist Church and has taught Sunday School.

Bee Cochran Stauffer and her husband, R.J. Stauffer are retired and living in Celina, Ohio. Their three sons are: R. Jay Stauffer, M.A., Superintendent of Schools, New Bremen, Ohio; Dr. Ronald J. Stauffer, principal of schools, Murfreessboro, Tennessee; and Robert J. Stauffer, M.A., athletic director in Kenton, Ohio. All are married.

Bee and Roger have three grandchildren: Ronald Jay, aeronautical engineer, Ohio State University, captain in the U.S. Air Force; Lt. Robert Jeffrey, an Air Force engineer at Wright Patterson; and Jaqueline Stauffer, a sophomore at Miami University majoring in computer science, also in the U.S. Air Force.

Bee's hobbies include antiques, "Flo Blue" dishes, genealogy, photography, oil painting, hooking rugs, traveling, and collecting autobiographies and Elsie Dinsmore books of the 1800's.

In 1983, Bee, her brothers, sister, and first cousins revived the "Cochran - Rose" reunion on Indiana.

COFFIELD

The Coffield history has been recorded since 1788, at the birth of James Coffield, a native of Ireland. He and wife, Jane (Craig) lived in Guernsey County, Ohio, where he served with the First Ohio Regiment in the War of 1812. In 1837, they and their son, Thomas, moved to Huntington County, Indiana. Jane, due to illness several years prior to her death, hired girls to help her in the home. One of these was Delilah, the daughter of David and Nellie (Roberts) Crawford. Thomas and Delilah later married and had a son. (David) Harrison Coffield, in 1861.

Harrison married Anna Carnes in 1887. Ann was the eldest daughter of John II and Caroline (Burgess) Carnes, who had relocated here from Guernsey County, Ohio. Anna's grandparents, John I and Anna Bell Carnes, migrated from County Cork and County Down, Ireland, in 1826, with John I's two brothers and her sister. John and I bought some land (now part of Salt Fork State Park) in Guernsey County, Ohio, where they lived and are buried.

Lona Mitchell - in wedding dress - 1927 Anna Coffield, Harrison Coffield, Nova Coffield (Lona Mitchell marriage to Gerald Mitchell July 2, 1927)

Harrison and Anna Coffield's first child was Nettie, born in 1888. Nettie later married (Alvin) Bert Custard and had two children: Glen Burr, in 1905, and Vernis Adelaid Custard, in 1911. Bert died in 1964 and Nettie died in 1979.

Harrison's and Anna's second child, Charlie, was born in 1892. He died in April of 1893, the last son in the Coffield lineage.

The third child, Lona, was born in 1897. Lona taught in one-room schools in Wells County for seven years prior to her marriage to Gerald Mitchell in 1927. They moved to Anderson in 1928, where Gerald worked at Delco until his retirement. He passed away in 1969, and Lona remained in Anderson until her death in 1975.

The fourth Coffield child is Nova, born in 1905. Harrison and Anna raised these children on their farm (west of McNatt), where Harrison was successful at farming threshing, and sawmill operation. Nova attended the Ebersol one-room school and finished at Warren High. Her childhood memories include a Christian home and activities centered at the Union Chapel. She married Carlin Schoeff in 1933 and raised two sons: Kyle Carlin, born in 1936, and David Coffield Schoeff, born in 1940.

Kyle married Lois Elaine Laymon, of Warren, and they had Nancy Elaine in 1958 and Thomas Kyle Schoeff in 1961. Nancy married Greg Clem of Fairmount. They live in nearby Jonesboro with their toddler, Courtney Elaine. Thomas married Denise Hotmire of Upland. They reside in Indianapolis with infant daughter Kara Denise.

David Schoeff married (Margaret) Anne Hartnett of Bluffton and had two children: Cynthia Jo, born in 1960, and Matthew David Schoeff, in 1967. Cynthia lives in Greenfield, Indiana, while Matthew resides in Greenville, Ohio, near Anne. David was killed in a work-accident eight days after his father, Carlin's death (a stroke victim) in June, 1977.

Nova resides in Wells County. She enjoys teaching and attending Sunday school and spending time with family, friends, and related social activities.

ISAAC CONFER FAMILY

Isaac Confer, son of Samuel and Susannah McClellan Confer, was born in Wells County on December 31, 1873. On February 24, 1894, he married Anna S. Bushee, born May 26, 1873, the daughter of Allen and Jane Woods Bushee. The Confers moved to a farm near Walkerville, Michigan, where they lived until 1916. While living in Michigan they became the parents of eight children: Zennie Alepheus (January 31, 1895), Curtis (September 18, 1898), James DeWayne (Dee) (May 25, 1900), Mary Ilo (November 25, 1903), Iva Elizabeth (October 24, 1905 to May 12, 1906), Samuel Eldon (April 13, 1909 to January 11, 1910), Hazel Ndora (April 27, 1912), and Erma Ivan (April 3, 1914 to March 20, 1915).

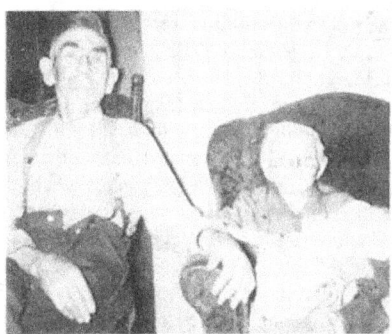

Issac and Anne Bushee Confer

In 1916 following the death of Anna's father, the family moved back to Wells County to a farm inherited from Anna's father. The farm was located one mile south of the Wells County -Allen County Line Road and three-fourths of a mile west of state highway 1. Isaac farmed and was an enthusiastic outdoorsman who loved to hunt and fish. Along with telling "tall but true" tales, he liked to cut out newspaper articles for sources of debate and was a "die-hard" Republican. Anna was a quiet "homebody," but still had a mind of her own. She worked hard gardening and caring for her family. It was not an easy life with three of her children dying in infancy and their daughter Hazel becoming developmentally handicapped after having the measles with a sustained high fever. Even though she remained childlike herself until her death (May 29, 1983), she loved attention and being around children. Zennie changed his name to John Z. Confer and married Hazel Lucille Rogers (February 4, 1899), daughter of Harry and Effie Ollie Tuttle Rogers, on September 23, 1919. They had six children as follows: Donald Edwin (March 30, 1922), Mary Ellen (July 8, 1920), Richard Dale (August 2, 1926), Dorothy Margaret (May 22, 1928), Betty Mae (April 5, 1930), and Daniel Eugene (March 29, 1934). Curtis married Margaret Kehrn (August 4, 1905) on May 22, 1930; they had no children. James DeWayne (Dee) married Dorcus Redding (November 11, 1905) and they had two daughters, Joan and Norma. Mary married Ross Wickliffe and had four children: Marjorie, Wayne, Mildred and Richard. After Isaac retired, he returned to his farm in Michigan each spring to hunt and can deer meat to bring back to his family for winter meat. Anna, "Little Grandma," died February 26, 1958, at the age of 85. Grandpa Ike passed away on December 21, 1963, at the age of 90.

JOHN Z. CONFER

At the age of fourteen Zennie Alpheus Confer (born January 31, 1895), the son of Isaac and Anna Bushee Confer, went to Detroit to seek work. he later changed his name to John Z. Confer and joined the Army during World War I, in which he was sent with forces to the shores of France. After returning to Detroit he met his wife-to-be, Hazel Lucille Rogers (born February 4, 1899) the daughter of Harry and Effie Ollie Tuttle Rogers, after dating her sister, Louisa. Hazel and John were married September 23, 1919, and moved to the Wells side of the Wells County-Allen County Line, just west of state highway 1. Their first home was about two miles west of highway 1 on the County Line Road; then they moved to a home just east of the railroad track on that same road. Their first son, Donald Edwin, was born at this home on March 30, 1922. They then moved about a a half mile west into the home of Samuel and Susannah McClellan Confer, Johns' grandparents, where the following children were born: Mary Ellen (July 8, 1924), Richard Dale (August 2, 1926), Dorothy Margaret (May 22, 1928), Betty Mae (April 5, 1930), and Daniel Eugene (March 29, 1934.

Most everyone who knew John called him Jack. jack was very sensitive; he loved to read and enjoyed good music. He farmed the eighty acres where they lived, worked at General Electric, and played violin in the GE orchestra in Fort Wayne. He worked very hard, and even though he frequently suffered from mastoid problems and "shell shock" as a result of his war experiences, he refused the available Army pension and aid offered to him, feeling the need to work things out on his own. He and Hazel were always willing to help anyone in need.

John Z. and Hazel Rogers Confer

Hazel was a busy homemaker, caring for her family and gardening and preserving food. They never left home much except to carry out necessary errands. For years Aunt Margaret, Mrs. Curtis Confer, took the children to Sunday school. Jack didn't feel the need for church and said, "You don't have to go to church to love the Lord." Donald married Phyllis Marie Schnurr (born July 8, 1923) on August 20, 1946, and they had eight children: Donna, Margaret, John, Raymond, Kenny, Norman, Mary, and Ted. Mary married Melvin Martin Hirschy (born October 19, 1920) on December 24, 1941, and they had nine children: Linda, Edward, Judith, Bonnie, Gary, Kathleen, Dean, Randy, and Lori. Richard "Dale" married Patsy Ann Scott (born August 4, 1932) on December 16, 1950 and they had five children: Beverly, Shari, Barb, Patrick, and Curtis. Dorothy married Marvin Eugene Wicks (born May 3, 1922) on October 19, 1951, and they had a son, Michael Daniel. Betty married Robert Kling (born October 12, 1927) on November 7, 1953, and they had four children, Larry, Pamela, Robin and Scott. On March 23, 1948, Jack died of a self-inflicted gun-shot wound. Hazel continued to live on the farm until her death on September 7, 1975.

DOUG AND JILL CONLEY

Brain Douglas Conley was born February 22, 1957, to George and Marcia Phyllis (Johnson) Conley. Jill Diane (Croy) Conley was born June 9, 1957, to Donald Lee and Phyllis Ann (Courtney) Croy. Both Doug and Jill attended the Bluffton School System, Doug living in Bluffton and Jill in Vera Cruz. They both graduated from Bluffton High School in 1975. Jill continued her education at Ball State University where she received a degree in Early Child Education, while Doug continued to work at Paul Ludwig's grocery in Bluffton as he had throughout high school.

Doug and Jill Conley

Doug and Jill were married in August of 1977, and their first home was in Bluffton. Jill's first teaching experience was at Head Start as teacher's aide. She continued to teach for a few years at the Bluffton Parent Cooperative while Doug worked for Moorman Manufacturing. They then moved to Vera Cruz where they continue to live, and Jill worked for her father at Croy Machine Shop for the next ten years. During these years Doug worked for the Keebler Company and Fretter Appliance, both in sales. Doug then got into the food broker business with H.J. Bodey, Inc. and then sales force of Fort Wayne which is his current employer. Jill's interest in art has reappeared during the last few years as she took oil painting classes and was involved with the Adams-Wells Art Association.

Doug and Jill are now focusing their attention on their son, Christopher Jay Conley, who was born August 23, 1990 at the Wells Community Hospital.

COOK

(The following history was written by Mary Williamson, daughter of Paul Cook's friend and partner Edward Bruce Williamson.)

Paul Howard Cook (January 27, 1891- November 7, 1963) was born near Poneto in Wells County, Indiana, to John and Elizabeth Howard Cook. He was the oldest of three children. A brother, Wayne, and a sister, Sylvia, preceded him in death. Paul's father was president of the Poneto Bank and owned a tile mill near their home. His mother had been a teacher before her marriage.

Both his father and mother stimulated his interest in plants. About 1910, after reading some books by L.H. Bailey, he began his first plant breeding with small fruits, then sweet peas and later a few iris.

World War I interrupted his iris breeding but did not lessen his interest in it. After his return from France, Emma Carnes, Paul's future wife, introduced Paul and E.B. Williamson. This was the beginning of a very stimulating friendship for both men.

On May 29, 1920, Paul Cook and Emma Carnes were married in Bluffton. Emma was a constant companion, helper, and partner in all of Paul's iris work. Emma (1895-November 8, 1982) was a warm, friendly, gentle woman who worked beside her husband. She had the same love for iris as he did. Together Emma and Paul introduced about 70 iris and several hemerocallis. In the mornings, Emma did the hybridizing according to the plans Paul had worked out, many of them thought out during the preceding winter. During the flowering season, Emma graciously entertained and offered refreshments to the many visitors that called at their gardens. After Paul's death, Emma continued to make her own crosses. Her first introduction was Compliment. Emma was an active member of the First Baptist Church, the Bluffton Garden Club, and the Northeaster Iris Association.

About the time for their marriage, Paul became a rural mail carrier, first out of Bluffton, then Uniondale. It was a most convenient occupation, giving Paul the full afternoon in his garden.

He was a charter member of the American Iris Society and a member of that society's Scientific Committee.

Paul Cook's method of iris breeding was purely scientific. In the winter, he studied the genetics of iris breeding, laid his plans for the next season's crosses, and figured, mathematically, the results of the crosses. When his seedlings blossomed, he would compare, mathematically, the flowering results with those he had made two years previously on paper. The results against the paper count were amazingly accurate. A scientist from Cornell University said, "Paul is one of the best geneticists in the country."

Paul felt his best field to be in hybridizing and, in the last few years of his life, he considered his greatest contribution might be in inspiring and stimulating the new and young hybridizers of iris. His simplest statements concerning iris were always given after careful judgment.

Paul was an iris grower, par excellence, and creator of the Dykes Medal winners, Sable Night, Whole Cloth and Allegiance. His iris breeding included not only all the different types (dwarf, median, and tall species) but also hemerocallis, daffodils, tree peonies, gladiolias, and true lilies. His last iris introduction was Ecstatic Night in 1963. His first iris introduced in 1937 was named E.B. Williamson. This iris took the Roman Gold Medal in 1938. Paul worked patiently and methodically for seventeen years before choosing one of his seedlings for introduction. Those that followed were winners. Paul was not only a member of the American Iris Society but the British Iris Society, The New Zealand Iris Society, The Dwarf Iris Society, the Median Iris Society, the Aril Iris Society, and the Northeastern Indiana Iris Society.

Mr. Cook also received the "Distinguished Service to the Citizens of Wells County" by the men of Wells County, March 16, 1960.

COOK

Great-grandfather John Cook came to Rockcreek Township in 1864. He was born in Greenbrier County, West Virginia, in 1833. He was a grandson of Zachariah and Martha (Andrick) Cook. Their children were John, Elizabeth, Mary, Nancy, Margaret, Susana, and Sara. Zachariah 1751-1846 was a Revolutionary War veteran and participated in many battles from 1781-1783.

Although lost records hinder us from definite proof it is believed that my great-grandfather was son of John and Nancy (Martin) Cook. The family moved to Pike County, Ohio, around 1833 where Zachariah died in 1846, as did his wife.

During the Civil War when the Confederates were raiding for men for the Southern Army, great-grandfather "disappeared" so he would not have to fight against a relative in the Union Army. We can find no record of his wife. When he came to Wells County, he brought with him three young sons, William Henry, 1859, Zachariah, 1860, and John, 1862. In 1865, he married Isabelle (Johnson) Saylor, 1841, daughter of Solomon and Sarah (Sanders) Johnson. They had two children, Josephine and Jonas. They lived on a farm east of Rockford. John died November, 1902, and was buried at Barber Mills Cemetery near Rockford.

Back (L to R) Paul Pugh, Frank Van Camp, Tom Pugh, Jim West ; Middle (L-R) Marilyn Pugh, Judy VanCamp, Kathy Pugh; Front (L-R) Charles and Esta Pugh

Zachariah, my grandfather, 1860-1953, married Mary Ellen Sills, 1865-1943, daughter of William 1839-1915 and Nancy Jane (Fuller) Sills, 1842-1880. Nancy Fuller's family can be traced through Chief James Godfroy to Rowan, France during the Crusades. Grandpa was a charter member of the Seventh Adventist Church at Rockford. Grandma joined soon after. Their children were: Arthur 1882-1904, John William 1884-1915, Clarence Courtney (1890-1971), Pearl Opal 1894-1980, Carl 1898-1942, Raymond Francis 1905-1979. Clarence was my father and told many stories of his early life. He and a cousin "Peck" went skinnydipping and crawdadding in Rockcreek near his home. He and another cousin saw "Granny" Johnson killing chickens at a chopping block so they decided to try it. She caught them just as "Biscuit" had the ax up ready to behead Dad. In 1900 they moved to Montpelier. Grandpa worked at Jackson Shovel Company as did my father who later was manager of Cook Ice and Coal Company.

In 1912 Clarence Cook married Martha Celesta Cook 1894-1964, daughter of William Douglas David Cook 1858-1924 and Celeste (Johnson) Cook 1854-1894. Their children were: Nora Ruanna 1913, married Alvin Walker, Arlie Price and Maurice Barrington; Mary Esta 1914; Thelma Marie 1916-1949, married Roger Myers; Russell 1918-1918; James Edward 1920 killed on Luzon 1945; William L. 1921-1921; David Arthur 1925-1976; Jack 1926-1980.

Mary Esta married Charles Edward Pugh 1911 in 1933. Their children: Paul Edward 1934 m-1955 Marilyn Ann Lloyd 1936; Thomas Dean 1937 m-1959 Kathleen Chick 1940; Mary Ellen 1938-1989 m-1957 James D. Wert 1936; Judith Ilene 1940 m-1958 Glen F. VanCamp 1936.

Charles and Esta Pugh are blessed with eleven grandchildren and eight great-grandchildren.

JOHN W. COOK

John W. Cook was born in Greenbrier County, West Virginia May 21, 1833. In his early childhood days he left his native state and came with his parents to Jackson County, Ohio. He married and had three children: John Jr., William, and Zachariah. John came to Wells County in 1864 after his wife died. There he met and married Isabella Jane Johnson Saylor, daughter of Solomon Johnson, November 1, 1865. Isabella was born June 25, 1841, in Wells County, the twelfth child of Solomon and Sarah Sanders Johnson. She had married Levi S. Saylor December 1, 1859. It is now known what happened to Levi.

Golden Wedding 1881-1931
Zachariah and Mary Ellen Cook, Raymond Cook, Pearl Stonerock, Clarence Cook, Carl Cook

Sarah Josephine was born to john and Isabella about 1867. She married Solomon F. Johnson June 26, 1886. Jonas Deliscus Courtney was born to John and Isabella in 1869. He married Jessie M. Braden.

John and Isabella joined the Christian Church at Bly in 1878. When a Seventh-Day Adventist Church was organized in Rockford in 1887, John and Isabella joined that church. Isabella owned land north of Rockford along the creek, which was given to her by her father, Solomon Johnson. The Seventh Day Adventist Church was built on a corner of this land and was later deeded to the Indiana Conference of Seventh-Day Adventists.

John died November 29, 1902. Isabella continued to live in her home at Rockford until her death. Her grandson remembers her sitting in the doorway of her home smoking a clay pipe when he was a child. Later he found one of her pipes near the site.

CORLE FAMILY

LaRelle "Charlie" Corle was born in Portland, Indiana, on May 7, 1933, to LaDrew and Lucille (Hardy) Corle. I was born Joy A. James, in Union City, Indiana, the second daughter of Harry W. and Thelma P. (Fields) James.

My family, which included my sisters Judy and Jackie, moved to Portland when we were quite small. Being neighbors to the Corle family, it was no surprise to our families when LaRelle and I married on August 18, 1955.

My father moved to Bluffton in 1957 to manage Thoma Furniture; mother was employed at the Stillman Store in Ft. Wayne. Father, needing someone to lay floor covering, hired LaRelle, and in 1959 we made the move to Bluffton.

Our first child, Curtis Wayde, was born July 28, 1958, in Decatur, Indiana, and Cassandra Lynn was born September 4, 1959, also in Decatur. By the time Cassandra was a year old, I had gone to work at Franklin Electric, to help pay for our new home that was now under construction at the corner of Horton and Morgan Street. Our home was completed in the spring of 1960.

Our third child, Christopher John, was born December 29, 1963. We almost had a New Year's baby! Carla Jo followed just 21 months later on September 27, 1965. Our family was not complete.

The Corle Family

We lived in our new home on Horton Street for nine years and then moved to 500 South 600 East in Harrison Township. Our love for the country could not be contained anymore. By the time we moved in August, we had already purchased eight bred gilts, a horse and five calves. We were also farming several acres in and around the Bluffton area.

The year 1974 was not a good year for our little family. LaRelle had come home from work on Monday feeling quite ill from what we thought was his ulcer. He died the same days in Wells Community Hospital, on November 10. We later learned he had had an aneurysm of the main artery. Our family was devastated!

My parents and sisters had left this area a few years prior to our move to the country. Mom, Dad, and my sis Jackie, moved to California and Judy to New Jersey.

Dad and Mom later retired to Parker, Arizona, where my father died in 1987. Judy now resides in Bakersfield, California, and Jackie in Palm Desert, California.

My children are scattered throughout the world; Curtis, his wife RaeJean (Decker), and their six daughters, reside south of Markle, Indiana. Cassi, her husband Mike Hill, and their daughter Sara, reside two miles from Curtis. Christopher is serving in the U.S. Army, stationed in SHAPE, Belgium. Carla is serving in the U.S. Navy, stationed in San Diego, California.

I married Douglas B. Patterson, son of Pat and Jane (Bulger) Patterson, and we just recently moved to our home on State Road #116 in Wells County. Doug is employed at Hower Tool in Ossian, and I am employed with the City of Bluffton. *(Joy A.(Corle) Patterson)*

COTTON-HOOVER

Joshua T. Cotton (born 1784), William W. Cotton (1811), Lewis C. Cotton (1847), Ernest S. Cotton (1869), and Forst G. Cotton and their spouses are all interred in Prospect Cemetery north of Uniondale.

Forst G. Cotton was born May 26, 1894 to Ernest S. and Fanny EuDora (Goshorn) Cotton. He had one sister, Sadonna (Cotton) Beck, who resides in Fort Wayne. They were raised on a farm in Union Township, which had been homesteaded by one of their grandfathers and the original land title was a grant from the Federal government.

Forst, in a Christmas Eve ceremony, married Cleona Hoover who was the daughter of William and Penelope J. (Norton) Hoover. Although farming was his first love as an occupation, the press of financial needs caused Forst to go to "the city" for work.

The General Electric in Fort Wayne gave him training in machining and toolmaking and that became his life's work. The Depression caused a lay off period during which he and a good neighbor butchered hogs then sold meat from door to door in order to support their families.

By this time three children had been to Forst and Cleona; Betty Eloyce (1919), EuDora Jane (1922) and Lyle J. (1928).

In 1933 Forst was hired by the International Harvestor at Fort Wayne, and he was a machinist in the transmission department for 28 years.

Forst was known for his singing ability and his son, Lyle, can remember going to various revival meetings and to CCC camps where Forst would be the song leader to provide solo music.

Cleona was a full-time homemaker but she always did more than just take care of her own family. As was the custom then, she took care of her mother and her father as their health failed in their declining years. Although this made life more confined for the young members of the family, there were memories formed and lessons learned that could not have been experienced in any other way.

Forst and Cleona were an integral part of the church community at Prospect Episcopal (now United) Methodist Church all of their married life until, in later years, they moved to Uniondale and joined the Methodist Church there.

Daughter Betty married Doyt E. Inman, daughter EuDora married Harold E. Yager and son Lyle married Gladys R. McAfee.

Refer to: Inman-Cotton, Yager-Cotton and Cotton-McAfee

COTTON-MCAFEE

Lyle J. Cotton was born April 3, 1928, to Forst G. and Cleona Hoover Cotton in Fort Wayne, Indiana. Sisters Betty E. (Inman) and EuDora Jane (Yager) greeted him with the parents. The Depression of 1929, and the resulting loss of employment at the General Electric Plant, caused Forst to move his family back near the home farm in Wells County in 1930.

All twelve years of Lyle's formal education were received in grade school, junior high school and high school at Ossian. His religious training was received at home and at church then known as Prospect Methodist Episcopal Church. Good people among his classmates and teachers helped formulate his life.

Front L. to R. Gladys & Lyle Cotton. Back L. to R. David Cotton, Claudia (Cotton) Gipson, Steve Cotton.

During his senior year he met Gladys R. McAfee and some of the questions about the future seemed to be answered. After graduation from Ossian High School in 1946, Lyle enlisted in the U.S. Marine Corps, but Gladys said that she would be waiting. They were married July 27, 1947.

Lyle had displayed some talent for singing so, as a birthday present Gladys paid for voice lessons for Lyle form Florence Starr in Bluffton. Therefore, he was invited to sing at many weddings and for entertainment throughout the area. He also freely used his voice for the worship of God.

Lyle was a representative for the sale of New York Life Insurance from 1954 to retirement. He served as judge of Bluffton City Court from 1964 through 1971 and 1988 through 1991. He received the honorary 33rd Degree from Scottish Rite Masonry in 1989.

Gladys R.McAfee was born June 13, 1928, the eighth child of nine born to John McAfee, Jr. and Hazel A. (McCleery) McAfee and was raised on a farm two miles west of the Rockcreek School.

Gladys' formal education was received at Rockcreek School where she attended all 12 years. She was a very active participant in all activities of school and was cheerleader for three years. After high school she attended Wayne University of Cosmetology and has continually been engaged in that profession. In 1973, she was president of the Fort Wayne Cosmetologists Association, the organization of the profession.

Twelve years she worked with youth in the International Order of Rainbow for Girls. She was instrumental in organizing the first group of "Candy Striper Girls." These young ladies worked in hospitals giving cheer to patients. Many continued to further studies and made nursing a career.

The First United Methodist Church has been the family's church home and Gladys has taught youth and adults as well as being active with United Methodist Women. Lyle has served many ways, singing in the choir for 40 years being his first love.

Three children came to the family. Claudia Ann (Cotton) Gipson was born July 21, 1948. She is married to Richard L. Gipson and has three children Jason Tait, Oliver Bryce and Alysa Shay Gipson. They lived in Dillsboro, Indiana. David McAfee Cotton was born August 5, 1949, is married to Kathleen (Stotts) Cotton, and they have two sons, Ian David and Dylan Stotts Cotton and they live in Lynnwood, Washington. Steven Forst Cotton was born October 1, 1950, was married to Judy Ann (Croy) Cotton who died suddenly in 1986. They had three sons, Matthew Shane, Joshua Forst and Daniel Croy Cotton. In 1988, he married Mal-Sook (Baek) Cotton whom he had met while working in Korea. They live near Vera Cruz, Indiana.

Refer to: Cotton-Hoover, Forst G. Cotton Family, John McAfee, Jr. Family

SAMUEL G. COTTON AND GEORGE W. COTTON

Samuel G. Cotton was born October 1819 Holmes County, Ohio, was son of James and Rachel Cotton of Pennsylvania. Samuel married Diannah McKinnon Fleming and they moved to Rockcreek Township, Wells County, Indiana, about 1844. He was considered to be a prominent and prosperous farmer in Wells County. Their children were: Cyrus S. (1840) married 1) Margaret Torrens, Phoebe Hart; James A. (1842) married Mary R. Johnson; Aaron Fleming (1844) married Harriet Henley; Mary A. "Molly" (1847) married John C. Marshall; Wiliam Franklin (1849) married Margaret; George W. (1851) married Josephine Lovely McDannel/McDaniel.

George Washington Cotton was born August 1, 1851, in Bluffton, Wells County, Indiana. He died in September 1925, and is buried in Fairview

Grandma and Grandpa Hamar 1945 (Bessie Cotton McKinney)

Cemetery. In April, 1875, he was married to Josephine Lovely McDannel, daughter of Elias and Sarah Rupp McDannel. Their children were: Bessie Pearl Cotton (1876) married Hamer McKinney; Marshal S. (1878) married Opal; Ralph Carlton "Carl" (1880) married Cecil Stuart; Franklin Fisk (1881) married Oral Bond, Grace Daugherty; Hazel B. (1885) married Mort Tiger; Ruby Dean Cotton (1888) married LeRoy Chester Wolfe; Waldo (1891-1891); George (1892-1896).

Josephine McDannel Cotton 1853-1920

George was a farmer and later engaged in buying and selling livestock. He was a hard working, truthful, and honest man and was moral in every respect. He and his wife were members of the Baptist church and were zealous in all charitable and Christian work. George was warm-hearted, merry, and jovial. In his earlier days he was known as "Cyclone Cotton." This name was given him as the result of his espousal of Prohibitions which was accompanied by such extreme measures as that of smashing saloon products. Josephine loved to wear hats, she always had one on in pictures.

STEVEN F. COTTON FAMILY

On October 1, 1950, Steven Forst Cotton was born to Lyle and Gladys Cotton. Growing up in Bluffton, he attended Park School (K through four), Central School (five through eight), and Bluffton High School, graduating in 1968.

At the beginning of his freshman year, when all of the eighth grades from the various schools of the township came to the high school, he met a pretty blonde young lady, Judy Ann Croy (born January 8, 1950). Judy, the daughter of Clarence and Geneva Croy, lived near Vera Cruz. Steven always felt that she was the girl for him, but romance didn't thrive until their senior year. Their relationship continued to grow, and after a year of his attending college, they were married in August of 1969.

He attended Purdue University-Fort Wayne studying Industrial Management. After marriage, he continued this studies while working for Mix-Mill Corporation in Bluffton. He accepted an opportunity to work for General Electric in Fort Wayne, but with an economic slow-down, he had to seek other employment. He found this at the American Hoist Company which manufactures earth moving machinery.

Matthew Shane Cotton was born September 30, 1972, and they became a family.

In 1976, Steven accepted a job with Bucyrus Erie, manufacturers of very large earth moving and mining equipment, in Pocatello, Idaho. While there, another son, Joshua Forst Cotton, was born March 4, 1978.

After three years in the West, Steven and Judy brought their family back to Indiana when he started employment with General Electric, at Decatur. On June 4, 1979, Daniel Croy Cotton was born in Bluffton. Now there were three boys to carry on the Cotton name!

While in Idaho, the family had attended a Methodist Church where Steven sang in the choir. Upon returning to Indiana, they resumed their membership at the First United Methodist Church in Bluffton. Steven joined the choir, and Judy became very busy in the church. She came to choir with Steven, took an active part with the hand bell choir, was president of the United Methodist Women, and taught Sunday School.

1980 found Steven working for the Sheller-Globe Corp., manufacturers of steering wheels. This is known as United Technologies Automotive. He is presently general plants manager of Howe, Indiana, and Monterrey, Mexico, plants.

Steven and Judy had a typical marriage with ups and downs, hard work, and times of play with lots of fun. During a fun time, while on a much anticipated Gulf of Mexico cruise with three other couples, without any warning, Judy had a cardiac arrest and died, April 11, 1988. She has been greatly missed.

Son Matthew graduated from Bluffton High School and is now attending Wright State University in Dayton, Ohio.

When Steven's work took him to Korea on business, Mal-Sook Baek (born on October 18, 1962) a resident of Seoul, was assigned as his interpreter. A friendship flourished and she came to America; and in August 1989, they were married.

The family continues to live near Vera Cruz. Josh and Dan are busy with school activities and their great love, baseball and basketball. Mal-Sook goes to school to improve her English, and Steven, in his leisure time, coaches PAL basketball, and assists with Little League baseball.

WILLIAM COTTON FAMILY

My great-grandfather, William Cotton, moved to Wells County from Austentown, Ohio and purchased land in Union Township in 1848. He married Hannah Rhinear and they raised six children: Jackson, Lewis, Mary, Elisabeth (Libby), Nancy and Sarah (Aunt Al), my grandmother. William was the seventh generation down from John Cotton who helped found and name the town of Boston in the 1600's. He was a well known religious leader often called the Patriarch of New England. William and his wife were co-founders and staunch members of the beautiful little Prospect Methodist Church located west of Uniondale. Twenty-five of his family members are buried in the cemetery across the road. This church is still serving the community today. My grandmother, Sarah Almira Cotton, married Carlisle Snider, March 26, 1868, in Ossian, Indiana. A short while later they headed west in a covered wagon across Iowa, Kansas, and Nebraska in search of freedom and prosperity until they settled near the town of Maywood, Nebraska, where they homesteaded and built a snug, warm sodhouse. They raised seven children, the oldest son, Charles, being my father.

Back (L to R) Forest Cotton, Wayne Brown, Ernest Cotton; Front (L to R) Wayne Brown, Lewis Cotton

Lewis Cotton married Mary Jane Templeton and their son, Ernest, fathered Forest Cotton. Two of his children Eudora and Lyle still live in the Ossian, and Bluffton area.

Carlisle and Sarah (Cotton) Snider, 1925 married in Ossian 1868

Another child of William and Hannah was Mary Jane who married Francis Wilmington. He later died from injuries suffered in the Civil War, and Mary then taught school to raise her children. Another daughter, Nancy (Nan), served as the postmaster of Belvidere, South Dakota. I have a photo showing the Sioux Indians having a Pow Wow in the streets of Belvidere in the early days there. Another daughter, Elisabeth (Aunt Libbie), married a Penquite and lived in Iowa. A son, Jackson, farmed in the area and is said to have furnished land for the Prospect Church. The old William Cotton homestead is located west on the road 950 N. two miles then south on road 100 E. one-half mile then west one mile to Meridian Road the one-fourth mile south on the west side.

Many descendants of this pioneer family reside in Indiana and elsewhere. In my case from Nebraska on west to Colorado.

COUCH FAMILY

The Couch family history in Wells County began when Harry Russell and Ruth Alma (Roberts) Couch moved to a farm on the McNatt Road, west of state road 3 in Jackson Township. The year was 1919, one year after their marriage in the town of Van Buren (Huntington County). Ruth's parents were Linzy and Atlanta (Denton) Roberts of Jefferson Township (Huntington County). On the day of Ruth's birth, June 11, 1900, a new barn was raised on her father's farm. Ruth, the youngest of six children, attended a one-room school called Ford's School. Linzy's parents, Samuel and Sophia (Wiley) Roberts came to Jefferson Township in 1849 from Darke County, Ohio. Atlanta's parents were James and Sarah (Carl) Denton also of Huntington County.

Harry was born May 15, 1897, in Salamonia Township (Huntington County). He was the son of Jessie and Mary (Meyer) Couch. He grew up and went to school in Warren. He met his future bride at a school event called a "ciphering match." Harry's grandfather, William Henry Couch, came to Indiana from Guilford, North Carolina, with his Quaker family in a covered wagon in 1853. He married Sarah, the daughter of John and Rachel (Ruggles) Buzzard in 1855. Because his Quaker upbringing forbade him to bear arms, William served in the Civil War as an ambulance driver with Company "C" of the 54th Indiana Volunteer Infantry. William Henry's parents were John and Mary (Pitman) Couch. John's father, Meshach, came to the state of Delaware from England in the mid 1700's and moved to North Carolina about 1780 after marrying Mary Welch of Kent County, Delaware, in 1773.

Five children were born to Harry and Ruth Couch: Robert Dean (1919), Mary Atlanta (1921), Paul Eugene (1925), William Jesse (Bill) (1932), and Harry Junior (1934). Mary died in 1933 of rheumatic fever, and Robert died as the result of an automobile/train accident in 1939.

Together, the family farmed in Jackson Township (Wells County) and Jefferson Township (Huntington County) and was active in the Mt. Zion United Brethren Church. Harry was the Sunday school superintendent for many years and Ruth was both a Sunday school teacher and accompanied the congregation on the piano. In 1951, Harry and Ruth moved to South Mulberry Street in Bluffton. He had become the insurance agency manager and saw the business grow rapidly throughout the county. Harry retired in 1962. He and Ruth returned to live on McNatt Road in Jackson Township on the first farm west of their original Wells County home.

Paul married Ethel (Harrold), daughter of Elmer and Nellie (Williamson) Harrold of Chester Township. They have three children: Larry, Steven (Steve), and Mara Jo.

Bill married Winifred Griffith, daughter of Sam and Helen (Arnold) Griffith of Jackson Township. They have five children: William Lee (Bill), Bruce Alan (deceased), Robert Lynn (Rob), Tresa, and Bryan Keith.

The Harry R. Couch Family - 1935
Back row (L to R) Ruth, Robert, Harry, Junior, and Harry Russell; Front row (L to R) Bill, Paul

Harry Junior married Shirley Weikel, daughter of Hervey and Isabel (Harrison) Weikel of Rockcreek

Township. They have five children: Mark, David, Lisa, Jeffrey, and Bradley.

Paul and Ethel began farming in Jefferson Township (Huntington County) but moved to their present home on Mt. Zion Road (Jackson Township) in 1953. The Couch family has farmed this land continuously since 1921. Paul and his sons, Larry and Steve, farm considerable acreage in Jackson, Liberty, and Chester Townships. Paul and Ethel spend their winters at their home in Sebring, Florida.

In addition to farming, Larry Couch and his wife Rosalie (Moorman) are employed by the Franklin Electric Company in Bluffton. Larry is the supervisor of technical services and computer operations and Rosalie is a credit specialist. Their home is in Chester Township. Their daughter Laura is married to Rod Sills, and their son Michael Dean (Mike) is a student at Purdue University.

Steve also works as a foreman at Franklin Electric in addition to farming. He married Judy (Sleppy) and has two sons, Kevin and Kyle Steven. Kevin is a student at Vincennes University. Steven then married Sharon (Martin) and they live in Liberty Township.

Mara Jo is employed as an accounting clerk at Franklin Electric and is married to Alan Williams. Alan works for Gaiser Construction Company. Mary Jo and Alan live in Harrison Township. They have two children, David and Rebecca.

After graduating from Huntington College, Bill began teaching at Roll High School. He became a principal, serving in various school systems throughout East Central Indiana, including Southern Wells School. He continued his education at Ball State University and became a superintendent of schools. He is currently at the Shelby County, Indiana School System. Winifred is a nurse at a geriatric health care center (The Manor) in Shelbyville.

Their oldest child, Bill, is married to Angela (Barton) and they have two children, Bruce Edward and Alyssa. Bill does architectural restoration for Boyce, Inc. Angela is a reading specialist at the Jay West Jr. High in Jay County. Bill and Angela live south of Muncie and are restoring their historic home.

Rob works for Harmon's Classics, an automobile restoration company, and is married to Elizabeth (Clements). Elizabeth (Beth) is the charge nurse at the Meadowvale Nursing Home. They have two children: Travis and Chad (deceased) and live in Bluffton.

Tresa is a teacher and is married to Steve Patz, the principal of Elwood Middle School. They have two children, Ross and Stephanie, and lived in Elwood, Indiana.

Bryan Keith works for the McCardle, Inc. and lives with his wife Sandra (Morgan) in Hartford City, Indiana. They have four children: Brandon, Candice, Kyle and Kendra.

Harry Junior graduated form Manchester College and is the manager of advanced composite engineering for the Delco Products Division of General Motors in Dayton, Ohio. He and Shirley live in Tipp City, Ohio.

Mark is a medical doctor in Vandalia, Ohio. He is married to Judy (Metz) who is head nurse in his office. They have two children, Mark and Kelly Brubaker. Kelly is a student at Wright State University.

David is the regional manager of sales and operations for Mayflower Transit, Inc. He is married to Elise (Mayhew), who is an obstetrical nurse at the Wadsworth-Rittman Hospital. They live in Medina, Ohio, and have five children: Michael Christopher, Phillip, Jordan, Matthew David, and Lisa Betheny.

Lisa is a home economist and is married to Mark Chastain, an accountant with Cincinnati Gas and Electric Company. They live in Hebron, Kentucky, and have two children, Audrey and Nathan.

Jeffrey is a captain in the 45th Medical Battalion of the U.S. Army and is medical evacuation helicopter pilot. He is married to Patricia (Cunningham) who is a librarian. They have two sons, Matthew Emerson and Brian David. Patricia (Patti) and the boys are living at Nelligen Army Base in Stuttgart, Germany, while Jeff is stationed in Saudia Arabia during "Operation Desert Storm."

Bradley is a district executive for the Lake Huron Area Council of Boy Scouts of America in Michigan. He is married to Sandra (Scott) who is a manager for Wal Mart. They live in Bade Axe, Michigan.

Ruth Alma (Roberts) Couch, in whose honor this history is written, resides at Swiss Village in Berne, Indiana. She will be 91 years young in June, 1991.

JIM AND GLORIA COURTNEY

Jim and Gloria Courtney owned and lived in one of Wells County's oldest houses for 22 years. Known as "Hannah's Place", and a landmark for nearly 150 years, the red brick house has been a familiar site to several generations of local residents. It was the subject of an outstanding water color done by Harry Lindstrand and now in the permanent collection of the Wells County Creative Arts Council. The Federal style house at 6200 SE State Road 116 was built in 1846 by William Studebaker. Bricks were made on the site from clay in the field west of the home. Sand from the adjacent creek bank was used for the mortar. The home has four fireplaces, one in the living room and one in each of the three bedrooms. From William Studebaker, the home went to the Oliver P. and Anna Louise Markley family, passing on to their daughter, Hannah, who married Manson Reiff. The Manson Reiffs continued to own the property until it passed to their son, Marion Reiff.

The William Studebaker house built in 1846

The MBG&E (Marion, Bluffton, Geneva & Eastern) traction line passed in front of the house. This interurban line went through Linn Grove and as far as Geneva, although the original plan was to reach Celina, Ohio. This section was abandoned about 1917, while the interurban continued between Marion and Bluffton. Riders on the car going to Linn Grove told of being able to reach out the car window and touch the iron fence in front of the home. The iron fence still fronts the property and evidence of the embankment for the railroad can been seen where the line crossed the creek east of the house.

Jim and Gloria Courtney

In the 1930's era, Hannah Reiff was known for chicken dinners served in the home, by reservation, to the public, thus gaining the reference, "Hannah's Place."

Dave and Linda Thompson, sons Shane and Jason King

Around 1958, Bill and Ray Kipfer purchased the farm's 150 acres and home at auction. The home with 1.88 acres was sold in July 1961 to James and Gloria Knoble. The Knobles were divorced in 1964, and Gloria and her four children: Linda, Jim, Pamela, and Tammy continued to live in the home. In July, 1968, Gloria Knoble married James L. Courtney, son of Howard and Mona Courtney. The Courtneys then owned the home until October, 1990, when they purchased a smaller home in the Inskeep addition, west of Bluffton. In December, 1990, they sold the property to their daughter, Linda and her husband, David Thompson. Linda has two sons, Shane King and Jason King. The Thompsons and their family are continuing to enjoy the William Studebaker Home that well may be the oldest in Wells County.

COX FAMILY

The Cox family moved to Indiana in 1916 from Vermillion County, Illinois. Lewis and Emma Burroughs Cox moved to Hoagland, Indiana, and, after a one-year stay, moved to Wells County in 1917.

During the remainder of Lewis and Emma's lifetimes, they lived on farms in Harrison and Nottingham Township. Like many other families in the early 1930's, they lost their farm in Harrison Township, but in 1936, they bought forty acres near Reiffsburg.

Lewis and Emma's only child, J. Raymond Cox, was born in 1915, just prior to the move to Indiana. Raymond attended school at Poplar Grove, Bluffton, and graduated in 1932 from Petroleum High School.

In 1937 he married Daisy Augsburger, a native of Adams County, and they initially lived with Lewis and Emma on the Reiffsburg farm. Near the end of 1940, Lewis bought a 40-acre farm just a few miles away, and Raymond and Daisey moved to a farm across the road, renting the land and house from Crella Gottschalk.

Here both families resided throughout the 1940's and 50's, jointly farming approximately one hundred and sixty acres. In addition to farming, Raymond served as the Nottingham Township trustee from 1951-1959. Two children were born during these years, Barbara, in 1940, and David, in 1943.

Raymond and Daisy Cox

In 1956 Raymond began his employment at the Cline Lumber Company in Bluffton, in addition to his farming and township trustee duties. He remained employed there until his retirement in 1980, serving as the manager for 25 years. Raymond and Daisy moved from the farm in 1959, and, after a brief stay in Linn Grove, they moved to Bluffton in 1961 where they bought the Aschbaucher residence at 712 North Main, in an area that has been restored historically as Villa North.

Both of the Coxes became involved in community affairs for many years.

From 1947-57, they both were active in the Wells County Men's Chorus, where Daisy served as pianist. Raymond joined the Kiwanis Club in 1958 and remained a member until his death in 1988. Daisy, who began teaching piano in 1927, has been the piano teacher for many local residents. She also served as the organist for the First Methodist Church and St. Joseph's parish. Both Raymond and Daisy were members of the Mennonite Choral Society in Berne. Raymond was an avid amateur photographer who exhibited his work locally and in Fort Wayne, where he was a member of the camera club. Daisy shared his hobby and also is an amateur photographer and member of the camera club.

The next generation of the Cox family included David, who is an associate professor of Political Science and director for the masters in the public administration programs at Memphis State University. He graduated from Ball State University, received his undergraduate and master's degree in Australia on a Rotary scholarship, and earned his Ph.D. at Indiana University. He also served as project director for Project Achieve, sponsored by the Kaiser Foundation. Barbara Cox Wind is owner/director of Bridges School, a day care center in Granger, Indiana. She is a graduate of Ball State University.

When Barbara and David lived in Wells County, they were longtime active 4-H members, exhibiting their projects. David was a graduate of Bluffton High School and Barbara was a graduate of Petroleum High School.

There are four grandchildren: Emily and Lauren Cox, daughters of David, and Brian and John Newell, sons of Barbara. Emily is a high school student in Memphis and Lauren is in grade school. Brian is completing a master's degree in Library Science at Indiana University in Bloomington, and John is completing an undergraduate degree in Microbiology at Indiana University.

JOSEPH CRAVEN FAMILY

The Joseph Craven family are descendants of John Craven, who fought in the Revolutionary War. John enlisted May 17, 1777, and was taken prisoner at the Battle of Germantown. He was completely deafened by artillery fire. He was an exchanged prisoner and he re-enlisted in the Company of Captain J.A. Barkley under the command of General Anthony Wayne.

An employee of the Handle Factory, Joseph Craven married Elizabeth Nixon and their children were Charles, Bertha, Orin, Elmo Inez, Evelyn and twins Clarence Edwin and Oliver R.

Charles was unmarried. Bertha married Homer Baker; their children were, Dean and Robert; Orin married Celeste Caston having no children; Elmo Inez married Fred Emshwiller; their children were J. Joe Craven, Fred Craven and Thomas; Clarence Edwin married Mabel N. Bower; their children were Herbert Edwin and Catherine Elizabeth; Oliver R. married Betty Barr having no children. Evelyn, twin of Edwin, passed away at an early age. C. Edwin was the purchasing agent at the Red Cross Manufacturing Company for 52 years, a challenging job during World War I, where windmills and cider presses were manufactured. Oliver was employed at General Motors in Flint, Michigan. He left his mark on Flint Bowling, for during his career he had nine 300 games and rolled more than 10 series of 700 or higher.

Orin O. retired from active work on daily newspapers, retiring from the *Evening-News Banner* on November 30, 1957, after 60 continous and uninterruped years of service. He became news editor of the *Evening Banner* in 1929, having started work as a reporter on the *Evening News* in 1897. Orin was the recipient of the "Community Service Award" in 1960.

CREEK

Our paternal grandparents were Jasper and Maremna (Roberts) Creek of Blackford County, Indiana. They were Quakers of German descent, farmers and parents of nine children. Jasper was one of twelve children. Rev. William Henry (Billy) and Ettie (Noe) Carnes our maternal grandparents, were Methodists, Irish-Scotch descent, farmers, parents of seven children. Both families came to this part of the country in the early 1800's.

Jasper and "Remmie" had nine children, Orie Melvin (1885-1941), was our father. Our mother, Alma Myrl (1887-1951), was the oldest of seven children born to "Billy" and Ettie.

Orie and Alma were married in 1906 and had six children. Four were born to them while they lived in Chester and Nottingham Townships, Wells County.

Around 1918, they purchased and moved to small farm one mile north of Rockford, Indiana. They lived there until the farm sold in 1950. The house is now occupied.

Herald Milton was born in 1908 and died in 1983. He married Grace Mussleman in 1929. They have two children and four grandchildren.

Helen Louise was born in 1911. She married Norval Kline in 1940. They have one son, two grandsons and one great-granddaughter.

Evert Leroy was born in 1913. He married Ruthella Furnas in 1935. The have four children and six grandchildren.

Ruth Azalia was born in 1915. She married Lloyd Shriner in 1937. They have four children, sixteen grandchildren (one deceased) and five great-grandchildren. There are five sets of twins in the family.

The four older children attended the one-room school at Rockford, where Russel Stinson taught until the consolidation of schools in 1922.

Leona Grace was born in 1922. She served as an Army nurse in World War II. She married Rev. Max Morgan in 1946. They have five children and twelve grandchildren.

Elma Lorraine was born in 1928 and married Edward Martz. They have three children and five grandchildren.

Orie and Alma Creek family 1928
Top row L to R: Herald, Helen, Evert and Ruth;
Seated L to R: Orie, Leona, Alma and Elma (baby)

All six of the Creek children graduated from Rockcreek, where their father was custodian for fifteen years. All were active in music and sports.

In summer, Orie farmed and was a "driller" at the Heller stone quarry. Raising a family during the "Great Depression" was not easy. The family was forced to do without or "make over." Having a large garden and "truck patch," an apple (and other fruit) orchard that Orie planted and carefully tended; chickens and hogs for eggs and meat, and cows for milk, helped the family to survive.

Alma, an expert seamstress, made all the girls clothes and some of the boys. She made some dresses from printed feed sacks, also pillow cases and sheets from bleached flour sacks.

The Creeks were members and regular attenders of the Rockford Methodist Church where Helen and Ruth served as pianists.

In the late 30's Orie raised corn for hybrid seed for Herman Miller. The de-tasseling, harvesting and processing were all done by hand.

CROOK-GEETING-SNIDER

In 1887 Lewis R. Crook was born at home in Markle. His first wife, Mabel Duhamell, died two weeks after the birth of their second child, Helen, in 1924. Their first child, Emmaline, was born at Christmas time in 1921. In the early 1920's Lewis and Mabel lived in the Nashville, Indiana, area. When his wife died Lewis brought his two little girls home to his parents' home in Uniondale. His mother was not well at the time, and a young girl by the name of Ethel Geeting was helping in the home of his parents. On March 20, 1926, Lewis and Ethel were married.

Over the years Lewis had several jobs. These included building cabins for tourists in Nashville, Indiana, and plowing the ground with his jenny mules at the site of the newly formed Ouabache State Park so the WPA boys could plant the trees. Lewis also worked for the Estey Piano Factory, the City of Bluffton as a weed inspector, and in later years the OK Modern Laundry. Lewis also enjoyed drawing and then embroidering pictures. Lewis died in January, 1990.

Mr. and Mrs. Lewis Crook

Ethel Ruby Geeting was born on September 11, 1903, in Huntington County. Her maternal great-grandparents (Stump) immigrated to the United States from Ireland. Her mother, Estella Stump Geeting, died when Ethel was seven years old. Ethel's great-grandpa Geeting married a Miami Indian woman from Wabash. Ethel's father was Austin Walse Geeting. Ethel had one brother, Alfred Geeting, who served in World War I and died March 12 in the 1950's.

Ethel's first marriage was to Clarence Counterdale Snider (born October 8, 1900) on December 31, 1918. Ethel and Clarence had one child, Carl Ray Snider, born August 23, 1919. Carl worked in a CCC Camp in Illinois around 1938-1939. He then joined the Army during World War II and was in the first Infantry Division. Carl was in five major battles during the war. His first Infantry Division took part in the invasion of North Africa, the campaign in Sicily, the D-Day Allied landing on June 6, 1944, and later that year in the Battle of the Bulge. The last battle was when the Allies broke through Hitler's Siegfried Line along the border between Germany and France. After the war, Carl worked with his father, owner of Snider Construction, in Flint, Michigan. While in Flint Carl also trucked coal for home owners. In the 1960's Carl worked for the OK Modern Cleaners in Bluffton. For a short time Carl was employed at the Corning Plant and then worked several years for Lynn Woods, operating cranes and other heavy equipment. Carl retired in 1989 with a retirement party in his honor at the Dutch Mill Restaurant in Bluffton. Carl now spends his time creating hand-made leather products.

CHARLES AND FERNE (WALKER) CROSBY

Charles Clifford Crosby was born on May 20, 1896, in Chester Township, the son of Fred A. and Agnes Elmira Shields Crosby and the grandson of Simeon and Mary Pace Crosby and Calvin Andrew and Caroline Lucy Deaver Shields.

Monnah Ferne Walker Crosby was born on June 30, 1904, in Chester Township, the daughter of Alvin and Bertha Alice Farlow Walker. Ferne's grandparents were William and Sarah Adams Walker and William Riley and Mary Alice Farlow.

Charles and had two sisters, Grace Speece and Ethel Huffman.

Ferne had three sisters, Chloe Carnes, Blanche Carnes, and Irene Thomas and four brothers, Wayne, Howard, Claire, and Jerome.

Two children, Verlice (Spud) and Agnes, were born to Charles and Ferne.

Verlice married Catherine Minnich and they reside in Chester Township. Verlice is a farmer and a past Chester Township trustee.

Agnes married William (Bill) Payne, and they live near Roll in Blackford County. Agnes attended many Chester Center and Southern Wells School activities, since her husband was the principal and superintendent of these schools.

Verlice and Catherine have three children, Marilyn, Richard, and Joy.

Charles and Ferne Crosby 50th Wedding Anniversary

Marilyn married John Maddox and they reside in Chester Township. They have three children, Michael, Dawn, and Mitchell and two grandchildren, Jordan and Casey.

Richard married Barbara Freeman and they live in Chester Township. They have four children: Kenneth (Kent), Karla, Kraig and Kyle, and one grandchild, John Michael.

Joy married David Liddy and they have two children, Sarah and Travis.

Agnes and Bill Payne have two children, Jill and Phillip.

Jill married James Schuhmacher, and they have three children, Jennifer, Jessica, and Justin. The Schuhmachers reside near Hartford City.

Phillip married Carol Mallory; they have one daughter Emily and the reside in Noblesville.

Charles and Ferne had a vocation of farming and raising livestock. Charles was known for his "threshing rings." One "ring" was called the "east ring" and operated mostly in Nottingham Township, while the second "ring" operated in the Chester Township area. Everyone, especially the children, looked forward to the ice cream supper which closed the threshing season.

Charles and Ferne were always interested in Chester Township affairs. They could ben seen at Chester Center basketball games and other school functions. Charles was a member of the Chester Township Advisory Board for twelve years (1944-1956). They attended the Chester Center Christian Church and were active in the township Farm Bureau.

Ferne worked before her marriage at the Bay Piano Factory in Bluffton, and in later years at the Warren Methodist Home. Ferne is a charter member of the "Chester Night Clubbers" Home Demonstration Club and was the club's first president. She is still an active member of the club.

Charles and Ferne were married in April of 1921, and have resided in the same home since that date. Their home is located one mile west of the Southern Wells School.

Charles passed away June 15, 1978, and along with his parents and grandparents is buried in the Miller Cemetery, which is located one-half mile west of the family home. Ferne continues to live at the same family farm home and enjoys visits from family and friends.

CROW-ROBINSON

The great-grandparents of Helen Robinson, James and Lydia Crow, were the first settlers and built the first building on the farm at the southwest corner of Hamilton and Indianapolis Roads, two miles north of Zanesville. They had two sons, Calvin and Michael. Calvin married Lora Swank of near Yoder and they had two children, Claude and Carrie. Claude married SaVella Caley of north of Markle, and they had two children, Kenneth and myself, Helen (Crow) Robinson. All four generations lived on that farm at various times.

After James Crow died, Calvin and Lora moved into the home place.

Returning home from Fort Wayne, in 1912, they had a bad auto accident just one-half mile north of their home. There were three doctors in Zanesville then and they all raced out there to assist via horse and buggies. That night Grandma Lora died at their home. Grandpa Calvin stayed with his mother in Zanesville while recuperating.

Claude and SaVella lived north of Markle near her parents, the Sam Caleys. Claude helped with the farming there, so not until spring of 1919 were they able to move in with Grandpa Crow. I (Helen) was born at the house just north of Markle where Bobby Caley now lives. Kenneth was born at the Crow farm in 1923. In 1929 our mother, SaVella, died and in 1933 Grandpa Crow died.

Claude remarried and later moved to near Ossian. His sister, Carrie Crow moved in to the homeplace. She died in 196?, and the farm was sold out of the family.

In 1935 I (Helen) married Wayne Robinson, whose parents had bought the first farm north of Zanesville on the Feighner Road, back the lane.

The following 25 years we lived in Waynedale and Fort Wayne. We had three children, Fred, Joe and Donna. Wayne worked at Bowsers for 26 years and at Magnavox for 15 years.

When we were newlyweds, Wayne found work at $.40 an hour. Our rent was $10 a month and food budget for the week was $4 to $5. We sometimes saved up a dollar to buy gas to come out and see our parents. In 1959 we bought the Fred Crow farm and moved back. By this time the children were teenagers. Fred was a senior in high school, so he graduated from Union, spent four years in the Navy, graduated from American University, University of Hawaii, and is now living in Perth, West Australia with his British wife, Jennifer, and two children, Justin and Fiona.

Joe graduated from Lancaster and Purdue University. He works for Case Power & Equipment Co. at Memphis, Tennessee. He married Carolyn Newhard of Uniondale and they have two children, Amy and Jason.

Our daughter, Donna is an L.P.N. at Huntington Hospital. She married Vernon Bradburn of near Markle. Vernon works for Preston Trucking. They lived just around the corner from our old place. They have three children, Matthew, Angela and Jennifer.

We sold our home in Union Township and

now winter in Florida and summer in an apartment in Waynedale.

CROWL-GRAY-KERNSTEIN FAMILIES

Theodore and Mary Belle Gibson Crowl lived on a farm south of Ossian. Their next to the youngest child was my grandfather Sherman Kennyson Crowl.

Sherman worked on the Interurban Railroad and farmed his land in Allen County. Sherman married Fern Ellen King. They raised five children of their own and one of his nephews. The children are Mary Ellen Crowl Woods, Sherman Kennyson Crowl, Jr., Warren E. Crowl, Phyllis Maxine Crowl Palmer and Robert Allison Crowl.

Sherman K. Crowl, Jr. is my father. During World War II Sherman was stationed in England. It was there he met and married my mother Crystal Marion Davidge Crowl. Sherman and Crystal have six children and they are Janet Elaine Crowl Gray, Karen Diane Crowl Burden, Lorene Ellen Crowl Barnes, David Sherman Crowl, Richard Gregory Crowl and Steven Terry Crowl. There are now eleven grandchildren.

Sherman and Crystal lived on a farm in Lafayette Township in Allen County. Crystal died in March of 1988.

Janet married William H. Gray in 1985, and they live west of Bluffton. Chris lives in Wells County and works in Fort Wayne. Tim has been in the Air Force since he graduated from high school. He has been stationed in Germany and Greece, and now he is in England. William Gray's only son, William, Jr., died in 1985 in Fort Wayne.

CLARENCE AND GENEVA CROY

Leah Elisa Gifford, from the family of Emil Baumgartner was born June 20, 1855 and died summer 1915. He was the son of Jacob and Elise (Kohler) Baumgartner of Souperswye, Switzerland. He married Lena Moser. She was born July 20, 1852, at Combio, Kt. Bem, Switzerland. She died January 28, 1895. Emil was a mason contractor. He taught school in Switzerland, and he loved music. He had nine children. Their fourth child was Leah Elise (Baumgartner) Gifford. She was born February 20, 1885, died June 17, 1967. She is buried at Six Mile Cemetery. She married Thomas Gifford August 1, 1903, in Warren. Thomas died in 1960. He is also buried at Six Mile Cemetery. They had seven children. Their fifth child was Geneva Lucille born April 1, 1913. Geneva's family lived in the Vera Cruz area. She married Clarence Oliver Croy, born September 11, 1911.

(L-R) Pauline Marie (Croy) Dubach, Donald Lee Croy, Jerald Lloyd Croy, Judy Ann (Croy) Cotton

Clarence was the son of George and Martha (Jones) Croy. He was raised east of Nottingham. He came to Vera Cruz with his brother, Howard Croy, who lived there. Clarence and Geneva had four children: Pauline Marie, born June 21, 1931; Donald Lee, born May 29, 1933; Jerald Lloyd, born November 9, 1934; and Judy Ann, born January 8, 1950, died April 11, 1988. She is buried at Six Mile Cemetery. Clarence opened the Croy Machine Shop in Vera Cruz on August 1, 1945. He operated the shop until he sold the business to his son Don in 1970. One of the machine shop's primary products in its early years was the rotary weed mower. They also had a constant business of farm machinery repair. Geneva died on November 1, 1969, and is buried at Six Mile Cemetery. On January 3, 1976, Clarence married Rosemond Booth. They made their home on the east side of Bluffton along the Wabash River. For several years now they have spent their winters in Cortez, Florida. Clarence will be buried at Six Mile Cemetery. Rosemond will be at Fairview Cemetery. Her children are Mrs. Don (Debbie) Bowman, Fred Booth, and Chad Booth.

DONALD LEE CROY FAMILY

I (Donald Croy), was born May 29, 1933, in Vera Cruz, at home, at 2815 Mulberry Street. My parents are Clarence Oliver and Geneva Lucile (Gifford) Croy. I am one of four children. At three years of age, we moved to my present home, 2736 S.E. Mulberry Street, where I lived for the next sixteen years. I attended Vera Cruz School until the eighth grade and then Bluffton High School. I graduated in 1951. My senior year I met Phyllis Ann Courtney.

Phyllis was born August 19, 1935. She is the daughter of James Howard and Mona Maxine (Stout) Courtney. She is the only daughter of five children. They lived in Bluffton. James died in 1966 and is buried at Stahl Cemetery. Mona will be buried at Elm Grove Cemetery.

Donald Lee Croy and Phyllis Ann "Courtney" Croy

We had our first date on Valentine's Day. After two years of dating and Phyllis' graduation, we were married on June 20, 1953. Our first home was on the second floor of the Markley apartment house at 416 W. Central Street, Bluffton. When I got home from my honeymoon my service papers were in the mailbox. At this time I left Phyllis, my first love, with my second love, my 1949 Ford V-8. I spent two years in the Army. I left for Germany on the last day of the Korean Conflict. When I returned home, my folks, owned the little grocery store that sat diagonally at the corner of Center and Wabash Streets in Vera Cruz. Phyllis was working there with my folks learning to know the community. We soon bought our first house at auction in 1955 from the Telsie Shendler estate. It had no indoor plumbing so that was my first evening job. I was working at Croy Machine Shop for my father.

We had two of our daughters at that house. Jill Diane born June 9, 1957, and Cheryl Ann, born July 24, 1960. In 1963 we moved to our present location (my parents home). There we had our third daughter, Penny Sue, born December 12, 1964. Jill married Brian Douglas Conley, on August 13, 1977. They have a son, Christopher, born August 23, 1990. Cheryl married Steven Taylor on January 25, 1986. They have a son, Mikel, born March 18, 1989. Penny married Kent Park on January 26, 1985.

I have lived all my life in Vera Cruz except for two months in Bluffton and my years in the service. I have been told my home was originally a buggy shop, where they made and displayed buggies. Several years ago when we remodeled, we found a poster of new buggies in one of our walls. This house is home to us and Vera Cruz is home to us. On July 1, 1970 I bought the Croy Machine Shop. That building was originally the second location of the St. John United Church of Christ.

I enjoy going to gas engine shows and Phyllis enjoys quilting. We are members of the Six Mile Church. We will be buried in the Six Mile Cemetery. *Submitted by Donald Croy*

CRUM

Samuel Crum was a progressive farmer residing in Rockcreek Township, as a native of Pennsylvania. He was born in Dauphin County, March 22, 1822. His parents, John and Elizabeth (Haynes) Crum, were natives of Pennsylvania and of German ancestry.

Samuel was reared on the home farm, and received such educational advantages as the rude log cabin subscription schools of that early day afforded. He lived with his parents until 19 years of age, after which he worked out by the day and month until his marriage.

He was married October 25, 1847, to Miss Mary Braham who was born in Dauphin County, Pennsylvania. Her father, John Braham, being a native of the same state was also of German descent. After his marriage he rented his father-in-law's farm for fourteen years.

He was bereaved by the death of his wife in 1851, who left at her death one child, a son, named John Henry.

In February, 1858, Mr. Crum came to Wells County, Indiana and bought 100 acres of land in Rockcreek Township which was only partially improved. He married again in 1863 to Miss Elmina Swartz, who was born in Lancaster County, Pennsylvania, coming with her father to Wells County, Indiana, in 1854.

To this union were born four children, Eli, Emmanuel, Aaron (deceased) and David.

Mr. Crum began life without capital and by his own industry and exertions he accumulated a good property, which he used in surrounding himself and family with all the necessary comforts of life.

In politics, Mr. Crum cast his suffrage with the Democratic Party. Mrs. Crum was a member of the German Reformed Church.

Samuel Crum died November 16, 1889.

John Henry Crum, of Banner City, was born near Harrisbruy, Dauphin County, Pennsylvania, January 14, 1848, a son of Samuel and Mary (Braham) Crum, also native of Pennsylvania. John H. was an only child, and when his mother died he was two and one-half years of age.

John was 14 years of age when he came to this county. He was educated here and for several years was engaged in agricultural pursuits, although he taught school for sometime previous to his marriage. This event occurred in April, 1870, to Miss Alice Gardenour.

After marriage they came to the farm which was purchased by Mr. Crum in 1869, upon a portion of which the Chicago and Atlantic Railroad passed.

In 1884, Mr. Crum built his fine farm house adjacent to the village of Banner. They had six children, who were Franklin, Charles, Delbert, Effie, Attie and Iva.

In 1882 Mr. Crum was elected Justice of the Peace of his township and was re-elected in 1886.

Mrs. Crum died January 9, 1887, and her remains were interred in St. John's Cemetery in Union Township, Wells County.

He then married Emma J. Preskey October 7, 1887, and to this union were born six children. They were Lela, Minnie, Hubert, Mary, Hazel and Pearl.

He then resided on a farm along the Wabash River in Rockcreek Township. He next moved his family to Bluffton where he became court bailiff. He died in May, 1929.

Delbert Crum was born February 16, 1878. He was married July 20, 1900, to Anna Durst. To this union were born four children: Baby Crum died at birth; Gerald Dale Crum, June 5, 1908; Wendell Burdette Crum, June 25, 1913; and Margaret Lucile Crum, December 1, 1918.

Anna died in 1938.

Delbert made his living by farming in Rockcreek Township and did so until he retired. He then married Mary Schwartz in 1942 and they lived in Bluffton and then to Uniondale until Mary's death in 1957 and Delbert's death in September 1972.

Gerald Crum and Laverne Yoder were married March 2, 1935. They lived in Uniondale, Indiana, and Gerald worked at General Electric until he retired from there in 1973 and still lived in Uniondale until Laverne's death in October, 1973, and Gerald's death in February, 1984.

Wendell Crum and Magdalene Wilson were married June 22, 1940, and to this union were born three sons: Benjamin Burdette Crum, October 1, 1940; Theodore Lee Crum, January 24, 1944; Timothy K. Crum, August 20, 1949.

Wendell and his family resided in Uniondale and he worked at General Electric until his retirement in April 1975. He and Magdalene still live in Uniondale. Benjamin is married to Sharon Weeks of Indianapolis, IN and to this union was born: Kimberly Rae, December 4, 1965; Jeffrey Benjamin, April 15, 1968; Molly Elizabeth, July 9, 1971.

Theodore is married to Mary Jane Coon from Fort Wayne and to this union were born: Jonathan David, May 30, 1971; and Jennifer Fo, November 4, 1972.

Timothy is married to Marilyn Bruns of New Haven and to this union was born: Matthew Martin, January 11, 1977; Andrew Ryan, February 16, 1979; and Renee Anna, October 23, 1981.

Lucile Crum and Loren Elzey were married October 8, 1938. Lucile and family lived near Uniondale, and Loren farmed, then had a filling station in Uniondale, then was Wells County treasurer until his death in July 7, 1985. To this union was born: Sharon Annette Elzey, July 16, 1941; Rebecca Diane Elzey, April 17, 1946.

Sharon is married to Larry Bowers of Paris, Illinois, and to this union were born: Bradley Dean, August 22, 1969; Kelly Ann, March 5, 1971.

Rebecca is married to Michael Walker of Markle and to this union were born: Quinn Renae, April 28, 1971; Kara Diane, January 15, 1973; and Krista Michelle, March 24, 1977.

CUPP FAMILY

Ray L. was born to Otto L. and Amy Lewellyn Cupp on October 17, 1889. Otto and Amy were the parents of twelve other children, all deceased. They were Lola, Clellah, Joseph, John, Everett, Orlo, Otis, Ruth, Dana, Paul, Willard, and Ernest. In 1908, Ray married Bertha Holcomb, daughter of Dr. J.H. and Charity Swaim Holcomb. Bertha was born in Elkin, North Carolina, in 1890, and is still living. To Ray and Bertha were born five children: Mary Harris, Helen Blue, Robert, Richard, and Ruth. All are deceased except Mary.

Ray Cupp, Helen Cupp, Homer Houtz - In front of Ray Cupp's Store

Mary was married to Fred Harris, deceased. They had one son, Frederick, who is also deceased. Frederick was the father of two children, Gretchen and John, both living in New Jersey, with their mother Nicki.

Robert was married to Margaret Miller. To them were born four children: Barbara married to Don Taylor; John married to Judy Brickley; Mick married to Connie Myers; an David.

Emmett Fisher (1st man), child unknown, Mary Cupp Harris, Roy Cupp (Mary's father). Roy Cupp Grocer around 1930-1931

Barbara and Don are the parents of three living children: Rose, Philip, and Karen; and Robert, who is deceased.

John and Judy have four children: Jeff, Jennie, Janice, and Jason. They also have two grandchildren.

Mick and Connie are the parents of three children: Michelle, Robert, and Tiffany.

David is the father of Shelli, Richard, and Melissa. Richard was married to Martha Huffman. They were the parents of two daughters: Penny, married to James Herber; and Pamela, married to Michael Fisher. Jamie is the daughter of Penny. Pamela, who is deceased, had one son Christopher.

CUSTARD

From the marriage of Susan Jones (daughter of Wm. and Rachel Jones), and William (Bill) R. Custard were born ten children. The names of the children were: Pearl (Custard) Trout, Alvin Bert Custard, Clifford Custard, Arzona Custard, Earl Custard, Hazel (Custard) McKay, Ethel (Custard) Samoff, Blanche (Custard) Roberts and Fern (Custard Sell. These children were scattered all over the Midwest.

Alvin Bert Custard was born on October 20, 1883, and died on November 22, 1964. He married Nettie (Coffield) Custard on December 31, 1904. Nettie was born on December 29, 1888, and died in April,l 1979. Bert was a piano tuner by trade. He also farmed near McNatt in Jackson Township. When they retired, they moved into the house next to the McNatt General Store. Bert and Nettie were members of the McNatt Methodist Church. Two children were born from this union, Glen and Vernis Custard.

Glen Custard was born on October 5, 1905. He graduated from Adrian College in Michigan with a degree in teaching. He taught in several schools around the area. His first marriage was to Ruth Patch on July 17, 1927, at Muncie, Indiana. Three children were born to Ruth and Glen: Shirley (Custard) Haines, Nancy (Custard) Conner, and Galen Custard. After the death of Ruth Custard on March 30, 1981, he married Besse Denny. Glen died on December 28, 1989.

A daughter, Vernis A., was born on May 23, 1911, at Rich Valley, Indiana. She graduated from Bluffton High School in 1929, and she attended Marion Business College in Marion, Indiana. She married Howard E. Baker on July 21, 1934, at Alexandria, Kentucky. They had two daughters, Sharon K. was born on March 10, 1943, and Lennyce E. born on April 3, 1946.

Sharon K. was married to Claire T. McMillan on May 16, 1964. They have two daughters: Clarice K. born on September 1, 1967, and Kristi L. born on January 10, 1971.

Lennyce was married to Laurence (Larry) Powers on November 22, 1969. They have one daughter named Emily.

CUTLER

My grandmother, Florence Irene Cutler was born in 1909 in Wells County, Indiana. She was the daughter of Earl Alexander Cutler and Olive May Close Cutler. She married Frederick Eugene McKinney and they had four children: Kathleen, Carol, Bill and Roger. After she and Fred divorced, she moved to Fort Wayne, Indiana, where she lived and worked until 1979. Her last residence address in Fort Wayne being 5117 McClellan. While in Fort Wayne she worked for the former Gerber Haus Motel and she was a devout member of the South Side Church of the Nazarene. After suffering a mild stroke, she was unable to live alone and moved in with her daughter, Kathleen, in Ossian, Indiana. She later took up residence at the Ossian Healthcare

Florence I. Cutler McKinney about 1970

Center where she resided until her death on June 21, 1988. She had 29 grandchildren at the time of her death. Her hobbies included any type of ballgames, hockey, and she collected salt and pepper shakers. She is buried at Oak Lawn Cemetery, Ossian, Indiana.

Earl Cutler was the son of Alpheus Jeremiah Cutler (1862) and his first wife, Nancy Gear. In 1889 Alpheus married Rosa McClain and they had nine children: Levina Josephine, Lillie May, David, Leona Fern, William, Livona, Clarence, Ireta Ethel, and Harold Raymond. Many were married in Bluffton, Indiana. Earl Cutler married Olive May Close in 1902, she being the daughter of George W. and Margaret Darwactor Close. Earl and Olive had thirteen children: Glenn (1903-1962) married Luella Tennison; Chester (1905-1959) married Marion Mills; and Esther; Luella (1907-1976) married Frank Duchateau and Paul Masson; Florence Irene (1909-1988) married Frederick E. McKinney; Elmer Leroy (1911-1981) married Virginia Shields and Kay -); Paul (1913) married Ruth Kite and Bonnis LaGette; Esther Pauline (1915-1985) married Ivan Cartwright; Helen (1917-1922); Forrest "Bud" (1919-1985) married Deloris Clanon; Ruth (1921) married Gail Hall; Earl Jr. (1923-stillborn); Gladys (1924) married Walter Porter and John McClellan; Kenneth (1928) married Rachel Sweet. Alpheus Jeremiah Cutler was the only child his mother raised after the death of his father. His parents were Fanny Reeves and Jonathan Cutler, born in 1834. They migrated to the Wabash County area in 1845 from Highland County, Ohio, with his parents, Abner (born 1792) and Mary Watson/Woten Cutler. The remaining children were placed in White's Institute in Wabash, Indiana. Alpheus and Rosa McClain Cutler are both buried in Fairview Cemetery, Bluffton, Indiana.

Earl Alexander Cutler
Olive May Close Cutler

Olive May Close Cutler (born 1881) was the first child of Margaret Darwactor and George Washington Close, a farmer in Root Township. Other children were Jane, Elizabeth, Gilbert, Laura, Harvey and one unnamed. George came from Holmes County, Ohio and Margaret from Muskegon County, Ohio. She was the daughter of Margaret Jones and Gilbert Darwactor of Pennsylvania, who lived in Wells County from 1880 until their deaths. They last resided at 709 W. South Street.

DOUGLAS L. DAILEY AND SUSAN M. DOTTERER DAILEY

Douglas L. Dailey was born on January 21, 1959, to Donald and Carol Dailey of Adams County, Indiana. Susan M. Dotterer was born on January 8, 1958, to Paul and Phyllis Dotterer of Bluffton. On June 19, 1977, Doug and Susan were married at the Apostolic Christian Church near Vera Cruz.

Doug came to Bluffton to work at the Sherwin-Williams Paint Store, which was located at the corner of Market and Johnson Streets. When the store closed in 1977, he was hired by Butler Brothers' True Value. While employed at True Value, Doug was active in the Bluffton Chamber of Commerce and served as its president in 1984.

Susan earned a degree in elementary education from Ball State University. She then returned to the Bluffton-Wells County Public Library, where she had worked during high school. In December, 1979, Susan was hired as the temporary manager of the newly opened Ossian Branch Library. She continued in this position until may, when her sister Kathy completed her degree.

On May 18, 1980, Doug and Susan became the parents of Stefanie Kay. Benjamin Douglas joined the Dailey family on June 14, 1983. A second son, Kevin Lynn, was born to Doug and Susan on August 8, 1985.

In November 1985, Doug became manager and part-owner of the Bluffton radio station, known as WCRD. At that time the call letters of the station were changed to WBGT and it was known as "The Bright Spot."

Doug changed careers in 1987 when he went to work as a salesman for Rubber, Inc. This Chicago-based company sold equipment and supplies primarily to tire dealers. Doug started Doug Dailey Sales in 1989 and became a self-employed factory representative for FMC, and automotive equipment company.

In 1981 Susan went back to work part-time in the children's department of the Bluffton-Wells County Public Library. In August, 1990, she was again named Ossian Branch Librarian. This full-time position allowed her to manage the Ossian Branch, which was in the process of moving from its storefront location at 105 South Jefferson to a converted house at 207 North Jefferson. However, the job also permitted her to continue working half her hours in the children's department of the main library in Bluffton. *Submitted by Doug Dailey*

VERLIN DALRYMPLE FAMILY

Verlin was born in Huntington County, July 30, 1909 son of Jesse Edward and Goldie Agusta Perry Dalrymple. He was a grandson of Henry E. Dalrymple, a well known pioneer of Wells County.

On May 17, 1930, Mr. Dalrymple married Mary Josephine Worster, daughter of C. Columbus and Lillie J. Shull Worster and the granddaughter of Wm. Thomas Worster, a well respected citizen of Wells County for many years.

Mrs. Dalrymple was born May 22, 1911 in Van Buren, Indiana.

Verlin and M. Josephine Dalrymple

Verlin and Josephine moved to 312 Roe Street, Ossian in 1939. Mr. Dalrymple was employed at Holsum Bakery in Fort Wayne at the time. Three children were born to them: Norma Jane, August 2, 1932, Robert Leroy, October 16, 1935, Connie Jo, May 29, 1941.

Verlin continued to work in Fort Wayne until 1944 when he landed a really good job at Springer's Mill in Ossian paying $30 per week. In 1949 he went to work for Kenny Rutledge at the Levy Elevator. He worked there until 1953.

The family moved to Warren in the summer of 1953 where they remained until 1967 when Verlin and Josephine having all their children married moved to Uniondale, where Verlin worked for Farm Bureau Elevator. He retired from Farm Bureau, July 1974.

In 1986 they sold their home in Uniondale and moved to Capri Meadows in Bluffton. A desire to be closer to their children led them to move to Markle in 1990, where they presently live.

Verlin and Josephine are members of the Order of the Eastern Star, the Masonic Lodge, and the Markle United Methodist Church.

Norma J. married Arthur J. Behning, they live near Zanesville, Indiana. Robert L. married Mary Louise Miller and lives near Huntington, Indiana. Connie J. married Bill L. Brubaker and they live near Uniondale, Indiana.

ROBERT MUNTON DARROW FAMILY

The first home in Wells county for the Robert M. Darrow family was the "Marybelle," located west of the Rockcreek School and owned by Harry and Dorothy Lindstrand. The school has been demolished but a plaque marks its place in history.

Bob (Robert M.) Darrow was born March 10, 1918, in Garrett, Indiana. Later, his family moved to Logansport and then returned to the Fort Wayne area. After his father's death, he and three of his sisters went to live in the Masonic Children's Home in Franklin, Indiana. After graduating from Masonic High School, Bob went back to Fort Wayne. he was in the first group of inductees drafted from Allen County for World War II. During training, he transferred from the 38th Infantry into the 727th Railway Operating Battalion. His duty took him from Africa to Germany, where remembers hearing Churchill's "victory speech" on radio while in a hospital in Mannheim, Germany.

Back (L to R) Jason Bush, Sara Holmes, Carey Holmes, Pamela Bush, Jane Darrow; Front (L to R) Emily Holmes, Sarah Bush, Angela Bush, Robert Darrow

Jane (Emma Jane Eldridge) Darrow was born in Rensselaer, Indiana, on April 10, 1921. She attended International Business College in Fort Wayne. During the war she worked in the expediting department at Farnsworth Corporation. She belonged to their ladies' bowling league, which came to Bluffton to bowl with the Farnsworth team here.

When he returned from overseas, Bob and Jane were married on August 30, 1945, at Forest Park Methodist Church. They had two daughters: Pamela Jane, born July 31, 1946; and Susan, born April 21, 1950. Bob was co-owner of Wells County Automotive Supply, Inc., which opened for business in Bluffton on June 14, 1957. The firm was located on the northeast corner of Washington and Johnson Streets. Thus, the Darrows moved from Fort Wayne to "Marybelle" on August 23, 1957.

Pamela and Susan attended Rockcreek School until the family moved into Bluffton in 1959. They went to Central School and Bluffton High, and both graduated from Indiana University in Bloomington. Pamela was married to Ronald G. Bush and they had three children: Jason Robert, 17, Angela Jayne, 15, and Sara Elizabeth, 9. Susan is marred to Carey Lynn Holmes, born January 22, 1950, a son of Francis and Wilda Holmes of Bluffton. Emily Anne, 10, is their only child. Both families reside in Church Southwest Allen County near Fort Wayne.

The Darrow family was active in the First United Methodist Church. Jane worked in the local Girl Scout Organization and, with Mrs. Jim (Rene) Zoll, directed the first day-camp for girl scouts at Oubache State Park. She is a past member of Bayview Literary Guild and Progressive Homemakers Club. She enjoys needlework and piecing quilts, and is known for her cornhusk dolls. Bob belongs to the Elks, Bluffton Lodge FA&M 145, where he is a trustee, and the Scottish Rite. Since retiring, Bob loves gardening and miniature trains, and spends lots of time working on his replica of Plymouth Plantation. Bob and Jane enjoy life in their rural home southeast of Bluffton, where they have lived for twenty-six years.

DAUGHERTY

To Grandfather Jesse were born six children, Edwin, Donna, Olean, Pauline, Harold, and last Raymond. Harold married Dorothy Wolf in 1942. After serving in World War II, Harold worked his way up through the accounting department of Dana Corporation (Ft. Wayne and Marion) to plant controller at the Lima, Ohio, facility prior to retirement. Dorothy, although schooled as a hairdresser, remained at home to raise their six children: Kay Janene (Williams), Gary Lee, Alan Duane, Dean Edward, Paul Leon, and Keith Lynn. The family home location was moved between births of each child and the next, but all are Wells natives. All but Keith were on their own when in January, 1974, Harold and Dorothy moved from Craigville to Elida, Ohio.

Dorothy and Harold Daugherty

Alan left home a year after Lancaster High School to attend Ball State University and married Regina Lee Bender soon after. Regina (sometimes called Doody) attended Rockcreek but later met Alan about the time the Rockcreek students were consolidated with Lancaster. The early years of their marriage were spent in Muncie earning the education degrees both later received. Regina also earned her elementary education Master's from Ball State University, while Alan completed a Master's in art at St. Francis College in Fort Wayne. Both have spent a number of years in the education field and Alan also spent several years in construction.

Regina was the youngest child of Merlin "Buzzy" Keith and Alice Elene (Martin) Bender. Gerry and Karen preceded Regina's birth. All but Elene (also called MeeMaw) were Wells natives, as were several generations of the Bender family. Merlin died when Regina was only three, leaving the children to be supported and raised by only their mother in their home in Uniondale.

Clockwise, Regina, Alan, Tyler, Deric Daugherty

Alan and Regina had their first child on June 4, 1970, in Muncie on the day Regina was to receive here college diploma. Due to a lung defect, Lance Stuart died the next day and was buried near his Grandfather Bender in Markle. Deric Ross was born February 9, 1972, after the couple moved to Bluffton. Deric followed his parents and attended Ball State University to study architecture. August 22, 1974, Tyler Leith joined the family and plans to attend college following a 1992 graduation from Bluffton School.

After living in a mobile home on the Ball State campus, Alan and Regina moved to Bluffton, as Alan had secured a teaching position with the Southern Wells Corporation. They purchased a house at 307 West Central. Through a several year process, and with the young couple doing nearly all of the work, the house was improved through electrical, plumbing and other alterations. The house was sold when the family moved to 513 West Market, a large Colonial Revival house built by Harry Studebaker in 1903. Over two years were spent by the entire family in restoring the beauty of this single family home, which earlier had been converted into a three unit apartment dwelling.

DAUGHERTY, CHARLES

Memory of mandolin folk music has become one legacy handed down to today's generations of ancestors following Charles Cecil Daugherty. His children, grand-children, cousins, nephews and nieces remember enjoyable evenings sitting at the feet of this man and his instrument. Family folklore handed down through Charley includes the story that his father, Ezekiel, often walked with his brothers behind a covered wagon and a spring wagon to look for rabbits as they made their way to Union Township from Trumbull County, Ohio. John B. and Millie Matildia (McGee) Daugherty brought a family of eight children (Ezekiel being the fifth) on this trip in 1866. "Zeke" was also a folk musician who could play lively folk tunes on the violin while clog dancing. Ezekiel lived for a time in a house located about a half mile north of his son's (Charley) farm. This house was later moved to Uniondale and lived in by Charley's nephew, Edwin Daugherty.

Charley was born the youngest of four children to Ezekiel and Winnie Etta (Double) Daugherty. Sister Iva married Albert "Dell" Shady and had seven girls plus a boy who died an infant. Brother Clarence lived less than four years. Brother Jesse married Mary Kleinknight and had six children but also lost one of them to a childhood accident. Infant and childhood deaths appear in every Daugherty generation which lived in Wells County including two sisters of Ezekiel. Charles married Fern A. Haflich on January 12, 1912, and eventually purchased a farm a couple miles south of Uniondale which is still owned by his son Junior. Charley was fatally injured in a 1964 farming accident on this farm.

Ervin Lamoin was the first child of Charley and Fern and married Ruth Maxine Taylor of Fort Wayne. Their children were daughter, Delores Marlies, who married Don Menke and produced two children (Danny Joe and David Edward), and their son, Larry Lee, who married Barbara Sprong and fathered two girls (Erika and Michelle). Ervin was a fifty year maintenance employee of the Northern Indiana Public Service Company and resided in Michigan City prior to his 1974 retirement to Bradenton, Florida.

Charles and Fern's second child, Mary Magdalene, wedded Max Donald Foreman in Wells County in 1936 and birthed two boys. Their first child, Donald Dee, married Anna Marie Deckard, they had three children, Jodi Lynette, Mark Alan and Lisa Marie. Their second son, Bertrand Ted, married Linda Jo Sacca. Their children were Troy David, Teresa Darlene, and Steven Joseph.

Ralph Finley married Charley's third child, Martha Bell. The only child from this marriage was Gemma SueAnn, who married Phillip Sickafus. They are parents of Tamara SueAnn, Heather LeAnn, and Schlaura Nicole. Gemma's family presently lives in her Grandfather Charley's final home which he built in Uniondale.

Charley and Fern's fourth child, Dornal Darlene, was born in 1921, died in 1947, and never remarried.

Junior Haflich Daugherty who married Marjorie Dickie was the last of Charley's children. Jimmie Wayne was the first child of this marriage but Jimmie died in infancy. Later children were Marilyn Sue who married John Legge, while Cathy Jo married Mark Coleman. *(See Photo on Page 607)*

DAVENPORT FAMILY

John Catlett Davenport, born May 1847 in Greene County Pennsylvania, was a teacher and came to Wells County as a young man. He married Sara Elizabeth McFarren and in the course of years they had six children. As each child married my great grandfather gave each one a Seth Thomas clock and twenty acres of land. "Our" clock still remains in good running order and is in the possession of my younger daughter, Jerry Ludeke in Bakersfield, California. Daughter Georgia Kegley lives in Charlottesville, Virginia.

Before Kansas became a state, Davenport was sent to what became Smith City as a government representative. Here he established the Davenport Church and on the opposite corner the Davenport School. Several years ago an article in our paper said the Rotary Club of Smith City was raising funds to restore both the church and school.

Several years later a friend wrote Davenport of the rapid growth of Radford, Virginia, where a large railroad bridge was being built across the river. John moved his family to Radford and my mother, Stella, was one of "four female" graduates in 1894 to graduate from Radford State Teacher's College. This has now become a large "University of Radford."

John Catlett Davenport died in July 1895 and is buried in the Old Cemetery in East Radford.

After John's death my grandmother's brother, George F. McFarren (Bob McFarren's grandfather) brought his sister and five of her children back to Wells County to live. The oldest son had married and lived in Knoxville, Tennessee.

Stella married "Ed" Reynolds and they became owners of The Progress store. Three children were born to this union: Deane-1902, Hillis-1904, Julie (me) in 1906. Julia graduated from Bluffton High School, attended Sweet Briar College in Virginia and graduated from Indiana University with a B. A. degree and taught for a year.

In 1927 Julia married Robert Dreisbach from Fort Wayne. They lived in New York for 5 1/2 years where their two daughters were born. They moved back to Fort Wayne in 1933 when Dreisbach, an acoustical engineer became responsible for the sound system for the Chicago World's Fair of 1933.

Since my daughters and I were in Bluffton with my parents, (Stella and Ed Reynolds') so often, we "helped" at The Progress Store and we still feel we are a loyal part of Wells County. On Saturday nights when "pay" envelopes were distributed, each of my girls received an envelope with 50¢ in it. I, alas, got nothing! But I did enjoy being in the store and seeing customers who had become friends through the years.

DAVIDSON

Thomas Barton Davidson was born April 25, 1906, in Poteau, Indian Territory, now Oklahoma, the son of William and Nancy (McDaniel) Davidson. About 1917, the Davidson family moved to Terre Haute, Indiana. Tom worked in coal mines in Indiana and Illinois. On April 1, 1930, he married in Crown Point, Indiana, Nondus Clova Cain, (born Gibson County, Indiana, October 27, 1912), the daughter of Osro and Millie (Thompson) Cain, natives of Grant County, Indiana.

Tom and Nondus located in Grant County, Indiana, where Clova Joanne was born February 12, 1931. After moving to Terre Haute, Peggy Ann Davidson was born February 21, 1933. When the coal mines closed due to the Depression, the family returned to Grant County where Nondus' parents resided and two sons, Thomas Osro (1935-1937) and James Robert (1938) were born. They lived in Hanfield, then purchased a small farm at Cole Station, southwest of Marion. Tom worked at the Anaconda Wire Company in Marion.

The family moved in the spring of 1943 to Chester Township, purchasing the Kunkel farm south of Poneto. Tom obtained a threshing machine to harvest wheat and oats. He always had a team of draft horses and also operated a sawmill on the farm.

Tom farmed his own land and also rented many acres from Travisville to Jackson Township over the years. This was the era of the two bottom pull type plows, two row cornpickers, wire tied baler and WC Allis Chalmers tractors. The discs and harrows were loaded on flatbed wagons to be moved from farm to farm. The wheat and oats were cut with a binder, placed in shocks, and cured until the grain could be threshed. The draft horses were used for cultivation, pulling the bundle wagons for threshing, making hay, and other farm uses. Tom had no older son, so Peggy was his assistant during harvesting and planting season.

Nondus and Tom Davidson

Two more sons were born, Richard Eugene (1944) and William Joseph (1950). The children all graduated from Chester Center High School except Bill who graduated from Southern Wells after the consolidation.

Clova Joanne Davidson married Richard Wentz of Blackford County. They were the parents of four children: Nancy Wentz (Dayton, Ohio) married Carl Fish and had two children, Greg and Stephanie; Patricia Wentz (Corpus Christi, Texas) married Richard Line and Richard Dolan, has a daughter, Tricia Line; Tim Wentz (Marion, Indiana) married Cheri Rettig, has two children, David and Sarah Wentz; and Douglas Wentz lives in Corpus Christi, Texas.

Jim Davidson (Palm City, Florida) married Connie Ford, and had three children: Barton (deceased), Julie, and Frank. Dick Davidson (Fort Wayne) married Shirley Bowman and had four children: Steven, Michael, Jeremy and Jennifer. Bill Davidson married Pat Fuller, has a daughter Becky Davidson.

Tom Davidson, who died April 27, 1974, spent the remainder of his life on the farm south of Poneto and worked for the county highway department. Nondus was employed as a geriatric technician at Swiss Village, Berne, until her retirement, and she died in October, 1990.

DONALD EUGENE DAVIS

Donald Eugene Davis was born June 22, 1920, at his grandfather Francis Marion Buckner's home near Poneto, Indiana. He is a son of Arch Sherman and Dale (Buckner) Davis. Both parents were teachers in the public schools.

Arch Sherman Davis was born in Wells County, Indiana June 24, 1892, died March 8, 1933, and is buried in Elm Grove Cemetery, Bluffton, Indiana. He served his country during World War I as a field artillery man, Hattisburg, Mississippi. He was a son of Sherman Davis of Poneto, Indiana, whose father was Amos Davis. His mother was Martha Jane Yarger, born in Wells County, Indiana, 1871, died 1942, and buried in Grove Cemetery near Poneto, Indiana. Amos Davis came from Wales.

Martha Jane Yarger was one of ten children whose parents were James Yarger and, wife, Martha (Roberts) Yarger. James Yarger was a son of Josephus Yarger who resided near Nottingham, Wells County, Indiana, and is buried in Nottingham Cemetery. James Yarger served in the Army for the Union in the War Between the States.

Dale (Buckner) Davis was born September 21, 1895, at Poneto, Indiana. She was one of three children born to Frances Marion Buckner, born 1867 and died 1938, and Stella (Doster) Buckner, born 1868 and died 1931. Dale (Buckner) Davis died in 1961.

Francis Marion Buckner is descended from Captain Phillip Buckner, of Revolutionary War fame, and a long line of pioneers dating back to the 1500's at Oxford, England. His wife, Stella Doster, was a daughter of Hezakiah Doster and Serepta Tewksbury, daughter of Simeon Tewksbury, born October 2, 1846, married September 27, 1866. Hezakiah was born at Summerset, England on July 6, 1843, and died May 10, 1910. The Tewksbury family, it is said, came to America on the Mayflower around 1635. George Doster, 1816-1886, and wife, Jane (Hardwidge) Doster, 1824-1908, and five year old son, Hezakiah Doster were immigrants from Summerset, England to the United States in 1848. Word has been handed down through the family that they were on the water in a sailing ship for six weeks making the voyage.

Donald Eugene Davis has one sister, Frances Marion (Davis) Walsh of Poneto, Indiana. Francis has two children, Cami Walsh of Fort Wayne, Indiana and David Dale Walsh of Poneto, Indiana.

Donald Eugene Davis graduated from P. A. Allen High School, Bluffton, Indiana class of 1938. He married Martha Rose (Courtney) November 11, 1942. He engaged in farming and also began a life long pursuit of drilling for and producing oil and gas. This business he had successfully followed for the past 52 years, having drilled many wells in the Mid Continent area. He commenced drilling his first well when he was nineteen years old.

Mr. and Mrs. Davis have resided the past forty-nine years on a farm acquired by Mr. Davis's great-great-grandfather, George Doster, in 1870 located in section six of Nottingham Township, Wells County, Indiana.

They have two daughters, Gloria Ann Davis and Cynthia Jo Davis. Gloria Ann (Davis) Doehrman, wife of Merlin Doehrman, is the mother of two daughters, Sheryl Ann (Patterson) Roush and Suzanne Patterson, who resides in Indianapolis, Indiana and is a speech pathologist by profession.

Sheryl Ann (Patterson) Roush is married to Kevin Roush, and they have two daughters, Tiffany Suzanne, five and Heather Ann, three. They reside near Poneto, Indiana.

Cynthia Jo (Davis) Cassell is married to Robert Cassell and they have three daughters, Melissa Rose Hinshaw, thirteen, Courtnie Lin Holloway, ten, and Bobbi Jo Cassell, three. They reside near Larwill, Indiana.

DAVIS-JONES

Philip Jones, my great-grandfather, was born near Warren, Indiana in 1838. Later, moving to a farm north of Liberty Center, he married Sarah Ruble with at least eight known children born to this marriage. After the death of his first wife, he married Nellie (Harrold) Cunningham.

When Liberty Center was a thriving community, even boasting an opera house, Philip Jones owned the blacksmith shop. At one time, he was known as the strongest man in Wells County.

He died October 20, 1905. Arsenic poisoning was strongly suspected as cause of death, but, examination failed to discover any.

One of his sons, Charles, my grandfather, married Luvetha Davis. She was the daughter of Cuthbert Davis, who ran a grocery store in Liberty Center and also did plastering. My grandparents were farmers. They had seven living children: Everett, George, Ernest, Robert, Harold and Virginia.

My grandfather died July 3, 1954 and my grandmother died in August of 1963.

My father, the youngest son, was Harold (nicknamed Mike).

To his first marriage to Florence Barker were born to daughters, Dorothy and Roberta.

His second marriage was to Ruth Garrison of Lansing, Michigan, who is my mother. Five children were born: DiAnne, Linda, Michael, Philip and Sue. They, also, raised Dorothy and Roberta.

My father farmed most of his life. Later, he was custodian of the Liberty Center High School.

Mike and Beth (Atkinson) and Chris, Erin, and Theresa

My parents managed the Liberty Center Restaurant for several months. It came to be a "family affair", but, with both parents working at other jobs as well, they had to give it up. Gone were the french fries and onion rings for lunch!

The year of his death, 1969, at the age of fifty-three, my father was custodian at the Wells County Courthouse.

My mother worked at Wells Community Hospital for ten years; thirteen years at the Bluffton Animal Clinic and is presently employed part time at the Markle Medical Center in Markle.

Dorothy (Jones) (Thompson) Stolte had five children by Donald E. Thompson of Bluffton: Dwight, Denise, David, Dennis and Deidre. Two still reside in Bluffton: Denise, married to Harry Mosure, has three sons: Andy, Adam and Donald. Deidre, married to Pat McKeone has a son, Cory.

Roberta (Jones) (England) Grubbs had twin daughters by Russell England: Melody and Melinda.

DiAnne is married to Bill Wafford of Bluffton and has a 4-year old daughter, Ashley. DiAnne is an LPN at Markle Medical Center in Markle.

Linda, married Bill Bourne and lives in Bluffton. Linda worked several years as a director of nurses and is now with Bi-County Services.

Philip lives in Niles, Michigan with his wife, Jeanne (Kloko) and their two-year old twin boys, James and Jason.

Sue married John Hinkle of Chicago and lives in Romeoville, Illinois with their three-year old son, Shea.

Mike lives in Bluffton with his wife Beth (Atkinson-Feltt of Keystone) and three children: Chris, Erin and Theresa. Mike is employed as coordinator at the Markle Medical Center in Markle.

Other descendants of my great-grandfather still reside in Wells County.

LINDA LUCILLE ENGLE DAVIS

Linda was born January 29, 1949, at Lackland Airforce Base in San Antonio, Texas. She is the daughter of Guy Edward and Helen Marie Shorter Grumble Engle. Linda came to Wells County when she was six months old. She moved, with her parents, to the Engle farm just east of Reiffsburg. She began her schooling at Poplar Grove School south of Bluffton. Upon the divorce of her father and mother, she attended school in Bluffton. When her father remarried, Linda came to live with him and finished elementary school in Petroleum. Then she went to Indiana Academy, Cicero, Indiana, a Seventh-day Adventist boarding high school for one year. The next fall, Linda went to school at Ashland City, Tennessee, where her mother was now living. During that time her father and stepmother and family moved to Broadview Academy in LaFox, Illinois. Linda spent her final years of high school with them at Broadview and graduated from there in 1967.

Leland Davis, Linda Engle Davis

Linda enjoyed the South and entered college in the fall at Southern College at Collegedale, Tennessee, where she spent two year studying business. The next summer she obtained a job at Hinsdale Hospital in Hinsdale, Illinois and began work. Later she determined to return to Southern College for more education. There she met Leland Wray Davis of Jacksonville, Florida, and they were married October 24, 1972, in Wells County. Linda and her husband worked for Hinsdale Hospital in Hinsdale, Illinois, for a year, then decided to return to Florida, where Leland studied court reporting. They are now living in Douglasville, Georgia. Leland is employed by a court reporting firm in Atlanta. They have three children: Edward Merle, born July 13, 1980, in Orlando, Florida; Jason Leland, born March 4, 1982, in Orlando, Florida; Susan Marie, born October 25, 1988, in Douglasville, Georgia.

MARTHA ROSE COURTNEY DAVIS

Martha Rose (Courtney) Davis was born in Bluffton, Indiana, November 11, 1921, to Gondola (Mowery) Courtney and Harry Courtney. She lived in Bluffton until just before starting to school, then her parents and brother, Roger Wendell, born August 22, 1923, moved about a mile out of Bluffton. She went through all eight grades at Poplar Grove Elementary School. She lived in Bluffton, Indiana again before graduating from P. A. Allen High School.

After graduation she went to Warner Beauty College in Fort Wayne, Indiana, and was a beautician at two large department stores in Fort Wayne, Indiana until her marriage.

On November 11, 1942, she was married to Donald Eugene Davis in Marion, Indiana, by her great uncle, Reverend Wesley Kemper and moved to a two story brick house built by Donald's great-great-grandfather. The house had been unoccupied for some time and needed a lot of tender-loving-care.

During the 48 years Martha and Donald have lived there they had two daughters, five granddaughters, and two great-granddaughter, as described in the account of Donald Eugene Davis.

Martha's father, Harry Courtney, was born in Wells County, Indiana, June 10, 1897. For a time while growing up, Harry, his two brothers, and parents lived in Michigan. After he and Gondola were married in 1918, Harry worked for the Ohio Oil Company for 25 years, and ten years at Franklin Electric Company in Bluffton, Indiana.

Harry's mother was Minnie Alice (Kemper) Courtney, born in Hocking County, Ohio, to Durias and Sara (Nutter) Kemper on May 17, 1876. Minnie passed away July 2, 1966. She and her husband, Monroe, had three sons. Monroe was born march 8, 1873, to Seth and Margaret Courtney. He was a farmer and oil field worker. Monroe passed away December 17, 1938. Seth Courtney passed away September 30, 1875.

My maternal grandmother, Docia ann Brittenham, was born June 2, 1871, to Isaac Johnson Brittenham and Nancy Emily Dudley. Docia Ann married Charles Gilbert Mowery in 1892. Charles was the son of David and Melinda Miller Mowery, born in Pendelton County, West Virginia, on August 12, 1869.

Isaac J. Brittenham was born in Ross County, Ohio, February 2, 1838 to David and Margaret Carmean Brittenham. He was a soldier and a member of Company K63D Regiment, Ohio Volunteer Infantry. Isaac later was engaged as a farmer and stock raiser in Wells County, Indiana. He married Nancy Emily Dudley, daughter of John and Docia Clevenger Dudley in Randolph County, Indiana in 1867.

RICK DAVIS

Rick was born in Bluffton, Indiana, October 15, 1989, to George and Julie (Flowers) Davis. Dawn was born March 25, 1959, at the Wells County Hospital in Bluffton to Robert and K. Jean (Platt) Gleim. They were married May 3, 1980, at the Markle Church of Christ. Rick attended Bluffton High School. Dawn graduated from Norwell High and attended Ivy Tech in Fort Wayne. Rick is employed at D. L. Frick and Son pallet repair in Zanesville, Indiana, and he is also employed at Richard's Restaurant in Bluffton. Dawn is employed at Caylor Nickel Medical Center in Bluffton. She has been employed there thirteen years as of this writing February 1991. Their home is west of Uniondale, Indiana on the Gleim property.

Dawn was a Girl Scout in Wells County Rockcreek Township for eleven years. She helped with the Klondike Derby one year in Fort Wayne, Indiana during her scouting years.

DAVIS-SCHWARTZ

My father's families were from Germany.

The Davis family moved to Indiana from Tennessee and settled in Wells County in 1837. My great grandfather, Leander Davis, was two years old when they settled in the then wilderness on the present site of Murray among the first six families.

Leander married Mrs. Mary Eichhorn in 1874, and they had four children. Mrs. Eichhorn had three children from an earlier marriage. They bought a farm two miles northeast of Markle. My grandfather, Orve, was born in 1883.

The Schwartz family settled in Rockcreek Township in 1852. My great, great grandparents, Jacob Farling and Elizabeth Crum, came from Pennsylvania. Jacob Farling's father, Abraham, was from Wittenberg, Germany, and fought in the American Revolutionary War. Jacob was born in 1822 and married in 1846. Jacob had nine children. A daughter Harriet married Levi Schwartz in 1867. Levi Schwartz was a farmer and owned a saw-mill in Murray. A daughter of Levi was Effie, born in 1886.

Orve Davis and Effie Schwartz were married in January, 1907. They lived on the Davis farm northeast of Markle. Orve died in 1952, and Effie moved to Bluffton where she died in 1966. Three sons were born in this marriage. Ray, 1907, was a lawyer who worked for the government and is retired and living in Santa Rosa, California. George, 1915, was a lawyer in Bluffton and is deceased. Robert, 1917, was an insurance agent and is deceased. Robert was my father. He married Hazel Rivers from Rockcreek Township and I was their only child. I was born in 1941. My parents also moved to Bluffton in 1952.

I graduated from Bluffton High School and then married Clyde Maggard who was from Liberty Township. We live in Lancaster Township. Clyde is employed by the K-Mart Corporation and has been involved with little league baseball many years. We have two children, Kathy born in 1960 and Kent born in 1963. Kathy graduated from Ball State University, is married and lives in Xalapa, Veracruz, Mexico. She and her husband, Adrian Carballo, have four children, Steffany, Clyo, Adriana, and Alan. Our son, Kent, graduated from Purdue University. Following graduation from college Kent played professional baseball in the Cleveland Indian's organization. Kent married Lynn Wright from Warsaw, and they live in Fort Wayne where he is employed at Fort Wayne National Bank.

My hobbies are traveling and singing. I was in the Wells County Choral Club many years. I sing in a ladies trio called "Harmony". I am a member of Sweet Adelines chorus "Towns of Harmony" of Harmony International, Incorporated. (*Judy Ann Davis Maggard*)

MATTHEW FOWLER DAVIS

Matthew Davis was the first of ten sons of Joseph Davis and Rachel Fowler. The story (not documented) is told that her father floated down the Ohio River to the Little Miami River on the second flatboat to navigate that river. He settled in the place where Cincinnati now stands and was a founder of that city. Matthew was born around 1808. It is believed that his first wife's name was Ruheme Vail. According to the 1850 census, he had a young wife named Lucy who was born in Kentucky. His children were: Mark, born in Ohio in 1830; Rachel, born in Clermont County, Ohio in 1838; Rebecca, born in Ohio in 1840; Mary, born in Ohio in 1842; Elizabeth, born in Indiana in 1844; Sarah, born in Indiana in 1846; Joel, born in Indiana in 1848.

Joseph Davis (this could have been Matthew's father or his brother, the third son of Joseph) homesteaded Southwest 1/2 of Southwest 1/4 Section 29 Township 27-N Range 11-E and Southeast 1/2 of Southeast 1/4 Section 30 Township 27-N Range 11-E in 1837. Six years later in 1837, Joseph sold this property to Matthew Davis. In 1849 Matthew Davis, along with Solomon Johnson, platted the town of Rockford from property owned by both men.

Matthew sold eighty acres in 1865 to Esther Johnson, wife of Jonas Johnson, which property eventually became owned by Francis Shull, whose wife, Ruth, was a granddaughter of Jonas and Esther. Matthew sold forty acres in 1867 which eventually became the property of Glessner Johnson and then Francis Shull. The whereabouts of Matthew Davis following this time are not known.

Two of Matthew's daughter married Nathan Johnson, son of Solomon Johnson.

Rachel married Nathan November 19, 1886. They had two sons: William Henry born January 7, 1857-died January 16, 1933, married Mary Alice Butler; James Louis born 1858-died 1925, married Mary S. Redding.

Sarah Davis married Nathan Johnson January 19, 1861. They had four children: Rebecca, Charles born October 27, 1866, John, and Jefferson.

VERLIN AND BARBARA (ECKELBARGER) DAVISON

Our earliest history of the Davison family dates back to Verlin's great-great-grandfather, Moses Davison (1804-1880), and his wife, Elizabeth. They had thirteen children and were living in Lancaster County, Pennsylvania. In 1844 they traveled to Miami County, Peru, Indiana, and lived there four years. In 1848 they relocated on a farm in east Jefferson Township of Wells County. Verlin's parents were Furl and Amy (Davis) Davison.

Amy was the daughter of Isaac and Lola (Jennings) Davis. There were twelve children in this family. They lived 1/2 mile north and a mile or so east of Ossian; I understand this is where Davis Road got its name.

Verlin's father was a farmer living in Jefferson and Lancaster townships. Verlin attended Lancaster High School.

The Eckelbarger family came from Germany in the early 1800's and to Wabash County, Indiana, in the 1840's. My grandparents were Charles and Minnie (Draper) Eckelbarger. My parents were Lawrence and Mary (Carter) Eckelbarger.

The Carters journeyed from new England, clearing the land and building homes. They moved into Grant County in the 1830's. My mother told me my ancestors were German, Dutch, Scotch, and Irish, and our forefathers were farmer, carpenters, bootleggers, teachers, and preachers.

We lived in Huntington and Grant Counties before moving to Wells County in 1935. We lived in Union Township, 3/4 miles east of the Prospect Methodist Church and 1/4 mile south. I graduated from Union County High School.

Verlin and Barbara Davison

Verlin and I were married on June 24, 1945, at the Wesleyan Church in Uniondale by the Reverend Floyd Titus. Verlin loved farming but in due time went to work at General Electric in Fort Wayne, retiring in 1985. During these years I worked away from home, the longest time being in the office at General Electric.

We are enjoying our grandchildren and traveling. Verlin likes gardening, and my hobbies are sewing, quilting, shopping and singing in the sanctuary choir.

We have six children:

Stephen married Nancy Johnson, and they are living in Ocala, Florida. He is a minister of the Gospel and has been serving at the Calvary Baptist Church for the past sixteen years.

Rebecca married Jerry Foreman of Decatur. She is a mother and homemaker and lives in Uniondale.

Mary Lynn married James Welch; she is a mother, homemaker, and a Wal-Mart employee. She lives in Decatur.

Dennis married Denise Eggert and they live in Lakeland, Florida. He is a piano technician and is the minister of music at the Heritage Baptist Church.

Chris married Toni Morris of Poneto, where they live nearby and he is employed by the Northern Wells School.

Milissa (Carney), and daughter Dannielle, live in Bluffton.

We have fourteen grandchildren, one step-granddaughter, and one great-grandson. We are members of the First Church of the Nazarene in Bluffton. We honor God, love our country, and display our flag proudly. It's been great living in Wells County. *Submitted by Barbara Davison*

DAWSON-BROWN FAMILY

Cyrus and Amelia (Pritchard) Dawson were my great-grandparents living in Morgan County, West Virginia (near Berkeley Springs), when my grandfather, Henry Markwood Dawson was born November 20, 1839.

At the age of 29, grandfather was courting a young maiden named Mary McIntire, a daughter of Harrison and Catherine McIntire. In the Spring of 1868, the family along with a sister, Dorcas, and a brother, William, and his wife Mary Ann, pulled stakes and headed west. Grandfather came with them as driver of the covered wagon. It is interesting to note the living arrangement the two families used before leaving. All family members lived in one brother's house during summer, then switched to the other brother's house in the wintertime.

They settled and bought land adjoining that of their brothers Nun and Dick who had migrated earlier. Grandfather also bought land nearby and married his sweetheart in June, 1868. Sometime later, William and his son-in-law, R. A. Kilander, purchased Harrison's interest which was one hundred-seventy acres. Harrison lent money privately.

My father was one of six children born of this union. He was named Harrison McIntire Dawson, apparently due to close ties with the in-laws. However, father used the nickname, Mack, throughout life. He married Corina Mae Brown and they reared fourteen children (one died a day after birth).

Grandfather died at age eighty-five, Grandmother at age ninety-two, Father at seventy-two and Mother at sixty. Ten children survive and all are over sixty years old. Mabel is the eldest at eighty-eight, followed by Faye, Floyd, Harvey, Glen, Charles, James Ray, Dale, Allison and Gene. Earl, Iva, Fern and Mary are deceased. James married Jacqueline Marie-Louise (Regnier) a French war bride and they reared four sons; William, Philip, Gary and Bruce.

A cousin has traced the maternal side of my family tree to a clan living in Denmark, never having known to be conquered. At the height of England's dominion over much of the world, the King made an unusual request to the King of Denmark. He wanted a regiment of Danish soldiers for His Majesty's Royal Guard. The Danish monarch considered it an honor and dutifully set about searching for a select unit.

"Mack" second from right, father of James Dawson, with a group of champion horseshoe players. 1920's

The regiment chosen had a crest in the form of a crescent in their coat of arms. Their service record was exemplary and they were greatly admired. When their term of service ended, they agreed to emigrate to England. The King thereupon offered them a land grant in exchange for services rendered. There was a unanimous vote for the English name "Moon" and was thus used in the deed.

William Penn emigrated colonies to the "new world" in 1682 and established the Moon's in Bucks County, Pennsylvania. Deeds of land were issued to John and Jasper Moon by William Penn. It was also noted that our ancestors were undoubtedly Quakers.

The clan later split, some going west and into New York state. Others opted to head south, to Virginia, thence to North Carolina, to Tennessee, finally settling in Clark township, Clinton, County, Ohio. Here, these ingenious settlers found their niche. They became cabinet makers, shoemakers, harness-saddlers, hatters, chairmakers, brick and stonemasons, lock and gunsmiths and worked in copper. Residents in Ohio and Indiana have in their possession gusn manufactured by William and Jesse Moon.

In the Spring of 1808, Daniel and Joseph Moon, along with their families, came to a site near Martinsville, Ohio. The following autumn, Samuel and John Moon and John Routh (a brother-in-law) with their families, settled in the Moon community. A daughter of Joseph Moon, Jane, had married John Routh and they reared five sons and eight daughters. A daughter, Charlotte, married John Brown whose parents were Elisha and Polly Alexander (daughter of James Alexander).

Four children were born of this union. Daniel Routh Brown, the youngest, married Sarah Emily Haynie, the parents of my mother, Corina Mae Dawson.

CHARLES DAY FAMILY

Charles Edward Day was born May 14, 1913, in the house his parents had built on a hill above the Mossburg Creek that circled around below and behind it in Liberty Township, about a mile from where his great-grandparents, the Reverend Henry and Jane Thrailkill Mossburg, had pioneered in 1837. Charles was the youngest of the three boys born to William Henry and Minnie Floretta Buckner Day. His oldest brother, Frank, was born November 15, 1902, and his brother, Paul, born on February 25, 1908, died when seventeen months old.

W. H. and Floretta Day

Charles' playmates were the Forest Prible children, who lived on a farm across the road. Since there were seven of them, there was never time to be lonely. They were cousins, as Forest and Charles' mother were first cousins. They all attended the school a quarter of a mile west in the little town of Bly where on each corner the Liberty Union Christian Church (sometimes called the Bly Christian Church), a store, a blacksmith shop, and the Bly School stood.

Charles and Birdena Day

Charles' father, William Henry Day, was the son of Ambro and Ethalinda Mossburg Day, who lived a half mile north of Bly. Ethalinda (1836-1915) had arrived in Wells County in 1837. Her father, the Reverend Henry Mossburg, born in Maryland (1777-1838) and his wife, Jane Thrailkill (1790-1871) were the second family to settle in Liberty Township, having come from Ohio to Indiana. They had twelve children, eight living and four deceased. The two oldest boys, Daniel who was eighteen, and Henry Jr., fifteen, had come ahead and built the log cabin for the family. Henry Sr. was in poor health and died of consumption the following year. He was buried on his land west of his home, and this became the Mossburg Cemetery where many of the pioneer families and their present-day descendents are now buried.

Ambro Day (1827-1900) with three brothers and a sister arrived in Indiana in 1850 from North Carolina. He and Ethalinda were married in 1859. They had two children, Nancy (1860-1930) and William Henry (1873-1959). Remembering the spiritual heritage of her father, Ethalinda had prayed to have a son, and she dedicated this child to the Lord before he was born. He became a Baptist minister and pastored the Poneto Baptist Church for fifteen years and the Pleasant Mills Baptist Church for thirty-four years. Before he owned a car, in order to get to Bluffton and Pleasant Mills, he would take the interurban and stay over the weekend in order to preach there.

William Day

Charles' mother, Minnie Floretta Buckner (1879-1978), was the only child of John and Lurana Prible Buckner. She grew up on their farm about a half mile east of Bly. John Buckner (1852-1933) was the oldest of nine children of William (1827-1851) and Amelia Margaret Yelton Buckner (1831-1916), who moved from Kentucky in 1855 to Wells County.

In Virginia, William Buckner's grandfather, Philip Buckner (1747-1820), had engaged in commerce with England, home of his ancestors. He held the position of Commissary in the Revolutionary War and used his private fortune in the cause of Virginia, paying for supplies for the army from his own means. After the war he was reimbursed with large grants of land in Kentucky and Ohio. He took his family and a group of settlers form Virginia with him and established the town of Augusta, Kentucky, in 1793, where he raised his family of nine children. His wife was Tabitha Ann Daniel (1756-1838), daughter of Captain William and Elizabeth Daniel of Port Royal, Virginia. Their son, Thomas (1796-1833), who married Matilda Hanson, were the parents of William Buckner, Floretta's grandfather.

Kent and Pam Day, Lindsey, Kevin and Mitch

Charles' grandmother, Lurana Prible Buckner (1858-1911), was the second child of John Jeptha (1832-1923), and Marian Becker Prible (1836-1909). John Jeptha's parents, Enoch Morgan (1807-1840), and Lydia York Pribble (1811-1903) came to Indiana in 1836, from Preble County, Ohio, when John Jeptha was four years old. (Members of the Prible family did not always spell their names the same way.)

Three of John Jeptha Prible's six children had been born when he enlisted in Company A, 13

went to work for the Ross Gear Division of T.R.W. Cindy is a registered nurse, and they have two children, Erica and Heather. In January, 1991, Mark's job as Principal Engineer required the family to move to Greenville, Tennessee.

Mark's maternal grandparents are Marvin and Helen (Hoppenhofer) Uhl of Fort Wayne. Marvin Uhl was raised most of his life in a home of Runion Avenue. Although Marvin's mother died when he was in his teenaged years, the family of three boys and three girls and their father, Edward J. Uhl, seemed to have a happy home, although there was never an abundance of money available to them. The family was quite musically oriented and would frequently have friends gather for a "musical" either during lunch hours or in the evening.

On April 21, 1932, Marvin married Helen Hoppenhofer, and the two of them raised their family of three children in Fort Wayne (Mary E. Day, Betty L. Barry and Edward J. Uhl). Marvin was a tailor and pattern maker and worked most of his working years at the Fort Wayne Tailoring Company. Marvin was very talented, musically, and could play any song he had ever heard on either his Hohner button accordion or his harmonica without the use of music. Their two daughters were encouraged to take music lessons and it turned out to be quite an admiration society. Marvin envied the girls' ability to read music and the girls envied Marvin's ability to play without music. Marvin provided the music at the wedding receptions of two of his grandsons - Mark and Mike Day.

Marvin died at the age of seventy on Good Friday in the year 1980. He is buried in Lindenwood Cemetery, Fort Wayne.

(See related articles under Melvin Day, Michael Day, Matthew Day, Mitchell Day, Frederick Day, and Albert Shadle.)

MARVIN DAY FAMILY

Marvin L. Day (1929-) was the only child of the 1923 marriage of Frank Day and Carrie Gordon Day.

Frank Day (1902-) was the oldest son of Henry (1873-1959) and Floretta Day (1879-1978). Carrie Gordon (1901-1989) was a daughter of John Oliver Gordon (1874-1954) and Dessie Thompson (1875-1969). She had a brother, Clarence Gordon, who married Beth Garrett. John "Ol" Gordon was a Rockcreek Township grain farmer and cattle man. He was one of the first in this area to own a gasoline powered farm tractor.

Carrie Gordon was a graduate of Liberty Center High School. She received training at Tri-State University which enabled her to teach in one-room school houses at Raber and Rockford in Wells County. She later attended Manchester College and Ball State University. Carrie finished her teaching career at Poplar Grove in Wells County in the early 1950's. She was a member of Daughters of American Revolution, Wells County Historical Society, and First United Methodist Church.

Marvin Day graduated from Bluffton High School in 1947. He then served in the United States Navy during the Korean Conflict aboard the U.S.S. Hooper Island. He was employed by Panhandle Eastern Pipeline Company in Bluffton for thirty years. Marvin is a member of Bluffton Lodge 145 F & AM, Scottish Rite, Mizpah Temple of Fort Wayne and Bluffton American Legion Post III.

In 1952, he married Betty Bayless (1930-) daughter of Kenneth and Mary Bayless. Betty is a 1948 Bluffton High School graduate. She is a member of Eastern Star, Psi Iota Xi Sorority and First United Church of Christ.

Marvin and Betty were born in Bluffton and have always resided there. In 1965, they moved to their present home at 425 Wayne Street where the mailbox for several years read "The Seven Days".

Marvin and Betty are the parents of five children. Susan (1952-) is a 1971 graduate of Bluffton High School and Purdue University. She currently lives in Lafayette, Indiana where she teaches and coaches at Tecumseh Middle School. Sally (1954-) is a 1973 Bluffton High School graduate and also a graduate of Purdue. She currently works and lives in Indianapolis. Sarah (1956-) graduated from Bluffton High School in 1974 and Ball State University. Sarah married David Seligman of Wilmington, Delaware in 1980. They have one son, Daniel Day (1986-). Sarah and her family live in Zionsville, Indiana where Sarah teaches. Scott (1957-) is a 1976 Bluffton High School graduate and a graduate of Ball State. In 1978, Scott married Pandora Squires of Bluffton. They live in Sturgis, Michigan with their two daughters, Jana (1978-) and Jill (1982-). Scott is company controller for Vanguard Industries in Colon, Michigan. Steve (1960-) is a 1978 Bluffton High School graduate and Purdue alumnus. Steve lives in Bluffton and works as a salesman for a Fort Wayne Company.

Refer to the Frank Day Family. Refer to the Kenneth Bayless Family.

MATTHEW LYNN AND MARCIA (MAST) DAY

Matthew L. Day is the third son of Melvin and Mary Day. Matt was born in Fort Wayne and attended Village Woods Elementary and Junior High School where he was active in Boy Scout Troop #306. Matt attained the Eagle rank in 1972 when he was thirteen years old. He attended high school at Paul Harding and was in the first class to go through all four years and graduate from Harding High School. After graduation, Matt began working at Magnavox as a photographer. He also had his own photography business - doing weddings and family group portraits. His hobby became his vocation and his avocation. Matt is presently the Video Sections Supervisor at Magnavox. He has an Associate Degree in Communications from Purdue University.

Matt married Marcia Mast (daughter of James and Barbara Mast of Fort Wayne) after Marcia's graduation from Indiana University School of Nursing. Marcia is presently employed by Lincoln National Life Insurance Company in Fort Wayne.

Edward J. Uhl approximately 1910 with his mandolin.

Matt and Marcia purchased nineteen acres of land on County Road 1100 just about one mile east of Zanesville where they built their home in 1991. Matt is an excellent wood craftsman, and has built many cabinets and much furniture for their new home, as well as the wood work. Some of the pieces are made from oak and cherry trees cut down when Matt's parents built their home. They have one daughter, Melanie Elisabeth.

Matt's great-grandparents were Edward J. and Dorothy (Blair) Uhl. E. J. and Dorothy were married on June 1, 1904, and they supported a growing family by running a grocery store in Venedocia, Ohio, owned by E. J. and his brother, Henry. After some years in the grocery business, Ed took a job with the Nickle Plate Railroad. The railroad job took the family to Pennfield, Michigan; Argos, Indiana; and finally to Fort Wayne. As a young man, E. J. learned to play the mandolin while Dorothy accompanied him on the "pump" organ. Many of their children were also musically inclined. Several of the children worked at the Knitting Mills which was only a few blocks from their home. Often co-workers would join family members for lunch or an evening of music. Ed left the railroad and worked for Allied Mills until his retirement. Allied Mills was also walking distance from the family home on Runion Avenue. Dorothy died in 1931, Ed in 1958. They are both buried in Venedocia, Ohio.

Dorothy (Blair) Uhl and her children always remembered Dorothy's mother and step-father with great fondness. They lived in an eight-sided house in Michigan which had been built as a dance hall and had a large open area on the second floor where dances had once been held. They also remembered Grandma Reese for her clay pipe, for huge family dinners containing home-made cottage cheese and ice cream, home-grown melons, dried corn, and honey from their own bee hives.

(See related articles under Melvin Day, Mark Day, Michael Day, Mitchell Day, Albert Shadle, and Frederick Day.)

MELVIN DEAN AND MARY ELLEN (UHL) DAY

In June of 1989, Melvin and Mary Day moved into their home just south of the County Line Road on 400 West (approximately one mile west of Zanesville). This move brought Mel back to the county in which his family has lived for many generations, dating back to 1850. Melvin is the son of Fred and Cecil (Shadle) Day. Although born in Kansas City, Missouri, Melvin and his mother returned to Wells County when he was approximately five years old due to the unexpected death of his father, Fred. After graduation form Allen High School in 1949, Mel enlisted in the army and served as a paratrooper in the 82nd Army Airborne. Upon discharge from the army, Mel went to work at General Electric Supply Company in Fort Wayne, where he met and later married Mary E. Uhl.

Mary, daughter of Marvin E. and Helen (Koppenhofer) Uhl, was born and raised in Fort Wayne. She graduated from South Side High School in 1953, took a thirty-five year break to raise her family, and graduated with a B. S. degree from Indiana Institute of Technology in 1991.

Melvin and Mary raised four sons (Mark, Michael, Matthew, and Mitchell) while living in the Anthony Wayne Village addition in Fort Wayne and in a home on the Old Decatur Road just outside of Fort Wayne. Mel is presently enjoying an early retirement from General Electric Company. Mary is the Manager of Benefits and Administration at Slater Steels.

One set of Melvins' great-great-great-grandparents, Philip and Mary (McGlade) Shadle, came to Chester Township in Wells County in 1847 where he farmed one hundred-ten acres of land. The following year, their son and daughter-in-law, Philip and Margaret (Donelly) Shadle, also moved to Wells County from Pennsylvania. Philip and Margaret raised a family of fifteen children and were among the organizers of the United Presbyterian Church at Warren, Indiana. Margaret preceded Philip in death in 1917 at the age of eighty-eight; Philip died at the age of ninety-three in 1919. Both are buried in Snow Cemetery.

Melvin and Mary Day taken in 1984

William Abner Shadle, the third son of Philip and Margaret, was born September 29, 1852. He married Hannah (Penrod) Shadle on October 12, 1871. Early in their marriage, William and Hannah and Jim and Elizabeth Brotherton (Hannah's sister and brother-in-law) decided to take their young families and homestead in Kansas. They traveled in a covered wagon to Kansas and began establishing their homesteads. One of the Brotherton children was bitten by a rattlesnake and died as a result of the bit. This death discouraged both couples; they packed their belongings and returned to Wells County where they spent the rest of their lives. William was a farmer and they raised their family of seven children on their 100-acre farm.

At the age of 55, William decided to retire from active farming. Even though his health was good, he sat and watched while his son (Albert) and grandson (Homer) farmed his one hundred acres. Hannah died in 1931 at the age of seventy-eight; William died in 1933 at the age of eighty-one. They are both buried in Woodlawn Cemetery in Montpelier, Indiana.

(See related articles under Albert Shadle, Frederick Day, Mark Day, Michael Day, Matthew Day, and Mitchell Day.)

MICHAEL EUGENE AND SHARON "SHERRY" (MERRYMAN) DAY

Michael E. Day is the second son of Melvin and Mary Day. Mike attended Village Woods Elementary and Junior High Schools and was active in Boy Scout Troop #306, attaining his Eagle Rank when fourteen years old. Mike was active in the band in Junior and Senior High School. He started high school at New Haven and was in the first class to graduate from Paul Harding High School.

Shortly after graduation from high school, Mike married Sharon "Sherry" Merryman (daughter of George Merryman of Fort Wayne and Kathleen Cardin of Yoder, Indiana). Sherry is a graduate of South Side High School and is presently an optician in the office of Dr. Scott Miller. Mike and Sherry have two daughters, Julie and Jennifer, who attend Norwell Jr./Sr. High School.

Mike has an Accounting Degree from Indiana University and is the Vice President of Finance at Midwest America Credit Union in Fort Wayne. The family moved to Wells County in July, 1990; they live on the County Line Road (1200 North) about a mile east of Zanesville. Mike is a Notary and a Tax Consultant.

Helen E. Uhl - taken at Christmas, 1990 at the home of Melvin/Mary Day

Mike's maternal grandmother is Helen (Koppenhofer) Uhl of Fort Wayne. Helen was one of the younger children in the family of seven children of John and Mary (Miller) Koppenhofer of Holgate, Ohio. after leaving high school, Helen made up her mind she was going to move away from the farm and go the the "big city." She debated between Toledo and Fort Wayne, deciding on Fort Wayne. She immediately found work at the Dudlo Plant (magnet wire manufacturing company) upon her arrival; but she had to return to Ohio after a short time as her parents had promised a neighbor that Helen would help them when their baby was born. After completing her obligation at home, Helen returned to Fort Wayne, this time bringing her youngest sister with her. The two girls applied for work at the Dudlo plant and both got jobs after Helen promised she would not quit work to return to Ohio again. The two lived in an apartment house that face McCormick Park and they walked to work each day. While two sisters moving away from their family home and into an apartment may not be a particularly unusual situation in this day and age, it was very adventurous thing to do in the 1920's.

Helen met and fell in love with Marvin Uhl. They were married on April 21, 1932, and raised their family of two daughter and one son in Fort Wayne. Their daughters are Betty Barry and Mary Day, their son is Edward Uhl. Although Helen knew how to drive before she was married, she did not drive after her marriage, always using public transportation or walking wherever she wanted to go. As a result of exceptionally good health and the regular exercise, Helen is an active, cheerful, delightful grandmother to six boys and great-grandmother to seven girls. She is still independent and active at eighty-nine years of age.

(See related articles under Melvin Day, Mark Day, Matthew Day, Mitchell Day, Frederick Day, and Albert Shadle.)

MITCHELL DEAN AND KAREN (MAUK) DAY

Mitchell, the youngest son of Melvin and Mary Day, was born on January 1, 1965. He was educated at Village Woods Elementary and Junior High Schools. Like his three older brothers, Mitchell also attained his Eagle Rank in Boy Scouts, Troop #353. The family moved to a home on the Old Decatur Road just outside of Fort Wayne in 1979,

and Mitchell graduated from Heritage High School. He attended Rose Hulman Institute of Technology in Terre Haute, Indiana, graduating in 1987 with a Chemical Engineering degree. After graduation, Mitchell was hired by Linde Division of Union Carbine Corporation. He was assigned to a Chicago location for a short period and then went to Bettendorf, Iowa for several years.

Mitchell married Karen Mauk (daughter of William and Rachel Mauk of Terre Haute) in 1989; they presently reside in West Bloomfield, Michigan, just outside of Detroit where Mitchell is the General Motors Corporate Account Representative for Linde Division. Karen, a registered nurse, works at Providence Hospital, Southfield, Michigan

John and Mary Koppenhofer

Mitchell's heritage is predominantly German. His grandmother's parents were John and Mary (Miller) Koppenhofer who lived in Henry County, Ohio. Both of them had been born in the United States, but both families had come from Germany. Mary's family settled in Virginia where her father had a small gold mine. Although the ore from the mine was not of the best quality, it was enough to support the growing family until the time of the Civil War. Not wanting to be involved in the war, the family left their gold mine and headed for Ohio. They made their home in Defiance County and that is where Mary was born.

Mary married John Koppenhofer when she was seventeen years old (1888) and they raised their family of seven children on a farm in Henry County, Ohio. Of course, as the practice at that time, all of the children were expected to help on the farm - the boys working in the fields and the girls helping with cooking and housework, only going to the fields to help during harvest if needed. John died in 1930 of cancer. Mary shared her home with one of the married daughters for several years. After that, Mary began visiting each of her children for a portion of the year. She made regular rounds and usually spent half of each year in Ohio with the families of Alf, Ed, Laurie Imbrock, and Elnora Cours. The second half of the year was spent in Fort Wayne with the families of Hanna Hockemeyer and Helen Uhl (the two youngest daughters). Memories of "Grandma" and her visits to Fort Wayne include her cooking potato dumplings, fried noodles, and sweetened rice. She loved to dip soda crackers into her coffee. Sometimes she would butter the crackers and sprinkle them with sugar before dunking them in the coffee. Grandma Koppenhofer died in 1953 in Fort Wayne, Indiana.

(See related articles under Melvin Day, Mark Day, Michael Day, Matthew Day, Frederick Day and Albert Shadle.)

EARL AND NELLIE DEAM

Earl and Nellie Deam were both born and raised in Wells County and lived here all their lives.

He was a farmer as well as a carpenter. He devoted much of his life to his church, agricultural, community service, and political government affairs. He was honored with the Community Service Award in 1972.

Nellie was a homemaker and was very active in church and civic matters. She was president of the Wells County Homemakers Extension Club 1949. She was a member of the County Choral Club. She played the piano for the Methodist Church in Reiffsburg.

They were both active members of the Historical Society and Farm Bureau. He helped relocate the log cabin to the 4H grounds. He was on the Wells County Selective Service Board. At his death on April 16, 1974, he was on the Harrison Township Advisory Board and previously had been a deputy county assessor. Each had their own special projects but their main concern was their love and devotion for each other and their children.

Earl's grandfather, John Deam, married Katherine McCance; three children were born to this union, but their father died very young, making it difficult for Kate to raise her family alone. Therefore she "let out" the boys to a Mr. Myers to keep until they were twenty-one. She married a Mr. Wells and moved to Fort Wayne, taking her daughter Harriet with her. One brother, Orland, died, but John Milton continued to live with Mr. Myers until he was twenty-one, as agreed by his mother.

John attended the Reiffsburg Church and it was there he met the very popular Mary Etta King, whom he courted and married on August 13, 1888. They raised four children: Rollie, Clara, Clarence, and Earl, my father. Earl help farm his father's farm, and I can remember spending many happy hours visiting them there. Grandma always had sugar cookies in the cupboard or bread butter and brown sugar for us to take home "in a poke."

Earl finished grade school and continued studying at the Bluffton Business College. He took a job at a meat market in Bluffton until the lure of the outdoors was too much for him. Back to the farm he went, working for Charlie Chalfant for $18.00 per month.

Earl attended Sunday school at Reiffsburg Church, and it was there that he caught the eye of a beautiful young lady, Nellis Beaty, who happened to be visiting her sister, Grace Dunwiddie. After a short courtship they were married in Poneto on April 14, 1909.

Earl purchased a farm five miles south of Bluffton and continued to raise his family. It was this farm that Arlue, Erma, James, Earl Jr., and Betty would call "the home place." We attended grade school and high school from here. We were a happy family and enjoyed sharing good times with each other. The family circle has been broken up in the past few years, but we stay in touch and have a family reunion annually. (Arlue Whitlock)

OPAL DAVIS DEAN

I am Opal Davis Dean, a 1926 graduate of the Liberty Center, Indiana, High School. My first seven years of school was spent attending the Roberts School, two miles west of Liberty Center. I was alone in the seventh grade when the school closed. I had two sisters, Edith (deceased) and Estalene Clark, who also attended Roberts School. Our father was Emery Davis, a farmer.

We attended Boehmer Methodist Church, on the Wells-Huntington County line, of which I am still a member, and I am very happy to say I attended

Roberts School 1921; Murial Boltin - teacher; Opal Davis - 2nd from left

Easter Sunday service with a grandson in 1991. *(Opal Davis Dean)*

VIRGIL A. DE ARMOND

Virgil a De Armond (born January 19, 1897, died September 17, 1957) was the son of James William and Lulu May (Walton) De Armond. He and his brother Iowa were raised mostly by their grandparents, Abe and Mary (Myers) Walton in Warren, Indiana. In 1918 Virgil enlisted in the army and served in France during World War I. He was in the 136 Field Artillery Division. He was discharged in April, 1919.

On September 14, 1920, Virgil wed Meryl Wilson (born April 23, 1898, died February 12, 1952). She was the daughter of Curtiss P. and Mary (Romine) Wilson of Pennville, Indiana.

In 1922 Virgil and Meryl moved to Bluffton, Indiana seeking work. He worked at the Red Cross Foundry, as a janitor at the Farmers and Merchants Bank, for WPA during the Depression and at Fruehauf Trailer Company in Fort Wayne. Although they moved several times during this time, four of their five children were born on West Cherry Street. The five children are as follows:

Virgil and Meryl De Armond

Wanda (De Armond) Tarr (born October 6, 1921) married Floyd Tarr (born July 13, 1916, died Mary 30, 1984) son of Daniel N. and Rosie (Jones) Tarr. Wanda currently resides in rural Wells County. Wanda and Floyd had five children: Dave Tarr of Bluffton, Gloria (Tarr) Kilmer of Marion, Don Tarr (Deceased), Elaine (Tarr) Tobias of Nebraska and John Tarr of Berne. Wanda has four grandchildren, Daniel M., Jessica, Jadriana Tarr and Nicholaus Tobias.

Rosamond (De Armond) Johnson (born July 25, 1923) was married to Richard W. Johnson (born April 18, 1922, died May 8, 1960) son of George A. and Gertrude Johnson. Rose currently resides outside of Ossian. Rose has two children, Tom of Phoenix, Arizona, and Mike of rural Ossian. There are seven grandchildren: Cheryl, Richard, Janelle, Christina, Shannon, Chad and Craig. Also there are two great-grandchildren: Tyson and Caley McBride.

Robert E. De Armond (born September 21, 1928) married Doris Hunnicutt, daughter of Jesse and Hazel (Edgar) Hunnicutt. They currently reside in Bluffton on West Cherry Street. They have three sons; Robert Jr., of rural Celina, Ohio, James, of Fort Wayne, and William, of Fort Myers, Florida. They have five grandchildren: Laura, Mara, Ross, Nicole and Rio De Armond.

Dick A. De Armond (born February 12, 1932) married Beverly Marshall. They have three children: Judy, Diane and Rick De Armond. They have six grandchildren: Tyson, Trina, Shannon, Tommy, Loring and Tricia.

Charles L. De Armond (born February 16, 1936) married Emma Faye Holloway, daughter of Ivan W. and Erma L. (Emley) Holloway. Charles and Faye live on West Cherry Street in Bluffton. They have three children: Randy De Armond, of Bluffton, Teresa Wagner, of Grand Rapids, Michigan, and Steve De Armond, of Ossian. They have two grandchildren: Amanda and Jared De Armond.

Although times were often tough, especially during the Depression, with hard work and perseverance the De Armond family has grown and prospered.

ALEXANDER RUBLE DE BOLT

Alexander Ruble De Bolt, born July 23, 1879 was the second son of George and Barbara Ellen (Ball) De Bolt of Decatur, Adams County, Indiana.

Alex De Bolt and his wife Esther Della (Robison) De Bolt, born January 31, 1878, moved to Vera Cruz, Wells County, about 1901. This move from Decatur, Adams County, was prompted so that Mrs. De Bolt could be near her father, John Robison, who had moved to Vera Cruz, having retired from farming in Adams County. Alex was a barber so he set up a shop in Vera Cruz, and barbered there for many years. There were six children born to the De Bolts. The first three, Marie, Guy and Vera, died at an early age. Following the death of the first three, Virgie, Elmer and Luther were born. They attended the local public school in Vera Cruz. When the children were old enough to attend high school the De Bolts were prompted to make a move, as Vera Cruz did not have a high school, and transportation to Bluffton could not be arranged. There were no school buses at that time.

Alexander R. De Bolt

In 1922, Alex closed his barber shop and sold his property in Vera Cruz, and moved to Ossian, where his children went to high school. Alex was employed at the Evin Hoover Barber Shop. He later bought the barber shop and the building and continued to barber until 1934, he then sold the building to Heyerlys who used it to expand their bakery business.

Alex then bought a farm southeast of Vera Cruz along State Road #116, where he resided until his death in 1935. Mrs De Bolt returned to Ossian where she remained until her death in 1937.

ELMER LLOYD DE BOLT

Elmer was born February 23, 1909, in Vera Cruz, Harrison Township, Wells County, Indiana. He was the second surviving child of Alexander R. and E. Della (Robison) De Bolt. Elmer's father was the local barber in the village of Vera Cruz.

Elmer was educated through the seventh grade at the local public school in Vera Cruz. The family then moved to Ossian, Indiana, where he completed high school, graduating the class of 1927. During the summer vacation between his junior and senior years at Ossian High School, Elmer volunteered for Citizen's Military Training at Fort Benjamin Harrison, near Indianapolis, Indiana. This experience improved his health and stamina. He won a marksman medal for the use of the Army rifle and an honorable discharge. Following high school he served as an apprentice barber under his father and became a licensed barber in 1933.

Elmer Lloyd De Bolt

In the meantime Elmer also started to work at the General Electric Company in Fort Wayne, Indiana. He completed necessary courses to qualify him for everything from production foreman, quality control engineer, and personnel and labor relations managerial positions. Elmer continued to work at General Electric until his retirement in 1971, after 42 years. He also barbered on a part time basis during this period of time.

After retiring from General Electric he enrolled at Indiana University, Fort Wayne Campus, taking the prescribed Business Course in Real Estate. Having passed the course and receiving his certificate, he passed the Indiana State exam and received his license to sell real estate in Indiana.

On a more personal basis, Elmer and Ruby I. Greek (born March 17, 1908) were married on July 23, 1930. To this union three children were born, Norma Jean (De Bolt) Ploughe, Carolyn Joan (De Bolt) Yager, and Larry Wayne De Bolt. They lived in Yoder, Allen County Indiana and Ossian, Wells County, Indiana, during their married life. The marriage of Elmer and Ruby was terminated by divorce in 1961.

Elmer was married again in 1963 to Anna L. (Betty Lash) Froebe. Anna (or Betty, as her friends called her) died of cancer in 1974. Elmer married again in 1975 to Goldia M. (Neuenschwander) DeLong and resided in Poe, Allen County, until Goldia's death by cancer in 1990.

Elmer is a United Methodist Christian, and member of Gideon's International. He is a past Master of the Ossian Masonic Lodge #297, and 32° Scottish Rite Mason in Fort Wayne, Indiana. He is also a past Patron of Emeral Chapter, Order of the Eastern Star. He was Scout Master for the Ossian boy Scout Troop in the early 1930's. Elmer now lives at 115 E. La Fever Street, Ossian, Indiana 46777.

DECKER-ROMEY

Davilla Nelson Decker and Della May Romey were both Wells County school teachers. They went to Valparaiso University for part of their training. They were married in 1910 and lived on a farm in Rockcreek Township. They had four children: Ivan, Dwight, Anna and a son that died soon after birth. There are fifteen grandchildren.

Michael Decker came to America in 1753 from Germany. He settled in Berks County, Pennsylvania. His eldest son, John Jacob Decker, was born in 1756. He served in the Army of the Revolution and took part in the battles of Brandywine, Germantown and Monmouth. He was at Valley Forge and was then discharged in December 1779.

This is the "First" Charles W. Decker in his tire and automotive shop then situated in Marie's Gifts location, way back in 1921.

John Jacob Decker first married Eva Barbara Zehring. One of their children was Christian who was born January 30, 1794. He was the ancestor of Davilla Nelson. Eva Barbara died soon after his birth of Christian, so Jacob married the sister of Eva Barbara, Catharine Zehring. They had several children and among them was Jonathan, born in 1808 who is the ancestor of some of the Deckers in Wells County.

Christian Decker married Anna Maria Albert, and one of their children was Isaac, born in 1819. In 1845 Isaac married Elizabeth Houser and a son, Edward, was born July 19, 1846. He married Rebecca Houtz, and they had nine children: Ella (Hoover), Davilla Nelson, George, Charles, John, Rufus, Otto, Jesse, and Orpha (Joray).

John Romey was born September 4, 1854 in Wayne County, Ohio. His parents Theophil and Anna (Musser) Romey, came to America from Switzerland. They went to Mt. Eaton, Ohio and later bought a small farm near Eaton where they lived until their deaths, which occurred within a year of each other.

Anna Widmer was born November 23, 1859 at Mulligen, Switzerland. The family came to America and settled in Eastern Ohio. Here she met John Romey, and they were married and had Della and Andrew. They moved to Indiana to a farm in Nottingham Township. Here Elma (Strahm), Grover, Reuben, Rosella (Davenport-Striker), and Clyde were born. After farming for many years they moved to Linn Grove. John Romey died in 1937 and Anna in 1951.

IVAN AND ELIZABETH BAILEY DECKER FAMILY

Ivan Decker was born in Rockcreek Township, November 21, 1912. His parents were Davilla Nelson Decker and Della Romey. Both were school teachers.

Anna Elizabeth Bailey Decker was born September 19, 1913, in Liberty Township, to John Bailey and Lydia Myrl Gilbert. Grandpa Bailey was a farmer, and Grandma Bailey was a paper hanger, and known for delicious baked goods.

Ivan and Elizabeth were graduated from Rockcreek in 1930 and 1931, respectively, and were residents of Rockcreek Township. Their home was a mile north of Rockford. They were married June 25, 1938, at St. Mark's Lutheran Church in Uniondale. They had eight children.

Jayne (1939) graduated from Rockcreek and Ball State. She is married to Dale Sullivan. They teach and live in Logansport, and have three daughters: Diann (Mrs. Thomas) Metz, who teaches in Logansport; Julie, a student at Indiana University of Kokomo; and Jennifer, a Caston High School Senior.

Joyce (1941) is a 1959 graduate of Rockcreek. She also attended Heidelburg College. Joyce is the Engrossing Clerk of the Ohio House of Representatives, and lives in Columbus, Ohio. She's been active in the Democratic Party.

Back (L-R) Ed, Myrl Jean, Betsy, Jayne, and Joyce; Front (L-R) Ivan R. Decker, Carol, Elizabeth, Phillip and Ivan J.

Mary Elizabeth (1943) graduated from Bluffton High School and attended Ball State. She lives in Columbus, Ohio, and works for the Ohio State Highway Patrol. She has three children: Nancy (Mrs. Steve) Wise lives in Florida; Elizabeth Ann (Mrs. Homayoun Honormandian) lives in California; and Richard Borne is a student at Purdue while living in Fort Wayne.

Edward (1944), who lives near Eaton, graduated from Rockcreek and Indiana Barber College. Ed is married to Christine Suzanne Chaney. They have four children. Cheri (Mrs. Garrett) Hamilton, has two children, Erin and Lucas, and lives near Montpelier. Tami, a Purdue graduate, works in Indianapolis. Clint and his wife, Jackie, are Ball State graduates, and live in Muncie. Dustin is a Purdue student. Ed and his family show "Spots" at Swine Shows and State Fairs.

Myrl Jean (1947) hold degrees from Bluffton, Ball State, St. Francis, and Illinois State. She's an administrator of special education service in Kewannee, Illinois, where she resides. She is a collector of Holstein cow and pig memorabilia.

Ivan Junior (1950) graduated from Huntington. He resides in Fort Wayne and works for General Telephone. He and his wife, Barbara, have three school age children: Cathy, Christopher, and

Michael. Ivan enjoys camping and canoeing in northern Minnesota.

Carol (1952) graduated from Huntington. She resides in Columbus, Ohio, where she is a member of the Carpenters' Union. Being a carpenter, she has worked on many interesting buildings and bridges.

Philip (1958) graduated from Huntington and Purdue. His degree is in Agricultural Mechanization. He's a Huntington County resident who works for Precision Soya in Rockcreek Township.

All the Decker kids showed cattle and swine at the 4-H Fairs. Ivan and Elizabeth, as farmers, were active in the Farm Bureau. He enjoyed showing "Spots" pigs, and Shorthorn and Holstein cattle, at the Street Fair. She was a member of Home Demonstration clubs. Both were members of the United Church of Christ, in Bluffton, and also attended St. Paul's Lutheran Church in Rockcreek Township. Ivan and Elizabeth were Historical Society members, and Ivan spent many of his retirement years working with genealogy. Elizabeth worked at Clinic Dietary for 17 years before retiring in 1979. Ivan worked 12 years at Corning before retiring in 1977.

DECKER-MCAFEE

Edward Decker was born 1846 and died 1916 at age seventy. He was a farmer in Rockcreek Township. His father was Isaac Decker, formerly from Montgomery, Ohio. His wife was Elizabeth. Edward married Rebecca (Houtz) Decker, born 1851, the daughter of John Houtz. She died in 1912, age sixty-nine. Their marriage in 1869 gave them nine children. They resided on the family farm in Rockcreek Township that was his father Isaac's farm. Children were Ella Decker (Hoover); D. Nelson Decker; George E. Decker; Charles W. Decker, who married Lillian McAfee; John F. Decker; Rufus L. Decker; Otto Decker; Jesse Decker; and Orpha Decker (Joray). Edward and Rebecca are buried in Emmanuel Cemetery near Rockford, Indiana.

Charles W. Decker was born 1877. He received his education in the county schools and the Valparaiso Normal School. He taught three years in the schools of Rockcreek Township. His marriage to Lillian M. McAfee August 13, 1899, took place in Bluffton. Lillian was the daughter of Mr. and Mrs. John McAfee, prominent farmer of Rockcreek Township. She was born in 1879. Three children were born in the Decker family: Verdi Decker (Ullman), Ruth Decker (French), and Charles Decker, Jr. Charles Decker, Sr. was a teacher, county surveyor, circuit court bailiff, city councilman, and business man. The Decker Overland Company was started in 1934, 112 North Main.

Mr. Decker died at age 62, 1939. Mrs. Decker died in 1964. They are buried at Elm Grove Cemetery, Bluffton, Indiana.

Charles W. Decker, born 1915, received his education at Bluffton High School. There he met and married Jean Crum, who was born in 1915. Charles W. Decker III was born in 1942. Mr. Decker continued to operate the Deck's Super Service Station, founded in 1934 by his father, Charles, Sr. Charles, Jr. was a business man, city councilman, Bluffton mayor, fire chief, executive secretary of chamber of commerce. He passed away in 1989 and is buried at Elm Grove Cemetery, Bluffton, Indiana. His wife Jean survives. A son, Charles (Skeet) Decker, married Rebecca Monroe, born 1943. They have two children, Kelli Decker, born 1964, and Charles W. Decker IV, born 1967.

Skeet Decker continues to operate the family business on N. Main Street, which has give fifty-seven years in service to the community.

Refer to John McAfee Sr. history.

DE HAVEN

Nathaniel and Jane DeHaven came to Bluffton from Summit County, Ohio, with their small family in 1854. He operated a shingle and lath factory in Bluffton.

Among his children were Margaret who married Dr. C. T. Melsheimer. They later moved to Elnora, Indiana where they spent the rest of the lives.

Nancy married William Woods. They had one son, Edward. They all spent their lives in a small house located on the corner where the Community Building now stands.

Nathaniel was a blacksmith and later an oil-well driller in Pennsylvania and Montana. He was Wells County's sheriff from 1861-1865. He left for Pennsylvania soon after his term ended. He was the father of the well known artist Frank Carter DeHaven, who was the father of the actress Gloria DeHaven.

Walter Brown DeHaven was one of the children born in Summit County, Ohio on May 38, 1843. Watt, as he was commonly known, fitted himself for work as a steam engineer, meanwhile working as head sawyer at the McDowell Lumber Company. In 1886 when the city of Bluffton erected the first municipal pumping station, Watt was chosen to have charge of the plant. His son, Lew, was appointed assistant. Watt continued with the waterworks and assumed general supervision of the electric lighting plant, when that was installed, until his retirement in 1911. He died in 1912.

Backrow (L to R) Winnie Elwell Ayres, Lois De Haven Shire, George Alshouse, Jacob Ayres, Water Shire; Front (L to R) Franklyn Shire, Letta De Haven Alshouse and Helen Alshouse

He married Dorothy Plessinger in 1864. They had four children.

Lew, married Minnie Leist. Lew became superintendent of the Electric and Water Plant when Watt retired in 1911. He later went to Fort Wayne State School where he was an engineer. They had two children, Frank and Bess.

Lon (Benjamin Loren) who married "Tot" (Mary) Kapp had one daughter, Katherine, who taught in the Bluffton Schools. After Lon's death in 1920, Tot and Katherine moved to Muncie and later to California.

Roy, played the cornet and was in several musical groups in Bluffton and the area. He soon joined a dog and pony show as a musician and went on to join Ringling Brothers Circus, which later combine with Barnum and Baily as a member of the Parade Band and also became manager of the Reserved Seat Ticket Sellers.

Letta, Married George Alshouse, a farmer in Rockcreek Township and had one daughter, Helen.

Dorothy Plessinger DeHaven died a couple years after Letta's birth.

Watt then married Mrs. Lavina Elwell, who had a daughter, Winnie, who married Jacob Ayres and moved to Greentown.

Watt and Lavina had five children.

Lois married Walter Shire, who was a baker at the old Star Bakery on West Market Street. They moved to Plainwell, then Watervliet, Michigan where they had a five and ten cent stores. They had two boys, Franklyn (Sam) who was a pianist and did a lot of playing in the Bluffton area, then after graduating from P.A. Allen High, he was a musician and artist in Kalamazoo, Michigan. Robert, who graduated from Watervliet, became a men's clothing store manager.

Robert DeHaven died in 1895.

Clark also worked at the Light Plant before going to General Electric in Fort Wayne. He married Emma Schaefer and had three children, Walter B., Ruth, and Dorothy.

Lenna worked in Cook's Grocery, around the corner on Johnson Street, until she married Gus Stahl. They had two children, Merriel and John. Both died as children.

George married Margaret Evans before serving in World War I. He worked in the office of H. C. Arnold and Son before opening his own coal yard on West Washington Street. He spent his entire life in Bluffton.

DEHAVEN-ALSHOUSE-GINGERICK

Jacob and Sarah Ditzler Alshouse and infant son Frank left Crawford County, Ohio, coming to Indiana in 1865. They settleed in Rockcreek Township, Wells County. Jacob ran a sawmill with his brother-in-law, George Ditzler, to get money to but some land and build a log cabin, where three children, Etta, George, and Rosa were born.

They built a large new house in 1881. To get the trim for the house Jacob went to the McDowell Sawmill in Bluffton where Walter (Watt) DeHaven was the head sawyer.

They became active in the Horeb Lutheran Church, which had been established in 1859 on the banks of the Wabash west of the Cover bridge.

The children attended the Haiflich School, which was located at the south edge of their farm.

Frank married Dicy Lesh and had two sons, Ross and Floyd. He was a partner of Robert Fox in a Hardware in Markle before his death in 1902.

Etta married Daniel W. Lesh and had two children, Joseph and Eulalia. They lived on the Lesh home farm across the Cover bridge on the south side of the Wabash.

Rosa studied music at Taylor University, then taught piano until her marriage to Sylvester Lesh. They had two daughters, Maxine and Ruth.

George received a diploma from Indianapolis Business College and attended Marion Normal School. He taught for two years at the Iron Bridge School on the Rockcreek Center Road.

George became interested in a Bluffton girl, LeEtta (Letta) DeHaven, a daughter of Watt DeHaven, who had left McDowells to become the first superintendent of the Bluffton Water Works, a position he held until his death in 1912.

George and Letta were married December 3, 1902, and on Watt's first visit to their home, he saw

317

his pattern decorating the large front porch. Jacob and Sarah retired and with Rosa moved to a large house on the hill in Markle and George assumed the farming.

They had two daughters who died at birth. Finally I, Helen, came. I went to Haiflich School, too, then to Markle for eighth grade and my freshman year while Rockcreek was being built. Following graduation, I finished a two-year course at Ball State and taught at Rockcreek and Bluffton before I was married to Donald Gingerick in 1935.

Donald's father, William had a foundry in Akron, Indiana, until he had a light stroke and retired. They moved to Wells County shortly before their oldest son, C. Marvin, M.D. opened offices in Liberty Center and Uniondale.

We lived in Union Township three years. Barbara Ann was born during that time. Donald was helping my father farm so we built a house on the Alshouse farm. Soon John Donald was born.

When Donald left, Barbara and John were Rockcreek students. I taught at Liberty Center eleven years. Then I went to Ossian and finally West Rockcreek and West Union for a total of thirty-seven years teaching.

George died in 1951. Letta, Barbara, John and I kept on farming with help from Tommy Morrisey. Letta died in 1965.

When Barbara graduated, she went to beauty school, then married Raymond Bolinger, who grew up near Waynedale. Ray took over the farming. They had eleven children. The oldest, Gene, and his family now live in "The house that Jake built."

When John graduated he went to Purdue, and served twenty-three years in the Air Force and Air Guard before becoming a State bank examiner in Illinois. John also has three daughters: Adair, who graduated from Augustana, then married Gregory Hunt and now lives in Appleton, Wisconsin and teaches autistic children; Audrey, who graduated from St. Olaf's and is now living and working in Minneapolis; and Erin, who is still in grade school in Springfield, Illinois.

DEIHL

William J. Deihl, our grandfather, whose ancestors came from somewhere in Germany, settled in Adams County and later moved to Craigville, Indiana, where he opened a lunch room and meat market in 1892. He met and married Rosa Tucker, who came from Tell City, Indiana. They had four children, Frank, Velma, Roy and Carrie. Frank, our father, took over the store after his father's death in 1917. After World War I, when Roy came home from the war, Frank and Roy purchased the store and all of the related businesses from their mother.

The businesses, besides running the store, were shearing sheep, buying and selling of wild game pelts and cow hides, butchering of cows and hogs, dressing all kinds of poultry for express rail shipment to Cleveland, Buffalo and New York City during the holiday seasons. In addition, our father owned and operated a theater featuring silent movies, medicine shows and vaudeville.

The Deihl's were among the first, in Craigville, to have a Delco Light electrical system, pressure water system and walk-in refrigeration. They also had a meat huckster serving the country side. The meat was transported in a home made ice box. The remaining space on the truck was devoted to live poultry which they purchased from local farmers. Frank bought Roy's part of the business in 1935. Our father was also the postmaster of Craigville for 21 years until his death in 1941.

Louise and Max Deihl, Betty and Robert Deihl

Frank married Marie Cotterly in 1917. She was the daughter of John Cotterly, who owned and operated a grocery and general store across the street from Deihl's. Our Grandfather Cotterly came from Bern, Switzerland as a child. Of this marriage there were three sons - Robert, Max and Dwight. Dwight died in 1937 while a small child. Our mother died in 1980.

Robert and Max both attended the Craigville Grade School and Lancaster High School. Robert married Betty Miller of Bluffton in 1940 and they have two children, Rebecca, of Massapequa Park, New York, and Michael, of Juneau, Alaska. Robert's working career was in aircraft, space and related electronics. During this time he lived in Michigan, Tennessee, Texas, and New York until retirement in 1981 in Bluffton. Max married Betty's sister, Louise Miller in 1942 and they have one son, William, of Richmond, Virginia. Max's working career started in Michigan in aircraft. After a short period he returned to Bluffton and began work at Zollner Piston of Fort Wayne. In 1982 he retired from Zollner's with 40 years of service to the company.

FRANCIS AND AMANDA DENNEY

Francis Denney was the son of Walter and Nancy Denney. The family immigrated to the United States from Ireland. Eventually, they settled in Union Township, Wells County. Frank, as he was called, Married Amanda Bell. They had six children. Ellis was the oldest. Next was a daughter, Golda, followed by another daughter, Myrtle. The came twins, Grover Cleveland and Laura, named for President Cleveland and his wife. The youngest was Gertrude.

Frank Denney said he could save money better if he was in debt, so when he would have forty acres of land paid for, he would buy another. He was able to give each of his children forty acres of bare land as a wedding gift.

One of the first automobiles in the community was an Overland belonging to Frank. He took the car to the pasture field behind the barn to learn to drive it. Neighbors didn't understand why anyone would want one of those "contraptions" and said, "Frank Denney has taken leave of his senses."

According to my mother, Amanda Bell Denney was a tiny woman and a meticulous housekeeper. She was very strict with her family, especially her daughters, allowing them to see only young men who met with her approval.

Frank and Amanda are buried in the Haverstock Cemetery at Zanesville. They, and many others like them, have contributed much toward making Wells County one of the best in the state.

GROVER AND VESTA DENNEY

Grover Cleveland Denney and was a son of Francis Denney and Amanda Bell. Vesta was the daughter of John Sands and Lucinda Mygrant. They lived on a farm on the west side of Union Township, Wells County. When they were married, Grover's family gave them forty acres. Grover bought another forty and they set about to have trees cut and the lumber sawed for the house and barn.

Grover and Vesta were the parents of three children. Argend, the oldest, married Aline Eichhorn. They had three children, Harold Dean, Colleen Denney Martin and Diane Denney Norris. Marybeth (Betty) married Luke Martin. Their children were Mona Lee Martin Talbert, Sharon Martin Lee, Duan, twins Dyrl and Byrl, and Jerolyn Martin Ozment. Joyle, the youngest, married Ralph Wilson. Their children were Sunya Wilson Sipe, Larry, and Denney.

Grover was a farmer and Vesta a housewife. They were active members of the United Brethren Church in Zanesville. Vesta was a good cook and always fixed extra for Sunday. If the preacher hadn't been invited anywhere for Sunday dinner, she knew Grover would invite the preacher and family to have dinner with them.

Grover served as trustee of Union Township for several years. At the time of his death, he was a salesman for an office supply firm. Grover and Vesta are buried in the Haverstock Cemetery at Zanesville. (Sunya Wilson Sipe)

AARON DERR FAMILY

Aaron Landis Derr was born in Wells County, Rockcreek Township, April 17, 1865. His parents were Joseph and Catherine Scott Derr. Joseph Derr was born in Pennsylvania, March 17, 1836. He moved to Crawford County, Ohio when he was a boy. Then moved to Indiana and Wells County in 1863. His first wife Catherine Scott died in 1879. There was ten children born to this union. Then in 1885 he was married to Sarah Connett. Joseph was a highly respected and active member of the Methodist Church in Markle. He lived on Lee Street in Markle, after moving from the Derr Homestead in Rockcreek Township.

Aaron Derr married Bertha Alice Haiflich on December 24, 1890. Bertha was born February 16, 1886 to Joseph and Parentha (Beal) Haiflich. Aaron and Bertha lived on the Derr Homestead, which is now the Dale Krinn Homestead. Aaron was a farmer.

To this marriage four daughters were born. Cressie was born in 1892 and died at the age of 28, she never married. Rela Key was born in 1894. She married Clarence McAfee in 1920. They had one son, Clarence Jr., born February 15, 1925. Hallie Faye was born in 1898. She married Wilfred Brown in 1923. They had one son Doyle, who was born July 5, 1924. Grace was born November 2, 1900. She married Clarence Platt November 24, 1920. They had five children (refer to Clarence Platt family).

The Derr girls all went to the one room Haiflich School which was about a half a mile from there home on old 303. Aaron Derr moved from the Homestead in 1914 to the present home of Grace Platt, corner of 303 and 224. He died March 19, 1950. His wife Bertha died October 17, 1946.

DEVOE-BEEKS

The Chester Township farm where I reside with my husband, Charles DeVoe, dates back to December 21, 1841, when it was homesteaded by my great-grandfather, Daniel Sills, Sr. (1804-1873). Daniel Sills, Sr. was married to Mary Blackford and they had ten children, one being Daniel Sills, Jr., my grandfather (1843-1919). My grandfather married Mary Dick, and they had fourteen children, one of whom was my mother, Mary Catherine (Katy, 1890-1956). As a child she attended Five Points School. She married Floyd Beeks, a Blackford County native, on June 26, 1919. They were married soon after he was discharged from the service after army service during World War I. Until their deaths, they lived on the same land that was homesteaded by my great-grandfather.

The two-story home we live in was built in 1880, and it was preceded by a log house. The outside structure remains the same, but changes to the inside room arrangements have been made. The farm is now recognized by the State of Indiana as a Hoosier Homestead Farm for being owned by the same family for over a hundred years. And that family tradition shall continue.

I have one brother, Daniel C. Beeks, born March 24, 1924, and we jointly own the farm. Daniel graduated from Chester Center High School. After being honorably discharged from the peace-time army due to the death of our father, he worked fourteen years at Indiana Box in Montpelier and then became a familiar and helpful face at Chaney Hardware (also in Montpelier) where he worked for twenty-six years. He is now retired and resides in Montpelier with his wife Sylvia, whom he married in 1968.

Upon graduating from Chester Center High School, I worked at Montgomery Ward in Hartford City. I married Charles DeVoe, then a Delaware County resident, in 1947. Charles is a Selma High School graduate and served in World War II; he received the Purple Heart and was honorably discharged. He retired from Warner Gear (now Borg Warner) in Muncie after forty-one years of work and continues to farm on a small scale. Charles and I are active member of the First Baptist Church in Montpelier where we attend regularly. Charles assists in a number of capacities, and I have served as organist over forty years.

We have two sons: Dean Alan, born April 5, 1950, and David Allan, born January 3, 1968. Dean graduated from Southern Wells High School in 1968 and attended Purdue University. A member of the Glee Club at Purdue,, Dean had the opportunity to travel abroad with this vocal organization, including trips to Europe and Hawaii. He married Jane Cleefman of Reynolds in 1972; she is also a Purdue graduate. Dean is General Manager of the Elkhart County Farm Bureau Co-op, and Jane teaches at Middlebury Elementary School. Residing in Goshen, they have two children, Dena Suzanne, seventeen, and Scott Allan, fifteen.

David graduated from Southern Wells in 1986 and from Purdue University in 1990. Throughout high school and college, he excelled in cross country and track. While at Purdue, he was named to the 1988 Academic All-Big-Ten Cross Country Team. On May 20, 1990, he married Lora Jo Geisman, a graduate of Norwell High School and of the Wayne Beauty School of Cosmetology in Fort Wayne. They currently reside near Markle. David is employed by the Huntington County Farm Bureau Co-op as a crops specialist, and Lora is a cosmetologist at Hair Junction in Bluffton. *Submitted by Martha Beeks DeVoe*

DEVORE

My grandfather, Ross DeVore, was born on December 12, 1857, in Hardin County, Ohio. In 1860, when he was two years old, his parents, Lewis and Rachel (McNutt) DeVore, moved to Rockcreek Township, Huntington County. Ross was one of eight children.

My great-grandfather, Lewis DeVore, enlisted and served in the Civil War until its end, returning to his Huntington County home.

Ross attended school until he was thirteen and then began to take care of himself, hiring out to farmers in the vicinity and give faithful service although his wage was small. He came to Wells County on April 13, 1889, to work for David Studabaker. On October 4, 1894, he married Sarah Studabaker, David's daughter. They had two sons, Homer and Robert.

My father, Homer, was born on January 21, 1896. He was a 1915 graduate of Bluffton High School. He attended Purdue University for one year and then returned home to farm.

My mother, Mildred Steiner, was born on October 21, 1897, in Adams County. She was a 1916 graduate of Bluffton High School as there was no fourth year at her high school.

My father and she were married October 21, 1919. She was an elementary school teacher for three years prior to her marriage. They lived on a farm adjoining the old Psi Iote Pool. In 1923 they moved to a farm at the junction of 116 and Harrison Road.

Homer and Mildred had two children: Ruth, who was married to Dale Luginbill, now deceased; and Glen, who married Marilyn Jo Kurtz from Pioneer, Ohio. They now live in Saline, Michigan. They had two children, Beth and David, and a granddaughter Amanda.

Our mother died on June 1, 1935, and our father died on June 25, 1954.

Ruth was a school cook for twenty-four years with the Bluffton Harrison Metropolitan School District, retiring in 1987.

All of the DeVore family were members of the Six Mile Church.

Dale and Ruth had four children, all graduates of Bluffton High School.

Judy has a Bachelor's and Master's Degree in Elementary Education from Ball State. She resides in Houston, Texas, and is married to Ray Roberson. They have five children, Elise, Ryan, Christopher, Leanne, and Timothy.

Carol has a Bachelor's Degree in Education from Taylor University. Currently she is librarian for four elementary schools in the Eastbrook District, Upland, Indiana, where they reside. She is married to Joe Romine and has two children, Kelli and Kyle.

Philip, after attending Taylor University and IPFW has a Bachelor's Degree in Economics from the University of Wisconsin-Eau Claire. He was the last man drafted from Wells County for the Vietnam War. He served two years in the army. Currently he's Vice-President of the combined business Rockton Lumber and Home Lumber of Rockford. He is married to Susan Farb and they have four children, Megan, Seth, Kiersten, and Peter. They reside in Rockton, Illinois.

Mark has a Bachelor's Degree in Aviation Mechanics from Purdue and a Master's in Business Administration from the Emery Riddle School of Aeronautics. He currently resides in Miami, Florida, where he's customer service supervisor for Airbus. He is married to Catherine Malan and they have a daughter, Lesley. *Submitted by Ruth DeVore Luginbill*

DICK FAMILY

The Dick Family has its early origins in Blackford County, mostly Washington Township near Roll. James I. Dick, the second son of Lawrence H. and Mona Irene Dick, was born in 1944. He was a member of the last graduating class of Roll High School. In the same year Glennis (Slusher) Dick was born at home in Jackson Township, Wells County, the second child of Glen L. and Violet (Banter) Slusher. The Slusher family roots are all in Jackson Township, where Glennis graduated from Jackson High School.

James Dick Family 1989

Jim and Glennis were married at the McNatt United Methodist Church in 1964 and lived most of their married life on a mini-farm on the Blackford/Wells County line in Jackson Township. Jim has spent his professional career in the field of electricity/electronics and is presently the senior resident engineer with Minnesota Mining and Manufacturing company in Hartford City. Glennis is a high school teacher and vocational coordinator at southern Wells High School.

Two sons were born to this marriage: Gregory Scott Dick, born in 1968, is a graduate of Southern Wells High School and Indiana University/Bloomington with a history degree. Christopher James Dick, born in 1970, is a graduate of Southern Wells High School and is in his third year of environmental engineering at Purdue University/West Lafayette.

PEGGY D. DICK

Peggy Davidson Dick was born in Vigo County, Indiana, on February 21, 1933, a daughter of Thomas and Nondus (Cain) Davidson (see entry for Davidson). The family moved to Grant County, Indiana, where Peggy attended the Radley one-room grade school. In 1943, they moved to Chester Township, Wells County. It was quite a change from a one-room grade school of thirty pupils to a large twelve-grade school of approximately two hundred students. After graduation from high school, Peggy pursued further studies in nursing at the Fort Wayne Methodist Hospital School of Nursing.

Edward and Peggy Dick Family; (L to R) Kara, Yvonne, Eric, Erin, Peggy, Ed, Bruce, Brian, Elizabeth, and Lori

On August 28, 1954, while employed at the Clinic Hospital in Bluffton, she married Edward Dick, the son of Albert Virgil (Andrews) Dick of Adams County, Indiana. In 1955 they moved to Monroe and Peggy was employed by a physician in Berne. Ed was farming and employed at the International Harvester in Fort Wayne. In 1956 they built a new home in Monroe, which they later exchanged for a farm in Washington Township.

Edward Dick (1927) graduated from Kirkland High School and served four years in the air force, spending three years Germany during the Berlin Air Lift. He is a retired air traffic controller, having worked for the Federal Aviation Administration at Baer Field, Fort Wayne.

Peggy and Ed Dick are the parents of four children: Eric Dick (1956) is employed by Pace Arrow, Decatur, and married Yvonne Brubaker, a nurse at the Clinic Hospital; they have two children, Erin Renee and Kara Sue. Brian Dick (1958) is a graduate of Indiana University in computer science, lives in Providence, Rhode Island, and is married to Elizabeth Sheridan, a primary school teacher. Bruce Dick (1960) lives at home and is engaged in farming and has a hog operation. Lori Dick (1963) graduated from Indiana University and Roosevelt University, Chicago, is a paralegal in Indianapolis, and attends the Indiana University School of Law.

Peggy worked many years as a registered nurse at the Clinic and Adams County hospitals, in a physician's office, and as an Adams County hospitals, in a physician's office, and as an Adams Central School nurse. She is now active in family history research and volunteer work, compiling records to place in libraries for the benefit of family researchers. She has also compiled and published family histories and records. She is a member of the Indiana Historical Society, Indiana Society of Pioneers, Indiana Genealogical Society and state registrar for the Women Descendants of Ancient and Honorable Artillery Company of Massachusetts.

The family is now living on a farm in Washington Township, Adams County, Indiana.

DICKASON

John Dickason (1806-1891) and Nancy Stanley Dickason (1806-1881) lived in Nottingham Township. Their children were: George Franklin, who married Caroline Hendershell; Jacob E. (1835-1920), who married Barbara Susanne Ifer; Angelina, who married George Priest; and Susan who married David Gill.

Jacob E. Dickason married Barbara Susanne Ifer in 1857, their large family consisted of: William H. who married Hettie Bell Dye; John F. (1860-1942), who first married Minnie Turner and then Lydia Elizabeth Schneider; George S; Walter P. who married Minerva (?); Naamon who married Maud Turner; Jacob, who married Mary E. Beckler; and Francis Marion whose first marriage was to Inez (?), and whose second marriage was to Evelyn Bergdoll; infant; Warren, who married Anna Lavenia Lambert; Samuel; who first married Cora Kizer and later married Hazel McCleery; Cyrus, who married Hattie Anne Lamber; Fitastus "Ora," who married Bessy (?); and Rosa who married William Clark.

Through John F. Dickason's marriage to Minnie Turner, a daughter, Rosa Elizabeth, was born. This marriage ended in divorce in 1891, and John was awarded custody of Rosa, who later married Henry Florey.

In 1894, John F. Dickason married Lydia Elizabeth Schneider (1865-1939). He was a farmer and a carpenter as well. He built their house, which featured a lovely wood stairway, hardwood floors, and built-in kitchen cabinets (a rarity for that time period). Their family: Susanah Barbara (1895-1899); Hazel Marie (1897-1975), who married Sanford Bunch. Their children were: Marguerite; Ardelia, who married Ed Thiesing; Elizabeth; Oscar, who married Martha Altsinger; Ruth, who married Donald Ingols; John, who married Adele Czerwin; Gene, who married Mable (?); Joe, who married Elda Mae (?); the third child of John and Lydia was Mable May (1898), who first married Thomas Bell and then Bert Cowman. Her children were Junior Thomas Dickason (1915-1986) married Doris King (Their children: Oscar Gene married Carol Cone; Nancy married John McCarthy; Sally married Robert Reyonds; Linda married Lawrence Walker) and Lois; the Fourth child of John and Lydia was Bonnie Lucille (1901-1975) married Donald Wayne VanCamp children; Mary Pauline married Earl Towns; Roger Wayne married Wilma Thomas; Marlin Eugene married Norma Boxell; Martha Louise married Donald Lenwell; James Howard; Glen Franklin married Judith Pugh; the fifth child was an infant (1903); sixth was Jasper E. (1904-1990) first married Nellie Marie VanCamp; second married Louise Richardson; seventh was Oscar Eugene (1907-1989) married April 26, 1927 to Leone C. Grove (1905-?).

Standing - Bonnie and Jasper Dickason, Seated - Lydia Elizabeth and John Dickason

Oscar and Leone Dickason later moved to Charlestown, Indiana. Their family: Barbara Gene, October 20, 1928 first married Herman Crockett Moore; second married Bill Frazier; third married Edwin Cruise. Son: Gary Wayne Moore, born September 27, 1947, married Lisa Seeders (Children: Melissa Suzanne, 1971; Jennifer Rene, 1975). Jerry Grove Dickason, August 8, 1940, married September 19, 1971, Elisabeth Catharina Groenendijk, born July 31, 1940 in Rotterdam, The Netherlands.

Jerry and Elisabeth "Elly" Dickason have two sons: Blaine Grove, November 9, 1972; Robert Myles, August 21, 1978; and they reside in Montclair, New Jersey. Jerry is a professor at Montclair State College and Elly is an editor.

DILLE-DILLEY FAMILY

There is a record of John Dillie being born in Hackney, at present a borough of London, in 1645. The 1659 court records of Essex County, Massachusetts state the same John Dillie made a deposition, aged about twenty-one years in 1664. He was one of the free-holders of Woodbridge, New Jersey; drawing a ninety-four acre lot. A number of transactions between 1669 and 1683 involving John Dillie show the surname spelled variously: Dillie, Dilley Dilly, and Dillie. Genealogists all know this is typical of the period.

John and Sarah Dille had four children. Susanna, born 1676; Sarah born 1677; John Jr., born 1681; and Jonathan, born 1684.

John Jr. Dille married Ruth Taylor. To this union were born; two children: Sarah, born 1706, died at age twenty; David, born 1718 and destined to become the patriarch of most of the Dilleys west of the Alleghenies. John Jr. died 1747 and Ruth in 1722. They are buried in Newarks oldest Presbyterian Church Cemetery.

David Dille born 1718 married Mary Elizabeth Wade. They were blessed with fourteen children, two daughters and twelve sons. William, born 1738; Isreal, born 1740; Aaron, born 1742; Sarah; Elizabeth, born 1744; John, born 1748; Isaac, born 1751; Samuel, born 1752; David Jr., born 1753; Price, born 1754; Asa, born 1755; Lewis, born 1756; Jonathan, born 1757; Caleb, born 1759. William, Jonathan and Sarah did not come with the family when they, with other pioneers, migrated to Washington County, Pennsylvania. The group settled on Ten Mile Creek. David died after 1793. Mary Elizabeth lived to be ninety-eight. Her obituary in an Ohio paper reads "she left nine children, ninety grandchildren, three hundred sixty-four great grandchildren and twenty-eight great-great grandchildren." They came to Washington County, Pennsylvania in 1776.

Isaac Dille (1757-1827) married Sarah and served in the Revolutionary Militia from Washington County, Pennsylvania. They had twelve children.

Steven Dille was their eldest son. Steven Dille was born July 1, 1781, died April 16, 1840. Rachel was his wife. At a meeting at his house August 2, 1832, Steven became a member of the committee that founded Bethel Cumberland Church in Washington County, Pennsylvania. Many of the Dilles migrated west to Belmont and Logan counties in Ohio. Here William L. Dille was born on March 8, 1808. It is not known when he came to Huntington County, Indiana, but he is buried in the Horeb Cemetery there.

William L. Dilley born March 8, 1808, Logan County, Ohio, married Sarah Chambus.

John A. Dilley, born December 20, 1832, died at Markle, Indiana September 12, 1884, married Caroline Haflich, born September 5, 1838 and they had one son. Caroline was one-fourth Indian from the Miami tribe. She died shortly after my grandfather, Joshua A. Dilley was born, December 7, 1862. Joshua Dilley died August 8, 1919, married Flormelia Selby of Markle, Indiana September, 1885. They lived in Markle all of their lives. My grandfather was a rural mail carrier out of Markle all of his working years. The first years he delivered the mail by horse and buggy. I still remember the Buffalo robe lined in grey wool that he wrapped about himself during the winter months. Joshua and Florella Amelia were blessed with three children: Carl Raymond Dilley, Opal Dilley, and Daris Dilley.

Carl Raymond Dilley, born May 19, 1886 at Markle, Indiana, died May 7, 1965 at Wells Community Hospital, married Maude Myrtle Maddux of Markle, Indiana, born May 21, 1887. My parents were blessed with six daughters.

Wilma Maxine, born September 25, 1908, died February 15, 1956, married Howard Mossburg.

Mildred Lucile, born July 15, 1911, died February 1, 1981, married Edward Kipfer.

Sarah Flo, born September 22, 1913, married Willard McKinney.

Gwendolyn Kathleen, born July 13, 1915, died January 17, 1923.

Euince Eileen, born August 23, 1917, married William Eli Haifley.

Glenna June, born January 27, 1925, died January 18, 1931.

Eunice Eileen Dilley married William Eli Haifley on January 1, 1939. We were blessed with three children; Heather Lea, born June 23, 1940, married Thomas Marvel Meisch in 1977; Linda Nell, born May 7, 1945, married William C. Fronk, June 22, 1982; and Thomas Dilley Haifley, born March 12, 1950, married Kathryn Ford King September 29, 1984.

I was born in Newville, Indiana. My father served on the town council when the name was changed to Vera Cruz. He was a blacksmith by trade when we first moved there. Autos and tractors were fast replacing horses. In 1924 he went to work for the Paton McCray Furniture Company in Bluffton, Indiana. In 1929 we moved to Bluffton. after Patton McCray went out of business in 1930 or 31, my father opened his cabinet and furniture business at 218 North Oak in Bluffton, Indiana. He worked at this until his death.

Grandchildren of William and Eunice (Dilley) Haifley: Kurtis Von Kaufman, born September 6, 1960 to Heather (Kaufman) Meisch; Karla Vey Kaufman, born September 19, 1963 to Heather (Kaufman) Meisch; Linda Eileen Meisch, born March 9, 1978 to Heather Lea and Thomas Meisch; William J. Fronk, born February 6, 1978 to William C. Fronk; Christopher Fronk, born September 5, 1975 to William C. Fronk; Katharine Elizabeth, born August 4, 1985 to Linda Nella and William Fronk; Kyra Nicole and Paul William, twins, born April 28, 1986 to Thomas Dilley and Kathryn Ford (King) Haifley; Mark Brigeforth, born November 1989 to Thomas and Virginia (Campbel) Haifley.

Great-grandchildren of William and Eunice Haifley: Greta Louise, born February 8, 1984; Samuel Lee, born February 29, 1985; Elijah Neil, born March 4, 1988; Jesse Alan, born January 8, 1990 to Karla and Don Heminger, Kurtis Von the II, born July 4, 1989; Konrad Vincint, born June 4, 1990 to Ensign Kurtis Von and Janene (McDermott) Kaufman.

William and Eunice Haifley were born not far from, and have lived in about Bluffton all of our lives. Though we have traveled extensively we call this home. We reside at 3716 East River Road, Bluffton, Indiana.

DITMAR-CARVER

On the day Charles J. Ditmar was born, December 28, 1885, his birthplace, Tonsburgs, Norway, was celebrating its one thousand year existence. At fourteen he stowed away on a ship and traveled all over the world, working as shipmate and cook. During World War I, Charles was unable to locate any of his family, his parents and twin sisters. At the outbreak of the war he was working on the Panama Canal and enlisted in the United States Army, receiving his United States Citizenship and serving in France, where he was disabled. After the war he returned to New York City and then moved to Washington D. C. He eventually settled in Cleveland, where in 1924 he married Harriett Elizabeth Burns Herbst, a widow from Ossian, Indiana. Elizabeth was a decedent of the Kizer and Grim pioneer families of Jefferson Township. Elizabeth and her six unmarried children had moved to Cleveland upon the death of her husband, William Herbst. The Herbsts had eight daughters and a son.

Two children were born to Charles and Elizabeth in Cleveland, a daughter and a son, Charles Norman, who was born in 1926. In 1929 the family, consisting of three of the Herbst children, a grandson, and the two Ditmar children, returned to West Ossian, where the parents resided until their deaths in the early 1960's. Norman served in the South Pacific and Korea during World War II, and upon his return he married Margie L. Carver in 1948. They had attended the Ossian School where Margie graduated in 1946.

Margie was born in 1928 at Echo, the youngest of nine children of Harry and Orva Roe Carver. Her grandparents were Charles and Cynthia Carver. The Carver families resided in the Echo, Prospect and Ossian vicinity. In 1929 Harry Carver died, and later Margie lived in the home of her aunt and uncle, William and Helen Carver Johnson. Helen died in 1933 and Margie soon entered the home of William's sister and her husband, Curtis and Hilda Quackenbush, and Curtis's father, John E., in West Ossian. Curtis served in World War I in France, leaving and returning to the Quackenbush home in West Ossian. Curtis's grandfather, Peter Quackenbush, was from an early pioneer family of Jefferson Township. Hilda was a decedent of James and Rebecca Johnson, early settlers of Jefferson Township and John and Elizabeth Stover Young, an early family of Ossian. When John E. Quackenbush died in 1955, at age ninety-nine, he was Ossian's eldest resident.

Back: (R-L) Claudia Coffield, Nichole Gaunt, Jennifer Coffield, Front: (R-L) Norman and Margie Ditmar (Taken in 1987)

Norman and Margie's daughter, Claudia, graduated in the last graduating class of Ossian in 1967, graduated from International Business College, married, and had Nicole Marie Gaunt and Jennifer Elizabeth Coffield. They reside in the old Quackenbush historical home in West Ossian. Claudia has worked in office positions and attends classes at IPU. Nicole graduated from Norwell Middle School.

Norman, a lineman for REMC, was injured severely in 1957. Later he was employed at Royal Lace and Tuthill Pump. Margie was employed as a secretary. Presently both are retired and residing south of Ossian.

DITZLER FAMILY

George Calvin Ditzler and wife, Cassiah Cassandra (Sarbaugh), came to Rockcreek Township, Wells County, Indiana, in 1864. They bought a farm near Murray. Mr. and Mrs. Ditzler married about 1840 in York County, Pennsylvania and lived in Adams County a few years. In 1851, George and family went to Crawford County, Galion, Ohio, where he was a carpenter. Later, he owned a farm in Morrow County, Ohio.

George was born April 17, 1817, in Adams County, Pennsylvania near Abbottstown. His parents were David and Anna Maria (Yohe) Ditzler, who had twelve children. David's ancestors arrived in Pennsylvania by 1740's and settled in Berks County.

J. Frank Ditzler and four sons; Vier C., Paul F., Hillard L., Ray F., J. Frank Ditzler (seated)

Cassiah was born August 11, 1820 in York County, Pennsylvania. Her parents were Jacob and Catherine Sarbaugh, who moved to Wells County with their only child. Mrs. Sarbaugh died in 1864 and Jacob died after 1883.

December 1918 Vier C. Ditzler and Mayme E. Ditzler owned farm in Jackson Township, Wells County in 1920-1966

The nine children of George and Cassiah were: Susannah Schory Briggans; Sarah Alshouse; Melinda Lines; Mary Schoch; Elizabeth Haflich; John; George, Jr.; Alice Taylor and Jacob Franklin. This family was recorded by Mr. Richard Hot in Higgins Ancestors. George, Sr. died May 6, 1892, and Cassiah's death occurred March 3, 1900, Rockcreek Township, Wells County, Indiana. Burial: Horeb Cemetery near Markle, Indiana.

Frank Ditzler and wife, Lulu (Sechler), married May 10, 1885, had eight children. Nell Cordelia moved to California in 1920. She was a bookkeeper. She was born February 10, 1886 in Bluffton, Indiana, married Otto Reed In Montpelier in 1908 and J. T. Smith in California and died December 28, 1969 in Venice, California. Her son was Robert Reed.

Vier Clenwood farmed in Jackson Township, Wells County. Merchant in Warren for forty years. He was born January 26, 1889, married Mayme Haynes in Huntington, Indiana, December 24, 1918 and died January 5, 1966 in Warren, Indiana. His children were: Vier, Jr.; June Glover; Virginia Neel; Gale (Don); Donna L. Bolinger and Barbara Breedlove.

Ray Franklin lived in the West. He was born July 27, 1890 in Wabash County, Indiana at Roann, married in 1920 to Florence Stevens and later to Lorene and died in Lebanon, Oregon in 1975. Daughter Genevieve Popick.

Hillard Lyle graduate of Bluffton High was a Chicago industrialist. He was born March 20, 1893 in Markle, Indiana, married Beatrice Douglas in

1920 in Chicago, Illinois and Lillian Jones and died January 31, 1974 in Fort Lauderdale, Florida.

Glendora moved to Idaho in 1918 and was a teacher in California. She was born April 15, 1895 in Montpelier, Blackford County, Montpelier, Indiana married Karyl Witty in Lewiston, Idaho and 1818 and died in Los Angeles, February 26, 1974.

Ruby Irene lived in Honolulu and Florida. She was born May 17, 1897, married Fred Rich May 22, 1916 and died in Tarpon Springs, Florida, July 31, 1988. Children: William, Paul and Dorothy Goodman.

Erma Laurietta moved to California in 1920. Her home is Brookings, Oregon. She was born August 9, 1898 in Montpelier, married Henry Stone and Guy Rice in Oregon and had a daughter, Nancy Stone Swingley.

Paul Fenwick moved to California in 1921. He was a businessman is Santa Ana, California. He was born February 5, 1904, married Martha Gable August 20, 1914 and died May 8, 1989.

Lulu (Sechler) born Huntertown, Indiana, December 17, 1864, died April 2, 1907, Montpelier, Indiana.

Frank Ditzler, born Morrow County, Ohio, September 19, 1861, died November 18, 1938, Warren, Indiana.

FREDERICK DIPPEL FAMILY

In 1945 Frederick and Mina (Schoppman) Dippel and their two children Wilma Lou and Rolland left Milwaukee and settled in Wells County on a farm at 5690 N. State Road 301, Craigville. Fred was a native of Australia, while Mina was born in the Hoagland area. They engaged in farming, and Fred was also employed at Franklin Electric, retiring in 1969. In 1971 Fred was injured in a farm accident, passing away in September 1971. Mina remained on the farm and kept busy with sewing, making many bridal outfits for area brides as well as other sewing. She now resides in Ossian. Both children graduated from Lancaster High School. Following graduation, Wilma Lou was employed at John A. Morris Co. In 1961 she married Delbert Bauermeister and moved to Fort Wayne. They have two daughters, Mrs. Vernon (Caryn) Clements and Mrs. Mark (Linda) Rekeweg.

Rolland Dippel, Frederick Dippel, Mina Dippel, Wilma Lou Dippel with "Flossie" the dog

After graduation Rolland was also employed at Franklin and farmed. In July of 1959, he married Charlotte Heinicke from Evansville, Indiana and moved into a home on U.S. 224 in Tocsin, Indiana. They have two sons, Carl and David. Both attended Bethlehem Lutheran School and Norwell High School. Carl attended IPFW in Fort Wayne, and is employed at Burlington Air Express in Fort Wayne. Davis is a Military Police officer with the U.S. Army Reserves, and is employed at Scott's Food Stores in Decatur. Rolland was employed at Franklin over thirty years. He was active in Local 802, serving as treasurer for many years, and also in the Quarter Century Club at Franklin, holding various offices. He passed away in April, 1989, following a short illness. Charlotte is employed at Jeffers, Hoffman & Niewyk in Fort Wayne, and remains in Tocsin with Carl and Dave. All were/are active members of Bethlehem Lutheran Church, Ossian.

HENRY DOTTERER & MARY REINECK DOTTERER

Henry Dotterer was born on a farm in Defiance County, Ohio on May 22, 1888, and moved to Wells County in the fall of 1912. He was married to Mary Reineck in Paulding County, Ohio, on September 17, 1916. Mary was born in Paulding County, Ohio, on September 17, 1888. Henry served as an ordained minister in the Apostolic Christian Church in Wells County.

Henry Dotterer originally came to Wells County in 1912 to assist Dan Gerber harvest crops. The Dan Gerber farm was located at the junction of 100 North and State Road #301. After the harvest Henry became employed at the Benedict Moser, John Hartman and William Fiechter tie barn located at 215 North Main Street. For the younger generation a tie barn was a parking garage for horses.

Front: Henry, Mary and Paul
Back: Caroline, Joseph and Marjorie

Henry purchased the business interests from Mr. Moser and Mr. Fiechter and the firm of Hartman & Dotterer was formed. With the invention of the automobile the need for a tie barn diminished, so they started a feed, seed, and coal business. In 1937 Henry purchased John Hartman's share of the operation and changed the name to Dotterer & Sons.

All of Henry and Mary's four children were employed in the family owned business sometime during their lives. However, their youngest son, Paul, after serving in the United States Army during World War II, returned to Bluffton and assisted Henry with the business. Although Henry suffered a stroke in 1955 and died on May 2, 1956, Paul continued the business until 1959.

The building at 215 North Main Street was erected in 1904 as a barn. The Incel Corporation was formed to manufacture cellulose insulation in 1959 and used the building for a few years. Incel then moved to Craigville and the building was used for storage until it was razed in 1984. The Hardee's Restaurant is now located on this site.

Mary Dotterer resided in an apartment building beside the Feed, Seed, and Coal Store until her death on October 13, 1968. She was a homemaker her entire life.

Henry and Mary had four children. The oldest, Joseph H. married LaVina Hodel of Roanoke, Illinois, in 1940. They are the parents of four children: Marilyn Graf, William, Carolyn Hoerr, and John. Joseph and his family moved to Phoenix, Arizona, in 1958.

Henry and Mary's second child, Marjorie M., married Earl Stucky in 1940. Earl was from Monroe, Indiana, where they still reside and own a business. Two sons were born to this marriage, Richard and Steven.

Caroline was the third of Henry and Mary's children. She married Larry Lantz of Bluffton in 1944. They still live here and are the parents of one child, Alan.

Henry and Mary's fourth child, Paul E., married Phyllis Gerber from Bluffton in 1950. Four children were born to this marriage: Kathryn Gerber, Susan Dailey, Sally, and Jeffrey.

PAUL E. DOTTERER AND PHYLLIS A. GERBER DOTTERER

Both Paul and Phyllis are natives of Bluffton, Indiana. Paul was born on May 15, 1926, to Henry and Mary Reineck Dotterer. Phyllis was the daughter of Joseph (Bud) and Sophia Isch Gerber. She was born on May 25, 1929.

Paul graduated from P.A. Allen High School in 1944. He was inducted into the United States Army on October 6, 1944. During his years in the service, Paul was assigned to the 77th Infantry, which served in Okinawa, the Philippine Islands, and Japan. He attained the rank of sergeant.

Paul returned to Bluffton during Street Fair Week in 1946. He rejoined Dotterer and Sons, which was a feed, seed, and coal store. This family business was located at 215 North Main Street, Bluffton.

Phyllis graduated from P.A. Allen High School in the class of 1947. After graduation Phyllis went to work as a secretary for the Bluffton Schools, which later became the Bluffton-Harrison Metropolitan School District.

Left to right: Kathy, husband Gordon Gerber, daughters Karyn and Sonya. Paul, Jeffrey, Sally, Stefanie and Phyllis. Susan, husband Douglas Dailey, daughter Stefanie (behind Phyl) sons Kevin and Ben.

On October 22, 1950 Paul and Phyllis were married at the Apostolic Christian Church. Shortly after the birth of their oldest child, Paul and Phyl moved to 504 west Market Street, where they still reside.

Paul was the sole proprietor of Dotterer and Sons after the death of his father in 1956, until it closed in 1959. Paul, along with other investors, started the Incel Corporation in 1959 to manufacture cellulose insulation at the former feed store location.

Paul left the insulation company and worked as a distributor for Quaker State Oil Company until

1965. He returned to the insulation business as a dealer in spray-on insulation and the application of urethene foam insulation.

Paul became a bus driver for the Bluffton-Harrison School District in 1971. On October 1, 1976, he was hired as the director of the Wells County Area Plan Commission. During his tenure the Rural Housing Numbering System was instituted in Wells County. He and his staff assigned 5,200 numbers to the residents of the county. The Rural House Numbering system is still in effect.

Phyllis continued working for the school system. She was the first secretary when East Side Elementary opened in 1965. During her career she worked at the superintendent's office, Bluffton High School, Central Junior High, Poplar Grove and Columbian, as well as East Side.

Both Paul and Phyl have been actively involved in the Bluffton schools. Besides their employment, they have served on the East Side PTA, the All-Night Prom Committee, and the Alumni Association.

Paul and Phyl are the parents of four children. Kathryn S. was born on February 16, 1954. Sh married Gordon Gerber of Adams County on July 12, 1981. They have two daughters, Karyn S. and Sonya R. Kathy is a librarian and Gordon is an engineer. They currently reside near Peoria, Illinois.

Their second daughter, Susan M., was born on January 8, 1958. She married Douglas Dailey of Adams County on June 19, 1977 and settled in Bluffton. There were three children born to this marriage: Stefanie K., Benjamin D., and Kevin L. Susan is a librarian. Doug is self-employed as a salesman.

Sally K. was born on March 14, 1963. She is employed as a chemist by the Eli Lilly Company in Lafayette, Indiana.

Paul and Phyl's youngest child, Jeffrey P., was born on August 7, 1968. He works for a computer consulting firm located in Chicago, Illinois.

LLOYD C. DOUGLAS

Did you realize that Lloyd Douglas, the famous author, used to live right here in Wells County? He lived in the small town of Uniondale when he was a lad of 13 and his father was the minister of St. Mark's Church there. His father was A.J. Douglas and he served as minister there from 1889 to 1892.

Among his writings are *The Robe, The Big Fisherman, Magnificent Obsession, Forgive Our Trespasses, Precious Jeopardy, Green Light, White Banners, Disputed Passage, Home for Christmas, Doctor Hudson's Secret Journal, Invitation to Live,* and last but not least, *A Time to Remember. A Time to Remember* was his last book, written because he was going crazy not writing. His family and his publishers suggested a book of remembrances. That is just what it is, and it includes his delightful memories of Uniondale!

The parsonage where Douglas lived in Uniondale

He mentions the Wabash River, the B&O Railroad and ran through town, Ormsby's Drug Store, Doctor English, Papa's church, Ditzler's saw mill, the school he attended, Mr. Longfellow his teacher, and his Uncle Worth who took him to Fort Wayne to see the circus!

The Uniondale Station where Douglas loved to watch luxury trains

The inside cover of this book sums up his feelings of three years in Uniondale. There is a drawing of a boy lying on the ground with a small church in the background and it says: "Some of my happiest memories relate to the hours I spent there (Uniondale) making pictures of the white clouds which hovered so close, wondering dreamily what was beyond the blue ceiling far away." Hoping to write a second volume, he died February 13, 1951, before he could begin it.

DOWTY FAMILY

A London youth in the service of his master, Edward Doty (1598-1655) came to America on the Mayflower in 1620. He was a signer of the solemn compact. After his term of service, he became a freeman, married, became prosperous, and raised nine children.

James W. Dowty (1815-1886), great-great-great-grandson of Edward Doty, moved to Indiana in the 1860's and settled on a farm in Wells County, Jefferson Township. James married Catharine Ledman, and they raised eight children.

Adam Dowty (1846-1900), the sixth child of James, married Lydia Meyers (1850-1932) in 1867. They had four children: Lillian (1869-1901), James (1873-1958), William (1873-1946), and Benjamin (1885-1963). Adam farmed with his father in Jefferson Township and later in Lancaster Township.

James Wilson Dowty, like his father, with a farmer and carpenter, lived in Lancaster Township and later moved a mile north of Ossian in Jefferson Township. He married Lena Carrysot (1879-1959) in 1897. They had nine children: June Marie (1898-1948), Paul Adam (1900-1981), Mary Janette (1903), Roberta Aldine (1908), James Kenneth (1910-1984), Hubert Vernell (1912), Erma Regine (1915), Wendell Francis (1918), and Marjorie Edith (1923).

June Marie Dowty married Philip Snider (1891-1957) in 1920. They had one child, Vera Maurene (1940). There are three grandchildren.

Paul Adam Adolphus Dowty married Marie Thieke (1897-1969) in 1936. There were no children. Paul then married Hilda Krieg (1906) in 1971.

Mary Janette Dowty married Paul Gilbert (1900-1975) in 1923. They had six children: Duane (1925), Margaret (1927), Lena (1929), Keith (1932), Gene (1934), Lyle (1936). There are sixteen grandchildren and seventeen great-grandchildren.

Roberta Aldine Dowty married Andrew Gilliom (1902-1990) in 1929. They had one child, Richard (1934). There are three grandchildren and three great-grandchildren.

James Kenneth Dowty married Esther Freuchtenicht (1912) in 1931. They had two children, Darlene (1932) and James (1941). There are four grandchildren and one great-grandchild.

The Dowty Family in 1940. Seated Erma Regine, Lena, James, and Marjorie. Standing: Roberta, Hubert, Paul, Wendell, James, Kenneth, Mary and June.

Hubert Vernell Dowty married Velma Vananda (1914) in 1933. They had two children, Don (1936) and Karen (1943). There are seven grandchildren.

Erma Regine Dowty married Claude Koons (1910) in 1933. They had two children, Kent (1935) and Lynne (1941). There are three grandchildren.

Wendell Francis Dowty married Mary Johnson (1921) in 1941. They had two children, Ronald (1947) and Jerrold (1953). There are eight grandchildren.

Marjorie Edith Dowty married Earl Sorg (1924) in 1947. They had two children, Michael (1947) and Sandra (1951). There are three grandchildren.

DRENNEN

The Drennen family moved to Wells County in 1949, where they purchased a farm in Jackson Township. My husband, Warren Vincent Drennen, was born in Blackford County on November 20, 1920. He and his father, Benjamin Harrison Drennen, born October 10, 1887, farmed together until his father's death, August 27, 1957, after which Warren took over the farming. His mother was Lucy May Leffingwell Drennen, who was born May 21, 1890. She died February 4, 1969. He had one sister, Forest Devona, born June 17, 1911, and died March 3, 1952.

His grandparents were James Samuel and Sarah Glover Drennen, who were born in Blackford and Grant Counties. His maternal grandparents were Hiriam and Sarah Townsend Leffingwell, who were both born in Blackford County. His ancestors came from Ireland and England.

I married Warren Drennen on August 26, 1962. We have one son, Rex Allen Drennen, who was born on August 30, 1967, in Blackford County. He graduated from Southern Wells High School in 1986. He was active in 4-H, band, FFA, and won the Auto Mechanics Award in 1986. He is employed as head technician at Hiday Chrysler in Bluffton, Indiana, and also helps with the family farming.

We live on the family farm, which Warren still farms. He was also employed in maintenance at Gripco in Montpelier, Indiana, for fifteen years before retirement in 1989. He enjoys the outdoors and raises a huge garden each summer. He graduated from Roll High School.

Warren, Edith, and Rex Drennen

I am a homemaker and Women's Leader for Jackson Township Farm Bureau in Wells County. I graduated from the Montpelier High School.

We are active members of the Independence Church of Christ in Blackford County. I was formerly Edith Lucile Spaulding, born in Blackford County, August 16, 1932. My father was LeRoy B. Spaulding, who was born July 14, 1903 in Blackford County. My mother was Ella Lucile Croft Spaulding who was born July 25, 1903 in Muncie, Indiana. They were married October 19, 1922. I have one sister Olive Gadbury, and two brothers, Gale and Gerald, living, and two brothers Gaylord and Glen, deceased. My father died October 4, 1965, and mother died May 1, 1981.

My grandparents were William Henry and Alice I. Beeks Spaulding and were born in Wells and Blackford Counties. My maternal grandparents were Charles Cory and Clara May Dawson Croft who were born in Springfield, Ohio, and Liberty, Indiana. My ancestors on the Spaulding side came to Blackford and Wells Counties from Vermont in a covered wagon in 1837. One of the five brothers who came here was my great-great grandfather, Franklin Benjamin Spaulding who died February 20, 1875.*(Edith Lucile Drennen)*

DUNWIDDIE FAMILY

The Dunwiddie family is of Scotch-Irish descent appearing in the 13th century on the west coast of Scotland. The first immigrants arrived in Kent County, Delaware, prior to the American Revolution. Records date back to 1774.

Henry Harrison Dunwiddie was born on a farm one mile south east of Reiffsburg, Indiana. His father was Benjamin F. Dunwiddie. His mother was Emma Valentine. He had three sisters and two brothers. Flossie, Marie and Ethel are all deceased. Clarance Dunwiddie lives in Selma, Indiana, and Merlin Dunwiddie lives in Reiffsburg, Indiana.

Henry married Grace Dyson, daughter of Levi and Lydia Dyson, in 1920. They had six children. Lela was born 1921 and is retired from Sterling Casting. She resides in Bluffton.

Vera was born in 1922. She married Glen Morehouse and has two daughters Diana and Georgina. They reside on a farm near Milford, Indiana.

Elizabeth was born in 1926 and married Harold Meyer. They have four sons: Rodney, Bruce, Greg and Randy. Elizabeth retired from the Caylor Nickel Clinic where she worked as a registered nurse. Harold is retired from the U.S. Postal Service.

Lloyd was born in 1930 and married Eleanor Fisher. They have three daughters, Suzanne, Kelly and Erin. Lloyd is a graduate of Purdue University and retired from General Electric.

George was born 1932 and married Nancy Sowards. They have four children: Julie, Marcia, Linda and Mark. George retired from Navistar after 33 years. He is employed now at General Manufacturing in Bluffton. Nancy is employed at the Wells County Clerks Office

Gerald was born in 1936 and married Betty Lesh. They have three children: Cynthia, Chris, and Cathy. He is a farmer in Rockcreek Township and drives a school bus. Betty is employed as secretary at General Manufacturing.

The Henry Dunwiddie family was raised on a farm seven miles southeast of Bluffton. Henry's wife Grace was raised on this farm. When she was a small child in 1907 her father built a large round barn on the farm. This barn is still standing in good condition. During the hard times of the Great Depression Henry and Grace bought the farm from her parents. Grace died an untimely death in 1943.

All of the field work on the farm was done with horses and mules until 1937 when he bought his first tractor. Our farm was similar to most other farms in the area. We had several cattle, sheep, hogs, horses and mules. All the water for the livestock was pumped from a well either by hand or with a windmill. Finally, in 1939 the power lines were finished and the power was turned on. Up to this time we had one radio that used a battery which had to be taken to Bluffton to get recharged. Henry continued to farm renting additional land, until about 1960 when he retired from farming.

GERALD DUNWIDDIE FAMILY

Gerald Dunwiddie was the sixth child born to Henry and Grace (Dyson) Dunwiddie. He was raised on a farm in Harrison Township, Wells County, and graduated from Bluffton High School in 1955. He was in the service from 1957-1959, serving one year in Germany as a tank mechanic.

In 1959, he married Betty Lou Lesh, daughter of Ernest and Ethel (Barlett) Lesh. They settled in Rockcreek Township so that Gerald could help Ernest with the farming. At that time, Gerald worked full-time at Graden's Recapping in Bluffton. Within a year, Gerald went to farming full-time. They raised feeder pigs and grain farmed.

Three children were born to Gerald ad Betty Lou: Cynthia Lou on February 18, 1963; Chris Allen on June 3, 1965; and Cathleen Sue on March 10, 1971. All three children graduated from Norwell High School.

Cynthia (Cindy) married Ryan Langford on September 7, 1985 and has since resided in Rockcreek Township on a farm west of Gerald and Betty's home farm. They have two children: Michelle Lynn, born on November 12, 1986; and Logan Michael, born on December 31, 1988. Ryan works at Slater Steel in Fort Wayne, and Cindy works for Traditions Restaurant in Bluffton.

Chris has worked at Weaver Popcorn since he graduated in 1984. He still resides at home, helping with the farm and bowling in his spare time.

Cathleen (Cathy) also resides at home and commutes to IPFW in Fort Wayne. She is in her second year, majoring in supervision /office management. She plays tennis for IPFW in the fall. She also continues to sing and play volleyball in her spare time.

Gerald has driven a school bus for Northern Wells Community Schools for eleven years. He also served on various 4-H committees when the children were still involved with the 4-H program.

Betty Lou was able to stay at home while the children were growing up. She now works full time at General Manufacturing in Bluffton.

The family attends Hope Missionary Church in Bluffton.

DOUG AND KIM DURR FAMILY

Palmer Douglas Durr, a child of the nineties is the latest addition to our family. Before his birth there were many speculations on what his name would be as his fifteen year old brother, Marshall Parr (born 1975), and six year old sister, Ti Mikkel (born 1984), both have unusual names. Because their father, Ray Douglas Durr (born 1945), has an avid interest in golf, the names Parr and Palmer were chosen, but mistakenly many assume Ti (pronounced Tee) is a golf related name as well. Ti, however, is a music term for the seventh note of the scale, do re me fa so la Ti Durr! The musical name reflects the love for music held by her mother, Monica Kim Mann Durr (born 1956). Parr and Ti have lived up to their names as Parr has enjoyed golf since he was old enough to hit a ball and is currently participating as a freshman on Norwell High School's golf team, and Ti sings and dances as a part of Pizzazz School of Performing Arts under the direction of her mother. It may be too early to tell if baby Palmer will aspire to golf or music, but whatever he chooses will receive the full support of his family. Our family has always lived in Wells County and many family members have also lived here through the generations. What follows is a brief outline of our children's maternal heritage.

It is easy to trace my father's arrival in Wells County. William August Mann (born 1936) came to Bluffton in 1954 with his parents, Loren Lockhart Mann (1909-1982) and Edith Adeline Clark Mann (1908-1969), when he and his father started the Duchess Pretzel Company (see related article). Gram and Grandaddy were members of the First Methodist Church where Gram was active in choir activities for several years until they moved to Reading, Pennsylvania in 1966. Dad met mom, Elizabeth Lou Barnes Mann, at Macy's Drive-In where she was a car hop. They were married in 1956 and had four children: myself, (Kim), Kami Jo (Osborne), Kelli Renee (Beisel), and Wiliam August II (Chip). Chip and Kami still live in Bluffton, Kami with her husband, Thomas Lee Osborne, and daughters, Kai Elizabeth age seven and Kamann Rae age three and a half. Kelli and her husband, James Beisel, live in Birmingham, Alabama.

Mother's family roots run much deeper in Wells County than dad's. Mom has one older brother, Charles Ray, who now resides in Fort Wayne. Her parents, Claude Oren Barnes (born 1907) and Josephine Parintha Markley Barnes (born 1907) have also lived their entire lives here although they currently winter in Florida. Grandma Jo graduated from Chester High School in 1926. Her older brother, Lewis, and sister, Bernice Baker, continue to reside in Wells County as well, all having moved to Bluffton from the Petroleum area. A younger sister, Charleen Roberts, resides in Marion Indiana. Their parents, Charley Dennis Markley (1882-1948) and Stella Grove (1883-1943) farmed their property in Chester Township on the Meridian Road. The old homestead was blown down in the tornado of 1966. Grandma was named after both her grandmothers. Her paternal grandparents were Jonathan Markley (born 1838) and Catharine Parintha Sturgis, and on the maternal side, Lewis Grove (1844-1894) and Josephine Stahl (1846-1926). Anna Stahl, Josephine Stahl's mother who died in 1893, is as far in the genealogy as we could trace Grandma's maternal lineage, all generations having lived in Wells County to the best of our knowledge. The Markley origins can be traced back to German, Gabriel Markley, and French, his wife whose maiden name was Dickensheet. Their son Jonathan 1780-1819) and his wife Rachel (1794-1820) bore a son also named Gabriel (1814-1873) who married Hannah Tuttle and in turn bore another son named Jonathan who was Grandma Jo's grandfather. Grandma's family tradition of hard work carries through to today.

Grandad Claude's genealogy can be traced through several generations who also made their lives in Wells County. His parents, Arthur Ray Barnes (1881-1971) and Emma Catharine Alberson (1882-1976), lived briefly in Wayside, Kansas, where Grandad was born before returning to Petroleum in 1908 to operate a general store. A sister, Thelma Naomi, was born before the general store was sold and Great Grandad Roy bought into the Petroleum Hardware in 1912. Thelma lives in Petroleum where she continues to style hair in Thelma's Beauty Shop as she has for well over 50 years. Following in Aunt Thelma's footsteps, my mother also became a beautician and has owned and operated the Fireside Boutique in Bluffton since 1968.

Great Grandad's Ray's ancestry can be traced back to Scottish descent when his great grandparents, William and Rosanna Searles Barnes, moved to Delaware County from Scotland in 1825. They embarked to move to Texas in 1852 but a flagstaff fell on William seriously injuring him, hence they returned to Pennville, Indiana. Their son James (1828-1906) and his wife Susannah (1830-1909) also made their lives in Pennville bearing a son also named William H. (1850-1921). He married Ella Cory (1862-1895), daughter of Nathan (1832-1893) and Elizabeth Cory (1833-1910). They had three sons, Joe, Clyde, and Ray, the oldest, who was my great-grandfather.

Great Grandma Emma's family contains some interesting side notes. Joshua Alberson (1794-1879) came to North Carolina from England. He and his wife, Catharine Deter (born 1808), later moved to Adams County near Domestic. Their son, Charles (1826-1878) married Mary Ann Brown (1821-1909) who was a daughter of squatters, Philip and Julia Taylor Brown from Jay County. Tales of Mary Ann Brown Alberson include a childhood encounter with a bear. Apparently, she treed the bear when she was about twelve years old while the men were out hunting. An obituary account refers to her as a kind and loving mother, never more pleased than when her children were gathered around and she was telling of her pioneer life. Charles and Mary Ann settled in Nottingham Township near Phenix, raising eleven children, one of whom was Philip B. Alberson (1854-1939), who married Sarah Olive Davis (1858-1939) daughter of Thomas F. and Alice Rogers Davis, and eventually purchased his fathers 230-acre estate where he farmed, raised stock and drilled twenty-three oil wells. An upstanding citizen, he was a member of Odd Fellows and Sarah was a member of the Rebekkah Degree. They owned a store in Phenix and were active in Republican politics. Accounts relate that Philip was highly respected and often approached for legal advice. Of their seven children, my Great Grandma Emma was one. Her obituary could have reach much like her grandmother's before her as she was also kind and loving, never happier than when children were gathered around. I baked many a pie and worked many a puzzle with my Great Grandmother Emma, the memory of her love still warming me. It is interesting to note that Great Grandmother Emma's sister, Violet Williams, still resides with family near Wolcottville, Indiana at the ripe age of ninety-seven.

In tracing this brief family history, it reiterates the fleeting quality of life. Should each of our children live to be as old as some of their ancestors, at ninety years of age they would see the year 2065, 2074 and 2080. Parr, Ti and Palmer, what does the future hold? What will your children's eyes behold?
(Kim Durr)

RAYMOND DURR FAMILY

Politics, the law, and sports are three concepts that characterize the lives of the members of the Raymond Durr Family.

Raymond "Daddy" Durr grew up on a farm in the Craigville area. He and his brothers soon made themselves known in the county, especially through their skill in basketball. They all played for the Lancaster Bobcats. We have been regaled with stories of close games, fights on the gym floor, and outrageous behavior at those contests. According to the family legend, Raymond's mother, (Mrs. Oliver (Cora Brown) Durr), suggested that the mascot of Lancaster Central should be "Bobcats." Her sons proceeded to shave their hair in the classic "Bobcat" cut. Those haircuts, and the ability to keep the "Bobcat" banner flying for a week, earned the right to be called "the Bobcats".

In 1939, he met and married a Tocsin girl by the name of Ellen, daughter of John and Genevieve (Rupright) Nash. They settled in that community and proceeded to raise four children, Marlyn Kaye (b. 1940), David Lynn (b. 1943), Ray Douglas (b. 1945), and Melanie Sue (b. 1948). Raymond joined the Masonic Lodge, and Ellen became a Pythian Sister. Tocsin, in those days, was a close knit community and a kind of paradise for children. There was a Tocsin Lumber & Grain Little League team, which "Daddy" coached, a horseshoe team, a Pythian Sister Lodge, who had great ice cream socials, and an active United Methodist Church, which we all attended regularly. There were also two "gasoline stations: in Tocsin which gave the men a place to "loaf." The soda pop in the ice-cold water, the peanut machine, and the checkerboard are part of the memories of the station.

The Durrs lived in Tocsin for approximately fifteen years. All of the children became Ossian Bears, delivered the *Bluffton Banner,* and pursued childhood dreams.

Our lives took an abrupt turn in the early 1950's. As interest in politics intervened and Raymond became the Democratic candidate for Wells County sheriff. The days were filled with campaign activities—canvassing Wells County voters, handing out campaign cards, and attending county-wide community events. It was an exciting time and our efforts were successful. We now faced the challenge of leaving Tocsin and moving into the Wells County Jail.

The next eight years of our lives were filled with memorable and enlightening events. All of us witnessed the sometimes tragic and sometimes comic behavior of humanity. We grew, we observed, and we learned from that experience, and many times our collective sense of humor carried us through.

Dave and Doug managed to carry on the tradition of basketball. Both played for the Bluffton Tigers, and both have treasured memories of those years. Dave became a teacher and coach, and now lives in Michigan. Doug is in manufacturing, and he and his family live near Bluffton. Melanie is a private secretary in a law firm in Bluffton, and is pursuing a degree in education. Marlyn is a teacher in the Northern Wells School System.

The Raymond "Daddy" Durr family posed for a final rememberance of their eight years in Wells County Jail. Sitting on the jail steps prior to the jail being demolished is left to right, Dave, Marlyn, and Ellen. Standing left to right is former Sheriff "Daddy", Doug and Melanie.

Upon leaving jail, Ellen and Raymond moved to a home southeast of Bluffton. Ellen went to work

Standing (L to R) Tom Osborne, Kami Osborne, Bill Mann, Betty Mann, Kelli Beisel, Jim Beisel, Kim Durr holding Palmer Durr, Doug Durr, Jo Barnes, Claude Barnes; Front: (L to R) Chip Mann, Kamann Osborne, Parr Durr, Kai Osborne, Ti Durr

at J.C. Penney Company in Bluffton. Measuring material, arranging displays, and learning the mysteries of a computerized cash register became part of her life. She retired from Penny's after twenty years, and still enjoys the deep and lasting friendship of fellow employees. Raymond spends his time helping Doug at his firm, going to basketball games at Bluffton, Southern Wells, and Norwell, and most of all visiting people.

They are the proud grandparents of six grandchildren. Marlyn's daughter, Angie, lives in Indianapolis, and carries on the political tradition by working in the governor's office. David and his wife, Sally, have two daughters, Sarah and Elizabeth, age sixteen and twelve. Sarah is a cheerleader for the St. Joe "Bears", and Elizabeth enjoys playing soccer and tennis. Doug and his wife, Kim, have three children. Parr is a student at Norwell High School and is already an accomplished golfer. Ti (pronounced tee) is an imaginative seven year-old who enjoys dancing and performing. The newest grandchild is a happy active baby boy named Palmer, whose particular talents are yet to be discovered.

Politics, the law and sports . . . all have helped mold us. We have also been blessed with good health, security, and solidity. We look to the future with optimism and believe that the members of our family will continue to attempt to make life a bit better for their human beings.

HENRY DURST

Mathias Durst, son of Henry and Elizabeth Durst, was born in Glarius, Switzerland, February 18, 1841. Mathias Durst was married in the year 1864 to Barbara Noble. He crossed the ocean in 1865 and located near Waterloo, Indiana.

To this union were born: Henry, Elizabeth, Fred, and Gus. Mathias' wife died in 1874; then he married Mary E. Nickleson in the year 1878, July 14. To this union five children were born: Jennie, Anna, Leona, Walter, and Amy. Mathias died December 17, 1905, and was buried in Fairview Cemetery at Bluffton, Indiana.

Mary Emmaline Nickleson, daughter of James and Regencia Nickleson, was born June 22, 1853, at Clarksville, Indiana, and married Mathias Durst July 14, 1878. After Mathias Durst's death, she married John Wright of Fort Wayne. After his death she was married to Amos Ivan of Bluffton on November 2, 1926.

FRANK EARL FAMILY

Frank and Margaret Earl lived in Wells County most of their lives. They lived near Murray and were active in the Murray Missionary Church. Later they moved near Zanesville.

Frank Earl and his binder

They were the foster parents of Letha who married Harmon Henry, Lois Tobias Swihart, and Paul Tobias. Harmon and Letha had a daughter, Margaret Ann. Frank passed away in 1952 and Margaret in 1980. She was 95.

EDRIS

The Edris family came to Rockcreek Township from Lancaster County, Pennsylvania sometime between 1864-1866. Henry Edris and his father-in-law, Laurer Weber purchased 159-acres from the heirs of Joseph Schnatterly. The farm is located one-half mile west of Rockford back the lane right on the curve of the road. Mr. Schnatterly had a homestead deed to one hundred sixty acres dated March 15, 1837 signed by then President Martin Van Buren. While traveling to his new land, his team of horses ran away, upsetting his wagon and killing him. Mr. Schnatterly was buried on the corner of the farm; The grave marker can be found against a tree on the north side of the cemetery. This one acre cemetery is now owned by the United Methodist Church.

Henry (born November 26, 1840) and Sarah (born 1843) Edris parented eight children: Mary Elnora Smeltzer (1864), Edwin (1866), Henry (1868), Aaron (1871), Milton (1873), Elizabeth (1876), Harry (1879) and Louis (1882). The youngest seven were born in the home they had constructed on their farm. Henry died Feb. 27, 1888 from pneumonia contracted while cutting timber in his woods for a new home. Sarah died Jan. 1, 1922. They are buried one-quarter mile north of the farm in the Emmanuel Cemetery along with her mother, four children, six grandchildren and two great-grandchildren.

Three sons continued the farming with the last being Milton, my grandfather. He purchased the family interest, married Nora Harnish in 1906 and they farmed until his death April 13, 1948. Their three sons, Homer (September 10, 1907) (my father), Lester (1909) and Chester (1914) were born there. In 1920 my grandfather built the brick home still located across the road from the rear of grandfather's farm. I have vivid memories of the homemade bread with freshly churned butter Grandmother made while grandfather kept the diversified fruit orchard and watermelon patch in good taste. After his death, son Chester farmed for a few years. Chester and family moved to Florida so the family farm was sold.

My father married Alta Sheets. I was born May 23, 1932, and sisters Beverly Skurner January 7, 1936 and Donna Bradley April 18, 1940. We were farmers as the family background has been. We all (the whole family) attended Rockcreek School. I married Bluffton resident Mary Ann Herrberg December 13, 1953. We have two daughters, Theresa born December 23, 1954, and Lorene born March 10, 1959. Theresa married Thomas Hoopingarner (son of former county resident Lee Hoopingarner), and they have one son, Steven, born September 27, 1983. They reside in Tucson, Arizona, while Lorene lives in Medford, Oregon.

The Edris family remaining in Wells County were John H., son of Aaron. John was a well-know Bluffton attorney. He had a daughter, Joan, and a son, John H. Jr. who continues the law practice. Grandchildren of Edwin were Lawrence, Ruth (Mrs. Dan) Freds and Martha (Mrs. Russell) Allen. Children of Henry in Bluffton were Dorothy (Mrs. Harold) Plummer and Kathryn (Mrs. Harold) Richey. Many descendants reside locally.

My family and I have resided in Tucson, Arizona, for over thirty-three years. I am a practicing CPA with my own accounting practice. Any success I have attained I attribute to the upbringing of my family, the educational system, good morals and hard-working ethics of my Wells County background. I am most proud to be an Edris and an Indiana native. *(Dale E. Edris)*

EDRIS-BOONE

We can date our paternal ancestors back to December 3, 1740. Johann (Eader) Edris sailed on the ship *Robert and Alice* from Rotterdam. The master of the ship was Walter Goodwin and it carried one hundred eighty five passengers to the new world. Johann and his wife, Dorothy, are buried at Klopp's churchyard, Berks County, Pennsylvania. Johann and Dorothy's only child, Andreas Edris, born February 1, 1741, married Margaret Noble, born March 6, 1744, and from this union came ten children. Andreas and Margaret's child, Johann, (July 19, 1769) married Magdalena Noll, (December 15, 1775) and from this union came twelve children. Johann and Magdalena's child, Leonard, (October 22, 1810) married Elizabeth Spittler, (Unknown) and from this union came four children. Leonard and Elizabeth's child, Henry Edris, born November 27, 1840, married Emaline Sarah Weber, born September 17, 1843, and from this union came eight children. From this union came our family.

We can date our maternal ancestors to the year 1750. John Henry Weber emigrated from Hochstadt Deutschaland in this year. He lived on a farm near Host Church, Berks County, Pennsylvania from 1770 until 1815. He served as captain of the Sixth Company, Pennsylvania from 1770 until 1815. He served as captain of the Sixth Company, Sixth Battalion, Pennsylvania Militia in the War of Independence 1777-1778. John Henry Weber, (May 28, 1735) married Elizabeth Filbert, (December 6, 1741). Their child John Peter Weber, (November 1, 1778) married Susannah Reber, (unknown). John Peter and Susannah's child, Lawrence Weber, (August 10, 1819) married Sarah Moyer, (January 31, 1825) and from this union came two children. Their child Emaline Sarah Weber, (September 17, 1843) married Henry Edris, (November 27, 1840) on January 12, 1863, and the union produced eight children. Henry and Emaline's child, Edwin Lawrence Edris, (September 17, 1866) married Ida Redding (June 21, 1867) and from this union came two children, Charles Lawrence Edris (April 2, 1889) and Winnie Merle Edris (July 30, 1891). Charles Lawrence Edris was my grandfather. My grandfather married Ethel Marie Fisher (March 24, 1891) and from this union came three children of which my father, Lawrence Ellsworth Edris (May 14, 1912) was one. Dad married my mother, Dorothy Pauline Boone, (November 8, 1915) a descendent of Daniel Boone's family, but then that can be another story.

Edwin L. Edris purchased the family farm in Rockcreek Township from Joseph High on August 8, 1906. It was on this farm that myself and three brothers grew up. I remember grandmother Ethel Marie Edris always teaching me new ways to do canning and cooking. Grandmother worked with the 4H Clubs in Wells County for years, so knew much about these things. When my father died December 21, 1970, it was my mother that helped hold us all together. Mother decided to keep herself busy working at Wells Community Hospital and is living in Bluffton at this time. My youngest brother, Max Leon Edris, and his wife, Connie Sue Davis, married July 30, 1966, and with their two children, Kelly Renie and Todd Allen, also live in Bluffton. Max works for the Southern Wells School Corporation.

The Garrett family in 1990
Front row: Charles Sean Garrett, Joseph Lawrence Garrett; Back row: Lisa Marie Garrett, Judith Edris Garrett, Charles Franklin Garrett

My brother, Reverend Gerald Lee Edris, and his wife, Cheryl Dianne Cargar, married June 13, 1970, and with their children, Lorie Elaine, Matthew Lawrence, and Debbie, live in Wabash, Indiana, where he is pastoring a church.

My brother Charles Lawrence (Larry) Edris and his wife Sharon Elaine Kochler, married October 26, 1968, and with their two children, Andrea Lynn and Stefanie Jo, live in Fort Wayne, Indiana, where Larry is Vice-President of Lincoln National Life Insurance Agency.

As for myself, I married Charles (Chad) Franklin Garrett of Liberty Center on October 24, 1960. From our marriage came three children. Our oldest, Joseph Lawrence, lives in Gore, Oklahoma, and works as a city police officer. Our other two children, Charles Sean and Lisa Marie, live with us in Washington, West Virginia, where Sean attends Glenville State College and Lisa Marie, Parkersburg Beauty College. Chad worked for Corning Engineering as a project engineer in Corning, New York. We spend our time traveling between our home in West Virginia and apartment in Corning. I am working as the Director of Educational Services at a West Virginia hospital and recently graduated with my Masters Degree in Nursing. Plans for the future include living in Shenzhen, China and north of Moscow, Russia with Chad's work over the next few years.*(Judith Kay Edris Garrett)*

EDWARDS-BENNETT

Pollyanna Edwards was born to Kenneth and Melba Edwards on January 24, 1962. She is the third child of the family, and was born at the Wells County Hospital in Bluffton after many false labor trips. Dr. Gingerick was the doctor and he was ill at the time. He always referred to Melba's labor as a "slow train through Arknasas." Unable to be with her at the time, another doctor was on call but didn't make the appointed hour. Melba had a good nurse standing by, who just happened to be on duty at least for ten more minutes. Besides being a good nurse, Barbara Caley Girvin was our neighbor in Markle at the time, and also one of our best friends. She brought Pollyanna into the world.

It came time for Pollyanna to go to kindergarten, and she spent a year in Fuhrer's Garage at Uniondale, along with several other Union Township children. In 1968, she entered first grade at Rockcreek and remained there until her family moved to Zanesville in 1973. Attending Lafayette School in the sixth grade, she graduated from Homestead in 1980. All this time of high school she had been cooking at LK Restaurant, and then in 1979, she went to work for her sister at Richards. She entered Ivy Tech's Culinary Arts School in 1981 and received her degree in 1982.

The Bennetts
Brice, Steve, Brock, Pollyanna, Baili

While employed at Richards, she met and married Stephen Bennett on July 18, 1982. Steve (born July 3, 1950) is the son of Charles and Nila (Scott) Bennett of Albion, Indiana. Charles' parents were Perry and Josie (Hively) Bennett, and Nila's were Archie Allen and Ruth (Beers) Scott. Steve graduated in 1969 from Churubusco High School. He attended Green Center during his elementary years. He has attended and holds degrees from Ivy Tech, IPFW, and IIT. For several years he taught mechanical engineering at ITT Technical Institute, and is now employed as a design engineer at Gencorp in Wabash, Indiana. Steve has a brother, Bob, and sister Karen. He was married before and has a daughter, Nicole, who is twenty one years old.

The Bennetts have always made their home in the Zanesville area and currently are living in Windfall Estates, just north of Zanesville on Feighner Road. Pollyanna's Uncle David McBride and his sons built the family a lovely new home there several years ago.

Pollyanna took time out from work when their first son, Brock, was born on May 14, 1983. Since her mother would babysit, she took the manager's job at the LK for a year in 1984, just before the restaurant closed for the building of the I-697-469 interchange and the coming of GM. On June 10, 1985, the Bennetts were blessed with another baby boy and they named him Brice Donald, after his great-grandfather Don McBride. It is to this day a fitting name for him. If you want to know his personality, refer to the Donald McBride writing in this book. On November 25, 1988, everyone was elated when they became parents of a baby girl. She is the spitting image of her mother. She has blond curls like Shirley Temple and a beautiful smile. They named her Baili.

Pollyanna still works part time for her sister and spends the rest of her time with her family. Her children attend Lafayette Central. They are the fourth generation of the family to attend the school. Grandma Mildred Garrison Edwards graduated from there in 1932, Kenny Edwards in 1955, and Pollyanna attended sixth grade there. They are the only ones presently holding this honor.

JAMES ELI ELLISON EARNEST FAMILY

Houston Henry Ringer, married Annabelle Owens. Houston and his wife lived on the farm place in Jennings County, and they had eight children: Phoebe (1898), Mary Catherine (1899), Carrie Alice (1900), Rauleigh (1903), William (1904), Houston (1909) and James (1910). Henry's wife, Annabelle, died in 1911 and he continued to live on the farm and raise his children.

James Eli Ellison Earnest Family
Back row: L to R, Ella Louise, John Franklin, Evelyn Eileen, and Mildred; Front row: Litia Ann, Virginia, Carrie Alice, and James Eli Earnest

Isaac N. Earnest (1818) was the great-grandfather of James Eli. With his wife, Susanna, he migrated from Tennessee in the early 1840's to Indiana. They settled in Madison County, Van Buren Township on a 160-acre farm where they lived out their lives. They had three children: John Redric (1844), William (1848), and Mary E. (1847).

John Redric Earnest, the paternal grandfather of James, married Litia Ann Ellison from West Virginia, daughter of the Reverend James Eli Ellison; they resided in Madison County and their seven children were: Ida (Flint) (1866), Sara (Brown) (1869), Isaac (1877), and Stella (Kaufman) (1879), Stella was the mother of the Reverend Ernest Kaufman, minister of the First United Methodist Church Bluffton from 1949 to 1953.

James's father, Isaac Newton Earnest, married Nellie Blanch Adams on August 29, 1900, with the Reverend James Eli Ellison officiating at Madison, Indiana. Their six children were: Stella and Ella, twins, born November 20, 1901; James Eli Ellison, born February 8, 1904; Mary Jane Lucille, born March 25, 1906; Hazel, born in February, 1908; and Martin W., born October 23, 1916. Isaac came to Wells County from Grant County in March of 1943. He purchased 22-acres in Jackson Township and lived out the rest of his life until his untimely death in a farm accident in 1947.

DOUG EDWARDS FAMILY

In January, 1956, Tamra Lynn Green was born to George and Betty (Moore) Green. She was the third of four children. Terry was born in March, 1948; Gary (Mick) in February, 1949; and Glenda, in September, 1957.

At the time of Tamara's birth, the family resided west of Murray until 1966, when they moved to a larger, new home in North Oaks Addition in Bluffton. After the kids had married, George and Betty moved to a smaller home in Willowbrook in Bluffton.

Terry, who is married to Kim Shaffer, has three children, Tod, Chris, and Ked, and they reside north of Bluffton. Mick has two children: Kara lives in Bluffton, and Mike lives with his dad in Nashville, Tennessee. Glenda has two children: Bruce and Colby, and lives in Bluffton.

Tamra attended elementary and middle school at Lancaster, and graduated from Norwell in 1974.

It was there that she met her future husband, Douglas Edwards, who graduated in the same class.

Douglas, Shane, Skip, and Tammy Edwards

They married in March, 1975, and lived in Zanesville, Indiana, in a house trailer beside Doug's parents, Kenneth and Melba (McBride) Edwards. In March, 1977, they bought a home in Bluffton, where they resided until moving to their current home in Uniondale in June, 1983.

At the time of their marriage, Doug worked at Wayne Metal in Markle. From there he worked at Franklin Electric in Bluffton. Later, he became self-employed with a janitorial service which then expanded to a lawn and janitorial service. Currently his business is mainly lawn service, employing three to five in a season. He also is a livestock equipment distributor for Moorman's.

Tamra hired on at J.C. Penney in Fort Wayne in November, 1975, as a Christmas employee. In a few months, she moved from sales clerk to personnel where she stayed until February, 1978. Since then she has been employed as a bookkeeper for James S. Jackson Company, Inc. in Bluffton.

Two children were born to the couple. Shane Kenneth arrived on July 7, 1977 and Skip Douglas on April 22, 1982. Both are students in the Northern Wells School System.

Summers are extremely busy with the family's first love—baseball. Doug coaches, both boys play, and Tamra is the fan club (and sometimes sideline coach!)

EDWARDS-MCBRIDE FAMILY

Kenneth Edwards and Melba McBride were married at the Zanesville Church of God on September 2, 1955. Kenneth is the son of D. Wayne Edwards and Mildred Garrison. His Garrison background may be found in the Garrison-Biberstine writing in this book. Kenny's father was the son of William Edwards and Lillie McNabb. Lilli's father was James McNabb and her mother was Hulda Johnson. Her grandfather was William McNabb, and her mother was his second wife, Susan White. William, the son of Manley and Mary McNabb, was born in Washington County, East Tennessee, on October 15, 1825.

The family moved to southern Indiana in 1833, and William grew to manhood in Lawrence County where he lived until 1887 when he "homesteaded" near Ulysses, Kansas. In 1889, he moved to Medicine Lodge, Kansas where he spent the remaining years of life. He died on May 28, 1909. During the Civil War he was a member of the Company K, 17th Indiana Volunteers.

William was married five times and had thirteen children. Melba is the daughter of Donald McBride and Mary Martin Botts. Kenny was born in Fort Wayne, Indiana, and when he was three years old his parents moved to the Crow School just one-half mile north of Zanesville. Melba was born on the McBride farm just one-half mile south of Zanesville. Both were born in 1936. Kenny spent all his schooltime at Lafayette Central graduating from there in 1955. Melba spent her school years at East Union Center, graduating in 1954. It was at Lafayette's graduation in 1954 that Kenny noticed Melba and later arranged through a mutual friend, Lynn Smuts, to meet her and ask her for a date.

That date turned into a proposal of marriage a year later and a wedding that fall. The wedding was a small one with only a Labor Day weekend for a honeymoon, because Kenny had been accepted into the General Electric Apprentice School and was to start classes on Tuesday. Melba was employed in the offices at S.S. Kresge at Baer Field. Their first home was a nineteen foot trailer with no bathroom and no running water. It was parked at Melba's folks on the farm, and they paid $5.00 a month utilities. In the spring of 1956, their first son, Douglas, was born. In 1957 the Edwards purchased their first home and moved on #224 in Markle. They paid $2500 for the house and the payment was $25.00 a month. The heat bill ran about $90.00 a year. It was while they lived there that a second child, Robin, was born in 1958.

The Edwards
Back: Jonathan, Douglas, Jennifer, James, Jeremiah; Front: Robin, Kenny, Melba and Pollyanna

Soon after, Kenny graduated from apprentice school as a full fledged tool and die maker. On graduation, along with their diplomas, they received $100.00 and their lay-off slips. He never returned to GE when they called him. He immediately was hired by Franklin Electric in Bluffton and a few months later took a better job at Model Engineering in Huntington. After a year there, he was laid off and was told he would be called back soon. In the meantime he had met Jerry Yeoman while working there and he knew that he had just recently opened a new shop on Etna Avenue. He went out to talk to Jerry who said he had six weeks work for him. After the six weeks were up he hired him permanently, and for many years after, Jerry would come around on his anniversary and tell Kenny that he had six weeks more work for him. He spent twenty eight happy and productive years working for Jerry and his son, Ed. The last four years of being employed there, he was shop manager. Ed had taken over for his father when he passed away, and then Ed was taken by a heart attack at the age of thirty-six. Kenny left Yeomans to take a new job at J.B. Tool in Ft. Wayne where he now works. Currently, he is their only moldmaker and he enjoys working with the younger guys and teaching them his "old ways."

In 1959, they bought a new house in Skyline Addition in Markle. They enjoyed many years there and added three more to the family. Pollyanna was born in 1962, Jennifer in 1965, and James in 1970. In 1973, the Edwards moved back to their hometown of Zanesville.

They now live in Melba's great-grandfather Michael's home which was purchased by him in 1857 when it was the Zanesville House Hotel. It has never been out of the family since. In Zanesville the family has enjoyed being involved in church work, Lions Club, many, many charity events, and writing the Zanesville History Book and heading up the Centennial Celebration in 1976. They are also involved in this book as co-ordinators for Union Township.

After moving back to the big house, they added two more to the family making a total of seven lovely children. The last two came at once in the form of twin boys, Johnathan Michael and Jeremiah Martin. They were an unexpected joy to all when they were born one week late, on April 18, 1977. Jimmy (James McBride) is 21 this year and will be entering his last year at Huntington College where he is studying business management. The twins will be entering Homestead High School this fall as Freshmen. They spent their junior high years at Saint Peters Lutheran School in Huntington. The rest of the children are on their own and you may read their stories elsewhere in this book.

EDWARDS-MILLER

Jennifer Louise Edwards was born on May 28, 1965 at the Wells County Hospital in Bluffton. She was the fourth child of Kenneth and Melba McBride Edwards. Jenny attended kindergarten, first and second grade at Rockcreek Elementary as her family lived in Skyline Addition in Markle at the time. In 1973, her family moved to Zanesville across the Allen-Wells County line and she switched to Lafayette Central. Attending Woodside for seventh and eighth grades, she then went to Homestead to high school. At that time as a freshman, you could make a descision to work a little harder and graduate in three years. Jenny made this option because she already had a full time job as waitress for her sister. Her dream was to be a housewife and mother. The principal and the guidance counselor thought that was very unusual, and they tried to persuade her to take all four years. She didn't give in and graduated in 1982 with very good grades and more credits than she needed. In 1983 on August 20, she married Jeffrey P. (J.P.) Miller. J.P. was born on July 6, 1963 in Wabash County. He is the son of Karl Miller and Judy Garrison. Both were from Clear Creek Township of Huntington County. J.P.'s grandpa, Guy Miller, was a frequent customer at Richards in Huntington where Jenny worked. Jenny's sister, Pollyanna, also worked at the restaurant, and Guy wanted J.P. to meet her. When he came to meet

The Millers
Andrew, J.P., Abigail, Amy, Jenny

Pollyanna, he picked Jenny who was there instead. After they were married they moved into a house on Grandpa Miller's farm.

Their house burned in March of 1984. Luckily, Jenny was at work and J.P. was at Huntington College where he was attending school at the time. They then rented a college house and lived on campus until February 1986 when they moved to Toledo, Ohio to help start a church there. On July 30, 1986, their son Andrew Emery was born, and in April 1987, they moved to Columbia, Missouri with the church. In Columbia, Abigail Helene was born on January 19, 1988 and Amy Christine on January 6, 1990. In late 1988, J.P. started his own pest control business. Jenny helps with the business but she has fullfilled her dream of being a wife and mother. She is a wonderful mother to three very special children. J.P.'s Grandpa Miller is deceased but his grandmother, Hollis (Schwartz) Miller, lives in Huntington. His Grandmother Garrison died when his mother, Judy, was young and Grandpa Kenneth Garrison lives just outside of Huntington. Besides the writings in this book, you may find Jenny's grandparents in the following: *Zanesville Indiana History-1976*, J.L. McBride-*Biographical Memoirs of Wells County-1903*, David Martin Sr.-*Griswold's 1917 Pictorial History of Ft. Wayne*, Samuel Clem and Jonathan Michael-*History of Allen County 1880*, and Jonathan Michael-*History of Allen County 1880*, and Jonathan Michael (page 798), Jonas Cline (page 285), Clems (page 327 and 444), all of the *Biographical and Historical Record of Adams and Wells County 1887*, and all the Michael grandfathers-*Sulz am Neckar Germany History-1984*.

EDWARDS-PHILLIPS

Robin Edwards Phillips was born at the Wells Community Hospital on August 17, 1958. She is the daughter of Kenny and Melba McBride Edwards, of Zanesville. Robin lives in Zanesville also, next to their parents. She has a mobile home on the spot where her great-great-great grandfather John Michael's house sat when he first came to town in 1866 from Clear Spring, Maryland.

Robin grew up in Markle spending school time at the Markle Kindergarten, East Union, Rockcreek, and Ossian. She attended Norwell in her freshman year. Her parents then moved to Zanesville and she graduated from Homestead.

Robin Phillips receiving ten year award from Ron Milholland as Don Strong looks on.

In the spring of 1980, Robin married Mike Phillips, son of Fred and Mildred Huffman Phillips of Union Township. After several years of marriage, they parted friends and Mike is remarried. Robin is single. Here is her story:

Whoever said young people don't know what hard work is these days hasn't met Robin Phillips. At thirty-three, she is the manager of Richards Restaurant in Huntington and a twenty-one year veteran of the food service business.

Robin grew up in Markle, and as a twelve-year old in the summer of 1971, she walked to the Gateway Inn on Indiana-3, where she asked the owner, Vera Yates, for a job. She went home disappointed after Mrs. Yates told her she was too young to hire. But the next evening, Mrs. Yates called and said she did have a job for Robin. So, Robin returned to the Gateway Inn, where she washed dishes by hand, and peeled forty pounds of potatoes every evening after school.

"Mom always had us kids working around the house, I wanted something new to do," Robin recalled, "I figure I was putting in just about a 30-hour-week at Gateway Inn, and was getting paid one dollar an hour."

In 1973, when Robin's family moved from Markle to Zanesville, she had to leave her job at the restaurant. But as soon as she got her driver's license, Robin was back in Markle, asking for her old job. She was rehired as a cook by the Gateway Inn's new owner, Kyle Legge.

Robin graduated as an honor student from Homestead High School in 1976, and enrolled in Huntington College that fall as a math major. The following year, Robin left the Gateway Inn to work at the LK Restaurant on Lafayette Center Road near I-69. She was employed there as assistant manager for almost two years. Early in 1979, Robin heard there was going to be a new unit in the Richard's chain built in Huntington. Through the help of a family friend, Mary Webber of Bluffton, she contacted Don Strong the owner, and was quickly hired as the assistant manager. Not long after the restaurant opened, she was promoted to manager. She graduated with honors from Huntington College with a degree in education in 1980.

"Richards like to have their managers 'come from the kitchen.' Robin said, "because if you know the kitchen, you can run the whole restaurant." Robin certainly has 'done her time' in the kitchen. As manager, she coordinates the operation of the restaurant, delegating some jobs to others, but always taking care of the food orders and scheduling of employees. It is sometimes more than a full-time job, because Robin is responsible for the restaurant even when she's not there.

"There is a reward here, because you can see people improve around you," Robin reflects. "I appreciate hard work, and I always try to tell my employees when they've done a good job."

Richards attracts a good lunch trade from Huntington offices and factories during the week, but the restaurant's busiest time is Sunday lunch.

She has developed a good rapport with her regulars. "I enjoy being with people and visting with the customers," she said. "Some of our morning customers come and sit at the counter just so they can watch us work up at the kitchen window!"

Since Richards considers itself a "family" restaurant, it is fitting that part of Robin's family works with her.

Her sister, Pollyanna Bennett, has been her employee off and on since the restaurant opened. A sister, Jennifer Miller, was her head waitress for several years. Her brother, Doug Edwards, contracts the cleaning. Brothers Jim and Doug also have worked for her at times in the kitchen and waiting tables. Mom Edwards does the decorating and Dad helps with repairs. This year two more Edwards became employees, as Jonathan and Jeremiah (twin brothers), are busing tables and washing dishes.

The restaurant is a large part of her life but she still takes time out to enjoy family and friends. She loves to travel and shop and several years ago treated her family, Mom, Dad, and brothers Jim, Johnathan, and Jeremiah to a cruise to the Bahamas. Her dream is to have all of the family go the next time.

EMIL AND MAGDALENA AMSTUTZ EGLY

Since the naturalization of the children follows that of the parent, it is believed that, when Emil Egly aplied for his final naturalization papers on August 18, 1913, there had never been another instance when so many citizens had been made by the naturalization of a single individual. Emil and his wife Magdalena were the parents of seventeen

Emil Egly family picture taken about 1911
Backrow, L to R: Edwin, Noah, Zella, Albert, Ida, Lewis, and Lydia.; Front row: Martha, Lizzie, Father Emil holding Levi, Edna, Clara, Mother Magdalena holding Ralph, Glen, and Emma. One son, Hugh, had died two years earlier and another son, Walter, was born one year after this picture was taken.

329

children, nine sons and eight daughters, who were born over a period of twenty-seven years. The first was born when the mother was nineteen and the father twenty-four; the last, when the mother was forty-six and the father fifty-one.

The father of this large family was born April 3, 1861, in the Canton of Bern, Switzerland. His parents were Benedict and Maria Blotter Von Gunten Egly. Emil and one or two of his brothers ran away from home to escape entering the Swiss Army and were stowaways on a cattle ship bound for America. Sailors befriended the boys on the third day at sea and made them work their way across the ocean. They landed in New York City on May 3, 1882. The Egly boys then traveled to the Swiss community of Berne, Indiana where they earned money to bring the remainder of the family to America.

While in Berne, handsome Emil, who had sandy red hair, met the pretty Magdalena Amstutz who was the sixth of Abraham and Elizabeth Augsburger Amstutz's twelve children. She was born April 3, 1866. Magdalena had come to Berne from her family's home near Beaverdam, Ohio, in 1884, and was making her home with Mr. and Mrs. John Gerber. After a whirlwind courtship, Emil and Magdalena were married in Berne on August 5, 1884.

After their marriage, the couple moved to Wells County where they lived back a long lane on the French farm in Nottingham Township. Thirteen of their seventeen children were born there. The names and dates of birth of the children area as follows: Albert, July 16, 1885; Ida, August 8, 1886; Lydia, December 25, 1887; Noah, April 10, 1889; Lewis, March 10, 1891; Zella, September 28, 1893; Elizabeth, January 13, 1895; Emma, April 9, 1896; Hugh, October 25, 1897; Edwin, January 27, 1899; Martha, November 25, 1901; Glen, January 4, 1903; Levi, September 27, 1905; Clara, October 1, 1907; Edna, October 23, 1908; Ralph, April 22, 1910 and Walter, April 12, 1912. The last four children were born after the family moved to a farm in French Township in Adams County. Later the family moved to a farm in Adams County near Peterson, Indiana.

The older children attended Warner School while they lived in Wells County. They also walked to the Nottingham Church for revival meetings.

All of the above mentioned Egly family members have now passed away; however, their descendents hold an annual reunion on the fourth Sunday in June.

EICHHORN

Robert and Mary (Bailey) Eichhorn were married November 20, 1937, in Bluffton, Indiana, at the parsonage of the Reformed Church by Reverend Matthew Worthman.

Robert was born November 14, 1914, in Lancaster Township, Wells County to John and Emma (Schoonover) Eichhorn. He graduated from Lancaster High School in 1931. Mary was born October 13, 1915, in Union Township, Wells County to John and Myrl (Gilbert) Bailey. She graduated from Rockcreek High School in 1933.

Robert and Mary live on the farm and in the same house where he was born. He has been a farmer all his life. He farmed with his father and brother Elco for a while. At one time they owned one of the first pull type combine and rubber-tired tractor in Wells County. Robert is still farming 200-acres with the help of his grandson, Kevin Morris, who is also employed at the Bob Bate Chevrolet Agency in Ossian.

Bob and Mary Eichhorn, Jim and Joan

Robert's father told us his great-great grandparents came to America crossing the ocean in a small boat.

Robert and Mary are the parents of two children, Jimmie Lee Eichhorn and Marilyn Joan Morris. Jim married Connie Booth in Bluffton on June 27, 1959. They live in Adams County. They have three children. Kent Alan was born on June 3, 1960, Cindy Sue was born on June 9, 1962, and Adam Lee was born on December 27, 1973. Cindy was married to Leslie Jay Smith on April 11, 1987. They have one son Jay Michael Smith born on September 27, 1990. Joan married Richard Allen Morris on June 1, 1963, and they live in Wells County. They have two children, Kevin Richard, who was born November 29, 1965, and Kami Jo, who was born May 18, 1970. Kevin married Deborah Meek on December 20, 1986. They have one son, Austin Mitchell, born on April 4, 1990. Kami will be married on June 22, 1991, to Marc Gavilanez. Marc is a son of Doctor Marcelo and Joan Gavilanez of Bluffton.

Bob and Mary have been active in the Wells County Farm Bureau several years, Mary being a county woman's leader for eighteen years, and Bob, Lancaster Township Chairman. They are active in the First United Church of Christ, and Mary is a member of the Friendly Neighbors Home Demonstration Club.

Bob and Mary both recall their first year of school as having to walk to school. Bob walked about one mile to Murray School and Mary about a mile to Sugar Grove, which is located one mile south of Uniondale. Mary also rode a horse drawn wagon hack for a few years to Murray School.

VON A. (PAT) EICHHORN FAMILY

Dad was one of eight children born to Charles and Harriet Jane Brickley Eichhorn. A brother and sister died in infancy and are buried at St. Paul Cemetery. Von had a twin brother Don. He was born two to three minutes before midnight and dad two minutes after midnight. When the doctor made it into the county seat to register the births, he remembered they had occurred on different days.

Von "Pat" Eichhorn

Von was married in 1927 or 1928 to Myrtle Anna Fairchild who graduated from West Rockcreek. Dad met Mom at Markle when she was taking violin lessons and playing in her high school orchestra. They have three children: Mary Jane, Gloria Anna, and Thomas Franklin. They all graduated from East Rockcreek High School. They have each married and each has three children.

Von worked for General Electric in Fort Wayne nineteen and one-half years and quit to start his own Electric, Heating, Plumbing, and Appliance Store in Uniondale. He first campaigned for joint State Senator of Wells, Adams, and Blackford Counties in 1928, and was Senator from 1930 to 1958. Many youngsters from this area served as Senate Pages through these years.

Mom says that you were lucky if you lived near a river. They had an ice house, it had double walls two feet thick, and the walls were filled with sawdust. The cut blocks of ice would keep all summer long.

We had an ice box on our back porch when I was young, and bought blocks of ice for fifteen, twenty and thirty cents each.

I can remember when Dad came home from the factory and put on old ear phones, dialed in a lot of static, and kept yelling at us kids to "keep quiet" while he listened to Father Coughlin, and politics, etc.

EISAMAN FAMILY

From post-graduate studies in New York and Philadelphia, Doctor Jack L. Eisaman and Mrs. Mary Alice Eisaman came to Bluffton in 1940. He was the third physician to join the Doctors Caylor and Nickel at the Caylor-Nickel Clinic.

Doctor Eisaman was a graduate of Columbia City High School and Indiana University School of Medicine.

Mary Alice Ringo Eisaman was graduated from Muncie Central High School, Ward Belmont Junior College, and Indiana University.

Doctor Eisaman served in an Evacuation Hospital Unit of the United States Seventh Army in Europe during the World War II.

The Eisamans are the parents of Mrs. Jean Eltaiby of Rapid City, South Dakota, Mrs. Judy Schroeder of Washington, D.C., and John Ringo Eisaman of Bluffton. Jean and Judy each have a son and a daughter. John and his wife, the former Roberta Gerber, are the parents of Jack W. and John, Jr., Mrs. Nicholas Ringger (Jeanette), and Julie—all in the Bluffton area.

Doctor Eisaman makes his home at Crooked Lake in Whitley County and Venice, Florida. He is board certified in Internal Medicine, a member of the American College of Cardiology and the American College of Physicians of the Chest. He is a past president of the Bluffton Kiwanis Club.

During her fifty years residency in Bluffton, Mary Alice Eisaman has been active in many community activities. She is a member of the First United Methodist Church.

In 1944, she was one of the founders of the Wells County Society for Crippled Children and Adults. For a number of years she was president of the organization. She was the first woman to be president of the Indiana Easter Seal Society for Crippled Children and Adults and served on the national level. She has been active in the elimnation of architectural barriers for the handicapped. As president of the local society she was influential in the formation of the Vera Cruz Opportunity School which has developed into ARC.

one from William Brindle at Zanesville, and one from Thurber and Salisbury. His son, Dale, joined him in business when he purchased the old Jefferson Township School on Mill Street after the new school on South Jefferson was put into use. He converted the building into several apartments, as well as Ossian's first funeral parlor. Until this time the embalming, viewing, and final ceremonies were conducted in the homes of the deceased.

Mr. Elzey, as an ordained minister, could perform weddings as well as funeral ceremonies, and was often called upon to speak at special occasions.

Abner S., Siddie, and daughter, Ilow, lived in the east apartment and Abner W. and Anne lived in the west one for fifteen years.

Abner White Elzey joined the firm as a full partner, and the furniture and funeral business continued until 1958 when the funeral home in Ossian, and the Waynedale branch, became Elzey, Dickey, Haggard Funeral Homes, and later Elzey, Haggard.

Dale's wife, Magdalene White, a daughter of David White and Emma Kreigh was one of the first women in the state to be certified as a licensed embalmer. Dale served on the board of the Ossian State Bank for 20 years, several of which as vice-president.

Dale and Magdalene had two children: Abner W. and Phyllis Ann. Abner married Anne M. Young in 1934, and Phyllis married Dr. Ernest a. Baade. The Baades had two children, Richard and Sheryl. Abner and Anne had three, Sandra, Dalene, and DeLynn (Dean).

A.S. Elzey was responsible for putting Waynedale on the map. It was named for son, Dale.

Anne, after serving as Jefferson Township Chairman for several years, was executive secretary to the Wells County Tuberculosis Association for fourteen years. She was a volunteer to the Fort Wayne Veterans Hospital Occupational Therapy Department, for nine years, as a representative of the American Legion Auxiliary.

Elisha V. (second) Elzey was born 1845 and died in 1933. Abner S. was born in 1867 and died in 1949. Dale E. was born in 1895 and died in 1983. Abner W. was born in 1915 and died in 1984.

ELZEY-DECKER

Ezkiel and Christina (Blosser) Elzey had seven sons, Daniel, Joseph, Emmanuel, John, Jesse, Calvin, and Isom. William and Isabella (Young) Decker had ten children, Wilson, John, Burris, Charles, Earl, Minnie, Anna, Olive, and twins, Zeffa and Effie.

The Elzey Family in 1932
L to R, Standing: Donald, Minnie, Earl, Lela, Byrl, Erma, Fred, Viva Sitting: Maxine, father Isom, Doris mother, Effie, Mary

Isom Elzey married Effie (Decker) October 31, 1896. Twelve children were born. Ruth died in infancy. Mary's (Virgil Davison) son, Charles, died age seven, daughter, Rowena, has daughters Rebecca, Connie, Sandra and Kathy. Erma's (Glen Ulmer) children are: Mary (Fred Weiland), Bette (Robert Knox), and William. Their children: Daniel, Scott and Ann Weiland; Robert, Mary Jo and Lisa Knox; William, Steve, Jodi and Lee Ulmer. Lela's (Deloss Ormsby) children are: Vaughn (Margie Glander), Max (Jayne Rigger), Ruth (Sabel Bates), Robert (Norma Noonan), Wendell (Janet Smith) and Donald (Sandra Blair). Vaughn's children are: Reggie, Tim, Julie and Jill; Max's daughter is Nancy and son, Tom. Ruth had daughters, Karen and Linda. Robert's children are: Danny, Keith and Kathy. Wendell's children are: Joti, Jeff, John and Jason. Donald's children are Lora, James, Greg, Kelli, Renae and Eric.

During World War II, Vaughn served with the U.S. Maines, Max and Robert with the U.S. Navy and Wendell with the U.S. Army. Fred never married and died at age 39. Minnie (Charles Rupright) had no children. Donald's (Eileen Blem) daughter is Anna Rose (Charles Brockelsby) and their children are Daren and Nick. Earl's (Lucille Nichelson) daughter is Dixie (Edwin Snider) and her children are: Lori, Michael, Lynette and Murray. Earl ("Peck") was a stand-out basket-ball player at Lancaster. Byrl's, twin to Earl (Olean Daughterty), daughter was Bette Rose. Her children are Debbie, Gary, David and Rae Lee.

Byrl served in the U.S. Army during World War II, where he was killed in action during the Battle of the Bulge on January 17, 1945. Viva's (Leon Falk) children are Richard (Sharon McFarren), Diane (Les Claghorn) twins, Denny (Lorraine Miller) and David (Terri Schortgen). Richard has twins, Jason and Justin, and Jennifer. Diane's children are Mark and Elizabeth Ann. Denny's children are Adam, Daniel and Jesse, step-daughter Lisa Contadeluci; Maxine's (Robert Dentel) children are Kent and Carol Ann (Jeff Rice). Kent's son is Shawn. Carol's children are Jeremy and Amanda. Dentel served four and one-half years in U.S. Army during World War II. He was wounded in the Philippines and received Purple Heart. Doris (Wendell Schwartz) has sons: Ronald (Dian Spencer), David (JoElla Ernst) and Stephen (Patty Moyer). Ron's children are Ron Jr., Julie, Christopher, Timothy, Suzanne, twins Michael and Catherine, and Sarah. David's children are Matthew, William, Rebecca and Kimberly. Stephen's children are Brian and Cliff. David served with the U.S. Army in Vietnam and received the Purple Heart.

The Elzey family lived one mile north of Murray for approximately twenty-five years. Their occupation was farming. Father also drove a school "hack" approximately twenty-five years, first by horses and later by motor bus. The route was later taken over by his son, Byrl, until he was drafted into the Army in 1944. The family operated a cider mill located in Murray. Later it was moved to the farm. The family drinking water was derived from a natural spring. Schools attended were Murray, Lancaster, and Bluffton. Mary and Erma attended Bluffton before Lancaster had a four-year high school. They attended the Murray Christian Church.

ELZEY-SNIDER

My father, J. Earl "Peck" Elzey was born in Wells County, Lancaster Township in 1913. He was one of twelve children born to Isam and Effie

Decker Elzey. He had a twin brother, Byrl, who was killed during World War II.

He graduated in 1932 and played basketball for the Lancaster "Bobcats" for four years of his high school. At his commencement address the speaker told the class he didn't know what their career choices could be unless maybe an undertaker, since this was during the depression.

In 1943, he bought a farm next to the Lancaster School and spent the remainder of his years in that location. He was a farmer, raised cattle and worked a few years at General Electric in Fort Wayne. Coon hunting was one of his hobbies.

Edwin and Dixie (Elzey) Snider, Michael and Lynette

He married N. Lucille Nichelson in 1937. Her father, Theodore Nichelson and mother, Deloress McBride Nichelson, along with a brother Claude, worked hard as share-croppers in Union, Rockcreek and Lancaster Townships. They belonged to the church of God in Zanesville, Indiana.

One child, Dixie Elzey, was born in 1938 to Earl and Lucille at Bluffton, Indiana. She started school at Lancaster in the fall of 1944 with Mrs. Leonora Byrd as the teacher. After nine years at Lancaster the last three years were completed at Salamonie Township School in Warren, Indiana.

Dixie married Edwin Snider of Grant County, son of George and Geraldine Boyer Snider. They lived five years in Jackson Township until they moved to their present home in Rockcreek Township on 300W, known as the Cover Place.

They are members of Saint Mark Lutheran Church in Uniondale, Indiana.

Four children were born to this union. Michael in 1958, graduated from Norwell and has an Associate degree from Ivy Tech. He is employed at K-K Tool and Design in Markle, Indiana. He obtained a private pilot license in 1986.

Lynette born in 1960, graduated from Norwell, attended Ball State, and dental hygiene in Gainesville, Florida. She is a dental hygienist living in Fort Wayne.

Laurie Ann born in 1963, died at the age of nineteen months. Murray born in 1966 died in 1976 of leukemia.

Edwin works at the Dana Corporation in Fort Wayne as head maintenance welder and enjoys flying their airplane with son Michael.

Dixie serves as a rural mail carrier at the Markle Post Office with service starting in 1975.

GLEN EMLEY FAMILY

In 1918, Fay and Harmon Emley, living in Clear Creek, Huntington County, traded their new Ford on forty acres in Union Township, Wells County. They had four children: Roscoe, Erman, Glen, and Dorothy, who grew up on this farm. They graduated from Union Center High School and went to church at Prospect. Through the years, they added eighty acres to their farm. Harmon drove a stock truck, hauling stock and moving people around Uniondale.

Glen and Doris Martin were married in 1940. At this time, Glen took over his father's business. Later Glen went to the Marine Corp., came home in July, 1946, and bought forty acres in Jefferson Township. In January, 1947, Glen went to work for International Harvester. We moved to Uniondale in November, 1948. Our daughter, Linda, was born in April, 1949. We bought our present home in June, 1951. Our daughter, Glenice, was born in June, 1957.

Linda and William LeBeau live in Fort Wayne. They both work at Lincoln National Life Insurance Company. Their daughter, Kelly Wolfe, is a sophomore at Concordia High School. Their son, Gordon Wolfe, lives with his father in Ossian and is a junior at Norwell High School.

Glenice and Steve Godsey live near Markle. They both work at K-Mart Fort Wayne Distribution Center and own and operate a used car lot in Markle. They have two children. Their daughter, Jeri Danielle Godsey, is a sixth grader at Norwell Middle School. Their son, Jeremy Glen Godsey, is a third grader at Lancaster Elementary School.

Glen and Doris are now both retired and spend their summers at the lake near Coldwater, Michigan, where Glen likes to fish. Glen is also a Past Master of Markle Masonic Lodge #453, a Past Patron of Markle Eastern Star #567, and a Past President of District 14 Association. Doris is a Past matron of Markle Eastern Star $567.

DANIEL ENGLE

Daniel Engle grew up on a farm the tenth of thirteen children, nine of whom grew to adulthood and married. His sister, Emma, died the day he was born.

On July 18, 1896, he married Emma Nevada Maurer from east of Geneva, Indiana. Daniel's brother "Link" (William) had a farm one-half mile south of Harper School. His brother "Mort" (Robert) had eighty acres one-half mile north of Harper School. Joe, Arthur, and Dan Engle acquired one hundred sixty acres (the home place) which was one-half mile west of Harper and one-half mile east of Phoenix. Dan bought out Joe and Arthur about 1900.

Five children were born to Dan and Emma: Harry born 1898, died January 8, 1967, married Gladys Romanie; J. Merle born January 3, 1900, married Mary Magdalene Deeds; Melvin Henry born 1902, married Ruth McConnel; Nellie born 1905, married Ivan Cash; Ethel born 1910, married Don Lightfoot.

Dan and Emma lived on the farm using horses, then steam. He at one time or another had a ditching machine, corn shredder, Clover huller, and a thrashing machine. These machines were uses on his own farm and to do custom work for the community. In 1912 Dan moved his family and belongings (including a team of mules) to Bayou Coden, Alabama. They arrived there December 25. He went there to clean and plant orange trees for another man. His son Merle remembers plowing new ground as a thirteen-year-old in the summer of 1913. Dan came back to the Indiana farm and brought Harry with him to thrash grain. The rest of the family was left in Alabama. Emma was not happy with the arrangement and told her husband. Dan said if she didn't like it to come back. So Emma packed up everything in September of 1913 and all moved back—including the mules. They moved into a house in the southeast corner of Pennville, Indiana. Dan invested in a cement block factory with Doctor Charles Caylor Sr. A storm destroyed it in 1915 or 1916. At that time Dan bought and moved into a brick house west of the elevator. He bought into the elevator with three other men and sold out in 1949.

Emma Engle died in January 1935. Dan died in February 1961. They are buried in the Odd Fellows Cemetery east of Pennville.

DANIEL LEE ENGLE

Daniel was born June 26, 1961, in the Wells Community Hospital in Bluffton. He is the son of Guy Edward and Jeannine Shull Engle. He lived with his parents at 4098E SR 218 until he was three years old. At that time, he moved with his family to LaFox, Illinois, where his father was building maintenance supervisor and his mother taught business courses at Broadview Academy, a Seventh-day Adventist boarding school for grades nine-twelve. Daniel attended elementary school at the Aurora SDA elementary school ten miles from home. He enjoyed home, school and church activities—especially camping with the Pathfinders (a church-sponsored club for children of grades five-ten). Following graduation from eighth grade, Daniel continued his education at Broadview Academy, where he not only studied but worked at various occupations on and off campus. He worked on grounds and maintenance and in the academy print shop, operated the public address system in the chapel, and worked at Harris Pine furniture plant off campus. He graduated in 1980.

Daniel Lee Engle

Daniel had obtained an interest in electronics, so when he entered Andrews University that fall, he began studies in electronics engineering technology. As part of his four year program, he was required to spend co-op time working in an actual work situation. Daniel spent two summers doing co-op work at Florida Hospital in Orlando, Florida and graduated with a BS degree from Andrews University in the fall of 1984. Florida Hospital hired him on a full-time basis and Daniel moved to Orlando. In the fall of 1986, Daniel's path crossed that of another Indiana native, Nancy Arlene Driscol, also a graduate of Andrews University. She was employed at Florida Hospital in the fund raising department. Daniel and Nancy were married September 27, 1987, in Columbus, Indiana. At the present time Daniel is employed by Florida Hospital in Information Systems as supervisor of PC support. Nancy is employed by the University of Central Florida in fund raising.

GUY EDWARD ENGLE

Guy was the son of J. Merle Engle and Mary Martha Deeds Engle. He was born November 29, 1926, on the Engle homestead near Phoenix in Wells County. He grew up in a rural setting and learned farming skills. Guy attended eleven grades of school at Pennville, then spent his twelfth year of schooling at Petroleum, where he graduated. After graduation, he was persuaded to enlist in the Air Force requesting training in airplane engine mechanics. He was sent to Lackland Air Force Base in San Antonio, Texas. The roster of men in which he was listed was split arbitrarily through the middle. Those in one half were sent to airplane engine mechanics school and the other half were kept as permanent personnel at Lackland. Guy was in the group destined to stay at Lackland. He spent time in the air police and the ended up working in the service club. Guy attained the rank of sergeant and left at the end of his three year stint.

Daniel, Jeannine, Linda, Guy, Sally

Guy married Helen Marie Shorter Grumbles April 2, 1948. On January 29, 1949, Linda Lucille was born to them. Guy and Helen bought a home in San Antonio but later sold it and moved back to Indiana. While in Texas, Guy joined the Seventh-day Adventist Church, of which Helen was already a member. On their return to Indiana Guy worked at a variety of jobs, including Warner Gear at Muncie, door-to-door selling of Seventh-day Adventist books, and electrical work with an electrician in the local church. Eventually they moved back to the farm near Reiffsburg, where Guy farmed for a time, then got a job at Dunbar Furniture in Berne, Indiana.

Helen divorced Guy in 1956. Later, Guy met Jeannine Shull at the local SDA Church. On June 30, 1957, they were married. Jeannine was the daughter of Francis Shull and Eunice Ruth Johnson Shull. Jeannine was born February 11, 1929, at Berrien Springs, Michigan. She, with her parents, moved in with her grandparents, Glessner and Rachel Johnson, in Wells County at the age of four during the depression. Jeannine attended Rockcreek Center School through grade ten. She then attended Indiana Academy, an SDA boarding school at Cicero, Indian, and graduated in 1947. She attended Andrews University at Berrien Springs, Michigan, and graduated in June 1951 with a BA degree in business education. Jeannine taught business education classes at Cedar Lake Academy, in Michigan five years and at Battle Creek Academy for one year.

After their marriage, Guy and Jeannine lived at the home place near Reiffsburg seven years, then moved to Broadview Academy, LaFox, Illinois, where guy was maintenance supervisor and Jeannine taught part-time. Guy and Jeannine had two children: Sally Anne, born August 3, 1959, married Kenny Ray Seymour; and Daniel Lee, born June 26, 1961, married Nancy Arlene Driscol.

In 1982, Jeannine and Guy moved to her parents home in Rockcreek Township to look after her mother and, later, her father.

ISAAC ENGLE

Isaac Engle traces his ancestry from his parents, William and Lutitia Engle, back through seven generations to four brothers who in 1683 came to the United States from Cambridgeshire, England, which is about sixty four miles from London.

Isaac married Ann Hopkins of Waynesville, Ohio, on December 23, 1857, and migrated with a brother to Wells County, Indiana, sometime in 1859 or 1860. He bought one hundred sixty acres of land east of Phoenix. It is related that the woods were so thick that, when Ann went to pick berries, she got lost. She "hollered" and Isaac answered until she found her way home.

Isaac was a farmer and was active in Republican politics. He was on the jury for the first murder trial in the county. He made one or two trips a year to Fort Wayne with hog meat and other goods to sell and trade for what he couldn't raise. He had a large orchard and a sorghum mill.

Isaac and Ann had thirteen children: Prudence, born May 11, 1859, died October 27, 1879; William "Link," born September 19, 1860, died April 11, 1942, married Mary E. Hilton; Emma F., born December 21, 1862, died September 1, 1876; Robert "Mort," born September 7, 1864, died May 24, 1945, married Roseta McLain; Hannah, born October 23, 1866, died March 29, 1901, married Samuel Fisher; James A., born July 30, 1869, died April 17, 1946, married Mary E. Shoemaker; Martha A., born October 22, 1871, died October 20, 1944, married E.W. Lewis; Charles R., born October 9, 1872, died December 31, 1873; Amanda E., born January 31, 1875, died August 25, 1875; Daniel, born September 1, 1876, died February 14, 1961, married Emma Maurer; Joseph C., born August 27, 1878, died May 21, 1907, married Mary Regester; Horrace E. born June 20, 1882, died October 25, 1882; Arthur Leslie, born February 9, 1884; died April 6, 1956, married Roseta Books.

Ann Hopkins Engle died March 7, 1891, and was buried in the old cemetery east of Pennville, Isaac died September 20, 1896, and was buried beside her.

J. MERLE ENGLE

J. Merle (the J was added when somebody told him he should have a third initial) grew up on the farm, driving, riding and working mules and steam equipment. He went to Alabama with is parents in 1912 and returned with his mother in 1913. He worked on his father's farm, in the block factory, and in the mill. Upon finishing school, Merle worked at a factory in Fort Wayne, then went west and worked in the Kansas wheat fields and the Oklahoma oil fields.

J. Merle Engle, Mary Deeds Engle

On January 12, 1924, Merle married Mary M. Deeds, who was born in Randolph County, Indiana, January 24, 1903. They started housekeeping in a little red house in the woods at the farm by Phoenix. In 1930, they moved to Doctor Charles Caylor's farm west of Pennville and farmed for him. In 1944, they bought a 160-acre farm one-half mile east of Reiffsburg in Wells County, where they did general farming. Merle served on the jury for the second murder trial in Wells County.

Merle and Mary had six children: Iris Marie, born October 20, 1924, married Max Reynolds; Naomi Mae, born October 29, 1925, married Fred M. St. John; Guy Edward, born November 29, 1926, married Helen M. Grumbles; his second marriage was to Jeannine Shull; Ray Carlton, born October 26, 1927, died December 31,1941; Wilma Jessie, born August 3, 1929, married Bill Fuller; Waneta June, born August 3, 1929, died September 30, 1930.

Merle and Mary joined the Reiffsburg United Methodist Church. They built a new house on four acres just east of Reiffsburg in 1949. Merle later retired and rented the farm out to be farmed. Mary died July 24, 1976. She is buried in the Odd Fellows Cemetery at Pennville beside Waneta and Ray. Merle continued to live at home. He sold the farm except for the house and one acre of land around it. His daughter Jessie and her family live in the house.

JEFF ESPICH FAMILY

Although we can't set an exact date, we know that the Espich family first came to Wells County some time just prior to the 1850's. They settled in the northern part of the county around the Zanesville area.

Our family has been traced back to Michael Espich, who was born in 1573 at Lilitz, Germany, and became the Duke of Silesia. Next of note came William Espich, born in 1703 in Germany, a farmer who brought the family to Pennsylvania to escape religious persecution.

A sad note, for me, is that the family name is likely to end soon in Wells County. That is, unless the young ladies who are the latest in the family line decide both to remain here and adopt the "novel" idea of keeping the family name through marriage and children. Those young ladies are our teenage daughters, Cari and Kimberly Espich, both of whom are fortunate to have attributes that should serve them well in life. The word "our" denotes myself, Jeff, and my wife and best friend, Sharon Cary Espich. Sharon came to Indiana from Illinois for a college education as a teacher and got a family in addition. I have really never left home, except for college and the U.S. Army.

Wells County has treated us well. A small family business has kept both Sharon and me gainfully employed, and the people of this area have elected me their state representative for the past twenty years. That government service has been most rewarding as we try to help prepare our neighbors and our state for the future.

My parents, Helen Keller Espich and Doyle Espich, have spent their lives in this community, though mom was born a county away. Dad was of the Zanesville family and Grandpa Keller was a railroader who brought mom to Wells County when he was working the "rails." The folks were good people who worked hard, followed their religion, and gave of themselves to their family and community. Daughter Marcia is a teacher and lives in Allen County with her husband, Steve Gabet and son Zac.

Four uncles and aunts were born in Wells County to dad's side, though only Uncle Ed Espich and wife, Reada, remain with most of their offspring nearby. Close relationships with these good people were important in our youth and remain a part of our lives. Grandparents on Dad's side were Effie Meeks and Walter Espich, born in Zanesville and Uniondale in the 1880's. Mom's parents were Virgie Brickley, a part of the Brickley family that remains in Wells County, and Clarence Keller, who was born in Whitley County and was my "buddy" during childhood years.

Great-great-grandparents were the ones who were the first Espichs to settle in Wells County, though I must admit the names get a little confusing. John William Espich, who died at Zanesville in the year 1851, is the first recorded Espich in Wells County, but records also indicate that there were dozens of Espichs in the area during the last half of the 1800's. A fruitful time. (Jeff Espich)

JOHN EVERSOLE FAMILY

The Jacob and Susannah (Miller) Eversole family came from Fairfield County, Ohio, in 1854 to Rockcreek Township Wells County, near Markle, Indiana. Then to Lancaster Township, near Murray, Indiana, about 1862 or 1863. Jacob was a mail carrier on horseback. His route was east of Murray about two miles, and then back to the Murray Post Office. They had eleven children.

William Henry Eversole was born in 1847, and killed by a Clover Leaf freight train at Bluffton, Indiana, July 26, 1926, age 79. He married Lucinda Freds. Eleven children were born to them: Charles, Oren, Bertha, Jennie, Mary, Minnie, Tena, John, Vera, and twins who died in infancy.

John Eversole, born November 28, 1900, died May 21, 1961, was a school teacher and surveyor. He was in World War I, and was sent to France and Germany. When he returned, he became Wells County Treasurer. In 1921, he married Vesta Linn Neff, born March 31, 1895 and died July 1975. She was superintendent of nurses at the Wells County Hospital in Bluffton, Indiana. Her father and mother were Mr. and Mrs. Nate (Elizabeth) Neff, who had seven children. Later, Mr. Eversole was a Realtor and an insurance salesman. He worked for the Louisville, Kentucky Land Bank for fourteen years. He owned a farm east of Bluffton, which is now the Marckres Addition. Mrs. Eversole was a registered nurse, doing some private duty, and she helped with the Red Cross classes during World War II. In 1923, a daughter, Nina Jane, was born to them. She became an registered nurse, also, and worked in surgery at the Lutheran Hospital in Fort Wayne, Indiana. She later helped start the Whitley County Hospital, Columbia City, Indiana, as superintendent of nurses in charge of surgery. In 1952, Nina Jane Eversole married Raymond E. Meyer (son of David and Margaret Engeler Meyer).

Raymond (Electrical Engineer of Purdue University) and Nina Jane live in Raymond's home place in Bluffton. They had two children. John E. Meyer (graduate of Indiana University as an Optician) is now in Indianapolis, Indiana, where he is the lab specialist for Lens Crafters. Karen (graduate of Indiana University in Respiratory Therapy) is married to Larry D. Strahm of Monroe, Indiana, and he is second vice-president and works in the Leasing Corporation for Manufacturers Bank, Detroit, Michigan.

On October 10, 1990, a daughter, Lauren Elizabeth, was born to Karen and Larry.

ROGER EYMER FAMILY

On a cold, snowy evening, November 21, 1959, Roger Henry Eymer and Jane Ellen Schrader repeated their marriage vows in a small Methodist Church in Centreville, Michigan.

Roger, born January 27, 1939, in Constantine, Michigan, was the sixth child and fourth son of eight children born to Dorothy (Gross) Eymer and Lester C. Eymer. Following his mother's death, Roger, at age four, lived first with relatives and then in many foster homes in Saint Joseph County, Michigan. Eventually, as a young teen, he settled in the Sturgis, Michigan area with Clarence and Marie Hagen and their two daughters, Ardith and Gloria. These loving people became family.

Jane, born October 7, 1940, was the third child and second daughter of four children born at Three Rivers, Michigan, to Agnes (Teller) Schrader and Louis G. Schrader. Until her marriage, she lived on a small farm near Nottawa, Michigan. Much to the delight of present family members, the one-room, stone schoolhouse Jane attended during her elementary years has become a museum. Many items displayed in the museum came from the Schrader farm.

Roger and Jane Eymer

The marriage of Roger Eymer and Jane Schrader produced three daughters: Kelly Diane, born January 24, 1961; Karen Marie, born April 25, 1963; and Karlene Ellen, born November 23, 1967. The girls were all born in Sturgis, Michigan, the community in which Roger and Jane set up housekeeping. (Future pets also proved to be female).

The Eymers lived in Sturgis for ten years, with Roger working as owner/operator of a canned milk route. Before the birth of their first child, Jane worked in the offices of the Kirsch Company in Sturgis.

As an army reservist, Roger was called into active duty during the Berlin Wall crisis. He was stationed during this time in Fort Lewis, Washington.

In 1969, the family moved south to the small community of LaGrange, Indiana, where Roger worked for the Standard Oil Company and later as co-manager of the Farm Bureau Cooperative. During this time, Jane worked as secretary and Christian Education Director in the LaGrange First United Methodist Church.

In October of 1980, the Eymer family, minus two daughters by this time, moved to Bluffton, Indiana following a job offer for Roger at the Wells County Farm Bureau Cooperative. Shortly after the move, Jane accepted the position of Christian Education Director and Administrative Assistant at the Bluffton First United Methodist Church. Roger presently manages Inland Oils in Fort Wayne.

In 1982, daughter Karen married Jeffrey L. Prible of Bluffton. This union has produced children: Michael David, Matthew Lynn, and Meghan Marie. The family is engaged in farming, residing at 4343S 200 East, Bluffton. Daughter Kelly married Taron W. Smith of Columbia city in 1983. They have two daughters, Malorie Marie and Maggie Jane. The family is associated with the Smith and Sons Funeral Homes in Columbia City and South Whitley. Daughter Karlene holds a management position with a Fort Wayne retail clothing store.

The family's migration "south" has contributed to the expansion of the once small Eymer family, which now numbers twelve at immediate family gatherings.

Roger and Jane currently reside at 1927S Hoosier Highway, Bluffton. is "home."

FAHL

The Fahl family ancestors were Pennsylvania Dutch. They were of German descent. Daniel, Mary and Henry Fahl lived on a farm east of Huntington on 900N.

Daniel married Lydia Lantis whose parents were of Swiss decent. They lived on a farm near Bly, a crossroads town now extinct. Three children were born to this union. Their names were Charles Elmer, Leah Samantha and Mary. The mother died when Mary was about two years old and Mary grew up in the grandparent Lantis's home. Daniel later remarried a younger sister of Lydia, Elizabeth. To this union Frank, Cora and Harmon were born.

Charles Elmer went with his parents to Iowa, where they bought a farm and Charles became a cattle herder in his early teens. During the panic of 1880, they lost both farms and they traveled back to Indiana in a covered wagon. Back here they settled in Browns Corners where Daniel set up a blacksmith shop. Charles found work among farmers and also worked in the blacksmith shop and the tile mill. He bought the tile mill at Uniondale and later traded it for forty acres near Roanoke, Indiana.

In the meantime, Charles met and married a lady from the Prospect community, Ada Longshore. To them was born a son who died shortly after birth. During the spring of 1911, the Fahls moved to the Hamilton farm west of Union Center in Union Township, Wells County.

Charles loved working with horses and along with farming managed to get matching teams. The doctors, undertakers, bus drivers and some farmers were interested in matching teams. A nice team of horses meant the same as a new automobile does to us.

Ada Fahl passed away in 1916 of a ruptured appendix. Roswell McDowell had been living in the home and he married Carrie Fusselman. They lived with Charles until March 16, 1918, when Charles married Mary J. Osborn. To this marriage was born two daughters, Desta Lucile and Genevieve. Charles continued to farm until the time of his death, October 27, 1943, of a heart attack. The daughter, Genevieve, married Wendell Diehl, who had joined in the farming operation in 1941 and continued after Charles's death until the farm sold in 1968. Lucile married John Sonnigsen and she still owns a corner of the Fahl farm. Mary Jane Osborn Fahl lived until August 28, 1988, just five months short of her 100th birthday.

FALK

My great-great-grandfather, Albert Falk (1806-1879), was born in Germany. He immigrated to the United States in 1834 and moved into Wells County in 1849.

His oldest son, Jacob (1835-1889), was born in Richmond County, Ohio. He was married to Rachel Jones (1841-1927). Jonathan "Shafe" (1870-1943), their third child and my grandfather, was born in Rockcreek Township. He married Nettie Ann Smith (1872-1962), the daughter of Jacob and Elizabeth Jane (Morris) Smith.

Jonathan and Nettie had five children. Guy Benjamin (1893-1974) and Justine May (1895-1968) were born in Liberty Township. Howard Fulton (1901-1972), Homer Floyd (1904-1970), and Leon Shafe (1911-1986) were born in Harrison Township. All of them lived and raised their families in Wells County.

Seated front: Bill Falk, Gene, Ilene, Laura Saalfrank (child) and Robert Falk Middle: Rebecca Saalfrank, Joseph, and Samuel Falk Standing: Homer, Cressie and Ruth Falk taken 1968

My father was Homer Floyd. Mother's maiden name was Cressie Irene McAfee (1906-1978). She was the daughter of Oliver Bert and Stella Alice (Sheets) McAfee. They were married in their pastor's house on January 1, 1929, the year the Great Depression began. They stayed with Grandma and Grandpa Falk until spring, when they moved to the farm in Rockcreek Township where they would spend the rest of their lives, and where I live now.

They had three children: Robert B. (1932), Ilene Alice (1938), and myself, William Homer (1946). Robert married Ruth Harris and had two sons, Samuel and Joseph. Ilene married Eugene Saalfrank and had two daughters, Rebecca and Laura.

I graduated from Rockcreek High School in 1964 and served in the Vietnam War from 1965-1967. I worked at Corning Glass Works for nineteen years, also farming during these years. I am presently farming full-time in partnership with my brother. *Submitted by William H. Falk.*

JACOB FATCHER

Jacob Fatcher was born in Rein Bayern, Germany on July 8, 1850. His parents were Jacob and Margaret Young Fatcher. The family emigrated from Germany to New York in 1851 and lived in Brooklyn. His father was a tailor and Jacob learned the trade from him. He married Elizabeth Bauman (born March 22, 1856, in Bucyrus, Ohio) on November 2, 1874, in Brooklyn, New York. In 1889, the family came to Ossian and Jacob set up a well-respected tailor's trade.

According to the 1900 census, there were four living children: Mary (also known as Mamie, Mrs. Adam Turner) born in New York in 1876; Henry born in New York in 1879; George, born in New York in 1882 and married to Edith Resler; Augusta, born in Indiana in 1891 and married to Charles Resler. In 1900, Henry was working for his father as a tailor and George was apprenticed as a blacksmith.

Augusta Fatcher married Charles Resler in

1915. They had five children: Phebe (born 1918-1989), George William (born 1919, died 1934), Wendell (born 1921), Betty (born 1924, died 1979), and Everett (born 1930). Everett and his wife Betty Jean Krill were married in 1951. They have three children: Cynda, born 1953 and married to John Bunting; Debra, born 1954 and married to Jack Springer; and Rick, born 1957 and married to Deborah May.

Deb and Jack have a son Eric, born 1985. Rick and Deb have a son Chad, born 1981 and a daughter Angela born 1986.

FATE

Samuel and Mary Fate were my great-grandparents and moved to Wells County, Indiana from what is now Crestline, Ohio, in 1854. They settled in the woods one and half mile east of Markle on what is now State Road 116. They were frontier people and cleared the land, so they could farm and build a frontier log home, which still stands today at that same location. To them were born Rebecca, Lucy, Emmanuel, Hugh and John Wesley Fate.

John Wesley Fate was born on September 2, 1852. John bought the homestead in Wells County and in 1888 married Julia Ann Roberts from Wells County. John and Julia were my grandparents and continued to farm the homestead. To them were born Blanch, Boston Hiramus Bartholomew, Dwight Bedford, Forest Graden, Voss Omer, and Hulda Augusta Fate. John died June 30, 1923, and Julia Ann died in 1920. All of these children are deceased.

December 24, 1950
Back (L to R) Junior, Sharlee, Avis Seated (L to R) Boston, Iva Bottom (L to R) Vanice, Robert

Boston Fate was born on September 1, 1891, and was raised on the homestead. He married Iva Buel in December 24, 1912. Iva Buel was born July 3, 1891, in Rockcreek Township, Huntington County, and her father was a farmer. To them were born Avis B., March 24, 1914, Robert Lowell, July 3, 1915, Anna Vanice, March 29, 1918, Boston Junior, June 22, 1920, and Sharlee Mae Fate, May 10, 1932. All five children graduated from the East Rockcreek High School in Wells County. Boston bought a fifty five acre farm in the far NW/4 of Rockcreek Township in Wells County, was a farmer most of his life, and he also farmed the homestead. He was employed with the United REMC for a few years. Boston died February 27, 1955, in Wells County, and Iva died March 7, 1982, in Huntington County. Boston and Iva were my parents.

Avis married Harry Wright and moved to Fort Wayne. Avis and Harry both worked in Fort Wayne, she as a registered nurse and he as a factory worker. They had three children: Louis Michael, Roseann, and Nancy Carol. Avis died February 15, 1985, and Harry in 1988.

Robert married Iva Marie Paxson and had five children: Catherine Elaine, David Lowell, Gary Lee, Rex Galen, and Paul Edward. Robert was a farmer and owned a farm in Union Township. Rex and Paul Fate still live on part of that ground that was their father's farm. Gary lives in Bluffton. Robert died October 23, 1982. Iva is a retired registered nurse living in Markle in Wells County.

Anna Vanice married C. James Atkinson and moved to Huntington where they still live today. They are retired factory workers. They had two children, Carolee Ann and Robert Eugene Atkinson.

Junior married Martha Blair and had six children. Mary Joan, Clarence Duane (Jim), Michael, Ronald, Richard, and Roger Fate. Joan Mahensmith still lives in Wells County. Junior worked in construction and as a land developer, etc. Martha, a homemaker, now retired, lives in Florida and Michigan.

Sharlee married Stuart R. Klefeker on October 27, 1951. Stuart's family also came to Wells County from around Greenville, Ohio. There were no children born to this marriage. They do have a foster daughter, two grand-daughters, a grandson and two great-granddaughters.

They live at 1637W US 224, just one-half mile west of Uniondale in Rockcreek Township. The home where Sharlee was born and grew up is still standing on Oak Road in Rockcreek Township. Sharlee has worked in the Wells County Area Plan Commission at the Courthouse for past eleven years and Stuart has worked for the State Highway Transportation Department out of the Markle Unit for twenty-three years.

FAUS-ARCHBOLD

Harry Samuel Faus was born on December 18, 1892, to John and Cora (Houtz) Faus in Wells County. His wife, Mary Letha Archbold, was born on June 3, 1899, to James and Sara (Mills) Archbold, in Wells County. They were married on July 12, 1917, at Ossian.

Harry was a farmer until they moved to Murray. He worked for WPA and Central Soya Company in Decatur, Indiana. His last place of employment was Erie Stone Company. He retired in 1957 due to ill health. Mary was kept busy raising fourteen children. When her husband passed away, she sold the big house in Murray and moved to a smaller home across the street.

The family attended the Murray Missionary Church where Mary was a member. Harry passed away on February 19, 1961, followed by his wife's passing away on February 20, 1983. There were fourteen children born of this marriage.

Oliver Basil, born March 12, 1918, died October 24, 1948.

Donald Brooks, born September 17, 1919, died August 17, 1962. Brooks was married to Louise Smith, daughter of Charles and Hazel (Miller) Smith on June 15, 1946. Children born of this marriage are: Keith Wayne, born June 8, 1953, died May 20, 1976, and Janice Sue, born March 27, 1956.

Ida Pauline, born July 27, 1921, was married to Galen Norman Ripple, son of Augustus and Lovina (Dunbar) Ripple, on November 15, 1941. Norman passed away on August 9, 1982. Children born of this marriage are: Galen Dee, born August 1, 1944, Sherryl Dian Nicholson, born November 21, 1951, and Norman Dennis born June 12, 1956. Pauline has eleven grandchildren and two great-grandchildren.

Harry Jr., born on June 3, 1923, and died July 10, 1986, was married to Marilyn L. Sliger, daughter of Earl and Winifred (Smith) Sliger, on September 9, 1944. Two sons born of this marriage are: William Lee born May 2, 1946, and Kenneth Bradley, born February 10, 1951. There are eight grandchildren.

Cora Maxine, born January 12, 1925, was married to Albert C. Cook, son of William and Pearl (Gause) Cook on October 15, 1949. Albert passed away on December 25, 1988. Two daughters born to this marriage are: Cynthia Maxine Burke, born February 7, 1951, and Shirley Alberta Shaffer, born July 17, 1952. There are six grandchildren.

Harry S. and Mary L. (Archbold) Faus

Paul Robert was born November 11, 1926.

Raymond Max, born September 27, 1928, and died on May 28, 1962, was married to Mildred J. Huffman on March 31, 1956. Later divorced, Mildred had two sons, Harry and Robert Huffman.

Betty Lou, born October 25, 1930, married Robert R. Graham, son of Theodore and Mary (Taylor) Graham on October 28, 1949. There are three children: Robert Michael, born on July 26, 1950, Vicki Lynn Reber, born January 25, 1953, and Terri Sue Runkle born on August 30, 1956. There are ten grandchildren.

Janet Rose, born September 4, 1932, married to Russell A. Ripple, son of Augustus and Lovine (Dunbar) Ripple on October 21, 1950. There are three sons: Daniel Russell, born on December 1, 1951, David Allen, born October 30, 1952, and Douglas Eugene, born January 30, 1959. There are four grandchildren and one great-grandchild.

Ruth Ann, born on October 21, 1934, married to Richard C. Coppess, son of Calvin and Marie (Jones) Coppess on December 31, 1953. There are two children born of this marriage: Franklin Richard, born May 8, 1957, and Karen Ann Loshe, born March 5, 1961. There is one grandchild.

Adrian Dean, born May 30, 1937, and died October 19, 1966, was married to Carolyn Linn, daughter of Walter and Helen (Gottschalk) Linn on January 31, 1964. They had one son, Linn Don, born on January 26, 1965.

Dale Eugene, born September 5, 1938, married to Sandra L. Campbell, daughter of Ira and Martha (Miller) Nicholson on March 27, 1971. They have one daughter, Angela Jean, born on January 14, 1972. Sandra's children are Deborah Lynn Campbell born on October 5, 1962, Douglas Linn Campbell, born on September 8, 1963, Jon Michael Campbell, born on June 12, 1966, and Jeffery Dean Campbell, born on October 7, 1967. There are three grandchildren.

Bertha Marie, born on April 7, 1940, was married to Douglas M. Williams, son of Adrian and Cynthia (Terry) Williams on May 28, 1961. They had two children, Rebecca Ann Williams, born on October 31, 1962 and Timothy Douglas, born on November 1, 1963. Later they divorced and she married Calvin F. Wyatt, son of Cecil and Kathryn (Mosure) Wyatt on September 1, 1984. Calvin's children are: Calvin J. Wyatt, born April 16, 1966, Tammy Sue Wyatt, born on October 31, 1969, and Shonda Lynn Wyatt, born July 31, 1975. There are seven grandchildren.

Donnie Kay, born on September 7, 1941, and died on July 15, 1990, was married to Patricia A. Campbell, daughter of Dale and Kathryn (Mazelin) Campbell on December 30, 1962. Later they divorced. There are three sons: Kent Adrian, born on October 13, 1963, Kelly Dale, born on September 26, 1966, and Kris Samuel, born on August 27, 1969.

Harry and Mary had five sons, three sons-in-law, nine grandsons, and three great-grandsons who have served or are still serving in the Armed Forces.

FAUS-SLIGER

Harry Faus was born June 3, 1923 in Wells County. The fourth child of Harry Samuel Faus (a farmer who later worked at the Erie Stone Company) and Mary Archbold Faus (a homemaker). They were the parents of fourteen children. Still living are Pauline, Maxine, Paul, Betty, Janet, Ruth, Dale, and Marie. Deceased are Basil, Brooks, Harry, Max, Dean, and Donnie. Harry Samuel died in 1961 and Mary died in 1983.

Marilyn Sliger was born July 16, 1928, in Bluffton to Earl A. Sliger and Winifed Smith Sliger. They were the parents of another daughter, Cleora Jocelyn, born in 1926.

Dad and mother met when they both worked at the H.C. Bay Piano Company. They were married in 1925 at Bluffton. Dad left the Bay Company and went to work as a molder at the Red Cross Foundry. Mother was a homemaker until my sister and I were well along in school. Then she started working at the Estey Piano Factory. When World War II started both went to work in defense plants. Dad at Freuhauf in Fort Wayne, mother at Farnsworth here in Bluffton. Dad passed away in 1975 and mother died in 1982.

It was during World War II that Harry Faus and Marilyn Sliger met. Before their marriage Harry worked for the Johnloz Grocery at Murray. Later he worked at the Erie Stone Quarry. During the war years, he worked at the General Electric Company in Fort Wayne.

Harry and Marilyn were married September 9, 1944, in Bluffton. Gas was rationed and you had to have coupon books for gas, kerosene, meat, canned goods and sugar.

Harry and Marilyn Faus

In May, 1946, our first son, William Lee, was born. In 1951, Kenneth Bradley was born. Both boys are graduates of Bluffton High School.

In 1948, the General Electric went on strike, so Harry put his application in to Franklin Electric one day and went to work for them the next day.

In 1945, we bought our home on Washington Street, where I still reside.

Harry joined the Volunteer Fire Department in 1979. He was certified as a Master Firefighter and served as the department treasurer until his retirement.

In 1984, Harry was elected to the City Council as councilman of the second district.

He retired from Franklin Electric in June, 1985, and from the Fire Department in January, 1986, because of ill health. He was still a member of the City Council until his death in July, 1986.

Our son Bill moved to Elkhart, Indiana, and is a police lieutenant in charge of the K-9 Division. He has three sons: Bill Jr., a K-9 police officer; Brad, a heavy equipment operator for Elkhart Company and Bob, an assistant manager with the Felpausch Grocery Chain in Elkhart. Bill is married to the former Sally Crane.

Our youngest son, Ken, is married to the former ReAnn Hinton from the southern Wells area. They are the parents of three sons: Brian thirteen, Kevin ten, and Kory one year old. They reside in Ossian, Indiana. Ken owns and operates the Majestic Style Salon at Southtown Mall in Fort Wayne.

We were all charter members of the Calvary Lutheran Church in Bluffton. We have had good times and bad, but I believe the epitaph on our tombstone sums it up. "We Loved, Laughed, Cried, and Believed Together. (Mari*lyn Sliger Faus)*

FAUSZ FAMILY

The family of Albert J. and Lela M. (Smith) Fausz first came to Wells County in 1932. He was a farmer, and an employee of the Majestic Company of Huntington. Before his marriage, he served in the U.S. Marine Corps and was a veteran of World War I.

Albert died October 27, 1964, and Lela died August 11, 1984. They were the parents of four children: George Barnett, Clare Louise, William D., and Londa Kay.

George graduated from Union Center High School in 1940. He is a veteran of World War II, serving in the U.S. Army Medical Department from August, 1942, to November 1945. George now lives in Denver, Colorado, and is married to the former Edna M. Wagner. He is a retired building contractor. They have one son, Kenyth Barnett of Denver, who is married to the former Diana Webb. They have two sons, Christopher of Phoenix, Arizona, and Andrew of Denver.

Clare Louise graduated in 1941 from Union Center High School, and now resides in Huntington County. She is married to Burl E. Pease. They are retired farmers, and Clare Louise was employed as a secretary at Kresge Warehouse in Fort Wayne for thirty-eight years. Burl is also retired from the Fox Musical Manufacturing Corporation of South Whitley, Indiana.

Burl is a veteran of World War II, having served in the Quartermaster Department from 1943 to 1945. They had no children.

William D. is married to the former Clara Mae Douglass. They both are graduates of Union Center High School, with the class of 1945. Clara Mae also graduated from the former Wayne Beauty College of Fort Wayne, Indiana. They still live in Union Township, Wells County, where they have always been engaged in farming. They have three children: Gary, Sherry, and Terry.

Gary is married to Roma Lee Moss. They live in Union Township, where they own and operate a Lawn and Garden Equipment business. Gary and Roma have one daughter, Amy Renee, who was born February 27, 1989.

Sherry Diane lives in Oxford, Indiana. She is married to Dale Lynn Jones, who is the vocational director of the Benton Central School District of Benton County. Sherry is a homemaker, and receptionist for the Asgrow Seed Company of Oxford, Indiana. They have one son, Kraig Michael, born December 8, 1978, and one daughter, Kristi Michelle, born June 28, 1982.

Terry L. and his wife, the former Pamela Ann Peden, reside in Union Township and are full-time farmers. They have three children: Brian Daniel, born April 20, 1978; Keith Matthew, born February 10, 1981; and Tami Marie, who was born May 7, 1985.

Londa Kay Fausz, the youngest daughter of Albert J. and Lela M., now resides in Marion, Indiana. She graduated from Huntington High School, Huntington, Indiana. Londa is employed as office manager for the Northeast Indiana District of the Nazarene Churches. She has never married.

FEEBACK-WELCH FAMILY

Until our move to Bluffton in 1976, my husband and I spent our growing up years in the suburbs of Fort Wayne. My roots are traced through several generations there since my parents, John N. Welch and Dorothea Lagerstrom Welch, were also born and raised there. My paternal grandfather, John J. Welch, was a Fort Wayne native and a graduate of Purdue University. He held a managerial position at General Electric Company for thirty years. He was married to Florence Giant, from Maples, Indiana, in 1924. Their marriage produced four sons; my father was the oldest and the only one who married. My maternal grandfather, Oscar Lagerstrom, migrated from Upgrenna, Sweden, in the early 1900's to Canada and began a journey south to the United States. He labored on farms as he traveled through Minnesota, Wisconsin, Illinois, and Indiana. In 1921, he married Nellie Young of Kokomo, Indiana, and they settled in Fort Wayne, Indiana, to raise their son and daughter.

Wedding portrait of John J. Welch (seated) and Florence Giant May 7, 1924 Attendants: Mary Welch and Lansing Giant

Fort Wayne was my birthplace in 1950, and my brother, John Michael Welch, completed our family in 1952. He remains unmarried and continues to reside in Fort Wayne, where he works for the Screen Art Advertising Company. My career as a registered nurse began after graduation from Purdue University in 1971. I have worked in the fields of geriatrics, intensive care, school nursing, industry, and family practice. My marriage to David Feeback took place on June 8, 1974.

Ohio is the state of origin for my husband's family; his parents, Allen Feeback and Marjorie Connors Feeback, were born in Urbana and Sandusky, Ohio. Paternal grandparents Ed and Alma Behnke Feeback lived in Toledo, Ohio, where David's father grew up as an only child. Maternal grandparents Ed and Alma Behnke Feeback lived in Toledo, Ohio, where David's father grew up as an only child. Maternal grandparents Harold Connors and Mary Galloway Connors raised their family of five daughters and two sons in Toledo also. David's mother was a twin and third in the birth order of her family.

Toledo was my husband's place of birth in 1951 and he moved to Fort Wayne with his family shortly before his sister, Valerie's birth in 1955. Valerie was married to Jeff Pelz in 1978 and they live in Fort Wayne, where she is employed by Pollution Control Systems. David completed undergraduate study at Wabash College and was graduated from the Indiana University School of Law in 1976. The relocation to Bluffton occurred as a result of a position offered to him as assistant prosecutor for Wells county. He joined the law firm of Edris, Brown, Hanselman and Johnson in 1981.

Bluffton is the birthplace for all of our children, beginning in 1979 when our oldest son Chad was born. 1983 brought the birth of Ryan, and Andrew arrived in 1989.

Our transition from big city to smaller town has been facilitated by our involvement in community organizations. My husband has been active in the Jaycees, Wells County Foundation, and the Wells County Bar Association. I am a past officer in the Beta Phi Chapter of Tri Kappa and a former member of Bluffton Community Women. We are both members of the Creative Arts Council and Friends of the Library.

FERGUSON

In 1838, James W. Ferguson purchased one hundred sixty acres in what is now Wells County's Jefferson Township. The site lies east of Ossian on Davis Road. At that early time, recording for the area was done in the courthouse at Fort Wayne.

James was born in Scotland on December 25, 1800, and was the son of John and Charlot (Miller) Ferguson. He became a baker, and in 1820 he, his father, and a younger brother, Thomas, sailed for Quebec, Canada. There they eventually bought a farm and settled down. Before their mother and their youngest sister, Janet, could join them, John died.

In 1833, James married Eliza Hume, who was born March 3, 1809, in Edinburg, Scotland. Her parents, John and Catherine (Louden) Hume, died when she was very young, and her grandparents, John and Genne (Bennett) Hume, followed. In 1818, she was taken by her uncle, George Hume, who emigrated to Canada with his family, also in 1820.

The Ferguson brothers became dissatisfied with Canada, and James followed his brother to the Fort Wayne area, where Thomas met and married Janet Yule. Working together on their new land, the brothers made a clearing and a cabin for Thomas and then for James.

Thomas died, and Janet, the mother of five children, married another early settler, neighbor Charles White, and had six additional children.

Just south of the James Ferguson farm was a great swamp. Rattlesnakes and wild animals abounded. Malaria was rampant, and strange plants were common. Indians made infrequent visits to the cabin in search of food and supplies, and to satisfy their curiosity.

Travel was difficult and sometimes dangerous in those early days, but the settlers enjoyed such pleasures as box socials and bees. Property for Elhanen Cemetery was donated by the family, and they attended the Elhanen Church for many years.

James and Evyline Ferguson at home on the occasion of their 50th wedding anniversary

James and Eliza had eight children, including James W., born at the homestead on March 4, 1846. He married Mary Barbara Wagner, born in Mansfield, Ohio, on June 8, 1853. they lived on the family farm. Their son, Victor, also resided on the family homestead until his death in 1971. Their other children were Lydia (Archbold), Ella (Daily), Grace (Gallivan), Clarence Henry, and Floyd.

Clarence married Artimishia Leaisure, daughter of Marcellus and Drusilla Jane Keller Leaisure of Kingsland, on January 9, 1902, and their children were James Marcellus (born January 4, 1903, in Jefferson Township), Mildred (Kahlenbeck), Churl Carlyle, and Joseph Vernon.

Residing in Wells County at this time are the widow of James Marcellus, Evyline (Brophy), born near Roanoke on January 23, 1904, his daughters, Mildred and Ann Dee Ferguson, his son, James Edwin, his grandson, Michael, and his great-grandchildren, Jennifer, Heather, and Michael.

Persons with common Wells County surnames such as Archbold, Ault, Best, Crowell, Daily, Drage, Gallivan, Koons, Wall, and White frequently trace their lineage to the Ferguson family. Ferguson Park in Bluffton and Ferguson Road at Baer Field are named for members of this early Wells County Family.

MAX FETTERS FAMILY

Max was the first child born to Ralph and Ruby (Goodspeed) Fetters. Max was active in the Boy Scouts and attained the rank of Eagle Scout. He also started a tradition carried on by his younger brothers and sisters of carrying the *News Sentinel* and was awarded a scholarship by the newspaper. After graduation from Bluffton High School, Max also graduated from Indiana University in Fort Wayne and the Northwestern University Dental School in Chicago. Max then entered a three year internship program with the United States Army. While stationed at the Presidio in San Francisco, he met a registered nurse, Elsa Fasser. They were married the next year in West Haven, Connecticut.

Elsa's grandmother, Hedwig (Walther) came to the United States from Germany in 1890, accompanied only by her little brother, Max. She was sixteen years old. They went to live in the household of John Hegel in New Haven, Connecticut. At the age of sixteen, John had joined the Second Connecticut Regiment to become a drummer boy in the Civil War. He was present when President Abraham Lincoln addressed his troops from the platform of a railroad car. After the war he joined a traveling circus as a trapeze artist. Elsa never met this adventurous grandfather, as he died before she was born. After his first wife died, John married Hedwig, and his three teen-aged sons went along on the honeymoon trip by train to the Chicago World's Fair. The couple had three daughters. Elsie Hegel married William Fasser. William was the youngest of eight children born to Leonard and Mary Fasser and the only one of the eight to have any children. He served in World War I and married Elsie on Armistice Day, November 11, 1919.

Front Row: L to R, Carolyn Fetters, Elsa, Max. Back Row: L to R, Cliff Fetters, Janine Fetters 1973

The first two years that Max and Elsa were married, Max was stationed at Ft. Ord, California. Their first child, Janine Patricia, was born at Fort Ord Army Hospital. After leaving the service, they lived in Napa, California, for one year before returning to Indiana. Their son, Clifford William, was born in Bluffton. Max practiced in Tipton, Indiana, for eight years, and their daughter, Carolyn Rose, was born there. Next, the family moved to Indianapolis while Max studied to become Board Certified in Pediatric Dentistry at Indiana University Medical Center.

Following graduation, Max, Elsa, and family moved to Fort Wayne. Max was elected president of the Isaac Knapp District Dental Society for the term 1983-1984. Janine graduated from Miami University in Oxford, Ohio. She is married to Michael Mettler and has a son, Michael. Clifford graduated from Indiana University Medical School and is a Board Certified family practice physician in Carmel, Indiana. Carolyn graduated from the University of Texas at Austin and manages an apartment complex in Houston, Texas.

FETZER-SHIVELY

J. Adam (1840-1882) and Mary Brodt Fetzer (1836-1882) (my great-great-grandparents), were the parents of three children: Mary Magdaline, born October 18, 1868, died at the age of eight months; John A. (1870-1903); and Barbara Catherine (Katie) 1876-1951), (my great-grandmother).

Mary, John A., and Katie were all born in the two-story log cabin on the old Fetzer home place on Indiana Highway 116 southwest of Uniondale (now the Herb Hill home).

John A. and Katie became orphans in 1882. With both parents dying months apart. After their parents' death, John A. went to live with Uncle John S. Harsh. Katie went to Ohio to live with Catherine and Lewis Wetzer, another aunt and uncle.

John A. married Lydia Sawyer in 1893. They

had one child. Homer L. in 1893. Lydia died in 1898.

John A. married Della F. Winger in 1899. They had one son, John E. Fetzer (1901-1991). John E. Fetzer owned several radio and TV stations in Kalamazoo, Michigan, and also owned the Detroit Tigers baseball team. On June 13, 1956, John organized the eleven-man syndicate which was the successful bidder in the purchase of the Detroit Baseball Club of the American League of Professional Baseball Clubs. As one-third owner he became the first chairman of the board of directors. November 10, 1960, he purchased control of the club by acquiring an additional one-third interest at which time he assumed the presidency of the club. By January 31, 1962, he purchased the final one-third interest and became the sole owner, there being only one other sole owner in either the American or National Leagues. John Fetzer, a member of the board of directors of the American League, as well as chairman of the radio-television committee, was also a member of the pension committee of baseball and sat on the executive council (the controlling body of baseball), under the chairmanship of commissioner Ford C. Frick. The Tigers were sold in 1983 to Tom Monaghan, owner of Domino's Pizza.

As for Barbara Catherine (Katie) Fetzer, she later returned from Ohio to Indiana. She married Frederick Shively (1870-1965) at Uniondale on April 2, 1896. They had four children. Carl (1897-1991), Lawrence (1899-1987), Burlene (1904-1988), and Floyd (1907) (my grandfather).

Floyd Shively married Dorothy Decker July 4, 1923, in Fort Wayne. She was the daughter of Jesse and Bertha Viola Decker.

They had three children: Beverly (1929), Richard (1936) (my father), Charles (1941). Beverly and Richard live near Uniondale. Charles lives in Bluffton.

November 1945
Beverly Shively, Dorothy, Floyd, Richard, Charles

Concerning the above Shively family, Beverly married Arland Bell (June 8, 1972). Richard married Carole Stellhorn (January 4, 1958). Charles married Sally Gerber (June 18, 1961).

The Shivelys have been farmers in Rockcreek Township for over one hundred years. My grandfather, Floyd, father of Richard and Uncle Charles, won many awards for corn and black angus cattle. Floyd was the Corn King, in 1957, in Wells County.

The following constitute the descendents of the above. Beverly and Arland have two sons. Michael Numbers (1961), and Mark Numbers (1964). Richard and Carole have one daughter Kim (1958). Charles and Sally have three children: Lisa (1962), Andrew (1962), Anthony (1964).

Michael has no children. Mark has one son, Marc. Kim has two children Scott and Jennifer (my children). Lisa has three children: Lance, Brittany and Logan. Andrew and Anthony have no children.

Kim Denise Shively married Joseph Scott Minnich on October 14, 1978, at St. Marks Lutheran Church (where the Shively family have been members since 1872) Uniondale, Indiana. I now live in Bluffton.

Our son, Scott Richard Minnich, was born June 8, 1980. Scott is a fourth grader at East Side Elementary School. He enjoys Chess Club and baseball, where he is catcher and third baseman for his junior league team. Scott also was on the soccer team. Our daughter, Jennifer Lynn Minnich was born August 8, 1981. Jenny is a third grader at East Side Elementary School. She enjoys Chess Club and Brownies. She is on the Girls Softball League, and also enjoys other sports. (*Kim Shively Minnich*)

JOHN J. FIECHTER

Andrew Fiechter of Bern, Switzerland, was a widower. Marie Wierman, a young girl, married him when he promised to take her to America. They came to America in about 1858 and settled in Wayne County, Ohio. He lost his life during the Civil War, leaving her to raise three children. John was one of these. When he was about ten they moved to Wells County.

John (1859-1947) married Lena Reinhard (1863-1942). Her parents also came from Berne, Switzerland. They were the parents of thirteen children. John J. (1890-1974) was their fourth child. He was born on a farm where Bill and Kathy Stoller now live. In 1893, this family moved to a farm one and one-half miles south and one-fourth mile east of Craigville. This is where John J. grew up. Today a grandson, Douglas Fiechter, and his family live there.

John J. and Lydia Fiechter farm.
Date of picture unknown, probably in the late 30's

On February 8, 1914, John J. married Lydia Gerber (1891-1971), daughter of Jeff (1866-1951) and Elizabeth Baumgartner Gerber (1867-1937). Their parents were born in Switzerland. Lydia was born in Adams County and was the oldest of nine children. They began their married life on a farm one-half mile east from where John J. lived. In 1920, they bought eighty acres joining east to this farm and west of the Adams County line. It had a barn and small home that they used for a summer home. A big home was built for about six thousand dollars. Some time later he offered to buy eighty acres across the road from Eli Moser for two hundred dollars an acre. This deal fell through, but during the depression he bought this same land for two thousand dollars. They farmed, milked cows, and raised hogs until they retired in 1958 and moved to Craigville, where they lived the rest of their lives. Their son John D. and family moved to the farm, but today a grandson Steve Fiechter and family live there.

John J. and Lydia raised eleven children:

Ervin (1915) married Ellen Neuenschwander. Their children are Louise Reimschisel and Rinda Ulrich.

Irene (1916) married Aaron Reinhard. Their children are Rosemary (deceased), Donnie, Jerome, and John.

Velma (1918-1976) married Carl Kipfer (1912-1990). Their children are: Ronald, Beverly Hodel, and Joleen Sinn.

Marie (1920) married Herman Drayer. Their children are Donna Vega, Jerry, Herman D., Dennis, and foster son, Rocky Giltner.

Alice (1922) married Millard Aschliman. Their children are Diane Heyerly, Loretta Smith, Derryl, Laura, and Lou Ann Kaeher.

Mildred (1924) married William Neuenschwander. Their children are Thomas, Nancy Schladenhauffen, Janice Schwartz, Darlene Habegger, Vickie Meyer, Carol Mock, Marcia Geisel, Terryl, Peggy Yergler, Jeff, and Rex.

Dale (1926) married Doris Tonner. Their children are Jennifer Schwartz, Gloria Grant, Anthony, and Kevin.

Doris (1928) married Charles Neuenschwander. Their children are Cynthia Cox, Sheryl Cress, Kathryn Freed, Andrea Sipe, Dee Charles, Debra, Daniel, and Dennis.

Lillian (1930) married Walter Bertsch. Their children are Lonnie, Jodi Towle, Thomas, and Jeanne Steffen.

John D. (1932) married Shirley Gerber. Their children are Steven, Timothy, Tamara, Stan, and Tricia.

Gerald (1934) married Eunice Beer. Their children are Michael, Teresa Earney and Douglas.

There are one hundred twenty eight great-grandchildren and one great-great-grandchild.

FLANINGAM-MUIR-NEUHAUSER

John Flaningam (1917-1985) was married to Dorothea Neuhauser (1919) in 1941. John, born at Thorntown, Indiana, was the son of Lester Flaningam and Edith Woody. Dorothea was the daughter of Amos Neuhauser and Marianne Rupp. Dorothea was a graduate of Bluffton High School and both she and John graduated from Indiana University.

John was a former high-school teacher and coach. He was in the Navy under the Gene Tunny physical education program. Their first son, Pat (1942), was born in Hampton, Virginia. John transferred to Pearl Harbor. While he was there, the second child, Ann, was born (1945) in Bluffton. It took much planning and official clearance before he could be called on the phone. No dates or number were to be given. When officials found the call was about a child's birth, it was okay to talk, but the conversation was not private.

John Patrick (Pat) graduated from Indiana University Medical School as a Doctor of Internal Medicine. He is presently with the Kaiser Hospital at Oakland, California. He married Christine Steichen of Indianapolis in 1967. They have two sons, Mike (1969) now at U.C. San Diego, and Jill (1973) who will graduate from Oakland High School in 1991.

Ann Flanigam (1945) married Richard Scott in 1967 in Bluffton. both graduated from Bluffton High School. They had two children, Shannon (1975) and Hilary (1978). Both are currently in the Bluffton School system. Ann and Dick were divorced in 1981. She took her maiden name again. Ann is a graduate of Indiana University with a B.S. in

Education. She earned her Masters degree in clinical psychology from Saint Francis College and is now working on her doctorate at the Alfred Adler Institute in Chicago. She was a psychotherapist four years and has now been at Caylor-Nickel in the same capacity for six years. She is currently a member of the Bluffton-Harrison school board.

Alexander "Sandy" Muir (1921) married Dorothea Naehauser Flaningam in June, 1990. Sandy was born near Bloomington and graduated from Indiana University in journalism. In World War II he was with the U.S. Army Signal Corps, stationed in the Pentagon at Washington. After additional study he was certified as an electronic engineer.

After the war he was employed with the Defense Communication Agency, performing duties involving missile and network communication, engineering, and research and development. He retired in 1973 after 32 years of service that required extensive travel. Sandy is a member of Kiwanis. Both he and Dorothea are active in volunteer work at Caylor-Nickel Hospital and the Methodist Church.

FLUKE-BRONNER

Linnie Elizabeth Bronner, although born in Huntington, Indiana, grew up on the farm corner of 300 West and 900 North in Wells County, Indiana. The Union Center School grounds were deeded from this acreage. Her mother was Anna Warner, seventh daughter of Lewis and Catherine (Sitze) Warner. They had come to the United States from Baden, Germany in 1853. After some time at Sandusky and Crestline, Ohio, and in Rockcreek Township, Wells County, the Warners settled at this location in 1870.

Jacob Bronner, also of Baden, married Anna in April, 1889. They brought the Warner farm from the heirs and moved there 1893. Here Linnie's sisters were born: Mina in 1895 and Guinevere in 1906.

50th anniversary reception for Herschel and Guinevere (Bronner) Lesh, June 21, 1981 Left to Right: Ralph and Elizabeth Walker, Denver and Anna Laura Slater, Frances and Hubert Smith, Eileen and Jacob Fluke

When Mina was a teenager and invited to a party, she was allowed to go only if Linnie, who was skilled in handling horses, would drive. There Linnie met Earl Fluke, recently come from Champaign, Illinois, with his parents and eight younger siblings. A married brother and a married sister had stayed behind in Illinois.

Early Fluke and Linnie were married in the home of the bride's parents in April, 1911. they began homemaking on a Huntington County farm where their first child, Frances Elenore, was born in 1912. Soon the couple moved just a mile north of the Bronner home. There Elizabeth was born 1914, Anna Laura in 1920, and Jacob Wayne in 1927.

Eventually Earl bought this farm from his father-in-law and also farmed the Bronner acreage. During busy summer days, Linnie prepared picnic lunches for Earl and the family. Bales of hay in the clean barn on Linnie's home place were the picnic grounds.

Coming from Illinois corn country, Earl was also a horse lover. This was evident in his showing of blue ribbon and championship Belgian draft horses at the Bluffton Street Fair.

Beginning with Anna Warner and her sisters, four generations of this family attended the Union Township Schools on the corner. First a one-room grade school was built at the crossroads. About 1904, the Bronners deeded ground to the township for the high school where Linnie and her sisters continued their education. Only one of the fourth generation graduated from Union Center, for progress decreed centralization of schools.

The Flukes moved one-mile east of Union in 1935. From there each of the children were married. Elizabeth, who did secretarial work, and Ralph Walker, later a postal employee, married in 1936. Their children are Stuart, Patricia, and Suanne. In 1940, Frances, a teacher, and Hubert Smith were wed. He was a feed salesman. Their daughter is Cynthia. Anna Laura, a nurse, and Denver Slater, engaged in construction, were married in her parents' home in 1942. Their children were Michael, Thomas, and Diane. Jacob and Eileen Flora were married in 1947. He was a farmer and active in Farm Bureau affairs. Eileen was a nurses assistant and the last of this generation to retire. Their daughters are Linda, Sandra, Cinda, Jaleen, and Dixie.

Ralph Walker, Denver Slater, and Jacob Fluke were in the services during World War II.

JACOB W. FLUKE FAMILY

The Jacob Fluke family resided on the family farm, located at 900 N 200 W in Union Township, until 1981.

Jacob, son of Earl F. Fluke and Linnie Bronner Fluke, married Bertha Eileen Flora, daughter of Robert C. Flora and Josephine Harrod Flora. Jacob was a graduate of Union Center High School, class of 1945. Eileen was a graduate of Hoagland High School, Allen County, class of 1945.

The Union Center School was located on farm ground owned by Jacob Bronner, grandfather of Jacob Fluke.

Chauncy Fluke, father of Earl Fluke, moved to the Markle area from the Champaign-Urbana area of Illinois and was married to a Dyson.

Robert Flora was a son of Irvin Flora, and was a native of the Flora, Indiana, area.

Josephine Harrod Flora was a daughter of Enos Harrod of Hoagland and a descendant of James Harrod of Harrodsburg, Kentucky. James was a companion of Daniel Boone.

Jacob and Eileen have five daughters and eleven grandchildren.

Linda Jo married Randal Plummer and lives in Nottingham Township. Both graduated from Purdue University.

Sandra Kay married Gilbert Young Jr. and lives in Huntington. Gilbert is a navy veteran, attended Purdue and graduated from Bethel College. Sandra attended Hixons School of Floral Design in Cleveland, Ohio.

Cinda Sue graduated from Purdue with a B.S. degree, and from the University of Cincinnati with a Masters degree. she is employed in Dearborn, Michigan.

Jalene Renee married Thomas Magnuson of Elkhart. Both graduated from Purdue University. They moved to Phoenix, Arizona, where Tom died at an early age of cancer. Jalen married Joel Jarale of Wisconsin, and they reside in Mesa, Arizona.

Dixie Dawn married Robert Wagner of Schereville, Indiana. Both are graduates of Purdue and reside in Phoenix, Arizona.

Jacob Fluke entered the navy and had boot training at Great Lakes Naval Training Station. From there he went to Hospital Corps School at Camp Faragut, Idaho. He served in the U.S. Naval Hospital in Seattle, Washington, and U.S. Naval Hospital 103 on Guam in the Mariana Islands.

He returned to the family farm and married Eileen in 1949. They lived there until 1981 when they moved to the Bluffton area of Lancaster Township. Jacob retired from Indiana Farm Bureau Incorporation in 1989. Eileen retired from Wells Community Hospital in 1990.

FLUKE-SLATER

Anna Laura Fluke, born in Union Township, Wells County, one of four children of Linnie E. (Bronner) Fluke and Earl F. Fluke, was married December 19, 1942, to Denver Paul Slater, born in Allen County, the fourth son of Burdell J. Slater and Hazel (Hoopingarner) Slater. They were married in the home of the bride's parents. Both Anna and Denver's parents were farmers in Union Township. Denver's mother died in 1923.

The grounds for Union Center School, at 300 West and 900 North, were deeded from acreage owned by the great-grandparents of Anna (Fluke) Slater. Linnie (Bronner) Fluke was in one of the beginning classes to graduate from the school and Michael Denver Slater, son of Anna and Denver, was in the last graduating class of the school in 1962.

Slater Family, October 1988
L to R: Michael Denver Slater, Diane Sue Foughty, Anna Laura Slater, Denver Paul Slater, Thomas Duane Slater

Anna L. graduated in 1938 from Union Center High School, attended Manchester College, and received her registered nurse's license through Lutheran Hospital School of Nursing in Fort Wayne. She worked thirty-five years at Caylor-Nickel Medical Center.

Denver P. also graduated from Union Center in 1938. A World War II veteran, he was engaged in construction, farming and was an employee at Cline Lumber Company. Both Anna and Denver retired in 1984.

Anna and Denver had three children who were all born in Wells County.

Michael Denver Slater, Fort Wayne, has four children. The eldest, Kirt Michael, married Tamera Oswalt (daughter of Max and Katherine Oswalt) in

1988. Kimberlie Anne lives in Warren. Mark Denver and Sara June both live in Fort Wayne.

Thomas Duane Slater married June McBride (daughter of Juanita and Roy McBride) in 1965. They live at 2668 E 250 N. They have three daughters. Tonya Michelle married Kent Ingle (son of Marlene and Richard Ingle) in 1988. They live in Ossian. Jodi Marie lives in Orlando, Florida, and Jennifer Diane attends Norwell High School.

Diane Sue Slater is married to Geoffrey Allen Foughty (son of Martha and Herman Foughty) and lives at 4356 W 200 N. Her oldest, Shelli Ann Cardin, is married to Michael Lee Jenkins (son of Judy and Carl Jenkins) and lives in Fort Wayne. They were married in 1988. Stefani Sue Cardin, the youngest, attends Norwell High School.

Anna and Denver Slater live at Coldwater Lake, Michigan, but spend time in Arizona and Bluffton.

FOLK-GRAHAM

Our grandfather was John Henry Folk, born August 31, 1830, in Pennsylvania. He married Christina Gleich on February 22, 1855. In 1855, they moved to Indiana on a farm located one mile west and one mile north of Uniondale. They had seven children: Hiram, Sarah, John, Ida, Frank, Anna and Emma.

Frank, born January 27, 1867, was our grandfather. On March 10, 1889, he married Liberta Brickley, the daughter of Andrew Brickley and Sarah Haiflich, born November 2, 1868. He was a farmer and they lived in the same house in which he was born (one mile west and one-mile north of Uniondale). She was a homemaker and loved to crochet when she had time. They had nine children: Ora, Clara, Hazel (died in infancy) Cressie, Charles, Beulah, Jesse, Mary and Joseph. Grandfather died on September 26, 1946 at the age of 79. Grandmother stayed on in their home alone, until she died in 1962 at the age of 94.

Our father, Charles, was born on October 28, 1890, near Uniondale. He married Hazel Graham, (May 21, 1894) on September 25, 1912. She moved from Howard County with her parents, Milton M. Graham and Amy Elizabeth Conner to a farm on State Road 303 (two miles south of East Center School). They had five children: Goldie, Mabel, Devona, Hazel and Carl.

Frank Folk Family
Back row: Buelah, Charles, Cressie, Jesse, Mary
Front row: Frank, Joseph, Liberta

My parents had ten children: Robert (1938) lived a few hours; Berneice married Kenny McBride and they have one daughter Judy and live in Markle; Helen Gearhart Solloway had three sons: Fred, Rex and Ned. She died August 9, 1941; Dorma, married Halden Greene and they have two sons Ron and David and live in Markle; Maxine Hilsmier Collins has one son, Larry, and lives in Fort Wayne; Faye married Everett Wilson. They have three children: Greg, Gaylene, and Garland and live in Markle; Margaret, married Chase Furnas. They have seven children: Sandy, Steve, Cindy, Joe, Mary, Robert, and Katie and live in Florida; Richard died August 22, 1982. He was married to Phyllis Veazey and they have a son Garry; Betty married Donald Rodenbeck. They have two sons: Mike and Randy. They live in Huntington; Phyllis (Peg) died July 30, 1975, she was married to John Kyle and they had one son Tom. My parents reared my nephew, Fred Gearhart, after his mother passed away.

All eight of us girls worked at General Electric, Fort Wayne. Richard farmed and in the later years of his life, he worked at Dana, Fort Wayne. Fred works on construction. In 1953, my parents bought a house in Markle. My father died January 3, 1963. My mother died June 27, 1969. She was a homemaker and also worked as a cook at East Union Center School for several years. My father worked on the farm most of his life. He retired after seventeen years at Baer Field as a maintenance operator.

I married Everett Wilson in 1950. We moved to Uniondale in 1951. The house we bought was across from the Town Hall. At this time the streets had no names. Now it is called Sugar Street. We have fond memories of Uniondale as our three children were born in and east of there. In the 1950's, my husband Everett managed the restaurant there. He worked at the vault plant and had a chance later to use the experience in buying his own vault plant. We lived east of Uniondale on thirty-five acres, which Everett farmed. While he worked these jobs, I was working at General Electric in Fort Wayne. I retired in 1987 with more than thirty-nine years of service.

We have three children and eight grandchildren. Greg married Bev Britt. They live east of Markle with their daughters Nilah (sixteen) and Melanie (fourteen). Gaylen married Roger Dalrymple and lives in Shoshone, Idaho with their children: Bradley (fourteen); Tiffany (eight); and Stephanie (seven); Garland lives in Markle and has three children: Miles (eight), Joel (seven) and Jenica (three).

In 1984 my husband and our sons bought National Cement, a burial vault plant. A short time later they formed a partnership and changed the name to Wilson Burial Vault. Although the business is in Huntington, we make our home in Markle. In 1989, we moved to the house my parents had bought and lived in as their retirement home at 335 Clark, Markle. (Faye *(Folk) Wilson*)

GEORGE FORST FAMILY

George Washington Forst, wife Henrietta, and son Alfred, moved to Bluffton in 1888. George was born in 1830 in Greentown, Ohio. He moved, with his parents, to Warren Township, Indiana, sometime before 1850. In 1850, he married Henrietta Miller, who was born in 1827 in Bavaria, Germany, and had come with her parents to America at age ten.

They lived with his parents until George acquired farm land near them. In September 1864, he was drafted for service in the Civil War, but was discharged a few months later with a back injury. They moved to Roanoke, then Huntington, and finally, to Bluffton.

Alfrieda (Effie) Stuver, a granddaughter, was married in their home, November 1891, to Frank Bayha. Effie's mother Melissa had died in childbirth when Effie was five. She spent most of her childhood living with her grandparents. Henrietta died in October, 1900, and George moved to 918 West Wabash, next door to Effie and her family.

Standing (L to R) Melissa and Emory Seated (L to R) George, Albert, Frank, Henrietta

George worked as a janitor at Columbian School until shortly before he entered the Soldier's Home at Marion, Indiana, where he died in 1910. My mother Mary Bayah Thomas, daughter of Effie and Frank, remembered visiting George in Marion with her mother or one of his sons. Sometimes they went by interurban or train, and sometimes by horse and buggy. Mother remembered George as white haired, clean shaven, medium height, and gentle nature. A few pieces of his hand-carved furniture are still in our possession.

Their oldest daughter Melissa married Alfred Stuver in 1869, parents of Effie. Sophia married James Wilson and had one child, Iva Hurtle.

Franklin Forst, oldest son, was born in 1855. He became a baker in Huntington, then moved to Bluffton to pursue this trade. Then he entered the grocery business with his brothers as partners. In 1900 the Forst Grocery was on Market Street across from the Court House.

He married Margaret Woodard in 1883. They had no children. Mother remembered Frank as a reserved man, quiet, good with children, progressive, a good business man. He owned a beautiful carriage with a matched team, and later a car. Mother spent many happy hours with them.

Emory was born in 1860, moved to Bluffton soon after Frank, married Fora Daub in 1883. They had two children, Dessie Wiltse and Earl. Emory was in business with Frank for eight to ten years. Mother remembered riding in his buggy to Huntington, with Emory on buying trips for the store. He would visit his Aunt Salomie and cousin Iva Hurile. His son Earl, a delivery boy for Forst Grocery, often took mother with him on deliveries in the buggy or, in winter, on the bob-sled.

Albert became a partner with his brothers in the early 1900's. He was born in 1867, married Lizzie Thomas; then, after her early death, married Myrtle Justus in 1900.

All of the Forst family were church members, quiet people, and good citizens. All are buried in Fairview Cemetery.

HERBERT AND LAWRENCE FOSTER FAMILIES

Since there are at least two distinct and separate Foster families in Wells County, these Fosters can be identified as coming from Fountain County in west central Indiana. Their ancestor was John Foster (1735-1800), a Methodist lay preacher from Maryland who fought in the Revolutionary War and was given a land grant in Ohio as a result. Other members of the family migrated to Indiana and settled in Fountain County near Attica.

Herbert Holford Foster (1902-1967) and his brother Stephen Lawrence Foster (1906-1959), known as Pete, came to Wells County a few years apart. Herb came first (1920) and was employed by the Bay Piano Company and the Starr Bakery. When Pete arrived on the scene in 1924, he was employed in the construction trade. Their mother, Edna Meeker Foster, had also come to Bluffton in 1923; She died in 1932 and is buried in Fairview Cemetery with Herb and Pete and their wives.

In 1928, Herb and Pete purchased the Parlor City Bakery from Frank Beatty. They operated from this S. Main Street location for a year before moving to Market Street and renaming the business The Foster Brothers' Bakery. In 1943, the Fosters expanded into the beer distributing business when they founded The Wells Distributing Company. It was located on W. Perry Street. The bakery was sold in 1949. Pete left his partnership with Herb shortly after and became a wholesale salesman for the Fort Wayne Drug Company He was employed in this capacity until his death. Herb continued to operate the Wells Distributing company until his death. That firm was sold in 1968.

One interesting sidelight to the Foster brothers' involvement in the baking business, in which the bulk of the work is done in the morning, was their interest in the game of golf. They were both among the earliest members of the Parlor City Country Club and maintained memberships there for the remainder of their lives. They were both excellent golfers. In addition, they were keenly interested in hunting and wildlife conservation. Both kept fine riding horses, which they stabled at the old livery barn on East Perry Street.

Herb Foster was married to Martha Boyd (1904-1925) of Bluffton in 1924. She died from the complications of childbirth. A daughter, Marion Boyd Foster, was born of this marriage. Marion graduated from Bluffton High School in 1943. She married Charles (Bud) Schmoll, of Bluffton, in 1946. They are divorced. Marion has three children: Sally, Steve, and Karen. She is a realtor and resides in West Palm Beach, Florida.

In 1927, Herb married Margaret Aline Smith (1909-1968) of Bluffton. Two children were born of this marriage: Phyllis Ann (1928) and Betty Lorain (1930). Phyllis graduated from Bluffton High School in 1946 and was married to Tom Byrd of Bluffton in 1947. Tom died in 1964. Phyllis has two children: Tim and Susan. Phyllis is an X-ray Technician at the Caylor-Nickel Clinic. Betty graduated from Bluffton High School in 1948 and was married to James Sands of Bluffton in 1953. They have five children: Jill, John, Julie, Jennifer, and Jane. Jim owns and operates the Sands Construction Company, located in Bluffton. (See entry for Sands family).

Stephen Lawrence (Pete) Foster was married to Mary Catherine Wiecking (1910-1972) in 1928. They had three children: James Wiecking (1929), Sally Ann (1931) and Stephen Lawrence Jr. (1936). Jim graduated from Bluffton High School in 1947 and from Indiana University in 1951 with a degree in history. He has an adopted son, Kevin, who lives in Los Angeles. Jim is retired from the Los Angeles School System and lives in Bluffton. Sally Ann graduated from Bluffton High School in 1949, attended Indiana University, and was married in 1956 to Patrick DeSantis of Los Angeles. Sally has three children: Christina, Alicia, and Andrea. She still resides in Los Angeles. She is divorced from Patrick. Steve graduated from Bluffton High School in 1954 and attended Indiana University. He was married to Carol Helmrich (1941) of Magley, Indiana, in 1968. Steve and Carol have three children: Michael, Matthew, and Patrick. Steve owned the Bluffton Package Store from 1972 to 1987. (See entry for Wiecking Family).

FRANK

John L. (Jack) and Patricia A. (Drussell) Frank moved their young family from Fort Wayne to Wells County in 1960 after Jack began a new position as accountant with the former Red Cross Manufacturing Company.

They had two sons when they moved to Bluffton: Geoffrey E., born October 23, 1955, and Charles R., born July 27, 1959. Both were born in Fort Wayne. A daughter, Catherine A., was born in Bluffton on May 4, 1962.

The family built a home at 1037 McCoy Road (later East Spring Street) across from a field where East Side Elementary School later was built.

Jack and Pat both were active in Saint Joseph's Catholic Church. Jack served on the building committee that led to the current church facility on North Main Street (Indiana 1).

Jack was a World War II and Korean War veteran. He was an active bridge player and earned life master status. A heart attack took him from the family at the age of 41 on January 21, 1965. Their oldest child was age nine at the time.

Pat filled the role of both mother and father and saw all three of her children graduate from area universities. In recent years, Pat was active in the church choir at Saint Joseph's.

Pat began to have problems from congestive heart failure in September of 1989 and died March 8, 1991.

Geoffrey is a former reporter and sportswriter for the Bluffton News-Banner. He became active in local government, serving as Wells County Auditor from June, 1981, through November 1985. Geoff currently is Public Affairs and Human Resources Director for Job Works, non-profit organization based in Fort Wayne.

Geoff married the former Mary Lynn Johnson, a caseworker for more than ten years for the state department of Public Welfare in Wells and Adams counties. Mary Lynn currently is Social Services Coordinator for the Head Start Program in Wells and Adams counties.

Both Geoff and Mary Lynn are Ball State graduates. They have two sons, John E., age six and Paul D. age one. They live in Bluffton and John attends Lancaster Elementary School.

Charles also graduated from Ball State University. he is a caseworker for the Marion County Department of Public Welfare at Indianapolis.

During his days at Bluffton High School, Chuck was active in the Wells County Teenage Republicans (TARS). He was secretary of the organization and active in publishing a newsletter for the local TARS that received national recognition.

An employment opportunity took Cathy to the Florence, Kentucky, area, near Cincinnati, to serve as a manager in the Frisch's Restaurant chain. She previously worked as a manager for the Rax Restaurant chain in Fort Wayne.

Cathy met and married August (Butch) Schroer. Their family includes two children, Sarah age ten, and Matt age four. They live in Florence, Kentucky.

Also a Bluffton High School graduate, Cathy was profiled in *Who's Who Among American High School Students*. She attended and graduated from Purdue University at West Lafayette.

JOHN FRANK FAMILY

John Frank with his wife, the former Dorothy Isch, and sons Herb and Ron moved to Wells County in March, 1952, to a farm in Section Ten in Liberty Township which they purchased from John and Helen Gregg in 1951.

John was born in Morton, Illinois, and later moved with his parents, Sam and Nettie Voepel Frank, to the LaCrosssse and Valparaiso areas where he was associated with the Home Oil Company until 1948. Then he, with his wife and son Herb, moved to Adams County, Indiana, the birthplace of Dorothy, who was the daughter of Ernest and Elise Meiss Isch, and was a former x-ray technician at Caylor-Nickel Clinic. At the time of their marriage, which took place at the Bluffton Apostolic Christian Church on June 15, 1941, she was living at 211 West Cherry Street, which is the present site of the Masonic Temple.

In September of 1964, they purchased a farm in Section Four in Liberty Township and after Herb's marriage to Nancy Gilliam of Bluffton in 1968, they became the owners of the farm in Section Ten. John and Dorothy then moved to the newly constructed home at 0746 South 300 West, and they currently reside at this address.

On September 7, 1972, their son Ron passed away suddenly at the age of 21 from a heart ailment on the campus of Huntington College where he was a senior and student teacher at Huntington North High School.

John and Dorothy are the grandparents of Nick Frank, a junior at Ball State University. Ross Frank, a freshman at Tri-State University, Janel Frank, a sophomore at Southern Wells High School, and Jay Frank, a seventh grader at Southern Wells.

FRANKE-MILLER

Erwin C. "Red" Franke was born April 16, 1910, to Christian and Sophie Mueller Franke, German immigrants who came to America in their teens. He married Velma W. Miller, born October 9, 1917, daughter of Herman L.G. Miller and Rosina Graft Miller, on May 1, 1938. They lived the next thirteen years on 900N, Ossian, in the same house where her grandparents, Fred and Marie Graft, had resided some forty years earlier.

After the death of Erwin's mother, Sophie, Erwin and Velma moved in to care for his father, Christian, where they live today on 800N, Ossian, Indiana. He continued to farm the ground until he retired in 1977, with traditional crops as well as tomatoes raised for the Ossian Canning Company.

In addition to farming, Erwin was a carpenter and general contractor. He has been active in community and church activities. Erwin was Wells County 4-H Director, precinct committeeman of the Republican Party for thirty-five years, township trustee, deputy assessor and assessor for two terms each. He has served in various offices of Bethlehem Lutheran Church and as chairman of the church building committee for the new church built in 1979. On May 13, 1988, he received the Sagamore of the Wabash and "Distinguished Hoosier" awards from the Governor of the State of Indiana.

Velma has been a homemaker, worked at General Electric for twelve years and has been active in church activities holding local and district offices in the Lutheran Women's Missionary League and Valpo Guild.

Erwin and Velma are the parents of four children. All four were baptized and confirmed at Bethlehem Lutheran Church, attended Bethlehem Lutheran day school and graduated from Ossian High School.

The Erwin C. Franke Family
Seated: Velma and Erwin Standing: Kathleen, Rosalie, Robert, and Junior. Taken on Erwin's 80th birthday, 1990

Rosalie Ann, born March 22, 1939, married Leroy E. Hilsmier, September 12, 1959. They had Michael, September 9, 1964; Mark, September 26, 1965; and Matthew, December 15, 1973. They were divorced in 1979; she then married Gary Van Dam, born April 7, 1943, on March 22, 1986. Rosalie received her R.N. and B.S. degrees and is currently vice president of Services for Professional Care Management, Inc. in Fort Wayne. Gary is a director of sales with Aircom of Indianapolis.

Robert Duane, born February 24, 1941, married Carolyn A. Hostetter, born December 11, 1943, on October 20, 1962. They had Curtis Dean, April 18, 1966, and Julia Ann, September 15, 1974. Robert joined the Air National Guard on his eighteenth birthday and is presently a colonel and jet fighter pilot with the 122nd Tactical Fighter Wing, Fort Wayne, Indiana. Carolyn is a Mary Kay Consultant.

Erwin C., Jr., born March 3, 1945, married Carol Kay Eibling, born September 28, 1945, on September 9, 1966. They have two daughters, Kristy Lyn, born May 17, 1969, and Angela Kay, born February 21, 1971. Erwin C., Jr. graduated from Valparaiso University and is a senior staff engineer with Navistar, Fort Wayne, Indiana. Carol is a dental hygienist.

Kathleen June, born June 30, 1949, married Rex E. Lepper, born February 24, 1949, on June 25, 1971. They have two sons, Adam Gabriel, born March 20, 1976, and Joshua Christian, born August 14, 1979. Kathleen graduated from Ball State University and is a speech pathologist with East Allen County Schools. Rex is a barber/stylist.

Three grandsons are married: Michael to Judi Alger, November 26, 1988; Mark to Kathryn Miller, August 13, 1988; and Curtis to Leigh Ann Jones, September 18, 1990.

FRANKE-MUELLER

Christian (Christ) Franke was born on September 21, 1875, in Todtenhausen #64, Kreis-Minden, Germany, to Friedrich Wilhelm Christian Gottlieb Franke and Marie Christine Friederika Meier, who were united in marriage on April 7, 1861, in Saint Marien Kirche, Minden-Westfalen, Germany. He had three brothers and two sisters, none of whom came to America. He came to America around seventeen years of age in about 1892. He spent those weeks working out his passage fare by taking care of horses in the hold of the ship.

After arriving in New York, he took a train to Decatur, Indiana, and from there walked the railroad tracks to Magley, where someone was to meet him. We believe a cousin, Henry Bauermeister, met him.

He spent the next three years working as a hired hand for Wiliam (Bill) Hilgeman on a farm in Adams County, Indiana, receiving his room and board plus one hundred dollars a year as his pay.

Christian Franke Family, 1921
Front row (L to R): Erwin and Ruth Middle Row (L to R); Sophie with Martha, Christ Back row: (L to R):Gerhard and Herbert

At age twenty-two, he returned to his homeland Germany to visit, leaving there on the *S.S. Trave* on March 15, 1898, from Bremen to return to America.

His marriage to Sophie Mueller, born May 23, 1884, the oldest of six children born to Konrad Mueller and Sophie Dammeyer Mueller Jossen, #27, Post Lahde, Kreis-Minden, Germany, took place on May 25, 1902, in Bethlehem Evangelical Lutheran Church, Tocsin, Indiana, with the Reverend William Ludwig officiating.

After arriving as a young girl in America, she lived with an aunt, Louise Werling, and her husband, John, until she married Christ Franke.

He brought his bride to the farm in Jefferson Township 28N, Wells County, Section Twenty-four, Range Twelve E, which he bought from Jasper Gossard October 3, 1898, consisting of forty acres.

The interesting part of this is that these acreages are listed on sheepskin as an original United States Land Grant, signed by then President Millard Fillmore on December 20, 1850.

Then on January 24, 1910, Christ added forty acres bought from Zacharriah B. Gossard (we call that the prairie, or back forty).

These original land grants were both executed in the Federal Land Grant Office Fort Wayne, Indiana, and signed by a Jacob King and a Philip King, both of Wells County, Indiana.

Christ and Sophie lived, worked, and raised their five children on this farm. Herbert born April 11, 1903, died December 4, 1984, married Martha Graft, April 27, 1930. Gerhard born March 18, 1906, never married. Erwin, born April 16, 1910, married Velma Miller, May 1, 1938. Ruth born August 30, 1912, married to Gilbert Ehlerding April 24, 1932. Martha born December 2, 1920, married Wilbur Selking, January 31, 1942.

Sophie returned to her homeland once, leaving America in 1935 and returning January, 1936, on the *Europa,* leaving from Bremen in Bremerhaven, Germany.

Christ and Sophie were members of the Bethlehem Evangelical Lutheran Church, M.S., Ossian, Indiana, north of Tocsin, where their children were baptized, attended church day school, and were confirmed.

Christ died February 12, 1958, and Sophie died February 1, 1951. Both were laid to rest in the Bethlehem Church Cemetery.

One son, Erwin, along with his wife, Velma, lives on the farm, and a grandson Erwin, Jr. and his wife, Carol Eilbing Franke, live in the wooded area of the aforementioned acreage.

Notes of Interest: (1) Before the R.E.M.C., the C. Frankes had a power plant called a "Delco Plant" in an outbuilding. This was purchased from L.L. Bender, Bluffton, Indiana. (2) Christ Franke and neighbors worked together to build the telephone lines in their area.

FRENCH-RUNYON-PARNELL

In 1835, Joseph French Sr. and his son Joseph Jr. came from Madison County, New York. Joseph had bought over fourteen hundred acres from the government. Being the first white family to settle, French Township was named for them. A short time later, Joseph's brothers, George and Smith French, and grandmothers, Dunbar and Sheldon, arrived.

They built their first cabin on the bank of the Wabash, near the edge of the water, knowing nothing about the overflow. They raised corn and vegetables, and Mrs. French planted the apple seed for a nursery. This was the beginning of most of the orchards between Bluffton and Portland, as newcomers came to Joseph for trees.

Ada (French) and David Runyon

All went well until the third spring, when the Wabash began to rise. Melissa French (Hall), the daughter of Joseph Jr. was born March 10, 1838. She was the first white child born in French Township. When she was three days old, the cabin was surrounded by water and the floor (which was made of puncheons) began to float. Joseph got his Indian boat (a hollowed log), rowed in at one door and placed his wife and baby in the canoe and went out the other door. They stayed at his father's place almost one-half mile from them until the water subsided. The woods were full of Indians who were quite friendly and curious about the new white baby, but didn't want to trade babies because she was a girl baby.

In the course of time, John Runyon and family settled in Hartford Township. He was a Democrat and a Baptist minister from Rockingham County, Virginia. His wife was Mary (Price) Runyon, and they had nine children, one of whom was David, born May 2, 1841. David married Ada Maloi French, born October 25, 1844, the daughter of George and Eliza French. Their children were Ella, Elroy Forrest, Sam, Talford, and Cora May Runyon. Sylvia French married Joseph Runyon and both families seemed inclined to inter-marry.

Joseph Sr. and Sally French are buried beside George and Eliza French in the French Cemetery on the Reynolds farm. David Runyon died in 1929, and

Ada (French) Runyon died in 1902. They are buried in Greenwood Cemetery in Linn Grove.

Cora May Runyon married William Clinton Parnell September 6, 1911. He was from Scott County, Virginia. Their children were May, Clifton, Forest, Frederick, twins David and Donald, Robert, Opal, and June Elizabeth. Dad Parnell died while serving his fourth term as county assessor of Blackford County in 1949. They raised most of their family in Montpelier. Cora died in 1956 and is buried in IOOF Cemetery in Montpelier.

I married David Clyde Parnell on September 18, 1943. He was named for his grandpa Runyon. We had one son (William Francis) born November 1, 1946. He married Janet Sue Koorsen and they have two daughters, Aislinn Alaina born October 3, 1984, and Elise Erienne born January 6, 1988. They live in Fort Wayne.

David died December 2, 1981, and is entombed in Brookside Cemetery. My name is Margaret Anne (Francis) Parnell. I live in Montpelier and winter in Winter Haven, Florida. Many French and Runyon descendants are still living in Bluffton and the surrounding area. *(Mrs. David Parnell)*

DWIGHT FRITZ FAMILY

Ancestors of the Fritz family emigrated from Germany and settled in Wells County in November, 1858. Family members engaged in farming, blacksmithing, and David Fritz was sheriff of Wells County at one time.

Dwight Fritz married Marie Markley after graduation form Bluffton High School and attending Indiana University. In 1926 Dwight started in the retail business selling Delco light plants, Maytag washers, and bicycles. The retail operation lasted for fifty-seven years known as Fritz Electric Company until it was closed in 1983. Dwight passed away in 1949 and Marie in 1956.

Children of Dwight and Marie were Robert, William, Joan and Carolyn (Lou).

Robert married Barbara Oda in 1942. Children were Sandra, born in 1943, and Jerry, born in 1948.

William married Mary Alice Wunder of Paulding, Ohio, in 1946. Children were Janelle, born in 1947, and James, born in 1949.

Joan married William Robertson of Indianapolis, Indiana, in 1952. Children were Claudia, born in 1956, Cynthia, born in 1958, and Catherine, born in 1961.

Carolyn married Virgil Reber in 1949. Children were David, born in 1950, Steven, born in 1951, and Craig, born in 1954.

Dwight Fritz was born in 1893 at home on Fritz Road (100 E). He graduated from Bluffton High School in 1911. He also played on the basketball team that participated in the first high school tournament ever held. He was a trustee of the Methodist Church and participated in many civic organizations.

Marie Fritz was born in 1895, the daughter of William D. and Margaret Dettinger Markley. She was active in the operation of Fritz Electric until her death.

Robert Fritz was born in 1918 and graduated om Bluffton High School in 1936. He served in he Air Force as bomber pilot trainer from 1942 to 1945, a first lieutenant. Active in American Legion, he was the post commander and in 1956 served as state commander, He was on the school board many years and in civic organization. He was in retail business in Bluffton more that forty-seven years. He passed away July, 1990.

William Fritz was born in 1922 and graduated from Bluffton High School in 1940. He attended Butler University, the University of Notre Dame, and graduated from Columbia University Navy Officers training school. He served in the U.S. Navy as an executive officer and navigator in the Pacific from 1943 to 1946 a lieutenant senior grade. He was post commander of the American Legion, a member of the Wells County draft board, and a director of Farmers and Merchants Bank. He was in the retail business thirty-eight years in Bluffton.

Joan Fritz Robertson was born in 1927. She graduated from Bluffton High School in 1945 and attended Butler University. She was active in the real estate business in Indianapolis. She passed away May, 1974.

Carolyn (Lour) Fritz Reber was born in 1930. She graduated from Bluffton High School in 1948 and attended butler University. She was secretary in Bluffton schools from 1960-1980.

The Fritz family has always felt that Wells County is a great place in which to live and work.

FRYBACK-PINNEY

Clifford Fryback was born in Wells County, on February 13, 1912. He was the son of John and Hazel Fryback. Since John was a cream buyer for Scholosser's Creamery, Cliff made many runs in Wells County picking up cream from the farmers. Cliff met Nellie Pinney (born May 1, 1913) on one of these cream runs. Nellie's parents were Ernest and Lucy Stout Pinney, who ran the Pinney Grocery Store in Mt. Zion. They dated, and were married on March 5, 1931.

Nellies Grand Representative Reception and Celebration of 60th wedding anniversary, March 5, 1991 Left to Right: Shellie Mossburg, wife of Mike Mossburg, Clifford and Nellie Fryback, Mike Mossburg, grandson of Cliff and Nellie

Cliff and Nellie have two daughters, Joyce Ann and Patricia Lou. Joyce married Ralph Smith and they have five children: Don, Judy, Cindy, Neal, and Sherrie. Patricia married Richard Mossburg, and they have three children: Scott, Mike, and Julie.

Nellie, since retirement from Franklin Electric, has been active in Crescent Chapter of Eastern Star, and has served as Worthy Matron. She now holds the office of Treasurer. She was appointed Grand Representative of Texas Grand Chapter last year, and had her reception in March, 1991. Cliff and Nellie also celebrated their 60th wedding anniversary in March, 1991.

WILLIAM AND CLIFFORD FRYBACK

The Frybacks came to Wells County from Maryland. My grandfather, William Addison Fryback, married Ida Alice Avery from Adams County, June 20, 1885. They had nine children, seven boys and two girls. My father was the third child. John Clifford Fryback was born in Uniondale, September 28, 1889. He married Hazel Van Camp in Decatur, August, 1911. They had two sons, Clifford B. Fryback, born in 1912, and William M. Fryback, born in 1921.

Grandpa Fryback lived in Murray when I was seven or eight years old. Cliff had a pony and spring wagon. We used to stay with grandpa and grandma and cut hay in the cemetery. When we would drive over the graves, it would make the springs squeak and my brother would say the spirits are crying because we were running over their graves. Scary!

Jennifer Fryback Hilgedag, James C. Fryback, Dorothy Fryback, William M. Fryback, George Fryback, John W. Fryback. Taken September 1990 at Jim's wedding

We went to Grandma Van Camp's for holidays. My dad had a touring car with snap-on ising glass windows. Often, in the winter, we couldn't get into the barn yard because of the snow. They would meet us with a horse and sleigh to bring us up to the house. When we finally got into the house, we were frozen. Cars at that time didn't have heaters. You had to wrap up in a bear skin robe. When we got into the house, we hurried to the stove, either the hard coal burner in the living room or the kitchen range. When grandma later got modern, she had a coal oil stove, but that wasn't nearly as warm as the old coal range. Grandma came from Switzerland when she was a little girl and one of the traditions that she brought with her was wine making. When we came in out of the cold, even the kids got a small glass. One day, the whole family was having their wine and the minister came to call. You never saw such scurrying in your life to get the wine glasses out of sight.

Our gang each built a canoe. We would take the hoops off of wooden barrels to make the ribs. At that time autos had fabric tops. Mr. Suddeth ran the junk yard that is still on State Road #1. He didn't like kids in his yard, so he had two big dogs. We would sneak over the back fence with a knife to cut the fabric, but we had to stay close to the fence. When we heard him call the dogs, we had to go like the dickens. I believe that you can outrun a dog when you are scared—at least, I did.

Clifford Fryback married Nellie Pinney, March 5, 1931. Nellie was one of four daughters of Ernest and Lucy Pinney who ran a grocery store in Mt. Zion. They have two daughters, Joyce Ann Fryback born November 14, 1931, and Patricia Lou Fryback born October 12, 1940.

Joyce married Ralph Smith on March 21, 1949. They have five children, Judith (August 16, 1950), Neil, (September 16, 1953), Donald (September 30, 1949), Cynthia (October 1, 1951) and Sheryl (June 24, 1960).

Patricia married Richard Mossburg on September 12, 1960. They have three children: C. Scott (June 23, 1961), Michael (August 17, 1965), and Julia (March 28, 1967).

William Fryback married Dorothy F. Dittmann from Lagrange, Illinois on April 10, 1943. They have four children, Jennifer Fryback (March 19, 1945), John (July 30, 1947), George (July 8, 1950) and James (February 4, 1955). Jennifer married William Hilgedag on January 28, 1967. They have three children, Elizabeth Suzanne (October 1, 1967), Stacy (March 7, 1975) and Stephanie (June 7, 1977). John married Theresa Sutton on February 14, 1981. They have two children, John Michael (March 6, 1988) and Jillian Elizabeth (April 17, 1989). George married Elaine Hughes from Wachula, Florida, on February 14, 1976. They have twins, Nicholas and Nicole (August 24, 1979) and Jessica (June 27, 1984). James married Stephanie Ruck on September 21, 1990. She has two children from a previous marriage, Cole and Brittany.

WILLIAM AND ESTHER FRYE

William F. Frye is the son of William Thestle Frye and his first wife, Evelyn Irene Harris. He was born October 12, 1947, in Decatur, Indiana. His father, William T. Frye, is the son of Oscar Ollis Frye and Grace Leisure of Bluffton. Other children of Oscar and Grace Frye were Forrest (Mary Ulmer), Ebert, Gerald, Virginia (Sow Kunihiro), Betty (Ob Hughes), Bernice (William T. Cash) and Berdilla (Edgar Hughes).

Evelyn Irene Frye was the daughter of Ernie and Mary (McFarren) Harris of rural Bluffton.

William F. Frye retired from the Marine Corp in 1985 after twenty years of service. In his spare time he enjoys bowling, reading a good book, enjoying country music and spending time with his family. His wife, Esther, is the daughter of Raymond L. and Violet Pearl (Lee) Hakes of Bluffton. She was born in December, 1945, in Bluffton and is the eldest of five children which includes Thomas (Cathy Lovell), Joyce (Donald Hastings), Rose (Michael Colvin) and Marion Charles (Karyn Wade) who was named after his two grandfathers. Esther graduated from Bluffton High School in 1966 and her hobbies include genealogy, bowling, and traveling. She is a member of the DAR in Bluffton. Bill and Esther have been married for sixteen years and have one son, William O. Frye.

Raymond L. Hakes is the youngest son of Charles and Gladys (Chronister) Hakes of Decatur. His siblings include: Dorothy (Clarence Roop) and Harold (Shirley Suddeth). He retired in 1965 after twenty years service in the Air Force. He is now serving as a Disabled Veteran Transportation Officer at the Veteran's Hospital in Fort Wayne. His wife, Violet, is the daughter of Marion and Martha (Baumgartner) Lee of Bluffton. They were married November 30, 1944, in Miami, Florida. In her spare time she enjoys gardening and having her family close by.

For both of these families, serving in the military and the fact that Bluffton has been a permanent home, has offered security, family and friends. It is a good place to raise a family and has a legacy to pass on to future generations.

JOHN ADAM FULK FAMILY

John Adam Fulk brought his wife, Nora, and two daughters, Helen and Marie, from a farm in Adams County to Bluffton in the fall of 1914 and started a wood-working and blacksmith shop. Another daughter, Lucille, was born to them.

The Fulks moved once from No. 1 Plat of town at 210 North Main Street to Lancaster Street to care for Grandpa Marcellus Norris. Then they moved back to the Main Street home, back of which, on Water Street, was the blacksmith shop. I remember watching my dad shoe horses. He was very strong and could handle the meanest horse. He also hammered out plow shares and iron on an anvil and then tempered the iron in a large slack tub of water. People would come to get this water to put on poison ivy. One of dad's specialties was building farm trailers. Mother died on August 30, 1971, and dad died on March 1, 1972.

After graduation from high school, I worked for over thirteen years at the News-Banner. Helen was employed at the Caylor-Nickel Clinic, and Lucile worked at Deam and Harris Drug Store.

Helen moved to New Haven after her marriage to F. Lyle Tustison and still lives in the house they built. Her husband died in August 1977. Their two children are Mrs. Charles (Judy) Lenderson, of Fairfax, Virginia, Purdue graduate nurse, who has a son Chuck and son Larry of Rossville, Illinois. He is a Purdue graduate engineer. His wife is Martha and his daughter is Mary. Lucile Wells now lives at Capri Meadows in Bluffton.

John A. Fulk, blacksmith (on left) Water Street, Bluffton, Indiana

I lived with my parents when my son Frank Wilson was an infant and worked for County Superintendent of Schools, Lloyd Lieurance. In 1963, I moved with Superintendent Lloyd Biberstine to Southern Wells Consolidated Schools and retired January, 1984, with thirty-one and one-half years of service.

In 1954, I was married to Roy Rice, of North Manchester, and moved to new home at 1115 Wayne Street. Roy was brought to Bluffton by Hoosier Milk Condensery as a butter maker. Our family was increased by Roy's son Gene, thirteen, and daughter Norma, eleven. Roy also had a married daughter, Mrs. Everett (Melba) Holmgren and a son, Ronald, who was a student at Purdue.

Gene is employed in quality control at Allen Dairy in Fort Wayne where he lives with his wife Sue. Their daughter Dawn is a junior at I.U.; son Gregg is a freshman at ITT in Fort Wayne. Mrs. Larry (Norma) Michael, a Ball State graduate, lives in Phoenix, Arizona, and is employed by Best Western International; her daughter Di-Anne is a college student.

The Holmgrens, who live in North Liberty, are Ball State graduates and are both in education. Their son Mark, a Purdue graduate engineer with Hershey Foods, lives in Pennsylvania with his wife Karen and daughter, Amy. Their son Carl, a Purdue graduate engineer, resides in Houston, Texas with his wife Martha and two stepsons, James and Jason. Their daughter, Dee, who is a Purdue graduate, is a nutritionist at Elkhart Hospital.

Ronald is vice president of the Kroger Company at Cincinnati, Ohio. He and his wife Di-Anne have two sons, Scott, who is with General Mills in Minneapolis where he lives with his wife Marjorie and son Aaron; and Brent, a student at Washington College in St. Louis.

Doctor Frank Wilson attended I.U. on a basketball scholarship and graduated from Indiana Medical School and a sports medicine fellowship at Columbus, Georgia. In 1991, he left his orthopaedic group and opened his own sports medicine office in Indianapolis. He and his wife Christine have three children: Matthew, thirteen; Tiffany, eight; and John, nine months.

Roy and I moved to our lake home on Little Barbee in 1985 and spent the winter months in Englewood, Florida. Roy died on August 15, 1988.

RINEAR-FUNK FAMILY

John Wesley Rinear was born in Cuyahoga County, Ohio, March 4, 1842. His family moved to a farm on Section 21, Liberty Township, in 1854. On September 25, 1861, he enlisted in the Indiana Volunteer Infantry during the Civil War. He was wounded at the mouth of the White river in Arkansas and honorably discharged October 7, 1862.

On April 2, 1863, he wed Sarah C. First. They were the parents of Hannah Sophia, born December 28, 1866. She was the first white child born in the town of Liberty Center. John was a staunch Democrat and was elected Justice of the Peace in 1872 in Liberty Center. In 1877, he was appointed postmaster and in 1894 was elected to the State Senate.

Absalom Funk was born near Chambersburg, Pennsylvania, February 12, 1839, and died July 9, 1875. he came to Wells County in November, 1866, from Wayne County, Ohio, and lived in Section 34 of Lancaster Township until his death. He was married to Ann Margaret Bower January 8, 1852. They had eight children, among whom were Susannah M., the wife of Doctor Frank Garrett of Liberty Center, and John Bower, who married Hannah S. Rinear.

Standing L to R: Eric Funk, Rinear Funk, Robert Funk Seated L to R: Trudy Dickason, Marian Funk, Susie Lambert

John B. Funk and Hannah Rinear were married April 2, 1885. They had three children: John A. J., born May 22, 1886, Sarah Ann Mabel, born December 13, 1888, and Charles Rinear, born February 2, 1892. John B. Funk was a self-taught druggist who passed the state licensing board and had a drug store and pharmacy in Liberty Center. He was also president of the Liberty Center State Bank until it was dissolved after the Bank Holiday. He and his wife were active members of the Liberty Center Baptist Church.

Charles R. Funk and Kitty E. Boltin were married April 2, 1913, in Liberty Center. Charles was a farmer. He was the first person in Wells County to die in the flu epidemic of 1918. Kitty became a teacher and raised her family. She died January 23, 1967. They had three children. John W. was born February 19, 1914, and died March 16, 1987. He graduated from I.U. Medical School and practiced medicine in Indiana and California. John and his wife, Ernestine Graber, had four sons: John, Joe, Jim and Jake. They all live in California. Crystal Ann was born March 16, 1916, and died October 13, 1938. Rinear was born September 11, 1918. He graduated from Liberty Center High School in 1936, International Business College in 1939, and joined the U.S. navy in 1940 and served World War II on active duty. On March 14, 1942, he married Marian Wolff. They had four children. Sue Hannah was born May 13, 1947. She is an registered nurse living in Florida. Eric Rinear was born December 17, 1948. He is a C.P.A. living in Florida. Robert Wolff was born October 7, 1950. He is married to Karen Fletchall and is an insurance broker living in Kokomo. Trudy Evelyn was born December 12, 1951. She is married to Joe Dickason. She works as a purchasing scheduler and lives with her family in Churubusco.

After World War II, Rinear purchased other heirs' interest and moved to the original farm settled by John Wesley Rinear, his great-grandfather.

DAVID W. AND JOAN C. FUREY FAMILY

David W. Furey, son of David J. and Adele R. (Tarr) Furey of Allegheny County, Pennsylvania, married Joan C. Brown, daughter of Robert L. and Thelma R. (Darr) Brown of Adams County, Indiana. They were married on March 25, 1967.

Both had earned their Bachelor's degrees from Huntington College in 1967. They later earned their Master degrees from Saint Francis College and Ball State University.

David has taught at Norwell High School since it opened in 1967. He is a business education teacher and has been the department head for twenty years. Joan has taught at Lancaster, Rockcreek, and Ossian Elementary schools.

Joan and Dave Furey, Lora, and Carolyn Jo

To this marriage two daughters were born: Lora Leigh Furey graduated from Norwell High School in 1986, and Carolyn Jo Furey graduated from Norwell High School in 1990. Lora earned her Bachelor's degree in elementary education from Ball State University in 1990, and is presently teaching in Las Vegas, Nevada.

Carolyn is a student at Ball State University. She is expanding her interest in Art and Advertising.

David is an active member of the Ossian Volunteer Fire Department and is presently assistant chief.

Joan's involvement with youth led her to be a charter member of Norwell's Dollars for Scholars. She has been president for two years (1989-91). She is also an active member of Ossian Psi Iota Xi sorority.

The family are active members of Saint Luke United Church of Christ in Adams County. David is an elder of the church. Joan has been the church organist for thirty-one years and has taught a young adult Sunday school class for twelve year.

In 1968, they purchased their home on Morton Lane in Ossian. They have resided there ever since.

FURNAS-CREEK

Everett Creek's parents were Orie and Alma Carnes Creek. He was born near Domestic, on August 1, 1913. His brother and sisters are Herald, (deceased), Helen Kline, Ruth Shiner, Leona Morgan, and Elma Martz. He graduated from Rockcreek School, Wells County, in 1931.

His marriage to Ruthella Furnas took place in their home, north of Rockford, on June 8, 1935. They have four children: Joseph Lee, born May 26, 1937; David Edwin, born August 25, 1939; James Everett, born May 20, 1944; Anita Alma, born December 19, 1950.

All of the children were born while living in or near Bluffton. They all graduated from Bluffton High School.

Everett's first job after graduating form high school was with Herman Miller, a seed corn raiser of Rockcreek Township. In 1937, he and his family moved to Bluffton. He had a country bread route for four years. He then worked for Graden's Service Station on Elm Street, and the Bluffton Rubber Works on East Market Street. In 1951, he became the agent for the Standard Oil Company. He retired in 1976.

He and his wife are active members of the First United Methodist Church in Bluffton.

Joseph, their first born child, married Carol Rose from Fort Wayne in 1968. They live southeast of Bluffton on a portion of the farm he was raised on with their daughter Lisa. He has retired from the Electrical Union in Fort Wayne.

David married Rebecca Dickerson of Decatur in 1971. They live in Decatur with their two sons, Joel and Daniel. James married Linda Tompkins of Fort Wayne in 1965. They live northwest of Fort Wayne, with their son Jeffery. Their daughter Shelli married Daniel Lipinski and they live near Fort Wayne.

Anita married Steve Blake of Upland, California in 1983 and they live near Upland with a daughter Emily.

GAISER

Two world wars have eliminated the records of the Gaisers in Germany. However, we know that George J. Gaiser (1835), and his younger brother David left home, near Stuttgart, in 1849. They stowed away in a barrel on a steamer, and after a thirty-five day journey, jumped ship and swam ashore in New York Harbor. After serving as an indentured servant for three years in the shoe cobbler trade, George ventured west to Dayton, Ohio, where his brother was living. Leaving his family in Ohio, George eventually settled on a farm in Chester Township, Wells County, Indiana.

George J. Gaiser married Martha A. Cloud in 1861 shortly before joining the Union Army to fight against the Confederacy. At the end of the war, he returned home from a prison camp, after having been mistakenly reported as killed in action.

George and Martin had five children, David H., Daniel, Melvin, Sarah, and William A. (1871).

William A. Gaiser married Emma Alice Crosby in 1893. William Gaiser was engaged in farming in Chester and Liberty Township, near Mount Zion, most of his life. William and Emma had five children: Belle (Cloud) in 1894, Oka M. in 1896, Cecile (Sheets) in 1902, and Garl Leon in 1910.

After returning from the Kansas oil fields in 1918, Oka M. Gaiser, my father, took up farming near the South Africa School in Liberty Township. Oka married Estella Lockwood in 1920, and had four children: Dorothy (Beitelshees) in 1921, died 1990; Doris (Burkhead) in 1924; Crystal (Lee) in 1927; and Noel in 1932. After Estella's death in 1939, Oka Gaiser married Marguerite Lewellen in 1942. In 1944 Oka and Marguerite moved from a farm on the Huntington side of the Wells and Huntington County line to Chester Township where Oka continued farming until his retirement in 1972. Marguerite taught school for a total of 37 years, including several one room schools in Adams County, and the Monroe School, prior to her marriage. After her marriage she continued teaching at the Warren Elementary School, Chester Center, Liberty Center, and Southern Wells Elementary Schools. Oka died in 1986, and Marguerite has lived at Swiss Village in Berne, Indiana, since that time, while renting out the family farm in Chester Township.

Oka and Marguerite Gaiser had two children. In 1946 Oka Leon was born, followed by Marilyn Lewellen in 1947. Marilyn married Paul G. Miller of Clay City, Indiana, while they were students at Purdue University in 1968. The Milers now reside in San Clemente, California, with their two children, Amanda Marguerite (1978) and Adam Paul (1981).

After obtaining a degree from Purdue in 1970, Oka Leon taught Industrial Arts at Norwell and Southern Wells High Schools. In 1975 he started a remodeling/construction business. This business, Gaiser Construction Inc., is still active in Wells County.

In 1977, Leon Gaiser married Susan K. Potts, a daughter of Ralph and Ruth Sturgeon Potts of Wells County. They are the parents of two children Hilary Linn (July 16, 1986) and Caleb Oka (November 23, 1988).

Leon and his family are the only Gaisers still residing in Wells County.

GALLIVAN

The first half of our family name is from a Gaelic word meaning "bright" and the second half means "white". This name appears on a map usually given tourists to Ireland. The family estate was located in County Kerry. The name Galvin also appears along side Gallivan. My great-grandfather's given name was Denis. My brother seemed to think that his given name had only one n instead of two. Prior to the time Denis Gallivan left the family estate, our name was O'Gallivan. Even today that is still true in the Gaelic tongue.

Denis Gallivan moved to a location six miles from Tralee on the Tralee to Cork road. He had three children whose names were John, Thomas and Mary. John was the eldest of the three and came to America first. Had Denis remained on the family estate during the potato famine, our family history might have been quite different. Since he had left the family estate, there was no obligation on the part of his family to aid him during this disaster. For a time, there was a public works program in place by the British Government in which he was in a supervisory position. This was all outside work, and he became ill due to the dampness of the climate. A physician advised that he must quit his job. Our great uncle Thomas looked very much like his father and, for a period of two weeks, impersonated him. The family, fearing reprisal from the British government, refrained from sending Thomas, so his father returned to work which quickly brought on his death.

L to R Back row: Mary C. Gallivan, Dwight Gallivan (married August 28, 1941) L to R Front Row: Grace Gallivan, Victor F. Gallivan, Carl Gallivan

My grandfather, John, when he was twenty years of age, made his way on a ship which landed in New Orleans on Christmas Day in 1851. They disembarked the next day. There was considerable snow on the docks, and for a few days he was able to work there in place of the slaves who could not work because they had no shoes. This, of course, was one of the very few times New Orleans has had snow. He came from there up the Mississippi River to the Ohio River to Cincinnati. On the way up the Mississippi they stopped at a plantation to refuel, where there they could have had work as slave supervisors. My grandfather was able to call one of the slaves aside and found out what kind of person his master was. The word was unprintable. Since he decided not to stay, his future brother-in-law, who was with him, didn't stay either.

Grandfather, who worked on the Wabash and Erie Canal and also on the Wabash Railroad, was able to pay for the passage to America of his brother Thomas. He and his brother together worked to bring their sister Mary and their mother to this country. He married and lived in Darke and Preble Counties in Ohio. He and his first wife, who died, had one son there by the name of Jeremiah. In 1869, he came to Wells County and purchased a farm which is still in the family at 6052 N 300E. He married Amarilla High, whose father was Ezekial High and whose mother was a Dailey. They had two sons, John Carl Gallivan and James Earl Gallivan. There was also a half-sister, Blanche.

My brother, Dwight Ferguson Gallivan, married Mary C. Campbell, who survives as of this writing. They had two sons, William and Robert, and a daughter, Bonnie, who is married to Phil Bayt and lives in Indianapolis. Both Bonnie and Phil are attorneys who have a daughter Catherine Marie.

My parents, John Carl Gallivan and Olive Grace Ferguson, were married in 1910. My brother, Dwight, was born on the family farm in 1912, in a log house which still stands, and I was born in Tocsin in 1919. Our parents were both school teachers before they became a farm family.

Dwight Gallivan's wife Mary, formerly Mary C. Campbell, graduated from Oak Park High School in Illinois, attended college at Oberlin, Ohio, then finished at Ball State in 1936. She started teaching at Lancaster and while Dwight was in FBI, taught at Liberty Center, Ossian, Bluffton and later at Adams Central, where she and Dwight accompanied the senior class on their trip to Washington, D.C. Dwight and Mary were married in 1941.

For nearly twelve years, Dwight Gallivan was court reporter for the Wells Circuit Court. During most of World War II, he was in the FBI. After an injury, he returned to Bluffton to join a law practice with John F. Decker. After a short time, A. Walter Hamilton joined the firm. In 1954 the former Knight of Pythias building was remodeled for a new law office as well as other offices. Victor Gallivan has also been practicing for many years at the same location as a public accountant.

Robert B. Gallivan has been employed at LICA of Berne and owns a home just south and west of Murray. William A. Gallivan attended Hillsdale College, Michigan and presently is self-employed. Both Mary and Dwight have been active in community affairs, including First United Methodist Church. Mary has participated in Church Women United, Wells Hospital Auxiliary, Foltz Reading Club. Dwight was extremely active in Kiwanis affairs, including being local club president, district governor in 1954 and later a Kiwanis International trustee for two terms. He also was a 32nd degree Mason as well as being a member of Elks and a charter member of the Wells County Historical Society. Dwight died May 28, 1989.

RALPH H. GALLOWAY

Ralph Herbert Galloway was born in Harlan County, Kentucky, May 2, 1921 and died September 12, 1991. He is the son of Roy and Annie Mae (Smith) Galloway. He has three sisters: Mildred, Pauline and Yvonne.

Ralph attended school in Kentucky and worked in the coal mines of Kentucky and Virginia.

When World War II came along he went into the armed forces. He was in the European Theatre of Operations. Most of the time he was a machine gunner on the front lines. He earned four campaign stars, a Bronze Star, and also a Good Conduct Medal. He was discharged from service on December 30, 1945.

He came home to Virginia and on January 10, 1946 married his sweetheart, who had been waiting for him, in Harlan County, Kentucky. This young lady was Mabel Fritz, the daughter of William McKinley and Tishia (Hall) Fritz. She was born to them on August 30, 1924.

Ralph and Mabel lived in Wise County, Virginia, until 1947. They left the coal fields of Virginia and came to Richmond, Indiana to seek employment elsewhere rather than work in the coal mines.

Ralph and Mabel's only child was born July 8, 1950, while they lived in Richmond. They named this child Fredonna Colleen Galloway. Ralph moved his family to a farm near Petroleum, Indiana, and they lived there for a short while, later moving to Liberty Center, Wells County, Indiana in 1954.

He and Mabel worked at Franklin Electric until retirement in 1984. Ralph has been very active in the community. He and his wife belong to the Liberty Center Baptist Church.

He received his license to preach the Gospel of Christ in 1959. He served as pastor of the Poneto Baptist Church from 1972 until 1983. He has held many offices in the Liberty Center Baptist Church. He was ordained into the ministry on February 10, 1991. A great honor was bestowed upon Ralph on this day by the Liberty Center Baptist Church.

Ralph and Mabel Galloway

Ralph and Mabel's daughter, Fredonna Colleen Galloway, married Carl Haler of Cambridge City, Indiana, and of this marriage two children were born. They are Justin Adam Haler, born November 4, 1974, and Sarah Grace Haler, born August 5, 1983. They also reside in Wells County.

GARRETT

The Garrett family sketch will begin at Joseph, born on January 17, 1814, in Maryland. One son was born to his first marriage. His name was Noah, born December 17, 1839. He later moved to Indiana in 1861. Noah married Leah Funk, born on April 29, 1836, and raised four children. Their names are I.V. Lester, born in 1862, Alice L., born in 1863, Frank C., born July 11, 1866, and Walter O. born in 1870.

I.V. Lester married Fanny (Howard) and had two children, Very I. and Bertha B. Alice married Alonzo F. Rittenhouse, and Walter O. married Ruie Sturgis.

In 1888 Frank C. married Mary Elizabeth Boltin, born in 1868. They lived and raised their family in the Liberty Center area. Their five children are Hattie Flo, Noah Mount, Lola M., Alonzo B., and Mary Alice.

Noah Mount was born on January 6, 1901, and married Jeanetta Ada Craig, born July 16, 1904 in Fairmount, Indiana. Ada was the daughter of Clarence Geno and Elizabeth Beershebe (Crawford). Her brothers and sisters were: Clarence Crawford, Arthur B. Thurman Thomas, Forrest Doyle, Ruba, Juanita, Chella, and Pauline.

Noah and Ada were married July 27, 1931, and lived and worked in Liberty Center all their life. Their children were Ruba Jane, Mary Elizabeth (Biddy) who married brothers Claude and Clyde Harris and are mentioned further on other pages of this book. Max Arthur (Pat) and Mount Eugene (Mike) are veteran bus drivers for Southern Wells.

Pat was born on September 9, 1925 and married Lorene Mae Ireland, born January 25, 1924. They are the parents of Larry Allen; Anthony Gray, deceased; Laurie Anne; and Michele Sue.

Larry was born on December 7, 1947 and married Diane Marie Claus and have two sons. Patrick Allen was born on November 24, 1970, and Jeremiah Jon was born on February 12, 1979. Larry's family lives in the Ossian area.

Laurie was born November 18, 1952, and married Michael Allen Russell. They have four sons: Anthony Michael was born July 22, 1979, Andrew William was born August 10, 1983, Adams James was born April 1, 1986 and Nicholas Allen was born June 26, 1988. Laurie's family lives in the Southern Wells District.

Michele was born on June 15, 1955, and married Harry Edward Summan. They have one son, Edward Gray, born February 2, 1988. Michele's family lives in Jay County.

Mike was born on September 22, 1926 and married in 1945 to Barbara Ann Baker, born on December 17, 1926. They have one daughter named Jennifer Ann who married Keith Allen Paxson from Keystone, Indiana. Their son Kim Lee is deceased.

Jennifer and Keith are parents of one deceased son named Todd Allen, and two daughters Dawn Michele, born February 4, 1972, and Alyssa Ann, born January 2, 1974.

GARRETT

Since the arrival of Noah Garrett in 1863, the Garrett family has been a prominent one in Wells County. Noah Garrett's mother died in Mahoning County, Ohio, where he was born. His father, Joseph Garrett, married Elizabeth Ciphers and to that union four more children were born: O.D. Garrett, Dr. Frank W. Garrett, and a daughter who married Isaac A. Smith.

Noah Garrett (1839-1908) had married Leah Funk (1836-1914) in Ohio on Christmas Day, 1860. Noah and Leah, the daughter of Benjamin and Elizabeth Rouch Funk, had four children: Ivan Von Lester (1862-1908); Alice Rittenhouse (1863-1950); Walter O. (1870-1950); and Frank Curtis. Ivan Von Lester died unexpectedly in 1908. While his estate was being auctioned, his father took ill and died days thereafter.

Frank Curtis Garrett (1866-1944) married Mary Elizabeth Boltin on January 31, 1889. Mary Elizabeth ("Lizzie") was the daughter of Wiliam J. (1842-1914) and Mary A. Richardson Boltin (1848-1925). William Boltin was the son of Stewart Boltin and Elizabeth King. Elizabeth King was the daughter of Johnston King, Jr., and Margaret Stanley of Wells County.

Frank Curtis Garrett and Mary Elizabeth Boltin Garrett
Wedding Photograph -1889

Frank and Lizzie Garrett had five children, four of whom survived to adulthood and who have numerous descendents in Wells County in 1991. Their first child, Lola Mabel (1890-1982) married Hiner Holmes Ellis (1888-1957) (See The Ellis family in this volume). Alonzo Boltin Garrett (1893-1968), Hattie Floe (1898-1902), Noah Mount (1901-1967), and Mary Elizabeth (1903-). The four children who lived to adulthood raised families in Wells County. Mary Elizabeth Garrett married Ralph Markley.

The Garret family has been noted for its conservatism in politics throughout its tenure in Wells County; however, this high calling could not withstand the fires of love. After Lola Garrett became the bride of Hiner Ellis, she soon came to decide that the old adage regarding politics and bedfellows had far deeper meaning than might first be observed. In the two generations that followed, the Republican Garretts and the Democratic Ellises served as county officials concurrently: In 1946, Curtis Ellis became Wells County Auditor, while his uncle, Alonzo Boltin Garrett, was Wells County treasurer. In 1991, as this essay is written, Alonzo's daughter, Betsy Noe, is Wells County recorder while Curtis' son, Ted, is a Wells County councilman.

GARRETT-POPEJOY

Joseph Garrett moved from Northeast Ohio about 1840 and homesteaded a farm one mile south of Liberty Center. His first wife died at the birth of Noah. Later he married Elizabeth Ciphers, also from Ohio. They had three children: Amanda (later Smith), Ora D., and Franklin W. Franklin graduated from Butler Medical University, and married Susan M. Funk. They had two sons, Joseph Parvin and Chase Orin. Dr. Franklin Garrett was Liberty Center's medical doctor until his death in 1922. He had a considerable interest in Liberty Center's development, including the bank, telephone company, flour and grain mill, and the Baptist Church. Susan loved raising flowers and graciously cut them for many local occasions.

Chase and Nellie Garrett's 50th Anniversary (1965) Left to Right: Royce Kurtz, Betty Kurtz, Chase Garrett, Nellie Garrett, Eleanor Garrett, Dean Garrett

Joseph Parvin married Elma Johnson. They had one son, James Richard. After Elma's death, Joseph married Leah Murphy. They had one son, Charles "Chad". James R, after graduating from Purdue, married Burnell Hillbert. They have daughters Rhonda and Cindy and five grandchildren. Chad married Judy Edris and they have daughter Lisa and sons Joseph and Sean.

Chase Orin married Nellie, fourth daughter of Christopher "Doc" Popejoy and Ida Noe. Christopher was a farmer and carpenter. Dr. Garrett had attended Nellie's birth; the birth of a girl was a real disappointment to a farmer who wanted a son. In friendly banter, Dr. Garrett said he would take her. Nineteen years later, he was blessed to have Nellie as a daughter-in-law. Chase was a farmer and agricultural businessman. As a young man, he sold and raced motorcycles successfully. Nellie devoted much time to church and community affairs.

Chase and Nellie had a daughter, Betty, and a son, Joseph Dean. Betty earned a diploma from Manchester College and taught at Rockcreek School. She married Royce E. Kurtz, also a graduate of Manchester. He was an educator and retired from Purdue as professor emeritus. They have three children, Garrett, Deanne and David. Garrett graduated from the University of Colorado, Boulder. David graduated from Purdue. Deanne married James R. Recker, from Appleton, Wisconsin and a Purdue graduate. Their children are: Jim, a Ball State student; Dan, a John Herron Art School student, and Elizabeth, still in high school.

J. Dean graduated from Purdue and married Eleanor McGuffie of Detroit. Dean was in automotive engineering and manufacturing. Their three children are Linda Kilgore of Anaheim, California, Gregory, and Richard of Liberty Center. Linda has a daughter, Janet, and Gregory has a daughter, Rebecca. Richard lives on the C.H. Popejoy homestead two miles South of Liberty Center with his wife, Wendelene Sweitzer (formerly of Sturgis, Michigan), and their four children: Brent, Taneka, Chase, and Samuel. Rich and Wendy attend IU-PU in Fort Wayne. Wendy is a Wells County deputy sheriff.

RAYMOND AND BERTHA B. GARRETT FAMILY

Raymond, son of Charley and Louella Priest Garrett of Penn Township in Jay County, and Bertha, daughter of Robert and Anna Hunt Brittingham of Washington Township in Gibson County, Indiana, moved to Wells County in the summer of 1950.

Both Raymond and Bertha were graduates of Ball State Teachers College in 1947. Raymond taught at Pennville High School during the year 1947-1948 and at Union Center, Wells Count, from 1948 through 1957. He finished teaching a total of 40 years at Elmhurst High School in Fort Wayne. He taught math, physics, physical education, and driver training at some time during those forty years.

Bertha taught at La Fontaine High School in Wabash County during the year 1947-48. She also taught at Lancaster High School in Huntington County, at Lancaster in Wells County, at Rockcreek in Wells County, and for several years has been teaching part-time at both Ivy Tech and IU-PU at Fort Wayne.

Garret Family
(L to R) David, (10); Joseph, (15); Karen, (5); Paul, (17)

The family lived just north of the Lancaster School Road on the east side of Highway One. Children of the family are: Paul B., born August 5, 1952; Joseph B, born May 2, 1954; David B., born May 6, 1959; and Karen Ann, born February 21, 1964. All the children were born at the Wells County Hospital, and Doctor Max Gitlin was the family doctor. The family attended the Methodist Church in Bluffton.

The two older sons attended Lancaster

Elementary School until the family moved to their new home on Ferguson Road in Allen County, in August of 1962.

Paul is a graduate of Purdue University, and received his Ph.D. degree in mathematics from Princeton University. He has been a part of the faculty at Yale University, Stanford University, and is currently at the University of Minnesota, at Minneapolis. His family is wife, Carol Brunzell, and two sons, Peter and Loren.

Joseph is a graduate of Purdue University. He has been with the City Securities investment firm in South Bend, since his graduation from Purdue. His family is wife, Elaine Penner, daughter, Natalie, and two sons, Joseph Ryan and Matthew Brian.

David is a graduate of Ball State University with a degree in cello performance. Also he has a master's degree from the University of Texas at San Antonio. He has played in the orchestras at Fort Wayne, Grand Rapids, New Orleans, Shreveport, San Antonio, and is currently in the Houston, Texas, orchestra. He married Debra Thomas and they have one son, Nathanial David. Since their divorce, Debra and Nate live in New Albany, Indiana.

Karen Ann is a graduate of Purdue University, with a B.S. degree in international agronomy. She also has a master's degree in both plant pathology and statistics from Colorado State University. She is married to Peter Garfinkel of Lafayette, Indiana.

GARRETT-SAWYER

George William (Bill) Garrett and Joan Sawyer were married June 15, 1940 at the parsonage of the St. John Reformed Church, Vera Cruz, Indiana, by the Rev. Herbert H. Meckstroth.

They first met, so to speak, in the first kindergarten class in Bluffton, Indiana. Years passed, and they were unaware of each other until the 1936-37 school year of Bluffton High School, when fate brought them together in Mary Shafer's first year typing class. Bill had received a double promotion at the Bluffton Columbian School, so he was a year ahead of Joan. At the end of the school year, Bill asked Joan to his senior class prom, and she accepted — the rest is history!

Joan worked in her Aunt Ruth Keplinger's business (Ruth's Dress Shop), from the time it was opened in 1936. The dress shop was located in the 100 block of South Johnson Street in Bluffton, where Dr. Louis Severin had his office until he moved his practice to a small house behind his residence. Joan worked until she and Bill started a family.

Times were hard, so after graduating from high school, Bill went to work for Mrs. George Morris as a driver/handyman. World War II came along, and with gas rationing, a driver wasn't needed. After being rejected by "Uncle Sam", Bill did his part for the war effort by working many long hours at the Farnsworth Plant in Fort Wayne, Indiana, where they made parts for the armed services. After the war, he worked for Steury Bottling Co., Bluffton, delivering soda pop.

In 1951, Bill bought the inventory stock of the Mobile Service Station, corner of Main and South Streets in Bluffton. Son, Jerry, helped after school and weekends, and during the summer months. After graduation from Bluffton High School, he worked at the station full time. In 1962, they moved to the Texaco station, corner of Main and Washington Streets in Bluffton. In 1968, Bill bought the Marathon Service Station, 127 South Main Street, located where the old Bliss Hotel used to stand. Due to ill health, Bill retired. Jerry continues to operate the business.

To Bill and Joan Garrett were born Gerald William (Jerry) December 3, 1942, and Sally Ann, December 6, 1943.

Gerald William (Jerry) Garrett married Darlene Suman, and they now reside at 10 Columbian Ave., Bluffton. They are the parents of Mark William, Lisa Ann, and Matthew Wayne. Mark William Garrett married Tamara Kaufman on June 21, 1986. They reside in St. Charles, Illinois, and both work in Chicago, Illinois. Lisa Ann Garrett married Lee Fonacier on June 30, 1990. They reside and work in Indianapolis, Indiana. Matthew Wayne Garrett resides and works in St. Louis, Missouri.

Sally Ann Garret married Floyd Lobsiger in 1961, and they now reside at 210 West Central, Bluffton. They are the parents of Kent A. and Amy Jo. Kent A. Lobsiger married Karen Patti on May 16, 1987. They reside and work in Columbus, Indiana. Amy Jo Lobsiger graduated May 12, 1991, from the Detroit School of Law; and she expects to pursue the law profession after passing the bar exam.

GARRETT-THOMPSON

John Howard and Mary Prentice were the parents of Frances (Fannie) Howard, born August 5, 1864, and died in November, 1951. They came from Ohio in 1865 to Wells County. Fannie married I.V.L. Garrett in 1886. I.V.L. Garrett was the son of Noah and Leah Funk Garrett. He was born in 1868 and died in 1908. Leah also came from Ohio. They joined and helped start the Liberty Center Baptist Church. I.V.L. Garrett was the first president of the Bluffton Street Fair in 1898. He and Fannie lived on a farm one mile south of Liberty Center which their granddaughter and grandson-in-law. Lois and Wendell Hamilton presently reside on.

They had two daughters Vera Ione and Bertha Blen.

Bertha was born October 8, 1895, and died in April, 1986. She never arrived. She taught in the Liberty Center and Jackson Schools for many years and also was a dietician at the Methodist Memorial Home in Warren. She was very active in the Liberty Center Baptist Church.

My mother, Vera, was born June 17, 1888, and died July 22, 1968. She married Charley Alvin Thompson on September 24, 1919. He was born on December 9, 1883, in Huntington County to George Howard and Armitta Angeline Fix Thompson. He died March 12, 1965. They had four children: Glen Elmer, Matha Irene, Doris Ann and Lois Blen.

Glen was born in Sulphur, Oklahoma, September 15, 1920 and then moved to Liberty Township in 1921. He was married to Wilma Idell Oldfield on December 5, 1947, and now reside in Markle, Indiana (Wells County). They have no children.

Matha was born May 30, 1924, and married Lozure Gene Wolfgang on July 5, 1952. He was born August 30, 1925. They were married in the new Liberty Center Baptist Church being the first couple married there following its completion in 1951. They have four children, all residents of Mesa, Arizona. Sally Jo was born May 1, 1956, Thomas Edward born September 2, 1958, Janice Kay born August 10, 1960 and John Adam born January 1, 1970.

Sally Jo married Fred Wells in November, 1984, and they had two daughters, Anna Catherine (Kitty) February 17, 1986, and Hayley Elizabeth October 20, 1987. They are now divorced. The other children are not married.

I was a twin born on March 22, 1927. I married James Medford Knuckles on November 20, 1971. We have no children.

Lois is my twin sister and she married Arthur Wendell Hamilton September 21, 1957. They have four children: Garrett Warren born August 11, 1958, Jill Marie born June 20, 1960, Marilyn Sue born July 20, 1962 and Lynn Kay born March 27, 1964.

Garrett married Cheri Rene Decker on July 26, 1986. They have two children, Erin Nicole born February 23, 1988, and Lucas Allen, born November 22, 1989.

Jill married Larry Clontz on July 22, 1989. They have one daughter, Gaberiella Marie, born December 25, 1989.

Marilyn married William Bradford on November 14, 1981 and they have one daughter Lydia Sue born March 19, 1988. Lynn is single.

GARRISON-BIBERSTINE

Elijah B. Garrison married Hannah Smith and they are the parents of Thomas Alexander Garrison. Thomas Alexander Garrison married Jane Brothers and they had six children: Ora Wesley, Maud, William, Winifred, Joseph I., and Israel Leonidas. A story passed down through the generations was that Thomas Alexander Garrison was a marshal from Wabash, Indiana, and he moved to a farm near Coffeeville, Kansas, and was a member of a posse that chased Jesse James and the Dalton Brother Gang.

Israel Leonidas married Grace Lindsey. She was the only child of Edward and Lydia (Shoemaker) Lindsey. To Israel and Grace were born: Dwight, Paul, James, Roger, Helen Stinson, Goldie Shatzer, Ruby Hine, and Mildred Edwards.

Paul married Martha Biberstine. Her parents were David and Mary (Moser) Biberstine.

David and Mary Biberstine had 14 children: Ida Hirschy, Jenna Bauman, Pearl Mankey, Edward, David II, Mary Strahm, Sadie Strahm, Rebecca, Mike, Andrew, Martha Garrison, Clara Hartman, Goldie Bauman, and Chris Biberstine.

Garrison Family
Back row: Lloyd, Junior, Paul, Carolyn and Larry
Front row: Doris, Martha and Joan

Paul and Martha Garrison have six children.

Lloyd married Norma Sutton. They have three children: Michael married Elaine Courtney and has three children: Rachel, Amber, and Christopher; Barbara Garrison; and Donna married Otis Smith and has two boys, Jonathan and Eric.

Junior married Elaine Rogers. They have five children: William, Kitty, Robert, Juanita, and Cynthia. William married Debra DeFord and has three children: Joshua, Timothy, and Cody. Junior is married again to Helen Creech. Kitty married John Prouty and has four children: Randy, Shane, Desiree' and Nichole. Robert married Sheila Elston and has two boys, Zachariah and Eric. Juanita married Greg Simpkins and they have two children, Jay and Jeremy. Cynthia has a daughter, Kristen.

Carolyn Garrison married Raymond Herman and they have six children: Mrs. Tim (Debbie) Glenn; Mrs. Rick (Beverly) Highlen and they have two children, Anika and Zachary; Mrs. Nelson (Linda) Broman and they have two daughters, Angela and Allison; Mrs. Kent (Sheila) Meyer and they have two children, Joshua and Jessica; Terry married Tina Beck; and Tony Herman.

Doris Garrison married Bill Young and had two children: Mrs. Brian (Julie) Etchison and they have two children Brian II (S.J.) and Bo Nathanial; and David Nathaniel.

Dayra Joan Garrison is the fifth child of Paul and Martha Garrison. Larry Garrison is the sixth child, and he has a son, Derek.

GARTON

An original copy of the first English Bible printed in the United States contained the Garton family records dating back to 1695. William Garton lived in Back Neck, Fairfield County, Bridgeton, New Jersey. According to Carl M. Williams, a curator of the Cumberland County Historical Society, New Jersey, there is a record which shows the early Garton family seal from the counties of Yorkshire, Sussex, and Kent which dated back in England's early history.

William E. Garton was born on August 9, 1888 in Michigan; he married Flossie Presdorf, born on May 21, 1894, and lived in Lancaster Township. They were the parents of five children. Wendell, the first child born October 25, 1910 married Anna Dubbs, born February 1, 1910. Their children were Barbara and Larry. Barbara married Eldon Bunch and they were the parents of four children: Keith, Karen, Kent, and Katherine, who attended Bluffton Schools. However, later they moved to Auburn where all graduated from high school. Keith and his wife Julie Knox Bunch had two sons. Karen married Dan Pfister and five children were born to them. Katherine Bunch married Randy Rufner and they were parents of a daughter.

The second child of William and Flossie Garton was Marvin who died in infancy.

The third child of William and Flossie was Donovan, born November 15, 1916. He married Lucile Shaffer, born June 20, 1918. They were married on February 17, 1940, and were the parents of two children, Sharon and Steven. Sharon married Donald Barger on March 7, 1964, and they became the parents of three children: Robert, Suzette, and Ann Marie. Steven Garton married Katherine Jacobus on June 19, 1971, and two daughters were born to them, Abigail and Amanda.

William E. and Flossie Garton

Wilborne (Bill) Garton was the fourth child of William and Flossie Garton. He was born on July 11, 1920, and married Ramona Murray June 21, 1941. They were the parents of three sons: Jack (June 21, 1946), Rick (May 15, 1950), and Dan (September 20, 1952). Rick married Jill Gemmer April 2, 1983, and they were the parents of three daughters, Cassidy (December 21, 1984), Courtney (October 22, 1986), and Chelsea (April 12, 1989).

The fifth child of William and Flossie Garton was Betty, born December 17, 1924. She married William Grove, Jr. on August 1, 1948. William was born January 9, 1925. They were the parents of two sons, Arlen February 17, 1951 and Mark December 11, 1955.

Arlen married Janette Lorenze on May 31, 1986, in Houston, Texas. Mark Grove married Cheri Fancher in Indianapolis on February 14, 1988. They are parents of a son, Benjamin, born on May 8, 1989.

William Garton was employed at the Estey piano factory in Bluffton and also was a painter. He and his older son, Wendell, painted the rooms in the Wells County Hospital. Wendell, Donovan and Wilborne (Bill) and retired from General Electric Corporation in Fort Wayne. Also included was William Grove, Jr., husband of Betty Garton Grove. The enjoyed many sports, including basketball, baseball and golf. Betty was employed at the Wells County courthouse and at the Caylor-Nickel Clinic Hospital before her retirement.

GAVILANEZ

Marcelo R. Gavilanez, the oldest of nine children, was born in Guaranda, Ecuador, South America, to Ramiro Gavilanez and Eloisa Falconi de Gavilanez, who were both school teachers.

Joan P. Hankey was born in Butler, Indian, to Henry Hankey and Gladys David Hankey, their second child. Henry was a farm owner and Gladys raised nine children.

Marcelo met Joan, who was serving in his hometown as a missionary nurse midwife following her graduation from Fort Wayne's Lutheran Hospital School of Nursing and the Maternity Center in New York City. Her duties in Ecuador included home deliveries and Bible classes. He worked at the missionary radio station HCJB preparing news for the Spanish radio broadcasts.

Left to Right: Juanita, David, Marcelo, Marc, Joan

Both returned to Indiana and were married (1965) in Joan's home church in Dekalb County. They lived in Fort Wayne while Marcelo completed his pre-medical degree and Joan worked as maternal and child care supervisor at Lutheran. A daughter, Juanita, (1967) and a son, Marcelo Jr. (Marc) (1968) were born at Lutheran Hospital during this time.

The family moved to Guadalajara, Mexico, for four years of medical school. Then followed clinical training in Hackensack, New Jersey, and Philadelphia, Pennsylvania, before spending four years in an obstetrics-gynecology residency program in Corpus Christi, Texas. A son, David, was born there in 1976.

In July, 1980, the family said good-bye to sunny Corpus and moved back north as Marcelo had joined the Markle Medical Center. David was three years old and Juanita and Marc were in middle school at Norwell.

A school project required a search of family roots and development of a family tree. It was discovered that Joan's grandmother, Emma Kline David, had been born in Newville (Vera Cruz) in 1891. Emma's mother, Rosa Klein Kline, was also born in the Vera Cruz area in 1858. Rosa's parents, Nicholas and Catherine Kline, had immigrated to that area from Germany around 1850.

The Gavilanez family feel at home in Wells County. They are active members at Hope Missionary Church, have helped with the summer migrant workers, and are never far from Wells Community Hospital.

Juanita graduated from Taylor University and is now training to be a physician's assistant. Marc graduates from Taylor University in 1991 and will marry Kami Morris this summer. David will start high school this fall.

GAY-VENIS

Richard Dwight "Dick" Gay (1898-1964) married Irene Venis (1900-1986) on Thanksgiving Day, 1919, in Bluffton. Dick was born in Adams County. Irene was born in Bluffton and graduated from Bluffton High School. She was a daughter of Roy Venis and Alta Steele.

Dick was a graduate of Tri-State College at Angola, Indiana. Irene took a secretarial course at Muncie, Indiana.

After a short stint in World War I, Dick taught at Bluffton High School. Irene had worked for Chandelier Company (later the site of Settegren Piano Factory). Son Jim was born (1921) while they were in Bluffton.

Dick and Irene moved to Midland, Michigan, in 1923 where they started a five and ten cent store that would eventually be a chai of six. Their second son Richard Dwight Gay, Jr. was born in Michigan.

In 1927 the family moved to Alma, Mighigan, as the chian of stores grew. The boys and Irene both had worked there in the stores. The sons eventually owned all, but later sold out.

As in most families, a new generation finds many different professions to follow. This is especially true of this family. Jim graduated from Central Michigan University at Mount Pleasant, Michigan. He served in the Air Force, ending as a navigator in World War II. After this he worked for Bell Telephone Company until returning to the Gay chain of stores in 1951.

Jim married Dorothy Malaney during the war. They had two sons: David and Doug. David graduated from University of Michigan, then earned his doctorate at Cornell University. He is now employed as a computer scientist at Providence, New Jersey. His wife Tanner is employed at a book publishing company and has written two books of her own.

Doug graduated from Michigan State, then from the University of Michigan Medical School. He is a pathologist at Burnes Clinic - a part of Northern Michigan Hospital. He lives in Potosky.

Dwight also graduated from Central Michigan

University. He married Barbara Carter during World War II. He served on a mine sweeper in the Navy. In 1947 he returned to Alma and the chain of five and ten cent stores.

Dwight and Barbara had three sons: Rick, Jeff and Tim. Rick graduated from the University of Michigan Law School and practices law in Alma, Michigan. He married Sue Kuschion. They have two children, Kegan and Kelsey. Jeff graduated from the University of Michigan Medical School as a doctor of internal medicine at Denver, Colorado. As of April 1, 1991, he will be with Kaiser Hospital there. Tim also graduated from Central Michigan University. He is now teaching in the high school at Weslaco, Texas, where they now live. He married Sue Bayne and they have three children: Jonathon, Christopher, and Stephanie.

MYRON GEARHEART FAMILY

Myron and Barb Gearheart moved to Wells County from Cass County in 1949. They first moved to an 80-acre farm with Myron's father, Alvah. After Alvah passed away they moved to the old Effie Lee farm home where they lived and their children grew up and attended the old Jackson Center School. In 1962 they bought the old Ed Merritt farm, with Mary and Bob still at home. Patty had married Dale Slusher and later Mary Lee married Philip Herr, and Bob was married to Darlene Banter.

Patty and Dale live on the late Johnnie and Ret Slusher farm on the corner, and have two children, Terrie and Scott. Terri and Scott attended Southern Wells School. Terrie married Larry Feemster, and they now have two children, Keith and Jennifer and another one to arrive in August. Scott married Angela Jayne Smith. They have two children, Josh and Melinda.

Terrie and Larry have a double-wide trailer on the old Ditzler farm and Scott and Angie have a trailer on the old Fred Oxley farm. all of their children attend Southern Wells School.

Mary Lee and Phil later bought the Kyler Runkle farm. They have two children, Jody Lin and Ben Herr. Jody was married to Brent Huffman. They had two boys, Kurt and Kyle. They were divorced, and Jody later married Rick Cooper of Daleville. The Huffman boys both go to Daleville School. Rick Cooper had two children, both at home. As of now, Bree, the daughters, is a freshman at Anderson College, and A.J. is a tenth grader at Daleville High School. Ben is an eighth grader at Southern Wells. Jody graduated from Southern Wells.

Bob married Darlene Banter, and had two boys, Wesley and Dustin. They were later divorced. Bob has been in the ministry for thirty years and is now a pastor at the First Methodist Church in Marion. Bob has earned his doctor's degree in religion and is married to Anita Dygert Brigham. She has four children and is a social worker.

Wesley works at Warsaw at Owens' Grocery, and Dustin is at Auburn Health Care Center in Auburn. Kris Brigham, Bob's step-son, is a student at Indiana University. Ben Brigham lives with his father in Fort Wayne. Nate and Cindy are both with Bob and Anita in Marion, and attend Justis School in Marion.

Myron and Barb, Patty and Dale, Phil and Mary and families all are members of the Dillman United Brethren Church.

CLARREN L. GEHRING FAMILY

Great-grandfather Joseph Gehring came to America with his half-brother Issak in 1868. Joseph moved to the Newville Community now called Vera Cruz, Indiana. Joseph married Anna Tonner and they had four sons: Joseph, Samuel, Issac and Joel.

Grandfather Joel was born in a log cabin, six miles east and three miles south of Bluffton, December 6, 1866. His father died when he was two or three months old. When he was thirteen, his mother died. The John Heyerly family took him in and raised him.

He lived with the Heyerlys and worked as a carpenter until his marriage to Elizabeth Baller on February 8, 1896. Elizabeth Baller was born October 3, 1864. They bought a farm four miles east of Bluffton, Indiana, and they had two children, Homer and Mary. Joel died February 17, 1960, and Elizabeth died November 28, 1964.

Father Homer, born June 7, 1897, married Ida Stauffer June 28, 1924. Ida was born October 29, 1903. They had four children: Lavera, DeWayne, Betty and Clarren. Homer and Ida bought the farm from Joel and Elizabeth when they quit farming. Homer died July 30, 1990.

Clarren, born February 5, 1932, married Joyce Grandlinard May 25, 1952. Joyce was born August 10, 1935. They had six children: Sharon, Kent, Scott, Bruce, Lynn, and Aleda. They also have fourteen grandchildren.

As of 1991, Sharon lives in California; Kent and Aleda live in rural Ossian, Indiana; Scott is serving in the army, stationed in Saudi Arabia with Desert Storm, Bruce and Lynn live in Bluffton, Indiana.

GEIGER/REED

Blanche M. (Reed) (August 22, 1906) and Clair E. Geiger (August 13, 1903, deceased December 29, 1987) were married in Zanesville, in 1934, by the Rev. Tracey of the Church of God.

Milo and Zeffie (Kitchen) Reed were Blanche's parents. Milo ran a butcher shop. Her grandparents were Sylvester and Elizabeth (Sink) Reed of Yoder and James and Emma Kitchen of Wells County.

Blanche went to work in 1920, at age fourteen, at the Sunshine Creamery owned by D.W. Keplinger, Zanesville. She worked twelve hours per day, six days a week, for ten dollars a week. She attended night school at Betty Gene College, to become a beautician. Blanche then opened a shop in her home in 1935.

Clair's parents and grandparents were Homer and Elsie (Siebolt) Geiger; Valentine and Sarah Geiger, of Huntington County; and David and Alvina Siebolt of Markle. Clair worked twenty-seven years at General Electric, beginning at age sixteen for sixteen cents per hour.

Clair Geiger at his Ham Radio base in his Zanesville home

In August 1945, Blanche and Clair opened the first plumbing, heating, radio, and appliance store in Zanesville, located in the Odd Fellow Lodge building. They operated their business for twenty-three years. Eugene and Glenna Cayot bought the business in August 1968. Following the sale of the store, Blanche and Clair bought and sold antiques for ten years.

Although Blanche and Clair had no children, they were, along with other business people, instrumental in the construction of the Zanesville Community Park. In 1947, the Zanesville Business Mens Association decided to buy land from John Jacobs for a softball diamond. Everett Gaskill, Dee Hoopingarner, and Clair signed a note to buy the land. Ira Baker loaned the money. Clair, through the Protective Electric Co. of Fort Wayne, was able to get an engineer to lay out the ball diamond for Zanesville, and also the east diamond at the Markle Ball Park. The Zanesville Park was one of the first to use underground wiring. In 1950, the ball park was incorporated with Lawrence Platt, president, and Blanche as secretary. Years later, the ball park was turned over to the Lions Club to maintain and operate.

When the park was first started, only $250 was donated. Dee Hoopingarner donated the concession stand. Labor and REMC work was donated, and most all other labor was paid by proceeds from concessions and collections at the ball games. Arlo Platt (barber), announced the games for many years. Blanche said there were very large crowds attending the games.

Clair was a ham radio operator who had received many awards from the American Radio Relay League Inc., and USAF Military Affiliated Radio Systems. Clair made it possible for many church mission people to talk to their families while serving overseas. He received cards from ham radio operators from every state in the USA and many foreign countries.

GENTIS FAMILY

"Daniel Gentes is born in Herrzogthum Zweybrucken (Province of Two Bridges) to Daniel Gentes and Gentesin Linderin. Eva Gentesin, one born in the year 1771 and her parents have Ben Christian Fogelgesand and the mother was Barbara born in Brackungerin."

Her the pieces would not fit, but one fragment was whole and it read: "Isaac Gentes is born in the year 1817." We do not know when Daniel and Eve left Germany for the United States, but it must have been some time after 1795, not long after the Revolutionary War. The *History of Clark County, Ohio*, gives much credit to Daniel and Eve and their family, speaking highly of Daniel and his sons for their assistance to newcomers in the clearing of land, building of cabins, and in helping to defend the settlers against the Indians. Daniel and Eve had built a brick house only five or six miles from Springfield, Ohio. The interior walls were at least a foot thick, and an old-fashioned cupboard was built in from ceiling to floor. Daniel had set aside two acres to be used as a burial ground, He, Eve, and three of the seventeen children are buried there, but there are no markers, and the area is farmed.

Family members were in Germany in 1979 and went to Breiffurth, the birthplace of Daniel Gentes. Gentis families still live there. No one knows when the spelling was changed from Gentes to Gentis.

One son of Daniel and Eve was John Gentis, born 1808, who married Catherine Zerkle, December 1832. Their son, Noah, married Sarah Hill. Their son, Samuel Gentis, born in 1873, married Rose Shoemaker.

Samuel and Rose had children, and one happens to by my Grandpa Daniel D. Gentis. Early in his teenage years he fell in love with Olive Carns, and they eloped in the hills of Kentucky. Dan loved everything about Kentucky; but chose to homestead in rural Nottingham Township as a prosperous farmer with many acres. He and Olive had eight children. Dick, Joyce, Dave, Jim, Jack, Rex, Bill, and Arlene.

L to R: Joyce, Dick, Dave, Jim, Jack, Rex, Bill, Arlene

The homestead was destroyed by the Psalm Sunday tornadoes in 1965, but they rebuilt in the exact same spot. Dan and Olive also had a winter home located in Sebring, Florida. Dan had a special love of horses along with his farming and hunting. Grandpa was an excellent storyteller, and this has been carried on by many of the boys.

The family grew to 31 grandchildren and 80 great-grandchildren who live mostly in and around Wells County to date.

GEORGE

Neither of us, Kermit George and Lillian Kesler George, are Wells County natives, but we have lived here over 40 years. Something of ourselves first, then some family background.

Lillian is a native Hoosier, but Kermit was originally a Buckeye. Lillian was born in Fort Wayne and graduated from Central High School in 1942. She and five classmates have met monthly for the 49 years since, perhaps something of a record. After secretarial training, Lillian worked eight years at Lincoln National Life Insurance Company, then in Bluffton a short time at Franklin Electric Company, and a shorter time as secretary of the First United Methodist Church, where they are members. Very limited eyesight for over 30 years and loss of sight since 1988 limits her activities but not her interests and enthusiasm.

Mr. and Mrs. Kermit H. George

Kermit was born near Hoytville, Ohio, and graduated from Jackson Township School there. In contrast to 325 graduates in Lillian's class, Kermit's class had 19 members. He started college at Indiana Institute of Technology, but World War II interrupted and he spent 38 months in the Army. He served as an officer in the Pacific Theater in the Combat and Airborne Engineers (Paratroopers) and was wounded in Okinawa. After discharge he completed his electrical engineering degree. He worked 36 years at Franklin Electric as and electrical engineer and retired in 1984.

Lillian and Kermit met at Calvary EUB (later Methodist) Church in Fort Wayne and were married there on June 7, 1947. During Kermit's 38 months in the Army, Lillian wrote him a letter every single day, and Kermit missed only a few in return. They lived three years in Fort Wayne, then moved to an apartment in Bluffton while building a house on Dustman Road all by themselves—every brick, board, shingle, plumbing and electrical fixture. They have lived on Parkway Drive in Bluffton since 1964.

Lillian's parents were Arthur and Marvel McClymonds Kesler; they lived first in Fort Wayne and later in Spencerville. Her father was a tool and die maker at International Harvester and died in 1965, just before retirement. Her mother died in 1982. Generations of grandparents back in 1837 include the names McClymonds, Souder, Harker, Farver, Zehendner, Wagers, and Bartholomew. Records show several of Lillian's and Kermit's grandfathers fought in the Civil War and War of 1812. Lillian has one sister in Fort Wayne.

Kermit's parents were Merritt and Bernice Dermer George of Hotyville, Ohio. His father served in World War I, was a farmer, and died in 1980. His mother died in 1987. Grandparent's names on his family tree include Dermer, Sholty, Darrow, Myers, Traul, Miller, McCollum, Gross, Wertz, Tosh, Knisley, Morrison, Woods, Hughes and Russel, back to Jacob Waltz who came from Germany in 1751 as an indentured servant. Kermit has a brother in Bluffton, one sister in Ohio, and another in Wyoming.

Most of our forebears were of German, English, Scot, Irish, and French extraction. Most lived in northeast Indiana and northwest Ohio and we believe they would agree that Wells County, Indiana, is an excellent place in which to live.

AMOS AND DEVONA (COLLINS) GERBER

Mrs. Amos (Devona Collins) Gerber was born in 1912, the second child of six children, of Lee R. and Clara Therkelsen Collins, my mother's people were from Denmark.

Amos Gerber was the eighth of nine children born to Gideon and Carline Kehrn Gerber. He was born in Adams County in 1911. Amie's grandparents were from Switzerland. Amie graduated from Lancaster Central High School in 1930 and was on the basketball team and the captain of the team. I graduated from Bluffton High School in 1930. Amie and I were married in Bluffton by the Rev. Matthew Worthman in 1938. We had already bought and furnished our home on East South Street, where we lived for thirty years.

Our son Tom was born in 1951 and is a musician in Indianapolis. His wife, Barbara Kalluar, a native of Canada, is also a musician.

Our son John, born in 1955, is a loan officer in the The Farmers & Merchants Bank. He is married to Joyce Moore of Dallas, Texas. We lost two daughters in infancy.

I am happy to be a good wife and mother and to help others.

Gideon Gerber started a bank in Craigville in 1917. Amie, being a good son, started working in the bank at the age of sixteen, but he managed to finish high school. Father and son moved the bank to Bluffton in 1933, into the old Wells County Bank building, and it is still in the same location, at 101 South Main Street. Amie was voted in as president in 1960, after his father's death. Amie held that position until the bank was sold in 1987. In addition to his position as president of Farmers & Merchants Bank, he worked untiringly as a civic and volunteer leader for Bluffton. Amie has received many honors and awards for his efforts to make Bluffton a better place to live. Amie's latest award was a framed certificate naming him a "Sagamore of the Wabash" from our Governor, Evan Bayh, in 1991. Of course, it hasn't been all work. We love to dance and travel too.

Amie and I have gone from horse and buggy days, one room-school houses, kerosene lamps, and much more, as well as the worst Depression in history.

Amie brought about the first street lights for Craigville. It was the first small town to light up. With help he built a tennis court in Craigville. Amie at the age of twenty-six held the title of the youngest Exalted Ruler of the Elks.

Amie is a devoted Bluffton Free Street Fair worker of over sixty years standing and was its president in 1949. Amie was also president of Bluffton Chamber of Commerce in 1941.

Amie has an office in downtown Bluffton where he is enjoying his retirement and greeting his friends. I must also tell you that he is a great fisherman and has lots of stories to tell.

I am still the devoted wife of fifty-three years, mother and homemaker. We both love our town, our friends, our family, and our home. *(Devona Collins Gerber)*

GERBER/ISCH

Alvin and Helen Isch Gerber were born in Adams County, Indiana. They were married in the Apostolic Christian Church on June 16, 1940. Alvin, born April 4, 1915, is a son of Jehu W. and Lydia Maller Gerber, one of fourteen children. Helen was born October 20, 1912, daughter of John and Katie Steffen Isch. She has two brothers, Harry and Roger Isch, of Bluffton. Alvin has four brothers: Gaius, Sylvan, Floyd, and Edward. Two brothers, Lloyd and Truman, are deceased. His seven sisters are: Mrs. Roy (Helen) Gerber, Mrs. Homer (Minnie) Aschliman, Mrs. Ervin (Anna) Isch, Mrs. Ralph (Leona) Schwartz, Mrs. Ervin (Alice) Schwartz, Mrs. Wm. (Sarah) Steffen, and Mrs. Edward (Josephine) Schwartz.

Alvin and Helen are parents of four children. Mary Kathryn (Mary K.) was born January 12, 1943; Jeanne Elizabeth was born September 14, 1945; Jay William was born November 27, 1953; and Mark Alvin was born September 4, 1955.

Mary K. Gerber graduated from Ball State with a teaching degree, and is married to Leon E. Gerber, owner of "Pet Rest", a crematory service for small animals, located on U.S. #224 west of Kingsland, Indiana, where they reside. Mary K. is still teaching at Adams Central School. They have two sons: Jeffery A. Gerber, married to Rhonda Nuest, parents of Jacob and Autumn Rose; and Bradley W. Gerber married to Shawn Burke, parents of Abraham and Josiah.

Gerber Furniture

Jeanne Gerber graduated from Ball State with a teaching degree, and is married to James (Jim) Rinkenberger of Cissna Park, Illinois, a teacher of mathematics. They both taught school in Park Forest, Illinois. In 1974, they moved to Bluffton and are currently residing at 2599 S.W. Church Road. They have three sons: James Lincoln (Linc) Rinkenberger, married to Catrina Westfall, parents of Chase Adam; the other two sons are Luke Allen Rinkenberger and Joel David Rinkenberger.

Jay W. Gerber graduated from Indiana University with a degree in marketing. He is married to the former Deborah Freiburger of Ossian. They have one daughter, Emily Jo Gerber, and three sons, Bryan Jay, Brant Wm., and Bruce Thomas Gerber. Jay is owner of Gerber Agri Systems in Bluffton. They reside at 3851 E.St. Road #124, Bluffton, Indiana.

Mark A. Gerber graduated from Indiana University with a degree in accounting. He is married to Barbara Hoffmann of Hoopeston, Illinois. They have three children, Seth David, Sarah Ann, and Leah Elizabeth Gerber. Mark is a partner in the Honegger-Ringger accounting firm. They live at 1789 E. 250 N. Rd., Bluffton, Indiana.

Alvin and Helen started housekeeping in a house they purchased at 122 E. Ohio Street, in Bluffton, for $1200.00. Alvin was working at the Bluffton Rubber Works. His salary was $12.00 weekly, averaging 12 hour days. A year later, he accepted a job at Thoma & Son Furniture Co., helping with deliveries, floor covering installations, and funerals. Helen continued working part-time in the laboratory at Caylor-Nickel Clinic where she has been employed since 1930.

In 1946, Alvin and his brother, Ed Gerber, opened an upholstery shop in the old Ratliff Grocery building at the corner of Arnold and Mulberry Streets. In 1947, they decided to build the Gerber Furniture building north of Bluffton on St. Rd. #1. The only established business north of the railroad in this mile was the R.S. & M Studio at the corner of Dustman Rd. and St. Rd. #1. Gerber Furniture opened its doors for business in March, 1948. It became necessary for Alvin to sell their home to raise money to build the store. They received a whopping $8,500.00 for it. They moved into Helen's parent's upstairs in the John Isch home in Villa North, where they lived for ten years with many pleasant memories. In 1958, they moved into their newly built home at 227 Northwood Drive, where they still live.

In the 1950, Ed Gerber decided to move to Ft. Lauderdale, Florida. He went into the real estate and orange grove business. Alvin took over the furniture store and continued in business until 1970, when he sold the business to Harry and Roger Longenberger, long time employees, who are present owners today.

JOSEPH E. GERBER AND SOPHIA H. ISCH GERBER

Joseph E. Gerber was born April 25, 1895, in Adams County, Indiana, and was known by the nickname Bud. He was the son of Jeff Gerber (1867-1951) and Elizabeth Baumgartner Gerber (1869-1937). He had five brothers: Aaron, Samuel, Elias, Jack and Melvin (Pete) and three sisters: Lydia Fiechter, Mary Steffen and Hulda Dubach Heinold.

Sophia H. Isch Gerber was born on January 1, 1899, in Gridley, Illinois, to Ernest Isch (1873-1920) and Elise Meiss Isch (1873-1964). Sophia's family consisted of five sisters: Ella Yergler, Bertha Moser, Clara Isch, Amelia Baine and Dorothy Frank and three brothers: Joseph, Elmer and and Harold. The Ernest Isch family moved to this area in 1906.

Joseph (Bud) and Sophia were married on November 20, 1921, at the Apostolic Christian Church in Wells County. Bud had served as a cook in the United States Army during World War I previous to their marriage. During his lifetime Bud worked as a farmer in both Wells and Adams Counties. He was also part-owner of a tile mill in Craigville, Indiana. For a while Bud and Sophia owned a restaurant in the 200 block of North Main Street. Bud was employed by National Oil and Gas as a tank truck driver; and at the time of his death on February 2, 1949, he was a cook at the Dutch Mill Restaurant.

Camp Breckinridge, Kentucky January 1949
L to R: Sophia, Donald, Phyllis, and Joseph (Bud)

During his life, Sophia worked as an aide at the Caylor-Nickel Hospital. She also worked as a housekeeper and cooked in several restaurants in Bluffton. "Soph" will be remembered as being one of the best cooks and bakers in the area. Sophia died on June 19, 1986, at the Meadowvale Care Center, where she lived the last ten months of her life.

She and Bud were the parents of two children who still live in Bluffton. Their oldest child, Donald G., was born in Craigville on July 25, 1925. He married Justine Fiechter of Wells County on December 4, 1949. They have three children: Douglas G., Jean A. and Kris A. Douglas married Ruby Habegger and they are the parents of five children: Molly, Joseph, Abby, William and Carson. Jean married Terry Neuenschwander. They have four children: Bethany, Alex, Kip and Rachel.

Bud and Soph's second child was born in Adams County on May 25, 1929, and was named Phyllis A. She married Paul Dotterer of Wells County on October 22, 1950. Four children were born to this marriage: Kathryn S., Susan M., Sally K., and Jeffrey P. Kathryn married Gordon Gerber. They are the parents of two daughters, Karyn and Sonya. Susan is married to Douglas Dailey. They have three children: Stefanie, Benjamin and Kevin.

LES GERBER FAMILY

Lester R. Gerber was born May 4, 1936, a son of Elmer and Emma (Sinn) Gerber. He lived on a farm in Adams County with his four sisters and five brothers until his marriage on June 15, 1958, then he moved to Wells County and has lived in this county since then. His marriage was to Rosemary Hartzler, daughter of John and Ella (Ramsier) Hartzler of Sterling, Ohio. She was born in Wayne County, Ohio, on April 29, 1934. She had six sisters and three brothers.

Les is self-employed as an insurance agent. He started the Les Gerber Insurance Agency in 1968 and has done business in Bluffton, Indiana since. Rosemary is part-time wallpaper hanger. We both enjoy volunteer work locally and away from the county.

Les and Rosemary's family circle is made up of three daughters: Peggy Elaine, born September 30, 1959; Jennifer Kay, born on her dad's twenty-fifth birthday, May 4, 1961; Lynn Renee celebrates on March 9, 1964 and one son, Perry Lester born May 23, 1967.

Peggy married Derryl Aschliman (April 13, 1956), son of Millard and Alice Aschliman, on September 13, 1981. They are dairy farmers in Adams County. They have three living children: two daughters, Elizabeth Rose, March 31, 1983; Tiffany June, October 23, 1984, and one son Taylor Max sharing a birthday with Uncle Perry on May 23, 1988. One son, Byron Ray, November 19, 1986, died August 2, 1990, as a result of a car and pick-up truck accident.

Les Gerber Family
Les, Rosemary, Jennifer, Peggy, Lynn and Perry.

Jenny's family began on August 26, 1979, when she married Jim Fiechter, (November 22, 1958), son of Carl and Mary Fiechter, of Adams County, where they are residents today. They are hog and grain farmers. Their children are Klint David, December 29, 1980; Quinn Alan, sharing a birthday with Aunt Lynn on March 9, 1982, and two daughters, Stacy Lyn, March 25, 1984 and Jamy Kay born October 22, 1989.

Lynn married Brad Fiechter (April 26, 1961), on September 19, 1982. He is the son of Charles and Maxine Fiechter. They reside in Wells County were he works as a tomato and grain farmer. Lynn does part-time clerking at Ellenberger Auction.

Perry attended and graduated in 1989 from Purdue University at West Lafayette. He is an industrial engineer and is employed at the present at Kitco, Inc. of Bluffton.

All of our children are graduates of Norwell High School and all of our grandchildren, at this time, attend or will attend Adams Central School, Monroe, Indiana.

GERBER-MOSER-SILLS

A late ice storm covered the area on March 30, 1928, affecting electricity and travel. The parents of Joan Moser Sills, Mabel Gerber and Dennis Moser, were married by kerosene lamps in their pastor's home. Residing in Craigville, Mabel was a telephone operator and Dennis taught at the Lancaster School.

Mabel was born March 23, 1907, to Gideon and Caroline Gerber, who were farming east of Bluffton. Early Gerbers left Switzerland and finally reached Wells County in the late 1850's.

Farmer, business man, and elevator manager, grandfather Gerber became cashier of Farmers State Bank, established in 1917 in Craigville, where the family then lived. When many banks failed, grandfather moved the bank to Bluffton. He was president of the Farmers and Merchants Bank when it opened for business on January 3, 1933.

Grandmother was a superb cook, and homekeeper who raised nine children with help of her older daughters. The Gerber grandparents were members of the Apostolic Christian Church. Grandfather compiled his autobiography, *The Gideon Gerber Story* in the 1950's. The book was published in 1964.

1967 Sills Family
(L to R) Joan, Kris Ann, Kathy, Dick, Karen. (Boys in Middle) Ted, Rick.

Dennis was born on October 29, 1900, to Peter and Jennie McBride Moser. Working his way through college, Dad completed his teaching degree at Indiana University. He taught elementary school for fifteen years, including Wells County Schools at Lancaster, Vera Cruz, and Poplar Grove. Employed by Farmers and Merchants Bank in 1939, Dad was assistant cashier. He continued at the bank until his 1965 retirement.

Dennis and Mabel enjoyed happy retirement years. Dad died on April 24, 1986. Mother is well and active.

After her parent's marriage in 1928, Joan was born on February 16, 1930, and Doris was born on January 21, 1932. The family moved to Bluffton in 1931.

Doris pursued a nursing career, and taught for many years. She married Lawrence Hall; they are the parents of Christopher, 22. They live in Alma, Michigan.

Joan Moser met Dick Sills in high school. Active in sports, Dick received the Robert Baumgartner Trophy presented in 1947 for outstanding student athlete.

Dick was born May 31, 1929, to James E. and Alvena Graham Sills. His grandparents were James Edgar and Carrie Hoskins Sills, and Harry and Emma Heller Graham of Bluffton.

Richard Sills and Joan Moser were married on July 10, 1949. Living on West Market Street, Dick worked at the Hoosier Condensed Milk Company (demolished). Joan was employed at the Bluffton-Wells County Airport, now Manville's location.

Kathryn was born on November 12, 1951. Kris Ann was born on April 10, 1953. Rick was born on November 2, 1955. The family moved to East Central Avenue in 1956. Ted was born on August 20, 1959, and Karen was born on November 27, 1965. All are Bluffton High School graduates, and all are now married.

Kathi and Dave Hartman of Marion, are the parents of Melanie, seventeen, Jeff, twelve, and Sean, four. Kris Ann Barger of Bluffton, is the mother of Nathan, thirteen. Rick and Cheryl Crandall Sills' children are Jamie, thirteen, Eric, eleven, and Laura, eight. Ted and Karen Reinhart Sills live in Decatur with Corey, eighteen, Casey, fifteen, and Lisa, thirteen. Karen and Kevin Reed, of rural Ossian, are the parents of Klayton, two, and Kourtney, ten months.

We still reside on East Central Avenue. We are active at the First Baptist Church. A kitchen designer, Dick manages the Cline Kitchen Center. He enjoys golfing in his spare time. Joan works part-time and likes gardening, sewing, and reading. *(Richard and Joan (Moser) Sills)*

GERWIG

On New Year's Day in 1922, a baby came to take up residence with Harry and Gladys (Wagner) Gerwig, Liberty Center. They named him Paul Eugene.

On February 10, 1924, another son, Kenenth, arrived.

Paul loved country life and spent most of his youth living with his uncle and aunt, William and Kate Reece, assisting with the farm work. He graduated from Liberty Center School in 1939.

In January 1941, he joined the U.S. Air Force. He was a ball turret gunner on an 8th Air Force B17 Flying Fortress, a member of the 487th Bombardment Group. Paul spent three years in Panama and a year in England.

T/5 Kenneth Gerwig had not seen his brother for four years (narrowly missing each other several times). Kenneth got permission from his colonel to go to London to see S/Sgt. Gerwig. He was driven across Belgium and France, took a boat to London and phoned Paul. He was on a mission, but it wasn't long until he called back. Paul got permission and took Kenneth on his first plane ride flying over England for four and one-half hours. He loved it!

S/Sgt. Gerwig was discharged from the U.S. Air Force in September 1945. He received EAME Theater Ribbon with three Bronze Stars, American Defense Service Medal, Good Conduct Ribbon, and Air Medal with three Oak Leaf Clusters. He transferred to the U.S. Air Force Reserve and retired January 1, 1971.

Paul Gerwig

S/Sgt. Gerwig married Dorothy Matson, daughter of Frank and Jessie Carlson Matson, July 27, 1945. They are the parents of Michael, born July 25, 1947, and Gloria Jean Gerwig Mayne, born December 3, 1950. They have seven grandchildren and two step-grandchildren.

After his retirement, Paul was employed at Tonner Body Works and Herman Reiff Construction Co.

Paul joined the Bluffton Police Department in August 1960. In 1966, Sgt. Gerwig became a deputy sheriff during the last year of Sheriff Alva Smith's term, and continued with Sheriff Miles Hoopengardner until 1968, when Mayor Carl Goodwin appointed him Bluffton's Chief of Police. In 1970, he gave up the post to run for sheriff. He was elected and then re-elected in 1974.

In 1975, Sheriff Gerwig formed the County Reserve Unit. Deputy Nyal Frantz was appointed to serve as the overseer of the group of 15 men.

He also launched Crime Stoppers in 1988, assisted by Chief Deputy Michael Smekens.

Following his eight years as sheriff, he became a security guard for Franklin Electric. When Sheriff Nyal Frantz resigned because of ill health, the Republican caucus chose Gerwig to fill the last one and one-half years of his term. In 1986, he won his final term which expired in 1990.

Sheriff Gerwig and his wife, Dorothy, served the County for thirteen and one-half years, by far the longest for any sheriff and matron in Wells County history. He was called "Father of Law Enforcement". Regardless of how much crime Sheriff Gerwig had seen in the years that he has been associated with the law enforcement agencies, he is certain that the bulk of kids are still good.

"Act like a man and you'll be treated like a man" was Gerwig's advice to his prisoners. Sheriff Gerwig was adamant for "Golden Rule" treatment.

Now retired, he is fishing, flying and farming a little.

GESLER

On the banks of Rockcreek north of Rockford stands the house where we three Gesler sisters were born. Grandfather Lewis Gesler, German descent, lost his father at age six and helped to support his mother. When he was 12 he came to Wells County. At 16 he worked for land owners and made enough money to buy 200 acres. He married Calista Johnson in 1876. They were parents of Homer, Inez, Grace and Wilma. Calista left with the two young girls and moved to Oregon.

Lewis later had a home built on the west bank of Rockcreek at Rockford where they had livestock, chickens, ducks, geese, fruit trees and a garden. Aunt Inez kept house for her father, Lewis.

Homer married neighbor Edna Kline in 1913. They had three daughters: Clella arrived in 1914, Martha, 1917, and Doris in 1920.

Clella's first year of school was in the little one-room school south of Rockford, under a fine teacher, Russell Stinson. In 1922, East Rockcreek consolidated was ready and that's where we graduated. Clella graduated from business college in Fort Wayne and worked in some small offices and then at International Harvester until 1943. In 1942 Clella married James K. Clark, an Indiana University accounting major who worked at Lincoln Life. He later took over Clark's Farm and Lawn Supply in Nine Mile, south of Fort Wayne. Four children: Richard, Jeannette, Sharon and Kathy made up the family. They are now all married and there are five grandchildren. James K died in 1978.

Sister Martha Gesler, a Lutheran Hospital Fort Wayne graduate became an industrial nurse at General Electric. She met Harold Britton, an electrical engineer, and they were married Christmas, 1942, and moved to Schenectady, New York, and later Syracuse, and are still with General Electric. They had five children, Wayne, Gary, Dale, Paul and Beth.

Doris Gesler worked at General Electric and played the organ at Salem Reformed Church Fort Wayne. She graduated as a piano major from Sherwood Music School in Chicago and met and married Harold Studer, an elementary school administrator. They lived in Oak Lawn, Illinois, where Jim, Jack, Dick and Ray were born. The family later moved to Cleveland, Ohio, and then settled in Harrisburg, Pennsylvania, where Doris continued piano and organ and Harold taught.

Our grandfather, Lewis Gesler, died in 1939, and our father, Homer Gesler, died in 1949, after having built a sandbox behind Clark's garage for grandchildren and neighbors. Aunt Inez Gesler continued the little farm in Rockford, always helping the needy or sick. She raised fruits, vegetables and beautiful flowers.

One cold winter eve in 1948, we enjoyed her delicious clothesline taffy. Little Richard Clark helped pull it across the dining room then let loose, giving us a big laugh. We enjoyed tossing bean bags at her homemade black cats hanging in the doorway, also playing her parlor organ.

Homer and Edna Gesler took us girls to Sunday School and Church every Sunday and we started our families that way. We all keep in touch with phone calls, letters, and visits.

Clella (Polly) Gesler Clark still lives since 1942 on old Hwy 3 at Nine Mile, member of United Methodist Church, likes needlework, gardening and traveling. She is a member of the Fort Wayne Southmoor Singers and the Indiana Master Gardeners Association.

LEWIS GESLER

Lew was born October 30, 1851. His parents were of German descent. Lew's father died when his son was six years old. This left his mother in straitened circumstances, so she placed the boy out at work when he was about twelves years of age. She continued to provide Lew with clothing and other necessities of minor character but kept for her own use his small earnings. At the age of sixteen, Lewis Gesler came to Wells County, Indiana and found employment with Henry Edris. He worked for him two years for fourteen dollars a month. He continued working out by the month for other people until he accumulated five hundred dollars. He invested this and some borrowed money in eighty acres of farmland in Rockcreek Township. He worked for Wierly Lamb three years and bought more land until he owned at one time two hundred acres.

Lewis married Calista Johnson, daughter of Jonas and Urania Barber Johnson and granddaughter of Solomon Johnson and Hallet Barber. Lewis and Calista had four children: Homer C. born 1879, married Edna, Eva Inez, never married, Wilna, and Virgil.

Calista took the younger two children and moved to Oregon some time later, leaving Inez to care for her father and brother.

Inez was a member of the Rockford Seventh-Day Adventist Church until her death. She lived by the creek on the north edge of Rockford on property originally settled by her great-grandfather, Solomon Johnson, and passed on to his daughter, Isabella. Some years later Inez's brother Homer lived with her until his death. Inez loved flowers and gardening. Every Sabbath she brought a basket of flowers to church if any were in bloom. She also loved music—played the organ and piano at church and sang. She died in a nursing home in Huntington and donated her body to research.

BELLE GIBSON, HARRY W. JOHNSON FAMILY

James K. Gibson (1844-1895) came to Pennsylvania and married Mary C. Sommers, (1853-1920) from Ohio. They died in Ossian and had eight children: John Gibson, (1875-1941) lives most of his life in Huntington; 2) James Lewis Gibson (1880-1956) lives most of his life in the Ossian/Kingsland area; 3) Clem Gibson (1882-1948) lived most of his life in the Kingsland area; 4) Grover Gibson (1884-1962) lived in Kingsland most of his life. 5) Minnie Gibson died as an infant; 6) Alice Gibson (1879-1948) lives mostly in Markle/Huntington area; 7) Harry Raymond Gibson (1895-1954) lived most of his life in Fort Wayne, where he was a policeman; 8) Belle Gibson (July 8, 1888 - September 5, 1974). When Bell was eight years old, she was taken to her aunt's house in Bluffton to live with Lewis Johnson and Nannete Johnson, who lived at the present address of 1868 E. Corning Rd. Belle graduated from Bluffton in 1908; during the World War II she worked at the General Electric Plant in Fort Wayne. In 1911 she had a son by Harry A. Johnson, Harry W. Johnson, born June 12, 1911, died November 6, 1984. He married Helen W. Johnston (born September 30, 1911), on June 18, 1932. Their children were: (1) Marylou Johnson, born July 28, 1933, married August 12,1951 (see Richard L. Bumgarner family); (2) Ted Lewis Johnson (born February 28, 1936, married February 6, 1955); Sally Jo Johnson (born December 6, 1940, married December 14, 1967).

Harry and Helen lived most of their lives on the 80-acre farm that is located at the western edge of Bluffton on Corning Road. Harry had many jobs; he employed the area teenagers to help with the harvest. He was the county milk inspector, and he was a sales representative for a walk-in cooler/freezer company that put up buildings all over the state of Indiana.

Helen was raised by Pearl Brown Johnston and John A. Johnston. Pearl was born in 1887 and died in 1976. John A (Joke) was born in 1881 and died in 1951. Helen's real parents were Sophia Kammyer, (1874-1956) and David Jacobs, who died in 1951 in California. Sophia's mother was Lousia Lizzette Rakhmy, born April 8, 1844, in Germany. Her death date is unknown. David Jacobs came from Pennsylvania via Germany; he had a brother who was a meat cutter in Utica, New York.

See Merril J. Miller family history and Ted L. Johnson family

JAMES GIBSON FAMILY

James Gibson married Mary Summers, January 4, 1871, and resided at Echo.

Their children and spouses are: Minnie, born about 1872; John (b. 1875), married Lida Elzey; Alice (b. 1878), married Nelson Biddle; John and Alice lived in Huntington. Clem, (b. 1882), married Ona Davidson. Their children are: Graydon, Evaline and Bonnie Lou. Grover, (b. 1888), married Jennie Mossy. Clem and Grove resided one mile west of Kingsland. Belle (b. 1888), one child, Harry Johnson, resided in Bluffton. Harry Raymond, (born 1895) married Esther Strahm and lived in Fort Wayne.

Addie and James Gibson

My father was James Lewis, (b. 1880), he married Zella Patten and had one daughter, Wanda. Zella died of tuberculosis in 1917.

He later married my mother, Addie Davison. Their children are: Bertalene, (myself) Nina, and Maxine. We lived at Kingsland and our father worked on the railroad and also at the Studebaker plant in Fort Wayne.

Wanda married Vern Frederick and resided at South Whitley. She died in 1977. Their children are: Joyce, Kent, Sharon, James (died 1959), Janet, Becky, Randy and Doug.

Bertalene married John Walsh and lives in Fort Wayne. Their children are: Rosalyn (Gordon Anthony) and John L. Walsh.

Maxine died in 1953. Her daughter, Connie (Jerry Houser), lives in Fort Wayne.

June 6, 1943 I (Nina) married Paul Johnson (cite Paul Johnson history).

DARRELL GILBERT FAMILY

John Bryan Gilbert (January 23, 1896 - January 20, 1973) and Reeta E. (Dowty) Gilbert (February 27, 1899 - May 5, 1989) raised their eight children on a farm in Rockcreek Township. Darrell E. Gilbert was the second child born to John and Reeta on September 18, 1922. He attended Rockcreek High School and graduated in 1940. After graduation, he served in the Army Air Force from January 1943 to February, 1946. He and Beulah Justine Freds were married on June 11, 1944.

Beulah (known as Boots) was born on January 4, 1923 and died September 10, 1991, in Wells County. Her parents were Ores Freds (March 21, 1890 - June 9, 1955) and Hazel (McBride) Freds (July 21, 1893-April 23, 1981). Boots also graduated from Rockcreek School in 1941. After graduation she worked at General Electric in Fort Wayne until her marriage to Darrell.

Darrell and Boots returned to Wells County after World War II and bought an 80-acre farm in Rockcreek Township. In 1946, Darrell took a job with the R.E.M.C. in Wells County. In 1973, he and Boots moved to Monticello, Indiana, where he worked for the White County R.E.M.C. He retired in 1986 and moved back to Wells County.

Darrell served on the Western Wells School Board and was on the first Northern Wells School Board. During their residency in Wells County, Boots and Darrell attended St. Paul's Lutheran Church.

Left - Bart and Vicki Seslar with Bret and Ashley Middle - Darrell and Boots Gilbert Right - Ron and Sara Gilbert with Kelly and Troy

Two children were born to the Gilberts: Ronald Darrell and Vicki Rae. Ron was born on March 13, 1949. He was raised on the farm in Rockcreek Township. He attended Rockcreek School (grades 1-9) and graduated from Lancaster School in 1967. Ron then attended the United Electronics Institute in Louisville, Kentucky, and graduated in 1969. It was there that he met his wife Sara.

Sara Francis Peterson was born on October 10, 1950, to Charles E. and Sara Alice Peterson in Lebanon, Kentucky. Sara attended the Sullivan Business School from 1968-1969. Ron and Sara were married in Kentucky on April 25, 1970.

Ron was employed by RCA in Marion, Indiana. They moved to Gas City, Indiana, in 1974. In 1986 he was transferred to the Thompson Consumer Electronics Plant in Bloomington, Indiana. Sara is employed by the Monroe County Community School System.

Ron and Sara have two children: Kelly Renee, born on January 7, 1974, and Troy Wade, born on September 21, 1977. They attend the Monroe County Community Schools.

Vicki was born on November 12, 1950. She attended Rockcreek School (grades 1-9), Lancaster School (grades 10-11), and then graduated from Norwell High School in 1969. She attended Indiana University and graduated with a degree in Elementary Education. Vickie taught school in Wells County and received a master's degree in 1978.

Vickie married Bart Jeffery Seslar on December 1, 1979. Bart was born to Gerald V. and Mary Lucille (Horn) Seslar on August 26, 1949, in Antwerp, Ohio. Bart graduated from Antwerp High School in 1967, then attended Tri-State College. He received a degree in drafting design technology. Bart served in the United States Air Force from 1969 to 1973. He was then employed by International Harvester in 1973.

Vicki and Bart have two children: Ashley Nichole, born December 5, 1980, and Bret Andrew, born on May 16, 1982. They both attend Lancaster Elementary School in Northern Wells. The Seslar family resides on the Gilbert farm in Rockcreek Township.

GILBERT, HOUTZ AND LESH FAMILIES

At the end of the first lane, west of St. Paul's Church in Rockcreek Township, Wells County, north one-half mile, is a large white frame five bedroom house and a big bank barn. Perry and Mary Ellen Valentine Gilbert bought the 160-Acre Mast farm, raised their three sons and one daughter there. After Howard married Masyl Houtz October 7, 1915, the older Gilbert's and Herman moved to Uniondale.

The Gilberts, Houtzs and Leshs all originated in Germany. December 25, 1709, ten ships sailed with four thousand on, among them was Belthazer, who died at sea. He was Isaac Lesh's grandfather and Isaac was Dwight Lesh and Masyl Gilbert's grandfather. The ships landed at New York June 11, 1710. They settled in Pennsylvania, later moved on to Indiana, and settled in Rockcreek Township, Wells County.

The name Loesch was changed to Lesh in fourth or fifth generation. Isaac and Samantha Cover Lesh had six boys and two girls. The boys were all carpenters, most of them cabinet makers, which they learned from their father. They were all musically inclined. Hattie Lesh married Simeon Houtz, (known as Sim). They had Masyl and Dorothy. Sim was a son of Jeremiah and Mary Ellen Jefferies. Sim had three brothers and four sisters.

Martin and Lyda Houtz Gilbert had fourteen children. One was Perry, who married Mary Ellen Valentine. They had three sons and one daughter. Harry married Gertie Schoonover. They had two sons, Lloyd and Dean, both died, leaving no male heirs. Herman married Evelyn Garman. They had no children. Howard, born April 26, 1894, married Masyl Houtz, born August 7, 1894, on October 7, 1915. They had two daughters so the Perry Gilbert branch name died when Howard died December 19, 1974.

My sister, Dorothy, born June 3, 1902. She married Charles Dunn. They had two sons. William married Susan Larkey. Kay married Karen Weitholter. They have Nicole and Mark.

Howard and I have two daughters. Cecile, born August 30, 1918, married Lamar Hite. They have four sons and two daughters. Ronald married Roseann Pierce. They have Paula who is currently serving in the U.S. Navy, Amy, and Steve. Donna Krauskopf Parquette has two daughters. Michelle, married Steve Milholland; and Tonya, married Tim Arnold. Jeanne married Al Saalfrank and have Chad. Gary married Sharon Hamilton. They have two daughters, Angie and Sandy. Doug married Linda Moulin and have Allison. Blain married Cathy Rettig. They have two sons, Eric and Kevin.

Herman and Evelyn Gilbert, Harry and Gertie Gilbert, Lela Lesh, Dwight Lesh, Howard Gilbert, Masyl Gilbert

Our other daughter, Arleen, born August 9, 1925, married Jack Smith. They have one daughter and two sons. Judy married Roger Lothamer. They have two sons and one daughter, Matthew, Jason ad Jenny. Jon married Brenda Masters. They have daughter Brook and son Andy. Jeff is Arleen and Jack's other son.

I went to a one-room school where one teacher taught all grades up to and including the eighth grade. There was no water system. There were outdoor toilets. Our drinking water was in a bucket in the all. We all drank out of same dipper. It must not have hurt us because here I am 96 years old. My uncle, Herman Lesh was my first teacher at Raver School, (two miles south of Rockcreek Center) and also my last teacher at Rockcreek Center where most of my school years were. Schools were two miles apart.

LOWELL GILBERT FAMILY

On the night of March 5, 1948, Lowell Eugene Gilbert, son of John B. and Reeta E. (Dowty), married Jeanne Ellen Hower, daughter of Clarence M. and Della I. (Betz) Hower, in Huntington, Indiana.

Lowell had worked for the R.E.M.C. based in Ossian, Indiana, but began farming as an occupation soon after marrying. The farm operation included grain, milk cows, hogs, and chickens.

The next few years saw six children born into this family. Teresa Ann Gilbert, now a math, P.E., and health teacher, is married to C. Douglas Carr of Rockford, Ohio. Doug also teaches swimming, P.E., and health, and does some coaching. Both are teachers at the Adams Central School. They are the parents of Jennifer Ann and Aaron Douglas.

John Martin Gilbert, an educator, married Susann Grabner of Monroeville. John taught elementary children and is now the principal of Northeastern Elementary School in Wayne County. They reside in Portland, Indiana. Susann teaches home economic classes at the Adams Central School. They have two children, Kathryn Christine and John David.

Lowell E. Gilbert Family - 1987 Back L to R - Charles, Robert, John, William Front L to R - Judy, Jeanne, Lowell, Teresa

Judy Marie Gilbert, a math and P.E. teacher, married John S. Brehob of Indianapolis, Indiana. John is a partner in a family business, Brehob Nursery, Inc. They have two daughters, Jonnelle Lynne and Julie Anne.

Robert Wayne Gilbert, math teacher and coach at Norwell High School, married Jacklyn J. Bunch. Jackie also teaches math classes at Southern Wells Schools. They have two children, Alicia Nicole and Kyle Robert.

William Hower Gilbert attended Purdue for two years and now lives in St. Louis, Missouri. Bill is employed in the construction business.

Charles Lowell Gilbert is an elementary teacher. He resides and works in Richmond, Indiana. Chuck has been active in the civic theater and the Whitewater Opera Company in that city.

Lowell discontinued raising any livestock, but branched out into doing farm drainage work as well as the grain farming. Jeanne began full-time teaching in 1962. She spent 29 years teaching fifth grade students at the Rockcreek and Lancaster building in Wells County, retiring May 30, 1990.

OLAN AND WALDENE GILBERT

William Gilbert II, pioneer of Wells County, and a farmer of Chester Township, was a native of Ypsilanti, Michigan, born May 24, 1837. His parents, William I. and Elizabeth (Moore) Gilbert, natives of East Kent, England, migrated to America in 1830, settling in Canada near Montreal. They left Canada and moved to Washtenaw County, Michigan, staying here until September 1837, when they came to Wells County; making the journey by team, following the Indiana Trail from Fort Wayne to Scuffle Creek. They settled in Chester Township, section thirty, on a tract of 264 acres, which the father had purchased the winter before. They camped on Henry McCulluch's land. While running the line of the land the father cut his foot severely, so he hired a space cleared for his cabin. Mr. Gilbert was no hunter so he bought thirteen deer the first winter and hauled provisions from the Griffin Mill on Walnut Creek about twenty-five miles distance, being obligated to make a road. The wheat was ground but not bolted.

First granddaughter of William Gilbert II, 1889 Olan Gilbert's first cousin Stan, Joe, Ralph, Carolyn's Aunt Mable Gilbert (Swaim)

William I died June 16, 1850, Elizabeth surviving until July 4, 1860. They were the parents of seven children. William Gilbert II, the subject, was three when they came to Wells County. He received his early education in the subscription schools and the public school two years. February 29, 1859, he married Elizabeth Hammond, a native of Ohio. Her parents moved to Jackson Township until the father died; then the mother moved to Chester. They were the parents of ten children. Herschel E., the ninth child, born April 2, 1874, the subject of this sketch, has resided on the land entered from the government all his life. He married Nora McIntire January 1, 1900. They were parents of three sons: Claude (born August 9, 1900), Robert (born August 27, 1906), and Olan Laverne (born March 13, 1911) the subject of this sketch. His father, Herschel E., died in 1930 and Olan continued the farming November 23, 1935, he married Blanche Waldene Booher. One son was born to this union, Glen Olan Gilbert (born August 29, 1937). December 23, 1963, Glen married Eda Ellen Maggard. They have two children: Vicki Ann (Gilbert) Haviland (born December 15, 1964) and Michael Dewayne Gilbert (born April 27, 1969). Glen lives on the Homestead, where we have lived for fifty years. Olan built a new home on the Homestead in 1985, where we live in retirement. There was one acre, known as "Little Chicago", which was designated for a school that never materialized. There was a blacksmith, a sawmill and a grocery store, all passe. This location is 10272 S.E. Jeff Road 90.

Dillinger stayed two nights at "Monkey Park," one mile north of us at Twin Bridges, where he hid in the undergrowth.

Olan L., his father, mother and two brothers went to Five Points School, built in 1876, still standing. The Grange and Horse Thief Detective Association met here.

GILBERT-PARK

Stanley Dean Gilbert born October 6, 1942, in Bluffton is the youngest son of Ralph Moffett Gilbert born September 14, 1891 - May 27, 1974 and Nellie Lavina (Walsmith) Gilbert born October 4, 1900 - May 9, 1985. Stanley was raised on a farm in Chester Township where his parents had lived since 1933. The farm had been in the Gilbert Family from the time it was homesteaded in 1837.

Stan has two brothers and a sister, Ralph W. Gilbert born August 26, 1922 who lives in rural Mooresville, Indiana; Joseph M. Gilbert born March 30, 1931, lives in Chester Township at Five Points, and Carolyn Jean (Gilbert) Saxman born April 26, 1935, and lives at Plainfield, Indiana.

Stan graduated from Chester Center High School in 1960 and Huntington College in 1966 and holds a teaching degree. He has been employed as a teacher in the Bluffton - Harrison MSD Schools since his graduation.

His marriage was to Carolyn Jo Park of rural Uniondale, daughter of George H. and Avis L. (Underhill) Park. Carolyn was born March 23, 1944, in Bluffton, Indiana.

Their home has been in Bluffton for most of the marriage except for three years spent in Huntington while Stan was going to college. Since 1972 they have lived at 624 W. Cherry Street Bluffton, Indiana.

Seated L to R - Christine, Cara, Julia. Standing L to R - Geoffrey, Stan, Carolyn and Angela

Born to their marriage are five children: Angela, Julia, Christine, Geoffrey and Cara.

Angela Rene (Gilbert) Oman was born August 29, 1962, in Bluffton, graduated from Bluffton High School and Purdue School of Nursing. She worked at Wells Community Hospital. She is married to Jon Steven Oman, the son of Wendell and Roberta (Campbell) Oman of Bluffton. Jon works for the City of Bluffton. Jon and Angela have three children: Derrick Matthew born November 8, 1980, Danielle Nichole born October 16, 1983 and Lauren Rebekah born January 18, 1989.

Julia Marie (Gilbert) Johnson was born June 6, 1967, in Bluffton and graduated from Bluffton High School and Ball State University. Julia holds an elementary teaching degree. She is married to David Michael Johnson of Ossian son of Larry and Faye (Conley) Johnson now of Ossian but born in Henry County, Indiana. David works for Fort Wayne Community Schools. They have a daughter, Caylynne Renee, born April 28, 1991.

Christine Kay Gilbert was born August 22, 1969 in Bluffton, graduated from Bluffton High School and will graduate from Ball State University in July, 1991. She will hold a four-year degree in paralegal law administration.

Geoffrey David Gilbert was born December 27, 1971, in Bluffton, graduated from Bluffton High School and is in his first year at Ball State University.

Cara Lynn Gilbert born June 25, 1977, and is in the eighth grade at Bluffton Harrison Middle School.

Along with teaching Stan coaches girls track and boys and girls cross country. Since 1974, Carolyn has worked for the Bluffton-Wells County Public Library.

The family are members of the First United Church of Christ in Bluffton.

For further information refer to Gilbert - Walsmith family and Park-Underhill family.

GILBERT-WALSMITH

The family of Ralph Moffett Gilbert can be traced to William Gilbert one of the pioneers of Wells County who immigrated to America in 1830, from East Kent, England, and settled in Canada within thirty miles of Montreal. From Canada they moved to Washtenaw County, Michigan and remained there until September, 1837, when they came to Wells County, Indiana, making the journey by team, following the Indian trail from Fort Wayne to Scuffle Creek. Here the family settled in Chester Township, section 30, on a tract of 264 acres of timber land, which had been purchased the winter before. The first three weeks after their arrival in the county they camped on Henry McCulluch's place. While engaged in running off he line of the land William cut his foot severely, which laid him up and he had to hire a space cleared on his land for his cabin, which he hired built. Mr. Gilbert was no hunter, but devoted all his time to clearing and improving his land. The first winter he bought thirteen deer, and all his provisions from the Griffin Mill on Walnut Creek, about twenty miles away, and had to make a road to get there.

William died June 16, 1850, and Elizabeth July 4, 1860. They were the parents of seven children: Eleanor, John, William, Eliza, Ann, Elizabeth, and Thomas who died in his infancy.

The young William Gilbert home and family

The young William Gilbert, Ralph's grandfather was three years old when brought by his parents to Wells County. He received his early education in the subscription schools, and for a couple of years in the public schools. He was married February 9, 1859, to a woman also by the first name of Elizabeth Hammond a native of Ohio, and a daughter of Joseph and Judith (Henson) Hammond. Her parents were born, raised, and married on the Guernsey Island, off the coast of Northern France. William and Elizabeth Gilbert had ten children. Douglass, February 19, 1860 - October 21, 1865; Emeline, December 25, 1862 - April 30, 1864; James McClellan, November 10, 1863 - June 15, 1947; Lois A., June 8, 1865; Matilda E., April 1, 1871; Herbert, August 30, 1872; Herschel E., April 2, 1873 and Martha Alice, August 23, 1876.

James McClellan Gilbert married Mary Catherine Moffett, November 1, 1865 - January 14, 1957, on December 26, 1885, and they were the parents of two children. Mabel (Gilbert) Swaim July 13, 1889 - February 11, 1976, and Ralph Moffett Gilbert born September 14, 1891 - May 27, 1974.

Ralph married Nellie Lavina Walsmith born October 4, 1900 - May 9, 1985. Nellie was the daughter of Joe born January 1, 1859 - November 1, 1935 and Susie Dolly (Crites) Walsmith born April 29, 1879 - February 17, 1963, of Montpelier, Indiana. Joe Walsmith had come to Montpelier from the oil fields of Pennsylvania and earned the reputation of being one of the best rig builders and pumping power contractors in the entire Western oil fields. Joe also explored for oil in Western oil fields including Old Mexico during the Mexican Revolution, and built ships in Texas before he retired. After retirement he ran a garage in Montpelier.

Ralph and Nellie Gilbert lived in Hartford City where Ralph worked 17 years at the Hartford Corrugated Box Inc. He returned to the Gilbert homestead to farm in 1933. Four children were born to the marriage; Ralph Walsmith born August 26, 1922, now of Mooresville, Indiana; Joseph McClellan Gilbert born March 30, 1931, of Chester Township Wells County; Carolyn Jean (Gilbert) Saxman born April 26, 1935, now of Plainfield, Indiana; and Stanley Dean Gilbert born October 6, 1942, living in Bluffton, Indiana.

For more information refer to Gilbert-Park.

GILBERT-ROBERTS

Our 80-acre farm in Rockcreek Township was purchased in 1911 by my grandparents, Martin (1869-1935) and Elizabeth (Harvey) Gilbert (1871-1954).

My parents, John Bryan (January 23, 1896-January 20, 1973,) and Reeta E. (Dowty) Gilbert (February 27, 1899-May 5, 1989,) lived here from their marriage on November 26, 1919 until their deaths. Reeta's parents were William and Myrtle Nellie (Bush) Dowty. John was a farmer and a World War I veteran. He helped build Rockcreek School. Their eight children graduated from there. They are Ruth Eloise (September 10, 1920), Darrell Everett (September 18, 1922), Lowell Eugene (May 21, 1924), Lois Eileen (August 26, 1926), Joyce Evelyn (December 2, 1930), John David (October 23, 1934), Carol June (June 1, 1936), and Janet Suzanne (January 5, 1939).

My husband, Lester's paternal grandparents were Lewearlie (January 25, 1885 - April 14, 1968) and Emma Ann (Reef) Roberts (September 6, 1888 - November 25, 1939). His parents were Francis Earl (October 5, 1906 - February 14, 1970) and Jennie Kathryn (Maddux) Roberts Bricker (April 28, 1909). Kathryn's parents were Arthur (1882/1944) and Rachael (McFarren) (1885/1949) Maddux. Earl and Kathryn had seven children: Betty Irene (December 30, 1928), Lester Eugene (December 7, 1930), John Edwin (January 28, 1935 - January 31, 1935), Frederick Earl (September 18, 1936), Lawrence Kaye (June 24, 1938), Walter Lavern (July 17, 1940) and Joyce Marie (November 19, 1941).

Lester Roberts and Joyce Gilbert were married on May 25, 1952, in Wells County. Their son, Kim Eugene (April 22, 1953) was born at the USAF base in Presque Isle, Maine, in Aroostook County where Lester was stationed during the Korean War.

Kim married Janice Rae Weikel (August 29, 1953), daughter of Hillard and Ruth (DeVoux) Weikel of Ossian. They have two sons, Jason Andrew (October 7, 1977) and Joshua Michael (December 22, 1982). They live in Indianapolis where Kim is a Kroger manager and Janice a manufacturing engineer with United Medical.

Lester and Joyce's five daughters were born in Wells County. Rita Sue (January 24, 1956) married David Brinneman (October 20, 1955), whose parents are Priscilla (Tarr) and Franklin Brinneman of Lancaster Township. They have three children: Steven Michael (January 4, 1979), Amanda Nicole (September 14, 1981) and Ted Franklin (March 31, 1983). They own Brinneman Construction on Dustman Road.

Amy Lou (May 4, 1959) married David Larry Kreigh (February 15, 1958), son of Larry and Opal (Bard) Kreigh. Opal died in 1990. David is terminal manager for Towne Air Freight in Indianapolis. They live in Brownsburg with their three children: Dustin David (August 5, 1982), Benjamin Larry (April 16, 1986) and Chelsea Renee (January 15, 1991).

Back row - Melissa, Rita, Lester, Kim, Lori Front row - Joyce, Jennifer, Amy

Lori Ann (January 14, 1961) married Ronald Joseph Knecht (January 10, 1959), son of Albert and Ruth (Sheidler) Knecht of Greensburg. Ron is an engineer for Johnson Controls in Indianapolis where they reside with their two children: Matthew Ryan (March 3, 1983) and Kelli Jo (April 12, 1986).

Mellisa Lee (June 14, 1965) married Larry Todd Graft (March 25, 1964), son of Larry and Sondra (LaCrone) Graft. Sondra died February 19, 1981 in Wells County. Larry lives in Paulding County, Ohio. Todd is employed by Kroger. Melissa is a cosmetologist in Fort Wayne. They live on the homeplace with their daughter, Cassondra Joyce February 3, 1989.

Jennifer Lynn graduated from Ball State in 1990 and is production assistant at WPTA Channel 21 in Fort Wayne.

At one time the Roberts children were enrolled in five different schools. Kim at Indiana University, Rita at Ball State, Amy and Lori at Norwell High, Melissa at Lancaster and Jennifer at Rockcreek.

GINGERICK-BOLINGER

Barbara Gingerick married Raymond C. Bolinger, son of Jesse J. and Alice Bosler Bolinger, on August 6, 1955.

We started our life together on the Chester Brown Farm in Rockcreek Township. After farming there three years we purchased the old Smeltzer place in northwest Union Township. Over the years we have added more ground to our livestock operation.

We are blessed with a large family, six boys and five girls. The tenth child, Peggy, died at three days of age. She was the last burial in the Horeb Cemetery before it was relocated in 1970. Gene, Edith, Dale, Nancy, Karl, Lucille, Marilyn, Mark, Mick, and Dann all graduated from Norwell High School.

Back L to R Helen Gingerick, Barbara Bolinger Front Gene Bolinger with twin daughters Chelsea Mari (left) and Brande Renae (right)

Gene married Vicki Shanks. Vicki had a son, Jason, and twin daughters, Chelsea and Brande. Gene has worked as a welder and truck driver. Edith married Charles Careins and has four children: Jennifer, Sarah, Andrew, and Chad. She is a homemaker and is involved in church work. Dale married Anita Fairchild. They have two daughters, Melissa and Samantha. A third daughter, Amanda, was stillborn. Dale is currently raising hogs and operating a welding shop with the family. Nancy married Kevin Fox and they have three sons: Matthew, Ethan, and Jordan. She is a homemaker and also is involved in her church. Karl is associated with the family farm. Lucille (Lucy) married Nick Van Hoozen and has two daughters, Hannah and Beth. They live west of South Whitley on a small acreage. Marilyn married Eric Juarez and has one son, Jacob. She is a beautician and now lives in Noblesville. Mark married Stacey Mullins and has a son, Levi and a daughter, Alyssa. He is an ironworker and lives on our farm in Huntington county. Mick married Malinda (Mindy) McCracken. He also is involved in the family farm operation. Dann is currently attending Purdue University, studying animal production. *Submitted by Barbara Bolinger*

GIROD-KOBER

The Oliver Girod family came to America from Berne, Switzerland, in April, 1855. Relatives from Ohio met them in New York with a team and wagon to bring them back. My grandfather, Peter, was born in 1856. He spoke only French when he started to school. Later he also spoke German and English. Grandma Louise Allman Girod also came from Switzerland. She was six years old when she arrived in America. She and Grandpa lived on a farm in Adams County, Indiana, and raised nine children, including my father, Alfred. All were members of the Reformed Church.

Dad worked in a large dairy in Illinois when he ws drafted in 1917. He served as a wagonneer in France hauling supplies to the trenches. After the war he married my mother, Marie Brickley. She was a teacher at Murray, a daughter of Minnie Mosure and Thomas Jefferson Brickley. Mother's family were pioneer residents of Wells County. Her grandmother Catherine Lesh Brickley, came to Iniana in 1848 from Berks County, PA at age three. She was married to Lewis Brickley, who came from Trumble County, Ohio, at age nine. Lewis was a private in the Indiana Volunteer Infantry of the Civil War. Catherine died at the age of 33, the mother of five children. Both were members of the Lutheran Church. Lewis lived to age 79. For a number of years he was engaged in farming and also had a hardware on West Market Street (where Linn & Saurer used to be). Mother's maternal grandparents were Maria Keely of Bluffton and Abner Mosure from Vera Cruz. They resided on South Main St. in Bluffton. Abner served in the Civil War also. When Abner was forty-four, his horse was frightened as he attempted to pick up a passenger. He fell from the buggy on South Main St. and was fatally injured in the runaway. Following her husband's death, Maria moved to West Washington Street, where she cooked meals for employees of the Red Cross Manufacturing Company. Maria, daughter of Katherine Shultz and Sebastian Keely, was born in Huntington County, Pennsylvania, in 1847. The family moved to Bluffton in 1850, where they operated a general store on West Market Street (where the Progress is).

Jack and Jean Kober 1988

Minnie Mosure, my grandma, married Jeff (Thomas Jefferson) Brickley in 1885 at the age of 15. They lived in Bluffton until after the birth of their first son, Harry Dwight Brickley. When Uncle Dwight was six weeks old, they moved to the country, a farm in Rockcreek Township where my sister, Joyce Grandlienard and her husband Brooks now live. My mother was born there in 1892. She attended a one-room school close to her home and then drove a horse and buggy to attend high school in Bluffton. After high school she attended teacher training courses at Valparaiso and Marion Colleges. Before her marriage, she taught at Rockcreek, Lancaster and Murray schools for 12 years. Her younger brother, Raymond, died in France in 1918 during the World War. I remember that we always went to the cemetery at Fairview and the American Legion would fire shots over his grave on Decoration Day. Grandpa Brickley was a member of the Wells County Council for eighteen years, serving from 1922 until his death in 1940.

My dad and mother raised five children on their Rockcreek Township farm. The three older girls, Hallie Pace and the twins, Joyce Grandlienard and myself (Jean Kober) were all registered nurses. The youngest daughter, Ina May Dormire, is a teacher and their one son, Don, is a children's heart doctor at Riley Children's Hospital in Indianapolis. After her family was grown my mother helped organize the Vera Cruz Opportunity School for handicapped children, where she served as principal for four and one-half years. From 1938-1964 she was a member of the Wells County Library Board.

My father continued to farm until his death in 1964. Mother died in 1967.

In 1948 I married Jack Kober, a Liberty Township farmer. Jack's parents were Jennie Lieurance Kober and Walter Kober. We have three children. Jill, born in 1950, married Jerome Markley, son of Clive and Dorothy Markley. They have three sons, Benjamin, Paul and Andrew. Jill teaches third grade at Southern Wells, and Jerome farms and teaches at Adams Central. Our son, Joseph (Joe) was born in 1952. He married Clarice Beechler, daughter of Willard and Beatrice Beechler. They have three children: Adam, Krista and Patrick. Joe is a farmer and Clarice teaches kindergarten at Lancaster. Judy, our youngest daughter, was born in 1958. She married William (Bill) Hogg, son of Bruce and Willmina Hogg. They have two sons, John and Peter. Judy is a registered nurse and works in Home Health Care at Caylor Nickel Medical Center. Bill farms and is a substitute rural mail carrier for Bluffton. Jack has served on the Liberty Center Volunteer fire Department for twenty-seven years and has recently retired from farming. I was a school nurse at Southern Wells for twenty years and have also retired. We are both members of the Boehmer United Methodist Church.

GIRVIN

As the great-great-granddaughter of Samuel B. Caley, the rural Zanesville mail carrier in 1850 (refer to Zanesville History Book), I will introduce myself as Barbara R. Caley Girvin, born in 1926, daughter of George Clifford Caley, born in 1889 and Cressie I. Haflich Caley, born in 1891. I was born and reared in Union Township, Wells County, attending all 12 years and graduating from East Union Center High School in 1944. I entered the Lutheran Hospital School of Nursing in September, 1944 and graduated in August, 1947. This was the era of World War II years - the nurse and the doctor situation was critical as many were in the service and as student nurses, we worked many long, hard hours to achieve our training. I belonged to the Cadet Nurse Corp - a government program that paid for your training completely, plus you had a small monthly allowance of $15.00. You had one weekend a month off and at that time nurses worked a six day week. You were to enter a branch of service at the end of your training if the war was still on. The war ended before my training, so I was entitled to seek my own employment.

I entered the job force eager and ready. I was employed as a surgical nurse at Wells County Hospital in September, 1947. I lived in the Nurses' Home there until December, 1947. At this time I married Hubert T. Girvin, born 1924, the oldest son of E.F. Girvin and Elizabeth (Mayne) Girvin of Markle. Our first Girvin household was at 135 Logan Street, Markle, Indiana. We had this home built by National Homes, one of the first pre-fab manufacturers (an early version of modular homes). This was the first new home built in Markle following World War II. We remained in this house in Markle until 1958, with the exception of a one year period when Hubert was recalled into active military service during the Korean War. Our first two sons were born when we lived in this home, Gary E., born 1951, and Larry L., born 1953. In 1958, we bought a forty acre farm at the north edge of Markle and moved our family there into the old farm house. We subdivided ten acres of this farm into what is known as Skyline Addition. Over the years nearly thirty new homes have been built in this quiet addition.

Zanesville's Main Street Looking West - 1920

We also made additions to our family, a daughter Lisa Ann, born 1963, and Vincent A., born 1965. The four Girvin children were reared in this home and we remained in Skyline Addition until 1985, when we sold our house and retired to a smaller home in Huntington, Indiana.

I worked as an R.N. part-time at Wells Community Hospital in the surgical and obstetrical departments for more than 26 years and retired in 1987. Hubert retired as plant manager for Wabash Magnetics, Huntington, in 1988.

Our oldest son, Gary E., served as an auditor of Wells County (one of the youngest auditors in the state of Indiana) from 1975 through 1982, before going with a computer company in Indianapolis, Indiana. Our second son, Larry L, lives in Markle and has a tree and aerial service. Our daughter, Lisa A. (husband - Brian Street), lives in Markle and has her own hair salon. The youngest son, Vince (wife-Lori Hamilton), resides in Huntington and he works at the NAPA Service Center in Fort Wayne, Indiana.

We have two granddaughters, Kerry Marie Girvin, born 1978, daughter of Larry and Deb Girvin, and Leah Paige Street, born 1990, daughter of Lisa and Brian Street. (*Barbara Caley Girvin*)

GLASGOW FAMILY

James I. Glasgow, son of James S. and Margaret Hogg Glasgow, with his wife, Betty Evans Glasgow and their eight month old son, James E., born June 25, 1940, moved from Jay County, Indiana, 1941 to a farm owned by Jim's uncle, Charles Hogg. The farm was located west of Bluffton on state road 124 in Wells County.

Jim was very proud of his Scot-Irish ancestry. His grandparents came from Ireland and Scotland in the early 1850's.

On June 29, 1943 Sherry was born and on November 30, 1945, Scott was born.

Many years were spent farming. Later Jim worked at Hoosier Grain Elevator, Corning Glass and G and H Fertilizer of Markle and Bluffton.

Betty started working in 1952 at Murphys 5 and 10 store, later at Lancaster School's Cafeteria for seventeen and one-half years and in 1968 started as food purchaser for Caylor-Nickel Clinic and

Hospital, continuing for thirteen and one-half years.

All three Glasgow children graduated from Lancaster Township School and Purdue University.

Left to Right
James E. (Jimmie), Betty (Mother) Sherry, Scott, James I. (Jim)

James E. received a Ph.D. from Rice University in Houston, Texas in microbiology and is now doing research at the University of Pennsylvania Medical Center in Philadelphia, Pennsylvania. He married Nadine Wise of Lancaster, Pennsylvania August 7, 1965. She received an M.S. degree in bacteriology at Purdue University, and is now employed as data coordinator for Merck Sharpe and Dohme Pharmaceutical Company, Blue Bell, Pennsylvania. They have two children, Karen, twenty-one, a student at Juniata College, Huntingdon, Pennsylvania, and Jamie, eighteen, a student at Wake Forest College in Winston, Salem, North Carolina.

Sherry had a degree in elementary education and speech and hearing therapy from Purdue and a master's in education from Indiana University. She was an International Farm Youth Exchange Student to Taiwan in 1965. She married Larry Kuntz from Good Field, Illinois in 1967. He graduated from Christian Theological Seminary, Indianapolis, Indiana, and received a Doctor of Ministry from United Theological Seminary, New Brighten, Minnesota, 1980.

Larry is a minister at the Christian Church in Martinsville, Indiana. Sherry teaches second grade at Post Elementary School in Martinsville. They have two children, Matthew, eighteen, a freshman at Purdue and Carrie, seventeen, a senior at Martinsville High School.

Scott received a BA degree in education from Purdue University January, 1969. He taught school in Florida three years, was a polygraphist in Louisiana and a teacher in New Orleans, Louisiana. In 1982, he bought a chicken farm near Russellville, Arkansas. He teaches high school English and speech at Adkins High School in Adkins, Arkansas.

Scott married Beatrix Drews, from Naples, Florida in 1969. She is a registered nurse and in administration at the hospital in Russellville, Arkansas. They have two children, Mollie, twenty, a junior at Arkansas Tech., and Ian, seventeen, a senior at Russellville High School in Russellville.

In 1968, Jim and Betty bought one-half acre of land just west of the farm they came to in 1941. They built a small house on this land.

Jim died June 9, 1990 at age, 74 years.

ROBERT AND GERTRUDE GLASGOW

Robert Scott Glasgow, was a veteran of World War II and farmer after service.

Gertrude Johnson Glasgow, was the first Wells County Extension Agent in Home Economics from April 13, 1953 to June 30, 1978.

Robert and Gertrude married May 14, 1948, moved to Wells County, Rockcreek Township, in 1950. Robert died October 3, 1966. Gertrude still lives in Rockcreek Township.

GEORGE E. GLASS

George E. Glass, son of E.A. and Edna Ella (Eckhart) Glass, was born September 19, 1905, in Wells County, Indiana. Though he lived only to the age of 45, his life was indeed a colorful one.

After graduating from Bluffton High School he attended LaCrosse Normal School of Physical Education in Wisconsin and served as assistant athletic director of the Community Club. His training in Physical Education led him to play professional basketball in the Lake Shore League, coach freshman football and teach swimming classes at the Lake Forest Military Academy. From here his adventures included: tramping steamers and oil tankers from the east and west coast and Great Lakes; performing a flying trapeze and a triple bar act on the vaudeville stage and with the Sells Floto circus; sailing through the Panama Canal with a crew engaged in mutiny; working as house detective at the Davenport Hotel in Spokane; and practicing football at Gonzga University; playing basketball and football at Wilammett University in Salem, Oregon; working as a guard in the violent ward at the state asylums in Salem and Richmond, Indiana; traveling to Canada on a gold rush; instructing at the state deaf and dumb school in Columbus, Ohio; and doing detective work at the Deshler-Wallick Hotel. He also worked as a harvest hand in the Kansas wheat fields and traveled the country with fairs as a "barker".

George and Mary Ellen (Somers) Glass and Sandra (Glass) Houlihan.

In his time George hitchhiked at least 40,000 mils and once left New York with only seven cents. In the chilly March weather of Green Bay, Wisconsin, George was challenged to dive thirty feet from a bridge into the icy waters of the Fox River. Despite the risk and potential injury from the chunks of ice floating in the river, George completed the dive, won the bet and repeated the feat the next day at the request of reporters and photographers from a variety of news services!

Of the six universities George attended, no two were in the same state. He earned his own way through all of them and his last experience at Indiana University began with "bustin' dishes" at the Kappa house. He was the spokesman for the Class of 1933, debated on the freshman and varsity teams, participated in drama production and was elected vice-president of the Jackson Club and the Junior Law Class of 1931-32. He was a member of the Senior Law Class, Acacia Social Fraternity, the Phi Delta Phi law fraternity and the Theta Alpha Phi drama fraternity.

George was elected Wells County's prosecuting attorney in 1933 and served for two terms. He was defeated in 1935 in his bid for a Congressional seat. He moved to Ft. Wayne in 1937 to practice law and married Mary Ellen Somers on April 17, 1938. To this union one daughter was born, Sandra (Glass) Houlihan.

George Glass' activities in fraternal circles included membership in the Moose Lodge 200 and the Bluffton Moose Lodge, service as governor of the local lodge, deputy general governor of the order and regional director in Connecticut. He was a member of the Kiwanis Club, the Bluffton Methodist Church, and the First M.E. Church in Fort Wayne.

George Glass died February 12, 1951 and is buried in the Fairview Cemetery in Bluffton, Indiana.

ROBERT MAX GLEIM FAMILY

Bob was born March 23, 1933 in Wells County to Walter and Roberta (Walmer) Gleim. He was a graduate of Bluffton High School in 1951. He married K. Jean Platt August 30, 1958. They had one daughter Dawn Denise; she married Ricky Lynn Davis of Bluffton. Bob served in the Korean War Conflict in the 1950's. He was a truck driver most of his adult life, driving for Dairy Queen, Blue Flame, Habig Trucking, and National Gas and Oil all of Bluffton. He was driving for National Gas and Oil when he met his death (See death article)

Knight of the Road

Wells Trucker Robert Gleim, 47, dies from injuries after swerve to save woman's life.

"Greater love hath no man than he lay down his life for his brother"

Robert M. Gleim, 47 of Uniondale, Indiana was a Wells County citizen who lived up to the highest calling of Christian brotherhood.

Robert Max Gleim

He died at 11:40 p.m. Tuesday March 10, 1981, of complications from surgery for severe injuries he received in a February 21, traffic accident at U.S. 37 and Bruick Rd. in Allen County just northwest of Fort Wayne and southwest of Harlan. In the episode, Gleim was driving a National Oil Gas Company tanker truck. A woman's car had come across the centerline. To avert what would have been almost certain death for the woman, and proving there are still "knights of the road" among truckers, Gleim risked his life to swerve and miss the auto, sending his tanker rig out of control, with the result that it overturned. The spilled gasoline from the tanker burst into flames. Nevertheless, it appeared the gallant trucker had cheated death as he emerged from the wreckage and the fireman extinguished the blaze. He was taken to Parkview Hospital with a large gash to the head that required more than thirty stitches to mend, plus other injuries that included cracked ribs and a collapsed lung. He was reported within a couple days as improving and was in a regular hospital room. However, in succeeding days at the hospital it was determined that Gleim had still more serious injury, a fractured neck. The first three cervical vertebrae at the top of the spine were broken. Gleim underwent a delicate and strenuous seven-hour operation on March 3, to attempt to deal with the highly serious fracture condition. He survived the operation and was placed in the intensive care unit. One week later he died amid the complications from that surgery and his injuries. An autopsy was being performed today at Parkview toward more specific determinations. However, his death in any case will become recorded as a traffic fatality in Allen County on basis of the injuries that resulted in the surgery attempts to save his life. Mr. Gleim was a driver of National Oil and was employed twenty-five years in trucking. He was a safety conscious truck rig operator who had the difficult experience a number of years ago of having been in a fatal accident in which he was no way to blame. In his action on the morning of February 21, it turned out that he gave up his life to spare another.

His wife Jean was a Scout leader and service team chairman for ten years in the late 60's, and early 70's and she also was a Sunday school teacher, at the Markle Church of Christ for twenty-five years. At present she is an employee of Richard's Restaurant in Bluffton and lives west of Uniondale, Indiana.

GODWIN-HARRIS

Blanche Lenora (Godwin) Harris was born in Chester Township on December 19, 1906, the youngest child of James Marion Hamilton and Anna Lenora (Stratton) Godwin. James was born 1866 in Springfield, Missouri, and died 1941 in Nottingham Township. He was the son of Nathan and Mary Godwin. Anna was born 1864 and died 1941, she was the daughter of Issac Stratton.

I am the only living child of seven children. My brothers and sisters were Pearl Nibarger, 1888-1963; Warner, 1890, who died in 1919 with the flu during the flu epidemic that year; Mary May Harris, 1891-1918; Clark Henry, 1899-1987: Chester Marion, 1904-1984 and Myrtle Smith, 1883-1976.

Seated: Martha Betz, William and Blanche Harris and Mildred Wells. Standing: Charles Harris, Ruth Falk, and Paul Harris. November 1985

I sewed a lot for my family. As a young girl I pieced a quilt top out of scraps that a neighbor did not want, this I later passed onto my oldest grandson Stephen Louis Wells. I raised fryers and hens and dressed them out myself and sold them in town. I worked at Sheller Dryden Rubber Company in Montpelier, tomato factories in Redkey and Bluffton, Duchess Pretzel Company in Bluffton and sold Avon products. I was active as a member of the Union Chapel Church of the Nazarene located on the Jay and Wells County line. My three daughters and a granddaughter were married in this church: Mildred in 1943; Martha in 1954; Ruth in 1956; and Paula in 1991.

I met William Robert Harris and married him on November 25, 1925. We enjoyed sixty-one and a half years together. We had ten children of which five are still living. They are: first child - Mildred E. Wells, 1926, of Connersville, her son Stephen, 1951, his sons are Jason, 1982, and Michael, 1986, of Ann Arbor, Michigan; Loueen Kirkendall, 1956, her children are Derk, 1977, and Courtney, 1987, of Morgantown; fifth child - Ruth, 1933, of Bluffton, her children are Samuel, 1959, his sons are Benjamin, 1982, Lucas, 1985, and Jacob, 1989, of Decatur and Joseph, 1961, at home; sixth child - Martha Betz, 1935, her sons are Steven, 1955, and his son Brandon, 1989; Jerry 1957 his children are Amber, 1984 and Andrew, 1989 all of Fort Wayne. Seventh child - Paul, 1937, of Bluffton his daughters MaDonna Butler of Fort Wayne, Paula Brown, 1971, of Pennville. Ninth child - Charles, 1941, of Middlebury, his children are Glenda Martin, 1962, her daughter Daysha, 1985; Jeffrey 1964 and Rhonda, 1967 of Marion. My third child - William Jr., 1931-1963, was ill eight years with Amyotrophic lateral sclerosis and remembered by friends during those years.

My husband, William was born January 27, 1904, and died June 13, 1987. He was the second child of eight children of George, 1872-1942, and Elva (Kershner), 1880-1972. His three sisters are still living - Hazel Ayers, 1901, and Esther Monroe, 1905, of Celina, Ohio and Mary Mitchell 1919 of Bluffton. His deceased brothers and sisters are Charles Albert, 1908-1970; Chester Burl, 1909-1984; Mearl L., 1915-1985 and Rosa C. Miller, 1921-1989. William did farming along with being employed at Hoosier Grain Elevator in Montpelier from 1943 until 1968 when he retired. Prior to that at Frazier Tile Mill and Tom McCabe Pipeline Construction Company. His grandfather was William L., 1843-1916, the brother of Phineas Ivy, 1847-1912, the sons of Henry 1817-1864. *Submitted by: Blanche L. Harris*

GOODMAN-STAIR

Missionary publisher G.D. Watson Goodman, born near Cincinnati, Ohio, on January 22, 1920, son of Rev. William Preston and Myrtie Viola (Martt) Goodman; and missionary publisher Rose Amelia (Stair) Goodman, born northeast of Plymouth, Indiana, on January 19, 1920, daughter of Harry Cyrus and Lillie Aurora (Beyler) Stair, were both graduates of Marion College, Marion, Indiana (now Indiana Wesleyan University), in 1942. Married August 30, 1943, their first home was a rented apartment above Mrs. Barrington in Bluffton. Watson pastored the Fiat Friends Church and due to men teachers called into military service he was asked to teach in junior high at Central High school in Bluffton. Rose taught at Poneto (first four grades) the last year of its existence.

Watson and Rose left Bluffton to serve nearly sixteen years on the mission field in South Africa. Their first three years were spent at Mount Frere in the Transkei from 1945-1948. Rose was principal of the post-primary Industrial Institute for native girls and taught on government salary. Watson was district superintendent of the Pilgrim Holiness Church (now Wesleyan), supervising thirteen outstations and pastoring the large Mount Frere Church. Under Watson's direction a new mission station was built about one hundred miles away in Pondoland. The natives names it Good Hope. Nine hundred Pondos came to the dedication.

Watson was then asked to help found and become the first president of Union Bible College in Brakpan on the Gold Reef where he served two years (1948-1950). Rose served on the faculty.

Watson and Rose Goodman

From 1951-1961 the Goodmans were directors of Gospel Centre Work (an interdenominational faith ministry) about ten miles from Johannesburg. They went five days a week into four townships: Edenvale, Natalspruit, Germiston, and Alberton where they reached no less than two thousand youth each week in their personal ministry. Large flannelgraph Bible figures were used so all could see and hear the Word of God at the same time. They also ministered in the public schools (black and white), and for ten years published a quarterly magazine, "JOY" for the whole of Southern Africa.

Watson began publishing a scripture booklet, "HELP FROM ABOVE", in the three languages to help reach the masses with the WORD and to help establish converts in their Christian faith. The Scriptures had such impact the Goodmans knew they must reach the nations of the World with "HELP FROM ABOVE" and other Scripture booklets.

In 1961 the Goodmans returned to the States to found World Missionary Press, an evangelical, interdenominational, faith service ministry, dedicated to publishing free Scriptures in the language of the people worldwide. In 1970 the press was moved from Winona Lake, Indiana to New Paris, Indiana, where over 500 volunteers came monthly from 67 different churches to donate their time in getting out Scripture booklets in over 230 languages, going into 179 countries at the rate of one and one-half tons per weekday. Watson was president there until 1987 at which time he and Rose felt they should transfer to Enterprises for Emmanuel which he had founded in 1985 in Elkhart, Indiana, where their youngest daughter, Ruth Goodman (now Johnson) highly qualified and dedicated to missions, was already working full time. Goodman's son-in-law, Jay Benson and his wife, Vicky, both also highly qualified and dedicated to missions now lead World Missionary Press.

Watson is chief executive officer of Enterprises For Emmanuel, also a non-profit, evangelical, interdenominational faith service ministry with two specific goals: supplying pastors and leaders with personal Bible study helps'. Thompson Chain

Reference Bibles, teaching aides, etc.; and reaching multitudes of boys and girls worldwide with illustrated salvation booklets on their level. "HE IS RISEN" which graphically portrays the basics of the Christian faith is having great impact and is now published in English, Spanish, Hausa, and Romanian. More than forty languages have been requested and are in various stages of preparation. Volunteers and contributions are increasing to help fulfill this God-given vision.

The Goodmans have four children (all born on Thursday): Victoria Raye, Donald Watson, Ruth Estelle, and Harry Woodrow: and three grandchildren: Jeff Benson (born in Indonesia while his parents were missionaries there), Jessica Flo and Grant Isaac Goodman.

The American Mothers Committee chose Rose as American Mother of the Year for the State of Indiana in 1975. Watson is listed in "WHO'S WHO IN THE WORLD" in the 1989-1990 Marquis publication. Also a one page biography with his picture appears in the 1990 edition of "International Register of Profile" published in England.

Both Watson and Rose were presented with an outstanding Achievement Award in the field of language and literature by Indiana Wesleyan University Alumni Association on October 5, 1990.

DONALD GOODSPEED FAMILY

Irene Teresa Irezze, but her father could not pronounce Teresa, was born on November 27, 1909. On November 6, 1926, she married Gerald Edwin Goodspeed, born August 13, 1909. Gerald Goodspeed retired from Delco Remy, located in Anderson, Indiana, in 1972. During World War II he drove daily from his home one mile west of Poneto, Indiana, to work in Anderson. He was written up in the company newspaper for having the longest commuter trip at fifty-two miles. Gerald died in 1974. Irene resides in Montpelier, Indiana. Gerald and Irene's children are: Robert, Donald, Glenn, and David.

Gerald's ancestry includes Richard Warren, a passenger on the Mayflower, Gerald's great-great grandfather, Nathan Goodspeed, was born June 9, 1795, in Massachusetts and came to Harrison Township, Wells County, in 1864 after spending many years farming in Athens County, Ohio. Nathan's father, Nathan Senior, was a seaman lost at sea. His children were bound out upon his death. Nathan Junior married Thankful Holwey. His mother was Thankful. Thankful Thomas was born in 1761 on Cape Cod and married Nathan Senior on January 25, 1782.

The second Nathan was joined in Wells County by his son, Ira B. Goodspeed, who was born ed aw y on January 29, 1949. To this union was born three children: Opal Helen, Elwin Ray and Werge, Francis, Daniel, and Thankful. Ira purchased his father's homestead and farmed until his death on May 31, 1911. Ira's son, Francis Marion Goodspeed, was born in 1863. Ira married Hannah Bell Markley on September 3, 1885. Their children were: Opal Lulu, Bertha, Vera, and Charles. Hannah Bell's father, Jonathan Markley, was born in Wells County on June 4, 1838. Jonathan was for many years the oldest living person born in Wells County. He died April 28, 1917. Jonathan married Catherine Sturgis and they had fourteen children. Jonathan's father, Gabriel, and his wife, Hanna Tuttle, came to Wells County in 1837 and farmed in Section eighteen of Harrison Township along the Wabash River.

Francis Goodspeed's son, Charles, was born on October 11, 1886. He married Zella Williams on May 18, 1904. Their children were: Leslie, Gerald, Ruby and Virginia. Zella's parents were John W. Williams and Henrietta Jones. Their children were: John, Samuel, Everett, Zella, Mattie, Jennie, Zehrn, and Dorothy. Henrietta's father and mother were Samuel Jones and Delilah Thompson. Samuel was a blacksmith in Poneto, Indiana. During the Civil War Samuel joined Company K Seventy-fifth Regiment at the age of thirty-nine. He joined twenty-three days after the birth of Henrietta. Charles Goodspeed was employed for many years by the Panhandle Pipe Line.

GORDON

Robert Ray Gordon, the youngest son of James T. Gordon and Priscilla (McAfee) Gordon, was born February 17, 1895. He was in the first draft from Wells County and served as sergeant during World War I from September 5, 1917, to February 18, 1919. He was stationed at Camp Zachary Taylor in Louisville, Kentucky where he met and later married Carrie Alice Foster on November 29, 1918. She passed away on July 23, 1936. Ray and Carrie lived in Louisville for several years, and Ray drove a Yellow Cab while they resided there.

Ray started going deer hunting in 1934. For years he and his two brothers, Howard Gordon and Verne Gordon, left every year on November 10 and traveled to Trenary, Michigan where they would hunt deer for two to three weeks. He only missed a couple of years of not being able to go deer hunting in Michigan. In 1970, he started going deer hunting with Al Huyghe, husband of his niece (Mary Alice Gordon) Huyghe. They traveled to Sundance, Wyoming every year to hunt deer and in 1975, when Ray was 80 years old, they all camped out that year.

November 1988 Alfred and Gloria Gordon. Daniel and Beth Gordon, Robert Ray 2 1/2, John Daniel 1 1/2, Tim and Connie (Gordon) Brennan, William Michael, 2, Michael Patrick 3 months

Robert Ray Gordon served as Republican Wells County surveyor in 1945-1946 and again in 1960-64. He passed away August 22, 1980. Robert Ray and Carrie lived in Rockcreek Township. Their children were: Alfred Ray Gordon, born June 6, 1928, and Arthur Lee Gordon, born May 23, 1929. Alfred married Gloria (Stoffel) November 26, 1949 and their two children are Daniel Ray Gordon, born August 30, 1951 and Connie Maie Gordon, born December 7, 1953. Alfred was born and has lived on the farm in Rockcreek Township that has been in the Gordon family well over 100 years. Alfred graduated from Rockcreek High School in 1946. He is now retired. Gloria served two terms as Republican Wells County recorder and is presently in the third year of her second term as Republican Wells County treasurer. They are members of St. Joseph's Catholic Church.

Daniel Ray Gordon, a local attorney, graduated co-valedictorian from Norwell High School in 1969 and from Harvard Law School in 1976. Daniel married Beth (Berghoff) on September 10, 1983, and they have three children, Robert Ray, born January 5, 1986, John Daniel, born March 23, 1987, and Elizabeth Christine, born March 13, 1989.

Connie Marie Gordon graduated from Norwell High School in 1972, and married Timothy P. Brennan on September 15, 1984. They have two children, William Michael Brennan, born November 18, 1986, and Michael Patrick Brennan, born August 12, 1988. They reside in Naperville, Illinois.

Arthur Gordon, a graduate of Rockcreek High School in 1947, retired from Franklin Electric Company and married Darlene (Slagle). Their children are: Tim, Terrie and Tammy. Arthur has three children from a previous marriage: Arthur, Jeff and Jean Ann.

GORDON FAMILY

Our great-grandfather, William Gordon, was born in Roxburshire, Scotland, in 1824 and emigrated to Rockford in Wells County, Indiana, in 1854, with his parents, Thomas and Margaret Gordon. He had six children: Andrew, Thomas, John, Christine, Archie, and William, who was our grandfather. Our great-grandfather, William, died in December, 1871, and was buried at Rockford, Indiana.

Our grandfather, William, had two children: Miles, who was commonly known as "Stokes", and our father, James. Grandfather was a contractor, livestock dealer and farmer. He was killed when his automobile was struck by a train in Liberty Center, Indiana.

L to R James O. Gordon, Pearl Gordon, Helen Gordon Gast

About 1963

Stokes married Vera Phillips, and they had one child, Joan. Stokes died before he was thirty years of age. His wife taught school for many years and is now retired and living with her daughter in Connecticut. Joan is a professor who did not marry. She received her degree from Rockford College and a Ph.D. from Columbia University.

Our father, James, married Pearl Stout, and they had two children: my sister, Helen, and myself, William. Our father was a contractor and farmer. He served for many years as a director of the Old First National Bank in Bluffton. Our parents were active in the Baptist Church until their death. Our father died in Florida in 1973 and our mother died at the Methodist Home in Warren, Indiana, in 1986.

Helen married David Gast of Warsaw, Indiana, and they had one child, Linda. Linda had two children, David and Alicia. Helen attended Indiana University, and for many years has been active in the Cardinal Learning Center for retarded children. David Gast received a B.S. degree from Indiana

University. Linda was graduated from Purdue University with an A.B. degree. She resides in Ventura, California. Linda's children, David and Alicia, are both college students and unmarried.

L to R - William S. Gordon, James K. Gordon, William S. Gordon, Jr., Taylor J. Gordon
April 1991

Laura Kenner and I were married in Huntington, Indiana, in 1935. We had two children, James and William Jr. Laura received an A.B. degree from Indiana University, and I have a B.S. degree from Indiana University and a J.D. degree from University of Michigan Law School. We were active in the Presbyterian Church in Huntington and served on the Boards of Directors of numerous community organizations. I was president of the Indiana State Bar Association in 1973-74 and in 1990 received the Indiana Lawyer 50-year Award made by the Fellows of the Indiana Bar Foundation. James received an A.B. and an M.D. degree from Indiana University. He has two daughters, Catherine Angela and Amy Carol, both of whom are in college and unmarried. James is an M.D. in Vero Beach, Florida. William Jr. obtained a B.S. degree from Ball State University and received an M.S. and a J.D. from Indiana University. He is an attorney in Huntington, Indiana, where he has served as Chief Deputy Prosecuting Attorney for a number of years. He had one son, Taylor James, a high school student, who is believed to be the last male descendant of our great-grandfather, who bears the name of Gordon. *(William Gordon)*

CHARLES (CHUCK) GORDON

Charles was next to the youngest son of James T. and Priscilla (McAfee) Gordon. They had four sons: Verne T., John Howard, Charles L. and Robert Ray. Charles was born April 15, 1892 in Rockcreek Township near Rockford, Indiana. He attended a one-room school house known as Raber School in Rockcreek Township. He went to Bluffton Business College in 1909 and graduated. He married Urania V. Johnson on September 7, 1911. He worked at the Rockford Stone Quarry a short time and then farmed, and raised and sold Belgian horses. He passed away on January 29, 1949. To this union was born three children: Opal Helen, Elwin Ray and Wendell J.

Opal Helen was born October 12, 1912, and married Robert C. Jones of Liberty Township on August 28, 1938. A daughter, Jane Ann, was born on September 12, 1948.

Elwin Ray was born on September 20, 1917, and passed away April 9, 1936. He was never married.

Wendell J. was born on January 22, 1926. He married Maxine Mertz of Bluffton and had a girl, Linda, and a son, James. He and Maxine separated and in 1957 he went to California and then settled in Nevada. He married Linda and had four children: Tina, Jim, Charles and Elwin Ray. Linda passed away and later he married Velma. No children were born to this union.

CHARLES LINCOLN GORDON

Chuck was born April 15, 1892, in Rockcreek Township the son of James Thaddeus and Priscilla McAfee Gordon. His grandfather, John Gordon, came to the States from Scotland as a child. His grandmother came from Ireland. Chuck attended school at the schoolhouse which was located at the corner of 300W 100N. He also attended and graduated from the business college in Bluffton. On September 7, 1911, he married Urania Vesta Johnson, daughter of Glessner and Rachel Butler Johnson. Urania was born in Rockcreek Township June 19, 1892. Both young people had been raised on farms about a mile from each other. Urania was a member of the Seventh-Day Adventist Church in Rockford and attended elementary school at the schoolhouse on the southeast corner of her father's property (100N 500W). D.N. Decker was her teacher.

Charles Lincoln Gordon and Urania

Chuck and Ranie moved into a house on Highway 124 between 100 and 200W. From there they moved to Rockford on the north east corner of Main Street and Mill Street. Opal Helen was born to them October 12, 1912. Elwin Ray was born September 20, 1917. Shortly thereafter Chuck and Raney moved in with Glessner and Rachel Johnson, Raney's parents, where Chuck helped farm. In 1922 they moved to a farm belonging to Chuck's father, located on Highway 124, and Chuck continued farming. A third child, Wendell Jay, was born to them January 22, 1926. Elwin Ray became ill at the age of eighteen and died of uremic poisoning April 9, 1936. Opal Helen married Robert Calvin Jones August 28, 1938.

Wendell Jay married Maxine Mertz. They had two children, Linda and James. After their divorce, Jay moved to Sacramento, California in 1957. He worked in an airplane factory and then for the Southern Pacific Railroad. He moved to Carlin, Nevada to be closer to his work. There he married Linda. They had five children: Tina, James, Charles, Linda, and Ray. At the present time he is retired and living in Carlin with his wife, Velma.

Chuck became ill with cancer and passed away January 29, 1949. He joined the Seventh-Day Adventist Church before his death. Raney moved from the farm to Liberty Center. She died at the home of her daughter July 7, 1975. Charles, Urania, and their son, Elwin Ray, are buried in the Elm Grove Cemetery at Bluffton, Indiana.

JOHN OLIVER GORDON FAMILY

John Oliver Gordon (1874-1954) was the son of John (Jack) Gordon and Katherine Brown. His father, John, came to America with his parents from Scotland and settled in Wells County, Indiana. He was married to Dessie Thompson (1875-1969) and they had two children, Carrie (Gordon) Day (1901-1989) and Clarence Oliver Gordon (1898-1978). They lived on 400W in Rockcreek Township, Wells County, Bluffton, Indiana, for many years. John Oliver and Dessie are buried in Elm Grove Cemetery, Bluffton, Indiana.

Clarence Oliver married Beth E. Garrett in June 1922, and they had two children - Marcia Phyllis (Gordon) Walburn (1924-) and Eugene Elmon (1925-1969). They lived at 3358 W 100 N, in Rockcreek Township Wells County, Bluffton, Indiana, from the time they were married.

Marcia married Roger Walburn on June 20, 1948 (Father's Day) at the Emmanuel Methodist Church and they had six children:

Cynthia Ann (Walburn) Biberstine who married Marvin Biberstine, and they had two children, Matthew and Carl.

Rosemary Lynn (Walburn) Risser who married Ned Risser, and they had two children, Brett and Kyle.

Lawrence Alan Walburn (1954-1981).

Sandra Kay (Walburn) Biberstine who married Cliff Biberstine, and they had three children: Casey, Jessica and Brittany.

Tamara Sue (Walburn) Smith who married Bryan Smith, and they had two children, Josh and Joel.

Debra Elaine (Walburn) Ruble who married Brian Ruble, and they had two children, Zack and Brock.

Eugene married Arlene Buel on June 19, 1949 (Father's Day). They lived across the road from John Oliver and Dessie Gordon at 0246 N 400 W, in Rockcreek Township, Wells County, Bluffton, Indiana, for almost 20 years. They had four children: Ned Eugene Gordon, Sr. (August 26, 1950 -) who married Jamie McClelland and they had two children, Ned Eugene Gordon, Jr. (called Gene after his grandfather) and Shaun.

Daryl Lee Gordon (October 11, 1952 -) who married Cathy Roberts, and then was divorced four years later.

Kathryn Ann (Gordon) Clements (May 23, 1954 -) who married Ronald Clements and they had two children, Jennifer Elizabeth and Jessica Lynn.

Barry Richard Gordon (May 9, 1958 -) who married Cynthia Ann Burke and they had two children, Blake Adam and Lauren Romaine.

Descendants of John Oliver Gordon are two children, three grandchildren, fifteen great-grandchildren and 21 great-great-grandchildren.

THOMAS GORDON

Thomas and Margaret (Smith) Gordon came to America from Roxburyshire, Scotland. They left Liverpool on July 8, 1854 on the "Columbia" and settled in Rockford, Indiana in Wells County with seven of their children. One son had come to American previously, and a daughter, Jennie, remained in Scotland. One of their sons, John (Jack) was our great-great-grandfather. On March 7, 1861, he married Katherine Brown.

John and Katherine were parents of James T., William D., Nancy J., Margaret, Fannie E., John O., Frank W. and Robert S.

Our grandfather, James T., married Priscilla McAfee on September 9, 1886. She was the daughter of Samuel and Elizabeth Lesh McAfee. They lived east of Rockford, Indiana. There they raised four sons: Verne T., John H., Charles L. and Robert R. All were farmers in Rockcreek Township. James T. Gordon passed away on May 20, 1949. Priscilla passed away on April 19, 1959.

John Howard married Fern Sparks and had no children. Charles L. married Urania Johnson and had three children: Opal Helen, Elwin Ray and Wendell J. Robert Ray married Carrie Foster and had two children: Alfred Ray and Arthur Lee.

Back (L to R) - Charles, Verne, Howard and Ray Gordon. Front (L to R) - Jams and Priscilla Gordon

Our father, Verne T., married Mary Estella Raber on March 14, 1911. She was the daughter of John C. and Maria Lucabaugh. Verne and Stella had two daughters, Verda May, born on December 7, 1914, and Mary Alice, born on May 22, 1923. They lived two miles west of Bluffton, which is now State Road 124. In 1923, they moved three and a half miles west of Bluffton on a farm purchased from Francis Hogg. Verne was a member of the Masonic Lodge and Elks Lodge of Bluffton. Verne passed away on August 28, 1956 and Stella passed away on October 2, 1932.

Verda M. married Claude A. Penrod of Chester Township on February 24, 1940. Claude served in World War II and passed away on February 8, 1954. A son, Jerry Lee, was born on November 7, 1943.

Verda M. was the postmaster of Uniondale, Indiana, from June 12, 1959, to October 2, 1987. On March 15, 1962, she married Gerald S. Wright. He passed away on August 23, 1982.

Jerry Lee married Joanna Jump on August 30, 1964, and had four children. Gregory Claude married Tonya Keplinger and had two children, Kyle Lee and Kristy Kay. Kathy Lyn married Keith Fiechter. They have no children. Patti Jo married Steven Teague and had two children, Anna Mersaydes and Spencer Lee. David William is the youngest.

Mary Alice married Albert Huyghe on March 8, 1945, and had three children. Albert passed away on April 21, 1976.

Marsalene married Kent Roush on May 17, 1968, and had two children, Tina Anne and Nicki Kay. Steven Albert married Wendy Wesenberg on March 9, 1979 and had one daughter, Kali Marie. Kali passed away at the age of eight months. Noreen Sue married Patrick M. Humerickhouse on April 14, 1979, and had two daughters, Carli Jo and Ashtyn Lane.

GORRELL-SWAIM

My maternal great-grandparents, (Esther) May Gorrell and David Hathaway Swaim, grew up together in Ossian, their families being involved in the town's early history.

The first Gorrells to settle in Wells County were Joseph and Esther Glass Gorrell, who arrived in 1840 from Trumbull County, Ohio. They were originally from Beaver County, Pennsylvania where Joseph' father, James (1770-1828), an Irish Insurrectionist, settled after being exiled by the English.

Joseph and Esther were charter members of the First Ossian Presbyterian Church, and it was on their farm southwest of Ossian that the congregation constructed its first building.

Their son, James, married Mary Ann Milliken in 1850, and one of their children was my great-grandmother, May, born in 1861.

*May Gorrell Swaim 1930's
David H. Swaim late 1930's*

William and Hannah Toy Swaim moved in 1857 from Troy, Ohio, to a farm near Ossian. They were born and married in New Jersey. William was descended from Tys Barentsz-Swaim of Holland, who in 1661 emigrated to America, settling in New Amsterdam. One of the five children born to William and Hannah Swaim was my great-grandfather, David Hathaway Swaim, born in 1858.

David was five years old when his father (by then Lt. Colonel Swaim), was mortally wounded in 1863 at the Civil War battle of Champion Hill, east of Vicksburg. Five years later Hannah moved her family into Ossian and became the proprietress of a millinery shop. Her death occurred in 1895.

Both May and David were educated and were teachers in the Ossian Schools, May being one of four comprising the first high school graduating class in 1881. After attending Valparaiso University and M.E. College in Fort Wayne, David became in 1879 assistant superintendent under P.A. Allen at the Ossian School, which later became the first high school. In 1884, he and his brother, W.T.T. (Tom) Swaim, graduated from the University of Michigan Law School and formed a law firm with Asbury Duglay in Bluffton. May Gorrell, then a Bluffton grade school teacher, became Mrs. David Swaim in 1885. Their home was at the corner of Wabash and Oak Streets.

David Swaim's 50 years in journalism began in 1888 when he, Tom Swaim, and Asbury Duglay bought the Bluffton weekly *Chronicle*. In 1890 David was appointed Bluffton postmaster, serving for three years while Tom managed the paper. The Swaims gave up their law practice to devote full time to the paper and in 1893 they also bought the Bluffton *Evening News*, a daily. Tom died in 1895 and David continued publishing both papers for 23 years, discontinuing the weekly in 1918. The News-Banner Corporation was formed with the 1929 merger of the two dailies, the *Evening News* and the *Evening Banner*.

A founding member of Bluffton's Chamber of Commerce, David Swaim was also an early supporter of the Street Fair. He was instrumental in the preservation of the city light and water plant as a municipally-owned utility. He held memberships in the Masonic Lodge and the Elks Club, the latter given in appreciation for his many bass solos in the Elks Minstrel Shows. Both May and David were active in the First Methodist Church, where David was a choir and quartet member.

Their two children were, Helen Swaim (Mrs. Frank) Thompson (1888-1931), and my grandfather, Roger Gorrell Swaim (1897-1976). May Gorrell Swaim died in 1936 and David H. Swaim died in 1939. *(Kathy Burleigh Denny)*

EVERETT GOSHORN FAMILY

The history of the Goshorn family in America began on August 24, 1750, when Johann Gansshorn (later Anglicized to Goshorn) and his family arrived from Germany at the Port of Philadelphia, twenty-five years before that famous document declaring the colonies' independence from England was drafted. The Goshorns became established as farmers in York County, Pennsylvania; it was there, in 1849, that Johann's great-grandson George moved to Jefferson Township in Wells County, where he farmed with his son William.

William Goshorn and his wife, Fannie Ogden Goshorn, had eight children. One daughter married William Woodward and another married Ernest Cotton, both of Wells County. A son, John Vincent, married Catherine Woodward in 1862.

John and Catherine Goshorn's first child, Elwin Francis, was born on June 12, 1881. Their other two sons, Homer Victor Goshorn and Raymond Woodward Goshorn, and their daughter, Erma, remained residents of Wells County their entire lives.

Elwin married Darlene Carr on December 22, 1904. Darlene's ancestors were also Wells County residents. Her first cousin is Nellie Bunn McNeal, who at 102 years of age has recently received a great deal of notoriety, having appeared on nation-wide television. Darlene's father, Clarence (C.D.) Carr, was a well-known Ossian businessman and entrepreneur around the turn of the century. In addition to selling insurance, he was a justice of the peace, a poet, and an inventor. His poems have been collected and printed. His business card read, "C.D. Carr, Justice of the Peace. Knots tied and untied." Justices of the Peace back then could married and divorce couples.

Back: (L-R) John Goshorn (son of William), Elwin Goshorn, (son of John), William Goshorn. Front: Everett Goshorn (son of Elwin)

Elwin owned a tie barn in Ossian and bred Belgian horses. He and Darlene had four children while they lived in Wells County: Catherine, Everett, John Carr, and Margaret. In 1915 Elwin and his family packed their belongings on two horse-drawn wagons and headed for Huntington, Indiana, where Elwin had taken a job with the Erie Railroad

Company. The family rode the interurban rail line to Kingsland and took the Erie Railroad from there to Huntington. Their belongings followed by wagon. Elwin and Darlene had three more children while living in Huntington: George Richard, Billy Wayne, and Betty Jane.

Before retiring in 1973, Everett was an educator and school administrator in Huntington County for 44 years, and his wife, Sophie, also taught school. Their daughter, Anne Marie Mitchell, resides in Bellevue, Washington, and has three children. Their son Everett Ewlin (Bill) Goshorn, obtained a law degree and returned to Wells County in 1970 with his wife, Margaret (Peggy), who is an elementary school teacher at Lancaster Elementary School. In 1980 Bill was elected judge of the Wells County Court and is currently judge of the Wells Superior Court. He and Peggy reside in Lancaster Township and have three children: Julie Ann (nineteen), who attends DePauw University, William Tighe (fifteen), who attends Norwell High School, and Mark Everett (11), who attends Lancaster Elementary School.

GOTTSCHALK'S

The family name of Gottschalk is quite familiar in the history of Nottingham Township, Wells County, Indiana. The Gottschalk families arrived in America in 1840, and after spending their first years in Montgomery County, Ohio, they came to Nottingham Township in 1846 and established the Gottschalk homestead farm.

Anna Maria Schnurle Gottschalk's passport was issued on April 29, 1840, for herself and three unmarried children. It stated her age as 60. Children listed on the passport were: Barbara, twenty; Michael, eighteen, and Magdelena, sixteen, all born in Unterhaugstett, Germany.

Anna Marie Schnurle Gottschalk was the daughter of Johann George and Anna Maria Kuberlin Schnurle. She married Jacob Frederick Gottschalk on February 5, 1811. Jacob Frederick was born on March 7, 1780, in Haugstett, Germany, son of Johann Jacob Gottschalk, a weaver by trade, and Sophia Adam. Sophia's father was John Michael Adam. Johann Jacob Gottschalk's father was John Michael Gottschalk, born in Monakam, Germany.

After the death of Jacob Frederick Gottschalk Sr. on April 5, 1828, in Germany, his widow Anna Maria left Germany for America, accompanied by her unmarried children and her oldest son, Jacob Frederick Jr., born November 19, 1808, along with his two daughters, Eva Barbara, born November 10, 1835, and Mary, born October 23, 1836. They were the children of his first marriage to Belinda Stahl. Belinda's parents were Johannes and Anna Marie Klug Stahl. After Belinda's death, Jacob Frederick Jr. married Christina Katharina Fuchs, born December 14, 1815. Her parents were Andreas and Christina Katharina Volle Fuchs. Their first son, George J., born September 10, 1839, also accompanied his parents to America. They spent almost their entire married life in America in Nottingham Township.

Anna Marie Schnurel Gottschalk's younger son, John, born November 23, 1813, married Sarah Hannah Mattis in Germany; they also came at the same time as the others and moved to Nottingham Township in 1846. They raised their family in Wells County. John passed away January 27, 1877. John and Sarah are buried in the Old Salem Church Cemetery adjacent to the original Gottschalk Homestead. They raised their family in Wells Daughter Anna Maria married John Michael Miller in Germany, and they spent most of their adult life in Nottingham Township.

Daughter Barbara, born in Germany in 1820, married Frederick Keller of Montgomery County, Ohio. They later moved to Miami County, Indiana. Both passed away and are buried in the Charpie Cemetery in Washington Township, Miami County.

Son Michael, born February 3, 1822, in Germany was married in Montgomery County, Ohio, to Hilda Curtner. They remained in Ohio and raised a family of eight.

Daughter Magdalena, born 1824 in Germany, was issued a marriage license in Montgomery County, Ohio, on February 3, 1851, and married Benjamin Shriner.

FREDERICK RANNELS GOTTSCHALK

Jacob and Christina Fuchs Gottschalk's son, Frederick Rannels, who was born on September 5, 1852, on the Gottschalk family farm in Nottingham Township, married Margaret Hook on January 25, 1874. They spent their entire married life on the family farm. Margaret Hook's father was George Hook, who was born in Germany. Her grandparents were George and Elizabeth Goss Ream. George Ream was born in Schulykill County, Pennsylvania on March 6, 1813, and died on February 21, 1879, in Fulton County, Indiana. Elizabeth Goss's father was Jacob Goss. The Ream and Goss families came from Germany through Pennsylvania into Fairfield County, Ohio. George Ream and Elizabeth Goss were married on June 7, 1835. The Ream and Goss families were both living in Fulton County, Indiana, during the 1850-60-70 censuses.

Frederick Rannels and Margaret Hook Gottschalk lived on the Gottschalk family farm adjacent to the Old Salem Church in Nottingham Township. Frederick R. passed away on January 26, 1907. Margaret, born on July 16, 1854, passed away on June 7, 1920. They both are buried in the Old Salem Church Cemetery.

Children born to this union were: Andrew (first born, on January 2, 1875; married Bertha Garret); Minnie (married Charles Cory and they had three daughters); George Wesley (married Minnie Durkes - no family); Edna Mae (infant); Luella (married Augustus Reynolds - two sons); Amanda (married Pearl Gentis - two sons); Della (married Henry Durkes - two daughters); Thurman (married Alice Druckemiller - one daughter); Nina (married Emil Moser - one son); Ruth B. (married Daniel Moser, seven children, which included triplet daughters born on Christmas Day); Clement R. (married Mahala Reusser - four children; served in World War I); Esther (last child, born November 29, 1897; married to Henry Pierce, two sons).

JACOB FREDERICK GOTTSCHALK, JR.

Jacob Frederick Gottschalk, Jr. came to America in 1840 along with his wife Christina Kathrina Fuchs with their first son, George J. (born September 10, 1839 in Germany) and Jacob's two small daughters from a previous marriage, Eva Barbara, born November 10, 1835, and Mary, born October 23, 1836. Jacob Frederick Jr. and wife Christina lived in Montgomery County, Ohio, until they moved to Nottingham Township, Wells County, in 1846.

Jacob Frederick Jr.'s oldest daughter, Eva Barbara, married Gabriel Schrock and raised their family in Wells County. Both are buried in the Old Salem Church Cemetery. Daughter Mary, married Peter Rose of Wells County. Mr. Rose served in the Civil War and died in a hospital in Nashville, Tennessee. Son George J., resided in Harrison and Chester Township. He passed away on April 14, 1917.

Back row L to R: Geo Gottschalk, Michael Gottschalk, Matthins Andrew, Fred, and Noah Front row L to R Mary Rose Shigley, Barbara Shrock, Amanda Gottschalk

Jacob and Christina's first child born in America was Sarah, born January 17, 1841. She married Jacob Betzner. Son Michael C. married Jennetta E. Shigley; they are both buried in the Old Salem Church Cemetery. Son Johannes, born August 8, 1844, married Elizabeth Stogdill of Adams County. Johannes served in the Civil War and his wife Elizabeth was an Army nurse. Son Jacob, born in Wells County on November 11, 1846, passed away on September 24, 1848. Son Michael married Eliza Baker. Son Andrew, born November 11, 1850, in Wells County, married Laura Sheets. Andrew and Laura's family were prominent citizens in Adams County. They owned and operated a drug store, a supply company, and a tile factory; postmaster in Berne, and other family accomplishments were treasurer of Adams County. One son was a state senator in Indiana and another son, True, was a physician.

Son Frederick Rannels, born September 5, 1852, married Margaret Hook on January 25, 1874. They spent their entire married life on the original family homestead. Son Noah, born November 27, 1860 married Sarah Heller. They spent their entire life in Nottingham Township. Both are buried in Old Salem Cemetery.

Jacob Frederick Gottschalk Jr.'s second wife Christina Katherina Fuchs passed away on November 18, and is at rest in the Old Salem Cemetery. After his second wife's death, Jacob Frederick Jr. married a third wife, Elizabeth Walter Shepperd. They were blessed with two daughters, Amanda, who remained single and Susanna, who married John Haecher.

Jacob Frederick Gottschalk Jr. passed away on January 26, 1877, and was buried in the Old Salem Church Cemetery. He and his second wife with their infant son and his two daughters from his first marriage had sailed from LeHavre, France, in April, 1840, for America. After 93 days on the ocean, they had arrived in New York City, and then had gone on to Montgomery County, Ohio, and finally to Nottingham Township, Wells County, Indiana. Here he and Christina had raised a large family. He had cleared the land for the family homestead and was now resting with his Lord in the Old Salem Church Cemetery. One will never know and much less understand all the efforts, time, sorrow, hardships, and happiness one man experienced in order to make a better life and a place to live not only for his beloved family but for the next generation of his family.

NOAH GOTTSCHALK

Noah Gottschalk was born in Nottingham Township, Wells County on April 13, 1854. He was the eighth son and ninth child of pioneers, Jacob Frederick Gottschalk, Jr. and Christena Catharina Fuchs. His parents were German immigrants; they came to the United States in 1840 and settled in Ohio for awhile before moving to Wells County in 1846. The farm where Noah was born is adjacent to the Old Salem Church.

Noah's mother died on October 18, 1855, when he was only one and a half years old. His father died January 27, 1877; both are buried in the Old Salem Church Cemetery.

On September 15, 1878, Noah was united in marriage with Sarah Heller, daughter of David Heller and Mary Ann Gentis. They settled on a farm less than a mile from his home place. He was a prominent farmer and loved to hunt. He purchased the farm in 1880 from his brother Mathias, who had migrated to Peru, Indiana.

Three children were born to them. A girl, Berthena, was born on January 14, 1880, and a son, Harry, on January 11, 1884. Both of these children died of diphtheria just twenty-seven days apart in 1886. Another son, Goldie Grover, was born on October 25, 1887. Goldie married Lottie Moeschberger in Wells County on February 5, 1910. They started married life in Wells County but later moved to Adams County on a farm only a mile and a half from his father's farm. They had two children, Loren and Ruth.

Noah Gottschalk and Sarah Heller married September 15, 1878

Later the husband of the oldest step-daughter (Ida Steiner) lost his life through an accident. Noah and Susan took her and her four small children into their home and he began to rear a third family. This was in October, 1924; but on February 22, 1925, Noah died after a seven day's illness of pneumonia. Susan died on May 27, 1939. All the family are buried in the Old Salem Cemetery.

Noah's grandson, Loren, born on July 21, 1921, was married on April 12, 1941, to Dorothy Lucille Stalter (born February 25, 1916) daughter of Norman and Cleo (Mosure) Stalter. After their marriage, they moved to the farm his grandfather had purchased in 1880. They have lived here for over fifty years. The farm has now been in the family one hundred and ten years.

They are the parents of one daughter, Bonita Irene, a graduate of Indiana University. She now lives in El Dorado, Kansas, where she is principal of the middle school. She has one son, Matthew, born April 27, 1974.

Noah's granddaughter, Ruth Gottschalk, lives in Berne and is retired from the First Bank of Berne.

GOTTSCHALK-SCHNUERLE FAMILY

It was in 1840, at the age of 60, that Anna Marie Schnuerle Gottschalk, a Lutheran and widow of Jacob Friedrick Gottschalk, Sr. came to America from near Calw, Germany, as did her six children: Jacob, Jr., John, Ann Maie, Barbara, Michael, and Magdalena. They settled first in Ohio, but in the mid 1840's the oldest three came to Nottingham Township, here in Wells County. They associated with the Evangelische Gemeinschaft, now known as the Old Salem United Methodist Church, in whose cemetery they and many of their descendants lie buried.

Jacob Friederick Gottschalk, Jr., born in 1808, cleared eighty acres for a farm. He had three wives: Belinda Stahl, Christina Fuchs, and Elizabeth Shepherd, and fathered sixteen children: Eva Barbara married Gabriel Schrock; Mary married Peter Rose; George J., Sarah married Jacob Betzner; Michael married Jeannetta Shigley; John married Elizabeth Stogdill, Jacob; Mathias married Eliza Jane Baker; Andrew married Laura Sheets; Frederick Rannels married Margaret Ann Hook, Noah married Sarah Heller, Catharina died as child; Susanna married John Haecker, Amanda; and two children died in infancy.

John Gottschalk, born in 1813, married Sarah Hanah Mattis in Germany. There is some confusion about their children, but it is thought their children were: Jacob married Catherine Heller; Lucinda married Jonas Coffman; George ("Big George") married Mary Eger; Mary Ann married Peter Mowery and then Jacob Furthmiller; Barbara married Seth Snider, Michael married Genevieve Power, Sarah married David Furthmiller and later Henry Dawkins; and John.

John Gottschalk and his wife, Sarah Mattis, and their children, Michael and Barbara.

Anna Marie Gottschalk was born in 1816, and married John Michael Miller. They had nine children, six of whom died in childhood: John, Magdalena, Mary, Michael married Louise Eger and had nine children, Barbara, Jacob, Lucinda married William Mertz, Sarah married Edward Heller, and Noah.

The three youngest immigrants, Eva Barbara Gottschalk, Michael Gottschalk (who changed the family named to "Gotttschall"), and Magdalena Gottschalk, settled, and remained, in Ohio.

Extensive information on the Gottschalk and related families is recorded in the book, GOTTSCHALK, GOTTSCHALL, published in 1987, and available in major genealogical libraries. It list 1,461 direct descendants of Jacob and Anna (Schnuerle) Gottschalk.

GRADEN-MOSER

In the early 1900's, John and Rosa Moser Graden moved to Wells County, near Vera Cruz, from Fort Wayne. Both Swiss immigrants, John had come to this country at the age of sixteen, arriving in New York in December, 1887. He became a citizen on September 20, 1906. Rosa Moser came to this country at the age of nineteen, arriving in New York on April 25, 1895. She traveled to Fort Wayne, where her brother, Fred Moser, lived. He had come to this country several years sooner. John Graden and Rosa Moser met for the first time in a Fort Wayne restaurant, where she was employed. They were married on June 10, 1897 at the Salem Reformed Church in Fort Wayne.

John farmed in the Bluffton and Vera Cruz area. They had nine children: Bertha, born April 8, 1898, married Charles Maddux, a car salesman, and they had two daughters, Dorothy and Marilyn. Albert, born January 26, 1900, was a builder of homes and a brick layer in the Wanatah area. He married Louise Welty and they had one daughter, Dorothy. Mary, born August 17, 1901, married Hugh Heller, an employee of the Ford Motor Company in Hammond, and they were the parents of six children, Dorothy, Robert, Wendell, Betty, Shirley, and Donald. John, born January 26, 1903, was a carpenter and built the original First Church of Christ at the corner of Spring Street and Clark Avenue in Bluffton. In later years, John and his wife, Bernice Hasty, moved to Hart, Michigan. Frederick, born January 18, 1906, along with his brother, Edward, started a service station on East Elm Street in the 1930's. In the 1940's, Edward left the business, and Frederick started a tire recapping business. Frederick married Florence Crowl and they had one daughter, Jean. Louise, born November 7, 1907, married Albert M. Bowers, Works manager of the International Harvestor in Indianapolis. Edward, born May 15, 1910, was elected Wells County sheriff in 1944 and served two two year terms. Later he moved to Kendallville and started a recapping business. He married Gertrude McAnnich and they had one son, Barry, (the only grandson to carry on the Graden name). Helen, born June 7, 1912, married Jules Toussaint, a restaurant owner in Fort Wayne. Esther, born June 27, 1914, married Walter F. Smith, and they had one son, Garry. At the time of their marriage, Walter was in the Navy; then later he became an engineer technician with the Army Civil Service. They were living in Honolulu, Hawaii, and he was stationed at Hickman Field at the time of the bombing of Pearl Harbor, December 7, 1941.

John Graden was from an Apostolic Christian family in Switzerland and Rosa was a member of the Reformed Church. John, in later years, joined the Reformed Church in Bluffton.

After John's death in 1934, Rosa lived in Bluffton and did house work and cared for children, and also kept busy quilting, crocheting, and knitting. She remained active in her church until her death in May, 1957.

GRAEFLIN

The Rev. Walter Graeflin pastored the Church of the Nazarene for 25 years, from 1957 to 1983. The church was then located at 327 W. Cherry, with the parsonage next door at 321 W. Cherry. Walter spearheaded the 1965 church remodeling, which also expanded the foyer to connect the church and parsonage. With the purchase of a new parsonage on Ellingham Pike in 1973, the old parsonage became Sunday-school rooms.

Walter, born to Swiss immigrants in Cleveland, was reared in Wellington, Ohio. He was educated at Eastern Nazarene College in Wollaston, Massachusetts, a small suburb of Boston, and Nazarene Theological Seminary in Kansas City, Missouri. Walter met his bride while they attended Eastern Nazarene College.

Iris, born and raised in the Washington, D.c. area, attended two years of college and then accompanied her husband to the seminary. While Walter attended classes and worked full-time at Bendix Aviation Corporation as a tool and dye maker, Iris was a full-time mother and homemaker.

Rev. Walter and Iris Graeflin

The Graeflin family arrived in Bluffton in August of 1958 with children Arlette, age seven, and Ron, age four. Bluffton was Walter's second pastorate following three years in Anderson, Indiana, at the Fairfax Church of the Nazarene. Iris graduated from Indiana University in 1967 and began teaching kindergarten at Poplar Grove School. Both of the children graduated from Bluffton High School and Olivet Nazarene College in Kankakee, Illinois.

Walter continues to pastor at his third assignment in Seymour, Indiana. He commutes from the Graeflin home in Bluffton. Iris has continued teaching kindergarten at East Side School since the merger of Poplar Grove and East Side. Arlett has returned to Indiana from Idaho to prepare for graduate work in Theatre Arts. Ron and his wife, Sheryl, reside in Muncie as associate pastors in charge of children at the Muncie Southside Church of the Nazarene.

GRAFT-BAUERMEISTER

Fredrich (Fred) Graft, sometimes called Kraft, Kraeft, or Graeft, born April 26, 1867, was the son of immigrant Rosina Werling, born March 10, 1837, who with her parents left their home in the Province of Rheinpfalz, Germany to come to the United States.

Rosina married Christian Graft, born February 17, 1828, in Zion Friedham Lutheran Church, Adams County, Indiana, May 20, 1858, and lived near Echo, Section twenty, Jefferson Township, Wells County (the house that is now the Wm. and Adele Roembke home, Road 900N). Fred was one of nine children.

Fred married Marie Bauermeister, born June 17, 1876, Loh #37, Petershagen, Germany, the daughter of Ernest Bauermeister, born August 11, 1841, and Sophie Wilhelmina Luise Limbach, born March 18, 1837, Loh #24, Petershagen, Germany, who were married October 5, 1862, in Windheim, Germany. Marie was one of eight children. She came to America at about fourteen years of age after her parents had already migrated.

They were married November 26, 1896, in Bethlehem Evangelical Lutheran Church, Tocsin, Indiana. He bought an eighty acre farm, Section thirty, Township 28N, Range 13E, from David A. Isnogle and Louisa, his wife, November 1, 1906.

The Fred Graft Family
First Row: Rosina, Fred, Lawrence, Marie and Luella. Hilda, Arthur, Elmer, Esther, and Martha.
(Fall of 1928)

Fred was in the grocery store business with John Kreigh located at Echo, circa 1900. There was also a post office in this same building. He also drove the huckster wagon with a team of horses on a regular tour through the community.

Fred also worked at the Echo Tile Mill a number of years before buying the farm, then devoted his life to farming. They were the parents of ten children: Paul, born September 29, 1897, died August 21, 1898; Rosina, born December 14, 1898, died July 12, 1976, who married Herman L.G. Miller, April 8, 1917; Elmer (Doc.), born September 29, 1900, died January 25, 1971, who married Ella Hoffmann, April 16, 1922; Esther born, November 4, 1902, died September 3, 1965, who married Herman Werling, November 7, 1920; Hilda, born July 27, 1905, died May 6, 1952, who married Morris B. Schull, May 26, 1928; Luella, born October 9, 1907, and living, who married Edwin Meyer, July 31, 1927; Martha, born May 23, 1910, died July 27, 1974, who married Herbert Franke, April 27, 1930; Arthur, born May 3, 1913; and living, who married Hildegarde Wente April 29, 1939; Lawrence (Deedle), born December 16, 1915, died September 4, 1970, who married Viola Ehlerding January 19, 1941; Lorine, born June 17, 1919, died March 6, 1922.

Their children were all baptized, attended the church day school, and were confirmed in Bethlehem Evangelical Lutheran Church, M.S., Tocsin, Indiana.

Fred died February 17, 1940, and Marie died March 9, 1952. They are both buried in the Bethlehem Church Cemetery, Ossian, Indiana.

GRAFT-WERLING

Among the early pioneers of Jefferson Township were Christian and Rosena (Werling) Graft. Christian Graft was born February 17, 1828, in Jossen #30, Germany. The name is spelled Krefft in the Windheim, Germany, church records. Some old local records spell it Kraeft or Kraft. A language barrier created the name Graft when Christian applied for his deed. Later, when the error was discovered, the family adopted the new spelling rather than change the deed.

Christian left Germany at age 25 and arrived in New York on April 26, 1853, on the ship *Meta*. He left immediately for Preble Township, Adams County, Indiana, where his half-sister, Christena, and her husband, Conrad Gallmeyer, were living.

On May 6, 1856, Christian applied for his naturalization papers in the Allen County Court. He labored a short while on the farm before getting a construction job on the Wabash-Erie Canal. With these wages and a loan from Conrad, Christian bought one hundred twenty acres in Section 20, Jefferson Township. A family story passed down through the generations states that Christian cut a large tree at just the right height for a table and small trees around it for seats. Over these he built his log cabin.

Graft Homestead 1899
L to R: Fred, Conrad, Ernst, Willie, Charles, Christian Jr., Mary, John, Christian Sr. and Rosena

Christian married Rosena Werling on May 20, 1858, in the Zion Friedeim Lutheran Church in Preble Township. The cabin served the family well until a disastrous fire burned it down along with the barn, corn-crib, and grainery. A two-story home replaced the log cabin. Despite hardships, Christian and Rosena wee able to accumulate a large estate which enabled them to leave each of their children forty acres or the equivalent in money.

Rosena was born March 10, 1837, in Lambsheim, Germany, to Johannes and Christena (Foltz) Werling. Rosena, her parents, and siblings —Andrew, John, Henry, and Elizabeth - immigrated on the ship Oneida and landed in New York March 23, 1842. They lived several years in Meigs County, Ohio, where David and Margaretha were born. David died from cholera during the Civil War and is buried in a National Cemetery in Tennessee. In the spring of 1853 the family moved to Preble Township where Johanne's brother, Andrew Werling, was living. Another brother, David Werling, remained in Meigs County. Johannes and his family joined the Zion Friedheim Lutheran Church where Christian Graft was also a member. Rosena died January 9, 1895, and Christian died December 5, 1904. They were laid to rest in the church cemetery. They were the parents of eleven children.

Christian and Rosena's first child, Wilhelmine Christine Elizabeth, was born March 6, 1859, and died 21 days later on March 27. She is buried in the same cemetery as her parents.

John C. Kraft/Graft was born March 12, 1860. He married Ida Forbrich September 9, 1886. They were the parents of Clara, Albert, Charles, Herman, Emil, Emma, Max, Ida, Paula, Laura, Gertrude, Paul, and Arnold. John C. Graft died June 30, 1936, and Ida died December 27, 1939, and were buried in the Bethlehem Lutheran Church Cemetery in Jefferson Township.

Christian J. Graft was born December 3, 1861. He married Maria Helene Steiner February 25, 1886. Their children were: Christian, Otto, Mary, Selma, Annie, Nora, Henry, Mathilda, Adele, and Peggy. Christian died April 8, 1945, and Mary

Helene died in 1965. They are also buried in the Bethlehem Cemetery.

A son, Heinrich Friedrich Wilhelm, was born September 23, 1863, and died December 1, 1863. He is buried in the Zion Friedheim Cemetery.

Marie "Mary" Christine Graft was born November 8, 1864. She was married November 1, 1885, to Conrad D. Gallmeyer. They were the parents of Frieda, Martha, Elenora "Ella", Martin, Johanna, Carl, Eulalia "Lily", Conrad, Maria, and Gerald. Mary died April 9, 1950, and Conrad died November 7, 1924. They were laid to rest in the Zion Friedheim Cemetery.

Friedrich Graft was born April 26, 1867. He married Marie Bauermeister November 26, 1896. Their children were: Paul, Elmer, Esther, Hilda, Luella, Martha, Arthur, Lawrence "Deedle", and Lorene. Fred died February 17, 1940, and Marie died March 9, 1952. Both are buried in the Bethlehem Cemetery.

Conrad F.W. Graft was born September 23, 1869. He moved to Chicago around 1900.

Wilhelm Graft was born February 3, 1872. He married Anna Bauermesiter April 30, 1896. The young couple lived with his parents on the homestead, and Willie assisted in the farming until tuberculosis took its toll on his health. Willie died February 14, 1901, and is buried in the Friedheim Cemetery. Willie's widow married William Roempke and they were the parents of Alvina, Else, and William Jr. William and Annie purchased the Graft homestead from Conrad and Mary Gallmeyer and it continues to be in the Roempke family today.

Ernst Graft was born March 24, 1874, and died March 23, 1927. He is buried in the Ossian Cemetery.

Helena Hanna Sophie Graft was born March 11, 1877, and died of tuberculosis May 8, 1895, at age 18. She is buried in the Zion Friedheim Cemetery.

Carl "Charles" Graft was born February 4, 1880. Charles remained single and is buried besides his brother Ernst in the Ossian Cemetery.

Lilly Gallmeyer, one of the grandchildren of Christian and Rosena Graft, married Herbert W. Kirchner October 1, 1922, in the Zion Friedheim Lutheran Church. They had four children: Vernice, Eldora, Ardena, and Marvin. Ardena married Don H. Burke on November 2, 1947, in the St. Paul's Lutheran Church, Preble. They have three children: Kathryn Kay, Ann, and David.

GRAHAM

Charles A. Graham was born in 1867. He married Mary Franklin who was born in 1873. They had eight children: Vernon, Ted, Carrie, Vida, Flossie, Cassius, Joseph and Bert. Charles owned a blacksmith shop in Petroleum which was sold in 1918. The family then moved to a farm near Petroleum and Charles started farming and continued until the late 1930's. Mary died in 1942 and at that time Charles moved to Petroleum and lived in a house behind his daughter, Flossie who had married Harold Clark. Charles died in 1947. Flossie and Vida, who both live in Bluffton, are the only living children.

Flossie Graham married Harold Clark in February, 1929. Harold's parents were David Clark and Josephine King Clark. David was a farmer and a minister at the Methodist Church in Bryant, Indiana. That church has now been moved to Bear Creek Farms. Both of Harold's parents died in the early 1940's.

Harold brought a milk route from Claude Grover in the late 1930's picking up milk from the farmers and taking it to Garrett for processing. Harold and Flossie lived in Petroleum and had one daughter, Carolyn Jean who was born May 17, 1940. She is now married to Donald Hay and they have two daughters, Jodi Ann Kaehr and Toni Lynn Hay.

Flossie bought O'Brien's Coffee Shop from Harry O'Brien in 1945. The family moved to Bluffton during this same time. She changed the name of the restaurant to Clarkie's Coffee Shop. It was located at 113 South Johnson St. She went out of business in 1962.

Harold died December 30, 1946 at the age of 41. Flossie married Eugene (Salty) Coulter December 12, 1959. Gene worked at General Electric and had two sons: David who is married and lives in Bluffton and Dick who was in the Air Force and stationed in Germany and was killed in an automobile wreck in 1974 while in Germany.

Gene and Flossie live at 225 East Wabash St. which is the site of the old Baumgartner Hatchery.

GRAHAM-FAUS

Robert Roosevelt Graham was born in the little town of Linn Grove, Indiana, Adams County, On May 2, 1929. He was the second child of Theodore R. and Mary M. (Taylor) Graham. Bob's dad, Ted, passed away on March 12, 1961.

Betty Lou Faus was born in a farm house near Boiling Springs, Murray, Indiana, on October 25, 1930. She was the eighth child of Harry S. and Mary L. (Archbold) Faus. Her dad passed away on February 19, 1961, and mom passed away on February 20, 1983.

Bob attended grade school at Linn Grove, Indiana and high school at Hartford High School. Betty attended grade school at Murray and graduated from Lancaster Central High School in 1948.

Bob and Betty were married by the late Rev. George G. Holston, formerly of Linn Grove, on October 28, 1949, at the Evangelical United Brethren Church parsonage at Kokomo, Indiana.

Bob had worked at United Milk Condensary at Berne, Indiana, and Meschberger Stone Company at Linn Grove, Indiana. He retired in 1990 from Food Marketing Corporation (formerly Bluffton Grocery Command) of Fort Wayne, Indiana, where he had worked 39 years as a truck driver.

Betty had worked in the offices of Morris 5¢ to $1 Stores of Bluffton, General Electric in Fort Wayne, Indiana, and various waitress jobs. Her land place of employed was Kitco, Bluffton, Indiana.

Bob's favorite past-time is watching Indiana University, Detroit Pistons, and other basketball games. We enjoy playing cards and games, especially with the grandchildren. Betty bowls on a Ladies League at the Bluffton Bowling Center.

Their son, Robert Michael was born on July 26, 1950, in Wells County. Mike and Debra Lynn Markley, daughter of Wayne and Winnie (Baller) Markley were married on April 7, 1973. Though divorced, three sons were born of this marriage: Michael Shane born November 24, 1973, Shannon Lynn born March 13, 1976, and Derek Ryan born June 10, 1977. Mike and Karen Sue Barger, daughter of John and Nancy (Beard) Baumgartner, were married on November 28, 1986. Karen has two daughters, Mandi Renee born May 18, 1975, and Alicia Kay born January 21, 1980.

Their first daughter, Vickie Lynn was born on January 25, 1953 in Adams County. Vicki and Raymond Dale Reber, son of Donald and Emma (Sider) Reber were married on March 19, 1971. Vicki and Ray have three children: Christi Ann, born October 5, 1971, Cami Raye, born April 17, 1975, and Cory Don who was born December 11, 1976.

Their second daughter, Terri Sue, was born on August 30, 1956, in Wells County. Terri and David Lester Runkle, son of Kyler of Amy (Booher) Runkle were married on June 15, 1975. Terri and Dave have two sons, Andrew Clayton, born May 1, 1977, and Aaron David who was born February 11, 1979.

All three children of Bob and Betty are graduates of Bluffton High School, Bob and Betty have been residents of Wells County for 39 years and are planning on spending their remaining years here as their children, most of their family and friends also live here. They hope to spend more precious time with their families as they know that they are richly blessed.

GRAHAM AND GOLDSBERRY

Our family of Grahams can be traced to our great-great grandparents. Grandfather Graham arrived in the USA in 1865 at the age of seventeen. In 1865 he came to Wells County and bought an

The family of Robert and Betty (Faus) Graham

eighty acre farm three miles east of Rockford. He married Maggie Wallace in 1877. She was the daughter of Thomas Wallace. They had three sons, Thomas, who was a school teacher and later a police lieutenant for twenty-five years in Los Angeles, Robert, my father, and John.

Robert married Ruby Babcock, who was a daughter, of James D. Babcock. He came to Wells County from Rennsalaer, Jasper County, to a farm on old 303 and later moved south of Petroleum, where he was a stockbuyer and farmer.

December 1984
The James Graham Family
Front L to R: Carolyn, Jim, Linda Back L to R: Peggy, Pat, Mike, Robert

Robert and Ruby, my parents, lived on the original eighty acre farm and Grandfather bought an eighty acre farm one and one-half miles east of the original. My sister Helen was born in 1910 and I was born in 1924. I graduated from Rockcreek School in 1942 and served in the Marines during World War II. In 1948 I was married to Carolyn Goldsberry, daughter of James and Thriece Goldsberry. I was one of the first employees of Corning Glass and retired in 1990.

We have five children. Linda graduated from Indiana University in 1973. She was married to Lew Kunkel and they have two daughters, Karmen, sixteen, and Katy, twelve. Michael graduated from Indiana University with a DDS degree in 1979 and is currently practicing at the Caylor-Nickel Clinic. He is married to Connie Walburn and they have two children, Courtney, twenty-one months, and Spencer, six months. Patrick graduated from Norwell High School and works at farming and at Fasson. He is married to Debra Osborne and lives on the original Graham farm at 100N and 200W. Peggy graduated from Norwell and International Business College. She is married to Duane Kuhn and they have two daughters, Brittany, four, and Jennifer, one and one-half. Robert graduated from Norwell and lives in Berne, where he worked for the Ford Garage. He also helps on the farm.

The Goldsberrys came to Wells County in 1906 from Clinton County. My grandfather Draper married Ethel McDonald Brown in 1903. They had two daughters, Dessie and Bessie, and a son James, my father. James married Thriece White in 1926. They had two daughters, Carolyn and Barbara. Carolyn married James Graham and Barbara married Jack Sprunger and they had three children, Suzanne, Scott, and Steven. *(James and Carolyn Graham.)*

GRAHAM-PLUMMER

We can trace the Graham to my great-great grandfather in Donegal County, Ireland. My grandfather William (1848-1926) came to America when seventeen with an uncle and worked on his farm until 1865. William then bought an eighty acre farm three miles east of Rockford. In 1877 he married Maggie Wallace (1856-1943), daughter of Thomas Wallace. They had three sons, Thomas, Robert, and John. Robert, my father (1884-1963), married Ruby Babcock (1891-1983), daughter of James D. Babcock (1849-1927), a stock-buyer. We can trace the Babcocks to 1624. They came to the U.S.A. from England eight generations ago. He lived on 303 and later near Petroleum. My mother was active in the Better Homes and Loyal Neighbor Clubs, the Presbyterian Church, and the D.A.R.

I, Helen, was born in 1910 in the same house as my father and my brother, James R., born in 1924.

Nancy, Jim (two years old), Tom Plummer

I attended Falk one-room school for seven years, where the teacher taught all eight grades, cleaned the floors and built the fires. I graduated from Rockcreek High School in 1927, and from Fort Wayne Lutheran School of Nursing in 1932 as an R.N. I retired from Wells Community Hospital after thirty years of general duty and twelve years of private duty. I have seen many changes in the medical field.

In 1936 I married Robert Plummer. We have three children: Thomas R., born in 1940, Nancy Joan born in 1943, and James R., born in 1947. Bob worked at Central Dairy until he became ill in 1961 with emphysema and died in 1969 at age fifty-nine.

Our children all graduated from Bluffton High School. Tom has two sons, Craig and Trent. Captain T. Craig graduated from Purdue University in 1985 and is currently serving with the U.S. Air Force in Saudi Arabia. He is married to Sandra Floyd and is living in Shreveport, Louisiana. Trent just completed four years in U.S. Air Force and has a daughter, Taylor Michelle.

Nancy married Frank Steffen in 1961 and has four children: Janice, graduated from International Business College, is married to Michael Nichter, has Benjamin, twenty-one months, and lives in Fort Wayne. Doug, married to Daphne Willett, lives in Bluffton. Scott, married to Carolyn Case of Decatur, graduated from Butler University, lives in Indianapolis, and is working in the computer field. Mark has a daughter, three, lives in Uniondale and works at Ossian for Gerber Grocery.

James attended Indiana University School of Technology, is married to Jennifer Mickley, has three sons: Shane, seventeen, Jared, thirteen, and Brett, ten. They live near Ouabache Park. Jim is a salesman for National Oil.

In 1974 I married Lloyd Romine, who is retired after many years as a meat cutter. We have done some traveling, are members of the First Presbyterian Church, where I first went with my grandparents in a horse and buggy. We've enjoyed our work and children and are now enjoying our grandchildren and great-grandchildren.

GRANDLIENARD-GIROD

Brooks Grandlienard was born December 4, 1920 to Charles E. and Marguerite Hinchman Grandlienard. He was the oldest of five children, and the family resided south of Vera Cruz on a farm that had been in the Grandlienard family since 1856. They were dairy farmers, proud of their Jersey cattle, often showing them at fairs. The children attended Poplar Grove grade school, and graduated from Bluffton High School. Brooks, Fred, and Kenneth have continued in dairy farming, with Brooks keeping the same Jersey cattle his father owned. Ruth was a teacher in the South Adams Schools; and Joe is a retired minister. The children remember getting a pony for Christmas with their dad parading it through the house.

Brooks and Joyce Grandlienard
Married 1948

Brooks served in the U.S. Army during World War II. On September 3, 1948, he married Joyce Girod, daughter of Alfred and Marie Brickley Girod. She, along with her twin sister, Jean, had just graduated from Lutheran Hospital School of Nursing. The Girods lived on a farm west of Bluffton. Jean and Joyce were born August 29, 1926. The children graduated from Rockcreek High School. Jean's sisters, Hallie, and Joyce are registered nurses. Sister, Ina May, is a teacher and brother, Don is a pediatric cardiologist at Riley Hospital. Alfred was a farmer and Marie, a school teacher.

Grandlienard kids school bus
Lewis Pence bus driver

Brooks and Joyce have five children. Their daughters, Beth, Amy, Meg and Jo were named after Louisa May Alcott's "Little Women". Beth was born May 12, 1951. She graduated from Ball State and is a registered nurse at Wells Community Hospital. She is married to Kent Decker and they live near Bluffton with their children, Katherine and Matthew, and grandson, Michael. Amy was born August 23, 1953. She graduated from I.U. and is an audiologist. She married Scott Jones and lives in Phoenix with their son, Will. Meg was born May 17, 1955. She graduated from Ball State and teaches music. She married James Heinzman. They have a son, Aaron and lives in Westfield. Mark was born August 14, 1957. He married Shari Confer. They have four sons, Jason, Joshua, Jared, and Jordan, and live in Bluffton. Mark works at Moorman Manufacturing Co. and is a student at Indiana University in Fort Wayne. He is a Judo instructor. Jo Maria was born February 9, 1962. She graduated from Indiana University, and works as a sales representative, calling on hospitals in the Chicago area. She is married to William Joy and lives in Wheaton, Illinois, with their daughter, Emma.

The family lived on the John Edris Farm, west of Bluffton, for many years. They purchased the family farm in Rockcreek Township, originally purchased in 1891 by Joyce's great-grandfather, Lewis Brickley. In 1980 they built a new home and moved "back home".

Brooks is active in Soil Conservation, serving on the board for many years. He was one of the earliest in the area to practice no-till farming. He was a director of the Federal Land Bank. Joyce continues to enjoy nursing at Wells Community Hospital. They are members of Old Salem United Methodist Church.

GRANDLIENARD-HINCHMAN FAMILY

Charles E. Grandlienard lived his entire life on the 80-acre farm his grandfather had purchased in 1857 for a total of $662.53. The farm is located southwest of Vera Cruz on County Road #75. It was there that Charles was born March 13, 1890, the third of four children, born to Henry and Catherine Winkler Grandlienard.

As a young man he operated a ditching machine until he was called into service during World War I. He served with an engineering company in France during the war.

On his return from overseas, Charles married Marguerite Hinchman, a school teacher from Nottingham Township, and the two took over the operation of the family farm following the death of his father in 1920.

The couple had five children: four sons and a daughter. Brooks married Joyce Girod, and they live on a farm in Rockcreek Township. Fred married Letitia Wilhelm, and they also live on a farm near Celina, Ohio. The youngest son, Joe, served as a minister in the United Methodist Church for a number of years and is now a counselor in a psychiatric hospital in Phoenix, Arizona. The daughter, Ruth, married Sherman Neuenschwander, of Berne. She was a public school teacher for more than 30 years. The Grandlienards had a total of 22 grandchildren, all of whom attended college.

The family was very active in the Old Salem Evangelical Church in southern Wells County, later known as the Old Salem United Methodist Church. Charles served as Sunday School superintendent in that church for more than 30 years. In addition to his work in religious circles, he was always very active in agricultural, extension, and civic affairs. He was also a big fan of Bluffton High School sports, attending their basketball, football, and baseball games until into his late 70's.

Charles Grandlienard died in 1970, at the age of 80. At the time of his death, his place of residence was still the home in which he had been born. Only during his Army service had he lived anywhere else.

Marguerite Grandlienard lived alone on the home farm until her death in 1976. Both are buried in the Six Mile Cemetery.

GRANDLIENARD-SAUNIER FAMILY

Abram-Louys (Abraham) Grandlienard came to Wells County with his second wife, Sophia Saunier, from the French-speaking section of Canton Bern, Switzerland. Arriving in Indianapolis on July 4, 1850, and unable to understand English, they could not determine the reason for the celebration. They settled first on what was later known as the Lewis Bilbee farm near Vera Cruz. The woods were so dense that when cattle strayed, it was necessary to take a compass when going to look for them in order not to get lost. In 1857, they purchased and moved to what in later years was known as the Charles Grandlienard farm on County Road 750 E. They were Lutherans and attended a church located where Indiana State Road 218 is met by the Adams-Wells County Line Road. Abraham died in 1864 after suffering a kick in the head from a horse while he was taking a wagon load of pigs to market in Fort Wayne. Sophia lived on as a widow for 48 years and died in 1912. They are buried in the cemetery at Vera Cruz.

They brought to America four children from Abraham's first marriage, Marianne-Emilie, Susanna-Sophia, Abram-Louys III, and Henriette Emiline. They also brought their first child, Paul. They later had four more children: Henry, Marie, Elise, and Edward.

Paul Grandlienard married Mary (or Martha) Jane Winkler. They had four children: Lewis, Mae (married Otto Blocker), William (married Ica French, and two whom were born twelve children), and Ora Ethel (married Chester Vernon Franklin). Many of this line dropped the "e" in Grandlienard.

Henry married Catherine Winkler, to which union were born four children: Dora (married Rueben Miller), Bessie (married Harvey Garboden), Charles (married Marguerite Hinchman), and Fred, who died during the flu epidemic in 1919 at the age of twenty-four and never married.

Elise married George Gottschalk; to this union were born two children, Carrie Eva (married Henry Schlagenhauf), and Orest (married Vada Druckemiller).

Edward, son of Abraham and Sophia, died when twenty four and never married.

Many of the family were associated with the Old Salem Evangelical Church in southern Wells County, later to be known as the Old Salem United Methodist Church, and many are buried in its cemetery.

The Home of Abraham and Sophia Grandlienard, and later of Charles and Marguerite Grandlienard

A book, *The Grandlienard Family In Switzerland and America*, published in 1985, traces the origins of this family to Perrefite, Switzerland, in the 18th century and lists descendants. It is available in major genealogical libraries.

The oldest part of this house was built in 1864. The floor beams, still in place 1984, were logs sixteen inches in diameter cut in two. The uprights were logs cut between three and four inches thick. Insulation consisted of soil scraped off the surface of the fields and filled in between the walls. When modern insulation was installed in the early 1960's, a county agent happened by and asked for a sample of the soil that had been used. After it had been analyzed at Purdue University, the analyst phoned in excitement to find out from whence the soil had come, as it had proven to be "perfect" — lacking no nutrients and needing no fertilizers!

GRANDLIENARD-WILHELM

Frederick D. Grandlienard, third child of Charles and Marguerite Hinchman Grandlienard was born April 2, 1923. Brooks and Ruth were older than Fred, and Kenneth and Joseph were younger.

Fred attended Poplar Grove Grade School and graduated from Bluffton High School in 1941. After completing a short course at Purdue in 1942 he was employed as a dairy herd improvement tester in Elkhart County for a year before being drafted in the Air Force in February, 1943. After he completed pilot training in the P-51 fighter plane, the war ended. He returned home to be separated from active duty but remained in the Reserve for eight years.

On March 9, 1946, he married Letitia "Tish" Wilhelm, eldest daughter of Edith High and Charles Wilhelm. The Wilhelms' second daughter, Bonnie Jean, died at the age of five, and Mary Janelda, third daughter, married Roger Neff, son of Edson and Esta Pennington Neff.

Fred and Letitia Grandlienard

Four children were born: Randolph "Randy", served in the Air Force four years and graduated from Ball State in 1974. He married Elizabeth Ponton from Bogota, Colombia, South America. He presently is employed with the Andersons Management Corporation at Poneto, Indiana. Bruce graduated from Purdue in 1972 and served as a pilot in the Air Force eight years. He is employed as a charter pilot at Smith Field, Fort Wayne. Janelda graduated from Indiana University School of Nursing in 1973 and married Gerry Towne of Bluffton. They have four children: Jenny, fourteen, Tyler, eleven, Philip, three and Luke, two. They reside northwest of Bluffton. Gary served in the Peace Corps in 1982 and married Ana Calderno from Cali, Columbia, South America. They have two children, Freddy, four and Lorena, two. He is self-employed and they reside at West Lafayette, Indiana.

Four generations have lived on the family dairy farm at 100N-100W since October, 1906, when Joseph and Margaret High purchased the land. The Falk one-room school, Rockcreek No. 8, stood on the corner of the farm until 1924, when it was demolished and students then went to the new East Rockcreek Township School.

The family have been involved in various community activities and are members of the Old Salem United Methodist Church.

DESSIE GREEK

A history of Wells County would be incomplete without the story of Dessie Greek. Her father, William Wallace Greek, was born in Pleasantville, Fairfield County, Ohio, on August 24, 1855, to John and Vinean (DeVol) Greek. Seven years later, the Greeks moved to Sheldon, Allen County, Indiana. By the age of eighteen, W.W. had gone into business with his father. On August 19, 1877, he married Elizabeth "Lizzie" Johnson, the daughter of Noah and Sarah (Thomas) Johnson of Union Township, Wells County, Indiana. This young couple's first child, William Pearl, was not born until January 29, 1882. By then, W.W. had begun his own insurance business in Sheldon. In 1886, he moved the business to Bluffton where Dessie was born March 20, 1887. Sadly, when Dessie was little more than two years old, her mother died. In less than a year, Dessie and her brother had as their step-mother, Laura V. Marsh; but she died in 1897. The next year their father again married, and Miss Maggie McBride became their second step-mother.

Another difficult period for Dessie began in 1907 when her grandfather, Noah Johnson, died in September. The following June, her brother, William Pearl, married Estella Bethel of Peru, Miami County, Indiana. Before summer's end, on August 20, 1908, William Wallace Greek died. Still another shock was in store for Dessie: her brother, who had gone west for his health, died at Denver, Colorado, June 2, 1910, just two years after his marriage.

One good thing happened. Dessie's grandfather, Noah Johnson, willed her over $400.00, a lot of money in those days. With it, she was able to enroll in nurse's training at Presbyterian Hospital in Chicago. Along came World War I, and in 1917 Dessie enlisted and served at Base Hospital 13 in France. After her discharge in 1919, she returned to Presbyterian Hospital where she served as supervisor of a floor until her retirement in 1953.

After the war, Dessie took the first group of Gold Star Mothers to Europe, and she helped secure legislation which enabled nurses who had served in the war to be admitted to veterans hospitals. Also Dessie served as commander of Chicago's Jane Delano Post, American Legion. After retirement, she resided in the Veterans Domiciliary at Dayton, Ohio, where she died June 16, 1962.

This remarkable visionary, a woman many years ahead of her time, was buried in Bluffton's Fairview Cemetery where an Army Nurse monument will soon mark her grave.

GREEN

Ralph and Alma Green moved to Wells County from Abottsfort, Wisconsin in 1940. Ralph worked from Fruehauf in Fort Wayne and Alma was a housewife. They made their home on East Arnold Street in Bluffton from 1940 to 1963.

Alma died in 1958 and Ralph was killed in a car accident in 1963.

Ralph and Alma were the parents of three daughters. Lila K. married Alfred Mittlestedt and had three children: Yvonne, (Bonnie), James and Donald. Johnny married Albert Goldamer and had one son, Alan. Shirley married Bud Lovett and had three children: Bill, Jane, and Susan.

BRUCE AND JOY GREGG

Bruce is the son of Linn and Betty Gregg of Bluffton and has been a lifelong resident of Wells County. His family has been a part of Wells County history for many years (see Linn and Betty Gregg). He graduated from Norwell High School, and holds a Bachelor of Science Degree in supervision from Purdue University, and Associate Degrees in Marketing and Management from Indiana University. Bruce is employed as a cost accounting supervisor.

Joy is a native of Jay County. She grew up in Dunkirk, Indiana. She is the daughter of Thompson Huffman and Carolyn Antrim Shroyer. Her father, Tom Huffman, resides in the Dunkirk area where his great grandfather, George Huffman Jr., settled in 1837. Tom is a direct descendant of the founder of Dunkirk. Carolyn's grandparents, Alasander and Ila Bennett, and her great-grandmother, Elizabeth Tharp, lived in Wells County.

Joy's parents divorced in the mid-1960's. Her mother, Carolyn, then married Dr. Herbert L. "Doc" Shroyer. Doc maintained a medical practiced in Dunkirk for 20 years, until forced to close the practice in 1970, due to failing eyesight. Many Bluffton residents may have known Doc Shroyer. He worked several years at the Caylor Nickel Clinic taking medical histories. He was the first blind doctor on the staff. He thoroughly enjoyed the work at Caylor Nickel! There were twelve children in Joy's family, ten of whom were raised by Doc and Carolyn.

Joy graduated from Dunkirk High School. After a year at Manchester College, she transferred to Ball State University where she earned a bachelors of science degree in mathematics and business education. She became a part of the Bluffton community during the fall of 1976, when she took a job with Franklin Electric. Joy is currently a self-employed tax preparer working from her home. She enjoys volunteer work at Lancaster Elementary. She is also a leader of the Lancaster Daisy Girls Scouts.

We were married in October, 1979. We have two children, Joshua, nine and Katie, six, who attend Lancaster Elementary School. Josh loves sports and math. Katie loves dance, gymnastics and baseball.

We are members of the First Presbyterian Church of Ossian where Bruce serves as a trustee and Joy teaches Sunday School, and is a co-leader of a children's after-school group.

The family resides at 5552E 100N, Bluffton.

LINN AND BETTY GREGG

We are both native Hoosiers. We have lived in Indiana all of our lives, except for a three year period when we lived in Illinois. We are both now retired and enjoy the freedom to travel more.

Linn was born in Bluffton and graduated from high school there. He served in the U.S. Navy from 1942 to 1945 during World War, and from 1950 to 1952 during the Korean War. He is an active member of Grover Sheets Post 111 of the American Legion in Bluffton.

Betty was born in Roanoke, in Huntington County, before her family moved to Wells County. She attended grade school in Poneto and high school in Bluffton.

We were married in December, 1942, and had fours sons. Our first child, Gene, died in 1956. We raised the remaining three sons, Bob, Bruce, and Bill in Wells County, and all three were graduates of Norwell High School.

Bob and his wife, Karen, live in Baltimore and have three daughters. Bruce and his wife, Joy Huffman Gregg, live in Bluffton and have a son and a daughter. Bill and his wife, Marcia Decker Gregg, live in Detroit, and are expecting their first child.

Betty's parents were Frank and Rosella James. Her father was a farmer and died in 1968. Her mother died in 1989. Her grandparents were John and Julie Pearl Ruble James and lived in Huntington County and in the Warren area. Betty has two sisters, Ruby Huffman and Thelma Lehman, and two brothers, Jack and John James.

Linn's parents were Linn Sr. and Nellie Jamison Gregg. Linn Sr. operated his own trucking firm in the 1940's, managed the Ouabache State Park in its early years and held various other jobs before retiring. Linn Sr. died in 1978 and Nellie currently resides at Westhaven Health Care. Linn had two brothers: Roger Gregg who died in 1990, and Jim Gregg who died in 1966. He had one sister, Helen Gregg Miller, who lives in New Castle, Indiana.

Linn's father, Linn Sr., had one brother, Levi Gregg, and one sister, Ruth Greg Captain. Both are now deceased. Linn Sr.'s parents were Richard and Louvina Linn Gregg. Richard was one of thirteen children of John Gregg, who came to the United States from Ireland in 1858.

WILLIAM GREGG

William Gregg, my great-grandfather, was born November 10, 1837, at Kilmacreman, County Donegal, Ireland. His parents were Richard Gregg (1780-1840) and Fannie McClure (1794-1881).

He was reared in his native Ireland and resided with his parents until the spring of 1855.

The voyage to America took five weeks and he landed at New York Harbor. He came directly to the virgin woods of Wells County, Indiana, because his older brothers, John and Daniel, had settled in Liberty Township earlier.

The young eighteen year-old Irishman with red hair and beard helped build the corduroy road from Bluffton to Fort Wayne. Trees about six to eight inches in diameter would be trimmed of their branches and laid crosswise down a path. To help make the first road smooth, dirt would be filled between the logs. This was rather successful until it rained and then the dirt would be washed out to leave the road rough and bumpy.

In 1857, he purchased eighty acres of heavily timbered wilderness for $600 from a land speculator. He began to clear and farm the land in Rockcreek Township three and one-half miles west of Bluffton, known today as State Road 124. He built a two-room log cabin and large barn from native timber.

On December 19, 1860, William married a neighbor girl, Agnes Gordon (1841-1920), daughter of Thomas Gordon and Margaret Smith. Agnes had immigrated with her family from Kelso, Scotland in 1854. They were both self-reliant, independent and dyed-in-the-wool Presbyterians.

From this union were born Fannie, Margaret (my grandmother), Eliza Ann, Jeannette, Mary, and Agnes. They were named for Williams mother and sisters in Ireland. All the girls were born in the log cabin.

In 1873, Wiliam built a kiln on the farm west of the barn where they clay was right to make brick. When enough bricks were fired, and river stone quarried for foundations, William and his brother John started to build identical two-story houses. Both of these houses are in use today.

Slavery and temperance over-shadowed all other political issues. William was drafted for Civil War service in 1865, but he paid a man $200 to go in his place. The war ended before the proxy arrived in camp.

Fannie never married. Margaret married Joseph High and to whom was born Edith (married Charles Wilhelm). Eliza Ann married Peter Barwiler. Jeanette married Louis Reiff to whom was born Agnes (married Gerald Russell). Mary married Charles Fritz to whom was born Dwight (married Marie Markley) and Agnes died at a young age.

William Gregg lived to be 84 years old and the family is buried in the Fairview Cemetery, Bluffton, Indiana.

GREGG-WORMAN

Our great-grandfather, John Gregg, was born in County Donegal, Ireland, on May 9, 1829, and died February 9, 1907. His parents, Richard and Fannie McClure Gregg, raised several children three of whom, John, William and Daniel immigrated to America in June 1851.

John first applied his trade of bricklaying in Philadelphia, Pennsylvania, then in Wayne County, Ohio. While in Ohio, he purchased a tract of wild land in Liberty Township, Wells County.

John visited Ireland a few times in his lifetime, the last time with his very young son Thomas. Upon his return to this country after his first visit to Ireland, he took up residence on his land in Liberty Township. He met Fannie Wallace there and they married on October 19, 1858. Fannie, daughter of Samuel and Susanna Jackson Wallace, was born on March 28, 1841. Her father was born in Ireland and came to this country in 1832. John and Fannie had thirteen children, eight of whom lived to adulthood.

Left to Right: Howard, David, Frank, John and Marion Gregg

Their son, Thomas D. Gregg, was our grandfather. Thomas married Ida I. Morris, daughter of David and Lochia A. Taylor Morris. They had five sons: John, David, Marion, Howard M. and Frank.

Howard was our father, born December 21, 1906, and died September 1, 1968. He worked as a mechanic most of his life. He preferred to work on farm equipment. In 1936 he married Margaret Worman, born December 31, 1913 and died December 2, 1978.

They had four children: Jane Kay, Jack H. Jerry Lou and Kathryn. Jane worked 31 years for Indiana Bell. Jack married Marcia Nicholson and has one son, Douglas Shawn, twenty eight years old. Jack has worked for Fisher Body for almost 30 years and lives in Liberty Township. Jerry Lou married Ray A. Shaw and is a teacher at the Bluffton High school. They have four daughters. Sherry Lyn, twenty-six, graduated from Purdue and now works for a Fort Wayne bank. She is married to Anthony Johnson and has one son, Blake Alan, born in 1990. They live in northern Wells County. Judy, twenty-four, Ann, twenty, and Carol, eighteen are currently attending Purdue University. Kathryn has remained at home.

The farm and the brick house that John built is still owned and operated by a descendant, our cousin Rex K. Gregg, son of David.

Our grandfather, Lloyd Worman came to Wells County about 1906. He was born in Noble County on June 17, 1886, and died September, 1959. He was in the Air Force in World War I, stationed at Langley Field, Virginia. The story goes that while at Langley Field, he decided that he was wasting his time and might as well be home with his wife and three children, but his commanding officer talked him out of going AWOL. He owned one of the first cars in the west end of Bluffton. He was something of a daredevil in his younger years.

He married Olive Emma French, daughter of Eugene and Eliza Reynolds. They were the first of their families to live in Wells County. Olive and Lloyd had six children, five of whom lived to adulthood: Margaret, LeRoy, Paul, Robert and Joan.

Our mother, Margaret, worked in the Wells County Public Library for twenty-two years.

ROBERT AND AMY (GORDON) GREINER

Robert S. and Amy Gordon Greiner arrived in Bluffton on the 4th of July weekend celebrating our nation's bicentennial. Bob was assuming the position of property manager at Ouabache State Park. They had come from Parke County, covered bridge capital of the world, where Bob had been assistant manager at Raccoon Lake State Recreation Area and Amy was the librarian at Rockville Junior-Senior High School.

They had met four years earlier in Winamac, Indiana, Amy's hometown. Bob, a native of Wabash, Indiana, came to Winamac after graduating from Purdue University, to begin his career with the Department of Natural Resources at Tippecanoe River State Park. After Amy graduated from Indiana University, they were married in August 1973 and moved to Park County, where they lived for three years before moving to Bluffton.

Until their first child, James Robert (Jay) was born, Amy worked with the youth programs at the County Extension Office. When Jay made his appearance on September 11, 1978, Bob was lucky enough to have the distinction of being the first non-medical father present at a caesarean birth in Wells County. Jay was delivered by Dr. Bud Keye at Caylor-Nickel Hospital.

Amy spent one year at Southern Wells as the K-12 librarian before their daughter, Rebecca Anne, was born on October 29, 1981.

In 1983, Amy began working at the Bluffton-Wells County Public Library in Children's/Outreach Services where she is still serving in that capacity (1991).

Since moving to Bluffton, the Greiners have been active members of the First United Methodist Church. One or more members of the family have also been active in other community organizations, including Boy Scouts, Creative Art Council, East Side PTO, Foltz Club, Girl Scouts, 4-H, League of Women Voters, Lions Club, and Tri Kappa.

SOPHIA A. AND ARTHUR J. GREWE FAMILY

The purchase of the first thirty-five acres of the farm unit founded by my grandparents is recorded February 14, 1896, the same date five acres of this tract (located corner of 750N and 650E) was sold to the charter members and trustees of the Bethlehem Lutheran Church of the Evangelical German Lutheran Congregation for $250.

My grandmother, Sophie, was born August 2, 1869, to Wilhelmina Gallmeier and Andrew Werling. My grandfather was born April 4, 1869, to Elizabeth Hildebrand and William Grewe. They married December 5, 1895, and my father, Arthur, was born to them on September 2, 1896. They also reared six foster children: Edith Pierce Rutz, Mabel Crosby Scheumann, Gustave Rutz, Theodore McBride, Alma Rutz Bauermeister, and Emilie Rutz. My mother, Sophia Anna, was born May 17, 1899, to Sophia Reasoner and Ferdinand Schaefer.

My parents' engagement was short, as mother lived northwest of Fort Wayne and primary transportation was horse and buggy. They married on December 22, 1921. After Christmas, they rode the inter-urban from Fort Wayne to Ossian and, in a snowstorm, walked the five miles home.

My parents were farmers. Dad was interested in new technology and conservation. He was instrumental in getting the REMC to our rural area so the church would have electric lights. Before electricity, every Christmas Eve day a huge evergreen was cut down and put in the church. It was decorated with candles and large lead balls in red, green, silver and gold. The candles provided the light for the Christmas Eve service. Each child received an orange and candy and nuts - a tradition continued today.

Left to right: Arthur (Father) Vera (daughter) Delores (daughter) Arnold (son) Sophia (mother)

My mom's "heart's desire" was a bathroom (once we had electricity) and an outdoor fireplace constructed to blue prints she'd ordered from the Majestic Furnace Co. My father thought it absurd to want to eat outdoors and go to the toilet indoors! She got the bathroom - I've still got the unused drawings.

Guests frequently dropped in for a meal or longer visits. I'm sure my brother remembers the summer that cousin Larry Scheumann vacationed with us and they were instructed to clean the cider press. Instead of carrying the pulp to the fields, they fed it to the hogs to save time. My parents watched their sick hogs stagger, fall down, and try to get up, until they realized the hogs were drunk from fermented apple pulp! The hogs recovered.

I was the youngest of four children. Frederich died in infancy. Vera married Arthur W. Hoffman, and they live near Monroeville, Indiana. Arnold married Martha Maxine Hoover (deceased) and they had three children: a son, James Arnold, who with wife Shirley have two daughters, Jennifer and Tammy; a daughter, Ginger, and her husband, Corwin Robertson, who have a daughter Allison Bree; Arnold's youngest daughter, Jeanette, lives with him at their home in Louisville, Kentucky.

Dad was a lifetime member of Bethlehem Lutheran Church and mom transferred her membership there following their marriage. Our lives revolved around the spiritual community and social life of the church. Dad died on February 25, 1952, and Mom died on August 27, 1981. *Submitted by Delores.*

GRIFFIS FAMILY

Lloyd Griffis, his wife Betty, and their three children, David, Elizabeth and Susan, moved to Bluffton from Marion, Indiana, in January of 1963. Their first home was in a rental property at 221 West Central Avenue. In July of 1963, the family moved to the home they purchased at 844 Parkway Drive. Lloyd and Betty Griffis still live at that home.

Lloyd came to Bluffton as a vice-president of Old-First National Bank and served as its president from 1968 until his retirement in January of 1986. He was active in the Indiana Bankers Association, serving as president in 1976. Locally he is a member of Rotary Club, The Masonic Lodge, the Elks Lodge, and the American Legion. He is also active in the Chamber of Commerce and Bluffton Revitalization.

Betty Griffis has been active in the Red Cross as a volunteer nurse at the Blood Bank and teaching Expectant Parent Classes. She is a member of Foltz Reading Club. All of the family have been active members of Calvary Lutheran Church.

David Griffis and his wife, Virginia and theirs sons, Michael and Edward, live in Tucson, Arizona. David graduated from Bluffton High School and Indiana University. He is executive director of Malloy, Jones and Donahue law offices.

Elizabeth Griffis Deemer lives in Stevensville, Maryland, with her husband Barry. She is a school psychologist for Anne Arrundel County. Elizabeth also graduated from Bluffton High School and Indiana University.

Susan Griffis Swenson resides in Indianapolis with her husband, Andrew, and daughter, Sarah Mills. Susan is a teacher at Harcourt School. She graduated from Bluffton High School and Kansas University.

HAROLD L. GRIMM AND LOLA (STAHAM) GRIMM

Harold was born in Nottingham Township, Wells County, October 4, 1927. He was the oldest son of Harold C. and Dorothy Grimm. Elic and Cora (Shannon) Grim were his grandparents. Harold has three brothers, Pete (deceased), Roger of Petroleum, Bob of near Poneto, and one sister, Mary Jane, Frauhiger of Bluffton.

Lola is the daughter of Levi and Ocie (Poling) Strahm. She was born in Wabash Township, Adams County, on May 9, 1928. She has been a housewife and helped on the dairy farm all her married life.

They both graduated from Petroleum High School in Nottingham Township, in 1946.

(L-R) Tim, Harold, Lola, Pam, Linda, Mark

Harold has been engaged in dairy farming all his married life. He has served on the Chester Township Advisory Board for 20 years, and served different terms as trustee at the Keystone United Methodist Church. He is presently a director for Milk Marketing, Inc., and also a director for Milk Promotion Service of Indiana. He served several years as Democratic precinct committeeman in Chester Township.

There were five children: Linda, the oldest, born in 1947, married Charles (Ez) Harris. They have three boys, Lance, Chad, and Chris. Linda is a teachers assistant at Southern Wells High School. They live close by. Charles works at Franklin Electric. Rodney (deceased) was born in 1950, and passed away in 1952. Tim, born in 1953, is a veterinarian at Berne, Indiana. He is married to Paula Carnall. They have three children, Ryan, Carlee, and Desmond. Paula is a speech teacher, and they live west of Berne. Pam, born in 1955, is married to Richard Schortgen. They have three boys, twins, Brad and Brent, and Jason. Pam is a respiratory therapist at St. Joe Hospital, Fort Wayne, and Rick works at Navastar in Fort Wayne. They live one-half mile south of Norwell School. Mark, born in 1957, married Jaimi Warthman. They have two girls, Leah and Stella. Mark graduated from Purdue with a degree in agronomy, and came back to dairying and farming. Jaimi is a Spanish teacher at Southern Wells High School. They live two and one-half miles south of Poneto.

MARK ALLEN GRIMM AND JAIMI LYN (WARTHMAN) GRIMM

Mark and Jaimi met May 29, 1977, while making laps through Bluffton, Indiana. They were engaged November 13, 1980, and married November 14, 1982.

Mark and Jaimi (Warthman) Grimm, Leah Marie (4 years) Stella Delanie (8 1/2 mo.)

Mark, the son of Harold Lloyd Grimm and Lola Belle (Strahm) Grimm, was born July 18, 1957, in Hartford City, Indiana. He is the youngest of four children. Linda Lou (Mrs. Charles) Harris, who lives in Poneto, Dr. Timothy Harold Grimm, who lives in Berne, and Pamela Sue (Mrs. Rick) Schortgen, who lives in Ossian, are his older siblings.

Mark graduated from Southern Wells High School in 1975, and Purdue University in 1980, with a degree in agronomy. He currently milks cows, and farms several acres.

Jaimi, the daughter of Joyce Marie (Miller) Warthman and the late Dale Warthman, was born September 25, 1959, in Decatur, Indiana. She has an older brother, James Neal Warthman, who lives in Bluffton, and a younger brother, Dr. Jerry Dale Warthman, who lives in Anderson.

Jaimi graduated from Bluffton High School in 1977, and Ball State University in 1981, with an art education, Spanish education degree, and a master's degree in 1988. She taught art at each level for a total of six years, and is currently teaching Spanish at Southern Wells Junior and Senior High School. Mark enjoys following options and commodities in the markets, and playing basketball, while Jaimi enjoys music and gardening.

Leah Marie was born on December 2, 1986, in Bluffton. Marie is a family name in Jaimi's mother's family.

Stella Delanie was born August 7, 1990, in Bluffton. Delanie is for Jaimi's father Dale and his mother Anna (Abbott) Warthman.

For more information on Jaimi's mother's family see Miller-Reaser article.

For more on Mark's family see Harold L. Grimm and Lola (Strahm) Grimm.

GROH-RAUCH

In 1906, Mabel Groh was born in Wells County to Jacob and Mary Reinhart Groh, in a brown shingled house which still stands along Thiele Road, just north of the railroad and Dustman Road. Mabel, who had one brother and one sister, remembers sitting on the railroad tracks waiting for her mother to come home from town. She graduated from Craigville School after the eighth grade, receiving a permit not to go on to high school because riding the school bus gave her side ache. Mabel could only speak German until age eight when she went to school. In 1933 Mabel married Jay (Jehu) Rauch, of Adams County, at the Apostolic Christian Church near Vera Cruz. They had one son, Jerome, born in 1936 in Berne where they lived for three years. Jay and Mabel, both being of German Swiss ancestry, taught Jerome to speak Swiss before he learned English. After farming in Adams County for sixteen years they moved to a home they built, in the Byrd Woods, two miles east of Bluffton along 124, in 1955. Jay worked at the former Bluffton Estey Piano Factory for seventeen years and has built over twenty grandfather clocks, one of which stands in Goodwin Funeral Home. Mabel has pieced, by hand, many quilts, some of which belong to her son and grandchildren. In 1954, Jerome married Virginia Neuenschwander of Berne and they have three children, living in or near Bluffton most of their married life. Jerome also worked at Estey Piano Factory and is a piano tuner technician. He also drove a school bus for Bluffton for seventeen years and works for the Indiana Department of Transportation. From 1967 to 1972 the Jerome Rauch family owned and operated a music store on South Main in Bluffton. Virginia works in the cafeteria at Bluffton Middle School. Their children are: Cynthia (Cindy) Geisel, married to Stan Geisel. They are parents of Rochelle, fifteen, Carissa, fourteen, and Zachary, eleven. Cindy is a cook at

Bluffton High School and Stan works at Hower Tool near Ossian. A son, Jerry, born in Wells County, is married to Kathy Gerber and their children are: Rachel, twelve, Jadon, eleven, Micah, eight, and Hannah one and a half. Jerry owns the Harvest Health Foods Store in Bluffton and together with Kathy, they home school their children. Another son, Michael, born in Wells County, is married to Susan Schladenhauffen and they have five children: Adam, fourteen, Nicole, thirteen, Ryan twelve, and Sarah, eleven. Michael works for the Indiana Department of Transportation in Fort Wayne and Susan is a bookkeeper for Reimschisel Ford. The above families all live in Harrison Township except Jay, age eighty-six, and Mabel, age eighty-four, who now reside in Christian Care Retirement Home on Dustman Road and in April, 1991, they will celebrate their fifty-eighth wedding anniversary.

GROVER

My great-grandfather was William Grover. He and his wife Mary had twelve children: Robert, Frank, John, Willie, Willard, Sylvester, Homer, Oscar, Charles, Jane, Elizabeth and Offie.

Their son, John was my grandfather. He married Adelia McCleery. They had three children: Glenn, Emery and Floyd. Glenn married Lawrence Williamson.

They had six children: DeWitt, Dorris, Nile, Eugene, Eugene, Veda and Frieda.

Emery married Myrtle Taylor. Their children were Howard and Harley.

Floyd married Ruth Brittenham on December 1, 1923. Twin sons, Cloyd and Lloyd, were born to them on November 1, 1924. Lloyd died when he was twelve due to an injury which he received while playing baseball. A daughter, Anna Louise, was born April 1, 1930. She graduated from Liberty Center High School in 1948. She married Ralph Cole on July 25, 1951. They live in Huntsville, Alabama. They had five children: Carol, Robert, Richard, Karen, and a baby who died at birth. Carol died at the age of 32 in 1985. Robert and Richard live in Huntsville. Karen is presently living in Italy.

Cloyd graduated from Liberty Center High School in 1942. On November 18, 1944, he married Marjorie Dennis. From April, 1945, until October, 1946, he served with the U.S. Army in Japan. In 1947 they bought their home in Liberty Center from Kenneth and Hilda Higgins.

Seated L to R: Lorena Best, Lora Grover, Mindy Grover, Brandon Best; Standing L to R: Cathy Best, Dennis Grover, Brian Grover, Cloyd Grover, Darrel Grover, Douglas Grover

On October 31, 1947, their first child, Cathy Marie, was born. She graduated from Liberty Center High School in 1966 and attended Indiana-Purdue University for three years. On July 18, 1981, she married Phillip Best. They have two children, Brandon Eugene, born August 2, 1983, and Lorena Marie, born October 16, 1984. They live in Huntington County.

Dennis Lee was born on January 2, 1950. He graduated from Southern Wells High School in 1967 and from Purdue University with an associate degree in architectural design. He served seven years with the Indiana Air National Guard. He married Rebecca Woodward on April 28, 1973. They have one daughter, Lora Jane, born December 14, 1975. They live in Jackson Township, Wells County.

A third child was born on May 17, 1953, Darrel Lyn graduated from Southern Wells High School in 1971. He attended Indiana Vocational and Technical College where he studied auto mechanics. He married Mary Katherine Lewis on January 21, 1973. They have two children, Melinda Kay, born October 9, 1973, and Brian Douglas, born July 26, 1978. They live in Liberty Center.

On March 30, 1961, Douglas Lon was born. He graduated from Southern Wells High School in 1979 and from Purdue University with a bachelor's degree in electrical engineering technology and a minor in supervision. He married Lona Meyer on June 22, 1985. They live in Bluffton.

Cloyd worked thirty years with Wells County Farm Bureau Co-op and is now employed with Southern Wells Community Schools. He is a member of the Liberty Center United Methodist Church, the Liberty Center Lions Club, and the Bluffton Masonic Lodge.

GROVER-NUSBAUMER

On October 16, 1928, in Jackson Township of Wells County, a son was born to Paul L. and Agnes L. (Ruse) Grover. He was named Herbert Eugene. He was the only child born to this union; however, eighteen years later they adopted a girl, Carol Sue.

Herbert's grandparents were Andrew Frank and Mary Louise (Jones) Grover of Liberty Township, and Amos Lloyd and Mary Catherine (Smith) Ruse of Huntington County.

The family lived in Mt. Zion until 1932. They moved into Warren, where Herbert attended his first two years of school. His father had a can milk route. In 1936, they bought a farm in Huntington County and Paul farmed and continued to haul milk until he sold the route in 1943.

Herbert graduated from West Rockcreek in 1946. He went to work at International Harvester. Later he decided that factory work was not for him, and he bought the milk route which his father had previously owned.

(L-R) Tamara, Marsha, Herbert and Phyllis, Daniel

In the meantime, in a large brick house in Nottingham Township, a sixth child was born to Jesse L. and Ora A. (Sawyer) Nusbaumer. She was born on October 20, 1931, and was named Phyllis Jean. She came into a family of two brothers, Kenneth and Cloid, and three sisters: Berneice, Nilah, and Juanita. Five years later another sister, Donna, was born.

Their grandparents were George and Catherine (Hunsinger) Nusbaumer and Amos W. and Mary E. (Strain) Sawyer.

Phyllis, along with her brothers and sisters, lived in the same home in which she was born and attended Petroleum School all twelve years. She graduated in 1949.

Phyllis worked at Wells County Hospital a short time until she met Herbert. They were married at the Poneto Methodist parsonage on May 20, 1950, and set up housekeeping in Markle. They lived there until 1954, when Herbert sold the milk route and bought the John Tarr farm in Liberty Township. In 1975, they built a new house on the property. Herbert has also been employed at Dana Corp. of Marion, and Mohr Construction and E & B Paving of Huntington.

There were three children born to this union. Daniel Eugene, born May 24, 1952, attended Liberty Center and Southern Wells Schools and graduated in 1970. He was married to Janean L. Brewster of Berne on March 23, 1974. They live near Poneto with their two sons, Robert Daniel, twelve and Terrance Eugene, ten, who attended Southern Wells School.

Marsha Diann was born October 12, 1953. She attended Liberty Center and Southern Wells School, graduating in 1972. She graduated from Parkview Methodist School of Nursing in 1975. While in nurse's training, she met Dennis Dean Powell, of Akron, Indiana. They were married on July 6, 1974. They live in Rockcreek Township, and their two children, Kristi Jo, eleven, and Kevin Dean, eight, both attend Lancaster School.

Tamara Kay came into the world on December 20, 1958. She attended Southern Wells School and graduated in 1977. She graduated from International Business College in 1981. She married Brian K. Mossburg of rural Bluffton on August 5, 1978. They live in Yoder, Indiana and have one child, Angela Reneé, age two.

GULDIN

The first records of Guldins in Wells County, Indiana, were the three children of Jerimiah and Amelia (Lamm) Guldin of Pennsylvania: Thomas, Clara and Irwin. Thomas was a school teacher and married Dee Ormsby of Union Township. They had two children and lived in Bluffton. Clara Guldin was housekeeper for the A.B. Cline family in Bluffton.

Irwin Guldin was a farmer in Huntington County. He married Minnie Kate Sheets. Their son Charles Jennings Guldin was born on March 3, 1897. His mother died when he was six months old and he was raised by his mother's parents, William and Melissa Jane (Thompson) Sheets. He graduated from Rockcreek High School, Huntington County in 1914. He married Anna May Nordyke, daughter of Jacob and Laura (McGahey) Nordyke, who had a farm near Toll Gate, Lancaster Township, which later became the site of the Pretzel Bits Company and a housing development on the north side of State Road 116 just west of State Road 1. They rented a farm near Buckeye, Huntington County, where Max Guldin was born in 1918. In 1919 they rented a farm from Allen B. Kline in Rockcreek Township, Wells County. In 1921 a daughter, Marjorie, was born. Both children started at

Rockcreek Township School, and continued there until 1929 when Charles bought a farm in Union Township, Wells County. The family lived here until the Depression caught them, as it did many others. They then moved back to Rockcreek Township, where both children graduated from Rockcreek High School, Max in 1936 and Marjorie in 1939.

Max married Martha Alice (Peachie) Sturgis, daughter of Dr. Earl Bruce Sturgis D.D.S. Max worked from 1941 to 1947 for the Allen-Wells County Rural Electric Membership Corporation when he became manager of the LaGrange County, R.E.M.C., from which he retired in 1984. They have four sons.

Marjorie married Carl R. Miller and now lives in Holland, Michigan. Marjorie sells real estate and Carl retired from General Electric in Holland. They have four children, two boy and two girls.

Following is a list of ancestors from 1529 to the present compiled by Isaac W. Guldin: 1. Hans Jochin Guldin married Susan Tribolet; 2. Hans Jochin Tribolet Guldin married Anna Maria Koch; 3. Samuel Koch Guldin (founder of the Reformed Church movement in America) married Mary Magdelene Malcarida; 4. Samuel Malcarida Guldin, (patriarch of all Guldins in America.) married Elizabeth Hilsaweek; 5. Daniel Hilsaweek Guldin married Catherine Elizabeth Gelback; 6. John Gelback Guldin married Mary Cranrath; 7. Daniel Cranrath Guldin married Elizabeth Strunk; 8. Amos Strunk Guldin married Magdelene Clauser; 9. Jerimiah Guldin married Amelia Lamb; 10. Irwin Frank Guldin married Minnie Kate Sheets; 11. Charles Jennings Guldin married Anna May Nordyke; 12. Max Irwin Guldin married Martha Alice Sturgis; 13 Marjorie Jean Guldin married Carl R. Miller; 14. Children of Max and Martha; Marjorie and Carl; grandchildren.

HABEGGER-BAHLER

Ben Habegger was born in Adams County on June 22, 1927. Ben is the great-grandson of Peter Habegger (1824-1894), the grandson of Benjamin Habegger (1863-1924) and the son of Edgar (1902-1942) and Savilla Roth Habegger, born in 1905 and still living. Ben married Arlene Bahler on March 20, 1949. Arlene was born in White County on March 17, 1927, to Jacob Bahler Jr. and Emma Steffen Bahler, both deceased. Their ancestors were predominantly Swiss, although Grandpa Roth was French.

Ben and Arlene moved to Wells County in 1957 from White County where they had lived for seven years. They purchased a farm west of Bluffton on Corning Road. Besides farming, Ben worked for Gerber Dairy a number of years and later at Mix Mill for nearly twenty-two years. He is now retired, and they live at 425 South Main, the former Baptist Church parsonage.

They raised their family in Liberty Township and their children all graduated from Souther Wells High School. They all reside in Wells County, except Martha, who lives in nearby Adams County.

Samuel J., born in White County, February 10, 1951, a graduate of Purdue University, worked as an engineer at Corning Glass for ten years. Since then he established Habegger Photography. He married Darlene Neuenschwander and they have three children: Jason, sixteen; Jill, fifteen; and Jeni, thirteen.

Rosemary, born in White County on May 22, 1952, married Rodney Mounsey. She is presently employed by Habegger Photography. Rod farms and is night-foreman at Moormans Manufacturing. They have four children: Russell, seventeen; Robin, fifteen; Ryan, thirteen and Rebekeh, ten.

L to R: Jane H., Ted H., Rosemary Mounsey, Rod M., Sam H., Ben H., Darlene H., Teresa H., Tim H., Ruby Gerber, Arlene H., Doug G., Keith Stoller, Martha S.

Ruby K., born in White County June 30, 1953, married Douglas Gerber. Doug is currently custodian of our country church. They own the Health Food Emporium in Huntington, which Ruby manages. They have five children: Molly, thirteen; Joseph, twelve; Abby, eleven; William, nine and Carson, six. Rita, born in White County, July 30, 1955, died February 3, 1957. She had Downs Syndrome.

Ted E., born in Wells County, June 8, 1958, married (Mary) Jane Martin. They own and operate Country Cabinets, a cabinet shop located on State Road 218, west of Poneto. Ted also farms our ground. They have three children: Leah, twelve; Elizabeth, ten; and Abraham, nine.

Martha, born in Wells County on August 1, 1959, married Keith Stoller, Adams County. She is a graduate of Indiana University, with a degree in nursing. Since graduation, she has been employed by Caylor-Nickel. He is a farmer and they have two children: Isaac, three and Emma, twenty-two months.

Tillman (Tim), born in Wells County on December 23, 1962, married Teresa Baughman. He is employed by Siemens. He is trained to install and repair CAT scanners in the northeastern Indiana region. They own our farm building, and Teresa mostly manages the 12,000-bird laying flock. They have three children: Benjamin, four; Sara, two; and Andrew, new-born.

Ben has a Mennonite background and Arlene is Apostolic Christian. Their family has been affiliated with the Apostolic Christian Church for many years.

HABIG

Janet Elizabeth Grimm was born on March 11, 1932, to Gerald Bryan and Cecile Bernice Nusbaumer. Janet had one brother Roderick and two sisters Beverlyee and Marianna. Janet was born at home and grew up on the family's farm at 0387 W 1100 S, Keystone, Indiana.

Janet has seen many changes in the world. Electricity came to their home in 1939, radio in 1940, indoor restroom facilities in 1943, and her dad's first tractor was a John Deere B.

Janet graduated from the Chester Center High School in 1950 with a class of eighteen students. Coca Cola cost five cents.

In 1960, Janet married Lewis John Habig, son of Harvey and Willa Habig. Lewis has one brother Jim and two sisters Donna and Ellen. Janet and Lewis had six children: Shirley Ann in December 1951; Kenneth Reed in July 1953, David Brian in June 1955, Mary Louise in March 1956, Penelope Lynn in September, 1957, and Jeffrey Lewis in June 1960. They set up housekeeping in Bluffton and then St. Petersburg, Florida.

In 1966, Janet moved her children to 1125, S. Meridian road, Keystone, Indiana, which was her grandfather's farm. Her parents lived just around the mile.

My name is Mary and Janet is my mother. The old farm house was heated by wood when we first moved in. Imagine a woman five foot three, one hundred ten pounds taking six children age six to thirteen to the woods with a little red wagon and cross cut saw for wood. This was an adventure for us children, but I'm sure mom didn't think so. The heating was later converted to oil.

Mom fried delicious rabbit dinners from those raised by the boys. A big garden provided vegetables all year long. This supplemented her income from a job at Sheller-Globe in Montpelier, Indiana. Summer Sunday afternoons were spent playing baseball in the barnyard and kite flying in the fall. In the winter we ice skated on the neighbors farm pond one-fourth mile south of us. Mom would pick us up in the car, knowing we would be too cold to walk home. Everyone had a new outfit for Easter Sunday

The Habig Family

and Egg Hunt was tradition. Everything was a family affair. Our grandparents took us to Sunday school at the Keystone Methodist Church. The boys farmed for Uncle Roderick and Aunt Naomi. Our Southern Wells School bus driver was Ben Soper and our mail man was Cliff Morrison. These people and many more made a big difference in our lives and to you we say thanks.

Shirley married Michael Meyer of Bluffton and now lives in Hoagland, Indiana with three children: M. Troy, sixteen; Michelle, fourteen; and Nicholas, twelve.

Kenneth married Nancy Bennett of Saint Petersburgh, Florida where they live with two children: Heather, thirteen and Kyle, ten.

David married Janalyn Nottingham of Union City, Ohio, and now lives in Indianapolis with two children: Joseph, three and Johnathan, one.

Mary married Jon Holloway of Poneto, Indiana and lives in Tocsin, Indiana with one son, Benjamin Heath, fourteen.

Penelope married Lee Gearheart of Keystone and lives in Henderson, Texas with three children: Logan, ten; Gabriel, eight and Paige, six.

Jeffrey married Stephanie Helms of McNatt, Indiana and lives in Petroleum, Indiana with two children: Jennifer, ten and Ryan, four.

In 1976, Mom married Gerald Grimm of Petroleum. Janet now has five step-children and their families that she considers her own. They set up housekeeping in 6858 S. 200 E. Bluffton, Indiana, where mother still lives. Pete died in September 1988. What I remember the most is his easy smile, his love for Indiana University Basketball, his love for family, and his insistence on a neat yard. And I appreciate his being a grandfather to our children.

But to my mother I say, thank you and we all love you. *(Mary Louise)*

WILLIAM E. HAIFLEY FAMILY

The William E. Haifley ancestors: John Hafflich (the original spelling), his wife Ann, and son Jacob, from the Palatine region of Germany, settled in York County, Pennsylvania, about 1771.

Jacob served in the Northumgerland Militia under Captain Michael Motez, serving in the General Continental Army during the Revolutionary War. About the year 1800, their son, Philip, and his wife, Hanna, moved to Wells County, Indiana and settled near Uniondale. He had changed the spelling of his name to "Haflich."

The German people from this region of Pennsylvania were know as Pennsylvania Dutch. Farming, hard work, and honesty made them good citizens, and they soon became well-respected residents in Wells County.

Two generations of Haflichs followed as farmers in the Uniondale area.

Philip's son, Isaac Haflich, his wife, Catherine, and family (1867).

Isaac's son, William A. Haflich, and his wife, Sarah, had a large family. William lived to be ninety-two years old (1924). All the children remained farmers except one. Eli C. Haifley broke ranks, moved to Bluffton, Indiana, and became a barber. He married Emma Gettle, and they were blessed with nine children: Ralph, Hervert, Elsie, Mary, Harry, and Lloyd. Three other daughters died as children. Eli and family then moved to Sturgis, Michigan, soon after World War I and returned to farming. They lived there for the remainder of their lives (1942). Eli changed the spelling to "Haifley."

The oldest son, Ralph, remained in the Bluffton area as he had entered his own business, "Haifley Construction Company." He had one of the first farm tile ditching machines, and was well-known and respected through-out Wells County.

Ralph married Cora B. Frauhiger in 1911, and they were blessed with four children: Irene, Justine, William, and Erma June. The Ralph Haifley home was in villa North near Bluffton, Indiana, and remained so until Cora's death in 1983. She was ninety-four years old, living twenty years beyond her husband, Ralph.

The great depression ended the Haifley Construction Company in 1929. During 1933, the Haifley family had started the Bluffton Custom Cannery. This business continued to be run as a family business until 1955.

William E. Haifley married Eunice E. Dilley Janaury 1, 1939. William left the canning business for a position with the General Electric Company, at Fort Wayne, Indiana. He later joined the army during World War II and served in the 126th Battallion until the end of the war. There were two daughters then, Heather, five years and Linda, two months. Thomas came along after the war in March, 1950. After returning from the war, William accepted a management position with an emerging company, Franklin Electric. He played a key roll in the early development as well as its later multi-plant world expansion until his retirement in 1979. His position in the last fifteen years was manager of Advance Manufacturing Engineering. His talents continued to be required by the company as he has continued to serve in a consulting capacity to this day.

The Haifley home is on the River Road one-quarter mile east of Bluffton on the "Banks of the Wabash." Eunice and William are lifelong members of the First Methodist Church, and belong to several community organizations. They have enjoyed several sports and hobbies through-out their lifetime. Eunice is best known as an Indiana artist and William was known in his early years as one of the first archers in Wells County. There were several articles published in the *Outdoor Indiana*, during the 1930's, of his hunting skills and expertise in making the archery equipment. Since retirement, William has taken up the hobby of creating authentic wood carvings of birds, and Eunice makes the birds come to life with her painting.

Eunice and William have nine grandchildren and five great-grandchildren. The oldest daughter, Heather L. Meisch, has three children. Kurtis V. Kaufman and his wife, Janene. They have two sons, Von and Conrad. Kurt is a Navy man with rank of Ensign. Heather and her husband, Thomas Meisch live in Bluffton and she owns and operates the Colonial Hair Care Salon.

Heather's oldest daughter, Karla Hemminger and husband, Don, have four children: Gretta, Samuel, Elijah, and Jesse. They live in Coldwater, Michigan. Heather's youngest daughter, Linda, is still in school.

William and Eunice's second daughter, Linda, and her husband, William Fronk, have one daughter, Katherine, six years old, and two sons, Christopher and William Jr., both adults. Linda is a graduate of Butler University, and has her own consulting business in Kansas City, Missouri.

Thomas D., the youngest Haifley child, has three children: Kyra and Paul (twins) five and one-half years old and Mark who is sixteen months. Thomas is a Clinical Psychologist. He lives and practices in Greensboro, North Carolina. He is a graduate of Indiana University.

The Haifley family is proud of our past heritage. We love our country, city, and land. Above all, we cherish and appreciate our freedoms of religion and speech that we inherited from our forefathers. We pledge to defend them as they have so courageously done.

HAFLICH

Ordeleden Donald Haflich was born November 26, 1903, on a farm west of Bluffton in Rockcreek Township, Wells County to Frank E. (1875-1956) and Bessie Z. (Bender) Haflich (1878-1972). He was the youngest of two sons, the older son being L. Vaughn Haflich (1900-1982). They moved to Liberty Township where "O.D.," as he was known from then on, attended Smokey Row Grade School on what is now Corning Road, and graduated from Liberty Center High School in 1921. As there were no school buses then, he and a friend took turns driving their horse and buggy to school.

As a young man, he worked for H.C. Arnold Seed Company for fifteen dollars a week and later in 1923 at the F.F. Engler Department Store, where Penney's is now located. It was in this store he learned his life's trade of shoe fitting. In the spring of 1927, he started work at L.R. Leopards, later known as Miller-Jones Shoe Store.

Mr. and Mrs. O.D. Haflich

In 1921, he met a young lady from Bluffton, Marjorie I. Little. She was the only child of John A. (1869-1949) and Linnie E. (Hupp) Little (1873-1966), born on May 16, 1904, in Warren, Indiana. She graduated from Bluffton High School in 1921 and worked for many years at the People Store in Bluffton. She also worked beside O.D. in the family business. Her death was in 1985.

On June 12, 1922, Marjorie and O.D. eloped to Hillsdale, Michigan, to be married. That was the custom with many young people then. Six years later on October 16, 1928, they had a daughter, Evelyn Deane, born at the Wells County Hospital. Evelyn's grandfather, Frank Haflich, was on the hospital board at the time. Evelyn went to Poplar Grove School for three years, then to Bluffton, and graduated from high school there in 1946. Late in 1928, O.D. moved his family to Fort Wayne where O.D. worked in the shoe department at Wolf and Dessauer Department Store.

Three years later, in 1931, O.D. and his family moved back to Bluffton and lived with his parents on a farm east of Bluffton. In September 1939, O.D. was able to start his own business, a family shoe store, in a room which was formerly the Vogue Hat Shop. He has remained there in that business with the help of his son-in-law, R. Dale Morrissey. O.D.'s daughter and Dale were married on February 14, 1952, in Saint Joseph's Catholic Church, Bluffton. They have four children, two girls and two boys.

O.D. and Dale were business partners in Bluffton and also opened a family shoe store in Decatur in 1950.

O.D. has four grandchildren: Nancy E., 1956; Janet M. 1958; Michael D., 1961; Patrick D., 1962. All graduated from Adams Central High School in Adams County, and Nancy and Janet graduated from Ball State University. Three of his grandchildren have come full circle, moving back to Bluffton to continue in the family business. Patrick remains in Decatur in the business there. Janet is married to Douglas A. Lehman, and they have two sons, Nathaniel and Gregory. Michael is married to Jill A. Flaugher, and they have two children, Nicole and Matthew, making O.D. a great-grandfather and also one of Bluffton's oldest businessmen still in business today.

HAILFLICH FAMILY

Our great-great-great-grandparents, Philip and Hannah (Shadle) Haflich, purchased land in Rockcreek Township in 1848. Philip was born in 1778, in Pennsylvania, the second child of Jacob and Margaret Haflich. Jacob, our great-great-great-grandfather, was a private in the Northumberland County Rangers of Pennsylvania during the American Revolution.

Our great-great-grandfather Isaac, born in 1811, was the second son of Philip and Hannah. Isaac and his wife, Catherine (Pletcher), came to Rockcreek Township in 1848, where Isaac was a prosperous farmer and able hunter. Isaac died in 1867, and his wife in 1890.

Our great-grandfather John was born in 1851, the youngest child of Isaac and Catherine's twelve children. He married Elizabeth Jane Ditzler in 1870.

The Jesse Haiflich Family in 1962
Back Row L to R: Lucile (Haiflich) Swaim, Dallas Haiflich, Norman Haiflich, John Haiflich, Doris (Haiflich) Kummer. Front Row L to R: Jennie (Haiflich) Kraft, Jesse Haflich (father), Edith M. (Wiser) Haiflich (mother), Rosalie (Haiflich) Hamilton

After great-grandmother Elizabeth's death in 1935, great grandfather reminisced to a granddaughter that their courtship started at a "Husking Bee." He shucked a red ear of corn and as was the custom, won the privilege of kissing the girl of his choice, he chose Elizabeth, who he felt was the prettiest girl at the "Bee." Both John and Elizabeth chose to be buried at Prospect Cemetery, rather that Horeb, like their parents and grandparents, so the survivor could walk to the grave of their spouse. John died in 1936.

Born in 1871, our grandfather, William E. Haiflich, was the first child of John and Elizabeth. In 1890, he married Ora Elsa Crismore, daughter of William and Lettitia (Longshore) Crismore. Elsa died in 1900. Grandfather subsequently married Mary Highlen and lived in Ashtabula County, Ohio, before returning to Union Township. Grandfather died in 1936, and he and Elsa are buried in Horeb Cemetery. Grandfather was a farmer and raised Newfoundland dogs.

Our father, Jesse Haiflich, born March 13, 1893, was the oldest son of William E. and Ora Elsa. He met and married Edith M. Wiser while living in Ashtabula County, Ohio. In 1923, they returned to Indiana with their children: Norman, Lucile, Dallas, and Doris, and settled in Huntington County where John, Rosalie, and Jennie were born. In 1935, we moved to Wells County, where dad worked several years as a telephone lineman for the Ossian, Uniondale, and Zanesville exchanges. In later years, he was an auto mechanic. Mom was a homemaker. Dad passed away in 1976 and Mom died in 1987. Both are buried in Horeb Cemetery.

Jesse and Edith had twenty grandchildren, thirty-two great-grandchildren, and two great-great-grandchildren. Of Mom and Dad's children and grandchildren, several still reside in Wells County. Doris Kummer (Mrs. Kenneth), Lucile Swaim (Mrs. James), Norman, and Louise (Guinn) Haiflich, who moved from Maryland in 1990. Susan Kummer, daughter of Kenneth and Doris, Orville, son of Dallas and Ruth (Richey) Haiflich, resides with his wife Laura (Jessen) and their children, Jodie, David, Andrew, Benjamin, Samuel, and Margaret in Jefferson Township. Dallas passed away in 1982. John and Marybell (Brown) Haiflich, and Jennnie (Mrs. Gerald) Krafft reside in DeKalb County, Indiana. Rosalie Hamilton (Mrs. R.W.) resides in Fort Wayne, Indiana. *(Rosalie E. Hamilton)*

HAFLICH

In Wells County there resided several Haflich families who all spelled the family name several different ways. This is the history of Samuel A. Haflich, born January 23, 1850 in Wells County. He was the son of Jacob Haflich, born in 1816, and Anna Hoover Haflich, born in 1821. They migrated to Wells County from Lewisburg, Pennsylvania, and Virginia. This Samuel A. Haflich married Sarah D. Lesh in 1874. She was the daughter of Jacob Lesh and Margaret Erhart Lesh. The Lesh family was rather large, six daughters and two sons, I believe.

Being a granddaughter of Sam and Sarah, I will try to compile some of their history as accurately as I can.

Their homeplace was in Rockcreek Township. They lived in a large two-story brick home with a big bank barn. Their home was close to the Wabash River and from their yard the Horeb Church and Cemetery could be seen. This house is still being lived in today and is in excellent condition. The walla are fifteen inches thick masonary. The covered bridge could almost be seen from their farm. No longer does the Horeb Church exist; at the time when the Reservoir was put in (around 1960), the land was taken over by the government. The church was torn down and not replaced. The cemeterey was moved about four miles to the intersection of 224 and 303. This was a Lutheran Church who's minister at one time was the father of Lloyd C. Douglas, author of *The Robe*. This church was a great part of the Haflich family.

Sam and Sarah had six children. Their oldest child, Clara, died early in childhood. The other children are as follows: Jacob, who taught at a one-room schoolhouse about one and one-half miles from the Haflich home, Jacob married Dora Eichorn who died shortly after the birth of their only child Ruth Haflich McClure. The second son was William (Fred), who married Mary Jane Daugherty. They had two children, Richard and Jane. the third son was Clifford, who married Winnie McAfee. Clifford and Winnie had a daughter Lucille Haflich Bobay. The fourth son was Curtis, who married Zoa Gaskill. They had two duaghters and two sons, Phyllis, Robert, JoAnne, and Gene. The second Haflich daughter, Cressie, married Geogre Clifford Caley and had two daughter and two sons, Jaunice, William (Bill), Samuel, Barbara, and Don Clifford.

The Haflich children all attended the one-room schoolhouse that was near their home. Many winter mornings while walking to school they would walk across rail fences that were covered by drifted snow. In the evenings they would ice skate on the Wabash River.

Their grandmother, Margaret Lesh, lived close by. The children called her "Grosmommy," and when she wanted to converse with the adults she would speak in Pennsylvania Dutch if it was not to be heard by little ears.

The covered bridge was also a great part of the community. It was the only way to cross the Wabash river for quite some distance. What stories that bridge could tell. Around 1957 the covered bridge was maliciously destroyed by fire.

Sam and Sarah moved from their farm to Markle in 1929 to live with their granddaughter Ruth. They had raised Ruth from infancy. Samuel died in 1931 and Sarah died in 1942.

Today there are only two Haflich grandsons living, Gene (Indianapolis) and Richard (Sarasota, Florida). Of these two grandsons, there are five great-grandsons carrying on the Haflich name.

JOHN HAIFLICH FAMILY

Spelling of the Haiflich name has caused much confusion in the effort to find ancestors. Some of the spellings are Haffelee, Haffley, Haifley, Hafflick, Haflich, Hoeflich, Hefleg, Hafleigh, Heffling, Hayslick. The variations in Wells County are Haiflich, Haflich, Haifley.

November 2, 1848, Philip Haflich of Richland County, Ohio, recorded in the clerk's office of Wells County, the purchase of one hundred eight acres along the Wabash River in Rockcreek Township. This marked the arrival of the Haflich family to Wells County. Over the next three years, sons Isaac, Jacob, and Samuel purchased farms near their father, and moved their families west. The 1860 census lists all as farmers, with several children in each household.

Amazingly, Philip (born November 28, 1779) and his wife Hanna (Shadle) (born July 24, 1782) were in their late 60's when they packed their belongings and moved to the newly opened Indian Territory of northeastern Indiana. Being of good stock, they both lived to celebrate a few birthdays beyond their eightieth years.

Philip's father Jacob Hafflick served in the American Revolution according to *Snyder County Pioneers* by Charles Fisher, page 35. Jacob's father, John Carl Haffelee, arrived in Philadelphia, Pennsylvania, October 31, 1737, on the ship *William*.

Isaac (born July 11, 1807) and Catherine (Pletcher) (born January 9, 1810) purchased a farm adjoining his father's land in May, 1850. It was here the last of twelve children was born. His name was John, and he was the first Hoosier-born Haiflich.

John (born February 6, 1851) married Elizabeth Ditzler (January 16, 1850) May 1, 1870, and lived on a farm one-mile south of Uniondale and the first place east. There they raised their four children, William E., George, Clare, and Harley A. George moved his family to Delaware, Oklahoma, to work in the oil fields. The initial after William's name was important. During the first quarter of this century, there were three William Haiflichs on R.R. 1, Uniondale.

William E. (born August 2, 1871) married Orie Elsie Crismore (born 1873) December 29, 1890. To this union was born four sons: Ray, Jess, John H., and Charles E. Tragedy struck this family twice. Twins, Dellie Irene and Nellie Lore, were born in 1897 and lived two weeks and four weeks respectively, taken by a flu epidemic that swept the community that year. Shortly after the birth of Charles, Orie passed away, leaving William with four small boys to raise. Mary Highland married William January 11, 1902, and helped raise the family and added two more, Freda and Ivan Howard.

John (born October 11, 1896) married Mayretha Beaber (born May 25, 1900) May 14, 1919. To this union was born Laura May, Richard E., and Thomas E. From 1933 to 1954, John supported his family by farming different farms in Union and Jefferson Townships. He was also one of the first hybrid seed corn dealers in the county, starting in the late 1940's. After moving to Uniondale in 1954, John served several terms on the Uniondale Town Board.

Seated: Mr. and Mrs. John Haiflich. Standing: George Haiflich, William Haiflich, Girl is Clara Haiflich, Tucker and smaller boy is Harley Haiflich of Uniondale, Indiana

Most deceased Haiflichs are buried in the Horeb Cemetery which was relocated to its present site two miles west of Uniondale on U.S. 224. Originally located on the banks of the Wabash River, it was moved in 1971 because of constructing the Huntington Reservoir. The Horeb Lutheran Church was started in 1860 on land donated by Samuel Haflich, and next to the church was a cemetery for members of the community and congregation.

Laura May (born April 23, 1920) married David McAfee (February 18, 1917) March 7, 1942. They reside on their farm in Rockcreek Township. David is a retired farmer and Laura May is a retired beautician.

Richard E. (born August 5, 1922) married Dorma Mae Hoopingarner (born April 10, 1925) March 10, 1945 and they presently reside at 228 North Bond Street, Bluffton. Thomas E. (born August 9, 1927) married Nancy Lee Numbers (born September 18, 1932) April 6, 1949. Currently Tom and Nancy reside in Hershey, Pennsylvania, where both are employed with the Hershey Foundation.

From 1950 to 1972, Richard and Thomas farmed together in Liberty Township on the Morris Farm. During the early 1960's, they developed one of the largest hog operations in Wells County, marketing two thousand head of fat hogs annually. Because of management decisions by the landowner, the operation ceased and both men found other employment. For approximately nineteen years, Richard worked at Graden's Tire in Bluffton until his retirement in 1987. While there he was known to many in the community as Farmer Dick.

To David and Laura may McAfee were born three girls: Mona Kay (deceased), JoAnn and Bonnie. JoAnn (born November 4, 1948) married Mark Click (January 31, 1945) December, 1969. They have three children Mark David (born November 28, 1970), Janna Michelle and Scott Matthew (born July 2, 1973). They reside in Culver, Indiana where Mark is an instructor at the Culver Academy. JoAnn is employed at the Academy, also.

Bonnie (born September 25, 1951) married Monte Fisher (born April 12, 1950) June 18, 1972. They have two daughters: Krista (born July 9, 1979) and Kami (born June 28, 1982). They live in Rockcreek Township. Monte is a deputy in the Wells County Sheriff's Department and Bonnie works at the Old-First National Bank.

To Richard E. and Dorma Haiflich were born two children, Stevan R. and Karen Sue. Stevan R. (born July 13, 1948) married Ruby O'Donnell (born October 25, 1942) December 18, 1977, and lives at Warren, Indiana where Stevan is senior pastor of the Huntington County South Parish. Ruby works at Norwood Nursing Center, Huntington, Indiana, as activities director. They have four children: Ramona Rudus (born April 29, 1964), David O'Donnell (born May 4, 1965), August 3, 1973, and Andrew (born February 15, 1975).

Karen Sue Reinhard lives at 4921 E. S.R. 124 with her son, Shawn. Karen is the secretary at Monarch Systems, Ossian. She is the cog that keeps the big wheels turning.

To Thomas E. and Nancy Haiflich were born two children, Mickey and Vickie. Mickey (born October 10, 1949) passed away March 17, 1963. Vickie (born August 29, 1951) married Norman Miller (born November 18, 1950) November 27, 1971, and lives in Hershey, Pennsylvania with their three: Benjamin (born may 28, 1975) Jon (born July 10, 1977), and Kimberly (born February 23, 1980). Norman is the manager of the Hershey Farms and Vickie teaches in the public schools.

Haiflichs with their roots in Wells County, literally span the nation from California to the nation's capitol. From Texas to Indiana, there are many representing the county well. However, none of the clan has been venturous enough to brave the cold north of Wisconsin, Minnesota, and similar environs.

DAVID AND MARJORIE HAINES

Dave is the oldest son of Roy and Darnella (Reed) Haines of Sabina, Ohio. He is a Vietnam War veteran, a graduate of Oklahoma Military Academy and Ohio State University, and is employed as a Regional Agronomist with DeKalb Plant Genetics. Dave is also a Realtor with McBride Realty and a member of the Optimist Club.

Marge is the oldest of six children of Alvin and Alma (Nieberding) Kaup of Fort Recovery, Ohio. She attended Wright State University and Ohio State University and is employed as a legal secretary with the firm of Dale, Gordon and Huffman. Marge is currently president of the Alpha Eta Chapter of Psi Iota Xi Sorority and secretary of the Wells County Republican Women. She is also a member of the Lancaster Township Board.

Dave and Marge Haines, Joe, Abby, Valerie, and Samantha

Between them there are six children: Randy and Renee, from Dave's previous marriage; Joseph Eley, from Marge's previous marriage; and Abigail, six; Valerie, five; and Samantha, two, all born of Dave and Marge. Randy is a 1987 Norwell High School graduate and is an Arizona State Highway Trooper, stationed in Yuma, Arizona. Joe is in the sixth grade at Norwell Middle School. Abby attends Lancaster Elementary School and Valerie attends the Presbyterian Church Nursery School. Samantha spends her days at home with the baby sitter. The family attends the First United Methodist Church in Bluffton.

Dave and Marge moved to Bluffton, Indiana, in February, 1984, and reside at 222 Briarcrest Place in the Willowbrook Addition. As a family, they enjoy weekends boating at the many Indiana lakes.

HALE-MARKLEY-EDINGTON

The most noted ancestor that I find was my great-grandfather, Bowen Hale. He was born in Kentucky on July 4, 1801. His father was John Hale, the son of James Hale, a native of England, who immigrated to America and located in Maryland. Bowen Hale settled in Wells County in the year 1835 and at that time only about twelve white families lived in the county. Mr. Hale entered forty acres of land near Murray and with the help of one of the earliest settlers, Henry Miller, soon had a comfortable cabin. Bowen Hale was elected the first auditor, clerk, recorder in Wells County and served a total of twenty years as clerk in the county. He also held the office of postmaster and filled the office of judge for three years. In the the year 1837, Wells County was formed.

In 1840, Bowen Hale married Mary Ann Deam, my great-grandmother, and they had eight children. Jane Hale, my grandmother and Bowen's daughter, married Daniel F. Markley, my grandfather and a son of Gabriel Markley, my great-grandfather. Gabriel had entered Wells County when only four families resided in the east part of the county in 1835 and settled east of Bluffton on seventy-two acres of land near the present State Park. He owned eleven hundred acres of land in Wells County later in his life.

Daniel Markley and Jane Hale had eleven children, and the home farm was the site of the present Grace Baptist Church.

My mother, Grace Markley, born September 29, 1889, married my father, Coulson Edington, in 1905 and raised six sons in the city of Bluffton. Coulson Edington's fathers was John Edington born in 1833 and immigrated to America from Scotland. He married Sara Lash in 1866.

Eugene Edington Family
Max, Gene, Phebe, Tom, Ned, Jack, Jo Ann, Rachel, Grace, Ben, Donovan, Kim, Libby, Sally, Vickie

Franklin Edington, born in 1906, married Betty Dunning. Larry, Kent, David, and John were also part of this family. Dick Edington, the oldest son, married Connie Pursley and lives in Harrison Township.

Paul Edington married Helen Young and their two daughters, Sibyl and Sue, grew up in the Frankfort area.

Coulson Edington, Jr., married Betty Mosure and they lived in Bluffton most of their years and now live in Florida.

William Edington married Betty Deihl and worked with Bell Telephone during his lifetime. They had two daughter, Diane and Carol.

James Edington married Mary Leitz and is retired from Food Marketing in Fort Wayne. They have one daughter, Katie, and three sons: Tim, Mike and Chris.

Eugene Edington married Phebe Rogers and four sons were born to this marriage. Jack Edington is an electrical engineer with Magnavox. He married Vickie Haffner of Bluffton. They have a son, Donovan, age five, and a daughter, Gena, age one, and lives in Harrison Township. Tom Edington is principal of Salamonie School in Huntington County. He has two daughters, Grace and Rachel in Bluffton. Ned Edington is a Federal probation officer in Fort Wayne. He married Sally Shanahan and they have two children: Benjamin, age nine; and Elizabeth, six. Max Edington married JoAnn Meehan, lives in Houston, Texas, and works for a French oil company. They have a daughter Kimberly who is four

HALL

George S. Hall was the eldest son in a family of eight children, six sons and two daughters. Joining him were five brothers, Charles, David, James, Oliver and Theodore, as well as two sisters, Kate (Hall) Way and Martha (Hall) Sowards. George was born in Cumberland County, New Jersey on November 6, 1849.

In 1855, he moved with his parents, Robert and Emily Hall, to Wells County, Indiana and continued there as a resident. In 1871, he married Nancy Ann Gilland. To this union were born two sons, John G. and William I. Hall.

George was affiliated with the old Salem U.B. Society. Then in 1875, the Emmaus M.E. Church was instituted and he became the first member, along with William Sowards. They remained members until the church was destroyed by fire in 1927. At that time, because many rural churches were being discontinued, it was thought best to not rebuild Emmaus. Though the church was not rebuilt, the surrounding area retained the name "Emmaus Neighborhood" indefinitely. George lived through the entire history of the church, fifty-two years, making it a rather unique experience. George and William then joined the M.E. Church in Ossian, Indiana.

My grandfather, George, and my father, William (known to his neighbors and friends as Bill), built a house on an eighty acre farm, two and five-tenths miles southeast of Ossian, where my grandparents lived until my grandfather, George, died in 1939. My father then bought the family farm and lived there the rest of his life.

L to R: Ruth (Culter) Hall, Gail Hall, Lucille (hall) Stout, Howard Stout, November 30, 1981

William married Flora Wilson on April 30, 1903. She bore their son, Irvin C. Hall. After graduating from Tocsin High School, Irvin moved to Toledo, Ohio, where he lived until his death on July 14, 1962. Flora died March 10, 1908.

On September 30, 1911, William married Hazel Fern Orr, daughter of J. and Martha Orr of Uniondale, Indiana. William and Fern had a son, Gail, and a daughter, Lucille. Gail married Ruth Cutler, also of Ossian, and moved to Britton, Michigan, where they worked and lived until Gail died on July 20, 1989. Ruth continues to live in Britton.

Gail and Ruth had three children: Beverly Ann, Brenda and Douglas. Beverly Ann was killed while crossing the street by her school in 1946. She was eight years old at the time of her death. Brenda lives in nearby Tecumseh, Michigan, and Douglas lives in Kalamazoo, Michigan.

Lucille married Howard Stout in Fort Wayne, Indiana, on November 30, 1931. We had two sons, Tom Howard, of Goshen, Indiana (born June 3, 1933), and Carlyn Neil (born June 28, 1940), who lived only twenty-eight hours. My husband, Howard, and I moved to Goshen, Indiana, in 1948, where we have lived and retired.

My brother Gail and I went to Tocsin School through the eighth grade. We were then transferred to Ossian High School. My mother, Fern, died April 16, 1951, and my father, William, died December 22, 1960.

My hobbies are keeping scrapbooks and photo albums. I have wedding and anniversary pictures of my school friends and may other people I knew in and around Ossian and Tocsin, as throughout all my single life I lived in Wells County.

I get many of my pictures from the *Ossian Journal*, which I have received for several years. *Submitted by Lucille (Hall) Stout.*

DANIELLE MICHELLE HALL

It was Good Friday, March 24, 1989, when Danielle Michelle Hall was born here in Bluffton. She is the great-granddaughter of Margaret L. Cossairt/Drabenstot (1919-1987). Born in Whitata, Kansas, Margaret was a life-long resident of Wells County. Danielle is the first born daughter of Daniel J. Hall (1961) and Suzanne Michelle Osborn Hall (1970). Danielle's parents were married March 26, 1988, in Copperass Cove near Fort Hood, Texas. Sergeant Hall was stationed at Fort Hood in the U.S. Army. Upon completion of his eight-year obligation to the military, he and Suzanne returned to Bluffton to reside.

Margaret Drabenstot

Danielle's mother, Suzanne, is the youngest daughter of Richard E. (1933) and M. Jean (Drabenstot) Osborn (1948). Suzanne has one brother, who is Danielle's uncle here in Wells County, Scott Osborn (1968).

Scott had performed on stage as a youth with the Indianapolis Junior Civic Theater. Since various family members had flirted with a performing career in the past, this inspired Danielle's grandmother, Jean Osborn to encourage Danielle's entrance into the Wells County 4-H fair baby contest at age four months. Danielle was carried to victory atop a tropical carriage complete with palm tree...a first for Bluffton. A true showman, Danielle knows how to smile and laugh.

Mrs. Osborn owns a downtown Bluffton shop, Bluffton Basket Company/Classy Wrap at 116 N. Main, a business she started in light of her granddaughters first place win at the 4-H fair. She is noted to say (with humor) that she is training her young granddaughter to be a clown, hoping to bring her up in a newly-formed family business. Joining in the mentor spirit, Grandpa Richard Osborn was seen sweeping the street attired in a clown suit at the shop's grand opening. Danielle continues to be entered in clown contests, and she wins.

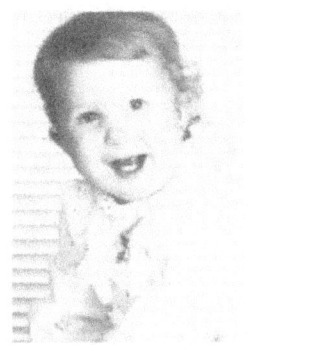

Danielle M. Hall

A sense of humor coupled with family business is not foreign to Danielle's family. Grandpa Richard, with father Marion, ran the family business, Osborn Plumbing at 627 W. Wiley, until Marion's death. Marion was also known for his civic service as Bluffton Fire Department Chief. Danielle's great aunt, Peggy Jo Drabenstot/Thompson, with her husband Charles and sons Kent and Kris, operates Fairway Floor Covering on Main Street, and son Kelly operates Carpet Care.

This sense of Wells County entrepreneurship stems back to Danielle's great-grandfather, Milo C. "Mike" (1915-1970) and Margaret L. Drabenstot. Born in Huntington, Mike came to Wells County as a youth and resided with John and Winnie Graham as a farm hand. Mike would gladly share the funny capers of youth with stories about his friends, Tom Graham and Ver Ash. these men were truly hard workers with a good sense of humor through the depression and hard times of the thirties. Mike became a mechanic at the Glen Marsh Ford dealership on West Washington Street. Margaret was a secretary for Smith Trucking Company. Mike and Margaret married and lived on West Market Street. They moved with daughters, Peggy Joe and Jean, to a farm on Lancaster Road, one and a half miles west of Lancaster School. Mike started his own business in the Falk Building on Main Street (presently occupied by Country Squire Florist).

Then in 1954, Mike and Margaret bought the farm and house at 1025 W. Lancaster. It was there that Mike started and operated the Bluffton Auto Body Shop until his sudden death in 1970. Margaret worked at the Dutch Mill Restaurant for sixteen years. Mike's business leaned heavily toward what was then a male dominated profession, but he loved his little girls. Peggy Jo was the little lady and Jean was the creative twirling tomboy. Peggy had three boys and Jean had a son and then came Mike's first granddaughter Suzanne. Mike died when she was only nine months old. Suzanne's daughter Danielle would have been the apple of her great-grandparents' eyes. Danielle's facial features, small physical features, largely favor those of her great-grandmother Margaret and the humor of great-grandpa Mike is starting to bud.

If the ability to laugh is inherited, Danielle Michelle Hall will surely be a jolly, hard working, struggling entrepreneur. At best she will be a clown in her own right.

HAMILTON

Ellis Hamilton (born October 25, 1854, died May 29, 1925) came from Ohio to Wells County and married Lavine Elizabeth Harter (born May 31, 1855, died June 30, 1931) on May 6, 1876. They had ten children: Bertha Myrtle (born May 31, 1883, died July 11, 1883); Armintha (born March 13, 1878, died June 20, 1965); Joseph Emery (born October 21, 1879, died June 30, 1953); Lennie Irene (born September 15, 1881, died November 30, 1953); Jesse Allen (born April 19, 1885, died July 31, 1964); George Reed (born April 15, 1887, died January 1, 1919); Samuel Earl (born March 15, 1890, killed in World War I in France August 4, 1918); Sarepta Pearl (born August 14, 1892, died May 21, 1946); Otto Sherman (born July 25, 1894, died September 19, 1963); and Leslie Merle (born February 16, 1897, died March 13, 1971).

Back Row (L to R) Lennie Irene, George Reed, Joseph Emery, Jessie Allen, Armintha. Front Row (L to R) Otto Sherman, Sarepta Pearl, Samuel Earl, Leslie Merle

The two youngest sons, Otto and Leslie, married the Brown sisters, Marie and Marjorie, on April 24, 1920, and lived on farms across the road from each other their entire married lives. Leslie, my father, married Marjorie May Brown (born December 2, 1895, died April 28, 1972), and had two sons, Wayne Edward (born September 22, 1924) and Richard Lee (born June 27, 1933).

Wayne Hamilton married Anna Jane Stinson (born May 31, 1928) on July 27, 1947. Their daughter, Cathyrn Elaine (born June 1, 1948) born in Hartford City, Indiana, and then moved to Colon, Michigan. Cathyrn married Tim Robert Creek (born April 4, 1946) on February 19, 1972, and have one daughter Laura Beth (born April 19, 1982), and they live in Indianapolis, Indiana. Wayne worked as a carpenter. While living at Colon, Michigan, Roger DeWayne (born July 18, 1950) and Robert Eugene (born February 7, 1952) were born. Roger married Georgia May (Erbacher) Whiteacre (born August 15, 1953) on September 16, 1973, and they have two sons: Jason Allen (born July 18, 1972) and Jeremy DeWayne "JD" (born May 10, 1975). They live at Nottingham, Indiana. Roger and Georgia drive semi-trucks for Schneider Trucking. Robert married Sandra Jo Lacoax (born January 18,1952, died January 25, 1991) on February 4, 1972, in Coldwater, Michigan; they eloped. Robert works at C and A Tool as a tool-and-die man. Sandra passed away January 25, 1991 in Churubusco, Indiana. They have two sons: Ryan Eugene (born March 21, 1975) and Chad Allen (born November 24, 1978). Wayne and Anna Jane's third sons, Mark LeRoy (born July 27, 1955), married Rhonda Lynn Kline (born June 20, 1955), on October 26, 1974, and had two daughters while living in Whiteville, North Carolina: Lesli Marie (born December 29, 1980) and Ashley Erin (born June 7, 1983). Mark works at Tokheim Corporation in Fort Wayne, Indiana, as an electronic engineer.

Wayne worked at Kitco Company, a rubber factory, as the third shift foreman from January 13, 1966 through January 13, 1979, and retired to start his own wood-working shop, specializing in picture frames. Anna Jane worked as a custodian at Franklin Electric Company for eleven years, and retired in July 1985.

HAMILTON

April 24, 1920, was the wedding day for Leslie Merle Hamilton and Marjorie Brown. It was also the wedding day for Otto Sherman Hamilton, Leslie's older brother, and Marie Brown, Marjorie's older sister.

Otto and Marie began their life together on a small farm in Poneto, Indiana. Otto drove a school

Mark, Ashley, Lesli, Rhonda, Jason, Georgia, Roger, JD, Jane, Wayne, Chad, Ryan, Sandy, Robert, Cathyrn, Laura, Tim Creek

bus and was also a farmer and dairyman. Marie was a school teacher in Bluffton. Born to them on May 30, 1923, was A. Wendell, who while growing up helped with farming and the cattle, as well as working with the state highway department. Later he married Lois Thompson of Liberty Center, on September 21, 1957. Born to them: Garrett, August 11, 1958; Jill, on June 20, 1960; Marilyn Sue, on July 20, 1962; and Lynn, on March 27, 1964. Garrett married Cheri Decker on July 26, 1986. They have two children: Erin Nichole, February 24, 1988; and Lucas Alan, November 22, 1989. Jill married Larry Clontz of Flint, Michigan, on July 22, 1989. They have one child, Gabrielle Marie, born December 25, 1989. Marilyn Sue was married to William Bradford of Buckeye, Indiana, on November 14, 1981. They have one daughter, Lydia Sue, born March 19, 1988.

Also born to Otto and Marie was Arden on May 17, 1932. From 1952-1955 Arden served in the Coast Guard. On December 24, 1955, he married Mary Jane Dalrymple. They had two children: Micheal, born January 17, 1964; and Patrick, born April 15, 1965. Micheal married Angie McCarver, and they have two children: Cassey and Arden Jaren. After attending college in Oklahoma, Patrick married and he and his wife, Lynn, now reside in Oklahoma.

Both Wendell and Arden were both born in Wells County and both still reside there. Wendell retired from Franklin Electric and is currently employed at the Wells County Jail. Arden remarried in August of 1986 to Joan Whitesell and is employed by Franklin Electric.

RICHARD LEE AND EMMA MAY HAMILTON FAMILY

Richard Lee Hamilton, son of Leslie and Marjorie (Brown) Hamilton, was born at home in rural Poneto, Indiana, on June 27, 1933. He was married to Emma May Hunt on April 11, 1954, in the Keystone United Methodist Church, by the Reverend Dwight Conrad.

Two daughters were born to Richard and Emma May Hamilton. Deborah Kay was born May 27, 1955, at the Fort Belvior Army Hospital in Virginia. Rebecca Sue was born on June 17, 1960, at the Blackford County Hospital in Hartford City, Indiana/

Deborah was married to Don Keith Swartz on May 25, 1974, in the Keystone United Methodist Church by the Reverend Larry Smith.

Rebecca married Bruce Whiteleather on September 28, 1985, in the Forest Park United Methodist Church in Fort Wayne, Indiana.

Don and Deborah Swartz have two children: Daniel Lee was born December 23, 1980, and Davina Jo was born May 1, 1985.

Richard Lee Hamilton graduated from Chester Center high School in 1952. Employed at Dryden Rubber in Montpelier, Indiana, from 1952 through 1954. Entered the U.S. Army in 1954, discharged in 1956, after being stationed at Fort Myer, Virginia, with the 4th MP (CI) Division. Upon returning from military service, Richard returned to Dryden Rubber and later was employed at Fort Wayne Corrugated Paper in Hartford City, Indiana. In 1958, Richard enrolled at Taylor University in Upland, Indiana. After transferring to Ball State University in 1960, he completed his BS degree in 1963 and his MA degree in 1968.

Richard began his teaching career in the Bluffton school system at the Central Junior High School in the area of Industrial Arts. After three years he transferred to the newly-built Southern Wells Junior-Senior High School. After teaching two years in the classroom, Richard was appointed assistant principal, held that position for twenty years, and then transferred into the classroom in 1990.

Richard has one brother, Wayne Edward Hamilton, residing at rural Poneto, Indiana.

Emma May (Hunt) Hamilton graduated from Chester High School in 1954. Entered Ball State University in 1966 earning her BS degree in 1970 and her MA in 1974 as a Home Economics instructor. Emma May has spent her entire professional career in the Northern Wells school system at Norwell High School from 1970 through 1991. She played the leading role in establishing and implementing a newly-formed child day-care program at the Norwell High School, started in 1990. Emma May is the daughter of Gilbert and Lucille (Tappy) Hunt.

Don Swartz attended and graduated from Purdue University in 1981. Before entering Purdue, Don served four years in the U.S. navy from 1973 through 1977. Upon discharge from the U.S. Navy, he entered the naval Reserves from 1977 to present.

Deborah (Hamilton) Swartz attended Fort Wayne Bible College in 1973, after graduating from Southern Wells High School in 1973. Deborah, "Debbie", attended Purdue and is presently attending Indiana Wesleyan University in Marion, Indiana.

HAMMOND

Donald Wade Hammond and his wife, Nadine Todd Hammond, came to Bluffton in 1937. Mr. Hammond was born in Kosciusko County, son of Mr. and Mrs. Charles Hammond. Nadine Todd Hammond was born in Madison County, Indiana, daughter of Mr. and Mrs. O.J. Todd.

In 1917, Don Hammond enlisted in the United States Army. He spent several months in France during World War I. He graduated from Purdue University in 1923 with a mechanical engineer's degree.

Nadine Todd Hammond graduated from Anderson Indiana High School and Ball State University. She was a teacher in the Bluffton City Schools for nineteen years.

In 1937, Don Hammond was appointed Superintendent of the CCC Camp located east of Bluffton. The CCC Camp later developed into the Ouabache State Park.

Don and Nadine Hammond had two sons, David Todd and Donald Wade Hammond II.

David Todd Hammond graduated from Bluffton High School in 1953, from Indiana University in 1957, and from Washington University School of Medicine in 1960. Doctor David T. Hammond is married to Jane (Thoma) Hammond. They have three children, Doctor Todd Hammond, Kristen Hammond, and Greg Hammond. Doctor David Hammond is a practicing physician in Saint Louis, and the David Hammond family are all in the Saint Louis, Missouri area.

Doctor Donald Wade Hammond II graduated from Bluffton High School in 1957, from DePauw University in 1961, and from Washington University School of Medicine in 1965. He is married to the former Jane Presnell. They have two children, Jennifer and David Wade. Doctor Donald Wade Hammond II is a practicing orthopedic surgeon and he and his family live in the Saint Louis, Missouri area.

Don Hammond died in 1966. Nadine T. Hammond later married Fred Arend.

HANNIE-SCHLAGENHAUF

Grandfather Gottlieb Hannie was the fifth child in a family of eleven children. He and grandmother Lisetta Rufenacht were married in Switzerland in 1885 and came to America in 1887 along with his parents. They settled in Adams County and farmed there. They were the parents of twelve children. My father, Karl, was their fourth child. He was born in Adams County in 1891. He and Matilda (Tillie) Reinhart married in Vera Cruz in 1916. The year of her birth was 1897 and she was the ninth child in a family of eleven. Her parents were Fred and Fannie (Ruff) Reinhart, who lived on a farm near Vera Cruz.

Kate and Lawrence Schlagenhauf 50th anniversary 1990

My parents were lifelong farmers in Adams and Wells Counties. Their four children were Kathleen (Kate), Robert, Kenneth, and Mary Jane, who married Ward Showalter in 1945 and are the parents of three children.

Kathleen married Lawrence Schlagenhauf in 1940; he has never lived farther than two miles from his birthplace in Wells County. Our home is on a 240-acre farm (SW 32-26-13) east of Reiffsburg. Farming has been a lifelong occupation. Lawrence also drove a school bus for Bluffton Harrison Schools for thirty-six years. We're 1937 graduates of Bluffton High School. I served as county president of Wells County Home Extension Clubs in 1961 and 1962 and was employed at Montgomery Ward and Buyer's Guide part-time.

Our children are Larry, born in 1944, and Rex, born in 1948; they share a December 24 birthday. Both are graduates of Purdue University. In 1967, Larry married Mary Anne Metz from Memphis, Tennessee, who is also a Purdue graduate. They both taught in the Bluffton Schools. They now live in Indianapolis, where Larry is employed in sales. Their children are John, a P.F.C. in the Marine Corp. and Lisa, a seventh grader.

Rex enlisted in the Air Force in 1971 and married Claudia Lamb of Lafayette in 1973. She is an I.U. graduate. In his career as a pilot they have served in several states and countries. Their most recent overseas assignment was in Germany for four and half years. He flies a KC135 tanker at Grissom Air Force Base and has the rank of lieutenant colonel. Their children are Michael, a seventh grader, and Chelsea, a fourth grader.

Lawrence's grandfather, John Schlagenhauf, was born in Germany in 1838 and came to America at age twenty. He lived in Linn Grove and Vera Cruz where he made caskets and furniture. He later moved to a farm east of Reiffsburg. He married Luticia Gentis in 1886 and fathered eight children. Lawrence's father, Henry, was the eighth child and his birth-date is 1885. He married Eva Gottschalk in 1906 and their children are Caroll, who married

Ralph Hook (they are parents of six children), and Lawrence. Father and son farmed together until Henry's retirement. Grandpa always had ponies for kids to ride and for several years, while younger, was the "engine man" for the threshing ring. He also purchased the first Fordson tractor in Wells County. Eva's parents were George and Elise (Gandlienard) Gottschalk. They lived to celebrate their seventieth wedding anniversary.

We are members of the Old Salem U.M. Church and the Historical Society. Lawrence enjoys Rotary, remodeling, and sports. I love quilt making and crafts. We celebrated our 50th wedding anniversary in October, 1990. (Kate and Lawrence Schlagenhauf)

WILLIAM J. HARBER FAMILY

William J. Harber was the son of Jacob A. Harber and Isabella G. Weller of Allen County, Pleasant Township, Indiana. His two brothers were Giles and James; his sisters were Rosalie, Eileen, and Regina.

He attended Saint John Grade School, and then Saint Aloysius, where he graduated from the eighth grade. Saint Aloysius was a two-story, two-room grade school with one large coal stove in each room and outside plumbing. The eighth grade class contained six girls and four boys. He went on to graduate from Central Catholic High School in Fort Wayne.

He served in the United States Navy during the Korean War and is a charter member of Ossian Post 2861, Veterans of Foreign Wars of the United States. He is employed at GTE in Fort Wayne.

Carolyn S. Harber is the daughter of Robert H. Butcher and Audrey G. (Perry) Butcher of Whitley County, Jefferson Township, Indiana. Her two sisters are Sharon and Nancy; her brothers are Robert, Larry, Charles, and Kenneth. She attended kindergarten at Hillcrest School in Fort Wayne and graduated from Jefferson Center High School in Whitley County, Indiana.

Their eight children: Sheila, Renee, Marjorie, Theodore, Peggy, Jacob, William and Kristin, all graduated from Norwell High School, Marjorie as valedictorian. Five children were in active military service: Sheila, Theodore, Jacob, and William in the United States Navy and Marjorie in the United States Air Force.

In July, 1970, they moved to Union Township, Wells County, Indiana. Their nine grandchildren are Justin, Alex, Allisyn, Joshua, Steffannie, Brittannie, Mellannie, Kyle, and Troy.

DAVID A. HARKLESS FAMILY

The David A. Harkless family ties to Wells County first began with Dave's parents, David C. Harkless and Marcille J. Helfrick, attending and graduating from Ossian High School. They married and set up housekeeping on a farm around Poe, Indiana. From this marriage were born three children: David A., Daniel J., and Diane K. The children attended Madison-Marion Consolidated High School at Hoagland, Indiana, where David A. met Judy Dietrich, daughter of Adolph and Ann Dietrich. Upon graduation from high school, David joined the U.S. Air Force, and Judy enrolled at Valparaiso University. After two years of college, Judy accepted a teaching position at Bethlehem Lutheran School. She taught first and second grade for the 1965-66 school year. On July 9, 1966, Dave and Judy were married and moved to San Antonia, Texas. While in San Antonio, Dave finished his four year obligation to the U.S. Air Force, and Judy started up a kindergarten for Immanuel Lutheran Church. She also served as the pastor's secretary during this time.

Standing (L to R) Lori, Lane, Matthew Mitchell, Lisa. Seated (L to R) Dave and Judy Harkless

When Dave had finished his military commitment on March 8, 1968, the couple again desired to move back to the Wells County area. Judy wrote to the principal at Bethlehem and was excited to find that they again had a vacancy and needed a first and second grade teacher. The couple moved to Truman and Lela Bell's apartment on South County Line Road when they returned from Texas. They lived on the Allen County side of the road. Also at this time Dave applied and was accepted in an apprenticeship program at Tokheim Corporation in Fort Wayne to become a tool and die maker. After teaching two years at Bethlehem School, Judy quit teaching to begin a family. A daughter, Lisa, was born to the couple on September 19, 1970. When Lisa was six months old, Dave and Judy bought the Paul and Clara Witte homestead on 800N in Wells County. In May of 1972, Dave graduated from his apprenticeship at Tokheim and became a tool and die maker. On September 5, 1973, the family was unexpectedly blessed with boy/girl twins, Lane and Lori.

When Lane and Lori were three years old, Judy continued her college education at Indiana University at Fort Wayne. In the fall of 1979, Judy did her student teaching in first grade at Ossian Elementary. She graduated from IPFW in December of 1979, and consequently got a fifth grade teaching job at Ossian School, and finished the 1979-80 school year. The following year, Judy got a third grade position at Ossian Elementary where she remains at the present time. Dave and Judy's oldest daughter, Lisa, graduated from Norwell High School in 1988, and International Business College in July of 1989. She married Matthew Mitchell, of Bluffton, on January 13, 1990. Lane and Lori are presently juniors at Norwell High School and both plan to further their education after high school.

HARNISH

Samuel Harnish, twenty-eight and wife Anna, twenty, left Germany in 1732, came to Philadelphia on the ship *Pink Plaisance* and settled in northern Lancaster County, Pennsylvania near Cocalico. Two cousins came a few years earlier and informed them of shortcuts and problems to avoid. Samuel and Anna had eleven children. They were farmers and had acquired a large amount of land by the time of his death in 1788, at age eighty-four. One son, John, and wife Anna had seven children. John fought in the American Revolution. John and Anna's son, Henry married Barbara Gearhart. They had twelve children and lived at Mt. Zion, Pennsylvania. Their son Samuel married Readocia Edris in 1852. They had nine children. In 1861, they moved to Wells County, first farm house south of Murray on State Road 116 on the east side. After Samuel's death in 1868, Readocia sold the farm and bought a farm one and one-fourth miles west of Murray bridge. She had the home built. In 1872, the barn was built. It is known as the "Harnish Homestead." Samuel and Readocia's son, John married Ida Shoemaker. They had four children. Rosa married Jesse Houtz. They had three children. Clara married Homer Nutter. They also had three children. Ella married Charles Wallace. Pierce Sr. married Iva Mae Holloway. They had seven children. In 1910 Pierce's father died. He then took over the farming. In 1944, Pierce Sr. became county commissioner for two terms, Democratic County Chairman from 1948-1952, and State Highway Superintendent (Bluffton District) from 1948-1952. He graduated from Bluffton Business College and served as vice president and director of Federal Land Bank for twenty years. In 1964, he became co-owner of the Dutch Main Car Wash at 1309 S. Main, with son Pierce Jr. He was active there until his death in 1974 at age eighty-three.

Pierce Harnish, Sr. hauling sugar beets from field in the 1930's

Pierce Jr. continued as owner and operator of the car wash. In 1979, he sold the gas station on north side of car wash to son Randy. Randy then rebuilt it into a convenience store known as "Country Cupboard." Children of Pierce Sr. and Iva Mae are as follows: John (deceased) married Rozada Hough. They had three children: Janice, Doyle and Darrell. Leroy (deceased) married Freda Fishbaugh (deceaed). They had two children, Marilyn and Morris. Gerald married Alice Riddile. They had three sons: Wayne, Dale and Jerry (deceased). Mabeline married Eldie Vickrey (deceased). They had two children, Ronald and Sue Anne. Her second marriage was to Harold Ryan. Mildred married Fred Corah (deceased). They had two children, James and Joseph. She later married Francis Lee (deceased). Fred (deceased) married Marcielle Highland. They had two children: Galen and Gloria. Pierce Jr. married Carolyn Faus. They had four children: Randy, Rinda, Rosanne, and Ronald. Pierce Jr. and his wife Carolyn still live in the house on the Homestead farm that our great-grandmother, Readocia Harnish, had built in 1868. They would tell how the men walked daily from Rockford, fourteen miles round trip, to do the plastering. The cost to build this two and one-half story house was one thousand dollars. The ground is now farmed by Richard Harnish, the sixth generation.

HARRIS

We start this history with Clyde's grandfather Edward Harris. He was born on October 7, 1858, in

West Virginia. His grandmother was Celia from Wells County, who was born on December 28, 1868, in Hamilton County, Indiana, to Joseph B. and Elizabeth (Kelly) Moore. They were married and had twelve children, who were Joseph William, Clyde's father Charley, Lee Otis, George Henry, Ray Everett, Rosa Belle, Omar Vernon, Edna Jane, Jenny May, Florence Irene, James Oral, Lillie Laverna, and Crystal Evelyn.

Clyde's father Charles was born in Wells County on April 3, 1889, and married in 1915 to Constance (Thompson), who was born on September 22, 1891 in England. Their children are Florence born on October 8, 1915, Claude born on August 15, 1920, Clyde born on April 18, 1922, and William Eugene born on August 27, 1933. They all are living in Wells County at the present time.

As a boy Clyde attended school at Bluffton but graduated from Liberty Center. Clyde and Claude both met their wives who also were sisters while at Liberty Center. They later had a double wedding on August 22, 1943. Clyde married Mary Elizabeth (Biddy) Garrett, born on October 31, 1923 and Claude married Ruba Jane Garrett. They were the daughters of Noah Mount and Jeanetta Ade (Craig) Garrrett and sisters to Max Authur (Pat) and Mount Eugene (Mike).

Clyde has farmed all his life and worked at Sterling Casting for nineteen years before retiring. Clyde and Biddy have lived on the same farm three miles west of Bluffton on State Road 124. Their five children are Robert Dale born August 21, 1944, Richard Kay born on July 28, 1946, Michael Clyde born on October 15, 1948, Ted Leon born on March 18, 1952, and Cheryl Sue born on August 18, 1961.

Robert graduated from Manchester College, married, and has two boys, Matthew Robert, twenty one, and James Adam, twenty. Bob married Bonnie L. Adams in 1974 and they have a son Jesse Cole, eleven. Bob and his family now live in Rockcreek Township and works as a computer programer.

Richard also graduated from Manchester College. While at Manchester he was an exceptional ball player and was on the NAIA College All American Basketball team. Dick was a teacher in Biology at Huntington Junior High before moving to Hawaii. He became a pilot while back in the states and was doing both teaching and flying before moving to Fresno, California where he enjoys flying for a charter company as a full-time career.

Mike graduated from Ball State University and became an industrial arts teacher. He has been currently teaching at Norwell for the last twenty years. Mike married Carolyn Sue Kunkel in 1970 and has three children: Mark Alan, fourteen; David Michael, twelve; and Michella Sue, nine.

Ted graduated from Manchester College in accounting. He married Linda Ann Price in 1985. They live in Colfax, Indiana and he works as an accountant.

Cheryl married soon after graduating from Southern Wells and has two children Richelle Nicole, ten, and Ryan Allan, five. She is now married to Barry D. Schantz and lives in Delta, Ohio.

HARRIS

This Harris family has resided in Wells County ever since James Harris and family came to Wells County from Jay County in 1857. This family has been traced back to the early 1700's in Hyde County, North Carolina. Where they originally came from, and when they arrived in the colonies, has not been determined. They are, however, of English descent and were Quakers. They were planters or farmers.

The first Harris on record died in 1713. This was William Harris. His grandson William served in the Revolutionary War.

In the census of 1790, we find Thomas Harris listed in Hyde County, North Carolina. He was the fourth generation on record up to this time. In 1804, Thomas moved his family to Columbian County, Ohio. Then in 1842, Benjamin Harris, a son of Thomas, moved his family to Northern Jay County, Indiana, near Balbec. The son, James, having been born in 1836, was six years old at this time.

In 1857, James married Loruhama McDorman. They moved to a farm one-mile north of Chester Center in Wells County.

The McDormans were Irish Quakers. They settled first in North Carolina, then moved, by way of Ohio to Jay County, Indiana.

L to R: Don V. Harris, granddaughter Leigh Harris, Mrs. Don Harris, granddaughter Meghan Harris

James had a brother Benjamin. In the winter of 1863 Benjamin enlisted in the union army, "Western." He was honorably discharged in 1865.

James and his wife had nine children. One of these was Benjamin A. Harris, born March 7, 1875. He married Myrtie Carnes, a daughter of William H. Carnes of Chester Township, on May 30, 1898.

William H. Carnes was one of the pioneer settlers of Chester Township having settled on a farm three miles west of Poneto in 1854.

Benjamin and Myrtie Harris had eight children namely: Hazel Harris Henschen, Don V. Harris, Hugh Harris, Vera Harris Repp, Gerald Harris, Pauline Harris Niblick, Wanda Harris King, and Frances Harris Nadolny.

The son Don, along with the older brothers and sisters, attended grade school at District No. 2-"Slacum" in Chester Township. Then the family moved into Nottingham Township; he attended Petroleum High School. After high school he obtained a degree in pharmacy from Butler University. He married Nellie Dukes, a daughter of Frank T. Dukes and Mary Naomi Wilson Dukes. Then, for some fifty years, they were involved in pharmacy and retail drug business in Bluffton, until retiring in 1972. They have one child, a son, Don V. Harris, Jr. This son is a lawyer in Washington, D.C. He and his wife, Joan (Haffler), have two daughters: Leigh, who is a teacher in special education in Washington, D.C. and Meghan who is an economist with the Department of Agriculture in Washington, D.C.

This briefly is some two hundred and seventy years of this "Harris" family branch.

CLAUDE L. HARRIS FAMILY

On August 15, 1920 Claude was born to Charles and Constance (Thompson) Harris in Griggs County, North Dakota. Charles was born and raised a farmer near Warren, Indiana. Constance was born in England and came to the United States with her parents and brother when she was seven years old. Claude has a sister, Florence, and two brothers, Clyde and William of Bluffton.

Ruba Jane (Garrett) Harris was born to N. Mount Garrett and Jeannetta Ada (Craig) Garrett on May 2, 1922. Mount Garrett was born and raised in and around Liberty Center. His descendents came from Pennsylvania and Ohio. Ada Garrett was born in Indiana and her descendents came from Kentucky and Virginia. Ruba Jane has a sister Mary E. Harris and two brothers, Max (Pat) Garrett and Mount E. (Mike) Garrett.

Claude, after graduation from Liberty Center High School, worked at Cline Lumber Company in Bluffton and also in construction of runways for Baer Field until going to the Army Air Corp in the fall of 1942. Ruba Jane attended Lutheran Hospital School of Nursing and graduated from there in the fall of 1943. On August 22, 1943, Ruba Jane and Claude and Mary E. (Biddy) and Clyde Harris were married in a double wedding ceremony at the Liberty Center Baptist Church. The couples were married by Reverend John Doyle.

The Harris Grandchildren
(L to R) Brad Thornburgh, Sarah Thornburgh, Kevin Harris, Philip Haiflich. Back row (L to R) Brian Harris, Andrew Haiflich

Claude and Ruba Jane lived in Kearney, Nebraska, where Claude was stationed with the Air Corps and was a mechanic on B-24 bombers. He was discharged in December, 1945. Since his discharge from the service, Claude has farmed and was the head of the maintenance department at Wells Community Hospital for twenty-seven years. He retired in January, 1989. Ruba Jane retired from nursing in 1983 after working at Wells Community Hospital for more than twenty-five years.

Five children were born to Claude and Ruba Jane.

Donald Lee Harris was born June 16, 1944, in Kearney, Nebraska. He graduated from Liberty Center High School, Franklin college, and Indiana University with a Masters degree in student personnel. Following graduation from Indiana University, he enlisted in the Army Medical Corp. During this time he married Marilyn Lucille Liechty from Wauseon, Ohio. He served in Seoul, Korea, while in the Army. Following his discharge, he attended Yale University where he received a degree in the Health Care field. He is now senior vice-president of Corporate Affairs, Inova Health Systems, Incorporation of Fairfax, Virginia. Don and Marilyn live in Burke, Virginia, with their two sons Brian, eighteen, and Kevin, fifteen.

James Craig Harris was born May 3, 1946, in Bluffton, Indiana. Jim graduated from Liberty Center High School and Franklin College. He was a member of the Liberty Center basketball team which played a memorable "nine overtimes" in the regional game with Swayzee in 1964. After graduating from college, he immediately enlisted in the Air Force. He became a pilot of A-37 bombers and was sent to Vietnam in January, 1970. Jim was killed in the crash of his plane in Cambodia on February 1, 1971. He was twenty-four years old.

Cynthia Ann was born on May 25, 1948 in Bluffton, Indiana. She graduated from Liberty Center High School, Manchester College, and the University of Kentucky. At present she is the Director of Dietetics and Food Services at Parkview Hospital, Forth Wayne, Indiana. Cindy has two sons, Philip, seventeen Andrew, sixteen.

Patricia Rae was born on December 7, 1950 in Bluffton, Indiana. Patty graduated from Southern Wells High School and Ball State University. Patty married Bruce Thornburgh of Eaton, Indiana in 1973. At present she is teaching in the Vicksburg, Michigan schools. Patty and Bruce have two children, Bradley, thirteen and Sarah eleven.

Sandra Kay was born October 21, 1954, in Bluffton, Indiana. Sandy graduated from Southern Wells High School and Taylor University. She worked as a volunteer for Youth for Christ/Campus Life for ten years and now works with young people in a church youth group. Presently, Sandy works in the business office of Fort Wayne Cardiology, Fort Wayne, Indiana where she is the head of the computer department.

HARRIS-FALK

Ruth Elva (Harris) Falk was born October 29, 1933 in Nottingham Township the daughter of William R. and Blanche L. (Goodwin) Harris. She attended Petroleum School and graduated from Pennville High School in 1952. She worked at Fryback's Confectioner, Morris Five and Ten Cents Store, Snug Restaurant, and Franklin Electric. She met Robert B. Falk while he was serving in the Army of the Korean War from 1952-1954. They were married June 10, 1956, and resided in Bluffton until they purchased a seventy acre farm in Rockcreek Township in partnership with his brother.

December 1989
Back (L to R) Ruth and Joan. Middle (L to R) Lucas and Joseph. Front (L to R) Samuel holding Benjamin, Robert, and Jacob

Robert was born May 10, 1932 in Rockcreek Township the son of Homer and Cressie. He played on the Rockcreek Dodgers basketball team and graduated in 1950. He worked at Franklin Electric a short time; then he went to International Harvester and was there for twenty-four and one-half years. He has been farming part time and with International Harvester closing the Fort Wayne plant in 1983, he and his brother purchased more land and farm full time.

Our first son, Samuel Robert, was born May 2, 1959. He attended Bluffton Eastside Elementary, Lancaster Junior High, and graduated in 1977 from Norwell High School. He graduated from Purdue University Fort Wayne in 1982. He met Joan Marie Winans, who was born November 8, 1962, in Adams County, the daughter of Ross and Sharon (Raber) Winans. They were married on May 15, 1982, at the Pleasant Mills Methodist Church. He now works at Fort Wayne Wire Die Incorporation and lives in Saint Mary's Township in Adams County where they purchased twenty acres and raise hogs from farrow to finish. They have three sons: Benjamin Lee was born October 19, 1982, and attends Adams Central Elementary; Lucas Robert was born September 30, 1985 and Jacob Ross was born June 7, 1989.

Our second son Joseph was born August 21, 1964. He attended Bluffton Eastside Elementary, Rockcreek Elementary, Lancaster Junior High, and graduated from Norwell High School in 1982. He graduated from International Business College in 1985. He worked at Safety Equipment from 1985-1990. He is presently working at Sears Telecatalog and West Central Neighborhood Ministry both in Fort Wayne. He enjoys refinishing antique furniture.

HARRIS-FISHER

Joseph Harris married Nancy Fisher and they lived near Uniondale. They were parents of seven children: Kirk, Dewey, Fred, Charles, Wilbur, Forrest, and Glendora.

Kirk married Carrie Gearhart and they were parents of two daughters, Ruth and Helen, who gave them sixteen grandchildren.

Charles never married.

Dewey married Nellie Woods and had one stepson, Bruce.

Fred married Mary Cupp. Their only son, Fred, had two children, John and Gretchen.

Forrest married Kathryn (last name unknown).

Wilbur married Nellie Haiflich, and they have one stepson and three grandchildren.

Glendora married John Numbers and they had a stepson, Don, and two daughters, Donna B. (McCormick) and Nancy L. (Haiflich) and five grandchildren and ten great-grandchildren.

HARRIS-WHEELER

My grandfather, Guy Harris, was born in 1883 in a log house at Nottingham. In his early twenties, he became a teamster, hauling pipe and tools in the oil fields, then numerous in the area, and hauling gravel to build many of the roads in southern Wells County in the early 1900's.

He married Retta McGeath, daughter of Franklin Pierce McGeath, and started farming in Chester Township, also working for the Indiana Pipe Line Company, driving sixty miles a day in a Model-T touring car. As it was before the days of antifreeze, in the winter the radiator was drained once you reached your destination for the day, then refilled for the trip home. He later purchased a farm in Nottingham Township, where he lived when he retired.

He continued to help my father, Roy Harris, with farming until the age of 81. One day in the field he remarked, "I intended to retire at eighty, but guess I'll have to change it to one hundred." During his later years, he spent three winters in California, making the trip home each time by air, after saying in the 1930's that the "only way an airplane will kill me is if it falls on me." Retta died in 1960, and Guy died in 1977.

Guy and Retta Harris 1955

"Gramp" and "Granny," as they were affectionately called by most who knew them, had three children: Helen Gordon, Kathleen Tappy and Roy Harris.

I was born on May 15, 1947, the daughter of Lillie Alberson Harris and Roy Harris. I graduated from Petroleum High School in 1965, and later married Harlow Hahn. We had one son, Jarrod, in 1975, and were later divorced.

In 1987, I married James Wheeler, who had three children: Sarah, James and Cassandra. In 1988, we had a daughter, Katherine. The older children attend Southern Wells School.

As I had always lived close to my grandparents, much of my childhood was spent at their house. As I grew up, I had visions of one day living in "Gramp's house," so it 1966 when he went to stay with his children, I rented it and finally purchased it in 1978. In 1988, we decided to remodel and by adding on increased the size of the existing house to fifteen rooms.

I am secretary to the Medical Director of Charter Beacon Hospital in Fort Wayne and Jim, a veteran of the Vietnam war, works at Franklin Electric in Bluffton. We spend much of our free time searching for and collecting antiques and finishing the new part of the house to look "old" by using wood trim, light fixtures, and other items found in our "antiquing expeditions."

ELMER AND DELMER HARROLD FAMILY

It all began when Ithamer Harrold moved to Indiana from Stokes County, North Carolina, with his family of ten in 1851 by ox cart. Of this family, a son, George Harrold married Sally Minnich and settled in Wells County. Their children were Isaac, Ross and James Roscoe.

James Roscoe Harrold (1867-1939), a farmer, married Amanda Murray (1868-1903). Born to this union were: Elmer Austin, James Delmer and Alma (1901-1903). James Roscoe remarried to Mary Hunnicutt who passed away in 1934.

Elmer Austin Harrold (February 10, 1894-November 8, 1976), a teacher and farmer, married Nellie May Williamson (January 30, 1900-September 13, 1974) on December 23, 1917. After serving his country in World War I, he returned to Chester Township where they bought a farm and raised their four children: Kenneth Maxwell, Thelma May, Ethel Berniece and Dee Allen.

After four years in the Army during World War II, Kenneth (January 6, 1919) married Blenda Lorene Mowery (October 17, 1922) on March 23, 1946. They have lived in Wells County all their lives. They currently live in Harrison Township. He is now retired from farming and Franklin Electric. They had twins, Janis Lee and Linus Kay (December 27, 1946).

Janis married Kenneth Deam and they reside in Ohio. They have two children: Natalie and Nathan.

Delmer and Elmer Harrold

Linus married Karen Kellogg and they reside in Harrison Township. They have two children: Sandra and Christopher. Linus is the owner of Lin's Lock and Key in Bluffton.

Thelma May (February 28, 1922) married Charles Richard Brown (August 30, 1920), a farmer, on November 28, 1946. They have lived in Huntington County all their married lives. They live in Warren, now. Born to this union were Shirley Jean (November 20, 1949) and Denise Jane (September 17, 1955).

Shirley Brown married Kenneth Stanley. He and Richard Brown (father-in-law) farmed together. They are the parents of Dawn and Douglas. She lives with her children in Warren and works at the Exchange Bank.

Denise Brown married Joseph Bucher. They have two children: Kristin and Kelly. They live on the Brown farm in Jefferson Township of Huntington County.

Dee Allen (June 27, 1941) married Penelope Louise DeBold (February 28, 1947) on September 26, 1965. Three children were born to this marriage: Craig Allen (May 11, 1967), Stacy Ann (February 5, 1970) and Kari Ann (November 9, 1972-August 2, 1984). Kari was killed in an automobile accident. Dee remarried to Rebecca Jo Skinner (August 20, 1941) on December 17, 1982. They reside near Bluffton and Dee is employed by Keeber Company, Incorporation.

Craig married Tina Moser and is serving in the Air Force in Saudi Arabia. They have a daughter Malorie. Mother and daughter are in Germany.

Stacy is attending Hunting College for further education.

Ethel (October 2, 1924) married Paul Eugene Couch (June 16, 1925) on April 16, 1944. They have lived near Mount Zion in Jackson Township thirty-nine years, which is most of their married lives. They have three children who all still reside in Wells County. They are: Larry Dean (May 22, 1945), Steven Eugene (November 12, 1949) and Mara Jo (July 4, 1952).

Larry married Rosalie Moorman of Jackson Township, and they have two children. Laura married Rodney Sills of Chester Township, and they reside in Lancaster Township. Michael is attending Purdue University in Lafayette.

Steven married Judy Sleppy of Chester Township, and they have two sons. Kevin is attending Vincennes University, and Kyle resides with his mother in Keystone. Steven has remarried to Sharon Martin Hunnicutt. They reside in Liberty Township.

Mara Jo married Alan Wiliams of Harrison Township. They have two children: David and Rebecca. They reside in Harrison Township.

Larry, Steve and Mara Jo all are employed by Franklin Electric in Bluffton, Indiana. Larry and Steve are also engaged in farming.

James Delmer Harrold (December 21, 1898-June 12, 1987) married Marie Gladys Mounsey (August 10, 1900-November 14, 1985) on May of 1919. She was the first daughter of Samuel and Minnie (Ustic) Mounsey. Delmer and Marie were staunch members of the church at South Liberty Christian until death. Delmer was an ordained minister in the Indiana Miami Reserve Christian Conference. He pastored churches in Madison, Delaware, Clinton, Tipton and Adams counties.

Delmer taught at various schools in Wells County: Mount Zion, Batson, Jackson, Rockcreek, Chester, and at Roosevelt in Madison County. After his school retirement, he worked at Franklin Electric in Bluffton, and at Wayne Metal in Markle. They had three children: Betty Alice, Bernard Eugene, and Paul Cleophas.

Betty Alice (November 23, 1919) married Ronald Noe in 1949. He passed away July 1956. She married Kenneth Thompson February 26, 1958. They live in Liberty Township.

Bernard Eugene (February 5, 1925) married Kathleen Walker November 1952. They have three children who are: Bernard James, Camilla Ruth and Renata Jane. Bernard James (June 8, 1954), resides in Findlay, Ohio. Camilla Ruth was born October 19, 1955. Renata Jane (November 11, 1963) married David Donnell September 4, 1988. They reside in New Jersey.

Paul Cleophas (August 10, 1934) married Martha Shaw June 18, 1954. There were three children born to their marriage. Melinda Sue was born June 15, 1954 and is attending Cal State College of California. Twins born to the marriage are Todd Andrew and Scott William born May 31, 1966. Todd is at Michigan State at Lansing and Scott is in college at Marquette, Wisconsin.

HARTIGAN-WOOD

Timothy Lee Hartigan and Cheryl Ann Wood were married on July 30, 1977, Uniondale Saint Marks Lutheran Church.

Timothy and Cheryl Hartigan, Kerri and Kelsy

They have two children Kerri Jo (August 2, 1983) and Kelsey Lee Ann (October 10, 1986).

Timothy Lee is the son of Richard and Barbara Tharpe Hartigan. Cheryl's parents were Robert Jr. and Eleanor Morris Wood.

HARVEY

West of Murray there is a large boulder with a bronze plate that reads: 1829. Doctor Joseph Knox, the first white inhabitant of Wells County settled on this quarter section in a cabin located north eighty two degrees twenty feet, west one thousand eight hundred twenty feet.

Henry Miller, who followed him in 1831, was the first permanent settler. Elizabeth Miller Harvey, the first white child, was born in the year 1834 in a cabin north 34 degrees zero feet, west one thousand four hundred thirty eight feet.

Elizabeth Miller was my great-grandmother, having married my great-grandfather, Jacob Richey Harvey September 20, 1855. They had five sons:

Henry McConel, born July 31, 1856, died August, 1859; William Sylvester, born November 3, 1863, died unknown; Jacob Ezra, born November 3, 1863, died unknown; John Robert, born October 17, 1867, died unknown; Charles Ezra, born November 5, 1871, died January 2, 1932.

Charles Ezra was my grandfather, he married Arrilla Mae Hege (born February 21, 1877 and died February 21, 1957) on October 6, 1894. They had one son, Henry Wells (Born October 16, 1895 and died August 7, 1964).

Charles and Arrila lived a short distance west of this boulder. As a child, I remember going past their home and seeing this stone and plate and being told of its history.

Just north of Murray is a cemetery with several members of the Harvey family buried there. Several had served in the Civil War. Just how they fit in the family I don't really know (but would like to know).

I was born in Bluffton and have returned on occasion to take in the Street Fair and look around. Does anyone remember the fish pond on the Court House Square? It had a wrought iron railing around it, and I loved watching those goldfish swimming among the lily pads. Also at the west end of Market Street, there was a field full of Iris flowers that filled the air with their scent.

Bluffton has grown over the years, but I am pleased that some things are still around: the street fair which signals the end to another summer of festivals and fairs and the cement tree and squirrel just north of the bridge over the Wabash River.

HARVEY-BENNETT

My great-great-grandfather, Robert Harvey, married Elizabeth Richey on March 19, 1818 in Butler County, Ohio. Robert was the fourth white man to settle in what became Wells County. He came with his family from Union County, Indiana, following the Indian trails and settled on the present site of Murray in 1832. The preceding winter he became totally blind from inflammation of the eyes. The troublesome times of 1832 (the year of the Black Hawk Indian War) induced his brothers, Samuel and John, to move him back to Union County where he stayed the following winter. He became the owner of three hundred acres of land in Lancaster Township. This Harvey farm remained in the possession of four generations of Harveys for one hundred forty years, until it was sold by Robert's great-granddaughter, Minnie Stover, in the 1970's.

Robert was the son of Henderson Harvey, a Revolutionary War veteran. Robert was in the War of 1812 and was a soldier in Captain John Farlow's Company of Militia in the 8th Indiana Regiment. Robert and Elizabeth had four sons: William Elzie (my great-grandfather), John, Jacob R., and Lorenzo D. The latter died in the Civil War at Mumfordville, Kentucky, on November 21, 1862. Jacob R. married Elizabeth Miller, the first white child born in Wells County. A marker identifying the cabin site where she was born is located one mile west and three miles north of Bluffton.

*Marjorie Harvey Petersen
Age 21, 1945*

Great-grandfather William Elzie Harvey married Saloma Russell on April 26, 1846. They, too, were farmers in Lancaster Township. Their grave marker can still be found in the old Bluffton Cemetery along the Wabash. Their son William E. married Alice Bennett, the granddaughter of Robert Collins Bennett, who named the city of Bluffton. They lived on forty acres of land near Stringtown until they moved with their nine children to Rusk County, Wisconsin, in 1905. My father, Victor Harvey, was the fifth child in that family and married Elizabeth Mead, and they lived for nearly a half-century in Cable, Bayfield County, Wisconsin, enjoying and working in the woods.

My great-great-grandfather, Robert Collins Bennett, one of the early pioneers of Wells County, was chosen for the first County Board of Commissioners in June, 1837, along with Solomon Johnson and James Scott. Only ten or twelve votes were cast in that election. According to the *Bluffton Evening News-Banner* (Centennial Edition, September 15, 1937), R.C. Bennett named the city of Bluffton; "It was not until 1838 that Robert Bennett, standing on a bluff which effects a bend in the Wabash River saw the advantages of the location for a town and from its situation gave Bluffton its name."

Abram Studabaker and R.C. Bennett both donated land for the city on part of which the present site of Blufffton stands, including the site of the present courthouse. And, together, they donated two hundred seventy dollars in cash. In March, 1838, the town site was surveyed and the original plot of one hundred ninety one lots laid out.

My husband, Eugene J. Petersen was a seminary professor for thirty years in San Francisco and Detroit, and we live in San Leandro, California.

A descendant of the early pioneers of Wells County—*Marjorie Harvey Peterson, who submitted the above.*

HAUENSTEIN/SCHOENAUER

John Raymond and Dorotha Rosemary Hauenstein were married in Huntington, February 13, 1949. They lived in Huntington County just north of Markle until they moved to Union Township, Wells County, in December, 1952. They have two children: Elizabeth Ann (Beth), born March 16, 1950; and mark Edward, born October 15, 1952.

John R's. great-grandfather, John Hauenstein, Sr. was born on September 8, 1820, and he immigrated from Tegerfelden, Switzerland, in 1845. He walked from New York to Huntington, Indiana. He located on a farm just north of Huntington. John Sr's. descendents continued to live on that farm until 1949 when John R. moved to the Markle area. John R. was born in Huntington County on July 28, 1922, to John Fredrick and Philabeana Meyer Hauenstein. He has a twin brother. He graduated from Huntington Township High School in 1940. he served in the Army during World War II from February 1943 to October 1945. John R. was in the European Theater of Operation for twenty-seven months. As a child of five years, he began to milk cows on his father's farm. He was a farmer until he retired in 1985. He tenant-farmed the Paul and Lillian McGuffey farms for thirty years.

Dorotha was born in Whitley County to Daniel Edward and Nellie Redman Schoenauer on October 1, 1924. She also was raised on a farm. She graduated from Roanoke High School in 1942. She worked for the Farm Credit Service before her marriage. She has been a homemaker and has volunteered as a Laubach Literacy tutor. Her grandmother, Elizabeth Zurcher Schoenauer immigrated from the Berne, Switzerland area in 1870 as a child of eleven years.

In 1972, John R. and Dorotha bought the Howe farm in Rockcreek Township. He removed the farm buildings. In 1982, they moved to their new home, built near a pond on the farm. Some of the wood salvaged from the old buildings was used in their home, including the mantle on the fireplace which was a hand-hewn barn beam.

During their adult years, they both attended classes to improve their skills and interests. In his retirement, John R. has enjoyed caring for a large lawn, gardening, and cutting firewood. He has planted more than two thousand trees on the farm.

Beth graduated from the Norwell School system. She attended Indiana and Purdue Universities and is a registered nurse at Lutheran Hospital in Fort Wayne. She was a Peace Corps volunteer from 1970 to 1973. She served in Pianco, Pariaba, Brazil. She also lived in Brazil from October, 1976 until May, 1980.

Mark graduated in 1971 from Norwell High School. He served in the Army from September, 1972 to September, 1974. He was stationed in Germany 20 months. He now works for Mossburg Masonry and lives with his family near Uniondale.

In September 1988, John R. and Dorotha traveled in Switzerland, the land of their ancestors. They spent a day in Tegerfelden and visited the church where John R's. ancestors worshiped. This church, built in the 16th century, is still used today.

HAUK

This history originates in Holland in 1790, when Philip Hauk I came to America. His great-great-grandson, Abner Absalum (1859-1937), came to Wells County in 1901 when he herded his cattle from Montgomery County to his farm southeast of Bluffton. Later, traveling in his first car, he became lost returning via the cow-path to his home county. When he retired to his West Central Street home in Bluffton, "Uncle Ab" became a basketball enthusiast. Every Saturday afternoon neighborhood pre-teen boys were inviteed to practice in his back yard. When these boys played high school basketball in the Cherry Street gym, he gave their coaches a run-down on the abilities of his proteges.

A.A.'s first wife was Emma Moore, and the children of that marriage were Irl and Ethel (Hauk) Steiner. His second marriage was to Eliza Watson (1872-1938), daughter of John Watson (born in York, England) and Margaret Downing (born in Sheffield, England). Their children were Ida (1891-1975), unmarried; and George (1893-1928), who married Fay Chalfant.

Fay L. (Chalfant) Hauk

Fay Chalfant Hauk, one of Wells County's most active citizens, was born December 15, 1891, to Mary Prillaman and Robert D. Chalfant. Fay Hauk's lifelong activities centered around family members, music, work, and church. When she was young, she helped care for a younger brother and sister and gave piano lessons, traveling around the county in a horse-and-buggy to do so. She was a noted pianist and at age eighteen received an honorary certificate from the Chicago Conservatory of Music.

She married George A. Hauk on October 25, 1912, and had two children, Mary (Shoup) and Max Hauk. Her husband died in 1928, and she managed to support herself and her children by sewing (she supervised a government sewing class); she also sold garden produce, resumed her music teaching, did factory work at the Farnsworth Plant in Bluffton, and was an employee of Caylor-Nickel Clinic for seventeen years.

Fay Hauk also actively participated in the religious life of the Six Mile Church. She was organist and pianist for over twenty-five years; she was the superintendent of the church's primary department for twenty-five years; she sang in the choir; she wrote and directed many children's programs, and took many neighborhood children to Sunday school. In 1974, the church's Youth Group presented a special "This Is Your Life" program to honor her for her years of service. In 1976, at the age of eighty-five, Fay was the featured speaker at the church's cornerstone dedication ceremony.

Fay's interests extended from her family and church to Wells County's history. She was an active member of the Wells County Historical Society and opened her home to the Society's "Home Walk," as her house, build in 1847, was one of the oldest in the county.

Mrs. Hauk is currently a resident of Swiss Village, where she is still able to remember and to sing clearly all of her favorite hymns. She remains an inspiration to her family and to her church.

Fay and George Hauk's children: Mary (see Shoup) and Max (married Eldred Williams in October, 1945). Max served as a captain in the U.S. Army Transportation Corps for four years; taught high school science for 35 years; and served as Assistant Superintendent of the Bluffton-Harrison MSD for eleven years. He retired in 1977. Their children are: Melinda (Mrs. Gene Leighty) and Cynthia (Mrs. Rodney Ehrlich). Their grandchildren are: Laura and Kim Leighty and Carrie and Mark Ehrlich.

DONALD AND CAROLYN HAY FAMILY

Donald E. Hay was born April 13, 1935, to Russell W. Hay and May Nixon (Hatfield) Hay in Rushville, Indiana. Don has two brothers, Russell Franklin (Bud) Hay and Charles Adam Hay.

After a few years in Indianapolis, Indiana, and Huntington, Indiana, the family moved to Bluffton in 1949 when Don was in the eighth grade. Don's father worked at Tokheim in Fort Wayne, Indiana, until his death in 1970 at the age of sixty-four. His mother retired from Eaton Corporation (now known as Kitco) in 1973 and still lives in Bluffton.

After graduation from Bluffton High School, Don enlisted in the Marine Corps. He served three years active duty. Basic training was in San Diego, California, and then he was shipped to Japan, Okinawa, and Iwo Jima. The last year was spent in the States at Camp Lejeune, North Carolina. He was assigned to Brig Company MP Battalion as a cross country chaser picking up AWOL(s). Don was honorably discharged July 1, 1957.

(L to R) Donald Hay, Carolyn Hay, Toni Hay, Jodi Kaehr, Jeff Kaehr, Ian Kaehr, Nikia Kaehr

January 1, 1958, he joined the Bluffton Police Department under Mayor Robert Venis. In April, 1960, he was appointed Chief of Police by Mayor Charles Decker at the age of twenty-five. At the time, he was the youngest Chief of Police in the State of Indiana. He served in this capacity for eight years. In 1971, he was appointed detective which was a newly created position for the Bluffton Police Department. Through promotions he attained the rank of Detective Sergeant, Detective Lieutenant, and Detective Captain before retiring in 1980 after twenty-two years. Don unsuccessfully ran for Wells County Sheriff in 1978.

Don married Carolyn Jean Clark October 18, 1958. Carolyn is a 1958 graduate of Bluffton High School and has worked at Carnall & Sons, Inc. for twenty-eight years. She is the daughter of Flossie Coulter and the late Harold Clark. Harold died December 30, 1946. Flossie married Eugene (Salty) Coulter on December 12, 1959. Flossie owned Clarkie's Coffee Shop on South Johnson Street until she went out of business in 1962.

We have lived at 1241 Stogdill Road for twenty-four years where we raised our two daughters.

Our oldest daughter, Jodi Ann Kaehr, graduated from Bluffton High School in 1977 and International Business College in 1980. She is married to Jeffrey Kaehr and they live in Marion, Indiana, where Jeff is a sales representative for Keebler Company. They have two children, Ian Phillip, age five and Nikia Marie, age three.

Toni Lynn graduated from Bluffton High School in 1987. She will graduate this year with a degree in Respiratory Therapy. She works at St. Joseph Hospital in Fort Wayne, Indiana and has signed a contract to continue employment there after graduation.

ELSIE ROEMBKE HECKMAN

Elsie Roembke was born September 19, 1905, in Lockwood, Missouri, to William Roembke Sr. and Anna Bauermeister. Elsie's parents had purchased an 80-acre farm in this community and lived there for several years in Missouri. A neighbor girl was swinging her in the yard swing, and Elsie fell out and broke her arm.

The Roembke's had a farm auction there before coming to Indiana. Anna and the girls, Meta, Alvina, and Elsie, rode on the train while William Sr. traveled in the box car with his team of horses "Dick" and "George," so he could feed and water them. They purchased a farm in Jefferson Township on road 700E between 900N and 1000N. Elsie first attended Jackson School on the corner of 900N and 700E because it was near home. Later she attended Bethlehem Lutheran School and then Friedheim Lutheran School. Meta was fifteen, Alvina was nine, and Elsie was seven years old when their brother William Roembke Jr. was born on March 19, 1912. In 1917, the family purchased and moved to the present Roembke farm at 7272E-900N near Echo. Parents and children worked hard planting, cultivating, and harvesting crops with horses or hand labor. They raised chickens, pigs, sheep, and milk cows. In 1919, a bad tornado struck this neighborhood. The Roembke farm was spared. They went to the cellar during the tornado and when they came up, they could look across the fields and see barns and houses of their neighbors destroyed. Elsie always had a fear of storms after that.

Carl and Elsie (Roembke) Heckman

As the Roembke girls grew up and were dating, their younger brother "Willie" would play tricks on their boyfriends, like tying the buggy wheel fast to the axle with a rope. In the early 1900's, the Roembke's bought their first car—a Ford. This car was stolen in Fort Wayne and was never found.

On September 19, 1925, Elsie married Carl W. Heckman at Zion Lutheran Church, Friedheim. The wedding reception and dinner were held at the home of the bride's parents, which was the usual custom of that time.

Elsie and Carl moved into his parents' farm home in Adams County about five miles from the Roembkes. Carl was a farmer for many years and Elsie was a homemaker. They moved to Fort Wayne in 1955. Carl was employed at Western Auto Warehouse and as a school bus driver, and was also employed by Roembke Electric before he retired. Carl and Elsie did volunteer work at Lutheran Hospital in Fort Wayne. Elsie was active in the Ladies Aid Quilting Society at Peace Lutheran Church in Fort Wayne.

Elsie and Carl had five children: Imogene married Gilbert Bultemeier. They had two children, Carla and Deanna. Maurice married Barbara Zock. They had four children: Cynthia, Bonita, Terry, and Pamela. Betty married Richard Schroeder. They had four children: Rebecca, John, Elizabeth, and James. Donna married Noel Fenner. They had three children: Gregory, Eric, and Matthew. Carl and Elsie had a stillborn son, born in 1936 and buried in Friedheim Lutheran Church Cemetery.

Elsie and Carl celebrated their Golden Wedding Anniversary in 1975. Elsie died at age seventy-four on March 5, 1980, following several strokes. She is buried in Oak Lawn Cemetery, Ossian, Indiana. Carl is living in Garrett, Indiana.

HEDGES FAMILY

The Wells County, Indiana branch of the Hedges family has been traced to Sir Charles Hedges who was born at Wanborough, Wiltshire, England in January of 1649. In 1673, he graduated at Oxford University and received his M.A. and L.L.D. degrees. He engaged in the profession of Civil law and acquired great eminence. He served as judge of the High Court of Admiralty and of the Prerogative Court of Canterbury. He was also legal counselor to King James II and was appointed Secretary of State by King William III and again by Queen Anne. He received the honor of Knighthood and served in Parliament for many years.

This information was obtained through the Genealogical Society of the Church of Jesus Christ of Latter Day Saints.

Charles Hedges, Gentleman, the son of Sir Charles, was the father of Joseph Hedges who emigrated to Maryland in 1710 and died at Monaquacy, Maryland in 1732. Joseph's will names Charles Hedges, Sr. as one of his sons and heirs.

Charles, Sr. moved to West Virginia, and he and relatives founded the town of Hedgesville. However, his son, Charles, Jr., moved to Brook County, West Virginia where his son, Elijah, my great-great-grandfather was born. These early Hedges were people of some means. They were, in fact, wealthy land holders. Charles, Sr., Charles, Jr., and Elijah all participated in the Revolutionary War. Elijah also fought on the frontier after the Revolution and was wounded at Wheeling Creek.

This information was taken from fully documented records of the DAR and from the National Archives. Elijah received a government pension for his military service and later moved to Fairfield County, Ohio, where he and his wife, Mary Baxter Hedges, are buried. Elijah died in 1844. His son, Robert McClure Hedges, was born in 1817. In 1846, he and his wife, Sophia Kirkwood Hedges, moved to Wells County, Indiana.

Soon after Robert arrived in Wells County, he purchased about two hundred acres of land in Harrison Township, about five miles south of Bluffton, just west of the Ellingham Pike. Here he developed a well improved farm and became a prosperous farmer. Thirteen children were born to Robert and Sophia. Their son, James Kirkwood Hedges, was my grandfather who married Eunice Neff in 1872. Eunice was the daughter of Levi and Rebecca Goodspeed Neff. Levi was the son of John Neff who was born in Pennsylvania. John was the son of Jacob Neff who was born in Germany and came to this country before the Revolutionary War. Eunice's lineage has also been traced to Richard Warren who came to America on the Mayflower in 1620. As a result of this relationship, I hold membership in the General Society of Mayflower Descendants. Nine children were born to James K. and Eunice. They were: Charles Franklin, Alice, Robert, Nathan, Elbert, Arthur, Harry, Ethel, and Earl.

Charles Franklin was my father. During his early years he became quite proficient at the art of

The James Kirkwood Hedges Family about 1910 - Front row (L to R) Nell, Glen, Harry, Hattie, Nate, Ethyl Rudy, Alf Rudy, Earl, Art, Majeska, Eugene, Bert. Back row (L to R) Bob, James Kirkwood, Eunice, Crystal, Charles Franklin, Josephine, James, Effie, Mary, Grace, Murray

square dancing and was well-know for this fete. He became active in Civic affairs and was a member of the Harrison Township Advisory Board for many years. He also assisted in the administration of the schools.

In 1899, my father married Josephine Shoemaker of Nottingham Township. My father then started working in the oil field in the souther part of the county. After a few years he resigned and bought a farm located near Poneto.

My sister, Crystal, and I graduated from Bluffton High School. I was a member of the class of 1926. I took teacher's training at Ball State University and taught in Harrison Township for several years. I also taught at Portland and Berne High Schools. I returned to New York City to study at Columbia University and received my M.A. degree in 1950 and started work in school administration at Highland, Indiana, located about twenty-five miles from the Chicago Loop. In 1956 while studying at Vanderbilt University, I met my wife, Vera Lee Hedges, nee Jenkins, a teacher from Bastrop, Louisiana.

After spending two years teaching in Bastrop, we returned to Highland, Indiana, where I opened a secondary school of sixteen hundred students and a staff of one hundred people. I also became active in the North Central Association of Colleges and Secondary Schools and was a member of their evaluation staff. My wife worked in a supervisory capacity in the Hammond, Indiana Schools. When I retired we moved first to San Diego, California and then returned to Bastrop.

We are the parents of four children: our oldest son, James K. Hedges, M.D. (O.B-Gyn.) lives in Rolling Hills, California; Colonel James E. Roper of the Air Force resides in Montgomery, Alabama; Carol Emsminger lives in Indianapolis and teaches in the Indianapolis City Schools; and Lee Anna Morris lives in San Marcos, California and is the Dean of Students in a high school in Vista, California. *(James A. Hedges)*

HEDGES

Our great-grandfather, Robert McClure Hedges, and his brother came from Fairfield County, Ohio in 1846 on horseback. Apparently they served as scouts for a wagon train. They settled on a farm located south of Bluffton, on the Ellingham Pike, in Harrison Township. He married Sophia Kirkwood, and they were the parents of thirteen children.

James Kirkwood Hedges, one of the thirteen children, was our grandfather. He married Eunice Neff. They were the parents of nine children: Frank, Alice, Hedges Shoup, Robert, Nathan, J. Elbert, Arthur, Harry, Ethel Hedges Rudy, and Earl.

Grandpa Hedges was a farmer and manufactured tile. The kiln stood just south of the house on the home place, and clay for the tile was taken nearby in the same field.

Arthur Hedges, our father, taught school in his early adult life. Some of the schools where he taught were: Frog Pond, Grove, old Poplar Grove, Gerber, and Shoemaker. He often remarked that he walked to school, built the fire, did the janitor work, and taught the eight grades.

Farming was his great love, so he quit teaching. He married Effa Smith from Sidell, Illinois, where they lived several years until they bought a farm in Harrison Township adjoining his parents home. He rented a railroad car and rode with his horses, horse-drawn farm implements, and household goods, to their new home.

They were faithful members of the Prairie Methodist Church for many years.

Three daughters were born to this union: Mary Hedges Erhart, Eunice Hedges Athan, and Ruth Hedges Bowman.

Seven generations of Hedges, and their descendents, have lived on this Ellingham Pike farm, namely Robert McClure Hedges, James Kirkwood Hedges, Arthur Hedges, Eunice Hedges Athan, Don Athan, Thomas Arthur Athan and Kedric Athan.

HEDGES-WISNER

We can date the Hedges family back to 1846 in Harrison Township, to our great-grandparents Robert and Sophia (Kirkwood) Hedges. Robert and Sophia's son, James K. Hedges, married Eunice Neff. Their son, James Elbert Hedges, was my father. James Elbert married Grace Bloxsom. Their children were Eugene, Modjeska, Murray, Hubert, and myself, Charles.

I married Louise Wisner on November 23, 1939. Louise's family in Wells County dates back to 1838 in Lancaster Township. The homestead was established by her great-grandparents, William and Mary Jane (Plummer) Wisner. Her grandparents were Silas and Jennie (Masterson) Wisner. Louise's parents were Alfred and Zola (Stewart) Wisner.

Louise and I have lived on our farm in Lancaster Township for over fifty years. Our daughter, Janet, was born on February 17, 1942. She is married to Archer Farmer and they live in North Carolina. Her daughter, Sheila Settle, born on November 19, 1963, is married to Troy Geisel. They live in the former home of Sheila's great-grandparents, Alfred and Zola Wisner. Sheila graduated from Norwell High School and is attending Indiana-Purdue University. She works at Caylor-Nickel Hospital, and Troy is employed at Thunderbird Products in Decatur. Janet's son, Douglas Settle, graduated from Norwell High School and lives in Fort Wayne. He is employed at Don Ayres Auto Mall in Fort Wayne.

Our second child, William Hedges, was born June 10, 1943. William received his masters in American History from Ball State University. He

The James Kirkwood Hedges Family taken approximately 1910

The Hedges family on the 50th wedding anniversary of Charles and Louise Hedges. November 23, 1989, Janet, Archer, Joyce, Dustin, Jennifer, Bryce, Cindy, SusanWilliam Hedges, Ryan, Douglas, Troy, Sheila, William Seck, Charles, Louise, Richard and Erin

has been employed at South Side High School in Fort Wayne for twenty-five years, where he is currently the assistant principal. William married Susan Tucker from Terre Haute. Their son, Ryan Hedges, was born April 7, 1971. Ryan graduated from Snider High School and is now attending Northwestern University. Their daughter, Erin Hedges, is a graduate of Snider High School in Fort Wayne. She plans to attend Butler University in the fall of 1991.

Eleven years later, our second son, Richard, was born on February 12, 1954. Richard received a Bachelor's degree in education from Ball State University. He married Cindy Lindemann from Tocsin, Indiana. They live with their daughter, Bryce, who was born September 24, 1988, in Longmont, Colorado. Richard is the assistant manager of a land development company in Boulder, Colorado.

Our second daughter, Joyce, was born on September 8, 1956. She received her Bachelor's degree in elementary education from Ball State University and her Master's degree in education from Indiana-Purdue University. Joyce has taught first grade at Lancaster School since 1978. Joyce and her husband, William Seck, live in Lancaster Township. A son, Dustin, was born on December 16, 1981, and a daughter, Jennifer, was born on January 19, 1984. *(Charles and Louise Hedges)*

NOTE: Charles Hedges passed away April 22, 1991 after this article was written.

HEINIGER

Ulich Heiniger was born in 1864 in Bern, Switzerland, and came to the United States in 1880 when he was sixteen years old. He went to Elgin, Iowa. He met and married Anna Baumgartner in Prairie Du Chen, Wisconsin in 1892. George was born in 1893, Fred was born in 1895, Henry in 1897, Clara in 1900, and Nellie in 1910.

George married Beulah Reinhold and lived in Fort Wayne, Indiana. He was in World War I. He was a mailman in Fort Wayne. Fred was in World War I and went to France. He came home, farmed, and married Clella Stahl from Murray, Indiana, December 29, 1921. Wayne was born August 30, 1922, in Vera Cruz, Indiana. Esther was born August 17, 1925. Wayne was in World War II, 94th Division of the 8th Air Force. He was stationed in England. He came home in 1945. He worked at GE in Fort Wayne. He met Phyllis Clark at Rural Youth.

Phyllis was born in Wisconsin. She came to work at the Caylor-Nickel Clinic. Her brother, Dick, married Beulah Kaehr from Adams County. That's how Phyllis came here. Wayne and Phyllis were married on November 30, 1947. They rented the Six Mile Parsonage, lived in Vera Cruz a year, and then moved to Bluffton, Indiana. They bought a house at 228 East Wiley. The Paul Wassons were their neighbors for several years. Wayne and Phyllis had four children: Bruce, Cynthia, Dale and Steven.

Bruce and Cynthia went to Park School before we moved to Curryville, Indiana. Bruce married Nancy and lives in LaOtto, Indiana. Nancy had four children and Bruce adopted them. They are: Kenny, Melvin, Cindy and Velvet. Velvet was killed in an auto accident five years ago. Kenny married Tonya and has Kelsey and Kenneth.

Cynthia married Carl Knueve and lives in New Haven. They have a son, Gregory, born January 29, 1991.

Dale married Diane Dishong. They have a son, Eric, born May 20, 1989.

Steve is at home with Phyllis and Wayne. Esther married Bernard Whonsetler. They have five children: Janet, Paula, Susan, Mary and Craig.

Janet married and lives in Denver, Colorado. She has a girl. Paula married and lives in Toledo, Ohio. She has a boy. Susan married and lives in Anchorage, Alaska and has three girls. Mary married and lives in Washington Center Courthouse, Ohio, and has a girl. Craig lives at home in Hicksville, Ohio. Henry Heiniger was a chiropractor in California. He had a daughter. Clara Heiniger didn't have children. Nellie Heiniger married Bert Moser and they had four children. Kenny married Wanda Mertz. Phyllis married Virgil Swartz. Betty married Shorty Mann. Frank married Norma Johnson. Bert Moser founded Moser and Son Heating. Kenny and Frank worked for Bert. Shorty Mann took over for Bert. Shorty retired and his son, Steve, took over and owns it now.

DAVID HELLER

David Heller was born November 7, 1830, in Cumberland County, Pennsylvania. His parents were German immigrants. The family moved to Nottingham Township in 1838 from Fremont, Ohio. The father, Levi Heller, purchased eighty acres at one dollar and twenty-five cents an acre. Later he purchased forty acres. At the second purchase he was looking for someone to split rails so that when they moved the following year they would be able to fence in their livestock. A neighbor woman (name unknown) heard of his request and said she would split one thousand rails for five dollars, which she did.

They arrived in Wells County the first week of August, 1838. They had to cut a road half a mile through underbrush to unload the household goods, five barrels of flour, and blacksmith tools.

David and Mary Ann Gentis Heller

Part of the rails that had been split were used to build a double rail pen for a house until they could build a log cabin. The rail pen had two sides and a back partition. The first two nights the roof was bed quilts until they could make clapboards. By the third day it was covered and ready for rain.

The next step was to dig a well. After that everyone who was big enough had to help clear ground so they could sow winter wheat for next year's bread. Then they were ready to fell trees for the log cabin.

The first winter the wolves came so close they could hear their teeth crack, and they would howl night after night. There was also plenty of deer, wild turkey, rabbits, and squirrels. There were some bears, lots of raccoons, opossums, porcupines, some wild cats, foxes and many snakes.

After the cabin was up, the rest of the winter was spent in clearing more land to plant corn in the spring.

When David was seventeen years old, the John Gentis family moved onto acres bordering the Hellers. They had a daughter, Mary Ann, who was fourteen years old. After four years of courtship, David and Mary Ann married in 1852. They rented forty acres from his father to help pay for the eighty acres he purchased across the road from his father.

They had two children. Edward was born September 21, 1856, and married Sarah Miller on November 28, 1880. They had three children, Bert C., Ollie, and Pearl. Edward's sister Sarah was born July 26, 1854, and married Noah Gottschalk on September 15, 1878. They also had three children: Berthena, Harry, and Goldie.

At this writing one grandchild still lives, Pearl Heller Smith, who was one hundred years old on December 26, 1990. There are four great-grandchildren. Loren and Ruth Gottschalk, Lois Heller Bohlke, and Mildred Rinebolt.

In the year 1876 (the centennial year), David, Mary Ann, Sarah, Edward and a fifth unknown person each planted a tree in honor of our country's birthday. Four of the trees are still alive. The farm is now owned by Dale and Delores Harvey.

The Hellers celebrated fifty-nine years of marriage. David died in 1919 and Mary Ann in 1912.

This history was taken from the autobiography written by David Heller in 1912 when he was eighty-one years old, seven years prior to his death.

PAUL HELMS FAMILY

Paul Dwight Helms was born August 29, 1919, in Warren, Indiana. Paul went to school in Warren and graduated from Warren High School in 1937. He served in the Army from January, 1942 through September, 1945, during World War II. While in the Army he met a young woman while stationed at Pine Camp, New York. He married Virginia Mae (Smith) born November 29, 1927, in Mercerville, New Jersey. They were married February 16, 1946, in Hamilton Square, New Jersey Baptist Church. He is a retired farmer and retired factory worker from Franklin Electric in Bluffton, Indiana. He worked at Franklin Electric in Bluffton from 1966 to 1976. Virginia is a housewife and from 1965-1984 went to work at the Corning Plant in Wells County near Bluffton.

They lived in Huntington County for six months after their marriage and then in Wells County for one year near Liberty Center. They moved back to Huntington County near Warren for about four years. Then back to Wells County in 1951 east of McNatt for about eight years. The next move was to just north of McNatt to where they live today.

Their present location is in Section 9 of Jackson Township in Wells County. They have seven children: Susan Kay Stone (April 19, 1847); Sandra Sue Archbold (September 11, 1949); Sheryl Ann Roush (July 11, 1953); Sharlene Alice Bumgarner, (September 6, 1956); Paul Dwight (November 1958), deceased; Sara Jane Betts (March 29, 1960); Stephanie Mae Habig (July 25, 1961). Susan graduated from Jackson Center High School in 1965, the rest of the girls graduated from Southern Wells High School.

Paul Helms Family
Top: Susan and Sandy. Middle: Paul, Virginia, and Sheryl. Bottom: Sara, Stephanie, Sharlene

Susan Kay Stone has two children, Dawn Richelle (August 18, 1971) and Shawn Everett (February 16, 1973).

Sandra Sue Archbold has two children, Tricia Lynn (August 1, 1970) and Gregory Michael (February 25, 1973).

Sheryl Ann Roush has three children, Joel Christopher (November 18, 1970), Chad Justin (April 9, 1973) and Julie Christine (March 7, 1977).

Sara Jane Betts has three children, Emily Dawn (April 7, 1984), Brandon Michael (January 22, 1986) and Corey Paul (July 28, 1988).

Stephanie Mae Habig has two children, Jennifer Mae (February 7, 1981 and Ryan Jeffrey (March 13, 1987).

Paul's father was Ernest Russell Helms, born April 19, 1890, and died October 24, 1974. He was a prosperous farmer in Huntington County, a Republican politician, serving on many committees for his party. He married Vera Mable Helms. She was born August 29, 1890, and died November 23, 1969. She was a housewife. They had four sons, Meredith, Paul, Vaughn and Max.

Ernest's father was William H. Helms born in Winchester in 1851 and later moved to Huntington County. He died in 1919. He married Eunice A. Irwin. She was born in 1849 and died in 1928. William was also a prosperous farmer in Salamonie Township, Huntington County.

Vera's father was Harrie C. Manring born November 4, 1866, and died May 13, 1953. He married Anna Laurie Cross. She was born April 4, 1867, and died June 18, 1963. Harrie was County Road Supervisor for two years and a farmer. They resided in Jackson Township in Wells County.

HENLEY-FRAVEL-LAMBERT

William Dowe Henley Jr. was born July 4, 1926. His parents are William Dowe Sr. and Lucile (Lambert) Henley and the family lived in Poneto. He has one sister, Lois, and one brother, Richard. His father is deceased and his mother, a retired school teacher, lives in Montpelier, Indiana.

In 1934, the family moved to Nottigham Township, one mile north of Phenix, where Bill worked on his parents' farm while attending school. Bill graduated from Petroleum High School in 1944.

As a youngster, Bill enjoyed the several days each summer spent with his grandparents, William and Leona Lambert, at their home just east of Poneto.

During World War II, Bill enlisted in the Army Air Corps, was stationed at Biloxi, Mississippi, for his basic training, and was at Las Vegas Air Base at war's end and his discharge in 1945.

On December 31, 1946, Bill married Madeline Fravel from Geneva, Indiana, daughter of William and Ruth (Christman) Fravel. Madeline's father was a building contractor, a school bus driver for twenty-eight years and Geneva street and water superintendent for many years. Madeline's mother was a homemaker.

Following their marriage, Bill and Madeline moved to Chicago, where Bill attended ITI and earned an associate degree in industrial electronics. They then moved to Bluffton and had two daughters. Bill worked for General Electric in Fort Wayne. In March, 1948, Bill started work with Montgomery Ward and Company. Bill and Madeline and their two daughters left Bluffton in 1954 when Bill was promoted to assistant manager of the Ward Store in St. Marys, Ohio. They then moved to Crawfordsville, Indiana; Decatur, Illinois; and then to Bloomington, Illinois, where their third daughter was born.

In October, 1959, Bill was named to store manager of the Wards Store in Kewanee, Illinois. Moves followed to the Chicago Roseland Ward Store; Jacksonville, Illinois; Taylorsville, Illinois; Rockford, Illinois; Janesville, Wisconsin; and Rhinelander, Wisconsin. Bill was active in the Chamber of Commerce, Rotary, and Kiwanis civic clubs. Madeline always worked in the school systems.

In January, 1983, Bill retired from Montgomery Ward after thirty-five years with the company. Bill and Madeline then moved to Geneva, Indiana, and built a home on Rainbow Lake. They both have kept busy buying, reworking and selling real estate. Bill has served on the Lake Board, the Geneva Town Board and the Chamber of Commerce. Bill is presently on the Geneva Library Board and the Adams County Foundation Board.

Bill and Madeline's daughters are Judith, living in Normal, Illinois. Judy attended Illinois State University and works for Grow-Mark, a division of Illinois Farm Bureau. She has two children, Tammy and Robert.

Diane lives in Ventura, California. Diana attended Patricia Stevens and the University of California at Santa Barbara, and is a drafter for an engineering firm in Santa Barbara, California. She has one daughter, Chanda.

Nancy lives in Thorp, Wisconsin. Nancy attended the University of Wisconsin at Whitewater and is a social services investigator for Clark County, Wisconsin.

HENSLEY-LAMBERT-BRODT

William Dowe Henley (April 20, 1901), son of Samuel and Malinda Ogalsbee Henley, and Mildred Lucile Lambert (October 8, 1900) were married May 19, 1923 at Huntington, Indiana. They became the parents of three children: Lois Clare Henley Mitchell, William Dowe Henley, Jr., and Richard Lambert Henley. Dowe and Lucile were graduated from Bluffton High School in 1918. Prior to their marriage, Lucile had attended Muncie Normal and Madam Blaker Teacher's College, Indianapolis, and taught five years in Wells County schools. Dowe farmed most of his life. In 1934, they bought a farm in Nottingham Township where the family lived for thirty-one years.

In 1954, Lucile began teaching first grade in Montpelier, where she taught until retirement 1968. In 1965, they moved to Montpelier. Dowe's death occurred on October 13, 1965.

Lucile Henley

Lucile's paternal grandparents were Robert P. (April 7, 1844), and Caroline Harding Lambert (March 31, 1849). They were natives of Queen's County, Ireland. In 1847 Robert P., age three, arrived in America with his father, William H. Lambert; his mother, Susan Pierson Lambert, had died at sea. William H. and son went to Butler County, Ohio, where the father married Matilda Moore. In reminiscing, Robert always recalled her kindness. Later the family moved to Wayne County, Indiana, where a daughter, Susan, was born. In 1859, they located on land previously purchased in Chester Township, Wells County.

In 1860 Robert lost by death, his father, stepmother and half sister. All are buried at Woodlawn, Montpelier.

After service in the Civil War, Robert was a member of the Lew Dailey Post G.A.R. at Bluffton.

At age 23, Caroline Harding, daughter of Arthur and Lavenia Dickinson Harding, natives of Ireland, came alone to visit relatives in America.

On May 12, 1872, Robert P. Lambert and Caroline Harding were married in Bluffton. They became parents of thirteen children. In 1882, they acquired land in Nottigham Township, one-fourth mile west of Herrman School, which their children attended. For several years they enjoyed revenue from oil wells on their farm. Their son, William A., was pumper for these wells. After the oil boom in this area, he was an oil driller in other states, including Oklahoma.

After retirement Robert and Caroline moved to Poneto where he died on June 16, 1935 and she on August 20, 1929.

The maternal grandparents, John and Emma Sechler Brodt, were of German Descent. John's parents, Gottlieb and Margaretta Seaman Brodt were members of Horeb Lutheran Church. They are buried at Horeb Cemetery. Gottlieb came to America in 1832.

Emma Sechler Brodt's parents, Benjamin and Eliza Moyer Sechler, were pioneers in Union Township. They were members of St. John Lutheran Church and are buried at St. John Cemetery.

Benjamin's parents were Jacob and Maria Fusselman Sechler. Jacob's father, Andrew Sechler, and Maria's father, Philip Fusselman, served in the Revolutionary War.

Lucile Henley is a member of Calvary Lutheran Church, Bluffton; Francois Godfroy Chapter National Society Daughters of the American Revolution; Order of Eastern Star; and Daughters of the Union Veterans of the Civil War.

HENLEY-MITCHELL

Lois Clare Henley Mitchell, born February 18, 1924, is the daughter of William Dowe Henley and Lucile Lambert Henley. A 1942 graduate of Petroleum High School, she received a nursing degree in 1945 from Lutheran Hospital School of Nursing at Fort Wayne, Indiana. For twenty years, she was employed as a nursing supervisor at the University of Chicago Hospital and clinics. Sine returning to Indiana in 1976, she has been employed as a psychiatric nurse at Veterans Administration Medical Center, Marion, Indiana.

She has three daughters: Ruth Lucile, married to Dennis Price, Vietnam veteran, has a B.S. degree in business administration, and is a supervisor at S K Tool Company in Chicago, Illinois. She has a daughter, Tina and a son, Lewis.

Linda Kay is a 1978 graduate of Blackford High School. In 1983, she received a B.S. degree in political science at Ball State University. After serving three years in the U.S. Army, she was married to Scott Bassett, a native of Nebraska, who had served seven years in the U.S. Army. He is employed at Veterans Administration Medical Center, Marion, Indiana. They have one son, Everett Bassett.

Susan was graduated from Blackford High School in 1978. She attended Indiana State University at Terre Haute, Indiana and received a B.A. degree, majoring in English and Education in 1983. After teaching a year at Francesville, Indiana, she was married to Chris Logan, an Intelligence Specialist in the U.S. Navy. They have two sons, Andrew and Joseph.

Lois has two Revolutionary War ancestors who served from Pennsylvania. Her maternal grandfather, William A. Lambert, was a player on the noted Keystone football team in 1904.

HENLEY-PEARSON

Richard L. Henley born November 18, 1941, son of William Dowe Henley and Lucile Lambert Henley, who were natives of Wells County, was married March 1, 1964, to Judy K. Pearson, born October 18, 1943, daughter of Jack and Joan Burklo Pearson. They are parents of four children: John Richard, December 31, 1965; Chris William, December 20, 1966; Lori K., February 5, 1968; and Jackie Lucile, May 8, 1970.

John Richard, after graduation from Norwell High School 1984, attended Andrews University, Berrien Springs, Michigan. After giving one year of student missionary service in Bangkok, Thailand, in 1988, he will complete an M.S. degree in biology at Andrews in June, 1991.

On July 29, 1990, John was married to Penny Sue Teeter, an registered nurse, who graduated from Southern College, Collegedale, Tennessee in 1990 and is employed at Memorial Hospital in South Bend. Penny, daughter of Larry and Tootie Teeter, was born March 22, 1969. John and Penny reside in Berrien Springs, Michigan.

Jackie, John, Judy K., Chris, Lori, and Richard

Chris William was graduated from Norwell High School in 1985. He was graduated from Walla Walla College in College Place, Washington, in 1989, receiving a B.S. degree in mechanical engineering. he is now employed with Boeing Aircraft, and resides in Seattle.

Lori K. Henley, after graduation from Norwell in 1986, is attending Walla Walla College in College Place, Washington, and will receive a B.S. degree in civil engineering in June of 1991.

Jackie Lucile Henley, a 1988 graduate from Norwell is a junior at Andrews University and plans to be graduated with a B.S. degree in chemistry in 1992.

Judy K. Pearson Henley is a 1961 graduate of Petroleum High School. She was graduated from Parkview Memorial Hospital School of Nursing in Fort Wayne in 1964. For the past ten years she has been employed as a certified psychiatric nurse at the Veterans' Administration Medical Center, Marion, Indiana. She has two Revolutionary ancestors who served from Virginia, and she is a member of the Captain William Wells Chapter, National Society Daughters of the American Revolution.

Richard L. Henley is a 1959 graduate of Petroleum High School. After attending college a year, he served in the U.S. Army for three years, October, 1963 to October, 1966. For twenty-nine years he has been employed as plumber and steam fitter at General Electric in Fort Wayne.

Richard is a descendant of Thompson Henley, native of Virginia, who took out a land patent in 1838 in Harrison Township, Wells County. His son, William Henley, was a soldier in the Civil War, enlisting at Indianapolis, with Company H 47th Regiment, Indiana Volunteers. He died in the Battle of Champion Hills, Mississippi, on May 16, 1863. He left two sons, Charles C. and Samuel Henley. On December 18, 1884, Samuel married to Malinda Ogalsbee. They became the parents of three children: Charles H., May, and William Dowe. Dowe and Lucile Lambert were married May 19, 1923, at Huntington.

Richard and Judy and family are members of the Chapel Hill Seventh Day Adventist Church at Markle, Indiana. Their home is in Rockcreek Township.

MICHAEL AND LENA BIBERSTEIN HENNEFORD

When Michael Henneford was seventeen years of age, he left his native Wurttemberg, Germany, embarking at Bremen, Germany, and landing at New York City on or about June 24, 1869. He then proceeded to Vera Cruz, Indiana and settled there. In Vera Cruz he met Lena Biberstein whom he married on June 22, 1873.

Michael was born March 6, 1852, in Breitenberg, Wurttemberg, Germany, which is near Stuttgart in the Black Forest. Michael was a blacksmith by profession. Lena, who was the fifteenth of Benedict and Rosanna Ritter Biberstein's sixteen children, was born on May 20, 1852 in Wayne County, Ohio.

Michael Henneford standing in front of his comfortable home in Vera Cruz

Michael was a member of the Saint John Reformed Church in Vera Cruz and was an ardent church worker. He served as a trustee and a member of the church's building committee. The depth of his religious convictions is indicated by the fact that in his sixty years of membership at the Saint John Reformed Church, he had only missed attending Sunday School and Worship Service twice. Both times he was ill.

In 1866, when Lena was fourteen, she was confirmed in the Saint John Reformed Church in

Vera Cruz. She was an active member of that church all her life. The Ladies Aid Society of the Church met at her house occasionally.

Michael and Lena had eight children, all of whom were born in Vera Cruz.

Amelia was born March 23, 1874. She played the piano and organ and made wedding dresses for brides-to-be. She married Emanuel Joray on her thirty-third birthday. They had two sons, Philip and William.

Kathryn was born May 1, 1876. In her twenties, she became a dry-goods clerk at the Niblick Department Store in Decatur and eventually married the owner, Daniel M. Niblick.

The eldest son, George, was born February 26, 1879. He married Jeanette Myers and they had two children, Walter and Romaine. In 1911, George and his family moved to Montana.

The next son, Otto, was born July 9, 1881. He married Charlotte Monroe and the couple had two daughters, Helen and Ethel. Otto was a school teacher and lived for awhile in Montana, also.

Martin was born September 5, 1883. He married Pearl Heche and they had two children, Donald and Marjorie. Martin raised hogs and milked dairy cattle on an eighty acre farm near Vera Cruz.

Mary Mathilda, who was know as Tillie, was born February 5, 1886. She married Frank McFarren and lived in Bluffton.

The seventh child, William, was born May 21, 1888 and died three and one-half years later.

Harold was born July 11, 1891. He graduated from Heidelberg College in 1913. He was an accomplished musician who played both piano and organ. Harold lived in Olympia, Washington, where he was appointed chairman of the State Board of Tax Commissioners and also served as state party chairman for the Democratic Party.

Lena died in the afternoon of Friday, October 17, 1930. The common testimony of her children was that she was a wonderful mother and that she labored in love for her children until her hands were stricken. Michael died on November 6, 1934. Both Michael and Lena Henneford were highly respected citizens of the Vera Cruz community.

HENSCHEN-YANEY

Ida Henschen was born in 1889, grew up and married Orville Yaney. They were both of Kirkland Township in Adams County. With three children, they moved to Oklahoma where Orville worked the oil wells. While in Oklahoma, six more children were added to the family. They eventually migrated back to Indiana.

Ida Yaney and daughter, Evelyn, with husband Ken Rutledge and daughter Janice, lived together in a house on West Mill Street in Ossian near the grain elevator and railroad.

Bill Yaney, wife Betty and four children: Marsha, Joy, Keven, and Mike lived just a few blocks from there.

Vera and husband Carl Easley raised their five children: Bob, Jim, Larry, Carol, and Don, in Ossian and Craigville.

Georgia and husband Paul Arnold raised three children, Barbara, Denny, and Ron, on the Arnold homestead in Kirkland Township, Adams County.

Margaret with three daughters, Donna, Mardell, and Dena; and Ed Yaney, with wife Mary Jane and three children, Doug, Susan, and Sally, settled and raised their families in Fort Wayne.

Ida outlived five of her nine children. She died at one hundred years, six months and one day old at Ossian Health Center on July 9, 1989.

HERBST

Albert Herbst, son of Joseph Herbst, and his wife, Martha Augusta (Perkins), lived in Bluffton and raised three children, Bertha Henrietta, Ralph, and Guy. Bertha married Earl Bruce Sturgis, who later became one of Bluffton's leading dentists. Ralph and his wife Ola lived in Richmond, Indiana, and had one son, Robert, who still lives there. Guy's wife was Irene, and they had three daughters: Catherine, Mary Louise, and Frances, they eventually moved to Gary, Indiana. Catherine is the sole survivor of her immediate family and now lives in Mesa, Arizona.

DONALD F. HERMAN FAMILY

Donald Floyd Herman was born February 4, 1920, in Adams County to Frank and Jessie Kaves Herman. He attended Hartford Center School. He served in the Army with the Transportation Corps during World War II. He is of German Ancestry.

He is married to Grace Madonna Liechty Herman. She was born in Adams County on October 28, 1931 to Amos and Della Nussbaum Liechty. She graduated from Monroe High School. Grace is from Swiss ancestry.

They farmed in Adams County near Linn Grove before moving to Nottingham Township in 1968, where they purchased a dairy farm at 10172 S 200 E. Keystone, Indiana.

They are the parents of the following: Ronald Dean (1950) who is married to Linda Bentley (1948) and they have two children, Amy Renee (1980) and Adam Wesley (1982). Ron is employed at EPC in Geneva. They reside in rural Keystone.

Steven Lynn (1955) who is married to Vivian Stiltner (1957). Steve is employed at Troxel Equipment. They reside in rural Keystone.

Sharlene Sue Morgan (1956) who is married to Glen Morgan (1955). They have two children, Jerome David (1978) and Melissa Sue (1980). Sharlene is a Realtor with Daniels Realty in Ossian. They reside in Bluffton.

Arlene Lou Herman (1956) is employed at Keebler and resides in Bluffton.

Brian Lee (1958) was married to Karen Buckland (dissolved). He has two children, Jill Madonna (1980) and Benjamin Jay (1983). Brian is employed with his father on the Dairy Farm. He resides in rural Keystone.

Joy Ellen Mygrant (1960) is married to Michael Mygrant (1956) and they have two daughters, Lisa Diane (1978) and Dawn Marie (1979). Joy is employed at Ames and they reside in rural Bluffton.

Jay Allen Herman (1960-1982) was killed in a farm accident in the fall of 1982.

Edward Ray (1962) is married to Celinda Luckey (1962) and they have two children, Jarrod Jay (1985) and Ashley Nicole (1988). Ed is the Wells County Highway supervisor and they reside in rural Keystone.

HERWICK-HALL

Frank Vance Herwick, a native of Zaleski, Vinton County, Ohio was born July 8, 1885. He attended grade and high school, and was enrolled in Rio Grande College in Ohio. He was employed by the Government Inspection Service and was assigned to Hoof and Mouth disease control in Indiana. This employment led to Frank meeting an Indiana school teacher, Miss Chloe Hall.

Frank was one of six Herwick children born to Valentine John Herwick and Violetta Reynolds Herwick. Valentine was born in 1845, but place of birth is not clear. His induction papers into the Civil War lists his place of birth as Germany. Census information of 1880 lists Louisiana as his birthplace. Violetta Reynolds was a member of a large colonial family migrating to Ohio from Maryland and Virginia. Her parents were George Reynolds and Elida Ann Jones Reynolds.

Chole Hall was the daughter of Nun Hall and Mary Habig Hall. This was Nun Halls second marriage. His marriage to Miss Ruth Ray ended in divorce leaving three young children: William, Eva, and Cora Hall. Mary Habig Hall raised these three children and three of their own: Chloe, Elizabeth and John. Nun Hall was the son of Reuben Hall and Elizabeth McIntire. Mary Habig was the daughter of Phillip Habig and Elizabeth Wisenfelder, both natives of Germany. Phillip emigrated with three other brothers during the Civil War: John, Peter and Jasper. They were following the Potters Trade in Missouri. Phillip located in Darke County, Ohio, Randolph and Wells counties in Indiana. Phillip was a farmer.

Ed Yaney in far back. Back (L to R) Bill Yaney, Margaret Beamer (Ross), Ida Yaney, Orville Yaney, Vera Easley, Homer Yaney, Georgia Arnold. Middle (L to R) Evelyn Rutledge, Bob Easley, Donna Beamer, Mardell Beamer, Jim Easley. Front (L to R) Janice Rutledge, Larry Easley, Barbara Arnold

John Habig, son of Phillip and Elizabeth, and brother of Mary Habig Hall farmed in Chester Township, Wells County. He was married to Minta Hamilton and they were the parents of twins, Howard and Inex Habig Grove, Alice Habig Merritt, and Harvey Habig. They also raised a nephew, Cletus Hamilton. John's second marriage was to Mrs. Meda Peck Miller.

Elizabeth Hall, born July 5, 1893, married Jesse Hamilton. They farmed in Wells County and retired in Bluffton. Elizabeth took care of her mother and they shared later years together.

John Hall, son of Nun and Mary Habig Hall, unmarried, died at age 26 and is buried in Keystone Friends Cemetery.

Chloe Hall was born August 31, 1891. She married Frank V. Herwick April 12, 1917, in Bluffton, Indiana. Their daughter Mary Violetta Herwick was born June 1, 1918 in Westerville, Ohio. She celebrated her Golden Wedding Anniversary with her husband Max C. Holloway on December 22, 1990. They are the parents of two children, Marcia Ann Holloway born in 1945 when her father was serving in the Pacific War in World War II and Vance Cary Holloway, born in 1950, unmarried and lives in a group home in Mishawaka, Indiana. Marcia Ann Holloway married Jack Michael Holloway of North Liberty, Indiana, August 19, 1967. They both graduated from Indiana University in 1967. They are the parents of two girls: Jennifer Leigh Holloway and Jessica Lynn Holloway. They attend McCutcheon High School in Tippencanoe County, Indiana.

Max and Mary Holloway have made their home in Columbia City, Indiana and since retirement have spent six months in Dunedin, Florida and six months in Indiana each year.

HETRICK

Peter Hetrick was just a young man of about twenty-six when he brought his family to Wells County from Perry County, Ohio. The year was 1844. Peter, wife Catherine (Drum), and sons David, Amos and Simon settled in the woods in what is now Lancaster Township and became one of the early pioneer families of the township. They purchased ground owned by Catherine's father, John Peter Drum of Ohio. The couple later had two daughters born in Wells County, Mrs. John Trostel and Mrs. Sara Ann Hartman. David and Simon married Margaret and Caroline Bender respectively. Amos married Catherine Diehl and, like David and Margaret, birthed no children.

A portion of the Hetrick farm was platted in April, 1879, by Peter in cooperation with his neighbor, William Hartman. Craigville became prosperous due to the railroad. The small town can boast of being the first dial system in the county, and had the only bank in the county to survive the 1929 crash. Craigville still has a post office.

Amos and Catherine adopted the youngest child of Samuel and Lucinda (Cline) Diehl because Lucinda died three days after childbirth. Amos Harlow Diehl was thus provided for by Samuel's sister and brother-in-law. On February 28, 1888, at the age of twelve, young Amos H. was legally adopted. Samuel and Lucinda had four other children: William, Franklin, Mary, Ellen (Brown), and Hannah Rosa (Uhrich) before Amos was born.

Clarissa Stultz became Samuel's second wife and with this marriage produced seven step-siblings for young Amos. They include: Samuel, Martha, Adam and Lillie, plus three who died in infancy.

William and Hannah (Billman) Diehl were the natural grandparents of the adopted Amos Hetrick. Besides Samuel and Catherine, they had a third child, Mary, who married James Ward.

Amos Harlow married Rosa Arretta Abbott in 1895. Rosa was a daughter of the Reverend Daniel William and Esther Jane (Lambert) Abbott. The Reverend Abbott was a circuit-riding preacher in a large area of Indiana and Ohio which included Wells County. Rosa was a charter member of one of her father's churches, the Craigville United Brethren. The Reverend Abbott was a Civil War soldier of the North; a preserved letter sent to his wife Jane places him in the trenches outside Richmond in the final few days before the fall of Richmond and the defeat of the Confederate Army.

Five children were born to Amos and Rosa. Arie Armintha married Harry Heckley. Tracy LaVera married Robert Nyle Wolf. Maynard Alton married Mary Thomas. Mable Irene married Roy Schlickman and lived in Gibson City, Illinois. Donald Robert married Madge Elnore Wasson and they lived most of their life in Fort Wayne and had two children, Darrell Gene and Steven Dee. It is only through Don that the Hetrick name continued from the adopted Amos.

RUBY JOHNSON PRUITT HICKS

Ruby June Johnson was born June 8, 1901, in Rockcreek Township, the ninth child of Glessner and Rachel Butler Johnson. Ruby attended the Seventh Day Adventist Church school and, after it closed, the one-room, eight-grade public school at the south end of her father's property (100N 500W). Upon finishing eighth grade, Ruby attended high school at Liberty Center one year, Beechwood Academy, a Seventh-day Adventist boarding high school near Indianapolis, one year, and graduated from Emmanuel Missionary Academy, Berrien Spring, Michigan. Ruby went on to get a college degree in home economics at Emmanuel Missionary College (now Andrews University) in Berrien Springs, Michigan. She then obtained a position as food service director and home economics teacher at Cedar Lake Academy, Cedar Lake, Michigan.

Howard H. Hicks and Ruby Johnson Pruitt Hicks

Ruby met Carl Pruitt from Peru, Indiana while at Emmanuel Missionary College and married him June 5, 1923. Carl had studied to be a minster, and their first home was a tent set up in Cheboygan, where Carl helped hold evangelistic tent meetings. From that beginning, Carl and Ruby moved around Michigan pastoring many churches. Carl and Ruby moved back to Indiana and Carl pastored seven churches in northeast Indiana, including the Rockford SDA church where Ruby first attended church and school. Carl died on September 25, 1962, following a move to Logansport, Indiana.

Ruby moved back to Rockford for a time, then moved to California. After a few years she came back to Indiana and lived with her sister Urania a couple of years. She lived in Florida one winter and decided to move to Florida. When she went to California to get her belongings, she changed her mind and stayed in California. It was there that she renewed acquaintance with Howard H. Hicks, who had been the president of the Northern Michigan Conference when she and Carl first set up housekeeping. Howard has been widowed and Ruby and Howard married and lived in Escondido, California. At Howard's death, Ruby moved back to Loma Linda, California and has lived there since.

HIGGINS

James H. Higgins and Lydia M. Chalfant were both born in Scioto County, Ohio. They were among the early settlers in Wells County. History tells us that James H. Higgins and Lydia M. Chalfant Higgins had several children. One of them was Chads Higgins (1858) He was our grandfather. Also we understand that James H. Higgins laid out the town of Newville (now Vera Cruz), loved animals, and rode around the county on horseback doctoring and caring for them.

Chads Higgins married Ida M. Cobbum in 1883. Reports tell us that the father of Ida Cobbum, James Cobbum, came with his parents in 1836 from Hocking County, Ohio. He was only two years old and his mother held him and rode horseback as they entered the Wells County wilderness. Chads and Ida M. had two sons, James Earl and Charles E. Higgins.

Doctor Earl Higgins

James Earl married Arnetta Pearl Ditzler in 1906. Pearl was the daughter of John Ditzler and Kathryn Bulinda Brickley from another pioneer family. Earl and Pearl first lived on the Brickley farm near Murray and Earl hauled logs to the Bricley sawmill. Earl Higgins and Pearl first lived in Rockcreek Township; Earl then worked along the banks of the Wabash River with his horses. In 1912, Earl build their home in Harrison Township five miles southeast of Bluffton on Six Mile Creek. This house was built from timber cut from the farm. Earl purchased this farm from his father, Chads. He farmed until 1914 when he decided there had to be a better way to make a living. Earl then enrolled in the Indianapolis Veterinary College, graduating on April 17, 1917. Dr. Earl Higgins was a practicing veterinary surgeon in Wells County for fifty-two years. Doctor Higgins served two different periods on the Wells County Board of Commissioners: 1928-1940 and 1956-1961. Doctor Higgins was also a great horseman; in 1936 he imported, with the Holbert Horse Importing Company, Belgian stallions from France. He bred, trained, sold, and swapped Belgian horses until the 1950's.

Earl Higgins was born 1887 and died in 1971. Pearl Ditzler Higgins was born 1886 and died in 1943. Both are buried in the Bethel Cemetery, Wells County.

Earl and Pearl were the parents of three daughters and three sons: Helen Lucile (1907-1917); Hermenia (1909), married Robert L. Schlagenhauf and their children are: Jane (Davidson), Ted Schlagenhauf, and Alice (Moore).

Kathryn (1911-1971), married Harold Hott who died in 1979 and their children are: Richard Hott, Don Hott, Janet (Krick), Joyce Hott, and Judy (Baumann).

Dale (1919-1976), married Mary Van Emon and their children are: David Higgins and Tom Higgins.

Joe E. (1922), married Betty Baumgartner, and their children are: Sandy (Wolker), Sharon (Suttleworth), John Robert Higgins, Sheila (Resinger), Sue Ellen (Brown), and Sindy (Cockriel).

James H. (1926), married Patricia Ifer and they are now living in Bluffton. Their children are James Michael Higgins and Connie Sue (Hose).

HIGGINS-THRAILKILL

Kenneth L. (Casey) Higgins and Hilda Jane Thrailkill were married at Noblesville, Indiana on September 1, 1935. The photograph of Mr. and Mrs. Higgins was taken in Fort Wayne, Indiana at their 50th wedding anniversary dinner party with many friends.

Kenneth is a retired Bluffton Postmaster, Wells County Auditor and County Councilman. He was also associated with food processors, H.J. Heinz Corporation, McNeil and Libby, and a co-owner of Bluffton Foods Incorporated. For thirty-five years, he and Mrs. Higgins resided on their farm at the Bluffton city limits, State Road 124 West. In 1972, they build and moved to a home at 1225 Sycamore Lane, Riverview addition in which they lived for seven years. They have spent the past fourteen years at the farm and in their home located in Bradenton, Florida.

Kenneth and Hilda Higgins
September 1, 1985

Kenneth L. Higgins is the son of Charles E. Higgins and Carrie B. Hower. Charles E. Higgins was the son of Chads Chalfant Higgins, and his mother was Ida Mae Cobbum. The Higgins, Chalfant and Cobbum families were natives and early residents of Harrison Township, Wells County. Carrie B. Hower, Kenneth's mother, was the daughter of Noah Hower and Ellen Clowser. The Hower and Clowser families resided in Jefferson and Lancaster Townships of Wells County.

Kenneth Higgins had three brothers all deceased, Harold, Garth and Roger. Roger served in World War II and during the last battle on Luzon, he lost his life. His body was returned to Elm Grove Cemetery, Bluffton where he is buried with Harold, Garth and their mother.

Hilda Jane Thrailkill is the daughter of William Ernest Thrailkill and Minnie Lydia Croasdale. She is a relative of and shares the same name with Jane Thrailkill, one of the earliest settlers in Liberty Township, Wells County. Jane Thrailkill is referred to in the first printed historical record of the county, *The Wells County Atlas*. William Ernest Thrailkill's father Joseph Thrailkill came to Liberty Township from Swayzee, Grant County, Indiana. The Thrailkills' were originally from Virginia. His mother was Millie Jane Buckner, daughter of William Buckner and Amelia Yelton. Millie Jane was born in Kentucky.

Hilda J. Higgins mother was Minnie L. Croasdale, daughter of Robert Walker Croasdale and Jennie Jane Ernst. Robert Walker Croasdale was the son of Ezra Croasdale and Ruth Ann Walker. Jennie Jane Ernst's parents were John Ernst and Mary Ellen Zeigler. The north sections of Liberty Center, Indiana were plotted by the Ernst and Croasdale families and are recorded at the county courthouse.

Kenneth and Hilda Higgins are members of the Liberty Center Baptist Church. Mrs. Higgins was responsible for compiling the Wells County marriage records from 1900-1976. There are nine volumes in each set that has been presented to the local library and libraries in several states.

Present address are 1286 Lakeview Court, Bluffton and 6099 Coral Way, Bradenton, Florida.

DANIEL WAYNE HIGHLEN

Daniel Wayne Highlen was born on October 7, 1922, at the Wells Community Hospital, Bluffton, Indiana. He was the son of Lee Roy Highlen and Mabel Esther (Thrailkill) Highlen, natives of Wells County, Indiana. Daniel was the second child of Lee and Mabel Highlen, the first of four boys. He had an older sister, Wanda Jane, and three younger brothers, Dick Eugene, Robert William, and Fredrick Lee. He passed his early life on the family farm at Liberty Center located at the intersection of roads 250 south and 350 west. The family lived on this farm until 1936 when Dan's father sold the farm and moved the family two and one-fourth miles south of Poneto on Meridian Road.

Daniel Wayne Highlen

Dan attended the Methodist Church at Liberty Center. He also attended Liberty Center grade school from 1928 to 1937. Then he attended Chester Center High School, Wells County, graduating in 1940. He was active in basketball, track, and 4-H while in school.

In 1933, he had raised a pig, "Grunty," and won Grand Champion in Durco Barrow at the Bluffton Free Street Fair. He and his pig then went on to competition at Indianapolis and also to the Chicago Livestock Exposition in Chicago. Many other ribbons were also won in the Durco Barrow division by Dan.

After graduating from high school, Dan joined the U.S. navy in which he served from 1943 to 1946. He received his basic training at the Great Lakes U.S. Navel Training Station, Great Lakes, Illinois. From there he attended radar school in Hingham, Massachusetts. He was in much action during World War II. He saw action in many battles. One instance was when he was in charge of a caravan of jeeps going across North Africa. They had to be be very careful or the Arabs would steal anything they could. Dan also endured much hardship while serving in the Navy, sometimes going three or four days without food or water. Another instance was when one of the ships Dan was on was damaged by a mine. It was in shark-infested waters, and Dan had to swim to safety. He said later that he never knew he could swim so long or so far. Dan was one of the few survivors. He was decorated with six battle stars and many medals for his duty, including a medal for his participation in the invasion of Southern France. He fulfilled his service in 1946 and was honorably discharged as a petty officer radarman S2/C.

On September 10, 1950, at Fort Wayne, Indiana, he was married to Helen Gracia Brandyberry, daughter of Floyd and Josephine (Karns) Brandyberry of Monroe, Indiana. After his marriage, Dan settled with his wife in Decatur, Indiana. He worked at many jobs but finally took up his profession as a factory worker at Rea Magnet Wire of Fort Wayne. He retired from there in 1984 after thirty and one-half years service.

Dan and Helen were married twenty-one years before her death in May, 1972, of colon cancer. They spent much of their lives living in a mobile home in Decatur, traveling, and raising their three children: Daniel Wayne Highlen II born February 20, 1951 at Monroe, Indiana, home of Helen's parents; Cindy Lou Highlen (Powell), born January 2, 1959 at Decatur, Indiana; and Linda Sue Highlen (Myers), born August 5, 1960 at Decatur, Indiana.

Dan was a good provider for his family and a loving husband. He became ill in December of 1985 with cancer and died at home in Decatur on May 25, 1986 at the age of sixty-three. He was buried alongside his wife at the Ray Cemetery at Monroe, Indiana.

DICK EUGENE HIGHLEN

Dick Highlen was born on November 7, 1925, at the Wells Community Hospital, Bluffton, Indiana, the son of Lee Roy Highlen and Mabel Esther (Thrailkill) Highlen, natives of Wells County. Dick was the third child and second son of Lee and Mable Highlen. He had a older sister, Wanda Jane, an older brother, Daniel Wayne, and two younger brothers, Robert William and Fredrick Lee.

Dick passed his early life on the family farm at Liberty Center. He attended the Methodist Church as well as the Liberty Center Grade School there. He later attended the Chester Center High School south of Liberty Center. While in grade school, Dick was active as a drummer in the Wells County Community Band.

After school, Dick continued to help work on the family farm, which was now near Fort Wayne on Leo road. For several years he did this before taking up the profession of construction work. He worked mainly in the Forth Wayne area on many big and small projects, including the Summit

Building in downtown Fort Wayne. He retired in 1981 due to a heart disability after thirty plus years.

Dick was married on December 15, 1950, at Fort Wayne to Alice Marie Books, daughter of Ray and Ruth (Evans) Books. After his marriage Dick settled with his wife in Fort Wayne. After many years, their marriage ended in divorce, though they remained friends until her death in 1986 of cancer.

In the spring of 1988, Dick moved from 4132 Warsaw Street, Fort Wayne, which had been his main address for most of his adult life, to U.S. 27 south, Country Court Estates, where he bought a mobile home.

On August 12, 1988, Dick Eugene Highlen passed away at his home due to a massive heart attack. He was buried at the Mossburg Cemetery in Wells County beside his mother, father, and brother Fredrick.

FREDRICK LEE HIGHLEN

Fredrick Lee Highlen was born October 13, 1930 in Liberty Center, Wells County, Indiana. The son of Lee Roy and Mable Esther (Thrailkill) Highlen, natives of Wells County, Indiana. Fred Highlen was the fifth and last child of Lee and Mabel Highlen, the fourth of four boys.

He spent his early life on the family farm at Liberty Center, roads 250 South and 350 West. Then his father sold it and the family moved to an eighty acre farm south of Poneto. Fred spent most of his youthful years on this farm. Later, his father sold this farm and moved the family again to a farm north of Fort Wayne in Allen County, Indiana.

Fred Highlen graduated from Huntertown High School in Allen County in 1949. He was active in track, pole vaulting and basketball. While in high school Fred worked evenings at a gas station.

Fredrick Lee Highlen was married August 6, 1949 at Fort Wayne to Jeanette Joan Julian. After his marriage they settled in Fort Wayne for one year. In 1950, Mr. Highlen and his wife moved to Corpus Christi, Texas, as Mrs. Highlen's parents lived there.

Here he got a job with C.P. & L, Citizens Power & Lighting Company. He worked a year for the company before getting drafted into the U.S. Army.

In 1952, he entered the U.S. Army, serving some time in Germany. Upon returning from the U.S. Army in 1954, he returned to Texas where he and his wife continued to make their home.

Mr. Fredrick Highlen lived in several towns in southern Texas including Kingsville, Gregory, Corpus Christi, and Sinton. At Sinton he built a house three miles north and a quarter mile west of town off Highway 66. Mr. Highlen also built a small trailer park on the west side of the six acres.

Mr. and Mrs. Highlen were married almost thirty-five years before divorcing on April 4, 1984. They had four children. The first-born was a baby girl born April 28, 1951, who lived only four hours. They then raised three other children: Kenneth Lee Highlen born November 15, 1959; Keith Sheldon Highlen born October 30, 1962; and Kay Louise Highlen born October 12, 1966.

Mr. Highlen had thirty-four years in with C.P. & L. Electric Company before retiring in 1985, due to a heart disability. On December 22, 1987, Mr. Highlen passed away at a Corpus Christi, Texas hospital due to a massive heart attack. He was cremated and his ashes sent to Indiana. He was buried July 23, 1988 at the Mossburg Cemetery in Wells County, Indiana. He lies beside his mother and father, Lee and Mabel Highlen, and his brother Dick Eugene Highlen.

HIGHLEN-PRIBLE

We have traced our family back to November 6, 1805. This was when John Highlen or Hiland married the former Christina Waldeck, (born April, 1806, died April 14, 1844.) It is thought they sailed in to the shores of Maryland then came through Pennsylvania and Ohio to Indiana. They had eleven children, one of them being Daniel Josephus (August 16, 1831, to November 8, 1910). He married Eliza Redding (February 23, 1834 to June 25, 1914). To them were born three children. Sarah, Frank, and Malinda. Frank, (October 2, 1864, to April 11, 1911), was my grandfather. Daniel enjoyed working with walnut wood; he made several pieces of furniture which various members of the family still have and use. He lived near Liberty Center, then moved to Markle where he was active in business circles until retirement.

Grandfather Frank married Elizabeth David (August 22, 1862, to August 20, 1893). To them were born two sons, Ora (September 1, 1884) and Lee Roy (March 10, 1886, to June 15, 1956). Lee, who later was my father, was seven years old when his mother died. Both boys were cared for by their grandparents until their father remarried on June 3, 1896. She was Sarah Wickliff (May 12, 1855, to May 6, 1920). She was a very good mother to the boys. To Frank and Sarah was born a son Glen (1898 to 1963).

The family lived north of Liberty Center in Rockcreek Township and the boys went through the eighth grade in the Raber School. My father was an avid baseball fan. He played in many games on the Murray diamond.

At age twenty-one father married Frances E. Johnson, whom he fondly called Frannie. She was born November 7, 1889, and died March 20, 1916. They had been married June 16, 1907. Their happiness was short-lived due to her early death. To this union were born three girls: Opal Ruth (April 14, 1908, to April 10, 1978), Helen, (April 20, 1911), Gelena, (December 7, 1913 to August 3, 1944). The girls attended school in Liberty Center, Opal and Gelena graduating. Opal lived her adult life in and near Warsaw, married to Francis Woods. Her daughter, Gloria Bradway, still lives in the area. Gelena was a registered nurse, having graduated from Methodist School of Nursing in Fort Wayne with high honors. Helen helped with the house work and cared for the young children of the ensuing family.

At the time of Gelena's birth we lived one mile west of Liberty Center. She was fifteen months old at the time of Mother's death.

Three years later Father remarried on February 26, 1919. Our new mother was born April 4, 1896, and died March 2, 1975. She was Mabel E. Thrailkill. Five children were born to this union: (1) Wanda Jane, (July 13, 1920), married to A. Scott Haynes on December 31, 1955 in Fort Wayne. He was born January 16, 1918. They have one daughter, Becky Jane, (November 28, 1957), a graduate of Brigham Young University; she is an accomplished dancer. They live in Orem, Utah. (2) Daniel Wayne (October 7, 1922, to May 28, 1986) had three children: Daniel Wayne II; Cindy Lou, (January 2, 1959) married to Kurt Powell; one daughter Crystal; and Linda Sue Highlen, married to John Myers of South Charleston, Ohio. (3) Dick Eugene (November 7, 1925, to August 12, 1988) was married to Alice M. Books (November 8, 1930. She is deceased). (4) Robert W. Highlen (October 11, 1928), married Julaine F. Rudney September 4, 1947. They have five sons: Robert William (Bill), Michael Eugene, Joseph Lee, Thomas Edward and James Christopher. (5) Fredrick Lee (October 13, 1930 to December 22, 1987). He was married to Jeanette Joan Julian August 6, 1949. She was born February 23, 1932. They have three children, Kenneth Lee, Kay Louise and Keith Sheldon, all living in the Dallas-Fort Worth Area in Texas.

Lee R. Highlen - Director of Livestock Marketing, Indiana Farm Bureau Federation

Our father farmed until the very early twenties. He helped organize the Production Credit Association in Wells County, an organization which enabled farmers to borrow money to buy livestock and then pay it back when the animals were sold. He was the first shipping manager for the Liberty Center Stock Yards. Most of the car loads of hogs or cattle went to Buffalo, New York, which was the best market.

His experience in this work prepared him for his later work with the Indiana Farm Bureau Federation. He first served as Field Man, then was selected for the position of Director of Livestock Marketing for the state. This position necessitated having an office in Indianapolis. His travels broadened greatly. He traveled throughout the state, attending meetings as well as serving on boards of directors for stockyards in Louisville, Buffalo, and Cincinnati. In 1931 he served as secretary-treasurer of Producers Livestock Marketing Association in Louisville. He held the Farm Bureau position for sixteen years. The family operated a hog farm northwest of Liberty Center. In 1941 father was appointed to the State Tax Board by Governor Henry Schricker. While living near Liberty Center the family attended the Methodist Protestant Church. I am still an active member there.

April 4, 1936, I was married to Harold Prible, (September 29, 1907). We were married by the Rev. James M. Baker in Anderson, Indiana. Harold is the second child of C. Forest Prible, (February 25, 1884, to July 14, 1949) and Dora Alice Miller Prible (February 9, 1885, to August 21, 1968). Harold worked all his growing up years with his father and after finishing high school worked full-time on the farm, doing field work and dairy work. The family was known for their love for Jersey cattle.

We lived on the Frank Day farm northwest of Liberty Center and followed in the Jersey tradition along with hogs and field work. After thirteen years we purchased a farm south of Bluffton, and in April, 1951, moved to our present home on the Ellingham Pike.

We have four children: Saundra Jayne, (May 7, 1937), David Gene (January 31, 1939), Sara Kay (November 17, 1941) and Susan Celeste (March 10, 1948).

Saundra owned and operated a beauty shop from 1958 through 1960 in the village of Keystone. She called it "The Beauty Nook". On March 1, 1959, she was married to Junior D. Bergman (March 1, 1937). They lived near Bryant, Indiana for three years. He was employed by Banker's Dispatch Inc. He was then transferred to Omaha, Nebraska, and in 1964 he was transferred to Detroit. He is now involved in the same type of work, being operations manager of Data Air Courier in the Detroit area. They have four children:

The Harold and Helen Prible Family, 1979 Sara, Saundra, Helen, Harold, David, Susan

Kerry Bergman (November 19, 1959) is married to the former Kimberly Thomsen (June 11, 1968). He has a daughter Kimberly May, (August 17, 1982) from a previous marriage. He is in construction.

Terry Bergman born November 13, 1960. He lives in St. Helena Isle, South Carolina. He has two children, Nicole Sheree (December 4, 1979) and Nathanuel (November 12, 1981). He is a Cadillac technician working on Hilton Head Island.

Ellen Frances Bergman (May 3, 1966) married Danny Lemilin (July 23, 1966). Marriage date, September 13, 1986. They have one child, Sarah Renee (August 17, 199). Danny works for Fife Electric Supply Company and Ellen is secretary for Data Air Courier, Detroit area.

Phillip Oren Bergman (June 26, 1967) is married to the former Tina Addaire (March 29, 1968). They were married September 21, 1985. They have two children, Anthony Phillip (September 2, 1986) and Timothy Allen (May 2, 1941). Phillip served as an enlisted man in the United States Marine Corps, being stationed in California, Missouri, North Carolina, and Okinawa. He was honorably discharged as Lance Corporal and is still in the Marine Reserves. He works for his father, Junior, in Data Air as does his wife Tina.

David Prible attended Tri-State College in Angola, Indiana, then came back to Bluffton and worked at Kitco Engineering as a production foreman several years. Like his father, he helped with farming all his growing up years and during the last several years has become a well-known grain farmer. He was married to the former Connie S. Allen (July 16, 1941) November 29, 1959. She is in her fifth year as Wells County assessor. In 1990 she was selected assessor of the year in the state. She served on the legislative committee, state level, and has testified at various times before our legislature. They have four sons: Jeffrey Lynn, (December 25, 1960). He is married to the former Karen Marie Eymer, (April 25, 1963). The marriage date, March 13, 1982. To this union were born: Michael David July 2, 1984), Matthew Lynn (November 15, 1986), and Meghan Marie (April 1, 199). Jeffrey has followed the farming tradition of his forefathers.

The second Prible son is Robert Allen (April 10, 1963). He is married to the former Lynette Irene Blevins (January 13, 1966). Marriage date, August 2, 1986. Daughter Katelyn Suzanne was born on January 5, 1991. Robert is employed by Isch Seeds as sales manager and Lynette is a certified medical assistant with the Markle Medical Center. The third son, Steven Douglas Prible (August 2, 1964), is married to the former Julia Ann Worthington (December 30, 1963). Marriage date, February 25, 1984. Steven is employed in the electrical department for the city of Bluffton. Julia is a medical secretary with Markle Medical Center. The fourth son, Mark David Prible, (December 31, 1967), is married to Julia Ann Dawson (April 21, 1972). Marriage date June 29, 1991. Mark is a journeyman tool and die maker with Kitco Engineering, Bluffton.

Sara Prible worked for Lincoln National Life of Fort Wayne until her marriage on July 15, 1961, to David M. Pursifull. They were divorced in 1980. She now works at Christian Care Center, Bluffton. Five children were born to this union: (1) Jerry Lee Pursifull (July 17, 1962); married Karen Sue Delaney (June 16, 1968). Marriage was December 13, 1988, now divorced. To this union a son Jacob Lee was born (November 13, 1989) Michigan. Jerry works on a dairy farm near Somerset Center. (2) Michael David (November 5, 1963) is married to the former Jennifer Myers (December 27, 1963), married April 28, 1984. Michael is a sales engineer for Rolf Heating and Air Conditioning in Fort Wayne. Jennifer works for Carnation Company at Baer Field as distribution center coordinator. They have one son, Andrew Michael (April 22, 1986) and a daughter Emily Suzanne (November 2, 1990). The family lives in Wells County, near Zanesville. (3) Teresa Kay Purcifull (October 14, 1965) married Brian Bothast (January 20, 1965). Marriage date, August 30, 1986. A son, Brett Lee, was born to the union August 27, 1987. Brian is a sales representative with Western-Southern Insurance. Teresa works for Caylor Nickel Medical Center as an out-patient records coder. (4) Brian Daniel Purcifull (September 9, 1971) a graduate of Rochester High School, will attended a technical school in Logansport. (5) Patricia Mae (Patti) (September 23, 1977) lives with her mother in Bluffton and is in seventh grade at middle school.

Susan Prible Ellison resides with her husband, Stanley E. Ellison, at the corner of Main and Plumb Streets in the Croasdale Addition of Liberty Center, Indiana. Their house was once owned by Susan's great-great-great-grandfather, John Jeptha Prible. Susan's birth date is March 10, 1948; Stanley's birth date is May 20, 1943. Marriage, March 21, 1964. Susan is a para-professional with Adams-Wells Special Services working in Bluffton Middle School. Stanley is a journeyman electrician at CPC (Chevrolet Pontiac Canada) Division of G.M. in Marion, Indiana. They have two daughters: Christina Linn (October 21, 1964) and Stacey Renee, (June 11, 1971). Christina married Keith Alan Masterson (May 7, 1964) marriage date January 28, 1983. They have one son, Kirk Alan (August 7, 1983). She is employed at Peyton Northern in the DDI Department and Keith is a research technician with CIBA-GEIGY Seed Division in Bluffton. They now reside in Liberty Center in the house once owned by Millie Jane Buckner Thrailkill, 1855-1941. Stacey is married to Matthew Shane Gearheart (March 23, 1968), marriage October 26, 1991. Stacey is employed by CIBA-GEIGY Seed Division as a secretary. Shane is employed by Peyton Northern in the shipping department.

As I scan through this piece of family history I find various fellowships of believers—Methodists, Church of Christ and Baptist. *(Helen Highlen Prible)*

HIGMAN-KING

Ralph K. Higman was born in Bluffton in 1919 and lived there most of his life. He was a graduate of Bluffton High School and Purdue University. After graduating from college with a degree in civil engineering, his first job was at Crane Naval Depot, working for the E.I. DuPont Co. In 1943 he enlisted in the Navy Construction Battalion, better known as the Seabees. He was stationed on Okinawa when World War II ended and received his discharge from the Navy in 1946. He then went to China as an employee of the United Nations Relief and Rehabilitation Administration.

In 1947 Ralph returned to Bluffton and was associated with Don Hammond and Frank Buckner in an engineering firm. He was later employed by Reiff Construction Co., before starting his own civil engineering and land surveying business, which he operated for more than twenty years.

Ralph King Higman

Reflecting his love of community, Ralph contributed much time to his many civic interests. As a youth he was active in scouting and after his return was an assistant scoutmaster with Bluffton's Kiwanis Troop #140. He held county, district and council posts during his scouting career. In 1967 he received the Silver Beaver award, the highest council level honor. He was a past president of the Lions Club; past commander of American Legion Post 111; and headed a committee in an attempt to save Wells County's last covered bridge, among other Historical Society interests. He served on the First Presbyterian Church board of trustees, and at the time of his death in 1978 had been appointed to a second term on the Bluffton-Harrison school board.

Ralph's great-grandfather, Clement Ross Higman, was born in Delaware, grew up in Ohio, and in the 1830's moved to Wells County, along with his mother, Sara (Ross) Higman, and a brother and sister. Clement married Martha Walker in 1840. One of their sons, George W., married Catherine Neff in 1876. Their son, John Wesley, and Faith (Kreigh) Higman were Ralph's parents.

On January 3, 1958 Ralph Higman married Marjorie E. King, daughter of Mason N. and Mary (Bever) King of Petroleum, Indiana.

The Kings trace their ancestors back to 1786, when John Christian and Anne Catherine (Baum) King came to America from Wittenburg, Germany. They settled in Perry County, OH. Their son, George, was the father of David, Henry, Adam and George W., who migrated to Wells County, where they homesteaded land in the Reiffsburg area. Henry's son, Henry S., married Mary LeChot. They were the

397

parents of six sons and one daughter, including Mason N., father of Galen E., Iris M., Nile L., Maxine A., Roger D. and Marjorie E. King.

Ralph and Marjorie Higman became the parents of two sons; Ted King Higman and John (Jack) Mason Higman. Both sons graduated from Bluffton High School and Purdue University. They each received a Ph.D. in electrical engineering from the University of Illinois in Urbana. Ted is an assistant professor at the University of Minnesota. Jack is a visiting research assistant professor at the University of Illinois.

ELIJAH AND SURILDIA HITE

Joseph Hite, son of Abraham and Hannah Hite, was born in what is now Page County, Virginia, near Luray, in the rich Shenandoah Valley. Most of the family moved to Fairfield County, Ohio about 1801-05. Joseph is said to have been the owner of the site at Thurston, Ohio. He participated in the War of 1812. He was a prominent member of the Primitive Baptist Church, and granted land to the church in 1832 for a meeting house when his first wife, Frances Berry Hite, died.

On May 17, 1835, Joseph married Sarah Biddle. Soon they moved to Rockcreek Township, Huntington County, Indiana. Children born to them were: infant son born February 12, 1884 and died February 13, 1884; Emily born February 2, 1845 and died October 7, 1852; Rebecca born July 7, 1847; Joseph Jr., born August 1, 1849 and died October 27, 1852; Sarah born April 27, 1851 and died October 21, 1852; Elijah born April 30, 1853 and died September 13, 1927; Jacob born January 29, 1855; Saffiah born May 12, 1857 and died September 6, 1860; William born January 22, 1859; Marion born March 19, 1861; Samantha born October 28, 1863; and Henry M. born September 11, 1866 and died May 6, 1910, unmarried.

Elijah married Surildia Call (born July 31, 1857) on May 10, 1876. Children born to this marriage: two sons, who died in infancy; Cora Elzena, born September 18, 1884, married Edward J. Walter on November 22, 1919; and Effie May, born January 30, 1890, married Arthur Smith on March 1, 1913.

Cora E. (died July 12, 1971) and Edward J. Walter (died November 22, 1927) had one son. Edwin Hite Walter, born July 4, 1921, married Imogene McCarty on May 27, 1941, and divorced in 1949. He married Lucille Shorey on March 29, 1954. They have a son, Keith Edwin, born January 11, 1956. They live in Bluffton (See Arthur Smith and Hite)

HOCKMAN

Gregory D. Hockman was born to the parents of Harold and Marilyn (Harmon) Hockman on December 6, 1956. Greg is the third son in a family of four boys. Greg grew up in the small town of Bremen, in Southeastern Ohio. In 1967 Greg's family started attending the Avlon United Brethren Church. Greg was very active in the church teaching Sunday School and attending youth group. In May of 1975 Greg graduated from Fairfield Union High School. After graduation Greg began working as a meat cutter for the Kroger Company and took some classes at Circleville Bible College.

Kimberly S. Gornall was born to the parents of James and Gloria (Burnworth) Gornall on May 28, 1962. Kim is the oldest daughter in a family of four children. Kim has two sisters and one brother. Kim grew up in the small town of Rushville in Southeastern Ohio. Kim's family has always attended the Avlon United Brethren Church. Her great-grandfather, Ira Newton Burnworth, was a United Brethren minister and helped to start many United Brethren Churches in Southeastern Ohio.

Greg and Kim met in church, and after Kim graduated in May, they were married in the Avlon United Brethren Church by Rev. Herbert Householder on June 27, 1980. Greg and Kim continued to be active in the Avlon Church. On April 5, 1981 they were blessed with the birth of their first son, Gregory Allen. With the ill-health of their pastor, Herbie Householder, Greg became the lay leader and assisted the pastor in many areas, including preaching. Once again Greg and Kim were blessed with a second son, Mark Andrew, born September 9, 1983.

In April of 1985 Greg and Kim answered the call to full-time service to God. In July of 1985 Greg gave up his job at Kroger and with their two sons, moved to Hartford City, Indiana. There Greg became the pastor of the Fairview United Brethren Church and went full-time to Huntington College. In May of 1989 Greg graduated with a bachelor of arts degree. Greg then entered the Graduate School of Christian Ministries at Huntington College. After four and one-half years of service at the Fairview Church, in January of 1990 Greg and Kim and their two sons moved to the Dillman Church parsonage in Jackson Township of Wells County. In May of 1990 Greg graduated with a master's degree.

The Hockmans are enjoying getting to know the residence of Jackson Township and the children are enjoying the new friends they are making at Southern Wells School and the Dillman Church. They are looking forward to being a part of the community for many years.

HOFSTETTER-KAHN

Dixie Kahn Hofstetter Smith was born to Bill and Vadis Kahn on December 30, 1937. Dixie was born at her home in Kingsland, Indiana, which at that time was not uncommon because the doctor would come to the house. Dixie was number five of the ten children that Bill and Vadis had. As did all the children, she attended Lancaster High School.

Dixie became a second mother to her five younger sisters since she had to help cook, clean and change diapers. Dixie's favorite pasttime was fishing and talking about the big one that got away. In the spring she always had her good mushroom woods and on Mother's Day the clan would gather at Bill and Vadis' house for the celebration. All the Kahn family would walk down the Nickel Plate (now Conrail) Railroad to hunt for mushrooms. If it was a nice day and the snakes were out, those snakes would chase a few home in a hurry.

Dixie married Carl D. Hofstetter on August 27, 1956. Carl is the son of Earnest Hofstetter and Twilla Sanders of Geneva, Indiana. Carl and Dixie had four sons: John born October 7, 1955; DeWayne born May 3, 1957; Kenny born March 25, 1959, and Tim born October 31, 1970.

John married Delores Bergman (born December 18, 1950) on July 13, 1974. John and Delores have four children: Vicky (born March 30, 1971); Michael (born August 29, 1972); Deb (born January 4, 1975); and Kevin (born November 2, 1976). Vicky married Ryan Neuenschwander on November 18, 1989 and gave John and Delores a grandson, James Robert on January 19, 1990. John works at EPC at Geneva, Indiana, and Delores is a housewife.

DeWayne married Peggy Bergman (born November 6, 1957) on March 5, 1977. DeWayne works at O & R Tool and Die at Geneva, Indiana, and Peggy is a housewife.

Kenny married Sherri Palmer (born February 11, 1961) on August 12, 1978. Kenny and Sherri have two daughters, Sheba (born February 22, 1979) and Monica (born January 23, 1986). Kenny works at EPC of Geneva, Indiana, and Sherri is a housewife.

Tim was a 1989 graduate of South Adams High School and works at All American Homes in Decatur, Indiana.

Dixie worked at EPC of Geneva, Indiana for twenty years and she also worked at Corning Glass of Bluffton, Indiana. Dixie married Wilbur Smith in June 1978 and they resided in Geneva, Indiana.

This is a tribute from son, John, to mother, Dixie, who passed away on August 25, 1989 from pancreas cancer. With this contribution, her memory will not be forgotten, and her grandchildren will know a little about her life in Wells County.

HOGG FAMILY

John Hogg, of Scottish descent, was born in 1803 at Letterkenny, County Donegal, Ireland; he married Margaret Torrens. She died in 1866. John and most of his family came to Wells County about 1873. A daughter, Margaret, married William Henry Park. His youngest son, John, married Fanny Torrens and later Catherine Park. His oldest son, James, married Fanny's sister, Elizabeth, and settled on a farm west of Bluffton. Elizabeth died in 1917. James spent his last years with his son, John.

James and Elizabeth Hogg had three children: Sarah, John Henry, and Francis Ward. Sarah married Wesley Woodruff. They had four children: James, Jennie, Gideon, and Willard. Francis married Grace Baker. They had four children: Milford, Anna Ruth, Robert and George.

John, born in 1877, married Gertrude Lee in 1900. She was the daughter of James Anderson and Delia Goodyear Lee; she died in 1908. In 1911 John married Mary Alma Mastin, a court reporter from Wilkes County, North Carolina. She was the daughter of Edward Olin and Mary Elizabeth Johnson Mastin. E.O. Mastin was a farmer and state legislator. He was the last of fifteen children, the only boy to survive, and was born when his mother was forty-eight. Alma died in 1918, and in 1920 John married her sister, Carrie May.

Standing L to R: Barbara Hadley, John Hogg, Bill Hogg, Judy Hogg. Seated L to R: Bruce Hogg, Peter Hogg, Willmina Hogg

John and Alma had three children: Bruce Lee, Gertrude Elizabeth, and Max Olin. Bruce, born in 1913, is a graduate of Rockcreek High School, and is a retired farmer and sub rural mail carrier. He married Willmina Monier in 1946. She was a member of the Rev. Paul Sharpe's U.P. Church, at

Sparland, Illinois, and is the daughter of Robert Halsey and Edith Waugh Monier. She was a teacher and first taught in a one-room school, at a salary of sixty-five dollars per month.

Bruce and Willmina have two children, Barbara Jean and William Bruce. Barbara born in 1951, graduated from Norwell High School in 1969. She attended Manchester College, and graduated from the Indiana University School of Nursing. She lives near Wabash. William, born in 1954, is a graduate of Norwell High School and Manchester College; he married Judith Gay Kober, daughter of Jack and Jean Kober, in 1975. She is a Southern Wells and Indiana University School of Nursing graduate and works with Caylor-Nickel Home Health Care. They have two sons, John Andrew, born 1980, and Peter Girod, born 1982. John is in the fifth grade and Peter is in the second grade at Lancaster Elementary. They live on the home place in Rockcreek Township. Bill farms and carries mail part-time.

Gertrude, born 1915, received her earlier education at Rockcreek and Ball State and taught in Rockcreek Elementary for several years. In 1940 she married the Rev. Paul Sharpe, pastor of LaPrairie U.P. Church, Sparland, Illinois. He was the son of Fred and Minnie Harnish Sharpe and served in World War as a chaplain. He died in the Philippine Islands in 1945. They had a daughter, Jane Ann, born 1942; she is an art teacher. She married Joseph Gildow and lives near Tipp City, Ohio.

In 1948 Gertrude married Harvey Milton Luce, a Lt. Colonel in World War II. He studied for the ministry at Xenia Seminary in Pittsburgh, and pastored a U.P. Church in Southfield, Michigan. He later became an administrator in the Michigan, Ohio and Kentucky Synod. He was killed in an auto accident in 1977. Gertrude also taught school in Michigan, Illinois, and Ohio, and now lives in Dayton, Ohio, and Clearwater, Florida.

They have two children, Carolyn Jean and Donald Milton. Carolyn, born in 1950, is a special education teacher; she married Lynn Christy, a veterinarian. They have two sons, Alex Harvey and Paul Edwin, and live in Vandalia, Ohio. Donald, born 1952, is a professional photographer in Cleveland, Ohio.

Max, born in 1918, is a graduate of Rockcreek High School and Ball State; he taught school in Ohio and served as a captain in World War II. He was a credit manager with R.C.A. in the Los Angeles area. In 1944 he married Dorothy Johnson (died 1989). Max lives in Downey, California. They have two children, John Douglas and Rebecca Jane. John, born in 1949, is a hospital administrator. He married Veronica McGraw. They have two children, Jeffrey Lee and Gregory Scott. They live in Downey. Rebecca, born in 1954, is a lawyer, practicing in the Los Angeles area.

John Henry Hogg was a farmer and seed corn salesman. He was an early advocate of the use of hybrid corn and more fertilizer. His son, Max, won the Wells County Five Acre Corn Growing Contest in 1930, '31, '32. His son, Bruce, won in 1933.

Descendants of the original John Hogg, through the next four generations, living in Wells County, are Fred F. Park and son, David; Wendell Hogg and daughter Susan Price; and Bruce Hogg and son William. There are also younger descendants.

HOGSTON FAMILY

James Allen Hogston and Betty Eileen Lee were united in marriage at Oak Chapel Evangelical United Brethren Church in eastern Grant County on August 31, 1956. James, a Van Buren High School graduate, was a son of James Frank and Mabel Swindell Hogston. Betty, a Roll High School alumna, was the daughter of LeRoy and Cecelia Leaming Lee. All of the parents were raised in the Marion-Grant County area. Betty had two brothers, Everett and Raymond. James had two brothers, Dicky and David and one sister, Mary, now Mrs. Robert Palmer.

Hogston Family Picture Left to Right: James, Erma, Jenny, Patty, DeAnn, Howard, Becky, Bob, Rene, Larry, Ann, Doris

Their first child, Doris Marie, was born in 1957. The family moved from the Oak Chapel Community to the present Hogston farm home in Wells County at 1883 West 1200 South in 1958. Karen Sue was born in 1959, and Howard Eli in 1960. Jim and Betty were expecting their fourth child when Betty, twenty-seven, was killed in a tragic traffic accident on State Road 18, eight miles east of Marion, on January 26, 1962. Interment was in Gardens of Memory, Huntington County.

On February 7, 1964, at Mt. Olive Church of Christ in Lawrence County west of Williams, Indiana, James married Ann Sarah Williams, daughter of Fay Fisher and Doris Asher Williams. The Williams ancestors came to Lawrence County from Sevier County, Tennessee. The Ashers were from Stilesville, Indiana. Ann, a graduate of Huron High School and Purdue, grew up on a farm near Williams. She has one brother, Absalom Fay. She taught at Rossville and Bedford before her marriage.

To this marriage were born six children: Robert Allen, 1966; Larry Fay, 1968; Jenny Lavonne, 1970; Patricia Grace, 1971; Erma Jean, 1974; and Rebecca Sue, 1976. All six grew up in the Hogston home with the loving care of the three older children. The first seven children graduated from Southern Wells. Erma and Becky are currently enrolled at Eastbrook High School

Back- Peter Stephan; Front (L to R) Shelly, Haley and Karen (Hogston) Stephan

Doris was married to Ted McCammon of Blackford County on March 15, 1975. She and their daughter, Rene, live in Bloomington, Indiana. Karen, a registered nurse, married Peter Stephan, M.D., from Los Angeles, California, on September 15, 1986. They have two daughters, Shelley and Haley. Howard married his Southern Wells classmate, DéAnn Patterson, on September 2, 1990. They are residents of Bluffton. Bob, an accountant with Marathon Oil, lives in Pandora, Ohio. Larry is a tool and die computer programmer, and Jenny is a physical therapy assistant. Both reside in Fort Wayne. Patty is studying accounting at Vincennes University.

Jim, a part-time farmer, has been employed at the General Motors Plant in Marion for thirty-four years. Ann, who decorated cakes as a hobby for many years, has worked in the bakery at Scott's Foods in Bluffton since 1984.

The family has attended Churches of Christ in Bluffton, Portland, and Woodland Hills in Marion.

HOLLOWAY FAMILY

William Holloway (born December 30, 1856, died May 16, 1909) visited relatives in Wells County where he met and married on March 27, 1886, Emma Evaline Pace (born September 26, 1865, died December 23, 1943). William was a native of Randolph County and taught school in his early life and was also trustee of Middle Creek Township.

William and Emma moved to Wells County in 1902 and settled in a log house in Harrison Township on eighty acres. They brought with them three children with two buried in Randolph County. William and Emma had two children in Wells County. Their children were Irly Ernestine (married Luster Haecker), Iva Mae (married Pierce Harnish, Sr.), Ivan William Sr. (married Erma Lucille Emley), Emma Marie, and Florence Susanna Holloway.

Ivan W. Holloway (71) Erma L. Holloway (57) taken at 4-H Park, Bluffton, Indiana, 1971

Our Aunt Marie and Aunt Florence were well known for their handicrafts. They received many ribbons at fairs, and sold many of their finished items. In May of 1953, Aunt Florence received a letter from Mamie Eisenhower thanking her for a set of crocheted pin and earring set.

Our parents, Ivan and Erma, bought the farm from our grandmother's estate in January, 1944, and lived there until their death. Ivan was born September 28, 1899, and died August 5, 1973. He enjoyed farming and was a farmer all of his life. Erma (born January 6, 1914, died January 5, 1986) was the daughter of Harmon and Faye (Kauffman) Emley from Union Township. They married in Markle on November 23, 1935. Their five children are: Emma Faye, Julia Kay, Ivan William Jr., Rex Eugene, and Jane May.

Emma Faye (born April 12, 1937) married Charles De Armond (born February 16, 1936) on November 17, 1957. They have three children: Randy Lee (born April 6, 1959), Teresa Lynn (born March 21, 1960), and Steven Leroy (born April 20, 1964). Teresa married Alan Wagner on October 1,

1988. Steven married Cristie Lutz on June 8, 1985. They have two grandchildren, Amanda Renae and Jared Michael De Armond.

Julia Kay (born December 24, 1940) married Louis C. Sauerwine on December 13, 1958. They had four sons: Lazerne C. (born January 10, 1958), Louis C. Jr. (born June 14, 1962), Michael Anthony (born November 5, 1963, died August 14, 1968) and Matthew William (born September 11, 1965, died February 19, 1966). Louis married Barbara Chilcate and has five children: Michelle, Brian, Tony Louis, Adam Charles, and Benjam Warren. Louis has one grandchild, Kyle Hendricks.

Ivan William Jr. (born July 14, 1943) married Anna Lynch on February 9, 1964. They have two children, Angela Louise (born January 14, 1972) and William Glen (born August 12, 1976). Angela married Michael Anderson on July 14, 1990.

Rex Eugene (born September 21, 1946) married Patricia Gaskill on October 5, 1968. They have three children, Rex E. Jr. (born November 14, 1969), Douglas (born October 2, 1971) and Dianna (born May 22, 1975). Rex married Machelle Yencer and has one child, Joshua.

Jane May (born February 2, 1952) married Dorrence Lewis on June 14, 1977. They have two sons, John P. (born May 17, 1965) and Kenneth R. (born April 6, 1973). John married Kimberli Steiner September 27, 1986 and they have three children: Nicole, Kelli, and Joshua.

Although all of Ivan and Erma's children have married and have children of their own, the two boys have farms of their own. Two of the girls live on the original land and one daughter owns part of the home land.

CARY HOLLOWAY-LUHAMEY MATSON

Book W, pp 287, Lands Records, Wells County, Indiana, shows transfer of March 6, 1873, of eighty acres from James Myers to Jonathan Cary and John Wesley Holloway. This farm is located south of Poneto on the Chester, Nottingham Township line in Chester Township. This entry marks the introduction of the Cary Holloway line in Wells County; however, other Holloways were living in Wells County.

Three brothers and one sister made the move from Ross and Fayette Counties, Ohio. The three brothers: John Wesley, Lemuel and Jonathan Cary had all served in the Civil War. The will of their father: William E. Holloway is Estate Case #3295 Ross County dated 1862-1864. Real estate of 153 acres located in Concord Township, Ross County, is the same land conveyed to Lemuel deceased, by Elijah Holloway, by deed dated July 18, 1818 and recorded in Lands Records of Ross County, Ohio, and by said Lemuel devised to William E. by will of record in Ross County probable court. William E. had met an accidental and untimely death, and the farm had to be sold to close the estate of Elijah Holloway, William E's grandfather; he was a Revolutionary soldier who moved his family to Ohio from the eastern shore of Maryland, Worcester County, with a party of early Methodists led by White Brown.

The wife and mother of the William E. Holloway family was Love Brittenham (Lovey Jane). Volume 2, Pickaway County, Ohio marriage records in March, 1835, lists a Wm. E. Holloway and Love Brittenham receiving a marriage license. She was not listed in the will or estate closing so we presume her death was prior to 1862.

Heirs of William E. listed in the will were: Lemuel, Mary Jane, Nancy Carmean and Joseph Carmean, John Wesley Holloway, Rebecca Willis and Franklin Willis, her husband, Jonathan Cary Holloway, a minor, and Ellen Holloway, a minor. Cary was listed as living in Tennessee, but was serving in the Civil War.

Cary Holloway was the only male family member to marry. Luhamey was born 1858 and married Cary Holloway March 6, 1879. She was the daughter of James Finley Matson, and Nancy Cook Matson. Nancy Cook Matson died during or shortly after the Civil War. James Finley served in the Civil War and they parented two children: Samuel, and Luhamey. James Finley married his second wife Rebecca Francis Roberts. Children born to this union were: Andrew, Erk, Christ, Ernest Matson, Stella Yeager, Allie Shinn, and Susan Teagle. Samuel Matson married Elizabeth Patterson and they lived in Montpelier, Indiana. Their children were: Merle, Foster, and Clarence. Sam died June 9, 1946.

Children born to Luhamey Matson Holloway and Jonathan Cary Holloway were: Cora Bell Holloway, born 1879, married Ray "Boss" Stookey; Ethel Mae Holloway, born 1891, married Isaac Otto Miller, August 16, 1909 and Lee Holloway, born August 8, 1882 who married Jennie Kirkwood, born October 23, 1879, died September 16, 1949; Carl and Dick Holloway were also sons of Cary and Luhamey who died in their teens due to tuberculosis. Jennie Kirkwood and Lee Holloway were married in 1900. She was the daughter of Henry (Harry) Kirkwood, and Sara Elizabeth King Kirkwood. Children born to this union were: Ruby born 1902, died 1904; Robert Carl Holloway, born 1950, died 1974; John Henry, born 1911, died 1986; Mary Jane, born 1916, Max Cary, born 1918; Joe Dean, born 1921, died 1981.

Lee Holloway took in his second marriage, Mrs. Virgie Alvords of Fort Wayne. Lee died April 23, 1952, and is buried in Stahl Cemetery.

S. JACK HOLLOWAY

A mile-long stretch of S.R. 218 in Chester Township has for many years been called by friends and family, The Holloway Mile. As it is here that stands the family of M. Ferne and Joe D. Holloway and their twelve children.

The original farm had been payment to a Civil War relative and has been passed down through the Starr family for several generations, with each generation leaving its mark, such as the barn built by O.O. Starr in 1893, and The Blanche Chapel, a tiny church built for a disabled Blanche Starr.

Also in this mile is the home of S. Jack Holloway, the third child born to Joe and Ferne. The oldest son, Jack graduated from Chester Center High School in 1964. He then enlisted in the U.S. Army as a paratrooper in the 101st Airborne Division. In April of 1966 he left for a year tour of duty in Vietnam. In early 1967 he returned home for a 30-day leave. It was at this time that he met Kathy (Campbell) Taylor. On October 28, 1967, Jack and Kathy were married. For service to his country Jack was given the Purple Heart and the Bronze Star. Jack and Kathy had two children Clifton (October 27, 1967) and Clinton (January 25, 1973). Jack and Kathy were involved in the Bluffton Jaycees, and for a short while they operated a pickle barrel concession wagon that they took to fairs and shows. Jack also worked for Hulchers Emergency Railroad Service and did a lot of construction work. Then, as often happens, they grew apart and were divorced in 1978.

On May 3, 1985, on the front of walk of their new home, Jack married Patricia J. Grabner. Together they built a beautiful ranch style home to replace the original home that was destroyed by fire in 1981. In 1988 a well-stocked pond was added, complete with a fountain and a quaint beach house where they spend their summer evenings. Together they manage Capri Meadows Apartments, which has 172 apartments for families, senior citizens, handicapped, and disabled people. It is located at the north end of Bluffton.

As for the next generation of Holloways, Clifton graduated from Vincennes University with an associate degree in Conservation Law in 1991. Clint graduated from Bluffton High School also in 1991. At this time he hopes to attend college and study business and political science.

JOE D. HOLLOWAY FAMILY

Joe, youngest son of Lee and Jenny Kirkwood Holloway, was born in 1921 in Nottingham Township and was a 1939 gradute of Petroleum High School. In May 1941 he married Ferne Starr, born 1923, a daughter of Ralph and Pauline Kean Starr. Making their home west of Poneto, Joe was employed for twenty-five years by Wells County, ABS. He then became superintendent of the Bluffton District, Indiana State Highway until his untimely death in 1981. Joe was civic minded and was involved with Boy Scouts, 4-H, Republican Party, and the Historical Society, to name a few. Ferne currently resides on Elm Drive in Bluffton, and is the Harrison Township assessor. She spends her free time visiting her eleven grown children, and twenty-one grandchildren.

Joe Holloway Family 25th Wedding Anniversary 1966

They are: Sally Jo Tinkel, born June 26, 1942, Ball State graduate, current president of Northern Wells School Board; mother of Scott, born August 7, 1966 (wife Janet Ulshafer), Julie born May 26, 1969, and Amy, born June 6, 1970, all Ball State graduates. Sally is a counselor at Homestead High School, Fort Wayne.

Sara Jane, born January 31, 1944, wife of Eric Jarrett, resides in Liberty Township, and is a member of Southern Wells School Board. Their children are Lindsay Jo and Emily Ann, students in Southern Wells.

Stanley Jack, born March 17, 1946, resides near Poneto and is married to Patricia Grabner. Jack served two tours of duty in Vietnam, with 101 Airborne Division. Jack's sons are Clifton, a student at Vincennes, and Clinton, president of his senior class at Bluffton High School.

Susan Jenelle Waters, born December 16, 1948, resides in Allen County, and has an extensive career in hotel and restaurant management. Her children, all graduates of Carroll High School include Troy, a student at IPFW, Stephanie, and Jeremy.

LeAnna Jill, born April 10, 1950 is married to Kenneth J. Ellenberger. They are parents of DeAnna, a student and tennis player at St. Francis, and Douglas and Angel, students at Bluffton. Jill enjoys a banking career.

Ferne (Starr) and Joe D. Holloway October 1980

Steven James born October 10, 1951, is married to Teresa Nash, and has one son, Jonathan, four years old. They reside in Chester Township and Jim is a longtime employee of M.L. Hulcher Company.

Martha Jerrideane, born April 17, 1953, married Don Lehman and lives near Toscin. Their daughter April is a student at Bethlehem Lutheran. Jerri works part-time at Caylor Nickel and drives a Northern Wells School Bus.

Jon Ralph, born November 14, 1954, married Mary Habig and has one son, Heath, a student at Northern Wells. They reside in the old Toscin School and Jon works at Franklin Electric.

Jeffrey Lyn, born September 27, 1956, lives on the old Starr Homestead near Poneto. He is married to Debra Bruner and is employed at Wayne Metal, Markle. Daughter Courtnie Lin attends grade school in Whitley County.

Jerome Max, born February 27, 1959, married Brenda Holloway. Residing in Bluffton, they are the parents of Heidi, Joseph, Jenni, and Janet. Jody is an auctioneer and realtor with Ellenberger Brothers, and a very dedicated Republican.

Jay Alan, born October 27, 1961, married Marie Bartlett, a farmer in Jay and Blackford Counties, they are building a new home near Trenton.

Daniel Gene Anderson, born February 20, 1946, made his home with us after the death of his mother Maxine. He married Rose Oswalt and sons Ashley and Anthony are students at Bluffton. He resides in Poneto, works at Fisher Body, Marion, and is very active in Boy Scouts.

HOLSINGER

John Holsinger, who had to come to America from Germany at a very early age, first settled in Ohio and then moved on to Liberty Township, Wells County, and settled on a farm, five miles west of Poneto, then first farm north on the east side of road. There he farmed and raised his family. He was also a carpenter by trade. They raised four children, two boys and two girls. The boys' names were Andy and Ben. John and Mary Holsinger went to the South Liberty Christian (Africa) Church. They attended regularly and he served as a deacon for several years. Ben met and married Linnie Welch in 1910 and to this union were born five children: Brooks, Ellen, Howard, Iris, and Richard. Clines owned a lumber yard in Poneto and Ben ran the lumber yard for several years. During the Great Depression, Clines closed the lumber yard, and Ben moved his family back to the Holsinger farm. Ellen and Brooks graduated from high school at Liberty Center. Ellen and Paul Osborn were married at the Holsinger farm house. Ellen and Paul had three children: J.P. Osborn Jr., Lynn E. and Ruth Ann. J.P. Osborn passed away August 11, 1988. Ellen and Paul Osborn have been married 54 years last October. John Holsinger and son, Ben did a lot of carpentry around the Holsinger farm. Margaret Sills lives on the Holsinger farm as of today.

HOOK-SAWYER

We can date the Sawyer family back to January 30, 1872, when Anna Muller wed Jacob Narr in Theringen, Germany. To this union seven children were born. The family came to the United States in 1882 and settled in Wells County. One of their daughters, Emma, married Emmanuel Sawyer in 1901 in Poneto, Indiana. Emmanuel came with his parents from Pennsylvania. His father was killed in the Kingsland Interurban wreck. To the Emmanuel and Emmas union were born three children. Marie Warner at Fort Wayne, Carl of Bluffton, and Howard of Bluffton. Howard was born May 11, 1909, in Wells County. He graduated from Petroleum High School. He was a milk hauler for the Hoosier Condensary and later a milk inspector for Wayne Co-op in Fort Wayne. He married Florence Miller on September 8, 1932, in Portland, Indiana. Her parents were John Edward and Myrtle (French). Florence graduated from Petroleum High School and the Methodist School of Nursing as registered nurse. She was the organist at the Evangelical and Reformed Church, now First United Church of Christ, for thirty years. She passed away in July, 1984. They had one daughter, Sonja O., born January 23, 1939. She graduated from Bluffton High School in 1957. First she was employed at Kresge Warehouse in Fort Wayne until becoming a homemaker, then later she became a school bus driver. Sonja wed Jerry Hook on September 6, 1958, in Bluffton. The Hook family can be dated back as far as 975. Jerry's parents were Ralph and Caroll (Schlagenhauf). Jerry graduated from Bluffton High School in 1957. He was employed at Rem Johnston Printing Co. for twenty-eight years. He is now assistant supervisor at the Wells County Highway Department. Jerry and Sonja had five children. Kristi, born July 29, 1959, graduated from Bluffton High School in 1977. She passed away in February 1985. Cindy, born December 10, 1960, graduated from Bluffton High School in 1979 and from the Academy of Hair Design in Indianapolis, and is a hair stylist barber in Fort Wayne. She has three children: Ryan, Matt and Abby.

They reside in Bluffton. Phil, born February 9, 1963, graduated from Bluffton High School in 1981 and Indiana Technical College in 1984. He married Susan Kimmer in 1984. They had one son, Nathan, born September 14, 1987. Susan was killed in a car accident on November 7, 1988. Phil married Jennifer Cullers on March 9, 1991. Phil is employed at National City Mortgage Company as a computer analyst. They reside in Miamisburg, Ohio. Jeff, born August 4, 1964, graduated from Bluffton High School in 1983 and Purdue University in 1988 as an electric engineering technologist. He is employed in Fort Wayne with Advance Electric Company. He married Shari Speheger on October 7, 1989, in Bluffton. They are expecting their first child in July, 1991. They reside in Bluffton. Kent, born August 24, 1966, graduated from Bluffton High School in 1985 and Academy of Hair Design in Indianapolis. He is employed at Hower Tool in Ossian and resides in Bluffton.

HOOK/SCHLAGENHAUF

Ralph Allen Hook (September 17, 1903 - April 29, 1970) was the son of Paul Dennis and Minnie Stover Hook. They were farmers near Eaton, Indiana. Ralph graduated from Eaton High School and attended Purdue University. Caroll Schlagenhauf (January 12, 1907) was the daughter of Henry and Eva Gottschalk Schlagenhauf. They were farmers in Wells County. Caroll graduated from the Hartford Township School in Adams County. A blind date, arranged by a girl friend, proved to be the beginning of this family tree. Ralph worked for the American Can Co. as a traveling mechanic at the time of their marriage on May 8, 1926. However, they settled in Bluffton in 1927, where they lived and raised their six children. Ralph opened his own garage in 1932 after working for the former Houser Garage. He operated this garage until his death in 1970. Caroll spent most of her married life being a housewife and mother, although she did work for J.C. Penney after her children were older. In 1937, they bought the house at 203 East Arnold Street, from the estate of Levi Heller, for $600.00. They sold this, in 1958, and bought the Walter Scholl residence at the corner of Silver and Bond. Ralph moved his garage there at the same time. In 1968, they remodeled and moved to the house on the farm that had belonged to her grandfather, George Gottschalk, on State Road 218 in Nottingham Township. Caroll was born and raised in this house and continues to reside there in 1991.

Ralph Hook
Caroll Hook

Their children are: Anna Lee (Mrs. Charles) Ault who has five sons: Stephen, Stanley, Scott, Stacey, and Stuart, and ten grandchildren, and lives in Wells County. Claudine (Mrs. James) Powell who has three daughters, Pamela Durdahl, Phoebe Zoll, and Caroll Ann Powell, and six grandchildren, and lives in Wells County. The Rev. James S. Hook, who married Mary Helen Naffziger of Washington, Illinois, has four children: James, John, Matthew and Mary Elise Dickerson, and five grandchildren. He is pastor of St. Mark's United Methodist Church of Decatur. Jack D. Hook, who married Joyce Johnloz of Murray, has two daughters, Diana Schwartz and Jan Bennett, and two granddaughters, and lives in Bluffton. Armatha (Mrs. Carl) Green who had three sons, Mark, Chad, and Gary, and two grandchildren, and lives in Fort Wayne. And Jerry K. Hook, who married Sonja Sawyer, has five children: Kristi (July 29, 1959 - February 17, 1985),

Cindy Cale, Phil, Jeff, and Kent, and four grandchildren, with another due the summer of 1991. He also lives in Wells County.

The Hook family has always been a close-knit family. Ice skating played a big part in their growing up. Ralph made skates for the little ones because none could be purchased small enough. They would go skating every night there was ice, regardless of the temperature. A five gallon bucket filled with the dirt thrown out by the dry cleaning plant burned to make a warm fire to warm cold hands. Ralph placed a spotlight on a tall pole attached to a battery, powered by a homemade generator, and placed it on the ice of Kunkel Lake to provide light to skate by. When they went home, often with a few extra skaters, Caroll would make hot chocolate to warm the insides. What a mound of clothes and boots on the floor! What good memories!

HOOPINGARNER

Rick D. Hoopingarner, son of Dale and Miriam Hoopingarner of Uniondale, was born March 9, 1962, and married Dana Louise Sadler, daughter of Tom and Louise Sadler of Uniondale, born December 22, 1963. We were married on a nice summer day, June 5, 1982.

Rick left for basic training for the U.S.A.F. at Lackland, Air Force Base in Texas that following September. Dana joined him at Wichita Falls, Texas at Sheppard Air Force Base. It was there that Darrick Thomas was born on November 17. He was named after his Grandfather "Tom" as it was his first grandson. Our next adventure was a transfer to Tampa, Florida at MacDill Air Force Base. This was very close to Dana's grandmother Frances (Smuts) Bradbury Freeland and step-grandfather, Don Freeland, who resided at Bradenton, Florida at that time. Cylie Nicole added more fireworks to our lives on July 6, 1984. This was the first granddaughter for Dale and Miriam.

Left to right: Cylie - age 6 1/2, Rick - age 26, Dana - age 27, Cole - age 2 1/2, Darrick - age 8

Our next military move was back to Fort Wayne Air National Guard Unit in Fort Wayne during the year of 1985. After a number of rental houses we are presently living in our first home in the Zanesville area at the Hoopingarner Addition. Cole Evan came along on Mother's Day, May 8, 1988, to bring sunshine and more laughter to the family.

With three beautiful children at our side we have become very active in our local Methodist Church in Zanesville and our children's activities at school. Time seems to move quickly and soon there will be more to add to our family history. In-laws? Grandchildren? More moving? I can't wait to see how it all is planned out!

DONALD L. HOOPINGARNER

John Hoopingarner, Don's great-great-grandfather came to the United States with is wife Elizabeth from Germany. He settled in Ohio. To this marriage, a son, Don's great-grandfather George, was born. George married Emily Smuts in 1857. In 1859, they moved to Union Township in Wells County where they set up housekeeping. George was a carpenter. He and his wife had four sons: Clarence Estep, Don's grandfather Joseph N., George Frank, and Ralph V. and a daughter Elmira.

The son, Joseph N., is the family we will be following. He was a carpenter like his father. Joseph married Mary Robinson and to this marriage nine children were born. Bertha married David Fritz and they had Jay and James. Roy (Don's father) born February 11, 1891 (died April, 1941) married Gola Smith, born December 27, 1893 (died July 1, 1980). Dee, who married Lura Campbell and had three sons, Nola, Ned and Neil. Paul, who married Freida Sunderman, had three children, Phil, George and Judy. Emma, who married Earl Neith, had three children, Sadonna, Mary Lou, and Dean. Dessie, who married Grover Carpenter, had four children, Zelda, Joseph, Max, and Fonda. Ross, who married Mabel Metts, and had four children, Lucille, Burwell (Jack), Vera, and Joquette. Hazel, who married Burdell Slater and had four children, Dewald, Dayton, Denver and Bobby (who died in infancy). Lastly Orpha, who married Russell Parker, had Russell, Jr.

In Roy's marriage to Gola in 1914, was blessed with seven children. Roy was a carpenter also. The first child was Helen, born February 7, 1915, who married Owen Allen. To this marriage, two daughters were born. Janet in 1957 was the first. She married Joe Briner and they had three children, with Susan being the first born. She married Michael Ormsby and they had a son Chase Michael. Susan is now married to Mike Bartlett. A second daughter was born to Janet and Joe and her name is Cheryl. Cheryl was married to Alan Burnett and they had a daughter Megan. The third child was a son, named Brian. The second child born to Helen and Owen Allen was Brenda, born in 1940. She married Marvin Bradburn, and they lived in Markle, Indiana for a number of years before moving to Muncie, Indiana. They have three children, the oldest child was a girl, named Teri Jo. She married Steve Best and had a daughter Trisha. Teri later married Kevin Allred and had Joel and Nikki. Teri is now married to Larry Klooze and lives in Muncie. Brenda and Marv's second child was a son Dirk and he married Cindy ___. The third child was another boy, named Trent. Trent is married to Stephanie _____.

The second child, born to Roy and Gola, was John H., born July 18, 1917. John graduated from Ball State University and was a teacher a period of time before working for the State of Indiana in Indianapolis before retiring. He married Lorene Butler from Helmer, Indiana. They lived in Ossian before moving to Indianapolis. To this marriage, two daughters were born. Kay lives in Florida with her husband Larry Combs. The second daughter Gail was married to Mark Filipow and they had a son Sean. Gail lives in Indianapolis. Marjorie was the third child born September 19, 1919. She married Fred Rabel. They lived in Fort Wayne for many years before moving to Albuquerque, New Mexico. Fred was a painter but also sang in many churches and Marjorie played for him. She was a graduate of International Business College. To this marriage two children were born, the first being Maris. Maris was married to Joe Loftus and had three children, Cindy, Joe and Marcie. Maris is now married to Don Cowgill and lives in California. The second child was a boy named John. He married Gloria Leach and they had three children, Anatasia, Monica, and Tommy. John is now married to Elena ___.

Betty was the fourth child born on June 5, 1921. She married Arden Gemmer who during most of their marriage was a dairy farmer in Roann, Indiana. To this marriage three sons were born. David married Shirley Brey. They live in California and have two sons, Scott and Brian. The second son was Jim who is married and has three children, Todd, Amy, and Andrew. The third son Bob, married Marsha Kauffman and has two children, Jason and Andrea. Betty and Arden now live in Sun City, Arizona. All three sons live in California. Everett Dale was the fifth son born October 24, 1927. Dale was a carpenter all his life. He married Miriam Highlen and they had three children, Karen is the oldest. She married Bob Sommers. They had two boys, Shane and Scott. Kent is the second child, married Susan Colescott of Marion. They live in Huntington, Indiana. They have two sons Kyle and Brett. The third child was a son Rick. Rick married Dana Sadler and they have three children, Darrick, Cylie, and Cole.

The sixth child born to Roy and Gola was Donald Lee born September 28, 1935. Don is the president of the State Bank of Markle and is married to Marlene Platt born March 15, 1936. They had two daughters, Pamela the oldest, born June 23, 1858, is married to Larry Boye, and they live in Florida. Both are music teachers. The second daughter, Shari Lynne born February 2, 1961 in living at home.

The seventh child was Ronald Dee born October 11, 1936. Ron has been a carpenter all his life. His first marriage was to Nancy Thurber. They had three children before Nancy passed away. Eric lives in Indianapolis, Amy is married to Phil Brown and they have two children, Matthew and Nancy. The youngest child is Aaron. He married Tina Greider. Ron is now married to Beverly Dorton Vannatter. Beverly has a daughter, Cammy Vannatter.

LEWIS HOOPENGARDNER

It is told that the first New World Hoopengardner, George, arrived in Philadelphia on November 2, 1752, on board the Phoenix from Rotterdam and Portsmouth. He paid taxes on a farm in Fulton County, Pennsylvania, Bethel Township, in 1798. It is also told that the first Hoopengardner came from Germany with William Penn and settled around the town of McConnellsburg (Fulton County, Pennsylvania). It is not certain that either of these situations is true or if they pertain to the Hoopengardner's that came to Wells County, but there is the possibility. It is known that Abraham (born 1842) enlisted in the Civil War at McConnellsburg, county seat of Beaver Falls. In the 1887 biographies of Wells County, it is said that the great-grandfather of Elizabeth Hege/Hage was Peter, who was born in Germany and was the first of that name to immigrate to America. He settled in Lancaster County, Pennsylvania where Elizabeth was born.

Lewis Hoopengardner married Elizabeth Hege/Hage (birth and marriage dates unknown but death dates were: Lewis, February 1867; Elizabeth, February 1853). They had eleven children: Susan (1830, married James Ross; John (1832), married

Elizabeth McCoy McMurray; Mary Jane (1833), married Matthew Allen; David (1835), married May Jane Ady; Elizabeth (1838), married Joseph McMurray; Lewis (1840), married Lydia Ann Lepper; Abraham/Abram (1842), married Mary Porter; George (1845), married Amanda Shafer; Rebecca (1848), married Andrew Apple; infant (1851); Sophia Catherine (1853). The last two probably died as infants/young children.

David and Lewis emigrated to Indiana before the Civil War. Abraham came after the war. All three served in the Civil War. At the time of Lewis' death is 1931, he was the last surviving Civil War veteran in Ossian.

Lewis (1840-1931) married Lydia Ann Lepper in 1866 in Wells County.

They had eleven children: 1. William Atwood (1867) married Amanda Young in 1890; 2. Marietta (Maive) Louise (1869-1927) married Alva E. Hughes in 1891 and then Benjamin F. Fryback; 3. Martha (Matt) Elizabeth (1870-1951) married William Goshorn in 1894; 4. John (1872-1932) married Martha Quackenbush in 1899; 5. Francis (1874-1876); 6. George (1876-1902) married Nellie Earl; 7. Jasper Burdell (1880-1955) married Bertha Robbins, Mabel Vicle, Ethel Melching; 8. Dora Elsie (1884-1982) married Clyde White in 1904; 9. Iva Marie (1886-1920) married Curtis Clyde Archbold in 1906; 10. Benson Hoopengardner (1889-1960); 11. David Hoopengardner (1891-1967) married Violet Jean Farell in 1925.

The descendants of Dora and Clyde White are listed in the biography of Charles White.

REX AND ZOA FOLK HOOPINGARNER

George Hoopingarner (born March 12, 1835) (died June 1934) came to Indiana from Ohio, and bought a farm northeast of Markle, Indiana, in Union Township. The land cost him $13.00 an acre. He and his wife, Emily, had sons Estep, Joseph, George Franklin, and Ralph, and a daughter, Ella Hoopingarner Caley.

Rex Hoopingarner (born May 18, 1889) (died April 23, 1961), son of George Franklin and Mary Nevada Grubaugh, married Zoa Ethel Folk (born January 15, 1891) (died August 29, 1970), daughter of Henry Folk and Amanda Jane Motz Folk, on August 6, 1910, at the home of the bride's parents.

They farmed in Union Township all except seven years, when they moved to Huntington County (1933-1935), and then back to Rockcreek Township, Wells County (1935-1940). In 1940, the family moved back to the original homestead for retirement.

Standing (L to R) Pauline (Hoopingarner) Snyder Heer, Carl Hoopingarner, Dorma (Hoopingarner) Haiflich. Seated (L to R) Julia (Hoopingarner) Burger, Zoa, Rex

To this union was born four children: Carl (born Ma 17, 1911), Pauline (born September 21, 1913), Dorma Mae (born April 10, 1925), and Julia Fae (born March 1927).

In the early 1930's, after Carl married and had his first son, there was an all male, five generations with the Hoopingarner name. So the Hoopingarner names goes on.

Carl married June Brentlinger (May 21, 1932). To this union was born five children. Carl Lee (born January 11, 1933), Jerry Dee (born May 16, 1935), Robert Joe (born September 8, 1938), Jan Lynn (born April 29, 1948), and Terry J. (born February 23, 1952).

Carl Lee married Patricia Michael (December 20, 1953) at Muncie, Indiana, and had three children: Sherre Lee, Michael Rex, and Thomas Carl. They have six children.

Jerry Dee married Kitty Thoma (October 10, 1956) at Zanesville, Indiana, and had had four children: Jeffery Allen, Rickey Lee, Jennifer Lynn, and David Scott. They are blessed with five grandchildren and two step-grandchildren.

Robert Joe married Marjorie May (November 2, 1957) at Zanesville, Indiana. They have three children: Randy Joe, Timothy J. and Kelly Sue. They have three grandchildren.

Jan Lynn married John Hyland (May 21, 1982) at Fort Wayne, Indiana. They have no children. John has four by a previous marriage, and two grandchildren.

Terry J. married Jeanne Martin (March 18, 1972) at Zanesville, Indiana. They have three daughters. Tracy, who died at age 18 months, and Jami and Tricia.

Pauline married Avon Dale Donald Snyder (April 30, 1932) and was blessed with six children: Bonnie Lou, Sharon Kay, Ronald Dean, Molly Jane, Dale Wayne, and Janice Ann. Avon was burned fatally in a welding accident (August 4, 1967) at Earth Construction in Fort Wayne, Indiana.

Standing (L to R) Carl Hoopingarner, Rex Hoopingarner; Seated (L to R) G.F. Hoopingarner holding Carl Lee Hoopingarner age seven months, and George Hoopingarner age 98.

Bonnie Lou married Larry A. Johnson (December 9, 1950) in Fort Wayne, Indiana, and had two daughters: Cynthia Diann and Julie. They have six grandchildren.

Sharon Kay married Kenneth Hormann (June 6, 1952). To this marriage was born four children: Christina, Gary, Regina, and Kenneth. They also have eight grandchildren, two step-grandchildren, and one great-grandson.

Ronald Dean married Janice Landrum (December 29, 1956) at Fort Wayne, Indiana, and they have four children: Craig, Robin, and Lisa. A daughter, Heidi, died at birth. They have three grandchildren.

Molly Jane married James Allen Stier (September 23, 1962) at Norfolk, Virginia, and they have three children: Lynn, Tere, and David. They have two grandchildren.

Dale Wayne married Marylin Eisenbarger (October 31, 1964) in Fort Wayne, Indiana, and they have four children: Jeffery Allen, Jill Elizabeth, Heather Marie, and Heidi Lynn, who died at birth on May 3, 1971.

Janice Ann married Thomas Forbing in Fort Wayne, Indiana (July 18, 1976). They have three children: Nicole R., Joshua, and Zachary J.

Pauline remarried (March 30, 1974) to Lester Raymond Heer at Fort Wayne, Indiana. Lester died July 26, 1977.

Dorma married Richard E. Haiflich (March 10, 1945) at Zanesville Church of God Parsonage. They are blessed with two children: Stevan Richard and Karen Sue, along with three grandsons and two step-grandchildren.

Julia married Calvin E. Burger (August 6, 1947) and have two daughters: Kathy Jo and Kimberly Rene. They have five grandchildren of which three granddaughters are deceased.

HOOVER

Felix Hoover, S.A.R. member (1752-1826), was the progenitor of this Jefferson Township family. He married Sarah and moved from Pennsylvania to Ohio by 1803. His son William H. Hoover, War of 1812 (1797-1874), married Sophia Young (1801-?) whose parents were Casper Young and Susannah Yost, Frederick County, Maryland. Her brother Levi Young was one of the first settlers in the Ossian area in 1839.

Third generation Levi Hoover (1826-96) married Catherine Heffner (born 1833 to Michael Heffner and Elizabeth Frey, Frederick County, Maryland) in the Methodist Church at Troy, Ohio. Elizabeth's parents were Michael Haffner (used earlier surname spelling) and Mary Snow. The Levi Hoover family with son Franklin Pierce (1852-1923) and daughter Adaline moved to Wells County in 1853.

The Swiss/German ancestry of Hoovers joined with the English/Irish ancestry when Franklin married Sarah Frances Norton (1860-1933) whose family had moved from Virginia in 1842. Her grandparents included James E. Norton and Elizabeth West, and William West and Sarah Arthur (both born in Virginia) and great-grandparents John Twibell (1760-1853) and Elizabeth Currier (1770-1849) who were married in Baltimore, Maryland. John came from North Ireland with the British but joined the American cause (D.A.R. record).

Evin Franklin Hoover (1881-1962) was the oldest of eight children in the Franklin Hoover family. He had four brothers: Robert who married Harriet Hower, Levi, who died at age three, Homer who married Verda Seward, and Dan who married Gertrude Louden; and three sisters: Georgianna who married Kirt Hatfield, Sarah, who married Earl Short, and Berniece, who married Chester Sheets. Evin married Bertha Orlinda Caston (1884-1959) in 1903. The family, who attended Ossian Methodist Church, were Helen (1904-89), who married Emmett Spindler, Corrine (1908-), who married William Geake, Dale (1910-), who married Esther Bates, Paul (1913-88), who married Virginia Schaper, Josephine (1915-), who married John Moore, Gene (1918-), who married Alice Koons, Lloyd (1921-), who married Geneva Richards, and Mark (1924-), who married Marjorie Barrett.

Wedding Photograph - Evin F. Hoover and Bertha O. Caston

The lively family lived on a farm the first home south of Ossian on the west side of today's State Highway 1. Evin also began a barber shop that soon grew to a five chair location just three doors south of today's Heyerly Bakery in Ossian. Young son Dale worked on Fridays and Saturdays giving numbers to waiting customers, shining shoes, selling candy bars, cigars, and chewing tobacco. Music was enjoyed with songs around the player piano in the parlor at grandparents, Franklin and Sarah's, as well as piano lessons by mother Bertha's sister Josephine. During World War I patriotic children marched behind a parade of the Home Guard carrying popguns and sticks. In the evening Ossian's Main Street was closed for movies such as the serial *Midnight Man* starring James J. Corbett.]

Long Saturday hours at the barber shop led Evin to study meat cutting and open a store in Fort Wayne where the family moved in 1923. Lloyd (Army) and Mark (Navy pilot) served in World War II. Observing Wells County roots, the close family, now including seventeen grandchildren, held a picnic at the Ossian Conservation Club in 1954. In 1988 almost one hundred family members gathered at the DeKalb County country home of Corrine's granddaughter. The annual affairs are attended by those living throughout the United States and England.

Many of the deceased Hoover clan are buried in Ossian.

HOOVER

Genealogy traces the name of Hoover to descendants of Andreas Huber, who came to America from the Palatinate in the year 1738. (The name was spelled in many different ways: Hover, Hoober, Huber, Huver, Hueber and Hoover.) The name Hoover is a Swiss family name found among the Mennonites of Germany and America. More than fifty Hubers emigrated to America before the Revolutionary War; they represented four different faiths: Mennonite, Lutheran, German Reformed and Moravian. The name Hoover also occurs among Quakers and Brethren in Christ.

The subject of this history is John M. Hoover, who was born April 27, 1817, in Landsville, Lancaster County, Pennsylvania. On September 10, 1841, he married Mary M. Kemp in Montgomery County, Ohio. Mary M. Kemp, born in 1820, was the daughter of Solomon and Magdelena Baker Kemp. John M. Hoover's parents were Daniel and Susan Moyer Hoover. Daniel Hoover was born on January 24, 1782, and passed away on August 26, 1851. His wife, Susan Moyers Hoover, was born On April 30, 1791, and passed away on November 29, 1869. Both Daniel Hoover and his wife Susan are at rest in the Landisville Reformed Mennonite Cemetery in Lancaster County, Ohio.

John M. Hoover and Mary Kemp Hoover had the following children: daughter Elizabeth (born 1842); son Benjamin (born 1844); Christina (born 1846); Catherine (born 1848, first married to Abraham S. Masterson, and second marriage to Ephraim L. Bowers, Catherine passed away in 1933); daughter Susanna (born 1850), George W. (born 1851); daughter Mary Ellen (born 1854 and married to Frank Christman); daughter Mahala (born November 25, 1856, married to John G. McCleery); and son John Edmond (born 1859). All but their first child, Elizabeth, were born in Harrison Township, Wells County, Indiana.

John M. Hoover passed away on February 1, 1892, and his wife Mary M. Kemp Hoover passed away on March 9, 1887. They were members of the Methodist Episcopal Church and both are at rest in the Six Mile Cemetery.

Mary Kemp Hoover's parents were from Clark County, Ohio, where Mr. Kemp was engaged in farming. In 1839 they came to Wells County, Indiana, where they purchased the Abe Studebaker farm of two hundred and twelve acres. They made this farm their home until his death on June 11, 1850. They were the parents of eight children, three boys and five girls. Solomon Kemp's family left a legacy for their ancestors to follow. As one of the pioneer families of Wells County, Indiana, the Solomon Kemp family has long been prominent in the history of Wells County. Solomon Kemp is buried in the old Bluffton Cemetery, located on Oak Road, north of Wabash Avenue in the city of Bluffton.

John M. Hoover and Mary Kemp Hoover raised their family in the rich farmland of Harrison Township in Wells County, Indiana. They were the parents of Mahala Hoover McCleery, the mother of Hazel Augusta McClerry McAfee. (Refer to John McCleery and John McAfee, Jr. histories.)

JAMES AND MARCIA JOHNSON HOTOPP

On a cool December day in 1975, James A. Hotopp and Marcia C. Johnson were married at the Six Mile Church. Most of the groomsmen were Southern Wells School coaches and had to leave the festivities early to attend a big game.

James was born in Wayne County to Anthony and Mina Hotopp. He played basketball for Richmond High School and Earlham College from where he graduated with a degree in history. He finished his master's degree at Ball State University. Jim teaches at Southern Wells High School.

Back (L to R) Marcia and Jim Hotopp; Front (L to R) Kelly, Kevin

Marcia, born in Allen County, is the daughter of Leon and Anna Johnson (see Leon Johnson history). Marcia graduated from Bluffton High School in 1971, Huntington College in 1974, and Ball State University in 1976 with a master's degree in elementary education. She taught first grade at Southern Wells until Kevin Andrew was born in 1981. Kevin enjoys school, chess, and farming. Daughter, Kelly Michelle, was born in 1983. She enjoys school, collecting stuffed animals, and learning new crafts.

Jim, Marcia, Kevin, Kelly, and Higgins (pet Golden Retriever) live on two and one-half acres in Harrison Township, Wells County.

HOUTZ

Philip Houtz was an emigrant from Germany in 1730. His great-grandson, Henry Houtz III (1815-1890), was my great-grandfather and came to Wells County in 1845. The family had moved west through Pennsylvania, Montgomery County, Ohio, Indianapolis, and then to Wells County. He built the first brick house in Wells County and fired his own brick. He also fired brick for the first brick St. Paul Church. He was one of the first to be buried at St. Paul Cemetery.

Henry III was married to Fanny Harp, and they had eleven children: Eli, Amanda, Philip, Christina, Eliza, Jacob, Angelina, Jeremiah, Sara, and Lydia. A son, Josiah, was killed in Vicksburgh in 1863. My grandfather Jeremiah (1842-1923), also buried at St. Paul, was married to Mary Ellen Jefferies. They had ten children: Jesse (my father), Jacob, Simeon, Frederick, Abe (all buried at St. Paul); Charles, a doctor, moved to North Dakota to the gold fields, and homesteading and on to Montana; Fanny to North Dakota; Rose to Terre Haute; Mary to Canada; and Elizabeth to New Jersey. Grandpa Jeremiah served in the Civil War from 1861 to 1865, and was a member of the Lew Daily Post GAR at Bluffton.

Jeremiah Houtz

My father, Jesse (1868-1953), was a farmer and carpenter in Wells County and, after retiring, lived in Bluffton. He was the eldest son of ten children. His mother died when he was young, and he worked and helped his brother, Charles, through medical school. In 1909 he married Rosa Harnish, daughter of John and Ida (Shoemaker) Harnish. They had three children. My sister, Ida, married Elmer Charters and lives in Montana. Their children are: Evelyn, Dale, Hazel, and Bill. My youngest sister, Martha, married Anthony Daniel, and lives in New Jersey. She has a daughter, Rosemary.

In 1934, I, John Jeremiah Houtz, married Mary Hunnicutt, daughter of John and Laura (Jackson) Hunnicutt. We have three daughters: Joyce (Dahlquist), her children: John DeLong, Joseph DeLong; Betty (Parker), her children: Joan (Paxson), Linda (Kellam), Kent Campbell, Lynn Campbell: Carol (Watkins), her children: Stacia (Cooper), Daphne (Starkey), Shawn Yount.

I have retired from farming, and Mary and I reside in Warren. *Submitted by John Jeremiah Houtz.*

HOUTZ-VENIS

Roy Houtz (1903-1991) married Mary Venis (1906) in Bluffton in 1924. Roy Houtz was the son of William Henry Houtz and Ida Blanche Sale of rural Uniondale. Mary was the daughter of Roy Venis and Alta Steele.

The children of Roy Houtz on Mary Venis Houtz are: William (Bill) (1928) married Elizabeth Campbell (Betty) (1932) in 1953. (1) Susie (1954) married John Tarascou (1952) in 1974. Children a. Anna 1983; b. Grant 1988. (2) Bill (1956) married Susan Chappell (1955) in 1978. He went to West Point and is now in government service in Brussels, Belgium. Children: a. Christina 1980; b. Christopher 1982. (3). Clifford 1958 married Stephanie Corgell (1959) in 1980. Children: a. Heidi 1982; b. Katie 1983.

Richard (Dick) (1930) married Betty Jane Nelson (1928) in 1952.

(1) Deborah (1953) married Scott Powers (1951) in 1974. Children: a. David 1977; b. Matthew 1979; c. Sarah 1987 (adopted). (2). Peter (1957) married Teresa Bracker (1958) in 1982. Children: a. Timothy 1984; b. Daniel 1986.

Roy Houtz and family moved to Alta Loma, California in 1952. Since most of his work was in sales of animal feed, he decided to start a chicken ranch.

Increases in population left them in the midst of the city instead of a rural area. The ranch was sold in the mid 1980's.

Their boys, Bill and Dick, worked with them from the very first. Eggs were sold to the main airlines. The Houtz homes form a compound - this property was not sold. Roy and his sons retired. Several of the girls are nurses. Two of the boys are pilots. Most of the family live near Alta Loma except Bill, Jr., who lives in Brussels, Belgium.

Many of Roy's relatives live in Bluffton or the near vicinity. Mary also has relation in Bluffton.

HUFFMAN-ELLIOTT FAMILY

Robert J. Elliott and Barbara Huffman Elliott reside on a farm south of Bluffton (Harrison Township Section 18) bordering the Wabash River which is a Studabaker homestead farm, given by Abraham Studabaker to his son William, a brother of John Studabaker and half-brother of Peter Studabaker. They reside in a home built in the 1860's by Abraham T. Studabaker for his wife Louisa Dewitt and their eleven children, the youngest of which was Minnie Myrtle, grandmother of Barbara Huffman Elliott. Minnie married Edward L. Huffman, grandson of David and Hannah (Pine) Huffman and son of John and Mary J. Runyon, who resided in Hartford Township, Adams County, Indiana. Dale Abraham Huffman, middle son of Edward and Minnie, was Barbara's father. Barbara's mother, Gwendolyn Long, was born in Wells County, Indiana, daughter of Orville Martin Long and Elise Amber Stout. Gwendolyn's grandparents were Marada Field Stout and George William Stout. The Long family was descended from Indian heritage near Eaton, Indiana.

Barbara and Bob met at Indiana University, where both were chemistry majors, and were married upon graduation in 1949. They lived in St. Louis, Missouri, Granada Hills, California, and Cincinnati, Ohio, before returning to reside in Indiana in 1974. Bob was employed for many years at Bristol Meyers in St. Louis, then by Max Factor in California, and by Richardson Merrill in Cincinnati. In Indiana, he worked at W.S. Shamban in Fort Wayne, and the Incel Company in Bluffton. A veteran of World War II, he served from February, 1942, to January, 1946, in the 536th Army Engineers Light Pontoon Company, 9th Army, in England, France, Belgium, Holland, and Germany. Barbara was head of technical information services at Mallinckrodt Chemical Works, Uranium Division, for fifteen years and at the Petrolite Corporation, Research Division, before their son Michael, was born. She received her master's degree in library science also from Indiana University. After returning to Indiana she was head of technical services at the St. Francis College Library and is currently library director at the Bluffton-Wells County Library.

Barbara Huffman held by Edward L. Huffman, Dale Huffman, Mary J. (Runyan) Huffman

Robert is the son of Virginia Lesejus Bibb and Joseph Angelo Elliott; he was born on October 24, 1923, in St. Louis, Missouri. The Elliotts trace their heritage from England to Rails County in northern Missouri. Joe Elliott's maternal grandfather was Michael Hartigan, who migrated from County Limerick, Ireland, to Monroe County, Missouri, in 1866. Virginia Bibb was the granddaughter of Charles William Damron and Sejus Gabriella Crank. Charles William was a descendant of Dunmore Damon, whose father migrated from Scotland to Virginia. Sejus Gabriella Crank, better known as Ma Sissie, lived to be over one hundred years old and could vividly recall events from her childhood during the Civil War in Virginia in the unusual role of daughter of a Union Army soldier who was a southern landowner. Ma Sissie was the granddaughter of Henry Forqueran and Susan Gaddy. Susan Gaddy's father, Bartholomew Gaddy, served in the Revolution and was at the Battle of Yorktown.

Joe Elliott, Virginia Bibb Elliott, Robert J. Elliott, Barbara Huffman Elliott, Gwendolyn Long Huffman, Dale Huffman

Michael Roger Elliott, son of Barbara and Robert was born in 1963 in St. Louis, Missouri. A graduate of the University of Chicago in 1985, he resides in East Newport, Maine, and works as chief statistician and researcher for Northeast Research in Orno, Maine. He is married to Amy Lesemann, daughter of Arthur and Joan Lesemann of Englewood, New Jersey. Amy teaches English composition and English literature in Fairfield Community School System in Fairfield, Maine. They have no children as of this writing.

HUNNICUTT FAMILY

John and Laura (Jackson) Hunnicutt started housekeeping December 15, 1897 at South Liberty located two miles south and two miles west of Liberty Center. There was a good school and church located there which made a good place to raise a family. They had four girls and three boys.

The Hunnicutt ancestors came from England and Scotland. Samuel, a Quaker minister, was our great-great-grandfather. He married Phearaby Block in Surrey County, Virginia, November 15, 1774. To this union our great-grandfather, Chappell was born September 11, 1807.

Chappell became a herb doctor and as the Quakers migrated westward; he married Elizabeth Roberts in Clinton County, Ohio on September 11, 1840. They later moved to Wells County around 1850. Their children were: James, Ezra, Neri, Anthony, Sarah, Phearaby, Eliza, Samuel, Robert, Chappel, Lindsley, Cathlene, Ulyssis and Mary. Ezra and Neri served in the Civil War from Wells County.

Neri was our grandfather, born July 25, 1842, died August 27, 1897, and he married Elizabeth Catherine Baker, daughter of John Baker, Jr., April 15, 1865. They resided in Jackson Township a few years before moving to South Liberty. Their children were: Sylvester, John, Elnora, Ida and James. Elizabeth died December 22, 1882 leaving Neri to raise a very young family with James being just three years old.

Our grandfather, Neri, had been a farmer and at one time had a small drug store in Mt. Zion.

Our father, John, was a farmer, hauled logs and oil well equipment and pulled oil wells with horses. He also found time to be janitor of the South Liberty Church for several years.

Our mother's parents were Joseph L. Jackson and Mary A. Thompson. Her grandfather, Hiram Jackson was perhaps the first white man to make a permanent residence in Liberty Township located one mile east and one mile south of Liberty Center.

Mother started a subscription summer school a few years prior to her marriage at South Liberty. She didn't teach after she was married. They had seven children:

Netti, born December 16, 1898, died December 4, 1900.

Rosa married Clifford Ruble, a farmer, their children are Robert Ruble and Phyllis (Pond).

Everett, born August 22, 1902, died October 18, 1918 of influenza.

Charlie married Florence Musselman of Wells County. He owned a confectionery wholesale store in Muncie. Their children are: John Roger, Wayne, Janice (King), Willis and Jerry.

Ida married John Collins, a salesman for Texaco Oil Co. Their children are: Billie, Sue (Poulson) and Ted.

Carl married Mary Meade, January 12, 1929, daughter of William Patton and Elizabeth (Addington) Meade. In 1933, we settled four miles west of Liberty Center, in Buckeye where we had a general store for twenty years; along with a huckster wagon that served Wells and Huntington Counties.

I also farmed, had an insurance agency and am now retired.

Our children are: Louella (Sproat), Kenneth, Louise (Campbell), Carlene (Griffin), Larry, Thomas, and James.

Mary married John Houtz on November 17, 1934, John was a farmer and we lived near Buckeye until retiring in 1985. We now reside in Warren. Our children are: Joyce (Dahlquist), Betty (Parker), Carol Ann (Watkins). *(Carl Hunnicutt and Mary Hunnicutt Houtz)*

EVERETT JOSEPH HUNNICUTT

Everett Joseph Hunnicutt was born to Laura (Jackson) and John Hunnicutt August 22, 1902. He died October 18, 1918 during the influenza epidemic. The 1918 flu epidemic was a terrible tragedy.

Everett Joseph Hunnicutt

ROSA EDITH HUNNICUTT

Rosa Edith Hunnicutt was born to Laura (Jackson) and John Hunnicutt on October 30, 1900. The family live one-fourth mile south of the South Liberty (Africa) Church on the west side of the road. Ancestors on both sides of the families were farmers. Rosa drove a horse and buggy to Liberty Center to attend high school after graduating from the South Liberty Grade School. In her senior year she was accepted as a student in the Huntington Business College. She worked her way through business college by living with the Samal family, helping with the housework and caring for their daughter. Upon graduation she was employed by the W.B. Company in Bluffton as a typist stenographer proficient in taking short hand.

The Interurban passenger railways were very popular at this time because the system was a great improvement over horse and buggy travel. However, as the personal gasoline powered motor car became more popular the Interurban lines were used less and less most lines became obsolete in the early 1930's. For her wedding in 1922, Rosa and her mother, Laura, rode the Interurban to Liberty Center, on to Bluffton and then on to Fort Wayne to buy her silk wedding dress at the Hutner's Paris dress shop.

Rosa Edith (Hunnicutt) Ruble and Clifford Edward Ruble wedding picture October 14, 1922

She married Clifford Edward Ruble, a Huntington County farmer, on October 14, 1922 and spent the rest of her life as a farmer's wife. Clifford and Rosa lived on a farm on road 800 S. in Huntington County owned by Marcus Thompson from 1922 until 1938. They then moved to the next farm west located at 4190E-800S, which they had recently purchased. A great event happened in 1938. Electricity came to the farm.

Their oldest son, Robert Edmond Ruble was born December 3, 1923 in a log house on the Marcus Thompson farm. Twin girls were stillborn on March 12, 1929. Their youngest child, Phyllis Joan (Ruble) Pond was born October 25, 1930.

Robert married Margaret (Peg) Wheatley July 28, 1957. They live on a farm one and one-half miles south of Buckeye in Huntington County.

Bob and Peg's children are: Susan Marie (Ruble) Osborne born January 3, 1959, Ned Eugene Ruble born April 11, 1961, and Barbara Rose Ruble born April 26, 1963. Susan is married to Rick Osborn and living in Iowa. She is a pharmacist. They have one daughter, Alyssa. Ned lives two miles south of Buckeye and farms with his dad. Barbara works and lives at home.

Phyllis married George Pond June 10, 1951 and they live at New Haven, Indiana. Their children are: Jean Ann (Pond) Grasmick born August 5, 1957. She is a respiratory therapist and lives in Indianapolis. Douglas Edward Pond born December 8, 1955. He is science director with the Indiana Department of Agriculture working under the direction of Lt. Governor Frank O'Bannon. William Walter Pond born October 9, 1953 married Brenda Kay Armentrout June 23, 1979. Dr. William Pond is an anesthesiologist in Fort Wayne. Their children are Gregory Clifford Pond born February 8, 1985, and Scott Everett Pond born March 2, 1988. Phyllis Ruble Pond presently teaches kindergarten at New Haven, Indiana. For the past 14 years she has also served the 15th and 20th districts as their state representative in the Indiana General Assembly. The 15th district included Union and Jefferson Townships of Wells County as well as the southern half of Allen County.

The last few years of their lives Clifford and Rosa spent the summers farming and the three winter months in Palmetto, Florida. Clifford died March 11, 1979 and Rosa died September 28, 1985.

HAROLD WAYNE HUNT FAMILY

Harold Wayne Hunt was born July 26, 1922 in Decatur, Indiana, to Theodore Oman and Eva Bowman Hunt. He graduated from Lancaster High School in 1940. He was employed at Central Soya forty-one years. For fifteen years he operated an appliance service in his spare time. He entered the U.S. Army Air Corps on November 4, 1942, completing forty-nine missions in B24 bombers in the South Pacific Theatre during World War II. He was awarded the Purple Heart, the Air Medal with three Oak Leaf Clusters, the Asiatic-Pacific Theater Ribbon, and the Philippine Liberation Ribbon with one Bronze Star.

On October 12, 1943, in the chapel at Biggs Field, El Paso, Texas, he married Dorothy Frances Watrous who was born in Riverside, Illinois, November 5, 1922, to Austin Augustus and Sadie Lagerpusch Watrous. She graduated from Bluffton High School in 1940 and worked at the Fort Wayne General Electric plant where slacks and hair nets were required for a woman to fill a man's job during World War II. When Wayne was discharged on September 5, 1945, they settled in Craigville so that their children could attended Lancaster School. While raising their family, Dorothy worked in the photography field and was postmaster of Craigville retiring in 1989 with twenty-six years of service with the U.S. Postal Service. The family belonged to the Presbyterian Church of Bluffton. Children born to Wayne and Dorothy are as follows:

Barbara Louise, born July 1, 1944, graduated Lancaster High School and International Business College, married Thomas Putman of Fort Wayne. Daughter, Angela Marie, was born September 17, 1969. Barbara has earned the CPA certificate and is employed by the accounting firm of Dress Perugini.

Janet Marie, born September 30, 1946, graduated Lancaster High School and Ball State University and married Michael Hawley of Winchester, Indiana. Their first son, Christopher Wayne, was born July 31, 1968, but died shortly after birth. Son, Ryan Michael, was born October 6,

Wayne and Dorothy Hunt Family - Back (L-R) Kim Strader, Daniel Hunt, Dorothy and Wayne Hunt, Tom and Barbara Putman. Middle (L-R) Matthew and Virginia Strader, Christine, Joshua and Jaime Hunt, Janet, Scott, and Michael Hawley. Front (L-R) Adam, Allison, Ben and Carrie Strader, Ryan Hawley, Angela Putman

1975, and son, Scott Patrick, was born January 23, 1979. Janet teaches business subjects at Snider High School, Fort Wayne, where Michael is also employed as a history teacher and football coach.

Virginia Ellen, born March 15, 1948, graduated Lancaster High School and Ball State University and married Captain Kim Jon Strader of Salt Lake City, Utah. Son, Matthew Wayne, was born December 25, 1971. Second son Jacob Donovan was born February 23, 1974, and died in 1976. Third son, Adam Lee, was born June 26, 1975, and first daughter, Allison Yvonne, was born January 20, 1978. Twins, Carrie Ann and Benjamin John, were born on July 31, 1979. Captain Kim Strader, a helicopter pilot, was killed at n air show at Ramstein Air Force Base, Germany, when burning planes fell among spectators and participants.

Daniel Wayne was born December 7, 1956, graduated Norwell High School, and operates an appliance repair service in Craigville. He is married to the former Christine Mae Hunteman. Their daughter, Jamie Lee, was born February 23, 1976, and their son, Joshua Daniel, was born February 26, 1981. Christine is postmaster at Uniondale, Indiana.

The family belonged to the Presbyterian Church of Bluffton.

Wayne Hunt died September 23, 1989, and is buried in Prairie View Cemetery, Tocsin, Indiana.

RALPH HUNT FAMILY

Ralph Hunt married Nancy Agnes Smith March 22, 1842, in Warren County, Ohio. Their children were Edwin Shannon, born December 3, 1842; Martha Emaline, born June 15, 1845, and died April 3, 1846; and Alexander Smith, born November 16, 1848.

Shannon married Lib Williams and had several children. He served in the Civil War.

The Ralph and Shannon families emigrated to Wells County after the Civil War. After Agnes died September 5, 1872, Shannon, his family and his father who was about sixty-five years old, left by wagon, then float boat to settle in Hunter, Arkansas. Ralph died on the Mississippi River and was buried at Memphis, Tennessee.

Alexander married Rachel Tribolet, a daughter of John and Elizabeth Ogle Tribolet of Delaware County. Children born to this union were:

Nora who married Ezra Burget. Their children were Dorothy and Helen.

James L., born September 2, 1874, married Lida Richey. Their children were: Ralph, Raymond, Violet and May. James died in 1948.

Oscar Ralph, a surviving twin, born July 29, 1876, married Dessie D. Nelson. Their children were Lela, Zella, Ethel, Hazel, Mayme, Emory, Sophia, twins Alma and Chalmer, and Walter. Oscar died in April 1959.

Agnes Smith, born July 24, 1878, married Martin Heckley February 12, 1898. They had twin sons who were still-born and a daughter, Emma. When Emma was about seven years old, her mother became an invalid. Martin worked his farm, raised his daughter and took care of his invalid wife until her death.

Alexander E. was born August 27, 1882. On April 12, 1910, he married Ethel Cherry. No children were born to this union. During the Depression, they lost their farm in Lancaster Township as did many others. Alex was a school teacher and trustee of Lancaster Township. He died January 6, 1948.

Theodore O. was born September 15, 1884. On November 8, 1911, he married Eva Myrtle Bowman. Their children were Berneice, Loren, Leon, Harold Wayne, Gaylord and Roberta. Theodore died April 1, 1961.

William John, the only child not born in Wells County, was born in Huntington County, September 23, 1886. He married Laura Thompson. Their children were Byrl, Dale, and Keith. William died May 1, 1954.

Millie Clementine was born August 25, 1889, near Tocsin. She married Clyde F. Scherrer. Their children were Delbert and Mary. Millie died January 30, 1978, and could not be buried for several days because of the blizzard of 1978.

At this writing, eleven great-grandchildren of Ralph and Agnes are still living; Helen Burget Doenges of Markle; Mae Hunt Crabill of Fort Wayne; Hazel Hunt Lewton of Craigville; Chalmer Hunt of Angola; Loren Hunt of Bluffton; Gaylord Hunt of Auburndale, Florida; Roberta Hunt Lockwood of Ossian; Byrl and Dale Hunt both of Decatur; Delbert Scherrer of Greenville, South Carolina; and Mary Scherrer Heuer Smith of Fort Wayne.

THEODORE O. HUNT FAMILY

Theodore Oman Hunt was born on September 15, 1884, in Wells County, a son of Alexander Smith and Rachel Tribolet Hunt.

On November 8, 1911, he married Eva Myrtle Bowman, who was born in Tocsin on August 7, 1889, a daughter of John Adam and Eliza Jane Archbold Bowman. They raised six children, and enjoyed a happy married life for just eight months short of fifty years. All four of their sons served in World War II.

Six children were born to Theodore and Eva. Abbreviated biographical information about each follows:

Berneice Elizabeth, born September 17, 1912, near Bingham in Allen County, married Paul Frantz of Liberty Center on March 18, 1944. Paul was a son of James Marion and Harriett Ann Boltin Frantz. Kent Hunt and James Paul were born to this union. Berneice died June 5, 1977.

The Theodore Hunt Family
Back (L to R) Leon, Loren, Gaylord, Wayne. Front (L to R) Roberta Lockwood, Eva, Theodore, and Berniece Frantz

Loren Wilmer, born September 17, 1915, married Oleta Paddock, daughter of George W. and Ilka Wilson Paddock of Darwin, Illinois, now lives southeast of Bluffton. Their children are Phyllis Lee, Jemetta, and Dr. Loren W. Hunt.

Leon Jay, born December 1, 1919, married Madge Cole of Liberty Center. Their children are: Margaret Ann, Donald, Timothy, Sally, and Joseph. They made their home in New Haven. Leon died in April, 1980.

Harold Wayne, born in Decatur on July 26, 1922, married Dorothy Frances Watrous, daughter of Austin Augustus and Sadie Lagerpusch Watrous. They lived in Craigville, and their children were Barbara Louise, Janet Marie, Virginia Ellen, and Daniel Wayne. Wayne died September 23, 1989.

Gaylord Vernell, born February 23, 1925, married Virginia Mae Latshaw of Pennsylvania, daughter of Albert Wiser and Edna Spahn Latshaw. Children born were Susan Marie, Theodore Albert, John Cameron, and Amy Diane. They now make their home in Auburndale, Florida.

Roberta Olene, born September 2, 1927, married Roger Joseph Lockwood, son of Cecil and Mary Stahl Lockwood. Children born were: Steven Rick, Kevin Charles, and Kevin Diane. They live in Ossian.

Theodore died April 1, 1961; Eva died August 14, 1966. They are buried in the Prairie View Cemetery near Tocsin.

HUSEMAN

We moved to Bluffton in June of 1977 from West Lafayette where John was a student at Purdue University.

John Alan Huseman grew up at Crown Point, Indiana on a dairy farm. He graduated from Lowell High School in 1970.

Linda Rios Huseman grew up in East Gary, now known as Lake Station, Indiana, and graduated in 1970 from River Forest High School.

We were married in 1973 and moved to West Lafayette where John was attending the School of Veterinary Medicine. Upon graduation, he joined the practice of Dr. Lou Schroeder at the Bluffton Animal Clinic and moved to Wells County with a new daughter, Angela, then one year old.

We lived for two and one-half years of Elm Grove Road, and during this time our son, Douglas was born. When Doug was six months old we moved to a tri-level house on Honeysuckle Lane, where our daughter Katherine was born in 1982.

We now live at 350 North, having moved here in 1989. Our children enjoy the country life style and their many live stock are used in 4-H projects.

In 1990 John purchased the Bluffton Animal Clinic from Dr. Lou Schroeder. We are members of St. Joseph's Catholic Church in Bluffton.

IFER

The Ifer ancestry dates to the arrival, by boat, of ten year old Peter Slutman who settled in Montgomery County, Ohio. His daughter, Elizabeth, married George Ifer. Their son Peter married Sarah L. Devoss and their family consisted of six males and two females (who died in infancy). The family settled in Nottingham Township. The six Ifer brothers were: George Wesley, Warren Henry, John William, Francis (Frank), Charles Wilbur and Earl.

Front (L to R) George, Warren, John; Back (L to R) Frank Charlie Earl

These six brothers were active in the community and engaged in farming and homesteading as well as oil-well related activities in the Nottingham area and in Oklahoma.

The families of these six are as follows: George (died 1954): his daughter, Flo (Chambers) had two children, Peggy and George W.; Warren (died 1927): his son Carl, who had a daughter Dorothy (Vary); a daughter Blanche (Johns) who had two sons, Keith (deceased) and Kent; a daughter Elsie (Houtz) (deceased), who had a son Clarence (Kay); John (died 1948): His son Homer (deceased), had a daughter Patricia (Higgins); and a daughter Mabel (Shinn) (deceased) with two daughters Phyllis and Gloria; Frank (died 1942): had two sons, Dowell, without children and Peter (deceased) who had a son Frank and a daughter Mary Precious (Stone); Charles (deceased 1945): had a son Dale (deceased), who had two daughters, Carolyn Joyce (Highlen) (deceased) and Loretta Sue (Sliger); a daughter Norma (Harter) who had a son Ron (deceased); and another daughter Ida Rose (Gerard) who has two daughters Priscilla (Hawks) and Jane (Schladen); Earl (died 1945): had two daughters, Irsel (deceased) without children, and Nellie (Carter) who had three children, Suzanne (Smith', Jamie (Rapp) and Julie (Hill).

Descendents currently living in and around Wells County include: Patricia Ifer (Jim Higgins) and son J. Michael. Phyllis D. Shinn (musician) and Gloria L. Shinn, M.D., engaged in the practice of general surgery at the Caylor-Nickel Clinic. Frank Ifer (wife, Ruth Bender) has two children, Kara and Kurt, the only male descendent in the sixth generation to carry the family name. Mary P. Ifer Stone (Wayne Stone). Dowell Ifer (wife, Louella Dougherty). Clarence Kay Houtz. Norma Ifer Harter (Earl Harter). Ida Rose Ifer Gerard (Charles Gerard) and their children, Priscilla Gerard Hawks and Jane Gerard Schladen (Tom Schladen). Loretta Sue Ifer Sliger (Fred Sliger) daughter of Dale.

INMAN-COTTON

Doyt E. Inman was born to Grover and Lola Inman while they lived in Willshire, Ohio. He was preceded by a brother, Dale, and followed by a sister, Maxine (Mrs. Ardis Crum). Grover was a barber by trade but he purchased a farm west of Uniondale and moved the family to Indiana. He continued barbering in Huntington as well as working the farm.

Betty Eloyce Cotton was born to Forst G. and Cleona (Hoover) Cotton and was followed by a sister, EuDora Jane, and brother, Lyle J. Cotton.

Doyt and Betty Inman - 50th Anniversary picture

Doyt graduated from Union Center High School in 1934 and Betty graduated from Ossian High School in 1937. They were married September 3, 1939. Two children were born to them: Sara Lee, who lived only a shore time after birth, and Lane Stuart Inman.

For a number of years, Doyt was an automotive parts salesman traveling out of Fort Wayne. In the early 50's the family was making their home in Uniondale, and he was appointed as the rural mail carrier out of the Uniondale Post Office (RR #1). Later his route was expanded to include RR#3 out of the Ossian Post Office. He retired from this service in 1979.

Betty was a fulltime homemaker until the Sears catalogue store announced its opening in Bluffton and advertised for employees. She was accepted as an employee and worked there continually until she retired. She and Doyt retired at the same time (1979). They now divide their living between Pretty Lake, Indiana and Sarasota, Florida.

Son Lane was in the last graduating class, 1968, from Rockcreek High School. Lane followed his grandfather's barbering profession and owns a shop in Fort Wayne. He lives there with his wife, Sidonnie. He has a daughter, Terena Kumfer, sons Chad and Scott, and a stepson and step-daughter, Kurt and Leslie Kerfoot.

(Refer to Cotton/Hoover, Yager/Cotton, Cotton/McAfee.)

INSKEEP

We can date the Inskeep family back to Judge John Inskeep (1677-1729) in Sadely Green, Staffordshire, Old England. Sometime in the early 1700's his son, James (born 1703) came to America and settled in the East. His descendants slowly moved west until my great-great-grandfather, Foreman (born 1830), became one of Wells County's earliest settlers when he came here from Gallion, Ohio in 1853.

Foreman was married to Margaret Shell (born 1826) and they bought two hundred forty acres of land in Rockcreek Township west of Bluffton. When Foreman died in 1891, his farm was divided up between his four children, Sarah C. (Sally) (born 1853), William H. (born 1855), Issac N. (born 1858) and Vause G. (born 1860).

Vause was my great-grandfather. He married Louisa Ness (born 1861) and had six children, Bessie, Fred, Harvey (born 1891), Issac (born 1892), Glenn (born 1894), and Garth. As far as I know all my ancestors were farmers and/or carpenters except for great-uncle Issac who was a handwriting expert living in California.

Glenn was my grandfather. He married Thelma Oleen Lesh (born 1897), the daughter of Milo Lesh and Minnie Decker. A sister, Viva Lesh married Harvey. Grandma and Harvey both died in 1955. Grandpa bought forty acres from great-aunt Sally west of his eighty acres and the other half of the farm was eventually sold. However, forty more acres are, in a way, back in the family, as recently Jay Langel, a grandson of Aunt Bessie bought this land.

Glenn and Thelma had three children, Richard Glenn (born 1924), Robert Lesh (born 1926) and Carolyn Sue (born 1936). Richard married Harriet Simmons and they have four children, Julia, Joseph, Thomas and Stephen. They live in Fort Wayne. Aunt Carolyn died in 1962 and never married.

Robert, my dad, married Marilyn Ruth Pence (born 1929) of Markle on June 21, 1947. They lived east of Markle close to where I live now and later moved to a farm west of Rockford where dad farmed and worked for Renner's Express. In 1962, they built a house just west of my Grandpa's house. Grandpa died a year later. The Inskeep name stops here as Mom and Dad had five daughters.

Candy (born 1948), graduated from International Business College and works for a law firm in Fort Wayne. She has two daughters, Toni (nineteen) and Jamie (fourteen). She lives in Ossian. Cathy (born 1950), married Don Booth in 1985. She works at Old First Bank and lives in Bluffton. Cindy (born 1952), married Gary Cook in 1977. She works at K-Mart Distribution Center and has two daughters, Abby (ten) and Amy (six). they live west of Bluffton. Cheri (born 1953), married Jerry Thomas in 1976. She works for Franklin Electric and has two children, Adam (twelve) and Traci (nine). They live northeast of Markle. Carla (born 1956), graduated from Ball State. She married Keith Claghorn in 1978. She is a nurse and lives in Indianapolis. They have three children, Nicholas (seven), Benjamin (three) and MacKenzie (two).

INSKEEP-VICKREY

Stephen D. and Sarah (Owen) Vickrey had three sons, Homer, George and Noah, and farmed along the Wabash River in Wabash County, Indiana. After successive crop failures because of flooding, they bought a Liberty Township, Wells County farm along present State Highway 124. Sarah passed away at age forty and Stephen did not remarry. The family was cared for by Stephen's mother and later by housekeepers. One was a widow, Dessie Sliger Eubank, who brought with her Helen Eubank born August 23, 1895, her daughter, born August 22, 1917. Son Noah, born February 11, 1892, married Dessie, born August 23, 1958, in 1925, having purchased the adjoining Johnson farm with a down payment from his World War I medical discharge settlement. At Stephen Vickrey's death, Noah purchased the homestead and lived there his lifetime. He like raising pigs. He farmed with horses, never owning a tractor. The farm was identified by the white horse in the roadside pasture that survived his owner by several years. Noah's second marriage, in 1954, was to Velma Anders Sliger. Noah and Dessie had one daughter, Doris E., born October 24, 1928. Helen and Doris graduated from Liberty Center.

Standing (L to R) Susan and Kent Inskeep; Seated (L to R) Jan, Doris and William B. Inskeep.

William Henry and Margaret (Dye) Inskeep, born in Ohio, lived on the Rockford Pike in Rockcreek Township, with their children, Anna, Harry, Forman, Elizabeth, Charles and Henry, William Henry died at age forty-five and his wife two years later, leaving the six children, who stayed together on the farm. Charles, born June 24, 1890, married Mary Elizabeth (Mollie) Reece in 1915. A trip to the Warren fair was their first date. Uneasy about riding on Charles' motorcycle, Mollie touched her foot to the ground often. On returning home she discovered her shoe sole worn through! They farmed the Inskeep homestead. During World War II, Charles worked at Zollner's in Fort Wayne, moving there in 1947. They had five daughters, Dorotha, born in 1918; Mary Esther, born in 1919; Virginia born in 1922; Emojean, born in 1923; Charlene, born in 1926; and one son, William B., born in 1928, all Rockcreek graduates. Mollie enjoyed gardening. She resided at the Warren Methodist Home after Charles' 1972 death until her death in 1979.

William B. Inskeep and Doris E. Vickrey married August 26, 1950, at Liberty center Methodist Church, where they remain members. They moved into the former Johnson farmhouse, Doris' birthplace. After Noah Vickrey's death, the Inskeeps moved to the Vickrey homestead, where they presently reside. William, employed by Northern Indiana Public Service for thirty-eight years, in addition to farming, enjoys raising sheep. The farm is now identified by the sheep in the roadside pasture. Doris, employed twenty-nine years at Wells Community Hospital, served as office manager and treasurer. Both William and Doris retired in 1988.

The three Inskeep children, Southern Wells graduates are as follows: Son Kent L., born June 24, 1951, attended IPFW, married Lana K. Buse, and resides in Bluffton. They have three daughters, Amanda S., born April 1, 1971, with the Army in Germany, Kathleen L., born October 2, 1974, and Natalie R., born January 6, 1977.

Daughter Susan K., born June 7, 1953, Ball State graduate, married Darrell K. Freds, rural Bluffton. They have a son, Will B., born December 20, 1974, and a daughter, Rebekah M., born December 6, 1977

Daughter Jan L., born January 16, 1956, Indiana State graduate, married James L. Miller, living in Redlands, California, with one son, Ryan, born August 2, 1987. Both Susan and Jan teach school and Kent is a machinist.

ISCH-MANGOLD

Harry and Clarice Isch are planning to celebrate their golden wedding anniversary. They were married fifty years ago, on June 1, 1941, in the Apostolic Christian Church at Roanoke, Illinois.

Clarice was the daughter of Ezra and Anna Leman Mangold, now deceased. She and her twin brother, Clarence, were bon on November 13, 1914. She had two younger brothers: Harley, of Fort Wayne and Willis, of Leipsic, Ohio. One sister, Melba, lives in Eureka, Illinois.

Harry, son of John and Katie Steffen Isch, also deceased, was born in Bluffton on March 4, 1917. His sister, Mrs. Alvin (Helen) Gerber, and a brother, Roger, both live in Bluffton.

Harry and Clarice had four children. John Harry was born November 25, 1942. Ann Catherine was born on his birthday, in 1945, but she soon left them. They were heart-broken when she died, after a short illness, on December 26, 1946.

But God is Good Catherine Jane came along January 19, 1948, and Connie Sue was born on March 7, 1949.

John showed an early interest in medicine. He had great respect and admiration for Dr. Harold Caylor, his mentor, when he worked at Caylor-Nickel Hospital, during several summers.

He received a B.S. degree from Purdue, an M. D. from Indiana University, and spent two years as a resident at Jackson Memorial Hospital at Miami, Florida. He is presently a cardiac surgeon with the Heart Institute at St. Vincent Hospital, in Indianapolis.

In 1967, he married Mary Jane Rager, a nurse, of Van Wert, Ohio. They have three children. Andy is a senior and Beth is a junior at Wheaton College. Katie is a freshman at Carmel High School. Their home is in Carmel, Indiana.

During her high school year, Cathy helped her dad in the store (when she had time). She attended Ball State a year before she graduated from the University of Indiana with a degree in nursing.

On June 6, 1971, Cathy was married to Keith Steffen, of Fairbury, Illinois. He finished his education, which had been interrupted by army duty in Vietnam, at Illinois State University, and is now an administrator at St. Franics Hospital, Peoria, Illinois. They have four children. Tom is a junior and Todd a sophomore at Washington High School. Abby is in the fourth grade, and Ann is in the second grade at Washington Grade School. Their home is in Washington, Illinois.

Connie, too, helped out at the store. After high school, she graduated from Indiana University with a degree in Special Education and taught briefly after her marriage on May 14, 1972, to William Witzig, for Gridley, Illinois. Bill served in the army in Europe after graduating from the University of Illinois. He is an engineer with Ault and Witzig of Indianapolis, where they reside. They have three boys: David, a sophomore at Heritage High School; Brian, in the eighth grade; and Robert, in the fourth grade at Heritage Grade School.

Harry and Clarice began their married life in a little brown house at 222 East South Street, in Bluffton.

Harry, always interested in hardware - and in people - opened Isch hardware in 1936, at the age of 19. His first cash register was a cigar box. He enjoyed his work, and valued his customers, for forty-one years. In 1977, he sold the store to Jim Geisel, a former employee.

Clarice, who had taught school for five years before their marriage, reluctantly agreed to "help out" for a year during the teacher shortage in 1955. In 1977, after "helping out" at Lancaster Grade School for 22 years, she and Harry both retired.

Their home address is 1760 Timberidge Road, Bluffton , Indiana.

JACKSON

The first white settlers of Liberty Township were James Jackson and Henry Mossburg in 1836. James Jackson's parents were Samuel and Hannah (Gibson) Jackson. James married Elizabeth Hooker and had a son Hiram (born 1817) who married Mary A. Logan on August 16, 1838. Hiram, with his father's family moved to near Economy, Delaware County, Indiana, when he was five years old, and resided there until he was nineteen years old, when they came from there to near Liberty Center. The first sermon preached in Liberty Township was in his father's house. Hiram and Mary (Logan) Jackson had twelve children: Elizabeth (born 1839), Rachael (born 1840), Samuel (born 1842), Mary Ann (born 1843), John (born 1845), Margaret (born 1846) Joseph Logan (born 1849), Nancy (born 1851), James (born 1854), Hiram (born 1856) Martha (born 1858, George Washington (born 1861).

Our linage is Joseph Logan (born April 13, 1849, died August 9, 1914) married Mary Alice Thompson (born September 21, 1851, died December 28, 1929) on August 25, 1872 and had eleven children Laura Jane (born 1873, died 1947), Lydia M. (died in infancy), Emma Alice (born 1876, died 1960), George (born 1878, died 1942), twins Mary Myrtle and Charles Howard (born 1882 and both died in less than one year), another set of twins Luster M. and Lulie M. (born 1886) Luster dying in infancy, Alma Anna (born 1887, died 1962), Augustine (born 1889, died 1897), and Lillie Merle (born 1892, died 1940).

Jackson Family: Standing back row: Emma Alice, Laura Jane, and George; Front row: Alma, Joe, Gussie, Merle, Mary Alice (Thompson) and Lulu

My grandmother Emma Alice Jackson (born April 20, 1876 in Liberty Township died September 15, 1960) married David Oscar Kingen (born February 13, 1877 died May 29, 1924) on February 21, 1896. Four children were born to this union, William Howard (born 1897, died 1973), Maudie Mae (born 1902, died 1988), Grace Larona (born 1907, died 1945) and Ralph (born 1916, died 1981). Emma Alice (Jackson) Kingen's second marriage was to William Gaiser on February 14, 1929.

My mother, Maudie Mae Kingen married Roy Elliott Stinson (born 1901, died 1978) and had six children Alice Rose (born 1923 lived two months), Martha Louise (born 1924), Kenneth Edwin (born 1926), Anna Jane (born 1928), Sarah Lou (born 1930) and Nellie Mae (born 1932).

There are many wonderful memories of my grandmother Emma Alice (Jackson) Kingen/Gaiser. She was a good christian woman, who enjoyed life and her pleasure was most complete when she could be of some service to a friend or neighbor as she always congenial and self-sacrificing. Grandma was of petite stature and had a lively step with a twinkle in her light green eyes. She loved pretty clothes and lots of jewelry. Grandma loved caring for the sick. The story is told that on occasion, during the Depression Days in the 1930's, she would quickly sew clothing so a deceased person would be properly dressed for burial. (*Anna Jane (Stinson) Hamilton*)

JACKSON-HOOKER

James Jackson (1785-1853) and wife Elizabeth Hooker Jackson (1797-1865) moved to Wells County, Indiana locating in Liberty Township, Indiana, January 1837. James Jackson, was born in Surry County, North Carolina, a son of Samuel Jackson, Jr. (1758-1834) and Hannah Gibson Jackson (1764-1841) were married January 23, 1782, near Dayton, Ohio. Samuel Jackson, Jr. was the son of Samuel Jackson (17?-1797) and Catherine Plankinhorn Jackson, who immigrated to Rowan (now Guilford) County, North Carolina, from Pennsylvania via Maryland. The Jacksons adopted the Quaker Religion while in Rowan County (the New Garden Monthly Meeting) and after moving to Surry County joined Tom's Creek MM and helped organize the Westfield MM.

James and Elizabeth Jackson had nine children, six sons and three daughters, one of which was Samuel J. Jackson (born January 4, 1834, Delware County, Indiana died 1918). Samuel J. Jackson married Sarah Foust (1834- ?) October 29, 1857. They had nine children, five of whom were, James U., Amos L., Rachael (Vore), Ida (Grove), and Charles W.

Samuel J. Jackson was the first postmaster in Liberty Center, Indiana (1874-1877). In 1862, he enlisted in the 75th Indiana Infantry and served until 1865 during the Civil War. His father, James Jackson, served in the War of 1812, and his grandfather, Samuel Jackson, Jr., served in the War of 1776.

James U. Jackson (1858-1947) married Sabina W. Smith (1873-?) January 16, 1892. They had five children: Cecil U. (1892-1952), Paul C. (18?-19?), Ethel (Schenider) (18?-19?), Charles S. (1900-1958), Ruth (Swartz) (19?-living). James U. Jackson was a prominent business man of Liberty Center for many years the leading lumberman of that locality. He also taught two terms in Liberty Township and was director of Liberty Center Deposit Bank.

Cecil U. married Nellie Ann Osborn September 10, 1914. Nellie Ann Osborn was born October 30, 1892, daughter of Breck and Mary Ann (Mounsey) Osborn. Nellie Ann died July 23, 1940. They had three children: Helen (Schmeling), James S., and Marti (Clark). Cecil Uriah Jackson was a prominent businessman of Huntington, Indiana.

Charles S. married Lois Marie Kyle on January 3, 1922. Lois Marie Kyle was born March 5, 1901, daughter of C. D. (Gene) and Grace (Trasher) Kyle.

Charles Spurgeon Jackson was an electrical and mechanical engineer, graduating from Tri-State College, Angola, Indiana. He worked at Fort Wayne and Bluffton, Indiana and Wright Field (Dayton, Ohio) from 1940 until 1958 as a guided missile development-control engineer. The names of their children are Charles Eugene, born August 18, 1923, and married Norma Lee Wampler; Dorothy Marie, born September 17, 1925, and married Courtney Clark Lubbes; Richard Harold, born September 4, 1929, and married Nancy Carolyn Ballinger, August 20, 1960.

JAMES JACKSON FAMILY

The James S. Jackson family can trace their ancestors into Wells County as James Jackson, born March 1, 1785, married Elizabeth Hooker, born in 1797, in Dayton, Ohio on October 6, 1816, and moved to Delaware County, and on to Liberty Township in 1837, where they were the first white settlers. They family spent their first winter in a house with three walls, the fourth wall covered by brush. They cleared land to farm. James Jackson was a warrior of 1812, taken prisoner at the time of Hull's surrender at Detroit. His father served five years in the War of 1776.

Samuel J. Jackson, born January 4, 1834, was three years old when his parents brought him to pioneer this territory. Transportation was by trails through woods. There were few people in the area, and as he grew, he attended subscription schools. He married Sarah Foust, born April 9, 1834, in Highland County, Ohio, on October 29, 1857. They settled in Liberty Township, Wells County, Indiana. He was a farmer, clearing land - also a merchant and a man of affairs. In 1862 he enlisted in Company E of the Seventy-fifth Indiana Infantry and served three years during the Civil War. He served the area as Postmaster from 1874 to 1877. Samuel J. and Sarah had nine children, the oldest son James Uriah, born October 13, 1858, grew up on the family farm. His father later bought a store where he worked at age fourteen, also attending school. His education was in the Bluffton Normal School. He was later a teacher in Liberty Township for two terms.

For many years, James U. was a lumber dealer, also owner of hardware store and an eighty acre farm. He was a Director of the Liberty Center Deposit Bank. January 16, 1892, he married Sabina Smith, born July 13, 1872. History shows they were members of the Liberty Center Baptist Church, where he was a trustee. Politically he supported the principles and policies of the Republican Party. James U. and Sabina were parents of five children: Cecil Uriah - December 6, 1892 to January 8, 1952; Paul Clayton - September 4, 1895; Ethel (Jackson) Schneider - December 12, 1897; Charles Spurgeon - July 18, 1900 to September 25, 1958; Ruth (Jackson) Swartz - March 16, 1910.

Cecil Uriah Jackson, born December 6, 1892, eldest son of James U. and Sabina Smith, married Nellie Ann Osborn, born October 30, 1892, daughter of Mary Ann (Mounsey) and S. Breckenridge "Breck" Osborn, married September 10, 1914. Both Cecil and Nellie attended schools in Wells County - after they wed they lived on their farms in Liberty and Jackson Townships. They also were owners of the grocery in McNatt, where they operated Model "T" Ford huckster wagons through the county for the convenience their customers. Later in 1923, they moved to Florida for the health of Cecil who had rheumatic fever.

The family returned to Indiana for a visit in 1925, and during this time their Florida home burned; they never returned to live there again. The Jacksons moved to Huntington where their children were educated through high school. For many years Cecil and Nellie owned and operated an Insurance Agency in Huntington. They were parents of three children: Helen Ilo - July 5, 1915; James S. - September 5, 1918; Martha M. - January 20, 1920 to January 12, 1991.

Nellie's death, on July 23, 1940, was a shock to all the Huntington community as she was a special lady, warm, outgoing, and civic minded. The Jacksons were members of the First Baptist Church.

In August 1947, Cecil married Esther (May) Webber in Huntington; a second marriage for both, she brought two children to the marriage: Marvin Webber - February 10, 1928; Barbara Webber - August 18, 1933.

Cecil and Esther continued to live in Huntington until Cecil's death, January 8, 1952.

James S. Jackson, born on a farm in Liberty Township, Wells County, Indiana on September 5, 1918, only son of Cecil U. and Nellie A. (Osborn) Jackson. An industrious youth, he sold and delivered Saturday Evening Post magazines in the Huntington city businesses. He, at the age of twelve, designed an insulated "Pop Wagon" and sold advertising space on the top and sides, and delivered ice cold pop to offices and business employees in Huntington. During his high school years, when he was old enough to drive, he ran a milk route with front door delivery service.

After graduation from high school, he worked as a construction laborer. Later his employer, W. R. Dunkin and Son, rewarded hard work with an opportunity to be a carpenter apprentice and learn a trade. He attended a year at Huntington College.

December 2, 1939, James S. and Mary Alice Krieg, born May 10, 1918, only daughter of Hazel L. (Mickley) and Wilbert A. Krieg, were married in Daleville, Indiana, by the Reverend G. Rollin Osborn, uncle of the groom. A year in Huntington where James S. continued working construction and Mary Alice was an assistant cashier for J. C. Penney Company.

A trip to Santa Monica, California, to take sister Martha to marry a high school sweetheart, and the Jacksons stayed in California for one and one half years. Continued education for James S. with a night school course in blue print reading and estimating, and a continuation of apprenticeship carpentry.

World War II was declared December 7, 1941, a move back to Huntington in February, 1942 and, in September of 1943, James S. volunteered in the United States Air Corp. He was accepted into the Air Corp Cadet Training Program and inducted December 21, 1943. After many months of training, he earned his wings as a Second Lieutenant Navigator and was assigned to a B-29 crew in Lincoln, Nebraska, for additional training. Peace was declared September 2, 1945. James S. was honorable discharged October 6, 1945.

A move to Bluffton, as a General Superintendent for W. R. Dunkin and Son Construction Company on the new Houser Engineering Factory (now Kitco).

In June 1947, James S. and Mary Alice started James S. Jackson Construction Company where it has grown from one wheel barrow to many. Beautiful buildings have taken shape and are our memorials to honest and hard work.

The Jacksons have five children and each one at some time has made a contribution to family and the family business.

Today all five children are married with families and live in the Bluffton area. There are sixteen grandchildren.

James D., born July 4, 1942, on March 28, 1962 married Celia Uptgraft born December 5, 1944, Jim and Celia have five children: James Todd, born November 4, 1962, on November 18, 1989, married Jill Ann Huse, born November 30, 1967; Heather Lyn, born August 1, 1966; Lara Ann, born December 5, 1968; Chelsea Rose, born March 6, 1982; Conor Samuel, born December 27, 1984.

Thomas Krieg, born January 14, 1947, on November 21, 1969 married Priscilla Fuller born August 10, 1949, Tom and Priscilla have a son: Thomas Andrew, born July 11, 1970.

Sally Ann, born February 12, 1952, on December 11, 1971 married Norman Kain, born October 11, 1949. Sally and Norm have three children: Norman Wade, born January 13, 1976; Jamie Lyn, born December 28, 1977; Brian Thomas, born January 1, 1982.

Michael Alan, born May 21, 1954, on March 1, 1975 married Suzanna Ernst, born January 10, 1955. Mick and Susie have three children: Matthew Alan, born February 1, 1978; Tifany Marie, born September 26, 1982; Shaun Michael, born January 21, 1985.

Cynthia Jayne born, March 2, 1959, on September 12, 1981 married Jeffry Lambert, born September 5, 1958. Cindy and Jeff have four children: Lynette Austin, born August 25, 1983; Lincoln Jeffry, born July 13, 1986; Saretta Marie, born March 24, 1988; Janelle Elizabeth, born February 13, 1990.

Life in Bluffton has been rewarding, and this Jackson family has come "full circle" in Wells County, Indiana.

JACOBS-BRICKLEY

Ralph Jacobs married Alice Brickley September 9, 1951, at the Liberty Center Methodist Church. God blessed them with three children. Robin, 1953; David, 1955; Susan Renea, 1962.

David has two children: one also named David, the other Shawn. David and wife Rosyleen, (Slone) and sons live at 5675E 500N Craigville. David served in the Navy. Robin has three children: Tisha, Todd, and Sarah. They all live in Fort Wayne. Robin served in the Marines. Susan Renea had two children: Joshua Vollmar and Amanda Rupright. Ralph and Alice's loving daughter Renea, and their dear granddaughter Amanda, were killed in a auto accident March 21, 1985. Her son Joshua was critically injured. Thank God he is now perfectly healthy and has only slight facial scars. Joshua lives with his father Michael Vollmar in Huntington. Renea graduated from Norwell.

Alice Brickley was in the class of 1950 at Liberty Center. Alice is one of seventeen children of Herbert and Gladys Brickley. Her youngest brother George died at age twenty. They were all born in Wells County. Alice's father Herbert and mother Gladys (Robaugh) lived and died in Wells County. (See Herbert Brickley History). Alice's paternal grandfather Chester Brickley and grandmother Zora (Weikle) Brickley farmed just west of Uniondale on old 224. Alice's maternal grandfather Curtis Rohbeugh, and grandmother Curtis Rohbeugh, and grandmother Astelle (Featherhoff) Rohbeugh farmed in Liberty Township. Alice lived with Floyd, Ruth and Annie Grover in Liberty Center at the time of her marriage.

Ralph was born in Centralia, Illinois, February 14, 1926. His father was Ernest Wise. Ralph's mother Erma (Adams) Wise moved to Fort Wayne in 1930. She eventually married Ray Jacobs of South Whitley. Ralph attended Washington grade school and Central High School. Ralph has two brothers Fayette, who is deceased, and David, formerly of Bluffton and now of Norwalk, Connecticut. Ralph's maternal now deceased, grandmother, Lulu (Jones) Adams-Davis lived in Bluffton.

While living in Fort Wayne and working for the General Electric, Ralph was drafted into the Army during World War II, serving in France, Belgium, Holland, Germany, Austria, Japan, and the Philippines. He received medals and the Combat Infantryman's badge. After World War II, Ralph's parents, Ray and Erma Jacobs, bought farm two miles north and two miles west of Liberty Center. While living there, Ralph met his future wife, Alice. During this period of his life, he was called to active Army duty for the Korean War. Ralph saw combat in both North and South Korea. Upon discharge, he received a second award of the Combat Infantryman's Badge along with the Silver Star and other medals. After Korean service, he returned to General Electric, married, and then carried mail. Due to military disability, he had to retire from the postal service.

Alice now works for Lutheran Hospital. They would like to travel when she retires. They operate Jacobs Ladder Statuary Supply. Ralph belongs to the Disabled American Veterans and Veterans of Foreign Wars, and the American Legion. They are members of Markle Church of Christ. They reside two miles east of Markle on Indiana 116.

ELIJAH JACOBS FAMILY

Elijah Jacobs had a family of twenty-one children. His first wife Susanna's children were: Mary Ann Iler, Melissa Ellen Settlemeyer, David Franklin, Sophia Manda (Snyder) Hanney, Swirilda, Porter, Louise Jane Miller, and Lize Jane. His second wife Lydia McGuire's children were: Isabella Schoeff, Angeline Redding, Naomi Curry, Lydia Viola (Kate) Weaver, Martha Jane (Jenn) Keplinger, Ameila Conner, Eddie Austin, Effie Anna, Rose Chaney, Cora (Edgar) Lantis, Clark, Maud, and William.

They lived one and one-fourth miles south of Zanesville, on Road three, on the southeast corner.

Melissa Ellen Jacobs married James Settlemeyer. (Refer to Settlemeyer family.)

David Franklin Jacobs married Irene Keplinger. (Refer Frank Jacobs family.)

Angeline Jacobs married Alfred Redding. (Refer to George Redding family.)

Naomi Jacobs married James Curry. (Refer to Robert Curry family.)

Lydia Viola (Kate) Jacobs married Jacob Weaver. (Refer to Jacob Weaver family.)

Jenn Jacobs married Frank Keplinger. They lived two miles south and one-half mile west on Road 303, the present home of Bethina Douglass.

Clark Jacobs married Perle Knight. (Refer to Knight family.) They lived next to Jenn and Frank at the present Clifford D. Fox Farm.

William Jacobs first married Lulu Jennings. His second wife was Nancy Redding. (Refer to George Redding family.)

ELIJAH JACOBS FAMILY

Elijah Jacobs was my great, great, great grandfather.

Elijah Jacobs was born October 14, 1827 (died January 20, 1915) and had a family of twenty-one children, eight by his first wife Susanna and thirteen by his second wife Lydia. His first wife Susanna was born September 9, 1825 (died April 7, 1862). Their children were Mary Ann born December 4, 1849 (died September 1928) married an Iler, Melissa Ellen born August 10, 1851 (died October 15, 1930) married James Settlemeyer, David Franklin (Marlene Platt Hoppingarner's great, great, grandfather) born August 13, 1853 (died January 9, 1933) married Irene Keplinger, Sophia Amanda Snyder Hanney born February 3, 1856, Surville Jacobs born April 7, 1858, Porter Jacobs born March 27, 1860 (died July 27, 1861) twins Louise Jane and Eliza Jane born March 28, 1862 (Eliza lived one day).

Elijah's second wife was Lydia McGuire, born September 25, 1835 (died June 16, 1890). Their children were: Isabella born Mary 29, 1864 (died June 29, 1934) married a Schoeff, Angeline born April 9, 1865 (died January 2, 1921) married Alfred Redding, Naomi born August 6, 1866 (died September 20, 1931) married James Curry, Lydia Viola (Kate) born December 2, 1867 (died September 20, 1931) married Jacob Weaver, Martha Jane (Jenn) born January 30, 1869 (died February 8, 1955) married Frank Keplinger, Amelia born April 15, 1870 (died September 2, 1947) married a Conner, Eddie Austin born April 28, 1882 (died October 15, 1947) Effie Anna (no details) Rosealie (Rose) born December 16, 1874 (died February 5, 1958) married a Chaney, Cora May (Edgar) born Mary 12, 1875 (died February 26, 1910, married a Landis, Clark born December 16, 1877 (died May 20, 1955) married Perle Knight, Mandy born February 23, 1879 (died November 25, 1887) William born December 2, 1881 (died October 14, 1966) married Lulu Jennings; his second wife was Nancy Redding.

David Franklin Jacobs married Irene Adina Keplinger and they had ten children. The first child born was Willie born February 17, 1878 (died March 24, 1878), Charles born March 10, 1879 (died September 14, 1886), Ora Lee born August 4, 1882 (died February 11, 1961) married Arthur Gaskill. Ora and Arthur had one son Everett born July 30, 1902 (died September 18, 1985). Everett married Genevieve Walker and they had a daughter Alice Lou. Arthur died at twenty-eight years of age and Ora married Charles Jones born December 25, 1879 (died August 3, 1947) and they had one daughter Mary born November 7, 1913.

She married Vernon Dafforn and they had four sons Danny Gene, Merrill Lynn, Kirby Allen, and Jackie Lee. Frank and Irene's next child was Della (Marlene's grandmother) was born July 20, 1885 (died November 4, 1962) who married Charles Smith born May 1, 1880 (died March 23, 1961). To this marriage two daughters were born, Vesta born February 22, 1905 who married Paul Parker. Paul was a minister during his lifetime. They had one son Merle Eugene born January 9, 1927 (died January 6, 1991). Merle married Mary Francis Redding and they had three children, Michael Lee, Mark Alan, and Marcy Ann. Wilma (Marlene's mother) was the next daughter born on February 20, 1912 and she married Arlo Platt born June 11, 1907 (died April 17 1985). Arlo was a barber in Zanesville, Indiana for 55 years. They had three children, Carolyn Rose born July 9, 1931, (died March 14, 1935) Halden Clair born December 1, 1933 and he married Carolyn Miller. They had two boys, Gregory and Gary. Gregory married Suzanne Cox, and they live in Florida and have two boys Gregory and Cameron. Gary married Cathy Wilson and they live in Grabill, Indiana, and have two children, Lyndsy and Matthew. The last child born to Arlo and Wilma was Marlene Louise born March 15, 1936 and she married Donald L. Hoopingarner. Marlene and Don have lived in Markle, Indiana most of their married years. Don is President of the Bank in Markle. They had two daughters, Pamela Le, was born June 23, 1958, and is married to Larry Boye. They are both music teachers and live in Florida. The second daughter born to Don and Marlene is Shari Lynne, born February 2, 1961 and still living at home.

Roy L., another son, was born December 23, 1888 (died January 15, 1889). Gary Dee was born April 8, 1890 (died February 9, 1975). He married Alma James, and they had two daughters, Dorthea and Marcella. Marcella married Michael Linta and they had two children, Michael and Tina. Clarence (John) born October 6, 1892 (died May 26, 1948) married Zola Platt. They had four children Darrell, Doris, Loris (Bud) and Donnabelle. Mary was born August 11, 1898 (died in infancy), another child died in infancy, not named and the last child born was Arlie born November 11, 1899 (died March 6, 1986). She married Mont Chaney and they had one daughter, Marilyn.

EDWARD J. AND RUTH M. JAMES

Ruth was born in Rock Creek Township, Indiana. She attended twelve years at Rockcreek and graduated in 1938. Edward J. was born in Chicago, Illinois, and graduated from St. Patricks High School in 1935. He went to work in the trucking business for seven years, then worked for the North Shore Electric Railroad until interrupted by World War II, serving overseas ETO in the Transportation Corp (rail) until 1946. He returned home and spent a year with the railroad at Great Lakes, Illinois yard before moving to Wells County.

Ruth and Edward were married in Bluffton on May 11, 1946, moving to Kenosha, Wisconsin, for one years. Our daughter, Marcelline J., was born at

Kenosha, and we moved to Rockcreek Township in September, 1947. Edward was affiliated with Renner Express (trucking) for thirty-four years, retiring in 1983.

Ruth was affiliated with the Caylor Nickel Hospital and Clinic for twenty years and retired in 1984.

Marcelline J. graduated from Bluffton and Methodist Hospital School of Nursing. She married Richard Hoy of Indianapolis and they have two sons, Randolph (Randy) William and Michael (Mike) Allen, ages twenty and sixteen years, respectively. Randy graduated form Bluffton and graduated from Vincennes University. Mike is completing his sophomore year. Ruth was the daughter of Orval and Vera (Miller) Dickie. Her grandfather and grandmother were Robert and Melisa (Pyle) Dickie of Rockcreek. Her great, grandfather and grandmother, who were William and Margaret (Tudy) (Gordon) Dickie, came from Scotland and homesteaded their home in Rock Creek, Wells County, Indiana.

Edward's mother and father, Edward and Margaret (Cronin) James met and were married in Chicago, Illinois. Edward's father was a Master Barber and his mother was a homemaker. His father had a brother, John, and they were born around Reading, Pennsylvania. His family came from Cardiff, Wales.

Edward's mother, Margaret had three sisters and four brothers. Her mother was Bridget Agnes Daly and was married to Thomas William Cronin. They both came from Ireland.

Edward had two brothers, Francis J. and George (Bud) A. and a sister Adele M. Dorsey.

Ruth has one sister, Marjorie J. Daugherty.

FRANCIS E. JAMISON

Francis E. Jamison, formerly of Bluffton, and now a resident of Decatur, was born in Chester Township, Wells County, on May 20, 1928. Francis is the oldest son of Revie W. and Mary M. (Gaiser) Jamison. Revie was born on November 28, 1904 in Chester Township, and married Mary on December 20, 1922. Mary was born May 25, 1906, and died in the Wells County Hospital on October 22, 1971. Children of Mary and Revie are: Francis, who married Vera Krick of Adams County, Indiana. They are the parents of Darline, Debra, Sherlie, David, and Robert, deceased. Dee A., who married Alma Pagowski of Michigan, had two children, Greg and Brenda. Dee later married Thelma Hatfield from Michigan, and was step-father to James and Tommy. Ruby J. married Ervin Martz of Fort Wayne, and their children were Sheila D., Keith, George, Nancy Lee, Betty Ann, Mary, Darla Kay, and Bruce. James L. of Warren, Indiana, was married to Louise Stoller, and had three children, Gary, Jimmy, and Diane. His marriage to Helen Flenor, presented him with two sons, Barry and Michael.

Francis' grandfather, Charles J. Jamison, who was born February 28, 1881, and died March 4, 1956, was a farmer all his life; he was the son of Allen and Elizabeth (Penrod) Jamison. Charlie was married to Leottie O. Carnes, who was born December 1, 1885, in Wells County; she died in 1935. Leottie was the daughter of Thomas and Hannah (Miller) Carnes. Francis' maternal grandparents were Melvin A. and Rachel (Huggens) Gaiser. Melvin was born March 21, 1869, and died at Okemah, Oklahoma in 1949. His parents were George (a Civil War soldier), and Martha (Cloud) Gaiser. Martha was the daughter of Joseph and Sarah (Sharp) Cloud.

Francis Johnson graduated from Bluffton High School in the class of 1946. After graduation, he enlisted in the United States Navy and served aboard a mine-sweeper as fireman and signalman.

Francis married Vera Krick on August 12, 1950. She is the daughter of Orley and Naomi (Ramsey) Krick. They live in Decatur, Indiana and had five children: Darline F. Schrock, born September 16, 1953, in Decatur, lives near Leo, Indiana; Debra Kaye Morence, born February 11, 1955, is the mother of Brande St. John, and Christopher Robin; Sherlie Marie Walter, wife of Charles, was born May 20, 1957 at Wells County Hospital. They have two children: Amanda Kaylyn and Matthew Jamison. They reside near Preble, Indiana. David William was born August 25, 158, at Wells County Hospital. He is married to Virginia Ertel, and is the father to three children: David Jr., Angela, and Andrea. Robert Glenn was born October 15, 1960, and died in a tragic accident in July 1970.

ERIC N. AND SARA JANE JARRETT FAMILY

Eric N. and Sara Jane Jarrett reside at 3393 West 200 South, Liberty Center, Indiana. They are restoring a home of historical value to Wells County. Built by O. D. Garrett around the turn of the century, it was purchase by the Jarretts in 1971. Gravel pits on this farm were worked to build some of the first roads in Wells County. Many senior citizens recall hauling gravel from this site.

Rick, as he is known, works in management at Sterling Casting. He loves the outdoors, has interest in farming and gravel business, and has as his hobbies carpentry and environmental and energy management. He has installed solar and geothermal systems in their home and is a pioneer in this field at this time.

He is the son of Bently B. and Loretta Schell Jarrett. Grandparents include Willard and Susan F. Gregg Jarrett and Arthur E. and Florence Nelson Schell.

He met his wife, Sara Jane, in the first grade at Liberty Center. It wasn't necessarily love at first sight, but by grade eleven, things became serious. The traditional order in the classrooms was alphabetical. She was the daughter of Joe E. and Ferne Starr Holloway, and Holloway and Jarrett went side by side. They graduated in 1962 and he went to electronics college and she got a job. After college money ran out, they decided to get married. They started out in 1963 with less than $300.00 worth of furniture, car payments and a lot of love.

Home being restored by Eric N. and Sara Jane Jarrett at 3393 West 200 South Liberty Center.

Things progressed well, they both had steady employment, and Jane retired at the age of thirty-three to work at home and play a little. Suddenly she launched a new career. Though all hope had expired in the first thirteen years of marriage, they were blessed by a daughter, Lindsay Jo, on June 25, 1977 and another, Emily Ann, on September 30, 1978. She is now a full time homemaker, doing volunteer work with children and elderly, and is currently serving on the Southern Wells School Board.

Lindsay and Emily are students at Southern Wells, grade eighth and sixth, and are typical teenagers. They play the piano, love swimming, and riding their ATV's, are 4-H members and in the church youth group.

Working and playing together is a priority. They attend the Liberty Center Baptist Church, where Rick is a deacon and Sunday School superintendent and Jane teaches and directs an after school program. Rick and the girls sing in the choir. They are currently helping to establish a family support group for Wells County: FUN, or Families Unite Now.

Both Eric N. and Sara Jane's families date back in Wells County history before 1850. They were both born here and have remained here throughout their lives.

SUSAN GREGG JARRETT 1902-1990

Susan Florence Gregg was born in Wells County in 1902 in a house built by her grandfather. She was third child of Joseph D. (1865-1960) and Rachel Brinneman Gregg (1869-1940). Her father worked for the railroad and later hauled gravel. The family consisted of Ben Gregg (1890-1982), who moved to Trenary, Michigan in the upper peninsula; Hazel J. (Hamilton) (1891-1982), she married James L. Hamilton, and lived at the site of the Southern Wells Elementary School; and Mary L., who married Clarence C. Craig and resided near Liberty Center.

Susan had blue eyes and red hair, a trait shown in all generations, and was known to be very determined–or stubborn. She graduated with the class of 1921 from Liberty Center High School, but refused to have her picture taken with the rest of the class. She married Willard C. Jarrett, (1893-1962). Willard was of Indian decent, a nephew of Chief Francis Godfroy. Susan did extensive research on the Indian heritage. She loved history and loved to tell her great-granddaughters Indian stories. She was equally proud to tell how her grandfather had came over to America from Ireland. This was John Gregg (1851-1922), who married Fannie Wallace and had several children.

Lindsay Jo Jarrett, Susan F. Gregg Jarrett (great grandmother), Emily Ann Jarrett

Susan and Willard Jarrett had five children. At the time of her death in 1990, she had buried four and had only one living.

Their children were: Bently B. Jarrett (1922-1974), a World War I and Korean Veteran. He married Loretta Schell of Fishers Station, Indiana and had three children, Eric Nelson, (1944), Clinton

E. (1946-1966), and Jane Ann (now Rupright) (1947).

Janet J. Jarrett Mejia, had four children and resides at Lake Elsinore, California. She cared for her mother the last five years she lived.

Joan Jarrett McMilon (1926-1989), mother of eight children, she resided in California all her married life.

Larry W. (1928-1958) served in Korean War, never married, and lost his life in a car accident near Montpelier.

Donald R. (1933-1979) lived at home with his mother and was ill for about thirty years before his death.

Susan Jarrett worked hard to raise her children and care for her sick child as well as make a living for the family. She retired from Franklin Electric in 1962. She had true grit, as the character line in her face showed, and a special fondness for anyone needing help, including all children, any animal, and anyone who looked Irish or Indian.

A disappointment to her was that the name Jarrett will not carry on after this generation. Her only grandson with the last name of Jarrett was blessed with two daughters. There are no other relatives with the same last name.

JENSEN-BIBERSTINE

Phyllis Elaine Jensen, daughter of Victor and Alice (Johnsen) Jensen, a graduate of Northwest Institute of Medical Technology, Minnesota, came to Bluffton to work at the Wells County Hospital. She also worked, later on, at the office of Dr's. Brickley, Mead and Hamilton.

In October of 1949 she married V. Ted Biberstine, son of Roy and Ethel (Hunnicutt) Biberstine, in Faribault, Minnesota. They moved into an apartment in the home of Ted's parents, one mile south on State Road One (brick home by pits). Ted drove a milk truck for Hoosier Condensery. June 18, 1950, Ted left for State Police School at Indiana University, and Victor Ked was born.

State Police work took the family to Decatur. November 18, 1951, Lowell Scott was born, and on a hunting trip to Minnesota, twins, Timothy Jay and Kris Ann were born on October 27, 1952. The family moved to the home of Ted's grandparents Frank and Netti (Durr), Biberstine on Dustman Road, Bluffton. On January 11, 1954, Cliffton Paul was born. Here Ted started Biberstine Trenching and in 1957 left the State Police to work for Ohio Farmers as an adjustor.

He became president of Ayres Adjustors, Incorporated, Fort Wayne, and retired in 1990 to enjoy more hunting and fishing.

In 1964 the family moved one mile west on Dustman Road to a new home built on twelve acres of the former Everett Tarr farm on "Old Buttermilk Cut". Brick trim on the house is from the old Bliss Hotel and Cafe (where Ted and Phyllis met). Lake Jensen, dug in 1955, has provided year round family entertainment.

Ked attended Sams Institute and is employed by General Motors. He and Terry Sue Vaughn, born January 2, 1954, to Jerry and Sue (Carnes) Vaughn, live in Lancaster Township with children Ashley Vaughn, ten, and Zachary Ked, eight. Scott, a graduate of Hobart Welding School, is employed at MPI Furnace Company. He and Deborah Siela, born July 9, 1952, to Leo, Jr., and Naomi (Yake) Shilling, live in the old Schocke farm on Elm Grove Road. A graduate of Indiana University and University of California at Los Angeles, Deb teaches inhalation therapy at Ball State University. Tim is employed at Quabache State Park. He and G. Jean Kaake, born July 21, 1953, to Gordon and Mary Jane (Hamilton) Kaake, reside in Harrison Township with daughter Quinn Nicole, age eleven. Jean is employed at Eastside School. Kris, is a graduate of Ball State University, and David J. Troxel, born July 24, 1951, to Ralph and Elsie (Frautchi) Troxel, reside in Lancaster Township, with children Clinton Jensen, twelve, Blake Austin, eight, Alex Conrad, three. Dave is a partner in Troxel Equipment Company and Kris operates a school of dance in their home. Cliff is an owner-operator semi-driver for Central Transport. He and Sandra Kay (Walburn), born June 13, 1956, to Roger and Marcia (Gordon) Walburn, live in Rockford Township, with Casey Alan, eight, Jessica Jo, six, and Brittany Kay, four.

Phyllis is a past president of Psi Iota Xi; all families attend Calvary Lutheran Church; children are involved in Scouts, swimming, and dancing, as were their parents. Everyone agrees Bluffton is a wonderful place to live and raise children.

REVEREND G. RAYMOND JEWEL

In June 1945, the Reverend G. Raymond Jewel, along with his wife Evelyn and six year-old daughter Donna Marie, was assigned as Pastor of the United Brethren in Christ Church located at the corner of Ohio and Bennett Streets in Bluffton, Indiana. The Reverend Jewel had formerly been Assistant Pastor to the Reverend Lloyd Eby at the Warrendale United Brethren Church and later pastored the Trailside United Brethren Church (both in Michigan). The Reverend G. R. Jewel and family moved in 1951 when he was appointed Pastor of the Third Street United Brethren Church in Fort Wayne, Indiana.

Daughter Donna Marie began school at Liberty Center, riding on a school bus driven by Gerold Penrod. Donna also attended Rockcreek and Lancaster Schools. Graduating from Northside High School, Fort Wayne, she went to Olivet Nazarene College, Kankakee, Illinois, graduating with a bachelor of science degree in elementary education. She received her master of science degree from Saint Francis College, Fort Wayne. She is in her thirtieth year of teaching and is regent of the John Houlton Chapter, Daughters of American Revolution in DeKalb County, Indiana.

The Reverend G. Raymond Jewel

Son Donald Ray was born January 27, 1947, at Wells County Hospital attended by Dr. Brickley. He attended school in Fort Wayne and graduated from MacIntosh High School, Auburn, Indiana. He served in the United States Army and later the United States Navy. He is a machinist and is currently employed as a press operator in Auburn, Indiana. D. Ray is secretary to the Anthony Halberstadt Chapter, Sons of the American Revolution.

Son David Bentley was born November 10, 1949, at Wells County Hospital attended by Dr. Brickley. His schooling included Fort Wayne, and Auburn, Indiana, where he graduated from DeKalb Central High School. He graduated from Indiana University with a degree in hospital administration. David married Rebecca Oswald and they have two children. David is employed in administration at the Veterans Hospital in Cleveland, Ohio.

The Reverend G. R. Jewel is deceased and his widow Evelyn lives in Auburn, Indiana.

JOHNLOZ

Fredrick Louis Johnloz was born in May, 1826, in Bavaria. His wife Emelia was born in France in December, 1818. They were married in 1848. Their son Julius, born December, 1853, and daughters, Juliann, 1858, and Emily, 1859, were all born in Kirkland Township, Adams County, Indiana.

In 1878, Julius married Elizabeth (Eliza) Walker, who was born in September, 1855. They had six children: Charles O., Jacob B., John A., Emma, Fredrick F. and Alexander.

Left back: Ked Biberstine, Terry B., Ashley B., Zachary B. Left front: Dave Troxel, Kris T., Clint T., Blake T., Alex T. Middle back: Tim Biberstine, Scott Biberstine, Jean, Quinn B. Right back: Ted Biberstine, Phyllis B., Cliff Biberstine. Front right: Sandy B., Casey B., Jessica B., Brittany B.

Charles married Lillie May Diehl. To them were born five sons: Hie Julius, who married Ellenor Franks; Alva Roman, who married Helen McKeefer; William Charles, who married Fay Jackson; Fredrick Raymond, who married Jane Elizabeth Walsh and Robert Eugene, who married Olive Elizabeth Morgan. Also five daughters: Dorothy May, who married William Caston; Florene, who married Herman Decker; Ann Catherine, who married Russell Berkhieser; Geraldine Mardell, who married Weisell Brooks Woodward and Lillian Marie, who married Oscar Brown.

The Charles Johnloz family resided on US 224, Wells County, for many years. Robert and Olive Elizabeth still reside on the original Johnloz farm. The home place and barn are still intact on the farm. There are numerous Johnloz descendents living in Wells County today.

HIE J. JOHNLOZ FAMILY

Hie Julius Johnloz was born to Charles E. and Lilly Diehl Johnloz in Adams County, Indiana, on December 17, 1904. He was the oldest of ten children. His brothers were Alva (deceased), William Frederick and Robert. His sisters were Dorothy (Mrs. William Caston), Florene (Mrs. Herman Decker), Ann (Mrs. Russell Berkheiser) Geraldine (Mrs. Weisell Woodward) and Lillian Marie (Mrs. Oscar Brown).

The Johnloz family moved to Wells County in 1919 and resided on the Carrosot farm five miles north of Bluffton along Road #1. Hie attended Lancaster Central School, played basketball and graduated in the class of 1924.

He began a career in the grocery business at Kingsland, Indiana, in the fall of 1924 working with C. A. Bell. He was transferred to Bell's store in Murray late in 1925 and continues to reside in Murray.

In June of 1927 he married Ellanor May Frink, a daughter of Lewis C. and Mattie Dunlap Frink of Jefferson Township. Ellanor was from a family of four girls. Her sisters were Martha E. Frink (deceased), Louis Johnson (deceased), and Juanita (Mrs. James F. Hixon).

Hie J. and Ellanor Johnloz November 1964

Hie and Ellanor lived in Murray and operated the grocery and general store as a family business. In 1933 they initiated a "Huckster" service which was a door-to-door grocery on wheels. They also bought eggs and poultry from the farmers of Rockcreek and Lancaster Townships. In 1954 they constructed a modern market and they continued the business as a family enterprise until they retired in 1970.

Their family consisted of two sons and two daughters. Mrs. Russell R. Diehl (Elizabeth), Mrs. Jack Hook (Joyce), Dr. David K. Johnloz and Charles L. Johnloz. David was married to Rebecca Johnston and was killed in a farm accident in 1988. Charles is married to Janeil Kipfer. Twelve grandchildren and eleven great grandchildren comprise the Johnloz family.

In 1941 the Johnloz's purchased the abandoned Murray School and had it torn down and a new home was constructed on the site in 1963. Some of the materials of the school building were used in the home. Many memories were preserved in the process.

Hie was involved in several community affairs. He drove a school bus for several years and served on the Wells County Council during the years 1960-1966 and 1970 through 1978. He served as the Secretary-Treasurer of the Murray Cemetery from 1947 until the present time. He is the caretaker of the Cemetery.

After retirement the Johnloz's spent several winters in Florida in the Bradenton area. Ellanor was ill with cancer over the years and they were not able to go for a few years. She went to be with the Lord in February, 1990.

They were active members of the Murray Missionary Church and served it well over the years. It has been a very important part of their lives. Hie loves to go fishing and continues to enjoy it even with his great grandchildren. The grandchildren of the family are: Jerry Diehl married to Lois Sullivan; John Diehl married to Margaret DeFillipo; Brian Diehl married to Debra Abbott; Diana Hook married to Robert Schwartz; Jan Hook Bennett; David K. Johnloz II married to Jennifer, son of David K.; Jennifer Johnloz, daughter of David; Christopher Johnloz, son of David K.; Daphne Johnloz Black, daughter of Charles L., married to Michael Black; Denise Johnloz Pope, daughter of Charles L., married to Mark Pope; Craig C. Johnloz, son of Charles L., married to Wendy Meeks; Dawn Johnloz Musselman, daughter of Charles L., married to Rodney Musselman.

The great-grandchildren are Melissa Hough, Scott Diehl, Lindsay Schwartz, Amber Bennett, Brady, Luke Brianne and Megan Diehl, Spencer and Kendra Johnloz and Saundra Musselman.

JOHNS-ADAMS

Henry E. Johns, 1870-1961, settled in Reiffsburg, Indiana. He married Clara (King) Johns (1874-1944). Henry had two sons, Raymond (1894-1963) and Fred (1898-1976). Henry and his wife bought farm land around the area. His grandson, Keith Johns, had fond memories of going to visit his grandfather. They farmed with horses and enjoyed riding those big horses. Keith spent most of his time with his grandfather. His farm lies just south of the Stahl Cemetery.

Fred Johns graduated from Petroleum High School and Purdue University. He married Balanche Ifer (1848-1939), daughter of Warren Ifer. They both became school teachers. His son Keith was the first born in 1929 and died in 1989. Later his brother Kent was born in 1938. Fred remarried after Balanche died. He was married to Lena Peel from Berne, Indiana. She has two daughters, Genevieve Wahman and Ellen Breedlove. In 1940 they had a son, Ronald.

Fred taught school for thirty-five years, while his wife worked as a nurses aid at the Wells Community Hospital.

Keith graduated from Petroleum High School in 1946. While in school he worked at the Shell Station owned by George Risser. For a year he worked at Houser Chevrolet and the railroad. Then in 1948 he started work at Bell Telephone, or "Ma Bell" as he called it.

In 1950 Keith married Betty Adams. Rhonda Kay came along in 1951 and at that time the family lived in Bluffton. Keith's grandfather gave him an acre west of Reiffsburg where he built a small home for the family. In 1953 brother Michael came along.

1987, Front (L to R) Brady Johns, Debra (Palmer) Johns, Betty (Adams) Johns, Heather Schlagenhauf, Rhonda (Johns) Schlagenhauf, Heath Schlagenhauf. Standing (L to R) Jermey Johns, Mike Johns, Keith Johns, Alan Schlagenhauf.

Rhonda Kay started school in 1956 at the same time her dad started to build a bigger home for his family. During Rhonda's sixth grade year, Keith finished the new home which gave the family a bigger home and Rhonda her own room.

Mike and Rhonda graduated from Southern Wells High School. After Rhonda's graduation in 1969 she attended Ravenscroft Beauty College and completed beauty college in February. She had a new job in March and married on April 25, 1970, to Alan Schlagenhauf. They began housekeeping and have always lived on Alan's mother's home place, five miles east of Reiffsburg. Heath came along in 1974 and Heather in 1980. Their two children kept them very busy as they both were in 4-H and sports.

Mike married Debra Palmer in 1973. They had two sons: Jermey in 1976 and Brady in 1977. Mike has a construction company while Debbie is a respiratory therapist.

Keith had the opportunity to buy his mother's farm in 1976 consisting of eighty acres west of Nottingham. He then retired in 1978 from the phone company. He and his friend, Jim Higgins, farmed together. Betty has worked at Service Finance and Old-First National Bank. She also helped build our homes by doing all the painting and sanding.

Alan and Rhonda also remodeled their old farm house with Rhonda doing the sanding and staining of the oak trim. They enjoy raising and showing Morgan Horses. Heather has her own horse for 4-H while Heath has his steer and pigs. The family have membership at the Old Salem Methodist Church which is two and a half miles south of their home.

JOHNSON

Issac Johnson was the father of Able Johnson. Issac was born about 1785. They came from Brooks County, West Virginia. He died in 1818 and she died in 1825. He married Martha Wheeler.

Our great-grandfather was Reverend Able Johnson. He was born in Harrison County, Ohio, February 6, 1814. He moved to Muskingum County, Ohio, at the age of ten years with his parents. He was left an orphan at the age of eleven, entirely dependent on his own energy and skill for support. He united with Adams Baptist Church at the age of sixteen and at once became an active member. He was licensed to preach the gospel at the age of nineteen and ordained to the full work of Gospel Ministry at Taylorville, Ohio, in the year of 1841.

He was united in marriage to Miss Sarah Smith, April 2, 1835, in Muskingum County, Ohio. They had eleven children, nine boys and two girls. Four sons and one daughter passed away early in life. They had five sons who responded to call of their country. Two of whom laid down their lives as sacrifices on the altar of their county.

Able moved to Indiana in 1850 and settled in Huntington County, where he remained until the spring of 1853, when he moved to Wells County and settled on his farm one mile south of Liberty Center, Indiana. He bought this farm from the government. It is Section 21 in Liberty Township. He later moved to the village of Liberty Center in 1884.

He organized the First Baptist Church of Liberty Center in the summer of 1855, of which he became a constituent member. He served as pastor thirteen consecutive years and in all about seventeen years.

Elder Johnson in his day was the leading minister in Northern Indiana. He passed away April 9, 1891, at age seventy-seven. Burial was in Mossburg Cemetery, Liberty Township, Wells County.

One of Able Johnson's sons was Adriman Johnson. This was Estel Johnson's father. He was born December 11, 1843, and died August 19, 1918, at age seventy-five. He married Jane Isadare Klingel. She died in 1944, at age ninety-three. Adriman was a Civil War Veteran, C.B. 101, Indiana Regiment. He was the first mail carrier in Liberty Center, Indiana. He drove a horse and mail wagon. This was after the Civil War.

They had ten children. Several died in infancy of typhoid fever. Some of the children lived to be a good age.

They were Maude Edington, Edith Mossburg, Mollie Mossburg, George Johnson and Estel Johnson.

The typhoid fever really hit the Johnson family. There were three children laying in caskets downstairs and the mother and two children were lying upstairs, ill with the epidemic.

Estel Johnson was a farmer. He married Orpha Armoninia Marshall, October 17, 1915. They had three children: Lucille Moser, near Laporte; Aileen Mertz, near Bluffton; and Paul, near Berne. Estel died May 4, 1954 and Orpha died January 15, 1949.

JOHNSON

William Clay Johnson was born December 7, 1850 in Jackson County, Ohio. He was the sixth of seven children of Robert and Nancy (Buckley) Johnson. He died November 22, 1925, in Nottingham Township, of chronic nephritis. William came to Indiana in 1874 and settled on a farm of one hundred fifty-three acres in Nottingham Township previously bought by his older brother Isaac B. Johnson in March 1868. Isaac died November 25, 1868 and is buried in Alberson Cemetery. Robert was born in Greenbrier County, West Virginia, in 1819 and Nancy was born in Ohio in 1821.

Charity Jurden Shigley was born September 21, 1856, in Nottingham Township, and was the third of five children. She was the daughter of John and Maria(h) (Reed) Shigley. Charity and William were married September 14, 1876, in Nottingham Township. Her father was born in Green County, Ohio, in 1826, and her mother was born in Ross County, Ohio. Her father came to Indiana in 1828 with his father and family. Charity died December 6, 1939, of a heart attack at her home and was buried Alberson Cemetery along side her husband. She never remarried. Charity had thirty-two grandchildren and one great-grandchild when she died.

William C. and Charity J. (Shigley) Johnson

William boarded with the John Shigley family while he was building a house and clearing timber. There were only fourteen acres cleared at the time he took over the farm. William and Charity had nine children, John (Minnie Grove), Lulu (George Bussell), Mollie (Mullins), Melvin, Hugh (Mary Stacey), Forrest (Edith Penrod), Clara (Charles Fosnaugh), Jessie (Virgil Lockwood) and Wiliam R. (Ray). Hugh and Forrest both married and moved to Los Angeles and Mollie married and moved to Hoopston, Illinois. Forrest and Ray were in World War I and both were overseas. Ray drove an ambulance in France and Forrest served in the Army in France.

During the oil boom several wells were drilled on the farm but only gas was found. It furnished lights for several years. Usually nuts and bolts could be found when shucking corn during the winter.

Ray married Pauline Goldsberry of Hartford City on September 1, 1928, and they had one daughter, Barbara Jean. They lived in Fort Wayne and he worked at the old Dudlo Plant. The depression hit them hard. Ray went back to the farm and Pauline to Hartford where she could get work. In May of 1936 the family finally returned to being under one roof - at Domestic. He helped other farmers and worked for a man who owned a threshing machine and a saw mill.

Ray bought a "filling station" in Reiffsburg in 1938 and ran it for thirty years. Over the years he turned it into a small grocery. Ray and Pauline moved to Reiffsburg in May of 1941 and lived there until they died, Pauline December 31, 1970, and Ray December 30, 1971.

Barbara married Harley McKuras September 1, 1949, and they have one son, Michael. She attended school at Petroleum, Poplar Grove and Bluffton High School (Class of 1947). Barbara worked after school during her senior year at the library and continued after graduation until her son was born. She has worked at Franklin Electric for thirty-two years.

Refer to McKuras, Shigley and Abbott/ McDaniel histories.

JOHNSON-DALE

Thomas Dale married Mary Ann Ball October 24, 1823. They had four sons, born in Eardisely, Herefordshire, Great Britain. William Dale married Selena Meredith in 1852 in Blaina Monmouth, Great Britain. They had nine children. They came to America July 7, 1853, leaving from Liverpool on the ship *Andrew Foster*. The ship arrived in New York in August 1853. John Dale married Ann Cooper September 2, 1867. Thomas Dale married Mary Evans and both remained in Great Britain throughout their lives. James Dale married Esther Bennett Dickens and came to America in 1856. They were the great grandparents of Loisellen (Dale) Johnson.

James and Esther had nine children: Mary Ann, James William, Charles Lorenzo, Minie Lucy, Arthur E., Alfred, Esther Lea, Hattie, and George W. Charles Lorenzo was born August 25, 1860, married Idella May Frazier and they were the grandparents of Loisellen Johnson.

Charles L. and Idella M. had four children: Fannie, Ada, Rachel and James Elihu, who was the father of Loisellen. He was born March 25, 1900, in Jay County. He married Neva Eileen (Mann) Dale, who is still living in Keystone, Indiana.

Paul and Loisellen (Dale) Johnson, Jr. and family

James Elihu lived most of his life in Wells County and was a farmer until he passed away May 16, 1961. They had two daughters. Annalue married Roland J. Pearson and they had three children. She passed away August 2, 1984. Loisellen is married to Paul Williams Johnson, Jr.

Loisellen worked at the Wells County Department of Health in Bluffton for eighteen years, retiring in 1985. Paul worked at Dana Corporation in Fort Wayne, Indiana, for thirty-nine years and retired in June, 1990. They live in Wells County and have two sons. William Lee Johnson works at CTS in Berne, Indiana and lives in Wells County. He has three children: Gregory L. Johnson, Pamela Kay (Johnson) Morris and Aaron Johnson. James Dale Johnson lives north of Fort Wayne, Indiana, and works at Lincoln National Life Insurance Company in Fort Wayne. He has one son, Jeremiah.

Paul and Loisellen also have four great-grandchildren: Ashley Nichole Johnson, Kyle Gregory Johnson, J. D. Morris and Joshua Morris.

JOHNSON-DIEHL

Eugene L. Johnson (1915) was born in Adams County to Thomas E. and Lucinda Beitler Johnson. He married Helen I. Diehl (1918), February 20, 1937. Her parents were Lawrence L. Diehl and Goldie Graham Diehl. Helen lived in Wells County most of her life and was employed by Keebler Company for eleven years.

Eugene was employed by Kraft Foods as a cheesemaker, General Electric, Standard Package and was a farmer. He served in the Navy during World War II. They are parents of eight children, all raised in Wells County and graduates of Lancaster Central and Norwell High School.

Eugene and Helen are living on the farm they purchased in 1950 and enjoy their children, grandchildren, and great-grandchildren coming home. They are members of Murray Missionary Church since 1946.

50th Anniversary 1987 - Back (L to R) David, Tim, Dennis, Tom, Steve, Stan; Front (L to R) Debra, Helen, Eugene, Janice

Janice Johnson Wagoner (1939) married David Wagoner from Elkhart. They live in Norwich, New York, and are owners of Stebbin House Bed and Board. He is employed by Proctor and Gamble. They have two children, Eric (1961) married to Jan Faulkner and they are Leather Artists living in Seattle. Rochelle (1964) married Tom Anderson and they have two children, Tyler and Lesley. He is employed by Proctor and Gamble.

Dennis G. (1941) served in the United States Navy four years, and was employed by International Harvester until it closed in 1983. He moved to Frenso, California, and was employed by Fresno Church of the Brethren as Caretaker. He married Karen Sue Nevius (1967). She had a daughter Ronda Bartrom who was adopted by Dennis. They had three children, Michael (1968), a graduate of Davis University, Kimberly (1970) a Supervisor, and Dane (1971) a student at Fresno Junior College. Ronda Wagner has a daughter, Amber (1986). Dennis as Karen were divorced and he married Karin Mazonni (1990). She has three daughters, Kimberly, Amy, and Tami.

Timothy A. (1947) enlisted in the United States Marines and served in Vietnam two years. He was employed by Renners Trucking and they lived in Bluffton and Bowling Green, Kentucky. He married Rebecca Ramp in 1971 and they have three daughters and a son, Greg Shilling serving in the United States Army in Italy, Jennifer (1972) a bank teller, Brandy (1976) and Nicole (1977). He is supervisor for Renners and they live in Indianapolis.

Thomas L. (1948) served in the United States Marines and was stationed in San Diego, California. He married Rebecca Lowry and they have a son Kevin (1970) serving in the United States Army. Thomas and Rebecca divorced and he married Caroline Betz Dedrick. She has three sons, John, Keith and Charles. Thomas is employed with Pace Arrow and lives in Bluffton.

David W. (1950) graduated from Ball State University and married Monica Dilger, also a graduate of Ball State. They have a daughter, Sasha (1980). They spent two years in Peace Corp in Ghana, Africa. They moved to Fresno, California in 1978 and he was self-employed as a gardener, while attending Fresno State University. David has a Master of Science in Counseling Degree.

Debra Johnson Gabbard (1952) graduated from Ball State in 1974 and is teaching French in East Nobel High School. She married Gary Gabbard, also a graduate of Ball State. He is third grade teacher in Garrett, Indiana. He is formerly from Valparaiso, Indiana. They have two sons, Joel (1980) and Sean (1981). They live near Kendallville on Cree Lake.

C/RM Stanley D. Johnson (1954) enlisted in the United States Coast Guard in 1973. He married Paula Trimble in 1974, and they have two sons, Aaron (1975) and Brian (1976). His present duty is United States Coast Guard, Long Beach, California. They live in Garden Grove, California.

Steven K. (1958) was employed by Pace Arrow in Decatur for several years. He married Julie Jackson (1959) in 1985. Julie was personnel with for Air Wisconsin and was transferred from Baer Field to South Bend to work for United Express. Steve is employed by Four Winds R. V. in Elkhart and attends Ivy Technical in South Bend, where they reside.

ELWIN BUTLER JOHNSON

Elwin was born March 13, 1895, in Rockcreek Township. He was the sixth child of Glessner and Rachel Butler Johnson. Elwin attended the local Seventh-day Adventist Church, school and the eight-grade public school at the south end of his father's farm. He graduated from Liberty Center High School. He married Charity Legg from Windfall, Indiana, June 11, 1917. Charity was born October 14, 1895, in Tipton County, Indiana. She graduated from Beechwood Academy. She had a farm at Windfall where she and Elwin lived. Shortly thereafter he was drafted into the army and sent to Camp Taylor near Louisville, Kentucky. The war ended before he was sent into active duty. Elwin and Charity both went to chiropractic school in Chicago, then moved to Emmanuel Missionary College (now Andrews University) at Berrien Springs, Michigan, where they set up a chiropractic office. Later they moved to Madison, Tennessee. Elwin pursued a pre-med course of study and Charity studied nursing. After their graduation, they moved to Loma Linda, California, and Elwin studied medicine and graduated as a medical doctor. They returned east and settled in Allegan, Michigan, where Elwin practiced general medicine from 1935 to 1969. He moved to Oak Haven, Michigan, and practiced medicine part time until he went into full retirement in 1979.

Elwin Butler Johnson

Elwin and Charity had a son, Hubert, who married and moved to Reno, Nevada. He had a son, Stephen, who lives in Sparks, Nevada. Elwin and Charity adopted two little girls, sisters, Hazel and Betty.

Hazel married Malcolm Gordon, and Betty married Girard Miller. Charity died in 1972. In 1975, Elwin married again. This marriage was to Dorothy Ann Morton. Elwin died May 30, 1980, and is buried in Allegan, Michigan.

GLESSNER JOHNSON

Glessner Johnson, son of Jonas and Urania (Barber) Johnson, was born in Rockford, Indiana, in 1854. A farmer all his life, he married seventeen year-old Rachel Jane Butler, daughter of Edward and Amanda (Catlin Gray) Butler, in 1881. Rachel, whose parents came from Ohio, was also a native of Rockford, where her sisters Martha (Mrs. George Minch) and Mary (Mrs. William "Spike" Johnson, a cousin of Glessner's) lived. Family tradition has Glessner and Rachel residing in a log cabin when their first child, Oren Glessner, was born in 1882. Shortly thereafter they moved across the road into the large two-story frame house recently built by Jonas, and lived there with Glessner's father and stepmother, Esther. Their next child, Aurie Opal, was born in 1884. She soon followed by Elsie Grace (1886), Everett Earl 1889), Urania Vesta (1892), Elwin Butler (1895), Lois Loretta (1897), Eunice Ruth (1900), Ruby June (1901), Vera Mabel (1904), and finally Verna May (1907). All but Vera survived infancy.

Glessner and Rachel Johnson

When the Rockford Seventh Day Adventist Church was organized in the spring of 1887, Rachel and her two sisters were among the eighteen charter members, with Glessner joining that summer. He served as a deacon and was a faithful member until his death. His children growing up in and around the church all joined between their ninth and fourteenth birthdays, several of them serving in various capacities. When the church needed a new roof in 1904, Oren, a former church clerk, lent a hand as carpenter. Twenty-year-old Aurie was the clerk that year. She later became a chiropractor and tragically died unmarried at the age of thirty in a house fire.

Aurie's younger brothers Everett and Elwin also became chiropractors and moved away from Wells County to practice, Elwin first serving in the Army during World War I and later becoming a medical doctor. Oren's departure from the area left no sons to help Glessner with the farm. Of his daughter, Lois married Paul Legg, a brother of Elwin's wife Charity, and moved to Michigan. Ruby lived in various places when she wed Carl Pruitt, an elder of the Seventh Day Adventist Church. Ruth went away to college, then taught school in Illinois, where she met her husband, Francis Shull. Verna remained in the area, marrying Olis Bradburn of Wells County. He was an upholsterer by trade, first in Bluffton and later on a farm north of town.

Elsie and Urania, however, married local farmers who were willing to help their father-in-law. Elsie became Mrs. Charles Roth on her birthday in 1907 and set up housekeeping on a farm a mile east of Rockford. Charles Gordon won Urania's had four years later. Ruth and Francis returned and lived with her parents until their deaths. Glessner died in 1937 and Rachel in 1943. They are buried together in Rockford Cemetery.

JAMES LOUIS JOHNSON

James Louis Johnson, son of Nathan and Rachel Davis Johnson, grandson of Solomon Johnson and Matthew David, was born in 1858. His mother died when he was an infant. His father married Sarah Davis, James' mother's sister, on January 19, 1861, in Wells County. They moved to Washington State. Later they returned to Kentucky with small children. The story is told that a stranger joined their camp and was a great help on the trip back east. He stayed until almost the end of the trip, then disappeared. It was always considered an act of Providence.

James married Mary Sabina Redding, daughter of Ransom and Miriam Highlen Redding, May 22, 1880, in Wells County, Indiana. Mary's grandfather, William Redding, had been born in Wilkes County, North Carolina and was one of the first settlers in Wells County. James and Mary had two infants who died and are buried in the ME Cemetery. They also had a daughter, Bessie, who grew to adulthood and married Charles Walter Grogg.

Mary died July 6, 1887, and is buried in Wells County in the ME Cemetery. Some years later James must have returned to Washington State, where his father had taken him as a child. He died in 1925 and is buried in Walla Walla, Washington.

JACOB JOHNSON FAMILY

Jacob Johnson, prosperous farmer, came to Allen County in 1853. For history of his parents and siblings, see entry, Calvin and Altha Johnson Scott. Jacob was born in Columbiana County, Ohio, March 13, 1834, died February 14, 1911. He married Elizabeth Biddle, daughter of John Biddle and Susannah Bevington, December 23, 1858, in Wells County. See entry, John Biddle.

They lived in a log home in Wells County and later built a brick home on their one hundred sixty acre farm, Allen-Wells County line, Jefferson Township.

They had ten children. James and Silas, infants, died in 1859.

John, born August 31, 1860, died March 19, 1923, married Elvira Dobbins, December 24, 1882. Children: Bessie, born 1883, married Ira Baker; Albert, born 1887, married Stella Nickolson; Effie, born 1895, married Brown; and William, born 1897, married Annie Woods.

Josiah, born April 27, 1862, died May 15, 1863.

Isaac, farmer and logger, Pleasant Township, Allen county., born May 2, 1864, died February 16, 1936, married Elizabeth Smith, March 31, 1887. Children: Wesley, 1888-1888; Curtis, 1889-1890; Susie, born June 3, 1891, died February 13, 1961, married Alexander Peake, 1923; Alfred, born December 13, 1894, died February 2, 1990, married Edith Counsellor, April 7, 1917; Ralph, born February 13, 1897, died October 27, 1981, married Tolles Leonard; Almira, born May 2, 1900, married Benjamin Taylor, April 6, 1919; James, born March 18, 1903, married Helen Forrest, March 13, 1924; Wilmette, born November 1914, died April 13, 1981, married Harold Messick, December 25, 1933.

Susannah, born October 17, 1866, died April 4, 1949, married Melvin McConkey, January 29, 1889, and resided Wauseon, Ohio. Their children were: Charlie, Frank, and Ralph.

Rebecca, born April 12, 1869, died November 12, 1944, married William Crow, December 27, 1890. Their children were: Nellie married Lloyd Parker; Frank, born April 1, 1898, died August 20, 1923; and Cleo, married Donna Barrett.

Charles, born August 10, 1871, died March 13, 1941, married Zina Merchant, December 31, 1890. Their children were: Mel, single; Lulla, born October 13, 1898, married Clyde Reed; Doris married Russell Grimm; Elizabeth married Max Graft; Emma married Fred Bennet and Snyder; Daniel, born 1899, died 1976, married Dorothy; Sylvia married Lewis Smith and Paul Graft; Robert married Neolla Grimm; Claude, born 1903, died 1974; Clarence, born May 13, 1910, died May, 1985; Charles and Zina lived on eighty acres of the Jacob Johnson farm.

Joana, born September 2, 1873, married Julian Pequignot, May 9, 1902. Children: Lawrence; Charlie; Arthur, died age seventy-nine, married Nellie Rice; Frank; John; Gertrude, married Joseph Kramer; Gary.

Henry, born February 23, 1876, died February 15, 1952, married Sophia Young, August 19, 1896. Their children were: Hilda, born January 8, 1897, died December 2, 1976, married Curtis Quackenbush, August 19, 1920; Thelma, born July 17, 1899, died September 21, 1989, married Loyall Weist, November 1, 1919; Russell, born May 4, 1902, died May 1, 1965, married Mae Schille, November 11, 1924; William, born May 28, 1908, married Helen Carver, 1929 and Kathleen Arick.

Elizabeth died January 2, 1902. Jacob marred Flora Augerbroght, August 11, 1904. Jacob died February 14, 1911.

JONAS JOHNSON

Jonas Johnson, son of Solomon and Sarah (Sanders) Johnson, was born in Wayne County, Indiana, in 1825. He was brought by his parents to Wells County at age of nine and helped his father clear and farm their one hundred twenty acres in Rockcreek Township. When he became twenty-one, he rented the home farm; then in 1848 married seventeen year-old Urania Barber, daughter of Hallet and Sarah (Vining) Barber. In addition to farming Jonas rented the grist and sawmill that Hallet had built in Rockford and operated it for seven years.

Meanwhile, his family began to grown. Before her death in childbirth in 1861, Urania bore eight children, five of whom survived infancy: Lavetha (born 1849), Deliscus (1850), Glessner (1854), Calista (1855), and Nora (1858). Six months after Urania's death, Jonas married her sixteen year-old niece, Esther Witham, daughter of Louis and Elizabeth (Barber) Witham. She and Jonas had no more children, but in 1865 they bought the eighty acre farm west of Rockford from Matthew Davis. There in the woods they erected a two-room house.

Jonas Johnson

Esther was mother to the children until they established their own homes. Lavetha, only three years younger than her stepmother/cousin, was the last to marry. In 1893 she became the wife of James Knudson, affectionately known as Uncle Jens to his numerous nieces and nephews. Calista, forbidden to marry her first cousin Cuthbert Davis, joined with Lewis Gesler, instead, in 1876 and had four children: Homer, Eva Inez, Wilna, and Virgil. Tragically, Calista later abandoned her husband and two older children and moved with Cuthbert and his children to Oregon. Her older brother, Deliscus, also lived in Oregon but never married.

With Deliscus gone, Glessner was the only son remaining to help Jonas with the farm. In 1881 Glessner married Rachel Jane Butler and the following year they had the first of their eleven children. About that time they moved with Jonas and Esther into a spacious two-story frame house that Jonas just had constructed on the northern edge of his property. To build it he hired a professional carpenter, Adam Korn, who in 1887 married Nora, built a house for her north of Rockford, and had six children: Charles, Fay, Cecil, Glessner, Delbert, and Lazern.

Described during that era as "a modern and commodius dwelling," Jonas' new house was finished by 1886 when Seventh Day Adventist brethren held a meeting in it. The following spring the Rockford Church was organized, enthusiastically supported by the Johnson family. Jonas' sister Isabella Cook donated land to build the church, and Adam Korn used lumber cut but from Jonas' woods to construct and furnish the building. Jonas was a deacon, and Esther, three of his sisters, and all his children and grandchildren who lived in the area became members. He also supported education, with the Rockford school located on the southern edge of his property. A democrat until 1875 and a Granger, Jonas died in 1904, fours years after Esther, and was buried in Rockford Cemetery.

JOHNSON

The Larry L. Johnson family moved to Ossian, Indiana, on August 15, 1973.

Larry is the oldest son of Fred and Mary Johnson of Straughn, Indiana, in Henry County. He attended elementary, junior high, and high school at Lewisville, Indiana, and graduated in May of 1958. He received his bachelor's degree from Butler University in 1963, his master's degree from St. Franics College in 1967, and his doctorate in educational administration in August, 1973, from Ball State University. Larry has been employed with the Fort Wayne Community Schools since June, 1963, and is currently a middle school principal at Kekionga Middle School.

Willa F. (Faye) was the youngest child of the late Benton and Stella Conley of Lewisville, Indiana, in Henry County. She attended elementary, junior high and high school at Lewisville and graduated in 1958. She was a homemaker for over twenty years. She has been employed by the Northern Well Community Schools for the past seven years.

The Johnson family in 1986 Larry, David, Faye, and Jeffrey

Larry and Faye were married on July 3, 1960, in the Lewisville Methodist Church. They lived in Indianapolis, Indiana, until June 1963, and in Fort Wayne until August, 1972. They lived in Muncie, Indiana, from August, 1972, until August, 1973.

The Johnson have two sons. David Michael was born February 11, 1964, in Fort Wayne, Indiana. He graduated from Norwell High School in May, 1982, and from Ball State University in May, 1987. He is employed as a computer programmer for the Fort Wayne Community Schools.

David was married to Julie Marie Gilbert, daughter of Stanley and Carolyn Gilbert of Bluffton, on August 12, 1989. Their first child, Caylynne Renee, was born April 28, 1991. They live in Bluffton.

Jeffrey Lynn was born on October 22, 1965, in Fort Wayne, Indiana. He graduated from Norwell High School in May, 1984. He attended Ball State University for two years and is employed by CMG, a construction company in Fort Wayne. Jeffrey was married to Cassandra Kay Polley, daughter of Wayne and Ella Polley of Fort Wayne, on August 27, 1988. They are expecting their first child in October, 1991. They live in Ossian.

LEON AND ANNA JOHNSON

In 1952, F. Leon Johnson and Anna L. Brown were married in Van Wert County, Ohio. They moved to Wells County in 1955.

Leon was born in Madison County to Charles R. and Hazel Johnson. He attended Manchester College and Canterbury College, graduating with a bachelor of science degree in elementary education.

Anna was born in Lucas County, Ohio, to Gordon and Hermina Brown. She graduated from Hoagland-Jackson High School, and then worked as a secretary at the Marsh Foundation in Van Wert, Ohio.

When Leon and Anna Johnson moved to their newly purchased farm in Harrison Township, they brought with them household goods, some farm equipment, a milk cow, a dog, and daughter, Marcia Colleen and baby, Stanley Gene. After the tiring day of moving, little Marcia put on her hat and was determined to return to her "real" home. Marcia was born in 1953.

Stan, born in 1954, demonstrated early his interest in farming when as a toddler he would escape from the house and crawl to the barn to see what Daddy was doing.

Elaine, Marcia, Teresa, Stan and Sheila Johnson

On moving to Wells County, Leon was immediately offered a teaching position at Rockcreek School. He taught sixth grade there for twenty-one years.

Next came daughter, Karen Elaine, in 1956. Elaine had a constant smile and could sing "Jesus Loves Me" more consecutive times than anyone cared to hear. In 1959 another blue-eyed, tow-head was born. Sheila Rochelle loved horses. Since a real horse was not to be, she quenched her love for them by reading horse books, and collecting horse models and figurines.

Then, in 1960 Teresa Ann was born. Teresa was blessed with many sibling "care givers." They may not have always been gentle but she did miss them when the school bus took all of them to school except her.

At Christmas and Easter, the four girls always had prettier dresses than any store handled. Their mother usually made the four dresses alike, only differing in color.

All five children were active in 4-H and in their church youth groups. All five graduated from college, married and now have children.

Marcia and Jim Hotopp live in rural Wells County with children, Kevin and Kelly. Stan and Diane Johnson also live in rural Wells County with children, Kyle and Chris. Elaine and Gary Seidner live in Blackford County and have children, Sharla, Nathan, Caleb, and Micah. Sheila and Greg Beckman live in Fulton County with children; Brian and Rochelle. Teresa and Bruce Ley live in Wells County with daughters, Jennifer and Rebecca. (See individual family histories.)

MARSHALL JOHNSON

Pearl and Marshall were married March 7, 1925, in Coldwater, Michigan. They traveled there in a Motel T Ford with side curtains. A Christian minister by the name of the Reverend Mesner performed the ceremony in his home. His wife and daughter stood as witnesses. Their honeymoon was the trip to Coldwater and back home the next day. They started housekeeping one mile west of Lafayette School where they lived until moving to Union Township, Wells County, in 1944.

Marshall Emery Johnson was born January 28, 1904. He was the son of Samuel P. Johnson and Lavina Florence Showalter. Samuel was from Ashland, Ohio, and Lavina was born in Jackson Township of Huntington County. The father and mother were farmers all their lives. They settled in Huntington County and it was there that Marshall was born. Marshall's father was number fifteen and the last child in his family. He was the last to pass away. Marshall attended Lafayette School when it was the old one room building.

Pearl Esther Sanders was born February 9, 1905. Pearl's mother, Jesse Cobb, was born in Indiana. When Jesse was a young girl, her family moved to Colorado. They made the trip in a covered wagon pulled by mules, and they settled on a ranch near Littleton, Colorado. When Jesse was fourteen, and after she had lost both parents, she returned to Indiana. In Indiana, she met and married Homer Sanders moving with him to Colton, Ohio, where he worked for the railroad. It was in Colton, Pearl was born. The Saunders moved back to Roanoke, Indiana in 1913. While in school at Roanoke, Pearl and Marshall met through some mutual friends. They dated for three years until they got the courage to make the big step. Homer Sanders worked as a freight and passenger agent for the Wabash Railroad in Huntington. He died in 1945 at age sixty-two. Pearl remembers how he used his telegraph to dispense his messages. The telegraph is a far cry from the computers of today. Jesse lived to be ninety-one. She passed her last years living with the Johnsons.

Marshall's mother died when he was a young boy, in 1920, of cancer. His father lived to be eighty-five. He passed away in 1945.

Marshall and Pearl's first farm is within a stone's throw of the new General Motors Plant in LaFayette Township. This land is now zoned for light industry. It was here that their only child, Richard Emery, was born during one of the winter's worst blizzards on November 6, 1927.

Marshall Johnson Farm

Marshall has farmed all his life. First he farmed with his father and later with his son for twenty-five years. He retired in 1979. Farming during the depression was their most remembered hardship. They had to "count the pennies" to but a loaf of bread, and they traded chickens and eggs for groceries.

Their son Richard (Dick) lives with his wife, Gene Hope, on the Johnson Farm. This farm is located in the southeast corner of section seven. This farm was preempted in 1848, by the Reverend David Thomas. It was in a cabin on this land where the United Brethren Church was begun in Union Township.

There are four grandchildren in this family. They are: Nancy Plummer of near Kendallville; Judy Quackenbush of rural Uniondale; Pattie Macias of south of Markle; and Richard Johnson of Stroudsburg, Pennsylvania. Three step-grandchildren include Diane Wilkinson of Auburn, John Eulitt of West Minot, Maine, and Nancy Bayout of Allentown, Pennsylvania. There are also nine great-grandchildren and nine step-great-grandchildren: Nikki, Ryan, and Kylie Plummer; Jeramy and Jessica Bear; Vincent III, Vanessa, and Alexandria Macias; Eric Johnson; Eric and Lindy Quackenbush; Erika and Zachary Wilkinson; Alena, Caleb, and Cathleen Eulitt; and Lee and Marc Bayout. In 1987, the Johnsons had the distinction of being one of the longest married couple in Union Township. They received a special award during Wells County's Sesquicentennial. In March 1991, they received congratulations on their sixty-sixth anniversary from President Bush and Barbara.

NOAH AND SARAH (THOMAS) JOHNSON

Noah Johnson was born in Washington County, Pennsylvania, April 27, 1826, the son of James and Rebecca (Baxter) Johnson. He was the oldest of fourteen children who are listed in this volume under Calvin C. and Altha Ann (Johnson) Scott. Noah's father, James, was the son of Solomon and Frances (Warne) Johnson. Solomon's father was Peter. The parents of Frances were Joseph and Dorcas (Miller) Warne. Joseph fought in the American Revolution as a private in Lieutenant Colonel Theophilus Phillips' Fifth Battalion, County of Westmoreland, Pennsylvania. Noah's mother,

Rebecca, was the daughter of James and Altha Mariah (Legg) Baxter of Washington County, Pennsylvania.

About 1831, Noah and three sisters moved with their parents, James and Rebecca (Baxter) Johnson, to Columbinana County, Ohio. There, on June 5, 1829, Enos and Margaret (Cameron) Thomas had their twelfth child, a baby girl, Sarah. Her father had been "commissioned a territorial justice of the peace" in 1798 and performed the first marriage in Columbiana County. For more of his achievements, see Genealogy of The Descendants of John Kirk by Miranda S. Roberts. Ms. Roberts traces Enos Thomas through his parents, Seth and Martha (Kirk) Thomas, to Joseph and Anne (Hood) Kirk of Darby, Pennsylvania. Joseph was a son of John and Joan (Ellet) Kirk. John Kirk was born June 14, 1660, at Alfreton in Derbyshire, England and was the son of Godfrey Kirk.

Noah and Sarah (Thomas) Johnson

Although we do not know when or how Noah Johnson and Sarah Thomas met, we do know that they were married on May 13, 1846 in Beaver County, Pennsylvania. Their first three children were born in Columbiana County: Emmitt Enos, December 25, 1847; Amizet, May 13, 1850; and Rebecca A., August 14, 1852. The the family moved to Wells County, Indiana. In fact, Noah's parents and all his siblings, single or married with families, also moved to this area.

Noah and Sarah purchased a large farm on 100 West, just south of County Line Road. At that time, the land was covered with dense forest which he had to clear. Five more children completed the family: Margaret R., born December 5, 1855; Bethena Icedene, born July 14, 1858; Elizabeth J., born April 23, 1860; Albert Lincoln, born October 17, 1862; and Ella May, born July 7, 1866.

When Albert Lincoln was only four days old, Noah, then 36, signed Civil War enlistment papers in Indianapolis with the Thirty-fourth Indiana Volunteers. A second enlistment was signed on December 14, 1863. Along the edge of this page, it says, Mustered into the service of the United States, in Company E, 34th Regiment of Full Veteran (sic) Foot Volunteers, on the 19 day of February, 1864 at Pass Cavallo, Texas." These papers describe Noah as 5 feet and 10 inches, blue eyes, black hair, with dark complexion.

Biographical Memoirs of Wells County, Indiana states, "He took part in the Vicksburg campaign, the battle of Port Gibson, the fight at Champion Hill, back of Vicksburg and at Jackson, all in Mississippi, and after the last campaign he was transferred to New Orleans, Lousiana (sic), where he did garrison duty until December, 1863. He also took part in the Red River expedition, and the fight at Brownsville, Texas." He was discharged September 26, 1865 at Saint Louis, Missouri.

It was after Noah's return from the Civil War that Ella May was born. The war had taken its toll from Noah's vision, and he was awarded a pension of one dollar per day. Gradually, his eyesight became so poor that he could not "distinguish a man from a woman 10 feet distant." He had to "hire a man to drive his reaper," and a neighbor drilled Noah's wheat. so, by December 30, 1903, when he signed his will, Noah and Sarah had sold their Union Township farm and moved to Ossian. There he died on September 23, 1907.

After a couple of years, Sarah moved to the home of her daughter, Rebecca "Belle" Babcock, in Fort Wayne and died there February 22, 1911. Noah and Sarah are buied in Oaklawn Cemetery at Ossian.

Of their eight children, only Bethena Icedene remains single. Marriages of the other were as follows: Emmitt Enos Johnson to Emma Catherine Smetzer, February 18, 1868; Amizet Johnson to Ida Belle Thompson, September 29, 1882; Rebecca A. Johnson to Thomas Zeph Babcock, June 18, 1876; Margaret A. Johnson, first to George David Rush, October 13, 1881, then to Frank Didier, May 15, 1898; Elizabeth J. Johnson to William Wallace Greek, August 19, 1877; Albert Lincoln Johnson to Lucinda Thurber, September 2, 1886; and Ella May Johnson, first to George Franklin Young, November 28, 1889, and then to William O. Lakey. There were eighteen grandchildren. For more information about the descendants of Noah and Sarah (Thomas) Johnson, see Johnson Tree; Branch One, by Mary Joan (Piatt) Lauer, also author of this family entry.

OREN JOHNSON, ROBERT O. JOHNSON, AND ROBERT C. JOHNSON

Oren Johnson, born in 1882 in a log cabin on the western outskirts of Rockford, Indiana, was the oldest of Glessner and Rachel (Butler) Johnson's eleven children. Shortly after his birth, the family moved into the large two-story frame house his grandfather Jonas Johnson recently erected on his farm. At the age of eleven, Oren joined the Rockford Seventh Day Adventist Church, served it as clerk when he was fourteen, and upon reaching adulthood became the proprietor of the Rockford General Store, having little taste for farming.

L to R. Kelsie Marie Johnson, 8 mo., Kathy Johnson, Richard Tuthill, Robert O. Johnson, Katherine Johnson, Nancy Tuthill, Robert C. Johnson.

In 1906, Oren married Bessie Pearl Armstrong, daughter of John and Ellen Diane (Sparks) Armstrong, who arrived in Indiana in 1886. They came from the same area of North Carolina as Oren's great-grandfather, Solomon Johnson. John rented farms in Wells and Huntington County, where Pearl was born in 1888, eldest of four sisters. Soon after she married Oren, he traded the store for a pop-bottling works in Warren, Indiana. There Pearl gave birth to Vera Marie in 1908 and Lawrence Armstrong in 1910. Two years later Oren was employed as a carpenter in the King Piano Factory in Bluffton, where Dorothy Elberta was added to the family. By 1915 they were living on the John Henry Hogg farm north of Rockford, and their fourth child, Robert Oren, was born.

When the baby was old enough to travel, they were off again, this time headed for California by way of Illinois oil fields. There the 1918 flu epidemic caught up with them, and Pearl succumbed at age thirty, worn out by the constant moving. Instead of continuing west, Oren took the children to Cincinnati, where they grew up. Oren died in Kentucky in 1967.

The only one of Oren's children to return to Wells County was Robert. He came back in 1930 to live with his childless aunt and uncle, Elsie (Johnson) and Charles Roth, on a farm just over the county line in Huntington County. Bob joined the Army during World War II, served in Alaska, and in 1947 brought his bride, the former Katherine Mae Buckley, and daughter Nancy back to Bluffton. There he was working for the power company when Robert Charles was born in 1949. The following year they bought a farm on the Wells County line across the road from Charlie and Elsie's.

When Elsie died in 1964, Bob moved his family into her house. He and his son continued to farm in both Wells and Huntington counties until 1985, when young Bob began operating a helicopter aerial applicator business. As of this writing, Bob is back living on the Wells County line farm, Katherine having passed away in 1989. In 1976 young Bob married Kathryn Renee Barringer, daughter of Marion and Louise Barringer, and now resides in Elsie's house. Their daughter Kelsie Marie, born in Bluffton in 1987, is the seventh generation Johnson to have a Wells County rural address.

PAUL JOHNSON FAMILY

We are fourth generation descendants of Able Johnson, (cite Able Johnson history).

Paul and Nina (Gibson) were married June 6, 1943 and resided one mile north and one mile west of Petroleum. In 1947, we moved to Rockcreek township on the Wells, Huntington County Line. In 1963, we moved east of Markle on State Road 116.

Our children are: Karen (Tom Hunnicutt), Gary (Judy Workman), Jerry and Steve (Joyce Masterson).

Karen graduated from Rockcreek in 1963. Due to consolidation, Gary graduated from Lancaster in 1966. Jerry and Steve graduated from Norwell High School in 1970.

Paul and Nina Johnson

We farmed and milked holsteins. Our children participated in school activities and 4-H. Paul served on the 4-H board in 1963 and was also a horse and pony project leader in 1966. Karen served as a horse and pony project leader also in 1966.

Paul is a member of the Bluffton Masonic Lodge and the Scottish Rite in Fort Wayne. I was active in Eastern Star and the Rockford Friendship Club. We are members of the Emmanuel (Methodist) Community Church north of Rockford.

Gary and Judy reside east of Liberty Center with their sons, Brian and Brad. Brian will be a senior, Brad a freshman.

Jerry resides at Route #1, Berne. Steve and Joyce reside in Berne.

Karen and Tom reside one-and-a-half miles from the Wells County Line near Warren. Their son Heath is attending California Institute of Technology in Pasadena, and daughter, Lisa, will be a freshman at Huntington North.

In1 1973, we moved west of Berne on State Road #218 where we now reside.

PAUL EDGAR JOHNSON

Paul Edgar Johnson was born September 20, 1912, in rural Adams County, Indiana, a son of Thomas Edgar and Lucinda (Beitler) Johnson. He spent his early childhood on a farm and attended school in Washington Township, Adams County.

His father died when Paul was fifteen years old, and the family moved to Decatur, Indiana. Included also were his sisters Eva Miriam and Eva Marie (twins), Mary Anna, and brothers Eugene, Lawrence, and Thomas, Jr.

On July 10, 1932, Mrs. Johnson lost her life in a swimming accident near Decatur that left the seven children without parents.

Paul married Bernice Elizabeth Thornton Green on July 25, 1933. Bernice was born in Fort Wayne on August 10, 1911, the daughter of William A. and Mary (Kelly) Thornton, who was of Irish decent. They resided in Adams County. Bernice had one brother, William, Jr., and two sisters, Ruth and Margery. Bernice attended school in Decatur.

Paul Edgar Johnson Family 1949
Front: L to R. Sharon, Jerry, Carolyn. Back: L to R. Ruth, Paul, Norma, Bernice, Paul W.

Paul and Bernice had six children: Ruth, Paul, Norma, Sharon, Jerry, and Carolyn.

The family lived in Adams and Allen Counties before moving to Wells County in 1949. Paul was a skilled core maker by trade and worked in various foundries in the area. He was an avid gardener and carpenter and built the home in which they lived in Fort Wayne.

Ruth Eileen was born March 15, 1934, and married Richard W. Stroud. They reside in Liberty Center. They have four children: Gerald Lee, Karen Jo (now Mrs. Gary Parsons), Keith Alan, and Gregory Charles.

Paul William was born May 10, 1935, and married Louis Belle Strahm. They reside in rural Decatur and have three children: Paul William, Jr., William Kenneth, and Jennifer Jean.

Norma Loreen was born December 7, 1936, and married Franklin D. Moser. They live at Bluffton and have two children, Cathy Sue (now Mrs. David Strain) and Chris Alan.

Sharon Kay was born February 6, 1939, and married Russell J. Ries. They reside at Fort Wayne and have five children: Stephen Paul, Russell J. Jr., Thomas Allen, Debra May (now Mrs. Homer Jacobs), and Raymond Edward.

Jerry Lee was born February 2, 1943, and married Sandra Wallace. They live in Brown City, Michigan, and have two children, Michael and Edward.

Carolyn Ann was born December 8, 1945, and married David Schaefer. They reside near Ossian and have two children, Sheryl Lee (now Mrs. Rick Lobsiger), and David Scott.

Bernice died suddenly at Bluffton on March 13, 1962, and is buried in the Decatur Cemetery.

On March 28, 1964, Paul married Elva (Carter) Baumgartner, daughter of Charles and Ala Magnola (Reeves) Carter of Grinnell, Iowa. Elva was born and raised in Grinnell.

Paul and Elva lived at Big Lake near Columbia City for several years before moving to rural Ossian in 1984. During retirement they enjoyed fishing, woodworking, and various crafts. Paul died after a short illness on February 17, 1989, and is buried beside Bernice in the Decatur Cemetery. Elva resides north of Ossian, Indiana.

RICHARD AND PHYLLIS JOHNSON

Richard and Phyllis Johnson moved to Rockcreek Township, Wells County, in December 1961, raising their three sons on their small place north of Rockford.

Richard was born in Allen County, Indiana, to Quincy and Madge Randle Johnson, the oldest of three children. He graduated from Huntington Township in 1953 and began working at International Harvester in Fort Wayne where he retired in 1983 and after 30 years service. He has worked several odd jobs through the years, the main one being a butcher at Wood's Locker in Zanesville.

Richard's ancestors came from England, settled in Virginia for a time, and then moved on the Wilkes County, North Carolina. He is very proud of his fifth great-grandfather, Samuel, who was a captain in the Revolutionary War.

Phyllis was born in Huntington County to Howard and Carrie Ward Burley, the youngest of four children. She graduated from Union Township, Huntington County, and married Richard on June 19, 1955. They remained in Huntington County until moving to their present home in 1961.

Phyllis was a homemaker during the years their children were growing up, and at the present time writes auction and show reports for an antique trade paper. She and Richard share a common interest in antiques, collecting, and selling. She also raises canaries and is active in the church, teaching classes of all ages.

Each of Richard and Phyllis' three sons graduated from Norwell High School. James Randle graduated in 1975, is married, and lives near Majenica with his wife, daughter, and son. Thomas Richard graduated in 1976 and spent three years in the Army after graduation. He lives in Fort Wayne and also has a son and a daughter. Donald Lee graduated in 1979, received his journalism degree in 1983 from the University of Evansville, is married, and lives near Knightstown, Indiana. He and his wife also share his parents' interest in antiques.

Richard and Phyllis Johnson

Phyllis' sister, Wanda Burley Pequignot, lived one-half mile north of the Johnson home for many years before moving to the Burley homeplace. An uncle and aunt, Jesse and Nora Cargar, lived across the road from the Pequignot home. Nora Cargar was a sister of Howard Burley. Jesse Cargar drove a school bus for Rockcreek Township for 32 years.

Richard's mother, Madge Randle, was born August 10, 1912. She died January 1, 1946, in Arizona, and is buried near Delphi, Indiana. His father, Quincy, was born December 23, 1904, in North Wilkesboro, North Carolina. He retired from International Harvester of Fort Wayne in 1966 and died February 27, 1983, in Huntington, Indiana.

Phyllis' mother, Carrie Ward, was born March 27, 1901, in Huntington and died February 5, 1977, at her home in Union Township, Huntington County. Her father, Howard, was born September 14, 1896, in Lancaster Township near Majenica, Huntington County, and was a farmer all his life. He died in Bluffton, Indiana, on December 27, 1970. They area both buried at the Star of Hope Cemetery, east of Huntington in Huntington County.

STAN AND DIANE JOHNSON

On an early spring day (March 30, 1985) - so as not to conflict with farming, Stanley G. Johnson and Diane L. Denney were married at the First Church of Christ in Bluffton.

Stan was born in 1954 in Defiance County, Ohio, to Leon and Anna Johnson (see Leon Johnson history). He graduated from Bluffton High School in 1973, and from Huntington College in 1977, with a BS Degree in Elementary Education. Stan has been farming since the mid 1970s.

Kyle (2 1/2) and Chris (7 mo.) Johnson

Diane was born in Wabash County to Max and Janet Denney, in 1961. She graduated from Huntington North High School in 1979, and from Parkview School of Nursing in 1983. Diane works part-time as an RN.

Son, Kyle Gene, was born February 22, 1988 - the year of the severe drought. The corn and soybeans were sparse and stunted but Baby Kyle grew like a weed. Now Kyle enjoys "helping?" his dad and playing with his puppies. Kyle's little brother is Chris Allen, born April 6, 1990. Chris is a happy, smiling baby who finds pleasure in following around his big brother.

Stan, Diane, Kyle, and Chris live and work on their Harrison Township farm.

SOLOMON JOHNSON

Among the earliest residents of Wells County was Solomon Johnson. He arrived in 1836, cutting his way through the woods for lack of roads, and bought an eighty-acre tract in Rockcreek Township from the federal government. He then put up a temporary shanty, soon to be replaced by a log cabin, to house his wife, the former Sarah Sanders, and growing family. They probably joined Solomon in 1837, after living a short time in Blackford County on the site of Montpelier. At that time he purchased an additional forty acres and cleared a patch to begin cultivation.

Sarah and Solomon, the son of Charles and Susannah (Sparks) Johnson, were originally from Wilkes County, North Carolina. There, one week short of her fourteenth birthday, Sarah gave birth to her first child, Appoline, in 1816. Two years later James Louis was born. Probably around 1820 the little family headed north and first settled in Wayne County, Indiana. They were there in 1825 when their second son, Jonas, was born, two years after their second daughter, Elizabeth. Shortly thereafter, they continued north to Delaware County and added Nathan (born 1827), Susiana (1829), Mary Jane (1831), and Solomon (1833) to the family, though the latter two and Elizabeth died in infancy. After Sarah Ann (Sally) was born in 1835, the family moved to Blackford County, then on to Wells County to have Ermina (1837), Henry (1839), Isabella (1841), and finally Charles (1846). Charles died in 1849, leaving nine of the thirteen children to attain adulthood.

With the help of his sons, Solomon cleared his land and soon had a thriving farm. He eventually bought 160 acres in Huntington County, too, which they cleared, farmed, and then sold. A member of the Democratic Party, Solomon also found time to be active in politics, serving as president on the first board of county commissioners from 1837 to 1840. Johnson Street in Bluffton is named after him, but Solomon's greatest interest seemed to be in a town closer to home. In 1849 he and Matthew Davis platted the town of Rockford (also known as Barber's Mills for the saw and gristmills built their earlier by Hallet Barber) located on their own property. Solomon watched the village grow until his death in 1864 at the age of seventy-one. He was buried with Sarah in the Rockford Cemetery.

Before he died, Solomon saw most of his children married. Appoline became the wife of William S. Clark in 1838, and James wedded Hannah Lawellen 1843. Two united with Hallet Barber's children - Jonas with Urania Barber in 1848, and Sally with Ibern Barber a year later. Nathan took two daughters of Matthew Davis in succession - Rachel in 1856 and then Sarah in 1861. Susiana became Mrs. Solomon Sparks in 18 46 and Ermina, Mrs. Isaac Price in 1853. After her father's death, Isabella married Levi Saylor in 1865 and later John W. Cook of Rockford. Jonas and Nathan also remained in the area and did their part to populate Wells County.

TED L. JOHNSON FAMILY

Ted L. Johnson was born on February 28, 1936. He married Marjorie J. Hahn who was born on October 16, 1936. They have three children. Cindy Sue Johnson was born November 30, 1955. Her children are Jason Jay Johnson, born July 7, 1972, and Jeremy Joe Turner, born August 18, 1973. Jacklyn Kay Johnson was born May 16, 1957, was married on August 19, 1980 to Dan T. Hoffman, born April 5, 1957, to Fred and Joan Hoffman of Decatur. Jacklyn and Dan have a son, Myles Frederick, born July 19, 1986. Douglas Shawn Johnson, born May 25, 1962, married in 1982 to Robin Berry, born in 1965.

WILLIAM HENRY JOHNSON

William Henry Johnson, son of Nathan Johnson and grandson of Solomon Johnson, was born January 7, 1857, in Kentucky. His mother was Rachel Davis, daughter of Matthew Davis. After his mother died and his father remarried, William moved with his parents to Washington State. They later returned to Kentucky with small children. The story is told that a stranger joined the camp as they were returning from the west. He was of great help on the trip. He stayed until almost the end of the journey, then disappeared. The family considered this stranger an act of Providence.

William (Spike) Henry Johnson and Mary Alice Butler Johnson, Jim, Susie, Lena, Edith, Annie, Merle

William (Spike) married Mary Alice Butler February 9, 1878, in Wells County. Mary was the daughter of Edward S. and Amanda Catlin Gray Butler, who were resident in Rockcreek Township at 100N and 450W. Edward was a glassworker and had immigrated from Hartford City, Pennsylvania. Mary was born September 21, 1856. Spike was employed at the Rockford stone quarry, and he and his family lived across from the entrance to the quarry. There were eight children in the family: Susan Delphina married George Schmidt; Edith Esther married Marion Raber; Sarah Ruhama married Carl Braden; James married Bessie?; Anna married Ed Schmidt; Lena married Oscar Harnish; Merle married Amos Phillips, then ? Bates; and Fred E.

William (Spike) Henry Johnson died January 16, 1933, and is buried in the Rockford Cemetery. His wife, Mary Alice Butler Johnson, was a member of the Seventh-day Adventist Church. She died October 5, 1939, and is buried in the Rockford Cemetery.

JONES FAMILY

Virgil Jones, whose parents were Phillip and Nellie (Harold) Jones, was orphaned at the age of seven and reared in the home of Cary and Bertha Roush in Jackson Township. Along with the Roush children, Alton (deceased), Helen (Mrs. Glen Schoeff of Lancaster Township) and Ruth (Mrs. William Deeter of Marion) he was a part of their immediate family for the next 15 years. In 1922, he married Audra Bardsley and four children were born to the union: Naomi (Mrs. Richard O. Martin of Liberty Township); Harold (deceased in infancy); Dean (of Kewanna) and Velma (Mrs. Sebert Souers of Liberty Township). It was only after Virgil's death in 1961 that the family became interested in learning more about the Jones line and an interesting story unfolded.

The earliest know ancestor of this line was Daniel. An immigrant from Wales, he was born in 1715. His wife's name was Mary and their son John was a Revolutionary War soldier. John and his wife, Linna, who had settled in Beaver County, Pennsylvania, and later lived in Scioto and Clinton Counties in Ohio, raised eight children to adulthood. Following in their father's military footsteps, four of their sons (Samuel, Daniel, Oliver and Isaac) were soldiers in the War of 1812. While passing thru Indiana they were so impressed with the beauty of the area that they vowed to return one day to make their homes. Samuel returned and became founder of the town of Warren in Huntington County. Daniel, along with Nathaniel Batson and Leander Morrison, was one of the first three permanent white settlers in Jackson Township. Oliver also became a resident of Jackson Township while Isaac settled in Madison County. Daniel had married a young lady by the name of Susanna Gardner and they reared a large family. Their son, Enoch, and his wife, Mary Elizabeth (Brinneman) became the parents of the earlier mentioned Phillip.

Daniel, Oliver, Enoch and Phillip Jones are all buried in the Batson Cemetery in Jackson Township. They, and their offsprings, have played influential parts in the settlement and development of Wells County as we know it today.

ROBERT CALVIN JONES

Bob was born November 27, 1913, in Wells County. His father was Charles Jones, his grandfather Phillip Jones (who killed the last bear in Wells County), and his great-grandfather was Enoch Jones. On his mother's side, his mother was Lydia Lavetha Davis, grandfather Cuthbert Davis, and great-grandfather George W. Davis, who was married to Delphinia Barber (daughter of Hallet Barber). Bob's great-great-grandfather was Joseph Davis, who came to Wells County from Ohio in 1837.

Bob obtained his education at Liberty Center consolidated school. On August 28, 1938, Bob married Opal Helen Gordon, daughter of Charles and Urania Johnson Gordon. Helen can trace her ancestry back to Solomon and Sarah Johnson in Rockcreek Township in 1836 and on back to John Johnson, who came to the new world from England prior to 1663. She is related to Hallet Barber through her mother, Urania Johnson Gordon. Helen was born October 12, 1912. She attended Rockcreek Center school.

Bob and Helen began life together living southeast of Reiffsburg. Then they moved to a house three or four miles north of Rockford and later lived from 1942-50 in the little house in the woods on the farm homesteaded by Bob's ancestors in 1837. They eventually bought the farm across the road at 1638S 300W. Bob and Helen adopted a daughter, Jane Ann, born September 12, 1948. Bob worked at a number of jobs including electrical, plumbing and county highway until his death May

10, 1977 of congestive heart failure. He is buried in the Mossburg Cemetery. Helen and Jane Ann continue to live on the farm.

Jane, Helen Jones 1986

Bob and his family enjoyed the out-of-doors. Early every spring would find them making maple syrup in the woods across the road. The school children from Liberty Center came every spring on field trips to watch the making of maple syrup and to enjoy tasting it on pancakes with hot chocolate. Bob and Helen enjoyed gardening, fishing and indentifying trees, plants, animals and birds. Both Bob and Helen were members of the Rockford Seventh-day Adventist Church and later of the Marion Seventh-day Adventist Church.

JORAY

Emanuel and Julie Grandlienard Joray sailed from northwestern Switzerland, near the French border, on April 19, 1844, bound for America. They were from the parish of Belphrohon, Canton of Berne, Switzerland, where their five children were born. The family arrived in New York City on July 4, 1848, and came directly to Wells County, Indiana. They were among the first seven settlers in the settlement of Newville, which in 1880 changed to Vera Cruz.

Charles Auguste was eight upon arrival. He became a cabinet maker and in 1866 married Elizabeth Sauter. They had five sons: Albert, Edward, Emanuel, Charles, and Frederick. Only Emanuel, the well driller, married and had children. There were also three daughters: Emma (Joseph) Moser, Mary Elizabeth (Oscar) Ehrsam, and Catherine (Charles) Servis.

Emilie was seven, and in 1862 married Christian Luginbill of Adams County.

Robert and Olive Sweeny - March 28, 1976 - 45th Wedding Anniversary

Elsie, three, only lived to age 13. David, who celebrated his first birthday after arriving in America, died at age 18. Justive, born in Vera Cruz in 1846, died young. These three and their parents are buried in Vera Cruz Cemetery.

The oldest child, Samuel, my grandfather, was ten upon arriving and, in 1864, married Esther Baughman, whose family had come to Wells County that same year from Neward, Ohio. He was a wagon and sled maker, having a shop for 35 years located north of the Reformed Church and across the street from Croy's barn, in Vera Cruz. for thirty years they were members of a Lutheran Church south of Vera Cruz. They then moved to a farm, south of the County Home, where they lived 25 years before moving to a farm east of Six Mile Church, where they were members at the time of their deaths.

All seven children were born in Vera Cruz. The oldest, Sarah born 1865, married Peter Shoemaker, and had one daughter Carrie, who was chief telephone operator in Bluffton from 1914 to 1956. She then retired and married Charles Lesh.

Victor, born 1866, died at age six; and a sister Sureldia, born 1872, died at age five. They and their parents are also buried in Vera Cruz Cemetery.

Robert Samuel, born 1869, married Cora VanEmon, daughter of Hiram (Amanda) VanEmon, of Wells County. Their daughter, Olive (Robert) Sweeny, currently resides in Bluffton. Olive's son, Paul (Barbara Binegar) Sweeny's children, Nancy (Keith) Cole, twins Dan and Dave, and Tim and Tom, all born in Bluffton settled in the Warsaw area. Olive's daughter, Evelyn (Gene) Pope, lives on the Sweeny farm in Harrison Township, has two children, Allen (Beth Wilson) Pope of Indianapolis, and Twila (Ron) Dubbeld, who with their children, Janella and Dion, live in Harrison Township.

Noah, born 1876, married Sarah Myers in 1897. They had two daughters, Harriet and Margaret; neither had children.

Twins born August 5, 1879, were George, who never married, but always lived with his twin, Harvey Elsworth, my father, who married Orpha Imo Decker in 1918. Their only daughter, Maxine Joray, is now a Bluffton resident.

AUGUSTE AND ELIZABETH MAUTE JORAY

Early in his life, Auguste Joray took up the trade of cabinet making. It was by this profession and that of farming that he supported his wife, the former Elizabeth Maute and their eight children.

Auguste, who was born in the Canton of Bern, Switzerland on August 18, 1836, was the second of six children of Emanuel and Julie Grandlienard Joray. He came with his parents from Switzerland to Vera Cruz, Indiana, when he was eight.

Elizabeth was the daughter of Martin and Mary E. Sauter Maute. She was born September 24, 1842 in Wurttemberg, Germany. In 1865, when she was nearly twenty-three years of age, she came to America and settled in Newville, Indiana, which was later called Vera Cruz.

Auguste and Elizabeth were married September 6, 1866, by Reverend John H. Stepler, pastor of the St. John German Reformed Church in Vera Cruz. They became the parents of eight children: Albert, Edward, Emma, Emanuel, Mary, Charles, Catherine and Frederick. The family lived in a house that was originally Auguste's parents' home on the north side of Vera Cruz. At the dinner table, the Joray children would speak French to their father, German to their mother and English to each other.

Albert, the oldest son, was born September 24, 1867. He only lived to be twenty-six years old.

Edward was born July 30, 1869. He never married and lived with his mother and his two other single brothers, Charles and Fred. Edward earned his living working as a well driller with his brother, Emanuel.

Emma was born January 2, 1872. She married Joseph J. Moser and the couple lived on a farm in Nottingham Township in Wells County. They had three children: Walter, Pearl (Mrs. Ralph Jahn) and Ruby (Mrs. Harold Greiner). Auguste Joray family on August 14, 1889

Back row L to R: Edward 20, Albert 21, Emma 17, Emanuel 15, and Mary 13. Front row: Auguste 52, Catherine 8, Frederick 6, Charles 11 and Elizabeth 47.

Emanuel, who was born February 3, 1874, was the only one of the five sons who married. He married Amelia Henneford and they had two sons, Philip and William. Emanuel starting drilling water wells in 1896. By the time of his retirement in 1945, he had drilled over two thousand wells, most of which were in Adams and Wells Counties.

Mary, the fifth child, was born April 27, 1876. She married Oscar Ehrsam and they had five sons: William, Harry, Melvin, Lester and Harley. The Ehrsams lived three miles west of Monroe.

Charles was born September 17, 1878. He worked as a carpenter and lived with his mother and brothers Ed and Fred in Vera Cruz.

Catherine, who was known as Kate, was born December 19, 1880. She married Charles Servis and the couple had one daughter, Violet. They lived on West Spring Street in Bluffton.

Frederick or Fred, the youngest child was born on March 2, 1883. He lived in Vera Cruz and was a painter and paper hanger by profession.

Auguste Joray died on July 26, 1891, three weeks before his fifty-fifth birthday. Elizabeth Joray, who wanted to live to be one hundred, died when she was eighty-nine on March 27, 1932. Both are buried in the Vera Cruz Cemetery.

CHARLES AND PEGGY KEIL JORAY

Although he was born at the Wells County Hospital on October 18, 1949, Charles Joray did not live in Wells County until July, 1975 when he began working as the director of the Bluffton-Wells County Public Library. His parents were William and Delores Egly Joray who lived on a farm near Linn Grove. For the previous two years before moving to Bluffton, Charles had been the director of the Hartford City Public Library.

Charles was newly married when he moved to Bluffton. He had married Margaret (Peggy) Keil, a daughter of Paul and Rosemary O'Brien Keil of Evansville on January 24, 1975 at the Mormon Temple in Washington, D.C.

Peggy had received a degree in dietetics from Purdue University in the spring of 1974, and she completed a dietetics internship at Indiana University Medical Center in Indianapolis in December, 1974. Charles had a Bachelor's degree in social studies from Ball State University which he received in 1971 and a Master's degree in Library Science that he received in 1973.

Charles Joray family, February 1, 1991. Back row (L to R) Charles 41, Craig 14, and Bruce 12. Front row: Molly 6, Elizabeth 9 and Peggy 39.

While in Bluffton, Peggy worked as a part-time dietitian at the Caylor-Nickel Clinic until the birth of the couple's first child, Craig, on July 8, 1976. After her son's birth, Peggy did dietetics consultant work at Cooper Community Care Center and Meadowvale Care Center.

When they moved to Bluffton, Charles and Peggy rented a house at 422 West Central which was located one block east of the high school. Then in May, 1976, they purchased a home at 18 Woodlawn in the Hi-Lo Subdivision.

While living in Bluffton, two more children were born to Charles and Peggy. Bruce was born on September 22, 1978, and Elizabeth was born on May 21, 1981. Three years later, after the family had moved to Kokomo, a fourth child was born on February 6, 1984.

The Joray family enjoyed the cultural aspects of the Bluffton community. They attended the house concerts sponsored by the Creative Arts Council and Charles participated in the Wells County Band while Peggy enjoyed involvement in Foltz, a literary study group.

The Jorays attended the Church of Christ of Latter-Day Saints in Fort Wayne until a branch of that church was begun in Decatur in March, 1977. They then were active members there for the remainder of their stay in Bluffton.

On January 11, 1982, Charles began work as the director of the Kokomo-Howard County Public Library and the Joray family then moved to Kokomo, Indiana.

EMANUEL AND JULIE GRANDLIENARD JORAY

In 1844 Emanuel Joray decided to emigrate to America from the parish of Belprahon, prefecture of Moutier-Grandval, canton of Bern, Switzerland. His family had lived in that area of northwestern Switzerland near the French border for generations. The parish registry of Moutier lists many, many Jorays in the baptism and marriage records which began in the 1630's.

Accompanying thirty-three year old Emanuel to America were his wife, Julie Grandlienard) who was ten years his senior, and their five small children. Samuel was the eldest having been born ten years before the voyage, Auguste was nearly eight, Emilie was soon to be seven, Marianne Elise was three, and the baby, David Solomon, would not be one until his family arrived in America in July.

Emanuel, who was a farmer, was a rather short man measuring five feet, five-and-one-half inches tall. He had brown hair and eyebrows and a high forehead. His face was oval-shaped, his chin round and his eyes were grey. Although his nose was large, his mouth was average in size. A distinguishing characteristic was that his upper front teeth were missing.

The Joray family set sail in April, 1844 and arrived in New York City in July. After landing in this country, they came at once to Wells County, Indiana, and settled in the dense forest six miles southeast of Bluffton along the Wabash River. This settlement became known as Newville; then later Vera Cruz.

On August 13, 1844, Emanuel Joray paid five hundred dollars to Christian and Martha Saurer for eighty acres of land. At a later date, the eastern portion of this land along the road dividing Adams and Wells Counties was donated by Emanuel to the church in Vera Cruz to be used as a cemetery. The agreement between Emanuel and the church was that he and his wife and their descendents could have any available lot free of charge or at a reduced rate as a burial site. Thus, one will find many Jorays buried in the Vera Cruz Cemetery.

Two years after setting up housekeeping in Wells County, on April 12, 1846, Julie Joray gave birth to her sixth child and third daughter, Justine. Julie was forty-four year of age at that time.

Three of Emanuel and Julie Joray's children died at a relatively early age. In 1854 Marianne Elise died on the 25th of September at the age of thirteen. David Solomon died on March 5, 1862, when he was eighteen. Justine died at the age of thirty on August 6, 1876. The other three children - Samuel, Auguste and Emilie - lived to a good age, married and had children.

Emanuel Joray died on April 10, 1877, at the age of sixty-six years.

When the Biographical and Historical Record of Adams and Wells Counties was published in 1887, Julie Joray was listed as one of the oldest residents of Vera Cruz. Julie was eighty-six in December of 1887. A little over a year later, she died on March 29, 1889.

Both Emanuel and Julie Joray are buried in the cemetery that they had given to the Vera Cruz community.

SAMUEL AND ESTHER BAUGHMAN JORAY

Samuel Joray, the eldest child of Emanuel and Julie Grandlienard Joray, was a wagon maker by profession. He was already well established in the business of making wagons and sleds in Newville (Vera Cruz) when he took as his bride Esther Ellen Baughman. She was a daughter of Isaac and Mary Ann McDowell Baughman and was born in Newark, Licking County, Ohio.

The Baughman family moved to Wells County in 1864 when Esther was seventeen years of age. In the fall of that year, thirty-year-old Samuel Joray married this young, new arrival to the Newville community.

Esther was a woman who very much loved to cook. She never used a recipe, but would use a pinch of this and a cup of that based on what she felt the mixture needed at the time.

For thirty-five years, Samuel worked as a wagon maker in a shop that was north of the Reformed Church and across the street from Croy's barn in Vera Cruz. Thus it was in that town that all seven of Samuel and Esther's children were born.

The children are: Sarah, Victor, Robert, Sureldia, Noah and twins George and Harvey.

Victor and Sureldia died before reaching maturity; Victor at the age of six in 1873 and Sureldia at the age of five in 1878.

Sarah, the eldest child, married Peter Shoemaker. They had one child, Carrie, who married Charles E. Lesh.

Robert married Cora Jane Van Emon, and they had two daughters: Edna, who died when she was five-and-a-half months old and Olive, who married Robert Sweeny. Robert Joray resided on a farm near Reiffsburg for fifty-three years. In 1948, he retired from farming and moved with his wife to 310 East Market Street in Bluffton.

Noah married Sarah Elizabeth Myers and they had two daughters: Harriet, who married Joseph Parrish and Margaret, who died at the age of nineteen.

George, the elder of the twins, never married. He was a farmer and resided in Wells and Huntington Counties.

Harvey, the younger twin, married Orpha Decker. They had a son who died in infancy and a daughter, Maxine. Harvey's farm was located eight miles west and one-half mile north of Bluffton on the Wells-Huntington County line.

Around the year 1883, Samuel moved his family to a farm east of Highway 1 and north of the Poplar Grove School near the Wells County Home. For twenty-five years he lived there farming and continuing to make wagons and sleds in his shop on the farm.

Five years before Samuel's death, he and his wife moved to a farm east of the Six Mile Church.

On October 29, 1912, Samuel suffered a stroke which left him paralyzed. He slowly declined and died on January 8, 1913. Esther survived her husband for four and one-half years. She died in the morning of July 24, 1917.

JOHN JUDD

John Judd was born September 2, 1806 in Shenandoah (Page) County, Virginia. He was the son of William Judd and Nancy Gander.

The date of John's arrival in Wells County in unknown. On April 12, 1836 he married Anna M. Double (the daughter of Jacob Double and Winifred Masters). They had ten children: Ellen (born 1837), Isabella (January 22, 1839-September 11, 1870), William (February 17, 1841-May 21, 1850(1?), George (born January 7, 1843), Ezkiah (May 26, 1846-February 12, 1926), Isaac (born December 16, 1848), Jacob (February 27, 1851-September 12, 1857), Mary A. (born August 2, 1854), Daniel W. (March 24, 1857-August 24, 1857), and Henry F. (January 18, 1860-1944). The mother, who was born April 14, 1816, died on May 11, 1887 and was buried in Elhanan Cemetery in northeast Wells County. John died on May 15, 1892 and was also buried in Elhanan Cemetery. Four of their children (Isabella, William, Ezkiah and Henry) are buried there as well.

John's ancestors have been traced back four more generations. John's father, William, was born in 1783 and died about 1863. He married Nancy Gander, who bore John. After her death he married Nancy Hershberger, with whom he had two more children. William or his father served as a lieutenant of the Virginia Line from Rockingham County, Virginia. William is buried in Ohio. William's father was Isaac Judd. He married Lettice (last name unknown) and had two children, William and Elizabeth. Isaac's parents were Michael and Mary

Judd. Will records from Virginia seem to indicate that Michael's father was also named Michael. Thus far, the Judd decendants have not been able to trace the family line back any further.

KAHN

There has been a family of Kahn's living in Kingsland for the last one hundred years.

Myer Kahn was born in Gemany on September 16, 1836. He came to America around 1853. Myer fought for the North in the Civil War, from April 12, 1861 to April 18, 1865. When he came home from from the war he married Christina Gilbert (1845-1939), who was from Dayton, Ohio, on April 5, 1866. Myer and Christina made their home at different locations in Wells County but at the time of his death on November 6, 1918, they lived in Root Township in Admas County. Myer made his living as a farmer and a horse trader. Myer and Christina had four children, Alonzo, Emma, Ella and Leo.

Alonzo David Kahn was born in Wells County on February 16, 1869. Alonzo started a scrap metal yard in Kingsland around 1890; also, like his father, he was horse trader. On May 4, 1904, he married a Wells County girl named Margaret Katherine Dishong, who was born March 10, 1886. Alonzo and Margaret had six children: Nellie, William L. (who died at three months), Clarence, William D., Erma, and Helen Bernice.

Alonzo died on December 5, 1932. Margaret died June 7, 1953. Both died in Wells County. Alonzo is buried at the Saint Paul Cemetery in Rockcreek Township along with his father and mother, Myer and Christina. Margaret's resting place is Fairview Cemetery in Bluffton.

Bill and Vadis Kahn

William David Kahn was born in Wells County on January 4, 1909. William married Vadis Olean Green, the daughter of Homer Green and Garnet Grutrude Richards, on June 17, 1929. Vadis also was born in Wells County on March 3, 1912. Bill and Vadis both grew up in Kingsland and it was there they raised their ten children: Paul, born in 1930, Bill born in 1931, Tom born in 1934, Jack born in 1935, Dixie born in 1937 and died in 1989, Connie born in 1939, Sally born in 1941 and died in 1989, Judy born in 1942, Becky born in 1943, and Linda born in 1945.

Bill and Vadis are the proud grandparents of forty grandchildren, fifty-one great-grandchildren and one great-great-grandchild.

Bill is retired from the Dana Corporation at Fort Wayne, where he was a tool grinder. Bill also owns the scrap metal yard at Kingsland in which as a boy he worked with his father Alonzo; he then continued with the business when his father died. Vadis was a homemaker and full-time mother. Vadis was quite busy in the summertime putting out large gardens and canning lots of fruits and vegetables.

Vadis passed away on December 11, 1987, in Wells County. She is resting at Oak Lawn Cemetery in Ossian.

KELLER FAMILY

Eli Martin keller (1881-1928) was born in Washington Township, the son of Benjamin C. and Sarah Angeline McConkey Keller. His great-grandfather, David Keller, was the founder of the name in this country, coming to Pennsylvania from Germany. Early history of the Keller family is recorded in the 1914 *Blackford-Grant County History*, page 196.

Eli Keller married Zina Nestleroad (1891-1964). They were the parents of seven children; Gladys, Cecil, Cleophus, Irene, Ruby, Leona and Wilma.

Gladys Keller, born October 20, 1910, married Jay Haiflich of Uniondale, Indiana. They have no children.

Cecil Keller, born August 9, 1912, married Alonzo Smith of Monroe, Indiana. They are parents of three children, all born in Adams County. Eloise Lucile Smith, born September 26, 1932, married Howard Neussbaum of Berne, Indiana. Their children are Steven born November 16, 1953, and Michael born July 17, 1956. Chester Smith, born January 1935, married Phyllis Mattax of Monroe, Indiana. They are the parents of Debra Smith, born July 15, 1963. Lester Smith, born November 23, 1937, married Pamela Walter of Decatur, Indiana. They are the parents of five children: Laura, born February 6, 1964; Janeen, born September 22, 1966; Leslie, born May 21, 1971; twins, Michelle and Melissa, born December 26, 1973.

Eli & Zina (Nestleroad) Keller and family

Cleophus Eli Keller was born in Howard County, Indiana, February 12, 1914, and died in August 8, 1981. His first marriage was to Mildred Platt of Wells County. Their children, both born in Wells County, are Doyle, born August 23, 1933, and Jerry born November 6, 1936. Cleophus Keller's second marriage was to Geraldine Klein of Fort Wayne, Indiana. Their children are Michael Eugene, born July 14, 1948, and Kathleen Keller, born June 30, 1953.

Irene Keller was born December 12, 1915. Her first marriage was to Earlyn Hoffman of Kendallville, Indiana. Their son is Dwight Hoffman, born August 13, 1937. Irene's second marriage was to Dale Death of Adams County. Their children are Roger, born February 5, 1945, and Patricia Irene Death, born August 23, 1943.

Ruby Josephine Keller was born in Blackford County, April 26, 1917. She never married. Her home is in Bluffton.

Leona Keller was born July 23, 1918. She married George Edward Miller of Wells County, August 16, 1937. Their daughter Barbara Miller, born October 7, 1940, married Charles French of Bluffton, Indiana. Their children are Michael, born January 4, 1961, Douglas, born August 15, 1962, and Angela, born March 18, 1965. Phyllis Jean Miller was born July 13, 1945 and died July 8, 1972. She married Richard Baller of Wells County, and their children are Jodi Leigh, born April 9, 1969, and Sarah Marie Baller, born January 26, 1978.

Juanita Keller was born March 22, 1923. She married Garl Eugene Masterson of Liberty Center, Indiana. Their daughters are Karen, born October 4, 1946; Shirley, born April 12, 1948; Monna, born June 28, 1951; Cheryl, born May 16, 1955.

MR. E. HOWARD KELLER-MARGARET KELLER

Howard Keller was born and raised in Chester Township, Wells County. He was the son of Marvin and Clara Richey Keller, born August 6, 1918. He attended school in Chester Center School graduating with the class of 1936. He farmed most of his life.

Margaret Shields was born October, 28, 1920, to Jesse and Mary Graf near Sharpsville, Indiana, Tipton County. She attended grade school at Ross School and two years at the Sharpsville High School. She moved with her parents to Blackford County and graduated from the Montpelier High School in 1938. Margaret moved to the Jackson Township, Wells County home in 1941. She and Howard were married March 7, 1943. They lived in Chester Township for fifteen years. They had a daughter, Martha L. Howard, farmed, raised hogs, and milked cows. They rented a farm from the Huddlestons, Mrs. Ellis, and Mrs. Burson besides farming for his father and father-in-law. Those years were years of neighborhood farming and working together.

As Howard became ill, the family moved to Winter Haven, Florida, in November, 1957. Howard passed away in Winter Haven Hospital, December 24, 1958. Margaret and daughter remained in Florida until 1970. Martha was married to William "Bill" Bair on July 3, 1970. They moved to Springfield, Missouri that fall. Margaret came to Indiana and helped care for her parents, Jesse and Mary Shields until their death. Martha and Bill are parents of a daughter, Cinnamon, a sophomore in Troy State College and a son, Eric M. a freshman at the Lake Wales High School where the family reside.

(L to R) Mildred Albertson, Mary Shields, Gretchen Garrett, Margaret Keller, 100th birthday of Mary Shields

Margaret has been a farm wife, homemaker and worked in several other positions. While living in Florida, she attended the Lakeland Beauty College and worked in a shop in Auburndale, Florida for fifteen years, coming back to Indiana in 1970 to live with and take care of her parents. She is a charter member of the Loyal Workers Extension Homemakers Club of Blackford County which was organized February 13, 1940.

She was in 4-H work for ten years and in the Extension Homemakers for fifty-one years. In Blackford County, she held all the offices of the then Home Demonstration clubs and was district representative in 1981-1983. She has held the state offices of Public Relations, Citizenship, Family Life, Logo and International.

Since selling the estate, Margaret purchased property in Montpelier, Indiana, in the spring of 1989 and has lived there since. She still helps care for patients, it seems there is a need for that type of work everywhere she goes.

She is a member of the First Baptist Church in Montpelier, Indiana, and also a member of the Past County Presidents Club of the Extension Homemakers of Blackford County.

MR. AND MRS. MARVIN KELLER

Marvin and Clara Keller lived all of their married life (fifty-six years) on the homestead where Marvin was born and raised. It was located on the Blackford-Wells County line in Chester Township, Wells County.

Clara met Marvin when she worked for his mother, doing housework at the age of thirteen or fourteen. In those days, young girls would go to peoples' homes to do work for extra money in order to buy clothing and books for school.

Marvin was born January 1, 1890, to Martin Vanburen Keller and Lalee Elizabeth Keller, who migrated to southern Wells County from Fairfield County, Ohio. Other children born to this union: Henry, Arthur, Bessie, and Cary.

Clara Edna was the daughter of Milton Loomis Richey and Estella M. Spaulding Richey. Clara was born November 20, 1896, in Harrison Township, Blackford County. Other children born to this union were: Raymond E.; Virginia Grace, who married George Cassell; Carl, died at age three weeks; Mary Lucile, married Floyd Petzel; George Marion; Chester Albert; Catherine Loraine, married Harley Hapner; Kenneth Warren; and an infant who passed away.

Estella Spaulding Richey's grandparents, Francis and Mary J. Hale Spaulding, migrated to Wells County and the Keystone area from the state of Vermont in the early 1800's. Marvin and Clara Edna Richey were married on December 4, 1913. They were farmers on the homestead; raised hogs and milked cows as most families did in that era. Clara always had a beautiful garden, which she always planted with both flowers and vegetables. Raising of chickens was a must, for meat and eggs to eat and to sell.

They were parents of Helen Irene (1915) who married Carl Leroy Allen and their children are Eugene and Charlotte Kay; Earl Howard (1918), married Margaret Shields and their daughter is Martha; Ralph Laverne (1926) married Gloria Garrett and their children are Karen Lee, Carl Duane, David Allen, and Barbara A., Elmer Ray (1931), married Mary Lou Prough and their children Judy Ann, Janet Rae, Michael Eugene and Eric ger.

Marvin and Clara were able to celebrate their fiftieth wedding anniversary on December 4, 1963, with most of their children and all of their grandchildren present. One son, E. Howard had passed away on December 24, 1958.

Marvin Keller passed away on September 5, 1969, from heart complications. He was seventy-nine years of age. Clara Keller followed her husband in a little over four months, passing away on January 21, 1970, from a blood clot that went to her heart due to a broken arm. She was seventy-three years old.

KELLEY-SMEKENS-GEELS

Basil C. Kelley and his sons, John and George, along with their families, moved to Bluffton from Adams County in 1907. They formed the B.C. Kelley and Sons Monument Works in Bluffton.

George's family later moved to Marshall County, and after the death of the elder Mr. Kelley, the business was carried on for many years as Kelley Monument Works. located on East Market Street.

After the death of B.C. Kelley, John and his family were the only family members remaining in Wells County. Before moving to Bluffton, John had married Bessie Kelly. Although they shared the same surname, they were not related. They had eleven children, six of whom died in infancy. Of the remaining five, daughters Martha and Marie continued to live in Wells County. Madelene is still living in Plymouth.

John Kelley was active in civic affairs. For many years a faithful member and trustee of Saint Joseph's Catholic Church, he was also a loyal Rotarian, twice a member of the the city council, and finished one term as mayor of Bluffton in 1920 and was again elected as mayor in 1929. He died in office in 1934. Mrs. Kelley died in 1968. They and their immediate family were buried in Fairview Cemetery amid hundreds of stones engraved and set by Mr. Kelley and his assistants.

Daughter Martha married Clemen (Bud) Smekens in 1936 and had five children, four of whom remained in Wells County. They have ten living grandchildren and one grandson, Scottie, who died in 1990. There are also three great-grandchildren.

A word of eulogy for Scottie Smekens. Physically handicapped from birth, he had a brilliant mind and an indomitable spirit. His philosophy as expressed to his grandmother was, "There are no cripples in heaven."

The parents of Clemen Smekens, who were both natives of Belgium were for many years residents of Wells County.

Clemen Smekens retired after forty years employment at O.K. Modern Cleaners. Martha Smekens retired after twenty years in the insurance department at Caylor-Nickel clinic.

Daughter Marie married Cletus Geels in 1933. His parents moved to Wells County in the early twenties. A watchmaker by trade, Cletus Geels operated the Geels Jewelry Store for twenty-six and one-half years, closing the store on January 1, 1956. He later was engaged in farming and trenching. Mr. and Mrs. Geels had four children, one of whom lives in Wells County. They have eleven grandchildren and six great-grandchildren. Mr. Geels died in 1989.

Ten members of the immediate Kelley family have served or are serving in some branch of the armed forces.

Children, grandchildren and great-grandchildren of Cletus and Marie Geels: son Bernard (Pete) Geels, married Linda Gilliom; their son Stephen married Nunzia Rapisarda and they have one son Bernard. Their daughter Catherine married Walter Van Betuw and their children are Sarah and Adam.

John Geels married Karen Kitt; their children are Joni and Darry.

Mary Alice married Norman Reuille; their children are Elizabeth (Sr. M. Clare O.S.F.), Michelle and Amy.

Rose Ann married Steven Hinesley; their children are Mark who married Vicky West; Ann who married Brent Hossinger, and whose children are Maria, Molly, Clinton.

Michael and Kristina.

The children, grandchildren and great-grandchildren of Clemen and Martha S. Mekens are as follows:

Son John married first Jana Heller and second Kathy Chamberlain. The children of his first marriage were Deborah who married Tim Gaunt, their children are Joshua and Jordan; Dean who married Michelle Johnson and whose daughter is Stephaine; and David.

Son Michael married Sue Cochran and their son was Scott (deceased), Michael married second to Melissa Gerber and their children are Amy and Chad.

Son Joel married first Karen Kunkel and second Barbara Fetters, his children are Angela and Brady.

Mary Suzanne Smekens married Gary Studabaker and their children are Brian and Nathan.

Jane Smekins married Gregory Waters and they have a daughter, Sara.

KENNEDY-WALKER

Jeremiah Kennedy came to the virgin forest of Chester Township, Wells County, in 1839 from his native Ireland. His son, John Kennedy, born March 1, 1836, married Lucinda Ann Harris, who was born October 24, 1845. Their children were: Francis, Nettie, Laura and Arthur. John Kennedy served in the Forty-seventh Indiana Infantry. His major action was at Champion's Hill and the siege of Vicksburg, Mississippi. He served three years without a wound or serious illness. He said it was because he was so short the bullets went over his head. John farmed eighty acres in Chester Township until his death on August 6, 1920. The farm had seven producing oil wells during the East Central Indiana oil boom.

Arthur Kennedy, born October 20, 1883, was a farmer and oil field worker. He married Margaret Walker, born October 30, 1883. Margaret was a graduate of the Keystone High School. Arthur completed his course of study at Keystone but did not graduate because he would not give the required speech. Margaret's father and mother were Calvin Walker, born in 1859, and Emily Jarrett, who was born in 1860.

Calvin's father, Alexander Walker, born in 1816, is reported to be the first white child born in Jackson Township, Wells County. Alexander's wife was Nancy West, who was born in 1815 in Kentucky. Arthur and Margaret's children are Ruth (deceased), Teresa Irene, Paul, Carl, Charles, John, and Kathleen.

KENNEDY FAMILY

Jeremiah Kennedy brought his family to the United States in 1839. After a short stop in Ohio, they came to Indiana. Two children were born to them: John (born March 1, 1836) and Winifred. Jeremiah bought eighty acres of land in Wells County in Chester Township.

John had helped his father on the farm but in September, 1861, he enlisted in the U.S. Army during the Civil War. At the end of the war, he returned and married Lucinda Harris McDorman.

They had four children: Frank, Laura, Nettie, and Arthur. Nettie and Laura never married.

Front Row: Helen, Cecile, Bonnie. Back Row: Leonard, Neldon, Glenn, Kenneth and Marguerite

Winifred married William Fitzpatrick and lived on a farm near Poneto. Winifred's daughter married Jack Moynihan of Bluffton, the grandfather of Senator Pat Moynihan who has been so active in government in Washington, D.C.

John's Frank married Mary May Lawry and went to housekeeping in a log cabin one-fourth mile north of what is not the Southern Wells School. Later they moved to a farm one-half mile south of the school. There he farmed and worked in the oil fields. In 1916, they bought and moved to a farm two miles west of Keystone. They were the parents of eight children: Cecile, Bonnie, Kenneth, Leonard, Glen, Neldon, and twins, Waldon and Weldon, who died in infancy.

Frank and Mary Kennedy with Sally (Leonard and Clara's daughter: Janet and Beverlyee

Cecile graduated from Keystone High School. She attended Muncie Normal College and taught school for one year. She and Gerald Nusbaumer were united in marriage in 1920. To this union was born four children: Marianna, Roderick, Janet, and Beverlyee. Gerald died in January, 1976.

Marianna married Ralph Wentz of Liberty Township, Wells County. They have one son, Dennis Guy. She now lives in Fort Pierce, Florida.

Roderick married Naomi Bloxsome and they live on a farm southeast of Keystone. They have two children, Barbara and Kay, five grandchildren, and one great-granddaughter.

Janet was married to Lewis Habig and has six children: Shirley, Kenneth, David, Mary, Penelope, and Jeffrey. She has thirteen grandchildren and lives south of Bluffton.

Beverlyee married William Mugg. They live in San Diego, California. They have two children, Mary and Patrick, and one grandchild.

Kenneth Kennedy married Marguerite Kocher. They have one son, Joe and two grandchildren. Joe lives in Fort Wayne and Marguerite lives on the farm one-half mile north of Five Points.

Leonard married Clara Lex. They have two daughters, Sally and Elizabeth. Clara has five grandchildren and lives in Harford City. Bonnie never married and died in 1989. She had worked for fifty years in the Henderson Clothing Store in Montpelier before retiring.

Glen married Helen Stallsmith and they have three daughters: Judy, Patti, Rose Marie and several grandchildren. They live in Alexandria, Indiana.

Neldon Kennedy spent two years in the Navy during World War II and worked at McIntosh Manufacturing in Berne until he retired. He lives on the home place, just over the bridge west of Keystone.

Arthur Kennedy, uncle of Cecile Nusbaumer, married Maggie Walker. They lived for several years in Chester Township, then moved to LaPorte, Indiana. They had seven children, most of whom live near LaPorte and Fort Wayne, except Irene Goodspeed, who still lives in Montpelier.

KEPHART

S. Bruce Kephart, M.D., moved with his family to Bluffton in July, 1951, to join eleven physicians and surgeons then on the staff of Caylor-Nickel Clinic. A board-certified specialist, he founded their Department of Obstetrics and Gynecology which he chaired during his thirty-eight and one-half years of practice in Bluffton until he retired on January 1, 1989.

Born August 21, 1917, in Reading, Pennsylvania, of German stock that had immigrated to the United States in the 1750's, Dr. Kephart was graduated from Bucknell University at Lewisburg, Pennsylvania in 1939, took his medical training at the Medical School of the University of Pennsylvania in the class of April, 1943, and entered active military service in Philadelphia in February, 1944. Serving with the 16th Armored Division in the ETO until victory in Europe, he then was enclave surgeon at the Nuremberg War Crimes Trials. He returned to the United States in August, 1946, and trained in his specialty of obstetrics and gynecology first at Chicago Lying-In Hospital and later at City Hospital of Akron, Ohio.

Mary Elizabeth "Betty" Eyler was born in Pittsburgh, Pennsylvania, on April 27, 1919, to German, English, and Scotch-Irish parents. She received the degree of A.B. in mathematics in 1940 from Bucknell University and on June 27, 1942, married Doctor Kephart in Philadelphia, where she was supervisor of the calculating division of Towers, Perrin, Forester and Crosby, Inc., a firm of pension consultants.

S. Bruce and Mary E. Kephart

The Kepharts built their present home at 910 Riverview Drive, moving in 1957 from the Kunkel farmhouse a half mile south of town on State Road 1. The four Kephart children are all graduates of Bluffton High School: 1966, Maryanne (Mrs. Patrick K. Michaels) now of Santa Rosa, California; 1967, John Eyler of San Ramon, California; 1969, Patricia, (Mrs. Rex L. Mahnensmith) of Providence, Rhode Island; 1970, James Eyler of Salem, Oregon, whose wife is the class valedictorian, Susan Rivar Kephart.

Doctor and Mrs. Kephart are active members of the Bluffton First United Methodist Church and of the North Indiana Annual Methodist Conference. Doctor Kephart is a trustee of the Indiana Area Foundation and Mrs. Kephart is a lay member of the Conference Board of Ordained Ministry. Doctor Kephart has served the local church in many capacities, including as chairman of the Board of Trustees. He has taught Sunday school for over thirty-five years. He now heads the United Methodist Men. Mrs. Kephart is a past president of the United Methodist Women and currently a member of their executive committee

Professionally, Dr. Kephart is a Fellow of the American Board of Obstetricians and Gynecologists, A Fellow of the American College of Surgeons, a Fellow of the International College of Surgeons. He was president of the Indiana Society of Obstetricians and Gynecologists in 1968, just before Mrs. Kephart became president of the Indiana State Medical Association Auxiliary in 1969. They are both past presidents of the organized medical societies in Wells County. Dr. Kephart is director emeritus of the Indiana Division of the American Cancer Society and twice served as president of the Wells County Unit.

Doctor Kephart is a past president of the Bluffton Rotary Club and served on the Anthony Wayne Boy Scout Council for many years. He is a member of Bluffton Chamber of Commerce, Bluffton Horizons, Mizpah Shrine, Scottish Rite of Fort Wayne, and Pennsylvania Masonic Lodge #227. The Kepharts are founding members of the Creative Arts Council. Mrs. Kephart was the only secretary of the Poplar Grove School Building Corporation 1957-1976. She is a member and past president of the Foltz Literary Club, the Bible Study Club; she is president of the Fort Wayne Chapter CX of P.E.O. for 1991-1992.

KEPLINGER FAMILY

The first record of a Keplinger family living in Indiana was of an Abraham Keplinger who came from Hagerstown, Maryland, and moved to Zanesville, Indiana, in 1854. He was married to Margaret Hoverstock, and they were parents of eleven children. He and his family worked diligently in the Zanesville United Brethren Church. Abraham served as Sunday school superintendent. They also worked hard clearing their farm to build a home. This, however, was a different Keplinger family than is now residing in Zanesville. James Wesley's father was Jacob, born in 1817, whose first wife was Catherine. They were parents of six children before she died in 1854. Wesley then married Anna Raiehart, who was the mother of three children, one of which was James Wesley. Also, from this large family came three soldiers who served in the Civil War.

In 1882, the James Wesley Keplinger family first became Hoosiers when he and his wife Mary E. Arbaugh, who were married in September of 1880, moved from Winfield, Ohio, to a small farm in Davies County, Indiana, near Epsom. Because of illness and deaths in the family, they were to return to Ohio for a period of time, but moved back in March, 1896 to Zanesville. He was employed with International Food Food Company and later

Farmer's Guide of Huntington. He also served as postmaster of Zanesville for 24 years, retiring in 1933.

To James and Mary were born four children. An infant son in 1882 who lived only a short while. A second son, Waldo Howard, born in 1885, who died in 1892 and a third son, Homer "Harry" Harrison, was born in 1888 and passed away in 1956. A daughter, Mila Mae was born in 1890 and passed away in 1984.

Mila married Leon Newhouse. Leon served in World War I, was a watchmaker, and worked at Homer Gettle Optical in Fort Wayne. They had no children but were devoted to caring for family members in their "golden years."

Homer "Harry" Keplinger married Amy May Brown of Lafayette Township in 1917. Amy was a school teacher in a one room school house. Harry was a painter, paper hanger and a very well known barber in Zanesville.

Harry and Amy were the parents of two daughters, Wilda Maxine, born in 1918, and Marceille Janell, born in 1929. Wilda operated her beauty shop on the opposite side of her father's barber shop. Wilda married Earl Kamm in 1944 and in 1948 moved to Albuquerque, New Mexico. They had no children and Wilda still resides in Albuquerque.

Marceille married Carl William Shelley of Bluffton in 1953 and resides in Fort Wayne where Bill is retired from teaching school after serving thirty-five years. They have four children and eight grandchildren. Twin girls, Karen and Kathy are the oldest. Karen and her husband Lee and their two children, Aaron and Christa reside in Denver, Colorado. Kathy lives in Tulsa, Oklahoma with her husband Kent and their five children: Dana, Darla, David, Devin and most recently Daren. Kevin is married to Jane, and they have no children yet. Karlene resides in Chicago with her husband Roc, and they have one child, Joseph.

In October of 1942, Harry Keplinger purchased the Albert Knight property in Zanesville. The Harry Keplinger family lived there until both daughters were married and Harry and Amy passed on. Kevin Keplinger Shelly is presently living in the "Knight" Keplinger house in Zanesville.

The Keplingers did not inherit monetary sums to make for luxurious living. They did, however, inherit the blessings of a devout Christian heritage with a strong faith which hopefully will be passed on to future generations.

ABRAHAM KEPLINGER FAMILY

Abraham Keplinger family-Great-great-great-grandfather of Marlene Platt Hoopingarner, John Adam and Margretha Keplinger are buried in Winfield, Ohio. They are my great-great-great-grandparents. They had a son named Joseph, who married Catherine Snyder in 1814. They spent the first of their married life near Hagerstown, Maryland, until 1830. In 1832, they moved to Tuscarawas County, Ohio, where they settled on a farm. Catherine was the daughter of Adam and Catherine Synder of Boonsborro, Washington County, Maryland. Her father was born in Germany.

Joseph and Catherine had twelve children, one of which was Abraham, my great-great-grandfather (died in 1888). He was born near Hagerstown on October 5, 1829. In 1832, his family came to Winfield, Tuscarawas County, Ohio. In 1850, he married Margaret Hoverstock (lived in Zanesville, Indiana in 1854)(died in 1915). Margaret was the sister of William Hoverstock (1816-1903) whose statue stands in the Zanesville Hoverstock Cemetery. His wife was Elizabeth.

Abraham helped in the United Brethren Church. He was superintendent of the Sabbath School for a number of years. On their farm in Zanesville, they had a raw sugar mill. To their marriage was born eleven children. They were, Laura Amanda, November 26, 1851; Cinderilla December 12, 1852; Martin Luther, May 30, 1855; Irene Adina July 27, 1857; Ida May, January 25, 1859; Jay Lincoln, October 12, 1860; Emma G., April 6, 1862; Ulysses W., October 28, 1865; Mary Catherine, September 12, 1867; Dayton Woodworth, May 7, 1869, and Charles Otto, September 15, 1871.

The member of the family that I am following is Irene Adina. She married David Franklin Jacobs on November 18, 1875 and had ten children. Frank and Irene were by great-grandparents. Their children were Willie born February 7, 1878 (died in infancy), Charles, March 10, 1878 (died September 14, 1886), Ora Lee, born August 4, 1882 (died February 11, 1961), Della May born July 20, 1885 (died November 4, 1962), Roy L., born December 23, 1889 (died in infancy), Gary Dee born April 8, 1890 (died February 9, 1975), Clarence John, born October 6, 1892 (died May 26, 1948) and Mary born August 11, 1898 (died in infancy).

Frank died in 1933 and Irene in 1939. The one daughter Della May was my grandmother. She married Charles Smith in 1904. Charles was a farmer who died in 1961 and Della died in 1962.

Della and Charles had two children. Vesta Marguerite was born February 22, 1905. She married Paul D. Parker in 1925. Merle Eugene was born to this marriage. The other daughter was Wilma Maxine born February 20, 1912. She married Arlo Platt who was a barber in Zanesville, Indiana for fifty-five years. Their first child was Carolyn Rose who died early in age. Halden Clair was born December 1, 1933. He married Carolyn Miller. To this marriage, two sons were born; Gregory married Suzanne Cox. They have two sons, Gregory and Cameron who live in Florida. Gary, the other son of Hal and Carolyn, married Cathy Wilson and they have Lyndsy and Matthew who live in Grabill, Indiana. The third child born to Arlo and Wilma was Marlene Louise March 15, 1936. She married Donald L. Hoopingarner in 1955. To this marriage, two daughters were born: Pamela Le who married Larry Boye and lives in Florida and Shari Lynne, living at home.

KINCAID

The Miles and Elizabeth Kincaid family moved from Cass County, Indiana, to Wells County on a farm near Uniondale in March 1937 along with six of their seven children. Miles was born September 21, 1889 in Lee County, Kentucky, and Elizabeth (Adams) Kincaid was born December 14, 1894, in Lee County, Kentucky. They were married April 16, 1912. Their oldest daughter, Gladys, born July 7, 1913, was married to William Hahn of Cass County and moved to Middletown, Ohio in 1932. The other six children were Russell, born February 11, 1918, Edward, born April 22, 1920, Ada, born November 3, 1922, Ruth, born December 8, 1924, Joyce, born September 30, 1929, and Larita, born February 27, 1932. Their daughter Gladys died from leakage of the heart October 31, 1941, at the age of twenty-eight, leaving two little girls and one boy. Miles and Elizabeth raised the two younger ones, Margie, born October 16, 1936, and Richard Hahn, born July 22, 1938. Their older sister, Carol, born February 4, 1934, remained in Ohio with her father.

In 1948 the Kincaid's purchased a farm in Chester Township near Mount Zion. While living there Elizabeth passed away July 14, 1959. In 1961, Miles married Ethel Morrison, widow of Alvie Morrison, and moved to Bluffton. Ethel was the mother of John Morrison, who lost his life in World War II, Ned Morrison, Lee Stanley Morrison, and Juanice Morrison Love.

1957 Kincaid Family
Front Row (L to R) Miles and Elizabeth Kincaid
Back Row (L to R) Russell, Edward, Ada, Ruth, Joyce, Larita

Our dad loved farming and always said he loved to turn the soil. He also enjoyed hunting. Mother loved quilting, working in the garden, and growing flowers, of which iris was one of her favorites. She also loved to raise chickens, ducks, and turkeys. She set chicken eggs and hatched them in an incubator. As a child I loved to look through the glass door of the incubator and watch the little chickens peck their way out of the shell into their new life.

Their two sons served in the Army during World War II in the European Theatre. Russell received the Purple Heart award from serving in the infantry.

Their son, Russell married Jean Baumgardner, Edward married Vyrena Weikel, Ada married William Herbst, Ruth married Brooks Heckley and after his death July 5, 1977, married James Dailey. Joyce married Johnnie Genth, and Larita married David Eckelbarger. Margie Hahn married Ted Johnson and Richard Hahn married Janice Guthrie. The Kincaids were blessed with many grandchildren before Miles passed away November 9, 1975.

KING

Basil was born August 23, 1922, to Ernest E. and Verda Duff King, in Wells County, Indiana. Jessie was born July 9, 1922, to Rufus E. and Mary Binegar Stauffer, in Adams County, Indiana. Basil and Jessie were married July 17, 1944 in Bluffton, Indiana, and are the parents of Mark A. King, born December 6, 1956, of Dayton, Ohio, and Joan Renee' Wentz, born May 24, 1958, of Garland, Texas. Basil and Jessie have two grandchildren, Amanda and Megan Wentz of Garland, Texas.

Our present house at 7012 S. SR 1, Bluffton, was built in 1857 by Henry S. King, Basil's great-grandfather, when his grandfather Amos S. King was one year old. In construction of the six-room two-story house, the corners are of one foot square hewed logs with one-fourth hewed out for the room corners. The rafters are part sawed and part hewed saplings. The interior is finished in walnut.

The King ancestors, John Christian King and

his wife Anne Catherine Baum King, came from Wittenberg, Germany, landing in America September 27, 1786. They first lived in Rockingham County, Virginia and later moved to Perry County, Ohio, in 1802 with part of the family later moving to Wells County, Indiana around 1830.

Basil worked for the U.S. Air Force at Wright-Patterson Air Force Base from 1941 through 1977 prior to returning to Wells County in 1978. Basil is a 1940 graduate of Petroleum High School and Jessie is a 1940 graduate of Hartford Township High School. The King's are members of Calvary Lutheran Church.

KING FAMILY

We trace our King roots from Wittenberg, Germany to America in 1786 and to Wells County in the 1850's and 1860's. From these German pioneers, a granddaughter, Lydia King Mowery, and three grandsons, David, Henry, and Adam migrated to Nottingham Township homesteads in the 1850's. Another grandson (and our great-great-grandfather), George W. King, with his wife, Catherine Grove King, and family came to settle in Harrison Township in November 1865. The primary occupation of nearly all of these ancestors was farming and livestock raising.

While serving as trustee of Harrison Township in the late 1880's, George W. and his family lived in the fine brick home he built in 1882. It is still in use today, and located at 3414 Hoosier Highway.

Everett K. and Kathleen L. Durham King

Our great-grandfather, Charles H. King (1870-1950) was the youngest of eight children of George W. and Catherine King. Charles married Abbie Booher and one son was born, Everett E. King (1899-1969). Abbie died in 1904 and Charley married Clara Bickel. Charley and Clara farmed one half mile west of Bluffton on State Road 124 for many years.

Everett E. King married Mabel E. Schwartz (1902-1976) and had three children, Ina Mae (1922-1977), Karl K. (born 1924), and Everett K. (born 1931). Although their first love was farming, Everett E. and Mabel both worked many years at and retired from General Electric Company in fort Wayne.

Ina Mae married Jason C. Dickerson. They had four daughters, Carolyn Kay, Darla, Karen, and Sherri. All four live in the Fort Wayne area.

Karl K. married Cleora J. Sliger and they have two sons. Barry and his wife, Rita, and their two children, Cherie Lynn and Shane, live in Bluffton on Sunset Drive. Kendis and his wife, Deloris and family, Jean, Nicholas, Matthew, and Elizabeth, live in Chester Township.

Everett K. and Kathleen Durham King live on West Cherry Street and have four children. Everett retired from the Magnavox Company in 1990. Their four children are Loronda K., Charles D., Kelli L., and Bruce D.

Loronda, formerly married to David Mahon, lives in Chester Township with her three children, Christopher R., Elizabeth A., and Cory D., Loronda is a registered nurse.

Charles D., a certified auto technician at Reimschisel Ford, is married to Tamara Kummer and lives with their daughter, Mallory R., on South Main Street.

Kellie L. lives in Fort Wayne with her husband, Michael Craighead, and they have five children: Adam, Aaron, James, Sheena, and Siarra.

Bruce D. married Cynthia Frederick, and with their son, Brent they live at 5914S-200E. Their residence on the road known as Ellingham Pike is located approximately eight hundred north of the birthplace of Everett E. King.

Tamara King, Cynthia King, Loronda Mahon, Rita King, and her daughter, Cherie Lynn, are all employed at Caylor-Nickel Medical Center.

GABRIEL H. KING AND BENJAMIN J. KING

Representing one of the first families established in the wilderness of Liberty Township in Wells County was Benjamin J. King. He was the son of Gabriel H. King, who was born in North Carolina, Stokes County, May 3, 1822, son of Johnson and Margaret (Stanley) King. About 1830, when he was eight years of age, his parents came westward and established a home in Delaware County, Indiana, securing land from the government. But the parents did not survive their removal to the West, and in the following year they both died within a month of one another. They left six children, Gabriel being the youngest.

Benjamin King

In the fall of 1837, when he was fifteen years old, Gabriel King and his older brother Johnson came to Wells County, where Johnson King entered eighty acres of land in Section 21 and 22 of Liberty Township. The Kings were the first family in the township, and theirs was the third cabin erected west of Liberty Center. At first they had no habitation at all, and their goods were unloaded from their wagons under an oak tree. Johnson King died in Wells County in 1843. Gabriel H. King bought eighty acres in Section 27 of Liberty Township. In 1857, he sold his farm and bought eighty acres of improved land in the same township. In 1865, he bought a tract of land upon which he erected a sawmill, and thereafter made farming and lumbering his joint occupation until 1879. Gabriel H. King moved to Liberty Center in 1879, where he conducted a store for a time, but in 1882 he turned this business over to his youngest son and then erected the first flouring mill at Liberty Center.

Gabriel King was prominent as a leader in the local Democratic Party and filled the offices of township clerk for seven years, magistrate for four years, county commissioner for three years, and township trustee for twelve years, besides other local offices. He was county commissioner of Wells County when the present court house was erected.

On February 25, 1841, Gabriel H. King married Susan Mendenhall, daughter of Benjamin and Margery Mendenhall. She was born in Miami County, Ohio, and came to Wells County in 1839. Mr. and Mrs. King had twelve children. The families these children married into were Foust, Bigbee, McNatt, Parmalee, Butterfield, Foreman and Haumesser.

Benjamin J. King was born August 27, 1848, grew up on his father's farm in Liberty Township, and after leaving the local schools, worked in farming and also with milling. He owned a good farm of eighty acres and had one of the best homes in that locality. On December 24, 1868, Mr. King married Jane McNatt, who was born in Guernsey County, Ohio, and came to Wells County in the fall of 1863. They had five children. One of these children, Anna King, and her husband, Arthur Thomas, are the ancestors of David Thomas, the founder of Wendy's. Other families that married into the Kings were Going, Mossburg and Boltin.

KIRKWOOD

The Kirkwoods can trace their name back to Scotland and Ireland, so we are known as Scotch-Irish. Our family migrated to the United States in 1797, settling in Pennsylvania.

My great-great-grandfather, William Kirkwood, was born in 1820 in Franklin County, Pennsylvania. He married Susannah Gehrett and in 1850 moved to Wells County and purchased 240 acres northeast of Petroleum. It took a day to make a round trip to Bluffton because of poor roads. He served four terms as county commissioner and two terms as township trustee.

My great-grandfather, George Kirkwood, was the second child of William and Susannah Kirkwood and owned one hundred twenty acres just north of Petroleum, Indiana. He married Mary Warner in 1868, and she died in 1878 leaving five little children. At her death, the children were placed in various homes. My grandfather, Franklin Kirkwood, was born in 1869 and he went to live with his grandparents, William and Susannah Kirkwood.

December 1989
L to R: Kent, Tod, Chad, and Linda Kirkwood

My grandfather, Franklin Kirkwood, married Mary Ellen Bouse in 1891. My grandfather was a farmer and a drill bit sharpener in the oil fields of Nottingham Township. He purchased forty acres southeast of Petroleum, where the family lived until 1911. He then purchased one hundred acres one miles south and three-fourths mile west of Petroleum. This farm had ten oil wells operating on it. He passed away in 1925.

My father, Dale Kirkwood, was born in 1911 and was only four months old when his family moved to this farm. He was thirteen years old when his father died, so many responsibilities were cast on him at an early age. In 1944 he married my mother, Genivee Frantz. My grandmother then moved to Petroleum and my parents started life together on the home place. At grandmother's death in 1951, they purchased the farm from the two other heirs and they farmed for many years. My father also worked as a fieldman for the ASCS Office and ten years for the State Highway Department and retired when he was sixty-five years old. My mother worked for the ASCS Office in Bluffton for twenty-five years and retired in 1979. My father died in 1984 and two years later my mother moved to Bluffton.

My sister, Karol Kirkwood, and I, Kent Kirkwood, are twins and were born on July 5, 1950. We both graduated from Southern Wells School in 1968. We also took further schooling in Fort Wayne. My sister married James Scott on October 4, 1970, and they live in Berne, Indiana. They have a son, Mark, fifteen years old and a daughter, Joyce, eleven years old.

I have worked at Franklin Electric twenty-one years and also farm forty acres. On July 6, 1974, I married Linda Johnson. We have two sons, Chad, fourteen years old, and Tod, eleven years old, who attend Southern Wells School. We live in Chester Township, one and one-half miles south and one mile west of Southern Wells School.

KIRTLEY FAMILY

After living in Huntington County for six years, John Willie and Irene Oda Kirtley moved their family to a farm in the Markle area of Wells County in 1929. The following year, they moved to the Birkett farm two and one-fourth miles north of Liberty Center on Road 303. Their children, Charlie, Annie, John, and Edward, all attended the Liberty Center School. The family attended the Baptist Church there.

Their oldest child, Charlie, married Leila Shafer and they were the parents of two children. Janet (Kirtley) and Jack McCallister live in Lebanon, Missouri. They have two children, Nancy, at home, and mark of Colorado. Bill Kirtley married Peggy Hess of Columbia City, and now lives in Michigan with their two children, Roger and Amanda.

Annie (Kirtley) married Dale Gover of Liberty Center, now deceased, and they have two daughters. Barbara (Grover) (Mrs. Merrill) Armstrong of Stuart, Florida, has three children, David, Tammy, and Patrick, and six grandsons. Joyce (Grover) (Mrs. Ken) Clay, lives in Three Rivers, Michigan, and has three children, Kathy, Ross, and Rodd. Annie now resides in Three Rivers, Michigan.

John Kirtley married Flora Morris of Peru, Indiana, and they have two children. Kenneth lives in Crossville, Tennessee. He has three children, Bob, Lesa, and Jody, and one grandson, all living in the Bluffton area. Karol (Kirtley) is married to Lee Poyser and they have three children, Tanya (Mrs. Tony) Evard of Kendallville, Kirt Slater of Bluffton, and Kim Slater of Warren.

James Edward Kirtley, now deceased, was married to Eileen McCune, and they were the parents of one daughter, Linda. She has three children and lives in northern Indiana.

Both Mrs. and Mrs. Willie Kirtley are now deceased.

KNOFF

Upon completion of his dental training at Northwestern University and the University of Chicago, Dr. Raymond G. Knoff began his practice of dentistry in the small communities of Berne and Geneva. It was not long, however, until he and his family moved to Wells County and established themselves in Bluffton. Dr. Knoff joined another dentist, Doctor Lew Dailey, with their offices located on the second floor of the Studebaker Bank Building in February, 1919.

On July 1, 1927, Dr. Knoff leased a suite of rooms in the Caylor-Nickel Clinic and continued his practice there. His practice grew to such an extent that he employed a working staff including a newly graduated dentist, Doctor James McPheeters, and three dental assistants.

Doctor Knoff was a member of the First Methodist Church in Bluffton, a member of the official board and secretary of the quarterly conference of the church. He also served faithfully as a choir member and as secretary and superintendent of the Sunday school.

Dorothy Knoff Rose and Ruthanna Knoff Pearson

Fraternally, he was a member of the Knights of Pythias lodge and the Kiwanis organization. Having enjoyed the observance of the many sports in the area and having once been an active tennis enthusiast, Doctor Knoff particularly enjoyed his association and membership on the City of Bluffton's Park Board.

Doctor Knoff was a member of the state board of dental examiners, a member of Isaac Knapp Dental Association, the Northern Indiana Dental Association, the Chicago Dental Association and of the Indiana Dental Association. he also was actively interested in the Students' Free Examination Program and received a presidential certificate of appreciation for having served as the examining dentist for the Wells County Local Board No. 1.

Raymond Gladstone Knoff was born October 9, 1886, in Pemberville, Wood County, Ohio, where his father Harrison Knoff (1839-1903) was principal of the school system. The family later moved to Decatur, Indiana, where Raymond graduated from high school. His mother was Eliza Jane Mann (Welty) born in Decatur (1847-1933), daughter of Justin and Rachel Ball (Reynolds) Mann. The Mann family descended from William (1830-1808) and Lydia Fleming Mann of Palmer, Massachusetts. Rachel Ball Mann was the granddaughter of James Ball (1751-1834) whose name was placed on the Revolutionary War Soldiers Memorial in Decatur.

Harrison Benton Knoff married Eliza Jane Mann August 13, 1868, in Decatur, Indiana. He was born in Coshocton County, Ohio to John (1810-1881) and Mary Reed Knoff. The Knoff family line has been proven to Sussex County, New Jersey to Frederick County, Maryland. Two brothers, John and Philip Knoff sailed from Rotterdam to America in 1743. The family originated in Norway through Silesia in the Holy Roman Empire.

Doctor Knoff, who practiced his dental profession until his death May 13, 1944, married Lulu Grace DeWeese (1889-1979) May 24, 1909, in Hammond, Indiana. Their children are Naomi Knoff Lewis (1910-1976) (Robert), Ruthanna Knoff Pearson (William Howard) and Dorothy Knoff Rose (Max O. 1921-1988).

KNOX FAMILY

We trace this family to 1840 when Great-grandpa John Knox migrated to the United States from Scotland and Great-grandma Harriet Knox came over from Holland. They worked their way across the country and settled in California, where Great-grandpa Knox died in 1940 at age ninety-five. Along the way they had five children, one girl and four boys.

Grandpa John Franklin Knox was one of the four boys and was born in Iowa in 1871. He married Anna Carrie Johnson who was born in 1873 in South Dakota. Her parents had migrated to the United States from Norway. They had six children: Ethel, Clarence, Hazel, Floyd, Williard and Harold.

Grandpa Knox worked all over the heartland while they were raising their family. He worked on farms in Kansas and Iowa. Then he worked in the oil wells in the Oklahoma territory. That's where our dad (Floyd, the fourth child) was born in a sod hut, dug out of a hill. The family then went to the Dakota territory where they lived in a log cabin and had to go outdoors and climb a ladder to get to the attic to sleep, which was terribly cold in the winter.

It was during these hard years that they lost two of their children. They then moved to Illinois, where the daughter Hazel married Willie Roberts and settled in Pontiac, Illinois. Grandpa Knox then moved his family to Indiana and settled on the Crow farm east of Vera Cruz in Adams County. Later they moved to a farm outside of Warren and then on to Bluffton where he retired from farming. He then took care of the concession stand at Washington Park and later the concession stand at the Psi Ota Pool.

The Knox Family
Seated, Mildred and Floyd. Standing, Hazel, Evelyn, Francis and Horace

Williard Knox, deceased, married Golda Flowers from Wells County and had two children: Viola and William. Williard was a preacher and lived several places but later came back to Wells County to live. Viola married and had three children. William married and had five children. Viola settled in Anderson, Indiana and William in California.

Harold Knox, deceased, married Helen Ruth Faulkner in Wells County and has lived here since. They have one son, Donald Wayne who married Patricia Cass. They have four children and settled in California.

Floyd Knox, deceased, married Mildred Dessie Gifford, deceased, daughter of Mr. and Mrs. Thomas Gifford, from Wells County on February 27, 1922. He helped build the State Park and later was in construction. They had four children: Hazel, (deceased), Horrace (Bud), Evelyn and Francis (Tom).

The oldest, Hazel, deceased, married Roy Stebing, deceased, and had three children: Larry (deceased), Diana and Becky. They lived in Fort Wayne. After divorcing Mr. Stebing, Hazel came back to live in Wells County.

Horrace (Bud), now retired, married Betty Shipley from Wells County. They had two children: Karen and Kevin. Karen lives in the Kingsland area with her two children: Misty and Mark Harris. Kevin lives in Bluffton and has two children: Mathew and Ryan Knox. Kevin Knox's boys are the only Knox boys left to carry on this Knox family name according to our research. Evelyn, the third child, married Vernon Brown who also was from Wells County, they had one son Ted, who married Diana Miller. They have two children: Michelle and Christopher. Michelle married Tony Mills and they have a new baby, Karrissa, which makes Evelyn and Vernon Brown great-grandparents. All of the Brown family lives in Wells County.

The youngest, Francis (Tom) married Deloris and they live in Lafayette, Indiana.

KOONS FAMILY

The Koons family moved to the Fort Wayne area in 1853 and started a saw mill business in Waynedale, sawing planks for the plank road that ran from Fort Wayne to Bluffton.

Philip, the sixth child of seven, started a saw mill in West Ossian in 1872. He then operated a livery stable and tie barn next to the interurban station. He married Elizabeth Jane Porter in 1868. They had five children, Edith (1869-1921), Sarah (1871-1955), Delbert (1874-1946), James (1878-1949), and George (1885-1958).

George Guy Koons spent his entire life in Ossian. He was active in sports and played center on the first high school basketball team in Ossian. After high school, he decided to follow his brothers Delbert and James into railroading, and enrolled in the Charles Carpenter Telegraph School located in Ossian. His railroad career started with the Chicago and Erie Railroad. He then transferred to the Lake Erie and Western Railroad, now the Norfolk and Southern.

Guy married Edna Hanna Swaim (1888-1982) in May of 1909. Guy bought a grocery store and was station and freight agent for the Interurban Railroad from 1910 to 1920. He delivered Standard Oil products for the next two years, then decided to resume his railroad career and became station agent in Yoder for the Nickel Plate Railroad. Around 1940 he became station agent in Ossian, where he worked until his death in 1958.

Guy and Edna had five children, Claude (1910), Ralph (1913-1915), Elizabeth (1916-1947), George (1917), and Barbara (1925).

Claude Swaim Koons followed his father into the railroading business and worked for the Erie Railroad as a station agent and tower operator for forty-five years. Claude married Erma Regine Dowty (1915) in 1933. Claude and Regine had two children, Kent D. (1935) and Lynne Claudette Colvin (1941). They have three grandchildren, Gregory Koons, Jill Koons, and Linda Koons.

Elizabeth Jane Koons married Harold Henry Johns (1912-1966) in 1938. They had one child, Kay Francis Hardie (1938). Harold and Jane ran a Five and Dime Store in Webberville, Michigan. There are three grandchildren, William Hardie, Lori Hardie, and Alison Hardie.

George Franklin Koons served in the army during World War II. After the war he became a watch maker and owned a jewelry store in Monteplier, Indiana. In 1945, he married Geraldine Leonora Mow. They have four children, Kathleen Annette Zentz (1947), George Allan (1949), Nancy Lou (1952), and Thomas Wayne (1954). They have four grandchildren, Roger Zentz, April Koons, Alison Koons, and Jared Koons.

Barbara Lou Koons married Norman Fremont Young in 1947. Norman served in the Navy during World War II. He worked for Field Crest Textile Mills as a chemist and plant manager in Eden, North Carolina. They have two sons, Norman Fremont Jr. and Douglas Koons.

KOONS

George Koons, the earliest of our ancestors to come to the United States, was born in 1803 in Buehl, Alsace, France (now Germany). He arrived in Philadelphia in 1830, accompanied by his wife, three children, and a brother and sister. They settled near Danville, Pennsylvania, where four more children were born. The family moved to Allen County, Indiana, in 1853, buying a farm along what is now Indiana State Road 1, opposite the northeast corner of the present Brookwood Golf Club near Baer Field. He was a teacher in the parochial school of Saint Mark's Lutheran Church in Pleasant Township, Allen County.

Philip Koons, the youngest son of George Koons, was born in 1837, near Danville, Pennsylvania. As a young man, he and his brothers operated a sawmill near the present site of Baer Field, with their mill output being used to build the roads in this part of Indiana. Philip married Elizabeth Jane Porter in 1868, in Wells County, and they lived northeast of Ossian, at the intersection of Wells County Roads 1050N and 500E, beside a sawmill he owned and operated with his brother, John. In 1872, they moved to Ossian, where Philip bought and ran a sawmill and a lumber business called Koons and Company. They were the parents of five children, Edith, Sarah, Delbert, James, and Guy.

George Guy Koons, was born on May 10, 1885 in Ossian, and he graduated from the high school there in 1903. He finished the telegraphy school in Ossian, before beginning work as an agent for the railroad in Mays, Indiana. On May 6, 1909, he married Edna Hannah Swaim, the daughter of James Polk Swaim and Celinda Alice Burnett, in a ceremony held in her home in Ossian. In 1910, he left the railroad, and they returned to Ossian, where they purchased a home, and the grocery store-interurban station next door. In 1923, he joined the Nickel Plate Railroad as station agent in Yoder, Indiana, and in 1940 he became the station agent of the depot in Ossian. Guy and Edna Koons were the parents of five children: Claude, Ralph, Jayne, George, and Barbara.

Barbara Lou Koons was born December 6, 1925, in Ossian and attended the public schools there, graduating from high school in 1943. She worked for Lincoln National Life Insurance Company in Fort Wayne, until 1947, when she married Norman Young in the Methodist Church in Ossian. They lived in Crawfordsville, Indiana, and Charlottesville, Virginia, where she worked while he attended school. In 1953, they moved to Leaksville (now Eden), North Carolina, where they have continued to live. They are the parents of two sons, and are members of the Leaksville United Methodist Church. Barbara is a member of the Daughters of the American Revolution and the Order of the Eastern Star, and she is active in church and community affairs.

JOSEPH KREIGH

Joseph Kreigh, who came to Wells County in the late 1840's, was born on October 31, 1797, the first born of Elias and Anna Marie (Polly) Gibbons

The Koons Family in 1918
Front Row: Esther Gorrell, Claude, Phillip, Gretchen. Middle Row: Jane, Sarah (Gorrell), Phillip, Elizabeth, and Edith (Hatfield). Back Row: George, Edna, George Guy, Robert Hatfield, Elizabeth Gorrell, James, Frank Gorrell, Delbert, Helen Hatfield, and Zulema Hatfield

Kreigh as recorded in the Reformed and Lutheran church records of Schafferstown, Lebanon County, Pennsylvania.

Joseph married Eva Marie Kessler in 1824, and their son William was baptized in July, 1825. Samuel, Joseph Jr., Rebecca, Jacob and Cyrus were also born in Pennsylvania, and then the family moved to Stark County, Ohio, in 1837, where Henry, Abraham, George, and Sarah were born. In the late 1840's, they moved once again. This time they settled in Wells County where Isaac was born in 1849. Their children married and prospered in their new home.

SAMUEL KREIGH

Samuel Kreigh was born on October 16, 1826, to Joseph and Eva Kessler Kreigh in Schafferstown, Pennsylvania. He met the family of Mathias and Roseanna Hoelle Beck, while living in Ohio, and came with them to Wells Country. He was so impressed with their daughter, Magdalene, (who was born in Leidringen, Wertemburg, Germany, in 1833, shortly before the family emigrated to America) that he married her January 17, 1850. Their children were Martin, born and died 1850, Samuel, Roseanna, Eliza, Mary Ann, Rebecca, John, Sara Emma, Charles, and Mildred.

Magdalene died, and Samuel married Hattie Archbold in 1888, and moved to Michigan. The children were mostly married by that time: Sam, Jr. to Elizabeth Rupright, Roseanna to Theo Melching, Mary Ann to Nicbolas Shorts, Rebecca to Sam Paulison, Eliza to Isaac Green, John to Lillie Rupright and Sara to David White.

LILLIAN KRIDER

Lillian Charlene (Osborn) Krider was born either September 12 or 14, 1939, at the family home in Jefferson Township, the fifth child of John Howard and Leita Ardella (Smith) Osborn. The date of her birth has always been a matter of debate. Her birthdate was celebrated on September 12, until she obtained a copy of her birth certificate in 1957, and discovered her birth date had been recorded as September 14 by her father. Her mother maintained she was born on September 12.

Early memories of the farm where she was born, included a large family garden and apple orchard. The family gathered to butcher and render lard, make apple butter, and can garden produce to provide a year round food supply. The farm sold in 1944 to settle the paternal grandparent's estate. That prompted a move to Union Township to a farm owned by Leita's mother. Lillian went to Union Center School the following year and her life then centered around activities at school, home, and the Prospect Methodist Church. Accepting responsibility for family duties was expected, not assigned. As in any large family, being a productive family member required doing the laundry in the "wringer" washing machine, hanging clothes or beating rugs on the clothes line, helping in the garden, churning butter, chopping thistles in the farm fields, picking cherries, or picking milk weed pods for the war effort. The kitchen had a wood cook stove and as modern conveniences arrived in the rural area, a kerosene stove replaced it. The boys did farm chores and worked in the fields.

Although money was never plentiful, we were always ready for some fun: a bicycle ride, picking wild flowers and berries in the woods, or listening to the "Fat Man" or "The Shadow Knows" on the radio and eating a bowl of popcorn. We played "This Old House" on the crank victrola until Leita simply could not tolerate it. When the record came up missing, she told us the record was broken. On Saturday nights, we went to Ossian for the "free show" in front of Hunter's Supply House. We sat on blankets in the street and watched whatever movie was showing. Afterwards, an ice cream cone from the corner drug store soda fountain tasted good.

Lillian, a member of Prospect Methodist Church, held various offices in the Methodist Youth Fellowship, and attended Epworth Forest church camp. She was a member of 4-H for seven years, doing food preparation and sewing. She participated in the 4-H honor dress review and was Union Center's 1957 Betty Crocker Homemaker of Tomorrow. Lillian earned spending money trimming grass at the Prospect Cemetery, raising geese, babysitting, and caring for the sick, which helped prepare her for a career in nursing. She graduated valedictorian in 1957 and received the Wells County Medical Auxiliary's nursing scholarship. She worked at General Electric that summer and then entered Parkview Memorial Hospital School of Nursing. In 1960, following graduation, she worked at the Caylor Nickel Clinic, Bluffton. She married Robert Krider on February 15, 1961.

Robert, born November 30, 1936 to Florence Waneta (Sonner) Krider and Kenneth Scott Krider of Forth Wayne, traces his roots to Wells County. His maternal grandmother Sonner spent her early years in Union Township and is buried in Wells County. Lillian continued at the Clinic until November, when she joined her husband serving in the 101st Airborne Division of the U.S. Army at Fort Campbell, Kentucky. In March, 1962, after the military service, they moved from the apartment in Clarksville, Tennessee, to a rental house in New Haven, Indiana, and Robert returned to his job at International Harvester Company.

Lillian was a nurse at Parkview Memorial Hospital until the birth of Teresa Renee, born December 23, 1962. In 1963, she worked for the American Red Cross Regional Blood Center, Allen-Wells Chapter, and resigned as Assistant Chief Nurse prior to the birth of their son, Kenneth Scott, born August 22, 1967. Scott died March 1, 1977, as a result of chickenpox.

Teresa once asked Lillian if she grew up wearing long dresses and riding in covered wagons. No, but her great-grandparents may have! Teresa attended Fort Wayne community schools and graduated from Snider High School (1982) and nursing school at Purdue University in Fort Wayne (1986). In 1983, Teresa married William Purdy, born May 2, 1961, to J. Wilbur and Mary Katherine (Reust) Purdy, Fort Wayne. Teresa and William have three children: Justin David and Jason Christopher (twins) born June 18, 1983, and John William born August 3, 1987. Teresa is a registered nurse in the Maternal Infant Child Care Division at Parkview Memorial Hospital, Fort Wayne.

William served an apprenticeship in the printing business and works at Precision Litho Inc., Fort Wayne. Bill was the youngest of his family and had little experience with new babies. Before the twins were born, in conversation with a lady at the birthing classes, she mentioned baby cereal. Bill asked, "What kind do you feed them, Rice Krispies or Puffed Rice?" because his grandfather had eaten that after he lost all his teeth. Wow, did Bill have to learn fast. Grandma Lillian tailored stories for the twins and they loved it: "Two little Indians went out hunting dressed just alike, with a bow and arrow just alike, etc." It was 1965 when Robert and Lillian purchased the home in the Maplewood Park, Fort Wayne, where they currently reside. They are members of Faith Baptist Church, Trier road. Robert is retired from Navistar, formerly International Harvester Company. Lillian has been with Parkview since 1968, and is currently an Infection Control Practioner. She completed her B.S. in Nursing (1985) and received her certification in Infection Control (1987). In the thirty years that Lillian and her husband have been married, they have traveled to various points, but she says her heart always feels it belongs in Wells County. (Refer to Levi Osborn for previous ancestry.)

KRINN FAMILY

"Your mother and I were married where they feed the pigs on Uncle Burr's farm," George Ami Krinn liked to tell his children. George Married Jessie Armentha Fordyce on November 26, 1903, in the home of this aunt and uncle, his father's sister Mary Elizabeth (Krinn) and her husband, Burr Druckemiller in Wells County, Indiana. Later the section of the home where George and Jessie married was converted to a barn. George was the son of Daniel and Elizabeth (Sliger) Krinn, both Hocking County, Ohio, natives. Daniel, a Civil War veteran, his wife, and her parents moved to Indiana between 1870 and 1875, spending time in both Grant and Wells Counties. George's wife Jessie was not born a Fordyce, but was raised with the name since her mother, Martha (Saxon), married William Franklin Fordyce when Jessie was just a year and a half old. Jessie's biological father is unknown, but her mother's people lived in the Converse, Indiana, area, near the Grant-Miami County line, from the mid-1800's.

L to R: Donald Letis Krinn, Charlene Audrey Krinn, Berneil Marcina Krinn, William Richard Krinn

George and Jessie lived in Wells County most of their lives, although two of their children were born in the state of Kansas, where the family lived briefly on two separate occasions. Besides the Krinn-Druckemiller farm, they lived on the Wiecking farm east of Bluffton, the Popejoy, Weaver, Falk, and Buckner farms, and on Indiana State Road 1 near Ossian. George was a farmer most of the time, but in Kansas he worked in the salt mines. The children of George and Jessie Krinn were: Donald Letis, born September 16, 1904, and died May 7, 1987; Berneil Marcina, born April 11, 1906 and died in July, 1987; William Richard, born October 14, 1911; Charlene Audrey, born March 20, 1913; Maxine Ardella, born July 2, 1916; Orest Albert, born August 23, 1918 and died March 29, 1975; Marguerite Betty, born May 14, 1919 and Frances Jean, born November 20, 1926. Of these children, five are still living. William Richard and Iva Irene

(Schelling) Krinn, Charlene (Krinn) Bender, and Verline and Frances Jean (Krinn) Suter live in Fort Wayne, Indiana; Luster and Maxine Ardella (Krinn) Roush live near Montpelier, Indiana; and Samuel H. and Marguerite Betty (Krinn) Eichhorn live in Zanesville, Indiana. Their descendants are scattered across the United States, but many live in Wells County and Allen County.

George died on September 23, 1941, and following his death, Jessie moved to Fort Wayne to live near several of her children. She died on March 13, 1960. George and Jessie are buried in the Six-Mile Christian Church Cemetery east of Bluffton.

Krinn descendants gather each August for a family reunion, usually in Wells County. Although the Krinn Family Association began as a reunion of the progeny of Daniel and Ellen (Sliger) Krinn, it has grown to include descendants of all three German immigrant Krinns: Daniel's father, Gottlieb Friederick Krinn, and his brothers, Johan Georg and Johan Michal. All three settled in Ohio in the early to middle part of the nineteenth century.

KUMFER-SMUTS

Robert Wayne Kumfer was born to Victor L. and Mary Ellen (Confer) Kumfer. His grandparents were Charles and Elizabeth (Bushee) Kumfer and Warren and Ollie (Fisher) Confer. Charles Kumfer was one of fifteen children.

Robert lived with his parents and brother, Forrest E., on the farm. Although he was born in Adams County, he has lived all his life in Union Township, Wells County. On the farm they had a variety of animals including milk cows, sheep, hogs, chickens and rabbits. They sold eggs and rabbits to the Kreigh and Hoover Grocery, now called the City Market, in Ossian, Indiana.

One special day on the farm was butchering day, which was on New Years Day. The children would be home from school to help. Friends and family worked together to accomplish the task. An outside fire was build at 4:00 a.m. to heat the water in an iron kettle. Four to six hogs would be butchered. The hogs were killed, scalded, scraped and hung in the morning ready to be cut up in afternoon. Granddad Kumfer usually made the lard. Cubes of fat were cooked in a large kettle and squeezed in a press. During the following days, the women cooked down the sausage and either canned it in glass jars or put it in crocks with hot lard poured over it, it was stored in the cellar. Hams were salt and sugar cured and hung in a cold room upstairs. Sometimes Granddad smoked the hams.

Rosemary and Robert Kumfer

Robert married Rosemary Smuts (see Smuts). On their wedding day, a bad snow storm blew in. About one third of the invited guest attended. By the time the ceremony and reception were over, the snow was drifted very high. Some of the guests stayed overnight at their neighbors' homes and had to have their cars pulled from the snow the next day. The bride and groom were stranded in Fort Wayne for three days.

Rosemary's parents were Ruthford and Bertha (Vollmar) Smuts. Ruthford was a school teacher for forty-two years. Her grandparents were Ira and Etta (Farrell) Smuts and Jacob and Stella (Settlemeyre) Vollmar.

Bob is a farmer and retired factory worker, and was the Union Township Trustee for sixteen years. He served in the U.S. Army during the Korean War. Rosemary is the Zanesville, Indiana, Postmaster.

Robert and Rosemary have four children: Stephen Robert has an associate degree from ITT Technical Institute in electronics. Joyce Ann married Robert E. Jeffries and lives in Rochester. Kay Ellen married Garry L. White. Their children are Jason Lee and Danielle Rose. Garry is a graduate of Indiana Vocational Tech. School with an associate degree in Automotive Mechanics. They live east of Ossian, Indiana. Jonathan Charles was born and died in 1964. Bob and Rosemary live on their own farm where they built a new house, southeast of Zanesville, Indiana. They are members of the Church of God, Zanesville.

KUMMER FAMILY

At the age of sixteen a young man by the name of Samuel Kummer Sr. packed his few possessions in a homemade chest, which a great-grandson still possesses, and came to the United States from Switerzland. He ended up in Ohio where he eventually married a girl by the name of Mary Woblett. They later moved to a farm near Poneto in Wells County. To this union were born four children: Edward, Samuel Jr., Clara, and Emma. At the age of eighty-five, after his wife passed away, while living alone, Samuel Sr. was believed to have been murdered at his home. His home was in a turmoil with drawers emptied on the floor, furniture was upset and Mr. Kummer had a large bump on his head. After investigation by Sheriff McClain, it was decided that it was not a murder as seventeen dollars was found on the victim and the lump was caused by a fall.

Back (L to R) Samuel Kummer, Clarissa (Merritt) Kummer Front (L to R) Mary Ann Kummer, Bill Kummer

In 1907, our father Samuel Jr (1882-1946) married Clarissa Merritt, (1889-1938). To this union were born seventeen children. Two died at birth. Living children are Earl Kummer, Kenneth Kummer, Thelma (Kummer) Kaufman, Edna (Kummer) Tschannen, of Bluffton, Donald Kummer, Wayne Kummer, Maxine (Kummer) Foltz, Norma (Kummer) Collett, and Goldie (Kummer) Wagner, (1907-1978) of Muncie, James Kummer and Betty Kummer (1924-1986) of Fort Wayne, Lester Kummer (1913-1990) of Elkhart, William Kummer (1912-1980) of Montpelier, Robert Kummer of Iowa, and Mary (Kummer) Chenoworth of Texas.

During World War II, five brothers served their country in the service: William in the Army, Earl and Kenneth in the Air Force, and Donald and Robert in the Navy. All returned home safely in 1945. All served overseas but William, who was injured in a mine explosion in Oklahoma.

There are still four brothers and sisters living in Wells County. They are Kenneth, Earl, Thelma, and Edna. There are four grandchildren in Wells County, Richard Kummer, Susan Kummer, Jack Kaufman, and Janice Hiester.

There are five great-grandchildren living in Wells County, Tammy King, Shellie King, Kim Hartman, Jimmy Pursley, and Teresa Pursley.

There are three great-great-grandchildren in Wells County, Mallory King, Ashley King, and Nathaniel Hartman.

There are many grandchildren, great-grandchildren, and great-great-grandchildren of Sam and Clarissa living in many parts of the United States.

One grandson, Dewayne Kummer son of Kenneth Kummer was killed in the Navy in 1966. Terry Kummer, son of Earl Kummer also served in Vietnam War.

I am sure if Samuel and Clarissa Kummer were still living today, they would be very proud of their Heritage they left in Wells County.

We have one cousin Coelia Kummer, daughter of Edward and Pearl Kummer living in Bluffton. Another cousin Cleola Shoemaker died in 1984. *(Earl Kummer and Kenneth Kummer)*

KUNKEL

We can trace our family roots back to Prussia, Europe. In 1750 Johann Heinrich Kunkel was born in Germany Kingdom of Hesse. He immigrated to the United States and lived in York County, Pennsylvania. He married Elizabeth Christina Kleinfelter. Her parents were Michael and Appollonia, (an Indian). Elizabeth was born on February 18, 1763, and died March 28, 1815. Johann died in 1827. We have listed that seven children were born in York County, Pennsylvania to Johann and Elizabeth. They were Michael born on February 12, 1782, Henry II born in 1785 and died in 1841, Elizabeth born in 1788, Barbara born in 1791, Rebecca, born in 1794, Eva born in 1796, and Christina born in 1799.

Following Michael's family line, we found that he married twice. His first marriage was to Elozabeth Myers. They had one son named Henry, born on February 2, 1814. Mrs Kunkel died in 1815. His second wife was Catherine Sentz. Their children are Mary, Lydia, Nancy, Polly Diana, Michael Jr. (September 1816-May 7, 1886, Eloza, Samual Daugherty, Matilda, and Rebecca. Michael Sr. died around 1846 in Richland County, Ohio. The wife of Michael Jr. (Julia Mason) died in 1847 in Crawford County.

In 1855, Cathrine moved with several children to Wells County, Indiana. Samual D. settled in Adams County. Rebecca moved to Wells County and married John Wasson on June 29, 1859. Michael Jr., also settled in Adams County but moved two years later to Bluffton to give his children the advantages of higher education. Michael Jr. and Julia had four children Sophia (1840-1879), Samual (1843-1935), Louisa who died in 1854, and Calvin (1846-1922). Samual; who married Elizabeth Blue, was distinguished along with his brother-in-law, Michael Blue, founder and originator of the town of Tocsin. Their mother, Catherine, died on June 13, 1870 and is buried at the Murray Cemetery in Wells County.

Michael's second marriage was to Mary Ann Kleinknight (December 3, 1827-February 27, 1913). Their children are Martha Ann who died in infancy, Dora A. who died at three years, John Oliver, Theodora Horton who later married Frances Keller, Lydia Matilda (1854-1929) and married Thomas Souders in 1872, Rebecca A. born in 1857 and married Henry Masterson, and William Albert (January 31, 1868-September 30, 1931).

JOHN OLIVER KUNKEL

The family line of John Oliver Kunkel born in Lancaster Township on December 23, 1852, continues the sketch turned in by Mrs. Norman (Betty) Kunkel. John Married Melissa M. Blue (January 16, 1854-March 8, 1921) a sister to Elizabeth (Blue) Kunkel, on November 11, 1876. They had six children who are Fred Alden (August 25, 1877-January 6, 1959), Mary Ann (June 23, 1880-July 28, 1956, Reuben Blue (October 10, 1882-February 2, 1952), Elzy Orne (June 16, 1887-?), Eva Dee O. (June 23, 1894-?), Claudine Myrean (March 13, 1898-?). John farmed the old homestead two years then engaged in the general merchandise business at Tocsin for nine years. He resumed farming in Lancaster Township before selling and moving to Chester Township.

The spouses of their children were as follows: Fred Alden married Nettie Mock in May, 1910, Mary Ann married Arthur Earl French on August 29, 1908, Reuben Blue married Blanche Olive Wolf on January 20, 1917, Elzy Orne married Grace Van Ella May, Eva Dee O. married Ralph Morford, and Claudine M. married Brooks E. Souders.

Reuben's wife Blanche (November 12, 1882-January 12, 1952) was the daughter of Isaac C. and Zelda V. (Essex). They lived south of Poneto in Chester Township. Their children graduated from Chester except for the youngest who graduated from Lancaster. Their children were Faith, stillborn June 18, 1918, Norman Wolf (June 5, 1919-December 14, 1981), John Isaac (January 14, 1921-May 14, 1982), Arden Gale (January 2, 1923-May 13, 1990), Avis Joan (born February 25, 1924), and Luster Ray (March 21, 1919-August 1, 1968).

Norman married Betty Marcille Eichhorn from Lancaster Township on July 5, 1947. Their children are Pamula Sue (born July 13, 1948), married and had two sons Troy Eugene Wilkin, born March 16, 1968).

Norman married Betty Marcille Eichhorn from Lancaster Township on July 5, 1947. Their children are Pamula Sue (born July 13, 1948), married and had two sons Troy Eugene Wilkin, born March 16, 1968, an Trent Allen Wilkin, born June 28, 1969. Trent is married to Nicole Tally and they have a son, Shane Michael, born January 29, 1990. Pam lives in Melbourne, Florida. Stephen Wayne, born July 2, 1951, married Cris Dorothy Sammons. They have four children: Jason Wayne born November 1, 1973, Kimberli Ann born June 26, 1975, Kellie Sue born December 3, 1977, and Jodi Lynn born August 17, 1981. Stanley Alan born on January 8, 1954, married Debra Ann Lockwood. Their children are Brent Michael, born July 11, 1983, and Chelsea Lynn born November 21, 1986. Timothy Dale, born October 21, 1955 married Jane Ann Hunterman. Their children are Jarrod Andrew born March 1, 1984, Sarah Ann, born February 8, 1986 and Jennifer Erin born November 8, 1989. All three boys live in Lancaster Township within a mile from where they grew up. Norman and Betty's youngest child was Patsy Ann (June 10, 1959-June 17, 1966) who died of leukemia. Norman helped manage the Bluffton Bowling Center, drove bus for the Northern Wells School Corporation, and farmed. Sons, Steve and Stan, are now active in the Bowling Center. Son, Tim, is farming the family farm on 300 North in Lancaster Township.

KYLANDER-KILANDER

Philip Cuylinger, who died in New Jersey in 1768 is the earliest known ancestor of the Kilander family in America. He was probably an emigrant for Sweden, as the Kilander family originated there. Papers of his estate list the name as Cuylinger, Caylinger, Cilliner, Kilinger and Killonger. Philip Kilinger is listed as beneficiary. In 1833, a Revolutionary War Pension application was filed by Phillip Kilander in Kentucky. Facts in the application coincide exactly with the records in New Jersey, so we can safely say that he was the son of Philip Cuylinger.

Phillip's children were Isaac, Abraham, Jacob, Sarah, Mathew, Ester and Phillip Jr. Jacob, a veteran of the War of 1812, and Phillip Jr. came to Wells County from Brown County, Ohio, in 1851. Jacob eventually owned 360 acres in Jackson Township, two hundred forty acres of which were on the north side of what later became Dillman.

Gravestone of Jacob Kylander, the first Kilander to come to Wells County

Jacob's children were David, Dillman, Sarah, Melvina, Perry and Calvin. Perry and Calvin also came to Wells County from Ohio. Perry purchased one hundred sixty acres in Jackson Township in 1854, and later owned three hundred twenty acres from which he gave the timber to build the Dillman Church. Perry and wife Sarah had twelve children. They were Polly, Sarah, Maria, Calvin, William, Mautrice, Olive, Robert, Geanettie, Jacob, Emma and John. Olive married Phanuel McIntire who was a commissioner when the courthouse was built, and they later lived where the Fryback's now live in Villa North. Robert built the "Kilander Brick House" in Jackson Township.

Another son, Jacob Marion and wife Eliza, were the parents of Jesse, Guy, Cary, Ruby and Lloyd. Guy was a veteran of World War I. He and wife Delpha were the parents of Wilma, Leon and Loren.

Leon and wife Mary are the parents of Leon, Jr., Deborah and Robert. They own one hundred sixty acres in Jackson Township, forty acres of which were in the original purchase of Perry.

Leon and Mary's farm was the first in Wells County to receive the Hoosier Homestead Award and was recognized in an article in the News-Banner of July 3, 1976 which was included in the time capsule in the corner stone of the courthouse.

Leon Sr. and Mary are retired. Leon Jr. and wife, Louella, live on an adjoining farm and have children David and Lisa. Deborah lives in Portland and teaches at East Jay Junior High. Robert is at home, farming the homeplace. Thus, David is the seventh generation, father to son, who has lived on this farm.

Although a biography in the library stated that Jacob came to Wells County with his son Perry, and stayed until death, no one now living knew where he was buried. In the fall of 1989, Leon Sr. and his cousin Ellen Huffman of Bluffton found the graves of Jacob and Polly Kylander and Phillip and Ellen Kilander in the Balsley Cemetery in the edge of Blackford County, less that three miles from Leon's home. Shortly thereafter they received much of the information about the early family from a newly found cousin in Tennessee. They now know that they have several relatives in southern Indiana and other states with variant spellings of the name. A "Gathering" is planned for June 28-29, 1991 in the Brown County State Park.

LADD-BRYANT

William and Olive Isabelle (Ladd) Bryant moved to Jefferson Township in Wells County to a farm two and one-half miles north and two miles east of Ossian in 1912, from Swayzee, Indiana, in Grant County.

William's parents were Edmond and Esther (Downing) Bryant. They were from Moreland, Indiana. William was born December 20, 1857, and died February 22, 1913. Olive was born July 6, 1863, and died October 1947.

Olive's parents were Mary (Powell) Ladd and Boyd Ladd. The ancestry of the Powell family goes back to Hay, Wales, where they worked in the woolen mills. They came to America in 1808 and settled in Virginia. From there the family slowly moved westward to Ohio and then to Indiana.

Olive Isabelle Bryant about 1924

Olive was the oldest of nine children and had the usual experiences of pioneer times including going to a log school and using the old McGuffey readers.

She finished her schooling at Marion Normal School and was engaged in teaching until her marriage to William Bryant in October, 1881. They lived on a farm near Swayzee, Indiana, until moving to the farm in Wells County.

William only lived about six months after they moved to Wells County. He died of pneumonia after working with his son, Ozro Bryant, who had purchased a farm on the Wells County-Allen County line. They had been clearing some land in the cold of February when he became ill.

433

Olive and William had eight children, and there were two teenage daughters to raise when William died.

Olive stayed on the farm for about three years and rented out the fields. She then sold it and purchased a home in Ossian. She struggled to make a living by selling Avon products house to house. At that time Avon was a fairly new company, manufacturing household and cosmetic products. She was so successful at selling that as soon as her girls were raised she was made a district sales manager. She traveled to most small towns in Illinois, Indiana, and Ohio, appointing sales ladies to sell Avon in their town. They had to buy a sample kit for $5.00 and then they were in business.

Olive was fifty-eight years old when she started traveling and she could not drive a car, so she rode on trains and busses and did lots of walking before she arrived at a town.

Olive could only returned to her family about two or three times a year, When she did, she had many interesting stories to tell of her travels. One story passed down was that when she could not get to one small town cross the Ohio River, she hired a man to row her across in a row boat. When they got to the middle of the river she became frightened and asked him if he could swim. He said no, and she told him she couldn't swim either. They made it safely after all.

She traveled well into her seventies and bought and paid for two homes in Ossian. One reason she was so successful at selling was her love of people and here interest in their lives. She worked all through the Depression, and if a lady wanted a kit to sell Avon but did not have the $5.00, she would trade anything she felt was of the same value. It might have been a quilt, fancy work, or jewelry. Many of these things she sent home to her family. Then she would sent the $5.00 out of her own money to the company. She was required to get a lady to sell before she could move on to the next town.

It was obvious that Olive was a liberated woman before Women's Lib became popular.

The farm where she lived and the house she bought are still being lived in at this time. Her grandson, Vernon Bryant lives on his farm near the place where her farm was located, and her great-grandson Ross Bryant also lives and owns a farm nearby.

LAMBERT-LUDE

Ted (1942) and Melanie (Lude) Lambert, born in 1944 in Wells County, both of Fort Wayne, were married in 1962. They had three children: Dawn (1963), Bryant (1966), and Tresa (1967).

They spent their first year living in a small bungalow in Fort Wayne. After Dawn was born they moved to the country where they could raise a garden and animals. The next year, they moved to a small farmstead near Ted's parents. Bryant and Tresa were born. The family lived there until 1975. The children helped with large gardens as well as a few hogs each year. Pumpkins were raised for Halloween. One 240-pound pumpkin, which was larger than all three children, was the focal point for Wayne Rothgeb's morning farm show and also at Lafayette Central School which the children attended.

On the way to the Wolf Family reunion at the 4-H Park, the family looked at some land, a portion of the Decker farm on Road 350N, which they ultimately purchased. Many hours were spent camping and fishing. Wildlife packets and thousands of pine trees were planted there.

In 1974, a home was started and the family moved in February 1975. The children attended Lancaster School.

Dawn graduated from Norwell in 1981. In December, 1981, she married Jack Gideon (1957) of Fort Wayne, where they now live. Their daughter, Jazmyn Nicole, was born on April 27, 1991.

International Harvester, where Ted worked, closed its Fort Wayne factory in July, 1983.

Bryant graduated from Norwell in 1984. Shortly after, the family moved to Urbana, Ohio, where Ted resumed work with International Harvester (Navistar) at Springfield.

Bryant attended Clark College at Springfield. He married Shelly Randall (1965) of Urbana in October, 1985. They have three sons, Steven (1982), Blake (1986), and Dylan (1990), and reside near Urbana.

Tresa graduated from Graham High in Saint Paris, Ohio in 1985. She married R. Scott James (1967) of Lena, Ohio and they reside in Saint Paris.

Ted and Melanie plan to return to Wells County after retirement.

Melanie's grandparents were Dewitt and Esther (Arnold) Wolf. They were farmers and owned a dairy farm on River Road. Both are buried at Elm Grove Cemetery. Robert and Aldine (Gerber) Lude are both buried at Greenlawn Cemetery in Fort Wayne. They farmed in Craigville and later lived in Fort Wayne.

Melanie's parents are John and Maxine (Wolf) Lude. After living at Craigville, then Fort Wayne, the Ludes have retired in Columbia City. Maxine is an accomplished seamstress and has created many quilts for her grandchildren. John is an expert wood craftsman.

Ted's grandparents are Howard and Merle (William), buried in Huntington County. They farmed Howard's parents farm all their married life. Also Ira (deceased) and Delsie Lambert. Delsie (1896) resides at Miller's Merry Manor in Huntington.

Ted's parents are Lester and Betty (Branstrator) Lambert. Betty is buried at Prairie Grove Cemetery at Fort Wayne, and Lester is a retired farmer living in Fort Wayne.

DANIEL C. LANTZ

In August, 1980, Dan and Gladys Lantz decided to retire from their farm in Adams County and take up residence in Bluffton. They purchased a home at 1003 Stogdill Road.

Daniel was a son of Gideon and Elizabeth (Reinhard) Lantz. They moved to Craigville from Leo, Indiana, when Dan was a child. He attended school at Craigville. In September 1938, he married Gladys Bertsch, and for the next forty-two years they were farmers in Adams County.

Since returning to Wells County, Dan has worked as a Federal crop adjuster for about three years and helps farm during planting and harvesting seasons. He also gives of his time as a volunteer at the Commodity Give Away. He enjoys his retirement, doing small repair jobs for relatives and friends, and visiting shut-ins.

Gladys was a daughter of Samuel and Rose (Minger) Bertsch. When she was a child her family was busy running the Bertsch Gas Station on State Road 124, about five miles east of Bluffton, and farming. In time she married the "boy around the corner," Dan Lantz. She spent the coming years helping milk cows, farming, doing household duties, and raising a family. She also worked as a volunteer at a Swiss Village in Berne for twenty years.

*Dan and Gladys Lantz
50th anniversary*

They have five children living in Wells County. Steve is at home with his parents. Daniel Jr. is married to Charlene Harrison, and they are the parents of Amy and Jason. Mary is a nurse and works in Fort Wayne. John is married to Sue Heyerly, and they are the parents of Shawna and Shelby. Rose is married to Ted Pfister and they have one daughter, Leonda, and four sons, Chris, Dan, Courtney, and Matthew. Jim lives on the home farm with his wife, Kathy Myers, and their children, Chad and Cybil.

Gladys keeps busy spreading cheer to her neighbors with visits and homemade goodies, and enjoys working with the World Relief sewing group. Dan and Gladys are very popular with their ten great-grandchildren, and spend many hours tending their thriving garden in the summer. They are members of the Apostolic Christian Church.

LAUTZENHEISER-STARR

We can date the Starr Family back to 1846, when great-grandfather Engle and Catharine Starr lived in Bluffton. December 30, 1846 Engle was the fourth county agent directed to sell lots seventy feet by one hundred forty feet. They owned 328 East Market and the three houses to the east. One of their six children was Lewis, born November 17, 1861, died November 27, 1929. Lewis was Bill's grandfather. He married Mary (Bovine) and they had two children Ethel and Harry. Lewis and son, Harry, owned the Starr-Pop, ice cream and candy factory at 328 East Market. They cut blocks of ice from the river for the ice house. This is where the famous "Jersey Lillies" were made (this was a taffy). Harry born May 21, 1888 and died February 5, 1964, married Florence (Sprunger) Starr, born December 22, 1889, and died February 5, 1974. They had three sons Harold, Donald and William.

Her parents were Elias Sprunger and Susanna (Riesen) Sprunger of Berne. Florence continued to live at 328 East Market after Harry's death. Note: Florence and Harry died on the same date. Bill was born in Bluffton on June 25, 1921 and died July 11, 1987 at his home at 1005 Elm Drive. He worked for the Farnsworth Company until it closed. He was in the photography business, R.S.M. Color Lab, and also owned the Candle Shoppe. Bill married C. Maxine (Lautzenheiser) Starr, born November 29, 1921. We both were born, married, and graduated from Bluffton High School. We have one son, Gregory Starr, born, June 14, 1945, who is Program Manager, Electronic Systems for Magnavox. He married Rebecca (Terhune) Starr, born December

6, 1944, daughter of Ray and Leota Terhune of Petroleum. She is a registered nurse at the clinic. They have a son Douglas, a junior at Norwell High School. They have a daughter Diana (Starr) Hiday, who will graduate from Indian University May 1991. Her new job will be a consultant for the Summitt Group, Incorporation of Fort Wayne. Diana married Gregory Hiday, son of Nedra and Larry Hiday. Greg also graduated from Indiana University. He is now manager of the Hiday Chrysler-Plymouth-Dodge.

Bill and Maxine Starr 1984

My grandfather, Jesse Lautzenheiser, born in Ohio in 1864, died in 1955, married Mary E. (Cline) Lautzenheiser, daughter of William and Jenny (Bovine) Cline from Bluffton. My father, George Sr., born October 7, 1891 and died September 20, 1968, married A. Sadie (Niblick) Lautzenheiser who was born June 6, 1893 and died, July 10, 1973. They had ten children: Helen, Harold, Robert, Mary, Eileen, Maxine, William, George Jr., Rosie, and Jack. My father owned the Bluffton Foundry and Machine Company on West Washington. he also owned the Kaiser-Frazer dealership at the corner of Main and Wabash. He was a councilman under Mayor John H. Waid, 1943-1948.

My mother's family of Niblick's came from Ireland in 1801. her father was George W. Niblick, born September 15, 1860 and died October 18, 1949. He married Anna J. (Lowdermilk) Niblick from Warren. We have extensive history on both the Niblick's and Lowdermilk's.

LEAS

In a farmhouse in Jackson Township, Ralph and Ruey (Slusher) Leas took up residence in 1918. This house became their homestead and they began their family. Their family, at completion included: Lillian (Bradford), Gail, James Cletus, Donald, Robert, Lois Jane (Carpenter), and Jackie.

The oldest Leas child, Lillian, began school in 1926. She went to the Eversole School in Jackson Township. Since that year, there has always been a "Leas" in the Jackson or Southern Wells school system. In fact, it appears that the future of this school system is secure because the Leas have nearly one hundred direct descendents and that number is steadily growing.

Both Ralph and Ruey have passed away, but their legacy is carried on by their descendents. The farmhouse in Jackson Township still stands as a constant reminder of the beginnings of the "Leas" legacy.

LEE

William A. Lee, a resident of Wells County, was well-known in the area as a farmer, educator, lawyer and deputy prosecutor. He was born to Alexander and Susanna (Tracy) Lee in Nottingham Township on August 20, 1855, and settled in Wells County to get his education in district schools and attended County Normal at Bluffton. At age seventeen, he was granted his first license as a teacher and for a number of years, he also filled the office of justice of the peace. He was the Sunday school superintendent at the Methodist Episcopal Church of Poneto, where he was in charge for over sixteen years. He actively practiced law from 1898 until his death in 1907. He was wed to Emma R. McFarren, who was born in Wells County, the youngest sister of the prominent Bluffton businessman, George E. McFarren. The couple had three children: Karl, Grace and Ralph. Karl A. acquired a good education in common school and commercial college and became a farmer living in Lancaster Township of Wells County. He married Cecile Kiser. The couple did not have children, although they raised Ralph and James Kiser in their home. Grace S. was a teacher and married Levi J. Nutter and later lived in the Chicago, Illinois area. The couple had one daughter, Joyce. Ralph Cleveland married Margaret Grace Fleming and lived his entire life in Nottingham Township. The couple had four children: Nina Virginia, Keith Eugene, Rosemary Ann, and Roger Carroll Lee.

Nina married Everett Schooley and the couple has four children: Donald Lee of Goshen, Indiana who is married to the former Nancy Wheeler and they have two children; Gale Eugene of Michigan City is married to Madeiline Habig and they have six children; Judith Ann of Indianapolis, married to Wendell D. Foster and they have two children; Teresa Lynn of Bluffton is married to Mark Dustman and they have three sons.

Keith Eugene now resides on the former Karl A. Lee farm in Lancaster Township and is married to the former Ruth Ann Randall. The couple has two children: Eric R. and Erin R.

Rosemary Ann who lives in the Dayton, Ohio area has three children, Rita Kay, David Alan and Pamela Lynn. She is married to Jim Harrold.

Roger C. Lee is married to the former Glenna L. Noble and the couple resides on the homestead farm south of Poneto where they raised two children, Randall C. and Carol A. The farm was the original home of the family since 1889 when Laura V. Fleming purchased the forty acres of land. She willed the farm jointly to Bertram P. Fleming and Margaret Grace Lee in November of 1932. At that date, the family of Ralph C. Lee lived continuously on the farm until it was acquired by Roger and Glenna Lee in 1957.

MARION AND MARTHA LEE

Martha Mae Baumgartner, the wife of Marion Ernest Lee, was born on August 18, 1894, the eldest daughter of Joseph and Salomet (Steffen) Baumgartner. Her brothers and sisters were: John (Mabel Penrod), Samuel (Mary Rhinehard), Ida Mae (Arthur Wolf) and Priscilla Mae (Daniel Steffen).

Martha was the granddaughter of Benedict and Anna (Hubacher) Baumgartner, German emmigrants who migrated to America to escape religious persecution during the early 1800's, and who finally settled in Vera Cruz, Indiana, during the middle 1850's. They donated part of their land where the Apostolic Christian Church now stands.

Marion Ernest Lee, born June 25, 1891, in Huntington County, Indiana was the first son of Samuel H. Lee and Mary Elisabeth Pugh. His brother and sisters were: Bessie (John Eichenberry), Eunice, and Raymond Leslie (Margaret Wooster). His mother was the great-granddaughter of a Revolutionary War soldier named William Dusenberry, who was born in Suffolk County, New Jersey, and settled in Perry County, Ohio.

Marion Lee and Martha Baumgartner were married in Bluffton at the courthouse on June 29, 1916. After the ceremony, the couple were "belled" by their friends and relatives. They became the parents of three daughters: Eunice Priscilla (June), born June 18, 1917; Violet Pearl, born December 6, 1919; and Maxine Lucille, born December 8, 1924. June married Otis Conner; Violet married Raymond Hakes, and Maxine married Clyde Farnsworth.

Times were hard during the depression, and to make ends meet, both Marion and Martha worked.

Martha (Baumgartner) Lee
June
Marion E. Lee
1917

One New Years Eve, Marion woke his three daughters and took them outside to the backyard. That year there was a meteorite shower, and it was quite an experience seeing the stars fall on the last night of the year.

During his spare time, Marion enjoyed doing carpentry as a hobby. He was able to supply their own furniture, with a clothes cupboard, china cabinet, rifle cabinet, an sturdy chairs that lasted a long time. He also enjoyed fishing and hunting. One of his favorite spots for fishing was close to the railroad trestle on the Wabash River. Martha enjoyed gardening and raising flowers. The gardening became a way of life, as it helped support the family and it brought in extra income during the fall and winter months.

During their lifetime, they and their children attended the Church of the Nazarene on Cherry Street in Bluffton. Marion died September 8, 1963 and Martha died January 9, 1989. Their final resting place is at Elm Grove Cemetery. Marion and Martha weren't able to leave much in material value to their children, but they left a legacy of love, hard work and self-sufficiency for them to follow.

WAYNE AND PEARL LEE FAMILY

Wayne Lee, son of Darwin and Hettie Lee, was born June 18, 1903 near Jackson Center School. Sylvia Pearl Minnich, daughter of William and Vila Minnich, was born October 18, 1905, just three miles north, across the Salamonia River. They attended different rural schools and didn't meet until they attended Warren High School. It was love at first sight; and after a four year courtship, they were married on April 11, 1925. Their total possessions consisted of a 1923 Model T. Ford, less than ten dollars in cash, and Wayne had a job teaching school in Jackson Township for eight hundred fifteen dollars per year. However, with the help of their parents, relatives, friends and a trusting furniture dealer, they were able to start housekeeping in a three room house near the banks of the Salamonia River. They spent their honeymoon with Pearl raising chickens, a large garden, and canning food for the winter. Wayne worked in the green lumber division of H.C. Bay Piano Company until school started.

The transition year was 1937. After teaching for fourteen years in grades one through twelve and going to night school, summer school, and on Saturdays, Wayne graduated from Indiana University with a Master's degree in school administration. Pearl quit milking cows, raising rabbits, and chickens, and hoeing in the garden. The principal's job at Chester Center was offered to him at a salary of fourteen hundred dollars per year, and thus began a career of thirty-one years as a school administrator in Wells County schools. After living in nine rented houses in twelve married years, with no electricity or indoor plumbing, they now rented a house with electricity but still no plumbing. In 1940, they purchased a house in Bluffton and lived there for eighteen years. In 1958, they purchased a farm on the Well-Huntington county line and moved to the country.

Pearl worked at the Wells County and Caylor-Nickel Hospitals for many years. She was a fifty year member of the Home Extension Clubs in Wells County and served as County President for two years.

Wayne and Pearl Lee

Wayne was the principal at Chester Center for four years, Rockcreek Center for fourteen years, Lancaster Central for five years, and Wells County Superintendent for eight years. Altogether, he worked for forty-five years for and with the best people in Wells County—the boys and girls.

Beginning in the early thirties and continuing to the present time, the Lee family has been a part of the Liberty Center Methodist Church, teaching Sunday School and serving as officers in most departments of the church.

Daughter Eleanor Kay was born October 18, 1936. She attended the Bluffton schools and Ball State College. In 1960, she married Willis Nussbaum, son of Rufus and Ida Nussbaum, from Adams County. Willis and Eleanor lived on a farm near Monroe for seventeen years and then moved to Monroe where they now reside. Willis has worked at Berne Furniture for thirty-five years and Eleanor has worked at the Berne Public Library for seventeen years. They have two daughters, Anne-Marie, born October 6, 1966, and Cheryl Lynn, born November 27, 1968. They graduated from Adams Central High School and Ball State University. Anne-Marie is an elementary teacher in the Penn-Harris-Madison school system at Mishawaka and Cheryl is a staff accountant at the corporate offices of Sycamore Shops in Indianapolis.

In 1968 the retirement years began. A cottage at Sechrist Lake and a home at Lake Placid, Florida were purchased. Summers were spent on the farm and at the lake cottage, and winters at Lake Placid. In 1990, Wayne and Pearl moved to Zermatt House at Swiss Village Retirement Home at Berne, Indiana. It has now been sixty-six years since Wayne and Pearl were married and today they are enjoying life and going strong.

CRAIG LEONARD FAMILY

The Craig Leonard family lives at 521 West Market Street, Bluffton, in the 1891 John Grove House, which Mr. Leonard restored in 1980-82; the house is individually listed on the National Register of Historic Places. Craig and Elizabeth (Betsy) Leonard, who are both natives of Fort Wayne, were married April 21, 1984, at the Unitarian Meetinghouse in that city, and they have since resided at their present address. The Leonards have two daughters: Sarah Julia, born March 14, 1987 and and Jane Elizabeth, born April 2, 1990; both girls were born in Bluffton.

The Craig Leonard family in 1990. (L to R) Elizabeth, Jane, Craig, Sarah

Craig Leonard was born October 28, 1949, the elder son of Philip Allen Leonard and Juanita Powell Leonard. Mr. Leonard has resided in Wells County since 1959. A 1968 graduate of Bluffton High School, he went on to earn a Bachelor of Architecture degree at Ball State University in 1976. That same year, he entered the field of historic preservation with his first project, the exterior refurbishment of the Wells County Courthouse.

Except for a year spent as the state architect for historic buildings, he has since been self-employed as a consultant in this field. To date his work has included the nomination of more Indiana properties (thirty-two) to the National Register than any other person, including historic districts in the cities of Fort Wayne, Columbia City, and Ligonier. He has authored all of the Wells County nominations to the National Register. His restoration projects include work on the Lanier House at Madison, Indiana, and the State Reception Room in the Kentucky Capitol Building. In 1988, he completed two years work in the role of preservation consultant for the restoration of the Indiana State Capitol. In that same year, he received a Master of Architecture degree at Ball State University, where he teaches on a part-time basis. Since the illness of his late father, beginning in 1989, Mr. Leonard has also assumed responsibilities as vice-president and treasurer of Standard Plastic Corporation.

Elizabeth Rose (White) Leonard was born April 26, 1952, the eldest child and only daughter of Tenney Glenn and Dorothy Phyllis Edna Semler Schuerenberg White. Mrs. Leonard is a lineal descendant of Peregrine White, one of the Pilgrim Fathers. She is a 1970 graduate of Elmhurst High School and in 1980 received the degree Bachelor of Fine Arts from Indiana University at Fort Wayne. Mrs. Leonard is a member of the Foltz Literary Club, Psi Iota Xi Sorority and the Fort Wayne Shuttlecraft Guild. Her interests include weaving, quilting, needlepoint, and especially gardening. She is presently a full-time homemaker who prefers to be called the "Lady of the Manor." She shares with her husband a love of history and art, as was well demonstrated in their collaboration on the 1986 book, *An Architectural Atlas of Wells County, Indiana.* This was the result of a two-year project, sponsored by the Wells County Historical Society, to research and inventory local historic properties. One of these, an 1853 farmhouse in Nottingham Township, was purchased by the Leonards in 1989.

PHILIP A. LEONARD FAMILY

Philip Allen Leonard was born in Chicago October 6, 1918; he was the son of Philip Haskell Leonard (1884-1968), a native of Boston, and Juliet Marguerite Richter Leonard (1883-1964), a Chicagoan. He was baptized at Saint John's Episcopal Church in Brookline, Massachusetts, of which his grandfather, Lucius Philip Leonard, was a deacon. During his childhood he lived in a host of places, starting with a ranch his father had near Rocky Point, Wyoming, followed by an island off Martha's Vineyard, then Ipswich, Massachusetts, Minneapolis, Chicago (where he graduated from Von Steuben High School in 1936), and finally Fort Wayne, Indiana, where his father decided to retire after working several years as a superintendent at the Wayne Knitting Mills.

After serving in the U.S. Army in England during World War II, Mr. Leonard returned to Fort Wayne, where he went to work for the Wayne Home Equipment Company. In 1948 he joined Wayne Plastics Company, where he was general manager from 1948 to 1956.

The P.A. Leonards in 1946, their wedding day

In 1956, Mr. Leonard founded Progressive Molded Products; with the aid of his father-in-law, he located a building in Bluffton (the former A.W. Cotton Cabinet Works at 1100 South Morgan Street) to house his venture. In 1959, after commuting from Fort Wayne for several years, Mr. Leonard moved his family to Wells County. The next year, the business was reorganized as Standard Plastic Corporation, as it is still known.

Juanita Powell Leonard was born in Marion County, Indiana, October 16, 1922, the daughter of Luther Earl Powell (1896-1960) and Mildred Marshino Powell (1901-). The Powell family moved to Wells County in 1940. After graduating from Carmel High School in 1940, Juanita attended International Business College at Fort Wayne, where she completed a two-year course of study in 1942. She then found employment as secretary to the Fort Wayne manager of the Greyhound Bus Company, where she worked for seven years.

The Leonards were married at Bluffton on September 18, 1946, and they initially resided in Fort Wayne. They have two sons, Craig, born October 28, 1949, and Philip Earl, born April 11, 1955. In 1964, the family moved to a farm in Harrison Township, where Mrs. Leonard still resides. Philip A. Leonard died September 19, 1990, after an illness of one year. Since that time, Mrs. Leonard and her sons have continued the family business, which since 1985 had been located at 850 Decker Drive, Bluffton.

LEPPER

John A. Lepper and his wife, Louisa Sarah Fairbanks Lepper, came to Wells County in 1848. He was born in Montgomery County, New York in August, 1808 and died in the Prospect community in September, 1884. His wife was born in New York in December, 1810, and died in the Prospect community in October, 1858. They resided in Trumball County, Ohio before coming to Indiana. John's parents were Jacob Lepper (born between 1774 and 1784 and died before 1817) and Mary Allen (born in Rhode Island). Mary Allen Lepper's second marriage was to William Quackenbush who was born in New York and came to Wells County in 1850. John A. Lepper was a charter member of the Prospect Church in Union Township.

John A. and Louisa had ten children: Sally M. (Lucy) (1837), married Orsen Jennings; Jacob (1838-1864), died a prisoner of war, Florence, South Carolina; Olive (1840), married Ellison Covert; Mary (1841-died an infant); Thomas P. (1843) married Nancy Dick, (Civil War veteran); James Ed (1844), married Martha Quackenbush in 1866, (Civil War Veteran); Lydia Ann (1847-1926), married Lewis Hoopengardner in 1866; William (Will) H. (1849-1938), married Minerva A. ?; John M. (1851-1928), married Lucy Hayes; Mary L. (1853), married Seymore Goshorn.

Most of the descendants of these siblings are no longer in Wells County except for those of Lydia Ann and Lewis Hoopengardner. Their daughter Dora Elsie married Clyde White and their descendants are listed under the biography of Charles White.

LESH FAMILY

The Lesh ancestors, or (Loesch), came from the country comprising the Lower Palatinate (Germany) with its capitol being Heidelberg. Our coat-of-arms dates back to 1653 when they were made barons.

They were under the rule of John William, who tried to compel the conversion of the people, who were mostly Protestant, to the Roman Catholic Church. Under his rule they suffered many hardships, impelling many of them to break off their attachment of the fatherland, and to make and seek new homes in distant America.

A large number went to Holland, and by invitation of Queen Anne, thousands were transported to England in 1707-8-9 where they encamped near London.

Ten ships left London December 25, 1709, with four thousand. Among them was Balthaser Loesch (our ancestor), his wife, and three sons. Balthaser Loesch died at sea. They reached New York, June 1, 1710. They settled around there but had to work for others before they were given land. In time, they left there for Pennsylvania and on farther west. Finally this family of Leshs settled in Wells County and Rockcreek Township.

Our great-grandfather was Isaac Lesh. He married Samantha Cover. They had eight children: Wilson, Harry, Clara, William Lewis (our grandfather), Harriet, Herman, and Milo.

William Lewis married Sadie Nash. They had two children: Irene, who married George Farling, and Dwight (our father) married Lela Gilbert. They lived in Rockcreek Township, east of the former Rockcreek School.

Their children are Helen, who married Loren Decker and lives in Huntington County. They have one adopted son, James. Gerald (lost at sea in World War II). Dale, who married Jane Gordon, and lives north of Uniondale. They have two children, Dennis and Marilyn Nyffeler. Ray married Roberta Milligan. They live in Rockcreek Township and have four children, David, Linda, Bruce, and Kent. Ruth married Max Fisher and lives in Fort Wayne. They have two children, Roger and Diann. Harold married Barbra Barrick. They live in Rockcreek and have four children, Nikki, Gary, Neal, and Perry.

LESH FAMILY

The Ernest Lesh family is of German origin. The most remote ancestors of whom we have records came from Heidelberg, Germany, being driven thence by French oppression. They came over from Rotterdam, Holland, on the ship *Restauration*, reaching New York in 1710. The first stopping place was Scharrie County, New York, which they left on account of excessive taxation by the Duke of York. After negotiating with William Penn, they located in Center County, Pennsylvania.

Jacob Lesh, with his father's family, left Pennsylvania in 1848 and settled in Wells County. At that time Rockcreek Township was a wilderness of trees and swamps. Jacob, at the age of twenty-one, took up the carpenter trade, and thus erected many buildings yet standing today. He married Elizabeth Gilbert, daughter of Martin and Lydia (Houtz) Gilbert, in 1872, and they were the parents of Charles E., George L., Fred C., H. Alva, Maggie C., and Esther J.

Ernest and Ethel Lesh

George Luther Lesh married Clara Farling, daughter of Jacob and Mary Anne (Haiflich) Farling, in 1900, and were the parents of Ernest, born in 1902, and Elizabeth, born in 1910. In 1902, When Ernest was born, they lived in a log cabin. Around 1909, they built the house which is still standing and being lived in by Ernest's youngest daughter, Betty Lou.

In August of 1923, Ernest married Ethel Barlett, daughter of Issac and Mollie (Ernst) Barlett. He always farmed and had livestock. In his younger days, he would travel with his truck and bring back produce, such as watermelons, peaches, or potatoes. He ran a sawmill to which many a neighbor would bring logs from their woods in order to have them sawed into lumber. Martha Jane was born June 2, 1924; Maxine was born on April 12, 1931; and Betty Lou was born on October 5, 1938. The family were members of Saint Paul's Lutheran Church. Ernest served as president of the Wells County Farm Bureau from 1966-1968, and was the Rockcreek chairman. He also served on the county board of directors for the Farm Bureau. He was the treasurer of the Rockcreek Township Mutual Farmers Insurance Company. his sister, Elizabeth, married Frank Lepper, who is deceased. They had two sons, William and Robert. Elizabeth had five grandchildren. She currently resides in Fort Wayne, Indiana.

Ernest's three daughters married farmers. Martha Jane married Paul Lauer from Bippus, Indiana. They have four children: Nelson, Paula, Alan, and Roger. All of them are married, and Martha has nine grandchildren.

Maxine married Charles Goebel from Andrews, Indiana. She has twin daughters, Linda and Dianne. They are both married, and Maxine has three grandchildren. Maxine and Charles recently moved to Huntington, Indiana.

Betty Lou married Gerald Dunwiddie of Bluffton, Indiana. As previously mentioned, she lives on the home farm in Rockcreek Township in Wells County. She has three children: Cindy, who is married; and Chris and Cathy, who reside at home. Betty has two grandchildren.

Ernest died of lung cancer on Friday, November 26, 1976. Ethel followed him on Sunday, July 24, 1977.

HERSCHEL AND GUINEVERE BRONNER LESH

This story will attempt to track the ancestry of Herschel Lesh and Guinevere (Bronner) Lesh, who lived from 1943 to 1981 just north of the Union Center School.

The Lesh (originally Loesch) family came to this country in 1710 from the Palatinate region of southwestern Germany. The Loesch who first arrived, six generations before Herschel, was Johann George. Johann's sons was Balthazer, and his direct link son was Peter. Peter served in the American Revolution.

June 21, 1981, 50th anniversary of Herschel and Guinevere. (L to R) Karen, Herschel, Guinevere, Donna, Larry, and Stephen

John Lesh (1800-1864), Peter's son, the great-grandfather of Herschel, was born in Berks County, Pennsylvania. John moved to Indiana in 1848 and eventually purchased a farm in Rockcreek Township. John's thirteenth (and last) child was George W. (1860-1926), Herschel's grandfather. George's mother was Harriet McAfee Cover, the second wife of John.

Lella (Otlella) Lesh (1879-1957) was the son of George W. Lesh and Christena Logan (1862-1910). Iva Lesh (Ditzler) and Curt Lesh were siblings of Lella. Lella and Effie Haflich (1886-1976) were married in 1905 and their only child was Herschel (1908-1985). Effie was the daughter of John Haflich (1845-1888) and Lavina Sink (1855-1930). Effie's siblings were Anna (1876-1878), John, and Jennie Haflich Roe (1878-1949). Lella and Effie lived on a farm about one and five-tenths miles north of Uniondale and for years Lella was the buyer for the Uniondale stockyards.

Herschel and Guinevere (1906-1990) were married in 1931 and lived until 1943 in Blissfield, Michigan, where Herschel was a teacher, coach and principal. Indiana schools where Herschel worked, either as teacher or administrator were: Ossian, Lafayette Central and three schools in Fort Wayne. He served fourteen years as principal at Brentwood Elementary School. Gunievere was an elementary teacher for about thirty years at Union Center and Rockcreek. They both retired in 1973.

All four of Guinevere's grandparents came to America in the 1850's from the Baden area in southwestern Germany. John George Bronner (1837-1916) and Fredrica Rheinacher Raber (1833-1885) were married in Ohio, where Jacob Bronner (1863-1936), Guinevere's father, was born. The family came to Wells County in 1869 before settling in Huntington County in 1871.

Guinevere's other grandparents were John Lewis Warner (1812-1883) and Elizabeth Sitze Warner (1821-1899). They were married in 1840 before coming to America. They moved from Ohio to Indiana in 1864 and bought the land that included the future Union Center School site. Their ninth child in a family of ten was Anna Warner (1863-1929), the mother of Guinevere.

In 1889, Jacob Bronner and Anna Warner were married. Guinevere was the youngest daughter of their three children. the two older sisters were Linnie Gronner Fluke (1890-1971) and Mina (Wilhelmina) Bronner Herran (1895-1988).

Herschel and Guinevere's son, Larry (1937) is a teacher in Fort Wayne. He was married in 1963 to Donna Keller (1939) from Clear Creek Township in Huntington County. They have two children, Karen (1965) and Stephen (1967).

LEVY

The Levy family dates back to 1752, when Friedrich Christian Levi came to Oberlingen, Switzerland, from Hanau, Germany. Born June 16, 1843, Frederich Wilhelm Levi was one of seven sons born to this stocking weaver, and, as a young boy, had the opportunity to immigrate to America with two of his brothers. After living in the United States, his name was written as William Levy. He served in the Civil War, and two years after his discharge, he married Christine Hoffer (1847-1918), a native of Bluffton, Ohio. They farmed in Paulding County, Ohio, and to this union were born eight boys and three girls.

Of these sons, my grandfather, David Levy (1873-1950) found his way to Bluffton, Indiana, and was employed by Adam Hartman of Vera Cruz, Indiana. Here he met my grandmother-to-be, Aldine Gilliom (1873-1947), a daughter of Isaac Gilliom, whose farm was just east from where David worked. Aldine's great-grandfather John and wife Elizabeth were born in Bern, Switzerland.

David Levy and Aldine Gilliom courted, eventually married on November 6, 1898, and lived in Aldine's childhood home. Ten children were born to this union: Mary, William, Henry, George, Alvin, Amos, Emma, Ralph, Walter, and Raymond. As a family, they attended the Apostolic Christian Church near Vera Cruz, and farming proved to be their livelihood. As a sideline, David was frequently called upon to pull the horse-drawn hearse in a funeral, since he had fine horses and fancy harnessers.

The Levy Family in 1990
Robert, Annie, Erika 14, Raegan 20

My father, Amos "Stook" Levy, was the sixth child born to David and Aldine Levy on December 15, 1908. After attending Kirkland High School, and drawing on his father's background, he, along with his brothers, farmed and milked until he declared independence. Soon, he was employed by a prominent Bluffton businessman, Ware Baker, whose many acres of ground he farmed.

After meeting my mother, Lucille Myers, daughter of Cleophas and Marie Risley Myers (Keystone, Indiana) their marriage was celebrated on March 8, 1941. Housekeeping began in the red brick house south of the Bluffton Bowling Alley, and they later moved one-half mile south to the original Kunkel farm. After thirty-eight years of farming, raising hereford and brahma cattle, dad retired and moved into town on East South Street.

I, Robert Allen, was the only child born to Stook and Lucille Levy (July 27, 1946). A 1964 graduate of Bluffton High School, I attended International Business College and have been employed by Franklin Electric, Incorporation, since 1967.

On October 4, 1975, I married Annette "Annie" Aschliman, the youngest daughter of Kenneth and Justine Heyerly Aschliman. We live on East South Street with our two daughters. Reagan is a sophomore attending Hillsdale College in Hillsdale, Michigan, and Erika is in the eighth grade at Bluffton Middle School

Sadly, my dad died on August 3, 1987, and Justine died on October 9, 1987. From these two special people, as well as from our two surviving parents, Lucille and Ken, we have been given the opportunity to see first hand what mutual love and respect can accomplish. *(Robert Levy)*

MANES AND HELEN (SMITH) LEVY

Manes Levy, son of Eli and Martha (Reinhard) Levy, was born in Dekalb County, moving to Wells County in 1921. His father died at the age of 51 years and his mother died at 46 years of age. He had four brothers and one sister who preceded him in death. The Levy brothers, with their father were quite well-known for their expertise with horses. They successfully won at the Bluffton Fair Horse Pulling contests, hauled logs and loaded them with their horses, dug basements with slip scoop, used their teams in helping lay the pipe line from Bluffton to Paulding, Ohio, in addition to other jobs within the area. They were also farmers.

Manes met Helen Smith in Uniondale at his brother, Grover's home. Grover was employed by Mrs. Jim Sales on her farm and Manes was visiting there. Helen was working for Mrs. Chester (Bessie) Osborn during her illness and they lived next door to Grover Levys. Helen was a daughter of James and Karah (Stine) Smith. She entered Union Center's first grade at the age of five years and graduated from there. She furthered her education at Fort Wayne Bible College, Saint Francis College and Purdue (Fort Wayne Campus).

Manes as a farmer, also working at various times at the Farm Bureau grain elevator in Uniondale, construction work, school bus driver, and for the Wells County Highway Department from which he retired. The Levys lived all but four years of their (to date) fifty-one years of their married life in Wells County.

Helen taught in a parochial school in Adams County for some years. She then taught at the Johnny Appleseed Center for mentally handicapped children, now the Association for Retarded Citizens of Allen County. Her position for the past fifteen years has been in the capacity of social work for young children and their families.

Manes and Helen Levy have two sons and one daughter. William David married Claudette Thomas, live in Chicago, and are the parents of Julia Lucile and Claudia Marie. William is employed as Health Club manager for the University Club of Chicago.

William lost most of his sight as a young child and graduated from the Indiana School for the Blind. James Eli married Carolyn Biberstein, and they live in Houston, Texas and are the parents of Lincoln James. James is employed by an air-conditioning firm specializing in commercial heating and air-conditioning. Linda Rose is married to Richard Teusch, lives in Union Township and is employed in their restaurant, Waynewood Inn, Fort Wayne. Linda has three children, sons Tracey and Jason Roth, and daughter, Sheila (Roth) Teusch. Sheila and Tom have two sons Thomas Jacob and Mitchell Lee. Sheila works as a teacher's aide for ARC-AC, Fort Wayne. They live in Uniondale. The Levys have been members of the Evangelistic Church in Craigville for many years. They moved from Union Township in 1986 to Bluffton due to Manes failing health.

BRUCE AND TERESA LEY

On a sultry June day in 1986, Bruce Calvin Ley and Teresa Ann Johnson were married at the First United Church of Christ in Bluffton.

Bruce was born in 1961 in West Burlington, Iowa, to Calvin and Mary Ann Ley. Bruce moved to Bluffton in 1965 when her father became pastor of the First United Church of Christ. After graduating from Bluffton high School in 1980, Bruce earned his BS degree in electrical engineering at Rose-Hullman in 1985. Bruce has been working at CTS in Berne as an electrical engineer since 1985.

Teresa was born at the Wells Community Hospital in 1960. Her parents are Leon and Anna Johnson (see Leon Johnson history). She graduated from Bluffton High School in 1979, and from

Parkview School of Nursing in 1982. Teresa continues to work part-time at the Wells Community Hospital.

Bruce and Teresa Ley with Jennifer and Rebecca

Daughter, Jennifer Marie, was born December 30, 1988. Jennifer enjoys swimming and listening to storybooks. Rebecca Michelle was born June 19, 1990. She enjoys the company of other children and playing peek-a-boo.

Bruce, Teresa, Jennifer, and Rebecca live north of Bluffton in Lancaster Township.

CALVIN AND MARY ANN LEY

On a cold January day in 1966, the Reverend Calvin Martin Ley and his wife Mary Ann, along with their children Wayne, Barbara, and Bruce (see Bruce Ley history) moved to Bluffton, Indiana, after serving pastorates in Portage, Wisconsin, and West Burlington, Iowa. The Reverend Ley had been called to be the new pastor of the First United Church of Christ in Bluffton.

Calvin Ley was born in St. Bernard, Ohio, and grew up in Wisconsin. He graduated from Lakeland College and Mission House Seminary, which are near Sheboygan, Wisconsin.

Mary Ann was born in Sheboygan, Wisconsin. After moving to Bluffton, she received her BS and MS degrees from Indiana University, Fort Wayne. She taught fourth grade at East Side Elementary School for nineteen years.

The Reverend Ley served as pastor of First Church in Bluffton for over twenty-five years, moving from Bluffton to Yorktown, Indiana, in April of 1991.

The Ley children graduated from Bluffton High School. Wayne graduated from Purdue University and married Kathy Beckler, daughter of John and Connie Beckler of Bluffton. Their children are Aaron (born 1981), Andrew (born 1984), and Allissa (born 1988).

Barbara graduated from Ball State University and married William Broyles of Muncie. Their children are David (born 1981) and Jonathon (born 1987).

Bruce graduated from Rose-Hullman and married Teresa Johnson, daughter of Leon and Anna Johnson of Bluffton. Their children are Jennifer (born 1988) and Rebecca (born 1990).

Calvin Ley has roots in Wells County because his grandmother, Mary Ellen Engeler (see Raymond Meyer history), who married his grandfather, Martin Vitz, was born in Vera Cruz. Calvin Ley's great-grandfather, Peter Vitz, established and served German Reformed churches in Wells, Adams, and Huntington counties. Among these are Saint John Church at Vera Cruz, Saint Lukes at Honduras, Salem at Magley, Saint Peters at Huntington, and Cross Church, Berne.

LICHTENBERGER-BLACKSTONE

This is a brief history of the parents and grandparents of John L. Lichtenberger, who was a prominent citizen of Bluffton and Warren, Indiana. His lineage is documented to 1610 in Germany.

*John L. Lichtenberger
Mary Blackstone Lichtenberger*

John Lichtenberger (father of John L, who came to Wells County) was named Johann in Germany. He was the son of Johann Michael and Anna Maria (Wurster) Lichtenberger and was born at Rudmerebach, Germany, on January 12, 1812. He came to America in January, 1833, and was naturalized on September 11, 1838 at York, Pennsylvania. On August 2, 1836, he married Maria Amanda (Mellenger). They had three children: Mary Amanda, born January 5, 1838; John L., born September 9, 1839; and Jacob, born January 5, 1841. It is said Mary Amanda had a twin, Barbara, but no documented proof.

John L. Lichtenberger, a carpenter/contractor, was a participant in the building of the business section of Bluffton. Before coming to Bluffton in the late 1800's, he was in Washington Courthouse, Ohio, where he took part in the construction of the local courthouse.

John L. married Mary Blackstone, born in 1838 at Sharon, Pennsylvania, the daughter of Jonas and Emily (Andrews) Blackstone. John L. died March 11, 1919, and Mary died November 15, 1925, and are both buried in Fairview Cemetery in Bluffton. They had two children, one daughter who died in infancy and Emma L. who married W.W. Wilhelm. The Lichtenbergers and Wilhelms had a small grocery at 527 West South Street in Bluffton before moving to Warren about 1911.

LLOYD C. LIEURANCE

Lloyd Lieurance first came to Wells County with his parents, brother and sister. He attended high school and graduated from Roll in Blackford County because Jackson Township had no high school at that time.

After high school he graduated from Muncie Normal College now Ball State University. He wrote the only history of that school and it is still in the Ball State Library.

During his college years, his parents deeded a small parcel of land to him in Jackson Township. Over the years he added to that land to make a total of four hundred acres.

Lloyd eventually remodeled an 1863 vintage house in 1938 giving it lights, a furnace and a basement. He build a dairy barn in 1950. He always called the farm home but he only lived there intermittently until 1949 when he remodeled it again making it his permanent residence.

After college, he taught in Hamilton County and then became principal of what is now Hamilton Heights School. It was at this time that he married Edna Shaffer of Arcadia, Indiana.

After obtaining his superintendents license from Indiana University, he ran for County Superintendent of the schools in Wells County. However, soon after he was sent to Europe to serve in World War II. Toward the end of the war, Captain Lieurance started a school for American servicemen in Berlin, Germany. On the twentieth anniversary of that same school it had served more than ninety thousand servicemen and is now affiliated with the University of Maryland.

Lloyd C. Lieurance Farm

After the service, he returned to Wells County to become Superintendent again. Since there were nine schools in his district, his hobby of flying was beneficial. he used a makeshift landing strip in the field behind the house and landed in nearby fields at each school.

Lloyd C. Lieurance felt his greatest reward was in starting the Vera Cruz Opportunity School. Since the school was not state funded, he spoke before clubs and organizations to raise the funds necessary to start the school. He and several other greatly dedicated individuals worked to accomplish what was considered the impossible at that time.

Lloyd C. Lieurance later retired from the Army as Major. Edna Lieurance died in 1874, Lloyd followed here in 1985. His home is still occupied by his daughter Jane Lieurance, an interior decorator in Hartford City. David Lieurance, the youngest son, along with his family still farms the land. The oldest son, Major Robert J. Lieurance is retired from the Air Force and resides in California. Mrs. Marianna Mounsey, the eldest daughter, of Fort Wayne, is actively involved in the family owned M and R Truck Sales Incorporated of Fort Wayne.

LINDSTRAND-MCAFEE

Harry Lindstrand was the son of Al and Anna Dahl Lindstrand. They were immigrants of Sweden. Their first home was in Chicago, where they moved to in 1905. Harry, their only son, was born there and when he was seven, they moved to Bluffton, Indiana. Two sisters were added to the family, Phoebe and Irene. He attended Bluffton High School from which he graduated. he did all the art work for the Senior Retrospect, in the year which he graduated, 1928. Upon graduating, he attended the Chicago Academy of Fine Arts, Art Institute and American Academy of Fine Arts.

He was employed by Montgomery Ward Company for six years. Harry and Dorothy (McAfee) Lindstrand were married December 24, 1936. Harry and his wife Dorothy moved to her father's farm in 1941. They farmed the family farm and raised a fine herd of Guernsey cattle. Mrs. Dorothy Lindstrand was the daughter of Ernest and Artie (Raber) McAfee of Rockcreek Township. She attended and graduated from Rockcreek High School in 1926.

In 1953, they moved to Bluffton where he engaged in the Art and Advertising business. He did work for Franklin Electric and Blue Flame Gas Company and other business accounts in the area. Blue Flame logo is seen nation wide on trucks and business buildings through out the United States.

Harry and Dorothy Lindstrand

After retiring, he devoted his time to the fine arts, especially water color paintings. He displayed his exhibits at Indiana University, Brown County, Indiana; Commerce, Texas College Show; Huntington College; Taylor University; Van Wert, Ohio; Warren, Indiana; Tempe and Scottsdale, Arizona. He was president of the Temple Art League in Airizona for two years.

He was president of Bluffton Kiwanis Club and a member of the Creative Art Club. He and his wife, Dorothy were members of United Church of Christ.

Mrs. Lindstrand was a graduate of Indiana University. She taught music and art in schools in Wells County for twenty-three years.

On December 24, 1986, they celebrated their 50th wedding anniversary. Harry passed away May 11, 1987. He is buried in the Elm Grove Cemetery, Bluffton, Indiana. *(Refer to John McAfee Sr. and John C. Raber histories)*

LINN

Seven brothers came from Northern Ireland to America, one of them being the father of Joshua Linn. Joshua Linn was born April 23, 1791 and died in 1837, at age forty-six. He married Rachel Linn who was born May 13, 1794. They were parents of twelve children, all born in Monroe County, Ohio, and later moved to Darke County, Ohio. The children were: Mary, born August 30, 1812; William, born October 28, 1814; Margaret, born May 11, 1816; John, born March 3, 1818; Sarah (Sally), born February 19, 1820; Samuel, born April 29, 1822; Mariah, born April 10, 1824; Manurva, born April 20, 1826; Lucinda, born May 19, 1828; Levi, born February 1, 1831; Andrew (Alexander) born June 18, 1833; and Ellen Jane, born November, 1836.

John, Samuel, Levi, Andrew, and Sarah came to Indiana from Darke County, Ohio. Each boy received a quarter-section of land and Sarah received two hundred dollars.

Levi married Mary Drum in 1854, in Monroe County, Ohio. They came to Indiana, Wells County, where she died November 5, 1857, at the age of twenty-five years, leaving a small daughter who died on April 23, 1861, at the age of six years and four months.

Levi's second wife was Caroline Meyers, born October 26, 1838, and died April 1, 1913, at age seventy-five years. Levi died October 27, 1874, at age forty-three years.

Levi and Caroline had seven children. Nancy, Alice, Lovina, and a son that died in infancy, Viola, Oliver Theodore, and Louisa.

Nancy married Will Echrote and divorced him, married Pete Pence who died and Tom Oakden who died. Children of Nancy's were Ethel Eckrote Sawyer and Berta Echrote. Berta died July 15, 1898, at fourteen years, six months and ten days.

Alice married David Gottschalk, Children were: Mabel, (Mrs. Harley Slack of Lagrange, Indiana); Thelma; Bruce; Mary Lou; Karol; and Dean.

Lovina married Richard Gregg and had three children, Lee, Linn (Red), and Ruth (Mrs. Charles Captain).

Viola married James A. Sturgeon and had two sons, Ray and Hugh. Hugh married Mimia Kleinknight and had three children, Ruth, Robert, and Wayne. Ruth married Ralph Potts, and had one daughter, Susan. Susan married Leon Gaiser and they have two children, Hilary Linn born July 16, 1986, and Caleb Oka born November 23, 1988. Robert K. married Jean Louise Spade and has three children, James Linn born in 1960, Steven Robert born in 1962, and Beth Anne born in 1970.

Oliver Theodore married Ellen hall. Their children are Grace Linn, Mary Linn Ellenberger (Mrs. Jesse), Justine Linn Sprunger (Mrs. David), Genevieve Linn Windmiller (Mrs. Harrold), and Walter H. Linn.

Louisa married George L. Caps, born November 13, 1874, and died July 1, 1948. They had four children: Gladys born May 21, 1897, and died December 15, 1973; Helen born December 17, 1901, and died February 7, 1905; Paul born December 31, 1905 and died August 28, 1983. Paul rebuilt player pianos, married Dessie Schwartz and had one child, Wendel, born in 1950. Betty born on December 4, 1916.

LINN-GOTTSHALK

Our great-great-grandparents, Josha and Rachel Linn, came from Ohio and were granted land under the Homestead Act signed by President Martin Van Buren in 1837. They had ten children, one whom was our great-grandfather Levi. He married Caroline and farmed the same homestead. Levi also made a beautiful quilt that is still in excellent condition. They had five daughters and our grandfather, Oliver. He married Cora Hall, his first wife and, they had four daughters, Mrs. William (Genevie) Windmiller, Mrs. David (Justine) Sprunger, Mrs. Jesse (Mary) Ellenberger, Grace, and our father, Walter (born 1908). After Cora's death, Oliver married Rosa Bears.

Back row (L to R) Marilyn Bardsley, Carolyn Faus. Front row (L to R) Walter and Helen, Cheryl Barnes

Walter Linn married Helen Gottshalk (born 1916). Helen's great-grandparents came from Wittenburg, Germany, and were farmers and carpenters. Their children were: William, who married Bertha Garrett; Mrs. Charles (Minnie) Cory; George, who married Minnie Durkes; Cora Hawks; Clara Blanchard; Etta May Gottshalk; Mrs. Augustus (Luella) Reynolds; Mrs. Henry (Della) Durkes; Mrs. Emil (Nina) Moser; Mrs. Daniel (Ruth) Moser; Mrs. Henry (Lillie) Pierce; Clement, who married Mahala Reusser; Mrs. Purl (Amanda) Gentis (who farmed and then retired to Bluffton, leaving the farming to their son Truman, who married Mildred Nutter); and our grandfather, Thurman.

Thurman married Alice Druckemiller, and our mother Helen was born in 1916. They farmed the same square as the Linns. He was a good carpenter and died in 1960. Our grandmother Alice is still living. Born February 10, 1892, she still retains her spunkiness and will soon be ninety-nine.

Three daughters were born to Walter and Helen. They live in Wells County. Marilyn, the oldest, married Max Bardsley and lives on the homestead. He farms and works in sheet metal. They have five children: Matthew; Mrs. Keld Tom (Teresa) Ibholm; Tina; and twins, Kristina and Mrs. Steve (Kathlina) Carney.

Carolyn married Adrian "Dean" Faus (deceased) and had a son, Linn, who is a sergeant in the U.S. Air Force. She works at C.T.S. of Berne.

Cheryl, the youngest, has a daughter, Angel Egner, and a son, Paul Barnes, Jr.

Walter liked to hunt, fish, and go barefooted. He also liked to drive his 1910 Model "T" Ford "horseless carriage," bought new by his dad, Oliver. Helen liked to fish; she also farmed and worked in factories. His death came in 1979 and hers came in a traffic accident in 1987.

LINN-SPRUNGER

Joshua and Rachael Linn's eleven children, William, John, Samuel, Levi, Andrew, Mary, Sarah, Mariah, Minerva, Lucinda, and Ellen Jane, didn't lack for things to do even though they didn't have cable TV. The energetic couple traveled from Monroe County, Ohio, to Wells County, Indiana, to lay claim to two sizeable tracts of land from the U.S. government in 1837 and 1838.

The Thomas Phillips Family 1991
Back row (L to R) Thomas, John, David, Edwin Arrance (son-in-law). Middle row (L to R) Sandra Arrance, Mary Lou, Pamela (John's wife). Front (L to R) Zachary (twin), Tom and Harold Arrance, and Caleb Phillips (Twin)

Through much hardship they labored to clear their land grant farm located approximately four miles northwest of Linn Grove, Indiana. Upon the death of Joshua in 1839, each son received a quarter section of land, plus horses and a new saddle. The girls each received money, a horse and a new saddle as they became of age.

Our great-grandfather, Levi Linn and his wife, Caroline, raised five daughters: Mary, Nancy, Lovina, Viola, and Louisa, and one son, Oliver Theodore. Upon their death, the land was equally divided among the six children.

The David Hughes Family, 1990
(L to R) Steven Hughes, Betty (Sprunger) Hughes, David Hughes, Pamela (Hughes) Simons

Our grandfather, Oliver Theodore Linn, known to his friends as "O.T.," married Cora Ella Hall, a teacher in 1900. Over time, he bought land from his sisters.

O.T. was an aggressive, enterprising, and well-to-do agriculturist in Wells County. In 1910, he built a five-bedroom house for his family with walk-in closets, inside plumbing and a dumbwaiter. He rigged up a motor on the washing machine and butter churn, had his own cider mill, made maple syrup, and built bobsleds. A welcome change of pace included an evening spent with friends and neighbors for a taffy pull and a songfest with O.T. accompanying on his accordian, Jew's harp, violin, bones, or harmonica. Every Sunday and Wednesday the family attended church at Old Salem where O.T. and Cora taught Sunday School.

This union was blessed by four daughters and one son: Grace, Mary, and Justine, all deceased; Genevieve (Peg); and Walter, deceased. Cora died at the early age of forty-four. O.T. then married Rose Bears, who became a beloved stepmother.

Grace Linn graduated from the Indiana University School of Nursing in 1921. She worked in several hospitals throughout the states during her career and also served in the U.S. Army Nurse Corps during World War II. One of her military assignments was in a Japanese interment camp in New Mexico.

Mary married Jesse Ellenberger and raised seven children: Donald (deceased); Robert; Nancy (Mrs. Paul Markel); Kenneth; Richard; and twins, Shirley (deceased); and Charlotte (Mrs. Bruce Mittlestadt). Jesse and his brother, Dale, founded the Ellenberger Brothers Auctioneers business in Bluffton.

Justine (1904-1982) was a beautician, wife, and devoted mother. She and her husband, David Sprunger (1896-1977), made a wonderful and loving home for their two daughters, Mary Lou and Elizabeth Ellen (Betty). David was in the plumbing and heating business. Mary Lou (Mrs. Thomas H. Phillips), Jamestown, Indiana, has three children: Sandra, David, and John. Betty (Mrs David Hughes), Fort Wayne, Indiana, has two children: Steven and Pamela.

Genevieve was also a beautician, housewife and mother of one son, Edwin. She married Harold (Bill) Windmiller, teacher, coach and a member of the Indiana High School Athletic Association.

Through Genevieve's ingenuity and perseverance, she and her sister, Justine, establishing a beauty shoppe in Bluffton in 1926. It was a thriving business for nearly twenty years.

Walter married Helen Gottschalk and had three daughters: Marilyn (Mrs. Max Bardsley), Carolyn (Mrs. Adrian Faus), and Cheryl (Mrs. Paul Barnes). Walter bought his father's farm. Today, this same land, which dates back to 1837, is being farmed by O.T.'s granddaughter and her husband, Marilyn and Max Bardsley.

The Oliver T. Linn Family
(L to R) Grace, Mary, Cora Ella, Walter, Oliver T., Justine, Genevieve (Peg)

In 1931, Justine (Linn) and David Sprunger purchased their first home at 504 West Market Street and lived thee for over twenty-five years. Although we were city folks, we got a taste of life on the farm once a year when the cow tents wee erected on West Market Street during Street Fair week. We parked cars in our backyard to earn spending money for the fair. For many years O.T. Linn drove his 1910 Ford in the fair's opening night parade. As a small child, Betty thought Street Fair was in celebration of her September 26 birthday.

Mary Lou and friend, Nancy Heemstra Yeager, were two of the first waitresses at the Dutch Mill, which was built by Nancy's father, Simon Heemstra, in the late 1940's. Our visits to Bluffton never seem complete without dining at the Dutch Mill.

Church camp at Epworth Forest, Lake Webster, Indiana, family pitch-in dinners and MYF at the First Methodist Church were always fun times. Many happy childhood memories, as well as a rich Christian heritage, always draw us back to Bluffton, our Indiana "home." *(Mary Lou Sprunger Phillips)*

STEPHEN A. LINN FAMILY

In the Joshua Linn family, there were twelve children, of whom four sons and a daughter came to Wells County from Darke County, Ohio, around the middle 1800's.

The brothers were John, Levi, who married Caroline Meyer, Andrew (Alexander), who married a Popejoy, Samuel, who married Jenny Shoemaker, and their sister Sarah (Sally), who married a man by the name of Trueax.

John, the oldest to come to Wells County, was born in 1818. He died in 1886. John married Nancy Ann Harmasan and had the following children: Washington, who went to Kansas to live and married out there, Joshua (Jack) who never married, William Milton, who never married, and Stephan Andrew, who was born in 1860.

John Linn bought three hundred acres along the present road 600E and 400S. Eventually, the acreage was sold except for sixty-six acres where Martha still lives.

Stephan married Eliza Jane Oglesbee and moved to the present location in 1885. They had

The Linn Sisters
Top Row: Pearl, Mary. Bottom Row: Ina Mae, Martha, Chloe. Taken April 1915

five daughters: Ina Mae, Chloe, Mary, Pearl, and Martha. The first four daughters were born in the log house. Later, a new house was built and Martha, the only living daughter, still lives in the same house in which she was born. Ina Mae married Herb Conner and had three children: Donald, Evelyn and Otis. Chloe married Robert Elliott and had four children: Stephan, Enid, Elia, and Enis, who died at the age of two months. Pearl married Ollie Kreps and had three children, Max, Martha Jane, and Esther Louise.

Eliza Jane Linn died in 1935. Stephan Linn died in 1945.

LIPKEY FAMILY

We can date the Lipkey family back to 1752 when our great-great-great-great grandfather, Henry Lipkey, was born in Germany. One of the six children of Henry and Mary Ann was our great-great-great grandfather, Charles Lipkey. One of the eight children of Charles and Margaret was our great-great grandfather Henry L. Lipkey, born in 1819 in Brooke County, Virginia. In 1850, Henry L. Lipkey bought a farm in Indiana, which is located one mile north of Uniondale and still owned by the Lipkey family. One of twelve children, of Henry L. and Elizabeth Rachel, was our great grandfather William Addison Lipkey.

In 1906, William Addison Lipkey was elected Sheriff of Wells County. His son-in-law and our grandfather, Charles V. Pierce, were his deputies. William Addison and Mary Williamson Friedline had two children, Clifford Ray, and Nova Grace who married Charles V. Pierce. They had three children, one stillborn son, Mary Margaret, and Charles Clifford Pierce, also known as Charles Clifford Lipkey, who was raised by his aunt and uncle Clifford R. and Lenore P. Lipkey, after the death of his mother when he was an infant.

Our father, Charles Clifford Pierce Lipkey, was married to Helen Justine Kumfer on December 20, 1941, and lived on the Lipkey farm all their married life. Our father passed away January 4, 1990, and my mother still lives on the farm. The farming is done by our brother-in-law, Tom Fisher, who is married to our sister Cathy. They have three children, Robin, who is married, Amy, and Todd. They live across the road from my mother. Our brother Jim, and his wife JoAnn, and two children, Jeff and Jessica, live in Fort Wayne. Our sister Kay and her husband, Rob Lyons, live in Fort Wayne.

My mother has the original sheepskin deed from President Millard Fillmore dated December 20, 1850, which is the date our parents were married in 1941. *(Rebecca L. Lipkey Swoverland)*

LOHMULLER FAMILY

When the Caylor Nickel Clinic needed an Internist/Hematologist, Doctor Herbert W. Lohmuller came to Bluffton in June, 1968, leaving private practice in Philadelphia, Pennsylvania to fill the position. His wife, Genevieve, and their ten children, ages sixteen and one-half to three years, followed on July 1. Bernard, Martin, and Mary were enrolled in Bluffton High School. John and Theresa attended Central Junior High and Paul, Joseph and Margaret went to East Side Elementary. Catherine and Elizabeth were too young to go to school.

The family was warmly received into the community and immediately became involved in youth and civic activities. They were also active in Saint Joseph's Catholic Church.

All the children graduated from Bluffton High School and most pursued higher education, accumulating one associate, nine bachelor, four master and one M.D. degrees. Schools attended include Dayton University, Indiana-Purdue Fort Wayne, Indiana University Bloomington, Purdue University, Ball State University, Kettering College of Medical Arts, University of Notre Dame and Saint Mary's College.

They are now established in a variety of careers, with Mary, Theresa and Margie in Elementary Education, Cathie in business administration and Beth in communications public relations. However, Mary and Margie are now homemakers. Bernie is director of the college cable access channel in Fort Wayne. Marty is a registered respiratory therapist and John is an over-the-road truck driver. Paul has his own construction company and Joe is a surgeon.

The family is now scattered in Iowa, Missouri, Louisiana, and in Bluffton, Fort Wayne, Huntington, South Bend, and Indianapolis in Indiana. Seven of the children are married and there are eighteen grandchildren.

In addition to their church activities, Herb and Genevieve volunteered in the Migrant Ministry for many years. Herb organized and worked in the St. Joseph's Migrant Worker Clinic. Genevieve helped in the clinic and volunteered in the Migrant Day Care Center for four years and then directed it for three years.

Herb retired from the Caylor Nickel Clinic in December 1989. However, he returned part time to the family practice department in January 1991. This still allows him time for traveling and visiting family. Genevieve keeps busy with needlework, visiting family, arranging family gatherings and church and club activities. Also, she coordinated ecumenical celebrations for Church Women United. Both Herb and Genevieve enjoy singing in the church choir.

Herb received his M.D. from Ohio State University School of Medicine and was a member of the American Medical Association and American College of Physicians. He was Director of Medical Education at the Clinic as well as chairman of the department of medicine and other boards and committees at various times. Genevieve received an A.B from Trinity College, Washington, D.C. and belonged to the Medical Auxiliary, League of Women Voters and Rosary Altar Society. She is still active in the Foltz Literary Club and Church Women United.

Even though scattered, the children all consider Bluffton and the big house at 1120 River Road "home." When all are together, there is no end to the "Remember when...'s."

RICHARD D. AND JUDITH M. LONGENBERGER

We have in our possession a land purchase certificate issued to a Jacob Harbster, dated August 20, 1838, and signed by President Martin Van Buren. This certificate is for eighty acres in Harrison Township, Wells County, Indiana. The price paid for the eight acres was one hundred fifty dollars. In 1853, the farm was transferred to a Christian Baumgartner. Dick's maternal great-grandfather Peter Meyer then purchased the acreage in 1862. On November 11, 1910, it was deeded to his daughter (Dick's great aunt) Lizzie Weinland. On February 14, 1958, Dick purchased the farm from the Weinland estate at public auction. It is a Hoosier Homestead farm, having been in the same family for well over one hundred years.

Richard Dean Longenberger was born December 15, 1936, the youngest of seven children, to Ernest and Pearl Frauhiger Longenberger. They lived on the Wells-Adams County line near Tocsin. On September 29, 1958, Dick married Judith Marie Nussbaum, oldest of three children of Jerome and Dorcas Liechty Nussbaum of Berne.

Dick and Judy Longenberger

We have spent our life, and raised our family on the farm. We have three children and two grandchildren. They are Thomas Richard, born September 21, 1959, who is a partner in the farming operation. He lives in Harrison Township. Our second child, Sheryl Ann, born February 12, 1962, married Timothy Gerber. They, along with their daughter, Lydia Rae, live at Louisville, Colorado. Our youngest, Linda Fay, born August 21, 1963, married Thomas Bushee. They, along with grandson Caleb Dean, also live in Harrison Township.

We are active members of the First United Methodist Church in Bluffton. We have participated over the years in Wells County Extension Homemakers, politics, and various other organizations. *(Judy Longenberger)*

ROGER AND MARILYN LONGENBERGER

After our marriage in 1953, we built a house on my parents farm in Adams County. In 1954, employment at Gerber Furniture brought us to Wells County. We remained living in Adams County and Roger drove the fifteen miles. Having grown up on the Adam and Wells County Line, Bluffton was no stranger to Roger. He was the sixth child of Ernest and Pearl Longenberger, rural Craigville. We both graduated from Adams Central High School.

Our oldest daughter Deborah, also graduated from Adams Central in 1972 and International Business College in Fort Wayne. She now lives near Ossian with her husband, Robert Cress and two daughters, Heather, age nine and Nicole, age four. They own and operate Villa North Motors on State Road 1, north of Bluffton.

Our second daughter, Cynthia, graduated from Adams Central in 1976 and Ball State University in 1980. She taught kindergarten her first year at Adams Central. After her marriage in 1981 to Michael Carr of Bluffton, they settled in Peoria, Illinois where she has taught second grade and Mike is a C.P.A. with Caterpillar. They have two sons, Ryan, age five and Matthew age two.

Third daughter, Sara, was born in 1964 and was enrolled at the new middle school in Bluffton. She was in the seventh grade and was excited about going to a brand new school. She became very active in tennis, golf, and basketball. After graduating from Bluffton in 1982, she also attended Ball State in Muncie, where she majored in Finance. After graduating she was employed at Union Federal Bank in Indianapolis. Her marriage in 1987 brought her back to Bluffton. She married Brent Imel, who has Imel Motors in Bluffton. That same year, the State Bank of Markle was opening a Branch in Bluffton. She was named manager and is still employed there. They have one son, Drew, almost one.

In 1970, Roger and his brother, Harry, purchased the furniture store from Alvin Gerber. Harry's wife, Devona became involved in the office work. I (Marilyn) after, taking Interior Design classes at I.U.-P.U. in Fort Wayne, started in sales.

In 1977, we decided we were making too many trips back and forth. We sold our home and purchased a house on Summit Avenue here in Bluffton.

We are both members of First United Methodist Church in Bluffton and Parlor City County Club, where Roger enjoys his favorite past time.

Marilyn is a member of Alpha Eta Chapter of Psi Iota Xi Sorority here in Bluffton.

LOVELL

Ralph David Lovell was born February 25, 1895, in Harrison Township, Wells County, Indiana. He was the fourth of four children born to Michael H. Lovell and Mary Almirtie King Lovell.

Mary King was born in Cedar County, Missouri. She died January 24, 1900, in Wells County. Her husband Michael was born March 17, 1865, in Jay County, Indiana and died August 8, 1945, in Jay County.

Ralph met and married Daisy Artlica Gierhart on February 16, 1916. After residing in Illinois and working in the oil fields, they returned to Domestic, Indiana. They then purchased a farm in Jay County, where they resided until the 1960's. Upon retirement they purchased a house on 224 West in Wells County, Indiana, where they lived out the rest of their days.

Daisy Gierhart was born October 9, 1897, in Bryant, Jay County, Indiana. She was the third of six children. She died February 5, 1978, in Wells County. Her father's name was George William Gierhart. He was born December 18, 1869, in Fairfield County, Ohio. He was the son of Eli and Elizabeth Ault Gierhart. He married Edna E. Daugherty on September 24, 1892. Edna was born September 24, 1871, in Adams County, Indiana, to George and Isabelle Fifer Daugherty. She died February, 1954, and was buried at Bryant, Indiana.

Daisy and Ralph had eight children born to their marriage.

Manford was born October 19, 1916, in Randolph County, Indiana and died four hours after birth. He was buried in Windsor, Indiana.

Lewis Alonzo, born August 11, 1917, in Jay County, Indiana. He married Mary Hassaniour December 28, 1947, and died November 1, 1983, in Wells County.

Fredora Pauline, born December 1, 1919, in Illinois, married Preston Beach. She died in a motorcycle accident in 1949.

Ralph D. Lovell and Daisy A. Gierhart Lovell Taken about 1972 at the Lovell Family Christmas Dinner

Iris Evelyne, born July 16, 1922, in Bridgeport, Lawernce County, Illinois. She married George Warner and resides in Petroleum, Indiana.

Edna Fern, born November 22, 1924, in Sumner, Lawrence County, Illinois, married Paul Hench and resides in Fort Wayne, Indiana.

Audrey Joan, born November 29, 1927, in Sumner, Lawrence County, Illinois, married Vernon C. Melton October 31, 1947, and resides in Bluffton, Indiana.

Ralph David Lovell Jr., born July 22, 1932, in Bluffton, married Carol J. Clifton. He died March 20, 1986.

Patricia Arlene, born December 15, 1939, in Domestic, Wells County, Indiana, married Floyd Harshman and resides in Marshall, Illinois.

LOWRY-FRIAR

The Lowry family dates back to 1852. Benjamin and Hannah (Morris) lived in Chester Township, Wells County, Jonathan was one of ten children born in 1841. He married Elizabeth (Edgar). They lived in Chester Township, Wells County one and one-half miles from Southern Wells School. Jonathan built his home around 1870, which is still standing and has had very little changes made. We have kept this home place in the family for five generations.

They had six children. One of the daughters was Jennie born 1868-1936. She was a school teacher. She married James Wood and they had two daughters: Edith and Ethel. Edith married Cary Mounsey, had two children and moved to California. Ethel, our grandmother, married Doctor Erman Williamson in 1915. He was a veterinarian. They had three children, Myron, Jane, and Richard.

Jane, our mother, married Olin Friar in 1936. they had three children, Suzanne, Jeffery, and Cheryl. Jane remarried in 1954 to John Nestleroad. They had a son, Charles.

Suzanne (1937-1965), married James Harris in 1955. They had three children, Deborah, Gary, and Dana. Suzanne and Deborah (1955-1965) were killed in 1965, Palm Sunday tornado in Keystone. Gary married Karen Meyer, had one son, Tyson, divorced. Dana married James Nash. They have two children, Melissa and Ryan.

Jeffery married Joyce Harrold in 1962. They had three children, Teresa, Jay, and Jennie. They divorced. Jeff married Karen Kunkle in 1989. Teresa married Neil Dollar in 1980. They have three children, Dustin, Nathaniel and Sierra.

Jonathan and Elizabeth Lowry

Cheryl married Jim Davis in 1963. They had two children Brenda and Timothy. They divorced, and Cheryl married Ted Powell in 1973 and they had one son, Blake. Cheryl and family live on the home place, and Ted has an excavating business and raises miniature horses and buffalo.

Brenda married Ronald Banter in 1990. They live in Grant County.

Charles Nestleroad married Carol Stewart in 1978. They had one son, Michael. They divorced in 1986. He is now married to Lisa Bowman (1990).

LOWRY-KUNKEL FAMILIES

We can date the Lowry family back to 1852, when our great-great-great-grandparents, Benjamin and Hannah (Morris) moved to Chester Township, Wells County. One of their ten children, Jonathan, born March 3, 1841, was our great-great grandfather. He married Elizabeth (Edgar) and they had six children, four daughters and twin boys. Levi Lewis, whose twin died at birth, was our great-grandfather. He married Neva Perry. They had only one son, our grandfather, Edgar Lewis. He married Floe Carnes. They had three daughters, Crystal, Helen, and Irene.

*Harris Family February 1991
Mike (43), Sue (42), Mark (14)
David (12) and Michella (10)*

Our mother, Helen, born May 24, 1924, married Arden G. Kunkel of Poneto on June 19, 1945, soon after he returned from World War II and after she had completed a nursing degree at Ball State. They lived in Fort Wayne where Sharon Kay was born on May 2, 1947, and Carolyn Sue on June 19, 1949. Later in 1949, they moved to Tocsin, Indiana. On January 20, 1951, twins, Linda Diane and Arden Lewis, were born.

Our father's parents, Rueben and Blanche (Wolf), who both died in 1952, lived on a farm west of Tocsin, at the corner of U.S. 224 and IN 301. Our parents later that year purchased the farm that is now known as "The Lazy K." On March 22, 1958, another set of twins, Robert Brooks and Roberta Annette were born.

Our father was engaged in farming and carpenter work in the Bluffton area and retired in 1986. he died May 13, 1990. Our mother worked for thirty-seven years as an RN and retired in 1979.

Our father, a private pilot, purchased his first airplane in the late 60's. He built hangers and made part of the farm into an airstrip, where he and other pilots could pursue their hobby. Later a flying club known as the Wells County Pilots Association was formed. As a club they have sponsored annual chicken BBQ's at "the Lazy K," with profits going to charities and high school scholarships.

Sharon, who graduated from Ball State as an RN, married Lynn Woods. They live near Zanesville with their two sons, Chris, seventeen, and Michael, twelve. Sue, a graduate of Ball State with a teaching degree, married Mike Harris. They live west of Bluffton with their three children, Mark, thirteen, David, eleven, and Michella, age nine.

Linda, also a Ball State graduate with an elementary education degree, married Kent Stephens. They live in Dublin, Ohio, with their two children, Kendra, twelve, and Joel, ten. Lew graduated from Lewis College in Joliet, Illinois, married, and later moved to Greeneville, Tennessee. He is employed as a corporate pilot for Diamond "G" Aviation. He has two daughters, Karmen, sixteen, and Katy, twelve.

Bob, a roofing contractor, married Linda Kimmel and lives in Kendallville with their three sons, David, thirteen, Grant, three, and Matthew Arden, five months. Annie, who is employed as a bank teller, married Terry Hoffmeier. They live west of Ossian and will soon move to "The Lazy K," the family homestead, with their three sons, Lee Arden, eight, Benjamin, six, and Jonathan, four.

LUSK

My grandfather John N. Lusk was born in Ohio, May 12, 1829, a son of James and Julia (Beeler) Lusk, natives of Tennessee and Virginia respectively. His father died and his mother married the Reverend D.H. Drummond, who died in Harrison Township about 1870. John purchased land in Lancaster Township, Section 31. In 1866, he married Martha Routh. They had two children, Mary Jane (1867) and Charles R. (1873), who was my father. John N. died in 1907. My father graduated from Purdue and was a pharmacist for a short time before coming back to the farm to help his parents. He married Margaret Ann Smith and they had two sons, James (1911) and Robert (1913) born in the same home as their father. The house still stands today. Charles died in 1954, a member of the First Baptist Church in Bluffton. My brother, who was a professor at Purdue for eighteen years is now retired and living in Tuscon, Arizona, with wife Anna. Our parents are buried in Elm Grove Cemetery.

I attended Murray School and graduated from Lancaster High School in 1929, right before the great depression. My mother had died in 1927. I worked for different farmers in Rockcreek Township, making my home with them. When no work was available, I lived with dad and we made it by hard work. In 1936, I went to work for the Ware Baker Implement Company, working up to a mechanic.

On May 29, 1936, I married Margaret Robbins, a daughter of W.G. Robbins, a native of Illinois, and May Sturgis Robbins. Margaret's grandfather was

Lemuel D. Sturgis, son of Thomas Sturgis, born in Ireland in 1802, who came to America in 1812 and to Lancaster Township in 1852. Lemuel was a farmer in Lancaster Township and also in Liberty Township, where he died in 1903. Margaret's father died in 1958 and her mother in 1969; both are buried in Elm Grove Cemetery. She has a sister, Joan, Mrs. Nevin Kendall of Liberty Center, and had a brother Bill, who died in November, 1990.

50th wedding anniversary, May 1986
Front Row: Robert and Margaret Lusk. Back Row: L to R: Robert W. Lusk, Ann German, Rebecca Swanson, Jackie Jack, John R. Lusk

Margaret graduated from Bluffton High School in 1934. We had five children: Robert W. who graduated from Bluffton High School in 1955; Ann, Jackie, John R. and Rebecca, all of whom graduated from Steuben County schools.

After I worked in Fort Wayne at the General Electric for a time I decided I wanted to farm. We lived on the Shoemaker farm west of Bluffton where the Peyton North on 100E now stands. I served on the board of directors of the 4-H Association and was president for two years. In 1955 and 1956 I was a Wells County Hospital trustee. In 1955, we bought a farm in Steuben County and moved there in late 1956.

The children are now all married and we have fifteen grandchildren and six great-grandchildren. I am retired, and our son John does the farming. Margaret still has membership in Poplar Grove Extension Club in Wells County and we still have our membership in the Bluffton Baptist Church. *Submitted by Robert and Margaret (Robbins) Lusk.*

THE REV. S.A. MACKLIN FAMILY

My parents, the Rev. S.A. Macklin and Ermah E. (Banghart) Macklin moved from Van Wert, Ohio, to Zanesville in the fall of 1923. Their two children were Wilma Theodore, a fifth grader, and Howard Addis, two years old. Father was pastor of the Middle Church, the United Brethren in Christ (Old Constitution).

Wilma attended the two-room school in Zanesville until it closed in 1926. Then she went to Union Center and graduated there in 1931. In 1931 our family moved across the county line to Allen County, and Howard attended Lafayette Central. He graduated there in 1938, the same year Wilma graduated from Huntington College. Howard also graduated from the college in 1942.

Wilma taught in northern Indiana for 23 years. Her subjects were vocal music in grades 1-12, English and Latin. She was also high school librarian.

Wilma received her MA from Ball State in 1949. She also attended summer school at Indiana University, Manchester College, and Purdue.

For eight years Wilma was assistant librarian at Huntington College. After nine years of retirement she went back to work at the college library in 1979 and is still there (April, 1991) part-time.

Howard was in World war II, serving with the army in the Pacific Theater. After the war he taught math for five years. He and his wife both have their master's degrees from Ball State in the field of math. Howard taught at Indiana Technical College for sixteen years, then went to Ferris States at Big Rapids, Michigan, where he taught until he retired.

Howard Macklin, Wilma Macklin

Our parents were both born in 1880. They met at Tri-State College and married on Thanksgiving Eve, 1913. Wilma was born October 6, 1914; Howard was born October 28, 1920. Wilma was married to Donald H. Dutcher at Winona Lake, Indiana, August 1, 1959. Howard married Helen Whitacre at Pennville, Indiana, August 20, 1950. They have one son, Larry Lee. He has two children, Chris and Staci, both in grade school

My parents retired and moved to Winona Lake in December, 1951. They moved to Huntington to be near us in 1962 and died in the mid sixties.

The Dutchers lived in Huntington in the 1960's, retired at Winona Lake in August, 1969, and moved back to Huntington in June, 1978, to be near my stepson and his three boys.

The Dutcher's have been active in church, school and college activities. Wilma played the piano and organ for many years, gave private lessons, and played for weddings, funerals and social activities. She was a paid accompanist for singers during her college years.

Donald was a tank-truck driver for the Shell for twenty-one years. After moving to Huntington, he drove a transport truck for Marathon. *(Wilma Dutcher)*

MADDUX

Our great-grandfather, John N. Maddux, was born in Wells County, Indiana in 1843. He was the son of Jacob and Anna Maddux, who emigrated from Ohio. John N. was a farmer, and lived in Lancaster Township in a small community named Eagleville. He served in the Union Forces during the Civil War. He married Elizabeth Platter in 1867, and died at the young age of thirty, in 1873. Elizabeth later married Augustus Raver in 1877. Elizabeth was born in Virginia to Nicholas and Malinda Platter. Nicholas and Malinda were married in 1842 in Shelby County, Ohio, and emigrated to Wells County in 1856. Nicholas was a farmer, and also ran a sawmill in Eagleville for twenty years. As an avocation, he made furniture and constructed rough boxes for undertakers. Elizabeth and John N. had two children, William E. and Chester J. H. Maddux. Chester was our grandfather.

Chester married Ida Hege, the daughter of Amos and Mary Patton Hege in 1894. Amos Hege served

L to R: Jack Zimmerman, Jane Stinson, Max Stinson. Seated L to R: Carolyn Zimmerman, Alta Maddux.

with the Union Forces as a private soldier in Company A, 30th Indiana Regiment, enlisting on February 10, 1864, and being discharged on November 14, 1865. Chester did some farming, and also worked in the general store in Kingsland. Chester and Ida had three children including our father Dwight E. Maddux. Dwight was a mechanic throughout his lifetime, and married Alta M. Studebaker in 1916. Alta was the daughter of George W. and Sara Huffman Studebaker, who lived on a farm near Kingsland in Lancaster Township. Dwight and Alta had two daughters, Jane and Carolyn. Jane married Max L. Stinson, and they reside on a farm in Wells County. They had one son, Michael, who is deceased. Carolyn married Jack R. Zimmerman, of LaGrange County, Indiana. Jack served in the military for twenty-two years, retiring in 1972, and has worked in civil service for the past seventeen years. They reside in Virginia. Jack and Carolyn are the parents of two daughters, Kathleen Himes, and Kristine Cassidy, both of Indianapolis; and one son, David, residing in Knoxville, Tennessee. There are six grandchildren in the family.

MADDUX-MINNICH

We can date the Maddux family back to August 1843, when our great-grandfather, John N. Maddux, was born in Lancaster Township. In August 1862, he enlisted in Company G, 101st Regiment, Indiana Volunteers to serve in the Civil War. While in the line of duty at Munfordville, Kentucky, he became ill, developing lung disease. He received a medical discharge in 1863 at Gallatin, Tennessee. In 1867, he married Elizabeth Platter, the daughter of Nicholas and Melinda Platter. John and Elizabeth had two sons, William Edwin and our grandfather, Chester Jacob Hamilton Maddux. In 1894, Chester married Ida Hege, the daughter of Amos and Mary Patton Hege. They had three children: Dwight, Charles, and Mildred.

Chester and Ida Maddux and Dwight, Charles and Mildred taken in 1912

Our father, Charles, married Bertha Graden in 1917. He was a car salesman and enjoyed horses, having a riding horse until the age of seventy. Our mother enjoys quilting and crocheting and has been an active member of her church since 1911. She was the daughter of John and Rosa Moser Graden, both Swiss immigrants. John came to this country in December 1887, at the age of sixteen. His first job was working on a farm which is now Riverview Addition in Bluffton. Rosa arrived in New York in April 1895, at the age of nineteen. They were married in 1897. Their other children were: Albert, Mary, John, Frederick, Louise, Edward, Helen, and Esther.

Our parents had two daughters, Dorothy, born July 31, 1919, and Marilyn, born October 7, 1932. Dorothy married Frederick D. Sprunger and they had two children, Susan and Thomas. Marilyn married Floyd Minnich on December 25, 1951. They had three children: Joseph, born August 25, 1958, Timothy, born March 17, 1960, and Cynthia, born May 22, 1962. Joseph married Kim Shively and they had two children, Scott and Jennifer. He is a quality control manager for Simpson Industries. Timothy married Lori James and they are the parents of three children: Andrew, Megan, and Nicholas. He is chief financial officer and vice president of Triple Crown, a trucking division of Norfolk and Southern. Cynthia is a student nurse at Lutheran Hospital in Fort Wayne.

Floyd Minnich was born September 16, 1928, to Oscar and Ethel Mowery Minnich. Oscar was a farmer and moved to Wells County with his parents, Samuel and Nancy Gump Minnich. He married Ethel Mowery, the daughter of Samuel and Mary Reynolds Mowery. Floyd, a co-owner of Graden Tire, served two years in the Korean War, attaining the rank of staff sergeant. One year of his service was spent in Germany. He served on the Bluffton Volunteer Fire Department, the Bluffton City Council, the Board of Works, the Bluffton Harrison Metropolitan School Board, and was vice chairman of the original Wells County Area Plan Commission. As a member of the First United Church of Christ, he served as president of consistory, elder, deacon, trustee, and on the building committee for the educational unit. He is also a member of the Wells County Historical Society, the American Legion, and a former member of the Lions Club.

Marilyn was employed for eight years by Indiana Bell Telephone Company, and since 1973, she has been the bookkeeper for Graden Tire. She is also a member of the First United Church of Christ, the Wells County Historical Society, the American Legion Auxillary, and an inactive member of Tri Kappa.

NATHAN MADDUX FAMILY

Nathan Henry Maddux (1910-1981) was born October 29, in Wells County, the only son of Lester and Rosella (Hilge) Maddux. He had five sisters: Mary (Miller), Genella (Hendricks), Edna Faye (Rice), Marjorie (Waters), and Harriette (Cary). His father, Lester, and grandfather, Nathan, were lifelong residents of Bluffton. His mother, Rosella, was the daughter of Henry Hilge and Katherine (Yager) Hilge from Honduras in Adams County. The Hilge family, with German origins, had migrated to Adams County from Pennsylvania.

Nate, as his friends called him, graduated from Bluffton High School, earning Major B letters in several sports. He was active in basketball, football, and track, setting a high jump record that lasted for several years.

He met and married Ruth Miller, who came to Wells County from Hannibal, Missouri. Together they raised four daughters: Diana D. (Captain), Marna Nadine (Brown), Kathy Jill (Boeslund), and Gay Ann (Isaksen). Diana and her family reside in Wells County (See Captain entry). Marna, Kathy, and Gay and their respective families reside in Fort Wayne, Indiana.

Marna has two sons: Christopher David and Kent Richard, two daughters: Michelle Lynn and Deborah Sue, and five grandchildren: Brandon Jeramiah, Nicole Michelle, Nathan Richard, Joshua Lyn, and Kyle Ray.

Kathy has two daughters: Cassandre Raeannan and Sarah Rebekah.

Gay has two daughters: Amanda Ruth and Amber Noel.

After graduating from high school Nate worked several jobs, including fireman at the Bluffton Municipal Plant. At the beginning of World War II, he accepted employment at the General Electric Company in Fort Wayne, Indiana, where he held the position of electrical engineer for thirty-two years before retiring due to ill health.

A man of firm convictions, Nate was active in local politics, serving on the city council from 1948 to 1968. He was a life-long member of Epworth Methodist Church where he was a board member for many years. Deeply dedicated to his God, family and community, he was constantly striving to make the world a better place in which to live.

MANKEY-FRAUHIGER

Forest Mankey, a son of Christian and Sarah Bridegan Mankey was born May 25, 1891. He had five brothers and sisters. They were: Wesley, James, Susie, Harve and Ervin.

On March 5, 1913, he married Nettie Frauhiger, daughter of Phillip and Bertha Meyer Frauhiger. She was born October 17, 1891. She had nine brothers and sisters. They were: Noah, Maggie, Emma, Cora, Della, Harry, Albert and Fannie.

They traveled to Bluffton in a horse and carriage to be married. They started their married life living on the Wells/Adams County line before moving to Montpelier. While at Montpelier, he drove horses to haul stone for road repair in addition to farming to support his growing family. By the time they decided to move from Montpelier back to Wells County they had six young children.

Standing: Carl, Patsy, Ralph, Mabel, Walter, Glen.
Sitting: Laura, Dorothy, Forest, Freda, Nettie, Mary.

Back in Wells County they continued farming. In addition to the usual crops, they also grew sugar beets, and he worked at the sugar beet factory in Decatur and, during World War II, at General Electric in Fort Wayne. Nettie was kept busy tending to her family and taking care of the large gardens she planted each year. She would make beds and paths in her gardens. Each bed would be planted with a different vegetable in the center and would be edged by lettuce on all four sides. She would grow enough to feed her large family and their families and many of their neighbors. She also milked their cows in addition to a large pickle patch which she would pick and sell to customers to take them to the pickle factory in Bluffton. There were never strangers to the Mankey family. Anyone was always welcome to join in for a meal or to spend time with them.

After making several moves in Wells and Adams Counties, in 1941 they made their final move to a farm in Lancaster Township where they lived the rest of their life. They had thirteen children

They are: Mrs. Wilford (Freda) McBride, who lives in Jefferson Township east of Ossian; Mrs. William (Violet) Hoffman (May 11, 1915 - January 24, 1946); Mrs. Jacob (Mabel) Denis of Fort Wayne; Ralph who lives near Magley in Adams County; Carl of Craigville; Glen (June 4, 1926 - February 2, 1983); Mrs. Sherman (Mary) Gould of Decatur; Walter of Craigville route; Lester who died in a motorcycle accident in 1950; Bonnie (September 8, 1935 - October 2, 1935); Mrs. Larry (Patsy) Dafforn who lives on the Allen-Wells County line north of Ossian and Mrs. Doyle (Laura) Werling who resides just north of Tocsin.

Nettie died June 9, 1974, and Forest died January 13, 1979. They leave behind a very large number of offspring which to this date adds up to thirteen children, fifty-three grandchildren, one hundred sixteen great-grandchildren, twenty-two great-great grandchildren and still growing. They are laid to rest in the Pleasant Dale Church of the Brethren Cemetery in Adams County.

MARVIN L. MANN FAMILY

Marvin Lee Mann, son of Wilson and Anoli (Walters) Mann of Monroe, Indiana, was born July 27, 1945, in Decatur, Indiana. He has an older brother, Frederick; a twin brother, Mervin; a younger brother, Bruce; and a younger sister, Beth. Marvin graduated in 1963 from Adams Central High School in Monroe. During high school, he had been active in the band. After high school, he worked at the Berne Furniture Company before starting in January 1965 at Corning Glass Works in Bluffton. He joined the Air National Guard in July 1965 and retired from it in October 1988. He has worked since September 1983 at the Greenville, Ohio, Plant of Corning, Incorporated.

The Marvin L. Mann Family
Front: Sandy and Marvin. Back: Jon and Katina

Marvin married Sandra Kay (Nihiser) Mann, the only daughter of Lawrence and Erma (Fackler) Nihiser of Van Wert, Ohio. Sandra, who was born August 7, 1948, in Van Wert, has two older brothers, Larry and Jerry. Sandra graduated in 1966 from

Van Wert High School. She had been active during high school in Junior Achievement and had her own School of Dance. Upon completion of high school, she attended Ohio State University. Sandra received a bachelor of science and a master of science in elementary education from Indiana University. She started teaching fifth grade for the Bluffton-Harrison School District in the fall of 1973 and is currently still in that position.

The Manns have two children. Jon Harlo was born December 4, 1969, at the Wells Community Hospital. Jon graduated in 1988 from Bluffton High School. In December 1990, he received an associates degree in applied science from the School of Engineering and Technology at Purdue University. He is currently working on his bachelor's degree in computer integrated manufacturing technology (robotics). Jon has been employed since December 1987 as a cashier at Scott's Grocery in Bluffton.

Katina Marie was born September 5, 1972, at the Wells Community Hospital. Katina (Tina) graduated in 1990 from Bluffton High School and is currently attending Ball State University, majoring in elementary education. She has been employed since August 1989 as a bulk food's clerk at Scott's Grocery in Bluffton.

The Manns, who reside at 1121 Ridgewood Lane, Bluffton, are members of the Pleasant Dale Church of the Brethren, in Adams County, Indiana.

KENNETH RICHARD MANNING FAMILY

Kenneth Manning was born in Miami County, Indiana, on January 10, 1922, the son of Joseph O. and Nina Hazel Edgerton Manning. Joseph died in November, 1948; and Hazel in April, 1928. Kenneth attended eleven public schools in northern Indiana before graduating from high school at Bluffton in 1940.

After two years at Heidelberg College, Tiffin, Ohio, Kenneth married Dorothy Ann Harward of Durham, North Carolina, and served three years in the U.S. Army Air Corps during World War II, attaining the rank of first lieutenant. Following military service, Kenneth completed requirements for the bachelor of arts degree from Duke University. Daughters, Nancy Carol and Brenda Kay, were born, respectively, in 1946 and 1948.

Following his graduation in 1949, Duke University employed Kenneth as a budget specialist which began a career in college and university business management and teaching, spanning a period of forty-one years. Institutions served during this time were, besides Duke, the University of Michigan, the University of Alabama, Winthrop College, South Carolina, and Indiana University. Son Douglas Keith was born in 1958. Kenneth earned the MBA degree in 1975, and a certificate in management accounting in 1979. He and Dorothy were divorced in 1983. He retired effective June 30, 1990, and now resides in Bluffton.

This brief biographical sketch was written primarily to facilitate the introduction of additional notes regarding Kenneth's family history, which may be typical of many Wells County residents if they took the time to investigate their backgrounds. Prior to 1988, Kenneth had no knowledge of his ancestry and their origins. Recent genealogical research has provided the information contained in these notes.

Thomas Edgerton, Sr. was born in England circa 1705. Thomas, Jr. was born in New Jersey circa 1740. Joseph, son of Thomas, Jr., was born in 1762, moved to North Carolina, thence to Indiana in about 1805. Joseph brought part of his family from North Carolina including his youngest child, Daniel. Daniel's son, Calvin, was the first Edgerton born in Indiana. The date was January 9, 1827. In 1847, Calvin and his new bride, Hannah, moved from their home in Wayne County to Miami County where they raised ten children, and were prominent in the affairs of the Amboy Friends' Church and Harrison Township. Calvin and Hannah's oldest son, Franklin, and his son, William, were Nina Hazel Edgerton's immediate forebearers. Kenneth, therefore, is a seventh generation Hoosier.

Other maternal ancestors arrived in America before the Edgertons. Among them were Edmund Nicholson (Massachusetts c. 1637), Mareen Duvall (Maryland c. 1650), William Bundy (North Carolina c. 1650), William Bogue (North Carolina c. 1710), Thomas Atwood, Joshua Perisho, and Benois Brasseur. Christopher Bundy, a fourth generation American, and Hazel's great-great-great-grandfather, was a veteran of the Revolutionary War. Still other maternal ancestors included surnames such as Oden, McFadden, Overman, Stubbs, Hill, Saint, Smith, Boyer, Wells, Penn, Jacob, Boyd, Stevens, and Cheney.

Joseph Manning's family has more recent American origins and is more difficult to trace but includes such surnames as Swope, Artsburger, Hannah, and McNeal.

Your family history, too, can be both surprising and rewarding.

MARSHALL

We don't have much history about these ancestors of mine. All our older ancestors that could tell us much about them are deceased.

I am Aileen Johnson Mertz.

My grandmother's name was Fidelia Carey Haughton.

Great-grandfather's name was Zebelom Carey. He was born in 1815 and died in January, 1883. He was seventy-three years old. Great-grandmother's name was Arzenith Carey. She died on January 30, 1886, at age seventy-three. They were buried in Friends Church Cemetery, at Rockford, Indiana.

Fidelia married James Marshall. This was my grandfather, who died January 17, 1892, at the age of thirty-six years, three months and eight days. He was buried in Friends Cemetery at Rockford, Indiana. Fidelia was born August 17, 1894, and died April 27, 1940. She was eighty-two years and ten days. She was buried at Emanuel Methodist Cemetery at Rockford, Indiana. They had three children. Luetta Marshall was born in 1887 and died in 1896. She was buried beside her father, James Marshall. Another daughter was Orpha Arominia Marshall. She married Estel A. Johnson. She was born October 10, 1890, and died January 15, 1949, at age fifty-eight. She is buried in Mossburg Cemetery, Liberty Township, Wells County, Indiana. They had three children: Lucille Moser, who lives near Laporte; Aileen Mertz, who lives near Bluffton; and Paul Estel, who lives near Berne, Indiana.

Another daughter was Stella Marshall Markley Redd. She was born March 24, 1884, and died July 22, 1973. She is buried in Six Mile Cemetery, Harrison Township, Wells County, Indiana. She married Oliver Markley. They adopted one boy. His name was Arthur Lawrence Street Markley. He was killed in World War II in an airplane crash in Texas. Mr. Markley died from a stroke. Later Aunt Stella married an old time friend of the family, George Redd. Mr. Redd passed away and is buried in Elma Grove Cemetery in Bluffton, Indiana. Aunt Stella attended Six-Mile Church and lived one-half mile east of it until she married Mr. Redd; then she moved into Bluffton. *(Aileen Mertz)*

MARSHALL-HAUGHTON

We don't have much history about these ancestors of mine. All our older ancestors that could tell us much about them are deceased.

I am Aileen Johnson Mertz writing this article.

My grandmother was Fidelia Carey Marshall Haughton. At one time she lived on Smokey Row Pike, which is now Corning Road.

Great-grandfather's name was Zebelom Carey. He was born in 1815 and died January 13, 1883. He was seventy-three years old. Great-grandmother's name was Arzenith Carey. She died on January 30, 1886, at age seventy-three years, nine months and two days. This was taken from a tombstone in the Friends Cemetery, Rockford, Indiana.

Fidelia married James Marshall. This is my grandfather. He died January 17, 1892, at the age of thirty six years, three months and eight days. Our mother was only two years old when her father died. Mr. Marshall is buried in the Friends Cemetery at Rockford, Indiana. They had three children. Luetta Marshall born in 1887 and died in 1896. She was buried beside her father, James Marshall, in Friends Cemetery at Rockford, Indiana. Fidelia was born August 17, 1858, and died April 27, 1940, age eighty-two years, eight months and ten days. She is buried in Emanuel Methodist Cemetery at Rockford, Indiana. The other children were Orpha Aromonia Marshall. She married Estel A. Johnson. She was born October 10, 1890, and died January 15, 1949, age fifty-eight. She is buried in Mossburg Cemetery, Liberty Township, Wells County, Indiana. They had three children: Lucille Moser, near Laporte; Aileen Mertz, near Bluffton; and Paul Estel, near Berne, Indiana.

Another daughter is Stella Marshall Markley Redd. Aunt Stella was born March 24, 1884, and died on July 22, 1973. She is buried in Six Mile Cemetery, Harrison Township, Wells County, Indiana. She married Oliver Markley. Later he died from a stroke and is buried in Six Mile Cemetery, Harrison Township, Wells County, Indiana. They adopted one boy. His name was Arthur Lawrence Street Markley. He was killed in World War II in Texas. He was a navigator on the plane. Later Aunt Stella married an old time friend of the family, George Redd. Later he died and is buried in Elm Grove Cemetery in Bluffton, Indiana.

We always called Stella, "Aunt Stell." That was a request by her when we were very young. She attended Six-Mile Church and lived east of it one-half mile. She lived there most of her married life until she married Mr. Redd; then she moved into Bluffton. Aunt Stella had a son earlier in life, Don Murphy. He is buried in the Friends Cemetery at Rockford, Indiana.

There was also another half sister raised in the home. She is Hazel Haughton. She was never married. She had typhoid fever when she was ten years old. Her body grew but her mind didn't. She was born August 17, 1894 and died June 13, 1985. She was ninety-one years old. She is buried beside her mother in the Emanuel Cemetery, Rockford, Indiana.

Fidelia had a son, Willis Deam. We don't have any dates of anything about him. He left home very young because he didn't care for his step-father. He got a job on the interurban in Marion, Indiana. Later he went to Madison, Wisconsin, to make his home. He joined the Klu Klux Klan, not realizing what it was like. He later withdrew from it. He saved his money and bought him a furniture store there. He married a woman in Wisconsin and is buried there. I remember Uncle Willis real well. (*Aileen Johnson Mertz*)

MARTIN-BENDER

George Cleveland ("Cleve") and Minnie Sarah (Frantz) Martin, with their children, Galen, Eulala, Alice Elene, and Alvada, arrived in Jay County about January 1919. They moved there from Greenbrier County, West Virginia. Already in the area were Minnie's two brothers, John and Joe Frantz, with their families.

Cleve was a farmer and always lived on rented farms. The family lived on five different farms in Jay County and three more children, Blendene, Theora, and Veva, were born there.

Merlin Keith Bender and Elene Martin Bender

Cleve moved his family to Wells County to the George Templin farm, east of Petroleum, in March, 1928. They lived there one year, then moved to what was known as the Ellingham farm, two miles west of Bluffton. Almost a year later when the farm was sold, it was moving time again. The youngest son, Fred, was born in October, 1929, before they left that farm in March, 1930. Next they moved to the Hurt Neff farm, one miles west of Union Center School in Union Township. They were able to live there until March, 1937, when they moved to the Humke farm, two miles north of North Manchester in Wabash County.

When the family moved to the Neff farm, Elene started at the Union Center School as a sophomore. There she met her future husband, Merlin Keith Bender, known as "Buzzy" by all who knew him well. They were not married until April 18, 1937, on Elene's twenty-first birthday at the home of her parents near North Manchester

Bender Family - August 1990
Back (L to R) Gerry Bender, L. Kay Roberts, Alan Daugherty. Front (L to R) Karen Roberts, Elene Bender, Regina Daugherty

They started housekeeping in Mrs. Waltz's three-room Uniondale apartment which rented for eight dollars per month. Buzzy ran Cupp's Cabin Filling Station, located just behind Cupp's Grocery in which Elene worked part-time. February, 1938, the young couple moved in with Buzzy's parents, William and Elva Bender, two miles north of Uniondale. The move was to help with the farming and remodeling of the house. Buzzy and Elene moved to the next farm south of Buzzy's folks in January, 1940, then one year later to the Harris farm, two miles north and one and one-quarter mile west of Uniondale. Due to Buzzy's failing health in September, 1950, Buzzy and Elene bought the Elizabeth Brickley property on South Main Street in Uniondale where Elene still lives. Buzzy passed away January 29, 1951, from a subarachoid hemorrhage. While living with Buzzy's parents on June 22, 1939, Elene had their first child, Gerry Lynn. Gerry started at Union Center School, but after the family moved, attended Rockcreek. He graduated from there in 1957, then went to Purdue, where he earned degrees in Horticulture and elementary education. He's taught elementary school twenty-eight years at Indianapolis.

Karen Kay was born second. She met Lawrence Kay Roberts while in school and then married in 1960. Their family history including children and grandchildren is in this publication.

Regina Lee was Buzzy and Elene's last child. She attended Rockcreek but graduated at Lancaster in 1966. She married Alan Daugherty. Additional family information is located in another family history.

C. MARTIN FAMILY

Cosie (Cozy) and Bessie Martin moved from the Gosport-Bloomington, Indiana, area to the Bash Farm Dairy between Roanoke and Fort Wayne in 1918. They moved to Zanesville, Indiana in 1922. They were blessed with ten children; two died shortly after birth. In Zanesville, "Cozy" as people called him, worked for the Keplinger Creamery & Dairy, driving the milk and butter truck to Fort Wayne.

Back row (L to R): Ruby, Kenneth, Ronald, Herbert, Larry. Front row (L to R): Shirley, Imogene, Bessie Martin, Pauline, Cosie Martin

After Keplinger Dairy was disbanded, farmers in the Zanesville community wanted a creamery in the area. They convinced Cozy to start one, which he did with very little financing. Being 1929, Depression time, it was really rough, but by hard work and long hours, he was successful.

The Zanesville Creamery, formerly the Klenke Grist Mill, was located across from the Pallet Co. The Martin family bought the Huldy Miller property, and made a buggy shop into a house where the Delm Shepler house now stands. Then he bought the Klenke property, next to the creamery, in 1930. Cozy built a filling station next to the creamery in 1934, operated by Harvey Snyder. In 1937, he built a modern Shell station on the main corner in Zanesville, operated by Larry Perkins. It is now owned and operated by Roebuck Bros.

Creamery - (L to R): Ed Seibolt, C. Martin, Red Stark, Velma Cavitt, Ernest Reed

Cozy and Bessie worked had and helped their children, who wished to stay in the area, built homes. Of course Cozy demanded they come by with a payment each month. After operating the creamery for a number of years, Cozy had a nervous breakdown, and in 1948, decided to sell out to the Sherman White Co. of Fort Wayne.

Cosie Martin home next to creamery

He had bought the Art Merriman farm, at the east edge of Zanesville, in 1946. After being raised on a farm in southern Indiana, along Bean Blossom Creek near Gosport (where, at one time, it was a noted hide-out for the famous bank robber, John Dillinger), he said he would like to go to the farm again.

He was successful on the farm, raising many hogs and employing all the young kids in Zanesville, among them, Tom Bailey and Steve Martin (others unknown).

Cosie Martin and son Kenny

Cozy and Bessie's children (oldest to youngest):

Ken Martin, retired married Pauline Middaugh of rural Uniondale. Now residing at Lake Livingston, Huntsville, Texas, he was in Houston many years with a welding supply business; owner of Alloy Welding Supply, and partner in Iweco Supply.

Pauline married Fred Young, retired, Bluffton, Indiana. He ran a farm equipment business in Zanesville. They reside in Florida six months; and at a lake in northern Indiana six months.

Imogene, married Robert Deam, Bluffton. Robert (deceased) worked at Joslyn Steel Mill as Superintendent of Maintenance.

Ruby married Dusty Rhoads, of Garrett, Indiana. Railroad man, lives in Auburn, Indiana. Retired from Magnavox.

Herbert Martin, rural Markle, married Juanita Colemen, Waynedale, Indiana. Insurance business many years; employed at L.S. Ayres, Fort Wayne.

Ronald Martin, Graham Dr., Fort Wayne, married Marlene Wildey, Waynedale. Employed many years at Zollner Piston Co., Fort Wayne.

Shirley married Phil Husband, Roanoke, Indiana. Shirley is employed at Fort Wayne Community Schools. Phil worked many years as foreman at International Harvester; employed as food marketing foreman, Fort Wayne.

Larry Martin, Ossian, Indiana, married Edie Sells. Years at Magnavox Co. Real estate Co. Now at Magnavox.

P.S.: one more memo... Cozy made us all, and our spouses, work in the creamery, or the younger ones on the farm, from early in the morning until late at night. But we never regretted it!

MARTIN CHILDREN

Galen C. Martin was the oldest child of "Cleve" and Minnie Martin (see separate family sketch). He worked on their rented farm doing all tasks that fell his lot. In 1930 he graduated from East Rockcreek, Wells County. While attended International Business College, Galen married Mary Harvey of Markle (1933). After he graduated his farming days were over. He worked for Gulf Oil Company doing everything from operating a station in Fort Wayne to doing office work in Bryan and Steubeville, Ohio to owning his own bulk oil plant in St. Clairsville, Ohio.

G.C. Martin family taken June 22, 1948 Back (L to R) Veva, Theora, Blendene, Alvada, Elene, Eulala. Front (L to R) Fred, Cleve, Minnie Galen

Galen and Mary had six children. First, Jacqueline, who became an RN, is married, has two children and lives in Wheeling, West Virginia. Second, Clark spent some time in the Army, is married with five children in Utah. Next, Carole died at two years. Eric became an architectural engineer, is married with two children and lives in St. Clairsville. Fifth, Brewster, attended Ohio State, is married with two children. Gordon, the last child, completed college, married, has three children and lives in St. Clairsville. Brewster and Gordon have a pre-cast concrete factory in Wheeling, West Virginia.

Galen died July 15, 1984 but Mary still lives in their home in St. Clairsville.

"Cleve" and Minnie's second child, first daughter, Eulala, did usual household duties and did a little farm work when necessary. She graduated from East Union High, Wells County, in 1931, and attended Manchester College. She became a teacher of elementary classes, earned her lifetime license and spent thirty-one years teaching public school, three years in third grade and fourth plus twenty-eight years in fifth and sixth.

On August 13, 1940, she and Robert McLean were married at Plymouth, Massachusetts. They had no children.

The next children Elene (Bender) and Alvada (Snyder) are covered in other family histories in this book.

Blendene lived with "Cleve" and Minnie, worked in Wabash, Indiana, was never married and still lives in North Manchester.

Theora graduated from Chester School, North Manchester, in 1940. She worked at Honeywell in Wabash, and married serviceman Charles Ellis April 20, 1945. Charles was stationed in Harlingen, Texas. Theora lived in Texas until Charles tour of service was finished. They moved to Anderson, Indiana. She did office work, and Charles worked for General Motors. Charles died in 1978. Theora remained in Anderson and ma.ried Don Welter December 12, 1980. She had no children.

Veva graduated from Chester High also. She is a widow and lives in Warsaw. Her three sons by Elmer Hackworth are Craig of Michigan, Steven in Colorado, and Laird in South Carolina. A later marriage was to Alex Shepherd.

Fred, the youngest of the Martin children, graduated from Chester High and entered the Air Force as soon as he was eighteen, serving eight years as a jet mechanic. Fred now owns Farmer's Mill in Zanesville. He has two step-children, Doug Jacobs in Wisconsin and Paula Jacobs Moore of Ossian. His son, Scott, is married and lives in California.

MARTIN-FRANTZ

About December, 1918, George Cleveland (Cleve) Martin and Minnie Frantz Martin with their four children: Galen six, Eulala four, Elene two, and Alvada four months, boarded the train in Rainelle, West Virginia. They came to Indiana to become Hoosiers.

John Frantz and Joe Frantz, two of Minnie's brothers, had settled in Indiana a few years before Cleve and Minnie arrived. They were kind enough to have a place for the newcomers to move into. This meant the Martins started their Hoosier life in Jay County.

Cleve and Minnie didn't buy a farm. Being a renter of land meant frequent moves for the family.

After nine years, five moves, and three more daughters: Blendene, Theora, and Veva, the family moved north to the Lawrence Templin farm located east of Petroleum in Wells County. The move meant changing schools. Galen and Eulala were in Poling High School while the younger children were in Liberty, a one-room school. Now they were all in the Petroleum School.

George Cleveland Martin and Minnie Sarah Frantz Martin 50th wedding anniversary September 1961

A 1929 move was from Templin farm to the Ellingham farm west of Bluffton. The most exciting event of this move happened in October, 1929. Finally, a baby brother came into the family. After six girls — what a change!! He was named Fred.

The Rockcreek School was blessed with six Martin students for one year and two months. In the spring of 1930 there was another move. The Neff farm in Union Township was the family's new home. Then... imagine, seven years in the same house!

Galen Martin graduated from Rockcreek School in 1930. Eulala graduated from Union Center High in 1931, Elene from there in 1933, and Alvada in 1936.

In 1937, Cleve and Minnie and the younger kids moved to the Humke farm north of North Manchester. Here they lived for ten years. After Cleve quit farming, they moved to Sidney for one year, then back to North Manchester in 1948. Cleve was caretaker of Manchester's Warvel Park for several years, and in September, 1961, Cleve and Minnie celebrated their golden wedding anniversary with a family dinner in Warvel Park. Many friends and relatives called at the park during that day.

Cleve died in Manchester, December 15, 1964, at age seventy-nine.

Minnie continued living in their house until the summer of 1980, when she was brought back to Wells County. She lived at Capri II almost a year. She lived at Meadowvale on her ninety-fifth birthday. In March, 1983, Minnie was taken to the newly opened Ossian Health Care. She celebrated her ninety-sixth birthday on May 4. She died there September 19, 1983.

MARTIN-LAMBERT

The Lambert name appears in English records as early as 1273 A.D. I am Orlu (Lambert) Martin, born June 28, 1903, daughter of William A. Lambert and Leona (Brodt) Lambert, life-long residents of Wells County. I graduated from Bluffton High School in the class of 1922. I attended Madam Blaker's Teachers College in Indianapolis and received my teaching degree from Ball State University in Muncie. I was a teacher in the Wells County Schools for five years (1923-1928).

On May 20, 1928, I married Raymond Guy Martin, son of Grant and Rachael (Thrailkill) Martin. Following our marriage we lived in Toledo, Ohio, for the next forty-two years. Upon my husband's retirement from the Libby-Owens-Ford Glass Company, we returned to Wells County, where he died on November 22, 1968. We were the parents of a son, Robert A. Martin, born June 25, 1930. Following his service in the U.S. Navy during the Korean War, he received his B.A. degree from the University of Toledo and M.A. and Ph.D. degrees from the University of Michigan, where he remained as a professor of English for twenty-seven years. Since 1986, he has been a professor of English at Michigan State University.

I have four grandchildren: John, born 1961, graduated B.A. from Harvard University, Phi Beta Kappa, Magna Cum Laude, and is presently an editor with a publishing firm in Boston. Douglas, born 1963, graduated B.S. from the University of Michigan as an electrical engineer and received his M.S. degree from the University of Missouri. He presently works for an aircraft company in St. Louis. Carolyn, born in 1967, is presently completing post-graduate work at Michigan State after receiving her B.S. degree there also. Her twin sister, Christine, received her B.A. from Albion College in psychology and presently works as a family and child counselor in the Lansing area.

My ancestors were largely immigrants. My paternal grandparents, Robert and Caroline (Hardin) Lambert were both born in Queen County, Ireland. He served in the Civil War and was a member of the Lew Dailey Post, Bluffton, Indiana. During the war he served under General William Tecumseh Sherman during his campaign in the South. My maternal grandparents, John and Emma (Sechler) Brodt, lived in Uniondale, Indiana. John was the son of Gottlieb Brodt and Margaretta (Seaman) Brodt. Emma (Sechler) Brodt was the daughter of Benjamin and Eliza (Moyer) Sechler, and was directly descended from the Everett family of Massachusetts and Lehigh County, Pennsylvania. Edward Everett was the president of Harvard University, U.S. Congressman and senator from Massachusetts, and Ambassador to Great Britain during his public career. Known as the finest orator of his time, he was the invited speaker at the dedication of Gettysburg Cemetery, and spoke for nearly two hours. His presence there is now somewhat eclipsed by Abraham Lincoln's two and one-half minute "Gettysburg Address."

The Everett family first came to this country in 1636 and settled in Dedham, not far from Boston, Massachusetts. My Revolutionary War ancestors were Andrew Sechler (great-grandfather of Emma (Sechler) Brodt), Phillip Peter Fusselman, and several members of the Everett family in Pennsylvania and Massachusetts. My affiliations are Calvary Lutheran Church, Bluffton; Audubon Society, Cardinal Chapter in Berne; Descendants of American Colonists; Daughters of the American Revolution, Lansing, Michigan chapter; Descendants of the American Civil War, Thomas Lampherd chapter; Fifty year member of the Order of the Eastern Star, Bluffton and Toledo, Ohio, chapters.

My fondest memories are of the days when my husband and I were young, his loving devotion to the well-being of his family, and his ability to meet each day with courage and grace.

MARTIN-SNYDER

Alvada Hope Martin is the daughter of "Cleve" and Minnie Martin who have their own family history in this book. Alvada graduated from East Union High School in 1936.

Dale Snyder, son of Harvey and Etta Snyder of Zanesville, also graduated from East Union in 1935.

Dale and Alvada were married in December, 1940, at Merlin and Elene Bender's (Alvada's sister) home near Uniondale. Alvada and Dale lived in Uniondale the first few of married life. During this time Alvada worked in a factory at Roanoke, then at Inca in Fort Wayne, and later several years at Ayres Tea Room. Dale worked at International Harvester in Fort Wayne.

Neil Snyder, first child of the couple, was born in May, 1942 in Uniondale. After moving away from there, a daughter, Candace, and two more sons, Kelly Joe and Kevin Dale, were born into the family.

The children attended the Markle School until the school was closed. The three older ones graduated from West Rockcreek (Huntington County). Kevin graduated from Heritage in Fort Wayne.

Dale and Alvada Snyder
50th Wedding Anniversary photo

Neil graduated in 1960, worked at International Harvester, and was trained in the apprentice school for machine repair. He also worked at Yeoman Engineering in Huntington, and Noll Printing. Neil and Carol Hosler, a graduate of Lancaster of Huntington County, were married in 1961. They have three children: Wendy, Jill, and Lonnie — all graduates of Huntington North High School in 1980, 1983, and 1985 respectively. Carol worked for Square D several years, but currently works in Fort Wayne.

Wendy and Jill both attended International Business College after high school.

Wendy married Doug Gower in 1983. Doug is employed at Fort Wayne Magnavox, and Wendy at Kresge's. Their two daughters are Brittany Lynn, four and Brandi Leigh, almost two.

Jill is married to Brian Conn, and lives in Fort Wayne. She works for ITT and has no children.

Lonnie is employed by Yeoman Engineering of Huntington and is not married.

Candy, only female child of Alvada and Dale, graduated from Manchester College, and married Tom PeGan. They adopted two children, Abby and Ryan. Abby graduated from Snyder High School and then attended IUPU in Fort Wayne. After a divorce, Candy married Ken Zimmerman, and together they own and operate Village Pools of Fort Wayne.

Joe graduated from General Motors Institute in Flint, Michigan, and now works for GM in Anderson. He married Vicki Carnes. Their child, Molly, attended Evansville University.

The youngest child of Dale and Alvada, Kevin, graduated from Ball State University, and taught a couple of years. He spent a few years in Arizona before returning to Indiana, and now also works for Village Pools.

After thirty-seven years at Harvester, Dale retired. He and Alvada spend their winters in Florida, and are in Indiana in summer, plus they go to Minnesota for good fishing.

ED MARTZ FAMILY

In the midst of the Great Depression, Edward Martz, at the young age of three, moved with his family from Monroe Township in Adams County to a farm near Ossian. Ed's parents were Webster and Louetta Mock Martz. Ed was the youngest of five children. The others were Marion, Ruth, Frances and Esther. The Monroe Township farm was sold to an Amish family for one hundred dollars per acre. Webster purchased 260 acres of farmland near Ossian for fifty dollars per acre.

Ed resided on this farm throughout his boyhood. He graduated from Ossian High School. At age twenty he married Elma Creek of Rockcreek Township in Wells County. Her parents were Orie and Alma Carnes Creek. Elma was also the youngest in her family. Her siblings included Herald, Helen, Everett, Ruth and Leona. Elma's family lived on a farm near Rockford. During Elma's youth, Orie and Alma tended their farm while Orie worked as custodian at the Rockcreek School. Elma is a Rockcreek High School graduate.

Ed and Elma were united in marriage in 1947 and resided in the farm house on the W.C. Martz farm, where Ed had grown up. Ed and Elma purchased the Martz farm from Ed's father as well as two hundred adjacent acres. They were kept busy over the years raising crops, feeding livestock and milking cows. In 1976 all livestock was sold and grain became the sole commodity of the Martz farm. Ed and his father worked together until W.C.'s death in 1975.

Ed and Elma are the parents of three children: Linda (born in 1947), Ted (born in 1953) and Kent (born in 1955).

Linda, a Huntington College graduate, married Stanley Reed from Wabash County and also a Huntington College graduate. They have two children: Jeffrey (born in 1969) and Lorraine (born in 1976). Linda is employed as guidance counselor at Norwell High School. Stan is a teacher and coach for Northern Wells also. They reside in Jefferson Township. Jeff Reed married Heidi Thiele, daughter of Ed and Connie Thiele, in July of 1990. Jeff is employed as a field manager for Weaver Popcorn.

Ted Martz, plant manager of the Fremont Company in Bluffton, married Cheryl Hiday, daughter of Malcolm and Justine Hiday of Ossian. Cheryl, and Indiana University graduate, teaches at Lancaster Elementary in Huntington County. They have three children: Heidi (born in 1976), Heather (born in 1978) and Robert (born in 1981). Ted is also engaged in farming with his father.

Kent, a graduate of Indiana University, resides near Roanoke, Indiana. He is employed by Southwest Allen County Schools as a counselor.

Although Elma was raised a Methodist, when they married she joined Ed's home church, First Presbyterian of Ossian. Both Ed and Elma remain active members of this church, having served over the years on various committees, as Sunday School teachers, Sunday School superintendent, and trustees; and both remain elders.

Ed has served thirty-five years as a director of the United R.E.M.C. He is also serving his fourteenth year as a director of the Ossian State Bank. Ed and Elma still live on the Martz farm and remain active in farming.

WARD L. MASON

"Ho! Ho! Ho! What would you like for Christmas?" Those who were kids in the 50's and 60's will remember the chubby, jolly Santa's lap they sat on at Murphy's Dime Store. Well, it was Ward who took their orders for the toys and goodies to be brought on Christmas Day.

Ward Leeder Mason was born in Omaha, Nebraska, in 1914 and grew up in Hammond, Indiana, where he graduated from Hammond Technical High School in 1933.

The country was in the middle of the Great Depression and jobs were nonexistent for men, young or old at that period of time. Ward joined the Civilian Conservation Corps in 1934. The CCC was set up as part of the New Deal program in 1933 to provide training and employment for young men.

January 12, 1936, Ward was transferred to the Bluffton State Park and Game Preserve (Ouabache State Park). He served as mess sergeant while helping build the shelter houses, dig the lake, build the roads and plant the trees that make our State Park what it is today.

He married Nancy Josephine Sales in 1937 and continued to make his home in Bluffton.

For more than sixty years Ward was an active member of the Boy Scouts. He became a member at the age of twelve, and an Eagle Scout by the age of fourteen. Many young Wells County men benefited from his expertise and love of the Boy Scouts. He organized the Sea Scouts in Wells County in 1937 and served as an adviser until 1941. He served on various committees and as an assistant troop leader until he became the leader of the Explorer Post in 1956. He took his scouts on canoe trips in Canada and "deep freeze" camping in the winter. In 1968 he was awarded the Silver Beaver, the highest council recognition which the National Boy Scouts of America gives to adults.

In addition to scouting, Ward served as head of Wells County Civil Defense for many years. He is a member of the First United Church of Christ, the Masonic Lodge, Scottish Rite, past Worthy Patron of Eastern Star, and a honorary lifetime member of the Rotary.

Ward is retired after thirty-seven years as a machinist for the General Electric Company.

Ward and Nancy Jo have three children: Richard, Edward, and Mrs. Jan (Alice) Curry.

MATSON

My great-grandparents, Robert and Harriet (Bates) Matson were natives of Ohio of Scottish ancestry. They lived in Washington Court House, Ohio, and were the parents of eight children. Their sixth child, Denial (1845-1923) was my grandfather.

In 1871 he married Margaret Halligan (1852-1925). She came to America from Dublin, Ireland when she was six years old with her brother and three sisters accompanied by their aunt. Grandma fell in the ocean when the ship docked and was rescued. The parents planned to come later, but the mother became ill and died. Their father never came, so the children were adopted.

Denial and Margaret became the parents of eleven children. They were Cora McLeod (1872-1954), Alma Hixon (1874-1956), Nancy (1876-1893), Worley (1878-1953), Frank (1880-1971), Maude Runyon (1883-1952), Irma Brinkman (1885-1967), Lena Honley (1887-1955), Robert (1890-1915), Homer (1892-1896), Ina Hollenbaugh (1894-1932).

Grandpa worked for the railroad and was transferred to Bluffton. Because of the size of the family, they lived in two adjoining homes in the 1000 block of West South Street. They had no carpets and the two oldest daughters told that they had to scrub the floors until the water was clear. The youngest said she had to go to the store every other week with a wooden bucket to be filled with brown sugar. Grandpa raised bees and Grandma used honey and brown sugar in her cooking.

Grandma was a devout Baptist and my cousin, Martha Hixon Clark, who resided with them after her father passed away said Grandma chided Grandpa for playing cards. Cousin Martha is ninety-six and has lived the longest of any in the Matson family. Every fall she comes from Detroit to visit. Bluffton is still her home.

*Mother's Day, May 13, 1962
Jessie and Frank Matson*

Grandpa was very thrifty and often told his children to watch their nickels and dimes and the dollars would take care of themselves.

In 1915 Uncle Rob, 25, had appendicitis. The doctor operated on him on his parent's kitchen table. He lived two days.

My two oldest aunts were widowed over fifty years. Aunt Cora never had a date, but Aunt Alma went "on a dare" to a show with fellow. She said she felt terrible for doing this and never had another date.

My father, Frank Matson, married Jessie Carlson from Royal Center, Indiana. Her parents were Swedish. Our folks had five daughters: Mrs. Leon (Eva) Shepard (1904-1990, Mrs. Carl (Marguerite) Cash (1906), Audrey Matson (1912), Mrs. John E. (Mary) Smith (1919) and Mrs. Paul (Dorothy) Gerwig (1921). They had seven children: Robert, William and Doris Shepard (Smith), Dixie Cash (Randol) and Janet Cash (Schoeff) and Michael and Gloria Gerwig (Mayne).

Dad worked in hoop mills in Arkansas and Louisiana. He was a very fast coiler and after his death I found a dozen letters from many states begging him to come work for them. However, he returned to Bluffton and had a restaurant for five years. Later he worked at Decatur for Frank McDowell, and then came back to Bluffton to superintend the McDowell Lumber Company. He retired at the age of seventy-five.

Mother was a wonderful Christian person, and I remember taking food and clothing to many poor people. Occasionally we meet someone who tells us they would not have had anything for Thanksgiving or Christmas if our Mother had not furnished it. How well I remember my sister, Dorothy, and I walking to the Central Dairy with our jug and a nickel for a gallon of milk for a needy family.

I never remember my Dad being out of work. When he retired Dr. Mead said he wouldn't live six months. He lived fifteen years and the only exercise he got was sitting on the front porch waving to everybody who passed our corner.

Now there are only four daughters left. We get together a couple times a week and sometimes more. We enjoy each others company!

MAYER

Jerry Mayer married Polly Jean McMillan in July of 1978. Jerry is the son of Robert and Sharon Mayer, and Polly is a daughter of Everett and Colleen McMillan. Jerry is employed by Triple-Crown out of Fort Wayne, and Polly is a homemaker. They are the parents of four children: Royce, Asa, Darrie, and Rhesse. The family resides in Jackson Township, Wells County and are members of Dillman United Brethren Church.

MCAFEE

In Rockcreek Township on February 17, 1925, Clarence Lloyd and Rela Kay (Derr) McAfee became the proud parents of a son. They named him Clarence McAfee, Jr., but he was known as "Junior" by his family and friends. He was their only child.

The McAfee family came from Ireland and settled in Virginia where Samuel, Junior's great-grandfather was born. He later moved to Pennsylvania before coming to Rockcreek Township. Samuel and Elizabeth (Lesh) McAfee were the parents of Jacob McAfee, Junior's grandfather, Jacob and Amanda (Lamm) McAfee had five children who reached adulthood. They were: Ulrich, Lovie (McAfee) Fishbaugh, Charles, Clarence and Lewis.

When Junior was two years old, his parents purchased eighty acres from his grandfather, Jacob, in Rockcreek Township located at 3892 West 300 North. There Junior grew up on the farm learning the hardships and blessings of farming. Today he is the third generation of McAfees to own and farm that acreage.

Junior attended Rockcreek School and graduated in 1943. He was active in sports. He began following in the footsteps of his father, grandfather, and great-grandfather, who had all been farmers. However, it was during World War II, and Junior was drafted to serve his country. He left in September 1944 for training and later fought with the 29th Infantry in Europe. He received the Combat Infantry Badge, the ETO Ribbon with two Battle Stars, and two Victory Ribbon. When the war ended in Europe he served in the military government in Germany until his discharge in April, 1946.

Junior began farming with his father and planning for the future. In January of 1948 he bought a forty acre farm from Charles and Anna Guldin located at 3983 West 200 North. He paid three hundred dollars an acre and many people thought that was a ridiculous price. He also bought Charlie's machinery, six gilts, eleven cows, and two hundred and fifty chickens.

Marjorie, Roger, Larry, Clarence, Jr., Connie

On March 21, 1948 Junior married Marjorie Maxine Geiger, daughter of W. Scott and Vera B. (Hite) Geiger. Marjorie was born in Rockcreek Township, Huntington County. She went to the West Union School for five months and then her family moved to 2670 North 500 West in Rockcreek Township, Wells County in January, 1934. She finished the 1st grade at Rockcreek and graduated from there in 1945. Marjorie had a brother Wilbur, who is deceased.

The Geiger family came from Germany, first settling in Pennsylvania and later in Ohio. They came to Indiana in 1864 and purchased land southwest of Markle near where the Rock Creek joins the Wabash River. It remained in the family until it became part of the Huntington Reservoir.

Junior and Marjorie began their life together on the forty acre farm and are living there today. Marjorie resigned her position in an insurance office when they were married and from then on was a support and helpmate in the farming operations. In the 50's and 60's Junior worked at various part-time jobs off the farm. Through the years they have purchased several more acres nearby the original "40". Today they have a farrow to finish hog operation along with the grain farming.

They have three children: Larry Lee, who married Elaine Blessing. Their children are Brent and Amy. Roger Wayne, who married Joyce Thompson. Their child is Troy. Connie Sue, who married Stephen and Orfer. Their children are Jessica and Kelli. They are all living in Rockcreek Township.

In 1970 Roger became a partner in the farming operation and in 1990 Larry became an employee.

Junior and Marjorie are members of the Uniondale United Methodist Church where they have been actively involved. They are Democrats. Junior was trustee of Rockcreek Township for four years and has served on the advisory board for eight years. He has been involved in other community groups too.

DAVID MCAFEE FAMILY

Peter McAfee was born in Rockcreek Township in 1854, the son of Samuel and Betsy (Lesh) McAfee. Samuel McAfee came from Ireland; Betsy from Pennsylvania. Peter lived all his life in Rockcreek Township.

Peter married Mary Conklyn, and they were the parents of seven children: Jennie (High), Bert, Clara (Harshman), Florence (Houtz), Chester, Nellie (Harshman), and Calvin.

Calvin C., the youngest of the children married Edna May Smeltzer, the oldest of William and Laura (Branner) Smeltzer August 16, 1916. (William Smeltzer coming from Pennsylvania). Calvin and Edna resided on a farm located on 300 North (known as McAfee Road), west of Old State Road 303. They were the parents of Samuel David.

Left to right: Monte Fisher, Bonnie (McAfee) Fisher, Laura McAfee, David McAfee, JoAnn (McAfee) Click, Mark Click and son Mark David Click

David attended Rockcreek School, which was constructed the year before his enrollment, for twelve years and has during his lifetime seen consolidation and final destruction. David married Laura May Haiflich (Shorty) daughter of John and Mayreatha (Beaber) Haiflich, March 7, 1942. She attended Ossian and Rockcreek Elementary Schools and graduated from East Union Center High and Wayne University of Cosmetology. They live approximately a mile from his birthplace on 400 W.

David spent his time farming and raising livestock and is best known for his interest in Angus cattle. Laura, a domestic engineer, aided with the farm chores while she also owned an operated a beauty shop in her home for twenty-five years.

They are the parents of three daughters: Mona Kay (deceased), JoAnn, and Bonnie Lou. Jo Ann, a 1968 graduate of Lancaster High School, married Mark William Click of Woodstock, Virginia, on December 27, 1969. Mark spent over twenty-four years serving the United States Army at nine different bases after their marriage with two tours in Vietnam prior to the marriage. They have three children, Mark David born at the Wells Community Hospital while his father served with 75th Ranger Division at Fort Richardson, Alaska, and Janna Michele and Scot Matthew (twins) born in Anchorage, Alaska. Upon retirement he located his family in Culver, Indiana, where he and Jo Ann are employed by Culver Academies. Jo Ann earned her degree in Business Administration over the many years of re-locating and parenting.

Mark David, CMA 1988, received his associates degree in computer science from Ancilla College and is currently working on a second degree in business administration. Janna and Scott will graduate in the spring of 199 from the Culver Community School and plan to attend Ancilla in the fall.

Bonnie Lou (1969 graduate of Norwell High School) married Monte Lynn Fisher (1968 graduate of Norwell High School South Campus), June 18, 1972. Monte is the son of Lee and Roberta (Nicklas) Fisher of Zanesville. Bonnie has been employed by the Old First National Bank in Bluffton for twenty-one years and has, since its opening, served at the Ossian Branch. Monte a three-year Marine veteran, has served as a Wells County deputy for fourteen years and also farmed.

They are the parents of two daughters, Krista May and Kami Lynn, who attended Lancaster Elementary School.

The McAfee family attends the St. Paul Lutheran Church, in Rockcreek Township, where David has served and held various positions within the church as has Laura, Bonnie and Monte. David has also served as secretary for the St. Paul Cemetery Association and president of the Rockcreek Township Farmers Mutual Insurance Company. All members of the family have been actively involved with the 4-H program at local through state levels.

Laura currently is serving on the Indiana State 4-H Foundation Committee for Wells County.

JOHANNES, SAMUEL, JOHN SR. AND JOHN JR. MCAFEE

John McAfee Sr. was born on January 6, 1854, in Wells County, Indiana. He was married on March 30, 1877, to Isabelle Light, born November 12, 1856. They were married in Grant County, Indiana, where she was a resident. They made their home in Rockcreek Township, Wells County, Indiana, where his prime interest was farming. John and Isabelle were faithful members of the St. Paul Lutheran Church and both are at rest in the church cemetery.

The subject of this article, John McAfee, Sr., was the son of Samuel McAfee. Samuel McAfee was born in Westmoreland County, Pennsylvania - January 3, 1825. On October 19, 1851, he married Elizabeth Lesh. In the 1850 census of Wells County, Samuel McAfee was listed as living with the A.B. Waugh family in Rockcreek Township. Mr. Waugh stated that he was a native of Scotland. Elizabeth Lesh McAfee was the daughter of John Lesh and Anna Marie Snavely. They resided in Lebanon, Pennsylvania. Elizabeth Lesh was the oldest of fourteen children. John Lesh was the son of Johann Peter and Maria Eder (Edris) Lesh. Elizabeth Lesh's mother, Anna Maria Snavely, was the daughter of Jacob Snavey and Salome Sabina Wild Snavely, both of Lebanon, Pennsylvania.

Samuel McAfee's father was Johannes McAfee, born March 14, 1789, and his mother was Susanna McAfee. John McAfee passed away at the home of his daughter Harriet McAfee Lesh, who was the second wife of John Lesh.

The death of Johannes McAfee was on August 24, 1870. He is buried in the St. Paul Lutheran Cemetery, Rockcreek Township Wells County, Indiana. His wife Susanna is buried in Tabor Reformed Cemetery in Lebanon, Pennsylvania. She passed away on April 14, 1864. Johannes and Susanna's family were: daughter Harriett (married to John Lesh); daughter Susan (married Mr. Hayes); Samuel (married to Elizabeth Lesh); and son James McMullen (married first to Mary Porch and after her death married to Arminda Redding).

L to R: Lillie (McAfee) Decker, daughter Verdi, Ernest McAfee, John McCafee Sr., Isabella (Light) McAfee, Winnie (McAfee) Haiflich, John McAfee Jr.

Johannes and Susanna McAfee's oldest son Samuel served in the Civil War. He was residing in Wells County and was one of the patriots who gallantly went to the front when the nation was in dire need of defenders. On August 20, 1862, he left his wife and family to enlist in Company G., 101st Indiana Volunteers Infantry under the leadership of Captain Wilson. Samuel took part (among others) in the following serious engagements: Perrysville, Chickamanga, Missionary Ridge, and Chattanooga; he was also all through the Atlanta Campaign and at the siege and fall of the fated city. He was at the battles of Peach Tree Creek, Georgia, and Bentonville, North Carolina, and was present at the surrender of Rebel General Johnston. Samuel McAfee was honorably discharged at the close of the war at Louisville, Kentucky. Samuel McAfee purchased his first farm in Wells County, Indiana, on April 17, 1850, from Aelis H. Farron.

Elizabeth Lesh McAfee passed away in Rockcreek Township, Wells County, in September, 1894, and is buried in the St. Paul Lutheran Cemetery. She was often called "Betsy," and was greatly admired by all who knew her; some called her

Blessed. After Elizabeth's death, Samuel lived among his children and passed away on March 18, 1909, at the home of his daughter, Catherine Jenkens. She was residing in Vigo County, near the city of Terre Haute, Indiana. His body was returned to Rockcreek Township to his final resting in the St. Paul Lutheran Cemetery beside his wife.

Samuel and Elizabeth McAfee had the following children: Son Jacob (born February 26, 1852, married first to Jane Logan; after her death he married Amanda Lamm); son John (married Isabelle Light); son Peter (married Mary Conklin); daughter Sarah and son James passed away as infants; son William (died at the young age of twenty-six); daughter Catherine (first married Chester Scotton and after his death married Clem Jenkins); daughter Priscilla (married James F. Gordon); daughter Hattie (married William D. Gordon); and son George (passed away at the young age of two years).

John and Isabelle Light McAfee along with his sons operated a saw mill in Rockcreek Township. They were active in the Democratic Party and helped in many ways in the development of their community. They had the following children: Son Othello (born 1877 passed away as an infant); daughter Lillie (married Charles W. Decker; they resided in Bluffton); Ernest (married Artie Raber); daughter Winnie (married Clifford Haiflich); and son John, their last born (married Hazel A. McCleery).

John Jr. and Hazel McCleery McAfee resided on the family homestead in Rockcreek Township and assisted his father John Sr. with the farming operations. (See entry for John McAfee, Jr.)

JOHN MCAFEE JR.

John McAfee Jr. was born on June 12, 1887, in Rockcreek Township, Wells County. He was the youngest son and child of John McAfee Sr. and Isabelle Light McAfee. He attended district schools in Rockcreek Township and later graduated from the Bluffton Business College with a degree in business. He was in the first class to graduate from the college.

On September 15, 1908, he was united in marriage to Hazel Augusta McCleery of Harrison Township, Wells County. The marriage was performed by H.B. Diefenbaugh, minister of the German Reformed Church. Hazel was the only daughter of John G. McCleery and Mahala Hoover McCleery. She was educated in the Harrison Township School District in Wells County.

John and Hazel McAfee spent their entire married life on the McAfee homestead in Rockcreek Township. They were members of the St. Paul Lutheran Church. John specialized in raising and breeding Belgian horses and pure-bred Guernsey dairy cattle. John and his children showed their prize livestock in 4-H shows, state and local fairs, winning many blue ribbons. He was dedicated to farming, specializing in corn and soybeans. He helped to organize the REMC Rural Electrification in Wells County. He was active all his adult life in the Democratic party; he served many years as precinct committeeman and also served on the election board in his township.

Hazel and John McAfee were blessed with nine children: son John born October 17, 1909, married Anna R. Otis; they had a family of seven children. John resided in Arizona at the time of his death on March 23, 1971. He is buried in the St. Paul Cemetery in Rockcreek Township, Wells County. His internment in this cemetery marks the fifth generation of John McAfee's in the St. Paul Cemetery. Son Donald, born September 15, 1911, married Helen Sorgen; he passed away on December 30, 1984, and was living in Fort Wayne at the time of his death; he was buried in the Greenlawn Memorial Cemetery. Son Robert was born on October 21, 1913; he married Betty Lindeman and resided in Toscin at the time of his death on February 9, 1971; his final resting place is in the Toscin Cemetery. Son Frederick was born on March 8, 1915; he married Miriam Beverly and lived in Rockford, Wells County; he passed away on July 2, 1969. He is at rest in the St. Paul Cemetery. Daughter Elizabeth, born June 10, 1916, resides in Wells County. She remained single. Son Harry, born August 6, 1918, married Betty Simon and resides in Phoenix, Arizona. Daughter Maxine, born on May 26, 1921, married Richard J. Moser and resides at Berne, Adam County, Indiana. Daughter Gladys, born June 13, 1928, married Lyle J. Cotton, resides in Bluffton, Wells County. Son Jack, the last child, was born on October 12, 1935; he resides in Fort Wayne, Indiana, and is married to Marlene Campbell.

Seated: Gladys (McAfee) Cotton, Donald McAfee, John McAfee, Jr., Hazel A. (McCleery) McAfee, John W. McAfee III, Maxine (McAfee) Moser. Standing: Elizabeth McAfee, Jack McAfee, Robert McAfee, Harry McAfee, Frederick McAfee.

John McAfee, Jr. passed away suddenly on May 4, 1951, as he was preparing to plant his fields in corn. He had several heart attacks prior to this date. Hazel McCleery McAfee continued living on the family farm until her death on May 4, 1956. Her death was unexpected, as she had been in good health prior to this date. Many friends and members of the family greatly mourn her death. Both John and Hazel are buried on the McAfee family plot in the St. Paul Lutheran Church Cemetery in Rockcreek Township. (See entries for John McAfee, Sr. and John McCleery.)

MCAFEE-ROBERTS

There is a farm in Rockcreek Township, Wells County, once owned by Jacob and Amanda (Lamm) McAfee. In the farm house at this location, Darwin Dwight McAfee, grandson of Jacob and Amanda, was born on May 25, 1926. He was the second of three sons born to Lewis Dwight McAfee and Bonnie Mae (Schell) McAfee. He has one older brother, Owen Oscar, and a younger brother, Arlin K. After graduating from Rockcreek High School in 1944, he worked for REMC, helped his father farm and also bought a truck for grain hauling. He continued his love for basketball by being a referee for thirteen years.

On February 26, 1948, our father married Betty Irene Roberts. Our mother, born December 30, 1928, in Lancaster Township, was the first child of Francis Earl Roberts and Jennie Kathryn (Maddux) Roberts. Later, mother and her parents moved to Rockcreek Township where her brothers, Lester Eugene, John Edwin (who died shortly after birth), Frederick Earl, Lawrence Kay, Walter Laverne, and sister Joyce Marie (Sills) were born. After graduating from Rockcreek High School in 1946, she attended Wayne Beauty College in Fort Wayne, graduating in November of 1946

Darwin and Betty McAfee February 26, 1948

Together, our parents owned and operated the Rockcreek Filling Station from November 1948 to August 1952. Our father continued to help his father with farming. For twenty-three years, beginning in 1948, he drove a school bus for Rockcreek School, which later became part of the Northern Wells Community School System. For several years our parents lived in the residence located at the filling station, during which time Sharon Kay was born on July 9, 1949.

In 1952 they moved to a farm three-fourth mile west of the Rockcreek School which they farmed for our father's uncle, Charles McAfee. They helped with two other farms at this time, one owned by an uncle, Ulrich (Dutch) McAfee, and one owned by our grandparents, Lewis and Bonnie, located just north of Rockcreek School. On June 24, 1953, Cathy May was born and a son, Michael Dee, was born June 22, 1959.

Our parents purchased a farm in East Rockcreek Township in 1962 and later moved to that location. Michael and his family live in one of the farm homes at 0615W-200N and our parents lives in the other farm home at 0862W - 200N. They purchased the farm formerly by Charles McAfee, west of the Rockcreek School in 1972, and in 1987 bought our grandparents' farm which included the former site of the Rockcreek School.

Sharon and her husband, Larry Lee Reed, purchased from our parents the farmhouse which was formerly owned by Charles McAfee. They reside at that location. Sharon works with the Northern Wells Community School System and Larry is director of materials management at Caylor-Nickel. Sharon and Larry have two sons, Todd Alan and Timothy Michael. Todd and his wife, Kelli Renee (Ratcliffe), live in West Lafayette, Indiana, where they both attend Purdue University. They have one daughter, Kelsi Renee. Tim attends Ball State University in Muncie.

Cathy is married to Robert Lawrence Hayden. They live in Harrison Township and own a decorative wood carving business. She has one son, John Matthew Langley, whose father is Michael Langley. Bob and Cathy have one daughter, Jennifer Marie

Michael is married to Brenda Louise (Shoaff) They have two children, Ryan Lewis and Sarah Renee. Michael is engaged in grain farming with our father. He also has a hog operation.

DAVID MCBRIDE

William David McBride was born on Valentine's Day 1943, in the farmhouse that still stands on the Michael-McBride Indiana Homestead, just one-half mile south of Zanesville on old #303. He and his wife, Karen Stotle (born August 4, 1943), still live on ten acres of that Indiana Homestead. David is the son of Don and Mary (Martin Botts) McBride. Karen is the daughter of Don and Hilda (Ditzenberger) Stotle, also of Union Township. David is a carpenter and owns McBride Construction. Karen is a housewife and keeps all the books for the company.

The McBrides have three children. Gregory David born Mary 23, 1963, Trent Andrew born July 26, 1965, and Tina Michelle born April 29, 1968.

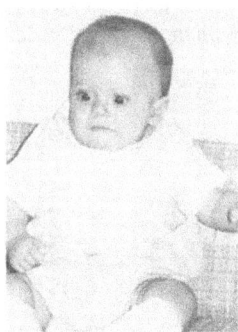

Joshua McBride

Dave McBride started his carpenter career at the age of fourteen when he built a chicken feeder in Union Center's shop class. He proudly brought it home to show his parents. After Dave was out of hearing distance, one parent said to the other, "One thing sure, Dave will never make a carpenter". Today he is one of the finest carpenters in the area. In 1961, just out of high school, Dave went to work for Frank Fine at Markle Lumber, where he helped built some of the first houses in Skyline Addition there. In 1962, he went in partnership with Jim Caley, and in 1965 started his own business. He works in all areas of construction and masonry work.

All through their growing up years Greg, Trent, and Tina helped their father on the job site. In 1988, Greg and Trent started their own business called McBride Brothers Construction.

McBrides: top Greg, David, Trent Middle: Karen, Molly, Tina; Front: Colette, Benjamin, Nicholas

Greg married Colette Marie Perkins on October 2, 1983, and they have two boys, Nicholas David born on November 22, 1986; and Benjamin Donald born on April 26, 1989. They live in a new house just across the road from the Prospect Church in Union Township. The house was built by the brothers and their father.

Trent was involved in helping his father move a home from it's original site to another lot, when he met his wife. GM was coming to the area and the Bunns of Lafayette Township were in the way, therefore their home had to go. Trent married Molly Bunn on March 5, 1988. They have one son named Joshua Bunn McBride. He was born on Christmas Day 1990. They live in a new house in RoseAnn Heights at Ossian. It also was built by the brothers and their father.

Tina is a graduate of Ball State University, and is a high school math teacher and softball coach at Norwell High School. She lives at home. The Stotles have lived in Union Township since Karen was three years old. Don is retired from International Harvester and farming. For the listing of David's ancestors refer to Edwards-Miller writing references.

DONALD MCBRIDE

April 11, 1894 was a happy day at the Zanesville House, the old hotel located in Zanesville on the Allen-Wells County Line. On that day in the back bedroom Donald McBride was born. He was the firstborn son of Dr. James Lowery McBride and Almissa Michael McBride. Delivered by his father in the house where his mother was born and where for fifty years his father would practice medicine. Don went to grade school in a little brick school in Zanesville on the Wells County side of town. Zepha Longshore Smith was his first grade teacher. She always gave him extra assignments to keep him from bothering the other children. He was sent to Fort Wayne at the age of thirteen so he could get his education. He graduated from Central in 1913. His parents paid one dollar fifty cents a week for his board and room at a house that still stands on Liberty Street.

Dad received a teaching license on March 6, 1914, from Muncie Normal Institute (Ball State) after satisfactorily finishing twelve weeks of study. He never used the license, as he preferred farming.

Don and Mary McBride - 40th Anniversary

He then went to Purdue University for two years: then in 1916 he was sent with the Indiana troops to the Mexican border under Gen. John Pershing against Panco Villa, a Mexican rebel leader. The next year, 1917, he was called to the first World War, as was his father, to serve as a wagoneer in France. He always joked that he got his best education at a local pool hall when he was boarding in Fort Wayne. When he told of the Mexican border incident, no one would believe him and he joked that when he landed in France, the enemy gave up. Maybe they didn't believe him because he also told that he helped Teddy Roosevelt storm San Juan Hill (this happened before he was born!)

Don returned from the war eager to start farming, so his father sent him south of Zanesville on one hundred acres that had belonged to his grandfather Michael. At thirty-five, he married Mary Martin Botts who at the time had three small boys, Darrell, Cedric, and Douglas. They took Cedric and Douglas with them to the Southern Indiana town of Nashville where they were married on November 21, 1930. They left Zanesville with five dollars, which paid for their trip, their marriage license, and their food and lodging for an overnight stay. Dr. McBride moved a house to the farm to be their home. In 1947 Don and Mary bought the farm from his mother. They were the third generation to own it. Don farmed the land and ran a dairy in the 40's. He delivered milk and Mary's homemade butter and cottage cheese to customers in the Zanesville and Markle area. They also had customers coming from as far as Fort Wayne. In 1933 the WPA, under the Roosevelt Administration, dug a lake on the farm. Don and Mary's first son Roger was born in 1932. At the age of eighteen months, during and outbreak of scarlet fever, he died of the disease. In 1934, Maurice was born, in 1936, Melba, in 1939 Mary Lou, and in 1943 David was born. David was the only child not delivered by his grandfather as Dr. McBride died in 1941.

Our father raised seven children on that farm, with the help of a lot of hard work from our mother. He farmed for years with horses, picking corn by hand, and threshing with a threshing machine long after everyone else went to combines. He loved his work and never once complained of being dissatisfied with farming. He never went to work in town, but made do with the money from the farm. After retiring from farming, he still kept busy doing odd jobs around the farms and fields. He was a little like Will Rogers - "He never saw a man he didn't like." He loved to come to town to visit at the station, the grocery, the garage, the mill, or the barber shop - anywhere he could tell a story, or talk about old times, or start an argument about politics. Dad's gone now. He passed away on January 26, 1980 a great loss to all of us.

In 1974 we started celebrating his birthday with an open house at "The Zanesville House" where we now live. We had such a crowd, about 200, that Kenneth Keller came down to interview Dad and take a few pictures. Keller, then the Sunday Magazine Editor for the paper, was so enchanted by Dad's enthusiasm for history that he wrote an article for two consecutive weeks. These appeared in the April 21 and 28 papers. There were many private publications after that. Beginning with a fake recall to the army with some questions on it as to what happened to some missing equipment during the Mexican skirmish. Later a fake sale bill was published privately announcing that Dad was selling out to return to active duty. The sale bill went over so good, we printed 700 of them that he handed out over the years.

We had started something that ended up being an every birthday and Christmas occurrence, for Dad and his friends liked the publications so that it took all my sister Mary Lou Burkhart's and my imagination to come up with something new each time. Since Dad thought he could probably run the country as well as anyone, we decided to run a fake campaign for president, with the campaign slogan being "Keep in stride, vote McBride" with an overboot as his campaign symbol. From 1975 on we published souvenir postcard, birth announcements, and many reports to the nation.

Dad saved lots of things that were his ancestors that are still housed in our home where they came from originally. He helped lots to keep history alive in Zanesville and without him the *Zanesville History Book* would not have been the same.

An old friend said her words of comfort at the funeral home that summed up his life. "No regrets," she said, "only happy memories!"

Mary, our mother, was born on October 24, 1905, to William David Martin and Mahala Disler when they lived on a farm near Monroeville, Indiana. Mom is in excellent health and she still resides on the farm just south of town. Although she only finished eighth grade, as most girls did in her time, she raised seven children, working as a farmer's wife most of her life. She has lived in Union Township for fifty-eight years, now in the house that her father-in-law had move to the farm. It was moved to the spot at the cost of one hundred and twenty five dollars by Griffin and before, sat on the Thomas farm, and belonged to Sean Thomas. Now Bob Thomas, Sean's grandson, farms our homestead as he has done for about thirty years. She has always been a wonderful mother to all of us.

MAURICE MCBRIDE FAMILY

Maurice Edwin McBride was born on May 25, 1934 in the house on the family homestead, just one-half mile south of Zanesville on old #303 (300N). He was delivered by his grandfather, Dr. J.L. McBride. Maurice spent all his growing up years on that farm. In 1952 he graduated from East Union Center as valedictorian of his class. He had helped with the farming all his life, starting to plow at the age of six. After high school he took a job with operators union oiling cranes, and later he went to work at Brudi's gravel pit in Waynedale. It was then that he got interested in running large equipment. He married (December 1952) Janet Steed, daughter of Chalmer and Marceile Steed, who are now residents of Union Township. They were formerly of Aboite Township of Allen County, moving to Lafayette Township and then down on Hosler Road in Union Township. They taught many people square and round dancing at their home called Melody Acres.

McBride-Michael Indiana Homestead

In 1957 Maurice and Janet and their small son, Tim, (May 29, 1954). Moved to a farm near Irma, Wisconsin to be near a family friend, Bill (Jum) Huffman. There he began McBride Excavating which he still runs today. After moving to Wisconsin a daughter, Kirsten, was born (May 2, 1958). Tim still lives at home and helps his father in the business. Kirsten is married to Pat Griffiths (1979), and they reside in Allen Park, Michigan where Pat is a youth minister. They have two children, David James (October 5, 1980), and Joanna Michael Elizabeth, (October 15, 1983) who dearly love to visit Grandma and Grandpa McBride in Wisconsin. The McBrides now own two hundred twelve acres in Wisconsin besides the Indiana homestead.

On October 23, 1984 a small segment of the Don McBride family ventured to Indianapolis to accept the Indiana Homestead Award from Governor Orr. The award was for the family farm just south of Zanesville in Union Township. In order to receive this award your farm has to be owned by the same family for one hundred years. The farm was homesteaded by John Wandel and the preemption certificate was signed by Zachary Taylor in 1849. John was a resident of Zanesville who became county treasurer from 1855 to 1859. Jonathan Michael, grandfather to Don McBride, bought the round in 1878 from Wandel. The farm had many trees on it then, and the land needed to be cleared. There were no buildings on it at this time. In 1892 a large bank barn was built from the timber off the land. Many of the timbers were hand hewn. In 1900, because of his age, (sixty-eight) Jonathan sold the farm to his daughter and son-in-law, Dr. J.L. and Almissa McBride. The land was still very poor. There were stones everywhere but Dr. McBride had great expectations, and he held on to the land. In 1931 he moved a house from three and one-half miles south on 303 to the farm so his son, Don, and his wife, Mary, and her three sons could have a home there. It wasn't until November of 1933 that they moved to the far. The land was still very poor and times weren't too good. The Botts Boys, Darrell, Cedric, and Doug, worked hard to help their stepfather, Don, with the crops and the livestock.

Then came the second World War, and all three boys had to go. By the time the war was over they were all married and then the McBride kids had to help. We had a dairy then and we delivered milk to the whole town of Zanesville. Mary made cottage cheese, butter and rolls, and cleaned chickens and sold eggs to the whole countryside, including some customers in Fort Wayne. One year we cleaned 3,000 chickens. Without this income the farm would never have survived. During the 30's, when the WPA was building the farm a pond, Mary served the men all kinds of good things to eat. She sold hamburgers for five cents buying the buns at the huckster wagon for one cent.

It took them about three years to hand dig the pond. All of Don's children were born on this farm. Roger, a first son, born in 1932 died at eighteen months during a scarlet fever outbreak. Maurice, the second born in 1934, purchased the farm February 3, 1987. Melba the third child, is married to Kenneth Edwards, and she is the Union Township co-ordinator for this book. A fourth child, Mary Lou, born in 1939, is married to Kenneth Burkhart and lives in Huntington County. David, the fifth and last child born on the farm lives on ten acres of the original homestead. Don McBride farmed the homestead for his father on shares. He farmed with horses, picking corn by hand, and threshing with a threshing machine. In 1947, after Dr. McBride's death, Don and Mary bought the one hundred acre farm from Almissa. Don farmed until his retirement in 1964, at which time he was seventy years old. Since then Bob Thomas has been farming for the McBrides.

Mary and Don sold their last cows in 1976. In the 1880's Jonathan Michael raised milk cows on the farm. Every day he drove his cows one mile into Zanesville to milk them in the barn in town since there was no barn on the farm. After milking he would drive them back to the farm.

In 1980 Don died and Mary continued to run the farm. Mary still lives on the farm. She has been there for fifty-eight years. In October 1991 she will be eighty-six years old. She quit handling the farm bills in 1987 when Maurice purchased the homestead. Maurice lives in Wisconsin but is hoping to return to Union Township to the farm in the future. He is the fourth generation to own the land.

MCCAGUE FAMILY

The McCague family connection to Wells County, Indiana, began about the mid 1850's when William Hamilton McCague and wife Margaret (Archbold) settled land some four or five miles east of the town of Ossian. There they lived out their lives farming and running a small country store and rearing their eleven children. William born March 15, 1882 in Mt. Pleasant, Ohio was apparently named after Dr. William Hamilton, the local physician who likely delivered him. Margaret was born January 17, 1829 to John A. and Elizabeth (Gibson) Archbold in Tuscarawas County, Ohio, and married William there on December 22, 1846.

William Hamilton McCague - Margaret Archbold McCague

The U.S. progenitor of the McCague family was John McKaig, who was said to have been born in Scotland in 1780 and apparently in fleeing authorities crossed the channel to northern Ireland in his early teens. However it cannot be proven that he was not born in Monaghan County, Ireland, for it was from there that he immigrated to Philadelphia about 1800 "with an uncle." No history of the latter has been discovered. John settled in Carlisle, Pennsylvania, where for a few years he worked as a freight wagon driver delivering goods across the mountains to the west for supplies for the settlers in eastern Ohio territory. On March 27, 1807 he married Mary Jane Holmes of Carlisle whose parents remain unknown. In that town they continued to live for a few years and had at least three children there: Ellinor, born/died 1808; James Fremont, born 1809, who in adult life settled in Hardin County, Kentucky; and Annabelle, born 1811, who married William P. Moore. In later years the latter sold his wife's parents a farm, but failing to provide a deed, cheated them from the ownership.

Marion and Sadie McCague Family - 1927
Back (L to R) Mable, Sadie, Kenneth, Minnie, Suzanna (holding Charles McCalla III), Arlene, Marion. Front (L to R) Wendell, Franklin, Wilson, Marceille, Mary

After 1811 John and Jane moved to Harrison County, Ohio, where they farmed for several years. In that place they had additional children including: Elizabeth, born 1813, married Harrison Moore (no known relationship to William P.); Ellen, born 1816, who married first Thomas W. Taylor and later William Wright with whom she lived in Lima, Ohio. Next, in 1819 was born Andrew Jackson, who married Mary Jane Moore, a sister of Harrison. They too moved to western Ohio, as did William H. and Margaret, who also lived around Lima prior to removing to and settling in Wells County, Indiana.

Sometimes before 1825, John and Jane removed from Harrison County, Ohio to another farm in Tuscarawas County, Ohio. No records have been found to establish any ownership of land in either place. It was in the latter county that were born Mary Jane in 1825, who married John Isnogel, and John Holmes, born 1830 who first married Rebecca Williams and later Lucinda Smith, and these later children also removed to the Lima/Paulding, Ohio area.

John is said to have died of pneumonia on January 1, 1851 after which Jane went to live with Ellen Wright in Lima, Ohio, where she died in 1859 and was buried.

William Hamilton McCague died in Wells County, Indiana April 1, 1906 and Margaret preceded him in death there on July 5, 1897. Their eleven children included: Elizabeth, 1849-1850; John Lafayette, 1851-1916, married Mary Daine Sutton and lived in Bluffton, Indiana; Andrew Commodore Perry, 1853-1924, married Lorena Dowty; Mary Ellen, 1860-1932, married Martin Bisson and lived in Fort Wayne; Charles Hamilton, 1861-1928, ran a livery stable in Fort Wayne where he died; Martha Alice, 1861-1884. William Frederick, 1863-1881; Marion General, 1868-1946, who married Sadie Valzetta Shimer and continued to live and die on part of the original McCague land; Ida Mae, 1869-1930, and James Francis, 1866-1931, neither of whom married and lived together their lives on part of the original land; and lastly Minnesota (1872-1953), married Charles W. Snarr and they too lived and farmed near her siblings.

MCCARTNEY-ECKELBARGER

Both families of Forrest and Anna Belle Eckelbarger McCartney have been interwoven in the building of this nation from colonial days. The two families had forefathers serving in the Revolutionary War. Members of our families were in the War of 1812, and the Civil War. They helped lay out Columbus, Ohio, took part in the Gold Rush of 1849, and the Land Rush of Oklahoma, and did some of the most gruelling work of all — clearing the land for farming.

Forrest and Anna Belle McCartney

The McCartneys emigrated from Scotland to Northern Ireland and then sailed to America after one generation. The McCartneys moved across the frontiers by ox-cart in a series of moves, arriving in Allen County, Indiana, in the 1830's. There they bought land from McCartney relatives whose land record appears in Allen County's first land book.

Albert McCartney married Marjorie Powers, who was a native of Wells County. He came to Wells County from Allen County with his family in 1930 to a farm south of Uniontown.

Marjorie's family is not traceable yet beyond her grandfather, but various members of the Powers family are buried in the old cemeteries of Wells County.

Departing southern Germany, the Eckelbarger family pushed westward and after various moved arrived in Wabash County, Indiana, in the 1840's. Anna Belle's grandparents, Charles and Minnie, came from Wabash County in different moved to Wells County, Union Township.

Anna Belle's maternal family, the Carters, came out of the Massachusetts Bay Colony. The journeyed from New England into the wilderness, cutting their homes and farms out of the forest several times; and moving to Grant County in the 1830's to do the same. Anna Belle's parents, Lawrence and Mary, lived in Grant and Huntington Counties before coming to Wells.

Anna Belle and I were reared in Wells County, and we both graduated from Union Center High School. I am a veteran of World War II, having served in the Air Force. After wards I entered college, and subsequently taught elementary school in Laporte County and Ossian. We were married in Bluffton in 1952. I received a ready-made family of two stepsons, Richard Dean and William Michael, from Anna Belle's previous marriage. Richard was murdered in 1968, leaving us three grandchildren. William lives in Bluffton and is married to Joye Deming. They have two daughters. We have four sons of our own: Jonathan, Randall, Ken, and Lane. Jonathan is not married but lives both in Bluffton and Fort Wayne. Randall married Beverly McAfee; they have three children and live in Rockcreek Township. Ken married Karla Grogg and lives in Bluffton with four children. Lane, of Bluffton, is not married but has three children.

Because of a low teaching salary and a growing number of boys, I left the field of education and became employed at International Harvester which is now Navistar. Eventually I went into management and retired in 1981. Because of the needs of our family, Anna Belle chose to seek a position at GE; she retired form there in 1985. We have been active during our married lives in churches, scouting, the local Gideon organization, and a political party.

As a result of research done for the Carter family genealogy, a volume was placed in the Bluffton Library entitled *The Edward Carter Family*. Also stated to appear is *The Isaac McCartney Family*.

MCCLEERY FAMILY

John McCleery was born in 1786 in Lancaster County, Pennsylvania; he moved to Fairfield County, Ohio, Greenfield, Township. Here he passed away in September, 1834. His wife Elizabeth (Ross) was born in Ohio in 1800. John McCleery and wife Elizabeth are buried in Fairfield County, Ohio.

John McCleery's grandfather James McCleery was born in Castlereagh, Down, Ulster, Ireland. He was married to Alice McGrew on June 21, 1769, in the St. James Presbyterian Church in Lancaster County, Pennsylvania. James McCleery passed away in 1813 in Lancaster County. They had one son, James, born in 1770 in Lancaster County. In 1786 he married Jane Jenetta McCleery. He passed away in 1826 at Fairfield County, Ohio. He was a member of the Trinity Lutheran Church.

James McCleery was the father of John McCleery, who married Elizabeth Ross. They were blessed with the following children:

Matilda (born October 28, 1823) she remained single.

James Ross was born on October 22, 1825. He married Margareta Gutelius on October 23, 1849, in Carroll Fairfield County, Ohio. James Ross McCleery became a doctor. He studied medicine under the celebrated Dr. Brusler at Lancaster and and completed his medical education at the University of Pennsylvania in the winter of 1848-49. He practiced his profession in Ohio up to the time of his emigration to Bluffton, Wells County, Indiana, on August 30, 1851. Shortly after he arrived in Bluffton he entered into partnership with Dr. Henry Courtney under the firm name of Courtney & McCleery, which continued harmoniously for several years. When the senior partner Dr. Courtney emigrated to Iowa, the partnership was dissolved. Dr. McCleery resided on his farm a few miles southeast of Bluffton. In the spring of 1861 he entered into partnership with Dr. Melsheimer in the drug business under the name of McCleery and Melsheimer. A fine three-story brick building was erected to house the business. The firm continued in business for several years until it was dissolved by the withdrawal of Dr. McCleery to assume the duties of clerk of Wells County. He was elected to this office in the fall of 1867, and was re-elected in 1871. He passed away on April 21, 1874, in his fifty-second years. Dr. McCleery was a man of fine social qualities which endeared him to all his acquaintances. He was a prudent and cautious practitioner of marked ability. He had a very extensive knowledge of the theory of medicine and possessed that very rare faculty of reducing it to a successful practice. In the spring of 1853 he united with the fraternity of Mason in Fort Wayne, Indiana, and continued to be a worthy member until his death. He and his wife Margaretta A. are both buried in the Fairview Cemetery, Bluffton, Wells County, Indiana.

Front row: Minnie Myrtle, Lucille, Mahola (Hoover) (Markley) McCleery Helen (granddaughter) John G. McCleery, Emona (Girod) McClerry, baby Dorothy Elizabeth. Back row: Hoover Ross, Mollie (Miller) McCleery, John Everett, John McAfee, Hazel A. (McCleery) McAfee, Frank Harold, Charles

John McCleery and Elizabeth Ross McCleery had a daughter Jane, born 1829, who was living in Fairfield County, Ohio, at the time of the 1850 census.

Son John S. McCleery was born on November 16, 1830. He was blind but this did not hinder him in his education, for he graduated from the Blind Institute of Columbus, Ohio in 1852. He came to Wells County, Indiana, and became a prominent school administrator until the time of his death on November 17, 1887. He is buried in the Fairview Cemetery, Bluffton Wells County. He remained single.

James Ross McCleery and Margaretta Gutelius McCleery had the following children: Maria Elizabeth, born August 20, 1850, married Henry Lyons; John Gutelius, born July 4, 1852, married Mahala Hoover; Susan Catherine (married Jerry North); Idaline Jane (married Arkansas Altdoeffer); Mary Alice (married Henry Stine); Cora Margaret (married Isaac Van Gorder); Anna Irma Augusta (Gussie) (married Howard Bennett); Lula Maude (passed away at the age of three years); and James Ross (passed away at one year of age on May 9, 1872).

John Gutelius McCleery, born July 4, 1852, married Mahala Hoover, who was born on November 25, 1856. They were married on her birthday in Bluffton, Indiana. They lived on a farm south-east of Bluffton in Harrison Township, where they raised the following children: Son Hoover Ross (born December 24, 1876, married to Minnie Myrtle Markley; they had one daughter Lucille); son John Everett (born September 1, 1879, married Mollie Miller; they had one daughter Helen Justine); son Frank Harold (born March 18, 1882, married Mary Beer, they had two daughters, Ruth and Margaret); son Charles Tinker (born July 12, 1885, married Emma Girod; they had two daughters, Dorothy Elizabeth and Pauline); their only daughter, Hazel Augusta (born December 30, 1888) married John McAfee on August 11, 1911; to this union were born nine children, six sons and three daughters.

John G. McCleery passed away suddenly on May 16, 1922, after a sudden heart attack at the age of sixty-nine. He was a very prominent farmer and a former Bluffton manufacturer. He was admired by his countless friends and relatives. He was known for his industrious habits and his sound integrity. He was engaged in the hub-spoke business with his brother-in-law, Jerry North. Their firm was located in the building which later housed the Red Cross Manufacturing Company.

For many years the name McCleery was identified with Wells County, where its associations were most honorable and where it was respected due to success in business, outstanding public service, and civic duties that were well-performed.

John G. McCleery was a member of the First Baptist Church in Bluffton, a member of the Free and Accepted Masons, Knights Templar and Knights of Pythias Lodge in Bluffton. The Bluffton Commandery held services at the time of his death. Interment was in the Six Mile Cemetery. Mahala Hoover McCleery passed away on March 3, 1943, and is at rest in the Six Mile Cemetery beside her loving husband. Mahala Hoover McCleery was the daughter of John M. and Mary Kemp Hoover, who lived in Wells County, Indiana. (Refer to John Hoover family history.)

MCCLURE-BIBERSTINE

Rebecca (Rhea) Watkins was born on September 1, 1859, and died on November 10, 1941. George Watkins, her husband, was born in 1859 and on July 25, 1935. They had a son and a daughter: William, born August 7, 1890; and Edna Esta, born October 30, 1893. They lived in Monongah, West Virginia until Edna was eight years old. Then they moved to a farm west of Petroleum. They farmed all their lives.

William had a son, William (born April 8, 1915), who lives in Berne at Swiss Village. He also had a daughter, Evelyn (Watkins) Boyle, (born September 17, 1912) who lives in Bluffton.

Orla McClure (born September 16, 1887, died February 27, 1972) married Edna Esta Watkins on June 12, 1912. He farmed and worked in the oil fields at Illinois.

March 1985 Left to right: Back - Margaret Biberstine, Matthew Biberstine, Edna McClure, Marvin Biberstine. Front: Cynthia Biberstine, Karl Biberstine

Orla and Esta had a son and a daughter: Arthur Burl (born May 24, 1915, died December 9, 1918) and Margaret Louise (born May 14, 1913). Margaret started to school in a one-room school at Herman, and next went to Frog Pond. She had to walk four miles a day to each school. Grades five and six were attended at Petroleum; she rode to school in a horse-drawn "hack" and took a lunch box each day. She graduated from Chester Center High School in 1931.

Margaret Louise married Martin Biberstine, son of Chester and Minnie Biberstine, on May 2, 1937, at Mellott, Indiana, by the Rev. Guy Walters. Martin worked as a mechanic, farmed, and was a great motorcycle man. He died on January 27, 1984.

Martin and Margaret had a son, Marvin Gene Biberstine. He was born on October 28, 1949, and died on November 17, 1988. He went to school at Southern Wells and worked at K-Mart for twenty years. He coached football and softballs teams.

Marvin married Cynthia Ann Walburn, a daughter of Marsha and Roger Walburn, on August 24, 1969. She was born on October 5, 1949. They lived east of Liberty Center until 1975, when they bought and moved to a home in Liberty Center.

Marvin and Cynthia had a son, Matthew Lee (born October 28, 1970), who graduated from Southern Wells High School.

Karl Robert, a son of Marvin and Cynthia, was born on March 30, 1977. He lives with his mother at Burton, Michigan and is in the eighth grade. He plays football, basketball, and softball and is in the band.

Matthew married Cindy Endsley, of Van Buren, on March 3, 1990. Brandon Marvin was born to them on January 18, 1991.

MCCORD

Eugene W. McCord (born 1921), a native of West Virginia, and Jeanne Vivian Smith McCord (born 1922), a native of Ohio, met while both were students at Kent State University, Kent, Ohio. They were married at Kent on January 30, 1944, and moved to Bluffton, Indiana in September, 1946, with their first son, Michael (born 1945), from the Ohio village of Windham, where they had resided since Eugene's discharge in March 1946 from Army service during World War II.

Eugene, a graduate of KSU, class of 1943, served with an Army evacuation hospital in Europe. He accepted a position in July, 1946, with the daily newspaper in Bluffton, the Evening News-Banner. He was a reporter and sports editor ten years, becoming in 1956 the newspaper's managing editor, a position he held prior to retiring on March 1, 1986. He returned to a part-time editorial position, holding that job to this time.

Eugene and Jeanne McCord had other children: David (1947), John (1949-1981), Jennifer (1956), Amy (1959), Dan (1961), and Susanna (1963).

In addition to being a wife and mother, Jeanne was active in church and volunteer social service programs.

The McCords were members of First Baptist Church (ABC-USA) and were affiliated with the Democratic party. Neither Eugene nor Jeanne sought or held public office, although both were active election campaign participants.

Both Eugene and Jeanne are of Scot-Irish ancestry. The McCord ancestry traces back to Chester County, Pennsylvania, and farther to Donegal County in Ireland. Records show the McCord clan owning land near the present Chambersburg, Pennsylvania, and at the former McCord's Fort, Pennsylvania, where, in 1756, an attack by Indians killed most of the occupants. The few survivors abandoned the area and fled to relatives in Albemarle County, Virginia. Ancestors of Eugene McCord held lands in Hardy County, Virginia, and Braxton and Lewis Counties, formerly Virginia, now West Virginia.

Jeanne Smith's ancestors, traced from Northern Ireland, settled first in New York and then spread westward to Ohio, settling initially in the Bryan, Ohio, area.

DAN RUSSELL MCCORD

My name is Dan McCord. I now live in Indianapolis but was born in Bluffton on February 19, 1961. Growing up in Bluffton during the 1960's and 1970's in a family that included parents, Eugene, and Jeanne McCord, three sisters, and three brothers was a good experience.

Our town was small enough to know many of the people you passed on the streets uptown and all of your neighbors within several blocks. As a matter of fact, none of the kids in our family could get away with anything. Our dad was managing editor of the *Bluffton News-Banner* and wherever any one of us was seen, Dad would be told who it was and when and where we were. I did many of the things other boys did, played in various baseball leagues, carried newspapers for many years, and took part in 4-H activities.

All of my brothers and sisters and I graduated from Bluffton High School We did a variety of activities which included publications and Thespians. For a span of twenty-five years, one or another of the McCord children was in a music department unit of the Bluffton-Harrison Metropolitan School District. All of us were in the Tiger Marching Band. Also, I sang in musical groups and did solo work sometimes.

A claim to belonging to a piece of history in Wells County probably belongs to the youngest in the family, Susanna. She graduated in the 100th class of BHS and had her name placed in the capsule interred at the high school and to be opened in the 200th year.

My only claim to being part of the community history was when I contributed to one of Mother's projects. The Ministerial Association decided to start a food bank/utility bank in late 1982. Mother got it organized and then worked as a volunteer for it. I was employed in a grocery store and realized that still usable but old bread had to be thrown away. I asked if the food bank could use it. My mother said yes and I talked to the store boss, who arranged for mother to pick up the bread.

Donations to the food bank grew rapidly and Mother couldn't do it alone. Jane Eymer from the First Methodist Church began to help and then Donna Handshoe and Randy Saunders, from the First Baptist Church. A few months after these people had loaded and unloaded many pounds of bread every week, the Reverend Donald Crellin of the First Baptist Church asked Mother to find something for retired teacher Frank Monroe to do. Monroe took over the bread bank, later turning it over to Harry Steffen.

The bread bank and food bank moved to the basement of a building uptown which the welfare department was utilizing. At this time, Mabel White and Connie Cupp, together with several other volunteers, kept this food help going, and now in 1991 the aid groups are still functioning.

Recently when I tried to get help for a burned-out fellow worker in Indianapolis, I learned that volunteers working together and commitments from large segments of the community do not happen so easily in big cities. I appreciate my memories of Bluffton. (*Dan R. McCord*)

MCCORD-DYKES

I was born in Bluffton. My parents are Jeanne and Eugene McCord. They named me Amy Jeanne. My bloodlines are a mixture of Scottish, Irish, English and German and Connecticut Yankee. But even with all that "melting pot" influence, I am without a doubt a product of Bluffton.

Bluffton in the 1960's was a safe, happy environment for a young girl's growing years. On Saturdays, my sister, Jennifer and I walked the seven blocks toward "uptown" and the movie theater. Right now the name of the theater escapes me, but I remember seeing all the classic Disney films there. Back then we could gain admission to the movie for twenty-five cents. Popcorn was about ten cents.

We were a reading family. Our parents read to us every night and as we developed reading skills of our own, they encouraged us to read to our younger siblings. Bluffton and Wells County provided excellent opportunity for growth. Thanks to the public library's stash of books, the whole world was an open arena for any young girl's imagination. We had 4-H, Girl Scouts, music lessons, and a host of other mind-broadening advantages.

My church home, First Baptist, at Cherry and Johnson Streets, weilded a tremendous influence as well. One of the fondest memories is of a Christmas time tradition. Each choir, beginning with the Cherub (the youngest), sang a verse of "The First Noel". As each choir sang its verse, we all stood patiently until all choirs together sang again the first verse. Nearly everyone had a lump in the throat by the conclusion of the beautiful song. It was at First Baptist Church that I was baptized.

Of all my Bluffton experiences, my proudest one is the education I received there. Bluffton, during the 1960's and 70's was a superb haven for educational nurturing. No matter where I have lived, people have made a point of asking me, "Where were you educated?" They expect to hear that I went to West Heath boarding school in England, or some such. But I happily report that I went to East Side Elementary, a public school in Bluffton, and that I am a 1977 Bluffton High School graduate. My learning experience at DePauw University did not supersede that which I gained in Bluffton's public schools. I am immensely proud of this.

Today my husband, Brad Dykes, and I live in Tell City, Indiana, with our three children, Alan, Lauren, and Megan. Brad is the C.E.O. of Perry County Memorial Hospital. I am a professional actress/announcer, and sometimes write articles. Brad and I are both active in Tell City's First Baptist Church. In addition to this, I serve as an officer on a Parent Advisory Board for my children's school, am a Brownie leader, writ for the American Cancer Society, and serve on the Hospital Auxiliary.

Perhaps the favorite of all my volunteer activities is reading to school children, grades K-2, in various schools throughout southern Indiana and northern Kentucky. After the reading session, I can always count on at LEAST a thousand hugs, and the question from the teacher. "Where in the world did you learn to read like that?"

In Bluffton, of course. (*Amy Jeanne McCord Dykes*)

MCCORMICK

Frank R. McCormick married Carrie Snow. They had a son, Howard. Howard married Cleo L. Grove, and they had three sons, Herman and Herbert, who were twins and Kenneth.

Herman married Rose Risser and had one daughter, Janis Kay. Janis Kay married Howard Jones.

Herbert married Donna Numbers and had three children, Melody, Michael, and Nancy. Melody married Alan Schwieger and had two children, Jennifer and Matthew. Michael married Carmen Quinoes and had four children: Chris, Ashley, Aaron, and Stephanie. Nancy married Gerald Schmaltz and had one son, Joseph.

Kenneth married Colleen Burns and had seven children: Robert, John, Debbie, David, Tim, Tammy, and Cindy. Robert married Penny Baxter and had two sons, Cliff and Brandon. John married Robin Smith and had two children, Joey and Taunya. Debbie has one daughter, Brandi. David married Vickie Mounce and has three children, Nick, Doug and April. Tim married Lisa Aschliman and has two children, Travis and Taran. Tammy married Andy Winning. Cindy married David Bates.

TILLIE HENNEFORD MCFARREN

Tillie Henneford McFarren had a beautiful philosophy of life. In a letter to her nephew, Philip Joray, she wrote that she believed the best things in life were free, such as a beautiful sunset, soft falling snow, red birds eating the seed she had put out, a little dog wanting to sit in the same chair with her, a good book on a cold evening in a warm room, popcorn and apples, the garden in spring, rain on the roof and a red, red rose.

Tillie, who was the sixth of Michael and Lena Biberstein Henneford's eight children, was born February 5, 1886, in Vera Cruz. She was named Mary Mathilda, but was always known as Tillie.

Tillie seemed to be little tomboyish while growing up. She loved to do stunts like balancing on a tree stump. She also enjoyed climbing old apples trees in Klein's orchard in Vera Cruz.

Tille Hennford McFarren

When she was a young woman, Tillie worked as a clerk in the Leader store on the northwest corner of Main and Market Streets in Bluffton. There she met Francis (Frank) McFarren. The two were married on December 31, 1913. Frank and Tillie did not have any children, but their nephew, Philip Joray, lived with them in their Bluffton home so he could attend high school in Bluffton.

Just before their marriage and for several years after, Frank and Tillie enjoyed going to the lakes in northern Indiana. They went to Lake James, Jimmerson Lake, Snow Lake and Crooked Lake. There they fished, went boating, wading, had water fights and looked for water lilies.

Tillie had well-appointed flower gardens in her backyard. Additionally, she had a talent for putting foliage and flowers in attractive arrangements. Tillie would often take flowers to the sick and "shut-ins." She was a member of the Bluffton Garden Club and for twenty-seven years was on the Flower Committee of the First Baptist Church in Bluffton.

Tillie possessed remarkable artistic talent, which she employed in drawing portraits and scenes in nature. She was also talented in writing and often wrote poems and short stories. An example of one of her poems is recorded below:

Woman's Weakness
I earned some money the other day,
And though the doctor want his pay,
And the baby needs a pair of shoes,
And hubby has many "unpaid dues",
So many places for money indeed,
I spent it all for some flower seed.

Tillie was baptized and confirmed in the St. John Reformed Church in Vera Cruz. However, since her husband was interested in the First Baptist Church in Bluffton, she and Frank joined that church soon after their marriage. For many years, she taught a Bible class and served in the various activities of the Women's Missionary Society. Tillie was a dedicated and faithful member of First Baptist Church for forty years.

Tillie died on March 24, 1955, at her home in Bluffton. Rev. Carleton Atwater, Tillie's minister, eulogized her as a good neighbor and an intelligent, inspiring and industrious person who loved people and people loved her.

MCFARRENS

John McFarren was born in 1797 in Westmoreland County, Pennsylvania and married Elizabeth Faust in 1824. He moved to Wells County in about 1840 and lived at first near Wells on Huntington County line, on what was known as the McFarren homestead located a mile north and a little west of what is now Poneto, Indiana. The current farm located just west of the Hoosier Highway is the location of the McFarren Cemetery.

John McFarren's father, John McFarren, a typical Irishman of Scot lineage, fled from Ireland and was shipwrecked on the way to America.

Jacob McFarren, with three brothers and three sisters, was raised on the homestead and was married in 1841.

George Francis McFarren had five brothers and five sisters. George married Martha Ann Miller in 1866 in Wells County and had a daughter Winnietta May. After the death of Martha Ann, George remarried in 1875 to Martha Jane Bennett with two sons born to the union, Harry Arthur and Earl.

George Francis moved to Bluffton where he established the McFarrens Clothing store, finally located on the north east corner of the intersection of Main and Market Streets. The McFarren home was built at 505 S. Main Street. Harry Arthur married Flo Morris in September of 1898. Children were: Harriett, Morris, George, Harry Arthur Jr., Martha and Robert William. Harry was secretary/treasurer of the Morris five and ten cents stores, which were later sold to G.C. Murphy. Harry Arthur Jr., with wife Pauline, resided in Bluffton for a number of years raising daughters Mary Lou and Judith Ann. After retirement, Mac and Polly moved to Tucson, Arizona.

Robert William, with wife Roma Evelyn Frankland (born in Murrumbeena, Australia) have resided in Bluffton since 1945 with children Sue Ann, Diana Kay and Gary Lee.

Gary Lee resides with wife Rhonda and their two sons, Robert William II and Joseph Madison, in southern Wells County at the south end of Keystone, Indiana.

MCINTIRE

Early Wells County McIntires were of Scotch-Irish descent. Ancestor Charles McIntire of colonial Virginia, born about 1724 in Ireland (died 1783), was a "Mariner." He was granted land in Virginia by Thomas Lord Fairfax in 1763 and 1766; he served in the Revolutionary War. His oldest child, Thomas, (1744-1820), purchased land from his father at Berkley Springs, Virginia, and established a grist mill. Thomas had nine children. The fifth child, Charles, was born in 1783 and died in 1858.

John Marion Burchard born September 25, 1851, died May 2, 1924, Eve (McIntire) Burchard born March 17, 1850, were married June 14, 1870

Charles, a blacksmith, raised some fine running horses; he served briefly in the War of 1812. He had ten children: the third child, Nun, was born 1809 in Frederick County, Virginia.

Five of Charles's boys left Virginia and went West. Nun and Dick were the first to sell out in Virginia and move West in 1836, after a preliminary round trip on horseback to Indiana. They made their own roads most of the way.

Nun was a pioneer farmer, served as probate judge until about 1851, and held other public offices in Wells County. Nun and Dick were issued land patents by the U.S. Government in 1837-38 for good farm land in what they thought was Chester Township, but which proved later to be Jackson Township. Both men are listed in 1840 Federal Census of Wells County.

Nun had married in Virginia. He had thirteen children and eleventh child, Eve (1850-1920), married John Burchard and also had thirteen children. Edith Burchard Williams was their fourth child, (1878-1968). She attended Marion College at Marion, Indiana, taught school, and was the mother eight children.

In 1868, Harrison, William, and sister Dorcas came by covered wagon and bought land close to their brothers on what is now county road #1100-700W. The settling became known as "McIntire Row." The Asbury church at road #3 intersection was known as McIntire at one time and the cemetery was McIntire Graveyard. Dick McIntire, who owned a sorghum mill, gave land where both are located to the community.

Eve attended McIntire School #7 at the corner 1100S-700W. Nun's house was east of the school. He and his brothers molded and dried brick for this home, which had three large rooms with fireplaces and large cupboards in each room. Great-grandmother told about the Miami Indians, mostly friendly, coming around her house to hunt, since it was close to swampy land and the Salamonie River. Nun died 1881; she died in 1901.

The five pioneer McIntires are all buried at Asbury Cemetery along with many of their family and descendants. This includes Eve McIntire Burchard and Edith Burchard Williams.

Edith's youngest child, Verda Williams Booth, was born 1914 and was a seamstress; her oldest child, Wanda Booth Smith, born in 1937, is a medical technologist at the Caylor-Nickel Clinic in Bluffton. Wanda's daughter, Kathy Smith Curry, born in 1957, is a Wells County social worker. Her daughters attended Ball State University at Muncie, Indiana. Great-great-grandchildren of Edith's are Nicole Renee Curry (eight years), Scott Andrew Curry (five years), and Jennifer Michelle Curry (newborn) who are the tenth generation and direct descendants of Charles McIntire of Colonial Virginia. The last four generations listed are residents of Bluffton.

MCKINNEY-COTTON

Hamer McKinney born February 13, 1874, in Fayetteville, Brown County, Ohio the son of Thomas and Martha Wilson McKinney. He married Bessie Cotton, in Wells County November 18, 1893. She was born January 15, 1876 and was the daughter of George Washington and Josephine McDanniel (McDannel) Cotton. Hamer spent his adult life in Bluffton where he engaged in farming and stock trading. He and Bessie lived two miles south of Bluffton on the Hoosier Highway. All of their children were born in Bluffton. They were Martha Esther (1894-1969) who married Glen Robinson; Ruth (1896-1900); John Wayne (1899-1955) who married Wilmetta Shirk; Beatrice Bell (1903-1988) who married Howard Weygand; Robert Lelan (1906-1940); Frederick Eugene (1908-1986) who married Florence Cutler and later Helen Ulmer); George "Jerry" Thomas (1911-1981) who married first Wanda Shipley and then Marie Murphy. Hamer, Bessie, Ruth, Beatrice, Robert Frederick and George Thomas are all buried in Fairview Cemetery in Bluffton, Indiana.

James William McKinney son of Thomas and Martha Wilson McKinney, was born September 14 1859 in Brown County, Ohio. He attended the county schools near his home and then entered the Bainbridge High School, Bainbridge, Ohio. He graduated from the teacher's college at Hillsboro, Ohio. He taught a few years at Liberty Center, Ohio, then attended the Starling Medical College at Columbus, Ohio, graduating in 1893 and on May 13, 1898, he entered the practice of medicine in Bluffton, Indiana. In 1923, after practicing medicine for twenty-five years, he attended the Quarto Centennial of his graduating class at Columbus, Ohio. Dr. McKinney's first office rooms were established with Dr. Edward Horton in the Kunkle-Vaughn block. In 1900, he located his offices in the I.O.O.F. building where he remained for twenty-five years, moving only a few months before his death to the late C.E. Brinneman building on Washington Street.

Jerry, Fred, Robert, Wayne, Hamer, Bessie, Beaty, Esther, McKinney, December 25, 1933

On January 11, 1902 he married Harriett Ogden "Aunt Hattie" in Bluffton, Indiana. She was born in 1876 in Bluffton, and died in 1941, daughter of Nancy Ann Brickley ("Jennie") and George S. Ogden. Harriet and "Doc" had no children. Aunt Hattie had real dark hair and big brown eyes. She was a milliner by trade. She made Grandma McKinney (Martha) a beaded hat with velvet which was later given to Esther (her daughter) and it was then given to the museum.

Dr. McKinney was a happy, jovial person. He was a member of the Methodist Church having been converted at the age of nineteen. He became a Mason at age twenty-one and was a 32nd degree Mason at the time of his death. He was a member of chapter council and Knight Templar, a member of the Benevolent and Protective Order of the Elks; the Moose Lodge and the Chamber of Commerce. He was president of the Tri County Medical Society and served as president of the Board of Pensions for thirty years, having been recommended to the post by Indiana senators, Albert J. Beveridge and J.A. Nemenway with a personal endorsement from Congressman J.A.M. Adair of the Bluffton district. Dr. McKinney died on August 15, 1930 of a cerebral hemorrhage. He had recently returned from Mt. Clemens, Michigan where he had taken treatments at a sanitarium. While at a local dentist office where he had his teeth x-rayed, he had a relapse and was removed from the office by ambulance to his home where he died two hours later. Both Dr. and Mrs. McKinney are in the mausoleum at Fairview Cemetery, Bluffton, Indiana.

THOMAS F. MCKINNEY-FREDERICK MCKINNEY-T. WM. MCKINNEY

Thomas Forseith McKinney born September 13, 1840 Brown County, Ohio son of William and Hannah Russell McKinney. On October 24, 1860 he married Martha Jane Wilson born September 5, 1830, Brown County, Ohio, daughter of William and Mary Fore (Foor) Wilson. The family moved to Liberty Township, Wells County, Indiana in about 1892. While in Ohio Thomas was a Methodist pastor. Upon moving to Wells County, he became a farmer. Thomas and Martha are both buried in Fairview Cemetery in Bluffton. Children were: Ada, born 1864, married Benjamin F. Snowhill; Charles Wesley, born 1865, married Rosella Miller; Clara "Clovie", born 1867, married first James Tudor and then Clem Holderbaum, #3 Curtis Walker; James W. "Doc", 1871, married Harriet Ogden; Edward S. 1872, married Ethel Lee; Hamer, born 1874 married Bessie Cotton.

Thomas was a conscientious worker, enjoyed the highest esteem of his neighbors, and the respect of all who knew him for his many excellent qualities. Martha was a woman to whom family ties made a wonderfully strong appeal. She was known among a wide circle of friends for a kindly, sunshiny disposition. In 1909, they sold their farm in Liberty Township, five miles west of Bluffton and moved to a new home which was located north of Poneto where they lived the remainder of his years. Thomas died April 28, 1911

Martha Wilson McKinney born September 5, 1830, died September 2, 1917

My grandfather, Frederick Eugene McKinney was born in Bluffton, Indiana in 1908. He married first Florence Irene Cutler daughter of Earl and Olive Mae Close Cutler and then Helen Naoma Ulmer, daughter of John Harrison "Harry" and Frances Hughes Ulmer all of Wells County. Children from these two marriages were Kathleen, Carol, T. William, Kenneth, Roger and Donna. Fred was in the poultry business.

Thomas William "Bill" McKinney was born October 12, 1935 in Bluffton, Wells County, Indiana. He was the third child of Florence Irene Cutler and Frederick Eugene McKinney. At one time the family lived two miles south of Bluffton on the Hoosier Highway and also lived at 928 Wabash. Bill who is president and partner of Collins Motor Company in Fort Wayne, was married to Betty Marie Hughes on April 22, 1955. She is the daughter of William and Frankie Caskey Hughes of Fort Wayne. Their children are:

Douglas William "Doug" born August 27, 1957 married first Tracy Purkhiser and then Linda Whitaker. One daughter, Karen Marie McKinney was born October 28, 1979 from first marriage. Doug and Linda live in Sidney, Indiana and are employed in the "Gold Rush" antique business in Pierceton, Indiana.

Daniel Frederick, born March 29, 1960, lives in Fort Wayne, Indiana and is employed at Collins Oldsmobile and also student at International Institute of Technology. He is not married.

Dawn Marie, born November 1, 1963 married Gregory A. Newport. They live in Stable Acres, Columbia City, Indiana. Dawn is employed at Magnavox, Greg at Collins. Their two children are: Casey Marie, born December 22, 1987 and Cody William, born August 16, 1990.

MCKURAS

Sean Michael (born December 31, 1976) and Megan Elizabeth McKuras (born April 24, 1980) moved to Apple Valley, Minnesota with their parents Michael Edward and Julie Ann (Fritz) McKuras in July 1984. Michael and Julie were married in Fort Wayne July 1972. Michael works for Pillsbury and Julie is a nurse. Michael is the only child of Harley Leo and Barbara Jean (Johnson) McKuras and was born in Bluffton, September 7, 1950. He graduated from Bluffton High School and IPFW. He worked at Wabash Avenue Greenhouse while in high school and then at Bachman's, Home Dairy, Lincoln Bank and North American Van Lines.

Harley is the youngest son of Leo and Nellie (Abbott) McKuras and was born at Fiat, Jay County on January 11, 1926. Genieve (Sylvan Studebaker), Wanda (Virgil Waters) and Murray (Ruth Carmen) are the other children. Harley graduated from Petroleum High School in 1944 and went into the Navy right away. He served in the Pacific Theater for two years on an LSM ship. He worked for Franklin Electric for two years, and he was a meatcutter for Kroger for several years before returning to Franklin. He worked there for twenty years before he died August 12, 1985. He was a member of the American Legion and a life member and past commander of the Veterans of Foreign Wars.

McKuras Family - Genieve, Wanda, Harley, Murray

Harley and Barbara were married in 1949. She is the daughter of William R. (Ray) and Pauline (Goldsberry) Johnson. Ray was born and raised in Nottingham Township. He moved his family back to Wells County in 1936.

Leo was born in Jay County, the youngest child of William Hugh and Isabelle (Suters) McKuras. He had two sisters and a brother, Leonidas (Sue Chenoworth), Hazel (Abe Sprunger) and Maude (Russell Lucas). He was born and raised on a farm in Jay County and later became a barber. He and Nellie were married in 1916 - she was the daughter of Andrew V. and Catherine (McDaniel) Abbott. He moved his family to Reiffsburg, Wells County in 1928 and worked in a factory for a while and then started farming on a farm east of Reiffsburg. He and Murray worked at Baer Field during World War II putting in runways and on other construction projects. Nellie died in 1962 and Leo in 1974.

William was the son of Hugh and Margaret Ann McKuras. He was born in Athens County, Ohio in 1849 and served in the Civil War for one year. During that year he traveled over 7,000 miles and most of it on foot. He married Kate Lewis, and she died shortly after Leonidas was born. He then married Belle Suters, and they had three children. Belle was born in Randolph County, a daughter of Washington and Susan (Ayers) Suters, who were born in Pennsylvania. Belle died in 1920 and William died in 1925.

Hugh was born in Scotland in 1810, and Margaret Ann was born in England in 1818. Hugh came to America in the early 1840's after having served on a whaling ship in the Arctic. His brother died on the ship coming to America. McKuras is a sept of the Ferguson Clan.

Refer to Johnson, Shigley and Abbott/McDaniel histories.

MCMILLAN

Paul and Zada E. (Banter) McMillan were married September 17, 1923, and had three sons born from this union. Paul died from tuberculosis on September 12, 1941. John James McMillan was born on October 17, 1932. His first marriage was to Janice (Barker) McMillan, and seven children were born. The children are: James R., J. Robert, Jennifer R., Joseph R., Jane, Julie and Jeremy. His second marriage is to Frances D. (Pearce) McMillan.

Sharon, Claire, Clarice, and Kristi

Twins, Claude B. and Claire T., were born on February 6, 1940. Claude B. is married to Judy (McClain) McMillan, and one son was born, Paul C. McMillan. He had two step-children, Randy McClain and Lorie (McClain) Bauermeister.

Claire T. McMillan is married to the former Sharon K. (Baker) McMillan. They were married on May 16, 1964. Sharon graduated from International Business College in Fort Wayne with an associate degree in business administration. Sharon is a rural carrier out of the Warren Post Office. Claire graduated from Purdue University with an associate degree in engineering. He is a supervisor at Franklin Electric. They are members of the Dillman United Brethren Church in Jackson Township. Both are members of the Eastern Star at Crescent Chapter #48 in Bluffton. Claire is a past Worshipful Master of King Lodge #246 at Warren, Indiana. He is also school board president of the Southern Wells School Corporation. They live on a

198-acre farm in Jackson Township, Wells County. The farm has been in Sharon (Baker) McMillan's family for one hundred years.

From this marriage two daughters were born, Clarice K., September 1, 1967 and Kristi L., January 10, 1971. Clarice graduated from Ball State in May 1990 with a degree in International Finance. Kristi is a student at Ball State University.

MCMILLAN

Randal Wayne McMillan married Janice Turner in 1974. Randal is the son of Everett and Colleen McMillan, and Janice is the daughter of Gerald and Genevieve (Thurman) Turner. Randal and Janice bought the home farm of Colleen's parents, Mr. and Mrs. Rhessa Slusher, and moved there in 1978. Randal farms and raises hogs. He also drives a school bus for Southern Wells Community Schools while Janice works for Weaver Popcorn at Van Buren. They are the parents of two children: Aaron Josiah and Kelly Ann.

CLAUDE AND JUDITH MCMILLAN FAMILY

The Claude Banter McMillan family was started August 6, 1966, in Van Wert, Ohio.

Claude, a twin born February 6, 1940, is the son of James Paul McMillan, born May 11, 1895 (died September 12, 1941) and Zada Elizabeth (Banter) McMillan, born January 10, 1902. Claude's marriage was to Judith Anne (Keipper) (McClain) McMillan born April 18, 1945. She was the daughter of Albert Raymond (Keipper) (born October 2, 1909-died April 29, 1970) and Dorothy Elizabeth (Wooley) Keipper (born January 26, 1922-died May 29, 1976.)

Claude and Judy have three children, two from a former marriage, Randy Alan McClain and Lorie Lynne (McClain) Bauermeister; and a son born to their marriage, Paul Chadler McMillan.

Randy Alan McClain was born September 9, 1961 in Bluffton, Ohio and is the son of William Allen McClain and Judith Anne (Keiper) (McClain) McMillan. Randy is married to Angela Jo Steffen, born December 7, 1962. She is the daughter of Roberta (Holloway) Steffen and Kenneth Steffen of Bluffton, Indiana. They are the parents of a daughter, Abby Kristin, born April 29, 1989, and are expecting their second child in July, 1991. Randy and Angela graduated from Norwell High School and own R.M.C. Auto Body Service. Angela also works at Caylor-Nickel Clinic.

Claude McMillan Family

Lorie Lynne (McClain) Bauermeister, born March 11, 1963 at Van Wert, Ohio, is the daughter of William Allen McClain and Judith Anne (Keipper) (McClain) McMillan. She is married to Jeffrey Laine Bauermeister, born May 3, 1961, son of Lester and the late (Elva Jo) Joey (Runking) Bauermeister. They have three children, Whitney Rae born November 2, 1985, Carlee Jann born September 18, 1989 and Brair Laine born January 25, 1991. Jeff and Lorie both graduated from Norwell High School and operate a swine production business in Jefferson Township. Jeff is also works at Melching Machine Shop and Lori has her own beauty shop.

Paul Chadler McMillan, born February 24, 1968, in Bluffton, Indiana to Claude and Judith Anne (Keipper) (McClain) McMillan is married to Gaye Lynn Sadler of Uniondale, Indiana. Chad and Gaye graduated from Norwell High School. Chad is employed at Pyromation Company, Inc., in Fort Wayne, and Gaye graduated from Purdue School of Dental Hygienist and is employed by Dr. Horsewood in Hoagland, Indiana. They live in rural Zanesville, Indiana.

Claude is employed at Franklin Electric Company as a manufacturing engineer, and Judy works as a receptionist for Dr. Huseman at the Bluffton Animal Clinic. They have lived in Wells County since their marriage on August 6, 1966.

EVERETT MCMILLAN FAMILY

Everett Edward McMillan married Frances Colleen Slusher in 1950. Everett is the son of Boyd and Julia McMillan and Colleen is the daughter of Rhessa and Martha Slusher. Everett was working for Salamonie Mills when they were married. They lived in a log cabin south of Warren on the farm which was farmed by his father. Later Everett drove a milk truck and picked up milk in ten gallon cans from farms.

After the birth of their second child in 1953, the moved to a farm in Huntington County where Everett helped farm and milk cows for Mr. and Mrs. Wayne King. In 1953, after the birth of their fourth child, they moved to a farm in Wabash County near La Fountaine. There they farmed and milked cows.

In 1960 they moved their six children and belongings back to Jackson Township, Wells County, just two miles from where Colleen grew up. They bought a farm just west of McNatt owned by Fred Williams. They milked cows until 1979 when Everett sold his entire herd at one time. They have continued to farm and raise cattle.

Everett enjoys woodworking in his spare time, and Colleen enjoys gardening and quilting.

They are the parents of nine children. Joetta Fay married William McElhaney and lives in Grant County. Trudy Ann married Ron Westfall and lives near Bluffton. Randal Wayne married Janice Turner of Grant County and lives in Jackson Township. Ginger Lou married Steve Arko from Elkart and lives near Goshen. Polly Jean married Jerry Mayer and lives in Jackson Township. Cherry Sue married Barry Story and lives near Bluffton. Daisy May married Darrel Groves from Pennsylvania and lives in Chicago, Illinois. Rebecca Rose married Kevin Page from Toledo, Ohio and lives in Jackson Township. Bonita Kay is engaged to Stefan Ekhardt from Fort Wayne.

Everett and Colleen enjoy their sixteen grandchildren and two step-grandsons.

They are members of Dillman United Brethren Church.

MCNAMARA

On December 16, 1967, Thomas Henry McNamara, his wife, Margaret, and four children moved to Bluffton from Marion, Indiana. Thomas had previously worked in the family Texaco station in Marion. He took a job with Irving Brothers Stone Company and moved here to manage Erie Stone in Bluffton, Markle, and later Montpelier Stone. He retired in December, 1988.

Thomas was born June 21, 1933, in South Bend, Indiana, to William and Avaline Probst McNamara. He married Margaret Louise Huber June 11, 1955, in Marion, Indiana.

Their first child, Thomas Henry Jr., was born May 20, 1956, in Pensacola, Florida, while his father served in the Navy. He married Brenda Kunkle August 1, 1990 in Bluffton.

Teresa Marie, born December 15, 1957, in Marion, married Randy Lee Melton on November 20, 1976, in Bluffton. They have two sons, Dustin Lee, born June 30, 1981, and Casey Austin, born February 6, 1983, in Bluffton.

Tamara Sue, born April 30, 1959, in Marion, married Douglas Eugene Gilbert on August 27, 1977, in Bluffton. They have two children: Ike Thomas born May 23, 1979, and Dominice Nikol, born December 31, 1980, in Bluffton.

Timothy Michael was born May 14, 1962, in Marion. He married Mary Taylor September 29, 1984. They have a daughter, Leslie Marie, born March 23, 1988, in Bluffton.

Margaret Huber was born January 13, 1938, in Marion, Indiana to John Golden Huber and Agnes Burniauskis, who were married December 5, 1931.

Agnes Dominice, born November 3, 1908, came to America about 1915 from Lithuania. Her father Ygnac Burniauskis arrived in Baltimore, Maryland, May 30, 1912, and settled in Marion, Indiana. He married Stephnia Gudelwiski, born December 25, 1888, in Russia and died February 10, 1923, in Marion, Indiana. Ygnac was born October 25, 1884 in Zorany, Russia, and he died January 17, 1972, in Indianapolis, Indiana.

John Huber was born November 29, 1902, the son of John F. and Amanda Jane Myers Huber. He died July 13, 1980, in Marion, Indiana.

John F. was born November 18, 1864, married Amanda September 23, 1890, in Marion, Indiana. He died April 23, 1918, in Marion.

Amanda was born September 18, 1863, in Dayton, Ohio, and died November 2, 1932, in Marion, Indiana.

Avaline Marie Probst, was born October 8, 1900 in South Bend, Indiana to Henry and Cynthia Nettie Singler Probst. She married William McNamara September 26, 1922. She died May 30, 1988, in Marion.

Henry Probst born September 11, 1863, in White Pidgeon, Michigan, married Cynthia, September 11, 1889. She was born May 30, 1864, in Millersburg, Indiana, and died August 19, 1938, in Sturgis, Michigan. Henry died June 3, 1941, in South Bend, Indiana.

William Carr Whitehead McNamara was born November 19, 1900, in Brownstown, Indiana, to Dr. William Erasmus Whitehead and Caroline Carr Colburn. He died June 6, 1985, in Marion, Indiana.

Dr. Whitehead was born December 4, 1846, in Lawrenceburg, Indiana, and married Caroline October 21, 1890, and died January 5, 1984, in Brownstown, Indiana.

Caroline was born September 19, 1874, in Medora, Indiana, and died August 10, 1957, in South Bend, Indiana.

WILLIAM "PAT" MEADE FAMILY

Henry and Emily (Rodgers) Meade came to Wells County in the late 1800's from Scott County, Virginia. They bought a farm south of Bluffton on

200 S. in Liberty Township. They were members of the Liberty Center Methodist Church.

As a result of Uncle Henry settling near the Addington's (cite Addington history), my father, William Patton "Pat" met and married my mother, Mary Elizabeth (Addington). They were married in 1904 and lived near Poneto. They later moved near Keystone. My father farmed, bought and sold livestock, and worked a short time in the Oklahoma oil fields. My mother did some wallpaper hanging after the children were older.

William Patton and Elizabeth Meade

My brothers and sisters and their families are: Vera (Phillip Shadle); Joyce, (Ivan, Ivans). Velma, (Claude Huffman); Irene, (Sidney Beaty II), Sidney served in World War II. Leon, (Joetta Fields); Donald, (Anne Henderson).

Arnet, (Elizabeth White); Janice, (Rene Roman),Judy, (Chuck Kelley), Sherry, (Michael Peneguy).

Alvis, (Vallera Gray); Pat, (Becky Tarr), Rex (Teresa Pratt), Mike, (Mary Dean Schlagenhauffen), Tim (Janet Larimer), Greg, (Dorothy Stidham), and Jeff. Tim is the Wells County Sheriff with Greg and Mike also residing in Bluffton. Pat served in the Vietnam War.

Dorothy, (Virgil Meyers), Deborah Mackey, (Edgar Carter), and Daniel Mackey.

I (Mary) married Carl Hunnicutt. We have seven children: (cite Hunnicutt history). Our son, Kenneth, and his family reside in Bluffton. Kenneth and sons-in-law, Richard Sproat and Harold Campbell, served in the Korean War, with our son, Tom, serving in the Vietnam War. Larry served in the National Guard, and Jim is presently serving in the National Guard.

Uncle Henry's sister, Pearl, and brother, Arnet, later settled in Wells County.

Aunt Pearl married Tom Smith, they had one infant, deceased. Uncle Tom drove a gasoline truck for Hartman's gas station, located at the corner of Wabash and Main Street.

Uncle Arnet married Laura Robinson and worked as a painter. Their children are: Lois (Rodney Prough), Mary Maxine (Ed Hiatt), Wanda, (Melvin Wall), Ralph (Anita Mosure), Keith, (Marilyn Brown), Keith lives in Bluffton. Rodney, Melvin, Ed and Ralph all served in the Navy.

Because of Uncle Henry and Aunt Emily's nerous hospitality, many friends and relatives came from Virginia to visit, resulting in several marriages.

Having no children of their own, they also enjoyed having their nieces and nephews visit them. I have many fond memories of Uncle Henry and Aunt Emily Meade. *(Mary Meade Hunnicutt)*

MELTON

Lawrence "Joe" Melton was born October 23, 1894, in Hyden, Leslie County, Kentucky. He was the fourth child of ten and the son of John Mitchell Melton and Martha Belle Valentine.

John Mitchell was born August 20, 1866, in Wooten, Kentucky; he married Martha December 24, 1885. He was the grandson of Tarry H. Melton, the first Melton to come to Kentucky. He died January 14, 1931, in Hyden, Kentucky.

Martha Belle was born September 17, 1870. She died May 30, 1948, in Grassy Branch, Kentucky.

Lawrence "Joe" Melton married Lillie Colwell after serving six years in the Army during World War I. Lillie was the daughter of Morris Colwell and Sarah Fugate Colwell. She was one of eleven children and was born October 13, 1901, in Hazard, Perry County, Kentucky. Joe and Lillie had seven children. They were Alvy, Edna, Joe, Vernon, James Marvin, Rancie and Loretta.

Lawrence Joe Melton and Lillie Colwell Melton - Photo taken in Lexington, Kentucky in approximately 1934 or 1935

In 1943 "Joe" sold his farm in Hazard and moved his family to Bluffton. They arrived May 15, 1943. They settled in the Travisville area and went to work in the fields for the Far Bureau. "Joe" worked and lived in the Bluffton area the rest of his life, and he died November 29, 1959, in Bluffton. His wife Lillie is currently residing in Bluffton.

Their fourth child, Vernon C., was born February 4, 1927, in Hyden, Kentucky. He worked hard and helped his family. Then on May 15, 1944, he was called to duty with the Army. He served his country well and was discharged December 23, 1946. Then on October 31, 1947, he married Audrey Joan Lovell. To their union five children were born.

Sonja Sue, born September 12, 1948, married William Habig. They have one son, David Emery.

Linda Lou, born July 4, 1949, married Ed Camomile. She has two daughters, Sabrina and Regina Miller, and one stepson, Travis Camomile.

Larry Eugene, born July 22, 1952, was married to Yuvonne Dillon. He has two daughters, Amy Steinhilber and Tiffany Melton, and one son, Aaron Melton.

Peggy Ann, born December 21, 1953, married Jeff Nash. She has two sons, Nathan and Jason Springer.

Randy Lee was born April 5, 1955, in Wells County. He married Teresa Marie McNamara November 20, 1976, in Wells County. They have two sons, Dustin Lee, born June 30, 1981, and Casey Austin, born February 6, 1983. Both were born in Wells County.

Vernon worked in and around the Bluffton area and then started Melton Construction. Then in 1981 he and his wife moved to Bonita Springs, Florida, to build 192 duplex units before returning to Bluffton in 1990.

MENDENHALL FAMILY

There's a small house in Chester Township in which Joseph W. Mendenhall and Lena R. Jacobs started housekeeping. Two daughters were born to this union: Vera Frances and Hilda Mary.

My father preferred to be called William Joseph, but most people called him Bill. His ancestors were English Quakers who came to America about 1657 and took up residence in Pennsylvania. The name Mendenall was originally spelled Mildenhall, which is the name of an English castle that was later converted into a college. My father was of the Mordecia line. He died on April 3, 1988.

Grandfather Eli was born January 4, 1857 in Liberty Township in Wells County. He married Mary Catherine Wagner, who was born November 22, 1859.

My mother was a Jacobs; her mother was Mary Eilar. Grandma was a devoted Quaker and nearly always wore a full long apron over her dress. Mother played the organ at South Liberty Church. My grandparents were farmers. James Mac Jacobs (my grandfather) was a janitor at the South Liberty Church. He lived just across the road, and ministers often stayed in their home. I believe the house is still standing and occupied.

Farming was short-lived for my father, as he was kicked by a horse. After weeks of recovery he went to the Illinois oil fields in his first car, a Ford with side curtains. Every vacation we spent at our grandparents' home and visiting with other relatives.

The oil field was certainly different from farming. We lived among six families, fairly close together. The houses were called shacks, but mother kept ours nice, clean and cozy. We had a cow, chickens, and a good sized garden and lots of friends.

Frances Clark, Barry Clark (son) Joseph W. Mendenall (father) and Diane Clark (granddaughter)

I attended a good two-room school (almost new) and the Methodist Church beside it. I adored my teachers, except one who was a "rufflie" and kept a cat-o'-nine-tails near his desk. There were no buses, so if bad weather showed up, someone from our village came to take us home. Otherwise we walked about a mile. My sister was about two years younger than I and often needed help, as all the younger ones did, but someone always came to the rescue. Blackman was a favorite game we played between the school and the church.

Father always liked the farm, and after about ten years in the oil field he decided to return to Indiana to help his parents, as they were elderly and sick. Death came soon for Grandma.

I spent my first seven school years in Petrolia, Illinois, then five years at Liberty Center, Indiana, and after that on to Ball State and teaching. I taught at Poneto, at Liberty Center, and Southern Wells, and all were enjoyable. My sister, Mary Chalfant, taught school at Poneto, at Liberty Center, and in Kentucky.

I married Harry Clark, a farmer, and have one son, Barry, who is also a farmer. Harry E. Clark died in June, 1970.

I'm a member of the D.A.R., the Home Economics Club, the Liberty Center Baptist Church, Historical Society, and the Wells County Community Hospital Auxiliary. I enjoy crafts and several hobbies. *(Vera Frances Clark)*

MENDENHALL-COMBS

Harry E. Mendenhall was born September 17, 1880, in Liberty Township, to Eli and Catherine Wagner Mendenhall. He was the oldest of nine children, seven boys and two girls. He married Tottie Stout (daughter of Sam and Sarah Ratliff Stout) in Bluffton, December 25, 1898. To this union was born five daughters; three dying in infancy. The two living are Hope and Faith; both graduates of P.A. Allen High.

Harry worked in the oil fields and later moved to Bluffton and built a house at 781 Clark Avenue, where they lived until their death. After moving to Bluffton he worked as custodian at the Old High, P.A. Allen, and Lancaster schools. He also operated a garage on Clark Avenue. He worked many places and drove trucks for Craig Trucking Company, and also worked for the county.

He and Tottie were members of the Moose and the Ladies Legion. They celebrated their fifty-seventh wedding anniversary.

Faith Mendenall Combs

Sam and Sarah Stout, my grandparents on my mother's side, lived on South Clark Avenue. They had four children, and raised four of their grandchildren. Sam was the custodian at the court house for many years. They lived at 315 W. Central Avenue until their death.

I married William Combs of Waynetown, Indiana, August 27, 1939. We moved to Hartford City, Indiana, where he worked for Montgomery Ward. During World War II we moved to Norwalk, Connecticut, where he worked for Machlett Laboratories, where they made tubes for the government - the tube that split the atom bomb.

After the war we moved back to Hartford City, Indiana, where we had radio and television business for twenty years. We later moved to Lafayette, Indiana, where we both worked at Purdue University. After the death of Bill I moved back to Hartford City, where I presently live.

We had one daughter, Rebecca Ann Combs. She married Jack Cain, and they live three miles south of Montpelier, Indiana. They have three children, Brian, Lori, and Beth, and five grandchildren. Jack works for 3M and Becky is a district manager for House of Lloyd.

Brian is an ex-Marine. He had a son Ryan. He is employed at Rem Johnston Printing in Bluffton, Indiana. They live in Montpelier.

Lori is married to Brett Townsend, and they have a son, Zachary. Lori has a beauty shop in Hartford City, Lori's Hair Trends.

Beth married Charles Watkins, and they have three children: Seth, Richard, and Amanda. Beth attends Amber's Beauty School.

I am a Past Matron of Purity Chapter of Eastern Star, member of Grace United Methodist Church, William Wells Chapter of D.A.R., Hartford City Historical Society, A.A.R.P., and a life member of Omega Nu Tau Sorority. *(Faith Combs)*

MENDENHALL-HURST

Our family dates back to Canterbury Court, England, 1633, where our tenth generation ancestor was born, Thomas Mendenhall, an English Quaker.

Mordecai Mendenhall was our Revolutionary War soldier born in Lancaster County, Pennsylvania in 1713.

Our grandfather Eli was born in Liberty Township in 1857, where he farmed. He was married to Mary Catherine Wagner, who was born November 23, 1859.

Our parents, Tottie Stout and Harry Mendenhall, were married on Christmas Day, 1898. They celebrated their fifty-seventh wedding anniversary in 1955. They were surprised with a gift from the Heinz 57 Varieties Company saying that was a special date for them too!

Two daughters were born in Bluffton, Hope Elizabeth and Faith Maxine.

Hope Mendenhall Hurst

Our father worked in the oil fields in Oklahoma, and Liberty Center, and Lost Lakes, Indiana.

After he returned to Bluffton the automobile was becoming popular here, so Father became a mechanic and started a garage, repaired cars and pumped gasoline. The highlight of the week was to go for a ride on Sunday, if we could leave before someone with a mechanical problem delayed us.

Mother was a daughter of Sarah Ratliff and Samuel Stout, who lived in Bluffton.

I attended Central School and graduated from P.A. Allen High School. After graduation I worked in Chicago, Illinois for two years at the Better Speech Institute.

In 1944 I started working at the Caylor-Nickel Clinic, first in the clinical laboratory for eleven years, then after becoming a registered medical technician, and with special training at Michigan University Hospital in Ann Arbor, Michigan, for nuclear medicine, I worked in the isotope laboratory for seventeen and one-half years. I retired from the clinic in 1976.

I worked in the nursery at the First Baptist Church, and sang in the choir for a number of years.

Harry (Pat) Hurst and I were married and built a home on South Scott Street. Pat worked for the Caylor-Nickel Clinic twenty-eight years. He had worked at Indiana Bell and Fruehauf Trailer Company during World War II. Pat died in August 1985.

I am a member of the First Baptist Church, Daughters of American Revolution, Wells County Historical Society, Eastern Star, and I am an American Red Cross Volunteer. I like to read, shop, travel, and do hand work. *(Hope Hurst)*

MERCHANT

Benjamin Manifold married Annabel Danger in November, 1730. They lived in York County, Pennsylvania. They had six children: William, Joseph, Edward, Elizabeth, Mary and Benjamin Jr. A seventh child, John, was born after the death of his father.

Frances and Raymond Merchant

Benjamin Manifold Jr., married Mary Payne in 1777. They lived in Hopeville Township, York County, Pennsylvania, until 1796, then moved to Knox County, Tennessee. Here he built a mill to grind wheat and corn and kept articles for sale. Later it became known as Manifold Station. The Manifold children were: George, William, Rachel, Elizabeth, Hannah, Joseph, Alice, Benjamin III, Henry, Mary, Sarah (born in October 1800,) and Martha.

Sarah Manifold married Thomas Scott in November, 1828. They moved to Madison County Indiana. Their children included: Mary (Birchfield), James, Joseph, and Margaret (Birchfield). James Scott married Elvira Crosley. They had three children: Emma (McCarty), John, and Attie (Gibson). John Scott married Etta Mingle. Their children included: Emma (Reese) (born July, 1887) Flossie (Ogle), Lloyd, Oma (West), Hanly, Martha and Frances.

Emma Scott married Leonard Reese September, 1909. They lived in Hancock County Indiana. Their children are: Laura Ruth (Williams), Esther (Oaks), Helen (Souder), Frances (Merchant (born August 1917), and Marjorie (Willie). Frances Reese married Raymond Merchant on June 20 1943, in Hancock County, Indiana. Raymond Merchant was born in December, 1919, in Hancock County. His parents were John and Laura (Zook) Merchant. John and Laura Merchant were married in December, 1912. They had twelve children Woodrow, Lewis, Raymond, William, James Robert, Ruth (Proudy), Jeanett (Holcomb), Mary (McCulloch), Elanore (Riley), Margaret (Smith) and Warren. Raymond's father, John, was born in Hancock County in August of 1883 to William and Alice (Walsmith) Merchant. William was born February 12, 1859, and Alice was born in Ma

1863. Raymond's mother was Laura (Zook). She was born in Johnson County in December 1887, to James and Utha (Lang) Zook. James was born in Morgan County in March, 1844, and Utha Lang was born in Morgan County in October, 1848.

In 1951 Frances and Raymond Merchant purchased fifty-seven acres in Wells County and moved to their present location in Chester Township. He worked for thirty years at Delco Remy in Anderson. They have three children: Sue, born in May, 1944; Joyce (Rupe), born in 1946; and Rhea Merchant, born in February 1955.

Sue Merchant lives in Wells County. She has a son, Kenneth Merchant, born in January of 1964. Joyce married David Rupe in 1968. They moved to Portland, Indiana and they have a son Mike, born in November, 1968. Rhea Merchant graduated from Taylor University in 1977. She is living in Chester Township and works at Indiana Glass. Kenneth Merchant married Jill Clouse (later divorced). They have three children: Kendra, born in October, 1981, and twin sons, Christopher and Andrew Merchant, born in November 1984. Kenneth and his children live in Chester Township.

MEYER

Our grandparents, Adam and Caroline (Saxman) Meyer came across from Germany in 1879. They were accompanied by four sons, Adam, George, Fred and Lou. They settled for a short time in Ohio, then moved to Jackson Township, Wells County. Four more sons were born there, William, Chris, Charles and Henry. Henry, the youngest was born January 6, 1887.

Our mother was born in Jackson Township, Wells County, November 24, 1892. She was the daughter of Joseph and Martha Ann (Allen) Jones. They were early settlers in Wells County. They had three sons and two daughters: Robert, Ed, Frank, Bertha and Lucy.

Henry Meyer married Lucy on May 1, 1913. Three of their children, Mildred, Anna and Henry A. were born in Jackson Township. They moved to Union Township in 1920 and had three more children Mary, Bertha Mae and Lucy E.

Our father farmed for a short time, then worked as a custodian for the Union Center School for four years. He then worked at Miller's elevator in Uniondale for four years before returning to Union Center as custodian. He was there until his death at the age of forty-six on March 20, 1933.

Our mother had to go to work to support us, doing custodial and cafeteria work at the Union Center School. Later she moved to Lancaster Township and worked in the cafeteria at Lancaster School. In 1959 she retired and moved to Bluffton where she was an Avon representative for many years. She lived in Bluffton until her death on January 11, 1990 at the age of ninety-seven.

Mildred married Elmer Keller in 1933 and has always lived near Flint, Michigan. They have one son, William, also a resident of Michigan. Elmer, a General Motors retiree, died in 1977.

Four of their children have always lived in Wells County. Anna married Rosco Lydy in 1939. They now live in Bluffton and have two daughters, Kay Ormiston of Bluffton and Georgia Schmidt of Fort Wayne. Anna is retired from the Caylor-Nickel Clinic, and Rosco is retired from International Harvester.

Henry A. (Bud) married Evelyn Morris in 1949. They had two sons, Richard Morris and Frank Morris, both of Bluffton. When Evelyn died in 1977, Bud married Gyneth Baker in 1979, and moved to Decatur. Gyneth, a CTS retiree, died January 15, 1991. Bud retired from the Eri Railroad after many years as a trackman.

Mary married Bernarr Biddle in 1941. They had two children, Thomas of Ossian and Jolene Heyerly of Decatur. Bernarr, who was employed by the Dairy Division of the State of Indiana, died in 1974. Mary retired from public employment in 1985.

Bertha Mae married Aden Strahm in 1944. They have two children, Daniel Strahm and Pat Wall both of Bluffton. Aden is retired from farming and carpenter work. Mae is employed at the Dutch Mill.

Lucy E., married Glen Fiechter in 1947, and lives in Tocsin. Lucy is retired from the General Electric Company, and Glen is retired from Berne Furniture.

ALVIN AND MINNIE MEYER

My grandparents, Alvin and Minnie Meyer, were married at Bethlehem Lutheran Church on October 9, 1932. Alvin Christian Meyer was born to Ernst and Marie Wiegmann Meyer on May 22, 1911. He graduated from Lutheran Institute, which was a business school. Wilhemina Marie Caroline Nahrwold, later legally changed to Minnie, was born to Karl (Charles) Frederick and Anna Werling Nahrwold on June 7, 1913.

They had four children: Wilbur of Ossian, born May 8, 1933 (Shelley, Stanley, Sanford, Sheldon Sherry); Kenneth of New Port Richey, Florida, born July 9, 1935 (Rhonda, Pamela, Amanda, Angela, Christina, Timothy, Misty); Doris of Orlando, Florida, born August 17, 1937 (Jeffery, Timothy); and Sandra of Kendallville, born February 14, 1943 (Kamilla, Richard). They also shared their home with Grandpa's brother, Marvin G. Meyer, for about 30 years.

Alvin and Minnie Meyer

They settled down on their farm on 600E in 1939 where Grandpa farmed at first with horses (one pair named "Jane and Belle") until he bought his first John Deere tractor. He raised hogs for thirty-four years until 1973, but also had dairy cows, sheep, and chickens earlier. I remember helping Grandpa load corn onto the truck; then we'd take the load into Tocsin to be ground into hog feed. Grandpa would give me a quarter and that bought a whole lot of candy!

Grandpa started working for Magnavox in 1937 and started out at forty dollars a week. He retired in 1973 and then he and Grandma started spending their winters in Florida.

My Grandma, Minnie, stayed home taking care of her family most of her life, except for the brief time she worked at Slick's Laundry, just long enough to earn enough money to buy a sewing machine. Grandma told me once that hamburger was three pounds for twenty-five cents when she and Grandpa were first married. She belonged to the Bethlehem Ladies Aid for about forty-five years and also sang in the choir. Grandma was a wonderful cook, and I get hungry just thinking of the good smells that used to come from her kitchen. She always had a homemade "goodie" and a nice, soft, warm lap for us grand-kids to curl up on when we came to stay.

Grandma passed away on April 2, 1983, and Grandpa on December 27, 1989. Many of my cousins and I spent most of our summer vacations with Grandma and Grandpa, and we have many, many fond memories of them. *Pamela Meyer Stinson*

CHARLES D. MEYER FAMILY

In 1870, Jorn and Franie Meyer moved from Ohio to Nebraska. Later they moved to the Bluffton area. They had six children: Javit, John, Obed, Elizabeth, Darmoris, and Fannie.

Obed was born April 15, 1866, and died November 5, 1908. He married Sarah Klopfenstein and they had fourteen children: Amelia, Ida, Sylvia, Adam, Lewis, Sophia, Elizabeth, Jacob, Mary, Charles, Stella, Alvie, Mahilda, and Theodore.

Charles ((born March 17, 1902), married Ida Bollinger on April 3, 1926. They had two children, Lester and Dorothy.

Lester (born March 3, 1931) married Carolyn Williams on September 16, 1956. They have two children, Kelli and Kent. Kelli (born January 20, 1960), married Kent Lesh on June 12, 1985. They have two children, Lindsey born January 5, 1985 and Courtney born May 18, 1988. Kent (born July 26, 1963), married Sheila Herman on March 3, 1984 and they have two children, Joshua born August 1, 1984, and Jessica born February 10, 1988.

Dorothy (born February 14, 1939), married Wayne Fiechter on June 22, 1958, and they have two children, Joni and Mark. Joni (born March 1, 1960), married Gene Longenberger on January 21, 1979. They have three children, Abbey born July 30, 1981, Mandy born March 2, 1984, and Katy born February 2, 1986. Mark (born May 28, 1963), married Shelly Kaufman on February 13, 1983. They have three children, Joel born December 12, 1986, Caleb born July 29, 1987, and Melissa born December 11, 1989. All of Charles' family live in the Bluffton area.

Charles and Ida celebrated their sixty-fifth wedding anniversary April 3, 1991.

CHARLES NEWTON MIDDLETON

In April 1937, Charles "Newt" and Louise Middleton moved to Wells County from Fort Wayne. Their home was three-fourths mile west of Zanesville on North County Line Road. They had two children. Floyd, thirteen years old and Ruth, eleven. There was another member of the household. Newt's Aunt LaVina Boals. She was seventy-four years old.

Living on the farm was a big change for the family who had spent the previous years in town. There was livestock to care for, garden to make and fields to plant. Plenty of work for all. In addition, Newt worked as a machinist at International Harvester.

In 1951 Newt and Louise sold this farm to Art and Hannah Rutenberg and moved to a farm they had previously bought on 400N. It was three-fourths mile south of North County Line Road.

Standing: Ruth Sullens, Floyd Middleton. Seated: Newton and Louise Middleton - 50th wedding anniversary.

In 1952 Newt opened a machine shop in the Uniondale feed barn. He named it Uniondale Machine Shop. Newt repaired many kinds of equipment in the next twenty years, from bicycles and lawn mowers to farm machinery and gravel pit equipment.

Floyd, Newt's son, did much of the farming until he enlisted in the Navy in 1943. In 1944, he married Susette Mitchell who lived near Uniondale. Both Susette and Floyd graduated from East Union Center in 1942.

After he was discharged from the Navy, Floyd finished his college education and became a teacher. He was a principal at East Union Center from 1956 to 1962.

From 1962 to 1974 he was an assistant principal in various Fort Wayne Community Schools. Susette was also a teacher in the Fort Wayne Schools until she retired.

Floyd passed away in February 1974.

Ruth graduated from East Union in 1944. After working at several different jobs, she married Calvin Sullens whom she met in San Diego, California. Calvin had remained in the Navy after World War II. The next sixteen years were spent in cities from the west coast to the east coast of the United States.

In 1966 Ruth, Calvin and their three daughters returned to Wells County. They first rented a house on Union Center Road where they lived for a year and a half. In 1968 Calvin and Ruth bought a house in Zanesville on Broadway. They still reside in Zanesville.

Newt and Louise Middleton remained at their farm on 400 N for nearly thirty years. Louise died in April 1981 and Newt passed away in February 1982.

Charles H. Middleton, Newt's grandson, purchased the farm and lives there at this time.

DAVID MEYER FAMILY

David Meyer was born in 1872 on a farm about one and one-half miles south of Vera Cruz, Indiana. His father was Peter Meyer II, who was born in Bern, Switzerland. His mother was Elizabeth Moser of Bern, Switzerland. David had three brothers and four sisters, Jacob, Albert, Joney, Bertha, Sarah, Elizabeth, and Ida.

David went to school about one mile south of his home. This schoolhouse is still standing. He finished the fifth grade at this school. He helped his father on the farm for a while and later, as a youth, started to build roads with his cousin, Jacob Klopfenstine.

In 1900, with the financial help of his father, he built the store building at 118 North Main Street in Bluffton. The name of the store was Meyer and Klopfenstine, and they sold harness, robes, whips, and buggies. One year, David would be out building roads and Jacob would run the store. The next year, they would reverse positions. Later Jacob left and went out on his own, and David Meyer had the store. Besides selling and repairing harness, he started selling Auburn automobiles, along with buggies. He later sold Oakland and Pontiac cars. Some of the employees were Adolph Witzeman, who had one-quarter interest, Harry Studebaker, Art Tremp, and Clem Williams. Ray Stalder and Ray Mossburg were automobiles mechanics.

David married Margaret Engeler, June 15, 1899. They were married by the Reverend Peter Vitz. They had three children: Margaret Meyer born July 1, 1901, died July 2, 1901; Ruth Rosanna Meyer, born 1904, died 1930; and Raymond E. Meyer, born 1912.

Margaret Engeler was the daughter of Frederick and Rosanna Biberstein Engeler. The Engelers lived in Vera Cruz and had ten children. Their daughter, Mary Ellen, who served as a school teacher in Vera Cruz, married Martin Vitz, a son of the Reverend Peter Vitz, who as a minister at the Reformed Church in Vera Cruz. Mary Ellen and Martin Vitz (who became a minister) had a grandson, Calvin Ley, minister of the Bluffton First United Church of Christ for twenty-five years.

Frederick and Rosanna Engeler's children were: Frank, Edward, Margaret, William Martin, Martha, Henry Frederick, Mary Ellen, Albert, Emma, and Charles.

Raymond E. Meyer, son of David Meyer and Margaret Engeler graduated from Bluffton High School in 1930, and from Purdue University in 1935 with a degree in electrical engineering. He worked in Owensboro, Kentucky, for Ken-Rad Tube and Lamp Corp. He worked for Farnsworth and Magnavox in Fort Wayne and Franklin Electric in Bluffton. On June 29, 1952, he married Nina Jane Eversole. From 1965 to 1974, Raymond and his wife, Nina Jane, operated Bluffton Fabrics at 118 N. Main Street, where yard goods and notions were sold. They have a son, John E. Meyer, born May 30, 1961, and a daughter Karen, born May 21, 1963. John graduated from Indiana University in 1984 and is working in Indianapolis for Lens Crafters as an optician. Karen graduated from Indiana University as a registered respiratory therapist in 1985, and married Larry Strahm of Monroe, Indiana, on June 29, 1985. They have a daughter, Lauren, and live in Canton, Michigan. Karen works part-time at Garden City Hospital and Larry is a second vice president of Manufacturers Bank in Detroit, Michigan.

MEYER-DUNWIDDIE

My great-grandfather homesteaded the farm where I grew up. His daughter, Lydia Ann Mowery, was my grandmother. She married Levi Dyson, and they farmed the same place. My mother, Grace Dyson, was born in 1902. My grandfather had the round barn built in 1907. It is in Harrison Township, southeast of Bluffton. My mother and my father, Henry Dunwiddie, were married in 1920. My parents bought the farm, and my grandparents moved to Bluffton. There were six children in my family: Lela, Vera, Elizabeth, Lloyd, George, and Gerald. We were all born in the same house as our mother.

Our mother died in 1944, after a fire in our home. Dad married Sallie Murray in 1948. he died in 1983.

Joe and Adella Meyer, Helen, Harold, and Kenneth

On August 31, 1952, I married Harold R. Meyer. He grew up in Riverside at the Meyer Milling Company. His grandfather built the mill. His parents were Adella Moser and Joseph Meyer. He has two brothers, Kenneth and Don, and had a sister, Helen, who died in 1936 when she was fourteen. Harold, as a boy, helped his dad in the mill. His mother died in 1963, and his dad in 1971. Harold was in the Army and served in the Korean War.

The Dunwiddie Round Barn
Lloyd, George, Gerald, Lela, Elizabeth, Henry

We have four sons: Rodney was born September 21, 1953. He is married to Carol McAhren and they live in Albany, Indiana.

Bruce was born December 20, 1954. He is married to Melody Williamson. They have two sons, Joe, nine, and Mike, seven. They live in Berne, Indiana.

Gregory was born March 22, 1956. He married Sarah Fleuckiger. They have two sons and live in Berne, Indiana. Their sons are Chad, ten, and Grant, six.

Randy was born September 10, 1964. He lives in Philadelphia, Pennsylvania. He formerly worked at WOWO Radio in Fort Wayne. He is working in radio in Philadelphia.

Harold worked thirteen years at General Electric in Fort Wayne and thirty-three years at the post office in Bluffton. I worked thirty-two years as surgical nurse at Caylor-Nickel Hospital. We are both retired. *(Elizabeth Dunwiddie Meyer)*

MEYER-JOHN SR.-JR.-OLIVER O.

The Meyer family, Dustman Road, Bluffton, dates to my great-great-grandparent Jakob Meyer, born 1755, and Barbara Zurflueh born 1755 and died 1804, union, Bern, Switzerland in 1779. Jakob's son Christian, 1789 to 1849, my great-grandfather, wed Elizabeth Schoeni, born 1770 in Switzerland, in April 1812. To this union was born grandfather

John Meyer, Sr., in May 1818. He died in 1901. He married Veronika Strahm (born 1819, died 1899), in Oberdiessbach, Bern. The Meyer's and Strahm families emigrated to America about 1850. John Sr., and Veronika resided in Kansas, and lastly in Indiana. In later years, they were with Obed Meyer, near Bluffton. They are buried in the Christian Apostolic Cemetery nearby.

1942 L to R: Alton B., Orel H., Lillian M., Corinne O., Oliver O., Laura E., Dr. Orlando (World War II uniform) Major, John W.

My grandparents were farmers. In 1895, they purchased eighty acres. In 1899, John H., and Laura acquired the acreage (later twenty acres were sold). They married in Decatur, Indiana in 1891, and built the two-story white frame house and red barn. Their children were: Aaron G., a Ohio farmer (1891-1967), and Orel, (1893-1976), teacher and oil jobber, were born in Adams County. The rest of the children were born on Dustman Road: John (1896-1973), in oil sales and a Studebaker dealer; Lillian M. (Daugherty) (1899-1973), telephone operator and business executive; Dr. Orlando (1901-1970), teacher and physician-surgeon; Robert (November 5, 1903), died November 15, 1903); Alton (1905-1985), teacher, coach, realtor, investment broker: Oliver 1908-1986, teacher, farmer, realtor; Corinne M. (Bond) born in 1911, an office clerk, personnel management; and Laura M. (Cochran) 1916-1988 a teacher.

My father, John H. Meyer, Jr. (1864-1934), born and grade schooled in Adams County, was a blacksmith, truck farmer, gardener, manager of Craigville Telephone Company, and honey bee keeper. He physically suffered hernias; was a baseball fan, ardent fisherman and hobbies, while mother was the ever faithful, supportive wife, mother, homemaker; born in 1870 in Neufchatel, Fenin Engellow, Switzerland; sailed with Jacob Millers (eight) (family grew to seventeen) from Le Havre - arrived USA, December 1877, via SS *Canada*. Mother spoke French, Swiss German, fluent English, could do sums, reading, and writing, although she had but nineteen days of schooling. A pastime pleasantry was French telephone conversations with the Girardt - Millers. My parents resided on Dustman Road until they passed away, with burial in Elm Grove Cemetery. Mother died in 1946, and was of the Reformed Church.

Our family was ecumenical, athletic, and somewhat patriotic. Orel (Lt.), served World War I; d John (Corp.) World War II. Dr. Orlando, physician surgeon A.A.C. Major. Alton (American Red Cross director, Bavaria.) Oliver flight instructor, Florida. Corinne, C of E Personnel D.C.

Oliver was the Meyer farmer. He married Elizabeth Shookman (1913-1959), a teacher and homemaker, in 1942. They had three daughters, born between 1949 and 1952. Laura (Farner) a teacher, Jeanne (Jeppson) a teacher and computer center director, and Marian (England), law. They resided on Dustman Road through University vacations until marriages.

In 1962, Oliver married Nancy Marie Strahm, a loving marriage of twenty-four years; a full-time mom, homemaker and Oliver's "right hand". Oliver's health began to fail in the 80's - farming retirement was about 1984. From 1934 to 1976, the farm ownership was claimed by Orel. In 1979, Oliver purchased the sixty acres to be known as the Oliver O. Meyer farm - the Little School property was purchased during his last marriage.

Upon Oliver's demise in 1986, his widow, Nancy, dismantled the house (served it's purpose well) and erected a two bedroom home on her three and one-half acre plot of the original farm property, near the barn that had been replaced earlier.

I left Indiana late in 1933, married a California man, Max, in 1949. Our jobs were O/S for thirty years. R and R's found us visiting California and Indiana. Our retirements were in 1979 when Max's health began to fail. He sees that I visit Wells County for there are pleasant memories that will remain always, relatives, neighbors, and friends we hold dear. (*Corinne Meyer Bond*)

MILLER

The Miller family's association with Wells County dates back to the 1830's when Frederick Miller bought three hundred and twenty acres of timberland in Harrison Township, Wells County. However, Frederick and his wife, Susan, who lived in Franklin County, Ohio, never came to Indiana to settle. They were farmers and the parents of fourteen children. Also, they were of German ancestry.

A grandson, Lemuel Walter Miller, was born in Wells County on May 12, 1853. Lemuel was married to Susannah Staver in 1879. They lived their entire married life on an 80-acre farm in Rockcreek Township. Their oldest child, Frederick Nelson Miller, born November 28, 1880, was my grandfather. He married Lulu Barcus in 1907 and they lived on a farm north of Liberty Center where Fred was a farmer and carpenter. They had three children, Helen, Vernon, and Ruth.

*The Miller Family in 1989
John, Shirley, Bryan (13), and Jana (5)*

My father Vernon, born February 6, 1914, married Fabiana Cathryn Johnson from Huntington, Indiana on June 7, 1941. Vernon and Fabiana lived on a farm southwest of Bluffton. Vernon is a farmer, a pilot, a flight instructor, an A and E (aircraft and engine) mechanic, and a FAA authorization inspector. He owns Miller Airport which is southwest of Bluffton, Indiana. He purchased his first airplane, a Piper Cub, in 1940, and they built the first airport hanger in 1954. Fabiana was employed as a teacher in the Bluffton-Harrison School System for twenty years until she died in January 1983.

Vernon and Fabiana had one son, John William Miller, born on November 2, 1951. While John was growing up he received flight instructions from his father, and he earned his private pilot's license at the age of seventeen. He graduated from Balls State University in 1974, and he married Shirley Springer on August 9, 1975. Shirley grew up on her parents' (Charles and Dorothy Springer) farm in Lancaster Township (just north of Bluffton). Shirley also graduated from Ball State in 1974 with a degree in mathematics and computer science. John and Shirley lived in Muncie, Indiana for a couple of years where their sons, Bryan Douglas, was born on September 24, 1976. Then in the spring of 1977, the moved to Wells County to the town of Ossian (where they currently reside). On December 12, 1984, a daughter, Jana Lynette, was born. John is employed as a mechanical engineer at Phelps Dodge Magnet Wire Company in Fort Wayne, Indiana and Shirley is employed as a programmer/analyst at Lincoln National Corporation in Fort Wayne, Indiana.

ADAM WENDELL MILLER

Adam was born to John D. and Catherine Houts Miller on September 27, 1862 in Lebanon, Pennsylvania and died June 26, 1949. Adam was fifth child of five girls and five boys. He came to Indiana in search of a place to make a home. He settled on two acres of land in Banner City in 1883, built a two story log house and married Louisa Jane Jacobs February 10, 1884. Louisa was born March 22, 1862, died September 26, 1946 in Huntington, Indiana and was buried in Zanesville, Indiana. Louisa was daughter of Elijah Jacobs, born November 14, 1827 Tuscarawas County, Ohio and died January 20, 1915, Zanesville, Indiana and Susannia Masters was born September 9, 1825 and died April 7, 1862. Family stories say she was a full blooded Indian. Adam had a large garden, strawberries and raspberries. I saw one time when eight strawberries filled a quart box. He had under the cellar storage for vegetables and cover from storms.

Wedding picture of Adam and Louise Jane Jacobs Miller.

There were three children born to the couple. Katie Alice, born September 11, 1885 in the log house. Ida E. born September 27, 1888, and George W. born July 25, 1896, both in new two story nearby. The area was heavily wooded so he did a lot of timber cutting for both houses. Each spring he built several hot beds for starting all kinds of garden plantings. Early 1900 Adam had a coal yard in Uniondale, Indiana and delivered coal for the folks.

Katie married Charles Dumbauld March 23, 1908, and the couple had three children:

a. Hersel Dumbauld born September 28, 1908 in Markle, Indiana and married Letha Rickert August

465

23, 1946. Hersel served in Navy Seabees Construction Battalion in World War II. b. Eva was born December 31, 1912, Markle, Indiana and married Melvin Daugherty who was born September 29, 1912. Divorced c. Erma born March 25, 1915, Markle, died February 17, 1976. She married David Gaskill November 16, 1946 and he died March 1980. There were no children.

Ida was born September 27, 1888 and died February 9, 1975. She married Ivan Weaver who was born October 5, 1891 and died May 29, 1964. Buried in Zanesville, Indiana. There were no children.

George was born July 28, 1896 and died May 31, 1952. He married Meta Riggers who was born February 23, 1896 and died June 19, 1973.

a. Ruby C. Miller, born September 2, 1919 and died June 7, 1967. Married Harry C. Aker September 6, 1942 and he died 1962 in Pittsburg, Kansas. Ruby is buried in Huntington. a. Glen A. Aker. Married Dorothy Carylon May 9, 1965. b. Daughter Kristen born February 1973.

b. Alden Frederick Miller born November 18, 1922. Married Sarah Emily Rudauph, born March 30, 1925. They live at Norcross, Georgia. a. Sarah Elizabeth Miller, born October 14, 1954; b. Alden Frederick, Jr., born February 7, 1957 c. John Gregory Miller, born August 18, 1959.

MILLER-BOUSE

Marion Ralph Miller and Lucille Irene Bouse were married on February 7, 1932. They lived most of there married lives at 807 South Williams, Bluffton, Indiana. Their four children and eight of their nine grandchildren were born here.

Marion was the son of Chester A. and Elsie (Hethcote) Miller. He was born January 5, 1911, in Howard County, Indiana and moved with his parents to Wells County in 1919. They made their home for many years in the Kingsland area. Marion was one of three children born to this union, they were Russel P., and Maxine (Motz). Chester was well known in his retirement years for his strawberries and raspberries which graced many a table in Wells County. Marion's ancestors were of German descent. His grandfather Henry Clay and father Chester were born in Rush County, Indiana, later moving to Howard County.

Marion graduated from Ossian in 1928 and made his living as a salesman, he belonged to the Masonic Lodge and was an avid fan of basketball and baseball (Cubs).

Marion R. Miller Family - 1947
1st Row left to right: Marion, Lucille, Shirley. 2nd row: Gloria, Connie, Ralph.

Lucille I. (Bouse) was born on March 19, 1912, in Petroleum, Indiana. She was the oldest child of Calmar Ray and Lottie (Twigg) Bouse. Their other children are: Mable (Faus), Virginia, Bessie (Fuller), Forest, Harriett (Mohler), Jack and Rex. Harriett, Jack and Rex still make their home in Bluffton. Lucille's great-grandparents Joseph and Francis (Gaskill) Bouse were married in 1855 in Ohio. They left there in 1867 with seven children including Lucille's grandfather Lemuel and traveled to Indiana by covered wagon to West Grove, Indiana, in Jay County where five more children were born before moving in 1877 to a mile east of Nottingham in Wells County. Then Lemuel married Susan (Harshman), and they had four children, the oldest being Lucille's father Calmar born June 9, 1889. Calmar married Lottie (Twigg) on October 21, 1911; her parents were John P. and Emmaline (Blair) Twigg. John P. was born to William and Amanda (Carr) Twigg in Adams County, Indiana. They passed away when he was eight. Afterwards he was raised in foster homes. Emmaline was the daughter of Robert and Catherine (Gehrett) Blair whose family's were in Wells County as early as 1860's.

Marion and Lucille Miller's children's and grandchildren's roots are in Wells County but have spread to the West Coast and Germany. Their oldest daughter Gloria (Demers), born July 15, 1932, has four daughters: Debra Meyers born August 5, 1954, (twins) Sherrie (Meyers) Paull and Terrie (Meyers) LaBreche, born February 4, 1956, and Elizabeth (Meyers) Hitch, born January 24, 1962. Gloria has two grandsons: Keith Paul and Greg Hitch. Gloria and her family make their home in the Anaheim, California area. Connie, born December 9, 1934, and her husband, Charles Confer, have one son Mike born November 10, 1965. They live in Corona, California. Ralph T., born December 25, 1943, and his wife, Nancy, live in Bluffton, and have two daughters, Lisa, born June 23, 1964, and her husband, Anthony Schwartz, who live in Germany, and Kimberly R., born November 28, 1965, who lives in San Francisco, California. Ralph has one grandson, Logan Miller Schwartz, born November 16, 1990 in Germany. Shirley J. born July 17, 1945, and her husband, Olin Moeschberger, live in Monroe, Indiana, and have two children, Deanna, born March 20, 1963, and her husband Mike live in Berne, Indiana. James D. born May 19, 1966, lives in West Lafayette.

Marion R. Miller passed away on October 25, 1969, and Lucille on March 30, 1985. They were laid to rest in the Oaklawn Cemetery at Ossian, Indiana.

ELAINE AND STUART MILLER

Our ancestors were from Switzerland. We were both born in Adams County Hospital in Decatur, Indiana. We were married on November 18, 1962, in Berne, Indiana. Our first home was at 814 Melody Lane, in Mobile Manor, in Bluffton. Elaine graduated from Lutheran Hospital School of Nursing in 1962. Soon after graduating in August, she started working full time as an RN at Caylor Nickel Hospital. She is currently working there in the Post Anesthesia Care Unit (or Recovery Room). We are members of the First United Methodist Church where Elaine sings in the Chancel choir and plays handbells with the Bellaires. Stu has worked in Berne at Smith Bros. Inc. as an upholsterer for twenty-three years. He also reupholsters part-time in the evenings at home.

Our daughter, Andrea, was born November 23, 1965. She graduated from International Business College in Fort Wayne. Our son, Jason, was born on June 11, 1967, and graduated from DeVry Institute in Columbus, Ohio. They both live and work in Columbus, Ohio.

Elaine, Stuart, Jason, and Andrea Miller

In July 1969 we moved to 428 W. Washington Street, and lived there until June 1989. We then moved to our present home at 343 East Dustman Road.

Elaine's parents are Percy and Arvada Gould. They have lived in Berne, Indiana for forty-seven years. Percy was a jobber salesman for the Gibson Company in Fort Wayne, Indiana. He called on many service stations and businesses in Wells County until his retirement. Stu's parents were Walter and Vera Corinne Miller. They had a bakery, called Miller's Bakery, in Warren, Indiana for many years. Walter died forty-eight years ago. Corinne ran the business for several years before selling it to the Kings and moving to Berne, Indiana, where she presently resides. *(Elaine and Stuart Miller)*

FLOYD E. MILLER

William Miller our great-grandfather, came as a stow-away from Germany at the age of fifteen. He worked his way west to Adams County. It was here William met Clarissa Bristol of Iowa, married and settled on a farm near Honduras (Henpeck). He cleared the land, built their home and farmed until drafted by the Army during the Civil War, leaving his wife and three children. Reuben (our grandfather), Albert and Mary. He died on his way home from the war. Clarissa was a seamstress, who wove cloth and made suits for prominent men in Bluffton and Adams County.

Our grandfather, Reuben, married Elizabeth Jean Gue Natt of Ohio in 1877. She was the daughter of Eugene Jean Gue Natt from France and Lavina Napp from Ohio. Her name was later shortened to Elizabeth Jennett.

Louise Deihl, George E. Miller, Betty Deihl

Reuben was a farmer and raised horses. Mr. Barnum from the Barnum and Bailey Circus approached Reuben to buy his dapple greys. He was refused, because the horses were needed on the farm.

Floyd and Lillian Miller - 1952

Reuben and Elizabeth moved several times. During the flood of 1913, their home near Murray was surrounded with water. The neighbors rescued the members of the household. Before they left the house, they put an old sow in the kitchen to avoid her drowning. Water filled the basement and washed cans of fruit from the shelves.

Reuben and Elizabeth had ten children: Ida, Charley, Dora, Mae, Clifford, Floyd, Blanche, Homer, Hazel, and Ocea. Our father, Floyd, married Lillian Watters in 1912. She was the daughter of George and Rena (Dewitt) Watters of Bluffton. Floyd was a member of the Honolulu Ramblers (a musical group) that played on WOWO Fort Wayne radio station. He worked at the Bay Piano Co. and also the Chandelier Co. After that he worked for Klopenstines Cigar Store. Later he worked with Ellenberger Auctioneers. He was a joking and jovial man who made many friends over the years. They had five children: George E., Byrlin, Betty, William, and Anna Louise. Lillian died in 1972, and Floyd died in 1981.

Honolulu Ramblers L to R: top row: Floyd E. Miller, Francis Slentz, Russell Harris, Roy Garr.

George E. married Leona Keller in 1937, and they had two daughters, Barbara and Phyllis. Phyllis died in 1972. Byrlin married Esther Hill, and they had three daughters, Bonnie, Judy, and Marilyn. Marilyn died at birth. Byrlin died in 1981; Betty married Robert Deihl in 1940 and they had two children, Rebecca and Michael; William married Ramona Sills in 1948 and they had seven children: Janice, James, Joyce, Steven, William, Richard and Timothy. Janice died as a small child. Their mother Ramona died in 1985, and their father William died in 1986; Anna Louise married Max Deihl in 1942, and they had one child, William.

GALE MILLER FAMILY

The parents of Gale Eldon Miller were Roy Jacob and Mary Evelyn Wilkin. They had an older daughter, Ina Marie Miller Grote, married to Richard Grote and living in Fort Wayne.

The parents of Gayle Elizabeth Hoeppner Miller were Fredrick Martin Henry Hoeppner and Cora Aretha Selby Hoeppner. To this union were born Eileen Evelyn and Gayle Elizabeth.

Eileen was married to Robert Gemmill and to this union were born: Selby, Gloria, and Julia. She later married Karl Huff, and to this union was born Steven Allen Huff. The Huff lives in Noble County, Indiana.

May 1988 - Cora Hoeppner's 90th Birthday Back Row, L to R: Gale Miller, Lanette Williams, Norman Miller, Lorraine Falk. Front Row, L to R: Diane Brown, Shari Miller, Gayle Miller, Monica Miller.

Selby married Joan Harrindean on February 10, 1961. To this union were born Todd, Teresa and Tony. Gloria married Tim Donovan and to this union were born Brian and Carrie. Julia married Jim Dotson, to this union were born Rachel and Katie. Steve Huff, married Anita Schoeff, and to this union were born Melanie, Merissa, and Matthew.

Gayle was married to Gale Eldon Miller on December 14, 1946. To this union were born: Dwight, Diane, Lorraine, Norman, Lanette, Shari, and Monica. Dwight (January 21) died in infancy.

Diane Marie (April 16, 1948) married Ted Allen Brown on June 18, 1966. To this union were born Kimberly, who died in infancy; Michelle Lynn, who married David Anthony Mills on September 9, 1989; to this union was born Karissa Michelle on January 27, 1991; and Christopher Allen Brown, born October 30, 1970.

Lorraine Evelyn Miller was married to Joseph Contadeluci and to this union was born Lisa Renee. Lorraine was later married (June 10, 1983) to Denny Falk.

Norman LeRoy Miller was born November 18, 1950. He married Vickie Haiflich on November 27, 1971. To this union were born Benjamin Thomas Miller on May 28, 1975, Johnathan Norman Miller on October 7, 1977, and Kimberly Kai Miller on February 23, 1980.

Lanette Coreene Miller married Paul Anthony Williams on February 10, 1973. To this union were born: David Paul on October 23, 1973, Pamela Jane on January 7, 1975, and Jason Roy on March 16, 1976.

Shari Joe Miller was born November 6, 1968 and Monica Gayle Miller was born on January 14, 1973.

The Gale Millers resided in Nottingham Township on road 900S from 1948 to 1987, when they moved to Gale's home place on 800S in Wells County.

Mr. Miller was a rural mail carrier for several years; he broadcast basketball and football games for Southern Wells for twenty years. His main occupation was farming.

Gayle Miller in later years worked as relief in Bi County Services group homes.

They belong to the First United Church of Christ in Bluffton. Gayle teaches classes and sings in the choir. She has also belonged to the Wells County Extension Homemakers Chorus since 1951, and to the Adams County Chorus since 1983.

Gale Miller was a charter member of the Petroleum Lions Club and a member for many years of the Petroleum Odd Fellows. He also belonged to the Bluffton Rotary Club at one time.

DR. GERALD AND MARY MILLER FAMILY

Dr. Gerald L. and Mary (Mishler) Miller and children, Shari (born March 2, 1958), Marlis (born May 22, 1962), and Stephen (born January 10, 1967) moved into Wells County in March, 1967. Three years earlier our family had moved to Markle (in Huntington County) to set up a medical family practice. Elmer Mossburg Construction built us a new home in a wooded area two miles east of Markle (5955 North 400 West, Uniondale). We bought this woods from Mrs. Dorothy Radkey. The Haiflichs from Bluffton owned this woods at one time and grew herbs.

Dr. Miller grew up in Shipshewana, Indiana, where his father, Perry J., was principal of the Shipshewana Grade and High School. His mother, Lucille, was a fourth grade teacher at the same school.

Back (Left to Right) Shea, Kevin, Marlis, Chuck, Shari, Steve, Sherri. Front: Dr. Gerald and Mary Miller.

Mary grew up on a farm in LaGrange County. Her parents, John and Ruth (Dintaman) Mishler owned their two hundred and sixty acre farm. She attended school at Shipshewana from sixth through twelfth grade. The first five grades were in a one room country school named Saylor. We both graduated from Shipshewana High School in 1955. We were married at Middlebury, Indiana, on August 25, 1956. Gerald graduated from Goshen College in 1959 and Indiana University School of Medicine in 1963. He interned at Lutheran Hospital in Fort Wayne.

Dr. Gerald Miller and Dr. LeRoy Kinzer founded Markle Medical Center, Inc., in 1963. The practice now has offices in Markle, Bluffton and Warren. It has expanded to eight physicians and has fifty-one employees.

Dr. Miller served on the Norwell High School Board from 1975 through 1983. he as been director of the State Bank of Marke since 1972. He has been medical director of EMS Services for Wells County from 1970-1990. He is also director of Wells County Home Health Care.

All three of our children attended Rockcreek Elementary and graduated from Norwell High School. Shari graduated from Goshen College in

1980 and married Charles Wagner from St. Louis, Missouri. They are presently living in Indianapolis and both teach in the English department at Butler University and Franklin College.

Marlis graduated from Taylor University in 1986 and married Kevin Castle from Marion, Indiana. They have one son (Shea) and live in Gurnee, Illinois. Kevin is a product manager at Wilson Jones and Marlis is a personnel officer at First of America Bank.

Stephen graduated from the University of Indianapolis in 1989 and married Sherri Wood from Indianapolis on April 27, 1991. Stephen is a programmer/analyst for ITT Aerospace/Communications at Fort Wayne. Sherri is a corporate paralegal for Biomet in Warsaw.

We are glad that we made our home in Wells County. It was a good place to raise our family.

HENRY MILLER FAMILY

Mrs. Harry (Catherine E.) Thomas is the great-great-granddaughter of Henry and Catherine Zeek Miller, who were the first white settlers to reside permanently in Wells County. They settled in November, 1832, near an Indian encampment close to the town of Murray on the Wabash River. Their's was the first farm settled between Fort Recovery and Huntington. Many stories of their hardships in the early years have been passed down. At one time, it was said, a year passed before Catherine saw another white woman. They moved into a small shack that a Dr. Knox and his son had built. Dr. Knox and his son could not tolerate the wild animals, unfriendly Indians, and loneliness, and soon returned to the East. Henry and Catherine became friendly with, and were trusted by, the Indians, however, and were able to survive in the wilderness. Their daughter, Elizabeth Miller Harvey, was the first white child born in Wells County and was the seventh of ten children. Four of their six sons served in the Union Army during the Civil War and one (William) died in Andersonville Prison.

Henry Miller and Catherine Zeek Miller

Mrs. Thomas's great-grandmother was Catherine Miller Weaver, the youngest of the ten children, who was born on September 9, 1842. Catherine Miller Weaver was married to Branson Weaver in 1863, during one of his two enlistments in the Civil War, first in Co. "G" 12th Regiment of Indiana Volunteers and then Co. "B" 53rd Regiment of Indiana Infantry Volunteers, who marched with General Sherman to the sea. The letters he wrote home to his wife during the Civil War have been preserved and are very interesting.

Branson Weaver was a school teacher and farmer and active in county fairs. Catherine Miller Weaver and Branson had five children: Lizzie Quick Grove, John Weaver, Hattie Weaver, and Maude Weaver Bender. Their youngest died in infancy.

Their daughter Hattie was Mrs. Thomas's grandmother; she died when her son Dwight was an infant. Dwight was adopted and raised by his Grandmother Catherine and his Aunt Lizzie Quick Grove. He was the father of Catherine Thomas. Dwight also had two sons, David Dwight (deceased) and John Richard, who resides in Gas City. David has two children, David D. Weaver and Kathy Weaver Sheridan, who reside in Marion, Indiana. He had six grandchildren.

Harry and Catherine Thomas have two sons, William Dale and Harry Dwight, and three grandsons. Jeffrey and Scott are in the Air Force, and Michael lives in Fort Wayne.

Mr. and Mrs. Thomas have remodeled and enlarged the old Weaver farmhouse, which was built in 1858, and now reside there.

JOHN MICHAEL MILLER-MICHAEL MILLER

John Michael Miller and his bride, Anna Maria Gottschalk, along with other relatives and friends, set sail for America on April 25, 1840, from their home in the Kingdom of Wüttemberg, Germany; a journey that would take ninety-three days. When they saw land, they cleaned their boat and threw overboard the straw in the hold which had been their beds. They didn't make it to shore by night and had to sleep on blankets over the hard boards. Landing in New York, they traveled through Pennsylvania and settled in Montgomery County, Ohio. John Michael applied for naturalization papers in 1844 and was naturalized in 1846. They came to Nottingham Township, Wells County, Indiana in 1847 and settled on a forty acre tract of woodland which he began to improve. They lived in a log cabin until a better habitation could be prepared.

Front L to R: Christina (Miller) Fosnaugh, Michael Miller, Glenna (Miller) Augsburger, Louisa (Eger) Miller, Clara (Miller) French. Back L to R: John, Ervin, Reuben, Jacob and Wesley.

His life was a ceaseless round of toil with hardships and vicissitudes calculated to test to the utmost his courage and endurance. The water supply was purely surface character, creating a noxious atmosphere; neither age, sex, or condition was spared its infections. Consequently, only three of their nine children grew to maturity. He lived to see his farm of one hundred twenty acres brought to a high state of cultivation. Their three children who lived to maturity were, Lucinda, born November 11, 1854, married William Mertz, a druggist of Vera Cruz and Fort Wayne; she lived to be just a few days less than one hundred one years old; Sarah born March 20, 1857, married Edward Heller of Berne. Their daughter Pearl Heller Smith lives at Swiss Village in Berne, Indiana and celebrated her one hundredth birthday December 26, 1900. She has a keen mind, reads the daily paper, and is a brilliant conversationalist; Michael, the subject of this review, was born on December 25, 1848, and married Louisa Maria Eger on November 21, 1872. They started housekeeping in the log cabin in which he was born and purchased forty acres from his father for one thousand five hundred dollars, going in debt for the entire amount. However, he was rich in a well-defined purpose to succeed and, being blessed with good health, in a few years purchased a threshing outfit, thus materially increasing his earnings. Five years after his marriage, he paid off all his indebtedness and purchased another forty acres. He accumulated considerable acreage by his good judgement and foresight, coupled with sterling honesty and tireless industry. Michael was known as one of the most successful agriculturists and stock raisers in the area. He was active in politics, citizenship, and religious activities. The Miller and Gottschalk families figured prominently in the life of the Old Salem Church, from its founding to the present time. The Michael Miller family was blessed with five sons and three daughters who grew to maturity. They were Jacob, who married Hermina Sell; John, who married Myrtle French; Reuben, who married Dora Grandlienard; Ervin who married Ada Watson; Christina, who married Frank Fosnaugh; Clara, who married Earl French; Wesley, who married Wilma Opliger; and Glenna, who married John Augsburger. *(Berneil French Amstutz, granddaughter of Michael Miller.)*

KERRY MILLER FAMILY

Kerry Wayne Miller and Shirley Jean Williams were married October 1, 1960, at Chester Center Church in Chester Township. Kerry was born April 12, 1942 in Bluffton, Indiana to John and Crystal (Murray) Miller. His parents are life-long residents of Wells County. Kerry, along with his brother and parents, lived on a farm which has been in the family for many years.

Shirley was born January 8, 1942, on a farm northwest of Piper City, Illinois, to Wayne and Margaret Williams. Legend tells that it was the coldest night of the winter and that the bed was pulled up against the cookstove. The Williams family moved to Chester Township from Illinois in December of 1952. They engaged in farming and milking cows.

Kerry and Shirley attended Chester Center School where they met in the fifth grade. They graduated in 1960. Both were members of the band, school newspaper, and yearbook staff. They were also eight-year 4-H club members.

The Kerry Miller Family
L to R: Mark, Laura, Kerry, Shirley, Diana, Michael.

Kerry was awarded an apprenticeship at Franklin Electric in June, 1960. He has been employed there since that time and is a maintenance electrician. He enjoys working on cars and buying older-model Chrysler cars.

Although she has been a housewife and mother for most of her marriage, Shirley has been employed at Franklin Electric since 1978 in the housekeeping department. She enjoys crafts - especially machine knitting and quilting.

The family has attended Hope Missionary Church since 1972.

They have four children and two grandchildren. Laura Jean was born May 4, 1961. She attended Fort Wayne Bible College where she majored in elementary education. She married Russell Iida of Kapaa, Hawaii, on July 25, 1987. Their son, Justin Stacy, was born on April 13, 1990.

Michael Wayne was born May 23, 1962. He graduated from Ball State University in 1987 with a degree in biology. On April 6, 1991, he will be married to Margaret Confer.

Diana Carol was born November 29, 1963. She graduated from Ball State University in 1989 with degrees in business administration and marketing.

Mark Evan was born July 1, 1966. He attended IPFW and is now employed at Franklin Electric. On December 24, 1987, he married Beth Flueckinger. Their daughter, Joy Nichole, was born March 14, 1989.

The Miller family resided in a mobile home in Chester Township until the beginning of 1971, when they moved to 404 W. Central Avenue in Bluffton. The large house, which was built in 1898, was quite a change from a mobile home. The children were afraid to go upstairs by themselves! There seems to be a resident ghost in the house, as footsteps have been heard several different times during the night.

The Miller family has been very active in the Wells County 4-H program. All four children were ten-year members, winning many honors, and Shirley was a 4-H leader for thirteen years.

Our family has been blessed with good health and is thankful that we have ben able to enjoy the rural and small-town life of Indiana. *Submitted by Shirley Miller*

LEE AND LOMA MILLER FAMILY

Lee Thomas Miller, son of William and Etta (Springer) Miller, was born September 25, 1904 in Mercer County, Ohio. He had two brothers. In 1906 his family moved to his grandfather's farm east of Decatur, Indiana. He was a welder at Central Soya Co. in Decatur, and at the General Electric Co. in Fort Wayne, where he retired and in 1969 after thirty-five years of service. He was a member of the Quarter Century Club.

Lee and Loma Luella Hahnert were married November 29, 1934 at her parent's home in Monroe, Indiana. Loma was born December 5, 1910 in Monroe, to George Alfred and Eliza Mae (Johnston) Hahnert. Her father was a Spanish-American War Veteran, and a rural mail carrier for thirty years from Monroe. Loma had five brothers and one ster.

Loma's grandfather (Frederick Hahnert), at e eighteen, came from Germany to the United States. He made harness, tanned leather, and made shoes for customers. Loma's grandmother (Melinda Ball Johnston) was a first cousin to the Ball Brothers in Muncie, Indiana.

On June 24, 1934, Ida (Markley) Tarr auctioned off her father's farm known as the Rev. Johnathon Markley farm in Wells County, near Murray, Indiana. He was a former pastor of the Murray Church.

L to R: Arthur Miller, Beatrice Miller, Loma Miller, Karen Miller, Lee Miller.

Loma and her father attended the sale and she purchased the farm for Lee Miller who was working in Fort Wayne. Lee and Loma moved to the farm December 31, 1934, but had no electric or telephone service until the 1950's.

In 1935, Lee built a farm bridge over the McCullough ditch. In 1938, we bought our first tractor and farmed evenings and weekends. Raised cattle, sheep, chickens, had a large garden, and worked with bees. In 1963, Lee built a large barn for machinery. The native lumber used for floors and trim was seasoned three years before the Rev. Markley built the house in 1897. The walls, inside and out, are made of three layers of brick. We later built a bathroom and removed part of the front porch.

Lee and Loma have three children who attended Lancaster High School. Arthur Gene was born January 15, 1940, graduated from Purdue University, and served in the U.S. Air Force. He is a rural mail carrier in South Whitley, Indiana. He married Martha Geist March 27, 1974. She is a medical technician at Lutheran Hospital in Fort Wayne. They have three daughters, Sarah, Margaret, and Amanda.

Beatrice June was born October 17, 1943, and graduated from Chapman College. She married Donald Anderson January 31, 1970. He is retired from the U.S. Air Force, and a graduate student at Purdue. They have one son, Gregory, and one daughter, Elizabeth.

Karen Joan graduated from Purdue and is a medical technician at St. Joseph Hospital in Fort Wayne.

Lee and Loma belong to the First United Methodist Church in Bluffton, Indiana. Lee died July 5, 1989. Loma belongs to the United Methodist Women's Society, Loyal Neighbors Home Extension Club, and does volunteer work. She enjoys sewing, reading and gardening.

MERRILL J. MILLER FAMILY

Merrill J. Miller was born on December 14, 1943, and was married on December 14, 1967, to Sally Jo Johnson, who was born on December 6, 1940. Their children are: (1) Patricia Dawn Johnson, born July 28, 1960, and married in 1982 to John E. Whitted, son of Betty and Thurman Whitted of Rockford, Ohio, born September 20, 1958. (2) HolliAyn Mayhew, born April 8, 1965, whose children are: Tanya Lynn Brown, born September 28, 1981, and Andrew Jeffery Brackin-Brown, born on September 7, 1986. (3) Shawn David Miller, born August 25, 1968, and married on February 5, 1990, to Catherine Lynette Owens, daughter of Betty Ownes born February 7, 1971. (4) Suzanna Noel Miller, who was born November 27, 1972.

MILLER-REASER

In 1926, Robert Neal Miller (1906-1990) married Emma Marie Reaser (1908-1969). Robert (Bud) Miller was the son of Ethel (Grove) (Miller) Shane (1888-1970) and Kit Carson Miller (1884-1912). One other son is Alton Don Miller (1904). Ethel's second husband was William Shane (1874-1928), and they had one son Lavon (1915). William brought to this marriage two sons, Herman (1900-1989), and Ernest.

Robert and Emma were the parents of Doris Ann (1930). She married Dwight Eugene Wilson (1926) in 1951 and has two children, Stanley Kent (1952) and Valerie Kaye Jackson (1954). The second daughter is Patty Lou (1932), and she married Richard E. Glenn (1930) in 1950, and they had five children: Judy Marie (1953), Timothy Earl (1955), Rick Alan (1957), Gary Lee (1959), and Susan Elaine (1962-1974). The third daughter, Joyce Marie (1936) married Dale Warthman (1934-1982) in 1957. They had three children: James Neal (1957), Jaimi Lyn (1959) and Jerry Dale (1961).

L to R: 1957 - Sylvia Wilson, Ethel (Miller) Shane, Stanley Wilson, Robert (Bud) Miller, Zelma (Tewell) Reaser, Valerie Kaye Wilson, Emma (Reaser) Miller.

Robert and Emma were both employed at the Bay Piano Company and later the Estey Piano Company. Emma later worked for the Farnsworth Radio Corp. and Robert retired from Indiana Michigan Electric Co. in 1970. Robert was Wells County Deputy Sheriff from 1940 to 1944.

Robert and Emma purchased the property at 1341 West Cherry Street from her parents in 1928 and Robert lived there until his death. Emma Marie (Reaser) Miller was the daughter of Ezra Levi Reaser (1886-1955), and Zelma Tewell (1891-1975). They also had two sons Levi (1913), and Lawrence Clayton (1911-1952), and a daughter Clara Lucille (1907-1908).

Ezra and Zelma also worked at the piano factories before moving on the Ellingham Pike to start farming. They later moved to the Reaser homestead on State Road 218 and farmed until Ezra suffered a paralyzing stroke in 1953. Levi Reaser still lives there.

ROY AND MARY (WILKIN) MILLER

Roy Jacob Miller's ancestors were among the early settlers of Wells and Blackford Counties. Isaac and Mary Ann (Bachtel) Miller came from Stark County, Ohio, in a covered wagon in 1863 to Rockcreek Township. Their son, Andrew J. married Luella (Lesh) in 1883, and to them was born Roy J., who married Mary E. Wilkin in 1921. Roy's great-grandparents, John and Mary (Snavely) Lesh, came to Rockcreek Township in 1854 from Bucks County, Pennsylvania. His second marriage was to Harriet (McAfee) Cover. There is a book at the Fort Wayne Library, published in 1914, concerning the Lesh (Loesch) family since their arrival in America. From the first marriage, a son Jacob Lesh married Mary Ann (Gregg) and they were the parents of Mary Luella Jacobs; his second marriage was to Amanda Gilbert. Mary Ann Gregg was a daughter of Robert and Elizabeth (Conner) Gregg from Donegal, Ireland, who arrived in America in 1832 and moved to Rockcreek Township in 1854 from Wayne County, Ohio.

Roy Jacob Miller and Mary Evelyn Wilkin Miller, married December 14, 1921. Photo taken December 1971.

Mary E. Wilkin Miller's parents were Nelson and Clara (Maddox) Wilkin. Nelson's father, William, and his father, Thomas, came from Harrison County, Ohio, in 1836 to Jefferson Township. William married Mary F.A. Trenary whose parents Richard and Matilda (Settle) Trenary came by horseback in 1838 to Jefferson Township form Loudon County, Virginia. Richards' second marriage was to Mahala Archbold. Nelson' wife Clara was born in Blackford County. Her parents were Michael and Sarah (Clapper) Maddox. His father, Silas, and Diademe (Embry) Maddox, and his father, Michael Maddox, came from Highland County, Ohio, to Blackford County in 1832. Clara's grandfather Jacob Clapper married Amanda Kemmer. Her parents were Peter and Catherine (Hech) Kemmer, who came from Fayette County to Blackford County in 1838. Peter's parents Nicholas and Sarah (Faylor) Kemmer came to Bracken County, Kentucky in 1800 from Berks County, Pennsylvania, after receiving a land grant for service in the Revolutionary War. Adding a bit of interest, we learn from a Fayette County biography, that Nicholas came from Germany to Boston, Massachusetts. He was at the Boston Tea Party disguised as one of the Indians who threw the famous tea overboard. He also was at the surrender of Cornwallis to Washington at Yorktown, Virginia. He is buried at Bentonville, Ohio. One of his descendants has his war medal and the knife used at the Boston Tea Party.

REUBEN AND ELIZABETH MILLER

Reuben Miller, son of William and Clarissa Miller, was born September 9, 1859, in Adams County, Indiana. He married Elizabeth Jean Gue Natt on April 22, 1877, in Decatur, Indiana.

Elizabeth Jean Gue Natt, born August 20, 1861, in Scioto County, Ohio, was the daughter of Eugene (Elizabeth's obituary states Francis) Jean Gue Natt from France and Lavina Napp from Scioto County, Ohio. Her family in Portsmouth, Ohio, were short, stocky, heavy people and all Catholics.

It is told that Elizabeth could only speak French until she was an adult, even though in later years there was no apparent accent when she spoke English. Her brother, who shortened his name to John Jennet, often visited in their home. He was a traveling musician, a violinist. Another brother came by regularly to stay a few days. It was necessary for Reuben and Elizabeth to supply him with a pillow made from hops to relieve his asthma. Elizabeth had also a half-brother, Chris Santa of Columbus, Ohio.

Front row: Floyd Miller, Reuben Miller, Elizabeth Miller, Charley Miller. Back row: Ocea Miller, Hazel Miller, Mae Stogdill Homer Miller, Dora Prible, Ida Merriman, Blanche Miller.

Elizabeth Miller was very generous, and would have given away everything she had, if it had been possible. She fed the workers form the quarries for a few years. Reuben is remembered for his jolly and joking manner.

When their son Charley was one and a half or two years old, they would often ride in a large wagon to the Wabash River, south of the old bridge at Murray, where they spent the day fishing. Because Charley was small, a pen was made from fence rails, in which he played while the others fished.

Floyd Miller used to relate an interesting story about the time old Mr. Barnum from the Barnum and Bailey Circus approached his father, Reuben Miller, and wished to buy his dapple gray horses. The offer was refused, because the horses were needed on the farm.

Approximately the last week in March, 1913, Reuben and Elizabeth were visiting relatives in Columbus, Ohio, for a few days, when a flood came. The waters completely surrounded their farm home near Murray, where they had left their son Floyd and his young wife with the three children still at home, Homer, Hazel, and Ocie. Neighbors came to their rescue with horse and wagon to remove them to their home. Before they left they sent an old sow swimming into the kitchen to avoid drowning. Water filled the basement and washed cans of fruit from the cupboard shelves. The water and mud combined made quite a mess. The flood of 1913 was one long remembered.

When he was assessor and lived in Stringtown (now Oak Street Extended, Bluffton), Reuben would start out early in the morning walking through he country on his wooden leg. (He was very accident-prone, and lost a leg through one of his misfortunes.) At whatever home he happened to be at noontime, he stopped lunch. The story is told that on one occasion no one answered his knock at the door, so he entered and sat down for a meal at the table where the family had already eaten but had not cleared the dishes from the table. While he was resting after his meal, a woman appeared from the bedroom where she had been napping, A surprise for both?

SUZANNE AND JOHN DAVID MILLER

John D. Miller, M.D., F.C.C.P (January 19, 1925-June 17, 1990), and Suzanne Eiler (June 30, 1925), came to Bluffton in 1979. Dr. Miller accepted a position with Caylor-Nickel Clinic as a pulmonary disease specialist. He served as president of the Clinic Board of Directors (1981-1985, 1987-1990), until his death. Early in his career, he was appointed superintendent of the tuberculosis facility, Sunnyside Sanatorium, Indianapolis. After the miracle cure of TB by streptomycin, Dr. Miller became co-director of the respiratory disease service at General Hospital (Wishard Memorial) and assistant director of hospitals, Health and Hospital Corporation, Marion County. He received appointments from Governor's Welsh, Branigan, and Whitcomb as chairman of the Tuberculosis Council. He was chairman of many state and national medical committees including those for the American Lung Association. He was an assistant professor at the Indiana University School of Medicine, clinician, lecturer for hospitals and professional organizations throughout the state.

Suzanne - John D. Miller

Beginning 1979 Miller received successive appointments to the Indiana Medical Licensure Board from Governors Bowen, Orr and Bayh. He was board president 1981-1989 and board member at the time of his death. Governor Evan Bayh proclaimed February 22, 1990 as *John D. Miller Day in Indiana* to honor his work in making the Indian Medical Licensure Board one of the premier boards in the country and for his service to the medical profession. He was the recipient of two Sagamores of the Wabash, awarded by Governor Orr and posthumously by Governor Bayh. Dr. Miller graduated in 1953, from the Indiana University School of Medicine and was a member of Tau Kappa Alpha, the medical honorary fraternity. Suzanne, who graduated from Manchester College in 1947, is a former schoolteacher. Their children are:

James Eric, PU '76 (born May 14, 1953), Cincinnati, Ohio. Delta Capt.: children: (1) John Edward, born April 9, 1981, (2) Brett Alan, born May 13, 1985.

Gail Leslie Suer, PU '78 (born April 11, 1955), Muncie, Indiana. homemaker: children: (1) Carly Jeanne Grissom, born August 13, 1982, (2) Matthew Thomas (born April 2, 1985, (3) Michael Jay (born October 27, 1986), (4) Allison Mae (born August 27, 1989). Married Robert P. Suer, M.D., internal medicine IU '77.

Lora Jeanne Jones, M.D. (Internal medicine) PU '78, IU' School of Medicine '83 (born June 27, 1956), Bluffton, Indiana children: (1) Jeffrey Eiler born June 29, 1984, (2) Kipp Cameron (July 9, 1988. Dr. Jones is in private practice with Robert Suer, M.D., Muncie. Married Larry G. Jones, M.D.

Internal medicine IU '78. Jones is an emergency physician with Caylor-Nickel Clinic.

Gretchen Joanne Ratliff Marion College '90 (born July 3, 1958), Indianapolis, Indiana. Manager Corporate Communications, Melvin Simon and Associates, Indianapolis. Children: (1) Kyle Tanner born June 27, 1989. Married Jim Ratliff, blacksmith, boilermaker, Amtrack.

Both Dr. and Mrs. Miller trace their genealogical lines to colonial America. Their forebearers, German Baptists, (later church of the Brethren), came with others of this devout group (Peter Becker, Alexander Mack) to escape religious persecution in Germany.

MILLER-TAYLOR

The descendants of Andrew Miller and Thomas William Taylor have lived in Wells County for many years. Andrew, born in 1816 in Pennsylvania, married Sarah Perkins. The 1850 census says he was a carpenter in Jefferson Township, Wells County, with real estate worth three hundred dollars. Known children are: William, James, Jacob, and Lucinda (Mrs. Daniel Todd). He and two of his three wives, who all died in their twenties or thirties, are buried at Elhanen, near Ossian.

William, (1847-1908), married Mary Elizabeth Clowser (1847-1921), daughter of John Henry Clowser and Sarah Schoch. William, a lay preacher at the Church of Christ in Christian Union in Craigsville, ran a sawmill. Their children were: Sylvester, Bertha Shady (Mrs. John), Sadie Waugh (Mrs. Frank), Louis Ellis, Minnie, and Laverne.

In 1910 Louis Miller (1882-1940), married Maude Rose Taylor (1884-1963). Both were teachers in one-room schools. They lived at Craigville, then Ossian, where later Louis graduated from International Business College and became a bookkeeper.

Louis Ellis Miller about 1920

Maude was the daughter of Joseph A.D. Taylor, (1842-1922). The son of Thomas Taylor and Ellen McCague, he served in the Civil War in the 99th Ohio Regiment, Sherman's Division, for three years until the end of the war, at which time he was twenty years old. A farmer and hardware dealer, he married Mary Jane Parke (1842-1922), and lived west of Ossian in what is now called Tiletown. The Parkers are traced to Robert Parker from England, who landed at Barnstable, Massachusetts, about 1640. Sisters of Maude were (Mrs. Edwin) Martha Hawley, (Mrs. Freeman) Annie Thayer, (Mrs. Otis) Ida Shafer. Her brother was Victor Carl.

Louis and Maude Miller had two daughters born in Ossian. Elaine (1914), and Rosemary (1916). Elaine, a teacher, married Woodrow Noe (1912-1990), in 1939. Their children are: Rosemary Ann, of Northfield, Ohio; Robert, of Warren, Ohio; and Timothy, of Long Island City, New York. Robert's children are Tonya Mentzer, of Poland, Ohio, and Danielle, of Bristolville, Ohio. Steven and Tonya Mentzer are parents of Steven, Jr. and Theresa. Robert is now married to Therese Creek.

Rosemary Miller graduated from Ossian High School and was a hospital secretary. She married Floyd Bell and they had four children: Donna Pauline and Diane Elaine are twins born in 1941. Donna graduated from a California university, and Diane from the University of Colorado. Both are hospital executives in Huntington Beach, California.

Diane Bell married Ray Wegener and they have a daughter, Cynthia (Mrs. Richard) Erickson, of Lakewood, Colorado. Her children: Jason and Jennifer. Diane married Lou Steinmetz, and Kurt and Jennifer are their children.

Phillip Bell, a mechanic, lives in Broomfield, Colorado. He has two daughters, Angela and Frances, and a son James. His wife was Linda Pelham.

Carol Lea Bell (1955), married Dieser Magin, and they, with their son, Daniel (1973), live in Lakewood, Colorado. Carol is a graphic artist.

After Floyd Bell's death Rosemary married Evart Cornum. They live in Denver, Colorado.

Elaine Noe lives near Bluffton, Indiana.

WILLIAM H. MILLER

William H. Miller, an enterprising and public-spirited citizen of Wells County, and justice of the peace of Chester Township, is a native of Indiana, born in Henry County, April 7, 1852, a son of John and Rachel (Rodgers) Miller. John Miller was a native of Boone County, Kentucky, and when a boy three years old was brought by his parents to Henry County, Indiana, May 29, 1852, he came to Wells County and purchased one hundred sixty acres of wild land on section 14, on which he located. Game was very plentiful, especially deer, wild turkeys and squirrels, when he first settled in the county, but he did not follow hunting except for fur animals, of which he hunted and trapped a considerable number. He made his home in Wells County until 1880, when he removed to Reno County, Kansas, remaining there until his death in June, 1885. William H. Miller was but seven weeks old when he was brought by his parents to Wells County, and here lived here with the exception of about three years, from 1880 until 1883, spent in Wexford County, Michigan. He was reared to the avocation of a farmer, his youth being spent in assisting on his father's farm and in attending the schools of Chester Township. November 1, 1875, he was married to Miss Amanda M. Miller, a native of Wells County, Indiana; a daughter of Henry G. and Francina (Morris) Miller, natives of Germany and Ohio respectively. Six children born to this union: William H., George E., Laura Ellen, Ida Elsie, Lewis Elmer and Helen Viola. Since 1878 Mr. Miller, in connection with his farming pursuits, followed blacksmithing and carpentering. His farm consisted of his interests as an heir in one hundred forty five acres of land which was mostly all improved. When the family first settled in the county settlers were few, and many were the hardships and privations endured by these pioneers. The road which ran past the home farm was then nothing but a trail through the woods, and the improvements of Chester Township had hardly commenced. When they could not go to mill, they would have to grate corn on an iron grater late into the night to get enough corn meal for the next day, or they would sometimes pound the corn in a mortar. Wheat was a great rarity in those days. For two or three years after coming to the county the father, John Miller, made a living by hunting minks and selling their skins. When John Miller first settled in this county he had a hard time making a living. The foxes would catch and carry off the pigs, and opossum would visit the hen roost. The howling of the wolves made the night hideous; so bold did they become that they would come near the house and fight the dog, and often when Mr. Miller would go out hunting for raccoon, the howling of the wolves would drive the dog back and he would be obliged to return. One hard winter when feed was scarce, he had to take his ax and cut down the elm trees for the cattle to browse upon to keep them from perishing. Their meat consisted principally of turkey and squirrel, and when the old gun got out of fix they had to do without even that. In politics Mr. Miller affiliated with the Democratic party, but in local elections voted independent of party ties. In the spring of 1884 he was elected justice of the peace, which office he filled with credit to himself and satisfaction to his constituents. He was a member of the old school Baptist Church, and Mrs. Miller was a member of the Christian church.

MILLER-WILLIAMS

I am a branch of the Williams and Boxell family tree. Our house is believed to be over one hundred years old. Dan Keplinger built our house. The ground was part of the Chapean Indian Tribe.

My grandfather Boxell owned it, and my dad and mother bought it from them in 1917. I was born in this house. I was one of five children. Mother died in 1925. My sister and I lived with our mother's parents for over two years, then my grandfather Boxell died.

Our farm is in Wells County, one and one-fourth mile west of Zanesville. My dad's parents lived across the road. When I was six years old, my dad took me to his parents and my dad's sister Lulu raised me. She was the only mother I can ever remember.

I went to Lafayette Central School all twelve years; our class will celebrate our fifty years, May 18th.

My great-grandfather Williams had a horse farm on the east edge of Zanesville on the Cozy Martin farm. My great-grandfather Young was trustee of Lafayette Township for several years.

I was married to Charles Miller in 1946. We moved here in 1949 to help take care of the folks. We had two boys. Our oldest son, Roger, has Millers Manor Nursery on Rd. 224. They have two boys, Kent and Nathan. DeWayne lives in the Sandalwood Addition at Ossian. He has two girls, Jodi and Christy, who live in Haver Hill Addition in Fort Wayne.

Charles and I, and the boys farmed almost four hundred acres when they were home. As the boys left home we cut back on the farming. Charles worked at International Harvester Truck Sales and Processing, and we farmed too. We quit farming in 1978. We also were in the Home Care Program for Veterans for fifteen years. We were forced to retire in 1983 when Charles had a heart attack. In 1984 he had to have a five by-pass surgery. I had a heart attack in 1986. Then we had to let the Veterans in our home go back to the V.A. in Marion.

Charles and I will be married forty-five years in June. We bought the farm in 1968 from mother. She and her brothers, Dee and Harley, had bought it from Manda Boxell (grandmother) in 1928.

Mother (Lulu) passed away in 1978. I thank God every day that I had a second mother. She was a member of Zanesville First Church of God. We had gone to the United Brethren for around thirty years. We started going to the Church of God in 1975 and joined the church 1979. *(Mrs. Charles (Elizabeth) Miller)*

MITTLESTEDT

The Mittlestedt family moved to Wells County from central Wisconsin in the early 1940's.

Alfred E. Mittlestedt and Lila K. Green were married in Abbotsfort, Wisconsin, on July 1, 1938. In 1941 the Mittlestadts moved to Bluffton, and Alfred (Al) started work in Fruehaf in Fort Wayne. He also served in the U.S. Army during World War II. Following his return to the U.S. in 1947, Al joined the maintenance department at Franklin Electric. He retired from Franklin in 1978.

Lila spent many years in the urology department at Caylor-Nickel Clinic. She and Al made their home in Bluffton. After Al's retirement they moved to Ocala, Florida. Al passed away there in 1986.

Al and Lila had three children: Yvonne M., graduated from Ball State with a degree in nursing. She married Bobbie A. Fisher, a Corning Glass employee, in Dallas, Texas, and they have three children and two grandchildren. David an architect in Dayton, Ohio; Vicki works in Greenville and has two children; and Deanna, a student at Ohio State University.

James G. Mittlestedt worked for Aerial Lift Industry in Fort Wayne and Waukesha, Wisconsin, for many years. He married Sally (Runyon) in 1963. Sally was a teacher in the Southern Wells System for twenty-eight years. They have two children. Laura K. was killed in a car accident in August, 1987. Patrick W. works for Disney and resides in Winter Garden, Florida. Jim and Sally moved to Winter Garden in November, 1990, and are employed there.

Donald Lee Mittlestedt has lived in Wells County all his life. He is married to Connie J. (McFarren), and they have five children and one grandchild. Robert A. works for Miller Body Shop in Bluffton. Matt L. married Connie S. (Jones). He is self-employed and works at Maxwell's Tree Service in Fort Wayne, and has one son, Steven. Lesia A. owns L and M Tree Service. Mike is employed by K-Mart Corporation. Christina M. is at home.

MOORE-CASSIDAY

My parents, Joseph Kelly Moore and Cleora Isabelle Russell Moore, was married February 6, 1925. My father, he was always called Kelly, was born in Hamilton County and was the fifth child of seven and the first son of Aaron Cornelius and Gertie Jones Moore. They later moved to a farm south and west of Liberty Center where Grandpa Moore farmed and also served as trustee for a period of time. My father died March 20, 1958.

My mother was the third child and second daughter of Charles Franklin and Martha Augusta Arnold Russell. For 48 years she operated a beauty shop out of her home and still works occasionally at the age of 85.

My Grandpa and Grandma Russell moved into a house north and east of Liberty Center where my mother and I were both born.

I graduated from Liberty Center High School in 1949 and September 5, 1951, married Dean Cassiday of Wabash. We have four children: Timothy Allen, born in 1954; Rebecca Lynne in 1955; Deana Sue in 1957 and Brian Kelly in 1960.

Upon the death of Grandma Russell in 1961 we moved into the home place and lived there until 1985, when we built a new house just to the west of the original house. Our son Tim and his family now reside in the home place making the fifth generation to live there. Tim is married to the former Kim Buckland, and they have four children: Katrina eighteen, Kari fifteen, Kelli twelve, and Kevin eight. Tim works at MoorMan Manufacturing Company and Kim works at Peyton's Northern Distribution Company. Becky lives in Casper, Wyoming, where her husband, Dave Foster of Huntington, is a geologist. She has a BS degree in biology. They have three sons, Mark nine, Danny six, and Adam three. Deana Melching lives near Bluffton with her son and daughter, Brett eleven and Shelby three. She works at the Farmers and Merchants Bank. Brian and his wife, Julie Ann Giek of Peru, presently live in San Antonio, Texas with their two sons, Joshua six and Zachary three. Brian is a captain in the Air Force and stationed at Kelly Air Force Base. Julie is an RN and works at the Medical Center Hospital in San Antonio.

I worked at the Wells Community Hospital for twenty two and one-half years and retired January 13, 1989. I was director of medical records. During that time I also was an EMT and rode and drove an ambulance for thirteen and one-half years. Dean served in the Army during the Korean War. He was first stationed at Fort Hood, Texas, where we lived for some time and then he was sent to Germany. On his return from there he was released from the service. His discharge was several years later. He served as a rural mail carrier for twenty eight years servicing first, Liberty Center and then expanding to Liberty Center and Poneto. He retired in 1986. We are both members of the Liberty Center Baptist Church where I am a pianist and Dean is a deacon. *(Phyllis Moore Cassiday)*

MOORE-GREEN FAMILY

My parents were Howard and Minnie (Gibson) Moore. They had eleven children. Marjorie married Manford Wise and lives in New Paris, Indiana. They have three children. Georgia married Albert Mast and lived in Goshen, Indiana; while raising three children. She now lives in Florida. Norma married Orlo Berkey and lives in Elkhart, Indiana. They have one child. Emily married Winfred Mishler and lives in New Paris, Indiana. They have six children. Jim married Ruth Stewart and lives in Elkhart, Indiana. They raised two children. Dick married Bea Raulston and lives in Ontario, California. They raised three children. Forrest was married and raised seven children. He passed away in Texas in 1989. Don married Lena Morand of Berne, Indiana. They lived in Richmond, Texas, and raised three children. Jean married Evert Blem out of Murray, Indiana. They raised three children. She passed away in 1970. Arvilla is deceased. Betty married George Green, son of Robert and Mary (Ramsey) Green, of Kingsland, Indiana and raised four children.

We moved to Wells County in 1934 from Adams County. Dad and mother bought a forty acre farm two miles east of Bluffton in 1936. They did a little bit of farming. Dad built a bakery on a corner of the property and baked and sold bread, rolls, cakes and cookies. They had bread routes throughout the county. They had to close the bakery in 1942 because of Dad's health and because of World War II. The older girls had already moved away from home, and the boys were called up for military service. Dick, Forrest, Don, and Norma were all in the military in World War II. Don also served in the Korean War.

Forrest, Don, Jean, and Betty attended school in Vera Cruz for elementary education. They graduated from Bluffton High School. Georgia, Norma, and Don graduated from Lancaster High School.

George and I were married in 1947 and have lived in Lancaster Township ever since. He worked at Franklin Electric in Bluffton for thirty-seven years and is now retired.

We raised four children. Terry married Kim Shaffer and has three children, Tod, Chris, and Ked, and resides north of Bluffton. He currently is in Wisconsin, serving in the military in Operation Desert Storm. Mick (Gary) has two children, Kara and Mike, and lives in Tennessee. Tamra married Douglas Edwards from Zanesville and has two sons, Shane and Skip, and lives in Uniondale, Indiana. Glenda lives in Bluffton and has two children, Bruce and Colby. *(Betty Moore Green)*

MOORE-LOUDEN

Joseph K. Moore, of 1126 Sycamore Lane, Bluffton, was born August 2, 1926. Graduated from Liberty Center High School in Liberty Center, Indiana; enlisted in the U.S. Navy in World War II; and attended Indiana University. He married Dorothea Louden of Bluffton on February 21, 1947. She was born August 13, 1924. They are the parents of a daughter, Jo Ann, and a son, George Kenneth.

Jo Ann was born August 9, 1948. Graduated from Bluffton High School in 1966, and went on to graduate in 1971 from Lea College in Minnesota, with a degree in physical education, and teaches at Norwell Middle School. She was married June 1, 1972 to Steve J. Ault. They have two sons, Andrew Charles, twelve, and Adam Joseph, five.

George Kenneth graduated from Bluffton High School in 1971, and went on to Indiana State University and graduated in 1975 with a degree in industrial arts, and teaches in the middle school in Bluffton. He was married December 28, 1985, to Michelle Call. They have a son Scott Joseph, born April 8, 1987, and a daughter, Jordan Louise, born March 14, 1991.

Dorothea graduated from Bluffton High School in 1943 and went to Christian College in Columbia, Missouri, and graduated in 1945. She is a homemaker and interested in needlework and golf. Member of the First United Church of Christ, Wells County Historical Society, and Tri Kappa Sorority.

Joseph is the son of the late Kenneth and Esther Smith Moore of Liberty Center, Indiana. He worked two years for Ware Baker Co., nine years for Goodin Motor Co., and sixteen years for Kaade Motor Sales before going into business for himself at Moore-Chevrolet Oldsmobile, Inc. He is a member of the Liberty Center Methodist Church, active in Bluffton Lions Club, Gun Club, and the Parlor City Country Club. He has one brother Deane of Ossian. He retired the end of 1986.

Dorothea is the daughter of the late George B. Louden and Louise Ashbaucher Louden. She has one sister, Alice Ann Nalle of Culpepper, Virginia. Mrs. Louden is now a resident of Swiss Village in Berne, Indiana.

GUY MORRIS FAMILY

Guy Jones Morris was born October 2, 1905 in Liberty Township, Wells County. He was the son of

Elmer E. and Effa (Jones) Morris and had two older sisters, Blanche (Mrs. Harry Minniear) and Fay.

Martha Elizabeth Prible was born September 19, 1906 in Liberty Township, Wells County, to Charles Forest and Dora Alice (Miller) Prible. She was the oldest of seven children, the others being Harold, Edwin, Mary (Mrs. William Moses), Paul, Esther, and John.

Both Guy and Martha graduated in 1924 from Liberty Center High School. Martha then attended Manchester College for two years to become an elementary teacher. Prior to her marriage, she taught school in Wells County. Guy attended Tri-State College at Angola, Indiana. At the home of Martha's parents, on June 30, 1929, they were united in marriage at a private sunrise wedding ceremony. They resided several years in Fort Wayne, where Guy worked at General Electric. In the early 1940's they returned to Wells County (living in Lancaster Township and then at 210 East Washington Street in Bluffton). On December 18, 1944 their only child, Janet Marie Morris, was born in Bluffton.

Martha and Guy Morris and daughter Janet (1951).

Active members of the Liberty Center Methodist Church, Guy served as Sunday School superintendent and Martha as pianist. In later years Martha became a member of the First United Methodist Church in Bluffton and of the local chapter of the Daughters of the American Revolution. Guy worked as a drafting engineer for Houser Engineering in Bluffton and later for Franklin Electric Co. He was not well for approximately nine years, and his death resulted on December 2, 1953 at the age of forty-eight from a very rare disease. After Guy's death, Martha began working in the office of Franklin Electric, where she was employed for several years. After retiring, her health caused her to become a resident of the United Methodist Memorial Home at Warren, Indiana, in 1973. On October 10 of that year she died of cancer and heart failure at the age of sixty-seven. Both Guy and Martha are buried in the Mossburg Cemetery in Liberty Township, Wells County.

Their daughter Janet graduated from Bluffton High School in the class of 1962. She then received a B.A. degree in mathematics education from Manchester College in 1966 and a M.S. degree from Illinois State University in 1968. In 1966 and 1967 she was employed as a computer programmer at Franklin Electric. After receiving her master's degree she was employed as a junior high mathematics teacher at Village Woods Junior High School in East Allen County for six years. Then she taught junior high and high school mathematics in the South Adams Schools for seven years. In 1981 she left the teaching profession and returned to computer programming. In 1983 she was hired by Kitco as a computer programmer, and currently is Information Systems (data processing) manager at Kitco. Janet is active in the Apostolic Christian Church and resides in Mobile Manor. She enjoys traveling, reading, walking, bicycling, genealogy, knitting, and music. (*Janet Morris*)

MORRISSEY

Thomas Michael Morrissey (1896-1967) and Hattie Marie Pruitt (1899-1953) were married in Gibson City, Illinois, in January, 1920, and moved to a 120-acre farm south east of Bluffton.

On February 11, 1921, Harold Frances was born, and on July 11, 1922, Robert Dale was born. They grew up on the farm and graduated from Poplar Grove eight grade. After moving to Rockcreek Township, the boys graduated from Rockcreek High School in 1939 and 1940.

They were drafted into the U.S. Army for World War II in 1942. Harold went to the European Theater and Dale to the Pacific Theater.

Harold Morrissey married Marcille Derr in 1943 before going overseas. After being discharged in late 1945 he went to work with his father-in-law, Brownie Derr, in the Ossian Locker Plant. Harold and Marcille raised three children, Carolyn Jane, born in 1948; Ann Louise, 1951; and James Kenneth, 1954. Harold joined O.D. Haflich and Dale Morrissey in the Haflich and Morrissey Shoe Store and moved his family from Bluffton to Winchester, Indiana in 1959. He later sold his Winchester Shoe Store in 1983 and retired to Punta Gorda, Florida.

R. Dale Morrissey was assigned to infantry combat units in New Guinea, the Philippines, and the Army of Occupation in Japan in 1944 and 1945; he was discharged a staff sergeant in January 1946. He then went back to work for O.D. Haflich in the Bluffton Brownbilt Shoe store until 1948, when he became a partner and the name became Haflich & Morrissey Shoe Store.

In August 1950, they opened a new shoe store in downtown Decatur with Dale as manager. He married Evelyn Dean Haflich on February 14, 1952. They purchased a new home south of Decatur, "Yost Woods," in 1956. Their children are, Nancy Elizabeth, 1956; Janet Marie, 1958; Michael David, 1961; and Patrick Donald, 1962. They graduated from St. Joseph Catholic Grade School and Adams Central High School in Monroe, Indiana.

Nancy, after graduating from Ball State University as a business major, lives in Bluffton and is president of Haflich & Morrissey Inc. She is manager of Nancy's Classic Image, a ladies' dress shop on west Market Street, Bluffton.

Janet is married to Douglas Lehman. Both are graduates of Ball State University. They live in Bluffton. Douglas works for Standard Federal Bank, as an assistant vice-president and branch manager, and Janet is employed by the Bluffton-Harrison M.S.D. as a secretary at East Side Elementary. They have two sons, Nathaniel, 1981; Gregory, 1988.

Michael lives in Bluffton and is married to Jill Flaugher. He is manager of the Haflich & Morrissey Shoe Store in Bluffton.

Jill is a beautician, employed by the Fireside. They have two children, Nicole, 1987; and Matthew, 1990.

Patrick lives in Decatur and is manager of Haflich & Morrisey Shoe Store, Decatur.

Dale and Evelyn Morrissey, in their retirement live on R.R. 4, Oakwood (Yost Woods), Decatur, Indiana.

B.H. MORTON FAMILY

Benjamin H. Morton was born May 26, 1903, in Muncie. He moved with his parents to Jackson Township in 1910. His father, Benjamin Monroe was born in Wayne County. His mother, Rosa Marie (Dupont) was born in Maine of French Canadian parents. They were married in 1900 in Minnesota. They lived in a small house in the woods near Duluth until moving back to Muncie.

In Muncie, Benjamin M. worked at a slaughter house. He sometimes herded hogs from the country right down the main streets of town. At that time Ball State was one building in the middle of a field and the Ball sisters drove their electric cars around town.

In 1910, he traded his house in Muncie for a forty acre farm in the middle of Section 22. The family moved in on St. Patrick's Day. They lived in this house until they bought the eighty acre farm that was between them and the road.

A daughter, Mildred, was born in 1916. She was married to Arthur Krumdick in 1941.

Benjamin H. married Oma Manring, daughter of Harry C. (Hal) and Annie Laura (Cross) Manring. The Manring farm has been in the family for 96 years. The marriage took place on March 12, 1939, in their present home at 9207 S. 900 W. They have spent their lives engaged in farming.

They have three sons, Stanley M. was born in 1940, and twins Warren H. and Marshall E. were born in 1942. They graduated from Jackson Township High School. Stanley and Warren graduated from Taylor University, and Marshall received his degree ad from Huntington College.

Stanley married the former Luanne K. Affolder of Berne in 1963. They have two sons, Benjamin M. and Thomas J.

Warren and Geraldine (Geri) Nelson were married in Curtis, Nebraska, in 1967. They are both teachers. He teaches at Salamonie Junior High and she is at the Berne Elementary School. They have twin daughters, Lisa and LeAnn, who are seniors at Grace College, Winona Lake.

Marshall was married to Marylee Sweet in Elyria, Ohio in 1966. He teaches elementary school in Lagrange, Ohio and she gives private piano lessons. They have two children, John seventeen and Jane thirteen.

The Morton families are all active in their respective churches.

STANLEY MORTON FAMILY

Stanley Manring Morton was born January 25, 1940 to Benjamin H. and Oma A. (Manring) Morton. He graduated from Jackson Township High School in 1957 and Taylor University in 1961. In 1963, he was married to Luanne Kae Affolder of Berne.

They lived in Linn Grove, Indiana until 1965 when the house they were renting was destroyed in the Palm Sunday tornado. They then built a new home at 9907 S. St. Rd. 3 where they still live.

Stanley taught mathematics at Hartford Center, Jackson Twp., and Southern Wells high schools for a total of nine years. He is currently a farmer and drainage contractor. He has also been a sales representative for Pioneer Hi Bred for twenty-five years. Luanne has been employed by Southern Wells High School as a bookkeeper for eight years.

They have two sons, Benjamin M., born in 1965, and Thomas J., born in 1968. Both graduated from Southern Wells High School and Ben is a graduate of Taylor University.

Ben and his wife Kelly (Koehlinger) formerly of Lynchburg, Virginia and also a Taylor alumnus, lived in Jackson Township. He is employed by Pioneer Hi Bred and she is assistant director at the Marion Boy's Club.

Tom lives in Bluffton and is employed by L.H. Carbide in Fort Wayne. He is a member of the Air National Guard and is currently on active duty in Saudi Arabia as a part of Operation Desert Storm.

NELSON L. MOSER FAMILY

Nelson L. Moser (July 1917 - February 1976), was the son of Joe and Martha Moser. He lived in and around Bluffton all his life. He served in the army during World War II and was a partner in the Moser Implement Company. Many farmers knew him; he loved driving the truck, picking-up and delivering equipment. In 1943 Nelson came home on a furlough and married Marie B. Steffen (August 1919 - November 1984), the daughter of Amos and Mary Steffen of Milford, Indiana. They had two daughters, Gloria Jean and Sheila Kay. Marie was a wonderful homemaker and at various times would work part-time at different jobs to help out. Nelson and Marie enjoyed people and entertained a lot. In the middle 1950's they bought the Nel-I Dress Shop on Johnson Street. Marie did all the purchasing and managed the store, while Gloria and Sheila helped out after school and on Saturdays. Nelson and Marie sold the store in the late 1960's and Marie went to work part-time at the Dutch Mill, where she remained as long as her health permitted.

Gloria married Terry Wayne Steffen, son of Norman and Lucille Steffen. They have three children, Jean Ann, Wayne Terry, and Joy Lynne. Terry worked at the Bluffton News-Banner for many years. In 1987 Terry and Gloria bought Quick Printing Service in Berne, Indiana, where both kept very busy. Quick Printing has turned into a family business where Jean, Wayne, and Joy (in the summer) all help out. Jean and Wayne are also part-time students at IPFW. Wayne is married to Jeanne Sue Bertsch, a full-time student at Ball State University. She is the daughter of Walter and Lillian Bertsch. Joy is a student at Bluffton High School.

Sheila married Kent Barger Sprunger, son of Adrian and Nadine Sprunger. They have four children: Marie Nadine, Jason Kent, Joseph (Joe) Nelson and John Adrian. Kent is a partner in the Moser Implement Company, and served on the Wells County Library Board for several years. Sheila is a homemaker, kept very busy organizing her children's various activities. Marie is a graduate of Ball State University. Jason is a student at Wabash College. Joe and John are students in the Bluffton Harrison School System.

One of the most important things to Nelson and Marie was doing things with their family. Their home was always open to their children and grandchildren, and all of their friends. The summers always consisted of picnics, kite flying, fishing, and a week or two for everyone together at a cottage on Lake Wawasee. Nelson and Marie were active in the Apostolic Christian Church, as are many of their family. They lived short lives here on earth, but left many good memories for their children, grandchildren and many friends.

WILLIAM MOSER SR.

Born December 26, 1903, in Wells County, he was the son of John and Priscilla (Steffen) Moser. His marriage to Emma Meyer, who survives, took place in Bluffton. He had one son, William Gene Moser who resides in Bluffton with his wife Edna (Reinhard) Moser. Also, five grandchildren who reside in Bluffton, Mrs. Ernie (Robin) Schwartz, Mrs. Gene (Melinda) Gilgen, Mrs. Blake (Fawn) Gerber, Drake Moser, and Trout Moser.

William Moser, Sr.

Mr. Moser was active in oil production most of his adult life. His early exploration ventures were in Michigan, Illinois, Kentucky and southern Indiana. Later pursuits took him to Oklahoma, Montana, Wyoming, and California. In 1930, he founded the Moser Oil and Gas Company which later became National Oil and Gas Company in the 1940's. The company is still a family-owned business which is now controlled by his son, William Gene. He also was an early investor and developer of real estate in the Disney area of Florida, where he bought and sold large tracts of land for development. Cattle ranching and citrus growing were among his Florida business interests. Mr. Moser founded and operated twenty-eight companies throughout the United States.

In August, 1981, the William Moser family presented the Caylor Nickel Medical Center with funds in excess of $800,000 to purchase a CT (computer tomography) scanner, which is advanced diagnostic equipment. In recognition of this gift, Mr. and Mrs. Moser were designated life Presidential Directors of the Caylor Nickel Foundation.

He was a member of the Apostolic Christian Church, where he served for many years on the board of the World Relief, Mennonite Central Committee. William and his wife, Emma, enjoyed many years of fishing and travels throughout the world. He also was an avid hunter.

MOSSBURG FAMILY

Rev. Henry Mossburg was born in Germany in 1776. His parents came to Maryland when he was six months old. In his early years he went to Virginia seeking work. While there he became a minister, met and married Jane Thrailkill.

From 1827 to 1837 they lived in Delaware County, Indiana. In 1837 they moved to Liberty Township, Wells County where the Mossburg Cemetery is located. His was the second family, and his was the first death in Liberty Township, November 2, 1838. He was buried near his cabin.

Daniel was the second son and fifth child born to the union. In 1840 he met Elizabeth Brown at an Indian dance where Rockcreek joins the Wabash River. They were married January 6, 1842. He was a farmer and also a cabinet maker. To them eight children were born. Daniel died March 21, 1900, and Elizabeth four days later. They rest in Mossburg Cemetery.

Daniel P. Mossburg, son of Daniel and Elizabeth was the fifth child of eight children. He was born April 23, 1852 in the cabin of his grandfather. He also became a lover of woodworking, but unlike his father, he became a hewer and a builder of barns. His marriage to Catherine Shoemaker took place at the brides home June 5, 1872. After the birth of ten children, Catherine died at an early age on November 28, 1899.

Daniel was married the second time soon after he moved to Warren, Indiana where he became town marshall, and remained such for twenty years. He died March 5, 1937, and lies beside Catherine in the Mossburg Cemetery. Emerson F. Mossburg was the first child of Daniel and Catherine born August 7, 1873. He worked as a farm hand until his marriage to Hannah Aby Irwin on October 6, 1900. He too, liked wood working and became a builder of houses and barns. Edith was born on October 28, 1901, and died February 20, 1920. Howard was born October 23, 1904 and died October 29, 1974. Elmer was born September 23, 1906 and died February 1987. Grace (Mossburg) Dolby was born February 18, 1911. Hannah Aby died January 17, 1941, and Emerson died February 15, 1953, and is buried with his wife, daughter and one son in Mossburg Cemetery. Elmer is buried at Markle.

Elmer, like the generations before him was a builder. His marriage to Alfreda Dennis took place September 20, 1930. To them were born four children. Jerry, who married Norma Jean Kinsey, is the father of Janelle and Jeffrey. Linda, who is married to Donavon Carl is the mother of three sons, Mitchell, Courtney and Patrick. Kirby, who married Shirley Merchant, is the father of Byron, Juli and Joni. James, who married Sandra Hahn, is the father of three daughters, Angela, Annette and Angenette.

Byron married Cindy Griffith and is the father of two sons, Caleb and Aaron.

Jerry and James are owners of Mossburg Construction. Kirby is the owner of Mossburg Masonry.

MOSSBURG

This account is in memory of Bob Mossburg, who worked on the "Mossburg" history for twenty years. These dates and information are all due to his many hours of work and dedication.

We can record the Mossburg's back to Baden, Germany when William and Mary started to America in 1777. Their son Henry, was six months old, and he probably had brothers and sisters, although there is no proof.

Henry became a chaplin in the "War of 1812". Rev. Henry married Jennie Jane Thrailkill on February 2, 1810 in Ross County, Ohio. They lived in Clinton County, Ohio, and also Wayne and Delaware Counties in Indiana and settled in Liberty Township in Wells County.

Back L to R: Cindy, John, Rod. Front L to R: Fran and Bob Mossburg May 1988.

By this time, they had twelve children: Rebecca, born in 1811, but never married; Matilda Ann, born in 1813, who married Johnson King and Isaac Marshall, but never had children; Able Morgan Sargent, born in 1815, who died as a teen-ager; Sarah, 1817, who married George Sparks and had six children; Daniel, 1819, who married Elizabeth

Brown and had eight children, including a set of twins. Henry William, 1821, married Rebecca Scotton, and had five children, only one of which lived over a year. He then married Mary Elizabeth Wiley, and had ten children. His third marriage was to Phariba Allen. Hiram, 1824, married Catherine Walker and had one son. Angeline, 1826, died in childhood. James Tolliner, 1827, married Isabella Mounsey and had ten children: Isabella died in childbirth. Then he married Mary Parker and Sarah Hogston. John, 1829 and Virganette, 1831, both died in childhood. Ethalinda, 1836, married Ambro Day and had two children.

You would probably guess that most of the Mossburg's in this area are descendants of these people.

Rev. Henry died on November 2, 1838, and was buried where he lived, which is now called the Mossburg Cemetery in Liberty Township.

Daniel his second son is our direct ancestor line from Rev. Henry. Daniel and Elizabeth's fourth son, John married Emily Irvin and had three children, but only one lived, Lloyd Lewis. Lloyd married Leah Dial, had three children, but one baby died. Leah died in 1927 and Lloyd married Martha Sheets in 1935. Lloyd's only son Ray Hugo, married Vivian Jackson from Morgan County, on October 11, 1924, and on May 29, 1929, they had their only child, Robert Eugene.

On October 14, 1950, Robert and Frances Macklin were married and had six children. Rodney, born March 4, 1952, married Deborah Thompson and had three children, Christopher, age nineteen, Anna, age sixteen, and April, age eleven. Randall, born June 5, 1953, married Debra Brandon, and had one daughter, Sonya, fifteen. Randy was killed in a motorcycle accident June, 1976. Debra and Sonya now live in Colorado. Cindy, born February 9, 1955, has twins, who are seven years old, Travis and Heather Richardson. Sharon died shortly after birth, January 17, 1959. Mark, born February 5, 1960, was visiting with my parents and they went fishing. Mark fell in the reservoir and drowned at the age of ten. John, April 8, 1961, married Christine Smith, and they have three children: Jacob, nine, Jennifer, five, and Laura, two. All of us live in Liberty Township.

Lloyd, Ray and Robert graduated from Liberty Center High School. Rodney, Randall, Cindy, and John graduated from Southern Wells High School. *(Fran Mossburg)*

RICHARD AND PAT (FRYBACK) MOSSBURG

The Mossburg family has been farming in Liberty Township since Rev. Henry Mossburg settled there in 1836. My lineage started from Rev. Henry's son, James T. Mossburg. About this period in history was when the name was changed from Mossberg to Mossburg. Hiram was the one of James T. Mossburg's sons who married Hannah First. One of his sons was Charles G. Mossburg. From his marriage were four children: Oscar, Howard, Ethel and Charles Homer.

Charles Homer married Ida Marie Wyant in 1930. Two boys were born to this marriage, James Richard and Robert Dale. C. Homer and Ida now reside in St. Petersburg, Florida since their retirement from farming. Oscar, Howard and Ethel are all deceased.

Robert and Linda Watson Mossburg now live in Milwaukee, Wisconsin. Linda Watson was from Fountaintown, Indiana. They have four children: Diane, Denise, David, and Dana and four grandchildren.

Richard and Pat Mossburg

Richard married Pat Fryback and is the sixth generation of Mossburg's still farming in Liberty Township. They have three children. C. Scott married Barbara Higgenbottom, and has one son, Thomas, and lives in Bluffton. Mike married Shelley Oliver and lives near Gas City. Both boys are in agriculture related occupations. Julie Mossburg married Ervin Puckett. They have two boys Jesse and Adam and live in Carmel, Indiana.

Richard belongs to the Farm Bureau, Masonic Lodge, Scottish Rite and Mizpah Shrine and the Order of the Eastern Star. He is active in PAHLS, and environmental groups. Pat belongs to Eastern Star and has been active as Worthy Matron of Crescent Chapter in Bluffton and has had other state appointments. *(James Richard Mossburg)*

ROY LEON MOSSBURG FAMILY

The history of Roy Leon Mossburg and Aenone Smith started when Rev. Henry Mossburg, (1777-1838) at the age of six months, came to the United States with his parents in the year 1777. He fought in the War of 1812 and there became a minister. When thirty-five years old he married Jane Thrailkill. They eventually had twelve children. They moved to Wells County and around 1836, the second white family to settle in Liberty Township. He died two years later.

James Toliver Mossburg, one of Henry's sons, was born in Ohio in 1827. He had three wives and a total of ten children: Mary Jane, Sara S., Elizabeth Ann, Isabell, Herman, Almira, James A., Imma, Ammalydia and Elijah.

James' youngest son, Elijah Palmer Mossburg (1869-1954), married Mollie (Mary) Johnson in 1892. They had three children: Lola Custer, Mabel Nahrwold and Roy Leon.

Roy Leon Mossburg (1897-1979), was born in Liberty Center. He was a school teacher, and cashier at the Liberty Center Bank at the time it was robbed by John Dillinger in April, 1930. He also served on the first grand jury convened in Wells County. In 1920 Roy married Aenone Smith.

Aenone's grandfather, William Wesley Smith (1841-1912), was born in Louisville, Kentucky. He moved to Howard County, Indiana, at the age of twelve. In 1863 he married Sarah Eva Spraker (1841-1902). They had six children: Addison Eugene, Amelia Martha, Charles Newton, Omar Jessie, Alma Emma and Harry D.

Charles Newton Smith (1873-1936), farmed, operated a dairy and owned a bakery. In 1897 he married Fayette Pearl Moore. Because of his wife's health they moved to Oklahoma. They had two children, Sharon LaMarr (1897-1951) and Aenone (1899-1978). After his first wife's death he married Bertha Anne Stamm Hatton (1881-1929), and moved to Poplar, Montana. One child was born, Wesley Warren Smith (1913).

Aenone Smith met Roy L. Mossburg while attending church in Liberty Center, Indiana. They were married in Poplar, Montana, but returned immediately to Liberty Center to live. They had five children: Louis G. (1921-1944), who was killed in World War II, Donald Leon (1925-1988), Dale Eugene (1927), Nancy Mae (1929), and Charles, who died at birth. In 1943 they moved to Warren, Indiana, where Roy worked at the grain elevator. They moved to Fort Wayne in 1945, where Roy was employed at the Fort Wayne National Bank until retiring.

Donald Leon Mossburg married Helen Durham (1925) in Huntington, Indiana, in 1947. Their children are Sarah Schweyer (1955), Ronald Leon (1959), and Dean (1962). Donald Leon served in the 82nd Airborne Division during World War II.

Dale E. Mossburg married Doris A. Stucky (1927), in Warren, Indiana, in 1949. Their children are Anne Tucker (1950), Jean Anne Becket (1952), Jo Linda Walters (1954), and Kay Davis (1956). Dale worked at General Electric in Fort Wayne and Holland, Michigan. He served as Military Police at Arlington Cemetery during World War II.

**See Campbell, William Henry for history of Nancy Mae Mossburg.

THOMAS MOSSBURG

I was born March 18, 1989, at the Wells Community Hospital in Bluffton, Indiana. My mom, Barbara Higginbottom, moved here from Waverley, Iowa, on July 4, 1976, with her parents A.J. and Jan Higginbottom and two brothers.

Four generations of Mossburgs
Left to right: Richard holding Thomas, Homer and Scott, July, 1990.

My dad, C. Scott Mossburg, was born at Ft. Knox, Kentucky, but moved to Wells County, six months later. His parents and my grandparents are Richard and Pat Mossburg. My great-grandparents are Home and Ida Wyant Mossburg who have lived in St. Petersburg, Florida, for many years. They were originally from Wells County. My other great-grandparents are Clifford and Nellie Pinney Fryback who just celebrated their sixtieth wedding anniversary in March, 1991, and who still live on Corning Road four miles outside of Bluffton.

MOSURE AND FRAUHIGER

We traced the Mosure and Frauhiger families back to the 1800's. John Mosure (our great-grandfather) was born to Jonathan and Elizabeth Krill Mosure on September 21, 1865, in Murray, Indiana. When he was six weeks old they moved to Vera Cruz, Indiana. In 1887 John and his father

475

started a blacksmith shop in Magley. In 1893 he married Della Yarger, daughter of Samuel and Kathrine Archbold. He sold his interest in the Magley business and bought into one in Vera Cruz. They also lived in Decatur and worked at a variety store. In 1903 they bought a farm in French Township, Adams County. This house was the first one east of the Adams and Wells Counties line on State Road 116.

John Mosure served as trustee and in 1915 was elected auditor of Adams County for four years. After retiring from office they moved to the farm. He was president of the French Township Fire Insurance Company until 1947.

Four children were born to John and Della Mosure: Ocie, who married Nathan Moesberger; Cleo, who married Norman Stalter; Harley, who married Nellie Flowers; and David H., who married Mabel Dedrick. The Mosures had seven grandchildren and nine-great-grandchildren.

Rod, Sue (Frauhiger), and Frank Dickason

David and Mabel Mosure (our grandparents) were married in 1916. Her parents were Dave and Ida Dedrick. The Dedricks had six children: Lulu, who married Homer Marshall; Jim, who married Ethel Bowman; John; Mabel, who married David H. Mosure; Ruby, who married Orville Stanton; and Mary, who married Milo Niblick. They resided on the 500 block of East Silver St. in Bluffton.

Two children were born to the union of David and Mabel Mosure: Wendell Eugene and Cecile Marie (our mother).

They lived on Silver St. and at 504 East Townley in Bluffton. David worked for Sherman White Produce Co., located on West Washington Street near Cline Lumber. Mabel made gloves at home for the glove factory. The children helped with grading of the eggs and testing the cream. David was also conservation officer. In 1935 they moved to Morrocco, Indiana, and lived out their lives there.

Cecile moved into the family home and worked at the Wells Community Hospital. She met Ora Frauhiger while working for her father. They married in 1937. Two children were born to this union: Carolyn Sue on June 22, 1940, and Donola Marie on June 5, 1944.

Our father's parents were William H. and Bertha Fiechter Frauhiger. He was a farmer and did carpenter work. They lived in Magley and moved to south of Monroe, Indiana. Fourteen children were born: Inez, who married Tim Bauman; Ora, who married Cecile Mosure; Erna, who married William Kipfer; Aldine, who married Clyde Clayton; Cathleen, who married Leonard Reynolds; Rose, who married Paul Scott; Sylvan, who married Doris Gilliom; William, who married Betty Neuenschwander; Earleen, who married Lewis Steffen and Delilah Brickley. The other children died at an early age. The family later moved to 124 East, the present home of Sylvan Frauhiger.

Our parents still live on East Townley Street in Bluffton. Dad worked for the Airplane Station, Moser Implement, and the high school, retiring in 1976.

Donola lives in Auburn with her husband, Richard Leon Markley, and son Derek. Donola is a preschool teacher at the YMCA. Richard is a data processing manager of the Reinaissance Publishing Company.

Carolyn Sue is married to Frank W. Dickason, and they reside west of Bluffton. They have one son, Rodney W., who is married to Mary E. Ferrell; they have one son, Zachary. They own and operate the family business, Dickason Truck and Equipment Inc., on US 224 in Uniondale, Indiana.

JOHN MOSURE

John Mosure was one of the sons of Johnathan Mosure of Vera Cruz, Indiana, and they were blacksmiths. Johnathan lived in Vera Cruz for forty-four years and was an evangelical minister.

John Mosure was a life long resident of Wells and Adams Counties. He married Bertha Idella Yarger. Along with his blacksmithing, he farmed. Later the Mosures moved to Decatur, Indiana, where John owned the American Store at 130 N Second St. In 1915 John was elected to a four year term as auditor of Adams County and also was elected trustee of French Township. He also served as president of French Township Fire Insurance Company for thirty-five years until his retirement. John and Bertha Idella Mosure celebrated their fiftieth wedding anniversary January 28, 1940. Both are buried at at Six Mile Cemetery at Bluffton, Indiana.

John Mosure

Johnathan Mosure was married to Elizabeth Krill and their children were Frank, John, Edward, Ella, Mary, Lulu, and three other children who died young.

Frank married Rose Gehrig and they adopted daughter Dessie, who married Raymond Reynolds.

John married Bertha Idella Yarger and their children were Ocie, Harley J., Cleo May, and Dave. Ocie married Nathan Meschberger, and their children were Harold (married Mildred Jacobs) and Josephine (married John Rathert). Harley J. Mosure married Nellie Flowers and they adopted Alfred. In later years Harley married a second time. Harley was superintendent of the Bluffton Power Plant. Cleo May married Norman S. Stalter, and their children were Dorothy Lucille (married Loren C. Gottschalk) and Kenneth Dwight (married Marie Valentine.)

David Mosure married Mabel Dedrick and their children were Cecil (married Ora Frauhiger) and Wendell (married Thelma Leverenz). Wendell was also called "Bud".

Edward married Mary Edith Clark and their children were Forrest (married Clara L. Reynolds), Raymond (married Mary M. Oliver) and Gladys (married Tinkle and second husband Harry Lockwood).

The daughters of Johnathan all married; Ella married Wiliam Spade. Mary married William Selby and Lulu married Otis Riley.

As stated before Johnathan and Elizabeth Mosure are both buried at Six Mile Cemetery, Bluffton, Indiana.

MOSURE-SELBY

Jacob Moser came from Berne, Switzerland, in 1765. He settled in Schuylkill County, Pennsylvania. He was the great-grandfather of Cora Selby Hoeppner. He had eleven children, one of them Jacob Jr., who was said to have been 6'2" and dark complected. Jacob Jr. died at thirty-five in 1854. He also had eleven children, one of whom was Jonathan, born in Ohio, on August 15, 1836. He was the father of Mary, born December 30, 1876. She was the mother of Cora Selby Hoeppner and was married to William Selby in 1893. They came to Vera Cruz in 1905.

Left to right: Johnathan Mosure, born August 15, 1836, married Elizabeth Krill. Born to this union were Edward, born December 18, 1869; Dave, born July 30, 1862. He was accidentally shot in a hunting accident when he was 21; Frank, born February 8, 1861; John born September 21, 1865, Ella born November 8, 1872, and Mary born 1876. She later married William Selby in 1893 and they became the parents of Cora Selby Hoeppner.

Johnathan Mosure, son of Jacob Moser, Jr. was born in Ashland County, Ohio on August 15, 1836. He and Elizabeth Krill were married in Bluffton, Indiana, by the Rev. Polly. To this union were born nine children:

Frank, born February 8, 1861, married Rosa Gehring 1884; David, born July 30, 1862, accidentally shot hunting; John, born September 21, 1865, married Idel Yarger. Their children are Osa, Harley, Cleo, David; Edward, born December 18, 1869, married Edith Clark 1893. Their children are Gladys, Forrest, Raymond, and one child who died in infancy; Ella, born November 8, 1872, married William Spade in 1893. Their children: Dessie, Nellie, Floyd, Glenn, Helen; Mary, born 1876, married William Selby in 1893. Their children are: George, Edna, Cora, Charle Albert, Bessie, Gladys Lucile, and twin sons Gerald and Harold who died in infancy; Lula, born August 30, 1881, married Otis Riley, their children are Clyde and Harold.

Mary was the mother of Cora Selby Hoeppner; her family moved to Vera Cruz 1905. The Moser name was changed to Mosure by Mrs. Jacob Mosure Jr. at Decatur. There were others by the name of Jacob Moser living nearby, and sometimes the mail would get mixed up. She wrote to her godson in Ohio and told them to spell her name Mosure. Jonathan Mosure died May 4, 1912. His wife died April 19, 1920. Cora was born May 4, 1898.

Some of my memories are of gifts at Christmas. There was a large bowl of candy, which they did not get often, one orange, and a gift I especially remember is a 10¢ ABC Book. Trees were decorated with strings of popcorn, colored paper chains, and real candles. The tree was a branch cut from a bigger tree and stood in the corner. There seemed to be more snow while I was growing up. I can remember snow over the fence posts many times.

Along health lines, most children wore a bag of asafoetida on a string around their necks. It was to help keep diseases away. It really had an awful odor. We rubbed goose grease and turpentine for colds, and in the spring chewed slippery elm bark to clean us out. Drinking sassafras teas was supposed to be good for your blood, and there was always a dish of sliced onions with sugar on the back of the wood range making a syrup used for colds.

In 1905 we moved to Vera Cruz, which had a population of around one hundred and twenty-five.

Twin sons were born to my mother and father. They only lived a short time, one for ten days. Many people came to see them because twins were not common. My father buried them. On the death certificate it said "undertaker, father."

Around 1902 my parents and I went to Michigan to visit my grandparents. They met up with a horse and buggy and we drove on corduroy roads. There were friendly Indians around and we played with their children. My grandparents lived in a log cabin. The Indians taught the white man to dry deer and bear meat.

In Vera Cruz my father had a meat market and grocery store. My mother baked bread and buns and sold them. Dad did the butchering. T-Bone steak and round steak sold for fifteen cents a pound, liver five cents.

We had no refrigerator, only a large walk-in cooler in the store. In the winter, ice in the nearby gravel pit was twelve to fourteen inches thick; this was cut into large fifty pounds blocks and packed the ice house in saw dust. It kept until the next winter.

My father caught fish and they were salted down and used all winter.

My parents rented rooms to peddlers and the line-men that put in the first cross-country telephone line through Vera Cruz in 1915. They charged twenty-five cents a meal.

Trapping was a necessity to supplement income. My father trapped muskrats and sent the meat by street car to Fort Wayne where it was served in a popular restaurant.

On Saturday girls and boys would get together and make clothes-line taffy. The older ones played post office and when there was a big snow we go bob-sledding.

In 1914 an Evangelist, Bob Jones, was Bluffton. Several young people went by bob sled to hear him. We played on the ice and the boys played hockey with a tin can and a stick.

In 1913 a plane landed in Bluffton. It was a big thrill to go see. There was an interurban that ran through Riverview and one-fourth mile south of Vera Cruz.

One of the jobs I did was wash barber towels for fifteen cents an hour, and clean houses. The lady I cleaned for had a sweeper for the carpets but it took two people to run it. We cleaned or carpet by spreading salt on it and sweeping it with a broom. We also made a rag rug for our floor, and put clean straw under it for warmth.

For entertainment there was square dancing almost every Saturday night, as well as church and box socials. Once a year, the Barnum and Bailey Circus came to Bluffton.

At eighteen I went to work at General Electric in Fort Wayne; I made sixty cents an hour.

In 1918 my brother George enlisted in World War I. On the ship there was an epidemic of flu, and several soldiers were buried at sea.

I married Fred Hoeppner October 21, 1922. Some neighbors boys put sand in the gas tank of Fred's Car when he was supposed to get married, and he had to borrow car.

We did not have a washer for two years. We bought furniture for $972.57 and it took five years to pay for it.

To this union were born Eileen Evelyn Hoeppner in 1924, and Gayle Elizabeth Hoeppner in 1929. We moved to Bluffton in March of 1926. Fred started a sheet metal business there.

In 1929, there were three banks in Bluffton when the depression hit. You couldn't buy a loaf of bread without cash. A lot of people lost their homes.

We moved to E. Wiley Avenue, paying $2500. It was then the only house on the block.

Sometimes Fred was paid for his work with ducks and pigs. We have lived in our present home sixty years to date. Fred passed away June 2, 1983. Cora Hoeppner still resides on East Wiley to date.

KAY MOUNSEY FAMILY

Kay was born April 2, 1931, the son of Victor and Grace (Lockwood) Mounsey of Poneto, Indiana. His father is deceased and his mother is living at Swiss Village in Berne, Indiana.

Kay married Shirley Platt, who was born February 25, 1932, the daughter of Clarence and Grace (Deer) Platt of Uniondale, Indiana. Her father is deceased, and her mother is living at her home of rural Uniondale.

Kay and Shirley married April 21, 1956, at the Church of Christ in Markle, Indian. They were the parents of four children.

Randy Kay was born March 16, 1957, and died at birth.

Kelly Jean was born March 15, 1959.

Kevin Lynn was born May 31, 1960, and he died from a car accident October 9, 1976. Kerry Lee was born September 19, 1963.

Kay and Shirley lived in Indiana the first twenty years of their married life. Kay working for the W.T. Grant Co. for seventeen years. When the company filed Chapter 11, Kay had to seek new employment. He took a job with the Lowell Supply Company in Bloomington, Illinois, and we moved to Danvers, Illinois in 1976.

Kelly graduated from Norwell High School in 1977. She lived with her Grandmother Platt, during her senior year. She moved to Illinois after graduation. She met and married Douglas Wellenrieter, on August 4, 1979, in Bloomington, Illinois. They have two daughters, Brooke age eight, and Bria age five. Doug is a school teacher and coach at Momence High School, and they are living in Kankakee, Illinois.

Kay took a job with Pioneer Hig-Bred International in January 1985, therefore moving to Princeton, Illinois.

Kerry graduated from Princeton High School in 1982 and from Illinois Community College in 1984. Kerry married Jodi (Schmidt) Mounsey, April 20, 1985, in Princeton, Illinois. They have two daughters, Megan, four and one-half, Cortney, two and one-half. Kerry started with Pioneer part-time in high school and is still working full-time for Pioneer. They live in Ankany, Iowa. Kay worked for Pioneer in Princeton for five years and when the company reorganized, the Princeton office was closed, and Kay was transferred to Pioneer in Johnston, Iowa. In June of 1986 we bought a home in Urbandale, Iowa where we now reside.

MOUNSEYS

James Perry Mounsey and Sarah Ann McNatt, married in 1879, lived two miles south and one and one-half miles west of Liberty Center. Perry's father, John, born in 1812 in Cumberland County, England, came to the states in 1830 with his older sister Mary and her husband, Atkinson Edgar. John settled in Wells County in 1840 with his wife Caroline Stratton. To them were born Thomas, Miami, Hiram, and John. After Caroline's death, he married Eliza Merriman, also of English descent. Their children were Elijah, James Perry, George, William Bruce, and Mary Ann (Osborne). One of John's favorite stories was how he crossed the Mississinewa River on the ice with a team of horses and a large sled on his way to Grant County for corn during the worst winter in memory, that of 1844.

James Perry Mounsey House in Liberty Township Wells County built 1895

Jams Perry and Sarah Ann (McNatt) Mounsey along Claude, Victor, Charles, their wives and children.

Perry and Sarah first settled on brother Elijah's farm, but three years later moved into an old hewed log house he bought and moved to eighty acres John had given him. Their fifth child, Claude, was born in 1894. In 1895, Perry built a handsome nine room, two-story house with a rambling porch on three sides, framed by "ginger bread" trim. The house had a water storage tank in the attic supplied by a windmill driven pump that also pumped water for the cattle. Thus Sarah had a sink and running water in the kitchen. The house was lathed and plastered by another early Liberty Township resident, John E. Beaty.

In those days, the stock came first so three years previously, Perry built a 40x70 frame barn with center entry and full length haymows. He raised beef cattle and work horses as well as practicing general farming. He wintered fifteen to twenty head of yearling draft horses for sale the following spring.

Perry and Sarah's children were Lillie, Lula, Floyd, Charles, Claude, Victor, and Mabel. Floyd and Mabel died as infants. Charles married and moved to Fort Wayne. Victor married Grace Lockwood and farmed all eighty-seven years of his life. Lillie married George Helms of Huntington County. Lula married Cyrus Pane of Chester Township. Claude married Mae Beaty, daughter of John and Belle Huffman Beaty, of Liberty Township. Claude and Mae bought a three-room frame house in Warren for $600, and moved it to Perry's farm. The house was never painted and had no insulation. When Claude was elected county treasurer, the family moved to Bluffton. During the 1929 Depression, Claude and the county sheriff transported checks and cash between and treasurer's office and the few banks that were open in surrounding towns. A loaded shotgun was their constant companion.

Perry remained healthy and active into his late seventies until he fell from the haymow and partially crushed his ankles. Walking was then a problem so he retired to his Morris chair smoking cigars and telling stories. One of these was of the corduroy road extending one mile west from the Africa school and church. Any buggy or wagon traveling that road could be heard a mile away.

After the treasurer's office, Claude worked for the Federal Land Bank of Louisville, Kentucky, for thirty years, eventually moving to Louisville. He retired at 70 and moved back to Bluffton where he and Mae resided at 1010 Summit until their deaths, Mae in 1978 and Claude in 1980.

Claude had kept the farm and added acreage for fifty years. Now he enjoyed spending time with the tenant farmer of many years, Bob Westfall, feeding the pigs and visiting about farm matters. Mae, who had become a nationally accredited flower judge, divided her time between her flowers and tracing the ancestors. Claudine, Robert, Claude, Jr., and Joyce remember their father as a cheerful, hardworking, and fun loving father. Their memories of Mae are of her concern for her children and her lifelong love of flowers.

MOWERY-MINNICH

Our family beginnings in Wells County date back to 1864, when Great Grandfather Peter Mowery came to Harrison Township. He purchased land in Section 25 in the year 1865. Great-grandfather Mower married Lydia King in Pickaway County, Ohio, in the year 1849. Their children were: Ezra, Allen, George Franklin, Williston, Minerva Catherine, Amos, Samuel Nathan and Lydia Ann.

Samuel Nathan, our grandfather, was born November 29, 1866, and was married in February, 1888, to Mary Reynolds, whose parents were William and Elizabeth Chalfant Reynolds. Children of Samuel and Mary were: Charles R., Ethel Mae, Edith Fay, Howard Amos, Bertha M, Walter W., and Earl R.

Front: Ethel (Mowery) Minnich and Oscar E. Minnich. Seated: Clara, Mary Jane, Wayne and Floyd. Standing: Clarence and Harold.

Ethel Mae, our mother was born July 27, 1891, and married our father, Oscar Earl Minnich, on December 11, 1909. Children born to this union were Clara Irene, who married Harold Perry Andrews and had eight children: Clarence Earl, who married Mildred Neuenschwander and had five children: Chester Wayne, who married Marjorie Stram and had two children, Harold Amos, who married Lucrecia Burger and had three children: Floyd LaVerne, who married Marilyn Maddux and had three children: and Mary Jane, who married David G. Park and had two children.

Sister Clara and brothers Chester Wayne and Clarence E. are now deceased. Harold is a resident of Wilshire, Ohio, and is retired from Meshberger Stone Company.

Our father, Oscar Minnich, came to Wells County in the year 1906 and settled on a farm in Lancaster Township near Craigville. He told about making at trip with his brother from Eaton in a wagon pulled by two horses and a work horse tied behind. The trip took two days.

Samuel and Nancy Manerva Gump Minnich, our grandparents, were married February 26, 1887, in Eaton, Indian. They had lived in Darke County, Ohio, and Delaware County, Indiana. Children of Samuel and Nancy were Martha Annie, Oscar Earl, Hugh, Ora J., John Ervin and Mary Elizabeth.

Our parents met at church services at Six Mile Church southeast of Bluffton. Dad was a farm hand on the "Hannah Reiff" farm. Hannah's brick house still stands on the curve on route 116 near Riverside. They lived all their married lives in Harrison Township and were married nearly fifty-three years.

Floyd, the next to the youngest of the family of Oscar and Ethel Minnich, has resided in Wells County all his life. He is married to Marilyn Maddux and they have three children: Joe, who is married to Kim Shively; Tim, who is married to Lori James; and Cynthia Minnich. Floyd is co-owner of Graden Tire Company on West Cherry Street, Bluffton.

Mary Jane, the youngest of the family, moved with her family to Illinois and back again to Bluffton. She is married to David G. Park and they have two children: Karen S. Karwoski, who is married to Don Karwoski; and Kent, who is married to Penny Croy. Mary Jane and Dave are owners of Carnall and Sons, Insurance Agency and John W. Carnall and Sons, Land Title Company, located on South Johnson Street in Bluffton.

JOHN K. MUGG

John Kerkoff Mugg came to Wells County in the fall of 1939 from Battle Ground, Indiana. John graduated from Purdue University with a teaching degree in Vocational Agriculture and Science. He secured his first teaching job at Lancaster Central School. John also worked with the 4-H program.

On May 10, 1941, John married Martha Beeker from Brookston, Indiana, near Lafayette. They took up permanent residence in Wells County following their marriage, living in various locations in Lancaster Township, Vera Cruz, and Bluffton. One of their locations was the former Jahn Funeral Home, now the home of the Wells County Historical Society Museum on Market Street.

John and Martha are the parents of three children. Becky was born in 1943, graduated from Lancaster Central in 1961, and attended Purdue University. Becky married and moved with her husband throughout the United States as he served in the United States Air Force. She has settled in Glendale, Arizona. Judy was born in 1947. She graduated from Lancaster in 1965 and from Ball

State University in 1969 with a degree in education. She moved to Warsaw, Indiana, to teach and is a school administrator for the Warsaw School System. The family name was continued when the fourth generation of John Mugg was born in 1952. John Steven, known as Steven, graduated in 1970, from Bluffton High School where his name appears in the record book in the area of cross country and track. Steve established a new mile record in his senior year. Steve graduated from Ball State University with a degree in elementary education. Steve married Rita O'Neil from Columbia City in June 1973. They established residence in Monroe, Indiana. Steve teaches at Adams Central School, and Rita is a science teacher at Norwell Middle School. John and Martha have three grandchildren: Chris Shady, the son of Becky; John Nathan, the fifth generation John Mugg, son of Steve and Rita; and Kelli Mugg, daughter of Steve and Rita.

John and Martha Mugg - 1990

John was involved in education at Lancaster Central for thirty years, teaching agriculture, shop, and science classes. While teaching at Lancaster, he was also involved in the Boy's 4-H program. Through school consolidation, John moved to Norwell High school, teaching there until he retired in 1979. John retired from teaching with a record that will be difficult to match. In his forty years of teaching he missed only one day of school for illness. In addition to teaching John has worked for J.C. Penney Company in Bluffton since 1951. He also assists at the Goodwin Memorial Chapel, the former Jahn Funeral Home.

Martha was a homemaker until all of their children were in school. She began working part time in the lab at the Hoosier Condensory on West Wilkey Avenue. She became a receptionist for Drs. Brickley, Meade, Hamilton, and Panos, on Main Street, where she worked until 1964. In 1964 she assumed the receptionist duties for Dr. Jess Scott, Optometrist. Martha retired from her receptionist duties with Dr. James VanWinkle, who took over from Dr. Scott in 1989.

Both John and Martha have been active in many civic and church groups within the Bluffton area. Martha is a dedicated blood donor and has received recognition for her generous contributions to the American Red Cross Bloodmobile, having donated over twelve gallons. Martha is also active in the Hospital Auxiliary at the Wells Community Hospital. John has been involved in various community projects with the Historical Society and currently serves on the Wells County Council. John was named Wells County Senior Citizen in May, 1988. They are members of St. Joseph Catholic Church in Bluffton, Indiana.

MULLES FAMILY

Claude E. Mulles was born October 10, 1910, to Sylvester E. Mulles and Bessie (B. Hoopingarner) Mulles, Claude E. Mulles married Ruby (Herndon) August 6, 1932. They lived most of their married life in Wells County. They had two children. Claude graduated from Union Center, Wells County in 1930.

Barbara A. Mulles married Dwight Jennings. Barbara lives in Bluffton, Indiana. They had one daughter, Debi, who married Scott Shepler. They live in Marion, Indiana. Debi graduated from Norwell High School in 1973. Barbara, her mother, graduated from Union Center 1952. The Scott Sheplers have two daughters, Heather and Ashlae. Debi has taught art in a Marion, Indiana school since she graduated from Marion College in 1977.

Claude and Ruby Mulles 55th Wedding Anniversary -1987

Ronald K. Mulles married Kathy Johnson. Ron graduated from Union Center in 1960, he lives in Sacramento, California. He is chaplain of Sutter Hospital there. Ron and Kathy have two children. Carrie married Paul Moreland. They have one son, Jonathan. They live in Portland, Oregon.

Rick Mulles also lives in Portland, Oregon. He graduated from Vancouver, Washington.

Claude E. Mulles retired from the Penn Central Railroad after thirty-two years of service. He and his wife, Ruby, live at Hobe Sound, Florida since 1983.

James E. Mulles, grandfather of Claude lived many years around Markle, Indiana. He married Mary Ann (Wolfcale). They had three children: Annie, Sylvester and Orla. James was born April 21, 1853. Mary Ann (Wolfcale) Mulles was born September 30, 1856.

William Isaac Mulles and Rebecca (Nicholson) Mulles are the parents of James E. Mulles. They were born in Irdle County, North Carolina. They moved to Indiana, October 6, 1867 near Markle, Indiana in Rockcreek, Wells County. They both are buried in Horeb Cemetery, Wells County.

Claude E. Mulles has a brother, Clarence, and two sisters, Wava and Doris.

MURRAY

In 1926 Phebe and Homer Murray came to Bluffton from the Panama Canal Zone. Her father, William B. Jordan, was a railroad conductor there. Homer had been a left-handed pitcher in the Western League and was sent by the government to Panama to organize a league there. They operated a jewelry store in Bluffton.

Homer died in 1944 after a long illness. Phebe, a nurse's aide at the clinic, later was city clerk treasurer. She died in office on June 27, 1958, of a stroke at age 62. They had tree sons: Homer, James, and Jordan.

Homer born July 12, 1915, graduated from Indiana University as a journalist. He was in the Canadian and U.S. Air Forces in World War II. He married Anna Jane McCammon. He was an editor for Fort Wayne Journal-Gazette when he died October 13, 1972. Jane works for the council on aging. They have three children:

David, born June 7, 1949, graduated from Murray State University and received JD and MBA degrees from Creighton University. He is president of Medical Mutual in Maryland. He married Cindy Pond and has three children: Patrick, born July 2, 1979, Gregory, born June 2, 1982, and Ben, born August 30, 1985.

Pierre, born May 14, 1951 earned a mechanical engineering degree from Rose-Hullman and MBA from Northwestern. He is vice-president of McLean-Fog (specialty fastener manufacturing) near Chicago. He married Sue Hiller and has three children: Brian, born July 19, 1979, Jennifer, born March 28, 1982, and Kevin, born August 1, 1984.

Laura, born September 1, 1953, a nurse, is married to Paul Zimmerman, a minister. They live in Colorado with their two boys, Timmy, born November 24, 1982 and Andrew, born August 20, 1984.

James, born August 25, 1917, graduated from Ball State, was a lieutenant, J.G., in the Navy in World War II, married Mary Tonner (graduate of Ball State and Bluffton Elementary teacher), and was a teacher and/or principal at Ossian, Union, Poplar Grove, Ft. Wayne schools, EBV in Maracaibo, Venezuela, and East Side Elementary. He was Lion's Club president, city councilman, and an American Legion baseball coach. Both were active in First United Church of Christ. Jim retired in 1978 to live on Lake Tippecanoe and in Englewood, Florida. On January 16, 1987, Jim died of cancer. On January 2, 1988 Mary married Charles Webb. Jim and Mary's children: Kay, born May 9, 1946, graduated from Ball State University. She lived five years in Spain, Germany and Peru and married Leonardo Villa-Garcia, whom she met in Peru while on Rotary Fellowship. They are Spanish and German professors in North Carolina. Kay had her first baby, Isabel Maria, on May 12, 1990, at age 44.

Phebe Murray with sons Homer, James and Jordan

Judy, born November 26, 1948, married Jerry Anderson. They both graduated from Ball State University and earned master's from St. Francis. Judy taught in elementary school and is now an admissions director. Jerry was a music director and is now a middle school dean-counselor in Fort Wayne. They have three children, Holli, born June 7, 1957, Jamie, born May 11, 1977, and Ben, born November 9, 1983.

Cathy, born April 30, 1952, graduated from Indiana University, married Greg Grigsby, and teaches art in Bridgton, Maine. Greg is a school counselor. She has one son Aaron, born April 6, 1978. Greg has two sons, Matt, born July 12, 1973 and Geoff, born October 11, 1975.

Ted, born February 14, 1954, was on the tennis team at Ball State three years before joining PBI and assigned to Hawaii, Jakarta, Mexico, Puerto Rico, and India as a teaching pro. He's now the tennis pro at a club near Atlanta. December 29, 1986 he married Shikha Naha, a teacher, from India.

Jordan, born July 9, 1919, graduated from University of Arizona as metallurgical engineer. He was an Air Force pilot in World War II. He married Betty Stafford, who worked at the News Banner. He worked for U.S. Potash in Carlsbad, New Mexico, and Davy Engineering in Lakeland, Florida, who sent him to Africa and Germany to design chemical plants. They have three children:

Susan, born March 3, 1946, a nurse married to Chuck Kirkeby lives in Colorado. Daughter Sonja, born October 25, 1970, is currently in the Air Force and stationed in Frankfort, Germany.

Melody, born April 21, 1949, now divorced, is a nurse working in Tampa.

Jimmy, born October 24, 1953, graduated from Rollins College and is working in the post office in Merritt Island, Florida. He married Mary Jockasch and has three boys, David, born September 29, 1979, Andrew, born July 13, 1981, and Joshua, born March 30, 1983.

Left to right: Raymond Johnston, Charley Snow, Josie Bennett, Alfred Murray, Stella Murray, Myrtle Snow, Ida Johnston, Zern Murray, Harry Bennett, Hamilton Murray, Sarah Murray holding Wilma Bennett, Grandmother Robey, Clarence Snow, Bob Snow, Garnet Snow.

MURRAY

Hamilton Murray was born July 31, 1860 and died January 14, 1933. Sarah Rhoby was born January 12, 1861 and died July 3, 1935. They were married on October 9, 1883 and were the parents of seven children. A daughter Carol died in infancy. So many families lost babies during those years.

Albert Ray (Jack) Murray born March 3, 1891 - died December 12, 1953

The oldest child was named Josie who was born August 15, 1885 and died January 1955. Josie married Harry Bennett and they were parents of four children. Wilma Bennett was their first child and she married a Ramseyer. They were parents of four children: Delores, Pauline, Howard and Marilyn.

Josie and Harry's second daughter was Faye who married a Hudson and they had three children: Sharon, Clyde and Rick.

Edna Bennett married a Gavin and they had five children: Bob, Betty, Bill, Jerry and Connie.

Nellie Bennett married Howard Miller and they were parents of Carolyn, Larry, Terry and Diana.

Myrtle Murray was born February 4, 1888 and died August 19, 1975. She married Charles Snow and they were the parents of Garnet, Clarence and Bob. Garnet married a Lehman who had one daughter, Barbara Ann. Clarence had no children. Bob had two children, Robert J. and Juaniece.

Alfred Murray was the third child of Hamilton and Sarah Murray and was born March 13, 1889 and died April, 1946. He married Stella Starr and they were parents of seven children. Four died, Ethel, Oscar, Virgil and Martha Rose. Wayne married and had two sons, Fred and Jerry. Fred had two children Jennifer and Jason. Jerry had two children also and they were Mike and Jill.

Virginia Murray married Paul Griffin. Robert Murray and his wife Rita had one daughter Linda.

The fourth child of Hamilton and Sarah Murray was Albert (Jack) Murray who was born March 3, 1891 and died December 12, 1953. He married Edith Howard and they were parents of one daughter, Ramona, born October 9, 1919. She married Wilborne Garton and they became parents of three sons, Jack, Rick and Dan.

Ida Murray was born November 17, 1894 and died November 23, 1990. Ida married Raymond Johnson and they were parents of two children. Eunice Johnson married Ray Beighler and they were parents of four children: Jim, Alice, Howard and Patricia. Ida and Raymond had a second child, a son, named Ira Eugene.

Zern Murray was the sixth child of Hamilton and Sarah Murray. He married Daisy Walker and they had one daughter, Wanda. Wanda married John Blair and they had three children: Sandra, Muriel and Tim.

Entertainment consisted of harnessing a calf to a cart and persuading a sister to climb in, then turning it loose in the apple orchard while it ran pell-mell between the trees, hopefully!

Churches were used for worship AND entertainment. Wheels were removed from buggies which were hoisted to the roof-top during 'meeting' times.

ELMO AND LENA MURRELL

In March of 1956, Elmo and Lena Murrell and their three children moved from Fort Wayne, Indiana, to Wells County. They purchased the one hundred twenty acre farm, located on county road 1000 North in Union Township, from the estate of Christian Rutenberg. From our house we could see the old Union Center School which all three children attended. They were all born in Fort Wayne, Indiana.

Son Richard Allen graduated from Lancaster High School in 1965, from Indiana University and then Indiana University School of Medicine. He is now a cardio-vascular surgeon living in Evansville, Indiana, with his wife, Kathy and two daughters, Lauren Allen and Sarah Allison.

Second son, Michael David, graduated from Norwell in 1970, from Indiana University and Christian Theological Seminary. He is an ordained minister. He served churches in Indiana and is now living in Fort Wayne with his wife, Debra and son Zachary and daughter Lindsey.

Our daughter, Rebecca Ann, was one year old when we moved to Wells County. She is a graduate of Norwell High School (1973) and has a teaching degree from Indiana University. She has taught in Wells County at Lancaster and Ossian Elementary. In June of 1973, she married Travis Holdman. They then served eighteen months on the mission field in Haiti. They returned to Wells County and Travis became the Welfare Director for the county. In September of 1988, they moved to Indianapolis so that Travis could attend Indiana Law School. He has graduated, passed his bar and is now affiliated with a Bluffton law firm. They are living in Wells County with their two children, LeAnne Renee and Wesley Travis.

Elmo was working for United States Rubber Co. when they decided to leave Fort Wayne. It was then that he formed his own company and operated in Fort Wayne as Protective Coatings from 1958 until his retirement in 1987. Michael is now very active in the business. Lena worked for North American Van Lines in Fort Wayne for twenty-five years, retiring in 1985. The family is very active in the Zanesville United Methodist Church.

MUTH, KELLOGG FAMILIES

Elizabeth Muth, born 1823, in Wheeling, West Virginia, was the daughter of Lewis Bayha, who was a double first cousin of George Bayha. George moved to Bluffton in 1852. Elizabeth's husband, John Muth, died in 1886. In May, 1888, she and two daughters, Louise and Elizabeth, moved to Bluffton to be near Mrs. F.N. Kellogg another daughter. A son, William Muth, lived in Montana. Rose married Dr. G.E. Fulton after they moved to Bluffton.

Francis Nelson Kellogg, born at the corner of Cherry and Main in 1843 was the son of Nelson and

Rachel Kellogg. He learned early the trade of printer on the People's Press, the first Republican newspaper in the county, published by his father.

Rose Kellogg and Billy

He served three years in the Civil War. When he returned he again joined his father in the newspaper trade. He was postmaster of Bluffton from 1869 to 1875. After 1875 he again engaged in the printing business until his death.

Nelson Kellogg, the father of Francis Nelson Kellogg, was born 1807 of Scotch and German ancestry, in Virginia. He moved to Bluffton in 1839, worked as a mason until 1856, then started a newspaper, The People's Press, which lasted until 1861. He became postmaster from 1861 to 1866. He was a Justice of the Peace for eighteen years. In 1849 he was elected the first mayor of Bluffton and again in 1868 he was mayor. He was deputy postmaster under his son F.N. Kellogg from 1869 to 1875.

F.N. Kellogg married Rose Muth, daughter of Elizabeth, in 1877. They had two children, Fannie and William Kellogg.

Fannie Kellogg born 1878, was a competent newspaper worker for the old Weekly Chronicle and the Evening News of Bluffton. She was the first woman typesetter in Bluffton. She composed news stories and ads by hand setting the type.

She learned to run the Simplex machine and then the Linotype. She was very skilled in her work. She was the first society editor as usually the Bluffton papers employed men and boys to scout the streets for news. She was an assidous worker, versatile and knew all phases of the newspaper work. She was seventy-eight at the time of her death.

The only son of F.N. and Rose Kellogg was William, born 1890, died 1946. He was a copy editor for the News Sentinel in Fort Wayne at the time of his death, but his early training started in Bluffton.

He was a newspaper man for thirty-seven years in Bluffton, Indianapolis, and Fort Wayne. He worked on the Bluffton News from 1909 to 1917, then joined the 344th Field Artillery, 14th Division in World War I. When he returned he worked on the Journal Gazette from 1914 to 1922. Part of the time he worked on the Evening Press edition of that paper as city editor.

He worked at Indianapolis on the News and Star from 1922 to 1929. He returned to Fort Wayne as city editor on the Journal Gazette then joined the News Sentinel as copy editor in 1936.

MYERS

We can date the Myers family back to 1823. Joseph Myers was born in Clark County, Ohio; his parents Abraham and Susannah Myers, were natives of Maryland and Pennsylvania. Joseph Myers worked as a farm laborer in Ohio until 1853, when he came to Wells County, Indiana. He located on one hundred sixty acres in Chester Township. In 1854 he was married to Nancy Jones, they had six children: James B. Myers, George R. Myers Nancy Elizabeth Myers, William Alfred Myers, Maggie Myers and Daniel Myers.

William Alfred Myers was born May 24, 1862, Wells County, Indiana. He married Anna E. Herrmann on May 4, 1889. William A. and Anna lived on one hundred sixty acres in Chester Township where he was a farmer all of his life. Anna died January 31, 1940 and William A. died June 20, 1944. They were the parents of two sons, Cleophas (C.E.) Myers born January 31, 1890 and Cary McKinley born November 22, 1899.

Cleophas married Virgie Nina Marie (Risley) daughter of Franklin and Mary Alice (Watson) Risley of Keystone, Indiana on March 23, 1912. They resided on a 160-acre farm in Chester Township until he retired and moved to Bluffton in 1971. Cleophas died February 17, 1985. Marie is ninety-five years of age and living at the Christian Care Center in Bluffton.

Their children were: Mary Lucille Myers born October 16, 1912, married Amos (Stook) Levy, March 8, 1941, passed away August 3, 1987. They had a son Robert Allen Levy born July 27, 1946, who lives in Bluffton. Winifred Elaine Myers born March 24, 1920, married Charles Weterick, July 5, 1945. They reside in Bluffton, and their three children are: Cheryl Combs of Decatur, Indiana, born April 28, 1947; John R. Weterick of Fort Wayne, Indiana, born July 14, 1951 and Joe N. Weterick of Bluffton, born October 14, 1958. Beth (Betty) Myers born May 12, 1922, passed away February 1, 1989. Herman Watson Myers born December 17, 1926 married Sandra A. Brotherton of Dunkirk, Indiana, on August 3, 1958. Their children are William Herman Myers of Portland, Indiana, born June 1, 1959, and Carolyn Jane Myers of Fort Wayne, Indiana, born September 19, 1961. Herman W. Myers, retired March 21, 1989, from the Old-First National Bank in Bluffton, having worked for the bank for forty years, retiring as senior vice-president and cashier. Herman is a member of the board of directors of the bank, a member of the board of directors of the Huntington Mutual Insurance Company of Huntington, Indiana. Herman is secretary of the Bluffton Free Street Fair having served for several years, also a member of the board. In the past he served as a director of the Wells County Foundation, the Chamber of Commerce, United Way of Wells county and on committees of various organizations of Bluffton and Wells County.

Herman and Sandra's son, William Herman Myers, followed his father footsteps in the banking profession, employed at the Peoples Bank, Portland, Indiana. William married Darci Gilbert of Portland, Indiana, August 8, 1988. They are the parents of twin boys George Herman and Jay William, born January 30, 1991.

MYERS 1823-1990

Joseph L. Myers (born July 13, 1823) came to Wells County, Chester Township in the fall of 1853 from Clark County, Ohio, his birthplace, to the one hundred sixty acres he had purchased on March 18, 1850.

His parents, Abraham and Susannah (Pence) Myers, were natives of Maryland and Pennsylvania.

In 1854 Joseph married Mary Jones, a daughter of Michael and Nancy Jones. Their six children were: James B., George R., Nancy E., William A., Maggie and Daniel. When William Alfred Myers, born May 24, 1862, in Wells County, married Anna E. Hermann in 1889, he was given the original house Joseph had built and some farm land. Their children were Cleophas and Cary M.

Cary McKinley Myers and Nellie Marie Carnes were married in 1923 and eventually moved with their son William Robert to the home place in 1944. William Robert and Bobette (Boswell) Myers married in 1960 and have three children.

Randall L. and Sandra K. (Myers) Slaughter and children, Clayton Harmon, age ten, and Tawny Marie, age seven, live near Sweester, Indiana. Richard K. Myers is from Brooklyn, New York, and Jeffrey L. and Linda F. (Collins) Myers and children, Kristen Rae, age two and Adam Robert, age one, live in the state of Washington.

MYERS FAMILY

The Myers family has been active in business in Bluffton for almost ninety years over three generations. In 1890, Asa and Anna Myers with their children Ora, Dillon, Earl, Gracia, and Eleia came to Bluffton from Warren and established a greenhouse business in the 600 block of West Market Street named City Greenhouse.

Asa Lemon Myers was born in Guernsey County, Ohio, on May 4, 1845, a son of Michael and Eleia (Lemmon) Myers. His brothers and sister were William, Nancy, and Frank. Asa Myers married Annalysa Luce on July 27, 1865, in Burnettsville, White County, Indiana. She was born in Green County, Ohio, on April 11, 1848, a daughter of Lucius and Nancy Ann (Ireland) Luce. Before coming to Bluffton, Asa Myers was in the sawmill business with his brother Frank in Warren and two other locations along the Salamonie River.

In 1902 the greenhouses were moved to a new location on Wabash Avenue (today North Oak Street Extended) and in 1911 the business was renamed Myers and Company. On June 7, 1921, Asa Myers died and Dillon Myers purchased the business from the heirs and renamed it Myers Floral Company. Anna Myers died August 26, 1932.

Dillon M. Myers was born on August 20, 1873, in White County, Indiana. He served in the Spanish-American War in Company E, 160th Regiment from Wells County. He married Katherine Mae Clark, daughter of Jacob and Henrietta (Kreisher) Clark on September 12, 1905, in Ashland, Ohio. She was born March 9, 1882 in Ashland, Ohio. Her brothers and sister were Harry, Charles and Jessie Clark.

Dillon Myers was very active in the business and civic affairs of Bluffton and was president of the Chamber of Commerce and Historical Society. He served as vice-president for the Wells County Centennial observance in 1937. He was active in the Kiwanis Club serving as its president and surveyed and marked the route of the Kiwanis Trail along the Salmonie River in Wells and Huntington County. Dillon Myers died on April 18, 1943, and the greenhouse business was sold to Herman Schumacker. Katherine Myers died February 2, 1956.

Dillon and Katherine Myers had two sons, Clark and Charles. Charles J. Myers was born in Bluffton on January 17, 1913, and graduated from Bluffton High School in 1930. He was married to his classmate Florence Mae Davison, daughter of Mont and Iva (Gourley) Davison on June 28, 1930. She was born May 9, 1912, in Uniondale. Charles Myers started Myers Gun Shop in 1940 and ran the business until his death on December 7, 1974. A skilled craftsman, his custom rifles are highly prized by gun collectors. Florence Myers continued the business until November 1978 when she retired. She died March 11, 1989.

Charles and Florence Myers had two sons, Charles J. Jr., born 1932, who is an electrical engineer and the superintendent of the electric utility at Anderson, Indiana, and Robert J., born 1935, of Fort Wayne who is now retired.

JACOB AND MARTHA MYERS FAMILY

Jacob and Martha Myers came from Pennsylvania to settle in Murray during the middle of the 1800's. Their children were Simeon, Joseph, Orran, Benjamine, James, William, Martha, Elizabeth, Lucy, Louise, and Sara. Some of the children died young. Simeon, Benjamine, and William migrated to the Chillicothe and Kansas City, Missouri area. The rest lived in the Wells or Allan County area. Several are buried in the Murray Cemetery.

Joseph moved to Bluffton and married Lucria Shreve. Their children were: Rose, Joseph, Grace, Martha, Jerry, and Lloyd. Two other children died early in life. Rose married Freeman Stroup and moved to Ottawa, Ohio. Joseph married Grace Grove and was a businessman in Huntington, Indiana. Grace married the Rev. Chalker and upon his death, William Wasson, living in Bluffton. Martha married John Lowry and lived in Fort Wayne, Indiana. Jerry married Mae Parrish and became a plumber in Bluffton for most of his life. Lloyd married Mary Dean Stech and was a traction line employee and later a postal employee. Rose Stroup had two children that lived to maturity, Devona and Helen. Jerry had a daughter, Emedele. Lloyd had two children, Robert Samuel and Sara Lee. Rose, Joseph, Grace, ad Jerry are buried in the Fairview Cemetery. Lloyd is buried in the Elm Grove Cemetery. Martha Lowry is buried in Lindenwood Cemetery, Fort Wayne.

The first Joseph was active in early Bluffton business circles, having owned and operated at times the stone quarry just east of Highway 1 on Highway 124. He housed the horses used to work it in a large barn on his property at 214 W. Central. He constructed the home there in 1881, and it is still owned by descendants. Stone from the quarry was used in the weights of the original court house clock. He also owned and operated a wooden hoop mill for making barrel hoops on the east side of Marion Street a half block north of Wabash Avenue. While gone for dinner one day, the steam boiler exploded landing well over on Wabash Avenue. He did not rebuild, but instead, purchased a more modern hoop mill at a location on West Wiley Street near the railroad. It became a good investment because of its modern efficiency. On the properties on Marion Street he constructed three identical houses. He was active as a commander of the local GAR post.

NAHRWOLD

Johann Daniel and Marie Christine Louise (Kolte) Nahrwold were the parents of Friedrich Christian Nahrwold, who was born on July 26, 1793, in Germany, and who later became a farmer in Germany. On July 22, 1812, Friedrich married Christine Wilhelmine (Meyers), and they had three children prior to her death on June 20, 1833. Thereafter, Friedrich married Christine Wilhelmine Louise (Reinking), who was born on January 27, 1811, the daughter of Johann Ernest and Marie Catharine Elisabeth (Westenfeld) Reinking. Friedrich and Christine (Reinking) Nahrwold were the parents of three children: Conrad Friedrich Wilhelm Nahrwold, who was born on July 21, 1838, in Westphalia, Germany; Christian Nahrwold (1842-1923); and Carl Nahrwold (1846-1913). Friedrich Nahrwold died on December 6, 1857.

Conrad Nahrwold immigrated to America in 1867, when he was twenty-nine years of age, and thereafter he was employed at the Pennsylvania Shops in Fort Wayne, Indiana, for thirty consecutive years. He married Sophie Wiegman, in Fort Wayne, Indiana, on June 13, 1870, who was the daughter of Karl Wiegman, and was born on April 22, 1848, in Germany, and came to America when she was sixteen years of age. Conrad and Sophie Nahrwold lived in Fort Wayne, Indiana, and were the parents of four children: Wilhelmine Nahrwold (April 13, 1871-August 22, 1886); Charles Fredrick "Karl F." Nahrwold (June 12, 1873-March 2, 1929); Sophie Nahrwold (March 12, 1878-December 4, 1881); and Carolina "Lena" (Nahrwold) Werling (February 14, 1892-April 10, 1981). (Carolina married Rudolph Werling on September 7, 1916, and they had five children). Conrad and Sophie purchased a one hundred-and-twenty acre farm in Jefferson Township, Wells County, Indiana, from William and Francina Rupright for $5, 600.00 on April 8, 1897, where they resided until their deaths. Conrad Nahrwold died on February 1, 1915, while Sophie Nahrwold died on March 26, 1931. Both are buried in Bethlehem Lutheran Cemetery, Ossian, Indiana.

NAHRWOLD-BULMAHN

On April 9, 1946, Dennis Lynn Nahrwold was born. He is the son of William C. and Marie E. (Franz) Nahrwold. He graduated from Ossian High School in 1964 and received a degree in tool and die making. He worked for Melching Machine Shop, Ossian, and General Electric, Fort Wayne, for several years. In 1982, he took up farming and gave up his job in town. His hobbies are trap and skeet shooting and bowling.

On August 12, 1967, he married Maxine Ann Bulmahn of Preble Township, Adams County, Indiana. She was born October 15, 1947, and is the daughter of Hugo and Florence (Marbach) Bulmahn. She graduated from Monmouth High School in 1965. She is a full-time homemaker and her hobbies are quilting, sewing, and gardening.

Dennis and Maxine have been blessed with three children, Diane, Julia, and Thomas.

Diane June was born July 4, 1968. She graduated valedictorian of her 1986 Class of Norwell High School. She graduated from Purdue University in 1990 with a degree in Mathematics/Statistics. Presently, she is employed as an Actuarial Consultant at Lincoln National Life Insurance Company in Fort Wayne. While at Purdue University, she served as president and treasurer of Purdue's Actuary Club.

Julia Kay was born March 24, 1970. She graduated in the top ten of the 1988 Class of Norwell High School. Presently, she is a junior at Ball State University pursuing a degree in Accounting. She is a member of the Accounting Club at Ball State University. She studied piano for many years under the direction of Mrs. John Pease.

Thomas Lee was born September 24, 1974. Presently, he is a sophomore at Norwell High School. His hobbies are hunting, trapping, and fishing. He is also a member of the 4-H Rifle Safety Club.

NAHRWOLD-FRANZ

William Conrad Nahrwold was born February 27, 1911. He was the sons of Charles and Anna (Werling) Nahrwold. On October 14, 1939, he married Marie Emma Franz. She was born on November 4, 1916, and was the daughter of Albert and Emma (Kukelhan) Franz. They have one son, Dennis Lynn, who was born on April 9, 1946. He married Maxine Bulmahn on August 12, 1967. They have three grandchildren, Diane, Julia, and Thomas. In 1989, they celebrated their 50th wedding anniversary.

William and Marie Nahrwold - 1987

At the time of William and Marie's marriage, they rented an 80 acre farm, two mile NE of Tocsin, from William's Uncle William and Aunt Mary Werling. In 1948, they purchased this farm and still reside there. He farmed all of his life and raised chickens, cows, horses, pigs, and sheep at one time. He presently is retired.

Marie is a full-time homemaker. She is a member of the Ladies' Aid and enjoys quilting with them. Her hobby is growing flowers, and has served 16 years on the Ladies' Aid Altar Guild.

They both are members of Bethlehem Lutheran Church.

NAHRWOLD-HEUER

Carl Nahrwold was born April 6, 1918, in Wells County, Indiana, to Charles Fredrick "Karl F." and Anna (Werling) Nahrwold. He was born on the family homestead and still lives there. "Karl F." and his sons, William and Carl, farmed the land.

Carl attended Bethlehem Lutheran and Tocsin School. When Carl's father, "Karl F." Nahrwold died March 2, 1929, William and Carl had to do the farming with the help of their mother. William was eighteen years old and Carl was ten. They farmed this way together even after William married Marie Franz in 1939. They split the partnership in 1984, each farming his own ground; William with his son Dennis, and Carl with his son-in-law, Tom Patrick.

Anna, Carl's mother, and her two daughters, Clara and Paula, still at home, moved to a new home she had built for them in Fort Wayne, Indiana on Winter Street. Carl married Helen Heuer, born April 5, 1920, the daughter of John and Amanda (Bleeke) Heuer, on June 22, 1946. Helen was born in Root Township, Adams County, Indiana. She attended St. Peter Lutheran School, and graduated from Monmouth High School in 1938. She was employed at the Federal Land Bank Office in Decatur, Indiana from 1938-1942. From 1942-1946 she worked at the First State Bank of Decatur.

Carl and Helen Nahrwold

They had three children. Colleen Sue Nahrwold, born May 18, 1949, attended Bethlehem Lutheran School, Ossian, for eight years. She graduated from Ossian High School in 1967. Colleen married Thomas Lynn Patrick, (born January 27, 1950) on February 12, 1972. Tom was employed at General Electric, Decatur, Indiana for over twenty years until the plant closed. He also farmed, and continues to do so. Colleen was employed at Fort Wayne Wire Die for nine years, then was a homemaker. They have three children: Mark Allen (August 3, 1972), Jodie Lynn (June 15, 1978), and Darren Thomas (May 6, 1988).

Cynthia Ann Nahrwold, born February 11, 1954, attended Bethlehem Lutheran School for eight years. She graduated from Norwell High School in 1972. She graduated from Ball State University with honors, and received a BA in English in 1977. She continued her education at Arizona State University in Tempe, Arizona, receiving her master's degree in English (Linguistics) and Composition in 1984 while teaching at ASU. Since 1984 she has been employed at Briar Cliff College in Sioux City, Iowa, where she holds the position of Assistant Professor of English/Writing and Linguistics, and Director of the Writing Lab.

Michael Dean Nahrwold, born April 10, 1957, attended Bethlehem Lutheran School for eight years, and graduated from Norwell High School in 1975. He started classes at ITT Technical Institute in September, 1975. He was employed at Fort Wayne Electronics from 1977-1979. He graduated from ITT August 26, 1977, and started teaching electronics at ITT October 1, 1979.

Mike married Kathy Lynn Worden, (born November 21, 1958) on June 5, 1981. Kathy graduated from Norwell High School in 1977. She is a graduate of Indiana University, and is employed as a dental hygienist for Dr. Robert Arnold in Fort Wayne. They have two children, Brian Michael (October 28, 1988), and Sara Nicole (January 4, 1991).

Mike and Kathy built a new home on the corner of Nahrwold farm in 1987. In March, 1990, Carl and Helen purchased a farm of thirty-eight acres at a public auction. This farm was owned by Carl's sister, Minnie and her husband, Alvin Meyer. Both are deceased. The farm is located across the road from the Nahrwold homeplace.

NAHRWOLD-WERLING

Charles Fredrick "Karl F." Nahrwold was born June 12, 1873 to Conrad and Sophie (Wiegman) Nahrwold in Fort Wayne, Indiana, graduated from International Business College, and lived with his parents on Lewis Street in Fort Wayne, Indiana, until they moved to their farm on April 8, 1897. He married Anna Sophia Werling (born October 30, 1879) the daughter of Wilhelm and Elizabeth (Bieberich) Werling, in Adams County, Indiana, on April 14, 1907. From this union, seven children were born:

Linda (April 28, 1908) married Paul Grewe (August 15, 1903-September 23, 1987) on February 1, 1930, and had two daughters. Bernice married Eugene Myers and has two sons, David and Martin, who married Wendy Slim, and has two sons, Colin and Mason. Leah Ann married Michael Fifer, and has two children, Koren and Jesse.

Charles F. and Anna S. (Werling) Nahrwold - 1927

William (February 27, 1911) married Marie Franz (November 4, 1916) on October 14, 1939, and has one son: Dennis, who married Maxine Bulmahn and has three children: Diane, Julia, and Thomas.

Wilhelmina "Minnie" (June 7, 1913-April 21, 1983) married Alvin Meyer (May 22, 1911-December 27, 1989) on October 9, 1932, and had four children: (1) Wilbur, who married Ilene Fackler; has five children, Shelley (married Ted Ambriole, has one son, Tyler), Stanley (married Patricia Sprunger, has two daughters, Laura, and Kristen, Sanford, Sheldon (married Cindy Bradtmueller), and Sherry (married Tim Moser, has a daughter, Alicia); (2) Kenneth (married Eleanor Baatz, had five daughters, Rhonda (married Ronald Smith, has one daughter, Sarah), Pamela (married Dan Stinson), Amanda (married Robert Coburn, has two children Jessery and Jacob), Angela (married Bruce Phillips, has two daughters, Erin and Lisa), and Christina (married Gregory Buckland. Kenneth and Eleanor divorced, and he re-married Sandra Johnston, and had two more children, Timothy and Misty; (3) Doris Ann (married Dale Graft, has two sons, Jeffery (married Sherry Bishop, has one daughter, Tiffany), and Timothy; and (4) Sandra (married Paul Lydy, has two children, Kamilla (married Mark Shire, has three sons, Matthew, Dustin, and Derrick), and Richard).

Helen (September 26, 1915) married Elmer Franz (August 25, 1914-May 19, 1985) on May 17, 1941, and has two children: Janice married Larry Bultemeier, and has two children, Marci and Brett); James married Loretta Strader, and has four daughters, Angela, Elizabeth, Amanda, and Jennifer.

Carl (April 6, 1918), married Helen Heuer (April 5, 1920) on June 22, 1946, and has three children: Colleen married Thomas Patrick and has three children, Mark, Jodie, and Darren; Cynthia; Michael married Kathy Worden and has two children, Brian and Sara.

Clara (March 19, 1920) married Lloyd Scherer (September 22, 1919-February 4, 1985) on April 10, 1948, and has two children: Karen, who married John Casey and has a daughter, Erin, and step-son, John, Jr.; and Dale, who married Judith Fox and has one daughter, Megan.

Paula (June 17, 1923) married Raymond Franz (November 21, 1921) on July 31, 1948, and has one daughter, Jean.

Charles Fredrick "Karl F." Nahrwold died on March 2, 1929, and Anna Sophia (Werling) Nahrwold died on July 7, 1968. Both are buried in Bethlehem Lutheran Cemetery, Ossian, Indiana.

The farm purchased in 1897 by Conrad and Sophie Nahrwold still remains in the Nahrwold name, and is owned by Carl and Helen Nahrwold.

NASH

The house where Reuben Henry Nash was born, October 21, 1870, is still standing and occupied on US 224 near Tocsin in Jefferson Township, Wells County. He married Edessa (Sowards) in 1894. She was born in February of 1875 and died in February of 1915. Reuben died on September 16, 1954. Both are buried in Prairie Grove Cemetery near Tocsin. One of their seven children, Harry Wendell, born October 26, 1909, was married to Marguerite (Smith), born January 5, 1914. They were married October 5, 1935, and have two sons, Merlin Ray born July 27, 1940, and Dale Duane, born September 6, 1944.

The Nash family taken in 1985. Front row L to R (seated) Douglas 10, Tonya-16, Todd-7, Donna, Jennifer-13, Anna, Scott-18, Stephen-16. Back row L to R Dale, Harry, Marguerite, Merlin.

Merlin attended Ossian School five years and brother Dale one year before their parents moved to Lancaster Township. They both liked to help their father farm, especially when he would let them drive the tractor. Both were 4-H members with their project being "hogs". Merlin graduated from Lancaster High School in 1958, but commencement was held at Ossian School because Lancaster School was badly damaged by fire on April 16, 1958. School ended that day for the rest of the term. He served in the National Guard. For the past 26 years he worked at Sears. On February 27, 1965, he married Anna (Niswonger) who is an L.P.N. employed with Markle Medical Center. They live north of Bluffton with their two sons, Scott Alan, 24, employed at Expert Transmission in Bluffton and Stephen Ray, 21, employed with Newell Construction. They are both graduates of Norwell High School.

Stephen married Tina Quackenbush in November of 1989 and they have a daughter, Alexa, born February 3, 1991. They live in Ossian.

Merlin's hobby is antique tractors and belongs to "Wheels of Yesteryear."

After the fire, the Lancaster School was rebuilt and Dale graduated from there in 1962. He played basketball four years. He served in the National Guard and was employed at Fruehaufs until acquiring a farm. He also raises hogs and has beef cattle. Dale married Donna (Murchland) on July 1,

1967. She is employed by Northern Wells School Corporation. They have two daughters and two sons. Tonya Fay, 21, is an agriculture major at Purdue in her third year. She will marry Timothy Weiss on June 29, 1991. Jennifer Jane, 18, graduated in May of 1991 from Norwell and will attend Purdue to study pre-law. Douglas Eugene, 15, is a freshman, and Todd Allen is in the sixth grade at Norwell. They both love to play basketball and help farm where they live near Tocsin.

NASH

Ellis and Minta Nash moved to Wells County in 1916, in Jackson Township, one and half miles north of Dillman. Ellis, son of Jesse and Mary Adaline (Betty) Nash was born April 15, 1862, near Wilmington, Ohio.

Richard Nash, the first of this line, came from the Nashes in Ireland. The first Richard was a "Boatwright" in Kent County, Maryland. His children's names: Richard Nash II and Thomasin Nash.

In 1693 "Nashe's Enlargement", land on Kent Island, is mentioned in the will of Samuel Wheeler, guardian of Richard Nash II. The will of Richard Nash II of Appoquinimink Hundred, New Castle County, Delaware, probated on May 4, 1787, states that he was a yeoman and owned extensive acreage. His wife Rebecca and seven children were listed.

Front row: L to R. Oscar, Ellis and Minta Nash. Back row: L to R. Lester, Raughlia and Herbert Nash 1908

The census of 1800 in Westmoreland County, Pennsylvania, lists Richard Nash IV, born about 1754. Richard IV was born in the state of Delaware and at the time of the Revolutionary War was engaged in carrying wheat, flour, and wood to Philadelphia from different points. He was taken prisoner at Delaware Bay and carried to the Island of Bermuda, where he was kept for some time and afterward reprieved and brought back to Philadelphia as a guide. After the war, he came to Pittsburgh, where he and Jane Barr were married. She was a native of Ireland, born in 1762. They settled in Westmoreland County, Pennsylvania, where they remained until 1804. They then moved to Mason County, Kentucky, and in 1810 to Adams County, Ohio: in 1831, they came to Fayette County, Indiana, where they remained until their death. They had ten children.

The fifth child was Jesse Nash. Jesse Nash married Mary Pike on March 7, 1816, in Adams County, Ohio. They then moved to Hamilton County, Ohio, around 1829, and he worked in a boat-yard there at $1.00 a day, for one year. He then moved to Brown County, Ohio, and lived three years on a rented farm. He then purchased 65 acres near Woodville, Ohio, on which he lived until 1847. He then sold and went to Howard County, Indiana, purchasing 150 acres. Here he remained until his death on November 20, 1856.

Jesse and Mary had eight children, the youngest being Jesse Nash, Jr. Jesse Nash, Jr., was born March 7, 1836, near Woodville, Ohio, and married Mary Adaline (Beaty) in May, 1859, in Clinton County, Ohio. They had eight children and lived most of their lives in Howard County on a farm. Ellis Nash was the second child.

Ellis Nash came to Tipton County about 1865, where he was married to Minta Burns on March 31, 1893. They established their home south of Greentown. They were the parents of four boys: Raughlia, Herbert, Lester, and Oscar Nash. All four boys were born in Howard County. In 1905 they moved to Washington County, near Salem, in a log house on 60 acres.

From 1916 they lived in Jackson Township until Ellis' death on December 10, 1937. Minta moved to Warren, where she lived until her death on September 13, 1961. Three of the boys served in World War I - Raughlia and Herbert in the army, and Oscar in the navy.

ESTEL AND LOIS (SHUMAKER) NASH

Estel Nash attended the Banner (one-room) School in Jackson Township, and Liberty Center High School, where he graduated in 1943. He served in the Army in World War II and was stationed in Germany for a while.

Estel Nash

On June 21, 1947, he and Lois M. Shumaker (born May 10, 1924, to Homer and Noami Shumaker) were married in the Jefferson Center Methodist Church, in Huntington County. They had two sons: Fredrick L., born January 19, 1949, and Joseph H., born June 7, 1950.

They lived in Huntington County before moving to Liberty Township and building a new home on 300 South. Estel worked at International Harvester in Fort Wayne and Lois taught school. They were members of the Liberty Center Methodist Church and Estel was a member of the Liberty Center Lions Club, Masonic Lodge, and Bass Club. Estel is now living near Bloomington, Indiana.

FREDRICK L. AND KAREN (ARNOLD) NASH

Fredrick attended the Liberty Center High School and Southern Wells High School where he graduated in 1967. He then served in the Air National Guard.

On August 12, 1972, he and Karen Arnold (born December 23, 1977, to Georgiana and Russell Arnold) were married in the Liberty Center Baptist Church by the Reverend Myron Hinton. They have two children: Daniel L. Nash, born December 11, 1973, in Wells County, and Devon L. Nash, born June 1, 1977, in Wells County.

Karen (Arnold) Nash, Fred Nash, Devon Nash, Daniel Nash

Fred is a member of the Masonic Lodge and works as a technician at the Air National Guard at Baer Field. Karen is a member of Psi Iota Xi sorority.

HERBERT AND ADDIE (CONWELL) NASH

Herbert Nash and Addie Conwell were married December 21, 1922, at the Methodist Parsonage at McNatt in Jackson Township. Herbert Nash, born February 9, 1896, in Howard County, was the son of Ellis and Minta Nash. Addie Conwell Nash, born December 10, 1898, in Grant County to Otto and Ida (Determore) Conwell.

Addie and Herbert Nash 30 year anniversary 1952

On June 4, 1917 in Rush County, Herbert volunteered for service in the Army in Company B, Fourth Indiana Regiment. In September of 1918 he left camp Shelly, Mississippi, for France. He returned in December, 1918, and on January 15, 1919, at Fort Harrison, Indiana, he got his discharge papers.

In 1921 he started farming in Jackson Township, Wells County. Herbert and Addie had two children: Estaleene J., born February 5, 1924, in Jackson Township and Estel L., born September 30, 1925, in Jackson Township. In 1935 Herbert and Addie purchased a farm in Liberty Township on 500 South, and lived there for the rest of their lives.

They were members of the Methodist Church in Liberty Center. Herbert was a charter member of the Lions Club in Liberty Center. Herbert was a farmer and carpenter.

Addie, a former school teacher, was a member of the Bluffton Garden Club and the Business and Professional Women's Club.

Herbert Nash was killed in an auto crash on the Hoosier Highway on September 20, 1963, and Addie Nash passed away on August 17, 1974, in Wells County.

JOSEPH H. NASH AND KAY ANN (HARSHMAN) NASH

Joseph H. Nash attended Liberty Center and Southern Wells High School, where he graduated in 1969. He then served in the Air National Guard.

On August 20, 1977, Joe and Kay Ann Harshman (born March 18, 1955, in Bloomington, Indiana to Harmon and Betty Harshman) were married in St. Paul United Methodist Church in Bloomington, Indiana. They live in Jackson Township, Wells County.

Amy Jo, Katy, Kay, Joe, and Jessica Nash

They have three children: Amy Jo Nash, born January 10, 1981, in Wells County: Jessica Ann Nash, born February 10, 1983, in Wells County; and Katy Elizabeth Nash, born November 18, 1984, in Wells County.

They are members of the Boehmer Methodist Church. Joe is a member of the Masonic Lodge. Kay is an O.B. Supervisor at the Wells Community Hospital, and Joe is a carpenter.

NASH-HANNI

My grandfather, Elihu Nash, was born in Starke County, Ohio January 27, 1833, (died November 30, 1902) and came to Jefferson Township, Wells County, with his parents in 1843. He married Margaret Shady of Adams County in 1858. Both are buried in the Murray Cemetery. Their seventh child, of nine, was my father Reuben Henry, born October 21, 1870. He attended school a half mile from home. The family were members of the Emmaus Methodist Church.

On Thanksgiving Day 1895 he married Sarah Edessa Sowards, born February 5, 1875, (died February 2, 1915). They farmed in Lancaster Township. I, Rachel, born June 23, 1906, was the fifth of seven children. In March 1913 we moved to a farm west of Tocsin that had been in the Sowards family, and where my mother's grandparents had lived many years. We walked one and one half miles to the Dailey School. The Erie Railroad was building the second track. Many strange people worked on the track and walked past our house to Kingsland where they had a place to stay. They would sing as they walked along. Often they stopped at our house for milk and eggs. After our mother died, my sister and I kept house until the younger ones grew up. In the late 1930's, the brick house, where the family was raised and where my father still lived, was heavily damaged by an explosion that occurred when someone blew up machinery being used to build what is now U.S. Highway 224. One wall was cracked and several windows were broken. My father died September 16, 1954. Our parents are buried in the Tocsin Cemetery.

On August 8, 1925, I married Edward "Pete" Hanni from Berne, whose parents were born in Switzerland, came to America and settled in Berne, where they met and were married. We lived in Wapakoneta, Ohio, where he was a motorman on the interurban lines until it went out of business. We moved back to Wells County in 1929. He then worked at General Electric until we bought a farm, and began farming south of Tocsin. He died in September, 1943.

Our children were Kenneth, born October 12, 1928, who married Colleen Messick in 1953. He died November 18, 1985. John, born November 14, 1933, married Evelyn Barrick in 1955. Theodore "Ted" was born October 26, 1936, and he married Jane Meyer in 1958.

I have eight grandchildren, one step grandson, five great-grandchildren and one step great-granddaughter.

NASH-MELTON-SUMAN

Estaleene Nash is the daughter of Addie and Herbert Nash. Estaleene attended the one-room Banner School in Jackson Township and the Liberty Center School, where she graduated in 1942. On September 11, 1943, she was married to Shelby Clyde Melton (born September 12, 1917, in the town of Kansas, Illinois, to John and Pearl Melton) in Marion, by the Reverend John Clawson. They had three children: Melvin F. Melton (born February 12, 1945 in Marion), Marcia J. Melton (born January 7, 1948, in Marion), and Max Allen Melton (born in 1953 in Wells County). In 1953 Estaleene and Shelby moved to Liberty Township and lived there until December, 1960. On February 24, 1979, Shelby Melton passed away in Paris, Illinois.

Melvin F. Melton attended school in Marion and Liberty Center. On June 8, 1963, he married Rachel Noblet (born January 18, 1945, in Jay County to John Noblet and Martha Fenters Noblet) at the First Methodist Church in Churubusco. They had three children: Kamie Sue (born January 15, 1964), Shawn Patrick (born October 3, 1966), and Dawn Marie (born January 11, 1971). A second marriage was to Rae Jean Martin on April 3, 1976 in Lakeland, Florida. They had two children: Jacob N. Melton (born September 19, 1977), and Sara Beth Melton (born September 19, 1980). Melvin is now living in Lakeside, Arizona.

Marcia J. Melton attended the Liberty Center School and Taylor University. Marcia married Jerry L. Dulworth on September 16, 1967, at the Liberty Center Methodist Church.

Marcia and Jerry Dulworth, Todd, Mark, Jerry E.

They have three children: Jerry E. (born April 10, 1968), Todd Lynn (born June 8, 1970), and Mark Allen (born August 1, 1971). They lived in Liberty Township and Nottingham Township before moving to Montpelier. Jerry L. Dulworth is employed by Sheller-Globe, and Marcia is employed by Franklin Electric. The children graduated from Blackford High School. Jerry E. is employed by Westerner Wheel, Huntington. Todd is in the Marine Corps, on duty in Operation Desert Shield. Mark is in the Army, training in Monterey, California.

Max Allen Melton attended Southern Wells School before joining the Navy in December, 1970. He served during the Vietnam War on the Ticonderoga.

Max Melton

He married Audra Skeritt (born September 30, 1952, in Ventura, California) on May 4, 1980, in San Diego, California. They had two children: Christopher J. (born April 5, 1981), and Faun C. (born June 10, 1983). Max is living in Liberty Center and is employed by Kitco.

On May 28, 1965, Estaleene Nash Melton and John W. Suman (born July 19, 1917, in Adams County to Harry and Bessie Suman) were married at the Liberty Center Methodist Church by the Reverend Dale Linhart.

John and Estaleene Suman

They built a home on 500 South in Liberty Township. Then in 1975, they moved to the Nash homeplace on 500 South. John and Estaleene both worked and retired from Franklin Electric Company. They are members of the Liberty Center Methodist Church; Estaleene is a member of the Bluffton Business and Professional Women's Club, and the Wells Community Hospital Auxiliary.

NEFF

The Neff family immigrated from Germany prior to the Revolutionary War. They settled in Franklin County, Pennsylvania, and John Neff moved to Well County in 1865. He located in Harrison Township on Section eighteen, where he followed farming until his death. He married Catherine Neff on May 28, 1827. The couple died within six hours of each other on March 19, 1872, and are buried in the same grave at Stahl Cemetery at Reiffsburg, Indiana.

Nine children blessed this union, one of whom is Levi (1823-1884). He is the father of John Nathan (1858-1945), who was a farmer and road builder in northern Indiana. Nate, as he was known, was very active in the Democratic Party.

Nate married Louisa Shoemaker on February 27, 1884. Samuel was their only child. After Louisa's death, he then married Rachel Linn in July of 1889. To this union were born six children. They were Edson, Vesta, Cora, Frank, Everett, and Lucile.

Edson Neff
Esta Neff

Edson Neff, "the second son of Nate" was born in 1890 and married Esta Pennington in 1915 at Bluffton. They resided in Harrison Township, Wells County. To this union were born Ruth, James, Roger, and Harold.

Ruth Eleanor married Russell Archbold on July 9, at Wabash, Indiana in 1942. They have resided most of their lives in Connersville, Indiana. They have one son, Ronald, who married Barbara Mackall on April 4, 1981. Ruth spent thirty-two years in the Fayette County school system as Director of Financial Accounting.

James married Marthiene Fletcher on July 8, 1945, in Paris, France. He chose a military career in the Air Force retiring in 1971 after thirty years in service. They reside in Hot Springs, Arkansas. Offsprings born to this marriage are Jeanne and Jayne. Jeanne married Benny Veteto on June 27, 1969, and they have two sons, James and Stephen. Jayne married Joseph Dierks on October 7, 1981, and they have two children, Kimberly and Andrew.

Roger married Mary Wilhelm on August 11, 1951, at Bluffton, Indiana, and now resides east of Pleasant Lake, Indiana. Roger spent most of his life in insurance sales and is an avid fisherman. Three children were born to this marriage: Katharine, Joseph, and Christina. Katharine married Jack Janasiak April 8, 1972, in Angola, Indiana. They have two children, Kristen and Jacob. Joe married Susan Maham on May 22, 1982, in Florida. Christina Neff remains unmarried and lives in Raleigh, North Carolina.

Harold married Carol Jean Costello on February 2, 1952, in Bluffton, Indiana. He was employed at Franklin Electric as an engineer and was very active in the local Democratic Party. To this marriage were born Cynthia, Victoria, and Mark.

Harold died in December of 1989.

Cynthia married William Mullins October 18, 1980. They have one son, Nathan. Victoria married Lon Knowles in Bluffton on June 5, 1976. Their children are Kain, Tana, and Samantha. Mark married Donna Burdjenski on November 11, 1989.

CHARLES NEUENSCHWANDER

Charles (Chuck) Neuenschwander was born on a farm northwest of Vera Cruz on October 20, 1927 to William G. and Elizabeth (Lizzie) Neuenschwander. Needed at home, he quit school at the beginning of his junior year to help his dad with the farming and milking.

On December 5, 1948, he married Doris Fiechter, born in 1928, daughter of John J. and Lydia. She graduated from Lancaster and worked at the Farmers and Merchants Bank. Soon after, they took over the farming operation and his folks moved into a new home on State Road 124. In 1964 they purchased 180 acres from the 310 acres they were farming.

Chuck, like his dad, liked to design things. One thing he designed was a grain handling apparatus that permitted converting conventional drying bins to a continuous drying operation. A company in Indianapolis, Farm Fans Inc., got interested in this and came to the farm in the spring of 1966 to see it. Chuck had a patent applied for and they agreed to purchase it. They asked him if he would work for them. He agreed to work for them for two years to continue testing and refining his invention. That November a change started for his family. Walter Jr. lived on a farm, owned by his father, just south of of the Apostolic Christian Church, and Walter Sr. lived in a small home across the road from his farm. Walter Jr. and his wife moved to the William G. farm, Walter Sr. and his wife moved back on their farm, and Chuck and his family moved into the small home, all in one day.

On November 8, 1966, Chuck started to work for Farm Fans. January 22, 1967, the family moved to Indianapolis. His farm background helped in the designing of grain dryers and handling equipment that he was involved in. He enjoyed the work and it was challenging. The two years turned into ten, then almost twenty-two, with many changes: They moved into a home in the country on July 4, 1972, another move on July 4, 1981, into a home built by the family, then back to Wells County, on an additional five acres purchased of the home farm, on September 14, 1988.

Front row: Dee Charles, Chuck holding Daniel, Doris holding Dennis, and Debra. Back row: Cynthia, Sheryl, Kathryn, Andrea. Photo taken in 1965.

This was the day Chuck was dismissed from the Indianapolis hospital where he had had bypass heart surgery on July 8, followed by a stroke which left him with left-sided weakness. This caused his early retirement.

Eight children were born to the couple.

Cindy, born September 2, 1950, married Tom Cox. They have two daughters, Tobi and Traci, and live near Fairland, Indiana.

Sheri Cress, born December 21, 1951, works for National Oil and Gas, and lives in Bluffton with her two daughters, Carla and Heather.

Kathy, born November 27, 1954, married Tom Freed. They live in Greenfield, Indiana and have four sons, Jeremy, Nathan, Joshua and Matthew.

Andrea, born October 16, 1956, married Keven Sipe. They are the parents of Janelle, Mindy, Kristopher and Nicole and live near Berne.

Dee Charles, born March 11, 1959, married Laura Gerber. They live in Bluffton and he works for Magnavox. Their children are Amy, Adam and Wendy.

Deb, born March 11, 1961, is a nurse at Wells Community and lives in the lower level of her parents' home.

Daniel, born September 21, 1964, married Tammy Adams. They have three sons, Johnathon, Joseph and Jacob and live in the lower level of the home built by the family near Morristown, Indiana.

Dennis, born September 21, 1964, married Cathy Sue Hargraves. They have one son, Brandon, and live in the upper level of the family home.

NEUENSCHWANDER-KUNKEL

Gladys Carol Neuenschwander and John Daniel Kunkel were married April 16, 1938, at St. John's Evangelical Church in Indianapolis. Both were employed in Indianapolis, at that time.

John, a graduate of Indiana Barber College, Indianapolis, served his apprenticeship there, then returned to his hometown of Poneto and opened his own business.

Gladys, a graduate of Indiana Business College, in Indianapolis, is retired from Farm Credit Services (formerly PCA's) after twenty-three years of service.

Gladys (Neuenschwander) Kunkel, born in Wells County May 16, 1914, is the daughter of Jesse W. and Ivy (Niblick) Neuenschwander.

John, the son of Fred A. and Nettie (Mock) Kunkel, was born May 28, 1913, in Bridgeport, Illinois. The parents of both John and Gladys are deceased.

Fred Kunkel worked in the oil fields in Illinois, later returning with his family to the Mock family farm in Chester Township, where he resumed the occupation of farming.

The parents of Gladys and John were farmers in Wells County near Ossian. Farming and love of the land were basic to most of the ancestry.

Two sons and two daughters were born to this marriage: Larry Gene, born October 30, 1939, Karen Kay, born November 25, 1944, Jill Anne, born August 3, 1948, and Randy John, born November 21, 1950.

Larry, a graduate of Texas Lutheran College and his wife Jackie (Shearer) Kunkel live in New Braunfels, Texas, where they own and operate Kunkel's Insurance Agency. He has two daughters, Kelly Renee' and Cammy Jo, both married and residing in Florida, one son, Jeffrey Scott Kunkel, a student at Texas A & M, and one stepdaughter, Tammy Shearer.

Karen (Kunkel) (Smekens) Friar, a graduate of Ball State University, with her husband, Jeff Friar, live in rural Blackford County in a recently restored farm home, vintage 1800's. Karen has two children. A daughter, Angela Kay (Smekens) Harris, was born August 10, 1966. Angela and her husband, Scott Harris, reside in the rural Poneto area. A son, Brady Joel Smekens, born April 24, 1970, is a student at Ball State University. Karen has three stepchildren and three stepgrandchildren.

Jill Anne (Kunkel) Johnson and husband James D. Johnson live on a farm in rural Allen County, just north of Fort Wayne. Jill attended Taylor University and has been sales manager for Victor Interim Services of Fort Wayne for eighteen years. Jim has a son, Jeremiah James, age fifteen. They enjoy country living with quick access to the city and their work.

Randy and wife, Connie (Wolfcale) Kunkel

live in Bluffton. Randy graduated from Indiana Barber College and Connie is a dental technician. Randy has two children, Kimberli, born January 8, 1969, and Kevin John, born June 29, 1973. Kimberli (Kunkel) (Noble) Hartman and husband Brad Hartman, also live in Bluffton. Kimberli has a son, Tyler John Noble, age three, and two stepchildren. Kevin is a student.

Top row: Karen, Larry, Randy, and Jill. Seated: Gladys and John

The family lived in Poneto. Kunkel's Barber Shop was operated there until 1944, when John joined Turners Shop in the Bliss Hotel, Bluffton, Indiana. In 1950 he became associated with Niblicks Barber Shop on East Market.

On April 11, 1958, Kunkel's Barber Shop was opened in the former Walmer building on North Main Street. Later John and his wife, Gladys, purchased the building, changing the name to the Kunkel Building. Son Randy joined his father in business in May of 1974. Randy now owns and operates the shop. The name of the barber and style shop was changed to Hairs The Latest.

The business extended to a third generation in April of 1986, when Angela (Smekens) Harris, a granddaughter of the elder Kunkel, joined the firm as a full time stylist. Angela is a graduate of Ambers Beauty College of Muncie.

Randy's daughter, Kimberli, became associated with the business in November of 1989 as a full time stylist. Kimberli is a graduate of Masters School of Cosmetology of Fort Wayne. The father and grandfather would be very proud to know his son and two granddaughters are continuing in the family business.

The Kunkel family moved to Bluffton in August 1967. John died in May of 1977. Mrs. Kunkel still resides in Bluffton. Church membership is with First United Methodist Church of Bluffton, where Gladys is still an active member.

WALTER NEUENSCHWANDER FAMILY

Walter Neuenschwander's great grandfather, Ulrich Neuenschwander (1822-1905), came to America from Switzerland with his wife, Elizabeth Steffen, 1828-1907, and lived in the vicinity of Vera Cruz

William G. Neuenschwander, was the son of their son, John Neuenschwander, 1895-1975. He married Lizzie Schwartz, 1887-1972. She was the daughter of Dan Schwartz, 1856-1939, and Anna Aeschliman Schwartz, 1855-1949. Walter W. Neuenschwander was the son of William G. Neuenschwander, born October 28, 1909, two-and-half miles west of Linn Grove, Indiana in Wells County. In 1917, he moved one mile west and one-half mile north of Vera Cruz and in 1931, started farming on a farm owned by Fort Wayne National Bank one-and-a-half miles west of Vera Cruz. In 1931, he bought 128 acres just west of this farm. In 1933 married Edna Irene Schaefer, daughter of Fred Schaefer and Martha Baumgartner Schaefer. We were married 57 years September 11, 1990.

In 1934 we bought 72 acres which made 200 acres in all. The average price of land was $23.00 per acre. In 1935, the state wanted to buy 1,000 acres around there, so these 200 acres were sold, which was the first ground that was purchased for a state park. This is now where the lake is in the Ouabache State Park. In 1935 we purchased 139 acres a half mile east of Vera Cruz, which was known as the Hostetter farm.

In 1944, we bought the Martin Henneford farm, which was one mile north of Vera Cruz. From 1944 to 1954 we milked some cows. In 1954 we put in a milking parlor and milked 45 cows. In 1969 we sold cows, and then the farm was sold to this brother, Bill. In 1972 we started to do custodial work for the Apostolic Christian Church north of Vera Cruz until 1978. In 1975 a new home was built two-and-a-half miles west and one half mile north of Vera Cruz.

Children of Walter and Edna are: Doris Ann - 1935-1935; Marilyn Jean - April 3, 1937, married Charles Gerber in 1964; Carolyn Irene - November 4, 1937, married John Meyer in 1956. Their children are: Mark - April 26, 1958, married Kristie Kipfer, children: Jonathan, Cecily, Stephanie; Lora - April 11, 1960, married Dan Kieser, child, Jerod; Lona - January 12, 1963, married Doug Grover; Michelle - July 24, 1966, married Kirk Johnson; Diann Kay - 1940-1940; Walter Junior - March 14, 1944, married Joyce Schoeff in 1964. Their children are: Karen - April 23, 1965, married Jeff Isch. Children: Kevin and Jason; Kristi - August 1, 1967, married Brian Curry; Kathy - December 4, 1968, married Jeff Bertsch. Child: Caleb.

WILLIAM G. NEUENSCHWANDER

The Neuenschwanders came to America from Switzerland. Ulrich Neuenschwander, Sr. (1822-1905) and his wife, Elizabeth Steffen Neuenschwander (1828-1907) lived in the vicinity of Vera Cruz, Indiana. They were the parents of eight children. One was John (1856-1928) who married Mary Barger (1860-1933). They were the parents of six children. William G. was their third child.

Fifty Golden Years
Seated: Virgil, Elizabeth, William G., Walter. Standing: Ellen, Anna, Ada, William Jr., Martha, John, Lucille, Charles, Betty, and Joyce

William G. (1885-1975) married Elizabeth (Lizzie) Schwartz (1887-1972) on November 25, 1908. She was a daughter of Dan Schwartz (1856-1939) and Anna Aeschliman Schwartz (1855-1949). This family came to America from Switzerland in 1853 and settled in Monroe County, Ohio. They moved to Bluffton, Indiana in the early 1870's. William was born in a log cabin on the road which is now called Dustman Road. This home was moved across the road and is occupied by Steve and Joan Kelly. Another home was built over part of the original foundation and is owned by Kim and Sue Yergler. The original barn is still standing.

They started their farming life west of Linn Grove inside the Wells County line. In 1917 they bought a farm about two miles northwest of Vera Cruz from Samuel Aeschliman. They built a temporary home which later was converted into a chicken house. William Strahm built their new home which cost about $5,000. They farmed and milked cows here until they retired in February, 1949, and moved to a new home, located east of Bluffton on 124, which they purchased from Earl and Anna Frauhiger. They lived there for the rest of their lives. Their son Charles and his wife Doris, lived on the farm. In 1967 Charles and his family moved to Indianapolis. Today a grandson, Dean Frauhiger, and his family live there and it's owned by William and Betty Frauhiger. William and Elizabeth Neuenschwander were the parents of twelve children: Walter (1909) married Edna Schaefer; children are: Marilyn Gerber, Carolyn Meyer, and Walter Jr. Virgil (1914) married Harold Isch; children are Janet Furrer, Jean Moser, Judy Kipfer, Leslie, and Laura Compton. Ellen (1915) married Ervin Fiechter; children are: Louise Reimschisel and Rinda Ulrich. Anna (1917) married Earl Frauhiger; children are: Dale, Doyle, Charles, Chauncey, and Wanita Laukhuf. Ada (1918) married David Gerber; children are: William, Ann Marie Reinhard, Leon, and Genevieve Isch. Martha (1920) married Luster Heyerly; children are: Herbert and Sue Lantz. Lucille (1922) married Walter Kaehr; children are Ronald, James, Rita Everett, and Keith. William (1924) married Mildred Fiechter; children are: Thomas, Nancy Schladenhauffen, Janice Schwartz, Darlene Habegger, Vickie Meyer, Carol Mock, Marcia Geisel, Terryl, Peggy Yergler, Jeff and Rex. John (1926) married Irene Isch; children are: Randolph, Michael, Linda McAfee, and Joe. Charles (1927) married Doris Fiechter; children are: Cynthia Cox, Sheryl Cress, Kathryn Freed, Andrea Sipe, Dee Charles, Debra and twins, Daniel and Dennis. Betty (1930) married William Frauhiger: children are: Steven, Dean, and Kris. Joyce (1932) married Howard Baumgartner; children are: Beverly Joloff, Mary Francesi, Julie Schwartz, Craig, and Joy Tonner. There are approximately 153 great-grandchildren and 40 great-great grandchildren.

NEUHAUSER-CLAYTON

Paul Neuhauser (1922) married Nancy Jane Clayton (1922) in 1943. He is the son of Amos Neuhauser and Marianne Rupp. She is the daughter of Dr. Homer Clayton, dentist, and Ethel Spaulding. Both Paul and Nancy and daughters Diane and Peggy were born in Bluffton and were graduates of Bluffton High School.

Paul graduated from Purdue in 1943. He worked for U.S. Steel until called into the service (1944-1946) with the Navy. He was based in San Diego, California.

He then returned to Bluffton and was employed at the Hoosier Condensed Milk Company. When Hoosier was sold to the Fort Wayne Co-op he continued with them until 1967. From 1967 to 1977 he operated Dairy Service. He then worked for

Wisconsin Dairies and Land-of-Lakes until his retirement in 1987; he still operated Dairy Service.

Nancy attended Franklin College at Franklin, Indiana, then followed Paul in the service, working in Monterey, Corpus Christi, and San Diego. After their return to Bluffton she helped part-time at Caylor-Nickel research for several years.

Diane (1947) and Peggy (1950) graduated from Miami University, Oxford, Ohio. Diane also went to Loyola University in Chicago and then Vanderbilt University. She served as a Unitarian Minister (1977-1983). Presently she has her consulting service in Chicago. She married Earl Bickett, a graduate of North Illinois University. He is owner of E. H. Bickett & Company. Diane and Earl operate out of the same office. They have two adopted sons, Keith and Craig.

After completing a degree at Miami University at Oxford she went to Exeter University in England on a Rotary Scholarship. There she studied psychology for a year. Before coming home she worked in kibbutz in Israel for the summer.

Peggy finished graduate school at San Diego in psychology. She then went to Nashville (1974-1988) working in a psychiatric hospital for children for three years. Next she was Director of Women's Resource Center at the Y.M.C.A. at Nashville, for two years. For five years, Peggy was with Hospital Corporation of America. The rest of the time she was in her own business - moving it to Boston in 1988. She also wrote a book, Tribal Warfare in Organization.

She married Scott Bridgeman (1951) in 1989. He has a degree from Springfield College in Massachusetts. He is now finishing his M.B.A. at the University of New Hampshire. He has a son Ryan (1979) from a previous marriage.

NEUHAUSER-RUPP

Amos Neuhauser (1884-1973) married Marianne Rupp (1881-1953) in March 1910. Amos was born in Adams County, the son of John Neuhauser and Christina Steiner. Marianne was born near Archbold, Ohio. Her parents were Daniel Rupp and Magdalena Gerber. Both were products of an eighth grade maximum education but desired for all their children to have much more. In fact Amos bargained with his teacher, Godfrey Bell, agreeing to keep the stove going, room swept, papers graded, etc. in return for all the extra math he could be taught. He did this for about three years.

Amos was manager of the Peoples Store (now Edelweis Flower and Gift Shop) at Berne in his late teens. Marianne stayed with relatives, Jesse and Clara Stauffer Rupp, while working for Amos in the general store. Her first wage was $9.00 per month. Two children were born, Maurice and Mildred, while at Berne.

Amos was sure for some time that he wanted a dairy of some kind. With financial help of friends and relatives, Riverside Dairy at Vera Cruz became a reality (1910). They moved and two more children, Lucille and Dorothea, were born at Vera Cruz in Wells County.

Because the traction line was removed and there was a need for shipping, in 1919 the business was moved to Bluffton. It was renamed Hoosier Condensed Milk Company and was located on West Wiley beside the railroad and across from the former H. C. Bay Piano Company.

Their home then was at 408 W. Wiley Avenue. The last son, Paul, was born here. All five children were Bluffton High School graduates, as were three of the spouses. The next generation will and does have more graduates of B.H.S. Times had changed and these children would mostly be college graduates. Sports were also affected. Six graduated or attended Purdue University, and nine were for Indiana University. Other spouses of later family members keep the contest going.

Both Amos and Marianne were members of the Defenseless Mennonite Church west of Berne. In 1930 their membership was changed to First Methodist in Bluffton. Marianne, whose father was a Mennonite minister, was agreeable - it would keep the children more active in church work.

Amos remarried after the death of Marianne. These two spent their last years at Swiss Village having the distinction of being the second couple to move there.

Amos and Marianne are buried at Fairview Cemetery. More information on the families can be found at the Wells County Library. This will include Neuhauser, Rupp, Steiner, Stauffer, and hopefully, soon also the Venis family.

NEUHAUSER-THEOBOLD

Maurice Neuhauser (1910-1973) married Clarice Theobold (1912) on October 1, 1933. He was the son of Amos Neuhauser and Marianne Rupp and was born at Berne. Clarice was the daughter of William Theobold (1874-1960) and Alice Britsch (1880-1973) and was born at Archbold, Ohio.

Maurice was a graduate of Bluffton High School and Purdue University in bacteriology. He worked at the Pioneer Ice Cream Company, then returned to the Hoosier Condensed Milk Company as a farm inspector. Still wanting to be in the medical field, he went to Michigan State to become a veterinarian.

He was a second lieutenant in the Army Reserves - Veterinary Corp. from 1942 to 1944, during World War II, and he was sent to Lafayette, Indiana by the U.S. Department of Agriculture for the State of Indiana. He established his own clinic after the war and kept it until 1960.

He was then sent to Fort Wayne in 1960, by the U.S. Department of Agriculture to work on TB control among cattle. Because of heart surgery, this was cut to eight counties until his retirement in 1972.

Clarice, musically talented, became a regular organist at thirteen in her church at Archbold. She had special extra training at Toledo University and some at Michigan State. From 1960-1973 she taught piano and organ for the Hedman Music Company in Fort Wayne. She was also organist for their church.

In 1976 Maurice and Clarice spent the summer in Switzerland working on the Neuhauser genealogy as a hobby. A copy is in the Wells County Library. Clarice is now living at Bellevue, Washington.

They had two daughters: Alice Ann and Barbara Jo. Alice (1944) married Charles Bailey (1943) in 1966 at Lafayette. They had two children, Michael (1968) and Jill (1973). Alice graduated from Purdue University in Speech and Hearing and then got a master's degree in Deaf Education at Kansas State University. She taught in the Kansas schools until 1985.

She was divorced in 1983 and married Ronald Spring (1951) at Washington in 1987. Ron was a graduate of the University of Washington and is now a bank examiner and computer specialist.

Barbara Jo (1948) was born in Lafayette. She earned double bachelor degrees in Electrical Engineering and Physics. She won a scholarship to Standford University where she completed her master's and doctorate. She is continuing research at San Francisco State University in Physics. While at Standford she also taught classes. She currently lives at Palo Alto, California.

STEPHEN NEWELL

Stephen Foster Newell, was born on March 21, 1939, in Fort Wayne, and Caroline Elizabeth Buckner was born on June 7, 1937 in Wabash County, Indiana, were married on October 3, 1959 in Fort Wayne. Steve moved to Bluffton in July, 1954, graduated from Bluffton High School and Indiana Institute of Technology, Fort Wayne. Steve is employed by the Indiana Department of Transporation as an engineer. Caroline moved to Bluffton in June, 1944, with my family. Caroline graduated from Bluffton High School and Indiana University and teaches in the Fort Wayne Community Schools, and currently serves as a Bluffton-Wells County Library Board Trustee, appointed in 1983.

Steve and Caroline have three sons. Christopher Stephen, born August 25, 1964, graduated from Bluffton High School and Butler University. He is employed as a research scientist at Boehringer Mannheim, Indianapolis and resides in Indianapolis.

Scott Foster, born November 11, 1967, at Fort Wayne, graduated from Bluffton High School and Indiana State University with a degree in Aviation Administration and Professional Pilot.

Jonathan Andrew, born February 19, 1974, at Bluffton, is a junior at Bluffton High School.

The Newell family has carried on the family interest in Standardbred race horses. Steve and all three boys have trained and raced horses, and Jon plans a career in the Standardbred horse industry. *(See entry for Joy Buckner family)*

NIBLICK-MONTICUE

Ross Niblick was born September 28, 1890 at Henpeck, in Adams County, to Bruce and Ellen Clark Niblick. Grace Milholland was born in Keystone on October 20, 1893 to George and Elizabeth Bartlemay Milholland. They were married on December 5, 1911 in Liberty Center. They were the parents of three children. Robert M., born June 18, 1913, Dwight E. "Steve", born September 14, 1919, and Melda E., born January 6, 1926. They lived most of their lives in Lancaster Township and farmed for a living. They are both deceased. Ross died November 29, 1967, and Grace on November 22, 1978.

Mr. and Mrs. Ross Niblick

Robert married Pauline Harris on September 5, 1931, and she still lives in Bluffton. He was a barber in Bluffton for many years. They had one son, James Robert, born June 20, 1933, and he lives east of Vera Cruz. Robert died January 4, 1984.

Dwight married Ruth Paxson on September 14, 1939, and they live in Lakeland, Florida. They had three daughters and one son. Rebecca Teachout, born April 16, 1941, Susan Topp in, born June 3, 1947, and both live in Florida. Patricia Lockwood was born June 6, 1950, and lives in Bluffton. Steve, born August 8, 1961, lives in Fort Wayne. Before retiring, Dwight worked as a heavy equipment operator.

Mr. and Mrs. Gene Monticue

Gene was born February 9, 1926, the second son to Ralph and Nellie Shaw Monticue, in Marion. He had an older brother, James, now deceased. Gene enlisted in the Marines and left in March 1944 for boot camp at San Diego, California. He served in the Second Marine Division, 6th Regiment Special Weapons Company. He was in the South Pacific and in Japan after the war ended. He came home a corporal in August, 1946. Gene and Melda both graduated from Lancaster Central School in 1944.

Melda married Gene on October 5, 1946, in Huntertown. They are the parents of on son, Michael Alan, born January 15, 1955. Michael married Cheryl Pierce on March 22, 1975, at Monroe. They are the parents of a son, Brandon Michael, born December 4, 1979. Michael lives in Ossian and works at Waynedale Radiator, Inc.

Gene farmed in Lancaster Township where the family home is located, and also 120 acres in Nottingham Township. He is now retired. Melda has worked for Erie Stone, Inc. as a bookkeeper for 45 years and is getting ready to retire.

NOBLE

George Marion Noble of Clinton County, Ohio, married Phoebe Jane MaGuire of Darke County, Ohio. The couple had seven children: Mertie, Ida, Ethel, Charlie, Lulu, Enzla, and Ora.

George and Phoebe lived in an area near 124 West in Liberty Township as a farm family. The seven children were raised on the farm and lived in the surrounding counties to raise their families, except the daughter, Lulu, who moved to Battle Creek, Michigan.

In 1902 Charlie Noble and Lena Pearl Shields were married in Rockcreek Township of Wells County. They generally lived in an area about six les west of Bluffton on 124, and attended the Rockford Friends Church. They raised two children, Marion Andrew and Leota Leona.

Marion married Luetta Trout of Huntington County. The couple had four children: Wilma, Glenna, J. Charles, and James L. Leota married but never had children.

Marion spent most of his years as a farmer, but was an employee of the Wells County Highway Department from which he retired, and spent his retirement years in Poneto, Indiana. Luetta was a homemaker.

Wilma married but did not have children, Glenna married Roger C. Lee and they have two children, Randall C. and Carol A. Charles married and had three children, Cynthia D., Edward W. and Charles Steven, who is deceased. James married Joyce A. Tappy and they have two sons, Brian K. and Kurt L.

Randall C. Lee married Nancy J. Stump and they have two children, Rob C. Lee and Andrea Jo Lee. Carol A. Lee married Michael L. Fisher and they have three children: Kelli J., Leah A., and Matthew L.

Cynthia Noble married Lee Coleman and they have three children: Angela, Amy, and Josh. Charles Steven Noble was killed in an auto accident June 6, 1982, and has one daughter, Jessica.

Edward W. Noble married Lori Ray. Edward's children are Max, Taffie Jean, Amber and Lindsay. The family lives in the Fort Wayne area.

Brian K. Noble married Cathy Cook, and Kurt L. Noble married Kristy Melick. Kurt has a son, John Tyler Noble. Both Brian and Kurt live in the Wells County area.

NOE

The Noe family descended from Andrew Noe (1760-1832), a French Huguenot from Noe, France. One of his thirteen sons, Saren, was the father of David Noe, a cooper barrel maker. He moved to Chester Township, Wells County, and purchased 80 acres of land for $3.00 an acre in 1837. David Noe married Harriett Goodnow. Oscar Noe (1857-1931), was one of their seven children.

Oscar married Tunie Foster. He was a school teacher many years in Wells County, and was known as a strict disciplinarian. Their descendants were: Carleton (1893-1959), Whitcomb (1897-1971), Lowell (1906-1955), and Woodrow (1912-1990).

1944
Woodrow, Whitcomb, Carleton, Lowell

Carleton graduated from Liberty Center as also did this three children. He served in the U.S. Army in World War I. He married Geneva Hess in White County and moved to Wells County in 1927. He farmed the Popejoy farm in Liberty Township many years before he purchased land nearby. Geneva was a school teacher. Children: Henrietta (Mrs. Harold Caylor) (1922) of Bluffton. She was a Registered Nurse for 17 years in Colorado, California, and Indiana, Nurse Anesthetist for 29 years at Caylor-Nickel Hospital. Her daughter, Carol, was born in 1945. Carol Anne Lee (Mrs. Hasan Gucluyildiz). Graduated from Bluffton High School and Franklin College, master's from Purdue. Evelyn Tunie (Daily Langdon) 1924, Hartford City. Registered Nurse. In Army Medical Corp Reserve, worked at Caylor Nickel Hospital and Hartford City Nursing Home. Children: Linda Evelyn, 1948, Mrs. Max Bennett) Has daughter Jennifer 1977, son, Ryan 1982. Susan Mary (Mrs. Randall Goroski) 1951. Has daughter Carrie 1981, son Randall 1983. John Hess Noe, 1931, Swanton, Ohio, is a graduate of International Business College. He served in Marine Corps during Korean War. Married Betsy Garrett. Their children: John Jr. (Jack) 1961, Jane Anne (Mrs. Steve Prescott) 1966. Jack married April Garcia, had daughter Maria, 1981. Later married Annette Workinger, had son, Jace, 1987.

Whitcomb was a printer and lived in the Lafayette area. He married Ethel Hollcraft and had four daughters.

Lowell was a printer and lived in Chester Township most of his life. In 1943 he married Mildred Carnes, who was a life-long first grade teacher in Wells County.

Woodrow, born in Ashtabula County, Ohio, was cared for after his mother died by Robert and Zella Ratliff. After graduating from Bluffton High School and traveling during the depression, he was a printer. He married Elaine Miller, of Ossian, in 1939. She graduated from Ball State University and taught twenty years in Wells County schools. The Woodrow Noes are active members of Epworth United Methodist Church, Bluffton. Their children are Rosemary Ann, Northfield, Ohio, born 1940 in Bluffton. She is a nurse practitioner in Cleveland. Robert Louis, born 1943 in Bluffton, is a millwright in a steel mill in Warren, Ohio. Timothy Lowell, born 1955, in Warren, Ohio, is a technical coordinator at a museum in Long Island City, N.Y. Robert married Diane Picuri of Warren, Ohio in 1962. Their children are Tonya Mentzer, Poland, Ohio, and Frankie Danielle, Bristolville, Ohio. Steven and Tonya Mentzer are parents of Steven Jr., born 1985, and Theresa, born 1987. Robert is now married to Therese Creek.

JACOB G. NORDYKE FAMILY

Jacob G. Nordyke, son of Daniel and Sarah Nordyke, was born in 1864. He married Laura B. McGahey, daughter of Mr. and Mrs. James McGahey, who was born in 1865. They were married January 7, 1888. They had an infant daughter born December 1, 1888, who died at birth. Daughter Lela Elma Nordyke was born June 28, 1890. Son Ernest Neal Nordyke was born July 29, 1892. Son Lewis Birch Nordyke was born October 21, 1894. Anna May Nordyke was born February 18, 1897. Maudie Ruth Nordyke was born October 21, 1898, and Edward William Nordyke was born September 6, 1900.

We lived in Tipton County, near Nevada, which was a very small town with a two-room school building. The nearest high school was at Windfall, Indiana. In 1906, we moved from Tipton to Wells County and bought a farm north of Bluffton. Lela attended high school in Bluffton, and the rest of us attended Toll Gate school one mile north of Bluffton. The farm, where we lived, was located where the Keebler's factory is now. The farm buildings were in the center of the farm with a lane from State Road 116 to the buildings. The buildings are not here anymore, and there are now residences facing State Road 116.

Lela Nordyke graduated in 1909 from Bluffton High School. She graduated from DePauw University in 1917, and was a school teacher. She then graduated from Chicago Training School in 1920, and later that year went to China as a missionary sent by the First United Methodist Church Women's Foreign Missionary Society. She served five years at WuKu China and returned home on furlough, but her health failed and she died June 31, 1927.

Jacob Nordyke home near Bluffton, Ind.

Ernest Nordyke married Neva Gilliom. Lewis Nordyke married Sadie Elzey. Anna Nordyke married Charles Guldin. William Nordyke married Margaret Bennett. Ruth Nordyke was a school teacher and later was employed at General Electric. Anna (Nordyke) Guldin after her husband's death, married Herman Miller and several years after his death she married Lloyd E. Roth, a retired teacher and minister.

The Nordyke family came to the United States from Holland. They came from the Northdykes of Holland. The McGahey family came from Ireland. Grandfather James McGahey came over on a freighter and landed in New Orleans, and came up the river to settle in Kentucky where our mother Laura was born. He moved later to Sharpsville, Indiana and later to Mt. Etna, Indiana.

Ernest died in 1953, Lewis died in 1966, William died in 1977. Ernest and Neva had three children: Helen (Marquart), Anna Louise (Handy), and Dale Nordyke, who is deceased. Lewis and Sadie had one son, Richard. William and Margaret had five children, Lela Pauline (Murray), Dorothy (Melton), Robert Nordyke, Phyllis (Emenhiser), and Edward Nordyke. Anna and Charles had two children, Max Irwin Guldin and Marjorie Jean (Miller).

We moved from the farm to a residence in Bluffton on West Wabash Street in 1940.

ALFRED J. NORRIS FAMILY

In May, 1961, Alfred J. Norris (July 13, 1937), age 23 moved his wife, Alice Ann (Stone) (June 28, 1940), age 20 and daughter, Mary Alice (May 30, 1960), age one, from Pennville, Indiana, in Jay County to Poneto, Indiana in Wells County. He came to manage Norris Feed Mills which was bought in partnership with his father, Alfred and brother, Dick on July 3, 1960. Dick had set up and operated the Liberty Township Feed Mill and grain elevator the first year.

The Norris family lived on East Washington Street in Harrison Township in Poneto. To this home was also born Toni Arlette (August 30, 1961), Alan Jay (December 19, 1962), and Betsy Annette (April 12, 1965) (night of the Palm Sunday tornado) all at the Caylor-Nickel Clinic Bluffton, Indiana. In May, 1967, they moved to a home at 0290W, State Road 218, bought from Virgil Morgan located in Chester Township in Greenville.

Mary Alice Norris married Stephen Michael Towne (March 20, 1956), 310 W. Wiley Street, Bluffton, Indiana on June 28, 1980, (her mother's 40th birthday) at the Church of the Nazarene, 321 W. Cherry Street, Bluffton. They established a home in Montpelier, Indiana, Blackford County. Michael Andrew (July 31, 1983) was born at the Caylor-Nickel Clinic. In 1984 they bought a house from Larry Tourney at 9455S 300W, Poneto, in Chester Township. Into this home was born Stefanie Michelle (October 5, 1985) and Elizabeth Linnea (September 5, 1988) at Caylor-Nickel Clinic.

Toni Arlette Norris married Christopher Todd Davidson, (September 28, 1963), rural Bluffton on November 29, 1986 at the Church of the Nazarene, 321 W. Cherry Street, Bluffton. They "house sat" in Huntington County for Roy Lahr for five months. In 1987, they moved to a rental property 2383 W SR 124, Bluffton in Liberty Township. In October, 1988, a property in Chester Township, 6772S 200E, Bluffton, was bought from Craig Wolfcale and became their home. To this home was born Christopher Todd Davidson II (September 1, 1989).

Alan Jay Norris married Tonya Sue Mitko (March 29, 1965) of Alpena, Michigan on July 14, 1984 at the Free Methodist Church in Alpena, Michigan. They established housekeeping in a house trailer at 0240W SR 218, Poneto, in Chester Township. In 1985 the trailer was moved to a 44-acre farm, 0774W SR 218, Poneto, in Chester Township, bought from Jack Terrell in 1984. To this home was born Nathan Alan (February 13, 1986) and Cory William (May 5, 1988) Norris at the Caylor-Nickel Clinic. On September 24, 1988 they moved to 0288W SR 218, after selling the trailer to Bob and Ruth Ford. In the fall of 1989 a home was built south of the trailer in the woods of the farm. Moving day was March 19, 1990. Into this home Jeremy Mark Norris was born (April 4, 19, 1990) at Wells Community Hospital.

Betsy Annette Norris married James Mitchell Evans (July 19, 1964) of Syracuse, Indiana on June 13, 1987 at the Church of the Nazarene, 321 W. Cherry Street, Bluffton. They established a home in Syracuse into which Jeffrey Mitchell Evans was born (October 4, 1989) at Goshen General Hospital in Kosciusko County.

NUMBERS-GRIMM

Albert Numbers married Mattie Grimm and they lived in Ossian. They were parents of five children: John, Roy, Martha, Helen, and Irene. Two of these children, Roy and Helen never married.

Martha married Harley Sparks. Irene married Lee Shepler. John married Thelma Parker, and they had one son, Don. She died and he married Glendora Harris.

John and Glendora had two children, Donna B. and Nancy L. Nancy married Thomas Haiflich, and they had two children, Mickey and Vickie. Mickey was ill from birth and died at age 13. Vickie married Norman L. Miller, and they are the parents of three children: Ben, Jon and Kimberly.

Don Numbers married Beverly Shively. Donna married Herbert McCormick and they had three children: Melody, Michael and Michelle. Melody married Alan Schwieger and they are parents of two children, Jennifer and Matthew. Michael married Kathy Reiff and they had one son, Christopher, before they divorced. A second marriage to Carmen Quinones brought forth three children: Ashley, Aaron, and Stephanie.

Michelle married Gerald Schmaltz and they are the parents of a son, Joseph.

NUSBAUMER

George and Catherine (Hunsinger) Nusbaumer were married January 27, 1866, in Wayne County, Ohio, and later migrated to Keystone, Indiana. One of their children, Alpha (Bert) Albertus, was born January 26, 1870.

Bert received his education in the Scott schoolhouse near their home. There were times he crawled onto fallen logs to stay out of water on the way to school.

At one time, he remembered hearing about an implement called a corn planter to be pulled by a team of horses. So, they got on their buckboard and traveled several miles to see it.

Gerald B. Nusbaumer and Cecile B. Nusbaumer

On August 29, 1896, at the age of twenty-five, Bert married Anna Esther Schooley, daughter of Oliver and Mary Schooley.

Children born to them were: Gerald B, born February 4, 1898, Hilda Octave, born November 7, 1899, Dorothy, born May 4, 1901, Frances Esther and Clayton, born October 4, 1914. Clayton died at age three and Dorothy when an infant.

Bert and Anna settled in Montpelier, where he drilled for oil with a set of tools that he and a brother (Ray) had purchased. After buying another set of tools they independently moved with it, as the oil fields developed to the west, until they got into Illinois. There, because of distance from home, they gave up and quit the business.

After buying a farm in Chester Township, Bert and Anna had attended Marion Normal College preparing to teach school, but she decided not the teach after all.

Roderick, Kay, Naomi, Barbara Nusbaumer

Gerald, their son, graduated from Keystone High School in 1916. He then went to Muncie Normal, and taught at Blackford and Matamoras in Blackford County, and at the Gavin school in Chester Township.

On August 14, 1920, Gerald and Cecile Kennedy were married. That ended Cecile's teaching career. She had graduated from Keystone High School in 1916, attended Muncie Normal, then taught at the Linn School in Harrison Township, Wells County. Gerald quit teaching and started farming with his father in 1921.

Gerald with Roderick, Bert, Anna Nusbaumer, Frances and Marianna

Frances, the younger daughter, went to Scott schoolhouse, then to Chester Center High School, where she graduated. Following graduation she enrolled at Ball State Teacher's College, attending there 1933-35. Following graduation she taught at Chester Center, Montpelier, Peru, and Huntington. She received her B.S. degree from Ball State in 1950. She and Ralph Buckner were united in marriage December 23, 1950. They made their home in Huntington. Ralph passed away in June of 1988.

Gerald and Cecile purchased their farm in 1927 and moved onto it. To them were born four children: Marianna, born May 6, 1921, Roderick, born June 24, 1924, Janet, born March 12, 1932, and Beverlyee, born May 27, 1937.

Roderick graduated from Chester Center School and enlisted in the Navy Air Corps during World War II. After the war he married Naomi Bloxsome on June 8, 1946.

Naomi was the daughter of Dr. Arthur and Irene Bloxsome of Pennville, Indiana. She attended the Pennville grade school, then came to Chester Center. After graduation, she entered nurse's training at Ball Memorial Hospital, graduating June 8, 1945. She was employed at Ball Memorial Hospital, Wells County Hospital, Caylor-Nickel Clinic, and a short time as a nurse at Corning Glass factory.

Roderick farmed his grandfather's farm as well as the land at their present home after 1951.

To Roderick and Naomi were born Barbara A., born April 28, 1949, and Kay T., born March 1, 1951.

Kay graduated from Purdue University with a MIT degree in 1973. He now operates his machine shop in Fort Wayne. He has two children: Nathan, born March 20, 1978, and Sarah, born August 12, 1984.

Barbara has three boys: Bryan, 22, Roderick, 15, and Kyle, 10, and also a granddaughter, Natasha, age two-and-a-half.

NUSBAUMER

Kenneth Earl was born to Jesse Lee and Ora Alice Nusbaumer on January 19, 1916, in Nottingham Township on the family farm. He is the oldest of seven children. Kenneth attended the one-room Scott schoolhouse until it closed, and started fifth grade at Petroleum. He rode to Petroleum School in a Model T school hack, and remembers getting stuck in the mud in front of the school! He graduated from Petroleum in 1934.

In 1933, Jesse went to the Chicago World's Fair. When he returned, he found that Kenneth had plowed up a one acre patch with a one bottom horse drawn plow to plant potatoes. Because of Kenneth's initiative they had over 180 bushels of potatoes in the cellar that fall. The next year, the Nusbaumer's (not wanting a good thing to get away) expanded the patch by an acre and a half. The four hundred bushel yield was taken to Kentucky where small potatoes (walnut size) sold for fifty cents a bushel; larger potatoes sold for $1.50.

Kenneth remembers making the trip to the Chicago World's Fair in 1934. They pitched a make-shift tent beside the car and slept on the grounds overnight. The excursions to the Indiana State Fair were a different story. They slept in or under the car, but fair officials requested that they leave and re-enter each morning paying the admission fee each time.

Kenneth farmed with his dad, but in 1935, decided to rent farm ground on his own. He supplemented his income by raising hogs and unloading coal at the Keystone elevator. His hard work allowed him to buy his first car, a 1929 Chevrolet. After some fast talking, his dad allowed him to have five gallons of gas a week. In 1940, Kenneth purchased his first tractor, a new Minneapolis Moline R. the tractor was bought in Kokomo and he drove it home to Wells County.

Kenneth met Mary Lou Thomas in 1944. Mary Lou had attended the Chester Center School, and was now working at Farnsworth for a salary of $32.00 per week. Mary Lou was active in the Chester Center Church, often singing and playing piano for funerals, weddings, and services.

Kenneth and Mary Lou married on January 27, 1945. They settled in Nottingham Township on one of Jesse's farms. Kenneth continued to farm with his dad and brother, and rented more ground. Their first cow was a wedding gift from Mary Lou's parents. The couple was still busy remodeling the house when Carol Kay was born on November 5, 1945. She was joined by a brother, Gary Lamoine, on April 5, 1948. Later that year the family purchased an 80 acre farm in Chester Township.

After extensive remodeling, the family moved to the homestead. Three years later, Linda Fern was born on January 23, 1951. The births of Rita Marlene on March 6, 1955, and Darrel Duane on August 22, 1958, completed the family.

Far back: Darrel. Back row L to R: Marlene, Linda, Carol, Lamoine. Front L to R: Mary Lou and Kenneth Nusbaumer

By 1958, Kenneth determined that the family farm needed more ditching. When he encountered difficulties in hiring someone to do the work, he decided to do it himself. He purchased a Buckeye Ditching Machine from Brazil, Indiana, and later started Nusbaumer Ditching. The small business supplemented his income until 1973. An additional eighty acres was added to the homestead in 1974.

The Nusbaumers have many memories of life on the farm. The children's first calf, Honey Belle, was given to them by Grandpa Thomas. Many other animals were to follow: sheep, rabbits, ducks, and even a pair of peacocks. Newborn lambs and pigs were often found nestled in a box next to the stove in the living room. Sundays were spent at church, followed with a fried chicken dinner, and drives around the countryside. A special treat were the family vacations taken to Washington D.C., Wisconsin Dells, and the Smokey Mountains. The children are all grown and have families of their own.

Carol married George Lugar on December 31, 1966. Two children were born to this marriage: a stillborn son, Kenneth, on February 13, 1969, and Tamara on September 3, 1970. Carol and George divorced in 1971. Carol works at CTS in Berne, and resides in Nottingham Township.

Lamonine purchased a 120 acre farm in 1976 in Chester Township. He married Joan Clark Kingery on December 15, 1979. Jody was born on February 24, 1982. He joined three other children, Barry, Tammy and Lisa Kingery. Joan is a second grade teacher at Southern Wells. Lamoine is Fire Chief of the Chester Township Fire Department, and continues to farm.

Linda marred Steve Haynes on August 5, 1972, and is an assistant to an oral surgeon. Two sons were born to this union: Nathan on September 7, 1973, and Gabriel on February 12, 1976. They reside in Fairfield, Ohio.

Marlene has served since 1985 as the Wells County Vital Records Registrar. She married Jim Hoag on June 8, 1974. They have two sons: Brad born October 7, 1978, and Brent, January 3, 1980. Jim is a conductor for the Norfolk Southern Railroad. In 1987, they build a home and reside near Tocsin.

Darrel is currently employed by France Stone Company as an equipment operator. He married Debbie Phipps Horn on February 9, 1980. They have three children, Clinton born May 1, 1978. Brandon on October 14, 1981, and Gregory on July 18, 1983. The family resides in Bluffton.

Kenneth and Mary Lou remain on the homeplace and farm approximately eight hundred acres with their son, Lamoine. They are both members of the Chester Center Church. Kenneth occupies his spare time with woodworking and Mary Lou enjoys playing the piano and nurturing her flowers.

NUSBAUMER

Mr. and Mrs. Joseph Nusbaumer and family came to the United States in June, 1842, and settled in Wayne County, Ohio. On August 11, 1842, their son George was born. In 1863, Joseph and his son John, moved to Wells county, Indiana, while George was serving in the Army during the Civil War. George sent money home in 1865 with which was purchased forty acres of land that is a part of the homestead today. He and his wife, Katherine, married in January, 1866, and moved into their log cabin in 1867. George also purchased forty more acres adjacent to them. In 1875, they built the still standing brick 24x28 house. It was a two-story house with an outside stairway. The bricks were molded and fired from dirt on the farm.

George was killed by a train in 1899. Katherine continued to live on farm, asking her third youngest child, (of eleven) Jesse Lee to stay and farm. In 1908, Katherine added a 12x24 addition to the back of the house, widened the upstairs, and put in an inside stairway.

Jesse and his wife, Ora (Sawyer) were married in 1913 and had seven children: Kenneth, Bernice, Cloid, Nilah, Juanita, Phyllis, and Donna. Their son, Cloid, married Ruthann Oswalt in 1946. Of their three children, Jerry Lee was born on October 8, 1949. Jesse lived on the farm until his death in 1974. His grandson, Jerry and his wife, Gretta (Lehaman), then purchased the homestead and live with their family in the brick house, farming the land and raising pigs. Jerry served in the Vietnam War before he married Gretta on July 15, 1972. Gretta is a daughter of Emerson and Corrine Lehman of Berne. She worked as a urology technician at Caylor-Nickel clinic until they started their family. She is employed part-time now. Their children are Joetta LeAnn born, October 11, 1975, Jesston LeeWayne born March 2, 1980, Janelle Lynn born January 17, 1985, and Jessica Lehman born July 10, 1990.

DONALD L. NYFFELER

The late Donald L. Nyffeler, a deceased resident of Tocsin, was a native of Allen county, Indiana. He was born in 1918 in Fort Wayne, Indiana, a son of Louis Nyffeler and Estella (Rhodes) Nyffeler. From the age of two, Donald was a resident of Pleasant Township, Allen County. Donald attended Pleasant Township No. 1, a one-room school called Meyers School, located at the intersection of Winchester Road and Ferguson Road thruway. After graduating form Elmhurst High School in 1935, he farmed for his father until 1943. He attended classes at Indiana University campus for a semester, then returned to Fort Wayne. He was employed at Isaly Creamery at Main and Broadway, Fort Wayne, near St. Joseph's Hospital. There he made cottage cheese and cheese of all kinds. He worked at the Harvester several years. Later he worked at the Peter Echrich plant in Fort Wayne. There they made cold meats, hot dogs, Canadian bacon, etc. He retired after thirty-two years. After retirement, he graduated from Reppert School of Auctioneering in Decatur.

In July, 1945, he married Betty Jean Hall of Fort Wayne. She was a daughter of Loren Haughton Hall and Helen Thompson Hall from Ispeming, Michigan. Orphaned at the age of two, she was raised by her grandmother, Jessie Haughton Hall, and Frank and Flora Haughton Pool of Fort Wayne. My great-grandfather, Doctor Haughton, was a country doctor around Spencerville and Huntertown. Betty attended South Wayne Grade School in Fort Wayne to the sixth grade. Seventh and eight grades at Hoagland School, and the South Side High School in Fort Wayne.

Don and Betty were parents of three children. Dean resides in Price, Utah, and is married to Madelain (Mason) Nyffeler, who was from Idaho Falls, Idaho. They have three daughters: Nicole, Lizanell, and Marenna.

Peggy, the oldest of the daughters, is married to Leonard Graft and they are the parents of Eric and Andrea. They reside in Bluffton, Indiana.

Beth, the youngest, married Randy Merriman and they have two sons, Shanon and Tony, and they reside in Preble, Indiana.

Don had two sisters, Evelyn Hissem, who died in 1968 and Leah (Nyffeler) Smith of Bloomington, Indiana.

Don's dad, Louis Nyffeler, was born in 1888 in Jay County, Indiana. He was a farmer and a long-time chiropractor in his Theile Road home near Fort Wayne, His parents, Charles F. Nyffeler, Sr. of Hutyl, Canton, Berne, Switzerland, and Rosina (Rufener) Nyffeler, of Blumstien, Canton, Berne, Switzerland, arrived in the U.S. on the *LaFrance* (six weeks by boat) in 1887. They had eight children: Charles, Jr., Otto, Paul, Louis, Edwin, William and Oswalt, Rosie (Nyffeler) Bracht of Fort Wayne, and Leah (Nyffeler) Speicher of Geneva, Indiana.

Don's mother Estella was descended from Pennsylvania German Huguenots. The Rhodes family (original spelling was Roth) were Welch-English settlers. The Thomas Ballingers and Wards and Papes were found on her maternal grandmother's side. Abigail Ballinger was a direct descendant of the Ballingers who settled in Pennsylvania with William Penn. William Ballinger, Abigail's father, left Camden, New Jersey, and settled with his family in Logan County, Ohio. One of her maternal ancestors was Stephan Paynter, who feuded with Oliver Cromwell over the rights of Quakers. Stephan Paynter, with two others, governed Bermuda for four months in the 1600's.

Peggy Graft graduated from Ossian School in 1968. Dean graduated from Ossian School in 1965, and Beth graduated from Norwell in 1972. Ossian and Lancaster were to have graduation together at Norwell's new gym, but students wanted to graduate from their respective alma maters.

Donald's dad died in 1974, and his mother in 1990. Don died in August 1990.

O'DOCHARTAIGH-DAUGHERTY

John B. and Millie Matildia (McGee) Daugherty were the progenitors of one Irish clan of O'Dochartaigh who presently reside in Wells County.

According to the "Origin of the O'Dohertys" by Anthony Mathews, O'Dochartaigh originates as a surname from one born in the 9th century who was named Dochartach. Dochartach was a son and heir of Maongal and a grandson of Fianan, Lord of Inishowen, the northern peninsula of Ireland. From this son, and when surnames became popular in northern Ireland, the origin of O'Dochartaigh began to be used as a line of descent. The name was anglicized in a wide variety of fashions of which O'Docherty; O'Dogherty; O'Dougharty; and O'Dougherty are but a few. Somewhere the O' was dropped and the Americanized version Daugherty, became existent and is in Wells County today. The ancestory of this clan is a prominent, interesting history in Donegal, Ireland.

John B. Daugherty, died 1883
Mrs. John B. Millie (McGee) Daugherty 1825-1909

The only memorial to John B. Daugherty and wife Millie, who brought this name into Wells County, is a weathered tombstone in Saint John's Cemetery, located in Union Township. A small recognition was awarded them in the Bluffton Chronicle on December 22, 1909, in Millie's obituary which read: "Mr. and Mrs. Daugherty were among the early settlers of Wells County."

Genealogical research places 1866 as the year in which John B. and Millie settled on their farm in Union Township. Their westward movement was from northwest Ohio, Trumbull County. Eight children had been born to them, and all must have accompanied them on that long and arduous journey. Mrs. John Rupright (Elizabeth Daugherty), a sister to John B., could have been the influence which brought them westward. The Ruprights, with their two children, had earlier come from Trumbull County, Ohio, and they settled in Preble Township, Adams County in 1852. This lineage of brother and sister seems to be of a John Daugherty and Isabella E.F. Campbell, who were natives of Westmoreland County, Pennsylvania. To them had been born a son, John B. (eldest child), and eight daughters. Elizabeth, the fifth child, was born in Mahoning County, Ohio. The parents are buried in Trumbull County, Ohio. This ascertains that they too had moved westward from Pennsylvania into northwest Ohio.

Ezekiel and Winnie Etta (Double) Daugherty married September 13, 1883

John B. and Millie Matildia had four daughters and four sons, Printhia Jane, Olive Elizabeth, Mary Ann, William, Ezekiel, Candice, Edward Alman, and John Franklin. Only Ezekiel, grandfather of this articles contributor, carried the family name forward.

Ezekiel Daugherty married Winnie Etta Double to whom was born a daughter, Iva Myrtle (Shady) plus three sons. Clarence died in early childhood. The remaining sons, Jesse and Charles, are the progenitors of certain Daugherty's who still reside in Wells County. Although "Charlie" had two sons, Ervin Lamoin and Junior H., only the grandchildren of Jesse have carried the name beyond.

If you are child, grandchild, or great-grandchild of either Jesse Elwin Daugherty (Mary Ellen Kleinknight) or Charles Cecil Daugherty (Fern A. Haiflich), your presence in Wells County is from those "early settlers" John B. Daugherty and Millie Matildia McGee.

FLOYD J. OLDFIELD

Floyd J. Oldfield (1924-1986), son of E. Floyd and Nora Froh Oldfield, married Jeanette Smuts, daughter of Ruthford and Bertha Vollmar Smuts, in 1945. Floyd was a farm boy, attended Lafayette Central School, and joined the Navy in 1944. He served as an AA gunner through 1946, earning American Area, Asiatic Pacific, Philippine Liberation, and Victory Bar. He worked in construction, plumbing, and started truck driving in 1955.

Jeanette attended Lafayette Central School and Fort Wayne Lutheran Hospital School of Nursing. She was an occupational health nurse for over twenty-three years at International Harvester Company in Fort Wayne, and she still works part time at Fort Wayne factories.

Their children attended school in Union

Township and graduated from Norwell High School. Linda lives in Bluffton, Dale lives in Pasadena, Texas, and has two children, Cristi and Brandon. Donna and Judy live in Houston, Texas, and Anita lives near Indianapolis.

OPLIGER

Christian and Maria Opliger, also spelled Oplinger, came from Switzerland in 1843 and settled in Wayne County, Ohio. In 1856, he purchased the town of Jericho, which had a saw mill, sugarcane mill, tannery, cider press, gristmill, and blacksmith shop. Christion was a skilled carpenter and built many structures in the area. He was born in 1822, died in 1893, and was a member of the Reformed Church.

They had seven children: Samuel, William, Christian, who died in the Civil War, John, who died aboard ship coming to America, Elizabeth Opliger Sowers, Emma Opliger Hofsteter, and Clara Opliger Locke.

Samuel Opliger was born on May 24, 1854, and married Sara Gable, the daughter of Elizabeth Shoup and Joseph Gable. Samuel built and lived in several homes in Wells County, Indiana. At Linn Grove he owned a hardware store and was one of the first car salesmen in the county. At Domestic he owned a country store and post office. In later years he built a Sears mail order home on Silver Street in Bluffton, worked for one of the local piano factories, and owned two of the first gas stations in the city. Sarah died on October 10, 1923. Samuel died on January 19, 1933.

1890 Opliger
Back (L to R) Harvey, Lawrence, Edward. Front (L to R) Wilma, Samuel, Lester, Sarah, Leona

They had seven children: Lawrence, Harvey E., Edward, Lester, Mary Almeda, Wilma, and Leona. All of Samuel's sons attended college.

Lawrence was born November 5, 1878, and died in 1947. He married Mary Baumgartner and was the county school superintendent in Adams county. They had two children: Velma, who married Grant Smith, and Faye, who married Newell Neuhauser.

Harvey was born October 9, 1883, and died on October 1, 1905. He was unmarried.

Edward was born March 27, 1889. He and his wife Ethel had three children: Lois, Clayton, and Curtis. After his wife's death he married Elizabeth Perves. He was a teacher in Linn Grove and later moved to South Dakota, where he was the school superintendent.

Lester was born on March 26, 1896, and died on May 29, 1982. After returning from World War I, he taught in South Dakota. After his marriage to Bertha Schaffter, he farmed in Wells County, Indiana and later worked for the Ford Motor Company in Detroit, Michigan. After his wife's death he retired to Bluffton. They had no children.

Mary was born December 29, 1890 and died on October 5, 1893.

Wilma was born August 17, 1892 and died in 1971. She married Wess Miller, who was the first county milk route carrier for Amos Neuhauser's condensery. They owned a farm north of Bluffton and later retired to town. They had no children.

Leona was born December 11, 1894 and died December 7, 1972. She married Clarence Edwin (Ed) Rose in 1912. They had two children: Leonard and Max. She was a member of the First United Methodist Church, Matron of Easter Star, and chairman of the county Democrats.

BERNARD L. OSBORN

Bernard Lee Osborn, was born at the home of his parents in Jefferson Township, Wells County, Indiana, on March 26, 1934, the second of eight children of John Howard Osborn, born June 3, 1903 and Leita Ardella (Smith) Osborn, born March 14, 1905, who were married on March 6, 1932 at the Methodist Church parsonage at Ossian, Indiana. The children of this marriage of John and Leita, from oldest to youngest are: Ellen May Armstrong, Bernard Lee, Estel Earl, Herman DeWayne, Lillian Charlene Krider, Rose Marie Williams, Frank Howard, and Glenna Irene Raber.

John Osborn's parents were William Wallace Osborn and Ida Mae (Sherer) Osborn of Jefferson Township, Wells County, Indiana. William Osborn was a farmer and also an insurance agent for the Huntington Farmers Mutual Insurance Company. He and his wife, Ida, raised a family of eight children of which John was the youngest.

In the Genealogy Department of the Allen County Public Library (Fort Wayne, Indiana) there is a book on the Osborn family tree, "Descendents of Levi Osborn, 1827-1913" by Parker. This book shows that Levi Osborn, father of William Osborn came to Wells County in September of 1848, from Trumball County, Ohio. This book also traces the ancestry back to the early 1400 and includes Nicholas Osborn, born in 1727 who, with two brothers, was in America prior to the Revolutionary War and states that all three brothers participated in that war, but no trace of the other two brothers has been found since that time. Variations of the spelling of Osborn are: Osburn, Osborne, Osbern, Osberne, Osbirn, Osbirne, Osbeorn, etc. In old Norse, or Norwegian language it is Asbjorn, and in German it is written Asbiorn or Aspirn.

Leita (Smith) Osborn's parents were Frank Syphers Smith, born May 10, 1881, and Zepha Pearl (Longshore) Smith, born May 24, 1883, of Union Township, Wells county. Frank Smith was a farmer and Zepha was a school teacher. They raised two children of which Leita was the oldest.

When using the 1983 Wells County road numbering system, the farm that had been the Osborn farm is now 0584 East 900 North, Ossian, Indiana and the Smith farm is now 1523 West 900 North, Markle, Indiana.

Due to a blizzard the evening Bernard was born, the doctor arrived the next morning and recorded the birth on the day he arrived. Therefore all school records and etc.; before 1952 will show a birthdate of March 25, and after obtaining the birth certificate, March 26, 1934 was used.

The Osborn family attended the Prospect Methodist Church located one mile west of the Osborn residence. Bernard can remember going to church by horse and buggy, although the family owned a 1928 Buick, which soon, due to changing times became the usual mode of transportation. The usual method of farming was with horses, and a McCormick Deering 1020 tractor was used primarily to supply power to belt driven stationary equipment.

During the summer of 1944, electricity replaced the kerosene lamps and some stationary gasoline engines around the farm. Also this was the year the farm was sold to settle the estate of William and Ida.

Bernard had attended the Ossian Grade School (Jefferson Township) and now during March of his fifth grade, he was to transfer to the Union Center School (Union Township). This transfer was necessary because the family moved to the Frank Smith farm. Frank had died in October, 1926, and later his widow, Zepha, had taken a job at Camp Atterbury south of Indianapolis to help in the World War II effort.

Bernard's father replaced William as agent for the insurance company in 1934. Therefore, it was Bernard's job to do a large share of the farm work during the summer. He also mowed several lawns in the community, including the Prospect Cemetery, and worked for several farmers during the planting and harvest season.

After his graduation from high school in 1952, he gained employment at Franklin Electric, a manufacturer of electric motors, in Bluffton. During the spring of 1956, he transfered from the production machine shop to the tool room as an apprentice tool and die maker. He also enrolled that fall at the Fort Wayne extension of Purdue University, to complete his educational requirements for the apprenticeship. Attending on a part time basis, he graduated in 1963, "With Distinction," having received his degree in the school of "Applied Arts and Sciences of Mechanical Engineering Technology."

On February 1, 1957, he married Carolyn Ann Keel, born September 19, 1936. The ceremony was performed by Reverend D.R. Hutchinson, at the home of the bride 1804 Etna Avenue, Huntington, Indiana. They established residence in an upstairs apartment at 404 West Market Street in Bluffton. Shortly thereafter, they moved to 918 South Main Street, and in January of 1959, they moved to a new home which had been constructed for them at 16 Woodlawn Street in a new Bluffton subdivision. Carolyn was employed as a telephone switchboard operator for Indiana Bell Telephone Company at Huntington, Indiana, at the time of their marriage. Carolyn Ann (Keel) Osborn has a separate entry in this book.

Carolyn and Bernard are the parents of one son, Michael Wayne Osborn, born July 28, 1957 in Huntington, Huntington County, Indiana. Michael graduated in 1975 from the Bluffton P.A. Allen High School. He received his degree in AASEET from Purdue University in West Lafayette, Indiana, in 1984. He lives in West Lafayette, Tippecanoe County, Indiana where he works at CTS Microelectronics. Michael W. Osborn has a separate entry in this book.

In March of 1967, Bernard accepted employment at Bowmar Instrument Company at Fort Wayne, where he worked in the Model Shop till July of 1971. On August 2, 1971, he started his employment at the Magnavox Company in Fort Wayne as a model maker in the Engineering Model Shop.

Bernard is a licensed "amateur radio operator," having received his license in 1976.

Fraternally, he, like his father, has been active

in many bodies of Freemasonary; each being a member (John was a fifty years member) and a past master of the Ossian Masonic Lodge #297, also members of the "Scottish Rite of Freemasonary, Valley of Fort Wayne." As a member of the Wells County York Rite, they served in many offices, of the Chapter, Council, and Commandery. Also, Bernard is a member of the Fort Wayne Shrine, Mizpah Temple.

CAROLYN A. (KEEL) OSBORN

Carolyn A. (Keel) and Bernard L. Osborn in 1989

Carolyn Ann (Keel) Osborn, Bluffton, Indiana, was born September 19, 1936 in Huntington, Huntington County, Indiana, oldest of four children of Leonard Wilbur Keel and Doris Oletha (Hoover) Keel. Her sisters and brother were Carol Jean (Keel) Bucher, Beverly Sue Keel, and Alan Wayne Keel, all living in Huntington County, Indiana.

Leonard Wilbur Keel, father of Carolyn Ann, was born August 8, 1910 in LaPorte, Midland County, Michigan, the fifth child of Maude (Haneline) Keel and Alfred Keel. He was reared in the Clear Creek and Dallas Township areas of Huntington County, and also spent some time in Midland County, Michigan. He attended school at Goblesville, Huntington County, Indiana. Some of his employment was working with the Wabash Railroad and at carpentry work in the Huntington County area.

His wife, Doris Oletha (Hoover) Keel, was born November 25, 1914, in Huntington County, the third child, of Melvin Hoover and Clara Alma (Gray) Hoover. She was reared in Lancaster Township, Huntington County, where her parents were farmers. She graduated from Lancaster Township High School, Huntington County, Indiana in 1933.

Carolyn was reared in Huntington County, attending grade school at Central Elementary School and Huntington Township. She graduated from Huntington Township High School in 1954.

Carolyn came to Bluffton, Wells County, Indiana, at the time of her marriage to Bernard Lee Osborn on February 1, 1957, and has lived her since that time. When she first came to Bluffton she was employed as a switchboard operator for Indiana Bell Telephone Company at Bluffton, having transferred here from the Huntington office of Indiana Bell Telephone. She later worked in the Bluffton-Harrison Metropolitan School District, as a secretary-receptionist in the superintendent's office. Then spent a few years working in Allen County at Masolite Concrete Products and North American Van Lines before returning in June 1986, to work in Bluffton at the Caylor-Nickel Medical Center in Telecommunications.

In 1981, Carolyn became a licensed amateur radio operator as is her husband, Bernard, and son, Michael.

Her husband, Bernard, is the son (second child) of John Howard Osborn and Leita Ardella (Smith) Osborn of Jefferson Township, Wells County, Indiana. Bernard was reared in Jefferson and Union Townships, Wells County, Indiana, attending both Ossian and Union Center Schools. He graduated from Union Center High School in 1952. Later he attended Purdue University, Fort Wayne Campus, where in 1963 he received his ASMET degree.

Carolyn and Bernard are the parents of one son, Michael Wayne, who was born July 28, 1957, in Huntington, Huntington County, Indiana. Michael was reared in Bluffton, attending Bluffton schools and graduating from Bluffton P.A. Allen High School in 1975. He then attended Purdue University in West Lafayette, Indiana, where he received his AAASEET degree in 1984. He lives in West Lafayette, Indiana where he works full time at CTS Microelectronics as a Technician in the Engineering Test Design Department. He is communications officer of Tippencanoe County Emergency Management and also works some with the emergency medical services of Mulberry, Indiana as an emergency medical technician. (See separate entries for Bernard Lee Osborn and Michael Wayne Osborn in this book.)

HERMAN OSBORN

Herman Dewayne Osborn, born in 1938 to John and Leita Osborn, was their first child to be born in the hospital. He attended Union Center School, where he graduated in 1956. To meet the morning school bus, he'd dash out the front door and leap over the wood banister and spirea bushes in one bound.

Sometimes he'd lie on his back in the living room, with Frank and Glenna bouncing on him, and tell Paul Bunyan stories. He said, "Babe Blue Ox was stretched out, taking a nap, when the road was built, and that is the reason for the hill where the church is built. His tail was in the way, and they paved right over it."

He played high school basketball, and contributed significantly to the farming operations: fixing equipment, driving tractor, planting, and plowing. If he was tired while plowing late at night, he stuck his arms through the steering wheel, so that he would awaken at the end of the row, when the wheels hit the ditch and turned.

After high school, while working in Huntington, he still did farming and enjoyed raccoon hunting. He hunted with Clyde Elsten, a friend from work, and later met his daughter, Peggy Joan, whom he married in 1959. Peggy, born in 1941, was the only daughter of Clyde M. and Josephine Elsten of Huntington and had one brother, Doyle (Butch). Herman and Peggy were active members of the United Brethren Church, and had four children: Dale DeWayne (1960), Chris Melvin (1962), Clinton Howard (1965), and Laura Jean (1971).

They vacationed in the Smokey Mountains several times, cooking on a kerosene stove and sleeping in the pop-up camper. One summer, vacationing in Michigan, Herman explained the origins of the Great Lakes: "Paul Bunyan and Babe Blue Ox went to the ocean, and on the way back, he drug his axe. That explains the Saint Lawrence River. It had been raining in Michigan, so their feet stuck in glops of mud and formed the Great Lakes. Then Paul Bunyan headed south, still dragging the axe, making the Mississippi River." Peggy argued with them and had the children convinced that it was a fairy tale, and Herman had been teasing them with his stories, again. Before they could drop the topic,

Herman swung the car into a parking lot displaying the huge statues of Paul Bunyan and his ox. Herman's eyes sparkled with elation, the kids were struck with amazement, and Peggy was furious. There was no way to argue with "reality," so everyone jumped out for a snapshot in front of these heroes.

In addition to full time work at Noll Printing, he operated a successful lawn mower and small engine repair shop out of his garage at 1429 Riverside Avenue. In the early 1980's, Herman reconstructed a huge farm home with full basement and outdoor swimming pool at 1021E 300N, Huntington. Herman, his brother Frank, and the three boys worked evenings and weekends on this project, summer and winter. They moved the two story house onto the basement, removed old plastering back to the studs, totally gutted the house, redoing it. It was beautiful when done. Also, they cut firewood on Saturdays in the winter to fuel wood stoves at both his home and the farm. By now he was a self-educated engineer and had been recruited by Lehigh Printing. For years, they had talked about moving south to a warmer climate, and Herman was enthusiastic about his new position. In December 1985, Herman, Peggy, and Laura, moved to Dallas, Texas, with Herman's new job. He left Noll Printing as maintenance engineer on computerized printing presses and sold the new home.

In June 1986, Herman, Peggy, and Laura died in Dallas. That same spring, the beautiful home near Huntington accidently burned to the ground, when a small garage fire spread through the entire home. All three boys graduated from Huntington North High School. Dale worked at Noll Printing until December 1986 as a journeyman pressman. Then, he joined the Huntington City Police Department as a police officer and is instructor for Defensive Tactics, Huntington County. Dale also operated a lawn service business. In 1982, he married Lisa Ann Denney (daughter of Max and Janet (Hodel) Denney), and even though the current trend is for mothers to work outside the home, it is significant that Lisa stays home to care for the children: Christine Louise (1985) and Matthew DeWayne (1987).

They visit Lisa's parents in Houston, Texas, each year, wearing home new cowboy hats and boots. In December 1990, before they left on their Houston vacation, they celebrated Dales's birthday with an 'Earthquake cake' by Aunt Glenna (split down the middle with toy cars and light post dropped at an angle), because an earthquake was predicted to occur that week on the New Madrid fault. What a laugh, when on their way home from Houston, news reporters announced that small tremors had been felt in Indianapolis, Indiana, and they had missed it after all. They are active members of the United Brethren Church.

Chris attended Vincennes University until 1988, and currently lives in Huntington. He works at M and R Truck Sales, Fort Wayne, and enjoys working on automobile engines and doing body work.

Clint played high school football and attended Purdue University, West Lafayette, and Huntington College. He joined the U.S. Navy in 1986, graduated from the Nuclear Power School, and currently resides in Ballston Spa, New York, with his wife Therese. They were married in 1989 by the pool at her parents' home, Hugh and Sandra Ridenour, Orlando, Florida. (Refer to Levi Osborn for previous ancestry.)

JOHN OSBORN

John Howard Osborn, the youngest of eight children, was born in 1903 to William and Ida Mae

Osborn. Until 1944, he lived with his parents at what is now 0584E 900N, located one mile east of the Prospect Methodist Church. As was customary at the time, he left high school his sophomore year to work the farm.

John married Leita Ardella Smith in 1932 and had eight children: Ellen Mae (Osborn) Armstrong (1932), Bernard Lee (1934), Estel Earl (1935), Herman DeWayne (1938), Lillian Charlene (Osborn) Krider (1939), Rose Marie (Osborn) Williams (1942), Frank Howard (1945), and Glenna Irene (Osborn) Raber (1948). They moved to 900 N 1523W in 1944. They were active in the Prospect Methodist Church, and Leita played the piano for the services for over fifteen years. She decided to resign the Sunday morning that her youngest child threw her bottle, and it rolled the length of the church pews and rested against the altar.

John Osborn was a farmer, an insurance agent for over forty years, and a jack of all trades in the community, fixing furnaces, pumps, and mechanical apparatus. He fired the furnace at the church on Saturday nights and Sunday mornings, and worked the furnace for a few years at the Union Center schoolhouse. On the coldest winter nights, he would put a load of coal or wood in the kitchen stove that heated the radiators at the farm house, then circle to the church for a couple of hours, then the school, and back to stoke the fire at the house. He and the children were caretakers of the church lawn and the cemetery for many years. When electricity came to the area, he wired the farm house and barn. He did the painting and papering, and expected the children to pitch in and help. With a forge, a welder, and a barn out back, if equipment broke, he and the boys fixed it.

John and Leita loved each other, and it was reflected in the raising of their children. John milked cows, putting most of it in the bucket, but squirting across the stalls to shoot a cup in the cat's pan and catch the kids if they were close by. In the 1940's and 50's, they had cows, pigs, chickens, one pet chicken, a pet rabbit, a dog, and cats too numerous to mention. (Leita was appalled when the pastor came to visit, and Rose was sitting in the living room rocking the chicken. She didn't allow animals in the house).

Leita and John Osborn

John was a faithful member of the Masonic Lodge and took pride in teaching the rites to new members. He had the gift of gab and was an historian of community events, relating tales of a humorous nature to all who showed interest. He and Leita both loved to laugh, and possibly it was their good nature that allowed them to be supportive and take a distinct pride in each of their children's individual accomplishments. Whoever was youngest always ate from the tin alphabet plate, raised letters running around the border, and while the children were in first and second grade, Leita attentively listened to them read. She wore a dress and full apron with pockets and black oxford shoes with a modest heel, every day, all day. She used the apron to gather eggs, pick beans in the the garden, catch a spill at the table. She involved the kids in canning: beans, cherries (fifty-four quarts one year), and peaches (dropped off by a neighbor).

Neighbors were good to the family and sometimes dropped off a bushel basket of clothes or some canned goods. (Nobody had garage sales then, and the kids all wore lots of hand me downs). There were exceptionally sweet green onions from the side ditch by the drive and raspberries in the garden and the woods. Trixie, the family dog, chased ahead of Leita as she met Meno Roth's meat truck, when he stopped out front. He swung open the back of the panel truck and tossed a small piece of bologna to get rid of the dog; he high tailed it to the barn with his prize.

Leita was an active member of the W.S.C.S. (now the UMW, United Methodist Women) and participated as an Eastern Star. As a get-away, she often spent the weekend in Bluffton at her mother's house, sometimes taking the youngest child along. Her mother had a backyard filled with tulips. Leita loved her own tulips, irises, lilac and rose bushes, sweet williams, and peonies.

Summer vacation was a Sunday spent at the family reunion, a visit to church camp at Epworth Forest, or a visit with relatives at a lake cottage. Leita had a stroke in 1974 and died in January 1975 after three months in the nursing home. In December 1985, John required constant care and moved to the Ossian Health Care facility where he died in March 1988.

Ellen married Chuck Armstrong. Bernard married Carolyn Keel. Estel, because of his disabilities, has been a resident of long term care facilities since the time that Leita was no longer able to care for him. Herman married Peggy Elston. Lillian married Robert Krider. Rose married Glenn Williams. Frank is the independent bachelor. Most of their histories are contained separately herein. Glenna married Donald Kent Raber.

Glenna graduated from Lancaster Central High School, Purdue University at Fort Wayne, B.S. in Mathematics, M.S., in Education, and continued her education in computers. She taught mathematics for Fort Wayne Community Schools four years, then switched to General Telephone for two years. Except for seventeen months at Xerox, she has been at Magnavox Government and Industrial Electronics since 1981, where she is a scientific programmer/analyst for computer aided design in engineering.

Glenna married Donald Kent Raber (born 1948) in 1970, three months before he left to serve in Pleiku Vietnam as an air traffic controller in the U.S. Army. He graduated from Lancaster Central High School, Indiana University at Fort Wayne, B.S. in business, and was an auditor for Lincoln National Corporation before switching to GTE. He has been with GTE since 1983, as an auditor and as a revenue analyst.

Glenna and Don moved often to stay near their school and work: to a trailer park south of Fort Wayne, an apartment, rented houses near IU-PU Ft. Wayne, in Markle, and in Cedarville. They bought their first home southwest of Fort Wayne in 1983, but were transferred to GTE, Westfield, in 1985, and moved to their current address in 1987: 16825 Darling Road, Woodburn, Indiana.

Don and Glenna have two dogs and no children. They are members of the United Methodist Church, where Glenna currently teaches Sunday School and is program chairman for a UMW Circle.

Don's parents (Earl Gilbert Raber, born 1921 in Rockcreek Township, and Monnah Blanche Carnes, born 1919 near Keystone) had two other children: Bruce Lee, born 1951, and Constance Sue, born 1957. (Refer to Levi Osborn for previous ancestry).

LEVI OSBORN

To pass on the Osborn history to future generations, this section includes a brief history of Frank Osborn, great-grandson of Levi Osborn, followed by nearly a word-for-word reproduction of the history of Levi Osborn as published in the 1887 Adams-Wells County History book. Frank Howard Osborn, seventh of eight children, was born in 1945 to John Howard and Leita Ardella Osborn (daughter of Frank S. and Zepha Pearl Smith). He grew up at the 900N 1523W address and lived in the house until October 1988, when it was sold at auction to settle John's estate. Frank did the upkeep and kept the house in good shape as his parents aged. While maintaining his professional career, he did everything from painting the house, to roofing it, to counting out John's daily medications, and bringing in the evening paper. He mowed several acres of lawn every week. After graduation from Lancaster Central High School in 1964, he worked while in college and received scholarships. He graduated from Purdue University in West Lafayette in 1969, and accepted an engineering position at Navistar (International Harvester), where he is currently a development engineer.

The following was reproduced from the 1887 Adams-Wells County History book: Levi Osborn, of Ossian, was born in Canfield, Trumbull County, Ohio, in 1827, son of Jacob and Elizabeth M. (Harris) Osborn. James Harris, father of Elizabeth M., was probably born in the town of Milford, Mifflin County, Pennsylvania, of Irish ancestry. His wife was Alice Woodard, and they reared a large family: Elizabeth M., Mary, John, Thomas, Margaret, James, Ann, David, Hannah, Joseph, Robert and Rachel. Margaret, Ann, James and Hannah came to Wells County. John settled in Adams County. John Osborn, grandfather of Levi, was a son of Nicholas Osborn, who came to America from England prior to the Revolutionary War. He was accompanied by two brothers, and all were soldiers in that war; but no trace of the two brothers has ever been found since the close of the war. Mrs. John Osborn, a German lady, had ten children: Conrad, Nicholas, Jacob, John, William, Jonathan, Amos, Andrew, Margaret, and Elizabeth.

Jacob Osborn was a soldier in the war of 1812. He was twice married. His first wife was Annie Babbitt, and their children were: Elias, Harmon, Mary A., and Aaron. After the death of his wife, Jacob married Elizabeth Harris, and their children were: Levi, James, Margaret and Elizabeth (twins), Eliza J., Anna, and William. They all married except for Elizabeth, who died in infancy.

The death of Jacob Osborn occurred when Levi was twelve years old, and when he was twenty-one years old he came to Wells County and pre-empted the northwest quarter of section 24, Union Township. He built a pole shanty on the land the day before it was entered, ate and slept in it. This was the western boundary of settlement at that date. He cut and burned the first pile of brush to cook his supper and may be said to have made the first clearing in the immediate neighborhood. During the first eight months of his stay in the county, Mr. Osborn worked by the month for William W. Cotton, who brought his family to this county at the same time Levi came. Levi returned to his old home in April, 1849, and remained until September of the following year, then returned to his home in the new country, bringing his wife, Catherine Ashburn, whom he married June 13, 1850. She was the daughter of Joseph and Elizabeth (Hart) Ashburn. Her father's people were German, and her mother's were Irish. They removed to this county in April, 1884, to make their home with their children.

Front Row (L to R) Joseph Nelson, Levi O. Osborn, Catherine Osborn, Sarah Elizabeth. Back Row (L to R) Margaret Anliza, Ettie May, William Wallace, Elias Emmett, Mary Ellen, Jacob Wesley

Mr. Ashburn died at the home of Mr. Osborn in 1886, aged eighty-six years. His wife remained with Mr. Osborn's family. Their children were: Catherine, William, Mary, Jesse, Nelson and Prossor. Mr. Osborn erected a log cabin on the spot where his fine farm house now stands, and they occupied it October 28, 1850. Under its roof, all their children were born except the youngest. Joseph N. married Albina Longshore; Elizabeth E. married O.C. Krewson; Jacob W. married Paulina Sowle; Mary E. became the wife of Orland J. Krewson, and after his death married his brother Thomas; Elias E., William W., Etta M. and Anna M. are unmarried and stayed with their parents.

Levi made all the furniture for their house. Blankets served for doors, and not a sawed board was used in the construction of the house, except the lid of a chest which was used in making a window. The bedsteads were made of poles, the seats of puncheon (split log) slabs, the table of clapboards and the floor of the same material.

Mr. Osborn worked for some of his neighbors by the day, for which he received corn and potatoes. Although the woods were full of game, he never hunted, or even killed a deer or turkey, but devoted all his time to the cultivation of this land.

They became members of the first Methodist Episcopal church organized in the neighborhood; this church is still in existence. Levi was an officer in the church for more than a quarter of a century. During the progress of the Civil War (1861-1865) he was drafted, but after being in camp two weeks at Indianapolis he was released, the township having filled its quota. In 1853, he was elected trustee of the township, and during his term of service the Centre schoolhouse was built, and several new roads laid out. He was a Republican and was one of the founders of that party in this county. January 1, 1885, he was injured when a saw fell on his left foot, resulting in its amputation by Doctor Stemen, at Saint Joseph's Hospital, Fort Wayne. Levi died in 1913.

(For further accounts, refer to other Osborns listed herein. For the most recent account, refer to the *Genealogical Record of the Descendants of Levi Osborn 1827-1913* on file at the Allen County Public Library.)

MICHAEL W. OSBORN

Michael Wayne Osborn was born July 28, 1957 at the Huntington County Hospital, Huntington, Indiana. He was the only child of Bernard Lee Osborn and Carolyn Ann (Keel) Osborn, who resided at 918 South Main Street and later at 16 Woodlawn Street, Bluffton, Indiana.

Michael was reared in Bluffton and attended school at Columbian Elementary, Central Junior High, and Bluffton P.A. Allen High School from which he graduated in 1975. While in high school, he was a member of the band including the Marching Band and Jazz Ensemble, Spanish Club, Honor Society, student manager for baseball team, freshman and sophomore years, and the football team during his junior and senior years, and also worked with the audio-visual, sound equipment, and stage lights during school functions.

During the summers of his junior high school years Michael operated the concession stand at Roush Park. He worked at the Bluffton Bowling Center during his junior and senior years of high school. During the summers he worked for the Wells Community Pool for three years in maintenance, and three years as assistant manager. After graduation he worked part-time at construction work.

1975 High School graduation picture of Michael Wayne Osborn

Michael was active in the Boy Scouts; he was a member of Columbian Cub Scouts Pack 3153, Baptist Church Troop 142 and then Jaycees' Troop 141, where he received his Eagle Scout award on July 18, 1977. In 1973, he was initiated into the Order of the Arrow, Kiskakon Lodge, Camp Little Turtle. He served as junior assistant scoutmaster of Troop 141 in 1975.

Michael was also interested in electronics and amateur radio having received his amateur radio license in 1976.

In the fall of 1975, he entered Purdue University, West Lafayette, Indiana, and graduated from the school of Applied Arts and Sciences of Electrical Engineering Technology in 1984.

While enrolled at Purdue, he worked part-time in the Lafayette area. Some of the places he worked included delivery at Let's Munch Out (LMO), Pin Pan Alley where he repaired electronic video and pinball games, and Wolfelt Electronics Security Systems as a Central Station Monitor. During the summer of 1980, he worked for Purdue University residence hall maintenance at Terry Courts, and residence hall food service at Shreve Hall.

Michael lives in West Lafayette, Tippecanoe County, Indiana and has been employed full time at CTS Microelectonics, Division of CTS Corporation, since 1981. He is an electronics technician in the Engineering Test Design Department.

July 1, 1980, he received his Emergency Medical Technician certification and has been a member with the Mulberry Volunteer Ambulance Service since November, 1986, at Mulberry, Indiana.

He is an Indiana Emergency Medical Service certified driver, and an American Heart Association Certified Basic Cardiac Life Support-Cardio Pulmonary Resuscitation (BCLS-CPR) instructor.

In August 1987, he was an Emergency Medical Technician with the Pan American Games held at Indianapolis, Indiana, and he was a member of the Purdue Stadium Rescue Squad at Purdue home football games 1984-90.

Michael is a member of the Tippecanoe County Emergency Management Agency serving as Communications Officer and has received training to the Operations Level for responding to hazardous materials incidents.

PAUL OSBORN

2738 West 800 South, Chester Township. In May, 1910, my mother, Maud Shadle Minnich moved up here on this farm and in this house with two children, Don Minnich and Mary Minnich. She had lost her husband a couple of years earlier in death. Then that fall she married John Osborn in November. To this union were born two children, Ruby and Paul Osborn and at this writing all are passed on but Paul Osborn who is writing this history.

My father was a farmer and also a carpenter by trade. My mother and father lived on this farm forty-five years, and then my mother passed on with a heart attack. But father lived on the full fifty years on this farm.

Ellen Holsinger and I were married in 1936 and we lived in with my folks a little over two years until I found a place to live. Our first son, John Paul Osborn Jr., was born in this house. I still own the family farm. Ellen and I were both born in Chester Township and have lived all our lives in Wells County. I am seventy-seven years old, and Ellen and I live at 8647 South 200 West, Poneto. *Submitted by Paul Osborn.*

DORTHEA LUCILE HAMILTON OSTRANDER

Dorthea Lucile (Hamilton) Ostrander, born November 3, 1918, is the youngest daughter of Joseph Hamilton and was raised by Joe Jamison. Joseph Emery Hamilton (October 21, 1879 to June 20, 1965) son of Ellis and Lavine E. (Harter) Hamilton married on September 9, 1906, Alice Rebecca Penrod, daughter of John and Mary A. Penrod.

Dorthea's son, Clarence Warren Ostrander (born August 7, 1942) married Ava Jean Minegar (born November 22, 1940) on November 29, 1972. Clarence Warren adopted the children of Ava Jean. Jeani Marie (born June 28, 1960) married John Bennett (born June 15, 1964) on July 19, 1989. Gregory Ros (born January 17, 1964) on July 15, 1985, married Theresa Dawn Markley (born July 1, 1962). Dorthea's last child, Jeffery Eugene (born September 18, 1965), married Kimberly King (born April 28, 1967) on September 16, 1989 and they have a daughter, Brittany Nichole, born January 29, 1990.

Dorthea has been hanging wall paper

professionally for forty-five years, covering a territory of northern Indiana from Muncie to Quincy, Michigan.

The business all evolved from decorating her own home, then to helping neighbors, then assuming the patrons of several "old time paperhangers" who retired at this time, and it became a thriving business. Besides the average of at least one hundred different homes each year, it has included restaurants, offices of lawyers and dentists, shoe and liquor stores, and church foyers all in the town of Bluffton.

Dorthea Ostrander

The wallpapering business at first was a spring and fall seasonal job due to the heating of homes. (There are lots of trials to putting paper over and around the old wood and coal heating stoves and in the kitchen around the wood ranges). As the years moved along, the papering became a five-day-per-week job. The week was rounded out by the need for a janitor at the Epworth United Methodist Church. That job has continued for twenty-four years, mainly on Saturday, along with teaching adult Sunday School classes for twenty-eight years. In the beginning, wallpapering was paper only, except for an occasional oil-cloth in a splash area. As people became more interested in decorating their homes new materials became available, such as grass cloths, bark cloth, vinyls, burlaps and vinyl coated paper.

It had been a detested chore in the past to use wallpaper cleaner every year to spruce up the wallcovering, but that has given way to the new washable materials.

Forty-five years ago, if the householder did not have the paste cooked and ready to use, the paperhanger cooked whatever type he/she desired, that is, cooking flour, brown sugar, vinegar and water to the right consistency for paste (with no lumps) or using Argo starch made up thicker than for starching clothes. Both concoctions were very sticky and held the paper on walls satisfactorily. If there was difficulty, you dissolved powdered glue and added it to the paste. Care was needed to avoid getting these pastes on the surface of paper, for they could stain the not so colorfast paper of those days and could not be washed.

All of the above have given way to prepared powdered pastes for the different types of papers, along with pre-mixed pastes and pre-pasted materials. Painted walls were in vogue for a short period, even over wallpapered walls. Removal of wallcovering by scraping and steaming was and is always a hot, messy time, consuming job, which was not scheduled in the bookings and often delayed the finished job. There are many "tricks" in the wallpapering trade, which cannot be learned at "lessons" and in literature. Spotting the match, aligning patterns to the best decorative use, bonding of seams, use of borders to advantages, and even the covering of accessories in the room.

Ceilings are seldom papered anymore, but they were the easiest part after the scaffolding was in place and the guide line for the first strip was made, for there were few things to fit around. Good equipment is a necessity. Sturdy ladders of different heights, extension planks, measuring tapes and yard sticks, brushes of different density and stiffness, trimmers, scissors, seam rollers, sponges and buckets were all used. A sturdy folding work table of comfortable height, straight-edge and level. Last but most important was "patience."

The "trickiest" covering is foil, allowing for no sharp folds or scratches and difficult trimming. The selling of wall coverings was not a part of the business. Thoroughly reading and following the paper company's instructions is a must, followed by experience with various types of walls. Trial and error, even the image of paper falling off as it is applied may become a sudden reality. With proper care, many wallcoverings may last from five to x number of years.

Ample time needs to be allotted for each job, to avoid delay for the the next customer. Personal quality time is when a job is finished and before the next booking. Always notify the next customer if the arrival will be late. Vacations have not been on the scheduling book. Yard and gardening are good therapy after being inside all day. The nicest part of the job is meeting people and serving them. Some customers are never met. Just do the job as per instructions left in the house, leave a bill and their check will follow. They trust and you trust. Only three times in forty-five years was a reimbursement lost. Trustworthy is the word for Wells County and Bluffton area people.

OSWALT

Gustin E. Oswalt was born on August 26, 1924, the first child of Faye and Minervia Gustin Oswalt. The Oswalt family ancestors came to America from Germany. Gustin Oswalt lived his entire life in Poneto, Indiana.

When he was quite young, Gustin spent most of his time helping his grandfather with farming. During this time he began to live with his grandparents Charles and Addie Tappy Oswalt.

Gustin Oswalt and Doris J. Shaw were married on December 24, 1943. They kept their marriage a secret until Doris graduated from Liberty Center High School in the spring of 1944. After graduation she moved to Poneto and they continued to live with Gustin's grandfather Charles Oswalt, who at this time was seventy-nine years old and a widower.

Rose Anderson (daughter), Charles Oswalt (great grandfather) Carolyn Melching (daughter), Gustin Oswalt (father) Faye Oswalt (grandfather), Marolyn Roth (daughter)

After Gustin Oswalt married he farmed, drove a truck hauling stock, tomatoes, etc. and had a service station in Poneto for a few years. In 1951, he leased ground and built what was known as Oswalt Grain and Milling. He operated this business with the help of his brother Charles Oswalt, until his death June 9, 1961. Gustin had a massive heart attack while working at their home in Poneto. He was thirty-six years old, leaving his wife and five living children, four daughters: Rose, twins Marolyn and Carolyn, and Vickie and one son Timothy.

Rose Oswalt married Dan Anderson and resides in Poneto with their two sons, Anthony age eighteen and Ashley age fifteen. Rose works at Columbia Elementary School as a reading aide. Dan Anderson works at Fisher Body in Marion, Indiana.

Carolyn Oswalt married Tom Mechling, their home is on Wiley Avenue, Bluffton. They have three children, Heidi, age twenty, Misty, age eighteen, both out of school and Brandon age fourteen. Tom works at Hartford Manufacturing in Adams County. Carolyn also works there part-time. Carolyn has two step-children Lea Ann and Brent Mechling.

Marolyn Oswalt, now married to Calvin Roth is living on Echo Lane with their two sons Eric C. Funk age fifteen and Gustin Curtis Funk age ten. Calvin Roth and Tony Oswalt (a cousin of Marolyn's) own and operate O & R Percision and Hartford Manufacturing both in Adams County. Marolyn Oswalt has three step-daughters Thesa, Tara, and Tess Roth.

Vickie Oswalt married Larry Boots. They have four children: Brent (married to Jamie Crowder); Brittany, age seventeen; Braden, age thirteen; and Bently, age eleven. Vickia and Larry live with their family on Market Street. They have a bed and breakfast at their home known as Victoria's Manor. Larry also works at Franklin Electric.

Timothy Oswalt married Deena Andrews, they have two daughters Brooke, age eleven, and Rhiannon, age nine. They reside on Elm Grove Road. Tim works at Hartford Manufacturing in Adams County and Deena works at Peyton Northern.

Mrs. Doris Oswalt lived and raised her children in Poneto. Doris Shaw Oswalt married Harold McFarren. Harold's first wife, Joan Oswalt, was a sister to Gustin Oswalt.

Joan Oswalt McFarren died in March 1975, but will always be remembered for her love of children and work in the Poneto church nursery. Harold and Joan had two children, Sharon and Jack.

Sharon McFarren married Richard Falk and resides north of Bluffton. They have three children: twins Jason and Justin, age twelve and Jennifer age seven. Richard Falk works at Lime City in Huntington, Indiana.

Jack McFarren resides in Poneto with his four children: Daniel, nine; Amber, eight; Amanda, six; and Michael, age four. Jack works at Keebler Company in Bluffton.

OSWALT

Jacob Oswalt our great-great-great-great-great-grandfather immigrated from Germany to Pennsylvania (born 1722, died September 1819). His son Jacob was born in Pennsylvania in 1765 and died in 1836 in Ohio. Jacob's son, Joseph, our great-great-great-grandfather, was born in Ohio in 1806. He married Fanny Shimberry and they had nine children, five born in Ohio and four in Wells County, Indiana. Joseph died August 11, 1873 and Fanny March 7, 1878.

Our great-great-grandfather, William, was born February 19, 1830. William married Martha Jane

Dickason. They had six children. William and his second wife, Pauline Ensley Shindler had five children. Great-great-grandfather William lived in Poneto for twenty years and died at the ripe old age of seventy-one years near Keystone. His obituary stated he was a robust man who endured many hardships raising his family while Wells County was still a wilderness. William spent much of his younger days hunting and was noted for having killed more deer and wild turkey than any other in the county.

Faye and Nervia Oswalt

Charles married Addie Tappy, who's parents, Simon and Henrietta Keyes donated the ground for the first Methodist Church in Poneto. Great-grandfather Charles was a farmer like his father and grandfathers, but is fondly remembered as spending his later days playing with us. He died in 1955 at the age of ninety-one. Charles and Addie had three children, Carrie Helen, Faye Everett and Wilford Samuel. Helen and her husband, Jess Barrington owned Barrington grocery store in Poneto for thirty years.

Faye, our grandfather, born October 31, 1897 died March 1979 and Manervia Angeline Gustin, born April, 1898 died July 1989, were married in 1923. They had only formal education through the seventh grade, but grandfather was very self-educated. Grandfather Faye worked in the Bluffton Piano factory for a time, but was known by many for his work and knowledge as a electrician.

Several years ago the Journal Gazette wrote a feature on Poneto. Grandfather's interview and picture were used in the article. He referred to himself as the old relic of Poneto. Grandmother Nervia was an aide at the Wells County Hospital for several years. She also taught Sunday school at Poneto Methodist for thirty years. She was highly respected by her family and many others. They had seven children: Gustin Everett; Ruthann (Mrs. Cloid Nusbaumer); Joan (Mrs. Harold McFarren); Glendon; Vera (Mrs. Delbert Alfeld); Marjorie (Mrs. Bert Brewster); Charles (wife Ruth) Oswalt.

Gustin Oswalt our father was born August 26, 1924. He married Doris Jean Shaw, our mother, born April 3, 1924. They eloped and were married on Christmas Eve, December 24, 1943. Dad served in World War II and was a member of Poneto Methodist Church. He built Oswalt Grain and Milling Elevator in 1951 which he operated with the help of our mother and his brother Charles until his death in 1961.

Our parents had seven children: Claude and Gustin died at birth; Rose (Mrs. Dan Anderson) is the mother of Anthony and Ashley; Carolyn (Mrs. Tom Mechling) has Heidi, Misty, Brandon and step children LeaAnn and Brent; Marolyn (Mrs. Calvin Roth) has Eric Culver Funk and Gustin Curtis Funk and step daughters Thesa, Tara and Tess; Vickie (Mrs. Larry Boots) is the mother of Brent, Brittany,

Braden and Bentley. Timothy (wife Deena Andrew) has Brooke and Rhiannon. We have a step-sister Sharon (Mrs. Richard Falk), her children are Jason, Justin, and Jennifer. Our step-brother, Jack McFarren has Daniel, Amber, Amanda and Michael.

OSWALT-ELLISON

Berta Elmer (Pete) Oswalt, born August 6, 1907, married Nevo Ellison on January 7, 1933, He was known as a fine carpenter. Nevo and Pete moved from Chester Township to Big Lake where they lived until his death in 1982. Nevo now resides near Keystone. They have two sons, Donald Fredrick Oswalt who married Adeline Lorine (Ruse) on June 5, 1955, and Gerald Duane Oswalt, who married Margaret Anne (Bowser) August 23, 1959.

Donald and Adeline have four children and live near Keystone, Indiana. Donald served in the U.S. Army and was based in Korea. Daughter Kathy Jo was born August 16, 1959. She married James Richard Smeltzer who is a career navyman based on the east coast. Karla Jean, born March 23, 1965, has married Daniel Ray Gephart and presently lives in Fort Wayne. Kenny Jay, born March 14, 1969, and Kerry Joe, born April 8, 1971, are unmarried. All four children are graduates of Southern Wells School.

Gerald and Margaret live in Warsaw, Indiana, and have three children. Gerald is in police work. Daughter Geri Anne married Hal Arden Heagy, and they have one daughter, Whitney Anne. Son Jeffrey Duane, who served in the U.S. Army in Korea, has a son Ryan Adam. Gerald's youngest is Keven Andrew Oswalt.

OSWALT-GERARD

Our father, Edward Lavere Oswalt, son of William Frederick and Ida Elsie (Miller) Oswalt, married our mother, Margaret G. Gerard, on June 1, 1946. She was the daughter of Lee Alfred and Ruth C. (Michael) Gerard.

Our father served four years in the United States Air Force in World War II. After returning, he worked as a bookkeeper for Wells County Farm Bureau Co-op, later took up farming in Liberty, Jackson, and Nottingham Townships. He also drove a school bus fifteen years for Petroleum and Southern Wells Schools.

From this union they had six sons. The first two sons were born in Liberty Township, James Edward and Daniel Kay. Jim was born November 7, 1947, and Dan was born June 24, 1949. The other four sons were born in Jackson Township: Thomas Lee born September 24, 1953, Terry Gene born January 20, 1955, David Allen born January 13, 1958, and Jeffrey Wayne born February 24, 1960.

Standing (L to R) Jim, Jeff, Terry, Dan. Seated (L to R) Edward and Margaret, Tom, David

They moved from Jackson Township to Nottingham Township in January, 1961. All their sons graduated from Petroleum and Southern Wells School.

Jim graduated from Indiana University, and married Judy Warner. They live in Nottingham Township with two daughters, Julie eighteen, and Jamie fifteen. He is engaged in farming and selling real estate.

Dan graduated from Purdue University, and married Jo Ellyn Jacobs. They live in Chester Township with three daughters, Susan thirteen, Amie eleven, and Kari nine. He is engaged in farming and tool and die.

Tom graduated form Southern Wells, and married Myra Bunch. He is employed at Franklin Electric, and helps his father farm. They live in Wells County with a son, Kreig fourteen, and a daughter Joey, eleven.

Terry graduated from Manchester College, and married Kimberly Porter. They live in Wabash, Indiana with a daughter Nicole eleven, and a son Kyle eight. He is a school teacher.

David attended Manchester College, and married Barbara Fair. They live in Nottingham Township, and have two daughters, Jennifer nine, and Sarah five. He drives an oil route for Steffen Oil Company.

Jeff, a graduate of Southern Wells, married Karen Bell. They live close to Winchester, Indiana. They have two sons, Jacob five and Jared three. He is manager of Producers Marketing in Winchester.

OSWALT-SURFUS

William Frederick Oswalt and Ida Elsie Miller of Chester Township, Wells County, were married April 28, 1906, and started housekeeping three/fourths mile east of the present Southern Wells School, formerly Chester Center School. They had four sons and three daughters. Berta (Pete) Elmer Oswalt married Nevo Ellison. Pete was a fine carpenter. He and Nevo lived many years at Big Lake where he enjoyed fishing. Pete died December 30, 1982. Edith Amanda (Oswalt) married Cecil Schwob of Warren, Indiana. Clyde Franklin married Areta Marie (Ogle) and farmed in Chester Township for many years before moving to the southern edge of Bluffton. Mary Irene Oswalt died of pneumonia in 1915, at the age of fourteen and one-half months. Paul (Barney) Wilbur Oswalt married Jennie Marie (Gray) and lived many years on Wabash Street. Barney worked many years for Fritz Electric store. He died December 31, 1964. Helen Catherine (Oswalt) married James Henry Surfus. Edward Lavere Oswalt married Margaret Grace (Gerard). They have been successful farmers and dairymen.

Frederick Oswalt worked in the piano factory in Bluffton. He was well-know in the area for his fine carpentry. A doll bed that he made for his daughter, Catherine, has now been given to her granddaughter, Patricia Surfus Makowski, local veterinarian, who lives in Bluffton.

Ida was know for her fine work as a seamstress, and loving Christian spirit. Ida and Fred were both members of the Chester Center Christian Church. A story is told: at one time when the church was closed, Ida was being driven past the church by her son, Clyde. She asked him to stop; then got out and knelt to pray on the church steps. A short time later the church was reopened. They were dedicated Christians. For many years, the stone church directory stood in honor and memory of Ida. In addition to raising a fine family, they kept Ida's father, William H. Miller, and Fred's mother, Pauline, when they became unable to care for themselves. and they eventually died in their home.

Daughter H. Catherine Oswalt married James Surfus in 1939, and remained living with her father, helping with household duties. Ida had died when Catherine was a senior at Chester Center. Catherine met the new blue-eyed boy, James Surfus, at school, her junior year. The high school sweethearts were later married and had two sons. Charles Frederick Surfus was born while they still lived in Chester Township. The family later spent many years living in Majenica, Huntington County, where son Roger Allen, was born. James was the employee and shareholder in Majenica Tile Company. The boys graduated from Lancaster Township, that county.

Charles married M. Dianne Gard; they lived in Majenica from 1960 until moving to the Inskeep Addition, Harrison Township, Wells County. Charles was the second local person hired at the new Corning Glass Works in October, 1964. They have three children: Patricia (Surfus) Makowski, David, and Cheryl.

Roger graduated from Purdue University with a Mechanical Engineering degree. He married Sandra Kilander, and has worked for McDonnell Douglas Aircraft in St. Louis for nearly twenty years. They have three children: Timothy, Scott, and Tammy.

OSWALT-NUSBAUMER

On October 31, 1897, Faye Everett Oswalt was born to Charles and Addie (Tappy) in Poneto, Indiana. Charles was a son of William and Jane (Dickason). The Oswalt family came to America from Germany prior to 1760 and settled in Virginia before coming to Indiana. Addie's parents, Simeon and Henrietta (Key) Tappy, moved to Wells County from Virginia. On October 31, 1923, Faye married Minervia Gustin, daughter of Joseph and Izella (Freels), from Chester Township. Nervia was born on April 10, 1898. Her grandparents were Allen and JoAnn (Carr) Gustin and William and Matilda (Bennett) Freels. Faye and Nervia lived in Poneto where they raised their family of three sons and four daughters: Gus, Glendon, Charles, Ruthann, Joan, Vera, and Marjorie. Nervia worked at the Wells County Hospital and faithfully attended the Poneto Methodist Church. She taught Sunday School for several years. Faye worked at the Estey Piano Factory.

In 1842, Joseph and Barbara Nusbaumer emigrated to America from Switzerland. Their youngest son, George, was born in Wayne County, Ohio, that same year and later served in the Civil War. George came to Nottingham Township in Wells County in 1865 and married Catherine Hunsinger. Of their family of twelve children, Jesse was born on April 12, 1884. After his father's death, Jesse began farming the homestead. His marriage to Ora Sawyer, a music teacher, was on October 11, 1913. Ora was a daughter of Amos and Mary (Strain), both Wells County natives. Amos' family came to Indiana from Pennsylvania in 1857. Jesse and Ora had a family of two sons: Kenneth and Cloid; and five daughters Bernice, Nilah, Juanita, Phyllis and Donna.

Jessie and Ora became members of the Poneto Methodist Church after the Airline Church closed. During this time their son Cloid, born September 20, 1919, was serving in the Army during World War II. While on furlough, he met Ruthann Oswalt, born November 22, 1925. After he had served his country for four and a half years, they were married at the church parsonage on October 19, 1946. They are still active members of this church. They lived in Nottingham Township, where Cloid engaged in farming with his father. In 1947, Rebecca was born on July 25. Their son Jerry was born on October 8, 1949. In October 1953, Cloid and Ruthann bought an eighty acre farm located on 1000 S, where they build their current residence in 1967. On January 1, 1955, Janice was born.

Becky married Bill Edmundson in 1971 and currently lives in Rockford, Illinois. Becky is a computer assistant in a school. They have three children: Billy eighteen, Carrie thirteen, and Aimee ten. Jerry married Gretta Lehman in 1972 after returning from the Vietnam War in 1971. They purchased the Nusbaumer Homestead in 1975 after the death of Jesse in 1974. Ora had died in 1970. Jerry and Gretta are the parents of four children: Joetta fifteen, Jesston ten, Janelle six and Jessica six months.

Jan graduated from Taylor University and is an elementary teacher. Ruthann's parents lived in Poneto until Faye's death in 1979 and Nervia's death in 1989. Cloid continued farming and raising hogs with his son Jerry until his retirement in 1986.

J.H. PAINTER FAMILY

J.H., as John Henry Painter was called, (1868-1961) was the oldest of eight children living in Lingelstown, Pennsylvania. He left home at fourteen and lived and worked on his grandfather's farm in Virginia for two years. The slogan "Go West Young Man" influenced him to take off, and lack of funds stopped his travels at Bluffton where he had two uncles, Joe and Sam Rose. After working at a variety of jobs ranging in pay from 25¢ a day to $84 a year, his Uncle Joe, a grocer, hired him as a clerk. A partnership was arranged until he finally purchased the store for the inventory price of $4000. He then bought the George Markley grocery on South Main Street. After two years, he moved his store to the south room of the Thoma building, 118 South Main Street, where he operated a very successful grocery until 1929.

John Henry Painter and his wife Ida with their children: L-R John Rose, Paul E., Dorothy, and Mary Elizabeth (Webber)

Before his marriage in 1891, J.H. built a four-room house at 502 E. South Street at a cost of $650 and furnished it for $120. His bride, Ida Rebecca Walmer, (1871-1947), was the youngest daughter of Jacob and Elizabeth Decker Walmer. Five children were born to them: Joseph, 1892, died age nine; John Rose, 1894, died in 1922; Paul E., 1896-1982; Mary Elizabeth, 1898; and Dorothy, 1900-1985. In 1902 J.H. bought a larger home at 906 South Main Street and moved his family there. He built a building across the back of the double lot to house a horse and Shetland ponies which were enjoyed so much by the children. Stories are told about Dorothy riding her pony through the grocery store uptown. J.H. also built bins for the winter storage of apples and potatoes for sale in his store. The children attended Park School on East Ohio Street, Central School at 502 W. Washington Street, and Bluffton High School at 508 West Washington Street, walking to and from school, including home at noon for dinner. In 1918 Mr. Painter bought the home at 424 West Washington Street where he lived until his death in 1961. His wife, Ida, died in 1947.

J.H. was a very hard worker and loved doing it from early morning to late at night. By the same token, he expected a lot from the people he employed. He paid his help very well but they were required to earn it. His wife Ida was equally industrious at homemaking and pies, cakes and goodies could always be found in her kitchen for the children's friends who came to play. The family was faithful in attendance and participation at the First Reformed Church on West Washington Street, and later to the First United Church of Christ at 301 West Cherry Street. The family established the Painter Memorial Chapel in the church as a memorial to them.

LELAND PALMER FAMILY

This family history goes back to 1809, when the ancestors were early settlers in Virginia and moved to Prairie County, Ohio, in 1828. In 1839, they settled in Jackson Township, Wells County, where some descendants still live today.

In 1899, Leland was born in Jackson Township to John W. and Lorinda (Cruse) Palmer. He worked one day in a factory, one year on the railroad, and from 1922 on, he was a farmer starting with eighty acres and two horses. He married Belva Garrett in 1922, and they raised four children:

Martelle, born in 1923 who still resides with her mother at their home in Van Buren, Indiana, when they moved from the Jackson Township farm in the mid-1970's; and Wilma, born in 1928, who operates her own upholstery business in her home in Jackson Township. Wilma and Don Lacey had three children who are:

Donna (Lacey) Runkle, who resides in Jackson Township with her husband Dale, and has two children, Kimberly and Mark, who live at home. David Lacey, who resides in Goshen, Indiana, with his wife JoAnn, and has four grandchildren. The third child, Timothy Lacey, was killed in a 1968 farm accident.

The Leland Palmer Family

Wilma currently lives in Dillman, Indiana, with her husband, James Crouch.

John, the third child of Belva and Leland, born in 1935, is a farmer and factory worker who still lives in Jackson Township with his wife, Carol

(Deemer). They have three children and five grandchildren. Their children are: Larry Palmer and his wife, Amy, and two children who live in Jackson Township; Pam (Palmer) Gehrke who lives with husband, Doug, and two children in LaPorte, Indiana; and Cathy (Palmer) Placheki, who lives in Kent, Ohio, with husband, Tate, and one child. Robert, the fourth child of Leland and Belva, was born in 1939, and is a high school teacher at Madison-Grant High School where he taught since 1961. He and his wife, Mary (Hogston), have two children. Julie (Palmer) Pearson, who resided with her husband, J.D., in Clarksville, Tennessee, and Michael Palmer, who resides in Sunnyvale, California.

This family is unique in "togetherness" since it has been their tradition to meet on Sunday afternoons each week for the past fifteen years to share good food and the times of their lives.

As you can see, the Leland Palmer Family roots are still well-planted in Jackson Township, but some of the newer shoots are branching out to the corners of our nation.

KENT AND PENNY PARK

Kent Leon Park was born October 8, 1962, in Decatur, Illinois, to David and Mary Jane (Minnich) Park. He is the grandson of Fred and Irene (Wall) Park and Oscar and Ethel (Mowery) Minnich. After a few years of moving around the Indiana and Illinois area, his parents moved the family back to Bluffton where he attended the Bluffton schools from fourth grade through his graduation from Bluffton High School in 1980. During his high school years, he was very involved in the Bluffton High School Band. Upon graduation he attended Ball State University for one year then transferred to Ferris State College for three years where he earned degrees in both Photogrammetry and Ornamental Horticulture. During his last year of college he met Penny Sue Croy.

Penny Sue Croy was born December 12, 1964, at the Wells Community Hospital to Don and Phyllis (Courtney) Croy. She is the granddaughter of Clarence and Geneva (Gifford) Croy and James and Mona (Stout) Courtney. She attended the Bluffton School System throughout her school years and graduated from Bluffton High School in 1983. She was as a life-time resident of Vera Cruz until her marriage to Kent. Growing up in Vera Cruz meant many summer days were spent at the Ouabache State Park either swimming, biking or climbing the "fire tower".

Kent and Penny (Croy) Park. Taken 1984 (engagement photo)

Kent and Penny were married on January 26, 1985, on a surprisingly sunny day as Bluffton received the worst snow storm of the year the day before their ceremony. A mere five weeks after their marriage they moved to Las Vegas, Nevada for two years. Upon Kent receiving new employment they moved to Pickerington, Ohio where they continue to live at this time. Although they are not presently living in Wells County. They will always think of Wells County as their home.

Both Kent and Penny enjoy fishing and camping. They also attend many antique gas and steam engine shows (a tradition in Penny's family).

PARK-PERRY

Our particular story focuses on our parents and their lives in and contributions to Wells County. However, in writing the family history, we are chronicling the arrival, settlement, and history of two families that have contributed to the historical tapestry of the county.

Sixty years after his great-grandparents, Thomas and Matilda Perry, and thirty-five years after his grandparents, William Henry and Margaret (Hogg) Park, came to Wells County, Frederick F. Park, our father, was born on the Perry homestead near the banks of Scuffle Creek in Chester Township in 1908. This is the same Scuffle Creek which the first survey party in this part of Indiana in 1822 recorded on their original plotting. It is also the same Scuffle Creek on whose banks the first commercial oil well in Indiana spouted forth. A majority of the Perry homestead is still in the hands of Thomas and Matilda Perry's descendants.

After completing elementary school in Keystone and attending Montpelier High School for two years, Fred Park graduated from Chester High School in 1925. He then earned a bachelor's degree from Ball State and received a master's degree from Indiana University. It was while attending Ball State that he met our mother, Irene Wall of Randolph County. They were married April 5, 1930, and have spent their sixty-one years of marriage in Wells County.

We can trace the Wells County beginnings of the Park side of the family back to 1873. William Henry and Margaret (Hogg) Park immigrated to the United States from Donegal, Ireland, on June 1 of that year. In the fall they traveled from New York to Wells County and settled near Murray, where they joined his uncles, Joseph, James and Matthew, who settled in the area in the 1850's. Some of Margaret (Hogg) Park's family also immigrated to the Murray area at that time. As a result, the Park and Hogg descendants residing in the county are related. Henry and Sarah (Gailey) Parke, the parents of William Henry, followed their son from Letterkenny, Ireland, in 1874. Besides William Henry, they had nine other children: Joseph, Charles, Martha, Rebecca, Catherine, Eliza, Andrew L., Alexander G., and John. George H. and Charles A. Park, sons of Alexander, resided in Wells County.

William Henry Park farmed for many years before moving to Bluffton, where he was engaged as a practical nurse for ten years before retirement. He and Margaret were members of the United Presbyterian Church at Murray throughout their lives. Great-grandmother Margaret died on February 8, 1900. Great-grandfather William Henry died on June 29, 1930, at the age of 84. Both were buried in the Elm Grove Cemetery at Bluffton.

Our great-grandparents had seven children. Harry Washington Park taught school at several one-room schools in the county. His last few years of teaching were in Chesterton, Indiana. He never married. John Alexander Park married Mary Bowers, and they lived most of their lives in Montpelier, Indiana. Their children were: Eldon, John Jr., Helen, Elizabeth, Robert, and Margaret Ann. Charles Gailey Park married Nora Harris. Uncle Charlie also taught at several schools in the county during his lifetime. Sarah (Sadie) Park married Frederick A. Turner. She, too, was a teacher at schools in the county, including the Dillman and Bluffton schools. After their marriage, the Turners lived the remainder of their lives in Chicago and Florida, where they raised their two children, Lawrence Lynn and Phyllis Jeanetta. Jennie (Jane) Elizabeth Park married Jay Josselyn. They lived most of their lives in Havre, Montana.

Francis (Frank) Torrence Park married Blanche Janney. Uncle Frank taught at the Shoemaker School and at Petroleum High School. He later taught in Dana, Yorktown, Ridgeville, and Richmond before retirement. Their son Byron is a retired orthopedic surgeon.

Our grandfather, James Garfield Park, was the middle of the seven children. He attended the Donaldson School in Lancaster Township. After graduation he earned a teaching diploma at the University of Louisville and began a nineteen-year teaching career (in addition to farming) in Chester and Harrison Townships. Wells County schools at which he taught include Batson, in Jackson Township, and Slacum, Keystone, Five Points, and Old Red in Chester Township. He married our grandmother, Mildred Perry, in 1907.

Her great-grandfather, Thomas Perry, was a member of Major Talbot's Pennsylvania Regiment that fought in the Revolutionary War. His son Thomas married Matilda Perry and moved to Wells County from Columbiana County, Ohio, in 1849. They purchased from the government 550-acres of land in Chester Township on which to settle and farm. Our grandmother's father was Daniel Perry, the eleventh of thirteen children born to Thomas and Matilda Perry. Daniel Perry married Esther Casterline of Blackford County. They lived on and farmed the Perry farmstead until his death in 1926. Esther preceded him in death in 1911. Both are buried in the Friends Cemetery at Keystone.

Our grandmother, Mildred Perry Park, had two brothers, Lawson and Fred, and a sister, Neva. Lawson married Glenna Brubaker and they resided in Chester Township all their lives. They had two children, Charles and Yolanda. Charles married Mary Kunkel and farmed the Perry land all his life. His son Thomas still farms a section of the Perry homestead. Mildred's brother Fred married Mary Oswalt. They raised five children in Chester Township: Evelyn (Perry) Biggs, Pauline (Perry) Wenrick, Dorothy (Perry) Kaeting, Ilene (Perry) Schmidt, and Warren. Grandmother Park's only sister, Neva, married Levi Lewis Lowry. They had one son, Edgar Lewis Lowry, who married Floe Carnes. Following the death of her first husband Neva married Ross Athan. She lived her entire life in the county.

James and Mildred Park had two sons, our father, Frederick F., and Hillard Eugene. Uncle Hillard married Helen Stone of Albany, Indiana, where they both taught school. He became interested in professional scouting and started a long career as an executive for the Boy Scouts of America. He served in scout executive posts in Ionia, Michigan; Pekin, Illinois; Bloomington, Indiana; Eau Claire, Wisconsin; and Bellville, Illinois. Aunt Helen and Uncle Hillard are both deceased and buried in Elm Grove Cemetery. They are survived by two children, Gene Edwin and Elizabeth. Gene is director of Parks and Recreation in New Berlin, Wisconsin.

Elizabeth (Park) Toth is a member of the faculty at Syracuse University.

Our mother, Irene (Wall) Park, was raised on a farm in Randolph County, near Deerfield Indiana, by her parents Fred Lee and Daisy (Jellison) Wall. Mother's great-grandparents, Allen and Sarah Wall, migrated to Randolph county from North Carolina in 1817. Allen and Sarah had ten children of which Allen B., Fred's father, was the youngest. He married Malinda Barnhart in 1858. Fred Lee was the ninth of their children. Their seventh child, Hiram, moved on to Wells County, where he purchased and farmed land in Nottingham Township. He is buried in the Alberson Cemetery.

The mother of Daisy (Jellison) Wall. Seattia Summerville Steed, moved from Virginia to Randolph County in a covered wagon and settled along the Mississinewa River in 1853. She later married James Jellison, whose family migrated from Pennsylvania to Randolph County.

Our parents devoted their professional and personal lives to education. After graduation from Ball State, Dad taught one year at the Deacon School in Cass County. He then returned to Wells County to teach mathematics and physics, and to coach baseball and basketball, at Rockcreek High School from 1930 to 1934. In the fall of 1934 he started a thirty-nine year career at Bluffton High School. He taught mathematics until 1946, when he was appointed principal, a position he held for twenty-seven years until his retirement. His love of mathematics, and his success at teaching the subject was demonstrated by the accomplishments of his students. Lois (Shepherd) Headings won the Indiana algebra contest in 1936 and Jean (Frazier) Redding was the state geometry champion in 1940. During his tenure as high school principal (during which he also served as athletic director), he completed a term as president of the Northeastern Indiana Athletic Conference (NEIAC), served a five-year term on the Indiana High School Athletic Board of Control (1967-72), and was a member for seven years of the activities committee of the Indiana North Central Association for Accreditation of Schools and Universities.

As we children graduated from Bluffton High School and were entering college, our mother turned from raising a family and keeping the home to teaching. In 1952 she accepted position at Poplar Grove Elementary School, where she taught until her retirement in 1970. She earned her bachelor of science degree from Ball State in 1961 and went through commencement with her son Don, who was also graduating that year. All six members of the family earned undergraduate degrees from Ball State.

Fred F. Park Family
Front row, Irene (Wall) Park, Don Larry, Norma Jane, Frederick F. Park, 2nd Row: David G., Marilyn Ann

Our parents had five children: Marilyn Ann, David Gene, Norma Jane, James Frederick (deceased), and Don Larry.

Marilyn married Robert Pickell of Muncie, Indiana. Both are middle school teachers at Yorktown, in Delaware County. They have three children: Robert Paul II, Randall Lee, and Leslie Carol. Robert Jr. married Christine Mathew of Highland, Indiana, and is director of choral music at Plymouth High School. They have one child, Ryan Mathew. Randall married Sally Weitendorf of Joliet, Illinois; they live in Lake Bluff, Illinois where Randy is employed as a marketing manager with Amersham Corporation, a pharmaceutical company. Sally is an account executive for Baxter Corporation, another pharmaceutical company. They have one son, Eric Park Pickell. Leslie married Jeffrey Bone of Valparaiso; they live in Chicago, where she works for Amersham Corporation in personnel development and Jeff is an architect.

David Park married Mary Jane Minnich, daughter of Oscar and Ethel (Mowery) Minnich of Wells County. After graduation from college, Dave served two years in the armed forces, eighteen months of which were in Korea. On his return, he entered professional scouting and served as an executive for the Boy Scouts of America at Decatur, Illinois; Terre Haute, Indiana; and Libertyville, Illinois. In 1971 they returned to Wells County and purchased the Carnall and Sons Insurance and Abstract Company. They have two children, Karen Sue and Kent Leon. Karen married Don Karwoski of Chicago; they reside in Fort Wayne. They have one son, Benjamin Richard. Don works as an independent contractor for the installation of wireless cable TV, and Karen is employed by Carnall and Sons. Kent married Penny Croy, daughter of Don and Phyllis Croy of Vera Cruz, in Harrison Township. They live in Pickerington, Ohio, where Kent works as a project director for Photogrametric Services, Inc. Penny is office manager for Lippert Abrasives in Reynoldsburg, Ohio.

Norma Jane married George Armstrong of Hebron, Indiana. They live in Valparaiso where Norma has taught mathematics for thirty-five years in the Portage, Hobart and Duneland school districts. George is an engineer with Meca Engineering. They have two sons, George Andrew (Drew) and Frederick John. Drew married Deborah Harless of Kokomo, Indiana. He works for a farm supply and elevator firm in Howe, Indiana, his interest being in animal health. Fred married Susan Abbott of Austin, Texas. He is employed as a field director for a construction firm in the Chicago area.

Don Park, the youngest, married Claire Swick of South Bend. After acquiring his master;'s and doctors of education degrees, he taught at Ball State University for eleven years before moving to Bloomington, Indiana, where he is associate executive director of Phi Delta Kappa, Inc., a professional education fraternity. Claire is coordinator of academic counseling for the School of Business at Indiana University. They have two daughters, Kristen Lynn and Jennifer Leanne. Kristen married Timothy Trella of Chesterton; and they live in Michigan City, Indiana. Kristen is a student at Indiana University Northwest. The Trellas have two children, Elizabeth Marie and Phillip James. Jennifer graduated from Indiana University and is employed by Enterprise Leasing Corporation in Chicago. Don and Claire's sons, Shawn Larry, and twins Eric Allan and Ryan Michael are deceased.

Wells County is reflected in our family and extended family. It has influenced each of us in our daily lives. Our parents have enjoyed living and working in Bluffton and have contributed to the fabric of the community. Both have been active in the United Church of Christ in Bluffton for over sixty years. Dad served as treasurer for forty-three years. Both have been active in the Wells County Historical Society. Mom served eleven years as a hostess at the historical museum and secured volunteers; dad served as president of the society from 1980 to 1989. Mother served on the board of directors of the Wells County Foundation and the Wells County Council on Aging. She has also been a member of Psi Iota Psi philanthropic sorority since 1937 and of the Bay View Book Club since 1943.

However, the real contributions of our parents have been to the youth of Wells County. Their leadership, participation in, and support of public education and of activities for young people have been a lifelong commitment. Much of this commitment is reflected in the community awards and recognitions they have received through the decades. Dad was presented the Wells County Community Service Award in 1965 and the Distinguished Alumni Award from Ball State University in 1973. Two of the most memorable recognition were the naming of the Bluffton High School football and track facility as the Fred F. Park Stadium and the award given him by nearly 400 graduates of Bluffton High School who received weekly newsletters from him while they were in the service during World War II.

We are proud to be a Wells County family. It is our hope that the Park/Perry ancestry will continue to be a part of the future historical tapestry of the county. *(Marilyn (Park) Pickell, David Gene Park, Norma Jane (Park) Armstrong, and Don Larry Park)*

PARK-UNDERHILL

Henry and Sarah (Gailey) Park came from Letterkenny, Ireland in 1874, on the steam ship SS *Utopia*. They had ten children. Two of the children came earlier to America seeking the "land of opportunity." They sent word back to Ireland for the rest of the family to come. This was great news for those yet in Ireland. It took them three weeks to cross the ocean.

My father, Alexander Park, born January 12, 1859, died September 26, 1952, was fourteen when they came to America and was the youngest in the family.

Henry and Sarah bought a farm two miles north of Murray and this land is still in the family. That was at a time when Uniondale was just a woods; it did not become a small town until 1882.

From L to R: George and Avis Park, Carolyn Gilbert. Back L to R: Rick and Don Park, Kim Byerly

My father, Alexander, went out west in the late 1800's and set up a homestead. He stayed there for about two years.

When his parents died, he bought the home and farmland. He was past fifty when he married. His wife was Jessie Hoopengardner. She was born October 12, 1881, died December 1, 1965; she was from New Galilee, Pennsylvania. Jessie's parents were George and Amanda (Shafer) Hoopengardner. Jessie was the youngest of five children.

Alexander and Jessie had two sons, Charles born February 23, 1914, died December 4, 1985, and myself, George Henry, born November 27, 1916.

My first year of school was in 1921; I went to Murray School. We rode in a horse drawn school hack driven by Isom Elzey. I graduated from Lancaster High School in 1934.

On December 25, 1939, I married Avis (Underhill) Park who was born near Uniondale February 27, 1920. She graduated from East Rockcreek High School in 1938.

Avis was the youngest daughter of Carlin, born December 25, 1886, died March 15, 1952 and M. Fern (Newhard) Underhill, born December 8, 1889 died June 27, 1979. Carl was from Mentone, Indiana, son of John and Emma (Whetsone) Underhilll. Carl had one sister, Flavia (Underhill, Myers) Tinkey. Fern was the fourth child of eight born to Frank and Celesta (Young) Newhard of near Uniondale.

Carl and Fern had four children: Ruby, Darrell, Garth and Avis. Carl was manager of the Farm Bureau Co-op elevator in Uniondale for several years until his death in 1952. Fern worked at Wells County Hospital for several years in the kitchen.

When Avis's grandparents (Newhard) died, my parents Alexander and Jessie Park bought the farm from the Newhard estate in 1937. The farm was known as the Sunnyside Subway Farm because the Erie Railroad subway was beside the farm one mile east of Uniondale. We were married at this home and have lived here ever since, fifty-two years.

There are four children born to this marriage. Donald E. born November 1, 1940, married to Pisamai (Thonghut) Park of Bangkok, Thailand. They have four children: Sakachia married to Angela (Villaneva); they have two children Shawn and Stacy. Madee (Park) Walker married to Donnell, they have one child Janelle. Malee (Park) Elrod married to Ned Elrod, they have one child Melissia. Donald's youngest son is Lawerence E.

Carolyn J. (Park) born March 23, 1944, married Stanley Gilbert from Chester Township. They have five children. Angela married Jon Oman and they are the parents of three children: Derrick, Danielle and Lauren. Julia married David Johnson and have one daughter, Caylynne. Carolyn's other children are, Christine, Geoffrey and Cara.

Richard Park, born July 24, 1951, married Sheila Byerly of Ossian. They have two children Katie and Abby.

Kimberly (Park) born November 23, 1959, married Kirt Byerly of Ossian and they have two daughters, Jenilee and Jessica.

I have farmed and worked at the Uniondale and Ossian Lumber Company until I retired. Avis worked several years for the Uniondale Telephone Company, until the company went to dial to keep up with modern times. *(George and Avis (Underhill) Park)*

GENE AND JUDITH ANN PARKER

Gene is the oldest son of Russell Parker and Irene (Henschen) Parker of Fort Wayne, Indiana. He graduated from North Side High School in 1961 and has been employed at Zoller Pistons since 1963.

Judy is one of three children of John L. and Lucille K. (Smith) Simerman of Ossian, Indiana. She graduated from Ossian High School in 1961. She worked at Lincoln Life three years, married Gene, born May 18, 1963 and helped her mother who owned Poe Florist in Poe, Indiana. In 1983 Judy and her mother opened the House of Flowers in Ossian.

They have two children: Laura Ann born October 23, 1964 and Michael Allen born June 12, 1969.

Laura played saxaphone in the Norwell Brass Impact for two years and in the marching band for six years. Laura was the 1979 Wells County spelling bee champion. She graduated from Norwell High and Purdue University with a degree in mathematical science. She will marry Neil Ainsley of Fort Wayne, Indiana, August 10, 1991.

Mike played baseball from minor league through teen league. Was on the cross country and track teams at Norwell and played saxaphone in the band. He worked at the McDonalds in Bluffton for years, received a degree in automotive technology from ITT Fort Wayne and currently works at Muffler Doctor in Bluffton. He married Amy Gerber the daughter of Jerry and Ann Gerber of rural Bluffton and has a daughter named Amanda Michelle born October 11, 1990.

PATRICK-NAHRWOLD

Colleen Sue (Nahrwold) Patrick is the daughter of Carl and Helen (Heuer) Nahrwold. She was born on May 18, 1949, and baptized on May 22, 1949, at Adams County Hospital by the Reverend Harry Behning. From 1955-1963 she attended Bethlehem Lutheran School, Ossian, Indiana. On April 7, 1963, she was confirmed by the Reverend A.O. Kaltwasser at Bethlehem Lutheran Church, Ossian, Indiana. Colleen was a member of the last graduating class of Ossian High School in 1967. After high school she worked at Fort Wayne Wire Die in Fort Wayne, Indiana for nine years.

On February 12, 1972, at Bethlehem Lutheran Church, Ossian, Indiana she married Thomas Lynn Patrick (born January 27, 1950), son of George Harrold (born September 23, 1920) and Betty Jean (Price) Patrick (born March 1, 1927) of Monroe, Indiana. Tom graduated from Adams Central High School in 1968. He worked at General Electric in Decatur, Indiana, from January 1969-October 29, 1988, when they closed the plant. Tom's great-grandfather, Daniel Patrick, was born July 9, 1844, at Clogham Parrish, Gallon, Kings County, Ireland. He came to America and established a homestead in Logan County, Ohio, near East Liberty. He and his wife Amanda Jane had seven children, one of whom was Pearl George (February 2, 1885-July 17, 1926). He married Daisy M. Benton (June 7, 1885-January 2, 1922). They had five children: Sam, Thelma, Maurice, Mildred, and George (Tom's father.)

Tom and Colleen are the parents of three children: Mark Allen (born August 3, 1972) a senior at Norwell High School, Jodie Lynn (born June 15, 1978) is in the seventh grade at Norwell Middle School, and Darren Thomas (born May 6, 1988).

In 1977 they purchased two and one-half acres to build a home from William Grewe. In June of 1989 they purchased twenty-seven acres from Edwin W. Grewe Sr.

Tom is now a full-time farmer, while Colleen is a homemaker.

PEARSON-BURKLO

Ancestors of the Wells County Pearson family date back to 1842, when Peter and Martha (Taylor) Pearson came to Indiana from Clinton County, Ohio. He was a native of Virginia; she was from North Carolina. Peter, a farmer, settled in Blackford County in 1844.

Gilead, son of Peter Pearson, was married in Minnesota in 1867 to Mariah Greenwood, daughter of Henry and Margaret (Farlow) Greenwood of Wells County. Gilead owned land and farmed in Minnesota. Heartbroken at the loss of three of their first four children, Gilead and Mariah returned to Indiana in 1876. After farming a few years, they bought a grocery store in Dillman. In 1894, the moved their family to Poneto. They are buried in the Grove Cemetery.

A native of Wells County, Tom Pearson, son of Gilead, married Maude Smith. She was the daughter of Peter W. and Dora (Forker) Smith. In

George and Avis Park Family

1919 they moved to Medford, Wisconsin, as homesteaders. After a farming accident, they returned to Poneto, Indiana. Tom and son, Jack, bought land in Notthingham Township in 1951. Tom and Maude are buried in Markle Cemetery. Their children are: Guyla (1916-1986), who married Virgil Davison and moved to New Mexico. Their children are: Linda, David, and James. Everett (1919-1988) married Iva Noonan and lived in Mississippi. They have one son, Kit. Roxy (1920-1964) married Glen Lynch and lived in Petroleum. Children: Anna, Mary, Tom, John, and Henry. Jack (1925) was born near Poneto and graduated from Jackson Center. He married Joan Burklo. Jack farmed until 1965 and retired from Kunkle Valve in Fort Wayne in 1987. They relocated to Union Township in Zanesville. He and Joan had two daughters: Judy (1943) graduated from Petroleum and Parkview School of Nursing. She is an R.N. working at the Veterans Hospital in Marion. Judy married Richard Henley, son of Dowe and Lucile (Lambert). They live in Rockcreek Township. Children: John, Chris, Lori, and Jackie. Nan (1948) graduated from Petroleum and Indiana-Purdue, Fort Wayne. She teaches at Bluffton High School. Nan married Kenneth Yake, son of Noah and Martha (Zirkle). They live in Lancaster Township. Children: Courtney and Jessica.

Joan Burklo (1925), daughter of Ed and Laura (Stotts) Burklo, graduated from Jackson Center and married Jack Pearson in 1943. She retired from General Electric Company in 1984. Joan had three older sisters: Cecil Gilbert (1902-1991), Stella Bush (1907), and Ruth Carnes (1917). Her maternal grandmother, Sara Jane (McIntire), married William Stotts. Sara Jane, daughter of Dick McIntire, was the niece of Nun, William and Harrison. These four brothers came from Frederick County, Virginia, during the years 1836-1868, settling in sections 25, 26, 35, and 36 in Jackson Township. This two mile area was referred to as McIntire row. The brothers, their wives, an unmarried sister, Dorcas, who was called Darkey, and many of their descendents, are buried in the Asbury Chapel Church Cemetery. They and their ancestors are recorded in *Charles McIntire of Colonial Virginia*, compiled by June R. (McIntire) Taylor and Lois M. (McIntire) Salisbury, daughters of Turner McIntire.

PENCE

One story is that two Pence brothers and a cousin came to America from Germany through Holland soon after the Dutch settled New York. Their name was spelled Pentz but in arriving in America, they changed their name to Pence.

Martin Pence (born March 19, 1790), and Mary Elizabeth Corder were married on February 7, 1812. They were both born in Virginia. They moved into Ohio and had several children, one of which was my great-great-great grandfather, David Pence (born 1815). He married Anna Smith in 1836 in Ohio where their first six children were born. He and his wife moved near Swayzee, Grant County, Indiana, when my great-great-grandfather, John Smith Pence was a small child. They had a total of thirteen children: Emily, Noah, Andrew, Louise, Louis John S., Sarah, Melissa, Jasper, Casmer, David, Mary Etta and a baby unnamed.

John S. Pence lost his first two wives early in marriage and in 1871 he married Mary Martha (Mattie) Watson (born 1846, died 1938) and had the following children, Rolla Daniel (born 1873), Earl D. (born 1874), Dora A. (born 1876), Henry (born 1879), Glen D. (born 1881) and Blanche Ethel (born 1885).

Rolla, my great-grandfather, married Minnie Luella Weeks, (born 1875) in 1894. They had ten children, Irel Vern (born 1895 married Anna Kelsey), Lola Fern (born 1897 married George Gilbert/ Clarence Brickley), Noah Lester (born 1899), Orus Russell (born 1903 married Mildred Kocher/ Margaret Weber), Ada Mildred (born 1906 married Harley Slane), John (born and died 1909), Nina Ethel (born 1910, married Maurice Roe), Frederick (born 1912, died 1913), Olive (born 1914, married Fred Divelbiss), and Woodrow Wilson (born 1918, married Patricia Kelley).

This 1911 or 1912 Ford belonged to the Rolla D. Pence family. Picture of Markle Baumgardner Buggy repair shop, Rolla at the wheel, 18 month, Nina in front, Mildred, Minnie with baby, Frederick on her lap and Lola next to her. The buggy in background was to be repaired as Irel had wrecked it the night before.

In 1908, Rolla and Minnie moved to the farm east of Markle in Union Township when my Grandpa Orus was five years old. When they moved, great-grandpa and the oldest boys walked their cattle from Swayzee to Markle and Minnie and the younger children took the train. In 1918 the home burned and Rolla (a carpenter) rebuilt the house in 1919.

Orus married Mildred Ruth Kocher (born 1902) on December 24, 1924. She was a school teacher. They lived in the old one-room schoolhouse on 116 east of Markle after they were married. They had one daughter, Marilyn Ruth (my mother) born March 20, 1929. Grandma died during childbirth. Grandpa then moved back home where he helped farm and Great-Grandma Pence helped take care of Mom. In 1951 Great-Grandma Pence died and Grandpa bought the farm. In 1958, after almost thirty years, Grandpa married Margaret Weber (born 1902) and they still live on the farm today.

Marilyn married Robert Inskeep (born 1926) on June 21, 1947 and had five children, Candy (born 1948), Cathy (born 1950), Cindy (born 1952), Cheri (born 1953) and Carla (born 1956).

Reference Inskeep family history.

PENCE-DOUGLASS

Harry and Nora (Retherford) Pence moved to Union Township from Grant County, in 1903. They decided to sell their farm here in 1918, and moved back to the Swayzee, Indiana, area. Their second daughter, Bethina, married Howard Douglass, also a farmer, and they have two children, Clara Mae and Rex. Upon learning that the farm where Bethina once lived in Wells County was for sale, they purchased it and moved her in 1936.

They were active in Farm Bureau; Markle United Methodist Church; Howard served on the Township Advisory Board; and Bethina was a charter member of the Union Center Happy Hour Home Extension Club.

Both children graduated from Union Center High School. Clara Mae married William Fausz, a farmer from Union Township. Rex farmed with his father and married Marilyn Harnish, daughter of Leroy and Fred (Fishbaugh) Harnish. They were also engaged in farming in Wells County. The newlyweds moved into the original farm house, as Howard and Bethina has remodeled a house for themselves immediately east on the same road.

Douglas Farm - Union Township

After farming for two years, Rex was drafted into the U.S. Army. An auction was held to sell livestock and selected equipment, and Marilyn went back to live with her parents and await the birth of their son, Philip. Rex spent is last year of duty in LaRochelle, France, and resumed farming at the same location after his discharge. Three more children were born and more acres were added to the original one hundred sixteen acres. All four children were graduated from Norwell High School and various colleges: Philip from Huntington College with an education degree. However, farming looked more appealing and he joined his father in the family operation. He married Marcia Kidd from Fort Wayne and moved into the Douglass farmhouse. Their children are Rachel, Paul, and Isaiah.

Patricia graduated from Ohio Wesleyan University, married Tim Baker, son of Bob and Carol Baker, and taught at Lancaster Elementary School. They lived west of Ossian with their two children, Ryan and Allison.

Susan graduated from Indiana University Business School, and was a secretary at Tuthill Pump, Fort Wayne. She married Stanley Rekeweg, son of Edgar and Rozella Rekeweg. They have two sons, Jason and Justin, and live north of Craigville.

Steven graduated from Northwest Business College with a degree in auto/diesel maintenance. After working in Fort Wayne, he also decided that farming looked better, so he joined his father and brother in farming. He married Leslie Helm from Montpelier, and they now live on Indianapolis Road, close to the farm.

Howard, Rex, and Philip have all served on the Township Advisory Board, a position still held by Philip. All the Douglass men are farmers, as are the sons-in-law. The Pence-Douglass Homestead is still owned by Bethina Douglass.

We are very proud of our heritage and strive to be good stewards.

HERMAN PENCE FAMILY

Herman Edward Pence was born in Bluffton, Harrison Township, Wells County, on July 17, 1910, the son of G. Wilford Pence and Ida R. Merkey Pence. He was married September 3, 1938 to Allene Emma Baumgartner of Fort Wayne, Allen

County, Indiana. She was born February 23, 1911, daughter of John E. Baumgartner and Edith Emrich Baumgartner.

Herman E. Pence graduated from P.A. Allen High School in Bluffton, in 1928, and enrolled in the Toolmaker Apprentice School at General Electric Company in Fort Wayne, Indiana. He graduated in November 1932, and continued with General Electric Company advancing as a manufacturing engineer, and trouble shooter in new plants until 1947. He worked as a manufacturing engineer with Franklin Electric Company in Bluffton, in 1947, and 1948, as he was starting a dairy farm operation in Harrison Township.

Herman and Allene Pence

He operated the dairy farm until 1959, selling a herd of one hundred purebred Holsteins after milking a ton of milk per day. He also operated one of the first confinement hog operations in Indiana.

In 1959, he started working with Mix Mill Inc., in Bluffton, as manufacturing engineer. He assumed responsibilities of manager of manufacturing and worked there until retirement in November 1974. Mix Mill employed up to one hundred people, and manufactured equipment to handle grain and prepare livestock feed.

Allene E. Baumgartner graduated from North Side High School in Fort Wayne in 1929. She enrolled in nurses training at Methodist Hospital in Fort Wayne in 1930, and graduated in 1933. She worked as a nurse in Indianapolis and in Brooklyn, New York, and was employed by the Public Health Department in Fort Wayne, until her marriage to Herman Pence on September 3, 1938.

Allene maintained a home and assisted with the farm work. She raised all the young stock in the dairy operation, as welled as helped with the milking chores. She operated the hog confinement operation with the assistance of the sons, during 1959, while Herman was disabled with a heart attack. She worked as a surgery supervisor at Wells Community Hospital in Bluffton from 1960 to 1974, when she retired. Herman and Allene continued to live on their farm in Harrison Township in the summer, and in a home in Englewood, Florida, in the winter. As this is written in 1991, they were both eight years old and active in their church and community.

Herman and Allene have three sons: Robert Edward Pence (July 1, 1939), David Allen Pence (April 10, 1941), and John Frederick Pence (April 29, 1945).

Robert E. Pence served in the U.S. Air Force from 1962 to 1966. He was employed at General Electric and later at Lincoln Life Insurance Co., as a computer programmer and specialist. He is a steam railroad buff.

David A. Pence completed a machine builder apprenticeship course at Franklin Electric, and attended Purdue University. He first married Janet Schreiber and had two children: Mathew A. (September 29, 1974) and Carrie Ann (August 28, 1978). He is to be married to Katherine Misegades Smith on June 28, 1991, this being a second marriage for both. Katherine has three children: Ellen Smith, twenty-two, James Smith, seventeen, and Rachel Smith, fifteen. David has owned and restored steam traction engines and other early farm tractors.

John F. Pence married Martha Pfister. To their union were born four children: John David (February 20, 1969), Jason Robert (September 4, 1970), Christa Leigh (January 29, 1972), and Cassandra (Cassie) Jeraldine (May 3, 1974). Christa gave birth to a son, Mason Andrew, on October 29, 1990. John completed an associate degree in business and science at Purdue University. John David Pence served in the Persian Gulf War in early 1991.

G. Wilford Pence was born March 31, 1875 to Peter Pence, Jr. and Lydia Ann Warner Pence. On October 14, 1909, he married Ida R. Merkey, who was born April 11, 1884, to Levi Merkey and Lydia Ellen Houtz Merkey. Peter Pence Jr. was born July 18, 1853, to Peter Pence Sr. and Sarah Sloan Pence.

Peter Pence Sr. was born in 1817. He moved to Logan County, Ohio, in 1826. In 1842, he came to Wells County and purchased eighty acres of land for $200. A few years later, he moved to Wells County and purchased an additional eighty acres for $200. Sarah Sloan was born in 1818 in County Armara in Ireland.

G. Wilford Pence, Peter Pence Jr., and Peter Pence Sr. are buried at Bethel Cemetery in Harrison Township.

Levi Merkey was born January 4, 1857, at Rehrersburg, Pennsylvania, and died June 30, 1931. Lydia Ellen Houtz was born May 5, 1864, and died July 30, 1943. Both are buried at Bethel Cemetery in Harrison Township.

Lydia Ann Warner was born May 20, 1851, and died in 1938. Her parents were John Warner and Lydia Moyer-Warner. The John Warner family came down the Ohio River to Cincinnati in 1850, and then cut their way through the forest to their homestead one mile east of Petroleum in Nottingham Township. They cut trees for a log cabin which was one room with a fireplace and a loft above with an outside ladder entrance, used as a sleeping room. In 1886, several of the family including the mother died from smallpox. In 1870, father John went to Iowa to locate a land grant, and on the way back, he got on the wrong train on double track. He jumped off into the path of another train and was killed. The Warners are buried in the Granard Cemetery one-half mile west of Reiffsburg in Nottingham Township.

One of Lydia A. Warner's ancestor's family was the Sara Warner kidnapped and raised by the Indians after the Deerfield (Massachusetts) Massacre. Her gravestone is in the Deerfield Museum.

PENROD

There was a small log house in Liberty Township in Wells County by the Blanche Chapel Church in which Chester Franklin and Rebecca Jane Hamilton Penrod started housekeeping. Three daughters, Bessie, Hattie, Lizzie and seven sons, Jim, Jack, Frank, John, Sam, George and Charlie were born to this union.

My father's ancestors were United Brethren and came from Pennsylvania. My father was born March 25, 1885, and died on August 27, 1925.

My mother was a Hamilton. Mother was a devoted Dunkard and nearly always wore a full and long apron over her dress and a bonnet. My father was a farmer and a blacksmith for fifty years. He said if he could be in the black smith for fifty years, he would lay down his hammer and hang up his tongs. He died at the age of seventy. My mother, Rebecca Jane was born December 21, 1860, and died April 23, 1949. My parents were farmers and my father was a janitor at the Blanche Chapel Church where he attended church. Our house was close to the church, but fire destroyed it some time ago. The church is still standing and there are still services there. We had one cow, a pair of mules, some goats, a good size garden and lots of friends.

I attended a good one-room school, called the Popejoy School, located two miles south of Liberty Center in Wells County. There were no busses, so in good weather we walked one and three-fourths miles. In case of real bad weather, someone from

50th Wedding Anniversary - September 3, 1988
L - R Back row: Robert Pence, John D. Pence, Jason Pence, Herman Pence, John F. Pence, Katherine Misegades Smith, Louise Misegades Smith, Paul Merkey. Middle Row: Mathew Pence, Christa Pence, David Pence, Allene Pence, Cassie Pence, Ethela Merkey. Front row: Cary Pence, two visiting children.

our community came after us in a bobsled pulled by mules.

Baseball was our favorite game, that we liked to play after school. There were quite a lot of Penrods that attended this school. The school has been torn down for many years.

This is where George W. Penrod was born in 1901. Left to right: John Penrod, Sam Penrod, George Penrod, Charlie Penrod - 1908

I was a string butcher and learned my trade in Freemont, Michigan. I worked for most of twenty-years at the Hoosier Grain Elevator in Keystone and at the highway garage in Bluffton. I am now retired and will be ninety this June 9, 1991.

I married Florence L. Bennett on October 31, 1936. We have three children: George Allan and Paul Edward and one daughter, Rebecca Ruth. We have six grandchildren; Ruth Elaine, Mark Allan, John Michael, Ronda Lee, Jeremy and Kyle. We are great-grandparents to Kayle Nicole Boice and Sarah Christine and Carrie Elizabeth Penrod.

I am a member of the Chester Center Church in Chester Township in Wells County. I enjoy having lots of flowers. (*George W. Penrod*)

PENROD

The history of the Penrod family in Wells County began on November 4, 1848, with Samuel and Elizabeth Penrod purchased a forty-acre homestead in Liberty Township from the United States. Nine years later Andrew J. and his wife, Joannah (Pace), assumed ownership and continued to farm the homestead.

In 1909 the ownership was transferred to John and Mary (Britt) Penrod. Children: Alice, Annie, Nellie, Perl, Rose, Edith, Mabel, Ada, Clell, Fred, Alva, Arch, and Ora. Of their children two survive: Perl and Ada.

Perl married Tom Falk. Children: David, Dale, Phyllis (Cobbs), Janice (Berry).

Ada married John Mitchell. Daughter, Kathleen Ann. They live in Burbank, California.

Ora "Dick" was born November 4, 1892. He married Sceloy Ayres. They had one son, Claude, who was born on February 11, 1917. Ora was a farmer and drove bus for Chester School. Sceloy died in 1945.

In March 1951, Ora purchased the original omestead from his father's estate. He farmed until his death in November 1960.

Claude graduated from Chester in 1935 where e lettered in basketball. On February 24, 1940, Claude married Vera Gordon who was a 1932 graduate of Rockcreek. A son, Jerry, was born on November 7, 1943.

Shortly after Jerry's birth, Claude went to Europe to serve in the 744th Railway Battalion with the U.S. Army for the duration of World War II.

Upon his return, he drove truck for the Panhandle Eastern Pipeline Company in Bluffton.

In 1951 the family moved to Uniondale. After Claude's death on February 8, 1954, Verda worked as a cook at Rockcreek School. Later she worked at the Uniondale Corner Market. Verda then became the Uniondale Postmaster for twenty-eight years until her retirement in 1987.

Andrew and Joanna Penrod Family in front of original Penrod home

Jerry assumed ownership of the original homestead in 1960 after his grandfather's death. He graduated from Rockcreek in 1961, and from Ball State University in 1965. Presently Jerry teaches history and coaches freshman basketball at Southern Wells. He also lives on and farms the original homestead.

On August 30, 1964, Jerry and Joanna (Jump) were married. Joanna is the daughter of Vernard and Mary (McIntosh) Jump. Joanna graduated from Lancaster in 1964, and later from Ravenscroft Beauty College. She had her own shop, but is now the owner and manager of Grandma Jo's Restaurant in Montpelier.

Their four children: Gregory (July 28, 1965), Kathy (February 6, 1967), Patti (October 18, 1968), and David (June 24, 1973) are graduates of Southern Wells.

Greg married Tonya (Keplinger) July 13, 1984. Children: Kyle (February 1, 1988) and Kristy (July 28, 1990). Greg works in Agri-business and Tonya works as a secretary.

Kathy married Keith Fiechter August 3, 1985. Kathy is a surgical technician while Keith assembles motor homes.

Patti married Steven Teague September 3, 1988. Children: Anna (October 3, 1989) and Spencer (December 27, 1990). Patti works on accounts at a grain elevator, while Steve works in agri-business.

David while a student at Southern Wells was active in the FFA Chapter. He plans to study telecommunications at Ball State University.

GEORGE W. AND FLORENCE L. PENROD

George W. Penrod is next to the youngest son of Chester Franklin and Rebecca Jane Hamilton Penrod of Wells County. He was from a family of ten. He was a string butcher by trade and enjoyed farming, worked at the Hoosier Grain elevator for twenty years and was employed at the State Highway Garage for many years.

He attended school at the Popejoy School in Liberty Township in Wells County. He had to walk to school in those days, but if the weather was too bad, someone from the community would come to take us home on a bobsled pulled by mules.

He is currently retired and will be ninety the June 9. He was born June 9, 1902.

Florence (myself) is next to the third oldest of nine children of Larry A. and Ruth Thomas Bennett of Wells County. I attended a one-room school at Noe in Wells County and then spent the rest of my school days at the Chester Center School. I graduated in 1936.

I was born June 29, 1916. We are the proud parents of three children. George Allan Penrod born, July 22, 1938, and is married to Jane Barner and they have two sons, Mark Allan, born September 24, 1960, and Jon Michael, born August 13, 1962. Jane and Alan have two grandchildren, Sarah Christine, four, and Carrie Elizabeth, one.

Paul Edward was born August 13, 1950, and is married to Sue Reimer and they have two sons, Jeremy Edward, born December 11, 1979, and Kyle Andrew, born July 24, 1982.

Rebecca Ruth was born May 24, 1942, and is married to Art Prentice. They have two daughters, Ruth Elaine Boice, born September 22, 1959, and Ronda Lee Mathew, born July 9, 1963, and one granddaughter, Kaye Nicole Boice, born October 3, 1986.

I am an active member of the Chester Center Christian Church of Wells County in Chester Township. I retired from CTS after eighteen years at Berne, Indiana, in 1979.

I enjoy reading, crafts and several other hobbies.
Submitted by Florence Leone Penrod

PEQUIGNOT

Ansel A. and Wanda Burley Pequignot lived in Rockcreek Township, Wells County, from January, 1956, until October, 1982.

They purchased the old Decker Home on what is now 500 W. north of 200 N from Carl and Muriel Freds. They had two children.

Carolyn graduated from Rockcreek in 1963. She married James Riley Beck, son of Freida and Louis Beck in 1964. He was also a graduate of Rockcreek in 1963. They lived in Zanesville across from the United Brethren Church from 1973-1977. They are the parents of four children. Brian Christopher graduated from Huntington County Schools in 1986 and from DePauw University in Greencastle, Indiana, in 1990 and now works at Magnavox in Fort Wayne.

Twins, Jamie Heather and Amber Denise, graduated from Huntington County Schools in 1990 and are living at home. Jamie married Edward Hartman, who is in the army.

Joshua Jay was born when they lived in Zanesville and is a freshman in high school this year.

Mark Alan Pequignot graduated from Norwell in 1973. He now lives in Union Township, Huntington County.

Ansel worked at Corning Glass Works and Wanda taught school at the Lincoln Elementary School in Huntington.

THEODORE W. PFISTER

William and Elizabeth Pfister had just settled on their farm in Wells County when they were blessed with the birth of their second son who they named Theodore William. The date was April 17, 1937. At about that same time, all the trees were planted in the CCC Camp (Ouabache State Park). As Ted grew up he was full of energy and quite a challenge for his parents. But he was reminded by his dad in a birthday card last week, he's glad to have him for a son, even though he gave him a few grey hairs.

Ted attended school in Vera Cruz, where his teacher was Eldon Sprunger. He had a great respect for Mr. Sprunger, also a little fear for sure. He finished his education at Bluffton High School. There he met another man he still admires a lot. Maybe he wasn't always on the same wave length as Fred Park, but he feels he received a good education. He graduated in 1955.

Ted and Rose Pfister

He tried two jobs in town, at Sterling Casting and Franklin Electric. But his heart was in farming, so he went into partnership with his dad.

On July 26, 1959, he married Rose Lantz from Adams County. Their first home was at 617 South Main Street in Bluffton. She was employed at Lincoln Life in Fort Wayne. With the birth of their first child, they moved to a house trailer on his parents farm near the Ouabache State Park. After the arrival of the third child, Ted's parents decided to let his family move into the farm home. So now Ted was sleeping in the bedroom he was born in. In 1973 the home was remodeled and added on to. The wonderful old bank barn is almost the same as when it was built in the 1890's. The hand hewed beams are as strong and beautiful as ever. The outside has been covered with many coats of paint. The bottom has had pigs every year since Ted lived there. The upstairs has hay, straw, and some equipment.

Ted now farms and raises hogs with his sons. The years have gone very fast and have been pleasant. Soon he may leave the old farm home to make room for the next generation.

Ted and Rose were blessed with five children. On April 29, 1960, they had their first and only girl, who they named Leonda Ann. She is married to Lynn Stieglitz and has four children: Amanda, Jeremy, Natalie, and Tianna. He is the manager of Milan Center Feed and Grain and the Feed Barrel. They live in New Haven.

Their first son was born on June 19, 1961. His name is Chris Theodore, and he is married to Shari Stoller from Craigville. They have a son named Kyle. Chris also has a "Little Brother", Shane Turner, who is like part of our family. He has helped on our farm a lot.

Next came along Daniel William on August 28, 1962. He is married to Cherry Stoller from Van Wert, Ohio, and they have two sons, Tony and Brett.

Courtney was the third son, born on August 6, 1964. He married Jodi Gerber from Adams County. They have three boys: Lance, Spencer and Ty.

Last but not least, there is Matthew Lane, who is a freshman at Bluffton High School.

Ted has been active in soil conservation, 4-H, and Gateway Woods in Leo. They are members of the Apostolic Christian Church.

THOMAS W. PFISTER FAMILY

The Thomas W. Pfister family had its beginning in Wells County in 1936, when Tom moved from Adams County, where he was born, to Wells County. He moved with his parents, William and Elizabeth Pfister, when he was two years old. He lived the next seventeen years across the road from the Ouabache State Recreational Area (then the CCC Camp) and watched workers plant the evergreen trees in the bare fields to make the park. He remembers easily viewing the "fire towner" in the park from his home when the trees were small.

Tom was the Wells County spelling bee winner when he was in the seventh grade. He graduated from P.A. Allen High School, where he met and dated his future wife, Barbara Pearson, youngest daughter of the late Jenner and Daisy Pearson. She had lived at 4901 South-State Road 1 all her life with her parents.

Barbara remembers many Saturdays when she helped her mother clean chickens and deliver them to customers in town. They got fifty cents for dressing and delivering each chicken. They would wash the chickens in Ivory soap to make them white before cutting them up. She can also remember going to the feed mill on West Water Street on Saturday with her Dad to get chicken feed ground when she was twelve years old. Then she could pick out the "printed feed sacks" she wanted to use to make herself a new dress. Her mother, Daisy, will be remembered by many for the homemade "cream candy" she made and sold in town.

Barbara was the winner of the Tuberculosis essay contest in grade school. She and Tom were both active members of Wells County 4-H clubs for several years. Barbara graduated from P.A. Allen High School in 1952. They were married July 12, 1953, at the Apostolic Christian Church by the late Sam Aeschliman. Barbara was then employed at the Dime Trust and Savings Bank in downtown Fort Wayne. Tom sprayed tomatoes for local farmers and helped his father farm. Later he futher his education by serving a tool and die apprenticeship program at Franklin Electric and attending IUPU in Fort Wayne in the evenings. He spent several years working in Bluffton factories. His first job paid approximately $1.00 per hour starting wage. He was one of the first employees of Star Engineering. During this time the Pfisters lived in a three-room apartment at 212 East Central, rented from John Painter for $40.00 a month. There they were blessed with the first daughter, Rebecca. The family soon outgrew the apartment, so they moved to the "Big Brick House" on South Main Street between the bowling alley and what was then the Ware Baker Implement Company. They rented the whole downstairs for $60.00 a month from Ware Baker. While living here two more daughters were added to the family tree, Joan and Carmon. While the family was living in the Big Brick House the back room was used as a precinct voting place.

Renting at this expensive price was not too practical, so the Pfisters decided to invest their money in a farm. In 1957 the John Oswalt farm at 6131 East-100 South was for sale for $200 an acre — an enormous price for a young couple with a family, but they decided to try it. Tom's father retired in 1972 from farming, and they purchased his share of equipment and were now full-time farmers! They also raised hogs. Hogs were about $16.00/CWT and corn was about $1.00 per bushel.

They had an eight-party phone line with their number being 822-4.

On the farm the Pfister family grew fast with the addition of three daughters, Patsy, Lisa, and Peggy, and one son, Timothy. In 1966 they built a chicken house for 10,000 layers; all the children soon became expert egg gatherers. It was always work, but many happy hours can be recalled working together as a family. The kids looked forward to Friday when "Lewie the Egg Man: came and gave them all "a stick of gum!" School years on the farm were busy and exciting with school activities and sports. All of the children graduated from Bluffton High School.

After twenty-eight years on the farm, the Pfister children were all out on their own, and the house soon became too big. In 1985 Tom and Barbara purchased a smaller home at 4800 Est-State Road 316, where they live today. They are the grandparents of sixteen children who keep them busy in their spare time. They have one grandson who will carry on the Thomas Pfister name, Timothy John (TJ) Pfister, the only son of Timothy and Angela (Hunt) Pfister. In January, 1991, Tom underwent open heart surgery. As of this writing he is farming part-time, is enjoying life, and is very thankful for the miracle God has performed in his life through medical knowledge. The Pfisters enjoy camping and traveling in their spare time.

WILLIAM PFISTER

The Pfister name became part of Wells County history when William and Elizabeth purchased the Dave Klopfenstein farm, located near the entrance of what is now the Ouabache State Park.

Elizabeth's claim to Wells County history goes back to a home at 404 East Cherry Street. Her family lived there while her father worked at the Cline, Zimmer, and Reed Hardware. She was employed in the Bruce Williamson home for eight dollars per week. Elizabeth was the ninth of twelve children born to Aaron and Aldine Klopfenstine Moser. Her brother, Bert Moser, was with the Bluffton Fire Department for thirty-two years, serving as fire chief for nine years.

Bill was born in Iroquois County, Illinois, and was living in Leo at the time of his marriage to Elizabeth. They spent their first months of marriage in Mansfield, Ohio. When they returned to Elizabeth's home are, they lived in Adams County for three years before moving to Klopfenstein farm. It was the location of a whiskey distillery. The mash left from making the whiskey was conveyed to the barn and fed to the cattle. In 1938, the whiskey aging building was taken down. It contained many large river rocks. These rocks were donated to the CCC Camp (Ouabache State Park) and used to make the fireplaces in the shelter houses.

Bill and Elizabeth became dairy farmers, and saw many ups and down in the economy during their working years. While living there, they raised four children: Thomas, Theodore, Julia, and Mary Joe. Bill often remarks and about the changes he experienced in the methods of farming.

In 1963, the built a home one and one-half miles west east of the present homestead. At eighty-eight years of age, Bill is still active sometimes driving a tractor and helping around the farm. Elizabeth keeps busy with cooking and housework. Every summer she has a beautiful, bountiful garden. She also has lots of trees, shrubs, flowers, and a neat looking lawn. They are both willing helpers for their extended family which now includes eighteen grandchildren and thirty-four great-grandchildren.

They are members of the Apostolic Christian Church near Vera Cruz.

PHEGLEY

Byrom J. and Marcella Phegley and sons, Noel and Mark, moved from Monticello, Indiana, to Bluffton, Indiana, in September 1957. They originally lived in Rensselaer, Indiana, their respective parents being James Byrom and Arno Prouty Phegley and Thomas and Marguerite Daugherty Eldridge.

Mr. Phegley was a co-owner of Wells County Automotive Supply, Inc., established in 1957 in the Fryback Building on South Johnson Street and later moved to 643 North Main Street. A second store, Adams County Automotive Supply, Inc. was opened in 1962 at 207 North Third Street in Decatur, Indiana.

The Phegleys built a home in 1961 at 3280E 350S (formerly Cobbum Road). They became members of the First United Methodist Church, Parlor City Country Club, and the Elks Lodge. Mrs. Phegley actively participates in United Methodist Women, Tri Kappa Alpha Associate Chapter, and Bay View Reading Club and Study Club. In 1987, she was chairman of Wells County's week long Sequicentennial celebration.

Noel and Mark Phegley attended Poplar Grove School, Central Junior High, and both graduated from P.A. Allen High School. After two years' additional schooling (Indiana University and Northwood Institute), Noel moved to Columbia City to open Columbia City Automotive Supply, Inc., in 1974. He married Gloria Pease of Bluffton in 1976. Their daughters are Abigail, eleven, and Jamie nine.

Mark Phegley joined his brother in business after attending Indiana University two years. He is now managing the Decatur store. He married Julia Adkins of Columbia City in 1984. Their children are Drew, six, Mollie, three, and Mallorie one week.

Mr. Phegley suffered a severe heart attack in 1981 and died in August, 1984, with burial in Elm Grove Cemetery.

PINNEY

World War I ended less than three years before Ernest and Lucy Pinney packed their four daughters and all their belongings and left Darke County, Ohio, for Indiana. Ernest had purchased a general store in the small town of Mt. Zion on the Jackson-Chester Township line in southern Wells County. Ernest, Lucy, and their family lived in the south half of the store and slept upstairs while maintaining their business in the remaining portion of the building. As late as 1958, Pinney's grocery was the center of the community. Saturday nights found the walls bursting with people who had come not only to buy groceries but to share gossip and trade lies around the still-present coal stove near the rear of the establishment.

A native Hoosier, Ernest Pinney was born June 9, 1885, in Jay County, Indiana, the eldest child of Hiram and Nina Bell Inskeep Pinney. Hiram Pinney (1861-1947) was the son of Wilson Pinney, who died before Hiram was born, and Lucinda Davis. Wilson's parents were Charles and Hannah Bailey Pinney.

Nine Bell Inskeep was the oldest daughter and second of twelve children born to Angus (1838-1920) and Susan Lindley Inskeep. Susan (who was called "Sarah") was born in 1842 near Piqua, Ohio, to Daniel and Eleanor Lindley. The Inskeep lineage stretches back to Staffordshire, England, where James Inskeep was born to John and Mary Inskeep. James, in oedipal fashion, married Mary Miller, lived almost a hundred years, and died in Hardy County, Virginia, which is now a part of West Virginia. His son, Abraham (1745-1825), married Susan Vause (daughter of William Vause and Jemima Hedges) in 1864. They named their son James (1765-1858) after his grandfather. James, the grandson, married Sarah Frye and also spent his life in what is now West Virginia. Samuel Inskeep (1802-1868), their son, moved to Piqua, Ohio, and married Ann Spencer. Angus Inskeep was born to them in 1838.

Ernest Clifton Pinney and Lucy Anna Stout Pinney 1957

Lucy Ann Stout Pinney was born in Randolph County, Indiana, on March 29, 1888, the younger of two daughters of Samuel (1949-1891) and Christina Barbara Daubenmier Stout (1859-1940). Samuel Stout was a native of Darke County, Ohio, the son of John (1806-1865) and Susannah Stout. Christina, named after her mother, was the daughter of Frank (1833-1925) and Christina Barbara Scholl Daubenmier (1835-1888). Christina Scholl's father, Mathias (1801-1879), was born in Germany, the son of Jacob Frederick (1778-1862) and Anna Barbara Weidner Scholl (1781-1848).

Ernest and Lucy Pinney were the parents of five children: Clifton, who died shortly after birth in 1905; Vera Lavina (1906-1971), who married Guy Oren Grove; Myrtle Beatrice (born 1909), who married Nelson Burr Huffman; Nellie May (born 1913), who married Clifford B. Fryback; and Mary Marie (born 1917), who married Curtis Osman Ellis (see "Ellis", this volume). Ernest died in 1960, just a few years after the store was sold. Lucy died in 1969, aged eighty years.

PITTS

The Pitts family are relative newcomers to Wells County, moving to Bluffton in 1966. Neal Chase Pitts, M.D., is the son of Guy Moseley Pitts and Nancy Salina Chase of Mexico, Audrain County, Missouri. Guy's father, William Pitts, was born in Lincolnshire, England and moved to Morrisonville, Christian County, Illinois with his father Richard as a child. Guy's mother, Lillian Moseley, descended from the Spears-Yarnall family of Harrison County, Kentucky and the Moseley family of Henrico County, Virginia. Nancy Salina Chase is a lineal descendant of John Throckmorton who with Roger Williams founded Providence, Rhode Island. Salina is also a descendant of William Chase an early settler of Brown County, and John Wilkinson, an early settler of Miami County, Indiana.

Neal was born December 6, 1933, in Jackson, Mississippi. He graduated in 1952 from Mexico High School and in 1956 from Culver-Stockton College in Canton, Missouri. In 1960 he graduated from the University of Missouri Medical School in Columbia, Missouri and subsequently did graduate medical studies at the University of Mississippi Medical Center in Jackson and the Mayo Clinic in Rochester, Minnesota. In 1966 he joined the staff of the Caylor-Nickel Clinic as a rheumatologist. A major in the U.S. Army Medical Corps from 1967-1969, he was stationed in Japan. He belongs to the Sons of the American Revolution, Sons of Confederate Veterans, Sons and Daughters of the Pilgrims, Order of the Crown of Charlemagne, the Military Order of the Stars and Bars, the Somerset Chapter Magna Charta Barons, the Colonial Order of the Crown, Society of Indiana Pioneers and the National Huguenot Society.

The Pitts Family 1981
Annette, Erin Pitts Scott, Neal and Heather Anne

On June 23, 1957, he married Nelia Annette Gnuse, the daughter of Solomon F. Gnuse and Faye Barkelew of Lewiston, Lewis County, Missouri. Solomon was the grandson of Herman Heinrich Gnuse who immigrated from Elverdissen, Westphalen, Germany to Quincy, Illinois in 1852. Herman's wife was Hannah Nagel who immigrated the next year. Faye was the granddaughter of Henry A. Barkelew from Middlesex County, New Jersey and Charlotte Louisa Spencer whose family came from Connecticut to Huron County, Ohio in 1824. Faye's maternal great-grandfather was John Duncan the son of Colin Duncan who immigrated from Scotland to Scott County, Kentucky in 1792. Annette was born October 19, 1937, in Durham, Lewis County, Missouri. She graduated from Lewistown High School in 1955 and later attended Culver-Stockton College in Canton, where she was a member of Chi Omega Sorority. She later graduated from Gem City Business College in Quincy, Illinois. Neal and Annette belong to the Presbyterian Church. They have two daughters, Erin Chase Scott, born September 13, 1964, in Jackson, Mississippi and Heather Ann Pitts, born April 16, 1967, in Bluffton. Both daughters graduated from Bluffton High School and Miami University of Ohio. On April 9, 1988, Erin married Gregory C. Scott, the son of Clyde and Vivian Scott of North Euclid, Ohio. Both Erin and Heather now live in Cleveland, Ohio.

PLATT

In a small, rural country home located north of the Arbaugh School in Union Township, a son was born to Clarence W. and Grace (Derr) Platt on July 20, 1925, and was given the name of Wendell Wayne. In the coming years he was joined by two sisters, Kathryn Jean, and Shirley Ann, and a brother, Dale (Butch). Their home was located close to their grandparents, Fred and Saloma Ann (Leavengood).

Wayne spent his childhood on the farm, where, in later years, he joined his father in the farming operation. He spent his entire school days at Union Center where he was active in softball, basketball, and track.

During high school days, he met Anna Louise Follis, who also attended Union Center, and they were married on December 7, 1947. Her parents were Virgil and Hazel (Miles) Follis, both of whom are now deceased. Anna Louise was born in Jefferson Township, Huntington County. She was the youngest of the family with three brothers, Alvin of Fort Wayne, Indiana, Eldon, and Ora of Rockcreek Township, Huntington County. Eldon and Ora are both now deceased.

After marriage, Wayne continued to farm and also was employed for thirty-four and one-half years at Tokheim Corporation, Fort Wayne, Indiana, from which he retired in 1987. Anna Louise was employed by the Wells County Superintendent of Schools, Wells County Nursing Service, and retired in 1988 from Caylor-Nickel Medical Center.

They are the parents of a daughter, Kayleen Anne, who was born on April 10, 1953. She attended Rockcreek School and graduated from Norwell High School. She is married to David Lynn Bushee, son of Kenneth (deceased) and Ada (Frauhiger) Bushee. They are the parents of two children, Jeremy David, fourteen, and Amy Jennifer, eleven, and reside north of Ossian. Kayleen is employed at Lincoln National Life Insurance Company, Fort Wayne, Indiana, and David is employed at Ossian Lumber Company.

They have resided in Uniondale for the past thirty-eight years and are members of the Markle Church of Christ.

CLARENCE PLATT FAMILY

Clarence was born August 12, 1898, in Union Township to Fredrick and Salmona Ann (Dell) (Leavengood) Platt. They both were born in Union Township. They cleared the ground and cut the logs, to build their home. Fred was born in 1872 to Manuel Platt. Manuel's paretns were John and Sarah Jean (Moyer) Platt. John rode his horse to Indiana from Warren, Ohio. He was born in 1815.

Salmona Ann's parents were Peter and Martha (Zimmerlee) Leavengood. She was born in 1873.

November 1990
Grace celebrating her ninetieth birthday with her grandchildren and great-grandchildren

Fred and Doll were the parents of three children. One daughter, Clella, died at an early age. Lawerence was born August 13, 1900. He first marriage was to Mary Allen, who died a few years after their marriage. A daughter was born to this union on May 27, 1917. She is a graduate of Union Center High School. She is married to John Allison, and they live in Bluffton. Lawrence's second marriage was to Forrest Woods. They had two daughters, Alberta and Clella. Their daughters graduated from Ossian High School. Lawrence died in January of 1973, at the age of seventy-two. Clarence and Lawrence attended a one-room school in Union Township, one-half mile east of their home. The school was called the Arbaugh School; it was located on what is 300W now in Union Township.

Clarence married Grace Deer on November 24, 1920 (refer to Aaron Landis Deer). To this union were born five children.

Clarence Jr. was born August 4, 1923, and died at birth. W. Wayne was born July 20, 1925 (refer to Wayne Platt family). K. Jean was born May 20, 1928 (refer to Robert Max Gleim Family). Shirley Ann was born February 25, 1932 (refer to Kay Mounsey family). Dale Eldon (Butch) was born May 24, 1941. (Refer to Dale Platt Family).

Clarence was farmer in Union and Rockcreek Townships and a school bus driver in both townships. He was a janitor at the East Union School for a short period of time in the late twenties and early thirties. He also worked at Kresge Warehouse at Baer Field at one time, and retired from Tokheim in Fort Wayne, at the age of sixty-two. He died in 1970, at the age of seventy-two. He is buried in the Horeb Cemetery, the ground for which was bought from Him and Grace. He was a very active member of the Markle Church of Christ.

Grace is a homemaker, and is pretty much confined at home since the amputation of her legs, the one in May of 1989. She still lives in Rockcreek Township where she has lived since 1914, except from 1920 to 1946, when she lived in Union Township. After the death of her mother in 1946, they moved back to look after her father. Clarence and Grace bought the Deer home in 1951. This home is on 300W or old 303. Grace is the oldest member of the Markle Church of Christ.

DALE ELDON PLATT FAMILY

Dale (Butch) was born in Union Township May 24, 1941, moving from UnionTownship in 1946. He is a graduate of Rockcreek High School, and played basketball and softball for the Rockcreek Dodgers teams in the late 50's. After graduation he was employed at Zanesville Lumber Company managed by Dee Hoopingarner. He is presently employed in the office of the Alltel Telephone Co. in Delphi, Indiana. He has worked for the telephone company for twenty-six years. He was a veteran of the Vietnam War in the 60's.

Dale is married to Dorothy Lee (Dottie) Faust, daughter of Kenneth and Pauline Faust. Kenneth is a resident of Wells, and Pauline is deceased. They have one daughter, Patricia Nicole, born August 26, 1972. She is a senior at Delphi High School in Delphi, Indiana. Dottie is a beautician and now is working at Thoughtful Impressions in Delphi.

Dale played several years in Little League and Junior League, at Ossian and Liberty Center, as a boy. Then in later years he played softball for the Markle Merchants in Markle, for several years.

JOHN PLATT FAMILY

My great-grandfather was John Platt, born in 1815 (buried at St. John, Wells County, Union Township). His first marriage was to Sarah Jane Moryers. They had eleven children: Mary, Lucy, Emmaline, Angeline, Cass, Jerry, Cornelius, Frank, John, Emanuel, and Sarah Jane.

John was married for the second time to Sarah Ann Crismore (died 1864) and had six children: Edward, who married Onie Edmunson; William, who married Effie Edmunson; Senus, who married Ella Meyers; David, my grandfather, who married Maud Little; George, who married Jennie Wright; and Maud Ellen, who died young.

Arlo Platt - Barber in Zanesville, Indiana for fifty-five years.

David, my grandfather, was born August 14, 1871 (died June 13, 1959). His wife, Maud Little, was born August 7, 1875 (died April 6, 1965). David ran a cream station in Zanesville, Indiana. To this married seven children born: (1) Forest (July 8, 1894 to October 5, 1918); (2) Zola (October 5, 1895 to June 3, 1985) married John Jacobs and they had four children: Darrel, who married Regina Klopfenstine; Doris, who married Dale Taylor and had two children, Karen Kay and Larry Dale; another child was Loris (Bud), who married Polly Stokes and had two children, Vickie and Gordon; the last child was Donnabelle, who married Richard Augspurger and had two children, Terry Joe and Patti. (3) Hershel (October 25, 1897 to September 26, 1984) was the third child born to David and Maud. He married Patty Smith and they had four children: Mary Louise (died young); James, who married Lois Ann Thompson and they had four children: James, Jeffrey, Teresa, and Cheryl; David, who married Patsy Overman, and they had three children: Michael, Chris, and Robin Marie. The last son was Bob, who married Sandra Behrens and had three children: Lianne, Allan, and Susanne. (4) Chancy (April 15, 1900 to October 11, 1972) was married to Edna Feist. They had one child, Joseph David (died in infancy). (5) Ermel born September 5, 1902, died young. (6) Arlo, born next, was my father (June 11, 1907 to April 17, 1985) and he married Wilma Smith, born February 20, 1912. They had three children: Carolyn Rose, who died young; Halden born December 1, 1933, who married Carolyn Miller. They had two sons: Gregory married Suzanne Cox and they have two boys, Gregory and Cameron. Hal's other son was Gary, who married Cathy Wilson, and they have Lyndsy and Matthew. Arlo and Wilma's last child was a daughter, Marlene, born March 15, 1936, who married Donald L. Hoopingarner. They lived in Markle, Indiana, most of their married life. They had two daughters Pamela Le, born June 23, 1958, who married Larry Boye and Shari Lynne born February 2, 1961, living at home. The last of David and Maud's family was (7) Isma, born June 7, 1910, who married Olaf Blauser. Their children were Janice, who married Daniel Wolfe and had Danny, Jr., Brian, and Allison; Nancy who married Gary hall, and they had Deana, Darla, Debby, and Denise; Clodella married Jim Darland and they had Paul David, and Joanna Kaye; Brenda married Keith Henline and they had Tracy Ann and Erin Elizabeth.

PAUL PLATT FAMILY

Paul E. Platt was born August 6, 1927 to Clayton L. and Rowena (Ertel) Platt. We lived on Gordon Farm, west of Bluffton for seventeen years. I was born there in 1927. Dad bought the Park farm in 1941, we moved there in 1945, west and north of Bluffton.

Paul and Helen Platt

In 1937, Amer Morris built a new barn on Gordon farm, where we lived. Fred Fuhrer set up his saw mill back in the woods and dad cut trees down. I set on saw horses, drilled holes in the log to mortise out for braces. Dad pulled each section up with horses. This is the barn that burned in 1971.

Gary and Carol (Platt) Mounsey (L to R) Eric, Brian and Trent

David and Dorothy Gregg, High and Grace Garton, and dad and mother used to butcher hogs and beef. Those were the days, when neighbors got together, even made clothes line taffy.

William and Jennifer (Stout) Platt (L to R) Elizabeth and James

On June 18, 1949, Paul married Helen M. White, daughter of George Ralph and Hazel B. (Cloud) White of Poneto. We had two children, a son, William E., born May 22, 1951 and a daughter Carol A., born June 28, 1956. William married Jennifer Stout, September 8, 1973. They live on a farm near Poneto. They have two children, a son, James M., born July 9, 1979 and a daughter Elizabeth L, born June 18, 1983. Carol A. married Gary A. Mounsey, September 15, 1974. They live five miles west of Bluffton. They have three sons, Brian, born October 21, 1980, Eric J., born August 17, 1983 and Trent M., born January 21, 1987.

RUFUS ELMER PLATT FAMILY

Rufus Elmer Platt born June 23, 1877, was the son of Jacob Platt, 1846-1898, whose grandfather was George Platt. George came from Marshall, Ohio, Trumble County, in the 1860's with two other brothers, John and Henry. They were Pennsylvania Dutch and they spelled their name Blott. Some Ohio people still spell it that way. George settled in Wells County. He had married Levina Moyer, May 8, 1845, in Lordstown Township. Their children were Jacob, Caroline, Frank, George Emanuel, Mary Lewis, and Elvira. Jacob married Sarah Elizabeth Mullis and their children were a baby boy who died in infancy, Rufus, Maria, Lottie and Ella.

Back row (L to R) Rufus, Lura, Jacob. Front Elmer Platt, Elton Taylor.

Rufus married Lura Elton Keller, July 1, 1900. She was born December 23, 1882, in Wheeling, Indiana, and at age three moved to Markle. Their children were Elton, Elmer, Ralph and Garth. They had purchased forty acres SE of Union on 303. Rufus bought an eighty acre from on 1000N. They farmed with horses and raised chickens, cattle and hogs to make a living and to payoff the debt. Rufus died June 19, 1941. Kenneth, a grandson stayed with Lura. He farmed and went to school until hospital debt was paid off in December, 1941. He finished his last year and a half at W. Rock Creek. She sold the farm to Roy Cayot in 1942 and moved into a house on Sparks Street in Markle. The farm dwellings are now torn down and the ground owned by Rex Douglas. Lura died December 30, 1971. Many memories were acquired at this home.

Rufus and Lura Platt

His children were Elton Elizabeth, born September 13, 1901, married Norman A. Taylor, a contractor from Union Township, Huntington County, December 23, 1925. A new home was built for her in Huntington on Etna Avenue. Their children were Mary Ethel, John R., Norma Elizabeth, Charlotte Jane and Alberta Ann. Norman's father and grandfather built several houses and mills with one mill still standing at Bellville. Elton died January 6, 1967 and Norman died May, 1974. There are ten grandchildren, one dead and twelve great-grandchildren, three dead.

Elmer, born December 5, 1902, married Vera Horn. She lived two miles south of Zanesville. Her mother had married Frank Prough. They farmed the Jeff Beaty farm on 1000N and Elmer drove a school bus for fifteen years. The moved to Nine Mile, then moved to Huntington County on the Phillip Davis farm in west Rock Creek and in 1948 to their present farm. Their children were: Kenneth, Keith, Ralph, and Betty Lou. Elmer died October 2, 1989. There are six grandchildren, one dead, four step-grandchildren, nine great-grandchildren and five step-great-grandchildren.

Ralph born November 4, 1905, died of a tonsillectomy blood clot October 23, 1928, the morning that Mary Ethel was born to Elton. He was twenty-three and attending Huntington College.

Garth born August 22, 1909, married Ethel Hoopengardner of Ossian. Her brother, Miles was former sheriff of Wells County. They had a daughter, Katherine who married Gene C. Friar and their children were Gene Jr. and Cheryl. She divorced and married James Gillie. Garth and Ethel lived in Waynedale most of their married life. He drove a stone truck for May's Stone and Gravel. Ethel taught school in Allen County. They have two great-grandsons. Garth died at the Caylor-Nickel Clinic while Norman died some hours later at Wells County Hospital, May 6, 1974.

His sisters: Marie 1878-1959 married Phillip Davis, a farmer from Rockcreek, Huntington County. Their only daughter, Nina, born 1909, lives at Millers Merry Manor in Huntington.

Lottie died at age seventeen in 1898.

Ella, 1882-1968, married Ora Wilcoxson, a farmer and they lived for years SW of the Union School on 303. They adopted a daughter, Virginia, who married Earl Mounsey. They lived in Decatur. Virginia died in 1976.

PLUMMER-RICHARDSON

Benjamin Plummer, born in 1797 was Pennsylvania Dutch. They settled around Flemingsburg, Kentucky. In 1820 Benjamin married Mary Waugh of Maysville, Kentucky. They were parents of ten, Evaline, Harriet, John, Sarah, Benjamin Abbot, Nancy, Mahala, Mary, James Ruben and Presley who were twins.

In 1857, Benjamin Abbot married Harriet Conrad of Maysville, Kentucky. Nine children were born to this marriage, John, Cornelia, Thomas, Mary, Lewie, Charles, Emery, William and a twin to Charles born dead. Sometimes before 1868 the family moved to Rush County, Indiana, where Charles was born. When he was seven the family moved to a farm north of Van Buren.

In December, 1892, Charles married Winifred Steel from Coesse, Indiana, in Whitley County. She was of Scotch Irish descent. They were parents of seven children: Mary, Ruth, Charles Ivan, Esther and Florence. Beulah and Francis died shortly after birth. They lived in Jefferson Township, Huntington County, until 1907, when Charles Ivan was two. They bought and moved on a farm in Jackson Township, Wells County, near the old Batson School.

Charles W. was trustee in Jackson Township for eight years. His brother William was the grandfather of Howard Plummer who resides in Wells County.

In January, 1934, Charles Ivan (Pinky) and Ruby Richardson of Warren were married. They are

509

parents of one daughter, Judith Ann born in March 1939, in Newark, Ohio. In July 1939 the family went to live in Huntington, West Virginia, where Charles was employed by Hoosier Engineering Company. In July, 1960, Judy married Donald Shaffer of Wells County and moved there. In 1970 Charles and Ruby moved to Petroleum. He died in 1980.

The John Richardson family of English ancestry settled in Campbell County in Virginia, then in Highland County, Ohio. In the 1840's they came to Jefferson Township in Huntington County. My great-grandfather was a circuit rider minister in the early days. He married my great-grandmother, Nancy Hart of Indian heritage, before leaving Ohio. He and another ordained minister started one of the first churches in the area.

My great-great-great-grandfather Richardson fought in the Revolutionary War. Great-grandpa John and Great-Grandma Nancy were the parents of six. My grandfather Francis was a son. He married Cynthia Ann Arnett. They were the parents of eight children, one of whom was my father Daniel Richardson. He and Cora Gage were married in 1911. They had five children. I was born in 1913. Gene and Emil served in World War II and both are deceased. Robert lives near Warren and Vivian in Arizona.

Michael Beck and Susan Hahn were married in Heidelberg, Germany, in 1804, came to America in 1805. They settled in Heidelberg, Pennsylvania, then to Hagerstown, Maryland. In 1835 the family moved by covered wagon to Hagerstown, Indiana. They were parents of seven children, a son, of which was William, my great-great grandfather. He was one of the first settlers in Jefferson Township, and a skilled craftsman in woodworking. He married Elizabeth Campbell of Kentucky. They had thirteen children: a daughter, Caroline married William Cook. They had three children, Elijah, Emma and Mary Elizabeth. Mary married Kent Gage of French ancestry in January, 1890. They had Cora Alice born February 1891, my mother.

Kent was a very talented musician and an accomplished harpist, a member of the orchestra that toured with "Blossom Time" play for several season. He died in 1938.

DR. BYRON K. POINDEXTER FAMILY

Dr. Byron K. Poindexter was born December 27, 1933 to Hattie McBride) and Ives T. Poindexter of Sandborn, Indiana. He was an only son in the family, with six sisters: Marjorie, Marilyn Jo, Patricia, Shirley, Jeane, and Linda. His father, Ives, his grandfather, Huett, and five of his six uncles were funeral directors. The Poindexter name was on many funeral homes in the southern Indiana area. Dr. Poindexter decided to follow a different drummer ad became a dentist. During his high school years his dentist, Dr. W.P. Stoetling, of Sandborn, introduced him to Patricia Gayle Hunley, the daughter of a friend. Patricia later became Mrs. B.K. Poindexter.

Patricia was born September 20, 1934 to her parents, William and Helen (Small) Hunley of Dugger, Indiana. She was an only daughter with two brothers, William and Robert. Her father was an electrical equipment contractor.

Patricia and Byron, known as Patty and B.K., dated through high school and college. B.K. spent his freshman year of college at Vincennes University, where he played guard on the VU basketball team. He transferred to Indiana University at Bloomington, the following September, where he and Patty were both students. They enjoyed the college scene of IU sports and all of the things college students enjoyed in the 1950's, such as black and white TV, white buck shoes, women's housing hours, and Stan Kenton music. They were married in June, 1954, and moved to Indianapolis where B.K. was a student at Indiana University School Dentistry at Indiana University Medical Center. He graduated with a D.D.S. degree in May, 1958. They moved to Bluffton in June, 1958, and in August, 1958, he opened his first dental office, located in the Gal-Ham Building. They have four children: a daughter, Devon K. (Mrs. Donald Willey), born August 17, 1958; a son, Byron Clay, born May 31, 1961; a son, Blake Theodore, born February 14, 1966; and a daughter, Gay Rachelle, born February 9, 1968. Their children grew up in Bluffton and have degrees from Hillsdale College and Indiana University. They have one grandchild, Carson Landis Willey, born November 12, 1985.

Left to right: Back row - Blake, Gay, Don, Devon, Clay. Front row - Dr. B.K. and Patricia 1983.

Dr. and Mrs. Poindexter served on many committees for college sorority and fraternity functions during their children's college years. They also served on the Parents Advisory Board of Hillsdale College.

Dr. Poindexter moved to his current office located 328 West Market in May, 1966. His building, which he owns, is a historic site that dates back to the early 1900's.

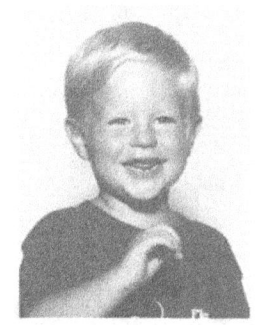

Carson L. Willey, 1989, grandson of Dr. and Mrs. B.K. Poindexter.

They constructed their home in Riverview in 1960, where they have lived for thirty-one years.

Mrs. Poindexter is past-president of Bluffton Newcomers organization, currently is vice-president of Alpha Associates Chapter of Tri Kappa, a member of the Order of Eastern Star, Isaac Knapp Dental Auxiliary, and Shrine Auxiliary. Dr. and Mrs. Poindexter are members of First United Methodist Church, Wells County Creative Arts, Wells County Historical Society, and Parlor City Country Club. They served two terms on the Bluffton High School All Night Party committee, and taught Sunday School during their children's growing up years.

Dr. Poindexter is a member of Isaac Knapp Dental Society, Indiana Dental Society, American Dental Society, Masonic Lodge, Elks, Delta Sigma Delta, Mizpah Shrine, Wells County Shrine, Scottish Rite, and Wells County Crime Stoppers. He is a past president of Wells County Crippled Children, and he is an active supporter of Big Brothers/Big Sisters, and Ducks Unlimited.

The Poindexters have a deep affection for Bluffton and feel that it is a wonderful place to live and rear a family.

POLDERMAN-MAJORS

Marinus Polderman was born July 30, 1907, Zeeland, Netherlands, to Cornelius and Anna Staal Polderman. Deciding to go away on a big ship at age sixteen. March 18, 1923, he arrived alone at Hoboken, New Jersey. Becoming a citizen September 11, 1929, at Kalamazoo, Michigan, he made his home in Scotts, Michigan; and worked at the Checker Cab Company and farmed. He met Anna Kooima, marrying in 1933 in LaGrange County, Indiana. She was born October 3, 1917, in Portage, Michigan to Thomas and Nettie Wheaton Kooima. Thomas had arrived in 1879 from Netherlands. They divorced and Anna remarried John Yankoskey.

Left to Right; Shona, Delores, Truques, Dixen, Neil.

Marinus remarried Sara Hamel Dabbelaar. Anna and Marinus had two children: Anna and Neil. Neil born January, 1939 at Portage, Michigan. When serving in the Air Force in Little Rock, Arkansas, he met Delores Majors. She was born February 6, 1940, in Malvern, Arkansas, to Tommie and Ruby Ashley Majors. After graduating from nursing school, they were married December 7, 1962, in Kalamazoo, Michigan, living there for three months. Neil was employed at Gibson guitar Factory. They moved to Oklahoma City, Oklahoma, while Neil attended FAA Aeronautical School, then to Milwaukee, Wisconsin where Neil worked at General Mitchell field and Delores worked at Trinity Memorial Hospital. Their children were born in Cudahy, Wisconsin: Truques, November 20, 1963; Dixen, November 14, 1964; and Shona, May 26, 1968. In September 1971, Neil was transferred to Baer Field, Fort Wayne, Air Traffic Control Tower. They lived at Ossian, Kozy Kourt in 1973, November 1973. They built a home on State Road 224. The years at Ossian have been filled with a lot of community activities, little league and teen league baseball, football, basketball, track, wrestling, band, winter guard, baton twirling, and cub scouts. All three graduated from Norwell High School.

Shona spent two years at University of

Oklahoma, then transferring and graduating from Middle Tennessee State University, 1990. Now she makes her home in Nashville, Tennessee. Truques married Wendy Welker, five, January, 1991, living in Fort Wayne. Dixen attended classes at Ivy Tech, working in Fort Wayne, Indiana, living in Ossian. Delores is involved in many community and school activities. Neil retired 1990, and they continue to live at their home in Ossian.

REVEREND AND MRS. ESTON E. POLING, SR.

Reverend Eston Poling was born and raised in Montrose, West Virginia. When he was seventeen years old, he came to Indiana to live with his sister. Not long after he came to Indiana, his sister passed away. He then moved to Richmond, Indiana, where he met his wife, Emma Englebert. They were married on November 13, 1937.

In 1943, Reverend Poling was drafted into the army to serve his country during World War II. He took his training in Denver, Colorado, and also served time in France and England as a medical technician.

Reverend Poling had accepted his calling to the ministry before entering the army. While in the army, he was able to do some of his first ministering as he and his buddies would hold their own church services.

Reverend and Mrs. Eston E. Poling, Sr. and Family

In 1948, Reverend Poling accepted his first pastorate of the First Pentecostal Church in Dunkirk, Indiana. He and his family pastored there for eight years. One of the highlights of his ministry there was when one of the lay members came out to their farm home with a truckload of smothered chickens. Times were hard; but they had all the chickens they could eat!

In 1955 Reverend Poling and his family accepted the call to pastor the First Pentecostal Church in Bluffton. Under his pastorate here, several remodelings were done to the church which resulted in actually remodeling the whole inside and outside of the structure. There have been many memories of his thirty-five years as pastor here in Bluffton which would be too numerous to elaborate on. On December 31, 1989, Reverend Poling retired as pastor due to their health. Upon his retirement, he was given an honor of "Honorary Member" of the United Pentecostal Church organization which is located in St. Louis, Missouri. During his pastorate here in Bluffton, he also served as a presbyter on the Indiana District Board of the United Pentecostal Church.

Reverend Poling has had the honor of being Dean of Ministers of Wells County.

Reverend Poling was also noted as the "sewing machine man." He along with his wife, Emma, operated the Singer Store here in Bluffton for several years. After the store was closed, Reverend Poling continued to repair sewing machines until failing eye sight caused him to have to give it up. This was a hobby he really enjoyed.

Reverend and Mrs. Poling have two sons: Eston Jr., and James Lenoard; and four daughters: Rita Marlene, Irene Louise, Martha Ann, and Marcia Joan. They have a son deceased, Robert Eugene. They are the grandparents of eleven grandchildren and six great grandchildren.

JOE POND

Joe was born in Chester Township, august 29, 1895, on a farm about a mile from Keystone. His folks were Frank and Effie Venham Pond. He walked to school his first two years, but when he was in the third grade his grandfather built him a two-wheel cart and acquired a little pony to pull it. When he reached high school he thought he was too big to still be driving a pony, so he secured a horse and buggy to take him to Keystone. Keystone was the first school in Wells County to have an organized basketball team. Joe didn't play on the team but remembered that around 1904 or 1095 Keystone scheduled a basketball game with Muncie and the boys went over on the train and Keystone won. Joe graduated from high school in 1915.

Joe Pond 1978

Three years he stayed on the farm helping his dad. The first time he ever voted was for Woodrow Wilson. Six months later he was drafted into the Army. He was sent to Beauregard, Louisiana, where he didn't get much training, and then went overseas as a member of a field hospital company. He landed in France, then moved into Luxembourg, where his unit stayed for three weeks. He did anything in the hospital that came along. He worked twelve-hour day shifts and he stayed here for about a month before he was relieved.

Each new move that Joe's unit made put hospital personnel closer to the front. His unit was on the front the very day the Armistice was signed.

After the war he was placed in the Army of Occupation in Germany where he worked in an evacuation hospital. It wasn't until July 9, 1919, that Joe got home. He came back to help his dad on the farm. His father died in 1922.

Joe stayed on the farm with his mother and married Letha Mann in 1926. Soon after this the country was in a depression. It was really tough. Farmers couldn't get enough out of a wagon load of corn to buy a load of coal. So they burned the corn in their stoves to keep warm. Joe sold hogs for three cents per pound. Nevertheless, he was able to pay off his dad's mortgage.

Joe drove a school bus for Chester Township and he also graded county roads. He worked teams of horses with the equipment until sometime shortly after 1935, when the county got trucks.

In 1961 he worked full time for the state highway department and retired in 1965 when he was seventy.

Joe and Letha had one daughter, who passed away in 1968. They had five grandchildren. Letha passed away in 1974. Joe passed away at the Warren Methodist Home on March 2, 1984.

POPE-DUBBELD

The dust storms and depression hit hard in 1936 in Raub, North Dakota. As a result, Harry and Grace (Snyder) Randol and adoptive son, Fred and his wife, Vivian (Olson) Pope, and children: Gene, four; and Violet, one; left their farm machinery in a corner of a field and loaded a small truck and a four-wheeled farm wagon with just their personal belongings. They traveled twelve hundred miles to Wells County and then settled in Union Township northeast of Markle.

Two more children were born to Fred and Vivian Pope. all four children: Gene, Violet, Wayne, and Richard, graduated from East Union High School. My father, Gene, went on to graduate from Manchester College and Saint Frances college of fort Wayne.

Ronald and Twila Dubbeld, Janella Joy, Dion Gene

My grandmother, Vivian, was widowed in 1967. She remarried in 1977 to Harold Scheele and they reside in Markle.

My father, Gene, has been a school teacher in Jay County School Corporation since 1964. My mother, Evelyn (Sweeny) Pope, has been a private music teacher of accordion, marimba, piano and organ since 1949. They have both been active in evangelistic music in numerous churches throughout Indiana and many other states since 1956. She is currently employed at H and R Block in Bluffton. They live on the same farm in Harrison Township where Evelyn was born. My grandparents, Robert and Olive (Joray) Sweeny, moved onto this farm when they were married in 1931.

I have one brother, Allen Pope, who is a 1971 graduate of Bluffton High School, a graduate of Marion college, and Indiana University School of Law. He is currently an attorney for the city of Indianapolis. He married Beth Wilson in 1982 and they have two adopted sons: Isaac Allen, four; and Enoch Allen, two.

I graduated in 1974 from Bluffton High School, attended Ft. Wayne Summit college and Penn View Bible College majoring in music. I married Ronald Dubbeld of Vicksburg, Michigan in 1978. He is currently an employee of the Bluffton Middle School. We have two children: Janella Joy, six, who is a student at East Side Elementary School; and Dion Gene, two. We reside on the same farm in Harrison Township as my parents.

Following a family musical tradition, I enjoy giving private voice lessons, and Ron and I are active in church music ministries. My grandmother, my mother, and myself all took lessons on the same piano. My daughter and son are the fifth generation to be active in church music. They are also the seventh generation to reside in Wells County.

Some of my fondest childhood memories are listening to my grandfather's favorite stories as we traveled the back roads of Wells County to his favorite fishing spots. My grandmother also had many family pictures to entertain me as a child. They established a pride of a Christian family heritage that is richly rooted in Wells County. *(Twila (Pope) Dubbeld)*

PORTER

Three siblings lived in Wells County in 1860: James Porter, Catherine Porter Clark (wife of Jeremiah), and Allie Ann Porter Houser (married to Martin). Their parents, names unknown, were both born in Ireland. One family member remembers it as County Cork and that they were Protestants. James was born 1816 in Pennsylvania, possibly the Doylestown area, and died in Wells County, in May, 1885. It is told that he left Doylestown in a covered wagon, selling household goods and notions to farm families. Allie/Alley was born 1820, in Ohio, possibly the Finlay/Delphos area, and died in Wells County in September, 1895. Catherine was born 1823 in Ohio and died in Wells County in September, 1897.

James and his wife Sarah Galehouse Porter had three children: Mary A. (Mrs. Abraham Hoopengardner) born 1841 in Ohio; Elizabeth (Lib) J. (Mrs. Phillip Koons) born 1945 in Ohio; Catherine (Kitty) Summers Wilgus born 1856 in Ohio; Erwin (I.A.) born 1858 in Indiana married Flo Wilgus.

Allie Ann and her husband Martin Houser had six children: Jane Sara (Mrs. Sam Milliken) born 1842, died 1927; John; Jacob; David (married Henrietta Besser) died at age ninety; Ella (Mrs. Fred Livingood); and Jane.

Catherine and her husband Jeremiah (Jerry) Clark had eight children: Virgil, born 1846, died 1928; Walter (married Rose Niriter) born 1852, died 1912; Lantz Alanson (married Amelia Caston) born 1855, died before 1914; James P. (married Dora Sutton) born 1851; Mary A. (Mrs. Charles R. White) born 1859, died 1927; Martha (Mrs. Elmer Allen) born between 1861 and 1866; Alice, born 1865, died 1887; Laura (Mrs. Lafayette Gorrell) born 1868, died 1935.

PORTER-MICKLITSCH

John and Ruth (Porter) Micklitsch were married in Bluffton, April 11, 1942. In May, 1942, John was inducted into the army. He served three years in the European Theatre and received seven Bronze Stars. After the war he went to Wayne University and joined Ruth in the beauty business and the Micklitsch Beauty Salon in Bluffton.

On May 10, 1947, their first child, Jan Carla was born. She died eight months and two days later of menningitis in 1948.

Terra Angela Micklitsch was born November 18, 1948. Their son, Jon Joseph Micklitasch, was born October 18, 1952. Terra married George Levy of Cortland, New York, on October 11, 1969. Their son Darryl was born on November 28, 1970. Son Gregory died at birth in 1972. Their daughter Nicole was born on January 12, 1974.

Jon Joseph married Cathy Beeks of Bluffton on November 24, 1974. Their son Carl Joseph was born on February 27, 1979. Their daughter Angela Ruth was born on December 3, 1985.

Left to right - Jon, Terra, Ruth, John

Vincent Porter came to Virginia from Scotland and then headed west to Kentucky. There he married Margaret Love. Their sons, George Andrew and Nickolas came to Indiana. George married Mary Smith of Wells County. Their children were James, Frank Arthur (Ruth's father), Charles, Ethel, and Mary. Vincent's grave is at the old cemetery at Bethel Church southeast of Bluffton.

Arthur married Genevieve Chronister of Decatur, daughter of George and Margaret (Fisher) Chronister. George's parents were Henry and Lydia (Miley) Chronister of Ireland and Margaret's parents were Henry and Ruth (Mallonee) Fisher of Ireland. To Arthur and Genevieve Porter, seven girls were born: Esther, Margaret, Thelma, Helen, Harriet, Ruth, and Georgiana.

Esther had one son, Robert Stewart. Margaret had three daughters, Phyllis, Gloria, and Carol from her marriage to Maurice Smith of Huntington. Thelma had a son from her marriage to Charles Anderson and a daughter, Mary Catherine, from her marriage to Albert Krock. Helen had two sons, Walter Clark, Jr. and Raymond from her marriage to Walter Clark of Chicago. Harriet had three sons from her marriage to Robert Dailey of Tocson: Phillip, Porter, and Dennis. Georgiana, the youngest was married to Russell Arnold of Liberty Center and had four children: Billy Ray, Karen, Keith, and Tony.

John Micklitsch's parents were Frank and Mary (Jesselnick) Micklitsch of Suchen, Austria. Mary's parents, Anton and Maria (Jereb) Jesselnick of the House of Suchen. Frank's parents were John and Katrina (Poje) of Micklitsch, Austria.

John's parents came to America in the early years of 1900. They had a candy factory in New York and then moved to Pennsylvania and settled in the village of Ralston in Lycoming County. They had eleven children: Frank, Mary, Sophia, Rose, Joseph, Albert, Max, Raymond, John, Louis, and Robert.

The fifth child, Joseph came to Indiana to attend college in Angola and married Geneva Henry. They came to Bluffton to live when he was transferred here as a civil engineer for the state of Indiana. John came to Bluffton in 1937.

ALVA AND NELLIE BOWMAN POTTER

Alva Potter was born on May 9, 1893, in Clinton County, Indiana, to Claude and Flora (Louks) Potter. In 1904, the Potters purchased a farm in Lancaster Township, Wells County, bringing Alva by horse drawn wagon along with a few personal possessions. Household goods were sent by railway to Tocsin.

Nellie Florence Bowman was born on July 14, 1892, the first child of John and Eliza Jane Bowman of Tocsin. She was raised in Tocsin and Lancaster Township, and attended Bender Grade School which was located on what is now 300N. It was there that she first met Alva Potter.

On March 21, 1914, Alva and Nellie were married. Alva was a farmer and Nellie was a homemaker. Four daughters and one son were born to this union. They are N. Pauline, who married Charles A. Myers (deceased); Doris Jane who married Clarence Castilow (deceased); Wilma Jean who married, first, Daniel Bailey (deceased) and second, Robert Lagemann; Iris B. married Clifford Owens. Only son James R. is married to Barbara Merrell.

Alva died March 9, 1951. At the time of Nellie's death on January 27, 1982, she had eleven living grandchildren and eighteen great-grandchildren.

Alva and Nellie were lifetime members of the Lancaster United Brethren Church which is now the Lancaster Chapel United Methodist Church.

POTTS

Ralph Potts, Sr. was born in England in 1869. He emigrated to the United States in his late teens. A glass blower by trade, he traveled across the United States, finally settling near Dunkirk where he worked in the glass factories. In June of 1897, he married Mary Alice Shuman, a daughter of Joseph and Louisa Smith Shuman, of Wells County. They were the parents of six children. Helen, born in 1900, died of cholera at six months. Joseph, born 1901, died of pneumonia at two years. Hugh, born in 1904, also died in infancy. All three of these children are buried at the Grove Cemetery near Poneta, Indiana.

Estella Potts Fisher was born March 11, 1911. She had one son, James Hoffacker, of Dayton. She spent most of her adult life living in Dayton, Ohio, where she died in February, 1978. James, and his wife Ruth, were the parents of two sons, Brett and Todd, both of Dayton.

Martha Potts, born August 21, 1906, married Gerald (Ted) Hayes. They were the parents of twin daughters, Miriam and Marilyn. Until their retirement and subsequent move to Florida, they lived near West Alexandria, Ohio, where they farmed, and Ted worked as a night watchman at General Motors. Martha died in December of 1982, and is buried in Brandenton, Florida. Marilyn Hayes Coble was the mother of three children, Donald, Cindy, and David. Mariam Hayes married James Sheriff, and they were the parents of three daughter, Susan, Pamela, and Connie Jo. Miriam, widowed, lives in Florida, as does her sister the present Mrs. Robert Davis.

By the time the last of their children, Ralph Potts, Jr. was born on March 9, 1919, Ralph, Sr. and Mary were residing near where the Southern Wells School now stands. In 1930, Mary Alice Potts married for a second time to Frank Chalfant of Harrison Township. My father spent his early adulthood helping his step-father in his farming operation, while graduating from Bluffton High School in 1938. Here he met his future wife, Ruth Ilene Sturgeon, the daughter of Hugh and Mima Kleinknight Sturgeon of Harrison Township. They were married in June of 1942, in Hattiesburg, Mississippi, prior to my father leaving for the South Pacific. he served with the 38th Division, U.S. 152nd, Infantry. Stationed in Hawaii, and then New

Guinea, he finally ended up serving as a mess sergeant on the front lines in the Philippines. It was at the Battle of Bataan, that he received three Bronze Stars for Bravery, while delivering food under attack to the men on the front lines, and to those in enemy territory.

At the end of World War II, he again farmed. Upon Frank Chalfant's death he and my mother moved to the Chalfant farm where he continued farming, and also worked as a tool and die maker in Berne, Indiana.

They were the parents of one child, Susan, born April 14, 1951, who married Leon Gaiser in June 1977. They are the parents of two children, Hilary Linn, born July 16, 1986, and Caleb, born November 23, 1988. After my father's death in March of 1987, due to cancer, we moved near my mother. *(Susan Potts Gaiser).*

EARL POWELL FAMILY

Luther Earl Powell (1896-1960) and his wife, Mildred (born 1901) came to Harrison Township, Wells County, in March, 1940. Mr. Powell, a native of Hamilton County, Indiana, was the eldest son of James Edmon Powell and Grace Sunderland Powell. He bought a farm here in 1937, when he became convinced that Indianapolis was growing too close to the Carmel, Indiana, area where he farmed. He chose his new farm from a catalogue of property that had been foreclosed during the Great Depression. Moving to Wells County at that time was a quite change for the Powell children, who were already accustomed to the blessings of rural electrification and indoor plumbing; they had to wait until about 1942 for the local advent of these advantages in their new neighborhood. The Powells attended the Old Salem Church in Nottingham Township.

*Earl Powell Family in 1957
(L to R) Guelda, Ted, Earl, Mildred, Juanita, Jim*

The Powells had four children, Juanita Wanda (born 1922), Guelda Luana (born 1924), James (1929-1985), and Ted (born 1934). Except for their oldest daughter, who completed high school at Carmel in 1940, all of the Powell children completed their education at Bluffton High School. Juanita graduated from Fort Wayne's International Business College in 1943 and married Philip A. Leonard of that city on September 14, 1946. Guelda married R.D. Williams, a native on Nottingham Township, on April 20, 1946. James married Claudine Hook of Bluffton on April 1, 1951. Ted married Roberta Poffenberger on January 13, 1951; his present marriage, to Cheryl Friar Davis of Chester Township, took place may 31, 1973.

Earl Powell was well known for his skills as a self-taught mechanic and maker of his own implements. From the workshop on his farm came a number of items of hardware, homemade farm equipment, and household goods, many of which can still be seen today on the family farm. In 1948 he added a shed to the north end of his barn to house a monoplane that his son Jim piloted, using the cow pasture as a runway. Other enthusiasms included fishing, boating, an go-carts. The farming operation included dairy cows, hogs (he called then his "mortgage lifters"), chickens, and grain farming, with several shifts in emphasis over the years. Earl Powell died suddenly in 1960 at age sixty-four of heart failure.

Mildred Kathryn Marshino Powell, a native of Osgood, Indiana, is the daughter of Edward Marshino and Mary Davis Marshino. Her father was a stone masonry contractor whose projects included work on the Indiana World War Memorial at Indianapolis. "Mil" is not only notable for her skills as a homemaker. She is also an accomplished needleworker whose crochet and quilting are the prized possessions of her children, thirteen grandchildren, twenty great-grandchildren, and one great-great-grandchild. Despite the size to which the family has grown, her home remains the natural center of family holiday celebrations.

LEONA V. RABER POWELL FAMILY

Leona Vita Raver, born July 11, 1892 and died March 14, 1979, was married to Ophel Hugh Powell February 27, 1917. He was born October 16, 1891 and died August 25, 1963.

Leona, was a daughter of Israel J. Raver, Rockcreek Township farmer, born June 30, 1865, a son of Augustus and Clementina Kapp Raber, died in 1926. His marriage was to Mary Alice Carrysott, born February 20, 1871, and died October 19, 1953. She was a daughter of Adlophus and Samantha Carrysott. The children were: Vivian, Leona, Lucile, Lewis, Esther, Lorin.

Vivian, born in 1891 and died January 24, 1990, was married to Harold Park, born September 27, 1887 and died in 1967. Their children were: Frederick, died March 15, 1988. His marriage was to Glenna Huffman. Children: Paul and Larry. There were five grandchildren. Mary Louise married James Deam, who died in March 1988. Their children were Marshall, Diana, Debbie, James Jr. Several grandchildren.

Leona and her husband, Ophel, had five children, Clifford, Herschel, Ophel Joseph Jr., Kathleen and Mary Birdella. Their family histories may be found in this publication under the Ophel Powell family history.

Lucile born September 17, 1896 and died September 12, 1976. Her first marriage was to Guy Ware and a second marriage was to Mr. Jaeger.

Lewis born in 1903 and died August 28, 1969, was married to Hilda. They had a daughter, Janet. His second marriage was to Sally.

Esther, born in 1907, and died March 29, 1958 was married to Dean H. Roe, who died February 20, 1985. They had a son, Robert Dean, born June 15, 1938.

Lorin, born January 16, 1911, died December 4, 1973, was married to Dorothy. They had two sons, Paul Charles and Judson Lorin. A second marriage was to Ruth.

POWELL-HOOK

In 1940, Leonard Earl and Mildred (Marshino) Powell moved from a farm in Hamilton County to a farm southeast of Bluffton that they had purchased.

James Edward was the third child of Earl and Mildred and was born October 14, 1929. Jim attended Bluffton High School and continued to help his father farm, milk, and raise hogs. While still in high school he owned his own airplane and flew if for pleasure and business such as hunting cows and hogs in the corn fields. All was not work on the farm because they would often go to Vera Cruz on a summer eve and watch free movies.

Claudine Hook (August 30, 1928) became his bride on April 1, 1951. Jim and Claudine purchased new furniture when they were married for the total of seven hundred dollars. This included kitchen table and chairs, dining room set, a couch, four end tables, two chairs, two rugs and pads for the living room. They had three daughters. Pamela Lee (July 5, 1952) married Joe Durdahl and they had two daughters, Ivy (April 3, 1972) and Misty (April 8, 1974). Phoebe Jo (June 7, 1953) married Jeff Zoll and had three children, Naundus (May 15, 1971), Bernard (May 6, 1975), and Etta (July 12, 1980). Caroll (October 20, 1959) has a daughter, Jamie (July 20, 1986).

Powell Bulldozing was formed in 1956 when Jim and his brother, Ted, bought their first bulldozer and went into land clearing and pond building along with farming.

When Jim and Claudine purchased a farm three miles southeast of Bluffton in 1963, Jim also purchased Ted's interest in the equipment and went into bulldozing full-time on his own. He built scores of farm ponds in the area as well as major projects such as: the lake and stadium at Taylor University, the Lake at Geneva, Indiana, excavating for Peytons and Scott's Grocery at Bluffton. During the major blizzards he would not only open County roads, but he would take a portable generator from farm to farm so that the farmers could milk their cows. One of his employees was his daughter, Caroll, who learned to run a bulldozer at a young age.

Besides his work, Jim loved dogs, motorcycles, and his grandchildren. He was actively engaged in the business until 1982 when cancer forced him to stop working. However the business continued until his death in December, 1985.

Claudine was primarily a mother and housewife, but she did have a home sewing business doing alterations and custom sewing. She is active in the Old Salem United Methodist Church and has served as organist for many years. She also is active in the Historical Society and the Bluffton High School Alumni Association.

OPHEL H. POWELL FAMILY

Ophel Hugh Powell, Rockcreek Township farmer, born October 16, 1891, in Boone County, died of a heart condition August 25, 1963.

He was a son of David Powell, Lancaster Township farmer, born September 1, 1869, in Boone County, son of Mr. and Mrs. David Powell and died of a heart attack in 1939. David's first marriage was to Birdella Bercaw, who died when Ophel was age five. David's second marriage October 7, 1901 was to Ocie D. Harvey.

To David and Birdella, were born Ophel Hugh, Buren A., Olive Etta.

Ophel's marriage February 27, 1917 was to Leona Vita Raver, born July 11, 1892, died of heart problems March 14, 1979. Their children were: Clifford, Herschel, Ophel Joseph, Kathleen, and Mary Birdella.

Clifford Milton, Rockcreek Township farmer, born February 12, 1918, died of sudden heart attack April 9, 1987. He married Betty Romaine Stauffer December 15, 1946. Their children were: Clifford

Hugh, born October 1, 1947, died October 8, 1947, Gerry Lee born May 13, 1949, Terry Lynn born October 13, 1951, Byron Ted born December 31, 1955. Gerry married Patricia Ann Lesh September 13, 1969. There sons were: Patrick David born July 18, 1970, John Michael born April 14, 1973, Scott Eric born May 30, 1977 and Timothy Jason born April 7, 1981.

Herschel Gene, Rockcreek Township farmer, real estate agent was born August 29, 1919, and died of sudden heart attack July 23, 1984. He married October 2, 1968 to Rebecca Jane Hiatt Durdahl born October 16, 1923. Adopted daughters are: Patricia Jane Durdahl Canfield Morrisey, March 29, 1955, Bonnie Jean Durdahl O'Gorman September 3, 1956.

Ophel H. and Leona V. Powell

Ophel Joseph Jr., manager of parts department Shepler Motors, Huntington, was born June 13, 1921 and died of sudden heart attack June 23, 1953. He married May 11, 1947 to Madlyn Iverne Carnes. Their children were: Stephen Joseph, born April 29, 1948, Suella Birdella born November 5, 1950. Stephen married Vicki Felts February 7, 1976. Their daughters are: Alissa Jo born November 15, 1976, Megan Ann, born January, 1983. Suella married Michael Wayne Southard on October 9, 1970. Their children wee: Michael Wayne Jr. born December 31, 1978, William Blue born March 18, 1973, and step-daughter, Robin Michele Southard born January 19, 1968.

Alma Kathleen, employed in offices of Kraft Company and Chamber of Commerce in Kendallville was born January 20, 1923 and married June 16, 1945 to Harold Adolph Hill who was born October 30, 1913 and died May 7, 1973. Their daughters were: Marsha Kay, born March 20, 1946 and Rebecca Jo, born June 23, 1948. Marsha married Durrell LeRoy McKenzie. Their daughters are: Debra Kathleen, born February 11, 1973, Shari Elizabeth born March 31, 1971. Rebecca married John Frederick Dykstra. Their sons are Gregory Stuart born December 1, 1970, Thomas Edwin born September 17, 1973. Kathleen's second marriage November 26, 1977 was to Vern Steckley, born June 8, 1913.

Mary Birdella, employed forty-four and one-half years at Bluffton News-Banner, born August 1, 1925, married April 18, 1948 to Rex Nathaniel Coffield born August 24, 1926. Their son, Philip Rex, born May 14, 1956, was married June 18, 1983 to Carol Noll, born July 17, 1953. A son, Nathan Lowell was born January 17, 1987.

Olive Etta, sister of Ophel, was born July 10, 1897 in Boone County, died June 4, 1971. She married Harold L. Bickel, who died March 7, 1944. Their children were Leah Mae, Harold Byron, Harriet Virginia, Carolyn Jean. Olive's second marriage December 22, 1951 was to William F. Oertel, born July 21, 1893, died December 11, 1966.

Leah Mae, born May 16, 1920 and died October 23, 1987, was married September 14, 1941 to Hillard Albert Shadle, born March 10, 1920 and died January 12, 1990. Their children were: Jimmy Lee, born July 27, 1942, was married December 19, 1964 to Karen Sue McFarland, born June 25, 1944. Their children were: Gail Sussanne born September 25, 1968, Amy Marlane, born August 28, 1973, Nancy Ellen, born December 18, 1947, married Walter Kelly. Their children were Douglas Allen born October 12, 1968, Cynthia, born February 7, 1970. Charles Hillard born June 13, 1949, and married Marsha Shaw. Their children were: Brent Allen, born June 4, 1974, Lisa Marie born August 29, 1977. Steven Dwight, born February 12, 1952, and married to Rhonda Perry. Their children: were Jason Paul, born December 31, 1973, Craig Steven, born January 30, 1977. His second marriage December 9, 1984 to Denise, their child was Paige Alene born November 1, 1987.

Harold Byron was born November 5, 1921, married December 25, 1947 to Ina May Hullinger, who was born October 3, 1924.

Harriet Virginia, born June 23, 1923, was married June 14, 1942 to Ralph J. Schlagenhauf, who was born February 17, 1922. Their sons were: Ralph Jared born June 1, 1945, married Ann Louise Fairbairn, born December 6, 1945. Their children were Kyle born February 11, 1969, Erick born March 11, 1975. Gary Byron, born July 18, 1948 and married June 14, 1969 to Judy Claire Wing. Their sons were Byron Jay, born May 31, 1976 and Ryan Gary born May 24, 1978.

Carolyn Jean, born March 4, 1931, married Robert Glen Lucas, born August 12, 1931. Children: Gregory Alan born January 27, 1956, Celia Ann born August 25, 1954, Jeremy Glenn born February 24, 1965.

Buren A., brother of Ophel, married Nellie. Their children were: Ray, Roger, Robert, Rex and Lolita.

PRIBLE

John J. Prible was born to Enoch and Lydia York Pribble in Preble County, Ohio in 1832. They moved to Indiana near Warren when John was four years old. In 1854, he married Maria Becker. In 1861 they moved to Wells County just east of Bly. John lived there until 1909, when he moved to Liberty Center and his grandson, Forest Prible, (our father) moved to the Prible farm.

John J. and Maria had five children: Byron (our grandfather), born 1855, Lurania (Mrs. John Buckner), Flory, who died at the age of four while John was fighting in the Civil War, Lucritia (Mrs. John Ware), and James. John J.'s name was Pribble until he was discharged from the army. On his discharge papers his name was Prible and he used that spelling from then on.

Byron was born partially blind from cataracts on both eyes, but that did not stop him. He graduated from blind school in Indianapolis. For a short time he delivered mail from Liberty Center to Bly. He farmed before working in the broom manufacturing business in Indianapolis. Later he and his wife ran a small neighborhood grocery in the west part of Bluffton. He died at the age of eighty-two.

In 1881, Byron married Martha Buckner. Born to Byron and Martha were Lydia A. (Mrs. Basil Gordon), Charles Forest (our father), George, Ardive (Mrs. Fred Payne) and Garrett.

Front row (L to R) Esther, Martha, Dora, Forest. Back Row (L to R) John, Mary, Edwin, Harold, Paul.

Forest married Dora Miller in 1905. They lived a mile south of Bly until they moved to the Prible farm east of Bly in 1909. Members of the family still live there. All of their children attended Bly School and Liberty Center High School. For twenty cents a week Paul would go to the Bly School to start fires in the pot-bellied stoves so it would be warm when the teacher and students arrived.

Born to Forest and Dora were seven children. Martha married Guy Morris. Their daughter, Janet, lives in Bluffton.

Harold married Helen Highlen. Harold farmed in Liberty Township and Harrison Township. They live on the Ellingham Pike. Their children are: Saundra (Mrs. Junior Bergman) who lives in Taylor, Michigan; David, who married Connie Allen and lives in Nottingham Township; Sarah, who married Davie Pursifull (divorced) and lives in Bluffton; and Susan (Mrs. Stan Ellison) who lives in Liberty Center.

Edwin married Crystal Eddington. They live in Bluffton. Their children are Jane (Mrs. Steve Givens) and Larry, who married Carol Mahnensmith. Jane lives in Richmond. Larry lives in Carmel, Indiana.

Mary married William Moses. Mary and Bill both worked at the GE Plant in Fort Wayne. Before moving to Fort Wayne, Mary gave piano lessons. Their daughter, Kathy, works for Goldstine-Northill, Inc.

Paul, a World War II veteran, married Mary Elizabeth Hooper. They had one son, Ray, who became a doctor. He married Linda Finney. Their children are Bill, Amy, Jonathan and Joshua. They live in Amherst, New Hampshire. After the death of Mary Elizabeth, Paul married Pauline Murden. They live in Rochester, Indiana. Paul taught school in Lancaster and later in Peru.

Esther taught school in Galveston, Indiana; Rockcreek; Montpelier; New Haven; and Village School in Fort Wayne.

John, a World War II veteran attended Purdue University, farmed, and worked in Bluffton at the John A. Morris Company. John and Esther live on the Prible farm in Liberty Township.

EDWIN PRIBLE FAMILY

Edwin E. Prible was born November 29, 1908, in Liberty Township, Wells County to parents Forest and Dora Prible.

Crystal (Eddington) Prible was born October 20, 1913, in Bluffton, Indiana, to parents Robert and Maud Edington.

Edwin and Crystal were married in Kentucky in 1941 with Mr. and Mrs. Cletus Johnson of Marion, Indiana, as best friends and witnesses.

Mr. Prible was a public school teacher and administrator throughout his professional career of forty-five years. Mrs. Prible was a homemaker. She did serve briefly as a bank teller in Warren and as church secretary of the First United Methodist Church in Bluffton.

Mr. Prible's professional career included athletic coaching and teaching at Union Center, Liberty Center, and Lancaster Center, Principal at Lafayette Central, Ossian, and Huntertown. He was superintendent of schools at Bluffton from 1956 through 1975, and retired from public life in 1975.

Edwin and Crystal Prible
November 1989

Some of the associations, clubs and organizations Mr. Prible was associated with are as follows: chairman of Wells County committee for reorganization of public school, member of Indiana State Board of Education, member of Indiana State Board of Vocational-Technical Education; Wells County Area Plan Commission member; Wells County Foundation Board member; Adams-Wells County Joint School Services Administrator; member of Indiana Association of Public School Administrators, National School Superintendents Association, Northern Indiana Superintendents Club. Mr. Prible is a member of the First United Methodist Church, Bluffton Masonic Lodge fifty year member, Scottish Rite member, Parlor City Country Club, and other professional associations.

Mr. Prible graduated from Liberty Center High School in 1926, Manchester College with an A.B. degree in 1930, and Indiana University in 1939 with an M.S. degree. He obtained additional credits from Ball State, Butler and Purdue University.

Edwin Prible's brothers and sisters were Martha (deceased), Harold, Mary Moses, Paul, Esther, and John Prible.

Edwin and Crystal had two children: Jane Prible Givens and Larry Prible.

Jane Prible married Stephen Givens of Anderson and their children are Stephanie and Gregory.

Larry Prible married Carole Mahnensmith of Bluffton, and their children are Patricia, Tom, Dan and Jay Prible.

Edwin and Crystal retired from public life in 1975 and now spend their summers in Bluffton and during the winter live in a retirement community in Bradenton, Florida, called Heather Hills Estates.

PRICE-BYNUM

James A. Price, born 1870, died 1941, and Hulda Bynum, born 1881, died 1961, were both born in Greene County, Indiana. They were married in Bloomfield, Indiana on July 11, 1900, and moved to Fort Wayne, Indiana where Mr. Price taught school.

Mr. Price's father, James Hamilton Price, born 1842 and mother, Levina Strauser, born 1851, were both born in Greene County, Indiana. His grandfather, Moses Price, born 1800, married Mary Wilson, born 1810, in Tennessee. They moved to Greene County, Indiana in 1831.

Hulda Bynum's father was Daniel Bynum, born 1846 in Greene County, Indiana and mother, Lois Bilbert, born 1853 in Williams County, Ohio. The Bynum family line has been traced back to John Bynum II who died in 1715 in Surry County, Virginia.

The following children of James and Hulda Price were born in Fort Wayne, Indiana. Calvin, born 1901, died 1973, married Aldene Church. Lucille, born 1904, died 1978, married Kenneth Due. James, born 1907, married Sally Arnovitz. Robert, born 1910, married Edith Yoho. Harvey, born 1914, married Harriet Swisher. Richard, born 1917, died an infant.

By this time the parents decided it was time to move to the country. They purchased the William Dowdy farm located five miles north of Bluffton on State Road #1, in Lancaster Township and moved there in February, 1918. There the following were born: Daniel, born 1919, married Martha Parr. William, born 1922, married Roberta Inskip.

James A. Price Sr. left the teaching profession in 1909 and went to work for the American Book Company and later the Row Perterson Company, selling school text books in Indiana until the time of his death.

The farming was done by the sons, who over the years developed a herd of prize winning Jersey cattle. Calvin, the first to operate the farm, later operated a fruit farm before moving to work in Fort Wayne.

Calvin and Aldene had two daughters. Mary Ann married Boyd Blake and they moved to Florida where she taught school. Their two daughters, Jenny and Judy, now live in Hollywood, Florida. Their other daughter, Patt married Lee Harter and they live in Fort Wayne.

Lucille, "Lucy," after attending Indiana University, taught in Lancaster Township and later in Fort Wayne schools. After marrying Kenneth Dye, they moved to Philadelphia, Pennsylvania. Kenneth died in 1941 and she married Robert Warfield in 1946. They lived in Frederick, Maryland until her death in 1978.

James attended Wabash College and then moved to Pennsylvania where he sold school textbooks until retiring in 1972. He now lives in Greensburg, Pennsylvania with wife Sally.

Robert attended Purdue University and worked as a application engineer for a national electrical equipment company in several states before being transferred to Indianapolis. He has a son, Robert Jr. born 1943.

Harvey attended Wabash College and later took up Boy Scout work. He finished his service as Chief Scout Executive of the Boy Scouts. They have a son, Harvey Jr. born 1940 and a daughter Kathrine born 1943.

Daniel attended Ball State and lives on the home farm on State Road #1. They have a daughter, Katherine Ann, born 1944 and a son, Daniel Jr. born 1949.

William served in the Army during World War II. He farmed the Doctor Brickley farms for many years. They have a son, William Jr. born 1942 and a daughter Andria, born 1947. William Sr. is now married to Barbara Brockman and lives in Florida.

EARNEST PULVER

Earnest Pulver (1884-1956) was born Ernst Pulver, son of Gottlieb (1856-1926) and Anna (Egli) Pulver (1860-1912). Earnest was born in Wattenwil, Switzerland, just south of Bern. When Earnest was only four years old he left Switzerland with his aunt, Mrs. Fritz (Rosetta) Hanni. They left Switzerland because of religious persecution, and for opportunities in the New World. They left from LeHavre port in France, on the ship *La Bourgne*. They arrived at the port of New York on April 16, 1888.

Once in America, the three settled in Elgin, Iowa, where there were other Apostolic Christian immigrants that had settled there as well. Earnest was a member of the Apostolic Church in Elgin. Earnest first heard of Bluffton, Indiana, when he talked to a family named Baumgartner who was visiting Elgin. They invited him to Bluffton and he accepted. He was amazed at how friendly the people were, and how humble and content they were. When he returned to Elgin, he collected his belongings, said his good-byes and moved Bluffton.

Earnest married Elizabeth Kipfer on April 20, 1913, Elizabeth's birthday. Elizabeth was the daughter of John Kipfer (1837-1915), and Rachel Steffen (1858-1923).

Earnest was a skilled carpenter and farmer in Bluffton. He and Elizabeth lived in Bluffton for many years, raising all of their six children here. They moved away from Bluffton in 1930, the time of the great depression. After moving a few more times the family finally settled in Churubusco, Indiana.

The children of Earnest and Elizabeth Pulver are: Amos John (1914-1970) who married Ethel Sauder. They have four children: Linda, Gary, Joyce and Nancy. Amos died in an automobile accident. He worked at Rea Magnet Wire Company. Ethel still lives in Forth Wayne, Indiana.

Lester Pulver (1916-) married Florence McKimmey (1923-1977). They have eleven children: Carole, Philip, David, Mary Ellen, William, Daniel, Steven, Stanley, Barbara, Karl and Christian. Florence died of a stroke at home on July 9, 1977. Lester remarried Aldulla Reinhard September 20, 1978. Lester retired from Rea magnet Wire Company and lives in Bluffton.

Raymond Pulver (1917-1980) married Mary Schweitzer (1917-). Raymond worked at Rea magnet Wire Company. He died on December 6, 1980. Mary still lives in the house that Raymond built for them in Ossian. They have nine children: Judith, Elaine, Karen, Diane, Dennis, Rebecca, Beverly, Kathy and Larry.

Sylvan Pulver (1918-) retired from the Hobby House Restaurant in Fort Wayne, Indiana. He resides at the homeplace in Churubusco.

Irene Helen Pulver (1921-) is retired from General Electric in Fort Wayne. She enjoys gardening and resides at the family hone place in Churubuso.

Sarah Jane (Pulver) Reinhard married Donald Reinhard (1930-). Sarah retired from Franklin Electric Company in Bluffton, Indiana. They reside in Bluffton and have two children, Doyle and Marcia.

PURSLEY

The Pursley family came from the Hartford City, Indiana area. The four brothers were orphaned at an early age, each reared by a different relative. John was section foreman in Tocsin. Henry came to

Tocsin at age 16, later living with Doctor Blue, farming his land and caring for livestock.

In 1912, Henry married Elva Kleinknight, daughter of George and Ida Yager Kleinknight. Doctor Blue built them a house in his orchard. Marjorie and Vernall were born here.

When World War I came along, John and Henry decided to farm together, renting two farms, one mile south and two east of Liberty Center in the Gavin neighborhood.

Farm machinery, small animals and chickens were moved to Liberty Township in wagons with sideboards. Cattle were herded. To miss Bluffton, they went down U.S. 224 to the Praire Road, which ran between the farms.

Henry and Elva (Kleinknight) Pursley 1912

Six years later, John's wife, Ida (Swift) inherited a farm near Hartford City. They moved there with their daughter, Mayro, about six. A son, Worth, born in Tocsin, died there of diphtheria at age five.

Henry remained in Liberty Township. Another daughter, Wanda, was born.

When Marjorie was in fifth grade and Vernall in second, they drove a horse and buggy to school, leaving the horse in the Tarr Livery Stable. The following year, Hiner Ellis built an enclosed bed on a Model T Ford with bench seats, which he called a "hack." He hauled all his children and those on the Pursley Road, about a dozen. It was great fun for the riders when Henry used his team of horses to pull the hack when it became stuck on muddy roads after spring rains.

Corn husking contests were held at the Pursley farm in the late 1920's. Food was prepared by the Liberty Center Baptist ladies and served in a freshly whitewashed cowbarn. Airplane rides were offered, sung the barnyard as a landing strip.

All the children graduated from Liberty Center.

Following World War II, Henry bought the Gavin Homestead House with eighty acres from Mrs. Charles Gavin. He died in 1958, and his widow moved to Bluffton. Following a heart attack in 1960, she moved to Fort Wayne with her daughter, where she died in 1965.

Marjorie attended North Manchester College and taught school at East Rockcreek, Liberty Center and Poneto.

She married contractor Leroy Kanning and resides in Fort Wayne. They are the parents of three children. IUPU graduate Bervia Jennings of rural McClure, Ohio, and Purdue graduates Mayro Kanning of Cincinnati and William of St. Louis. They have three grandchildren.

Vernall Pursley married the former Ruth Roberts, whose death occurred in 1946. They were the parents of four children, Sandra Stroup of Gas City, Connie Edington and William Henry Pursley, both of rural Bluffton, and Judy Craig of rural Liberty Center. He has twelve grandchildren and seven great-grandchildren.

A second marriage was to Vernia Pugh, who died in 1974. He now resides with his wife, the former Ruth Edgell, on the farm he bought from his father's estate in 1960.

Wanda married Harlan Hasler and resides on their farm in rural Uniondale. They have three children, all Purdue graduates. Marilyn Oliver and David Hasler live on farms in rural Uniondale, and Marjorie Reinke at Lansing, Michigan. They have six grandchildren.

JOHN C. RABER

John C. Raber, our grandfather, was born in Lebannon County, Pennsylvania, on October 16, 1849. His parents were Joseph and Elizabeth Raber. They came to Wells County in March 1861. John C. was twelve years old at the time.

Our grandmother, Maria Lucabaugh, moved to Wells County from Wayne County with her parents, Henry and Mary Leonard Lucabaugh. They settled in Rockford, Indiana, where they operated a grocery store and post office of which he was postmaster.

John C. Raber and Maria Lucabaugh were married February 21, 1878, and lived almost two miles east of Rockford in a large frame house. In 1917, they built a smaller house across the lane for themselves and a son, Homer, moved into the larger house. The one room Raber School, where all eight grades were taught, was built on the corner of their land, which is the northwest corner of 300 West and Rockford Pike. Eight children were born to this union.

Lewis died at age ten.

Charles married Oddessa Iona Eichhorn and a daughter, Vadas, was born. Charles was killed on September 21, 1910, at the Kingsland Train Wreck.

Ada married Frank Hoffacker and had a son, John. They were owners of the Snug Restaurant for a number of years.

Artie married Ernest McAfee and had a daugther, Dorothy Lindstrand.

Henry married Eva McClure and had three children, Berniece Armstrong, Ruth Eileen Archbold and Paul.

Mary Estella married Verne Gordon and had two daugthers, Verda May and Mary Alice.

Cora married Arden Fishbaugh and had five children, Leslie, John, Frieda Harnish, Richard and Joan Wiekel.

Homer married Maude Gilbert and had two sons, Wayne and Earl.

Our parents, Verne and Estella (Raber) Gordon were married March 14, 1911, and lived two miles west of Bluffton, which is now known as State Road 124. In 1923, they moved three and a half miles west of Bluffton on a farm they purchased from Francis Hogg.

Verda M. was born December 7, 1914, and married Claude A. Penrod of Chester Township on February 24, 1940. Claude served in World War II and passed away February 8, 1954. A son, Jerry Lee, was born November 7, 1943.

Verda was postmaster of Uniondale, Indiana, from June 12, 1959, to October 2, 1987. On March 15, 1962, she married Gerald S. Wright. Gerald passed away on August 23, 1982.

On August 30, 1963, Jerry married Joanna Jump and had four children.

Gregory Claude married Tonya Keplinger and had two children, Kyle Lee and Kristy Kay.

Kathy Lyn married Keith Fiechter.

Patty Jo married Steven Teague and they have two childen, Anna Mersaydes and Spencer Lee.

David William is the youngest.

Mary Alice was born May 22, 1923. On March 8, 1945, she married Albert Huyghe. Albert passed away on April 2, 1976. Three children were born to this union.

Marsalene married Ken Roush on May 17, 1968, and had two daugthers, Tina Anne and Nicki Kay.

Steven Albert married Wendy Wesenberg on March 9, 1979, and had one daughter, Kali Marie. She passed away at age eight months.

Noreen Sue married Patrick M. Humerickhouse on April 14, 1979, and has two daughters, Carli Jo and Ashtyn Lane.

JOHN WAYNE RABER FAMILY

J. Wayne Raber was born in 1919 in Wells County, the eldest son of Homer O. and Maude (Gilbert) Raber. He had one brother, Earl. The Raber homestead in Rockcreek Township was built by J. Wayne's great-grandfather and remains in the Raber family. Wayne married Lea Beth Cook, daugther of William and B. Grace Cook from Monroeville, Indiana, in 1944. A farm was purchased in Liberty Township where they lived their entire married life. Three children were born and loved. Cynthia married Larry Lieurance and have four children; Luann, Rex, Jan and Nick. Larry died October, 1990, of cancer. An interesting fact of this marriage is the history of their home in Chester Township. In 1909, while Fred Crosby was residing in the home, it burned and a new home was rebuilt on the same foundation. The Lieurance's purchased the home in 1964, which was somewhat of a landmark because of its structure and supposedly being on the highest point in Wells County. In 1985, this house also burnt and a new residence was built around the one room left standing and some of the foundation was used again. In 1990, the large barn on this site burned.

A son, John Randall Raber, married Mary Kelly and they have two sons, Kelly and Drew. They reside in Bellevue, Washington. Sidney Wayne Raber, son, married Susan Foster and have two children, Tobie and Zachary, and live on the Raber homestead. J. Wayne was a farmer and owned a swine operation. He developed an incinerator and was part owner of R. & K. Incinerator Company until his death in December, 1989, of cancer.

RANDALL

My great-grandfather, Addison Randall, served as an apprentice in New York before coming to Bluffton. In 1861, he purchased one hundred and sixty acres in Lancaster Township, described at the time as one of the finest in the county. He and my great-grandmother, who, incidently, dropped over dead at the kitchen door while calling the men in for dinner, were the parents of a daughter and four sons. Maria, who married Isaac Clowser of rural Craigville, David, George, William and Frank, my grandfather. Frank married Loretta Bowman of Adams County. Their children were my father, Homer, Elva and Ervin.

My grandfather, father and uncle hauled stone with their horses and mules for the county roads. My great uncle, David, was caretaker of the horses for the Fort Wayne Fire Department. The family was well known for their fine horses and horsemanship.

Elva married Daniel Brinneman of Bluffton. Ervin married Fanny Neuenschwander of rural Berne. Homer married Goldie Clowser of Craigville. Goldie was a school teacher. After graduating from the Craigville School, she completed the senior year at Bluffton High School. While attending high school in Bluffton, she stayed at the home of John Carnall and his wife and family. Her means of travel to and from Bluffton was by train. After graduating from Marion Normal School and Valparasio College, she taught school in Craigville, the Bender School and the school one and one half mile south of Craigville. The school south of Craigville is still standing and was the only school of the three that had a furnace. Her parents were Joseph Warren Clowser and Almeda Elizabeth Anderson of rural Craigville. Joseph Warren and Isaac Clowser were brothers. Goldie and Homer's children were Richard and Ruth Ann. Richard was killed in 1929. Ruth Ann graduated from Lancaster High School and is employed at Frankln Electric. I, Ruth Ann, married Keith E. Lee of rural Poneto. His parents were Ralph Lee and Grace Fleming of rural Poneto. Keith graduated from Petroleum High School. He served in World War II in the Air Force. He was in the second day of the invasion of Normandy. Keith is a carpenter. Our children are two sons, Eric and Erin. Eric graduated from Norwell High School, Northwestern University and DePaul University. He is a professional musician, primary instrument the tuba. He is living in California. Erin graduated from Norwell High School. The summer of 1988, during the drought and high temperatures, he marched with the Northern Aurora Drum and Bugle Corp of Saginaw, Michigan, playing on the horn line. He is a senior at DeVry Technical Institute in Columbus, Ohio, studying to be a compter stystems analyst.

The farm has remained in our family for 130 years in this year of 1991.

REASER

John and Sarah Reaser purchased forty acres of land southwest of Bluffton and there they moved their family from Wayne County, Ohio, in 1853. John was born in Pennsylvania in 1807, Sarah in 1815. Their children were John James (born 1836) married Cynthia Lane, Nancy (born 1838) married John W. Quick, Margaret (born 1840) married Levi Neff, Elizabeth (born 1842) married Henry Wagner, Cornelius (born 1845) married Elizabeth Valentine, Tamer (born 1852) married Henry Benton Nute, Joseph George (born 1856) married Emma Ochsenrider. They lived in Nottingham and Harrison Townships.

Joseph was a farmer and a schoolteacher. He and Emma had five children: Clarence (born 1881), John Eli (born 1883) married Ella Hoad, Charles, Ezra D. (born 1886) married Zelma Tewell, Margaret (born 1888) married John W. Williams, Joseph and his second wife, Mary Ann Bennett, had two children, Joseph, Jr., and George, who married Alice Whitten.

Joseph's son, Ezra, was my grandfather. For many years, he lived on a farm two miles east of Poneto that we call the homeplace for it was originally purchased by his great-grandfather, John. Ezra's son, Levi Reaser, now owns and lives on the farm. It will soon have been in the Reaser family one hundred years.

Ezra and Zelma were the parents of four children, Clara Lucile (born 1907) deceased, Emma Marie (born 1908) deceased, Lawrence (born 1911) deceased, and Levi W. (born 1913).

Emma married Robert (Bud) Miller (deceased) who was a descendant of Henry Miller, the father of the first white child born in Wells County. They had three daughters, Doris Ann, Patty Lou and Joyce Marie. They lived in Bluffton, Indiana.

Levi married Iris Micheal. They have two daughters, Connie Kay and Jacqueline Sue. He is retired from farming and resides on the homeplace east of Poneto in Nottingham Township.

Lawrence married Nellie Noble. They had two children, Janet Lucille and Jerry L. He was a farmer and owner of L & G Equipment Sales. He resided on a farm two miles south and one-fourth mile east of Poneto. He died in a vehicle collision at the age of forty years, nine months.

Janet married James E. Smith. They live in Nottingham Township. Their children are Randall, Larry, Christofer, and Heidi (Smith) Bryant. They have eight grandchildren. Janet currently works in the County Recorder's Office, Jim is a former partner in Wells Mold & Machine Company, Bluffton, Indiana. He was the owner/operator of the Petroleum Shell Station for a number of years.

Jerry married Peggy Swagart. They live in Petroleum, Indiana. Their children are Brian, Rodney and Gregory Reaser. Brian lives in Allen County. He is married to Thea Marie Barnes. They have two children, Liara and Jaron. Rodney lives in Petroleum and has two daughters, Maranda and Beth Ann. Gregory lives in Petroleum and has one son, Brandon Lee.

Jerry and Peggy are the owners of Wells Mold & Machine Company and Emenar Leasing Company, Inc. They began their business at their residence in 1972.

EVERETT J. REASER

It's a long way from Illinois to Texas, to Wells County, Indiana, back to Texas, Louisiana, Wyoming, Argentina, Dubai, Australia, Italy, Singapore, Thailand, South Africa, and finally, returning to Wyoming! That is the colorful path that Everett, with his roots in Wells County, has traveled.

Born September 9, 1912, to John Eli Reaser and Helen Icylean (Hoad) in Bridgeport, Lawrence County, Illinois, the family soon moved to the Texas oil fields. Everett's mother died when he was only six years old. Everett and his two sisters, Nellie Helen (Winstead) and Virginia Lou (Burdge), came to Wells County to be cared for as the oil field was no place to be without a mother.

Everett spent about two years with his grandparents, Joseph George Reaser and Emma (Ochsenrider). During that time in Wells County, he tells about attending school, then coming home at night and getting additional schooling from his grandfather.

Born in Wells County, Joseph George was a well-known local farmer and educator. Joseph George Reaser was the youngest of three sons and four daughters of long-time Wells County residents, John Reaser and Sarah (Goodman), who settled herein about 1855. Joseph George's siblings were: John James, Nancy (Quick), Margaret (Neff), Cornelius, Elizabeth (Wagner), and Tamar (Nute).

Joseph George's children by Emma (Ochsenrider) were: Clarence E., John Eli, Ezra D., and Charles. His children by his second wife, Mary A. (Bennett), were George Bennett and Joseph.

At age eight, Everett took the train from Indianapolis, all by himself, to rejoin his father who had remarried. John Eli was now a foreman with what was later to become Continental Oil Company (Conoco). They lived in an "Oil Town Shanty" and Everett walked four miles each way to the country schoolhouse. His father (unlike his grandfather) did not seem to have much use for "schoolin" and, when Everett was twelve years old, pulled him out of the classroom and put him to work as an oil field hand. Everett's formal education ended at the eighth grade. The oil seemed to infuse into Everett's blood, and his whole life, from then on, was to revolve around oil drilling.

Everett J. Reaser and wife, Naida Theola (Taylor) Reaser, April 1990, Casper, Wyoming.

Everett's first "real job" was tending thirteen pumping oil wells. His pay was $1.00 per day and he "batched" in a two-room shack. At this same time he was hiring men who earned $.42 per hour! Everett was a dedicated and loyal hard worker, and a fast learner. He was soon transferred to Olney, Texas, with a pay raise to $75.00 per month. His continued hard work was rewarded within six months with a pay raise to $120.00 per month (a very good wage in 1932).

He met Naida Theola Taylor at the company picnic, and they were married February 22, 1937. They have no children and she has been by his side through all his oil drilling adventures all over the world.

By the time he was twenty-six years old, he was the Drilling Superintendent of Louisiana, operating out of four offices, and in charge of some seven hundred men. His wages had skyrocketed to $385.00 per month. In 1948, he became Vice-President, Exploration, for the state of Wyoming with Continental Oil Company.

He got tired, after a while, of the corporate life and started his own company, the Reaser Drilling Company, operating out of Casper, Wyoming. After seven years of being "his own boss", Conoco enticed him to come back and work with their Overseas Operations, in 1963.

The next eleven years, he barely set foot in the United States. Instead, he and Naida lived for six months to two years at a time wherever he was called upon to drill for oil. He retired from Conoco in 1974, and currently lives in Wyoming.

He has always been an avid sportsman and continues to make an annual trek to pheasant hunt in South Dakota. He is also interested in history items. He still has the organ from the church in Wells County that played at his father's and grandfather's funerals. He rescued it from going to the dump when the church was being razed or remodeled.

REBER-GRAHAM

Raymond Dale Reber and Vicki Lynn Graham were united in marriage March 19, 1971, at the Epworth United Methodist Church in Bluffton, Indiana, by the Reverend Carl Brookshire.

We are Bluffton High School graduates and have lived our entire lives in Wells County. For the last ten years, Ray has been employed by J.P. Foodservice of Fort Wayne, Indiana, as a truck driver. He was a member of the Bluffton Volunteer Fire Department from 1973 to 1984. For the last two years, I have been employed by the City of Bluffton as the SenioRide bus driver, and also as a substitute bus driver for the Bluffton-Harrison Schools.

Ray and I have three children. Christi Ann was born October 5, 1971. A 1990 graduate of Bluffton High School, she is currently employed at Burger King. She enjoys reading, crocheting, playing softball, and watching basketball games. Cami Raye was born on Aporil 17, 1975, and is a sophomore at Bluffton High School. She is a member of the Spanish Club and participates in basketball, softball, volleyball, and tennis. Cory Don was born December 11, 1976, and is an eighth grade student at Bluffton Middle School. He likes to read car magazines, work on motors, and help with the lighting system at school plays and programs.

Left to Right: Cory, Christi, Cami (standing), Vicki, Ray, Dusty (dog). February 1986

Ray's parents, Donald E. Reber (December 31, 1924-January 24, 1975) and Emma V. Siders (July 6, 1929) were married March 28, 1946, at Emma's grandmother Pflueger's house in Fort Wayne, Indiana, by the Reverend Roy Scott. They lived in Bluffton and had four children: Carol Ann (September 1, 1946), Gloria Jean (September 12, 1948), Katherine Sue (May 16, 1950), and Raymond Dale (October 29, 1951).

Don Reber served in the Army during World War II. He was the son of Geroge and Hazel (Shady) Reber who lived in Bluffton. Emma's parents were Clifford and Edna (Bass) Siders of Fort Wayne, Indiana.

My dad, Robert R. Graham (May 2, 1929), was the son of Theodore and Mary (Taylor) Graham of Linn Grove, Indiana. My mom, Betty L. Faus (October 25, 1930), was the daughter of Harry and Mary (Archbold) Faus of Murray, Indiana. Dad and Mom were married on October 28, 1949, in Kokomo, Indiana, by the Reverend George Holston. They moved to Bluffton in 1952. The children born of the marriage were: Robert Michael (July 26, 1950), Vicki Lynn (January 25, 1953), and Terri Sue (August 30, 1956). *(Vicki (Graham) Reber)*

RECORD

The family of William Jackson Record, Jr., moved to Bluffton in October of 1973, from Martinsville, Indiana. William took a position as a Vice-President and Loan Officer at Old First National Bank.

William (Bill) Record was born and raised in Martinsville. He received a B.S. and M.S. in Agriculturual Economics from Purdue University, West Lafayette. He is the son of William J. Record, Sr., from Valley Mills, Indiana, and Clara (Kraft) Record, formerly of Medaryville, Indiana.

Jo Ann Record, who was born and raised in Indianapolis, Indiana, received B.S. and M.S. degrees in Elementary Education from Indiana University, Bloomington. She is the daughter of Dr. John Louis Kixmiller, DVM, from Freelandville, Indiana, and Gayle (Hill) Kixmiller formerly of Deedsville, Indiana. Jo Ann is a teacher in the Bluffton-Harrison school system.

All three Record children graduated from Bluffton High School. The oldest child, Robin Beth, also graduated from Purdue University, West Lafayette, with a B.A. in Visual Design. Jeanne Gaylan received a B.S. in Elementary Education from Indiana University, Bloomington. William Jackson, III (Bill) earned a B.S. in Mechanical Engineering from Purdue University, West Lafayette.

REDDING

The Redding families of Wells County were Quakers, and can be traced back to Halifax County, and Wilkes, North Carolina, to a William Redding, who died before 1768. He had four children, Joseph, John, William, and Sarah. William, born November 1, 1750, married Martha Martin, whose parents were Ambrose and Sarah Martin. William and Martha are the parents of John, Ambrose, Sally, William, Rebecca, Nathan, Elizabeth, Nancy, James, and Martha. John, born May 10, 1777, died December 19, 1869, Wilkes County, North Carolina, married Polly Brown on February 24, 1803. They were the parents of Martin, Patsy, William, Allen, Williams, Mary, John M. (Whistle), Delpha, and Hiram.

Martin, born January 25, 1804, died September 17, 1866, Wilkes County, North Carolina, married Sara Martin, December 15, 1824, and were parents of Thurston W., Patsy, John, Thomas, Angline, Hiram, William, James, Sarah, Nathan, Mary, and Daniel. Thurston Washington Redding, born September 21, 1826, died May 30, 1898, Wells County, Indiana, and married Claressa Walker January 15, 1850, Wilkes County, North Carolina. They were parents of James, Sina, Martha, Richard, Wesley, Sarah, Geroge, Alfred, John O., Thomas, Mary, Leander, and Nancy A.

John Oliver, born August 3, 1866, died April 19, 1924, married Mary Ann Sheets on March 11, 1893. Her parents were William and Malissa Jane Thompson Sheets of Wells County. They were the parents of Charles, Josie, Edna, and Eldon. Josie, born May 11, 1896, died November 4, 1967, married Omer Creviston on September 7, 1915, and were the parents of Paul, Opal, John and Ralph. Opal Justine born March 13, 1920, married Harry Burnett Lund August 20, 1940, and are parents of Janet, Coleen and Connie.

Janet, born February 20, 1942, married Donald Wolf. They are the parents of Thomas, born October 15, 1961, who married Sandra Hamilton; Richard, born December 14, 1962, married Malinda McDonald; and Randal, born November 15, 1965. Janet then married Ripton Dudley. Coleen, born July 14, 1944, married Kent Klipser. They are the parents of Camilla Rae, born November 15, 1965, married Kenneth A. Taylor June 6, 1987. Coleen then married Eldon Rybolt, and they are the parents of Timothy Martin, born June 15, 1969. Coleen then married C.K. Robbins. Connie, born Septmber 5, 1949, married Dennis Day, August 16, 1969, parents of Ginger Renee, born May 22, 1970, Jeffery Michael, born June 28, 1971, and Jeremy Matthew, born April 6, 1979.

Edna Marie, born February 1, 1899, married Jasper Waters, February 5, 1921, and were parents of Harold, Gerald, and Loren. Harold, born June 16, 1922, married Martha Allen, September 12, 1947, and were parents of Wayne, born October 14, 1948, and Gregory, born October 31, 1953, married Jane Smekens November 17, 1984, parents of Sara Lynn, born May 25, 1990. Gerald, born July 16, 1924, married Dorothy Harris, November 18, 1951, and they were parents of Gary, born January 23, 1953, married Donna Garbbard on March 24, 1990.

Janice was born February 27, 1956. Linda was born April 5, 1957, married Bryan Peterson, May 21, 1983. Loren was born January 12, 1928, married Elizabeth Smith, September 12, 1952, and were parents of Michael, born March 30, 1955, died December 5, 1982. He married Alicia Oestreich December 14, 1975, and were parents of Chad, Tracey, and Nicolle. Kenneth was born October 7, 1959, married Teresa Knowles April 5, 1980, and were parents of Lindsey and Eric. Donald was born January 26, 1961, married Marvel Mason June 1, 1979, and were parents of Donald, Marisa, and Kasey. Donna was born January 26, 1961. Effie Marie was born November 13, 1962, married Todd Eschenbacker May 5, 1984, and were parents of Abbey.

William Eldon was born February 28, 1902, died November 9, 1970, married Halcyon Pitzer August 17, 1933, and were parents of Carol Jean, born August 11, 1941. Carol married David Neuenschwander July 26, 1959, parents of Kenneth Wayne and Crystal Ann.

CHARLES FRANKLIN REDDING FAMILY

Charles Franklin Redding, (my deceased husband's) father, James Grover as a child, and his parents, James Franklin and Mary Alice (Caudla) Redding, came to Huntington County, Indiana, from Wilkes County, North Carolina. Later they moved to Wells County. They were farmers. Grover, as he was known, was born September 19, 1893. He had three sisters, Eller, Bessie, and Fern.

Grover's father died at the age of forty-four, in 1909, and his mother died in 1929 at age sixty-five. Both were buried in the M.E. Cemetery (Spider Hill) Rockford, Wells County.

Being sixteen, Grover had a lot of responsibility farming the home place, along with his mother and sisters. February 17, 1917, he married Grace Leo Hoover from Huntington County, and their residence was a farm which his mother owned and is now known as Road 500W in East Rockcreek Township.

A son, their only child, was born to them in this house, July 2, 1919. He was Charles Franklin, my deceased husband. Several years later, they sold the farm and bought another farm with more acreage, located in the northeast corner of Junction 303 and 116 in Rockcreek Township, Wells County. From here, Charles attended his first three grades of school at Rockcreek. Later, he and his parents moved to a farm one mile south of Markle and one-half mile east, in West Rockcreek Township, Huntington County. He graduated from Markle High School in 1938. His first job after graduation was driving a Bakery Company truck. Later, he worked for a bridge construction company and then went into farming with his father.

Front Left to Right: Michelle 4-3/4, Enid, Tracy 15, Charlie. Back Left to Right: Claudia, Gary, Clifford 12, Jay, Marlene. November 1985

Januray 29, 1941, Charles married Enid Slusser, daugther of Clarence and Minnie (Shock) Slusser from Clear Creek Township, Huntington County, a 1938 graduate of Clear Creek High School. A son, Gary Wayne, was born to us, May 5, 1946.

In 1950, Charlie and I and his parents, J. Grover and Grace, purchased the home place on 500W. By then the acrage had expanded and there were two sets of buildings. Four days before Christmas, Charlie and family moved into one set of buildings and farmed. A couple of years later, his parents retired from farming and moved in to the other house. Grover worked a number of years at Wayne Metal Company in Markle, and Grace was a cook at East Rockcreek School.

In 1977, Charles' parents became residents of the Warren Home, Warren, Indiana, in the hospital unit. Grover passed away in 1978, and Grace in 1979. They were members of Markle United Methodist Church and are buried in Markle Cemetery.

Our son, Gary, attended all twelve years at East Rockcreek School and graduated in the last graduating class in 1964. He was active in sports and 4-H. He received an Electrical Engineering degree from Purdue University and a Masters from Lake Forest College, Chicago. He married Claudia Lynn Mathews, daughter of Jack and Lillian (Lane) Mathews, Indianapolis, Indiana, on June 2, 1968. She graduated from Lawrence Central High School and a Beauty College; presently employed as a bank teller. Gary is employed as sales representative with an electronics component firm. They have three children: Tracy Lynn 20, Clifford Franklin 17; and Michelle Lee 10. Residence is north of Westfield, Indiana.

October 10, 1959, another son, Jay Alan, was born to us. He attended his school years at East Rockcreek, Lancaster and graduated from Norwell in 1978. He was active in 4-H, sports, and band. He received a Secondary Education degree, cum Laude in 1983 from Taylor University, a Masters in Science from Indiana University and held coaching positions at Findlay College and Kent State University. He is presently a pharmaceutical sales representative. Jay married Marlene Jo Rogers, daughter of Jesse and Kathryn (Waltz) Rogers, Chester Township, Wells County, December 18, 1982. She is a graduate of Southern Wells High School and holds a degree in Elementary Education from DePaul University. They have a daughter, Janet Marie, two and one half years, and reside on Till Road, Fort Wayne, Indiana.

My husband, Charlie, received great pleasure from farming, fishing and sports. After retirement, he enjoyed working with wood in his shop also. In later years, arthritis prevented him from doing many of the things he enjoyed and on August 5, 1989, he passed away suddenly from a heart attack while sitting on the patio at his farm home where he was born. He is buried in Markle Cemetery. He was a good and loving husband, father, and grandfather. He and his family were members of the Markle United Methodist Church, where he served as trustee several years.

GEORGE REDDING FAMILY

The George Redding Family came to Wells County from Rush County and purchased one hundred sixty acres east of Zanesville shortly after 1840. George had married Nancy Sparks, the daughter of Joshua Sparks and Rachel McGray. George's parents were William Redding and Delphia Brown who lived on top of Redding Mountain in Wilkes County, North Carolina.

George and Nancy were the parents of ten children: William, John, Rhoda, George Jr., Joseph, Samuel, Joshua, Phinias, Malinda, and Sarah.

George William Redding

Five children from this union married. William married Eliza Pressler; Rhoda married my grandfather, James T. W. Smith; Joseph married Catherine Bell; Joshua married Elizabeth Wickliff; Phineas married Barbara Ellen Baker; and Sarah married Frank Hyland. Malinda Jane never married, but stayed at home and took care of her mother, who was paralyzed. Nancy died January 21, 1908. George died April 24, 1885. Both are buried at Uniontown Cemetery.

Nancy and George were both good, God-loving people. They were pioneers in organizing the Baptist faith in Wells County. One of their granchildren, Freeman White, who is now 92 years old and lives in Fort Wayne, told me that they held church meetings in a field across the road from where they lived and that George and Nancy donated the ground where Uniontown Church stands.

My Grandmother Rhoda, the oldest daughter, was disinherited because she was wearing a hoop skirt and was getting out of a buggy when the skirt got hooked on the second hoop and showed her leg just above the ankle. This is found in George's will written in 1876.

Rhoda and James Smith lived two miles west of Sheldon (Yoder) in Allen County, but two of their children married and lived in Wells County. Robert Smith, who married Bertha Courson, had a daugther, Fernie Bell MacDonald, who lived in Wells County and now lives in Fort Wayne, Indiana; and Rebecca, who was married to Will Reed. They had three children who were born in Wells County: Herschel, Earl, and Bessie, who married John D. Archer.

PHINEAS REDDING

Phineas Redding was the youngest son of George and Nancy Sparks Redding. He married Barbara Ellen Baker on February 15, 1874. They were the parents of eight children: Ores, Pirlie, Jasper, Raymond, Alford, Nora, Millie, and Perry. They lived on a farm one and one-half miles east of Sheldon, Indiana (now Yoder), on the old Springer farm. Phineas made his living on the farm until he took a job working for P. Morgan and Company in Fort Wayne, Indiana. The family attended the Fairview Church. Phineas passed away December 12, 1918, in Fort Wayne, Indiana, and his wife, Barbara died in 1928. They are both buried at Uniontown Cemetery, Wells County. Phineas' oldest daughter, Nora, married Alonzo White. Lon, as he was called, signed up for the United States Army to fight in the Spanish-American War. He was sent to the Phillippine Islands and didn't return to the United States for six years. After Lon left for the army, Nora bore him a son, Freeman. His father saw Freeman for the first time in Fort Wayne, Indiana, near Wayne and Harrison Streets.

George and Nancy Redding's oldest daugther, Rachel, married James T. W. Smith. They lived west of Sheldon about two miles. They were the parents of George, William, Eberly, Rhoda, Jane Sink, Ella Snider, Robert, Tine, Rebecca Reed, and Adaline Smith. Their son, Robert, and his wife, Bertha Courson, and youngest daughter, Fernie Bell, were born in Wells County. They lived off the Smith Road about one and one-half miles from the Bell School. Fern recalls the big oak tree in the front yard where she spent many hours in her swing hanging from one of the limbs, and in the winter riding on a bob sled to church. She said her father, Robert, would stop and pick up the neighbors, and they would sing all the way to church. After Robert left the farm in Wells County, he worked for Dudlo Manufacturing Company in Fort Wayne, living on Packard Avenue. Robert passed away April 30, 1930.

JOHN A. REECE-MARY EMILINE (KIMMER) REECE

John Alexander Reece and Mary Emiline (Kimmer) were married February 8, 1885, in North Carolina. John Kimmer, a brother of Mrs. Reece, first moved to Indiana in 1894, followed by the John Reece family. My grandmother (daugther of Mr. and Mrs. Reece) was a baby. John Reece first moved to Plumtree, Indiana, and was a farmer in Liberty and Rockcreek Townships. John A. Reece's parents were James and Mary Melissa Reece. Mary Reece's parents were Henry and Laura Kimmer. John and Mary Reece were buried in Spider Hill Cemetery north of Rockford, Indiana.

Back - William, Arthur, James. Middle - Vada, Molly, Gertie, Lottie, Anna. Front - Charles, John, Mary Reece.

Children of John and Mary Reece were: James Reece born 1886, who married Etta Stroud. (Their children: Noel Reece married Nina Haines, Cleora Reece, Bluffton, Ruth (Mrs. Alva) Cheeseman, Roger Reece.); Carrie Nevada (Mrs. Charles) Walker born 1889. (Their children were John Reece who married Helen Masterson and Roberta (Mrs. Robert Harris).

My grandmother, Mary Elizabeth (Molly), married Charles B. Inskeep. My mother, Anna Emojean Inskeep (Mrs. Edwin V.) Brown is the fourth of their six children. Mary and Charles Inskeep's children are: Dorotha (Mrs. Seved) Rochon, Mary Esther (Mrs. Arthur) Line, Virginia (Mrs. Joe) Lieurance. Charlene (Mrs. Warren) Young, William Inskeep who married Doris Vickrey.

Taken 1984
Back Row - Herman and Golda Osborn, Emojean and Ed Brown. Front Row - Julie Ann Osborn, Bruce, Gloria, Josh Osborn, Jenni Osborn.

William Reece married Kathryn Wagner. His second marriage was to Della Gerber Grover, Bluffton. HIs chldren were: Gertrude (Mrs. Luster) Arnold; (Their children are Dale, Robert, Marjorie, Harold, and Max. Gertie's second marriage was to Raymond Crist.) Lottie (Mrs. Bernard) Kramer; (Their chldren were Leeanne, Peggy and Cynthia.); Charles Kimmer Reece, born 1907, married Myrtle McLaughlin. (Their children were Nila Ann and Kahlia.); Anna, born 1902, (Mrs. Menno) Amstutz; (Their children were Betty, Roger, Joyce, Eugen and Keith).

The children of my parents, Edwin Vernon Brown and Anna Emojean Inskeep Brown, are Darrell, who married Connie Williams, (Their children are Michelle and Craig.) and Marvin, who married Angela Moore. (Their children were Eric and Jason.) His second marriage was to Mary Bosstick. Marcia married Tom Davey. (Their children are Beniah, Lydia, Amos, Anna, Naomi, John, Magdalen, Elizabeth.) Cynthia married James Young. (Their children are Christina, Beth and Phillip.) Saundra has three chldren, Amber, Jarred, and Levi. Gloria married Bruce K. Osborn in 1973. Our children are Jennifer, Joshua and Julie.

REIFF-ROBBINS

John Karl Reiff (1799-1861) my great-great-grandfather, established his family of nine on a farm south of Bluffton. This land grant was issued to Reiff by President Van Buren. Our son-in-law, Morris Harnish, has this original grant, as he is now owner of the land.

This area attracted so many Reiffs that it became known as Reiffsburg. Reiff had a saw mill here and furnished logs for the original road between Fort Wayne and Connersville.

My grandfather, George E. Reiff (1856-1940), was a farmer and road contractor. He and his wife, Rose Bay (1864-1935), had three children, Elizabeth Bender, Jesse L. Reiff, and John E. Reiff.

Hersh and Virginia Robbins
November 1990

Jesse Reiff (1887-1944) was a carpenter at a very young age, building barns, houses, furniture and anything needed. He married Virgie Souerwine (1888-1923) daughter of Peter Souerwine. They were parents of four children: I am the oldest; Herman, who died in 1976; Thelma Swisher Rector; and Jess J. Reiff. We lived on a farm west of Bluffton. By this time my father drew plans and made his blue prints for any large building. Herman and I walked to school at Smokey Row.

My mother was a musician and entertained different groups by playing the piano. My father was interested in music also, and in his thirties, he bought a violin. He sent for lessons from the U.S. School of Music in Chicago and learned to play. My father drove an Overland Touring car, and many Sundays, he would go into Bluffton and bring my grandparents to the farm. One sunday they surprised my grandparents by entertaining together.

In the early twenties, my father built the Rockcreek and Chester Center Schools. They have since been torn down. He was in the Liberty Center Lumber Company with James and Stokes Gordon. Later, he built and remodled stores for Morris Five and Ten Company in Indiana, Illinois, Ohio, and Michigan.

Hersh Robbins came to Indiana in 1911 from Spokane, Washington, with his parents, James Garfield Robbins (1880-1927) and Louella Dougherty (1880-1966). They had four children, the oldest dying in infancy, Hersh, Joe A. (1913-1977), and Mary Jane McCreery, who now lives in Gaston, Indiana. Hersh attended Buckeye School, north of Uniondale, and after moving to Bluffton graduated from high school and attended Purdue University until the Depression.

We were married in 1933 and bought this house at 203 West South Street, which still remains our home. We have two children, our daughter, Kay (Mrs. Morris Harnish), lives east of Bluffton. They have four grown children: Ginny Stocker, Richard, David, and Caryn Harnish. Our son, James, married Rinda Decker, and lives near Indianapolis; they have two grown daugthers: Julie and Penny Robbins.

We have had a very happy life together and have been most fortunate living near our children and their families.

ARLAND GALE REINHARD

Arland Gale Reinhard and his twin brother, Carlton Dale, were the first-born children of Howard (born 1919) and Ilene (Ehrman) Reinhard. Although born in Decatur, Indiana, on September 5, 1947, Arland's parents resided at 419 East Silver Street in Bluffton, Indiana. In 1952, shortly after the birth of his sister, Arvilla, his family moved to Craigville. His other sister, Carla, was born in 1956. His parents still reside just south of Craigville.

After graduating in 1965 from Lancaster High School, Arland received a BS in Business (1970) and an MS in Education (1971) from Indiana University in Bloomington. While working towards his Master's degree, he served as a Teaching Associate and Graduate Assistant at the IU School of Business. From 1970-1990, Arland was a business education teacher at Fort Wayne Community School's Elmhurst High School, where he also served as Department Head from 1974-1990. In the fall of 1990, Arland welcomed a career change by accepting a business education teaching position at Southwest Allen County's Homestead High School.

Back (Left to Rigth) Carmen, Marc. Front (Left to Right) Arland, Ruth, Aimee, Eric.

Since 1972, Arland has also operated Arland Reinhard Tours, Inc. Having escorted tour groups to six continents, his business specializes in cruises and group travel.

On March 30, 1974, Arland married Ruth Arlene Von Gunten at the First Mennonite Church in Berne, Indiana. Born October 11, 1946, in Decatur, Indiana, Ruth is the daughter of Paul and Marguerite (Kitson) Von Gunten of Berne. Ruth has three brothers, Stephen, Lee, and a twin brother, Ronald Arlyn. (Lee is married to Arland's sister, Carla.) Ruth works as a Registered Nurse in the Intensive Care Unit at the Caylor-Nickel Medical Center.

Ruth and Arland's four children, all born at the Caylor-Nickel Hospital, include Carmen Ruth (5-11-75), Marc Arland (6-18-76), Aimee Joyce (11-14-78), and Eric Von (4-18-80). The family resides north of Bluffton at 2470 North State Road 1. All are active members of the Pleasant Dale Church of the Brethren in Adams County. The children attend Lancaster Elementary, Norwell Middle School, and Norwell High School.

While researching the Reinhard genealogy, Arland discovered that his grandfather, Adolph (1879-1976), left his Hinterwil, Switzerland, home at age 9. He boarded the French Line's ship "La Bourgogne" in Le Havre, France, and arrived at the Port of New York on April 16, 1888, with his father, cheesemaker Andreas (1841-1924), his mother, Rosina (Zimmermann), and brother, Gottfried. An older brother, Albert, had preceded them to Indiana. (The family came to Indiana at the encouragement of Lancaster Township cousin Dan Reinhard.) Other ancestors include Johannes (1801-1859) b. Eriswil, Switzerland; Ulrich (17670-1863) b. Eriswil, Switzerland, d. Heimenhausen, Switzerland; and Daniel (born about 1740 in Canton Bern, Switzerland). Arland is in contact with the Reinhard cousins still living in Switzerland and visits them when he escorts tour groups to Europe.

CARLTON DALE REINHARD FAMILY

I was born September 5, 1947, the oldest child of Howard and Ilene (Ehrman) Reinhard. Less than a minute later I had an identical twin brother Arland Gale. On February 12, 1952, my sister, Arvilla Jean (Rodenbeck), was born, and on October 11, 1956, sister, Carla Jane (Von Gunten), was born. I lived in Bluffton until age five, when the family moved to Craigville. Having attended Lancaster Central School for the entire twelve years of schooling, I graduated in 1965.

I worked at the Dutch Mill Restaurant during my high school and early college years. Also working at the Dutch Mill was a young, attractive waitress named Julia Baker. Her parents, Clifford Junior and Mary Imogene, sister, Diana Sue, and brother, Jerry Wesley, moved to Bluffton from Yorktown, Indiana, during Julia's 1964-65 senior year. Julia stayed in Yorktown and graduated from Yorktown High School in 1965. Jerry graduated from Bluffton High School in 1967 and Diana graduated from Bluffton in 1969.

Carlton Reinhard Family
Carleen 8-1/2 months, Nathan 6-1/2 years, Julia, and Carlton.

Julia graduated from Indiana University with a degree in Elementary Education in 1969. We were married in Bluffton at the Park United Brethren Church on July 5, 1969. The first couple of years as newlyweds, we lived in Columbus, Indiana, where Julia taught fourth grade at Petersburg Elementary School.

I finished my Bachelors degree in Business Education in January, 1970, at Indiana University by doing my student teaching at Columbus High School. Fortunately, I was immediatley hired by Brown County High School to fill an unexpected second semester vacancy. The following year, I taught at Edinburg High School at Edinburg, Indiana.

During the 1971-72 school year, we moved to Boulder, Colorado, where we attended the University of Colorado and each of us earned a Master's degree. From there we spent two years as Peace Corps volunteers teaching on the Eastern Caribbean Island of St. Vincent. In 1974, we returned to the United States and settled in our current home in Hamilton, Indiana.

I have taught business subjects at Hamilton High School since 1974. Julia taught at South Milford Elementary School during the 1974-75 school years and then at Hamilton Elementary School until our son, Nathan Carlton, was born July 11, 1983.

In 1984, Julia took a nine hour a week teacher/director position at Angola Community Nursery School in Angola. In 1989, she resigned to take the same position at the Rainbow Preschool in Hamilton.

July 11, 1989, our daughter, Carleen Julia, was born. The four of us are active members of the Cedar Lake Church of the Brethren west of Auburn. Nathan is currently in the first grade at Hamilton Elementary School and Carleen continues to explore theworld and increase her vocabulary every day.

Although we do not live on big Hamilton Lake, we do live on Terry Lake, which is just one-half mile from the Hamilton School. Terry Lake provides lots of opportunity to share family time year round and we enjoy the relaxing view from our home.

EZRA REINHARD

Ezra Reinhard was born on June 20, 1894. Ezra's grandfather, Daniel Reinhard, II (1833-1898), emigrated to the United States from a town near Bern, Switzerland. Daniel married Fannie Frauhiger (1829-1905) in 1854. Together they moved to the Bluffton community, and raised their family here. Ezra's father was Daniel Reinhard, III. Daniel (1861-1930) married Rosie Hartman (1866-1948).

Daniel Reinhard owned a horse and feed business on the banks of the Wabash in Bluffton, Indiana. The business was located at the parking lot across from the Country Squire Florist shop. Ezra worked for his father at the mill loading wagons and collecting money on accounts. Ezra was a member of the Apostolic Christian Church.

Ezra Reinhard (1894-1967) married Delva Aschliman (1895-1976) on January 4, 1920. Together they have eleven children. They are:

Harry Edward Reinhard (1920-1975) married Catherine Steffen (1916-1974). Harry was a farmer in Bluffton, and also worked at Franklin Electric. He married Catherine Steffen on May 4, 1952. They had five children: Larry, Joan, Roger, Linda, and Mary Jo.

Aldulla Marie Reinhard (1922-) married Lester Pulver. Dulla retired from General Electric in Fort Wayne. She is known throughout Bluffton as a professional caterer and cake decorator. Dulla and Les reside at the Reinhard home place in Bluffton. Their children are: Carole, Philip, David, Mary Ellen, William, Daniel, Steven, Stanley, Barbara, Karl and Christian.

Mildred Louise Reinhard (1924-) married Elmer Badiac. Mildred worked at General Electric, and retired from Lincoln Life, Inc. Mildred and Elmer reside in Fort Wayne. Their children are: Marilyn, Carolyn, Gloria, James, and Sam.

Ezra, Jr. (1925-) married Doris Ellen Clause, who passed away on July 9, 1989. Ezra is a farmer in Bluffton. He and Doris lived in Bluffton all their lives. Their children are: Wayne, Jerry, Tony, and Mona.

James Paul Reinhard (1927-) married Ruth Stoller. Jim is a farmer, and worked at Star Engineering in Bluffton. Jim and Ruth had five children: Edward, Pauline, LouAnn, Herbert, and Tom.

Dale Walter Reinhard (1928-) married Martha Lobsiger on April 18, 1990. Dale is a lifetime farmer in the Bluffton community. Martha worked as a banker for several years. They reside in their new home south of Bluffton. Their children are: Rick, Greg, and Michele (Lobsiger).

Kenneth Orval Reinhard (1932-) married Ann Gerber. Kenney is a liftime farmer in the Bluffton community. Kenney and Ann live southwest of Bluffton. Their children are: Kevin, Kent, Lanae, Kris, and Lynette.

Betty Jane Reinhard (1932-) married Carl Macklin. Betty retired from Franklin Electric and farming. Betty and Carl live north of Bluffton near Norwell. Their children are: Debra, Alan, Connie, and Ronnie.

Edna Lucille Reinhard (1936-) married William Gene Moser. Edna is a professional seamstress, and Gene is the President of National Oil and Gas Company. They are life-long residents of Bluffton and the parents of five children: Robin, Melinda, Fawn, Drake, and Trout.

Daniel Simon Reinhard (1938-) married Delores Sauder. Dan and Delores have lived in Bluffton, Kansas, and now reside in Detroit, Michigan. Their children are: Rebecca, Sherry, Tim, Rhonda, Marlene, Doug, Mike, and Jeff.

TONY REIFF FAMILY

The Tony Reiff family has deep roots in Bluffton, and in Australia.

Tony was born in Sydney, Australia, to Jack and Doreen (Luestner) Reiff on April 30, 1945. Jack had met Doreen while in the Army during World War II. Jack brought his wife and new son to the United States shortly after Tony's birth. The rest of the Reiff family was here in Wells County. Jack's parents, Johnny and Gladys Reiff, and siblings, Verdane, Bob, Joyce, and Joan, made their home on the family farm in Section 6 of Liberty Township.

Tony grew up in Bluffton on Miller Street. A daughter, Angela, joined the family. They moved to Decatur in 1960, and Tony graduated from Decatur High School in 1963, and Angie from Adams Central in 1969.

Linda has deep roots in Bluffton as well. Her grandfather, Richard Cherry, was born in Bluffton. It is thought that his birth was in the hosue on the corner of 124 East where Kenneth Steffen now resides. Richard was a half-brother to Homer Byrd, who was Circuit Judge in Wells County in the 1960's.

Linda was born and grew up in Charlotte, Michigan, the daughter of Maurice and Rebecca Cherry. She was the oldest of five children: Eric, Bonnie, Calvin, and Maurine. Linda graduated from Charlotte High School in 1966, and went that fall to Huntington College, where she graduated with a Bachelor of Science in Elementary Education in 1970. She began teaching elementary education in 1971, at Southern Wells, where she still is employed. She received a Master of Science in Education from Indiana University in 1976.

Tony and Linda Reiff, Benjamin, Christopher

Tony's education included Purdue University, and Tennessee Technological University where he graduated in 1973, with a degree in Natural Resource Management. He also served four years in the United States Air Force, and worked as an Air Traffic Controller. Tony took a job with the Ralph Higman Surveying firm in 1973, and continues to the present in the same employment. Ownership of the firm transferred from Mr. Higman, to Christopher Lewis, and it is presently owned by Joseph Stoody.

Tony and Linda met in 1974, and were married on June 26, 1976, at Zion Lutheran Church in Decatur, Indiana. Both are outdoor enthusiasts–

Tony being an avid fisherman, and Linda a walker and biker. Two sons born into the family also share these interests.

Benjamin John joined the family in 1979. He was born in Huntington, Indiana, as was Christopher Lucas, who was born June 30, 1981.

Both boys are students in the Bluffton-Harrison Schools. They are involved in sports and other school activities.

The family attends Calvary Lutheran Church where they are all active–Linda is organist and choir dircector and a member of the church council; Ben and Luke are involved in the "Joyful Noise" (youth choir) and other Sunday School and Youth activities. Tony is involved with Men's activities and ushering.

The family resides at 125 West Wabash where they have lived since September of 1978. The house is part of the original subdivision of Bluffton. They are currently in the process of restoring the exterior of the house to the original siding and color. The project should be complete in the summer of 1991.

The Reiffs are a Bluffton Family and intend to remain a Bluffton family for many years to come.

HOWARD AND ILENE (EHRMAN) REINHARD

Howard Franklin Reinhard was born to Adolph and Lydia (Meyer) Reinhard on November 11, 1919, in Adams County. He was the youngest child of ten. His brothers and sisters are as follows: Arnold Reinhard, deceased; Grace (Reinhard) Nussbaum, deceased; Herman Reinhard, deceased; Harry Reinhard, deceased; Esther (Reinhard) Lehman, Berne; Carl Reinhard, LaPorte, Indiana; Ruth (Reinhard) Dynes, Bryant, Indiana; Mary Reinhard, Bluffton; and Alice Reinhard, Fort Wayne. Howard grew up in Washington Township of Adams County and graduated from Kirkland High School in 1937. After graduation, he worked on his father's farm until 1941, when he went to serve in World War II. For thirty-nine months he served in the Coast Artillery, being stationed most of the time on the Aleutian Islands of Alaska. After returning from the service, he started working at Fruehauf's in Fort Wayne. During this time, he met Ilene Ehrman and they were married October 29, 1946. After their marriage, they resided at 419 East Silver Street, Bluffton. In 1952, Howard came to the Craigville Telephone Company, serving as telephone lineman and repairment. He later became the General Manager, and is still serving the company after thirty-nine years. Along with the job change, he moved his family from their Bluffton home to the house located at 2409 North Main Street, Craigville, which at the time, housed the telephone company upstairs. In 1965, the family moved to their present location at 1683 North State Road 301, Craigville.

(Left to Right) Carlton, Arland, Howard, Ilene, Arvilla, Carla.

Ilene May (Ehrman) Reinhard was born on November 24, 1924, to Floyd and Lola (Barger) Ehrman in Adams County. She was the oldest child as well as their only daughter. Her brothers are Hugh Ehrman of rural Decatur, and Floyd Kenneth, deceased. She grew up on a farm in Kirkland Township in Adams County. She was a junior leader in 4-H, and one year, was the Adams County Milking Champion. She graduated from Kirkland High School in 1944. After graduation, she worked at the GE in Fort Wayne, and married Howard in 1946. She also helped with the office work at the Craigville Telephone Company, when needed as operator, and wrote out all the toll statements by hand for the billing, before they switched to computerized billing.

On September 5, 1947, they were doubly blessed with twin sons, Carlton Dale and Arland Gale Reinhard, who graduated from Lancaster High School in 1965. Carlton married Julia Kay Baker on July 5, 1969, and they have two children. Nathan Carlton, born July 11, 1983; and Carleen Julia, born May 11, 1989. They now reside at Hamilton, Indiana. Arland married Ruth Arlene VonGunten on March 30, 1974, and they have four children: Carmen Ruth, born May 11 1975; Marc Arland, born June 18, 1976; Aimee Joyce, born November 14, 1978; and Eric Von, born on Apr1 8, 1980. They reside in rural Bluffton.

On February 12, 1952, they had their first daughter, Arvilla Jean, who graduated from Norwell High School in 1970. Arvilla married Stephen Charles Rodenbeck on November 29, 1980. They have three children: Mycal Charles, born July 21, 1982; Myshel Jean, born August 30, 1984; and Mylinda Jean, born December 23, 1987. They reside in rural Bluffton.

To complete the family, Carla Jane was born on October 11, 1956, and graduated from Norwell High School in 1975. On September 16, 1977, she married Lee Franklin VonGunten. They also have three children: Ryan Howard, born December 25, 1980; Kyal Paul, born December 17, 1982; and Lynae Elizabeth, born January 21, 1988.

RENNER-ELLIOT

Everett L. "Luke" Renner, born December 23, 1907, son of Samuel and Elizabeth McDaniel Renner, natives of Jay County, Indiana, and Kathryn Lambert, born August 9, 1907, daughter of William L. Lambert and Leona Brodt Lambert, were married August 6, 1932, in Toledo, Ohio.

They became parents of four children: Lynn A. Christopher L., and twins, Matthew Luke and John Mark.

Lynn (Elliott), John, Kathryn, Matthew, and Christopher

Luke attended schools in Bryant and Portland, Indiana, and was a graduate of Muncie Normal School (now Ball State University). He was basketball coach and teacher at Ossian High School and Petroleum High School. He taught Business at Berne-French Township High School for over twenty-five years. All of the Renner children graduated from Berne (South Adams) and were transported daily by their father. His death occurred March 11, 1973, while vacationing in Florida.

Kathryn Lambert Renner was a 1926 graduate of Bluffton High School. After graduating from Muncie Normal School, she taught for five years in Wells County Schools, prior to marriage. She returned to teaching in 1957 and taught until retirement in 1972. She was a member of Captain William Wells Chapter, NSDAR. Kathryn exemplified her patriotism and love of country by her obsession in flying the U.S. Flag every day at her home in Poneto. One of her last acts was to put up a new flag, which was lovingly donated by her sister, Lucille. Her death occurred July 14, 1990.

Lynn Renner Elliott, a graduate of Fort Wayne Business College, is employed as secretary/treasurer of Southern Wells Schools. She is a member of Francois Godfroy Chapter NSDAR. She was married to Jerry J. Elliott and they became parents of a son, James Lee, whose life was ended by a tragic accident. Their daughter, Shannon, graduated from Ball State University with a B.S.N. degree and lives in Cincinnati. She is married to Richard J. Skertic, an engineer with General Electric. They have two sons, William and Jacob Skertic.

Christopher L. Renner received an M.S. degree from Ball State University. He is currently teaching in the New Castle Schools. He is married to Cherlyn "Sucee" Brown, who teaches in the Muncie Schools. They have twin daughters, Sarah Kathryn and Portia Jane Renner.

Matthew Luke Renner served in the United States Army stationed in Vietnam. He is married to Deborah Eyanson, of Adams County, and they have two sons, Lucas T. and Clint M. Renner, and a daughter, Paige Fenstermaker.

John Mark Renner served in the United States Army, stationed in Korea. He has two daughters, Angie and Amy Kathryn Renner.

REYNOLDS FAMILY

The Reynolds Family name has been known in Wells County for well over a century and a half. There have been several branches of the family as the wilderness that became Indiana opened up and the more adventurous moved west from Pennsylvania and Ohio.

Our branch of the family started with William Reynolds, who married an Elizabeth Chalfant. Their son, Robert C., was born June 4, 1854, and died September 18, 1909. He was a farmer, a real estate dealer, and landowner.

Robert married Julia Ellen Quick in 1874, and they lived on a farm on Road #126, where their four children were born: J. Edwin, Harry, Della, and Arla. Della died in her teens and is buried in the family plot in Fairview Cemetery. Harry died years later after marrying Lona Merriman, a talented musician, and they had three children: Wilbur, Doyle, and Max. Arla married William Porland and after living for years in Muncie and Detroit, came back to Bluffton. They're buried in Fairview.

John Edwin Reynolds, who was my father, grew up on the farm and came into Bluffton for his schooling. While "Ed", as he was known, was in high school, his parents divorced and his father remarried Alma Oliver. They had no children and both are buried in a separate plat in Fariview from the Reynolds family plot. Ed attended Franklin College one year with his friends, Frank Bachelor and Harry McFarren. Ed, who had always loved accounting and record keeping, became a teller at the bank across Main Street on the corner. I think it was called the Wells County Bank.

Our family is intermixed with the McFarren and Davenport families, so I must digress a bit and give some of my mother's background. The McFarren family at that time, my great-grandfather's time, owned and lived on a large farm somewhere near Poneto and Liberty Center. I can drive to the farm, but can't tell you how to get there except to say our family cemetery is on the farm and very well kept up.

My great-grandfather, Jacob McFarren, and wife, Rachel (Faust) had ten children and on their marriage gave each child twenty acres and a Seth Thomas clock. Their daughter, Sarah, married John Catlett Davenport.

J.C. Davenport was an educated man and when they lived in Smith City, Kansas, he started a Davenport school and Davenport church. Sarah and J.C. had six children, on of whom was my mother, Stella Mae Davenport Reynolds. A son, George, was the father of Audra Paxson; and Mother's Uncle George was grandfather to Bob McFarren. When J.C. Davenport died in Radford, Virginia, where he is buried, Uncle George moved his sister Sarah and five of her children to Bluffton.

In Bluffton, my mother, Stella, and father, Ed (J. Edwin) Reynolds, met and married. Their children were Deane, Hillis, and Julia (me). Around the turn of the century, Dad bought the Progress Store, which he ran until he was in his seventies. Deane had a photography studio, Hillis died at age two, and I married Robert H. Dreisbach from Fort Wayne, an acoustical engineer. We have two daughters, Georgia Lee, now Mrs. Jack Kegley of Charlottesville, Virginia, and Jerry Lou, now Mrs. John Ludeke of Bakersfield, California.

WILLIAM RICHARDSON FAMILY

On February 18, 1946, the John Smuts Grocery, located in the Southeast corner of the Odd Fellows Building in Zanesville, was sold to two young men, Tom Bomar and Bill Richardson. They called it the B and R Grocery.

All went well, but the store was small so on January 1, 1947, Tom sold his half of the business to Bill. The store became the Richardson Grocery. Housing was impossible, so Bill, Faith, and two small daughters, Kathrine and Marcia, moved into the back rooms of the store. On July 4th of that year, the house directly behind the store became available, so Bill and his family moved, leaving the store its much-needed space.

Bill and Faith Richardson

William Lee Richardson (Bill) was born June 12, 1916, near Paris, Tennessee, and grew up in that rural community, graduated from high school, and attended one year of college at Martin, Tennessee. At nineteen, he joined his brother-in-law, Lee Hill, driving a produce truck from Florida to Fort Wayne. In 1936, he started living in Fort Wayne and there he met his future wife, Faith Clark.

Faith Clark was born June 5, 1920, in Dekalb County, Indiana. When she was six months old, her family moved to Fort Wayne, where she grew up. In 1936, she met her future husband, Bill, and they married June 30, 1940. To them were born two daughters, Kathrine in 1942, and Marcia in 1944. In 1947, they moved to Zanesville, becoming residents of Wells County.

After living in the back room of the store for six months, they moved to the house behind the store, living there eight years. On July 4, 1955, they moved across the street in to a new house. It was a miserable day, being the hottest July Fourth on record.

Kathrine attended Union Center and International Business College. She graduated from both with honors and now lives and works in Fort Wayne.

Marcia graduated from Lancaster School and Huntington College. She taught school two years. In June, 1970, she married John Wilson. They now live near Minneapolis, Minnesota, and have one daughter, Christy, born in 1981.

Bill and Faith spent twenty-five years in the original store and did well. In 1970, they bought the Gaskill Grocery, which was across the street, and consolidated the two stores and moved into the larger Gaskill Building. In 1981, they sold the store to Monwell and Donna Sheley, and retired.

Bill and Faith are enjoying retirement. Bill's chief enjoyment is bowling in Senior Citizens Leagues. Faith is a quilt maker. She has entered many quilt shows and won several ribbons. In 1990, she had two of her quilts published, one in a magazine and another in a quilt calendar. She also is active in the Wells County Historical Society Quilt and Craft Show.

JOHN ROGER AND ROSEMARY LORRAINE RICHEY

In 1921, Roger was the second child born to John and Carrie Richey, 127 East Silver Street, in Bluffton, Indiana. He has a sister, Josephine Warner. Roger graduated from Bluffton High School in 1939. He attended International Business College in Fort Wayne, then worked for Packard Motor Car Company in Detroit, Michigan, for two years.

Then came World War II. Roger enlisted in the United States Marine Corps in 1942, went through boot training in San Diego, Parachute Training School at Camp Gillespie; Fleet Marine force at Camp Pendleton; then into the Pacific Theater of war. He was wounded on Iwo Jima.

After his discharge from the United States Marine Corp in 1945, he worked at International Harvester in Fort Wayne, Indiana, for nine years, then Franklin Electric Company in Bluffton, Indiana, for twenty-eight years. He retired from there in 1982.

Rosemary was born in Indianapolis, Indiana, to Paul and Lorraine Lucas, in 1924. Paul was a mortician and Lorraine was a registered nurse. Rosemary and Lorraine moved to Bluffton in 1930. Lorraine was the superintendent of Wells County Hospital for a number of years.

Rosemary graduated from Bluffton High School in 1942, worked at General Electric Company in Fort Wayne for one year, then Baer Field Post Exchange for two years.

Roger and Rosemary were married by the Reverend Matthew Worthman in 1945. They have two children, Diana (Richey) Hay, and Douglas Richey. Five grandchildren: Natalie (Hay) Bassett, John Nathan Hay, Stacey, Meghann, and Kathryn Richey.

Grandparents of Roger's were Emanuel and Martha Ellen (Heller) Heche from Vera Cruz, Indiana; he was a building contractor. Harlan G. and Mary Jane (Rowe) Richey; he was a mail carrier in Bluffton.

Rosemary's grandparents were Nathaniel and Rosetta (Plummer) Mentzer from Bluffton and Joe and Sena Lucas from Advance, Indiana. Her great-grandparents were Henrietta Dare Trullender and George Washington Plummer, who lived two miles south of Tocsin, Indiana.

RIEDDLE

The surname of Rieddle has had many different spellings or mis-spellings whichever the case may be. In the old records it was not spelled as it is today, but it is difficult to determine which way is definitely correct.

Elmo Blaine Rieddle was born February 6, 1923, in Bluffton, Indiana. The home where the family lived was located at 322 East Horton Street. His father, Christian Rieddle, was born in Barton County, Kansas, September 6, 1885, and his mother, Cora Inez Hottel Rieddle, was born in Mercer County, Ohio, May 5, 1895. They also had a daughter, Crystal Bess Rieddle, (Mrs. W.R. Kleinknight, Jr.) who was born February 26, 1921, in Rensselaer, Indiana. Mr. and Mrs. Chris Rieddle made their home there for a time early in their marriage. Inez Rieddle's mother, Blanche Hottel, made their home with the Rieddles for many years.

Elmo and Verna Rieddle

Elmo and Crystal started school in Park Elementary on East Ohio Street; went on to Central Junior High on West Washington Street and graduated from P.A. Allen High School.

After graduation, Elmo worked locally at various jobs. Soon he was taken into service in World War II and served in the Eighth Army Air Force as a mechanic. His service included a tour of duty in England.

June 15, 1947, Elmo Rieddle and Miss Verna M. Linnett were married in Danebod Lutheran Church in Tyler, Minnesota. The Danish community of Tyler was her home town as well as the home area of her father and his family. Her father, Harald A. Linnett married Laurine Matson Linnett who was from the Danish settlement at Withee, Wisconsin. Verna had an older brother, Lawrence, who passed away in May, 1987. He lived in Mankato, Minnesota, where his wife and two sons continue to live. Lawrence and Verna began school in St. Paul; later went to school in Minneapolis and graduated from Tyler High School.

Elmo and Verna have lived in Toll Gate Heights since 1955. Their son, Christian Linnett Rieddle, was born June 17, 1957. He started school in 1975. In 1982, he received an MBA from Indiana University, Bloomington.

Chris took employment at Marathon Petroleum in Findlay, Ohio, then moved on to Society National Group in Indianapolis. At this time, he is employed at Indiana National Bank as a trust officer.

November 28, 1987, Christian and Debra Krompegel, from the Youngstown, Ohio area, were married in Carmel Lutheran Church, Carmel, Indiana. Debra is a graduate from Findlay College. Chris and Debra have a son, Matthew Christian Rieddle, born July 11, 1990.

Elmo has worked at Lincoln Foodservice Products, Inc. for twenty years.

RIEDDLE

The Rieddle family, Christian, Inez, and Crystal moved to Wells County in May, 1921. Christian was born September 6, 1885, in West Bend, Kansas, and grew up in North Dakota. As an adult, he was a dredge engineer working on the draining of swamp areas in Ohio, Indiana, Illinois, and Missouri. Inez was born May 5, 1895, in Mercer County, Ohio, and grew up in that area. Crystal was born February 26, 1921, in Rensselaer, Indiana, where her paternal grandmother lived.

With our maternal grandmother, we lived on East Horton Street in Bluffton. A son, Elmo, was born February 6, 1923. After moving to Bluffton, Christian was employed at the Erie Stone Company until his retirement. For a short time during World War II, he was employed in defense work at the General Electric Plant in Fort Wayne.

Since they lived across from Jefferson Park, Elmo grew up to be interested in baseball. There were many good softball and baseball games played there, both school and other organizations. Lights were erected and night games were played. They were especially popular during the years the Civilian Conservation Corp was at what is now Ouabache Park.

Crystal and Elmo attended Park Elementary School on East Ohio Street; Central Junior High on West Washington Street; and graduated from P.A. Allen High School.

After high school, Crystal was employed in the insurance department of John W. Carnall and Sons. January 18, 1947, she married Wilmer R. (Wid) Kleinknight, Jr., also a Wells County resident. They lived in Albuquerque, New Mexico, where two daughters, Anne and Mary, were born. Anne married David Watters, son of Earl L. (Bud) and Maenette Watters, Wells County residents. They live with two daughters, Kristen and Rebecca, in Sturgis, Michigan. Mary is married to Kevin Fleming and they live in Albuquerque. Crystal now lives in Truth or Consequences, New Mexico.

RITCHEY FAMILY

My great-grandfather, William Duckwall, walked to Jackson Township, Wells County, in 1834 from Highland County, Ohio. He built a lean to and stayed in the wilderness all winter. A few years later, he married Sarah Cloud, who was born on a flatboat as the family and others were coming to Indiana from Ohio on the Ohio river. The Clouds settled in Rush County. Some years later they came up to Grant County. When William Duckwall and Sarah Cloud were married, they lived in their log cabin on the land he had acquired from the United States government, north of Dillman in Jackson Township. He was a farmer. This land is still owned by descendants. They were the parents of four daughters: Elizabeth; Amanda; Nancy, who died as a child; and Margaret Kisiah, who was my grandmother. Margaret Kisiah married Ben Williamson and they had one daughter, Sarah Pearlie, my mother, born April 6, 1881. She married William Ritchey in 1901. They had two children, a son Lauren, who died in 1985, and a daughter, Violet.

My father's mother, Mary Almeda Allen, came to Jackson Township, Wells County, as a baby in 1850 with her parents, Zephaniah and Sarah Allen. His father, John Ritchey, came to Jackson Township at the age of seven in 1851 with the Calvin Kilander family from Ohio to a farm north of Dillman. This is the place of my birth. John Ritchey was a veteran of the Union Army in the Civil War. John Ritchey and Mary Almeda Allen were married in 1868. They had four children, Clara, William, Lena, and Pearl. all are deceased.

My father, William Ritchey, worked in the oil field as a rig builder during the oil boom here. Then later he was a farmer north of Dillman where I was born December 29, 1910. My father and mother, Sarah Pearlie, were both faithful members of the Dillman United Brethren Church where his father and mother were charter members. Also my great grandfather, William Williamson was one of the founders. My father went to school at Dillman. Mother went to Dillman two years, then went to Eversole School, all in Jackson Township.

I went all my elementary school years to Dillman School. Then I graduated from Warren High School, as Jackson Township had no high school then. *Submitted by Violet Banter*

GEORGE AND NINA RITTENHOUSE

In 1963 George and Nina Rittenhouse brought their family to Wells County and purchased a five-acre home place east of Bluffton on State Road 116, near Quabache State Park. They raised their four children there with the love and responsibilities of a family of six, with lots of mowing, a garden, a small orchard, trees, birds, and deer from the park.

When a young friend came home with one of our kids and joined in on the chores and routine. We overheard a comment at the meal table: "I wish my parents wanted me home after school; this is fun."

George left Randolph County to Purdue University in pharmacy, marriage in 1952, and R.O.T.C. military program. He then served in the U.S. Air Force as a pilot for three years, then came back to drugstore management in Muncie and Lafayette, Indiana. He came to Caylor-Nickel as pharmacist for five years and then opened the Bluffton Pharmacy at 312 South Main, and served the community with family pharmacy service for twenty years.

Nina also left Randolph County to Purdue University, majoring in home economics, and marriage in 1952. She had a good background in 4-H, and obtained some of her fashion training in New York. George calls her a multi-talented person. She says she just has a lot of ideas! Nina began with custom designs, then developed girls' dresses which sold to department stores and specialty shops. That was the beginning of a small design and manufacturing family business.

The Ritten-House Restaurant at 218 South Main became a family business about 1979, with home being on the upper two floors. It was developed with turn-of-the-century antiques and decor. The house was the former home of L.C. Davenport, another local druggist.

The Rittenhouses have four children:

Kent - graduated from Ball State University in business administration. He became a captain with a major airline. His pilot training came through the Air National Guard at Fort Wayne and through the U.S. Air Force.

Linda - graduated from Purdue University in hotel and restaurant management. She married Ralph Lies, Jr. They have an ice business and home products business in LaPorte, Indiana. They have two daughters; Brittany and Marlina.

Greg - graduated from DePauw and Southern Methodist Universities. He was an exchange student in Greece. He married Janice Glass, became a Methodist Minister, and has two sons; Justin and Joel.

Brock - started in landscape architecture at Purdue University. He changed to the restaurant business with experience in Indianapolis and Fort Wayne. He married Lynda McArdle and they have three sons: Andrew, Benjamin, and Aaron. He returned to the family business, the Ritten-House Restaurant, in 1990.

At present we have seven grandchildren with two more on the way.

GEORGE AND MILDRED RISSER

I, George Risser, was born in Petroleum and spent most of my life there until 1970. I married Mildred Luttman in 1934, and worked in the Shell Station for Brent Nutter for a short time. Any kind of work was hard to find during the depression, so we moved to Lafayette, where I worked at Fairfield Manufacturing Company until World War II, when we moved to Fort Wayne. I worked for Studebaker, and Mildred worked for International Harvester. In 1946 I bought the Shell Station in Petroleum and ran it for twenty-one years, retiring in 1971. Mildred worked for K-Mart Distribution Center near Baer Field, Fort Wayne, for sixteen years.

After we both retired in 1971, we bought an Airstream Trailer and traveled all over the United States, Canada, and Mexico. We bought a home in Florida and spend our winters there, and our summers either traveling or staying in Indiana.

Mildred's parents were Olin and Alda Luttman. They were farmers and owned a farm one mile east and one mile south of Petroleum. They retired from the farm in 1965, and spent their retirement in Petroleum until both their deaths in 1969.

George and Mildred Risser
May 3, 1988

My parents were Calvin and Lovina Risser. May father ran the Petroleum Hardware Store, along with his partner, Ray Barnes. Calvin died in 1944 and Lovina died in 1970.

My eldest sister, Irene, married Jack Stoner, and they raised their four children in Petroleum. Jack worked for the Nickle Plate Railroad, and Irene was the Postmistress for many years in Petroleum. She spent her later years with her daughter (Beverly) and son-in-law in Calhoun, Georgia, where she passed away in 1990.

My brother, Lloyd Risser, was married to Emma Blocker. They had one son, Max. Lloyd also had two daughters, Pamela and Lynda, from his second marriage. Lloyd drove a trolley car for many years in Indianapolis. After Lloyd's second wife, Pat, passed away, he married his third wife, Mariam. Lloyd passed away in 1987 and Mariam is living in Greensburg, Indiana.

My second sister, June, married Raymond Michael. They raised their four children in Dayton, Indiana, where they are spending their retirement years.

My third sister, Helen, worked for many years at General Electric, Fort Wayne, and was married to Joe Burnam, who worked for the Pennsylvania Railroad. Joe passed away in 1984. Helen recently married Art Crowe. They make their home in Fort Wayne and Winter Haven, Florida.

Mildred and I are the parents of one daughter, Norma Jean. Norma Jean grew up in Petroleum. Her first marriage was to Joe Monce. Joe and Norma had two sons. John, who is married and has two daughters, works for the 3-M Company in St. Paul, Minnesota, but has recently accepted an assignment for two years near Genoa, Italy. Larry is married and has a four-month old son. He works for UpJohn in Kalamazoo, Michigan. Norma is presently married to Dr. David Stone, who is an industrial doctor for the Fort Motor Company in Detroit, Michigan.

My father's parents were William Henry and Mary Alice Rose Risser and my mother's parents were George and Ocie Shellabarger Marsh. Most of my ancestors were from Pennsylvania, Ohio.

Mildred and I bought the Robert Niblick home at 726 Sycamore Lane, Bluffton, Indiana, in June 1988. *Submitted by George Risser*

MARSHALL A. RIX FAMILY

Marshall A. Rix, son of Moses M. Rix, married Catherine E. Craven, daughter of Edwin and Naomi Craven, in November, 1934. No children were born to the union. Both graduated from Bluffton High School. Marshall went on to the Apprentice School at the General Electric Company in Fort Wayne. Catherine was a secretary in the Bluffton High School for ten years, then went to the office of Dr. Jesse T. Scott, Optometrist, as his secretary-bookkeeper here, five years; then back to the high school office for five years more. Marshall volunteered in the Navy at the start of World War II and was stationed on a destroyer in the South Pacific. His ship had just captured a Japanese ship, camouflaged as a Red Cross ship, when the atomic bomb was dropped by the U.S.

After his discharge, he was employed twenty-seven years as an optician in the office of Dr. Jess T. Scott, Optometrist, and retired from there.

Catherine worked for sixteen years in the Superintendent's office of the Bluffton-Harrison Metropolitan School District as secretary and treasurer of the board. She retired from there.

Catherine served on the Bluffton-Wells County Public Library Board for eight years. She was very active in the Indiana State Educational Secretaries Association holding numerous offices. She was a member of the Daughters of the American Revolution and a member of the Fort Wayne Toastmistress Clubs for seventeen years.

After retirement, Marshall and Catherine spent twelve winters in Sarasota, Florida.

MOSES M. RIX FAMILY

Having been a rural mail carrier in Pennville, Moses M. Rix moved his family to Bluffton in 1917, where he received employment in the H.C. Bay Piano Company. He was married to Clarabelle Evilsizer and they had five children and one deceased. Namely, Wilbur, who married Pauline Collins; Eldon married to Mary Harmon; Marshall married to Catharine Craven; Mary married to George Zirkle; and Robert married to Connie Rousseau.

Wilbur's children were: Lewis, Don, Roger, and Evelyn. Lewis is a commercial artist. Don, Roger, and Evelyn are all employed by Marsh Foods; both Don and Roger hold executive positions. Eldon had one daughter, Mevalyn. Marshall has no children. Mary has two sons and a daughter living: William, Keith, and Jean (Mrs. Dave Noll). A son, Eddie, was killed in an auto accident shortly after discharge from the service. Robert, now deceased, had three children, Michael, Sonja, and Debra.

After the closing of the Bay Piano factory, Mr. Rix worked at the Muncie Warner Gear factory, where he commuted daily on the interurban. Several years later in Bluffton, he managed a filling station owned by Hartman and Son. At the time of his death, he was employed at the Red Cross Manufacturing Company.

Always active in the Democratic party, Mr. Rix at one time was employed by the city.

Mr. and Mrs. Rix were supportive of Street Fair activities and Mr. Rix always helped Wid Kleinknight in the Chicken Display tent, while Mrs. Rix was busy as a cook in the Church of Christ Food Tent.

ROBERTS-BENDER

Lawrence Kay Roberts, son of Francis Earl and Jennie Kathryn Maddux Roberts, was born June 24, 1938. He has resided in the little town of Rockford, Indiana, in Rockcreek Township all of his life and attended Rockcreek School where he graduated in 1956. He graduated from Manchester College in 1962 and started his teaching career in 1966 in the sixth grade at Lancaster School in Wells County. He later taught Social Studies and Physical Education in the junior high and moved to the Norwell Middle School in 1979, when the middle school opened, where he teaches Social Studies in the seventh and eighth grades.

Karen Kay Bender Roberts, daughter of Merlin Keith and Alice Elene Martin Bender, was born April 20, 1942. She attended Union Center School two years, moved to Uniondale and attended Rockcreek School and graduated in 1960. She met Kay in high school and they were married on July 23, 1960. They moved to North Manchester and she attended Manchester College one year while her husband was finishing his education. Kay and Karen had three children. Kerry Lee was born December 14, 1961. He married Laura Busche from Leo in 1984 and they have four children: Danielle Linn (February 24, 1985), Andrea Kay (August 13, 1986), Jarred Lee (January 23, 1989), and Jordan Edward (March 20, 1990). He graduated from Purdue University in 1991 with a degree in electrical engineering. They reside in Leo.

Douglas Kirk was born October 18, 1964, attended Purdue University and is pursuing a career in landscape architecture. Kelli Rae was born October 23, 1966 and married Brian Reifel in 1990. both are graduates of Indiana University. She is employed with Nestle's Brands-Carnation and he with Johnson and Johnson. They reside in Fishers, a suburb of Indianapolis.

EARL AND KATHRYN ROBERTS FAMILY

The Earl Roberts family started with the marriage of Francis Earl (Earl) Roberts to Jennie Kathryn (Kathryn) Maddux on April 7, 1928, in Wells County, Indiana. Earl was born on October 5, 1906, to Lewearlie Roberts and Emma Anna (Reef) Roberts in LaSalle County, Illinois. Kathryn was born on March 24, 1909 (although her legal birth date is April 28, 1909) to James Arthur Maddux and Rachel (McFarren) Maddux in Harrison Township, Wells County, Indiana. The reason for the birth date difference is that recording births was something new when Kathryn was born, and the recording of her birth was taken on the date that it was reported rather than the actual birth date.

At the time of their marriage, Earl was farming in Lancaster Township, Wells County, Indiana, with his father; and Kathryn was working at the H.C. Bay Piano Factory in Bluffton, Indiana. They started house keeping around Montpelier, Indiana, with Earl still farming with his two horses. He farmed eighty acres in the Montpelier area. In 1928 a daughter, Betty Irene was born on December 30, in Lancaster Township, Wells County, Indiana. Then in the year of 1929 they moved to Rockford, Indiana, where he started working at the Heller Stone Quarry. In 1930 they moved to Bluffton for a very short time and then moved back to Rockford where they lived until 1965.

After Earl and Kathryn moved back to Rockford, fine sons and one daughter were born. Lester Eugene was born December 7, 1930. John Edwin (Jackie) was born January 28, 1935, and died January 31, 1935; cause of death was being born a blue baby. Jackie is buried at Pennville, Indiana, in a cemetery on the east side of town. On September 18, 1936, Frederick Earl was born, and less than two years later Lawrence Kay was born, June 24, 1938. The last son was born July 17, 1940, and named Walter Lavern. A daughter, Joyce Marie was born on November 19, 1941.

All six children attended and graduated from Rockcreek High School, Rockcreek Township; Wells County, Indiana. The oldest child started school in the fall of 1934, and the youngest graduated in the spring of 1959.

All six children are now married and have families of their own. Betty married Darwin D. McAfee of Rockcreek Township, Wells County, Indiana, on February 26, 1948; and they have three children: Sharon, Cathy, and Michael. They also have six grandchildren and one great grandchild. They live in Rockcreek Township, Wells County, Indiana.

Lester married Joyce E. Gilbert of Rockcreek Township, Wells County, Indiana, on May 25, 1952; and they have six children: Kim, Rita, Amy, Lori, Melissa, and Jennifer. They also have eleven grandchildren. They live in Rockcreek Township, Wells County, Indiana.

Frederick E. (Fred) married Janet C. Dolby of Rockcreek Township, Wells County, Indiana, on July 4, 1959; and they have three children: Richie, Toni, and Dawn. They also have two grandchildren. They are residents of Fort Wayne, Indiana.

Lawrence Kay (Kay) married Karen K. Bender of Rockcreek Township, Wells County, Indiana, on July 23, 1960; and have three children: Kerry, Douglas Kirk, and Kelli. They have four grandchildren and live in Rockcreek Township, Wells County, Indiana.

Walter married Sue Maxwell of Fort Wayne, Indiana, on May 28, 1966; and they have two children: Kristin and Melinda. They now live in Auburn, Indiana.

Joyce married Jack B. Sills of Liberty Township, Wells County, Indiana, on August 4, 1963. They have three children: Travis, Jean, and Jan; and also have three grandsons. Jack died on September 30, 1989, and is buried in the Mossburg Cemetery, Liberty Township, Wells county, Indiana. Joyce resides in Liberty Township, Wells County, Indiana.

During the war years, Kathryn worked at the General Electric Company in Fort Wayne, Indiana, starting work in 1942. Then in 1946 she started working at Franklin Electric Company in Bluffton, Indiana, and retired from there in 1965. Earl worked at Heller Stone Quarry from 1929 until retiring in 1963, because of bad health. After retirement, Earl did carpenter work part-time until 1968.

After retirement, Earl and Kathryn lived in Tucson, Arizona, in the winter months (because of bad health) and came back to Wells County for the summer months. Earl died February 14, 1970, in Bluffton, Indiana is buried at the Rockford Friends Cemetery, Rockford, Indiana. Kathryn is still living and has remarried. She and her present husband, William Bricker, live in Lancaster Township, Wells County, Indiana.

STEPHEN AND ARVILLA RODENBECK FAMILY

On November 29, 1980, Stephen Charles Rodenbeck escorted Arvilla Jean Reinhard down the aisle of matrimony in the Pleasant Dale Church of the Brethren in Adams County. Reverend Dwight Hargett and the late Reverend Kenneth Bauman officiated the wedding.

Stephen, born July 26, 1955, only child of Edwin and Justine (Meyer) Rodenbeck, graduated from Bluffton High School in 1973, and from Huntington college in 1977, with an Elementary Education degree. Besides being engaged in farming, Stephen has worked with his father on carpentry, worked at Troxel Bins, and is currently employed full time at the Craigville Telephone Company, Inc.

Left to Right; Mycal, Stephen, Myshel, Mylinda, Arvilla

Arvilla, born February 12, 1952, to Howard and Ilene (Ehrman) Reinhard is the third child of four. She has two brothers; Carlton Dale Reinhard of Hamilton, Indiana; Arland Gale Reinhard of rural Bluffton; and a sister, Carla Jane (Reinhard) VonGunten of rural Bluffton.

After graduating from Norwell High School in 1970, Arvilla worked at the Ouabache State Park, was office secretary for the Wells County Republican Central Committee, and worked at the Bluffton License Branch for approximately seven and one-half years, the last four as manager. After resigning her position at the license branch, she started working at the Farmers and Merchants Bank. She worked at the bank for over ten years and left when their third child was born. She now works as part-time secretary at the Craigville Telephone Company Incorporated. The rest of her time is spent caring for their son and two daughters. Mycal Charles was born July 21, 1982; Myshel Jean, August 30, 1984; and Mylinda Jean, December 23, 1987. All three being delivered at the Wells Community Hospital.

In 1980 the Rodenbeck household was located in Riverside, and after five years they moved to their present home that was primarily built by Stephen, his father, Edwin, and Arvilla's father, Howard; located at 5998 SE State Road 116, Bluffton.

Stephen and Arvilla are members of the Pleasant Dale Church of the Brethren, rural Decatur, where their family attends.

WILLIAM AND ANNA ROEMBKE

William Roembke Sr. was born in Windheim, Germany, July 28, 1874; to Friedrich Roembke and Minna Dammeyer. Friedrich was a storekeeper in Germany, selling dry goods, groceries, and hardware. William worked in his father's store. William had four sisters: Minna, Doretta, Marie, and Sophia. He came to the United States of America as a young man. He traveled by ship to New York, then took a train to Decatur, Indiana. From Decatur he walked to Tocsin following the Erie Railroad tracks. From Tocsin he walked to the nearby farm house of his sister, Mrs. William (Sophia) Kammeyer in Jefferson Township.

Anna Bauermeister Graft Roembke was born in Loh, Germany, on October 28, 1878, to Ernest Conrad Diedrich Bauermeister and Sophie Limbach. Anna was the youngest of eight children: Ernest, Fredrick, Henry, Karl (Charles), Sophie Werling, William, and Maria Graft. Anna came to the United States of America with her parents at the age of thirteen. They came by ship from Bremen, Germany. The voyage was so stormy and rough, Anna was tied in her bunk to keep her from falling out. The voyage lasted so long that the relatives here in America thought their ship had been lost at sea. After their safe arrival, Anna and her parents settled on a farm in Jefferson township near Anna's brothers and sisters, who had settled here earlier. She attended Egypt School where she learned some English. Later she kept house for the Christian and Rosina Graft family.

In 1896 Anna married their son William Graft at Zion Lutheran Church, Friedheim, Indiana. William and Anna lived with Christian Graft and his sons after their marriage, as Rosina had died. Anna and William took a baby girl, Meta McGlen, to raise in 1897. After being married not quite five years, William Graft died of pneumonia in 1901. He is buried in Friedheim Lutheran Church Cemetery.

In 1902, Anna married William Roembke Sr. at the Bethlehem Lutheran Church, Wells County.

William, Anna, and Meta first lived on a rented farm on road 700N, near the present state highway. Here a daughter, Alvina, was born in 1903. Later they moved to Lockwood, Missouri, where they bought a farm. Elsie was born there in 1905. Three years later the family moved back to Wells County and purchased a farm on Road 700E between 900N and 1000N. William Roembke Jr. was born here in 1912. In 1917 the family moved and purchased the present Roembke farm near Echo on Road 900N, where Mrs. William Roembke Jr. still resides.

William Roembke Sr. and Anna Roembke; 1951

William Sr. and Anna farmed their entire working years. William Sr. maintained an active interest in politics and current events. Anna also assisted women at the birth of their babies who were born at home during these years. She also did beautiful handwork: spinning and knitting wool, crocheting and making quilts.

Meta married Christian A. Graft. They had seven children: Albert, Edwin, Walter, Christian Jr., Alma Weaver, Loretta Hunicutt, and Rosemary Osborne. They lived in Wells County.

Alvina married Victor Werling. They had four children: Viola Schwarz, Juanita Springer, Bernadine Scherrer, and Norman. They lived in Wells County. Elsie married Carl W. Heckman and had four children: Maurice, Imogene Bultemeier, Betty Schroeder, and Donna Fenner. They lived in Adams County. William Roembke Jr. married Adele Buuck and had two children: John and Sharon Ewell. They lived on the Roembke farm where Adele still resides.

William Sr. and Anna were members of Bethlehem Lutheran Church, Wells County. William Sr. died in 1958 and Anna died in 1977; both are buried in Oak Lawn Cemetery in Ossian, Indiana.

ROSCO AND WAHILLA ROHRER

A resident of Liberty Center for most of seventy-three years, Mrs. Roscoe (Wahilla) Rohrer lives just south of the Liberty Center Baptist Church (West Street) in Mrs. Rohrer's parents' home. Wahilla Max Merriman Rohrer, daughter of Selurious and Adelia Merriman, was born in Huntington County in 1910 and lived one-half mile north and one-half mile west of Mt. Zion, before coming to Liberty Center in 1918. Selurious Merriman taught school in Huntington County and worked in the local oil fields. Adelia was a housewife. Wahilla had one sister, Waneita, who was four years older. Roscoe Alfred Rohrer was born in Peru in 1913 and raised in New Haven. His parents were Wayne and Cora Rohrer, factory workers.

The union of Roscoe and Wahilla on January 2, 1940 produced one daughter, Patricia Ann, in 1950; the couple had moved to Liberty Center in 1949. Subsequently, the daughter died at the age of three of a virus, possibly pneumonia.

Wahilla has worked in various factories during her life in Fort Wayne, Marion, and Huntington; while Roscoe was employed by the Dana Corporation in Marion and has retired from there. Neither was able to finish high school; since both had fairly serious surgeries during those years.

In Liberty Center Mrs. Rohrer attended the Baptist Church near her home. She recollects traveling on the interurban that went from Bluffton to Marion (passing near Liberty Center) to shop and visit in Marion. A passenger train could be caught in Liberty Center at that time, too, where the present track remains.

ROHRING-WOOD

Stephen Lynn Rohring, son of Gilbert and Virginia Jones Rohring, and Lynette Marie Wood, daughter of Robert Jr. and Eleanor Morris Wood; were married July 27, 1974 at Uniondale St. Mark's Lutheran Church.

Steve and Lynnette Rohring, Matthew and Kelly

There children are: Matthew Robert, December 9, 1977; and Kelly Lynn, August 14, 1984.

JESSE ROGERS FAMILY

Jesse Rogers and his bride of three months moved to the farm in southeast Chester Township formerly belonging to Elmer Tewsksbury, in May 1954. Later the adjoining farm of Ralph Weatherholt was purchased. The one hundred and sixty-acre farms main operation is a fifty-cow milking herd. Additional land is farmed in Blackford County.

Jesse is the second son of Walter and Opal Schwarzkopf Rogers, both deceased, of Blackford County. Kathryn is the third daughter of Walter and Sarah William Waltz, both deceased, of Blackford County. Jesse attended the Montpelier schools, where he graduated in 1949. He was active in sports, FFA judging, and 4-H. In 1940 and 1966 he attended the Purdue Short Course and received the Farm Management Award and the Top Scholar Award. From 1952-54 he served in the army with the 1st Cavalry Division and was stationed in Japan. In addition to farming he has been active in Farm Bureau, serving as county president for ten years. He was a member of the Board of Zoning Appeals and has held various church council offices at Zion Lutheran Church. In the election of 1990 he was elected Wells County Commissioner from the 1st district.

His wife Kathryn was born in Jackson Township, Blackford County, where the first eight years of schooling were at Dildine. Her high-school days were at Montpelier. After graduation she worked as a telephone operator for Indiana Bell. She has been active in home demonstration work, serving as an officer in her local club and for the Blackford County unit. In 1989 she was honored to be named Farm Bureau District Four Woman of Achievement. Jesse and Kathryn were county coordinators for the LABO Exchange and also hosted IFYE's from Costa Rica and India.

They are the parents of four daughters. All graduated from Southern Wells with honors in 1973, 1975, 1976 and 1979 respectively. Karen received the county DAR award and received her degree from Purdue University. She married Guy Studebaker, who is a minister. They have one son, Jesse, eleven; and one daughter, Geny, twenty months.

January 26, 1990 - Jesse Rogers Family
Jordan, Danielle, Janet, Lydia, J.J., Jesse, Geny, Kathryn, Kelly, Bob, Kay, Greg, Louise, Guy, Karen, Marlene, Jay

Louise was a Hoosier 4-H Ambassador to Europe in 1974. After graduating from Vincennes University she married Gregory Reynolds, who is a printer-artist. They have three children: Danielle, eleven; Lydia, eight; and Jordan, three.

Loretta Kay was Southern Wells FFA Sweetheart and later Miss Wells County, 1977. She has an Associate's degree from Ball State and is married to Robert McCormick, extension agent for Howard County. They have a daughter, Kelly, age four; and a son, John, three months old.

Marlene toured with the American Musical Ambassadors Band in Europe. She holds a degree from DePauw University and is married to Jay Redding, a pharmaceutical representative. They have a daughter, Janet, two years of age.

We are grateful for the challenges and opportunities we have experienced in Wells County.

ROMINE

We do not have too much information on the Romine family. My father died of typhoid fever when I, Lloyd Romine was three years old. He was Charles Romine, 1875-1914. His parents were Nate and Elizabeth Romine. Nate was a Civil War veteran. Charles was married to Sarah Brown, daughter of Soloman and Hanna Brown. Sarah had six brothers and sisters: Amos, Lewis, William, Charles, Jess, and Anna.

Charles and Sarah had three children: Clarence (1900-1978), married to Clara Hamilton; Arthur (1902-1959), married to Lottie Hanna; Minnie (1898-1955), married to Allie Howdyshell; and Lloyd. My mother remarried in 1915 to Augustus Brinneman. They had one son, Vernon who is married to Mildred Killingbeck. They have three children: Jim, married, lives in California; Loren, married, lives in Berne; and Cathy, married, lives near Bluffton.

In 1936 I married Cora McAdam, R.N. (1912-1973), daughter of Arthur and Mable Allen McAdam. Arthur's father was a son of Charles and Rena McAdam. I was a meat-cutter for Kroger, Ratliff, Heyerlys' and Maloley's. Cora was a registered nurse at Wells Community and the Clinic Hospitals. Cora died in 1973 from a brain tumor. We have three children: Judy, graduated from International Business college is married to Ivan Thornburg. She has one daughter, Pamela Kahn Caldwell, and has one son, Joey, and four stepchildren. Sue is married to Robert Riley. They have Penny, who has two daughters; Amanda and Kayla Marie. Michael attended Ball State and lives in Muncie. Rob attended automotive school in Lima, Ohio. Joe graduated from Taylor and has a doctor's degree from Ball State University. Joe is married to Carol Luginbill. They have Kellie, fifteen; and Kyle, thirteen. They live in Upland, Indiana, where Joe is athletic director at Taylor University.

Lloyd and Helen Romine
1989

I retired from Maloley's in 1973. After Cora's death I worked for Pinkerton Security and later for D and D until I had a corneal transplant. I retired in 1986.

In August, 1974, I married Helen G. Plummer, R.N. We are both retired and enjoying it.

ROSE

In 1851 Peter Rose, my great-great-grandfather, and his brother Abraham came to Wells County. They were from Pickaway County, Madison Township, Ohio; where their parents, Anthony and Mary Rose; and grandparents, John and Dorothy Rose, had lived since the late 1820's. Abraham bought eighty acres of land in Nottingham Township, but he and Peter returned to Ohio after a few years.

Abraham married Sarah Crum in Ohio, and they lived the remainder of their lives there. But Peter returned to Indiana and married Mary Gottschalk and bought Abraham's land in July, 1856.

Peter Rose and wife, Mary Gottschalk
Wedding picture, 1856

Peter's other brothers and his sister also came to Indiana. They were: William and his first wife Eliza Billman, who went to Noble County around 1850 (after Eliza's death he married Sophia Baus); Catherine and her husband, Josiah Weist, who came to Wells County in 1860, where they raised their family; Isaac and his wife, Catherine Dunmore, who lived in Wells County in 1850; John and his wife, Rachel Teegardin, who came to Wells County in 1861, where they raised their family; Samuel and his wife, Sarah Weist, who lived in Wells County in 1854. Peter's mother, Mary, came to Indiana and lived with her children after her husband Anthony's death. Her parents were Peter and Margaret Woodring of Northampton County, Pennsylvania; and later of Fairfield County, Ohio. He was a Revolutionary War soldier.

Peter and Mary Rose farmed the Rose property and had five children: John Edward, who married Elizabeth Bebout; George Nathaniel, who married Elizabeth Mary Aiegenhain; James Monroe (Monroe), who married Sarah Bistauffer; Jacob Perry (Perry), my great grandfather; Barbara Elizabeth (Lizzie), who was unmarried. In 1865 Peter died of typhoid fever while serving in the Civil War. He was buried in Nashville, Tennessee.

Margaret Rose Bond, Lauren Delane Bond, Roy Jackson Bond

Mary's parents were Jacob and Belinda Gottschalk. After Peter's death she married John Shigley. Peter's son Perry married Mary Christina (Tine) Holloway in 1885. Tine's parents were John and Louvica Holloway. In 1897, Perry and Tine bought forty acres of land in Nottingham Township, which they later sold, and in 1903 bought the old Rose farm from Perry's mother. Perry and Tine had two children: Cleopus Earl (Earl) and Clarence Edwin (Ed), my grandfather.

Earl married Alta J. Cowens and had one child, Lloyd, who married Geneva Snow.

Ed, my grandfather, was a state detective in northern Indiana. During his life he also sold cars and was one of the county's top salesmen. He inherited the Rose family farm in Nottingham Township. He also purchased an additional farm just north of the original Rose property.

His wife, Leona, was the daughter of Samuel and Sarah Opliger. Samuel built a mail order house from Sears Roebuck in Bluffton. Ed and Leona moved into the Opliger home in 1923. Both Ed and Leona were active in Democratic politics and were members of the Methodist Church. Leona was the vice chairman of the county Democrats and a member of Eastern Star. They had two children: Leonard and Max, my father.

Leonard married Bette Bebb and had two children: Diana, who married Rick White and later Robert Sanden; and Geoffery, who married Sharon Krull. Kelle Ann was Leonard's child from his second marriage to Mary Licker.

Max married Dorothy Marie Knoff, the daughter of Raymond and LuLu (Billie) Knoff. Dorothy attended DePauw and Ball State Teachers College, receiving a teacher's license in both music and English. She taught in the county and city school systems; and now resides in Montgomery, Texas.

Max received a bachelor's degree in business from Indiana University and a teacher's certificate from Ball State College. He was a full lieutenant in the Navy during World War II. After the war he worked as a hardware jobber for the Schaefer firm. He later moved to his father's farm (north of the original property) and taught at Pennville Junior High in Jay County. In 1958 Max built a home in the Riverview section of Bluffton and began teaching at Lancaster High School (now Norwell). After his father's death, he inherited both of his father's farms in Nottingham Township, which he farmed until his death in 1988. Max had two children: David Alan, and me, Margaret (Marg).

David married Anne Parker, daughter of Dr. Sterling and Marge Parker of Decatur, Illinois; and is a graduate of Purdue University and Indiana University Law School. He is a partner with the Butler-Binion Law Firm of Houston, Texas. He has two children: Adam and Collin.

I graduated from Purdue University with a major in interior design and worked as a contract interior designer in Washington, D.C. In 1970 I married Roy Jackson (Jack) Bond, son of Reverend Roy J. and Ruth Bond of Savannah, Georgia; and now live in Bowie, Maryland. Jack is a graduate of Davidson College and works for the National Security Agency. We have one daughter, Lauren Delane. I have held positions in 4-H and Camp Fire. As an amateur genealogist, I have written papers on the Rose family. Following in the tradition of his forbears, my father Max willed the original Rose farm in Wells County, Nottingham Township, Indiana, to me. The property that my great-great-grandfather Peter purchased back in 1856 has been in the Rose family for one hundred and forty years.

RUDY

The ancestors of the Earl F. Rudy family initially appeared in Wells County around 1845 when his grandfather, Frank Rudy, of German descent, came on foot through forests to Indiana from Ohio. He was a barn builder and carpenter. He married Molly Ehle. They were parents of four children, one of whom was Edward M. Rudy.

Earl and Vera Rudy

Edward M. Rudy (1882-1971) helped build the first streets in Bluffton, Indiana, and was a farmer for many years. He married Della Lee Gerwig (1887-1985) of Robert E. Lee lineage in 1906. They had a son and two daughters, the eldest being Earl F. Rudy, born September 26, 1907. Earl became interested in agriculture, and when a teenager was crowned "corn king." He attended Purdue University. In 1930 he married Gretchen Hubner, daughter of Frank and Dessie Spade Hubner. They had two children: Donald B., born December 23, 1930, and Carolyn E., born July 21, 1932. Gretchen died in February, 1933.

Earl worked in the Wells County ASCS office for several years and assisted his father in farming. In 1937 he married Vera Neuenschwander, born May 13, 1911, to Simon and Caroline Hofstetter Neuenschwander. Her great-grandparents immigrated to Adams County from Switzerland. She lived in Fort Wayne and was employed at the Lincoln National Life Insurance Company. They started housekeeping south of Bluffton. A daughter, Rebecca J., was born to this union on May 24, 1941.

In 1937 Earl started Rudy's Hybrid Seeds business, producing small seeds, particularly corn. He and Vera continued this business until 1963, when Earl became one of the founders of Migro Company (composed of seventeen growers throughout Indiana). This was sold in 1979 to North America Plant Breeders; Mission, Kansas.

Donald Rudy attended Northwestern University and graduated from Indiana University Medical School. In 1961 he and his wife, Ruth Cox Rudy, left to spend fifteen years in Zimbabwe, Africa, as a missionary doctor and surgeon. At present he is in a clinic partnership with five other physicians in Glencoe, Minnesota, but has returned to Africa four times in the past five years to help for a month during each visit. He and Ruth are parents of two children: Mary Rudy Chapman and Mark.

Carolyn was Junior Miss America in 1949, attended DePauw University, and is a registered nurse, having graduated from Presbyterian Nursing School in Chicago. She married John W. Brill and resides in Indianapolis, Indiana. They have two sons: John W. II and Robert E., and one grandson, Corey Brill.

Rebecca graduated from DePauw University, received her masters from Purdue and her Ph.D. in psychology from Ball State. She maintains an office in the Madison Clinic in Muncie, Indiana, where she lives with her husband, Jay W. Troyka, and their two sons; Jay, Jr., and Matthew.

Earl and Vera have been active in community and civic affairs, and primarily in the First United Methodist Church, where Earl was trustee during the building of the present sanctuary. Vera was a member of the Chancel and Bell Choirs for numerous years. After fifty-three years on their farm, both are enjoying retirement at 1284 Lakeview Court, Bluffton, Indiana.

RUNKLE-GENTIS

Randall Scott Runkle, son of Kenneth and Imogene (Weaver) Runkle of rural Jackson Township, and Yvette Kay Gentis, daughter of Jack and Barbara (Slusher) Gentis of rural Nottingham Township were married on a hot eighty-four degree autumn Sunday afternoon on October 3, 1976 by the Reverend David Terhune at the Petroleum United Methodist Church, Petroleum, Indiana.

Randy and Yvette were high school sweethearts from the class of 1974, Southern Wells High School. Randy worked at Kitco during his senior year on the ICE program through school. Kitco laid him off weeks before graduation, because of the energy crunch. Yvette worked at the Bank of Montpelier on the COE work program through school.

Wedding bells were put aside, for a couple of years until the energy crunch let up a bit and Randy was hired at Majestic Corporation Huntington, in January 1976. We rented a small house from Jerry and Peg Reaser of Petroleum.

December 1987
Randy and Yvette Runkle, Tanner (eight), Brandy (seven), Cheyenne (four)

We became parents of our first son, Tanner Shay, born June 29, 1979. Followed just fifteen months later by our first daughter, Brandy Lace. Times grew tough once again. Randy was driving sixty-four miles a day on a three to four day work week. Christmas in 1980 looked really bleak. Christmas Eve was spent at Grandpa and Grandma Gentis', and when we arrived home, Santa had visited our home. A wooden red barn was under the tree Tanner's name on it. It was later learned that Paul and Judy Herring were the elves that saved our Christmas.

We moved closer to Huntington, on a small farm at Rockford, renting from Junior and Marjorie McAfee. Randy's job improved and Yvette worked full time at the Bluffton K-Mart. A third child, a daughter, was added to the family in July 1983; Cheyenne Cinnamon.

The family enjoys camping and classic car shows. Randy is presently restoring a 1956 Chevy from the frame up. Yvette enjoys sewing for proms and weddings. She also helps with the Harrison 4-H Club and teaches CYC at Sonlight Church. The children attend Bluffton school district.

God blessed us by providing access to our first home located at 226 North Marion Street in Bluffton, May of 1986. We find living in Bluffton very nice along with the convenience of running the children to all their activities. Randy is currently in his sixteenth year at Majestic Corporation, and Yvette now works full time as a bookkeeper at J and R Products, Craigville.

ROSCOE O. RUPEL AND E. MAXINE SMITH RUPEL

On November 5, 1914, Isaac and Lola Belle Loveless Rupel were blessed with a baby boy, Roscoe, the seventh child born to that union. They resided in Jay County, Indiana, and owned and operated The Union Stock Farm. The Rupel family moved from there to New Madrid, Missouri, and then to Huntertown, Indiana, where Roscoe graduated from Eel River Perry High School in 1935. They then moved to a farm west of Ossian, Indiana, where Roscoe met and later married E. Maxine Smith on October 5, 1940.

Maxine was born June 18, 1923, the tenth child to James J. and Karah Stine Smith of near Uniondale, Indiana. Maxine attended East Union Center School and lived on her parents' farm all her life until she married Roscoe. Roscoe and Maxine were blessed with seven children: James Isaac, who died in infancy; Kathryn L. Gunn, of Grand Rapids, Michigan, who with her husband owns and operates an excavating business; Patricia A. Brown, an employee of Lutheran Hospital in Fort Wayne; Susan D. Schafer, Orlando, Florida, an employee of R.J. Reynolds, Company; Captain Frederick M. Rupel, a Chaplain with the U.S. Army, having served in Turkey, Germany, (twice), the U.S. and presently in Saudi Arabia, participated in Operation Desert Storm; Ted M. Rupel, a former teacher in the Huntington County, Indiana, school system, currently residing in Nashville, Tennessee, where he teaches school; Joyce D. Sanders Hipsher of Zanesville, Indiana, an employee of Franklin Electric Company in Bluffton. There are twelve grandchildren and six great-grandchildren.

Roscoe and Maxine and Family; July, 1985

Roscoe worked at General Electric in Fort Wayne for thirty-six years. He was an avid sports person, mainly hunting and fishing, and greatly enjoyed life. Roscoe died March 16, 1989 at seventy-five years of age. Maxine never straying far from her birthplace, lives at 5855 Main Street in Uniondale, where the family has lived for twenty-four years. Her interests are her church, children, and grandchildren. She loves to travel, having gone to Europe and England twice, to tour the country and visit friends and relatives. Maxine has been a devoted mother, housewife, and a former employee of Kitco Incorporated of Bluffton and the CGal-Ham Corporation, also of Bluffton.

CHARLES RUPRIGHT FAMILY

The Charles (Chuck) Allen Rupright family resides at 7411 N 300 W, Markle, Indiana. Chuck is married to Kathy J. (Burger). She is a daughter of Calvin E. and Julia F. (Hoopingarner) of 7327 N 300 W, Markle, Indiana. A sister, Kimberly, resides in Huntington. She is married to Charles Chapman. They have a son, Christopher C., born January 7, 1986.

Chuck and Kathy have resided at the above address since their marriage, May 4, 1968. A daughter, Amy, born November 17, 1969, is a junior at Ball State University, Muncie. A daughter, Lori, was born March 6, 1961. She died on February 8, 1989.

Chuck and Kathy's home was originally built by John Folk, Kathy's great-grandfather. He was married to Amanda (Motz).

The whole of Wells County area shared the grief and sorrow of the Rupright and Burger families at the death of Lori. Lori, a senior at Norwell High School, was killed in a traffic accident on her way to school, February 8, 1989. Her car slipped on a patch of ice on highway #224, just one mile from her destination, throwing her into the path of Eric Milholland, who was just a mile from home, and on his way to work.

Lori was born on March 6, 1971, and would have celebrated eighteen years of life the next month. In eighteen short years she touched so many lives. Lori and her older sister, Amy, helped Grandpa Cal mow the cemeteries in Zanesville, and sometimes you would run into Cal at the station buying what he called "refueling" supplies for the girls. He would have pop and candy in his hands and remark that he had to keep them satisfied to keep them working.

Lori, who spent her grade school time at Rockcreek and Lancaster, was an honor student at Norwell where she achieved straight A's the last nine weeks. She was a member of the girl's varsity volleyball and basketball teams, and the pep club. She received the mental attitude award for volleyball, the sport she loved the most. Her teammates signed the sectional volleyball, and as a memorial to her, it was laid in the casket and buried with her.

Connie Caley Bowman, a native of Zanesville and close friend of the family, wrote a poem of Amy and Lori's younger days which she presented to the family as a memorial. The Norwell students were crushed at her death. This was the sixth death in her class this school year. Schools from all over the area sent flowers to the funeral attended by four hundred people. The funeral was held at the Markle Methodist Church. The Reverend John Parks gave a fitting tribute to Lori by using the letters of her name for the sermon. "L," was for her love. "O," was for her feeling and caring for others. "R," was for us to remember her. "I," was to remind us that she is in his arms. The funeral was attended by scores of young people. The school song was played, and fifteen to twenty of her girlfriends sang the song "Friends." The ballplayers from Norwell acted as pallbearers and wore their letter jackets in tribute to her. They were Tom Brickley, Scott Burke, Scott Douglas, Corey Gerber, Darron Johnson, Mike Miller, Shawn Reinhard, and Mike and Steve Sonnenberg.

Motz Reunion—Home of Amanda Folk, 1910

Lori is gone but she is not forgotten by the people whom she touched while she was here. Eric Milholland was not seriously injured in the crash. Eric, who was twenty five at the time, and his wife were residing with his parents, the Don Milhollands, during the winter months near Norwell. Eric was a catcher in the Chicago White Sox baseball organization at the time.

Every year the Ruprights present the Lori Rupright Mental Attitude Award to a deserving senior girl in sports at Norwell. A memorial brick also bears her name at the Indiana Basketball Hall of Fame courtyard.

RUSSELL-MOORE

My great-grandparents, August and Augusta Arnold, came from Saxony, Germany in 1846. In 1848 they settled in Vera Cruz.

My grandfather, William Arnold, was born in 1853 in Vera Cruz, living there until 1881 when he came to Liberty Center. His marriage to Henrietta

Isabella Higman took place in Liberty Center. He soon built a home on a large plot of ground which he later sold off lots for other homes. He also bought land a mile north and a quarter east of Liberty Center and later had a house built there.

They had two children: Martha Augusta and Lewis; and raised a grandson, Russell Arnold.

Grandfather Arnold was trustee of Liberty Township when the high school and also a school in Poneto were built in 1896. He and Bert Tinkel owned the hardware and in later years he operated a cider mill on his property. The apples were brought by teams of horses and wagons.

My mother married Charles Russell, a farmer and they had three children: Gerald, Ruth, and Cleora. Gerald owned a confectionery in Auburn and Ruth was a telephone operator at Liberty Center for several years.

I started to school in the old school house in Liberty Center. A new school was built and I continued there until graduation. My brother, sister and I drove a Storm King buggy, an enclosed buggy, and there were livery barns near the school where the horses were kept all day. After my brother and sister were out of school I continued to walk the mile and a quarter. There was finally a horse drawn bus, but only those living over one and one-half miles could ride the bus so I had to walk.

I graduated from high school in 1923. After graduation I worked as a telephone operator for six years and later graduated from beauty school in Fort Wayne in 1938. I operated a beauty shop in my home for forty-eight years and still work occasionally.

In 1925 I married Kelly Moore who was a farmer and also a star basketball player in high school. We lost one daughter and have a living daughter, Phyllis, who is married to Dean Cassiday.

Cleora (Russell) Moore, Great-Grandma Arnold, Grandma Russell and Phyllis (Moore) Cassiday

At the death of Kelly's parents, Aaron and Gertie Moore, Kelly and his brother Kenneth bought the Moore farm which I still own one half with Kenneth's sons, Joe and Deane Moore. The house at this location southwest of Liberty Center burned in 1960. I also have half interest with my daughter and son-in-law in my mother's home place. The Cassiday's moved into my mother's home following her death in 1961 and lived there until 1985 when they erected a new home on the farm. Their son, Tim Cassiday, his wife Kim and their four children now live in the original home.

I am active member of the Liberty Center Baptist Church and live in the home my grandfather built in 1881. *(Cleora Russell Moore)*

C.C. RUTENBERG FAMILY

In 1925 Christian C. (Crist) and Ida W. (Jahnke) Rutenberg moved from Huntington County to Wells County. Crist was born in Huntington (1873-1955) and Ida in Germany (1876-1947). She came to the United States when eleven years old. They were married in 1895. The move to Wells County was made by horse and wagon to a farm two miles east of Uniondale, Indiana, Lancaster Township. Norwell School was later built on a part of this farm.

The family that moved with them included Herb, Marie, Art, Frank, and Ruth. Older family members included Lena, Carl, and Edna.

Ida and Crist Rutenberg (1932)

The family later moved to Jefferson Township, near Echo, in 1929; and in 1931, to a farm at the west edge of Ossian. They then bought a farm, and moved to Union township in 1935 to what is now 2580 West 1000 North. These were depression years and hogs once sold for two and one-half cents per pound. Family members attended school at Murray, Lancaster, Ossian, and Union Center.

Crist was formerly a machinist at the Erie roundhouse in Huntington, as well as a farmer in Wells County. He and his wife, who was a homemaker, lived to celebrate their golden wedding. They were God fearing, loving parents, who raised eight children to adulthood, and were an asset to the community in which they lived. They were members of St. Peter's Lutheran Church in Huntington, and are buried at the Pilgrims Rest Cemetery, north of there. Crist had helped organize this cemetery many years before.

RUTENBERG FAMILY

At some time in their adult life each of the children of the C.C. Rutenberg family lived in Wells County. You will now meet Lena, Carl, Edna, and Herb.

Carolina (Lena; 1896-1990) took nurses training first at Huntington Hospital, and then graduated at Methodist in Indianapolis. She moved to Denver, Colorado, where she met and married Dean McClenny in 1927. She lived in Colorado about twenty-five years. There was one daughter, Beverly. Lena and Beverly moved back to Indiana in 1946. Lena became a nurse at the Caylor-Nickel Hospital, and worked there until her retirement. Beverly, after graduating from Union Center, became the wife of Ronnie Merchant. They now live in Markle. Lena is buried at Pilgrims Rest Cemetery.

Carl (1901-) and Clara Riggers were married in 1921. Carl learned the machinists trade at the Erie roundhouse and worked at Ortons Machine Shop, both in Huntington. He was also a farmer for many years. They had two daughters: Edith Lorene, who married Adrian Vebert; and Mary Louise who married Orlo Gephart. Both girls graduated at Union Center. Carl and Clara celebrated their golden wedding several years ago. Carl now lives in Lancaster Township, Huntington County, Denver, Colorado; where she graduated from Barnes Business College. While there she met and married Henry Dinsmore in 1926. They later lived in Portland and Waldport, Oregon. They had one daughter, Lois Kelley. Just a few years ago Edna moved back to Indiana and now lives at Capri II in Bluffton.

Herb, Carl, Frank, Ida, Crist, Edna, Ruth, Art, Marie (1936)

Edna (1903-) as a young adult found her way to Denver, CO, where she graduated from Barnes Business College. While there she met and married Henry Dinsmore in 1927. They later lived in Portland and Waldport, OR. They had one daughter, Lois Kelley. Just a few years ago Edna moved back to Indiana and now lives at Capri II in Bluffton.

Herbert (1906-) lived in Wells County for many years. He managed farms for others as well as later owning his own farm. He also worked at Wabash Fibre Box and retired from there. He married Doris (Brumbaugh) Ripley in 1951. Her family lived north of Markle. He has three step-children: Carolyn Reilley (Mrs. Jack), Ronnie Ripley, and Bob Ripley. They sold their farm in 1990, and moved to a mobile home at Woodlake Estates, Yoder. They enjoy both their summer home at Blue Lake and their winter home in Palmetto, Florida.

In their adult life, these later children of the C.C. Rutenberg family also lived in Wells County. They are Marie, Art, Frank, and Ruth. You will now meet them.

Marie (1910-) graduated at Ossian in 1930. After working in Huntington a short time, she moved to Fort Wayne, and graduated from International Business College in 1933. Her working years were as a ledger clerk at Indiana-Michigan Electric Company. She retired from there and lives in Fort Wayne.

Frank, Art, Ruth, Herb, Edna, Carl, Marie, and Lena (1979)

Arthur (1915-) graduated at Ossian in 1933. He met and married Hannah Lucas in 1946. Hannah was teaching at Union Center. They first lived south of Zanesville where they farmed and milked cows. After this experience, Art became a Surge Dairy

Farm Equipment dealer. They have one daughter, Chris Ann, who married Allan Johnson. She graduated from Norwell and I.U. Chris and Allan live west of Zanesville. Hannah is retired from Norwell and Art is semi-retired. They also live just west of Zanesville, and their winter months are spent in Palmetto, Florida.

Frank (1918-) graduated at Union Center in 1938. After several years working with both his father and brother; Art, in the business of farming, Frank worked at several places in Fort Wayne. He married Rose Vebert in 1979. Rose was a teacher at Norwell, and retired from there. Frank retired from Wabash Fibre Box Company. He now lives west of Ossian.

Ruth (1921-1984) graduated at Union Center in 1939. She then did her college work at Ball State, graduating in 1943. She soon came to teach at Union Center. Later she went to work on the Evanston Review, a paper in Illinois. There she met and married John Redmann, in 1950. They soon moved to Mississippi where she taught in the schools at Ocean Springs. They had three children-Greg, Jean, and Connie. Ruth is buried in the military cemetery at Biloxi, Mississippi. She will be remembered by several of her former students in this area.

SADLER

Tom and Louise (Bradbury) Sadler married in 1960 after being neighbors, and high school sweethearts at Lafayette Central in Allen County. Tom is the son of Harley and Irene (Rushart) Sadler. Louise is granddaughter of Ira and Etta Smuts, a homebuilder in the Zanesville area in the early 1900's, and the daughter of Edward "Ted" and Frances (Smuts) Bradbury. Three daughters blessed their marriage: Christine Ann Sadler was born in 1962, while living in the house presently known as the Zanesville House; Dana Louise was born in 1963, while renting the Clarence Roebuck homestead located just into Allen County; and Gaye Lyn was born in 1967, while renting a home owned by Herb and Eleanor Lunz. Tom and Louise jumped back and forth across the Allen/Wells County line before buying their present home in Wells County from Bob and Margaret Cupp in 1972.

In 1980 Tom dug the basement, with a crane, for the present brick sanctuary of the Zanesville United Methodist Church. He worked twenty-nine years for John Dehner, Inc. in Fort Wayne, as a heavy equipment mechanic/operator until the company closed in 1990. Louise has worked as a secretary at the K-mart Distribution Center for the past twenty years, until the plant closure in 1991-92.

Christine married Todd A. Hoffman, from Bluffton, in 1982; presently living in Texas, they have two children, Shauna and Ryan.

Dana married her neighbor and high school sweetheart, Rick Hoopingarner in 1982, and lives in Zanesville. They have three children; Darrick, Cylie, and Cole.

Gaye married Chad McMillan, a Bluffton gentleman, in 1989.

GEORGE SALTER FAMILY

George Salter was born in 1827; his first wife, Philenia Bump, was born in 1835. To them was born Amanda (1855, Mary Ann (1856), Frances (1858), John (1863), Ida Heiny (1869-1891), and Val. George's second wife, Magdaline Weibel, bore him one child; Sarah (1879), who died young.

Amanda married the Reverent William Mygrant. Mary Ann married James F. Walker; they had two children: Nettie Wofe and Murlie Chaney. Frances married George Farrell in 1875. Their children were: Ida Smith, Amy Woods, Etta Smuts (see entry for Smuts family), Earl, and Everett. William had three sons: Fred, Robert, and Herbert.

SANDS

My great grandparents were Daniel Sands and Alice May Sands who resided in Murray. They had three children: Floyd Everett Sands, Verna Sands, and Dessie Sands Edington, who are now deceased. My grandfather was Floyd who married Mary Helen Loretta Dennis on May 8, 1923. They resided in Bluffton at 905 W. Market until the time of their deaths.

They had five children: Margaret Alice, Donald Daniel, James Floyd, Robert Dennis and Joseph George. Peggy resides in Fort Wayne and has three children. Don lives in Palm Springs, California. Bob lives in North Hollywood, California and has five daughters. Joe lives in Gaffney, South Carolina, and has four children.

My father, Jim married Betty Loraine Foster on September 26, 1953 at St. Joseph's Rectory, in Bluffton. He is the owner of Sands Construction and works as a carpenter. Betty works part-time as a sales clerk at the Rose. They live at 118 East Wiley Ave., Bluffton. They have five children: Jill Marie, Jon Foster, Julie Ann, Jennifer Gay, and Jayne Michelle. They also have thirteen grandchildren.

Jon married Paula Maxwell on September 29, 1978. They have three children: Isaac, eight; Cole, six; and Leah, four. Jon is employed by Kinder Construction as a carpenter. Paula is a Licensed Practical Nurse. They live in Ossian at this time.

Julie married Rollyn Coverdale on June 24, 1978, and resides in Ossian. They have three children: Lauren, eleven; Phillip, eight; and Emma, four. Julie works as Education Director at the First Presbyterian in Bluffton. Rollyn works at Wayne Metal as an engineer.

Jennifer is married to Rob Biggs. They were married April 8, 1989, and have one child, Lillian, born October 18, 1990. Rob works for Allen County Highway Dept. Jennifer is staying home with Lillian at this time.

Jayne married Terry Ivins on October 17, 1986. They live in Bluffton at 905 W. Market Street. This was our grandparents home. They have two children. Daniel is two and Luke is one year old. Jayne graduated from Patricia Stevens in 1985. She is employed in the Sales Department at Bluffton Agri/Industrial Corporation. Terry works as a welder at Wayne Metal.

I, Jill Spencer, married Rex Spencer on November 21, 1975. We have four children; Zachary, fourteen; Justin, eleven; Margaret, eight; and Katherine, six. We live at 120 W. South Street, Bluffton.

I graduated from St. Joseph's Hospital School of Nursing in February 1975. I am employed at Caylor Nickel Hospital in the Intensive Care Unit. Rex works as a carpenter for Sands Construction. We are members of St. Joseph's Catholic Church. We are actively involved in Girl Scouts and in AAU Freestyle Wrestling.

Front, L to R; Louise, Gaye, Tom. Back, L to R; Dana, Chris.

This family enjoyed country living, and Tom always made sure their girls had a motor-driven toy of some nature! (toy or contraption?). Their girls went to Lancaster Elementary and Norwell High School. Their bus drivers, Denny Houtz, John Cupp, and Sharon Crozier, were special people to them. Fond memories of being #1 State Fair Band Contest Winners, as well as accepting invitations to Disney World and the Orange Bowl were special highlights in the late 1970's.

Back, L to R; Terry Ivins, Daniel Ivins, Jayne Ivins, Jim Sands, Betty Sands, Jennifer Biggs, Rob Biggs, Jill Spencer, Rex Spencer, Zachary Spencer, Julie Coverdale, Rollyn Coverdale, Emma Coverdale. Front, L to R; Paula Sands, Jon Sands, Leah Sands, Cole Sands, Issac Sands, Katie Spencer, Maggie Spencer, Justin Spencer, Lauren Coverdale, Phillip Coverdale. Not Pictures; Luke Ivins and Lillian Biggs.

SANQUIST

Lloyd David Sanquist was born on January 23, 1924, at Hines, Minnesota, the son of Spencer Oliver and Olive Lovetta Mae (Goble) Sanquist. Lloyd (Sandy) originally came to Indiana in 1950 with Indiana Construction while building the McMillan silo's in Decatur. On September 3, 1950, he married Esther May Gould, daughter of Odes Ray and Bessie Blanch (Lichtenberger) Gould.

In 1959, Sandy was employed by Hagerman Construction of Fort Wayne, Indiana. After the birth of their daughter, Nancy Lynne, on September 25, 1959, they purchased a home in Lancaster Township, Wells County, and moved here on December 17, 1960. In 1978, he joined the James S. Jackson Construction Company of Bluffton and in 1986 he retired.

Ester, Nancy, and Floyd Sanquist. (Insert) Nancy and Wayne Weis.

Nancy went to Adams Central for her kindergarten year, as Lancaster Elementary did not yet provide that service. She graduated from Norwell in 1977 and went to IU-PU Fort Wayne, graduating in 1979 with an Associate degree.

She is now a claims adjuster for SECURA Insurance Company of Appleton, Wisconsin. On May 5, 1990, she married Wayne Jay Weis, born October 14, 1952, in Allen County, son of Garfield (Gary) and Patricia May (High) Weis of Altamonte Springs, Florida. Wayne has one son, Clint Chandler Weis, born April 24, 1982, in Allen County.

In 1973, Wayne became a partner with Larry Baker at Baker's Marathon in Fort Wayne. Prior to that, he attended Ivy Tech and became an ASE certified technician in six areas. Wayne has also been a member of the army reserve for nineteen years. He is currently a chief warrant officer with the 221st Ordnance Company in Fort Wayne.

SAWYER-SEAGRAVE

William Steven Sawyer and Laura Elizabeth Seagrave were married on June 12, 1971, in the First United Methodist Church in Bluffton, Indiana. Our daughter, Amy Elizabeth, was born June 19, 1972. She graduated from Bluffton High School in 1990, and currently attends Masters College of Cosmetology in Fort Wayne. On November 30, 1976, our son, Brad Michael, was born. He is an eighth grader at Bluffton Middle School and enjoys most sports.

Steve was born at the Wells Community Hospital on September 18, 1948. He graduated in 1966 from Bluffton High School and has worked for twenty four and one-half years at the K-Mart Distribution Warehouse at Baer Field, Fort Wayne.

Steve's father, William Draper Sawyer, was born in Bluffton on February 12, 1924, to Dana Franklin and Dessie Goldsberry Sawyer. Dana Sawyer fought in Europe during World War I. Bill Sawyer graduated from Bluffton High School in 1942. He has a brother, Tom Sawyer. On January 31, 1948, he married Betty Alice Coffield. She was born November 26, 1928, to Clyde and Emma Fryback Coffield in Bluffton. She has two brothers, Rex and Ronald, both of Bluffton. She graduated in 1946 from Bluffton High School. In 1980, Bill retired from the Indiana National Guard after thirty-two years of military service. During World War II, while in the U.S. Army, he spent time in the Aleutian Islands. He retired in 1987 from Monarch Foods. Betty retired from Franklin Electric Company, in 1990.

Steve and Laura Sawyer, Brad and Amy

Steve has one brother, Douglas Alan, who is married to Connie Wolfe. They have three daughters, Michelle Ann, Kimberly, and Shannon. Doug now owns and operates Sawyer Realty, in Bluffton.

Laura Elizabeth Seagrave was born in Wabash, Indiana on June 11, 1951. She graduated from Bluffton High School in 1969, and Fort Wayne School of Practical Nursing in 1970. She worked as Activity Director at Meadowvale Care Center from 1985 to 1990.

Laura's father, John Affleck Seagrave, was born in Kokomo, Indiana, July 30, 1915, to Willard E. Seagrave and Emma Affleck Seagrave. He had one sister, Alice Mendenhall. John graduated from Kokomo High School, and attended the University of Illinois; then served in the U.S. Army Air Corps during World War II. My great-grandfather, John Gaston Affleck, came from Castle Douglas, Scotland. My dad worked for the Ditzler-Kelly Lumber Company, in Huntington, and owned the Culligan Soft Water Service in Bluffton for several years. He died on November 19, 1989. My mother, Elizabeth (Betty) Ditzler Seagrave was born in Markle, Indiana, on February 7, 1919, to Ray L. and Fern Rarick Ditzler. She had a brother, Edward, who died in 1952, and a sister, Alice Ditzler Petrie, who currently lives in Fort Wayne.

Betty Ditzler graduated from Huntington High School, attended Indiana University, and taught bridge to many people in the Bluffton area. Betty (Ditzler) Seagrave died November 12, 1988. She and my father are both buried in Mt. Hope Cemetery in Huntington.

Steve's great grandparents were: Sarah J. Hayden and Alexander Kurt Coffield, Ida May Avery Fryback and William Addison Fryback, Samuel Draper and Ethel Guy Brown Goldsberry and Curtis and Atta Robinson Sawyer.

Laura's great grandparents were: John Henry and Lizzie Shively Rarick, Laura Teeple and George Calvin Ditzler, Harriet Coomer and John Gaston Affleck, and Andrew Jackson and Elizabeth Chandler Seagrave.

For seventeen years Steve and Laura lived on South Williams Street but now reside on Summit Ave.

SAM SCHAEFFER FAMILY

Our family began May 18, 1975, with the marriage of Katherine Kay Shaffer (myself), daughter of Archie and Mildred (Earnest) Shaffer of rural Bluffton, to Samuel Robert Schaefer, son of Kenneth and Alice (Studebaker) Schaefer near Vera Cruz, Indiana.

As time went on, we had an addition to our family of two. Jennifer Rose Schaefer was born on November 4, 1978, at 11:34 p.m. Our number changed from three to four with the coming of Angela Kay Schaefer, arriving on October 2, 1980, at about 12:45 a.m.

Back; Samuel and Katherine Schaefer. Front; Angela and Jennifer.

Today, both our daughters attend school in the Bluffton-Harrison School District. Jennifer is active in the 4-H program in Wells County, and also is a part of the junior high track team. Angela is a Girl Scout, takes piano lessons, and also is in 4-H.

We are active members of the First Church of Christ in Bluffton. Katherine teaches Sunday School, the first grade class, and is also a member of the church choir.

Sam and Katherine are dairy farming, at the present time, with the name of our dairy being "S and K Dairy." Sam also has a livestock trailer he uses to haul cattle for other farms. He is also a part-time milk hauler for Allen Dairy.

At the present time we reside on a farm about five miles east of Bluffton.

(Katherine Schaefer)

SCHEUMANN-STOPPENHAGEN

Edward Scheumann and Helen (Stoppenhagen) Scheumann began their married life in Jefferson Township, Wells County, in 1946. Edward, son of Julius and Rosa (Luttman) Scheumann, came from the Hoagland area located in Allen County. Helen, daughter of Fred and Frieda (Bultemeier) Stoppenhagen, was born in Jefferson Township, Wells County, east of Ossian, Indiana.

Edward and Helen became full time farmers in Jefferson Township. Their home is located five miles east of Ossian near the Adams and Wells County line.

We have seven children. Dennis, born in 1948, married Sylvia Hoover on April 4, 1970. They have three children: twin boys, Jason Matthew and Joshua David, born in 1974, and Holly Lyn, born in 1975. They attend Bellmont High School in Decatur, Indiana. Dennis, Sylvia and family operate Mid States Food, Inc. in Decatur, Indiana.

Diana Kay, born in 1950, married Lynn Dishong on December 12, 1969. They have four daughters. Tisha Kay was born in 1970. She is in college at IPFW in Fort Wayne. Tina Lynnett, born in 1973, is a senior at Norwell High School. Twins, Tiffany

Dawn and Tonya Renee were born in 1976, and they are students at Bethlehem Lutheran School. Diana Kay and Lynn owned and operated the Thrifty Delivery Service in Fort Wayne, Indiana, until the death of Lynn on September 9, 1989.

Dalene Sue Coffield, was born in 1952. She has two daughters, Tracy Renee, born in 1979, and Joni Marie, born in 1981. They attend Bethlehem Lutheran School. Dalene is a prominent cosmetologist in Ossian, and is employed at Mel's Tips for Beauty, beauty shop.

Donna Renee, born 1952, lives at home. She is a custodian at Bethlehem Lutheran Church.

Dorothy Jo, born 1955, married Keith Kriok on January 31, 1976. They have two children, Alicia Alane, born in 1980 and Nicholas Paul, born in 1982. They attend Bethlehem Lutheran School. Keith is employed at Food Marketing, Inc. in Fort Wayne and drives a semi-truck there.

Dean Alan, born in 1956, lives in Adams County. He is employed and affiliated with Mid States Tool, Inc. in Decatur, Indiana.

Denise Alane, born in 1964, married Ted Schumm, November 26, 1986. They have one daughter, Lauren Nichole, who is sixteen months old. Ted is employed at Pace-Arrow, Inc. at Decatur, Indiana, and Denise Alane is a cosmetologist and owner of the Hair Junction Beauty Shop in Bluffton, Indiana.

We still live here on the same farm and in the same home for nearly forty-three years. (*Helen Scheumann*)

SCHLAGENHAUF-JOHNS

The Schlagenhauf name has had many variations. We have found from ancient tax rolls, some of the first persons to bear the name have been recorded from 1365 A.D. The name is well established in Austria.

My great-grandfather Johannes (John) Schlagenhauf was twenty when he immigrated to America in 1858. He lived at New Villa now (Vera Cruz) where he made caskets and furniture. His first marriage was to Catharina Gerken who died. His second marriage was to Luticia Gentis who had eight children: Katie Ann; George W., who is my grandfather; Emma; Minnie; Edwin; Freddy; Mary Effa, and Henry. My grandfather married Minni Dunbar on August 19, 1899. Minni's father, L. L. Dunbar was founder of Dunbar Furniture Company of Berne. Their children were Homer, my dad; Hobart, born and died in 1900; Mary; Von; Robert; Max, died at birth; and John Henry, killed in action defending Saipan.

My father married Anna Virgina Beeler January 7, 1923. They met at the Linn School which is still standing one-fifth of a mile west of where we live, which was my mother's home place. Dad went to the eighth grade but Mom went on to Bluffton High School, then to Fort Wayne Business College. They had five children: Mary Ann married Gene Hoover, had nine children; June married Richard Yager, had six children; George married Marlene Beer, had four children; Beth married Larry Myer, had two children; Alan married Rhonda Johns, had two children. My mother and father moved quite a bit before starting on east of 116. Dad farmed for a living from horses to a modern John Deere tractor. We have been farming for three generations. I farm with my brother, George, his son Jerry and my son Heath. Dad also drove a school bus for thirty-two years. Mom was a homemaker, good cook, and played the organ at Six Mile Church.

Alan, Heather, Rhonda, and Heath Schlagenhauf-August 1989.

I married Rhonda Johns in 1970. Rhonda went to Beauty College in Fort Wayne. Our son, Heath, was born January 27, 1974. Our daughter, Heather was born March 13, 1980. I served on the board of directors for United REMC, which I enjoyed. Rhonda served as the County President for the Extension Homemakers. Rhonda opened up a Beauty Shop in Vera Cruz in 1986. We both enjoy raising and showing Morgan Horses, our daughter Heather enjoys riding, and our son Heath enjoys his cattle.

We are members of Old Salem United Methodist Church. My folks are buried in Six Mile Cemetery and that is where me and my wife shall also be. (*Alan and Rhonda Schlagenhauf*)

GLEN AND HELEN SCHOEFF

Glen Schoeff and Helen Roush were married in 1934 and spent most of their early years together in the Jackson Township area. Helen is the daughter of Cary and Bertha (Friar) Roush and grew up around the Warren, Indiana, area, graduating from the old Warren High School. Glen, son of Charles and Bessie (Newhard) Schoeff, spent his childhood years around the Zanesville and Uniondale areas before moving to the Dillman area in Jackson Township. They both came from farm families although Helen's father, Cary Roush, also worked in the oil fields in his early days.

They had four children while living in Jackson Township: Carol, Frances, Roy and Joyce. In 1949, they moved to Lancaster Township northwest of Bluffton where a fifth child, Glennis, was born. They purchased a farm on Road 100N in the early 50's and still reside there at this writing. All five children attended Lancaster High School.

Glen was a farmer and worked many years at the Hoosier Grain and Supply in Bluffton until recently retiring. Helen is a homemaker who helped her children with 4-H club work in their younger days, and has always been active in home economics club work and church activities at Epworth United Methodist Church. Helen is an expert seamstress and an avid reader.

Daughter Carol married John Meeks, son of Marion and Edna (Gilbert) Meeks, in 1954, and they have four children: Michael (married Pam Thompson), Marilyn, Richard, and Linda (Mrs. Terry) Masterson. They live on State Road 1 north of Bluffton in Lancaster Township. John served with the U.S. Armed Forces in Korea in 1954-55.

Frances married George Junior McIntosh, son of George and Hazel (Rayl) McIntosh, in 1966, and they have two daughters; Lesli and Heather. They reside on Lower Huntington Road near the I-69 interchange in Allen County.

Roy married Janet Cash, daughter of Carl and Marguerite (Matson) Cash, in 1964 and they have three daughters: Cara, Shelley (Mrs. Todd) Preston, Sheryl (Mrs. Carl) Lusher, and a son, Brad. They live in Poneto, Indiana.

Also in 1964, Joyce married Walter Junior Neuenschwander, son of Walter and Edna (Schaefer) Neuenschwander. They are the parents of three daughters: Karen (Mrs. Jeff) Isch, Kristi (Mrs. Brian) Curry, and Kathy (Mrs. Jeff) Bertsch, and reside in Jefferson Township.

Glennis married Wayne Henly, Jr., son of Wayne and Naomi (Woodward) Henly, in 1972, and they have three children: Lori, Patrick, and Ryan. Wayne was in the U.S. Army in 1970-71 and was stationed in Germany. They currently reside in Lancaster Township.

PETER C. SCHOTT FAMILY

Peter C. Schott, son of George and Margaretta Bauman Schott, was born December 20, 1844, in Logan County, Ohio. George Schott was born in Bavaria. In 1930 they migrated to the United States and settled in Lorain County, Ohio. On December 16, 1863, Peter enlisted for three years in the Civil War as a private in Hoffman Battalion #128, Ohio Infantry, Company D. He was discharged at Camp Chase, Ohio, on July 13, 1865. He received a pension until his death. In 1867 Peter moved to Wells County, Nottingham Township. He married Martha Ann Watson on October 25, 1868. Their child, was born on July 13, 1871, near Domestic, Indiana.

The children of John G. Schott were Mildred Inez (Mrs. Lewis Markley); Catherine (Mrs. Joseph Frank Powell), who had one son, Michael, stillborn; and Terrell Watson Schott, born April 22, 1911. Terrell Watson Schott was married to Viva F. Chalfant on October 24, 1932, at the Baptist parsonage by Dr. Horace N. Spear. The parsonage was where the southwest corner of the Caylor-Nickel Clinic now stands.

Peter Schott's home was south of Domestic. He was a carpenter; he and his brother built buildings and also their home in Domestic. Peter was very talented. he worked in a glass factory in Ohio, and he also built furniture. His farm was in the oil well district. His son, John, worked in the oil fields around Petroleum. John and Sarah Schott owned the farm that Norman Gerber now owns. John's daughter, Mrs. Mildred Inez Markley, had six children, all living: Kenneth W. Markley, Roderick D. Markley, Phyllis Inez Markley Poling, Anna Lou Markley Walton, James M. Markley, and Richard Lewis Markley. Mildred Inez and Lewis Markley now reside at Christian Care Center.

Terrell Watson Schott worked with his father on the farm until his father died. Later he married Viva Chalfant Schott. He was a farmer and later worked as a butcher and meat cutter. Before his marriage, he was in the National Guard at the Portland, Indiana, 152nd Infantry. He later became a member of the First Baptist Church, the Masonic Lodge, and Eastern Star. He was a Thirty-second Degree Mason.

Viva and Terrell Schott were the parents of John Terry Schott, born December 8, 1935. He graduated from P.A. Allen High School in Bluffton. He enlisted in the U.S. Air Force and served from 1955 to 1960 when he received a medical discharge from Lackland Air Force Base, Texas.

The children of John Terry Schott and Nancy Aker Schott are: Margaret Faye, Zachary Alan, Victor Duane, John Douglas, and Amanda Lee Aker Schott (adopted). Margaret married Donald

Yates and had two sons, Chad and Bradley; she divorced and later married Sam McAfee, and they have one son, Andrew Dean. Zachary Schott has no children. Victor Duane married Julia Rhodes and they have two daughters, Jessica and Alyssa. He served in the U.S. Marine Corps at San Diego, California and is now in the National Guard at Bluffton. John Douglas married Tina Rhodes and they have one son, John Paul Julian. Adopted daughter Amanda married Cleodis Brown and they have three girls.

Peter Schott's daughter was Amanda Elanor Schott, who married Brookhart and had one daughter Natalie, who married Ben Lockwood.

My husband Terrell, better known at "Bud," collected guns as a hobby. He had his grandfathers Civil War musket. The gun and the discharge are at the Wells County Museum.

Viva Schott now lives at Capri II in Bluffton, where she takes an active part in Capri Friends, a resident's club.

SCHWARTZ FAMILY

Everett Schwartz married Maudie Julian in 1914 and lived in Lancaster Township, Wells County. In 1919 they bought a home located north of the Lancaster Chapel Church. About a year later a son was born to them in this home. His name was Lloyd L. Schwartz.

He grew up on this farm and spent his school years at the Lancaster High School. After graduating in 1939, he spent a few years farming and working for George Gerber to learn the plumbing, heating, and electric trade. During his farming years, Lloyd used horses to do his farm work. He used a one-bottom plow which was pulled by either two or three horses. To plant corn he used a two-row planter which had a wire to drop the corn in rows so it could be cultivated crossways. The corn was plowed with a one-row plow, one row at a time. He remembers milking his cows by hand. He was also a part of a threshing ring, which consisted of several neighbors who would cut oats and wheat with a binder, which cut the grain and tied it into small bundles. These were hauled on wagons to a threshing machine, which removed the grain from the straw and blew the straw into what were called "straw stacks."

Lloyd and Katherine Schwartz

After school and on Saturdays he would cut corn and put it in shocks to earn money for street fair. Yes, he would get 10 cents for each shock. The ears of the corn were removed and the fodder was fed to his cows.

Lloyd married a school classmate, Katherine Howard, a daughter of Frank and Pearl (Trenary) Howard. A daughter, Judy, married Alan Crull and lives near Poneto, Indiana. She is a part-time employee of the Caylor Nickel Clinic. A son, Dan Schwartz, is married to Nancy Shure. They are living in Caracas, Venezuela, where he is a representative of the Proctor and Gamble Company A second son, Joe Schwartz, is married to Janice Neuenschwander. He is the manager of Schwartz Plumbing, Heating, and Air Conditioning Company. A second daughter, Jean, is married to Robert Weber. She is a manager of the Long John Silvers Restaurant at New Haven.

Lloyd started his own business at the old Mill Building on the corner of Lancaster and Oak Streets, Bluffton, Indiana. From there the business was moved to the former John Fulk Building on the corner of Main and Water Streets.

In 1972 a plot of ground was purchased from Oliver Meyers and a new metal building was erected. It was opened for business on March 1, 1973, and is located at 610 North Main Street. It is now Schwartz Plumbing, Heating, and Air Conditioning Company, Inc. Over the years, Lloyd has employed a large number of people. Lloyd and Katherine are still living at the family home.

ERVIN SCHWARTZ

Ervin R. Schwartz was born March 9, 1917, in Wells County, Indiana, to Levi and Sarah Reinhard Schwartz.

Ervin was born as an artist in woodworking, making different kinds of toys out of wood.

He worked on his dad's farm, which was located one and one-half miles east and one-half mile north of Vera Cruz, Indiana until he went to work at John Baumgartner's Hatchery. From there he hauled milk to the United Milk Products Company at Berne, Indiana. In his spare time, he worked with his Dad as a carpenter for about three years. He then sold his milk route after about three years.

Schwartz Custom-Built-Cabinets truck

In 1941, he started at McMillen Feed Mills at Decatur, Indiana, driving a semi into the many states of Michigan, Illinois, Ohio and Indiana.

In 1943, he was inducted into the military service. He served in the United States one year before going to E.T.O. He served overseas twenty-five months in England and France. He was a First Cook in the General Hospital, Paris, France with at least two thousand patients. When World War II ended in 1945, he came home with an Honorable Discharge in February 1946. He married Alice Gerber on March 3, 1946.

My dad was a cabinet-maker, when I came home from service. I worked with my dad for one year, then I started making kitchen cabinets at Gerber Furniture in the basement, then owned by my two brother-in-laws, Alvin and Edward Gerber. I was there for twenty-two years, making cabinets. I left Gerbers and started my own business, "Schwartz Custom-Built-Cabinets," the name it holds now. I built cabinets for businesses and residential in 6 states. I am still very active in doing cabinet work after forty-five years. We live at 4199 S.E. St. Rd. 116.

My wife, Alice and I have five children. Mrs. Richard (Sharon) Meister of West Lafayette, Indiana. They are the parents of three sons, Robin, Ryan, and Rustin. Richard is a teacher at West Lafayette Schools. Ernest Schwartz is married to Robin Moser of Bluffton. They are the parents of three sons, Tiercell, Gyrkin and Lanner. Ernest is an Air Traffic Controller at Baer Field, Fort Wayne, Indiana. Mrs. Glen (Carol) Martin is of Benson, Illinois. They are the parents of three children, Jesse, Benjamin and Cassandra. Glen is a farmer and will be teaching school this fall. Sidney Schwartz is married to Sheryl Lesh of Bluffton. They are the parents of two children, Sean and Heather. Sid has been employed in sales and finance for Eley TV and Appliance in Bluffton. Additionally, he has been in real estate sales for twelve years and past President of the Chamber of Commerce. Tracy Schwartz and Tami of Bluffton have one child, Danielle. Tracy works for his brother, Ernie in Silk Screen Printing and part time does the woodwork finishing for his dad.

SCHWARTZ-FOLK

Oscar Levi Schwartz and Minerva Anna Folk were married August 24, 1890 in Wells County. Oscar's parents were Elias and Esther Moyer Schwartz and were of German descent, born in Pennsylvania. Minerva Anna's parents were John Henry Folk, born August 31, 1830, in Lehigh County, Pennsylvania, and Christina Gleich (Leich), born August 31, 1838, in Linn County, Ohio. Oscar was born July 8, 1868 in Rockcreek Township and died November 3, 1955. Minerva Anna was born August 21, 1872 and died June 1, 1951. Both were of German Lutheran and Reformed background. They are both buried at St. Paul Lutheran Cemetery in Rockcreek Township. They had five children: Bertha, David, Selah, Charles Otis and twins, Ida and Iva. Bertha, born February 23, 1891, married Forrest Riddile, and divorced in 1938. She was a seamstress and died at age sixty nine. They had six children; Lloyd, Alice Harnish, Martha Maines Clark, Anna Bailey, Sam Riddile and Joyzella Hosier. Lloyd drowned at age twenty. Alice had three sons (one deceased). Martha was an R.N.; her two husbands died. She had twin stepdaughters, and she died in 1990 at age seventy two. Anna has two children. Sam married Marilyn Fluke, had four daughters, and died at age thirty in an electrical accident. Joyzella had three children (Kevin died at age twenty six in a farm accident at their home). Joyzella died at age forty six in a car accident on her way home from her school nurse job.

Oscar and Anna Folk Schwartz

David, born February 28, 1893, married Iva Porter and had two children, George E. and Julia

May. He died of cancer at age fifty eight while serving as County Treasurer. Selah, born November 27, 1896, a teacher and music instructor, married Edward Fogwell and died at age eighty six. Charles Otis, born September 23, 1899, a teacher and farmer, married Gladys Roe, a Registered Nurse, had one child, Max, and died at age eighty five. Ida, born August 1, 1905, married Howard Harberson, had two children, John and Karen, divorced and is now married to Hyman Shaw and lives in Kalamazoo, Michigan. Iva, also born August 1, 1905 started in nursing with her twin at Lutheran Hospital, Fort Wayne, but gave it up to marry Arthur Fisher. They had three sons: Robert, Maurice and Wendel. Arthur died and Iva lives by herself in an apartment in Cincinnati, Ohio. Minerva Anna's brothers and sisters were: Henry, Hiram and Frank Folk, Sarah Griffin, Ida Crum and Emma.

SCHWARTZ-FOX

Brian D. Schwartz and Kay L. Fox were married May 17, 1975 at Union Church, Huntington, County. He is the youngest of the four children of George E. and Adeline (Dody Rebber) Schwartz of Uniondale, Union Township. She is the eldest of the five daughters of Clifford D. and June Beaver Fox of Union Township, Wells County, but formerly of Allen and Huntington Counties. Brian was born at Wells County Hospital, delivered by Dr. C. M. Gingerick. He was born on February 23, 1955, his Grandpa Rebber's sixty-fifth birthday. He attended seven grades at Union, eighth grade at Ossian (during the school consolidations) and graduated from Norwell in 1973. He graduated from Purdue University, Fort Wayne Campus, with a degree in mechanical engineering and is an engineer at Magnavox at Columbia City. Kay was born October 7, 1954, at Huntington County Hospital. She started school at Union Township, Huntington County, and finished the first year and the following seven years at Lafayette Central in Allen County.

Brian and Kay Schwartz; David, Leah, and Deborah.

The family then moved to Wells County, Union Township, and she graduated in 1973 from Norwell, where she and Brian met. Brian and Kay set up housekeeping in a trailer at Kozy Kourt, Ossian, and in 1978 bought a house in Ossian, where they still live. Kay was a secretary at Lincoln Life, Fort Wayne, and now is a teacher's aide at Ossian School. They have three children, all born at Wells Community Hospital. David was born October 2, 1979, and named after his great-grandfather, David E. Schwartz. Leah was born April 9, 1981 and Deborah, November 5, 1983. They attend Ossian School. The family is active in their church, First Missionary at Fort Wayne, and in community work. Brian is of German and English descent. (See Schwartz/Rebber for his history and family). Kay is of German heritage. Her grandparents are Clifford and Louella Prather Fox and Charles and Cholesta Frech Beaver, all from Huntington County. Kay's father, Clifford D. Fox is a farmer and construction worker. Her mother June is a secretary in Huntington. Kay's sisters are: Diane who married Mark Bonner from Huntington County, has two children and lives in Union Township, Wells County; Pam who married Chris Fulton of Wells and Huntington counties, has two children and lives in Fort Wayne; Brenda who married Ron Jones from Huntington, has three children (the first by a previous marriage) and lives in Huntington; and Karen who married Curt Foughty of Ossian, has four children and lives in Ossian.

SCHWARTZ-MOYER

Elias, twin sister Elmina, sister Carolyn, and brothers Levi and Edward were born in Lancaster County, Pennsylvania. They came to Wells County, Rockcreek Township, in 1854, with their parents, Mikel and Mary Magdalene Schwartz. Elias married Esther Moyer, who was also a native of Pennsylvania. They were farmers and of German Lutheran and Reformed background. They had nine children: Sarah, Davilla, Oscar, Agustus, Mary, David C., Wm. Henry, Jefferson, and Laura.

Sarah married Jacob Weisseise and had no children.

Davilla, born in 1865, married Lena Boyer, had no children, and died at age eighty nine.

Oscar, born in 1868, married Minerva Anna Folk, had five children (set of twin girls), and died at age eighty seven.

Agustus, born in 1970, married Artis Braner, had three children: Glen, Nettie Wright (Nettie had a set of twin boys, one died at birth), and Lula Caley. He died at age seventy four.

David C., born in 1872, married Bertha Powell, had six children: Everett, Hazel Pace, Winifred Miller, Damon, Dessie Caps, and Chester. Chester, who never married, was a minister and was killed in 1929 in a car accident in Ohio.

Henry, David C., Oscar, Davilla Schwartz

David died at age eighty five.

Mary, born in 1874, married Davis VanZant, had six children: Herman, Hubert, Howard, Stella Smoot, Ellen Lydy, and Catherine. Mary died at age sixty six.

Wm. Henry, born in 1876, married Lota Watson, had six children: Leah Clotine Spade, Gertrude Klein, Paul, Mark, Chester, and Lorin. Wm. Henry died at age eighty four.

Jefferson died at the age of thirteen, following surgery, on the kitchen table of their home, for a ruptured appendix.

Laura, born in 1883, married Charles Crum, had two children: Ardis and Woodrow. Laura died at age fifty one.

Most of the Schwartzes are buried at St. Paul Lutheran Cemetery, with Elias' father, Mikel, the first to be buried in this cemetery in 1861.

Elias' twin sister, Elmina, married Samuel Crum, whose first wife died two and one-half years after their only child, John Henry, was born. Elmina and Sam had four children: Eli, Emmanuel, Aaron (deceased), and David. Elmina died in the home of Ardis and Woodrow Crum, and is buried in St. John's Lutheran Cemetery in Union Township.

Sister Carolyn, married a Rahrer.

Brother Levi's son, Thomas—born in 1876, married Lula Myers. They had one daughter, Jean, who died at an early age. Thomas operated the Uniondale Lumber Yard, and built their house in Uniondale, where Lorin and Dorothy Schwartz now live. Levi's other son, Edward, married Mary Lucabaugh. They raised Ivah Miller. Levi's daughter, Effie, married Orve Davis. They had three sons: Ray, George, and Robert. Levi's other daughter, Margaret, never married. She died in the late 1980's. Margaret was the last of the cousins of Elias' brothers and sisters.

SCHWARTZ-PORTER

David Elias Schwartz, born in 1893, and Iva May Porter, born in 1895, were married June 12, 1920, in Uniondale after he returned from duty in France after World War I as an airplane mechanic. He was the son of Oscar and Minerva Anna Folk Schwartz of union Township, Wells County. His father was farmer, operator of Schwartz Threshing Ring (one run by Oscar, one by his son David and one by Oscar's brother Henry), and a railroader. Iva's father, Charles Edward Porter was born, November 23, 1897, to George E. and Anna Porter in New York. He moved to Osseo, Michigan, as a young boy and lost his right arm attempting to jump between the cars of a train. he learned teletype and became a station agent. He married Blanche Vande Bogart from Osseo, Michigan, and they came to Uniondale, where he was the Station Master for Uniondale's Station and Freight House combined for Erie Railroad for fifty-seven years and died at age ninety two. Charles and Blanche had three children: Iva, Laurence, and a daughter Nina, who died in infancy.

David Schwartz, was a Treasurer of Wells County. Iva Schwartz, was a Treasurer of Wells County.

Charles then married Alma Fryback Stroupe (who had one son, Kenneth Stroupe). They had Martha Beth, who married Jack McBride; they had one son, Phillip. Martha and Jack are both deceased. Philip has four sons and lives in Wren, Ohio. Iva and David both attended the Arbaugh School, one mile north of Uniondale, as did Laurence. (Iva recalled that the Schwartz children spoke German.) Dave then went to Union Center, Iva went to Bluffton Business School and Laurence graduated from Bluffton. They all went to St. Mark's Lutheran Church in Uniondale, with Dave and Selah Schwartz and Iva and Lawrence Porter playing in the church orchestra. Later Iva played the piano and organ at church. Iva worked nine years in the office at Morris Company in Bluffton, riding the CB&C.. Laurence married Marie Rose from Lima, Ohio, had one child, John (who has three children). Laurence is deceased. His wife, Marie, still lives in their home in Warren, Michigan. Dave and Iva had two children, George Edward and Julia May. (See Schwartz-Rebber or George's history.) Julia married George G. Hansen, a dentist from Baltimore, Maryland. They met when she was in the Army Nurse Corps at Fort Knox, Kentucky. They have two children, David Eric and Karen Lee. David, born September 1, 1949, graduated from college with business majors and is an insurance agent in the eastern states. He married Mary Cavalier, a teacher from West Virginia, on June 11, 1983. They live in Berkeley Springs, West Virginia. Karen, born July 4, 1951, graduated from college with an Occupational Therapy major. She lives and works as an O.T. in Bethlehem, Pennsylvania. David Schwartz had been co-owner/operator of a Garage/Implement business in the Lockwood garage building in Uniondale, Rockcreek Township. They lost the business due to the Depression and Dave bought the garage north across the RR tracks for $900.00 which was his WW I Veteran's bonus. This was the former Red Mans Lodge building, with the lodge upstairs and a theater downstairs. Dave and family lived upstairs. Dave later was a bus driver and trustee in Union Township. He died at age fifty eight while in office as Wells County Treasurer. Iva was appointed treasurer and was elected for the four year term. She died at the age of eighty four.

SCHWARTZ-REBBER

On Easter Sunday, April 21, 1946, George E. Schwartz and Adeline (Dody) Rebber were married at First Lutheran Church, Louisville, Kentucky. He had returned from Germany (he had been in the Battle of the Bulge during World War II) after about four years in the 324th Army Medical Battalion of the 99th Infantry Division. She was still in the Army Nurse Corps at Fort Knox, Kentucky. They had met when Dody and George's sister Julia May were at Lutheran Hospital School of Nursing, Fort Wayne, Indiana. He was the son of David E. and Iva Porter Schwartz of Uniondale, Indiana. She was the daughter of Herman F. and Clara Moeller Rebber of New Haven, Indiana. George and his sister were born in the Union Township farm home belonging to their grandfather, Oscar Schwartz. They started school in Rockcreek Township and graduated from Union. Dody was the middle child of a family of nine children, two sets of twins. They were all born in their farm home on Hartzell Road, New Haven. They attended Martini German Lutheran School on Moeller Road and graduated from New Haven High. They are all living except Robert, who died at age twenty four after an appendectomy. One of Dody's sisters, Mrs. Fred (Eleonora) Newhouse (also a nurse) lives in Wells County, south of Ossian

George and Dody set up housekeeping in an apartment above his parents garage, Schwartz Garage in Uniondale, Union Township. In 1954 they bought a house next to Legge Elevator, where they still live. This is one of the oldest houses in Uniondale and had belonged to the Gardenour estate. George worked for his father at the garage; when he became a partner the name was changed to Schwartz and Son Garage. After his three sons were born it became Schwartz & Sons Garage. George is still working there part-time. Dody worked as an RN for forty-one years, the last eighteen as Public Health Nurse of Wells County. She had attended IU School of Nursing, Fort Wayne. In 1977 she was honored as Public Health Nurse of the Year for the State of Indiana. She retired in 1987. George and Dody had four children: Jacqueline, born June 16, 1948; Geoffrey, March 21, 1950; Timothy, March 1, 1954; Brian, February 23, 1955. Jacquie attended IU, Fort Wayne. She married K. W. Evans from Buena Vista, Virginia, has one child, Justin Scott, 7, and lives and works in Richmond, Va, as an executive secretary. Geoff graduated from Taylor at Upland, Indiana, and from Ball State for his masters. He worked eight years for Wandering Wheels, a Christian bicycling group out of Taylor. He married Carolyn Breedlove from Marion, Indiana. They both teach: he, Industrials Arts, at Blackford County Junior High; she, 4th grade at Marion. They live in Upland. Tim attended Ball State, Taylor and IU, Indianapolis. He works at Indiana National Bank, Indianapolis, as Internal Security Investigator. He is married to Elizabeth Barret of Greenwood, Indiana, and lives in Indianapolis. He has one child, Jennifer, nine, by his first marriage. (For Brian, see Schwartz-Fox.) George and Dody are active in church (St. Mark's, Uniondale) and community; George still a volunteer fireman, Dody in nursing and health.

JAMES SCHWARZKOPF FAMILY

In the early 1970's James Schwarzkopf, who was born and raised in Blackford County, was employed as the high school principal of The Hamilton Community Schools of Dekalb County (1970-76). When traveling from that northern Indiana community to visit relatives living in Blackford County, he would admire a school building located in Chester Township, Wells County, for its structural attractiveness. In July, 1976, he became the Junior-Senior high principal of that educational facility known as The Southern Wells School Corporation and moved to Wells County with his wife, Sandra, also of Blackford County and their children, Dennis and Denise. They purchased a house located a short distance south of the school. It remains their home.

Both James and Sandra graduated from Montpelier High School, Montpelier, Indiana. James is also a 1959 graduate of Purdue University and received a Master of Arts degree from Ball State University, 1963. His educational career began in Eaton, Indiana, of Delaware County where he was a teacher for eight years and an administrator for three years (1959-1970).

Sandra is employed as office co-ordinator for The Andersons Management Corporation, Poneto, and for twelve years was the office secretary of the Bluffton First Church of the Nazarene, where both are active members.

In recent years they have enjoyed traveling the state of Indiana together enabling James to complete his goal to jog three miles in every county seat in the state, at the same time he collected pictures of the court houses and high school buildings and gathered interesting information about those areas.

James and Sandra Schwarzkopf

Son, Dennis, is married to Sherry Ailes. They live in Hartford City, Indiana, with their children; Steven, eight; and Brittany, one.

Daughter, Denise, lives in Terre Haute, Indiana, where she works with the mentally handicapped. She is a graduate of Vincennes University.

NORMAN RAY SCHWEIKHARDT

The Norman Ray Schweikhardt home was established in Jackson Township on May 13, 1951, when Norman Ray and Peggy Dehn Shultz were married at the Asbury Chapel Church.

Norman was the youngest child of Frank B. and Lovie (Roush) Schweikhardt, born on May 13, 1932. Peggy was the oldest child of Galen H. and Shirley (Allen) Shultz, born on October 1, 1933. Norman grew up on the farm with three brothers; Franklin, Fred, and Boyd, and one sister, Vera. Over the years they grew a variety of crops; corn, beans, wheat, oats, hay, tomatoes and sugar beets. They milked cows, raised hogs and chickens.

Norman and Peggy Schweikhardt

Norman attended and graduated in 1950 from Jackson Center School. Peggy moved to Jackson Township in 1946 with her family. She also attended and graduated in 1951 from Jackson Center School.

Norman and Peggy farmed and in 1965 Norman started working at Corning Glass Works, a new factory near Bluffton, Indiana. While there he became a journeyman electrician-instrument man. He continued there until the plant closed in 1983. In March, 1984, Norman was hired as an electrician at Dana Corporation in Marion, Indiana.

There were four children born in this family: Michael Ray on March 4, 1953, Michelle Ann (Shelley) on May 25, 1954, Matthew Dean on October 23, 1956, and Melinda Jo (Mindy) on August 30, 1964. Our children are all married, and we have eight grandchildren.

George and Adeline (Dody) Schwartz

Mike married Bridget Jean Brauchla on November 26, 1977, and they have one daughter, Emily Jean, born on January 21, 1983. Mike is employed at Salamonie Mills, a feed mill, in Warren, Indiana, and Bridget is employed at Eckman Motors, a car dealer. They live in Jackson Township in the house where Mike's parents lived when they were first married.

Shelley married Timothy Arthur Huffman on June 26, 1970, and they live in Liberty Township. They have two children, a daughter, Tracy Lynn, born on October 17, 1970 and a son, Timothy Joseph, born on May 2, 1975. Tim farms and Shelley works for the ASCS in Bluffton, Indiana.

Matthew married Melanie Lynn Kellogg on September 4, 1976, and they live in Chester Township. Matthew works for Farm Bureau Insurance and Melanie is a homemaker. They have two daughters, Lesli Lynn, born November 5, 1981, and Leah Lynae, born February 25, 1985.

Mindy married Troy Duane Drayer on April 30, 1983. They live in Wabash County and are houseparents at White's Institute (a correctional institution). They are parents of three daughters, Amanda Michelle, born March 22, 1984; Natalie Joy, born December 26, 1985; and Suzanne Kathleen, born September 12, 1987.

Norman and Peggy moved to Warren, Indiana, in March of 1982. Norman continues to work at the Dana plant and Peggy has been employed at the United Methodist Memorial Home, in the Activity Department since 1982. They are active members of the Asbury Chapel Church. They were active 4-H members as were each of their children. Music has always been an important part of their family and they continue to share it.

CALVIN AND ALTHA ANN (JOHNSON) SCOTT

In 1836, Calvin C. Scott was born in Ohio, and on October 29, 1871, in Allen County, Indiana, he married Altha Ann Johnson, the daughter of James and Rebecca (Baxter) Johnson, who had a total of fourteen children. The first four were born in Washington County, Pennsylvania; the other in Columbiana County, Ohio.

Noah (1826-1907) married Sarah Thomas; Frances (1827-1912) married Daniel Edwards; Isabella (1828-1860) was the wife of Samuel Woods; Harriet (1830-1907) married Charles S. Foulks; Isaac (1832-1911) was the husband of Douglas Jane Gordon; Jacob (1834-1911) first married Elizabeth Biddle, then Flora Brookwalter Angelbright; Abraham (born 1836) lived only four months; Harvey (1837-1917) married Phoebe Myers; Elizabeth (1839-1918) was the wife of William Henry Carbaugh; Lewis (1840-1905) married Nancy Farrell; Josiah (1842-1923) took as his wife Elizabeth Glass; Martha (1845-1906) was Mrs. William E. Angevine; Altha Ann (1847-1925) was the thirteenth child; and John Jackman (1849-1864) did not live long enough to marry. Of the twelve survivors, the six boys became farmers, and the six girls married farmers.

Although many lived out their lives in Allen County, Altha Ann, after marrying Calvin, became a resident of Union township, Wells County. There, he and Calvin reared four children: Harry A., Arleva J., James Franklin, and Amanda J. Sadly all four died before their parents. Further, Altha Ann, who survived until July 20, 1925, outlived not only her parents but also all of her siblings. Less than a year after Altha's death, Calvin died, February 17, 1926. This couple and all four of their children are buried in Uniontown Cemetery, Wells County. Also buried there are Altha Ann's parents and six siblings: Isabella, Jacob, Harvey, Lewis, Martha, and John Jackman.

Back, L to R; Mrs. James Franklin Scott, James Franklin Scott, Amanda J. Scott, Gibson W. Rogers, and Arleva (Scott) Rogers. Front, L to R; Calvin C. Scott, holding Scott Gray Rogers, Altha Ann (Johnson) Scott, holding Russell Calvin Scott.

After 1910, Calvin and Altha moved from their Union Township farm to one near Pleasant View, two miles south of Bluffton on the Hoosier Highway. After his wife's death, Calvin sold the property and household goods at public auction.

The first child of this couple, Harry A. Scott (1873-1897), died at the age of twenty four of consumption.

Arleva J. Scott (1877-1912) married Gibson W. Rogers on December 11, 1897 in Wells County, and this couple had one son, Scott Gray Rogers. Scott married Lucille Sophia Yager; and at the time of this writing, April 1991, lived in Brooklyn, Michigan. Scott and Lucille had no children.

James Franklin Scott (1879-1924) and Isora May Hoag were married October 8, 1902 in Huntington County, Indiana. They also had only one child, Russell Calvin Scott. On October 17, 1926, he married Helen Lorene Maples. Their only child, Kenneth Franklin Scott, married Mary Elizabeth Gard on July 27, 1952, in Lafayette, Tippecanoe County, Indiana. Kenneth and Mary Elizabeth had three sons: Steven Alan, David Earl, and Russell Wayne, and four grandchildren.

Amanda J. Scott (1885-1923) married first Melvin M. Reynolds, then Francis A. Reavis. There were no children.

CHARLES S. SCOTT FAMILY

In Wells County the Scott family history began on farms near Zanesville where Charles Sumner Scott was born in 1873 and Dora Ellen Peck in 1875. After they were married on February 25, 1897, Charles rode a bicycle to Ohio to attend barber's school. He heard that there was no barber in Keystone, so they moved to Keystone where he set up a barber shop in their home, and she later became the Postmistress there. Their children Don, Amy, Jess, and Fred were born in Keystone, and the family was raised close to the Methodist Church. They moved to Bluffton in 1919 where Charles was a jeweler and watchmaker. Always creative and inventive, he had numerous patents, including "Scott's Patented Click Springs" which provided a shortcut to clock repair.

Although all four children followed in the trade, Don and Amy also became teachers. Don married Mary Shofer in 1933, lived in Richmond, Muncie, and Texas, and died in 1980. Amy and Dewey Freeze were married in 1928 and owned a jewelry store in North Manchester for twenty years before moving to Wabash where she taught school. In 1983 she returned to Bluffton for five years and now lives in Swiss Village, Berne, where she is enjoying oil painting. Fred B. married Dorthy Leimgruber in Bluffton in 1937, lived in several other states; had two children, Mrs. Everett Dye (Sharon) of Jacksonville, Florida; and Fred C. of Humble, Texas; five grandchildren and three great-grandchildren. Fred B. died in Florida in 1989, and Dorthy now lives in Jacksonville, Florida.

Charles S. Scott Family
Front-Charles, Fred, Dora. Back-Don, Amy, Jess.

Jess was graduated from Northern Illinois College of Optometry in Chicago. In 1935 he began to practice optometry in the office of Homer R. Gettle. In 1943 he purchased the practice and in 1947 located at the corner of Johnson and Washington Streets until his retirement in 1987. Dr. James Van Winkle joined the practice there in 1967 and later became a partner.

Dr. Scott was active in many phases of community life until his death February 7, 1991. Perhaps most dedicated to the First United Methodist Church, his church affiliation since 1919, he was also active in Kiwanis for sixty years and was a member of the Masonic Lodge, Scottish Rite and Shrine. Photography was his main hobby.

His marriage in Vincennes on July 20, 1936, was to Mary Hilma Sappenfield. Mary Hilma was a teacher of Home Economics in the County Schools, Lancaster and Chester. She was active in many civic organizations and held office in church groups, Tri Kappa and Study Clubs. They had two children: Mrs. Grant Annable (Eleanor) of Stamford, Connecticut; and Richard J. of Arlington, Virginia; and four grandchildren: David Annable living in California, Susan Annable in Stamford, Shannon and Hilary Scott in Bluffton.

JAMES SCOTT

One of Wells County early pioneers, my great-grandfather, settled in Union Township, Wells County, Indiana. Born in 1825 in Trumble County, Ohio, he was the son of John and Debby McCorkle Scott. He, along with John Wilson and family, James Harris and Nancy Horn, all traveling in one wagon, settled this region in 1849. James had enough money to purchase one hundred sixty acres of land on the Indian Reserve which was open for settlement a short time earlier. The log house was located not far from where the present home now stands, but his real first home in Wells County was a "pole shanty" for eighteen months where he kept bachelors quarters. It took several months to make a small clearing since the trees had not been cleared nor roads built.

James and Elizabeth Scott

The Wolfcale family came and settled one mile east of James and he married one of the daughters, Belinda in 1851. They started married life in a log cabin with the ground as the floor and no mud plaster between the logs. Belinda died early in life, leaving James with one daughter, Eliza Jane, who eventually married Thomas Burneau.

James married, 1856, Elizabeth Wright from Vigo County, Indiana. Her father, Ira Wright and the father to the Wright brothers were brothers. Elizabeth taught school prior to her marriage to James. The couple had four children: Clark Ira, William Pearl, Alva, and Alma Belenda. Alma was my grandmother who married John Ertel of Ruth County, Indiana. They had a family; one of their daughters, Mary Ethel, was my mother. The family eventually returned to Wells County where alma and children shared many a happy time with the Scott clan. I can remember as a young child going visiting there, and it was always a treat to go inside the brick spring house where it was always so cool and pleasant, and grandmother would keep "vittles" such as milk, cream and butter.

The farm and most of the buildings are still in existence today and is located one mile west of Uniondale and two miles north in Union Township; Wells County, Indiana, and presently owned by the Noble Mitchell family.

NATHAN MACY SCOTT

Nathan Macy Scott, Nottingham Township, Wells County, was born February 21, 1842, in Penn Township, Jay County, Indiana. He was the son of Stanton and Esther (Edmundson) Scott. His grandparents were Joshua and Abigail (Stanton) Scott, a native of Scotland. Abigail was an aunt of President Lincoln's Secretary of War, Edwin M. Stanton. Stanton Scott, was born June 26, 1807, grew to manhood in Clark County, Ohio, and there married Esther Edmundson, daughter of Thomas and Elizabeth (Morsel) Edmundson, of English ancestry. After their marriage on September 21, 1836, the Scotts settled in Logan County, Ohio. In 1841 he moved to Jay County, Indiana, and lived there on a rented farm. While still renting in Jay County, he purchased 80 acres of land in Wells County, the same on which Gerald Scott now lives, and built a log cabin. In 1845 he moved to his farm, at that time there was no human habitation all the way to Pennville. Being but three years old at the time, Nathan M. Scott well remembered the neighbors and where their homes were located. Joseph Williamson lived one and a fourth miles south east. Darius Shinn's home was a mile south, John Dawson lived one and one-half miles northwest. Stanton Scott died August 24, 1855, leaving a widow and seven children. The children were Mary; Thomas; Nathan; Elizabeth, married B. L. DeWeese of Balbec; Joshua; Elma J. Rebecca.

Esther died July 4, 1896, all her surviving children comfortably settled in life. Before her marriage, she was a school teacher.

The Wells County schools furnished Nathan M. Scott his education, mainly the Scott School in Nottingham Township. In spring of 1864 he attended Liber College, near Portland, Indiana. He entered the school in September, but on October 13, 1864, he entered the U.S. service as a volunteer, enlisting in the 53rd Regiment, Indiana Volunteer Infantry. He was mustered out in the fall of 1865.

On October 11, 1873, Mr. Nathan Scott was married to Miss Tracy J. Lewis, born May 8, 1855, in Jay County, Indiana, a daughter of Lorenzo and Elizabeth (Haines) Lewis. Lorenzo's parents were Emery and Rachael (Thomas) Lewis of Welsh ancestry, and Elizabeth's parents were Timothy and Hannah (Tomlinson) Haines, of English ancestry.

After their marriage, Mr. and Mrs. Nathan Scott moved to their farm of one hundred and sixty acres in Nottingham Township, Wells County. He taught one term of school after his marriage, then devoted his time entirely to his farm. In 1873 he was elected justice of peace and serving four years, never holding an official position again. To them two children were born, viz: Elveretta, born February 5, 1875; William Tarlton, born August 13, 1878, attended the Eastern Indiana University at Muncie. Elveretta graduated from Pennville High School and was quite proficient in music.

The Scotts were members of the Friends Church. In politics he was an active Republican. As a member of Lew Dailey Post, G.A.R. at Bluffton, he never lost an opportunity to benefit a veteran of the Civil War. Nathan died October 3, 1940, and Mrs. Scott on May 17, 1930; both in Wells County.

SECHLER

Benjamin Frederick Sechler and wife, Eliza (Moyer), bought land in Union Township, Wells County, Indiana, by 1869. They had lived in Allen County, Indiana, from 1863. Benjamin and Eliza married in Lordstown, Trumbull County, Ohio, January 27, 1853, where he was a blacksmith and a farmer. Mr. Sechler sold smoked meats in his neighborhood of Uniondale.

Benjamin Frederick Sechler-Eliza (Moyer) Sechler. Early Settlers of Union Township, Wells County. Photo from 1890's.

Benjamin was born January 27, 1829, Bucks County, Pennsylvania. Names of his ancestors appear in Pennsylvania records by 1731. Some children and grandchildren of Andrew and Elizabeth Banks Sechler, Lehigh County, Pennsylvania, went to northeastern Ohio in 1830's. Later, Ben's relatives settled in northeastern Indiana.

Eliza was born February 15, 1834, in Stark County, Ohio. Her father was Jacob Moyer, of Lehigh County, Pennsylvania, and her mother was Catherine (Bechtel) of Stark County, Ohio. Eliza's sisters; Lydia Bailey, Lovina, and Sarah Platt, resided in Union Township.

Lulu (Sechler) Ditzler. Daughter of Benjamin and Eliza Sechler, May 1885.

Two young Sechler sons, Charles and Jacob, died in Ohio. Edward and Sarah died at a young age in Indiana. Seven children were raised near Uniondale.

Emma Catherine, born October, 1857, Trumbull County, Ohio, married John Brodt, June 15, 1873, in Wells County, Indiana, and died April 7, 1932, in Grant County, Indiana. The Brodt children were: Frederick, Charles, William, John, Rutherford, Euclair and Emma (twins), Leone Lambert, Estelle Thompson, Arla Hill, Jessie Winters, and Eva Logan. William H. farmed, worked at Bluffton foundry and was a butcher in Eureka, California. He was born November 20, 1859; married Emma Ensly, August 30, 1884, in Wells County; and died April 23, 1940 in Humboldt County, California. Mary Ella was an artist in Bluffton. She painted on glass. She was born March 17, 1861; married George W. Sigler, September 20, 1881, in Wells County; and died January 26, 1894. Ella's children were: Junie Dora Sigler, born December 24, 1884—died August 4, 1905; Anita Sigler, born about 1886—died March 14, 1887; Carl Sigler, born about 1888—died at about four years of age; Henry H. Carlisle, born May 11, 1890—died February 21, 1929.

Lulu Mae (researcher's grandmother) was born December 17, 1864, in Huntertown, Indiana; married Jacob Franklin Ditzler May 10, 1885, in Wells County, Indiana; and died April 2, 1907, in Montpelier, Indiana, Blackford County. The Ditzler children were: Nell Smith, Vier, Ray F., Hillard, Glendora Witty, Ruby Rich, Erma Rice, and Paul.

Dora Ida was a teacher in country schools who was born December 6, 1873, in Wells County and died September 17, 1903. John C. was a fiddler, painter, plasterer and decorator who was born September 17, 1875, in Wells County; married Minnie Laturner November 3, 1906; and died May 1, 1929 in Ft. Wayne, Indiana, Allen County. One child, Velma, died after one month, October 22, 1907, in Wells County, Indiana.

Lottie was a bright popular girl in Bluffton. She was born November 6, 1877, and died March 4, 1897 in Wells County, Indiana. Benjamin F. died March 21, 1908; Eliza died March 4, 1912, both in Wells County. Five Sechler children had consumption. Many family members were buried at St. Johns Cemetery, Union Township, Wells County, Indiana.

WILBERT SEIBOLD

In 1989, Mark Seibold of Huntington made the news by being invited to the White House to help break in the new forty-foot horseshoe pit, built near the White House swimming pool. He even got his picture in the Fort Wayne paper with President George Bush. Mark is one of the top horseshoe pitchers in the United States. Maybe just a little bit of Zanesville went with him to the White House!

Mark's grandmother, Edith, was a daughter of Nelson Bailey (1852-1920), who farmed all his life just one mile north of Zanesville on the northwest corner of Indianapolis Road. The same house is still standing there. Mark's grandfather, Charles Seibold, was her husband. He was a brother to Minnie (Mrs. Jack) Caley. Mark's father, Wilbert, was one of their three children. Charles and Minnie lived between here and Roanoke, near Little River, when they were growing up. Wilbert lived his high school years near the northwest corner of the intersection of Zubrich and Yoder Roads. There is no house there now. He attended Lafayette Central School then. During grade school at Union, he lived just three miles east of here on the County Line Road. At that time, he remembers the free shows that were held in Zanesville on Wednesday night. He also said he could attend the Monday night free show at Uniondale and Thursday night at Ossian! He had a great time coming to town and being able to play with the other kids. He grew up and married Bonnie Beeks.

Wilbert and his wife, Bonnie, have been pitching horseshoes for a very long time; therefore, their children also joined in. Their son Paris, who teaches in Huntington, pitches horseshoes with them. Wilbert has pitched in top groups of horseshoe pitchers all over the country. His wife, Bonnie, has won the State Tourney seventeen times, and was second in the World Tourney one year. Their daughter, Bonita Price, was Junior Girls' World Champion in 1967. And then, Mark got invited to the White House!

Samuel Seibold (1854-1915) was a large man. He weighed two hundred and twenty pounds and wore a size twelve shoe. His death was caused by falling out of an apple tree while picking apples. He married Emma Hoopingarner (1863-1940). Born in eastern Ohio near Winfield, she came to Zanesville when she was ten years old. She was twenty one when she and Samuel Seibold were married.

They had five children. The first child died in infancy. Charles (1885-1948) married Edith Bailey (1897-1973). He was a farmer in the Zanesville area all of his life. Minnie married Jack Caley. Pearl married Mr. Beck and moved to the Indianapolis area, where she is buried. Edward never married.

Wilbert, the son of Charles and Edith, served in the U.S. air Force during World War II, and was a prisoner of war for eighteen months. He retired from Dana Corporation in 1979 after thirty-two years of service. He married Bonnie Beeks of Andrews, Indiana, and they have four children: Shelley lives in Phoenix, Arizona, and she has one son, Peter. Bonita teaches school at Andrews, Indiana. She is married to Byron Price and they have two sons, Adam and Erik. Mark is single and works at Dana Corporation. He has been World Horseshoe Pitching Champion twice in the Junior Division, and twice in the Men's Division. Paris teaches school at Huntington North High School. he married Jean Arwett and they have two daughters, Kelli and Ashley, and one one son, Lee.

For more information, refer to the Zanesville history Book - 1976, Nelson Bailey Family.

GARY AND ELAINE SEIDNER

Gary Lee Seidner and Karen Elaine Johnson were married at Six Mile Church on June 9, 1979.

Gary was born in 1953 in Jay County to Gerald and Dorothy Seidner. He graduated from Delta High School in 1971. Gary earned his BS degree from Ball State University in math and his Master's degree in Physics from the same school. Gary teaches math related subjects at Delta High School near Muncie.

Sharla, Nathan, Caleb, and Micah Seidner

Elaine, born in 1956, is the daughter of Leon and Anna Johnson (see Leon Johnson history). She graduated from Bluffton High School in 1974, and from IU of Fort Wayne as a dental hygienist in 1977.

Daughter, Sharla Lee, was born September 11, 1982. Sharla is an excellent Montpelier Elementary School student. Nathan Daniel was born February 6, 1986. He is a little farmer who enjoys his pint-size chores. Caleb Adam was born January 22, 1988. Caleb has a constant smile that is only lost when a sibling takes his toy tractor away. Micah Philip, born July 20, 1989, is well known for his ability to climb "anything." His favorite pastime is chasing chickens.

Gary, Elaine, Sharla, Nathan, Caleb and Micah live in Blackford County on a small farm.

LARRY AND DIANA SELL

The family of Larry and Diana Sell began residence in Wells County in August 1965, one mile west of Bluffton on the old River Road and here commenced their teaching careers. A science teacher and coach for twenty-six years, Larry taught science at Chester and Petroleum prior to the consolidation into Southern Wells School Corporation. Diana started teaching at Lancaster High School in the area of physical education and health. Two afternoons a week she would travel to Union (on 303) to teach physical education to seventh, eighth, and ninth graders. The following year, 1966, she taught the same subjects at Bluffton High School for five months and left because of pregnancy. The following years included one year of kindergarten at Liberty Center Elementary and two and one-half years of physical education at Lancaster and Ossian Junior High Schools.

There were three children born to this couple: Michelle (Shelly) Marie, 24; Terry Lynn, 19; and Wendy Elaine, fourteen. Larry's aunt and uncle, Betty and Paul Sell, have resided in Wells County since their marriage and now live near Craigville. They had two sons, Don and David. Paul had careers in weather and insurance, while Betty had a banking position for many years. Both are now retired.

Diana has one sister who is also a resident of Wells County, Karen Sue Foy. She married Richard Markley Foy in 1964; they live near Southern Wells School on 800 S. with their three daughters: Stephanie, twenty; Angela, sixteen; and Suzanne, fourteen. Both Karen and Dick are teachers.

Larry's family can be traced as far back as the Revolutionary War when John Vian came to America in the 1700's as part of the British army. He married here and his relatives eventually settled in Knox County, Ohio. Many of Larry's ancestors were ministers, farmers, and teachers, and others were involved in politics; many of the women were housewives. His parents, Carl and Pauline (Book) Sell, live in Celina, Ohio, while two of his brothers reside in Rockford, Ohio, and one in Deltona, Florida.

Diana's earliest known ancestor came from Germany in 1749 and settled in Pennsylvania. Her mother, Mary Juanita Shoemaker Bonewitz, resides in Huntington, and her father, Robert Raymond Bonewitz is deceased; both were factory workers. Some of the ancestors were farmers, teachers, and businessmen, and several served in the Revolutionary War and World War II. One relative in her mother's family served in three wars. One brother, Bob, and one brother-in-law, Steve Updike, of Huntington, spent time in Vietnam as members of the army.

The couple is now divorced; Larry living in Bluffton, and Diana in Liberty Center.

THE PAUL SELL FAMILY

Paul and Elizabeth (Betty) Sell, of Lancaster Township, have lived in Wells County since 1952. They were married at Nine Mile EUB Church near Baer Field, and lived near Ossian until 1957, when they built a home in the Tollgate Addition of Bluffton. In 1969, they moved to their present home.

Paul is a native of Rockford, Ohio. He served in the U.S. navy in World War II, and later worked as a weather observer in Alaska. He lived at Barrow, Alaska, and had several adventures hunting whales, polar bears, walrus, and seals with the Eskimos. As a private pilot, he flew with the Civil Air Patrol over various parts of Alaska. Through his hobby of amateur radio, he made contacts over the world as well as regular contacts with friends and family in Ohio and Indiana.

Sell Family
Standing, L to R; Don and Dave. Seated, L to R; Betty holding Jennifer, Kelly and Matthew, Valarie holding Nathaniel, Paul holding Ciara.

Elizabeth (Betty Kelly) was born in Warsaw, Indiana, and grew up in Allen County, graduating from Lafayette Central High School. Her father, J. D. Kelly, was an engineer on the Pennsylvania Railroad. They have two sons, Donald and David. Don is married to the former Kelly Fischer of Bluffton, and they have a son, Matthew, and daughter, Jennifer. Dave is married to the former Valarie Nyenhuis of Iowa, and they have a daughter, Ciara, and son, Nathaniel.

When their children were in school, Paul and Betty were active in various community affairs.

Betty started as a Den Mother and Paul followed as a Boy Scout Leader. He also taught Sunday School over twenty years, as they were both participants in church functions.

Paul has continued in his life insurance business for many years and also worked for the National Weather Service. Betty worked for First Federal/Standard Federal Bank for 16 years, beginning as a branch counselor, and retiring as Branch Manager/Assistant Vice President. They enjoy traveling in their motor home, working in their garden, and enjoying numerous other hobbies.

Betty's roots go back to Ireland (Kelly) and to Europe on her Mother's side (Stamats), as the families settled in Pennsylvania and were derived from the Pennsylvania-Dutch. They moved in the mid 1800's to Indiana.

Paul's family goes back to northern Europe in medieval times, as in 1066, they went from Normandy to England with William-The-Conqueror. Paul's great-grandfather, Dr. Charles T. Sell, came to Indiana in the early 1800's, living in Adams County, later moving to Ohio. On his mother's side, the Boice family arrived in America in 1661, migrating with time to Pennsylvania, West Virginia, then Ohio and Indiana, settling on what is now known as Amishville. Paul's family is the fifteenth generation in America. Many generations of stalwart pioneers from both family branches, as detailed by old family records, provide an enviable background of which we are proud.

SELLERS-BAY

Charles Sellers cooked hamburgers at Mac's Cigar Store and Pool Room and clerked at Dal Wandel's grocery in Bluffton. Mary Jane Bay was a telephone operator. Their marriage in 1922 brought together two long-time Wells County families.

Charles' grandfather, K. B. Sellers, moved to a farm in Rockcreek Township in 1850, bringing his first wife and at least one child. He was a son of Frederick Sellers of Berks County, Pennsylvania. His first wife died after the birth of their sixth child. He then married Eliza Miller, daughter of John Miller and Mary Vrandt, and fathered seven more children.

Charles' father, also Charles E. Sellers, a Smith and Bell teamster, died in 1902 at age 27 from lockjaw from a splinter in his thumb. Six months later his only son was born. In 1899 he had married Louisa May Neff, daughter of Jacob Neff and Sarah Zirkel; Sarah's father was Noah Zerkle of Mason County, West Virginia, said to be a great-grandson of Ludwig Zirckel, a Palatine who died in 1747 in Pennsylvania.

The Bay family also has long resided in Wells County: William and Rebecca Bay, Janey's great grandparents, moved there after their 1832 marriage in Allen County and residence as one of three families in southern Adams County until 1834. Rebecca was a daughter of Christena Studebaker and Abraham Miller, also early residents of west central Ohio and eastern Indiana.

Janey's father was Charles Harrison Bay, who helped build the Bluffton bridge; his father was Harrison Bay. Janey's mother was the former Mary Elizabeth Barton and her grandmother was Mary Ann Sprowl Barton, wife of James Barton and granddaughter of Joseph Sprowl, "American," whose family in 1834 was first to settle in Lancaster Township of Huntington County, Indiana. Joseph's father, William Sprowl, came from Ireland with the British Army and Stayed in the New World after the Battle of Quebec in 1756.

Related names also include Wagner, Derr, Hamilton, Shoemaker, Johnson, Gilbert, Gross, Acton and Bumgarner. The graves of many of those mentioned are in Wells County cemeteries: St. Paul and Old St. Paul in Rockcreek Township, Mossburg in Liberty Township and Old Bluffton in Lancaster Township.

After the Sellers-Bay marriage, Charlie Sellers went to work for the Railway Express Agency; most of his forty-five years with REA he worked midnights and drove from the Bay family farm in Liberty Township to Fort Wayne, rarely missing work. Charlie died in 1977, Janey in 1985. Charles and Mary Jane had three children: a son who did not survive; a daughter, Mildred, who died in 1985; and a daughter, Charlotte, who resides in Jackson County, Indiana.

Charlotte, a former newspaper reporter who now freelances stories about law enforcement, is tracing her direct and collateral ancestors, including those believed to have come through Kentucky from Virginia. The search has taken her on several interesting trips; some of the most interesting have been back to Wells County, where old records hold many stories.

SELLERS FARM

FIRST GENERATION: Leroy "Lee" McKendose Sellers, age twenty five, and his first cousin, Finley H. Rhodes (Corporal-Civil War), age twenty two, Somerset, Perry County, Ohio, traveled by horseback to Zanesville, Muskingum County, Ohio, June 4, 1866. They bought land: section six, Nottingham township, Wells County, Indiana, at $10.00 an acre from the original owners, Jacob and Aciah Lane, who had purchased the land, 1850, from the government.

Starting July 14, 1866, land was cleared to build a log cabin. Leroy and family lived in the cabin until 1904 when his son, Emory Bing, built the present Sellers home.

June 6, 1878, Leroy, four neighbors, County Surveyor Finley Rhodes, presented a petition to the Board of Commissioners for the establishment of an open ditch, known as Sellers Ditch. Leroy helped to build the early roads, which many called corduroy roads. Later, Leroy was a Nottingham Township Road Supervisor.

Back, L to R; Dorotha D. Sellers, Margaret Sellers, Ruth Sellers. Front; Nora (Doyle) Sellers and Emory Bing Sellers.

February 1, 1871, Leroy married Mary M. Rush, daughter of John B. and Lydia (Stanforth) Rush. Two children were born to this couple: Matilda E. and Daniel Emory Bing Sellers. Leroy's wife, Mary M., died November 7, 1883, at age thirty one. The daughter's death occurred October 3, 1887, at age fifteen.

One-half acre was sold (1874) to Nottingham Township Trustee, where the Sellers School House was built. Later it was replaced by a brick school house named Frog Pond School.

Leroy died January 22, 1905, age sixty four and was buried in the Sellers Family plot, Grove Cemetery.

SECOND GENERATION: During the 1890 oil boom in this area, Emory Bing left farming to work as a driller, receiving about $65.00 a month. In 1904 he left the oil fields near Van Buren, and with his new bride, Nora Leah (Doyle) Sellers, daughter of Thomas and Margaret (Kessinger) Doyle, returned to the Sellers farm and to his newly built house. Four children were born to this couple: Leroy Thomas Sellers (born August, 1907, died August 25, 1907), Margaret, Dorotha, and Ruth Sellers.

Emory's farming was done by horses and later by a Farmal tractor. He joined the neighbors in threshing grain. With his experience as a driller, he was called upon to repair many broken ropes during hay-making season. In 1921, a new barn was built, put together with wooden pegs. During the years, many additions were added to the original house. Emory's last farming chore was shucking corn. He suffered a stroke and died on April 27, 1955, at age eighty years.

Nora Sellers was a homemaker, an excellent cook, and a seamstress. She was very active in the Poneto Baptist Ladies Aid. Her death occurred October 26, 1959, at age seventy-nine years. Both Emory and Nora Sellers were buried in the Masonic Cemetery, Van Buren, Indiana.

More family information may be found in The Doyle History Book, Grant County, 1984 and Sellers History Book, Wells County, 1991.

THIRD GENERATION: This Sellers house continued to be the residence of Sellers family since 1904. All three daughters, Margaret, Dorotha, and Ruth, graduated from Petroleum High School. Their teaching degrees were granted from Manchester College and Ball State University, with extra graduate work at Indiana University and University of Colorado. They taught a combined total of 133 years. They were members of Delta Kappa Gamma Society International for Women Teachers and Honorary members of Psi Iota Xi Sorority.

Margaret retired in 1979 with forty-seven years of teaching: Vera Cruz (grades one to four with forty-eight students), Poplar Grove (grades three and four), and Montpelier, Blackford County (fourth grade).

Dorotha taught music and art at Vera Cruz, Poplar Grove and Poneto Elementary Schools, forty years at Lancaster Central School, retiring in 1986 after forty-three years of teaching. In 1968 she received the Wells County Community Service Award, and in 1970 the Distinguished Service Award from Indiana Music Educators Association.

Ruth retired in 1986 after forty-three years of teaching in Wells County: 14 years (one year as third and fourth grade, 13 years as first grade teacher) at East Rockcreek School, twenty-nine years as first grade teacher in Bluffton (8 years at Central and twenty-one years at East Side School). In 1970 she received the "Outstanding Educators of America" Award.

The Sellers farm was recognized, 1976 in Indianapolis as a Hoosier Homestead Farm, having been in the same family name for over one hundred (110) years. Nineteen hundred and ninety one marks its one hundred and twenty-fifth year as being the Sellers farm.

SETTLEMEYER HOMESTEAD

Located two miles southwest of Zanesville, the name was originally spelled Settlemyre. James changed his branch of the tree sometime after 1880. In beautiful penmanship on an upstairs door you can still read: "James M. Settlemyre, October 16, 1880. Hurrah for Garfield!", as of January 1991.

In 1869 James (born December 30, 1845) moved from Ohio to rent a one hundred and sixty acre tract of land from his parents, William and Ann (Wilkerson) who bought it from the government. James cleared land, built a house, and married Ellen Jacobs, a daughter of Elijah and Susanna Jacobs. Elijah married three times and had twenty-one children.

Clean up sale; Nov. 28, 1983

August 19, 1876, a son, Lawrence, was born. He attended college in Valparaiso. In 1895, Lawrence married Etta Roe, daughter of Jeremiah and Mary Ann Garnand Roe. Lawrence joined his father in farming and raised shorthorn cattle.

A son, Kenneth Wilkerson Settlemeyer, was born June 29, 1902. Kenneth graduated from International Business College, and attended Huntington College, until their tow barns burned. He then assisted his father in farming, raising shorthorn cattle, and Poland China hogs. Kenneth also made "Nobite" equipment for muskrat and mink farmers. Current evidence relates his customers lived from Long Island, New York, to California, thirty-six states, Washington D.C., and eight Canadian addresses. Minnesota lead the list with forty-eight customers.

Kenneth married Alice, daughter of Jesse and Bertha Elick Decker on February 14, 1939, Valentines Day. Alice's parents married on New Years Day, a sister married on July 4, and the other sister married on Thanksgiving.

Two children were born to this union. Wayne (born January 23, 1941) married Bonnie, daughter of Jerold and Opal Milholland Gilbert. Their children: twins (born Dec. 3, 1964) Krista Kae and Kelly Rene, and Shari (born December 10, 1969). Krista married Victor Dudash on June 13, 1988. They had a daughter, Danielle, born July 21, 1990. Kelly married John Eden on June 3, 1989. Wayne is vice-president FHP and DC Manufacturing for MagneTek, St. Louis, Missouri. Lois (born September 30, 1943) graduated from Anderson College and Seminary. She is now a trustee for the college and a project leader for Dow Chemical, Midland, Michigan.

SALLY ANNE ENGLE SEYMOUR

Sally was born August 2, 1959, in the Wells Community Hospital in Bluffton. She is the daughter of Guy Edward and Jeannine Shull Engle. She lived with her parents at 4098E SR 218 until she was five years old. At that time she moved with her family to LaFox, Illinois, where her father was building maintenance supervisor and her mother taught at Broadview Academy, A Seventh Day Adventist boarding school for grades nine through twelve. Sally attended elementary school at the Aurora SDA elementary school ten miles from home. Sally enjoyed home, school and church activities; especially camping with the Pathfinders (a church sponsored club for children of grades five through ten). Following graduation from eighth grade, Sally continued her education at Broadview Academy, where she not only studied but worked at various occupations on and off campus. At various times, she worked in custodial work in the dormitory, worked in the library, did clerical work in the office, assisted in classroom tasks, and worked at Harris Pine furniture plant off campus. Sally graduated in 1978.

Kenny Seymour, Sally Anne Engle Seymour

Sally entered Andrews University to become an elementary school teacher, graduating in the fall of 1982. She immediately found employment in a Seventh-day Adventist elementary school at LaPorte, Indiana. Sally met and fell in love with Kenny Ray Seymour. Ken's home was Knoxville, Tennessee. At that time he was a seminary student attending Andrews University, and his assignment was to obtain practical experience in the church at LaPorte under the observation of the local minister. They were married December 25, 1984. Sally finished out that year of teaching. Ken graduated from seminary and they moved to Perry, Michigan, where Ken had been given three small churches to pastor.

Ashley McKenna was born May 6, 1986, in Lansing, Michigan. Ken and Sally were transferred to Cadillac, where Ken gained experience as assistant pastor of the Cadillac church and two smaller churches. A year later Ken was assigned to pastor three churches south of Cadillac. Kelly Rae was born Deember. 19, 1990.

ALBERT AND MINNIE DALE (GRAVES) SHADLE

Albert was the third child in his family of seven children. His parents, William and Hannah (Penrod) Shadle, were both Indiana natives and farmers, residing on a one hundred acre farm near Mount Zion, Indiana. Albert frequently recalled his family going west in a covered wagon, pulled by a horse. Albert must have been about five years old when he made this trip (see story under Melvin Day).

Albert met Minnie Dale Graves and they were married in 1894 when he was nineteen years old and she was twenty. Bert, like his father, was a farmer and rented various farms in the area while raising his family of two children. Homer was the oldest child and Cecil was the second. A third child, Lillie, died as an infant.

Albert and Dale frequently had their grandchildren staying with them for varying periods of time. Bert was particularly familiar with the grandsons as they frequently helped him with the farm work. Homer's children were: Hillard, Herman, Eugene, Wilbur, Dwight, Irene, and Sharon. Cecil's only son was Melvin Day.

Albert and Minnie Dale Shadle. Taken at their home approximately 1920.

Bert was a short, very heavy-set man who got that way because he loved to eat, particularly very fatty meat (cholesterol was no problem in those days). He ate with his knife and frequently had Pepto-Bismol with his meals to help his digestion. He also enjoyed snacking on hard candies, ring bologna, and peanuts.

Dale was an excellent cook. She never used a cookbook. When she found a new recipe that the family liked, she prepared it daily until the recipe was remembered. Family members have very fond memories of her fried chicken, sugar cookies, and orange pie.

Their grandchildren have well remembered the unique personalities of these two very special, very delightful people and many of the stories have been written down in the family genealogy by Mary Day. Their stories are also told in *The Shadle Family Cookbook* written and published by Mary Day in 1982.

Bert's normal clothing was bib overalls. In his farming years, he carried garlic in the pocket of his overalls, chewing on it during the day as he worked. Bert and Dale also had little faith in banks, they kept their money hidden or buried in tin cans. On birthdays and Christmas, it was their tradition that each of them gave each of the grandchildren $1.00. It was always obvious the money had been taken from a moist storage spot as it frequently carried a mildew odor that was covered up with perfume.

Minnie Dale died of a heart attack in 1958, Albert followed her in death in 1964. They are both buried in Woodlawn Cemetery, Montpelier.

(See related stories under Frederick Day, Melvin Day, Mark Day, Michael Day, Matthew Day, and Mitchell Day)

HOMESTEAD HISTORY OF PHILIP SHADLE

My great grandfather and his wife lived at 5065 West, 800 South, a homestead farm. They had 15 children and they never lost a baby at birth. He was a farmer and also a carpenter by trade in Chester Township. He must have been real successful because he got a farm and place for all his children to live, within a four or five mile radius of home base. I believe there were thirteen boys and two girls in this family. This farm has been in the Shadle family one hundred and forty years, with Francis Huffman living there now. There was a Snow Cemetery just across the section, you could see from home base, and the older Shadles were all buried there. My parents were both born in log houses. This is Paul Osborn reporting this news. I am a great grandson of this Mr. and Mrs. Philip Shadle.

Fern Crosby, Verlice and Catherine Crosby,;Marly and John Maddox, children: Michael, Dawn and Mitchell,;Richard and Barbara Crosby, children: Kent, Karla, Kraig and Kyle; Joy and David Liddy, children: Sarah and Travis-Taken 1983

SHADLE-STARR-MINNICH-CROSBY

Philip Shadle, 1825-1919, was a carpenter by trade. He hewed the logs to build the first substantial home of its kind in Chester Township. In 1845 he married Margaret Donnelly. He and his wife were the parents of fifteen children. Philip, with the assistance of his children, cleared 150 acres of virgin land, which he then farmed. He was interested in public affairs and became Trustee of Chester Township. Ada (1874-1959), one of his daughters, married Frank Starr, who was a farmer in Chester Township. Frank built a home for his family two and one-fourth miles north of keystone in 1900. Frank and Ada were the parents of eight children. Frank gave considerable attention to raising good horses. He displayed Percheron and Belgian horses in the "Horse Barn" at the Bluffton Street Fair in the '30's. One of these large teams pulled a wagon in the Street Fair parade which carried the band through the downtown streets of Bluffton.

Stella Murray, one of their eight children, was the mother of the late Wayne Murray

Pearl (1908-1976), another daughter, married Howard Habig, and together, they started "Habig Trucking" in Bluffton in 1935, a business which is still in operation.

Margaret (1900-1976), another daughter, married John Minnich, a farmer. They were the parents of six children: Ralph, Vera, Catherine, Robert, Roger and Nancy. Ralph (1918-1985), an employee of Meshberger Brothers married Berteen Stepp, and they have four children, eleven grandchildren and two great grandchildren. Vera (1921-1984) married Ernest Cochran. They have two daughters, seven grandchildren and two great-grandchildren. Scott Smekens (1964-1990), a young man well-known in Wells County, was a grandson of Vera and Ernie.

Catherine, the present bookkeeper of Habig Trucking, married Verlice Crosby, a farmer and former trustee of Chester Township. They moved to their present home at 2441W, 900S, Poneto, in 1945. They have three children, nine grandchildren and three great grandchildren. Their oldest daughter, Marilyn, a teacher in the Blackford County school system, married John Maddox, who farms and is an employee of Dana Corporation at Marion. They have three children: Michael, Dawn, and Mitchell; and also two grandchildren: Jordan and Casey. Their son Richard, a farmer, married Barbara Freeman, an employee of Peyton Northern. They have four children: Kent, Karla, Kraig, Kyle; and one grandson, John Michael. Their youngest daughter, Joy Liddy, is an x-ray technician in the Adams County Memorial Hospital in Decatur. She is the mother of Sarah and Travis Liddy.

Other children of Margaret and John Minnich are: Robert, living in Arizona with his wife Edith and three children and two grandchildren; Roger, a Franklin Electric employee, lives in Arkansas with his wife Lois, two daughters and two grandchildren; Nancy Thompson, their youngest daughter, is an employee of Wells Community Hospital and has two sons, James and Michael; and a daughter, Phyllis, who is a nurse at Lutheran Hospital. Phyllis is married to Reggie Hayes and has two daughters, Alice and Erin.

SHADY

On the south side of U.S. 224, about 1/2 mile east of State Road 1, in Lancaster Township, is a farm. On the front of the big red barn is painted the name "Shady."

This was the homestead of James Theodore Shady and Celesta (Davison) Shady. James always went by the name "Seat," and Celesta was known as "Lesta." James was born September 28, 1873 and died November 2, 1952. His parents were Martin and Margaret (Leeper) Shady, who lived near Tocsin. Celesta's parents were Milferd and Mary Ann (Gibson) Davison.

The Shady family dates back to William Shady in 1804 at Pennsylvania, parents unknown. He was bound out to a farmer with whom he lived until he was twenty-one years old. He spoke the German language, so he was either of German descent or he learned it from the farmer with whom he lived.

James and Celesta purchased forty acres of timbered land, clearing ten acres right away. In order to build the barn, they moved in a saw mill to cut the timber, which of course came from the farm itself. The barn was built first. They lived with a neighbor while the house was moved onto the land. It was during this time that they had their two oldest children. Later they again moved in the saw mill to cut timber to add on to the house. The rest of their children were born on the farm. They walked to the Eagleville one room schoolhouse on state Road 1. Their mother worried that they would freeze in the winter, but they all grew up and were educated.

James Theodore Shady and Celesta (Davison) Shady. 50th Wedding Anniversary picture

James and Celesta had ten children, five boys and five girls. The eldest was Cleo, a school teacher. She married Roy Davis. Harley, second in line, was a Methodist minister in the Northeastern district for sixty years. He married Mae Keller. Their third, Nellie, died as an infant. Mary worked at the Wells County Hospital, and married Scott Biddle. Leona lived most of her life around Murray and Bluffton and married Herman Gearhart. David married Elizabeth Duff and they live in Bluffton. Robert never married and lived at home until he died. Wendell Martin married Gaynell Bryant and worked for Zollner machine Works for thirty-two years. Wayne took over the farming for his father in 1932. He married Ruth Kizer. Nina was a telephone operator for Indiana Bell until she retired. She married Vance Davison in her later years.

James raised many turkeys and chickens. He was awarded numerous prizes at the Bluffton Street Fair. One of his prizes was a pump organ. It was shipped to Kingsland on the train and he went and picked it up with a wagon. It was a surprise to his family when he brought it home.

James never learned to drive a car, but was proud of the fact that he milked the cows until he was eighty-one years old. His youngest son, Wayne, now resides at the homestead. He has lived in a mobile home set behind the house since the death of his wife in 1987. His daughter, Linda, lives in the house with her husband and their four daughters.

MRS. DWIGHT (DOROTHY) SHADY

My grandfather, George Markley (1861-1941), was born in Wells County. He married Mary Ellen Arnold (1863-1888). Their children were Vernon, Jesse, and August. Later he married Lillian Gettle.

George and Lillian Markley

He taught school until 1893 when he started a grocery on West Market. He was on the official board of the Methodist Episcopal Church, and served twelve years on the Bluffton School Board. Their children were Harold, Paul, Edna, and Herman. Edna(1896-1976) was my mother.

My grandfather, Gillian Farling, was born in Nebraska, and married Sarah Elizabeth Houtz. They moved to Bluffton and opened a butcher shop on South Main. Grandma baked cakes and sold them on Saturdays. Their slaughter-house was on State Road 124 east. They had six children: Jane, Cloyd, Earl, Ethel, Skitz, and Edna. Cloyd (1891-1961) was my father.

Gillian and Elizabeth Farling

Dad took over this business and added groceries. It was Farling and Sons, first on Main, then West Market, and then north on Highway 1. (now Gerber Bros. Super-Valu)

Cloyd and Edna had five children: Harold, Dorothy, Lois, Cloyd Jr., and Betty.

Cloyd and Edna Farling

I, Dorothy, was born in 1914. While a junior at Ball State I started teaching dancing. My first recital was Nik Naks of 1931 and continued to 1941. I started school teaching at Covington, Indiana. In 1936, I married Carl (Shuey) Shewalter (1912-1941), son of Nancy and Harry Shewalter, a post office employee. They had another son, Hesper. Our daughter, Marcia Kay, was born in 1939. Shuey

Harry and Nancy Shewalter

was killed in an automobile accident. I went back to teaching for a total of thirty years at Lancaster, Rockcreek, Union, and Norwell.

At Lancaster I met Dwight Shady (1915-1979) son of John Shady and Bertha Miller. Bertha (October 18, 1879) was the first baby girl born in Craigville. They worked their two farms in Lancaster Township. Their children were Brooks, Helen, and Dwight. Dwight had two girls, Nancy and Sally, and I had Marcia. We married in 1944, and later added Linda and Terri. Dwight started his teaching as principal at Craigville in 1936., He taught 5th and 6th grades for thirty years at Lancaster, and six at Willshire, Ohio. He worked the two farms and sold life insurance. He was very active at Lancaster Chapel.

John and Bertha Shady

Nancy (1939-) married Linus Gerber who has Gerber Bros. Super-Valu at Bluffton, Ossian, and Berne. They have three children: Jackie married Rick Jenkins and has son, Chad and Benji; Jill married Mark Middaugh and has children, Megan and Jacob; and Jarrod.

Father of the year 1962

Sally Gomez (1941-) lives in Fort Wayne. She has four children: Jenny, who has served in the Gulf War 1991, Chris, Jason, and Michael.

Linda (1945-) taught school in Indianapolis and Greenwood. She married Gary Gearhart, and lives in Minneapolis. They have four children: Andrea, Anna Lisa, Angelina, and Andrew.

Terri (1953-) married Gary Worden who is in the construction business. She teaches at Norwell. They have two children, Nick and Kay.

I live on the farm in Lancaster township. Presently, my descendants are five children, fourteen grandchildren, four great-grandchildren, and many more to come!

(Mrs. Dwight (Dorothy) Shady)

LOUIS EDEN SHAFFER

Louis Eden Shaffer an his wife, Elva, came to Wells County (Bluffton) in 1931 from Fort Wayne, Indiana, during the depression to work for Claude Smith's father, David, a painter. Louis had worked for Bowser Manufacturing in Fort Wayne as a welder, until work went down to two days a week. They moved into an old cheese factory in Bluffton, after losing their home in Fort Wayne. Louis then worked as a hired hand on different farms in the area and later was employed by the State Forest, now Ouabache State Park. The Bluffton High School employed Louis as a janitor from 1943 until his retirement eighteen years later. An active member of the Epworth Methodist Church, he was treasurer for some time in the thirties and taught Sunday School. Louis lived out his life in Bluffton until his death in March, 1983, at ninety-seven years.

Lewis E. Shaffer and Elva Essa Woods Shaffer

Louis E. Shaffer was born at Dixon, Van Wert County, Ohio, December 20, 1885. He grew up in Van Wert County and as a young man worked on farms and was employed by the LE&W Railroad in 1903, until employment at Bowser Manufacturing in Fort Wayne, Indiana in 1917, when he moved to Fort Wayne. Louis E. Shaffer married Elva Essa Woods October 1, 1927, at Ohio City, Ohio. Their son, Archie James, was born August 1, 1929, in Ohio City, Ohio, on his grandfathers farm, and he grew up in Bluffton.

Archie James Shaffer married Mildred M. Earnest December 12, 1949, and they live near Murray, Indiana. Archie is an accomplished inside electrician and worked on the Southern Wells School when it was built. Now he works in control wiring, Phelps Dodge, Fort Wayne. They have five children: Gregory A., born October 23, 1952; Katherine Kay, born December 31, 1955; David Earnest, born August 21, 1958; Archie Jr., born November 17, 1959; and an adopted grandchild, Gregory Jr., born April 15, 1974. Gregory married Petra Baynes August 25, 1985, and they have one child, Christa Nicole, born May 11, 1987. Katherine Kay married Sam Schaefer May 18, 1975, and they have two children; Jennifer, born November 4, 1978, and Angela Kay, born October 2, 1980. They dairy farm near Vera Cruz, Indiana. David Earnest married Teresa Miller March 14, 1980, (divorced) and they have one child, Annett Marie, born September 2, 1981. David lives in Bluffton. He is employed by the Ouabache State Park and serves in the National Guard.

Louis's wife, Elva Essa Woods, was born February 6, 1893, in Highland County, Ohio. She was the daughter of James Fenton Woods and Clara Mae Boring Woods. Elva worked as a domestic as a young woman in Van Wert, Ohio. During the depression years in Wells County she took in laundry, and later was employed by General Electric in Fort Wayne as a matron until her retirement in 1958. She lived the rest of her life in Bluffton working and caring for families until her death September 20, 1967.

Joseph Fenton Woods, the paternal grandfather of Elva Essa Woods Shaffer, was born in Tyrone County, Eskelem, Ireland in 1834, the son of the Rev. Joseph Woods, who migrated to the United States with his two sons in 1842. Joseph married Rachel Ann Stout on March 30, 1858, and moved into a log cabin in Highland County, Washington Township, Ohio. They had seven boys and one girl: John William, born 1856; Henry, born 1858; Benjamin, born 1860; James Fenton, born 1862; Charles, born 1866; Frank, born 1867; Lavina, born 1872; and Joseph Jr., born 1874.

Elva's father, James Fenton Woods, was born in Sugar Tree Ridge, Highland County, Ohio, on March 9, 1862. He married Clara Mae Boring, February 17, 1886, at Wilmington, Ohio. They settled on a farm in Highland County, Concord Township, Ohio, until 1900 when they purchased a farm in Van Wert County, Ohio, and there they raised their six children to adulthood: Harry E., born June 27, 1887; Halder B., born August 7, 1890; Elva Essa, born Feb. 6, 1893; Dicie May, born Feb. 28, 1896; Dollie Elnore, born April 16, 1899; and Mary Marie, born November 4, 1901. They retired to Ohio City, Ohio, in 1933 to live out the rest of their lives.

SHAFFER-PLUMMER

Donald Wayne Shaffer (Jake) was born in Allen County but moved to Wells County in 1940. He grew up in Domestic and graduated from Petroleum High School. Don served in the Army from 1955 to 1958, and has been employed at Franklin Electric since 1955.

Judith Ann Plummer was born in Newark, Ohio, and grew up in Huntington, West Virginia, graduated from Huntington High School and attended Century College of Commerce. Judy has been employed at Moser Implement since 1979.

Don and Judy were married July 25, 1960, in West Virginia and moved to Bluffton. We moved to Petroleum in 1963. They are the parents of three children, all born in Wells County. They all attended Petroleum Elementary and graduated from Southern Wells High School. They have one grandson.

Mark Wayne born in 1961 is single, and has a son Tyler Wayne, born in 1982. Mark lives in Petroleum. Tyler attends Southern Wells Elementary.

Katherine Elizabeth, born in 1962, married Richard Garr from Los Angeles, California in 1990. They live in Bluffton.

Michael Charles, born in 1965, married Tonya Sue Nussbaum in 1988. They live in Berne. See Shaffer-Zuber and Plummer-Richardson.

SHAFFER-ZUBER

John Allen Shaffer 1875-1946, son of Lemuel Shaffer and Mother Steiner, and Harriet (Hattie) E. Markley, daughter of Jonathan Markley and Elizabeth R. Allen, were married in Wells County February 8, 1899. They were the parents of eleven children, Olga, Goldie, Herman, Leonard, Marie, Freida, Frances, Esther, Benny, Wayne, and Edward. Herman 1903-1964, was born in the village of Hen Peck in Wells County. His great-great-great-grandfather was Gabriel Markley who came from Germany about the time of the American Revolution.

Joseph Zuber 1874-1954, son of Mary Krummelvine (Germany) and Jacob Zuber (Switzerland), married Jessie Mills, 1879-1960, daughter of Catherine Kelley, born in Ireland 1839-1921 and William Mills, born in England 1839-1903. One of their children was born during their voyage. Joseph and Jessie had two children, Catherine Irene in 1908 and Louise.

Catherine married Herman Dwight Shaffer on April 7, 1926. They moved to Wells County in 1940, from Fort Wayne to begin farming.

Their children are Betty Louise, born 1927; Joseph John, 1929-1933; Robert Dwight 1931-1944; Eugene Burl, 1933; Donald Wayne, 1936; Lola Mae, born 1938; Judith Ann, born 1943; and James Allen, born 1951.

Betty married John Schlichter. They have three children: Larry, Connie, and Tom; and ten grandchildren. They make their home in Fremont.

Gene is married to Karen Heinzer from Germany. They have four children: Peggy, Linda, Jean Ann, and Jay; and five grandchildren. They live in Waukegon, Illinois.

Don married Judy Plummer from West Virginia, and they have three children: Mark, Kathy and Mike; and one grandson, Tyler. They are Petroleum residents.

Lola married Bob Myers, also of Wells County, and they have a son Robert and a daughter Ronda and two grandchildren. They live in Fort Wayne.

Judy married Don Huffman, also of Wells County, and they have three sons: Kevin, Brian and Travis. They live in Bluffton, as well as Catherine and Jim.

SHEETS

This Sheets family can be traced to two brothers, Andrew and Martin Sheets of Dauphin County, Pennsylvania. They left Pennsylvania and went to Rowen County, North Carolina, for a short time, then to Montgomery County, Ohio.

Martin Sheets died March 25, 1810. His wife, Margaret, died November 19, 1820. They were the parents of David, William, Martin, Susannah, Elizabeth, Henry, and Frederick.

Frederick Sheets, born July 1, 1781; died October 5, 1853, is buried at Bethel Church Cemetery, Phoneton, Miami County, Ohio. He married Margaret Niece. They were the parents of Jacob, John, Nancy, Eliza, Benjamin, and Catherine.

John Sheets, born June 4, 1816; died February 17, 1902, married Julia Ann Wyatt July 12, 1838. They were the parents of Sarah, Margaret, William, and Frederick.

William Sheets, born August 4, 1848, died January 2, 1926, married Malissa Jan Thompson on March 9, 1872. They were the parents of Mary Ann, Ella, Marie, Minnie Kate, Charles Frances, Stella Alice, Julie, Bessie, and Josie.

Mary Ann Sheets, born March 21, 1874, died December 11, 1957, married John Oliver Redding March 11, 1893. They were the parents of Charles, Josie, Edna, and Eldon.

Josie Redding, born May 11, 1896, died November 4, 1967, married Omer Creviston on September 7, 1915. They were the parents of Paul, Opal, John, and Ralph.

Opal Justine Creviston, born March 13, 1920, married Harry Burnett Lund August 20, 1940. They were the parents of Janet, Coleen, and Connie.,

Janet Lund, born February 20, 1942, married Donald Wolf. They were the parents of Thomas, born October 15, 1961, married to Sandra Hamilton; Richard, born December 14, 1962, married Malinda Mc Donald; and Randal, born October 10, 1965. Janet then married Ripton Dudley.

Coleen Lund, born July 14, 1944, married Kent Klipser. They were the parents of Camilla Rae, born November 15, 1965, who married Kenneth A. Taylor June 6, 1987. Coleen then married Eldon Rybolt, and they were the parents of Timothy Martin, born June 15, 1969. Coleen then married C. K. Robbins.

Connie Lund, born September 5, 1949, married Dennis Day August 16, 1969, parents of Ginger Renee, born May 22, 1970; Jeffery Michael, born June 28, 1971; and Jeremy Matthew, born April 6, 1979.

Edna Marie Redding, born February 1, 1899, married Jasper Waters February 5, 1921. They were the parents of Harold, Gerald, and Loren. Harold Waters, born June 16, 1922, married Martha Allen September 12, 1947. They are parents of Wayne, born October 14, 1948; and Gregory, born October 31, 1953. Gregory Waters married Jane Smekens November 17, 1984; and they are parents of Sara Lynn, born May 25, 1990.

Gerald Waters, born July 16, 1924, married Dorothy Harris November 18, 1951; and they are parents of Gary, born January 23, 1953, who married Donna Garbbard March 24, 1990; and Janice, born February 27, 1956; Linda, born April 5, 1957, married Bryan Peterson May 21, 1983.

Loren Waters, born Jaaury. 12, 1928, married Elizabeth Smith, September 12, 1952; and they were the parents of: (1) Michael, born March 30, 1955, died December 5, 1982; married Alicia Oestreich, December 14, 1975; parents of Chad, Tracey and Nicolle (2) Kenneth, born October 7, 1959; married Teresa Knowles, April 5, 1980; parents of Lindsey and Eric (3) Donald, born January 26, 1961; married Marvel Mason, June 1, 1979; parents of Donald, Marisa and Kasey (4) Donna, born January 26, 1961 (5) Effie Marie, born November 13, 1962; married Todd Eschenbacker, May 5, 1984; parents of Abbey.

William Eldon Redding, born February 28, 1902, died November 9, 1970; married Halcyon Pitzer, August 17, 1933; and they were the parents of Carol Jean, born August 11, 1941. Carol married David Neuenschwander, July 26, 1959; parents of Kenneth Wayne and Crystal Ann.

CARL OLDFATHER SHELLEY FAMILY

Carl O. Shelley was born October 19, 1900, the fourth child of David A. and Laura Etta Oldfather Shelley. He had three brother, Raymond, Paul and Lavere; and one sister, Glenn. Carl lived most of his life in Bluffton, graduating from Bluffton High School in 1918. His first job was at Starr's Ice Cream. Later he went to work for H. Thoma & Son.

During the Christmas season of 1918, he married Ila Mae Oswalt in Hillsdale, Michigan. Her parents were John and Christena (Ulmer) Oswalt. She was born in the Poneto area. She had three brothers: William, Clarence, and Cecil; all are now deceased.

Carl and Ila went to housekeeping in a three-room house at the back of the lot at 117 E. Cherry Street. All three of their children: Robert Eugene, Born in 1920; Carl William, born in 1925; and Elizabeth Ann (Betty), born in 1926, were born in the Cherry Street home. Later they moved to their home at 123 E. South Street.

While working for Thoma's, Carl served on the City Council for approximately six years. He continued to work at Thoma's until his death on April 3, 1958.

Carl's parents, David A. and Laura Etta (Oldfather) Shelley were charter members of what was then known as the Reformed Church. Carl and Ila were faithful members of the church now known as The First United Church of Christ.

Carl and Ila Shelley

After Carl's death, Ila stayed on at the home on South Street. Tt was much too large for one person, so she used the empty bedrooms to rent to relatives of patients who were in Caylor-Nickel Hospital. She made many friends who were so glad to have a room so close to their ill relatives. She continued to take in these people until her illness and death on August 26, 1978.

Their first child, Robert, graduated from Bluffton High School in 1938. He married Jessie M. Weist on November 2, 1941. He served in the U.S. Army from January, 1943, to December, 1945. After his discharge from the Army, he continued his work on automobiles and trucks until 1980. They are the parents of Janis Shelley Kaehr and James Carl. Janis has three children: Leanne, Kristen, and Clint. James has two children: Robert Douglas and Brian James.

Carl and Ila's second child, Carl William, graduated from Bluffton High School in 1943. He served with the U.S. Army during World War II and was a prisoner of war for seven months. He graduated from Indiana University and received his Master's degree from Ball State. He married Marceille Keplinger in 1953. He taught school in Noblesville and Fort Wayne until his retirement. They are the parents of: (1) Kathryn Kay whose children are: Dana Marie, Darla Kay, David William, Devin Anthony, and Daren Michael; (2) Karen Jean, whose children are: Aaron Lee and Christa Leigh; (3) Kevin Keplinger Shelley; and (4) Karlene Sue who has one son, Joseph William.

Carl and Ila's third child, Elizabeth Ann (Betty) graduated from Bluffton High School in 1944. She worked at the main office of the Morris Store after graduation. She married Ned Hoopingarner on November 24, 1948. Their children are: (1) Bruce E., whose children are: Scott Brian and Marc Bruce; (2) Nancy Jane, whose children are: Amanda Leigh and Megan Lynn; (3) Brian Dee; (4) Brice Wayne, whose children are: Kyle William, Travis Wayne, Kelli Ann, Caleb Brice, Allison Joy and Jordan Lane; (5) Brent Kevin, whose children are Cole Joseph, Jerod Michael and Chad Kevin; (6) Barry Joe, whose children are: Tyler Matthew and Wade Joseph; and (7) Bart Lane. Betty and her family moved to Florida where they still reside.

SHELTON-MALONE

Lisa Malone was born on December 12, 1969, youngest daughter of Jim and Marjorie Shelton of rural Ossian. Lisa attended Norwell High School and graduated mid-term of 1988. She was active in the 4-H Club and showed pigs and sheep several years along with homemaking and craft projects. After graduation she joined the Fort Wayne National Bank in their proof department, and a year later she transferred to the bookkeeping department full-time.

Lisa and Jeff Malone

On June 4, 1988, she was married to Jeffery Lynn Malone of Fort Wayne in the Zanesville United Brethern Church, where she is a member. Jeff and Lisa both play softball on the men's and ladies' church teams. Jeff is the son of Sue and Bill Conover, and Bill and Harriett Malone of Fort Wayne. Jeff graduated in 1984 from Wayne High School. For several years he worked for Scotts Food Stores; then in February of 1990 he joined the Manville Sales Corporation of Bluffton.

Jade Malone

Lisa and Jeff have a daughter, Jade Marissa, born on December 22, 1988. Jade stays in her grandma Shelton's day-care center each day while her parents work. They are expecting another addition their little family sometime in July.

JEFFREY SHELTON

Jeffrey Shelton, son of Jim and Marge Shelton of Ossian, was born on September 21, 1964, in Fort Wayne. He resided in Waynedale at 7206 Beaty Avenue and attended Waynedale School until he was eight years old. His parents moved to rural Ossian in 1973. Jeff then attended the Norwell schools and graduated from Norwell High School in 1984. While at Norwell he was vice president of his junior and senior classes. He also swam on the Aqua Knights Swim Team and while on the team he broke and held the backstroke record for several years. Jeff was also an active member of the 4-H Club. While in 4-H he showed pigs, sheep, cows, and participated in several other projects. He also showed the grand champion ewe for three years. While growing up Jeff played Little League, Teen League, and on the Zanesville United Brethern Church team. Jeff was also instrumental in organizing a slow pitch softball team which was sponsored by Mill Supplies. Jeff attended and graduated from Ball State University in May of 1988. There he received his Bachelor Degree in Business Management. After graduation he worked for Mill Supplies for two years as a salesman. In 1990 he joined the Prudential Insurance Company in their Fort Wayne Sales Department.

Jeff and Jill Shelton-February 1990

On April 28, 1990, he was married in the Zanesville United Methodist Church to Jill Spahr of Warren. Jill, the daughter of Max and Lois Spahr, graduated from Huntington High in 1984, and in May of 1988 graduated from Ball State School of Nursing in Muncie, Indiana. Jill now works for Lutheran Hospital in their Intensive Coronary Care Unit. Jill is the second of four daughters; her parents are farmers and big in the hog operation. Jill's mother is Director of Nursing at the Warren Methodist Home.

In 1988 Jeff purchased a house in Zanesville from Tom Ponsot at 10712 S. County Line Road. Jeff and Jill both reside there now and are very busy remodeling their own little home.

JIMMIE D. SHELTON

Jimmie Duade Shelton was born July 21, 1931, in Ripley, Mississippi, to a cotton and dairy farmer, John E. Shelton and Dessie Shelton. He moved to Bartlett, Tennessee, at age eleven. There he and his five brothers and five sisters helped on the family dairy farm and attended Bartlett School. After graduation in 1951, Jim joined the Air Force; he was stationed at Lackland Air Force Base in San Antonio, Texas; Warner Robins Air Force Base in Warner Robins, Georgia; Travis Air Force Base in California; and then in 1953 he was stationed at Loring Air Force Base in Limestone, Maine (which is seven miles from the Canadian Border). While stationed in Maine he met his wife Marjorie.

Jim and Marge Shelton-March 1990

Marjorie was born in Caribou, Maine, on April 2, 1936, and is the oldest of six daughters of J. Kenneth and Bertha Blackstone. She graduated from Caribou School in 1953. While growing up she helped on her parents' potato and dairy farm. She could swing a John Deere tractor around and slap a milker on a cow as well as any young man.

Matter of fact, she says she was more at home outside working than inside. All that changed after she and Jim were married on September 6, 1954.

While still in the Air Force and in Maine, a daughter, Mary Lou (see Rethlake) was born on June 27, 1955. In July, 1955, Jim was given an honorable discharge from the Air Force and they moved to St. Louis, Missouri, where Jim worked at MacDonald Aircraft until Delta Airlines called that they had an opening. Jim started working for Delta Airlines October 26, 1955, as a ramp service agent. In January, 1959, he was offered a promotion and transferred to Fort Wayne, Indiana. In 1990, Jim completed thirty-five years with Delta as a senior customer service agent. Jim is planning retirement in 1993. After moving his family to Fort Wayne, a son Jeffrey Allan (see Shelton, Jeff) was born. In May, 1973, they bought the Edwin Confer home on southeast corner of 1100 N. and 100 W. Marjorie runs a licensed Day Care Center out of their home. She is licensed for ten full-time and five part-time children and rarely has an opening.

Jim and Marjorie are members of the Zanesville United Brethern Church of Christ. Jim is also a member of the Zanesville Lions Club. Both are looking forward to retirement, as they love to travel and have been to Hawaii and other interesting places several times.

SHELTON-RETHLAKE

Mary Lou Rethlake, oldest daughter of Jim and Marjorie Shelton of Ossian, was born on June 27, 1955, at Loring Air Force Base in Limestone, Maine. When she was one month of age, the family moved to St. Louis after Jim was discharged from the Air Force. When Mary Lou was three, Jim was transferred to Fort Wayne. They moved into a house in Zanesville. They joined the Zanesville United Methodist Church in 1960. Mary Lou started school at Union Center, then they moved to Fort Wayne where she attended Waynedale School. In June, 1973, she graduated from Wayne High School. One week after graduation they moved back to Wells County. For three years she worked as a secretary at the Kresge Warehouse near Baer Field. In May, 1974, she married Kenton Howard Rethlake at the Zanesville United Methodist Church. They have resided in Waynedale since their marriage.

Kent is the oldest of two sons and two daughters of Phyllis and Harold Rethlake of Roanoke. He attended Indiana University (DGTS) of Fort Wayne, where he received his Associate degree in accounting. He works for Mill Supplies of Fort Wayne as their accountant. Ken also organized a farm league baseball team; the Zanesville Merchants have sponsored them for a second Little League since 1975.

May 1889-15th Anniversary
Kent and Mary Lou Rethlake, Jason (11 yrs.), Jessica (7 yrs.)

Mary Lou and Kent have two children: Jason Kyle, born May 11, 1978, a student at Miami Middle School; and Jessica Lyn, born May 17, 1981, a student at Waynedale School. Mary Lou is employed by Waynedale School as a Prime Time Aide.

In 1989, Mary Lou started experiencing severe headaches; within a month she underwent surgery at Lutheran Hospital. They were unsuccessful in removing the tumor and unsuccessful in attempting radiation treatment, so she went to the Mayo Clinic at Rochester, Minnesota. There Dr. Kelly rediagnosed the tumor as a central neurocytoma, an extremely rare tumor. Hers was the third they would do there, and there had been only twenty worldwide. The surgery was quite successful, and at this writing everything is fine. The clinic asked Mary Lou for permission to do blood samples for research, etc., and also wanted to write her case up in the Medical Journal. All her family members greatly praise medical science, but most of all rejoice and praise the Lord for his great miracles of healing and love.

MR. AND MRS. JESSE SHIELDS

Although Jesse and Mary Shields were not born and raised in Wells County, they spent the latter half of their life living in Jackson Township, Wells County.

Jesse Lawrence Shields was born March 26, 1888, to James and Eliza Grishaw Shields near Sharpsville, Indiana, Liberty Township, Tipton County.

Mary R. Graf was born September 30, 1885 to Joseph and Sarah Richards Graf, Windfall, Indiana, Wildcat Township, Tipton County.

Mr. and Mrs. Jesse Shields

Jesse Shields and Mary Graf were married August 4, 1909 in Tipton, Indiana. To this union three daughters were born: Gretchen L., Mildred V., and Margaret L.

Jesse was a farmer all of his life. While living in Tipton County near Sharpsville, Indiana, he was one of the first farmers in that area to grow soy beans. He also raised sugar peas for the canning factory in Tipton. In March, 1936, the family moved to Blackford County on a farm a mile west of Montpelier on State Road 18. They lived there for five years before moving to the farm in Jackson Township, Wells County on March 10, 1941, known as the Robert Kilander homestead. They rented the farm for five years before purchasing the eighty acre farm from Catherine Kilander Arnold and Cleo Kilander.

A tornado came through on March 19, 1948, striking the buildings....taking the beautiful big barn, garage and other storage buildings. The three story home withstood the storm damage.

As Jesse was a farmer all his life, his interest and hobby were in corn and small grains. He won many prizes at fairs and corn shows for his exhibits of single and ten ear displays. He was a member of the Indiana Corn Growers Association and a certified judge for five acre corn plots and small grains. He grew hybrid seed corn for many years and later sold hybrid seed for other growers. His livestock loves were the Brown Swiss cattle and Poland China hogs. He always had a few sheep around.

Mary was a farm wife and homemaker. She loved her flowers and garden and raised chickens for eggs, eating and selling. Her only work outside of the home was in tomato canning factories. She started in Sharpsville, then to Montpelier and retired from the Hartford Packing Plant, Hartford City. At the age of seventy-five, she had to give up working there due to the loss of the sight in her eye. She had worked for fifty years. She was a charter member of the Loyal Workers Extension Homemakers Club of Blackford County almost forty eight years.

Jesse passed away April 16, 1977, at age eighty-nine, after ten years of arthritis and finally a stroke. The livestock had been disposed of and they had rented the farm to neighbors.

Mary carried on with the farm until her death at age of one hundred and two, November 23, 1987.

The Shields home (known as the Kilander home) was the scene of many tours through the years, including the Wells County Historical Society, September 13, 1981; Blackford County Extension Homemakers clubs, September 21, 1978; plus many individual clubs and school tours.

When the estate was sold to Jay and Julia Tucker, the farm goes back to the McIntire side of the family. Jay's grandmother, Floy McIntire Tucker Rothenbush was a relative to Emily (Mrs. Robert) McIntire Kilander.

The love of Jesse and Mary's life was their children, grandchildren and great-grandchildren.

Gretchen married Earnest ""Earnie"" Garrett on June 30, 1940. They celebrated their fiftieth wedding anniversary June 30, 1990. They did not have children. They reside in Fort Wayne, Indiana.

Mildred married Wayne Albertson December 23, 1939. They had one son Robert. They lived in Montpelier, Indiana. Wayne passed away January 16, 1950. Robert lives in Fort Wayne, Indiana. He had a daughter, Michella, who passed away October, 1981; and a son Michael, also lives in Fort Wayne.

Margaret married E. Howard Keller March 7, 1943. They had a daughter, Martha. Howard passed away December 24, 1958. Martha lives in Lake Wales, Florida, with her husband, William Bair and children: Cinnamon Lee (twenty), and Eric M. (fifteen).

SHIGLEY

John Shigley married Barbara Potts in Jefferson County, Virginia in 1798. They migrated to Greene County, Ohio in 1803. They had five children: John L., Robert, Mary, William L., and George W. Their son George was born in 1806 and he married Barbara Fogle, September 2, 1826, in Greene County. Barbara was born in 1808. They had six children: John, Frederick, Susan (Israel Courtney), George, Rachel (Henry Alberson), land Samuel (Minerva Dewitt). Their son John was born in 1827 in Greene County and in 1828 the family came to Indiana (this was John and Barbara and George and Barbara). They settled in Tippicanoe County first and they bought their first land in Wells County January 16, 1851.

John Shigley

John and Maria's children were Janetta (Mike Gottschalk), George D. (Mollie Smith), Charity Jurdan, Lemual Orlando (Anna Lopp), and Martha (Nelson Rose). Lemual and Martha moved to Tippicanoe County but the other three stayed in Wells County. Charity married William Clay Johnson September 14, 1876, in Nottingham Township and they had nine children. They lived all their married lives on the farm of one hundred and fifty three acres across the road from the Shigley homestead and cleared by William. Janetta lived on a farm of one hundred sixty acres just to the east of William's farm (both in Section eighteen).

George (died April 8, 1900) and Barbara lived in Nottingham Township also. They paid Jacob Fogle (Barbara's father) five hundred thirty seven dollars for eighty acres of land in Section fourteen in Nottingham Township.

Charity and William's farmstead was very nice. The barn was very large and is listed in the Wells county Architectural Atlas. There was a large granary, a machine shed that was also a combination wood shed and garage, a summer kitchen and workshop (two rooms) that was over a cellar with river-rock walls and a smokehouse for their hams and bacons.

Marie died in 1876 and John married Mary (Gottschalk) Rose April 6, 1879. John's children were already married or almost but Mary had several small ones to be raised. Refer to Johnson, McKuras, Abbott/McDaniel histories.

SHIMER FAMILY

Obediah and Suzanna (Robinson) Shimer entered Wells County, Indiana after 1880 and settled on a farm about one mile south of Tocsin. They came from Richland County, Ohio, where they had both been born: he on December 9, 1840 to Mary C. (Catherine?) Dean and father undetermined, and Suzanna to Alexander and Margaret (Detwiler) Robinson on June 5, 1846. Alexander was the son of John Robinson, who was born in Ireland, immigrated to Westmoreland County, Pennsylvania, with his parents in 1784, and after fighting in the War of 1812 under General Anthony Wayne, removed to Richland County, Ohio, to settle, farm and rear his family. Alexander's mother was Margaret Nelson, also an Irish immigrant to Westmoreland County, Pennsylvania, and his wife, Margaret Detwiler, was born in 1818 in Franklin County, Pennsylvania, daughter of John and Anna (Ebert) Detwiler, who had also migrated to Richland County, Ohio, about 1838.

The father of Obediah Dean being unknown gives a mystery to his early life. Richland County Township school enrollment records in the 1840's do indicate his mother and the fact that she had two other children, Levi and Eliza Ann, believed to have been older than Obediah, who was referred to as "Obed. R." on several of the school records between 1843 and 1848. It was in October of that last year that he was recorded as living with Daniel and Maria (Aungst) Shimer, and he remained with them, assuming their surname as he approached manhood. Daniel and Maria were unable to have children of their own and had also taken another foster child, Nancy Underwood, age nine in 1850. A few years later they accepted into their home a third child, Asa Theo Myers, a nephew of Maria whose father had perished.

Rear, Left to Right; Verdie, Meadie, Ellen, Margaret, Clara, Florence. Middle, Left to Right; Obediah, Effie, Suzanna. Front, Left to Right; Sadie, Walter, Edith, Charlie, Emma

In August, 1862, Obediah Shimer enlisted into Company E, 102nd Ohio Infantry Regiment as a private as Belleville, Ohio. He served in military operations in Kentucky, Tennessee, and Alabama, and during that service contracted the measles, which left him considerably ill the last six or seven months of service prior to discharge in June, 1865. The illness left him with a residual damage to his lungs with which he suffered the rest of his life and also allowed his claim for a disability pension from the United States government in later life.

On September 3, 1867, Obediah married Suzanna Robinson and they began their lives farming and rearing their thirteen children in Worthington Township, Richland County, Ohio. The Ohio born children included: Effie Adaline (1868-1957) married to Joseph Richey and John Crowe; Margaret Maria (1869-1900); Asa Theo (1871-1873); Elmira Ellen (1872-1913) married to Daniel Webster Smalley; Verda Jane (1875-1916) married to Jacob Barger; Anna Almeda (1878-1933) married to Nelson Steele and John Gilbert; Clara May (1880-1963) married to Joseph Madison Breiner. The next child born establishes their time of removal to Wells County, Indiana, sometime between summer 1880 and summer 1882, and their remaining Indiana children included: Olivia Florence (1882-1896); Sadie Valzetta (1884-1975) married Marion General McCague in 1902 and lived their lives about three miles east of Ossian; Emma Henrietta (1886-1955) married Ernest F. Vanada; Charles Nelson Robinson (1888-1959) married Laura Louise Beck; Walter Ernest (1890-1911) who suffered a tragic death late on New Years morning while asleep in his buggy and was drawn in front of a passing train by his unrestrained horse; and their last born, Edith Adell (1894-1895). Almost all of their children remained to live for a time at least in Wells County, Indiana with their families.

Obediah was an industrious farmer and skilled carpenter who "raised" many local barns for his neighbors. He was a fastidious dresser and enjoyed having his picture taken in later years, especially with an automobile in his last years which he took much pride in. Suzanna died March 7, 1913, and around 1915 Obediah remarried, to the widow Martha Jane Haskell. She also preceded Obediah in death in 1919. He was accepted into Glory for a well earned after-life on October 8, 1923, a beloved father and husband, friend and neighbor; leaving a legacy of life for his many, many descendants that will proceed for time unknown.

SHIMER-MUSSER FAMILY

We date the arrival of the Musser family to 1941 when our father, Raymond "Buss" Musser came to Bluffton from Adams County. Dad met Theo Marie Shimer at the office of Drs. Brickley, Hamilton, and Mead, where Mom worked. Buss and Theo were married in November, 1942.

They lived in a couple of apartments before buying their only house at 727 S. Williams in 1944. They had three children: Monty in 1944; Michael "Mick" in May, 1947; and me, Rebecca "Becky" in March, 1953.

Dad always worked for the local General Motors dealership, first with Goodin Motors, then Kaade Motors until the time of his death in September, 1974.

Theo Marie and Raymond "Buss" Musser; September, 1973

In 1959, our mother went to work at the same place as our father, first in the bookkeeping department and then with our dad in the parts department. Mom continued to work for Kaade Motors and then Hiday Motors, until she retired on June 1, 1984. During her retirement she traveled and continued to play in a local bridge club which she had done for almost forty years. In 1987 Mom sold the house on Williams Street and moved to Lancaster Senior Apartments, where she lived until her death in May, 1989.

One of our fondest memories of having both parents work at the same place downtown was Street Fair week. At the garage my brothers were able to ride in the new cars during the Industrial Parade. We also were able to watch all the parades from the second story of the garage. During the week, I would go to the garage after school and Mom would let me ride the Merry-Go Round since it was right in front of the garage. After I rode it a few times she would take me down the block to play bingo and the duck game, as well as the coin toss for plates. We always had plenty of new plates and glasses after Street Fair. This was one of the best weeks of school!

My brother Monty also worked for Kaade Motors in the late 1950's and early 1960's, at which time he learned the body shop car repair trade. He now lives in Ocala, Florida. He has eight children and eight grandchildren, most of whom live in the Fort Wayne area.

My other brother, Mick, lives in Riverview, Florida, and works at Busch Gardens in the refrigeration department. He has a son and daughter along with two grandchildren. At this time, in February, 1991; his son is in Saudi Arabia in the army.

I married Paul Eugene Johnson from Uniondale in 1973. We live on South Marion Street which is only four blocks from where I grew up. My husband works at Franklin Electric. I have been working the last four years in the Harrison Township assessor's office at the Court House. My husband and I like to travel. At this time we have no children but we enjoy our time with our nieces and nephews.*(Becky Musser Johnson)*

SHOUP

This ancestry has been traced to Sebastian Schaub (1704) who came in 1740, from Switzerland to America on the ship "Friendship." His great-great-great-grandson, Thomas Nathaniel Shoup (1875-1946), was a son of Wells County by choice. His father, William H. Shoup married Adaline Myers (born in Wells County), daughter of John Myers and Nancy Griffin of Geneva. After Tom's early education in Elkhart County, he was issued a teacher's license (1895-1898). In 1897 he was issued a license in Wells County by County Superintendent, Robert W. Stine, in 1906 by a. R. Huyette, and in 1907 by Finley Geiger in Blackford County (Harriett Thoma's father). His teaching career spanned seventeen years, during which time he continued his education by correspondence and at Terre Haute University. In 1905 he spoke at the Teacher's Institute in Bluffton on "Race Relations." He taught at Petroleum along with his wife, Alice Hedges (died 1901), as well as at Nottingham, Hoover School (Melching Home on 116 S.E.), Smokey Row School (330S-600E) and the Poor Farm School in 1908 (near corner of 350 S. and County Farm Road). Here he introduced one of the earliest, if not the first, manual training courses in the Indiana schools. A picture of this work is displayed at the Wells County Historical Museum.

Roseann and Thomas N. Shoup

Thomas Shoup is also remembered for his teaching of music in all his one-room schools. The text, *American School Songs* (1908 by Hope Publishing Company, five cents per copy) included "a synthesis and practical set of exercises for review and drill in the Science of vocal music." Teacher Shoup expected all pupils to read music in all keys. In his Smokey Row School, a mahogany organ, adorned with red velvet stood across from the library.

Having an inadequate text for mathematics, he wrote one for all grades.

Literature, both prose and poetry, were loved by Tom, whose oral reading brought concepts to life. This was exemplified by his "library," which extended two shelves deep across one side of the schoolroom. History and geography were very important, as shown by pull-down maps. Also in that room, hanging above the maps, was George Washington's picture. A fly had crawled under the glass and had died right on his nose!

At times when Tom was reading poetry or prose, and loud singing of an inebriate with horse and wagon drove by the school, teacher Tom rushed out of the building and used prose of a different style to send the frightened rider on his way.

This teacher enriched the lives of many people in Wells County. His head was full of innovative ideas for which he had the ability to put into action.

In 1904 he married Roseann L. Biberstine, daughter of Emmanuel and Albertine (Bovine) Biberstine. In 1912 they retired to Rose's farm (6430E-350S) where they continued raising their family, all of whom became teachers: Mildred (Chiles) in Ohio, Edith (Bleezarde) in Massachusetts, and Robert in Ohio and Indiana.

Robert (1913-1975) a life-long resident of Harrison Township, Wells County, taught at Poplar Grove and Central School (1939-1946). In West Unity, Ohio, he was assistant high school principal. At Adams Central he was middle school principal before his retirement and death. He married Mary E. Hauk on December 24, 1938. Mary taught for thirty two years in elementary classes in Ohio and Indiana. At her retirement in 1979, she had taught twenty-two years at Columbian School. They have two children, Carol Ann Adams (Mrs. Charles) and William Shoup (married Judy Thinnes). Carol has Tom and Anne Link; Bill and Judy have Douglas, Steven, Scott, and Troy.

SHOWALTER

The Showalter family history in Wells County goes back to 1853.

William Showalter and his wife Polly (Brower) purchased land in Chester Township in November 1853. William was a full-time farmer. He and his wife had eleven children, one of whom was Abraham.

Abraham was born June 26, 1846, and married Mielma (Roberts) on February 17, 1870. They purchased land north of his parents place. He and his wife had nine children.

Ward and Mary Jane Showalter

William Elmer, son of Abraham, was born January 31, 1873. He married Eliza Jane (Jennie Macy) on August 20, 1902. Will was a farmer and a teacher who taught grades one through eight at the Scott School. He served as superintendent of the Keystone United Methodist Church for many years. He was Wells County recorder in 1932. His wife was a teacher also; she taught at the Keystone School and gave piano lessons. They purchased the land owned by Will's grandparents in February, 1908. They built a new house there in 1917. Will and Jennie had three children: Ruth, Keith, and Ward.

Ruth was born June 19, 1905, and died when she was twelve years of age.

Keith was born may 21, 1917, and graduated from Chester in 1933 and from Ball State in 1936. He married Grace (Grinstead) from Tipton, Indiana on December 27, 1936. They returned to Keystone to live with his parents. Keith taught social studies and coached basketball. Keith led the Chester Indians to their first basketball sectional championship in 1940. He was inducted into the Indiana Basketball Hall of Fame in 1978. Keith and Grace had two children Dalen and Wayne.

Dalen is Superintendent of schools in Glen Falls, New York. He was inducted into the Basketball Hall of Fame in 1987. Keith and Dalen were recognized as the first father and son to be inducted into the Hall of Fame.

Wayne is assistant principal at North Judson Schools in Indiana.

Will and Jennie's youngest son, Ward, was born on February 3, 1923. He graduated from Chester in 1941. On November 10, 1945, Ward married Mary Jane (Hannie). They lived in the home built by his parents. In addition to farming Ward sold insurance. In 1956 he started working for the Dana Corporation in Marion. He gave up farming in 1960 due to health reasons. Ward served as superintendent and on various committees of the Keystone United Methodist Church. He also served on the Chester and Southern Wells School Board. Ward and Mary Jane had three children: Ted, Kathy, and Kenneth.

Ted graduated from Southern Wells and Ball State University. He married Tamara (Dick) on November 2, 1974. They have two children: Eric and Amy. Ted and Tamara moved back to Wells County in 1984 and bought the family home when Ted's mother decided to move to Bluffton. Ted teaches social studies at Southern Wells School.

Kathy graduated from Southern Wells and Fort Wayne Bible College. She lives in Dayton, Ohio, and works for NCR.

Kenneth graduated from Southern Wells in 1980. He lives in Bluffton and works for the Manville Sales Corporation.

ELWIN DEE SHULL

Elwin was born April 22, 1931, at Berrien Springs, Michigan. He is the son of Francis and Ruth Johnson Shull. His identical twin brother, Edwin Lee, died two days after birth. At the age of two Elwin moved with his parents and older brother and sister to Rockcreek Township, Wells County, Indiana, to the home of his maternal grandparents, Glessner and Rachel Butler Johnson. Elwin attended Rockcreek Center School through eighth grade. He then transferred to Indiana Academy at Cicero, Indiana, a Seventh-day Adventist boarding school for high school students. Elwin graduated from there in May 1949. That fall he enrolled at Emmanuel Missionary College (now Andrews University) at Berrien Springs, Michigan.

While at Indiana Academy Elwin became friends with Marilyn Broglin, a fellow classmate from Bedford, Indiana, and they were married. Elwin continued his education, and Marilyn worked. Their first child, Teresa Kay, was born November 22, 1952. A son, Mark Edwin, was born July 27, 1954. Elwin graduated from Andrews University in June of 1954 with a Bachelor's degree specializing in chemistry, math, and education. Elwin obtained a job teaching in the Seventh-day Adventist elementary school in Muncie, Indiana. Their third child, Kurtis, was born May 14, 1956, in Muncie.

Marilyn, Kurt, Teresa, Ed, Elwin

Elwin taught in a number of different elementary school, including South Bend and Indianapolis, Indiana, and Riverside, California. He also taught science at his alma mater, Indiana Academy, and at Broadview Academy in LaFox, Illinois. For two years Elwin was principal of Broadview Academy. He finished his teaching career back at Indiana Academy and bought a home in a rural setting, four miles west of the Academy.

FRANCIS ELLSWORTH SHULL

Francis Shull was born in Galesburg, Illinois, December 8, 1903. His father was John Howard Shull; his grandfather Frederick A. Shull, born in Pennsylvania. His paternal grandmother was Emma Ellsworth, born in Vermont. Francis' mother was Rachel Estella Giveler. Her father and mother were Samuel M. Giveler and Frances M. VanDivinder of Pennsylvania. Samuel Giveler's father and mother were Jacob and Rachel Giveler.

Francis married Eunice Ruth Johnson, daughter of Glessner and Rachel Butler Johnson, September 1, 1925, at her home in Rock Creek Township in Wells County.

Francis Ellsworth Shull, Eunice Ruth Johnson Shull

Ruth was born April 7, 1900. She attended two years at the Rockford Seventh-day Adventist elementary school; then she finished at the Rockford School at the back of her father's property. She recalled walking to school through the fields on the crusted snow, which sometimes covered the rail fences. She was a bright student and was allowed to skip one grade. She graduated from Liberty Center High School in 1916. Ruth entered school at Emmanuel Missionary College (now Andrews University) in Berrien Springs, Michigan, that fall and graduated in 1920 with a degree in English and education. She began teaching at Fox River Academy near Ottawa, Illinois, where she met Francis, who was a student.

Following their marriage, they moved to Emmanuel Missionary College and Francis began ministerial study. Four children were born to them there: Vivion Earl, Jeannine, Elwin Dee, Edwin Lee. Edwin Lee lived only two days.

In 1933, entrapped by the great depression, Francis left college to find support for his family. They moved to the farm in Wells County, Indiana, where his wife had been born and reared. He helped his father-in-law on the farm cutting wood, milking cows, etc. Francis worked eight weeks in Tennessee, returned to Indiana, and obtained work with Jesse Dunn, a local carpenter, for about a year. When the United REMC brought electricity to rural Wells County, Francis supplemented his income by wiring houses, then plumbing. Occasionally he helped Charles Roth with the farming of the home place. Francis bought the Johnson home place upon the death of Rachel Johnson in 1943. He began farming but continued to do electrical and plumbing work. After the children left home, Francis attended school in Fort Wayne, learning to repair radios and TV's and Ruth refreshed her teaching skills at Ball State University. Ruth taught third and fourth grades in Markle one year; fifth grade at Union Center, eight years; and Kindergarten at Rock Creek Center, two years before retiring. Ruth passed away February 3, 1986 from congestive heart failure.

Francis and Ruth were lifelong members of the Seventh-day Adventist Church.

VIVION EARL SHULL

Vivion was born May 26, 1927, at Berrien Springs, Michigan. He is the son of Francis and Ruth Johnson Shull. At the age of six he moved with his parents, younger sister Jeannine, and younger brother Elwin to Rock Creek Township in Wells County. There they lived with his maternal grandparents, Glessner and Rachel Butler Johnson, on their farm just north and west of Rockford. Vivion attended Rock Creek Center school from grade one through nine. He went to boarding school at Cedar Lake Academy in Cedar Lake, Michigan, for grades ten through twelve and graduated in May, 1945. Viv was drafted into the armed forces near the close of World War II and spent a year in the navy at Great Lakes Naval Training Station near Chicago and at Treasure Island Naval Base in San Francisco Bay, California. At the close of his service in the armed forces, he used the GI bill and enrolled at Emmanuel Missionary College (now Andrews University) near Berrien Springs, Michigan.

Donn, Julie, Virginia, David, Vivian

During his schooling at Cedar Lake Academy, Viv met Virginia Strudwick from Muskegon, Michigan. They were married August 22, 1948, after his second year of college. Ginny had also completed a year of college. Ginny worked while Viv completed his college education. He graduated in August, 1951, with a Bachelor's degree in chemistry. Viv worked as a chemist for Studebaker Corporation in South Bend, Indiana, and they lived in Niles, Michigan.

A daughter, Sandra Sue, was born to them, May 5, 1950. On February 21, 1952, another daughter, Julie Jo, was born in Niles. Sandra Sue was stricken with polio and recovered. However, on January 26, 1953, she died of spinal meningitis and was buried in the cemetery in Niles.

Viv was laid off work when Studebaker auto sales dropped drastically. The family moved to Chattanooga, Tennessee, where Viv worked for Combustion Engineering for six years and then for Tennessee Products Chemical Corporation for four years. Donn Alan was born April 14, 1955; then David Scott was born January 20, 1961. In 1964 they moved to Livonia, Michigan, where Brian Douglas was born March 15, 1966. In 1968 Viv took a position with Michigan State University and moved to Holt, Michigan. He is an academic specialist, teaching and doing research in analytical electron microscopy for the Center for Electron Optics and the physics/astronomy department.

Viv purchased a home and two acres of fruit trees south of Holt and is enjoying his hobby of fruit farming. Julie Jo married Donn Clark of Owosso, Michigan. They have two children: Matthew Arden and Candace Jennifer. Donn Alan married Laila Mashni of Detroit, Michigan. David Scott married Judy VanDuinen of Berrien Springs, Michigan. They have two children: Eric Scott and Adam David.

SHULTZ

The Galen H. Shultz family moved into Jackson Township on April 26, 1946. Our roots are from Huntington County. The name Shultz means mayor of the town in its original home of Germany, and Galen was the name of a famous German doctor.

Our family came to Wells County from Sycamore, Illinois, where Galen had been transferred during World War II. He was a foreman at Anaconda Wire and Cable in Marion, Indiana, before going to a defense plant in Illinois.

The farm we live on, known as the Amos Swope Farm, is owned by Repco Farms, Inc., originally owned by members of the Weaver Popcorn Company, VanBuren, Indiana.

Galen and Shirley Shultz

Galen Hoover was born September 10, 1914, to Charles and Jeanette (Hoover) Shultz. Shirley Bell was born April 21, 1914, to E. Russell and Glagie (Myers) Allen. They attended school in Huntington County and graduated high school at Lancaster and Jefferson schools.

They were married December 24, 1932, and lived in Lancaster Township until 1943. Two of the four children were born in Huntington County.

Peggy Dehn was born October 1, 1933; and Donald Edwin, June 8, 1935. After the family moved to Illinois Jo Anne was born February 3, 1945. When World War II ended in 1945, we moved back to Huntington County before moving to Jackson Township. Mack Harrison was born December 11, 1947.

Galen and Shirley spent their years farming and raising popcorn as a principal crop. Galen also worked off season at Salamonie Mills, Warren, Indiana, and Weaver Popcorn Company at VanBuren, Indiana.

They are both active members of the Asbury Chapel Methodist Church. Galen is a Mason, Scottish Rite and Shrine member; Shirley is an active member of local and county Wells Extension Homemaker Club, Past President of Wells County 4-H Association and Wells County Extension Homemakers.

Our family numbers forty five at present::

Peggy Dehn married Norman Ray Schweikhardt May 13, 1951. They are the parents of Michael Ray, Michelle Ann, Matthew Dean, and Melinda Jo. All are married, and adding one grandson and seven granddaughters.

Donald Edwin married Shirley Ann Williams July 21, 1956. They are the parents of Kris Edwin, Kelli Ann, Kevin Ray, and Kerry Lynn. All are married and have added one granddaughter and seven grandsons.

JoAnne married Bruce Albert Stanton October 18, 1969, and they have two daughters, Jan Marie and Katie Jo.

Mack Harrison married Valerie Margaret Knecht on May 15, 1971, and are parents of Mack Harrison, Jr. Mack was a Marine pilot who lost his life off the coast of Beaufort, South Carolina, on March 14, 1974.

Our children and grandchildren live in Warren, Fort Wayne, Garrett, and Wells Counties, Indiana.

Our family occupations are farming, farm related milling company, insurance, factory, retirement home, truck driver, flower shop, computer related, office equipment, lawyers, school teacher, school secretary, government, correctional institution.

We, the parents spend our summers in Indiana,and winters in sunny Florida.

(Galen and Shirley Shultz)

SHUTT-MILLER

The Shutt family dates back to the early years of Huntington County. Guy and Ethel (Yates) Shutt moved to Union Township, Wells County in 1923. Both Guy and Ethel had a farm background and Guy worked the H. W. Lipkey farm near Uniondale until his death in 1940. To this union were born three sons: Max, Rex, and Guy, Jr. Max lived most of his life in Wells County working as a contractor and is now deceased. Guy, Jr. lives in Kentland, Indiana, and works for the Garst Seed Company after having been a private contractor and an employee of Standard Oil Company.

The Miller family was instrumental in the early development of Wells County. Being farmers, William and Susan Miller settled in Rockcreek Township. A son, John B. married Etta Ditzler and moved to Bluffton. He was employed by the Studabaker Grain Company for a few years. Later he moved his family to Uniondale, where he owned the Miller, Brickley Grain Company for many years. From the union of John B. and Etta were born six daughters and one son: Lela, Mabeline, Naomi, Mary, Margaret, Marceille, and John.

Rex and Marceille Shutt
Fiftieth Wedding Anniversary; November 2, 1990

Marceille worked for several years in the office of Morris 5 & 10 in Bluffton. Rex Shutt was engaged in farming with his father on the Lipkey farm. He took over the farming operation upon the death of Guy, his father, in 1940.

Rex and Marceille were married in November, 1940, and continued the operation of the Lipkey farm until 1951, when they purchased their own farm in Union Township.

They had one son, Jerry L., who received his Bachelor's degree from Indiana University and his Master's degree from the University of Michigan. He is now Vice President of Marketing Service in the office of Bradford Life Insurance Company at Lexington, Kentucky. He married Gloria Pace in 1971 and they have two children: Randall S. and Anita M.

Rex and Marceille spent a busy life on the farm and working for their church, St. Mark's Lutheran Church in Uniondale.

Rex was a member of the Wells County school reorganizational committee that formed the plans for the three school systems we have operating at this time. He served on the first school board of Norwell School for four and one half years.

Agriculture being his life, Rex was a member of the Wells County A.S.C.S. committee for twenty-four years and served several years as chairman.

Rex and Marceille, being dairy farmers, were confined by the operation until 1966, when they sold their dairy herd and continued grain farming. They retired in 1980 and live on the farm during the summer months. They purchased a home in Bradenton, Florida, in 1980 and have since spent the winter months there.

LEO AND EMMA SIELA FAMILY

Leo and Emma Nelson Siela made a home in Wells County in the early 1920's. They lived in several locations in Bluffton, Nottingham Township and Union Township. With a growing family they moved in and out of the county over a period of years. In 1935 they purchased a farm in Rock Creek Township.

They became the parents of thirteen children. Times before 1935 were hard and diseases were very prevalent. In the early 30's rheumatic fever and pneumonia claimed the lives of some of their children.

Mr. Siela, who became known for his apple orchard, passed away in 1956. Mrs. Siela passed away in 1981.

Five of their sons, Delmar, Bob, Dwight, Gerald, and John; and a daughter, Beverly, are still in the area with four of them still living in Wells County.

A daughter, Beverly and her husband, Claron Boots, still live on the family farm in Rockcreek Township.

SILLS FAMILY

Two Sills brothers came to America from Hesse-Darmstadt, Germany, in the late 1700's. They settled in Bedford County, Pennsylvania. The second brother, Michael, was the ancestor of Claude Lowell Sills, my father; and the first brother was the ancestor of the Claude Mendenhall Sills and his family in the southern part of Wells County.

Albert D. Sills and Ethel King Sills

My great-grandparents, Michael Sills and Mary Elizabeth Murray Sills, lived south of Warren. After Michael's death in 1907, his widow lived her last years at the homes of her children, passing away at the home of her daughter, Sarah Jane Batson, in Wells County near Mt. Zion.

Michael and Mary Sills' son, Albert D. Sills, my grandfather, married Ethel King, daughter of Benjamin and Jane McNatt King, in 1900. Their children were Jesse, Russell, Ralph, Cletus, Claude, Hugh and Inez. At this time, Claude L. Sills is the only surviving sibling.

Claude L. Sills married Mary Jane Stogdill in 1934 and they started their family of two girls, Constance (Connie) and Carolyn. Now there are six grandchildren and five great grandchildren.

Claude has been a mechanic, truck driver, and car salesman prior to his retirement.

When the State Road 1 bridge was being built, Claude worked for Habig Trucking. One day, he decided to paint his truck and shine it up. He just got finished and he got a call to make a delivery to the bridge construction sight. Mr. Habig never let him live down how his freshly painted truck looked after hauling in all that dirt and dust.

In 1942, our family moved to follow job transfers and in 1955 we moved back to Bluffton, when Claude was working for Renner's Express Trucking. After retiring from truck driving, he sold cars several years before completely retiring.
(Connie Sills)

SILLS-HITE

On November 15, 1903, a son, Claude M., was born to Leander P. and Della Mae Mendenhall Sills. She was a daughter of Eli and Catherine Wagner Mendenhall. Leander's parents were Phebe Jane Fuller (1853-1898) and Daniel Sills (1855-1877).

Claude had the misfortune of losing his mother at the age of six years in 1909. He started his schooling at Popejoy School in Liberty Township. He later went to Slacum in Chester Township. He graduated at Liberty Center High School in 1923. He was active in sports and always interested as a spectator all of his life.

After high school he obtained work at Bluffton in one of the piano factories as a polisher. From there he went to an auto factory in Toledo, Ohio. In Toledo, Ohio, on September 17, 1934, he married

Margaret Joann Hite, daughter of Samuel V. and Ella Broyles Hite of Huntington County. Both of my parents were born in Fairfield County, Ohio, but moved to Huntington County, Indiana, at an early age. My father's people were Swiss-German, and my mother's were Irish.

In 1934, Claude started farming; then in 1937 he purchased the Holsinger farm on 500W Liberty Township. There he lived until his death on September 16, 1982.

Born in Bluffton on December 14, 1941, was their only child, Jack B. Sills. Jack, too, attended Liberty Center School and graduated from there in 1959. After that he did factory work for eight years and then went into farming.

On August 4, 1963, he married Joyce M. Roberts, daughter of Earl and Kathryn Maddux Roberts of Rockford, Indiana.

On July 30, 1964, Travis J. was born and on August 22, 1966, twin daughters were born; Jan Marie and Jean Ann sills.

Travis farms for his mother. Jan is a certified public accountant in Fort Wayne; and Jean is married to Gary Halcomb of Knightstown, Indiana. They have three sons, Jared Keele, Nathan Tyler, and Mitchell Evan.

On September 30, 1989, Jack died at Wells Community Hospital of a heart attack.

In 1895 my parents moved to Jackson Township, Wells County, on the Lounsbury Lease. Housing was hard to find, so they lived in a two-room log cabin until my father built two rooms onto it. He worked for the Ohio Oil Company until 1903, then went to the Grant County fields for seven years. My older four brothers and sisters lived in Wells County, but my younger brother, Wayne D. Hite, and I did not until later. In 1910 they moved back to Huntington County, then later to the Oklahoma fields, where I spent part of early schooling. I then graduated in 1930 at West Rockcreek High School. *(Margaret Hite Sills)*

JACK B. AND JOYCE M. SILLS FAMILY

The Jack B. Sills family started with the marriage of Jack B. Sills to Joyce M. Roberts on August 4, 1963. Marriage vows were recited at the South Liberty Christian Church, in Liberty Township, Wells County, Indiana. Jack was the son of Claude M. Sills and Margaret J. (Hite) Sills and was born on December 15, 1941, in the Wells County Hospital, Wells County, Indiana. Joyce was the daughter of Francis Earl Roberts and Jennie Kathryn (Maddux) Roberts and was born on November 19, 1941, at their home in Rockford, Indiana.

They started housekeeping in Salamonie Township, Huntington County, Indiana. Joyce was working at the Caylor-Nickel Clinic in Bluffton, Indiana, at the time of marriage, and Jack was working at the 3-M plant in Hartford City, Indiana, and farming part time with his father.

While they lived in Huntington County, a son named Travis J. was born on July 30, 1964, at the Caylor-Nickel Hospital, Bluffton, Indiana.

Jack changed jobs in 1965 and started working at Franklin Electric Company in Bluffton, Indiana, while still farming part time.

In January 1966, Jack and Joyce purchased a farm located in Liberty Township, Wells County, where Joyce is still residing. They moved from Huntington County to Liberty Township on July 4, 1966. Twin daughters, named Jan Marie and Jean Ann were born on august 22, 1966.

All three children attended and graduated from Southern Wells High School. All three children also attended Purdue University, where Jan graduated.

Jean was married to Gary Halcomb from Henry County, Indiana, on June 23, 1986. They have three sons, Jared Kele, born January 9, 1987; Nathan Tyler, born June 15, 1988; and Mitchell Evan, September 7, 1990.

Jan is a certified public accountant working and living in Fort Wayne, Indiana. Travis lives in Liberty Township, Wells County, Indiana, on the home farm and is engaged full time in a grain farming and beef cow-calf operation.

Jack worked for a short period at CTS in Berne, Indiana, and also for Baker Implement Company in Warren, Indiana. He started farming full time in 1970 and farmed until the time of his death. He suffered a severe heart attack in the fall of 1986, and thereafter slowed down a bit. Instead of farming full time, he farmed part time, worked as a grain buyer for NFM of Poneto, Indiana, and helped with a straw baling operation which sold straw to the Campbell Fresh Company for growing mushrooms.

Joyce did not work outside the home after her children were born, until the year 1977 when she started working for Federal Land Bank Association, Bluffton, Indiana, and worked there until the fall of 1985. In the spring of 1986 she started working for the Wells County Agriculture Stabilization Conservation Service, which is a branch of the United States Department of Agriculture where she is still presently employed.

Jack suffered another heart attack in the fall of 1989 which was the cause of his death. He died September 30, 1989, and is buried in the Mossburg Cemetery, Liberty Township, Wells County, Indiana. Joyce stills lives on the home farm in Liberty Township, Wells County, Indiana.

SIMERMAN

Roger and Mary Belle Simerman live at 11585N 600 East, Wells County.

Roger is the son of Burr and Dollie Simerman, whose home was on 1100 East, Roger's birthplace. Mary Belle is the daughter of Ermal and Anna Hodson of Fort Wayne. She was born in Delaware County near Muncie, Indiana.

They were married on June 18, 1944 (Father's Day), in the Hebron United Brethren Church. It was located on the corner of 1050N and 500 East. Roger's grandfather Snyder helped build the church; it was later sold to John Simerman and torn down by Roger, his two sons, and John's two sons. June 18, 1944, was the hottest June 18 on record and the record still stands!

Two sons, R. Stephen (Steve) and Lanny L.; and a daughter, Janice S., were born.

Steve graduated in 1963 after twelve years at the old Ossian Grade and High School. Lanny also graduated from Ossian in 1964. Janice was a freshman when the new Norwell School opened, graduating in 1971.

Steve was a member of National Air Guard after graduation, and later married Sue Nycum, a graduate of Elmhurst of Fort Wayne. They live on the Allen-Wells County Line Road and are the parents of three children: Robin, Shelly, and Ronald.

Robin graduated from Heritage (near Hoagland) in 1989, and is now a student at Ivy Tech studying electronics. Shelly graduated from Heritage in 1990, and is now a student at I.P.F.W. at Fort Wayne, studying Medical Research. Ronald is a student at Heritage and will graduate in May, 1991. He then plans to go to college.

Lanny was drafted into the U.S. Army after graduation. Janice Henry, a graduate of Ossian, became his wife. Lanny served one year in Vietnam. They live on 200W in Wells County. Lanny and Janice are the parents of three children: Kimberly, Jeffery, and Jerry.

Kimberly graduated from Norwell in 1988, and is now a third year student at St. Frances College in Fort Wayne, studying psychology. Kimberly will be married to Quent Thompson on June 1, 1991. Quent is the son of Norman and Caroline Thompson, formerly of Zanesville.

Jeffery graduated from Norwell in 1990, and is now a student at North Manchester College, studying accounting.

Jerry is a sophomore at Norwell, and likes to farm.

Janice enlisted in the U.S. Navy after graduation. She later served at the San Diego Naval Base where she met her future husband, Michael Tryon of Michigan, also in the U.S. Navy. They were married at the Chapel on the base. Jan and Mike are the parents of two sons: Stuart and Eric.

Stuart is finishing his sophomore year at Cassopolis, Michigan, High School. Eric is in the sixth grade at Cassopolis, Michigan. The family resides near Union, Michigan.

Roger was a farmer and has now retired. Roger and Mary Belle purchased their farm on 1100N in 1947, and they still reside there.

BURR IVAN SIMERMAN

Burr was born October 21, 1890, the oldest of three sons of Mary Lula Summers and John Henry Simerman. His mother died from complications of child birth when he was nine. He then went to live with his mother's parents, William Henry Summers and Margaret Pierce; and later his Uncle Park Summers, until his father married his wife's cousin, Lilly Smith Niblick, who had two children of a previous marriage. They moved into 10618N-600E and lived as one family.

Burr married Dollie Snyder October 27, 1909, and later bought a farm at 6195E-1100N. He was a prominent farmer and on the school board when the Ossian High School was built. He died November 25, 1961, of colon cancer and was buried in Oaklawn Cemetery in Ossian.

Dolly Snyder Simerman, the daughter of Lewis Snyder and Mary A. Caston was born September 16, 1889, lived at 11216N-500E with three brothers and three sisters. She married, then moved a mile east to live the rest of her ninety years in the same house.

She was a very religious person, was very active in church and attended every Sunday as long as her health permitted. She was very interested in family history and collected stories, pictures, dates, and names so that she left behind a great legacy of family information.

She was also interested in every one around her and kept many scrap books of newspaper clippings dating back to the 1920's. She fell at the age of ninety and broke a hip. The doctors felt she was to old and frail for an operation and she finally died, January 20, 1988, outliving practically all her generation and too many of the next, of which she was fond of reminding you.

JOHN F. SIMERMAN

John F. Simerman was born September 14, 1831. Reportedly he came to Indiana from Virginia along with two brothers. On February 6, 1862, he married Isabella Judd, the daughter of John Judd and Anna M. Double. They had two sons, John Henry and George H.

Isabella died on September 11, 1870. She is buried in Elhanan Cemetery in northeast Wells County under her maiden name.

John married two more times and had two other sons, Everett and Marcellus. His other wives' names are not known. We know that he died from injuries received from a kick from a horse and that his coffin cost $15.00, but the date of his death and his burial place are unknown.

JOHN HENRY SIMERMAN

John Henry Simerman was born on November 8, 1862. He was the elder of two boys born to John F. Simerman and Isabella Judd at their home on 1000N near the Adams-Wells County line. His mother died when he was seven years old.

John Henry married Mary Lula Summers and had three sons: Clem Henry (May 12, 1893-October 4, 1965), Burr Ivan (October 21, 1890-November 25, 1961), and Vance Vernon (June 13, 1895-January 4, 1964). Mary Lula was the daughter of William Henry Summers and Margaret Pierce, who lived just south of the Allen-Wells County line on 750E. She died on June 9, 1900, at the age of thirty one; and was survived by three days by her infant daughter, Margaret. They are buried side by side in Elhanan Cemetery, east of Ossian. The boys were "farmed out" to relatives until John Henry's second marriage to his wife's widowed cousin, Lillie Smith Niblick. They set up housekeeping at the house presently at 10618N 600E with John Henry's sons and Lillie's two daughters, Iva and Ethel. Six more children were born to this couple: Marvin, Denver, Lawrence, Iliff, Esther, and Ellery. John Henry farmed until his death in 1928. He was buried in Oak Lawn Cemetery in Ossian.

JOHN L. AND LUCILLE SIMERMAN

John is one of five children born to Burr Ivan and Dolly Snyder Simerman. John attended the Beck country school until on the last day of school it burned down. He remembers that he was in the fourth grade. He then attended and graduated from Ossian High School. When he was eighteen he traveled on the train around the west picking apricots, cherries, and seeing the country.

He married Lucille Kansas Smith September 5, 1940, in Alexandria, Kentucky. He bought a farm located at 10612N-500E and worked at Zollner Pistons thirty-four years. He got up at four thirty and fed up to two hundred and fifty hogs, then picked up six riders and drove them to work, worked eight hours, drove them home, and ate supper. Then he would feed the hogs, milk the cows and farm eighty acres. Because of all this endeavor he was able to purchase more land and property. He retired from Zollners and spent his time fixing up old houses and renting them.

He had a great love of travel and every year he took his family from state to state. He was a great inventor, he holds a patent on a new type of step ladder. He was very active in church, never missing a Sunday if possible.

Lucille Kansas Smith, the daughter of Wayne Smith and Rose Wilson, lived at 16707 Winchester Road, walked to school in Poe, Indiana. Her father was burned to death when she was fourteen, leaving her with her mother and two younger sisters to farm during the depression era. She helped work the farm with a team of horses. She graduated from Ossian High School.

She met John on a blind date and they were married. She raised three children: David, Judy, and Lew, and kept very busy on the farm. In 1963 all three children left home within five weeks of each other by marriage or air guard.

Instead of becoming depressed, she and John took a chicken coop, cleaned it out, lined the walls with knotty pine and shelves and picked weeds which she made into flower arrangements. She put a notice in the paper and started selling them. The business grew till she decided to move it to Poe where she and john bought Poe Grocery. This kept growing till it was mostly flowers with some bread and milk. When John retired from Zollners he wanted to travel, so she closed the florist shop and they traveled.

She got bored in 1980, so she and her daughter, Judy, went back to the original shop on the farm and opened it again. This grew until they moved the House of Flowers to Ossian. Besides the flower business, she was very active in church; as organist, teacher, head of women's groups, and singing in the choir.

John is six feet two inches with black wavy hair and wiry frame. Lucille is barely five feet, very petite with brown hair. John and Lucille spend Sunday afternoons at their cottage on Big Lake where they enjoy their blossoming family, which at last count was twelve grandchildren and four great grandchildren.

MAURICE SIMPSON FAMILY

Frederick and Frances Beckner Simpson and their son and daughter-in-law, Curtis Avery and Lillian Stark Simpson, came to Chester Township in 1929 from Goshen, Indiana, and settled on the present Simpson farm. Curtis and Lillian had three children, Luana, Hollis, and Maurice. The family set to work expanding an excellent registered Jersey herd.

In the 1930's and '40's the herd won several awards. The Indiana State Jersey Cattle Club gave an award for top butter fat in two-year and four-year olds and lifetime production. The Indiana State Dairy Association awarded a gold medal for proven sire. The herd also won highest average production of butter fat over all breeds in the Wells county D.H.I.A. Testing Association.

Left; Jack and Beth (Simpson) Buie. Right; Maurice and Donna Simpson.

The family was invited to the Montpelier Methodist Church which they still attend. Lillian was well known as an excellent Sunday school teacher. Luana completed a teaching degree at Ball State and taught at Chester Center. She married Kenneth Lefforge and resides in Wabash County. Hollis earned a nursing degree at Ball State and worked as an R.N. at Wells Community Hospital and now lives at McLean, Virginia, with her husband, Dr. B. D. Blood.

While his sisters were busy with their projects, Maurice was actively playing basketball for the Chester Center Indians, a sport he still enjoys with enthusiasm.

Maurice followed closely in his father's footsteps. After his father's untimely death in 1949, Maurice was left at an early age with full responsibility of the farm. Maurice decided to change over to feeding choice beef cattle which was his pride and joy. Maurice served on the first committee for the Wells County Feed Lot Cattle Tours.

Farm improvement has always been foremost in his accomplishments. He also found time to work for community improvement. Many hours were devoted to bringing Southern Wells Schools together and he was secretary of the holding company until the high school debt was paid. He also worked at Dana Corporation, sold concrete silos, grain bins and drying equipment. He enjoys working with young boys of the community and thus has ample help around the farm.

Maurice married Donna Smith of Pitsburg, Ohio, in June, 1948. Donna earned a Master of Arts Degree at Ball State University and taught thirty seven-years at Troy, Ohio, Chester Center, Liberty Center and Southern Wells.

Their daughter, Carolyn Beth, was born February 22, 1953. She was graduated from the School of Pharmacy, Purdue University and is Pharmacy Manager at St. Joe Hospital, Kokomo. Beth has done extensive work on family genealogy. She is married to Jack Buie, a Purdue graduate in electrical engineering, and he is employed at Delco Electronics, Kokomo, Indiana.

The family remains active and proud of the farm, has been a part of various organizations, and has traveled extensively. They have many hobbies and are proud to be a part of Wells County.

ABRAHAM SINK FAMILY

Sophia and Abraham Sink built the present home of Mrs. LaRue Roudebush (3/4 mile south on Rd. 303, west side), where they lived until 1877, when they moved to a little house in town beside the U. B. parsonage. (Other people who have lived there are the John Smuts and Zola Shepler.) Their children were Ella Beaber, Emma Sink (mother of Alf Sink), Emmett Sink, Frank Sink, and Kate Swyhart.

Sophia and Abraham's daughter, Ella, married Joyce Beaber. They lived on the north side of Hoverstock Cemetery (the house was moved to town and is presently the home of James Ausman), they then moved to the S.E. corner of Main Street and Rd. 303. Later they lived in Mary Tarr's present home.

Ella and Joyce's daughter, Effie, married George Roudebush. They lived across from the U.B. Church, present home of James Beck. Their son LaRue married Jenny Waikel, and they they have a daughter, Helen Bates, who lives at Markle.

Alf Sink married Bertha Zion. (Refer to William Zion family). They had four children: Ethel (deceased), who married Roy Wilcoxson. They had four children and seven grandchildren. Garry E. had nine children: Everett (deceased) married Lyda

Davis. They had two children: Betty Wheeler and Dean, and five grandchildren. Wanda (of Zanesville) married Firman Burgess. They have one child, Larry, who married Sharon Richards, and they have two children; Shannon and Nicole, and live north of Zanesville.

Garry E. Sink married Lorena M. Haney. Their nine children are: Mary Beth, Richard, Lois Ann, Gary Lee, Norma Jean, Carol Sue (deceased), Jerald, Janet, and Kent.

Mary Beth, of near Zanesville, married Doyle Bowman. Their children are Mary Ann Bender, Jim Bowman, and Carol Jean Robison; and they have five grandchildren.

Richard married Lois Beaver, and their children are: Sharon, Dettmer, and Rosie Whitfield; and they have two grandchildren. They live in Florida.

Lois Ann of Zanesville married Calvin Smith. Their children are Cynthia Waldman and Kevin. They have one grandchild. Garry Lee of Zanesville married Nancy Bender. Their children are Douglas and Sandy. Norma Jean of Minnesota married Len Grotnes. Their children are Tamarah, Laurie, Stephen, and Sarah. Jerald of Zanesville married Darlene Smith. Their children are Susan and Pamela. Janet of Minnesota married Lyle Dahigren. Their children are Brian and Heide. Kent of Zanesville married Karen Maitlen. Their children are Kimberly Kay and Kirby.

SLATER

I was born July 7, 1949, in Marion, Indiana, to Oliver Farren and Joan (Tinsley) Slater. I have an older sister, Gloria Jean, who now lives in South Whitley and a younger brother, Paul Joe, who lives in Maine.

When I was four years old, I went to live with my aunt and uncle, Harry and Violet Ramseyer of Nottingham. I attended Petroleum School until Southern Wells was built, then transferred to Southern Wells.

I lived with Harry and Violet until I joined the Marine Corps in November 9, 1967, and served in Vietnam from 1968 to 1969.

I have two sons, Yancy Christopher of Montpelier and Dale, Jr. of Bluffton. In 1988, I married Jane Holmes and we now reside in Bluffton.

My wife is employed by the City of Bluffton and I work for the State of Indiana at the National Guard Armory. *(Dale Eugene Slater)*

SLATER FAMILY

While feeding cattle and hogs, gathering eggs from hens' nests, and tending to the chores always beckoning in a turn-of-the-century farm house, Constance Lee (Krinn) Slater was going through the age-old motions her grandmother and great-grandmother before her had performed on farms in Wells County, Indiana. Only she may not have realized it at the time. Her father had moved from the farm to the city as a young man, and following her grandfather's death when Connie was just two, her grandmother also moved from Wells County to Fort Wayne. Only as an adult did Connie, the daughter of William and Iva Irene (Schelling) Krinn, move to the county and the life of her father's childhood.

Connie Krinn, a 1957 graduate of Elmhurst High School in Fort Wayne, married her high school sweetheart, Laurie Francis Slater, on November 21, 1959. They lived in Fort Wayne until 1967, then decided to try their hands at farm life and bought one of the Eiffer farms on 1100 South, west of Nottingham. Laurie farmed most of the eighty acres with the help of his step-father, Ward Beecher Slater, and still drove into Fort Wayne each day to work at his job as an electrical engineer at Bowmar Electronics. Connie cared for the animals, which at times included beef cattle, hogs, chickens, cats, a beagle, and a Saint Bernard. She also cared for daughter Dawne, born in 1962, and son, Marion, born in 1969. Dawne attended school at Petroleum Elementary until the Slater family moved to the Huntertown, Indiana, area in 19733, the same year the school was razed.

After moving to the Huntertown area, Laurie and Connie Slater had a third child, daughter Jennifer, born in 1974. Laurie and Connie divorced in 1977 and both remarried. Connie, now widowed, lives in Fort Wayne and works in an alterations shop. She enjoys crafts of all kinds, both creating them from patterns and designing her own. Laurie and his wife, the former Grace (Addis) Skinner, live in the Tampa Bay, Florida, area, where Laurie works in the electronics field.

Daughter, Dawne Slater-Putt, has a bachelor's degree in journalism and a master's degree in history from Ball State University. She worked five years as a feature writer and assistant feature editor for the Kokomo, Indiana, *Tribune*. Currently Dawne is completing a master's degree in library science through Indiana University and works in the Historical Genealogy Department of the Allen County Public Library as supervisor of a nationally-known periodicals indexing project. In 1986 she married Fort Wayne native, Rodney Lee Putt, the son of Robert J. and Thelma (Keith) Putt; and they live south of Zanesville, Indiana. Marion is a junior at the University of Southern Florida, Tampa, majoring in electrical engineering. Jennifer is a junior at Dixie Hollins High School in the Clearwater, Florida, area.

SLEPPY (SCHLEPPI)

The Sleppy family tree has been researched back to Friedrich Schleppi of St. Stephan, Canton Bern, Switzerland. Benedikta Schleppi (1692) widow of Friedrich Schleppi, in 1728 emigrated with her three sons: Stephan, Johannes Ulrich, and Samuel; from Lenk, Canton Bern, Switzerland to Bodingen, Germany (possibly now Homburg-Beeden).

Our lineage Johannes (Hans) Ulrich Schleppi (1720-1789) arrived in America on August 28, 1750, locating in Philadelphia, Pennsylvania. Johannes Ulrich Schleppi, his sons, Michael, Daniel, Jacob, John and his son-in-law, Jacob Kemmerer (husband of Eva Elizabeth Schleppi) served in the Revolutionary War.

Jacob Schleppi (1756-1849) married Barbara Maurer on August 14, 1781, and their son John George ((1793-1871) married Mary Fransine (1803-1875). Jacob Schleppi was spelled Jacob Sleppy in the 1790 U.S. Census. There were no set rules for spelling in the colonies and to this was added the problem of English clerks spelling German names. The clerks of the time relied on phonetic spelling to record names and events.

John George and Mary Sleppy's son John Sleppy (1818) married Catherine Ruby on July 3, 1851, in the state of Pennsylvania. She was sixteen and he was thirty years old, and they came to Wells County in a covered wagon in 1851, and took a homestead close to Keystone, Indiana. They had a family of six boys and one girl. John Sleppy died March 18, 1874; therefore, Catherine Sleppy raised the family with the help of the older sons.

Sleppy Family
Parents standing: Altha and George. Children: Marcelle, Joe, Leon, and Everett.

One of the sons, Samuel Ruby Sleppy (1867) married Mariah Ellen Hartz on June 3, 1890. Samuel and Mariah Sleppy (my great grandparents) had five children, one being my grandfather George Paul Sleppy (1899). George Paul married Altha Irene Toman on March 4, 1922. Their children are: Everett Paul (1923), Melvin Leon (1926), Marcelle (1927), and Joseph Samuel (1930).

Everett Paul married Barbara Ellen Reff and they have no children. Melvin Leon married Ruth Ilene Graham and they have three children: Judy Ilene (1950), Gary Leon (1952), and Jerry Lee (1957). Marcelle married Robert Keith McFarren and they have a daughter Connie Jo (1948). Joseph Samuel married Nellie Mae Stinson and they have two daughters, Cindy Jo (1951) and Sandra Lynn (1952). Judy Ilene Sleppy married Steven Eugene Couch and they have two sons: Kevin Eugene (1972), and Kyle Steven (1980). Gary Leon married Kandice Lynn Booher and they have five children: Benjamin Leon (1974), Angela Lynn (1977), Amanda Mae (1980), Caleb Nathaniel (1984), and Brittani Nichole (1985). Jerry Lee Sleppy married Joyce Kay Poulson and they have three children: Melissa Kay (1983), Holly Joy (1985), and Joshua Lee (1986). Connie Jo McFarren married Donald Lee Mittlestedt and they have five children: Robert Allen (1964), Matthew Lee (1967), Lesia Ann (1969), Michael Joe (1970), and Christina Marie (1984). Cindy Jo Sleppy married Richard Allen Horrom and they have two children Amy Jo (1974), and Kristopher Allen (1977).

The four Sleppy households remaining in Wells County are Leon and Ruth, and Jerry, Joyce and family all of Keystone; Joe and Nellie of Poneto; and Gary, Kandy, and family of Liberty Center. There are one hundred and five Sleppy households in the United States according to a computer search in 1988. It is unknown to us how many there are spelled Schleppi, which is the original and correct spelling.

SLEPPY HOMESTEAD

There is an eighty acre farm one half mile south of Poneto that has been known to me as the Sleppy Homestead. It was believed for years that my great-grandparents Mariah and Sam Sleppy started there, which is true. However, through research it has been found that my great-mother Mariah Miller came to Ohio from France with her brother Peter sometime in the 1850's. Her father was a doctor and he and his wife stayed in France. Mariah Miller married John Frederick Knoble, and they had five children, but only John Frederick, Jr. survived. Mariah Knoble bought the farm south of Poneto on September 17, 1868, after her husband died.

Mariah Knoble's second marriage was to Charles M. Hartz on May 8, 1870. They have five children (three girls and two boys), and one of their daughters, Mariah Ellen Hartz married Samuel Ruby Sleppy on June 3, 1890. Mariah and Sam Sleppy had five children: Carl Franklin (1891), Homer (1892), Kathyrn (1897), George Paul (1899) and Carrie (died in infancy).. Carl Sleppy married Florence Snyder May 4, 1924, with no children. Homer Sleppy never married. Kathyrn Sleppy married Francis Marion Dickason and had Samuel Warren (Bud) (1917), Crystal Marie, and James Frederick. George Paul Sleppy married Altha Irene Toman on March 4, 1922 and had Everett Paul (1923), Melvin Leon (1926), Marcelle (1927), and Joseph Samuel (1930).

Samuel Warren (Bud) Dickason married Geraldine Lincoln February 7, 1939, and they had six children: Francis Warren (1940), Kathyrn Marie (1942), John Edward (1944), Linda Sue (died in infancy), Richard Lee (1949), and Joe Robert (1952). Bud Dickason died on October 8, 1968. Crystal Marie married Orland Bates, and they live in Iowa where two of her three daughters also live. James Frederick died in a motorcycle accident at the age of eighteen. Jerry Dickason still lives in Wells County, as do her children: Frank Dickason, Katie Stinson, and Richard Dickason.

Everett Paul Sleppy married Barbara Ellen Reff, with no children. Melvin Leon married Ruth Ilene Graham and had three children: Judy Ilene (1950), Gary Leon (1952), and Jerry Lee (1957). Marcelle married Robert Keith McFarren, and had a daughter Connie Jo (1948).. Joseph Samuel married Nellie Mae Stinson and had two daughters: Cindy Jo (1951), and Sandra Lynn (1952). All of the above presently live in Wells County except Everett and Barbara Sleppy, and Cindy Jo Horrom who lives in Montpelier, Indiana; and Sandra Lynn Sleppy lives in Indianapolis, Indiana.

The Sleppy Homestead is owned by my parents, Nellie and Joe Sleppy, and they were married June 3, 1940, just sixty years to the day after my dad's grandparents, Mariah and Sam Sleppy, were married and lived on the same farm.

There are three water wells on this eighty-acre farm, the reason being there were different dwellings on this farm. The first house was back a long lane by the railroad track. The present house was moved in two parts by Mariah and Sam Sleppy. The house has been changed by additions and remodeling. It is hopeful this farm will continue to be property of heirs of the Sleppy family.

SLIGER FAMILY

My grandparents, George Ammi and Susan Gordon Sliger, were born in Perry County, Ohio. I don't know the date they moved to Liberty Township, one half mile east of Mossburg Cemetery. It was always a pleasure to visit them. I loved their garden, which was made in small beds with walking paths all around. I remember the trumpet vines and hollyhocks and the many hummingbirds around them. My grandparents' children were: Nellie May Prible; Charley and Rose, both of whom died in 1899; Flora Carroll, who taught school in Wells County and moved to Florida in the 1920's; Francis E. (Frank); and Mary Alice Davis.

Our grandfather William Cole married Florence Ayres on December 25, 1881. She was a daughter of Caleb and Martha (Sutton) Ayres. Her father, Caleb, was killed in the Civil War. Their children were: Minnie Kasler, Ed Cole, Etta Holcolm, Martha Sheets Mossburg, Elzey, and Lula A. Our father, Francis E. Sliger, married Lula in 1908. My parents graduated from Liberty Center in 1906. At that time there were only three years of high school. Dad was on the first basketball team. The games were played outside and the players wore padded uniforms similar to football players today. Dad kept his interest in sports all his life.

George Ammi Sliger and Susan Gordon Sliger

My parents' children were: Nina Blair, Helen Raver, Ruth Johnson, Esther Ross, Ona Mae Johnson, Edwin Dale, Robert Wayne, and George William. We lived in several places in our younger days. One of these was one mile north and one and a quarter mile east of Liberty Center. We attended Smoky Row, a one room school which was three-fourths miles east and one mile north of us. We walked to school, except in real bad weather, when Dad would take us. Sometimes we went in the bob sled. This was pulled by the horses and had straw and blankets to keep us warm. We would pick up neighbors as we went. I recall stopping for Hilda Thrailkill who lived around the corner from us. Our teachers were Morgan Rowe and later Clive Markley. There were eight grades and one teacher taught all of them. They gave us a good basic education, and as we went to higher classes we all did quite well. The last day of the term, we had a carry-in dinner and the parents came. That school was closed in 1923, and we went to Liberty Center to school.

My parents had a Model T Ford which cost $360.00, FOB Detroit. It had side curtains we buckled on for winter. It had no starter and had to be cranked. In winter, a tea kettle of hot water poured over the engine was a big help in getting it started.

In those days sugar beets were a good cash crop, and we raised them for several years. Our Uncle Herb Kasler was the Sugar Beet Company field supervisor, and our grandfather Cole ran the railroad depot in Liberty Center. The beets were shipped out there.

I remember the grain threshing which was done by a threshing ring of neighbors and the Gavins who owned the engine and thresher. They always announced their arrival by blowing the whistle. Everybody had a job to do. Some loaded the shocks in the field, others unloaded them in the thresher, and others unloaded the grain. The ladies in the neighborhood always helped one another cook the big meals. It is a nice memory but I'm sure no one wants to go back to it. At the end of the season, all met and had ice cream and cake. The ring bought several five-gallon cans of ice cream and it was so good.

Another memory is of the Barnum-Bailey Circus coming to Bluffton. Everyone went, and it was like a holiday. We always went to the Street Fair and could hardly wait for fall, but somehow it doesn't seem the same now.

I remember the first airplane we saw; we all went outside to watch. It flew rather low and was a small winged plane.

A lot of years have passed since our youth. I will always remember our parents' advice to always vote, be a good neighbor and never feel sorry for yourself. These are pretty good morals to live by today.

These memories were written by Ruth Johnson and shared with her niece, Mrs. James (Rose Marie Blair) Harris, who is the oldest grandchild. (*Rose Marie Harris*)

SLIGER-SMITH

Earl Ammi Sliger was born September, 1898, in Grant County, Indiana. He was the son of John Moomaw Sliger and Lily Jane Conn Sliger. He had two older sisters. Essie Elizabeth married Raymond Ellis Johnson; both are deceased. Another sister was Dessie May Sliger; her first marriage was to Cecil Eubank. After he died, she married Noah Vickey. They are both deceased.

Earl was the third child and oldest son. There were two other sons. Russell David married Velma Anders; they are both deceased. Dwight Elmoody married Nellie Marie Huss; after she died, he married Helen Werts. Dwight is deceased but his widow, Helen, resides in Bluffton.

Earl and Winifred Sliger

Earl A. Sliger married Winifred Cleora Smith, who was born in Adams County, Indiana, in 1907, a daughter of William Smith and Florence Etta Chronister. William Smith operated a Music Store in Decatur, was a talented musician who played the piano, organ, clarinet, saxaphone, and drums. He also wrote several songs, two of them were published with copyrights. They had two daughters and a son older than Winifred. Ralph Marion Smith married Florence Twigg. Ralph served in the army during the first World War. Ralph and Florence are deceased. Next was Euriel Iretta, her first marriage was to Marion R. Barnthouse; a second marriage was to Otto Gase. All three are deceased.

The second daughter was Florence Mae, whose first marriage was to William LaTurner. After his death, she married Hugh Elston. They also are deceased.

Winifred was the youngest. Her father died when she was only eighteen months old. Her mother then moved the family to Bluffton and took a job as a cook in a restaurant, which now houses the State Farm Insurance Agency. Florence Etta died in October, 1928.

When Winifred got out of school she went to work for the H. C. Bay Piano Company, where she met Earl sliger. They were married in 1925. Their first daughter, Cleora Jacelyn was born in 1926. She married Karl King in 1946. She died March 6, 1991. They were the parents of two sons, Barry Earl and

Kendis Keene. Barry is married to the former Rita Penrod and they have two children, Cheri and Shane. The family resides in Bluffton. Kendis is married to the former Delores Driscoll, and they are the parents of four children: Jeanne, Nicholas, Matthew, and Elizabeth. They reside in the southern Wells County area.

The youngest daughter, Marilyn L., was born in 1928 and married Harry Faus, Jr. in 1944. They have two sons. William Lee whose first marriage was to Sue Sark, and they are the parents of William Jr., Bradley K., and Robert M. His second marriage was to the former Sally Crane, who has two sons: Dean and Ben. They all reside in Elkhart, Indiana. William served as a postman and a police officer in Bluffton before moving to Elkhart.

Their second son, Kenneth Bradley, is married to the former ReAnn Hinton. They are the parents of three sons: Brian, Kevin, and Kory; and they live in Ossian. Kenneth served two years in the army. After graduation from Bluffton High School, he attended National Barber College in Indianapolis and is the owner of Majestic Style Salon, South Town Mall.

Earl Sliger passed away February, 1975, and Winifred died in June, 1982. They and their daughters, sons-in-law and grandchildren were all members of Calvary Lutheran Church.

JOSIAH SLUSHER FAMILY

Mr. Josiah Slusher married Naomi Morgan in 1869. Josiah was the son of William and Hettie (Cale) Slusher, and Naomi was the daughter of Charles H. and Mary Morgan, natives of South Carolina.

After marriage Mr. and Mrs. Slusher lived on rented land in Jackson Township, Wells County, for a considerable time and then lived on Dr. Good's farm in Huntington County for three years. He then made a sale of his personal effects and went to Arkansas in November, 1876, but, not liking the country, returned to Wells County the following February and purchased forty acres on which he lived, which was then a wilderness and had no improvements except an old log cabin containing one room. In 1886, Mr. Slusher erected a comfortable house in which he and his family lived until 1901. In the meanwhile he worked at clearing off the land from its timber and converting it into a fruitful and profitable farm.

By 1901, Mr. Slusher had acquired the means with which to purchase the parental homestead. He owned one hundred and twenty acres of some of the finest farm land to be found in Wells County, and had seven oil wells which yielded him about $40 per month. He carried on general farming and at the same time devoted much of his attention to the breeding of livestock, Jersey cattle and Poland China hogs.

Mr. and Mrs. Slusher had nine children: Emma Eliza, who married Oliver Williams; William C., who married Daisy Riggs; Samuel, who died as a child; Leora, who died as a child; Charles, who married Chloie Godfrey; Mary Lena, who married Eugene Cruse; James Ross, who married Maggie Godfrey; and Goldie, who married Edward Jones.

In politics in his earlier manhood, Mr. Slusher did not identify himself with any particular party, but voted for such candidates as were best suited in his opinion to fill the various offices for which they were nominated. Later he became a strict Prohibitionist. With his family he was a member of the Radical United Brethren Church, was an active worked in the congregation, and was a trustee in the church since its erection. Too much credit cannot be given to Mr. Slusher for the prudence he exercised throughout life and the care with which he and his wife reared their children. (*Taken from 1903 Wells County history*)

MR. WILLIAM SLUSHER FAMILY

Mr. William C. Slusher married Daisy May Riggs in 1898. William was the son of Josiah and Naomi (Morgan) Slusher; and Daisy was the daughter of Trimbley and Catherine Riggs.

They lived on a farm in Dillman in Jackson Township where they had a homemade lighting plant. William owned a Fordson tractor. Their farm was called Progress Farm.

They were members of Dillman United Brethren Church and were very active in it.

They were the parents of eight children. Ruey Glee married Ralph Leas in 1918, and had seven children: Lillian Ruth, Gail Eugene, James Cletus, Donald Keith, Robert Dale, Lois Jane, and Jackie Lee.

Ronald T. married Leota Risinger in 1926 and had four children: Wilma Marie, Wilda May, Wilber Ervin, and Willis Risinger.

Ruth Faye married Merle Little in 1921 and had two children: Roger and Adriana.

Clara M. died as a baby.

Ransom T. married Thelma Daugherty in 1924 and had twelve children: Doris Ula, William Anderson, Kenneth Wayne, Phyllis Joan, Mary Jane, Laura Lavone, Anna Geneva, Thomas Wilber, Danny Earl, John Charles, Richard Lee, and Nancy May.

Rhessa Josiah married Martha Wagoner in 1930. They had three children: Frances Colleen, Ruth Eileen, and Barbara Jean.

Rapheal married Elretta Zoda and had five children: Gladys Elnora, Waneta Jean, Franklin, Dale Keith, and Karen Kay.

Roscoe married Helen Kahn in 1931. They adopted twins: Don and Donna. In 1959, Roscoe divorced Helen and married Nina Kariger.

SMITH

My father, John Earl Smith, was born in Bluffton, Indiana, May 31, 1890, son of George W. and Lula Viola (Baker) Smith.

He married Limpa E. Baxter February 6, 1909. They were the parents of two sons: Sherman (1909-1915) and Herschell (1911-1977). Herschell married Gertrude O'Connor, Columbia City, in 1940. They were the parents of a son, Larry Edward, born September 24, 1944. He married Janice Terry. They are the parents of two sons: Steven and Tim. They reside in Fort Wayne.

John Earl worked at the W. B. Brown Chandelier Factory.

His wife died in 1914, and on February 26, 1916, he married my mother, Marie Barton of Hartford City. They had three children: George Arnold (1917-1919); John Eugene, May 28, 1918; and Beverly Earlene, November 29, 1932.

My father also worked in Frankfort buying and cutting timber. When we returned to Bluffton he was employed at the H. C. Bay Piano Factory and B.K. Settergren Piano Company until his death June 4, 1933, at the age of 43.

John Eugene Smith married Mary H. Matson September 2, 1940. They reside at 227 North Bond Street.

John worked at Estey Piano Corporation, McDowell Lumber Company, and Franklin Electric Company.

Mary worked at McDowell Lumber Company, Gerber's Central Dairy, and John W. Gallman, Inc.

Beverly Earlene married James F. Niblick June 17, 1950, and they are the parents of three children: Kathy Ann, Cindy Lou, and Steven James. They returned to Bluffton after James retired from the Marine Corps after twenty-three years. He now drives a truck.

Kathy married Ronald Garner of Gary (a retired Marine who received the Purple Heart) and they have one son, Ronald. They reside in Bluffton.

Cindy married William Priester from New York. He is a warrant officer in the Marines and served in the Gulf War in Desert Storm. They have two children: Amy and Jeffery. They live in Hubert, North Carolina.

Steven married Katherine Taylor from Holly Ridge, North Carolina. They have three children: Carrie, Heather, and Steven II. They live in Kannapolis, North Carolina. Steven is an employee of the Phillip Morris Company. (*John E. Smith*)

SMITH

In 1837 Fleming Johns bought a quarter section of land from the government and came from Charlottesville, Virginia, to possess it. With him came his wife, Betsy (Walker); her father and her brother-in-law, Jacob Smith, whose wife Mary died in Virginia; Jacob's father, James, and Jacob's family (Jacob Austin, James, John, Lewis, Sarah Jane, and Mary). Jacob Austin was twelve then and walked the trip from Virginia to Fort Recovery, Ohio. They stayed there until they had found the land and knew where to go, then moved to Wells County.

Grace, Johntz, Austin, and Frances Smith. On the spot where the Gracys lived before they came to Wells County.

Meanwhile, Robert Gracy left Dublin, Ireland, where he had lost two sons named Samuel. The third Samuel, born in America in 1798, married Rachel Snively, came to New York state then to Washington Court House, Ohio. Their children

555

were: Mary (Shobe), Emily (Smith), Clarissa (Shepherd), Elizabeth (Smith), Harriet (Risley), Nancy Jane (Jones), Joseph, Sarah (Jones), Jullietta, and Samuel.

In 1848 the twins, Emily and Clarissa, came to Wells County where the family had purchased land. When the family came, Emily had already married Jacob Austin Smith on September 23, 1849 and lived on forty acres which Jacob had purchased for $150, the amount he earned for helping Fleming Johns clear his land. Four children died of diphtheria. Others were Mary (Shigley), Rachel Jane (Conrad-Sickler), Harriet (Walser), Louisa (Sickler), Ida (Warner), Andrew Johnson, Pheobe (Courtney) and Irene (Leslie-Davies).

In 1893 Andrew Johnson (born 1867), now called Johnts, went to St. Clair County, Missouri, to study law with his uncle, Samuel Gracy. There he met Minnie Alice Walker, daughter of David and Frances Kellerman Walker, married her in 1894, and brought her to Wells County. In 1898 they moved to their three-room house on the forty acres owned by Jacob Smith, with Edna Grace (born November 7, 1894) and David Austin (born September 14, 1897). Jacob and Emily now lived on twenty-six acres they had purchased across the road from their first cabin. Frances Lavera was born November 6, 1906.

Education was the interest of this family. Emily taught school before she was married. She taught her husband to read. Her daughters, Mary and Rachel Jane, were teachers.

Grace graduated from Bluffton High School in 1912, studied one summer at Marion Normal School, and taught that fall at "Poor Farm" one room school, then second grade at Park School, Bluffton. She then majored in Home Economics at Defiance College, taught at Liberty Center, Lancaster, Ossian, and Tipton County. She worked in the 4-H program and organized the first Girl Scout troop in Wells County.

Austin graduated from Bluffton High School in 1914, went to Muncie Normal School, taught four years in one room schools of Harrison Township, then attended Defiance College, majoring in mathematics and science. He taught at Liberty Center and coached the basketball team that played in the State Tournament in 1924. He was principal of schools in Warren, Albany, and Lynn; and was county superintendent in Huntington County.

Frances graduated from Liberty Center High School in 1923, attended Defiance College majoring in music. She taught piano privately until 1948, then taught at Hartford School in Adams County, Poplar Grove, and Vera Cruz in Wells County; and East Side and Park in Bluffton. She now resides on the farm where her grandparents established a home in 1849.

The family has been associated with Six Mile Church since the time of Jacob and Emily Smith.

Neither Grace nor Frances married.

Austin married Ninetta Boltin, daughter of Charles and Minnie Stahl Boltin in 1926. They had one son, Thomas Austin, who attended DePauw and Indiana Universities and now is a psychologist in Indianapolis. He married Janice Edwards, daughter of Russell and Maude Ritter Edwards of Winchester, Indiana. They have two daughters. Sheryl, wife of Jon Hays, and mother of Suzanne, John, and Susan. Both daughters are graduates of DePauw University.

SMITH FAMILY

Our branch of the Smith Family can trace their roots back to 1657 in Bavaria, Germany. After the Thirty Year War our forefathers came to the United States, landing in Philadelphia and eventually moving to Louisville, Kentucky, where William Wesley Smith was born in 1841. He moved with his parents to Howard County, Indiana, when he was twelve. He later married Sarah Spraker. They had six children, one being Omar Jessie Smith, born January 17, 1876. He married Caroline Catherine (Deisch) in 1901. O. J. and Caroline, (nicknamed Susie) had two children, William Henry and Gladys, while living in Miami County. They moved to Howard County where Howard Earl, Amelia Mae, and Walter Fielding were born. In 1912 the family moved to Wells County, where they purchased a farm on the corner of state roads 303 and 218. They farmed until 1940, when they moved into the edge of Liberty Center, where O. J. died on December 16, 1955. Susie died on May 23, 1964.

Back, Left to Right; Jon Wayne Smith, Judy Ann Lothamer, Jeffrey Howard Smith. Front, Left to Right; Arleen G. Smith, Jack Wayne Smith.

Howard Earl Smith born August 7, 1904, married Mary (Roof), born October 29, 1905, in Wells County. They started housekeeping in the "little red house" on a corner of his father's farm, where Jack Wayne was born on September 18, 1924. They moved into Poneto, Indiana, where Howard opened a garage. He is still in the Smith Trucking and Garage business within a block of where it all began. Three children followed Jack; Robert Lawrence, born September 26, 1927; Caroline Jane, born August 26, 1929; and Wendell Allen, born December 3, 1936.

Our parents, Jack and Arleen (Gilbert) were married on January 12, 1947. They rented a farm south of Liberty Center on S.R. 303, which they later bought. He supplemented the farm income by driving a semi-tanker for National Oil and Gas for twenty-nine years with no chargeable accidents. our mother, after raising us into our teens went back to work at Old-First National Bank, retiring after twenty-five years.

Judy Ann was born on September 6, 1947. Judy graduated from Liberty Center High School. She married Roger Joseph Lothamer on April 11, 1970. She graduated from Purdue University as a registered nurse and works at Lutheran Hospital. Roger is a robotics technician at the General Motors Plant. They have three children: Matthew Joseph, born June 5, 1971; Jason Howard, born May 27, 1974; and Jenny Ann, born July 11, 1975.

Jon Wayne was born June 7, 1950. He graduated from Southern Wells High School and Taylor University. He is an elementary school teacher at Adams Central in Adams County. He served six years in the National Guard. He married Brenda (Masters) on July 9, 1977, earning two masters in the same year, one by marriage and one at IUPU in Fort Wayne! They have two children: Brooke Nicole, born March 14, 1979; and Andrew Wayne, born October 22, 1982. Andy is presently the only male of his generation to carry on the Smith name.

Jeffrey Howard, the third child, was born on May 11, 1952. He graduated from Southern Wells High School and Ball State University. He is employed at the Fort Wayne State Developmental Center.

SMITH AND HITE

Ephriam Smith was born September 1, 1851, to Henry and Sara (Walker) Smith at Springfield, Ohio. He married Matilda Alice Feighner, who was born June 18, 1858, to Daniel and Mary (Barnes) Feighner at Philadelphia, Pennsylvania. Mary was born in 1818 in Somerset County, Pennsylvania. Her father was born in Adams County, Pennsylvania, near Gettysburg in 1804. They moved in Morrow County, Pennsylvania, in the early 1850's. Then they moved to Indiana. They were married on January 11, 1877, at her parent's home, seven miles east of Huntington, in Union Township. Ephriam died August 26, 1926, and Mary died October 11, 1909.

Arthur and Effie Smith

Their seventh child, Arthur Elsworth, was born August 7, 1889, and he helped his father run the tie barn at Roanoke. Arthur met a very beautiful young lady, Effie May Hite, who worked at Benders Dry Goods Store in Markle. (See Elijah Hite). This picture shows the buggy they used to court in. Arthur tells that going home after a date, he would lay down the reins and go to sleep, and the horse would take him home. One night the doctor and his horse tried to pass them but Arthur's horse would not let him pass. Arthur did not waken, and the doctor told him about it the next day.

Arthur and Effie were married March 1, 1913. This was the year of the flood in the Markle and Zanesville areas. Arthur farmed and also worked on the Erie Railroad. He had helped his brother-in-law (Oscar Lantis) on his farm in Rockcreek Township, and then he started farming on his own about two miles east of Markle. Their daughter, Helen Leona, was born December 16, 1913, and their son, Leonard E., was born on October 31, 1914.

They moved to a farm just west of 303 on 700N and a son, Jay Hite, was born December 17, 1916. Another son, Glen Waldo, was born June 11, 1919, and then Vaughn Eugene was born March 6, 1922. They moved about five miles west—just into Huntington County, and lived there thirty-five years. Arthur was a good farmer and also helped haul gravel to build roads and later drove a school bus for many years. A daughter, Hope Delean, was born November 18, 1923, and Delight Mae was born August 20, 1926. Arthur was musically inclined and played the mouth harp and rattled the bones. The family was very active in the Markle Church of Christ.

Their daughter, Helen, married Harold D. Fusselman on October 19, 1935. He was the son of Otis and Rose (Kuntz) Fusselman. Harold was born July 23, 1913, in Union Township. Their children are Charlotte, Dollie, Jerry, and Betty. Harold retired from International Harvester and their home is in Liberty Center. Harold died on June 29, 1990.

Leonard married Opal Vollmar September 2, 1938. She was the daughter of John and Lulu (Bryan) Vollmar of Union Township of Huntington County. They have a daughter, Luwona and son, Ronald. Leonard farmed and worked at Wayne Metal in Markle. Their home is at the east edge of Markle. Leonard died on December 21, 1983.

Jay married Ruth Brumbaugh on December 25, 1940. She is the daughter of Ed and Pearl Brumbaugh of Union Township. Their children are Ardith, Sonja, and Cheryl. Jay farmed and drove a school bus in Union and Rockcreek Townships.

Glen married Maxine Dolby on March 14, 1942. She was a daughter of Clarence and Tessie Dolby of Huntington County. Children born to them are Sharon, Marvin, and Kathy. Glen was a farmer.

Vaughn married Mary Weaver on May 23, 1942. She was the daughter of Floyd and Leota Weaver. Their five sons are Phillip, Keith, Duane, Fred, and Jeff. (See Smith and Weaver)

Hope married C. Garl Worster on July 28, 1945. He was the son of Cecil and Pearl Worster of Wells County. Their children are Joe, Max, Curtis, Vicki, Larry, and Patty. Garl is retired from Dana.

Delight married Guy Wiley on April 26, 1947. He was the son of William Everet and Mary Hutchinson of Liberty Center. Their children are Gregory, Mona Jean, and Ted. Guy retired from Magnavox and Delight from Square D.

As Arthur and Effie neared retirement age, they bought a farm back in Union Township of Wells County on the corner of State Road 303 and 700N.

Effie died December 13, 1959, at the age of sixty nine. Arthur died on June 5, 1971, at the age of eighty one. They have one hundred and seventy three decedents as of February 15, 1991.

JACOB CLIFFORD SMITH/-ARZONA FAY CLOUD

Clifford Smith, as he was known, was born in Greentown, Indiana, January 18, 1897. His father, David Harrison Smith, was born in Pennsylvania. Later, he became a glassworker and moved the family to different areas to work. Clifford's mother, Emma Jones, was the youngest daughter of Robert F. and Lavina Tripp Jones. The Jones family located in Chester township from Jackson County, Ohio, in 1853.

When Clifford was in his early twenties, he came from Wisconsin to help his uncle William "Lon" Jones farm in Section Five, Chester Township. He attended the Mt. Zion United Brethern Church in Christ where he met Arzona Cloud.

Arzona Fay, born February 28, 1902, was the daughter of Henry S. and Martha Lowry cloud of Mt. Zion. The Lowry and Cloud families were early farming residents of Jackson and Chester Townships. Part of mt. Zion was the farm of Henry Cloud.

Clifford and Arzona were married June 30, 1923, in Mt. Zion. They were the parents of three children. Lawrence Eugene was born June 10, 1924, at the William Jones farm in Chester Township. Mary Louise born April 23, 1928, died April 24, 1928. Robert Marlin, born September 9, 1937, died March 21, 1938.

They lived in and around mt. Zion all their married lives. He retired in 1963 as a semi-truck driver and Arzona was a homemaker. They both were members of the Mt. Zion United Brethren in Christ. Clifford served in World War I and was a farmer member of the Bluffton American Legion Post III.

Clifford passed away May 2, 1972, and Arzona passed away June 28, 1987. Both are buried in the Woodlawn cemetery in Warren, Indiana.

Lawrence Eugene graduated from Chester Center High School in 1943. he served in the U.S. Navy from 1943 to 1946. On November 6, 1954, he was married to Phyllis L. Hackenjos of French Township, Adams County, Indiana.

They are the parents of two children: Lester Ray and Rhonda Sue. Lester, born November 29, 1958, married Rhonda Kay Bennett of Hartford City, Indiana. They have two children. Daniel Benjamin was born January 12, 1988, and Jennifer Faith was born march 22, 1990. The family lives near Marion, Indiana. Rhonda Sue married Jerry Paul Orem of Richmond, Indiana, and they live in Indianapolis.

Lawrence and Phyllis live near Hartford City. He retired from Warner Gear, Muncie, Indiana, on March 31, 1990, after working there for forty-two years and ten months.

SMITH-JACOBS

William H. (Bill) Smith and Mary Gavin were married in 1926. William was the oldest child of Omer and Susie Smith, who moved from Howard County to Wells County at William's early age in 1914. Mary was the second daughter of William and Anna Howard Gavin of Wells County. Bill was a farmer who died in 1980. Mary is a member of Markle Health Care. They were the parents of two children: Thomas E., and Suzanne.

Tom, who graduated from Liberty Center in 1945, then entered military service of World War II, he lives in Huntington and is now retired from Refiners Transport. He married Susan Hall and they have two children: Amy Niswander of Huntington, and Thomas R. from Auburn.

Suzanne, who also graduated from Liberty Center and Wayne University of Cosmetology, now resides in Warren to be nearer her employment for twenty-three years as a beautician. In 1950 Suzanne married Joe Mark Jacobs, son of James Ralph and Hazel McElhaney Jacobs. Ralph, as he was most often called, was a son of Mack and Mary Eilar Jacobs—all of Wells County. Hazel's parents were Elijah and Ida McElhaney from Warren.

Joe enjoyed life and being with people. After graduating from Liberty Center in 1944, he entered military service of World War II. Returning to Wells County, he was a farmer, auctioneer/realtor and will be remembered by many as a Wells County surveyor. After nearly twelve years he resigned that position for work at the Wells County jail. He died in 1981.

A daughter, Jo Ellyn, was their first child born in 1952. She graduated from Southern Wells High School in 1971. Working formerly in the office of Dr. Bill Gitlin, she is now employed at pharmacy of Wells Community Hospital. In 1973 Jo married Daniel K. Oswalt, son of Ed and Margaret Oswalt. Dan is employed at L. H. Carbide Corporation in Fort Wayne. Their children are: Susan Lyn, thirteen; Amie Jo, eleven; and Kari Ann, nine; all students at Southern Wells School.

Carol Ann was born in 1957. She graduated from Southern Wells High School in 1975 and from Huntington Beauty College. She is presently employed at Vector Systems in Fort Wayne. Her children are: Mark Wilson, thirteen; and Kimberly Ann Wilson, eleven; students at Southern Wells.

James William was born in 1959. Also a graduate of Southern Wells in 1978, he began employment at Moorman Manufacturing Company. At present he is employed at Hulcher Emergency Railroad Service. In 1981 he married Denise Knight, daughter of Waldo and Margaret Knight from Warren. She is employed at Payton's Northern Distribution Center. Their children are: Diane Marie, seven; John Mark, six; students at Southern Wells School; and Jared William, one year of age.

SMITH-KUNKEL

The Smith and Kunkel families of Wells County moved from the East, through Pennsylvania and Ohio, and were among the first settlers in Indiana. James Wesley Smith was born in Killbuck Township, Holmes County, Ohio, in 1847. He moved to Magley, Wells County, and in June, 1871, at the age of twenty four, he married Mary Ann Barnhart, a descendent of the Andrews and Cecil families of Adams County, Indiana; Tuscarawas County, Ohio and the state of Maryland. They raised a family of nine children: Richard of Bluffton (1937), Melvin of Fort Wayne, Murtle of Decatur; Daniel; Charles of Fort Wayne; Frank C. who retired from the Huntington Fire Department in 1947; Florence of Fort Wayne; Laura and my grandfather John Henry who was born in 1885. In 1903 John Henry married Nellie Pearl Kunkel, daughter of Calvin and Sarah A. (Plummer) Kunkel. Calvin was the son of Michael Jr. and Julia Mason. (The Kunkel ancestors' history is covered elsewhere in this book.) Sarah, born in Ohio 1842, was the daughter of John and Lydia (Neidlinger) Plummer. John Plummer, of Richland County, Ohio, was a farmer and pioneer settler of Wells County, moving there around 1855.

Brothers; Gerald R. Smith and Calvin Kunkel Smith July, 1915

John Henry and Nellie were the parents of nine children, two of whom died at a young age. All the children were raised in the Bluffton area. My father, Gerald Ross (Red) Smith, was born in 1905 and married Marian Eloise Miller in 1927. He worked for many years as a Purchasing Agent for the Indiana Service Corporation in Fort Wayne and later was Purchasing Director for American Rock Wool Corporation of Wabash. He served several years as an officer of the National Association of Purchasing Agents. A great athlete (1935 State wrestling champion), fisherman, Shriner, and pilot, he had a successful and full life, remaining very active until his death in 1989. I have many fond memories of our rabbit and pheasant hunting in the Bluffton area during the 1940's around the stone quarry near Murray.

Calvin Kunkel Smith was born 1910. He married to a Maxine and had two children; then married Catherine Chase, and had two children.

Ardola Mae was born in Petroleum in 1912. She married Lea Roy Smith in 1928 and had five children. She then married Floyd Earl Sproat in 1941, then married Charles E. Martin in 1965 and is now living in Fort Wayne.

Donald J. was born in Tocsin in 1915. He began working for the Indiana Service Corporation in the 1930's. He married Beatrice Kirby in 1940 to 1961 and had three children. He advanced to the position of General Foreman and retired after over forty years with the company. He is living in Fort Wayne with his wife Margaret (Olsen).

Bernice Evelyn was born in 1916 in Tocsin and married Al Tomaini in 1936. She now lives in Gibsonton, Florida.

Jack Morris was born in Bluffton in 1919. He has lived most of his life in Fort Wayne, served many years on the Fort Wayne Police Department and presently is a security guard for one of the banks.

The youngest of the family, Lester Dale was born in 1924 in Bluffton. He married Margaret Olsen in 1942 and has four children. He retired from the Kellogg Company and is presently living in Battle Creek, Michigan.

SMITH-LOGAN

Galen Rolandues Smith (June 7, 1899-February 15, 1975), the son of Zachaus and Nellie Denny Smith of Allen County, and Lucille Hazel Logan (May 9, 1903) the daughter of James G. and Ollie Jane Johnson Logan of Allen County, were united in marriage on November 26, 1919, by the Reverend J. H. Hughes, judge at the Allen County Court House in Fort Wayne, Indiana.

Four children were born to this union: Wayne (December 24, 1920); Alma (September 1, 1923); Nona (March 15, 1930); and Nancy (September 11, 1941). The first three children were born in Allen County and Nancy was born in Wells County.

After their marriage they lived and farmed in Allen County, until the Spring of 1938, when the farm was purchased for the construction of Baer Field Airport. Galen and Lucille moved to Wells County where they rented the South Wind Farm located at the south edge of Ossian. The last of the four children, Nancy, was born while they lived at the South Wind Farm.

*Galen and Lucille Smith
Fiftieth Anniversary*

In search of his own farm Galen attended a farm sale, just to see what land was selling for. He purchased eighty acres on 700N near Uniondale, for $4000 (without Lucille's knowledge). It took weeks for Lucille to even look at what he had purchased. When she finally viewed his purchase, she thought it looked like a little WPA toilet on a hill. After a lot of hard labor, cleaning, and polishing, the house became their home in the spring of 1942.

Galen raised pigs and cattle land farmed the land. He also worked at the General Electric in Fort Wayne for a short time during World War II. Galen was known in the area for his pulling teams, with which he won many ribbons.

Galen and Lucille were active members of Fairview Church of God in Yoder, Indiana. Lucille was the typical farm wife, helping her husband and operating all the machinery.

Then in 1954 they sold their farm for $25,000 and purchased two hundred and fifty acres at Burr Oak, Michigan. Galen did custom farming while living in Indiana and Michigan.

For several years they wintered in Florida and then in Arizona. Galen passed away while in Arizona on February 15, 1975. Lucille continued to live on the farm in Michigan until 1978, when she moved back to Ossian. Lucille has always been an active member of the Extension homemaker's organization both while in Indiana and Michigan.

Galen's five siblings are: Clayton, Flossie, Velie, Leota, and Dorothy. Lucille's five siblings are: Chalmer, Goldie, Flossie, Edna, and Clifford, who died at age ten.

Galen and Lucille's family: Wayne married Rosemary Coovert on November 20, 1941, and they have three daughters: Pam, born June 9, 1946; Jean, born March 30, 1950; and Lynne, born May 15, 1951.

Rosemary died in 1976; and Wayne married Claudine Kummer on October 8, 1977.

Alma married Robert C. Swank on August 23, 1941, and they had one daughter, Joyce, born November 11, 1942.

Nona married Richard Neuenschwander on March 27, 1948, and had one son, Larry, born October 25, 1948.

Nancy married Stanley Davis on October 13, 1957, and had four children: Galen, born May 20, 1958; Deborah, born June 3, 1959; Priscilla, born May 19, 1960; and Kevin, born May 21, 1961. In 1971 Nancy and Stanley divorced and she married Donald Harkness on June 4, 1974.

SMITH FAMILY

In 1865 Jacob James Smith, native of Fairfield County, Ohio, son of Bartholomew and Mary (Eversole) Smith, having served with the Company F, Seventeenth Ohio Volunteer Infantry, moved to Wells County, Indiana to pursue farming. His marriage to Elizabeth Morris, daughter of Mitchell and Elizabeth (Hardesty) Morris produced four daughters and two sons. The younger son, James Jacob married a country school teacher, Karah Stine, daughter of William and Nancy (Spence) Stine, native of Carroll County, Ohio. Karah's father, veteran of the Civil War, served with Indiana Company A of the Seventeenth regiment, held as a prisoner of War, was the well-known blacksmith in Ossian who, together with his brother, patented the Stine plow.

James and Karah lived most of their married life in Wells County. James and his father farmed together and moved to a farm near Ashtabula, Ohio, for a short time when Grandmother Smith became ill and upon the doctor's advice they all moved near Mobile, Alabama, where she died eighteen months later. The families returned to Wells County and settled in Union Township two miles north of Uniondale. Grandpa Smith lived with James, Karah and children until his death at age ninety-two years.

To the union of James and Karah were born four sons and nine daughters of which two sons and one daughter died as infants. Mary lived to be twenty years of age and was the first traumatic experience with death that the rest of the children experienced. The older son, Everett, served his country as a career soldier. His experiences included service with General McArthur in the Philippines during World War II where he was wounded in action. Further service included government quality control in Japan and Alabama factories after retirement and working at the Astrodome in Houston where he settled. His remains lie in the National Cemetery near Houston. Everett had one daughter and one granddaughter. Goldie Ballard, deceased, retired after forty years with General Electric. Ruth Mosbarger has one daughter and one son, six grandchildren and two great grandchildren. Rose Richmond, deceased, had two sons, one daughter and six grandchildren. Her son, John, retired from active service as an airforce pilot, now teaching new pilots. Helen Levy has two sons, one daughter, six grandchildren, and one great grandchild. Maxine Rupel has two sons and four daughters, twelve grandchildren, and six great grandchildren. Captain Fredrick Rupel is serving as a Chaplain in current Desert Storm. Virginia Willig has one son, one daughter, and four grandchildren. Edwin has four children, six grandchildren, and one great grandchild. Thus, the direct descendents of James and Karah (Stine) Smith number eighty five.

All of the Smith children attended school in Union Township, some at the Buckeye school, the rest at Union Center, both now extinct. They weathered wars, the Great Depression and loss of loved ones, but have proven to be resilient with a great sense of humor, more wisdom, love for God and one another, and a sense of appreciation for the joy of living.

SMITH-NASH

The grandfather of Marguerite Nash, George Smith, was born in Portage County, Ohio, in August 18, 1849, but his parents, Leonard and Nancy (Caston) came to Jefferson Township when he was six weeks old. He was one of twelve children, four of which were born in Jefferson Township. Their ancestors were English Puritans who came to America in 1630, settling in Massachusetts. His mother died in 1879, and his father in 1884. They are buried in the Elhanan Cemetery east of Ossian. George married Lydia Snyder (born, April 27, 1852) in 1872. She was of "Pennsylvania Dutch" descent. They were farmers and lived on the same farm their entire life. They had six children, the youngest was Charles Ray (born July 18, 1889, died May 12, 1986), father of Marguerite Nash. Charles was called Ray. They attended the Hebron United Brethren Church and were active members for many years. His wife was born in Jefferson Township but moved across the road into Allen County when a young girl. They were married on March 16, 1910, and had one daughter, Marguerite. Ray farmed and worked the carpenter trade with his uncle for many years. Laura raised chickens, milked cows, and had a garden. she sold butter and eggs to regular customers. Marguerite's grandparents lived with them.

A vacation was an afternoon of fishing in the Wabash, and a picnic lunch once or twice each summer. The Bluffton Street Fair was a big attraction that everyone enjoyed. Their house burned down on February 20, 1920, when the temperature was fifteen degrees below zero. A new house was built that summer.

Marguerite attended a one-room school known as the Beck School. When the weather was bad someone took her, sometimes in her grandpa's "Storm King" buggy. Otherwise, she walked one and three-fourths mile. The schoolhouse burned down on December 23, 1925. The next semester they were taken by bus to the new Ossian School, from which Marguerite graduated in 1931. Her grandmother died June 9, 1932, and a grandfather died April 7, 1934, with both being buried at Elhanan.

Ray worked a few years at Ossian Plumbing and Heating.

In 1935, Marguerite married Harry Nash. His parents were Reuben and Edessa (Sowards). They had two sons, Merlin and Dale. They farmed and had dairy cows, chickens and pigs. Harry also worked several years at the Wells County Co-op in Bluffton and Uniondale. Both are now retired but live on the farm in Lancaster Township and are members of Lancaster Chapel United Methodist Church.

SMITH-SUMNER

We were born to "farmer" parents, whose ancestors had been long time residents of Hamilton County. My parents lived on a farm on State Road 31, two miles north of Westfield, which is twenty miles north of Indianapolis, where this writer was born on July 27, 1921. One-half mile east, Jim was born on March 31, 1920. We attended the Westfield schools in Washington Township where I graduated in 1939, after twelve years there. For two years following graduation, I was secretary to the principal, before marriage to James Eli Smith on March 14, 1942. We have always farmed and milked cows.

We moved to KEY-PET FARM in Nottingham Township from a big dairy farm we rented, MODEL MILL FARM located on State Road 38, two miles northwest of Noblesville. Our next door neighbor was Earl Powell's brother. (Earl was Craig Leonard's grandfather and Claudine's father-in-law.) We became acquainted with Earl through his brother, Harley, and when we got interested in buying a farm of our own, we decided to accept Earl's invitation to come to Wells County and let him show us around. (Earl had moved up from Hamilton County about thirteen years earlier.) He took us around to see some farms, and in the late fall of 1951, we purchased a farm from former Bluffton Mayor Charles Decker and his wife Jeanne, located on State Road 318, now County Road 1000 S. We moved on February 22, 1952, Washington's birthday.

We had two sons at the time; Stephen Frederick, born July 22, 1943, at Noblesville; and James Daniel, born March 18, 1948, at Indianapolis.

James Eli and Amanda S. Smith

We brought seven Holstein cows and some young stock with us. We had a drought that first summer, so Jim worked at extra jobs for a few years. He worked on the Bluffton City State Department, and for the County and State Highway departments, until he went into full-time dairying in 1959.

We were blessed three more times with the arrival of Joseph Alan, born December 19, 1953,; Mark Sumner, born May 19, 1955; and William Philip, born January 2, 1961, who was Wells County's first baby of the year. all were born in Wells County Hospital and all graduated from Southern Wells High School: Joe in 1972, Mark in 1973, and Bill in 1979.

Steve graduated from Petroleum High School in 1961, and from Huntington college in 1965. He has taught in the Montgomery County schools for several years. Dan graduated from Petroleum High School in 1966, and attended Taylor University for one and one-half years before serving in the U.S. Army for three years; one in Vietnam from July 15, 1969 to July 18, 1970.

We have ten grandchildren (nine living) and three step-grandchildren. Six were born in Wells County Hospital.

Dan married Cassidy Gwen Price September 29, 1984; their children are: Meredythe Katheryne, born January 10, 1986; Ethan Michael, born May 31, 1987; Anthony Morgan, born October 15, 1988; and Nathanael Matthew, born July 1, 1990. All four were born in Pinellas County, Florida.

Joe married Marita K. Cayot August 18, 1984, their children are: Adam Joseph, born August 8, 1985, died August 16, 1985; Clayton Jake, born March 3, 1988; and Shawn Joseph, born March 15, 1979 (by adoption).

Mark married Karen Elaine Carey, February 18, 1978, their children are: Jennifer Marie, born April 23, 1980; Joshua Seth, born March 27, 1974 (by adoption); and Glenn Nathan, born February 4, 1976 (by adoption).

Bill (married Michelle Fahl in 1982, divorced in 1989), their children are: Ashley Rebecca, born September 21, 1982; Megan Kimberly, born May 9, 1985; Kristan Jenee, born March 5, 1987.

Still actively engaged in dairying with son Bill, Jim holds Life Memberships in the National Holstein Association and Dairy Shrine. Also, the has held office in the following organizations: Indiana Holstein Association, District IV Holstein Club, Wells County Holstein Association, and Dairy Herd Improvement Association, and he has been a member for over forty-five years in the Farm Bureau. This writer has been a member of Wells County Hospital Auxiliary since its beginning, a former member of None Such (Extension Homemakers) Club, and a Sunday School teacher at Keystone Friends Church and Petroleum E.U.B. and United Methodist. We were members of Grace Bible Church for eleven years (in Berne), but attend the Petroleum United Methodist Church at the present time.

The Sumner genealogy has been traced back to Charlemagne (742-814) and the Smith to 1090. Wells County has been home for forty years, long enough to write a short history. (*Amanda Sumner Smith*)

SMITH AND WEAVER

Vaughn E. Smith (see Arthur Smith) married Mary V. Weaver (granddaughter of Jacob and Katie Weaver, great granddaughter of Elijah Jacobs). They have been farmers in Liberty and Union Townships and are the parents of five sons and eleven grandchildren.

Phillip E. was born October 6, 1943. He graduated from Union Center and Ball State University. There he met Wanda K. Orr from Kokomo, and they were married August 29, 1964. Phil is a teacher at Wayne High School in Fort Wayne. Wanda was a teacher's aide at Homestead High School. She died on January 21, 1990. They had three children. Brent E. was born may 3, 1966, and married Rachel Moreland on September 20, 1986. They lived just south of Zanesville until January of 1991 and then moved to a home south of Markle. Brian T. was born June 14, 1967, and married Jennifer S. Linn on December 18, 1987. They live in Cincinnati, Ohio. Brian has been to Haiti and Zaire, Africa, on Missionary Internships. Kimberly J. was born April 22, 1973, and is senior at Wayne High School. She has enrolled in Lutheran School to study radiological technology.

The Vaughn Smith Family

Keith E. was born June 16, 1947. He graduated from Lancaster Center, and General Motors School in Detroit. He worked as an auto mechanic, and then went into farming. He is a salesman now with McBride Realty in Bluffton. He married Linda L. Crum (daughter of Ardis and Maxine Crum of Uniondale) on June 5, 1971. Linda is a teacher at Ossian Elementary School. They have three children. Cory B. was born June 9, 1973, and is a senior at Norwell. He has been drum major for their marching band the past two years. He is enrolling at Ball State University in the fall to study music. Mindy J. was born May 15, 1974, and is a sophomore at Norwell. Craig E. was born September 21, 1977, and is in the Middle School at Norwell. Keith and his boys seem to have inherited their grandfather's (Arthur Smith) musical talents as they sing and play several musical instruments.

Duane L. was born April 14, 1952, and graduated from Norwell in 1970. He also has musical talent and led the Norwell Band as drum major. He also played in many of the musicals and plays at school and in Fort Wayne at P.I.T. and Civic Theaters. Duane spent twelve years in Washington D.C., working and learning the floral industry. He now is employed as a florist and lives and works in Fort Wayne.

Fred L. was born May 14, 1954. He drove a semi-truck for several years, and is now working as a mechanic for a trucking firm in Fort Wayne. He married Nancy Schober on March 2, 1974. They have three children. Sandi M. was born August 28, 1974, and is a junior at Norwell High School. She is also enrolled in the School of Cosmetology at the Career Center in Fort Wayne. Amy L. was born June 1, 1977, and is in the eighth grade at Norwell Middle School. Jeremy A. was born April 8, 1987.

Jeffrey A. was born November 10, 1964. His senior year at Norwell, he enlisted in the U.S. Marines and is still serving his country as a jet mechanic. He married Tonya Wagner (daughter of Robert L. Wagner and Janis L. Baker and granddaughter of Homer E. Blair) on June 16, 1984. They have two daughters. Christine A. was born December 18, 1984. Sara M. was born September 29, 1986. Jeff and his family live in Lexington Park, Maryland.

We have four grandchildren not in this picture.

IRA C. SMUTS

Ira C. Smuts (1873-1957), son of Jacob and Lavina Kessler Smuts, was united in marriage in 1896 to Etta E. Farrell (1877-1973), daughter of George and Frances Salter Farrell. Ira and Etta lived in Fort Wayne for about two years, where Ira worked for the streetcar company. They moved back to the Zanesville area, on the two-acre homesite on old Indianapolis Road, where they continued to live with slight interruptions, until their family of eleven was reared. Their home was a log frame building until they built a new, ten room, cement block home in 1911. In 1932 they moved to a new brick home they built in Zanesville, where a granddaughter, Jeanette Oldfield, now lives.

Ira Smuts was a general contractor and builder for some fifty-five years in Zanesville and the surrounding area. He was also very active in the construction of the first telephone system in the area. In his later years, he developed the Ira C. Smuts Addition on the west edge of Zanesville. Mr. and Mrs. John Walmsley now live in the last house he built. The Smuts' sons, most of the sons-in-law, and grandsons learned much from Ira in the contracting and building business by working with him. Ruthford and Estal continued in the trades during the summertime, along with teaching industrial arts during the school year. Jacob, the youngest son, taught at Indiana University in Bloomington and operated his company, National Homes, in Tyler, Texas. He owns the Jacob Smuts homestead that has been in the family for over one hundred years.

The children of Ira and Etta Smuts all grew up in the Zanesville area, except Robert, who passed away at the age of five.

Grace and Carson Priser (deceased) had two children: Joseph (deceased), and Daniel. Ruthford E. (deceased) and Bertha Vollmar Smuts (deceased) had six daughters: Jeanette Oldfield, Gene Geringer (deceased), Glenna Cayot, Barbara Peterson, Rosemary Kumfer, and Sharon Chilcote.

Hansel and Imo Zeigler Smuts had two children, Jerry and Nancy Beiser. Marie (deceased) and Raymond Line (deceased) had two children: Harold (deceased), and Caroline Peek.

Cecile and Wilbur Haines (deceased) had three children: David, Alice Pile, and Vesta Daffron. Cecile is now married to J. W. Haley. Vesta (deceased) married Vaughn Johnson (deceased).

Estal c. and Elizabeth Scott Smuts (deceased) had two sons: Lynn, and Lex. Estal was married to Justine Pfeifer (deceased) and is now married to Betty Brubaker.

Jacob G. and Pauline Spaulding Smuts had four children: Suzette key, Michael, James, and Steven

Frances and Edward Bradbury (deceased) had four children: Robert, Thomas, Louise Sadler, and John. Frances was married to Don Freeland (deceased).

Josephine and Warren Crowl had three children: Frederick, Rebecca Fones, and Jane Ann Kashdan.

JACOB SMUTS FAMILY

Jacob was reared on the farm which his parents, Robert and Elizabeth (Kohr) Smuts owned. Robert, of German extraction, was a native of Pennsylvania, moved to Ohio, then to Union Township, Wells County, Indiana.

Jacob was trained in agriculture. He was educated in the district schools of his neighborhood. He made his way by working as a hired hand. He married Lavina Kessler, who was reared in the home of Jacob Barnett. To Jacob and Lavina were born seven children: Frank, Ulysses G., Ira C., John M., Homer V., Cora B., and Jennie P. Jacob, a hard worker who earned himself a one hundred and four acre farm in Union Township, built himself a handsome brick dwelling in 1894, which still stands today, and is owned by his grandson, Jacob G., of Tyler, Texas.

Jacob also owns the parcel of ground just south of Zanesville, where there is a woods that the great blue herons call their home. In February each year, they return here to nest and spend the summer. We have documented proof that the herons have returned to this place for the past fifty-two years, because Alice Settlemeyer has seen them every year since her marriage to Kenneth in 1939. In a very old 1911 *Book of Knowledge* is found this startling information: "In the following tables the extreme age of things like the whale and eagle and tortoise are not given. The tables merely set out the age to which the certain animals often live, not the age to which very fortunate animals among them may possibly reach. The number of years that birds live: The heron—sixty years." According to the book, the heron's life span is only topped by the crow, the swan, and the eagle which are listed at one hundred years. Possibly some that we see in 1991 were hatched here in 1931. There are as many as fifty nests high up in the trees. They are highly visible in winter, being made of large twigs and being very large themselves. In 1991, we see many of the birds at area ponds and creeks. They fly with their necks crooked and their legs straight behind them and they are probably the largest bird you will see in Union Township. We have no idea how many years they have been returning to this spot. It is said that in the winter months the herons fly as far south as South America. *(Jacob Smuts)*

A Union Township Heron and Its Nest

SNIDER

For one hundred and fifty-four years, a farm northeast of Ossian near the Allen-Wells County Line has remained in the Snider name, passing down through four generations.

Henry Virginia Snider came to Allen County, at the age of twenty two, from Botetourt County, Virginia, where he was born May 13, 1812. He was a hauler, ferrying cargo from Virginia to Cincinnati, Ohio. After living a short time in Allen County, Indiana, he moved to Jefferson Township in Wells County. He was granted a one hundred and sixty acre tract of land; the deed was signed by Martin Van Buren, November 2, 1837. He returned to Virginia and met Lurana Catherine Morris in Clark County, Ohio. They married June 11, 1840, and returned to Wells County to begin housekeeping in a twelve foot by twelve foot log cabin. As soon as the land could be cleared, crops of potatoes and corn were planted.

John Chapman who was universally known as Johnny Appleseed soon became a frequent visitor and overnight guest. He knew Henry was a sure source of burlap shirts and the rough shoes he wore. In return, Johnny brought trees and the farm ended up with four acres of Appleseed's finest. One of these seedlings was a stunted little pear tree that Henry's four-year old daughter dragged around with her, insisting that he plant the seedling. The

Ira Smuts Family
Back row: Vesta Johnson (deceased) Hansel, Cecil Haines Haley, Estal, Frances Bradbury Freeland, Rutherford (deceased), Grace Priser. Front: Marie Line (deceased), Etta, Josephine Crowl, Ira, Jacob

seedling was planted directly in front of the second homestead and it survives today!

Johnny Appleseed Pear Tree at Wilson Snider Farm at R. 1, Ossian, Indiana. This was the Henry Snyder farm deeded to him 1837. Snyder relatives in picture, Sunday, July 19, 1987

Henry and Lurana had seven children. Nathan, born April 20, 1862, was our grandfather. Shortly after Henry's death on November 7, 1887, the farm was bought by Nathan Snider. Nathan married Ardella Eva Smith, May 5, 1887, and they were the parents of two children: Bertha; and Wilson, born June 7, 1892, and died June 3, 1984.

Our grandfather Nathan farmed all his life and lived on the farm until Wilson, our father, married Louise Catherine Elett, born November 23, 1918, died July 2, 1973. Nathan and Eva moved to Ossian, and Wilson and Louise moved into the homestead which was built in 1904.

Wilson attended Tri-State College in Angola and became a teacher. He taught a couple of years and then took over the farming. He was on call to go to the U.S. Army during World War II when the Armistice was signed. He also worked for the state and General Electric during World War II. Wilson and Louise had three children: Walter, born march 18, 1921, died November 22, 1973. Walter married Margaret Botruff and had two children, Paul and Jennifer; and lived in Huntington, Indiana.

Irene Louise, born July 11, 1923, married Martin Burkholder and had three children: Pamela, Gary, and Jayne. They live on a farm near Lima, Ohio.

Carol, born December 9, 1934, married Kenneth Harrington and had two children, Kelly and Laura; and now lives in Florida.

When we were small, we attended the Methodist church in Poe and later joined the Grace Lutheran Church in Fort Wayne. (*Irene L. (Snider) Burkholder*)

JOHN SNIDER FAMILY

My great-grandfather, John Snider, was born in Ross County, Ohio in 1801, married Delila Beard on June 12, 1820, and farmed with his father Henry, on Paint Creek (now known as Union Township) in Fayette County, Ohio.

He is shown on the 1826 tax rolls as having paid taxes on two horses, two cows, and one hundred sixty acres of land. After his father's death in 1834, he moved his family to northern Indiana, arriving in the Williamsport (Poe) area in 1835. He served as the postmaster and founded the M.E. church which is still a very active body of believers. While his home was just across the Wells County line to the north, he farmed extensively in Jefferson Township a short distance to the south. When the family arrived in 1835, the area was still inhabited by the Sac, the Fox, and Miami Indians. A trip to Fort Wayne for groceries or other supplies meant traveling right by a large settlement of Indians that lived near the Winchester Trace, a short distance southeast of Fort Wayne. When the tribe was engaged in a war dance or other festivities a very wide detour was necessary.

John Snider, age fifty six; 1857. A dageurrotype

John and his family had to clear most of their acreage of the large hardwoods found in abundance. While many of the logs were used to build a home and the necessary outbuildings, there remained a large number of trees and stumps that had to laboriously removed. Of necessity, the first crops were planted in between the huge stumps, which took considerable energy to remove since all labor was done by hand, with the help of a team of oxen or horses on the heavier work. Another problem for the settlers in northeastern Indiana was the extensive swamps that had to be drained before any farming could occur. John and Delila brought thirteen children into the world and several of their descendents still live in the area. The firstborn was Mary Jane who married into the McLain family, Rachel also married a McLain, Dr. Evan married a McLain girl. William, spouse unknown, Henry, Maranda, Elizabeth, who married Philip Snyder (name changed to Snider), a large landowner in the area, John Wesley, whose wife died in Poe, moved to old Mexico, but is buried near Poe. Emily, (Aunt Emma) has a large number of descendents in Indiana. Sarah died in infancy, Phylena died at seven months, Carlisle married Sarah Cotton in Ossian, in 1867, and the youngest, David, died quite young. Carlisle, my grandfather, enlisted in the 130th Regiment, Company F, of the Indiana Volunteer Infantry. He fought in many of the battles across the south, one of the bloodiest being the Battle of Franklin, Tennessee, where several thousand men were killed in the course of the five-hour battle. In the Battle of Lookout Mountain, he is listed as being among the first to reach the top. He was involved in the string of bloody engagements down across Georgia, known as the Campaign for Atlanta, which ended in the siege and eventual defeat for the Rebels.

After his discharge in 1865, he returned to the farm, but his experiences in the Union Army made his restless and eager to conquer new frontiers to the West. After his marriage, he and his wife Sarah traveled in a covered wagon across Kansas, Iowa, and eastern Nebraska until he found the land he wanted near the little town of Maywood, where he farmed until his retirement. He is remembered as a strongly patriotic man who always led the Independence Day parades playing his drum of fife. he had watched so many men die for freedom that he always valued his own freedom greatly. A grandson, Wesley, still farms the old homestead, but the well-built soddy house has long since melted into the soil from whence it came. A recent trip back to my roots in Indiana revealed the land still being farmed and well cared for by the families descended from John land Philip Snider. The rural families still form much of the backbone and strength of this nation. Many of our leaders have come from this sort of background. A grandson, Morris Snider, LaVeta, Colorado.

SUEL SNOW

This branch of the Snow family are descendents of Nichols Snow of Plymouth, Massachusetts, who came from England in the year 1623 on the good ship A*nn* and married Constance Hopkins in 1627. She had come to America with her father on the *Mayflower*. Although staying in the east (mostly in Massachusetts), Snows started moving west to Pennsylvania and Ohio in the middle 1700's.

Suel Snow, one of the earliest settlers in southern Wells County, Chester Township, came from Ohio in the early 1800's. He and his wife homesteaded on a farm two miles west of what is now Southern Wells School. They had three children. A daughter died in infancy and was the first one buried in what is now known as the Snow Cemetery. Mr. Snow donated the ground and gave it to the county as a free burial ground. A son, Johnnie Snow, died in the civil War.

The other son, Henry Snow, married Elizabeth Booth (also from Ohio) around 1860. They homesteaded a farm one-half mile east of what is now Southern Wells School. They had three children: George, Giffon, and Mollie (Stahl) Snow.

Giffon Snow married Sarah Ellen Goodin in 1893 and also lived on the Henry Snow farm. They had two sons, George Henry and Vertner. Vertner moved to Florida in 1932, and all his descendents are there.

George Henry Snow married Mary Minnich in 1924, and they had six children: Catherine, Kenneth, Crystal, John, Max, and Clyde. They also lived on part of the original Henry Snow farm most of their lives.

Their descendents still living in Wells County are Crystal Krieg, Max Snow, Brad Snow, Elizabeth Haynes, Jacob Snow, and Sarah and Suzanne Haynes.

HENRY SNYDER

Henry Snyder, the son of John Snyder and Elizabeth McDonnell, was born in Stark County, Ohio, and came to Wells County in 1837. He married Mariah Fertig, the daughter of Samuel Fertig and Susan Mumuller, and had nine children: Lewis B. (February 23, 1849—December 31, 1931), John W. (January 1, 1843—1928), Lydia (April 27, 1852—June 9, 1932), Charles, Sarah, and Fanny. Mariah died on August 6, 1856, at the age of thirty nine and is believed to be buried in the Old Ossian Cemetery.

Henry remarried in 1867 to a woman whose name has been lost. They had seven children: Catherine, Lucy, Annie, Mary, George, Martha, and Harland. Our family history tells us that Henry was a cabinetmaker. He died in 1883 and is believed to be buried in Waterford Cemetery in Elkhart County, Indiana.

JOHN SNYDER

John Snyder was born in Germany in 1802. He came to America about 1803, presumably with his parents (whose names are unknown). They stayed in Pennsylvania for a while. John married Elizabeth

McDonnell, a native of Scotland, and moved to Ohio. They came to Wells County about 1838. The Snyders had six children: Henry, Alfred, John, Sarah, Rebecca, and a third daughter whose name is unknown. The unknown daughter married Squire LaFever, for whom Ossian's LaFever Street is named. Rebecca married Peter Kiser, who owned an early butcher shop in Fort Wayne. Peter was born around 1805, and came to Fort Wayne in 1822 driving hogs. He issued rations to the Indians from his butcher shop on Calhoun Street while treaties were being made. He was reportedly six feet tall, weighed three hundred pounds, and is buried in Lindenwood Cemetery.

John Snyder was a cabinetmaker and like everybody else probably farmed to make a living. He died November 15, 1865, and was buried in the Old Ossian Cemetery. His wife Elizabeth was born in 1817 and died February 17, 1859. She is also buried in the Old Ossian Cemetery.

LEWIS F. SNYDER

Lewis F. Snyder, the son of Henry Snyder and Mariah Fertig, was born February 23, 1849. He married Mary A. Caston on August 5, 1875. She was the daughter of Abraham Caston and Clarissa (Sisson) Caston. They bought the farm whose present-day address is 11216 N. 500 E. from Chloe Freeland Caston, who was Mary's stepmother and Lewis' mother-in-law. They had seven children: Celia Jane (June 24, 1877—April 24, 1932), Charles (June 17, 1880—September 28, 1881), Harland V. (August 23, 1883—October 10, 1904), Dora Alice (October 16, 1884—January 24, 1945), Leary Lewis (September 14, 1886—December 2, 1972), Dollie (September 16, 1889—January 20, 1988), and Chloe Ann (September 28, 1893—).

Reportedly, he farmed until his daughter Dollie left home to marry. Since there was no one to milk the cows, he moved to Ossian. He was a Republican and a member of the United Bretheren church. After his death on December 31, 1931, he was buried in Oak Lawn Cemetery in Ossian. His wife was an invalid for two years and ten months before her death on June 4, 1941. She lived with her daughter Chloe. She is buried next to her husband.

SONNIGSEN

John V. Sonnigsen, a young man born of German ancestry, October 21, 1882, in Ottawa County, Ohio, moved to Paulding County, Ohio, and married Meda Gillette on February 26, 1908. She was born may 25, 1885, of Welsh and English parentage. The families were farmers.

They moved to an Ossian, Indiana, farm in February, 1937. During World War II, he worked in a factory in Fort Wayne along with farming. Their children included three daughters: Agnes, Pearl, and Eunice, all married by that time; and a son John Junior, still in high school, graduating from Ossian High School in 1939. He also farmed and drove semi-tractor trailers. Meda, the mother, died April 22, 1945 and John, the father, died in October 1956.

On March 24, 1945, John Jr. married Desta Lucile Fahl, eldest daughter of Charles and Mary Jane (Jennie) Osborn Fahl. Lucile was born December 29, 1919, in Union Township. Her father was a livestock and grain farmer and her mother had been a schoolteacher, but after marriage, at that time, women could not teach.

John and Lucile lived in Jefferson Township, and their family of five included Penelope (Penny) Suzanne, born December 27, 1951; Sara Elizabeth, born April 23, 1953; James (Jim) Leslie, born March 16, 1957; and twins, Jayne Anne and Jerrold (Jerry) Wayne, born January 12, 1959. This marriage ended in divorce in 1961, and the mother and children moved to Union Township, where the children attended school and each graduated from Norwell high School. Penny and Jayne each attended IPFW, Fort Wayne. Lucile retired in December, 1985, after nearly twenty years, from Triad-Utrad in Huntington, Indiana. This family continues to live in Wells County, except James, who owns his home and lives with his family in Fort Wayne, and the father, John Jr., retired from Perfection Biscuit Company as head garage mechanic, lives in Fort Wayne.

One member of the Sonnigsen family, Lieutenant Lynn Rothenbuhler, son of Agnes Sonnigsen Rothenbuhler, gave his life in the Vietnam War, serving as a helicopter pilot. He was buried in Fort Wayne with military services. The husband of Penny Sonnigsen, Richard Steinhilber, served in the air Force during the Vietnam War, later in the National guard, and then in the Navy aboard a frigate with duty in the Persian gulf as a lieutenant. They have a daughter, Amy, who joined the army Reserves and started training in a medical unit after graduating from Norwell High School in 1990, during which time many service people were taking an active part in Desert Storm.

SOWARDS

The Sowards family originated from Scotland and settled in eastern Ohio. John Sowards and Sarah Cole, born in Ohio in early eighteen hundred, were married and had two sons, Albert and Thomas J. Thomas Jefferson Sowards, born 1844—died 1922, was a civil war veteran, farmer, and then went into banking. He owned the Tocsin bank and resided on a farm near Tocsin. He married Rachael Dailey. her brother Frank Dailey ran for the governor of Indiana on the Democratic ticket in 1928, but lost by a small margin. They had three daughters, Lydia, Emma, and Ida; and two sons, Joseph D. who died in 1889 at the age of six, and John Randolph, born 1877—died 1963. He was my grandfather and was a kind and gentle man and loved children. He was raised on a farm near Tocsin and worked for the railroad, then as a rural route mail carrier until retirement. He drove a horse and buggy and then a car on his mail route, which was south-east of Bluffton. I now reside on a farm on his old mail route. He married Estella Kreigh on October 12, 1898. She was from a farm near Ossian and was born in 1876 and died in 1966.

Joseph Alonzo Sowards, two years; John R. Sowards, thirty years. T. J. Sowards, sixty-three years.

Four children were born from the marriage of John and Estella Sowards. Joseph Alonzo was born December 30, 1904, and died March 30, 1988. He married Bertha Baughman of Decatur in August of 1931. They were married fifty-six years and lived in the same house on main Street in Bluffton. He managed the Sinclair gas stations in Bluffton and was the Harrison Township Assessor during 1975 to 1986. He always gave treats to kids that came into the gas stations and was a good friend to everyone in the community. Justine, born May 6, 1907—died 1980, was married to Cletis Railing and had two daughters, Lynn and Cheri. Donna, born August 30, 1911, married Don Dillon and resides in Cambridge City, Indiana. Dale, born June 12, 1915, married Vera Pontius and resides in North Fort Myers, Florida.

From the marriage of Joe and Bertha Sowards four children were born. Arleen, born January 10, 1934, a graduate of St. Joe Hospital of X-ray technology and LPN school from Fort Wayne; married Don W. Harvey and had one child, Steve. Don and Steve are engaged in farming. Steve married Dawn R. Stone.

Nancy, born March 27, 1932, married George Dunwiddie and works at the County Clerk's office. George retired from International Harvester and they have four children. Juli married David Kaplan and lives in Arlington, Virginia. Marcia married Eric Steffen and has one daughter, Amber. They live in Bluffton. Linda married Mark Grush and lives in Leo, Indiana. Mark is a senior at Norwell.

Ned, born January 9, 1941, graduated from Purdue and married Myrna Boren. He is employed at Kirsch in Sturgis, Michigan. They have one son, Michael, age sixteen.

John, born February 8, 1943, lives in Fort Wayne and is employed at Office Depot. He has one daughter, Lynn, age seventeen.

WALTER SPEHEGER AND MARY (MCAFEE) SPEHEGER

The Speheger ancestors came from Switzerland to America by sailboat in the early 1800's. To have milk for the children they brought a cow on the boat with them. They then came by covered wagon to Wells County. Ben Speheger, one from this family, married Eliza Dubach.

The Dubachs came from Switzerland to this country by steamboat. A daughter, Eliza, was twelve years old. They settled in Wells County, where Ben and Eliza were married.

Ben and Eliza cleared the ground and built their home in Lancaster Township over one hundred years ago.

Occasionally, they would see an Indian come from the woods to drink water from the hog trough. Ben and Eliza had twelve children. The youngest son, Walter, was born in 1910 and married Mary McAfee from Rockcreek Township.

Speheger Hoosier Homestead Farm

William McAfee, of Irish descent, married Sarah Lamm. Her ancestors came from Heidelberg, Germany. William McAfee and Sarah Lamm married and settled in Liberty Township. Coulson, one of their four sons, married Myrl Miller.

The Miller descendants came from Pfatz, Germany, and settled in Pennsylvania. They brought with them a twenty-five pound Bible. The lids were board covered with leather, with brass corners. It is said to be well preserved to this date. A descendant, Lemuel Miller, married Elizabeth Staver, and they lived in Rockcreek Township. They also cleared the ground for their home. Their youngest daughter, Myrl, married Coulson McAfee. Their only child married Walter Speheger in 1941.

Walter and Mary live on the Speheger Homestead farm. They are members of the Apostolic Christian Church. When Walter cared for his parents and farmed, the farming was done with horses, and the ground was plowed with a one-row walking plow. Wheat was shocked and then thrashed, and corn was husked by hand. He also worked nine years in the AAA office. He then worked in the Old-First National Bank until he retired. They both attended one-room schools and walked there with the neighborhood children. They graduated from high school in their townships. Mary graduated from Anthony Wayne Institute business college in Fort Wayne and worked in the office of the Bluffton Grocery Company until 1943. She later was cashier at many auction sales.

Their two children are Stevan and Susan. Stevan graduated from Purdue with a degree in electrical engineering. he now is manager of Christian radio station WCFY in Lafayette. He married Monica Sutton, a registered pharmacist from Lafayette. Their oldest son, Douglas, is a graduate of Jefferson high School and also from Purdue in Meteorology. He is now doing research and studying for his Master's degree in Oklahoma. Roger is a student at Jefferson high School in Lafayette. His interests are baseball and coaching little league teams.

Susan (Speheger) Frauhiger is a licensed beautician, having graduated from Ravenscroft Beauty College. She practices her profession at her home. She married Leon (Pete) Frauhiger of Lancaster Township. He is a sales representative for Energy Control, Inc. in Ossian. They live in a home they built in the west end of the woods on the Speheger homestead. Their son, Jeffery, is a student at Norwell high School. His hobbies are wrestling and competitive horsemanship.

CHARLES B. AND RHODA A. SPENCER FAMILY

I am Retha Spencer Waters writing this. We moved from Roanoke to Union Township, Wells County, March 1, 1931. We lived three fourths of a mile south of the Allen-Wells County line, one mile east of Wells-Huntington County line, back a long lane. The neighbors north were the Tom Chaney family. The one south was the George Farrell family on Markle R.R. 1.

There were eight of us children: Bernard, Glen, William, Leota, Retha, Charles, Ruth, and Iva. Bernard graduated from Union Center in 1935. Ruth and Iva started school at Union.

In this picture from left to right are Mother Spencer, Glen, William, Leota, Retha, Ruth, and Iva. Father Spencer, Bernard, and Charles went to Markle with a load of wheat that day.

February 14, 1933, the house you see in the picture burnt to the ground. Father and Glen went to Roanoke that morning. The only ones home were Mother and Iva. The rest of us were in school. Mother saved a few things, but didn't want to take any chances. She didn't want Iva out in the cold too long, so she took Iva to the Farrell home. The neighbors around there took us in two nights. Then the trustee opened up the old schoolhouse in Zanesville, where we lived for a couple of months. We attended Mt. Zion church on the Wells-Huntington County line while we lived there. Mt. Zion used kerosene lamps that hung from the ceiling. They used coal and wood stoves to heat it.

Left to Right; Mother Spencer, Glen, William, Leota, Retha, Ruth, and Iva.

Father fixed a tool shed over for a house. We lived there until fall and moved one mile south of Zanesville until March 1st. Then we moved over near Uniondale. We attended Prospect Church when we lived there. The Jim Scott family lived north of us and the Oscar Schwartz family south. We lived there until March 1937.

My husband, Edward A. Waters, and I, Retha Spencer, were married July 25, 1940. My husband drove a bus into Bluffton for Huntington City lines and Twin City lines. Walter Moffitt owned the bus lines.

Our father died March 11, 1940. Mother died May 15, 1963. Bernard died March 29, 1975. his wife died November 9, 1989. Bernard married Rose Waters, May 15, 1949. Glen married Ada Kendall, October 8, 1941. William married Mary Earl, November 17, 1955. Leota married John Gougel, April 10, 1955. Charles married Donna Vincent, May 25, 1947. Ruth married Bill Young, December 25, 1957. Iva married Hank Brooks, July 1955. All have children but William and Leota. We have a grandson, Kelly A. Kipp, living on South Street in Bluffton. He married Vickie Curtis from Pennville. They have two daughters. (*Retha spencer Waters*)

SPRINGER

My great great grandfather, George Michael Springer, was born May 27, 1828, in Steinhart, Heidenheim District, Kingdom of Bavaria, Germany. He was married September, 1852, in Orange County, New York, to Maria Katharina Krauter, born February 7, 1833, in Ehingen, Wassertrudingen District, Kingdom of Bavaria, Germany.

My great, great grandfather was a Lutheran in Steinhart, Bavaria. I have the addresses of my living relation in Steinhart, Bavaria. They still are members of the same Lutheran church. The church in Steinhart is a newer church built today.

He came from the Port of Bremen to the Port of New York. The name of ship was Brem Barque Juno. It was a sailing ship. He arrived around New York City on September 13, 1852, with his future wife and his older brother, George Leonard Springer, and his wife Maria Sybil Krauter. They both married Krauter sisters. He stayed one year and seven months in Orange County, New York, as a farm hand and blacksmith. His trade was a blacksmith. They saved enough money for the canal boat ride and farm land to move to northern Indiana.

At Orange County, New York, they got on the Erie Canal, took that all the way to Toledo, Ohio, or maybe Mohawk Trail, then Lake Trail to Toledo, Ohio. From Toledo, Ohio, they took the Wabash and Erie Canal to Fort Wayne, Indiana. From there, they took the Plank Road, now called highway #1, or Bluffton Road, to southern Allen County, arriving April, 1854.

From there, my great, great grandfather eventually bought thirty acres on Yoder Road, near Highway #1. They lived in a log cabin for ten years. He and his older brother, George Leonard Springer, helped to start St. Mark's Lutheran Church on the Thiele Road just in Allen County, known as 450 E in Wells County. He saved more money those ten years. Then on May 16, 1864, he bought 65.84 acres in Wells County, on Highway #1 and the corner of 1200 North. By the 1890's he owned all four corners, Allen and Wells County line. In Allen County, it is known as South County Line Road.

My great, great grandfather's old wood house stands today. It has been remodeled with many additions. The address is 11820 north, State Road #1, Jefferson. Township, Wells County, Ossian, Indiana.

My great, great grandfather's intent for naturalization was October 10, 1854, Old Courthouse, Allen County, Indiana. His final naturalization was recorded October 11, 1888, Wells County court House.

I am Gordon L. Springer, working on the Springer family tree, with my aunt Della (Springer) Hilsmier, also along with Virgil Springer and Opal (Mahon) Thiele. The book will be available in the Bluffton and Ossian Libraries by 1993.

My great, great grandfather had thirteen children. The oldest, George Frederick Springer, was my great grandfather. He married Mary Louise Moshammer, on November 19, 1878. They had five children. Their third child was Gust Ernst Springer, who was my grandfather. He married Annetta Louise Marie Dettmer on January 2, 1908. They had twelve children, with my father, Kenneth L. Springer, being the eleventh child. He married Edna Eileen Felger on June 17, 1956. They had six children, four sons and two daughters.

My father, Kenneth L. Springer, graduated in 1951, from Indiana University. He was in real estate, and recently retired from the Ossian State Bank, as Senior Vice President. My mother, Eileen Springer, graduated in 1953 from Capital University, Columbus, Ohio, and taught four years an an elementary teacher in the Fort Wayne Community Schools.

Gordon, the oldest, has worked at the K-Mart Distribution Center, Fort Wayne, Indiana, since October 1978. His job title is Maintenance Class B.

Bradley Springer is a firefighter for the City of fort Wayne. He is also working on his fire science degree through a correspondence school, University of Cincinnati, Ohio. He was also in the Marine Corps from 1979-86, with a rank of E4 Sergeant, ground radio repair. His wife, Karen, graduated from Germania college, Quantico, Virginia. She is a nurse manager at the Lutheran Hospital, Fort Wayne. Her great grandmother is Bertha Cupp, who is one hundred and one years old in 1991. They

563

Kenneth and Eileen Springer family; their six children, four sons and two daughters, with their son and daughter-in-laws and grandchildren. Back, left to right; Bradley Springer, his wife, Karen (Taylor) Springer; Phillip Shappell, his wife Sharon (Springer) Shappell; Marshall Springer, his wife Jan (Detwiller) Springer; Paul, Kay, Gordon Springer. Front, left to right; Bradley Springer, Jr.; Mother Eileen (Felger) Springer, holding Gregory Shappell; Zachary Springer; Father Kenneth Springer; Shane, Justin Springer. Picture taken November 12, 1989.

have one son, Bradley, Jr., who attends grade five at Maplewood Elementary School in Fort Wayne.

Marshall Springer was in the Air Force, 1980-84, jet engine mechanic, rank E5 or Staff Sergeant. He works at the Air National Guard, Baer Field. His wife, Jan, is going to Lutheran College of Health Professions, Fort Wayne, toward a degree in nursing. They have three sons:. Zachary in grade two, Ossian Elementary School, enjoys playing soccer. Justin, grade one, is also at Ossian, and Shane at home.

Sharon (Springer) Shappell graduated from Ivy Tech and is a medical secretary for the Lutheran Hospital, Fort Wayne. Her husband, Mike Shappell, was in the Marine Corps from 1982-86, rank E4, radio operator. He now is employed with Bushey's, Inc., Fort Wayne, Indiana. They have one son, Gregory, at home.

Paul Springer graduated from I.T.T., Fort Wayne, and is employed with General Electric Aircraft Division, Taylor and Brooklyn, Fort Wayne, Indiana.

Kay Springer is attending I.U.-Purdue, fort Wayne, working toward a degree in communications. On her father's side, she is the youngest of fifty cousins.

Near 1200 North, on Highway #1, is my great, great grandfather's home. On 1200 north, the Allen County side, is my great grandfather's home, George F. Springer's. The house has been abandoned since the mid 1950's. Continuing on east is my grandfather's home, Gust E. Springer, and then my father's home, Kenneth Springer. My father's home is near his brother's apple orchard. The orchard is owned by Raymond and Roberta Springer. All of these homes are within a mile distance.

ARTHUR SPRINGER FAMILY

Our parents, Arthur and Minnie Springer, were born about a half mile apart. They lived most of their lives on the farm where Dad was born, northeast of Ossian.

My father's parents were Leonard Martin Springer and Marie Emile Dettmer. This is covered in another article under Leonard Martin Springer.

Our mother's father was John Michael Lipp, who was born February 13, 1862 in Wells County, son of Michael (1834) and Anna Margaritha (Fuchshuber) (1841) Lipp. Michael and Anna were born in Wurtemburg, Germany. Anna died in 1873.

In 1874 Michael Lipp married Eve Young, who gave birth to Margaret, who married Michael Springer (1894); Gust, who married Clara Hilsmier in 1901; Maria Caroline, who married Ferdinand Springer in 1899; and Fred, who married Clara Brase in 1903. Michael and Ferdinand Springer were my grandfather Leonard's brothers.

Virgil, Herbert, Gerald, Chalmer 1982

Our mother's mother was Caroline Young, born October 28, 1860 in Rhineburg, Germany. She was daughter of Valentine and Caroline (Kiefer) Young. Her older sister was Eve, born 1853, who married John Michael Lipp's father.

Valentine and Caroline Young also had a son, Gustave (1863), in Germany. Valentine and family emigrated in 1964. Then they had Jacob, who was born in Wells County (1868). He married Christina Lahrman in 1890.

John Michael Lipp married Caroline Young in 1887 at St. Mark's Lutheran Church in Allen County. All of our grandparents and great grandparents went to St. Mark's. Some of them helped start the church.

Their children were Michael (1888), who married Cora Springer in 1909; Edith, who died as a young woman; Minnie Rose, who was our mother and was born March 25, 1891; Charles (1892) who married Magdalena Springer in 1914; John (1894), who married Edna Lahrman in 1915; George (1895) who married Alvina Hilsmier in 1917; and Edward (1897), who married Mae Wallace in 1919.

During the depression of the early thirties, the Lipp families and our family had many great family get-togethers. We hunted, butchered, played cards, and ate together. My father drove a school bus for eight years at this time. He said that this job saved his farm.

Our parents, Arthur Springer, born July 10, 1889, and Minnie Lipp, were married on October 17, 1912. They owned and farmed one hundred and ten acres on the same road where they were born.

They had four sons: Herbert, born September 29, 1913, married Beryl Rodda (who was the daughter of Ossian's blacksmith) in 1937; Gerald, born November 11, 1915, married Ann Bloom of Garrett in 1939; Chalmer, born March 6, 1921, married Emma Jean Young of Fort Wayne in 1943; Virgil, born November 5, 1927, married Donna Ballinger of Fort Wayne in 1951.

Herbert retired from General Electric. Gerald and Virgil retired from Navistar. Chalmer retired from the vending machine business.

Herbert and Beryl's children were Bill, Lenard, Herbert Charles, and Cheryl. Gerald and Ann had Jim and Bonnie. Chalmer and Jean had Dan, Norman Dale, and Stanley. Virgil and Donna's children are Steven, Kathleen, and Lori.

Chalmer and Jean live on the back of the old home place. (*Virgil Springer*)

LEONARD MARTIN SPRINGER

My grandfather, Leonard, was born December 18, 1856, in Pleasant Township in Allen County. When he was eight years old his family moved to the northeast quarter of Section Four of Jefferson Township, Wells County. This is the southwest corner of Highway #1 and the Allen and Wells County Line.

His father was George Michael Springer, born May 27, 1828 in Steinhart, Germany, son of George L. and Maria (Mince) Springer. George L. was a farmer and a blacksmith. Other children were George Leonard, John Martin, Christina, Barbara, and Catherine. Only the boys and Catherine, of this family, came to this country. Catherine married Conrad Thiele (1859). John married Eva Fuchshuber (1858). George Leonard married Maria Sybilla Krauter.

Leonard Martin Springer's mother was Maria Katharina Krauter, born 1833, in Bayern, Germany. Her parents were George and Eva Maria Krauter. George Michael and Maria Katharina (Krauter) Springer were married in Germany in 1852, and came to Orange County, New York, the same year. After two years they came to Allen County. They had thirteen children, most of them born in Wells County. Leonard Martin Springer, my grandpa, was married to Marie Emile Dettmer on December 9, 1879, at St. Mark's Lutheran Church by F. A. Born. This church is about one mile east and on-fourth mile south of Yoder.

Maria Dettmer was born in Orange County, New York on August 11, 1857. Her father was John Diedrich Dettmer, who was born August 15, 1823 in Braunschweig, Germany, son of John D. and Sophia (Bachman) Dettmer.

John Diedrich Dettmer came to New York in September 1851. In March of 1855, he married

Mary Barbara Engelhard. She was born September 24, 1831 in Germany, and had come to New York in 1852.

In 1867 the Dettmers came to Wells County and cleared two hundred and twenty-three acres north of Ossian. Their other children were Anna, who married Charles Lahrman (1876); Maggie, who married Andy Springer 1891), Leonard Martin Springer's brother; Julia, who married John Ernst Witte; John who married Ida Macky; and Friedrich, who died as a child.

Leonard Martin and Mary (Dettmer) Springer had four children, all born northeast of Ossian. They were: Albert (1880) who married Mary Herbst (1902); Emma (1883) who married Friedrich Schinkel (1905); Jennie (1886) who married Jasper Redding (1905); and Arthur (my father) who was born on July 10, 1889. He married Minna Lipp on October 17, 1902.

Leonard was a farmer and a cobbler. I remember seeing his bench and cobbler tools upstairs in their house across the road from our farm. When I was young, we farmed his land. I can remember the aroma of eggs and fried potatoes almost every morning when we went by their house to go to the fields. They had a small hand pump in the kitchen for water. They also had oil lamps, and always drove a horse and buggy to church.

My grandparents had a home in Ossian on the southwest corner of Roe Street and Highway #1, where they retired. (*Virgil Springer*)

ADRIAN SPRUNGER FAMILY

Adrian and Nadine Sprunger have lived their life together in Wells County. They were married in 1940 and have raised one daughter, Camelia; and four sons, Jack, Kent, mark, and Ted. Adrian and Nadine have been living one-half mile east of Poplar Grove School on 350 South since 1954.

Adrian was associated with Masterson Clothing Store from 1941 to 1987. After he served his country in World War II, he resumed as a salesman and eventually bought the store in 1977. During the years when Adrian worked at Mastersons, he was involved with the Bluffton Chamber of Commerce, and a leader in many functions of the Retail Merchants Association.

Adrian was active in raising his children. He worked with the Bluffton Junior League and Teen League baseball programs. He was very active in athletics, and has maintained a vigorous interest in sports during his adult lifetime. Along with being a member of the First United Methodist Church, he has been active in various church, school, and community activities, including the Lions Club.

Adrian and Nadine Sprunger

Along with the above activities, Adrian has been interested in government affairs. He was elected to the Harrison Township Trustee position for three consecutive terms beginning 1971 until 1983. In 1987 he was elected Wells County Commissioner, and is serving in this position at the present time.

Nadine has been busy raising and supporting their children and grandchildren in various school activities. Along with providing her family with a loving home, she worked for the Bluffton Harrison School lunch program from 1963 to 1986. She always had an encouraging word and smile for the school children.

All the children are Bluffton High School graduates. They were active in high school athletics and all received a major B in sports.

Their daughter, Camelia, married Donald Clark, son of Mr. and Mrs.. John Clark of Angola, Indiana, where they now reside. They have four children: Matthew, Amy, Beth, and Julie.

Jack married Barbara Goldsberry, daughter of Mr. and Mrs. James Goldsberry of Bluffton. They now reside in Stafford, Virginia, and have three children: Suzanne, Scott, and Steven.

Kent married Sheila Moser, daughter of Mr. and Mrs. Nelson Moser of Bluffton. They have four children: Marie, Jason, Joseph, and John.

Mark married Sherrill Fahl, daughter of Mr. and Mrs. Ross Fahl of Markle, Indiana. They have two children, Todd and Jennifer.

Ted married Mary Lou Van Winkle, daughter of Mr. and Mrs. Clyde Van Winkle of Goshen, Indiana. They have two sons, Benjamin and Daniel.

The Kent, Mark and Ted families all now reside in Bluffton.

OTTO SPRUNGER FAMILY

It was in the fall of 1926, when Otto and Lila Lehman Sprunger moved to Bluffton from Berne, Indiana, with their three sons; Orison, Frederick, and Adrian. Otto had come to Bluffton to work as an engineer at the Hoosier Condensery Milk Company. In 1928 another son was born, Vaughn; and in 1931, another son, Curtis. The Sprunger and Lehman families both migrated to Berne, Indiana, from Switzerland in 1852, and all the parents and grandparents of this family were of Swiss descent.

The Otto Sprunger family lived on West Wiley Street until their death. Otto died in September of 1953, and Lila in June 1955. The Sprunger family was a Protestant Christian family of the Mennonite Faith and later joined the Reformed Church, now known as the United Church of Christ. Otto and Lila Sprunger knew the Lord and then demonstrated it daily, not with eloquent words, but with a welcoming spirit, charity, and love that their lives were lived to the glory of God.

Their five sons graduated from Bluffton High School. They had a great interest in sports, music, and all the fine arts. All five sons received a letter B in all the various sports.

The mother of the family was very talented in music. She spent hours playing the piano, and making her sons sing hymn. Mother Sprunger was also known for her baking, and was famous for her sugar cookies, cakes, and noodles.

In 1940, Orison married Miriam Liechty, daughter of Mr. and Mrs. Jerry Liechty from Berne. They had five children. Their eldest son is now deceased.

Also in 1940, Adrian married Nadine Barger, daughter of Mr. and Mrs. Herman Barger of Kirkland, Township, Adams County. They had six children, two daughters and four sons; the youngest child lived only five months. Adrian and his family was the only one of the five sons to make his home in Bluffton.

In 1941, Frederick married Dorothy Maddux, daughter of Charles and Bertha Graden Maddux of Bluffton, and had two children, Susan and Tom. After returning from World War II, Fred started working for Franklin Electric and was an early employee in the early growth of Franklin Electric. Later he was sent to Siloam Springs, Arkansas, where they now make their home.

Vaughn, married Arlene Habegger, daughter of Sylvan and Martha Habegger of Berne, Indiana. Vaughn is now, and has been, pastor of the Community Baptist Church at South Bend, Indiana. They have two children.

Curtis married Nyla Hicks, daughter of Mr. and Mrs.. Clyde Hicks of Yankton, South Dakota. Curtis and his family, one daughter and two sons, live at Mt. Clemens, Michigan, where he and his wife are both teaching.

RAY A. STAIR

Ray A. Stair was born on May 29, 1917, to Harry C. Stair and Lillie A. (Beyler) Stair in Marshall County, Indiana. He has one brother, Victor, living in Enid, Oklahoma, and four sisters living in Indiana. Rose Goodman lives in Elkhart. Vera Klatt lives near Plymouth. Vida and Tressie Stair live here in Bluffton. We all grew up on farms between Plymouth and Bremen, Indiana.

Ray graduated from Plymouth High School in 1935 and is thankful for all the Marshall County friends God has blessed him with. Our parents brought us up in Wesleyan Methodist Churches of Plymouth and Shiloh. Ray came to a living faith in Jesus Christ at Shiloh in 1936. God has given him a good and varied life with good fellowship with His Spirit and His people. Praise God from whom all blessings flow!

After high school, Ray worked for some of the best farmers between Plymouth dn Bremen, Indiana. Then he started working his way through Marion College (now Indiana Wesleyan University) until being drafted into the U.S. Army in 1944. The winter of 1945-46 he had charge of a First Aid Station in Camp Punch Bowl on the edge of Honolulu, Hawaii. He was honorably discharged in 1946, went back to Marion College for a year, and then transferred to Taylor University and graduated in 1948. He then went to Asbury Seminary for a year, after which he pastored a small Friends' Church in southwest Kansas during the winter of 1949-50.

After that, Ray went back to Marion, Indiana, and started dating Clara Ellen Brady. They were married December 30, 1950. Clara Ellen and Ray were both school teachers and taught in Indiana, Ohio, and Wisconsin. They had one son, Timothy Ray, who now has two sons, Joel and David. They all live in Elkhart, Indiana. Clara Ellen died of cancer and went to be with the Lord in 1970 while we lived near Augusta, Wisconsin. Before leaving Augusta, the Lord made it possible for Ray to give one hundred and sixty acres of woods to the New Tribes Mission. They are still using it as a boot camp.

After leaving Augusta, Wisconsin, Ray worked for the World Missionary Press at New Paris, Indiana, for over nine wonderful years.

In February of 1976, Norma Ann Grove and Ray were married. Her first husband, Hershel, died in an auto accident and went to be with the Lord in 1973. Norma grew up here in Bluffton, and we live at 739 W. Horton Street. Norma has two sons: Keith, living in Florida; and Neil, living in Fort

Wayne. Norma and I together have eleven grandchildren and two great grandchildren; all with great potentials.

After working over eight years at Meadowvale Care Center as Maintenance Supervisor, Ray retired, being past seventy years of age. Norma and Ray enjoy reading, bicycling, and traveling. They attend the Hope Missionary Church.

VICTOR STAIR FAMILY

Harry C. and Lillie A. Stair lived on a farm north of Plymouth, Indiana, before moving to Bluffton, Indiana. They were the parents of seven children. Six of them grew to adulthood, but Virginia died at the age of two and one half.

Victor is the oldest and now lives in Enid, Oklahoma. He was married to Thelma Bennett in April, 1945, while he was still in the Air Force; later they moved to Bluffton where their four children were born. Thelma died in 1960.

In November of 1960 he was married to Betty Stevens, of Enid, Oklahoma. She had one daughter, Susan, seven years old. They were married in Bluffton, but the following July they moved, bag and baggage, to Enid, Oklahoma. All five children graduated from Enid High School, and later they all went to the college of their choice.

Chuck, the oldest son and his wife, Wanda, live in New Paris, Indiana, with their two children: Jonathan, eleven; and Joanna, eight. Chuck works at the World Missionary Press, and Wanda is director of a nursery school.

Roger lives in Tulsa and is employed for the R.L. Hudson Company as a salesman selling sealing devices and rubber products. They have three boys: Aaron is fourteen; Brett is twelve; and Todd is two; and as I write, another little one arrived—a daughter, Kellie Jan!!

Rose Marie is married to Dwight Robart. They were both in the Navy when they met. They were married here in Enid, but now live in Readsboro, Vermont. Tami, thirteen, and Timmy, eleven, complete their family, unless one would want to count their family of cats!! Dwight works for a nuclear plant in Rowe, Massachussettes.

Tom is the youngest son and lives in Enid with his wife, Cathy, and their two sons: Jordan, eight; and Taylor, one. Tom is employed at the United States Post Office as a clerk.

Our daughter, Sue, graduated from the Oklahoma University School of Nursing and was employed at the hospital in Stillwater, Oklahoma. On the morning of May 12, 1982, she was on her way to work when, during a flash flood, her car was swept off the road and she drowned.

Vic and Betty attend the Cedar Ridge Wesleyan Church. They are both retired from their places of employment, Vic from the post office and Betty from J.C. Penney's. They keep quite busy with their part-time job of delivering medicines for a local drug store and pursuing their hobbies. Vic enjoys his electric guitar, and Betty enjoys working with plastic canvas.

VIDA STAIR AND TRESSIE STAIR

Vida Stair was born in 1927 and Tressie Stair was born in 1929 in Marshall County, Indiana, to Harry C. Stair, 1882-1951, and Lillie (Beyler) Stair, 1888-1982. We are the seventh generation descendants of Johannes Stohr, who arrived in Philadelphia on September 26, 1737, with his sons Johann Heinrich and Johann Philip on the ship St. *Andrew Galley* with John Stedman as master. The figures at the right of the name indicate the generation to which that person belongs: as Johannes (1) would be the first generation in this country; thus: Harry (6) Stair (Reuben (5), Jacob (4), John (3), Heinrich (2), Johannes (1) Stohr).

Harry, son of Reuben and Emma (Funk) Stair, and Lillie Stair, daughter of Moses and Matilda (Zimmer) Beyler, sold their farm near Plymouth, Indiana, in 1950 and moved to 227 East Horton Street, where Vida and Tressie now live. Harry's uncle, Walter Funk, was a judge of St. Joseph circuit court twenty-four years until his retirement in 1924. Harry's uncle, Nelson Funk, designed the Funk eight-color web perfecting press used by Miles Laboratories.

Harry and Lillie Stair's other children are: Victor, Ray, Rose, Virginia (in 1923 died from pneumonia when two years old), and Vera. Victor married Thelma Bennett (a first-grade teacher in

December 29, 1941 at Plymouth Indiana. Front, Left to Right; Tressie Stair, Lillie Stair, Harry Stair, Vida Stair. Back, Left to Right; Vera (Stair) Klatt, Ray Stair, Victor Stair, Rose (Stair) Goodman.

Bluffton) and lived in Wells County several years. Their children; Charles, Roger, Rose Marie, and Tom Stair were born in Bluffton. Thelma Stair passed away May 19, 1960. Later Victor married Betty (Maddux) Stephens and they now live in Oklahoma. Ray married Clara Brady and their son, Timothy, was born in 1955. After Clara passed away in 1970, Ray married Norma (Little) Grove in 1976 and they now live in Bluffton. Rose married Watson Goodman and both lived and taught in Wells County. Their oldest child, Victoria, and youngest child, Harry, were born in the United States—while Donald and Ruth were born in South Africa when Rose and Watson were missionaries there. They co-founded World Missionary Press in New Paris, Indiana, and now pioneer a new work, Enterprises for Emmanuel in Elkhart. Vera married Robert Klatt and they pastored various churches in New York, Michigan, Illinois, and Indiana. They lived awhile at 1020 South Bennett Street with their preschooler sons: Mark, Philip, and David. Later Vera taught first grade at Union Center. Vera and Robert Klatt now live near Plymouth, Indiana, and pastor the Davis Wesleyan Church.

Left to Right; Tressie Stair and Vida Stair (1983)

Vida became a Christian at an early age. Her brother, Vic, paid for her first piano lessons until her teacher offered a scholarship and subsequently a job teaching in one of her studios. Vida later took piano at Houghton college (New York) and Marion college, where she served as music assistant. Her aspiration to become a second grade teacher while still a second grader became a reality after graduating from Marion college (now Indiana Wesleyan University) and Ball State University—seven years at Poplar Grove with the remainder in the Fort Wayne Community Schools.

At the age of nine, Tressie accepted Jesus Christ as Savior at Shiloh Church near Linkville, Indiana. Tressie graduated from LaPaz High School, Marion College (now Indiana Wesleyan University), and Ball State University; she also studied violin a

Vic Stair
Back, Left to Right; Dwight Robart, Tom Stair, Chuck Stair, Wanda Stair, Roger Stair. Middle, Left to Right; Rose Robart, Tami Robart, Cathy Stair, Betty Stair, Vic Stair. Front, Left to. Right; Timmy Robart, Jordan Stair, Joanna Stair, Jonathan Stair, Brett Stair, Aaron Stair, Kay Stair holding Todd Stair.

summer at Houghton College (New York). Tressie taught kindergarten at Bluffton and second grade at Berne and Ossian.

Vida and Tressie have ministered in music for churches, nursing homes, banquets, weddings, receptions, twenty-fifth anniversaries, funerals, various organizations, and "in memoriam" concerts. In 1988 the Stair sisters made a recording and cassette tape with Clifty Studios at Paris, Tennessee.

STANTON-MINNIEAR

Albert Minniear, born in 1869 at Niptite, Indiana, Huntington County, walked to Boehmer in Wells County, at the age of fourteen to visit a sister, Nora Erwin. While visiting Nora, he gained employment with John I. Clark, who had a large farming operation nearby. While working for John T. Clark, he attended the Roberts School and later, Danville College. While working for Clark, he hauled logs to the Jones Saw Mill (located one mile north of Boehmer), which were cut to construct the Boehmer Methodist Church. In 1893, he married Viola Perlina Clark, the oldest daughter of John I. Clark, and moved to the fifty-seven acre farmstead, one mile north of Boehmer, which was purchased from George Melling. This farm, adjoined the Clark farm to the north, and had a log house with two stories. In order to go upstairs, it was required to go outside to access the stairs to the second floor. To this marriage four sons were born: Vaughn, Lloyd, Clarence, and Ernest; and one daughter, Bertha. In 1901 a new house was constructed, and later in 1910 and 1921, Albert purchased a total of one hundred and ten acres across the road in Huntington County.

Viola died in 1919, and Lloyd, the second son, continued to live on the farm and pursue an occupation in farming with his father. The oldest son, Vaughn, became a teacher after graduating from Liberty Center High School. He served in the U.S. Army in World War I, and taught at Petroleum, Tocsin, Plano, Illinois, and Monroeville, Indiana. Later he became superintendent of the schools in Garrett, Indiana. Ernest and Clarence moved to Gary, Indiana, where Clarence worked for the Public Transportation Company, and Ernest was a policeman. Ernest became Chief of Police after attending the J. Edgar Hoover School of the Federal Bureau of Investigation. Later, Ernest held executive positions with the state excise office. In 1930, Albert's only daughter, Bertha, married Harold Stanton after both graduated from Liberty Center High School. Harold was working on construction of one of the large steel mills in Gary, Indiana. As a result of the Great Depression, and the temporary closing of that mill, they moved back to the family farm in 1931. While engaged in farming in Huntington County near Plum Tree, Harold and Bertha purchased the home farmstead upon Albert's death in 1946. In September, 1947, they moved to the Minniear farm with their sons; Max, Larry and Bruce.

Active in Community service, Albert was a school board member when the Liberty Center High School was erected in 1913. Albert was active in development of the Liberty Center Telephone Company and the Farmer's Grain Elevator in Liberty Center. He was a director of the Huntington Mutual Insurance Company. Additionally, he served as superintendent of the Boehmer Sunday School for several years, and was a fifty-year member of the Odd Fellows Lodge in Liberty Center. As an avid outdoorsman he, along with three other comrades, built the first cottage on the eastern shore of Lake Webster in Kosciusko County prior to 1900.

With the advent of rural electrification provided by the REMC, Harold and Bertha improved the farm with the help of their sons, by remodeling the farmhouse and adding a modern water system. Soon the farming operation grew to include a full dairy herd, hog production, and poultry. Many of the family traditions continued as all of the Stantons graduated from Liberty Center High School, and three sons attended Indiana University with the supporting resources of the family farm. Also, all were members of the Boehmer Church where Harold served as superintendent. Also active in community and civic organizations, Harold and Bertha were members of the Wells County Farm Bureau, Home Economics Club and Masonic Bodies in Warren, Indiana, where they helped organize the Chapter of Rainbow.

The oldest son, Max, was an engineer in the electronics industry, after serving in the United States Air Force, and eventually retired in Pinehurst, North Carolina. He and his wife, the former Margret Edminsten, have three daughters and one son. Larry, who married Ester Moeller, became an medical doctor and radiologist. After serving the U.S. Navy, they reside in Washington, D.C. Larry and Ester have three sons and one daughter. Bruce, the youngest son, married Joanne Shultz, and after serving in the U.S. Army in Germany, and Vietnam, resides in Fort Wayne where he is in the contract furnishings business. Bruce and Joanne have two daughters.

Currently with six great-grandchildren, Bertha continues to reside on the family farm where she sleeps in the same bedroom where she was born. Harold died in 1970. Several family reunions have been held to include the fall ritual of making ketchup outdoors in a copper kettle and, most recently, to celebrate Bertha's eightieth birthday in 1989.

STARR-MURRAY

We can date the Starr Family back to 1846, when my great-great-grandfather, Engle, and Catharine Starr lived in Bluffton. December 30, 1846, Engle Starr was the fourth county agent directed to sell logs seventy feet by one hundred and forty feet. They owned 328 East Market and the three houses to the east. One of their six children was Lewis, born November 17, 1861, died November 27, 1929. Lewis was my great-grandfather. He married Mary Bovine and they had two children, Ethel and Harry. Lewis and son Harry owned the Starr Pop ice cream and candy factory at 328 East Market. Harry married Florence (Sprunger) Starr and they had three sons, Harold, Donald and William. Florence taught music and was a very talented lady. Florence continued to live at 328 East Market after Harry's death, February 5, 1964. Florence died February 5, 1974.

My father Harold, born July 15, 1911, died May 22, 1974; married Dorothy Hamje of Bluffton on September 1, 1945. Dorothy was born May 29, 1925, daughter of Edwin J. and Jessie Irene (Ormsby) Hamje. They had one daughter, Trudy L. (Starr) Murray, born February 26, 1947. Trudy attended International Business College and started working September 6, 1966 for Sunier and Lockwood, Incorporated (Insurance office) Trudy married Fred W. Murray, October 18, 1969. Fred was born March 11, 1940, son of Wayne and Ruth Murray. Fred attended Ball State University and teaches Social Studies at Bluffton Harrison MSD. We live at 1035 Stogdill Road, Bluffton. We have two children, Jennifer L. Murray, born June 6, 1971, currently a sophomore at Ball State University majoring in accounting; and Jason F. Murray, born August 8, 1974, currently a sophomore at Bluffton High School.

Fred's parents, Wayne Alfred Murray, born December 31, 1911, died July 30, 1989, and Ruth Lenore Jarrett, born August 17, 1914.

RALPH STARR FAMILY

Born April 15, 1898, in Chester Township, Ralph was the son of Otis and Flora Ulmer Starr. His grandparents were Benjamin F. and Sabina Nutter Starr and Henry and Catherine Edington Ulmer. They were all Wells County residents.

Ralph attended the Poneto School and graduated from Keystone in 1916. He farmed two miles west of Poneto on land that was homesteaded by the Starr family in 1836. He milked Ayrshire cows, raised Percheron horses and grain farmed.

Ralph married Mary Pauline Kean in 1919. She was the daughter of Leroy W. and Gertrude Cole Kean. They were members of the Blanche Chapel Church.

They were the parents of two daughters; Martha Ferne and Doris Elinor.

Ferne married Joe D. Holloway in 1941. They always lived close to her parents and their children were much a part of Ralph and Pauline's lives. (See Joe Holloway history.)

Doris attended Ball State and married Michael Drake. They had one son, Mike. Mr. Michael Drake was the principal of Ossian School in 1976, at the time of his death.

Doris is retired after forty years of teaching primary classes and is now Mrs. Richard Miller, 9182 West Harper Lake Road, Kimmell, Indiana.

After selling the cattle operation in 1960 to his son-in-law, Joe D. Holloway and Sons, Mr. Starr worked as a janitor at the Caylor-Nickel Clinic Hospital for fifteen years.

NORMAN E. STEFFEN FAMILY

Norman E. Steffen(August 1913-November 1961) was the son of John and Lydia Steffen. In 1945 he married Lucille E. Baumgartner (June 1925), the daughter of Louis and Ida Baumgartner. They had three children: Judy Marlene, Terry Wayne, and Ted Louis. Norman and Lucille lived on a farm in Adams County. After Norman passed away the family continued to work on the farm for ten years, at which time it was sold, and they moved to Wells County. Lucille went to work in Bluffton at Bachman's Pretzels, now Keebler's, and worked there for twenty years until retiring in 1990.

Judy married Donald Gene Isch, son of Ervin

Norman Steffen Farm

and Anna Isch. don is employed at Bluffton Rubber Company in Bluffton and delivers the Journal-Gazette daily. Judy is employed at Kitco in Bluffton and just recently celebrated her twenty-fourth anniversary of employment there.

Terry married Gloria Jean Moser, daughter of Nelson and Marie Moser. They have three children: Jean Ann, Wayne Terry, and Joy Lynne. Terry worked at the Bluffton News-Banner for many years. In 1987 Terry and Gloria bought Quick Printing Service in Berne, Indiana, where both are kept very busy. Quick Printing has turned into a family business where Jean, Wayne, and Joy (in the summer) all help out. Jean and Wayne are also part-time students at IPFW. Wayne is married to Jeanne Sue Bertsch, a full-time student at Ball State University; she is the daughter of Walter and Lillian Bertsch. Joy is a student at Bluffton High School.

Ted is married to Rosie Marie Lange, daughter of Donald and Betty Lange, They have six children: Diane, James, Barbara, Claude, Maria, and Ricky J.; and two grandchildren, Jessica and Elizabeth. Ted is employed at Quick Printing Service in Berne, Indiana. Diane, Jessica and Elizabeth reside in Florida.

STEINER

Henry Steiner arrived in Wells County, Harrison Township, from Pennsylvania in the 1800's. He purchased a half section of land and built a log cabin. His wife, Anna Kirchhofer, came to Berne from Ohio. Their son, Albert, was born in the log cabin in the late 1800's. Henry then built a frame barn and a house, both of which still stand (on 350 South, two miles east of Poplar Grove School).

Albert remembered that when he was a small child Annie Oakley visited several times while they lived in the log cabin. He attended Valparaiso College where he met Dr. H. Brown. They became life-long friends. In 1904, he married Ethel May Hauk.

Albert was the first person in Wells County to buy a four-door Buick. It had a cloth convertible top and snap-on side curtains. All trim was brass, including the lights. Later he purchased from the Heche family and operated the brick grocery store in Vera Cruz.

Albert and Ethel had three children: George, Ada, and Helen. George attended Purdue and retired from the Dana Company. He is now living in North Webster. Ada (Mrs. Clarence Miller) retired from Franklin Electric, and is now living in Bluffton and Florida. Helen was an aide at Wells County Hospital for nineteen years. She was also an aide at Davis Care Center, from which she retired. She is now living at the Meadowvale Care Center in Bluffton.

STEPP

Abraham Stepp was born April 16, 1793, in Virginia. He married Mary Wolfe, born July 31, 1801. Abraham and his wife and children: Phoebe, Rebecca, Michael, Abraham, and George moved to Henry County, Indiana, with an ox team and cart as transporation, and settled there for a short time. Another son, John, was born October 27, 1841. Sometime in the 1840's the Abraham Stepp family moved to Nottingham Township, Wells County. Abraham and Mary's sons later owned and lived on the same land. Michael, "who was a carpenter and built the house now standing two and one-half miles east of Keystone," later moved to Muncie. Abraham Stepp died June 26, 1871, and is buried along with his wife, Mary, in Woodlawn Cemetery east of Montpelier.

George, son of Abraham, became a blacksmith and lived in Nottingham Township. George and his wife, Clarissa Wright, lived in a house built by their son-in-law. That house now stands at 10455 South Meridian Road. They had eight children: Mary, Rebecca, Jane, James, Melvin, George, Maritta, and Thomas.

C. Birt Stepp

Back; John Stepp, Bert Stepp, Berteen Minnich, Charles Stepp, Frances Brown, George Stepp, Alice Shannon, Mike Stepp. Seated; Lydia Martin, C. Birt Stepp, Carrie Stepp, Parker Stepp.

Michael, Abraham's son, married Mary Swearingen, April 27, 1859. They had six children: John R., Mary, Emily, Abraham, Anthony, and Levi. Michael and Mary are buried in Stahl Cemetery. John, Michael's son, and his wife, Lucinda Hunter, owned and operated a store on road 50 East between 1000 South and 1100 South. that building now stands two and one-half miles east of Keystone. John R. had five children: Goldie, John, William, George, and Mary. John R. died June 15, 1926, and is buried in Stahl Cemetery.

John, Abraham's son, was born in Henry County, October 27, 1841. He married Maritta Swearingen May 24, 1860. They lived two miles east of Keystone. John was a shoe cobbler by trade and also served as community dentist. John and Maritta had seven children. Three died at an early age. The four living children were: Lydia, Enoch, Cbirt, and Evaline. John died April 9, 1907. His wife died nine days later. They are buried in the Keystone Cemetery.

Lydia married Thomas Rhea. They lived south of Poneto before moving to Parma, Missouri. They had three children: John, Thomas, and James. Lydia died February 26, 1950.

Enoch Stepp was born April 22, 1868. He married Louella Phillips June 15, 1900. They had one child. Louella died at child birth in 1902. The child died February 15, 1905. Enoch worked in the oil field as a driller. He died June 28, 1941.

Evaline married Bert Phillips September 27, 1895. Bert worked in the oil fields of upper Burma for British Oil. Evaline and Bert had no children. She died December 17, 1956.

Cbirt Stepp was born August 4, 1870, in Nottingham Township, Wells County. Cbirt worked in the area oil field and later farmed. Cbirt married Carrie Karns, daughter of George and Marjorie Harris Karns. Cbirt and Carrie both are buried in Woodlawn Cemetery near Montpelier. They had twelve children: Lydia Martin (deceased); Parker, in Redkey; John in Keystone; Michael in Florida; Marjorie in Ohio; George in Montpelier; Frances Brown in Montpelier, Rural Route; Alice Shannon in Montpelier; Berteen Minnich in Berne; Bert in Auburn; Bobby (deceased); and Charles, Meridian Road, Keystone.

STERN-PAGEL

We have been able to trace our family back to Noblesville, Indiana, to John Stern, born December 23, 1848, who married Mary E. Richart, born 1840, and to this union Jacob A. was born November, 1870. Mary E. passed away in 1874. John then married Leanna, born 1856, and to this union four boys and five girls were born. John died June 26, 1927, and Leanna 1932.

Grandpa, Jacob A., and Rosa Ann Webb, who was born November 19, 1870, were married in Winterset, Iowa. They then moved to Karney, Oklahoma, where Earl, Kathryn and Nelson were born. Aunt Kathryn remembers dragging cotton sacks for picking cotton. The family moved back to Noblesville, Indiana, where Jacob had come from originally. There Arthur Lloyd, our dad, was born May 11, 1907. The family moved to Huntington County by train. Jacob died August 30, 1944, and Rosa, June 20, 1940.

Doyle Stern, Carol Barger Stern, Ashley N. Stern, Suzanne McGaughy Stern,]Mark N. Stern, Elizabeth Broyles Stern, and Tim Stern.

Arthur "Art" met and married Esther Marie Emley, born June 17, 1907. Two sons were born in Huntington County; Arthur Lloyd II, December 21, 1930; and Doyle Robert, June 12, 1932. They then moved to Bluffton, Indiana, and Diane Kay was born August 18, 1939; and Ronald Wayne, September 27, 1941.

Art worked for Glen Marsh and John Gallman in auto repair, then started in business on his own in 1946 on Perry Street in Bluffton, Art's Body Shop. In 1941 Art moved his business to a new building he had built on State Road #1 North. He had the Nash dealership; then later it was Art's Rambler Sales. Art died September 7, 1972, and Ester, April 12, 1985.

Arthur Lloyd III "Lloyd" married Joan Walsh, born April 9, 1929. They have two sons. Arthur Lloyd II, born June 25, 1947, who married Susan Kaminke and has two children: Jennifer and Jeffery. And Steven Kent, born June 2, 1959.

Diane Kay married Frank Tayrien, born 1938, and they have two daughters, Kim Marie, born May 5, 1970 and Kristie Jo, born May 4, 1972.

Ronald "Ron" married Sandy Kiefer, born March 9, 1941; and they have three children: Angela Renee, born February 18, 1964, married Mike Wilkins; Cary Edward born August 25, 1966; and Andrew Wayne, born January 26, 1969.

Doyle married Carol N. Barger, born May 19, 1933. They have two children: Timothy Robert, born January 22, 1955; and Mark Nathan, born February 5, 1957. Doyle went to work for his father in the auto repair business in 1951. Then in 1965 he went into a business of his own, Stern's Body Shop, located about two miles north of where Art had his business. During the summers when school was out there were three generation of Sterns working in the shop. Timothy "Tim" graduated from Purdue and Art Center of Pasadena and is in industrial design. Tim married Elizabeth Broyles, born September 10, 1960; and they are expecting their first child.

Mark graduated from Norwell and Purdue and

is in marketing with a firm in Kewanee, Illinois. Mark married M. Suzanne McGaughy, October 4, 1957; and they have a girl, Ashley Nicole, born April 28, 1988.

STINSON

It has been suggested that when shaking the "Old Family Tree" not to shake the old tree too hard as some may be a little overripe.

Some sad but interesting incidents have come to me while tracing the Stinson family tree to great-great grandfather Robert Manley Stinson (1804-1877), who married Polly Bray (1804-1858) on June 2, 1825, at Ramseur, North Carolina. They had ten children. Polly Bray Stinson committed suicide by hanging herself on the rail fence in the backyard of their home on September 14, 1858. Robert Manley Stinson had a sister Anna (Stinson) Welsh. Anna, with an old maid invalid daughter, lived alone. One night a Negro man named Alidy Wren knocked on their door. They wouldn't unlock the door to let him in, so he took an axe from the woodpile nearby and broke the door down. Anna ran out of the back to her son's house nearby, but by the time they returned Wren had assaulted the invalid girl, and she later died. Alidy Wren was later hanged for the deed.
Stinson Family

Left to Right; Nellie, Roy, Anna Jane, Kenneth, Martha, Mae, and Sarah.

One of the ten children was my great-grandfather, John Manley Stinson (August 11, 1833-December 11, 1893) who married Hannah Mary Cassady (July 18, 1842-February 19, 1911) on April 30, 1857, and to this union fifteen children were born. Hannah Cassady's grandparents came from Ireland in 1793 to Pennsylvania. Her parents had nine children, and her grandparents had eight children. John Manley Stinson was in the Civil War, and Hannah had many hardships caring for the many children during his absence.

My grandfather, Eli Marshall Stinson (1866-1946) and a cousin, Paten Cox, came to Indiana in February of 1887 and worked on a farm near Liberty Center. They later moved to Bridgeport, Indiana, and met and married the Lehman sisters. Eli and Rosetta (Lehman) Stinson had three children: Chester (1893-1946), Clara (1895-1932) and Roy Elliott (August 28, 1901-February 15, 1978). Rosetta (Lehman) Stinson inherited a farm, and Eli farmed the place and raised and sold vegetables.

My father, Roy Elliott Stinson, moved to Wells County and married Maudie Mae Kingen (December 7, 1902-July 25, 1988) on October 21, 1922, and to this union were born six children: Alice Rose (1923, died at two months), Martha Louise (1924), Kenneth Edwin (1926), Anna Jane (1928), Sarah Lou (1930), and Nellie Mae (1932). Martha married Joseph Haines (1922-1985) and had three children: Connie Jo (1947); and twins, Susan Louise and Steven Louis (1953). Kenneth married Peggy Lou Ely (born 1932) and had two children: Linda Lou (1951), and Robert Edwin (1953). Anna Jane married Wayne Hamilton (born 1924) and had four children: Cathryn Elaine (1948), Roger Dewayne (1950), Robert Eugene (1952) and Mark LeRoy (1955). Sarah married Charles Garrett (born 1930) and had four children: Larry Dean (1951), Rita Kay (1954), Rea Allen (1958), and Lisa Mae (1969). Nellie married Joe Sleppy 91930) and had two daughters Cindy Jo (1951) and Sandra Lynn (1952). *(Nellie Mae (Stinson) Sleppy)*

MARK STINSON AND BETTY JANE BAKER STINSON

Mark and Betty have been residents of Wells County all their lives. Mark Elwin was the second child of Manley E. Stinson and Pearl O. Gordon Stinson. Manley was the son of Wiley Stinson, who was killed in an auto accident. Pearl was the only daughter of Will and Hattie Gordon. All were residents of Wells County. Betty J. Baker Stinson is the oldest child of Boyde L. Baker and Josephine Meyers Baker. Boyde L. Baker was the youngest child of T.S. and Stella Grimes Baker. The T.S. Bakers were residents of Oklahoma, Iowa, and Texas. Later they moved to Wells County and settled in Nottingham Township. Josephine Meyers Baker was the third child of Fred and Emma McCullick Meyers. Fred Meyers came to the United States at the young age of four years from Litzlestna, Germany. The Meyers residence was on a McCullick farm in Chester Township.

Mark E. and Betty Jane have five children: Rebecca Kay, Jeffrey Deane, Bruce Wayne, Kathy Ellen, and Bradley Lynn. Rebecca Kay married J. Dale Musselman and they have three children: Linda Kay Conner, (Linda having married Mark Conner); Randy Leon, single, living in Warren; and Rodney Allen, who married Dawn Johnloz—they have a daughter, Saundra Brooke, Mark and Betty's first great-grandchild. Becky and Dale also had a daughter, Brenda Kay Musselman, who was laid to rest at Warren at the age of seven days.

Jeffrey Deane married Susan Mechling. They have two children: Brian Jeffrey, born on his great-grandfather's birth date; and Kendra Susan, their second child.

Bruce Wayne married Cheryl Riggs. They have three children: Aaron Wayne; Heather Ann; and Ryan Manley, who was named after his great-grandfather.

Kathy Ellen married John W. Briles, Jr., and they have two children: Kristy Denise, and Nathan Wayne, both residents of Huntington County.

Bradley Lynn was the youngest child of Betty and Mark. Bradley lives at Huntington and attends college.

When Mark and Betty were married they moved to their present residence and have now lived there forty-seven years. They have been farm people their entire married life. Betty is a homemaker and practiced nursing a short time. They are still farming, although they are semi-retired.

JAMES W. STOGDILL

Life for James W Stogdill (the "W" stands for nothing, though he stands for much) started on February 13, 1897, on a farm northwest of Bluffton, Indiana. He was the youngest of four children born to George Washington Stogdill (1862-1950) and Lucinda Jane Vardmen (1863-1926). The oldest was Homer Bert Stogdill (1883-1943), then Glen Zepha Stogdill (1886-1966), then Ethel Stogdill (1892-1966), and finally, Jim. Their parents were both born during Abraham Lincoln's administration.

The family moved to the Studebaker farm north of Bluffton when Jim was three and where his father was a tenant farmer. Before school age, he would often go with Ethel to the Tollgate Public School at the northeast corner of State Road #1 and Dustman Road. The family moved to Bluffton when Jim was seven, and then he started attending Park School. He was class treasurer for each of his four high school years, perhaps portending his future career in banking. During high school he was a "fizz-jerker" (soda jerk) at Davenport and Ehle drugstore on West Market Street, as well as a messenger boy for the Western Union. It was at Western Union that he learned code that he would later use in amateur radio, a hobby he enjoyed and which he shared with both of his sons.

Two weeks after his Bluffton High School graduation in 1915, he started work at the Studebaker Bank. World War I was declared on April 6, 1917, and his banking career was interrupted when he and several friends volunteered on May 2, 1917. After the war, he continued at the Studebaker Bank until it closed in 1927. He then worked for the Citizen's Bank until it was sold and then on to the Old National Bank (organized in 1929) until it merged to become the Old-First National Bank in 1931. He was president at the Old-First from 1938 to 1968, when he retired.

While roller skating at the rink that used to occupy the space between the north half of the Post Office and the Elks Lodge, he met a dark-haired beauty, Mabel Lois Bryan. She was living with her parents in Linn Grove, Indiana, and commuted to Bluffton High School via the B.G. and C. (Bluffton, Geneva and Celina) interurban. They were married in Kentucky (they eloped) on December 13, 1919. Jim and Mabel had two sons who both became physicians: William James Stogdill (1921-) and Thomas Bryan Stogdill (1935-).

In 1987 Jim was honored as the Chamber of Commerce "Citizen of the Year" which was the year marking the seventy-fifth anniversary of his banking career. The Governor of the State of Indiana bestowed upon Jim the highest citizen's award, "Sagamore of the Wabash."

Jim was active in the Methodist Church, American Legion, Kiwanis, and the Masonic Lodge. If he had his life to live over, he has said that there's very little he would change. His strongest personality assets included industry and hard work. He was never without a job.

His was a life of caring and of service to his family, friends, neighbors, as well as customers of the bank.

Traits he has said he'd like to see his children emulate include: honesty, truthfulness and ambition. He has truly enjoyed every minute of his life. He'll long be remembered for his positive attitude, his happy spirit, and cheery disposition.

STORY

Barry J. Story married Cherry Sue McMillan in September of 1980. Barry is the son of Nelson Thomas and Evelyn Darlene Story; and Cherry is the daughter of Everett and Colleen McMillan. Barry is employed with the Wells County Sheriff Department, and Cherry is a homemaker. They have three children: Jasmine, Summer, and Tayler. The family resides at 0633 West 100 South.

WILLIASON STOUT

Williason Stout (1876-1965) farmer, hunter, trapper, fur trader, was born in Stoutsville, Fairfield County, Ohio. His parents, Peter and Sarah Conrad Stout, moved to Harrison Township, Wells County, Indiana, in 1880. He married Carrie Almer (1881-1955) and had six children. They were Pearl Ebnit, Mary Imler, Walter, Ben, Nelson, and Paul. He lived at the Wells County Home until his death. At present his youngest son, Paul, lives there. Paul married Mary Alice Bender, daughter of V. O. and Jennie Christman Bender.

Left to Right; Nelson Stout, Mary Stout, Ben Stout, Carrie Stout, Walter Stout, Williason Stout, Paul Stout, Pearl Stout.

His great-great-great-grandfather, John Michael Staudt (Stout) came from the Palatinate to Berks County, Pennsylvania, on the English ship, "Samuel," in 1760. John's grandson, George, moved to Fairfield County, Ohio, in 1808. George changed the name to Stout. His son, Benjamin Franklin Stout, laid out the present town of Stoutsville, Ohio, in 1854.

ADEN STRAHM FAMILY

Aden Strahm, born March 17, 1914, is the son of Daniel and Lydia (Klopfenstine) Strahm, and the grandson of Ulrich Strahm. Ulrich came to the United States from Switzerland with his family in 1850.

Aden married Bertha Mae Meyer in 1944. Bertha Mae is the daughter of Henry Meyer and Lucy (Jones) Meyer. Henry was the son of Adam Meyer who came to the United States from Germany in 1879.

Aden and Mae had two children. Patsy, born January 6, 1946, married Dale Wall, born august 21, 1945. They had two children. Michele, born November 29, 1968, is a graduate of Bluffton High School and University of Indianapolis. Heather, born February 14, 1973, is also a graduate of Bluffton High School and is pursuing a career in the health field. Daniel D. born September 23, 1947, married Trudith Dunn, born September 26, 1952. They had two children: Jeremy, born June 2, 1975, and Megan, born November 28, 1976. both Jeremy and Megan are students at Norwell High School. Dan was later divorced and was married to Donna Harris on August 31, 1990. They reside with her three children: Randy, born February 6, 1979; Darlene, born September 10, 1980; and Ryan, born May 4, 1986.

Aden Strahm, owned and operated a one-hundred acre dairy farm in Lancaster Township and worked as a carpenter throughout Wells County. Mae works as a waitress at the Dutch Mill Restaurant.

DANIEL STRAHM FAMILY

Daniel Strahm, born September 27, 1857, was one of four sons of Ulrich Strahm, and the grandson of Matthias Strahm. Matthias came to the United States from Switzerland in 1850. Daniel was a carpenter by trade. Daniel married Margaret Baumgartner in 1883. They had three children: Emma, born January 17, 1884, married Aaron Minger. They had no children. William, born February 19, 1885, married Nettie Minger; and they had one child, Agnes Sarah, born March 31, 1886, married Joel Keahrn and they had no children. Margaret Strahm, Daniel's first wife, died in 1886.

In 1887, Daniel married his second wife, Lydia Klopfenstine. They had fourteen children.

Eva, born December 20, 1888, married Ben Blume and had one son, James.

Edward, born March 9, 1890, married Fern Buckle and had four children. Their children were: Veda, Donald, Eugene, and Mona.

Martha, born march 12, 1892, married Ernest Gerber and they had two children. Their children are: Ethel and Ralph.

Esther, born October 13, 1893, married Harry Gibson and had three children. They are: Virginia, Patrick, and Betty.

Elizabeth, born August 18, 1895, married Dewey Caley. They had one child, George.

Aldine, born April 26, 1897, married Anthony Metzger and they had two children. Their two children are Polly and Nancy.

Jacob, born May 11, 1901, married Marcella Huser and had two children. Their children are Phyllis and Roderick.

Harry, born April 24, 1903, married Ida Bauman and they had one child, Gladys.

Albert, born January 8, 1905, married Genivieve Ormsby and had one child, Patricia.

Herman, born October 11, 1906, married Lola Lobsiger, and they had five children. Their children are DuWayne, Carol, Sharon, Kay Lynn, and Nancy.

Nelson, born February 13, 1909, married Josephine Moser and had three children. Their children are Virgil, Zenith, and Daisy.

Aden, born March 17, 1914, married Bertha Mae Meyer and had two children. They are Patsy and Daniel.

Ida and Homer, children of Daniel, both died at a young age: Ida at twenty four; and Homer shortly after birth.

All of the children of the Daniel Strahm family were born in Wells County. Through time, as the children grew older and married, they moved to various parts of the United States. Aldine to New York, Martha to Connecticut, and later Albert settled in Michigan. The remainder of the children stayed in Wells, Adams, and Allen County areas.

REVEREND FRANKLIN STRINE FAMILY

Reverend Franklin Strine was born in 1925 at Goshen, Indiana. He married Phyllis Fredrick in 1951 and born to them were: Devon-1952; Bruce-1955; Madelynn-1956; and Donalynn-1958. All of the children graduated from Huntington College, with Devon and Donalynn living in Wells County, and Bruce and Madelynn in Michigan.

Franklin entered the ministry at age forty serving in four Michigan churches of the United Brethren in Christ during the next twenty years. Frank and Phyllis have directed the Golden Years and Young at Heart camps (for fifty years and above) over the last ten years. She also played in a Gospel music group called the "Salvation Sounds" for nine years. This group consisted of four mothers playing accordion, piano, organ, guitar, drum, and melodica, giving concerts in the Tri-State area.

Back, Left to Right; Madelynn Grubbs, Reverend Devon Strine. Front, Left to Right; Reverend Bruce Strine, Phyllis Strine, Reverend Franklin Strine, Donalynn Strine.

Devon married Kathy Mallory in 1973 and their children are: Kelly-1975, April-1978, and Cory-1981. Devon won many medals both in high school and college track. Both are employed at Lincoln Life. He ministered at three Indiana churches and one in Florida.

Bruce married Paulette Moore in 1978, and their children are: Aimee-1979, Kristy-1982, Chad-1985, and Stacie-1987. He is pastoring in Michigan and has built two new parsonages and two new churches in the first eight years of ministry. Bruce and Paulette also conduct marriage seminars, JOYNT Ministries.

Madelynn married Britt Grubbs in 1978 and they have a son, Britt Charles-1981, and a daughter, Nichole-1984. Madelynn is Waterfront Director at Camp Michindoh near Hillsdale, Michigan, and also works with her husband, Britt, who is Operations Manager. Camp Michindoh (Michigan, Indiana, and Ohio) is a retreat center owned by the United Brethren churches of that area, and is their home year-round.

Donalynn is an ADC case worker at Bluffton Welfare Department. Due to her father's illness, she built a home in Markle where her parents have resided with her since 1986. She is involved in Good shepherd United Brethren Church activities and is co-director and quizmaster of the Central Conference Bible Quiz teams.

In the last four generations, there have been six secretaries, five teachers, two social workers, and eight in Christian service.

CHARLES L. STROUD

Charles Leon Stroud was born in Liberty Center, Wells County, Indiana, on October 6, 1901, the son of Milas J. and Jennie Cloe (Gaskill) Stroud. He had one sister, Athelma Beatrice. He attended Liberty Center High School, graduating in 1924. He was active in sports and played basketball for Liberty Center during their trek to the state semi-finals in 1924. He also played several musical instruments as a young man.

On July 29, 1926, he married Stella Lurana Ward, daughter of William J. and Myrtle L. (Spraker) Ward, originally of Kokomo, Indiana. She was born in Kokomo on July 5, 1908, and the family moved to rural Liberty Center in 1926.

Charles and Stella made their home in Liberty Center for many years, where he first operated a barber shop and later was employed by the Nickel Plate Railroad. They attended the Liberty Center methodist Church. Four children were born while they resided at Liberty Center: Richard Ward on September 20, 1929; Virginia Mae on August 11, 1931; and twins, Joseph Leon and James Lyle, on August 2, 1943.

Charles Stroud Family in 1948
Richard, Virginia, Charles, Stella, and twins, Joe and Jim.

Richard married Ruth Eileen Johnson. They live in Liberty Center and have four children: Gerald Lee, Karen Jo, Keith Alan, and Gregory Charles.

Virginia married Charles J. Booher and they had three children: Kandice Lynn, Debra Sue, and Terri Anne. Her second marriage was to Walter L. McMillen, and they live in rural Bluffton.

Joseph Leon married Veronica C. Stratton, and they had one son, Michael Joseph. His second marriage was to Sharon Rose Springer, and they have a daughter, Shari Jo, and a son, Jonathon Andrew. They live in rural Markle, Indiana.

James Lyle married Judith Ann Milby and they had a son, Troy Lee. A son, Jeffrey Allen, died soon after birth. His second marriage was to Stella Lee (Loy) Crain, and they have a daughter, Amy Renee. His family, including a stepson, Scott J. Crain, resides in rural Poneto.

Mr. Stroud was transferred by the railroad to Sims, Indiana, in 1943, and the family lived there for four years, where the two older children attended Swayzee high School. Richard graduated there in 1947. The family returned to Wells County in 1947, with Virginia graduating from Liberty Center in 1949 and Jim and Joe graduating from Bluffton in 1961.

Charles Stroud worked forty-two years for the Nickel Plate and N and W railroads, retiring as the N and W section foreman at Decatur, Indiana, in 1970. Stella has been a long time member of the Rebekah Lodge and is a member of the Daughters of the American Revolution.

Charles Stroud died November 4, 1988 and is buried in the Mossburg Cemetery. Mrs. Stroud resides in Bluffton, Indiana. *(R. Stroud)*

MILAS J. STROUD

M.J. (Joe) Stroud was born on September 15, 1883, near Wilksboro, North Carolina. At the age of fifteen he and several brothers moved to Wells County, Indiana. Their parents, Robert and Emma (Winkler) Stroud, along with a younger brother and sister, followed a short time later. Joe soon found employment with the Cloverleaf Railroad, an occupation he pursued for fifty-two years until his retirement from the Nickel Plate Railroad in 1951. He was presented a fifty-year service award from the railroad by his grandson, who was the local agent at that time.

On October 23, 1901, Joe married Jennie Cloe Gaskill in Liberty Center, Indiana. Jennie was born April 23, 1883, in Liberty Township, a daughter of John and Mary (Worster) Gaskill. Joe and Jennie lived all their married lives in Liberty Center.

M.J. Stroud Family in 1915
Joe, Athelma, Charles, and Jennie

A daughter, Athelma Beatrice, was born on October 13, 1903, and a son, Charles Leon, was born on October 6, 1905. Athelma was married to Noble Wagner, Hilliard Brickley, and to Glenn D. Wiley. No children were born of these marriages. Charles was married to Stella Lurana Ward, and they had four children: Richard Ward, Virginia Mae, Joseph Leon, and James Lyle.

Mr. and Mrs. Stroud attended the Methodist Church and were active in the Rebekah and Odd Fellow Lodges. Both were avid gardeners. Together they maintained a large flower garden and rose gardens at their home for many years. As a young woman Jennie carried the mail locally by horse-drawn buggy from Liberty Center to outlying post offices then in the area.

In 1966, at the age of eighty three, Joe was able to return to the area of his early childhood in Wilkes County, North Carolina, and to visit with friends, including now-elderly children of former slave families who were freed by his grandfather many years earlier. He had played with them as a young boy, and they had a tearful reunion.

Jennie Cloe Stroud died May 20, 1965, and Milas Joe Stroud died February 11, 1971. They are buried in the Mossburg Cemetery

RICHARD W. STROUD

Richard Ward Stroud was born on September 20, 1929, in Liberty Center, Wells County, Indiana, a son of Charles and Stella (Ward) Stroud. He had one sister, Virginia, and two brothers, Joseph and James. He attended school through the eighth grade at Liberty Center and graduated from Swayzee High School in 1947. He was active in high school sports and played varsity basketball four years with the Swayzee "Speedkings."

On December 26, 1952, he married Ruth Eileen Johnson of Bluffton. Ruth was the oldest daughter of Paul E. and Bernice E. (Thornton) Johnson, originally of Adams County, Indiana.

The Strouds set up housekeeping just north of Bluffton Indiana, but after a few months moved to Decatur, Indiana, to be nearer to his work as a telegraph operator for the Nickel Plate Railroad at their Decatur office. A son, Gerald Lee, was born at Decatur on July 11, 1954, and a daughter, Karen Jo, was born there on September 26, 1955.

Dick accepted employment with an electronics company at Huntington, Indiana, and the family moved there shortly after Karen's birth in 1955. They returned to his home town of Liberty Center in 1958 and Keith Alan was born on December 23, 1959. Gregory Charles was born on June 1, 1961.

Richard W. Stroud Family, 1990
Front, Left to Right; Karen, Ruth. Rear, Left to Right; Keith, Greg, Gary, Richard.

Gerald (Gary) married Rebecca Lynn Wilson on September 29, 1973, and they have three children: Craig Lee, Natalie Diane, and Blake Alan. They reside in Leesburg, Virginia.

Karen married Gary Lynn Parsons on June 3, 1978, and they have one son, Joshua Lynn. They reside in Fort Wayne, Indiana.

Keith married Fawn Elysse Browning on March 21, 1981, and they had two daughters, Stephanie Ann Marie and Kera Lurana. His second marriage was to Tamara Sue Cowgill on February 13, 1988, and they have one son, Kory Alan. They live in Bluffton, Indiana.

Gregory (Greg) resides at Huntington, Indiana.

Ruth managed the cafeteria at Southern Wells Schools and retired in 1990 after twenty years service. Dick was employed as an electrical engineer and retired in 1990 after thirty years with the Magnavox Company. He served in the army signal corps Engineering Laboratories from 1941 to 1952 and was involved with atomic testing at Bikini and Eniwetok atolls. Both Ruth and Dick are avid amateur radio operators. He is also a private pilot. Together they built their home at Liberty Center where they presently live

ABRAHAM STUDABAKER

Abraham Studabaker was a descendent of an old German family that had settled in the Colonies long before the Revolutionary War. They moved to Darke county, Ohio, in 1808, where Gettysburg now stands. A few years later he moved to a farm near Greenville, Ohio. He was a patriot in the War of 1812. He had seven children. Honorable John Studabaker donated the Bluffton Cemetery land in 1837. He and Abraham were full brothers. His father had married twice and he had three half-brothers and two half-sister.

William Studabaker, born February 7, 1807, and died march 9, 1883, was the eldest of seven children. He was born in Warren County, Ohio. In 1898 he moved to Darke County, Ohio, and lived on a farm near Greenville, Ohio, until he was twenty-one years old. He married Sarah A. Thompson in March, 1828. They lived on a farm near Greenville, the one known as the county farm, for eleven years. In 1839, they moved to Wells County, Indiana, on a farm owned by Lewis Markley and lived here six years. In 1845, they moved across the river to his farm where he lived until 1883. In 1875, he joined the Six Mile Christian Church. He owned two thousand acres of land in the upper valley of the Wabash.

William and Sarah had ten children: John, Ben, William T., David D. (Bluffton), George W. (Tipton), Abram T., J.M. and Anna Louisa who were twins, Mariah, and Mary A. In 1883 his wife and three of his children passed away. After his wife's death, he lived with his only surviving daughter and her husband, Anna Louisa and Oliver P. Markley, on West South Street in Bluffton, Indiana.

ABRAM T. STUDABAKER

Abram T. Studabaker was born on July 18, 1830, in Darke County, Ohio. He came to Wells County, Indiana, with the family in 1839. He taught three terms in the Wells County Schools.

On March 6, 1853, at the age of twenty three, he married Louisa DeWitt, daughter of Moses and Sally (Westbrook) DeWitt. Louisa was born April 17, 1828, and died October 10, 1911. The DeWitts were natives of New York and New Jersey.

Her erected a home on his farm in June 1853. His business was raising, purchasing, and sales of livestock. He bought more stock than any other man in Wells County. He was also a contractor and built twenty miles of gravel roads in Wells and Grant Counties. He supported the cause of prohibition.

Abram and Louisa had eleven children: Harriette (Mrs. Marion French) born March 3, 1854; Louis and Henry, twins, born August 4, 1855, and died in infancy; William L. (lived in Ottumwa, Iowa) born April 4, 1857; Mary J. (lived in Marion, Indiana) born December 13, 1858; Noah E. (purchased grain) in Van Buren, Indiana, born February 23, 1860; Idah (Mrs. Charles Helms) (lived near Decatur, Indiana) born November 28, 1861; Abby (Mrs. W. A. Bauman) lived near Decatur, (Idah and Abby were twins); John D. Studabaker, lived in Harrison Township, born July 31, 1864; Lilly (Mrs. L.L. Baumgartner) born August 3, 1866; and Minnie M. (Mrs. Ed Huffman) born February 1873, who lived in the old home place.

Abram T. Studabaker died at home, 607 South Main Street in Bluffton, Indiana. Other survivors, other than the children, were two brothers, David (of Bluffton), George (of Kansas) and a sister Mrs. O.P. Markley (Louisa).

DAVID D. STUDABAKER

My great-grandfather, David D. Studabaker, is a descendent of Peter Studabaker who came from Soligen, Germany, on the ship Harle. They arrived in Philadelphia, Pennsylvania, September 1, 1736. The descendents of Peter Studabaker settled in Hagerstown, Maryland. As time past they moved to Ohio then Indiana.

David D. Studabaker was born May 4, 1840, in Harrison Township, Wells County. He died December 2, 1924.

He was married to Esther E. Stahl on January 5, 1865. Esther Stahl was born November 5, 1837, and died July 27, 1921.

Left to Right; Sarah DeVore and Norah Studabaker

They had three sons and three daughters. Sons Fred and William, and daughter Nellie died at a very young age. Son, Hugh, lived to be fifty-two years old.

David's other two daughters were Sarah and Norah Studabaker.

Sarah was born April 11, 1868, in Wells County. Sarah was married to Ross DeVore on October 4, 1894. She lived to be ninety-one years old and died January 24, 1960.

Norah was born November 18, 1878. She never married, but was a piano teacher many years in Wells County. In her early years of teaching she went from house to house in a horse and buggy. The horse was named Pete. Later she went by automobile to teach.

Norah decided in 1934 to spend her winters in Winter Haven, Florida, coming back to Bluffton for a few weeks in the summer. In later years she was unable health-wise to do this. She was still giving piano lessons in 1969 (age ninety one) in Florida. She passed away in Florida on December 14, 1971, and she was brought back here for burial in Six-Mile Cemetery where other members of the family are buried.

David Studabaker and family lived on the farm where the old Psi Ote Pool was located. He owned and operated a stone quarry which was the site of the old Psi Ote Pool.

Back in 1912, after the death of his Uncle John Studabaker, David Studabaker purchased what is now the Wells County Historical Museum.

He and his wife lived there until their death. After the death of their son-in-law, Ross DeVore, on May 15, 1923, his widow, Sarah, and son Robert moved into the home with them.

Sarah and Norah then rented sleeping rooms to people needing them. At one time Warnock Spain, manager of Morris Dime Store, now Murphy's rented a sleeping room. He stayed there until his marriage.

As a small child, my family and I spent Thanksgiving and Christmas in this house where I have fond memories. It was also fun to go to the very top part of the house and look at the surrounding homes and area.

In May 1928 the house was sold to Ralph Jahn. This ended my visits as a child to this beautiful home.

The Studabaker family was among the early settlers of Wells County. They took an active part in the affairs of the community.

All were members and took an active part in the affairs of Six Mile Church.

STURGEON

The Sturgeon family traces its roots to Ireland and Suffolk County of England in 1524. They immigrated to the United States in 1730 and settled in Lancaster County, Pennsylvania.

Our branch of the Sturgeons in Wells County began with John Poultney Sturgeon. He was born May 15, 1810, in Mifflin County, Pennsylvania, and was brought to Perry County, Ohio, in 1817 by his parents. He married Mercy Chalfant (born 1848) in Perry County. She was the daughter of Chad and Nancy Ferguson Chalfant, originally of Perry County, but who moved to Wells County in 1837. The young couple joined her parents in 1865, settling within a few miles of each other on the present-day County Home Road.

John and Mercy were the parents of Clarinda (1849), Henry (1856), Sedora (1858), James (1861), and twins Mary and Nancy (1865). John and Mercy are buried at Bethel Cemetery.

James married Viola Linn, a daughter of Levi and Carolyn Myers Linn in 1889. They were the parents of two sons, Charles Raymond (1890-1969) and Hugh Linn (1891-1974). They are also buried at Bethel Cemetery.

Hugh married Mima Elizabeth Kleinknight in 1917. She was the daughter of Andrew and Anna (Schock) Kleinknight. Mima died in 1946. They were the parents of three children: Ruth Ilene (1918), Robert K. (1921), and Alfred Wayne (1926).

Ruth married Ralph Potts, Jr., in 1942, and they were the parents of one child, Susan, born in 1951. Susan married Leon Gaiser in 1977. They are the parents of Hilary Linn, born in 1986, and Caleb Oka, born in 1988.

Robert married Jean Louise Spade on November 6, 1948, following naval service during the Second World War. Jean was the daughter of Floyd R. and Leah Clotene Schwartz Spade. They are the parents of three children: James Linn, born in 1960; Stephen Robert, born in 1962; and Beth Ann, who was born in 1970.

Alfred Wayne never married. After U.S. Army service in World War II, he farmed with his brother on the family farm. In addition to farming, Robert was employed in the U.S. Postal Service from 1962 to 1987.

At the present time, James and Stephen are continuing the farming operation, in addition to their present jobs at Dunwiddie Heating, and Peytons Northern, respectively. Stephen is currently engaged to marry Linda Badger, daughter of Lowell and Nellie Badger, of Sullivan, Indiana. Beth is currently a junior at DePauw University, Greencastle, Indiana.

The original portion of the current farm that was settled in 1865 by John and Mercy Sturgeon was listed as a Hoosier Homestead in 1986 by the State of Indiana, marking over one hundred years of ownership as a family farm.

STURGIS

Earl Bruce Sturgis was born October 24, 1877, to Thomas Sturgis, Jr. and wife Alice White Sturgis. Thomas Jr. was the son of Thomas Sr. and wife Elizabeth Brazier Sturgis. His father was Reverend William Sturgis and her father was Reverend Jacob Brazier.

Thomas Sturgis, Jr. was a dentist in Bluffton. Earl Bruce Sturgis married Bertha Henrietta Herbst who was the daughter of Albert Herbst and wife Martha Augusta Perkins Herbst. Dr. E.B. Sturgis graduated from Ohio State University in dentistry and joined his father, Thomas, in the practice and continued until 1945 when illness forced his retirement. His offices were upstairs at the southeast corner of Johnson and Market streets for many years. He was active in church, civic, and fraternal organizations. Dr. Sturgis and wife, Bertha, raised five children: Vera (Jeffery) Sturgis, Kent L. Sturgis, Thomas A. Sturgis, Martha Alice (Guldin) Sturgis, and Don Kay (Bud) Sturgis.

Vera married Kenneth Jeffery and they had one son, Don Kenneth, who became a dentist and is now retired in Naples, Florida. Kent married Daisy Barlow of Marion and they had two children, a daughter Jean Rose who died in infancy and Jim E.C. Sturgis who lives in Onalaska, Wisconsin. Thomas A. married Ada (Peg) Kaehr and they had one son, John, who lives in Lebanon, Indiana. Don Kay married Betty Biberstine and they had four children: Tom, Linda, Rita, and Ted. He was killed tragically while driving a semi for Hoosier Condensary in New York. This leaves Martha (Peachie) who married Max I. Guldin son of Charles and Anna Guldin. Three of their four sons were born in Wells Community Hospital, Charles Bruce, Kay Sturgis, and David Eugene. A fourth son Kent Lee was born after moving to LaGrange county.

Martha is the sole survivor of Dr. and Mrs.. E.B. Sturgis, sister Vera, and brothers Kent, Tom, and Bud Sturgis.

DOYLE AND BONNIE SULLIVAN

Doyle and Bonnie Sullivan were married October 7, 1950, at the Methodist Parsonage in Poneto, Indiana. They have resided in Bluffton since July, 1969, at 1209 Stogdill Road.

Doyle was the son of the late Orville Sr. and Loretta (Crismore) Sullivan of Poneto, Indiana, and formerly of Uniondale, Indiana. He is a World War II veteran and a graduate of Liberty Center High School with the class of 1944. He was employed with Franklin Electric in Bluffton for thirty-five years. Five of those years was spent at the Siloam Springs, Arkansas plant from 1964 to 1969. He retired in 1986. He has a brother, Orville Jr. of Poneto, a sister, Barbara Prough of Bluffton. A half-brother, Paul Falk is deceased.

Doyle and Bonnie Sullivan

Bonnie was the daughter of the late Edson and Clara (Goodin) Bennett of Chester Township, Wells County. She graduated from Chester Center High School (where the Southern Wells school now stands) in 1946. She was employed at Bachman Foods for nine and one-half years and now is employed at the Bluffton News Banner. She has two sisters, Ruby Gentis of Huntington, and Cleo Aker of Craigville, and three brothers: Ralph Bennett of Portland, Claude E. Bennett of Bluffton, and Robert Bennett who is deceased. Bonnie and Doyle are members of the Park United Brethren Church in Bluffton.

There were three children born to Doyle and Bonnie: Terry Wayne, Athena June, and Jeffery Allan.

Terry Wayne, the oldest, graduated from the Siloam Springs, Arkansas High School and the Sequayah Polytechnic Trade School in Fayetteville in 1969. He was employed at Corning Glass in Bluffton. He has been employed with the Dalco Company for seventeen years, eight of those years at the Wenatchee, Washington, plant, but is now back at the Decatur plant. He lives on a farm near Decatur.

Athena June, the middle child, graduated from the Bluffton High School in 1973. She also graduated from Ivy Tech Culinary Arts School in Fort Wayne. She was employed at several restaurants and the Clinic Hospital in Bluffton. She now resides in Hayward, Wisconsin, with her husband, John Dedrick of Travisville, Indiana, and two sons from a previous marriage. He is self-employed as a taxidermist and she is a supervisor at Hardee's in Hayward. Athena's oldest son, Christopher James Hanson, is a sophomore at the Hayward High School and is also employed at Hardee's. Joshua David Hanson, the youngest, is a sixth grader at the Hayward Middle School.

Jeffery Allan Sullivan, the youngest child passed away in 1960, at the age of three and one half.

SUMMERS-HAMILTON

Jacob Summers, the father of Felix Summers, was born near Fredricksburg, Virginia, on February 16, 1816. He came to Indiana with his father's family as a young man. "An old deed shows that he bought eight acres of land in Wells County from Levi Hartzell in 1839 for $225," states a family history written by Matilda Summers in 1938. Jacob married Phebe Ann Sturgeon of Ross County, Ohio, on January 7, 1857. Jacob and Phebe Ann had three children: one being Felix Judd. Jacob died when Felix was nine years old, and his mother died when he was twelve. After the death of his mother he went to live with an aunt and uncle and remained there until he was grown.

Felix J. Summers (October 11, 1857-July 28, 1936) married Matilda Jane Rupright (January 18, 1860-January 20, 1950) on June 27, 1878. Matilda was the daughter of John and Elisebeth Daugherty Rupright of Adams County, Indiana.

Felix and Matilda started housekeeping on the original Jacob Summers farm in 1878. Their entire married life was spent in or around Ossian. Felix and Matilda had eight children, one being Lulu Alice Summers.

Lulu A. Summers was born on October 12, 1890. She was a graduate of Ossian High School and the Cincinnati School of Nursing and Health. She began her nursing career at the Wells County Hospital (Wells Community) in Bluffton in 1919. In 1922 she assumed the position of superintendent of the hospital and held that position until January, 1925. Lulu married Orville Grant Hamilton on October 4, 1925, in Bluffton.

O.G. Hamilton was born on August 21, 1891, in Washington County, Indiana. He was a graduate of Pekin High School, Central Normal College of Danville, Indiana, and the Indiana University School of Medicine. He started his practice in Bluffton in August of 1922. He first officed with Dr. C.H. Mead. Eventually Mead and Hamilton joined H.D. Brickley and the firm became, "Dr's. Brickley, Mead and Hamilton." (This long-term relationship was established with a gentlemen's agreement and a handshake.) In the 1950's, Dr. Constantino Panos joined the group and he and O.G. officed together until Dr. Hamilton's death on April 18, 1967. Lulu Hamilton remained in Bluffton until June, 1972, when he moved to the Towne House Retirement Home in Fort Wayne, Indiana. Lulu died June 27, 1990, about three and one-half months short of her one hundreth birthday.

The Hamiltons had two daughters, Jane Summers (July 16, 1929) and Mary Lou (August 14, 1926). Jane married Thomas L. Hiatt, also of Bluffton, on December 26, 1948. They moved to Michigan in 1949 and then to California in 1955. They currently reside in Vista, California. Mary Lou married E. William Kalt, Jr. of Elm Grove, Wisconsin, on April 7, 1951. They moved to Beloit, Wisconsin, following their wedding and still reside there. The Kalts have four children: Cynthia Anne; E. William, III; Thomas Hamilton; and Jane Elisebeth.

SURFUS FAMILY

Andrew and Betty (Harless) Surfus resided in Senca County, Ohio. They had one son, John, born in 1812.

John moved to Perry Township, Allen County, Indiana, in 1833. He was not educated because the family was poor and he needed to work. He possessed a yoke of cattle, table, chest, set of chairs, oven, and a bed made of sticks and bark. He married Ellen Delong in 1842. They lived surrounded by Indians and wild beasts. His success was attributed to his energy, perseverance, and his wife's assistance. They had twelve children (ten living in 1889): Stephen, George, Samuel, Andrew, John E., Mary, Harriet, Ellen, Salina, and Julia. He accumulated over one thousand acres of good land, gave his children a good home, and lived to see them all comfortably situated. He lived in elegance, surrounded by all the comforts of life. They were members of Methodist Episcopal Church, and were buried in Cedar Chapel Cemetery, Butler Township.

Andrew, John's seventh child, was a prosperous farmer and specialized in raising graded stock. He was born September 8, 1850, received a common school education, and lived with his parents till age twenty five. His father gave him one hundred and forty acres of good farming land. In 1875 he married Mary Snyder, born November 18, 1854, daughter of Jacob and Sarah Snyder. They had three children: Jerry, October 16, 1876; Orville, July 11, 1878; and Eva, July 25, 1880. Andrew died in 1927 and Mary in 1932.

Orville, a rural mail carrier, married Mary Burrell, born August 2, 1882, daughter of William and Emma Shoaf Burrell, on June 10, 1903, at the home of her parents. They had four children: William, August 29, 1905; Chester, February 1, 1907; Ruth, January 12, 1916; and Mabel, March 29, 1920. In 1919 they moved to Auburn, Indiana, where he later worked as a tool and die mechanic at Auburn Auto Company. They both died in 1965 and were buried in Woodlawn Cemetery in Auburn.

Mabel married a local boy, Floyd E. Miller (born August 24, 1918) September 2, 1943. They both attended McIntosh High School. Mabel also attended Wayne Beauty College. They had two children: Mary Marie, born February 28, 1944; and Donald Lee, born June 29, 1951. They moved to Bluffton, Indiana, in 1953. Floyd was employed at Montgomery Ward, and later at Almco Steel. Mabel was employed at Caylor-Nickel Clinic over thirty-three years (twenty-four years in Tumor Registry). They were First Methodist Church members. Floyd died in 1973 and was buried in Woodlawn Cemetery.

Mary married Charles T. Smith (born October 28, 1943) from Plumtree, Indiana, on July 17, 1965. They had two children: Nancy Marie, born August 20, 1969; and Tracy Donald, born July 28, 1973. Donald married Deborah Pitts (born September 19, 1950) on August 9, 1980. Mary and Donald were both married in the First Methodist Church in Bluffton.

Mabel was Vice President (three years), and Board Member Co-ordinator (fourteen years) of the Wells County Cancer Society's Reach to Recovery Program. She is a member of United Methodist Women and the National Tumor Registry Association.

CHARLES AND DIANNE SURFUS FAMILY

Charles was born in Chester Township, Wells County, in 1940, but grew up in Lancaster Township, Huntington County. James H. Surfus and Catherine (Oswalt) were his parents.

Charles attended Ball State University, Industrial Arts classes, for two years. Marjorie

Dianne (Gard) Surfus attended Ball State University and Ball Memorial School of Nursing, graduating with a BSN. Dianne was born in Wayne Township, Huntington County. Her parents are James Arthur Gard and Marjorie (Knight) Gard. Dianne is the second of seven children. The family moved to Lancaster Township, Huntington County, in 1943.

Dianne and Charles started married life in Huntington County, December, 1960. Patricia Rene (Patty) was born at Ball memorial Hospital December 6, 1961. In 1964, Corning Glass Works came to Wells County, where "Chuck" worked first in the order department, and then as shift supervisor. After missing the outdoor life, he returned to work at Majenica Tile Company, often ditching farms, or doing government waterways, in Wells and Huntington counties.

On a cold January 1, 1965, the family moved to the fourth house built in the Inskeep Addition, west of Bluffton. At the time, David Alan was thirteen days old. Cheryl Marie was born April 19, 1967.

Left to Right; David Surfus, Dianne Surfus, Patty Surfus Makowski, Joel Makowski, Cheryl Surfus.

Dianne worked as eleven-seven Pediatric Nurse at Caylor-Nickel Hospital for one and one-half years until resigning to establish the first Indiana Migrant clinic located at Plumtree.

She worked at Wells Community Hospital and in April, 1968, became the Director of Nursing. She has served on the boards of American Heart Association and Cancer Society. In 1988 she was elected President of the Indiana Organization of Nurse Executives.

The family has been members, and Sunday School teachers, at the First United Methodist Church, Bluffton.

Patty taught tap and jazz dance with Mary Lynn Lautzenheiser for two years. She attended Purdue University, and is a veterinarian at Honegger Animal Clinic, Ossian. Patty and her husband, Joel Patrick Makowski, live in Bluffton.

Dave enjoyed sports and played on the Franklin Electric Little League Team coached by his father. He was on Bluffton's high school wrestling and baseball teams, and the winning football team in 1982. He attended Purdue University graduating with a Bachelor's degree in meat science December, 1989. His first job is with Louis Rich Meat Company, Tulare, California.

Cheryl enjoyed track and gymnastics at Bluffton High School. Her senior year, she was first in uneven bars, until wrecking a snowmobile and collapsing a lung during the February 14, 1985, blizzard. She attended Purdue University and graduated August, 1990, with a Bachelor's degree in Environmental/Interior Design. In October, 1990, she moved to Visalia, California, with brother, Dave.

Charles died June 22, 1986, of a heart attack. Many friends from the church, work, neighbors, and family finished building a garage he had started. Years ago they had barn raisings—it still happened in Wells County, 1986.

CURTIS SURFUS FAMILY

Charles Curtis Surfus, son of William Howard and Emma Catherine (Dobbins) Surfus, was born in Noble County, Indiana, October 30, 1887. He married Christina Vedith Michaud, November 26, 1919. Her parents were Albert and Estella (Sackett) Michaud of Adams County, Indiana. Vedith was born January 25, 1898. In 1938 Curtis and Vedith moved from Jackson Township to Chester Township, Wells County, to a home one and one-half miles west of Chester Center School. The home on the property was destroyed by a tornado. They moved a house from Keystone to the present home location now owned by the youngest son, Marvin. Curtis served in World War I and was honorably discharged June 6, 1919. Their six children were all born before moving to Chester Township.

Vedith was ill and went to Mayo Clinic. She was sent home to die with a severe kidney problem. She gave Dr. Harold Caylor permission to do surgery. He told her it was the first kidney he ever removed. She lived many years after the surgery.

James Henry, the oldest son, was born October 15, 1920 in the old Surfus homestead of William H. and Emma at the "Surfus Sugar Camp" along SR 124 in Huntington County. James attended his senior year at Chester Center High School, where he met and later married H. Catherine Oswalt. They had two sons, Charles Frederick and Roger Allen. James died May 24, 1982. James often told of moving livestock from the Jackson Township farm to the Chester Township farm. It was in the days of fences. They drove livestock down roads, walking many miles. They would station family and neighbors at yards, and crossroads, to keep the animals on the road.

William Howard, second son, was born July 30, 1922. He was drafted into the U.S. Army November 20, 1942. He served in Africa, Sicily, and England, and lost his life in the World War II Invasion of Normandy, on his twenty-second birthday. he was laying communication lines to a forward company, and was killed by sniper fire. His country awarded him the Purple Heart posthumously., He is buried in a military cemetery in New Albany, Indiana.

Albert Richard was born October 26, 1924. Albert married Darlene Cecelia (Boxell). They presently live and farm in Rock Creek Township, Huntington County. They had four daughters and two sons: Donna, Linda, Richard, Alan, Kathy, and Carol. Donna is deceased.

Francis Maxine Surfus, born June 7, 1926, died of influenza as an infant, February 13, 1927.

Marjorie Estella (Surfus) Perry was born November 1, 1929. She married Warren Westley Perry. They farm in Chester Township and both worked at Franklin Electric, Bluffton. Daughters Christina Mae and Sherri Lynn both attended Southern Wells School.

Marvin Fredrick Surfus, born September 6, 1932, has continually farmed the home place. He married Norma Lee (Hopkins). Their children are Michael Wayne and Jeanette Susan. Jeanette served in the U.S. Air Force.

SUTILEF-BARRICK

In the late 1860's, Mary Rodgers, a young immigrant from County Cork, Ireland, journeyed from New York to Ohio. There she met Jacob Bailey, a Pennsylvania Dutchman working on the Erie Canal. They married and became the parents of Elizabeth, Catherine, and Willie while they lived in Paulding, Ohio. Catherine Marie, called "Kit" all of her life, was born August 5, 1880. Sometime in the 1880's the family moved to a farm one mile north of Uniondale, Indiana.

On August 25, 1877, Franklin Campbell (always known as "Pat") was born, the second son of George and Phoebe Campbell Barrick, descendants of Scot-Irish settlers in Huntington County, Indiana. Eventually, the family included four sons and five daughters, and the Barrick clan moved near Banner City, Wells County.

Pat Barrick and Kit Bailey married on September 28, 1902. On July 15, 1903, Clayton Leroy (Tate) was born. James Garth (Eddie) arrived in 1904, Jacob Raymond (Gabe) in 1907, and Jennie Justine (Teeny) in 1913. Pat Barrick was a postmaster, barber, and carpenter in their hometown of Uniondale. all of the children were known by their nicknames.

Back, Left to Right; Clayton Barrick, Mary Barrick. Front, Left to Right; Barbra Barrick Lesh, Beverly Barrick Hunter. June 1935

In neighboring Adams County, Hattie Viola Baumgartner, the youngest of ten children of Peter B. and Mary Hawkins Baumgartner, was born on June 24, 1889. Peter was born in Switzerland in 1842, and Mary Hawkins was a native West Virginian of English ancestry.

John W. Sutilef, born in London, England, in 1852, sailed to America with his parents in 1858. His father died at sea. When John was grown, he met and married, Maryann Bracker, an Ohio native, born in 1854. To this union were born ten children. The fourth son, William Willard, was born February 12, 1881, in Missouri. Sometime before 1886 the family moved to Adams County, where William later met and married Hattie Baumgartner on October 11, 1905. On May 16, 1918, William succumbed to tuberculosis. His widow and four children: Beulah, Minnie Louise, Mary Ellen, and Waldo, moved to Bluffton which became their hometown.

Mary Ellen Sutilef, born January 18, 1910, married Clayton Barrick in 1927. Their first daughter, Barbra Lou, arrived on December 11, 1927. Beverly Sue completed the family on December 10, 1930. From 1933 until 1942, Tate and Mary Barrick owned and operated Tate's Tavern in Uniondale. Tate worked for General Electric in Fort Wayne for forty years. He died on October 29, 1970. During World War II Mary also worked in General Electric's defense plant. The marriage ended in divorce in 1948, and both remarried. Mary retired from the Caylor-Nickel clinic in 1970. The widow of Nile Reynolds, she resides in Ossian.

Barbra and Beverly barrick grew up in Uniondale, attended Union Center, and graduated from Rock Creek High School. The Barrick sisters frequently sang and danced on the town hall stage in Uniondale in community amateur productions. A favorite show during the Depression years was the local version of WLS National Radio Barn Dance. However, World War II halted these diversions, and television brought down the final curtain on them.

SUTILEF-BARRICK

On April 21, 1946, Barbra Barrick married Harold Lesh, son of Dwight and Lela Lesh. They moved into a one-hundred year old farmhouse in Rock Creek Township. There they raised four children: Mary Nicole Lesh (Nicki), born on August 20, 1948, married Paul Mills, a Lancaster Township dairy farmer, in 1967. Their children are David Anthony (Tony), twenty three, and Mary Elizabeth (Beth), twenty.

Gary Dwight Lesh, born January 10, 1951, married Marlene Graft in 1976. They and their children: Jennifer, fourteen; Jason, twelve; and Nicholas, ten; live in Uniondale. A Franklin Electric employee, Gary attends IPFW.

Barbra (Lesh) and Beverly (Hunter) Barrick; 1958

Neil Kay Lesh, born October 3, 1955, an anesthesiologist in South Bend, married Dr. Cheryl Wibbens in 1984. They have two boys: Zachary, three, and Andrew Barrick, one.

Perry William Lesh, born November 17, 1958, married Cheryl Lash in 1981. He is an Indiana Department of Transportation employee. They live in Rock Creek Township with their children: Jacklyn Nicole, eight, and Clinton, four.

Barbra continued her education, graduating from Saint Francis College, Fort Wayne. She is a reading tutor at Lancaster Elementary School and an organist for Saint Paul's Lutheran Church, rural Bluffton. Harold, after thirty years at Zollners, retired to farm. He is active in the Masonic Lodge, Scottish Rite, Shrine Foot Patrol, and Saint Paul's Lutheran Church.

Beverly married Bruce Hunter on December 31, 1948, and moved to Ossian. Suellen was born on January 3, 1953, and Jeffrey Tad arrived on December 12, 1955. Beverly was graduated from Saint Francis College and earned her doctorate from Ball State. Dr. Hunter teaches first grade in Ossian Elementary School. Bruce was a partner for many years with his late father, Halden, in the Hunter Supply House in Ossian. In 1990, he retired from Farm Bureau Insurance. He is an avid golfer. The Hunters are members of the First United Methodist Church, Ossian.

Suellen Hunter, a graduate of IPFW, lives and teaches in New York City, attending Hunter College. she has appeared in off-Broadway theater.

Tad Hunter, manager of Personal Finance Company, Fort Wayne, married Lori Wichman, a registered nurse, of Huntington. They live near Craigville with their son, Gabriel Halden.

With the exception of Nicki Lesh Mills, who was graduated from Lancaster High School, all children of the Barrick sisters are graduates of Norwell High School, as are two grandchildren, Tony and Beth Mills.

Tony Mills, son of Paul and Nicki Mills, married Michelle Brown, daughter of Ted and Diane Brown, in September, 1989. Their daughter, Karissa Michelle, born January 27, 1991, is the latest branch on this family tree.

ELIJAH SUTTON

Elijah Sutton received as a land grant from the United States of America one hundred and thirty five point forty-eight acres on October 28, 1837.

He was active in settling Wells county. He preached the first sermon on the west side of the Wabash River. There is a plaque in the Courthouse commemorating his name.

He had eight children. His daughter, Mary Ann Sutton married Jacob Miller. They had six children. She inherited twenty-nine acres.

Jacob was also instrumental in making Bluffton the county seat. There is a plaque at the Courthouse in his name also.

Henry, their son, married Nancy. In 1874 he bought seventy acres from his family for six hundred eighty dollars. This is the south half of the southwest quarter section now bordering Tocsin and State Road 224.

They had six children: Matilda C. Archibold, Lydia V. Richey, Daniel J. Miller, Mary Ellen Shady, Samuel E. Miller, and Sarah Bell Michaels.

Henry died in 1876. Nancy, his wife, in 1882 sold land, thirty-three yards wide and the length of the farm to Chicago and Atlantic Railway Company.

Daniel J. Miller, their oldest son, purchase land from his sisters, a brother and a nephew for one thousand dollars from 1878 to 1892. He borrowed two thousand dollars from the Bank of Tocsin in 1916 to help pay the balance. Amos L. Byrd and James Trullender among others signed the contract.

Daniel J. married Sarah Malinda Heckley. They had eight children: Belle, Sadie, Garnet, Oliver, Annie, Dessie, Hazel, and Chauncey.

Times were hard and money scarce. Daniel sheared sheep, farmed and did custom butchering. A new barn was built from lumber out of his woods. The railroad was sold to Chicago and Erie, later Erie-Lackawana.

Then came the Great Depression and in 1932 Chauncey W., their youngest son, and Mira M., his wife, had to help financially to keep the farm.

In 1935, the State of Indiana bought land for fifty one dollars and twenty cents for State Road 224.

Mira and Chauncey worked as janitor and cook in the 1930's at the Wells County Hospital. Chauncey retired from the State Highway Department.

Mira died in 1972 and Chauncey in 1975. They had no children so the farm was left to William Beryl Miller, a nephew. Beryl, who died in 1990, was the son of Oliver and Iva (Palmer) Miller. His wife, Loretta H. (Jarrett) Miller still lives on the farm.

They moved into the house in April, 1976, as the birthday of the United States was being celebrated.

Someone of the six generations have lived on the farm for one hundred fifty-four years. Elijah was Beryl Miller's great-great-great grandfather

SWAIM-ANDREWS

A wedding at the Decatur First Methodist Church was the occasion for the first meeting of Celia Andrews of Decatur and Roger Swaim of Bluffton. She played the pipe organ for the ceremony and accompanied Roger, the baritone soloist. They were married in Decatur on May 31, 1924, and resided together at 405 West Market Street in Bluffton for the next fifty-two years. Two daughters were born to them: Janet on August 8, 1926, and Doris (Dodie) on December 12, 1927.

Roger was born in Bluffton on March 9, 1897, to May and David H. Swaim. He was a 1915 graduate of Bluffton's P.A. Allen High School, where his older sister, Helen, was on of his teachers. Roger attended DePauw University (class of 1920) where he was president of his junior class. He served in the Navy at Great Lakes Naval Station during World War I.

Roger G. Swaim and Celia M. Swaim, about 1964

In 1919, as reporter and sports editor, he joined his father full time at the "Evening News" and they worked at adjoining desks until David H. Swaim's death in 1939. He became advertising manager of the "Evening News-Banner" following the 1929 merger of the "Evening News" and the "Evening Banner." In the 1930's he took on the duties of general manager and editor, becoming publisher and president upon his father's death.

A member of Sigma Delta Chi (journalism fraternity), Roger served on the boards of the Inland Daily Press and Hoosier State Press Associations. He was a Mason and member of the American Legion. In 1949 he received the Old Gold Goblet, DePauw's highest alumni honor, and in 1962 he was presented with the Wells County Fish Fry's Distinguished Service Award. Like his father, he enjoyed all sports. He played high school varsity basketball and baseball and at one time he and Robert Cummins were city doubles tennis champions.

Celia M. Swaim was born March 8, 1897, in Monroe to Dr. Oliver Perry Morton Andrews and Mary Agnes Rainier Andrews. Dr. Andrews died when Celia was only three weeks old, leaving also a fourteen-month old daughter, Celia. In 1902, Agnes moved with her daughters to Decatur. The girls very early became interested in music, Celia in piano and pipe organ, Ceclia as a soprano soloist.

A 1916 graduate of Decatur High School, Celia attended the European School of Music in Fort Wayne and was an accompanist for David Baxter, well-known voice teacher of many singers in the area. In Decatur she taught piano and pipe organ and served for seven years as the First Methodist Church organist. She played for many social functions and also for silent movies.

Following her marriage, Celia immediately became involved in the newspaper, writing society news and feature articles. She later became the corporation's bookkeeper, serving in that capacity for many years. She always took a dedicated and active interest in the "News-Banner," becoming publisher upon Roger's death in 1976.

Among her community activities were Tri Kappa, Study Club, and Bluffton's first Girl Scout troop, for which she was an assistant leader.

Both Roger and Celia were supporters of the First Methodist Church, particularly in the music program. Roger sang for many years in the choir and Celia was substitute organist. Celia was accompanist for many local singers and both participated in community musical events. A highlight for Roger, as a young man, was singing at the Street Fair, accompanied by the Hartford City Band.

Though his health was failing, Roger and Celia took great satisfaction in the 1976 completion of the new "News-Banner" building at Johnson and Wabash streets. He died October 10, of that year, and Celia continued as publisher until the paper was sold to the present owners in June of 1986. Her death occurred September 10, 1988.

JAMES E. AND LUCILE M. SWAIM

James was born and raised on a farm bordering the town of Yoder, Indiana. He was the son of Lumley Tanton and Grace Lumley Swaim. James graduated from Ossian High School in 1934 and one week following graduation, he joined the Civilian Conservation Corps. He then was detailed to Springmill State Park in June, 1934, where he spent one year. James then enrolled in Tanner Barber School in Fort Wayne, Indiana, on September 17th. He served his apprenticeship in Ossian in Ernest Platt's barbershop and received his master's license in 1937. He was then employed by Tokheim Corporation, Fort Wayne, Indiana, and was part-time barber in 1937.

Lucile Haiflich, daughter of Jesse and Edith Wiser Haiflich, graduated from East Union High School, Wells County, in 1936 and was later employed at Culver Glove Factory, Bluffton, Indiana.

James and Lucile were married April 16, 1938, in the parsonage of the Reverend D. C. Souder, Huntington, Indiana, and lived in an apartment at the A.S. Elzey Funeral Home, Waynedale, Indiana, now known as the Elzey-Dickey-Haggard Funeral Home. James then worked in the A.S. Elzey barber shop and Lucile was employed by Metting's department store. In 1939 James was rehired by Tokheim Corporation and in 1941 worked in the tool room.

In September, 1943, the Swaim's purchased the home they are still residing in at 209 E. Lafever Street in Ossian. Two children blessed this union: Rex Eugene on February 14, 1942; and Rita Lou on April 17, 1944.

After graduating from Ossian High School in 1960, Rex served his tool and die-maker apprenticeship at Franklin Electric, Bluffton, Indiana, then journey man tool and die worker at J. C. Thompson Tool and Die, Fort Wayne, later to be purchased by CTS. He is now employed at Tokheim Engineering Department, Fort Wayne.

Rex and Patricia Davis, daughter of Gerald Emery and Thelma Renbarger Davis, were united in marriage at the Presbyterian Church in Ossian, Indiana, July 29, 1962. They are the parents of Kent Eugene, born November 23, 1965, now serving with the U.S. Air Force in Misawa, Japan, and later to be stationed at RAF Rhein Mein Air Force Base in Germany. Kurt Daniel was born May 24, 1968, and is now enrolled at IPFW Campus, Fort Wayne, Indiana.

Rita Lou Swaim was employed at Midwest Life Insurance Company and G.E. Corporation, Fort Wayne, after graduating from Ossian High School in 1962. Rita was married to Russell James Jr., son of Russell and Corrine Fryer James of Fort Wayne, February 8, 1964, at the Trinity Methodist Church, Putnam Street, Fort Wayne. Russell Jr. a graduate tool and die designer from CTS of Berne, Indiana, is now president of ZANXX Incorporated, Avilla, Indiana. They now reside on a farm near LaOtto, Indiana, and are the parents of two children. Wade Allen, born March 17, 1965, a graduate tool maker of ZANXX Incorporated and still employed there, resides in Swan, Indiana. Lara Lynne married Kenneth Amstutz III, June 20, 1986, son Kenneth and Karen Kummer Amstutz of Avilla, Indiana. Kenneth III is a skilled auto mechanic for Steve West Motors of Kendallville, Indiana. Lara is employed at Sacred Heart Nursing Home, Avilla, Indiana, as a QMA. They are the parents of one child, Larissa Marie, born January 4, 1987. The Amstutzes live on a second farm home of Russell and Rita James.

James and Lucile are retired. Lucile had worked for the Ossian Journal for seven years and James retired from Tokheim Corporation in 1981, having worked in the toolroom and quality assurance department for forty years.

SWEENY

The John Wesley and Jemima (Cary) Sweeny family came to Wells County from Wayne County, Ohio, in 1879 with their six children. They settled on Thiele Road in Lancaster Township. My grandfather, Willet, was sixteen. They built their home from native lumber, even making shingles. Bears were seen behind their home. After my grandparents' Willet Cary and Ida (Sowards) Sweeny, marriage in 1892, they also lived on Thiele Road. The house still stands where my father, Robert John Sweeny, the oldest of five children all born in Wells County, was born, November 27, 1893. He told of hearing, and then seeing the cloud that followed the explosion of the nitro-glycerin plant in the woods, close to their home. A man and team of horses, and wagon were blown up into the air and killed.

Gene and Evelyn Sweeny Pope

They were very much involved in the services at the "Pugney Church." The children walked to a school on State Road 1, north of Bluffton. They attended Craigville High School but Robert transferred to Bluffton High School, riding the interurban, where he graduated in 1913. He later graduated from Indiana University, in Bloomington, with a teacher's license.

During World War I, Robert was in active duty in France. He would tell of happenings on the boat, going and coming; and of the troops devouring a berry patch; and rats scaring the guards late at night; and all the tears on sighting the Statue of Liberty. His demonstrations of marching, snapping his heels together and maneuvering his gun shall not be forgotten. I felt well protected.

Upon his return he settled into helping his father farm southeast of Bluffton. He took a team of horses with a sled and hauled gravel to complete State Road 218, one to two miles east of Reiffsburg. With the coming of electricity, Robert sold Hinman Milkers to farmers following the depression.

A sister, Mae DeRuyscher, had two daughters: Lois Nelson of Muncie; and Ruth (Roscoe) Wall, along with children Dale, David, and Pat (Ron) Mayer, and their families, live in Bluffton. Daughter, Lois Carol (Tom) Carnall, lives in Preble.

His youngest sister, Esther, taught school for many years in Harrison Township. Sister, Nellie (Garth) Double, lived southwest of Ossian. Children Robert, Marjorie, and Don graduated from Ossian High School. Don's son, Don (Tina Sullivan), and children Michelle, Dawn, and Donald Andrew live in Poneto.

A musical, church-going family, they attended Myers Chapel Church, south of the County Home. Robert met Olive Joray while attending a cottage prayer meeting. They married in 1931. For years they were active members of the Wesleyan Church. Many years Olive was pianist, and Robert, chorister and Sunday school teacher. The next three generations are following in their footsteps.

Their children graduated from Bluffton High School. son Paul served in the U.S. Navy during the Korean conflict; married Barbara Binegar; moved and settled in Warsaw after Nancy, Dan and Dave, and Tim and Tom were born. Daughter Evelyn (Gene) Pope had two children, Allen and Twila, who were also Bluffton High School graduates.

The farm where Robert and Olive started housekeeping is still family run by Gene (Evelyn) Pope and Ron (Twila) Dubbeld and children Janella and Dion.

SWIHART-TOBIAS

Harold and Lois Swihart were married in the Church of God, Zanesville, April 24, 1954. They are parents of Dan and Sonja. Dan married Julie Stephenson, March 7, 1982. They have a son Jared Patrick born March 17, 1987. Sonja married Ray Burniston, Jr., July 24, 1987. They have a daughter Amanda Renee born August 24, 1988.

Lois Annette (Tobias) Swihart was born in Loveland, Colorado, to Ed and Merle Stuart Tobias. There were five other children: Joyce, Johannah, James, Stanley and Paul. Paul was one year old when Merle died. In 1937, before Merle died, Mrs. Frank Earl took the Zepher train to Colorado and brought Paul back to Indiana. In 1938, Lois (age four) and Stanley (age three) came on the Greyhound bus to Indiana. Stanley went to Arch and Hazel Tobias' and Lois went to stay with Frank and Margaret Earl. These dear people raised Paul and Lois.

Paul graduated from Huntington college and attended Findlay College; Findlay, Ohio. He is now pastoring at the German Town Church of God, Cascade, Maryland.

Mrs. Frank (Margaret) Earl, Stanley and Lois Tobias and bus driver.

Lois lives in Zanesville and is active in Church work and does child care.

In 1942 Ed Tobias came to Indiana with his family and Stanley returned with him. Ed passed away in 1953.

RALPH R. AND FLORENCE TAYLOR

In 1951, Florence Banter with two small children, located on an 80-acre farm in Jackson Township, Wells County. She had lived only two miles east of this farm but because of a corn picker accident and the death of her husband, Byron Banter, she was forced to find a new home.

The two small children were Bill Banter (February 24, 1946) and Janice Banter Babcock (October 11, 1947). Bill grew up on this farm, graduating from Jackson Center and Purdue University. After graduating from college, he returned to Jackson Township to farm. He married Dianna Rody, school teacher, and remained on Howard Baker's farm. They have two sons, Will Byron, (November 1, 1973) and Brent Aaron, (April 19, 1976), who are both students at Southern Wells.

Janice also grew up on the same farm, graduated from Jackson Center and Purdue University. She married Dr. George Babcock and has two children, Timothy Kent, (December 19, 1973) and Lisa Lynn, (April 1, 1977), who are both students in Bluffton schools. Janice, a nurse, and Dr. George, a surgeon, work at the Bluffton Clinic.

Back L to R: Robey, Bill. Front L to R: Janice, Ralph, Florence

While Bill and Janice were still very young, their mother, Florence Banter, married Ralph R. Taylor. He had served in the Navy and returned to his trade as a plasterer. To this union a son, Robey R. Taylor (September 12, 1953), was born. Robey also attended Jackson Center, but because of school consolidation, he graduated from Southern Wells. He also graduated from Purdue University.

Robey is the manager of a large mall in Elyria, Ohio. He married Anita Glasgow, an accountant, and they have two children, Megan Ruth (December 31, 1981), and Brandon Robert (September 16, 1983). Both are students in the Elyria schools.

We have lived on our present farm for 40 years, and by the way, Bill farms the farm now. We attend Oak Chapel U. M. Church in Grant County and spend a few winter months in our home in Florida. *(Florence Taylor)*

STEVE AND CHERYL TAYLOR

Cheryl Ann (Croy) Taylor was born July 24, 1960 at the Wells Community Hospital. She is the daughter of Donald L. and Phyllis A. (Courtney) Croy. She was the second daughter of three. Her grandparents are Clarence and Geneva (Gifford) Croy of Vera Cruz, and James Howard and Mona (Stout) Courtney of Bluffton. She lived on Sycamore Street in Vera Cruz.

When Cheryl was three years old they moved to 2736 S E Mulberry Street, just one-half block from her first home. This home was the same house in which her father was raised.

Cheryl went to Poplar Grove Elementary School then on to Central Junior High. She graduated in 1978 from Bluffton High School. One year later she was married to Joe William Neuenschwander (son of John and Irene Neuenschwander) on June 30, 1979.

Steve and Cheryl Taylor

Over the next two years they lived in two homes in the Vera Cruz area. In 1981 Joe joined the Air Force. They then moved to Denver, Colorado. This was their first time to live outside of Wells County.

After eight months in Denver they were stationed in Omaha, Nebraska. To get away from the city they rented a home across the Missouri River in Iowa. About one year later they were divorced. At that time Cheryl moved to Glenwood, Iowa. This was where she met Steve.

Steven Ray Taylor was born on October 19, 1958 in Minnesota. He is the son of Altonya and Harley Taylor. Steve was the youngest of three children. Harley was in the Navy, and they moved to Boston when Steve was five. When Steve was eight they moved back to their hometown of Farragut, Iowa. In 1967 they went to Naha, Okinawa for three years. Then back to Iowa.

After graduation from high school Steve moved around the area of Iowa he calls home. He working as a farm hand and also driving a truck. In November of 1980 Steve's first love was born, a Golden Retriever named Honey Bear. Soon after Steve and Cheryl met, Steve got a job offer in Dallas, Texas, so they were off to Texas.

On January 25, 1986 they were married. They lived in Texas for almost two years. The promise of jobs with the General Motors Plant opening just south of Fort Wayne (and encouragement from Cheryl's family) brought them back to Wells County and right back to Vera Cruz.

In October of 1987 they bought the Dwight and Lilly Reynolds farm, just south of Vera Cruz, near Riverside Warehouse. On March 18, 1989 they had a son, Mikel Ray Taylor.

Steve presently is employed by his father-in-law, Don Croy, as office manager at Croy Machine Shop in Vera Cruz. Cheryl is the manager of the Bluffton License Branch. They attend Six Mile Church. For a time they were the custodians of the Six Mile Cemetery.

They both enjoy fishing and camping. Steve is active in the Summit City Bassmasters.

TERRELL-HARMON

My great-grandparents were Mary Ann (Murray) and Harris Osborn and Alford and Lucy Terrell from the Wells/Huntington Counties area.

Born to Mary and Harris Osborn were several children, one being Amanda Edith, who was my grandmother. Born to the Terrell family were also several children, including Earl Wilford who was to become my grandfather. Grandma and Grandpa Terrell lived in Decatur for as long as I can remember, but my mother remembers when they were children they lived in Majenica and attended the Lancaster School in Huntington County. At that time my grandfather worked at the tile mill in Majenica for Joe Mills and for the WPA and PWA, building state road 5 during the Depression.

The family consisted of my Uncle Harris (later married to Mary First), Aunt Lucy (married to Woodrow Call), Uncle Von (married to Marjorie Weldy), and my mother, Lillian Edith.

L to R Back: Myrl, Jr., John, Janet, Jack, Jane. Front: Lillian, LaVon, Myrl, Sr.

Sometime in 1938 the Terrell family moved to Decatur on Mercer Avenue and my grandpa worked at the Decatur Tile Mill until it burned down; he then worked at the Rubber Works in Fort Wayne.

My father, Myrl Edward Harmon, was born to Admiral Dewey and Myrtle (Rumple) Harmon in Ohio City, Ohio. Grandpa Harmon worked for the railroad for a number of years, but then the family moved to Decatur and my grandpa went to work for Central Soya.

The Harmon family consisted of Ruth, Dorothy, Betty, Marie, Kenneth, and my dad. Kenneth died at the age of 12.

My mother and dad met in school in 1938 or 1939 and were married in 1943. My dad worked for McConnell and Son's delivering tobacco products until he was drafted during World War II and left in November, 1944. I was six months old at that time.

We lived at several places in Decatur, the last was on Patterson Street beside the railroad. We left there after I finished the fifth grade. By that time I was no longer an only child. I had three brothers, Jack Allen, born in 1948, John Arthur, born in 1951, and Myrl Edward, Jr., born in 1953, and a sister, Janet Arline, born in 1949.

In 1956 we moved from Decatur to rural Liberty Center, where another sister, LaVon Marjory, was born in 1957.

We then attended school at Liberty Center until I was 16, then moved again to rural Bluffton. I then attended Bluffton High School, my brothers and sisters going to Poplar Grove.

In 1960 we moved to a house on State Road #124, the first house in Huntington County where the younger children went to Warren to attend school and the older ones to Huntington.

Back L to R: Janet Wyatt, Jack Harmon, Myrl Harmon, Jr., John Harmon. Front L to R: Jane Slater, Lillian Morris, Jack Morris, La Von Hosler

During that period of time my dad worked at Salsibury (Dana Corp.) in Fort Wayne, Sterling Casting, and part-time at Earl Settle's gas station at the corner of Main and Spring. My mother worked at the Dutch Mill for five years, known to everyone there as "Shorty". She then went to work at Utah in Huntington until it burned down and then on the Utrad. In 1966 both my parents went to work at Corning Glass in Bluffton.

My father was employed there in 1974 when at the age of 47, he passed away. My mother retired from Corning in 1981 after 15 years. Mom was remarried in 1984 to Jack Morris; he died on March 4, 1988. They had resided in rural Montpelier. Two years ago, Mom bought a home on Dustman Road and moved to town.

I married Stephen Holmes and we had two children, Darryl Duane (married Linda Hale from California, has one daughter, LaVon) and Lora LuAnn (married John Lee, two children, Ashlie and Joshua). I remarried in 1988 to Dale Slater, Sr. and we reside in Bluffton. He is employed at the National Guard Armory and I work for the City of Bluffton as the mayor's secretary.

My brother Jack married Sheryl Ruse from Warren; they have two children, Andrea and Jason, and live in rural Warren. My sister Janet married Sam Wyatt from Mt. Zion and they have two children: Tim (married to Nancy Shannon from Bluffton, one son, Lincoln) and Tonya. Sam and Janet now live in Mom's former house in rural Montpelier. My brother John was married to Ruth Bustos from Warren and they had three daughters, Monica, Starr, and Jessica. Myrl Jr. married Sandra Smith from Warren and they have three children: F. Michael, Shannon, and Terri, and live in Huntington. LaVon married David Hosler from Huntington and has two children, James and Vanessa. They reside in Huntington.

THOMA FAMILY

In the year 1848 a lad of seventeen years by the name of Henry Thoma sailed from Edersdorf, Germany, across the Atlantic to America. They journey took 30 days. The same ship in which he sailed sank in the Atlantic on its return trip.

Young Thoma was in search of a better life. Alone in this new world, he apprenticed himself to a cabinet maker in Findly, Ohio. When this apprenticeship was completed (1848-1853), he started looking for a good location in which to start a business of his own. Going west he sailed on the Wabash River and came to a beautiful bluff on its bank. Here he started his cabinet making and the town which grew up became Bluffton. He prospered and was quite content with his life here.

He married Matilda Deaver (1835-1898). They had one son whom they named Herman William. By this time the cabinet makers had been led into the undertakers work as makers of coffins. So Herman joined his father in the combined business.

Herman was a very active citizen of Bluffton. He was a trustee in the Methodist Church, an officer holder in many branches of the Masonic Lodge, and played flute and piccolo in Bluffton orchestras. Herman was never too busy to visit with anyone or to listen to their troubles. He would rather visit than eat, which made his eating hours unpredictable.

William Henry (Bill) Thoma

Herman married Emma Flora (1876-1957). Emma's mother died when she was two and her aunt, Mrs. William Biberstine, took her. When Mr. Biberstine died in 1885, Emma continued living with and caring for her "Auntie" in her elder years.

Emma, too, was very active in the life of Bluffton. She belonged to all the Methodist missionary societies, was a Matron of Eastern Star, and served as secretary for years on the Board for Welfare Children.

Herman and Emma had two children: William Henry (1901-1974) and Mary (1904-1929).

William graduated from DePauw where he was a member of Phi Delta Theta. He then joined his father, and the firm became Thoma and Son Funeral and Furniture. He was very active in the Methodist Church, being a long time trustee and active participant in the extensive remodeling of the church in 1952. Bill (as he was known) was a loyal Mason, holding offices in the Bluffton lodge and a member of the Fort Wayne Scottish Rite and Shrine. For years he was on the Bluffton Library Board. In Fort Wayne he was on the Board of Directors of Brotherhood/Mutual Security Life Insurance.

Their daughter Mary graduated from Oberlin College as an outstanding flutist. She became a member of the Fort Wayne Philharmonic and numerous orchestras. While taking advanced work in Chicago, she contracted pneumonia which caused her untimely death at an early age.

William married Harriet Geiger, also a graduate of DePauw. In college, she was a member of Kappa Kappa Gamma, Phi Beta Kappa, Mortar Board, and was a Rector Scholar. She came to Bluffton as a history teacher.

After deciding to stay in Bluffton as Mrs. Thoma, she joined the city's activities. She was the first woman trustee of the Methodist Church and a president of the Women's Society. She was active in TriKappa and served twelve years as a Girl Scout leader. She also assisted at the Funeral Home, both before and after the death of her husband.

William and Harriet had three daughters: Betty Jean, Mary Jane and Patricia. All three attended DePauw where they were members of Kappa Kappa Gamma and campus activities. In 1954, Betty married George Weikert who was with AT&T in Minneapolis. In 1957, Jane married David Hammond who is a doctor in St. Louis. In 1961, Pat married Jim Mallers who is in the Northwest Allen School system in Fort Wayne.

Eight grandchildren have been born to these couples. All are college graduates and work in their special fields.

The Thoma family has been part of Bluffton history. Although no decendents live here permanently, they hold their lives in Bluffton as a great asset and are grateful for the privilege of having lived here.

THOMAS

James Thomas was born January 8, 1872, in Wells County. He and Louisa Greenwood, born February 1, 1877, were married on May 12, 1897. They began housekeeping with Louisa's mother, Alinda Ann, on a farm in Chester Township, near Poneto. On November 2, 1898, a son, Charlie, was born and a daughter, Fern, on March 31, 1902. Fern married Frank Phillips on May 22, 1937, and still resides in the Greenwood residence.

James died on August 29, 1951; Louisa died on June 14, 1959. They are both buried in Miller Cemetery, Chester Township.

Due to the oil boom, the Thomas' moved to Oklahoma when Charlie was about 16 years old. James found opportunity to be plentiful, and Charlie got his start as a water boy. Charlie stayed to work in the oil fields after his parents returned to Wells County.

Standing L to R: Jim, Peggy, Charlie. Seated L to R: Jane, Fern, Mary Lou.

In 1919, Charlie met Fern Florence Roll at a ball for the oil field workers. They married just six weeks later, on April 24, 1919, in Big Heart, Oklahoma. Fern was born July 28, 1896 in Avon, Iowa, to Henry Bingham Roll and Mary Elizabeth McKee Roll. Fern taught Indian children in a one-room schoolhouse, traveling several miles by horseback to get to school. A son was stillborn to this union on March 5, 1921, in Cleveland, Oklahoma.

Charlie and Fern returned to Chester Township in the spring of 1921, and settled in Section 17. In April, 1922, Charlie bought forty acres in Section 21 for a homestead. They were unable to move to this property because the house had recently burned. Three months later, Mary Louise was born on July 9, 1922. The couple purchased a house in Keystone and moved it to the homestead. This house still remains on the land today.

Charlie and Fern raised hogs, chickens, and milk cows on the small farm. "Pearl" and "Nellie" were retired to the pasture when the first modern machinery came to the farm in 1938, an F12 Farmall tractor with cast iron spade wheels.

Three other children were born on this farm: Jane Ann, January 31, 1924; Peggy Jean, August 16, 1931; and James Roll, October 9, 1939.

In 1941, Charlie purchased the forty acres in Section 21 that belonged to his parents. He purchased an adjoining forty acres in 1943.

Charlie was often confused with another Charlie Thomas in the area. Because of this confusion, Charlie was advised to add an initial to his name. He added the letter G., (for Greenwood) and was known from that point on as Charlie G. Thomas.

Charlie and Fern were both members of the Chester Center Christian Church, since 1923. The couple raised their children in the church, and remained active through the years.

On holidays, the whole family gathered at Charlie and Fern's. The grandchildren especially remember the Easter egg hunts. Charlie and the uncles would hide coins in the shingles of the house and in the bark of trees. The grandchildren enjoyed listening to the fascinating stories of Fern's early life as a teacher and neighbor to the Indians.

Mary Lou is the only child remaining in Wells County. She and her husband have raised five children here, and are the owners of the homeplaces. Their grandchildren have extended the Thomas' family to the fifth generation born in the County.

Many memories have been made through the years with Charlie and Fern. Charlie died at home on March 26, 1983. Fern remained at the homeplace until October, 1983, and then lived with her children until 1988. She died in Swiss Village in Adams County on January 29, 1990 at the age of 93. They are both buried in Miller Cemetery, Chester Township.

DAVID F. THOMAS FAMILY

David F. Thomas, his wife, Anne; sister Magaline, her husband, Abraham Beaber; sister Anna Mary, her husband Henry Beaber; oldest brother, Isaac, Jr. and wife, Barbara, youngest brother, John L. F., and his wife, Elizabeth, and all their families came to Indiana between the years 1845 to 1850 from Tuscarawas County, Dover Township, Ohio where their father Isaac, Sr. had homesteaded in 1810. All settled in the Zanesville area of Wells County.

Some came by canal, some by covered wagon, but for all the journey was long and difficult. They came to unchartered, uncleared land, but they settled and endured all the hardships of early pioneers to raise their families.

David moved to his pre-empted land in May, 1847, with his wife and three children, Sampson, age four, Lydia, three and Shalter, one year old. He built a log cabin, one room, no windows, and a door made of skins into which his family moved in January, 1848. In this cabin three more children were born, but none lived to adulthood. Between 1870 and 1872, David built a new home for his family. This home is still standing and is the home of Marshall Johnson.

David F. Thomas

In 1849, David started classes for U.B. members in his home. He, his sisters and brothers were all well acquainted with the United Brethern Church. Their father had donated land and helped build an early church, which still stands. Christian Newcomer, an early circuit rider from Fredrich's County, Maryland for the church, was a visitor in their home when he made the trip to Tuscarawas County.

David was granted his first license in 1859. Together with his two sisters and their husbands, they helped build the College Corners Church and later the school which served the small community for many years. David was a circuit rider on the Bluffton circuit and later minister at College Corners.

Isaac, Jr., moved to land David sold to him. There he raised five children. John L. F. moved to Zansville, where he worked at blacksmithing. He was a Justice of the Peace for several years. He was also a volunteer in the Civil War. He raised six children. Both sisters and their husbands lived close to Zansville, were active in school and church.

David's wife Anne died in 1873. His oldest son, Sampson, had married in 1866. Shalter had purchased land in Union Township, Huntington County and was farming there. David remarried in 1884 to Mahalia Jackson Black. She had two children from a previous marriage. Lydia married Reverend S. T. Mahon in 1884 and moved to Ohio.

David was very active in the conferences and many years held offices. He wrote several papers for the church. But in 1885 he tendered his resignation because of needing to spend more time on his farm.

David was a large man, stern, tall and energetic. He had a deep gruff voice and was a forceful speaker. Space does not permit the stories learned from many years of research about my third great-grandfather, but he left his family and descendants a heritage of hard work and dedication of which they may be proud.

JOHN LUCAS FLACK THOMAS FAMILY

John Lucas Flack Thomas was born in the year 1817. He became a blacksmith by trade and lived and worked and raised his family a number of years in Zanesville, Indiana from back in the early 1850's.

John L. F. and his wife, Elizabeth, raised seven children, two boys and five girls, two of which were twins. Elizabeth was born in 1824.

John and Elizabeth Thomas family taken in the early 1870's. Standing behind parents (L to R) are Lee, Anne, Laura, and Georgianne. Children in front are John H.G., Ida, and Emma.

Eldest child was Lee Richard Thomas who born in 1847. Georgianne followed next and was born in 1851. Georgianne married into the Karns family. She was the mother of Blanche Karnes who was a long time teacher in the Bluffton school system.

Ida was born in 1856 and was herself a teacher in the Bluffton grade schools for many years. Her birth was followed in 1858 by John H. G. The following year, 1859, a set of twin girls were born into the family. They were named Laura and Anne. Emma was the last of the seven children born into the John and Elizabeth Thomas family. She was born in 1864.

THOMAS-MILLER

In 1991, the United States is in the throes of another war. All talk is of patriotism and prayers for those in service. Both the Thomas and Miller families can be proud of members who answered the call to duty prior to 1991.

William Miller, my grandfather, volunteered for the War of the Rebellion, serving in one of the bloodiest battles, Chickamauga, in which he was wounded and a brother was killed. The 101st Regiment of Indiana Infantry served with Sherman's Army. In his three years in service, William marched 3507 miles, by rail traveled 759 miles, and sailed by steamer 650 miles, a total of 4,916 miles.

John B. Miller, Jr., World War II gunner, was missing for six months after being shot down over Yugoslavia. Raymond A. Haflich, a brother-in-law, served in France in World War I.

Ralph C. Thomas served in Cuba in the Spanish-American War. Howard Thomas was drafted in both World War I and II.

William Miller, born in 1824, came to Rockcreek Township, Wells County, in 1851. In 1859, he married Susan Rebecca Bender. Both Benders and Millers were natives of Essenheim, Germany. John Bender Miller, my father, was youngest of six: Franklin, William, Barbara Ellen Staver, Lydia Zoll, and Ada M. Decker.

John Bender Miller married Mary Etta Ditzler, the daughter of John R. and B. Catherine (Brickley) Ditzler. For several years the Ditzlers, my grandparents, managed the Wells County Home. Children: John Calvin, Elnora Myers, Pearl Higgins, and Mary Etta Miller. In 1911, John B. Miller

579

purchased the north elevator in Uniondale and in 1915 moved to Uniondale, purchasing the south elevator. Both were sold to Legge Elevator in 1942. His early training in the grain business was with Studebaker Grain and Seed of Bluffton. Children: Lela Haflich, Mabeline Keplinger and Naomi Boulware, both deceased, Mary L. Thomas, Margaret Cupp, Marceille Shutt, and John B. Miller, Jr., of Searcy, Arkansas.

Howard E. Thomas (Tommy), son of Ralph Courtney and Ethel (Masterson) Thomas, was employed for more than fifty years in Bluffton banks. He retired as a Direction, Vice President, and Load Officer of Old-First National Bank. For several years, he clerked sales for the bank. His family: Dorothy Rippe, Mary Hetrick, Martha Speheger, Kathryn Clowser, and Ruth Martin are all deceased. His death occurred in 1969. As was written of his grandfather Thomas, so it can be said of Tommy that "over the years he had the faculty of binding to himself scores of close and intimate friends."

Ralph C. Thomas was postmaster at Bluffton for nine years. Prior to his appointment, he was caretaker of the Elm Grove Cemetery for 25 years.

On June 30, 1945, Mary L. Miller and Howard E. Thomas were married at St. Mark's Lutheran Church, Uniondale. Mary (Miller) Thomas worked for 19 years at Bluffton banks. For 15 years, she helped clerk sales, and for several years was treasurer of the Wells County 4-H Association. For 21 years, to 1987, she was secretary-treasurer for Wells County Soil and Water Conservation District and the Rockcreek Conservancy District. Children of Howard and Mary Thomas are John Ralph Thomas, born May 22, 1948, and Rebecca Thomas Main, born June 14, 1949. John married Martha Maurer of Botkins, Ohio, and now lives at Jackson Center, Ohio. John is Credit Manager for Provico, Inc., of Botkins, Ohio. They own eighty acres where they breed Horned Dorset sheep. They also have a herd of goats and sell milk to a cheese factory. Their children are Catherine, 9, Caleb, 8, and Zebulon, 3. Rebecca married John A. Main of Fort Wayne. "Becky" has taught second grade and then kindergarten in Bluffton for 19 years. John has taught history at Bishop Luers High School, Fort Wayne, for 18 years. Their children are Mollie, 14, Lindsay, 11, and Abbie, 7. *(Mary L. (Miller) Thomas)*

SAMPSON THOMAS FAMILY

Sampson Thomas, oldest son of David F. and Anne Wieble Thomas, was born in Tuscarawas County, Ohio in 1843. He came to Indiana at age four and settled with his family in the Zanesville area of Wells County. He went to school at Caley School and College Corners after it was built.

In May, 1864 he joined the 137th light infantry volunteer regiment for 100 days of service in the Civil War. He was in the Georgia campaign and then was released in December, 1864. He came home to farm with his father. In April, 1866, he married the widow of Simon Kohr, Susanne Caley Kohr. Susanne had two children, Jacob and Madgalene. They lived in a log cabin on fifty acres of land purchased by Simon from his father when he married.

Sampson and Susanne had five children. Two died in infancy. Allie, a victim of rheumatic fever, died in 1888 at age fifteen. Lewis, the oldest was born in 1868. Monroe was born in 1878. Lewis moved to Huntington County, Union Township when he married Rose Anna Smith in 1890. They had two children, Floyd and Merle. Floyd married Mary Alice Bayha, had five children, two of which survived. Merle married Charles Paul, had three children, two of which still survive.

Home that Sampson Thomas built in early 1880's using his father's, David F. Thomas, tools. Located on 900 E. in Union Township, Wells County.

Sampson built a new home for the family sometime in the early 1880's. He built the house himself with lumber from his land. He drilled a new well and improved living conditions for the family. The house was heated with a wood stove in the kitchen and a coal stove in the living room. It was a luxury after the log cabin. Lewis used to tell of shaking snow from the covers on winter mornings when he was young. In comparison to our heated homes of today, it was crude but a wonder to them.

Sampson taught in several of the schools close to him in the winter. There are records of his payments which were at most one dollar and twenty-five cents for a week's work. The school year was short, but conditions improved when, through efforts of early dedicated pioneer men and women who wanted better education for their children, time and money became available.

Sampson was a reader and spent hours with his Bible and other books. He taught Sunday School at both College Corners and Zanesville, was a lay minister and served the church in other ways. He was able to blow fire from burns and healed many bad burns according to some of the older people of the community who knew him. He was a water dozer, and many of the wells in the community were ones he helped doze. The well for the log cabin was some way from the house, but the new well was just outside the door.

Lewis told many stories of his early youth. He worked hard, but learned much of his spelling, and reading, not from school, but from the spelling bees, the Bible quizzes and games of Bible verses taught at school and church. They had husking bees, quilting bees for all the families, and barn raisings were a community affair for newcomers or for someone who had the misfortune of losing a barn through fire. Singing school was a part of church and school.

Sampson was five foot six inches according to his service records, with hazel eyes and dark complexion. His later pictures show him with a beautiful head of white hair and full beard. The horse he rode was not gentle. He used the buggy only to make long trips into Ohio to visit relatives after Susanne's death in 1908. Sampson died in 1920.

Susanne was a small, gentle woman, greatly loved by her son Lewis' children. They had many stories of delightful visits with her.

Sampson helped many people with financial aid with food and material goods. He, along with his brother Shalter and son Lewis, never wanted thanks or notice of what they gave or did for others. It was done through real Christian brotherhood.

DAVID SWAIM THOMPSON

The Swaim family in Wells County dates back to 1857 when Lt. Col. William Swaim located with his wife, Hannah Toy Swaim, on a farm near Ossian. They were parents of five children, one of whom was David Hathaway Swaim, who later lived in Bluffton and became a publisher of the News-Banner. D.H. Swaim married Esther May Gorrell in Ossian, Indiana on September 16, 1885.

To them were born Helen Swaim, November 19, 1888-December 11, 1931, and Roger Gorrell Swaim, March 9, 1897-October 10, 1976.

On December 15, 1913, Helen, a teacher, married Frank G. Thompson. He was born January 5, 1890 in Montgomery County, Indiana and had come to Bluffton to teach Industrial Arts. Helen, a member of a literary club, Foltz Club, was also active in the choir of the First Methodist Church. Frank worked at the News-Banner for a while, then, as a Democrat, was elected mayor of Bluffton, a member of the Indiana House of Representatives and State Auditor. He later was appointed to the State Board of Tax Commissioners. He retired to Bluffton to manage his farm, and lived four of his last years with the David Swaim Thompson family. He died November 1, 1968.

David Swaim Thompson, July 25, 1916-October 31, 1984, and Barbara Thompson Kinnally, September 24, 1914-August 12, 1978, were children of Frank and Helen.

Barbara married William Joseph Kinnally, born in Gary, Indiana on January 30, 1915, son of Mr. and Mrs. John Francis Kinnally, in Bluffton, July 17, 1937. To them were born Sue Kinnally, December 28, 1941, and Joanne Kinnally, October 16, 1943. This family lived in Indianapolis, Indiana and Dallas, Texas, but mainly in Milwaukee, Wisconsin. Barbara and Bill retired to Scottsdale, Arizona, where Barbara died August 12, 1978.

Mary Jo Carlson, Clarabelle Thompson, Dave Swaim, Kathy Bailey, Judy Russ and "Sugar". 1959

David Swaim Thompson lived all his years in Bluffton, except when attending Wabash College and Indiana University. On June 17, 1939, in the First Methodist Church in Fort Wayne, Indiana, David married Clarabelle Chenoweth, born November 27, 1916 to George E. and Cora Edith Chenoweth of Fort Wayne, Indiana. She also had attended Indiana University. Mrs. Roger G. (Celia) Swaim played the organ and Reverend Schuyler A. Mow, grandfather of Clarabelle, assisted in the wedding ceremony.

David S. Thompson worked at the New Banner and then had his own insurance business, before teaching English at Liberty Center. He finished his teaching career as Guidance Counselor at Bluffton High School. He represented his 1934 class of Bluffton High in giving the address at its

50th reunion, 1984. Dave, an Eagle Scout, shared his interests in the outdoors and in sports with his family, but also helped youth in Little League as an umpire and some scouting activities. He and Clarabelle maintained interest and support in the First United Methodist Church and other civic interests as in Rotary, the Liberty Board, Wells County Fish Fry and Juvenile Officer for Dave. He was honored in 1964 as Father of the Year in Wells County. Dave died October 31, 1984. Clarabelle, an elementary school teacher in the Bluffton schools for 20 years, had civic interests including Tri Kappa, Church Women United, Wells County Literacy, The Study Club, and was a Girl Scout leader for three years.

Born of this marriage were: Judith (Judy) Ann Thompson - December 14, 1940; Mary Jo Thompson - July 25, 1943; Kathryn (Kathy) Thompson - March 16, 1946 to May 29, 1990.

The family enjoyed picnics in the State Park (Ouabache), athletics and other school events, visits with friends and relatives, and eventually shared a cottage at Little Crooked Lake. Fishing had always been a favorite activity of the Thompsons and the Chenoweths, and was shared with the grandchildren. Jeffrey Alan Steele and Angela Jean Steele were children of Judy Thompson Ross and Bob Steele. Charles David Sturgis, Jennifer Diane Sturgis, and Stephanie Dawn Sturgis were born to Kathy Thompson Bailey and Tom Sturgis. The children of Mary Jo Thompson and Don Carlson are: Dee Ann Carlson, Elizabeth Carlson, and Chip Carlson (Don F. Carlson II).

Jeff Steele and Mary Wanetta Perry were married August 31, 1985. Children born to them were Sara Brittney Steele, March 6, 1987, and David Jeffrey Steele, December 16, 1989 to December 21, 1989, great-grandchildren of Dave and Clarabelle Thompson.

DONALD E. THOMPSON FAMILY

My father, William O. Thompson (1892-1970), and his father, William M. (1863-1953), were both natives of Wells County. I remember Dad having scalded feet, after being in the large tank, after the Bracey Oil fire; how he hunted wild game and all the hides that covered the end of the barn. This was food and income during the Depression years. He drove the WPA workers to work in an old International truck and put hot coals under the motor, in order to get it started in the cold winter months. Dad cut and built the first roads thru the Qubache State Park and worked along with the WPA and the CCC boys, constructing buildings, bridges, quail pens, etc. I recall standing inside the roller wheel that Dad used on road construction.

I, Donald (Earl) Thompson, born in 1922, contacted polio at the age of eight, affecting both legs and was bedfast. My friends would play in the next yard outside my window, for my entertainment, during the quarantine. Later, we would play under the Florence Hot Blast stove, on the stove board, using the border for the roads for our cars. A new way of getting around was achieved, by holding to the edge of the round dining room table, a kiddie cart, and my loving mother (Hazel), that pulled me to the Park school in a coaster wagon. I rode a bike to the Central school and would stop at George Honley's Cafe, for a meatloaf sandwich and milk at noon. I did art work on the walls of the Park school, for the "Comet" school paper, and the 1940 Retrospect.

I married Lois King in 1945, and had two son, Thomas Dewayne (1946-1950) and Ted Lorin (1948), now in California. We had an early Christmas for Dewayne, due to a nine-month battle with leukemia.

My second union was with Dorothy Jones (1956) and we had five children: Dwight (1958), now in New Jersey: Denise (1960), married Harry Mosure in Bluffton; Dennis (1962), now in Florida; David (1964-1987), killed in an auto accident; and Deidre (1967), married Pat McKeone of Bluffton. I have four grandsons: Andy, Adam, Cory and Donald.

My sister, Mary A. (1912), married Joe Schlagenhauf (1913-1983), and had four children: JoAnn (1940), married Don Cline; Sandra (1944), married Jim Powers; Rea (1946), married Jerry Oxendine; and Johnny (1950), married Vickie Stepp. There are seven grand and great-grandchildren: Jenna, Greg, Whitney, Hayes, Ashley, Mathew, and Cortney. All reside in North Carolina.

I worked two years at Houser Engineering; three years Indiana State Highway; two years Studebaker war plant making parts for the Flying Fortress planes; and 36 years at Franklin Electric, building prototype, samples, Direct Current, cut-a-ways, and show display motors. The last few years, I moved into Drafting, after my department was terminated. I did hand engraving and art work for retirement parties and various occasions.

I retired in 1985 and helped the Boy Scout Troop 148 in the old Bluffton Cemetery clean up in 1986. Being a shutter-bug is my hobby, so I have an album of the clean-up with pictures of Mayor Fryback, Councilmen Ralph Santon, Clair Bush, and numerous others that helped.

JOHN THOMPSON FAMILY

John Ware Thompson and Maxine Markley wed in 1939 and have resided up the lane in Liberty Township on the Hoosier Homestead Farm of John's great-grandfather, Thomas Ware.

John, son of Guy and Nora Thompson Ware, was adopted by Uncle Ora and Nellie Burman Thompson after the death of his mother, Nora, when he was just an infant. John, a 1938 graduate of Liberty Center High School, was a participant in all athletics and a farmer and mechanic after graduation.

Ralph and Mary Alice Garrett Markley, the parents of Maxine, owned Markley Brothers' Grocery located on West Market Street. Maxine graduated from Bluffton High School in 1939.

Lee and Maggie Bartlemay Markley were Maxine's grandparents and lived on a farm with gravel pits out by the Six Mile Church. Upon Maggie's death and Lee's retirement, he moved to Bluffton.

Frank and Elizabeth Boltin Garrett were grandparents who owned a hardware store and lived in Liberty Center.

We are proud of our family, our three sons who served in the U.S. Army and our daughter.

Jim, our oldest son and a 1958 graduate of Liberty Center, is the rural mail carrier for Liberty Center and Poneto Route One. William, a 1963 graduate of Liberty Center, lives in Bluffton and has worked at General Electric in Fort Wayne for 28 years. He married Cheryl Conner, daughter of Kenneth and Patricia Grove Conner, and they have given us three wonderful grandchildren. Jeffrey Keith Thompson is married to Sara Spann. They have a son, Jobe Daniel Thompson. Jami Kay married Timothy Prough, and their son is Derek Michael Prough. Jennifer Karol Thompson, our granddaughter, is engaged and planning a July wedding.

Our son, Richard E. Thompson, lives in Bluffton and is a computer operator at Gerber's Grocery. He was a 1969 Southern Wells graduate. Our daughter, Joyce Ann, a 1975 graduate of Southern Wells, married Roger Wayne McAfee. They live on a farm in Rockcreek Township where he has a large hog operation and farms many acres with our farm included. Their son, Troy Jacob McAfee, is one year old. Roger is the son of Junior and Marjorie Geiger McAfee.

We are now retired. With us now are just cats and the family pony, King, yet there is never a dull moment.

THOMPSON-HARRIS

William (born 1867) and Fannie Marie (Marson) Thompson (born 1865) imigrated to the United States in May 1901 from England. Their two children were Constance (born September 22, 1891) and Willie (born 1901).

Constance married Charley Harris of Wells County on January 13, 1915. They had seven children, three died in infancy. The other children still live in the Wells County area. Florence Belle, born in North Dakota on October 8, 1915, now lives

Picture given to Maxine Thompson by Aunt Lorene (Marley) Erhart. School on Washington Street.

at Meadowvale Care Center. Claude Leroy was born in North Dakota on August 15, 1920. Clyde Harold was born in Wells County on April 18, 1922 and William Eugene was born in Wells County on August 27, 1933. Claude and Clyde's family sketches appear elsewhere in this book.

William (Bill) married Joyce Ann Keller, daughter of Albert Keller, Jr., and Evelyn M. (Captain) on May 27, 1951 at the Six Mile Church. Four children blessed this marriage: Deborah Joan (born April 16, 1952); Pamela Kay (born September 28, 1953); Steven Dean (born January 22, 1955); and Dennis Lee (born March 11, 1959).

Debbie married David Anthony Morse on September 17, 1977, and now lives in the Fort Wayne area. They have three children: Rebecca Joan (born February 10, 1979); Kevin David (born October 19, 1981); and Catherine Maria (born April 30, 1984).

Pam is married to Thomas DeMartino, and they have three children. They also make their home in the Fort Wayne area. Their children are: Christopher Erin McKee (born October 31, 1972); Michelle Evangeline McKee (born December 4, 1973); and Thomas Albert DeMartino (born September 8, 1982).

Steve lives in Bluffton and has one son, Corey Lee, born on November 9, 1979.

Dennis lives in Bluffton, also, with his wife, the former Ellen Marie Ullman. They have three daughters: Laura Marie (born on July 7, 1980); Sara Beth (born May 27, 1982); and Melinda Diane (born February 13, 1984).

THOMPSON-WERKING

Roberta A. Thompson Werking taught for 36 years in Fort Wayne, Indiana. She graduated from Liberty Center High School in 1943, Manchester College, and Indiana University. She was born in Wells County Hospital on February 14, 1925, the only child of Chester R. Thompson and Winifred Falk.

Her paternal grandfather, James Thompson, Sr., was born in Edinburgh, Scotland, May 16, 1747. It is not known when he came to this country, but he married Ann Perry from Rhode Island on March 16, 1768. Soon after the outbreak of the Revolution he enlisted, in 1776, with the Colonials and served in a Maryland regiment. How long he lived in Maryland is not known, but family records state that his children were born in Virginia. In about 1800 the family moved to Bracken County, Kentucky, where he and his wife died.

The Thompson's then moved to Huntington County, Indiana. On February 20, 1867, Robert H. Thompson married Eliza C. Stroup and moved to Liberty Township, Wells County. Upon his wife's death, September 10, 1910, he moved back to Warren, Indiana. His sons, Alfred P. and Ernest Elza and his grandsons, Chester R. and Kenneth B. Thompson lived all their lives in Liberty Township as farmers.

Ernest E. Thompson, born November 11, 1869, and died January 28, 1946. May 2, 1891, he married Etta M. Burman, a daughter of George W. and Lydia (Trimmer) Burman, of Warren, Indiana. Four children blessed the union: Mable (Don Merriman) deceased; Chester R., deceased; Buelah (Russel Wise of Union City, Indiana); and Kenneth B. of Liberty Township.

Chester R. Thompson was born October 2, 1898, died August 15, 1986. After graduating from Liberty Center High School in 1918, he went to Wabash College to be a teacher. He taught at Bly, Roberts, and Africa all in Liberty Township. He later turned to farming and was a farmer for 60 years.

He married Winifred Falk, September 8, 1923 (daughter of Sherman and Ida (Ludwig) Falk) in Louisville, Kentucky. Winifred was a first and second grade teacher at Rockcreek Center, Wells County, when it first opened in 1923. They had one child, Roberta A. Thompson.

Roberta married, May 30, 1948, Vernon E. Werking of North Manchester, Indiana. Vernon was a graduate of North Manchester High School, Manchester College, and Indiana University. Vernon taught in the Fort Wayne schools for 36 years. They have one child, Stephanie Werking Neill (James), and three grandsons: Stuart, Jason, and Joseph Neill, of Fort Wayne.

The Werkings lived in Fort Wayne for 40 years before moving back to Wells County, where they live on the farm and in the house that Roberta's great-grandfather, Joseph Falk, built in 1899, for $100. The lumber came from woods on the farm and the carpenters were from Kansas. The carpenters lived with the family that summer.

WILLIAM G. AND CHERYL ANN (CONNER) THOMPSON FAMILY

Thomas Ware, a farmer and plasterer, came to Wells County from Bracken County, Kentucky, among a group of early settlers. He had two daughters and seven sons.

Guy Ware, a carpenter, was the son of Dora and Anna (Redding) Ware and the grandson of Thomas Ware. He married Nora Lucrillia Thompson and they became the parents of a daughter and a son, John Ware. Nora died when the son was only six weeks old. Nora's brother, George Ora Thompson and wife adopted the infant, naming him John Ware Thompson.

George Ora was the son of George Howard and Armitta Angeline (Fix) Thompson. George Ora married Nellie Edith Burman and in 1937, purchased from the Ware heirs, the family farm, located northwest of Liberty Center. The Thompson family raised Brown Swiss dairy cows.

John Ware Thompson married M. Maxine Markley on October 3, 1939. She is the oldest daughter of Ralph E. and Mary Alice (Garrett) Markley. Prior to her marriage, Maxine worked with her father in the family-owned Markley Brothers Grocery, which business Ralph was involved in for over fifty years. John Ware farmed and worked in the implement business for Ware Baker and later for John Flaningam. When the family was grown, Maxine went to work as a clerk for the Progress Store and J. C. Penney, retiring from the latter.

Four children were born to John Ware and Maxine Thompson: Jimmy Lee, of rural Liberty Center; William G. and Richard E., both of Bluffton; and Joyce Ann, who is married to Roger McAfee. They have one son, Troy Jacob, and reside in Rockcreek Township.

William G. and Cheryl Ann (Conner) Thompson were married February 5, 1966, in Bluffton. They have one son and two daughters. Jeffrey Keith and Sara Kay (Spann) Thompson reside in Bluffton and have one son, Jobe Daniel. Timothy Derek and Jami Kay (Thompson) Prough reside in Bluffton and have one son, Derek Michael. Jennifer Karol Thompson, the youngest, also lives in Bluffton.

Cheryl Ann (Conner) Thompson is the daughter of Kenneth D. and Patricia (Grove) Conner, residents of Bluffton. In 1944, her father began employment with the Bluffton Grocery Company, which later merged with the Bursley Company to form the present Food Marketing Corporation of Fort Wayne. Her mother was employed many years at the Wabash Avenue Greenhouses and as co-owner of the Posy Pot Flower Shop.

Maternal grandparents of Cheryl (Conner) Thompson were Russell and Ruth (Henkel) Grove. Her paternal grandparents were Benjamin Franklin and Veda (Masterson) Conner. Frank Conner was employed by James A. Crosbie on his farm and as an employee of his bridge construction gang. He was on the gang which constructed the present Bluffton bridge. Veda Conner was employed many years in the housekeeping department at the Wells County Hospital, now known as the Well Community.

LOWELL AND LESLEY TILLMAN

Lowell is the oldest son of Russell and Inez Tillman of Coleta, Illinois. He is a graduate of Huntington College and is employed at the Lincoln National Life Insurance Company in Fort Wayne, Indiana. He is active in Boy Scouting, Ossian Conservation Club, and Ossian Lions Club, and a consistent Red Cross blood donor (21 gallons).

Lesley is the daughter of Earl and Almeda Lyons of Rockcreek Township (Huntington County). She is a graduate of Huntington College, and is employed at Poly-Hi in Fort Wayne. She sings in the Wells County Chorus.

Lowell and Lesley were married April 1, 1961, at the Buckeye Christian Church (Huntington County). They moved to 1514 E. 950 N., Ossian, Indiana in 1962, where they presently reside. Both have been active in scouting, both boys and girls, and also enjoyed camping as a family. They are active members of the Zanesville United Brethren in Christ Church. Their time now is spent with their expanding family.

They have three children. Larry is married to Lynne Ann (Rigby) and resides in Niles, Ohio, where he works for the local utility company. They have two sons, Curtis and Steven.

Lance is a graduate of Huntington College, and is employed at Farm Bureau Life Insurance Company in Indianapolis. He is married to Julia Noble of Indianapolis.

Lorraine is a graduate of Huntington College, and is finishing her Bachelor's Degree at Ball State. She is married to Todd Musick from Scotland, Pennsylvania.

All three are Norwell graduates, as well as Lynne Ann, Larry (1981), Lance (1983), and Lorraine (1987).

They also enjoy making Karmel Korn over an open flame in a cast iron kettle, a skill they picked up in their early scouting days. They can be seen popping "Karmel Korn" at some of the local events such as Ossian Days, Zanesville's Homespun Days, Bluffton Street Fair, Warren's Salamonie Festival, Johnny Appleseed Festival, and Huntington's Forks of the Wabash Festival.

TINKEL

Albert and Myrtle Tinkel moved to Liberty Center when "Bert" bought the local hardware store. He later bought eighty acres on the south edge of Liberty Center and started farming. He had one of the few round barns in Wells County built on his land.

About 1919, he rented the farm to Mr. Johnson and started to work at the Bay Piano factory. They moved to Bluffton and bought a home on West Wiley Avenue and lived there until he returned to farming about 1927.

Albert and Sarah Myrtle Pope were married in Grant County where their families lived. Albert's father was a Dunkard minister. Myrtle was born in Clinton County, Ohio, but moved to Landess while young. They had four sons: Homer A., Vaughn B., Justin C., and Dale D. The oldest three sons lived in Bluffton for a period of time after they married.

Homer married Gradus Mosure and they had four sons and one daughter: Everett, Max, Eddie, Evaleene, and Raymond. They all made their homes in Fort Wayne after marriage. Eddie now owns Tinkel Inc., Restaurant Equipment and Supplies in Fort Wayne. Vaughn and Justin had no children.

Dale D. married Mary E. Brown, daughter of G.W. (Bert) Brown and Mamie Ruble Brown in 1935. At that time Dale was farming with his father at the south edge of Liberty Center. We moved in the house across the street from his home. We later bought that farm and have lived there since.

Because of poor health, the doctor ordered "Tink" to quit farming. We bought the drug store in Liberty Center and operated it until he regained his health. He worked in different positions, including manager of Farmer's Grain, Production Credit, and lastly Huntington Mutual Insurance where he was president and field man until he retired in 1975. He died three years later of a heart attack.

We have two children, Bert Thomas and Sarah Sue. Tom graduated from Liberty Center High School, Purdue, and Ball State. He is a psychologist and the Director of Special Education in Huntington and Whitley Counties. Tom married Sally Jo Holloway, daughter of Joe and Fern Starr Holloway. They have three children. Scott, who married Janet Ulshafer in October, 1989, graduated from Norwell High School and Ball State University. He now lives in Louisville, Kentucky and is associated with the Xerox Company. Julie and Amy both graduated from Norwell High School and are students at Ball State University.

Sarah Sue married C. Darrel Huffman, son of Clyde and Mary Thompson Huffman, and is living on a farm in Liberty Township where he has a gun and fur shop. She attended both Purdue and Ball State a short while, then worked in the Gallivan and Hamilton law firm. She now works in the office of Siles Inc. in Ossian. They have three sons: Doug, Brian, and Michael. Doug is employed in an office at Baer Field. Brian married Beverly Dawson Schafer, daughter of Max and Jackie Dawson. They have three children: Tyler, Brett, and Andrea. He is employed in Fort Wayne and lives in rural Liberty Center. Mike married Lynne Freck of Warren. They have a daughter, Kaitlyn. Both Mike and Lynne work in the office of Siles Inc. in Ossian and have a home in Liberty Center. Doug, Mike, and Brian have formed a country/western band named The Mountain Dew Boys.

TOMAN

Joseph and Mahala (Parker) Toman came to Wells County in March of 1913, and founded the Toman Grocery Store in Poneto, Indiana. This store was under their proprietorship from 1913 to 1945. They had a Huskster Wagon with a sign on the side of the truck "Toman Store at Your Door". It went out in the country to the homes in Chester, Liberty, Harrison, and Nottingham townships in Wells County and parts of Blackford and Jay County and delivered groceries, dry goods, and hardware to those unable to travel to town to get supplies. They bought eggs and poultry while on the route from the people, sometimes as payment for groceries and sometimes to sell the merchandise for them. They had free drawings for groceries and other things every other Saturday night. They also had free out door shows every Monday night May to August. The merchants of Poneto sponsored the shows. Families came from all over to see the show and they would bring their blankets and chairs to gather for a family fun night.

L to R. Clyde and Ethel Toman, Altha Sleepy, George Sleppy, Mahala Toman, Leon Sleppy, Joe Toman, George Sleppy, Everett Sleppy seated with child between legs.

Joseph Clarence Toman was born in Rose Hill, Ohio in 1874. The Toman family ancestors have been traced and originally came from Baden, German. Joseph was the son of Phillip Toman (born 1847) and Susan Newbauer (born 1847). He came to Indiana in the early nineteen hundreds. He married Mahala Florence Parker (born 1875-died 1950), daughter of James A. Parker (born 1842-died 1929) and Nancy Smith (born 1840-died 1918) from Harford City, Indiana. They had five children: Clyde Leroy (born 1898), Joseph Clarence, Jr. (born 1901), Altha Irene (born 1903), Florence (born 1907 stillborn) and Selvan Chalmer (born 1912). Clyde married Ethel Fetter on December 22, 1922 with no children. Jospeh Clarence, Jr. married Catherine A. Hage and had three children: Nancy Elaine, Joseph Clarence III and Thomas Eugene. Nancy lives in Gainsville, Florida and has a son and a daughter. Joseph Clarence III has two daughters and a son. Thomas has a son and daughter. Joe III and Tom both live in Hamilton, Ohio. Joseph Clarence, Jr.'s first wife died in November 1949 and in 1950 he married Dorothy Jacobs. Altha Irene Toman (my mother) married George Paul Sleppy on March 22, 1922. They had four children: Everett Paul (born 1923), Melvin Leon (born 1926), Marcelle (born 1927) and Joseph Samuel (born 1930). Selvan Chalmer Toman (born 1912) married Mary Katherine Hill on August 24, 1940 and had no children.

I am the daughter of Altha and George Sleppy and married to Robert Keith McFarren (born 1924), the son of Clarence Eugene McFarren and Mamie L. Yager. We have one daughter Connie Jo (born 1947). She married Donald Lee Mittlestedt, and they have five children: Robert Allen (born 1964), Matthew Lee (born 1967), Lesia Ann (born 1968), Michael Joe (born 1970) and Christina Marie (born 1984). Robert Allen Mittlestedt married Christa Meier. Matthew Lee married Connie Sue Jones, and they have a son, Steven Allen (born 1988).

TODD-BOYER

The Todd family dates back to after the Civil War. Our great-grandfather, Valentine Todd, came to Wells County after serving in the Army. He married Belenda Archbold in 1866. Both families came from Ohio. They lived northeast of Tocsin and farmed beside her parent's farm.

They had one living son, our grandfather, George W. Todd. He was a school teacher, farmer, and trustee of Jefferson Township when the Ossian school was built in 1925. He married Carrie Hendry of Jefferson Township in 1896. They had a son and daughter. Their daughter, Imo Todd Simerman, who is now 92 years old, was a school teacher at Tocsin and Ossian schools. She spent her life in Jefferson Township. Their son, Forrest, who is now 88 years old, was born on their farm at 4349 E 1000 North in Ossian and is still living on the same farm. He married Hazel Eichhorn in 1924. They had three children: Marilyn Grove of Bluffton, Richard, who lives west of Ossian, and Doyle. Doyle, the oldest,

Doyle and Betty in center. Left: David and Ronda with children Emily, Joshua, Andy, Jessica. Center: Mike and Karen with children Robin and Eric. Right: Ron and Cindy with children Kelli, Nicole and Kevin.

was born in 1926. He married Betty Boyer in 1949 and farmed and worked in a factory. They have lived all of their married life at 4134 E 1000 North in Ossian.

Doyle and Betty had three sons: David, owner of Todd's Garage in Ossian, Michael, a farmer and presently a member of the Northern Wells school board, and Ronald, a machinist at Melching Machine and also a farmer.

David married Ronda Ellenberger, and they have four children: Emily, Joshua, Andrew, and Jessica. Michael married Karen Kaehr, and they have two children: Robin and Eric. Ronald married Cynthia Freiburger, and they have three children: Kelli, Nicole and Kevin.

Five generations of Todd family have lived their whole lives in Jefferson Township and have been and presently are members of the Presbyterian Church in Ossian.

Betty has been active in the Wells County home demonstration clubs. Doyle is retired from Tuthill Pump Company, but is still farming and enjoying life among family, friends, and Wells County.

TONNER

In 1920 Sylven Andrew Tonner purchased a repair shop in Bluffton. He was the son of John and Mary Tonner, who were farmers in Adams County. (Mary was born in Switzerland) Sylven had one sister, Irene, who married Lee Wittwer.

On June 13, 1920, Sylven married Esther Speicher from Berne, Indiana, where she had a hat store. (Her mother was also born in Switzerland.)

Sylven expanded his business to include building truck bodies. (Details of the Tonner Body Works are in another section of this book.) He was also a volunteer fireman. At age 53, only June 3, 1950, Sylven was killed in a plane crash. Esther ran the business for seven years after his death, then sold out and rented the building to Mix-Mill. Esther died in 1978 at age 82. Both were members of the First United Church of Christ. They had three children: Martin, Mary and Paul.

Wedding picture of Sylvan Tonner and Esther Speicher Tonner

Martin, born on May 26, 1921, was a BHS star basketball player. He worked for his dad until World War II. On January 10, 1943, after becoming an army first lieutenant, he married Virginia Bevens from Colorado. He spent time on Saipan in the Pacific. After the war he worked at Tonner Body Works. In 1949 he was commanding officer of Bluffton's National Guard. Later he moved to Detroit and now lives in Louisville, working for Truck Equipment. Virginia died of cancer in 1984 at age 63. They had four children:

John, born October 31, 1950, graduated from Ball State. He works for Digital and lives in Detroit.

David is a career servicemen, a captain in the army and helicopter pilot, presently stationed in Korea. On December 28, 1978, he married an Ok Yon (Angie) whom he met in Korea. She's at home in Savannah with their two children, Bobby, born March 3, 1979, and Diana, born September 29, 1981.

Robert is a dress designer and doll maker living in New York City. Bob and Dave, are twins and were born on July 14, 1952.

Mary Ellen, born June 11, 1954, is a speech therapist and is married to Sheldon Cousino, a computer programmer in Columbus, Ohio. They have three children: Adam, born March 28, 1978; Amanda, born July 29, 1982; and Katie, born on February 3, 1986.

Mary Tonner married Jim Murray and is included with the Murray family history.

Paul Tonner was born on February 9, 1928. He attended Defiance College before joining the Air Force for four years. While stationed in England he met Elizabeth Brunning, whom he married on February 27, 1954. He worked at the Tonner Body Works, Central Dairy, and International Harvester. They have three children.

Michelle, born December 29, 1954, graduated from Tri-State in Angola, Indiana. she married Roger Wolfe, who is now a minister. They live in Glendale, Arizona, with their two daughters, Rachel, born on February 14, 1983, and Monica, born on January 14, 1988. They are hoping to become missionaries in Spain.

Jane, born February 21, 1958, married Rick Mick from Angola. He attended Indiana University. She is an export secretary and he is a salesman in Angola.

Debra, born on October 28, 1964, married Blake Steury. She formerly managed Bandidos Restaurant in Fort Wayne and now works for Barkalow Midwest. Blake has a degree in theatre and plans to pursue an acting career. Their daughter Kala was born on December 20, 1989.

ROBERT B. TURNER FAMILY

Robert B. Turner, born in Pennsylvania in 1799, came to Wells County in the late 1830's. He was the grandfather of my grandfather, Charles Franklin Turner, who once pointed out land just north of Bluffton (then known as the Kunkel farm) and said, "My grandfather once owned that farm." Early records verify that Robert bought one hundred sixty acres in Section 34 in 1849.

Simeon Turner

However, he had arrived in the county before that time. Land near Murray (the northwest quarter of Section 18) that he sold to Jonathan Warner in 1849 was probably his first purchase. In September of 1841 he bought the site from which he ran the first mill in Bluffton, described as "lying east of Main Street and north of Wabash Street and bounded on the north and east by the Wabash River." At first it was a saw mill, but later, burrs were added for grinding grain.

Robert was active in the community and was one of the organizers of the first Sunday School of the Methodist Episcopal Church. It was this group that later organized the church, according to a 1900 Yearbook of the church which I have.

At the time of the 1840 Census, Robert's household included three sons and two daughters. The older daughter, Elizabeth, was born in Pennsylvania; John and Joseph were born in Ohio in 1833 and 1837 respectively. The mother, Bergata, a native of Pennsylvania, died in 1843 and is buried in the old Bluffton Cemetery beside an infant daughter, Amelia. Two Turner children, Edwin, ten, and Martha, seven, died in 1850. Elizabeth married Jacob V. Gary (Geary) on February 4, 1847.

In 1844 Robert married Catherine McMullin, a native of Pennsylvania in Jay County, Indiana. Their children were Lewis Lindley, born March 27, 1847; Oran (ge) Lemuel; Missouri, born on December 7, 1852; and Simeon, born on December 7, 1852.

The census of 1860 indicates that Robert had moved his family from Bluffton to the farm north of town. Then in 1866 they moved to Warren, Huntington County, Indiana. Catherine died there in September 1876, Robert, two years later. Both are buried in the Masonic Cemetery there.

Huntington County records reveal the marriages of Lewis L. Turner to Malinda Crandall on October 3, 1869; Orange L. Turner to Sarah Hart, August 5, 1876 and to Mary C. LaFever, November 10, 1880; Missouri Turner to Henry J. Coles April 6, 1871; and Simeon Turner to Emily Jane Brown on April 26, 1877.

Charles Turner, (1877-1961), my grandfather was the oldest of nine children of Simeon and Emily Jane Brown Turner. The others were: Cordelia, Nellie, Robert, Alice, Edward, George, Daisy, and John. All of them married, and all except Daisy and Charles left Indiana — most of them going to Oklahoma to work in the oil fields.

On March 4, 1904, Charles married Leuie Arnold (1887-1977) in Huntington. For a while they lived in Jackson Township, Wells County, where Edith Mildred was born on January 24, 1905. Their only son, Earl Simeon, was born in Warren on February 15, 1907. Then in 1909 the family moved to Bluffton. A daughter, Mary Lucile, was born on February 27, 1913; Esther Elizabeth was born on November 29, 1915.

In Bluffton Charles worked as a barber, except for a brief time while he was employed at the Bay Piano Factory. He worked many years as an employee and later as a partner of Frank Wisner in a basement shop at the southeast corner of Market and Johnson Streets. Later he retired from his own shop on Jersey Street near Wiley Avenue.

My father, Earl, who married Artha Kline on April 22, 1927, followed his father into the barber trade, I, too, learned and worked at this trade for a number of years.

As far as we know, the only descendants of Robert B. Turner now living in Bluffton are my aunt, Edith Roselius; her daughter, Doris Lutz; my daughter, Kathy; and me, Jon Turner—all of us natives of Wells County. *(Jon E. Turner)*

ULMER-MCKINNEY

John Ulmer, Sr., born 1805, and Elizabeth Geisinger, born June 1813, were married in Germany. In about 1835, they left Germany to go to the United States where they settled in Pike and later Fayette Counties, Ohio. Around 1850, the family migrated to Wells County where John and Elizabeth spent their remaining years. They were both buried in Six Mile Cemetery in Wells County. Children were: Phoebe (1832-1835); Jacob "Joe" (1838-1907); Andrew (1840-1907); John Jr. (1842-1917) Married Sarah Jane Hughes; Peter (1844-); Frank Phillip (1847); George (1853); and Nicholas (1855).

John Ulmer, Jr. born November 2, 1842, married November 19, 1865 Wells County, Indiana to Sarah Jane Hughes, daughter of Robert S. and Sarah Lanning Hughes. Children were: Robert S. (1872); William "Bill" (1873-1895); John Harrison "Harry" (1886-1952) married Frances Hughes; and Sadie.

Fred and Helen (Ulmer) McKinney

John Harrison "Harry" Ulmer married Frances Hughes, daughter of Thomas Paschal and Lucinda Fox Hughes. Their children were: Helen Naoma, born 1913, married Paul E. Nickelson and later Frederick Eugene McKinney; Anna Bell, born 1914; Esther L., born 1916, married Jack Mossburg; Mary Alice, born 1918, married Forrest "Bud" Fry; Wanda, born 1920, married Robert Davis and then Ken Speece; John, born 1925, married Mary Mitchell; and Frances Joan, born 1930, married Gerald Ramseyer.

Helen Naoma Ulmer married her second husband Frederick Eugene McKinney, son of Hamer and Bessie Cotton McKinney of Bluffton, Indiana. Children of their marriages include: Kathleen Marceile, born 1926, married Roy Stuff (1927-1952) and then John Blackman, Jr. Kathleen had nine children, retired from K-Mart and now lives in Washington. Phyllis Carol "Carol", born 1929, married Grady Grounds, Jr., they have five children and live in Texas. Thomas William "Bill", born 1935, married Betty Marie Hughes. They live in Fort Wayne, and have children Douglas, Daniel, and Dawn. Kenneth Eugene, born 1938, married Maybelle Correct, and then Caroline McIntosh. He lives in Georgia, has son, Robert and daughter, Kimberly. Roger Wayne, born 1940, married Patricia Frankenburg. Their children are Michael and Debra, all living in Fort Wayne. Donna Elaine, born 1945, married Ralph Braun. They live in Leesburg, Indiana, and have two children, Bruce and Hope.

Lucinda Fox was married in 1881, Wells County, Indiana, to Thomas Paschal Hughes. Their children were Clara, Jesse, Merl, John, Frances Lillie, Mary Ella, Indiana, and Paul. Lucinda was the daughter of John Henry and Polly Wilson Fox. In 1874 Polly died and John Henry Fox and children moved to Wells County, Indiana, northeast of town. In 1875, John married Caroline Knerehm.

Thomas Paschal Hughes was the fourth child of Thomas and Elizabeth Frances Dowell, daughter of William and Lucinda Dowell. Thomas was born January 30, 1823 in New Jersey and died August 28, 1886; Elizabeth was born June 1, 1821, Orange County, Virginia and died June 12, 1897, in Markle, Indiana. Children were infant son, died young; Henrietta (1851-1864); Samuel Wellington (1853-1928), Thomas and Indiana Lucinda (1862-1864).

VALENTINE-SMITH-ELY

We have traced our family back to 1715 from Mutterstadt, Germany. Johan George Valentine sailed from Holland via Plymouth, England, to Pennsylvania. He was a casket maker in Germany. He was granted fifty acres called Swiving Swamp in 1752. In 1758 he bought an additional one hundred acres. He became a naturalized citizen in 1758 and was buried on his homestead.

Johan's great-great-great grandson, Joseph Valentine, moved from Ohio to Bluffton, Indiana, in July, 1817. Joseph's grandson was in the Civil War from 1863 to 1865.

Barbara Valentine Shoemaker's son lived near Reiffsburg. He attended normal school at Bluffton in 1890 and graduated from DePauw University. He was a Methodist minister of sixteen pastorates and built four churches.

Elvin Laverne Valentine was born in 1895 and lived near Geneva. He enlisted in the army and was sent to France in 1918. He graduated from DePauw University in 1922 with a BA in History. He was a teacher and a principal at Kirkland High School.

Clona Valentine
Keith Smith
Married May 25, 1917

Ruth Valentine Shoemaker was born in 1890. She graduated from DePauw University and taught in Kokomo and Muncie schools.

Our great-grandfather John Valentine farmed near Poe, Indiana. He died in 1945 at the home of his daughter, Clona Valentine Smith, south of Murray.

John was married to Anna Snarr and had four children, Merle, Rheua, Clona, and Snarr. Rheua lived on a farm near Poe, Indiana, and married Chloe Snyder. They had three daughters: Evelyn Valentine Hilsmier, who lived near Poe; Pauline Valentine Miller, who lived near Ossian; and Joan Valentine Nau of New Haven. Rheua currently resides at the Ossian Health Center. He is ninety-seven years old. Merle of Ohio and Snarr of Fort Wayne are both deceased.

Clona continued to live on the farm at Murray. She was married to Keith Roscoe Smith. He graduated form Ossian High School with the first graduating class. He had two sisters, Garnet Smith Wait of Warren and Nellie Smith Showalter of Poneto, both school teachers; and one brother, Clem, a farmer south of Bluffton. Keith died in 1946. They had two children; Eugene Valentine Smith and Alice Eleanor Smith Ely. Clona was a member of the Murray Missionary Church, and attended South Side Farmers Market in Fort Wayne with flowers, vegetables, and poultry for fifty-seven years. Clona died in 1983 at the age of eighty-seven.

Eugene was married to Maxine Louise Byerly in 1945. They have two daughters, Penny Smith Barstow of Fairfax, Virginia, a graduate of Lewis University at Romeoville, Illinois, who is a registered nurse; and Rebecca Smith Schinderle of Denton, Texas. Becky graduated from the University of Illinois and is a teacher. Eugene graduated from Purdue University and was a Lieutenant in the U.S. Air Force and a pilot instructor in 1943. He was a chemical engineer for Amoco Chemicals in Wyoming and Texas for twenty-eight years. They have two grandchildren. They are retired, and he and his wife live in Ocala, Florida.

Alice Smith Ely has continued to live on the family farm near Murray since 1937. She graduated from International Business College in 1971 and is employed as a secretary at the Scottish Rite Temple in Fort Wayne. She is a member of the Murray Missionary Church. She has one daughter, Linda Jane Ely, who graduated from DePauw University with a masters degree in English and teaches English in Libertyville High School in Illinois. Linda plans to be married to Daniel Mark Falotico in June, 1991, in Deerfield, Illinois. She still comes home to Murray each summer and helps her mother with the family project, preparing produce for the South Side Market, which she enjoys, having sold flowers since the age of three.

VANCAMP-DICKASON

My great-grandfather John T. Vancamp (1851-1924) farmed in Liberty Township, Wells County. His parents were Abraham and Lucy Betts Vancamp, both born in Ohio. John married in 1871 (Wells County) Sarah J. Scott (1853-1934). Children: Jennie, Joseph, and twins James Charley and Eva (1880-1961). Eva's children: Donald, Russell and Catheline.

Russell (1902-1946) married Geneva Roberts (died 1984). Children: Janice, married Robert Osmundson (Children: Steven, Kathe); Gloria, married Milton Asbell; Max, married Carol Borcherding (Children: Lisa, Barry); Phyllis, married Franeback (Children: Teresa, Kimberly, Curtis).

Donald Wayne Vancamp and Bonnie Lucile Dickason about 1920

Catheline, married Zehner/Gearhart/ Borcherding son: Edwin Zehner.

Donald Wayne Vancamp (1899-1939) married (1920) Bonnie Lucile Dickason (1901-1975), children: (1) Mary Pauline, June 23, 1924, married Earl Towns, divorced, children: Ralph Edward, 1943, married Phyllis Parker, children: Timothy, 1966, married Lindsay Aker; Scott Howard, 1971; Jeffrey Dee, 1972, and Paul Eugene "Butch," (1945-1958); (2) Roger, 1925 married Wilma Thomas, children: Donald Wayne, 1949, married Mary Lou Rickord, children: Jeffrey, Amy); Marsha Kay, 1950, first married George Heilman, then Steven Ratliff, children: Jessica Heilman, Jacob Heilman; Ronald Alan, 1957, married Deborah Heffelfinger; (3) Marlin, 1929, married Norma Boxell, children: Tony, 1951-1957; Charles, 1953; Cathy, 1956; Gregory, 1959-1959; (4) Martha, 1931 married Donald Lenwell, divorced, children: Valerie; James; Gary; Franklin; (5) James 1933 and (6) Glen Franklin, 1936.

Bonnie Dickason's parents were John F. (1860-1942) and Lydia Schneider Dickason (1865-1939), who lived in Nottingham Township. Children: Susanna, 1875; Hazel, 1897; Mabel, 1898; Bonnie, 1901-1975; Jasper, 1904-1990; and Oscar, 1907-1989.

Bonnie's maternal grandparents Charles Schneider (1837-1906) and Barbara Walters (1841-1904) were born in Switzerland. Barbara's mother was Rosa Walters.

Bonnies' paternal grandparents, Jacob (1835-1920) and Barbara Susanne Ifer Dickason (1841-1916) were the parents of William; John F.; George S.; Walter; Naman; Jacob; Francis Marion "Doc"; Warren; Samuel; Syrus; Ora; and Rosa. Barbara Susanne Ifer's parents were George Ifer, born Pennsylvania, died 1891, and Elizabeth Slutman, born Ohio, died 1891.

The paternal great-grandparents of Bonnie Dickason, John W. (1806-1891) and Nancy Stanley Dickason (1806-1881), are buried in Stahl Cemetery.

I was born August 31, 1936 to Donald and Bonnie Dickason Vancamp and married June 1, 1958 Judith Ilene Pugh 19 January 19, 1940. We lived in Chester Township, Wells County, until late 1960, when we built our home near Montpelier. My occupation is a tool and diemaker, and I served over twenty years in the Indiana National Guard with the units in Hartford City, Bluffton, and Headquarters in Marion. My wife is a legal secretary. Our daughter Lois Lorraine (December 15, 1964) married Ronald Berman and their son Jesse Lee Bergman was born June 17, 1986. Our son Bradley Allen Vancamp was born June 23, 1973 and attends Blackford High School.

VANEMON

A pioneer family settling one mile south of Bluffton, with land on both sides of Road 1, were my great-grandparents, James and Matilda (Walker) Vanemon. They arrived in Wells county from Trumbull County, Ohio in 1847 with eight children.

Martha, then fourteen, later married John Williams and had three children. Amanda was eleven. Mary Ann, ten, later married Sam Riddle and had three children. Lawrence, seven, later married Susan Conrad and had four children. Rhoda, six, later married Ed Markley and had one child. Elizabeth was four. Absalom, one, later married Martha Evans and had three children. They lived in a brick house, south of Bluffton. The VanEmon School was located on their property, on the northwest corner of State Road 1 and 200 South.

Andrew was born in Wells County, January 16, 1848; married Emmarillis Hale; had five children; and lived a half-mile east of the VanEmon School.

Sophia Vanemon Deam, Cora Vanemon Joray, Twila Pope Dubbeld, Allen Pope

Hiram, my grandfather, who was thirteen when they arrived in America, married Amanda Lowrey in Bluffton, November 30, 1869. Twins were born November 3, 1870. One twin, Nora, lived eight months; and along with her brother, James, who died as a child; and grandparents are buried in the old Bluffton Cemetery on the banks of the Wabash. Twin, Cora, my mother, married Robert Joray of Vera Cruz in 1895. A daughter, Sophia (Ed) Deam, born April 7, 1875, loved flowers and lived her entire life on the family farm, a mile east of VanEmon School, which Cora and Sophia attended.

The land had been divided by James VanEmon to each son, eighty acres a "high forty" and a "low forty". After the marriage of Hiram and Amanda, they built their home on the "high forty" and it still stands today.

Hiram was a Corporal of Captain William Wilmington's Company A, the 34th Regiment of Indiana, in the Civil War. He was given a disability discharge on February 26, 1863. He was very proud of the American flag.

I, Olive Joray Sweeny, remember riding in a horse drawn carriage and singing all the way to Six Mile Christian Church, of which we were faithful members.

My parents, Robert (Cora VanEmon) Joray, purchased a farm in Nottingham Township, where two daughters were born. Edna lived only five months and was buried in Six Mile Cemetery. Later, grandparents and parents were buried beside her. I, Olive Gladness, born August 18, 1900, in a log cabin, later married Robert Sweeny, a Wells County farmer, and still live in Bluffton. Both our children, Paul and Evelyn, all seven grandchildren, and two great-grandchildren were born in Wells County.

Piano lessons were taken by three generations on the same piano. Olive Sweeny, Evelyn Pope, and Twila Dubbeld have been pianists in different local churches. Church music was our enjoyment and entertainment.

I, Olive Joray Sweeny, am the fourth generation, my daughter; Evelyn Sweeny Pope, the fifth; her daughter Twila Pope Dubbeld, the sixth; and her children, Janella Joy and Dion Gene Dubbeld, are the seventh generations to live in Wells County.

VAUGHN-CARNES

Jerry Lee Vaughn married Carolyn Sue Carnes on December 13, 1953, in Bryant by the Reverend Dewey Zent. Jerry is the son of Alvin Harrison Vaughn, born July 13, 1888 and Anna Mae Vancamp, born October 17, 1903. He was born at home, 503 East Central Avenue, delivered by Doctor Morris on July 5, 1933. Sue is the daughter of Everett Wayne Carnes, born 1885, and Mabel Chloe Walker, born November 17, 1898. She was born at home in rural Keystone.

Jerry is the youngest of four children, Betty, born 1924, Donna Mae, born 1927, Barbara Kay, born 1930, and Jerry, born 1933. He graduated from Bluffton High School in 1951. He joined the service in 1953 and was stationed at Fort Broughton, Pennsylvania.

Sue is the youngest of six children: Yvonne, born 1918; Monnah, born 1919; Berthetta; born 1921; Mary Magdaline, born 1923; Jack Walker, born 1926; and Sue, born 1935. She graduated from Chester Center High School in 1953.

When they were first married they lived in Pittsburgh, Pennsylvanin, because Jerry was in the service there. They lived there for two years. While they were living in Pittsburgh, their first child was born. Theresa Joan (Terry Jo) was born on January 2, 1955. She graduated from Bluffton High School in 1973. She was married to V. Ked Biberstine on February 28, 1976, at the First Church of Christ in Bluffton. Ked is the son of V. Ted and Phyllis Biberstine of Bluffton. He graduated from Norwell High School in 1968 and from Sams Institute in 1970. They live in Rockcreek Township. They have two children, Ashley Vaughn, born August 18, 1980 and Zachary Ked, born November 20, 1982. Both of their children were born in Bluffton.

Jerry and Sue had their second daughter on March 1, 1959, in Bluffton. Sandra Lee graduated from Bluffton High School in 1977 and also from Indiana State University. She was married to Kurt Rudoph Reiners on January 28, 1984. He is the son of Rudy and Jean Byers Reiners of Elkhart. He graduated from Elkhart Memorial High School and Indiana State University. They have one son, Andrew Christopher. He was born on May 30, 1988, in Elkhart.

Jerry and Sue's third child was a son. Scott Alan was born on December 6, 1960 in Bluffton. He graduated from Bluffton High School and Ball State University.

EDWIN CLARK VAUGHN

The scene was the First Baptist Church in Bluffton, Indiana. The time was the evening of May 18, 1925. The strains of the wedding march rang out, played by Betty Robinson, violin, and Edwina Patton, cello, granddaughters of the two couples who were being honored. Mrs. Lona Reynolds accompanied them on the piano. Stella Vaughn Patton and Nell Robinson Snyder preceded the honored couples down the aisle.

The event was the double celebration of the golden wedding anniversary of Judge Edwin Clark Vaughn and Sarah Elizabeth Trostel Vaughn, whose history this is, and Dr. Peter L. Robinson and Willamette Merriman Robinson. The two couples were married the same year and came to Bluffton at about the same time. They remained good friends as long as they lived.

Edwin Clark Vaughn was born in Medina County, Ohio, on February 14, 1853, to the Reverend Henry Warner Vaughn and Adelia Clark Vaughn. A family tradition says that she attended Oberlin College, in Ohio, but this has not been documented. Four children were born to the Vaughns: Helen Adelia, who married Norman Lynch and had one daughter, Hattie, and two sons, George Henry, born in 1870, and Ray, born in 1888; Russell Whitman, who married Lidah Rice and had no children; Edwin Clark, who married Sarah Elizabeth Trostel and had one daughter, Stella Adelia; and William (Willie), who never married, for he died when he was a young man.

Edwin grew up in Ridgeville, Indiana, where his father was the Baptist minister. he attended Ridgeville College and then taught school at Fairview, near Ridgeville.

On October 28, 1875, he married Sarah Elizabeth Trostel, the oldest daughter of Emmanuel Trostel and Rachel Mock Trostel.

They came to Bluffton and moved into a house on the southwest corner of Williams and Miller Streets. He traded his pocket watch for a kitchen table, two kitchen chairs, and a clock. Sarah brought with her several peony bushes, the gift of her grandmother, Ruth Mock (Mrs. Emsley Mock). She took those peonies with her every time they moved; and in the spring of 1991 they bloomed as usual.

At first, Edwin taught school. He became principal and then superintendent, before he turned to studying law in Levi Mock's office. In 1880 he opened his own office in the Curry block, with a library composed of four law books, all gifts. The first year of his practice, he collected forty-eight dollars in fees.

In 1881 he was elected mayor and served one four-year term in that office.

On July 30, 1876, their only child was born - Stella Adelia Vaughn.

In 1893 he was appointed judge of the Wells-Blackford circuit court, to finish the unexpired term of Judge J. S. Dailey, who had been appointed to the Indiana Supreme Court. He was re-elected to the bench twice, serving thirteen years and four months in all. His election to one of these terms was close; and he went to bed thinking he had been defeated. Before midnight, he was awakened by shouts of "Hooray for Vaughn!" He hurried out on the front porch to receive the cheers of the crowd.

Edwin Vaughn and John Decker became partners and established their own law firm, Vaughn and Decker. Their office was on the floor above the Walmer and Engeler store (now J. C. Penney store); and in November, 1918, when the wild celebration of the false armistice of World War I broke out, he took his family up there to listen to the bells ringing and look down at the people waving flags and shouting for joy in the street below.

He practiced law in Bluffton the rest of his life. He was city attorney during the last years of his life. At the time of his death on July 9, 1935, he was president of the Wells County Bar Association and was known as dean of that group. Abram Simmons succeeded him as both president and dean.

What he might have considered his most notable achievement came at the end of his life, when he was over eighty. One of his cases began in circuit court, was appealed, went to appellate court, was appealed, and wound up in the Supreme Court of Indiana. He argued the case before the Supreme Court, and after long deliberation, the Court decided in favor of his client. Ironically, the news of his victory came out in headlines the day after he died.

VAUGHN-PATTON

Stella Adelia Vaughn was born in Bluffton, Indiana, on July 30, 1876, the only child of Edwin Clark Vaughn and Sarah Trostel Vaughn.

She grew up in Bluffton in a house they built on West Central Avenue. After graduating in 1894 from Bluffton High School (at that time a brick building on West Washington Street), she went to college, first at State Normal School at Terre Haute and then Indiana University. She graduated from Indiana University, where she was a member of Kappa Kappa Gamma Sorority, in 1901; but even more important than her graduation was her meeting William Alexander Patton there. He was from Hebron, Indiana. They ate at the same boarding house, fell in love, and were married on May 7, 1903.

Before their marriage he worked for American Telephone and Telegraph Company in New York City. Neither of them wanted to bring up a family in the city; so when he was offered a job with the United Telephone Company in Marion, Indiana, he left New York and they began their married life in Marion. Their older daughter, Elizabeth Vaughn, was born there on February 9, 1905, on a twenty below zero day. Will worked so hard stoking the fire in the stove to keep it warm enough for the baby and the new mother that Stella was afraid he would burn the house down!

Will left the United Telephone Company in Marion to become manager of the United Telephone Company in Bluffton, and in 1910, just after the Kingsland interurban wreck, they moved to Bluffton. Elizabeth has always remembered being taken by her parents to one house after another where a family was grieving for the dead.

In 1913, Will became manager of the Marion and Bluffton Traction Company, and then in 1916, office manager of the W. B. Brown Company. In 1923 he and Morris McCray formed the Patton-McCray Company, which made bedroom furniture. He continued in this organization until 1942.

A few years after they moved to Bluffton, Stella, who had been a teacher in the Bluffton schools before her marriage, was appointed to the school board, on which she served for over ten years. She was the first woman in Bluffton to hold this position. Of course, being a woman, she was chosen as secretary of the board, and in those days the secretary had to take the school enumeration every year. This meant that she had to knock on every door in Bluffton and ask how many children of school age lived there. This was an important task, for the amount of state money coming to the school depended on the number of students enrolled.

She was also active in the League of Women Voters, and worked enthusiastically for the cause of woman suffrage. She was delighted when Indiana women got the vote; and she cast her first ballot for Cox in 1920.

On July 7, 1913, another daughter was born to Will and Stella Patton. She was named Edwina Josephine, for her two grandfathers; later, when she went to Indiana University, she added Vaughn to those names.

Both Elizabeth and Edwina became teachers. Elizabeth taught home economics in Bluffton for three years and then went to Fort Wayne to teach until she retired in 1967. Edwina taught English for one year in Fort Wayne, nine years at Union Center in Wells County, sixteen years full time, and three years part time at Huntington College, retiring with the title of Associate Professor Emeritus.

Will was a charter member of the Rotary Club in Bluffton. He served as its first president, and twenty-five years later was elected president again.

Both Will and Stella Patton suffered serious illness in their last years. Stella died on February 18, 1952, and Will died the next year, on April 22, 1953. Both are buried in Fairview Cemetery.

SARAH TROSTEL VAUGHN

Sarah Elizabeth Trostel was born October 4, 1856, the daughter of Emmanuel Trostel and Rachel Mock Trostel. Emmanuel's family owned land at Gettysburg, Pennsylvania; and the Trostel farm there was stained with the blood of soldiers. Emmanuel had come west to Indiana well before the Civil War, however. His wife, Rachel, was the daughter of Emsley Mock and Ruth Watson Mock.

Emmanuel had a farm in Randolph County, near Deerfield, Indiana; and it was said that when he plowed the land, his whistling could be heard for miles around. The musical talent he undoubtedly had has been passed down to many of his descendants.

(L-R) Judge Edwin C. Vaughn, Stella Vaughn, Sarah Vaughn

They raised tobacco on the farm, and when Sarah was a little girl she was given the task of picking tobacco worms off the leaves. Her father saw no reason why she shouldn't gather up the worms with her fingers (as he probably did occasionally); but her mother stepped in. "That child is not going to pick up those worms with her bare hands," she said; and thereafter the worms met their death at the end of a stick.

During the Civil War, Emmanuel moved his family to Canada, near Sarnia, and stayed until the war was over. Neither he nor the Mocks had much use for Abe Lincoln; their sympathies were with the South.

Sarah's brother Austin Orlando, born June 18, 1858, lived for a time in Wells County and then left his wife and daughter and moved to Missouri. After he and his wife were divorced, he remarried and reared a second family in Missouri. He returned only once, in 1923, to visit his brother and sister.

Her brother John Henry, born September 15, 1863, remained close to her all their lives. In Bluffton, when the Vaughns lived on Central Avenue, John and his family lived just south across the alley, on Wiley Avenue; and when the Vaughns built their home in Villa North, the Trostels lived next door. Their closeness was natural, for when Rachel Trostel died in 1884, John came to live with his sister's family. He always seemed like an older brother to Stella.

Another addition to Sarah's family occurred when Emsley Mock died in 1881, and his widow, Ruth Watson Mock (known to the family as Mammy) came to live with her granddaughter.

April 21, 1889, John Trostel and Isbelle Hartman were married. Three children were born to them: Edna Devona, born April 20, 1891, Gus Edwin, born June 12, 1892, and Lois Irene, born July 9, 1900. Gus died in 1951. Devona lived to be a hundred, and died on April 25, 1991, just five days after her hundredth birthday. Lois is still living, in June, 1991.

587

John had a fine voice, and he was famous in Wells County for his singing of campaign songs. Emmanuel's musical talent reappeared most noticeably in John and his family, for his daughter Lois had the gift of a beautiful voice. Her daughter Barbara and her granddaughters Robin and Beth share this gift of song.

Sarah Trostel Vaughn died on September 16, 1938, and is buried beside her husband in the mausoleum in Fairview Cemetery.

VAUGHN-VANCAMP

Alvin Harrison Vaughn, born July 13, 1888, married Anna Mae VanCamp, born October 17, 1903. Alvin is the son of Turner and Anna Ward Vaughn. Turner is the son of John Vaughn and his mother is named Mary. Alvin had four sisters. Minnie was married to Walter Meriky; Myrtle was married to Fred Keifer; Stella was married to Robert Watkins and Don Chaiphin; Anniebell was married to Joseph Call.

Anna is the daughter of William Worley VanCamp, born September 20, 1877, and Emma Jones, born in 1881. William was the son of Rolly VanCamp, born 1835, and Elizabeth Lesure, born 1836, who was the daughter of Ben and Lizzie Lesure. Emma was the daughter of Martha Reed and Arizona Jim Jones. Martha was also married to John Harris II. William Worley was married a second time to Flossie Evers.

William and Emma had four children: Anna Mae was married to Alvin Vaughn; Nellie Marie, born 1905, was married to Jasper Dickason; William Henry (died in childhood); and James Alexander, born 1910, married Ruth Turner. William's marriage to Flossie Evers produced two children, Evelyn, born 1930, who married Norm McFarren, and Edward, born 1925, was married to Mary Ann Elick. Emma, who is Anna's mother, was married a second time to Herb Manules but they had no children.

Alvin and Anna have four children. Betty, born 1924, was married to Doc Grover and then to Ora Baker, Jr. Donna Mae, born 1927, was married to Bill Baumgardner. They have two children, Steven and Jill. She also was married to Bill Turner and they had no children. Barbara Kay, born 1930, was married to George Nestle and they have six children: Fred, Kay, Gary, Christine, Karen and Kim, and they have ten grandchildren. They are no longer married. Jerry Lee, born 1933, is married to Carolyn Sue Carnes, born 1935, and they have three children: Terry Biberstine (Ked), Sandy Reiners (Kurt), and Scott, and three grandchildren, Ashley Vaughn Biberstine, Zachary Ked Biberstine, and Andrew Christopher Reiners.

VENIS-NEUHAUSER

Harold Venis (1914) married Lucille Neuhauser (1916) on December 24, 1937. He was the son of Roy Venis and Alta Steele; she the daughter of Amos Neuhauser and Marianne Rupp. Both graduated from Bluffton High School during the Great Depression of 1933.

Harold's first job was at A.E. Boyce Company in Muncie, Indiana. It was of short duration. Room rent was $2.00 per week, breakfast 25 cents, lunch and dinner each 35 cents. As he was only making $9.00 per week, he was left with five cents per week. He hitchhiked home on weekends in an attempt to keep even. Banks were closing, so he skipped school one morning to get his meager savings out.

Harold had worked several places in Bluffton and was employed by Franklin Loan when he and Lucille were married at Richmond, Indiana by the Reverend P. B. Smith, a former Methodist minister in Bluffton. She was teaching at Beech Grove, Indiana; hence a secret wedding known by immediate families only. Had the school known, she could have lost her job ($1,035.00 per year). No married women could teach unless the husband was disabled because of the depression.

Harold moonlighted for M.G.M. checking attendances at theaters. Pictures such as "Boys Town" were priced according to ticket sales. During this time their daughter, Karen, was born. He got home just in time to take his wife to the hospital. Karen was born January 1, 1939 - first birth of the year. Their second daughter, Barbara (1947), was born in Bluffton.

Lucille substituted in Bluffton and county high schools and finished some years for male teachers called into the service. She taught at Lancaster (1943-45) and also took Mr. Broman's place full time the first semester and mornings the second semester.

Harold and Lucille moved to Fort Wayne in 1957. Harold continued in sales until the three companies (Hoosier, Central Dairy and Pioneer Ice Cream) were sold. Both were active in starting the Aldersgate Methodist Church at Time Corners, Fort Wayne.

Lucy started her teaching in Fort Wayne Schools (1958-1972) with the exception of one year (1966-1967) when she got her master's degree in guidance and counseling at St. Francis.

Harold's next job was counselor and part owner of International Business College. He continued with them for two years after it was sold (1965). In 1968 he became a partner in Safety Equipment until it was sold in 1976. He often laughed about the number of times he was temporarily unemployed because of the business being sold.

Harold and Lucille moved back to Bluffton in 1974. Harold concentrated on investments. Lucille opened the Cotton Patch in November, 1973. This was the first quilt shop in Indiana. She sold this on December 31, 1983. It was recently closed by the second owner.

Now we have more time to spend with our daughters, grandchildren, and great grandchildren.

Our first daughter, Karen Venis Irvin Gibson, graduate of Bluffton High School, lives in St. Cloud, Florida. Karen attended Purdue and Fort Wayne Art School. Since moving to Florida she has worked for airlines Eastern, Florida Express, Piedmont and U.S. Air. Changes were the result of mergers, etc. She married Harley Gibson in Las Vegas on February 23, 1989. Her children are Tami, Michelle, and Scott.

Tami Irvin Klopfenstein (1958) is a graduate of Bluffton High School and Purdue University. She is currently employed by U.S. Air. She married David Klopfenstein of Angola in 1989. He was assistant manager of Scott's Grocery when it opened in Bluffton. Drake Klopfenstein is the son of Dave by a previous marriage.

Michelle Irvin Burkhart (1961) is a graduate of Bluffton High School, attended Indiana University, and then graduated from barber's school in Indianapolis. She worked at PJ's Beauty Shop, Fort Wayne. Dave was manager of Scott's Grocery when it opened in Bluffton and is now the manager of Scott's at Village of Coventry. They were married 1985 in Bluffton. Their children are Jullian (1987) and Ashley (1988).

Scott Irvin (1965) is a graduate of Bluffton High School. He attended college in Florida and is now in Phoenix, Arizona, completing his work for a degree.

Barbara Venis Parrish, our second daughter, lives in Fort Wayne, Indiana. She attended Bluffton Elementary School for three years. She and her husband, Donald Parrish, Jr., half owner of Parrish Truck Leasing of Fort Wayne, attended Indiana University. They were married in 1967. They have five children.

Don Parrish III (1968) is a graduate of Wheaton College. He married Kristen Carlson in November, 1990. He is currently working at the Chicago Mercantile Exchange. Holly Parrish (1972) was born in Bluffton and will graduate from Homestead High School in 1991. She will enter college this fall. Brandon (Chip) (1974) was born in Bluffton. Jacob was born in 1980 and Brooke was born in 1986.

VENIS-REDDING

Robert Venis (1910-1984) married Ruth Redding (1910) on Christmas Day in 1929 at Bluffton, Indiana. Robert was the son of Roy Venis and Alta Steele. Ruth was the daughter of Willis Brown Redding and Dora Henderson. They had two daughters, Donna Venis Collom (1935) and Carol Venis Booth (1939). Both were born in Muncie, Indiana, and all four plus Carol's husband were graduates of Bluffton High School.

Robert worked as a teller in a Muncie bank and the furniture department of Sears in Lexington, Kentucky. He and Ruth returned to Bluffton in the 1940's. He had the Western Union franchise and combined it with the Office Supply Store at 115 South Johnson. During this time he was active in the Street Fair committee and was Mayor of Bluffton (1956-1960). After closing the Office Supply Store he worked with Fred Booth, son-in-law, as a realtor. Robert worked at the Clinic Hospital as head orderly until they moved to California in 1976.

Ruth was secretary to Superintendent Craig from 1928 to 1929. She also worked at the receiving desk at the Clinic Hospital (1957-1976) and is now living with her daughter, Donna, at Alta Loma, California.

Donna (1935) attended Ball State College and later completed work for her teaching license in California. She married Jim Collom (1930-1983) in Bluffton. Jim was in the Air Force as hospital administrator at various locations including Alaska. After retiring from the Air Force he was hospital administrator in a California hospital. They had two sons, David and Jeff.

David attended Chaffey College in Alta Loma. He married a California girl and they have one child. Jeff's wife is also a California girl. He went to Cal Poly University and is currently a civilian aerospace engineer for the Navy. They have two children, Lori Lynn (1980), adopted, and Sara (1990).

Carol (1939) went to Ravencroft Beauty College. She took additional work in specialties and was a beauty operator until they moved to Upland, California (1975). She is now active in a personal ministry for the poor and needy. Her husband, Fred, is the son of Frank Booth and Rosemond Rix Croy. Both parents were graduates of Bluffton High School. Since moving to California, he is an independent home building contractor. They have two sons, Mark and Bill. Both went to Bluffton schools in the elementary grades. They have both married California girls.

Mark (1961) is an independent minister and works for Hertz Car Rental in Upland, California. They have two children, Timothy and David.

Bill attended Chaffey College and is now practice-teaching. He was married in 1990.

VENIS-STEELE

Leland Leroy (Roy) Venis (1880-1946) married Alta Steele (1881-1951) in 1899. Roy was the son of George Venis and Ellen Stonebrook and was born in Bluffton. Alta, daughter of Robert N. Steele and Minnie Stevens, was born near Peterson in Adams County.

Their four children, all born in Bluffton, were: Irene Venis Gay, Mary Venis Houtz, Robert Venis (Ruth Redding), and Harold Venis (Lucille Neuhauser). All four were graduates of Bluffton High School.

Roy was a partner with his father, George, in a shoe store and repair shop on North Johnson Street. While there George fell from a small ladder while trying to get a box from the top shelf for a customer. He died a few hours later at his residence, 517 West Wabash Street, Bluffton, Indiana. (1912).

About the time of World War I, Roy purchased the building at 115 South Johnson for his shoe and repair shop. (This building is still owned by a family member).

After Roy experienced several heart attacks, the front room was rented and the shoe shop business was sold to Charles Smith. He used the room facing Walnut Street until his death. The present owner moved back to North Johnson as a shop repair shop.

Both Roy and Alta were members of the First Reformed Church - now known as the United Church of Christ. Roy and Alta are buried at Fairview Cemetery.

LEE AND CARLA (REINHARD) VONGUNTEN

On September 16, 1977, Lee Franklin VonGunten and Carla Jane Reinhard started a new family unit in Wells County. They were married at the Pleasant Dale Church of The Brethren in rural Decatur, with the Reverend Kenneth Bauman and the Reverend Dwight Hargett officiating. After the wedding, they took up residence in a mobile home in Kozy Kourt, at Ossian, Indiana. In March of 1979, they moved to their new home at 4889 East State Road 124, Bluffton.

October, 1989
(L-R) Lee and Carla, Ryan (8), Lynae (6), Kyal (21 months)

Lee, the youngest child of Paul and Marguerite Kitson) VonGunten of Berne, Indiana, was born in Adams County on February 14, 1958. He had two older brothers, Stephen and Ronald VonGunten, both are living in Ohio now, and his sister, Ruth (VonGunten) Reinhard, who married Carla's brother Arland Reinhard, lives in Bluffton. Lee graduated from South Adams High School in 1976, and after graduation began working for the Craigville Telephone Company, Inc. In 1981, he became a salesman for Northwestern Mutual Life Insurance Company, and during the nine years of working with insurance, obtained both the Chartered Life Underwriter (CLU) and the Chartered Financial Consultant (CHFC) designations. In 1990, he chose to return to the Craigville Telephone Company, Inc. to assist with management responsibilities. Lee enjoys singing with a Christian male quartet named Sonrise, from Berne, Indiana.

Carla, the youngest child of Howard and Ilene (Ehrman) Reinhard of Craigville, Indiana, was born in Wells County on October 11, 1956. Her brothers are Carlton Reinhard of Hamilton, Indiana, and Arland Reinhard, of Bluffton; her sister, Arvilla (Reinhard) Rodenbeck, is also from Bluffton. Carla graduated from Norwell High School in 1975. After graduation, Carla worked at the Wells County Court House in the offices of the Surveyor, Area Plan Commission, and the County Clerk. She also worked for one-and-a-half years in the Abstract Department of John W. Carnall and Sons Inc. of Bluffton. In 1980, she began working at the Craigville Telephone Company as its secretary.

On December 25, 1980, Lee and Carla were blessed with a special Christmas present, Ryan Howard, their first son was born. Two years later, on December 17, 1982, they had their second son, Kyal Paul. Then Lynae Elizabeth joined her big brothers on January 21, 1988. All three children were born at the Wells Community Hospital at Bluffton, Indiana.

The family attends and are involved in many different activities at the First Mennonite Church of Berne, Indiana.

VORE
1630 TO 1990

The first Vores came from the Palatinate area of Germany to America in 1630, settled in Dorchester, Massachusetts and later at Windsor, Connecticut. In later westward movement, they settled in Wellsville, Pennsylvania (1713), Guernsey County, Pennsylvania (1815), and Chesterhill, Ohio (1830). John H. Vore, my great-great-grandfather, was a Civil War veteran of the 89th Ohio Regiment and was captured at Goldsboro, North Carolina in 1865. In 1878, John moved with his family of five sons to Bluffton, Indiana. His son, Frank C. Vore, became a traveling salesman for International Harvester Company and later was in the restaurant business as were my parents in the late 1930's.

Our homeplace became 1028 W. South Street in 1939 until 1973 when my parents moved to Murray, Indiana, where Fred and Gerry Vore still reside. Their children are Victor, a M.D. in Portland, Oregon; Patricia, a banker in Portland, Oregon; Della, with the Federal Reserve in Cleveland, Ohio; Don, Dana Corp. and living in Bluffton, and Rolland has Vore Realty in Bluffton.

WAGNER

The Wagner family arrived in Wells County in 1976, with Steve's new position as biology teacher at the newly-opened Bluffton Middle School. His family, originally from Sweden and Germany, located in Waterloo, Wisconsin. His parents, Victor Gustav and Mary Ann Veith, married and moved their young family to Speedway, Indiana, for Victor to pursue a career as a professional engineer. They raised six children.

Steve attended Brebeuf Prep and graduated from Wabash College in Crawfordsville. He married Nancy Carroll in 1975. She was an art student at St. Mary of the Woods College. They spent the first eight months in London studying and enjoying the British countryside.

The Carroll family came from England and located in Huntington County. Nancy's father, Jim Carroll, married Ann Stoffel, whose family came from Luxembourg in the late 1800's and also settled in Huntington. They moved to Fort Wayne, where he pursued a career in education and played professional clarinet and saxophone. They raised four children.

Josh, Ben, and Peter Wagner

Steve and Nancy now have three boys: S. Joshua, born April 3, 1978, Benjamin Carroll, born February 27, 1980, and Peter Remington, born December 3, 1983. All were born in Wells County. We all live at 700 South Nottingham Township in a one hundred year old farmhouse that we continue to work on.

Josh enjoys all sports, art, and boyscouting and would like to go into the Air Force Academy. Ben intends to go to Harvard, but at this time, enjoys Nintendo, baseball, and trumpet. Peter plans on a career as a singer dancer, enjoys reading, school, and bike riding.

Our entire family enjoys traveling, having spent a year in southern London on a Fullbright Program exchange in 1986. We also travel frequently to the beach in North Carolina and enjoy the Smoky Mountains, with illusions of someday becoming "good" campers.

We are all active members of St. Joseph's Catholic Church and are involved in the Sunday School program there.

WALMER FAMILY

The Walmer (Volmer-Wampler) family originated in Germany. Because of religious persecution they migrated to England, where they became large land owners. There is a Walmer Castle on the English channel—now a museum. Its picture was featured on the front of Life Magazine several years ago. Becoming dissatisfied they moved on to Rotterdam. From there they sailed for America, landing at Philadelphia, Pennsylvania. Being farmers they settled near Lancaster, in Lebanon County. Peter Walmer and his six sons built a log church in six days. It had a dirt floor and slab seats. The church was built in 1750 and was known as the Walmer Church. Records were lost or burned about the second church. In 1850 a large two-story brick church was built. It is still used on alternate Sundays by both Lutheran and Dutch Reformed denominations. On special occasions, they have combined services. It is located at Indiantown Gap, Pennsylvania.

David Walmer married Barbara Shuey. David died November 11, 1859, and is buried in the Walmer Cemetery, in Indiantown Gap. Barbara died November 19, 1865, while visiting her son Henry in Bluffton and is buried in Fairview Cemetery, Bluffton.

Walter & Roberta Walmer Gleim Golden Wedding Anniversary June 16, 1979

In late 1840's, two brothers, Jacob and Henry Shuey Walmer, left home to seek their fortunes. They arrived in Bluffton by way of Cincinatti. Henry was my grandfather. Henry married Catherine Krill on March 6, 1851. They were the parents of ten children. He was a cobbler and bought several parcels of land around Bluffton, including a farm at the west edge of town. He built a large brick house on this farm, which is now on West Cherry Street and occupied. As the town grew, he had lots laid off and built several rental houses. William Kunkel, Sr. was the surveyor.

The Walmer's first home was in the first block of West Washington Street. The area on the west side of town became known as Walmerville. There is still a short street there named Walmer Street. My grandfather died June 6, 1900.

Two of Henry's sons entered the mercantile business, first at Montpelier and then at Bluffton. David Allen (D.A) with partner Frank Engler owned the Walmer and Engeler Department Store where the present Penny Store is now located in Bluffton. E.S. Walmer owned the Peoples Store located at the corner of Johnson and Market Streets. The Walmer and Engeler store had the only passenger elevator in town. All three floors were utilized.

The third son, my father, William Walmer, started as a teamster and farmer. In 1906 he bought a small farm two miles south of town. For eleven years he drove a horse drawn "hack" to carry the children to school. He married Anne L. Greenfield on March 8, 1888. They were the parents of four children: Henry Homer (May 14, 1889), Dwight G. (March 31, 1891), Victor Glen (May 12, 1894), and Roberta (January 21, 1910). Glen fought in World War I and was awarded many medals. For five years I attended the Poplar Grove one-room school, where one teacher taught all eight grades, and then I went to the consolidated school. I graduated from Bluffton High School in 1927.

Two years after graduating from high school, I married Walter Gleim on June 16, 1929. We were parents of six children, Richard D. (July 21, 1930), Robert Max (March 23, 1933), William Rex (May 14, 1939), Carolyn C. (September 14, 1941), Janet C. (June 21, 1945), and Stephen Kay (August 27, 1949). Walter died February 26, 1986.

I am a member of the First United Methodist Church, Bluffton, The D.A.R., chapter member of the Daughters of Union Veterans of the Civil War, and the Wells County Historical Society. My hobbies have been quilting, collecting antiques, and raising flowers. I am now a resident of the Neal Home at Logansport, Indiana.

REVEREND H. L. WALMSLEY FAMILY

Harry Louis Walmsley was born in Pittsburgh, Pennsylvania, on March 7, 1900. He dropped out of school and later enrolled at the Gettysburg Prep School in Gettysburg, Pennsylvania. He went on to graduate from Gettysburg College and Gettysburg Seminary. He was ordained in the Lutheran Church in America. While in Gettysburg, he met and married Helen Elizabeth (Rummel) Walmsley. Helen was born January 19, 1906.

Harry and Helen's first child, Grace Anna (Harter) Walmsley was born August 26, 1930. Reverend Walmsley served as an assistant pastor in Cleveland, Ohio, for about six months. He came to the Uniondale Lutheran Parish in the spring of 1931. There were five churches in the parish: St. John's, Mount Zion at Nine Mile, St. Mark's at Uniondale, St. Paul's near Rockcreek, and Mount Horeb near the old Cover bridge.

Harry Walmsley Family

Other children born to Harry and Helen were: John Morris Walmsley, August 23, 1933; Lois Ruth (Walmsley) Shutt, April 29, 1935; Dorothy June (Walmsley) Howell, January 2, 1936 (deceased); Phyllis Ilene (Walmsley) Betz, January 19, 1939; and Betty Lou (Walmsley) Daugherty, July 24, 1940.

The St. John's church was removed from the parish after a short time. After many years of ministry, the Horeb church was closed because of the Wabash Reservoir project. The Mount Zion congregation was combined with Monroeville to form a new parish. Rev. Walmsley served the Uniondale parish for thirty-three years until his death on February 28, 1965. He gave of himself to his ministry and many still remember the sincerity of his service. He was recognized as a recipient of the Wells County Citizens of the Year for his ministry to the community.

JOHN MORRIS WALMSLEY FAMILY

John Morris Walmsley was born in Bluffton, Indiana, on August 23, 1933. His parents were Reverend H. L. Walmsley and Helen Elizabeth (Rummel) Walmsley. John had five sisters: Grace Anna, Lois, Dorothy, Phyllis, and Betty.

John graduated from Rockcreek Center High School in 1951. He attended Purdue University and graduated in 1955. John served two years on active duty with the United States Naval Reserve aboard the U.S.S. Wasp, CVA-18. He has completed twenty years of service with the Naval Reserve. John received his Master's Degree from Ball State University in 1963.

John married Jean Garlsnd (Saufley) Walmsley on December 25, 1959. They have three children: Janice Lynn VanMeter, born April 13, 1963; Joyce Ann Kitchin, born August 16, 1966; and James Philip Walmsley, born August 26, 1970.

John taught at Union Center for five years, Northern-Wells Community Schools for four years, and is completing twenty-six years with Fort Wayne Community Schools. Jean graduated from Huntington School, Huntington College, and physical therapy school at the Cleveland Clinic. She has worked as a physical therapist in Cleveland, Fort Wayne, Bluffton, and Huntington. John and Jean have lived in Zanesville since their marriage.

WARE-GREGG

My great grandfather John Gregg came to the United States in 1851 from Ireland. He was twenty-two years old. He lived briefly in Philadelphia, Pennsylvania. He moved near Wooster, Ohio, for four years, then moved to his farm in Liberty Township four miles west of Bluffton on State Road 124. He married Fannie Wallace in 1858. They lived in a log house until he and his brother William each built a brick house in 1873. William's house is in Rockcreek Township one-half mile east of John's. John was a bricklayer by trade. They made their own bricks and quarried the stone for the foundation from the Wabash River.

John and Fannie had thirteen children of whom four died as infants. My grandfather, Thomas, was born to them in 1874. He married Ida Morris in 1899. They bought eighty acres south of the home place and that is where they lived and raised their five sons: John, David, Marion, Howard, and Frank. David is my father. He married Dortha Penrod in 1924. David was a farmer all his life. He and Dortha had five children: Betty (died as an infant), Tommy, Rex, Patrick, and Bonnie. David bought his father's and grandfather's farms and moved there in 1937. Rex married Joyce Ware in 1952. While serving in the army for two years, Rex was stationed most of that time in Alaska. Joyce worked as office manager at Bob Bate Chevrolet for several years. They moved to the family farm in 1968 and purchased it in 1975 and are still farming. They have two sons, Ronald and Timothy. Timothy is married to Rosella Straley. They have three children: Paula Straley, Randy McClain, and Brittany Gregg. They live on what was grandfather Tom's farm. Timothy helps Rex farm and also works at NFM in Poneto.

Ronald married Lisa Dobson. They have three children: Jeremy and Julie Hinshaw, and Jessica Gregg. Ronald's occupation is auto body shop repairman. Ronald lives on his mother's family farm.

Anna Benton Hunt came to the United States from Ireland. She and her husband, Richard Hunt, lived for a time in Ohio, where he died. She and their five children, John, James, George, Douglas, and Mary Ann, moved to Liberty Township, where she bought eighty acres in 1883. Mary married Charles Ware. She became the owner of the farm in 1933. Charles and Mary had one son, Frank. Frank married Loretta Osborn in 1922. They has two daughters, Helen and Joyce. Frank became the owner of the farm in 1944. This was also where he was born. Helen married John Glass and they have three children: Norman, Karen, and Ervin. Joyce purchased the family farm in 1986.

WASSON FAMILY

George and Sarah Wasson were natives of Ireland and of Scotish descent. They were reared and married in their native country and, shortly after their marriage, came to the United States. After a short residence in Strark County and Wayne County, Ohio, they established a home on Section 11 in Lancaster Township, Wells County, Indiana, in 1841. In 1878, following the death of George, the property was deeded to son John. He married Rebecca Kunkle in 1859. Their children, Wililam Henry, married to Etta McAfee, and Sarah, married to Norval J. Kleinknight, owned and operated the land until 1909 when William became the sole owner.

William and Etta were the parents of Lantz and Edna. Edna married William Grim and they had one daughter, Marjorie. She is married to Cecil Lockwood and has two sons.

Lantz married Mae Clowser and they became the residents and owners of Section 11. They were the parents of three children: Katherine, born in 1979, Ner William, born in 1919, and Marilyn, born in 1931. Lantz died in 1947, and Mae in 1974.

The Wasson Family 1988

Katherine married Chester Shady in 1936. They had three children: Clyde Lee, Dell (Bud), and Adell. Clyde married Phyllis Farling. They live in Sparta, Wisconsin, and have three children: Kent, Kendra, and Kurt. There are two grandchildren. Bud married Gwen Hill and they have two children: Scott and Lori. They live north of Bluffton on a farm. Adell lives at home. Chester died in 1978.

Ner William married Irene Smith in 1938. They have six daughters: Suzanne, Janet, Rosemary, Rebecca Jean, Debra Lynn, and Merianne. Suzanne married David Beeler and they have five children: Joanna, Sandy, Tim, Julie, and Mark. They also have seven grandchildren. They all reside in Arizona. Janet married Richard Johnson and they have three children: Michelle, Mike, and Matt. Janet and Rich live in Waynedale. Rosemary lives in Swayzee and has two daughters: Stephanie and Paige. Becky married Terry Tyler and they live in Westchester, Ohio. They are the parents of Jeremy, Jeff, and Kelsey. Debbie is married to Don Lockwood. They have two children: Lindsay and Kyle. They live north of Ossian. Merianne is married to Larry Dewitt and they reside in Austin, Indiana.

Marilyn married Richard Gerber. They live in Portland, Indiana, and have five children. Carlene is deceased. Marlene, married to Randy Saunders, has two daughters and lives in St. Maries, Idaho. Cindy lives in Maitland, Florida. Lynn married J. B. Bender and they are the parents of three girls and one boy. They reside in Fuguay Springs, North Carolina. Jeff married Jackie Gerber and lives in Berne, Indiana. They have one son.

Ner William and Irene have owned the Wasson property since 1974. Bill still does the farming. He also drove a school bus for thirty years.

WATERS

We can trace our family back to Lincolnshire, England, where great-great-grandfather, Henry Waters, lived. We know of four children, Elizabeth, Henry, William and Matthew, our great-grandfather. Matthew, born February 12, 1836, left Liverpool, England, and arrived in New York in June, 1853. He stopped in Ohio a short time before coming to Union Township, Huntington County, where he married Nancy Agnes Swain September 12, 1861. Her parents were Louman Swain and Nancy Waters. August 6, 1862, Matthew was mustered into the Seventy-Fifth Indiana Infantry volunteers and was wounded during the battle of Chickamauga. Later, he was a prisoner of war and was released April 2, 1865.

Left to right: Linda Kay Waters Peterson, Gary Lee Waters, Janice Elaine Waters. Bottom: Left to right: Dorothy Jean (Harris) Waters, Gerald Clarence Waters

Matthew and Nancy Waters were the parents of twelve children: Mary Elizabeth, John Henry, William I, Nancy Catherine, Philip Isham, Elizabeth Jane, Charles Valentine, Daisy Belle, Hannah Elle, Benjamin Franklin, Joseph M. and Clida Eveline. Philip Isham, our grandfather, married Sylvia Jane Harshner June 19, 1893. Her parents were Andrew Harshner and Elizabeth Weaver, who farmed in Rockcreek Township, Wells County, near Bluffton, Indiana. They were the parents of Jasper Clarence, Dessie Marie, Earl Glen, James LeRoy, Kenneth and Virgil E. Our father, Jasper Waters, was born October 21, 1895, and died September 27, 1975. He married Edna Marie Redding February 5, 1921. Her parents were John Oliver Redding and Mary Ann Sheets, who have lived in both Union and Rockcreek Townships, of Wells County, Indiana. From the spring of 1930, they lived in Rockcreek Township, on a farm located at the corner of Indiana one hundred sixteen and three West until November, 1973, when they moved to Markle. They are the parents of Harold William, Gerald Clarence, and Loren Eugene. Harold William, born on June 16, 1922, in Rockcreek Township, Wells County. He married Martha Waneta Allen September 12, 1947, and are the parents of Wayne Allen born on October 14, 1948, and Gregory Kent, born October 31, 1953. Gregory married Jane Teresa Smekens November 17, 1984. They are the parents of Sara Lynn, born May 25, 1990. Gerald Clarence was born July 16, 1924, in Union Township, Wells County. He was in World War II from August 4, 1944, to July 3, 1946. After he returned, he married Dorothy Jean Harris November 18, 1951. Her parents were Walter Monroe Harris and Freda Mae Divelbiss. They live on a farm north of Markle in Union Township, Wells County. They are the parents of Gary Lee, born January 23, 1953, who married Donna Marie Gabbard on March 24, 1990. Janice Elaine was born February 27, 1956. Linda Kay was born April 5, 1957, and married Bryan Walter Peterson May 21, 1983. Loren Eugene was born January 12, 1928, in Union Township, Wells County. He married Elizabeth Mae Smith September 12, 1952. They are the parents of Michael Eugene born March 30, 1955, and died December 5, 1982. He married Alicia Marie Oestreich April 5, 1980. They are the parents of Chad Paul, Tracey Elizabeth, and Nicolle Marie. Kenneth Dean, born October 7, 1958, married Teresa Lea Knowles April 5, 1980. They are the parents of Lindsey Rachel and Eric Michael. Donald Raye, born January 26, 1961, married Marvel Louise Mason June 1, 1979. They are the parents of Donald Jr., Marisa Lynn, and Kasey Kathleen. Donna Faye was born on January 26, 1961. Effie Marie was born November 13, 1962, and married Todd Alan Eschenbacker May 5, 1984. They are the parents of Abbey Michelle.

SADIE LAGERPUSCH WATROUS

Sadie Heinz Lagerpusch was born in Keokuk, Iowa, on June 14, 1895, a third generation American, descended from Ludwig Lagerpusch, who was born in Germany, January 14, 1824, and emigrated to New York City in 1849. She was also a third generation descendent of John Hanson who was born March 22, 1820, in Yorkshire, England.

Austin Augustus Watrous was born in Cortlandville, New York, July 20, 1890, a ninth generation American, descended from Jacob Waterhouse, who arrived in New England in 1635. He was also an eighth generation descendent of William Tuttle of New Haven, Connecticut.

Austin and Sadie were married February 1, 1919, at Keokuk, Iowa. Early years of their marriage were spent in Cook County, Illinois. Their daughter, Dorothy Frances, was born in Riverside, Illinois, November 5, 1922; and son, Austin Augustus, was born August 26, 1926, also in Riverside. During the Depression, the family, along with Sadie's mother, Isabella, moved to New York state. For three years, they lived in Messengerville, New York, on property owned by Austin's mother, Emily Tuttle Watrous.

Sadie L. Watrous

In 1934, Austin was employed by the Department of the Interior, and moved his family to Decatur, Indiana, to oversee the construction of the Homesteads, a government project to enable those with insufficient capital to buy a home.

Austin and Sadie were divorced in 1937. Austin continued his career with the U. S. government, and died in Arlington, Virginia, in 1948. In 1938, Sadie brought her family to Bluffton. Dorothy graduated from Bluffton High School in 1940, and married

591

Harold Wayne Hunt of Lancaster Township. Austin, or "Buzzie" as he was always called, graduated in 1944, and married Doris Luedtke of Bluffton.

Sadie earned her living by working at Inca Wire Company in Fort Wayne during World War II. She spent many years taking care of children and invalids in their homes, and then was employed by Cooper Community Care Center, and the Caylor-Nickel Clinic, until her retirement in 1962. She lived on West Central Avenue the last thirty years of her life, and died in 1983, at the age of 88 years.

WATSON

I was born in Liberty Township Three, November 1935, to Elroy and Vera (Bender) Watson. My father came to Rockcreek Township about 1930, and worked as a hired hand for "Joke" Johnson, neighbor to Bender and Christman families. Elroy was born in DeKalb County to Willard and Pearl (Firgusson) Watson April 4, 1911, being the oldest of four children: Irvin Hilkert, deceased and formally lived in Wells County, Nellie, (wife of Waldo Krinn) Harrison Township, and Annabelle (Dunlap) Allen County. Parents dying when Elroy was six years old.

Patricia (Dyson), Vera (Bender), and Elroy Watson

It was at "Joke" Johnsons' that he met and married Vera Bender, oldest daughter of V. O. and Jennie (Christman) Bender, December, 1934, at Liberty Center Baptist Church. Prior to coming to Wells County, Elroy worked for Auburn Cord in Auburn, and was transferred to Connersville. At the closing of that plant, they moved back to Liberty Township and worked as a hired hand for George Vickery. In 1938, it was on to Noble County, and working on a farm near Albion. He moved back to Wells County and rented the Jessie and Audrey Prough Farm east of Ossian where I started school. When I was in fifth grade, we moved back to Liberty Township, on one of the L. L. Bender Farms. In 1949, Dad and Mom bought the Ves Landis Farm in Chester Township near Poneto, where they still live and farm. Elroy was a DeKalb Seed Corn Dealer in the 50's and 60's.

I graduated in 1953 from Chester Center High School, accepting an office position with the Farm Bureau Co-op in Bluffton. In the 1940's, Dad held positions from Township, Farm Bureau Chairman, Wells County Farm Bureau President, and served on the Co-op Board of Directors. From 1950's through 1960's, he was substitute Poneto rural carrier. Mother held the S. and E. office in the Farm Bureau, and was head cook at Southern Wells School until 1972, when a broken leg forced her to retirement.

I was a 4-H member, Jr. leader and in Wells County band. I was active in Rural Youth, where I met my husband, Robert Dyson, of Wabash County. After marriage on January 31, 1954, we lived in Wabash, Allen, Whitley, and presently Noble Counties. We have one son, David, Columbia City, three daughters, Lois (Brandenburg) at Columbia City, Lorinda, California, DeAnn, at home, and Dawn, attending Ball State University. Four grandchildren: Christina and Dean Dyson, Carrie and Heather Brandenburg.

In June, 1990, I donated a two-volume set of our FAMILY TREE, Roots-Branches-Twigs, Genealogy, to the Wells County Library. Copies can be found in Allen, Noble, DeKalb, Whitley, Wabash, and Huntington Counties. (Pat*ricia (Watson) Dyson)*

WATTERS-JOHNSON

Earl L. "Bud" Watters of 945 Ranch Road, Bluffton, was born November 3, 1922. He married Maenette Johnson, of Bluffton, on July 6, 1947. She was born January 18, 1924. Both have always lived in Bluffton. They are the parents of a son, David Earl Watters, who was born February 13, 1949, in Bluffton. David graduated from Bluffton High School in 1967, and Indiana University in 1971. On October 21, 1972, in Albuquerque, New Mexico, he married Anne Christine Kleinknight, a daughter of Crystal Rieddle Kleinknight and the late Wilmer R. Kleinknight, formerly of Bluffton. They are the parents of two daughters, Kristen, 16, and Rebecca, 13. They reside in Sturgis, Michigan, where David is Senior Vice-President and Trust Officer of AmeriTrust National Bank in Sturgis.

Earl graduated from Bluffton High School in 1940, enlisted in the Army Air Corps in December, 1941, and was discharged November 1945, with the rank of Technical Sergeant. He was employed at the Bluffton Post Office for 32 years, retiring January 11, 1980, as Postmaster of Bluffton. He was the first Postmaster named under the merit system, appointment being made June 7, 1975. His hobbies are golf and stamp collecting.

Maenette graduated from Bluffton High School in 1941, and was employed for twenty years in the office of John W. Carnall & Sons, Inc., as an abstracter. Working on the family genealogy is on of her interests.

The Watters are members of the First United Church of Christ and Wells County Historical Society. He is a member of the Bluffton Lions Club and the American Legion.

Earl is a son of the late Chauncey Earl and Helen Mae (Helms) Watters. His grandparents were George W. and Rena (DeWitt) Watters and John L. and Cordelia (Ratliff) Helms. His great-grandfather, Daniel Ratliff, was one of the last four surviving Civil War veterans of Wells County, Indiana. His great-great-grandfather, Moses DeWitt, who came from New York, was in the War of 1812, and is buried in the old Bluffton Cemetery. Earl has two brothers, George D. and Huston D., and two sisters, Lovina Mae Hunnicutt and Mary Lou Barger. The Watters family name is believed to be associated with the Welsh and English.

Maenette is the daughter of the late Harry Abraham and Edith G. (Grove) Johnson. Her grandparents were Walter B. and Nora Belle (Mettler) Johnson and Thomas Wilson and Lillian L. (Kline) Grove. She had two brothers, Thomas Richard and Donald D., and two sisters, Helen Jean Gilbert Lesh and Harriette L. Case, all deceased. Her great-grandfather, Abraham W. Johnson, came from Beaver County, Pennsylvania, and was of Scotch and Irish ancestry. He was one of the early settlers of Wells County, Indiana, having entered real estate in Harrison Township. Maenette's great-grandfather, Clemens John Kline (Klein), came to the United States as a young man from Main, Germany.

JACOB A. WEAVER FAMILY

One of the pioneer families of Wells County, Indiana, was the family which Jacob A. Weaver is today representing in Allen County, where he settled in young manhood. The Weavers were of Ohio birth, David Z. Weaver, father of the subject, being born in Monroe County, and there was reared to manhood. His first independent venture took him to Indiana, where he settled on land in Wells County. He was without means and was unable to buy improved land, but he compromised with fortune by homesteading a tract of government land, which he improved and patented in due time. His early life was not void of hardships, and with no near neighbors, loneliness in those first years was a foregone conclusion. He was friendly with the Indians, who were numerous, and with whom he frequently traded, buying his first team of horses from them.

Jacob and Katie Weaver

He married Susanna Kohr, and together they attained a pleasing measure of success in their work. In later years, Mr. Weaver owned and operated a grist mill at Zanesville, and was for some time engaged in stock buying. They were the parents of six children: John B., Catherine, Elizabeth, Emma, Jacob A., and Alice. Jacob A. Weaver was born in Wells County, Indiana, October 13, 1863. His young life was uneventful as that of most farmer boys, and he divided his time, until his later teens, between the work of the home farm and his studies in the village schools. When he was twenty-three years old, he left the family home and began farming on his own responsibility, beginning operations with an eighty-acre farm, to which he later added one hundred and two acres, so that he then had a considerable acreage under cultivation. Stock farming held his attention during most of the time, and he experienced a commendable success in that departure.

In 1902, he withdrew from active farm life, and settling in Fort Wayne, identified himself with the Fort Wayne Lumber Company, with which establishment he was associated until March 1917, when he returned to his farm.

In 1886, Mr. Weaver was married to Kate V. Jacobs, daughter of Elijah Jacobs, an old Wells County pioneer, and they had five children: Merlie E., who married Fred Fisher; Goldie M., who married Roy Keplinger; Ivan O., who married Ida Miller; Lela F., who married Elmer Minton; and Floyd A.

Floyd Allen Weaver married Eva Leota Gaskill (daughter of William and Altha Van Wormer Gaskill) on February 25, 1918. Children born to them were: Bessie L.; Marjory (Mrs. Richard

Stephens); Floyd Jr. (married Betty Thayer, daughter of Andrew/Margie Thayer); Mary V. (Mrs. Vaughn Smith), (See Smith and Weaver); Esther M. (Mrs. Max Poling); Ralph A. (married Norma Hoch), their children are Phyllis and Allen of near Ossian; Gerald (married Doris Warkentien); William R. (married Marcia Kaiser); Harold L. (married Jane Keister); and Carol Sue (Mrs. Gary Hoch). This family were mainstays in the Zanesville Church of God.

WEBBER FAMILY

Justus Morton Webber (1894 - 1988) was the only child of Agnes L. Justus and Harry C. Webber. The family was living in Warren, Indiana, at the time of his birth, where Harry worked for the railroad. Justus lived in Marion and Toledo, Ohio, where he worked until being called to serve in World War I. He served in a motorized division in Alabama and was on the battlefield in France driving an ammunition truck at the time of the Armistice. He returned to Bluffton where he went into business with his father, who managed the Bliss Hotel. His grandparents, Zachary Taylor Webber and Emma Angstedt Webber, lived on East Cherry Street. His maternal grandfather, M.M. Justus, also lived in Bluffton.

In Bluffton, he met and married Mary Painter on June 29, 1922. The three o'clock service in the Painter home at 424 West Washington Street, was performed by Reverend W. A. Alspaugh, pastor of the First Reformed Church. After a wedding trip to Montreal via the Thousand Islands of the St. Lawrence River, they set up housekeeping in the Bliss Hotel.

Left to right: Bud Webber, Dot Wilkey, Mary Webber, Justus Webber. Fiftieth anniversary celebration for Webbers and twenty-fifth for Wilkeys wedding

Two children were born to them: a premature son, Justus Painter (Bud) Webber, on February 21, 1923, and a daughter, Dorothy Jane Webber, on April 20, 1926. Both children graduated from Bluffton High School and entered college. Bud left school to serve in the Marines in World War II. Bud married Betty Heck from Ft. Wayne in July of 1947, and Dorothy (Dot) married Richard F. Wilkey in June of 1947. Bud's career as a disc jockey and musician took him to Indianapolis, Omaha, Nebraska, and San Francisco. He became a radio and TV program director in Seattle where they continued to rear their four children: Jane, born in 1948; Dan in 1949; Mike in 1951; and Tim in 1953.

The Wilkey family completed schooling at Purdue and moved to Colorado State University where Dick completed his Masters Degree, and a son, John, was born. Accepting employment in California, they moved to San Jose, San Diego, and Sacramento. A son, Frank, was born in 1952, and another son, David, in 1963. Dot, Dick, and David moved back to Bluffton in 1971.

Justus Webber was a salesman for the Bluffton Grocery Company, and later for Canterbury House Furniture out of Peru. Mary was Executive Secretary of the Wells County T. B. Association and an Occupational Therapist at Irene Byron Hospital in Ft. Wayne. In 1957, she became an elementary school teacher, teaching at Union Township school and at Poplar Grove School and serving as a substitute for fifteen years. An interest in the Wells County Historical Society was a retirement avocation for both Mary and Justus.

The Webber family lived at three Bluffton locations: 228 West Central Avenue, 424 West Washington Street, to assist in the care for Mary's parents; and, since 1961, at 412 West Market Street. The Wilkeys also live in an apartment at 412 West Market Street.

Mary and Dot are members of National College Sorority, Kappa Alpha Theta, and Indiana sorority, Tri Kappa, and are both past presidents of Easter Seal Society.

WEILEMANN-NEUHAUSER

Luzerne (Zernie) Weilemann (1908) is the son of Otto Weilemann (1888-1966) and Gertrude Parrish (1891-1969). He was born in Adams County, but was a graduate of Bluffton High School (1925). He married Mildred Neuhauser (1912) in 1938. She was the daughter of Amos Neuhauser and Marianne Rupp. Born in Berne, she attended first grade at Vera Cruz, then attended Bluffton schools and graduated in 1930.

Zernie was a graduate of Purdue (1929) and worked for Lyon Metal Products at Aurora, Illinois, returning to Bluffton in 1931. Through the Depression, he was a partner with his father in the plumbing business until 1937, when he started working at the Hoosier Condensed Milk Company.

He was in the Air Force stationed on Tinian as a propeller specialist. After the bomb was dropped, he flew over Hiroshima to witness the results. Various times he had to go up in a plane he had said was ready for duty.

After peace was declared in 1945, he returned to Bluffton and the Hoosier Condensed Milk Company. In 1947, he and a brother-in-law moved to Central Dairy in Fort Wayne, commuting daily until he and his wife moved to Fort Wayne in 1956.

When the companies were sold, he worked for Erie Materials. After the merger with a New Haven company, the name was changed to Erie-Haven. He continued employment there until 1973, when he retired. He served on the Board of Directors of Anthony Wayne Bank from 1958-1979.

Mildred attended Ward-Belmont in Nashville, Tennessee, for one year and then Indiana University for one year. She was bookkeeper at Hoosier Condensed Milk Company from 1932-1942, and from 1943-1946.

Mildred and Zernie had three children: Monica, Bill, and Cindy. All three were born in Bluffton, but just Monica and Bill attended school in Bluffton.

Monica (Posy) Weilemann (10-15-42) married Dale W. McMillen (Terry) (1-8-43) on August 8, 1943, at Fort Wayne. Both graduated from Indiana University. Terry, formerly part-owner and employed by Central Soya, is now self-employed in electrical supply sales in Texas. Posy started teaching needlepoint and worked up to doing national seminars and designing. They now live at Fort Worth, Texas.

They have two children: Megan (1969) and John Peter (5-5-80). Megan was married to Cleve Todd Perry on June 17, 1988.

Jon William (Bill) (11-2-46) was married to Lydia Ann "Edie" Hughes (10-11-47) on June 7, 1969. Both graduated from Indiana University - he in Business Administration. Bill was commissioned in the Air Force during the Korean War. He spent two years in service, but the war ended just as he was ready to be shipped out. He then worked for Continental Can until its merger with another company. He is now with Packaging Corporation of America at Evanston, Illinois. Edie has done finishing (sewing) for several craft stores in Chicago and Naperville, Illinois, where they now live. They have two children: Jon William (1971) and Christopher Edward (1983). Jon is now at the University of Illinois.

Cynthia (12-29-50) married Merrill Phillips (3-12-51) on June 21, 1974. Merrill graduated from the University of South Florida at Tampa. He worked for Central Soya and is now self-employed at Ingredient Exchange in Fort Wayne. Cindy went to Green Mountain College at Poultney, Vermont, for one year. She transferred to the University of Evansville, then graduated from the University of South Florida. She was employed at Anthony Wayne Bank in Fort Wayne and at a Madison, Wisconsin, Bank. She is now a teacher's aid in Fort Wayne. They have two children: Kiersten (1977) and Monica (1980).

JOSIAH (JESSE) WEIST FAMILY

My father, Josiah Weist, was born April 15, 1866. The family name was formerly spelled Wist. Josiah was known as Jesse, and was the youngest of nine children born to the first Josiah, born 1825, died December 10, 1900, and Catherina (Rose) Weist, born December 30, 1824, died December 2, 1897. Josiah (Jesse) lived in Vera Cruz for some time, but most of his life was spent in Bluffton. He did carpenter work, was custodian of Old Central School on West Washington Street for many years, and was Street Commissioner of Bluffton for several years.

Josiah and Laura Weist

His first marriage was to Mary Bossert, born March 20, 1868. They were married September 22, 1888. They had four children: Emma Nina, born June 5, 1891; Melvin Merl, born January 12, 1892; Olus Jane, born October 12, 1894; and Sarah Matilda, born June 21, 1896. Mary (Bossert) Weist died October 15, 1899. She was only 31 years old. She is buried in Old Salem Cemetery which is just east and south of Reiffsburg. The first Josiah, my grandfather, and Catherina (Rose) Weist, my grandmother, are also buried in Old Salem Cemetery.

On September 27, 1901, Josiah (Jesse) Weist, my father, married my mother, Laura Viola O'Donal, who was born February 26, 1883, in Jay County. Her parents were Charles Madison O'Donal and Lydia Ann (Stults) O'Donal.

Two children were born to this union. Raymond O'Donal, born June 6, 1906, and Jessie Mae, born May 26, 1922. On October 20, 1923, Raymond O'Donal married Ella Monroe. They had one little boy named Robert. Raymond O'Donal died July 8, 1958. On November 2, 1941, Jessie Mae married Robert E. Shelley. We have two children. The first was Janis, born June 2, 1949, and then James Carl, born February 21, 1955.

Janis married Steven Kaehr on September 7, 1974. They have three children: Leanne Shelley, born September 23, 1976; Kristen Marie, born October 16, 1978; and Clinton Michael, born March 12, 1982. They live in Adams County.

On September 1, 1973, James Carl married Patricia Lynn Adkins. They have two children: Robert Douglas, born March 15, 1982; and Brian James, born October 21, 1984. They live in Bluffton.

Josiah (Jesse) died August 5, 1945, and Laura died September 11, 1953. They were members of the First Baptist Church and are buried in Fairview Cemetery at Bluffton.

WELCHES

The Welches family have resided in Wells County since 1890. My father, Albert L. Welches, moved with his parents to a farm one-half mile east of Markle, when he was twelve years old. They formerly had lived in Huntington County. My grandfather came to America from Germany.

The farm has been in the family since that date. At the present time, my daughter, Phyllis, lives in the same house.

My father, Albert L., married Cora Miller in 1896. They had five children: Harry, Russell, Neva, Mark, and Wayne.

Patty Boots, Mark Rittenhouse, Angie Boots, Mary Welches, Tina Boots, Phyllis Rittenhouse, Kenneth Boots, Amy Rittenhouse, Eddie Stauffer, William Rittenhouse, and Wayne Welches

I (Wayne) married Mary E. Blair September 26, 1942. Two daughters were born to this union. Phyllis, born August 4, 1947, married William Rittenhouse, August 16, 1968. Patty, born November 11, 1951, married Kenneth Boots, September 4, 1970.

Phyllis has a son, Mark, who attends Norwell Middle School. She also has a daughter, Amy, who will become Mrs. John E. Stauffer, April 27, 1991.

Patty lives in Bluffton and has two daughters, Angie and Tina. They both attend Bluffton High School.

Both sons-in-law work for Franklin Electric. Phyllis works for the State Bank of Markle, and Patty works at the Dutch Mill.

I work for the Indiana Department of Transportation, and have for twenty years. Mary, my wife, is retired but has worked as a bookkeeper for twenty-five years at Home Products Cabinet Company, and Gulf Farm Center in Markle, and Fort Wayne Wilbert Vault in Fort Wayne.

We live just down the road from the home farm and have for five years, but we also lived on the home farm for thirty-five years.

WENTZ-DRUCKERMILLER

Harold Guy Wentz, born November 13, 1892, was the son of John Andrew and Alice Rebecca Lamm Wentz. John and Alice came from Pennsylvania to a farm west of Bluffton in Liberty Township in 1894. John's family came from Palatinata, Germany, in the mid-1800's. Alice's family, records show, came from Heidelberg, Germany, in 1740.

Harold Guy Wentz married Inez Druckermiller. Inez was the daughter of Allen Burr and Mary Krinn Druckermiller, born November 13, 1898. They moved to a farm in Liberty Township from Grant County, Indiana, in 1908. Notice an unusual fact–their birthdays were the same month and day.

Harold Guy and Inez had four children: My husband, Ralph Guy, born August 5, 1918, and three daughters, Doris, Betty, and Martha. Doris died at age ten. Betty married Wesley Sheets and resides in Fort Wayne. They have four children: Roger, Timothy, Rita, and John. Martha married Bill Pursifull. They have four children: Sherry, Bill, Vickie, and Robert. After a divorce, Martha later married Dean Houtz. They reside at Avon Park, Florida.

Ralph graduated from Liberty Center High School and then from Purdue University in 1941.

Ralph married Marianna Nusbaumer (Chester Township) on June 14, 1941. Ralph taught Vocational Agriculture at Wolf Lake High School near Albion, Indiana, for one year. In 1942, Ralph began teaching at the Bluffton High School as Agricultural Director. He was in that school system until 1954. A son, Dennis Guy, was born July 29, 1952.

In 1954, the family moved to Fort Pierce, Florida, where Ralph was a math teacher for twenty-six years. Ralph passed away February 15, 1987.

Dennis Guy graduated from the University of Florida in 1974. Following graduation, he moved to San Diego, California. He married Laura Larsen and has his own motorcycle business. They now live east of San Diego near Jamul with their two children, Andrew Guy, seven years old, and Katharine Marianna, who is three.

WERLING-GRAFT

The Werling ancestry for this branch was traced back to John Werling, born November 27, 1804, and Anna Christena, born April 15, 1805, in Germany. Their third son, John, came to America in 1841, with his two brothers, Andrew and Henry. John was born November 18, 1833, and on October 28, 1858, married Marie Schueler, born February 14, 1840.

They had twelve children and reared six: George, Fred, Wilhelm, Charles, August, and Susanna.

George, born March 5, 1860, married Anna Bremer, born November 14, 1866. They had four children: Ada, Martin, Herman, and Susanna. Their third child, Herman, was born January 20, 1896, and he married Esther Graft, daughter of Frederic and Marie (Bauermeister) Graft on November 7, 1920. They were married at the Bethlehem Lutheran Church, located two miles northeast of Tocsin. Esther was born November 4, 1902.

Herman's grandfather, John, bought their home place, located at what is now 750E 7500N, from the government. Just small patches of land were capable of being farmed at that time, as most of it was woods and would have to be cleared first. It was easy to till because the ground was loose and could be plowed with a small team of horses.

Herman Werling Family 1954, Father of the Year 1954. Back row: Joyce, Bonnie, Donald, Lois, Wanda, and Doyle. Seated: Carol, Bernice, Jean, Herman, Esther, and Phyllis

They lived in Wells County all their lives. He was a farmer and raised draft horses and had a great interest in horses all his life. They had five or six cows which they would milk by hand. They had chickens, also, and would sell eggs and cheese.

During World War II, Herman worked at American Coal and Supply Company in Fort Wayne where they made crates to put motors in for the U. S. Navy. For many years, he also hauled cattle to livestock markets for neighboring farmers.

In 1946, they purchased a 40-acre farm from Kenneth Neuenschwander, which is located north of Tocsin on 600E. This is where they lived the remainder of their lives.

He was on the Bluffton Street Fair committee for many years and was also a Wells County Councilman for sixteen to eighteen years. In 1954, he was nominated Father of the Year by Raymond (Daddy) Durr, (then Sheriff of Wells County).

They had ten children. They are: Donald (8-11-22/10-22-87); Mrs. Alfred (Bernice) Miller (12-25-24/6-6-66); Mrs. Robert (Phyllis) Jackson (8-13-27) of Silver Lake; Mrs. Delmar (Joyce) Heckman (10-12-29) of Decatur route; Mrs. Gene (Lois) Boyts (10-19-31) of New Paris; Mrs. Albert (Bonnie) McDowell (1-14-34) of Goshen; Mrs. Larry (Carol) Curry (1-28-36) of Ossian; Mrs. Tom (Wanda) Eichhorn (3-24-38) of Lafayette, Colorado; Doyle (4-19-40) of Tocsin, and Mrs. Ron (Jean) Anderson (8-5-47) of Bluffton.

Esther died September 3, 1965, and Herman on October 12, 1985. Both are laid to rest in the Bethlehem Lutheran Cemetery in Wells County.

WERLING-MANKEY

Doyle H. Werling was born April 19, 1940, to Herman and Esther Graft Werling. Doyle went to Bethlehem Lutheran grade school until eighth grade, then attended Ossian High School, where he graduated in 1958. After graduating, he began work at Kresge Warehouse at Baer Field and later left there to work at General Electric in Decatur. After the closing of that plant in 1989, he transferred to Fort Wayne General Electric Broadway plant, where he is now employed. He also farms and enjoys working on and restoring antique cars and tractors.

He is a member of the Vintage Chevrolet Club of America and usually has one or two antiques in the Bluffton Street Fair parade. He had one brother, Donald (deceased) and eight sisters: Bernice Miller (deceased), Phyllis Jackson, Joyce Heckman, Lois Boyts, Bonnie McDowell, Carol Curry, Wanda Eichhorn, and Jean Anderson.

Troy, Cammi, Laura, and Doyle Werling - 1987

On February 11, 1962, Doyle married Laura Mankey at the Lancaster Chapel EUB Church. Laura was born June 12, 1942, to Forest and Nettie Frauhiger Mankey. She graduated from Lancaster High School in 1960. After graduation, she worked in the office at Almco Steel in Bluffton until 1967. She is now employed part time at Kamco, Inc. near Poe. She has twelve brothers and sisters: Freda McBride, Mabel Denis, Violet Hoffman (deceased), Ralph, Dorothy Hoffman, Carl, Glen (deceased), Mary Gould, Walter, Lester (deceased), Bonnie (deceased), and Patsy Dafforn.

Doyle and Laura have two children, Cammi, born May 17, 1968, who attended Bethlehem Lutheran grade school and graduated from Norwell High School in 1986, and Purdue University in 1990. She is presently employed in Vail, Colorado, as an interior designer. Their son, Troy, born August 11, 1970, also attended Bethlehem and is a junior at Manchester College majoring in accounting.

Doyle and Laura live north of Tocsin on 600E in a home they built in 1965 on his father's farm. When this land was originally purchased from the United States of America in 1839 by Dian Jarushy Sutton, it was a plot of eighty acres. In 1883, Tocsin was platted on forty acres of this section. His father bought this in 1946 from Kenneth Neuenschwander. After Doyle's father's death in 1985, he inherited the farm. In 1972, they bought sixty acres on the east side of 600E in Section Thirty-One just north of Tocsin from James Dailey. This land was originally purchased from the United States of America in 1837 by Elijah Sutton.

They are members of Bethlehem Lutheran Church northeast of Tocsin.

WEST

Eulis West and Karen F. Kreigh were married on June 8, 1956. His parents were Alice Owens and Jess West; he was the seventh child of eight that grew up near Jonesboro, Arkansas. After serving in the Korean War, he came to live in Wells County with one of his brothers, Carl.

By this time, Karen's family had lived in Wells County for a couple of generations. Originally Pennsylvania Dutch, her paternal grandparents were Gerald Glendon (Pete) and Viola Desco (Smith) Kreigh. He worked at the city light plant, and she taught Sunday school at the Presbyterian Church for many years.

Karen's maternal grandparents were also from this area. They were Benjamin Harrison and Fern (Faith) Freeland. He was the light and water superintendent for the city of Bluffton. He supervised the construction and installation of both the water storage tank and the diesel power generators at the Water Works on the east side of town. Later in life, Fern graduated from Indiana University and briefly taught at Poplar Grove.

Karen was the oldest of two girls born to Everett Kreigh and Marian Freeland (McFarren) Kreigh. Everett was a telegrapher for the railroad. Marian was a switchboard operator at Caylor-Nickel Clinic. After their marriage ended, they both were happily remarried. Karen grew up on Horton Street in Bluffton and attended Bluffton High, class of 1956.

After briefly living in Lafayette, Eulis and Karen settled in North Oaks Addition on the north side of Bluffton. They have three daughters: Mary Alice Miller, Kathy Sue Musco, and Abigail West. Mary Alice married Bruce W. Miller in 1977. They have one son, Nicholas, who was born in 1981. Kathy married Victor J. Musco in 1983. They have two sons, Michael, born in 1985, and Matthew, born in 1989. Abi, a member of the First Baptist Church, will graduate with a degree in secondary education from Indiana University.

ROBERT WESTFALL FAMILY

Robert Eugene and Edith Lou (Trotter) Westfall were born and raised in Grant County, Indiana, in different rural areas. They both graduated from Van Buren High School, Van Buren, Indiana, in April 1947.

They were married in a little country church in Landess, Indiana, March 20, 1949, on a cold snowy but beautiful Sunday afternoon. They had a partnership in dairy farming with his parents for two years in Washington Township, Grant County, Indiana, where Ronald Eugene was born March 3, 1950. He was the first grandchild of Earl and Edith Westfall.

Moving to Licking Township, Blackford County, in 1951, they cash rented two hundred acres and dairy farmed there for three years, where Roger Allen was born August 31, 1953. Their desire to expand their dairy herd came about in a partnership with Claude L. Mounsey, who owned farm land in Wells County. They moved to Liberty Township, Wells County, on December 20, 1954, and spent thirty-four years dairy farming where Roberta Sue was born September 16, 1958.

Bob and Edith Westfall - Thirtieth wedding anniversary - 1979

Ronald is a Quality Assurance Manager at Kitco, Bluffton, and lives near Bluffton with his wife, the former Trudy McMillan, who is an RN at the Wells Community Hospital. She has two children, Chad and Jennifer Cardin, by a previous marriage (Brent Cardin) and he has two children, Eric and Nathan Westfall, by a previous marriage (Debra Yager). Roger attended Marion College, Marion, Indiana, and is employed at Wayne Metal, Markle, Indiana, as a forklift driver and sheet metal handler and lives in Warren with his wife, the former Jill Rennaker, who is a hair stylist. She and Roger have three children: Joy, Jared, and Jennifer. He has two children, Aaron and Jason Westfall, by a previous marriage (Nina J. Douglas). Roberta graduated from Huntington College, Huntington, Indiana, with a BSA in Business Administration and Education. Her husband, Brian K. Carnahan, holds a degree in Business Administration and Mortuary Science. They reside in Spencerville, Indiana, where they own and operate a mortuary business. They have three children: Robert, Magdalene, and Nicholas. Ronald, Roger, and Roberta attended the Liberty Township School and graduated from Southern Wells High School.

Bob and Edith retired from farming in March of 1987, and now reside in Chester Township. They are members of and hold offices in the South Liberty Christian Church. He has been a 4-H Council member, a past president and director of the Wells County DHIA, and is a Farm Bureau member. She has been a Liberty Township teacher's aide, director, and craft teacher of the Liberty Center Community Bible School and is a Wells County Extension Club Homemaker. She is presently working on family trees. They joined the Appraisal Research Corporation, Findlay, Ohio, in 1987.

WESTFALL

Ronald and Trudy (McMillan) Westfall were married July 5, 1980, at Epworth Methodist Church. Ron is a son of Robert and Edith Westfall, and Trudy is a daughter of Everett and Colleen McMillan. They reside at 2639 East Street Road 218. Ron is employed at Kitco as the quality control manager, and Trudy is employed at Wells Community Hospital as a registered nurse. They have four children: Chad and Jennifer were born to Trudy in a previous marriage to Brent Cardin, and Eric and Nathan were born to Ron from a previous marriage to Deb Branch.

WETERICK FAMILY (WUTHERICH)

John Weterick was born in Hettesville, Switzerland, in 1859, to Niklaus and Elizabeth Braun Wutherich. John married Elizabeth Jenni in 1882, in Bern, Switzerland.

The couple immigrated to the United States in 1883. John and Elizabeth were to escort a young boy to Ohio, for which service their passage to the United States was paid. They intended to settle in Ohio; however, enroute they met and became friends with a family who were coming to Indiana, and they encouraged John and Elizabeth to accompany them. After leaving their charge in Ohio with relatives, they proceeded to Indiana where they settled in the Vera Cruz area. John followed his trade as a carpenter, specializing in barn construction. Eventually, the couple acquired a small farm near Vera Cruz where they raised a family of eight children. Rose was the first born followed by Carl (who later changed his name to Charles), John, Frank, Frances, Elizabeth, Edward, and Anna.

Charles enlisted in the Navy and served four years. Upon discharge in 1910, he settled in Wolcott, Indiana, where he worked as a mechanic and later became owner of his own garage. In Wolcott, he met and married Berta McDonald in 1916. One son, Charles, was born to the union in 1917. In 1924, on a family visit to Bluffton, Charles became sick and after a lengthy illness died at the home of his sister, Rose McGill.

John and Elizabeth Jenni Weterick

Berta, along with son, Charles, and her aunt, Mrs. Carrie Clark, remained in Bluffton and eventually made it their home. Berta attended a beautician's school in Fort Wayne, and upon graduation, opened her own beauty shop in Bluffton at 107-1/2 South Main which she operated until 1971. Son Charles graduated from Bluffton High School and attended Indianapolis College of Pharmacy, graduating in 1941. In 1942, he enlisted in the Navy and served until the end of World War II, being discharged in 1945. Upon returning to Bluffton, he became associated with the Deam and Harris Drug Store. He had worked in the store for several years prior to his navy service. Eventually, he became a partner in the store with Don V. Harris. The firm was known as Harris and Weterick Drug Store. The store closed on November 18, 1972, with the building being sold to the Farmers and Merchants Bank. Charles went to work for the Hook Drug Company, retiring in 1982.

While working in the Deam and Harris Drug Store, Charles met and married Winifred Myers of Chester Township in 1945. Winifred was the store bookkeeper. Three children were born to the couple: Cheryl, Jon and Joe. Cheryl, Mrs. Jesse Combs, resides in Decatur; Jon lives in Fort Wayne; and Joe lives in Bluffton.

WETZEL

Martin Vanburen Wetzel, son of Martin M. and Elizabeth Seibert Wetzel, was born February 12, 1854, in Monroe County, Ohio. His parents soon moved to Ravenswood, Jackson County, West Virginia, where he grew to young manhood. His father served in the Union Army as an ambulance driver, pension #339545 and #326127.

The family left Virginia and settled in Wayne County, Indiana, by 1880. There Martin V. married Willia Frances Benson April 28, 1882.

Willia Frances Benson, daughter of William C. and Elizabeth Hays Benson, was born January 12, 1865, in West Virginia, probably Greenbrier County. Her father died January 22, 1865, and her mother married William A. Loudermilk in 1869. The family moved to Wayne County, Indiana, in 1877. Elizabeth Hays Benson Loudermilk died July 12, 1913, at Darke County, Ohio. She is buried in Hopewell Cemetery, Wayne County, Indiana.

Soon after their marriage, the Wetzel family moved to Chattanooga, Tennessee, where Elizabeth Seibert Wetzel died December 12, 1889. She is buried in Forest Hill Cemetery there. The family returned to Wayne County, Indiana, about 1893.

Martin M. Wetzel returned to West Virginia, where he died at Pt. Pleasant, Mason County, September 15, 1897. He is buried in Lone Oak Cemetery there.

Front left to right: Martin V. , Willia Frances Benson Wetzel. Back left to right: Harvey, James, Ethel, Inez, Nellie Marie Wetzel (children of Martin and Frances Wetzel)

After leaving his work in the oil fields, Martin V. took up carpentering until injuries received in the running away of a team forced him to give up this line of work. He then turned to lighter work around home and workshop. The family treasures the chairs, baskets and other items made with a pocket knife and loving hands.

The family arrived in Wells County around 1900 and settled at Nottingham. Seven children were born to the union: Therasia Belle, born October 21, 1884, died of burns March 9, 1900, buried Hopewell Cemetery, Wayne County, Indiana; Ethel May, born April 4, 1886, married Lunie Murle Hardwick, November 30, 1899, Wayne County, Indiana, died May 29, 1949, Wayne County, buried in Economy Cemetery; James Clarence, born November 10, 1893, married Amy _____, died April 7, 1958, Wayne County, Indiana, buried Willow Grove Cemetery; John H., born July 12, 1895, died February 3, 1896, buried Hopewell Cemetery, Wayne County, Indiana; Nellie Marie, born February 4, 1897, married Ray Penn, died of influenza October 24, 1918, in Tulsa, Oklahoma, buried Twin Hills Cemetery, Pennville, Jay County, Indiana; Harvey E., born October 3, 1898, married Elsie Koon March 25, 1918, Wells County, Indiana, then Ida Bell Bossard, died December 11, 1958, Wayne County, Indiana, buried Goshen Cemetery; Inez M., born August 20, 1902, Nottingham, Wells County, Indiana, married Martin Samuel Norton November 9, 1918, Wells County, living.

Martin and Frances left Wells County in 1920 and settled in Jackson County, Indiana, where Martin died December 17, 1927, in Redding Township.

Frances married Elmer Wilson August 8, 1931, but was separated from him when she died January 27, 1933, at Seymour, Indiana. She is buried beside Martin in Reddington Cemetery, Jackson County.

Martin's great and great-great-grandfathers, Martin and Captain John Wetzel, served in the Revolutionary War, as did Frances's great-grandfather, Levin Benson, pension #R777.

CHARLES WHITE

Charles and Isabelle Campbell White, accompanied by their children, immigrated to Philadelphia, Pennsylvania, from Glasgow, Scotland, in 1842. (A diary quotation stated: Waterloo – Philadelphia – June 21, 1842). They had been married in Gaelic Chapel in Glasgow in June, 1815. Charles was born in 1792. Isabelle's birth, 1789, was found recorded in Glasgow records.

Their children were: David (1816), Duncan (1818), Charles (1821), Daniel (1824), Agnes (1826), Margaret (1829), Isabelle (1832), and Mary (1837).

In 1849, the third son, Charles, headed west and found a Scottish settlement south of Fort Wayne. He stayed and soon married Janet Yule Ferguson (June, 1851) who was the widow of Thomas Ferguson. Janet was born in Glasgow in November 1819. She had five children: Ellen (1840), Eliza (1842), John Y. (1845), Anna (1846), and James T. (1848). Janet's parents, Robert and Helen Easton Yule, were married in Glasgow, July 1810, and had been in the Ossian area since the 1830's. They were both associated with Elhanan Presbyterian Church. (Corner of 600E 1000N; merged with the Ossian Presbyterian Church in 1926.)

Charles and Janet had six children: Alexander (1851), Duncan (1852), Isabella (1854), Andrew (1857), Charles (1859), and David (1865). They lived where Koons and Elsie Melching currently live (5850E 1000N). Charles was a farmer and church deacon.

Charles White and his wife, Mary Agnes Clark (married February, 1881), had one son, Clyde Olen (born March, 1883), who married Dora Elsie Hoopengardner in June, 1904. They had five children: Aubrey Olen (1908), Anna Kathleen (1912), Mary Adahleen (1912), Edwin (Buss) Eugene (1916), Elizabeth (Betty) Isabelle (1922).

Aubrey married Rosella Barrick Shull in 1952. Their children were: Karen Kay (1946), Cheryl Ann (1953), Larry Tim (1954), Debra Sue (1956), and Garry Lee (1957). Aubrey still farms land acquired by his great-grandfather in the 1850's.

Kathleen married George W. Auer in 1936. Their children were: Robert William (1945) and John Charles (1947). Her husband was an executive with General Electric for many years. They were living in Decatur, Indiana, at the time of her death in 1958.

Mary Adahleen married Richard J. (Jack) Barnes in 1942. Their children were: Elizabeth (Betty) L. (1942), Karen Ann (1947), and Richard C. (1951). She is a registered nurse who graduated from St. Joseph's School of Nursing in Fort Wayne. She worked in LaPorte, Indiana, and was a pediatrics nurse at Lutheran Hospital in Fort Wayne at the time of her retirement.

Edwin (Buss) married Lauretta Krauss in 1939. Their children were: Leilani Lou (1944) and Gregory Lynn (1949). He worked in the wire mill at the General Electric plant on Taylor Street in Fort Wayne for many years and also farmed. He died in 1984.

Elizabeth (Betty) married Robert Sheenan (1944). Their children were: Mary Kathleen (1946) and James Michael (1949). Robert was Missing in Action as a pilot in the Korean War. Her second marriage was to Phillip Dybbro (1954). Their children were: William (1954) and Julia (1956). Betty was a pilot in the WAC's during World War II. After living in the Seattle, Washington, area and Fairbanks, Alaska, she is now living on Vachon Island, Washington.

Several great-great-grandchildren of Charles and Janet White are now living in Wells County. Garry White is currently farming the acreage in northeastern Jefferson Township that his great-great-grandfather acquired in the 1850's. Elizabeth (Betty) Barnes Oakes teaches at Columbian Elementary School in Bluffton. Leilani White Mahnensmith is the trust officer at Ossian State Bank.

DAVID YULE WHITE

David Yule White, youngest son of Charles and Janet (Yule) Ferguson White, married on March 18, 1888, Sara Emma Kreigh, daughter of Sam and Magdalene (Beck) Kreigh. They lived on the family homestead until the first World War. They had seven children: Zain 1889, Hugh 1890, Lawson 1892, Magdalene 1895, Janet 1899, and twins, Duncan and David 1905.

Zain married Ted Michel of Fort Wayne in 1914, and had Ruth Irene, and twins, Janet and James, in 1923. Ruth married Bud Vincent and had three daughters, Melanie, Ruth Ann, and Michele, ten grandchildren, and several greats. Janet married Art Zapel and had four children, Linda Zain, Mark, Ted, and Shelly. Jim has a girl, Janet Ruth.

Hugh Yule was wounded in World War I and never married.

Lawson Yule married Velma Crowl in 1916.

Magdalene Yule married Dale Elzey in 1913. Their son, Abner, and daughter, Phyliss, have kept their ties with Ossian.

Janet Yule married Edwin Mueller in 1929. She was everyone's beloved Auntie.

Duncan Yule married Rose Poncha in 1931. Son, Duncan Jr., married Nancy White and had Douglas and Rebecca. Daughter, Sara Ann, married John Baker and had David, Sharon, and Diane.

David Yule was married to Cleta Hixon in 1928. Their four children are Fay, David, Tom, and Lawson. Fay married Len Johnson, and has four children and eight grandchildren; David and Annette (Sebree) have four daughters and six grandchildren; Tom is married to Debra Hanson. He has two children and two grandchildren. Lawson (L.D.) married Lana Pape. They have four children and one grandchild.

RUEBEN WHITE

Rueben White kept a saloon in Poneto about 1880. He died as a result of broken bones left untreated. The story is told of a barroom brawl, but that story has not been proven. Rueben had several children, among them, Josephine and others that live in or near Montpelier.

A son, Charles White, is buried at Ossian in Oaklawn Cemetery. He worked on the railroad as a young man, but he was hurt in an accident which left him crippled. He then became a teacher, doing most of his teaching in Jefferson Township in a one-room school and in the school of Toscin. The family claimed that he named the town of Toscin. He worked in Fort Wayne during World War II and died soon after.

Charles White married Bertha Judd and is buried at Oaklawn Cemetery, Ossian. (See family of Hezekiah Judd.)

Judd White as a lad became a telegrapher on the railroad and as an adult, he became a funeral director in Iowa. Ralph White lived in Lincoln, Nebraska, and was a salesman. Ruth White married a career soldier and lived in Georgia. Frank White married May Morton. Frank was a veteran of World War I. May was a piano teacher. Nelle White Hawk lives in Gaston, Indiana, where her family is engaged in large-scale farming. Janet White is married and lives in Florida. Frank married Mae Quakenbush. was a barber and she ran successful restaurants in Ossian and Yoder. Velma White died as a young oman and she is buried at Ossian by her parents and brother, Frank. Lucina White married Harry Coudret. They lived in Fort Wayne and in Sidney, Ohio. Justine Coudret is a white-collar worked in Fort Wayne. Bertha Rose Coudret married Robert Tindall and she worked for Lincoln Life in Fort Wayne.

(Charles) Garth White (1907-1960) married Mildred Stewart. Garth was a farmer in the Markle area and later near Reiffsburg. Both are buried at Ossian. Duane Arnold White married Camille Meadows and they were later divorced. He is a truck driver and lives in Fort Wayne. Duane Alan White was married to Tammy Shov (deceased and buried at Ossian). Brenda White married the Reverend Doug Rogers who has a church at Berne. They have two children, David and Angela. Kenny White married Laura George. Kenny is a truck driver and Laura works at Caylor-Nickel as a secretary. Their children are Tyler, Trent, Traydon, and Allison. Pam Whit works as a receptionist for Dr. Burry. Kevin White worked at Pizza Hut and then became a truck driver.

In 1950, Garth White married Mabel Anderson, a teacher at Petroleum who later taught at Rockcreek, Lancaster, and Norwell.

Klyda White trained as a medical technologist and went on to specialize in blood banking. She is now enrolled in medical school in California College of Osteopathic Medicine of the Pacific (COMP).

WIECKING FAMILY

Ernst Herman Frederick Wiecking was born in 1858 in Bramsche bei Osnabrueck in what was then the Kingdom of Hannover in Germany. At the age of 20, he joined his elder brother, Herman (1849-1915), in the United States, settling shortly thereafter in Bluffton. Herman lived in the Ernst Wiecking household for most of his life, although he was a great traveler. He never married. He is buried in the family plot in Elm Grove Cemetery, together with his sister, Hermine Dorothea (1844-1921), who also never married.

Ernst and Mate Wiecking with their children, Wilbur, Herman, Fred, and Hermine. (Taken about 1920.)

Ernst married Mary Frances "Mate" Studabaker in 1886; they had four children: Hermine (1888), Herman (1890), Frederick August (1892), and Wilbur Ernst (1895). In addition to a large tract of land in the south part of Bluffton, the family owned farms on the River Road and at the south end of the Hoosier Highway. Ernst and Herman Wiecking were successful merchants and cigar manufacturers in Bluffton for many years. They built the Wiecking Block on West Market Street in 1898. "Mate" Wiecking founded the Wiecking Florists in 1900; the firm was subsequently owned by her eldest son, Herman S. Wiecking. Ernst Wiecking died in 1934; his wife, Mary "Mate" Studabaker Wiecking, died in 1944.

Hermine was educated in the Bluffton schools and at Glendale College near Cincinnati. She attended Cornell University and received her BA degree from New York University and her MS degree from Butler University. She spent much of her career as a public school teacher and administrator, not only in Bluffton, but also in Ohio and West Virginia. Before retiring from full-time teaching, she was supervisor of music for the Anderson, Indiana, city school system. Following her retirement, she returned to live in the family home on West Wabash Street in Bluffton. She was active in many civic organizations until her death in 1980.

The Wiecking Cigar Factory in the early 1890's, located on the northwest corner of Market and Johnson Streets.

Hermine married Floyd D. Colson of Ashtabula, Ohio, in 1921; they were divorced in 1928. Twin children, Robert and Helen (born 1911), previously adopted by Mr. Colson and his first wife, became Hermine's wards upon the divorce.

Herman married Sarah Arnold in 1909; they had three children, Mary Catherine (Foster) (1910-1972), Herman Arnold (1911-1980), and Margaret Jean (Harper) (1915-1975). Herman was educated in the Bluffton schools and, after his marriage, took over the management of Wiecking Florists, a wholesale and retail greenhouse operation first established by his mother in 1900. He was a member of the Blue Lodge and Knights Templar of the Masonic Order. He died in 1953; Sarah Arnold Wiecking died in 1961. (See entry for Lawrence Foster Family.)

Frederick August married Marie Margaret White in 1920; they had two children: Frederick August, Jr. (1921-1963), and Charles White (1925). Fred was educated in the Bluffton schools; following graduation, he spent one year at the Noellische Handelschule in Osnabrueck, Germany, and subsequently entered Indiana University. His university career was interrupted by the First World War; he was separated as a first lieutenant at the war's end. Returning to Indiana University, he graduated from the Law School in 1919 and was admitted to the bar. He practiced law in Bluffton from 1929 until 1932, when the family moved to Hartford City and later to Indianapolis. He was appointed as First Assistant Attorney General of Indiana in 1933, later as Public Counsel to the State Public Service Commission, and finally as Judge of the Indiana Appellate Court in 1935. He was active in the Masonic Order (Scottish Rite), the Elks Lodge (of which he was Grand Esteemed Lecturing Knight) and the American Legion. He was Indiana State Commander of the American Legion in 1929. He died in 1936; his wife, Marie White Wiecking, died in 1990.

Wilbur Ernst was educated in the Bluffton public schools, spent a year at the Noellische

Handelschule in Osnabrueck, Germany, and graduated from Purdue University. He was employed for many years by the Bell Laboratories as an electrical engineer and was the holder of several patents in the communications field. He married Audrey Normo in 1923; they had three sons: William Ernst (1924-1944), Robert Wilbur (1926), and Kenneth David (1931). After the death of Audrey Normo Wiecking in 1961, he married Iantha Weinland Parrish (1902-1988). Wilbur Wiecking died in 1986.

WILEY-BERGMAN

Great-grandfather, Robert Wiley, came from Virginia to Jackson Township, Wells County, when he was thirteen. He married Sarah Jones on April 29, 1854, and moved to Liberty Township to farm and reared eleven children. My grandfather, John, was born January 21, 1855. He grew up to continue farming and was well-known as an agriculturist, using most modern methods of management in those days. He married Nancy Jane Day, daughter of Ambro and Ethelinda Mossburg Day, on March 9, 1882. Ethelinda was a granddaughter of William and Nancy Day from Halifax County, North Carolina. Ambro came to Wells County from Wilkes County, North Carolina in 1848, and was a veterinarian in Liberty Township. He and Ethelinda, the twelfth child of William and Mary Mossburg (born in 1836), were married in 1859. One of John and Nancy Wiley's six children was my father, William Everett, who was born in 1885. He became a mason and was well-known for his building skills. He built a home on grandfather's farm, north and east of Liberty Center. In 1922, he married Melissa Hutchinson, daughter of Alice and Augustus Hutchinson, from Grandview, Spencer County, Indiana. They had three children: Ermina (1923), Iona (1924), and Guy (1926). Ermina died March, 1926, and Melissa died April 22, 1926, when Guy was eleven days old. My grandparents reared him until their deaths in the early 1930's. We attended school in Liberty Center the first few years and then completed our schooling in Bluffton.

Iona married Donald Bergman, son of Christopher and Estella Pearl Bergman, on January 8, 1943. Don's grandfather, Christian Bergman, came from Hanover, Germany, in 1840, and settled in Pennsylvania. Don's parents were from Saxonburg and Mars, Pennsylvania. They moved to Wells County in 1915, and Don was born December 19, 1915. His father was a telegrapher for the Ohio Oil Company, then worked at Bracey's, and later owned a bread truck route during the 1930's. Don grew up to be a master mechanic and operated his own shop for over 45 years in Bluffton. We have four children.

Linda Kay was born July 13, 1947. She graduated from Indiana University and has taught school in the Bluffton district since 1969. She married Gene Worman in 1968. They have two sons: Jason Allan, born March 5, 1972, and Lance Adam, born March 19, 1975.

Chris William was born December 15, 1948, and graduated from ITT. He married Donna Hill on June 27, 1970. Their two daughters are Carmen Sue, born October 31, 1974, and Melissa Heather, born January 23, 1978.

Anne was born on September 18, 1953. She married John Patterson in 1974, and a son, John Christopher, was born on April 5, 1979. They divorced in 1987. Russ Minton and Anne were married July 28, 1990.

Jean was born February 12, 1958. She also is an I.U. graduate and teaches English. She married Hiroyuki Takahashi on September 25, 1982. In 1985, they moved to Osaka, Japan, where son George was born on October 7 1985, and Thomas was born on April 30, 1987.

WILHELM/LICHTENBERGER

William W. Wilhelm was born February 20, 1863, in Findlay, Ohio, and died July 23, 1918, in Warren Indiana, the son of Simon P. and Elizabeth (Minard) Wilhelm. William married Emma L. Lichtenberger on May 26, 1892, in Wells County. Emma was the daughter of John L and Mary (Blackstone) Lichtenberger, born January 16, 1871, Sharon, Pennsylvania, and died April 30, 1959, Warren, Indiana.

Left - Emma Wilhelm holding baby Mary. Right - William Wilhelm. Bottom - Harold and Raymond Wilhelm

The first child of William and Emma was Harold B., born October 31, 1894, and died January 23, 1958. Harold was a veteran of World War I, a second lieutenant with Company G, 335th Infantry Division, and is buried along with his second wife, Lutie, in Arlington National Cemetery in Washington, D.C. William and Emma then had a son, Raymond, no birthdate available, and a daughter, Mary E., born July 22, 1903, in Wells County. Mary was an organist for the United Methodist Church and the Brown Funeral Home in Warren. She died at Warren on October 11, 1973, and was buried in Fairview Cemetery in Bluffton. Their fourth child was Caroline Frances, born June 24, 1911, and died November 18, 1913, at Warren.

Mr. Wilhelm was in business with his father-in-law before taking the agency for the M and B Electric, moving to Warren about 1911.

DONALD L. AND DEVON POINDEXTER WILLEY

My family came to Bluffton in 1958. Mom was a Hunley from Dugger, Indiana. Dad was from Sandborn. Dad has six sisters, three older, three younger; he was in the middle. His father, Ivis, a funeral director, had six brothers; all but one of these men were funeral directors. I have sixteen aunts and female cousins on this side of the family and out of the sixteen, six of us are school teachers. Grandma Poindexter was a truant officer in Gary, Indiana, until age twenty-six, when she married Grandad. Her maiden name was McBride. My mother has two brothers and no sisters. Her father, my Popie, William Hunley, owned a heavy electrical equipment contracting firm. Grandma Hunley's maiden name was Small.

My parents, B. K. and Patty Poindexter, married in 1954, in Linton, Indiana. After my dad graduated at age twenty-four from Indiana University's Dental School, they came to Bluffton. "Dr. B. K." started his dental practice in the Gal-Ham Building in June, 1958. At a later date, in the early 1970's, Dad, along with John Sr. and Jack Edris purchased the old A. B. Cline home at 328 West Market for the location of their offices. Jack Edris sold his interest in the building to my father in 1988.

I was born in August of 1958. I graduated from Bluffton High School in 1976, the year of the national bicentennial. I recall the "all-community" church service held at the 4-H park in celebration of the occasion. It felt like a Victorian "day in the park", except everyone wore polyester clothing instead of cotton. It was fashionable for men at this time to wear leisure suits. How my students of today laugh to think that anyone would actually wear that kind of suit. They also think that it is hysterical that up to eighth grade, I had to wear dresses to school.

I can remember that in 1972 several of the older girls were called to the office at Central Junior High because the administration wanted to make sure their skirts weren't more than two inches above the knee. How I wish that was one of the types of memorable events occurring in schools today. How things have changed! One day, the girls of the Freshman class decided that they were going to make their own protest statement. Remember, these were the days of Viet Nam. They were all called to the office because they had worn bell-bottomed jeans. The legs of those jeans could have served as sail for the entire fifth fleet. The principal sent them home. They were considered for suspension, but after much heated controversy with their parents, it was decided that we could wear matched pant suits. It is interesting to think today what would happen if we outlawed jeans in schools or if administrators tried to dictate dress codes.

After graduating from high school, I attended Indiana University in Bloomington and earned a B.S. in Speech and English Education. I also met my husband, Don, a student there. He is originally from Elkhart, Indiana, the son of Frank and Doris Willey. Frank was a tool and die maker until his retirement in 1986. Don also graduated in 1980 from I.U.'s School of Business with a major in marketing. We were married on June 7, 1980, in Bluffton.

Our reason for coming back to Bluffton stemmed from a combination of family ties and the 1980 recession. Fortunately, Southern Wells High School was in need of a freshman English teacher. I was in need of a job. Don worked in Fort Wayne as a field manager for Hickory Farms of Northern Indiana. In 1983, we bought a local restaurant and owned that until 1988. In 1984, I finished my M.S. in education.

We have one son, Carson, who was born in November of 1985. About a year before we sold the restaurant, Don enrolled at IPFW and earned a certificate in quality control from Purdue. He works as a quality engineer for a company in Huntington. And ten years later, I'm still working at my desk here, at Southern Wells. (Devon *Poindexter Willey*)

DONALD WILLIAMS

On December 22, 1908, the first Bank of Petroleum opened. The President of that bank was my great-great-grandfather, Amos R. Williams.

Amos and his wife, Mary, were parents of nine children, one being my great-grandfather, Samuel Williams. Born on September 22, 1889, Samuel and his siblings grew up with the best advantages available to them.

My great-grandfather, Samuel, married Nettie Gertrude Montgomery. They became parents of six children, one being my grandfather, Donald Williams, who was born right here in Nottingham Township. Sam farmed and worked in the oil fields to raise his family.

Donald graduated from Petroleum in 1928. Later he served on the Advisory Board, and on the Southern Wells School Board.

He married Frances Hinshaw at Waterloo on September 6, 1936. Donald and Frances were parents of eight children. Seven of these children still reside in southern Wells County.

Helen is married to Ray Cale. They are the parents of two boys. Mark is married to Michelle Boltemeier. They are the parents of one daughter, Gabriel. Curt is Helen and Ray's second son. They also have two girls, Marilyn and Shari.

Nancy is employed by IBM and lives in Irvine, California.

Theodore Wayne is married to Lou Ann Way. They are the parents of two daughters, Julie, who is married to Brian Reusser; and Bonnie.

Thomas Dean is married to Becky Kiser. Tom has two daughters, Trudi and Tammi. Tammi is married to Steve Miller; they are the parents of one son, Nathaniel, and two daughters, Nichole and Taryn. Becky has one son, Andy, and one daughter, Karry.

Carolyn Joan is married to Galen Gray, and they are the parents of Dawn and Gay Lynn.

Rebecca, my mother, is married to Barry Penrod. I have one brother, Brad, who helps my father and grandfather farm.

Michael is married to Renata Ruble, and they are the parents of Travis and Joshua.

Amos, Samuel, and Donald, all moved to Petroleum in their later years. Donald and Frances moved to Petroleum in October 1978.

On October 27, 1988, Frances passed away. (*Beth Penrod*)

JOHN WILLIAMS FAMILY

John Washington and Henrietta Jones Williams moved to Wells County in the mid-1800's. Their children were Zella Goodspeed, Dorothy Swigert, Zehra Helms, Martha Barrington, Jane Goodwin, Emma, Everet (Cricket), Hugh, Sam, Edward, and John.

John (1889-1969) and Margaret Reaser (1888-1974) Williams were married in 1911. They had five children, one of whom is my father, Clarence. The other children are Wendell of El Paso, Texas; Joseph of rural Bluffton; Vivian Ecker (deceased); and Norma Miller of New Berne, North Carolina.

John W. and Margaret Williams - 1950

The John and Margaret Williams family lived on present day State Road 218 in Poneto across from the Norris Feed Mill. In the late 1920's, Margaret inherited a farm in Harrison Township. They lived there until their deaths. The Joseph Williams family still lives there. Clarence and Mary Williams built a home on a section of the farm in 1968. They still reside there.

Joseph Williams married Velma Ludington on November 3, 1945. Velma is a daughter of Eber and Bertha Diptman Ludington. They had two sons: Joseph, born November 16, 1952; and John, born August 26, 1955. Joseph and John reside in Harrison Township with their parents. Joseph Williams, Junior, has two daughters, Lisa (October 23, 1978), and Laura (October 23, 1982), who reside in the Valparaiso, Indiana, area with their mother.

Clarence married Mary Geraldine Grosjean December 19, 1948. Mary is a daughter of Victor Grosjean (11/16/1884 - 01/12/1972) and Elizabeth Edington (11/21/1888 - 12/06/1971). Victor came to Wells County from Switzerland around 1905.

Elizabeth's mother, May Gazille Porter (May 21, 1858 - January 12, 1931), moved to Bluffton from Ohio, when she was 19. Four years later, in 1881, she married Enestes Edington. They had five children: Elizabeth, Jennie Matson, Gladys Nicholas, Theodore, and David. David was a World War I veteran.

Clarence and Mary Williams had their first child, Judith Ann, on November 19, 1949. Three years later, Alan Stanley was born on November 13, 1952. Both were born at the Wells County Hospital. Clarence and Mary are life-long residents of Harrison Township.

Judith married Robert Maxwell on June 5, 1971. Robert's mother, Juanita, resided for a few years in Bluffton prior to her death. Robert and Judith have two children: Ryan Robert, born February 10, 1978, and Joshua Adam, born august 30, 1982. The Maxwells reside in Bluffton.

Alan Williams married Mara Jo Couch of Jackson Township, Wells County, on December 18, 1976. Mara Jo is the daughter of Paul and Ethel (Harrold) Couch. They had two children: David Alan, born April 12, 1980, and Rebecca Jo, born January 27, 1983. Alan and his family reside in southern Harrison Township.

ROBERT F. WILLIAMS FAMILY

Born on September 7, 1932, on a farm near Mount Summit, Indiana, Robert Franklin Williams was the youngest of three children and the only son of Walter and Lucy (Waters) Williams. While attending Indiana State Teachers College in Terre Haute, Indiana, Bob met Janice Lee Dinkel. Janice, born October 13, 1932, was the youngest of four daughters born to Herbert Klein and Bettie (Vice) Dinkel. Upon graduation from college, Bob and Janice were married on June 13, 1954.

Back (left to right) Christopher, Betsy, and Brian Front: Janice and Bob Williams

They moved to New Castle, Indiana, where both taught elementary school. On June 9, 1956, their first son, Jeffrey Dinkel, was born. In 1957, the family moved to Fort Wayne, Indiana, where Bob taught. On April 20, 1959, their second son, Brian Douglas, was born. That same year, Bob received his master's degree from Ball State University.

Bob assumed his first principalship at Deacon, Indiana, in Cass County in 1964, and the family moved to Logansport. Tragedy struck the family on June 21, 1965, when Jeffrey died of leukemia.

In 1966, Bob was appointed principal of three Wells County schools - Liberty Center, Petroleum, and Jackson - and the family moved to a home east of Liberty Center. Janice taught Kindergarten half days at Liberty Center and half days at Petroleum. Janice received her master's degree from Indiana State University in 1967.

Christopher Robertson, born October 15, 1967, joined the family through adoption when he was five days old. To make the family complete, Elizabeth Anne (Betsy), born June 25, 1969, was adopted into the family when she was three days old.

Bob became principal of the new Southern Wells Elementary School when it was constructed in 1973. Janice taught Kindergarten there until 1987, when she initiated the Gifted and Talented program for the school system.

In 1977, the family built a home in a wooded area northwest of Liberty Center. The family were all members of the Liberty Center United Methodist Church where both Bob and Janice were Sunday School teachers. Bob was also active in the Liberty Center Lions Club.

All three of the Williams children graduated from Southern Wells High School. Brian graduated from Ball State University in 1981, and from Notre Dame University Law School in 1984. Christopher served in the United States Air Force from 1986 to 1988. Elizabeth graduated from Ball State University in 1991.

ROSE WILLIAMS

Rose Marie (Osborn) Williams was born at 0584E 900N in 1942, to John and Leita Osborn, and went to Union Center School, where she graduated in 1960. She never liked school, and on the first day, told the family "Okay, I'll go one week, but then quit." Leita told her she could not do that. So she said, "I'll go two weeks and then graduate." That story stuck with her for life, along with another one: Rose was angry with Lillian, grabbed a framed wall picture that said "In God We Trust", and hit her over the head. The glass broke, and it hung on the wall that way for years. After high school, Rose worked in factories and was laid off after fourteen years with Corning Glass Works when they closed the plant. She currently works at the Bluffton Rubber Plant on West Lancaster Street. Rose married Glen Williams in 1964, son of Hobart and Pauline Williams, Bluffton. They divorced in 1970, and she raised the boys by herself: Glen Eugene (1964), David Logan (1965), and Gerald Wayne (1968). Christopher Allen (1970) was adopted at birth by Jim and Barb Betz, Rose's sister-in-law. He grew up in Bluffton. Barb was divorced later, and remarried Dale Kyle, who adopted Chris. Chris attended Bluffton High School and works as a security guard. Rose and Glenn lived in Ossian, Bluffton, and Dayton, Ohio, before she settled with the boys in Bluffton. David and Gerald were in PAL Club (Police Athletic League) and played Little

League. Gene graduated from Poplar Grove Learning Center in 1986, and lives at home. David attended Bluffton High School then worked at a refinery, Bluffton Rubber Company, and Sterling Casting. He married Teresa Marie (Purvis) in 1985, and has three children: Jeremy James (1983), Jessica Rene (1986), and Jacklyn Kay (1988). Gerald also attended Bluffton High School, then worked at the Bluffton Clinic Hospital before switching to the Bluffton Rubber Company in 1984. He married Lisa (Kemp), in 1988, daughter of Kenneth and Nancy Kemp, Warren, and has a daughter: Kristen Marie (1990). They all live in Bluffton, and Rose and Gene reside at 720 South Morgan. (Refer to Levi Osborn for previous ancestry.)

WILLIAMSON

I have been living in a retirement home in Evanston, Illinois, for the past eleven years and have no access to past family records, therefore, have to rely only on what my memories bring to mind.

My father was Edward Bruce Williamson, the son of Lent A. Williamson and Dorothea Kellerman. Lent and Dorothea lived in Villa North and raised a family of four – namely Bruce, Dwight, Ethel, and Paul. Bruce and Dwight spent all of their lives in Bluffton. Ethel married Earl Merriman and moved to Indianapolis. They had one daughter, Dorothy Hoagland, who now lives in Florida. Paul married and had four children and lived in Albuquerque. Bruce married Anna Tribolet and they adopted three girls – namely myself, then Mary and then Jane. The latter two are deceased.

Bruce was president of the Wells County Bank and was a well-known entomologist and botanist. He hybridized some of the finest iris in the world, for which he received four Dykes medals. It all started as a hobby, but later became The Longfield Iris Farm. His other hobby was collecting dragonflies. He became affiliated with the University of Michigan and made four trips to South America collecting. At his death, he left this collection to the University, where it remains on display.

Mary carried on with the iris business for several years after our father died. Then she sold out and turned to teaching biology and Spanish at Adams Central High School. She was also interested in and worked for the Museum. She died in 1987. Jane was in poor health and died in 1966, leaving two children.

Our mother, Anna, was the daugther of John Wesley Tribolet and Mary Bayha. They lived all of their lives in Bluffton and had six children.

I attended Indiana University, where I met and married Leland Thomas. We had three children, all of whom are living and who have given me eleven grandchildren and nineteen great-grandchildren.

WILLIAMSON-FRIAR

Myron Ora Williamson (1859-1935) was the son of Benjamin F. and Sarah (Layton) Williamson. Myron married in 1890 to Emma (Carnes) Williamson (1864-1896). They lived one and one-half mile south of Mount Zion in Wells County. They had three children, Erman (1891-1941), Nova (1894-1894), and Mearl (1895-1939). Mearl never married, and was in World War I. Erman graduated from Indiana Veterinarian College in 1915, and married Ethel Wood in 1915. He had a veterinarian office in the basement of their home, which was the Jonathan Lowry homeplace. Jonathan was Ethel's grandfather. They had three children, Myron, Jane, Richard. Myron (1916-1985) also was a veterinarian, married and had one daughter, Cindy. He divorced. Cindy had two daughters and lives in Florida.

Ora and Emma Carnes Williamson

Richard (1919-1980), also a veterinarian, married Virginia Goodspeed. They moved to Shenandoah, Iowa. They had four children: Karen, Steven, Sandy, and Dennis. Karen married and had two sons and one daughter, and now lives in Kansas City. Steve married and had a daughter and a son. Steve lives in Shenandoah, Iowa. Sandy married and had a son and a daughter, and lives in Kansas City. Dennis married and had two sons and he lives in Durango, Colorado.

Jane (Williamson) Friar married Olin Friar in 1936, and had three children: Suzanne, Jeffery, and Cheryl. Jane divorced and married John Nestleroad and had a son, Charles Nestleroad. Jane's family history is in the Lowry-Friar section.

WILSON

In 1916, John Alva Wilson (born 1897, died 1943) married Sylvia Jane (Rigby) Wilson (born 1895, died 1964). John was a product of the Wilson-Platt families and Sylvia a product of the Rigby-Miles families.

In 1922, Ronald Keith Wilson was born to this union and Dwight Eugene Wilson was born in 1926. Both boys attended the Poling School in Jay County.

In 1933, the family moved to an eighty-acre farm in Nottingham Township near Domestic in Wells County. The farm life included farming with horses, and their livestock included milking cows, chickens, sheep, and hogs.

Left to right: Dwight W. Wilson, Doris Ann (Miller) Wilson - Date: 1956

As the boys grew, they attended the Petroleum School. Ronald became an outstanding softball pitcher and graduated as 1939 class president and salutorian. Dwight also pitched softball, played basketball and also was class president and salutorian of his 1944 class. Both boys entered the service in World War II. Ronald emerged as captain in the Air Corps and Dwight as a sergeant in the Army Engineers.

Ronald graduated from Indiana University and spent most of his working career with Armstrong Cork Company. On his retirement, he was plant manager at their home plant in Lancaster, Pennsylvania. He now lives in retirement in Dunedin, Florida, with his wife, the former Bette Frailey of Lancaster, Pennsylvania. They have three children in California, Pennsylvania, and Georgia.

Dwight married the former Doris Ann Miller of Bluffton and spent most of his working career as manager with Franklin Electric Company of Bluffton. He is now retired and living in Bluffton. Son Stanley Kent Wilson lives in Indianapolis with his wife, Darla Lamberty Wilson, and children, Melanie and Diana. Daughter, Valerie Kaye Jackson, now lives in Ossian.

CHARLES WILSON FAMILY

My name is Charles J. ("Chick") Wilson. I was born at New Hebron, Illinois, on January 5, 1917. My parents were Orel and Ida Wilson. Orel Wilson was born on January 21, 1882. Ida Wilson was born on January 22, 1882. My brother, Harry F. Wilson, was born on October 10, 1901.

Mr. and Mrs. Charles J. Wilson

My father was born at Nottingham and carried the U.S. mail horseback from Nottingham to Geneva at 16 years of age. My mother was born at New Straitsville, Ohio.

After returning from the oil fields of Illinois, we rented the Dr. F. M. Reynolds Farm No. 2, one and one-half miles east of Keystone, which was 160 acres. My dad, brother, and I farmed that acreage with four sorrel mules until more modern equipment was available.

I graduated from Chester Center High School in 1935. I strung pianos at the Estey Piano Company in Bluffton during 1938-39. I entered the U.S. Air Force and attended Aeronautical University, Chicago, and the Packard Rolls-Royce Engine School in Detroit. After 30 and one-half years I retired from Franklin Electric where I had worked as a maintenance electrician.

My wife is Elois (Brewster) Wilson and is also a Franklin Electric retiree. I have a daughter, Victoria Mae Jenkins, who resides in Fort Wayne. *Submitted by Charles J. Wilson*

WILSON-HATFIELD

Sarah Haswell, born in Ohio on March 12, 1843, was my great grandmother. On May 25, 1861, in Dekalb County, Indiana, she married William Van Wormer. He was born July 10, 1840, in Pennsylvania. He was a farmer by choice, served in the Civil War with the 100th Infantry (IN). He died in 1920. She died in 1931. My grandmother, Janette Van Wormer, was born July 16, 1874, in Dekalb County, Indiana. She married James Sylvester Wilson, born December 22, 1863, on May 29, 1890. They were farmers. They had eight children: Altha, Bessie, Charles, Della, Edith, Cleo, Ida, Helen, and Eldon. He died in 1927; she died in 1960.

Charles Wilson Family
Back row: (L to R) Dick, Bob, Everett, Max, Phillip, Agnes: Center: Phyllis, Betty, Nancy. Front: Magdalene, Margaret, Charles, Janet

My father, Charles A. Wilson, was born (south west of Zanesville) on September 14, 1894. He married Margaret Ruth Hatfield (born October 3, 1918) on November 20, 1915.

My grandfather (on my mother's side), born in 1867, was Robert Lowery Hatfield. He married Mary Sarah Miliken (born in 1875). His father was John Hatfield; his mother was Ann Harter. Her father was James Miliken; her mother was Susan Dafforn. My grandfather was a carpenter and farmer, and especially liked working with fruit trees. My grandmother was a homemaker. She died in 1935, and he died in 1953.

My father (Charles) was primarily a farmer. The place he called home for nearly 63 years is located three-and-a-half miles north of Uniondale. The farm was called Butter Milk Ridge. To support his growing family, he farmed, did carpenter work, and also ran a portable seed cleaner that he took from farm to farm throughout Wells County, cleaning and treating seed for planting. My mother was a homemaker; working very hard as a farmer's wife, she still found time to play the piano. She loved to quilt, crochet, and knit, and she made many beautiful things through the years. In her spare time she cared for twin boys and nine other children.

Janet married John R. Cooper. She graduated from Lutheran Hospital as an R.N. and in 1953 opened the first nursing home (Cooper Rest Home) in Wells County. They have three children: Dan, Susan and Bonnie, and live near Bluffton.

Magdalene married Wendell Crum. She worked in an office as a receptionist. They had three boys, Ben, Tim, and Ted and live in Uniondale.

A twin, Robert, married Laurel Falk. He retired (after 33 years) from Kresge Ware House (K Mart). They have six children: Bruce, Deborah, Stacey, Jim, Steve and Roger. Robert lives in Uniondale.

Richard, twin of Robert, helped farm and lived his later years at the Soldier's Home at Lafayette. He died September 5, 1990.

Betty Blew was a hair dresser. She owned and operated her own shop. She died in July, 1984. She had five children: Judy, Donna, Gary, Mike, and Gwyndolyn.

Everett married Faye Folk. He farmed, worked at Baer Field, and the Wilbert Vault Plant, and also for the town of Markle; currently he is in partnership with his sons at Wilson Burial Vault.

We have three children: Greg, Gaylene, and Garland, and live in Markle.

Max married Babe Eichhorn. He graduated from Palmer Chiropractic College with a degree of Doctor of Chiropractic (D.C.). He lives in New Mexico, where he has his own practice. He has four children: Jon, Jake, Jennie and Jeff, all living in New Mexico.

Phyllis married Harley Confer. She graduated from Palmer Chiropractic College with a degree of Doctor of Chiropractic (D.C.). She has her own practice (Wilson-Confer Chiropractic Center). She has four children: Peter, Matt, Margaret and Sarah, and lives north of Uniondale.

Agnes married Robert Baker. She graduated from Huntington College with a degree in teaching. She left teaching to open her own businesses, The Bobbin, which serves all sewing needs, including sewing machines, and a clothing store, The Brass Giraffe. They have two daughters, Pamela and Linda, and live in Huntington.

Phillip had five children: Cindy, David, Tammy, Terri, Tonya, and Todd, and lives in Florida, working in the neon sign business.

Nancy married Gerald Johnson. She works for the Norwell school system. They have seven children: Scott, Lani, Rick, Lori, Deana, Darrin, and Deidra, and live in Ossian.

Our father died November 18, 1964. My mother felt the house was too big for one person and moved into a mobile home after selling the farm. After nearly 19 years, she was unable to stay alone. In 1983 she went into a nursing home. She has been there eight years and will be 93 on October 3, 1991. *(Everett Wilson)*

JOHN AND MARY WILSON

John Wilson was the youngest son of Gibson and Nancy Ann Harris. He was born in 1852, just one year after the family came to Indiana and purchased their farm from the United States government. John married a neighbor girl, Mary Eliza Housel.

They agreed that he would name the daughters and she would name the sons. The first child born was Charley Absolm Housel. He was the "apple of his parents' eye", but at age three months, he became ill and died. The parents were heart-broken. A year and a half later, Mary Alice was born. John named her for his wife and his grandmother, Alice Harris.

It would be a long time before John would name another child. Next was a son, Truesal Cyrus, followed by Cloyd. Another son was born, Victor James. The fourth son was Enos Church. Next was Raymond, who only lived two or three days. Then Arlo Clark was born. The last of the children was another girl, Harriet Jane.

John and Mary lived on the home place and cared for his mother until her death. The family had been living in a log cabin. John and Mary decided to build a house for the family. Grandmother wanted the house built her way, but in the end, John and Mary were able to have the windows and things they wanted.

John and Mary were Methodists and active in the Methodist Church, but John's mother was Presbyterian. She attended her church and the rest of the family attended theirs. John and Mary are buried in Oaklawn Cemetery, Ossian. *(Harriet Wilson Redding)*

RALPH AND JOYLE WILSON

Ralph and Joyle Wilson live on a farm at the west edge of Ossian. Ralph is the youngest of six children of Victor and Fannie Higley Wilson. Joyle is the youngest child of Grover and Vesta Sands Denney. Both Ralph and Joyle are life-long residents of Wells County.

Ralph and Joye purchased their farm from Ralph's mother several years after the death of his father. The farm was originally bought by Gibson and Nancy Ann Harris Wilson from the United States government in 1851. They came to Indiana from Trumbull County, Ohio. Two years ago, Ralph and Joyle sold the farm buildings and built a modular home and pole building on the farm. The new house gives them more room for their ever-growing family.

Ralph and Joyle raised three children: Sunya Sue, Larry Lionel and Denney Ralph. Denney passed away on January 21, 1987.

Sunya married Gerald Lee Sipe. They live near Decatur and had three children: Randall Wayne, Marcia, who was stillborn, and Jani Lynn. Gerald is employed by Dolco Packaging, Decatur, and Sue is employed by Lakeside Manor, Decatur.

Randy married Teresa Sudduth. They live in Decatur and are the parents of three sons. Jered is in junior high. Randy Joe and Andrew are in grade school. Randy is employed by Mullinix, Fort Wayne, and Teri is a full-time homemaker. They also serve as foster parents.

Jani married Tony Mann. They live in Bluffton and are the parents of a son, Steven James, and a daughter, Ashley Lyn. Tony is employed by Pretzels, Inc., Bluffton, and Jani is employed by Lincoln National Bank, Fort Wayne.

Larry married Norma Jean Bailey. They live near Decatur. Their two children are Mark Regan and Melissa Kay. They own and operate Wilson's Furniture Clinic, Decatur. Mark is single, lives in Decatur, and is employed by the family business. Melissa married Thomas Rorick. They live near Decatur with their daughter, Katrina. She is an elementary student in Decatur. Tom is employed by Rorick Electric, Decatur. Melissa is employed by both the Furniture Clinic and Rorick Electric.

Denney married Constance Hilsmier. They had three daughters. Diana Dee is married to Tim Osterhouse. They live in Fort Wayne, where Diana is employed by a food distributor and Tim is employed by Bowmar. Lori Ann is married to Mark Nevil. Lori is a photographer for Watters Studio, Fort Wayne, and Mark is the choral director and assistant band director at West Noble High School. They live in Churubusco. Stephanie Lyn is a student at Indiana University, Bloomington. She is engaged to Brent Hiday of rural Bluffton.

Ralph and Joyle celebrated their fiftieth wedding anniversary in 1990. They are retired, active in the Living Faith Missionary Church near Ossian, and enjoy fishing, gardening, and visiting with their children, grandchildren and great-grandchildren.

CHANCY WILSON

Chancy Wilson was born June 6, 1889, in Lancaster Township, Wells County, Indiana, the sixth child of eight children of James Woodward Wilson and Lydia Belle (Fleming) Wilson. James Woodward Wilson was born August 31, 1846 in Trumble County, Ohio, son of Gibson Wilson and Nancy Ann (Harris) Wilson, and died March 30, 1921. Lydia Bell (Fleming) Wilson was born November 8, 1851 in Wells County, Indiana, daughter of Aaron Fleming and Sarah Belle (Kirkpatrick) Fleming, and died December 28, 1937.

Chancy's parents lived on a 120 acre farm in Lancaster Township in Wells County, where he was born and grew up. He went to Fort Wayne, where he worked for Vesey Florists. On August 28, 1912, he married Pearl Ruby, the second daughter of Valentine Ruby and Mary (Heckley) (Ruby) Shoe. While he was working at the greenhouse the 1913 flood occurred, flooding the greenhouse. He and others went into the greenhouse in row boats trying to save the plants.

In 1914 their daughter, Mary Belle, was born. In 1915 they moved to Ashtabula County, Ohio, for a couple of years or so, then came back to Wells County to his parents' farm. His parents had moved to Ossian by this time.

Chancy and Pearl Wilson

In 1919 their second daughter, Ruby, was born. They farmed for several years until the early 1930's when he became manager of the Farm Bureau grocery store and creamery, located on East Market Street in Bluffton, Indiana.

In early 1932 he moved with his family to 515 W. Cherry Street in Bluffton and took over the Cloverleaf Creamery, buying cream from farmers in the surrounding area and shipping it to Decatur, where they made butter and other creamery products for the markets.

In 1934 he entered politics and ran for Clerk of the Wells Circuit Court and was elected. He served as clerk through two terms. After leaving the clerk's office he served as Deputy Auditor for three years.

He later worked in the insurance office of Frank Thompson and later in the Lockwood Insurance office. After that he went to work as shipping clerk for the Morris Five and Ten Cent Store. After a few years there he went to work for the Bluffton Auto Supply Company selling parts.

About 1962 he went back into politics and served for twelve years as Harrison Township Assessor, after which he retired at the age of 85.

During his life in Bluffton he attended the First United Methodist Church. He belonged to the Bluffton Kiwanis Club and in 1946 was elected its president. He was also a member of the Bluffton Elks Club and served as Exalted Ruler. He was president of infantile paralysis drives, president of the T.B. Association and active in the Crippled Children's Organization. He died February 10, 1978, and his wife, Pearl, died July 1, 1978.

VICTOR AND FANNY WILSON

Victor James Wilson was the third son of John and Mary Housel Wilson. He was a fun-loving boy, but he had a serious side. He loved children, even as a young person, and spoiled his youngest sister, Harriet. When he began courting Fanny Higley, Harriet was a little jealous. One evening, after Fanny left, Harriet could not find her favorite doll. At Christmas, the doll reappeared in a beautiful new outfit made by Fanny. From that time on, Harriet thought Fanny was all right.

Victor married Fanny. She was the daughter of Martha Hause and Edward Higley. They were the parents of six children. The oldest son, John, died in infancy. Mary, the oldest daughter, lived in the Chicago area all of her adult life. She had two sons, Alvin Collins and Lenard Hermer. Thelma married Harry Johnson. They live in Muskegon, Michigan, and have a daughter, Joretta Graves. Clara married Robert Sowards. Their children were Larry LeRoy, who died when he was 13 and Beverly Stuck. Paul married Mary Armstrong. They live in Ninnekah, Oklahoma, and have two children, Stanley and Paula Richards. Ralph married Joyle Denney. They live in Ossian and had three children, Sunya Sipe, Larry, and Denney. Denney passed away on January 21, 1987.

Victor and Fanny lived on the home place at the west edge of Ossian. They were active members of the Ossian Methodist Church. Both are buried in the Oaklawn Cemetery, Ossian.

WITWER

Dianne and George Witwer were married in Wells County on September 10, 1988. The service was held at St. Joseph's Catholic Church and the reception was held at the lodge by the lake in the Ouabache State Park. They are expecting their first child three years after their wedding anniversary.

George came to Wells County from Noble County in May, 1986. At that time, he and Jim Barbieri purchased the News-Banner. Born April 13, 1959, George grew up in a newspaper family with three older sisters in Kendallville. He graduated from East Noble High School in 1977, and Amherst College in 1981 with a Bachelor of Arts degree with a double major in philosophy and economics. He graduated from the University of Chicago in 1984, with a Master's Degree in Business Administration.

Dianne and George Witwer

Diane was born in Norton County, Kansas, on July 26, 1960. One of 11 children, she grew up on a wheat farm. She graduated from Lenora High School in 1978, and Benedictine College in 1982 with a math major. She graduated with George from the University of Chicago Graduate School of Business in 1984.

Both Dianne and George took jobs at Proctor and Gamble Company, in Cincinnati, in Brand Management. There they started dating. George coaxed Dianne to move to Bluffton in the summer of 1987, and proposed to her December 19 of that year. Dianne became Marketing Director of Caylor-Nickel Medical Center and became the first female member of the Bluffton Rotary Club. In 1991, she was promoted to Senior Director for Business Development.

George's family came to Indiana in the early 1880's. The founder of the Studebaker Automobile Company, J.M. Studebaker, had several children, including a daughter who married a Witwer. This couple gave birth to George Witwer, who became involved in the management of the Studebaker Company in South Bend. His son was George Mohler Studebaker Witwer, and his grandson is George Osburn Witwer. Mohler Witwer went into the insurance business. His son, who loved to write, bought the Kendallville News-Sun newspaper.

The original Witwers came to Indiana from Pennsylvania. They settled there in the 1720's. They came from around Switzerland as farmers.

Dianne's maiden name is Hickert. Her family has farmed in Kansas for several generation. Her mother's name is Beautrice and her father's name is Barney.

WITZEMAN

My grandparents, Mathias and Christina Witzeman, left Germany in the mid 1800's and settled in Newville, Indiana (now called Vera Cruz), east of Bluffton. Mathias, a furniture maker, also made coffins for McBride's and Thoma's mortuaries. Christina made the shrouds for the coffins. In the summer grandad worked outdoors on the coffins and we grandchildren played hide and seek in them.

My grandparents had four children: William, Adolph, Mary, and Emma. Will never married. Mary married Levi Beeler from Fort Wayne; they had three children: Eldon, Gladys, and Lillian. Emma married Harry Studebaker; they had no children.

1939
Howard and Opal Witzeman, Robert, age 10, Elizabeth, age 7

Adolph, my father, married Emma Meyers, from Berne, Indiana. The Meyers were cheese makers. Adolph was a harness maker. My parents moved to Bluffton from Fort Wayne in 1904 and my father worked for Meyers and Klopfenstine - dealers in buggies and harnesses. When tractors replaced draft horses, Adolph finished his working years as a spot welder for Houser Engineering; they manufactured auto accessories.

My parents had three children: Howard, Lulu, and Harold. Lulu married Willard Miller; they had one son, Willard, Jr. After their divorce, Lulu married Nile Vore. Harold married Josephine Beeler; they farmed east of Bluffton on the River Road. They had three children: Joan, Raymond, and Dorothy.

Howard married Opal Johnson, daughter of Roscoe and Mattie Summers Johnson. Opal worked at the glove factory on East Washington Street before she had children. They had two children, Robert and Elizabeth. Robert, a senior at Eden Theological Seminary, died of acute leukemia in 1953. Elizabeth graduated from Ball State in 1953 and is a Speech/Language Clinician in Rochester, Minnesota. Opal died of a stroke in 1970. Since

1974 Howard has lived with his daughter in Minnesota.

For sixty years Howard worked for family-owned businesses in Bluffton. He quit high school in 1910 to work at Stogdill and Dettinger's grocery. There he operated a steam engine peanut roaster and popcorn popper in front of the grocery and met farmers who came in their horse-drawn buggies with produce of butter and eggs to trade for groceries.

Howard served in World War I. After the armistice he came back to Bluffton and worked as a mechanic for Otis Schaefer's first Ford Agency in town and later for Fritz Electric Company. He worked for Fred Humphrey's Midland Oil Company in a small room on East Washington Street back of the Bliss Hotel, where he pumped gas and drove a tank wagon delivering gas to farmers. He worked for Lib Costello at the Parlor City Creamery on North Marion Street back of Herman Ulmer's grocery and at Cline's Lumbar Company. When the gymnasium was built on the high school on Jersey Street, he was a janitor there. His last job was a janitor at Harold Bowman's Bowling Center. At the age of 75 he retired. He has wonderful memories of many good friends in Bluffton and Wells County. *(Howard Witzeman)*

WOHLFORD

Max Vernon and Wanda Lee (Shideler) Wohlford moved to Wells County in March of 1978, natives of Huntington County, Roanoke, Indiana, residing at 2591 W. Rock Hill LN, Zanesville, Indiana. Their marriage took place in Roanoke, Indiana, Huntington County, on August 3, 1958.

Max Vernon Wohlford was born July 29, 1935, in Huntington County, the son of Walter Vernon and Grace Louise (Christ) Wohlford, Roanoke, Indiana.

Wanda Lee (Shideler) Wohlford was born November 1, 1935, in Huntington County, the daughter of Daniel Ernest and Opal Malissa (Ruble) Shideler, Roanoke, Indiana.

One daughter of this marriage, Lanette Louise (Wohlford) Wedding was born May 30, 1964, in Allen County, Fort Wayne, Indiana, and married Brian Wayne Wedding on October 29, 1988, son of Robert Edward and Carolyn Ann Wedding, Bluffton, Indiana, Wells County. One daughter of this marriage, Briana Louise Wedding, was born August 31, 1990, Wells County, Bluffton, Indiana. Malissa Rene (Wohlford) Pettit was born April 1, 1968, in Champaign County, Champaign, Illinois and married Robert Gayle Pettit V on May 25, 1991, son of Robert Gayle IV and Deana Pettit, of Utica, Kentucky.

WOLF

Andrew Wolf came to the United States from Germany in 1764 and married Eva Crebs five years later. They birthed eight children in Pennsylvania before moving to Ohio. Their oldest child, Christopher, married Rhoda Dorr and had ten children. Christopher's oldest child, William married Mary Matheny and had eleven children of their own. Large families were common for the Wolf families in the southeastern counties of Ohio.

Charles Campbell Wolf was the third child of William. He became important to Wells County history because three of his children settled here. He married Emily Patton and also had ten children. Charles' two older brothers fathered 18 children between them. It must have become clear to Charles C.'s children that Hockling and Athens Counties of Ohio were getting full of Wolfs because three sons chose to move westward. Issac Carthage, Samuel M., and Charles Albert Wolf all moved to Lancaster Township where they purchased and settled on adjoining land east of Tocsin.

Robert Nyle Wolf, Charles Albert Wolf, William Winfield Wolf, Rose Trullender Wolf, Albert Raymond Wolf, (baby) Minnie Maria Wolf

Decendants remain in Wells County from these men. Samuel had a large family while Issac married Zelda Essex and had only one child, Blanche Olive, who married Reuben Kunkle. Their Wolf decendants began to carry the Kunkle name.

Charles ("Hick") Albert Wolf married Rosetta Trullender, a native of Pugney in Wells County. Her parents were Rueben and Mary Trullender. Hick's family was of average size. Their first child, Mary Emily, died young while the next child, William Winfield, moved to Philadelphia serving on that city's police force. He had no children.

Robert Nyle Wolf, the third child was a 1913 graduate from Tocsin High School in a graduating class of four. He co-owned and operated a grocery in Craigville with Amos Hetrick sometime in the 1920's. Bob also worked for Standard Oil delivering fuel and oils to the Craigville community. He escaped serious injury when his truck was struck by a train at a Craigville crossing. At his death he was employed by the State Highway Department. Bob married Craigville native Tracy (Tracey) LaVera Hetrick in Boston, Massachusetts, where Bob was stationed in the military in World War I. Tracy was a graduate of Craigville High School in the 1916 graduating class of nine students. Their first child was Dorothy Louise who married Harold Daugherty (identified in another family sketch in this publication). Evelyn Lucile married Vernon Reed, while last child, Patricia Joan married Charles "Ted" Emenhiser.

Albert Raymond, fourth child of "Hick", married Nettle Strohm in 1919. Both presently reside at a Bluffton nursing home. Mrs. Homer (Wilda Mae) Dailey of rural Craigville and Mrs. Thurman (Marjorie Jean) Haggerty of Decatur were their children. Ray was a well known and long time employee of Tocsin Lumber and Grain Company.

Roy Thompson married Minnie Maria, the youngest of "Hick's" children. They had three boys: Charles R., David E., and Carl D.

Although many decendants of Charles Albert Wolf still reside in Wells County, this Wolf family named ended with "Bob" and "Ray". His sons fathered no male children.

WOOD-NICHOLAS

Robert H. Wood and Ethel J. Nicholas were married in 1931.

Their home was in Monroe County, West

Robert and Ethel Wood

Virginia until 1942, when they moved to Liberty Center. They resided there until moving to their present home in Poneto.

Children: Robert H. Wood, Jr., Willie L. Wood, Juanita J. Ivins and Judy A. Haver.

ROBERT AND ELEANOR WOOD

Wood, Robert H. Jr./Morris, Eleanor J.

(L to R) Lynnette and Steve Rohring, Matthew and Kelly, Robert Jr. and Eleanor Wood, Cheryl and Timothy Harigan, Kerri and Kelsey, Carla Wood

Married: April 19, 1953, Liberty Center Baptist Church. Children: Lynnette M. Rohring, January 3, 1955; Cheryl A. Hartigan, April 25, 1957; Yale Robert; born June 16, 1965, died June 19, 1965; Carla J. Wood, July 17, 1967. Parents: Robert H. and Ethel Nicholas Wood and James D. and Nettie Giltner Morris of Bureau County, Illinois.

WOODS-YOUNG

The Myron Wayne Woods family first became a part of Wells County history in October, 1956, when he and his wife Mary Elizabeth purchased the locker plant in Zanesville. They devoted many hours to their locker business, for almost thirty years serving many folks in Wells County as well as Allen and Huntington Counties. Myron, Mary, and family also raised mink for 15 years and were one of the few mink ranchers from the midwest who sold to the Hudson Bay Company.

Myron was born August 12, 1918, in Yoder, Indiana, to Erma Cleveland and Nora Beatrice McDowell Woods. Mary was born September 10, 1921, in Roanoke, Indiana to Russell Allen and Wilda Irene Koch Young. Myron and Mary have three children, Reida Kathleen, born January 7, 1942; R. Lynn, born March 21, 1947; and Douglas Dayton, born December 25, 1952. Myron and Mary celebrated their 50th wedding anniversary in September, 1990, with a gala event at the Union Church in Huntington County, where they are members.

Reida graduated from Union High School. She married John R. Zezula on May 15, 1965. John's father was an immigrant from Czechoslovakia when he was just a young boy. John and Reida have two sons, Chad Eric, 22, and Shannon Todd, 21. Both Chad and Shannon graduated from Norwell High School and both are attending Purdue University. Reida has been a dental assistant for thirty years with William A. Kunkel III, DDS, who also has roots in Wells County. John works for General Telephone Electronics in Fort Wayne.

*Myron Woods Family
Lynn, Reida, Doug, Myron, and Mary*

Lynn graduated from Lancaster High School and Greer Technical Institute. Lynn also served with the United States Navy "Seabees" on the DMZ in Vietnam for thirteen months. Lynn married Sharon Kay Kunkel on March 7, 1970. Lynn and Sharon have two sons Christopher Douglas, 17, and Michael Wayne, 12, both students at Norwell. Lynn has been in the heavy equipment/earth moving business for twenty years. His company's name is Lynn Woods Contracting, Inc. Sharon is an RN Specialist in Gastroenterology/Nutritional Support at Lutheran Hospital in Fort Wayne.

Doug graduated from Norwell High School and married Debrah Kay Sheets on March 11, 1978. Doug and Deb bought the Woods Locker from Myron and Mary when they retired and have expanded their business to include a meat retail and deli store. Doug is also in partnership with his brother, Lynn. The name of this partnership is called Specialty Conveyance Service, Inc., which is an environmental remediation corporation. Doug and Deb have two children, Dawn Marie, nine, and Dustin Dayton, seven. Both children attend Lancaster Elementary School.

ABRAHAM WOODWARD

Abraham and Mary (Brickly) Woodward moved to Wells County, Jefferson Township, in 1850, from Trumbull County, Ohio.

Abraham was the fourth child of Thomas and Margaret (Shievely) Woodward of Trumbull County, Ohio. Mary was the daughter of George and Belinda (Wolfcale) Brickly of Wells County, originally from Trumbull County, Ohio.

The Woodward's first settled on a tract of 80 acres on what is now State Road 1 and 700 N. The land had been partially cleared and Abraham completed the clearing. In 1854, he sold this land and moved to another farm located on 700 N and Meridian Road. Here they raised their children: Loretta, who married George Wasson; Olive Orlina, who married William Beatty; Laura, who married William Wilkin and later Dr. William Beatty; George Thomas, who married Mary Josephine Glass; Samantha E., who married L. T. Fryback; William, who married Mary J. Goshorn; John, who married Dora McBride; Wilson A., who married Ella Somers; and Alice, who married E. E. Derr.

George Thomas and Mary stayed on the family homestead. They had Clint, who married Eva Mills; Alva, who married Lucille Foster; Irene, who married Osborne Gilpin; Dorcas, who married Jesse Newhard; Ellis, who married Hazel Mahnensmith; Annis, who married Edgar Hunter; Alda Jane, who married Howard Carson; and Rosco, who married Lela Crowl.

Ellis and Hazel had three children: Ruthell, who married Charles Andrews: Weisell, who married Geraldine Mardell Johnloz, daughter of Charles and Lillian Deihl Johnloz; and Mary Lou, who married Charles Raymond Peck.

Weisell and Geraldine had two sons: Thomas Brooks, who married Mary Lou Baughman; and Fredrick Kay, who married Vera Keller.

Thomas and Mary Lou have three children: Cherese Mardell, Thomas Brooks II, and Jeffrey Shawn.

Some of Abraham's decendents still living in the Ossian area are Weisell, Frank, Amaline, Thomas, Thomas II, Jeffrey, Kevin, Scott, Brock and Stephanie Woodward; Ruthell Andrews; Sherwood Hunter; Rosemarie Milholland; Brian, Amy and Julie Dettmer and Melody Newell.

CHARLES AND ALMA WOODWARD

Charles born in Huntington, and moved to Markle at age seven. He was the son of John and Inez (Morrical) Woodward. After graduation from East Rockcreek, he worked in road construction. Later he worked at General Electric in Fort Wayne. He retired in 1978 with 37 years of service. Charles has four brothers. At this time the four older boys have celebrated their 50th wedding anniversaries, totaling over 257 years of marriage for five brothers.

Charles and Alma Woodward

Alma (Thayer) Woodward moved to Wells County in 1923, living east of Bluffton and attending Poplar Grove School until mid term of fifth grade, then attending and graduating at Rockcreek. Her parents were Andrew Baker and Margie (Wolfe) Thayer. Both parents were born and raised in Virginia. Alma has three sisters and a deceased brother, Shirley.

Charles and Alma met at school and also the Markle Church of Christ. Both have been members of the Markle Church over sixty years. We were married June 3, 1939. Charles spent 15 months in the Army in World War II, nine months were spent in Italy.

We have three children. Clara graduated from East Rockcreek and worked at the Markle Medical Center over fifteen years. She is now the library assistant at Lancaster Central School. She is married to Duane Cart of Huntington County. He is a Senior Scientific Analyst at Magnavox. Their son, Kevin, is a graduate of Norwell High School and is employed at Fort Wayne Toyota. They have a daughter Kimberly, a sophomore at Norwell. They live in Markle.

Our son, Ray, married Diane Vickrey of Huntington County. Ray is also a graduate of Rockcreek School. He spent three years in the Navy. He has twenty years of service at K-Mart Warehouse. They have a daughter, Mrs. Mark (Sally) Lewellen of near Hartford City, a part time nurse at Caylor Nickel Hospital. They have two daughters Elizabeth and Natalie, which make us proud great-grandparents. Their second daughter, Mrs. Jim (Sarah) Stoffel, lives in Huntington County. She works at Markle Medical Center at Warren. Their third child a son, Shawn, attends Huntington North High School. He enjoys all sports and works part time for Blair Excavating.

Elizabeth (3 1/2 yrs.) and Natalie (1 1/2 yrs.) Christmas 1990. Daughters of Mark and Sally Lewellen and great granddaughters of Charles and Alma Woodward.

Our second daughter, Mrs. Dennis (Becky) Grover, of Jackson Township is office manager at the Markle Medical Center in Warren. She is married to Dennis Grover, son of Cloid and Marjorie Grover of Liberty Center. He is the owner of Grover Construction Company. Their daughter, Lora, is a freshman at Southern Wells and enjoys sports. They live south of Mt. Zion.

Charles and Alma live on 550W near Markle in a mobile home. We have lived at this residence since 1967, our former home was taken for the Huntington Reservoir After the family grew up, Alma worked for ten years at receptionist for Myers Funeral Home in Markle.

The past twelve winters we have enjoyed living in Sebring, Florida. We enjoy the many friends from Wells County that also go to Sebring, Florida. Charles is an avid fisherman, and Alma does "quilt as you go" quilts. She gives each grandchild a hand made quilt when they graduate from high school. Also each child will receive a quilt for their 25th wedding anniversary.

We are very thankful for good health and for being able to enjoy a good life with family and friends.

CHRISTOPHER COLUMBUS WORSTER

Christopher Columbus Worster was born in Liberty Township on May 22, 1875, to William and Ellen Thrillkill Worster. Columbus, as everyone called him, married Lillie Jane Shull on January 21, 1897. Lillie was the daughter of Daniel and Margaret Hinkle Shull. She was born February 19, 1882 in Wells County.

Four children were born in to the union: Cecil, December 21, 1898; Margaret Ellen, February 15,

1900; William Palmer, August 23, 1904; and Esther Belle, March 30, 1907.

The Worsters lived in Bly, Indiana. Although closed up now, the house still stands on the corner of 500W and 100S. Mr. Worster was a farmer at the time.

Columbus and Lillie Worster taken in about 1950

Around 1910 the family moved to Van Buren, Indiana, where they added two more children to their family. They were Mary Josephine, May 22, 1911, and Otis Elbridge, December 18, 1918. While in Van Buren, Mr. Worster hauled logs to various saw mills in the area.

The family moved to Laud, Indiana, near Roanoke. They lived there for about one year and moved to Warren, Indiana, in abut 1920.

Mr. Worster was, in his later years, one of the pioneer sanitary engineers or the "junk man". He would drive his old horse and wagon around town and gather unwanted junk and take it to the dump for those who desired the service. Because of this travels, Mr. Worster was well known and well liked by most all the town's people.

They were members of the Wesleyan Methodist Church.

Mr. Worster died in 1956, and his wife died in 1962. Both are resting in the Taylor Cemetery in Huntington County.

As this story is being written today, two of the children are still living. Mary Josephine lives in Markle and Otis Elbridge lives in Warren. Decendents number six children, fourteen grandchildren, 33 great-grandchildren and numerous great-great-grandchildren, including this story's writer, granddaughter Connie Dalrymple Brubaker. Additional photo page 607.

WILLIAM THOMAS WORSTER

Born in Randolph County, March 31, 1835, son of Robert and Nina Elizabeth Marshall Worster. William came to Wells County about the time of the outbreak of the Civil War and enlisted in the 34th Indiana Volunteer infantry.

While at home on furlough William married Ellen Trailkill. He finished his enlistment and was honorably discharged. He returned to Liberty Township and took up farming and later became a mail carrier. He was a credit to the community.

William was well known throughout this community and held in high respect among the wide circle of friends. He was a member of the Lew Daily Post G.A.R. and the Methodist Protestant church.

William and Ellen had four daughters: Esther Bell, Jane, Elizabeth, and Lucy, and one son, Christopher Columbus.

William died January 30, 1918, aged 83, at home one mile north of Liberty Center, from pneumonia, having been ill only one week.

Mr. Worster's decendants numbered 17 grandchildren and 19 great-grandchildren at his death.

Brothers and sisters of Mr. Worster are Mrs. Charles McCrain, Mrs. Ann Brumbaugh, Mrs. Prescilla Ernest, Mrs. Sarah Ladd, Louise Worster; James, Jeremiah, Samual, Melissa Worster.

His resting place is in the Mossburg Cemetery.

Ellen Trailkill was born in 1845 and died in 1921. No information about her family is available to me at this time.

WYANT FAMILY

Reverend Ora and Emma Unger Wyant were originally from Russiaville in west central Indiana. They moved to Wells County in the early 1930's. Reverend Ora had preached in the Liberty Center Methodist Church. At one period of time during the early 1940's they ran a grocery store in Poneto, as well as a huskster wagon throughout the community.

They had four children, Lucile, Ida Marie, Arthur, and Donald.

Lucile retired from working at the Warren Methodist Memorial Home and is now living at the Markle Health Care Center.

Wyant Reunion, August 1990
Seated Lucile Wyant. Standing L to R: Homer and Ida Mossburg, Bernadine and Donald Wyant, Arthur and Simone Wyant.

Ida Marie married Homer Mossburg and they had two sons, Richard and Robert. Richard farms near Liberty Center and Robert lives in Milwaukee, Wisconsin and works for Briggs and Stratton Small Engine Company. Ida and Homer are retired and live in St. Petersburg, Florida.

Wyant store located in Poneto 1940's

Arthur married Simone Hilaire from Metz, France. She was a telephone operator in Carentan, France when he met her during World War II. They have three children, Steven, Carol Wyant Stoppenhagen, Lisa Wyant Saylor, who all live and work around Fort Wayne.

Donald married Bernadine Carr who was originally from Akron, Ohio. They met while they were both serving in the U.S. Navy. They have two daughters, Brenda and Debrorah, and live in Lynchburg, Virginia where Donald works for Bridgeport Brass.

YAGER-COTTON

Harold E. and EuDora Jane (Cotton) Yager have resided on a farm south of Ossian on State Road 1 since 1955. They were married December 28, 1941 at the Prospect Methodist Church west of Ossian. Both graduated from Ossian High School in 1940. Harold played on the Ossian Bears team that defeated Fort Wayne South Side in the Regional Tourney at Huntington in 1939.

In his youth, Harold aided his parents, Luster and Edith (Milholland) Yager, in farming and the operation of the Hillcrest Dairy. In October 1941 he began working for the Pennsylvania Railroad. He served in the U.S. Army for forty two months during World War II, twenty eight months in the European theater. When he returned home, he and EuDora lived in Fort Wayne for ten years, and he worked for the Pennsylvania Railroad, his seniority continuing from October, 1941.

EuDora is the daughter of Forst G. and Cleona (Hoover) Cotton who lived in Uniondale during

William Worster Family - north of Liberty Center

their later years. She was employed as a secretary/bookkeeper but has been a fulltime homemaker in the rearing of their five children.

Their children are; Carol J., a U.S. Air Force veteran who now works in the nursing profession and lives in Indianapolis.

Harold and EuDora Yager

Janice L. Neuenschwander, an executive secretary lives in Pandora, Ohio with her husband, John and children, Nathan C. and Marcy J..

Ray F. is a supervisor at the Dana Corp. in Syracuse, Indiana and lives there with his wife Amy Jo (Lewis) and three sons, Carter W., Tyler N., and Chase L..

Kevin W. is a toolmaker and works for Bowmar, working and living in Fort Wayne with his wife Rebecca (Dinius) and children Mariah and Derek.

Brent H. Lives at home and is employed by Fort Wayne Pools, manufacturers of fiberglass products.

Harold has two brothers, Dale and Lloyd, and a sister, Evelyn Isnogle, all of the Ossian area.

EuDora has a sister, Betty E. (Cotton) Inman who lives with her husband, Doyt E. Inman at Sarasota, Florida, Lyle J. and Gladys Cotton, a brother and his wife, live in Bluffton.

Harold retired from farming in 1979 and, after forty and one half years, retired from the Conrail Railroad in 1982.

The Ossian United Methodist Church is their Church home and EuDora belongs to the Jefferson Township Extension Homemakers Club and the Wells County Extension Choral Club.

They are quietly enjoying retirement.

Refer to: Cotton/Hoover, Yager/Milholland, Inman/ Cotton, Cotton/McAfee.

NOAH YAKE FAMILY

Lancaster Township in Wells County is home to the Noah Yake family. Of German and Swiss descent, Noah is the son of Lewis (1886-1972) and Della Frauhiger Yake (1889-1968). He has lived within a five mile radius of Craigville his entire life. Noah was born near Tocsin in 1919. When he was one year old, the family purchased a farm south of Peterson in Adams County, where Noah lived for twenty years, along with his brother, Evan, and sisters, Ruth (Henschen), Hazel (Leichty), and Naomi (Shilling). During this time the Lewis Yakes farmed and raised turkeys.

Noah returned to Wells County after his marriage to Martha Zirkle (1920), daughter of Cary (1892-1943) and Effie Studebaker Zirkle (1891-1973) in 1940. Martha, along with her brother, George Zirkle and sister, Mary Zirkle, were raised on various farms near Murray, Indiana. Cary worked for the Indiana Service Corporation (the interurban) and also International Harvester. Effie spent many years as a cook at Lancaster school.

Noah and Martha's first home is still, their current residence, located near Craigville in Lancaster Township. This farm had been owned by Noah's maternal grandmother, Bertha (Meyers) Frauhiger. The Yakes have lived on this farm for fifty one years. During this time they raised three sons: Frederick, Kenneth, and Donald. They supported their family by dairy farming and raising turkeys. Noah was also a mail carrier in the Craigville and Ossian areas for many years. Even though Noah and Martha are deeply grounded in Wells County, they have traveled extensively within the United States, visiting all fifty States during their married life.

Noah and Martha's sons graduated from Lancaster High School and reside in Lancaster Township. Their grandchildren have graduated from or are still attending Norwell. Frederick (1942) also graduated from Purdue University. He has been employed at International Harvester and is engaged in farming and trucking. In 1963 he married Patricia Callison (1942) of Bippus, Indiana. Their children are Kimberly (1966), Angelia (1968) and Kari (1975). Kenneth (1945) graduated from Indiana Barber College, served in the United States Navy, and operates a barbershop in Bluffton. In 1969 he married Nan Pearson (1948) of Petroleum, Indiana. Nan earned a degree in secondary education from Indiana University (Fort Wayne campus). She teaches at Bluffton High School. Their daughters are Courtney (1975) and Jessica (1977). Donald (1949) served in the United States Army and has been employed at Wayne Metal and farmed. In 1973 he married Sue Walton (1951) of Delphi, Indiana. Sue received a registered nursing degree from Lutheran School of Nursing and is employed by Caylor/Nickel Hospital. Melinda (1975) and Martin (1978) are their children.

Notice should be taken that the spellings of the Yake and Frauhiger names were Americanized. The German spelling of Yake was Yoeck. The Swiss spelling of Frauhiger was Frauchiger.

YOUNG

Henry Jacob Young, the first of our ancestors to come to Wells County, was sixty nine years old when he arrived. Born in 1791 in Knopp, Rhineland/Pfalz, Henry and his second wife settled near Ossian in Jefferson Township in 1860.

Valentine Young, the eldest child of Henry, was born in 1817, in Hettenhausen, Rhineland/Pfalz, and wed Carolina Kiefer in Pfalz in 1852. They came to America in 1864, and located northeast of Ossian. Later, they bought a farm at the intersection of Wells County roads 1100N and 500E.

April 3, 1987 Norman and Barbara (Koons) Young

Jacob Young, their fifth child, who was born at home in 1868, married Christine Lehrman in 1890, in her home in Pleasant Township, Allen County. They lived in Jefferson Township five years, then moved to her home place after her father died in 1895. Jacob farmed their land and worked as a blacksmith in Hessen Cassel, as they reared five children.

Arthur Jacob Young, the eldest son of Jacob and Christine, was born in 1891, in Jefferson Township, and attended the eight grades of St. Mark's Lutheran Church School. In 1912, in Pleasant Township, he married Alma Louise Springer, a daughter of George Frederick Springer and Mary Louise Moshammer. They lived in, or near, Ossian, all of their married lives, where Arthur worked as a painter. They had six children: Evelyn, Delbert, Darlene, LaVera, Dale, and Norman.

Norman Fremont Young was born September 12, 1925, in Jefferson Township. He graduated from Ossian High School in 1943, and served in the Navy from 1943 to 1946. He wed Barbara Lou Koons, a daughter of George Guy Koons and Edna Hannah Swaim, on June 28, 1947, in the Ossian Methodist Church. The couple lived in Crawfordsville, Indiana, until Norman graduated from Wabash College in 1949, then moved to Charlottesville, Virginia, where he graduated from the Institute of Textile Technology with an MS degree in 1951. He was recalled to active duty by the Navy, and upon release in 1953, they moved to Leaksville (now Eden), North Carolina, where he worked for Fieldcrest Mills, serving as division vice-president and general manager of blanket and automatic blanket manufacturing for many years. He retired in 1985, after thirty two years service with Fieldcrest Mills. Norman and Barbara live in Eden, are members of Leaksville United Methodist Church, and are active in community affairs. They are the parents of two children, Norman, Jr., and Douglas,

Norman Fremont Young, Jr., was born September 10, 1954, in Danville, Virginia. He graduated from the universities of North Carolina and George Washington University and Virginia Polytechnical Institute. He married Helen Margaret Swartz in 1983, in Fairfax, Virginia, and they live in Falls Church, Virginia, where he works as an engineer for Autometrics, and she is a paper conservator for the Smithsonian Institute.

Douglas Koons Young was born January 3, 1959, in Leaksville, North Carolina. After graduation from the University of North Carolina in 1981, he worked for the Department of Defense at Fort Meade, Laurel, Maryland, for nine years. In the fall of 1990, he enrolled in the law school at the University of Washington, Seattle.

ZEHNER

The first Zehner of our line to come to America was Adam Zehner. He was a Swiss, born in 1726, Swortzwolt, Germany (Black Forest).

Adam Zehner worked his way through the wilderness until he reached the Little Schuylkill River, four miles south of Tamaqua, Pennsylvania. There he built the first saw and grist mill in 1763. He had numerous encounters with the Indians, who feared him because they thought he was bullet-proof! Every morning Adam repeated the 91st Psalm, then prayed. He served in the Revolutionary War; in 1785 Adam married Mary Mertz, in Berks County Pennsylvania.

Adam and his wife Mary had fifteen children. His third son was David, born 1763. He married

Elizabeth Henrich. David and Elizabeth had fourteen children. The fourteenth was a son, Benjamin, born 1815. Benjamin married Hester Hoppes. They had nine children. They moved across Ohio, settling eight miles north of Muncie, Indiana, in Sharon (now extinct). The third son of Benjamin and Hester was Daniel.

Daniel Zehner born 1842, married twice: first to Sarah Bantz, near Albany, Indiana. The second marriage took place to Elizabeth Gabriel. To the first marriage were born three sons. To the second marriage were born nine children. Daniel decided to go west. Later he returned after his father's death, to run the water-powered flour mill in Sharon. To Daniel and second wife Elizabeth was born Lyman, their first son.

Lyman Zehner, born 1875, in Marshall County, Indiana made the trip west with his parents and returned July 25, 1893. He married Daisy Reynard. They bought a farm in Chester Township—8265S. 450W. Poneto. Lyman and Daisy had three children, a daughter and two sons, Lester and Gerald.

Lester married Jenny Zimmerman. They also resided in Chester Township. They had three children, Lyman Jr., Max, Nondes.

Gerald, son of Lyman and Daisy, was my grandfather. He married Faye Hiser. They helped farm the family farm. Gerald also drove a school bus, for Chester Center School. They were members of the Chester Center Church. They had three children, Jack, Bob, Joyce (now Mrs. Clyde Hudson). Gerald died at an early age of forty-two, followed shortly by Faye his wife, of who it was said she died of a broken heart from the loss of her beloved husband Gerald. The family farm was sold at auction and bought by Bill and Nondes Weatherholt. Nondes was a niece to Gerald, formerly Nondes Zehner, daughter of Lester and granddaughter of Lyman.

My father is Bob Zehner of Bluffton. He is a driver for Franklin Electric. He married twice, first to Yvonne Pond, second to Ellen Garn. To the first marriage were born two daughters, Camelia and Tonya.

I, Camelia, married Anthony Robles of Bluffton. We have six children: Joshua, Rachel, Isaiah, Hannah, Solomon, and Amos. We pastor Harvest Time Bible Church, in Bluffton. Our children attend Southern Wells School.

My sister Tonya married Stan Jenkins and resides in Ossian. They have four children: Shanda, Dustin, Nicholas, and Cherish.

I never met my Grandparents, Gerald and Faye, but I plan to see them in Heaven, along with many more of my ancestors. I would say unto my children and grandchildren to be: Go forth in the spirit of our ancestor—Adam Zehner of 1726: "I will say of the Lord he is my refuge and my fortress, my God in Him will I trust!"

WILLIAM C. ZION FAMILY

William C. Zion of Zanesville, was born in Madison County, Indiana, on February 10, 1845, the son of John P. and Nancy (Crismore) Zion. John and Nancy were married in Rush County, Indiana, and their children were all born in Indiana. The children were Jacob S., William C., George W., Thomas J., and John H.

Jacob married Susan Somer; George married Rebecca Bell; Thomas J. married Mary Ellsworth; John H. married Ida Hindman; and William C. married Mary C. Wagner. Mrs. Nancy Wagner Zion was the daughter of Martin and Catherine (Welbaum) Wagner.

The Zion family came to Wells County on October 20, 1863, purchasing a farm in Wells County. John P. was born in 1818 and Nancy in 1823. (Refer to Sink Family).

William C., a well-educated man, spent his life on the farm, which he purchased in 1870. At that time it had only a small clearing and no house. He improved his 120-acre farm, which was well-stocked and made convenient. William C. and Mary had three children; Ida E., Jason C., and Franklin A.

In 1884, Mr. Zion was elected township trustee, serving four years. The Needmore Schoolhouse and the Zanesville School were erected during the time he held office. The Iron Bridge, between Section twelve and thirteen was built, as were also two frame bridges over Flat and Davis creeks.

Note: Jacob S. was previously married to a Mary, who was the mother of Bertha Zion, wife of Alf Sink. Bertha was very small when her mother died.

ZODA-RUPLEY

Jerry and Mary Jo (Rupley) Zoda reside in Jackson Township on a farm west of Dillman which was settled by Jerry's great-grandparents, John Henry (1857-1918) and Emily (Wilkinson) (1853-1914) Schweikhardt, who moved from Henry County, Indiana in 1898. John and Emily were married September 22, 1878 and had eight children. Carolyn (Callie) Schweikardt (1886-1961), the fifth child, married Marvin E. Zoda (1882-1943) on August 27, 1904. They had six daughters and one son, Marvin J. (Bud), born March 24, 1914, who is Jerry's father.

December 24, 1990
Back (L to R) Jack Zoda, David and Jacob Harriett, Joe Zoda, Jerry Zoda, John Zoda
Front (L to R) Mary Jo Zoda, Wilma Zoda, Bud Zoda, Judy Harriett

Marvin J. (Bud) Zoda married Wilma Louise Thompson (born April 4, 1918), daughter of J. Elbridge and Lena (Beerbower) Thompson of Huntington County on December 24, 1939. They were the parents of four children: Jerry Lee, Richard Wayne, Timmy Joe, and Cathy Sue (Zoda) Wright.

Jerry Zoda (born October 26, 1940) wed Mary Jo Rupley (born December 25, 1939), daughter of Marion Emanuel (1908-1975) and Alice Lucille (Lash) (1910-1959) Rupley of Marion, Indiana. Jerry and Mary Jo, married on August 4, 1962, are the parents of four children: Joseph Wayne, born June 17, 1963; Jack Eugene, born September 4, 1964; Judith Ann, born October 15, 1970; and John Marvin, born September 30, 1973.

Judith Ann Zoda married David Michael Harriett (June 13, 1966), son of Mr. and Mrs. David W. Harriett of Bluffton, on March 17, 1990. They are the parents of Jacob David Harriett, born September 5, 1990.

Columbus and Lillie Worster home in Bly, Indiana. Liberty Township house is still standing. Taken about 1900. (See story on page 605)

Charles and Fern Daugherty (See story on page 306)

Index

Every effort has been made to include in this everyname index, all names as they appear throughout the historical sketches of this book. However, with over 35,000 individual names included in this volume it is possible one or more may have been ommitted through human error.

The intent of this index, is to provide a useful tool for family history researchers. This index also includes the listing of understood, but unwritten, married names in instances where only a maiden name appeared in the history sketch. When brackets are used around a name, they indicate the indexers inability to determine whether that name is a maiden name, middle name, former married name, etc.

Page numbers listed in the index refer to beginning locations of historical sketches which contain the indexed name in question. If the length of the history extends beyond a single page, the indexed name may actually be found on the adjoining pages.

ABBOTT, Alfred 161, Amanda 238, Andrew V. 238, 459, Anna 374, Catherine (McDaniel), 238, 459, Charles 238, Daniel William 394, Debra 414, Esther Jane (Lambert) 394, Eva 287, Eva Luesynda 238, George Washington 238, Hugh 281, Lola May 238, Nellie Florence 238, Osper 238, Rosa Arretta 394, Ruth 44, Ruth 45, Susan 500, Willie Arthur 238
ABNER, Gloria Kay 265
ABNET, Frances 268
ABSHIRE, Ed 86
ACCAVALLO, Anthony Jr. 238, Carmela 238, Charles 238, Charles Anthony 310, Charlie 6, Dennis 6, 310, Dennis James 238, Frances 238, Joyce, 6, 310, Joyce (Day) 238, Kenny 238, Mary 238, Nick 238, Rose (Samele) 238, Vincent 238
ADAIR, Congressman J.A.M. 458
ADAM, John Michael 366, Sophia 366
ADAMS, Anne Link 548, Betty 414, Bonnie L. 383, Burt 122, Carol Ann 548, Charles 548, Connie 270, Ed 122, Elanda 279, F. P. 185, Judy 150, Nellie Blanch 327, Ronald 145, Tammy 486, Tom 548
ADAMS-DAVIS, Lulu (Jones) 410
ADDAIRE, Tina 396
ADDINGTON, Alivs Patton 239, Belle 239, Carl 239, Carson 239, Charles Cromwell Jr. 239, Charles Cromwell Sr. 239, Dennis 239, Drusilla 239, Henry Ellington 239, Homer 239, John 239, Joseph 239, Lona 239, Mary Elizabeth 239, Mary Elizabeth 460, Nancy 239, Nancy Esterling 239, William 239, William Perry 239
ADDIS, Grace 553
ADKINS, Julia 507, Patricia Lynn 593
ADY, Hannah 103, Mary Jane 402
AESCHLIMAN, Sam 144, Sam 506, Samuel 487
AFFLECK, John Gaston 532
AFFOLDER, Charles 240, Charles 255, Corey Lee 239, Corey Lee 240, Daniel Edward 240, Elmer 240, Gary Lee 239, 240, 255, Jill Ellen 239, 240, Judith Ellen Hirschy Beer 240, Kathy 255, Kriss Shannon 240, Luanne K. 473, Luanne Kae 473, Mary Ellen (Beck) 239, Mary Ellen Hendricks 240, Michelle Minnette 240, Penny Jo 240, Samuel Melvin 240, Steve 239, Steven Lynn 240, Steven Lynn 255, Virgil Leroy 239, 240, 255
AGAR, Ina 269, Jessie McGuire 269, William Hoyle 269
AIEGENHAIN, Elizabeth Mary 527
AILES, Sherry 536
AINSLEY, Laura Ann 502, Neil 502
AKER, Amanda Lee 533, Blanche R. 239, Cleo 573, Dorothy 465, Glen 465, Glenn L. 239, Harry C. 465, Harry E. 239, Kristen 465, Lindsay 585, Nancy 533, Ruby C. 465, V. H. 239, William 239
ALBERDING, Edward 206
ALBERSON, Charles 240, 324, Clyde 240, Emma Catharine 324, Joan 240, Joshua 240, Joshua 324, Kenneth 240, Lillie 240, Mary Ann Brown, 240, 324, Milo 240, Philip 240, Philip B. 324, Raleigh 240, Sarah 240, William 240
ALBERT, Anna Marie 316, David 254, John Nicholas 254, Lydia 254, Henry 546, Michael 546, Michella 546, Mildred 546, Robert 546, Wayne 546
ALBERTUS, Alpha 490
ALBRIGHT, Jacob 91
ALEXANDER, 179, Almedia 241, Antoinette 241, Ben 241, Carl 241, Carolyn 241, Catherine 200, Charity 241, Clellah Tribolet 241, Dan 241, Dessie 241, Doris 241, Doris Joan 273, Frank 241, Gerald 241, Hugh 15, Hugh 241, James 241, James 309, Joe 241, John 241, Katie 241, Lenchen 241, Lester 25, Lester 241, Mary Ellen 241, Polly 309, Rhoda 241, Richard 241, Robert 71, Rowena 241, Virgile 241
ALEXANDER BROS, 179
ALFELD, Delbert 497, Vera 497
ALGER, Judi 343
ALLEN, Brenda 402, Carl Leroy 425, Charlotte Kay 425, Chris 243, Connie 514, Connie S. 396, Cyrus 242, E. Russell 549, Elizabeth R. 544, Ellen 289, Elmer 292, 512, Emma 242, Eugene 425, Georgiana 152, Gilbert 382, Glagie Myers 549, Hezekiah 103, Hezekiah 242, Ida 242, Isaac 242, Janet 402, Jasper N. 242, Jonathan 242, Leah 243, Margaret 247, Martha 326, 512, 518, 544, Martha Waneta 591, Mary 437, Mary Almeda 524, Mary J. 242, Matthew 402, Matthew Allen 242, Owen 402, P. A. 120, 200, 208, Phariba Allen 474, Philemon A. 128, Ransom 242, Richard 151, Roger 130, Roy 45, Russell 326, Sarah 242, Sarah 524, Shirley Bell 549, Theodore 79, Zephaniah 524
ALLISON, John 508
ALLPORT, Edward 214
ALLRED, Coleen 228, Joel 402, Kevin 402, Nikki 402
ALLSTON, Raymond 84
ALLYN, Florence 242, Frank 242, Golden 242, Hazel 242, J. B. 81, John 242, Mary Ann Kindel 242, Myrtle Bessie 242, Rozelle (Guy) 242, William 242
ALMDALE, Howard 146, Howard 219, Howard Mrs. 146, James 145, James C. 145, Jeane 154, Jim 219
ALMER, Carrie 570
ALSHOUSE, Etta 317, Floyd 317, Frank 317, George 317, Helen 317, Jacob 317, Rosa 317, Sarah 321, Sarah (Ditzler) 317
ALSPACH, W. A. 85
ALSPAUGH, W. A. Rev. 593
ALTDOEFFER, Arkansas 455
ALTSINGER, Martha 320
ALVORDS, Virgie 400
AMBRIOLE, Shelly 483, Ted 483, Tyler 483
AMSTUTZ, Abraham 329, Anna 519, Berneil French 468, Betty 519, Elizabeth (Augsburger) 329, Eugene 519, Joyce 519, Karen Kummer 576, Keith 519, Kenneth II 576, Kenneth III 576, Lara Lynne 576, Larissa Marie 576, Magdalena 329, Menno 519, Roger 519
ANDERS, Velma 408, Velma 554
ANDERSON, Almeda Elizabeth 516, Anthony 400, 497, Ashley 400, 497, Beatrice June 469, Ben 479, Beulah 243, Carl 37, Chloe 243, Cora 37, Dan 497, Daniel Gene 400, Delores 242, 373, Donald 469, Donna 243, Elizabeth 469, George 242, Georgianna Mae 243, Gregory 469, Holli 479, Howard 228, James Victor 243, Jamie 479, Jean 594, Jean 594, Jerry 479, John 34, Judy 479, Kim Roberta 242, Lauretta 264, Lesley 415, Mabel 597, Maxine 400, Michael 399, Naomi 243, Paul 95, Robert 243, Rochelle 415, Ron 594, Rose 497, Ruth Joanne 243, Tom 415, Tyler 415, Vic 92
ANDES, Harry 139
ANDESON, Charles 512
ANDORFER, Connie Sue 450, Jessica 450, Kelli 450, Stephen 450
ANDREW, Deena 497, Grace 263, James W. 263, Max 94, Sarah E. 263
ANDREWS, Aaron Lewis 271, Celia 575, Charles 604, Clara Irene 478, Deena 497, Harold Perry 478, Hazel 244, Lee 271, Lorene 546, Mary Agnes 575, Melinda 244, Merle Couldtrip 271, Oliver Perry Morton Dr. 575, Perry 244, Ruthell 604, Suzannah Marie 271
ANGEL, David 202
ANGELBRIGHT, Flora Brookwalter 537
ANGEVINE, William E. 537
ANGLEMEIRE, Rev. 82
ANGSTEDT, Emma 593
ANGUISH, Florence 293
ANNABLE, David 537, Grant 537, Sharon 537, Susan 537
ANTHONY, Gordon 356
ANTRIM, Andrew 243, Bruce 243, Edgar 243, Jan 243, Joy 243, Lucas 243, Marge 6, Marge 243, Rhea 243, Steve 243, Thomas 243
APPLE, Andrew 402, Lynne 152
APPLEGATE, Edna Blanch (Kistler) 276, Otto Ward 276, Zedda M. 276, Glenn 75
APPLESEED, Johnny 560
ARBAUGH, Mary E. 426
ARCHBOLD, Ann 244, Barbara 485, Belenda 583, Curtis Clyde 402, Dean 244, Denny 113, Edna 269, Eliza Jane 267, Emmett 244, Evelyn Joan 269, Forrest 244, Francina 244, George 244, George W. 583, Glen 244, Gregory M. 391, Harold 244, Hattie 244, 430, 431, James 337, Joan 244, John 244, John A. 244, John E. 269, Joseph 244, Katherine 475, Lettice 244, Lou Ann 263, Lovina (Yarger) 267, Luella 244, Lydia 339, Lyle 244, Marilyn 244, Martha 244, Marvin 244, Mary 244, Mary Dafforn 244, Mary Etta Valentine 244, Mary (Kent) 244, Mary Letha 337, Ned 244, Nellie 244, Patrick 244, Paul 244, Rebecca 244, Ronald 485, Rosa 244, Russell 48, Ruth Eileen 516, Ruth Eleanor 485, Sabertha 244, Samuel 475, Sandra S. 391, Sarah 244, Sarah Ann 244, Sarah (Mills) 337, T. W. 252, Thomas 244, Thomas W. 121, Tricia L. 391, Wendell W. 263, William 244, William John 267
ARCHER, John D. 519
ARCHIBOLD, Elizabeth 454, John A. 454, Mahala 469, Margaret 454, Matilda C. 575
AREND, Erma 244, Fred 145, 178, Fred 244, Fred 382, James 244, Jami 244, Kenneth 244, Linda 244, Lori 244, Nadine Todd 244, Ruth Ellen 244
ARICK, Kathleen 417
ARKO, Steve 460
ARMENTROUT, Brenda Kay 406
ARMITAGE, Harriet N. 363
ARMSTRONG, Barbara 429, Berniece 516, Bessie Pearl 419, Charles Ray 244, Christina Lynn 244, David 429, Deborah 500, Douglas Howard 244, Elizabeth Ann 244, Ellen Diane (Sparks) 419, Ellen Mae Osborn 244, Ellen May 493, George 500, George Andrew 500, Houston Tillman 244, John 419, Katrina Denise 244, Kent Douglas 244, Larau Elaine 244, Mark Steven 244, Mary 602, Norma 136, Norma Jane 500, Opal Mae 244, Patrick 429, Philip Doyle 244, Ross Howard 244, Susan 500, Susan Elizabeth 244, Tammy 429
ARNETT, Cynthia Ann 509
ARNOLD, Adam 245, Affie 245, Albert 245, Alice A. 259, Anna 245, August 529, Augusta 529, Barbara 393, Billy Ray 512, Catherine 546, Charles A. 245, Charles Russell 529, Chloe 245, Cleo B. 259, Cleora 529, Curtis 107, Cynthia 265, Dale 245, Dale 519, Denny 393, Dick 245, Donald 245, Dustin 245, Edith 266, Edith Charlene 259, Edith Miller 259, George 169, 208, 216, 245, George L. 145, 245, George Sr. 185, Gerald 529, Gertrude 245, 519, H. C. 20, 185, H. T. 75, Harold 245, 519, Helen 299, Henrietta 245, Henry 51, Henry C. 188, Henry Clay 245, Jacob 245, James T. 188, Joel 245, Julia 245, Karen 484, Karen 512, Keith 512, Lelia 245, Leuie 584, Lewis 529, Linda 245, Lindsay 245, Lorrie 245, Luster 245, 519, Margaret 245, Marjorie 245, Marjorie 519, Marjorie Carol 259, Martha Augusta 529, Mary Ann 245, Mary Ellen 542, Matilda (Masterson) 275, Max 245, Max 519, Moses 245, Nathan 245, Paul 393, Pauline 275, Rhonda 245, Robert 245, 482, 519, Ron 393, Russell 512, 529, Ruth 529, Sarah 245, Sarah 597, Sarah L. 245, Sherman 245, Sue 245, Tera Sue 245, Theodore 275, Thomas 13, 18, Tim 357, Tom 245, Tony 512, Wanda Eileen 245, William 529, William C. 113
ARNOVITZ, Sally 515
ARTHUR, Sarah 403
ARTMAN, Charlotte 252
ARWETT, Jean 538
ASBAUCHER, Lillian 152
ASBELL, Gloria 585, Milton 585
ASCHLIMAN, Alice 354, Annette Annie, Byron Ray 354, Delva 521, Derryl 340, Derryl 354, Elizabeth Rose 354, Homer 353, Justine (Heyerly) 438, Kenneth 438, Laura 340, Lisa 457, Millard 340, Millard 354, Minnie 233, Minnie 353, Taylor Max 354, Tiffany June, 354
ASH, Jack 130, Ver 380
ASHBAUCHER, Gedfrey 188, Ida 8, Ida 200
ASHBAUGER, Ben 64, Fred 64
ASHBURN, Catherine 495, Elizabeth (Hart) 495, Joseph 495
ATHAN, Don 98, Don 389, Donald Rosel 246, Elsie 246, Eunice Hedges 246, Eunice (Hedges) 389, Evangeline Barton 246, Francis Jane 246, John 246, John Wilson 246, Karen Santon 246, Katrina Marie Brown 246, Kedric 389, Linda Lou Rigby 246, Malinda 246, Mark 98, 246, Martha 246, Mary Jane 246, Michael Andrew 246, Nancy 246, Neva 500, Rex Arthur 246, Rosel Benjamin 246, Ross 500, Stephen Allenw 246, Thomas 246, Thomas Arthur 246, 389, William 246
ATHEY, Doris 136
ATKIN, Robert 64, Robert 96
ATKINSON, C. James 337, Carolee Ann 337, James 94, Robert Eugene 337
ATKINSON-FELTT, Beth 307
ATWOOD, Thomas 446
ATWOOD, Thomas 446
ATZ, John 68
AUER, George W. 596, John Charles 596, Kathleen 596, Robert William 596
AUGERBROGHT, Flora 417
AUGSBURGER, Daisy 300, Glenna 468, John 468, Donnahelle 508, Patti 508, Richard 508, Terry Joe 508
AULT, Adam Joseph 246, 472, Agnes 58, Anastasia Catherine 246, Andrew Charles 246, Andrew Charles 472, Anna Lee 154, C. F. 171, Charles 170, 401, Charles E. 246, Charles Fredrick 246, Charles William 246, Chuck 137, Edith 58, Fred 178, Fredley 58, Jo Ann 472, Jonathan Charles 246, Mary 58, AULT, Olivia Margaret 246, Samantha Marie 246, Scott 401, Scott Aaron 246, Scott Alan 246, Shannon Morae 246, Shawna Leigh 246, Stacey 401, Stacey Charles 246, Stanley K. 246, Stephen 401, Stephen J. 246, Steve J. 472, Stuart Henry 246, Sydney Nicole 246
AUMAN, James 552
AUNGST, Maria 547
AVERY, Ida Alice 345
AVILES, Victor 79
AYERS, Hazel 362, Jacob 317, Caleb 554, Florence 554, Martha Sutton 554, Seeloy 504
BAADE, Ernest A. Dr. 332, Richard 332, Sheryl 332
BAATZ, Eleanor 483
BABB, Gerald L. 223
BABBITT, Annie 495
BABCOCK, Becky 247, Elmer 247, Emmalee 247, Evelyn 280, Frank 247, George 247, George Dr. 577, Harold G. 247, Homer 247, James D. 247, 369, 370, James L. 247, Janice 577, Julia 247, Lisa 247, Lisa Lynn 577, Lynn 150, Lynn 154, Malinda McCart 247, Michael 247, Peleg III 247, Rebecca "Belle", Ruby 369, 370, Thomas 247, Thomas Zeph 418, Timothy 247, Timothy Kent 577
BABER, Frederica 22, William 22, 272
BACHELOR, Frank 522
BACHMAN, Sophia 564
BACHTEL, Mary Ann 469
BACON, Harriett 254, Joan 150
BADGER, Linda 572, Lowell 572, Nellie 572
BADIAC, Carolyn 521, Elmer 521, Gloria 521, James 521, Marilyn 521, Mildred Louise 521, Sam 521
BAEK, Mal-Sook 298
BAHLER, Arlene 376
BAILEY, Alice Ann 488, Anna 534, Anna Elizabeth 247, Anna Elizabeth 316, Catherine 574, Charles 488, Daniel 512, Edith 538, Elizabeth 574, George 59, Hannah 507, Jacob 574, Jill 488, John 316, 330, John Elgin 247, Kathy Thompson 580, Kit 574, L. H. 175, Lydia 538, Lydia Myrl (Gilbert) 316, Madiline 150, Mark Regan 601, Mary 157, Mary 330, Mary 574, Mary Jane 247, Melissa Kay 601, Michael 488, Myrl (Gilbert) 330, Nelson 538, Norma Jean 601, Ray 48, Willie 574
BAINE, Amelia 354
BAIR, Cinnamon 424, Cinnamon Lee 546, Eric M. 424, 546, Martha 424, Martha 546, Mildred Coverdale 289, William "Bill", William 546
BAIRD, Hershel 140
BAKER, Alexandria Louise 249, Allison 503, Allison Mae 249, Amy 264, Barbara Ann 348, Barbara Ellen 519, Benjamin Franklin 248, Berneice 240, Bernice 324, Betty 152, Betty J. 569, Bob 503, Boyde 249, Boyde L. 569, Carol 503, Charles 140, Clifford Junior 520, Dan 280, Dana 294, David 597, Dawn 294, Dean 301, Diana Sue 520, Diane 597, Doris Elaine 248, Eliza 366, Eliza Jane 367, Elizabeth 248, Elizabeth Catherine 405, Ethel 248, Evert 83, Grace 398, Grace E. 279, Gus 117, Gyneth 463, Hazel 248, Helen 248, Homer 144, Homer 301, Howard E. 248, Howard E. 304, Hugh 248, Inez 248, Ira 352, Ira 417, Ira Glenn 248, J. E. 248, Jacob 248, James M. 396, James W. 248, Jan 280, Janis L. 559, John 597, John Jr. 248, John Jr. 405, John Sr. 248, Josephine 249, Josephine 569, Judith 251, Julia 520, Julia Kay 522, Julie 142, Lennyce E. 304, Lester 259, Lewis 324, Louisa 267, Lula Viola 555, Lydia 248, Martin 248, Mary A. 248, Mary Imogene 520, Maxine 248, Michael Alan 249, Mildred 248, Mollie (Hudson) 248, Ora Jr. 588, Oscar E. 248, Patricia 503, Phil 294, Ralph 200, Ralph 207, Robert 301, Robert L. 249, Ryan 503, Ryan Patrick 249, Samuel 249, Sarah 248, Scott David 249, Sharon 597, Sharon K. 304, Sharon K. 459, Shelley 264, Staci Danielle 249, Stella 569, Steven Douglas 249, Susan (Hower) 248, T. S. 569, Timothy Martin 249, Ware 113, 142, 145, 146, 248, 438, 506, Ware Mrs. 146
BALAGURAS, Dianne 136, Nicholas J. 269
BALENTINE, C.J. 196
BALL, James 429, Mary Ann 415
BALLARD, Thomas 75
BALLER, Elizabeth 352, Jodi Leigh 424, Mark 202, Richard 424, Sarah Marie 424
BALLINGER, Abigail 492, Donna 564, Nancy Carolyn 409, Thomas 492, William 492
BANGHART, Ermah E. 444
BANGS, Jane 136, Owen R. 109
BANNISTER, Ken 286, Bill 577, Brenda 443, Brent Aaron 577, Byron 577, Claramae 249, Cora Belle 249, Dan 249, Darlene 352, Dianna 577, Ellen 249, Elmira Jeffries 249, Elsie 249, Florence 577, Frank 249, Gene 249, Harley 249, Howard 249, Ileen 249, Jack 24, Janice 247, 577, Jason 249, Jay 249, Jesse 249, Joan 249, John W. 249, Joseph 249, Joyce 249, Katie 249, Lillie Herring 249, Linda 249, Mae 249, Maria 249, Mike 249, Oscar 79, 249, Rex 249, Ronald 449, Roy 249, Sam 249, Sara 249, Violet 79, 249, 319, 524, Walter 249, Will Byron 577, Zada 249, Zada E. 459
BANTZ, Sarah 606
BAPST, John 95
BARBER, Alhern 421, Celestia 249, Chauncey 249, Delphina 249, 421, Elder 94, Elizabeth 249, Emerson 21, Emerson 249, Hallet 249, Hallet 356, Hallet 417, Hallet 421, Harrison 249, Ira Albern 249, Lovinia 249, Nancy Jane 249, Nina 249, Orin 249, Rosalinda 249, Sarah (Vining) 417, Urania 249, Urania 421
BARBIERI, Ashley Ann 250, Barbara 6, 136, Barbara 152, Barbara 200, Brent Edward 250, Charles Edward 250, Cynthia Jean 250, James C. 208, James Charles 250, Jim 6, 250, 602
BARCHMAN, Henry 172
BARCUS, David Leon 250, Helen 250, Herman Morris 250, Jack Leon 250, James Allen 250, James Ross 250, Janice Elaine 250, Lily Morris 113, Lula 250, 465, Tammera Sue 250, William 250, William E. 250
BARDO, Reggie 140
BARDSLEY, Audra 421, Kathlina 440, Kristina 440, Marilyn 440, Matthew 440, Max 440, Teresa 440, Tina 440
BARENTSZ-SWAIM, Tys 365
BARGER, Aleta 250, Alicia Kaye 369, Alta 250, Ann Marie 351, Carol N. 250, 568, Carol Natalie 250, Cynthia Sue 250, Debra Louise 250, Donald 221, 351, Doyle 250, Ed 44, 45, Elliot Samuel 250, Floyd 250, Glen 250, Herman 565, Jacob 547, John 221, John H. 250, John, Richard 250, Karen Sue 369, Kathryn Ann 250, Keith Allen 250, Kris Ann 355, Lamoin 221, Lola 250, Mandi Renee 369, Marry Neal 250, Mary 487, Mary Lou 592, Nadine 565, Nancy (Beard) 369, Nathan 355, Orval 250, Robert 351, Suzette 351, Way 221, William Keith 250
BARKELEW, Faye 507, Henry A. 507
BARKER, Florence 307, Janice 459
BARKLEY, J. A. 301
BARLETT, Ethel 437, Issac 437, Mollie (Ernst) 437
BARLOW, Daisy 572
BARNER, Jane 505, Minnie 86, Anna 251, Arthur 32, Betty 25, Betty L. 596, Charles Ray 324, Cheryl 440, Claude 182, Claude Oren 324, Clyde 130, David 251, Derek 251, Dick 251, Elizabeth 251, 596, Elizabeth Lou 324, Ellen Jeanne 251, Ian 251, Jack 140, 172, James 324, Jane Ann

264, John 251, Josephine Parintha 324, Judith 251, Karen 251, Karen Ann 596, Katharine 251, Linda 251, Lorene Ellen (Crowl) 303, Mary Adahleen 251,596, Maurice J. 251, Myah 251, Paul 440, Paul Jr. 440, Ray 182, Ray 524, Richard C. 251, Richard C. 596, Richard J. 251, Richard J. 596, Rosanna (Searles) 324, Sofronia (Dubbs) 251, Susannah 324, Thea Marie 517, Thelma Naomi 324, William 324
BARNETT, Caroline 82, Jacob 82, 560, Rachel 90
BARNHART, Malinda 500, Mary Ann 557
BARNTHOUSE, Euriel Iretta 554
BARNTHOUSE, Marion R. 554
BARR, 66, Betty 301, Bruce 122, Jane 484, W. R. 181, Will R. 145, William R. 8
BARRETT, Donna 417, Elizabeth 536, Marjorie 403
BARRICK, Barbra 437, 575, Barbra Lou 574, Beverly 575, Beverly Sue 574, Clayton Leroy 574, Debra 262, Diana 262, Eddie 574, Evelyn 485, Franklin Campbell , 574, Gabe 574, Garth 574, George 574, Jacob Raymond 574, James 574, Jennie Justine 574, Mary Ellen 574, Merlin 262, Millie 262, Olive 262, Pat 574, Phoebe 574, Shari 262, Tate 574, Teeny 574, Vicki 262
BARRICK-MARKLEY, Vicki 262
BARRIE, Barbara June Rice 271, Bruce Leon 271, Ian Bruce 271
BARRINGER, Kathryn Renee 419, Louise 165, Louise 419, Marion 419
BARRINGTON, Helen 497, Jess 497, Jesse 20, Martha 599, Maurice 296
BARRY, Betty 314, Betty L. 312
BARSTOW, Penny Smith 585
BARTH, David 145
BARTLEBAUGH, G.A. 82
BARTLEMAY, Mary Ann 245
BARTLETT, Marie 400, Mike 402
BARTON, Angela 299, J. F. 60, James 540, Marie 555, Mary Ann 540, Mary Elizabeth 540
BARTOS, Emil 64, II, Emil 96
BARTROM, Ronda 415
BARWILER, Frank 95, Joe 95, Louise 185, Peter 95, Peter 372
BASS, F. Kaye 146, F. Kaye Mrs. 146
BASSETT, Everett 392, Natalie 523, Scott 392
BASUMAN, Jenna 350
BATDORFF, David 250, Rachal Elaine 250
BATE, Robert 202
BATES, Aaron 264, David 457, Esther 403, Harriet 450, Helen 552, Justin 264, Orland 553, Ruth 333, Sabel 333
BATSON, Nathaniel 421
BATSON, Sarah Jane 550
BAUER, Ed 288
BAUERMEISTER, Adolph 252, Agnes 251, Alma Rutz 373, Amy 251, Anna 252, Anna 368, 388, Arline 251, Arthur 251, August 252, Brair Laine 460, Brenda Lee 252, Brian 251, Brian Keith 252, Briar 251, Carlee 251, Carlee Jann 460, Dawn 251, Delbert 252, 322, Elva Jo "Joey" (Runking), Emma 251, Ernest 73, 251, 368, 526, Ernest Jr. 73, 252, Ernest Konrad D. 252, Ernest Sr. 73, 252, Ernst 251, Fred 252, Fredrick 526, Fredricke Breier 251, Frieda 251, Friedericke 73, Glenn 251, Halden 252, Heidi 251, Henry 73, 251, 252, 252, 344, 526, Hulda 252, Jeffrey 251, Jeffrey Laine 460, Jodi Lynn 252, Karl "Charles", Karoline 73, Kurt 252, LaVon 251, Leona 252, Lester 216, 251, 460, Lori 252, Lorie 459, Lorie Lynn (McClain) 460, Louise 73, Luella 252, Luella Glenora Young 252, Marie 73, 252, 368, Marla 252, Martha 251, Mildred 251, 252, Minna 251, Norbert 251, Norman "Butch", Norman 252, Norman Robert "Butch", Norwin 252, Norwin Richard 252, Otto 73, 252, Otto David Karl 73, 252, Paul 251, Rod 251, Ronda 251, Scott 251, Sophia 252, Sophie 251, Terry 251, Tim 251, Tony 251, Whitney 251, Whitney Rae 460, William 252, 526
BAUGHAN, Benjamin Thomas 332, Jill Ann (Ellis) 332, Bertha 562, Esther 422, Esther Ellen 423, Isaac 423, Jill Ann (Ellis) 348, Mary Ann McDowell 423, Mary Lou 604, Nancy (Grove) 60, Teresa 376
BAUM, Anne Catherine 427
BAUMAN, Abby 572, Elizabeth 336, Goldie 350, Ida 570, Inez 221, Judy Hott 394, Kenneth Rev. 526, Kenneth Rev. 589, Margaretta 533, Tim 475, W. A. 572
BAUMAN/BAUGHMAN, Eliza 292
BAUMANN, Judy (Hott) 394
BAUMGARDNER, Bill 588, Jacob J. 188, Jean 427, Jill 588, Steven 588
BAUMGARTNER Ala Magnola (Reeves) 419, Allene Emma 503, Anna 390, Anna Hubacher 435, Benedict 435, Betty 394, Beverly 487, Charles 419, Christian 70, Christian 442, Cliff 233, Clifford Mrs. 95, Clifton 145, Craig 487, David 70, Edith Emrich 503, ELise (Kohler) 303, Elmer 170, 187, 233, Elva (Carter) 419, Emil 303, Ernestine 136, 154, Eunice Priscilla 435, Hattie Viola 574, Howard 487, Ida 567, Ida Mae 435, Jacob 303, John 369, 435, John E. 503, John H. 41, Joseph 435, Joy 487, Joyce 487, Julie 487, L.L. 572, Leah Elisa 303, Lilly 572, Louis 567, Lucille E. 567, Margaret 570, Martha Mae 435, Mary 487, 493, 574, Maxine Lucille 435, Nancy (Beard) 369, Peter B. 574, Priscilla Mae 435, Salomet Steffen 435, Samuel 435, Violet Pearl 435
BAXTER, Altha Mariah (Legg) 418, David 280, David 575, Deane 214, James 418, Limpa E. 555, Penney 457, Rebecca 537
BAY, Charles Harrison 540, Harrison 540, Mary Elizabeth 540, Mary Jane 540, Rebecca 540, William 540
BAYHA, Agnes 253, Charles 253, Eliza Jane "Lude", Elizabeth 253, 480, Emma 253, Frank 253, 342, Franklin 253, George 161, 253, George 480, George Jr. 253, Johann George 253, John 253, Lewis 480, Lou 253, Lydia 253, Martha 253, Mary 253, 600, Mary Alice 580, Miss Lydia 121, Paul 253, Ralph 253, Ruth 253, Sarah 253
BAYLESS, Amanda (Amy) 253, Ancil 254, Ancil Louis 255, Andrew 253, Ann 253, Benjamin 253, Betty 254, 311, 313, Braden 253, Brent 253, Brittany 253, Charles Homer 253, Charles Homer 254, 255, Charles Larry 253, 254, Emma 64, 254, 255, Ethel 64, 254, Frances 6, Gay 253, George 253, George Hays 253, Gerald 255, Gerald Dean 253, 254, Homer 254, 255, James O. 254, James Oscar 254, John 254, John Allen 255, Kathryn 253, Keith 253, 254, Kenneth 313, Kenneth Oscar "Kay", Kristina 255, Kristofor 255, Laura Ethel Hoffacker 253, 254, Lauren 253, Lori Jo 253, Loye 64, 161, Loye Marie 254, Lyle 253, Marjorie 254, Mary 313, Max 253, 254, Max Henry 254, 255, Megan 253, Oscar 64, 254, 255, Peggy 253, 254, Seth 253, Steve 253, Sue 254
BAYNE, Sue 351
BAYNES, Petra 543
BAYOR, Charles R. 271, Gregory Adam 271, Hosea 271
BAYOUT, Lee 418, Marc 418, Nancy 418
BAYT, Catherine Marie 347, Phil 347
BEABER, Abraham 579, Effie 552, Ella 552, Henry 579, Joyce 552, Mayretha 378
BEABERS, Abraham 99, Henry 99
BEACH, Preston 442
BEADSLEY, C.W. 202
BEAL, Chester Hayes 273, Mildred Gertrude 273
BEAM, T. J. 83
BEAN, James 98
BEAR, Jeramy 418, Jessica 418, Joe 89
BEARD, Delila 561, George 15
BEARDSLEE, Bethany 249
BEARS, John 19, 102, Rosa 440, Rose 440
BEATTY, William Dr. 604
BEATY, Belle 477, Cletus Vane 255, Dawn Rene 255, Douglas 279, Douglas N. 145, Douglas Neil 255, Douglas Neil III "Kip", Douglas Neil Jr. 255, Jared Neil 255, Jeff 509, Jessica Lee 255, John E. 477, Kevin Mack 255, Mae 477, Mary Adeline 484, Nellis 314
BEAVANS, Auhry I. 291, Brenda 292, Chris 292, David 61, David 292, Debra 292, Dee Moine 292, Donna 292, Eric 292, Hubert 292, John 101, Lester A. 292, Lisa 292, Michael 292, Morris 292, Nancy 292, Ryan 292
BEAVENS, 66
BEAVER, Charles 535, Cholesta Frech 535, Lois 552, Rich 145
BEBB, Bette 527
BEBOUT, Elizabeth 527
BECHTEL, Catherine 538
BECK, Agnesia 256, Amher Denise 505, Ancel 262, Anna 256, Anna Marie 256, Brian Christopher 505, Bryan 262, Bryan Michael 262, Carl 505, Caroline 509, Carolyn 255, Charles 255, Charles 256, Charles Sumner 255, Daniel 255, Edith 255, Elaine 84, Elaine 262, Emma 256, Ernie 84, Freida 505, James Riley 505, Jamie Heather 505, Jason 262, Jason Ryan 262, John 256, John Michael 256, Joshua Jay 505, Josiah 256, Josiah Larimer 240, 255, Laura 255, 256Laura Louise 547, Llewellyn 256, Louis 505, Lydia 256, Magdalene 430, 431, Magdelena 256, Martin 256, Mary 256, Mary Ellen 240, Mary Ellen 255, Mathias 430, 431, Mattheis 256, Maude 255, 256, Michael 509, Nancy Larimer 255, Nellie Lorinda Stogdill 240, Pearl 538, Richard 262, Roseanna Hoelle 430, 431, Rosina 256, Ruth 262, Sadonna (Cotton) 297, Samuel 256, Shannon 239, 256, Shannon Larimer 240, 255, Tina 350, Velma 255, William 509
BECKER, Ben 207, George 181, George P. 188, Henry 73, Henry 331, Maria 514, Peter 470
BECKET, Jean Ann 475
BECKLER, Alison 272, Anna 272, Benjamin 272, Connie 439, Elizabeth 272, Frank 272, Gary 272, John 82, John 272, 439, John W. 272, Kathy 272, 439, Laura 272, Louis 272, Mary E. 320, Pauline 272, Timothy John 272, William 272
BECKMAN, Brian 418, Brian Matthew 256, Greg 418, Gregory B. 256, Rochelle 418, Rochelle Alaine 256, Sheila 256, Sheila 418, Teresa 418
BECKSTEIN, Jim 130
BEECHER, Beulah Callaway 257, Garry 75, 257, Grant College 257, Greg Allen 257, Henry Ward 257, Howard Jr. 257, Lyman 257, Martha (Tharp) 257, Melody Renee 257
BEECHLER, Beatrice 359, Clarice 359, Williard 359
BEEKER, Martha 478
BEEKNER, John 58
BEEKS, Bonnie 538, Cathy 512, Daniel C. 318, Floyd 318, Katie 137, Mary 152, Sylvia 318
BEELER, Anna Virginia 533, David 591, Eldon 602, Gladys 602, Joanna 591, Josephine 602, Julie 591, Levi 602, Lillian 602, Mark 591, Mary 602, Sandy 591, Suzanne 591, Tim 591
BEER, Eunice 340, Marlene 533, Mary 455
BEERBOWER, Mary Elizabeth 279
BEHNING, Arthur J. 305, Harry Rev. 502
BEHNKE, Alma 338
BEHRENS, Sandra 508
BEIGHLER, Alice 480, Eunice 480, Howard 480, Jim 480, Patricia 480, Ray 480
BEISEL, James 324, Kelli Renee 324
BEISER, Nancy 560
BEITELSHEES, Dorothy 347
BEITENHAUS, Amy 268, Earl 268, Heather 268, Sara 268
BEITENHOUSE, Earl 21
BEITENHOUSE, Julie 21
BELGER, John 95
BELL, Amanda 318, Angela 471, Arland 339, Beverly 339, Carol Lea 471, Catherine 519, Diane Elaine 471, Donna Pauline 471, E.B. 82, Floyd 471, Frances 471, Fred 178, Gigi 25, Godfrey 488, Gracie 221, James 16, 471, John 61, Karen 498, Lela 383, Levi 121, Opal 61, Phillip 471, Rebecca 607, Sherman 61, Thomas 320, Truman 383, Wilda 248, William 121
BELLA, Joseph 70
BELLMAN, 179
BELSLEY, Larry 229, Marcia 229
BENAVIDES, Helen Norton 293
BENDER, 66, Advanti 258, Alice Elene 306, Alice Elene (Martin) 525, Amanda Staver 258, Barbara Mast 257, Barbara (Mast) 258, Bessie 258, Caroline 394, Charlene 431, Charles Wilson 257, Della Jane 257, Donald Rev. 99, Elene 448, 449, Elizabeth 172Elizabeth 520, Elizabeth Maro 257, Elva 447, Fredrick Adonis 257, Georgiana 115, 116, 258, Gerry 306, Gerry Lynn 447, J. B. 591, Jennie 592, Jennie (Christman) 570, John 257, John 258, John Daniel 257, John Henry 257, John Urban 241, Jonathan 257, 258, Karen 306, Karen K. 525, Karen Kay 447, 525, L.L. 172, 180, 344, 592, Lawrence 258, Lawrence L. 257, 258, Lilah 258, Linda Maro 257, Louis Nelson 257, Lynn 591, Malcolm Dean 257, Margaret 394, Marjorie 258, Maro 6, Mary Alice 570, Mary Ann 552, Maryalis 258, Maude 468, Merlin 449, Merlin Keith 306, 447, 525, Merlin Keith (Buzzy) 257, Nancy 552, Paul 6, Paul 8, Paul 140, Paul 210, Paul L. 257, 258, 268, Paul L. Jr. 268, Paul Lee Jr. 257, Regina Lee 306, 447, Ruth 407, Sam 163, 181, 257, Susan Rebecca 579, V. O. 570, 592, V. O. (Vergie) 258, Valley 258, Velma L. 257, Vera 258, 592, W. P. (Will) 257, William 447, William Henry 257, Winnifred 258
BENNET, Fred 417
BENNETT, Alasander 372, Alice 386, Amber 414, Baili 327, Bob 140, 327, Bonnie 573, Brice Donald 327, Brock 327, Charles 327, Charles William 259, Clara 573, Claude E. 573, Crystal Avis 259, Doris 280, Edna 480, Edson 573, Evelyn Ilene 259, Faye 480, Florence 505, Florence L. 504, Florence Leone 259, Floyd 36, Garnet Viola 259, Harry 480, Howard 455, Ila 372, Jack D. 280, Jan 401, Jan (Hook) 414, Jennifer 489, John 496, John A. 259, John Edward 259, Josie 480, Josie (Hively) 327, Karen 327, Larry A. 505, Larry Arment 259, Linda Evelyn 489, Margaret 489, Marjorie Rose 259, Martha Jane 457, Mary A. 517, Mary Ann 517, Max 489, Melissa 256, Nancy 376, Nellie 480, Nicole 327, Nila (Scott) 327, Perry 327, Peter 280, R. C. 386, Ralph 573, Rhonda Kay 557, Robert 140, Robert 573, Robert Collins 386, Ruth (Thomas) 505, Ryan 489, Sally 280, Stephen 327, Thelma 566, Thelma Irene 259, Verla Mae 259, Wilma 480
BENSON, Elizabeth Hays 596, J. McLean 130, Jay 362, Jeff 362, Levin 596, Willia Frances 596, William C. 596
BENTLEY, Linda 393
BENTON, Daisy M. 502
BENTZ, Isabelle 267
BENZ, H. Rev. 68
BERCAW, Birdella 513
BERG, Joseph 255, Marcella 255, Nellie 255
BERGDOLL, Evelyn 320
BERGER, James 144
BERGHOFF, Beth 363
BERGHORN, Henry 73
BERGMAN, Anne 598, Anthony Phillip 396, Carmen Sue 598, Chris William 598, Christian 598, Christopher 598, Delores 398, Donald 598, Ellen Frances 396, Estella Pearl 598, Iona 84, Jean 598, Jessie Lee 585, Junior 514, Junior D. 396, Kerry 396, Kimberly May 396, Linda Kay 598, Lois Lorraine 585, Melissa Heather 598, Nathanuel 396, Nicole Sheree 396, Peggy 398, Phillip Oren 396, Ronald 585, Saundra 514, Terry B. 396
BERKEY, Norma 472
BERKEY, Orlo 472
BERKHEISER, Ann 414, Russell 414, William Russell 413
BERLING, Will H. 145, William 95
BERRY, Pamela 292, Patty 292, Robin 421, Steven 292, Thomas 292
BERTSCH, Alice 259, Caleb 487, Carmon 506, Gladys 434, Jeanne Sue 474, Jeanne Sue 567, Jeff 487, 533, Kathy 487, Kathy 533, Laura 230, Lillian 474, 567, Lonnie 340, Michael 506, Rose 434, Samuel 434, Sylvan 259, Thomas 340, Walter 340, Walter 474, Walter 567
BESER, Henrietta 512
BEST, Bevan 228, Brandon Eugene 375, Lorena Marie 375, Phillip 375, Steve 402, Trisha 402
BETHEL, Estella 372
BETTS, 66, Brandon M. 391, Corey P. 391, Emily D 391, Gene 78, Lucy 585, Sara J. 391
BETZ, Amber 362, Andrew 362, Barb 599, Brandon 362, Charles 415, Chris 599, Christopher Allen 599, Harold 144, Jerry 362, Jim 599, John 415, Keith 415, Martha 362, Phyllis Ilene 590, Steven 362
BEVENS, Jacob 366, Jacob 367, Virginia 584
BEVERIDGE, Albert J. 458
BEVINGTON, Ray 111, Susannah 260, Susannah 417
BEYER, Lillie 566, Matilda 566, Moses 566
BEYERER, C.C. 89
BEYMER, Jess 15
BIBB, Virginia Lusejus 405
BIBERSTEIN, Alexander 259, Alexander Martin 259, Benedict 259, 392, Carolyn 438, David 259, Emanuel 259, Ferdinand 259, Frederick 259, Jacob 259, John Ferdinand 259, Julia 259, Lena 259, Lena 392, Maria Louise 259, Maria Susannah 259, Philip 259, Rosanna 259, Rosanna Lena 259, Rosanna (Ritter) 392, William 259
BIBERSTINE, Albert 260, Albertine Bovine 548, Amy 260, Andrew 350, Ashley 586, Ashley Vaughn 285, Ashley Vaughn 413, 588, Barbara Kay 260, Becky Jo 260, Benedict Jr. 260, Betty 259, 572, Betty Eileen 259, Brandon Marvin 456, Brittany 364, Brittany Kay 413, Carl 364, Casey 364, Casey Alan 413, Charles 260, Chester 260, 456, Chris 350, Cindy 456, Cliff 364, Cliffton Paul 413, Cynthia Ann 456, David 350, David II 350, Don 259, Doris Marie 259, Edith Bleezarde 548, Edward 350, Emanuel 260, Emmanuel 548, Ethel (Hunnicutt) 413, Frank 259, Frank 260, Frank 413, Fred 260, Ida 260, Jean 259, Jessica 364, Jessica Jo 413, Joan 260, Jogene 259, Judith Ann 260, Karl Robert 456, Ked 285, Ked 588, Kenny 259, Kris Ann 413, Laura 260, Linda 259, Lisa 260, Lloyd 132, Lloyd 260, Lloyd 346, Lowell Scott 413, Margaret Louise 456, Marie 259, Martha 350, Martin 456, Marvin 364, Marvin Gene 456, Mary (Moser) 350, Matthew 364, Matthew 456, Matthew Lee 456, Michelle Renee 260, Mike 350, Mildred Chiles 548, Minnie 456, Netti (Durr) 413, Nora 9, Phyllis 259, Phyllis 586, Ralph 259, Rebecca 350, Richard Wayne 260, Robert 548, Rose 260, Roseann L. 548, Roy 259, 413, Steve 132, Steven Wayne 260, Terry 588, Theresa 150, Tim 259, Timothy Jay 413, V. Ked 586, V. Ted 259, V. Ted 413, 586, Victor Ked 413, William 136, 260, 578, William Lloyd 260, Zachary Ked 285, 413, 586, 588
BICKEL, Carolyn Jean 513, Clara 428, Harold Byron 513, Harold L. 513, Harriet Virginia 513, Leah Mae 513
BICKERS, Patricia 288
BICKETT, Craig 487, Diane 487, Earl 487, Keith 487
BIDDLE, Alexander 260, Angeline 260, Bernarr 463, Elizabeth 260, Elizabeth 417, Elizabeth 537, Fredrick 64, Henry 260, Jacob 260, James 260, John 260, John 417, Mary 260, Mary 542, Nelson 260, 356, Rachel 260, Sarah 398, Scott 542, Thomas 463, Victor 260
BIEBERICH, Edwin 252, Eileen 252, Luella Young 252
BIERIE, Abe 243, Elise 243
BIGGS, Evelyn 500, Lillian 531, Rob 531
BILBEE, Lewis 371
BILHEIMER, C. A. 75
BILLER, Kent Rev. 97
BILLMAN, Eliza 527
BINEGAR, Barbara 422, 576
BINGAM, Ruth 150
BINKLEY, Char 204, Steven 204, Victor 204
BIRCHFIELD, Margaret 462, Mary 462
BIRK, I. C. 64, 96
BISHOP, John 181, Sherry 483, Wayne 140, 165
BISS, Rev. 60
BISSON, Martin 454, Mary Ellen 454
BISTAUFFER, Sarah 527
BITTLE, Andreas 260, Andrew 260, Jacob 260
BIXLER, George 233, H. C. 64, 96
BLACK, Adrienne 274, Adrienne 289, Angela 289, C. S. 287, Carol 274, Carole Deane 289, Carrie 289, Catharine B. 294, Cecile 289, Charles 289, Daphne 289, Daphne (Johnloz) 414, Demonthese 289, Evah 289, George 289, Herbert 274, Herbert W. 289, Hobart 107, Inez 289, Kenneth 289, Laura 289, Mahalia Jackson 579, Martha 289, Michael 274, Michael 414, Michael Travis 289, Minnie 289, Rose Ellen 289, Ruth 289, Sarah 289, Suzanne 287, Tonya 289, Wendy 289, William Herbert 289
BLACKFORD, Mary 318
BLACKLEDGE, Jason B. 109
BLACKLEGE, Joseph 117
BLACKMAN, Dr. Charles J. 145, Lucille 156, JR, John 585
BLACKSTONE, Bertha 545, Emily Andrews 439, J. Kenneth 545, Jonas 439, Marjorie 545, Mary 439, Wm. 202
BLAIR, Alvin 261, Belvin 26, Carl 261, Carrie Elva (Blocker) 261, Catherine (Gehrett) 466, Erma 261, Ervin 261, George M. 261, Hannah E. 262 Hannah E. (Holloway) 261, Harold 261, Homer E. 559, John 480, John Jr. 261, John Oscar 261, Martha 337, Mary E. 594, Mary Louise 261, Muriel 480, Nina 554, Raymond 261, Robert 466, Russell 261, Sandra 333, Sandra 480, Sean 542, Sterling 261, Tim 480, Walter 261, Wanda 480
BLAKE, Anita 347, Boyd 515, Emily 347, Jenny 515, Judy 515, Mary Ann 515, Steve 347
BLAKESLEE, Abbey Lynne 262, John Alvin 262, Julie Elise 262, Lucas Paul 262, Seth Bonham 262
BLANCHARD, Clara 440
BLANTON, Patty 156
BLAUSER, Olaf 508
BLAZIER, Bonnie 277, Joseph 277, Joseph 277
BLEEKY, Chad A. 265, Rohin Franze 265, Scott A. 265
BLEM, Evert 472, Jean 472
BLESSING, Bev 84, Elaine 450
BLEVINS, Irma 292, Lynette Irene 396
BLEW, Betty 600, Donna 600, Gary 600, Gwyndolyn 600, Judy 600, Mike 600
BLINN, Doris 15, Ethel 15, Ethel 79
BLISS, Jeffery 216, Jeffrey 162, 185, 188
BLOCK, Phearaby 405
BLOCKER, Bill 243, Dequestney "Cassie", Ella 243, Emma 524, George W. 261, Otto 371, Susanna Bierie 367
BLOOD, B. D. Dr. 552, Hollis 552
BLOOM, Ann 564
BLOSE, Luverne 270
BLOSSER, Christina 333
BLOXSOM, Grace 389, Wm. 121
BLOXSOME, Anna 262, Arthur Dr. 490, Arthur William 262, Grace 262, Irene 490, James 262, Naomi 262, Naomi 425, Richard 262, William 262
BLUE, Catherine 432, Elizabeth 432, Helen 304, Mary 276, Melissa M. 433, Michael 432, Michael C. 121
BLUME, Ben 570, Eva 570, James 570
BLUMENHORST, Ollie 239, Violet 239
BLUNT, Joseph 538
BLY, Nellie 13
BLYTHE, Marilyn 250
BOALS, Lavina 463
BOBAY, Edward 273, Lucille (Haflich) 378, Marie 273
BOCKMAN, John 89
BODINGER, Charles 271, Martha Mitckess 271
BOEHM, Anna Maria 254, John Philip 85, 254, Martin 58
BOEHMER, Joseph 13
BOESLUND, Cassandra Raeannan 445, Kathy Jill 445, Sarah Rebekah 445

BOETIN, Kitty E. 346
BOGAART, Blanche Vande 535
BOGUE, William 446
BOHLKE, Lois Heller 390
BOHME, Mike 285
BOICE, Kayle Nicole 259, Kayle Nicole 504, 505, Ruth Elaine 259, 505
BOLINGER, Abraham 68, Alice (Bosler) 359, Alyssa 359, Amanda 359, Brande 359, Chelsea 359, Dale 359, Dann 359, Donna L. 321, Edith 359, Gene 317, Gene 359, Jesse J. 359, Karl 359, Levi 359, Lucille 359, Marilyn 359, Mark 359, Melissa 359, Mick 359, Nancy 359, Peggy 359, Ray 64, Raymond 317, Raymond C. 359, Samantha 359,
BOLLINGER, Ida 463
BOLTIN, Charles 555, Mary A. (Richardson) 348, Mary Elizabeth 348, Minnie Stahl 555, Murial 315, Ninetta 555, Stewart 348, William J. 348
BOLTMEIER, Michelle 598
BOLTON, R.H. 82
BOMAR, Tom 523
BONAR, Judith 251
BOND, Corinne M. 464, Lauren Delane 527, Margaret 527, Max 464, Oral 298, Roy J. 527, Roy Jackson 527, Ruth 527
BONE, Jeffrey 500, Leslie Carol 500
BONEWITZ, 107, Bob 539, Bob Rev. 89, Diana 539, Karen Sue 539, Mary Juanita 539, Robert 107, Robert Raymond 539
BONHAM, Asa Emma Thompson 262, Burdain 262, Carey W. 262, Carl 214, Julie Anne 262, Lauren Gayle 262, Nancy 137, Nancy Joan Howard 262, Paul Irvin 262, Richard 262, Robert William III 278, Robert William Jr. 278, Sarah E. 262, Vivian Lynne 262, William "Bill"
BONNER, Diane 535, Mark 535
BOOHER, Abbie 428, Blanche Waldene 358, Charles J. 570, Debra Sue 570, Kandice Lynn 553, Kandice Lynn 570, Pauline 15, Terri Anne 570, Virgil 15, Virginia 570, William 144
BOOK, Pauline 539, Alice M. 396, Alice Marie 395, Andrew Jackson 262, Cory Jane 262, Edna 262, Elaine Kay 262, Gary Wayne 262, George Andrew 262, George Washington 262, Horton Hamilton 262, James Grover 262, Jeremy LaVaughn 262, Joyce Ann 262, Laura L. 262, Learna E. 262, Leota Ethel 262, Lesty Ann 262, Loreta E. 262, Marcia Lynne 262, Mary Elizabeth (Holloway) 262, Perry Alexander 262, Ray 395, Roseta 335, Ruth (Evans) 395, Thommas 262, Virgil LaVaughn 262
BOONE, Ann (Packer) 263, Daniel 43, Daniel 326, Dorothy Pauline 326, Gary 145, 227, 263, Gary L. 145, Harold 263, June 263, Scott Aaron 263, Stacie Lynn 263
BOONSTRA, Charles 140
BOOROR, Lauretta 84
BOOTH, Abby 408, Amy 408, Bill 588, Carol 588, Cathy 503, Chad 303, Connie 330, Connie Mae 247, David 588, Don 408, Elizabeth 561, Frank 588, Fred 303, Fred 588, Mark 588, Rosemond 303, 588, Timothy 588, Verda Williams 458
BOOTS, Angie 594, Bentley 497, Beverly 550, Braden 497, Brent 497 Brittany 497, Claron 550, Jamie 497, Kenneth 594, Larry 497, Patty 594, Tina 594, Vern 100, Vickie 497
BORCHERDING, Carol 585
BORDONARO, Kim 264
BOREN, Myrna 562
BORGMAN, Richard 98
BORING, Clara Mae 543
BORN, F. A. 564
BORNE, Catherine Wagner 263, Charles Conrad 263, Christ 263, Elizabeth 263, Elizabeth Ann 247, Grace 263, Jacob 263, James Henry 247, Louise 263, Louise Katherine 263, Nancy Elaine 247, Patricia Jean 263, Richard James 247, W. E. 81
BORROR, Allen 264, Danny 264, Dee 264, Dennis 264, Earl Richard 264, Edward 264, Eric 264, Erin 264, Evelyn Jane 264, Glenn 264, Glenn Jr. 264, Jarrett 264, Jenny 264, Jill 264, 279, Jobe 264, Judy 264, Justin 264, Lee 264, Lenna 264, Lisa 264, Lucille (Steffen) 279, Manda 264, Mike 264, Randy 264, Richard Earl 264, Ross 264, Sean 264, William 130, Wrenn 264, Wrenn 279
BORTON, Dolores E. 235, Isabel 244
BOSSARD, Ida Bell 596, Jacob 68
BOSSERT, Mary 593
BOSSTICK, Joe 275, John 275, Mary 519, Mary (Spore) 275, Ronald 275, Shane 275
BOTHAST, Brett Lee 396, Brian 396
BOTLIN, Ralph 293
BOTRUFF, Margaret 560
BOTTS, Benjamin 264, Cedric 454, Cedric R. 264, Chris L. 264, Cynthia 265, Darrell 264, 454, Darrell B. 264, Darrell Steven 264, David 264, Doug 454, Douglas 264, Douglas S. 265, E. H. Dr. 264, Ellenor (Fordyce) 264, Erica 264, Jason 264, Kelly 265, Mark 265, Martin 453, Mary Malinda (Martin) 264, Mary (Martin) 265, Mary Martin 328, Mary Martin 453, Michael V. 264, Neenah S. 264, Nilah J. 264, Patrick C. 264, Raven 264, Rita 265, Sandra 264, Sheila 265, Susan 264, Vernon 264, Vernon 265, Vernon F. 264
BOTTSCHALK, Ruth 367
BOULWARE, Naomi 161, 579
BOURNE, Bill 307, Linda 307
BOUSE, Calmar Ray 466, Forest 466, Francis (Gaskill) 466, Jack 466, Joseph 466, Lemuel 466, Linda Sue 290, Lottie (Twigg) 466, Lucille Irene 466, Mary Ellen 428, Rex 466, Virginia 466
BOVINE, Albertine 260, Mary 567
BOWEN, B.F. 6
BOWER, Angela R. 265, Ann Margaret 346, Carrie 266, Charles 266, Clara 265, Cynthia 265, Dennis A. 265, Dewhite 265, Diana K. 265, E. J. 265, Ella Mae 265, Ephraim L. 266, Frank 265, Gary A. 265, George E. 265, Gerald 265, Hannah 265, Henry 265, Irvin R. 265, Israel 265, Jacob 265, Joel 265, Joel D. 265, Judy 265, Kari 265, Kent P. 265, Lavelle 265, Linda 265, Mabel N. 301, Mabel Naomi 266, Mahlon 265, Marvin C. 265, Micael L. 265, Noah 265, Paul 265, Paul L. 265, Rebecca 265, Simon 265, Sondra S. 265, Viola 265, Willison 265, Zeffa 266
BOWERFIND, Henry 216
BOWERS, Albert M. 367, Bradley Dean 303, Ephraim L. 404, George 71, George W. Rev. 74, Kelly Ann 303, Larry 303, Mary 500, Mrs. 60
BOWERSOCK, Donnabelle Bolinger 251, Gail 251, Gary W. 251, Pamela J. 251, Scott W. 251
BOWMAN, Adam 267, Adam Bruff 266, Adam Jr. 266, Alice (Sauthine) 267, Ballard 99, Bert 320, Blake 266, Bonnie Albert 267, Bret 266, Byrl 266, Byron 266, Byron 266, Byron Washington 267, Catherine Lucile 266, Cathryne 266, Charles 266, Charles A. "Pop", Connie Caley 529, D. E. 266, Daniel Booker 266, Daniel Booker Bowman 266, Debbie 303, Dious 266, Don 303, Donald 266, Dorothy Elizabeth 267, Doyle 552, Ed 266, Eliza Jane 512, Eliza Jane (Archbold) 407, Elizabeth Spicer 267, Ellis 266, Elmer Laverne 267, Ethel 475, Eva Myrtle 267, Eva Myrtle 407, Eva Myrtle 410, Frank 266, Gail R. 267, George Dewey 267, George Oren 266, George Oren 266, Gideon 267, Harold 266, 602, Harry Oliver 267, Hellie Florence 267, Henry 266, Herman J. 267, Howard 266, 271, Howard McKinley 267, James 266, James L. 267, James Lewis 267, James W. 267, Jeffrey Lee 267, Jennie 266, Jennifer 266, Jeromy Edward 267, Jerry 271, Jesse Winfield 267, Jim 552, Joanna 266, Jodie 266, John 266, John 266, John 271, John 512, John Adam 267, John Adam 407, Karolyn May 267, Kasandrea Michelle 267, Keith Murray 267, Kenneth 266, Kenneth E. 267, Lewis Claude 267, Lisa 443, Loretta 516, Luster 266, Lydia (Bond) 266, Mary 266, 271, Mary Beth 552, Mary Lavina 267, Mary Shaffer 266, Mattie 267, Nancy 271, Nellie Florence 512, Oren 207, 266, Patricia 266, Rachael Funk 266, Ralph Wilmer 267, Rebecca 271, Richard 266, 267, Richard S. 266, Robert 266, Robert Wilson 267, Roy 266, Ruth (Hedges) 389, Samuel 266, Shirley 307, Vera 266, Viletta Jane 267, Virgil Ray 267, William 266, William A. 267, William Charles 267, William E. 266, William E. 266, Zola May 267, Zora 266 Jr. Adam 266, Sr. Adam 266
BOWSER, Margaret Ann 498
BOXELL, 66, Darlene Cecelia 574, Manda 471, Norma 320, Norma 585
BOYD, J.W. 82, Martha 342
BOYE, Larry 402, Larry 411, 426, 508, Pamela Le 508
BOYER, Betty 583, Davilla 535, Lena 535,
BOYLE, Ellen 331, Evelyn Watkins 456, Jennie 331, Mollie 331, Patrick 331, William 331
BOYTS, Gene 594, Lois 594, Lois 594
BOZE, Phoebe Ann (Buel) 279
BRAAKSMA, Marty 140
BRACHT, Rosie (Nyffeler) 492
BRACKE, Sally 150
BRACKER, Maryann 574, Teresa 405
BRACKIN-BROWN, Andrew Jeffery 469
BRADBURN, Angela 302, Cindy 402, Clifford R. 257, 268, Dirk 402, Gladys 268, Irene 268, Jane 268, Jennifer 302, Maro 268, Maro L. 257, 258, Marvin 402, Matthew 302, Olis 416, Ruby 268, Ruth 268, Stephanie 402, Teri Jo 402, Trent 402, Vernon 302, William 268
BRADBURY, Edward "Ted", Edward 560, Frances 560, Frances (Smuts) 531, John 560, Louise 560, Robert 560, Thomas 560
BRADEN, Ardis A. 268, Carl 421, Edna M. 268, Frances Harris 268, Franklin C. (Cad) 268, Jessie M. 297, John 268, John Charles 119, Neil 268, Ralph D. 268
BRADFORD, Lillian (Leas) 435, Lydia Sue 350, Lydia Sue 381, Marilyn 350, Marilyn Sue 381, William 350, William 381
BRADLEY, Donna 326, Louis 146, Louis Mrs. 146, Martha 136
BRADTMUELLER, Cindy 483
BRADWAY, Gloria 396
BRADY, Clara 566, Clara Ellen 565
BRADYBERRY, Bessie 283
BRAGG, Earl 58, Mary 244
BRAHAM, John 303, Mary 303
BRANCH, Deb 595
BRAND, Carl 271, Donald 271, Helen Brinkman 271, James 271, Robert 271, Rosemary 271
BRANDENBURG, Carrie 592, Heather 592, Lois 592
BRANDON, Deborah 474
BRANDYBERRY, Floyd 395, Helen Gracia 395, Josephine (Karns) 395
BRANER, Artis 535, Elis 78, Elizabeth 331
BRANIGIN, Roger 42
BRANNING, Henry Jr. 281
BRASE, Clara 564
BRASSEUR, Benois 446
BRAUCHLA, Bridget Jean 536
BRAUN, Bruce 585, Elizabeth 595, Hope 585, Ralph 585
BRAY, Clyde 140, Polly 569
BRAZIER, Jacob (Rev.) 572
BREECE, C. A. 145, 163
BREEDLOVE, Arthur 268, Barbara 321, Betty 268, Carolyn 536, Coralee 268, Deleen 268, Ellen 414, Emil 268, Ivan Eugene 268, Judy 268, Karen 268, Linda 268, Oather 268, Theresa 268
BREGE, William R. 73
BREHOB, John S. 357, Jonnelle Lynne 357, Julie Ann 357
BREIER, Fredericke 252, Friedericke 73
BREINER, Joseph Madison 547
BREMER, Anna 594
BRENDEL, Greg 98
BRENNAN, Michael Patrick 363, Timothy P. 363, William Michael 363
BRENNER, Tom 140
BRENTLINGER, June 403
BRESSER, 331
BRETZ, J. L. 85
BREWER, Bryan 269, Camille 244, Camille Elise 269, Dorothy 269, F. Hale 269, F. M. 269, Forace Hale 244, Forace Hale 269, Forace Mahlon 269, Jennie 269, Jennie Evelyne (March) 269, Joan 269, Kay 244, Kayleen Janele 269, Lyn 244, Lynette Elaine 269, M. Max 269, Moro 269, Phyllis 269, Rosalda 269, Ruth 269, Virginia 269, W. Ray 269, Wanda 269
BREWSTER, Bert 497, Janean L. 375, Marjorie 497
BREY, Shirley 402
BRICE, George 266
BRICKELY, Bryce A. 265
BRICKELY, Jessica L. 265, Kent P. 265, Sondra S. 265
BRICKER, Betty Irene 359, Francis Earl 359, Frederick Earl 359, Jennie Kathryn (Maddux) 359, John Edwin 359, Joyce Marie 359, Kathryn 525, Lawrence Kaye 359, Lester Eugene 359, Walter Lavern 359, William 525
BRICKLEY, Adaline 270, Alan Chandler 270, Alfred 270, Alice 270, Alice 410, Alyssa L. 270, Andrea K. 270, Andrew 13, Andrew 270, Andrew 270, Andrew 342, Andrew John 269, Arnetta 270, Athelma 571, Barbara Haiflich 270, Beatrice 270, Bertia 270, Bill 270, Bob 233, Brian L. 270, Brooks F. 270, Bryce 270, Bryce 270, Brynn Crystal 270, Bulinda 270, Catherine Lesh 359, Chester 270, 410, Clarence 270, 503, Cora 270, Darrel K. 270, David 270, Dean 270, Delilah 475, Dinah Marie 269, Dixie 270, Dorothy Lewis 270, Douglas 270, Effie 270, Elizabeth 270, 447, Frank 48, Frieda 270, George 270, Gladys (Robaugh) 410, Gladys Rohrabaugh 270, H. D. 136, 214, 269, 280, 573, Harry 216, Harry Dwight 263, 269, Harry Dwight 359, Harry Dwight Jr. 269, Herb 270, Herbert 270, Herbert 410, Hilliard 571, Ina Agar 263, J. A. 161, James A. 270, Janet Marshall 270, Janice 270, Jared Clinton 270, Jason Paul 270, Jean Diann 269, Jeffrey Thomas 269, Jerry 270, Joan 270, John 270, John Dwight 269, Jonathan 270, Joshua 270, Joshua A. 270, Judy 304, Kathryn Bulinda 394, Kevin L. 270, Laura 270, Laura Jean 269, Lester 270, Lewis 270, Lewis 359, Lewis 370, Liberta 342, Louise Kay 270, Marie 269, Marie 359, Mary 270, Maude Edna 257, Maxine Caley 99, Mick L. 270, Milo 270, Minnie Mosure 269, Nancy Ann (Jennie) 458, Nicole Lynn 270, Ola I. 270, Olan 165, Patricia 270, Peter 270, Peter 270, Rachel Marie 270, Raymond 269, Raymond 359, Richard 269, Richard 270, Richard Agar II 269, Richard D. 270, Rick E. 270, Robert W. 270, Sarah 270, Sarah Jane 269, Scott A. 270, Stephen M. 270, Thomas Jefferson 269, Thomas Jefferson 359, Thomas Raymond 269, Thomas W. 270, Tom 529, Virgie 335, William 270, William 270, William Herbert 270, Zelah 161, Zora Weikle 270
BRICKLY, Belinda Wolfcale 604, Effie 281, George 604
BRIDGE, Henry Rev. 97
BRIDGEMAN, Peggy 487, Ryan 487, Scott 487
BRIDGES, Henry 98
BRIGGANS, Susannah Schory 321
BRIGHAM, Anita Dygert 352, Ben 352, Cindy 352, Kris 352, Nate 352
BRIGHT, J.F. 58, Ruth 134
BRILES, John W., Jr. 569, Kathy Ellen 569, Kristy Denise 569, Nathan Wayne 569
BRILL, Carolyn 528, Corey Brill 528, John W. 528, John W. II 528, Robert E. 528
BRINDLE, William 332
BRINEMAN, Ingabee (Bee) 271, Jeffery Daniel 271, Vernosha Belle Croasdale 271
BRINER, Brian 402, Cheryl 402, Corvin 145, Joe 402, Susan 402
BRINKMAN, Barbara 271, Carl 271, Edward 271, Edward Jr. 271, Ellen 271, Helen 271, Henry 271, Irma (Matson) 271, Mildred 271, Norman 271, Rodney 271, Sandra 271
BRINNEMAN, 66, Agustus 527, Amanda Nicole 359, Amber Dawn 272, Ashley Nicole 272, Augustus Newton 272, Carl 98, Cathy 527, Clara 272, Daniel 272, 516, David 359, Edward Marcellus 272, Eliza Allen 272, Elva 516, Emmanuel 239, Franklin 359, Ida Ellen 272, Iliph Elmore 272, James Edward 272, Jefferson 272, Jefferson Daniel 272, Jessica Dianne 272, Jim 527, Kathryn Sue 272, Laura Jean 272, Lawrence Ross 272, Loren 527, Lorin Richard 272, Margaret Katherine 272, Mary Elizabeth 421, Mary Etta 272, Mathias Emanuel 272, Medora 272, Oscar Homer 272, Priscilla (Tarr) 359, Rachel Rebecca 272, Rebecca (Shaufer) 272, Shawn Ross 272, Shawna Lea 272, Solomon Wilmore 272, Steven Michael 359, Ted Franklin 359, Thomas Edward 272, Vernon 527, Vernon Edward 272
BRISTOL, Clarissa 466
BRITSCH, Alice 488
BRITT, Bev 342
BRITTENHAM, David 308, Docia Ann 308, Isaac Johnson 308, Margaret Carmean 308, Ruth 375
BRITTINGHAM, Anna (Hunt) 349, Bertha 349, Robert 349
BRITTON, Beth 355, Dale 355, Gary 355, Harold 355, Paul 355, Wayne 355
BRNKKMAN, Edna 271
BROCKELSBY, Anna Rose 333, Charles 333, Daren 333, Nick 333
BROCKMAN, Barbara 515
BROCKMANN, William F. 145
BRODT, Catherine 272, Charles 538, Christena 272, Elizabeth 272, Emma 538, Emma Sechler 391, Emma (Sechler) 448, Euclair 538, Frederick 538, Gottlieb 272, 391, 448, Hans 272, Jakob 272, Johann 272, John 272, 391, 448, 538, Lana 272, Margaretta Seaman 391, Margaretta (Seaman) 448, Mary 272, Rachel 272, Rutherford 538, William 538
BROGLIN, Marilyn 548
BROMAN, Allison 273, 350, Angela 273, Angela 350, Barbara 273, Benjamin 273, Carl Edward 273, Corey 273, David Alan 273, Eric 273, Joseph 273, Nancy Christina 273, Nelson 350, Nelson Arthur 273, Ralph 273, Robert Eric 273, Rosa 273, Roy 273
BRONNER, Anna 109, Guinevere 109, 341, 437, Jacob 109, 341, 437, John George 437, Linnie Elizabeth 341, Linnie Gronner 437, Mina 341, Mina Wilhelmina 437
BROOKHART, Amanda Elanor 533
BROOKMYER, Carol Ann 249
BROOKS, Hank 563, Lt. Nyal 43
BROOKSHIRE, Carl Rev. 517
BROPHY, Evyline 339
BROTHER, Jane 350
BROTHERS, Erma 273, John 273, Lance 273, Lawrence <Larry> 273, Lora 273, Lorena 273
BROTHERTON, Elizabeth 313, Jim 313, Sandra A. 481
BROUGH, C. 83
BROWER, Polly 548
BROWN, 66, Alice Erminnie 274, Amber 519, Amber D. 275, Amos 274, Amos 527, Amy May 426, Anna 527, Anna Emojean 519, Anna L. 418, Arthur Shriver 275, Asa 214, Asa Dr. 280, Bert 582, Bertha 274, C.I. 82, Carol Edwin 273, Charles 274, Charles 527, Charles Richard 385, Cherlyn "Sucee", Christie R. 265, Christopher 429, Christopher Allen 467, Christopher David 445, Clarence 274, Cleodis 533, Clyde 275, Clyde 275, Corina 274, Corina Mae 309, Craig 519, Craig M. 275, Craig Matthew 274, Cynthia 519, Cynthia E. 275, D. A. J. 98, Daniel Routh 274, 309, Darrell 519, Darrell E. 274, 275, David 204, 274, Deborah Sue 445, Delphia 519, Denise Jane 385, Derrick 275, Diane 575, Diane Marie 467, Dortha 274, Doyle 318, Earl 275, Edewin 274, Edith 274, Edna 155, Edna V. 267, Edwin 275, Edwin V. 275, Edwin V. 519, Edwin Vernon 519, Effie 417, Elisha 309, Elizabeth 474, Emily Jane 584, Emojean 274, Eric 519, Eric A. 275, Ethel McDonald 369, Everett 37, Evert 107, Frances 568, Frank T. 275, G.W. 582, George Wilbert 274, Gloria 519, Gloria J. 275, Gordon 418, H. Dr. 568, Hanna 527, Harold 275, Harold 275, Harold Dean 273, Harry 144, Hermina 418, Hilary 274, Howard 275, J.E. 202 Jacob 274, 275, Jarred 275, 519, Jason 519, Jason P 275, Jayson 275, Jess 274, Jess 527, Joan C. 347, John 309, John Sloan 274, Joy 275, Joy L. 275, Julia Taylor 324, Katherine 364, Katherine 364, Kathryn L. 529, Kent 275, Kent Richard 445, Kimberly 467, Larry Wayne 273, Levi 519, Lewis 274, Lewis 527, Lillian Marie 414, Lois 270, Mae 274, Mahlon Dehold 273, Mamie 582, Marcia 519, Marica E. 275, Marie 381, Marilyn 460, Marjorie 381, 382, Marjorie May 381, Marna Nadine 445, Martha Rose (Shriver) 275, Marvin 519, Marvin G. 275, Marvin Lewis 273, Mary 155, 240, Mary Ann 324, Mary E. 582, Mary Ellen 394, Mary Jane 274, Matthew 402, Michelle 429, 519, 575, Michelle Lynn 445, 467, Michelle R. 275, Michelle Rene 274, Nancy 402, Oscar 413, 414, Paula 362, Pearl Bell (Marker) 275, Phil 402, Philip 324, Phillip 275, Polly 518, Randall 265, Ray 145, Ray P. 178, Robert 274, Robert L. 347, Robert Leon 273, Sarah 274, 527, Saundra 519, Saundra A. 275, Shirley Jean 385, Soloman 274, 527, Sue 204, Sue Ellen (Higgins) 394, Tad 429, Tanya Lynn 469, Ted 575, Thelma R. (Darr) 347, Travis R. 265, Vernon 429, Violet 274, Violet 582, W.B. 163, 184, Wayne 299, Wesley 275, Wilfred 318, William 275, William 275, William 527, Willima 274, Zelah 161
BROWNING, Fawn Elysse 571
BROWNS, Anna 274
BROYLES, Barbara 439, David 439, Elizabeth 568, Elizabeth Ellen 250, Jonathon 439, William 439
BRUBAKER, Amanda 150, Amanda Caroline 276, Angela Kay 276, Benjiman Joseph 276, Betty 560, Bill 130, Bill L. 305, Billy Lee 276, Connie 6, Connie Dalrymple 150, 604, Glenna 500, Harmon 165, Kelly, Lionel Kent 276, Mark 299, Mary A (Watson) 276, Mary Elizabeth 276, Matthew Lee 276, Matthew Lee II 276, Pamala Lynn 276, Ralph D. 276, Virgie 180, Yvonne 319
BRUCKERT, John 89
BRUMBAUGH, Ann 605, David Henry 276, Ed 556, Edna Pearl 276, Edward Merl 276, Isaac 276, Martin G. 276, Melissa 240, Pearl 556, Rebecca (Waltz) 276, Ruth 556, Steven 240
BRUNEGRAFF, H. R. 107
BRUNER, Debra 400
BRUNNER, George Rev. 91
BRUNNING, Elizabeth 584
BRUNO, John 155
BRUNS, Marilyn 303
BRUNZELL, Carol 349
BRUSLER, Dr. 455
BRYAN, Elias 82, Mabel Lois 569
BRYANT, 331, Betty 277, Bonnie 277, Bonnie Lynne 277, Brenda 277, Brenda Lee 277, David 277, Deanna 277, Duane 277, Edmond 433, Elizabeth Ann 264, Erin 277, Esther (Downing) 433, Frances 277, Gaynell 542, Gaynelle 277, Geneva 277, Guilia 277, Heidi 517, Lee 277, Myrl 277, Olive Isabelle (Ladd) 433, Ozro 433, Ozro (O.L.) 277, Paul 264, Paul Jr. 264, Robert 264, Ross 277, Ross 433, Ross Wayne 277, Vernon 277, Vernon 277, Vernon 433, William 277, William 433
BRYSON, D.A. 86
BUCHER, Carol Jean (Keel) 494, Dr. Wendell 160, Joseph 385, Kelly 385, Kristin 385
BUCKLAND, Christina 483, Gregory 483, Helen 15, Howard (Red) 15, Karen 393, Kim 472
BUCKLE, Fern 570
BUCKLES, Ilow 245, J.H. 202, Lewis 102
BUCKLEY, Katherine Mae 419
BUCKNER, "Jimmy", Amelia Margaret 310, Amelia Margaret (Yelton) 278, Barbara 279, Beverly 146, 279, Bradley 279, Bruce 279, Caroline Elizabeth 278, Caroline Elizabeth 488, Charles Nicholas 279, Daisy Beulah 279, Dale 278, Doster 278, Edward Adams 279, Emma Adams 279, Frances Esther 490, Francis Marion 278, Francis Marion 307, Frank 160, 397 Franklin 144, 202, Franklin B. 279, George W. Dr. 279, John 238, 279, 310, John 514, John T. 311, Joy 127, Joy 278, Joyce 8,

Joyce Terry 278, Kathryn Annahelle 278, Lurana 310, Lurania 514, Martha 514, Millie Jane 395, Minnie Floretta 310, 311, Philip 311, Phillip 307, 310, Sally 279, Sarah Josephine 279, Stella (Doster) 307, Tahitha Ann 310, William 310, 395, William Nicholas 278, 279

BUCKSOT, Harry 242, Shirley Ann 242, Jr. Olin Ranchell (Jim) 242

BUEL, Arlene 364, Charles Emery 279, Della Mae Hime 279, Edward 279, Emma Luella 279, Faye Irene 279, George Brooks 279, George Emery 279, Howard Lemuel 279, Iva 337, Marvin 279, Roger Lee 279

BUGH, Miss Laura 121

BUIE, Carolyn Beth 552, Jack 552

BULGER, Dail 279, Dennis 234, Dennis D. 279, Eliza 245, Jane 279, Joseph S. 279, Judy 279, Milton Claire 279, Robert D. 279, Roger Claire 279, Sandra K. 279, Sarah E. (Guthrie) 279, Theodore D. <Ted> 279, Thomas Martin 279, Tom 279, Tom Jr. 279. William B. Bill, 279, William Daily 279

BULL, Charles Emery 279, George Brooks 279, George Emery 279, Howard Lemuel 279, Leota Irene 279, Mary Elizabeth 279

BULLOCK, Rollie 264

BULLOCK, Tony 264

BULMAHN, Florence 482, Hugo 482, Maxine 482, 483, Maxine Ann 482

BULTEMEIER, Brett 483, Carla 388, Deanna 388, Gilbert 388, Janice 483, Larry 483, Marci 483

BUTEMEIR, Clarence 77

BULTER, D. E. 147

BUMGARNER, Carrie Jo 279, Joe 279, Jordon Keith 279, Keith Richard 279, Kelli Marie 279, Michael Joe 279, Richard L 279, Richard L. 356, Sharlene A. 391, Steven Lee 279

BUMP, Philenia 531

BUMPUS, Joseph 82

BUNCH, Ardelia 320, Elda Mae 320, Eldon 351, Elizabeth 320, Gene 320, Jacklyn J. 357, Joe 320, John 320, Karen 351, Katherine 351, Keith 351, Kent 351, Mable 320, Marguerite 320, Myra 498, Oscar 320, Ruth 320, Sanford 320

BUNDY, Christopher 446, William 446

BUNN, Althea Ade 280, Darya 280, Evelyn 280, Henry 280, Jacob 106, Molly 453

BUNSOLD, Doris 265

BUNTING, Cynda 336, John 336

BURCHARD, F.D. 144, John 458

BURDEN, Karen Diane (Crowl) 303

BURDGE, Virginia Lou 517

BURDJENSKI, Donna 485

BURGAN, C.S. 202, David 112, George F. 259

BURGER, Cal 38, Calvin E. 403, 529, Julia F. 529, Kathy J. 529, Kathy Jo 403, Kimberly 529, Kimberly Rene 403, Lucrecia 478

BURGESS, Dick 182, Firman 552, Larry 552, Lou 182, Nicole 552, Shannon 552, Wanda 552

BURGET, Dorothy 407, Ezra 407, Helen 407

BURKE, Ann 368, Cynthia Ann 364, Cynthia Maxine 337, David 368, Don H. 368, Kathryn Kay 368, Scott 529, Shawn 353

BURKETT, Paul 58

BURKHALTE, Edward 98

BURKHART, 66, Bera Caroline (Walker) 280, Beth Ann 280, Dave 588, Kenneth 264, Kenneth 454, Kenneth W. 280, Kimberly Kay 280, Mary Lou 453, Mary Lou (McBride) 280, Michelle 588, Scott 588, Williard E. 280

BURKHEAD, Doris 347

BURKHOLDER, Gary 560, Irene Louise 560, Jayne 560, Martin 560, Pamela 560

BURKLO, Cecil 502, Ed 502, Joan 502, Laura 502, Ruth 502, Stella 502

BURLEIGH, Andrew James 280, James F. 280, Janet 280, Timothy Swaim 280

BURLEY, Carrie (Ward) 420, Howard 420, Phyllis 420

BURMAN, Charlotte 277, George W. 582, Lydia Trimmer 582, Zora 293, Joe 524

BURNAU, Eldie 234

BURNEAU, Eliza Jane 537, Thomas 537

BURNETT, Alan 402, Celinda Alice 430, Mary (Cochran) 294, Megan 402

BURNIAUSKIS, Agnes Dominice 460, Ygnac 460

BURNISTON, Amanda Renee 576

BURNISTON, Ray Jr. 576

BURNS, Brandon 457, Carolyn 283, Cliff 457, Coleen 457, Conor Patrick 281, Ed 281, Edmund 281, Joey 457, John 457, Logan Timothy 281, Merlin John 281, Minta 484, Morgan Lewis 281, Robert 457, Ronald 281, Susie (Mussetter) 281, Taunya 457, Virgil 281

BURNSIDES, John 193

BURNWORTH, Ira Newton 398

BURRELL, Emma Shoaf 573, Mary 573, William 573

BURROUGHS, Douglas Lynn 260, Lynn 260, Tanya Michele 260

BURTON, Diana Sue 255, Lillian 255, Roger 255, Yvonne 58

BURWELL, Molly 121, Newton 202

BUSCH, Claire 581

BUSCHE, Daniel Mark Hardy 242, Laura 525, Mark William 242, Matthew Jerome 242

BUSE, Lana K. 408

BUSH, Angela Jayne 305, George 38, 538, Jason Robert 305, Myrtle 245, Ronald G. 305, Sarah Elizabeth 305, Stella 502

BUSHEE, Ada 507, Allen 295, Amy Jennifer 507, Andrew 281, Anna S. 295, Betty 281, Caleb Dean 442, David Lynn 507, Edward 281, George 58, Gregory 281, Harley 281, Jacob 281, James 281, Jane (Woods) 295, Jeffrey 281, Jeremy David 507, Kayleen Anne 507, Kenneth 507, Mandy 281, Meggan 281, Olive (Cave) 281, Tavis 281, Thomas 442

BUSHONG, David 58

BUSSELL, George 415

BUSTOS, Ruth 577

BUTCHER, Audrey G. (Perry) 383, Carolyn S. 383, Charles 383, Kenneth 383, Larry 383, Nancy 383, Neil 98, Robert 383, Robert H. 383, Sarah 239, Sharon 383

BUTLEMEIER, Imogene 526

BUTLER, Amanda 416, Amanda Catlin Gray 421, Edward 416, Edward S. 421, H.E. 58, Lorene 402, MaDonna 362, Martha 416, Mary 416, Mary Alice 309, 421 Rachel Jane 416, 417

BUTT, Richard 113

BUUCK, Adele 526, John 526

BUYER, Jos 89

BUZZARD, Brenda 15, John 299, Rachel Ruggles 299, Sarah 299

BYANSKI, Tom 140

BYERLY, Jenilee 501, Jessica 501, Kimberly 501, Kirt 501, Maxine Louise 585, Sheila 501, Theo 221

BYNUM, Daniel 515, Gilbert 130, Hulda 515, Jeanne 165, John II 515, Lois 515

BYRD, Amos L. 575, Homer 521, Isabel 134, Jack 266, Leonora 333, Richard E. 36, Susan 342, Tim 342, Tom 342

CAIN, Beth 462, Brian 462, Jack 462, Lori 462, Millie (Thompson) 307, Nondus Clova 307, Osro 307, Rebecca Ann 462, Ryan 462

CALDERON, Ana 371

CALDWELL, Pamela Kahn 527

CALE, Cindy 401, Curt 598, Gabriel 598, Helen 598, Hettie 555, Marilyn 598, Mark 598, Michelle 598, Ray 598, Shari 598

CALEY, Barbara 281, 378, Cressie I (Haflich) 360, Don Clifford 378, Donald 281, Dwight 570, Elizabeth 570, Ella (Hoopingarner) 403, Elsa 281, G. C. 281, George 570, George Clifford 281, 360, 378, George Francis 281, Jack 538, Jane 281, Jaunice 281, 378, Kent 282, Kevin 282, Kirby 282, Kriss 282, Lula 535, Marjorie 282, Minnie 538, S. M. 109, Sam 302, Samuel 378, Samuel B. 281, 360, Samuel M. 281, SaVella 302, Vella 281, William 282, William <Bill> 378, William Samuel "Bill"

CALL, Alverta Belle (Vaughn) 282, Edward 147, Edward Joseph 282, Helen (Lister) 155, Joseph 588, Joseph W. 282, Lucy 577, Michelle 472, Surildia 398, Woodrow 577

CALLISON, Patricia 606

CALVERT, Jane 273

CAMOMILE, Ed 461, Travis 461

CAMPBELL, Andrew J. 283, Anthony 284, Ashley Linn 283, Bill K. 283, Brett Alan 283, Brian K. 283, Burt 283, 284, Carey 283, Carol 284, Charles 283, 284,, Christina Louise 283, Claudia Diane 283, Cleo 283, Cloe 284, Cory 283, 284, Dale 284, 337, Dale Leveral 283, David Kay 283, Deborah Lynn 337, Debra Lynn 283, Denisa 284, Dennis 284, Derek Evan 283, Dian Kay 283, Donna 284, Doris Valeria 283, Douglas Linn 337, Douglas Lynn 283, Doyle 283, 284, Doyle H. 283, Elizabeth "Betty", Elizabeth 509, Harold 460, Heidi 284, Helen 283, Isabella E. F. 492, Isabelle 596, Jackie Ray 283, James Alan 283, Jeffery Dean 337, Jeffery Deane 283, Jeremy 284, Jess 283, Jess 283, Jess 284, Jim 283, JoAnn 290, Jon Michael 283, Jon Michael 337, Judy Ann 283, Kathryn (Mazelin) 337, Kent 404, Kiersten E. 283, Liane R. 283, Linda 284, Louetta 284, Louise 239, Louise 405, Lura 402, Lynn 404, Margaret 283, Margaret 284, Marlene 452, Marna Sue 283, Mary C. 347, Matthew R. 283, Nicole Roseanne 283, Oleo 283, Patricia A. 337, Patricia Ann 283, Peggy Jo 283, Phillip 284, Phoebe 574, Randy Joann 283, Richard Lee 283, Robert 76, 284, Ronald 284, Rory Michelle 283, Ruth 284, Ruth Elizabeth 283, Sandra Kay 283, Sandra L. 337, Sara Jade 283, Sherry 284, Stacy M. 283, Tracie 284, Valeria 284, Virgil 283, Virgil 283, Virgil 284, Walter 284, Walter Sr. 284, William Dean 283, William Henry 283, William Henry 283, William Henry 284, Willie 283, Willie 284, Willie Henry 283

CAMPTON, Richard 98

CAPIN, Tom 98

CAPP, Delia 283

CAPS, Amos 284, Betty 440, Christopher 284, Christopher W. 284, Dessie 535, Dora 284, Edward 284, George L. 284, George L. 440, George W. 72, George William 284, Gladys 440, Helen 440, John 284, Lydia 284, Paul 440, Rineholt 284, Tillie 284, William 284

CAPTAIN, Bradley Lee 284, Charles 289, Charles 440, Charles Frederick 284, Charles Henry 284, Charles Nathan <Chad> 284, Diana 445, Diane 289, Evelyn 136, Ida 288, Ida May 288, John E. 284, Lewis 136, Lewis 140, Margaret 284, Myrtle 136, Ruth (Gregg) 372, Solomon 284, Timothy Linn 284

CARAVETTA, G. John 142

CARBALLO, Adrian 308, Adriana 308, Alan 308, Clyo 308, Kathy 308, Steffany 308

CARBAUGH, William Henry 537

CARDIN, Brent 595, Chad 595, Jennifer 595, Kathleen 314, Shelli Ann 341, Stefani Sue 341

CAREINS, Andrew 359, Chad 359, Charles 359, Jennifer 359, Sarah 359

CAREY, Arlene 37, Arzenith 446, Fidella 446, Karen Elaine 559, Willet 576, Zebelom 446

CARGAR, Cheryl Dianne 326, Jesse 420, Nora 420

CARL, Courtney 474, Donavon 474, Linda 474, Mitchell 474, Patrick 474, Sarah 299

CARLISLE, Freeman 538, Henry H. 538, Mary Ella 538

CARLSON, Dee Ann 580, Don 580, Don F. II "Chip", Elizabeth 580, Jessie 450, Kristen 588

CARMEAN, Joseph 400, Nancy 400

CARMICHAEL, Ed 107

CARNAHAN, Brian K. 595, Magdalene 595, Nicholas 595, Robert 595

CARNALL, John 516, John W. 102, John W. 145, Lois Carol 576, Ned 140, Ned 146, Ned Mrs. 146, Paula 374, Tom 576

CARNES, Alice Erminnie 274, Alma 285, Alma Myrl 301, Anna 295, Anna Belle 295, Berthetta 285, Berthetta 586, Blanche 302, Caroline (Burgess) 295, Carolyn Sue 285, Carolyn Sue 586, Carolyn Sue 588, Chad 285, Chloe 302, Clyde 285, Eldon 285, Emma 175, Emma 296, Ettie (Noe) 301, Everett 107, Everett Wayne 285, Everett Wayne 586, Floe 443, 500, Hannah (Miller) 412, Jack Walker 285, 586, Joe 285, 289, John I 295, John II 295, L. G. 98, Leottie O. 412, Madlyn Iverne 513, Mary Magdaline 285, Mary Magdaline 586, Mick 285, Mildred 285, 489, 285, 586, Monnah Blanche 494, Myrtie 384, Nellie Marie 481, Olive 352, Ralph 285, Ruth 502, Thomas 412, Travis 285, Vicki 449, William H. 384, William Henry 285, William Henry <Billy> 301, Wilma 244, Yvonne 285, 586

CARNEY, Dannielle 309, Linda 244, Lowell Adrian 244, Lucille (Lawson) 244, Milissa 309, Steve 440

CARPENTER, Fonda 402, Grover 402, Joseph 402, Lois Jane (Leas) 435, Max 402, Zelda 402

CARR, Aaron Douglas 357, Bernadine 605, Brenda 605, C. Douglas 357, Clarence (C.D.) 365, Cynthia 442, Darlene 365, Deborah 605, Jennifer Ann 357, Matthew 442, Michael 442, Ramona F. 265, Ryan 442

CARROL, John Mrs. 121, Susan 292

CARROLL, 66, A. L. 13, A.L. 76, Amos 13, Arthur 285, Clyde A. 285, Elbridge 285, Flora 285, Flora 554, Jane 240, Jim 589, Nancy 589

CARRYSOT, Lena 323

CARRYSOTT, Adolphus 513, Mary Alice 513, Smanatha 513

CARSON, Alta 155, Howard 604

CART, Christian 286, Duane 603, Herley 286, Kevin 603, Kimberly 603

CARTER, Barbara 351, Clyde 240, Flossie 240, Flossie 240, Harold 107, James 117, James 240, John 240, Kenneth 240, Lillie 240, Martha Sawyer 240, Maybelle Addington 239, Milo 240, Nellie Ifer 407, R. V. 75, Raleigh 240

CARTRIGHT, Stephen 23

CARTWRIGHT, Ivan 304, James S. 285, John 285, Matthew 285, Peter 285, Susan Frances 285

CARVER, Charles 321, Cynthia 321, Harry 321, Helen 417, Margie L. 321, Orva Roe 321

CARY, Ella L. 287, Harriette 445, L. M. 179

CARYLON, Dorothy 465

CASE, Carolyn 370, Harriette L. 592, Janis 248

CASEY, Erin 483, John 483, John Jr. 483, Karen 483

CASH, Carl 286, Carl 450, Carl 533, Charles Alonzo 286, Dixie 450, Dixie Carleen 286, Ethel 286, Hilda 286, Ivan 334, Janet 450, Janet 533, Janet Ann 286, Johnny 239, June (Carter) 239, Marguerite 450, Marguerite 533, William T. 346

CASS, Patricia 429

CASSADY, Hannah Mary 569

CASSELL, Bobbi 307, Cynthia Jo 307, George 425, Robert 307

CASSIDAY, Brian Kelly 472, Dean 472, Dean 529, Deana Sue 472, Joshua 472, Julie Ann 472, Kari 472, Katina 472, Kelli 472, Kevin B. 472, Kim 472, Kim 529, Phyllis 529, Phyllis Moore 472, Rebecca Lynne 472, Tim 529, Timothy Allen 472, Zachary 472

CASSIDY, Kristine 444

CASTERLINE, Esther 500

CASTILOW, Clarence 512

CASTLE, Kevin 467

CASTON, Abe 107, Abraham 286562, Ada 285 Amelia 292, Amelia 512, Amilia 286, Bertha 285, Bertha Orlinda 403, Betsy 286, Bonnie 289, Cassy 286, Catherine 286, Celeste 301, Charles 285, Chloe Freeland 562, Chris 289, Clarissa Sisson 562, David 289, Dorothy 414, Elizabeth Jane 286, Henry 286, John 58, 285, 286, Josephine 403, Josephine Frances 285, Josephus 285, Leslie 285, Lewis 286, 292, Mamie 289, Martha 286, Mary A. 286, 562, Nancy 286, Nancy Crem 286, Ned Leslie 285, Ollie 286, Richard 99, Russell E. 285, Samuel 286, William 286, 413, 414

CAVALIER, Mary 535

CAVITT, Velma 155, 447

CAYLOR, Alice 287, Alice (Shockley) 287, Bessie 287, Carolyn 287, Carolyn Alice 287, Charles 146, 216, 335, Charles Dr. 280, Charles E. 287, Charles Eli 287, Charles H. 287, Charles Homer 287, Charles Mrs. 146, Charles Sr. 334, Constance 287, Constance Joyce 287, David Samuel 287, Dr. Charles E. 145, Dr. Truman 145, Elias 287, Ella 155, Eva 287, Harold 146, 409, Harold D. 287, Harold Dr. 280, 489, Harold Mrs. 146, Henrietta 489, John 287, Julia 287, Patricia 287, Phyllis 287, Rebecca 287, Sarah 287, Suzanne 287, Suzanne B. 287, Truman 146, Truman 287, Truman Dr. 280, Truman E. 287, Truman Mrs. 136, 146

CAYOT, Adam 287, Bradley 287, Bradley 288, Brian 287, Carla 287, Carol 287, Carol 288, Carolyn 287, Cathleen 287, Cheryl 287, Clark 287, Craig 287, Dale 287, Debra 288, Dennis 287, Ellen 287, Ellen 288, Eugene "Gene", Eugene 288, 352, Glenna 352, 560 Harold 287, Ileen 287, James 287, Janell 287, Karen 287, 288, Kathy 287, Leslie 287, 288, Lewis 287, Linda 287, Manford 287, Marcella 287, Marcia 287, Marilyn 287, Marita 287, Marita K. 559, Martha (Heubner) 288, Michael 287, Mildred 287, Paige 288, Patricia 287, R. Edward 287, Rachel 288, Richard 287, Robert 287, Ronald 287 Roy 287, Roy 288, Roy 509, Steven 287, Thomas 287, 287, Yvonne 287

CHAFANT, Viva F. 533

CHAIPHIN, Don 588

CHALFANT, Abner 288, Aimie Lee 288, Alfred 288, Alice 288, Brent 288, Chad 572, Chadds 288, 289, Chads 288, Charles "Ray", Charlie 314, Clarinda 288, Cleo Lewis 288, Daniel 288, Elizabeth 288, Elizabeth 522, Elizabeth A. 288, Emma (Schock) 288, Eva 136, Eva 288, Evan L. 16, Fay 387, Faye Hauk 288, Frank 288, Frank 512, Harry 288, Henry 288, Howard 288, Howard 289, Hugh Linn 288, J. C. 288, James 288, Joseph 288, Joseph F. 288, Julie 288, L.F. 59, Lois 136, Lois 288, Lydia 288, Lydia M. 394, Mary 288, 461, Mary J. 288, Mary (Prillaman) 387, Mellie Pearl 288, Mercy 288, Mercy 288, Mercy 572, Nancy 288, Nancy Ferguson 572, Reason 288, Reason 289, Robert 288, Robert 288, Robert D. 287, 387, Ruth 288, Sarah 288, Sedora 288, Senior P. 288, Wayne 288, Wendell 288, Wendell C. 288, William 288

CHALKER, Rev. 482

CHAMBERLAIN, Andrew 254, Bradley 254, Kathy 425, William 254

CHAMBERS, Flo 407, George W. 407, M. W. 102, Peggy 407

CHAMBOUR, Rev. 68

CHAMBUS, Sarah 320

CHANEY, Charlene 285, 289, Christine Suzanne 247, 316, James 289, James Otho 289, Jim 285, Ked 285, Kendric 289, Marilyn 411, Mont 411, Murlie 531, Nick 279 289, Otho 289, Ron 289, Rose 411, Rosealie 411, Susie 289, Tim 285, Tom 563

CHAPMAN, Charles 529, Christopher C. 529, John 560, Kimberly 529, Mary 528

CHAPPELL, Susan 405

CHARLES, T. P. 107

CHARTER, Bill 404, Dale 404, Evelyn 404, Hazel 404

CHASE, Catherine 557, Nancy Salina 507, William 507

CHASE & BAKER, 179

CHASTAIN, Audrey 299, Lisa Couch 299, Mark 299, Nathan 299

CHEESEMAN, Alva 519, Ruth 519

CHENOWETH, Clarahelle 580, cora Edith 580, George E. 580, Mary (Kummer) 432

CHERRY, Bonnie 521, Calvin 521, Eric 521, Ethel 407, Ida 266, Linda 521, Maurice 521, Maurine 521, Rebecca 521, Richard 521

CHICK, Kathleen 296

CHIDESTER, Rosey

CHILCATE, Barbara 399

CHILCOTE, Sharon 560

CHIPP, W. D. 81

CHRISMORE, Sarah Ann 508

CHRIST, Gertrude 519, Grace L. 603, Raymond 519

CHRISTMAN, Berneice (Bunn) 280, Don 280

CHRISTMAN, Elizabeth Wirth 258, Frank 258, 404, Frederick 258, George 258, Iva (Faus) 280, Jennie 592, John 258, Mary Alice (Masterson) 258, Peter 258, Verl 258

CHRISTY, Alex Harvey 398, Lynn 398, Paul Edwin 398

CHRONISTER, Florence Etta 554, Genevieve 512, George 512, Henry 512, Lydia Miley 512, Margaret Fisher 512

CHUPP, Clark 28, Edith Florence 289, Elizabeth 289, Ellen 289, Forest 289, Gideon 289, Jake 289, Laura 289, Marguerite 289, Mary 289, Mildred 289, Platt 289, Roy 289, Wanda 289

CHURCH, Aldene 515

CHURCHILL, L. Henry 84

CIPHERS, Elizabeth 348, 349

CIRWITHEN, Issac 243, Sarah Emily 243

CLAGHORN, Alan Kent 290, Amy Lee 290, Andrea Fay 290, Angela Jo 290, Anna Louise 290, Benjamin 408, Benjamin Robert 290, Berta E. (Duvall) 290, Berta E. (Duvall) 290, Bradley Wayne 290, Bradley Wayne Jr. 290, Bret W. 290, Britton Lee 290, Christopher Robert 290, Christopher Wayne 290, Constance Elaine 290, Cynthia Sue 290, Daniel Daron 290, Debra Kay 290, Diane 333, Dustin Jo 290, Elise Annette 290, Elizabeth Ann 290, Elizabeth Ann 333, Emily Lynn 290, Erin Nicole 290, Gale Brian 290, Gerry 290, 291, James Kennedy 290, James Lee 290, James V. 291, James William 290, Jean Ann 290, Jeanette Lynne 290, Jeffery Lee 290, Jerry Lyle 290, John Jay 290, Jordon Glenn 290, Keith 408, Keith Alan 290, Kent Roger 290, Kristine Nicole 290, Larry Wayne 290, Les 333, Leslie Ann 290, MacKenzie 408, MacKenzie Jo 290, Mark 333, Mark Allen 290, Matthew Kent 290, Nicholas 408, Nicholas Keith 290, Pamela Sue 290, Robert 290, 291, Robert G. 291, Robert William 290, Ronald Eugene 290, Sorinna Lynn 290, Stephanie Jo 290, Ted Michael 290, Timothy Lee 290, Walter E. 290, 291, Walter E. Jr. 290 291, Walter E. Sr. 290, Wesley Walter 290, William David 290

CLAIRE, Judy 513

CLAMPITT, Charles 79, Florence 79, Thomas 60

CLANIN, Clyde 291, Florence Lugar 291, Maxine 291

CLANNEN, William Clannen 13

CLANON, Deloris 304

CLAPPER, Jacob 469, Sarah 469

CLARK, Aaron 292, Abraham 292, Alice 292, Allen 112, Amanda 82, Amelia 292 512, Amy 565, Aubry I. 292, Barry 291, 461, Barry E. 292, Beth 565, Brett 292, C. A. 81, Camelia 565, Candace Jennifer 549, Carolyn Jean 369, 387, Carrie 595, Catherine 292, Catherine Porter 512, Charles 121, 481, Clarence 82, Clifford 109, David 369, Deb 84, Diana 292, Diane 461, Dick 390, Donald 565, Donn 549, Dora 512, Edith 293, 476, Estalene 315, Ethel 152, 292, Ethel L. 291, Eunice (Irwin) 291, 293, Faith 523, Faye 293, Florence 155, Flossie 387, Frances 6, 461, Frances (Mendenhall) 292, George 292, Harmon 293, Harold 369, 387

CLARK, Harry 292, 461, Harry E. 291, Henrietta Kreisher 481, Henry 481, Homer 291, 292, Howard R. 293, Jack 294, Jacob 242, 481, James K. 355, James M. 292, James P. 512, James Porter 292, Jeannette 355, Jeremiah "Jerry", Jeremiah 292, Jeremiah 512, Jessie 481, John 565, John B. 292, John I. 13, 76, 291, 292, 567, John Irwin 293, Josephine (King) 369, Julie 565, Julie Jo 549, Katherine Mae 481, Kathryn 292, Kathy 355, Kelli 294, Lantz Alanson 292, 512, Laura 292, Lester 291, 292, Lester E. 292, 293, Margaret 292, Margaret DeGroff 292, Martha 291, 292, 512, Martha Hixon 450, Martha Maines 534, Marti 409, Mary 293, Mary A. 512, Mary Agnes 292, 596, Mary Edith 476, Mary J. 292, Mathias 260, Matthew 565, Matthew Arden 549, Myrtle 292, Myrtle

(Shadle) 292, Nancy 292, Nancy Ann (Helm) 293, Norma 292, Phyllis 390, Polly 355, Raymond 512, Richard 355, Robert 82, Rose 512, Roseann (Accavallo) 238, Rufus 76, Rufus 291, Rufus B. 293, Sargent 291, 293, Sharon 355, Sue 137, Susan 292, Traci 294, Vera Frances 461, Vicki 290, Viola Perlina 567, Virgil 292, 512, W. D. 190, Walter 292, 512, Walter B. 292, Washington 292, William 320, William S. 421, Jr, Walter 512
CLARKE, Stanley 175
CLAUS, Diane Marie 348
CLAUSE, Doris Ellen 521
CLAUSER, Magdelene 375
CLAWSON, John Rev. 485
CLAY, Joyce 429, Kathy 429, Rodd 429, Ross 429
CLAYTON, Clyde 475, Ethel 487, Homer Dr. 487, Nancy Jane 487
CLEEFMAN, Jane 318
CLEM, Courtney Elaine 295, Greg 295, Samuel 328
CLEMENTS, Caryn 322, Elizabeth "Beth", Jennifer Elizabeth 364, Jessica Lynn 364, Ronald 364, Vernon 322
CLEVELAND, Keith Eugene 435, Margaret Grace 435, Nina Virginia 435, Ralph 435, Roger Carroll Lee 435, Rosemary Ann 435
CLICK, Janna Michelle 451, Jo Ann 451, Mark David 451, Mark William 451, Meda 248, Scott Matthew 451
CLIFTON, Bob 234, Carol J. 442
CLINE, Abram 46, Albert B. 232, Albert Bradbury 293, Ann 283, Anne (Beatty) 276, Anthony M. 293, Bessie Wadsworth 293, Bethany 293, Betty 111, 154, Betty L. 293, Charlie 232, David M. 276, David Robert 293, Doris Arlene 276, Duane 276, Edward Fay 276, Florence B. 265, Fredrick 265, Harriet Chaffee 293, Harry 276, James 276, James W. 276, Jane (Steinhauer) 293, Jayde S. 276, Jenny (Bovine) 434, Jesse 276, JoAnn 276, John David 276, Jonas 328, Joseph 293, Josephine 152, Judy (Ellenberger) 293, Lloyd M. 232, Lloyd Maxwell 293, Lois 146, Lois Shirey 232, 293, Mark Ray 276, Martha 293, Mary Josephine 232, Mary Kay 276, Melinda 276, Ner William 293, Paul Martin 276, Robert 146, 293, Robert A 293, Robert Mrs. 146, Russell Ray 276, Ruth Maxine 276, Sandy 293, Vickie Marie 276, William 216, 434, William L. 145, 232, William Lloyd 293, William Wadsworth 293, William Washington 293
CLONTZ, Gaberiella Marie 350, 381, Jill 350, 381, Larry 350, 381
CLOSE, Elizabeth 304, George Washington 304, Gilbert 304, Harvey 304, Jane 304, Laura 304, Margaret Darwactor 304, Olive May 304, Robert 189
CLOUD, Agatha 293, Arzona Fay 557, Belle 347, Debra 293, Dollie 293, Ethan James 293, Henry S. 557, James Ethan 293, John 293, Joseph 412, Josie 293, Lucy Francis 293, Marguereta (Welch) 293, Martha A. 347, Martha Lowry 557, Melody 293, Rex 293, Samual 18, Sarah 524, Sarah (Sharp) 412
CLOUSE, Jill 462
CLOWSER, Almeda Elizabeth 516, Ellen 395
CLOWSER, Goldie 516, Isaac 43, 516, John Henry 471, Joseph Warren 516, Kathryn 579, Mae 591, Maria 516, Mary Elizabeth 471
COBB, Jesse 418
COBBUM, Alison 294, Brooks 294, Curtis 294, Don Alan 294, Faith 294, Graham 294, Ida M. 394, Ida Mae 395, James 394, Joe 288, LaRoy 98, Leona 106, Lewis 98, Margie 294, Norman 294, Vernon 294
COBLE, Cindy 512, David 512, Donald 512, Marilyn Hayes 512
COBURN, Amanda 483, Jacob 483, Jessery 483, Robert 483
COCHRAN, Bee 294, Benton C. 294, Chad 229, Ed 122, Edgar D. 294, Edger B. 294, Edward 107, Elizabeth Mae (Fleming) 294, Ernest 542, Ernest H. 294, Estella 294, Eula B. 294, Ezra H. 294, Gloria Sue 294, Kent Alan 294, Laura M. 464, Lucy J. (Rose) 294, Mary Elizabeth 294, Melvin Russell 294, Pamela Kay 294, Sharon Diane 294, Sue 425, Vera 542, William J. 294
COCKREIL, G. C. 75, Marjorie 281, Marjorie 282, Sindy (Higgins) 394
CODDINGTON, Albert 86
COERS, Morris 81, Morris Rev. 272, Vernice 136
COFFIELD, Alexander Kurt 532, Betty Alice 532, Charlie 295, Claudia 321, Clyde 532, Darlene Sue 532, David Harrison 295, Delilah 295, Emma Fryhack 532, Harrison 17, James 295, Jane (Craig) 295, Jennifer Elizabeth 321, Joni Marie 532, Lona 295, Luetta 283, Nathan Lowell 513, Nettie 295, Nova 295, Philip Rex 513, Rex 532, Rex Nathaniel 513, Ronald 532, Thomas 295, Tracy Renee 532
COFFMAN, Jonas 367
COLBERT, 66, Charles 18
COLBURN, Caroline Carr 460
COLE, Addie (Oppenheim) 154, Carol 375, Dan 422, Dave 422, Ed 554, Elizabeth 127, Elzey 554, F.E. 83, Florence 554, Karen 375, Keith 422, Lula A. 554, Madge 407, Melba 137, Nancy 422, Ralph 375, Richard 375, Robert 375, Sarah 562, Tim 422, Tom 422, William 554
COLEGROVE, Marjorie 270
COLEMAN, Amy 489, Angela 489, Cynthia 489, Harry 107, J. J. 75, James 60, Josh 489, Juanita 447, Lee 489, Mark 306, Roscoe 75
COLEN, Anna Louise McAfee 288, James 140
COLES, Henry J. 584, Missouri 584
COLESCOTT, Susan 402
COLLETT, Norma (Kummer) 432
COLLINS, Billie 405, Clara (Terkelsen) 353, Devona 353, Jack 140, 146, Jack Mrs. 146, John 111, 113, John 405, Larry 342, Lee R. 353, Linda F. 481, Maxine Hilsmier 342, Pauline 525, Ted 405
COLLOM, Donna 588, Jeff 588, Jim 588, Lori Lynn 588, Sara 588
COLSON, Floyd D. 597, Helen 597, Martha Cline 232, Robert 597, U. Gordon 293
COLVIN, Michael 346,
COLWELL, Lillie 461, Morris 461, Sarah Fugate 461
COMBS, Cheryl 481, Cheryl 595, Faith 462, Jesse 595, Larry 402, Rebecca Ann 462, William 462
COMER, A. J. Rev. 59, Laura 558
COMPTON, Laura 487
CONE, Carol 320
CONFER, Anna (Bushee) 295, Barb 295, Betty Mae 295, Betty Mae 295, Beverly 295, Charles 466, Connie 466, Curtis 295, 295, Daniel Eugene 295, Donald Edwin 295 295, Donna 295, Dorothy Margaret 295, Edwin 545, Erma Ivan 295, Hazel 60, Hazel Ndora 295, Isaac 295, Iva Elizabeth 295, James DeWayne (Dee) 295, Joan 295, John 295, John Z. (Zennie) 295, Kenny 295, Margaret 295, 468, Mary 295, Mary Ellen 295, Mary Ilo 295, Mike 466, Norma 295, Norman 295, Ollie (Fisher) 432, Patrick 295, Peter 234, Phyllis 130, Raymond 295, Richard Dale 295, Samuel 295, Samuel Eldon 295, Sarah 260, Shari 295 370, Susannah (McClellan) 295, Ted 295, Zennie Alpheus 295
CONKLIN, Mary , 451
CONKLYN, Mary 451
CONLEY, Benton 417, Brian Douglas 296, 303, Christopher 303, Christopher Jay 296, George 296, Jill Diane (Croy) 296, Marcia Phyllis (Johnson) 296, Stella 417, Willa F "Faye"
CONN, Brian 449, Jill 449
CONNER, Amelia 411, Amy Elizabeth 342, Cheryl 581, Cheryl Ann 582, Donald 441, Evelyn 441, Garnet 259, Herb 441, Ina Mae 441, Kay 165, Kenneth 581, Laurence 165, Linda Kay 569, Mark 569, Nancy (Custard) 304, Otis 435, Otis 441, Patricia (Grove) 581
CONNERS, Harold 338, Mary 338
CONNETT, Sarah 318
CONNORS, Marjorie 338
CONOVER, Bill 545, Sue 545
CONRAD, Harriet 509, Susan 586, Walter 221
CONRAD-SICKLER, Rachel Jane 555
CONROY, James 95
CONTADELUCI, Joseph 467, Lisa 333, Lisa Renee 467, Lorraine Evelyn 467
CONWELL, Addie 484
COOK, Albert C. 337, Archie 169, Arthur 296, B. Grace 516, Bruce 265, Buffy 265, Carl 296, Carrie Mae 268, Cathy 489, Celeste (Johnson) 296, Clarence Courtney 296, Cynthia Maxine 337, Daivd Arthur 296, Elijah 509, Eliza 147, Elizabeth 296, Elizabeth Howard 296, Emma 175, 509, Franklin 175, Isabella 417, J. B. 98, J. W. 20, Jack 296, Jacob 268, James Edward 296, John 296, John 296, John W. 297, John W. 421, John W. Jr. 297, John William 296, Jonas 296, Josephine 296, L.H. 214, LeaBeth 516, Leander (Chaddock) 154, Margaret 296, Martha (Andrick) 296, Martha Celesta 296, Mary 296, Mary Elizabeth 509, Mary Esta 296, Matthew 265, Nancy 296, Nora Ruanna 296, Paul 175, Paul Howard 296, Pearl (Gause) 337, Pearl Opal 296, Raymond Francis 296, Russell 296, Sara 296, Sarah Josephine 297, Sherley Alberta 337, Susana 296, Sylvia 296, Thelma Marie 296, Wayne 296, William 297, 337, 509, 516, William Douglas David 296, William Henry 296, William L. 296, Zachariah 296, 297
COOMER, Harriet 532
COON, Mary Jane 303
COONS, Max 140
COOPER, A. J. 352, Ann 415, Bob 140, Bonnie 600, Bree 352, Dan 600, Janet 152, 600, Jody 352, John R. 600, Mr. 221, Rick 352, Stacia 404, Susan 600
COOVERT, Rosemary 558
COPE, Dean 84
COPPER, Bill 15
COPPESS, Calvin 337, Franklin Richard 337, Karen Ann 337, Marie (Jones) 337, Richard C. 337
CORAH, Fred 383, James 383, Joseph 383, Mildred 383
CORDER, Mary Elizabeth 503
COREY, Peter 15
CORGELL, Stephanie 405
CORLE, Carla Jo 297, Cassandra Lynn 297, Christopher John 297, Curtis Wayde 297, La Relle "Charlie", LaDrew 297, Lucille (Hardy) 297
CORNUM, Evartl 471
CORRECT, Mayhelle 585
CORY, Charles 366, 440, Claude 324, Elizabeth 324, Ella 324, Minnie 440, Nathan 324, Ray 324, Willie 324
COSSAIRT, 66, Lela 156
COSTELLO, Carol Jean 485, Kevin 253, Lib 602, Michael 253, Patrick 253, Philip 253, Virginia 155
COTTERLY, John 318, Marie 318
COTTINGHAM, John O. 145
COTTON, Ancil W. 160, Bessie 458, Bessie 459, Bessie Pearl 298, Betty E. 605, Betty E. (Inman) 298, Betty Eloyce 297, 408, Carlton 271, Cleona 408, 605, Cleona (Hoover) 298, Crystal 248, Cyrus S. 298, Daniel Croy 298, David McAfee 298, Dylan Stotts 298, E.F. 121, Elisabeth "Libby", Ernest 299, 365, Ernest S. 297, Eudora 299, 605, EuDora Jane 297, 408, EuDora Jane (Yager) 298, F. A. 127, Fanny Eudora (Goshorn) 297, Forest 299, Forst G. 297, 298, 408, 605, Franklin Fisk 298, George 298, George Washington 298, 458, Gladys 147, 152, 298, 452 605, Gladys (McAfee) 232, Hannah 103, Hazel B. 298, Ian David 298, Jack 271, Jack Jr. 271, Jackson 299, James 298, James A. 121, 298, John 299, Josephine McDannel 458, Joshua 297, Joshua Forst 298, Judy Ann 303, Judy Ann (Croy) 298, Kathleen (Stotts) 298, Larry 271, Leota Irene 279, Lewis 103, 299, Lewis C. 297, Lyle 6, 8, 147, 148, 202, 298, 299, Lyle J. 297, Lyle J. 298 Lyle J. 408, Lyle J. 605, Mal-Sook (Baek) 298, Margaret 298, Marshal S. 298, Mary 299, Mary A. (Molly) 298 Matthew Shane 298, Max 271, Miss Mary 121, Nancy 299, Opal 298, Patricia 271, Rachel 298, Raph Carlton (Carl) 298, Robert 271, Ruby Dean 298, Samuel G. 298, Sarah 299, 561, Sarah Almira 299, Steven Forst 298, Susan A. 283, Waldo 298, William 103, 299, William W. 297, 495
COTTRILL, Henry 16, 86
COUCH, Alyssa 299, Angela Barton 299, B. L. 75, Bradley 299, Brandon 299, Brian 299, Bruce Alan 299, Bruce Edward 299, Bryan 299, Candice 299, Chad 299, David 299, E. L. 75, Elise Mayhew 299, Elizabeth Clements 299, Ethel Harrold 299, Ethel (Harrold) 599, Harry 142, Harry Russell 299, Jeffery 299, Jesse 299, John 299, Jordan 299, Judy Ilene 553, Judy Metz 299, Judy Sleppy 299, Kendra 299, Kevin 142, 299, 385, Kevin Eugene 553, Kyle 299, 385 Kyle Steven 299, 553, Larry 299, 385, Larry Dean 385, Laura 299, Lisa 299, Lisa Betheny 299, Mara Jo 299, 385, 599, Mark 299, Marry Junior 299, Mary Atlanta 299, Mary Meyers 299, Mary Pitman 299, Mary Welch 299, Matthew David 299, Matthew Emerson 299, Meshach 299, Micahel Christopher 299, Michael 385, Michael Dean 299, Patricia Cunningham 299, Paul 599, Paul Eugene 299, 385, Phillip 299, Robert Dean 299, Robert Lynn "Rob", Rosalie Moorman 299, Ruth 60, Ruth Roberts 299, Sandra Morgan 299, Sandra Scott 299, Sarah Buzzard 299, Sharon Martin 299, Shirley Weikel 299, Steven "Steve", Steven Eugene 385, 553, Travis 299, Tresa 299, William Henry 299, William Jesse "Bill", William Lee "Bill", Winifred Griffith 299
COUDRET, Bertha Rose 597, Harry 597, Justine 597
COULSON, Hermine Wiecking 8
COULTER, David 369, Dick 369, Eugene "Salty", Flossie 387
COUNSELLOR, Edith 417
COURS, Elnora 314
COURSON, Bertha 519
COURTNEY, Elaine 350, Gloria 300, Gondola (Mowery) 308, Harry 308, Henry 153, Henry Dr. 455, Israel 546, James 500, James Howard 303, James Howard 577, Jim 300, Margaret 308, Martha Rose 307, Minnie Alice (Kemper) 308, Mona 500, Mona Maxine (Stout) 303, Mona (Stout) 577, Monroe 308, Phoebe 555, Phyllis 303, Phyllis 500, Roger Wendell 308, Seth 308
COUSINO, Adam 584, Mary Ellen 584, Sheldon 584
COVAULT, Orpha 214
COVER, Christina 260, Hariet McAfee 437, Harriett 469, Samantha 437
COVERDALE, Emma 531, Julie 84, Lauren 531, Phillip 531, Rolland 84, Rollyn 531
COVERT, Ellison 437, Olive 437
COWANS, Emmarelis 243, John 243
COWENS, Alta J. 527
COWGILL, Don 402L, Tamara Sue 571
COX, Cindy 486, Cynthia 340, 487, Daisy 152, David 300, Emily 300, Emma Burroughs 300, J. R. Mrs. 95, J. Ray 232, J. Raymond 300, James M. 34, Lauren 300, Lewis 300, Paten 569, Ruth 528, Suzanne 411, Suzanne 426, 508, Tobi 486, Tom 486, Traci 486 Viola Jane 247
CRABILL, Mae Hunt 407
CRAIG, Clarence C. 412, Clarence Geno 348, Edward Ermal 242, Elizabeth Beershebe 348, Jeanetta Ada 348, Judy 515, Mary 6, Robert 18, William 18
CRAIGHEAD, Aaron 428, Adam 428, James 428, Kelli 428, Sheena 428, Siarra 428
CRAIN, Scott J. 570
CRAMER, David 239, DeWayne 239, LeRoy W. 239, Willie 239
CRANDALL, Malinda 584
CRANE, Ben 554, Dean 554, Sally 338554
CRANK, Sejus Gabriella 405
CRANRATH, Mary 375
CRAVEN, Bertha 200, Bertha 301, C. Edwin 266, Catharine 525, Catherine E. 525, Catherine Elizabeth 266, Catherine Elizabeth 301, Charles 301, Clarence Edwin 301, Edwin 525, ELmo Inez 301, Evenlyn 301, Herbert Edwin 266, Herbert Edwin 301, Joseph 301, Naomi 525, Oliver R. 301, Orin 301, Orin O. 208
CRAVENS, Edwin 106
CRAWFORD, 66, Arthur B. 348, Chella 348, Clarence 348, David 295, Delilah 295, Forrest Doyle 348, Juanita 348, Nellie (Roberts) 295, Pauline 348, Roy Rev. 241, Ruba 348, Thurman Thomas 348
CRAWLEY, Clyde 127
CREBS, Eva 603
CREECH, Helen 350
CREEK, Alma (Carnes) 347, 449, Anita Alma 347, Carol 347, Cathryn 381, Daniel 347, David Edwin 347, Elma 347, Elma 449, Elma Lorraine 301, Everett 347, 449, Evert Leroy 301, Helen 347, 449 Helen Louise 301 Herald 347, 449, Herald Milton 301, James Evertt 347, Jasper 301, Jeffery 347, Joel 347, Joseph Lee 347, Leona 347, Leona Grace 301, Linda 347, Lisa 347, Loena 449, Luara Beth 381, Maremna (Roberts) 301, Orie 347, Orie 449, Oric Melvin 301, Rebecca 347, Ruth 347, Ruth 449, Ruth Azalia 301, Shelli 347, Therese 471, Therese 489, Tim Robert 381
CREIGER, Martha 293
CRELLIN, Donald 81, 456
CREM, Nancy 286
CRESS, Carla 486, Deborah 442, Heather 442, 486, Nicole 442 Robert 442, Sheri 486, Sheryl 340, Sheryl 487
CRESSMAN, Sarah Elizabeth 250, Scott Joseph 250, Terry A. 250
CRETOR, Catherine 136
CREVISTON, John 518, John 544, Josie 544, Omer 518 544, Opal 544, Opal Justine 518, Paul 518, 544, Ralph 518, 544
CRISMORE, Ann 150, Lettitia (Longshore) 378, Loretta 573, Ora Elsa 378, Orie Elsie 378, William 378
CRIST, Betty 244
CROASDALE, Ezra 395, Minnie Lydia 395, Robert Walker 395
CROFT, Charles Cory 323, Clara May (Dawson) 323
CROMER, A. Rev. 64
CROMWELL, Margaret 239, Oliver 492
CRONIN, Thomas William 411
CROOK, Emmaline 301, Helen 301, Lewis R. 301
CROSBY, Agnes Elmira (Shields) 302, Alvin 302, Barbara 542, Bertha Alice (Farrow) 302, Catherine 542, Charles 107, 285, Charles Clifford 302, Emily 302, Emma Alice 347, Fern 78, Fred A. 302, Jacob 86, John Michael 302, 542, Joy 302, 542, Karla 302542, Kenneth <Kent> 302, Kent 542, Kraig 302, 542, Kyle 302, 542, Marilyn 302, 542, Marjorie Thomas 259, Mary (Pace) 302, Monnah Ferne Walker 302, Richard 302, 542, Simeon 302, Steve 251, Verlice 107, 542
CROSDALE, Ellen 250, Robert 87, Ruth 113
CROSLEY, Elvira 462
CROSS, Annie Laurie 391, Rev. 78
CROUCH, James 499, Jim 15, Wilma 15
CROW, Calvin 302, Carrie 302, Claude 302, Cleo 417, Frank 417, Helen 302, James 302, Kenneth 302, Lydia 302, Michael 302, Neal 45, Nellie 417, Vaughn 228, William 417
CROWDER, Jamie 497
CROWE, Art 524, John 547
CROWL, Crystal Marion (Davidge) 303, David Sherman 303, Florence 367, Frederick 560, Jane Ann 560, Josephine 560, Lela 604, Mary Belle (Gibson) 303, Rebecca 560, Richard Gregory 303, Robert Allison 303, Sherman Kennyson 303, Steven Terry 303, Theodore 303, Velma 597, Warren 560, Warren E. 303
CROY, Cheryl Ann 303, Clarence 289, 298, 500, 577, Clarence Oliver 303, Don 8, Don 500, Donald L. 577, Donald Lee 296, 303, Geneva 298, 500, Geneva (Gifford) 577, Geneva Lucile (Gifford) 303, Genevace 289, George 303, Howard 25, 303, Jerald Lloyd 303, Jill Diane 303, Judy Ann 298, 303, Martha (Jones) 303, Pauline Marie 303, Penny 478, 500, Penny Sue 303, 500, Phyllis 303, 500, Phyllis A. (Courtney) 577, Phyllis Ann (Courtney) 296, Rosemond 588
CROZIER, Sharon 531
CRUISE, Edwin 320
CRULL, Alan 534
CRUM, Aaron 303, Aaron 535, Alice 241, 270, Andrew Ryan 303 Ardis 64, 535, 559, Attie 303, Baby 303, Ben 600, Benjamin Burdette 303, Charles 303, Charles 535, David 303, David 535, Dean 241, Delbert 303, Effie 303, Eli 303, 535, Elizabeth 308, Elizabeth (Haynes) 303, Elmina 535, Emmanuel 303, 535, Franklin 303, Gerald Dale 303, Hazel 303, Hubert "Buck", Hubert 241, 303, Ida 534, Iva 303, Jean 317, Jeffrey Benjamin 303, Jennifer Fo 303, Johathan David 303, John 303, John Henry 241, 303, 535, Kimberly Rae 303, Laura 535, Lela 303, Linda L. 559, Magdalene 600, Margaret Lucile 303, Mary 303,, Mary Braham 241, Matthew Martin 303, Maxine 408 559, Merl 241, Minnie 303, Molly Elizabeth 303, Pearl 303M, Renee Anna 303, Samuel 241, 303, 535, Sarah 527, Ted 600, Theodore Lee 303, Tim 600, Timothy K. 303, Wendell 600, Wendell Burdette 303, Woodrow 535
CRUSE, Eugene 555, Luther 15, Mary Lena 555
CULBERSTON, C. L. Rev. 99
CULLERS, Jennifer 401
CUMMINS, Bob 127, Edna 266, Forrest 266, Robert 266
CUMP, D. J. 15
CUNNINGHAM, Nellie 307, Patricia "Patti"
CUNNINGTON, Steven 103
CUPP, Amy Lwellyn 304, Barbara 304, Bertha 563, Bob 166, 531, Clellah 304, Connie 456, Dana 304, David 304, Ernest 304, Everett 304, Janice 304, Jason 304, Jeff 304, Jennie 304, John 304, 531, Joseph 304, Lola 304, Margaret 531, 579, Mary 385, Michelle 304, Mick 55, 130, 304, Orlo 304, Otis 304, Otto L. 304, Pamela 304, Paul 304, Penny 304, Ray 166, Ray L. 304, Richard 304, Robert 304, Rosemary 290, Roy 304, Ruth 304, Tawnya Sue 290, Tiffany 304, Willard 304
CURRIER, Elizabeth 403
CURRY, 66, Alice 449, Brian 487, 533, Carol 594, James 411, Jan 449, Jennifer Michelle 458, Kathy Smith 458, Kristi 533, Larry 594, Naomi 411, Nicole Renee 458, Scott Andrew 458
CURTIS, Vickie 563
CURTNER, Hilda 366
CUSTARD, A. Bert 248, Alvin Bert 295, 304, Arzona 304, Clifford 304, Earl 304, Galen 304, Glen 304, Glen Burr 295, Nettie (Coffield) 248, Nettie (Coffield) 304, Vernis 304, Vernis A. 248, Vernis Adelaide 295, William R. (Bill) 304
CUSTER, Hilas Rev. 99
CUTLER, Abner 304, Alpheus Jeremiah 304, Chester 304, Clarence 304, David 304, Earl 304, Earl 459, Earl Alexander 304, Elmer Leroy 304, Esther Pauline 304, Florence 458, Florence Irene 304, Florence Irene 459, Forrest "Bud", Gladys 304, Glenn 304, Harold Raymond 304, Helen 304, Ireta Ethel 304, Jonathon 304, Leona Fern 304, Levina Josephine 304, Lillie May 304, Livona 304, Luella 304, Mary Watson/Woten 304, Olive Mae Close 459, Olive May Close 304, Paul 304, Ruth 304, 380, William 304, Jr. Earl 304
CUTSHALL, Frank 216
CUYLINGER, Philip 433
CYLKOWSKI, Joyce 273
CZERWIN, Adeled 320
DABBELAAR, Sara Hamel 510
DAFFORN, Danny Gene 411, Della 4[illegible], Jackie Lee 411, Kirby Allen 411, Larry 445, Lynn 38, Merrill Lynn 411, Patsy 594, Susan 600, Vernon 411
DAFFRON, Cindy Ann 249, Jesta 560, Timothy James 249
DAHIGREN, Brian 552, Heide 552, Janet 552, Lyle 552
DAHL, Anna 439
DAHLQUIST, Joyce 404, Joyce 405
DAILEY, Benjamin 354, Benjamin Douglas 305, Benjamine D. 322, Carol 305, Charles

G. 145, Dennis 512, Donald 305, Douglas 322, 354, Douglas L. 305, Emma 154, Esther Anna 267, Frank 208, 562, Homer 603, J. S. 586, James 103, 427, 594, Jess 45, 112, Kevin 354, Kevin L. 322, Kevin Lynn 305, L.W. 214, Lew 429, Lew Mrs. 116, Lew. W. 145, Phillip 512, Porter 512, Rachel 562, Ralph 207, Robert 512, Stefanie 354, Stefanie K. 322, Stefanie Kay 305, Susan 322, Wilda M. 603, Ella 339, Jess 44
DALE, Ada 415, Alfred 415, Annalue 415, Arthur E. 415, Charles Lorenzo 415, David 145, Esther Lea 415, Fannie 415, George W. 415, Hattie 415, James 415, James Elihu 415, James William 415, John 415, Mary Ann 415, Minie Lucy 415, Neva Eileen 415, Rachel 415, Thomas 415, Thomas 415, William 415
DALRYMPLE, Bradley 342, Connie J. 276, Connie Jo 305, Goldie Agusta (Perry) 305, Henry E. 305, Jesse Edward 305, Mary Jane 381, Mary Josephine (Worster) 276, Mollie 310, Norma 150, Norma Jean 305, Robert Leroy 305, Roger 342, Stephanie 342, Tiffany 342, Verlin 305, Verlin J. 276
DALY, Bridget Agnes 411
DAMMEYER, Minna 526
DAMRON, Charles William 405, Dunmore 405
DANGER, Annahel 462
DANIEL, Anthony 404, Elizabeth 310, Matilda 310, Rosemary 404, Tabitha Ann 310, Thomas 310, William 310
DANIELSON, Randy 140
DARLAND, Clodella 508, Jim 508, Joanna Kaye 508, Paul David 508
DARROW, Gladys 111, Jane 305, Pamela Jane 305, Robert M. 305, Susan 305
DARWACTOR, Gilbert 304
DARWIN, Charles Jr. 81
DAUB, Flora 342
DAUBENMEIR, Christina Barbara 507, Frank 507
DAUGHERTY, Alan 6, 8, 140, 447, Betty Lou 590, Candice 492, Cathy Jo 306, Charles Cecil 306, 492, Charlie 239, Clarence 306, Clarence 492, Dean Edward 306, Delores Marlles 306, Deric Ross 306, Donna 306, Dornal Darlene 306, Dorothy 306 603, E. J. 109, Edith 239, Edna E. 442, Edward Alman 492, Edwin 306, Edwin 306, Elizebeth 492, Elizebeth 573, Erika 306, Ervin Lamoin 306, Ervin Lamoin 492, Eva 465, Ezekiel 306, 492, Fern A. 492, Gary Lee 306, George 442, Grace 298, Harold 306, 603, Harold A. 492, Isabellah 492, Isabelle Fifer 442, Iva 306, Iva Myrtle 492, Jesse 306, Jesse Elwin 492, Jimmie Wayne 306, John 492, John B. 306, 492, John Franklin 492, Junior H. 492, Junior Haiflich 306, Kay Janene 306, Keith Lynn 306, Lance Stuart 306, Larry Lee 306, Lillian M. 464, Marilyn Sue 306, Marjorie J. 411, Martha Bell 306, Mary Ann 492, Mary Ellen 492, Mary Jane 378, Mary Magdalene 306, Melvin 465, Michelle 306, Millie Matildia 492, Millie Matildia (McGee) 306, Olive Elizebeth 492, Paul Leon 306, Pauline 306, Printhia Jane 492, Regina 6, Regina Lee 306, 447, Thelma 555, Tyler Leith 306, William 492, Willie Etta (Double) 306, Winnie Etta 492
DAUGHTERTY, Olean 333
DAVENPORT, Colonel "Louis C.", Addie 147, E. P. 112, E. R. 112, George 522, John Catlett 306, 522, L. C. 147, 163, 523, Sarah 522, Stella Mae 522
DAVENPORT-STRIKER, Rosella 316
DAVEY, Amos 275, 519, Anna 275, 519, Beniah 275, 519, Elizabeth 519, John 275, 519, Lydia 275, 519, Magdalen 275, 519, Naomi 275, 519, Thomas 275, Tom 519
DAVID, Emma Kline 351, Grace Eldeva Wamsley 257
DAVIDSON, Barton 307, Becky 307, Bill 307, Clova Joanne 307, Diane 307, Frank 307, James Robert 307, Jane (Schalgenhauf) 394, Jennifer 307, Jeremy 307, Jim 307, Julie 307, Michael 307, Nancy (McDaniel) 307, Ona 356, Peggy Ann 307, Richard Eugene 307, Steven 307, Thomas Barton 307, Thomas Osro 307, William 307, William Joseph 307
DAVIES, Adrienne 289, Doyt 289, Robin 289
DAVIS, Alice (Rogers) 324, Ameret Isophene 279, Amos 307, Arch Sherman 307, Bonnie 150, Brenda 443, Cheryl 443, Cheryl Friar 513, Cleo 542, Connie Sue 326, Cuthbert 307, 417, 421, Cynthia Jo 307, Dale (Buckner) 307, Deborah 558, Donald Eugene 307, 308, Edith 315, Edward 202, Edward Merle bles 308, Effie 308, 535, Elizabeth 309, 396, Emery 315, Estalene 293, Galen 558, George, 308, 535, George W. 249, 421, Gerald Emery 576, Gloria Ann 307, Hazel 308, James 228, Jason Leland bles 308, Jim 443, Joel 309, John 18, 58, John W. 91, Joseph 309, 421, Judy Ann 308, Julie 308, Kay 475, Kevin 558, Leander 308, Leland Wray bles 308, Linda 308, Lucinda 507, Lucinda (Richey) 279, Lucy 309, Luvetha 307, Lyda 552, Lydia Lavetha 421, Marie 509, Mark 309, Martha Rose (Courtney) 308, Mary 309, Mary Alice 554, Matthew 21, Matthew 309, Matthew 417, Matthew 421, Nina 509, Orve 308, 535, Patricia 576, Phillip 509, Priscilla 558, Rachel 309, Rachel 421, Ralph 144, Ray 308, 535, Rebecca 279, 309, Rick 308, Ricky Lynn 361, Robert 37, Robert 308, 512, 535, 585, Robert Mrs. 37, Roy 542, Sarah 240, 309, 417, 421, Sherman 307, Stanley 558, Susan Marie bles 308, Thelma Renbarger 576, Thomas F., 324, Timothy 443, Tommy 140, William P. 279
DAVISON, Addie 356, Amy (Davis) 309, Barbara 309, Celesta 542, Charles 333, Chris 309, Christopher Todd 490, Christopher Todd, II 490, David 502, Dennis 309, Elizabeth 309, Florence Mae 481, Furl 309, Guyla 502, Isaac 309, Iva Gourley 481, James 502, Linda 502, Lola (Jennings) 309, Mary 333, Mary Ann (Gibson) 542, Mary Lynn 309, Milford 542, Milissa 309, Mont 481, Moses 309, Nina 542, Rebecca 309, Stephen 309, Vance 83, 542, Verlin 309, Virgil 333, 502
DAWKINS, Henry 367
DAWLEY, Frances 238
DAWSON, Allison 309, Amelia (Pritchard) 309, Beverly 582, Charles 309, Corina Mae 309, Cyrus 309, Dale 309, Dehra 270, Earl 309, Faye 309, Fern 309, Floyd 309, Gary 309, Gene 270, 309, Glen 15, 309, Harvey 309, Henry Markwood 309, Irene 270, Iva 309, Jackie 582, James Ray 309, John 538, Julie Ann 396, Mahel 309, Mary 309, Max 582, Philip 309, William 309
DAY, Ambro 310, 311, 598, Ambrose 311, Bill 113, 310, Birdena 6, 310, Birdena (Voigt) 238, Carrie 313, 364, Carrie Gordon 254, Cecil 312, Cecil (Shadle) 313, Charles 6, 107, 200, 238, Charles Edward 310, 311, Connie 544, Daniel 310, 311, Dennis 518, 544, Edmond 311, Erica 312, Ethalinda 310, 474, Ethelinda Mossburg 598, Floretta 311, 313, Floretta (Buckner) 238, Frank 6, 254, 268, 310, 313, 396, Frank E. 311, Fred 312, 313, Frederick 312, 313, 314, Ginger Renee 518, 544, Heather 312, Henry 311, 313, Henry Jr. 310, Henry Sr. 310, Jana 313, Jeffery Michael 518, 544, Jennifer 314, Jeremy Matthew 518, 544, Jesse 312, Jill 313, Joyce 6, 310, Joyce Deanne 310, Julie 314, Kent 238, Kent Owen 310, Kevin Ross 310, Lindsey Marie 310, Marcia 313, Mark 312, 313, 314, Mark Alan 312, Maro 311, Martha 311, Marvin 310, Marvin L. 256, 311, 313, Mary 312, 313, 314, Mary E. 312, Matt 312, Matthew 312, 313, 314, Matthew L. 313, Melanie Elisabeth 313, Melvin 312, 313, 314, 541, Melvin Dean 312, Michael 312, 313, Michael E. 314, Mike 312, Minnie Floretta 310, Mitchell 312, 313, 314, Mitchell Kent 310, Nancy 310, Nancy 598, Nancy Jane 598, Pam 310, Paul 310, Paul Mason 311, Sally 254, 311, 313, Sarah 254, 311, 313, Scott 254, 311, 313, Steve 313, Steven 254, 311, Susan 254, 311, 313, Wilhorn 311, William 238, 311, 598, William Edwin 310, William Henry 6, 310, 311
DAY, Jr, William Henry 310
DAYTON, A. B. 75, Douglas 236
DE BOLT, Alexander R. 316, Alexander Ruble 315, Barbara Ellen (Ball) 315, E. Della 316, Elmer 315, 316, Esther Della (Robison) 315, George 315, Guy 315, Larry Wayne 316, Luther 315, Marie 315, Vera 315, Virgie 315
DEAM, Abram 38, Adam 38, Arlue 314, 154 169, 180, 253, Charles C. 8, Clara 314, Clarence 314, Debbie 513, Diana 513, Earl 314, Earl R. 9, Erma 314, Harriet 314, Harrison 38, Herbert 38, Imogene 447, J. P. 38, James 310, 513, James Jr. 513, John 314, John Milton 314, Kenneth 385, Marshall 513, Mary Ann 379, Mary Louise 513, Natalie 385, Nathan 385, Nellie 314, Robert 38, 447, Rollie 314, Sophia 586, Stella 116, W. H. 18, Willis 446
DEAM, Jr. Earl 314
DEAN, Eliza Ann 547, John 113, Levi 547, Mary C. 547, Obediah 547, Opal Davis 315
DEARMOND, Amanda 315, Amanda Renae 399, Charles 399, Charles L. 315, Diane 315, Dick A. 315, James 315, James William 315, Jared 315, Jared Michael 399, Judy 315, Laura 315, Loring 315, Lulu May (Watson) 315, Mara 315, Nicole 315, Randy 315, Randy Lee 399, Rick 315, Rio 315, Robert E. 315, Ross 315, Shannon 315, Steve 315, Steven Leroy 399, Teresa Lynn 399, Tommyon 315, Tricia 315, Trina 315, Tyson 315, Virgil A. 315
DEARMOND, Jr, Robert E. 315
DEATH, Dale 424, Patricia Irene 424, Roger 424
DEAVER, Matilda 578
DEBAILLIE, Alberic 281, Betty 281, Martha (Colpaert) 281
DEBOLT, Penelope Louise 385
DECHANT, Frederick 68
DECKARD, Anna 306
DECKER, Ada 64, Ada M. 579, Alice 541, Anna 316, 333, Anna Elizabeth 316, Barbara 316, Bertha Elick 541, Bertha Viola 339, Bob 87, Burris 333, Carol 316, Carol June 247, Catherine Joanna 247, Cathy 316, Charles 202, Charles 316, Charles 333, 387, Charles III 317, Charles IV 317, Charles Jr. 140, 317, Charles W. 317, 451 Cheri 316, 381, Cheri Rene 247, 350, Christian 316, Christopher 316, Christopher Joseph 247, Clint 316, Clinton Edward 247, D. N. 268, 364, D. Nelson 317, Dale 144, Danny 288, Davilla Nelson 316, Dorothy 339, Dustin 316, Dustin David 247, Dwight 316, Earl 333, Ed 289, Edward 316, 317, Edward David 247, Effie 333, Elizabeth 317, Elizabeth 499, Ella 316, Florence 414, George 316, George E. 317, Herman 413, 414, Isaac 317, Isaac Marie 316, Isabella 333, Isabelle 64, Ivan 316, Ivan Junior 316, Ivan Ralph 247, Ivan Ralph Jr. 247, Jackie 316, James 437, Jayne 316, Jayne Rosalyn 247, Jeanne 559, Jess 288, Jesse 316 317, 339, 541, John 316, 333, 586, John F. 8, 317, John Jacob 316, Jonathan 316, Joyce 316, Joyce Elaine 247, Katherine 370, Kelli 317, Kent 370, Lillie 64, 451, Loren 64, 437, Mary Elizabeth 247, 316, Matthew 370, Michael 316, 370, Michael William 247, Minnie 333, 408, Myrl Jean 247, 316, Olive 333, Orpha 316, 423, Orpha Imo 422, Otto 316, 317, Philip 316, Philip Martin 247, RaeJean 297, Rebecca (Houtz) 317, Richard Borne 316, Rufus 316, Rufus L. 317, Samuel 202, Skeet 317, Tami 142, 316, Tami Suzanne 247, William 333, Wilson 333, Zeffa 333
DEDRICH, Ethel 102
DEDRICK, Athena June 573, Caroline Betz 415, Dave 475, Ethel 266, Ida 475, James 144, Jim 475, John 475, 573, Lulu 475, Mabel 475, 476, Mary 475, Ruby 475
DEEDS, Mary M. 335
DEEDS, Mary Magdalene 334
DEEMER, Barry 374, Carol 499
DEERING, Mischelle 249
DEETER, Catherine 240, William 421
DEFILLIPO, Margaret 414
DEFORD, Debra 350
DEHAVEN, Benjamin Loren "Lon", Bess 317, Clark 317, Dorothy 317, Frank 317, Frank Carter 317, George 317, Gloria 317, Jane 317, Katherine 317, LeEtta <Letta> 317, Lenna 317, Letta 317, Lew 317, Lois 317, Margaret 317, Nancy 317, Nathaniel 317, Robert 317, Ruth 317, Walter 317, Walter B. 317, Walter Brown 317, Watt 317
DEIHL, Betty 318, 379, Bob 140, Carrie 318, Dwight 318, Frank 318, Louise 318, Max 318, Michael 318, Rebecca 318, Robert 318, Roy 318, Velma 318, William 318, William J. 318
DEISCH, Caroline Catherine 556
DELACOUR, Charles 164, Terrell 164
DELANEY, Karen Sue 396
DELONG, Alexander 112, Ellen 573, Goldia M. (Neuenschwander) 316, John 404, Joseph 404, Mary 116
DEMARTINO, Thomas 581, Thomas Albert 581
DEMERS, Gloria 466
DEMNING, Adeline 13, John T. 13, Oliver Bryan 13
DEMPSEY, R. H. 98
DENIRO, Robert 332
DENIS, Jacob 445, Mabel 594
DENNEY, Argend 318, Dianne L. 420, Ellis 318, Francis 318, Gertrude 318, Golda 318, Grover Cleveland 318, Harold Dean 318, Janet 420, Janet (Hodel) 494, Joyle 318, 602, Laura 318, Lisa Ann 494, Marybeth (Betty) 318, Max 420, 494, Myrtle 318, Nancy 318, Vernon 89, Walter 318
DENNIS, Alfreda 474, Marjorie 375, Mary Helen 531
DENNY, Besse 304, Gordon 280, Kathryn Burleigh 280, Kathy Burleigh 365
DENTEL, Carol Ann 333, Kent 333
DENTON, Atlanta 299, James 299
DERR, Aaron Landis 318, 508, Brownie 473, Catherine (Scott) 318, Cressie 318, E. E. 604, Grace 318, 477, 507, 508, Hallie Faye 318, Joseph 318, Marcille 473, Rela Kay 450, Rela Key 318
DERTING, Sarah Ellen 239
DERUYSCHER, Mae 576
DESANTIS, Alicia 342, Andrea 342, Christina 342, Patrick 342
DETER, Catharine 324
DETTMER, Amy 604, Anna 564, Annetta Louise Marie 563, Brian 604, Friedrich 564, Ida 564, John 564, John D. 564, John Diedrich 564, Julia 564, 604, Luther 73, Maggie 564, Marie Emile 564, Mary Barbara 564, Sharon 552, Sophia 564
DETWILER, Anna 547, John 547, Margaret 547
DETWILLER, Jan 563
DEVOE, Charles 318, David Allan 318, Dean Alan 318, Dena Suzanne 318, Martha (Becks) 318, Scott Alan 318
DEVORE, Amanda 319, Beth 319, David 319, Glen 319, Homer 319, Lewis 319, Rachel (McNutt) 319, Robert 319, 572, Ross 319, 572, Ruth 319, Sarah 572
DEVOSS, Sarah L. 407
DEWALT, Verdella 103
DEWEESE, B. L. 538
DEWEESE, Dr. 122
DEWEESE, Elizabeth 538, Lulu Grace 429
DEWEY, Thomas 34
DEWITT, Larry 591, Louisa 267, 405, 572, Merianne 591, Minervia 546, Moses 572, 592, Sally (Westbrook) 572
DIAL, Leah 474
DIAN, Sue 152, 200
DICK, Albert 319, Brian 319, Bruce 319, Christopher James 319, Daniel 318, Edward 319, Eric 319, Erin Renee 319, Glennis Slusher 319, Gregory Scott 319, James I. 319, Kara Sue 319, Lawrence H. 319, Lori 319, Mary Catherine <Katy> 318, Mona Irene 319, Nancy 437, Nondus (Cain) 319, Peggy (Davidson) 319, Tamara 548, Thomas 319, Virgil (Andrews) 319
DICKASON, Angelina 320, Barbara Gene 320, Barbara Suzanne 585, Bessy 320, Blaine 320, Bonnie 320, 585, Carolyn Kay 428, Crystal Marie 553, Cyrus 320, Darla 428, Donald 585, Fitastus "Ora", Francis Marion 320, 553, 585, Francis Warren 553, Frank W. 475, George Franklin 320, George S. 320, 585, Hazel 585, Hazel Marie 320, Inez 320, Jacob 320, 585, Jacob E. 320, James Frederick 553, Jason C. 428, Jasper 585, 588, Jasper E. 320, Jerry Grove 320, Joe 346, Joe Robert 553, John Edward 553, John F. 320, 585, John W. 320, 585, Junior Thomas 320, Karen 428, Kathryn Marie 553, Linda 320, Linda Sue 553, Lois 320, Lydia 585, Mable 585, Mable May 320, Martha Jane 497, Minerva 320, Naamon 320, Naman 585, Nancy 320, 585, Nancy (Stanley) 320, Ora 585, Oscar 585, Oscar Eugene 320, Oscar Gene 320, R.M. 214, Richard Lee 553, Robert Myles 320, Rodney W. 475, Rosa 320, 585, Rosa Elizabeth 320, Sally 320, Samual 320, 585, Samuel Warren 553, Sherri 428, Susan 320, Susanah Barbara 320, Susannah 585, Syrus 585, Trudy 346, Walter 585, Walter P. 320, Warren 320, 585, William 585, William H. 320, Zachary 475
DICKENS, Esther Bennett 415
DICKENSON, Hattie 155
DICKERSON, Mary Elise 401, Rebecca 347
DICKEY, Janette 150
DICKIE, Donald 268, Janice 268, Margaret "Tudy" (Gordon), Marjorie 306, Melisa (Pyle) 411, Orval 411, Robert 411, Vera (Miller) 411, William 411
DIDIER, Frank 418
DIEFENBACH, H. B. 85
DIEFENBAUGH, H. B. 452
DIEHL, Adam 394, Amos Harlow 394, Brady 414, Brian 414, Brianne 414, Catherine 394, Elizabeth 414, Franklin 394, Genevieve 103, Goldie (Graham) 415, Hannah (Billman) 394, Helen I 415, Jerry 414, John 414, Lawrence L. 415, Lillian 221, Lillie 394, Lillie May 413, Lucinda (Cline) 394, Luke 414, Martha 394, Mary 394, Megan 414, Roy 221, Russell R. 414, Samuel 394, Scott 414, Wendell 103, 336, William 394
DIERKS, Andrew 485, Jayne 485, Joseph 485, Kimberly 485
DIETRICH, Adolph 383, Ann 383, Judy 383
DIFF, Sade 264
DILGER, Monica 415
DILLE, Aaron 320, Asa 320, Caleb 320, Carl Raymond 320, Daris 320, David 320, David Jr. 320, Eunice Eileen 320, Glenna June 320, Isreal 320, John 320, John Jr. 320, Jonathan 320, Joshua A. 320, Lewis 320, Mildred Lucile 320, Opal 320, Price 320, Rachel 320, Samuel 320, Sarah 320, Sarah Flo 320, Steven 320, Susanna 320, Swendolyn Kathleen 320, William 320, William L. 320, Wilma Maxine 320
DILLEY, Eunice E. 377, Timothy 147
DILLINGER, John 216, 280, 447
DILLMAN, Ed 79, Jacob 79, John 79, Sidney 15, 79, Tess 145
DILLON, Don 562, Donna 562, Earl 145, Yuvonne 461
DINIUS, Rebecca 605
DINKEL, Betty (Vice) 599, Herbert Klein 599, Jancie Lee 599
DINSMORE, Edna 530, Henry 530, Lois Kelley 530
DIONNE, Maurice 140
DIPPEL, Carl 322, Charles Norman 321, Claudia 321, David 322, Frederick 322, Mina (Schoppman) 322, Rolland 322, Wilma Lou 322
DISHHONG, Tonya Renee 532
DISHONG, Diana Kay 532, Diane 390, Lynn 532, Margaret Katherine 424, Tiffany Dawn 532, Tina Lynnett 532, Tisha Kay 532
DISLER, Katrhyn (Campbell) 283
DITMAR, Charles J. 321
DITTMANN, Dorothy F. 345
DITZLER, Anna Maria (Yohe) 321, Arnetta Pearl 394, B. Catherine (Brickley) 579, Cassiah Cassandra 321, David 321, Edward 532, Elizabeth "Betty", Elizabeth 378, Elizabeth Jane 378, Erma Laurietta 321, Etta 550, Fern Rarick 532, Frank 321, Gale <Don> 321, George 317, George C. 22, George Calvin 321, 532, George Jr. 321, Glendora 321, Hillard 538, Hillard Lyle 321, Iva 437, Jacob Franklin 321, 538, John 270, 321, 394, John R. 579, June 538, Lorena 321, Lula 321, Lulu Mae 538, Mary Etta 579, Nell Cordelia 321, Paul 538, Paul Fenwick 321, Ray 532, Ray F. 538, Ray Franklin 321, Robert 321, Ruby Irene 321, Vier 538, Vier Clenwood 321, Vier Clenwood Jr. 321, William 177, 321
DIVELBISS, Fred 503, Freda Mae 591
DOATY, Anna 239
DOBBINS, Elvira 417
DOBSON, Lisa 590
DOCHANDT, A. G. 64
DODDS, 331
DOEHRMAN, Gloria Ann 307
DOEHRMAN, Merlin 307
DOENGES, Helen Burget 407
DOLAN, Richard 307
DOLBY, 66, Clarence 556, David 66, Grace Mossburg 474, Janet C. 525, Maxine 556, Tessie 556
DOLD, Anita 154
DOLLAR, Dustin 443, Nathaniel 443, Neil 443, Sierra 443, Teresa 443
DONAGHY, Richard 91
DONALDSON, W.M. 59
DONALDSON, W. M. Rev. 58
DONALDSON, Wilson 90
DONALDSON, Wilson E. 90
DONALDSON, Wilson M. 60
DONNELL, David 385
DONNELLY, Margaret 542
DONOVAN, Brian 467, Carrie 467, Tom 467
DOOLEY, D. C. 75
DORMIRE, Don 359, Ina May 359
DORR, Rhoda 603
DORSCH, Otto 64
DORSEY, Adele M. 411
DOSTER, Dr. 20, Hezakiah 307, Jane (Hardwidge) 307, Stella 278, 307
DOTSON, Jim 467, Katie 467, Rachel 467
DOTTERER, Caroline 322, Henry 322, Jeffrey 322, Jeffrey P. 322, 354, John 322, Joseph H. 322, Kathryn S. 322, 354, Kathy 305, Marjorie M. 322, Mary 322, Mary (Reineck) 322, Paul 305, 322, 354, Paul E. 322, Phyllis 305, 322, Phyllis A. 354, Sally 322, Sally K. 322, 354, Susan M. 305, 322, 354, William 322
DOUBLE, Anna M. 423, 552, Dawn 576, Don 221, Don 576, Donald Andrew 576, Garth 576, Jacob 423, Marjorie 576, Michelle 576, Nellie 576, Robert 576, Tina 576, Winnie Etta 492
DOUGAL, Phyllis 270
DOUGHERTY, Hugh 163, 185, 202, 216, John 188, Lois 248, Louella 407, 520
DOUGLAS, A. 98
DOUGLAS, A. J. 64, 96, 323, Beatrice 321, Lloyd 96, 323, Nina J. 595, Rex 509, Scott 529, T. G. 64
DOUGLASS, Barbara Louise 250, Bethina 503, Clara Mae 338, 503, Howard 503, Isaiah 503, Leslie 503, Marcia 503, Marilyn 503, Patricia 503, Patricia Joan 249, Paul 503, Philip 503, Rachel 503, Rex 503, Steven 503, Susan 503
DOWDY, William 515
DOWNING, David 75, Margaret 387
DOWTY, Adam 245, 323, Benjamin 323, Darlene 323, Don 323, Edward 323, Erma Regine 323, 430, Hubert Vernell 323, Ilow 245, James 323, James Kenneth 323, James Wilson 323, Jerrold 323, June Marie 323, Karen 323, Lillian 323, Lona 245, Lorena 454, Marjorie Edith 323, Martha (Belle) 155, Mary Janette 323, Myrtle 245, Myrtle Nellie (Bush) 359, Paul Adam 323, Roberta Aldine 323, Ronald 323, Vernon 234, Virginia 245, Wendell Francis 323, William 245, 323, 359
DOYLE, Margaret Kessinger 540, Thomas 540
DRABENSTOT, Margaret L. 380, Margerret L. Cossairt 380, Milo C. "Mike"
DRACHMAN, 179

DRAGE, Clover 150
DRAGONETTE, A. J. 231
DRAGOO, Chauncey E. 181
DRAKE, Doris 567, Michael 567, Mike 567, P.A. 78
DRAPER, Samuel 532, Amanda Michelle 536, Dennis 340, Herman 340, Herman D. 340, Jerry 340, Mindy 536, Natalie Joy 536, Suzanne Kathleen 536, Troy Duane 536
DREISBACH, Georia Lee 522, Jerry Lou 522, Julia 306, 522, Robert 306, Robert H. 522
DRENNEN, Benjamin Harrison 323, Forest Devona 323, James Samuel 323, Rex Allen 323, Sarah Glover 323, Warren Vincent 323
DREW, Clara 127
DREWETT, Elizabeth 259
DREWS, Beatrix 360
DRISCOL, Nancy Arlene 334
DRISCOLL, Delores 554
DRUCKEMILLER, Alice 366, 440, Burr 431, Mary Elizabeth 431, Vada 371, Allen Burr 594, Inez 594, Mary Krinn 594
DRUCKWELL, Elizabeth 293
DRUM, George 15, J. P. 15, John Peter 394, Mary 440, Opal 221
DRUMMOND, D. H. 443
DUBACH, Amos 221, Christine 221, Eliza 562, Linda 150, Pauline Marie 303
DUBBELD, Dion 422, 576, Dion Gene 511, 586, Janella 422, 576, Janella Joy 511, 586, Ron 422, 576, Ronald 511, Twila 422, 576, 586, Pope 511
DUBBS, Anna 351, Carol Kettenburg 249
DUBOIS, Isobel 200
DUCHATEAU, Frank 304
DUCKER, Paul 58
DUCKWALL, Amanda 524, Elizabeth 524, Margaret Kisiah 524, Nancy 524, William 524
DUDASH, Danielle 541, Krista 541, Victor 541
DUDLEY, Docia (Clevenger) 308, Janet 544, John 308, Nancy Emily 308, Ripton 518, 544
DUFF, Elizabeth 542
DUGLAY, Asbury 208
DUGLAY, Asbury 365
DUHAMELL, Mabel 301
DUKE, Karey 290
DUKES, Anna 155, Frank T. 384, Mary Naomi Wilson 384, Mearl 262, Nellie 384
DULIN, John 68
DULWORTH, Jerry E. 485, Jerry L. 485, Marcia 485, Mark Allen 485, Todd Lynn 485
DUMBAULD, Charles 465, Erma 465, Eva 465, Hersel 465, Katie 465, Letha 465
DUNAWAY, Dale 187
DUNBAR, Hobart 533, Homer 533, John Henry 533, L. L. 533, Mary 533, Max 533, Minni 533, Robert 533, Von 533
DUNCAN, Colin 507, J. C. 83, Jacob 112, John 507
DUNLAP, Annabelle 592
DUNMORE, Catherine 527
DUNN, Cecile 357, Charles 357, Howard 357, Jesse 267, 548, Karen 130, Kay 357, Marie 279, Mark 357, Nicole 357, Trudith 570, William 357
DUNNING, Betty 379
DUNPHY, Ray 148
DUNWIDDIE, Benjamin F. 324, Cathleen Sue 324, Cathy 324, 437, Chris 324, Chris 437, Chris Allen 324, Cindy 437, Clarence 324, Cynthia 324, Cynthia Lou 324, Elizabeth 324, 464, Erin 324, Ethel 324, Flossie 324, George 84, 324, 464, 562, Gerald 324, Gerald 437, 464, Grace 314, 464, Grace (Dyson) 324, Henry 324, 464, Henry Harrison 324, Juli 562, Julie 324, Kelly 324, Lela 464, Linda 324, 562, Lloyd 324, 464, Marcia 324, 562, Marie 324, Mark 324, 562, Merlin 324, Nancy 562, Suzanne 324, Vera 324, Vera 464
DUPIN, C. Wesley 80
DUPP, Dana 64
DURDAHL, Ivy 513, Joe 513, Misty 513, Pamela 401, Pamela Lee 513, Rebecca Jane Hiatt 513
DURHAM, Helen 475, Kathleen 428
DURKES, Della 440, Henry 366, 440, Minnie 366, 440
DURR, Cora (Brown) 325, David Lynn 325, Elizabeth 325, Kim 84,182, 325, Marlyn Kaye 325, Marshall Parr 324, Melanie Sue 325, Nettie 259, Oliver 45, 325, Palmer 325, Palmer Douglas 324, Parr 325, Ray Douglas 324, 325, Raymond "Daddy", Raymond 594, Sally 325, Sarah 325, Ti 325, Ti Mikkel 324
DURST, Amy 326, Anna 303, 326, Elizabeth 326, Fred 326, Gus 326, Henry 326, Jennie 326, Leona 326, Mary E. 326, Mathias 326, Walter 326
DUSENBERRY, William 435
DUSTMAN, Mark 435, Teresa 435
DUTCHER, Donald H. 444, Wilma 444
DUVALL, Berta E. 291, Mareen 446
DWENGER, Joseph 95
DYAR, E. W. 234
DYBBRO, Elizabeth 596, Julia 596, Phillip 596, William 596
DYE, Everett 89, 537, Hettie Bell 320, Lucille 515, Margaret 408, Sharon 537
DYKES, Alan 457, Brad 457, Lauren 457, Megan 457
DYKSTRA, Gregory Stuart 513, John Frederick 513, Thomas Edwin 513
DYNES, Ruth (Reinhard) 522
DYSON, Christina 592, David 592, Dawn 592, Dean 592, DeAnn 592, Grace 324, 464, Jesse 144, Levi 324, 464, Lois 592, Lorena 93, Lorinda 592, Lydia 324, Lydia Ann 464, Patricia 258, 592, Robert 592
EARL, Eva 109, Frank 326, 576, Letha 326, Margaret 326, 576, Margaret Ann 326, Mary 563, Nellie 402
EARLE, Charles 281
EARLEY, B.B. 163
EARNEST, Ella 327, Hazel 327, Ida 327, Isaac 327, Isaac N. 327, James 327, James Eli 327, James Eli Ellison 327, John Redric 327, Martin 327, Mary E. 327, Mary Jane Lucille 327, Mildred 532, Mildred M. 543, Sara 327, Stella 327, Susanna 327, William 327
EARNEY, Teresa 340
EASLEY, Bob 393, Carl 102, 393, Carol 393, Don 393, Jim 393, Larry 393
EASTON, Aldula 152, Helen Easton 596, Janet 596, Robert 596
EATON, Charles 185, James 185, Olney 64, T.A.R. 121
EBERLY, C.M. 58
EBERT, Anna 547
EBERTS, Ducky 36
EBNIT, Pearl 570
EBY, Lloyd 92
EBY, Lloyd Rev. 413
ECHELBARGER, Laura Effie 277
ECHOLS, Karen 273
ECHROTE, Berta 440
ECHROTE, Will 440
ECKELBARGER, Anna Belle 455, Charles 309, David 427, Lawrence 309, Mary (Carter) 309, Minnie (Draper) 309
ECKER, Vivian 599
ECKROTE, Eugene 142
EDDINGTON, Crystal 514
EDDY, Jonathan 18
EDEN, John 541, Kelly 541, R.D. 82
EDGAR, Almeda 246, Atkinson 246, 477, Elizabeth 443, Jane 246, John 246, Mary 246, 477, Mary Ann Mounsey 246, Minnie 246, Nora 246, Ruth 246, Sarah 246, Zelda Ann Poling 246
EDGELL, Ruth 515
EDGERTON, Calvin 446, Daniel 446, Frankliln 446, Hannah 446, Joseph 446, Nina Hazel 446, Thomas Jr. 446, Thomas Sr. 446, William 446, Benjamin 379, Betty 155, Carol 379, Catherine 567, Chris 379, Connie 208, 515, Coulson 379, Coulson Jr. 379, David 379, David 599, Dessie (Sands) 531, Diane 379, Dick 379, Donovan 379, Elizabeth 379, 599, Enestes 599, Eugene 202, 379, Franklin 379, Gena 379, Gene 140, Grace 379, Jack 379, James 379, John 379, Katie 379, Kent 379, Kimberly 379, Larry 379, Maud 514, Maude 414, Max 379, Mike 379, Mrs. 75, Ned 379, Paul 379, Rachel 379, Rebecca 506, Robert 514, Sibyl 379, Sue 379, Theodore 599, Tim 379, Tom 379, William 379
EDMINSTEN, Margaret 567
EDMUNDSON, Aimee 499, Bill 499, Billy 499, Carrie 499, Elizabeth (Morsel) 538, Esther 538, Thomas 538
EDMUNSON, Onie 508
EDRIS, Aaron 326, Andrea Lynn 326, Andreas 326, Beverly 326, Carolyn 200, Charles Lawrence <Larry> 326, Chester 326, Dale E. 326, Debbie 326, Donna 326, Dorothy 326, Edwin 326, Edwin Lawrence 326, Elizabeth 326, Ethel 142, Gerald L. 101, Gerald Lee 326, Harry 326, Henry 326, Henry 356, Homer 326, Jack 598, Joan 326, Johann 326, Johann (Eader) 326, John 216, 370, John H. 326, John H. Jr. 326, John Jr. 140,146, 216, John Jr. Mrs. 146, John Sr. 598, Judith Kay 326, Judy 349, Kelly Renie 326, Lawrence 326, Lawrence Ellsworth 326, Leonard 326, Lester 326, Lorene 326, Lorie Elaine 326, Louis 326, Maria Eder 451, Martha 326, Mattbew Lawrence 326, Max Leon 326, Milton 326, Readocia 383, Ruth 326, Sarah 326, Stefanic Jo 326, Theresa 326, Todd Allen 326, Winnie Merl 326
EDWARDS, D. Wayne 328, Daniel 537, David 79, Doug 329, Douglas 327, 472, James McBride 328, Janice 555, Jennifer 328, Jennifer Louise 328, Jeremiah 329, Jeremiah Martin 328, Jim 329, Jonathan 329, Jonathan Michael 328, K. 264, Kenneth 327, 328, Kenneth 454, Kenneth W. 280, Kenny 25, 329, Maude Ritter 555, Melba 6, Melba 25, 327, Melba L. 280, Melba (McBride) 327, 328, 329, Mildred 155, Mildred 350, Mildred Garrison 327, Pollyanna 327,328, Russell 555, Shane 472, Shane Kenneth 327, Skip 472, Skip Douglas 327, Tamra 472, William 328
EFFINGER, Ferdinand 95
EGBERT, Elizabeth 90
EGER, Louisa Maria 468, Louise 367, Mary 367
EGGERT, Denise 309
EGLY, Albert 329, Benedict 329, Clara 329, Edna 329, Edwin 329, Elizabeth 329, Emil 329, Emma 329, Estelle 329, Glen 329, Ida 329, Levi 329, Lewis 329, Lydia 329, Magdalena 329, Maria Blotter Von Guten 329, Martha 329, Ralph 329, Walter 329, Zella 329
EGNER, Angel 440
EHLE, Molly 528
EHLER, Jacob 95
EHLER, Roy 144
EHLERDING, Gilbert 344, Viola 368
EHRHARDT, Leo 89
EHRLICH, Carrie 387, Mark 387, Rodney 387
EHRMAN, Floyd 221, 522, Floyd Kenneth 522, Hugh 522, Ilene 522, Keith 221, Lola 221, Lola (Barger) 522
EHRSAM, Harley 422, Harry 422, Lester 422, Mary Elizabeth 422, Melvin 422, Oscar 422, William 422
EIBLING, Carol Kay 343
EICHE, Milo 140
EICHENBERGER, Vic 224
EICHENBERRY, John 435
EICHHORN, Adam Lee 247, Adam Lee 330, Aline 318, Beatrice 267, Betty Marcille 433, Charles 330, Cindy Sue 247, 330, Don 330, 378, Elco 330, Ellen 64, Elva 248, Emma (Schoonover) 330, Gloria 279, Gloria Anna 330, Harriet Jane (Brickley) 330, Hazel 583, Henry 154, Jimmie Lee 247, 330, John 142, 330, Joseph , Judge 146, Kent Alan 330, Kent Allen 247, Marguerite Betty 431, Marilyn Joan 247, Mary 308, Mary (Bailey) 330, Mary Jane 330, May 200, Mrs. 146, Oddessa Iona 516, Phillip 258, Robert 330, Robert Eldon 247, Samuel H. 431, Thomas Franklin 330, Tom 594, Von 22, 330, Wanda 594
EICHORN, Ada Azora 257
EICHORN, Joseph 200
EILAR, 66, Mary 461
EILER, Suzanne 470, Ves 13, 76
EISAMAN, Jack 146, 330, Jack Mrs. 146, Jack W. 330, John Jr. 330, John Ringo 330, Julie 330, Mary 152, Mary Alice 200, Mary Alice (Ringo) 330
EISENBARGER, Marylin 403
EISENHOWER, Mammie 399
EISHER, Bonnie 150
EKHARDT, Stefan 460
ELDRIDGE, Emma Jane 305, Marguerite (Daugherty) 507
ELETT, Louise Catherine 560
ELEY, Cheryllee 331, Elmer Dean 331, Jack Richard 331, Janet 331, Joseph 379, Myrtle (Hizer) 331, Patricia 331, Terri 331
ELICK, Andy 44, Mary Ann 588
ELKINS, Debbie 84
ELLENBERGER, Angel 400, Angel Michelle 331, Charlotte 440, Dale 440, DeAnna 400, DeAnna J. 331, Donald 440, Douglas 400, Douglas Jess 331, Jesse 331,440, Kenneth 440, Kenneth J. 400, Kenneth Joe 331, LeAnna Jill 400, Mary 440, Mary Linn 331, Mary (Linn) 440, Nancy 440, Richard 440, Robert 440, Ronda 583, Shirley 440
ELLENBURG, Vera 150
ELLERMAN, Judy 150
ELLINGHAM, Ann 331, Caroline 331, Charles 331, Charles (son of charles) 331, Dinah 331, Elizabeth (Bessie) 331, Hannah 331, Horace 331, James 331, John 331, Laura 331, Theodore 331, William 331
ELLIOT, D. L. 60
ELLIOTT, Barbara 6, Barbara 8,152, 154, Barbara Huffman 405, Barbara J. 200, Chloe 441, Elia 441, Enid 441, Enis 441, Ernest D. 332, Goldie (Kemp) 332, James Lee 522, Janice Sue 332, Jerry J. 522, Joan 137, Joe 81, Joseph Angelo 405, Kenneth E332, Lynn Renner 522, Michael Roger 405, Robert 441, Robert J. 405, Shannon 522, Sherry Lee 332, Stephan 441, Walter 84
ELLIS, Andrew William 332, Charles 448, Curtis Osman "Pete", Curtis Osman 507, David 332, Edward Osman 332, Ella Holmes 332, Hiner Holmes 332, 348, Luther Edward 332, Mary 184, Mary Marie 507, Pete 184, Rebecca Jane 332, Ted Leon 332, Theodore 151, Theora 448, Tim Ray 332, Tom Kay 332, Viola 332
ELLISON, Christina Linn 396, James Eli 327, Litia Ann 327, Nevo 498, Nevo 498, Stacey Renee 396, Stan 514, Stanely E. 396, Susan 514, Urshell 294
ELLSWORTH, Lydia S. 262, Mary 607, William 16
ELROD, Malee 501, Melissia 501, Ned 501
ELSTEN, Clyde M. 494, Doyle "Butch", Josephine 494, Peggy Joan 494
ELSTON, Florence Mae 554, Henry 81, Hugh 554, Peggy 494, Sheila 350
ELTAIBY, Joan 330
ELWELL, Lavina 317, Winnie 317
ELY, Alice Eleanor Smith 585, Linda Jane 585, Peggy Lou 569
ELZEY, Abner 597, Abner S. 332, Abner W. 332, Byrl 333, Calvin 333, Charles 58, Charley 58, Christina 333, Christine 246, Dale 332, Dalene 332, Daniel 333, DeLynn <Dean> 332, Dixie 333, Earl "Peck", Effie 333, Effie Decker 333, Elisha V. 332, Emmanuel 333, Erma 333, Ezkiel 333, Frank 210, Ilow Ruth 332, Isam 333, Isom 333, 501, Jesse 333, Joe 144, John 333, Joseph 333, Lida 356, Loren 303, Magdalene 597, Mary 333, Phyliss 597, Phyllis Ann 332, Rebecca Diane 303, Rowena 333, Ruth 333, Sadie 489, Sandra 332, Sharon Annette 303, William 333
EMENHISER, Charles 603, Patricia J. 603, Phyllis 489, Ted 603
EMERITUS, Pastor 96
EMLEY, Dorothy 333, Erma 333, Erma Lucille 399, Esther Marie 568, Fay 333, Faye (Kauffman) 399, Glen 333, Glenice 333, Harmon 333, 399, Linda 333, Roscoe 333
EMON, James 216
EMSHWILLER, Fred 301
EMSHWILLER, Fred Craven 301
EMSHWILLER, J. Joe Craven 301
EMSHWILLER, Ned 140, Thomas 301, Cindy 456
ENGELER, Albert 464, Charles 464, Edward 464, Emma 464, F. F. 188, Frank 216, 464, Frederick 259, 464, Henry Frederick 464, Margaret 464, Martha 464, Mary Ellen 439, 464, Rosanna 259, Rosanna Biberstein 464, William Martin 464
ENGLAND, Melinda 307, Melody 3, Roberta 307, Russell 307
ENGLE, "Mort", "Link", Amanda E. 335, Ann 335, Arthur 334, Arthur Leslie 335, Charles R. 335, Daniel 334, 335, Daniel Lee 334, Dean 84, Emma 334, Emma F. 335, Ethel 334, Guy 334, Guy Edward 308, 334,335, 541, Hannah 335, Harry 334, Helen Marie Shorter Grumbles 308, Horrace E. 335, Iris Marie 335, Isaac 335, J. Merle 334, 335, James A. 335, Jeannine (Shull) 334, 541, Jill 142, Joe 334, Joseph 61, Joseph C. 335, Lillian 142, Linda Lucille 334, Lutitia 335, Martha A. 335, Mary 335, Mary Martha (Deeds) 334, Melvin Henry 334, Naomi Mae 335, Nellie 334, Prudence 335, Ray Carlton 335, Robert "Mort", Robert 334, Sally 541, Sally Anne 334, Waneta June 335, William "Link", William 334, 335, Wilma Jessie 335
ENGLEBERT, Emma 511
ENGLEDOW, Jack 270, Judy 270, Tracy 270
ENGLEHARD, Mary Barbara 564
ENGLER, Frank 589
ENRIGHT, Hansey 121, Timothy 95
ENSLEY, Emma 538
ENSMINGER, Carol 388
ERHART, Mary (Hedges) 389
ERICK, Leone 8
ERICKSON, Jason 471, Jennifer 471, Richard 471
ERNEST, Prescilla 605
ERNST, Eliza Jane (Ball) 266, George 266, Jennie Jane 395, JoElla 333, John 16, 87, 266, 395, Netta Belle 266, Suzanna 410, W.H. 163
ERTEL, Alma 537, John 537, Mary Ethel 537, Virginia 412
ERVIN, Rev. 60
ERWIN, Cheryl 257, Eunice A. 391, Nora 567
ERXLEBEN, Bette 152
ESCHENBACKER, Abbey 518, 544, Abbey Michelle 591, Effie Marie 544, Todd 518, 544, Todd Alan 591
ESMOND, R.D. 202
ESPICH, Cari 335, Doyle 335, Ed 335, Helen (Keller) 335, Jeff 335, Jeffery 22, 216, John William 335, Kimberly 335, Marcia 335, Michael 335, Reada 335, Sharon (Cary) 335, Walter 335, William 335
ESSEX, Zelda 603
ESTEY, Colonel Jacob 168
ETCHISON, Bo Nathaniel 350, Brian 350, Brian II 350
EUBANK, Cecil 554, Dessie 408, Dessie May 554, Helen 408
EUBANKS, Dave 13
EULITT, Alena 418, Caleb 418, Cathleen 418, John 418
EVAN, Margaret 317
EVANS, Alferd 242, Corey Dr. 13, Earnest 242, George 242, Jacqueline 536, James Mitchell 490, Jeffrey Mitchell 490, Justin Scott 536, K. W. 536, Lovina 242, Martha 586, Mary 415, Nellie 242, Rob Dr. 84, Samuel 242, Teresa 154, Theodore 242, Tom 13, William Charles 242
EVARD, Tanya 429
EVENS, J.H. 89
EVERETT, Edward 448
EVERETTE, Rita 487
EVERS, Flossie 588
EVERSOLE, Bertha 335, Charles 335, Jacob 335, Jennie 335, John 335, Kenneth Mrs. 154, Mary 335, 558, Minnie 335, Nina Jane 335, Nina Jane 464, Oren 335, Susannah (Miller) 335, Tena 335, Vera 335, Vesta 214, William Henry 335
EVILSIZER, Clarabelle 525
EWELL, Robert 58, Robert 59, Sharon 526
EWING, Bernice 152
EWINGS, Miss T. 121
EYANSON, Deborah 522
EYLER, Betty 426
EYMER, Dorothy (Gross) 336, Jane 456, Karen Marie 336, 396, Karlene Ellen 336, Kelly Diane 336, Lester C. 336, Roger Henry 336
FACKLER, Irene 483, John David Paul 73, Louise 73, Martin 73, Paul 73
FAHL, Charles 562, Charles Elmer 336, Cora 336, Daniel 336, Desta Lucile 336, Desta Lucile 562, Frank 336, Genevieve 336, Harmon 336, Henry 336, Kenneth Rev. 97, Leah Samantha 336, Mary 336, Mary Jane 562, Michelle 559, Ross 565, Sherrill 565
FAIR, Barbara 498, Harry 216, Jerry 58, William 140, William Mrs. 136
FAIRBAIRN, Ann Louise 513
FAIRBANKS, Louisa Sarah 437
FAIRCHILD, Anita 359, Myrtle Anna 330
FAIRFIELD, Janice 287
FALK, Adam 333, Albert 336, Benjamin 362, Benjamin Lee 385, Cressie 119, 385, Dale 504, Daniel 333, David 333, 504, Denny 333, 467, Diane 333, Diane Kay 290, Guy Benjamin 336, Homer 385, Homer Floyd 336, Howard Fulton 336, Ida Ludwig 582, Ileen Alice 336, Jacob 336, 362, Jacob Ross 385, Janice 504, Jason 333, 497, Jennifer 333, 497, Jesse 333, Jonathan "Shafe", Joseph 336, 362, 582, Justin 333, 497, Justine May 336, Laurel 600, Leon 333, Leon Shafe 336, Lorraine 333, Lucas 362, Lucas Robert 385, Paul 573, Phyllis 504, Richard 333, 497, Robert 385, Robert B. 336, Ruth 362, Ruth Elva (Harris) 385, Samuel 336, 362, Sharon 333, 497, Shawn 333, Sherman 582, Terri 333, Tom 504, Viva 333, William Homer 336, Winifred 582
FALOTICO, Daniel Mark 585
FANCHER, Cheri 351
FARB, Susan 319
FARELL, Violet Jean 402
FARLING, Abraham 308, Betty 542, Char 150, Clara 437, Cloyd 542, Cloyd Jr. 140, 542, Dorothy 542, Earl 542, Edna 155, 542, Ethel 542, George 437, Gillian 542, Harold 542, Harriet 308, Jacob 308, 437, Jane 542, Lois 542, Lucile 157, Mary Ann (Haiflich) 437, Phyllis 591, Sarah Elizabeth 542, Skitz 542
FARLOW, Bertha Alice 285, John 386, Margaret 502, Mary Alice 302, William Riley 285, 302
FARMER, Archer 389
FARNER, Laura 464
FARNSWORTH, Clyde 435
FARR, A. J. 169, Pauline 155
FARRELL, Amy 531, Earl 531, Etta 531, Etta E. 560, Everett 531, Frances 531, 560, Fred 531, George 531, 560, 563, Herbert 531, Ida 531, Nancy 537, Robert 531
FARRON, Aelis H. 451
FASSER, Elsa 339, Hedwig (Walther) 339, Leonard 339, Mary 339, William 339
FATCHER, Augusta 336, Edith 336, George 336, Henry 336, Jacob 336, Margaret (Young) 336, Mary "Mamie"
FATE, Anna Vanice 337, Avis B. 337, Blanch 337, Boston Hiramus Bartholome 337, Boston Jr. 337, Catherine Elaine 337, Clarence Duane (Jim) 337, David Lowell 337, Dwight Bedford 337, Emmanuel 337, Forest Graden 337, Gary Lee 337, Hugh 337, Hulda Augusta 337, John Wesley 337, Lucy 337, Mary 337, Mary Joan 337, Michael 337, Paul Edward 337, Rebecca 337, Rex Galen 337, Richard 337, Robert Lowell 337, Roger 337, Ronald 337, Samuel 59, 337, Sharlee Mae 337, Toni 290, Voss Omer 337
FAULKNER, Everett 202, Helen Ruth 429, Jan 415
FAUS, Adrian "Dean", Adrian 440, Adrian Dean 337, Angela Jean 337, Basil 338, Bertha Marie 337, Betty 338, Betty L. 517, Betty Lou 337, 369, Bob 338, Brad 338, Bradley K. 554, Brian 338, Brooks 338, Carolyn 383, 440, Cora (Foutz) 280, Cora (Houtz) 337, Cora Maxine 337, Dale 338, Dale Eugene 337, Dean 338, Donald Brooks 337, Donnie 338, Donnie K. 283, Donnie Kay 337, Harry 338, 517, Harry Jr. 337, 554, Harry Samuel 337, 338, Ida Pauline 337, Janet 338, Janet Rose 337,

Janice Sue 337, John 280, 337, Keith Wayne 337, Kelly Dale 283, 337, Ken 338, Kenneth Bradley 337, 338, Kent Adrian 283, 337, Kevin 338, Kory 338, Kris Samuel 283, 337, Linn 440, Linn Don 337, Mable 466, Marie 338, Marilyn L. 554, Mary Archbold 338, 369, 517, Max 338, Maxine 338, Oliver Basil 337, Paul 338, Paul Robert 337, Pauline 338, Raymond Max 337, Robert M. 554, Ruth 338, Ruth Ann 337, Sally 554, Sue 554, William Jr. 554, William Lee 337, 338, William Lee 554, Jr,
FAUST, Dorothy Lee 508, Elizabeth 457, Kenneth 508, Ora 285, Pauline 508, Rachel 522
FAUSZ, Albert J. 338, Amy Renee 338, Andrew 338, Brian Daniel 338, Christopher 338, Clare Louise 338, Gary 338, George Barnett 338, Keith Matthew 338, Kenyth Barnett 338, Lela M (Smith) 338, Londa Kay 338, Sherry 338, Tami Marie 338, Terry 338, William 503, William D. 338
FAYLOR, Sarah 469
FEAR, Betty Lou 284
FEEBACK, Allen 338, Alma 338, Andrew 338, Chad 338, David 202, 338, Ed 338, Marjorie 338, Ryan 338, Valerie 338
FEEMSTER, Jennifer 352, Keith 352, Larry 352, Sharon 267, Terrie 352
FEIGHMER, Edna 58, Daniel 556, Mary (Barnes) 556, Matilda Alice 556
FEIST, Edna 508
FELBER, Jake 187
FELGER, Edna Eileen 563
FELTON, Billy 17
FELTS, Vicki 513
FENIG, Bryce 98
FENNEMAN, William 68
FENNER, Donna 526, Eric 388, Gregory 388, Matthew 388, Noel 388
FENSTERMAKER, Paige 522
FENTERS, Martha 485
FENTON, William 279
FERGESON, Nancy 288, Ann Dee 339, Anna 596, Artimishia 339, Charles 58, Charlot (Miller) 339, Churl Carlyle 339, Clarence 339, E. 83, Eliza 339, 596, Ella 339, Ellen 596, Evyline 339, Floyd 339, Grace 339, Heather 339, Henry 339, James 18, 58, 59, James Edwin 339, James Marcellus 339, James T. 596, James W. 339, Janet 339, Janet Yule 596, Jennifer 339, Jesse 134, John 112, 339, John Hume 292, John Y. 596, Joseph Vernon 339, Lydia 339, Margaret 292, Mary Barbara 339, Michael 339, Mildred 339, Nancy 288, Olive Grace 347, Sanford 82, Thomas 339, Thomas 596, Victor 339, W.R. 202
FERREE, Bessie 287
FERRELL, Mary E. 475
FERRIS, Lt. J. 43
FERTIG, Mariah 561, 562, Samuel 561, Susan 561
FETTER, Ethel 583
FETTERHOFF, Estella 270
FETTERS, Barbara 425, Carolyn Rose 339, Charles 185, Clifford William 339, Janine Patricia 339, Jerry 8, Lee 185, Luke 60, Max 339, Paul 92, Ralph 339, Ruby (Goodspeed) 339, W. L. 155, Z. T. 98
FETZER, Barbara 272, Barbara Catherine "Katie", Della F. 339, Homer L. 339, J. Adam 339, John 272, John A. 339, John E. 339, Mary (Brodt) 339, Mary Magdaline 339
FIECHTER, Alice 340, Andrew 340, Anthony 340, Brad 354, Caleb 463, Carl 354, Charles 354, Cyndee 150, Dale 340, Doris 340, 486, Douglas 340, Ellen 487, Ervin 340, 487, Gerald 340, Glen 463, Irene 340, Jamy Kay 354, Jim 354, Joel 463, John 250, 340, John D. 340, John J. 340, 486, Joni 463, Justine 354, Kathy Lyn 516, Keith 364, 504, 516, Kevin 340, Klint David 354, Lillian 340, Louise 487, Lydia 354, 486, Marie 340, Mark 463, Mary 354, Maxine 354, Melissa 463, Michael 340, Mildred 340, Queenie H. 250, Quinn Alan 354, Rinda 487, Stacy Lyn 354, Stan 340, Steve 340, Steven 340, Tamara 340, Timothy 340, Tricia 340, Velma 340, Vicki , Wayne 463, William 322
FIELDS, 66, Curtis 106, Joetta 460
FIFER, Koren 483, Leah Ann 483, Michael 483
FILBERT, Elizabeth 326
FILIPOW, Mark 402, Sean 402
FILLMORE, Millard 344
FINK, Samuel 61
FINLEY, Gemma SueAnn 306, Ralph 306
FINNEY, Linda 514
FIRGUSSON, Pearl 592
FIRST, 66, Hannah 475, Jacob 16, Mary Ann 577, Sarah C. 16, 346
FISCHER, Mary C. 268, Steve 140
FISH, Carl 307, Greg 307, Stephanie 307
FISHBAUGH, Arden 516, Clarence 34, Cora 516, Florence 155, Freda 383, 503, John 516, Leslie 516, Lovie 34, 450, Luzern 165, Luzerne 140, Richard 516
FISHER, Amy 441, Arthur 534, Bobbie 472, Bonnie Lou 451, Carol A. 489, Charles 19, Chastity 265, Christopher 304, Cynthia 274, David 472, Deanna 472, Diann 437, E. S. Dr. 264, Eleanor 324, Emmett 304, Ethel Marie 326, Fred 592, Henry 512, Iva 534, Kami Lynn 451, Kelli J. 489, Kelly 539, Krista May 451, Leah A. 489, Lee 451, Matthew L. 489, Maurice 534, Max 437, Michael 304, Michael L 489, Michele 265, Millicent (Ann) 274, Monte Lynn 451, Nancy 385, Omer 87, 274, Paul 207, Robert 534, Roberta (Nicklas) 451, Robin 441, Roger 437, Ruth Mallonee 512, Samuel 335, Stephen 274, Steve 265, Todd 441, Tom 441, Vicki 472, Wendel 534
FITCH, Viola 292
FITZPATRICK, R. N. 146, R. N. Mrs. 146, Raymond 216, William 95, 425
FIX, Armitta Angeline 582
FLACK, Cheryl 154, Gerald 331, Jarrod 331, Jon 331
FLANINGAM, Ann 340, Dorothea 340, Jill 340, John 202, 340, 582, John Patrick 340, John T. 145, Lester 340, Mike 340
FLAUGH, Chris 294, Danny 294, Francis Joseph 294, Francis Joseph, Jr. 294
FLAUGHER, Gary 15, Jill 473, Jill A. 377
FLECTCHALL, Karen 346
FLEMING, Aaron 601, B. A. 83, Bertram P. 435, Grace 516, Lydia Belle 601, Margaret Grace 435, Sarah Belle 601
FLEMMING, Kevin 523, Marion 157
FLENOR, Helen 412
FLESCH, David 251, Joshua 251, Lindsay 251
FLETCHER, Marthiene 485
FLICK, Susanna 270, Susanne 270
FLORA, Bertha Eileen 341, Eileen 341, Emma 578, Irvin 341, Jacob 259, Josephine (Harrod) 341, Maria Louise 259, Robert C. 341
FLOREY, Henry 320
FLORY, Wilmer 175
FLOWERS, Golda 429, Joe 77, Julie 308, Ken 234, Nellie 475, 476, Paul 264, Paul Mrs. 154
FLOYD, Halleck 60, Sandra 370
FLUECKIGER, Sara 464, Beth 468
FLUKE, Anna Laura 341, Chauncy 341, Cinda 341, Dixie 341, Earl 341, Earl F. 341, Elizabeth 341, Frances Elenore 341, Jacob 341, Jacob Wayne 341, Jaleen 341, Linda 341, Linnie (Bronner) 341, Linnie E. (Bronner) 341, Linnie Gronner 437, Marilyn 534, Sandra 341
FOGLE, Jacob 546
FOGWELL, Edward 534, Selah 534
FOLK, Amanda 529, Amanda Jane (Motz) 403, Anna 342, Berneice 342, Betty 342, Beulah 342, Charles 342, Clara 342, Cressie 342, Donna 342, Emma 342, 534, Faye 342, 600, Frank 342, 534, Garry 342, Hazel 342, Helen 342, Henry 403, 534, Hiram 342, 534, Ida 342, Jesse 114, 342, John 342, 529, John Henry 342, 534, Joseph 342, Margaret 342, Mary 342, Minerva Anna 534, 535, Ora 342, Phyllis "Peg", Richard 342, Robert 342, Sarah 342, Zoa Ethel 403
FOLLIS, Alvin 507, Ann Louise 507, Eldon 507, Hazel 507, Ora 507, Virgil 507
FOLTZ, Maxine (Kummer) 432
FOLTZ, May 154
FONACIER, Lee 350
FONACIER, Lisa Ann 350
FONES, Rebecca 560
FORBES, H. E. 98
FORBING, Joshua 403, Nicole R. 403, Thomas 403, Zachary J. 403
FORBRICH, Ida 368
FORD, Bob 490, Connie 307, Ruth 490
FORDYCE, Jessie Armentha 431, Martha 431, William Franklin 431
FOREMAN, 66, Bertrand Ted 306, Don 251, Donald Lee 306, Eli 169, Elizabeth 240, Jerry 309, Jodi 251, Jodi Lynette 306, Lisa Marie 306, Marie 251, Mark Alan 306, Max Donald 306, Ray 20, Steven Joseph 306, Teresa Darlene 306, Troy David 306, Ulmer 20
FOREST, Linda 150
FORKER, Dora 502
FORNSHELL, Robert 15
FORNWALT, Scott 265
FORQUERAN, Henry 405
FORREST, Helen 417
FORSELL, Barbara Carolyn 250
FORST, Albert 168, Alfred 342, Earl 168, Emory 168, Frank 168, Franklin 342, George Washington 342, Henrietta 342
FOSNAUGH, Charles 415, Christina 468, Frank 468
FOSTER, Adam 472, Becky 472, Betty 342, Betty Lorain 342, 531, Carrie 364, Carrie Alice 363, Catherine 200, Danny 472, Dave 472, E. M. 98, Edna 342, Herbert Holford 342, J. L. 98, James 8, 200, James Weicking 342, Jim 6, 140, John 342, Judith Ann 435, Kevin 342, Leonard 78, Lucille 604, Marion Boyd 342, Mark 472, Mary Catherine Wiecking 597, Matthew 342, Michael 342, Patrick 342, Phyllis Ann 342, Sally Ann 342, Stephen Lawrence "Pete", Steven Lawrence Jr. 342, Susan 516, Tunie 489, Wendell D. 435
FOUDY, Ron 145
FOUGHTY, Curt 535, Diane Sue 341, Geoffrey Allen 341, Herman 341, Karen 535, Martha 341
FOULKS, Charles S. 537
FOUNTAIN, Charles Jr. 83
FOUST, Harold 111, Helen 142, Sarah 409, 410
FOWLER, Rachel 309, Walter N. 36
FOX, Brenda 535, Clifford 535, Clifford D. 411, 535, Diane 535, Ervin 130, Ethan 359, John Henry 585, Jordan 359, Judith 483, June Beaver 535, Karen 535, Kay L. 535, Kevin 359, Louella Prather 535, Matthew 359, Pam 535, Polly Wilson 585, Robert 317, Angela 539, Karen Sue 539, Richard Markley 539, Stephanie 539
FOY, Suzanne 539
FRAILEY, Bette 600
FRANCESI, Mary 487
FRANEBECK, Curtiss 585, Kimberly 585, Phyllis 585, Theresa 585
FRANK, Catherine A. 343, Charles R. 343, Dorothy 354, Geoffrey E. 343, Herb 343, Janel 343, Jay 343, John 343, John E. 343, John L. "Jack", Nettie Voepel 343, Nick 343, Patricia A. (Drussel) 343, Paul D. 343, Ron 343, Ross 343, Sam 343
FRANKE, Carol Eibling 344, Christian "Christ", Christian 73, 343, Erwin 134, 344, Erwin C. "Red", Erwin Jr. 344, Friedrich Wilhelm 344, Gerhard 344, Herbert 344, 368, Martha 344, Ruth 344, Sophie Mueller 343
FRANKENBURG, Patricia 585
FRANKLAND, Roma Evelyn 457
FRANKLIN, Chester Vernon 371, Mary 369, William 298
FRANKS, Ellenor 413
FRANSINE, Mary 553
FRANTZ, Charley 292, Dan 68, Donald 142, Donald E. 145, Douglas 174, Genivee 428, Grant 272, Harriet Ann (Boltin) 407, James Marion 407, James Paul 407, Jim 113, Joe 447, Joe 448, John 447, 448, Kent Hunt 407, Lawrence 87, Minnie 448, Nyal 355, Paul 407, Robert 202, Samuel Rev. 88, Sara Lynn 174
FRANZ, Albert 482, Amanda 483, Angela 483, Dennis 482, Elizabeth 483, Elmer 483, Emma (Kukelhan) 482, Helen 483, James 483, Janice 483, Jean 483, Jennifer 483, Loretta 483, Marie 482, 483, Marie E. 482, Marie Emma 482, Paula 483, Raymond 483
FRANZMAN, Chad Michael 271, Kathryn Dene 271, Nellie Robinson 271, Oscar 271, Russell Floyd 271, Russell Hampton (Rusty) 271
FRAUGHIGER, Rose 150, Ada 507, Albert 445, Aldine 475, Anna 487, Bertha 606, Bertha (Fiechter) 475, Bertha (Meyer) 445, Betty 487, Carolyn Sue 475, Cathleen 475, Charles 487, Chauncey 487, Cora 445, Cora B. 377, Dean 487, Della 445, 606, Donola Marie 475, Doyle 487, Earl 207, 221, 487, Earleen 475, Emma 445, Erna 475, Fannie 445, 521, Harry 445, Inez 475, Jeffery 562, Kris 487, Leon 562, Maggie 445, Mary Jane 374, Nettie 445, Noah 445, Ora 207, 475, 476, Pete 562, Phillip 445, Renee Rachelle 260, Rose 475, Rudy 228, Steven 487, Susan 562, Sylvan 475, Wanita 487, William 207, 475,487, William H. 475
FRAVEL, Madeline 391, Ruth (Christman) 391, William 391
FRAYER, Frank 60
FRAYER, Sarah 60
FRAZIER, Bill 320, Idella May 415, Jacob 78, Jean 500, L. N. 179, Marjorie 239
FRECK, Lynne 582
FREDERICK, Cynthia 428, Dick 79, Becky 356, Doug 356, James 356, Janet 356, Joyce 356, Kent 356, Paul 58, Phyllis 570, Randy 356, Sharon 356, Vern 356
FREDRICKS, Elizabeth 289
FREDS, Beulah Justine 356, Carl 228, Carl 505, Dan 326, Darrell K. 408, Hazel (McBride) 356, Lucinda 335, Muriel 505, Ores 356, Rebekah M. 408, Ruth 326, Susan K. 408, Will B. 408
FREED, Jeremy 486, Joshua 486, Kathryn 340, Kathryn 487, Kathy 486, Matthew 486, Nathan 486, Tom 486
FREEL, Delilah 259, Monica 132
FREELAND, Benjamin Harrison 595, Chloe 286, Don 402, 560, Fern "Faith", Frances 560, Frances (Smuts) Bradbury 402
FREELS, Matilda Bennett 499, Ralph 221, William 499
FREEMAN, Barbara 302, 542, William 153
FREEZE, Amy 537, Dewey 537
FREIBURGER, Cynthia 583, Deborah 353
FREIDINGER, Dee 229
FRENCH, Ada Maloi 344, Angela 424, Arthur Earl 433, Charles 424, Clara 468, Douglas 424, Earl 122, 468, Eliza 344, Eugene 373, Fleming 144, George 344, Harriette 572, Ica 371, J. H. 98, Joseph Jr. 344, Joseph Sr. 344, Marion 572, Michael 424, Myrtle 468, O. P. 16, Olive Emma 373, Ruth (Decker) 317, Sally 344, Smith 344, Sylvia 344, Tom 147
FREUCHTENICHT, Esther 323
FREY, Elizabeth 403
FRIAR, Bertha 533, Charley 241, Charyl 509, Cheryl 443, 600, Donald 241, Gene C. 509, Gene Jr. 509, Geneva 241, Jane 443, Jane Williamson 600, Jeff 486, Jeffery 443, 600, Joaquin 241, Karen 486, Katherine 509, Marianna 241, Olin 443, 600, Robert 241, Ruth 241, Suzanne 443, 600, Victor 241
FRICK, Dave 25, Sandy 25
FRIEDLINE, Mary Williamson 441
FRINK, Ellanor May 414, Lewis C. 414, Martha E. 414, Mattie Dunlap 414
FRISBIE, M. M. 181
FRITZ, Barbara 345
FRITZ, Carolyn Lou 345, Charles 372, David 345, 402, Dwight 345, 372, James 345, 402, Janelle 345, Jay 402, Jerry 345, Jim 140, Jo 136, Joan 345, Mabel 348, Margaret 15, Mary Alice 345, O. V. 87, Paul 15, Robert 144, 345, Sandra 345, Tishia (Hall) 348, William 144, 345, William McKinley 348
FROEBE, Anna L 316Betty 316
FROH, Nora 492
FROHLICH, Samuel 70
FRONK, Christopher 320, 377, Katharine Elizabeth 320, Katherine 377, William 377, William C. 320, William J. 320, 377
FRUTH, Harvey 58
FRY, Ellen 293, Forrest (Bud) 585, Homer 45, Joel 112
FRYBACK, Benjamin 59, Benjamin F. 402, Beth 200, Bill 168, Cliff 168, Clifford 166, 184, Clifford 345, 475, Clifford B. 345, 507, Earl 168, Evan 59, George 59, 345, Hazel 345, Ida May Avery 532, James 59, 345, Jennifer 345, Jessica 345, Jillian Elizabeth 345, John 168, 345, John Clifford 345, John Michael 345, Joyce Ann 345, Levi 59, Nellie 147, Nellie May 507, Nellie Pinney 475, Nicholas 345, Nichole 345, Pat 475, Patricia Lou 345, William 140, 146, 202, William 581, William Addison 345, 532, William M. 345, William Mrs. 146
FRYE, Berdilla 346, Bernice 346, Betty 346, Ebert 346, Forrest 346, Gerald 346, Oscar Ollis 346, Sarah 507, Virginia 346, William F. 346, William O. 346, William Thestle 346
FRYHOVER, Harold 140
FUCHS, Andreas 366, Christena Catherine 367, Christina 366, 367, Christina Katharina 366, Christina Katharina (Volle) 366, George J. le) 366, John 89
FUCHSHUBER, Anna Margarietha 564, Eva 564
FUDGE, Henry 60, Joe 140, Joe 165, Joe 268
FUENTES, Barbara Delores 247
FUHRER, Fred 508
FUHRMAN, Henry 256
FULK, Helen 346, John Adam 346, Lucile 346, Marie 346, Nora 346
FULLER, Bessie 466, Bill 335, Francis 15, Goldie Pearl (Hizer) 274, James Harley 274, John 312, Mary Godfrey 279, N.W. 82, Noreen 15, Pat 307, Phebe Jane 550, Priscilla 410, Sarah A. 312, Sarah Elizabeth James 274
FULLHART, Anna 103, Anna 200
FULTON, Chris 535, G. E. Dr. 480, George 214, J.C. 214, Pam 535, Rose 480
FUNK, Absolom 346, Ann Margaret 346, Benjamin 348, Charles Rincar 346, Crystal Ann 346, Elizabeth (Rouch) 348, Emma 566, Eric 346, Eric C. 497, Eric Culver 497, Ernestine 346, Gustin Curtis 497, Jake 346, Jim 346, Joe 346, John 346, John A. J. 346, John B. 16, John Bower 346, John W. 346, Karen 346, Kitty E. 346, Leah 348, Marian 346, Nelson 566, Rincar 346, Robert Wolff 346, Sarah Ann Mabel 346, Sue Hannah 346, Susan M. 349, Susannah M. 346, Trudy Evelyn 346, Walter 566
FUREY, Adele R. (Tarr) 347, Carolyn Jo 347, David J. 347, David W. 347, Lora Leigh 347
FURNAS, Chase 342, Cindy 342, Joe 342, Katie 342, Mary 342, Robert 342, Ruthella 301, 347, Sandy 342, Steve 342
FURRER, Janet 487
FURTHMILLER, David 367, Jacob 367
FUSSELMAN, Betty 556, Charlotte 556, Dollie 556, Harold D. 556, Jerry 556, Otis 556, Philip 391, Phillip Peter 448, Rose (Kuntz) 556
FYSON, Ralph 102
GABET, Steve 335, Zac 335
GABLE, Elizabeth Shoup 493, Joseph 493, Martha 321, Sara 493
GABRIEL, Elizabeth 606
GADBURY, Olive 323
GADDY, Bartholomew 405
GADDY, Susan 405
GAEKE, William 403
GAGE, Cora 509, Cora Alice 509, Kent 509
GAGLE, Paul 144
GAHMAN, Enid 221, Robert 221
GAILEY, Sarah 500, Sarah 501
GAISER, 66, Belle 347, Caleb 288, 512, Caleb Oka 347, 440, 572, Cecile 347, Daniel 347, David 347, David H. 347, Don 13, Garl Leon 347, George 412, George J. 347, Hilary Linn 288, 347, 440, 512, 572, Leon 288, 289, 440, 512, 572, Marguerite 347, Marilyn Lewellen 347, Martha (Cloud) 412, Melvin 347, 412, Noel 347, Oka Leon 347, Oka M. 347, Rachel (Huggens) 412, Sarah 347, Susan 289, 572, William 409, William A. 347
GALBRAITH, H. C. 98
GALLARD, Goldie 558
GALLIVAN, 43, Blanche 347, Bonnie 347, Denis 347, Dwight 134, 140, 149, Dwight Ferguson 347, Grace 339, James Earl 347, Jeremiah 347, John 347, John Carl 43, 347, Mary 154, 347, Robert B. 347, Thomas 347, Tom 95, Victor 144, 146, 347, Victor E. 43, William A. 347
GALLMAN, John 568
GALLMEIER, Wilhelmina 373
GALLMEYER, Carl 368, Christena 368, Conrad 368, Edna 251, Elenora 368, Eulalia 368, Frieda 368, Gerald 368, Johanna 368, Lily 368, Maria 368, Martha 368, Martin 368
GALLOWAY, Annie Mae (Smith) 348, Fredonna Colleen 348, Mary 338, Mildred 348, Pauline 348, Ralph 87, Ralph Herbert 348, Ray 348, Yvonne 348
GAMBRILL, Paul M. 271, Sarah Anne Anderson 271, Virginia Anne 271
GANDER, Nancy 423
GANSSHORN, Johann 365
GANT, Ray 79
GANT, Ray 79
GARBBARD, Donna 518
GARBBARD, Donna 544
GARBODEN, Harvey 371
GARCIA, April 489
GARD, James Arthur 573M. Dianne 498, Marjorie (Knight) 573, Mary Elizabeth 537
GARDENOUR, Alice 303, Elva 257, Frank 270, John 270
GARDINER, Lisa Renee 263, Mattie 147, Ray C. 263
GARDNER, Sarah 260, Susanna 421
GARFINKEL, Peter 349
GARMAN, A. B. 96
GARMAN, Evelyn 357
GARN, Ellen 606
GARNER, Kathy 555, Ronald 555
GARNSEY, George 164
GARR, Katherine Elizabeth 544, Richard 544
GARRETSON, 66
GARRETT, Alice L. 348, Alonzo B. 348, Alonzo Boltin 348, Amanda 349, Amos 61, Anthony Gray 348, Barbara Ann 249, Belva 499, Bertha 200, 366, 440, Bertha B. 348, Bertha Blen 350, Beth 313, Beth E. 364, Betsy 489, Betty 349, Bill Mrs. 40, Brent 349, Charles "Chad", Charles 569, Charles Franklin <Chad> 326, Charles Sean 326, Charley 349, Chase 349, Chase Orin 349, Darlene 350, David B.. 349, Earnest 546, Eleanor 349, Elizabeth 349, Elizabeth (Boltin) 581, Elma 349, Fannie 87, Frank 581, Frank C. 348, Frank Curtis 332, 348, Frank W. 348, Franklin W. 349, George William "Bill", Gerald William 350, Gloria 425, Gregory 349, Gretchen 546, Hattie Flo 348, I. V. L. 350, I. V. Lester 348, Ivan Von Lester 348, Jeanetta Ade (Craig) 383, 384, Jennifer Ann 348, Jeremiah Jon 348, Jerry 350, Joan 350, Joe Mrs. 87, Joseph 87, 348, 349, Joseph B. 349, Joseph Dean 349, Joseph Lawrence 326, Joseph Parvin 349, Joseph Ryan 349, Judy 349, Karen 350, Karen Ann 349, Kim Lee 348, Larry 113, Larry Allen 348, Larry Dean 569, Laurie Anne 348, Leah 349, Leah (Funk) 350, Linda 349, Lisa 349, Lisa Ann 350, Lisa Mae 569, Lisa Marie 326, Lola M. 348, Lola Mabel 332, 348, Loren 349, Louella (Priest) 349, Mark William 350, Mary Alice 348, 582, Mary Elizabeth "Biddy", Mary Elizabeth 348, Mary Elizabeth (Boltin) 332, Matthew Brian 349, Matthew Wayne 350, Max "Pat", Max Arthur <Pat> 348, Michele Sue 348, Mount 87, Mount E. "Mike", Mount Eugene "Mike", Mount Eugene <Mike> 348, N. Mount 384, Natalie 349, Nathaniel David 349, Nellie 349, Noah 348, 349, 350, Noah Mount 348, 383, O. D. 332, 348, Ora D. 349, Patrick Allen 348, Paul B. 349, Peter 349, Raymond 349, Rea Allen 569, Rebecca 349, Richard 349, Rita Kay 569, Ruba Jane 348, 383, Sally Ann 350, Samuel 349, Sarah 569, Sean 349, Susannah M. 346, Taneka 349, Vera Ione 350, Very I. 348, Walter O.

348, Wendelene 349, Wendy 349
GARRISON, 66, Amber 350, Barbara 350, Carolyn 350, Christopher 350, Cody 350, Cynthia 350, Dayra Joan 350, Derek 350, Donna 350, Doris 350, Dwight 350, Elijah B. 350, Eric 350, Israel Leonidas 350, James 350, Joseph I. 350, Joshua 350, Juanita 350, Junior 350, Kitty 350, Kristen 350, Larry 350, Lloyd 350, Martha 350, Maud 350, Michael 350, Mildred 328, Ora Wesley 350, Paul 350, Rachel 350, Robert 350, Roger 350, Ruth 307, Thomas Alexander 350, Timothy 350, William 350, Winifred 350, Zachariah 350
GARRY, Leilani 596
GARTON, Abigail 351, Amanda 351, Barbara 351, Betty 351, Cassidy 351, Chelsea 351, Courtney 351, Dan 351, 480, Donovan 351, Grace 508, Haldah 103, High 508, Jack 351, 480, Larry 351, Lu Ann 210, Lucy 134, Margaret 103, Marvin 351, Ramona 8, Rick 351, 480, Sharon 351, Steven 351, Wendell 351, Wilborne 480, Wilborne (Bill) 351, William 351, William E. 351
GARVEY, Bill 196, Eileen 154, William 146, William Mrs. 146
GARWOOD, Melissa Sue 250
GARWOOD, Tim 250
GARY, Elizabeth 584, Jacob V. 584
GASE, Euriel Iretta 554, Otto 554
GASKILL, Alice Lou 411, Altha Van Wormer 592, Arthur 411, Chas. 193, David 465, Erma 465, Eva Leota 592, Everett 352, 411, Genevieve 109, Jennie Cloe 570, 571, John 571, Mary 571, Patricia 399, William 592, Zoa 378
GASS, Herbert 289, Nancy Chupp 289
GAST, David 363, David 363, Linda 363
GAUNT, Jordon 425, Joshua 425, Nicole Marie 321, Tim 425
GAVILANEZ, David 351, Eloisa Falconi 351, Joan 204, 330, Juanita 351, Marc 330, Marcelo 204, 330, 351, Marcelo Jr. "Marc", Ramiro 351
GAVIN, Anna Howard 557 Betty 480 Bill 480 Bob 480 Connie 480 Edna 480 George 98 Harry 144 Jerry 480 Mary 557 Robert F. 121 Victor 285 William 557
GAY, Christopher 351, David 351, Doug 351, Irene 589, Jeff 351, Jim 351, Jonathon 351, Kegan 351, Kelsey 351, Richard Dwight "Dick", Richard Dwight Jr. 351, Rick 351, Stephanie 351, Tanner 351, Tim 351GEAR, Nancy 304
GEARHAERT, Barb 15, Myron 15
GEARHART, Barbara 383, Carrie 385, Herman 542, Leona 542
GEARHEART, Alvah 352, Andrea 542, Andrew 542, Angelina 542, Anna Lisa 542, Barb 352, Bob 352, Darlene 352, Dustin 352, Fred 342, Gabriel 376, Gary 542, Lee 376, Linda 542, Logan 376, Mary Lee 352, Matthew Shane 396, Myron 352, Paige 376, Patti 352, Philip 352, Wesley 352
GEARY, Jacob 584
GEELS, Bernard 425, Bernard (Pete) 425, Catherine 425, Cletus 95, 425, Cletus Mr. 162, Cletus Mrs. 154, 162, Darcy 425, Herman 95, John 425, Joni 425, Mary Alice 425, Rose Ann 425, Stephen 425
GEETING, Alfred 301, Austin Wales 301, Estella (Stump) 301, Ethel 301, Ethel Ruby 301
GEHRETT, Samuel 117, Susannah 428
GEHRIG, Rose 476
GEHRING, Aleda 352, Betty 352, Bruce 352, Clarren 352, DeWayne 352, Elizabeth 352, Homer 352, Ida 352, Isaac 70, Isaac 352, Issak 352, Joel 352, John 68, Joseph 352, Joyce J. 352, Kent 352, Lavera 352, Lynn 352, Mary 352, Rosa 476, Samuel 352, Scott 352, Sharon 352
GEHRKE, Doug 499, Pam Palmer 499
GEIGER, Clair E. 352, Elise (Siebolt) 352, Finley 548, Harriet 578, Homer 352, Marjorie Maxine 450, Sarah 352, Valentine 352, Vera B. 450, W. Scott 450, Wilbur 450
GEISEL, Carissa 374, Cynthia 374, Marcia 340, Marcia 487, Rochelle 374, Stan 374, Troy 389, Zachary 374
GEISINGER, Elizabeth 585
GEISMAN, Lora Jo 318
GEIST, Dick 140, John 154, Martha 469
GELBACK, Catherine Elizabeth 375
GEMMER, Amy 402, Andrea 402, Andrew 402, Ann 402, Arden 91, Ardin 402, Bob 402, Brian 402, Cecile 289, David 402, Ed 289, Jason 402, Jill 351, Jim 402, Maurine 289, Scott 402, Todd 402
GEMMILL, Gloria 467, Julia 467, Robert 467, Selby 467, Teresa 467, Todd 467, Tony 467
GENTES, Daniel 352
GENTESIN, Barbara 352, Christian Fogelgesang 352, Eva 352
GENTH, Johnnie 427
GENTIS, Amanda 440, Arlene 352, Barbara 528, Bill 352, Brenda 246, Charles 288, Clara Alice (Chalfant) 288, Daniel D. 352, Dave 352, Dick 352, Jack 352, 528, Jim 352, John 352, 390, Joyce 352, Luticia 382, 533, Mabel McAfee 288, Mary Ann 367, 390, Noah 352, Pearl 366, Purl 440, Reathel 241, Rex 352, Ruby 573, Samuel 352, Thurman 440, Truman 440, Yvette Kay 528
GEORGE, Bernice Dermer 353, Kermit 146, Kermit 353, Kermit Mrs. 146, Laura 597, Lillian Kesler 353, Merritt 353
GEPHART, 66, Amanda 310, Cliff 284, Daisy 310, Daniel Ray 498, Henry 310, Jacob Frank 310, Kenneth 284, Madalyn Lavonne 276, Mary Louise 530, Mollie 310, Orlo 530, Ryan 284, Tammy 284
GERARD, Charles 407, Ida Rose Ifer 407, Lee Alfred 498, Margaret G. 498, Margaret Grace 498, Ruth C. (Michael) 498, Susannah 285, Thomas Dr. 285
GERBER, Aaron 354, Abby 354, Abraham 353, Ada 221, Alice 353, 534, Alvin 233, 353, 409, 442, 534, Amos 8, 140, 223, 353, Amy 502, Ann 502, 521, Ann Marie 487, Anna 353, Autumn Rose 353, Barbara 353, Blake 474, Bradley W. 353, Brant William 353, Bruce Thomas 353, Bryan Jay 353, Carlene 591, Carline (Kehrn) 353, Caroline 355, Carson 354, Charles 487, Cindy 591, Corey 529, Dan 322, David 487, Deborah 353, Devona 353, Donald G. 354, Douglas G. 354, Ed 233, 353, Edward 353, 534, Eli 206, Elias 354, Elizabeth (Baumgartner) 340, 354, Elmer 354, Emily Jo 353, Emma (Sinn) 354, Ernest 570, Ethel 570, Fawn (Moser) 474, Floyd 229, 353, Gaius 353, Genevieve 487, Gideon 223, 353, 355, Gordon 322, 354, Helen 353, 409, Helen (Isch) 353, Jack 354, Jackie 542, 591, Jacob 353, Jarrod 542, Jay William 353, Jean A. 354, Jeanne Elizabeth 353, Jeff 221, 340, 354, 591, Jeffery A. 353, Jehu W. 353, Jennifer Kay 354, Jerry 502, Jill 542, Jodi 505, John 329, 353, Joseph "Bud", Joseph 354, Joseph E. "Bud", Josephine 353, Karyn S. 322, Kathryn 322, Kathy 374, Kris A. 354, Laura 486, Leah Elizabeth 353, Leon 233, Leon E. 353, Leona 353, Lester R. 354, Linus 542, Lloyd 353, Lydia 340, Lydia (Maller) 353, Lydia Rae 442, Lynn 591, Lynn Renee 354, Mabel 355, Magdalena 488, Marie 221, Marilyn 487, 591, Marilyn Jean 487, Mark Alvin 353, Marlene 591, Martha 570, Mary Kathryn 353, Melissa 425, Melvin "Pete", Minnie 353, Molly 354, Nancy 542, Norman 533, Peggy Elaine 354, Perry Lester 354, Phyllis 322, Phyllis A. 354, Ralph 570, Rhonda 353, Richard 151, 591, Roberta 330, Roy 353, Russell 233, Sally 339, Samuel 354, Sarah 353, Sarah Ann 353, Seth David 353, Shawn 353, Shirley 340, Sonya 354, Sonya R. 322, Sophia (Isch) 322, Sylvan 353, Tillman 151, 206, Timothy 442, Tom 353, Truman 353, Vernon 233, Victor 233, Viola 233, William 354, 487
GERBERS, Karen 150
GERGER, Abby 376, Carson 376, Douglas 376, Elise (Meiss) 354, Ernest 354, Joseph 376, Molly 376, Sophia H. (Isch) 354, William 376
GERHARD, Jesse 18
GERHOLD, Gary 174, Jennifer 174, Michael 174, Steven 174
GERINGER, Gene 560
GERKEN, Catharina 533
GERMAN, Ann 443
GERMANN, Frederick 273, Mildred 273
GERWIG, Della Lee 528, Dorothy 450, Gladys (Wagner) 355, Gloria 450, Harry 355, Kenneth 355, Michael 355, Michael 450, Paul 450, Paul Eugene 355
GESLER, Clella 355, Doris 355, Edna 356, Eva Inez 356, 417, Grace 355, Homer 355, 417, Homer C. 356, Inez 355, Lew 356, Lewis 355, 356, 417, Martha 355, Virgil 356, 417, Wilma 355, Wilna 356, 417
GETTLE, Emma 377, Homer 80, 225, Homer Mrs. 80, Homer R. 145, Julia 287, Lillian 542, Sarah 80
GIANT, Florence 338
GIBBONS, Anna Maria 430
GIBSON, Alice 260, 356, Attie 462, Belle 356, Bertalene 356, Betty 570, Bonnie Lou 356, Brian Wayne 260, Clem 356, Elizabeth 244, 454, Esther 570, Evaline 356, George W. 244, Graydon 206, 356, Grover 356, Harley 588, Harry 570, Harry Raymond 356, James 356, James K. 356, James Lewis 356, Joe Rev. 101, John 90, John 356, Karen 588, Maxine 356, Minnie 356, Nina 356, Patrick 570, Rebecca (Reed) 244, Robert 260, Todd Alan 260, Tom 84, Tricia Renee 260, Virginia 570, Wanda 356
GIBSON, Wilson 90
GIDEON, Jack 434, Jazmyn Nicole 434
GIEK, Julie Ann 472
GIERHART, Daisy Artlica 442, Eli 442, Elizabeth Ault 442, George William 442
GIFFORD, Geneva 500, Geneva Lucille 303, Leah Elisa 303, Mildred 136, Mildred Dessie 429, Thomas 136, 303
GILLIOM, Kenny 259
GILBERT, "Boots", A. T. 15, Alicia Nicole 357, Amanda 469, Angela 501, Angela Rene 358, Ann 358, Arlene 556, Bonnie 541, Cara 501, Cara Lynn 358, Carol 245, Carol June 359, Carolyn 417, Carolyn J. 501, Cecil 502, Charles Lowell 357, Christina 424, Christine 501, Christine Kay 358, Claude 358, Dan 160, Darci 481, Darrell 130, 245, Darrell E. 356, Darrell Everett 359, David 245, Dean 357, Dominice Nikol 460, Dottie 15, Douglas Eugene 460, Douglass 358, Duane 323, Ed 13, Edna 533, Eleanor 358, Eliza 358, Elizabeth 245, 358, 437, Elizabeth (Moore) 358, Ella 64, Emeline 358, Francis 107, Geoffrey 501, Geoffrey David 358, George 245, 503, Glen Olan 358, Harry 357, Herbert 358, Herman 96, 357, Herschel 107, Herschel E. 358, Howard 64, 357, Ike Thomas 460, Isabel 134, James McClellan 358, Janet 245, Janet Suzanne 359, Jeanne 64, Jerold 541, Joe 358, John 358, 547, John B. 245, 357, John Bryan 356, 359, John David 357, 359, John Martin 357, Joseph M. 358, Joseph McClellan 358, Joyce 245, Joyce E. 525, Joyce Evelyn 359, Julia 501, Julia Marie 358, 417, 357, Kathryn Christine 357, Keith 323, Kelly Renee 356, Kyle Robert 357, Lela 437, Lena 323, Lloyd 357, Lois 245, 515, Lois A. 358, Lois Eileen 359, Lowell 245, Lowell Eugene 357, 359, Lyda (Houtz) 357, Lydia 245, Lydia (Houtz) 437, Lydia Myrl 247, 316, Lyle 323, Margaret 323, Martha 245, Martha Alice 358, Martin 245, 357, 359, 437, Mary Ellen (Valentine) 357, Matilda E. 358, Maude 245, 516, Michael Dewayne 358, Myrl 245, Nellie Lavina (Walsmith) 358, Olan Laverne 358, Olin 107, Opal Milholland 541, P. E. 161, Paul 245, 323, Perry 357, Ralph 358, Ralph Moffett 358, Ralph W. 358, Ralph Walsmith 358, Reeta 64, Reeta E (Dowty) 356, 357, 359, Robert 358, Robert Wayne 357, Ronald Darrell 356, Ruth Eloise 245, 359, Santley Dean 358, Stan 8, 358, Stanley 417, 501, Stanley Dean 358, Terena Ann 357, Thomas 358, Troy Wade 356, Vicki Rae 356, William 358, William Hower 357, William I 358, William II 358
GILBSON, George 244, William 244
GILDOW, Joseph 398
GILGEN, Gene 474, Melinda (Moser) 474
GILHAM, Oliver P. 153
GILL, David 320, Richelle Nicole 383, Ryan Alan 383
GILLAND, Nancy Ann 380
GILLEM, 66
GILLESPIE, Ines M. 269, Robert 269, Robert 272
GILLETTE, Meda 562
GILLIE, James 509
GILLIE, Katherine 509
GILLILAND, John S. 185, N.A. 82
GILLIOM, Aldine 438, Andrew 323, Becky 259, Doris 475, Elizabeth 438, Isaac 438, John 438, Linda 425, Loyd 207, Nancy 343, Neva 489, Richard 323
GILLOM, Amy (Ellerman) 150
GILMER, Michael 241
GILPIN, Osborne 604
GILTNER, Rocky 340
GINGER, Doug 234
GINGERICK, Adair 317, Audrey 317, Barbara 359, Barbara Ann 317, C. M. Dr. 535, C. Marivn 317, Donald 317, Erin 317, John Donald 317, William 317
GINTER, Esther (Pease) 14, Harve 14
GIPSON, Alysa Shay 298, Claudia Ann (Cotton) 298, Jason Tait 298, Oliver Bryce 298, Richard L. 298
GIRARDOT, Charles 95
GIROD, Alfred 359, 370, Don 370, Emma 455, Hallie 370, Hallie Marie 279, Ina May 370, Jean 370, Joyce 370, 371, Louise Allman 359, Marie 200, Marie (Brickley) 370, Oliver 359, Patti 142, Peter 359
GIRVIN, Barbara Caley 327, Barbara R. (Caley) 360, Deb 360, E. F. 360, Elizabeth (Mayne) 360, Gary E. 360, Hubert 281, Hubert T. 360, Kerry Marie 360, Larry L. 360, Lisa Ann 360, Vincent A. 360
GITLIN, Dorothy 136, Dorothy 200, Dr. William A. 160, Max 216, Max Dr. 349William 146, William Mrs. 146
GIVELER, Frances M. VanDivinder 548, Jacob 548, Rachel Estella 548, Samuel M. 548
GIVENS, Gregory 514, Jane 514, Jane Prible 514, Stephanie 514, Stephen 514, Steve 514
GLANDER, Margie 333
GLASGOW, Anita 577, Betty Evans 360, Gertrude 142, Gertrude Johnson 361, Ian 360, James E. 360, James I. 360, James S. 360, Jamieta 360, Juniata 360, Karen 360, Margaret Hogg 360, Mollie 360, Robert Scott 361, Scott 360, Sherry 360
GLASS, Alice 242, Daniel 272, E. A. 361, Edna Ella (Eckhart) 361, Elizabeth 537, Emma McCorkle 242, Ervin 590, George 272, George E. 361, Jacob 272, James 111, Jane 523, John 18, John 90, 242, John 272, 590, John T. 60, Karen 590, Katherine 272, Mary Josephine 604, Mary (Kesner) 272, Mathias 272, Norman 590, Sandra 361, Solomon 272, Susan Ann 272
GLAUS, Christian 89
GLEICH, Christina 342, 534
GLEIM, Bob 361, Carolyn C. 589, Dawn 308, Dawn Denise 361, Janet C. 589, K. Jean 308, Richard D. 589, Robert 308, Robert Max 508, Robert Max 589, Roberta (Walmer) 361, Stephen Kay 589, Walter 361, Walter 589, William Rex 589
GLENN, Gary Lee 469, John H. Jr. 231, John Jr. 231, Judy Marie 469, Patty Lou 469, Richard E. 469, Rick Alan 469, Susan Elaine 469, Tim 350, Timothy Earl 469
GLIME, Jean 150
GLOCK, Conrad 256
GLOVER, June 321, June 538
GNUSE, Herman Heinrich 507, Nelia Annette 507, Solomon F. 507
GODARD, I.A. 202
GODFREY, 66, Chloie 555, Jacques 312, James "Jacco", Maggie 555, Mary 312, Nancy (Hunter) 312
GODFROY, Chief Francis 412, James 296
GODSEY, Jeremy Glen 333, Jeri Danielle 333, Steve 333
GODWIN, Anna Lenora (Stratton) 362, Chester Marion 362, Clark Henry 362, James Marion Hamilton 362, Mary 362, Nathan 362, Warner 362
GOEBEL, Charles 437, Danette 287, Debra 287, Delain 287, Dianne 437, Linda 437, Rod 287
GOETZ, Edward J. 130
GOINGS, David 16
GOLDAMER, Alan 372, Albert 372
GOLDSBERRY, Barbara 369, 565, Bessie 369, Carolyn 369, Dessie 369, Draper 369, Ethel Guy Brown 532, James 369, 565, Pauline 415, 369
GOLDSMITH, Priscilla 285, Robert (Capt.) 285
GOLDWATER, Barry 34
GOMEZ, Chris 542, Jason 542, Jenny 542, Michael 542, Sally 542
GOOD, Anna 248, Ben 15, John J. 121
GOODIN, Clara 573, Golda 8, J.L. 145, S. 81, Sarah Ellen 561
GOODMAN, Donald 362, 566, Dorothy 321, G. D. Watson 362, Grant Isaac 362, Harry 566, Harry Woodrow 362, Jessica Flo 362, Myrtie Viola (Martt) 362, Rose 565, 566, Rose Amelia (Stair) 362, Ruth 566, Ruth Estelle 362, Sarah 517, Victoria 566, Victoria Raye 362, Watson 566, William Preston 362
GOODNOW, Harriett 489
GOODSPEED, Bertha 363, Charles 363, Daniel 363, David 363, Donald 363, Francis 363, Francis Marion 363, George 363, Gerald 363, Gerald Edwin 363, Gestie 102, Glenn 363, Harriet 102, Ira B. 363, Irene 363, Leslie 363, Lulu 363, Nathan 363, Opal 363, Robert 363, Ruby 363, Thankful 363, Vera 363, Virginia 363, Virginia 600, Zella 599
GOODWIN, Brad 174, Carl 202, Carl 355, Erica 174, Jane 599, John 92, Walter 326
GORDER, Isaac Van 455
GORDON, Agnes 372, Alfred Ray 364, Amy Carol 363, Andrew 363, Archie 363, Arlene Rose (Buel) 279, Arthur 363, Arthur Lee 364, Barry Richard 364, Basil 514, Blake Adam 364, Carrie 311, 313, 364, Catherine Angela 363, Charles 364, Charles 416, 421, Charles L. 364, Christine 363, Chuck 364, Clarence 313, Clarence Oliver 364, Connie Marie 363, D. F. 75, Daniel Ray 363, Daryl Lee 364, Dessie 364, Douglas Jane 537, Edwin 81, Elizabeth Christine 363, Elwin Ray 364, Elwin Ray 364, Eugene Elmon 364, Fannie E. 364, Frank W. 364, Gregory Claude 364, Hattie 569, Helen 363, 385, Howard 363, James 87, 216, 363, 364, James 520, James T. 363, James Thaddeus 364, Jane 437, Jean Ann 363, Jeff 363, Jennie 364, Jerry Lee 364, Jim 364, Joan 363, John "Jack", John 363, 364, John Daniel 363, John H. 364, John Howard 364, John <Jack> 364, John O. 364, John Oliver 313, 364, Josephine 152, Judge Frank 37, Kathryn Ann 364, Kathy Lyn 364, Kristy KAy 364, Kyle Lee 364, Lauren Romaine 364, Linda 364, Linda 364, Lydia A. 514, Malcolm 416, Margaret 363, 364, Margaret (Smith) 364, Marica Phyllis 364, Mary Alice 516, Mary Estella 516, Miles "Stokes", Nancy J. 364, Ned Eugene Jr. <Gene> 364, Ned Eugene Sr. 364, Opal Helen 364, 421, Patti Jo 364, Pearl O. 569, Priscilla, Priscilla (McAfee) 363, 364, Ray 364, Robert R. 364, Robert Ray 363, 364, Robert S. 364, Shaun 364, Stokes 520, Tammy 363, Taylor James 363, Terrie 363, Thomas 363, 364, 372, Tim 363, Tina 364, Urania Johnson 421, Velma 364, Verda 504, Verda May 364, 516, Verne 363, 516, Verne T. 364, Wendall J. 364, Wendall Jay 364, Will 569, William 363, William D. 364, William Jr. 363
GORMAN, William 241
GORNALL, Gloria (Burnworth) 398, James 398, Kimberly S. 398
GOROSKI, Carrie 489
GOROSKI, Randall 489, Randall Jr. 489, Susan Mary 489
GORRELL, Esther 90, Esther (Glass) 365, Esther May 365, 580, James 365, Joseph 60, 90, 365, Karen 251, Lafayette 292, 512, Laura 512, May 365, Milo 60, Richard 251
GOSHORN, Betty Jane 365, Billy Wayne 360, Catherine 365, Elwin Francis 365, Erma 365, Everett 365, Everett (Bill) 145, Everett Elwin (Bill) 365, Fannie Ogden 365, George 365, George Richard 365, Homer Victor 365, Johann 365, John Carr 365, John Vincent 365, Julie Ann 365, Margaret 365, Margaret (Peggy) 365, Mark Everett 365, Mary J. 604, Mary L. 437, Raymond Woodward 365, Seymore 437, Sophie 365, William 365, William Tighe 365, Willamn F. 402
GOSS, Jacob 366
GOSSARD, Zachariah B. 344
GOTTSCHALK, Amanda 366, 367, Andrew 366, 367, Anna Maria 366, 468, Anna Maria (Schnurle) 366, Anna Marie 367, Anna Marie Schnuerle 367, Barbara 366, 367, Belinda 527, Berthena 367, 390, Bonita Irene 367, Carrie Eva 371, Catharina 367, Christina (Fuchs) 366, Clement R. 366, David 440, Della 366, Dorothy Lucille 476, Edna Mae 366, Elise (Grandlienard) 382, Esther 366, Eva 246, 382, Eva Barbara 366,367, Frederick Rannels 366, 367, George "Big George", George 371, 382, 401, 366, 367, George Wesley 366, Goldie 390, Goldie Grover 367, Harry 367, 390, Helen 440, Jacob 366, 367, 527, Jacob Frederich 366, Jacob Frederick Jr. 366, Jacob Frederick Sr. 366, Jake 89, Johann Jacob 366, Johannes 366, John 89, 366, 367, John Michael 366, Loren 367, 390, Loren C. 476, Lucinda 367, Luella 366, Mabel 440, Magdalena 366, 367, Mary 366, 367, 527, Mary Ann 367, Mathias 367, Michael 366, 367, Michael C. 366, Mike 546, Minnie 366, Nina 366, Noah 366, 367, 390, Orest 371, Ruth 367, 390, Ruth B. 366, Sarah 366, 367, 390, Susanna 366, 367, Thurman 366, True 366
GOTTSCHALK, Jr. Jacob Frederick 367
GOTTSCHALK, Sr. Jacob Friedrick 367
GOTTSCHALK/ROSE, Mary 546
GOTTSHALK, Clement 440, Etta May 440, George 440, Helen 440, William 440
GOUGEL, John 563
GOULD, Arvada 466, Bessie Blanch 532, Elaine 466, Esther May 532, Mary 594, Odes Ray 532, Percy 466, Sherman 445
GOWER, Brandi Leigh 449, Brittany Lynn 449, Doug 449, Wendy 449
GRABER, John 259, Susannah 259
GRABNER, Patricia 400, Patricia J. 400, Susann 357
GRACY, Clarissa 555, Elizabeth 555, Emily 555, Harriet 555, Joseph 555, Julietta 555, Mary 555, Nancy Jane 555, Rachel 555, Robert 555, Samuel 555, Sarah 555
GRADEN, Albert 367, Barry 367, Bertha 367, 444, Dorothy 367, Edward 367, Esther 367, Frederick 367, Helen 367, Jean 367, John 367, 444, Louise 367, Mary 367, Rosa (Moser) 367, 444
GRAEFLIN, Arlette 367, Iris 367, Ron 367, Sheryl 367, Walter 83, Walter Rev. 367
GRAF, Jesse 424, Joseph 546, Marilyn 322, Mary 424, Mary R. 546, Russell 146, Russell Mrs. 146, Sarah 546
GRAFT, Adele 368, Albert 368, 526, Andrea 492, Annie 368, Arnold 368, Arthur 368, Carl "Charles", Cassondra Joyce 359, Charles 368, Christian 368, 526, Christian A. 526, Christian J. 368, 526, Clara 368, Conrad F. W. 368, Dale 483, Doris Ann 483, Edwin 526, Elmer "Doc", Elmer 368, Emil 368, Emma 368, Eric 492, Ernst 368, Esther 368, 594, Fred 252, Frederic 594, Frederick 73, Fredrich "Fred", Friederich 368, Gertrude 368, Heinrich Friedrich 368, Helena Hanna Sophie 368, Henry 368, Herman 368, Hilda 368, Ida 368, Jeffery 483, John C. 368, Larry 359, Larry Todd 359, Lawrence "Deedle", Lawrence 368, Leonard 492, Lorene 368, Lorine 368, Luara 368, Luella 368, Maria 526, Marie (Bauermeister) 594, Marie Christine 368, Marlene 575, Martha 344, 368, Mary 368, Mathilda 368, Max 368, Max 417, Nora 368, Otto 368, Paul 368, 417, Paula 368, Peggy 368, 492, Rosena (Werling) 368, Rosina 368, 526, Selma 368, Sherry 483, Sondra (LaCrone) 359, Timothy 483, Walter 526, Wilhelm 368, Wilhelmine Christine 368, William 252

GRAFT, William 526
GRAHAM, A.B. 142, Bert 369, Carl 342, Carolyn 369, Carrie 369, Cassius 369, Charles 369, Courtney 369, Derek Ryan 369, Devona 342, Emma (Heller) 355, Eva 287, Flossie 369, Goldie 342, Harry 355, Hazel 342, Helen 369, James 369, John 258, 369, 380, Joseph 369, Linda 369, Mabel 342, Mary M. (Taylor) 369, Mary (Taylor) 337, 517, Michael 369, Michael Shane 369, Mike 151, Milton M 342, Patrick 369, Peggy 369, Robert 369, Robert Michael 337, 369, 517, Robert R. 337, Robert Roosevelt 369, Robert T. 517, Ruby 247, Ruth Ilene 553, Shannon Lynn 369, Spencer 369, Ted 369, Terri Sue 337, 369, 517, Theodore. 337, 517, Theodore R. 369, Thomas 369, Tom 380, Vernon 369, Vicki Lynn 337, 369, 517, Vida 369, William 370, Winnie 380
GRAMM, Karen 229
GRANDLIENARD, Abram-Louys (Abraham) 371, Bessie 371, Beth 370, Brooks 359, 370, 371, Bruce 371, Catherine (Winkler) 371, Charles 371, Charles E. 371, Dora 371, 468, Edward 371, Elise 371, Fred 370, 371, Freddy 371, Frederick D. 371, Gary 371, Genriette Emiline 371, Henry 371, Ica (French) 239, Janelda 371, Jared 370, Jason 370, Jo 370, Joe 370, 371, Jordan 370, Joseph 371, Joshua 370, Joyce 136, 359, Joyce J. 352, Kenneth 370, 371, Lewis 371, Lorena 371, Mae 371, Marguarite (Hinchman) 371, 370, Marianne-Emilie 371, Marie 371, Mark 370, Max D. 239, May 370, Meg 370, Ora Ethel 371, Paul 371, Randolph "Randy", Ruth 370, 371, Susanna-Sophia 371, Vicki 239, William 239, William 371
GRANDLIENARD, III, Abram-Louys 371
GRANT, Gloria 340
GRASMICK, Jean Ann (Pond) 406
GRAVE, Ruth 289
GRAVES, Dale 312, Delsey 312, Denton 312, Emerson 312, Ernest 15, Hiram 312, John 312, Joretta 602, Lavaria 312, Mary 312, Minnie 312, Minnie Dale 541
GRAY, Amy Leona 286, B.J. 137, Barb 210, Beryl J. 200, Carolyn Joan 598, Dawn 598, Galen 98, 258, 598, Gay Lynn 598, Harry 142, Janet Elaine (Crowl) 303, Jennie Marie 498, Vallera 460, William H. 303
GREEK, Dessie 372, Flossie 277, Floyd 277, Geneva 277, Geneva Geraldine 277, John 372, Ruby I. 316, Vincan (DeVol) 372, W. W. 235, William Pearl 372, William Wallace 372, 418
GREEN, Alma 372, Armatha 401, Bernice Elizabeth Thornto 419, Betty 472, Betty (Moore) 327, Bonnie 289, Carl 401, Carole H. 85, Chad 401, Chris 327, 472, Clyde 83, Earl 289, Eliza 431, Eva Mae (Buel) 279, Evah 289, Gary 401, Gary <Mick> 327, George 327, 472, Glenda 327, 472, Isaac 430, 431, J. H. 81, John 221, Johnny 372, Kara 327, 472, Kathy 150, Ked 327, 472, Kenneth 259, Kim 472, Lila K. 372, 472, Mark 401, Martha 136, Mary 472, Mick 472, Mike 327, 472, R. Edwin Rev. 91, Ralph 372, Robert 472, Shirley 372, Tamra 472, Tamra Lynn 327, Terry 327, 472, Tod 327, Vadis Olean 424
GREENAWALT, Dick 59, H. L. 96
GREENE, Cathy 204, David 342, Halden 342, Joe 204, Ron 342
GREENFIELD, Anne L. 589, Charles 15, Nathaniel 112
GREENWALT, H. L. 64
GREENWOOD, Alinda Ann 578, Henry 502, Louisa 578, Margaret 502, Mariah 502
GREER, William Rev. 100
GREGERSON, Mickie 249
GREGG, Anges 372, Ben 412, Betty 372, 590, Bill 372, Bob 372, Bonnie 590, Brittany 590, Bruce 372, Daniel 372, 373, David 508, 590, Dorothy 17, 508, Elisbeth Conner 469, Eliza Ann 372, Fannie 372, Fannie (McClure) 373, Frank 590, Gene 372, Hazel J. 412, Helen 343, Howard 590, Jeanette 372, Jessica 590, Jim 372, John 284, 343, 372, 373, 412, 590, Joseph D. 412, Joshua 372, Joy 372, Joy Huffman 372, Karen 372, Katie 372, Lee 440, Levi 372, Linn 144, 153, 372, Linn (Red) 440, Linn Sr. 372, Louvina (Linn) 372, Marcia Decker 372, Margaret 372, Marion 590, Mary 372, Mary Ann 469, Mary L. 412, Nellie Jamison 372, Patrick 590, Rachel (Brinneman) 412, Rex 590, Richard 284, 372, 373, 440, Robert 469, Roger 372, Ronald 590, Ruth 284, 440, Susan Florence 412, Thomas 590, Thomas D. 373, Timothy 590, Tommy 590, William 372, 373, 590
GREIDER, Tina 402
GREINER, Amy 154, Amy (Gordon) 373, Bob 140, Edward 89, Harold 422, James Robert "Jay", Rebecca Anne 373, Robert 289, Robert S 373
GREWE, Andrew 373, Arnold 373, Bernice 483, Christian 73, Delores 373, Edwin W. Sr. 502, Frederich 373, Ginger 373, James Arnold 373, Jeanette 373, Jennifer 373, Karl 73, Leah Ann 483, Linda 483, Paul 483, Shirley 373, Tammy 373, Vera 373, William 373, 502
GRIDER, Pam 310
GRIFFIN, Carlene 239, Carlene 405, Nancy 548, Paul 480, Sarah 534, Virginia 480
GRIFFIS, Betty 154, 374, C. Lloyd 145, David 374, Edward 374, Elizabeth 374, LLoyd 216, 374, Michael 374, Susan 374, Virginia 374
GRIFFITH, Cindy 474, Helen Arnold 299, Sam 299, Winifred 299
GRIFFITHS, David James 454, Joanna Michael Elizabeth 454, Pat 454
GRIGSBY, Aaron 479, Carolyn 262, Cathy 479, Geoff 479, Greg 479, Matt 479
GRIM, Bill 207, Edna 591, Marjorie 591, Orville 207, William 591
GRIMES, George 169, Martha 81, Stella 569
GRIMM, Bob 374, Carlee 374, Cora (Shannon) 374, Desmond 374, Dorothy 374, Elic 374, Gerald 376, Harold 374, Harold C. 374, Harold Lloyd 374, Jaimi 374, Janet 376, Janet Elizabeth 376, Leah 374, Leah Marie 374, Linda 374, Linda Lou 374, Lola Belle Strahm 374, Mark 374, Mattie 490, Neolla 417, Pam 374, Pamela Sue 374, Pete 374, Rodney 374, Roger 374, Russell 417, Ryan 374, Stella 374, Stella Delanie 374, Tim 374, Timothy Harold 374
GRIMSLEY, Betty 293, Olive 293
GRINSTEAD, Grace 548
GRISHAW, Eliza 546
GRISSELL, Delores 286
GRIVIN, Barbara 281
GROENENDIJK, Elisabeth Catharina 320
GROGG, Charles Walter 417, Gene 132, Karla 455
GROH, Bob 259, Fred 144, Jacob 374, Mabel 374, Mary Reinhart 374
GROMAN, Dorothy 332
GROSJEAN, Mary Geraldine 599, Victor 599
GROSS, Earl 81
GROSSMAN, Catherine 258
GROTE, Ina Marie 467, Richard 467
GROTNES, Laurie 552, Len 552, Norma Jean 552, Sarah 552, Stephen 552, Tamarah 552
GROUNDS, Jr. Grady 585
GROVE, Arlen 351, Benjamin 351, Bob 292, Chloe 285, Cleo L. 457, Earl 111, Ethel 469, Floyd E. 127, Grace 482, Guy 184, Guy Oren 507, Hershel 565, Ida 409, Inez (Habig) 393, John 436, Keith 565, Lewis 208, 324, Lillian L. (Kline) 592, Lizzie Quick 468, Loene C. 320, Margaret (Blair) 262, Marilyn 583, Mark 351, Mary 292, Minnie 415, Nancy Cheryl 292, Neil 565, Neva 262, Norma 566, Norma Ann 565, Oliver 262, Stella 324, Thomas Wilson 592, Vera 60, Vera Lavina 507, Jr. William 351GROVER, Agnes L (Ruse) 375, Andrew Frank 375, Anna Louise 375, Annie 410, Barbara 429, Becky 603, Brian Douglas 375, Carol Sue 375, Cathy Marie 375, Charles 375, Claude 369, Cloid 603, Cloyd 375, Dale 429, Daniel Eugene 375, Darrel Lyn 375, Della Gerber 519, Dennis 603, Dennis Lee 375, DeWitt 375, Doc 588, Dorris 375, Doug 487, Douglas Lon 375, Elizabeth 375, Emery 375, Eugene 375, Floyd 375, 410, Frank 375, Frieda 375, Glenn 375, Harley 375, Herbert Eugene 375, Homer 375, Howard 375, Jane 375, John 375, Joyce 429, Lloyd 375, Lona 487, Lora 603, Lora Jane 375, Marjorie 603, Marsha Diann 375, Mary 375, Mary Louise (Jones) 375, Melinda Kay 375, Nileis 375, Offie 375, Oscar 375, Paul L. 375, Robert 375, Robert Daniel 375, Ruth 410, Sylvester 375, Tamara Kay 375, Terrance Eugene 375, Veda 375, Willard 375, William 375, Willie 375
GROVES, Darrel 460
GROW, Frank 58
GRUBAUGH, Mary Nevada 403
GRUBBS, Britt 570, Britt Charles 570, Madelynn 570, Nicole 570, Roberta 307
GRUMBLES, Helen M. 335, Helen Marie Shorter 334
GRUSH, Linda 562
GRUSH, Mark 562
GUCLUYILDIZ, Carol Anne 489
GUDELEWISKI, Stephnia 460
GUE NATT, Elizabeth Jean 466, Eugene Jean 466
GUILER, Ralph 187
GULDIN, Amelia Lamm 375, Amos Strunk 375, Anna 450, 489, 572, Charles 450, 489, 572, Charles Bruce 572, Charles Jennings 375, Clara 375, Daniel Hilsaweek 375, David Eugene 572, Hans Jochin 375, Hans Jocin Tribolet 375, Irwin Frank 375, Isaac W. 375, Jerimiah 375, John Gelback 375, Kay Sturgis 572, Kent Lee 572, Marjorie Jean 375, 489, Max I. 572, Max Irwin 375, 489, Samuel Koch 375, Samuel Malcarida 375, Thomas 375
GULLEY, Elizabeth 239
GUNN, Kathryn L. 529
GUSTIN, Allen 499
GUSTIN, Izella Freels 499
GUSTIN, JoAnn Carr 499, Joseph 499, Manervia Angeline 497, Minervia 499
GUTELIUS, Margareta 455, Will B. 145
GUTHRIE, Janice 427
GUTWEIN, Dawn E. Dr.
HABAGGER, Darlene 340, Arlene 565, Martha 565, Sylvan 565
HABEGGER, Abraham 376, Andrew 376, Ben 376, Benjamin 376, Darlene 487, Edgar 376, Elizabeth 376, Grant 168, Jason 376, Jeni 376, Jill 376, Leah 376, Martha 376, Peter 376, Rita 376, Rosemary 376, Ruby 354, Ruby K. 376, Samuel J. 376, Sara 376, Savilla (Roth) 376, Ted E. 376, Tillman "Tim"
HABIG, David 425, David Brian 376, David Emery 461, Donna 376, Ellen 376, Harvey 376, 393, Heather 376, Howard 393, Howard 542, Jasper 393, Jeffery Lewis 376, Jeffrey 425, Jennifer 376, Jennifer M. 391, Jim 376, John 393, Johnathan 376, Joseph 376, Kenneth 425, Kenneth Reed 376, Kyle 376, Lewis 425, Lewis John 376, Madeiline 435, Mary 400, 425, Mary Louise 376, Pearl 542, Penelope 425, Penelope Lynn 376, Peter 393, Phillip 393, Ryan 376, Ryan J. 391, Shirley 425, Shirley Ann 376, Stephanie M. 391, Willa 376, William 461
HACKENJOS, Phyllis L. 557
HACKWORTH, Craig 448, Elmer 448, Laird 448, Steven 448, Veva 448
HADLEY, Douglas L. 91, Jo 150
HAECHER, John 366, 367, Luster 399
HAEGLER, Oscar 113
HAFFELEE, John Carl 378
HAFFLICH, John 377
HAFFLICK, Jacob 378
HAFFNER, Adaline 403, D. L. 171, Franklin Pierce 403, Michael 403, Vickie 379
HAFLICH, Anna 437, Anna Hoover 378, Bessie Z. (Bender) 377, Catherin 377, Clifford 378, Cressie 281, 378, Curt 281, Curtis 378, Effie 437, Evelyn Deane 377, 473, Frank E. 377, Gene 378, Isaac 377, 378, Jacob 59, Jacob 378, Jane 378, Jennie 437, JoAnne 378, John 437, L. Vaughn 377, Lavina 437, Lela 579, Lella 437, O. D. 473, Ordelden Donald "O.D.", Philip 377, 378, Phyllis 378, Raymond 144, Raymond A. 579, Richard 378 Robert 378, Samuel 59, 378, Samuel A. 378, Sarah 377, William A. 377, William <Fred> 378, Zoa 281, Frank 258
HAGE, Catherine A. 583
HAGEN, Ardith 336, Clarence 336, Gloria 336, Marie 336
HAGGERTY, Marjorie J. 603, Thurman 603
HAHN, Carol 427, Jarrod 240, Margie 427, Marjorie J. 421, Richard 427, Sandra 474, Susan 509, William 427
HAHNERT, Eliza Mae (Johnston) 469, Frederick 469, George Alfred 469, Loma Luella 469, Daniel 121
HAIFLEY, Ann 377, Eli C. 377, Elsie 377, Erma June 377, Hanna 377, Harry 377, Heather 377, Heather Lea 320, Hervert 377, Irene 377, Jacob 377, Justine 377, Kyra 377, Kyra Nicole 320, Linda 377, Linda Nell 320, Lloyd 377, Mark 377, Mark Brigeforth 320, Mary 377, Paul 377, Paul William 320, Philip 377, Ralph 377, Thomas 377, Thomas Dilley 320, William 377, William E. 377, William Eli 320
HAIFLICH, Andrew 378, Benjamin 378, Bertha Alice 318, Caroline 320, Catherine (Pletcher) 378, Charles 378, Clare 378, Clifford 451, Dallas 378, David 378, Dellie Irene 378, Doris 378, Edith Wiser 576, Elizabeth 321, Elizabeth 378, Fern A. 306, Fern A. 492, Freda 378, George 378, Hanna 274, Hannah (Shadle) 378, Harley A. 378, Isaac 378, Ivan Howard 378, Jacob 378, Jay 424, Jennie 378, Jess 378, Jesse 378, 576, Jodie 378, John 97, 378, 451, John H. 378, Joseph 318, Karen Sue 403, Laura (Jessen) 378, Laura May 378, 451, Louise (Guinn) 378, Lucile 378, 576, Margaret 378, Marybell (Brown) 378, Mayreatha (Beaber) 451, Mickey 378, 490, Nancy L. 385, 490, Nellie 385, Nellie Lore 378, Norman 378 Orville 378, Parentha (Beal) 318, Philip 378, Ray 378, Richard E. 378, 403, Rosalie 378, Samuel 378, Sarah 342, Stevan Richard 403, Thomas 490, Thomas E. 378, Vickie 378, Vickie 490, Vicky 467, William E. 378, William E. 378, Winnie 451
HAINES, Abigail 379, Alice 560, Cecile 560, Connie Jo 569, Darnella (Reed) 379, Dave 379, David 560, Ellen (Rose) 294, Goldie 93, Hannah (Tomlinson) 538, J. M. 98, Jesse 155, Joseph 569, Marge 6, 379, Martha 569, Mayme E. 321, Nina 519, Randy 379, Renee 379, Roy 379, Ruth 240, Samantha 379, Shirley (Custard) 304, Steve 93, Steven Louis 569, Susan Louise 569, Timothy 538, Valerie 379, Vesta 560, Wilbur 560
HAKES, Charles 346, Dorothy 346, Gladys (Chronister) 346, Harold 346, Joyce 346, Marion Charles 346, Raymond 435, Raymond L. 346, Rose 346, Thomas 346, Violet 346, Violet Pearl (Lee) 346
HALCOMB, Gary 551, Jared Kele 551, Jean Ann 551, Mitchell Evan 551, Nathan Tyler 551
HALE, Bowen 18, Bowen 379, Dan 294, Delia 147, Delia (Wilson) 154, Emmarillis 586, J. P. 147, James 200, James 202, James 379, Jane 379, John 379, Roger Rev. 99
HALER, Carl 348, Justin Adam 348, Sarah Grace 348
HALEY, Cecile 560, E.E. 89, J. W. 560
HALL, Betty Jean 492, Beverly Ann 380, Brenda 380, Charles 380, Chloe 393, Christopher 355, Cora 393, 440, Cora Ella 440, Daniel J. 380, Danielle Michelle 380, Darla 508, David 380L, Deana 508, Debby 508, Denise 508, Douglas 380, Elizabeth 393, Ellen 440, Emily 380, Eva 393, Gail 304, 380, Gary 508, George S. 380, Helen Thompson 492, Irvin C. 380, James 78, James 380, Jessie Haughton 492, Joan 355, John 393, John G. 380, Lawrence 355, Loren Haughton 492, Lucille 380, Marvin 81, Mary (Habig) 393, Melissa (French) 344, Nancy 508, Nun 393, Oliver 380, Robert 380, Rueben 393, Tammy 253, Theodore 380, William 393, William I. 380
HALLIGAN, Margaret 450
HAMILTION, Dolly 155,
HAMILTON, A.W. 202, A. Walter 169, A. Walter 347, A. Wendell 381, Adam 100, Angie 381, Anna Jane 381, 569, Anna Jane Stinson 409, Arden 381, Arden Jaren 381, Armintha 381, Arthur Wendell 350, Ashley Erin 381, Bertha Myrtle 381, Cassey 381, Cathryn Elaine 381, 569, Chad Allen 381, Cheri 316, 381, Cheri Rene 350, Clara 527, Cletus 393, Deborah Kay 382, Ellis 381, Ellis 496, Emma May 382, Erin 316, Erin Nichole 247, 350, Erin Nicole 381, Garrett 316, 381, Garrett Warren 247, 350, George Reed 381, Georgia May 381, James L. 412, Jane 6, 136, 154, Jane Summers 573, Jason Allen 381, Jeremy DeWayne 381, Jesse 393, Jesse Allen 381, Jill 381, Jill Marie 350, Joan 381, Joseph Emery 381, 496, Lavine E. (Harter) 496, Lavine Elizabeth 381, Lennie Irene 381, Lesie Merle 381, Lesli Marie 381, Leslie 107, Leslie 382, Leslie Merle 381, Lois 381, Lois Blen 350, Lucas 316, Lucas Alan 381, Lucas Allen 247, 350, Lulu 214, Lulu A. 573, Lynn 381, Lynn Kay 350, Marie 381, Marilyn Sue 350
HAMILTON, Marilyn Sue 381, Marjorie 381 382, Mark LeRoy 381569, Mary Jane 381, Mary Lou 136, 573, Michael 381, Minta 393, O.G. 214, Orville G. Dr. 269, Orville Grant 573, Otto Sherman 381, Patrick 381, Phyllis 152, R. W. 378, Rebecca Sue 382, Rhonda Lynn 381, Richard Lee 381, 382, Robert Eugene 381, 569, Roger DeWayne 381, 569, Rosalie 378, Ryan Eugene 381, Samuel Earl 381, Sandra 518, 544, Sandra Jo 381, Sarepta Pearl 381, Sharon 357, Wayne 569, Wayne Edward 381 382, William Dr. 454
HAMITON, Lori 360
HAMJE, Dorothy 567, Edwin J. 567, Jessie Irene 567
HAMMOND, Carolyn 288, Charles 382, David 578, David Todd 382, David Wade 382, Don 397, Donald 144, Donald Wade 382, Donald Wade II 382, Elizabeth 358, Greg 382, Ivan 288, Jane 578, Jane (Thoma) 382, Janet 288, Jennifer 382, Joseph 358, Judith (Henson) 358, Kristen 382, Lois D. Chalfant 288, Marianne 288, Nadine 244, Nadine (Todd) 382, Todd 382
HANCOCK, Ruth 156
HANDLEY, F. T. 98
HANDSHOE, Donna 456
HANDWORK, Bertrand 127
HANDY, Anna Louise 489
HANES, Frank 182
HANEY, Joe 103, Joseph Rev. 97, Lorena M. 552, Maxine 291
HANKEY, Gladys David 351, Henry 351, Joan P. 351
HANKS, Mary 331
HANN, Lottie 527
HANNA, Daniel K. 16, Henry 75, John 234
HANNAH, Bill 111, William 112
HANNEY, Sophia Amanda 411, Sophia Manda Snyder 411
HANNI, Edward "Pete", Fritz 515, John 485, Kenneth 485, Rachel 485, Rosetta 515, Theodore "Ted"
HANNIE, Gottlieb 382, Karl 382, Kathleen "Kate", Kenneth 382, Mary Jane 382, Mary Jane 548, Robert 382
HANRAHAN, Ed 145
HANSELMAN, David L. 145, Vicki 130
HANSEN, Barbara Louise 263, David Borne 263, Elaine Jean 263, James Myron 263, Patricia Marie 263, Stanley 263
HANSON, Christopher James 573, David Eric 535, Debra 597, George G. 535, John 591, Joshua David 573, Julia May 535, Karen Lee 535, Mary 535, Matilda 310
HANUSIN, Ronald 151
HAPNER, Harley 425
HARBER, Carolyn S. 383, Eileen 383, Giles 383, Jacob 383, Jacob A. 383, James 383, Kristin 383, Marjorie 383, Peggy 383, Regina 383, Renee 383, Rosalie 383, Sheila 383, Theodore 383, William 383, William J. 383
HARBERSON, Howard 534, Ida 534, John 534, Karen 534
HARBSTER, Jacob 442
HARDEN, Velma 25
HARDIE, Alison 430, Kay Frances 430, Lori 430, William 430
HARDIN, Dean 107, Marcella 228
HARDING, Arthur 391, Caroline 391, Lavenia Dickinson 391, Silbert 107, U. E. 83, U. E. Mrs. 83, Warren 34
HARDWICK, Lunie Murle 596
HARDWIDGE, John 20, Kenneth 242, Lucy Evans 242
HARDY, Olin Ranchell 242
HARE, Jessie 102
HARGETT, Dwight Rev. 526, 589
HARGRAVES, Cathy Sue 486
HARKLESS, Daniel J. 383, David A. 383, David C. 383, Diane K. 383, Lane 383, Lisa 383, Lori 383
HARKNESS, Donald 558
HARLESS, Betty 573, Deborah 500
HARMAN, Irv 140
HARMASAN, Nancy Ann 441
HARMON, Andrea 577, Betty 577, Dewey 577 Dorothy 577, F. Michael 577, Jack Allen 577, Janel Arline 577, Jason 577, Jessica 577, John Arthur 577, Kenneth 577, LaVone Marjory 577, Lillian Edith 577, Marie 577, Mary 525, Monica 577, Myrl Edward 577, Myrl Edward Jr. 577, Myrtle 577, Ruth 577, Sandraa 577, Shannon 577, Sheryl 577, Starr 577, Terri 577
HARNISH, Alice 383, 534, Anna 383, Barbara 383, Carolyn 383, Caryn 520, Clara 383, Dale 383, Darrell 383, David 520, Doyle 383, Ella 383, Fred 383, Freda 383, 503, Frieda 516, Galen 383, Gerald 383, Ginny 520, Gloria 383, Henry 383, Ida 383, Ida (Shoemaker) 404, Iva Mae 383, James 520, Janice 383, Jerry 383, John 383, John 404, Kay 520, Leroy 383, 503, Mabeline 383, Marcielle 383, Marilyn 383, Marilyn 503, Mildred 383, Morris 383, 520, Nora 326, Oscar 421, Pierce Jr. 383, Pierce Sr. 383, Pierce Sr. 399, Randy 383, Readocia 383, Richard 520, Rinda 383, 520, Ronald 383, Rosa 383, 404, Rosanne 383, Rozada 383, Samuel 383, Wayne 383
HAROLD, David 58
HARON, William 270
HARP, Fanny 404
HARPER, Dora 275
HARPER, Margaret Jean Wiecking 597
HARRIETT, David W. 607, Jacob David 607, Judith Ann 607
HARRINDEAN, Joan 467
HARRINGTON, Kelly 560, Kenneth 560, Laura 560
HARRIS, 66, Adam 90, Angela Kay 486, Ann 495, Arthur 165, Beatrice 241, Benjamin 384, Benjamin A. 384, Bertha 240, Blanche E. (Godwin) 385, Blanche Lenora (Godwin) 362, Bob 234, Brian 384, Bruce 385, Carolyn 267, Celia 383, Chad 374, Charles "Ez", Charles 362, 374, 384, 385, Charles Albert 362, Charley 383, 58, Cheryl Sue 383, Chester Burl 362, Chris 374, Christina 72, Claude 348, 383, 384, Claude Leroy 581, Clyde 348, Clyde 383, 384, Clyde Harold 581, Constance (Thompson) 384, Crystal Evelyn 383, Cynthia Ann 384, Dana 443, Darlene 570, David 443, 495, David Michael 383, Deborah 443, Dewey 385, Dick 113, Don 145, Don V. 169, 384, 595, Donald Lee 384, Donna 570, Dorothy 518, 544, Dorothy Jean 591, Edna Jane 383, Edward 383, Elizabeth 495, ELva (Kershner) 362, Ernie 346, Evelyn Irene Harris 346, Florence 383, 384, Florence Bell 581, Florence Irene 383, Forrest 385, Fred 304, 385, Frederick 304, Gary 443, George 266, 362, George Henry 383, Gerald 267 384, Ginger 267, Glendora 385, 490, Gretchen 304, 385, Guy 240, 385, Hannah 495, Haslyn 150, Helen 34, 240, 385, Henry 362, Hugh 384, Iona 78, Ivy 240, James 90, 384, 443, 495, 537, 554, James Adam 38, James Craig 384, James Oral 383, Jarrod 385, Jay 443, Jennie 443, Jenny May 383, Jesse Cole

383, Jessica 72, Jim 113, John 304, 385, 495, John II 588, Joseph 385, 495, Joseph William 383, Joyce 344, Karen 443, Kathleen 240, Kathryn 385, Katie 72, Kevin 384, Kirk 385, Lance 374, Lee Ann 267, Lee Otis 383, Leigh 384, Lillie Alberson 240, Lillie (Alberson) 385, Lillie Laverna 383, Linda Lou 374, Lucinda Ann 425, Margaret 495, Marjorie 568, Mark 64, Mark 443, Mark Alan 383, Martha 362, Mary 304, 495, Mary E. 384, Mary May 362, Mary (McFarren) 346, Matthew Robert 383, Mearl L. 362, Meghan 384, Michael Clyde 383, Michella 443, Michella Sue 383, Mike 443, Mildred 362, Nancy Ann 601, Nicki 304, Nora 500, O.A. 78, Omar Vernon 383, Patricia Rae 384, Patrick 72, Paul 362, Paula 362, Pauline 488, Phineas Ivy 362, Rachel 495, Randy 570, Ray Everett 383, Richar Kay 383, Robert 495, 519, Robert Dale 383, Roberta 519, Ronald 267, Rosa Belle 383, Rosa. C. 362, Roy 240, Roy 38, Ruba Jane (Garrett) 384, Russ 78, Ruth 336, 362, Ruth 385, Ryan 570, Sandra Kay 384, Scott 486, Sharon 267, Stephanie 72, Sue 443, Suzanne 443, Ted Leon 383, Teresa 443, Thomas 384, 495, Tyson 443, Vivian 240, Walter Monroe 591, Wilbur 385, William 384, William Eugene 383, William Eugene 581, William Jr. 362, William L. 362, William R. 385, William Robert 362, Jr, Don V. 384, Jr, Joan Haffler 384
HARRISON, Charlene 434, Isabel 299
HARROD, Cinda Sue 341, Dixie Dawn 341, Enos 341, Jalene Renee 341, James 341, Linda Jo 341, Sandra Kay 341
HARROLD, 66, Alma 385, Bernard Eugene 385, Bernard James 385, Betty Alice 385, Camilla Ruth 385, Christopher 385, Craig Allen 385, Dee Allen 385, Elmer 299, Elmer Austin 385, Ethel 299, Ethel Berniece 385, George Harrold 385, Isaac 385, Ithamer 385, James Delmer 385, James Roscoe 385, Janis Lee 385, Jim 435, Joyce 443, Karen 84, Kari Ann 385, Kenneth Maxwell 385, Linus Kay 385, Malorie 385, Melinda Sue 385, Nellie Wiliamson 299, Paul Cleophas 385, Reneta Jane 385, Rosemary Ann 435, Ross 385, Sandra 385, Scott William 385, Stacy Ann 385, Thelma May 385, Todd Andrew 385
HARSH, Cora 272, Daniel 112, Edward 272, John 97, John 272, John S. 339, Mary 272, Theo 202
HARSHMAN, Betty 485, Clara 451, Floyd 442, Harmon 485, Kay Ann 485, Nellie 451, Richard Rev. 97, Shirley 137, 155, Susan 466
HARSHNER, Andrew 591, Sylvia Jane 591
HART, Delmar 275, Dinah Coverdale 289, Flora (Martin) 275, Frances (Stepp) 275, Ilah 155, Jeffrey 275, Jerry W. 275, John W. 275, Marcella 152, Nancy 509, Phoebe 298, Sarah 584
HARTER, Ann 600, Earl 407, Lavine Elizabeth 381, Lee 515, Michael 90, Norma Ifer 407, Patt 515, S. F. 98
HARTIGAN, Barbara (Tharpe) 386, Cheryl A. 603, Kelsey Lee Ann 386, Kerri Jo 386, Michael 405, Richard 145, Richard 386, Timothy 603, Timothy Lee 386
HARTMAN, Adam 438, Brad 486, Clara 350, Dave 355, Edward 505, Hoyt 144, 216, Isabelle 587, Jeff 355, John 322, Kathi 355, Kemberli 486, Kim 432, Melanie 355, Nathaniel 432, Sara Ann 394, Sean 355, Shirley 45, William 394
HARTMEN, Rosie 521
HARTNETT, Margaret Anne 295
HARTZ, Charles M. 553, Mariah Ellen 553, Mariah Ellen 553
HARTZLER, Ella (Ramsier) 354, John 354, Rosemary 354
HARVEY, Arleen 562, Charles Ezra 386, Dale 390, Delores 390, Don W. 562, Elizabeth 245, Elizabeth 468, Elizabeth (Miller) 88, 386, Henderson 386, Henry McConel 386, Jacob Ezra 386, Jacob R. 386, Jacob Richey 386, John 386, John Robert 386, Lorenzo D. 386, Mary 448, Ocie D. 513, Robert 386, Samuel 386, Steve 562, Victor 386, William E. 386, William Elzie 386, William Sylvester 386
HARWARD, Dorothy Ann 446, Dorothy Ann 446
HASHMAN, Elizabeth 242
HASKELL, Martha Jane 547
HASLER, David 515, Harlan 515, Wanda 515
HASSANIOUR, Mary 442
HASSLER, A.L. 85
HASTINGS, Donald 346
HASTY, Bernice 367
HASWELL, Sarah 600
HATFIELD, Adam 60, Adam Jr. 90, Adam Jr. 90, Daniel 90, Dennis 331, Hiram 60, 90, I.N. 214, James 412, Janet 331, John 600, Joseph 90, Kirk 403, Margaret 90, 109, Margaret Ruth 600, Martha 60, Mary Sarah 600, Robert Lowery 600, Robinson 168, Sarah (Brickley) 270, Thelma 412, Tommy 412
HATTON, Bertha Anne Stamm 475
HAUENSTEIN, Dorotha Rosemary 387, Elizabeth Ann "Beth", John Fredrick 387, John Raymond 387, Mark Edward 387, Philabeana (Meyer) 387
HAUGHTON, Fidella 446, Hazel 446
HAUK, Abner Absalum 387, Cynthia 387, Ethel May 568, Fay 94, 136, 289, 387, George 136, 387, Ida 387, Irl 387, Mary 136, Mary E. 548, Max 387, Melinda 387, Philip 387
HAUSE, Martha 602
HAVEN, James 265
HAVENS, Camille 244, Elbert E. 267, Ron 269
HAVER, Judy A. 603
HAVERFIELD, Thomas 275, Nathan 274
HAVERFIELLD, Tom 274
HAVERSTOCK, Jacob 82, Phoebe 82
HAVILAND, Vicki Ann (Gilbert) 358
HAWKINS, Mary 574
HAWKS, Cora 440, Priscilla Gerard 407
HAWLEY, Christopher Wayne 406, Edwin 471, Martha 471, Michael 406, Ryan Michael 406, Scott Patrick 406
HAY, Carolyn J. 387, Carolyn Jean 369, Charles Adam 387, Diana 523, Donald 369, Donald E. 387, John Nathan 523, May Nixon (Hatfield) 387, Natalie 523, Russell 165, Russell Franklin "Bud", Russell W. 387, Toni Lynn 369, 387
HAYDEN, Cathy 452, Jennifer Marie 452, Robert Lawrence 452, Sarah J. 532
HAYES, Alice 542, Erin 542, Gerald Ted, Lucy 437, Marilyn 512, Miriam 512, Phyllis 542, Reggie 542, Susa 451n
HAYNES, Becky Jane 396, Elizabeth 561, Gabriel 491, Nathan 491, Rebecca 145, Richard 202, Sarah 561, Scott 396, Steve 491, Suzanne 561
HAYNIE, Sarah Emily 309, Sarah Emilyh 274
HAYS, Carolyn Gearheart 253, John 555, Jon 555, Sheryl 555, Suzanne 555
HAYWARD, Mary Hannah 248
HAZELTON, Philip 84
HEADINGS, Lois 500
HEAGY, Arden 498, Whitney Anne 498
HEASTON, Katherine 200
HEATH, Bryan 262, Hubert 262, Kim 262, Kyle Heath 262, Natasha 262, Roderick 262, Sylvia Gephart 113
HECH, Catherine 469
HECHE, Emanuel 523, Martha Ellen 523, Pearl 392
HECK, Betty 593
HECKLER, Alice 268
HECKLEY, Brooks 427, Emma 407, Geneva 244, Harry 394, Martin 256, 407, Mary 601, Ruth 58, Sam 45, Sarah Malinda 575
HECKMAN, Betty 388, Bonita 388, Carl W. 388, 526, Cynthia 388, Delmar 594, Donna 388, Imogene 388, Joyce 594, Joyce 594, Maurice 388, Maurice 526, Ora 87, Pamela 388, Robert 144, Terry 388
HEDGES, Adeline 102, Alice 388, 548, Art 102, Arthur 388, Arthur Clay 246, Bryce 389, Charles 389, Charles Franklin 388, Charles Jr. 388, Charles Sr. 388, Crystal 388, Earl 388, Effa Belle Smith 246, Elbert 388, Elijah 388, Erin 389, Ethel 388, Eugene 389, Frank 389, Harry 388, Hubert 389, J. Elbert 389, James 389, James A. 388, James Elbert 389, James K. 388, James Kirkwood 388, 389, Janet 389, Jemima 507, Jonas 102, Joseph 388, Joyce 389, Mary (Baxter) 388, Modjeska 389, Murray 389, Nathan 388, 389, Richard 388, 389, Robert M. 102, Robert McClure 389, Rudy 389, Ryan 389, Sophia 102, Sophia (Kirkwood) 388, 389, Vera Lee (Jenkins) 388, William 389
HEDRICK, David 92
HEEMSTRTA, Simon 440
HEER, Lester Raymond 403
HEFFELFINGER, Deborah 585
HEFFLEFINGER, Cora Elen 257
HEFFNER, Catherine 403, Michael 403
HEFTY, Tom 165
HEGE, Amos 444, Arrilla Mae 386, Henry Wells 386, Ida 444, Mary 444, Mary Patton 444
HEGE/HAGE, Elizabeth 402
HEGEL, John 339
HEGNAUER, Robert 239
HEIGN, Pat 84, 152, Stacie 286
HEIL, D.R. 89
HEILMAN, George 585, Jacob 585, Jessica 585, Marsha Kay 585
HEINICKE, Charlotte 322
HEINIGER, Bruce 390, Cindy 390, Clara 390, Cynthia 390, Dale 390, Eric 390, Esther 390, Fred 390, George 390, Henry 390, Kelsey 390, Kenneth 390, Kenny 390, Melvin 390, Nancy 390, Nellie 390, Steven 390, Tonya 390, Ulrich 390, Velvet 390, Wayne 390
HEINOLD, Hulda Dubach 354
HEINZER, Karen 544
HEINZMAN, Aaron 370, James 370, Owen 75
HELFRICK, Marcille J. 383
HELLER, Bert C. 390, Betty 367, Catherine 367, David 367, David 390, Donald 367, Dorothy 367, Drew 264, Edward 367, Edward 390, 468, Gerald 145, Gunnar 264, Hugh 367, Jana 425, Levi 390, 401, Martha Ellen 523, Mary Ann Gentis 390, Ollie 390, Pearl 390, Robert 367, Sarah 366, 367, 390, Sarah 468, Shirley 367, Walter 95, 145, Walter W. 259, Wendell 367
HELM, Leslie 503
HELMRICH, Carol 342
HELMS, Bill 172, Carl 172, Charles 572, Cordelia (Ratliff) 592, Ernest R. 391, Everett 172, George 477, Harry 172, Harry 284, Idah 572, John L 592, Max 391, Meredith 391, Nancy 291, Paul 279, Paul D. 391, Sharlene 279, Stephanie 376, Vaughn 391, Vera M. 391, Virginia 279, Virginia M. 391, William H. 391, Zehra 599
HEMINGER, Don 320, Elijah Neil 320, Greta Louise 320, Jesse Alan 320, Karla 320, Samuel Lee 320
HEMMINGER, Don 377, Elijah 377, Gretta 377, Jesse 377, Karla 377, Samuel 377
HENCH, Paul 442
HENCHELL, Floyd 83
HENDERSHELL, Caroline 320
HENDERSON, Dora 588
HENDERSON, G.W. 83
HENDRICH, Elizabeth 606
HENDRICK, Mary Ellen 255
HENDRICKS, Genelle 445, Kyle 399
HENDRY, Carrie 583
HENKLE, Larry 140
HENLEY, Charles C. 392, Charles H. 392, Dowe 502, Harriet 298, Judy 502, Lois 391, Lucile 122, 502, Lucile (Lambert) 391, Lucile (Lambert) 392, Malinda Ogalsbee 391, May 392, Richard 391 502, Richard L. 392, Richard Lambert 391, Samuel 391392, Thompson 392, William 392, William Dowe 391, 392, William Dowe Jr. 391, William Dowe Sr. 391, Jr, William Dowe 391
HENLEY-PEARSON, Judy K. 392
HENLINE, Brenda 508, Erin Elizabeth 508, Keith 508, Tracy Ann 508
HENLY, Glennis 533, Lori 533, Naomi 533, Patrick 533, Ryan 533, Wayne 533, Wayne Jr. 533
HENNE/ROBINETTE, 331
HENNEFORD, Amelia 392, Amelia 422, Donald 392, Ethel 392, George 392, Harold 392, Helen 392, Kathryn 392, Lena 259, Lena Biberstein 457, Marjorie 392, Martin 392, Martin 487, Mary Mathilda "Tillie", Mary Mathilda 457, Michael 259, Michael 392, Michael 457, Otto 392, Romaine 392, Tillie 457, Walter 392, William 392
HENNY, Geneva 512
HENRY, Camilla 292, George 252, Harmon 326, Janice 551
HENSCHEN, Hazel Harris 384, Ida 393, Irene 502, Ruth 606
HERBER, James 304, Jamie 304
HERBST, Albert 393, Bertha Henrietta 393, Catherine 393, Frances 393, Guy 393, Harriett Elizabeth Burns 321, Irene 393, Joseph 393, Martha Augusta Perkins 572, Mary 564, Mary Louise 393, Ola 393, Ralph 393, Robert 393, William 321
HERBST, William 427
HERDDEEN, H.G. 82
HERMAN, Adam Wesley 393, Amy Renee 393, Arlene Lou 393, Ashley Nicole 393, Benjamin Jay 393, Beverly 350, Brian Lee 393, Debbie 350, Donald Floyd 393, Edward Ray 393, Frank 393, Grace Madonna (Liechty) 393, Jarrod Jay 393, Jay Allen 393, Jessie Kaves 393, Jill Madonna 393, Joy Ellen 393, Linda 273, 350, Raymond 350, Ronald Dean 393, Sharlene Sue 393, Sheila 350, 463, Steven Lynn 393, Terry 350, Tony 350
HERMANN, Anne E. 481
HERNDON, John 144, Ruby 479
HERON, Elizabeth 270, Janice 290
HERR, Ben 352, Jody Lin 352, Philip 352
HERRAN, Mina Wilhelmina 437
HERRBERG, Mary Ann 326
HERRING, Judy 528, Judy (Hart) 275, Lillie Ann 249, Paul 528
HERRMANN, Anna E. 481
HERRON, Alexander 331, George 331, William 331
HERSHBERGER, Nancy 423
HERSHER, Bert 263, Debra 288, Frederick 263, Josephine 263
HERTEL, George 89
HERWICK, Frank Vance 393, Mary Violetta 393, Valentine John 393, Violetta (Reynolds) 393
HESLER, George 121, John 121
HESS, Geneva 489 Peggy 429
HETRICK, Amos 394, 603, Amos Harlow 394, Arle Arminitha 394, Catherine (Drum) 394, Darrell Gene 394, David 394, Donald Robert 394, Mabel Irene 394, Mary 579, Maynard Alton 394, Peter 394, Simon 394, Steve Dee 394, Tracy LaVera 394, 603
HEUER, Amanda (Bleeke) 482, Carl M. 257, Helen 482, Helen 483, John 482, Linda Bender 268
HEUSSER, Henry 68
HEWITT, Jeff 140, Nancy 154
HEYERLY, Albert 224, Diane 340, Galen 224, Herb 224, Herbert 487, Herman 224, Jennifer 293, John 352, Jolene 463, Laura 293, Luster 224, Luster 487, Lynn 224, Ray 224, Ron 224, Stacy 293, Stan 224, Stanley 293, Sue 434, Sue 487
HIATT, Ed 279, 460, Jane S. 573, June 136, Mary Maxiene 460, Thomas L. 573
HICKERT, Barney 602, Beautrice 602, Dianne 602
HICKS, Clyde 565, Howard H. 394, Nyla 565, Thelma 15, W. W. 81
HIDAY, Brent 601, Cheryl 449, Diana (Starr) 434, Gregory 434, Justine 449, Larry 145, Larry 434, Malcolm 449, Nedra 152, Nedra 434
HIESTER, Janice 432
HIGGENBOTTOM, Barbara 475
HIGGINBOTTOM, A. J. 475, Barbara 475, Jan 475
HIGGINS, Amy 293, Arnetta Pearl Ditzler 394, Betty Baumgartner 394, Carol (Cline) 293, Chads 48, Chads 394, Chalfant 395, Charles E. 394, Charles E. 395, Dale 394, David 142, David 394, Garth 395, George 275, Harold 395, Helen Lucille 394, Hermenia 394, J. Michael 407, James 288, James Earl 394, James H. 394, James Michael 394, Jim 407 414, Joe E. 394, John Robert 394, Joy 293, Kathryn 394, Kenneth L. (Casey) 395, Linda Kay 273, Margaret E. 275, Mary Van Emon 394, Nellie (Thomas) 275, Patricia Ifer 407, Pearl 579, Tom 394, Tom L. 293, William 120
HIGH, Amarilla 347, Edith 371, Ezekial 347, Francis 224, Jennie 451, Joseph 326, 371, Lorraine 221, Margaret 371, Mearl 144, Ott 45
HIGHLAND, Marcielle 383, Mary 378
HIGHLEN, Anika 350, Carolyn Joyce Ifer 407, Cindy Lou 395, Cindy Lou 396, Cohn John 396, Daniel Josephus 396, Daniel Wayne 395, Daniel Wayne 395, Daniel Wayne 396, Daniel Wayne II 395, 396, Dick 395, Dick Eugene 395, 396, Frank 396, Fredrick Lee 395 396, Gelena 396, Glen 396, Helen 396, Helen 514, James Christopher 396, Joseph Lee 396, Joyce 407, Kay Louise 396, Keith Sheldon 396, Kenneth Lee 396, Lee 113, Lee Roy 395, 396, Linda Sue 395, 396, Mabel Esther (Thrailkill) 395, 396, Malinda 396, Mary 378, Michael Eugene 396, Miriam 402, Opal Ruth 396, Ora 396, Rick 350, Robert 64, Robert W. 396, Robert William 395, 396, Sarah 396, Thomas Edward 396, Wanda Jane 395, 396, Zachary 350
HIGHLEY, D. T. 45
HIGLEY, Edward 602, Fannie 601, Fanny 602, Martha 602
HIGMAN, Clement Rose 397, Faith (Kreigh) 397, George W. 397, Henrietta Isabella 529, John Mason "Jack", John Mrs. 154, John Wesley 397, Ralph 140, 144, 521, Ralph K. 397, Sara (Ross) 397, Ted King 397
HILAIRE, Simone 605
HILDEBRAND, Elizabeth 373
HILE, Conde Rev. 97
HILGE, Henry 445, Katherine 445, Roselle 445
HILGEDAG, Elizabeth Suzanne 345, Stacy 345 Stephanie 345, William 345
HILGEMAN, Bill 252
HILGEMANN, William "Bill"
HILL Arla 538, Constance 272, David 79, Donna 598, Harold Adolph 513, Herb 339, Julie 407, Lee 523, Marsha Kay 513, Mary Katherine 583, Mike 297, Rebecca Jo 513, Sara 297, Sarah 352
HILLBERT, Burnell 349, Cindy 349, Rhonda 349
HILLER, Sue 479
HILSMIER, Alvina 564, Clara 564, Constance 601, Della 563, Evelyn Valentine 585, Leroy E. 343, Mark 343, Matthew 343, Michael 343, Mrs. 150, Rosalie Ann 343
HILTON, Mary E. 335
HIME, Della Mae 279
HIMES, Kathleen 444
HIMLER, M. M. 83
HIMMELSTEIN, Max 165
HINCHMAN, Marguerite 371
HINDMAN, Ida 607
HINE, Ruby 350
HINES, Sherman 15
HINESLEY, Ann 425, Kristina 425, Mark 425, Michael 425, Steven 425
HINKLE, John 307, Shea 307
HINOTE, Rochelle 272
HINSHAW, Frances 598, Jeremy 590, Julie 590, Melissa Rose 307
HINTON, Myron 484, ReAnn 338, ReAnn 554
HIRSCHY, Bonnie 295, Dean 295, Edward 295, Gary 295, Ida 350, Judith 295, Judy 239, Kathleen 295, Kathleen Jo "Kathy", Kathleen Jo 240, Linda 295, Lori 295, Mary Ellen (Confer) 239, Mary Ellen Confer 240, Melvin 240, Melvin Martin 239, Melvin Martin 295, Paul 92, Randy 295
HISER, Faye 606
HISSEM, Charles 200, Evelyn 492
HITCH, Elizabeth (Meyers) 466, Greg 466
HITCHCOCK, Samuel 200
HITE, Abraham 398, Cora Elzena 398, Effie May 398, 556, Elijah 398, Ella Broyles 550, Emily 398, Frances Berry 398, Hannah 398, Henry M. 398, Jacob 398, Joseph 398, Joseph Jr. 398, Lamar 357, Margaret J. 551, Margaret Joann 550, Marilyn R. 200, Marion 398, Rebecca 398, Robert 202, Saffiah 398, Samantha 398, Samuel V. 550, Sarah 398, Vera B. 450, William 398
HITZEMAN, F. Wm. 216
HIXON, Cleta 597, James F. 414, Juanita 414
HIZER, Aaron M. 274
HOAD, Helen Icylean 517
HOAG, Brad 491, Brent 491, Isora May 537, Jim 491
HOAGLAND, Dorothy 600
HOBBS, Emma 150
HOBLITIZEL, Agnes 253
HOCH, Gary 592
HOCKEMEYER, Hanna 314
HOCKENBERRY, Sheryl 265
HOCKMAN, Greg 79, Gregory Allen 398, Gregory D. 398, Harold 398, Marilyn (Harmon) 398, Mark Andrew 398
HODEL, LaVina 322
HODSON, Anna Hodson 551, Ermal 551, Mary Belle 551
HOELLE, Agnesia Strohler 256, Martin 256, Rosina 256
HOELM, Mathias 89
HOEPPNER, Cora 476, Cora Aretha 467, Eileen Evelyn 467, 476, Fred 8, 476, Frederick Martin 467, Gayle Elizabeth 467, 476
HOERR, Carolyn 322
HOFFACKER, Ada 516, Brett 512, Candace L. 289, Carole Deane 289, Etta Gilbert 254, Frank 516, Henry 254, James 512, John 516, Laura Ethel 254, 255, Ruth 512, Sarah 289, Scott 289, Stacy Lee 289, Stanley 289, Steven 289, Todd 512, Winnie 64
HOFFER, Christine 438
HOFFMAN, Arthur W. 373, Barbara 353, Christine 531, Dan T. 421, Dorothy 594, Dwight 424, Earlyn 424, Fred 421, J. H 64, J. H. 96, Joan 421, John 89, Myles Frederick 421, Ryan 531, Shauna 531, Todd A. 531, Violet 594, William 445
HOFFMEIER, Annie 443, Benjamin 443, Jonathan 443, Lee Arden 443, Terry 443
HOFMANN, Pauline 251
HOFSTETER, Emma 493
HOFSTETTER, Carl D. 398, Caroline 528, Deb 398, DeWayne 398, Earnest 398, John 398, Kenny 398, Kevin 398, Michael 398, Monica 398, Sheba 398, Tim 398, Vicky 398
HOGG, Anna Ruth 398, Barbara Jean 398, Bruce 359, Bruce 398, Bruce Lee 398, Charles 200, Charles 360, Francis Ward 398, George 398, Gertrude Elizabeth 398, Gregory Scott 398, James 398, Jeffrey Lee 398, John 359, 398, John Andrew 398, John Douglas 398, John Henry 398, 419, Magdalene 142, Margaret 398, 500, Max Olin 398, Milford 398, Peter 359, Peter Girod 398, Rebecca Jane 398, Robert 398, Sarah 398, Wendell 398, William 398, William (Bill) 359
HOGG, William Bruce 398, Willmina 359
HOGSTON, David 399, Dicky 399, Doris Marie 399, Erma Jean 399, Howard El 399, James Allen 399, James Frank 399, Jenny Lavonne 399, Karen Sue 399, Larry Fay 399, Mabel Swindell 399, Mary 399, Mary 499, Patricia Grace 399, Rebecca Sue 399, Robert Allen 399, Sarah 474
HOLCOLM, Etta 554, Bertha 304, Charity Swaim 304, J.H. 304, Jeanett 462
HOLDEN, William 193
HOLDERBAUM, Clem 459
HOLDMAN, LeAnne Renee 480, Rebecca Ann 480, Travis 25, Travis 480, Wesley Travis 480
HOLLCRAFT, Ethel 489
HOLLINGSWORTH, Ethel 58
HOLLOPETER, B.S. 98
HOLLOWAY, Angela Louise 399, Benjamin Heath 376, Brenda 400, Car 400, Christina 262, Clifton 400, Clinton 400, Cora Bell 400, Courtnic Lin 307, 400, Dianna 399, Dick 400, Douglas 399, Elijah 400, Ellen 400, Emma Faye 315, 399, Emma Marie 399, Erma L. (Emley 315, Ethel Mae 400, Fern 582, Ferne

(Starr) 412, Florence Susanna 399, Hannah E. 262, Heath 400, Heidi 400, Irly Ernestine 399, Iva Mae 383, Iva Mae 399, Ivan W. 315, Ivan William Jr. 399, Ivan William Sr. 399, Jack Michael 393, Jane May 399, Janet 400, Jay Alan 400, Jeffrey Lyn 400, Jenni 400, Jennie Kirkwood 261, Jennifer Leigh 393, Jenny (Kirkwood) 400, Jerome Max 400, Jessica A. 262, Jessica Lynn 393, Jody 140, Joe 400, 582, Joe D. 400, 412, 567, Joe Dean 400, Joe Deane 331, John 262, 527, John H. 261, John Henry 400, John Wesley 400, Jon 376, Jon Ralph 400, Jonathan 400, Jonathan Cary 400, Joseph 400, Joshua 399, Julia Kay 399, LeAnna Jill 331, Lee 400, Lee 400, Lela Marie Blair 261, Lemuel 400, Louisa 262, Louvica 527, Love Brittenham 400, Lovey Jane 400, Lydia S. 262, M. Ferne 400, Marcia Ann 393, Marlene 208, Martha Ferne 567, Martha Ferne (Starr) 331, Mary Christina 527, Mary Jane 400, Max C. 393, Max Cary 400, Milton F. 262, Rex E. Jr. 399, Rex Eugene 399, Robert Carl 400, Ruby 400, S. Jack 400, Sally Joe 582, Stanley Jack 400, Steven James 400, Vance Cary 393, William 399, William E. 400, William Glen 399
HOLMES, Bill 17, 269, Carey Lynn 305, Charles 17, 269, Darryl Duane 577, Doris 17, E. Jean 269, Emily Anne 305, Francis 305, Jane 553, Josie 17, Kitty 17, LaVon 577, Linda 577, Lora LuAnn 577, Stephen 577, Wilda 305, William 17
HOLMGREN, Amy 346, Carl 346, Dee 346, Everett 346, James 346, Jason 346, Karen 346, Mark 346, Martha 346, Melba 346, Mary Jane 454
HOLSINGER, 66, Andy 401, B. 20, Ben 401, Brent 425, Brooks 401 Clinton 425, Dick 151, Ellen 401, Ellen 496, Howard 401, Irisr 401, John 401, Maria 425, Mary 401, Molly 425, Richard 401, Wendy Lee 290
HOLSTON, George 89, George G. 369, George Rev. 517
HOLWEY, Thankful 363
HONARMADIAN, Homayoun 247
HONEGGER, Kenneth 130,146, Kenneth Mrs. 146
HONEYWELL, A. A. 96
HONLEY, George 581
HONORMANDIAN, Elizabeth Ann 316, Homayoun 316
HOOK, Anna Lee 246, Anna Lee 401, Caroll (Schlagenhauf) 401, Cindy 401, Claudine 401, 513, Diana 414, George 366, Jack 414, Jack D. 401, James 401, Jeff 401, Jerry 401, Jerry K. 401, John 401, Joyce 414, Kent 401, Kristi 401, Margaret 366, Margaret Ann 367, Matthew 401, Minnie 246, Minnie (Stover) 401, Nathan 401, Paul D. 246, Paul Dennis 401, Paula 142,152, Phil 401, Ralph 170, 382, Ralph 401, Ralph A. 246, Ralph Allen 401
HOOKER, Elizabeth 409 410
HOOPENGARDNER, Abraham 402, Amanda 501, Benson 402, David 402, David 402, Dora 251, Dora Elsie 402, 596, Elizabeth 402, Ethel 509, Francis 402, George 402, 501, Iva Marie 402, Jasper Burdell 402, Jessie 501, John 402, Lewis 402, Lewis 437, Lydia Ann 437, Marietta Louise 402, Martha Elizabeth 402, Mary Jane 402, Miles 355, Miles 509 Peter 402, Rebecca 402, Sophia Catherine 402, Susan 402, William Atwood 402, Abraham 512, Mary A. 512
HOOPER, Mary Elizabeth 514
HOOPGARNER, Everett Dale 402, Karen 402
HOOPINGARDNER, Donald 228
HOOPINGARNER, Aaron 402, Allison Joy 544, Amanda 245, Amy 402, Barry Joe 544, Bart Lane 544, Bertha 402, Betty 402, Brett 402, Brian Dee 544, Brice Wayne 544, Brittany 245, Bruce E. 544, Burnwell "Jack", Caleb Brice 544, Carl 403, Carl Lee 403, Clarence Estep 402, Cole 402, Cole 531, Cole Evan 402, Craig 403, Cylie 402, Cylie 531, Cylie Nicole 402, Dale 402, Dana 531, Darrick 402, Darrick 531, Darrick Thomas 402, David Scott 403, Dee 352, Dessie 402, Don 402, Donald L. 411, 426, 508, Donald Lee 402, Dorma Mae 378, 403, Elizabeth 403, Elizabeth Ann Betty, Elmira 402, Emily 403, Emma 402, 538, Eric 402, Estep 403, Gail 402, George 402, 403, George Frank 402, George Franklin 403, Hazel 402, Heather Marie 403, Heidi 403, Heidi Lynn 403, Helen 402, Jami 403, Jan Lynn 403, Jeffery Allen 403, Jennifer Lynn 403, Jerry Dee 403, Jill Elizabeth 403, John 402, John H. 402, Joquette 402, Jordan Lane 544, Joseph 403, Joseph N. 402, Judith Diane 273, Judy 402, Julia F. 529, Julia Fae 403, Kay 402, Kelli Ann 544, Kelly Sue 403, Kent 402, Kyle 402, Kyle William 544, Lee 326, Lisa 403, Lucille 402, Marc Bruce 544, Marjorie 402, Marlene 426, Marlene 508, Marlene Platt 411, Michael Rex 403, Miriam 402, Nancy Jane 544, Ned 402, Ned 544, Neil 402, Nola 402, Orpha 402, Pamela 402, Pamela Le 411, Pamela Le 426, Pamela Le 508, Paul 402, Pauline 403, Phil 402, Ralph 403, Ralph V. 402, Randy 245, Randy Joe 403, Rex 403, Rhonda 245, Rick 402, Rick 531, Rick D. 402, Rickey Lee 403, Robert Joe 40, Robin 403, Ronald Dee 402, Ross 402, Roy 402, Scott Brian 544, Shari Lynn 426, Shari Lynne 402, Shari Lynne 411, Shari Lynne 508, Sherre Lee 403, Steven 326, Terry J. 403, Thomas 326, Thomas Carl 403, Timothy J. 403, Tracy 403, Travis Wayne 544, Tricia 403, Tyler Matthew 544, Vera 402, Wade Joseph 544
HOOPS, Minerva 258
HOOVER, Benjamin 404, Berniece 403, Catherine 404, Christina 404, Clara Alma (Gray) 494, Cleona 297, 408, 605, Corrine 403, Dale 403, Dan 403, Daniel 404, Elizabeth 404, Ella (Decker) 317, Evin Franklin 403, Felix 403, Franklin 403, Gene 403, 533, Georgianna 403, Grace Leo 518, Hahala 404, Helen 403, Homer 403, John Edmond 404, John M. 404, Josephine 403, Karla 264, Levi 403, Lloyd 403, Mahala, 451, 455, Mark 403, Martha Maxine 373, Mary Ann 533, Mary Ellen 404, Mary Kemp 455, Melvin 494, Paul 403, Penolope J (Norton) 297, Robert 403, Ruth 150, Sarah 403, , Susan (Moyer) 404, Susanna 404, Sylvia 532, William 297, William H. 403
HOPKINS, Ann 335, Constance 561, Norma Lee 574
HOPPES, Hester 606
HORAN, William 142
HORMANN, Christina 403, Gary 403, Kenneth 403, Regina 403
HORN, Debbie Phipps 491, Nancy 537, Vera 509
HORNADAY, B.F. 98
HORROM, Amy Jo 553, Cindy Jo 553, Kristopher Allen 553,, Richard Allen 553
HORST, Karl 77
HOSE, Connie Sue (Higgins) 394, Connie Sue Higgins 407
HOSIER, Joyzella 534
HOSLER, Carol 449, David 577, James 577, LaVon 577, Vanessa 577
HOSTETTER, Carolyn A. 343
HOTMIRE, Denise 295
HOTOPP, Anthony 404, James A. 404, Jim 418, Kelly 418, Kelly Michelle 404, Kevin 418, Kevin Andrew 404, Marcia 8, Marcia 94, Marica 418, Mina 404
HOTT, Bishop 102, Don 394, Harold 234, Harold 394, Joyce 394, Kathryn Higgins 394, Richard 321, Richard 394
HOTTEL, Blanche 523
HOUDYSHELL, Allie 527
HOUGH, Melissa 414, Rozada 383
HOULIHAN, Sandra 361
HOUSE, Walter 58
HOUSEHOLDER, Herbert Rev. 398, Phillip 266
HOUSEL, Ahsolem 103, Mary 602, Mary Eliza 601, Rhoda 103
HOUSER, Allie Ann Porter 512, Connie 356, David 512, Elizabeth 316, Ella 512, Henrietta 512, Jacob 241, 512, Jane 512, Jane Sara 512, Jerry 356, John 512, L.t. Wayne 43, Martin 512, Mary 214
HOUTS, Catharine 465
HOUTZ, Abe 404, Amanda 404, Angelina 404, Betty 404, Carol 404, Charles 404, Christina 404, Clarence (Kay) 407, Dean 594, Denny 531, Dorothy 357, Ed 64, Eli 404, Eliza 404, Elizabeth 254, 404, Elsie Ifer 407, Fanny 404, Florence 64, 451, Fredrick 404, Henry 64, Henry III 404, Homer 304, Jacob 404, Jeremiah 357, 404, Jesse 383, 404, John 317, John 405, John Jermiah 404, Josiah 404, Joyce 404, Lydia 245, 404, Martha 404, Martha 594, Mary 404, Mary 589, Masyl 357, Philip 404, Rebecca 316, Rosa 383, Rose 404, Roy 405, Sara 404, Sarah Elizabeth 542, Simeon 357,404, William Henry 405
HOVERSTOCK, Elizabeth 426, Margaret 38, Margaret 426, Margaret 426, William 38, William 426, William 99
HOWARD, Edith 480, Fanny 348, Frances "Fannie", Frank 534, John 350, Katherine 534, Mary 350, Pearl Trenary 534, Vane E. 262, Vane R. 262, Vivian Ellis 262
HOWELL, Dorothy June 590, Howard 15, Imo 15, Lester 78, Steven 92
HOWELLS, Henrietta 277
HOWER, Annetta (Foshnight) 150, Carrie B. 395, Clarence M. 357, Della I. (Betz) 357, Harriet 403, Jeanne Ellen 357, Noah 395
HOY, Marcelline J. 411, Randolph William 411, Richard 411
HUBBARD, George 66
HUBBERT, Rev. 66
HUBER, Amanda Jane Myers 460, Andreas 404, John F. 460, John Golden 460, Lewis 61, Margaret 460, Margaret Louise 460
HUBNER, Dessie 528, Frank 528, Gretchen 528
HUDDLESON, Leroy Rev. 97
HUDSON, Benjamin 248, Clifford David 243, Clyde 480, 606, Faye 480, Joyce 606, Katie Ann (Mullen) 248, Rick 480, Sharon 480
HUEBNER, Martha 287, William 287
HUETISON, Floyd 255, Madge 255
HUFF, Anita 467, Karl 467, Matthew 467, Melanie 467, Mercissa 467, Steven Allen 467
HUFFER, Lindsey 281
HUFFMAN, 66, Andrea 582, B.E. 214, Beatrice 111, Beatrice 270, Belle 477, Beverly 582, Bill <Jum> 454, Brent 352, Brett 582, Brian 544, 582, C. Darrel 582, Carl 107, Claude 460, Clyde 582, D. P. 60, Dale Abram 405, David 405, Don 544, Doug 582, Dr. 20, E. L. 136, Ed 572, Edward L. 405, Elijah 60, Ellen 433, Esther 214, Ethel 302, Frances 78, Francis 541, Fred 144, Glen 111, Glenna 513, Hannah Pine 405, Harry 337, Joan 241, John 270, Joy 372, Judy 544, Kaitlyn 582, Keith P. 145, Kenny 113, Kevin 544, Kurt 352, Kyle 352, Levi 214, Louis 60, Lynne 582, Madeline 136, Martha 304, Martin 76, Mary 582, Mearl 111, Michael 582, Mildred 165, Mildred J. 337, Minnie 136, 572, Myrtle Beatrice 507, Nelson 184, Nelson Burr 507, Oris 144, Richard 144, Robert 337, Roger 162, Ruby 372, Sara 444, Sarah S. 582, Shelley 536, Thompson 372, Timothy Arthur 536, Timothy Joseph 536 Tracy Lynn 536, Travis 544, Tyler 582, Velma Meade 239, Ward 145
HUGGINS, Bill 210, Steve 210, William 210, Alva E. 402, Betty 440, Betty Marie 459, Betty Marie 585, Clara 585, David 102, David 440, Edgar 346, Elaine 345, Frances 585, Frances Lillie 585, Frankie Caskey 459, Indiana 585, Jesse 585, John 585, Lucinda Fox 585, Lydia A. 593, Mary Ella 585, Merl 585, Ob 346, Pamela 440, Paul 142, Paul 585, R. S. 98, Sara Jane 585, Sarah Lanning 585, Steven 440, Thomas Paschal 585, Wanda Wheeler 289, William 459
HULL, Virgil 92
HULLHORST, Rev. 68
HULLINGER, Ina May 513, Les, Sandra J. Dr., Barry 76
HUME, Catherine (Louden) 339, Eliza 339, Genne (Bennett) 339, George 339, John 339
HUMERICKHOUSE, Ashtyn Lane 364, Ashtyn Lane 516, Carli Jo 364, Carli Jo 516, Edith 155, Noreen Sue 516,, Patrick M. 364, Patrick M. 516
HUMPHREY, Diane 154, Fred 602, James 162
HUMSINGER, Catherine 490
HUNICUTT, Loretta 526
HUNLEY, Helen (Small) 510, Patricia 222, Patricia Gayle 510, Robert 510, William 510,598
HUNNICUTT, 66, Anthony 405, Carl 239, 405, 460, Cathlene 405, Chappel 405, Chappell 405, Charlie 405, Delcie 259, Doris 315, Earl 259, Edson 259, Eliza 405, Elnora 405, Ethel Leona 259, Everett 405, Everett Joseph 406, Ezra 405, Frank 259, Freddie 259, Haxel (Edgar) 315, Heath 419, Hugh 259, Ida 405, James 239, 405, Jerry 405, Jesse 315, John 404, 405, 406, John Roger 405, Kenneth 239, 405, 460, Larry 239,405, Laura (Jackson) 404, 405, Laura 406, Lindsley 405, Lisa 419, Lovina Mae 592, Mary 239, 385, 404, 405, 460, Nellie 259, Neri 405, Netti 405, Phearaby 405, Robert 405, Rosa 405, Rosa Edith 406, Samuel 405, Sarah 405, Sharon Martin 385, Sylvester 405, Thomas 239, Thomas 405, Tom 419, Ullysess 259, Ulyssis 405, Wayne 405, Willis 405
HUNSINGER, Catherine 499
HUNT, A.E. 44, 45, 112, Agnes Smith 407, Alexander E. 407, Alexander Smith 407, Alma 407, Angela 506, Anna Benton 590, Barbara Louise 406, 407, Berneice 407, Berneice Elizabeth 407, Byrl 407, Chalmer 407, Dale 407, Daniel Wayne 406, 407, Donald 407, Dorothy 84, Dorothy Watrous 591, Douglas 590, Edwin Shannon 407, Emma May 382, Emory 407, Ethel 407, Eva (Bowman) 406, Everett 273, Gaylord 407, Gaylord Vernell 407, George 590, Gilbert 382, Gregory 317, Harold Wayne 406, 407, 591, James 590, James L. 407, Jamie Lee 406, Janet Marie 406, 407, Jemetta 407, John 590, John Cameron 407, Joseph 407, Joshua Daniel 406, Keith 407, Lela 407, Leon 407, Leon Jay 407, Loren 407, Loren W. 407, Loren Wilmer 407, Lucille 382, Margaret Ann 407, Martha Emaline 407, Mary Ann 590, May 407, Mayme 407, Millie Clementine 407, Nellie 273, Nora 407, Oscar Ralph 407, P.F. 202, Phyllis Lee 407, Rachel Tribolet 407, Ralph 407, Raymond 407, Richardnton 590, Roberta Olene 407, Ruth 249, Sally 407, Samuel 273, Sophia 407, Susan Marie 407, Theodore Albert 407, Theodore O. 407, Theodore Oman 267, 406, 407, Timothy 407, Violet 407, Virginia Ellen 406, 407, Walter 407, William John 407, Zella 407
HUNTEMAN, Christine Mae 406, P. R. 96, Paul 64, Paul 96
HUNTER, Bev 150, Beverly 574, 575, Bruce 575, E. E. 75, Edgar 604, Faye 139, Gabriel Halden 575, Halden 575, Jeffrey Tad 575, John Rev. 91, Lori 575, Lucinda 568, Sherwood 604, Suellen 575
HUNTERMAN, Jane Ann 433
HUPP, 66, John 16, Zipporah E. 267
HURST, Harry "Pat", Hope 462
HURTLE, Iva 342
HUSBAND, Phil 447, Shirley 447
HUSE, Jill Ann 410
HUSEMAN, Douglas 407, John Alan 407, Katherine 407, Linda Rios 407
HUSER, Marcella 570
HUSKINS, Jon 250, Jordan 250, Natalie 250
HUSS, Nellie Marie 554
HUTCHINS, David 86
HUTCHINSON, Alice 598, Augustus 598, D. R. Rev. 493, Melissa 598
HUVENDICK, Carolyn 152
HUYETTE, A. R. 111, 112, 113, 548, Anne 152, Erma 136, Irene 155
HUYGHE, Al 363, Albert 364, 516, Alfred Ray 363, Arthur Lee 363, Kali Marie 364, 516, Marsalene 364, 516, Mary Alice 364, 516, Mary Alice (Gordon) 363, Noreen Sue 364, 516, Steven Albert 364, 516
HYLAND, Frank 519, John 403
IBHOLM, Keld Tom 440
IDDINGS, Grace 136
IFER, Balanche 414, Barbara Susanne 320,585, Carl 407, Charles Wilhur 407, Dale 407, Dowell 239, 407, Earl 407, Elizabeth 407, 585, Francis (Frank) 407, Frank 407, George 407, 585, George Wesley 407, Homer 407, John William 407, Kara 407, Kurt 407, Louella 155, Louella 239, Patricia 394, Peter 407, Peter S. 407, Warren 414, Warren Henry 407
IHRCKE, Carl 226
IIDA, Justin Stacy 468, Laura Jean 468
ILER, Mary Ann 411, Mary Ann 411
IMBROCK, Alf 314, Ed 314, Laurie 314
IMEL, Brent 442, Drew 442, Sara 228, Sara 442
IMLER, Mary 570
INGLE, Kent 341 Marlene 341, Richard 341
INGOLS, Donald 320
INLOW, Grace 255
INMAN, Betty 408, Betty E. 605, Chad 408, Dale 408, Doyt E. 297, Doyt E. 408, Doyt E. 605, Grover 408, Lane Stuart 408, Maxine 408, Sara Lee 408, Scott 408, Sidonnie 408, Terena 408
INSKEEP, "Molly" (Reece), Abraham 275, 507, Amanda S. 408, Andrew Robert 270, Angus 507, Ann 507, Anna 408, Anna Emojean 519, Bessie 408, Candy 408, 503, Carla 290, 408, 503, Carolyn Sue 408, Cathy 408, 503, Charlene 408, Charles 408, Charles B 275, 519, Cheri 408, 503, Cindy 408, 503, Doris E. 408, Dorotha 408, Elizabeth 408, Emily Roseanne 270, Emojean 275, 408, Foreman 408, Forman 408, Fred 408, Garth 408, Glenn 408, Harry 408, Harvey 408, Henry 408, Isaac 408, Isaac N. 408, James 408, 507, James E. 270, Jan L. 408, John 408, 507, Joseph 408, Julia 408, Kathleen 408, Kent L. 408, Lana K. 408, Margaret 408, Margaret (Dye) 275, Mary 507, Mary Elizabeth "Molly", Mary Elizabeth 408, Mary Elizabeth (Reece) 275, Mary Esther 408, Natalie R. 408, Nina Bell 507, Richard Glenn 408, Robert 503, Robert Lesh 408, Roberta 515, Samuel 507, Sarah 507, Sarah C. 408, Stephen 408, Susan 507, Susan K. 408, Susan Lindley 507, Thomas 408, Vause G. 408, Virginia 408, William 275,275, 519, William B. 408, William H. 408, William Henry 408
IRELAND, Lorene Mae 348, Nancy Ann 481
IRICK, Harvey 60
IRVIN, Anniah 86Emily 474, Jimmy 13, Karen 588, Michelle 588, Samuel 86, Scott 588,Tami 588
IRWIN, Hannah Aby 474, Jim 132
ISAKSAN, Gay Ann 445, Amanda Ruth 445
ISAKSEN, Amber Noel 445
ISCH, Andy 4091, Ann Catherine 409, Anna 353, 567, Beth 4091, Catherine Jane 409, Clara 221, 354, Clarice 409, Connie Sue 409, David 282, Donald Eugene 567, Dorothy 343, Elise Meiss 343, Elmer 354, Ernest 343, Ervin 353, 567, Genevieve 487, Harold 354, 487, Harry 353, 409, Janet 487, Jason 487, Jean 142, 487, Jeff 487, 533, John 353,409, John Harry 409, Joseph 354, Judy 487,567, Karen 533, Katie 233,409, Katie (Steffen) 353, 409, Kevin 487, Laura 487, Leslie 487, Roger 353, 409, Virgil 487
ISENBERG, Emma 82
ISNOGLE, David A. 368, Evelyn 605, Louisa 368 Mary Jane 454
ITCHNER, Judi 283
IVAN, Amos 326, Mary E. 326
IVINS, Daniel 531, Juanita J. 603, Kaye 280, Lucille 261, Luke 531, Terry 531
JACK, Jackie 443, Lona 245
JACKS, Bachmann 162, Merrill 142
JACKSON, 66, Alma Anna 409, Amos L. 409, Augustine 409, Catherine (Plankinhorn) 409, Cecil 17, Cecil Uriah 409, 410, Celia 410, Charles Eugene 409, Charles Howard 409, Charles S. 409, Charles Spurgeon 410, Charles W. 409, Chelsea Rose 410, Conor Samuel 410, Cynthia Jayne 410, Dorothy Marie 409, Elizabeth 409, 410, Elizabeth (Hooker) 409, Emma Alice 409, Esther 410, Ethel 410, Fay 413, George 409, George Washington 409, Hannah Gibson 409, Heather Lyn 410, Helen Ilo 410, Hiram 405, Hiram 409, James 16, 17, 84, 146, 210, 233, 409, James D. 145, 410, James Mrs. 146, James S. 145, 409, 410, James Todd 410, James U. 409, James Uriah 410, Jill Ann 410, Jim 233, John 409, Joseph L. 405, Joseph Logan 409, Julie 415, Lara Ann 410, Larua Jane 409, Laura 406, Lillie Merle 409, Lulie M. 409, Luster M. 409, Lydia M. 409, Margaret 409, Martha 409, Martha M. 410, Mary 233, Mary Alice 410, Mary Ann 409,410, Mary Myrtle 409, Matthew Alan 410, Michael Alan 410, Nancy 409, Nellie Ann 410, Paul C. 409, Paul Clayton 410, Phyllis 594, Priscilla 84,410, Rachel 409, Richard Harold 409, Robert 154, 594, Ruth 410, Sabina 410, Sally Ann 410, Samuel 409, 410, Samuel J. 16, 409, Sarah 410, Shaun Michael 410, Suzanna 410, Thomas 233, Thomas Andrew 410, Thomas Krieg 410, Tifany Marie 410, Tom 84, 140, Valerie Kaye 469, 600, Vivian 474
JACOBS, Alice 270JACOBS, Altha Irene 583, Amelia 411, Angeline 411, Arlie 411, Carol Ann 557, Charles 411,426, Clarence John 426, Clark 411, Cora May 411, Darrel 508, Darrell 411, David 356, 410, David Franklin 411,426, Della May 426, Diane Marie 557, Donnahelle 410, 508, Doris 411, 508, Dorothy 583, Dorthea 411, Doug 448, Eddie Austin 411, Effie Anna 411, Elijah 411,465, 541, 559, 592, Eliza Jane 411, Ellen 541, Emma (Detrick) 276, Emojean 276, Erma 410, Fayette 410, Gary Dee 411,426, Gordon 508, Hazel McElhaney 557, Homer 419, Irene Adina 426, Isabella 411, James Mac 461, James Ralph 557, James William 557, Jared William 557, Jo Ellyn 498, Joe 144, Joe Mark 557, JoEllyn 557, John 352, 508, John Mark 557, Kate V. 592, Lena R. 461, Lize Jane 411, Loris "Bud", Louisa Jane 465, Louise Jane 411, Lydia 411, Lydia Viola "Kate", Mack 557, Mandy 411, Marcella 411, Martha Jane "Jenn", Mary 411,426,461, Mary Ann 411, Mary Eilar 557, Mary Luella 469, Maud 411, Melissa Ellen 411, Mildred 476, Naomi 411, Naomi 411, Ora Lee 411,426, Polly 508, Porter 411, Ralph 270, 410, Ray 410, Regina 508, Robert John 276, Robin 410, Rosealie 411, Rosyleen (Slone) 410, Roy L 411,426, Sarah 410, Shawn 410, Surville 411, Susan Renea 410, Susanna 411, 541, Swirilda 411, Tisha 410, Todd 410, Vickie 508, William 411, Willie 426, Zola 508
JACOBUS, Katherine 351
JACOBY, J. C. 96 J. G. 64
JAHN, Ralph 9, Ralph 422, Ralph 572
JAHNKE, Ida W. 530
JAMES, Alma 411, Corrine Fryer 576, Edward 411, Edward J. 411, Elizabeth 293, Francis J. 411, Frank 372, George A. "Bud", Harry 187, Harry W. 297, Isaac 293, Jack 372, Jackie 297, Jesse 350, John 372, 411, Joy A. 297, Judy 297, Julie Pearl (Ruble) 372, Lara Lynne 576, Lori 444,478, Marcelline J. 411, Margaret (Cronin) 411, R. Scott 434, Rita Lou 576, Rosella 372, Russell 576, Russell Jr. 576, Ruth 411, Thelma P. (Fields) 297, Wade Allen 576
JAMISON, 66, Allen 412, Andrea 412, Angela 412, Barry 412, Brenda 412, Charles J. 412, Darline 412, David 412, David William 412, David William Jr. 412, Debra 412, Dee A. 412, Diane 412, Elizabeth (Penrod) 412, Francis 412, Francis E. 412, Gary 412, Gerg 412, James L. 412, Jimmy 412, Joe 496, Mary M (Gaiser) 412, Michael 412, Revie W. 412, Robert 412, Robert Glenn 412, Ruby J. 412, Sherlie 412
JANASIAK, Jack 485, Jacob 485, Katharine 485, Kristen 485
JANNEY, Blanche 500
JARRETT, Bently 279, Bently B. 412, Clinton E. 412, Emily 425, Emily Ann 400, 412, Emmaline 279, Eric 400, Eric N. 412, Eric Nelson 412, Ethel 279, Jane

Ann 412, Jane (Fuller) 279, Janet J. 412, Joan 412, Lindsay Jo 400, 412, Loretta (Schell) 412, O. D. 412, Rex 142, Rick 412, Ruth Lenore 567, Sara Jane 400, 412, Susan F. 412, Willard 412, William B. 279, Williard C. 412

JAYNE, Nannie 200

JEAN GUE NATT, Elizabeth 470, Eugene 470

JEFFERIES, Mary Ellen 357, 404, Don Kenneth 572, Kenneth 572, D.W. 144

JEFFRIES, Robert E. 432

JELLISON, Daisy 500, James 500, Seattia Summerville 500

JENKENS, Cherish 606, Dustin 606, Nicholas 606, Shanda 606, Stan 606, Tonya 606

JENKINS, Benji 542, Carl 341, Catherine 451, Chad 542, Clem 451, Jackie 542, Judy 341, Michael Lee 341, Rick 542, Victoria Mae 600

JENNETT, Elizabeth 466, John 470

JENNINGS, Barbara A. 479, Bervia 515, Debi 479, Dwight 479, Lulu 411, Orsen 437, Sally M. "Lucy"

JENSEN, Alice (Johnson) 413, Phyllis 259, Phyllis Elaine 413, Victor 413

JENSON, Jep Rev. 97

JEPPSON, Jeanne 464

JERALE, Joel 341

JERSILD, Dianne 290

JESSELNICK, Anton 512, Maria Jereb 512

JETT, John 516

JEWEL, David Bentley 413, Donald Ray 413, Donna Marie 413, Evelyn 413, G. Raymond Rev. 413, R. G. 92

JEWETT, Isabel 273, Josiah 273

JOCKASCH, Mary 479

JOCOBS, 66

JOHNLOZ, Alexander 413, Alva 414, Alva Roman 413, Ann 414, Ann Catherine 413, Charles 604, Charles E. 414, Charles L. 414, Charles O. 413, Christopher 414, Craig C. 414, David K 414, Dawn 569, Dorothy 414, Dorothy May 413, Emelia 413, Emily 413, Emma 413, Florence 414, Florene 413, Frederick 414, Fredrick F. 413, Fredrick Louis 413, Fredrick Raymond 413, Geraldine 414, Geraldine Mardell 413, 604, Hic Julius 414, Jacob B. 413, Jennifer 414, John A. 413, Joyce 401, Juliann 413, Julius 413, Kendra 414, Lana Jane 262, Lillian Deihl 604, Lillian Marie 413, 414, Lilly (Diehl) 414, Olive Elizabeth 262, Robert 130, Robert 262, 414, Robert Eugene 413, Spencer 414, William 414, William Charles 413

JOHNS, Betsy 555, Blanche Ifer 407, Brady 414, Clara (King) 414, Elizabeth 81, Fleming 81, 555, Fred 268, 414, Harold Henry 430, Henry 111, Henry E. 414, Jermey 414, Kay Frances 430, Keith 268, 407, 414, Kent 268, 407, Kent 414, Michael 414, Raymond 414, Rhonda 533, Rhonda Kay 414, Ronald Henry 268, Roswell 103

JOHNSLOW, Daphne 289

JOHNSON, Aaron 415, Abel 81, Able 414, 419, Abraham 537, Abraham W. 592, Adriman 414, Aileen 446, Albert 417, Albert Lincoln 418, Alfred 417, Allan 530, Almira 417, Altha Ann 537, Amizet 418, Anette (Sebree) 597, Ann 537, Anna 256, 404, 420, 421, 438, Anna 439 Anna 539, Anna Carrie 429, Anthony 373, Appoline 421, Ashley Nichole 415, Aurie Opal 416, Barbara Jean 415, Becky 547, Bernice E. 571, Bessie 417, 421, Bethena Icedene 418, Betty 416, Blake Alan 373, Brad 419, Brandy 415, Brian 415, 419, Calista 355, 356, 417, Calvin C. 418, Carolyn Ann 419, Chad 315, Charity 546, Charles 309, 417, 421, Charles R. 418, Cheryl 315, Chris 418, Chris Allen 420, Chris Ann 530, Christina 315, Cindy Sue 421, Clara 415, Claude 417, Cletus 514, Craig 315, Curtis 417, Dane 415, Daniel 417, Darron 529, David 501, 597, David Michael 358, 417, David W. 415, Debra 415, Deliscus 417, Dewitt 98, Diane 418, Donald K. 592, Donald Lee 420, Doris 417, Dorothy 398, Dorothy Elberta 419, Douglas Shawn 421, Edith Esther 421, Edith G. (Grove) 592, Edward 419, Effie 417, Elise Grace 416, Elizabeth "Lizzie", Elizabeth 255, 417, 421, 537, Elizabeth J. 418, Ella May 418, Elma 349, Elwin 416, Elwin Butler 416, Emma 417, Emmitt Enos 418, Ermina 421, Essie Elizabeth 554, Estel 414, Estel A. 446, Esther 309, 416, Eugene 419, Eugene L. 415, Eunice 480, Eunice Ruth 416, 548, Eva Marie 419, Eva Miriam 419, Evelyn 155, Everett Earl 416, F. Leon 418, Fabiana Cathryn 465, Fay 597, Faye (Conley) 358, Forrest 415, Frances 537, Frances E. "Frannie", Frances (Warne) 418, Fred 417, Fred E. 421, Garold L. Dr., Gary 419, Gene Hope 418, George 78, 414, George A. 315, Gerald (Lois) 136, Gertrude 315, Glessner 309, 334, 364, 394 Glessner 416, 417, 419, 548, 549, Greg Shilling 415, Gregory L. 415, Guy 98, Harriet 537, Harry 356, 602, Harry A. 356, Harry Abraham 592, Harry W. 356, Harvey 537, Hazel 416, Hazel 418, Helen (Carver) 321, Helen W. 356, Henry 417, Henry 421, Hilda 417, Homer 87, Hubert 416, Hugh 415, Hulda 328, Ida 480, Ira Eugene 480, Isaac 414, 417, Isaac 537, Isaac B. 415, Isabella 356, 421, 537, J.A. 113, Jacklyn Kay 421, Jacob 260, 417, 537, James 321, 417, 418, 421, 537, James D. 486, James Dale 415, James Louis 309, 417, James Randle 420, Janelle 315, Janet 591, Jason Jay 421, Jefferson 309, Jeffrey Lynn 417, Jennifer 415, Jennifer Jean 419, Jeremiah 415, Jeremiah James 486, Jerry 419, Jerry Lee 419, Jessie 415, Jill Anne 486, Joan 234, Joana 417, John 309, 417, 421, John Jackman 537, John R. 415, Joke 592, Jonas 249, 309, 356, 416, 417, 419, 421, Jonas Deliscus Courtney 297, Joretta 602, Joseph 244, Josiah 417, Josiah 537, Julia 358, 501, Karen 419, Karen Elaine 418, 539, Katherine 419, Kathy 419, 479, Kelsie Marie 419, Kevin 415, Kimberly 415, Kirk 487, Kyle 418, Kyle Gene 420, Kyle Gregory 415, Larimer 255, Larry 358, Larry L. 417, Lavetha 417, Lawrence 419, Lawrence Armstrong 419, Lawson <L.D.> 597, Len 597, Lena 421, Leon 256, 404, 420, 438, 439, 539, Lewis 356, 537, Linda 428, Lois 156, Lois Loretta 416, Loisellen 86, Loisellen (Dale) 415, Lola 239, Louise 414, Lucinda Beitler 415, Lucinda (Beitler) 419, Lulla 417, Lulu 415, Lyndon 34, 42, Madge (Randle) 420, Maenette 592, Marcia C. 404, Marcia Colleen 418, Margaret R. 418, Marshall 99, Marshall Emery 418, Martha 239, 537, Mary 323, Mary 417, Mary Anna 419, Mary Jane 421, Mary Lynn 343, Mary R. 298, Marylou 279, Marylou 356, Matt 591, Mel 417, Melvin 415, Merle 421, Michael 415, 419, Michelle 425, 487, 591, Mike 315, Mike 591, Mollie "Mary", Mollie 415, Nancy 309, 419, Nancy (Buckley) 415, Nannete 356, Naomi 134, Nathan 309, 417, 421, Neola 155, Nicole 415, Nina (Gibson) 419, Noah 372, 418, 537, Nora 417, Nora Belle (Mettler) 592, Norma 390, Norma Loreen 419, Ona Mae 554, Oren 419, Oren Glessner 416, Pamela Kay 415, Paul 356, 414, 419, Paul E. 571, Paul Edgar 419, Paul Estel 446, Paul Eugene 547, Paul William 419, Paul William Jr. 415, 419, Pauline (Goldsberry) 459, Pearl 99, 418, Peter 418, Phyllis 420, Quincy 420, Rachel 334, Rachel (Butler) 364, 394, 416, 419 548, 549 Rachel (Davis) 417, Ralph 417 Ray 415, 459, Raymond 480, Raymond Ellis 554, Rebecca 309, Rebecca 321, 417, 537, Rebecca A. 418, Rebecca (Baxter) 418, Richard 315, Richard 418, 420, Richard 591, Richard Emery 418, Richard W. 315, Rieklef B. 267, Robert 134, 415, 417, Robert Charles 419, Robert J. 80, Robert Oren 419, Rosamond (DeArmond) 315, Roy 140, Ruby June 394, 416, Russell 417, Ruth 362554, Ruth Eileen 419, 570, 571, Sally Jo 356, 469, Samuel 420, Samuel P. 418, Sara (Sanders) 296, Sarah 94, 421 Sarah Ann "Sarah", Sarah Ann 249, Sarah Ruhama 421, Sarah (Sanders) 297, 417, Sarah (Thomas) 372, Shannon 315, Sharon Kay 419, Sheila 256, Sheila Rochelle 418, Silas 417, Solomon 21, 94, 249, 296, 297, 309, 356, 386, 417, 418, 419, Solomon 421, Solomon F. 297, Stanley D. 415, Stanley G. 420, Stanley Gene 418, Stephen 416, Steve 419, Steven K. 415, Susan Delphina 421, Susannah 417, Susannah (Sparks) 421, Susiana 421, Susie 417, Sylvia 417, Ted 427, Ted L. 421, Ted Lewis 356, Teresa 439, Teresa Ann 418, 438, Thelma 417, 602, Thomas E. 415, Thomas Edgar 419, Thomas Edgar Jr. 419, Thomas L. 415, Thomas Richard 420, 592, Timothy A. 415, Tom 315, 597, Urania 364, 394, Urania (Barber) 356, 416, Urania V. 364, Urania Vesta 364, 416, Vaughn 560, Vera Mabel 416, Vera Marie 419, Verna May 416, Vesta 560, Walter 146, 255, Walter B. 592, Wesley 417, William 321, 416, 417, William C. 546, William Clay 415, William Henry 309, 421, William Kenneth 419, William Lee 415, Wilmette 417JOHNSTON, "Joke"

JOHNSTON, Anges Gordon 266, Anna 266, Betty 152, Betty Jr. 136, Helen W. 356, John 202, John A. 356, Melinda Ball 469, Pearl 356, Raymond 480, Rebecca 414, Rem 165, Robert 266, Sandra 483

JOLOFF, Beverly 487

JONAS, Clarence 175

JONES, 66 331, Alder 107, Arizona Jim 588, Bertha 463, Bill 78, Bob 421, Brenda 535, Charles 307 411 421, Chris 307, Connie S. 472, Connie Sue 583, Dale Lynn 338, Daniel 421, Dean 421, DiAnne 307, Dorothy 307, 581, Ed 463, Edward 555, Emma 557, 588, Enoch 421, Enola 155, Erin 307, Ernest 307, Everett 307, Frank 463, Garry 216, George 274, 307, Goldie 555, Harold "Mike", Harold 421, Henrietta 363, Howard 457, Isaac 421, James 13, 76 307, Jane 274, Jane Ann 364, Jane Ann 421, Jason 307, Jeff 15, Jeffrey Eiler 470, Jennie Rev. 88, Joan 274, John 15, 421, Joseph 463, Kipp Cameron 470, Kraig Michael 338, Kristi Michelle 338, Larry G. Dr. 470, Lavina Tripp 557, Leigh Ann 343, Len 17, Lillian 321, Linda 307, Linna 421, Lora Jeanne Dr. 470, Lucy 463, Lucy 570, Margaret 304, Martha Ann Allen 463, Mary 411, 421, Michael 307, 481, 538, Nancy 481, Nancy Jane 555, Naomi 421, Nellie (Harold) 421, Oliver 421, Philip 307, Phillip 421, Rachel 304336, Ralph 98, Roberet Calvin 421, Robert 307, 463, Robert C. 364, Robert Calvin 364, Robert F. 557, Roberta 307, Ron 535, Roy 107, Samuel 363, Samuel 421, Samuel T. 13, Sandra J. Dr., Sarah 555, 598, Scott 370, Sue 307, Susan 268, 304, Theresa 307, Velma 421, Virgil 421, Virginia 307, Von 107, Wilbert 274, Will 370, William "Lon", William 20,304

JORAY, Albert 422, Auguste 422, 423, Bruce 422, Catherine 422, Charles 25, 200, 422, Charles Auguste 422, Cora 586, Craig 422, David 422, David Solomon 423, Dores (Egly) 422, Edna 423, 586, Edward 422, Elise 422, Elizabeth 422, Emanuel 392, 422423, Emilie 422, Emma 422, Frederick 422, George 422, 423, Harriet 422, Harvey 423, Harvey Elsworth 422, Julie Gandlienard 422, 423, Justine 423, Justive 422, Margaret 422 423, Marianne Elise 423, Mary 422, Maxine 422, Maxine 423, Molly 422, Noah 422, Noah 423, Olive 423, 576, Olive Gladness 586, Orpha (Decker) 317, Philip 392, Philip 422, 457, Robert 423, Robert 586, Robert Samuel 422, Samuel 422, 423, Sarah 422 423, Sophia 586, Sureldia 422, Surelia 423, Victor 422, 423, William 392, 422

JORDAN, William B. 479

JOSSELYN, Jay 500, Jennie Elizabeth 500

JOSSEN, Sophie Dammeyer 344

JOY, Emma 370, Wiliam 370

JUAREZ, Eric 359, Jacob 359

JUDD, Anna M. 552, Bertha 597, Daniel W. 423, Elizabeth 423, Ellen 423, Ezkiah 423, George 423, Henry F. 423, Isaac 423, Isabella 423, 552, Jacob 423, John 423, 552, Lettice 423, Mary 423, Mary A. 423, Michael 423, William 423

JULIAN, Jeanette Joan 396, Jeanette Joan 396, Kenneth 283, Maudie 534

JUMP, Joanna 364, 504516, Mary (McIntosh) 504, Vernard 504

JUSTUS, M. M. 593

KAAKE, G. Jean 413, Gordon 413, Mary Jane (Hamilton) 413, Quinn Nicole 413

KAEHER, Ina 136

KAEHR, Ada (Peg) 572, Beulah 390, Clint 544, Clinton Michael 593, Gloria 255, Ian Phillip 387, James 487, Janis 544, 593, Jeffrey 387, Jodi Ann 369, 387, Karen 583, Keith 487, Kristen 544, Kristen Marie 593, Leanne 544, Leanne Shelley 593, Lou Ann 340, Lucille 487, Mary 190, Mary Lou 285, Nikia Marie 387, Phil 255, Rita 487, Ronald 487, Sara Lee 255, Steven 593, Walter 487

KAETING, Dorothy 500

KAHLENBECK, Mildred 339

KAHN, Alonzo David 424, Becky 424, Bill 270, 398, 424, Clarence 424, Connie 424, Dixie 424, Ella 424, Emma 424, Erma 424, Helen 555, Helen Bernice 424, Homer 424, Jack 270, 424, Judy 270, 424, Leo 424, Linda 424, Myer 424, Nellie 424, Paul 270, 424, Sally 424, Tom 424, Vadis 398, Vadis Green 270, William D. 424, William L. 424

KAIN, Benjamin 331, Brian Thomas 410, D. F. 64, 96, Gene 259, Jamie Lyn 410, John 109, Norm 145, Norman 410, Norman Wade 410, Sally 84, Sally Ann 410, W. H. 109

KALLUAR, Barbara 353

KALT, Cynthia Anne 573, F. W., III 573, F. Wm. 573, Jane Elizebeth 573, Mary Lou 573, Thomas Hamilton 573

KALTENMARK, Douglas 287, Eric 287, Robert 287, Sheri 287

KALTWASSER, A. O. Rev. 502

KAMINKE, Susan 568

KAMM, Wilda 426

KAMMEYER, Sophia 526, William 526

KAMMYER, Sophia 356

KANNING, Leroy 515, Marjorie 515, Mayro 515, William 515

KAPLAN, David 562, Juli 562

KAPP, Harrison 216, Kate 147, Mary "Tot", W. S. 147

KARIGER, Nina 555

KARNES, Blanche 579, Georgianne 579

KARNS, Carrie 568, Fern 283, George 568, Georgia 147, Lucy 147, Marjorie Harris 568, S.R. 202, Samuel 147

KARWOSKI, Benjamin Richard 500, Don 478, Don 500, Karen S. 478, Karen Sue 500

KASHDAN, Jane Ann 560

KASLER, Herb 554, Minnie 554

KASSLER, Ila 155

KATTELL, Sherman 90

KAUFFMAN, Bethany Jane 279, Bradley Joseph 279, Brandon Gregory 279, Greg 68, Gregory 279, Marsha 402, Richard 68, Verlin 68, Verlin 144

KAUFMAN, Conrad 377, Ernest 327, Jack 432, Janene 377, Janene (McDermott) 320, Karla Vey 320, Konrad Vincint 320, Kurtis V. 377, Kurtis Von 320, Shelly 463, Tamara 350, Thelma (Kummer) 432, Thurl Mrs. 288, Von 377

KAUP, Alma (Nieberding) 379, Alvin 379, Marge 379

KAUTZ, Paul 144

KAY, Riley 144

KEAHRN, Agnes Sarah 570, Joel 570

KEAN, Gertrude Cole 567, Leroy W. 567, Mary Pauline 567

KEEL, Alan Wayne 494, Alfred 494, Beverly Sue 494, Carolyn 494, Carolyn Ann 493, Doris Oletha (Hoover) 494, Leonard Wilbur 494, Maude (Haneline) 494

KEELY, Maria 359, Sebastian 359

KEGLEY, Georgia 306, Georia Lee 522, Jack 522

KEHOE, Ruth 196 T.W. (Wayne) 196, Wayne 95

KEHRN, Goldie 221, Margaret 295

KEIFER, Fred 588

KEIL, Margaret "Peggy", Paul 422, Rosemary O'Brien 422

KEIPPER, Albert Raymond 460

KEIPPER, Dorothy Elizabeth (Wooley 460

KEISTER, Jane 592

KEITH, Homer 90, Thelma 553

KEK, J.A. 58

KELLAM, Linda 404

KELLER, Albert Jr. 581, Alfred Dr. 269, Arthur 425, Benjamin C. 424, Bessie 425, Cary 425, Cecil 424, Clara 425, Clara Richey 424, Clarence 335, Cleopus 424, David 424, Donna 437, Doyle 424, E. Howard 546, Eli Martin 424, Elmer 463, Evelyn M. (Captain) 581, Frances 432, Frederick 366, Gladys 424, Henry 425, Howard 424, Irene 424, Jerry 424, Joyce Ann 581, Kathleen 424, Kenneth 453, Kevin 102, Lalee Elizabeth 425, Leona 424, Lura Elton 509, Mae 542, Margaret 424, 546, Martha 546, Martha L. 424, Martin Vanhuren 425, Marvin 424, 425, Michael Eugene 424, Nicholas 95, Ruby 424, Sarah Angeline (McConkey) 424, Vera 604, William 463, Wilma 424

KELLERMAN, Dorothea 600

KELLEY, Basil 95, Basil C. 425, Catherine 544, Chuck 460, George 425, John 95, 425, Madelene 425, Marie 425, Martha 425, Patricia 503, William 226

KELLOG, Harvey 142, Nelson 202

KELLOGG, Fannie 480, Francis Nelson 480, Karen 385, Melanie Lynn 536, Nelson 480, Rachel 480, William 480

KELLY, Bessie 425, Betty 539, Cynthia 513, Douglas Allen 513, Elizabeth 539, J. D. 539, Joan 487, John 202, John W. 202, Jolly 254, Mary 516, Steve 487, Walter 513

KELNER, Michael 95

KELSEY, Anna 503

KELSO, Donald 142

KEMMER, Amanda 469, Catherine 469, Nicholas 469, Peter 469, Sarah 469

KEMMERER, Jacob 553

KEMP, Fredrick 82, Kenneth 599 Kristen Marie 599, Lisa 599, Magdelena (Baker) 404, Mary M. 404, Nancy 599, Solomon 404

KEMPER, Anna (Nash) 290, Durias 308, George 290, Sarah (Nutter) 308, Wesley 308

KENAGY, Luella 152

KENDALL, Ada 563, Nevin 443

KENNEDY, Arthur 425, Beverlyee 490, Bonnie 425, Cecile 425, 490, Elizabeth 425, Elizabeth Ann 290, Francis 425, Frank 425, Glen 425, Janet 490, Jeremiah 425, Joe 425, John 425, John F. 34, Judy 425, Kenneth 107, 425, Laura 425, Leonard 425, Lucinda Ann 425, Margaret 425, Marianna 490, Naomi 490, Neldon 425, Nettie 425, Patti 425, Roderick 490, Rose Marie 425, Sally 425, Waldon 425, Weldon 425, Winifred 425

KENNER, Laura 363

KENNERK, Gerald 140

KENT, Archie 79

KEPHART, Betty 154, 426, Bruce 146, Bruce Dr. 145, Bruce Mrs. 146, James Eyler 426, John Eyler 426, Mary Elizabeth 426, Maryanne 426, Patricia 426, S. Bruce Dr. 426, Susan 426

KEPINGER, Ralph 107

KEPLINGER, Abraham 426, Amy May 426, Anna 426, Barbara 150, Catherine 426, Charles Otto 426, Cinderilla 426, Conrad 82, D. W. 352, Dan 471, Daniel 82, David 82, Emma G. 426, Frank 411, Frank 411, George 228, "Harry", Homer Harrison 426, Irene 411, Irene 411, Irene Adina 426, Jacob 426, James 82, James Wesley 426, Jay Lincoln 426, John Adam 426, Joseph 426, Laura Amanda 426, Mabeline 579, Marceille 544, Marceille Janell 426, Margaret 426, Margretha 426, Martha Jane "Jenn", Martin Luther 426, Mary 82, Mary Catherine 426, Mary E. 426, Mila Mae 426, Roy 592, Ruth 350, Tonya 364, 504,516, Ulysses M. 426, Waldo Howard 426, Wesley 426, Wilda Maxine 426, Woodworth 426

KERFOOT, Kurt 408, Leslie 408

KERN, Barbara 287, Carolyn 25, Charles 140, Connie 287 Dean 287, Judy 287, Lisa 287

KERNS, Sandy 150

KERSHNER, Emma 283, Frank 45, 283, Helen J. 283, Henry 283, Ray 283, Ruth 256, W.K. 86, William Henry 283

KESLER, Arthur 353, Marvel McClymonds 353

KESSLER, Eva 430, Eva Maria 430, Lavina 560, Lavina 560

KETTERING, Charles F. 172

KETTERMAN, Rev. 60

KETTRING, Judy 150

KEY, Freida 270, Roland 270, Suzette 560

KEYE, Bud 373

KIBELE, Cuno 72

KIBELE, Cuno 164

KIDD, Marcia 503

KIEFER, Carolina 606

KIEFER, Caroline 564, Sandy 568

KIESER, Dan 487, Jerod 487, Lora 487

KIGER, W. L. 190, 200

KILANDER, Abraham 433, Calvin 433, 524, Cary 433, Cleo 546, David 433, Deborah 433, Delpha 433, Dillman 433, Eliza 433, Ellen 433, Emily 546, Emma 433, Esther 433, Geanettie 433, Guy 433, Isaac 433, Jacob 433, Jacob Marion 433, Jesse 433, John 433, Leon 433, Leon Jr. 433, Lisa 433, Lloyd 433, Loren 433, Louella 433, Maria 433, Mary 433, Mathew 433, Mautrice 433, Melvina 433, Olive 433, Perry 79, 433, Phillip 433, Phillip Jr. 433, Polly 433, R. A. 309, Robert 433, 546, Ruby 433, Sandra 498, Sarah 433, William 433, Wilma 433

KILDOW, Glen 175

KILGORE, Janet 349, Linda 349

KILINGER, Philip 433

KILLINBECK, Mildred 527

KILLINGBECK, Dovie (Bellville) 272, Mildred Luella 272, William 272

KILMER, Gloria (Tarr) 315

KIMBLE, 66

KIMMEL, Lee 20, Linda 443, Rev. 60

KIMMELL, Mary Shafer 9

KIMMER, Henry 519, John 519, Laura 519, Mary 245, Mary Emiline 519, Susan 401

KINCAID, Ada 427, Edward 427, Elizabeth Adams 427, Ethel (Morrison) 60, Gladys 427, Joyce 427, Larita 427, Miles 427, Russell 427, Ruth 427

KING, A. J. 183, Adam 397, 428, Amos S. 427, Ann 249, Anna 428, Anna Catherine (Baum) 397, Anne Catherine 427, Ashley 432, Barry 428, Barry Earl 554, Basil 427, Benjamin 550, Benjamin J. 428, Brent 428, Bruce 428, Bruce D. 428, Catherine Grove 428, Charles 45, 112, Charles D. 428, Charles H. 428, Cheri 554, Cherie Lynn 428, Chris 249, Cleora Jacelyn 554, Cynthia 428, David 397, David 428, Delores 554, Deloris 428, Doris 320, Elizabeth 348, 428, 554, Ernest 93, 427, Ethel 550, Everett E. 428, Everett K. 428, Fern Ellen 303, G.H. 16, Gabriel H. 428, Galen E. 397, Gary 249, George 397, George W. 397, 428, Henry 397, 428, Henry S. 397,427, Ina Mae 428, Iris M. 397, Jacob 344, Jane McNatt 550, Janice 405, Jason 300, Jean 428, Jeanne 554, John B. 121, John Christian 397, John Christian King 427, Johnson 16, 428, 474, Johnston Jr. 348, Karl 554, Karl K. 428, Kathleen 288, 428, Kathryn Ford 320, Kelli 428, Kellie L. 428, Kendis 428, Kendis Keene 554, Kimberly 496, Les 182, Lois 581, Lora 249, Loronda 428, Loronda K. 428, Lydia 428, 478, Mallory 432, Mallory R. 428, Margaret Stanley 428, Marjorie E. 397, Mark A. 427, Mary 117, Mary (Bever) 397, Mary Etta 31, Mason N. 397, Matilda Ann 474, Matthew 428, 554, Maxine A. 397, Nicholas 428, 554, Nile L. 397, Philip 344, Rita 42, Rita 554, Roger D. 397, Shane 300, 428, 554, Shellie 432, Sue 249, Tamara 428, Tammy 432, Verda 93, Verda Duff 427, Vernie S. 283, Wanda Harris 384, Wayne 460, Wendell 249

KINGEN, David Oscar 409, Grace Larona 409, Maudie Mae 409, 569, Ralph 409, William Howard 409

KINGERY, Barry 491, Joan (Clark) 491 Lisa, Tammy 491

KINNALLY, Barbara Thompson 580, Joanne 580, John Francis 580, Sue 580, William Joseph 580
KINSEY, Lori 283, Norma Jean 474
KINZER, Dawn 204, LeRoy 204, LeRoy 467
KIPFER, Beverly 340, Bill 300, Carl 340, Edward 320, Elizabeth 515, Janeil 414, Jay 206, John 515, Judy 487, Kristie 487, Ray 300, Ron 68, Ronald 340, Ulrich 70, William 475
KIPP, Kelly A. 563, Vickie 563
KIRBY, Beatrice 557
KIRCHHOFER, Anna 568
KIRCHNER, Ardena 368, Eldora 368, Herbert W. 368, Marvin 368, Vernice 368
KIRK, Anne (Hood) 418, Godfrey 418, Joan (Ellet) 418 John 418, Joseph 418
KIRKEBY, Chuck 479, Sonja 479, Susan 479
KIRKENDALL, Courtney 362, Derek 362, Loueen 362
KIRKPATRICK, Sarah Belle 601, William 15
KIRKWOOD, A. H. 185, Arthur 117, Carrie 155, Chad 428, Dale 428, Franklin 428, George 102, 428, Helen V. 291, Henry 400, Jennie 400, John 19, Karol 428, Kent 428, Sarah Elizabeth (King) 400, Sophia 389, Tod 428, William 428
KIRTLEY, Amanda 429, Annie 429, Bill 429, Bob 429, Charlie 429, Edward 429, Flora 429, Irene Oda 429, James Edward 429, Janet 429, Jody 429, John 429, John Willie 429, Karol 429, Kenneth 429, Lesa 429, Linda 429, Roger 429
KISER, Andy 598, Becky 598, Cecile 435, James 435, Jerome 239, Peter 561, Ralph 435, Rebecca 561
KISTLER, Don 132, J.M. 89
KITCHEN, Emma 352, James 352
KITCHIN, Joyce Ann 590
KITE, Ruth 304
KITSON, Alice 155
KITT, Jefferson 342, Karen 425
KIXMILLER, Gayle (Hill) 518, Jo Ann 518
KIZER, Charlotte 93, Cora 320, James 243, Jerry 140, Kenneth 122, Linda 243, Paul 93, Rena 20, Ruth 542, Sharon 243
KLAER, Lt. Louis 43
KLATT, David 566, Mark 566, Philip 566, Robert 566
KLATT. Vera 565, Vera 566
KLEFEKER, Stuart R. 337
KLEIN, Geraldine 424, Gertrude 535, Nicholas 68, Robert 270
KLEINEKAS, Rev. 68
KLEINFELTER, Appollonia 432, Elizabeth Christina 432
KLEINFELTER, Michael 432
KLEINKNIGHT, Andrew 572, Anna Schock 572, Anne Christine 592, Craig 274, Cyrstal Rieddle 592, Elizabeth Miller 255, Elva 515, Jacob 255, Kimberly 274, Krista 274, Lydia Jane 255, Mark Alden 274, Mary 306, Mary Ann 432, Mary Ellen 492, Mima 288, Mima Elizabeth 572, Mimia 440, N.J. 44, 45, N. J. 112, Norval J. 591, Sarah 591, W. R. Jr. 523, Wid 525, Wilmer R. 592
KLINE, Allen B. 375, Artha 584, Catherine 351, Clemens John 592, Edna 355, Ethel Mae 250, Hazel Gertrude (Brumbaugh 240, Helen 347, John Frederick 240, Laura Belle 58, Nicholas 351, Norma Lou 240, Norval 301, Rhonda Lynn 381, Rosa Klein 351
KLING, Larry 295, Pamela 295, Robert 295, Robin 295, Scott 295
KLINGEL, Jane Isadare 414
KLINGER, Russell 75
KLIPSER, Camilla Rae 518, Camilla Rae 544, Coleen 544, Kent 518, Kent 544
KLOKO, Jeanne 307
KLOOZE, Larry 402
KLOPFENSTEIN, Dave 506, David 588, Drake 588, Sarah 463, Tami 588, J. J. 167, Jacob 464, Lydia 570, Lydia 570, Regina 508
KNABE, Rev. 68
KNAPP, Grace Buckner 248, Harry J. 279
KNECHT, Albert 359, Kelli Jo 359, Matthew Ryan 359, Ronald Joseph 359, Ruth (Scheidler) 359, Valerie Margaret 549
KNEINKNIGHT, Anne 523, Mary 523, Wilmer R. Jr. "Wid"
KNEREHM, Caroline 585
KNIGHT, Albert 121, 214, 426 Denise 557 Jack 231 Jack W. 231 Joan 270 John 231 John W. 231 Margaret 557 Perle 411 Phyneal 270 Rebecca 82 Shirley 231 Waldo 557
KNOBLE, Gloria 300 J. F. 185 James 300 Jim 300 John Frederick 553 Linda 300 Mariah 553 Pamela 300 Tammy 300
KNOFF, Dorothy 527, Dorothy Marie 527, Harrison Benton 429, John 429, Lulu 527, Mary Reed 429, Philip 429, Raymond 527, Raymond Gladstone 429
KNOTT, 66
KNOWLES, Kain 485, Lon 485, Samantha 485, Tana 485, Teresa 518, Teresa 544, Teresa Lea 591, Victoria 485
KNOX, Bette 333, Clarence 429, Donald Wayne 429, Ethel 429, Evelyn 429, Floyd 429, Frnacis 429, Harold 429, Harriet 429, Hazel 429, Horrace 429, John 429, John Franklin 429, Joseph 18, Joseph Dr. 386, Karen 429, Kevin 429, Lisa 333, Mary Jo 333, Mathew 429, Michelle 429, Robert 333, Ryan 429, Vantress 18, Viola 429, Warner 18, Willard 429, William 429
KNUCKLES, Doris Ann 350, James Medford 350
KNUDSON, James 417
KNUEVE, Carl 390, Gregory 390
KOBER, Adam 359 Daniel 260 Jack 359, 398, Jean 136, 269, 359, Jean 398, Jennie Lieurance 359, Jill 359, Joseph (Joe) 359, Judith Gay 398, Judy 359, Kelly 146, Krista 359, Maria 260, Patrick 359, Walter 359
KOCH, Anna Maria 375, Becky 270, Ralph 85, Wilda I. 603
KOCHER, Flo 147 G. T. 147, Marguerite 425, Mildred Ruth 503
KOCHLER, Sharon Elaine 326
KOEHLER, John 287
KOEHLINGER, Kelly 473
KOERS, Eugene 95
KOHR, Elizabeth 560, Jacob 580, Magdalene 580, Simon 580, Susanna 592, Susanne Caley 580
KOLTE, Marie Christine Louise 482
KOLTER, Barry 250, Ed 45 Jared 250, John Max 250, Kristen 250, Travis 250
KOOIMA, Anna 510, Nettie Wheaton 510, Thomas 510
KOOMJOHN, Derek 251, Dirk 251, John 251, Lisa 251
KOON, Elsie 596
KOONS, Alice 403, Alison 430, April 430, Barbara 430, Barbara Lou 430, 606, Claude 323, 430, Claude Swaim 430, Delbert 430, Douglas 430, Edith 430, Edna Hannah 430, Elizabeth J. 512, Elizabeth Jane 430, George 430, George Allan 430, George Franklin 430, George Guy 430, 606, Gregory 430, Guy 430, James 430, Jared 430, Jayne 430, Jill 430, John 430, Kent 323, Kent D. 430, Linda 430, Lynne 323, Lynne Claudette Colvin 430, Nancy Lou 430, Philip 430, Phillip 512, Ralph 430, Sarah 430, Thomas Wayne 430
KOORSEN, Janet Sue 344
KOPPENHOFER, Helen 312, John 314, John 314, Mary 314, Mary (Miller) 314, Mary (Miller) 314, Arthur 84
KORN, Adam 417, Cecil 417, Charles 417, Delbert 417, Fay 417, Glessner 417, Lazern 417
KOWALKE, Ward 140
KRAFF, Gerald 378, Jennie 378
KRALICEK, Jennie V. 269, John 269
KRAMER, Bernard 519, Cynthia 519, Joseph 417, Leeanne 519, Lottie 519, Peggy 519
KRAUSS, Lauretta 596, Paul 96
KRAUTER, Maria Katharina 563, Maria Syhil 563, Maria Sybilla 564
KREIGH, Abraham 430, Anna Maria 430, Benjamin Larry 359, Billy May (Beaty) 255, Charles 430, Charles 431, Chelsea Renee 359, Cyrus 430, David Larry 359, Dustin David 359, Elias 430, Eliza 430, 431, Elizabeth 431, Emma 332, Erin Neille 255, Estella 562, Eva 430, Eva Kessler 431, Everett 595, George 430, Gerald Glendon "Pete", Glenn 262, Hattie 431, Henry 430, J. Roger 255, Jacob 430, John 430, 431, Joseph 430431, Joseph Jr. 430, Karen F. 595, Larry 359, Lillie 431, Lucile Mackey 255, Magdalene 431, Magdalene (Beck) 597, Marian Freeland McFarren 595, Marjorie Edith 262, Martin 430, 431, Mary Ann 430, 431, Mildred 430, 431, Opal (Bard) 359, Rebecca 430, 431, Regan Ann 255, Rex Alan 255, Roseanna 430, Roseanna 431, Sam 597, Sam Jr. 431, Samuel 256, 430, Samuel 431, Sara Emma 430, 431, 597, Sarah 430, Viola Desco (Smith) 595, William 430
KREISHER, Don 15, Mary 15
KREPPERT, E. A. 64, 96
KREPS, Esther Louise 441 Father 89 Martha Jane 441 Max 441 Ollie 441 Pearl 441
KREWSON, O. C. 495, Orland J. 495, Thomas 495
KRICK, Alicia Alane 532, Dianne 284, Dorothy Jo 532, Janet (Hott) 394, Janet Hott 394, Keith 532, Naomi (Ramsey) 412, Nicholas Paul 532, Orley 412, Vera 412, Walter 107
KRIDER, Florence Waneta 431, Kenneth Scott 431, Lillian 431, Lillian Charlene 493, Robert 431, Robert 494
KRIDER, Teresa Renee 431
KRIEG, Crystal 561, Hazel L. (Mickley) 410, Hilda 323, Mary Alice 410, Wilbert A. 410
KRILL, Betty Jean 336, Catherine 589, Elizabeth 476, Elizabeth 476, Nelle 167
KRIN, Mike 130
KRINN, 66, Berneil Marcina 431, Charlene Audrey 431, Constance Lee 553, Dale 318, Daniel 431, Donald Letis 431, Elizabeth 431, Ellen 431, Frances Jean 431, George Ami 431, Gottlieb Friederick 431, Harry 107, Iva Irene 431, 553
KRINN, Jessie Armentha 431, Johan Georg 431, Johan Michael 431, Leonard 107, Marguerite Betty 431, Mary Elizabeth 431, Maxine Ardella 431, Nellie 592, Orest Albert 431, Waldo 592, William 553, William Richard 431
KROCK, Albert 512, Mary Catherine 512
KROMPEGEL, Debra 523, Hertha M. 269, Kenneth 269
KRUEGER, Michael 89
KRULL, Sharon 527
KRUMDICK, Art 15, Arthur 473, Mildred 15, 473
KRUMMELVINE, Mary 544
KUHN, Brittany 369, Duane 369, Jennifer 369
KUKELHAN, Alice 251
KUMFER, Charles 432, Elizabeth (Bushee) 432, Elva 246, Forrest E. 432, Garry 432, Helen Justine 441, Jonathan Charles 432, Joyce Ann 432, Kay Ellen 432, Mary Ellen (Confer) 432, Robert Wayne 432, Rosemary 25, Rosemary 560, Stephen Robert 432, Terena 408, Victor L. 432
KUMMER, Betty 432, Clara 432, Claudine 558, Coelia 432, Dewayne 432, Donald 432, Doris 378, Earl 432, Edward 432, Emma 432, James 432, Kenneth 378, 432, Lester 432, Pearl 432, Richard 432, Robert 432, Samuel Jr. 432, Samuel Sr. 432, Susan 378 432, Tamara 428, Terry 432, Wayne 432, William 432
KUMPF, Michael 279, Scott 279, Sherman T. 279
KUNIHIRO, Sow 346
KUNKEL, 167, Arden G. 443, Arden Gale 433, Arden Lewis 443, Avis 239, Joan 433, Barbara 432, Betty 433, Blanche Wolf 443, Bob 443, Brenda 460, Brent 284, Brent Michael 433, Calvin 432, 557, Cammy Jo 486, Carolyn Sue 383, 443, Chelsea 284, Chelsea Lynn 433, Christina 432, Claudine Myrean 433, Connie 486, David 443, Dora A. 432, Elizabeth 432, Elizabeth (Blue) 433, Eloza 432, Elzy Orne 433, Eva 432, Eva Dee 433, Faith 433, Fred A. 486, Fred Alden 433, Grant 443, Helen 443, Henry 432, Henry II 432, Jarrod Andrew 433, Jason Wayne 433, Jeffery Scott 486, Jennifer Erin 433, Jodi Lynn 433, Johann Heinrich 432, John 20, John Daniel 486, John Isaac 433, John Oliver 432, 433, Julia (Mason) 432, 557, Karen 425, Karmen 369, 443, Katy 369, 443, Kay 280, Kelli Sue 433, Kelly Renee 486, Kevin John 486, Kimberli 486, Kimberli Ann 433, Lew 369, Linda 443, Linda Diane 443, Lois 156, Louisa 432, Luster Ray 433, Lydia 432, Lydia Matilda 432, Martha Ann 432, Mary 432, Mary 500, Mary Ann 433, Matilda 432, Matthew Arden 443, Michael 432, Michael Jr. 432, 557, Nancy 432, Nellie Pearl 557, Nettie 486, Norman 433, Norman Wolf 433, Pamula Sue 433, Patsy Ann 433, Polly Diana 432, Randy 486, Rebecca 432, Rebecca A. 432, Reuben Blue 433, Robert Brooks 443, Roberta Annette 443, Rueben 443, Samual 432, Samual Daugherty 432, Samuel 22, Sarah A. (Plummer) 557, Sarah Ann 433, Sharon Kay 443, Sophia 432, Stanley Alan 284, 433, Stephen Wayne 433, Theodora Horton 432, Tim 433, Timothy Dale 433, W.A. JR. 145, W. A. Sr. 145, William A. Jr. 162, William A. Sr. 162, William Albert 432, Sr. William 589,
KUNKEL, Blanche O. 603, Evaa 285, Jackie 486, Jill Anne 486, Karen 443, Karen Kay 486, Larry Gene 486, Randy John 486, Rebecca 591, Reuben 603, Samuel 267, Sharon Kay 603, William A. III 603
KUNTZ, Carrie 360, Larry 360, Matthew 360
KURTZ, David 349, Deanne 349, Garrett 349, Marilyn Jo 319, Royce E. 349
KUSCHION, Sue 351
KYLANDER, Polly 433
KYLE, Bob 151, C. D. <Gene> 409, Dale 599, Grace (Thasher) 409, John 342, Lois Marie 409, Marie 142, Tom 342
LABRECHE, Terrie (Meyers) 466
LACEY, David 499, Don 499, Donna 499, JoAnn 499, Timothy 499
LACLAIRE, Evelyn 265
LaCOAX, Leon 98, Sandra Jo 381
LACY, Henry 98
LADD, Boyd 277, 433, Mary (Powell) 433, Sarah 605
LAFEVER, Mary C. 584, Squire 561
LAFOLLETTE, Robert 90
LAGERPUSCH, Isabella 591, Ludwig 591, Sadie Heinz 591
LAGERSTROM, Dorothea 338, Oscar 338
LAGETTE, Bonnis 304
LAHR, Roy 490
LAHRMAN, Anna 564, Charles 564, Christina 564, Edna 564,
LAKEY, William O. 418
LAM, Hai 97, Minh 97, Son Hong 97
LAMARR, Sharon 475
LAMB, Claudia 382, Wierly 356,
LAMBERT, Anna Lavenia 320, Betty (Branstrator) 434, Blake 434, Bryant 434, Caroline Harding 391, 448, Cynthia 410, Dawn 434, Delsie 434, Diana 391, Dylan 434, Harriet 155, Hattie Anne 320, Howard 434, Ira 434, Janelle Elizabeth 410, Jeffry 410, Judith 391, Kathryn 522, Leona 391, Leona (Brodt) 448, 522, 538, Lester 434, Lincoln Jeffry 410, Lucile 392, 502, 522Lucile (Henley) 111, Lynette Austin 410, Melanie (Lude) 434, Merle (Williams) 434, Mildred Lucille 391, Nancy 391, Robert 448, Robert P. 391, Saretta Marie 410, Steven 434, Susan 391, Susan Pierson 391, Ted 434, Tresa 434, William 122, 391, William A. 391, 392, 448, William H. 391, William L. 522, Darla 600
LAMM, Amanda 450, 451, 452, Ethel 9, Leota 254, Opal Marie 254, Ora 8, 254, Rex 254, Sarah 562, Vadis 254
LAMPTON, Beth 137, Joseph 82, Kenneth 146, Kenneth Mrs. 146
LAMSON, Mary 247
LANCASTER, 179
LANDIS, 66, Cora May 411, Ella 221, Mary Ann 84, Mary Thompson 165, Ves 592
LANDRUM, Angie (Brubaker) 150, Branley L. 276, Janice 403, Lacey Jo 276
LANE, Aciah 540, Cynthia 517, Ed 15, Jacob 540
LANG, Mary 270, Pat 270, Utha 462
LANGDON, Daily 489, Evelyn Tunie 489, Linda Evelyn 489
LANGE, Betty 567, Donald 567, Rosie Marie 567
LANGEL, Jay 408
LANGEMANN, Robert 512
LANGFORD, Logan Michael 324, Michelle Lynn 324, Ryan 324
LANGLE, Isaih 258
LANGLEY, John Matthew 452, Michael 452
LANNING, Julia 245
LANTIS, Cora 411, Edgar 411, Elizabeth 336, Lena 34, Lydia 336, Orve 34, Oscar 556
LANTZ, Alan 322, Amy 434, Chad 434, Charlene 434, Cybil 434, Daniel C.434, Daniel Jr. 434, Elizabeth 434, Gideon 434, Gladys 434, Harry 322, Jason 434, Jim 434, John 434, Kathy 434, Mary 434, Rose 434, 505, Shawna 434, Shelby 434, Steve 434, Sue 434, 487, Sue (Heyerly) 224
LAPHAM, E. B. 175
LARGER, 331
LARIMER, Janet 460, Shannon 240
LARKEY, Susan 357
LARMORE, Wendell 140
LARRIMER, Elizabeth 171
LARSEN, Laura 594
LASH, Betty 316, Charles 45, Cheryl 575, Sara 379
LATSHAW, Albert Wiser 407, Edna (Spahn) 407, Virginia Mae 407
LATURNER, Florence Mae 554, Minnie 538, William 554
LAUDERMILK, Ray Rev. 91
LAUER, Alan 437, Mary Joan (Piatt) 418, Nelson 437, Paul 437, Paula 437, Roger 437
LAUKHUF, Wanita 487
LAUNER, F.W. 89
LAUTZENHEISER, A. Sadie (Niblick) 434, Eileen 434, George Jr. 434, Harold 434, Helen 434, Jack 434, Jesse 434, Mary 434, Mary E. (Cline) 434, Mary Lynn 573, Maxine 434, Robert 434, Rosie 434, William 434
LAWELLEN, Hannah 421
LAWERENCE, David 142
LAWRENCE, Ora 17
LAWRY, Edgar Lewis 500, Floe 500, Levi Lewis 500, Mary May 425
LAWSON, Michael 59, Michael M. Rev. 58, William 196
LAYMON, Lois Elaine 295
LEACH, Gloria 402
LEAISURE, Artimishia 339, Drusilla Jane Keller 339, Marcellus 339,
LEAS, Barb 15, Devonna (Campbell) 435, Donald 435, Donald Keith 555, Gail 435, Gail Eugene 555, Jack 15, Jackie 435, Jackie Lee 555, James Cletus 435, 555, Jim 111, Lillian Ruth 555, Losi Jane 555, Ralph 435, 555, Robert 435, Robert Dale 555, Ruey Glee 555, Ruey (Slusher) 435
LEAVENGOOD, Martha 508, Peter 508, Saloma Ann 507, 508
LEBEAU, William 333
LECHLEITNER, Lorane 150
LECHOT, Mary 397
LEDBETTER, Orpha 113
LEDMAN, Catharine 323
LEE, Alexander 98, 102, 435, Andrea Jo 489, Ashlie 577, Bessie 435, Betty Eileen 399, Carl 91Carol A. 435, 489, Carol Anne 489, Cecelia Leaming 399, Cecile 435, Crystal 347, Darwin 435, Delia Goodyear 398, Effie 352, Eleanor Kay 435, Emma R. 435, Eric 516, R. 435, Erin 516, Erin R. 435, Ethel 459, Eunice 435, Everett 399, Francis 383, George 579, Gertrude 398, Glenna 489, Glenna L. 435, Grace 435, 516, Hattie 435, James Anderson 398, John 577, Joshua 577, Joyce (Hart) 275, Karl 435, Keith 78, 79, Keith E. 516, LeRoy 399, Lora LuAnn 577, Margaret Grace 435, Marion 346, Marion Ernest 435, Martha (Baumgartner) 346, Mary 79, Mildred 383, Nancy J. 489, Ralph 435, 516, Ralph C. 435, Randall C. 435, 489, Raymond 399, Raymond Leslie 435, Rob C. 489, Robert E. 528, Roger 78, Roger 79, 98, Roger C. 435, 489, Ruth Ann 435, 516, Samuel H. 435, Sharon (Martin) 318, Susanna 102, 435, Sylvia Pearl 435, Wayne 107, 435, William A. 435
LEETH, Mike 221
LEFEVER, Squire 18
LEFFINGWELL, Hiriam 323, Lucy May 323, Sarah Townsend) 323
LEFFORGE, Kenneth 552, Luana 552
LEGG, Charity 416, Charity 416, Paul 416
LEGGE, John 306, Kyle 329, Robert 234
LEHMAN, April 400, Barbara Ann 480, Corrine 491, Don 400, Douglas 473, Douglas A. 377, Eli 569, Emerson 491, Esther (Reinhard) 522, Garnet 480, Gregory 377, 473, Gretta 491, 499, Janelle Lynn 491, Janet 473, Jessica 491, Jesston LeeWayne 491, Joetta LeAnn 491, Lila 565, Martha Jerrideane 400, Nathaniel 377, 473, Rosetta 569, Thelma 372
LEHRMAN, Christine 606
LEICHTY, Hazel 606, Gene 387, Kim 387, Laura 387
LEIMGRUBER, Augustus 95, Dorthy 537, Frank 95, Herman 95, Jerry 144, Lawrence 95
LEIST, Ben 93, Helen 111, James 98, Lizzie 93, Minnie 317
LEISURE, Grace 346
LEITZ, Mary 379
LeMASTER, Douglas Jr. 228
LEMILIN, Danny 396, Sarah Renee 396
LEMMON, Eleia 481
LENDERSON, Charles 346, Chuck 346, Judy 346, Martha 346, Mary 346, Ross 346
LENHART, E. Burt 267, John H. 267, Orval 267, Velma O. 267
LENNINGTON, Jacob 121
LENWELL, Craig 38, Donald 320, 585, Franklin 585, Gary 585, Glenda 38, James 585, Kim 38, Martha 585, Valerie 585
LEON, Jennifer JoAnn 283, Maria 266, Robert 283, Tara Michelle 283
LEONARD, Craig 9, Craig 164, 436, 559, Elizabeth 154, Elizabeth Rose "Betsy"Jane Elizabeth 436, Juanita Powell 436, Juliet Marguerite(Richtr 436, Lucius Philip 436, Philip A. 513, Philip Allen 436, Philip Earl 436, Philip Haskell 436. Sarah Julia 436, Tolles 417
LEPPER, Adam Gabriel 343, Frank 437, Jacob 437, James Ed 437, John 103, John A. 437, John M. 437, Joshua Christian 343, Louisa Sarah 437, Lousia 103, Lucy 437, Lydia Ann 402, 437, Martha 437, Mary 437, Mary L. 437, Minerva A. 437, Nancy 437, Olive 437, Rex E. 343, Robert 437, Sally M. "Lucy"Thomas P. 437, William 103, 437, William H. 437
LESEMANN, Amy 405, Arthur 405, Joan 405
LESH, Ada 270, Andrew Barrick 575, Balthazer 437, Barbra 6, Barbra 574, Barbra 575, Betty 64, Betty 324, Betty Lou 437, Bruce 437, Charles 422, Charles E. 423, 437, Cheryl 575, Christena 437, Clara 437, Clinton Nicole 575, Courtney 463, Curt 437, Dale 437, Daniel W. 317, David 437, Dennis 437, Dicy 317, Donna 437, Dwight 6, 435, 575, Edna 64, 270, Elizabeth 437, 450 Ella 64, Ellen 270, Ernest 64, 324, 437, Esther J. 437, Ethel (Barlett) 324, Etta 111, Eulalia 317, Fred C. 437, Gary 437, Gary Dwight 575, Gelana 232, George L. 437, George Luther 437, George W. 437, Gerald 64, 437, Grace 270, Guinevere 109, Guinevere Bronner 437, H.Alva 437, Harold 437, 575, Harriet 437, Harry 437, Hattie 357, Helen 437, Helen Jean Gilbert 592, Herman 357, 437, Herschel 109, 437, Irene64, 437, Isaac 357, 437Iva 437, Jacklyn Nicole 575, Jacob 378, 437, James 270, Jason 575, Jennifer 575, Jim 258, Johann George 437, Johann Peter 451, John 437, 451, 469, Joseph 317, Karen 437, Kent 437, 463, Larry 437, Lela 64, 575, Lella 437, Linda 437, Lindsey 463, M.J. 112, 437, Margaret 378, Margaret Erhart 378, Maria Eder Marlene 575, Martha Jane 437, Mary 469, Mary Cecile 270, Mary Luella 469, Mary Nicole 575, Maxine 317, 437, Milo 112, 408, 437,

Minnie 270, Mr. 221, Neal 437, Neil Kay 575, Nicholas 575, Nikki 437, Orlo Ervin 270, Patricia Ann 513, Perry 437, Perry William 575, Peter 437, Ray 437, Rosa 64, Ruth 317, Ruth 437, Sadie 64, Samantha (Cover) 357, Sarah D. 378, Sarah (Staver) 270, Sheryl 534, Stephen 437, Sylvester 317, Thelma 185, Thelma Oleen 408, Viva 408, William Horton 270, William Lewis 437, Wilson 437, Zachary 575
LESLIE-DAVIES, Irene 555
LESTER, C. S. 81, Will 120, William 95
LESURE, Ben 588, Elizabeth 588, Lizzie 588
LEURANCE, 66
LEVENSON, Ben 167Ezra 167
LEVERENZ, Thelma 476
LEVI, Fredrich Wilhelm 438, Friedrich Christian 438
LEVY, Alvin 438, Amos 438, Amos Stook 481, Ben 179, Carolyn 438, Claudette 438, Claudia Marie 438, Darryl 512, David 438, Eli 438, Emma 438, Erika 438, George 438, 512, Gregory 512, Grover 438, Helen 558, Henry 438, James Eli 438, Julia Lucile 438, Lincoln James 438, LindaRose 438, Manes 438, Martha 438, Mary 438, Mary Lucille 481, Myrna 132, Nicole 512, Raegan 438, Ralph 438, Raymond 438, Robert Allen 438, Robert Allen 481, Walter 438, William 438, William David 438
LEWANDOWSKI, Catherine Jean Smurdon 271, David 142, John J. 271, Susanne Marie 271
LEWELLEN, Marguerite 347
LEWIS, 156, Amy Jo 605, Autie Jr. 130, Autie Jr. 234, Christopher 144, 521, Cleo 214, 289, Dorence 399, Dorothy 270, E. W. 335, Elizabeth (Haines) 538, Emery 538, Harley 102, John P. 399, Joshua399, Kelli 399, Kenneth R. 399, Lorenzo 538, Mary Katherine375, Naomi (Knoff) 429, Nicole 39O, rval 122, Rachel (Thomas)538, Tacy J. 538
LEWTON, Hazel Hunt 407
LEX, Clara 425
LEY, Aaron 272, Aaron 439, Allissa 272, 439, Andrew 272, Andrew 439, Barbara 439, Bruce 418, 439, Bruce Calvin 438, Calvin 85, 438, Calvin Martin Rev. 439, Catherine 254, Christopher 254, Clavin 464, Ethel 152, Jennifer 418, 439, Jennifer Marie 438, Kathy 439, Mary Ann438, 439, Rebecca418, 439, Rebecca Michelle 438, Teresa 418, 439Teresa Ann 438, Wayne 272, 439
LICHAU, William 84
LICHTENBERGER, Anna Maria 439, Barbara 439, Emma L. 439, 598, Jacob 439, Johann 439, John L. 439, John L. 598, Maria Amanda 439, Mary 439, Mary Amanda 439, Mary (BLackstone) 598
LICKER, Mary 527
LICKING, Betty Sue 174, Bill 331, Brenda 174, Jacqueline 174, Linda174, Nicole 174, Ruth 174, Tom 174, William 174
LIDDY, David 302, Joy 542, Sarah 302, 542, Travis 302, 542
LIECHTY, Amos 393, Della (Nussbaum) 393, Jerry 565, Marilyn Lucille384, Miriam 565
LIES, Brittany 523, Linda 523, Marlina 523, Ralph Jr. 523
LIEURANCE, Cynthia 516, Jan 516, Jane Joe 275, 519, Larry 516, Lloyd 111, 346, Luann 516, Nick 516, Rex 516, Robert J. Virginia 275, 519
LIGGETT, Mary 244
LIGHT, Isabelle 452
LIGHTFOOT, Don 334
LILEY, Art 145
LIMBACH, Sophia Wilhelmine 252, Sophie 526, Sophie Wilhelmina Luise 368
LINCOLN, Geraldine 553, T. W. 98
LINDBLOM, Leonard C. 226
LINDEMAN, Betty 452
LINDEMANN, Cindy 389
LINDERIN, Gentesin 352
LINDLEY, Daniel 507, Eleanor 507
LINDQUIST, Marilyn 244
LINDSAY, Martha 154, Marty 145
LINDSEY, Edward 350, Grace 350, Leon 144, Lydia (Shoemaker) 350
LINDSTRAND, Al 439, Anna Dahl 439, Dorothy 305, 439, 516, Harry 8, 221, 300, 305, 439, Irene 439, Phoebe 439
LINE, Arthur 275, 519, Caroline 560, Harold 560, Marie 560, Mary Esther275, 519, Raymond 560, Richard 307, Tricia 307
LINES, Melinda 321
LINHART, Dale Rev. 485
LINN, Alice 440, Andrew 440, 441Andrew <Alexander> 440, Caroline440, 441, Carolyn 337, 440, Myers 572, Cheryl 440, Chloe 441, Cora Ella 440, Eliza Jane 441, Ellen Jane 440, Geneviene 115, Genevieve "Peg"Grace 440, Helen (Bottschalk) 337, Ina Mae 441, Jennifer S. 559, Jenny 441, John 144, 440, 441, Josha 440, Joshua "Jack"Joshua 441, Justine 115, 440, Lavina 284, Levi 284, 440, 441, Levi 572, Louisa 440, Lovina 440, Lucinda 440, Manurva 440, Margaret 440, Mariah 440, Marilyn 440, Martha 441, Mary 440, 441, Minerva 440, Nancy 441, Nancy Ann 41O, .T. 115, Oliver 440, Oliver Theodore 440, Pearl 441, Rachel 441, Rachel 485, Rose 440, Sally 441, Samuel 440, 441Sarah 440, Sarah Ellen (Siddie) 332, Sarah (Sally) 440, Solomon 332, Stephan Andrew 441, Theodore 440, Viola 288, Viola 440, 572, Walter 337, Walter 440, William 440, William Milton 441
LINNETT, Harald A. 523, Laurine Matson 523, Lawrence 523, Verna M. 523
LINTA, Michael 411, Tina 411
LINTON, Ellen 268, Genevieve 268, John A. 268
LIPINSKI, Daniel 347, Shelli 347
LIPKEY, Cathy 441, Charles 441, Charles Clifford 441, Cliff 44, Clifford R. 441, Clifford Ray 441, Elizabeth Rachel 441, H. W. 16, 1214, Henry 441, Henry L. 441, Henry W. 22, James 103, Jeff 441, Jessica 441, Jim 441, JoAnn 441, Kay 441, Laura 289, Lenore P. 441, Margaret 441, Mary Ann 441, Nova Grace 441, William Addison 441
LIPP, Alvina 564, Anna Margarietha 564, Charles 564, Clara 564, Cora564, Edith 564, Edna 564, Edward 564, Eve 564, Fred 564, George564, Gust 564, John 564, John Michael 564, Mae 564, Magdalena 564, Margaret 564, Maria Caroline 564, Michael 564, Minnie 564, Minnie Rose 564, Vaughn 142
LIST, Thelma 279
LITTEN, Lynette 264
LITTLE, Adriana 555, John A. 377, Linnie E. (Hupp) 377, Marjorie I. 377, Maud 508, Merle 555, Norma 566, Roger 555, Ruth Faye 555
LIVINGOOD, Ella 512Fred 512
LLOYD, 15, Dana 287, Danny 287, Darlene 287, David 287, Dean 287, Dianna 287, Donald 287, Donna 287, Marilyn Ann 296, Ralph 90
LOBISGER, Martha 521, Amy Jo 350, Floyd 350, Greg 521, Kent A. 350, Lola 570, Loren 145, 187, Michele 521, Rick 419, 521, Sally Ann 350
LOCKDALL, Matthew Bonham 262, Randall Lee 262
LOCKE, Clara 493, Roxie 294
LOCKWOOD, Ben 533, Cecil 407, 591, Cecil C. 235, Debbie 591, Debra 284, Debra Ann 433, Delma 145, Don 591, Donald 283, 284, Estella 347, Esther 239, Gladys 476, Grace 477, Harry 476, Henry 283, 284, James 239, Karen Diane 407, Kevin Charles 407, Kyle 284, 591, Lindsay 284, 591, Marge 152, Marjorie 591, Mary (Stahl) 407, Natalie 533, 533, Patricia 488, Philip K. 235, Richard 144, Rober Joseph 407, Roberta Hunt 407, Steven Rick 407, Thomas R. 235, Tom 140, Virgil 415
LOESCH, Balthaser 437
LOFTIN, Bernie 285, Jack 285, Jamie 285, Janet 285, Joy 285, June 285
LOFTUS, Cindy 402, Joe 402, Joey 402, Marcie 402
LOGAN, Andrew 392, Chalmer 558, Chris 392, Christena 437, Clifford 558, Edna 558, Eva 538, Flossie 558, Goldie 558, James G. 558, Jane 451, Joseph 392, 409, Lucille Hazel 558, Mary A. 409, Ollie Jane (Johnson) 558
LOGSIGER, Mamie 283
LOHMULLER, Bernard 442, Catherine 442, Elizabeth 442, Genevieve 154, 442, Herbert 146, Herbert Mrs. 146, Herbert W. 442, John 442, Joseph 442, Margaret 442, Martin 442, Mary 442, Paul 442, Theresa 442
LONG, Gwendolyn 405, Isaac 58, Mrs. 15, Orville Martin 405
LONGDEN, Fred. J. 145, Fred Mrs. 8
LONGENBERGER, Abbey 463, Cynthia 442, Deborah 442, Devona 233, 442, Ernest 442, Gene 463, Harry 233, 353, Harry 442, Katy 463, Linda Fay442, Mandy 463, Marilyn 233, Pearl 442, Pearl (Frauhiger) 442, Richard Dean 442, Roger 233, 353, 442, Sara 442, Sheryl Ann 442, Thomas Richard 442
LONGSHORE, Ada 336, Albina 495, Zepha Pearl 493
LOPP, Anna 546
LOPSHIRE, Zetta 155
LORENZ, Jan 351
LOSHE, Karen Ann 337
LOTHAMER, Jason 357, Jason Howard 556, Jennie Ann 556, Jenny 357, Judy Ann 556, Matthew 357, Matthew Joseph 556, Rober Joseph 556, Roger 357
LOUDEN, Dorothea 472, Dottie 136, George 232, George R. 472, Gertrude 403, Louise 136, Louise Ashbaucher 472
LOUDERMILK, Elizabeth Hays Benson 596, William A. 596
LOVE, Charles A. 273, Clara 273, E.M. 82, James III 288, Jim 111, Juanice Morrison 427, Malcolm 179, Margaret 512
LOVELESS, Lola Belle 529
LOVELL, Audrey 442, Audrey Joan 461, Cathy 346, Edna Fern 442, Fredora Pauline 442, Iris Evelyne 442, Lewis Alonzo 442, Manford 442, Mary Almirtie King 442, Michael H. 442, Patricia Arlene 442, Ralph David 442, Jr, Ralph David 442
LOVETT, Bill 372, Bud 372, Jane 372, Susan 372, W.W. 82
LOW, Brad 268, James 268
LOWE, Frank 144, Maxine 270, Ruth 84
LOWER, J.W. 58
LOWMAN, 167
LOWREY, Amanda 586, Tami 246
LOWRY, Benjamin 443, Benjamin 443, Crystal 443, Edgar Lewis 443, Elizabeth 443, Floe 443, Hannah 443, Hannah Morris 443, Helen 443, Irene 443, Jennie 443, John 482, Jonathan 443, 600, Levi Lewis 443, Martha 482, Neva 443, 500, Neva Perry 246, Rebecca 415
LOY, Stella Lee 570
LUBBES, Courtney Clark 409
LUCABAUGH, Henry 516, Maria 516, Mary Leonard 516, Mary 535
LUCAS, Celia Ann 513, Chester 160, Cora V. 250, Gregory Alan 513, Hannah 530, Helen 136, Jeremy Glenn 513, Lorraine 523, Paul 523, Robert Glen 513, Rosemary 523
LUCE, Annalysa 481, Carolyn Jean 398, Donald Milton 398, Harvey Milton 398, Lucius 481, Nancy Ann 481
LUCKEY, Celinda 393
LUCKY, Charles 15
LUDE, Aldine (Gerber) 434, Robert 434
LUDEKE, Jerry 306, Jerry Lou 522, John 522
LUDINGTON, Bertha Diptman 599, Eber 599, Velma 599
LUDLUM, Edward 78
LUDWIG, William 73, William Rev. 344
LUEDTKE, Doris 591
LUGAR, George 491, Kenneth 491, Tamara 491
LUGENBILL, Linda 270, Carol 319, Carol 527, Christian 422, Dale 319, Judy 319, Kiersten 319, Lesley 319, Linda 424, Mark 319, Megan 319, Peter 319, Phillip 319, Seth 319
LUND, Coleen 518, Coleen 544, Connie 518, 544, Harry Burnett 518, 544, Janet 518, 544, Opal Justine 544
LUNZ, Eleanor 531, Herb 531
LUSHER, Carl 286, Carl 533, Colin 286, Sheryl 533
LUSK, Ann 443, Anna 443, Charles 45, Charles R. 443, James 443, Jaskie 443, John N. 443, John R. 443, Julia (Beeler) 443, Mary Jane 443, Rebecca 443, Robert 443, Robert W. 443
LUTHER, Albert 228
LUTTMAN, Alda 524, Mildred 524, Olin 524
LUTZ, C.M. 144, Christie 399, Doris 584
LYDY, Ellen 535, Kamilla 483, Paul 483, Richard 483, Rosco 463, Sandra 483
LYLE, Roxy 285, Bob 290, Chad Daniel 290
LYNCH, Anna 399, 502, Glen 502, Gregory Henry 586, Hattie 586, Henry 502, Homer 89, John 502, Mary 502, Norman 586, Ray 586, Roxy 502, Tom 502
LYNN, Sheri 150
LYONS, Almeda 582, Earl 582, Henry 455, Ira E. Dr. 264, Lesley 582, Roh 441
MACDONALD, Fernie Bell 519
MACIAS, Alexandria 418, Patti 418, Vanessa 418, Vincent III 418
MACK, Alexander 470
MACKALL, Barbara 485
MACKLIN, Alan 521, Betty Jane 521, Carl 521, Chris 444, Connie 521, Debra 521, Ermah E. 444, Frances 474, Helen 444, Howard Addie 444, J.C. 76, J. C. Rev. 13, Larry Lee 444, Ronnie 521, S. A. 92, 444, Staci 444, Wilma Thedore 444
MACKY, Ida 564
MACNAMARA, Avaline Probst 460, Thomas Henry 460, William 460
MACON, Perry 64
MACY, Jennie 548
MADDOX, Casey 302, 542, Chloe 245, Clara 469, Dawn 302, 542, John 302, 542, Jordan 302, 542, Marilyn 542, Michael 302, 469, Mitchell 302, 542, Sarah 469, W.R. 142
MADDUS, Maude Myrtle 320
MADDUX, Albert 444, Anna 444, Arthur 359, Bertha 444, Bertha Graden 565, Betty 566, Carolyn 444, Charles 367, 444, 565, Chester J. H. 444, Chester Jacob 444, Diana 284, Diana D. 445, Dorothy 367, 444, 565, Dwight 165, 444, Edna Faye 445, Edward 444, Edwin 444, Elizabeth 444, Emma Anna 525, Esther 444, Frederick 444, Gay Ann 445, Genelle 445, Harriette 445, Helen 444, Ida 444, Jacob 444, James Arthru 525, Jane 444, Jennie Kathryn 452, 525, 551, John 444, John N. 444, Kathy Jill 445, Lester 445, Lewearlie 525, Louise 444, Marilyn 367, 444, 478, Marjorie 445, Marna Nadine 445, Mary 444, 445, Mildred 444, Nathan Henry 445, Rachel 525, Rachel (McFarren) 359, Roselle 445, Ruth 445, William 444, William E. 444
MAGGARD, Arnold 87, Clyde 308, Eda Ellen 358, Judy Ann 308, Kathy 308, Kent 308, Lynn 308
MAGIN, Daniel 471, Dieter 471
MAGLEY, Conrad 263, Ellen Jane 263, George 144, Rosana (Betzberger) 263
MAGNUSON, Thomas 341
MAGOR, E. J. 98
MAGUIRE, Phoebe Jane 489
MAHAM, Susan 485
MAHENSMITH, Harold 292, Joan 337
MAHLIE, Rhonda 276
MAHNENSMIETH, Leilani 596
MAHNENSMITH, Carol 514, Carole 514, Hazel 604, Leona 156, Lillian 150, Patricia 426
MAHON, Christopher R. 428, Cory D. 428, David 428, Elizabeth A. 428, Loronda 428, Opal 563, S. T. Rev. 579
MAID, Cherokee 175
MAIN, Abbie 579, John A. 579, Linday 579, Mollie 579, Rebecca Thomas 579
MAISH, Lynn 247
MAITLEN, Karen 552
MAJORS, Delores 510, Ruby Ashley 510, Tommie 510
MAKOWSKI, Joel Patrick 573, Patricia Surfus 498, Patty 573
MALAN, Catherine 319
MALANEY, Dorothy 351
MALCARIDA, Mary Magdelene 375
MALCOLM, Zander 95, Zoe 155
MALEY, Jeffrey Lynn 260, Michael 260
MALLER, Joel 207, Levi 207
MALLERS, Jim 578, Pat 578
MALLORY, Carol 302, Kathy 570
MALMSTEN, Anna 273
MALONE, Bill 545, Harriett 545, Jade Marissa 545, Jeffery Lynn 545, Lisa 545, Lisa Marie 545, Sue 545
MALOTT, Frank 15
MALSON, Bertha Jean 273
MAN, Tran 97
MANES, C.E. 82, J.C. 82
MANGOLD, Anna Leman 409, Clarence 409, Ezra 409, Harley 409, Melba 409, Willis 409
MANIFOLD, Alice 462, Benjamin 462, Benjamin III 462, Benjamin Jr. 462, Edward 462, Elizabeth 462, George 462, Hannah 462, Henry 462, John 462, Joseph 462, Martha 462, Mary 462, Rachel 462, William 462
MANKEY, Bonnie 445, Bonnie 594, Carl 445, 594, Christian 445, Ervin 445, Forest 445, 594, Freda 445, Glen 445, 594, Harve 445, James 445, Laura 445, 594, Lester 445, 594, Mabel 445, Mary 445, Nettie Frauhiger 594, Patsy 445, Pearl 350, Ralph 445, 594, Sarah (Bridegan) 445, Susie 445, Violet 445, Walter 445, 594, Wesley 445
MANN, Anoli (Walters) 445, Ashley Lyn 601, Beth 445, Betty 182, Bill 210, 210, Bruce 445, Chip 324, Christie 248, Craig 144, Edith Adeline (Clark) 324, Eliza Jane 429, Elizabeth Lou 324, Frederick 445, Jani 601, Jon Harlo 445, Justin 429, Kami Jo 324, Katina Marie 445, Kelli Renee 324, Letha 511, Lisa , Lisa 506, Loren Lockhart 324, Lorim Jr. (Jake) 210, Lorin L. Sr. 210, Lorin Sr. 289, Lydia Fleming 429, Martha 289, Marvin Lee 445, Mervin 445, Neva Eileen 415, Rachel Ball (Reynolds) 429, Sandra Kay Nihiser 445, Shorty 390, Steven James 601, Tony 601, Velma (Grove) 60, William 429, William August 324, William August II 324, William II 210, Wilson 445
MANNING, Brenda Kay 446, Brenda Kay 446, Dorothy Ann 446, Douglas Keith 446, Joseph O. 446, Kenneth 446, Nancy Carol 446, Nina Hazel Edgerton 446
MANNIX, Frances 254, 255, James 255, Nellie Cole 255
MANRING, Annie Laura (Cross) 473, Harrie C. 391, Harry C. Hal"", Oma 473
MANULES, Herb 588
MAPLES, Helen Lorene 537
MARBACH, Florence 482
MARCY, Julia 80
MARKEL, Nancy 440, Paul 440
MARKER, Daniel Monroe 275, Mary Augusta (Haverfield) 275
MARKLEY, 66, Andrew 359, Anna Lou 533, Anna Louise 300, 571, Arthur Lawrence Street 446, Augusta 542, Benjamin 359, Charley Dennis 324, Clive 359, 554, Daniel F. 379, Debra Lyn 369, Derek 475, Dorothy 136, 359, Ed 586, Edna 542, Eunice 154, 200, Frank 291, G. F. 155, Gabriel 202, 324, 363, 379, 544, Gary 202, George 177, 542, Grace 379, Hannah Bell 363, Harold 542, Harriet E. Hattie"", Herman 542, Homer 140, 177, Homer Mrs. 140, James M. 533, Jerome 113, 359, Jesse 177, 542, Johnathon Rev. 469, Jonathan 324, 363, 544, Jonathan J. 121, Jonathan J. Rev. 88, Josephine Parintha 324, Kenneth W. 533, Kent 262, Lee 136, 581, Lewis 533, 571, Lillian 542, Louisa 572, M. Maxine 582, Maggie (Barthlemay) 581, Margaret (Dettinger) 345, Marie 345, Marie 372, Mary 152, Mary Alice 582, Mary Alice (Garrett) 581, Mary Ellen 542, Max 145, Maxine 581, Mildred 136, Mildred Inez 533, Minnie Myrtle 455, O.E. 102, O. P. 572, Oliver 113, 446, Oliver P. 300, . 571, Paul 359, 542, Phyllis Inez 533, Rachel 324, Ralph 177, 348, 581, Ralph E. 582, Rhoda 586, Richard Leon 475, Richard Lewis 533, Roderick D. 533, Ruth 285, Sarah 94, 258, Stella 446, 446, Theresa Dawn 496, Vernon 542, Wayne 369, William D. 345, Winnie (Baller) 369
MARKS, Alice Mae 332, Ken 140, Mary Elizabeth 284
MARQUART, Helen 489
MARSH, Anna 154, Fred 122, Glen 140, 380, 568, Jane 292, Laura V. 372
MARSHALL, Beverly 315, Fidella 446, 446, Homer 144, 475, Issac 474, James 446, Janet 270, John C. 298, Luetta 446, Matilda Ann 474, Orpha Armoninia 414, 446, Stella 446
MARTIN, Cleve"", 66, Alice Elene 257, 306, 447, Alvada 447, 448, Alvada Hope 449, Ambrose 518, Ardola Mae 557, Ben 45, Benjamin 534, Bessie 447, Blendene 447, 448, Brewster 448, Byrl 318, Carol 534, Carole 448, Carolyn 448, Cassandra 534, Charles E. 557, Christine 448, Clark 448, Cleve 448, Coleen (Denney) 318, Cosie 447, David Sr. 328, Daysha 362, Doris 333, Douglas 448, Duan 318, Dyrl 318, Elene 448, 449, Eric 448, Eulala 447, 448, Fred 447, 448, Galen 447, Galen 448, Galen C. 448, George 92, George Cleveland Cleve"", George Cleveland 448, Glen 534, Glenda 362, Gordon 448, Grant 448, H.L. 202, Herbert 447, Imogene 447, Jacob N. 485, Jacqueline 448, Jeanne 403, Jeffrey 362, Jesse 534, John 448, Juanita 447, Ken 447, Larry 447, Luke 318, Lydia 568, Marlene 447, Martha 518, Mary 448, Mary Jane 376, Mary Melinda 264, Minnie 448, 449, Minnie Frantz 448, Minnie Sarah (Frantz) 447, Mona Lee 318, Orlu (Lamhert) 448, Pauline 447, Rachael (Thrailkill) 448, Rae Jean 485, Raymond Guy 448, Rhonda 362, Richard O. 421, Robert A. 448, Ronald 447, Ruby 447, Ruth 579, Sarah 518, Scott 448, Sharon 299, Shirley 447, Sylvester 92, Talbert 318, Theora 447, 448, Vera 447, 448, W. C. 81
MARTS, Edward 234
MARTZ, Betty Ann 412, Bruce Wayne 412, Cheryl 449, Darla Kay 412, Edward 301, 449, Elma 347, 449, Ervin 412, Esther 449, Frances 449, George 412, Heather 449, Heidi 449, Keith 412, Kent 449, Linda 449, Louetta (Mock) 449, Marion 449, Mary 412, Nancy Lee 412, Robert 449, Ruth 449, Sheila D. 412, Ted 449, W. C. 449
MARTZ, Webster 449
MASHNI, Laila 549
MASON, Alice 449, Angie 249, Edward 449, Elizabeth 200, Marvel 518, 544, Marvel Louise 591, Mary 147, Richard 449, W. D. 147, 253, Wanda 249, Ward 145, Ward Leader 449
MASSON, Paul 304
MAST, Abraham 64, Albert 472, Barbara 313, James 313, Marcia 313, Marjorie 472
MASTERS, Brenda 357, 556, Susannia 465, Winifred 423
MASTERSON, 66, Abraham S. 404, Byrl 164, Carl Eugene 424, Catherine Hoover 266, Cheryl 424, Chloe 258, Dorothy 136, Frank 266, George 45, Hazel 258, Helen 519, Henry 432, Jennie 266, Joyce 419, Karen 424, Keith Alan 396, Kirk Alan 396, Linda 533, Mary 266, Mary Alice 258, Maude 258, Monna 424, 258, Shirley 424, Terry 533, William Henry 258
MASTIN, Cary May 398, Edward Olin 398, Mary Alma 398, Mary Elizabeth (Johnson) 398
MATHENY, Mary 603
MATHEW, Chrstine 500, Anthony 492, Claudia Lynn 518, Jack 518, Lillian (Lane) 518, Ronda Lee 259, 505
MATSON, Alma Hixon 450, Andrew 400, Audrey 189, 450, Christ 400, Clarence 400, Cora McLeed 450, Denial 271, 450, Dorothy 355, 450, Erk 400, Ernest 400, Eva 450, Foster 400, Frank 177, 189, 189, 286, 355, 450, Frank Mrs. 177, Frank Mrs. 189, Harriet 450, Homer 450, Ina Hollenbaugh 450, Irma 271, Irma Brinkman 450, James Finley 400, Jennie 599, Jessie 189, 450, Jessie Carlson 286, Jessie (Carlson) 355, Lehamey 400, Lena Henley 450, Margaret 271, 450, Marguerite 286, 450, Marguerite 533, Mary 450, Mary H. 555, Mary (Smith) 189, Maude Runyon 450, Merle 400,

Nancy 450, Nancy Cook 400, Rob 450, Robert 189, 450, Samuel 400, Werley 450
MATTAX, Phyllis 424
MATTHEWS, Mr. 18
MATTIS, Sarah Hanah 367, Sarah Hannah 366
MATTLOCK, William 13
MATTOX, Jane 287
MATZEN, Richard 146, Richard Mrs. 146, Richard N. 145
MAUK, Karen 314, Rachel 314, William 314
MAUPIN, E. J. Rev. 80, Sandra 290
MAURER, Barbara 553, Emma 335, Emma Nevada 334, Jeanne 270, Martha 579
MAUTE, Elizabeth 422, Martin 422, Mary E. Sauter 422
MAXWELL, Barry 277, Douglas 277, Hugh 277, Joshua Adam 599, Juanita 599, Lisa 249, Paula 531, Robert 151, 599, Ryan Robert 599, Sherri 277, Sue 525, William 249
MAY, Deborah 336, Grace Van Ella 433, Marjorie 403, Nelson 265
MAYER, Asa 450, Darrie 450, Deborah 267, Jerry 267, 450, 460, Pat 576, Polly Jean 450, Rhesse 450, Robert 267, 450, Ron 576, Royce 450, Sharon 450, Sheri 267
MAYHEW, Elise 299
MAYNARD, John 187
MAYNE, Ellen 152, Gloria 450, Gloria Jean (Gerwig) 355
MAYOCK, Peter 146, Peter Mrs. 146
MAZELIN, Kathryn Anna 283, Amy 415, Karin 415, Kimberly 415, Tami 415
MC AFEE, Hazel Augusta (McCleery) 404
MC CLEERY, John G. 404
MC DORMAN, Lucinda Harris 425
MC GRAW, Veronica 398
MC KEEFER, Helen 413
MC MILON, Joan 412
MC MURRAY, Elizabeth McCoy 402
MC PHEETERS, James 429
MCADAM, Arthur 527, Charles 527, Cora 527, Mable Allen 527, Rena 527
MCAFEE, Amanda , Amanda 450, 452, Amy 450, Andrew 288, Andrew Dean 533, Arlin K. 452, Arminda , Artie 516, Artie Raber 439, Bert 451, Betsy (Lesh) 451, Betty 525, Betty Irene 452, Beverly 455, Bonnie Lou 451, Bonnie Mae 452, Brenda Louise 452, Brent 450, Bruce 207, Calvin 451, Catherine , Cathy 525, Cathy May 452, Charles 450, 452, Chester 451, Clara 451, Clarence 318, 450, Clarence Jr. 450, Clarence Lloyd 450, Connie Sue 450, Coulson 562, Cressie 119, Cressie Irene 336, Darwin D. 525, Darwin Dwight 452, David 64, 378, Donald , Dorothy 439, Edna 64, Edna May 451, Elaine 450, Elizabeth , 232, 450, Elizabeth (Lesh) 364, Ernest , 439, 516, Etta 591, Florence 451, Frederick , George , Gladys , Gladys R. 297, 298, Harriet 155, 469, Harry , Hattie , Hazel A. , Hazel A. (McCleery) 298, Hazel (McCleery) 232, Helen , Isabelle , 64, Jack, Jacob 452, James , James McMullen , Jane , Jennie 451, Jo Ann 451, Johannes , John 317, 455, John Jr. . . , 232, 298, Joyce 450, Joyce Ann 582, Junior 450, 528, 581, Larry Lee 450, Laura May 451, Lewis 450, Lewis Dwight 452, Lillian 317, Linda 487, Lovie 450, Margaret 533, Marjorie 528, Marjorie (Geiger) 581, Marjorie Maxine 450, Marlene , Mary 451, 562, Maxine , Michael 452, 525, Michael Dee 452, Miriam Beverly , Mona Kay 451, Myrl 562, Nellie 451, Oliver Bert 336, Oscar Owen 452, Peter 451, Priscilla , Priscilla 364, Rela Kay 450, Roger 582, Roger Wayne 450, 581, Ryan Lewis 452, Sam 533, Samuel , Samuel 364, 450, 451, Samuel David 451, Sarah 562, Sarah Renee 452, Sharon 525, Sharon Kay 452, Stella Alice (Sheets) 336, Susanna , Troy 450, Troy Jacob 581, 582, Ulrich 450, 452, William 562, Winnie 378, Jr. Clarence 318
MCAHREN, Carol 464
McALHANEY, Ralph 68
MCANNISH, Gertrude 367
McARDLE, Donald 146, 216, Donald Mrs. 146, Lynda 523
McBARNES, Glennis 14
MCBRIDE, Almissa 280, 454, Almissa Michael 453, Benjamin Donald 453, Caley 315, Carolyn 152, Cedric 453, Cora (Prillman) 289, Darrell 453, David 264, 327, 453, 454, Don 264, 265, 453, 454, Donald 264, 328, 453, Dora 606, Douglas 328, 453, Fred 289, Freda 594, Gregory David 453, J.A. 137, . 214, J. L. 121, 264, . 328, 454, Jack 535, James 8, James Lowery 453, Johathan Michael 454, John 130, Joshua Bunn 453, Juanita 341, Judy 342, June 341, Kenny 342, Kirsten 454, Maggie 372, Martha Beth 535, Mary 281, 453, 454, Mary Lou 264, 453, 454, Maurice 264, 453, 454, Melba 25, 264, 328, 453, 454, Michael 453, Nicholas David 453, Philip 535, Robert 23, Robin 328, Roger 264, 453, 454, Roy 341, Theodore 373, Tim 454, Tina Michelle 453, Tonya Michelle 341, Trent Andrew 453, Tyson 315, Warren 8, Wilford 445, William 144, William David 453, Wm. C. 181
MCCAGUE, Andrew Commodore Perry 454, Carrie 289, Charles Hamilton 454, Elizabeth 454, Ellen 471, Ida Mae 454, James Francis 454, John Lafayette 454, Lorena 454, Margaret 454, Marion General 454, 547, Martha Alice 454, Mary Daine 454, Mary Ellen 454, Minnesota 454, Sadie Valzetta 454, William Frederick 454, William Hamilton 454
MCCAIG, Ellen 454
MCCALLISTER, Jack 429, Mark 429, Nancy 429
MCCAMMON, Anna Jane 479, Rene 399, Ted 399
MCCANCE, Katherine 314
MCCANN, Alice 283, 284
MCCARTHY, John 320, Albert 455, Anna Belle 455, Beverly 455, Forrest 455, Jonathan 455, Karla 455, Lane 455, Marjorie 455, Randall 455
MCCARTY, Charlie 232, Emma 462, Imogene 398, Judith Gay Vivian 262
MCCARVER, Angie 381
MCCLAIN, Abby Kristin 460, Angela 230, Francina 244, Joan 156, Joseph 244, Judith Ann (Keipper) 460, Judy 459, Lorie 251, 459, Lorie Lynn 460, Randy 459, 590, Rosa 304, William Allen 460
MCCLEERY, Adelia 375, Alice 455, Anna Irma Augusta 455, Charles Tinker 455, Cora Margaret 455, Dorothy Eliabeth 455, Elizabeth 455, Frank Harold 455, Hazel 320, Hazel A. , Hazel Augusta 455, Helen Justine 455, Hoover Ross 455, Idaline Jane 455, J.R. 202, 121, James 455, 455, James R. 153, James Ross 455, James Ross Jr. 455, Jane 136, 455, Jane Jenetta 455, John 455, John Everett 455, John G. , John Gutelius 455, John S. 455, Lucille 455, Lula Maude 455, Maggie 147, Mahala , Maria Elizabeth 455, Mary Alice 455, Matilda 455, Pauline 455, Ruth 455, Susan Catherine 455
MCCLELLAN, John 304
MCCLELLAND, Jamie 364, Rev. 82
MCCLENNY, Beverly 530, Carolina 530, Dean 530, Lena 530
McCLERRY, 66
MCCLINTIC, Jack 281
MCCLOUD, Edith 248, Edith Baker 113
MCCLURE, Arthur Burl 456, Belle 75, David B. 153, Eva 516, Fannie 372, Margaret Louise 456, Morgan 241, Orla 456, Ruth (Haflich) 378
MCCOLLEY, J.E. 82, Charlie 417, Frank 417, Melvin 417, Ralph 417
MCCONNEL, Ruth 334
MCCORD, Amy 456, Amy Jeanne 457, Dan 456, David 456, Eugene 6, 8, 162, 208, 456, 457, Eugene W. 456, Jeanne 456, 457, Jeanne Vivian 456, Jennifer 456, 457, John 456, Michael McCord 456, Susanna 456, 456
McCORKELL, J. E. 66
MCCORKLE, John 285
MCCORMICK, Aaron 457, April 457, Ashley 457, Beth 241, Chris 457, Cindy 457, Courtney 241, David 457, Debbie 457, Donna B. 385, 490, Doug 457, Frank R. 457, Herbert 457, 490, Herman 457, Howard 457, Janis Kay 457, John 527, Kelly 527, Kenneth 457, Loretta Kay 527, Melody 457, 490, Michael 457, 490, Michelle 490, Nancy 457, Nick 457, Robert 175, 527, Stephanie 457, Tammy 457, Taran 457, Tim 457, Travis 457
MCCRACKEN, Malinda 359
MCCRAIN, Charles 605
MCCRAY, Morris 145, 162, 187, 587
MCCREERY, Ann 275, Mary Jane 520, Robert H. 275, Sarah 275
MCCROY, Evelyn 115, Morris W. 181
MCCRUM, Mary 285
MCCULLICK, Emma 569
MCCULLOCH, Mary 462, 358
MCCUNE, Eileen 429
McCURDY, Viola 155
MCDANIEL, Alexander 238, Amos 238, Catherine 238, Elmer 243, Enid 266, Lewis A. 267, Mary A. 267, Elias 298, Elizabeth 285, Sarah Rupp 298
MCDANNEL/MCDANIEL, Josephine Lovely 298
MCDERMOTT, Andrew 331, W. M. 181
MCDONALD, Berta 595, Gelene 270, Ida Leulva 283, 284, 283, Jos. 121, Malinda 518, 544, Marguerita 200, William 102
MCDONNELL, Elizabeth 561
MCDORMAN, Loruhama 384
MCDOWELL, Albert 594, Bonnie 594, Frank 177, Frank 185, Nora B. 603
MCELHANEY, Elijah 557, Eulalia Lesh 59, Harry 107, Ida 557, Marion 107, Minnie Bundy 113, Ona 107
MCFADDEN, F.M. 121, John 202, Mrs. 75, Robert 15, 121
MCFARLAND, Karen Sue 513
MCFARREN, Amanda 497, Amanda 497, Amber 497, Amber 497, Bob 306, 522, Clarence Eugene 583, Connie J. 472, Connie Jo 553, 553, Connie Jo 583, Daniel 497, Della 284, Diana Kay 457, Earl 457, Earl R. 145, Earnest 284, Elizabeth 457, Emma R. 435, Esther 241, Flo 171, Flo 457, Francis Frank"", Francis 145, Frank 392, G.F. 121, Gary Lee 457, George 457, George A. 188, George E. 435, George F. 306, George Francis 457, Harold 497, Harriett 457, Harry 522, Harry A. 171, 178, Harry Arthur 457, Harry Arthur Jr. 457, Jack 497, Jacob 457, 522, Joan 497, John 16, 457, Joseph Madison 457, Judith Ann 457, Marcelle 553, Marion 165, Martha 457, Martha Ann 457, Mary Lou 457, Michael 497, Mildred 284, Morris 457, Norm 588, Pauline 457, Rachel 522, 525, Ralph 165, Rhonda 457, Robert 102, Robert A. 472, Robert Keith 553, 583, Robert William 457, Robert William II 457, Roma 154, Roma Evelyn 457, Sarah 522, Sarah Elizabeth 306, Sharon 333, 497, Sue Ann 457, Tillie Henneford 457, Winnietta May 457
MCGAHEY, James 489, Laura B. 489
MCGAUGHY, M. Suzanne 568, Mary Suzanne 250
MCGEATH, James 240, Pierce 240, Retta 240, 385
MCGEE, Millie M. 492
MCGILL, Rose 595
MCGLEN, Meta 526
MCGRAY, Rachel 519
MCGREAVY, Brian 267
McGREGOR, D. R. 81
MCGREW, Alice 455
MCGUFFEY, Lillian 387, Paul 228, 387
MCGUFFIE, Eleanor 349
MCGUIRE, Lydia 411, 411
MCINTIRE, Catherine 309, Charles 458, Dick 458, 502, Dorcas 309, 502, Dwight 268, Elizabeth 393, Emily 546, Eve 458, Floy 546, Harrison 309, 502, June R. 502, Lester 268, Lois M. 502, Mary 309, Nora 358, Nun 458, 502, Phanuel 433, Sara Jane 502, Thomas 458, Turner 502, William 309, 502
MCINTOSH, Caroline 585, Frances 533, George 533, George Junior 533, Hazel 533, Heather 533, Lesli 533
MCKAIG, Andrew Jackson 454, Annabelle 454, Elizabeth 454, Ellinor 454, James Fremont 454, John 454, John Holmes 454, Lucinda 454, Mary Jane 454, Rebecca 454
MCKAY, Hazel (Custard) 304, O. R. 81
McKEE, 66, Christopher Erin 581, Ellen 266, Jerry 234, Michele Evangeline 581
MCKENZIE, Debra 513, Durrell LeRoy 513, Kathleen 513, Shari Elizabeth 513
MCKEONE, Cory 307, Pat 307, 581, Charles 82
MCKIERNAN, Thomas 216
MCKIMMEY, Florence 515
MCKINLEY, George Rev. 101, Ada 459, Beatrice Bell 458, Bessie Cotton 585, Bill 304, Carol 304, 459, Charles Wesley 459, Clara (Clovie) 459, Daniel 585, Daniel Frederick 459, Dawn 585, Dawn Marie 459, Debra 585, Donna 459, Donna Elaine 585, Douglas 585, Douglas William (Doug) 459, Edward S. 459, Frederick Eugene 304, 458, 459, 585, George Thomas (Jerry) 458, Hamer 298, 458, 459, 585, Hannah Russell 459, Harriet 152, J.W. 214, James W. (Doc) 459, James William 458, John Wayne 458, Karen Marie 459, Kathleen 304, 459, Kathleen Marcelle 585, Kenneth 459, Kenneth Eugene 585, Kimberly 585, Martha Esther 458, Martha Wilson 458, Micahel 585, Phyllis Carol 585, Robert 585, Robert Leland 458, Roger 304, 459, Roger Wayne 585, Ruth 458, Thomas 458, Thomas Forseith 459, Thomas William 585, Thomas William (Bill) 459, William 459
MCKINNON/FLEMING, Diannah 298
McKNIGHT, James 98
MCKURAS, Barbara Jean (Johnson) 459, Genieve 238, Harley 238, Harley 415, Harley Leo 459, Hugh 459, Isabelle (Suters) 459, Julie Ann (Fritz) 459, Kate (Lewis) 459, Leo 238, 459, Leonidas 459, Margaret Ann 459, Megan Elizabeth 459, Michael 415, Michael Edward 459, Murray 238, 459, Nellie (Abbott) 459, Sean Michael 459, Wanda 238, William Hugh 459
MCLAIN, J.E. 39, Rachel 561, Roseta 335
MCLAUGHLIN, E. Wayne 84, Myrtle 519, Patricia 154
McLEAN, Eulala 44, Eulala 448, Robert 448
MCLIN, J.C. Rev. 86
McMAHON, J. H. 98
MCMCLAIN, Randy Alan 460, Aaron Josiah 460, Bonita Kay 460, Boyd 460, Chad 531, Cherry Sue 460, 569, Claire 248, Claire T. 249, 304, . 459, Clarice 248, 282, Clarice K. 304, . 459, Claude B. 249, 459, Claude Banter 460, Colleen 450, 460, 569, Colleen 595, Daily Mae 460, Everett 450, 460, 569, 595, Everett Edward 460, Frances D. 459, Gaye 531, Ginger Lou 460, J. Paul 249, J. Robert 459, James Paul 460, James R. 459, Jane 459, Janice 459, 460, Jennifer R. 459, Jeremey 459, Joetta Fay 460, John 249, John James 459, Joseph R. 459, Judy 459, Julia 460, Julie 459, Kelly Ann 460, Kristi 248, Kristi L. 304, 459, Paul 459, Paul C. 459, Paul Chadler 460, Polly Jean 450, 460, Randal Wayne 460, 460, Rebecca Rose 460, Sharon 6, 142, Sharon 248, Sharon K. (Baker) 248, Trudy 595, 595, Trudy Ann 460, Zada E. 459, Zoda Elizabeth (Banter) 460
MCMILLEN, Dale W. 593, John Peter 593, Megan 593, Monica 593, Terry 593, Virginia 570, Walter L. 570
MCMULLIN, Catherine 584
MCNABB, James 328, Lillie 328, Manley 328, Mary 328, William 328
MCNAMARA, Leslie Marie 460, Tamara Sue 460, Teresa Marie 460, 461, Timothy Michael 460, William Carr Whitehead 460, Jr. Thomas Henry 460
McNARY, J. H. 98
MCNATT, Jane 428, Sarah Ann 477
MCNEAL, Nellie 280, Nellie Bunn 365, Tom 280
McNOWN, Grace 136
MEAD, C. H. 200, C. H. 573, C.S. 214, Clarence 9, 146, Clarence S. Dr. 269, Elizabeth 386
MEADE, Alvis 239, Alvis 460, Arnet 239, 460, Dorothy 460, Elizabeth (Addington) 405, Emily 239, 460, Franklin 175, Greg 460, Harry 102, 102, 239, 460, Keith 460, Marilyn 137, Mary 405, 460, Mary Elizabeth 460, Mike 460, Tim 460, Velma 460, Vera 460, William Patton 239, 405, 460
MEADOWS, Camille 597, Clo 15
MECHLING, Brandon 497, Brent 497, Carolyn 497, Heidi 497, LeaAnn 497, Lora 246, Misty 497, Tom 497
MECKSTROTH, Herbert 68, Herbert H. Rev. 350
MEDCHEIMER, C. T. 20
MEEHAN, JoAnn 379
MEEK, David 204, Deborah 330, Deborah Eileen 247, Peg 204
MEEKS, Bill 166, Carol 154, 533, Cynthia 142, Edna 533, Effie 335, John 533, Linda 533, Marilyn 533, Marion 233, 533, Michael 533, Pam 533, Richard 533, Sara Jane 272, Wendy 414
MEIER, Christa 583, Donald 287, Marie Christine 344
MEISCH, Heather L. 377, Linda 377, Linda Eileen 320, Thomas 377, Thomas Marvel 320
MEISTER, Robin 534, Rustin 534, Ryan 534, Sharon 534
MEJIA, Janet J. 412
MELCHING, Brett 472, Deana 472, Elsie 596, Ethel 402, Isaiah 45, Koons 596, Roseanna 431, Shelby 472, Susan 569, Theo 430, 431
MELDORF, 179
MELICK, Fred 20, H. C. 98, Kristy 489, Robert 111
MELLENGER, Maria Amanda 439
MELLING, George 567, William 13, 76
MELLODY, Hawthorn 168
MELSHEIMER, C. T. 317, Dr. 455
MELTON, Aaron 461, Alvy 461, Casey Austin 460, 461, Christopher J. 485, Dawn Marie 485, Dorothy 489, Dustin Lee 460, 461, Edna 461, Estaleen 485, Faun C. 485, James Marvin 461, Joe 461, John 485, John Mitchell 461, Kamie Sue 485, Larry Eugene 461, Lawrence Joe"", Linda Lou 461, Loretta 461, Marcia J. 485, Max Allen 485, Melvin F. 485, Pearl 485, Petty Ann 461, Rancie 461, Randy Lee 460, 461, Shawn Patrick 485, Shelby Clyde 485, Sonja Sue 461, Tarry H. 461, Tiffany 461, Vernon 102, 461, Vernon C. 442
MENDENHALL, 66, Addie 279, Alice 532, Benjamin 428, Bill 461, Catherine 550, Catherine Wagner 462, Della Mae 550, Eli 461, Eli 462, 550, Faith Maxine 462, Frances 291, H. Mary 288, Harry 462, Harry E. 462, Hilda Mary 461, Hope Elizabeth 462, Joseph W. 461, Lena (Jacob) 292, Lena R. 461, Margery 428, Mary Ann 243, Mary Catherine 461, Mordecai 462, Susan 428, Thomas 462, Tottie 462, Vera Frances 461, William 292, William Joseph 461
MENDETH, Charley 285
MENKE, Danny Jo 306, David Edward 306, Don 306
MENTZER, Nathaniel 523, Rosetta 523, Steven 471, 489, Steven Jr. 489, Theresa 471, Tonya 471, 489, Jr. Steven 471
MEO, Anne Colson 293, Kristen 293, Nicholas Rae 293
MERCER, Fielding L. 178
MERCHANT, Alice 462, Andrew 462, Carolina 530, Christopher 462, Don 37, Elanore 462, Frances 462, James 462, Jeanett 462, John 462, Joyce 462, Kendra 462, Laura 462, Lena 530, Lewis 462, Margaret 462, Mary 462, Raymond 462, Rhea 462, Robert 462, Ronnie 530, Ruth 462, Shirley 474, Sue 462, Warren 462, William 462, Woodrow 462, Zina 417
MEREDITH, Selena 415
MERIKY, Walter 588
MERKEY, Charles 102, John 283, John 284, Levi 102, 503, Lydia Ellen (Houtz) 503, Peter Sr. 503, Sarah (Sloan) 503
MERKLE, George 146, George Mrs. 146
MERLEY, Anna 251
MERRIMAN, 66, Adelia 526, Art 447, Beth 492, Don 582, Eliza 477, Emery 122, John 13, 76, Lona 522, Randy 492, Selurious 526, Shanon 492, Tony 492, Wahilla 526, Waneita 526, William 112
MERRIMANN, Dorothy 600, Earl 600, Ethel 600
MERRITT, Alice (Habig) 393, Clarissa 432, Ed 352, Gary 151
MERRYMAN, George 314, Sharon Sherry""
MERTZ, Aileen 446, Aileen 446, Alleen Johnson 414, Mary 606, Maxine 364, 364, Wanda 390, William 367
MESCHBERGER, Harold 476, Josephine 476, Mildred 476, Nathan 476, Ocie 476
MESSICK, Coleen 485, Harold 417
MESSINGER, N. Venita 269
METCALF, Brian Alan 270, David 270, Kimberly Sue 270
METTLER, Michael 339, Robert 140, 144
METTS, Fred 144, Fred 214, Mabel 402
METZ, Diann 316, John L. 145, Judy 299, Mary Anne 382, Thomas 316, Thomas Lee 247
METZGER, Aldine 570, Anthony 570, Nancy 570, Polly 570
MEYER, Aaron G. 464, Adam 463, 463, 570, Adella 464, Albert 252, Albert 464, Alton 464, Alvie 463, Alvin 463, 482, 483, Amanda 463, Amelia 463, Angela 463, 483, Bertha 464, Bertha Mae 570, Bruce 324, 464, Caroline 441, Caroline Saxman 463, Carolyn 487, Carolyn Irene 487, Cecily 487, Chad 464, Charles 463, 463, Chris 463, Christian 464, Christina 463, 483, Cindy 483, Corinne M. 464, Darmoris 463, David 145, 167, 216, 335, 464, Don 464, Doris 463, Doris Ann 483, Dorothy 463, Edwin 368, Eleanor 483, Elizabeth 463, 464, Emma 474, Ernest 73, Ernst 463, Fannie 463, Franie 463, Fred 463, George 463, Grant 464, Greg 324, Gregory 464, Harold 324, Harold R. 464, Helen 464, Henry 463, 570, Ida 463, 464, Irene 483, J. Frank 200, Jacob 463, J 464, Jacqueline Michelle 247, Jakob 464, Jane 485, Javit 463, Jeanne 464, Jessica 350, 463, Joe 464, Johathan 487, John 463, J 487, John E. 335, . 464, John H. 464, John Jr. 464, John Sr. 464, Joney 464, Jorn 463, Joseph 464, Joshua 350, 463, Joyce 487, Justine 184, Karen 335, 443, 464, 487, Kelli 463, Kenneth 463, 464, 483, Kent 350, 463, Kristen 483, Kristie 487, Laura 464, 483, Laura M. 464, Lester 25, Lester 463, Lewis 463, Lillian M. 464, Lona 375, 487, Lou 463, Luara 464, Lucy 570, Mable C. 184, Mahilda 463, Margaret 464, Margaret (Engeler) 335, Marian 464, Marie 463, Mark 487, Marvin G. 463, Mary 463, Melody 464, Michael 376, Michelle 376, 487, Mike 464, Minnie 463, Minnie 482, Misty 463, Misty 483, Nicholas 376, Nina Jane 154, Nina Jane 464, Obed 463, 464, Oliver 464, Orel 464, Orlando 464, Pamela 463, 483, Patricia 483, Peter 68, 442, Peter II 464, Randy 324, Randy 464, Raymond E. 335, . 464, Reuben C. 184, Rhonda 463, 483, Robert 216, 464, Rodney 324, 464, Ronald 221, Ruth Rosanna 464, Sandra 463, 483, Sanford 463, 483, Sara 464, Sarah 464, Sheldon 463, 483, Shelley 463, 483, Sherry 463, 483, Sophia 463, Stanley 483, Stella 463, Stephanie 487, Sylvia 463, Theodore 463, Timothy 463, 483, Troy 376, Vickie 340, 487, Wilbur 463, Wilbur 483, Wilhelmina Minnie"", William 463
MEYERS, Bertha 606, Caroline 284, 440, Christine Wilhelmine 482, Cleophas 107, Debra 466, Dorothy 239, Ella 508, Emma 602, Lucy 109, Lydia 323, Mary 299, Ruth 185
MICHAEL, DiAnne 346, Hannah 294, Jonathan 328, Larry 346, Norma 346, Raymond 524
MICHAELS, Jay 121, Joyce 287, Maryanne 426, Sarah Bell 575
MICHAUD, Albert 574, Christina Verdith 574, Estella (Sackett) 574
MICHEAL , 66, Iris 517
MICHEL, James 597, Janet 597, Janet Ruth 597, Ruth Irene 597, Ted 597
MICHLITSCH, Albert 512, Frank 512, John 512, Joseph 512, Katrina Poje 512, Louis 512, Mary 512, Max 512, Raymond 512, Robert 512, Rose 512, Sophia 512
MICK, Jane 584, Rick 584
MICKINNEY, Willard 320

MICKLEY, Jennifer 370
MICKLITSCH, Angela Ruth 512, Frank 512, Jan Carla 512, John 115, John 512, Jon Joseph 512, Mary Jesselnick 512, Ruth 115, Ruth Porter 512, Terra Angela 512
MIDDAUGH, Ernest 58, Jacob 542, Jill 542, Mark 542, Megan 542, Pauline 447
MIDDLETON, Beatrice 287, Charles Newt"", Floyd 463, Louise 463, Ruth 463, Susette 463
MILBY, Judith Ann 570
MILES, Charles 286, Hazel 507
MILHOLLAND, Edith 605, Elizabeth Barthlemay 488, Eric 529, George 488, Grace 488, Steve 357
MILIKEN, James 600, Mary Sarah 600
MILL, Gwen 591
MILLER, Abigail Helene 328, Abraham 540, Ada 468, Ada 568, Adam 465, Adam Paul 347, Agnes 142, Albert 466, Alden Frederick 465, Alden Frederick, Jr. 465, Alfred 594, Alton Don 469, Amanda 469, Amanda M. 471, Amanda Marguerite 347, Amy Christine 328, Andrea 466, Andrew 469, 471, Andrew Emery 328, Angela Kay 343, Anna 489, Annie 575, Arthur Gene 469, Barbara 258, 367, 424, Beatrice June 469, Belle 575, Ben 490, Benjamin 273, 378, Benjamin Thomas 467, Bernice 594, 594, Bertha 471, 542, Betty 318, Billy 66, Blanche 466, Brett Alan 470, Brian 268, Bruce 145, Bruce W. 595, Bryan Douglas 465, Carl R. 375, Carolyn 411, 426, 480, 508, Catharine 465, Catherine 468, Catherine Lynette 469, Charles 95, 471, Charley 466, 470, Chauncey 575, Chester A. 466, Christena 540, Christina 468, Christy 471, Clara 468, Clarence 568, Clarissa 466, 470, Clifford 466, Cora 594, Coralee 268, Crystal 468, Curtis Dean 343, Daniel J. 575, Deb 204, Dessie 575, DeWayne 471, Diana 429, 480, Diana Carol 468, Diane 467, Doc 137, Donald Lee 573, Dora 466, 468, Dora 514, Doris 567, Doris Ann 469, 517, 600, Duane 200, Dwight 467, Eddie 82, Eileen 266, Elaine 466, 471, Elaine 489, Eliza 540, Elizabeth 386, 468, 471, Elizabeth 562, Elsie (Hethcote) 466, Emma 517, Emma Marie 469, Ervin 468, Erwin C. Jr. 343, Ethel 469, Etta 550, Etta (Springer) 469, Fabiana Cathryn 465, Ferris 58, Florence 401, Floyd 466, 470, Floyd G. 573, Frances Rose 259, Francina Morris 471, Franklin 579, Fred 250, Fred Jr. 268, Frederick 465, Frederick Nelson 465, Fuhrman 89, G.W. 78, Gail 154, Gale Eldon 467, Garnet 575, Gayle Elizabeth 467, George 78, George E. 471, George Edward 424, George W. 465, Gerald 96, 204, 228, Gerald L. 467, Girard 416, Glenna 468, Guy 328, Hazel 466, Hazel 470, Hazel 575, Helen 136, 465, Helen (Gregg) 372, Helen Viola 471, Henrietta 342, Henry 18, 379, H 386, 468, 517, 575, Henry Clay 466, Henry G. 471, Herman 301, 489, Herman L. G. 343, 368, Hermina 468, Holliayn Mayhew 469, Hollis (Schwartz) 328, Homer 466, 470, Howard 480, Huldy 447, Ida 466, 592, Ida E. 465, Ida Elsie 471, I 498, Ina Marie 467, Isaac Otto 400, Issac 469, Iva (Palmer) 575, Ivah 535, J. B. 270, J.S. 58, J. U. 81, Jacob 18, 89, 112, 259, 367, 464, 468, 471, 575, James 471, James Eric 470, James L. 408, Jan L. 408, Jana Lynette 465, Janene 150, Jason 466, Jeffrey P. <J.P.> 328, Jennifer 329, Jess 78, Jess 107, Jodi 471, John 367, 468, 468, 471, 540, 550, John B. 550, John B. Jr. 579, John Bender 579, John Calvin 579, John D. 465, John D. Dr. 470, John Edward 401, 470, John Gregory 465, John Michael 366, J 367, 468, John William 465, Jon 378, Jon 490, Jonathan Norman 467, Joy Nichole 468, Joyce Marie 374, J 469, 517, Judy (Garrison) 328, Julia Ann 343, Karen Joan 469, Karl 328, Kathleen June 343, Kathryn 343, Katie Alice 465, Kent 471, Kerry Wayne 468, Kimberly 378, 490, Kimberly Kai 467, Kimberly R. 466, Kit Carson 469, Kristy Lyn 343, Lanette 467, Larry 480, Laura Ellen 471, Laura Jean 468, Laverne 471, Lee Thomas 469, Lela 550, Lemuel 258, 562, Lemuel Walter 465, Lewis Elmer 471, Lillian 466, Lisa 466, Lizzie 64, Loma Luella 469, Loretta H. (Jarrett) 575, Lorraine 333, 467, Louis Ellis 471, Louisa Jane 465, Louise 318, Louise Jane 411, Lucille 467, Lucinda 367, 468, 471, Lulu 465, 602, Mabel 573, Mabeline 550, Mae 466, Magdalena 367, Marceille 550, Margaret 304, 469, Margaret 550, Mariah 553, Mar-an Eloise 557, Marilyn Gaiser 347, Marion Ralph 466, Marjorie Jean 489, Mark Evan 468, Marlis 467, 467, Martha 469, Martha Ann 457, Mary 204, 256, 285, 367, 445, 466, 507, 540, 550, Mary A. 332, Mary Alice 595, Mary Ann 469, Mary E. 469, Mary Etta 579, Mary Evelyn 467, Mary L. 579, Mary Louise 305, Mary Luella 469, Mary Marie 573, Mary (Mishler) 467, Maud 64, Maxine (Motz) 466, Meda (Peck) 393, Merril J. 356, 469, Meta 465, Michael 89, 367, Michael Wayne 468, Mike 142, 529, Minnie 471, Mira M. 575, Mollie 455, Myrl 64, 562, Myrtle 468, Myrtle (French) 401, Nancy 466, 575, Naomi 161, 550, Nathan 471, Nathaniel 598, Nellie 480, Nicholas 595, Nicole 598, Noah 144, Noah 367, Norma 599, Norman 378, 467, Norman L. 490, Ocea 466, Ocie 470, Oliver 575, Patricia Dawn 469, Patty Lou 469, 517, Paul G. 347, Pauline Valentine 585, Perry J. 467, Peter 553, Phyllis Jean 424, Rachel Rodgers 471, Ralph T. 466, Rebecca 540, Regina 461, Reuben 371, 466, 468, 470, Richard 567, Robert Bud"", Robert 517, Robert Duane 343, Robert Neal 469, Roger 471, Rosalie Ann 343, Rosella 459, Rosemary 471, Rosina Graft 343, Roy Jacob 467, 469, Ruby 239, Ruby C. 465, Russell P. 466, Ruth 445, 465, Ryan 408, Sabrina 461, Sadie 471, 575, Sally Jo 469, Samuel E. 575, Sarah 367, 390, 468, 469, Sarah Elizabeth 465, Sarah Emily 465, Shari 467, 467, Shawn David Miller 469, Shirley J. 466, Shirley Jean 468, Stephen 467, 467, Steve 598, Stuart 466, Susan 64, 257, 465, 550, Susannah 465, Suzanna Noel 469, Sylvester 113, 471, Tabitha 268, Tammi 598, Taryn 598, Teresa 543, Terry 480, Treva (Sharp) 155, Velma 344, Velma W. 343, Vera Corinne 466, Vernon 465, Vickie 490, Vicky 467, Walter 283, 466, Wes 190, Wesley 468, Wess 493, Willard 602, Willard Jr. 602, William 466, 469, 470, 471, 550, 579, William Beryl 575, William H. 471, 498, William Mertz 468, Wilma 468, 493, Winifred 535
MILLIGAN, Dean 216, Dean E. 145, Roberta 437, W.V. 58
MILLIKEN, Jane Sara 512, Mary Ann 365, Sam 114, 512
MILLS, Barber 21, Beth 575, David Anthony 467, 575, Eva 604, Evelyn 271, Jessie 544, Joe 577, Karissa Michelle 467, 575, Karrisso 429, Marion 304, Mary Elizabeth 575, Michelle 575, Michelle Lynn 467, Nicki 575, Paul 262, 575, Sarah 374, Scotty 168, Tony 429, 575, William 544
MILLTER, Gerald 130
MINCE, Maria 564
MINCH, George 416
MINEGAR, Ava Jean 496
MINGER, Aaron 570, Edith (Mallonee) 290, Emma 570, Jay 290, Lela Kathryn 290, Nettie 570, Rose 434
MINGLE, Etta 462
MINN, Loren B. 13
MINNICH, 66, Andrew 444, Berteen 542, 568, Catherine 302, 542, Chester Wayne 478, Clara Irene 478, Clarence Earl 478, Cynthia 444, 478, Don 496, Edith 542, Ethel 500, Ethel Mae 478, Ethel Mowery 444, Floyd 444, Floyd LaVerne 478, Harold Amos 478, Hugh 478, Jane 500, Jennifer 444, Jennifer Lynn 339, Joe 478, John 542, John Ervin 478, Joseph 444, Joseph Scott 339, Kim 444, 478, Kim Denise 339, Lois 542, Lori 444, 478, Lucrecia 478, Margaret 542, Marilyn 6, 367, 444, 478, Marjorie 478, Martha Annie 478, Mary 496, 561, Mary Elizabeth 478, Mary Jane 478, 500, Maud Shadle 496, Megan 444, Mildred 478, Nancy 542, Nancy Gump 444, Nancy Manerva Gump 478, Nicolas 444, Ora J. 478, Oscar 444, Oscar 500, Oscar Earl 478, Ralph 542, Robert 542, Roger 542, Sally 385, Samuel 444, 478, Scott 444, Scott Richard 339, Sylvia Pearl 435, Tim 478, Timothy 444, Vera 542, Vera Mae 294, Viola 435, William 435
MINNIEAR, Albert 271, Albert 567, Bea 9, Bertha 567, Blanche 472, Clarence 567, Clarence Hampton 271, Clayton 134, Doris Marie 271, Ernest 567, Harry 472, L.A. 113, Lloyd 567, Phyllis Dene 271, Vaughn 567, Viola (Clark) 291, Viola Perlina Clark 271, Violet 293
MINSTERMAN, Louis 68
MINTON, Elmer 592, Russ 598
MISER, Roxianne 150
MISHLER, Emily 472, Harold 82, John 467, Ruth (Dintaman) 467, Winfred 472
MITCHEL, Patricia 403
MITCHELL, Anne Marie 365, Gerald 295, John 504, Kathleen Ann 504, Linda Kay 392, Lois Clare Henley 391, 392, Mary 152, Mary 362, 585, Matthew 383, Noble 537, Ruth Lucile 392, Susan 392
MITKO, Tonya Sue 490
MITTLESTADT, Bruce 440, Charlotte 440, Alfred 372, Alfred E. 472, Christa 583, Christina M. 472, Christina Marie 553, 583, Connie Jo 553, 583, Connie Sue 583, Donald 372, Donald Lee 472, 553, 583, James 372, James G. 472, Laura K. 472, Lesia A. 472, Lesia Ann 553, 583, Matt L. 472, Matthew Lee 553, 583, Michael Joe 553, Michael Joe 583, Mike 472, Patrick W. 472, Robert Allen 553, 583, Steven 472, Steven Allen 583, Yvonne Bonnie"", Yvonne M. 472
MOCK, Carol 340, Carol 487, Charles 243, Emsley 586, Emsley 587, George, Jenny 243, John 202, L. Farrell 146, L. Mrs. 146, Levi 202, Levi 586, Nettie 433, 486, Ruth 586, Ruth (Watson) 587, Timothy N. 145
MOELLER, Ester 567
MOESBERGER, Nathan 475, Deanna 466, James D. 466, John 68, Lottie 367, Olin 466, Shirley J. 466
MOFFETT, Mary Catherine 358
MOFFITT, Walter 563
MOHLER, Harriett 466, M. R. 96, Robert 202
MOHLOR, M. R. 64
MONCE, Jack 17, Joe 524, John 524, Larry 524
MONGER, Cathryn 136, Edith Waugh 398, Robert Halsey 398, Willmina 398
MONROE, Charlotte 392, Ella 593, Esther 362, Frank 456, Rebecca 317, Stella 189
MONTGOMERY, Isabell 285, Nettie Gertrude 598, William 112
MONTICUE, Brandon Michael 488, Cheryl 488, Gene 488, James 488, Michael Alan 488, Nellie (Shaw) 488, Ralph 488
MOOMAW, Earl 127
MOON, Daniel 309, Gerald 144, Jane 309, Jasper 309, Jesse 309, John 309, Joseph 309, Samuel 309, W. G. 75, William 309
MOORE, Aaron 76, Aaron 529, Aaron Cornelius 472, Alice (Schlagenhauf) 394, Alice Schlagenhauf 394, Angela 275, Angela 519, Annabelle 454, Arvilla 472, Betty 472, Cleora 529, Cleora Isabelle Russell 472, David 145, Deane 472, 529, Dick 472, Don 472, Dorothea 472, Elizabeth 454, Elizabeth (Kelly) 383, Emily 472, Emma 387, Esther Smith 472, Fayette Pearl 475, Forrest 472, Gary Wayne 320, George Kenneth 472, Gertie 529, Gertie Jones 472, Harrison 454, Herman Crockett 320, Howard 472, Jean 472, Jeniffer Rene 320, Jim 472, Jo Ann 472, Jody 246, Joe 140, 529, John 403, Jordan Louise 472, Joseph B. 383, Joseph K. 472, Joseph Kelly 472, Joyce 353, Kelly 472, 529, Kenneth 472, 529, Kenny 207, Lena 472, Marjorie 472, Mary Jane 454, Matilda 391, Melissa Suzanne 320, Michelle 472, Mike 79, 79, Minnie 472, Norma 472, Paula Jacobs 448, Paulette 570, Phyllis 529, Ruth 472, Scott Joseph 472, Susannah 239, William P. 454
MOORMAN, Rosalie 299, Rosalie 385
MORAND, Lena 472
MOREHOUSE, Diana 324, Georgina 324, Glen 324
MORELAND, Carrie 479, Jonathan 479, Paul 479, Rachel 559
MORENCE, Brande St. John 412, Christopher Robin 412, Debra Kaye 412
MORFORD, Ralph 433
MORGAN, Charles H. 555, Glen 393, Jerome David 393, John 153, Leona 347, Mary 555, Max 98, Max (Rev.) 301, Melissa Sue 393, Naomi 555, Olive Elizabeth 413, Rita Kellogg 596, Sandra 299, Virgil 490
MORMON, Martha 120
MORRIS, A.G. 127, Aaron 415, Amer 508, Austin Mitchell 330, Blanche 472, David 373, Douglas Shawn 373, Effa (Jones) 472, Eleanor J. 603, Elizabeth 558, Elizabeth Hardesty 558, Elmer E. 472, Evelyn 463, Fay 472, Flo 457, Flora 429, Frank 373, Frank 463, George 178, 214, 350, George S. 145, Guy 514, Guy Jones 472, Hannah 443, 443, Howard M. 373, Ida 590, Ida I. 373, J. D. 415, Jack 577, Jack H. 373, James D. 603, Jane Kay 373, Janet 514, Janet Marie 472, Jerry Lou 373, John 373, John A. 171, 178, Joshua 415, Judith 260, Kami 351, Kami Jo 247, 330, Kathryn 373, Kevin Richard 247, 330, Lee Anna 388, Lilie L. 250, Lillian 577, Lochia A. (Taylor) 373, Lurana Catherine 560, Marilyn Joan 330, Marion 373, Maro 311, Martha 514, May 255, Mitchell 558, Pamela Kay 415, Rachel 163, Richard 463, Richard Allen 247, 330, Toni 309, William 163
MORRISEY, Patricia Jane Durdahl 513, Tommy 317
MORRISON, Alvie 427, B. Y. 175, Cliff 376, Dr. 18, E. 60, Ethel 427, John 427, Leander 421, Lee Stanley 427, M. S. 64, Ned 427
MORRISSEY, Ann Louise 473, Carolyn Jane 473, Dale 473, Evelyn Deane 473, Harold Francis 473, James Kenneth 473, Janet M. 377, Janet Marie 473, Jill 473, Marcille 156, 473, Matthew 377, 473, Michael D. 377, Michael David 473, Nancy E. 377, Nancy Elizabeth 473, Nichole 377, Nicole 473, Patrick D. 377, Patrick Donald 473, R. Dale 377, Robert Dale 473, Thomas Michael 473
MORROW, Mary Jane 266, Ralph 216
MORSE, Catherine Maria 581, David Anthony 581, Kevin David 581, Rebecca Joan 581
MORTON, Benjamin H. 473, Benjamin H. 473, Benjamin M. 473, 473, Benjamin Monroe 473, Dorothy Ann 416, Geraldine Geri"", Jane 473, John 473, Kelly 473, LeAnn 473, Lisa 473, Luanne K. 473, Marshall E. 473, Marylee 473, May 597, Mildred 473, Oma 473, Oma A. (Manring) 473, Rosa Marie (Dupont) 473, Stanley M. 473, Stanley Manring 473, Thomas J. 473, Warren 132, Warren H. 473
MORYERS, Sarah Jane 508
MOSBARGER, Ruth 558
MOSER, Aaron 506, Adella 464, Aldine (Lkopfenstein) 506, Alicia 483, Audrey 239, Benedict 322, Bert 390, 506, Bertha 354, Cathy Sue 419, Chris Alan 419, Cleo 476, Daniel 230, 366, 440, 230, 476, Dennis 140, 355, Dina 230, Doris 355, Drake 474, 521, Ed 192, Edna Lucille 521, Edna (Reinahrd) 474, Edward 476, Eli 340, Elizabeth 464, Ella 476, Ellen 294, Emil 366, Emil 440, Emily 230, Emma 422, Fawn 521, Forrest 476, Frank 476, Franklin D. 419, Fred 367, Gene 146, Gene Mrs. 146, Gladys 476, Glen 230, Gloria Jean 474, 567, Harley 476, Ivan 187, 239, Jacob 476, Jacob Jr. 476, Jean 487, Jennie (McBride) 355, Jim 233, Joan 355, Joe 474, John 474, J 476, Jonathan 476, Joseph 422, Joseph J. 422, Josephine 570, Julie 230, Lena 303, Lucille 414, Lucille 446, Lula 476, Marie 567, Martha 474, Mary 476, Maxine, Maxine Lavon 273, Melinda 521, Nelson 565, 567, Nelson L. 474, Nina 440, Osa 476, Pearl 111, 422, Peter 355, Priscella (Steffen) 474, Raymond 476, Richard J., Robin 521, 534, Rose 230, Ruby 111, 422, Ruth 440, Sheila 474, 565, Sheila Kay 474, Sherry 483, Tim 483, Tina 385, Trout 474, 521, Walter 422, William 146, 206, William Gene 474, 521, William Mrs. 146
MOSES, Kathy 514, Mary 472, 514, 514, William 472, 514
MOSHAMMER, Mary Louise 563, 606
MOSIMAN, Ferdinand 190, George 259
MOSS, David 145, Jerry 262, Marjorie 262, Roma Lee 338, Walter 262
MOSSBURG, Aaron 474, Able Morgon Sargent 474, Aenone 475, Alfreda 474, Alice 13, Almira 475, Ammalydia 475, Angela 474, Angela Renee 375, Angeline 474, Angenette 474, Anna 474, Annette 474, April 474, Barbara 475, Bob 474, Brian K. 375, Byron 474, C. Scott 475, 475, Caleb 474, Catherine 474, Charles 40, 475, Charles G. 475, Charles Homer 475, Charly 13, Christine 474, Cindy 474, Custer 475, Dale Eugene 475, Dana 475, Daniel 474, Daniel P. 474, David 475, Dean 475, Deborah 474, Denise 475, Diana 475, Donald Leon 475, Doris A. 475, Edith 414, 474, Elijah Palmer 475, Elizabeth 474, Elizabeth Ann 475, Elmer 64, 474, Emerson F. 474, Emily 474, Ethalinda 310, 474, Ethel 475, Ethelinda 311, Frances 474, Grace 474, Hannah Aby 474, Helen 475, Henry 16, 409, Henry 474, Henry Rev. 40, 310, 311, 474, 475, 475, Henry William 474, Herman 475, Hiram 474, Homer 475, 605, Howard 320, 474, 475, Ida Marie 605, Ida Wyant 475, Imma 475, Isabell 475, Isabella 474, Jack 585, Jacob 474, James 40, 474, James A. 475, James Richard 475, James T. 475, James Toliver 475, James Tolliner 474, Jane 310, 475, Janelle 474, Jeffrey 474, Jennifer 474, Jerry 474, John 474, 474, Joni 474, Juli 474, Julie 345, 475, Kirby 474, Laura 474, Leah 474, Linda 474, 475, Lloyd Lewis 474, Lola 475, Louis G. 475, Mabel Nahrwold 475, Mark 474, Martha 474, Martha Sheets 554, Mary 474, 598, Mary Elizabeth 474, Mary Jane 475, Mike 345, 475, Mollie Mary"", Mollie 414, Nancy M. 283, Nancy Mae 475, Norma Jean 474, Oscar 475, Pat 475, Patricia 147, Patty 6, Phariba Allen 474, Randall 474, Ray 464, Ray Hugo 474, Rebecca 474, Richard 345, 475, 605, Robert 605, Robert Dale 475, Robert Eugene 474, Rodney 474, Ronald Leon 475, Roy L. 475, Roy Leon 475, Sandra 474, Sarah 474, Sarah S. 475, Scott 345, Sharon 474, Shelley 475, Shellie 345, Shirley 474, Sonya 474, Thomas 475, Thomas Steven 475, Virganette 474, Vivian 474, William 311, 474, 598
MOSSER, Hans Adam 254, Nicholas 254
MOSSIS, Nettie Giltner 603
MOSSY, Jennie 356
MOSURE, Abner 359, Adam 307, Alfred 476, Andy 307, Bertha Idella 476, Betty 243, 379, Cecil 476, Cecile Marie 475, Clara L. 476, Cleo 475, Cleo May 476, Dave 476, David H. 475, Dessie 476, Donald 307, Edward 476, Elizabeth 476, Elizabeth (Krill) 475, Ella 476, Forrest 243, 476, Forrest Jr. 243, Frank 476, Gladys 476, Gradus 582, Harley 475, Harley J. 476, Harry 307, 581, John 475, 476, Johnathan 476, 475, Lulu 476, Mabel 476, Madeline D (Bowman) 267, Mary 476, Mary Ann 243, Mary Edith 476, Mary M. 476, Minnie 359, Nellie 476, Ocie 475, 476, Raymond 476, Rose 476, Thelma 476, Wendell Bud"", Wendell Eugene 475
MOTEZ, Michael 377
MOTT, John R. 106
MOTZ, Amanda 529, Mary 82, Philip 82
MOULIN, Linda 357
MOUNCE, Vickie 457
MOUNCIE, Miss M. 121
MOUNSEY, Brian 508, Bruce 61, 78, Cary 107, 112, 443, Charles 477, Claude 477, Claude L. 595, Claudine 477, Clayton 66, Clyde 290, Cortney 477, Earl 509, Edith 443, Elijah 477, Eric J. 508, Floyd 477, Gary A. 508, George 477, Grace 477, Hiram 477, Isabella 474, J. L. 112, J. Perry 66, James Perry 477, Jeremy 142, Jodi 477, John 16, 66, 477, Joyce 477, Kay 477, 508, Kelly Jean 477, Kerry Lee 477, Kevin Lynn 477, Lewis 45, Lillie 477, Lula 477, Mabel 477, Marianna, Marie Gladys 385, Mary 474, 477, Mary Ann 477, Megan 477, Miami 477, Minnie (Ustic) 385, Minnie (Ustick) 290, Naomi Faye (Kemper) 290, Opal (Schemehorn) 60, Randy Kay 477, Rebekeh 376, Robert 477, Robin 376, Rodney 376, Russell 376, Ryan 376, Samuel 385, Samuel T. 290, Thomas 477, Trent M. 508, Victor 107, Victor 477, Virginia 509, William Bruce 477
MOUNT, Carrie 241, Carter 241, James 241
MOW, Geraldine Leonora 430, S. A. 75, Schuyler A. Rev. 580
MOWERY, Allen 478, Amos 478, Bessie 283, Blenda Lorene 385, Charles Gilbert 308, David 308, Ethel 444, 500, Ezra 478, George Franklin 478, Lydia 428, Lydia Ann 464, 478, Mary Reynolds 444, Melinda Miller 308, Minerva Catherine 478, Peter 367, 478, Rena 155, Samuel 444, Samuel Nathan 478, Velma 111, Willistonanklin 478
MOYER, Benjamin 243, Catherine 538, Dorcas 243, Eliza 538, Esther 535, George 243, Jacob 538, Kimberly 279, Levina 509, Patty 333, Rose 243, Saloma Ann 508, Sarah 326
MOYNIHAN, Jack 425, John 95, Pat 425
MUDRONY, Jeno 146, Jeno Mrs. 146
MUELLER, Edwin 597, Konrad 344, Mr. 68, Sophie 344
MUGG, Becky 478, John Kerkoff 478, John Nathan 478, John Steven 478, Judy 478, Kelli 478, Martha 478, Mary 425, Patrick 425, Rita 478, William 425
MUIR, Alexander Sandy"", Dorothea 152
MULLEN, Mullen 154, Thomas 244
MULLER, Anna 252, 401
MULLES, Annie 479, Barbara A. 479, Bessie Hoopingarner 479, Carrie 479, Clarence 479, Claude E. 479, Doris 479, Isaac 479, James E. 479, Kathy 479, Mary Ann 479, Orla 479, Rebecca Nicholson 479, Rick 479, Ronald K. 479, Ruby 479, Sylvester 479, Sylvester E. 479, Wava 479
MULLINS, Cynthia 485, Mollie 415, Nathan 485, Stacey 359, William 485
MULLIS, Sarah Elizabeth 509
MUMULLER, Susan 561
MURCHLAND, Donna 483
MURDEN, Pauline 514
MURPHY, A. W. 75, Billy 286, Don 446, James 268, Karen 268, Leah 349, Lydia 75, Marie 458
MURRAY, 66, Albert Jack"", Alfred 480, Amanda 385, Andrew 479, Ben 479, Betty 479, Brian 479, Carol 480, Carolyn Joan 267, Cathy 479, Charles Rev. 97, Crystal 468, David 479, Earl 78, Edna Brown 266, Ernest 266, Ethel 480, Fred 480, Fred W. 567, Gene E. 267, Gregory 479, Hamilton 480, Harley 122, Harold 266, Harold E. 267, Herb 20, Homer 479, Ida 480, Irene 266, James 140, 158, 479, James E. 267, Jason 480, Jason F. 567, Jennifer 479, 480, Jennifer L. 567, Jerry 480, Jill 480, Jim 136, 584, Jimmy 479, Jordan 479, Joshua 479, Josie 480, Judy 479, Kay 479, Kevin 479, Laura 479, Lela Pauline 489, Linda 480, Martha Rose 480, Mary 479, 584, Mary Ann 577, Melody 479, Mike 480, Myrtle 480, Oscar 480, Patrick 479, Phebe 479, Pierre 479, Ramona 351, 480, Rita 480, Robert 480, Rosco E. 267, Roscoe 266, Ruth 567, Ruth Lenore 567, Sallie 464, Sarah 480, Shikha 479, Stella 542, Susan 479, Ted 479, Trudy 235, Trudy L 567, Vaughn 78, Virgil 480, Virginia 480, Wanda 261, 480, Wayne 542, 567, Wayne Alfred 567, Zern 480
MURRELL, Debra 480, Elmo 228, 480, Kathy 480, Lauren Ann 480, Lena 480, Lindsey 480, Michael David 480, Rebecca Ann 480, Richard Allen 480, Sarah Allison 480, Zachary 480

MUSCO, Kathy Sue 595, Matthew 595, Michael 595, Victor J. 595
MUSICK, Todd 582
MUSKOFF, George 261
MUSSELMAN, 66, Brenda Kay 569, Dawn 569, Dawn (Johnloz) 414, Dayton 234, Florence 405, Grace 301, J. Dale 569, Linda Kay 569, Randy Leon 569, Rebecca Kay 569, Rodncy 414, 414, Rodney Allen 569, Sandra Brooke 569, Saundra 414
MUSSER, Michael 256, Michael 547, Monty 256, 547, Raymond 256, 547, Rebecca 256, 547, Theo Marie 256, 547
MUTH, Elizabeth 480, John 480, Louise 480, Rose 480, William 480
MYER, Beth 533, Larry 533
MYERS, Abraham 481, Adam Robert 481, Agnes E. 246, Anna 481, Anna E. 481, Asa L. 481, Asa Theo 547, Barbara 150, Benjamine 482, Bernice 483, Beth Betty"", Bob 544, Bobette (Boswell) 481, Carolyn Jane 481, Cary McKinley 481, Charles 121, Charles A. 512, Charles J. 481, Charles J. Jr. 481, Clark 481, Clayton 481, Cleophas C.L."", Cleophas 438, 481, Colin 483, Connie 304, Daniel 481, Darci 481, David 483, Debby 285, Dillon 8, Dillon 481, Dillon M. 481, Earl 481, Eleia 481, Elizabeth 482, Elnora 579, ELozabeth 432, Emedele 482, Emma 569, Ethelbelle 246, Eugene 483, Frank 481, Fred 569, George Herman 481, George R. 481, Grace 482, Gracia 481, H. C. 98, Harmon 481, Henry 93, Herman 6, 216, Herman W. 481, Herman Watson 481, Howard 285, Jacob 112, Jacob 482, James 400, 482, James B. 481, Jay William 481, Jeanette 392, Jeffrey L. 481, Jenniffer 396, Jerry 482, John 396, 548, Joseph 86, Joseph 481, 482, Joseph L. 481, Josephine 569, Kathy 434, Kristin Rae 481, Linda 285, Linda F. Collins 481, Linda Sue 395, Lloyd 482, Lola 544, Louise 482, Lucille 438, Lucria 482, Lucy 482, Lulu 535, Mae 482, Maggie 481, Marie (Resley) 438, Marjorie 221, Martha 482, Martin 483, Mary Dean 482, Mary Lucille 481, Mason 483, Michael 481, Mike 140, Nancy 481, Nancy E. 481, Nancy Elizabeth 481, Ora 481, Orran 482, Phoebe 537, Randall L. 481, Richard K. 481, Robert 544, Robert J. 481, Robert Samuel 482, Roger 296, Ronda 544, Rose 482, Ross 132, Ross Mrs. 137, Sandra A. 481, Sandra K. 481, Sara 482, Sara Lee 482, Sarah 422, Sarah Elizabeth 423, Simeon 482, Susannah 481, Susannah (Pence) 481, Tawny Marie 481, Virgie Nina Marie 481, Virgil 460, Wendy 483, Wiliam Robert 481, William 246, William 481, 482, William A. 481, William Alfred 481, William Herman 481, Winifred 595, Winifred Elaine 481
MYGRANT, Amanda 531, Dawn Marie 393, Lisa Diane 393, Lucinda 318, Michael 393, William Rev. 531
MYNATT, Dick 140
NADOLNY, Frances Harris 384
NAFFZIGER, Mary Helen 401
NAGEL, Hannah 507
NAHA, Shikha 479
NAHRWOLD, Colleen 483, Helen 483 ,Anna 463 ,Anna (Werling) 482, Brian 483, Brian Michael 482, Carl 482, Carl 502, Carolina Lena"", Charles 482, Charles Fredrick Karl F"", Christian 482, Christine Wilhelmine 482, Colleen Sue 482, Conrad 483, Conrad Freiedrich Wilhelm 482, Cynthia 483, Cynthia Ann 482, Dennis 483, Dennis Lynn 482, Diane 482, 483, Friedrich Christian 482, Helen (Heuer) 502, Johann Daniel 482, Julia 482, 483, Karl (Charles) Frederick 463, , Kathy 483, Kathy Lynn 482, Marie 483, Marie Christine Louise 482, Marie E. 482, Maxine 483, Maxine Ann 482, Michael 483, Michael Dean 482, Minnie 463, Sara 483, Sara Nicole 482, Sophie 482, Sophie (Wiegman) 483, Thomas 482, Thomas 483, Wilhelmina Marie Caroline 463, Wilhelmine 482, William 482, William C. 482, William Conrad 482
NALLE, Alice Ann 472
NAPP, Lavina 466, Lavina 470
NARHWOLD, Carl 483, Charles Fredrick Karl F"", Clara 483, Helen 483, Linda 483, Paula 483, Wilhelmina Minnie"", William 483
NARR, Emma 401, Jacob 401
NASH, Addie 484, Alexa 483, Alice 270, Amy Jo 485, Dale 558, Dale Duane 483, Dana 443, Daniel L. 484, Devon L. 484, Douglas Eugene 483, Elihu 485, Ellen 325, Ellis 484, Estaleene 485, Estaleene J. 484, Estel 484, Frederick 484, Frederick L. 484, Genevieve (Rupright) 325, Harry 558, Harry Wendell 483, Herbert 484, 485, James 102, 443, Jeff 461, Jennifer Jane 483, Jesse 484, Jesse Jr. 484, Jessica Ann 485, John 325, Joseph H. 484, 485, Karen 484, Katy Elizabeth 485, Kay Ann 485, Lester 484, Lois 484, Marguerite 558, Mary Adeline 484, Melissa 443, Merlin 558, Merlin Ray 483, Minta 484, Minta Burns 484, Oscar 484, Raughlia 484, Rebecca 484, Reuben Henry 483, Reuben Henry 485, Richard 484, Richard II 484, Richard IV 484, Robert 95, Ryan 443, Sadie 437, Scott Alan 483, Stephen Ray 483, Teresa 400, Thomasin 484, Todd Allen 483, Tonya Fay 483
NAU, Joan Valentine 585
NEEL, H. D. 98, Virginia 321
NEFF, Carol Jean 485, Catherine 397, 485, Christina 485, Cora 485, Cynthia 485, Donna 485, Edson 371, 485, Elizabeth 335, Esta 485, Esta (Pennington) 371, Eunice 388, 389, Eunice 389, Everett 485, Frank 485, H.H. 44, Harold 485, Hurt 447, Isaac 18, Jacob 388, 540, James 485, Jayne 485, Jeanne 485, John 13, 388, 485, John Nathan 485, Joseph 485, Katharine 485, Levi 102, 388, 485, 517, Louisa 485, Louisa May 540, Lucile 485, Margaret 517, Margaret 517, Mark 485, Marthiene 485, Mary 485, Nate 335, Rachel 485, Rebecca 102, Rebecca (Goodspeed) 388, Roger 371, 485, Ruth Eleanor 485, Samuel 485, Sarah 540, Silas 202, Susan 485, Vesta 485, Vesta Linn 335, Victoria 485
NEHER, John 76, Samuel 19, Samuel 61
NEILL, James 582, Jason 582, Joseph 582, Stephanie Werking 582, Stuart 582
NEITH, Dean 402, Earl 402, Mary Lou 402, Sadonna 402
NELSON, Alta 254, Betty Jane 405, Brainard 254, Dessie D. 407, George 20, Geraldine Geri"", Gloria 136, James 112, Jenny 254, John 273, Lois 576, Margaret 547, N. W. 179, Philip E. 254, Rebecca 260, Sarah 260
NEMENWAY, J. A. 458
NESS, Louisa 408, Nathan James 249
NESSBAUM, Howard 424, Michael 424, Steven 424
NESTLE, Christine 588, Fred 588, Gary 588, George 588, Karen 588, Kay 588, Kim 588
NESTLEROAD, Carol 443, Charles 443, 600, Jane 443, John 443, 600, Lisa 443, Michael 443, Zina 424
NETHERLAND, Brian 221
NEUENSCHWANDER, Ada 487, Adam 486, Alex 354, Amy 486, Andrea 486, A 487, Anna 487, Bethany 354, Betty 475, 487, Brandon 486, Carol 487, Carol Jean 544, Caroline 528, Carolyn 487, Carolyn Irene 487, Cathy Sue 486, Charles 340, 486, 487, , Cindy 486, Crystal Ann 518, 544, Cynthia 487, Daniel 340, 486, 487, Darlene 376, 487, David 518, 544, Deb 486, 340, 487, Dee 487, Dee Charles 340, 486, Dennis 340, 486, 487, Diana 292, Diann Kay 487, Doris 487, 487, Doris Ann 487, Ed 25, Edna 533, Edna Schaefer 487, Elizabeth 486, 487, , Ellen 340, 487, Fanny 516, Gladys Carol 486, Gordon 89, Irene 487, 577, Ivy 486, Jacob 486, James Robert 398, Janice 487, 534, Janice L. 605, Jean 354, Jeff 340, 487, Jesse W. 486, Joe 487, Joe William 577, John 487, 487, 487, 577, John 605, Johnathon 486, Joseph 486, Joyce 487, Joyce 533, Karen 533, Kathryn 487, Kathy 486, 487, 533, Kenneth 594, 594, Kenneth Wayne 518, 544, Kip 354, Kristi 487, 533, Larry 558, Laura 486, Linda 487, Lucille 487, Marcia 487, Marcy J. 605, Marilyn 487, Marilyn Jean 487, Martha 487, Mary 487, Michael 487, Mildred 478, 487, Nancy 487, Nathan C. 605, Peggy 487, Rachel 354, Randolph 487, Rex 340, 487, Richard 558, Ryan 398, Sheri 486, Sherman 371, Sheryl 487, Simon 528, Steve 84, Steven 146, Tammy 486, Terry 354, Terryl 340, 487, Thomas 340, 487, Ulrich 487, Ulrich Sr. 487, Vera 528, Vickie 487, Virgil 487, Virginia 374, Walter 487, 487, 533, Walter Jr. 487, Walter Junior 487, 533, Wendy 486, William 340, 487, William G. 486, . 487, 487, William W. 487
NEUHAUSER, Alice Ann 488, Amos 170, 340, 488, , 493, 588, Amos 593, Christina 488, Clarice 488, Diane 487, Dorothea 340, 488, Faye 493, John 488, Lucille 488, 588, 589, Marianne 488, 488, 588, 593, Maurice 488, , Mildred 488, 593, Nancy 152, Newell 493, Paul 140, 487, 488, Peggy 487, Tom 103
NEVIL, Floyd 102, Lori Ann 601, Mark 601
NEVINS, John 59, John Rev. 58
NEVITT, Virginia 245
NEVIUS, Karen Sue 415
NEWCOMB, Julie Renee' Athan 246, Rich 246
NEWCOMER, Christian 579
NEWELL, Brian 300, Caroline 200, Caroline Elizabeth 488, Christopher Stephen 278, 488, John 300, Jonathan Andrew 278, 488, Melody 604, Scott Foster 278, 488, Stephen 278, Stephen Foster 488
NEWHARD, Bessie 533, Carolyn 302, Celesta 501, Flavia 501, Frank 501, Jesse 604, Oscar 22
NEWHAUSER, Amos 487, Marianne 487, Nancy Jane 487
NEWHOUSE, Eleonora 536, Fred 536, Leon 109, 426, Mila Mae 426
NEWPORT, Casey Marie 459, Cody William 459, Gregory A. 459
NIBARGER, Pearl 362
NIBLICK, Anna J. (Lowdermilk) 434, Beverly Earlene 555, Bruce 488, Carrie 555, Cindy Lou 555, Daniel M. 392, Dwight E. Steve"", Ellen Clark 488, Ethel 552, George W. 434, Heather 555, Iva 552, Ivy 486, James 287, James F. 555, James Robert 488, Katherine 555, Kathy Ann 555, Lillie Smith 552, 551, Melda E. 488, Milo 475, Patricia 146, 488, Pauline 488, Pauline Harris 384, Rebecca 488, Robert 524, Robert M. 488, Ross 488, Ruth 488, Steve 488, Steven II 555, Steven James 555, Susan 488
NICELY, Rachel 102
NICHELSON, Cluade 333, Deloress McBride 333, Lucille 333, N. Lucille 333, Theodore 333, James 326, Mary Emmaline 326, Regencia 326
NICHOLAS, Debbie 270, Ethel J. 603, Gladys 599
NICHOLS, Robert 146, Robert Mrs. 146
NICHOLSON, Edmund 446, Edmund 446, Ira 337, Marcia 373, Martha (Miller) 337, Rose Ellen 289, Sandra 283, Sherryl Dian 337
NICHTER, Benjamin 370, Janice 370, Michael 370
NICKEL, Allen Dr. 280
NICKELSON, Paul E. 585, Stella 417
NIECE, Margaret 544
NIEDERHAUS, John 68
NIERMAN, Wendel 265
NIEZER, Charles 216
NIGEL, Wayne Everett Mrs. 58
NIHISER, Erma (Fackler) 445, Jerry 445, Larry 445, Lawrence 445, Sandra Kay 445
NIMMONS, Ebenezer 179, Mary (Wright) 154, William 179
NIRITER, Rose 292, Rose 512
NISWANDER, Amy Smith 557
NISWONGER, Anna 483
NIX, Edith 287
NIXON, Bob 196, Elizabeth 301, Richard 34, Robert 146, Robert Mrs. 146
NOBLE, Amber 489, Barbara 326, Bergie 107, Brian K. 489, Cathy 489, Charles Steven 489, Charlie 489, Claude 107, Cynthia D. 489, Edward W. 489, Enzla 489, Ethel 489, George 111, George Marion 489, Glenna 489, Glenna L. 435, Ida 489, J. Charles 489, James L. 489, Jessica 489, John Tyler 489, Joyce A. 489, Julia 582, Kemberli 486, Kristy 489, Kurt L. 489, Lena Pearl 489, Leota Leona 489, Lindsay 489, Lori 489, Luetta 489, Lulu 489, Margaret 326, Marion Andrew 489, Max 489, Mertie 489, Nellie 107, 517, Ora 489, Phoebe Jane 489, Sarah 289, Taffie Jean 489, Tyler John 486, Wilma 489
NOBLET, John 485, Martha 485, Rachel Noblet 485
NOE, 66, Andrew 489, Annette 489, April 489, Bernard 385, Betsy 348, 489, Carleton 489, Danielle 471, David 285, 489, Diane 489, Elaine 489, Ethel 489, Etta 285, Evelyn Tunie 489, Frankie Danielle 489, Geneva 489, Harriett 285, 489, Henrietta 489, Ida 349, Jace 489, Jane Anne 489, John Hess 489, John Jr. 489, Lowell 489, 489, Maria 489, Mildred 489, Oscar 113, 489, Robert 471, Robert Lewis 489, Rosemary Ann 471, 489, Saren 489, Therese 489, Timothy 471, Timothy Lowell 489, Tonya 489, Tunie 489, Whitcomb 489, Win 107, Woodrow 471, 489
NOLIN, Milton 90
NOLL, Carol 513, Dave 525, Jean 525, Lois 136, Magdalena 326, Wilma 267
NOONAN, Iva 502, Norma 333
NORCROSS, Allen 18, Isaac 18
NORDYKE, Anna Louise 489, Anna May 375, 489, Dale 489, Daniel 489, Dorothy 489, Edward 489, Edward William 489, Ernest 45, Ernest Neal 489, Helen 489, Jacob 375, Jacob G. 489, Laura B. 489, Laura McGahey 375, Lela Elma 489, Lela Pauline 489, Lewis 45, Lewis Birch 489, Margaret 489, Maudie Ruth 489, Neva 489, Phyllis 489, Richard 489, Robert 489, Ruth 489, Sadie 489, Sarah 489
NORMO, Audrey 597
NORRIS, Alan Jay 490, Alfred 200, 490, Alfred J. 490, Alice Ann (Stone) 490, Betsy Annette 490, Cory William 490, Diane (Denney) 318, Dick 490, Ed 145, H. L. 169, Jeremy MArk 490, Marcellus 346, Mary Alice 490, Nathan Alan 490, Toni Arlette 490
NORTH, Jerry 455, John 147, Mattie 147
NORTON, James E. 403, Martin Samuel 596, Sarah Frances 403
NOTTINGHAM, Janalyn 376
NOWAK, Ralph 140
NOWAKOWSKI, Jean 253
NUEST, Rhonda 353
NUMBERS, Albert 490, Beverly 490, Don 385, 490, Donna 457, Donna B. 490, Glendora 490, Helen 490, Irene 490, John 385, 490, Martha 490, Mattie 490, Nancy L. 490, Nancy Lee 378, Thelma 490
NUSBAUM, Emanuel 167
NUSBAUMER, Alpha 490, Anna Esther 490, Barbara 262, 425, 499, Barbara A. 490, Berneice 375, Bernice 491, 499, Beverlyee 376, 425, Brandon 491, Carol Kay 491, Catherine 490, Catherine (Hunsinger) 375, Cecile 490, Cecile Bernice 376, Clayton 490, Clinton 491, Cloid 491, 497, 499, Darrel Duane 491, Donna 375, 491, 499, Dorothy 490, Ferdinand 95, Frances Esther 490, Gay Lamoine 491, George 375, 490, 491, 499, Gerald 425, Gerald B. 490, Gerald Bryan 376, Gloid 375, Gregory 491, Gretta 491, Hilda Octave 490, Janelle 499, Janet 425, Janet Elizabeth 376, Janice 499, Jerry 499, Jerry Lee 491, Jesse L 375, Jesse Lee 491, Jessica 499, Jesston 499, Jody 491, Joetta 499, John 491, Joseph 491, 499, Juanita 375, 491, 499, Katherine 491, Kay 262, 425, Kay T. 490, Kenneth 78, 375, 491, 499, Kenneth Earl 491, Lamoine 491, Linda Fern 491, Marianna 376, 425, 594, Marlene 491, Nathan 490, Nilah 375, 491, 499, Ora 491, Ora A. (Sawyer) 375, Ora Alice 491, Phyllis 491, 499, Phyllis Jean 375, Rebecca 499, Rita Marlene 491, Roderick 262, 376, 425, Ruthann 491, 497, Sarah 490
NUSSBAUM, Anne-Marie 435, Cheryl Lynn 435, Dorcas (Liechty) 442, Eleanor Kay 435, Grace (Reinhard) 522, Jerome 442, Judith Marie 442, Tillman 98, Tonya Sue 544, Willis 435
NUSSDORFER, Fern (Crabbs) 251, John 251, Katharine June 251
NUTE, Henry Benton 517, Tamar 517,
NUTTER, Brent 524, Clara 383, Grace S. 435, Homer 383, Joyce 435, Levi 122, Levi J. 435, Mildred 440, Sabina 567
NUWBAUER, Susan 583
NYCUM, Sue 551
NYENHUIS, Valarie 539
NYFFELER, Beth 492, Betty 492, Betty Jean 492, Charles F. Sr. 492, Charles Jr. 492, Dean 492, Donald L. 492, Edwin 492, Estella (Rhodes) 492, Lizanell 492, Louis 492, Madelain (Mason) 492, Marenna 492, Marilyn 437, Nicole 492, Oswalt 492, Otto 492, Paul 492, Peggy 492, Rosina (Rufener) 492, William 492O'BANNON, Frank 406
O'BRIEN, Harry 369
O'CONNER, Joe 71, Barb 25, Gertrude 555
O'DAY, Henry 37
O'DELL, R. L. 98
O'DONAL, Charles Madison 593, Ella 593, Jesse Mae 593, Laura Viola 593, Lydia Ann (Stults) 593, Raymond 593, Robert 593
O'DONNELL, Ada B. 239, Charles D. 239, Edwin Clyde 239, Randolph L. 239, W. Ray 239
O'GORMAN, Bonnie Jean Durdahl 513
O'LAVERTY, Betty 152, Elizabeth 200, Glen 145, 146, Glen Mrs. 146
O'NEIL, Rita 478
OAKDEN, Tom 440
OAKES, Betty 251, DeWayne 251, Elizabeth 596, Jodi 251, John 251, Mary Anne 251, Richard E. 251, Ted 251
OAKLEY, Annie 568
OAKS, Esther 462
OBERHOLTZER, W. S. 64, 96
OCHSENRIDER, Emma 517, Emma 517, Vaughn 283
ODA, Barbara 345, William 58
ODELL, C. E. 81
ODIER, Marguerite 289
OERTEL, William F. 513
OESTREICH, Alica 544, Alicia 518, Alicia Mariee 591
OETING, Lizetta 252
OGALSBEE, Malinda 392
OGDEN, George S. 458, Harriet 459, Harriett (Aunt Hattie) 458, J.A. 90, John 18
OGLE, Areta Marie 498, Flossie 462, James 107, James R. 265, Linda 265
OGLESBEE, Eliza Jane 441
OGLESBY, Cecile 289, Charles 289
OKULY, DeLora 276
OLDFATHER, Allen 258, Eliza 64, Michael 254
OLDFIELD, Anita 492, Brandon 492, Cristi 492, Dale 492, Donna 492, E. Floyd 492, Floyd J. 492, Jeanette 492, 560, Judy 492, Linda 492, Nora 492, Wilma Idell 350
OLDS, Morton 181
OLESON, Robert 68
OLFATHER, Emma Blanche 254
OLIVER, Marilyn 515, Mary M. 476, Shelley 475
OLSON, Elaine 230, Tobias 230
OMAN, Angela 358, Angela 501, Bobbie 154, Danielle 501, Danielle Nichole 358, Derrick 501, Derrick Matthew 358, Jon 501, Jon Steven 358, Lauren 501, Lauren Rebekah 358, Paul 98, Roberta (Campbell) 358, Wendell 358
OMEN, Dana 168, Emma Bayha 168, Jacob 253
OMEROD, John 98
ONWELLER, Edith 111, Howard 111, Olive 111
OPLINGER, Bertha 493, Christian 493, Clara 493, Clayton 493, Curtis 493, Edward 493, Elizabeth 493, Emma 493, Ethel 493, Faye 493, Harvey E. 493, John 493, Lawrence 493, Leona 493, 527, Lester 493, Lois 493, Maria 493, Mary 493, Mary Almeda 493, Samuel 493, 527, Sara 493, Sarah 527, Velma 493, William 493, Wilma 468, 493
OPPENHEIM, A.P. 163
OREM, Jerry Paul 557, Ed 78
ORMBSY, Danny 333, Donald 333, Eric 333, Greg 333, James 333, Jason 333, Jeff 333, Jill 333, Joti 333, Julie 333, Kathy 333, Keith 333, Kelli 333, Lora 333, Nancy 333, Reggie 333, Renae 333, Sandra 333, Tim 333
ORMISTON, Kay 463
ORMSBY, Chase Michael 402, Deloss 333, Genivieve 570, Janet 333, Jayne 333, Jessie Irene 567, John 208, John H. 121, Lela 333, Margie 333, Max 333, Michael 402, Norma 333, Robert 333, Ruth 333, Vaughn 333, Wendell 333
ORR, Daddy 36, Fred Rev. 89, Hazel Fern 380, J. 380, Martha 380, Wanda K. 559
OSBORN, 66, Aaron 495, 495, Albina 495, Alyssa 406, Amos 495, Andrew 495, Anna 495, Bernard Lee 493, 494, 496, Bernice 292, Bessie 438, Breck 409, Bruce 275, Bruce K. 519, Carolyn Ann 493, Carolyn Ann (Keel) 494, 496, Catherine 103, 495, Chris Melvin 494, Christine Louise 494, Clinton Howard 494, Conrad 495, Dale 243, Dale DeWayne 494, Dixie 270, Elias 495, Eliza J. 495, Elizabeth 495, Elizabeth M. (Harris) 495, Ellen 244, Ellen Mae 494, Ellen May 493, Estel Earl 493, 494, Frank 494, Frank Howard 493, 494, 495, G. Rollin Rev. 410, Glenda Irene 493, Glenna 285, 494, Glenna Irene 494, Hank 270, Harmon 495, Herman 107, Herman DeWayne 493, 494, Ida Mae 493, I 494, J. P. Jr. 401, Jacob 495, James 495, Janet 243, Jean 380, Jeff 102, Jennie 562, Jennifer 519, Jesse 495, Joan 243, John 107, 244, 494, 495, 496, 599, John H. 61, John Howard 431, 493, 494, , J495, John Paul Jr. 496, Jonathan 495, Joseph N. 495, Joshua 519, Joshua K. 275, Julie 519, Julie Ann 275, Laura Jean 494, Leita 244, 599, Leita Ardella 431, 493, 494, 495, Leita Ardella (Smith) 494, Letia 494, Levi 103, 244, 493, 495, Lillian 431, Lillian Charlene 493, 494, Lisa Ann 494, Loretta 590, Lynn E. 401, M. Jean (Drabenstot) 380, Margaret 495, Marion 380, Mary 495, Mary A. 495, Mary Ann 61, 477, 577, Mary Ann (Mounsey) 409, 410, Mary J. 336, Matthew DeWayne 494, Michael Wayne 493, 494, Michael Wayne 496, Nellie Ann 409, 410, Nelson 495, Nicholas 493, 495, Paul 61, 401, 496, 541, Pauline 243, Prossor 495, Richard E. 380, Rick 406, Roland 66, Rose Marie 493, 494, Ruby 496, Ruth Ann 401, S. Breckenridge Breck"", Scott 380, Susan Marie (Ruble) 406, Suzanne Michelle 380, Therese 494, William 494, 495, William Wallace 493
OSBORNE, Debra 369, Kai Elizabeth 324, Kamann Rae 324, Kami Jo 324, Rosemary 526, Thomas Lee 324
OSBURN, Mary Ethel 23, Willis 23
OSMUNDSON, Janice 585, Kathe 585, Robert 585, Steven 585
OSTENDARP, 331
OSTERHOUSE, Diana D. 601, Tim 601
OSTRANDER, Brittany Nichole 496, Clarence Warren 496, Dorthea 155, Dorthea Lucile (Hamilton) 496, Gregory Ross 496, Jeania Marie 496, Jeffery Eugene 496
OSWALD, Rebecca 413
OSWALT, 66, Addie (Tappy) 497, Addie Tappy 499, Adeline Lorine Ruse 498, Amie 498, Amie Jo 557, Ann (McCreery) 275, Berta Elmer Pete"", Berta Elmer 498, Brooke 497, Carolyn 497, Carrie Helen 497, Cecil 544, Charles 497, 499, Christena (Ulmer) 544, Clarence 544, Claude 497, Clyde Franklin 498, Courtney Anne 275, Dale 269, Daniel K. 557, Daniel Kay 498, David Allen 498, Deena 497, Donald Fredrick 498, Doris Jean 497, Doris Shaw 497, Ed 557, Edith Amanda 498, Edward Lavere 498, 498, Fanny 497, Faye 497, Faye Everett 499, 497, Gerald Duane 498, Geri Ann 498, Glendon 497, 499, Gus 499, Gustin 497, Gustin E. 497, Gustin Everett 497, H. Catherine 498, 574, Helen Catherine 498, Ida Elsie (Miller) 498, Ila Mae 544, Jacob 497, 498, James Edward 498, Jamie 498, Jane Dickason 499, Jared 498, Jeffrey Duane

498, Jeffrey Wayne 498, Jennifer 498, Jesse 499, Jill Ann 283, Joan 497, 497, J 499, Joey 498, John 506, 544, Joseph 497, Julie 498, Kari 498, Kari Ann 557, Karla Jean 498, Katherine 341, Kathy Jo 498, Kenny Jay 498, Kerry Joe 498, Keven Andrew 498, Kreig 498, Kyle 498, Lorene F. 269, Manervia Angeline 497, Margaret 557, Margaret Ann Bowser 498, Marjorie 497, 499, Marolyn 497, Marolyn 497, Martha Jane 497, Mary 500, Mary Irene 498, Max 341, Minervia (Gustin) 497, Nervia 497, Nicole 498, Paul Wilbur Barney"", Pauline 498, Pauline Ensley 497, Rhiannon 497, 497, Ronald Keith"", Ronald Lee 283, Rose 400, 497, Ruth 497, Ruthann 491, 497, 499, Sarah 498, Susan 498, Susan Lyn 557, Tamera 341, Terry Gene 498, Thomas Lee 498, Timothy 497, Timothy 497, Vera 497, 499, Vickie 497, 497, Wilford Samuel 497, William Todd"", William 497, 499, 544, William Frederick 498, 498
OTIS, Anna R.
OTTERBEIN, Phillip William 58
OVERMAN, Hannah 446, Patsy 508
OWEN, Sarah 408
OWENS, Alice 595, Annabelle 327, Catherine Lynette 469, Clifford 512
OXLEY, Fred 352
OZEE, Sam 214
OZMENT, Jerolyn (Martin) 318
PACE, Bonnie Jean 279, Brian Robert 279, Emma Evaline 399, Gina Marie 279, Gloria 550, Hallie 359, Hazel 535, Hazel Bell (Schwartz) 290, Herman 290, Herman Harry 279, James Dwight 279, James Girod 279, Mary Jane (Stine) 260, Nora 260, Robert Edwin 279, Robert Harry 279, Stephanie Ann 279, Thomas Dwight 279, Veda Maxine 290, William 260, Zepha 265
PACKER, Charles 263, Phyllis 263
PADDOCK, George W. 407, Ilka Wilson 407, Oleta 407
PAGE, Blanche Helen 288, Kevin 460, Robert Wiley 288
PAGOWSKI, Alma 412
PAINTER, Dorothy 180, Ida Rebecca 499, J. H. 499, John 180, 187, 506, John H. 165, John Henry 499, Mary 180, 593, Paul 165
PALMER, Amy 499, Cathy 499, Debra 414, John 499, John W. 499, Julie 499, Larry 499, Leland 499, Lorinda (Cruse) 499, Martelle 499, Mary 499, Michael 499, Pam 499, Phyllis Maxine (Crowl) 303, Robert 399, 499, Russell 137, Sherri 398, Wilma 499
PANE, Cyrus 477
PANOS, Constantine 146, Constantine 269, Constantino 573, Deno 140, George 145, Pat 84
PAPE, Lana 597
PARK, Abby 501, Alexander 501, Alexander G. 500, Andrew L. 500, Angela 501, Avis 501, Avis L. (Underhill) 358, Blanche 500, Byron 500, Carolyn J. 501, Carolyn Jo 358, Catherine 398, 500, Charles 200, 500, 501, Charles A. 500, Charles Gailey 500, Clair 500, Dave 6, 140, David 398, 500, David G. 478, David Gene 500, Don 500, Don Larry 500, Donald E. 501, Eldon 500, Eliza 500, Elizabeth 500, Eric Allan 500, Frances Torrence 500, Fred 43, 140, 500, 505, Fred F. 10, .398, Fred Mrs. 140, Frederick 513, Frederick F. 500, Gene Edwin 500, George H. 358, 500, George Henry 501, Harold 513, Harry Washington 500, Helen 500, Henry 501, Hillard Eugene 500, Irene 152, 500, James 500, James Frederick 500, James G. 500, James Garfield 500, Jane 500, Jennifer Leanne 500, Jessie 501, John 500, John Alexander 500, John Jr. 500, Joseph 500, Karen S. 478, Karen Sue 500, Katie 501, Kent 303, 478, Kent Leon 500, 500, Kimberly 501, Kristen Lynn 500, Larry 513, Lawrence E. 501, Madee 501, Malee 501, Margaret 500, Margaret Ann 500, Marilyn Ann 500, Martha 500, Mary 500, Mary Jane 6, 478, 500, Matthew 500, Mildred 500, Nora 500, Norma Jane 500, Paul 513, Penny 478, 500, Pisamai 501, Rebecca 500, Richard 501, Robert 500, Ryan Michael 500, Sakachai 501, Sarah 500, 501, Shawn 501, Shawn Larry 500, Sheila 501, Stacy 501, William Henry 398, 500
PARKE, Henry 500, Sarah 500
PARKER, Amanda Michelle 502, Amy 502, Anne 527, Betty 405, Delight 17, Delight 111, Ellis 17, Gene 502, 502, Irene 502, James A. 583, Laura Ann 502, Lloyd 417, Mahala Florence 583, Marcy Ann 411, Marge 527, Mark Alan 411, Mary 474, Mary Jane 471, Merle Eugene 411, 426, Michael Allen 502, Michael Lee 411, Paul 411, Paul D. 426, Phyllis 585, Robert 471, Russell 402, 502, Russell Jr. 402, Sterling Dr. 527, Thelma 490, Vesta Marguerite 426, Wilma 411, Wilma Maxine 426
PARKHURST, Fred 39
PARKISON, Sarah Louise 249
PARKS, John Rev. 529
PARNELL, Aislinn Alaina 344, Clifton 344, David Clyde 344, Donald 344, Elise Erienne 344, Forest 344, Frederick 344, June Elizabeth 344, Margaret Anne (Francis) 344, May 344, Opal 344, Robert 344, William Clinton 344
PARR, Flo Evelyn 332, Frances Elizabeth 272, Martha 515, Philip 89
PARRISH, Barbara 588, Brandon 588, Brooke 588, Chip 588, Don III 588, Donald Jr. 588, Gertrude 593, Holly 588, Iantha Weinland 597, Jacob 588, Joseph 423, Kristen 588, Mae 482, Rebecca 332
PARSONS, Gary 419, Gary Lynn 571, Joshua Lynn 571, Karen 571
PASCHALL, J. W. 98
PASQUITH, Margaret 243
PASTORE, Cindi 84, Jennifer Kristen 250, Michele, Nick 250, Stephen 250, Stephen Nicholas 250
PATCH, Ruth 304
PATRICK, Amanda Jane 502, Betty Jean (Price) 502, Colleen 483, Colleen Sue (Nahrwold) 502, Daniel 502, Darren 483, Darren Thomas 482, 502, George 502, George Harrold 502, Jodie 483, Jodie Lynn 482, J 502, Mark 483, Mark Allen 482, 502, Maurice 502, Mildred 502, Pearl George 502, Sam 502, Thelma 502, Thomas 483, Thomas Lynn 482, 502, Tom 482
PATTEE, T. A. 64, 96
PATTEN, Robert 277, Tracy 277, Troy 277, Zella 356
PATTERSON, Amanda Renee 249, Bert 181, Bob 45, Charles 45, DeAnn 399, Douglas B. 297, Douglas Bert 279, Elizabeth 400, Esther 44, 45, Jane (Bulger) 297, John 598, John Christopher 598, Pat 297, Suzanne 307
PATTI, Karen 350
PATTON, Edwina 6, Edwina 8, 154, 181, 586, Edwina Josephine 587, Elizabeth 154, 587, Emily 603, Mary 444, Stella (Baughn) 586, W. A. 8, 145, 162, 163, 216, William A. 181, William Alexander 587
PATZ, Ross 299, Stephanie 299, Steve 299, Tresa Couch 299
PAUL, Charles 580, Henry 216
PAULI, August 68
PAULISON, Rebecca 431, Sam 430, 431
PAULL, Keith 466, Sherrie (Meyers) 466
PAXON, Audra 522, Froan 255
PAXSON, Alyssa 132, Alyssa Ann 348, Dawn Michele 348, Iva Marie 337, Joan 404, Keith Allan 348, Kent 248, Mahlon 39, Mahlon Irey 248, Orville (Joe) 248, Ray 151, Rodney Dallas 248, Ruth 488, Sherman 45, 248, Telfer 44, 45, 248, Todd Allan 348
PAYNE, 66, Ardive 514, Fred 514, Jill 302, Joan 150, Mary 462, Phillip 302, William 107, 132, 302
PAYNTER, Stephan 492
PEAKE, Alexander 417
PEARCE, Frances D. 459
PEARSON, Barbara 506, Chris 502, Chris William 392, Daisy 506, Elizabeth Nelson 272, Everett 502, Gilead 502, Grace 272, Guyla 502, Iva 502, J. D. 499, Jack 392, 502, Jackie 502, Jackie Lucile 392, Jenner 506, Joan 502, Joan Burklo 392, John 502, John Richard 392, Judy 502, Julie 499, Kit 502, Lori 502, Lori K 392, Mariah 502, Martha 502, Maude 502, Nan 502, 606, Peter 502, Roland J. 415, Roxy 502, Ruthanna (Knoff) 429, Tom 502, William Harvey 272, William Howard 429, Woodard 15
PEARY, Robert E. 36
PEASE, Burl E. 338, Gloria 507, Harriett A. 331, John 482, Walter S. 331, William A. 331, William A (son of William) 331
PECK, Charles Raymond 604, Dora Ellen 537, Edwin 208, Greg 82, Mary 260
PECKHAM, Ethel Anson 175
PEDEN, Pamela Ann 338
PEDERSEN, Eric 245, Linda 245, Robert 245
PEEK, Caroline 560
PEEL, Joseph Marion 268, Lena 414, Lena M. 268
PEGAN, Abby 449, Candy 449, Ryan 449, Tom 449
PELHAM, Linda 471
PELLECHIO, Juestina (Samele) 238, Sal 238
PELZ, Jeff 338, Valerie 338
PENCE, Ada Mildred 503, Andrew 503, Bethina 503, Blanche Ethel 503, Carrie Ann 503, Casmer 503, Cassandra Jeraldine 503, Christa Leigh 503, David 503, David Allen 503, Dora A. 291, 503, Earl D. 503, Emily 503, Frederick 503, G. Wilford 503, Glen D. 503, Harry 503, Henry 503, Herman 8, 288, Herman Edward 503, Ida R. (Merkey) 503, Irel 44, Irel Vern 503, Jason Robert 503, Jasper 503, John 503, John David 503, John Frederick 503, John S. 503, John Smith 503, Lola Fern 503, Louis 503, Louise 503, Lydia Ann (Warner) 503, Marilyn Ruth 408, 503, Martin 503, Mary Etta 503, Mason Andrew 503, Mathew A. 503, Melissa 503, Nina Ethel 503, Noah 503, Noah Lester 503, Nora 503, Olive 503, Orus Russell 503, Pete 440, Peter Jr. 503, Robert Edward 503, Rolla Daniel 503, Sarah 503, Woodrow Wilson 503
PENDROD, Claude 504
PENEGUY, Michael 460
PENN, M. Ray 596, William 402, 492
PENNER, Elaine 349
PENNINGTON, Esta 485
PENNY, 66
PENQUIGNOT, Wanda (Burley) 420
PENQUITE, Elisabeth 299, Jackson 299
PENROD, 66, Adae 504, Alice 496, 504, Alva 504, Andrew J. 504, Annie 504, Arch 504, Barry 598, Bessie 504, Beth 598, Brad 598, Carrie Elizabeth 259, Carrie Elizabeth 504, 505, Charlie 504, Chester Franklin 504, Claude A. 364, 516, Clell 504, Dave 224, David 504, David William 516, Dortha 590, Dristy 504, Edith 415, Edith 504, Elizabeth 504, Florence L. 259, Florence Leone 505, Frank 504, Franklin 505, Fred 17, 504, George 15, 259, 504, George Allan 259, 505, 504, George W. 504, 505, Gerold 413, Gregory 504, Gregory Claude 516, Hattie 504, Helen 15, Jack 504, Jeremy 259, 504, Jeremy Edward 505, Jerry 142, 504, Jerry Lee 516, Jim 504, Joanna 516, Joannah (Pace) 504, John 496, 504, John Michael 504, 259, 505, Kathy 504, Kathy Lyn 516, Ken 15, Kristy Kay 516, Kyle 259, 504, Kyle Andrew 505, Kyle Lee 516, Lizzie 504, Lula 15, Mabel 435, 504, Mark Allan 259, 505, 504, Mary A. 496, Mary (Britt) 504, Nellie 504, Ora 504, Patti 137, 504, Patti Jo 516, Paul Edward 259, 504, 505, Perl 504, Ray 15, Rebecca 598, Rebecca Jane (Hamilton) 504, 505, Rebecca Ruth 259, 504, 505, Rita 554, Ron 15, Ronda Lee 504, Rose 504, Ruth Elaine 504, Sam 504, Samuel 504, Sarah Christine 259, 504, 505, Tonya 516, Verda M. 516
PEOPLES, Elizabeth L. 250
PEQUIGNOT, Ansel O 505, Arthur 417, Carolyn 505, Charlie 417, Frank 417, Gary 417, Gertrude 417, John 417, Julian 417, Lawrence 417, Marl Alan 505, Wanda Burley 505
PERING, Orman 18
PERISHO, Joshua 446
PERKINS, Colette Marie 453, Larry 447, Martha Augusta 393, Sarah 471
PERRY, Ann 582, Charles 500, Christina Mae 574, Cleve Todd 593, Daniel 500, Dorothy 500, Earl 165, Esther 500, Evelyn 500, Fred 500, Glenna 500, Golanda 500, Ilene 500, Kenneth 165, Lawson 500, Marjorie Estella 574, Mary 500, Mary Wanetta 580, Matilda 500, Megan 593, Mildred 500, Neva 443, 500, Pauline 500, Rhonda 513, Sherri Lynn 574, Thomas 500, Warren 500, Warren Westley 574
PERSON, Geri 152
PERVES, Elizabeth 493
PETERS, Marion 287
PETERSON, Barbara 560, Bryan 518, 544, Bryan Walter 591, Charles E. 356, Eugene J. 386, Isabelle 267, Linda 544, Marjorie Harvey 386, Sara Alice 356, Sara Francis 356, Wm. 96
PETRIE, Alice Ditzler 532
PETT, Harold 77, 144
PETTIT, Deana 603, Malissa Renc 603, Robert Gayle IV 603, Robert Gayle V 603
PETTYJOHN, Chella 136, Harold 171, 178
PETZEL, Christie 202, Floyd 425
PFEIFER, Anne 84, Francis 249, Justine 560, Angela 506, Barbara 506, Brett 505, Carmon 506, Chris 434, Chris Theodore 505, Courtney 434, 505, Dan 351, 434, Daniel William 505, Elizabeth 505, 506, Jean 154, Joan 506, Julia 506, Lance 505, Leonda 434, Leonda Ann 505, Lisa 506, Martha 503, Mary Jo 506, Matthew 434, Matthew Lane 505, Patsy 506, Peggy 506, Rebecca 506, Rose 434, Shane Turner 505, Spencer 505, T. J. 506, Ted 434, Theodore 506, Theodore William 505, Thomas 506, Thomas W. 506, Timothy 506, Tony 505, Ty 505, William 505, 506
PHEGLEY, Abigail 507, Arno (Prouty) 507, Byrom J. 507, Drew 507, James Byrom 507, Jamie 507, Mallorie 507, Marcella 152, 507, Mark 507, Mollie 507, Noel 507
PHILIPPI, Myrtle Lorene 268, Peter 268
PHILLABAUM, James 202
PHILLIPPS, Aloysius 95, A. N. 140, Amos 421, Angela 483, Bert 568, Bruce 483, Cynthia 593, David 440, Erin 483, Evaline 568, Fern 578, Frank 578, Fred 329, John 440, Kiersten 593, Lisa 483, Louella 568, Mary Josephine 293, Mary Lou 440, Merrill 593, Mike 329, Mildred (Huffman) 329, Monica 593, Ner H (Rev.) 293, Robin (Edwards) 329, Sandra 440, Thomas H. 440, Vera 363
PHINNEY, E. 75
PHIPPS, Tammy 272
PICKELL, Chrstine 500, Eric Park 500, Leslie Carol 500, Marilyn 136, Marilyn Ann 500, Randall Lee 500, Robert 500, Robert Paul II 500, Ryan Mathew 500, Sally 500
PICKERING, Audrey 111
PICKFORD, Cheryl 145
PICURI, Diane 489
PIEPER, Cynthia 312, Lois 312
PIERCE, Charles Clifford 441, Charles V. 441, Cheryl 488, David 43, Henry 366, 440, Lillie 440, Margaret 551, 552, Mary Margaret 441, Roseann 357
PIETZ, David 146, David Mrs. 146, Jacquelyn 154
PIFER, Connie 248
PIKE, Mary 484
PILE, Alice 560
PINGRY, Calista 249
PINNEY, Beatrice 184, Charles 507, Clifton 507, Ernest 332, 345, 507, Hannah 507, Hiram 507, Lucinda 507, Lucy 345, 507, Lucy Anna 507, Lucy (Stout) 345, Mary Marie 332, 507, Myrtle Beatrice 507, Nellie 184, 345, Nellie May 507, Nina Bell 507, Vera 184, Vera Lavina 507, Wilson 507
PITTS, Deborah 573, Guy Moseley 507, Heather Ann 507, Neal 146, Neal Chase 507, Neal Mrs. 146, William 507
PITZER, Halcyon 518, 544
PLACHEKI, Cathy Palmer 499, Tate 499
PLANK, Vera 37
PLASTERER, Evelyn 155
PLATT, Alberta 508, Allen 508, Angeline 508, Ann 140, Anna Louise 507, Arlo 352, 411, 426, 508, Betty Lou 509, Bob 508, Brenda 508, Cameron 411, 426, 508, Carol A. 508, Caroline 509, Carolyn 426, 508, Carolyn Rose 411, 426, 508, Cass 508, Cathy 426, 508, Chancy 508, Cheryl 508, Chris 508, Clarence 318, 477, 507, 508, Clarence Jr. 508, Clayton L. 508, Clella 508, Clodella 508, Cornelius 508, Dale 507, 508, Dale Eldon 508, David 508, David Borne 263, Dorothy Lee 508, Edna 508, Edward 508, Elizabeth L. 508, Ella 508, 509, Elmer 509, Elton Elizabeth 509, Elvira 509, Emanuel 508, Emmaline 508, Ermel 508, Ernest 576, Ethel 509, Forest 508, Forrest Woods 508, Frank 508, 509, Fred 507, Frederick 508, Garth 509, Gary 411, 508, George 508, 509, Goerge Emanuel 509, Grace 477, 507, 508, Gregory 411, 426, 508, Halden 508, Halden Clair 411, 426, Henry 509, Hershel 508, Isma 508, Jacob 509, James 508, James M. 508, Janice 508, Jeffrey 508, Jennie 508, Jerry 508, John 508, 509, Jon 268, Jon Stephen 263, Joseph David 508, K. Jean 308, 361, 508, Karen 150, Katherine 509, Kathryn Jean 507, Kayleen Anne 507, Keith 509, Kenneth 509, Kenneth D. 263, Lawerence 508, 352, Levina 509, Lianne 508, Linda 268, Lois Ann 508, Lottie 509, Lovina 538, Lucy 508, Lura Elton 509, Lyndsy 411, 426, 508, Manuel 508, Marcia Ellen 263, Marcile 260, Maria 509, Marie 509, Mark Andrew 263, Marlene 402, 426, 508, Marlene Louise 411, Mary 508, Mary Allen 508, Mary Lewis 509, Mary Louise 508, Matthew 411, 426, 508, Maud 508, Maud Ellen 508, Michael 508, Mildred 424, Nancy 508, Olaf 508, Onie 508, Patricia Nicole 508, Patsy 508, Patty 508, Paul E. 508, Ralph 509, Robin Marie 508, Rowena (Ertel) 508, Rufus 509, Rufus Elmer 509, Saloma Ann 507, 508, Sandra 508, Sarah 538, Sarah Ann 508, Sarah Elizabeth 509, Sarah Jane 508, Sarah Jean 508, Senus 508, Shirley 477, Shirley Ann 507, 508, Stephen 268, Susanne 508, 508, Teresa 508, Teresa Louise 263, Vera 509, W. Wayne 508, Wendell Wayne 507, William 103, William 508, William E. 508, Wilma 508, Wilma Maxine 426, Zola 411, Zola 508
PLATTER, Elizabeth 444, Malinda 444, Nicholas 444
PLATZ, Nimrod 89
PLESSIGNER, Dorothy 317, B. F. 160, C.H. 163, Fred 167, Gus 167, James 202
PLETCHER, Catherine 378
PLOUGHE, Norma Jean (DeBolt) 316
PLUMMER, Benjamin 509, Benjamin Abbot 509, Beulah 509, Charles 509, Charles Ivan 509, Corneila 509, Dorothy 326, Emery 509, Esther 509, Evaline 509, Florence 509, Francis 509, George Washington 523, Harold 326, Harriet 509, Helen 370, Helen G. 527, Howard 509, James R. 370, James Ruben 509, John 509, 557, Judith Ann 509, 544, Judy 544, Kylie 418, Lewie 370, Lydia (Neidlinger) 557, Mahala 509, Mary 509, Nancy 418, 509, Nancy Joan 370, Nikki 418, Presley 509, Randal 341, Rayn 418, Robert 370, Rosetta 523, Ruby 509, Ruth 509, Sarah 509, T. Craig 370, Taylor Michelle 370, Thomas 509, Thomas R. 370, Trent 370, William 509
POFF, Brandi Jeau 279, Bret Lane 279, David Lauren 279, Deborah Jane 279, Joseph Lauren 279, Loren 144, Mark Andrew 279
POFFENBERGER, Roberta 513
POINDEXTER, B. K. 146, B. K. 598, B. K Mrs. 146, Blake Theodore 222, 510, Byron Clay 222, 510, Byron K. Dr. 510, Devon K. 510, Dr. Byron K. 222, Gay Rachelle 222, 510, Hattie (McBride) 510, Huett 510, Ives T. 510, Jeane 510, Linda 510, Marilyn Jo 510, Marjorie 510, Patricia 510, Patty 598, Shirley 510
POIRSON, Bunard 114
POLAND, Arla 522, William 522
POLDERMAN, Anna 510, Anna Staal 510, Cornelius 510, Delores 6, Dixen 510, Marinus 510, Neil 510, Shona 510, Truques 510
POLING, 66, Emma 511, Eston Jr. 511, Eston Rev. 511, Irene Louise 511, James L. 511, Jim 224, Marcia Joan 511, Martha Ann 511, Max 592, Phyllis Inez 533, Rita Marlene 511, Robert Eugene 511, Silas 60
POLLEY, Cassandra Kay 417, Ella 417, Wayne 417
PONCHA, Rose 597
POND, 66, Cindy 479, Douglas Edward 406, Effie Venham 511, Frank 511, George 406, Gregory Clifford 406, Joe 107, Joe 511, Phyllis 405, Phyllis Joan (Ruble) 406, Ralph 144, Scott Everett 406, William Walter 406, Yvonne 606
PONDER, Quentin D. 196
PONSOT, Tom 545
PONTIUS, Vera 562
PONTON, Elizabeth 371
POOL, Flora Haughton 492, Frank 492
POPE, Allen 422, 511, 576, Denise (Johnloz) 414, Enoch Allen 511, Evelyn 422, 576, 586, Evelyn (Sweeny) 511, Fred 511, Gene 422, 511, Gene 576, Isaac Allen 511, Mark 414, Richard 511, Sarah Myrtle 582, Twila 422, 511, 576, 586, Violet 511, Vivian (Olson) 511, Wayne 511
POPEJOY, C.R. 113, Christopher Doc"", Ida Noe 349, Matilda Jane 240, Nellie 349
POPICK, Genevieve 321
PORCH, Mary
PORTER, Alice 512, Anna 535, Blanche Vande 535, Catherine Kitty"", Catherine 292, Charles 193, 512, Charles Edward 535, Dick 45, Elizabeth J. Lib"", Elizabeth Jane 430, Erwin 512, Esther 512, Ethel 512, Frank Arthur 512, George Andrew 512, George E. 535, Georgiana 512, Harriet 512, Helen 512, Iva 534, 535, Iva May 535, James 512, Jim 266, Kimberly 498, Laura 512, Laurence 535, Margaret 512, Mary 402, Mary 512, Mary A. 512, May Gazille 599, Miss Mary 121, Nickolas 512, Nina 535, Ruth 512, Sarah Galehouse 512, Thelma 512, Vincent 512, Walter 304, Alva 267, 512, Claude 512, Doris Jane 512, Flora (Louks) 512, Iris B. 512, James R. 512, N. Pauline 512
POTTER, Wilma Jean 512
POTTHOFF, Fred 216
POTTS, Barbara 546, Estella Potts 512, Helen 512, Hugh 512, Joseph 512, Martha 512, Mary 288, 288, 347, 440. Ralph Jr. 288, 512, Ralph Jr. 572, Ralph Sr. 512, Ruth 572, Ruth Sturgeon 347, Susan 288, 440, 512, 572, Susan K. 347
POULSON, Carl 86, E. 81, Freddie 72, Harrold 72, Joyce Kay 553, Sue 405, W. C. 87
POWELL, Alissa Jo 513, Alma Kathleen 513, Bertha 535, Blake 443, Buren A. 513, Byron Ted 513, Carol Ann 401, Caroll 513, Catherine 533, Cheryl 443, Cindy Lou 395, Claudine 6, 8, Clay 145, Clifford 513, Clifford Hugh 513, Clifford Milton 513, Crystal 396, Dave 44, 45, David 45, 513, Dennis Dean 375, Earl 513, 559, Edward 513, Elizabeth 171, Flo 171, George S. 171, Gerry Lee 513, Grace Sunderland 513, Guelda Luana 513, Harley 559, Herschel 513, Herschel Gene 513, J. Orr Rev. 91, James 401, 513, James Edmon 513, James Edward 513, Jamie 513, John Michael 513, Joseph 277, Joseph Frank 533, Juanita Wanda 513, Kathleen 513, Kevin Dean 375, Kristi Jo 375, Kurt 396, Lolita 513, Luther Earl 436, 513, Margaret 277, Mary 277, Mary Birdella 513, Mary Davis 513, Mary E. 171, Megan Ann 513, Michael 533, Mildred 513, Mildred Kathryn Marshino 513, Mildred Marshino 436, Mildred (Marshino) 513, Nellie 513, Olive 277, Olive Etta 513, Ophel Hugh 513, Ophel Joseph 513, Ophel Joseph Jr. 513, Pamela Lee 513, Patric David 513, Phoebe Jo 513, Ray 513, Rex 513, Robert 513, Roger 513, Scott Eric 513, Stephen Joseph 513, Suella Birdella 513, Ted 443, 513, Terry Lynn 513, Thomas 277, Timothy Jason 513, William D. 171
POWER, Genevieve 367

POWERS, Bennie 272, Beulah 272, Charles 455, David 405, Emily 248, 304, Jacob 272, Jerrad 272, Jerry Wayne 272, Laurence 248, 455, Laurence <Larry> 304, Lennyce E. (Baker) 248, Margaret 8, 200, Marjorie 455, Mary 455, Mathhew 405, Minnie 455, Sarah 405, Scott 405
POYSER, Lee 429
PRATT, Teresa 460
PREMER, Hi 167
PRENTICE, Art 505, Mary 350
PRESCOTT, Jane Anne 489, Steve 489
PRESDORF, Flossie 351
PRESKEY, Emma 241, Emma J. 303
PRESNELL, Jane 382
PRESSLER, Elizada 519
PRESTON, Shelley 533, Todd 286, 533
PRIBBLE, Wayne 107
PRIBLE, Amy 514, Ardive 514, Bill 514, Byron 514, C. Forest 396, Carol 514, Carole 514, Charles Forest 472, 514, Clare 293, Connie 514, Crystal 514, Crystal (Edington) 514, Dan 514, David 514, David Gene 396, Dora 514, Dora Alice (Miller) 396, 472, Edith 293, Edwin 107, 472, 514, Edwin E. 514, Enoch 514, Enoch Morgan 310, Esther 472, 514, Flory 310, Flory 514, Forest 310, 514, Garrett 514, George 514, Harold 107, 396, 472, 514, 514, Helen 514, James 514, Jane 514, Jay 514, Jeffery Lynn 396, Jeffrey L. 336, John 472, John 514, John J. 238, 514, John Jeptha 310, 396, Jonathan 514, Joshua 514, Katelyn Suzanne 396, Larry 514, Linda 514, Lucritia 514, Lurana 310, 311, Lurania 514, Lydia A. 514, Lydia (York) 310, Lydia York 514, Mariah (Becker) 310, Mark David 396, Martha 107, 514, Martha Elizabeth, 472, Mary 107, 472, Mary 514, Mary Elizabeth 514, Matthew Lynn 336, 396, Meghan Marie 336, 396, Michael David 336, Nellie May 554, Patricia 514, Paul 472, 514, Pauline 514, Ray 514, Robert Allen 396, Sara Kay 396, Sarah 514, Saundra 514, Saundra Jayne 396, Steven Douglas 396, Susan 514, Susan Celeste 396, Tom 514
PRICE, Adam 538, Aldene 515, Andria 515, Arlie 296, Barbara 515, Bonita 538, Byron 538, Calvin 515, Daniel 515, Daniel Jr. 515, Dennis 392, Edith Yoho 515, Erik 538, Harriet 515, Harvey 515, Harvey Jr. 515, Hulda 515, Isaac 421, James 515, James A. 515, James Hamilton 515, Katherine Ann 515, Kathrine 515, Kathy 150, Levina 515, Lewis 392, Linda Ann 383, Lucille 515, Martha 515, Mary 515, Mary Ann 515, Moses 515, Patt 515, Richard 515, Robert 515, Robert Jr. 515, Roberta 515, Sally 515, Shelley 142, Susan 256, 398, Tina 392, William 515, William Jr. 515
PRICHARD, Connie (VanEmon) 257, Jennifer 257, Jeremy 257
PRIDDY, Evelyn 152, Harold 83
PRIEST, George 320, Robert Rev. 91
PRIESTER, Amy 555, Cindy 555, Jeffery 555, William 555
PRILLAMAN, Mary L. 289, Sarah 94, William 94, Lewis 289, Maria (Masterson) 289
PRIMROSE, J.E. 82
PRISER, Carson 560, Daniel 560, Grace 560, Joseph 560
PRIVETT, Kathy 150
PROBST, Avaline Marie 460, Cynthia Nettie Singler 460, Henry 460, Pamala 150
PROUDY, Ruth 462
PROUGH, Arlene 37, Audrey 592, Barbara 573, Clint 37, Derek Michael 581, 582, Frank 509, Harrison 127, Jessie 592, Lois 460, Mary Lou 425, Pharol 37, Rodney 460, Timothy 581, Timothy Derek 582
PROUTY, Desiree 350, John 350, Nichole 350, Randy 350, Shane 350
PRUITT, Carl 394, Carl 416, Hattie Marie 473
PUCKETT, Adam 475, Ervin 475, Jesse 475, Julie 475
PUGH, Charles Edward 296, Judith 320, Judith Ilene 296, 585, Mary Elisabeth 435, Mary Ellen 296, Paul Edward 296, Vernia 515, Wesley Rev. 97
PULVER, Aldula Marie 521, Amos John 515, Anna (Egli) 515, Barbara 515, Barbara 521, Beverly 515, Carole 515, Carole 521, Christian 515, 521, Daniel 515, 521, David 515, 521, Dennis 515, Diane 515, Earnest 515, Elaine 515, Ernst 515, Gottlieb 515, Irene Helen 515, Judith 515, Karen 515, Karl 515, 521, Kathy 515, Larry 515, Lester 515, 521, Mary Ellen 515, 521, Philip 515, 521, Raymond 515, Rebecca 515, Sarah Jane 515, Stanley 515, 521, Steven 515, 521, Sylvan 515, William 515, 521
PURCELL, 179, Lawrence 146, Lawrence Mrs. 146
PURDY, J. Wilbur 431, Jason Christopher 431, John Williams 431, Justin David 431, Mary Katherine 431, William 431
PURKHISER, Tracy 459
PURSIFULL, Andrew Michael 396, Bill 594, Brian Daniel 396, David M. 396, Davie 514, Emily Suzanne 396, Jerry Lee 396, Martha 594, Michael David 396, Patricia May Patti"", Robert 594, Sarah 514, Sherry 594, Teresa Kay 396, Vickie 594
PURSLEY, Connie 379, Donald 127, Ernest 78, Henry 515, Ida 515, Jimmy 432, John 515, Leo 95, Marjorie 515, Mayro 515, Teresa 432, Vernail 515, Wanda 515, William Henry 515, Worth 515
PURVIS, Teresa Marie Purvis 599
PUTNAM, Angela Marie 406, Thomas 406
PUTT, Robert J. 553, Rodney Lee 553, Thelma 553
QUACKENBUSH, Curtis 321 417, Eric 418, Hilda 321, John E. 321, Judy 418, Lindy 418, Mae 597, Martha 402, Martha 437, Peter 321, Phebe 103, William 437
QUACKENBUSN, Tina 483
QUADE, Larry 290, Robert Ryan 290
QUICK, C.G. 202, John W. 517, Julia Ellen 522, Nancy 517, Nancy 517
QUINN, Clarence 83
QUINOES, Carmenw 457
QUINONES, Carmen 490
QUISNO, Edward 15
RAABE, Arthur W. 84
RABEL, Anesthesia 402, Elena 402, Fred 402, John 402, Maris 402, Monica 402, Mr. 68, Tommy 402
RABER, Ada 516, Artie 439, 516, Bruce Lee 285, 494, Charles 516, Connie Sue 285, Constance Sue 494, Cora 516, Cynthia 516,, Donald Kent 285, Donald Kent 494, Drew 516, Earl 285, 516, Earl Gilbert 494, Elizabeth 516, Eva 516, Fredrica Rheinacher 437, Glenda Irene 493, Henry 516, Homer 516, Homer O. 516, J. Wayne 516, John C. 364, John C. 516, John Randall 516, Joseph 516, Kelly 516, Lewis 516, Maria (Lucabaugh) 364, Marion 421, Mary 516, Mary Estella 364, Maude 516, Maude (Gilbert) 516, Oddessa 516, Odessie 64, Paul 516, Randy 113, Sidney Wayne 516, Tobie 516, Vadas 516, Wayne 516, Zachary 516
RADKEY, Dorothy 467
RAFFA, Carolyn 248
RAFNEL, H. T. 81
RAGER, Mary Jane 409
RAHRER, Carolyn 535
RAIEHART, Anna 426
RAILING, Cheri 562, Cletis 562 Justine 562 Lynn 562
RAINEY, Mr. 179
RAINIER, Ceclia 575
RAINS, 66
RAKHMY, Lousia Lizzette 356, Rebecca 415
RAMSEY, Bonnie 154, Ida 20, J. H. 98, J. L. 98, Mary 472
RAMSEYER, Delores 480, Gerald 585, Harry 553, Howard 480, Marilyn 480, Pauline 480, Sue 229, Violet 553, Wilma 480
RANDALL, Addison 516, David 516, Dewey 84, Elva 516, Ervin 112, 516, Fanny 516, Frank 516, George 516, Goldie 516, Homer 516, Loretta 516, Maria 516, Richard 516, Ruth Ann 435, 516, Shelly 434, William 516
RANDLE, Madge 420
RANDOL, Billy 228, Billy Joe 286, Brian 286, Carly 286, Courtney 286, Dixie 450, Douglas 286, Gabriel 286, Grace (Snyder) 511, Harry 511, Holly 286, Julie 286, Morgan 286, Richard 228, Stacie 84, Zachary 286
RANSFORD, Nettie 147
RANSOPHER, Mollie 16
RANSPHER, I.F. 86
RAPISARDA, Nunzia 425
RAPP, Emelia 273, Jamie 407
RAPSON, Eugene 98
RARICK, John Henry 276, 532, Lizzie (Shively) 276, Lizzie (Shively) 532, Pearl 276
RASH, R. W. 92, 99
RASOR, Catherine 292
RATCLIFF, C. B. 185, Denton 45, Elmer 45
RATCLIFFE, Kellie Renee 452
RATHERT, John 476, Josephine 476
RATLIF, Evelyn 239
RATLIFF, Daniel 592, Gretchen Joanne 470, Jim 470, Kyle Tanner 470, Olive 293, Olive Grimsley 280, Otto 224, Robert 489, Sarah 462, Steven 585, W.C. 145, William C. 293, Zella 489
RAUCH, Adam 374, Hannah 374, Jadon 374, Jarrod 374, Jay (Jehu) 374, Jerome 374, Jerry 374, Micah 374, Michael 374, Nicole 374, Rachel 374, Ryan 374, Sarah 374
RAULSTON, Bea 472
RAUNER, Doris 221
RAVER, Augustus 444, 513, Clementina Kapp 513, Dorothy 513, Eliza 257, Esther 513, Helen 554, Hilda 513, Israel J. 513, Janet 513, Judson Lorin 513, Leona Vita 513, Lewis 513, Lorin 513, Lucile 513, Paul Charles 513, Ruth 513, Sally 513, Vivian 513
RAY, Larry 145Lori 489, Ruth big) 393
RAYER, Leona Vita 513
RAYL, Hazel 533
REAGAN, Ronald 34
REAM, Elizabeth (Goss) 366, George 366
REASER, Alice 517, Beth Ann 517, Brandon Lee 517, Brian 517, Charles 517, Clara Lucile 517, Clara Lucille 469, Clarence 517, Clarence E. 517, Connie Kay 517, Cornelius 517, Cynthia 517, Elizabeth 517, Ella Hoad 517, Emma 111, 517, Emma Marie 517, Everett 111, Ezra D. 517, Ezra Levi 469, George 517, George Bennett 517, Gregory 517, Jacqueline Sue 517, Janet 517, Janet Lucille 517, Jaron 517, Jerry 528, Jerry L. 517, John 517, John Eli 517, John James 517, Joseph 517, Joseph George 517, Joseph Jr. 517, Laurence Clayton 469, Lawrence 111, 234, 517, Levi 234, 469, 517, Levi W. 517, Liara 517, Maranda 517, Margaret 517, 599, Mary A. 517, Mary Ann 517, Naida Theola 517, Nanch 517, Nellie 517, Nellie Helen 517, Peg 528, Rodney 517, Sarah 517, Tamar 517, Thea Marie 517, Virginia Lou 517, Zelma 517, Zelma Tewell 469
REASONER, Sophia 373
REAVIS, Amanda J. 537, Francis A. 537
REBBER, Adeline Dody"", Clara Moeller 536, Herman F. 536
REBER, Cami Raye 369, 517, Carol Ann 517, Carolyn 345, Charles 165, Christi Ann 369, 517, Cory Don 369, 517, Craig 345, David 345, Don 165, Donald 369, Donald E. 517, Emma (Siders) 369, George 517, Gloria Jean 517, Hazel (Shady) 517, Katherine Sue 517, Raymond Dale 369, 517, Steven 345, Susannah 326, Vicki Graham 517, Vicki Lynn 337, Virgil 345
RECKER, Dan 349, Deanne 349, Elizabeth 349, James R. 349, Jim 349
RECORD, Clara (Kraft) 518, Jeanne Gaylan 518, Jo Ann 518, Robin Beth 518, William Jackson III 518, William Jackson Jr. 518, William Jackson Sr. 518, J. A. 60, Thelma 520
REDD, George 446, Stella 446
REDDING, Alford 519, Alfred 411, 518, Allen 518, Ambrose 518, Angeline 411, Angeline 518, Anna 582, Arminda , Bessie 518, Carol Jean 518, 544, Charles 518, 544, Charles Franklin 518, Claire 137, CLifford Franklin 518, Daniel 518, Delpha 518, Dora 588, Dorcas 295, Edna 518, Edna Marie 518, 544, 591, Eldon 518, Eldon 544, Eliza 396, Elizabeth 518, Eller 518, Fern 518, Gary Wayne 518, George 518, George 519, Grace 518, Halcyon 544, Hiram 518, Ida 326, J.L. 214, James 518, James Franklin 518, James Grover 518, Janet 527, Janet Marie 518, Jasper 519, 564, Jay 527, Jay Alan 518, Jean 500, Jennie 564, John 518, 519, John M. 518, John Oliver 518, 544, 591, Joseph 518, 519, Josie 518, Josie 544, Leander 518, Malinda 519, Marlene 527, Martha 518, Martin 518, Mary 518, Mary Alice (Caudla) 518, Mary Ann 544, Mary Francis 411, Mary S. 309, Mary Sabina 417, Michelle Lee 518, Millie 519, Miriam Highlen 417, Nancy 411, 518, Nancy A. 518, Nancy (Sparks) 519, Nathan 518, Nora 519, Ores 519, Patsy 518, Perry 519, Phineas 519, Phinias 519, Pirlie 519, Rachel 519, Ransom 417, Raymond 519, Rebecca 518, Rhoda 519, Richard 518, Ruth 588, Ruth 589, Sally 518, Samuel 519, Sarah 518, 519, Sina 518, Thomas 518,, Thurston Washington 518, Tracy Lynn 518, Wesley 518, William 417, 518, 519, William Eldon 518, 544, Willis Brown 588, Jr. George 519
REDMANN, Connie 530, Greg 530, Jean 530, John 530, Ruth 530
REECE, Anna 245, 519, Arthur 245, 519, Carrie Nevada 519, Charles 245, Charles Kimmer 519, Cleora 519, Eva 519, Gertrude 245, Helen 519, James 245, 519, John 245, 519, John Alexander 275, 519, Kahlia 519, Kate 355, Lottie 245, Marjorie 283, Mary 245, 519, Mary Elizabeth Molly"", Mary Elizabeth 408, Mary Emiline (Kimmer) 275, Mary Melissa 519, Molly 245, Nila Ann 519, Noel 519, Roberta 519, Roger 519, Ruth 519, Vada 245, William 245, 355, 519
REED, Andrew 112, Bessie 519, Blanche M 352, Clyde 417, Dennis 98, Earl 519, Elizabeth (Sink) 352, Ernest 447, Evelyn L. 603, Hershel 519, Jeffrey 449, Karen 355, Kellie Renee 452, Kelsi Renee 452, Kevin 355, Klayton 355, Kourtney 355, Larry 130, Larry Lee 452, Laura 289, Linda 449, Lorraine 449, Maria 546, Martha 588, Mary A. Jennings 242, Melvina 155, Milo 352, Otto 321, R. S. Rev. 97, Rebecca 519, Richard 140, Robert 321, Sharon Kay 452, Stanley 449, Susan 6, 154, Sylvester 352, Timothy Michael 452, Todd Alan 452, Vernon 603, Walter 221, Will 519, Winniet 161, Zeffie (Kitchen) 352
REEF, Emma Anna 525, Jean 150
REEMSNYDER, B. E. 85
REES, John 89
REESE, Emma 462, Esther 462, Frances 462, Helen 462, Laura 462, Marjorie 462, Ruth 462
REEVES, Carl 127, Dennis 240, Don 151, Fanny 304
REFF, Barbara Ellen 553, Barbara Ellen 553
REGESTER, Mary 335
REGNIER, Jacqueline Marie-Louise 309
REHBEIN, Vicki Patterson 279
REHM, Sally 270
REID, Chauncey K. 232, Romanell 259
REIDDLE, Elmo 137
REIDLINGER, Ed 95
REIFEL, Brian 525, Kelly Rae 525
REIFF, Agnes 372, Angela 521, Benjamin John 521, Bob 521, Christopher Lucas 521, Doreen (Luestner) 521, Elizabeth 520, Elizabeth A. 257, 258, Elizabeth Alice 258, George E. 520, George L. 258, Gladys 521, Hannah 300, 478, Herman 520, Jack 521, Jess J. 520, Jesse L. 520, Joan 521, John E. 520, John Karl 520, Johnny 521, Joyce 521, Kathy 490, Lizzie 258, Louis 372, Manson 300, Marion 300, Paul 160, Rose Bay 258, Rose Bay 520, Thelma 520, Tony 521, Verdane 521, Virgie 520, Virginia 520
REIHARD, Shawn 529
REILLEY, Carolyn 530, Jack 530
REIMER, Sue 505
REIMSCHISEL, Louise 487
REIMSCHISESL, Louise 340
REINCHIELD, Cecil 312, Lester 312
REINECK, Mary 322
REINERS, Andrew Christopher 285, 586, 588 Jean (Byers) 586, Kurt 285, 588, Kurt Rudolph 586, Rudy 586, Sandy 588
REINHARD, Aaron 340, Adolph 520, 522, Aimee Joyce 520, 522, Albert 520, Aldula Marie 521, Aldulla 515, Alice 522, Andreas 520, Ann 521, Arland 221, 589, Arland Gale 520, Arland Gale 522, 526, Arnold 522, Arvilla 520, Arvilla Jean 520, 522, 526, Betty Jane 521, Carl 522, Carla 520, Carla Jane 520, 522, 589, Carleen Julia 520, Carlton 221, 589, Carlton Dale 520, 522, 526, Carmen Ruth 520, 522, Dale Walter 521, Daniel 520, Daniel II 521, Daniel III 521, Daniel Simon 521, Delores 521, Donald 515, Donnie 340, Doris Ellen 521, Doug 521, Doyle 515, Edna Lucille 521, Edward 521, Elizabeth 434, Eric Von 520, 522, Eriswil 520, Ezra 521, Ezra Jr. 521, Gottfried 520, Harry 522, Harry Edward 521, Herbert 521, Herman 522, Howard 221, 520, 526, 589, Howard Franklin 522, Ilene 221, Ilene (Ehrman) 520, 526, 589, Ilene May 522, James Paul 521, Jeff 521, Jerome 340, Jerry 521, Joan 521, Johannes 520, John 340, Kenneth Orval 521, Kent 521, Kevin 521, Kim , Kris 521, Lanae 521, Larry 521, Lena 340, Leota 190, Linda 521, LouAnn 521, Lydia (Meyer) 522, Lynette 521, Marc Arland 520, 522, Marcia 515, Marlene 521, Martha 438, 521, Mary 522, Mary Ann 221, Mary Jo 521, Mike 521, Mildred Louise 521, Mona 521, Nathan Carlton 520, 522, Pauline 521, Rebecca 521, Rhonda 521, Roger 521, Rosemary 340, Rosie 521, Ruth 521, Ruth (VonGunten) 589, Sarah Jane 515, Sherry 521, Tim 521, Tom 521, Tony 521, Ulrich 520, Wayne 521
REINHART, Daniel 68, Fannie (Ruff) 382, Fred 382, Matilda Tillie""
REINHOLD, Buelah 390, Hugh 142
REINKE, Marjorie 515
REINKING, Christine Wilhelmine 482, Elva Joey"", Johann Ernst 482, Marie Catherine Elisabeth 482
REKEWEG, Edgar 503, Jason 503, Justin 503, Linda 322, Mark 322, Rozella 503
RENBARGER, Martha Harter 291
RENDRICKS, Mary 150
RENNAKER, Jill 595
RENNER, Amy Kathryn 522, Angie 522, Christopher L. 522, Clint M. 522, Elizabeth McDaniel 522, Everett L. Luke"", John Mark 522, Kathryn Lamhert 522, Lucas T. 522, Lynn A. 522, Matthew Luke 522, Portia Jane 522, Samuel 522, Sarah Kathryn 522
RENNOLLET, Ray 178
RENOLLET, Ray 145, 171, Vergil 145
RENTSCHLER, Marilyn L. 403
RENWICK, Rea 258
REPP, Vera Harris 384
RESINGER, Sheila (Higgins) 394
RESLER, Angela 336, Augusta 336, Betty 336, Betty Jean 336, Chad 336, Charles 336, Cynda 336, Deborah May 336, Debra 336, Edith 336, Everett 336, George William 336, Phebe 336, Rick 336, Wendell 336
RETHERFORD, Nora 503
RETHLAKE, Harold 546, Jason Kyle 546, Jessica Lyn 546, Kenton Howard 546, Mary Lou 545, Mary Lou 546, Phyllis 546, Tom 132
RETTIG, Cathy 357, Shari 307
REUILLE, Amy 425, Elizabeth 425, Michelle 425, Norman 425
REUSSER, Amanda Kay 269, Brian 598, Christopher John 269, Edna 241, James 290, John 269, Julie 598, Kay 244, Lindsay Nicole 269, Mahala 366, Mahala 440
REUST, Mary Katherine 431
REYNARD, Daisy 606
REYNOLDS, Alma Oliver 522, Amanda J. 537, Arla 522, Augustus 366, Augustus 440, Clara L. 476, Cleme 200, Danielle 527, Deane 145, 306, 522, Della 522, Dessie 476, Doyle 522, Dwight 577, Ed 306, Elida Ann (Jones) 393, Eliza 373, Elizabeth 522, Eva M. 288, Eva May Chalfant 288, F. M. 600, George 393, Gregory 527, Harry 522, Hillis 306, 522, Hugh Jack"", J. E. 115, J. Edwin 8, 145, 522, Jerry A. 145, Jim 15, John Edwin 522, Jordan 527, Julia 306, 522, Julia Ellen 522, Leon 288, Leonard 475, Lilly 577, Lona 522, 586, Louise 527, Luella 440, Lydia 527, Max 335, 522, Melvin M. 537, Mikel Ray 577, Raymond 476, Robert 320, Robert C. 522, Stella 306, Stella Mae 522, Sylvester 288, Wilbert 185, Wilbur 522, William 522
RHEA, James 568, John 568, Lydia 568, Thomas 568
RHINEAR, Hannah 299
RHINEHARD, Mary 435
RHOADES, S.A. 58
RHOADS, Dusty 447, Ruby 447, Sara 258
RHOBY, Sarah 480
RHODES, Bill 140, Estel 151, Finley H. 540, J. N. 98, Julia 533, Tina 533
RHODIFER, Beverly 99, George Rev. 99
RHOTEN, Festus 178
RICE, Aaron 346, Amanda 333, Brent 346, Carol Ann 333, Dawn 346, DiAnne 346, Edna Faye 445, Erma 538, Gene 346, Gregg 346, Guy 321, Jeff 333, Jeremy 333, Lidah 586, Marjorie 346, Nellie 417, Norma 346, Ronald 346, Roy 346, Scott 346, Sue 346
RICH, Beverly 154, Fred 321, Howard 145, 146, 187, 212, Howard Mrs. 146, Paul 321, Ruby 538, William 321
RICHARDS, Garnet Grutrude 424, Geneva 403, Paula 602, Sarah 546, Sharon 552
RICHARDSON, Bill 523, Cindy 474, Daniel 509, Emil 509, Faith 523, Francis 509, Gene 509, Goldie (Earhart) 264, Heather 474, Jean 264, Katherine 523, Louise 320, Macbride 264, Marcia 523, Robert 509, Ruby 509, Travis 474, Vivian 509, William Lee 523
RICHART, Mary E. 568, O.L. 58
RICHEY, Barbara A. 425, Carl 425, Carl Duane 425, Carrie 523, Catherine Loraine 425, Chester Albert 425, Clara Edna 425, David Allen 425, Diana 523, Douglas 523, Earl Howard 425, Elizabeth 386, Elmer Ray 425, Eric Roger 425, Estella M (Spaulding) 425, George Marion 425, Harlan G. 523, Harold 326, Helen Irene 425, Janet Rae 425, John 523, Joseph 547, Josephine 523, Judy Ann 425, Karen Lee 425, Kathryn 326, 523, Kenneth Warren 425, Lida 407, Lydia V. 575, Martha 425, Mary Jane 523, Mary Lucile 425, Meghann 523, Michael Eugene 425, Milton Loomis 425, Ralph Laverne 425, Raymond E. 425, Roger 523, Stacey 523, Virginia Grace 425
RICHHART, O.L. 58
RICHMOND, John 558, Rose 558
RICKERT, Letha 465
RICKORD, Mary Lou 585
RIDDILE, Bertha 534, Forrest 534, Lloyd 534, Sam 534
RIDDLE, Alice 383, John 90, Mary Ann 586, Sam 586
RIDENOUR, Hugh 494, Sandra 494, Therese 494
RIDER, C.O. 144, Compton 171, 200, Compton O. 178 Compton O. 223, J. H. 81
RIEDDLE, Christian 523, Christian 523, Christian Linnett 523, Cora Inez Hottel 523, Crystal 523, Crystal Bess 523, Elmo 8, Elmo 523, Elmo Blaine 523, Inez 523, Matthew Christian 523
RIES, Debra May 419, Raymond Edward 419, Russell J. 419, Russell J. Jr. 419, Stephen Paul 419, Thomas Allen 419
RIGBY, Lynne Ann 582, Stan 145, Sylvia J. 600
RIGGERS, Clara 530, Meta 465
RIGGS, Catherine 555, Cheryl 569, Daisy 555, Daisy May 555, Trimbley 555
RILEY, Elanore 462, James Whitcomb 164, Lulu 476, Michael 527, Otis 476, Penny 527, Robert 527
RILLING, James 89
RILY, Clyde 476, Harold 476, Otis 476
RINEAR, Charles 87, Ellen 266, Ellen McKee 266, George F. 266, Girthie 266,

Hannah S. 16, Hannah Sophia 346, John W. 16, John Wesley 346, Sarah 242, Sarah C. 346
RINEBOLT, Mildred 390
RINEHART, Brenda 277, Lena 250, Mark 277, Mark Alan 277
RING, Norma 244
RINGER, Carrie Alice 327, Houston 327, Houston Henry 327, James 327, Mary Catherine 327, Phoebe 327, Rauleigh 327, William 327
RINGGER, Jeanette 330
RINKENBERGER, Catrina 353, Chase Adam 353, James 353, James Lincoln 353, Jeanne 353, Joel David 353, Luke Allen 353
RIPLEY, Carolyn 530, Carolyn Ruth 276, Doris (Brumbaugh) 530, Rob 530, Robert Edward 276, Ronald Mark 276, Ronnie 530, Ward 276
RIPPE, Dorothy 155, 579
RIPPENGER, Maryann 150
RIPPLE, Augustus 337, Daniel Russell 337, David Allen 337, Douglas Eugene 337, Galen Dee 337, Galen Norman 337, Lovina (Dunbar) 337, Norman Dennis 337, Russell A. 337, Sherryl Dian 337
RIQPE, Dorothy 155
RISINGER, Leota 555
RISLEY, F.P. 86, Franklin 481, Hariet 555, Mary Alice (Watson) 481, Virgie Nina Marie 481
RISSER, Alice (Rose) 294, Brett 364, Calvin 182, Calvin 524 George 414, George 524, Helen 524, Irene 524, June 524, Kyle 364, Lloyd 524, Lovina 524, Lynda 524, Mariam 524, Mary Alice Rose 524, Max 524, Ned 364, Norma Jean 524, Pamela 524, Pat 524, Rose 457, William Henry 524
RITCHEY, Clara 524, John 524, Lauren 524, Lena 524, Mary Almeda 524, Pearl 524, Sarah Pearlie 524, Violet 249, 524, William 524
RITT, Paul Dr. 269 Paul J. 145
RITTENHOUSE, Aaron 523, Alice 348, Alonzo F. 348, Amy 594, Andrew 523, Benjamin 523, Brock 163, 523, Cora Alice 273, George 146, 151, 163, 523, Greg 163, 523, Jane 523, Joel 523, Justin 523, Kent 163, 523, Linda 163, 523, Lynda 523, Mark 594, Nina 163, 523, Olin 87, Phyllis 594, William 594
RITTER, Rosanna 259, 260
RIVAR, Susan 426
RIVERS, Hazel 308
RIX, Catherine 136, 200, Catherine E. 525, Clarabelle 525, Debra 525, Don 525, Eldon 525, Evelyn 525, Lewis 525, Marshall 525, Marshall A. 525, Mary 525, Mevalyn 525, Michael 525, Moses M. 525, Robert 525, Roger 525, Rosemond 588, Sonja 525, Wilbur 525
ROARK, Carl 75
ROBART, Dwight 566, Rose Marie 566, Tami 566, Timmy 566
ROBB, Amos 106
ROBBINS, Bertha 402, C. K. 518, 544, H.H. 202, Hersh 8, 520, James Garfield 520, Joe A. 520, John 78, Julie 520, Kay 520, Linda 264, Louella 520, Margaret 443, Mary Jane 520, May (Sturgis) 443, Penny 520, Rinda 520, Virginia 136, 520, W. G. 443
ROBERSON, Christopher 319, Elise 319, Leanne 319, Ray 319, Ryan 319, Timothy 319,
ROBERTS, Amy 525, Amy Lou 359, Andrea Kay 525, Atlanta Denton 299, Betty 525, Betty Irene 452, Blanche (Custard) 304, Brenda 244, Cathy 364, Charleen 324, Danielle Linn 525, Dawn 525, Douglas 525, Douglas Kirk 525, Earl 525, Elizabeth 405, Emma Anna (Reef) 359, Francis Earl 452, 525, 551, Frederick Earl 452, 525, Geneva 585, Janet C. 525, Jarred Lee 525, Jason Andrew 359, Jennie Kathryn 452, 551, Jennie Kathryn (Maddux) 359, 525, Jennifer 525, Jennifer Lynn 359, Joe 244, John 118, 268, John Edwin Jackie"", John Edwin 452, Jordan Edward 525, Josua Michael 359, Joyce E. 525, Joyce M. 550, 551, Joyce Marie 452, 525, Julia Ann 337, Julie 244, Karen K. 525, Karen Kay 447, Karen Kay Bender 525, Karla 244, Kay 525, Kelli 525, Kelli Rae 525, Kerry 525, Kerry Lee 525, Kim 525, Kim Eugene 359, Kirk 525, Kristin 525, Laura 525, Lawrence Kay 447, 452, 525, Lester 359, Lester Eugene 452, 525, Lewearlic 359, Linzy 299, Lori 525, Lori Ann 359, Mark 244, Mary Jane 268, Melinda 525, Melissa 525, Melissa Lee 359, Miranda S. 418, Rebecca Francis 400, Richie 525, Rita 525, Rita Sue 359, Robert D. 268, Ruth 299, Ruth 515, Ruth Ellen 244, Samuel 299, Sophia Wiley 299, Stella 268, Sue 525, Toni 525, W.Z. 58, Walter Lavern 525, Walter Laverne 452, William 92, Willie 429
ROBERTSON, Catherine 345, Claudia 345, Corwin 373, Cynthia 345, Joan 345, Ruth 134, William 345
ROBINSON, Uncle Bed"", Alexander 547, Amy 302, Ann 262, Charles Nelson 547, Donna 302, E. E. 83, E. Rev. 13, Fiona 302, Fred 302, George 175, Glen 458, Helen 302, Jason 302, Jennifer 302, Joe 302, John 547, Justin 302, Laura 460, Margaret 547, Mary 402, Rev 76, Suzanna 547, W. W. 81, Wayne 302
ROBISON, Andrew 292, Betty 586, Carol Jean 552, John 315, Peter L. 586, Willamette Merriman 586
ROBLES, Ames 606, Anthony 606, Camelia 606, Hannah 606, Isaiah 606, Joshua 606, Mary 150, Rachel 606, Solomon 606, Tony 78
ROCHON, Dorotha 275, 519, Seved 275, 519
ROCKWELL, Maria Perrin 258
RODDA, Ann 564, Beryl 564, Gerald 564
RODENBECK, Arvilla 221, Arvilla Jean 520, Arvilla (Reinhard) 589, Donald 342, Edwin 526, Justine (Meyer) 526, Mike 342, Mycal Charles 522, 526, Mylinda Jean 522, 526, Myshel Jean 522, 526, Randy 342, Stephen 221, Stephen Charles 522, 526
RODGERS, Emily 460, Mary 574
RODRIGUEZ, Cynthia 277
RODY, Dianna 577
ROE, Dean 130, Dean H. 513, Etta 541, Gladys 109, 534, Jennie 437, Jeremiah 541, Mary Ann (Garnard) 541, Maurice 503, Robert Dean 513
ROEBUCK, Don 25, 38, Peggy Thoma 38
ROEDERER, George 89
ROEMBKE, Adele 368, Alvina 388, 526, Anna Bauermeister Graft 526, Doretta 526, Elsie 388, 526, Ernest Conrad Diedrich 526, Friedrich 526, Marie 526, Meta 388, Minna 526, Sophia 526, William 252, 368, 388, William Jr. 388, 526, William Sr. 526
ROEMPKE, Alvina 368, Else 368, William 368, William Jr. 368
ROESLER, John 95
ROGERS, Angela 597, David 597, Doug Rev. 597, Effie Ollie Tuttle 295, 295, Elaine 350, George 90, Gobson W. 537, Harry 295, Hazel Lucille 295, Jesse 518, 527, Karen 527, Katheryn 527, Kathryn (Waltz) 518, Loretta Kay 527, Louisa 295, Louise 527, Lucille Sophia 537, Marlene 527, Marlene Jo 518, Opal 527, Scott Gray 537, Thurl 107, W. W. 185, Walter 527, Whorton 145
ROHBEUGH, Astelle (Featherhoff) 410, Curtis 410
ROHRABAUGH, Curtis Elmer 270, Gladys 270
ROHRER, Cora 526, Patricia Ann 526, Roscoe Alfred 526, Wahilla 526, Wayne 526
ROHRING, Gilbert 527, Kelly Lynn 527, Lynette M. 603, Matthew Robert 527, Stephen Lynn 527, Steve 603, Virginia Jones 527
ROLL, Fern Florence 578, Henry Bingham 578, Mary Elizabeth (McKee) 578
ROLLI, Magdalina Gottlieb 40
ROLLIE, Godlip 25
ROMANIE, Gladys 334
ROMEY, Andrew 316, Anna (Musser) 316, Clyde 316, Della 316, Della 316, Della May 316, Earl 43, Elma 316, Grover 316, John 316, Reuben 316, Rosella 316, Theophil 316
ROMINE, Arthur 272, 527, Charles 272, 527, Clarence 272, 527, Cornelius 262, Eliza Jane Brown 262, Elizabeth 527, Irene 262, Joe 319, 527, Judy 527, Kelli 319, Kellie 527, Kyle 319, 527, Lloyd 272, 370, 527, Margaret Singer 262, Minnie 272, 527, Nate 527, Noah 262, Sarah Catherine (Brown) 272, Sue 527, William 262
ROOF, Mary 556
ROOP, Clarence 346, R.M. 142
ROOSEVELT, Franklin D. 34
ROPER, James E. 388
RORICK, Katrina 601, Melissa K. 601, Norma Jean 601
ROSE, Abraham 527, Adam 527, Alta J. 527, Anne 527, Anthony 294, 527, Barbara Elizabeth 527, Bette 527, Carol 347, Catherine 527, Christina 262, Clarence Edwin 493, 527, Cleopus Earl 527, Collin 527, David Alan 527, Diana 527, Dorothy 8, 278, 527, Dorothy (Knoff) 429, Dorothy Marie 527, Eliza 527, Elizabeth 527, Elizabeth Mary 527, Geneva 527, Geoffery 527, George Nathaniel 527, Issac 527, Jacob Perry 527, James Monroe 527, Joe 499, John 294, 527, John Edward 527, Kelle Ann 527, Leona 493, 527, Leonard 493, Leonard 527, Lloyd 527, Margaret 527, Marie 535, Mary 527, Mary Christina 527, Max 493, 527, Max O. 429, Nelson 294, 546, Perry 527, Peter 366, 367, Peter 527, Rachel 527, Sam 499, Samuel 527, Sarah 527, Sharon 527, Sophia 527, William 294, 527
ROSELIUS, Edith 584
ROSIE, Don 145, Donald 146, Donald Mrs. 146, Eunice 152
ROSIER, Ed Rev. 97
ROSS, Elizabeth 465, Esther 554, Hebert 78, James 402, Judy Thompson 380, Lawrence 274, Marilyn 274, Mort 78, William 274
ROSSMAN, Randy 85
ROTH, Anna 489, Calvin 497, Charles 416, 419, Charles 548, Clarence 150, Elsie (Johnson) 419, Jacob 438, Lloyd E. 489, Marolyn 497, Meno 494, Sheila 438, Tara 497, Tess 497, Thesa 497, Tom 438
ROTHENBUHLER, Agnes 562, Lynn 562
ROTHENBUSH, Floy 546
ROTHERMAL, Mary 200
ROTHGEB, Wayne 434
ROUDEBUSH, Effie 552, George 552, Helen 552, LaRue 552, Walter 58
ROUSH, Alton 421, Bertha 421, Bertha 533, Cal 25, Cary 421, Cary 533, Chad J. 391, Heather Ann 307, Helen 421, 533, Joel C. 391, Julie C. 391, Kent 364, 516, Kevin 307, Lillian 258, Luster 431, Marsalene 516, Maxine Ardella 431, Nicki Kay 364, 516, Ruth 421, Sheryl A. 391, Sheryl Ann (Patterson) 307, Tiffany Suzanne 307, Tina Anne 364, 516
ROUSSEAU, Connie 525
ROUTH, Charlotte 309, John 309, Martha 443
ROWE, Hugh 20, Mary Jane 523, Morgan 554
ROWLAND, Virginia 152
ROY, Jesse 266
RUBLE, Barbara Rose 406, Berthena Tharp 274, Brian 364, Brock 364, Clifford 405, Clifford Edward 406, James 274, Mamie 582, Mamie Irena 274, Ned Eugene 406, Opal M. 603, Reneta 598, Robert 405, Robert Edmond 406, Sarah 307, Zack 364
RUBY, Catherine 553, Mary 601, Pearl 601, Valentine 601
RUCK, Brittany 345, Cole 345, Stephanie 345
RUDAUPH, Sarah Emily 465
RUDNEY, Julaine F. 396
RUDY, Carolyn E. 528, Della 102, Della Lee 528, Donald 528, Donald B. 528, Earl F. 528, Edward M. 528, Ethel (Hedges) 389, Frank 528, Gretchen 528, Mark 528, Mary 528, Molly 528, Rebecca J. 528, Ruth 528, Vera 152
RUFENACHT, Lisetta 382
RUFNER, Randy 351
RUGGLES, Rachel 299
RUMPLE, Myrtle 577, Rufus 78
RUNKLE, Aaron David 369, Amy (Booher) 369, Andrew Clayton 369, Brandy Lace 528, Cheyenne Cinnamon 528, Dale 499, David Lester 369, Donna 499, Imogene 528, Kenneth 528, Kimberly 499, Kyler 352, 369, Mark 499, Nelson 15, Randall Scott 528, Tanner Shay 528, Terri Sue 337, Yvette <Gentis> 352
RUNYON, Carrie 264, Cora May 344, David 344, Ella 344, Forrest 344, John 344, 405, Mary J. 405, Mary (Price) 344, Sally 472, Sam 344, Talford 344
RUPE, David 462, Joyce 462, Mike 462
RUPEL, E. Maxine 529, Frederick M. 529, Fredrick 558, Isaac 529, James Isaac 529, Joyce D. 529, Kathryn L. 529, Lola Belle 529, Maxine 558, Roscoe 529, Susan D. 529, Ted M. 529
RUPERT, Gertrude Mitchel 332, Harvey 332, Helen Maxine 332
RUPLEY, Alice Lucille (Lesh) 607, Marion Emanuel 607, Mary Jo 607, William Henry 162
RUPP, Clara 488, Jesse 488, Magdalena 488 Marianne 340, 487, 488, 588, 593
RUPRIGHT, Amanda 410, Amy 529, Barney 45, 112, Charles 333, Charles Allen Chuck"", Elizabeth 430, 431, 492, 573, Francina 482, Hank 332, John 492, 573, Kathy J. 529, Lillie 430, 431, Lori 529, Matilda Jane 573, Minnie 333, William 482
RUSE, 66, Adeline Lorine 498, Amos Lloyd 375, Mary Catherine (Smith) 375, Sheryl 577,
RUSH, Caroline 234, Dennis 98, Diane 150, Eura Anna 265, George David 418, Ishumal 265, John B. 540, Lydia Stanforth 540, Mary M. 540, Steve 98, 234
RUSS, John 84
RUSSELL, Adam James 348, Andrew William 348, Anthony Michael 348, Charles Franklin 472, Cleora Isabelle 472, Emma (Cochran) 294, Gene 294, George 75, Gerald 372, Martha Augusta (Arnold) 472, Mary Ann 294, Michael Allen 348, Nicholas Allen 348, Ricky 294, Robert 202, Saloma 386, Sue 245
RUST, William E. 16
RUTENBERG, Art 530, 530, C. C. 530, Carl 530, Carolina 530, Chris Ann 530, Christian 480, Christian C. 530, Clara 530, Crist 530, Doris 530, Edith Lorene 530, Edna 530, Frank 530, Hannah 530, Herb 530, Ida W. 530, Lena 530, Marie 530, Mary Louise 530, Rose 530, Ruth 530
RUTENGERG, Christian Conrad 276, Herbert 276, Ida (Johnkey) 276,
RUTLEDGE, Eph 16, Evelyn 179, Janice 179, Janice 393, Ken 179, Ken 179, Ken 393
RUTZ, Alma 252, Edith Pierce 373, Emillie 373, Gustave 373
RYAN, Harold 383, Mabeline 383
RYBOLT, Coleen 544, Eldon 518, Eldon 544, Timothy Martin 518, Timothy Martin 544
SAALFRANK, Al 357, Chad 357, Eugene 336, Laura 336, Rebecca 336
SACCA, Linda Jo 306
SADLER, Christine Ann 531, Dana 402, Dana Louise 402, 531, Gaye Lyn 531, Gaye Lynn 460, Harley Irene (Rushart) 531, Louise 402, Louise 560, Louise Bradbury 531, Tom 402, 531
SAILSBERY, Michael R. 130
SALA, Rev. 60
SALE, Ida Blanche 405, James W. 163
SALES, Jim 438, Nancy Josephine 449
SALISBURY, Earl 142, Lois M. 502, Martha 142
SALMONS, 331
SALSCHEIDER, Becky 152
SALTER, Amanda 531 Frances 531, Frances 560, George 531, Ida 531, John 531, Magdaline 531, Mary Ann 531, Philenia 531, Sarah 531, Val 531
SAMELE, Vincenzio 238
SAMMONS, Cris Dorothy 433
SAMOFF, Ethel (Custard) 304
SAMUEL, W. D. Rev. 259
SANDA, Christian 82
SANDEN, Robert 527
SANDERS, Diana 527, Homer 418, Joyce D. 529, Pearl Esther 418, Sarah 421, Twilla 398
SANDERSON, Edna (Brickley) 270
SANDS, Alice May 531, Cole 531, Daniel 531, Donald Daniel 531, Floyd 95, Floyd Everett 531, Isaac 531, James 342, James Floyd 531, Jane 342, Jayne Michelle 531, Jennifer 342 Jennifer Gay 531, Jill 342 Jill Marie 531, John 318, John 342, Jon Foster 531, Joseph George 531, Julie 342, Julie Ann 531, Leah 531, Margaret Alice 531, Robert Dennis 531, Verna 531, Vesta 318
SANFORD, Arthur M. 153
SANQUIST, Esther 598, Lloyd David Sandy"", Nancy Lynne 532, Olive Lovetta Mae Goble 532, Spencer Oliver 532
SANTA, Chris 470
SANTON, Ralph 581
SAPPENFIELD, Mary Hilma 537
SARBAUGH, Cassiah Cassandra 321, Catherine 321, Jacob 321
SARK, Midred Boltin 113, Sue 554
SAUDER, Delores 521, Ethel 515, Gary 515, Joyce 515, Linda 515, Nancy 515
SAUER, Christian 68, Ed 64, Gottieb 64, 68, John 89,, Louise 64
SAUERWINE, Adam Charles 399, Benjamin Warren 399, Brian 399, Lazerne C. 399, Louis C. 399, Matthew William 399, Michael Anthony 399, Michelle 399, Tony Louis 399
SAUNDERS, George 208, George L. 145, Marlene 591, Randy 456, 591
SAUNIER, Sophia 371
SAURER, Alfred 188, Alfred G. 145, Christian 423, Martha 423
SAUTER, Elizabeth 422
SAWYER, Amos 499, Amos W. 375, Amy Elizabeth 532, Atta Robinson 532, Betty Alice 532, Bill 137, Brad Michael 532, Carl 401, Connie 6, 532, Curtis 532, Dana Franklin 532, Dessie Goldsberry 532, Douglas Alan 532, Earl 144, Emmanuel 401, Ethel (Echrote) 440, Goldie 232, Howard 401, Joan 350, John 102, Joseph 102, Kimberly 532, Laura Elizabeth 532, Lewis 119, Lydia 339, Marl 72, Mary E. (Strain) 375, Mary Strain 499, Michelle Ann 532, Ora 491, Ora 499, Rebecca 102, Shannon 532, Sonja 401, Sonja O. 401, Tom 532, William Draper 532, William Steven 532
SAXMAN, Carolyn Jean (Gilbert) 358
SAXON, Martha 431
SAYLOR, Isabella Jane Johnson 297, Isabelle (Johnson) 296, Levi 421, Levi S. 297, Lisa 605
SCHAEFER, Alice 532, Angela Kay 532, 543, David 419, David Scott 419, E. J. 146, E. J. (Ed) 196, E. J. Mrs. 146, Edna 533, Edna Irene 487, Edward 216, Eva (Wagner) 267, Ferdinand 373, Fred 487, Hildegarde 196, Jennifer 543, Jennifer Rose 532, John W. 267, Katherine Kay 543, Kenneth 532, Martha (Baumgartner) 487, Mary 267, Sam 543, Samuel Robert 532, Sheryl Lee 419, Sophia Anna 373
SCHAFER, Beverly 582, Susan D. 529
SCHAFFER, Agnes 221
SCHAFFTER, Bertha 493
SCHALGENHAUF, Ted 394
SCHAMERLOH, Carol 152, Kerry 174
SCHANTZ, Barry D. 383
SCHAPER, Virginia 403
SCHARLACH, Arthur 144
SCHAUB, Sebastian 548
SCHAUSS, Joan 506
SCHEELE, Harole 511
SCHELL, Arthur E. 412, Bonnie Mae 452, Florence (Nelson) 412, Loretta 412, Mary 283, 284
SCHELLING, Iva Irene 431, 553
SCHENIDER, Ethel 409
SCHENKELS, Dale 288
SCHERER, Anna M. 254, Barry 251, Bruce 251, Dale 483, Judith 483, Karen 483, Keith 251, Kevin 251, Lloyd 483, Megan 483, Robert 251, Robyn 251
SCHERRER, Bernadine 526, Clyde F. 407, Delbert 407, Forrest 244, Mary 407, Orville 244, Rosa 58, Russell 244, Verlin 244
SCHERRY, Edna 136, John 136, Otto 68
SCHEUMANN, Darlene Sue 532, Dean Alan 532, Denise Alane 532, Dennis 532, Diana Kay 532, Donna Renee 532, Dorothy Jo 532, Edward 532, Helen Stoppenhagen 532, Holly Lyn 532, Jason Matthew 532, Joshua David 532, Julius 532, Larry 373, Mabel Crosby 373, Rosa (Luttman) 532, Sylvia 532
SCHICK, Charlotte 266
SCHILLE, Mae 417
SCHINDERLE, Rebecca Smith 585
SCHINDLER, Brian 84
SCHINKEL, Emma 564
SCHINKEL, Friedrich 564
SCHLADEN, Jane Gerard 407
SCHLADEN, Tom 407
SCHLADENHAUFFEN, Marjorie 190, Nancy 340, 487, Susan 374
SCHLAGENHAUF, Alan 414, 533, Anna Virginia 533, Beth 533, Byron Jay 513, Caroll 246, 382, 401, Catharina 533, Chelsea 382, Edwin 533, Emma 533, Erick 513, Eva (Gottschalk) 401, Freddy 533, Gary Byron 513, George W. 533, Heath 414, 533, Heather 414, 533, Henry 246, 371, 382, 401, 533, Hermenia Higgins 394, Johannes John"", John 382, June 533, Katie Ann 533, Kyle 513, Larry 382, Lawrence 382, Lisa 382, Luticia 533, Marlene 154, 533, Mary Ann 533, Mary Effa 533, Michael 382, Minnie 533, Ralph J. 513, Ralph Jared 513, Rex 382, Rhonda 533, Robert L. 394, Ryan Gary 513, Ted 394
SCHLAGENHAUFFEN, Mary Dean 460
SCHLEPPI, Barbara 553, Benekikta 553, Daniel 553, Eva Elizabeth 553, Friedrich 553, Jacob 553, Johannes Ulrich 553, John 553, John George 553, Mary 553, Michael 553, Samuel 553, Stephan 553
SCHLICHTER, Betty 544, Connie 544, John 544, Larry 544, Tom 544
SCHLICKMAN, Roy 394
SCHMALL, Charles 165
SCHMALTZ, Gerald 457, 490, Joseph 457, 490, Michelle 490
SCHMECKEBIER, Marcia 154
SCHMELING, Helen 409
SCHMIDT, Ed 421, Frank 293, George 421, Georgia 463, Ilene 500, Janet 137, Jodi 477
SCHMOLL, Charles Bud""
SCHMOLL, Karen 342, Sally 342, Steve 342
SCHNATTERLY, Joseph 326
SCHNEIDER, Barbara 585, Charles 585, Ethel (Jackson) 410, Lydia 585, Lydia Elizabeth 320
SCHNEPP, Phyllis 277
SCHNITZ, Helen Bernicce 273
SCHNOONOVER, Amos 18
SCHNURLE, Anna Maria (Kuberlin) 366, Johann George 366
SCHNURR, Phyllis Marie 295
SCHOBER, Nancy 559
SCHOCH, Mary 321, Sarah 471, Jack 36
SCHOEFF, Anita 467, Bessie 533, Brad 286, 533, Cara 286, 533, Carlin 295, Carol 533, Charles 533, Cynthia Jo 295, David Coffield 295, Floyd 279, Frances 533, Glen 421, 533, Glennis 533, Helen 533, Isabella 411, Janet 450, Joyce 487, Joyce 533, Kara Denise 295, Kyle Carlin 295, Matthew David 295, Nancy Elaine 295, Nova 17, Roy 533, Roy D. 286, Shelley 286, 533, Sheryl 286, 533, Thomas Kyle 295
SCHOENAUER, Daniel Edward 387, Elizabeth (Zurcher) 387, Nellie (Redman) 387
SCHOENI, Elizabeth 464
SCHOEPFLE, Christian 68
SCHOLL, Anna Barbara 507, Christina Barbara 507, Jacob Frederick 507, Mathias 507, Walter 170, 401
SCHOOL, Bonnie 253
SCHOOLEY, Anna Esther 490, Donald Lee 435, Everett 435, Gale Eugene 435, Judith Ann 435, Judy 142, Madeiline 435, Mary 490 Nancy 435, Nina 435, Oliver 490, Teresa Lynn 435
SCHOONOVER, Gertie 357
SCHORTGEN, Brad 374, Brent 374, Jason 374, Pamela Sue 374, Richard 374, Rick 374, Terri 333

SCHOTT, Alyssa 533, Amanda Elanor 533, Amanda Lee 533, Bud 533, Catherine 533, George 533, Jessica 533, John Douglas 533, John George 533, John Paul Julian 533, John Terry 288, 533, Julia 533 Margaret Faye 533, Margaretta 533, Martha Ann 533, Mildred Inez 533, Nancy 533, Natalie 533, Peter C. 533, Terrell W. 288, Terrell Watson 533, Victor Duane 533, Viva Chalfant 288, Viva F. 533, Zachary Alan 533
SCHRADER, Agnes (Teller) 336, Jane Ellen 336, Louis G. 336
SCHREIBER, Janet 503
SCHRICKER, Henry 281
SCHROCK, Darline F. 412, Emma 288, Gabriel 366, Gabriel 367
SCHROEDER, Betty 526, Carroll 140, Elizabeth 388, James 388, John 388, Judy 330, Lou 407, Rebecca 388, Richard 388
SCHROER, August Butch"" Matt 343, Sarah 343, W. H. 68
SCHUELER, Marie 594
SCHUHMACHER, James 302, Jennifer 302, Jessica 302, Justin 302, John 25
SCHULL, Morris B. 368
SCHULTZ, James 8, Max 68
SCHUMACKER, Herman 481
SCHUMAN, Dawn 294, Karen (Cobbum) 294, Kim 294
SCHUMANN, 179
SCHUMM, Denise Alane 532, Lauren Nicole 532, Ted 532
SCHWARTZ, Adeline Dody"", Adeline Doty"", Agustus 535, Alice 353, Anna 487, Anna (Aeschliman) 487, Anthony 466, Artis 535, Bertha 534, 535, Brian 333, 536, Brian D. 535, Carolyn 535, 536, Catherine 333, 535, Charles Otis 534, Chester 535, Christopher 333, Cliff 333, Damon 535, Dan 487, 534, Danielle 534, Dave 48, David 34, 109, 136, 333, 534, David C. 535, David E. 535, 536, David Elias 535, Davilla 535, Davis 535, Deborah 535, Dessie 440, Dian 333, Diana 401, Doris 333, Edward 353, Edward 535, Effie 308, 535, Elias 534, 535, Elizabeth 487, 536, Elmina 535, Ernest 534, Ernie 474, Ervin 233, 353, Ervin R. 534, Esther Moyer 534, Everett 534, Everett 535, Geoffrey 536, George E. 534, 535, 536, George Edward 535, Gladys 109, 534, Glen 535, Gyrkin 534, Harriet 308, Harry 280, Heather 534, Henry 535, Herman 45, 535, Howard 233, 535, Hubert 535, Ida 534, Iva 34, 534, Iva C. 254, Iva Caroline 253, Iva May 535, Iva Porter 536, Jacqueline 536, Jan 150, Janice 340, 487, Jean 534, Jean 535, Jefferson 535, Jennifer 340, 536, Joe 534, JoElla 333, John 144, Josephine 353, Judy 534, Julia May 534, 535, 536, Julie 333, 487, Kimberly 333, Lanner 534, Larry 98, Laura 535, Leah 535, Leona 353, Levi 308, 534, 535, Lindsay 414, Lisa 466, Lizzie 487, Lloyd L. 534, Logan Miller 466, Lorin 535, Lota 535, Lulu 535, Mabel 136, Mabel E. 428, Margaret 535, Marilyn 534, Marilynn 146, Marilynn 154, Mark 535, Martha Beth 535, Mary 303, 535, Mary Magdalene 535, Matthew 333, Max 534, Michael 333, Mikel 535, Minerva Anna 535, Monic 233, Oscar 535, 536, 563, Oscar Levi 534, Otis 109, Patty 333, Paul 535, Ralph 353, Rebecca 333, Robert 414, Robin (Moser) 474, Ron Jr. 333, Ronald 333, Sarah 333, 535, Sarah (Reinhard) 534, Sean 534, Selah 534, Selah 535, Sephen 333, Sidney 534, Suzanne 333, Thomas 535, Tiercell 534, Timothy 333, 536, Tom 84, Tracy 534, Wendell 333, William 333, William Henry 535
SCHWARTZKOPH, Diane 150
SCHWARZ, Viola 526
SCHWARZKOPF, Brittany 536, Denise 536, Dennis 536, Dianne 84, James 536, Opal 527, Sandra 536, Sherry 536, Steve 84, Steven 536
SCHWEIKHARDT, Boyd 536, Bridget Jean 536, Carol Callie", Emily Jean 536, Emily (Wilkinson) 607, Frank 79, Frank B. 536, Franklin 536, Fred 142, 536, Leah Lynae 536, Leslie Lynn 536, Lovie (Roush) 536, Matthew Dean 536, 549, Melanie Lynn 536, Melinda Jo Mindy"", Melinda Jo 549, Michael Ray 536, 549, Michelle Ann Shelley"", Michelle Ann 549, Norman Ray 536, 549, Peggy Dehn 536, Peggy Dehn 549, Vera 536
SCHWEIZTER, Mary 515
SCHWEYER, Sara 475
SCHWIEGER, Aaron 490, Alan 457, Alan 490, Ashley 490, Carmen 490, Christopher 490, Jennifer 457, Jennifer 490, Kathy 490, Matthew 457, Matthew 490, Melody 490, Stephanie 490
SCHWOB, Cecil 17, Cecil 498
SCOTT, Abigail (Stanton) 538, Alma Belinda 537, Altha Ann 537, Altha Ann (Johnson) 418, Altha Johnson 417, Alva 537, Amanda J. 537, Amy 537, Andrew 225, Anna Gertrude 247, Archie Allen 327, Arleva J. 537, Arthur 16, Attie 462, Belinda 537, Bernadine 292, Betty 225, Calvin 417, Calvin C. 537, Catherine 318, Charles Sumner 537, Clark Ira 537, Clyde 507, David Earl 537, Debby McCorkle 537, Don 537, Dora Ellen 537, Dorthy 537, Eleanor 537, Eliza Jane 537, Elizabeth 120, 537, 538, 560, Elma J. Rebecca 538, Elma Jane 120, Elveretta 538, Emma 462, Erin Chase 507, Esther 538, Flossie 462, Frances 462, Fred 537, Geo. W. 121, Gerald 538, Gregory C. 507, Hanly 462, Harry A. 537, Helen Lorene 537, Hilary 340, 537, James 13, 242, 386, 428, 462, James Franklin 537, Jennifer 225, Jess 146, 169, 225, 537, Jess Dr. 478, Jess Mrs. 146, Jesse T. 525, Jim 563, John 462, 537, Joseph 17, 462, Joshua 120, 538, Joyce 428, Kenneth Franklin 537, Lloyd 462, Margaret 462, Mark 428, Martha 462, Mary 152, 462, 537, 538, Mary Elizabeth 537, Mary (Hilma) 136, Mary Hilma 537, N.M. 121, Nathan 538, Nathan M. 120, Nathan Macy 538, Ogle 462, Oma 462, Pat 150, Patsy Ann 295, Paul 45, 475, Pearl 242, Perkins 242, Richard 340, Richard J. 537, Roy Rev. 517, Russell Calvin 537, Russell Wayne 537, Ruth (Beers) 327, Sandra 299, Sarah J. 585, Shannon 340, 537, Sharon 537, Stanton 109, 117, 120, 538, Steven Alan 537, Tacy J. 538, Thomas 462, 538, Vaughn 161, Vivian 507, William Pearl 537, William Tarlton 538
SCOTTEN, Charles 112, Hannah 331, Catherine, Chester, Rebecca 474
SEABOLD, Joe 8
SEAGLEY, Amanda 310, John 310, Julia (Dannamiller) 310
SEAGRAVE, Andrew Jackson 532, Elizabeth Betty"", Elizabeth Chandler 532, Emma Affleck 532, John 145 John Affleck 532, Laura Elizabeth 532, Williard E. 532
SEAMAN, Jonathon 109, Margaretta 272
SECHLER, Andrew 391, Andrew 448, Andrew 538, Benjamin 391, 448, Benjamin F. 538, Benjamin Frederick 538, Charles 538, Dora Ida 538, Eliza 538, Eliza Moyer 391, Eliza (Moyer) 448, Elizabeth (Banks) 538, Emma 272, Emma 538, Emma Catherine 538, Jacob 391, Jacob 538, John C. 538, Lottie 538, Lulu 321, Lulu Mae 538, Maria Fusselman 391, Mary Ella 538, Minnie 538, Velma 538, William H. 538
SECK, Dustin 389, Jennifer 389, William 389
SEEDERS, Lisa 320
SEIBOLD, Ashley 538, Bonita 538, Bonnie 538, Charles 538, Edith 538, Emma 538, Jean 538, Kelli 538, Lee 538, Mark 538, Minnie 538, Paris 538, Pearl 538, Samuel 538, Shelly 538, Wilbert 538, Ed 447
SEIDNER, Caleb 418, Caleb Adam 539, Dorothy 539, Elaine 418, Gary 418, Gary Lee 539
SEIDNER, Gerald 539 Micah 418, Micah Philip 539 Nathan 418 Nathan Daniel 539, Sharla 418, Sharon Lee 539
SEITZ, Lorie 250
SEKAR, Thomandram 145
SELBY, Bessie 476, Charles Albert 476, Cora 476, Cora 476, Cora Aretha 467, Edna 476, Flormelia 320, George 476, Gerald 476, Gladys Lucille 476, Harold 476, Mary 476, William 476, William 476
SELF, Erwin 83
SELIGMAN, Daniel Day 313, David 313
SELKING, Wilbur 344
SELL, Betty 539, Carl 539, Charles T. Dr. 539, Ciara 539, David 539, Diana 539, Don 539, Donald 539, Elizabeth 539, Fern (Custard) 304, Hermina 468, Jennifer 539, John Vian 539, Kelly 539, Larry 539, Matthew 539, Michelle Marie 539, Nathaniel 539, Paul 539, Pauline 539, Terry Lynn 539, Valarie 539, Wendy Elaine 539
SELLERS, Charles 540, Charles E. 540, Charlotte 540, Dorotha 150, Dorotha 540, Eliza 540, Emory Bing 540, Frederick 540, K. B. 540, Leroy McKendose Lee"", Leroy Thomas 540, Louisa May 540, Margaret 111, Margaret 540, Mary Jane 540, Matilda E. 540, Mildred 540, Nora Leah Doyle 540, Ruth 540
SELLS, Edie 447
SENTZ, Catherine 432
SERVIS, Catherine 422, Charles 422, Violet 422
SESLAR, Ashley Nicole 356, Bart Jeffery 356, Bret Andrew 356, Gerald V. 356, Vicki 6
SETTERGREN, B.K. 168, 183
SETTLE, Douglas 389, Earl 577, Huber 107, Lela 155, Matilda 469, Sheila 389
SETTLEMEYER, Alice 541, Bonnie 541, Etta 541, James, 411, Kelly Rene 541, Kenneth Wilkerson 541, Krista Kae 541, Lawrence 541, Lois 541, Melissa Ellen 411, Shari 541, Wayne 541
SETTLEMYRE, Ann 541, James M. 541, William 541
SEVERIN, Louis 214, Louis 350, Louis Dr. 145
SEWARD, Verda 403
SEWELL, May (Wright) 156
SEYMOUR, Ashley McKenna 541, Kelly Rae 541, Kenny Ray 334, 541, Sally Anne 541
SHADLE, 66, Ada 542, Albert 312, Albert 313, 314, 541E, Amy Marlane 513, Bert 541, Brent Allen 513, Calvin 107, Caroline (Penrod) 291, Cecil 541, Cecil Victoria 312, Chambers 121, Charles Hillard 513, Craig Steven 513, Denise 513, Dwight 541, Eugene 541, Gail Susanne 513, Hanna 378, Hannah (Penrod) 313, Hannah Penrod 541, Herman 541, Hillard 541, Hillard Albert 513, Homer 313, 541, Irene 460, 541, James Newton 291, Jason Paul 513, Jimmy Lee 513, Lillie 541, Lisa Marie 513, Margaret 542, Margaret (Donelly) 313, Mary (McGlade) 313, Minnie Dale 312, 541, Minnie Dale (Graves) 312, Myrtle 291, Nancy Ellen 513, Paige Alene 513, Philip 313, 541, 542, Phillip 460, Sharon 541, Steven Dwight 513, Vera 239, 460, Wayne 64, Wilbur 541, William 541, William Abner 313
SHADY, Adell 591, Albert Dell"", Bertha 542, Brooks 542, Bud 591, Celesta Davison 542, Chester 591, Chris 478, Cleo 542, Clyde Lee 591, Curtis 45, David 542, Dell 591, Dorthy 150, Dwight 542, Elizabeth 542, Gaynell 433, Gaynell 542, Gwen 591, Harley 542, Helen 542, Isaac 112, Iva Myrtle 492, James Theodore 542, John 44, 45, 471, John 542, Katherine 591, Kendra 591, Kent 591, Kurt 591, Leona 542, Linda 542, Lori 591, Mae 542, Margaret 485, Margaret (Lepper) 542, Martin 542, Mary 542, Mary Ellen 575, Nancy 542, Nellie 542, Nina 542, Phyllis 591, Robert 542, Ruth 542, Sally 542, Scott 591, Steve 221, Terri 542, Wayne 542, Wendell Martin 542, William 542
SHAEFER, E. J. 95, Emma 317
SHAFER, Amanda 402, Amanda 501, Ida 471, John 45, Leila 429, Otis 471, Sarah 285
SHAFFER, Jake"" Annett Marie 543, Archie 532, Archie James 543, Archie Jr. 543, Benny 544, Betty Louise 544, Catherine Irene 544, Christa Nicole 543, David Earnest 543, Donald 509, Donald Wayne 544, Donald Wayne 544, Edna, Edward 544, Elva 543, Esther 544, Eugene Burl 544, Frances 544, Freida 544, G. H. 83, Gene 544, Goldie 544, Gregory A. 543, Gregory Jr. 543, Herman 544, Herman Dwight 544, Jabec 64, Jabez 96, James Allen 544, Jay 544, Jean Ann 544, John Allen 544, Joseph John 544, Judith Ann 544, Judy 544, Karen 544, Katherine Elizabeth 544, Katherine Kay 532, 543, Kathy 544, Kim 327, 472, Lemuel 544, Leonard 544, Linda 544, Lola Mae 544, Louis Eden 543, Lucile 351, Marie 544, Mark 544, Mark Wayne 544, Mary 150, Michael Charles 544, Mike 544, Mildred 532, Mildred M. 543, Olga 544, Paul 216, Peggy 544, Petra 543, Robert Dwight 544, Sherley Alberta 337, Teresa 543, Tonya Sue 544, Tyler 544, Tyler Wayne 544, Wayne 544
SHALLABARGER, George 524, Ocie 524
SHANAHAN, Sally 379
SHANE, Ernest 469, Ethel 469, Herman 469, Karen Sue 250, Lavon 469, William 469
SHANKS, Daniel 61, Jason 359, Vicki 359
SHANNON, Alice 568, Nancy 577
SHAPPELL, Gregory 563, Mike 563, Phillip 563, Sharon 563
SHARI, Lanette 467, Monica 467
SHARP, Donna May 272, Donovan 272, Laruel 272, Rollie 265
SHARPE, Fred 398, Jane Ann 398, Minnie (Harnish) 398, Paul 398
SHATTO, Allen 130, Roger 162
SHATZER, Goldie 350
SHAUFFER, Mary 155
SHAW, Ann 373, Carol 373, Dell 142, Doris J. 497, Doris Jean 497, Gary D. 145, Glenn 146, Glenn Mrs. 146, Hyman 534, Ida 534, Judy 373, Kelly 287, Lucy 134, Marsha 513, Martha 385, Ora 287, Peggy 287, Ray 151, Ray A. 373, Robin 287, Russell 287, Sandy 287, Shad 287, Shane 287, Sherry Lynn 373, Sonia 84, Susan 287, Tammi 287, Vickie 287
SHEAD, Walter 95
SHEARER, Jackie 486, Tammy 486
SHEENAN, Elizabeth 596, James Michael 596, Mary Kathleen 596, Robert 596
SHEETS, Alta 326, Andrew 544, Benjamin 544, Bessie 544, Betty 594, Boyd 64, Catherine 544, Cecile 347, Charles Frances 544, Chester 403, David 544, Debrah Kay 603, Eliza 544, Elizabeth 544, Ella 544, Frederick 544, Henry 544, Jacob 544, John 544, 594, Josie 544, Julia Ann 544, Julie 544, Laura 366, Laura 367, Malissa Jane (Thompson) 518, Margaret 544, Margaret Niece 544, Marie 544, Martha 474, Martin 544, Mary Ann 518, 544, 591, Melissa Jane Thompson 375, Minnie Kate 375, 544, Nancy 544, Rita 594, Roger 594, Stella Alice 544, Susannah 544, Timothy 594, Wesley 594, William 375, 518, 544
SHELEY, Donna 523, Monwell 523
SHELL, Margaret 408
SHELLEY, Brian James 544, 593, Carl 187, Carl O. 544, Carl William 426, Carl William 544, David A. 544, Elizabeth Ann Betty"", Glenn 544, Ila Mae 544, James Carl 544, 593, Janis 544, 593, Jessie Mae 593, Karen 426, Karen Jean 544, Karlene Sue 544, Kathryn Kay 544, Kathy 426, Kevin Keplinger 426, Kevin Keplinger 544, Lavere 544, Luara Etta Oldfather 544, Marceille 426, Marceille 544, Patricia Lynn 593, Paul 544, Raymond 544, Robert Douglas 544, 593, Robert E. 593, Robert Eugene 544, William 280
SHELPER, Zola 552
SHELTON, Dessie 545, Jeffrey 545, Jeffrey Allan 545, Jill 545, Jim 545, Jim 545, 546, Jimmie Duade 545, John E. 545, Lisa 545, Lisa Marie 545, Marge 545, Marjorie 545, 546, Mary Lou 545, Mary Lou 546
SHENDLER, Telsie 303
SHEPARD, Doris 450, Eva 450, Leon 450, Robert 450, William 450
SHEPHERD, Albert 267, Alex 448, Clarissa 555, Elizabeth 367, Lois 500, Veva 448
SHEPLER, Ashlae 479, Debi 479 Delm 447, Heather 479, Irene 490, Lee 490, Marlowe 130, Scott 479
SHEPPERD, Elizabeth (Walther) 366
SHERER, Ida Mae 493, Roger 142, Roger 151
SHERIDAN, Elizabeth 319, Kathy 468
SHERIFF, Connie Jo 512, James 512, Pamela 512, Susan 512
SHERMAN, William Tecumseh 448
SHERRY, Erin 251, Kyle 251, Mary Anne 251, Mary Anne 512, Scott 251
SHEWALTER, Carl 542, Harry 542, Hesper 542, Marcia Kay 542, Nancy 542
SHIDELER, Ardith 15, Ardith 249, Chuck 15, Daniel Ernest 603, Mel 15, Opal Malissa 603, Wanda Lee 603
SHIDLER, Aaron 276, Lavina 276, Nancy (Strickler) 276
SHIELDS, Andrew 302, Caroline Lucy (Deaver) 302, Eliza 546, Gretchen L. 546, James 546, Jesse Lawrence 546, Katherine Jane 263, Lena Pearl 489, Margaret 424, Margaret 425, Margaret L. 546, Mary 424, Mary 546, Mildred V. 546, Noble 263, T.M. 78, Virginia 304
SHIFFERLY, Arlene 229
SHIGLEY, Charity 546, Charity Jurden 415, Frederick 546 George W. 546, Jeannetta 367, Jennetta E. 366, John 61, 415, John 527, John 546, Maria (Reed) 415, Martha 546, Mary 546, 555, Mary Gottschalk/Rose 546 Rachel 546, Robert 546, Samuel 546, Susan 546, William 546
SHILLING, Leo Jr. 413, Naomi (Yake) 413
SHIMBERRY, Fanny 497
SHIMER, Alice 255, Alice 256, Almedia 256, Anna Almeda 547, Asa 256, Asa Theo 547, Charles 255, Charles 256, Charles Nelson Robinson 256, Clara 256, Clara May 547, Daniel 547, Edith 256, Edith Adell 547, Effie 256, Effie Adaline 547, Elmira 256, Elmira Ellen 547, Emma 256, Emma Henrietta 547, Florence 256, Laura 256, Lawrence 255, Lawrence 256, Margaret 256, Margaret Maria 547, Maria 547, Martha Jane 547, Obediah 256, Obediah 547, Olivia Florence 547, Ruth 256, Sadie 256 Sadie Valzetta 547 Susanne 256, Suzanna 547, Theo 255, Theo Marie 256, Verda Jane 547, Verdie 256, Walter 256, Walter Ernest 547
SHINDLER, Pauline Ensley 497
SHINER, Ruth 347
SHINKLE, Carl 145
SHINN, Allie 400, Darius 538, Gloria L. 407, Mabel Ifer 407, Phyllis 152, Phyllis D. 407
SHIPLEY, Betty 429, Wanda 458
SHIRE, Derrick 483, Dustin 483, Franklyn Sam"", Kamilla 483, Mark 483, Matthew 483, Robert 317, Walter 317
SHIRK, Wilmetta 458
SHIRLEY, Wendy 277
SHIVELY, Andrew 339, Anthony 339, Barbara Catherine Katie"", Beverly 339, 490, Burlene 339, Carl 339, Carole 339, Charles 142, Charles 339, Dorothy 339, Floyd 339, Frederick 339, Kim 444, Kim 478, Kim Denise 339, Lawrence 339, Lisa 339 Richard 339, Sally 339, Rachel 555
SHOAFF, Brenda Louise 452
SHOBE, Mary 555
SHOCH, B. W. 98, J.B. 82
SHOCKLEY, Alice 287
SHOE, Mary 601, Pauline 134
SHOEMAKER, Barbara 93, Barbara Valentine 585, Carrie 422, Carrie 423, Catherine 474, Cleola 432, Edith 146, Henry 265, Ida 383, Jenny 441, Josephine 388, Louisa 485, Mary E. 335, Mary Juanita 539, Peter 422, 423, Rose 352, Ruth Valentine 585, S.A. 214, Sarah 265, Susannah Susan""
SHOFER, Mary 537
SHOOKMAN, Elizabeth 464
SHOREY, Lucille 398
SHORT, Earl 403, H. H. 136,, Martha Ellen 136, Musetta 136
SHORTS, Mary Ann 431, Nicbolas 430, 431
SHOUP, Alice (Hedges) 389, Douglas 548, Edith 136, Jacob 82, John 82, Mary (Hauk) 387, Mildred 136, Rachel 82, Rose 136, Scott 548, Steven 548 Thomas 136, Thomas Nathaniel 548, Troy 548, William 548, William H. 548
SHOV, Tammy 597
SHOWALTER, Abraham 86, Abraham 548, Amy 548, Dalen 548, Eliza Jane 548, Eric 548, Grace 548, Kathy 548, Keith 107, 548, Kenneth 548, Lavina Florence 418, Mary Jane 548, Mielma 548, Nellie Smith 585, Polly 548, Ruth 548, Tamara 548, Ted 548, Ward 107, Ward 382, 548, Wayne 548, William 548, William Elmer 548
SHOYER, Carolyn Antrim 372, George Jr. 372
SHREVE, Lucria 482
SHRINER, Benjamin 366, Lloyd 301
SHROYER, Herbert L. Doc""
SHUEY, Barbara 589
SHULL, Adam David 549, Brian Douglas 549, Daniel 604, David Scott 549, Donn Alan 549, Edwin Lee 548
SHULL, Elwin 548, Elwin Dee 548, Eric Scott 549, Eunice Ruth 548 Eunice Ruth (Johnson) 334, Francis 309, 334, 416, 548, 549, Frederick A. 548, Jeannine 334, 335, Jeannine 548, John Howard 548, Judy 549, Julie Jo 549, Kurtis 548, Laila 549, Lillie Jane 604, Margaret (Hinkle) 604, Marilyn 548, Mark Edwin 548, Rachel Estella 548, Rosella Barrick 596, Ruth 309, Ruth Johnson 548, 549, Sandra Sue 549, Teresa Kay 548, Virginia 549, Vivion 549, Vivion Earl 548SHULTZ, Bertna 310
SHULTZ, Catherine 310, Charles 549, Donald Edwin 549, Fred 310, Galen H. 536, Galen Hoover 549, Jeanette Hoover 549, Jo Anne 549, Joanne 567, Katherine 359, Kelli Ann 549, Kerry Lynn 549, Kevin Ray 549, Kris Edwin 549, Mack Harrison 549, Mack Harrison Jr. 549, Peggy Dehn 536, Peggy Dehn 549, Shirley (Allen) 536, Shirley Ann 549, Tina 310, Valerie Margaret 549
SHULTZ, William 310
SHUMAKER, Homer 484, Lois 484, Noami 484
SHUMAN, Joseph 512, Louisa (Smith) 512
SHUMAN, Mary Alice 512
SHUMM, Clark 144
SHURE, Nancy 534
SHUTT, Anita M. . 550, Ethel Yates 550, Fred 244, Gloria 550, Guy 550, Guy Jr. 550, Hattie 58, Jerry L. 550, Lois Ruth 590, Marceille 550, 579, Mary 244, Max 550, Randall S. 550, Rex 130, 550, Richard 151, Robert 244
SHUTTLEWORTH, Sharon (Higgins) 394
SICKAFUS, Heather LeAnn 306, Phillip 306, Schlaura Nicole 306, Tamara SueAnn 306
SICKLER, Louisa 555
SICKS, Alice 292
SIDERS, Clifford 517, Edna (Bass) 517, Emma V. 517
SIEBERT, Ella 86
SIEBOLT, Alvina 352, David 352
SIELA, Beverly 550, Bob 550, Deborah 413, Delmar 550, Dwight 550, Emma Nelson 550, Gerald 550 John 550, Leo 550
SIEVEKING, Suzanne Fudge 268
SIFORD, Mary 155
SIGLER, Anita 538, Carl 538, George W. 538, Junie Dora 538, Mary Ella 538
SILLS, 66, Albert D. 550, Alvena (Graham) 355, Brian 292, Camela 292, Carolyn 550, Carrie (Hoskins) 355, Casey 355, Cheryl (Crandall) 355, Claude 550, Claude Lowell 550, Claude M. 550, Claude Mendenhall 550, Cletus 550, Cluade M. 551, Constance 550, Corey 355, Daniel 550, Della Mae 550, Dick 355, Eric 355, Harold 292, Hugh 550, Inez 550, 551, James E. 355, James Edgar 355, Jamie 355, Jan 525, Jan Marie 550, 551, Jean 525, Jean Ann 550, 551, Jesse 550, Joan 355, Joyce 525, Joyce M. 550, 551, Joyce Marie 452, Karen 355, Karen (Reinhart) 355, Kathryn 355, Kris Ann 355, Laura 355, Laura Couch 299, Leander P. 550, Lisa 355, Margaret J. 551, Margaret Joann 550, Mary Elizabeth Murray 550, Mary Ellen 296, Michael 550, Nancy Jane (Fuller) 296, Phebe Jane 550, Ralph 550,

Richard 355, Rick 355, Rod 299, Rodney 385, Roger 17, Russell 550, Ted 355, Travis 525, Travis J. 550, 551, William 296, Jr, Daniel 318, Sr, Daniel 318
SIMERAL, Martha 283
SIMERMAN, Burr 551, Burr Ivan 552, Clem Henry 552, David 552, Denver 552, Dollie 551, Dolly Snyder 552, Ellery 552, Esther 552, Ethel 552, Everett 552, George H. 552, Iliff 552, Imo Todd 583, Isabella 552, Janice 551, Janice S. 551, Jeffery 551, Jerry 551, John 58, 551, 552, John F. 552, John Henry 551, 552, John L. 502, Judy 502, 552, Kimberly 551, Lanny L. 551, Lawrence 552, Lew 552, Lucile 58, Lucille K. 502, Lucille Kansas 552, Marcellus 552, Marvin 552, Mary Belle 551, Mary Lula 551, 552, R. Stephen 551, Robin 551, Roger 551, Ronald 551, Shelly 551, Snyder 551, Steve 551, Sue 551, Vance Bernon 552
SIMISON, Robert 279
SIMMONS, Abram 8, 145, 162, Harriet 408, Jennie 200, V.M. 162, Virgil 280
SIMON, Betty
SIMONS, P. M. 98
SIMONTON, Catherine 82, James 82
SIMPKINS, Greg 350, Jay 350, Jeremy 350
SIMPSON, Carolyn Beth 552, Curtis Avery 552, Donna 552, Frances Beckner 552, Frederick 552, Hollis 552, Lillian Stark 552, Luana 552, Maurice 552, R. J. 227
SINGER, Dowell 234, O.W. 97, Rhoda Connett 262, William 262
SINK, Abraham 552, Alf 552, 607, Bertha 552, Carol Sue 552, Clara 241, Corinthia Ann Gorman 241, Darlene 552, Dean 552, Douglas 552, Elizabeth 82, Ella 552, Emma 552, Emmett 241, 552, Ethel 552, Everett 552, Frank 99, 552, Garry E. 552, Gary Lee 552, Henry 82, Jane 519, Janet 552, Jerald 552, Karen 552, Kent 552, Kimberly Kay 552, Kirby 552, Lavina 437, Lois 552, Lois Ann 552, Lorena M. 552, Lyda 552, Mary Beth 552, Norma Jean 552, Pamela 552, Richard 552, Sandra L. 270, Sandy 552, Sophia 552, Susan 552, Wanda 552
SINKS, Roberta 276
SIPE, Andrea 340, 486, 487, Gerald Lee 601, Janelle 486, Jani Lynn 601, Kevin 486, Kristopher 486, Marcia 601, Mindy 486, Nicole 486, Randall Wayne 601, Sunya 602, Sunya S. 601, Sunya (Wilson) 318, Sunya Wilson 318
SIPES, Allie 102, Allie 102
SISSON, Clarissa 286
SIXBEY, Charles C. 164
SKERITT, Audra 485
SKERTIC, Jacob 522, Richard J. 522, William 522
SKILES, Deeda 137, Edna 155, K.B. 177, Robert 146, Robert Mrs. 146, Steve 140
SKINNER, Carol 284, Don 145, 293, Don K. 232, Edith Florence 289, Gordon Scott 293, Grace 553, Rebecca Jo 385, Sara Elizabeth 293, Sue 154, Sue Colson 293
SKURNER, Beverly 326
SLACK, Bruce 440, Dean 440, Harley 440 Karol 440, Mary Lou 440, Thelma 440
SLAGLE, Darlene 363
SLANE, Harley 503
SLATER, Anna Fluke 341, Bobby 402, Burdell 402, Burdell J. 341, Cal 17, Constance Lee 553, Dale Eugene Jr. 553, Dale Eugene Sr. 553, Dale Sr. 577, Dawne 553, Dayton 402, Denver 341402, Denver Paul 341, Dewald 402, Diane 341, Diane Sue 341, Gloria Jean 553, Grace 553, Hazel (Hoopingarner) 341, Jane 553, Jennifer 553, Jennifer Diane 341, Joan 553, Jodi Marie 341, Kathern 15, Kim 429, Kimberli Anne 341, Kirt 429, Kirt Michael 341, Laurie Francis 553, Marion 553, Mark Denver 341, Michael 341, Michael Denver 341, Oliver Farren 553, Paul Joe 553, Robert 15, S. E. 64, 96, Sara June 341, Thomas 341, Thomas Duane 341, Ward Beecher 553, Yancy Christopher 553
SLATER-PUTT, Dawne 553
SLEASMAN, Earl 82
SLEPPY, Altha Irene 553, Amanda Mae 553, Angela Lynn 553, Barbara 553, Barbara Ellen 553, Benjamin Leon 553, Brittani Nicole 553, Caleb Nathaniel 553, Carl Franklin 553, Carrie 553, Catherine 553, Cindy Jo 553, Cindy Jo 569, Everett Paul 553, 583, Gary Leon 553, George Paul 553, George Paul 583, Holly Joy 553, Homer 553, Jacob 553, Jerry Lee 553, Joe 189, 569, John George 553, Joseph Samuel 553, 583, Joshua Lee 553, Joyce Kay 553, Judy 299, 385, Judy Ilene 553,, Kandice Lynn 553, Kathryn 553, Marcelle 553, 583, Mariah Ellen 553, Mary 553, Melissa Kay 553, Melvin Leon 553, 583, Nellie 189, 569, Nellie Mae 553, Ruth Ilene 553, Samuel Ruby 553, Sandra 189, Sandra Lynn 553, 569
SLIGER, Brian 554, Charley 554, Cleora J. 428, Cleora Jacelyn 554, Cleora Jocelyn 338, Dessie 408, Dessie May 554, Dwight Elmoody 554, Earl 337, Earl 554, Earl A. 338, 554, Edwin Dale 554, Elizabeth 431, Ellen 431, Essie Elizabeth 554, Esther 554, Flora 285, 554, Francis E. Frank"", Fred 407, George 13, 76, George Ammi 554, George William 554, Helen 554, John Moomaw 554, Kenneth Bradley 554, Kevin 554, Kory 554, Lily Jane Conn 554, Loretta Sue Ifer 407, Lula 554, Marilyn 338, Marilyn L. 337, 554, Mary Alice 554, Nellie Marie 554, Nellie May 554, Nina 554, Ona Mae 554, ReAnn 554, Robert Wayne 554, Rose 554, Russell David 554, Ruth 554, Susan Gordon 554, Velma 408, 554, Winifed Smith 338, Winifred Cleora 554, Winifred (Smith) 337
SLIM, Wendy 483
SLUSHER, Angela Jayne 352, Anna Geneva 555, Barbara 528, Barbara Jean 555, Charles 555, Clara M. 555, Claudine 15, Daisy May 555, Dale 352, Dale Keith 555, Danny Earl 555, Don 555, Donna 555, Doris Ula 555, Elretta 555, Emma Eliza 555, Frances Coleen 460, 555, Frank 15, Franklin 555, Gladys Elnora 555, Glen L. 319, Glennis 319, Goldie 555, Helen 555, Hettie 555, James Ross 555, John Charles 555, Johnnie 352, Josh 352, Josiah 555, 555, Karen Kay 555, Kenneth Wayne 555, Laura Lavone 555, Leora 555, Martha 460, Martha 555, Mary Jane 555, Mary Lena 555, Melinda 352, Nancy May 555, Naomi 555, Nina 555, Patti 352, Phyllis Joan 555, Ransom T. 555, Rapheal 555, Ret 352, Rhessa 460,, Rhessa Josiah 555, Richard Lee 555, Rick 15, Ronald T. 555, Roscoe 555, Ruey Glee 555, Ruth Eileen 555, Ruth Faye 555, Samuel 555, Scott 352, Terrie 352, Thelma 555, Thomas Wilber 555, Violet Banter 319, Waneta Jean 555, Wilber Ervin 555, Wilda May 555, William 555, William Anderson 555, William C. 555, Willis Risinger 555, Wilma Marie 555
SLUSSER, Clarence 518, Enid 518, Minnie (Shock) 518, Susanne 269
SLUTMAN, Elizabeth 585, Peter 407
SLYE, Judith 285, II, Robert 285
SLYTER, A.B. 82
SMALL, Judith 274, Karen 274, Kathryn 274, Kenneth 274, Timothy 274
SMALLEY, Daniel Webster 547
SMEKENS, Amy 425, Angela 425, Angela Kay 486, Brady 425, Brady Chad 425, Clemen 95, Clemen 254, Clemen (Bud) 425, David 425, Dean 425, Deborah 425, Henrietta 254, Henry V. 254, Hubert 254, Jane 425, 518, 544, Jane Teresa 591, Joe 140, Joel 6, 208, 425, John 425, Juliette 254, Karen 486, Martha 425, Mary 254, Mary Suzanne 425, Michael 355, 425, Scott 294, 542, Scottie 425, Stephanie 425, Victoria 254
SMELTZER, Edna May 451, James Richard 498, Laura (Branner) 451, Mary Elnora 326, William 331, William 451
SMETZER, Emma Catherine 418
SMITH, Susie"", A. J. 136, Adaline 519, Adam Joseph 559, Addison Eugene 475, Aenone 475, Al 34, Alice Cross 251, Allen 20, 234, Alma 558, Alma Emma 475, Alma Priscilla 252, Alonzo 424, Alva 355, Amanda 559, Amelia Mae 556, Amelia Martha 475, Amy L. 559, Andrew Johnson 555, Andrew Wayne 556, Andy 357, Angela Jayne 352, Anna 503, Anthony Morgan 559, Ardella Eva 560, Ardith 556, Ardith Jay 276, Ardola Mae 557, Arizona (Cloud) 60, Arlene 556, Arthur 276,398, Arthur Elsworth 556, Ashley Rebecca 559, Bartholomew 558, Beatrice 557, Bernice Evelyn 557, Beverly Earlene 555, Bob 234, Brenda 556, Brent E. 559, Brian T. 559, Brooke 357, Brooke Nicole 556, Brooks 251, Bryan 364, Byron 89, C. L. 71, C. Scott 345, Calvin 552, Calvin Kunkel 557, Carol 512, Caroline Catherine 556, Caroline Jane 556, Carrie 283, Cary 246, Cassidy Gwen 559, Catherine 266, Catherine 557 Catherine Lucile 266, Catherine Lucile 266, Catherine Taylor 266, Charles 146, Charles 337, 411,426, 557, 589, Charles Mrs. 146, Charles Newton 475, Charles Ray 558, Charles T. 573, Cheryl 556, Cheryl Ann 276, Chester 68, Chester 424, Chrisofer 517, Christine 474, Chrstine A. 559, Cindy 345, Claude 543, Clayton 558, Clayton Jake 559, Clem 585, Clifford 557, Clona Valentine 585, Cory B. 559, Craig E. 559, Cynthia 341, Dallas 492, Daniel 266, 557, Daniel B. 266, Daniel Benjamin 557, Daniel H. 266, Darlene 552, Darren P. 251, David 102, 202, 543, David Austin 555, David Harrison 557, Deborah 573, Debra 424, Delight Mae 556, Della May 426, Derek 98, 234, Dixie 270, Dixie Kahn (Hofstetter) 398, Dolly 87, Don 345, Donald J. 557, Donna 552, Dora 502, Doral 140, Doris 450, Dorothy 155, 558, Duane ,556 Duane L. 559, Durand L. 251, E. Maxine 529, Eberly 519, Ed 78, Edna 155, Edna Grace 555, Effa 389, Effie May (Hite) 276, Elizabeth 417, Elizabeth 518, 544, 555, 558, Elizabeth Jane 336, Elizabeth Mae 591, Ellen 102, 503, Elmer 89, Eloise Lucile 424, Emily 555, Ephriam 556, Eric 350, Esther Sophia 266, Ethan Michael 559, Eugene Valentine 585, Euriel Iretta 554, Everett 558, Fernie Bell 519, Florabelle 165, Florence 554, Florence 557, Florence Etta 554, Flossie 558, Frances Lavera 555, Frank 103, 202, Frank C. 557, Frank S. 495, Frank Syphers 493, Fred 556, Fred L. 559, Galen Rolandues 558, Garnet 293, Garnet (Clark) 291, Gary 367, George 58, 82, 519, 558, George Arnold 555, George W. 555, Gerald Ross Red"", Gertrude 555, Gladys 556, Glen Waldo 556, Glenn Nathan 559, Gloria 512, Gola 402, Grace 94, Grace 136, Grace 288, Grant 493, H. Brooks 145, Hannah 350, Harry D. 475, Hazel (Miller) 337, Heidi 517, Helen 438, Helen Leona 556, Henry 556, Herschell 555, Hope Delean 556, Hott 20, Howard 20, 61, Howard E. 234, Howard Earl 556, Hubert 341, Ida 531, 555, Irene 555, 591, J.D. 58, J.T. 321, Jack 357, Jack Morris 557, Jack Wayne 556, Jacob 102, 336, Jacob Austin 555, Jacob James 558, James 438, 503, 555, James Daniel 559, James E. 145, 517, James Eli 559, James J. 529, James T. W. 519, James Wesley 557, Janeen 424, Janet 333, 517, Janice 555, Janice 555, Jason Bradley 246, Jay H. 276, Jay Hite 556, Jay Michael 247,330, Jean 558, Jeanette S. 251, Jeff 357,556 Jeffrey A. 559, Jeffrey Howard 556, Jennifer Faith 557, Jennifer Marie 559, Jennifer S. 559, Jeremy A. 559, Joel 364, John 6, 140, 177, 228, 450, 555, John Earl 555, John Eugene 555, John Henry 557, Jon 357, Jon Wayne 556, Jonathan 350, Joseph Alan 559, Josh 364, Joshua Seth 559, Judy 345, Judy 357, Judy Ann 556, Julia 345, Karah 438, Karah 558, Karen Stine 529, Katherine Misegades 503, Kathy 556, Keith 556, Keith E. 559, Keith Roscoe 585, Kenneth 98, 266, Kevin 552, Kristan Jenee 559, Larry 382, Larry Edward 555, Larua 557, Laura 424, Lawrence Eugene 557, Lea Roy 557, Leah 492, Leita Ardella 431, 493, 494, 495, Len 234, Leonard 558, Leonard E. 556, Leota 558, Leslie 424, Leslie Jay 247, 330, Lester 424, Lester Dale 557, Lester Ray 557, Lewis 417, 555, Limpa E. 555, Linda L. 559, Lois Ann 552, Lois (Whitacre) 251, Loretta 340, Louisa 337, 555, Lucille Hazel 558, Lucille K. 502, Lucille Kansas 552, Lucinda 454, Lula Viola 555, Luwona 556, Lynne 558, M.S. 142, Maggie Jane 336, Malorie Marie 336, Margaret 372, 462, 557, Margaret Aline 342, Margaret Ann 443, Margaret (Olson) 557, Marguerite 483, 558, Marian Eloise 557, Marie 555, Mark Sumner 559, Marvin 556, Mary 6, Mary 8, Mary 177, 234, 450, 512, 555, 556, 558, Mary 573, Mary Ann 557, Mary Ann Athan 246, Mary H. 555, Mary Louise 557, Mary Scherrer Heuer 407, Maude 502, Maurice 512, Max W. 251, Maxine 556, 557, Megan Kimberly 559, Melissa 424, Melvin 557, Meredythe Katheryne 559, Mervin 144, Michael 345, Michelle 424, Mindy J. 559, Minnie 136, Mollie 546, Murtle 557, Myrtle 362, Nancy 558, 559, 583, Nancy Agnes 407, Nancy (Caston) 558, Nancy Marie 573, Natalie D. 251, Nathanael Matthew 559, Neal 345, Nell 538, Nellie (Denny) 558, Nellie Pearl 557, Nettie Ann 336, Ninetta 555, Nona 558, O. J. 556, Omar 107, Omar Jessie 475, 556, Omer 557, Otis 350, P. B. Rev. 588, Pam 558, Patty 508, Pearl 460, Pearl 556, Pearl Heller 390, 468, Peter 68, Peter W. 502, Pheobe 555, Phillip 556 Phillip E. 559, Phyllis 154, 512, Rachel 503, 559, Rachel Jane 555, Ralph 345, Ralph Marion 554, Randall 517, Ray 558, Raymond 251, Rebecca 519, Rhoda 519, Rhonda 483, Rhonda Sue 557, Richard 557, Robert 20, 98, 519, Robert Lawrence 556, Robert Marlin 557, Robin 457, Ronald 246, 483, 556, Rose 58, Rose 552, Rose Anna 580, Rosemary 150, 156, Sabina 410, Sabina W. 409, Sandi M. 559, Sandra 577, Sara M. 559, Sara (Walker) 556, Sarah 414, 483, 556, Sarah Jane 555, Seth Rev. 72, Sharon 556, Shawn Joseph 559, Sherman 555, Sherrie 345, Sheryl 555, Smithy 102, Sonja 556, Sonja Sue 276, Stephen 146, Stephen Frederick 559, Steven 555, Susan 555, Susan Hall 557, Susie 557, Suzanne Carter 407, Suzanne (Susie) 557, Taron W. 336, Ted 84, Ted 200, Thomas 208, Thomas Austin 555, Thomas E. 557, Thomas R. 557, Tim 555, Tine 519, Tom 460, Tonya 559, Tracy Donald 573, Vaughn 592, Vaughn E. 559, Vaughn Eugene 556, Velie 558, Velma 493, Vesta 411, Vesta Marguerite 426, Viola 262, Walter F. 367, Walter Fielding 556, Wanda Booth 458, Wanda K. 559, Wayne 552, Wayne 558, Wendell Allen 556, Wesley Warren 475, William 519, 554, William H (Bill) 557, William Henry 556, William Philip 559, William S. 102, William Wesley 475, 556, Wilma 508, Winifred Cleora 554, Zachaus 558, Zepha Longshore 453, Zepha Pearl 493, 495
SMOOT, Stella 535
SMUTS, Barbara 560, Bertha 492560, Bertha (Vollmar) 288, Bertha (Vollmar) 432, Betty 560, Cecile 560, Cora B. 560, Elizabeth 560, Elizabeth Kohr 560, Emily 402, Estal C. 560, Etta 531, Etta E. 560, Etta (Farrell) 432, Frances 560, Frank 560, Gene 560, Glenna 287, 288 560, Grace 560, Hansel 560, Homer V. 560, Imo 560, Ira 432, 531, Ira C. 560, Jacob 560, Jacob G. 560, James 560, Jeanette 492, 560, Jennie P. 560, Jerry 560, John 523, 552, John M. 560, Josephine 560, Justine 560, Lavina 82, 560, Lex 560, Lynn 560, Marie 560, Michael 560, Nancy 560, Pauline 560, Robert 560, Robert 560, Rosemary 432, 560, Ruthford 288, 432, 492, 560, Sharon 560, Steven 560, Suzette 560, U. G. 96, Ulysses G. 560, Vesta 560
SNARR, Anna 585, Charles W. 454, Minnesota 454
SNAVELY, Anna Maria , Jacob, Mary 469, Salome Sabina Wild
SNIDER, Bertha 560, Carl Ray 301, Carlisle 299, 561, Carol 560, Charles 299, Clarence Counterdale 301, David 561, Delila 561, Dixie 333, Edwin 333, Elizabeth 561, Ella 519, Evan 561, George 333, Geraldine (Boyer) 333, Henry 561, Henry Virginia 560, Irene Louise 560, Jennifer 560, John 561, John Wesley 561, Laurie Ann 333, Lori 333, Lynette 333, Maranda 561, Mary Jane 561, Michael 333, Morris 299, Morris 561, Murray 333, Nathan 560, Paul 560, Philip 323, Phylena 561, Rachel 561, Sarah 299, 561, Seth 44, 45, 367, Vera Maurene 323, Walter 560, William 561, Wilson 560
SNOW, Bob 480, Brad 561, Carrie 457, Catherine 561, Charles 480, Charley 480, Clarence 480, Clyde 561, Crysal 561, Garnet 480, Geneva 527, George Giffon 561, George Henry 561, Henry 561, Jacob 561, John 561, Johnnie 561, Juaniece 480, Kenneth 561, Mary 403, Max 561, Mollie (Stahl) 561, Myrtle 480, Nichols 561, Robert Jr. 480, Suel 561, Vertner 561
SNOWE, Edyreth (Judith) 285 John 285, Susannah 285
SNOWHILL, Benjamin F. 459
SNYDER, Abraham 426, Adam 426, Alfred 561, Alvada 448, 449, Amos 182, Annie 561, Avon Dale Donald 403, Bonnie Lou 403, Candace 449, Catherine 426, 561, Celia Jane 562, Chalmer 207, Charles 561, 562, Chloe 585, Chloe Ann 562, Cora 256, Dale 449, Dale Wayne 403, Dollie 551, Dollie 562, Dora Alice 562, Elizabeth 561, Etta 449, Fanny 561, Florence 553, George 561, Harland 561, Harland V. 562, Harvey 449, Henry 113, 561, 562, Jacob 573, James 20, Janice Ann 403, Jill 449, Joe 449, John 18, 561, John 561, John W. 561, Kelly Joe 449, Kevin Dale 449, Leary Lewis 562, Lewis B. 561, Lewis F. 562, Lonnie 449, Lucy 561, Lydia 558, Lydia 561, Mariah 561, 562, Martha 561, Mary 561, 573, Mary A. 562, Molly 449, Molly Jane 403, Nell 449, Nell (Robison) 586, Philip 561, Rebecca 561, Ronald Dean 403, S. U. 85, Sarah 561, 573, Sharon Kay 403, Ted 162, Vicki 449, Wendy 449
SOLLOWAY, Fred 342, Helen (Gearheart) 342, Ned 342, Rex 342
SOMER, Susan 607
SOMERS, Ella 604, Mary Ellen 361
SOMMERS, Bob 402 Mary C. 356, Minnie 289, Scott 402, Shane 402
SONNENBERG, Mike 529, Steve 529
SONNER, Florence Waneta 431
SONNER, Joseph 103
SONNIGSEN, Agnes 562, Desta Lucile 562, Eunice 562, James Leslie 562, Jayne Anne 562, Jerrold Wayne 562, John 336, John Junior 562, John V. 562, Meda 562, Pearl 562, Penelope Suzanne 562, Sara Elizabeth 562
SOPER, Ben 376, Floyd 250, Rena 152, Sharon Kay 250, Susan Lynn 250,
SORGER, Earl 323, Michael 323, Sandra 323
SORG, Sorg Jr> 234
SORGEN, Helen
SOUDER, Bill 258, Carol 235, D. C. Rev. 576, G. H. 85, Helen 462, Robert 112, Willis 258
SOUDERS, Brooks E. 433, Thomas 432
SOUERS, Sebert 421, Velma (Jones) 421
SOUERWINE, Peter 520
SOUERWINE, Virgie 520
SOUTHALL, Harriett Pease 331
SOUTHARD, Michael Wayne 513, Michael Wayne Jr. 513, Robin Michele 513, William Blue 513
SOVINE, Frederick 284, Mary Ann 284 Sophia (Garbar) 284
SOWARD, 179
SOWARDS, Albert 562, Arleen 562, Bertha 562, Beverly 602, Clara 602, Clinton Jr. 146, Clinton Jr. Mrs. 146, Dale 562, Donna 562, Edessa 483, Emma 562, Estella 562, Ida 562, John 562, John Randolph 562, Joseph Alonzo 562, Joseph D. 562, Justine 562, Larry LeRoy 602, Lydia 562, Lynn 562, Martha (Hall) 380, Michael 562, Myrna 562, Nancy 324, 562, Ned 562, Rachel 562, Robert 602, Sarah 562, Sarah Edessa 485, T. J. 112, Thomas Jefferson 562, Vera 562, William 380
SOWERS, Elizabeth 493
SOWLE, Paulina 495
SPADE, Dessie 476, 528 Ella 476, Floyd 476, Floyd R. 572, Glenn 476, Helen 476, Jean Louise 440, Jean Louise 572, Leah Clotene Schwartz 572, Leah Clotine 535, Nellie 476, William 476SPAHR, Jill 545
SPAHR, Lois 545, Max 545
SPAIN, Warnock 572, William 216
SPAKE, Don B. 168, John 87, Robert 140
SPAN, E. T. 75
SPANGLER, Daniel 89
SPANN, Jobe Daniel 582, Sara 581, Sara Kay 582
SPARKS, Abigal Redding 268, Fern 364, Harley 490, Joshua 519, Martha 490, Nancy 519, Sarah 474, Solomon 421
SPAUGH, E. E. 75
SPAULDING, Alice I. (Beeks) 323, Edith Lucile 323, Ella Lucile Croft 323, Ethel 487, Francis 425, Franklin Benjamin 323, Gale 323, Gaylord 323, Gerald 323, Glen 323, L. 214, LeRoy B. 323, Mary J. (Hale) 425, Pauline 560, William Henry 323
SPEAR, H. N. 81, Horace N. Dr. 533
SPEECE, Esta (Cochran) 294, Grace 302
SPEHEGER, Ben 562, Douglas 562, Eliza 562, Frances 291, Inez 214, Martha 579, Monica 562, Roger 562, Shari 401, Stevan 562, Susan 562, Walter 130, 140, 562
SPEICHER, Esther 584, Leah (Nyffeler) 492
SPENCER, Ann 507, Bernard 563, Charles 563, Charlotte Louisa 507, Dian 333, Glen 563, Iva 563, Justin 531, Katherine 531, Leota 563, Margaret 531, Retha 563, Rex 531, Ruth 563, William 563, Zachary 531
SPICE, Juanita Irene 257
SPICHIGER, Brandi Janelle 290, Gary Michael 290, Jennifer Jo 290, Lloyd 283, Michael L. 290
SPIECE, Ken 585
SPIECER, Elizabeth 266
SPILLER, C.A. 58
SPINDLER, Emmett 403
SPITTLER, Elizabeth 326
SPIVEY, Deamand 169, James R. 145, James R. 169
SPRAKER, Myrtle L. 570, Sarah 556, Sarah Eva 475
SPRAY, Madge 155
SPRING, Ronald 488
SPRINGER, Alma Louise 606, Andy 564, Annetta Louise Marie 563, Arlin 287, Arthur 564, Barbara 564, Ben 249, Beryl 564, Bill 564, Bonnie 564, Bradley 563, Bradley Jr. 563, Catherine 564, Chalmer 564, Charles 465, Cheryl 564, Christina 564 Cora 564, Dan 564, Debra 336, Della 563, Donna 564, Dorothy 465, Edna Eileen 563, Edward 287, Emma 564, Emma Jean 564, Eric 336, Eva 564, Ferdinand 564, George 92, 249, George Frederick 563, 606, George L. 564, George Leonard 563, 564, George Michael 563, 564, George Mrs. 92, Gordon L. 563, Gust Ernst 563, Hal 287, Herbert Charles 564, Herbert 564, Jack 336, Jan 563, Jason 461, Jennie 564, Jim 564, John Martin 564, Juanita 526, Justin 563, Karen 563, Kathleen 564, Kay 563, Kenneth L. 563, Lamoine 92, Lavina 92, Lee 287, Lenard 564, Leonard 234, Leonard Martin 564, Lori 564, Magdalena 564, Maggie 564, Margaret 564, Maria 564, Maria Caroline 564, Maria Katharina 563, Maria Sybil 563, Maria Sybilla 564, Marie Emile 564, Marshall 563, Mary 564, Mary Louise 563, Minnie 564, Nathan 461, Norman Dale 564, Paul 563, Raymond 563, Roberta 563, Scott 287, Shane 563, Sharon 563, Sharon Rose 570, Shirley 465, Stanley 564, Steven 564, Susan 249, Virgil 563, 564, Zachery 563
SPROAT, Ardola Mae 557, Edward H 274 Edward Jr. 274, Floyd Earl 557, Louella 239, 405, Patricia 274, Richard 460
SPRONG, Barbara 306
SPROWL, Joseph 540, Mary Ann 540, Will 75, William 540
SPRUNGER, Adrian 140, 565, Arlene 565, Barbara 369, 565, Benjamin 565, Camelia 565, Curtis 565, Daniel 565, David 115, 440, Dorothy 444, 565, Eldon 505, Elias 434, Elizabeth Ellen Betty"", Florence 567, Frederick 565, Frederick D. 444, Hazel (McKuras) 459, Jack 369, Jack 565, Jason 565, Jason Kent 474, Jennifer

565, John 565, John Adrian 474, Joseph 565, Joseph Nelson 474, Justine 440, Justine (Linn) 440, Kent 200, 565, Kent Barger 474, Lila Lehman 565, Marie 565, Marie Nadine 474, Mark 565, Mary Lou 440, 565, Miriam 565, Nadine 474, 565, Nyla 565, Orison 565, Otto 565, Patricia 483, Scott 369, 565, Sheila 474, 565, Sherrill 565, Steven 369, 565, Susan 444, 565, Susanna (Riesen) 434, Suzanne 369, 565, Ted 565, Thomas 444, Todd 565, Tom 565, Vaughn 565
SQUIRES, Pandora 313
SROWL, Roy 263
SROWL, Wayne 263
ST JOHN, Fred M. 335
STACEY, Mary 415
STACKHOUSE, Hugh 86
STAFFORD, Betty 479, Nelson 112
STAGER, Ralph 233
STAHL, Anna 324, Anna Marie (Klug) 366, Arista L. 267, Belinda 366, 367, C. Rosalee 265, Cathryn E. Dolby 265, Clella 390, Elizabeth Ann (Liz) 253, Esther E. 572, Gus 317, Johannes 366, John 317, Josephine 324, Lester V. 265, Merriel 317, Rebecca 81, Rosalyn A. 270, Thomas P 267
STAILEY, Polly 152
STAIR, Aaron 566 Betty 566 Brett 566 Cathy 566 Charles 566 Chuck 566 Clara 566 David 565 Emma 566 Harry C. 565, 566 Harry Cyrus 362 Heinrich 566 Jacob 566 Joanna 566 Joel 565 John 566 Jonathan 566 Jordon 566 Kelli 566 Lillie 566 Lillie A. 566 Lillie A. (Beyler) 565 Lillie Aurora (Beyler) 362 Norma 566 Ray 566 Ray A. 565 Reuben 566 Roger 566 Rose 566 Rose Marie 566 Sue 566 Taylor 566 Thelma 566 Timothy 566 Timothy Ray 565 Todd 566 Tom 566 Tressie 565, 566 Vera 566 Victor 565, 566 Vida 565, 566 Wanda 566
STAKER, Glynn 127
STALDER, Ray 464
STALEY, Jayne 146
STALLSMITH, Helen 425
STALTER, Cleo May 476, Cleo Mosure 367, Dorothy Lucille 367, Dorothy Lucille 476, Kenneth Dwight 476, Marie 476, Norman 367, 475, Norman S. 476
STAMBAUGH, Dale 15, Inez 15
STAMPER, Kathy Low 268
STANFIELD, Edna 285
STANFORD, Lydia 265
STANLEY, Charles 233, Dawn 385, Douglas 385, Kenneth 385, Luana 269, Margaret 348, Nancy 585, Richard 385
STANTON, Blanch Ruth 243, Bruce 113, Burce 549, Cora 243, Dallas 243, Edith 243, Edwin M. 538, Fred Ivason 243, Harold 567, Iva Mariah Fish 243, Jan Marie 549, JoAnne 549, Katie Jo 549, Larry 567, Lena Esther 243, Max 567, Orville 475, Robert Howard 243, Robert Riley 243, Rose 243, Ruth Joanne 243, Thurman JEnnings 243, Zebulon 243
STARK, Christy 15, Red 447
STARKEY, Daphne 404
STARR, 66, Ada 542, B. F. 98, Benjamin 240, Benjamin F. 567, Blanche 400, Catharine 434, 567, Donald 434, 567, Doris Elinor 567, Dorothy 567, Douglas 434, Engle 434, 567, Ethel 434, 567, Fern 582, Ferne 400, Flora Ulmer 567, Florence 298, 567, Florence (Sprunger) 434, Frank 542, Gregory 434, Harold 434, 567, Harry 434, 567, Lewis 434, 567, Margaret 542, Martha Ferne 567, Mary 165, 567, Mary (Bovine) 434, Matilda Jane 240, Maxine (Lautzenheiser) 434, O. O. 400, Otis 107, Otis 567, Pauline 567, Pauline Kean 400, Pearl 542, Ralph 400, Ralph 567, Rebecca (Terhune) 434, Sabina 567, Stella 480, 542, Trudy L. 567, William 434, 567
STATLAR, John 13
STAUDT, George 570, John Michael 570
STAUFFER, Amy 594, Basil 427, Betty Romaine 513, Clara 488, Dwight 146, Dwight Mrs. 146, Ida 352, Jacqueline 294, Jessie 427, John E. 594, Margaret 266, Mary Binegar 427, R. Jay 294, Robert J. 294, Robert Jeffrey 294, Roger J. 294, Ronald J. 294, Ronald Jay 294
STAVER, Amanda 258, Barbara Ellen 579, Eliza Jane 258, Elizabeth 562, Elizabeth 562, John H. 258, Lydia 258, Mary 258, Minervia 64, Samatha E. 258, Sarah 258, Susannah 465, Susannah E. 258
STAVOR, Ella 64
STEAD, John 145
STEBING, Becky 429, Diana 429, Don 244, Gina 244, Larry 429, Linda 244, Roy 429
STECH, Mary Dean 482
STECKBECK, Robert 151
STECKLEY, Vern 513
STEDCKE, F.J. 89
STEDMAN, John 566
STEED, Chalmer 454, Janet 454, Marceile 454, Seattia Summerville 500
STEEL, Winifred 509
STEELE, Alta 351405, 587, 588, 589, Angela Jean 580, Bob 580, Clayton 98, David Jeffrey 580, George 112, Jeffrey Alan 580, Minnie 589, Nelson 547, Robert N. 589, Sara Brittney 580
STEFFEN, Abby 409, Allen 229, Amber 562, Amos 474, Angela Jo 460, Ann 409, Barbara 567, Brian 229, Catherine 521, Claude 567, Daniel 435, Dee 137, 150, Denise (Heyerly) 224, Derrell 229, Diane 567, Don 229, Doug 370, Elizabeth 487, 567, Elizabeth (Schwartz) 190, Elmer 229, Eric 562, Ervin 353, Frank 370, Gloria 474, Gloria Jean 567, Harry 456, James 567, Janelle M. 283, Janice 370, Jean Ann 474, 567, Jeanne 340, Jeffery 230, Jessica 567, John 567, Joy Lynne 474, 567, Judy Marlene 567, Karen 229, Keith 409, Kenneth 230, 460, 521, Lewis 475, Lucile 474, Lucille E. 567, Lydia 567, Marcia 562, Maria 567, Marie B. 474, Mark 370, Martha (Baumgartner) 229, Mary 354, 474, Nancy 370, Norman 474, Norman E. 567, Peter 190, Rachel 515, Randall G. 283, Rickey J. 567, Roberta 230, Roberta (Holloway) 460, Rosie Marie 567, Russel 190, Sarah 353, Scott 370, Ted Louis 567, Terry Wayne 474, Terry Wayne 567, Tobias 229, Todd 409, Tom 409, Wayne Terry 474, 567, William 190
STEGEKEMPER, Kate 155
STEICHEN, Christine 340
STEINER, Ada 136, 568, Albert 136, 568, Christina 488, Dan 140, Daniel L. Rev. 77, Ethel 136, Ethel (Hauk) 387, George 568, Helen 568, Henry 568, Ida 367, Kimberli 399, Maria Helene 368, Mary Elizabeth 247, Mildred 319
STEINHAUER, April 293
STEINHIBER, Amy 461
STEINHILBER, Amy 562, Penny 562, Richard 562
STEINKRAUS, Joan 270
STEINMETZ, Jennifer 471, Kurt 471 Lou 471
STEIR, David 403, James Allen 403, Lynn 403, Tere 403
STELLE, J. R. 98
STELLHORN, Carole 339
STEMEN, F.D. 89
STENGEL, Paul 77
STEPHAN, Haley 399, Peter 399, Shelley 399
STEPHENS, Alan Lee 252, Betty 566, Cleo 252, David 92, Evona Montfort 252, Joel 443, Kendra 443, Kent 443, Linda 443, Richard 592, Zachary Robert 252
STEPHENSON, Julie 576, Paul 98
STEPLER, John 68, John H. 422
STEPP, Abraham 568 Alice 568 Anthony 568 Bert 568 Berteen 542, 568 Bobbie 568 C. Bert 275 Carrie 568 Carrie Karns 275 Cbirt 568 Charles 568 Clarissa 568 Emily 568 Enoch 568 Evaline 568 Frances 568 George 568 Goldie 568 James 568 Jane 568 John 568 John R. 568 Levi 568 Louella 568 Lucinda 568 Lydia 568 Maritta 568 Marjorie 568 Mary 568 Melvin 568 Michael 568 Parker 568 Phoebe 568 Rebecca 568 Thomas 568 Tim 142 William 568
STERN, Andrew Wayne 568, Angela Renee 568, Arthur Lloyd 568, Arthur Lloyd II 568, Arthur Lloyd III 568, Ashley Nicole 568, Carol N. 568, Cary Edward 568, Diane Kay 568, Doyle 145, Doyle Robert 250, Doyle Robert 568, Earl 568, Elizabeth 568, Esther Mary 568, Jacob A. 568, Jeffery 568, Jennifer 568, Joan 568, John 568, Kathryn 568, Leanna 568, M. Suzanne 568, Mark Nathan 250, 568, Mary E. 568, Nelson 568, Nicole 250, Polly 152, Ronald Wayne 568, Rosa Ann 568, Sandy 568, Steven Kent 568, Susan 568, Timothy Robert 250, Timothy Robert 568
STERNER, S.V. 82
STEUBE, Charles 98,
STEURY, Becky 84, Blake 584, Debra 584, Kala 584
STEVENS, Betty 566, Eva E. 267, Florence 321, L.B. 202, LaVergne B. 163, Martha 268, Minnie 589, Phoebe H. 268, Solomon 268, Susan 566
STEVENS, Tillie 267
STEVENSON, Betty 277 Betty Lou 277, Mildred 277, Walter 277
STEWARD, Edward 251, Joy 251, Lavonne 251
STEWART, Alvin 9, Carol 443, J. M. 98, Jon 58, Mildred 597, Robert 512, Ruth 472
STICKLER, Talitha 155
STIDHAM, Dorothy 460
STIEGLITZ, Amanda 505 Harold 68 Jeremy 505, Lynn 505, Natalie 505, Tianna 505
STILLBERGER, Mary Jean 371
STILTNER, Vivian 393, L. E. 112
STINE, Cora 123, Henry 455, Karah 438, Karah 558, Mitchell 558 Nancy Spence 558, Robert W. 548
STINSON, 66, Aaron Wayne 569, Alice Rose 409, Alice Rose 569, Anna 569, Anna Jane 381, 409, 569, Betty 569, Betty J. 569, Betty Jane 249, Bradly Lynn 569, Brian Jeffrey 569, Bruce Wayne 569, Cheryl 569, Chester 569, Clara 569, Dan 483, Eli Marshall 569, Forest 165, Hannah Mary 569, Harold 165, Heather Ann 569, Helen 350, Jane 444, Jeffrey Deanne 569, John Manley 569, Kathy Ellen 569, Katie 553, Kendra Susan 569, Kenneth Edwin 409, 569, Linda Lou 569, Manley E. 569, Mark Elwin 569, Martha Louise 409, 569, Maudie Mae 569, Max 8, Max L. 444, Michael 444, Nellie Mae 409, 553, 569, Pamela 463, 483, Pearl O. 569, Peggy Lou 569, Polly 569, Rebecca Kay 569, Robert Edwin 569, Robert Manley 569, Rosetta 569, Roy Elliott 409, Roy Elliott 569, Russell 119, 268, 301, 355, Ryan Manley 569, Sarah Lou 409, 569, Susan 569, Wiley 569
STIPP, J.A. 144
STIREWALT, M. L. 96
STOCK, Art 99
STOCKER, Ginny 520
STOETLING, W. P. Dr. 510
STOFFEL, Ann 589, Gloria 363, Jim 603, Sarah 603, Shawn 603
STOFFER, Lorrie 245
STOGDILL, Elizabeth 155, 366, 367, Ethel 569, George Washington 569, Glen Zepha 569, Homer Bert 569, J. W. 185, James 144, 216, James W. 569, Lucinda Jane 569, Mabel Lois 569, Mary Jane 550, Matthew Russel 255, Nellie Lorinda 255, Rachel Ann Flum 255, Thomas Bryan 569, Wiliam James 569
STOHR, Johann Heinrich 566, Johann Philip 566, Johannes 566
STOKES, Polly 508
STOLLER, Bill 340, Cherry 505, Emma 376, Isaac 376, Kathy 340, Keith 376, Louise 412, Ruth 521, Shari 505
STOLTE, Dorothy 307, Eugene 98
STONE, David Dr. 524, Dawn R. 391, Helen 500, Henry 321, Mary Precious Ifer 407, Shawn E. 391, Susan K. 391, Vernon 234
STONEBROOK, Ellen 589
STONER, Jack 524
STOODY, Joseph 521
STOOKEY, Ray Boss""
STOPPENHAGEN, Carol 605, Fred 532, Frieda (Bultemeier) 532, Karl 73
STORGEON, James A. 72
STORK, Ronald 268
STORMBERG, Larry 151
STORY, Barry 460, Barry J. 569, Evelyn Darlene 569 Jasmine 569, Nelson Thomas 569, Summer 569, Tayler 569
STOTLE, Don 453, Hilda (Ditzenberger) 453, Karen 453
STOTTS, Laura 502
STOUT, Ben 570, Benjamin Franklin 570, Bill 137, 224, Carlyn Neil 380, Christina Barbara 507, Elise Amber 405, Ernest 184, Faith 462, George 570, George William 405, Hope 462, Howard 380, Jennifer 508, Jerry 89, John 507, John Michael 570, Lucy 184, Lucy Anna 507, Marada Field 405, Mona 500, Nelson 570, Paul 8, Paul 258, 570, Pearl 363, Peter 570, Rachel Ann 543, Sam 462, Samuel 462, 507, Sarah Conrad 570, Sarah Ratliff 462, Susannah 507, Thomas 144, Tom Howard 380, Tottie 462, Walter 570, Williason 570
STOVER, Minnie 246, Minnie 386
STOWE, Harriet Beecher 257
STRADER, Adam Lee 406, Allison Yvonne 406Benjamin John 406, Carrie Ann 406, Jacob Donovan 406, Kim Jon 406, Loretta 483, Matthew Wayne 406
STRAHM, Aden 463, 570, Agnes Sarah 570, Albert 570, Aldine 570, Bertha Mae 570, Carol 570, Daisy 570, Daniel 463, 570, Daniel D. 570, Donald 570, Donna 570, DuWayne 570, Edward 570, Elizabeth 570, Elma 316, Emma 570, Esther 356, 570, Eugene 570, Eva 570, Fern 570, Genivieve 570, Gladys 570, Harry 570, Herman 570, Ida 570, Jacob 570, Jeremy 570, Josephine 570, Karen 464, Kay Lynn 570, Larry 464, Larry D. 335, Lauren 464, Lauren Elizabeth 335, Levi 374, Lois Belle 419, Lola 374, 570, Lola Belle 374, Lydia 570, Lydia 570, Marcella 570, Margaret 570, Martha 570, Mary 350, Matthias 70, 570, Megan 570, Mona 570, Nancy 570, Nancy Marie 464, Nelson 570, Ocie (Poling) 374, Patricia 570, Patsy 570, Phyllis 570, Roderick 570, Sadie 350, Sharon 570, Trudith 570, Ulrich 570, Veda 570, Veronika 464, Virgil 570, William 487, 570, Zenith 570
STRAIN, David 419, Joseph 95
STRALEY, Paula 590, Rosella 590
STRAM, Marjorie 478
STRASBERG, Phyllis 287
STRASSWEG, Elsa 200 Caroline 477
STRATTON, Isaac 362, Veronica C. 570
STRAUSBAUGH, Emmet 193, Margarette B. 22
STRAUSER, Levina 515
STRAW, 66
STREATER, August 146, August L. (Augie) 196, August Mrs. 146
STREET, Brian 360, Leah Paige 360
STREHLER, Don 146, Don Mrs. 146
STRICKER, Fred 241
STRINE, Aimee 570, April 570, Bruce 570, Chad 570, Cory 570, Devon 570, Donalynn 570, Franklin Rev. 570, Kathy 570, Kelly 570, Kristy 570, Madelynn 570, Paulette 570, Phyllis 570, Stacie 570
STRING, J. H. 85
STROHM, Nettie 603
STRONG, Don 55,329, Lewis 58, Amy Renee 570, Athelma Beatrice 570, 571, Blake Alan 571, Charles 571, Charles Leon 570, 571, Craig Lee 571, Emma 571, Etta 519, Gerald Lee 419, 570, 571, Gregory Charles 419, 570, 571, James 571, James Lyle 570, 571, Jeffrey Allen 570, Jennie 155, Jennie Cloe 570, 571, Joe 571, Jonathon Andrew 570, Joseph 571, Joseph Leon 570, 571, Judith Ann 570, Karen Jo 419, 570, 571, Keith Alan 419, 570, 571, Kera Lurana 571, Kory Alan 571, Michael Joseph 570, Milas J. 570, Miles Joe 571, Natalie Diane 571, Rebecca Lynn 571, Richard W. 419, Richard Ward 570, 571, Robert 571, Ruth 137, Ruth Eileen 570, 571, Shari Jo 570, Sharon Rose 570, Stella 571, Stella Lee 570, Stella Lurana 570, 571, Stephanie Ann Marie 571, Tamara Sue 571, Troy Lee 570, Veronica C. 570, Virginia 571, Virginia Mae 570, 571
STROUP, Devona 482, Eliza C. 582, Frank 20, Freeman 482, Helen 482, John 144, Rose 482, Sandra 515
STROUPE, Alma Fryback 535, Kenneth 535
STRUDEBAKER, J. M. 602
STRUDWICK, Virginia 549
STRUNK, Elizabeth 375
STRYKER, Phillip 142
STUART, Cecil 298
STUCK, Beverly 602, Ruth 150
STUCKY, Doris A. 475, Earl 322, Glen 519, Richard 322, Steven 322
STUDABAKER, Abraham 571, Abram T. 571, 572, Anna Louise 571, Ben 571, Brian 425, David 319, 572, David D. 571, 572, Esther E. 572, Fred 572, Gary 425, George W. 571, Henry 572, Homer 98, Hugh 94, Hugh 572, J. M. 571, John 162, 185, 202, 216, 245, 571, 572, John D. 572, Louis 572, Louisa 572, Mariah 571, Mary A. 571, Mary Frances Mate"", Mary J. 572, Minnie Myrtle 405, Nathan 425, Nellie 572, Noah E. 572, Norah 572, Peter 81, 147, 185, Peter 405, 572, Sarah 147, 319, 572, William 571, 572, William L. 572, William T. 571
STUDEBAKE, Emma 602
STUDEBAKER, Abbagail 267, Abraham 405, Abram 267, 386, Alice 532, Alta M. 444, Christena 540, Effie 606, Genieve (McKuras) 459, Geny 527, George 61, George W. 444, Guy 527, Harry 464, 602, Jesse 527, John 9, 405, Karen 527, Sara 444, William 300, William 405
STUDER, Dick 355, Harold 355, Jack 355, Jim 355, Ray 355
STUFF, Roy 585
STULTZ, Clarissa 394
STUMP, Nancy J. 489, Samuel 61
STURGEON, Alfred Wayne 572, Beth Ann 572, Beth Anne 440, Charles Raymond 572, Clarinda 572, Henry 572, Hugh 440, 512, Hugh Linn 572, James 92, 572, James A. 440, James Linn 440, 572, Jean Louise 572, John 288, John Poultney 288, 572, Mary 572, Mercy 572, Mima Elizabeth 572, Mima Kleinknight 512, Nancy 572, Phebe Ann 573, Ray 440, Robert 440, Robert K. 572, Ruth 440, Ruth Ilene 512, 572, Sedora 572, Stephen Robert 572, Steven Robert 440, Viola 572, Wayne 440
STURGIS, Alice White 572, Betty 259, Bill 443, Catharine Parintha 324, Catherine 363, Charles 262, Charles David 580, Charles E. 8, 200, Clara 200, Don Kay (Bud) 572, E. Y. 147, 208, Earl Bruce 393, 572, Earl Bruce Dr. 375, Elmore 144, 147, Jean Rose 572, Jennifer David 580, Jim E. C. 572, Joan 443, John 572, Kent L. 572, Lemuel D. 443, Linda 572, Martha Alice 572, Martha Alice (Peachie) 375, Matilda 147, Rita 572, Ruie 348, Stephanie Dawn 580, Ted 572, Thomas 443, Thomas A. 572, Tom 259, 572, 580, Vera Jeffery 572, William (Rev.) 572, Jr. Thomas 572, Sr. Elizabeth Brazier 572, Sr. Thomas 572
STUVER, Alfred 342, Alfrieda Effie"", Effie 253, Melissa 342
SUDDETH, Argo 92, Argo Mrs. 92, Shirley 346
SUDDUTH, Teresa 601
SUER, Allison Mae 470, Gail Leslie 470, Matthew Thomas 470, Michael Jay 470, Robert P. Dr. 470
SULLENS, Calvin 463, Ruth 463
SULLIVAN, Athena June 573, Barbara 573, Bonnie 573, Charles 151, Dale 316, Dale Lee 247, Diann Jayne 247, Doyle 573, Jayne R. 316, Jeffery Allan 573, Jennifer 316, Jennifer Lee 247, Julie 316, Julie Ann 247, Lois 414, Loretta 573, Orville Jr. 573, Orville Sr. 573, Shirley 137, Terry Wayne 573, Tina 576
SUMAN, Darlene 350, Estaleen 485, Estaleene 152, John 485
SUMMAN, Edward Gray 348, Harry Edward 348
SUMMERS, David 271, Erskin 214, Felix 573, Jacob 573, John G 271, Joshua Craig 260, Karen 271, Lulu Alice 573, Margaret 551, 552, Mary 356, Mary Lula 551, 552, Matilda 573, Mattie 602, Megan Marie 260, Michael 271, Park 551, Phebe Ann 573, Roger 260, Thomas 271, William Henry 551, 552
SUMNER, Amanda 559
SUNDERMAN, Freida 402
SUNDLING, Mary 154, Mary 154
SUNIER, E. E. 8, 235
SURFACE, Earl 75, Rose 75
SURFUS, Alan 574, Albert Richard 574, Andrew 573, Betty 573, Carol 574, Catherine (Oswalt) 573, Charles 573, Charles Curtis 574, Charles Frederick 498, 574, Cheryl 498, Cheryl Marie 573, Chester 573, David 498, David Alan 573, Donna 574, Ellen 573, Eva 573, Francis Maxine 574, George 573, Harriet 573, James 498, James H. 573, James Henry 498, 574, Jeanette Susan 574, Jerry 573, John 573, John E. 573, Julia 573, Kathy 574, Linda 574, Mabel 573, Marjorie Dianne (Gard) 573, Marjorie Estella 574, Marvin Fred 574, Mary 573, Michael Wayne 574, Orville 573, Patricia 498, Patricia Rene Patty"", Richard 574, Roger Allen 498, 574, Ruth 573, Salina 573, Samuel 573, Scott 498, Stephen 573, Tammy 498, Timothy 498, William 573, William Howard 574
SURGAN, W. Mrs. 39
SUTER, Frances Jean 431, Verline 431
SUTERS, Susan (Ayers) 459, Washington 459
SUTILEF, Beulah 574 Hattie 574, John W. 574, Mary Ellen 574, Maryann 574, Minnie Louise 574, Waldo 574, William Willard 574
SUTTON, Dian Jarushy 594, Donald 140, Dora 292, 512, Elijah 575, 594, Elijah Rev. 259, Mary Ann 575 Mary Daine 454, Monica 562, Norma 350, Theresa 345
SWAGART, Janet 517
SWAIM, Alberta 156, Celia 136, 208, 280, Celia 575, Celia 580, Celinda Alice 430, D. H. 185, 190, David 208, David H. 575, David Hathaway 365, 580, Doris Dodie"", Doris 575, Edna Hanna 430, Edna Hannah 430, 606, Grace Lumley 576, Hannah Toy 365, 580, Helen 365, 575, 580, James 378, 576, James Polk 430, Janet 280, 575, Kent Eugene 576, Kurt Daniel 576, Lucile 378, Lumley Tanton 576, Mabel (Gilbert) 358, May 575, Patricia 576, Rex Eugene 576, Rita Lou 576, Roger 9, Roger 136, 208, 280, 575, Roger Gorrell 365, 580, W. T. 208, W. T. T. Tom"", William 365, 580
SWAIN, Louman Agnes 591, Nancy Agnes 591, Phil 145
SWANK, Carrie Summers 268, Charles 268, Joyce 558, Joyce Ann 252, Julia 268, Lora 302, Mark 268, Robert C. 558, Robert Christopher 252
SWANSON, Rebecca 443
SWARTZ, Daniel Lee 382, Davina Jo 382, Deborah 382, Don 382, Elmina 303, Helen Margaret 606, Mikel 64, Ruth 409, Ruth (Jackson) 410, Virgil 390
SWEARINGEN, Maritta 568, Mary 568
SWEENEY, Earl-Arn 244, Janet Faye 244, Nellie 244
SWEENY, Barbara 576, Dan 576, Dave 576, Esther 576, Evelyn 576, 586, Ida Sowards 576, Jemima Cary 576, John Welsey 576, Nancy 576, Olive 422 576, Olive Gladness 586, Olive (Joray) 511, Paul 422, 576, 586, Robert 422, 423, 511, Robert John 576, Tim 576, Tom 576
SWEET, Marie 276, Marylee 473, Rachel 304
SWEITZER, Wendelene 349
SWENSON, Andrew 374
SWICK, Clair 500
SWIFT, Ida 515
SWIGERT, Dorothy 599
SWIHART, Dan 576, Harold 576, Hilden 241, Jared Patrick 576, Lois 576, Lois Tobias 326, Paul Tobias 326, Sonja 576
SWINFORD, Mike 145
SWINGLEY, Charles 78, Nancy (Stone) 321
SWISHER, Fred 178, George 178, Harriet 515, Harry R. 178, Harry W. 178, Marie 127, 178, Richard 140, Thelma 520
SWOPE, Amos 549
SWOVERLAND, Jack 441, Rebecca L. Lipkey 441
SWYHART, Kate 552
SYBERT, John 89
SYMMES, Jayne 294
SYMON, William E. 287

TADDOTA, Antonett 238
TAFT, William H. 34
TAKAHASHI, George 598, Hiroyuki 598, Thomas 598
TALBERT, Pierre 146, Pierre Mrs. 146
TALLY, Nicole 433
TANGEMAN, F.J. 216, Frank 95, Fred 8, Fred 95, Fred J. 223, Frederick 146, Frederick Mrs. 146, Justine 154, Mayme 136, John 77
TAPPY, Addie 497, Henrietta 98, Henrietta Key 499, Henrietta (Keyes) 497, Joyce A. 489, Kathleen 385, Lucille 382, Simeon 98, 499, Simon 20, 497
TARASCOU, Anna 405, Grant 405, John 405
TARR, Beatrice 107, Daniel M. 315, Daniel N. 315, Dave 315, Don 315, Everett 413, Floyd 315, Ida (Markley) 469, Jadriana 315, Jessica 315, John 315, 375, Mary 552, Oscar 107, Rosie (Jones) 315, Wanda (DeArmond) 315
TATE, Clo Lucile 332, Hugh 107, O.F. 107
TAYLOR, Alberta Ann 509, Alice 321, Altonya 577, Anita 577, Benjamin 417, Brandon Robert 577, Bruce 83, Camilla Rae 544, Catherine 266, Charlotte Jane 509, Cheryl Ann (Croy) 577, Dale 508, Don 304, Doris 508, Ellen 454, Elton Elizabeth 509, Florence 577, Harley 577, Isaac 59, John 151, John R. 509, Jordan 99, Josseph A. D. 471, June R. 502, Karen 304, 563, Karen Kay 508, Katherine 555, Kathy (Camphell) 400, Kenneth A. 518, 544, Larry 99, Larry Dale 508, Lester 98, Martha 502, Mary 460, Mary Ann 99, Mary Ethel 509, Maude Rose 471, Megan Ruth 577, Mikel 303, Myrtle 375, Naida Theola 517, Norma Elizabeth 509, Norman A. 509, Philip 304, Ralph 79, Ralph R. 577, Robert 304, Robey R. 577, Rose 304, Ruth 320, Ruth Maxine 306, Scott 99, Steven 303, Steven Ray 577, Teresa 290, Thomas 471, Thomas W. 454, Thomas William 471, Victor Carl 471, Zachary 454
TAYRIEN, Diane Kay 568, Frank 568, Kim Marie 568, Kristie Jo 568
TEACHOUT, Rebecca 488
TEAGLE, Everett 400, Nathan 400, Samuel 400, Susan 400
TEAGUE, Anna 504, Anna Mersaydes 364, 516, David William 364, Patti Jo 516, Spencer 504, Spencer Lee 364, 516, Steven 364
TEAGUE, Steven 504, 516
TEAS, Edward 243, Emily Maria 243, George Hallowell 243
TEEGARDEN, Aaron T. 294, Abraham 294, Christian 294, Daniel 294, Rachel 294, Rachel 527
TEEPLE, Laura 532
TEETER, Larry 392, Penny Sue 392, Tootie 392
TEMPLE, Benton A. 331, Clara May 331, Donna M. 270, Sylvanus 331, Sylvester 331
TEMPLETON, Mary Jane 299, W. H. 16, W.H. 86
TEMPLIN, Carey 102, George 447, L. E. 140, L. E. Mrs. 140, Lawrence 145, 448, Meiry 155
TENNISON, Luella 304
TERHUNE, 66, Albert 268, David 528, Gladys 257, 268, Leota 434, Ray 434, Thomas 202
TERRELL, Alford 577, Amanda 577, Earl Wilford 577, Harris 577, Jack 490, Lillian E. 577, Lucy 577, Von 577
TERRY, Janice 555, Winifred Morse 278
TEUSCH, Jason Roth 438, Linda Rose 438, Sheila 438, Tracey 438
TEWELL, Zelma 517
TEWKSBURY, Serepta 307, Elmer 527
THARP, Elizabeth 372, James W. Sr. 257
THATCHER, Warren 66
THAYER, Andrew 592, Andrew Baker 603, Annie 471, Betty 592, Freeman 471, Margie 592, Margie (Wolfe) 603, Shirley 603
THEIM, Tran Nham 97, John R. 145
THEOBOLD, Alice 488, Clarice 488, William 488
THIEKE, Marie 323, Catherine 564, Connie 449, Conrad 564
THIELE, Ed 449, Edward 252, Frieda 252, Heidi 449, Martha 252, Opal 563
THIESING, Ed 320
THINNES, Judy 548
THOMA, Betty Jean 578, Bill 578, Emma 152, Emma 578, Harriet 154, 578, 136, 548, Henry 187, 212, 578, Herman 55, 187, Herman W. 212, Herman William 578, Kitty 403, Mary 44, 45, 578, Mary Jane 578, Matilda 578, Patricia 578, William 187, 200, 212, William Henry 578
THOMAS, Adam 408, Allie 580, Anna Mary 579, Anne 579, Anne Wiehle 580, Anthony 283, Arthur 428, Barbara 579, Bob 454, Bobbie 253, Caleb 579, Catharine 78, 468, 579, Charlie 578, Claudette 438, David 99, 428, David F. 579, 580, David F. Rev. 100, David Michael 579, Dean 253, Debra 349, Dick 38, Donald 285, Dorothea 600, Eli 112, Elias 86, Elizabeth 579, Emma 579, Enos 418, Ethel (Masterson) 579, Fern 578, Floyd 228, 253, 580, Floyd Jr. 253, Georgianne 579, Harry Dwight 468, Howard 216, 579, Howard E. Tommy"", Ida 579, Irene 302, Isaac Jr. 579, Isaac Sr. 579, JAcob C. 283, James 107, 578, James Roll 578, Jane Ann 253, 578, 580, 253, Jeffrey 468, Jerry 408, Jesse 78, Jessie 86, John H. G. 579, John L. F. 579, John Lucas Flack 579, John Ralph 579, Laura 579, Lee Richard 579, Leland 600, Lewi 580, Lewis 580, Linda V. 542, Lizzie 342, Lyde 253, Lydia 579, Magaline 579, Margaret (Cameron) 418, Martha 155, Martha (Kirk) 418, Mary 155, 394, Mary (Bayha) 253, Mary Bayha 342, Mary L. 579, Mary Lou 491, Mary Louise 578, Merle 580, Merrie E. 283, Michael 468, Monroe 580, Peggy Jean 578, Phil 253, Ralph C. 579, Ralph Courtney 579, Rhoda 86, Ruth Mabel 259, Sampson 579, 580, Sarah 418, Scott 468, Seth 418, Shatler 579, 580, Susanne 580, Thankful 363, Traci 408, William Dale 468, Wilma 320, 585, Zebulon 579
THOMET, Patricia Ann 331
THOMPKINS, Linda 347
THOMPSEN, Kimberly 396
THOMPSON, Alfred P. 582, Armitta Angeline 582, Armitta Angeline Fix 350, Buelah 582, Carl 284, Carl D. 603, Caroline 551, Charles 380, Charles R. 603, Charley Alvin 350, Cheryl Ann 582Chester R. 582, 582, Clarabelle 154, 580, Constance 383, 581, Corey Lee 581, Curt 284, David 278, 300, 307, 581, David E. 603, David S. 200, David Swaim 580, Deborah 474, Deborah Joan 581, Deidre 581, Delilah 363, Denise 307, 581, Dennis 307, 581, Dennis Lee 581, Dessie 313, 364, Diedre 307, Donald 307, Donald Earl 581, Doris Ann 350, Dorothy 307, Dwight 307, 581, Ernest Elza 582, Estelle 538, Falk 142, Fannie Marie (Marson) 581, Frank 145, 202, 365, 601, Frank G. 190, 580, George Howard 350, 582, George Ora 582, Glen Elmer 350, Helen 580, Howard 76, Ida Belle 418, J. Elbridge 607, James 542, Jami Kay 581, 582, Jeffrey Keith 581, 582, Jennifer Karol 581, 582, Jim 581, Jimmy Lee 582, Jobe Daniel 581, John Howard 262, John Ware 581, 582, Joyce 450, Joyce Ann 581, 582, Judith Ann 580, Kathryn Kathy"", Kelly 380, Kenneth 385, Kenneth B. 582, Kent 380, Kimberly 551, Kris 380, Laura 136, 407, Laura Marie 581, Lena (Beerbower) 607, Linda 300, Lois 293, 381, Lois Ann 508, Lois Blen 350, M. Maxine 582, Mable 582, Marcus 406, Mary 582, Mary A. 405, Mary Alice 409, Mary Jo 580, Matha Irene 350, Melida Diane 581, Michael 542, Minnie M. 603, Nancy 542, Nellie Burman 581, Nora Lucrillia 582, Norman 551, Ora 581, Pam 533, Pamela Kay 581, Peggy Jo (Drabenstot) 380, Phyllis 542, Quent 551, Richard E. 581, 582, Robert H. 582, Roberta A. 582, Roy 603, Sara Beth 581, Sara Kay 582, Sarah A. 571, Steven Dean 581, Ted Loren 581, Terry 284, Thomas DeWayne 581, Tim 284, Todd 284, Vera Ione 350, William 581, William G. 582, William M. 581, William O. 581, Willie 581, Wilma Idell 350, Wilma Louise 607, Sr. James 582
THONGNUT, Pisamai 501
THORN, Charles A. 100, Mariah 273, Marva 268, Taylor 273
THORNBURG, Ivan 527, Joey 527, Bradley 384, Bruce 384, Sarah 384
THORNE, Wilbur 98
THORNELL, Kenneth 92
THORNETT, Amy 249, Don 249, Eric 249, Julie 249
THORNTON, Bernice E. 571, Margery 419, Mary (Kelly) 419, Ralph 82, Ruth 419, William A. 419, William Jr. 419
THORPE, Chester 185
THRAILKILL, Hilda 554, Hilda Jane 395, Jane 310, 475, Jennie Jane 474, Joseph 395, Mabel 396, Millie Jane Buckner 396, William Ernest 395
THROCKMORTON, John 507
THURBER, Lucinda 418, Nancy 402
TICE, Elias 48
TIGER, Mort 298
TILLMAN, Curtis 582, Inez 582, Lance 582, Larry 582, Leslie 150, Lorraine 582, Lowell 150, 582, Russell 582, Steven 582
TILMAN, Maria 294
TINDALL, Robert 597
TINKEL, Albert 582, Amy 400, 582, Bert 529, 582, Bert Thomas 274, 582, Dale 87, 274, Dale D. 582, Dale Mrs. 87, Eddie 582, Evaleene 582, Everett 582, Gradus. 582, Homer A. 582, Janet 582, Julie 400, 582, Justin C. 582, Mary E. 582, Max 582, Myrtle 582, Raymond 582, Sally 130, Sally Jo 400, 582, Sarah Sue 274, 582, Scott 400, 582, Vaughn B. 582
TINKER, W. W. 81
TINKLE, Gladys 476
TINSLEY, Christena 262, Joan 553
TISDALE, Robert 81
TITUS, Floyd Rev. 309
TOBIAS, Ed 576, Elaine (Tarr) 315, James 576, Johannah 576, Joyce 576, Lois Annette 576, Merle Stuart 576, Nicholaus 315, Paul 576, Stan 98, Stanley 576, Tim 151
TOBIN, Ray 226
TODD, Andrew 583, Daniel 471, David 583, Doyle 583, Elizabeth 242, Emily 583, Eric 583, Forrest 583, J. J. 147, Jessica 583, John 260, Joshua 583, Kelli 583, Kevin 583, Mary 147, Michael 583, Mike 130, Nicole 583, O. J. 382, R. S. 106, R. S. 185, Rachel 260, Ralph S. 145, Richard 583, Robin 583, Ronald 583, Samuel 260, Valentine 583
TOMAINI, Al 557, Bernice Evelyn 557
TOMAN, Altha Irene 553, 583, Clyde Leroy 583, Florence 583, Joe 20, Joseph Clarence 583, Joseph Clarence III 583, Joseph Clarence Jr. 583, Mahala Parker 583, Nancy Elaine 583, Phillip 583, Selvan Chalmer 583, Thomas Eugene 583
TOMLIN, Judy 154
TONNER, An Ok Yon 584, Angie 584, Anna 352, Bobby 584, David 584, Debra 584, Diana 584, Doris 340, Elizabeth 584, Esther 187, 584, Irene 584, Jane 584, John 584, Joy 487, Martin 140, Martin 187, 584, Mary 479, 584, Mary Ellen 584, Michelle 584, Paul 584, Robert 584, Sylven 187, Sylven Andrew 584, Virginia 584
TOPPIN, Susan 488, Elizabeth 398
TORRENS, Fanny 398, Margaret 298, 398
TOTH, Elizabeth 500
TOURNEY, Larry 490
TOUSSAINT, Jules 367
TOWLE, Jodi 340
TOWNE, Elizabeth Linnea 490, Gerry 371, Jenny 371, Luke 371, Michael Andrew 490, Philip 371, Stefanie Michelle 490, Stephen Michael 490, Tyler 371
TOWNS, Earl 320, 585, Jeffrey Dee 585, Mary P. 585, Paul Eugene 585, Phyllis 585, Ralph Edward 585, Scott Howard 585, Timothy 585
TOWNSEND, Amos 185, 216, Brett 462, Lori 462, Zachary 462
TRACY, O.O. 82, Susanna 435
TRAILKILL, Ellen 605, Jane 474
TRAUB, Robert 95
TRAVIS, DeVota 274, John 102, Martha 274, 289, Rachel 102, Ralph 274, Robert 16, Robert 86, William 274
TRELLA, Elizabeth Marie 500, Kristen Lynn 500, Phillip James 500, Timothy 500
TREMAINE, Dan 253
TREMP, Art 464
TRENARY, Mary F. A. 469, Matilda 469, Richard 469,
TRIBOLET, Anna 55, 600, Elizabeth Ogle 407, Harry 208, J.W. 147, Jacob 55, 147, 187, Jacob 212, John 175, 253, 407, John Wesley 600, Margaret 147, 175, Mary 147, 600, Maude 175, Rachel 407, Susanna 375
TRICKER, Chrystal 266
TRIMBLE, Paula 415
TRIPLETT, Nancy 311
TROSTEL, Austin Orlando 587, Edna Devona 587, Emmanuel 586, 587, Gus Edwin 587, John Henry 587, John Mrs. 394, Lois Irene 587, Rachel (Mock) 586 587, Sarah Elizabeth 586, 587
TROUT, Luetta 489, Pearl (Custard) 304
TROUTMAN, Henry 144, Mildred 147
TROXEL, Alex Conrad 413, Blake Austin 413, Clinton Jensen 413, David J. 413, Elsie (Frautchi) 413, Ralph 413, Robert 55, Terry 140
TROYER, Enow R. 89, J.K. 89
TROYKA, Jay Jr. 528, Jay W. 528, Matthew 528, Rebecca 528
TRUBEY, Barbara 84, 136, Bill 140, C. William
TRUEAX, Sally 441
TRULLENDER, Henrietta Dare 523, James 575, Mary 603, Rosetta 603, Ruehen 603
TRUMAN, Harry S. 34
TSCHANNEN, Albert Anthony 263, Edna (Kummer) 432, Elizabeth Borne 263, Marie 221
TUCKER, Anne 475, Floy 546, Jay 546, Julia 546, Rosa 318, Susan 389
TUDOR, James 459, Ron 277
TURESDALE, David 90
TURNER, Adam 336, Alice 584, Amelia 584, Arthur 584, Bergata 584, Bill 588, Catherine 584, Charles Franklin 584, Cordelia 584, Daisy 584, Earl Simeon 584, Edith Mildred 584, Edward 584, Edwin 584, Elizabeth 584, Emily Jane 584, Esther Elizabeth 584, Frederick A. 500, Genevieve (Thurman) 460, George 584, Gerald 460, Janice 460, Jennie Elizabeth 500, Jeremy Joe 421, John 584, Jon 584, Joseph 584, Kathy 584, Lawrence Lynn 500, Leuie 584, Lewis L. 584, Lewis Lindley 584, Malinda 584, Martha 584, MAry Mamie"", Mary C. 584, Mary Lucile 584, Maud 320, Minnie 320, Missouri 584, Nellie 584, Oran Lemuel 584, Orange L. 584, Phyllis Jeanetta 500, Robert 584, Robert B. 584, Ruth 588, Sarah 500, 584, Simeon 584
TUSTISON, F. Lyle 346
TUTHILL, Nancy 419, Richard 419
TUTTLE, Hanna 363, Hannah 324, William 591
TWIBELL, John 403, Luther 16, Luther 86, William 107
TWIGG, Amanda (Carr) 466, Charles 243, Eleanor Purcell 243, Emmaline (Blair) 466, Florence 554, John P. 466, William 466
TYLER, Becky 591, Jeff 591, Jeremy 591, Kelsey 591, Mary Jean 294, Myron 249, Richard 249, Terry 591
TYNDALL, L. C. 75, Ralph 216
TYRON, Eric 551, Janice 551, Michael 551, Stuart 551
UDELL, Rev 86
UHL, Dorothy (Blair) 313, E. J. 313, Edward 314, Edward J. 312, 313, Helen 314, Helen (Koopenhofer) 312, 313, 314, Henry 313, Marvin 312, 314, Marvin E. 313, Mary E. 313
UHRICH, Hannah Rosa 394, Connie 284
ULERY, Kent 68
ULLMAN, Ellen Marie 581, H.M. 216, Howard 145, 184, J. A. 184, Verdi (Decker) 317
ULMER, Andrew 585, Anna Bell 585, Catherine 567, Erma 333, Esther L. 585, Flora 567, Frances Hughes 459, Frances Joan 585, Frank 585, George 585, Glen 333, Helen 458, Helen Naoma 459, 585, Henry 567, Herman 602, Jacob (Joe) 585, Jodi 333, John 585, John Harrison (Harry) 459, 585, Lee 333, Lloyd 8, Margaret 266, Mary 333, Mary 346, Mary Alice 585, Nicholas 585, Peter 585, Phillip 585, Phoebe 585, Robert S. 585, Sadie 585, Steve 333, Wanda 585, William 333, William (Bill) 585
ULMER, Jr, John 585
ULMER, Sr, John 585
ULRICH, Rinda 340, 487
ULSHAFER, Janet 400, 582
UNDERHILL, Avis 501, , Carlin 501, Darrell 501, Emma 501, Flavia 501, Garth 501, John 501, M. Fern 501, Ruby 501
UNDERWOOD, Doctor 15, Nancy 547
UNGER, Emma 605
UPDIKE, Alan 244, Steve 539, Wallace 244
UPHAUS, Rev. 89
UPTGRAFT, Celia 410, James Weisell <Jim> 279, Janice 279, Janice Elaine 255, Laura 279, Mary 255, Mary (Bulger) 279, Sheila 279, Weisell 255, 279
UPTON, Samuel 208
URBAN, Fran 241
URSHEL, Gina 150
VACHON, Alfonso 95
VAIL, Ruheme 309
VALENTINE, Clona 585, Elizabeth 93, 517, Elvin Laverne 585, Emma 324, Johan George 585, John 585, Joseph 585, Marie 476, Martha Belle 461, Mary C. 288, Mary Ellen 357, Merle 585, Phebe 244, Rheua 585, Ruth E. 291, Samuel 93, Snarr 585
VAN BETUM, Adam 425, Sarah 425, Walter 425
VAN EMON, Mary 394
VAN HOOSE, Edith Grace Toddie"", Mack 255
VAN METER, Mildred 277
VAN WINKLE, Betty 154, James 151
VAN WORMER, Janette 600 Sarah 600, William 600
VANANDA, Ernest F. 547, Velma 323
VANBUREN, Martin 560
VANCAMP, Abraham 585, Amy 585, Anna Mae 586, 588, Barry 585, Bonnie Lucile 585, Bradley Allen 585, Carol 585, Catheline 585, Cathy 585, Charles 585, Deborah 585, Donald 585, Donald Wayne 320, 585, Edward 588, Eva 585, Evelyn 588, Geneva 585, Glen F. 296, Glen Franklin 320, 585, Gloria 585, Gregory 585, Hazel 345, James 585, James Alexander 588, James Charley 585, James Howard 320, Janice 585, Jeffrey 585, Jennie 585, John T. 585, Joseph 585, Judith Ilene 585, Lindsay 585, Lisa 585, Lois Lorraine 585, Lucy 585, Marlin 585, Marlin Eugene 320, Marsha Kay 585, Martha 585, Martha Louise 320, Mary Lou 585, Mary Pauline 320, Mary Pauline 585, Max 585, Nellie Marie 320, 588, Norma 585, Phyllis 585, Roger 585, Roger Wayne 320, Rolly 588, Ronald Alan 585, Russell 585, Sarah J. 585, Tony 585, William Henry 588, William Worley 588, Wilma 585
VANDAM, Gary 343, Rosalie Ann 343
VANDIVINDER, Frances M. 548
VANDUINEN, Judy 549
VANEMON, Absalom 586, Amanda 422, 586, Andrew 586, Cora 422, 586, Cora Jane 423, Elizabeth 586, Emmarillis 586, Hiram 422, Hiram 586, James 185, 586, Lawrence 586, Martha 586, Mary Ann 586, Matilda 586, Nora 586, Rhoda 586, Susan 586
VANHOOZEN, Beth 359, Hannah 359, Nick 359
VANHORN, Amaziah 244, Elyla 244, Rachael 94, Tom 94
VANMETER, Janice Lynn 590, Jerald 130
VANNATTER, Beverly Dorton 402, Cammy 402
VANWINKLE, Clyde 565, James 146, 225, 537, James Dr. 478, James Mrs. 146, Mary Lou 565
VANZANT, Davis 535
VARDAMAN, V. A. 75
VARDMEN, Lucinda Jane 569
VARNER, Daniel 268
VARY, Dorothy Ifer 407
VAUGHN, 167, Adelia Clark 586, Alvin 588, Alvin Harrison 586, 588, Anna Ward 588, Anniebell 588, Barbara Kay 586, 588, Betty 586, Betty 588, Donna Mae 586, 588, E.C. 163, 202, Edwin Clark 586, 587, Helen Adelia 586, Henry Warner 586, Jerry 413, Jerry Lee 285, 586, 588, John 588, Mary 588, Minnie 588, Myrtle 588, Russell Whitman 586, Sandra Lee 285, 586, Sandy 588, Sarah Elizabeth 586, Sarah Tostel 587, Sarah (Trostel) 587, Scott 588, Scott Alan 285, Scott Alan 586, Stella 587, 588, Stella Adelia 586, 587, Sue (Carnes) 413, Terry 588, Terry Sue 413, Theresa Joan Terry Jo"", Turner 588, William 586
VAUSE, Jemima 507, Susan 507, William 507
VEAZEY, Phyllis 342
VEBERT, Rose 530
VEGA, Donna 340
VEITH, Mary Ann 589
VENIS, Alta 588, 589, Barbara 588, Bill 405, Carol 588, Christina 405, Christopher 405, Clifford 405, Daniel 405, Deborah 405, Donna 588, Ellen 589, George 589, Harold 588, 589, Heidi 405, Irene 351, 589, Karen 588, Katie 405, Lelard Leroy 589, Lucille 588, 589, Mary 405, 589, Peter 405, Richard 405, Robert 202, Robert 387, Robert 588, Robert 589, Roy 351, 405, 588, 589, Ruth 588, 589, Susie 405, Timothy 405, William 405
VERBERT, Adrian 530, Edith Lorene 530
VETETO, Benny 485, James 485, Jeanne 485, Stephen 485,
VETTER, Jack 289, Larry 289, Lynn Ann 289, Maurine 289, Sandra 289
VICKERY, George 592, Mabeline 142, S.B. 113
VICKEY, Dessie 554, Noah 554
VICKREY, Diane 603, Doris 275, 519, Doris E. 408, Eldie 383, George 408, Homer 408, Mabeline 383, Noah 408, Ronald 383, Sarah 408, Stephen D. 408, Sue Anne 383, Velma 408
VICLE, Mabel 402
VILLA - GARCIA, Isabel Maria 479, Kay 479, Leonarda 479
VILLANEVA, Angela 501
VINCENT, Bud 597, Dale 264, Melanie 597, Michele 597, Ruth Ann 597
VINING, Sarah 249
VINSON, Jim 25
VITZ, Martin 439, 464, Oswald 68, Otto 68, Peter 68, 439, Peter Rev. 464
VOIGT, August 310, Bertna 310, Birdena 310, 311, Daisy 310, Edwin 310, Lloyd 310, Marguerite 310
VOLLMAR, Bertha 492, 560, Jacob 432, John 556, Joshua 410, Lulu (Bryan) 556, Michael 410, Opal 556, Stella (Settlemeyre) 432
VOLLMER, 179
VONGUNTEN, Carla 221, Carla Jane (Reinhard) 526, Kyal Paul 589, Lee 221, Lee Franklin 589, Lynae Elizabeth 589, Marguerite (Kitson) 589, Paul 589, Ronald 589, Ryan Howard 589, Stephen 589, Carla Jane 520, Kyal Paul 522, Lee 520, Lee Franklin 522, Lynae Elizabeth 522, Marguerite (Kitson) 520, Paul 520, Ronald Arlyn 520, Ruth Arlene 520, 522, Ryan Howard 522, Stephen 520
VORE, Della 589, Don 589, Frank C. 589, Fred 589, Gerry 589, John H. 589, Lulu 602, Nile 602, Patricia 589, Rachel 409, Rolland 589, 589
VOUGH, 179
VRANDT, Mary 540
WABER, Alvin 268
WADE, Karyn 346, Mary Elizabeth 320, Norman 247, Sarah 247, Scott 247, Susan 247
WADLINGTON, Herman 287
WAFFORD, Ashley 307, Bill 307
WAGNER, Alan 399, Amber 415, Athelma 571, Benjamin Carroll 589, Catherine 550, Catherine (Welbaum) 607, Charles 467, Darya 280, Edna M. 338, Elizabeth 517, .

Goldie (Kummer) 432, Henry 517, Janis L. 559, Kathryn 519, Lucy 279, Martin 607, Mary Barbara 339, Mary C. 607, Mary Catherine 461, Mary Catherine 462, Nancy 6, 154, Noble 571, Peter Remington 589, Robert 341, Robert L. 559, Ronda 415, S. Joshua 589, Steve 589, Teresa 315, Tonya 559, Victor Gustav 589
WAGONER, David 415, Dennis G. 415, Eric 415, Janice Johnson 415, Martha 555
WAHL, Kate B. 245, Richard 331, Terri 331
WAHMAN, Genevieve 414, Lee 95, Lee 144
WAID, Jim 166, John 146, John 202, John H. 434, John Mrs. 146
WAIKEL, Jenny 552
WAIT, Garnet Smith 585
WAKSMAN, Alberto 146, Alberto Mrs. 146
WALBERT, Emma 200, Martin 202
WALBURN, Connie 369, Cynthia Ann 364, 456, Debra Elaine 364, Eugene 364, Lawrence Alan 364, Marcia (Gordon) 413, Marica Phyllis 364, Marsha 456, Roger 364, 413, 456, Rosemary Lynn 364, Sandra Kay 364, 413, Tamara Sue 364
WALDECK, Christina 396
WALDMAN, Cynthia 552
WALDO, L. K. 102
WALKER, Agnes 302, Alexander 425, Alvin 296, Betsy 555, Blanch 285, Calvin 425, Carl 425, Carrie Nevada 519, Catherine 474, Charles 58, 425, 519, Claire 285, 302, Claressa 518, Clark 37, Curtis 459, Daisy 480, David 555, Dollie 37, Donnell 501, Edward 98, Elizabeth Eliza"", Eva 519, Fern 285, Frances Kellerman 555, Genevieve 109, 411, H.T. 44, 45, Howard 285, 302, Irene 285, J.W. 121, James F. 531, Janelle 501, Jerome 285, 302, John 425, John W. 289, Joseph R. 16, Kara Diane 303, Kathleen 385, 425, Krista Michelle 303, Lawrence 320, Leonard 23, 25, Mabel Chloe 586 285, Madee 501, Maggie 425, Margaret 425, Martha 397, Mary Ann 531, Matilda 586, Michael 303, Minnie Alice 555, Murlie 531, Nancy 425, Nettie 531, Patricia 341, Paul 425, Quinn Renae 303, Ralph 341, Rebecca 248, Rowena 519, Ruth 425, Ruth Ann 395, Sarah (Adams) 302, Sarah M. 239, Stuart 341, Suanne 341, Teresa Irene 425, Verlice <Spud> 302, Vine 37, Wayne 285, 302, William 302, William Alvin 285
WALKO, Harry 145
WALL, Allen 500, Allen B. 500, Bonnie 189, Daisy 500, Dale 570, 576, David 576, Fred Lee 500, Heather 570, Hiram 500, Irene 500, Malinda 500, Melvin 460, Michele 570, Norman 189, Pat 463, 570, 576, Roscoe 576, Ruth 576, Sarah 500, Wanda 460, Warren 78
WALLACE, Brett 370, Charles 383, Ella 383, Fannie 284, 373, 412, 590, George 34, Helen 370, James R. 370, Jared 370, Jennifer 370, John 370, Mae 564, Maggie 369, 370, Mary 18Robert 370, Samuel 373, Sandra 419, Shane 370, Susanna (Jackson) 373, Thomas 370, William 90, D.A. 163, David 589, David Allen (D. A.) 589
WALMER, Dorothy 499, Dwight G. 589, E. S. 589, E. W. 181, Elizabeth Decker 499, Henry Homer 589, Henry S. 188, Henry Shucy 589, Hillard 127, 181, Ida Rebecca 499, Jacob 499, 589, John Rose 499, Mary Elizabeth 499, Paul E. 499, Peter 589, Roberta 589, Victor Glen 589, William 589
WALMSLEY, Betty 590, Betty Lou 590, Dorothy 590, Dorothy June 590, Grace Ann 590, H. L. 96, H. L. Rev. 59, 590, Harry 64, Harry Louis 590, Helen Elizabeth (Rummel) 590, Howell 590, James Philip 590, Jean Garland (Saufley) 590, John 560, John Morris 590, Lois 590, Lois Ruth 590, Phyllis 590, Phyllis Ilene 590
WALSER, Harriet 555
WALSH, Cami 307, David Dale 307, Frances Marion (Davis) 307, Jane Elizabeth 413, Joan 568, John 356, John L. 356, Rosalyn 356
WALSMITH, Alice 462, Joe 358, Nellie Lavina 358, Susie Doll (Crites) 358
WALTER, Amanda Kaylyn 412, Charles 412, Edward J. 398, Edwin 144, Edwin Hite 398, Keith Edwin 398, Mable C. 184, Matthew Jamison 412, Pamela 424, Merlie Marie 412
WALTERS, Barbara 585, Charles 25, Clyde 89, Emma Luella 279, Francis 170, Guy 94, Guy Rev. 456, J. W. 98, Jo Linda 475, John 15, Kenny 25, Linda 15, Mel 44, Rosa 585, Staci 132
WALTMAN, William 64, Wm 96
WALTON, Abe 315, Anna Lou 533, Mary (Myers) 315, Sue 606
WALTZ, Jacob 353, Sarah Willman 527, Walter 527, Gilda 279
WAMPLER, Norma Lea 409
WAMSLEY, Catherine (White) 60
WANDEL, Dal 540, John 454
WAPPES, Sarah (McCreery) 275
WARD, Carrie 420, Duree 286, Howard 420, James 394, Myrtle L. 570, Rebecca 274, Ruth Mary 274, 571, William J. 570, William R. 274,
WARE, Anna 582, Charles 590, Dora 582, Edna 107, Frankes 590, Guy 513, 581, 582, Helen 590, John 514, 582, Joyce 590, Lucritia 514, Mary 101, Morgan 101, Nora Lucrillia 582, Nora (Thompson) 581, Sally 248, Thomas 581, 582
WAREHOUSE, Elizabeth 603, Mark 603, Natalie 603, Sally 603
WARFIELD, Lucille 515, Robert 515
WARNER, Anna 109, 341, 437, Catherine Sitze 341, Elizabeth Sitze 437, George 442, Ida 555, Jacob 61, Jenny (Bassett) 154, John 503, John Lewis 109, 437, Jonathan 584, Josephine 523, Judy 498, Lewis 341, Lydia Moyer- 503, Mary 428, Mary (Sawyer) 401, Sam 182,
WARREN, Jim 294 Richard 363, 388
WARTHMAN, Anna 374, Dale 374, Jaimi 374, James Neal 374, Jerry Dale Dr. 374, Joyce Marie 374
WASHINGTON, John (Col.) 285
WASSON, Bert 266, Clem 44, Clem 45, David T. 16, Debra Lynn 284, 591, Edna 591, Elizabeth 266, Etta 591, George 591, 604, Grace 482, Irene 150, 591, Irvin 103, James 112, Janet 591, Jas. 121, John 266, 432, 591, Katherine 591, Lantz 44, 45, 591, Leo 112, Madge Elnore 394, Mae 591, Marilyn 591, Merianne 591, Ner William 591, Paige 591, Paul 390, Ray 45, Raymond 112, Rebecca 591, Rebecca Jean 591, Rosemary 591, Sarah 591, Stephanie 591, Suzanne 591, T. J. 83, Vern 165, William 112, 482, William Henry 591
WATERHOUSE, Jacob 591
WATERS, Alica 544, Benjamin Franklin 591, Chad 518, 544, Chad Paul 591, Charles Valentine 591, Clida Eveline 591, Daisy Belle 591, Dessie Marie 591, Don 175, Donald 518, 544, Donald Raye 591, Donna 518, 544, Donna Faye 591, Dorothy 544, Earl Glen 591, Edma Marie 544, Edward A. 563, Effie Marie 518, 544, 591, Elizabeth 544, 591, Elizabeth Jane 591, Eric 518, 544, Eric Michael 591, Gary 518, 544, Gary Lee 591, Gerald 518, 544, Gerald Clarence 591, Gregory 425, 518, 544, Gregory Kent 591, Hannah Elle 591, Harold 518, 544, Harold William 591, Henry 591, James LeRoy 591, Jane 544, Janice 518, 544, Janice Elaine 591, Jasper 518, 544, Jasper Clarence 591, Jeremy 400, John Henry 591, Joseph M. 591, Kasey 518, 544, Kasey Kathleen 591, Kenneth 518, 591, Kenneth Dean 591, Linda 518, 544, Linda Kay 591, Lindsey 518, 544, Lindsey Rachel 591, Loren 518, 544, Loren Eugene 591, Marisa 518, 544, Marisa Lynn 591, Marjorie 445, Martha 544, Marvel 544, Mary Elizabeth 591, Matthew 591, Michael 518, 544, Michael Eugene 591, Nancy 591, Nancy Catherine 591, Nicolle 518, 544, Nicolle Marie 591, Philip Isham 591, Retha Spencer 563, Rose 563, Sara 425, Sara Lynn 518, 544, Sara Lynn 591, Stephanie 400, Susan Jenelle 400, Teresa 544, Tracey 518, 544, Tracey Elizabeth 591, Troy 400, Virgil E. 591, Wanda (McKuras) 459, Wayne 544, Wayne Allen 591, William 591, William I. 591, Jr, Donald Raye 591
WATKINS, Amanda 462, Beth 462, Carol 404, Carol Ann 405, Charles 462, Edna Esta 456, George 456, Karen Denise 244, Rebecca Rhea"", Richard 462, Richard E. 268, Robert 588, Seth 462, William Pete", William 456
WATROUS, Austin Augustus 406, 407, 591, Dorothy Frances 406, 407, 591, Emily (Tuttle) 591, Sadie (Lagerpusch) 406, 407
WATSON, Ada 468, Annabelle 592, Dan 265, Eliza 387, Elroy 258, 592, Ian 265, Irvin Hilkert 592, John 387, Josephine C. Godbow 276, Linda 475, Lota 535, Martha Ann 533, Mary Martha Mattie"", Nellie 592, Patricia 592, Pearl 592, Tom 75, Vera 592, Willard 592
WATTERS, Bud 140, Chauncey Earl 592, David 523, David Earl 592, Earl 140, Earl L. Bud"", Earl L. Bud"", George 466, George D. 592, George W. 592, Helen Mae (Helms) 592, Juston D. 592, Kristen 523, 592, Lillian 466, Maenette 523, Rebecca 523, 592, Rena (Dewitt) 466, 592
WATTROUS, Austin (Buz) 165
WATTS, Miss Molly 121
WAUGH, A. B. , Frank 471, Mary 509, W.H. 121
WAY, Kate (Hall) 380, Lou Ann 598
WAYNE, Anthony 301, Anthony 547, Myron 236
WEATHERHOLT, Bill 606, Nondes 606, Ralph 527
WEAVER, Alice 592, Allen 592, Alma 526, Bessie L. 592, Branson 468, Carol Sue 592, Catherine 468, 592, David D. 468, David Dwight 468, David Z. 592, Elizabeth 591, 592, Emma 592, Esther M. 592, Floyd 556, Floyd Allen 592, Floyd Jr. 592, George 289, Gerald 592, Goldie M. 592, Harold L. 592, Hattie 468, Ida 465, Imogene 528, Ivan 465, Ivan O. 592, Jacob 411, 559, Jacob A. 592, John 468, John B. 592, John Richard 468, Kathy 468, Katie 559, Katie 592, Lela F. 592, Leota 556, Lizzie Quick 468, Lydia Viola Kate"", Marjory 592, Mary 556, Mary V. 559, 592, Maude 468, Merlie E. 592, P. H. 64, Phyllis 592, Ralph A. 592, Ronnie 202, William R. 592
WEBB, Charles 479, Diana 338, Mary 479, Rosa Ann 568
WEBBER, Agnes L. 593, Barbara 410, Betty 593, Bud 593, Dan 593, Dorothy Jane 593, Dot 136, Dot 593, Emma 593, Ether May 410, Harry C. 593, Jane 593, Justus 165, Justus Morton 593, Justus Painter 593, Marvin 410, Mary 136, 329, 593, Mike 593, Tim 593, Zachary Taylor 593
WEBER, Emaline Sarah 326, Herman 36, John Henry 326, John Peter 326, Laurer 326, Lawrence 326, Margaret 503, Robert 534
WEBKER, Carol 267
WEBSTER, Dosha Letha 281, George 202, W. C. 103
WEDDING, Brian Wayne 603, Briana Louise 603, Carolyn Ann 603, Lanette L. 603, Robert Edward 603
WEEKS, Minnie Luella 503, Sharon 303
WEGENER, Cynthia 471, Ray 471
WEGMAN, 179
WEIBEL, Magdaline 531
WEIDNER, Anna Barbara 507
WEIDTHOLTER, Robert 140
WEIKEL, Hervey 299, Hillard 359, Isabel Harrison 299, Janice Rae 359, Levi 13, Ruth (DeVoux) 359, Shirley 299, Vyrena 427, William 13, Zora May 270
WEIKERT, Betty 578, George 578
WEIKLE, Zora 410
WEILAND, Ann 333, Bette 333, Daniel 333, Fred 333, Mary 333, Scott 333
WEILEMANN, Bill 593, Christopher Edward 593, Cindy 593, Cynthia 593, Edie 593, Gertrude 593, Jon William 593, Jon William Jr. 593, Josephine Hersher 263, Luzerne 593, Lydia Ann 593, Mildred 593, Monica 593, Otto 593, Posy 593, Zernie 593
WEILMANN, Otto 263
WEINLAND, Lizzie 442
WEIS, Clint Chandler 532, Garfield Gary"", Patricia May (High) 533, Wayne Jay 532
WEISEL, Dr. 121, Mary 116, Will W. 145
WEISMAN, Gale 243, Raymond 243, Sharon 243
WEISS, Timothy 483
WEISSEISE, Jacob 535, Sarah 535
WEISSER, Anna 272, Jacob 272, Catherina Rose 593, Catherine 527, Emma Nina 593, Jessie M. 544, Josiah Jesse"", Josiah 527, Loyall 417, Mary Bossert 593, Melvin Merl 593, Sarah 527
WEIST, Sarah Matilda 593
WEITENDORF, Sally 500
WEITHOLTER, Karen 357
WELBAUM, Vada 150
WELCH, Dorothea 338, James 309, John J. 338, John Michael 338, John N. 338, Linnie 401, Mary 299, Walter 175
WELCHES, Albert L 594, Harry 594, MArk 594, Neva 594, Patty 594, Phyllis 594, Russell 594, Wayne 594
WELDON, John 13
WELDY, Dan 84, 140, Marjorie 577, Wendy 510
WELLENRIETER, Bria 477, Brook 477, Douglas 477
WELLER, Isabella G. 383
WELLMAN, Walter 36
WELLS, Anna Catherine Kitty"", David 98, Fred 350, H. Rev. 59, Hayley Elizabeth 350, Hugh 64, Jason 362, Michael 362, Mildred E. 362, Sally Jo 350, Stephen Louis 362, Stephen 362
WELSH, Anna 569
WELTLER, Don 448
WELTLER, Theora 448
WELTY, Ann Maria 245, John B. 245, Louise 367
WEMHOFF, Gregory 267, Michael 267, Ted 267, William 267
WENGER, Jack 68
WENRICK, Pauline 500
WENTE, Hildegarde 368
WENTZ, Alice Rebecca (Lamm) 594, Amanda 427, Andrew Guy 594, Betty 594, David 307, Dennis Guy 425, 594, Doris 594, Douglas 307, Harold Guy 594, Inez 594, Joan Renee 427, John Andrew 594, Katharine Marianna 594, Laura 594, Marianna 594, Martha 594, Megan 427, Nancy 307, Patricia 307, Ralph 425, Ralph Guy 594, Richard 307, Sarah 307, Tim 307
WERKING, Vernon E. 582, Ada 594, Allison Kate 242, Andrew 368, 373, Andrew 594, Andrew Jr. 73, Andrew Sr. 73, Anna 463, Anna Christena 594, Anna Sophia 483
WERLING, August 594, Bruce 242, Cammi 594, Carolina Lena"", Charles 594, Christena (Foltz) 368, Christian 73, Clara 482, David 73, 252, David 368, Donald 594, Doyle 445, 594, Doyle H. 594, Elizabeth 368, Elizabeth (Bieberich) 483, Esther 594, Esther Graft 594, Fred 594, George 73, 594, Henry 368, 594, Herman 368, 594, Johannes 368, John 73, 344, 368, 594, Karoline 73, 252, Kelli 264, Louise 73, 344, Margaretha 368, Martin 594, Mary 482, Nicole Renae 242, Norman 526, Paula 482, Rosena 368, Rosina 368, Rudolph 482, Ryan 264, Sophie 526, Susanna 594, Terry 264, Troy 594, Victor 526, Wilhelm 483, 594, 482
WERNER, Marie Leffel 258
WERT, Elizabeth 156, James D. 296, Sarah 270, William 59
WERTZ, Helen 554
WESENBERG, Wendy 364
WESLEY, John 91
WESSLING, Christian 89
WEST, Abigail 595, Carl 595, Dorothy 139, Elizabeth 403, Eulis 595, Jess 595, Nancy 425, Oma 462, Vicky 425, William 403
WESTENFELD, Marie Catherine Elisabeth 482
WESTFALL, 66, Aaron 595, Bob 477, Catrina 353, Earl 595, Edith 595, Edith Lou (Trotter) 595, Eric 595, Eric 595, Jared 595, Jason 595, Jennifer 595, Joy 595, Nathan 595, Robert 595, Robert Eugene 595, Roberta Sue 595, Roger Allen 595, Ron 460, Ronald 595, Ronald Eugene 595, Trudy 595
WESTMAN, Andrew 280, Sally 280
WETERICK, Anna 595, Berta 595, Carl 595, Charles 6, 140, Charles 169, 595, Charles E. 481, Cheryl 595, Edward 595, Elizabeth 595, Elizabeth Jenni 595, Frances 595, Frank 595, Joe 595, Joe N. 481, John 595, Jon 595, Jon R. 481, Niklaus 595, Rose 595, Winifred 595, Winifred Elaine 481
WETTE, Jacob 259
WETTER, Julia 259
WETZEL, Amy 596
, Elizabeth Seibert 596, Ethel May 596, Harvey E. 596, Inez M. 596, James Clarence 596, John 596, John H. 596, Martin M. 596, Martin Vanburen 596, Nellie Marie 596, Therasia Belle 596
WETZER, Catherine 339, Lewis 339
WEYGAND, Howardta 458
WHALEY, Lawrence 281, Patricia (Wilbanks) 281, Terry 281
WHARTON, Paul 142
WHEATLEY, Margaret Peg""
WHEELER, Ann 240, Ann (Harris) 385, Betty 552, Cassandra 385, James 385, Katherine 240, 385, Martha 414, Nancy 435, Sarah 385
WHETSTONE, Emma 501
WHICKER, Jennifer 84, John 140, Jolin 84
WHIELER, Samuel 484
WHITACRE, Helen 444
WHITAKER, Linda 459
WHITE, 66, Agnes 596, Albert Pete"", Alexander 58, 59, Alexander 596, Allison 597, Alonzo 519, Andrew 256, 596, Andrew McMillan 256, Anna Kathleen 596, Aubrey Olen 596, Bertha 597, Brenda 597, Charles 58, 256, 339, 596, 597, Charles Garth 597, Charles R. 292, 512, Cheryl Ann 596, Clyde 251, 402, Clyde Olen 596, Daniel 596, Danielle Rose 432, David 332, 430, 431, 596, 597, David Yule 597, Debra Sue 596, Diana 527, Dora 251, 402, Dora Elsie 596, Douglas 597, Duane Alan 597, Duane Arnold 597, Duncan 596, 597, Duncan Jr. 597, Edwin dahleen 596, Elizabeth 460, Elizabeth Isabelle 596, Elizabeth Rose 436, Eugene 596, Fay 597, Frank 597, Freeman 519, Garry L. 432, Garry Lee 596, George Ralph 508, Gregory Lynn 596, Harry L. 145, Hazel B. (Cloud) 508, Helen M. 508, Henry J. 267, Hugh 597, Isabella 596, Janet 339, 597, Janet Yule 596, Janet Yule Ferguson 597, Jason Lee 432, Joe 78, Josephine 597, Judd 597, Karen Kay 596, Kenny 597, Kevin 597, Klyda 597, Larry Tim 596, Lauretta 596, Lawson 597, Leilani 596, Leilani Lou 596, Lon 519, Lucina 597, Mabel 155, 456, Magdalene 332, 597, Margaret 596, Marie Margaret 597, Mary 596, Mary A. 512, Mary Adahleen 251, 596, Mary Agnes 596, Nancy 597, Pam 597, Peregrine 436, Phyllis Edna 436, Ralph 597, Rebecca 597, Rick 527, Rosella 156, Rosella Barrick 596, Rueben 597, Sara 431, Sara Ann 597, Sherman 168, Susan 328, Tenney Glenn 436, Thriece 369, Tom 597, Traydon 597, Trent 597, Tyler 597, Velma 597, Vera L. 267, Zain 597
WHITEACRE, Georgia May (Erbacher) 381
WHITEHEAD, William Erasmus 460
WHITELEATHER, Bruce 382, Rebecca 382
WHITESELL, Joan 381
WHITFIELD, Rosie 552
WHITLOCK, Arlue 314
WHITLOCK, Nicholas J. 269, Todd 269
WHITTED, Betty 469, Patricia Dawn 469, Thurman 469
WHITTEKER, J. E. 96
WHITTEN, Alice 517
WHONSETLER, Bernard 390, Craig 390, Janet 390, Mary 390, Paula 390, Susan 390
WIBBENS, Cheryl Dr. 575
WICHMAN, Lori 575
WICKLIFF, Dell 44, Elizabeth 519, Sarah 396
WICKLIFFE, Marjorie 295, Mildred 295, Richard 295, Ross 58, 295, Wayne 295
WICKS, Marvin Eugene 295, Michael Daniel 295
WIDMER, Anna 316
WIECKING, Charles White 597, Ernst Herman Frederick 597, Fred 144, Frederick August 597, Herman 253, 597, Herman Arnold 597, Herman S. 245, 597, Hermine 597, Kenneth David 597, Mary Catherine 342, Robert Wilbur 597, Wilbur Ernst 597, Willliam Ernst 597, JR, Frederick August 597
WIEGMAN, Karl 482, Sophie 482
WIEGMANN, Marie 463
WIEKEL, Joan 516
WIERMAN, Marie 340
WILBAUM, Veda 139
WILBURN, Lorena 247, Robert D. Rev. 97, Ruth 156
WILCOXSON, Ella 509, Ethel 552, Ora 509, Roy 552, Virginia 509
WILDEY, Marlene 447
WILE, William Jr. 206
WILEY, Athelma 571, Delight 556, Ermina 598, Glen D. 571, Gregory 556, Guy 556, 598, H. W. 164, Iona 598, Irene 155, John 598, Lyle R. 200, Mary Elizabeth 474, Mary Hutchinson 556, Mona Jean 556, Robert 598, Sophia 299, Ted 556, William Everet 556, 598
WILGUS, Catherine 512, Flo 512
WILHELM, Bonnie Jean 371, Caroline Frances 598, Charles 371, Dr. 151, Elizabeth (Minard) 598, Emma 598, Emma L. 439, Harold B. 598, Letitia Tish"", Letitia 371, Lutie 598, Mary 485, Mary E. 598, Mary Janelda 371, Raymond 598, Simon P. 598, W. W. 439, William W. 598
WILKERSON, Ann 541
WILKEY, David 593, Dick 140, Dorothy 593, Frank 593, John 593, Richard F. 593
WILKIN, Clara 469, Mary E. 469, Mary Evelyn 467, Nelson 469, Shane Michael 433, Theodore 95, Thomas 469, Trent Allen 433, Troy Eugene 433, William 469, William Dr. 604, Angela Renee 568
WILKINS, Mike 568
WILKINSON, Diane 418, Erika 418, John 507, Zachary 418
WILLETT, Daphne 370
WILLEY, Carson 598, Carson Landis 222, 510, Devon K. 510, Devon Kay 222, Don 598, Donald 222, 510, Doris 598, Frank 598, Ruth 154
WILLIAM, Thomas 103
WILLIAMS, Absalom Fay 399, Adrian 337, Alan 299, 385, Alan Stanley 599, Amos R. 598, Ann Sarah 399, Annabelle (Shivers) 274, Becky 598, Bonnie 598, Brian Douglas 599, Carolyn 463, Carolyn Joan 598, Christopher Robertson 599, Clarence 599, Clem 464, Connie 275, 519, Connie Sue 274, Cynthia (Terry) 337, David 299, 385, David Alan 599, David Logan 599, David Paul 467, Dequestney Cassie"", Donald 598, Dorcas 458, Doris Asher 399, Dorothy 363, Douglas M. 337, Edith Burchard 458, Edward 599, Eldred 387, Elizabeth Ann Betsy"", Elizabeth Emeline 267, Emma 599, Emma Eliza 55, Ernest 289, Everet 599, Everett 363, Fay Fisher 399, Frances 598, Fred 460, Gerald Wayne 599, Geraldine 111, Gladys Louise 289, Glen 599, Glen Eugene 599, Glenn 494, Harrison 458, Helen 598, Henrietta Jones 599, Hobart 599, Hugh 599, Ivan A. Sr. 274, Jacklyn Kay 599, James A. 153, James S. 267, Janice 179, Jason Roy 467, Jeffrey Dinkel 599, Jennie 363, Jeremy James 599, Jessica Rene 599, John 363, 517, 586, 599, John W. 363, John Washington 599, Joseph 599, Joseph Jr. 599, Joshua 598, Judith Ann 599, Julie 179, 598, Justine 111, Kay Janene 306, Lanette Coreene 467, Laura 599, Lib 407, Lisa 599, Lou Ann 598, Lucy (Waters) 599, M.D. 19, M. O. 102, , Maggie 15, Mara Jo Couch 299, Margaret 468, 517, 599, Martha 586, Mary 598, 599, Mary (Fuller) 274, Mattie 363, Michael 598,

Michelle 179, Nancy 598, Nettie Gertrude 598, Oliver 17, 555, Pamela Jane 467, Paul Anthony 467, Pauline 599, R. D. 513, Rebecca 299, 385, 454, 598, Rebecca Jo 599, Reneta 598, Robert 98, Robert Franklin 599, Rose Marie 493, Rose Marie (Osborn) 599, Rosemary 152, Ruth 462, Sam 599, Samuel 363, 598, Shirley Ann 549, Tammi 598, Teresa Marie Purvis 599, Theodore Wayne 598, Thomas Dean 598, Timothy Douglas 337, Todd 249, Tommy 92, Travis 598, Trudi 598, Violet 324, Walter 599, Wayne 468, Wendell 599, William 274, 458, Zehm 363, Zella 363

WILLIAMSON, 66, Anna 55, Anna 600, Ben 524, Benjamin F. 600, Bruce 180, 506, 600, Cindy 600, Dennis 600, Dorothea 175, 600, Dorothea (Kellerman) 154, Dwight 600, Edith 250, Edward 175, Edward Bruce 296, 600, Emma (Carnes) 600, Erman 600, Erman Dr. 443, Ethel 443, 600, George 145, Ivan 17, Jane 443, 600, 600, Joseph 538, Joseph D. 250, Karen 600, Lawrence 375, Lent 175, Lent A. 600, Margaret Kisiah 524, Mary 136, 175, 296, 600, Mearl 600, Melody 464, Minta 60, Myron 443, 600, Myron Ora 600, Nellie 299, Nellie May 385, Nova 600, Paul 600, Richard 443, 600, Sandy 600, Sarah (Layton) 600, Sarah Pearlie 524, Steven 600

WILLIE, Marjorie 462

WILLIG, Virginia 558

WILLIS, Franklin 400, Rebecca 400

WILMINGTON, Francis 299

WILSON, Altha 600, Andrew 601, Arlo Clark 601, Barbara Nettie 257, Bessie 600, Beth 422, 511, Bette 600, Bruce 600, Cathy 411, 426, 508, Chancy 282, 601, Charles 600, Charles A. 600, Charles J. Chick"", Charley Absolm Housel 601, Christine 346, Christy 523, Clara 602, Cleo 600, Cloyd 601, Constance 601, Curtiss P. 315, Darla 600, Deborah 600, Dellaes 600, Denney 318, 602, Denney Ralph 601, Diana 600, Diana Dee 601, Donaldson 16, Doris Ann 600, Dwight Eugene 469, 600, Edith 600, Edward 216, Eldon 600, Elmer 596, Elois (Brewster) 600, Enos Church 601, Everett 342, Fanny 602, Faye 600, Flora 380, Floyd L. 100, Frank 346, Frannie 601, Fred 172, Garland 342, 600, Gaylene 342, 600, Gibson 601, Greg 342, 600, Gwen 204, Harold 98, Harriet 602, Harriet Jane 601, Harry F. 600, Helen 600, Ida 600, James 342, James Sylvester 600, James Woodward 601, Janet 600, Janette 600, Jenica 342, Jered 601, Jim 600, Joel 342, John 204, 346, 523, 537, 601, 602, John Alva 600, Joyle 601, 602, Kent 600, Kimberly Ann 557, Larry 318, 602, Larry Lionel 601, Lori Ann 601, Lydia Belle 601, Magdalene 303, 600, Marcia 523, Margaret Ruth 600, Mark 557, Martha Jane 459, Marty 152, Mary 515, 602, Mary Alice 601, Mary Belle 282, 601, Mary Eliza 601, Mary Fore (Foor) 459, Mary (Romine) 315, Matthew 346, Melanie 342, 600, Meryl 315, Miles 342, Nancy 242, Nancy Ann 601, Nancy L. 267, Nilah 342, Norma Jean 601, O. M. 79, Orel 600, Paul 602, Paula 602, Pearl 601, Pearl (Ruby) 282, Ralph 318, 601, 602, Randy Joe 601, Raymond 601, Rebecca Lynn 571, Richard 600, Robert 600, Ronald Keith 600, Rose 552, Stacey 600, Stanley 600, 602, Stanley Kent 469, Stephanie Lyn 601, Steve 600, Sunya 602, Sunya Sue 601, Sylvia Jane 600, Teresa 601, Thelma 602, Tiffany 346, Truesal Cyrus 601, Valerie Kaye 600, Victor 601, Victor James 601, 602, William 459, Woodrow 34

WIMMER, Ronald 216

WINANS, Joan Marie 385, Ross 385, Sharon (Raber) 385

WIND, Barbara (Cox) 300

WINDMILLER, Arthur 130, Edwin 440, Genevieve 440, Genevieve (Linn) 440, Harold Bill"", Harold (Bill) 115, Harrold 440, William 440

WINDSTEAD, Nellie Helen 517

WINEGART, Blanche Johnson 251, Elwood I. 251, Illie 251

WINELAND, Keturah 150

WINES, J. W. 83, Mattie 83

WINGER, Della F. 339

WINKLE, Amberly 273, Jeffrey 273

WINKLER, Catherine 371, Emma 571, Martha Jane (Mary) 371

WINNING, Alan 457

WINTERS, Jessie 538, Mae 152

WIRT, William 128

WISE, Erma (Adams) 410, Ernest 410, J.G. 82, Jeff 264, Nadine 360, Nancy 316, Ralph 410, Russel 582, Stephen Clifford 247, Steve 316

WISENFELDER, Elizabeth 393

WISER, Edith M. 378

WISLEY, Milton 78

WISNER, Alfred 389, Catherine 245, Frank 584, H. L. 147, Jennie (Masterson) 389, L. C. 98, Louise 389, Maggie 147, Mary Jane (Plummer) 389, Silas 389, T. D. 147, T. L. 147, William 389, Zola (Stewart) 389

WITHAM, Elizabeth (Barber) 417, Esther 417, Louis 249, Louis 417

WITTE, Clara 383, John Ernst 564, Julia 564, Mike 142, Paul 383

WITTERN, Perl 207

WITTHOF, C. F. 85

WITTWER, Irene 584, Lee 584

WITTY, Glendora 538, Karyl 321

WITWER, Dianne 145, Dianne 602, George 145, George 602, George B. 208, George Mohler Studebaker 602, George Osburn 602, Mohler 602

WITZEMAN, Adolph 464, Adolph 602, Christina 602, Dorothy 602, Elizabeth 602, Emma 602, Harold 602, Howard 602, Joan 602, Josephine 602, Lulu 602, Mary 602, Mathias 602, Opal 602, Raymond 602, Robert 602, William 602

WITZIG, Brian 409, David 409, Robert 409, William 409

WIVELY, D.E. 58

WOFE, Nettie 531

WOHLFORD, Grace Louise 603, Lanette Louise 603, Malissa Rene 603, Max Vernon 603, Walter Vernon 603, Wanda Lee 603

WOLETT, Mary 432

WOLF, Albert Raymond 603, Andrew 603, Arthur 435, Blanche 443, Blanche Olive 433, 603, Bob 192, 603, Charles Albert 603, Charles Campbell 603, Christopher 603, Dewitt 434, Donald 518, 544, Dorothy 306, Dorothy Louise 603, Emily 603, Esther (Arnold) 434, Eva 603, Evelyn Lucile 603, Hick 603, Isaac C. 433, Issac Carthage 603, Janet 544, Jason Edward 272, Jeremy Daniel 272, Kent Duane 272, Malinda 544, Marjorie Jean 603, Mark 228, Mary 603, Mary Emily 603, Melvin 193, Michelle Renee 272, Minnie Maria 603, Nettie 603, Patricia Joan 603, Randal 518, 544, Rhoda 603, Richard 518, 544, Robert Nyle 394, 603, Rosetta 603, Samuel M. 603, Sandra 544, THomas 518, 544, Tracy 195, Wilda Mae 603, William 603, William Winfield 603, Zelda 603, Zelda V. (Essex) 433

WOLFCALE, Belinda 537, Bulinda 270, Connie 486, Craig 490, Irvin 228, Mary 270, Mary Ann 479, Richard 266, Richard D. 266

WOLFE, Allison 509, Brian 508, Connie 532, Daniel 508, Danny Jr. 508, Gordon 333, Jacob 102, Janice 508, Kelly 333, LeRoy Chester 298, Mary 568, Michelle 584, Mildred 267, Monica 584, Rachel 584, Roger 584, Tracy 221

WOLFF, Marian 346

WOLFGANG, Jacob 258, Janice Kay 350, John Adam 350, Lozure Gene 350, Matha Irene 350, Sally Jo 350, Thomas Edward 350

WOLKER, Sandy (Higgins) 394

WOMAN, Wea Indian 312

WOOD, Carla J. 603, Cheryl Ann 386, Clara 244, Dewey J. 244, Edith 443, Eleanor J. 603, Eleanor Morris 386, 527, Ethel 443, 600, Ethel Nicholas 603, Gary 279, J.A. 82, J. J. 56, James 443, Jennie 443, Jenny 56, Kelsey 603, Kerri 603, Linda 251, Lynette Marie 527, Richard 82, Robert H. 603, Robert H. Jr. 603, Robert Jr. 386, 527, Sherri 467, Teresa Marlene 244, Willie L. 603, Yale Robert 603

WOODARD, Alice 495, Margaret 342, Mary Lou 6

WOODRING, Margaret 527, Mary 294, 527, Peter 527

WOODRUFF, Ferris 98, Gideon 398, James 398, Jennie 398, Wesley 398, Willard 398

WOODS, Amy 531, Annie 417, Benjamin 543, Charles 543, Chris 443, Christopher Douglas 603, Clara Mae Boring 543, Dawn Marie 603, Debrah Kay 603, Debrah Kay Sheets 236, Dicie May 543, Dollie Elnore 543, Douglas Dayton 603, Dustin Dayton 603, Edna 244, Edward 317, Elva Essa 543, Erma Cleveland 603, Francis 396, Frank 543, Halden 204, Halder B. 543, Harry E. 543, Henry 543, Iva 244, James Fenton 543, John William 543, Joseph Jr. 543, Joseph Rev. 543, Lavina 543, Lynn 301, Lynn 443, Mary Elizabeth 603, Mary Elizabeth Young 236, Mary Ellen (Crowl) 303, Mary Marie 543, Michael 443, Michael Wayne 603, Myron Wayne 603, Nellie 385, Nora Beatrice 603, R. Lynn 603, Reida Kathleen 603, Samuel 537, Sharon 443, Sharon K. 603, Sue 443, Vergie 155, William 317

WOODSWORTH, James 90

WOODWARD, Abraham 604WOODWARD, Alda Jane 155, 604, Alice 604, Alma (Thayer) 603, Alva 604, Amaline 134, 604, Amry Brickly 604, Annis 604, Becky 603, Brock 604, Catherine 365, Charles 603, Cherese Mardell 604, Clara 603, Clint 604, Dana 188, Dorcas - 604, Ellis 604, Forrest M. 259, Frank 604, Fredrick Kay 604, George Thomas 604, Geraldine 414, Hazel 292, Inez (Morrical) 603, Irene 604, Jeffrey Shawn 604, John 603, Kevin 604, Laura 604, Loretta 604, Margaret Shievely 604, Mary Lou 604, Naomi 533, Olive Orlina 604, Ray 603, Rebecca 375, Rosco 604, Ruthell 604, Samantha E. 604, Scott 604, Stephanie 604, Thomas 130, 604, Thomas Brooks 604, Thomas Brooks II 604, Thomas II 604, Weisell 414, 604, Weisell Brooks 413, William 365, William A. 604

WOODY, Edith 340

WOOLARD, Lois McIntire 268

WOOSTER, 66, Jim 113, Margaret 435

WORDEN, Gary 542, Kathy 483, Kathy Lynn 482, Kay 542, Nick 542, Terri 542

WORKINGER, Annette 489

WORKMAN, Judy 419, Gene 598, Jason Allan 598, Joan 373, Lance Adam 598, LeRoy 373, Lloyd 373, Margaret 373, Paul 373, Robert 373

WORSTER, C. Columbus 305, C. Garl 556, Cecil 556, 604, Christopher Columbus 604, 605, Curtis 556, Ellen (Thrillkill) 604, Esther Bell 605, Esther Belle 604, Hope 556, James 87, Jane Elizabeth 605, Jeremiah , Joe 556, Larry 556, Lillie J. (Shull) 305, Louise , Lucy 605, Margaret Ellen 604, Mary 571, Mary Josephine 305, Max 556, Melissa , Nina Elizabeth (Marshall) 605, Patty 556, Pearl 556, Robert 605, Samual , Vicki 556, William 604, 605, William Palmer 604, William Thomas 305

WORTHINGTON, Julia Ann 396

WORTHMAN, Chauncey 45, Francilc 136, Jaimi 374, James Neal 469, Jerry Dale 469, Joyce Marie 469, Matthew 85, Matthew Rev. 353, Mattnew Rev. 523

WREN, Alidy 569

WRIGHT, Avis 142, Cathy Sue 607, Clarissa 568, E. E. 98, Elizabeth 537, Ellen 454, Gerald S. 364, 516, Harry 337, Ira 537, Jennie 508, John 326, Kathryn 175, Larry 15, Linda 150, Louis Michael 337, Lynn 308, Mary E. 326, Milton 79, Nancy Carol 337, Nettie 535, Roseann 337, Sheldon 25, Verda M. 516, William 454

WULLIMAN, Grace 290

WUNDER, Mary Alice 345

WURSTER, Anna Maria 439

WURTENBERGER, Anna Catherine 284

WURTS, Clara 285

WYANT, Arthur 605, Bernadine 605, Carol 605, Donald 605, Emma 605, Ida Marie 475, 605, J. K. 98, Lisa 605, Lucile 605, Ora 605, Simone 605, Steven 605

WYATT, Calvin F. 337, Calvin J. 337, Cecil 337, Garry 66, James 140, Janet 577, John 268, Jonathon 165, Julia Ann 268, 544, Kathryn (Mosure) 337, Lincoln 577, Lucinda Tam 268, Nancy 577, Sam 577, Shonda Lynn 337, Tammy Sue 337, Tim 577, Tonya 577

WYNEKIN, Frederick 68

WYSS, Angel 265, Les 265

XANDERS, W. H. 85

XXXXXX, Julie 351

YAGER, Amy Jo 605, Brent H. 605, Carol J. 605, Carolyn Joan (DeBolt) 316, Carter W. 605, Chase L. 605, Dale 605, Debra 595, Derek 605, Edith 605, EuDora Jane 605, Evelyn 605, Florence 139, George 515, Harold E. 297, 605, Ida 515, Janice L. 605, June 533, Katherine 445, Kevin W. 605, Lloyd 605, Lucille Sophia 537, Luster 605, Mamie L. 583, Mariah 605, Ray F. 605, Rebecca 605, Richard 533, Tyler N. 605

YAKE, Angelia 606, Courtney 502, 606, Della 606, Donald 606, Evan 606, Frederick 606, Hazel 606, Jessica 502, 606, Kari 606, Kenneth 502, Kenneth 606, Kimberly 606, Lewis 606, Martha 502, 606, Martin 606, Melinda 606, Nan 502, 606, Naomi 606, Noah 8, 221, 502, 606, Patricia 606, Ruth 606, Sue 606

YANEY, Betty 393, Bill 393, Doug 393, Ed 393, Evelyn 393, I.F. 61, Ida 179, Joy 393, Keven 393, Margaret 393, Marsha 393, Mary Jane 393, Mike 393, Orville 393, Sally 393, Susan 393, Vera 393

YANKOSKEY, John 510

YARGER, Bertha Idella 476, Della 475, Idel 476, James 307, Josephus 307, Martha Jane 307, Martha (Roberts) 307, Omar 144

YATES, Bradley 288, 533, Chad 288, 533, Donald 533, Margaret 533, Vera 329

YEAGER, B.T. 82, Nancy Heemstra 440, Stella 400, Victor 82

YELTON, Amelia 395, Amelia Margaret 310

YENCER, Machelle 399

YEOMAN, Elizabethrude 247

YERGLER, Ella 354, Peggy 340, 487, Robert 233, Sue 487

YOCUM, Dean 243, Forrest 243, Gene 243, George 243

YODER, Laverne 303

YOEMAN, Ed 328, Jerry 328

YOQUELET, Eugene E. 242, Mary 23, 537, Mary A. Osborn 242

YOST, Karla 250, Susannah 403

YOUNG, Abe 289, Adelia 252, Alma 252, Amanda 402, Anne M. 332, Arthur Jacob 606, Barbara 430, Beth 519, Beth Ann 275, Bill 207, 350, 563, Caroline 564, Casper 403, Celesta 501, Charlene 275, 519, Charles 89, 252, Christina 275, 519, 564, Columbus 121, Dale 606, Darlene 606, David Nathaniel 350, Delbert 606, Douglas Koons 606, Elizabeth (Stover) 321, Emma Jean 564, Evah 289, Eve 564, Evelyn 606, Frank 119, Fred 447, Fredrick 252, George Franklin 418, Gilbert Jr. 341, Gustave 564, Helen 379, Henry Jacob 606, Ida 264, Isabella 333, Jacob 564, 606, James 275, 519, Joe 121, John 264, 321, Julie 350, LaVera 606, Levi 18, 403, Ludwig 252, Mary 603, Norman 430, Norman Fremont 430, 606, Norman Fremont, Jr. 430, Pauline 447, Phillip 275, 519, Russell Allen 603, Sophia 403, 417, Sophia (Furhmann) 252, Valentine 564, 606, Warren 275, 519, Wilda Irene 603, Jr, Norman 606

YOUNGBLOOD, Beverly 241

YOUNT, Shawn 404

YULE, Helen Easton 596, Janet 339

ZAGROCKI, Diana (Barrick) 262

ZANE, Ebenezer 25

ZAPEL, Art 597, Linda Zain 597, Mark 597, Shelly 597, Ted 597

ZARTMAN, D. Walter Rev. 100

ZBOROWSKI, Robert 145

ZEDDIS, Bradford 265, Clayton Linn 265, Rita 25, Rodney 265

ZEEK, Catherine 468

ZEHNER, Adam 606, Benjamin 606, Bob 606, Camelia 606, Catheline 585, Daisy 606, Daniel 606, David 606, Edwin 585, Elizabeth 606, Ellen 606, Faye 606, Gerald 606, Hester 606, Jack 606, Jenny 606, Joyce 606, Lester 606, Lyman 107, 259, 606, Lyman Jr. 606, Mary 606, Max 606, Nondes 606, Sarah 606, Tonya 606, Yvonne 606

ZEHRING, Catharine 316, Eva Barbara 316

ZEIGLER, Imo 560, Mary Ellen 395

ZENT, 66, Dewey 78, Dewey Rev. 586, Jacob C. 13

ZENTZ, Kathleen Annette 430, Roger 430

ZEPS, Herman 145, Herman 162

ZERKLE, Catherine 352

ZEZULA, Chad Eric 603, John R. 603, Reida 603, Shannon Todd 603

ZIEGLER, J. C. 71

ZIKE, G. W. 75

ZILKIE, Hanna 287

ZIMMER, Matilda 566

ZIMMERLEE, Martha 508

ZIMMERMAN, Andrew 479, Candy 449, Carolyn 444, David 444, Jack R. 444, Jenny 606, John 272, Kathleen 444, Ken 449, Kristine 444, Paul 479, Rosina 520, Timmy 479

ZINNEL, Jonathon P. 73

ZION, Bertha 552, Bertha 607, Franklin A. 607, George W. 607, Ida E. 607, Jacob S. 607, Jason C. 607, John H. 607, John P. 607, Nancy (Chrismore) 607, Nancy Wagner 607, Thomas J. 607, William C. 607, William C. 607

ZIRCKEL, Ludwig 540

ZIRKEL, Noah 540, Sarah 540, Cary 606, Eddie 525, Effie 606, George 525, George 606, Jean 525, Jessica 502, Keith 525, Martha 606, Mary 606, William 525

ZODA, Carol Callie"", Cathy Sue 607, Elretta 555, Jack Eugene 607, Jarvin J. Bud"", Jerry 607, Jerry Lee 607, John Henry 607, John Marvin 607, Joseph Wayne 607, Judith Ann 607, Marvin E. 607, Mary Jo (Rupley) 607, Richard Wayne 607, Timmy Joe 607

ZOLL, Bernard 513, Cheryl 272, Doris 266, Etta 513, James 144, Jeff 513, Lydia 64, Lydia 579, Marshall 272, Mitch 272, Naundus 513, Pauline 272, Phoebe 401, Phoebe Jo 513, Rachel 272, Rene 305, Sebert 272, Stelphanie 272

ZOOK, Barbara 388, James 462, Laura 462, Utha 462

ZUBER, Catherine Irene 544, Jacob 544, Jessie 544, Joseph 544

ZURFLUEH, Barbara 464

How To Begin Your Family Tree

There is no need to panic at the thought of collecting the data necessary for a family tree. It is not as difficult as one might think and it often proves to be one of the most enjoyable and rewarding experiences a person can have. To begin your family tree (alias genealogy chart) simply write down your own name. With that accomplished you are underway.

Now you are ready for the next step which is to include, along with your name, some vital information. This normally includes your date and place of birth, date and place of marriage(s), and residence. Most record pages, used by those looking for their roots, also asks for the name of your spouse and a list of your children with similar information regarding them.

With this information now completed the next step is to record the names of your parents and gather identical vital record information about them. Move on to your paternal and maternal grandparents along with their information. Maybe you're catching on now. Next add your great-grandparents. You will normally have eight units at this level, but, if adoptions or second marriages have occurred in the family, you probably will want to include these additional lineage members. You should always proceed from the present to as far as you wish or can go into the past.

Understandably your memory may be as short as this writer's memory so you probably will have to rely on records to obtain dates and locations for people other than yourself. One of the most enjoyable ways of obtaining the necessary data is by interviewing the older living members of your family. Start with Dad and Mom. Move on to Grandpa and Grandma or aunts and uncles. Not only can you find the facts you desire, but the conversations and the renewing of family relationships are highlighted with folklore and historical trivia which you will find yourself passing on to new generations. It's a great opportunity to begin a family photo album to go along with the genealogical facts you record.

Old family photo albums can be a helpful source of information when people have forgotten dates or names, provided someone in the past saw fit to record information for future generations. Other family documents, such as wills, certificates, licenses, bibles, and other items, will often provide accurate details and dates. Going beyond this, the local Wells County Public Library houses many record books and microfilm resources. The library also has a very good collection of newspapers on microfilm. These can provide a source of information through news articles and obituaries.

What's it all for? It is for the enjoyment of the search, renewed relationships in the family, sharing finds and facts with other family members and friends, and preserving family history for future family researchers.

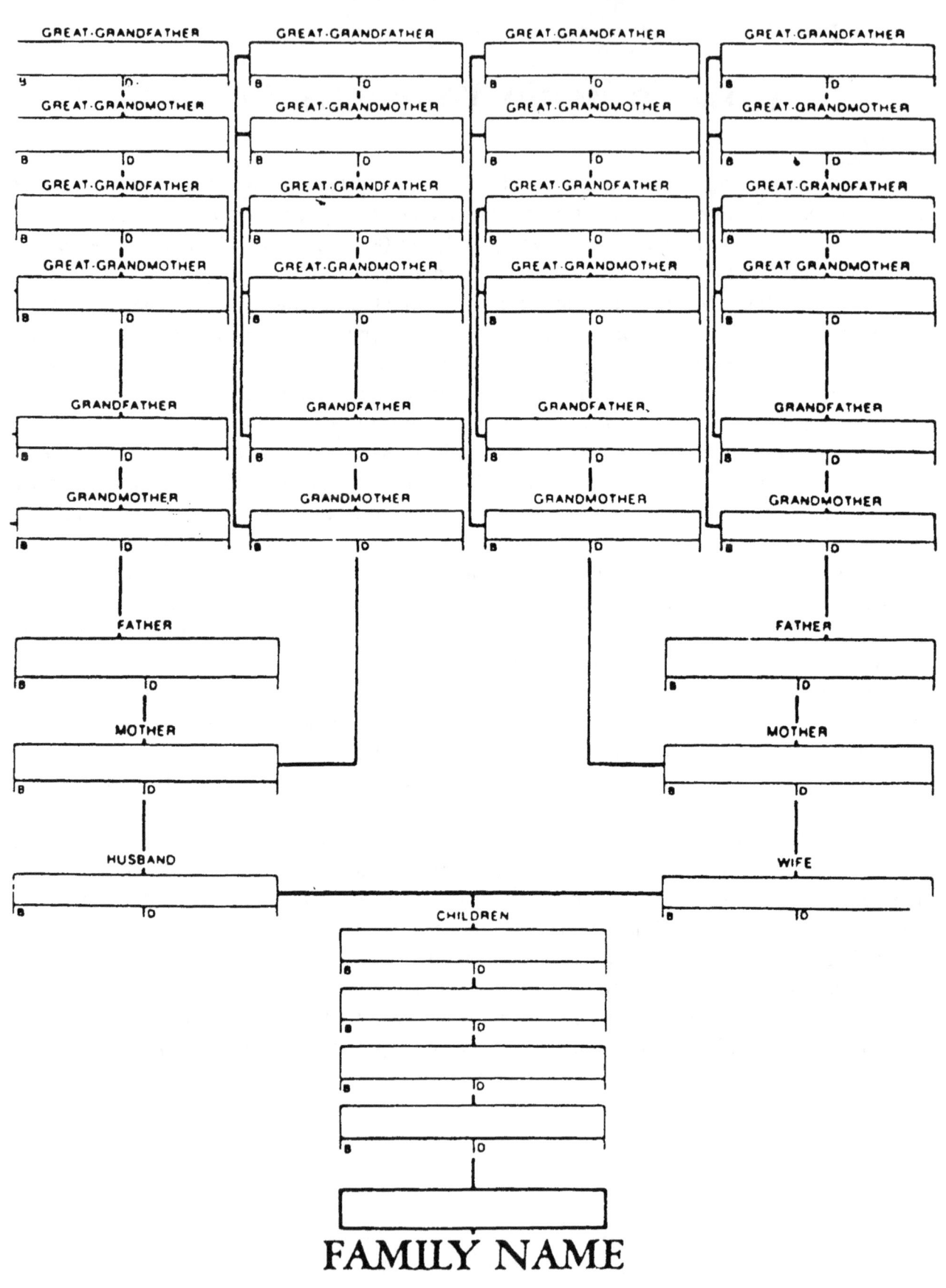

FAMILY RECORD

NAME	BIRTH		DEATH	
	Date	Place	Date	Place

NOTES

NOTES

NOTES

Unidentified group on the north steps of the courthouse. Believed to have been taken during Street Fair as the traditional flags ascending to the courthouse tower are reflected in the window. Photo from glass plate negative courtesy of Don Welch.

www.ingramcontent.com/pod-product-compliance
Lightning Source LLC
Chambersburg PA
CBHW080751300426
44114CB00020B/2691